KT-522-987

Handbook of Neurological Rehabilitation

Handbook of Neurological Rehabilitation

Second Edition

Edited by

Richard J. Greenwood

Consultant Neurologist, National Hospital for Neurology & Neurosurgery, London, UK and Homerton Regional Neurological Rehabilitation Unit, Homerton Hospital, London, UK

Michael P. Barnes

Professor of Neurological Rehabilitation, Hunters Moor Regional Rehabilitation Centre, Newcastle upon Tyne, UK, Clinical Director of Neurorehabilitation Services for Northgate and Prudoe NHS Trust, UK

Thomas M. McMillan

Professor of Clinical Neuropsychology, Department of Psychological Medicine, University of Glasgow, Gartnaval Royal Hospital, Glasgow, UK

Christopher D. Ward

Professor in Rehabilitation Medicine, Head, Division of Rehabilitation and Aging, School of Community Health Sciences, University of Nottingham, UK

Foreword by
Lord Walton

Psychology Press
Taylor & Francis Group
HOVE AND NEW YORK

First published 2003 by Psychology Press
27 Church Road, Hove, East Sussex, BN3 2FA

Simultaneously published in the USA and Canada
by Psychology Press
29 West 35th Street, New York, NY 10001

Psychology Press is a member of the Taylor & Francis Group

© 2003 Psychology Press

Typeset in Times by Newgen Imaging Systems, Chennai, India
Printed and bound in Great Britain by The Cromwell Press Ltd,
Trowbridge, Wiltshire

Cover design by Richard Massing

All rights reserved. No part of this book may be reprinted or reproduced or utilised in any form
or by any electronic, mechanical, or other means, now known or hereafter invented, including
photocopying and recording, or in any information storage or retrieval system, without
permission in writing from the publishers.

British Library Cataloguing in Publication Data
A catalogue record for this book is a available from the British Library

Library of Congress Cataloging in Publication Data

Handbook of neurological rehabilitation/Richard Greenwood ... [et al.] – 2nd ed.
    p. cm.
  Includes bibliographical references and index.
  ISBN 0-86377-757-0
   1. Nervous system–Diseases–Patients–Rehabilitation–Handbooks, manuals, etc. I.
  Greenwood, Richard, MD
  RC350.4 .N484 2002
  616.8′043–dc21

                                  2002068204

ISBN 0-86377-757-0

Contents

Contributors

Nick Alderman PhD CPsychol
Consultant Clinical Neuropsychologist, The Kemsley Division, St Andrew's Hospital, Northampton, UK

James Allibone BSc FRCS(SN)
Consultant Spinal Neurosurgeon, The Royal National Orthopaedic Hospital, Stanmore, UK

Michael P. Barnes MD FRCP
Professor of Neurological Rehabilitation, Hunters Moor Regional Rehabilitation Centre, Newcastle upon Tyne, UK, and Clinical Director of Neurorehabilitation Services for Northgate and Prudoe NHS Trust, UK

Rolfe Birch FRCS Eng by election
Orthopaedic Surgeon, Royal National Orthopaedic Hospital, Honorary Consultant, Royal Postgraduate Medical School and the Hospitals for Sick Children, Great Ormond Street, UK, Civilian Consultant to the Royal Navy, and Visiting Professor to UCL and Imperial College, London, UK

Paul W. Burgess PhD
Wellcome Trust Senior Research Fellow and Reader in Cognitive Neuroscience, UCL Institute of Cognitive Neuroscience, London, UK

Sally Byng PhD FRCSLT
Chief Executive of CONNECT—the Community Disability Network, London, UK

Trudie Chalder SRN RMN Dip Beh Psychotherapy MSc PhD
Senior Lecturer and Cognitive Behavioural Therapist, Academic Department of Psychological Medicine, King's College School of Medicine and Dentistry, London, UK

Barbara J. Chandler BMedSci MD MRCP
Consultant in Rehabilitation Medicine, Hunters Moor Rehabilitation Centre, Newcastle upon Tyne, UK

Jagdish C. Chawla MD FRCS
Consultant and Honorary Lecturer, Welsh Spinal Injuries and Neurological Rehabilitation Unit, Rookwood Hospital, Cardiff, UK

Linda Clare MA MSc CPsychol
Lecturer in Clinical Psychology, Sub-department of Clinical Health Psychology, University College London, UK

Charles Clarke FRCP
Consultant Neurologist, National Hospital for Neurology and Neurosurgery, London, UK and Whipps Cross Hospital, Whipps Cross, UK

George Cochrane MA FRCP FRCPE
Former Medical Director, May Marlborough Lodge Rehabilitation Centre for Severely Disabled People, Oxford, UK

Leonardo G. Cohen MD
Chief, Human Cortical Physiology Section, National Institute of Neurological Disorders and Stroke, National Institutes of Health, Bethesda, MD, USA

Christine Collin MBBS(Hons) FRCP
Consultant in Rehabilitation Medicine, Rehabilitation Centre, Battle Hospital, Reading, UK

Peter Critchley MD FRCP
Consultant in Neurology and Rehabilitation Medicine, Leicester Royal Infirmary, Leicester, UK

Elizabeth Davies PhD MFPHM
Honorary Lecturer and Specialist Registrar in Public Health, Department of Palliative Care and Policy, Guy's, King's and St Thomas's School of Medicine, London, UK

Nicholas Davies MBChB MRCP
Wellcome Trust Clinical Research Fellow, Muscle and Neurogenetics Section, Institute of Neurology, London, UK

Nicholas R. Dennis MB FRCP
Senior Lecturer in Clinical Genetics, University of Southampton, Southampton, UK

Alison Dunnachie SRD
Chief Dietitian, Southampton University Hospital NHS Trust, Southampton, UK

Stephen B. Dunnett
Professor, The Brain Repair Group, School of Biosciences, Cardiff University, Cardiff, UK

Sue Edwards FCSP, SRP
Consultant Physiotherapist, Muswell Hill, London, UK

D. El Kabir MB MRCP
Specialist Registrar, Lane Fox Unit and Sleep Disorders Centre, The Lane Fox Respiratory Unit, Guy's and St Thomas' Hospital Trust, London, UK

Pamela Enderby PhD MSc FCSLT MBE
Professor of Community Rehabilitation, Institute of General Practice and Primary Care, Community Sciences Centre, Northern General Hospital, Sheffield, UK

Clare J. Fowler MB BS MSc FRCP
Reader and Consultant in Uro-Neurology, The National Hospital for Neurology and Neurosurgery, London, UK

Neil C.M. Fyfe MChir FRCS FRCP
Consultant in Rehabilitation Medicine, Freeman Hospital, Newcastle upon Tyne, UK

Laura H. Goldstein PhD MPhil
Reader in Neuropsychology, Department of Psychology, Institute of Psychiatry, London, UK

Richard J. Greenwood MD FRCP
Consultant Neurologist, National Hospital for Neurology and Neurosurgery, London UK and Homerton Regional Neurological Rehabilitation Unit, Homerton Hospital, UK

Mark Hallett MD
Chief, Human Motor Control Section, National Institute of Neurological Disorders and Stroke, National Institutes of Health, Bethesda, MD, USA

Michael G. Hanna FRCP
Reader in Neurology, Muscle and Neurogenetics Section, Institute of Neurology, London, UK

Richard J. Hardie TD MD MA FRCP
Clinical Director, Neurological Rehabilitation, Defence Medical Services Rehabilitation Centre and Honorary Consultant Neurologist, St George's and Atkinson Morley's Hospitals, London, UK

Colette Haslam RGN
Clinical Nurse Specialist and Continence Advisor, The National Hospital for Neurology and Neurosurgery, London, UK

Dominic Heaney MB BCH MRCP
Research Fellow, Epilepsy Research Group, The National Hospital for Neurology and Neurosurgery, London, UK

Jacqueline Hochstenbach PhD
Neuropsychologist, and Head of the Centre for Brain Damage Aftercare, University Hospital Groningen and University of Groningen, The Netherlands

Allan House BSc MBBS MRCP MRCPsych DM
Professor of Liaison Psychiatry, Leeds General Infirmary, Leeds, UK

Robin S. Howard FRCP PhD
Consultant Neurologist, The Batten Unit, The National Hospital for Neurology and Neurosurgery, London, UK and Consultant Neurologist, St Thomas' Hospital, Guy's and St Thomas' Hospital Trust, London, UK

Tom Hughes MD MRCP
Consultant Neurologist, Rookwood Hospital, Llandaff, Cardiff, UK

Iqbal F. Hussain BSc FRCS MSc (Urol)
Research Fellow in Uro-Neurology, The National Hospital for Neurology and Neurosurgery, London, UK

Garth R. Johnson FREng, CEng, FIMechE
Director, Centre for Rehabilitation and Engineering Studies, University of Newcastle, and Hunters Moor Regional Neurorehabilitation Centre, Newcastle upon Tyne, UK

Eirian Jones FRCSLT
Speech and Language Therapist (retired), Cambridge, UK

Douglas M. Justins MB BS FRCA
Consultant in Pain Management and Anaesthesia, Pain Management Centre, St Thomas' Hospital, London, UK

Christopher Kennard MB.BS PhD FRCP FMedSci
Professor of Clinical Neurology and Head, Division of Neuroscience and Psychological Medicine, Faculty of Medicine, Imperial College of Science, Technology and Medicine, London, UK

Richard Langton Hewer MB FRCP
Honorary Professor of Neurology, University of Bristol and Emeritus Consultant Neurologist to the North Bristol NHS Trust, Bristol, UK

Andrew J. Larner
Consultant Neurologist, Cognitive Function Clinic, Walton Centre for Neurology and Neurosurgery, Liverpool, UK

Sue Mawson MCSP BSc(Hons) PhD
Senior Lecturer in Physiotherapy, School of Health and Community Studies, Sheffield Hallam University, Sheffield, UK

E.J.W. McClemont FRCP
Consultant in Rehabilitation Medicine, Lincoln District Health Care Trust, Lincoln, UK

Shona McIntosh MA Dip
Clinical Psychologist, Rehabilitation Research Unit, University of Southampton, Southampton, UK

Thomas M. McMillan MAppSci PhD FBPsS
Professor of Clinical Neuropsychology, Department of Psychological Medicine, University of Glasgow, Gartnaval Royal Hospital, Glasgow, UK

H. Merskey DM
Professor Emeritus of Psychiatry, London Health Sciences Centre, University of Western Ontario, Ontario, Canada

Frederick Middleton MD FRCP DPhys Med
Director, Spinal Injuries Unit, Royal National Orthopaedic Hospital, Stanmore, UK

Theo Mulder PhD
Experimental Psychologist, Professor of Movement Sciences and Director of the Institute of Human Movement Sciences, University of Groningen, the Netherlands

Christian Murray-Leslie MB BS FRCP
Consultant in Rehabilitation Medicine, Derbyshire Royal Infirmary, Derby, UK

Michael Oddy MA MSC PhD FBPsS
Head of Clinical Services, Brain Injury Rehabilitation Trust, Burgess Hill, UK

Malcolm Paes FRCA [deceased]
Formerly Pain Fellow, Pain Management Centre, St Thomas' Hospital Trust, London, UK

Alidz Pambakian MRCP
Lecturer in Neurology, Department of Neurology, Charing Cross Hospital, London, UK

L.E. Panton MRCSLT
Head of Speech Therapy, Hunters Moor Hospital, Newcastle upon Tyne, UK

Brian Pentland BSc MB ChB FRCP(ED) FRCSLT
Consultant Neurologist, Astley Ainslie Hospital, Edinburgh, UK, and Senior Lecturer in Neuroscience and Rehabilitation Studies, University of Edinburgh, Edinburgh, UK

Lorraine L. Pinnington Dip COT BA MSc PhD CPsychol
University of Nottingham Rehabilitation Research Unit, Derby City General Hospital, Derby, UK

E.D. Playford MD FRCP
Senior Lecturer/Consultant, Institute of Neurology, University College London, National Hospital for Neurology and Neurosurgery, London, UK

Mary Reilly MD MRCPI
Senior Lecturer and Consultant Neurologist, National Hospital for Neurology and Neurosurgery and St Mary's Hospital, London, UK

Philip H. Richardson PhD
Professor and Head of Outcome Research, The Tavistock and Portman NHS Trust and University of Essex, Colchester, UK

Ian H. Robertson PhD
Director, Trinity College Institute of Neuroscience, Dublin, Eire

John C. Rothwell MA PhD
Sobell Department, Institute of Neurology, London, UK

David N. Rushton MD FRCP
Consultant in Rehabilitation Medicine, Frank Cooksey Rehabilitation Unit, King's College Hospital, London, UK

Lynne J. Sandles PhD SROT
Head Occupational Therapist, Disability North, Newcastle upon Tyne, UK

Michael Saunders FRCP
Emeritus Consultant in Neurology and Neurological Rehabilitation, Newcastle City and Northallerton NHS Trusts, UK

Pamela J. Shaw MD FRCP
Head, Academic Neurology Unit, University of Sheffield, Sheffield, UK

Simon Shorvon MA MD FRCP
Professor of Clinical Neurology, Institute of Neurology, University College, London, UK

Michael V. Sofroniew
Department of Neurobiology, Brain Research Institute, UCLA, Los Angeles, USA

Benjamin Taylor MCh Orth FRCS
Consultant Orthopaedic and Spinal Surgeon, Royal National Orthopaedic Hospital, Stanmore, UK

Alan Tennant BA PhD
Professor of Rehabilitation Studies, Rheumatology and Rehabilitation Research Unit, University of Leeds, Leeds, UK

Pamela Thompson PhD CPsychol AFBPsS
Head of Psychological Services, National Society for Epilepsy, Chalfont St Peter, UK and Honorary Lecturer, Department of Experimental and Clinical Epilepsy, Institute of Neurology, University of London, UK

Derick T. Wade MD FRCP
Consultant and Professor in Neurological Disability, Oxford Centre for Enablement, Oxford, UK

Christopher D. Ward MD FRCP
Professor in Rehabilitation Medicine, Head, Division of Rehabilitation and Ageing, School of Community Health Sciences, University of Nottingham, UK

Simon Wessely MA BM Bch MRCP MRCPsych MSc MD FRCP FAcadMedSci FRCPsych
Professor of Epidemiological and Liaison Psychiatry, Academic Department of Psychological Medicine, King's College School of Medicine and Dentistry, London, UK

Jane Whitaker RegMRCSLT
Acting Head of Adult Services, Adult Speech and Language Therapy, St Richards Hospital, Chichester, UK

Arnold J. Wilkins BSc DPhil CPsychol FBPsS
Visual Perception Unit, University of Essex, Colchester, UK

A. J. Williams MB FRCP
Director, Lane Fox and Sleep Disorders Centre, The Lane Fox Respiratory Unit, Guy's and St Thomas' Hospital Trust, London, UK

Barbara A. Wilson OBE PhD CPsychol FBPsS
MRC Cognition and Brain Sciences Unit, Addenbrooke's Hospital, Cambridge, UK

Roger Ll Wood BA DCP PhD CPsychol FBPsS
Clinical Director, Brain Injury Rehabilitation Trust, West Heath, Birmingham, UK

Robert T. Woods FBPsS
Professor and Director, Dementia Services Development Centre, University of Wales, Bangor, UK

Gavin Yamey BA MB BS MRCP
Regional Neurological Rehabilitation, Homerton Hospital, London, UK

Foreword

When I began the practice of neurology more than 50 years ago, clinical neurology was regarded, with some justification, as being a purely diagnostic specialty with relatively little emphasis on treatment in the broadest sense. At that time, rehabilitation was a word which was barely ever mentioned and my own personal clinical experience soon demonstrated to me the appalling consequences of neglect of patients with chronic and progressive neurological disorders, many of whom, once diagnosed, remained at home with no physical, pharmacological or psychological support save for that derived from occasional visits by a caring general practitioner. In particular, I well remember that when I began a survey of all patients with muscular dystrophy in the Northern Region of the United Kingdom, I found many boys with dystrophy of the Duchenne type who had become appallingly deformed with multiple muscular contractures, gross scoliosis and other substantial disabilities because of failure to undertake simple supportive measures which might well have alleviated some of the worst consequences of the disease. In consequence, few boys suffering from that condition then survived beyond the age of 15 or 16 years, since gross spinal deformity commonly resulted in impairment of thoracic movement with consequential fatal respiratory infections.

During and after the Second World War, there was, however, growing emphasis upon rehabilitation, not least of those brain injured in combat; in the United Kingdom, the Military Hospital for Head Injuries based at what is now St Hugh's College in Oxford did excellent work in this respect, and of course the pioneering work of Ludwig Guttmann in the Spinal Injuries Unit at Stoke Mandeville Hospital in Buckinghamshire received considerable medical and public attention. Even so, when I was appointed a consultant neurologist in 1958, rehabilitation facilities for patients suffering from neurological disease were, in the Northern Region and in most other parts of the United Kingdom, rudimentary and I and my colleagues working in clinical neurology soon became convinced that a major effort to improve such services was urgently required. Happily, within the last 40 years many rehabilitation centers for the neurologically disabled have been opened in the United Kingdom and many consultants have been appointed specifically to work in the field of neurological rehabilitation, often alongside colleagues in rheumatology and what used to be called physical medicine.

The first edition of the *Handbook of Neurological Rehabilitation* received very favourable reviews, as it was perceived to fill an important gap in the medical literature. I have been pleased and honoured to have been invited to write a Foreword for this second edition, which seems to me to be a quite outstanding publication – comprehensive, detailed and well referenced, but so organised that specific areas likely to be of interest to individual readers are readily accessed. As the editors indicate in their Preface, the book is organised in three sections dealing specifically with principles of practice, assessment and treatment of functional deficits, and specific disorders; in the latter section, individual neurological diseases and syndromes are considered in detail. And it is good to see that the biological and scientific background to clinical practice is well covered in the section dealing with mechanisms of recovery, while in the section on assessment and treatment, mobility, other physical disabilities, cognitive function, personality and behaviour are all handled effectively. And it is notable that the contributions of other members of the healthcare team apart from neurologists and consultants in rehabilitation are given due weight in the rehabilitative process. Hence, there is much here of interest not only to doctors but also to physiotherapists, occupational therapists, speech and language therapists, nurses and clinical psychologists. We also find substantial coverage of biomechanics and rehabilitation engineering and the design and usage of what the authors call assistive technology, including aids to mobility, environmental control systems and communication aids.

In preparation of this second edition, the editors have assembled a distinguished team of contributors, most from the UK but a certain number from overseas, including within their number many internationally renowned experts. This revised and expanded edition highlights, as the editors say in their Preface, the importance of adding to medical responsibility in the field multi-disciplinary working with an expanding evidence base. Due attention is paid throughout to hospital in-patient and out-patient services, but also to those based in the community, and happily, too, objective evaluations of progress and outcome are included.

I commend this volume warmly to the greater medical and other professional audiences who will, I believe, find it an invaluable guide and reference source.

John Walton TD, MA, MD, DSc, FRCP, FMedSci
(Lord Walton of Detchant),
Detchant, Northumberland
August 2002

Preface to the second edition

Neurological damage still accounts for about 40% of people most severely disabled, and the majority of people with complex disablement resulting from physical, cognitive, and behavioural impairment. David Marsden's "simple truth that neurologists should take a leading complementary role in neurological rehabilitation", in his Foreword to this book's first edition, thus continues to be a vision to which we hope the second edition contributes. We are indebted to Lord Walton for the Foreword on this occasion.

Over the last 10 years technology, particularly neuroimaging, has continued to progress everyday diagnostic neurology, providing an expanding opportunity to explore the "so what" in the clinical management of neurological disorders. Class I trials, particularly after stroke, have demonstrated the effectiveness of rehabilitation therapies and its "black boxes"; new drug treatments, sometimes in tandem with therapy techniques, have been shown to be effective in the context of complex disablement and chronic neurological disease; and studies of neural reorganisation and plasticity have emphasised the reality of neurological change.

These developments make it increasingly possible to replace any perceived threat to medical responsibility by multidisciplinary working with an expanding evidence base. This should be mirrored by the growth of locally available inpatient and community-based services, enabled by objective evaluations of progress and outcome. We want this second edition to contribute to this process by facilitating the biological/clinical interface, providing a structure for managing the consequences of neurological damage, and focusing those involved in service provision, to the ultimate benefit of the disabled person and their family.

R.J.G., M.P.B., T.M.McM., C.D.W.
London, Newcastle upon Tyne,
Glasgow, and Nottingham, 2001

Preface to the first edition

This book describes those aspects of the process of rehabilitation applicable to the 2% of the population with disabling neurological disease. It has been directed towards a readership of neurologists, but naturally calls on expertise of a number of well-known authors from a variety of disciplines. It is hoped that it will be of value to all professions who work with patients suffering from neurological disorders. It assumes certain knowledge of neurological pathology and the diagnostic process in order to focus more sharply upon problem areas presented by the patient, and describes "all means aimed at reducing the impact of disabling and handicapping conditions and at enabling disabled people to achieve optimal social reintegration" (World Health Organization). At times, a description of solutions may appear banal, but their achievement in the real world is frequently difficult and complex. The negotiation and social and political brokerage necessary for the successful application of the rehabilitation process, not only in individual cases, but also in populations as a whole, should not be underestimated.

The book is divided into three sections. The first describes the epidemiological, social, political, and biological principles that underpin the practice of rehabilitation. The second describes the techniques necessary to this practice, including assessment and evaluation, and the characteristics and remediation of physical, cognitive, affective, and behavioural disorders. The third highlights the use of these techniques in the context of specific diseases. We hope the text emphasises the fact that rehabilitation is an on-going process involving problem solving and education, in which assessment, goal setting, intervention, and reassessment are necessarily reiterative and require multidisciplinary input. Where possible, evidence in support of the use of these techniques is described, but in many instances evidence of benefit, or otherwise, does not exist. This lack of evidence often does not represent the ineffectiveness of rehabilitation or absence of clear technique, but rather underlines the difficulties of researching into the area of multiple disability in contrast, for example, with trials of drugs or operations. Opportunities to rectify this situation are pointed out in the text.

We hope the book also emphasises and contributes to the understanding of other aspects of practice in neurological rehabilitation, including a perspective upon the icon of the randomised trial and a view that admits the usefulness of other group or single-case methodologies; some instances in which the needs of patients and their carers take precedence, in the end, over issues of cost containment, important though these are; the need for undergraduate or postgraduate training of doctors in neurological rehabilitation; and a breakdown of professional barriers within rehabilitation to facilitate the use of combined treatment techniques. Finally, we hope the reader can be persuaded that using the skills of diagnostic and medical neurology in conjunction with those of neurological rehabilitation is ultimately to the greater satisfaction of the practitioner and the greater benefit of the patient.

R.J.G., M.P.B., T.M.McM., C.D.W.
London, Southampton, and Newcastle upon Tyne, 1993

Principles of practice

Clinical aspects

1. The epidemiology of disabling neurological disorders

Richard Langton Hewer   Alan Tennant

INTRODUCTION

Virtually all significant neurological diseases can cause short- and long-term disability. For this reason, every locality must contain provision for this important clinical group. This chapter deals with some of the issues, including the nature and extent of the problem.

Epidemiology is concerned with the distribution and determinants of disease in health. The term clinical epidemiology is applied to the systematic approach to the gathering and interpretation of clinical data. Applied epidemiology, which is the subject of this chapter, incorporates the principles of clinical epidemiology but adopts a somewhat different approach. Rather than starting with the search for risk factors for disease, applied epidemiology starts with the presence of disease and describes the result of the disease and the potential effects of interventions. It also covers the economic and organisational implications of the epidemiological evidence.

What is a neurological disorder?

A neurological disorder can be defined as one that involves a recognisable anatomical and/or physiological disorder of the nervous system. However, not all disorders fulfil the criteria. For instance, some cases of epilepsy, headache, chronic fatigue syndrome, and sleep disorders have no obvious structural or physiological basis.

An important distinction is made between neurological and psychiatric disorder. Some conditions such as schizophrenia and manic-depressive conditions are generally regarded as being the province of psychiatry. Others, such as endogenous depression, occur in patients with neurological disorder and in many other situations. The borderline between neurology and psychiatry is recognised by the expanding subspeciality of neuropsychiatry. There are other important interfaces. One is between orthopaedics and neurology, exemplified by backache and sciatica. A vast number of neurological problems are encountered in general medicine.

A neurological disorder is not necessarily one that is the "province" of clinical neurology. Thus, the majority of patients with mental subnormality/learning difficulty have structural brain damage. In the UK these patients are looked after by a separate learning disability service. Clinical neurology has not traditionally been concerned with the disabling consequences of diseases such as stroke, multiple sclerosis, and Parkinson's disease, although the situation is changing.

What are the consequences of these disorders?

The problems experienced by patients may have several dimensions. Some way of dividing these into meaningful components is required. Analysis has been facilitated by the introduction of the World Health Organisation *Classification of Impairments, Disabilities and Handicaps* (ICIDH; WHO, 1980). This system has provided a useful framework for epidemiologists, clinicians, and others who are concerned with the consequences of disease.

The ICIDH classification identifies three concepts as consequences of disease:

Impairment. This is "any loss or abnormality of psychological, physiological or anatomical structural function". Impairment refers to parts or systems of the body that do not work. According to the ICIDH, pain and suffering generally are seen as consequences of disease or disorder, which may lead to activity limitations and are therefore viewed as impairments.

Disability. Disability is "any restriction or lack (resulting from an impairment) of ability to perform an activity in the manner or within the range considered normal for a human being". Basically, disabilities are things that people cannot do. Disability is concerned with the performance of activities, with tasks, skills, and behaviours, and the way the performance of activities departs from the norm.

Handicap. Handicap is "a disadvantage for an individual, resulting from an impairment or disability, that limits or prevents the fulfilment of a role (depending on age, sex and social/cultural factors) for that individual". Handicap refers to the interaction with a particular environment and relationship with other people. It can be experienced in several dimensions. For instance, there may be loss of physical independence with the need to rely on the help of other people. Mobility, the ability to move around effectively, may be curtailed. Employment, leisure, and obligations in the home may be affected, as may social integration. There may be reduced economic self-sufficiency.

The term "disablement" has been used to refer to all consequences of disease, that is, it embraces all three concepts (Badley, 1995). Likewise, "health status" has been used extensively to describe these three domains. On the other hand, "quality of life" has been described as extending beyond the disease/handicap continuum, mediated by a number of other factors including age, gender, ethnicity, self-confidence, coping skills, and self-esteem (Tennant, 1995).

A recent proposed revision has given the ICIDH classification a more positive nomenclature of impairment, activities, and participation with a greater emphasis upon extrinsic factors limiting activities and participation. However, the available epidemiological evidence is firmly rooted within the original version and this will be used in the present chapter.

Symptoms

A symptom may be defined as "a subjective experience of disease or physical disturbance observed by the patient" (*Webster's Third International Dictionary*, 1971). There are scores of disabling neurological symptoms, each generating its own management issues. One of the most important tasks of health professionals is to deploy techniques to control distressing symptoms. Some knowledge of the frequency, nature, and severity of symptoms is essential. However, symptoms do not fit comfortably into the ICIDH classification. Most are probably best classified as impairments. Thus, the impairment of attention may lead to personal hygiene disability, which may in turn lead to a handicap that involves restricted social life and, subsequently, reduced quality of life.

Problems and stages

A problem may be defined as "a difficult matter requiring a solution" (*Oxford Concise Dictionary*, 1997). Problems are an important component of need for patients in the acute and chronic phases of their disorders. Symptoms are an example of the problems faced by patients. All diseases involve a series of stages. Each stage embraces its own problems and needs. Thus, a patient with Parkinson's disease may present with deteriorating handwriting and tremor. Medication may be helpful. Five years after onset the problems may include deteriorating drug effectiveness, unsteadiness, as well as secondary problems involving employment and driving. Ten years after onset the initial medication may well be ineffective and the clinical problems may now involve dementia, incontinence, frequent falls, and pressure sores. Respite care and good nursing are all important. It is obvious that problems/needs and interventions will differ according to the stage of disease reached. It is also clear that staging is an essential element of comprehensive disease management planning. All this may appear obvious but there is little published literature on the subject of staging. Standard textbooks usually concentrate on diagnosis and acute treatment.

SOME IMPORTANT NEUROLOGICAL DISORDERS

Stroke

Stroke is a clinically defined syndrome involving the rapid development of symptoms and/or signs of focal loss of cerebral function with no apparent cause other than of vascular origin (Warlow, 1998). The loss of function can be global; for example, if the patient is in deep coma as a result of intracerebral or subarachnoid haemorrhage. Symptoms last for at least 24 hours or lead to death. The condition is heterogeneous and its numerous causes influence the prognosis, the interventions required and the preventive strategies.

Stroke incidence has been reliably studied in various white populations. The rates are similar, approximately 2 first ever strokes per 1000 population overall (Bamford et al., 1988; Carolei et al., 1997; Ellekjaer, Holmen, Indredavik, & Terent, 1997). The rate rises steeply with increasing age and for people aged 45–85 is approximately 4 per 1000 annually. About 75% of cases occur after the age of 65. However, there are important geographical variations. For example, there is a high incidence in Russia and a low incidence in France (Warlow, 1998). The stroke recurrence rate is approximately 5% annually, although the figure is higher than this during the months post stroke. There is also an increased risk, 3% per annum, of myocardial infarction.

The prevalence of survivors of stroke in the community depends upon the incidence and the death rate. Studies of prevalence are difficult and there have been few of them. One study in northern England estimated the prevalence of stroke at 47 per 1000 amongst those aged 55 years and over, and 15 per 1000 all ages (Geddes et al., 1996). Another study in New Zealand gave estimates of prevalence at 8 per 1000 aged 15 years and over (Bonita, Solomon, & Broad, 1997). In the former study an estimated 6 per 1000, all ages, reported dependency in aspects of mobility or self care following stroke. There was a highly significant age difference in the proportion reporting disability and dependency, ranging from 24.7% of those aged 55–64 years, to 75.3% of those aged 85 years and over. In the latter study, approximately 2 per 1000 aged 15 years and over required assistance in at least one self-care activity.

The measurement of stroke induced disability is particularly difficult because of the overlapping disabilities occurring in a largely elderly population. However, some problems such as dysphasia and unilateral arm paralysis are reasonably disease specific. The topic is of considerable importance for health-care planners. A recent national UK study (Harris, 1971) found that stroke survivors constituted about 25% of all severely disabled people living in the community.

The evidence suggests that the majority of stroke patients are admitted to hospital (Bamford, Sandercock, Warlow, & Gray, 1986; Wade & Langton Hewer, 1985). However, there is some variation from locality to locality (Geddes et al., 1996). The cost of stroke is considerable to individuals and to the State. Thus, in 1992/1993 stroke accounted for 5.55% of hospital in-patient expenditure. This figure was only exceeded by accidents (7.03%) and learning disability (6.91%) (National Health

Service Executive, 1996). A major paradox is that despite this large expenditure there is considerable disquiet at the quality of services which are often perceived as being poor (King's Fund Forum, 1988; Wilkinson et al., 1997).

Trends in incidence, prevalence, and consequences of stroke are equivocal. Some studies report a decline in incidence (Truelson, Prescott, Gronbaek, Schnohr, & Boysen, 1997), whereas others report a period of decline followed by unchanged incidence more recently (Shahar et al., 1997). There are no studies to date on the changing consequences of stroke.

Head injury

Just as stroke incidence at the international level can be shown to vary by a factor of three, likewise head injury incidence, leading to admission to hospital, has been shown to vary between 1.5 and 4.7 per 1000, all ages (Tennant, 1995). This variation is a function of the differing ways of case ascertainment as well as demographical and socioeconomic influences. However, incidence leading to hospital admission in one English region showed variation by a magnitude of four over 18 health districts, ranging from 1.5 to 6.2 per 1000, all ages. For the ages 15–60 male rates are twice those for females. The peak incidence is in males in the 15–30 age band.

In Britain the death rate from head injury has been falling since 1968 and was estimated to be seven per 100,000 in 1994 (Jennett, 1998). A similar trend is noted in the USA (Sosin, Sachs, & Smith, 1989). Those who survive a head injury contribute to the lifetime prevalence. Unfortunately, to date, there are only a few population-based estimates of the prevalence of any type of head injury. One study in Sweden looked at three cohorts of males and asked about their previous experience of head injuries. Almost one-quarter (24%) of 60-year-old males reported at least one head injury with unconsciousness; similar rates were found in the other cohorts with 21% of 50-year-old males and 23% of 30-year-olds reporting a similar experience (Silverb & Carlsson, 1986).

Details on the impairments, disabilities, and handicaps of those who have survived a head injury are almost always derived from small hospital-based studies. However, some national surveys provide relevant data. One influential study in the United Kingdom suggested that the prevalence of disabled survivors will be at least 1 per 1000 population report (Medical Disability Society, 1988). Another recent study attempted to determine the prevalence in the Canadian population, using data from the Canadian Health and Activity Limitations Survey (HALS; Statistics Canada, 1988). The weighted estimate implies a prevalence (associated with memory and learning problems) of approximately 0.6 per 1000 adults. As memory problems are reported by a majority of those surviving moderate to severe injury (Tennant, Macdermott, & Neary, 1995) this estimate can be considered to be of the same magnitude as the UK figures. The Canadian study provided a point prevalence estimate of 0.2 per 1000 adults for hearing disability, and 0.15 per 1000 for speaking disability following head injury (Moscato, Trevisan,

& Willer, 1994). There is little doubt that the most common form of sequelae associated with head injury is a set of symptoms referred to as the post-concussive syndrome. The syndrome includes poor concentration and memory, irritability, headache, fatigue, and depression (Mittenberg & Burton, 1994). However, there are no population-based estimates of the prevalence of these symptoms following a head injury, or any other cause.

Admission to hospital following head injury is common in many Western industrial societies. Thus, annual hospitalised incidence rates are a useful way of helping to plan the likely need for services. Some 80% are categorised as mild and only 5–10% as severe (Jennett, 1998). However, analysis of the US National Health Interview Survey (Sosin, Sniezek, & Thurman, 1991) found that only 16% of those with such head injuries were admitted to hospital. Children, members of families with low incomes, and those injured at home or school, were less likely to be admitted to hospital than others. Although in the USA health payment mechanisms may have played a part in the choice of treatment location, it seems that hospital statistics alone may not provide a comprehensive picture of the demand for health care following head injury.

Parkinson's disease

The incidence of Parkinson's disease varies between about 0.12 and 0.18 per 1000 population per year (Brewis, Poskanzer, Rolland, & Miller, 1966; Kusumi, Nakashima, Harada, Nakayama, & Takahashi, 1996; Rajput, Offord, Beard, & Kurland, 1984; Sutcliffe & Meara, 1995). Increasing exponentially with age, there is some debate as to whether or not it may be less common today in younger age groups (Ben-Shlomo, 1997).

The prevalence of Parkinson's disease is not easy to estimate. One major reason for this is that many patients receive treatment that, in the early stages of the disease, may virtually abolish the clinical features. Given this, a recent European study has estimated the prevalence of Parkinson's disease to be 16 per 1000 aged 65 years and over (de Rijk et al., 1997). Prevalence was found to be similar in men and women. There was a six-fold difference in prevalence from the 65–69-year-olds (6/1000) to the 85–89-year-olds (35/1000). Another recent study in Japan found prevalence to be 1.2 per 1000, all ages (Kusumi et al., 1996). In this study prevalence amongst females was found to be twice that of males (1.59 : 0.73). In contrast, a Norwegian study found prevalence (age adjusted) in males (1.21) to be 34% higher than in females (0.90) (Tandberg, Larsen, Nessler, Riise, & Aarli, 1995). Finally, a UK study found prevalence to be 1.2 per 1000 all ages (Sutcliffe et al., 1995), showing a 12% increase in a decade. This review assumes a prevalence of 1 per 1000, all ages.

Multiple sclerosis

The incidence of multiple sclerosis varies between 0.02 and 2 cases per 1000 population per year (Bencsik, Rajda, Klivenyi, Jardanhazy, & Vecsei, 1998; Brewis et al., 1966; Millar, 1980;

Pina, Ara, Modrego, Morales, & Capablo, 1998; Rothwell & Charlton, 1998; Shepherd & Downie, 1980). For the purpose of this review, an incidence of 0.04 per 1000 per year is assumed. However, incidence figures are of limited value as many patients will experience symptoms long before the correct diagnosis is made.

Both the incidence and prevalence of multiple sclerosis depends on a number of factors including ethnic background and distance from the equator. Kurtzke (1982) used a prevalence of 0.6 per 1000 for his calculations for the USA, similar to recent estimates from a number of countries (Bencsik et al., 1998; Pina et al., 1998). Figures for the UK vary between 0.8 and 2 per 1000, with higher rates reported in Scotland and Northern Ireland than England (Ford et al., 1998; McDonnell & Hawkins, 1998; Rothwell & Charlton, 1998). This review assumes a prevalence of 1 per 1000 persons.

A number of studies have involved the examination of cross-sectional data relating to the distribution of disability at different time points. However there are no studies in which the rate of progression of disability has been recorded from the onset of the disease in population-based samples. A number of studies suggest that about 50% of patients are independent and still able to walk after 15 years of disease duration. Up to 70% of patients living at home with a diagnosis of multiple sclerosis may have a disability (Harris, 1971; Martin, White, & Melter, 1989). Recent work has suggested that physical function and psychological well-being are most affected (Murphy et al., 1998).

Overall, the figures suggest that each year, 4 people per 100,000 will be diagnosed as having multiple sclerosis. Many more, however, will present to neurologists and other doctors with a variety of neurological symptoms that are probably not due to multiple sclerosis. There are still major gaps in our knowledge about the epidemiology of multiple sclerosis and there is still inadequate data to enable reliable prognostications to be given early on in the course of the disease.

Motor neurone disease

The average crude incidence rates for motor neurone disease ranges from between 0.004 and 0.02 cases per 1000 persons (Chancellor & Warlow, 1992; Dean, Quigley, & Goldacre, 1994). About half of all patients with motor neurone disease die within 2 years of the diagnosis, but probably about 20% survive 5 years or more. Prevalence figures vary quite widely between 0.001 and 0.11 per 1000 persons (Fong et al., 1996; Kurtzke, 1982). The rate for England and Wales varies between 0.04 and 0.07 per 1000 persons (James, Harper, & Wiles 1994; Roman, 1998).

One of the few epidemiological studies that reported impairment and disability found that swallowing speed was reduced (< 10 ml/s) in 67%. Vital capacity was < 70% of predicted value for age, sex, and height in 67% (James et al., 1994). Depression and pain have been reported to be at least as common as amongst those with multiple sclerosis (Tedman, Young, & Williams, 1997). An earlier British survey (Newrick & Langton

Hewer, 1984) showed that 57% of patients with motor neurone disease at any one time had significant dysphagia, and about 25% were totally dependent in all aspects of care. Indeed, it has been suggested that the loss of independence in self care and failing mobility may occur more rapidly than the current medical and social care agencies can accommodate (Young, Tedman, & Williams, 1995).

Once again, there are major gaps in our knowledge about the frequency of disabling problems in motor neurone disease. An important feature of the disease is that it is uncommon and yet the problems are complex, distressing, and to some extent disease specific. Day-to-day supervision by a Neurological Centre is often impossible. Expert help is therefore often required in the locality where the patient lives.

Epilepsy

The incidence rates for epilepsy vary between 0.2 and 1 case per 1000 persons, all ages (Shorvon, 1996; Zielinsky, 1982). Epilepsy presents particular epidemiological problems. Much depends on the definition of epilepsy and this centres around diagnostic accuracy, classification, medication, and the issue of the single fit or febrile convulsion. For instance, some studies include single fits and others do not. Kurtzke (1982) estimated an annual incidence 0.5 per 1000, with a further 0.5 having febrile convulsions and 0.2 a single fit. Recent figures for the UK in a series of papers give estimates ranging between 0.48 and 0.63 per 1000 persons (Cockerell, Eckle, Goodridge, Sander, & Shorvon, 1995; Cockerell et al., 1996; Goodridge & Shorvon, 1983). The present review will use an estimate of 0.7 cases per 1000 per year, to include those who are referred with a single fit.

The prevalence of epilepsy is also a matter for discussion and debate. A distinction may need to be drawn between those people who have had a fit at some point in their lives and those who are still on treatment. Zielinsky (1982) found a prevalence of active epilepsy of between 2.3 and 7.8 per 1000 persons, with a lifetime prevalence as high as 60 per 1000, including those who have had at least one non-febrile convulsion. This estimate is similar to another from Rochester, Minnesota, in the USA where the age-adjusted prevalence of active epilepsy was found to be 6.8 per 1000 (Hauser, Annegers, & Rocca, 1996). Prevalence rates for the UK in recent studies have been found to be between 4.2 and 5.3 per 1000 persons (Shorvon, 1996). Overall, the studies indicate that about 0.43 persons per 1000 of the general population have fits every week, and that about 1 per 1000 will be on anticonvulsant treatment. The disabling effect of epilepsy at the population level is unknown. The most recent UK disability survey estimates that 2% of all disabled people report epilepsy as a cause of their disability (Martin et al., 1989). This would imply a prevalence of 2.7 per 1000 whose disability was associated with epilepsy. On this basis, extrapolating to the earlier prevalence estimates, approximately 50% of those with epilepsy would experience some disability. However, the extent of that disability is unquantified, and may be associated with brief periods of lack of consciousness. Of those experiencing "consciousness disabilities" in the survey, 73% were attributed to epilepsy.

From the organisational point of view, it is necessary to identify those patients who are likely to need the specialised services offered by neurologists, neuropsychiatrists, and others who specialise in epilepsy.

Cerebral palsy

There is a long-term increasing trend in the incidence of cerebral palsy linked to distinct trend eras for preterm births (Hagberg, Olow, & Van Wendt, 1996; Pharoah, Platt, & Cooke, 1996; Topp, Uldall, & Langhoff-Roos, 1997). The rate is usually reported between 1.8 and 2.3 per 1000 live births but this can vary from as many as 80 in extreme preterm children, to 1.4 in term children (Boyle, Decoufle, & Yeargin-Allsopp, 1994; Hagberg et al., 1996; MacGillivray & Campbell, 1995). Incidence is also elevated in multiple births (MacGillivray & Campbell, 1995; Petterson, Nelson, Watson, & Stanley, 1993).

Prevalence estimates in the total population are rare, and are more likely reported as rates within a specific cohort of children. One population study reported a prevalence of 1.24 per 1000 (Razdan, Kaul, Motta, Kaul, & Bhatt, 1994). Another, 1.23 per 1000 survivors at the age of 3 (Grether, Cummins, & Nelson, 1992). Yet another, 2.4 per 1000 children aged 3–10 years (Boyle et al., 1996). A study based upon a register of all children born with cerebral palsy within a regional health boundary in the UK reported a high prevalence of approximately 4 per 1000 (Sinha, Corry, Subesinghe, Wild, & Levene, 1997).

Disability can be extensive. One study, which aggregated data from several regional sources, found that a third of those with cerebral palsy had no independent walking, and almost a quarter were incapable of dressing or feeding unaided (Pharoah, Cooke, Johnson, King, & Mutch, 1998). Almost a quarter had a severe learning disability (IQ < 50) and one in twelve had severe visual disability.

Migraine

Migraine is common at all ages. It has been suggested that approximately 50% of the variance in liability to migraine is attributable to genetic factors (Larsson, Bille, & Pedersen, 1998). In population studies of school children a positive family history of migraine has been reported to be between 50% and 89% (Bille, 1997; Lee & Olness, 1997; Palencia & Sinovas, 1997).

For children, prevalence of migraine, using International Headache Society (HIS) criteria for migraine, is reported to be 70–90 per 1000, and most children experience their first attack by the age of 10 years (Lee & Olness, 1997; Orji & Iloeje, 1997). There has been some suggestion that paediatric migraine differs from adult migraine in its epidemiology and symptom profile (Lipton, 1997).

For adults, the prevalence of migraine (using HIS) has been reported with a range of 70–130 per 1000 (Lavados & Tenhamm, 1997; Michel et al., 1996; Russell, Rasmussen, Thorvaldsen, &

Olsen, 1996; Sakai & Igarashi, 1997). Migraine without aura has been reported at a prevalence of 60–140 per 1000 (Sakai & Igarashi, 1997) and with aura with a prevalence of 20–80 per 1000 (Lavados & Tenhamm, 1997; Sakai & Igarashi, 1997). Prevalence amongst females can be up to twice that reported for males (Russell et al., 1996).

Accounts of the consequences of migraine are rare, and are usually presented as its impact upon work. Work loss appears to be affected differentially, with those most disabled by migraine accounting for approximately 80% of all work loss (Lipton, Stewart, & von Korff, 1997; Von Korff, Stewart, Simon, & Lipton, 1998). One study estimated time off work to be about 1 day every 3 months (Von Korff et al., 1998). Another study reported that 11% of those with migraine were bedridden for an average 1.6 days within a 2-week period, and that almost one in ten were restricted from normal activities for an average 2.4 days within that period because of migraine (To & Wu, 1995).

Dementia

With an ageing population, problems associated with dementia, including Alzheimer's disease, are presenting the health- and social-care services, and families, with ever increasing demands. The incidence of dementia increases sharply with age but no overall differences are found for gender (Kokmen, Beard, O'Brien, & Kurland, 1996; Letenneur, Commenges, Dartigues, & Barberger-Gateau, 1994). The incidence of vascular dementia has been estimated to be 6–12 per 1000 persons aged 70 years and older (Hebert & Brayne, 1995). In France, estimates for dementia and Alzheimer's disease were 16.3 and 11.4 per 1000 aged 65 years and over respectively (Letenneur et al., 1994).

The estimated prevalence of dementia in North America is 60–100 per 1000 persons aged 65 years and over, with Alzheimer's disease accounting for two thirds of these cases (Hendrie, 1997). A study in Japan reported a similar prevalence of 67 per 1000 of those aged 65 years and over (Ogura et al., 1995). Very high prevalence rates were found amongst those aged 90–99 years, 414 per 1000 for females, 212 per 1000 for males. Reported increases in the prevalence of dementia and Alzheimer's disease over time is probably a result of multiple factors, not just changes in underlying demographics (Beard, Kokmen, O'Brien, & Kurland, 1995). There appears to be an elevated risk of developing dementia in those with Parkinson's disease, particularly younger patients (Breteler, de Groot, Van Romunde, & Hofman, 1995).

Approximately 2% of disabled adults reported dementia as a cause of their disability. However, given the peak age of onset and the level of comorbidity in that population, it is very difficult to estimate the disabling effect of dementia alone.

OTHER NEUROLOGICAL DISEASES

There are many neurological diseases. It is not possible to deal with each one individually. Many are uncommon, but taken together they represent a major workload. For example, the

Table 1.1. Incidence, prevalence, and consequences of the major disabling neurological disorders. Expressed as a rate per 1000, all ages, unless otherwise specified. Ordered by age at peak onset, where possible

Peak onset	Condition	Incidence	Prevalence	Disability
0–15	Cerebral palsy*	2	3	3
	Meningitis	0.07		
	Muscular dystrophy		0.09	
16–24	Head injury	3**		
	Epilepsy	0.7	5	
	Migraine		70	7
25–54	Multiple sclerosis	0.04	1	0.7
	Cerebral tumour	0.16	0.45	0.16
	Guillain–Barrè	0.01		0.002
55–74	Stroke	2	15	6
	Parkinson's disease	0.15	1.2	
	Motor neuron disease	0.01	0.05	0.05
75+	Dementia***	15	67	

* Per 1000 live births; ** requiring hospital admission; ***aged 65 years and over.

Carlisle study (Brewis et al., 1966) suggested that the combined prevalence of optic atrophy, ophthalmoplegia, cerebellar ataxia, Huntington's chorea, muscular dystrophy, syringomyelia, and cerebral tumour was 1 per 1000—equivalent to the prevalence of Parkinson's disease in that survey. The consequences for the neurology and rehabilitation services are not known, but are likely to be considerable.

Cerebral tumour

The incidence of all primary brain tumours in the USA in 1973 was estimated to be 0.08 per 1000 persons per year (Walker, Robins, & Weinfeld, 1985). The Carlisle study found an incidence of 0.07 per 1000 per year, and other studies (Walker et al., 1985) have found a rate as high as 0.15 per 1000. About 20% of the patients presenting with tumours in the USA had meningiomas.

It seems reasonable to use an estimated incidence of 8 primary and 8 secondary tumours per 100,000 population per year, requiring diagnosis and management. Four (20%) of the twenty patients with primary tumours are likely to have meningiomas and a further four will have a malignant tumour. There will be about 0.45 persons per 1000 with a cerebral tumour; the number who are disabled is unknown.

There is a major need for further surveys of the epidemiology of disabling problems that occur in people with primary and secondary brain tumours. Personal experience indicates that the long-term management of this clinical group leaves much to be desired (see Chapter 43).

Guillain–Barrè syndrome

Guillain–Barrè syndrome has an incidence of about 0.01 per 1000 persons per year (Bak, 1985). About 35% will have respiratory insufficiency and 17% will require ventilatory support. One recent study following up patients at a median 7 years after onset found that 73% were symptom free. About one-fifth have some disability (Vedeler, Wik, & Nyland, 1997).

Encephalitis and meningitis

Bacterial meningitis has an incidence of about 0.095 per 1000 per year (Brewis et al., 1966). Viral encephalitis has an incidence of 0.074 per 1000. Herpes simplex encephalitis is uncommon, but produces major long-term problems. The prevalence of long-term disability due to encephalitis and meningitis is unknown.

"General medicine"

A very large number of neurological problems are generated within the bounds of general medicine. A major book on this subject was published in 1989 (Aminoff, 1989). This book has 780 pages and covers a vast range of disorders including, for instance, the neurological associations of diabetes, sarcoidosis, fungal infections, haematological disorders, and pregnancy. It is impossible to estimate the epidemiological size of this large clinical area.

DISCUSSION

Age and neurological disability

No discussion of the epidemiology of neurological disability is complete without a mention of the influence of age, which has been apparent throughout the review of incidence and prevalence given in this chapter. Warren (1975) has suggested that, in terms of broad age groups for planning, a case can be made for looking at adult disability in four age groups:

(1) 16–24 (school leavers and young people)
(2) 25–54 (those developing families, jobs, and careers)
(3) 55–74 (those reaching the end of employment and in active retirement)
(4) 75 and older, of whom half have disabilities due to multiple causes.

Disabled school leavers and young adults are a particularly important group, but there are few published studies. There were over 340,000 young people between the ages of 16 and 29 years with a disability severe enough to be included in the UK OPCS national disability survey (Chamberlain, Guthrie, Kettle, & Stowe, 1993). They are expected to pass through the same developmental stages as their non-disabled peers, to leave home, develop a clear sexual identity, and define a role for themselves in the community through employment or other activities (Hallum, 1995). For those with complex impairments this is clearly difficult. To facilitate the transition to adulthood one study identified a clear need for reliable, accessible, and high-quality services that addressed all aspects of adult life, for example, health status, adult education, recreation, residential and vocational needs (Hanley-Maxwell, Whitney-Thomas, & Pogoloff, 1995). Another study of a large sample of physically disabled 18–25-year-olds who had serious health needs concluded that these needs were not being met by current "ad hoc" arrangements (Thomas, Bax, & Smyth, 1989). It found that the transition from school to adult life was being attempted without the necessary skills to foster independence. Worse, the young adults' health was deteriorating, they were isolated from their peers, and not receiving all the state benefits to which they were entitled. From epidemiological evidence we would expect 2 per 1000 young adults aged 16–18 years leaving school each year with physical or complex disability (Kettle, 1993).

In the study by Thomas et al. (1989) undertaken in two English health districts, one urban and one semi-rural, 111 people between the ages of 18 and 25 were identified. Of these, 42% had cerebral palsy; 17% spina bifida; 6% rheumatoid arthritis; 3% multiple sclerosis; 20% were unspecified. The remaining 15% comprised single instances of uncommon disorder such as Friedreich's ataxia, muscular dystrophy, tuberose sclerosis, and spondylitis.

It is likely that neurological disorders underlie the disability in most young adults. This preponderance would probably have been even more marked if epilepsy had been included in the study.

The problems occurring in disabled school leavers are of much importance. Thomas et al. (1989) found that about 56% were incontinent of urine and 54% incontinent of faeces; 30% had a kyphoscoliosis. Contractures of the legs were found in more than 50% of the sample, and 26% had upper limb contractures. Some 34% had problems with skin care. Communication problems were present in 56%—especially those with athetosis. An estimated 41% were completely unable to walk.

Planning implications of the epidemiological data

The data in this chapter have been collected with a view to providing information for those whose task it is to set up high-quality services for people with neurological disabilities. Some of the main points are listed here:

(1) The epidemiology of neurological disorders is characterised by the following:
   (a) There are a few common disorders, e.g., stroke and migraine.
   (b) There is a large number of uncommon disorders, which, taken together, comprise a substantial number and generate a major workload.

(2) Many patients have more than one problem. For instance, epilepsy may be accompanied by evidence of intellectual impairment. Many neurological disorders occur amongst elderly people, the resultant disability being due to a combination of factors including age-related problems, general frailty, as well as the neurological disorder itself.

(3) The number and range of disabling neurological disorders and symptoms is very large. There are over 100 disabling neurological symptoms, in marked contrast with other specialities, e.g., respiratory and cardiac disease, which each cause only 6 or 7 disabling problems.

(4) Many neurological disorders can now be treated. Therapies are available for some, previously untreatable, conditions such as multiple sclerosis, motor neurone disease, and intractable epilepsy. Additionally there is now the potential for reducing the incidence of some inherited conditions such as Huntington's disease. However there are still a huge number of patients who face many years of continued disablement. It is important to recognise that most conditions can be ameliorated in one way or another. However, this requires time, the ability to assess and reassess as necessary, considerable expertise, and knowledge of the likely course of the relevant disorder.

(5) Because some disorders are uncommon, the appropriate knowledge/facilities may not be available locally. Thus, for instance, hereditary ataxias and uncommon forms of muscular dystrophy and difficult epilepsy may require specialist expertise at supradistrict or subnational level. This must be allowed for in planning.

One in eight of all disabled people in the UK have a disability associated with nervous system disorders (Martin et al., 1989). However, nearly two in five of those most severely disabled report these disorders as a cause. Some of the disabilities/handicaps experienced by neurological patients are the same, or similar, to those experienced by a large number of patients with non-neurological disorders. For instance, major mobility problems can occur in patients with asthma, rheumatoid arthritis, and chronic back pain. All these groups require the advice and help of a local mobility service with regard to housing, transport, footwear, wheelchairs, etc.

Similarly, many disabled people have major problems relating to education, employment and recreation. This is the basis for the suggestion made elsewhere regarding generic provision (Royal College of Physicians, 1986). The rehabilitation of neurological patients, amongst others, will rely to a considerable extent on the availability of these services. Some neurological disorders do need to be dealt with locally—despite being uncommon. Thus, a patient with severe bulbar palsy due to motor neurone disease will be unfit to travel far. Local expertise is required to deal with dysphagia and other problems associated with bulbar/pseudobulbar palsy.

The previous analysis can be used as a basis for planning neurological disability services. It will be recognised that the analysis is to a considerable extent incomplete, and it is clear that there is much scope for research in this area, particularly for the rarer conditions, but also for some aspects of the more common conditions. For instance, reliable data are required on the prevalence of impairment and disability due to head injury. Current studies, based on small clinical samples, tend to have differential case ascertainment, which makes comparison very difficult. Similarly, data are required about the number of people who have major disorders of, for example, swallowing.

The epidemiological evidence strongly supports the need both for specific neurological expertise (relating to diagnosis, specific treatment, the giving of an accurate prognosis, and the management of the impairment such as spasticity), and also for rehabilitative input, which might be concerned with other matters such as wheelchair provision and advice regarding employment and driving. It is important that those concerned with planning should clearly recognise that much can be done to lessen the disabling and handicapping results of neurological disease.

Some other current issues

A chapter of this type is most likely to be used if it illuminates and informs debate about some of the contentious issues of the day. It must also provide the basis for planning in clinical practice. For this reason, it seems worth identifying some of the issues that are currently having to be addressed by the National Health Service.

Organisation of service

(1) Should neurological rehabilitation be a defined discipline? If so, why? What should be the relationship to clinical neurology and to rehabilitation medicine?
(2) What should be the relationship to allied disciplines such as geriatrics and palliative care? Can the boundaries of the subject be defined?
(3) What should be the role of primary care in the management of this important group?
(4) Should the notion of a community rehabilitation service be supported? What is it? What epidemiological evidence supports the concept?
(5) What is the present use of nursing homes and younger disabled units by this group? Are the needs of clients being met? What should the use of these facilities be in the future?

Professional input

(1) What is the role of doctors? Can the role be defined? Should it be increased or reduced?
(2) Should the present arrangement of separate professional (physiotherapy, occupational therapy, and speech therapy) input be changed? Is a generic training programme indicated? Is there scope for generic therapists?
(3) How can social workers be incorporated into the picture?

   Psychology. Psychological problems are generally recognised as being important. The nature of the psychological changes occurring in disease are not well described. How can psychological skills be made more available? What are the training implications for doctors, therapists, and nurses? What are the research implications? Should there be a substantial increase in the number of psychologists?

Audit

Audit standards and care pathways are being developed. How can a knowledge of the epidemiology assist this process?

Age

(1) How should the problem of disabled school leavers be dealt with? How many clients are there? What are their needs?

(2) How should the 65+ interface be approached. Is such an age demarcation justified on any grounds—practical, historical, biological, epidemiological?

Problem orientation

It appears that patients with different diseases often generate similar problems. (A patient with multiple sclerosis may experience problems related to mobility, self care, and continence. Similar problems occur in patients with Parkinson's disease and traumatic brain injury as well as with non-neurological conditions such as rheumatoid arthritis.) Is there a case for organising some services on this basis rather than of disease? What epidemiological data exist? If it is true that most diseases follow a reasonably predictable course involving defined stages involving a particular set of problems, why is this not used for longitudinal planning?

Hospitals

(1) What use is currently made of hospitals by patients with neurological disability? What problems are experienced? What are the needs of patients?
(2) What are the training and resource implications?
(3) Should there be defined rehabilitation wards in major hospitals? Should these be structured on the basis of age, disease, problems, or a combination of two or more of these?
(4) What use could/should be made of community hospitals by this group of patients?

Costs

(1) What NHS costs are generated by patients with neurological disability? Can the costs be broken down into meaningful groups?
(2) Is there the opportunity for the more effective use of resources (opportunity costs)?

   These questions represent some of those currently being asked. Each one has an epidemiological dimension. However, no attempt is made in this chapter to deal comprehensively with each question. Rather it is hoped that the contents of the chapter may provide a basis for debate.

Finally

The epidemiology of disabling neurological disorders is clearly of much importance. Data needs to be made available for planners and others in an easily understandable form. There is much scope for further research as outlined in the chapter, particularly on the consequences of the disorders at the population level. Disabled people, particularly, have a vested interest in ensuring that the amount and quality of information is improved so that they have the evidence with which to support the case for improved services.

REFERENCES

Aminoff, M.J. (Ed.). (1989). *Neurology and general medicine*. New York: Churchill Livingstone.

Badley, E.M. (1995). The genesis of handicap: Definition, models of arrangement, and role of external factors. *Disability and Rehabilitation, 17,* 53–62.

Bak, P. (1985). Guillain–Barrè syndrome in a Danish County. *Neurology, 35,* 207–211.

Bamford, J., Sandercock, P., Dennis, M., Warlow, C., Jones, L., McPherson, K., Vessy, M., Fowler, G., Molyneux, A., Hughes, T., Burn, J., & Wade, D. (1988). A prospective study of acute cerebrovascular disease in the community: The Oxfordshire Community Stroke Project 1981–86. 1. Methodology, demography and incident cases of first-ever stroke. *Journal of Neurology, Neurosurgery and Psychiatry, 51,* 1373–1380.

Bamford, J., Sandercock, P., Warlow, C., & Gray, M. (1986). Why are stroke patients admitted to hospital? The experience of the Oxfordshire Community Stroke Project. *British Medical Journal, 292,* 1369–1372.

Beard, C.M., Kokmen, E., O'Brien, P.C., & Kurland, L.T. (1995). The prevalence of dementia is changing over time in Rochester, Minnesota. *Neurology, 45,* 75–79.

Bencsik, K., Rajda, C., Klivenyi, P., Jardanhazy, T., & Vecsei, L. (1998). The prevalence of multiple sclerosis in the Hungarian city of Szeged. *Acta Neurologica Scandinavica, 97*(5), 315–319.

Ben-Shlomo, Y. (1997). The epidemiology of Parkinson's disease. *Baillieres Clinical Neurology, 6,* 55–68.

Bille, B. (1997). A 40-year follow-up of school children with migraine. *Cephalalgia, 17,* 488–491.

Bonita, R., Solomon, N., & Broad, J.B. (1997). Prevalence of stroke and stroke-related disability: Estimates from the Aukland stroke studies. *Stroke, 28,* 1898–1902.

Boyle, C.A., Decoufle, P., & Yeargin-Allsopp, M. (1994). Prevalence and health impact of developmental disabilities in US children. *Pediatrics, 93,* 399–403.

Boyle, C.A., Yeargin-Allsopp, M., Doernberg, N.S., Holmgreen, P., Murphy, C.C., & Scendel, D.E. (1996). Prevalence of selected developmental disabilities in children 3–10 years of age: The Metropolitan Atlanta Developmental Disabilities Surveillance program, 1991. Morbidity and mortality weekly report. *CDC Surveillance Summaries, 45,* 1–14.

Breteler, M.M., de Groot, R.R., van Romunde, L.K., & Hofman, A. (1995). Risk of dementia in patients with Parkinson's disease, epilepsy, and severe head trauma: A register-based follow-up study. *American Journal of Epidemiology 142,* 1300–1305.

Brewis, M., Poskanzer, D.C., Rolland, C., & Miller, H. (1966). Neurological disease in an English city. *Acta Neurologica Scandinavica, 42*(Suppl. 24) 1–89.

Carolei, A., Marini, C., Di Naploi, M., Di Gianfilippo, G., Santalucia, P., Baldassarre, M., De Matteis, G., & di Orio, F. (1997). High stroke incidence in the prospective community-based L'Aquila registry (1994–1998): First year's results. *Stroke, 28,* 2500–2506.

Chamberlain, M.A., Guthrie, S., Kettle, M., & Stowe, J. (1993). *An assessment of health and related needs of physically disabled people*. Manchester, UK: Health Publication Unit.

Chancellor, A.M., & Warlow, C.P. (1992). Adult onset motor neuron disease: Worldwide mortality, incidence and distribution since 1950. *Journal of Neurology, Neurosurgery and Psychiatry, 55,* 1106–1115.

Cockerell, O.C., Eckle, I., Goodridge, D.M.G., Sander, J.W.A., & Shorvon, S.D. (1995). Epilepsy in a population of 6000 re-examined: Secular trends in first attendance rates, prevalence and prognosis. *Journal of Neurology, Neurosurgery and Psychiatry, 58,* 570–576.

Cockerell, O.C., Goodbridge, D.M.G., Brodie, D., Sander, J.W.A.S., & Shorvon, S.D. (1996). Neurological disease in a defined population: The results of a pilot study in two general practices. *Neuroepidemiology, 15,* 73–82.

Dean, G., Quigley, M., & Goldacre, M. (1994). Motor neuron disease in a defined English population: Estimates of incidence and mortality. *Journal of Neurology, Neurosurgery and Psychiatry, 57,* 450–454.

de Rijk, M.C., Tzourio, C., Breteler, M.M., Dartigues, J.F., Amaducci, L., Lopez-Pousa, S., Manabens-Bertran, J.M., Alperovitch, A., & Rocca, W.A. (1997). Prevalence of parkinsonism and Parkinson's disease in Europe: The EUROPARKINSON Collaborative Study. European Community Concerted Action on the Epidemiology of Parkinson's disease. *Journal of Neurology, Neurosurgery & Psychiatry, 62,* 10–15.

Ellekjaer, H., Holmen, J., Indredavik, B., & Terent, A. (1997). Epidemiology of stroke in Innherred, Norway, 1994 to 1996: Incidence and 30-day case fatality rate. *Stroke, 28,* 2180–2184.

Fong, K.Y., Yu, Y.L., Chan, Y.W., Kay, R., Chan, J., Yang, Z., Kwan, M.C., Leung, K.P., Li, P.C., Lam, T.H., & Cheung, R.T. (1996). Motor neuron disease in Hong Kong Chinese: Epidemiology and clinical picture. *Neuroepidemiology, 15,* 239–245.

Ford, H.L., Gerry, E., Airey, C.M., Vail, A., Johnson, M.H., & Williams, D.R. (1998). The prevalence of multiple sclerosis in the Leeds Health Authority. *Journal of Neurology, Neurosurgery and Psychiatry, 64,* 605–610.

Geddes, J.M., Fear, J., Pickering, A., Tennant, A., Hillman, M., & Chamberlain, M.A. (1996). Prevalance of self-reported stroke in a population in Northern England. *Journal of Epidemiological and Community Health, 50,* 140–143.

Goodridge, D.M.G., & Shorvon, S.D. (1983). Epileptic seizures in a population of 6,000: Part 1. Demography, diagnosis and classification, and the role of the hospital services. *British Medical Journal, 287,* 641–644.

Grether, J.K., Cummins, S.K., & Nelson, K.B. (1992). The California Cerebral Palsy Project. *Paediatric and Perinatal Epidemiology, 6,* 339–351.

Hagberg, B., Hagberg, C., Olow, I., & van Wendt, L. (1996). The changing panorama of cerebral palsy in Sweden: VII. Prevalence and origin in the birth year period 1987–90. *Acta Paediatrica, 85,* 954–960.

Hallum, A. (1995). Disability and the transition to adulthood: Issues for the disabled child, the family and the paediatrician. *Current Problems in Paediatrics, 25,* 12–50.

Hanley-Maxwell, C., Whitney-Thomas, J., & Pogoloff, S.M. (1995). The second shock: A qualitative study of parents' perspectives and needs during their child's transition from school to adult life. *Journal of the Association of Persons with Severe Handicaps, 20,* 3–15.

Harris, A.I. (1971). *Handicapped and impaired in Great Britain: Part 1.* London: Office of Population Censuses and Surveys, Her Majesty's Stationery Office.

Hauser, W.A., Annegers, J.F., & Rocca, W.A. (1996). Descriptive epidemiology of epilepsy: Contributions of population-based studies from Rochester, Minnesota. *Mayo Clinic Proceedings 71,* 576–586.

Hebert, R., & Brayne, C. (1995). Epidemiology of vascular dementia. *Neuroepidemiology, 14,* 240–257.

Hendrie, H.C. (1997). Epidemiology of Alzheimer's disease. *Geriatrics, 52*(Suppl. 2), S4–8.

James, C.M., Harper, P.S., & Wiles, C.M. (1994). Motor neurone disease: A study of prevalence and disability. *Quarterly Journal of Medicine, 87,* 693–699.

Jennett, B. (1998). *The Epidemiology of neurological disorders*. London: BMJ Books.

Kettle, M. (1993). *Evaluating the Leeds Young Adult Team*. Leeds, UK: Rheumatology & Rehabilitation Research Unit.

King's Fund Forum. (1988). Treatment of stroke. *British Medical Journal, 297,* 126–128.

Kokmen, E., Beard, C.M., O'Brien, P.C., & Kurland, L.T. (1996). Epidemiology of dementia in Rochester. *Mayo Clinic Proceedings, 71,* 275–282.

Kurtzke, J.F. (1982). The current neurologic burden of illness and injury in the United States. *Neurology, 32,* 1207–1214.

Kusumi, M., Nakashima, K., Harada, H., Nakayama, H., & Takahashi, K. (1996). Epidemiology of Parkinson's disease in Yonago City, Japan: Comparison study with 12 years ago. *Neuroepidemiology, 15,* 210–207.

Larsson, B., Bille, B., & Pedersen, N.L. (1995). Genetic influence in headaches: A Swedish twin study. *Headache, 35,* 513–519.

Lavados, P.M., & Tenhamm, E. (1997). Epidemiology of migraine headache in Santiago, Chile: A prevalence study. *Cephalalgia, 17,* 770–777.

Lee, L.H., & Olness, K.N. (1997). Clinical and demographic characteristics of migraine in urban children. *Headache, 37,* 269–276.

Letenneur, L., Commenges, D., Dartigues, J.F., & Barberger-Gateau, P. (1994). Incidence of dementia and Alzheimer's disease in elderly community residents of south-western France. *International Journal of Epidemiology, 23,* 1256–1261.

Lipton, R.B. (1997). Diagnosis and epidemiology of paediatric migraine. *Current Opinion in Neurology, 10,* 231–236.

Lipton, R.B., Stewart, W.F., & von Korff, M. (1997). Burden of migraine: Societal costs and therapeutic opportunities. *Neurology, 48*(Suppl. 3), S4–9.

MacGillivray, I., & Campbell, D.M. (1995). The changing pattern of cerebral palsy in Avon. *Paediatric and Perinatal Epidemiology, 9,* 146–155.

Martin, J., & White, A. (1988). *OPCS surveys of disability in Great Britain: Report 1*. The prevalence of disability among adults. London: OPCS Social Survey Division, Her Majesty's Stationery Office.

Martin, J., White, A., & Melter, H. (1989). *OPCS surveys of disability in Great Britain: Report 4. Disabled adults: Services, transport and employment*. London: OPCS Social Survey Division, Her Majesty's Stationery Office.

McDonnell, G.V., & Hawkins, S.A. (1998). An epidemiologic study of multiple sclerosis in Northern Ireland. *Neurology, 50*, 423–428.

Medical Disability Society. (1988). *The management of traumatic brain injury*. London: The Development Trust for the Young Disabled.

Michel, P., Pariente, P., Dura, G., Drefus, J.P., Chabriat, H., Henry, P., & Drefus, J.P. (1996). MIG-ACCESS: A population-based nationwide, comparative survey of access to care in migraine in France. *Cephalalgia, 16*, 50–55.

Millar, J.H.D. (1980). Multiple sclerosis in Northern Ireland. In F.C. Rose (Ed.), *Clinical neuroepidemiology* (pp. 222–227). London: Pitman Medical.

Mittenberg, W., & Burton, D.B. (1994). A survey of treatments for post-concussive syndrome. *Brain Injury, 8*, 429–437.

Moscato, B., Trevisan, M., & Willer, B. (1994). The prevalence of traumatic brain injury and co-occurring disabilities in national household survey of adults. *Journal of Neuro-Psychiatry and Clinical Neurosciences, 6*, 134–142.

Murphy, N., Confavreux, C., Haas, J., Konig, N., Roullet, E., Sailer, M., Swash, M., Young, C., & Merot, J.L. (1998). Quality of life in multiple sclerosis in France, Germany, and the United Kingdom. *Journal of Neurology, Neurosurgery and Psychiatry, 65*, 460–466.

National Heath Service Executive. (1996). *Burdens of disease*. London: NHS.

Newrick, P.G., & Langton Hewer, R. (1984). Motor neurone disease: Can we do better? *British Medical Journal, 287*, 539–542.

Ogura, C., Nakamoto, H., Uema, T., Yamamoto, K., Yonemori, T., & Yoshimura, T. (1995). Prevalence of senile dementia in Okinawa, Japan. *International Journal of Epidemiology, 24*, 373–380.

Orji, G.I., & Iloeje, S.O. (1997). Childhood migraine in Nigeria: I. A community-based study. *West African Journal of Medicine, 16*, 208–217.

Oxford Concise Dictionary. (1995) (9th edn) Oxford: Clarendon Press.

Palencia, R., & Sinovas, M.I. (1997). Prevalence of migraine in a sample population of school children. *Revista de Neurologia, 25*, 1879–1882.

Petterson, B., Nelson, K.B., Watson, L., & Stanley, F. (1993). Twins, triplets, and cerebral palsy in births in Western Australia in the 1980s. *British Medical Journal, 307*, 1239–1243.

Pharoah, P.O., Cooke, T., Johnson, M.A., King, R., & Mutch, L. (1998). Epidemiology of cerebral palsy in England and Scotland, 1984–9. *Archives of Disease in Childhood—Fetal and Neonatal, 79*, F21–25.

Pharoah, P.O., Platt, M.J., & Cooke, T. (1996). The changing epidemiology of cerebral palsy. *Archives of Disease in Childhood—Fetal and Neonatal, 75*, F169–173.

Pina, M.A., Ara, J.R., Modrego, P.J., Morales, F., & Capablo, J.L. (1998). Prevalence of multiple sclerosis in the sanitary district of Calatayud, Northern Spain: Is Spain a zone of high risk for this disease? *Neuroepidemiology, 17*, 258–64.

Rajput, A.H., Offord, K.P., Beard, M., & Kurland, L.T. (1984). Epidemiology of Parkinsonism: Incidence, classification and morality. *Annals of Neurology, 16*, 278–282.

Razdan, S., Kaul, R.L., Motta, A., Kaul, S., Bhatt, R.K. (1994). Prevalence and pattern of major neurological diorders in rural Kashmir (India) in 1986. *Neuroepidemiology, 13*, 113–119.

Roman, G. (1998). Amyotrophic lateral sclerosis. In *The epidemiology of neurological disorders*. C.N. Martyn & R.A.C. Hughes (Eds.). London: BMJ Books.

Rothwell, P.M., & Charlton, D. (1998). High incidence and prevalence of multiple sclerosis in south east Scotland: Evidence of a genetic predisposition. *Journal of Neurology, Neurosurgery and Psychiatry, 64*, 730–735.

Royal College of Physicians. (1986). *Physical disability in 1986 and beyond*. London: Author.

Russell, M.B., Rasmussen, B.K., Fenger, K., & Olsen, J. (1996). Migraine without aura and migraine with aura are distinct clinical entities: A study of four hundred and eighty four male and female migraineurs from the general population. *Cephalalgia, 16*, 239–245.

Russell, M.B., Rasmussen, B.K., Thorvaldsen, P., & Olsen, J. (1996). Prevalence and sex distribution of different forms of migraine. *Ugeskrift for Lager, 158*, 1369–1372.

Sakai, F., & Igarashi, H. (1997). Prevalence of migraine in Japan. *Cephalalgia, 17*, 15–22.

Shahar, E., McGovern, P.G., Pankow, J.S., Doliszny, K.M., Smith, M.A., Blackburn, H., & Luepker, R.V. (1997). Stroke rates during the 1980s: The Minnesota Stroke Survey. *Stroke, 28*, 275–279.

Shepherd, D.I., & Downie, A.W. (1980). A further prevalence study of multiple sclerosis in North-East Scotland. *Journal of Neurology, Neurosurgery and Psychiatry, 43*, 310–315.

Shorvon, S.D. (1996). The epidemiology and treatment of chronic and refractory epilepsy. *Epilepsia, 37*(Suppl. 2) S1–S3.

Silverb, A.G., & Carlsson, G. (1986). Head injuries in a population study. *Acta Neurochirurgica, 36*, 13–15.

Sinha, G., Corry, P., Subesinghe, D., Wild, J., & Levene, M.I. (1997). Prevalence and type of cerebral palsy in a British ethnic community: The role of consanguinity. *Developmental Medicine & Child Neurology, 39*, 259–262.

Sosin, D.M., Sachs, J.J., & Smith, S.M. (1989). Head injury associated deaths in the USA from 1979–1986. *Journal of the American Medical Association, 262*, 2251–2255.

Sosin, D.M., Sniezek, J.E., & Thurman, D.J. (1996). Incidence of mild and moderate brain injury in the United States in 1991. *Brain Injury, 10*, 47–54.

Statistics Canada. (1988). *The health and activity limitations survey: Users guide*. Ottawa, Canada: Disability Database Program, Statistics Canada.

Sutcliffe, R.L., & Meara, J.R. (1995). Parkinson's disease epidemiology in the Northampton District, England. *Acta Neurologica Scandinavia, 92*, 443–450.

Tandberg, E., Larsen, J.P., Nessler, E.G., Riise, T., & Aarli, J.A. (1995). The epidemiology of Parkinson's disease in the county of Rogaland, Norway. *Movement Disorders, 10*, 541–549.

Tedman, B.M., Young, C.A., & Williams, I.R. (1997). Assessment of depression in patients with motor neuron disease and other neurologically disabling illness. *Journal of the Neurological Sciences, 152*(Suppl. 1), S75–79.

Tennant, A. (1995). Epidemiology of head injury. In M.A. Chamberlain, V.C. Neumann, & A. Tennant (Eds.), *Traumatic brain injury rehabilitation: Services, treatments and outcomes* (pp. 12–24). London: Chapman & Hall.

Tennant, A., Macdermott, N., & Neary, D. (1995). The long-term outcome of head injury: Implications for service planning. *Brain Injury, 9*, 595–605.

Thomas, A.P., Bax, M.C.O., & Smyth, D.P.C. (1989). *The health and social needs of young adults with physical disabilities*. Oxford, UK: Blackwell.

To, T., & Wu, K. (1995). Health care utilisation and disability of migraine: The Ontario health survey. *Canadian Journal of Public Health, 86*, 195–199.

Topp, M., Uldall, P., & Langhoff-Roos, J. (1997). Trends in cerebral palsy birth prevalence in eastern Denmark: Birth-year period 1979–86. *Paediatric and Perinatal Epidemiology, 11*, 451–460.

Truelson, T., Prescott, E., Gronbaek, M., Schnohr, P., & Boysen, G. (1997). Trends in stroke incidence: The Copenhagen City heart study. *Stroke, 28*, 1903–1907.

Vedler, C.A., Wik, E., & Nyland, H. (1997). The long-term prognosis of Guillain–Barre syndrome: Evaluation of prognostic factors including plasma exchange. *Acta Neurologica Scandinavica, 95*, 298–302.

Von Korff, M., Stewart, W.F., Simon, D.J., & Lipton, R.B. (1998). Migraine and reduced work performance: A population-based diary study. *Neurology, 50*, 1741–1745.

Wade, D.T., & Langton Hewer, R. (1985). Hospital admission for acute stroke: Who, for how long, and to what effect? *Journal of Epidemiology and Community Health, 39*, 347–352.

Walker, A.E., Robins, M., & Weinfeld, F.D. (1985). Epidemiology of brain tumours: The national survey of intracranial neoplasms. *Neurology, 35*, 219–226.

Warlow, C.P. (1998). Epidemiology of stroke. *Lancet, 352*(Suppl. 111), 1–4.

Warren, M. (1975). The prevalence of disability. *Journal of the Royal College of Physicians of London, 23*, 171–175.

Webster's. (1971). *3rd International Dictionary*. Encyclopedia Britannica Inc. Pub. GeC Merriam & Co.

Wilkinson, P.R., Wolfe, C.D., Warburton, F.G., Rudd, A.G., Howard, R.S., Ross-Russell, R.W., & Beech, R.R. (1997). A long-term follow up of stroke patients. *Stroke, 28*, 507–512.

World Health Organization. (1980). *The international classification of impairments, disabilities, and handicaps*. Geneva: Switzerland, Author.

Young, C.A., Tedman, B.M., & Williams, I.R. (1995). Disease progression and perceptions of health in patients with motor neurone disease. *Journal of the Neurological Sciences, 129*(Suppl.), 50–53.

Zielinsky, J.J. (1982). Epidemiology. In J. Laidlaw & A. Richens (Eds.), *A textbook of epilepsy* (pp. 16–33). Edinburgh, UK: Churchill Livingstone.

2. The rehabilitation process: A neurological perspective

C.D. Ward   S. McIntosh

The aim of this chapter of this book is to describe rehabilitation from the point of view of a neurologically trained physician. After considering some defining principles, we outline the stages of the team-based rehabilitation process and then discuss referral criteria for rehabilitation programmes. Finally, we describe rehabilitation neurology as a clinical activity.

DEFINING PRINCIPLES

International classification of dimensions of disablement

The World Health Organisation (1980) distinguished three dimensions of disablement. These are linked by the concept of function, which is fundamental to rehabilitation. *Impairments* are defined as alterations in anatomy or physiology (bodily structure or function), for example fracture of the femur or recurrent laryngeal nerve palsy. *Disabilities* are restrictions in the performance of functions, such as walking or communicating. A recent revision of the scheme (WHO, 2001) terms this dimension as "activity". *Handicaps* are defined in the WHO classification as restrictions in fulfilment of social functions (for example paid employment), referred to in the revision as "participation". The revised scheme usefully draws attention to environmental factors as a fourth dimension of disablement. A primary aim of rehabilitation is to optimise function. This is achieved through measures designed to reduce the impairments and disabilities which in various ways impede social function. Disabilities can often be reduced by changes in the physical and social environment rather than in the individual.

Disadvantage, reflected in the frustrations experienced by individuals as a result of disease or injury, is a rehabilitation concept that extends somewhat further than handicap as defined by the WHO. Difficulties in social participation ("handicap") are usually a dominant source of disadvantage but negative personal experiences—for example, grief, shame, or pain—also cause disease-related disadvantage. The literature on *quality of life* attempts to capture the idea that personal experience as well as objective function should be taken into account in assessing the full impact of disease or injury.

Definitions of rehabilitation

Rehabilitation is difficult to define in a medical context (McLellan, 1997) and there is no generally accepted definition. WHO concepts of disablement suggest a definition such as: "the use of all possible means to reduce the impact of disease, and to maximise the social participation of people with impairments and disabilities". Other definitions are broader in scope, referring to maximising an individual's potential, or to optimising "physical, psychological, and social function". McLellan (1997) emphasises the active nature of rehabilitation and its educational basis, but does not adequately capture the processes of change that can occur around a disabled person as a result of rehabilitation, even when no change can occur in the individual. Some definitions implicitly assume that rehabilitation is a process of returning to a former level of function, but for practical purposes a definition should also cover the similar processes required for people with static or deteriorating conditions. We define rehabilitation as follows: "Rehabilitation is the active participation of a disabled person and others to reduce the impact of disease and disability on daily life."

Attributes of rehabilitation

Several attributes distinguish rehabilitation from other healthcare processes. First, in contrast to much medical treatment, rehabilitation focuses on differences as well as similarities between people. We can define impairments in terms of norms for biological characteristics, and disabilities/activities in terms of population norms such as the time to drink a given volume of cold water, or the time to walk 10 metres. It is even possible (although more difficult) to devise norms for levels of social participation, based on evidence such as employment levels in a relevant population of able-bodied people. However, it is much more difficult to think of individuals' levels of disadvantage normatively: Lack of social contacts, or unemployment, may be far more disadvantageous for one individual than for another. The implication for rehabilitation is that its starting point is an assessment of an individual's specific feelings and aspirations (Maitz & Sachs, 1995; Watts & Perlesz, 1999).

A second characteristic of rehabilitation is that it requires the active engagement of a client (or "patient") with at least one individual who is capable of helping to achieve a chosen goal. As an active process, rehabilitation is distinguished both from services supplied to the non-participating patient (care) and from spontaneous improvement in the patient (recuperation). The client's ability to cooperate may be limited, for example following severe brain injury, but rehabilitation can never, by definition, be forced on an unwilling subject. Professionals are not sufficiently aware of the fact that many disabled people seek support and care without wishing for any form of rehabilitation: they have no desire for changes or improvements in their daily lives.

Rehabilitation brings about change through time-limited *interventions*, which have foreseeable and measurable outcomes. Outcomes can take the form of (1) a quantal improvement in a previously static situation or (2) a steepening or a qualitative change in the process of recovery from an acute injury. The first rehabilitation services were developed to "fix up" physically injured troops for either combat duty or civilian employment, but our definition of rehabilitation also includes processes designed to improve the outcome (in terms of function, quality of life, and disadvantage) of a deteriorating condition such as Parkinson's disease (Ward, 2000). An important aspect of the rehabilitation programme for people with chronic disability is the prevention of future impairment and disability.

To summarise, the aim of rehabilitation is to reduce disadvantages associated with disease and disablement. An intervention (which is always time-limited) can be classified as a component of rehabilitation provided it is active and collaborative. Rehabilitation in its broadest sense may be needed by people with any neurological impairment—whether psychological or physical, static, deteriorating, or improving, mild or severe—which interferes with daily life.

Does rehabilitation work?

Since the previous edition of this book there has been a rapid accumulation of evidence that rehabilitation is effective (Sinclair & Dickinson, 1998; Turner-Stokes, 1999). Nevertheless, it is still widely believed that the benefits of rehabilitation are unproven. There are several reasons for this unjustified reputation: conceptual confusions regarding the nature and aims of rehabilitation, the complexity of rehabilitation processes, methodological shortcomings of much published research, and also, perhaps, prejudices against scientific evaluation on the part of some rehabilitation clinicians.

As we have tried to show, rehabilitation is not a unitary process but is based on a complex cluster of concepts. Moreover, rehabilitation can occur in many social and medical settings and may have very diverse goals. For these reasons the question "Does rehabilitation work?" needs a specific context: What processes are effective, and in what way? One type of answer to these questions is very general. The principles of rehabilitation are those of good management, which depends on a coordinated, goal-directed, "client"- or "customer"-centred approach (Mearns & Thorne, 1988). Good business management is justified by increased profits, but does good rehabilitation improve outcomes for neurological patients? There is increasing evidence that it does, for example in spinal injury (Inman, 1999), brain injury (Rice-Oxley & Turner-Stokes, 1999; Rose & Johnson, 1996), and multiple sclerosis (Ko Ko, 1999).

There have been many investigations of the effectiveness of component rehabilitation processes such as speech therapy. This approach provides more focus than merely asking "Does rehabilitation work?" but can still pose similar problems. For example speech therapy, like other types of therapy, involves a range of activities applied to a range of different impairments, disabilities, and disadvantages. The question "Is speech therapy effective?" could be as meaningless as asking "Is abdominal surgery effective?" Randomised controlled trials (RCTs) with negative results—for example on the effectiveness of aphasia therapy in stroke (Lincoln et al., 1984)—are easily over-interpreted. More sophisticated research designs are needed, particularly to produce evidence that individual rehabilitation goals have been achieved (Pentland & Macpherson, 1994; Wood, McRea, Wood, & Meeriman, 1999).

Many RCTs have demonstrated the efficacy of unidisciplinary interventions, but they too must be interpreted cautiously. When an intervention ameliorates an impairment it does not necessarily constitute rehabilitation.

Should neurologists be involved?

The speciality of rehabilitation medicine can never provide a comprehensive service for all people with disabilities and since neurological disorders account for a large proportion of all severe and complex disabilities, neurologists should expect to make a significant contribution to medical rehabilitation. Many neurologically trained physicians do in practice become skilled in small-scale rehabilitative programmes, for example in outpatient clinics, but are inhibited from larger scale activities partly by lack of resources and partly because of the medical culture in which they are trained and work.

Historically, British neurology has developed as a small speciality providing diagnostic services largely concentrated in regional units. Neurologists have not routinely been involved in the rehabilitation of people with neurological impairments (Langton Hewer & Wood, 1992).

The rehabilitation milieu is different from that of conventional clinical neurology. In the first place, the objectives of assessment are different. Neurological training is primarily concerned with the pathological significance of symptoms and signs: monocular visual loss with pain perhaps suggests optic neuritis, possibly multiple sclerosis; hemiplegia suggests a hemispheric lesion, perhaps a stroke; and so on. For rehabilitation purposes problems must be translated into functional terms: the symptoms of optic neuritis might cause anxiety, or perhaps loss of driving ability; hemiplegia has specific implications for walking and for transfers. To put it another way, neurological assessment classically seeks answers to two questions: "Where?" (what is the site of the lesion?); and "What?" (what is the pathological basis?). But rehabilitation neurology entails a third question, "So what?": what are the psychological, social, and physical consequences?

Interprofessional teamwork is a second aspect of rehabilitation that is in sharp contrast to the working practices of many neurologists. Nurses, therapists, clinical psychologists, social workers, and others have an important role in assessment as well as in treatment. The conventionally private doctor–patient relationship has a place in rehabilitation but there can be no doubt of the need to share much information between professionals and to be aware of the limitations of any one point of view.

A third distinctive feature of rehabilitation medicine is the close association of assessment and treatment. Neurology usually involves a *linear* process in which diagnosis (often achieved within 10 or 20 minutes) is followed in some patients by specific treatment. The clinical work of a British neurologist largely involves single clinical encounters for the purpose of diagnosis (Hopkins, Menken, & DeFriese, 1989). Rehabilitation assessment is more protracted, and is achieved *pari passu* with treatment. Members of the rehabilitation team adopt an empirical approach in which a session of treatment is itself a form of assessment: There is no absolute distinction between the two, no defined step from diagnosis to prescription to treatment. Moreover, in most conditions the diagnostic baseline is constantly changing as a result of deterioration, natural recovery, or response to treatment. The rehabilitation neurologist must therefore have a non-linear conception of management. Rehabilitation assessment initiates a programme that is repeatedly revised to take account of changes in the client and/or in the client's environment; such a reflexive approach does not necessarily come naturally to a conventionally trained neurologist.

A fourth point of distinction between conventional neurology and its rehabilitation counterpart is that it frequently strays into non-medical domains. It cannot ignore banalities such as garages and toilets that are not discussed in medical textbooks. This has discouraged many neurologists from what they see as a misuse of their specialised training. At the same time some non-medical professionals and some pressure groups have decried the "medical model" of disability. The claim in this chapter is simply that the medical model provides a perspective that is necessary in some situations. The medical model is incomplete in itself: Medical and non-medical factors are indissolubly linked in some situations, and particularly in those which neurologists most frequently encounter.

Thus, despite some features on the rehabilitation landscape seemingly alien to clinical neurologists, there is scope for neurological expertise to make contributions at all stages of the rehabilitation process. There is evidence that a substantial proportion of British neurologists currently provide rehabilitative services. Involving more neurologists in rehabilitation would require a large expansion of the speciality and, equally importantly, a radical change in training programmes (Ward, 1992).

To be clinically effective in rehabilitation, a neurologist will need to acquire expertise in the psychiatric as well as the behavioural and cognitive consequences of cerebral impairment. These aspects have been marginal to the training curriculum for British neurologists (neurological specialists in some countries, such as the US and Germany, at least routinely receive a broad grounding in general psychiatry). In addition to the crucial contribution of a clinical psychologist, the involvement of a neuropsychiatrist can greatly increase the quality of multidisciplinary rehabilitation, particularly for people with brain injury.

THE REHABILITATION PROCESS

This section outlines the successive stages of the rehabilitation process from referral to outcome. Although we will often have specialised hospital rehabilitation units in mind, the same principles apply to the whole range of environments in which neurological rehabilitation can and does take place—including routine neurology outpatient clinics.

The first step in rehabilitation is the identification of a patient or "client", which, as we shall see, is less straightforward than might be imagined (Webster, Daisley, & King, 1999). Then the rehabilitation issues must be identified and categorised—a process requiring specific clinical skills (some of which are mentioned in the final part of this chapter) as well as interprofessional collaboration. The next stage is the establishment of an overall plan to meet the individual's needs. This should involve the setting of outcome criteria for audit purposes. Usually, the plan is implemented through discrete steps or goals. The achievement of each goal represents an interim outcome. Meanwhile, monitoring of interim and final outcomes proceeds (Bauer, 1989; Chamberlain, 1988).

Who is the "client"?

The term "patient" is unfortunate because it implies a passive subject to whom treatment is applied by a doctor or therapist. We retain the word here for the sake of convention, but it is as well to remember that people even with severe disabilities may regard themselves as without medical problems and should not be termed "patients". Rehabilitation is subject to severe criticism when it fails to recognise the limitations of the medical model (Barnes, 1991; Oliver, 1990).

A person who is unconscious or who has impaired comprehension and communication needs an advocate to maximise the possibility of the person's own viewpoint being understood and respected. The advocate is usually a spouse or close relative, but may for example be a social worker or solicitor who is involved in negotiations with professionals on a client's behalf.

A divorced man aged 59 had hemiplegia and global aphasia. None of his children were prepared to care for him at home, but they mistrusted a woman who described herself as his common-law wife and offered to accommodate him; they claimed that prior to his stroke the relationship with this woman had not been close and suspected that she was trying to gain control over his money. She gave every appearance of being devoted to him. No-one could be sure of the man's own preferred future plan—institutional care or home life with his "girlfriend"? The situation was further complicated by the fact that a single social worker was an energetic advocate both for the man and the girlfriend: They were both her clients. With advice from a solicitor, the family eventually accepted the home solution.

It is important to recognise that the person with neurological deficits—the "patient"—is not the only legitimate focus of rehabilitation. Those who come into daily contact with the person, especially carers, may have their own requirements for information and practical advice (Gronwall, Wrightson, & Waddell, 1999; Harrison, 1987; Powell, 2001; Stewart, 1985). Some people with severe brain damage may be perceived as more or less "hopeless cases", and yet the full range of rehabilitative services, including clinical assessment, may be appropriate if the carers thereby gain more effective support.

A middle-aged woman who had had a haemorrhage from an anterior communicating artery aneurysm was resistant to all forms of structured therapy on account of her limited attention span, amnesia, behavioural problems, and lack of insight. Her desire was to return home and the staff of the hospital rehabilitation unit devoted most effort to liaising with her family, providing information, helping to resolve disagreements between her brother and her husband, and setting up a package of post-discharge services. These were designed to give a weekly programme of structured occupation that would interest her as well as providing relief for her husband. In this situation the husband and the brother were clients of the service in their own right, but the woman herself stood to gain by the arrangements that were agreed.

Channelling of rehabilitative effort towards the carer is legitimate provided it benefits the patient at least indirectly. On the other hand, there is a very real risk that the needs of carers may conflict with those of the person who is impaired. For every rehabilitative goal, therefore, the "client" must be clearly defined.

Who has the problem?

Perhaps the most critical step in the rehabilitation process is the identification of problems, since these are the raw material from which goals are derived. Consistent with the requirement to identify who is the client, we often need to ask ourselves who has the problem. Who perceives the need for a solution? The prime motivation for an intervention may come directly from the patient but there are other potential sources.

A young woman with severe disabilities due to multiple sclerosis was referred for insertion of a percutaneous endoscopic gastrostomy (PEG) tube. It transpired that many factors had led to the referral, including not only the anxieties of some professionals about the risk of food aspiration, but also practical issues concerning the time and effort required in assisting her with oral feeding. The woman herself was able to express a clear preference for continued oral feeding, even when the risks were explained to her. The "problem" in this case resided with professionals and carers rather than with the patient.

In assessing problems and establishing goals we can never fully realise a client-centred perspective, but we should make a constant effort to do so. Disability and disadvantage must be interpreted in terms of a complex network of physical, social,

and psychological elements forming the individual's "system" (Frude, 1991; Maitz & Sachs, 1995; von Bertanlanffy, 1968).

A previously confident middle-aged woman with Parkinson's disease found that her life was becoming restricted. She had recently completed a thesis and was under-occupied. She was reluctant to go out and meet people, or even to answer the phone. She found it increasingly difficult to join in conversations. These were symptoms of anxiety. But during the interview her husband repeatedly interrupted her own account of the problem, and contradicted her. He felt that she had sufficient occupation at home. Many of her difficulties stemmed partly from her husband's denial, and he was unconsciously contributing to her anxiety and social withdrawal. Her problems were located within a system comprising herself, her husband, and her social milieu. The situation improved without the use of drug treatment.

A person's system encompasses the social environment where concepts of "normality" and "disability" are defined, and hence there is a political aspect to the identification of problems. For example, policy decisions about the design of school buildings often determine whether wheelchair-users will have educational problems. Similarly, people with neurological impairments must contend with health and social services departments whose structures and policies may either create or remove problems. According to the social model of disability, the problem often resides not with the individual but with society.

A young man with severe epilepsy was referred to a day centre for people with physical disabilities. It was said that the centre could not accommodate him because his seizures would be a hazard to other users of the centre. It transpired that other people with epilepsy had been accepted at the centre, but that people with epilepsy were a cause of general anxiety among the staff, some of whom also felt that the centre should cater for "physical disability", which excluded seizures. In this case the epilepsy was a problem not just for the young man but also for part of his system, and the solution did not lie solely in drug treatment to reduce the frequency of seizures but required a change in the attitudes and policies of day centre staff.

Identifying and classifying problems

The WHO framework is necessary because the different dimensions of disablement are not reliably predictive of each other (Badley & Lee, 1987a,b; Bernspang, Asplund, Eriksson, & Fugl-Meyer, 1987; Granger, 1985). The neurologist can play a leading role in characterising impairments but must appreciate their human significance in the context of the individual's daily life and aspirations.

A man aged 38 with multiple sclerosis was deteriorating although still fully employed. He had a walking *disability* (his impairments affected the *activity* of walking) since he failed to meet normative criteria for walking such as the ability to walk unaided; to walk a standard 10 metre distance within a few seconds; to walk over rough ground at a normal pace; or to walk several miles without undue tiring. His multiple sclerosis could have caused this disability through a number of *impairments* In his case there was no cerebellar or sensory ataxia. The principal impairments were "scissoring" due to adductor spasm, and toe-striking due to excessive plantar flexion. Fatigue was due partly to the much higher energy requirement for his highly abnormal gait. To add to these impairments he had early flexion deformities of hips and knees, and also impaired confidence following a fall.

Assessment of his impairments allowed physiotherapy and botulinum toxin injections to be planned rationally.

Good medical practice has always given priority to the presenting complaint. In a similar way rehabilitation gives priority to the subjective impact of disease—the *disadvantage* it confers. Disadvantage is difficult to quantify and cannot be reliably inferred from disability. For example, inability to climb stairs is not often a severe disadvantage to a bungalow-dweller. Inability to speak would not be a disadvantage for a Trappist monk unless, as well might be the case, he suffered from a sense of loss of freedom to break his vow of silence at will. Situations of this type can often be translated into the revised WHO terminology, in which the concept of disadvantage is equated with limitations in social participation (WHO, 1997).

The man just described was not grossly disadvantaged at work, since his job was sedentary (he was able to *participate* in his occupational role). Walking difficulties restricted his family life since even the simplest shopping expeditions were slowed down. Physical exhaustion reduced his role (*participation*) at home. His abnormal gait constantly reminded him of his medical problems and of anxieties about the future. These factors sapped his confidence, affected his mood, and psychological as well as physical aspects of life were disadvantaged. These insights influenced the therapeutic programme.

A common medical response to disability is to focus exclusively on impairment, as though this was the person's "problem". According to this view the purpose of medical interventions is to "normalise" the patient. The disability movement rejects this form of medical normalisation as oppressive (Man, 1999; Oliver, 1990) because it makes unjustified assumptions about individuals' aspirations.

A young woman with cerebral palsy had undergone multiple operations in childhood because the main aim of both the parents and the doctors was to "normalise" her gait. At 26, her gait is awkward and effortful over even the shortest distances. In retrospect she believes that she should have been encouraged to make more use of a wheelchair at an earlier stage, and she wonders how much of the social and educational disruption caused by intensive medical management could have been avoided.

Whilst the terms "normal" and "abnormal" can have negative connotations in the context of impairments, there is no denying that disabled people seek to lead personal and social lives as rich in possibilities as those of others. This has implications for the types of residential, educational, employment, and recreational facilities that are planned. Medical rehabilitation could learn much from concepts of "normalisation" and "social role valorisation" that have been developed in the field of learning difficulties (see Flynn & Lemay, 1999; Wolfensberger, 1983).

Another unjustified assumption often made in rehabilitation is the equation of disability with dependency. Degree of dependency has a crucial influence on quality of life, and on the costs (both human and financial) of care. When it reduces autonomy, a fundamental human goal, dependency can often be assumed to be a source of disadvantage. However, endeavours to increase physical independence may sometimes conflict with other goals, including social fulfilment; moreover, for some people dependency is not altogether a disadvantage.

Many ethical and political issues are raised by concepts of disability, disadvantage, and dependency (Oliver, 1990). The disability movement disparages the all too ready assumption that it is always the patient/client who must adapt, and that our "normal" world is immutable. The rehabilitation programme should give priority to the client's interests, removing the source of a problem where possible, even if this involves changes in the human and physical environment (Rothwell, LaVigna, & Willis, 1999).

The WHO classification is too complex to be usable as a routine framework for classifying rehabilitation goals and outcomes. Simpler approaches have been proposed, for example Brown and Gordon's (1986) division of "rehabilitation indicators" into three domains: "skills" (which would include aspects of mobility and self-care), "activity patterns" (which are behavioural choices, reflecting psychological and social functioning), and "status" (including roles and occupations).

Disadvantage should form the focus of rehabilitation, and a classification scheme for disadvantages would simplify the process of routine assessment, documentation, and goal planning, and should ensure that major life domains are not overlooked. For many rehabilitation teams the agenda for rehabilitation planning is determined largely by the major categories of daily living activities (self care, mobility, etc.). These tend to form a short-list concerned with activities (disability) rather than with participation (handicap). When the list is extended to include more personal concerns it becomes long and unwieldy, with little chance of being applied routinely. The result is that crucial issues are not addressed.

A woman aged 22 had a subarachnoid haemorrhage just prior to the delivery by Caesarian section of her (first) baby. The child's father and grandparents proved highly capable of providing for the baby. Although the baby was brought to see her mother most evenings and occasionally stayed overnight, she did not feature explicitly in her mother's rehabilitation programme. The identified rehabilitation issues included communication, dressing, walking, etc., but not parenting.

The case history illustrates how an emphasis on function (especially physical function) fails to take future risks into account systematically. Risks of future psychological problems (e.g., alienation of a parent from a child) or of physical complications (e.g., falls or skin sores) should be routinely appreciated as part of the spectrum of disadvantages that rehabilitation can address. In our view, the lack of emphasis on risk as a component of disadvantage is a defect in the WHO classification.

Rehabilitation issues are often classified as "physical, psychological, social, or spiritual". The drawback with this scheme is that it is too close to the impairment domain, in which the functions of the mind and the body can be clearly separated. When disadvantages are considered, there is an intimate relationship between physical, psychological, social, and spiritual issues. We suggest that disadvantages—and rehabilitation targets—fall into four main groups, which correspond to a didactic mnemonic, "PILS": Prevention, Independence, Lifestyle, and Social context. "Prevention" refers to risks (see earlier). "Independence" refers to the traditional domain of rehabilitation, self care and mobility. "Lifestyle" signifies the roles and values that are unique to the individual. "Social context" refers to the human and physical environment, which has been given increased recognition in the 1997 WHO framework. These categories can be used as a framework first for describing presenting problems; second for summarising the present situation as a whole, including degree of dependency, taking account of assets as well as problems; and third for establishing a therapeutic plan, including a preventive strategy where relevant.

The rehabilitation contract

Effective rehabilitation is always based on an implicit contract, between the identified client (see earlier) and all others—professionals and non-professionals—who will be involved in the rehabilitation process. The agreement recognises a shared aim, based on a shared understanding of the client's aims and also of what can feasibly be achieved within a defined timescale. Where the client's (or professionals') understanding is limited or where expectations are thought to be unrealistic, a signed agreement is helpful. For example, someone with chronic pain might need to realise that a programme is designed to offer improved means of achieving a strategic goal such as a more normal social life, rather than total symptomatic cure. Whether the rehabilitation contract is implicit or explicit, aims must often be renegotiated as rehabilitation proceeds.

Can the professional team ever implement a rehabilitation strategy at variance with a client's own perceptions of needs? The possibility of conflict between professional and patient perceptions arises in many situations, but conflicts are especially difficult to resolve when a patient has reduced insight into the true nature of a problem. This may be because of organic brain damage (McGlynn & Schacter, 1989) or because of maladaptive psychological disorders. However, no rehabilitation programme is exempt from the need for a therapeutic contract and some common ground must be found between the client's and professional viewpoints. For example, a patient with hysterical paralysis might agree to the plan "to reduce the physical and psychological burden to other members of the family"; or "to resume a role in the community". In such circumstances the modalities chosen by the rehabilitation team (e.g., occupational therapy input, or advice) might not be those which the patient intuitively prefers (say, neurosurgery). Nevertheless, the therapeutic relationship remains viable provided the overall aim is shared by all parties: there can be differences about tactics, but not, ultimately, about strategy.

The rehabilitation aim

There is some confusion in the literature between an aim and a goal. As we define it, the rehabilitation aim is the *proposed* *overall outcome* that the client and others believe should be achievable in the long run. The rehabilitation aim is thus a composite picture of how things will turn out if the rehabilitation programme as a whole has been a success. To use political/military terminology, rehabilitation aims correspond to a *policy*. The policy is implemented through a *strategy* with stated objectives which are known as goals in rehabilitation. Subgoals correspond to the *tactics* that are used from day to day to carry out the strategy.

Without one overarching aim, therapy and nursing may continue indefinitely with no specific outcome and there are likely to be radical differences in purposes and expectations between clients and professionals. The concept of "life planning" has been developed for people with learning difficulties and is equally applicable in neurological rehabilitation.

For a mildly impaired person, the rehabilitation aim may be highly specific. For example in a person with neuropathy involving the hands the aim might be to remain at work, which might involve achieving a specific level of key-board skill through improved hand and arm posture. For a young man with severe closed head injury the aim might be to return home sufficiently independent for his parents to care for him while continuing to work full time; in another case, the goal might be full independence and sheltered employment.

Although it is essential to agree on an aim, reaching a consensus can be difficult. A person's aim often appears to professionals to be over-ambitious, for example the aim to resume training as a medical student following a severe head injury, or the aim of someone with chronic low back pain to be totally pain-free and fully employed in manual work. Nevertheless, such an aim might have to be accepted as a starting point. The rehabilitation aim is modified continuously by an educational process that involves not only the client but also professionals: outcomes often defy professional expectations.

At the outset, rehabilitation aims depend on the predicted prognosis. If a situation seems irretrievable, professionals often question whether it is "kind" to embark on rehabilitation. The answer must be that the plan should suit the context, but that there must *always* be an overall aim. Sometimes the prognosis is so poor that there might be reasons for an agreement among staff and family that active medical measures will not be taken in the event of an emergency such as a cardiac arrest. Nevertheless, medical staff have a responsibility to devise a plan to ensure that if the person does survive the outcome will be as satisfactory as possible. Early prognostication is often wrong and needs to be reviewed during the "reflexive" rehabilitation process we characterised earlier in this chapter.

A 17-year-old boy survived a severe head injury but remained in coma for several weeks, after which his responses remained very restricted. There were good reasons for assuming that survival was unlikely. Attempts to prevent or correct limb contractures caused him great distress and were not vigorously pursued by the staff responsible for the first phase of his management. On reaching the rehabilitation unit he had severe flexion contractures, which remained a major problem thereafter. On admission he was anarthric and dependent in all care. On discharge he had virtually normal verbal comprehension and conversational ability, was wheelchair independent, independent in many ADL tasks, and continued to improve subsequently. Aggressive early management of contractures would have hastened his discharge and improved the ultimate outcome.

In addition to prognosis, rehabilitation aims must take account of available resources. If someone following a stroke aims to return home, is it likely that the accommodation will be suitable, or more importantly that carers and helpers will be available? These questions recur in the detailed negotiation of specific goals but must be asked from the outset, lest a rehabilitation aim be predicated on false assumptions. This raises important ethical questions:

A young man was severely injured in a car driven by his 19-year-old girlfriend. He had multiple impairments due to brain injury. She was a very frequent visitor to the ward and eagerly participated in all care. She agreed to take him home for weekends. The possibility of her taking on his long-term care suggested itself, but it was found that they had not had plans to co-habit prior to the accident, and there was a danger that her own guilt about the accident would combine with pressure from the professional rehabilitation team to force her into a major long-term commitment.

Family support usually varies with age. Older patients are likely to have relatives of similar ages living with them who, although often expected and willing to care or nurse the person, may themselves have physical or cognitive impairments which increasing years can bring. Other relatives of older adults may take on a "carer" role for their family member while continuing employment and bringing up a family. Many women especially may find themselves looking after a parent with a neurological disability while also caring for young children and perhaps having to work part time. Similarly the younger children (under 18) of people with neurological impairments may find themselves in the role of "chief carer" and lose a part of their normal childhood years to caring.

There has been insufficient research on the emotive subject of effects of caring on children both as youngsters and later as adults. The nature of a rehabilitation programme, and its setting and duration, must take account of such factors if it is to be relevant to the person's future needs and the programme must not be based implicitly on the exploitation of unwilling or unsuitable carers. Once again there is an underlying political issue, concerning the role of carers, especially women, in relation to state-funded services.

Rehabilitation goals

Having agreed on one overall aim, the client and team must devise a workable strategy, typically consisting of a sequence of pragmatic, achievable goals. The process of negotiating goals (the term "goal-*setting*" is too prescriptive) is fundamental to rehabilitation. A rehabilitation aim such as "to return home" is mediated through many discrete short-term goals that should be formulated by a rehabilitation team. Goals can be categorised in hierarchies, with lower levels contributing to intermediate levels and so, ultimately, to the final outcome corresponding

to the overall rehabilitation aim. For example, the short-term goal "to achieve independent sitting without support" may be a preliminary to achieving standing balance, and then safe standing transfers, with a view to a planned discharge to live with a single carer. Thus, progress is monitored by the achievement of discrete, measurable gains.

Rehabilitation goals should be:

- directly *or indirectly* beneficial to the person (this condition allows for carer-centred aims)
- agreed between the rehabilitation team and the client or advocate (advocacy is required when a brain-injured person is incapable of entering into an agreement).

Many rehabilitation teams use the SMART acronym, requiring each goal to be:

- **S**pecific
- **M**easurable (at least in principle)
- **A**chievable (i.e., feasible both for the client and for the rehabilitation team, and timely)
- **R**elevant to rehabilitation aims
- **T**imed: achievable within a defined period of time.

In a hospital-based rehabilitation unit a short-term goal might be achieved within one or 2 weeks. Some short-term goals such as prevention of contractures are on-going, but interim outcome criteria (e.g., measures of range of joint movement) can be achieved within the suggested timescale.

Some supposed goals have no explicit relationship to the rehabilitation aim, or they may be too nebulous to be achievable or measurable. For example, a stated plan "to continue physiotherapy" is meaningless; and even relatively specific goals such as "to practise walking" need to be justified in terms of the programme as a whole. Is walking a strategic goal? What is the next relevant short-term goal for walking?

Each short-term goal requires at least one action. Each goal is the primary responsibility of an individual such as the client, a family member, or a professional: for example, the achieving of sitting balance might be assigned primarily to a physiotherapist.

Often, a major goal is approached by means of a programme of subgoals in which several or all team members participate. Thus, nurses or relatives (as well as the patient) could be involved in a programme to improve sitting balance. Similarly, although a speech therapist might be the prime mover in achieving the goal "to set up a structured speech exercise programme", family members and all members of the team should also be aware of their supportive roles. One of the difficulties in describing the essence of therapy is that a therapeutic programme usually combines specific professionally based elements with less specific components that are nevertheless important. In a well coordinated team, therapists and nurses pursue common therapeutic purposes through a variety of different activities. Routine procedures such as dressing or washing may often be implicated in several goals at once: promotion of independence, communication, remediation of hemi-neglect, prevention of contractures, prevention of shoulder pain, and so on.

Monitoring progress

Standard documentation encourages a systematic approach to rehabilitation, provides a record of progress and facilitates all forms of audit. An ideal documentation system has yet to be developed. The record should be headed by an explicit statement of the overall rehabilitation aims, which are updated at intervals, to reflect changing expectations. There should be an updatable list of problems, a serial record of impairments and disabilities, and a record of goals, actions, and outcomes. These stipulations are not unique to rehabilitation, being consistent with the principles of problem-oriented medical records (Petrie & McIntyre, 1979). There are clearly dangers in reducing the process of assessing an individual to checklists: real people can never be fully categorised. Effective rehabilitation requires all those involved to make a constant imaginative effort not to be constrained by prescribed routines.

One method of record keeping that we have experienced illustrates the process of goal-directed rehabilitation. In this model, a numbered list of problems was accumulated (see excerpt in Figure 2.1a for the following case):

John, a college student aged 19, suffered diffuse brain injury in a motorcycle accident on 20 January with a prolonged period of coma, and post-traumatic amnesia followed by steady recovery of function but with dysarthria, left spastic hemiparesis, and cognitive impairment, plus moderate behavioural difficulties. The aim was to return him to live with his parents and then to return to college. He continued to improve.

A continuing record of short-term goals was kept and reviewed weekly by the entire team (Figure 2.1b). The first column of the record refers to a numbered problem from the master list; the second column specifies a short-term goal relevant to the problem. The third column specifies the *action*, and who is responsible for carrying it out. The last column specifies the *date* at which the goal is to be achieved, and records whether

(a)

PROBLEM LIST		
No.	Problem	Date identified
7	Dependent in dressing	20 Feb
8	Impaired communication & social skills	20 Feb
9	Urinary incontinence	20 Feb
10	Left arm flexion contracture	27 Feb
11	Under-nourished	20 March
12	Mother's health problems	10 May
13	Uncertainty about which college course to register for	25 May

(b)

Rehabilitation aim:		*To return to college in September requiring minimal assistance in ADL; discharge to parents' care July*		
DATE	PROBLEM	GOAL	ACTION	BY WHEN
17 May	12	Find out if parents will be able to cope at discharge	Talk to father (Dr.)	24 May *(achieved)*
24 May	10	Full range of passive movement	Progressive splinting (OT)	13 June
24 May	7, 10	Place arm in sleeve independently	Supervised practice sessions, physio/OT	31 May *(achieved)*
24 May	9	Dry for 5 successive nights	Alter fluid + toilet regime (nurse)	31 May *(not achieved)*
31 May	11	Accept prescribed dietary supplements in full	Offer different menu of supplements (dietitian; nurse)	6 June
31 May	8+13	(i) Information about course options (ii) John to carry out phone enquiry	John to phone college for course brochure, prompted by speech/language therapist	
31 May	9	Dry for 5 successive nights	Meet patient + night staff to improve compliance with advice (nurse; psychologist)	6 June

Figure 2.1. Excerpts from (a) a list of problems identified during rehabilitation of a young man with head injury, and (b) his goal record-sheet.

it has been achieved at the agreed review date. Commonly, one action addresses two different problems and goals. In Figure 2.1, practising placing the arm in a sleeve was intended both as a form of ADL training and as a contribution to a programme to reduce flexion contracture. The patient's phoning for a college brochure was part of a programme to improve his social skills as well as a means of helping him to reach a decision about his future courses.

All members of the rehabilitation team, including doctors, should use the notes as a central information resource, and to record progress in a concise, standardised format. At the end of a programme of rehabilitation the notes should enable the original aims to be compared with recorded outcomes, and with the results of questionnaires administered to patients and/or carers. The results should be reviewed by the team as a whole at regular audit meetings.

Follow-up and outcome

A major weakness of many inpatient rehabilitation programmes is that professional input ends abruptly at the time of discharge. Since the rehabilitation plan is inevitably concerned with post-hospital life, its implementation often depends on factors beyond the immediate control of the hospital-based team. During the rehabilitation process it is usually essential to identify a group of professionals who can comprise a community rehabilitation team, and to hold case conferences with these, the patient, and the family prior to discharge. At the time of discharge full clinical details must be communicated and follow-up arrangements established.

Hospital-based teams need post-discharge follow-up for their own education. Without it they may fail to appreciate the limitations of hospital-based rehabilitation.

A 41-year-old Punjabi lady was transferred to a Community Rehabilitation Unit from a Spinal Injuries Unit to continue rehabilitation following a cervical cord and brachial plexus injury that had left her severely disabled. Despite many attempts to alleviate her problems during her lengthy stay in both units she was generally depressed, negative, withdrawn, and unambitious, and reported multiple physical symptoms for which no basis could be found. The family showed many signs of failure to understand her future needs, and there was a series of practical and financial difficulties, which it was felt would very likely prevent her ever being re-settled in the community. Eventually she did return to a suitably adapted home. At a late stage a family friend came from India to help care for her. When she returned a few months later her mood and attitude were transformed and it was found that arrangements for her care were working smoothly. Cultural factors and the effects of long-term institutionalisation had misled her, and also the rehabilitation team who under-estimated her potential for a positive outcome.

In evaluating the rehabilitation process we must ask: What is an economically justifiable outcome, given available resources? How large an effect must occur? Who must be affected: must the patient benefit directly? Must the effect be objective, or may it be merely subjective? Must it be measurable? If loss of autonomy is assumed to be a source of disadvantage how is increased autonomy to be measured? Freedom includes the freedom to reject opportunities, and a person's inactivity could be a positive but intangible outcome. This suggestion is difficult to square with the market metaphor for health provision, but what *behavioural* measures—what "product"—could be used as an index of freedom, or of justice, for individuals? Achieving realistic measures of outcome requires us to assess the potentialities of the person's social system as a whole, rather than merely to look at the individual's behaviour within it. Assessing quality of life is difficult, but necessary (Fallowfield, 1990; Rose & Johnson, 1996).

We must also ask: When should outcomes be measured: at time of discharge from a rehabilitation programme or later—and how much later? Sometimes a phase of active rehabilitation is an intermediate stage in a long-term plan to be achieved months or even years in the future.

REHABILITATION: WHO, WHERE, AND WHEN?

Currently, the decision to accept people for rehabilitation, whether as in-patients or as out-patients, is all too often made intuitively, without any objective assessment of therapeutic goals and without reference to explicit policies. Decisions about discharge also tend to be haphazard (Haas, 1988). Because of pressure on resources, three groups of questions need to be asked when selecting candidates for rehabilitation. They are required when a patient is referred to a hospital rehabilitation programme, for example a stroke unit, but are equally applicable to other settings. We should first ask: Is the rehabilitation resource (for example a hospital unit) designed for the person's needs? Second: What is the potential for rehabilitation and by how much can the natural history be changed? A third question, closely related to the second, is: What will happen *without* rehabilitation?

Is the rehabilitation resource designed for the client's needs?

The *sine qua non* for accepting a referral is compliance with operational criteria (e.g., age, type of clinical problem, etc.). A useful by-product of recent NHS reforms has been to clarify the contractual obligations of medical services. Explicit operational policies for hospital and community-based rehabilitation programmes can be used when selecting patients for rehabilitation and again when deciding whether to continue a programme, for example if the needs of a new referral are in competition with those of someone else who is continuing to make gains after a long period of in-patient rehabilitation.

Problems most often arise when there are multiple disabilities involving combinations of physical, behavioural, and cognitive problems extending beyond the expertise of a specific rehabilitation team. The occurrence of this combination for example in head injury or in Huntington's disease creates a strong argument for the existence of specialised units to meet complex needs (e.g., traumatic brain injury; see Stuckey, 1995). Units lacking the required expertise will be incapable of meeting the client's needs. Inappropriate admissions do no good, and indiscriminate acceptance of referrals disrupts the work of the unit. Where a new area of need is defined, a unit must take a conscious decision to adapt its policies to accommodate a new class of referrals or, where necessary, to add its voice to demands for the development of new facilities.

One factor that distinguishes the operational policies of different units is the pace or intensiveness of rehabilitation. Intensive programmes are not always what is needed even if they are available. Physical fitness, and behavioural factors such as attention span and self-awareness, influence an individual's ability to benefit from intensive therapy programmes. Elderly people and for those with severe multiple disabilities sometimes benefit from a relatively slow pace of rehabilitation. In establishing a unit's case-mix we must take account of the rehabilitation staff, who may not easily adjust to widely differing timescales required for different people.

The timescale of the proposed strategic goal is another important consideration. Chronic neurological conditions may be associated with maladaptive behaviours such as inappropriate gait patterns, long established behaviour disorders, or dysfunctional family dynamics that have been established for years. It may be possible to devise strategic goals to address such problems, but it would be unreasonable to expect changes to occur within a few weeks or months. A "water-on-a-stone" approach may be more effective than a "blitzkrieg".

Geography is another key factor. For some people the advantages of an intensive programme based in a regional centre are outweighed by its remoteness from the location of home and community. The hospital's work is then hampered because of limited access to the family, ignorance of the system, including home conditions, and difficulties in setting up appropriate post-discharge plans. People from outlying areas are sometimes impressed at first by the expertise of the large centre and then all the more disappointed by its inability to achieve outcomes relevant to community conditions.

What is the potential for rehabilitation?

Having established that a referral is appropriate in principle, we need to ask how the client is likely to benefit from rehabilitation—how much difference will it make? Much work has been done on the relationship between specific *medical* factors and outcome. A number of medical variables have been shown to predict poor outcomes, for example in stroke (Wade, Wood, & Langton Hewer, 1985). Such evidence from group studies is of limited value in predicting the rehabilitation potential of individuals. There are, however, neurological deficits that are intrinsically obstructive to the rehabilitation process. For example, receptive aphasia removes the potential for verbally based education and there is evidence that high-order perceptual deficits following right hemisphere damage are associated with poorer outcomes (e.g., Bernspang et al., 1987).

It seems reasonable to assume that rehabilitation potential is related to learning capacity and there is evidence that this is so

(Tondat Carter, Oliveria, Duponte, & Lynch, 1988). However, routine methods of assessing learning are poor predictors of skill-learning ability (see Chapter 10). Since it is unlikely that skill learning is a single faculty, it is arguable that the only way to assess a patient's capacity to benefit from specific types of re-educative therapy is through a trial period of rehabilitation. Rehabilitation potential should be reassessed at intervals.

Premorbid factors undoubtedly affect outcome (Brooks, 1984; Klonoff, Costa, & Snow, 1986). Outcomes are influenced by a wide range of factors including financial situation, social class, place of residence, local community facilities, the nature of previous employment and employers, and intellectual ability. Premorbid psychiatric and psychological factors often reduce a person's ability to make and maintain a meaningful therapeutic contract.

A man aged 59, believed to have been of low premorbid intelligence, suffered a severe head injury as a pedestrian. He had led a solitary existence in a bed-sit, and had always been vulnerable. He drank heavily and tended to neglect himself. He had never related well to other people, especially authority figures. It was therefore not surprising that he continued to reject the advice of the rehabilitation team and could not be motivated by attempts to increase his independence. He was socially out of his element in the rehabilitation ward and attempts at structured rehabilitation were for the most part futile.

What will happen without rehabilitation?

Rehabilitation potential cannot be considered in isolation from another question which bears on the ability of a rehabilitation programme to make a difference: What would have been the outcome without rehabilitation? The natural history of the impairment and the consequent disabilities and disadvantages play a major role in eventual outcomes of rehabilitation. Some conditions recover spontaneously and early intervention may give the false impression that therapy has been efficacious (Dombovy et al., 1987; Legh-Smith, Denis, Enderby, Wade, & Langton Hewer, 1987). On the other hand, early intervention may be associated with an improved outcome where full recovery does not occur (Oakes, Wilmot, Hall, & Scherk, 1990).

The risk of recurrence or of early death must be considered. The management of a cord lesion due to metastatic spinal disease is necessarily different from that of cord trauma. Such people nevertheless do need rehabilitative programmes.

Social and other premorbid factors may indicate the situation in such a way that the proposed rehabilitation input could only have a negligible effect on outcome. It is sometimes clear that the level of disadvantage (e.g., dependency) would be roughly the same with or without rehabilitation. For someone with a spouse willing to act as carer, rehabilitation might make the difference between home life and institutional care, whereas a similar person with no spouse might be destined for a nursing home even after intensive rehabilitation. Giving priority to people with a wider range of possible outcomes seems logical but is ethically hazardous since it leads to the suggestion that some categories—for example, older single men without capital or income—are inherently less worthy of rehabilitation than others in more fortunate circumstances. The principles advocated throughout this chapter should be applicable to all potential clients; the rehabilitation plan must be tailored to individual needs, to enable people as far as possible to gain or resume direction of their own lives, for their own purposes. The required plan must be matched with available resources.

CLINICAL NEUROLOGY IN A REHABILITATION SETTING

Initial assessment

The neurological patient is usually referred initially to a clinic, which rarely allows for joint assessment by a doctor and therapists, although this would often be the most efficient way of reaching decisions about further management. The complicated interrelationships between impairments, activities, participation, and quality of life call for a wide range of medical skills. Assessment must involve non-medical aspects of the situation as well as the narrower set of data required to answer the "Where?" and the "What?" of conventional diagnostic neurology.

Although assessment is obviously centred on the patient, additional information should always be gleaned from family members or professional helpers. There may be a nurse, therapist, or social worker who is a *de facto* or officially designated "key-worker" and hence a vital source of background information.

The first priority is a clear statement of what the patient (and/or carer) expects to gain from contact with the physician, and a listing (in order of subjective priority) of the *specific problems* to be addressed. The medical history is important but crucial information is often revealed by outlining the personal history in terms of major life events. These include landmarks in the life of a disabled person such as first use of a walking aid, loss of job, etc. It is important to have a picture of the *home situation* including arrangements for care if required, the state of health of carers, and a summary of the daily routine. This is especially useful in variable conditions such as Parkinson's disease. Day care, respite care, and other support services should also be summarised.

A functionally based *survey of abilities and disabilities* provides further background information. One time-saving method is to ask the patient (aided if necessary by a nurse) to complete an ADL checklist prior to meeting the physician. This, combined with a comprehensive report on symptoms, provides a framework for the consultation.

Special features of the neurological examination

Neurological assessment often makes a crucial contribution to rehabilitation assessment by identifying impairments which cause disabilities. The clinical question is often "Where?" is the lesion in a physiological rather than anatomical sense:

In a woman aged 56 with cerebral SLE, medical management was largely focused on establishing the diagnosis and organising drug treatment. Her case attracted the academic interest of junior doctors, students, and others. She had bilateral posterior hemisphere lesions on CT scan. She behaved as though she was blind, failing to grasp objects in front of her, and navigating the ward with caution and uncertainty. She failed standard tests of acuity and visual fields. She was labelled as "cortically blind". No counselling or rehabilitation for visual impairment had been planned. Detailed bedside neurological examination confirmed normal visual acuity complicated by Balint's syndrome. Apart from its intrinsic interest, this information allowed doctors and others to appreciate to some extent their patient's visual experience, and to offer appropriate counselling to her and to her carers.

This example of the location of functional deficits illustrates how neurological assessment can alter the way in which the patient as a whole is viewed. A less exotic example of a similar diagnostic synthesis would be the effect of a neurological assessment in establishing that fluctuations in mobility in a patient with Parkinson's disease are physiological rather than behavioural. Still more mundanely, the question often arises as to whether a pattern of disabilities is predominantly neurological or not. For example: is mobility impaired primarily by neurological deficit or by cardio-respiratory factors? Is weakness mainly due to pain? Is cognitive failure due to depression? The neurologist contributes at several levels to the process of mapping impairments onto disabilities.

Certain aspects of clinical examination are especially important in rehabilitation, but are often neglected in the assessment of people with neurological disabilities. One often reads elaborate neurological reports, with charts of muscle power, maps of sensory loss, etc., but with no written evidence of whether (let alone how) the patient walks, or talks, or reads; of course writers of textbooks are not guiltless in this respect. The assessment must include basic assessments of cognitive function, communication, hearing, and vision; and of standing, transferring, and walking. Some neurological abilities that do not figure at all in routine examination need to be tested in order to understand functional deficits. Such abilities may be routinely tested by therapists, although rarely by doctors: for example, swallowing, non-verbal aspects of communication, sitting balance, and responses to postural perturbations. The neurologist can also devise non-routine examinations as needed: for example, depth perception in relation to binocular vision, localisation of sounds in space, awareness of position of body parts, or control of voluntary movements and posture of the neck.

Functional observations are often more telling than formal tests. Gordon Holmes, who did much to establish the modern clinical routine, was well aware of the limitations of routine neurological examination:

More can often be learned of a patient's disabilities by observing his ordinary actions, as dressing or . . . walking when apparently unobserved, and his use of tools, as a pen, scissors or a knife and fork, than by special tests, though they usually produce a more complete analysis of symptoms.   (Holmes, 1946, p. 3)

Localisation of a lesion to the cervical cord and detection of upper motor neurone signs such as spasticity can be achieved without watching the patient walk, but in rehabilitation the emphasis is on the functional impact of spasticity on balance and gait. To take another example, different manifestations of unilateral neglect have similar localising significance, but their functional consequences may be different. No single neglect phenomenon is reliably predictive of others (Halligan, Marshall, & Wade, 1989), and understanding the effect of neglect in daily life requires direct observation of ordinary actions. Similarly, "bedside" tests of memory give only limited information about learning ability. Throughout the second section of this book there are examples of specific, functionally orientated neurological assessments that complement routine diagnostic examination.

Other aspects of physical examination

The spine and joints are important and often-neglected aspects of the general examination of heavily disabled people. Spinal deformities should be recorded and the range of passive joint movements should be measured and recorded unambiguously. There is no general agreement as to how this should be done, but the upper and lower limits of the range can be expressed in degrees of flexion, taking the anatomical position as zero. In people at risk of pressure sores the skin should be examined, especially vulnerable areas such as the feet and sacrum. Abdominal and rectal examination are of obvious importance in patients with sphincter disorders.

Although wheelchair seating, footwear and orthoses, and other equipment fall outside the scope of routine medical examination, the physician should at least be capable of screening for evidence of wear or misuse, for sources of pain and other symptoms, and for causes of actual or potential skin ulceration; not to mention simple, correctable problems such as stiletto heels in an ataxic patient or flat tyres on a troublesome wheelchair.

Summarising the data and creating a rehabilitation plan

Despite its limitations, medical assessment is usually helpful and is sometimes the only means of understanding a complex situation. In some respects medical assessment is more superficial, but also more general than the detailed examinations used by nurses, therapists, social workers, and others. It should touch on most aspects of the patient, including psychometric assessment, linking diverse clinical phenomena to a common biological basis. Although often maligned as failing to see the whole person, doctors are (or should be) trained to provide a unifying perspective (Ward, 1992). To achieve this the neurologist must draw on all available sources of evidence, and engage in a continuing clinical dialogue with the patient and family as well as professional colleagues.

Initial assessment is rarely definitive. The doctor who is accustomed to making snap diagnoses often jumps to wrong conclusions when attempting to identify key issues for rehabilitation. Medical assessment must be combined with information from other sources such as home-based assessments, and reports from nurses, therapists, and others (Table 2.1). An initial picture must often be revised as therapy and natural recovery proceeds.

Table 2.1.   A scheme for neurological assessment in a rehabilitation context

History
  Presenting functional problems: Purpose of assessment
  Medical history and diagnosis
  Personal history
  Home situation
  Survey of everyday abilities
  Record of carers, and professionals and others involved.

Examination
  Functional assessments relevant to presenting problems, e.g.:
  ● mood, personality, behaviour
  ● cognitive function
  ● functional vision
  ● communication (not merely speech)
  ● functional mobility (e.g., transfers, walking)
  ● relevant self-care activities (e.g., dressing)
  ● swallowing.

  Further routine examination as required to confirm pathological diagnosis and also to establish functional diagnoses.

  Additional assessments often required, e.g.:
  ● nutritional status
  ● spine and joints
  ● seating
  ● orthoses and other aids
  ● skin, especially sacral areas.

Summary of rehabilitation issues
  ● Prevention
  ● Independence
  ● Lifestyle
  ● Social context and physical environment.

The type of rehabilitation plan that emerges from assessment depends on the resources available. In its simplest form a plan can be negotiated between a solitary neurologist and a patient/client. More complex multidisciplinary planning and goal negotiation has been described earlier in this chapter. At neither end of the spectrum is there an accepted framework for creating a rehabilitation plan. Objectives are expected to emerge from the assessment, based on the individual's stated aims and taking account of professional observations. The PILS scheme (see earlier) is a useful *aide-mémoire*. Rehabilitation objectives, whether formulated in a multidisciplinary team or negotiated in an out-patient clinic, should take account of:

● preventable impairment and disability (for example, falls, or pressure sores)
● independence (mobility and functional activities)
● lifestyle (personal roles and aspirations, often affected by communicative ability)
● social context: carers, and also material resources.

Within a multidisciplinary rehabilitation team, the physician contributes along with the client and professional colleagues to the selection of goals first through an assessment (and reassessment) of disease prognosis. Initial assessment of impairment is crucial (see earlier) but during rehabilitation reassessment is often helpful.

A patient with a right hemisphere infarct failed to learn the sequence for side-to-side transfer within a reasonable time. The failure might have been related to visuospatial deficits but more detailed clinical analysis suggested the presence of pre-existing multi-infarct dementia. The revised neurological diagnosis suggested a poor prognosis and led to the adoption of a less ambitious rehabilitation plan.

Medical roles in the rehabilitation process

Doctors provide a range of specific interventions (for example, in the management of epilepsy or of spasticity). These should be component parts of a rehabilitation plan, subject to evaluation by the client/patient and by the rehabilitation team as a whole. In many cases the direct therapeutic role of the doctor is limited. The physician must however remain involved, maintaining a therapeutic relationship with the patient/client and with the family, providing information about progress and prognosis.

A consultant often assumes the role of team leader for historical and political reasons rather than on account of special expertise. There are advantages in non-medical leadership and a neurologist can make an effective clinical contribution to a rehabilitation team in a non-leading role.

CONCLUSION

This chapter has described the rehabilitation process with neurological rehabilitation in mind. The key stages in the process are: Identification of the client; identification of presenting problems; strategic planning; setting of short-term goals; monitoring progress; and evaluation of outcome. All of these usually require the collaboration of the client and family with several professionals forming a rehabilitation team, but the process can be adapted to many environments, including out-patient clinics.

A clear concept of the rehabilitation process, with its emphasis on a negotiated contract between professionals and clients, calls for defined operational policies. Any environment where rehabilitation is attempted would benefit from the establishment of such policies. The decision to accept referrals and to discharge clients should be based on the operational policy and should take account of the likelihood that rehabilitation will make a major difference. The envisaged benefits may be for a client other than the "patient". Judgement of the likely benefits of rehabilitation is a difficult art but it is open to objective evaluation, beginning with a number of basic criteria such as those discussed in the previous section of this chapter.

Rehabilitation neurology is a clinical activity based on diagnostic skills acquired through clinical neurological training although involving other skills in addition. It requires the neurologist to consider functional as much as anatomical localisation, and to move from the two questions, "Where?" and "What?" to a third: "So what?" Suitably trained physicians can make a unique contribution to a multiprofessional team. They can also apply the principles described in this chapter to other environments such as the out-patient clinic, by helping their patients to achieve chosen objectives under categories such as those encapsulated in the PILS scheme: prevention of future disability, independence, lifestyle (social participation), and context.

REFERENCES

Badley, E.M., & Lee, J. (1987a). Impairment, disability and the ICIDH (International classification of impairments, disabilities and handicaps): Model I. The relationship between impairment and disability. *International Rehabilitation Medicine, 8*, 113–117.

Badley, E.M., & Lee, J. (1987b). Impairment, disability and the ICIDH (International classification of impairments, disabilities and handicaps): Model II. The nature of the underlying impairment and patterns of impairment. *International Rehabilitation Medicine, 8*, 118–124.

Barnes, C. (1991). *Disabled people in Britain and discrimination: A case for anti-discrimination legislation.* London: Hurst & Company.

Bauer, D. (1989). *Foundations of physical rehabilitation.* Melbourne, Australia: Churchill Livingstone.

Bernspang, B., Asplund, K., Eriksson, S., & Fugl-Meyer, A.R. (1987). Motor and perceptual impairments in acute stroke patients: Effects on self-care ability. *Stroke, 18*, 1081–1086.

Brooks, N. (1984). *Closed head injury: Psychological, social and family consequences.* Oxford, UK: Oxford University Press.

Brown, M., & Gordon, W.A. (1986). Rehabilitation indicators: A complement to traditional approaches to patient assessment. *Central Nervous System Trauma, 3*(1) 25–35.

Chamberlain, A. (1988). The rehabilitation team and functional assessment. In C.J. Goodwill & M.A. Chamberlain (Eds.), *Rehabilitation of the physically disabled adult.* London: Croom Helm.

Dombovy, M.L., Basford, J.R., Whisnant, J.P., & Bergstralh, E.J. (1987). Disability and use of rehabilitation services following stroke in Rochester Minnesota, 1975–9. *Stroke, 18*, 830–836.

Fallowfield, L. (1990). *The quality of life: The missing measurement in health care.* London: Souvenir Press.

Flynn, R.J., & Lemay, R.A. (Eds.). (1999). *A quarter century of normalisation and social role valorisation.* Ottawa, Canada: University of Ottawa Press.

Frude, N. (1991). *Understanding family problems: A psychological approach* (pp. 28, 38–53). Chichester, UK: John Wiley.

Granger, C.V. (1985). Outcome of comprehensive rehabilitation: An analysis based on the impairment, disability and handicap model. *International Rehabilitation Medicine, 7*, 45–50.

Gronwell, D., Wrightson, P., & Waddel, P. (1999). *Head injury: The facts— a guide for families and caregivers.* Oxford, UK: Oxford Paperbacks.

Haas, J.F. (1988). Admission to rehabilitation centers: Selection of patients. *Archives of Physical Medicine and Rehabilitation, 69*, 329–332.

Halligan, P.W., Marshall, J.C., & Wade, D.T. (1989). Visuospatial neglect: Underlying factors and test sensitivity. *Lancet, 2*, 908–910.

Harrison, J. (1987). *Severe physical disability.* London: Cassell.

Holmes, G. (1946). Introduction to clinical neurology (p. 3). Edinburgh, UK: E&S Livingstone.

Hopkins, A., Menken, M., & DeFriese, G. (1989). A record of patient encounters in neurological practice in the United Kingdom. *Journal of Neurology, Neurosurgery and Psychiatry, 52*, 436–438.

Inman, C. (1999). Effectiveness of spinal cord injury rehabilitation. *Clinical Rehabilitation, 13*(Suppl.), 25–32.

Klonoff, P.S., Costa, L.D., & Snow, W.G. (1986). Predictors and indicators of quality of life in patients with closed-head injury. *Journal of Clinical and Experimental Neuropsychology, 8*, 469–485.

Ko Ko, C. (1999). Effectiveness of rehabilitation for multiple sclerosis. *Clinical Rehabilitation, 13*(Suppl.), 33–42.

Langton Hewer, R., & Wood, V.A. (1992). Neurology in the United Kingdom: I. Historical development. *Journal of Neurology, Neurosurgery and Psychiatry, 55*(Suppl.), 2–7.

Legh-Smith, J.A., Denis, R., Enderby, P.M., Wade, D.T., & Langton Hewer, R. (1987). Selection of aphasic stroke patients for intensive speech therapy. *Journal of Neurology, Neurosurgery and Psychiatry, 50*, 1488–1492.

Lincoln, N.B., Mulley, G.P., Jones, A.C., McGuirk, E., Lendrem, W., & Mitchell, J.R.A. (1984). Effectiveness of speech therapy for aphasic stroke patients. *Lancet*, 1197–1200.

Mahoney, F.I., & Barthel, D.W. (1965). Functional evaluation: The Barthel index. *Maryland State Medical Journal, 14*, 61–65.

Maitz, E.A., & Sachs, P.R. (1995). Treating families of individuals with traumatic brain injury from a family systems perspective. *Journal of Head Trauma Rehabilitation, 10*, 1–11.

Man, D. (1999). Community-based empowerment programme for families with a brain injured survivor: An outcome study. *Brain Injury, 13*, 433–445.

McGlynn, S.M., & Schacter, D.L. (1989). Unawareness of deficits in neuropsychological syndromes. *Journal of Clinical and Experimental Neuropsychology, 11*, 143–205.

McLellan, D.L. (1997). In D.L. McLellan & B.A. Wilson (Eds.), *Rehabilitation studies handbook* (p. 1). Cambridge, UK: Cambridge University Press.

Mearns, D., & Thorne, B.J. (1988). *Person-centred counseling in action*. London Beverley Hills, CA: Sage Publications.

Nirje, B. (1970). The normalization principle: Implications, and comments. *British Journal of Mental Subnormality, 16*, 62–70.

Oakes, D.D., Wilmot, C.B., Hall, K.M., & Scherk, J.P. (1990). Benefit of early admission to a comprehensive trauma center for patients with a spinal cord injury. *Archives of Physical Medicine and Rehabilitation, 71*, 637–643.

Oliver, M. (1990). *The politics of disablement*. London: Macmillan.

Pentland, B., & McPherson, K. (1994). An attempt to measure the effectiveness of early brain injury rehabilitation. *Health Bulletin, 52*, 438–445.

Petrie, J.C., & McIntyre, N. (1979). *The problem orientated medical record*. Edinburgh, UK: Churchill Livingstone.

Powell, T. (2001). *Head injury: A practical guide*. Oxford, UK: Speechmark Publishing.

Rice-Oxley, M., & Turner-Stokes, L. (1999). Effectiveness of brain injury Rehabilitation. *Clinical Rehabilitation, 13*(Suppl.), 7–24.

Rose, F.D., & Johnson, D.A. (1996). *Brain injury and after: Towards improved outcome*. New York: John Wiley & Sons.

Rothwell, N., LaVigna, G., & Willis, T. (1999). A non-aversive rehabilitation approach for people with severe behavioural problems resulting from brain injury. *Brain Injury, 13*, 521–534.

Sinclair, A., & Dickinson, E. (1998). *Effective practice in rehabilitation*. London: King's Fund Publishing.

Stewart, W. (1985). *Counselling in rehabilitation*. London: Croom Helm.

Stuckey, N. (1995). A national service for brain injured with severe behavioural disturbance—referrals, treatment and outcome in the first two years. *Health Bulletin, 53*, 40–46.

Tondat Carter, L., Oliveira, D.O., Duponte, J., & Lynch, S.V. (1988). The relationship of cognitive skills performance to activities of daily living in stroke patients. *American Journal of Occupational Therapy, 42*, 449–454.

Turner-Stokes, L. (1999). The effectiveness of rehabilitation: A critical review of the evidence. *Clinical Rehabilitation, 13*(Suppl.), 1–82.

von Bertanlanffy, L. (1968). *General systems theory*. New York: Braziller.

Wade, D.T., Wood, V.A., & Langton Hewer, R. (1985). Recovery after stroke—the first 3 months. *Journal of Neurology, Neurosurgery and Psychiatry, 48*, 7–13.

Ward, C.D. (1992). Medical education and the challenge of neurological disability. *Journal of Neurology, Neurosurgery and Psychiatry, 55*, 54–58.

Ward, C.D. (2000). Rehabilitation in Parkinson's disease and Parkinson syndrome. In R. Meara (Ed.), *Parkinson's disease and Parkinsonism in the elderly*. Cambridge: Cambridge University Press.

Watts, R., & Perlesz, A. 1999. Psychosocial outcome risk indicator: Predicting psychosocial outcome following traumatic brain injury. *Brain Injury, 13*, 113–124.

Webster, G., Daisley, A., & King, N. (1999). Relationship and family breakdown following acquired brain injury: The role of the rehabilitation team. *Brain Injury, 13*: 593–603.

Wolfensberger, W. (1983). Social role valorisation: A proposed new term for the principle of normalization. *Mental retardation, 21*, 234–239.

Wood, R.L., McRea, J.D., Wood, L.M., & Meeriman, R.N. (1999). Clinical and cost effectiveness of post acute neurobehavioural rehabilitation. *Brain Injury, 13*, 69–88.

World Health Organisation. (1980). *The international classification of impairments, disabilities and handicaps—a manual of classification relating to the consequences of disease*. Geneva, Switzerland: Author.

World Health Organisation. (2001). WWW3.WHO.int/icf

3. Organisation of neurological rehabilitation services

M.P. Barnes

INTRODUCTION AND BASIC PRINCIPLES

The process of rehabilitation is based on the principles of education and enablement. These principles are at variance with medical practice in general which often, of necessity, is based on the need to care for a sick individual. The fundamental difference between conventional medical practice and rehabilitation can be summarised as the former being "hands on" and the latter being "hands off". Many organisations of disabled people argue strongly against a medical model of management. It is argued that a disabled person is not sick and thus does not require to be "looked after" by health professionals (Oliver, 1990; Wolfensberger, 1972). This approach is undoubtedly valid for disabled people with relatively static, long-term disabilities but is it valid within the context of the acute situation or for people with deteriorating conditions? This chapter explores the role of the health-care system in the management of disabled people and attempts to define an appropriate structure for a neurological service. It is proposed that there is a continuum of service delivery from a health-oriented rehabilitation model in the acute phase working towards a client-centred psychosocial model for the later stages of rehabilitation.

The chapter will concentrate on the 16–65-year-old population. The provision of services for children with neurological disabilities and for elderly people can be based on the same principles as outlined in this chapter but are further complicated by the special provisions needed for these two client groups. In the UK it is the younger disabled adult for whom there is a paucity of services despite significant numbers of young people with disabling neurological conditions.

PRINCIPLES OF SERVICE DELIVERY

In 1985 the Living Options Working Party set out some key principles for disabled people (Prince of Wales Advisory Group on Disability, 1985). These principles can be summarised as follows:

- *choice* as to where to live and how to maintain independence, including help in learning how to choose
- *consultation* with disabled people and their families on services as they are planned
- *information* clearly presented and readily available to all disabled consumers
- *participation* of disabled people in the life of local and national communities with respect to both responsibilities and benefits
- *recognition* that long-term disability is not synonymous with illness and that the medical model of care is inappropriate in the majority of cases
- *autonomy*—freedom to make decisions regarding a way of life best suited to an individual disabled person's circumstances.

These principles are broadly compatible with a similar list produced by Silburn (1988) who, from a survey of disabled people, determined that there were seven basic needs: information, counselling, housing, aids/equipment, personal help, transport, and access.

It would seem reasonable to add that a person with a neurological disability has the right of access to information, advice, and treatment from an appropriate clinical expert. Such access should as far as possible be without undue delay, within a freely accessible environment, and within a reasonable geographical distance of the individual's home.

SPECIFIC SERVICE REQUIREMENTS

Local rehabilitation service

A report by the Royal College of Physicians (1986) identified a number of generic services felt to form a central part of a health-oriented rehabilitation resource. These recommendations have been adapted in the UK to local needs by a number of different health authorities (e.g., Northern Regional Health Authority Advisory Committee on Disability, 1989; North Western Regional Health Authority, 1990; Wade, 1990; Yorkshire Regional Health Authority, 1989). Further details and suggestions were more recently contained in the report of a UK Working Party on the subject (British Society of Rehabilitation

Medicine, 1992) and by a large umbrella organisation representing many UK-based neurological charities (Neurological Alliance, 1996a,b). Detailed purchasing suggestions have been made in a British Society of Rehabilitation Medicine document published in 1993.

A fundamental requisite is for a rehabilitation team, preferably housed within an accessible rehabilitation unit. Specific models of service delivery, including delivery of community services, are further discussed later in this chapter. In addition to an appropriate neurological rehabilitation team, a range of specific health services should be provided at a local level. These should certainly include:

- a continence service
- an orthotic service
- a pressure sore policy and service
- a prescription and maintenance service for basic wheelchairs
- a counselling service, particularly sexual counselling.

It is likely that these services will fall within the remit of health authority purchase. Other services needed at a local level could be purchased or provided on a joint basis between the health authorities and local authorities obviously depending on national statutes. Such services would include an aids and equipment display and loan facility (e.g., disabled living centre), an information service, and access to a broad range of housing, respite, and day-centre facilities. These issues are discussed later within the context of the longer term needs of people with physical disabilities.

Specialist rehabilitation centres

Some specific services cannot realistically be provided within every locality. The expertise required to run such services may not be widely available or alternatively the number of disabled people involved may be so small that local provision is not an economic proposition.

It is generally agreed (e.g., British Society of Rehabilitation Medicine, 1992, 1993; Northern Regional Health Authority Advisory Committee on Disability, 1989) that there is a need for specialist rehabilitation centres, which, in the UK, could serve a population of approximately 3 million people. Such centres would run along the same interdisciplinary lines as the local rehabilitation unit (and indeed may act as a local unit for their own locality) and would obviously need to maintain very close liaison with the local rehabilitation network. Ideally such regional centres should be seen as a resource to be used by disabled people, their key workers, and therapists, to learn from the expertise contained within the regional centre or to make use of specialist equipment and facilities. These centres would also act as a major focus of education, training, and research, which is important if the speciality of rehabilitation medicine is to develop on a firm academic base. Specific services contained within the specialist centres are likely to encompass

the following:

(1) A specialist rehabilitation service for people with the most complex multiple disabilities.
(2) A specialist rehabilitation service for people with brain damage of various causes who require in-patient rehabilitation. Such a service would include specialist expertise in the management of psychological and behavioural problems to cater for patients with severe behavioural difficulties (who may number about 1 per 100,000 population; Andrews, 1989). Specialist behavioural units offer one solution to this problem (Eames & Wood, 1985). Small behavioural units could be established in a segregated section of a brain injury unit so that as the patients with behavioural disturbance improve they could be integrated back into the more general rehabilitation environment and, hopefully, from there back into the community.
(3) A specialist service for complex wheelchair and special seating requirements.
(4) A bioengineering service.
(5) A communication aids centre.
(6) An information, advice, and assessment service with regard to car driving.
(7) A prosthetic service.
(8) A spinal injury service. The UK has seen the development of a network of spinal injury rehabilitation centres. These offer excellent examples of the value of interdisciplinary rehabilitation (e.g., Heinemann et al., 1989). It is a pity that such centres have developed in isolation as much of the expertise required would be similar to that needed in a broader based specialist rehabilitation centre.

Finally, there is a need to consider provision of facilities for the residential care of people with the most severe disabilities who realistically cannot be looked after in the community. This population would include people in a vegetative state or prolonged coma.

SERVICE DELIVERY

There is no single ideal model for the delivery of neurological rehabilitation services. There will need to be variations according to local needs and resources. There will be differences of emphasis between the needs of an acute rehabilitation service for people with acute stroke or post head injury and for a service that caters for the requirements of people with longer term disabilities. Services must adapt to the more intensive requirements of people with progressive disorders, such as motor neurone disease and multiple sclerosis, and the less intensive but still important requirements of people with relatively static conditions, such as head injury or spinal cord injury. Admission criteria to any neurological rehabilitation service need to be carefully defined, particularly with regard to age limits. Many rehabilitation centres in the UK cater for the needs of the working age population (16–64), leaving paediatric and geriatric neurological rehabilitation to appropriate colleagues.

Acute rehabilitation services

Acute rehabilitation teams—successful or not?   It would seem common sense that gathering together a group of interested and skilled professionals to provide a joint approach to the rehabilitation of a neurologically disabled individual should produce benefit for that individual over and above a more fragmented service. However, until recently there has been very scant evidence to prove this hypothesis. There is now emerging a reasonable quantity of evidence that confirms the efficacy of a holistic and interdisciplinary approach to acute rehabilitation. This is the case with regard to spinal injury rehabilitation (Heinemann et al., 1989) and head injury (Brooks, 1991; Cope, Cole, Hall, & Barkan, 1991; Cope & Hall, 1982) but more particularly to stroke rehabilitation (Dennis & Langhorne, 1994; Garraway, Akhtar, Hockui, & Prescott, 1980; Ottenbacher & Jannell, 1993; Reding & McDowell, 1989; Smith, Garraway, Smith, & Akhtar, 1982; Strand et al., 1985).

Although this recent research is encouraging there is undoubtedly a need for further research to confirm the scope, size, base, and operational policies of the acute neurological rehabilitation team.

Early intervention and advice.   There is some evidence of the efficacy of early rehabilitation intervention after an acute disabling neurological event such as stroke or head injury (Cope & Hall, 1982; Tobis, Turi, & Scheridon, 1982). The advice of the rehabilitation team can be useful in the acute phase particularly with regard to the prevention of complications. Nutritional requirements, swallowing problems, positioning, and other measures to reduce the complications of spasticity are a few examples of strategies that can alleviate difficulties at a later stage. There is evidence that relatives need information and support at this time (Oddy, Humphrey, & Uttely, 1978). There is a strong argument for the rehabilitation team to be an integral part of, or at least have close liaison with, the acute medical, neurological, and neurosurgical services.

Rehabilitation team.   It would seem appropriate that in the acute phase management is based on the medical model, at least until the patient has achieved medical stability. Other professionals begin to assume increasing importance in the post acute phase and a multidisciplinary team model becomes more appropriate. The gathering together of professionals from different backgrounds is not sufficient to merit the term "rehabilitation team" (see Chapter 4). The goal-setting process may tend to be organised on a departmental basis that could simply compartmentalise the patient's recovery. The rehabilitation team should seek to adopt an interdisciplinary approach in which departments become more integrated and the goal-setting process becomes more patient centred. Goals should be set which are relevant to an individual's recovery within their premorbid social situation and within their (realistic) postmorbid aspirations, interests, and abilities.

How then should the team be structured? It is clear that there needs to be representation from a core of disciplines—physiotherapy, occupational therapy, speech and language therapy, clinical psychology, nursing, rehabilitation medicine, and social work. There is a need for occasional input from dieticians, chiropodists, activity organisers, vocational trainers (see later) and a variety of medical specialist on an ad hoc basis. The precise composition of the team would depend on the size of the unit, admission criteria, discharge policy, availability of community support services, and so on. There have been attempts to define ideal compositions and staff/patient ratios for neurological rehabilitation units (e.g., Medical Disability Society, 1988; Pentland & Barnes, 1988). A recommendation in the UK is for a 1 : 5 physiotherapy and occupational therapy/patient ratio and 1 : 20 ratio for speech and language therapy, clinical psychology, and social work. A 1 : 1 nurse/patient ratio is also generally accepted. There will need to be senior and junior medical staff support. The problem with such recommendations is that the staff levels will depend on the scope and type of unit as well as the experience of the staff and qualified/unqualified staff mix in each department. A danger is that such recommendations will serve to emphasise the departmental ethos, whereas the philosophy should be more client oriented than department oriented. This problem has been overcome in some private units in the UK and more widely in the USA by the employment of rehabilitation officers/therapists who are not attached to particular departments but are responsible to a certain number of disabled people. The advantage of such an approach is to emphasise the client-centred functional goal-setting process. The rehabilitation officer would normally be responsible for carrying out the rehabilitation process with the guidance of a small number of specialist therapists from each discipline. The efficacy of such an approach over the departmental model remains unproven although the success of role blurring within the special circumstances of a behavioural modification unit should be noted (Eames & Wood, 1985). It is possible that the success, at least in lay terms, of the conductive education programme in Hungary may in part be due to the close therapeutic relationship of the rehabilitation therapist (conductor) with the disabled individual.

An alternative to the rehabilitation therapist model is the adoption of a key-worker system. In the context of the acute rehabilitation unit the role of the key worker would normally be to act as a channel of communication between the patient and family and the rehabilitation team as a whole. The key worker would be the individual who is most aware of the interests, abilities, and family dynamics of the patient both before injury and during rehabilitation. The key worker, with the patient and family on one hand and advice from therapy staff on the other hand, would help to determine the functional goals. The key worker would also act in a liaison capacity between the hospital/rehabilitation unit and the community support services to help ensure a smooth transition at time of discharge.

The key worker would ensure that the patient and family have ready access to information, explanation, and counselling as required and, perhaps most importantly, provide continuity of support. The background of the key worker could be from any of the therapies, nursing, or social work. There is no reason why cognitively intact patients should not act as their own key worker. The system used in the rehabilitation centre at Newcastle-upon-Tyne is for junior staff to act as key workers, with senior staff support. The process can be seen as educational for the key worker as well as beneficial for the patient. At the present time there is little evidence of the efficacy of the key-worker system compared to the standard multidisciplinary team model.

Rehabilitation unit. Does a rehabilitation team need a defined physical base? It would be entirely possible for an acute team based within a hospital to support patients directly on the medical or surgical wards. The same team could provide continuity of care and continue the person's rehabilitation once returned to the community. However, there do seem to be advantages in the creation of rehabilitation units. Wade et al. (1985) summarise the advantages of stroke rehabilitation units within a district general hospital setting. They propose that the potential benefits are that: The physical structure could be made more conducive to rehabilitation; the team approach is facilitated; staff morale should be higher; research should be stimulated; voluntary help is more likely; routine record keeping and follow-up (and thus audit) are more easily managed. There are no studies comparing the roving team approach with a rehabilitation unit but the latter is generally recommended (British Psychological Society Working Party, 1989; British Society of Rehabilitation Medicine, 1992, 1993; Oddy, Bonham, & McMillan, 1989; Royal College of Physicians, 1986; Wade, 1990).

The geographical site of the rehabilitation unit is probably less important than the internal design. However, one can envisage psychological advantages in moving from an acute hospital setting to a separate rehabilitation unit as a step towards a return to the community. Appropriate design can also be facilitated on a separate site. Units should be accessible by public transport and within or close to a local community setting in order to allow functional goals to be introduced in a realistic community environment. The internal design should facilitate independence and should preferably include single rooms, accessible patient kitchens, and dining facilities, large and small day rooms, and space to allow spouse and family to stay with or near the patient and thus participate in the educational process. It is axiomatic that all facilities within the unit should be fully accessible as should the building itself. The rehabilitation centre in Newcastle-upon-Tyne has two bungalows in the grounds, which act as transitional living and independence training facilities, and these have proved most useful.

The number of beds required in the unit is a difficult question. It would obviously depend on the population served, admission policy, discharge policy, and age or diagnostic criteria. It has been estimated that a unit of 20 beds would be required to meet the acute needs of the 16–65-year-old population with neurological disabilities in a typical English health district with a population of 250,000 (Northern Regional Health Authority Advisory Committee on Disability, 1989).

It is a vexed question whether local rehabilitation units should admit only certain categories of patients. There are differences in skill requirements for physically oriented rehabilitation (e.g., musculoskeletal and orthopaedic disabilities) compared with the more complex nature of rehabilitation when there are combinations of physical and psychological problems such as encountered in neurological rehabilitation. A case could be made for a separate neurological rehabilitation unit in order to cater for the specific and rather different requirements of people with neurological disabilities (Eames, 1987).

Transition to community. Many problems for disabled people occur at times of transition from one service to another. This is often apparent at the time of discharge from a rehabilitation unit when the hospital-based rehabilitation team hands over to community support services. Similar problems occur in a different context when school leavers with disabilities leave the educational and paediatric environment for a less organised adult support service (Bax, Smythe, & Thomas, 1988; Parker & Hirst, 1987). The importance of continuity must be stressed. Ideally the acute rehabilitation team should continue to be associated with the disabled person and family at and beyond the time of discharge. A phased discharge policy with periods of overnight stays at home, weekend leave, and perhaps trial periods in independence rooms or bungalows within the hospital are all desirable. It would seem sensible for hospital-based rehabilitation units to have day units where disabled people could continue to attend, for defined reasons, on an out-patient basis. A single point of contact with the rehabilitation team, perhaps through the key-worker system, would also be desirable. The same principles apply to discharge from regional centres and to handover for the disabled school leaver.

Geddes, Clayden, and Chamberlain (1989) report an innovative scheme to overcome the problem of transition. They discharged some people who had had a stroke into the care of "substitute families". These were lay carers who were recruited from the community and trained by staff at the rehabilitation unit. These people received care from their substitute families for an average of 8 weeks and during this time specific goals were met and the phased return to home was organised. Close contact was made with the rehabilitation unit via the key worker, who in this case was an occupational therapist with counselling skills. The study demonstrated an improved rehabilitation outcome at 1 year post stroke in those people who had been through the family placement scheme compared with a control group.

Cole, Cope, and Cervelli (1985) have bridged the transitional period in another way. Disabled people discharged from a hospital head injury rehabilitation unit attended an adult development centre based in a local church hall. The centre was staffed by an adult education teacher working with a variety of volunteers. The clients underwent a combination of individual and small group instruction in basic self care, home skills, and social skills development. Initially all clients were unable, due to their disability, to participate in higher level community vocational programmes, but after a period ranging from 1 to 12 months 47% of attendees obtained an improved level of function so that referral to a higher level of vocational programme was possible. This is a low-cost transitional programme but unfortunately did not contain a control group. Further work in this area is needed.

Young and Forster (1992) conducted a well-designed study of continuing stroke rehabilitation following discharge from the hospital unit. They randomised individuals to continuing attendance at a day hospital or to receipt of physiotherapy in the home. A total of 124 people was recruited. Both treatment groups had significantly improved functional abilities between discharge and 6 months, but the improvements were significantly greater for those treated at home despite the fact that the home-treated individuals actually received slightly less treatment. They concluded that home physiotherapy was probably more effective and more resource efficient than day hospital attendance and was the preferred rehabilitation method for continuing therapy after acute discharge.

A further problem on discharge is the lack of information about community services, follow-up arrangements, use of prescribed drugs, and other issues. Sandler, Mitchell, Fellows, and Garner (1989) demonstrated that the simple provision of an information booklet at discharge from hospital improved the accuracy and thoroughness of recall of important medical details.

Longer term rehabilitation

Basic principles

The author has discussed the requirements of an acute neurological rehabilitation service and some of the problems associated with transition from an acute unit to the community. People with longer term disabilities, either static or deteriorating, have different perspectives and requirements. Many people with longer term disabilities do not wish to perceive themselves as ill and in need of health care. Some organisations of disabled people have firmly rejected the medical model of disability management (Brisenden, 1986; Oliver, 1986). Disabled people's aspirations are commonly centred around the principles of normalisation as propounded by Wolfensberger (1972). Society at large is viewed as the disabling agency. Oliver (1990) illustrates this point of view by rewording the questions of the Office of Population Censuses and Surveys (OPCS) survey of disability (Martin, Meltzer, & Elliot, 1988). For example, the question "What complaint causes your difficulty in holding, gripping, or turning things?" could be reworded as "What defects in the design of everyday equipment like jars, bottles, and tins causes you difficulty in holding, gripping, or turning them?" "Does your health problem/disability make it difficult for you to travel by bus?" could perhaps be reworded as "Do poorly designed buses make it difficult for someone with your health problem/disability to use them?" Ultimately, "Can you tell me what is wrong with you?" could be revised to "Can you tell me what is wrong with society?" These are valid points and ones that should be

taken forward in the realm of political lobbying in an attempt to improve society's attitude towards disabled people. However, such longer term aims should be not be allowed to obscure the more immediate requirements of disabled people, which should be centred on enabling them to reduce their disability, and consequent handicap, within society as it exists today. A more useful concept in the short term, proposed by Bauer (1989), is the Least Restrictive Alternative. This concept recognises that some people will need to have their freedom, opportunity, or access restricted but requires that services be provided that facilitate the most normal living arrangement possible.

Is there a role for a neurological rehabilitation service within these principles? The author believes that the answer must be in the affirmative. There is a need for medical and health-oriented information regarding natural history, prognosis, treatment, and update on research. Many disorders have a need for on-going medical treatment (e.g., Parkinson's disease, epilepsy). In static, but more particularly in deteriorating, conditions there is a need to prevent unnecessary complications (e.g., contractures, pressure sores). There is a need for help and advice with regard to the provision of equipment, particularly more specialist equipment such as communication aids. In addition, there could be the requirement for further periods of active rehabilitation, such as following a relapse in multiple sclerosis.

There may well be a need for counselling, either peer counselling or professional intervention from psychologists or specialist counsellors. It is well recognised that the difficulties perceived by carers in the longer term are not particularly those related to physical disability but to psychological and more especially emotional and behavioural problems in the disabled person (McKinlay et al., 1981). Until recently many psychological and in particular higher executive functions were not felt to be amenable to therapeutic intervention. It is now clear that problems with memory, visuospatial function, and higher executive functions are amenable to a variety of interventions (see Chapters 32 and 33). There is a need, particularly after head injury, for relatively long-term rehabilitation for the cognitive and psychological sequelae of injury. This is particularly the case following brain injury when retraining of independence and social skills is required as well as specific vocational rehabilitation (see Chapter 38).

Service requirements

The author has summarised the importance of the continued involvement of the neurological rehabilitation team in longer term disability. However, there are other service requirements that are important but are normally outside the remit of the health service alone.

Housing and residential care. Provision is required of an appropriate range of housing varying from simple housing adaptations through adapted housing and a variety of sheltered living schemes to forms of residential care. In the UK the choice of housing is particularly limited and the next step from modest house adaptations is often residential care. There is much to be learnt from a wide variety of disability-friendly housing in Scandinavia (Development Trust for the Young Disabled, 1985).

It is a matter of considerable debate whether there is a need to provide residential accommodation for the most severely disabled people. It is theoretically possible for someone with any degree of disability to remain within their own home but often the degree of support required is not economic or practicable in a world with limited financial resources. It is likely that a very small number of residential beds will be needed in a health district. The numbers would depend on the degree and adequacy of community support services. Any such beds should be provided in as "homely" an atmosphere as possible, preferably with single-room accommodation. There is also probably a small need for residential and semicustodial care for people with severe and long-term behavioural disturbance. The needs of people in long-term coma (vegetative state) also need to be addressed. Andrews (1989) estimates the prevalence of vegetative state to be 0.3 per 100,000 population. Placement for such people is very difficult as they require a considerable level of clinical and nursing expertise. A few specialist units exist in the UK. Such units are ideal for maximising the person's long-term survival but are less than ideal given the often great distances from home. One option is to reserve a small number of beds in the specialist regional rehabilitation centre for these individuals.

Respite. There is considerable documented evidence of stress on the carers of disabled people (Kinsella & Duffy, 1979). Such stress can be alleviated by periods of respite for the disabled person. Preferably this should be on a planned basis but respite accommodation should provide access in a crisis situation. Social respite should be provided in a non-institutionalised environment. It is unfortunate that most respite facilities are contained within a hospital or institutional setting. A compromise solution is to provide the disabled person with a period of in-patient rehabilitation and reassessment of needs with a secondary purpose of providing a break for carers. A number of rehabilitation units now operate such a policy of "intermittent rehabilitation" for people with longer term disabilities.

Terminal illness. The hospice movement has provided a much-needed service but this is usually confined to people with cancer. Rehabilitation units should give consideration to providing a facility for people with terminal physical disabilities along the lines of the hospice movement. A joint scheme in Newcastle-upon-Tyne between the rehabilitation centre and the local hospice has proved a useful resource for people with motor neurone disease. The hospice provides day-centre and home care whereas the rehabilitation centre provides the facility for respite and terminal admission.

Practical help at home. Caring for a disabled person at home normally falls to close family members. The stress upon carers can be alleviated by the provision of practical help within the home. It is entirely possible for people with severe disabilities to live alone supported by a variety of care attendants. Many local authorities provide home-help and home-care schemes as well as such simple provisions as meals on wheels. The district nursing service also has a role to play but often the statutory schemes lack flexibility with a tendency to impose regimes upon disabled people. Schemes within the voluntary sector, at least in the UK, tend to be more flexible; examples are the Crossroads Care Attendant Scheme and the Cheshire Family Support Scheme. Perhaps the ultimate solution would be disabled people buying in care attendant staff to suit their own requirements (see later).

Recreational pursuits. Independence and social skills training can often be achieved through the medium of recreational pursuits. Rehabilitation teams should be aware of local and accessible opportunities for recreation and leisure.

Finance. Disabled people and their families need to be made aware of the bewildering array of state financial benefits. Disability brings additional costs (Martin & White, 1988). The rehabilitation team should be aware of available benefits and sources of appropriate information and advice.

Employment. In economic terms the main cost of disability to a national economy is lost employment. For example, O'Brien (1987) estimated the annual cost of multiple sclerosis in England and Wales to be £125,400,000 at 1986/87 prices; £100,000,000 of this figure represented the estimate of lost earnings. In the UK vocational rehabilitation is organised by a separate government department (Department for Work and Pensions). There are separate benefits and work adaptation systems and separate employment rehabilitation centres. There is often little liaison between the employment rehabilitation services and health and social rehabilitation services. Stambrook et al. (1990) demonstrated that only 55% of individuals who suffered a severe head injury and were in full-time employment before the injury were able to return to full-time work afterwards. In addition, those who did return to work only did so at a reduced level of occupational status. In the USA vocational counsellors are often an integral part of rehabilitation teams. This can produce improved employment prospects for disabled people. Wehman et al. (1989) demonstrated an excellent re-employment rate in a group of 20 severely brain-injured young men with an average coma length of 68 days. The key to their success seemed to be on-site training accompanied by a job coach who stayed with the head-injured individual until job performance stabilised. A variety of behavioural and social skills as well as cognitive retraining strategies were developed on site. This was followed by the gradual removal of the job coach but with continuing long-term support. This paper and others (Wehman et al., 1995) emphasises the need for rehabilitation to be based within the community and further implies the importance of vocational rehabilitation as an integral part of the whole rehabilitation process.

MODELS OF SERVICE DELIVERY

Chapter 2 outlined the epidemiology of disablement and illustrated that in any locality around 14% of the adult population have a disability and at least 2–3% of the population have a severe disability (Martin et al., 1988). The adequate and equitable delivery of health care to this population is clearly a logistic problem. The patchy and fragmented delivery at the present time is amply illustrated by Beardshaw (1988) and Edwards and Warren (1990). What are the options available?

Medical model

A traditional and still prevalent model for the longer term management of people with neurological disabilities has been the hospital out-patient clinic. This is unsatisfactory on a number of grounds. There is often very little continuity of care. The follow-up clinics tend to be run by junior medical staff who rotate on a regular basis. The sheer numbers of patients involved means that very little time can be spent with any individual who in turn could normally be seen every 3–6 months or at even longer intervals. There is normally little or no involvement from other members of an interdisciplinary rehabilitation team. This model may have some relevance to the management of certain disabilities (e.g., epilepsy, Parkinson's disease) but in general fails to meet the principles of service delivery as outlined earlier and is an unsatisfactory experience for both the doctor and the disabled person.

Disease-specific clinics

There are a number of examples of disease-specific clinics: for example, multiple sclerosis (Scheinberg, Holland, & Kirschenbaum, 1981) and minor head injury (Wrightson, 1989). These clinics have the advantage of providing an expert multidisciplinary team familiar with the problems specific to that disease or disability. Appropriate information and counselling support can be provided and self-help groups can be involved. The clinic setting can provide a social function as well as supplying a core of support for carers. The logistic difficulties with such arrangements are the number of clinics that would need to be held and the possibility of ignoring the requirements of disabled people with rarer conditions.

Community disability teams

It is theoretically possible for the acute rehabilitation team to remain in touch with the disabled person post discharge and continue a watching brief. This would provide continuity of support and ready access to appropriate staff and health resources. The disadvantage of this model is that a single rehabilitation team would soon be overwhelmed by the numbers of people involved and several different teams would need to be established. Strict discharge and review policy becomes necessary. Regular review would be useful but quickly places unacceptable demands on the service. The experience of the present author with an open access review system is that it allows reduction of the number of attendees per clinic and means that people can be seen when they have some difficulties they wish to discuss. No system is perfect and an open access review can mean that preventable complications arise that have not been recognised by the disabled person.

A further disadvantage of the acute rehabilitation team continuing an overview is that such a team is usually health oriented and may not have the expertise with regard to social and vocational rehabilitation. A solution to this problem is the development of a broader based multidisciplinary team with input from social services, employment rehabilitation, and other bodies. A team along these lines was developed in a London borough (Hunter, 1988) with an original remit to provide assessment, advice, and treatment to severely disabled individuals between the ages of 16 and 55. However, it soon became evident that it was not possible for the disability team to carry out treatment as well as fulfilling its other functions. It thus developed more of a coordinating role within the community, ensuring that existing services were delivered effectively to the clients as and when needed. The team also took on a planning role and became particularly involved in times of transition from hospital to community or from paediatric to adult services.

A further example is that designed in Cornwall within a rural setting (Evans, 1987). Referrals are made to community rehabilitation teams that have members drawn from health authority, social services, and employment services. They are based within smaller geographical areas within one health district and the team as a whole designs an active planned programme of continuing rehabilitation. Clients are discharged from the team fairly quickly but can be reintroduced at any time. These teams are largely established within existing staff levels by regrouping of resources and thus this is a relatively low cost option.

In the UK and other developed countries there has been a recent drive to reduce spiralling health costs by reducing the emphasis on acute hospitals and placing more resources in the community. This has led to a number of experiments with different formats of service delivery for disabled people in the community. We are beginning to see joint purchasing of such community teams by health and social service purchasers, although formalising this change has required new primary legislation, which has significantly delayed this process. A number of models of good practice for different disability groups are now available (Marks, 1991). It is likely, although not yet proven, that comprehensive disability teams based within the community and having a good working knowledge of the problems of the disabled families can prevent acute hospital admission and keep disabled people at home for longer as well as preventing, or at least reducing, the incidence of unnecessary complications. Much disability, even acute disability such as stroke, can be managed at home with appropriate support staff and resources. An extension of the concept of the community disability team is the liaison nurse or nurse practitioner, which is discussed later.

Primary care team

In the UK a base for longer term overview of disabled people is the general practitioner and the primary health-care team. A typical group general practice has a population of around 10,000. The numbers of disabled people are thus reduced to a more practical level. The primary care team could keep a watching brief and make referrals to a local rehabilitation team as appropriate. The system provides a practical solution to the logistic difficulties of large numbers of disabled people but has a number of disadvantages. Many disabilities, particularly neurological, are relatively rare. As an example, a general practitioner is likely to see one new person with multiple sclerosis only once every 20 years, and even commoner conditions, such as stroke, may be seen by a general practitioner only three or four times a year. This reduces the level of expertise and experience. Important points of management may be missed and questions left unanswered. The interests of general practitioners also vary considerably and it is likely that such a system will produce a patchy and uncoordinated service to the community as a whole. This was illustrated in Harris' (1971) study. There is still considerable evidence of patchy and unmet need in the care of severe physically disabled adults as amply demonstrated in the recent survey by Williams and Bowie (1993).

It would be possible for the primary health-care team to be supported by visiting members of a specialist rehabilitation team. Such a project was designed in Southampton with the support of the Parkinson's Disease Society. In this project a consultant in neurological rehabilitation attended meetings with primary care teams in four different group general practices for discussion of specific patients with Parkinson's disease. A wide range of recommendations were made at the meetings although the effect and take-up of such recommendations were not assessed. Limited conclusions can be drawn from this pilot project but the concept of a primary care team supported by visits from one or more members of the more specialist disability team is worth pursuing in future research.

The recent introduction of fundholding in general practice has produced a further dimension in the array of service purchasing options. General practitioner groups can now effectively hold their own budget and purchase a range of services themselves for their practice including purchase of acute hospital care and community health care. This may improve the possibility of the primary care team purchasing appropriate additional expertise and thus provide a better and more locally responsive disability service. However, a significant potential drawback is that the provision of local disability services will be further fragmented as purchase would be dependent upon the whim and the interest of the local general practitioner. The need for joint planning and joint purchase, particularly with local social services, may also be lost and overall there is cause for considerable concern within this new system for the provision of services for disabled people.

Case manager

The concept of the case manager has been given credence in the UK following the publication of the National Health Service and Community Care Act (1990). The discussion document that preceded the Act stated that "where individuals' needs are complex or significant levels of resources are involved (there is) considerable merit in nominating a case manager to take responsibility for ensuring that individuals' needs are regularly reviewed,

resourced and managed effectively and that each service user has a single point of contact . . . Case management provides an effective method of targeting resources and planning services to meet specific needs of individual clients."

There are many different models of case management (Hunter, 1988; McMillan et al., 1988). The emphasis of case management is to design packages of care that are applicable to an individual's needs rather than assessing for a range of available (or not available) services. In the USA and Canada the system is further developed with a number of models which vary in scope according to the position and level within the service of the case manager: whether or not they have authority to coordinate resources and most particularly whether they are responsible for individual client budgets. Case management can include:

(1) simple coordination within a single agency
(2) coordination across agency boundaries
(3) service brokerage, in which the case manager negotiates with key agencies on the client's behalf
(4) budget holding responsibility where services can be purchased on behalf of the client from statutory bodies, or from the voluntary or private sector.

Cooperation between different statutory bodies, particularly in terms of joint budgets, is difficult but not impossible to achieve. Attempts have been made in Winchester and Darlington (Beardshaw & Towell, 1990). The latter project on the severely disabled elderly in the community resulted in reduced burden on carers and, compared with a control group, substantial cost savings, improved quality of life, and improved quality of care outcomes, and a decrease in numbers of people requiring long-stay hospital care.

There is a number of, largely unpublished, examples of individual disabled clients holding budgets in order to purchase their own personally designed package of care, including home helps, equipment, and therapy input.

The concept of case management is not well developed in the UK and the widespread application of case management must await the establishment of properly based training programmes.

Nurse practitioner

A recent concept is the development of the role of the specialist nurse. The role and purpose of such a nurse varies widely and there needs to be considerably more research work regarding the most cost effective role for such a specialist as well as more specific and clear guidelines on training and educational requirements. Some early studies have shown modest benefit of such a specialist nurse working in the community (Forster & Young, 1996), whereas other studies (Kirker, Young, & Warlow, 1995) have shown more marked benefit and appreciation both from health professionals and from clients. The Foster and Young study evaluated whether a specialist nurse was able to enhance the social integration and perceived health of people after stroke or could alleviate stress in the carers. A stratified randomised controlled trial involving 240 stroke people failed to show significant differences in perceived health, social activity, or stress among carers between the treatment and control groups, although mildly disabled people with stroke had an improved social outcome at 6 months following specialist nurse intervention. The Kirker et al. study evaluated a multiple sclerosis liaison nurse in the community and demonstrated a high rate of appropriate referral to other therapists and improved coping, mood, confidence, and knowledge of multiple sclerosis among the client group. Carers reported similar benefits and general practitioners also found the specialist nurse helpful. Specialist nurses have now been trained to manage the most complex disabilities in the community such as the manipulation of anti-Parkinsonian drugs and administration of botulinum toxin for people with dystonia and spasticity. Much of the benefit probably derives from a key-worker role and a single point of contact into the complex array of community and hospital services. Such individuals could and should be trained in counselling skills, a much undervalued role in community services in general.

Independent living movement

The logical extension of case management is for the disabled person or family themselves to act as a case manager. There are examples in the UK of local authorities giving disabled people their own budget to buy services as required. This model is firmly supported by the Independent Living Movement and by disabled persons' groups such as the British Council of Organisations for Disabled People (Brisenden, 1986). This may be a workable solution for certain groups of disabled people, particularly for those who are cognitively intact, but becomes rather less satisfactory when dealing with people with cognitive disturbance. There are some disabled people who would clearly be unable to manage their own affairs. Who is to manage the affairs of these individuals and who is to decide on the required level of cognitive ability of the disabled individual? Is this to be a legal decision? Wider implementation of this model must certainly await legislation given the present dichotomy between health and social services and the lack of a clear boundary between health and social requirements.

Resource centre—towards a solution?

A solution to some of the difficulties encountered in service provision could be the creation of community resource centres. These centres would be local and accessible, particularly in terms of public transport. They could house an information service and perhaps provide a base for a disabled living centre with display of aids and equipment. They could provide a base for self-help groups and as such provide a social and peer counselling function. It is possible for the neurological rehabilitation team to be based within or visit the centre on a regular basis. Disabled people could be reviewed on a regular basis or access members of the rehabilitation team at specified times to discuss particular problems. It would be possible for disease specific clinics to be held within the centre. The centres could also act

as a base for social and recreational activities and it would be entirely possible for vocational counselling and training to be based within the same building. The centres could be managed by disabled people with the support of volunteers and some paid staff drawn from appropriate health and local authority community resources. A centre along these lines has been established in Liverpool in the UK and elsewhere. There are no published reports of the efficacy or perceived usefulness of such resource centres and such studies are to be encouraged. However, they would seem to offer potential solution to the problems of service delivery particularly with regard to the formation of close partnerships between disabled people and health professionals.

LIAISON AND MANAGEMENT

The requirements of a longer term rehabilitation support service go well beyond the boundaries of responsibility of health authorities. Different departments in the local authority (e.g., housing, social services) have an important role to play, as does the Department for Work and Pensions (financial benefits) and the Department of Employment (vocational rehabilitation). Other government departments (e.g., Education and Skills; Transport, Local Government and the Regions), and particularly voluntary bodies and private organisations, all have a role to play in service provision. The main problems of disability in the longer term are coordination between these different bodies. There is a need for close and formal liaison between different statutory and voluntary bodies, particularly for planning and coordination. The importance of involving organisations for disabled people and disabled people themselves in the planning process cannot be understated. There are now a number of guidelines and suggestions regarding the best way to involve users and disabled people in service planning and evaluation (Fletcher, 1995). Preferably the different managerial and financial structures within the different bodies should come together in a single managerial and financial entity so that the whole service provision for disabled people within a given locality is given some degree of coherence. Major change must probably await government legislation.

CONCLUSION

The organisation of disability services is complex. There is no single solution. This must depend upon identification of local needs and assessment of local resources and possibilities. There is a strong case to be made for a neurological rehabilitation team to be created within each locality, preferably sited within a rehabilitation unit. The network of such units needs to be linked to a specialist regional rehabilitation centre, which would cater for more specific and complex needs and provide a focus for education, training, and research. Longer term rehabilitation requirements are different from the post-acute situation with more emphasis on psychological and emotional problems. There is a need for close involvement with non-health resources for amelioration of handicap. There is a need for continuing involvement of a neurological rehabilitation team for assessment and review. There are a number of possible models for service delivery. An attractive proposition is the creation of resource centres to be developed within a community to provide an information, counselling, and support service as well as a single point of contact with rehabilitation professionals and facilities. Close links would need to be made between the rehabilitation team and the resource centre, which could be in the same physical base. However, the perceived requirement of disabled people to receive services in a non-medical non-hospital environment should be borne in mind. This chapter has summarised some possibilities and offered tentative solutions. The lack of research in this area prevents any firm conclusions. A single solution is neither possible nor desirable but research into the relative merits of different systems is a central prerequisite for future service development.

POSTSCRIPT

In recent years organisations of disabled people and many disabled individuals have voiced dissatisfaction with disability and rehabilitation health services. Health professionals who are planning or who are involved with such services need to be aware of the different viewpoints and emphases that are being proposed. Accordingly, the editors of this book asked Professor Michael Oliver to write a critique of this chapter. The editors welcome his contribution, which follows, and hope that this stimulates debate on this important subject.

A DIFFERENT VIEWPOINT—WHO NEEDS REHABILITATING?
Michael Oliver

Rehabilitation can be defined in many ways, but what is certain is that a whole range of practices stem from the definition adopted. This is not contentious but the problem is that none of the definitions adopted can be shown to be in accord with the experience of disability.

To put matters bluntly, all is not well in the kingdom of rehabilitation, whether it be rehabilitators expressing their anxiety (Royal College of Physicians, 1986) or the rehabilitees expressing their discontent (Beardshaw, 1988; Oliver et al., 1988). We could argue, as indeed Professor Barnes does in his chapter, that the problem centres around inadequate knowledge, poor skills, or defective organisation, or, more likely, a combination of all three.

Let me say at the outset I did not disagree with this analysis, but for me it is only a partial disagreement. It is the failure to address the issue of power and to acknowledge the existence of ideology that is the main problem. Hence, for me, rehabilitation is the exercise of power by one group over another and that that exercise is shaped by ideology. The exercise of power involves

the identification and pursuit of goals chosen by the powerful and shaped by ideology of normality, which goes unrecognised. Let me further emphasise here that I am not suggesting that we can eradicate the influence and effects of power and ideology in rehabilitation, but that our failure even to acknowledge their existence gives rise to a set of social relations and a range of therapeutic practices that are disabling for all concerned.

Space will not permit a detailed, sustained, and comprehensive critique of rehabilitation so in order to illustrate my argument I shall focus on the topic of the heart of the rehabilitation enterprise—walking.

What's so wonderful about walking?

Rehabilitation reproduces the concept of walking uncritically in that it is never analysed or discussed except in technical terms—what operations can we perform, what aids can we provide and what practices can we use to restore the function of walking. Walking is more complex and complicated than being either a simple physical act or indeed a social symbol, as the following quotation demonstrates (Turner, 1984):

Walking is a capacity of the biological organism, but it is also a human creation and it can be elaborated to include the "goose-step", the "march" and "about turn". Walking is rule following behaviour, but we can know a particular person by his walk or by the absence of a walk ... my way of walking may be as much a part of my identity as my mode of speech. Indeed, the "walk" is a system of signs so that the stillness of the migrainous person or the limp of the gouty individual is a communication.

The influence of ideology

A classic example of the way the ideology of normality linked to an uncritical concept of walking informs rehabilitation practice is this description and analysis of these practices by a person with a spinal injury (Finkelstein, 1981):

The aim of returning the individual to normality is the central foundation stone upon which the whole rehabilitation machine is constructed. If, as happened to me following my spinal injury, the disability cannot be cured, normative assumptions are not abandoned. On the contrary, they are reformulated so that they not only dominate the treatment phase searching for a cure but also totally colour the helper's perception of the rest of that person's life. The rehabilitation aim becomes to assist the individual to be as "normal as possible". The result, for me, was endless soul destroying hours trying to approximate to able-bodied standards by "walking" with callipers and crutches.

Such a devastating critique should not be individualised, for many people with spinal injuries are critical of the "physicality" of their rehabilitation (Oliver et al., 1988).

The operation of power

There are two dimensions to the operation of power: power to control the individual body and power to control the social body. The connections between the two are encapsulated in the work of the French philosopher Michael Foucault, whose discussion of health-care systems has been summarised as follows (Rabinaw, 1984):

An essential component of the technologies of normalisation is the key role they play in the systematic creation, classification and control of anomalies in the social body. Their raison d'être comes from two claims of their promoters: first, that certain technologies serve to isolate anomalies; and second, that one can then normalise anomalies through corrective or therapeutic procedures, determined by other, related technologies. In both cases, the technologies of normalisation are purportedly impartial techniques for dealing with dangerous social deviations.

For "technologies of normalisation" read "rehabilitation practices" and uncomfortable questions are raised.

Power and ideology in the rehabilitation enterprise

Again, space will not permit a sustained critique of the permeation of power and ideology into the rehabilitation enterprise, but I shall assume that Professor Barnes' chapter represents a generally accepted, consensual, and forward-looking description of that very enterprise. Therefore, my criticisms of his chapter can be regarded, for practical purposes, as a critique of rehabilitation.

According to Lukes (1972), central to the operation of power in society is what is not placed on the political (with a small "p") agenda. Hence, Professor Barnes rightly emphasises the importance of choosing goals for rehabilitation. But, who chooses those goals and what if the powerless chose goals different from the powerful, or indeed, reject the opportunity to choose any goals at all? This point is never even discussed. Similarly, his discussion of teamwork, the fact that teams do not work at all from the perspective of the powerless, and that we have known that for many years (Beardshaw, 1988; Blaxter, 1980) is not even mentioned. Approaches to and locations of multidisciplinary work are discussed in absence of the fact that such teamwork has been called "a familiar face" and has been shown to benefit the team members more than those who can constitute the work of teams (Oliver, 1991).

Like power, ideology is at its most influential when it is invisible and the ideology of normality permeates Professor Barnes' chapter. One example of where it surfaces is the comment on the "success", in lay terms, of conductive education. Many disabled people are profoundly disturbed by the ideology underpinning conductive education. Lest anyone should be unclear about what is wrong with conductive education—if rehabilitation attempted to set a range of goals that was unachievable for most of its clientele, that in order to pursue these unachievable goals great stress was placed on family life, and that physical progress was emphasised to the detriment of psychological health and social development, then it would be out of business quickly (Oliver, 1989). What can be pernicious about ideology is not simply that it enables these issues to be ignored but sometimes it turns them on their heads. Hence, conductive education is regarded as something meriting social applause, as something to make laudatory television programmes about, and finally as something that should be funded by government and business.

Conclusion

This critique should not be regarded as an attempt to throw out the baby as well as the bath water. Rather it is an attempt to force on to the rehabilitation agenda issues that have barely been considered. It is my belief that properly addressing these issues will make rehabilitation a more appropriate enterprise for all concerned—not only will the bath water be clearer but the baby healthy as well. In this critique, I have not addressed the important issue of what the rehabilitation enterprise will look like if we address the issues of powers and ideology, for I do not know. What I do know is that the enterprise will look very different from how it does now and that the issues involved are much broader than those discussed in this book. At the end of the day: "To 'rehabilitate' rehabilitation (and other human service agencies), we need to 'rehabilitate' ourselves" (Higgins, 1985).

REFERENCES

Andrews, K. (1989). *Provision of services for severely brain damaged patients in the United Kingdom*. London: Royal Hospital & Home Putney.

Bauer, D. (1989). *Foundations of physical rehabilitation*. Melbourne, Australia: Churchill Livingstone.

Bax, M.C.O., Smythe, D.P.L.T., & Thomas, A.P. (1988). Health care for physically handicapped young adults. *British Medical Journal, 296*, 1153–1155.

Beardshaw, V. (1988). *Last on the list: Community services for people with physical disabilities*. London: King's Fund Institute.

Beardshaw, V., & Towell, D. (1990). *Assessment and case management: Implications for the implementation of "Caring for People"*. London: King's Fund Institute.

Blaxter, M. (1980). *The meaning of disability* (2nd ed.). London: Heinemann.

Brisenden, S. (1986). Independent living and a medical model of disability. *Disability Handicap and Society, 1*, 173–181.

British Psychological Society Working Party. (1989). *Services for young adult patients with acquired brain damage*. Leicester, UK: British Psychological Society.

British Society of Rehabilitation Medicine. (1992). *Neurological rehabilitation in the United Kingdom—a report of a working party*. London: British Society of Rehabilitation Medicine.

British Society of Rehabilitation Medicine. (1993). *Advice to purchasers—setting NHS contracts for rehabilitation medicine*. London: British Society of Rehabilitation Medicine.

Brooks, N. (1991). The effectiveness of post acute rehabilitation. *Brain Injury, 5*, 103–109.

Cole, J.R., Cope, D.N., & Cervelli, L. (1985). Rehabilitation of the severely brain injured patient: A community based, low cost model program. *Archives of Physical Medicine and Rehabilitation, 66*, 38–40.

Cope, D.N., Cole, J.R., Hall, K.M., & Barkan, H. (1991). Brain injury: An analysis of outcome in a post acute rehabilitation system: Part 1. General analysis. *Brain Injury, 5*, 111–125.

Cope, D.N., & Hall, K. (1982). Head injury rehabilitation: Benefits of early intervention. *Archives of Physical Medicine and Rehabilitation, 66*, 38–40.

Dennis, M., & Langhorne, P. (1994). So stroke units save lives: Where do we go from here? *British Medical Journal, 309*, 1273–1277.

Development Trust for the Young Disabled. (1985). *The care of disabled people: Residents or residential care—the need for assessment and classification*. London: Development Trust for the Young Disabled.

Eames, P. (1987). Head injury rehabilitation: Time for a new look. *Clinical Rehabilitation, 1*, 53–57.

Eames, P., & Wood, R. (1985). Rehabilitation after severe brain injury: A follow up study of a behaviour modification approach. *Journal of Neurology, Neurosurgery and Psychiatry, 48*, 613–619.

Edwards, F.C., & Warren, M.D. (1990). *Health services for adults with physical disabilities*. London: Royal College of Physicians.

Evans, C.D. (1987). Rehabilitation of head injury in a rural community. *Clinical Rehabilitation, 1*, 133–137.

Finkelstein, V. (1981). *Disability and professional attitudes*. Sevenoaks, UK: Naidex Conventions.

Fletcher, S. (1995). *Evaluating community care—a guide to evaluations led by disabled people*. London: King's Fund Institute.

Forster, A., & Young, J. (1996). Specialist nurse support for patients with stroke in the community: A randomised, controlled trial. *British Medical Journal, 312*, 1642–1646.

Garraway, W.M., Akhtar, A.J., Hockui, L., & Prescott, R.J. (1980). Management of acute stroke in the elderly: Follow up of a controlled trial. *British Medical Journal, 281*, 827–829.

Geddes, J.M.L., Clayden, A.D., & Chamberlain, M.A. (1989). The Leeds Family Placement Scheme: An evaluation of its use as a rehabilitation resource. *Clinical Rehabilitation, 3*, 189–197.

Harris, A.I. (1971). *Handicapped and impaired in Great Britain*. London: Her Majesty's Stationery Office.

Heinemann, A.W., Yarkony, G.M., Roth, E.J., Lovell, L., Hamilton, B., Ginsburg, K., Brown, J.T., & Meyer, P.R. (1989). Functional outcome following spinal cord injury: A comparison of specialised spinal cord injury centre versus general hospital short term care. *Archives of Neurology, 46*, 1098–1102.

Higgins, P. (1985). *The rehabilitation detectives: Doing human service work*. London: Sage.

Hunter, D.J. (1988). *Bridging the gap: Case management and advocacy for people with physical handicaps*. London: King Edward's Hospital Fund.

Kinsella, G.J., & Duffy, F.D. (1979). Psychosocial re-adjustment in the spouses of aphasic patients. *Scandinavian Journal of Rehabilitative Medicine, 11*, 129–132.

Kirker, S.G.B., Young, E., & Warlow, C.P. (1995). An evaluation of a multiple sclerosis liaison nurse. *Clinical Rehabilitation, 9*, 219–226.

Lukes, S. (1972). *Power: A radical view*. London: Macmillan.

Marks, L. (1991). *Home and hospital care: Re-drawing the boundaries*. London: King's Fund Institute.

Martin, J., Meltzer, H., & Elliot, T. (1988). *OPCS surveys of disability in Great Britain: Report 1. The prevalence of disability among adults*. London: Her Majesty's Stationery Office.

Martin, J., & White, A. (1988). *OPCS surveys of disability in Great Britain: Report 2. The financial circumstances of disabled adults living in private households*. London: Her Majesty's Stationery Office.

McKinlay, W.W., Brooks, D.N., Bond, M.R., et al. (1981). The short term outcome of severe blunt head injury as reported by the relatives of the injured persons. *Journal of Neurology, Neurosurgery, and Psychiatry, 44*, 527–533.

McMillan, T.M., Greenwood, R.J., Morris, J.R., et al. (1988). An introduction to the concept of head injury case management with respect to the need for service provision. *Clinical Rehabilitation, 2*, 319–322.

Medical Disability Society. (1988). *The management of traumatic brain injury*. London: Development Trust for the Young Disabled.

Neurological Alliance. (1996a). *Living with a neurological condition—standards of care*. London: Author.

Neurological Alliance. (1996b). *Providing a service for people with neurological conditions*. London: Author.

Northern Regional Health Authority Advisory Committee on Disability. (1989). *Services for people with a physical disability in the Northern Region*. Newcastle-upon-Tyne, UK: Northern Regional Health Authority.

North Western Regional Health Authority. (1990). *Report of the working group on guidance for specialised health services for those people with severe or multiple disabilities*. Manchester, UK: Author.

O'Brien, B. (1987). *Multiple sclerosis*. London: Office of Health Economics.

Oddy, M., Bonham, E., & McMillan, T. (1989). A comprehensive service for the rehabilitation and long term care of head injury survivors. *Clinical Rehabilitation, 3*, 253–259.

Oddy, M., Humphrey, M., & Uttely, D. (1978). Stresses upon the relatives of head injured patients. *British Journal of Psychiatry, 133*, 507–513.

Oliver, M. (1986). Social policy and disability: Some theoretical issues. *Disability, Handicap and Society, 1*, 5–17.

Oliver, M. (1989). Conductive education: If it wasn't so sad it would be funny. *Disability, Handicap and Society, 4*, 197–200.

Oliver, M. (1990). *The politics of disablement*. London: Macmillan.

Oliver, M. (1991). Multi-specialist and multidisciplinary—a recipe for confusion? "Too many cooks spoil the broth". *Disability, Handicap and Society, 6*, 65–68.

Oliver, M., Zarb, G., Silver, J., et al. (1988). *Walking into darkness: The experience of spinal injury*. Basingstoke, UK: Macmillan.

Ottenbacher, K.J., & Jannell, S. (1993). The results of clinical trials in stroke rehabilitation research. *Archives of Neurology, 50*, 37–44.

Parker, G., & Hirst, M. (1987). Continuity and change in medical care for young adults with disabilities. *Journal of the Royal College of Physicians, 21*, 129–133.

Pentland, B., & Barnes, M.P. (1988). Staffing provision for early head injury rehabilitation. *Clinical Rehabilitation, 2*, 309–313.

Prince of Wales Advisory Group on Disability. (1985). *Living options*. London: Author.

Rabinaw, P. (1984). *The Foucault reader*. New York: Panthian.

Reding, M.J., & McDowell, F.H. (1989). Focused stroke rehabilitation programs improve outcome. *Archives of Neurology, 46*, 700–701.

Royal College of Physicians of London. (1986). *Physical disability in 1986 and beyond*. London: Author.

Sandler, D.A., Mitchell, J.R.A., Fellows, A., & Garner, S.T. (1989). Is an information booklet for patients leaving hospital helpful and useful? *British Medical Journal, 298*, 870–874.

Scheinberg, L., Holland, N.J., & Kirschenbaum, M.S. (1981). Comprehensive long term care of patients with multiple sclerosis. *Neurology, 31*, 1121–1123.

Silburn, R. (1988). *Disabled people: Their needs and priorities*. Nottingham: Benefits Research Unit, University of Nottingham.

Smith, M., Garraway, W., Smith, D., & Akhtar, A. (1982). Therapy impact on functional outcome in a controlled trial of stroke rehabilitation. *Archives of Physical Medical Rehabilitation, 63*, 21–24.

Stambrook, M., Moore, A.D., Peters, L.C., Deviaene, C., & Hawryluk, G.A. (1990). Effects of mild, moderate and severe closed head injury on long term vocational status. *Brain Injury, 4*, 183–190.

Strand, T., Asplund, K., Eriksson, S., Hagg, E., Lithner, F., & Wester, P.O. (1985). A non-intensive stroke unit reduces functional disability and the need for long term hospitalisation. *Stroke, 16*, 29–34.

Tobis, J.S., Turi, K.B., & Scheridon, J. (1982). Rehabilitation of the severely head injured patients. *Scandanavian Journal of Rehabilitation Medicine, 14*, 83–85.

Turner, B. (1984). *The body and society*. Oxford, UK: Blackwell.

Wade, D.T. (1990). Designing district disability services—the Oxford experience. *Clinical Rehabilitation, 4*, 147–158.

Wade, D.T., Langton-Hewer, R., Skilbeck, C.E., & David, R.M. (1985). *Stroke—a critical approach to diagnosis, treatment and management*. London: Chapman and Hall.

Wehman, P., Kreutzer, J., West, M. Sherron, P., Diambra, J., Fry, R., Groah, C., Sale, P., & Killam, S. (1989). Employment outcome of persons following traumatic brain injury: Pre-injury, post-injury and supported employment. *Brain Injury, 3*, 397–412.

Wehman, P.H., West, M.D., Kregal, J., Sherron, P., & Kreutzer, J.S. (1995). Return to work for persons with severe traumatic brain injury: A data-based approach to programme development. *Journal of Head Trauma Rehabilitation, 10*, 27–39.

Williams, M.H., & Bowie, C. (1993). Evidence of unmet need in the care of severely physically disabled adults. *British Medical Journal, 306*, 95–98.

Wolfensberger, W. (1972). *The principle of normalisation in human services*. Toronto, Canada: National Institute on Mental Retardation.

Wrightson, P. (1989). Management of disability and rehabilitation services after mild head injury. In H.S. Levin, H.M. Eisenberg, & A.L. Benton (Eds.), *Mild head injury*. New York: Oxford University Press.

Yorkshire Regional Health Authority. (1989). *Services for younger physically disabled adults*. Harrogate, UK: Author.

Young, J.B., & Forster, A. (1992). The Bradford community stroke trial: Results at six months. *British Medical Journal, 304*, 1085–1089.

4. The rehabilitation team

Rodger Ll. Wood

INTRODUCTION

Historically, neurological rehabilitation has relied upon several disciplines working together to achieve therapeutic goals. Indeed, a basic premise of rehabilitation medicine is that optimal patient recovery is built upon the concerted effort of several different treatment disciplines working as a team. Originally, the three professional *groups* comprising the rehabilitation team were medicine, nursing, and the clinical therapies (speech, occupational, and physiotherapy). With the passage of time, other professional groups became involved, such as psychology, recreational therapy, social workers, and, most recently, non-professional "therapy care assistants". Not only has the number of different disciplines comprising a team increased, but the balance of "power" has changed, in the sense that responsibility of leadership is no longer automatically the province of the medical doctor, but has passed to psychologists or other health workers, according to the type of rehabilitation being provided. The evolution of rehabilitation teams has therefore been slow and fragmented, partly because neurological rehabilitation is a broad church (in respect of its range of subspecialities) and partly because some specialities have resisted giving ground to others. There is, however, growing support for the development of teams in a number of health-care areas. They have been advocated in primary care (Dingwall, 1980), psychiatry (Ovretveit, 1986; Royal College of Psychiatrists, 1984), and, more recently, in health care generally (Furnell, Flett, & Clarke, 1987).

Published references to team approaches in physical or neurological rehabilitation remain scarce but several recent publications have recognised their importance. McMillan et al. (1988) claim that the subtle and diverse needs of patients with neurological and neuropsychological disability are unlikely to be met by one discipline. Wade (1987), in a discussion on neurological rehabilitation, recommends that "Hospitals and communities should develop teams or groups of specialist staff which concentrate upon managing patients with neurological disorders" (p. 47). He feels that there are enough patients of this kind in every district "to warrant specialist teams". Chamberlain (1988) also makes the comment that "a team approach is vital

in rehabilitation" (p. 49), but does not follow up that remark with recommendations of how the team should operate, except to discuss the roles of some team members. The Report of the Working Party on the Management of Traumatic Brain Injury (Brooks et al., 1988) comments on the need for consultants to meet regularly with other members of the team to ensure that observations from staff and relatives are considered during the assessment of a patient's needs but, yet again, there is no attempt to translate such an aim into a set of procedures that can be adopted in clinical practice.

Although treatment teams may have become a common feature of many medical specialities, their structure and complexity in neurological rehabilitation is possibly unique (although they admittedly share some characteristics with psychiatric teams). If neurological rehabilitation is dependent upon the effectiveness of the treatment teams, good clinical practice demands that we have a better understanding of how teams are structured and organised, in order to appreciate their function. This chapter therefore attempts to explore the dynamics of treatment teams to understand what motivates and directs their activities, and how they need to be managed and led.

WHAT IS A TEAM?

To begin with, it is necessary to differentiate between teams and workgroups. Workgroups exist when people are brought into relationships with one another by virtue of the fact that they work together. In this relationship, however, they do not necessarily share either work tasks or responsibility and they do not use the fact that they work together to enhance what they are doing.

In health care, workgroups are often misconstrued as a team, either because "teams" are supposed to exist within the organisation or because it is convenient to refer to a collection of individuals as "a team". The problem with such misconceptions is that by designating a "group" as a "team", expectations will emerge, both from the group members themselves who begin to perceive themselves differently, as well as from those outside the group who expect it to operate in certain ways and achieve superior performance targets. The definition of a team provided by Furnell et al. (1987) combines the main characteristics of a neurological rehabilitation team:

- professionals from different disciplines who meet regularly
- the allocation, by each member, of a significant proportion of his/her time to the pursuit of a team's objectives
- agreement on explicit objectives for the team that determine the team's structure and function
- adequate administrative and clinical coordination to support the work of the team, although not necessarily by the same person on all occasions
- a defined geographical base
- a clear differentiation of, and respect for, those skills and roles that are specific and unique to individual members, as well as a recognition of those roles that may be shared.

These components of a team reflect the views expressed by Brill (1976), who described a team as "a group of people, each of whom possesses particular expertise; each of whom is responsible for making individual decisions; who together hold a common purpose; who meet together to communicate, collaborate, and consolidate knowledge, from which plans are made, actions determined and future decisions influenced" (p. 22). These convenient definitions of a team need to be construed in a more critical perspective however. Dingwall (1980) made the comment that teams are thought of as a way of *coordinating* individual activities. This implies that the work to which the team has been directed was not being properly coordinated in the first place!

WHY HAVE TEAMS?

The benefits of teamwork are based on the notion that organising people into teams will:

(1) improve communication between the individuals involved in treatment
(2) lead to shared knowledge between individuals of different disciplines allowing more efficient treatment of the individual patient
(3) allow a more consistent goal-oriented approach and better continuity of care, for the patient as a whole
(4) promote a broader perspective for health-care provision (see Pollock, 1986; Watts & Bennett, 1983)
(5) provide a stimulating environment enhancing the contribution of team members, improving motivation, and increasing individual effectiveness
(6) create an *esprit de corps* that leads to a mutually supporting atmosphere.

In addition to these positive claims for teamwork it is also hoped that this approach will reduce weaknesses present in any health-care system. For example, any person working alone may suffer from limitations of knowledge or experience, whereas a team of different but interrelated workers can ameliorate these weaknesses and offer a framework to provide a holistic approach to the development of therapeutic plans for patients.

The value of a team approach is, however, based on assumptions and not upon any evaluation of outcome. To do this the "team model" would need to be tested against the "medical model", a virtually impossible task considering the overlapping elements of each model system and the fact (in practice) that quality of care transcends any kind of theoretical model. Given the complex nature of modern medicine there is, of course, a prima-facie argument for a team-based approach to patient care. This is based on the fact that medical technology is keeping people alive longer, saving life where previously death would have been inevitable, or giving life when *nature*, in terms of foetal or congenital abnormalities, would have prevented it occurring. Consequently health care is rapidly becoming a system where *quality* of life has become equal in importance to the preservation of life. The effectiveness of neurological and neuropsychological rehabilitation is increasingly being judged in terms of *social outcome*, a notion that incorporates quality of life because it addresses those disabilities that result in social handicap (World Health Organisation, 1980). This means that our work is ultimately directed towards community reintegration, a task that, of necessity, incorporates a variety of skills and where the importance of specific disciplines shifts as the evolution of recovery takes place.

WHAT TYPE OF TEAM?

Early approaches to team development in rehabilitation were based on the notion of *multidisciplinary* teams (disciplines working together but with separate roles and rehabilitation goals). It is the team structure most prevalent to (and suitable for) hospital-based rehabilitation, addressing relatively circumscribed goals with patients at an early stage of recovery. A multidisciplinary team approach was developed to provide a comprehensive assessment of a patient's disability pattern, helping to focus attention on specific treatment needs. However, as Mullins, Keller, and Chaney (1994) and Woodruff and McGonigal (1988) point out, there are limitations to this approach because independent team functions can lead to fragmented care if communication between team members is ineffective. Linder (1983) has argued that a multidisciplinary approach does not facilitate a holistic view of the patient, increasing the possibility that team members from different disciplines could end up working against each other if fragmented perceptions lead to divergent treatment plans, goals, and expectations (Mullins et al., 1994).

Notions of an *interdisciplinary model* developed largely as a result of the experiences of teams working in brain injury rehabilitation, addressing complex *neurobehavioural sequelae*. This type of rehabilitation, especially in later stages of recovery, exposed the limitations of the multidisciplinary approach. Wood (1989), for example, placed an emphasis on communication and coordination of care when working towards treatment goals. Mullins et al. (1994), in their analysis of team structures, suggests that an interdisciplinary approach incorporates formal methods of communication between team members, usually in the form of team meetings coordinated by a team leader/case manager.

The essential difference however, between multi- and interdisciplinary teams is that the roles and functions of the former are distinct, whereas in the latter they overlap. Eames (1989) describes this as a "blurring and sharing of roles", which may require staff to "learn and develop new skills which may be outside their normal professional requirements and experience" (p. 52). This approach is not without problems, however. The emphasis is on team members collaborating, to negotiate priorities and responsibilities. This largely depends upon the ability of team members to communicate openly and objectively. This ability varies according to the experience and personality of individual team members. The nature of this working process does not suit many personality types. A person may be a good therapist but lack the ability to be assertive in discussions about clinical priorities and treatment methods. Other therapists may feel uncomfortable stepping outside their professional role. Pressure to do so can lead to resentment and a breakdown of the team structure, possibly reflected by staff saying one thing but doing another when they feel they are not being watched. Consequently, although an interdisciplinary approach may be the best way of addressing certain types of rehabilitation programmes, it should not be considered the preferred approach for all types of rehabilitation and should not be introduced without careful staff selection and training.

The description of interdisciplinary team work given by Eames (1989) would now be understood as a description of *transdisciplinary* teamwork and is gaining ground as a method of teamwork in the social rehabilitation of people with neurobehavioural disability. This approach to teamwork involves the sharing of responsibilities by all team members, often with one discipline teaching some of its skills to other disciplines. This is done in order that more staff members are familiar with therapy procedures that are employed frequently as part of the overall rehabilitation programme. Mullins et al. (1994) describe the hallmark of this approach as "role release", something which Woodruff and McGonigle (1988) describe as "the sum of several separate but related processes, including role extension, role enrichment, role expansion, role exchange, role release and role support" (p. 168). The ultimate goal of this approach is to promote an integrated assessment and develop a unified treatment plan that is jointly carried out by all team members. It demands maximum group interaction and a focused treatment effort. It is an approach that incorporates the patient and family as part of the team, potentially eliminating any confusion about treatment procedures and goals.

In theory, this approach allows staff to integrate all working activities, learn from each other, and generate a greater understanding about theories and methods employed by other disciplines to the greater good of the patient in particular, and rehabilitation in general. In practice, however, the approach has the same strengths and weaknesses of the interdisciplinary model. The weakness of any team approach lies in the personality of the team members themselves. To facilitate the operational effectiveness of treatment teams we need to maintain a constant awareness of at least two things: (1) the organisational structure in which the team functions, and (2) the interpersonal dynamics of the teams.

ORGANISATIONAL ISSUES

One of the first considerations in the development of a team approach is the way the team, as a separate clinical unit, fits into existing organisational frameworks and management systems. Specialist teams need to have the kind of autonomy that makes it difficult for them to operate within large hospital systems organised departmentally and hierarchically. Some of the reasons for this will be touched on later when the functions and roles of team members are discussed but, primarily, a team needs to organise itself into a unit which has its own timetable of activities and a flexible style of operation that allows the changing needs of patients to be continuously addressed. To achieve this the team needs to establish its own staffing patterns, hours, or schedules of work, and responsibility or reporting structure.

These organisational issues often conflict with the more traditional management systems that operate in hospitals. For bureaucratic and professional reasons, team members are also members of departments and departmental procedures may conflict with team needs. Some therapy departments choose to rotate staff through different specialities in order to increase experience of staff and prevent boredom. This may be a good management procedure but it conflicts with the notion of a team, where consistency of staffing is needed to help develop a team identity and provide continuity of care. This may be one reason why nurses have difficulty integrating into a multidisciplinary team. They are always subject to their own management hierarchy and may be moved on and off teams in order to maintain staffing levels in other hospital areas. This maintains (on paper) adequate nursing cover for a hospital but causes havoc with treatment continuity and the integration of a multidisciplinary team, such that other team members may feel that they cannot rely on the continuous involvement of nursing staff and find it easier to delegate responsibility for the more important treatment activities to other therapy staff, relegating nursing to a secondary "caring" role.

The problems imposed by traditional management systems led many brain-injury rehabilitation teams in America to break away from large hospitals and become completely autonomous with regard to staffing, budget, and management systems. Based on his own clinical experience in Britain, a similar move was recommended by Eames, Turnbull, and Goodman-Smith (1989) and also (less directly) by Evans and Skidmore (1989). Healthcare managers must therefore recognise that if they advocate a team approach they must create a system that allows the team to operate effectively and with the confidence that their procedures or working methods are not going to be unnecessarily overturned by a departmental head or line manager.

The neurological rehabilitation team

Lack of coordination or organisation often increases as a function of the complexity of the task. This is one reason why neurological rehabilitation is best provided in a team context. The modern concept of neurological rehabilitation is based on a broad and comprehensive view of the limitations imposed upon an individual's lifestyle by the various disabilities that follow neurological impairment. The *Oxford English Dictionary* defines "rehabilitation" as a process that helps an individual with mental or physical handicap return to society. Many rehabilitation specialists may consider this definition to be axiomatic, but it is one that presents special problems for neurological rehabilitation because brain damage or central nervous system disease may result in some combination of physical disability, diminished cognitive resources, alterations of behaviour, and emotional instability; all or any of which can impose serious constraints upon community re-entry.

To address these diverse problems, it is necessary for a number of different professions to share the rehabilitation workload, promoting not only the clinical recovery of individual patients, but helping to ensure that clinical recovery becomes translated into good social outcome. To achieve this aim, teamwork in neurological rehabilitation involves the definition of common goals and the development of a plan to which each member makes a different but complementary contribution. The clinical rationale for this approach in brain-injury rehabilitation was outlined by Wood (1989) and one way of integrating staff to achieve good results has been offered by Eames et al. (1989).

The structure and function of a neurological rehabilitation team

For most individuals, the composition of a neurological rehabilitation team would be a medical doctor, therapists from the various disciplines, nursing staff, a social worker, and a clinical psychologist. In America, where the rehabilitation team is more established, they would add at least a vocational specialist, a clinical coordinator, and a case manager to this list. (There is of course a question as to whether or not relatives should be considered a part of the rehabilitation team, especially after the acute recovery phase of head injury or stroke. Constraints on space prevent a full consideration of this possibility, however.)

This introduces the concept of the *nuclear team* and the *support team*. The former comprises those individuals most involved with the patient on a day-to-day basis and usually consists of nursing staff, physiotherapists, speech therapists, occupational therapists, and clinical coordinator. A support team (which exists in theory, although not necessarily in practice) includes a doctor, clinical psychologist, social worker, vocational specialist, and case manager. These are in some respects more peripheral to the workings of the rehabilitation team because (1) their role is different (not having the same "hands-on" quality as the nuclear team), (2) they may not be in daily contact with either patient or team, (3) they are often perceived differently by patients and relatives, and (4) they may direct their time to acting as liaisons between either the team and family/employer, or the patient and the social environment to which he/she will return.

The point to be emphasised here is that the composition of the rehabilitation team and its mode of operation must reflect how the team perceives its goals of treatment. In a team that is rigidly structured according to professional boundaries, treatment will be *discipline oriented*. If, however, the goals of treatment are considered collectively by the team, the wider needs of a patient often emerge, forcing staff to realise that to achieve certain goals treatment must be conducted in a way that cuts across discipline boundaries and, as such, becomes *outcome oriented*.

Team goals

The rehabilitation of people with neurological disorders evolves through several stages, depending on the underlying clinical problem and pattern of handicap. However, the eventual discharge goals are more often determined by the kind of psychosocial environment to which the person will return rather than any clinical criteria (Wood, 1989). In the early stage of recovery the goals are primarily clinical, aimed at establishing medical stability, bowel and bladder control, skin care, and recovery of motor function. There will be an emphasis on nursing care and the reduction of physical disability. At this stage, the team *per se* may need only consist of doctors, nurses, physiotherapists, and occupational therapists. At a later stage of rehabilitation, however, the goals shift from clinical, to social or vocational. The primary aims of treatment become focused upon how a person uses skills, rather than the continued pursuit of the skills themselves. Emotional, behavioural, and cognitive factors become emphasised at this stage, requiring (1) psychological input to the team to identify learning difficulties and/or help the patient adjust to permanent disability, (2) speech therapy to optimise the person's communication skills, and (3) a vocational assessment to determine alternative work opportunities. Social work assistance may be required at any time to liaise with relatives and determine their needs *vis-à-vis* the patient or the employer but, during this period, they may help the treatment team recognise the social goals of treatment by illustrating the type of environment and support systems available after discharge.

Any discussion of team goals would be incomplete without some consideration of when team decisions need to defer to expert, individual decisions. The most obvious example would be deference to a physician on some matter of clinical safety or medical stability. Less obvious deferments would be to (1) a psychologist, in circumstances where learning difficulties have been identified that alter the way a patient responds to rehabilitation procedures, (2) a physiotherapist, in respect to advice on matters of mobility and balance, and (3) a social worker, when family needs have been identified that cut across the stated team's goal. There are many other situations when the team needs to acknowledge the expertise and experience of its own members and not force a utilitarian decision simply because the mechanism for one is available.

Team roles

The goals of the team at any stage of recovery will largely determine the roles of its members. As implied previously, these can be reduced to two broad categories—clinical recovery or social re-entry. The latter depends to a large extent upon the former, but the former is not sufficient (as a criterion for rehabilitation outcome) without the latter.

The prominence of different team members changes as recovery progresses. In post-acute stages, therapists need to be concerned with the application of function in real-life settings. This often proves a major obstacle to teamwork because some therapists (perhaps physiotherapists in particular) find it very difficult to leave the clinic and extend training in mobility or coordination out in the community. Nursing staff also seem unable to throw off the shackles of a shift system or the need to carry out other "statutory" procedures, which are often unnecessary or less important to community training. Speech therapists hardly ever see if their client can communicate as fluently at the supermarket check-out as they do in therapy sessions! Clinical psychologists are often too tied to standard test procedures to assess cognition by observing how patients respond in functional or community settings.

The moral of this rather critical perspective is that, in the course of applying rehabilitation training, therapists often lose their way and pursue objectives that have little social value to the patient. Teare and McPheeters (1970) found that in most working environments staff organise their time and activities to suit their own convenience rather than the employer or the project on which they work. Health-care staff of any discipline are as vulnerable to this problem as anyone else; therefore, in order to keep staff focused on the priorities of treatment on a day-to-day basis, clinical coordinators have come into being.

Clinical coordination

Noon (1988) has referred to an interdisciplinary team as a group consisting of "persons trained in different fields of knowledge with different concepts, methods, data, and terms, organised for a 'common effort' on a 'common problem' with continuous intercommunication among the participants from the different disciplines" (p. 1160). This diversity of disciplines, knowledge, working procedures, and attitudes can be a recipe for disaster unless the individual roles of team members are properly integrated and continuously directed to the "common problem". Those experienced in team development and management will recognise that Noon's notion of "common effort" may exist as a precarious entity, and the idea of a "common problem" often seems more an illusion than a reality.

Rehabilitation goals are often difficult to define and can vary according to who is offering the definition. Pollock (1986, p. 128) points to the "variety of perceptions of health goals and the assortment of pathways to reach these goals". She proposes that the different perspectives and approaches to their solution can be divisive and "militate against effective team functioning". Her "key concepts" for effective teamwork therefore become (1) coordination of several people, (2) cooperation, and (3) working towards a common aim. The appointment of a clinical coordinator in each multidisciplinary team can help achieve these aims. The role of a coordinator is to facilitate the interdisciplinary process by keeping track of treatment goals, thereby improving the continuity between different aspects of treatment. The coordinator should try and help team members evaluate their treatment methods with respect to those outcome goals that have social significance for the patient. The coordinator can also take some of the burden off the clinical team by acting as a link between them and certain outside agencies who may need to offer services to the team on an occasional basis. Coordinators may also assume a personnel role, arbitrating between members of the team when differences of opinion prevail.

Case managers

Whereas a clinical coordinator provides continuity at each stage of recovery, a case manager provides a continuous link throughout the whole recovery/rehabilitation continuum (Aronow, Desimone, & Wood, 1986). In this respect, therefore, case managers are the ultimate coordinators. In America, case managers become involved as early as possible in order to ensure that patients and their families receive information about treatment opportunities that can maximise recovery during the acute phase. Later they are responsible for identifying and coordinating services between hospital and the community, providing, where necessary, advice on long-term residential placement.

McMillan et al. (1988) emphasise the importance of a case manager in promoting recovery and reducing the burden of stress on families. They argue that the case management role cannot be subsumed by other members of the therapy team on an occasional or temporary basis. They also seek to distinguish this role from that of a social worker. Most social workers become involved at a particular stage of recovery, rather than throughout the continuum, and may lack the knowledge of rehabilitation procedures or patterns of recovery from different types of brain injury necessary to evaluate progress and advise families on alternative treatment opportunities.

TEAM DYNAMICS

How team members see themselves and their role often determines how they relate to other individuals in the team which, in turn, determines the quality of communication and the operational effectiveness of the team. Several things influence this perception: the first is the commitment of an individual to the "team concept" as opposed to a "discipline concept"; the second involves role and status factors affecting the cohesion between team members; the third comprises personality and motivational factors, which determine whether a team member works towards team goals or their own personal (covert) goals.

Team oriented or discipline oriented?

Many team members also belong to departments within a hospital and this may influence their sense of priority and feelings of allegiance. For example, a therapist may feel a responsibility to work in a certain way that fits in with the activities of the team but remains accountable to a head of department who demands a style of working, time keeping, and reporting that is incompatible with the team concept.

This can be a significant source of stress and tension to a team member who, in trying to address the requirements of two masters, succeeds in satisfying neither and antagonising both. In some respects the solution to this dilemma is relatively simple because it is a management or administrative problem which should be referred to (and resolved by) a higher level of authority. In practice, however, the bureaucratic nature of organisations prevent such decision making, protracting and compounding the problems experienced by clinical staff, often to the detriment of their work. Such conflicts should be considered during the early planning stage, before members of a team are identified, in order that a proper frame of reference can be adopted by the team members once they are brought together.

It must be realised, however, that discipline-oriented behaviour amongst team members may reflect feelings of anxiety on the part of individuals who find it difficult to adjust to teamworking. As Snyder (1981) points out, there has been a lack of educational preparation for teamwork amongst health-care professionals, which means that the different therapy disciplines are not sure how to relate to each other in a team context, allowing divisions between therapists and nursing staff to become particularly pronounced, acting as a major constraint to the continuity of care and the total integration of the treatment team.

Because young therapists, newly qualified, are not trained to work in teams, they often feel more comfortable in a departmental structure, surrounded by professional colleagues to whom they can turn for advice and support. In an interdisciplinary team, one may be seen as the "expert" for specific areas of activity, creating anxieties about one's ability to produce innovative solutions to complex clinical problems. Alternatively, experienced therapists, who should have no difficulty adapting their skills to suit new situations, often feel threatened by having their ideas questioned, or being asked to change a well-established work pattern in order to accommodate what the team sees as a better style of working.

The cohesiveness of a team may depend largely on the methods used to integrate different skills, methods and concepts that traditionally have separated individuals. Problems arise when people lack a clear conception of what their role entails, or when other people's expectations of them are different from their own (Kahn, Wolf, & Quinn, 1964). The implications of role ambiguity according to Chell (1987) are: (1) inappropriate behaviours and actions become wrongly associated with a particular role, (2) decisions may be taken by the wrong people, and (3) conflict both within and between role occupants may arise.

One way of avoiding role ambiguity is to avoid roles! Some exponents of the rehabilitation team advocate a "blurring of roles" (Eames et al., 1989), even to the point of using collective titles, such as rehabilitation officer, to avoid discriminating between disciplines (Eames, 1989). Other writers (Lewis, 1984;

Payne, 1982) feel that this may not be the best practice, however, because many individuals find role ambiguity very stressful and therefore avoid working in team-oriented centres. However, as Eames et al. point out, roles can be blurred without losing sight of a person's skills or when those skills should be utilised to advise and lead the teams thinking about a problem.

To achieve the kind of cohesiveness that promotes interpersonal activity, increases communication, and improves treatment delivery, teamwork must include: (1) a process for deciding on goals, (2) a process for helping members adapt their personal skills and responsibilities to achieve these goals, and (3) a process of dividing up and distributing the work. Consideration must also be given to the personal and career development of team members allowing some integration of their personal expectations with those of the parent organisation.

Personality and motivational issues

The fact that a rehabilitation team consists of a variety of disciplines and traditions makes its internal cohesiveness quite fragile and provides conditions where personality differences achieve a significance out of all proportion to the problems which precede them. Unless these differences are attended to, the "continuous intercommunication" Noon (1988) refers to will never happen and the group will never function as a team, capable of coordinating their efforts to achieve a common goal.

Chell (1987) argues that team management should reflect the twin objectives of any organisation: to achieve operational goals and satisfy individual needs. Payne (1982) claimed that personal development and team development are inseparable in any kind of collaborative team. Consequently, team development must include efforts to establish a good level of interpersonal activity between individuals in order for them to function properly as a team and be effective. This is one reason why Dyer (1984) described a team as "a collection of people who must rely on group collaboration if each member is to experience the optimum of success in goal achievement" (p. 4).

If motivation and personal development are such important factors in team development the team leader should hold a series of interviews with team members to identify their personal needs and, where possible, accommodate these in terms of training or counselling. This exercise can lead to alternative courses of action. One alternative is to do nothing! This may be chosen if only one individual presents a problem and when that person's needs are so out of line with the team's needs that it is easier to lose the individual than restructure the team. The other alternative, a teambuilding exercise, needs to be considered if several team members (especially key members) have personal needs that are not being met by the team's needs.

One procedure for teambuilding was proposed by Dyer (1984) and consists of the following procedures:

(1) Take at least 1 day off for teambuilding and get away from the hospital or clinic so that there will be no interruptions. Also, the change of environment may create a change of

ambience that will help blur divisions between disciplines and reduce status differentials.

(2) Each person should write his or her answers to the following set of questions and be prepared to discuss these answers with the other members of the team:

    (a) What keeps you from being as effective as you would like to be in your position?

    (b) What keeps the staff in the rehabilitation unit or in your department from functioning as an effective team?

    (c) What do you like about this unit/team that you want to maintain?

    (d) What suggestions do you have for improving the quality of working relationships and the functioning of the team with respect to achieving patient goals or providing better patient care.

(3) At the meeting, each person should present his or her responses to the questions in (2) and these responses should be written on a blackboard or flip chart. Responses are categorised under four headings:

    (a) blocks to individual effectiveness

    (b) blocks to team effectiveness

    (c) things people like

    (d) suggestions for improvement.

(4) The group should list, according to priority, the problems they want to address and this will form the agenda for the rest of that meeting and subsequent meetings.

(5) The group should try to eliminate as many obstacles to team development as possible. This may include clarifying roles, resolving misunderstandings about interpersonal attitudes, and sharing more information on each other's discipline activities.

The point of this exercise is to engage the team in a regular examination of its own effectiveness and to encourage the development of solutions to its own problems. This can be a complex process and the group will require some guidance to address pertinent issues and not become sidetracked into unproductive arguments. Someone therefore needs to facilitate the exchange of views and the elucidation of ideas and procedures that will promote internal cohesiveness and the achievement of team goals.

TEAM LEADERSHIP

Multidisciplinary teams obviously pose problems of status and leadership. As Kane (1980) pointed out, any team with a doctor in it tends towards a leader-centred pattern with the doctor as leader, either because the other members of the group are used to a subordinate position and the group process reflects this (Odhnar, 1970) or because doctors argue that they are legally responsible for decisions about patients and therefore resist the involvement of others.

Most clinical references to a rehabilitation team represent the "consultant in charge" concept as the automatic criterion for leadership. The Report of the Working Party on the Management of Traumatic Brain Injury (Brooks et al., 1988) states that "the ward rehabilitation team should be led by the Consultant in charge of the case . . ." followed by the statement that "this task must not routinely be delegated" (p. 11). Chamberlain (1988) and Wade (1987) point to the medical consultant as the natural leader or manager by virtue of "clinical responsibility". However, in the context of a multidisciplinary team, Furnell et al. (1987) ask: "Who is responsible to whom, for what, and under what circumstances?" (p. 15).

Responsibility and leadership

Furnell et al. (1987) describe the general concept of responsibility as "the expectation, obligation or duty of individuals or groups to perform certain functions and their culpability for neglecting these" (p. 15). There are, however, social and professional expectations of responsibility and these are often confused with formal organisational or legal definitions of responsibility. It is necessary to discriminate between these different perspectives if the question of responsibility and leadership is to be properly understood.

One cannot confuse or contest the concept of medical responsibility. It is based upon the formal training that every doctor receives and their ultimate qualification in medicine. In addition, the legal responsibilities of medical practitioners are incorporated in the National Health Service Act of 1946. However, rehabilitation, especially in the later stages of recovery, is not actually medical. If anything, the type of activity carried out at most stages of rehabilitation is "clinical", although at later stages rehabilitation becomes essentially social. "Clinical rehabilitation" covers a variety of skills, professions, and settings. This changes the perspective of treatment from medical care to health care, shifting what may be construed as legal responsibility away from the medical doctor and establishing within every professional discipline a responsibility for the patient's treatment and quality of care.

The organisation and infrastructure of neurological rehabilitation has not received formal consideration by government working parties, either in Britain or America, but one could possibly make comparisons with the Nodder Working Group (Nodder, 1980) who reported to the Department of Health and Social Security on the organisation and management problems of mental hospitals. They concluded that there was "no basis in law for the commonly expressed idea that a consultant may be held responsible for negligence on the part of others, simply because he is the 'responsible medical officer' " (p. 23). Within the context of a multidisciplinary team it would seem that no professional can be held responsible for another professional's actions, except in part by negligent delegation or referral.

Team leadership and team membership

What is the position of a doctor as team member? Most doctors, especially consultants, will recognise that their actual involvement with the team is quite limited, particularly in the later stages of rehabilitation. Once medical stability has been achieved doctors spend little time giving "hands-on" treatment (if they do any at all). Therapists, on the other hand, spend all their work-ing hours in the rehabilitation unit and several hours each day with individual patients. Doctors, by virtue of their different role, have duties that take them away from the rehabilitation unit, giving them less opportunity to involve themselves with day-to-day rehabilitation activities. Consequently they tend to see less of patients than other members of the rehabilitation team and, by implication, are less involved in the total rehabilitative care of a patient. This peripheral involvement can have a detri-mental effect on the internal cohesiveness of the group, breeding resentment and disharmony, which can destabilise the team at times of pressure and stress.

One example illustrating this was recently given by a consult-ant neuropsychiatrist in charge of a neurological rehabilitation team in Houston, Texas (Cassidy, personal communication). He explained how different therapy disciplines contributed each morning to the dressing and personal hygiene programmes of patients with various forms of disability. The medical staff, however, did not become involved until later in the morning when the progress of each patient was presented to them dur-ing a team conference. This created a division of labour not appreciated by the other members of the clinical team. Eventu-ally the consultant-in-charge recognised this and accepted the responsibility of helping to wash and dress one of the patients each morning as part of his contribution to his schedule of activities. His greater involvement with the more routine and "menial" activities of the unit increased the motivation of the other team members, altered the perceptions of patients about the importance of morning hygiene activities, made him feel a more central part of the team, and seemed to elevate morale and team performance generally, making this an effective use of his time.

Generally speaking, the skills and efforts of the various ther-apy disciplines are the ones that determine whether or not a patient will achieve his or her rehabilitation potential and, in most respects, the doctor's primary function is to act as a consult-ant for the team, advising them on medical issues and pointing out how certain conditions may impose constraints upon treat-ment. If one therefore determines leadership by the amount of involvement with the team or the contribution of team members to achieve team goals, the doctor would hardly be in the running in comparison with other disciplines.

Characteristics of a leader

Chell (1987) states that "Leadership is not a set of personal-ity characteristics per se, nor a style of operating which can be learned, but the ability to respond appropriately to the contin-gencies of a situation" (p. 133). This definition distinguishes between *what* leadership *is* as opposed to *how* to lead. With respect to what makes a leader, several reviews of leadership research find no substantive evidence to demonstrate that a leader has any distinctive quality (or set of qualities) that separate him or her from other members of the group (Chell, 1987; House & Baetz, 1979; Yetton, 1984). House and Baetz suggest that there

are three "invariant characteristics" of all leadership situations: (1) social skills, (2) the ability to influence others, and (3) the ability to fulfil task requirements and organisational goals. In specifying these characteristics the focus shifts from personal-ity traits to skills and abilities (what Mischel, 1968 refers to as *competencies*).

The principles of leadership appear to be the same at whatever level in the leadership hierarchy one operates or whatever the circumstances of the leadership role. The set of skills which an effective leader must have and exercise are (1) an ability to diagnose situations, (2) an ability to exercise judgement about what needs to be done and to do it, and (3) to have an adapt-ive personality, flexible enough to behave in ways demanded by the situation in order to maintain appropriate social skills and exercise influence. Belbin (1981) reduces the characterist-ics of a leader to "someone tolerant enough to listen to others but strong enough to reject their advice" (p. 53). In this respect a fundamental aspect of leadership is perception. Leaders have to protect themselves from the tendency to perceive aspects of the situation selectively, possibly distorting what appears to have happened, placing an incorrect interpretation on events.

Team structure and decision making

If the doctor is seen as the one who makes all the decisions, then a hierarchical structure automatically develops within the team and this tends to create an inflexible style of working. Burns and Stalker (1961) argue that hierarchical control can be effective when the problems that arise are predictable, but when staff are required to find innovative solutions to problems a hier-archically organised system can prevent (1) the right kind of staff interaction, (2) the production of ideas, and (3) the sense of responsibility that may be required to establish and achieve groups goals. Wilkinson (1973) found that resistance to innov-ation is less strong when there is a high level of interaction amongst staff, implying that a leader-centred structure is the least desirable system for a rehabilitation team.

A number of experts on team development have commented upon the need for a leader to be open to influence (Ends & Page, 1977; Likert, 1961; Payne, 1982). Ends and Page claim that the amount of influence a leader has over a team depends on how much the team think they can influence the leader. Likert felt that if team members were allowed to influence the leader's decisions they would have more commitment to them, based on his principle of *interaction influence*. The value of this to the leader is that if the team members adopt his decisions as their own, the leader will actually (but covertly) have more control over their subsequent actions.

Vroom and Yetton (1973) proposed a decision-making model that would help balance the quality of a decision and its accept-ance by team members. This model enables the team leader to decide which management style to adopt according to the demands of a situation. Five leadership styles were identified.

(1) The leader makes an executive decision autonomously, based upon an appraisal of the situation.

(2) The leader asks team members for information and their perceptions of the situation before making a decision.

(3) The leader shares the problem with team members individually, obtains their opinion, and then makes a decision that may or may not reflect the ideas of team members.

(4) The leader shares the problem collectively with all team members, obtains their views, but again makes a decision that may or may not reflect these views.

(5) The leader shares the problem with the group, encourages them to discuss it and collectively reach alternative solutions. Once consensus is reached, the decision is implemented.

The decision on which style to adopt depends upon (1) the time available to reach a decision, (2) the amount of knowledge available to the group to help them reach a sensible decision, (3) how important it is to have the team adopt the decision, and (4) the general level of agreement existing in the group at any given time. In a multidisciplinary team dealing with clinical issues, these factors will always vary and therefore the model seems to reflect the reality of most leadership situations.

SUMMARY

Instead of providing a clinical utopia, attempts to establish and implement rehabilitation teams often flounder on the rocks of personality conflict, role ambiguity, status problems, or the lack of a clinical model that will provide a framework for team activities and direct efforts in a way that unifies clinical staff rather than fragments them. Management ideology often overlooks the fact that there are "teams within teams" and that team members also belong to departments. Team membership is not therefore an all-or-none thing, and some consideration must always be given to the multiple identities shared by some members of a clinical team in order to understand how the team's structure and its position in a broader health care system may influence the dynamics of team membership.

The development of teams in any health-care system has never been easy and more effort is needed during staff training to convey their value. It is also important to educate qualified staff in the potential advantages (to patients) of a team approach. Part of this education will inevitably involve disabusing some clinical staff that working under the same roof or sharing treatment on the same patient may be necessary, but not sufficient criteria for a team approach to neurological rehabilitation.

REFERENCES

Aronow, A., Desimone, B., & Wood, R.Ll. (1986). Traumatic brain injury, discharge and beyond. *Continuing Care*, December, 14–16.

Belbin, R.M. (1981). *Management teams*. London: Heinemann.

Brill, N.I. (1976). *Team work: Working together in the human services*. Philadelphia: J.B. Lippincott.

Brooks, D.N., Eames, P.G., Evans, C., et al. (1988). *Report of the Working Party on the Management of Traumatic Brain Injury*. London: Medical Disability Society, Royal College of Physicians.

Burns, T., & Stalker, G.M. (1961). *The management of innovation*. London: Tavistock.

Chamberlain, M.A. (1988). The rehabilitation team and functional assessment. In C.J. Goodwill & M.A. Chamberlain (Eds.), *Rehabilitation of the physically disabled adult*. London: Croom Helm.

Chell, E. (1987). *The psychology of behaviour in organisations*. London: Macmillan.

Dingwall, R. (1980). Problems of team work in primary care. In S. Lonsdale, A. Webb, & T. Briggs (Eds.), *Team work in the personal social services and health care*. Croom Helm: London.

Dyer, W.G. (1984). *Team building: Issues and alternatives*. Reading, MA: Addison Wesley.

Eames, P.G. (1989). Head injury rehabilitation: Towards a "model" service. In R.Ll. Wood & P.G. Eames (Eds.), *Models of brain injury rehabilitation*. London: Croom Helm.

Eames, P.G., Turnbull, J., & Goodman-Smith, A. (1989). Service delivery and assessment of programmes. In M. Lezak (Ed.), *Assessment of the behavioural consequences of head trauma*. New York: Alan R. Liss.

Ends, E.J., & Page, C.W. (1977). *Organisational team building*. Cambridge, MA: Winthrop.

Evans, C., & Skidmore, B. (1989). Rehabilitation in the community. In R.Ll. Wood & P.G. Eames (Eds.), *Models of brain injury rehabilitation*. London: Chapman & Hall.

Furnell, J., Flett, S., & Clarke, D.F. (1987). Multidisciplinary clinical teams: Some issues in establishment and function. *Hospital and Health Services Review*, January, 15–18.

House, R.T., & Baetz, M.L. (1979). Leadership, some empirical generalisations. In B. Straw (Ed.), *Research in organisational behaviour* (Vol. 1, pp. 341–423). New York: Grune and Stratton.

Kahn, R.L., Wolf, D.M., & Quinn, R.P. (1964). *Organisational stress*. New York: Wiley.

Kane, R.A. (1980). Multidisciplinary team work in the United States: Trends, issues and implications for the social worker. In A. Lonsdale, A. Webb, & T. Briggs (Eds.), *Team work in the personal social services and health care*. London: Croom Helm.

Lewis, P. (1984). *Multidisciplinary clinical teams* [Discussion paper]. Manchester, UK: Northwestern Regional Health Authority, Psychology Advisory Committee.

Likert, R. (1961). *New patterns of management*. New York: McGraw-Hill.

Linder, T. (1983). *Early childhood special education: Program development and administration*. Baltimore, MD: Brookes.

McMillan, T.M., Greenwood, R.J., Morris, J.R., et al. (1988). An introduction to the concept of head injury case management with respect to the need for service provision. *Clinical Rehabilitation, 2*, 319–322.

Mischel, W. (1968). *Personality and assessment*. New York: Wiley.

Mullins, L.L., Keller, J.R., & Chaney, J.M. (1994). A systems and social cognitive approach to team functioning in physical rehabilitation settings. *Rehabilitation Psychology, 39*(3), 161–178.

Nodder, P. (1980). *Working group on the organisation and management problems of mental illness hospitals*. London: Her Majesty's Stationery Office.

Noon, M. (1988). Teams: The best option? *Health Services Journal*, October, 1160–1161.

Odhnar, F. (1970). Group dynamics of the interdisciplinary team. *American Journal of Occupational Therapy, 24*(7), 484–487.

Ovretveit, J. (1986). *Organisation of multidisciplinary community teams*. Uxbridge, UK: Health Services Centre, Brunel University.

Payne, M. (1982). *Working in teams*. London: Macmillan.

Pollock, L. (1986). The multidisciplinary team. In C. Hume & I. Pullen (Eds.), *Rehabilitation in psychiatry*. London: Churchill Livingstone.

Royal College of Psychiatrists. (1984). The responsibility of consultants in psychiatry. *Bulletin of the Royal College of Psychiatrists, 8*, 123–126.

Snyder, M. (1981). Preparation of nursing students for health care teams. *International Journal of Nursing Studies, 8, 18*(2), 115–122.

Teare, R.J., & McPheeters, H.L. (1970). *Manpower utilisation in social welfare: A report based on a symposium on manpower utilisation and social welfare services*. Atlanta, SA: Social Welfare Management Project, Southern Regional Educational Board.

Vroom, V.H., & Yetton, P.W. (1973). *Leadership and decision making*. Pittsburgh, PA: University of Pittsburgh Press.

Wade, D.T. (1987). Neurological rehabilitation. *International Disability Studies, 9*, 45–47.

Watts, F., & Bennett, D.H. (1983). *Theory and practice of psychiatric rehabilitation*. London: Wiley.

Wilkinson, G.S. (1973). Interaction patterns and staff response to psychiatric innovations. *Journal of Health and Social Behaviour, 14*, 323–329.

Wood, R.Ll. (1989). Salient factors in brain injury rehabilitation. In R.Ll. Wood & P.G. Eames (Eds.), *Models of brain injury rehabilitation*. London: Chapman & Hall.

Woodruff, G., & McGonigle, J.J. (1988). Early intervention team approaches: The transdisciplinary model. In J.B. Jordon (Ed.) *Early childhood special education*. Reston, VA: Council for Exceptional Children.

World Health Organisation. (1980). *International classification of impairments, disabilities and handicaps*. Geneva: Author.

Yetton, P. (1984). Leadership and supervision. In M. Grunberg & T. Wall (Eds.), *Social psychology and organisational behaviour*. Chichester, UK: John Wiley.

5. Measurement of disability and handicap

Christine Collin

INTRODUCTION

Assessment of disability and of handicap begins with an appraisal of the patient, in a hospital bed, in an out-patient department, or at home. It may be clarified or confirmed in those with communication disorders or cognitive impairment, by an interview with an immediate carer or next of kin. Other members of the rehabilitation team will contribute more detailed information. Assessment demands a knowledge of the tools available for the job but, more fundamentally, requires a recognition of disability and handicap. The diagnostic approach to disease militates against the careful functional analysis required in neurorehabilitation. It is difficult to remember that the patient dying with a paraneoplastic peripheral neuropathy may have independent upper limb function extended for weeks or months by the use of mobile arm supports or elbow coasters, when most medical enthusiasm is directed towards finding the primary lesion or considering the merits of cancer therapy.

This chapter aims to present a guide to the measures used in disability and handicap. The 1970s onwards have seen an explosion of these measures and most serious researchers in this field have now called for an end to the development of new measures suggesting that research interests can be focused on validation and reliability studies of existing measures, and a clear definition of their use, range, and limitations. An important application of their use is in the development of clinical audit.

Measures of disability and handicap are not confined by their descriptors. Some disability scales include impairments and many handicap measures record disability. There are four main categories of global disability and handicap measures. There are the early Activities of Daily Living (ADL) scales, which tend to record best the more severe levels of disability and are more relevant to hospitalised patients. Instrumental or extended Activities of Daily Living (IADL) are the second group and measure physical skills, but also reflect social skills and roles, and function within an environment or community. There is a third small group of measures, which are very short (five or six items only), easy, and quick to use, and are used to measure outcome in large medical trials. Last, there are many global health and life status questionnaires that cover physical, emotional, and social aspects of life, and attempt to record well-being or quality of life. These scales are usually long and may be used to compare communities, or groups of patients undergoing different treatments. Focal measures of ability, measuring one attribute or function such as gait speed, will not be covered in this chapter.

ICIDH AND ICIDH-2

The *International Classification of Impairments Disabilities and Handicap* (ICIDH) developed by Philip Wood of the World Health Organization (WHO, 1980) attempted to shed light and order on disabling experiences and has been revised. The original three terms used in Wood's 1980 ICIDH nomenclature—impairment, disability, and handicap—are attributed to Riviere (undated). They have become an accepted and useful framework within which to consider disablement.[1] Vreede (1988) commented on the negative aspect of these terms, preferring the more positive terms "activities of daily living" and "instrumental activities of daily living", and this suggested a continuum of experience.

Premorbid health and social status is rarely quantified in assessment scales although it is often the perceived rehabilitation goal of the patient and his family. The new ICIDH-2, begun in 1993 (WHO, 1997), tries to take this into account and removes some of the negative nomenclature, but changes two of the three terms, disability and handicap (Gray & Hendershot, 2000; WHO, 1997). The aim of the revision was make the tool more capable of use in different countries and cultures, and more acceptable to different sociological and health-care disciplines.

"Impairment" (I) has survived unchanged and is defined as a loss or abnormality of body structure or of a physiological or psychological structure. Abnormality is defined as a significant variation from a measured population norm.

"Activities" (A) replace "Disability" and are defined as the "nature and extent of functioning at the level of the person. Activities may be limited in nature duration and quality". This is a positive reframe of disability, removing the negative terminology, and concentrates on ability or *doing*.

---

[1] Disablement is a term that can be used less restrictively than the ICIDH-defined term "disability".

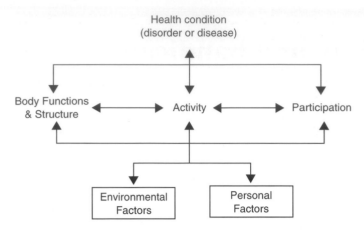

Figure 5.1. Current understanding of interactions between the constructs of ICIDH-2. (From β-I draft June 1997 with permission from WHO.)

"Participation" (P) replaces "Handicap", and like handicap deals with the societal consequences of the health condition. It is defined thus: "Participation is the nature and extent of a person's involvement in life situations in relation to Impairments Activities Health Conditions and Contextual factors." As before this still concentrates on *being*.

In practical terms in the health environment it was always difficult to achieve precise use of the terms disability and handicap, and it is likely that similar problems will be evident with the use of the new nomenclature. It retains the three-level classification and it improves on the understanding of the interactions and limitations of the model by including contextual factors in the new diagrammatic representation (Figure 5.1). It also removes the unidirectional and inevitable implications of the previous model. Inclusion of contextual factors is an attempt to acknowledge the premorbid status of the individual.

In ICIDH-2, participation emphasises interactions within society and the environment but still focuses on seven areas: personal maintenance; mobility; exchange of information; social relationships; education, work, leisure, and spirituality are the fifth area; economic life is the sixth; and the seventh is civic and community life. Survival roles are abandoned and there is a separate grading of contextual factors in recognition of the influence of premorbid and external factors on the generation of handicap.

It has taken many years for the original ICIDH nomenclature to enter common usage. The new terminology has been explained in this chapter but as it is not yet clear whether it will be accepted the original terms are retained.

WHY MEASURE?

Measurement in most specialities assists clinical management, research evaluation, and medical audit. In neurorehabilitation ADL assessment leads to the identification of significant disabilities. Regular measurement leads to the monitoring of change and frequent review of the treatment programme. This has a cascade effect and prompts both decision making and the determination of an accurate prognosis. This is a practical and educational exercise for all members of the rehabilitation team. Use of an appropriate ADL measure also permits long-distance, postal, or telephone follow-up.

In research evaluation use of a well-known and widely used ADL scale such as the Barthel (Mahoney & Barthel, 1965) means that entry and outcome data from different trials can be pooled or compared. Communication between research workers and different centres is enhanced if the same measurement tools are being used. The results of different interventions or no intervention can be more easily compared.

Attempts at audit in acute specialities have revealed many difficulties which are relevant to the problems posed in rehabilitation medicine. Defining endpoints is particularly difficult and can only be attempted with the use of appropriate measurement tools. The efficiency of different units can be compared. Audit of progress and management of specific disease processes becomes an integral part of the medical workload. If health service funding becomes insurance based then American experience suggests that scored disability assessments will play a vital part in securing remuneration for rehabilitation services. This was the reason in 1983 for the development of the prototype of the Functional Independence Measure (FIM) by Hamilton, Granger, and colleagues. The FIM is now one of the more widely used global measures of personal and extended ADL (Hamilton, Granger, & Sherwin et al., 1987). Other reasons for measuring include population screening, goal setting, selection of patients for clinical trials, and prioritisation or selection for specific treatments.

WHAT IS A GOOD MEASURE?

In the same way as one selects a screwdriver for screws or a hammer for nails, a good measure is only good if it is the most appropriate tool for the job. It is important to understand the strengths and limitations of the measuring tools available. Does it measure what you want? Does it measure it in units that you understand? The mathematical characteristics of scales should be understood before attempting statistical analysis (Collin, 1992). A scale might be ordinal, measuring magnitude, or nominal, describing rather than quantifying the data. Weighting might be added to give more emphasis to certain characteristics. Scores of disparate functions are often added together to give a single rating—the summed score. This defies mathematical logic but is all too often accepted in rehabilitation. Imagine asking what fruit and vegetables were left in the food store and being told, forty-three. Many disability scales are like this. Attempts have been made to develop hierarchical scales with Guttman scaling properties (Guttman, 1950) and interval scales with Rasch analysis (Rasch, 1980). Tennant, Geddes, and Chamberlain (1996) applied Rasch analysis to the Barthel Index to test its appropriateness as an interval measure, and found that a change in ability at the upper end of the scale was three times greater, unit for unit, than an apparently similar change in the middle of scale. This simply confirms that it is an ordinal scale and requires non-parametric statistical methods.

The more complicated or sensitive a measure is, the less reliable it is. A good scale is usually simple, measures the characteristic you are interested in or has a valid relationship to it, and is reliable. Repeating the test yields the same score and different people applying the scoring or doing the test, also achieve the same answer. There are many statistical methods of analysis in use to establish these properties. The pitfalls of measurement are expertly reviewed by McDowell and Newell (1996) and Wade (1992).

DISABILITY

Activities of daily living (ADL) are central to the measurement of disability. What are they? They are the basic self-care skills necessary for personal independence. The first published disability index that included everyday activities necessary for normal living was reported by Marjorie Sheldon in the *Journal of Health and Physical Education* in 1935. Judith Buchwald was the first user to publish the term "activities of daily living" in the *Physical Therapy Review* (1949), although some attribute the term to George Deaver (Deaver & Brown, 1945). Analysis of 25 ADL indices by Donaldson et al. in 1973 revealed that there were 10 essential activities in any ADL assessment. These are:

 (1) dressing
 (2) bathing
 (3) transfers
 (4) grooming
 (5) managing stairs
 (6) walking
 (7) feeding
 (8) going to the toilet
 (9) wheelchair skills
(10) continence.

The most important characteristics of any assessment are that it should be reliable, valid, sensitive, and simple to perform. Unfortunately, pursuit of individuality and sensitivity has led to the proliferation of longer and longer assessments, with more intricate scoring, covering a wider range of activities, that overlap into handicap. These are instrumental ADL scales and are discussed later.

Feinstein, Josephy, and Wells (1986) reviewed 43 functional disability indices and identified several problems. They pointed out that there is an absence of attention to the collaborative role of the patient, and suggested that complex psychosocial attributes are difficult to coordinate with physical ratings. Partridge and Johnston (1989) devised a rating of locus of control, which indicates whether the patient is passive (external) or self-motivated (internal). This can be used to predict collaborative effort and subsequent reduction of disability and handicap. Feinstein observed that patients' preferences about the relative importance of different disabilities was not sought. Other problems he noted included difficulties in measuring change, the use of transitional indices, the absence of reliability data, the

misinterpretation of summed scores, and the frequent absence of conceptual justification and criterion validity.

Law and Letts (1989) found similar problems in a critical review of over 20 ADL scales. After analysing the appropriate functions of different scales, they recommended that no further ADL scales should be developed. The Barthel index was the most consistently recommended scale.

McDowell and Newell (1996) selected the seven ADL scales with the best published evidence on validity and reliability, from more than 50. They drew attention to the difference between simple ADL scales such as the Barthel, measuring only the central activities necessary for independence in personal care, and measures of instrumental or extended ADL (IADL or EADL), such as the FIM and the Nottingham Extended ADL—which extend the disability theme into handicap with the inclusion of social adjustment and environmental factors. This group of measures could be renamed Participation ADL (PADL) in line with ICIDH-2. These measures are often coupled with the basic ADL scales because they retain ADL items in their content. In similar vein the OPCS national survey of disability arrived at 12 categories, including seeing, hearing, consciousness, disfigurement, and reaching in addition to more basic ADL items (Martin, Meltzer, & Elliot, 1988).

The recent development of PADL scales reflects first a trend in rehabilitation towards focusing treatment programmes on reduction of disability and handicap, with the aim of achieving patient-oriented goals; and second the perceived requirement for a single outcome measure to demonstrate the effectiveness of the programme. The ADL scale is not a global outcome measure, but can be used with a number of other specific tools of assessment to record change (e.g., Rivermead Behavioural Memory Test, Boston Aphasia Tool, Hospital Anxiety and Depression Scale). None of the measures used explain why change has taken place or whether it is environment specific. If the perfect disability measure was available, then clinical assessment and skill at suggesting interventions might become redundant.

ADL scales

Barthel ADL index

In this I will suggest that the Barthel ADL index (BI; Table 5.1) be adapted as a standard against which other measures should be evaluated. The BI is most useful when monitoring progress in an acute rehabilitation unit. It cannot stand alone, because it does not measure communication, cognition, mood, or motivation.

Wade and Collin (1988) proposed that the Barthel index should be in widespread use as the preferred measure of physical disability. Why? The BI contains the 10 activities usually considered to be the core of any ADL assessment. It has been used in more research than any other scale, and has covered a wider range of conditions. In 1980 Gresham, Phillips, and Labi showed that the BI was superior to both the Katz ADL index and the Kenny self-care evaluation when considering completeness, sensitivity to change, and amenability to statistical evaluation; the BI also had greater familiarity because of its widespread

Table 5.1. The Barthel ADL Index (from Mahoney & Barthel, 1965)

Item	Categories
Bowels	0 = incontinent (or needs to be given enemata) 1 = occasional accident (once per week) 2 = continent *If needs enema from nurse, then "incontinent".* *Occasional = once a week.*
Bladder	0 = incontinent/catheterised, unable to manage 1 = occasional accident (max once every 24 h) 2 = continent (for over 7 days) *Occasional = less than once a day.* *A catheterised patient who can completely manage the* *catheter alone is registered as "continent".*
Grooming	0 = needs help with personal care 1 = independent face/hair/teeth/shaving (implements provided) *Refers to personal hygiene: doing teeth, fitting false teeth,* *doing hair, shaving, washing face.* *Implements can be provided by helper.*
Toilet use	0 = dependent 1 = needs some help but can do something alone 2 = independent (on and off, dressing, wiping) *With help = can wipe self, and do some other of above.*
Feeding	0 = unable 1 = needs help cutting, spreading butter, etc. 2 = independent (food provided in reach) *Help = food cut up, patient feeds self.*
Transfer	0 = unable—no sitting balance 1 = major help (one or two people, physical), can sit 2 = minor help (verbal or physical) 3 = independent *Dependent = no sitting balance (unable to sit); two* *people to lift.* *Major help = one strong/skilled, or two normal people.* *Can sit up.* *Minor help = one person easily, OR needs any* *supervision for safety.*
Mobility	0 = immobile 1 = wheelchair independent (includes corners) 2 = walks with help of one (verbal/physical) 3 = independent (may use any aid, e.g., stick) *Refers to mobility about the house or ward, Indoors.* *May use aid. If in wheelchair, must negotiate corners/doors* *unaided.* *Help = by one, untrained person, including supervision/moral* *support.*
Dressing	0 = dependent 1 = needs help, does about half unaided 2 = independent, includes buttons, zips, shoes *Should be able to select and put on all clothes, which* *may be adapted.* *Half = help with buttons, zips, etc. (check!), but can put on* *some garments alone.*
Stairs	0 = unable 1 = needs help (verbal, physical), carrying aid 2 = independent *Must carry any walking aid used to be independent.*
Bathing	0 = dependent 1 = independent (may use shower) *Usually the most difficult activity.* *Must get in and out unsupervised, and wash self.* *Independent in shower = "independent" if* *unsupervised/unaided.*

use. They commented, "The Barthel ADL Index reflects the pragmatism and long clinical experience of its designers in its frankly preferential weighting of mobility and continence above other variables."

In 1996, 31 years after Mahoney and Barthel's first publication, McDowell and Newell are still recommending its use. "The Barthel Index is wisely respected as a good ADL scale: it also occupies an important place in the development of this field. Validity data are more extensive than those for many other ADL scales, and the results appear superior to others we review" (p. 62). They describe the original and the most used modified versions, including Granger's 15-item version, the modified 10-item version of Collin and Wade scoring 0–20 (Collin, Wade, Davies, & Horne, 1988), and a revised scoring of the 10-item version by Shah (Shah, Vanclay, & Cooper, 1989).

Does the BI have clinical utility? Is it quick and easy to use? Are the instructions clear? Is the scoring straightforward and can the results be communicated easily to others and over time? The BI is certainly easy to use. The score is a summed aggregate and there is preferential weighting of mobility and continence. Both self-report and taking information from nurses or carers were shown by Collin, Wade, Davies, and Horne (1988) to be reliable and rapid (less than 5 min.). The BI has also been shown to be reliable when obtained over the telephone (Shinar et al., 1987) and by post (McGinnis, Seaward, DeJong, & Osberg, 1986).

The BI is a 21-point scale, either 0–20 in one-point increments or 0–100 in five-point increments, and zero represents the worst score. Wade and Langton Hewer (1987) showed that in the 21-point scale the items showed a hierarchical tendency and suggested that this should be the preferred scoring. Barer and Nouri (1989) suggested that if the preferential weighting was removed and each item simply scored "pass" or "fail" then Guttman criteria are satisfied and it forms an ordinal scale of at least 10 points. However, this modification would reduce sensitivity and would be undesirable since one common criticism is that the BI lacks sensitivity.

Is the BI valid? Because it contains all the items usually included in ADL indices it can be said to have as much face validity as any other ADL measure. Concurrent and predictive validity have been established (Granger, Dewis, et al., 1979; Wade & Langton Hewer, 1987; Wylie, 1967). They related BI scores to the extent of motor loss, mortality, overall stroke severity, depression, accommodation, social activities, clinical judgement, and need for support in the community.

Factor analysis has confirmed that the BI is measuring a single domain. In stroke patients there seems to be a predictable progression through items as recovery occurs. The BI has also been shown to correlate closely with functional outcome in amputees (Collin, Wade, & Cochrane, 1992; Kullmann, 1987).

Is it reliable? High test–retest reliability correlations have been reported (Granger, Albrecht, & Hamilton, 1979). A well-designed formal study, performed as part of a large-scale study into stroke, found good reliability between different observers and telephone reporting (Shinar et al., 1987). Our study found an acceptable degree of reliability between testing observers and asking observers, and established what appeared to be genuine score changes (Collin et al., 1988).

Sensitivity signifies the smallest change detectable. Having only 21 different values the Barthel would seem to be relatively crude. Wade and colleagues (Wade & Langton Hewer, 1985; Wade, Wood, & Langton Hewer, 1987) and Granger, Dewis, et al. (1979) found that it was sensitive to change and determined that independence and dependence in selected items correlated with total score. Granger, Hamilton, and Gresham (1989) in a large multicentre stroke outcome study confirmed its ability to detect change and its use as a predictor of eventual outcome, but showed that there were no single cut-off scores that were specific or sensitive enough to use as a sole criterion for admission or discharge from rehabilitation services. A trade-off for its robust reliability is the presence of ceiling and floor effects, a lack of sensitivity at the extremes of scoring. This is not important as the main clinical purpose of the Barthel is to detect when someone starts to need personal help and quantify this need to the level of total dependence.

These are convincing arguments in favour of accepting the Barthel as the standard index of disability. Its use does not preclude the use of other more detailed assessments which may be necessary for the development of a particular course of treatment. All assessments used should ideally have been tested for validity and reliability. Therapists frequently suggest that it is a crude measure and ignores quality of movement or safety, but as these factors are usually associated with the ability to perform the act independently, it does measure some aspects of quality.

There is always a great temptation to modify a good measure in line with particular needs and, as described, this has happened with the Barthel. It has been extended with more complex scoring to give it greater sensitivity (Fortinsky, Granger, & Seltzer, 1981; Granger, Albrecht, & Hamilton, 1979; Shah, Vanclay, & Cooper, 1989) and simplification of the scoring to only 10 points has also been suggested (Barer & Nouri, 1989). As most of the research confirming its validity and reliability was performed on the original 21-point scale it seems sensible to continue using this version. The guidelines and modifications (Table 5.1) suggested by Collin and Wade et al. (1988) are recommended because they have been widely tested and shown to be reliable. When using the Barthel it is important to know which version it is, and this one can now be regarded as the English version. In practice it is now used widely in rehabilitation and is also used by geriatricians, nurses, and social workers. It forms the core of many assessment and protocols that govern nursing home and community care allocations.

Katz ADL index

This was developed on orthopaedic and elderly patients. Katz et al. (1963) observed that loss of functional skills occurs in a particular order, the most complex skills being lost first. Components measured include bathing, dressing, toileting, transfer, continence, and feeding. It omits mobility, wheelchair skills, grooming, and the use of stairs. The scoring is hierarchical but is cumbersome, and not easily amenable to statistical analysis.

Patients are assigned to one of seven categories according to the activities in which they are independent. If they break the ranking order more than once, then they are assigned to a separate unclassified category. The Katz ADL index has been widely used. It records the lowest level of function over a 2-week period of observation and takes 1–2 hours to perform. Although it has been used widely there has been little published evidence on reliability and validity.

Kenny self-care evaluation

This was developed by Hubert A. Schoening and staff of the Sister Kenny Institute in 1965 (Schoening et al., 1965). It includes trunk control, transfers, mobility, dressing, personal care, excretion, and feeding. Each of these seven categories have up to four activities with up to eight component tasks for each activity. It does not rate continence or toileting. In all there are 17 activities and 85 tasks. Each task is rated on a three-point rating scale: "independent", "requires help", and "dependent". Task scores are combined to produce an activity score between 0 (dependent) and 4 (independent). These are averaged to produce category scores. The Kenny provides great detail, but statistically has not been shown to be of superior discriminative ability to the Barthel. The scoring system is complex. The test takes up to 2 hours to perform and relies on direct observation.

PULSES

This is an acronym and was derived from earlier assessment methods used to estimate fitness for military duty. It means:

P = physical condition
U = upper limb functions
L = lower limb functions
S = sensory components (speech, vision, hearing)
E = excretory functions
S = mental and emotional status

Each subcategory is graded from "1" (completely independent) to "4" (severely disabled and dependent). When first introduced by Moskowitz and McCann (1957) it required a full medical examination and access to appropriate social information, but it was adapted in 1975 by Granger et al. so that the criterion throughout was the need for assistance.

The scoring system gives a numerical score from "6" (fully independent) to "24" (maximally dependent). PULSES differs from the Barthel in that it contains a psychosocial measure and a combined measure of speech, vision and hearing. The Barthel in contrast measures independence in individual functions (e.g., eating), that have direct implications for providers of care, by giving a clear assessment of need. PULSES has been found to be a reliable and valid measure when compared with the Barthel (Granger, Albrecht, & Hamilton, 1979), but when used to predict vocational status (Goldberg, Bernard, & Granger, 1980) was found to be inferior.

The Barthel and the PULSES profile were incorporated by Granger into the Long Range Evaluation System with a group of psychosocial measures. Using computer methodology he produced feedback reports, to permit rapid programme evaluation and comparison of individuals at different times in different locations (Granger et al., 1975). It is a very simple measure but is not used a great deal.

HANDICAP

The ICIDH format describes handicap as a disadvantage resulting from an impairment or disability, that limits or prevents the fulfilment of a role that is normal, depending on age, sex, social, and cultural factors, for that individual. It describes handicap in terms of its interference with what can be designated as survival roles. These are classified into six categories: orientation, physical independence, mobility, occupation, social integration, and economic self-sufficiency. A seventh category "other" has been included to allow coding of other areas of disadvantage not included in the six survival roles.

Handicap has been regarded as the mismatch between disability and environment. Critics of this simple concept of handicap have developed a broader image of handicap. This takes into account the contributing factors of impairment, disability, self, physical environment, cultural environment, and their interaction. Identical disabilities can result in differing handicaps due to cultural factors and it becomes increasingly important in a multicultural society to identify the important rehabilitation goals for each patient taking into consideration the aims and intentions of the family.

These criticisms were responsible for the ICIDH-2 and the development of a new language in which the societal consequences of a state of health and its interaction with the environment are described as participation.

Simple social and environmental measures can be astonishingly effective in reducing handicap and it may require government legislation, as in Canada, to make it happen (Hahn, 1987). This would ensure that wheelchair users had freedom of access to all public places and use of public transport. Many young tetraplegic patients face a horrendous barrage of difficulties before successfully achieving the transition from hospital to independent status in the community and some are not successful. The simple removal of physical barriers cannot remove handicap entirely because of the broader social and cultural factors involved. It is disappointing that environmental mountains are encountered so frequently when attempting to rehabilitate patients back into the community.

Many of the following scales infer handicap from disability measures. Handicap is a personal experience and it is probably unreasonable to suggest that it can be measured in a reliable way using any scales. A concert pianist will have enormous handicap if unable to perform because of a tendon injury in the hand, but will probably score maximum points on most extended ADL scales. It is difficult to believe that any scale can satisfactorily measure handicap due to its subjective content.

It can be argued that all human activity is modified by limiting conditions, which can be interpreted as handicap. It would be difficult to develop a score that could encompass or express this range. Quality of life or satisfaction with life measures come closest to measuring handicap but are not truly synonymous.

Instrumental or participating ADL

These usually include a wider range of activities that encompass domestic, leisure, and work spheres. The result obtained is a useful outcome measure. It infers "something" about handicap—usually a subjective judgement by the assessor—rather than an appraisal by the person with the disability. Assessment of mobility restriction is usually included by asking whether the patient walks outside, crosses roads, uses public transport, or drives a vehicle and does his or her own shopping. Some measure social interaction by asking the frequency of social outings, use of telephones, and writing letters. A few preclude the use of a separate ADL scale by including self-care activities, but these areas are better assessed separately because ADL scores are usually used during an acute event, whereas IADL measures are usually used during out-patient or distant follow-up. Many of the combined measures are simply too long to have any clinical utility. The Frenchay Activities Index and the Nottingham Extended ADL Scale are two similar assessments and both have demonstrated reliability and clinical utility.

Frenchay activities index

The Frenchay activities index (Table 5.2) was developed by Holbrook and Skilbeck (1983) and concentrates on social activities that span domestic, leisure, and work interests, indoors and outdoors. They recorded the frequency of 22 activities in stroke patients and then used factor analysis, which reduced the number of activities to 15. It is quick and easy to use, taking only 5 min to score and can be completed by interview or be used as a postal questionnaire. It gives a single summary score or can be used to give separate domestic, leisure, and social scores. Factor scores were produced to account for potential sex differences. These are rarely used in clinical practice.

Nottingham extended ADL scale

Nouri and Lincoln (1987) looked at activities undertaken by stroke patients and ranked them hierarchically. The Nottingham extended ADL scale (Table 5.3) is organised in four sections: mobility, kitchen, domestic, and leisure. The Guttman scaling procedure showed that all sections were valid unidimensional scales except for mobility which narrowly missed with a coefficient of reliability of 0.85 instead of 0.9 or above. The scale was developed very rigorously and the kappa coefficient was used to estimate test–retest reliability. This was excellent for 19 of the 22 questions, but was lower for some of the housework questions.

As the discrepancies were only observed in male respondents, it may be another example of the "he can, but does he" issue. This activities scale is also useful because the scoring, which is simple to understand, records whether the activity is performed

Table 5.2. Frenchay activities index (from Holbrook & Skilbeck, 1983, 'An activities index for use with stroke patients', *Age and Ageing*, 12, 166–170, by permission of Oxford University Press)

	Score
In the last 3 months:	
Preparing main meals	0 = never
Washing up	1 = under once weekly
	2 = 1–2 times/week
	3 = most days
Washing clothes	0 = never
Light housework	1 = 1–2 times in 3 months
Heavy housework	2 = 3–12 times in 3 months
Local shopping	3 = at least weekly
Social occasions	
Walking outside longer than 15 min	
Actively pursuing hobby	
Driving car/going on bus	
In the last 6 months:	
Travel outings/car rides	0 = never
	1 = 1–2 times in 6 months
	2 = 3–12 times in 6 months
	3 = at least twice weekly
Gardening	0 = never
Household/car maintenance	1 = light
	2 = moderate
	3 = all necessary
Reading books	0 = never
	1 = one in 6 months
	2 =< one per fortnight
	3 => one per fortnight
Gainful work	0 = never
	1 = up to 10 h/week
	2 = 10–30 h/week
	3 = over 30 h/week

The aim is to record activities which require some initiative from the patient. It is important to concentrate upon the patient's actual frequency of activity over the recent past, not his distant past performance or his potential performance. One activity can only score on one item.

independently, independently with difficulty, with help, or not at all. Scoring for each activity can be 4 points or 2 points (independent/dependent) and statistical evaluation was carried out on the two-point scale.

The use of either of these two scales as social activity measures is recommended because they have been carefully developed, are quick and easy to use, and are equally reliable as self-report measures. The Frenchay activities index includes gainful work and therefore has a wider range than the Nottingham extended ADL. The strength of the extended ADL is its demonstrated hierarchical properties.

Functional status index and questionnaire

Jette (1980) developed the Functional Status Index to provide a comprehensive assessment of non-institutionalised adults. It measures pain and difficulty in performing tasks as well as level of dependence, reflecting its original purpose which was to evaluate a programme of care for elderly arthritics. The original version was very long, and a shortened version (20–30 min)

Table 5.3. Nottingham extended ADL scale (from Nouri & Lincoln, 1987 with permission from Hodder/Arnold Ltd)

Response categories:	*2 points*	*4 points*
"no", "with help"	Scores 0	
"on my own with difficulty", "on my own"	Scores 1	

Questions:

Mobility
1. Do you walk around outside?
2. Do you climb stairs?
3. Do you get in and out of the car?
4. Do you walk over uneven ground?
5. Do you cross roads?
6. Do you travel on public transport?

In the kitchen
1. Do you manage to feed yourself?
2. Do you manage to make yourself a hot drink?
3. Do you take hot drinks from one room to another?
4. Do you do the washing up?
5. Do you make yourself a hot snack?

Domestic tasks
1. Do you manage your own money when you are out?
2. Do you wash small items of clothing?
3. Do you do your own housework?
4. Do you do your own shopping?
5. Do you do a full clothes wash?

Leisure activities
1. Do you read newspapers or books?
2. Do you use the telephone?
3. Do you write letters?
4. Do you go out socially?
5. Do you manage your own garden?
6. Do you drive a car?

that covers five areas, mobility, personal care, hand activities, home chores and interpersonal activities was produced. Results of validity testing were rather low.

The functional status questionnaire (Jette et al., 1986) was then developed and is attractive because it is self-administered, but unattractive because it requires computer analysis to produce a single-page report including six summary-scale scores and six single-item scores. It is a screening tool to detect levels of disability in the community and addresses psychological well-being, work performance, and social and personal factors in addition to physical function. Little attention has been paid to it in the UK, possibly because it is dependent on dedicated software available from one American source.

FIM and FIM + FAM

The Functional Independence Measure (FIM) and the Functional Assessment Measure (FIM + FAM) were barely mentioned in the first edition of this book but in a recent survey of 180 rehabilitation units in the UK (Turner-Stokes & Turner-Stokes, 1997) 123 reported that they were using some form of global measure of which the commonest was the Barthel index (78%) and the next was the FIM or FIM + FAM (45%).

The FIM was started in 1984 by a national task force from the American Congress of Rehabilitation and the American

Academy of Physical Medicine and Rehabilitation in response to fiscal pressure to form a reliable assessment system on which to base payment for rehabilitation services. The Uniform Data System for Medical Rehabilitation (UDS) was developed by Granger Hamilton and Sherwin and included demographic data, length of stay, hospital changes, and the FIM data. There are 18 items in FIM of which 13 are personal care, continence, and mobility and were derived from the Barthel, and 5 are concerned with communication and social cognition. Each item was originally scored on a four-point scale which has now been expanded to seven points.

During the implementation phase of the four-point scale score sheets bore the inscription "copy freely". The current FIM is copyright to UDS, training programmes are provided, and users of the system subscribe annually to UDS and are provided with newsletters containing details of difficult or unusual scoring situations. Participating units report their FIM data allowing outstanding documentation of the use of FIM and also of the rehabilitation settings in which it is used.

Reliability and validity have been established by Dodds et al. (1993), Hamilton et al. (1994), and Kidd et al. (1995) but the five social and cognitive items were found to be less reliable by Davidoff et al. (1990), who found a low ceiling effect. He used specific neuropsychological assessments for comparison which he found more reliable. The most robust and reliable items in the FIM are those based on the Barthel, and the FIM physical components can be transformed into a Barthel score. It takes a long time to score and in the UK is usually done as a team effort. This facilitates communication and other aspects of teamwork. There are still ceiling and floor effects and the total score is difficult to interpret.

Granger has used FIM scores to demonstrate that a change of one point is equivalent to a change in help of 2.2 minutes per day. This is a dangerous philosophy. It implies an accuracy that does not exist and gives a double-edged tool to managers of health-care systems.

The Functional Assessment Measure (FIM + FAM) was developed as an extension of FIM to measure outcome in brain injury. It includes 12 additional subscales on cognitive and psychosocial interaction. These have also proved difficult to score, and where there is disagreement between team members the lower score is adopted. Turner-Stokes and colleagues (1999) have developed the UK FIM-FAM taking out the 10 most troublesome items and revising and testing them. There was only slight improvement achieved in accuracy over the 10 items, although on some individual items there was significant improvement.

The most entertaining aspect of the scale is the software that has been developed to support it. The FAM-splat (Microsoft Excel) might remind some physicians of shady ink blots but gives an instant impression of the change observed during a rehabilitation programme with admission scores, the goals, and the discharge scores all clearly represented in one diagram. There is a UK FIM + FAM users group coordinated by the Regional Rehabilitation Unit at Northwick Park

Table 5.4.   The modified Rankin scale (from Rankin, 1957)

Grade	Description
0	No symptoms at all
1	No significant disability despite symptoms: able to carry out all usual duties and activities
2	Moderate disability: requiring some help, but able to walk without assistance
3	Moderately severe disability: requiring some help, but able to walk without assistance
4	Moderately severe disability: unable to walk without assistance, and unable to attend to own bodily needs without assistance
5	Severe disability: bedridden, incontinent, and requiring constant nursing care and attention

Original Rankin scale did not contain grade 0, defined grade 1 as "no significant disability: able to carry out all usual duties", and defined grade 2 as "slight disability: unable to carry out some of previous activities" (Van Swieten et al., 1988).

and they provide training programmes for new users and support.

Short outcome scales

These are included as a separate category because they were specifically developed as reliable outcome measures for use in multicentre trials in which some aspects of early management of acute illness or injury were being evaluated. They were not designed to be sensitive measures that record change on a week-by-week basis but were developed as simple, coarse, long-term outcome measures with high reliability. The two most well-known measures are the Rankin scale and the Glasgow outcome scale, which were developed respectively to record outcome after stroke and head injury.

Rankin scale

Rankin developed his scale in 1957 (Table 5.4). Warlow and colleagues (UK-TIA Study Group, 1988) modified it to take into account language disorders and cognitive deficits. Using six grades it measures overall independence but also refers to previous activities and abilities. Van Sweeten et al. (1988) found acceptable interobserver reliability with most disagreement occurring in the middle grades. He suggested that this may be because of the assumption in this scale that there is a constant relationship between walking skills and ability to lead an independent life. Condensing it to three or four grades would improve its reliability but would reduce its sensitivity and ability to detect clinically significant differences between patients. It is used widely.

Glasgow outcome scale

Jennett and Bond (1975) expressed the need for an objective scale to describe the ultimate results of early management of head injury after observing the frequently overoptimistic and vague reports of outcome. He designed a simple five-point scale. The points are 1—death, due to head injury, 2—persistent vegetative state, 3—severe disability (conscious but disabled), 4—moderate disability (disabled but independent), 5—good recovery (resumption of normal life but not necessarily work). In 1981 Jennett, Snoek, Bond, and Brooks subdivided grades 3 to 5 into a better and worse level to improve sensitivity.

Both versions have acceptable levels of reliability, and repeated assessments at 3-monthly intervals have shown a predictable pattern of recovery. This is a widely used and respected epidemiological measure of outcome after head injury.

GLOBAL HEALTH AND LIFE STATUS MEASURES

Quality of life, health status, well-being, and satisfaction with life are all terms that tend to be used interchangeably in health literature. This loose use of terms creates confusion. These have all been used as titles of health measures and sound different, but are they measuring the same concept? In practice three dimensions are usually incorporated in each measure relating to physical, psychological, and social functioning. Measures of health status, or health-related quality of life, are by definition more restricted than those of quality of life, and measure how people feel about their physical and mental health, whereas measures of well-being focus on feelings of depression, anxiety, energy, and positive well-being: Health status and well-being may not correlate with quality of life.

There has been an explosion of these measures in the last 20 years, not least because health economists link quality of life measures with resource allocation.

Quality of life measures should not be confused with quality adjusted life years (QALYS). These are numerical values designed to demonstrate the cost effectiveness of different forms of treatment by assigning values to changes in well-being resulting from treatment, considering the cost of treatment and the increased time of survival resulting from it. Treatments not associated with increased survival are obviously disadvantaged in this analysis. The cost of not treating patients is not considered in this monetary policy, although this can be high if as a result of no treatment a patient requires a nursing home bed. Another important flaw in this area of health economics is that health-care needs may be overlooked in favour of cost-effective procedures when resources are purchased.

Spitzer (1987) draws an interesting distinction between health status and quality of life measures. He says that health status measures should be used on healthy, unselected, geographically defined populations, whereas quality of life measures should be reserved for those who are definitely sick. Fallowfield (1990) does not differentiate between health status and quality of life measures in her treatise on quality of life issues, but their differentiation is discussed by Andressen and Meyers (2000) and Dijkers, Whiteneck, and El-Jaroudi (2000), and emphasised by Bradley (2001).

Two health status measures that demand attention, because of the thoroughness with which they have both been evaluated, are the sickness impact profile and the Nottingham health profile. The major difference here is that the Nottingham health profile asks about feelings and emotional states directly rather than through changes in behaviour. The sickness impact profile (Bergner, Bobbitt, Carter, & Gibson, 1981) comprises 136 statements in 12 categories concerning the impact of sickness on behavioural function. The functional limitation profile is the British version. Its role is in research evaluation and in community surveys. It is less good at detecting individual change. It is a time-consuming measure, which prevents it being used repeatedly as a clinical measure of handicap.

The Nottingham health profile (Hunt & McEwen, 1980; Hunt, McEwen, & McKenna, 1985) consists of 38 statements on health problems and 7 statements on areas of daily life affected by health problems. One problem with it is that it only expresses negative states of health and cannot indicate feelings of well-being. Both these measures have been shown to have a high level of reliability and have established content validity. They have been used to measure the outcomes of care or treatment in a wide variety of clinical situations.

Quality of life measures include indicators of psychological well-being and satisfaction with life ratings. Some of the interest in their development stems from the observations of poor quality of life experienced by terminal cancer patients undergoing heroic treatment, and the trend in geriatric medicine to determine management according to the philosophy "adding life to years, not years to life". Quality of life is influenced by many factors, including personality, personal expectations, family or their absence, illness impairment and disability, psychological factors including coping ability, and physical and cultural environment.

This list bears a close similarity to the factors that influence handicap (participation) and other social outcomes, and the two concepts are very similar. Dijkers et al. (2000) and Fallowfield (1990) explore these issues in a valuable contribution to the literature, and a collection of key articles can be found in a 1987 special issue of the *Journal of Chronic Diseases*, entitled "Measuring Quality of Life in Clinical and Epidemiological Research", with an editorial by Katz (1987a).

The EuroQol (EQ5D; 1990) and the Short Form 36 (SF-36) Health Survey (Wade, 1992) are two recently developed questionnaires that are comprehensive but brief. They have been extensively researched and are now well validated and have been shown to be reliable, but they do have floor and ceiling effects. The EQ5D has two parts: The first has five questions about mobility, self care, usual activities, pain, and anxiety, and a second "thermometer" requiring an overall rating of health status. It may be less sensitive to change than the SF-36. Originally American, an English version of the SF-36 is now available (Brazier et al., 1992). It has been used successfully as a population survey tool (Sullivan et al., 1994) and as an outcome measure. Domains include physical function, role limitations, pain, social function, mental health, energy, and general health perceptions. It was drawn from work of the Rand Corporation of Santa Monica and the Medical Outcome Study. There is also a shorter 12-item form (Ware, Kosinski, & Keller, 1995). SF-36 has become a well-used tool in a remarkably short space of time reflecting its careful development and is now available as an "international version", SF-36 V2 (Jenkinson, Stewart-Brown, Petersen, & Paice, 1999). Permission to use it should be sought from the Medical Outcomes Trust, PO Box 1917, Boston, Massachusetts, 02205, USA.

SUMMARY

It sometimes appears that measurement is done for its own sake—"If it moves, count it". In any situation, research or clinical, one must decide which attribute is of greatest interest and choose the most suitable accredited measure for the purpose. Handicap remains an elusive concept and anyone interested in measuring it would benefit from studying the ICIDH-2 classification first and considering whether it could be used, rather than using a global measure with poor definition. Transforming a handicap into a numerical score does not improve it or explain it, although it may be the only feasible way of doing population studies.

Outcome measures are required in clinical and research practice. The global measures described are often not very sensitive to change, or the total score obscures the dimension that has changed. Many global measures are time consuming to use and have low clinical utility. Simple focal measures like gait speed often have greater reliability and consistency and are more likely to reflect change due to a specific intervention or recovery. A simple disability measure, the Barthel, retains a central role in monitoring change in disability particularly in those patients in the early acute phase of their illness. It requires supplementing with other measures of cognition, memory or communication, and it remains to be seen whether all-inclusive measures like the FIM or FIM + FAM continue to rise in popularity, or whether more reliable and specific measures, described elsewhere in this book, retain their role in measurement of aspects of disability, alongside the Barthel.

REFERENCES

Andressen, E.M., & Meyers, A.R. (2000). Health-related quality of life outcomes measures. *Archives of Physical Medicine and Rehabilitation, 81*(Suppl. 2), S30–S45.

Barer, D., & Nouri, F. (1989). Measurement of activities of daily living. *Clinical Rehabilitation, 3*, 179–187.

Bergner, M., Bobbitt, R.A., Carter, W.B., & Gilson, B.S. (1981). The sickness impact profile: Development and final revision of a health status measure. *Medical Care, 19*, 787–805.

Bradley, C. (2001). Importance of differentiating health status from quality of life. *Lancet, 357*, 7–8.

Brazier, J.E., Harper, R., Jones, N.M.B., et al. (1992). Validity: The SF-36 Health Survey Questionnaire new outcome measure for primary care. *British Medical Journal, 305*, 160–164.

Buchwald, E. (1949). Functional training. *Physical Therapy Review, 29*, 491–496.

Collin, C. (1992). Scales and scaling techniques used in measurement in rehabilitation medicine. *Clinical Rehabilitation, 6*, 91–96.

Collin, C., Wade, D.T., & Cochrane, G.M. (1992). Functional outcome of lower limb amputees with peripheral vascular disease. *Clinical Rehabilitation, 6*, 13–21.

Collin, C., Wade, D.T., Davies, S., & Horne, V. (1988). The Barthel ADL index: A reliability study. *International Disability Studies, 10*, 61–63.

Davidoff, G.N., Roth, E.J., Haughton, J.S., et al. (1990). Cognitive dysfunction in spinal cord injury patients: Sensitivity of the FIM subscales vs neuropsychology assessment. *Archives of Physical Medicine and Rehabilitation, 71*, 326–329.

Deaver, G.G., & Brown, M.E. (1945). *Studies in rehabilitation: 1. Physical demands of daily life: An objective scale for rating the orthopaedically exceptional.* New York: Institute for the Crippled and Disabled.

Dijkers, M.P.J.M., Whiteneck, G., & El-Jaroudi, R. (2000). Measures of social outcomes in disability research. *Archives of Physical Medicine and Rehabilitation, 81*, S63–S80.

Diseases 1987, entitled Measuring Quality of Life in Clinical and Epidemiological Research with an editorial by Katz.

Dodds, T.A., Martin, D.P., Stolov, W.C., & Deyo, R.A. (1993). A validation of the FIM and its performance among rehabilitation inpatients. *Archives of Physical Medicine and Rehabilitation, 74*, 531–536.

Donaldson, S.W., Wagner, C.C., & Gresham, G.E. (1973). A unified ADL evaluation form. *Archives of Physical Medicine and Rehabilitation, 54*, 175–179.

EuroQol Group. (1990). EuroQol: A new facility for the measurement of health-related quality of life. *Health Policy, 16*, 199–208.

Fallowfield, L. (1990). *The quality of life: The missing measurement in health care.* London: Souvenir Press.

Feinstein, A.R., Josephy, B.R., & Wells, C.K. (1986). Scientific and clinical problems in indexes of functional disability. *Annals of Internal Medicine, 105*, 413–420.

Fortinsky, R.H., Granger, C.V., & Seltzer, G.B. (1981). The use of functional assessment in understanding home care needs. *Medical Care, 19*, 489–497.

Goldberg, R.T., Bernard, M., & Granger, C.V. (1980). Vocational status: Prediction by the Barthel index and PULSES profile. *Archives of Physical Medicine and Rehabilitation, 61*, 580–583.

Granger, C.V., Albrecht, G.L., & Hamilton, B.B. (1979). Outcome of comprehensive medical rehabilitation: Measurement by PULSES profile and Barthel index. *Archives of Physical Medicine and Rehabilitation, 60*, 145–153.

Granger, C.V., Dewis, L.S., Peters, N.C., et al. (1979). Stroke rehabilitation: Analysis of repeated Barthel index measures. *Archives of Physical Medicine and Rehabilitation, 60*, 14–17.

Granger, C.V., Greer, D.S., Liset, E., et al. (1975). Measurements of outcomes of care for stroke patients. *Stroke, 6*, 34–41.

Granger, C.V., Hamilton, B.B., & Gresham, G.E. (1989). The stroke rehabilitation outcome study—Part 1: General description. *Archives of Physical Medicine and Rehabilitation, 69*, 506–509.

Gray, D.B., & Hendershot, G.E. (2000). The ICIDH-2: Developments for a new era of outcomes research. *Archives of Physical Medicine and Rehabilitation, 81*(Suppl. 2), S10–S14.

Gresham, G.E., Phillips, T.F., & Labi, M.L. (1980). ADL status in stroke: Relative merits of three standard indexes. *Archives of Physical Medicine and Rehabilitation, 61*, 355–358.

Guttman, L. (1950). The basis of scalogram analysis. In S.A. Stouffer & F. Osborne (Eds.), *Measurement and prediction.* New York: Wiley.

Hahn, H. (1987). Adapting the environment to people with disabilities: Constitutional issues in Canada. *International Journal of Rehabilitation Research, 10*, 363–372.

Hamilton, B., Laughlin, J.A., Fiedler, R.C., & Granger, C.V. (1994). Inter rater reliability of the 7-level FIM. *Scandinavian Journal of Rehabilitation Medicine, 261*, 115–119.

Hamilton, B.B., Granger, C.V., Sherwin, F.S., et al. (1987). A uniform national data system for medical rehabilitation. In M.J. Fulmer (Ed.), *Rehabilitation outcomes: Analysis and measurement* (pp. 137–147). Baltimore: Paul H. Brookes.

Holbrook, M., & Skilbeck, C.E. (1983). An activities index for use with stroke patients. *Age and Ageing, 12*, 166–170.

Hunt, S.M., & McEwen, J. (1980). The development of a subjective health indicator. *Social Health Illness, 2*, 231–246.

Hunt, S.M., McEwen, J., & McKenna, S.P. (1985). Measuring health status: A new tool for clinicians and epidemiologists. *Journal of the Royal College of General Practitioners, 35*, 185–188.

Jenkinson, C., Stewart-Brown, S., Petersen, S., & Paice, C. (1999). Assessment of the SF-36 version 2 in the United Kingdom. *Journal of Epidemiology and Community Health, 53*, 46–50.

Jennett, B., & Bond, M. (1975). Assessment of outcome after severe brain damage: A practical scale. *Lancet*, i, 480–484.

Jennett, B., Snoek, J., Bond, M.R., & Brooks, N. (1981). Disability after severe head injury. Observations on the use of the Glasgow Outcome Scale. *Journal of Neurology, Neurosurgery and Psychiatry, 44*, 285–293.

Jette, A.M. (1980). Functional status index: Reliability of a chronic disease evaluation instrument. *Archives of Physical Medicine and Rehabilitation, 61*, 395–401.

Jette, A.M., Davies, A.R., Cleary, P.D., et al. (1986). The functional status questionnaire: Reliability and validity when used in primary care. *Journal of General Internal Medicine, 1*, 143–149.

Katz, S. (1987a). Measuring quality of life in clinical and epidemiological research [Special issue]. *Journal of Chronic Diseases*.

Katz, S. (1987b). The science of the quality of life. *Journal of Chronic Diseases, 40*, 459–463.

Katz, S., Ford, A.B., Moskwitz, R.W., et al. (1963). Studies of illness in the aged. The index of ADL: A standardised measure of biological and psychosocial function. *Journal of the American Medical Association, 185*, 914–919.

Kidd, D., Stewart, G., Baldry, J., et al. (1995). The FIM: A comparative validity and reliability study. *Disability and Rehabilitation, 17*(1), 10–14.

Kullmann, L. (1987). Evaluation of disability and of results of rehabilitation with the use of the Barthel index and Russek's classification. *International Disability Studies, 9*, 68–71.

Law, M., & Letts, L. (1989). A critical review of scales of activities of daily living. *American Journal of Occupational Therapy, 43*, 522–528.

Mahoney, F.I., & Barthel, D.W. (1965). Functional evaluation: The Barthel index. *Maryland State Medical Journal, 14*, 61–65.

Martin, J., Meltzer, H., & Elliot, D. (1988). *OPCS surveys of disability in Great Britain Report 1: The prevalence of disability among adults*. London: Her Majesty's Stationery Office.

McDowell, I., & Newell, C. (1996). *Measuring health: A guide to rating scales and questionnaires*. New York: Oxford University Press.

McGinnis, G.E., Seaward, M.L., DeJong, G., & Osberg, J.S. (1986). Program evaluation of physical medicine and rehabilitation departments using self-report Barthel. *Archives of Physical Medicine and Rehabilitation, 67*, 123–125.

Moskowitz, E., & McCann, C.B. (1957). Classification of disability in the chronically ill and ageing. *Journal of Chronic Diseases, 5*, 342–346.

Nouri, F.M., & Lincoln, N.B. (1987). An extended activities of daily living scale for stroke patients. *Clinical Rehabilitation, 1*, 301–305.

Partridge, C., & Johnston, M. (1989). Perceived control of recovery from physical disability: Measurement and prediction. *British Journal of Clinical Psychology, 28*, 53–59.

Rankin, J. (1957). Cerebral vascular accidents in patients over the age of 60: 2. Prognosis. *Scottish Medical Journal, 2*, 200–215.

Rasch, G. (1980). *Probabilistic models for some intelligence and attainment tests*. Chicago: University of Chicago Press.

Riviere, M. (undated). *Rehabilitation codes: Progress report 1957–1962*. New York: Office of Vocational Rehabilitation.

Schoening, H.A., Anderegg, L., Bergstrom, D., et al. (1965). Numerical scoring of self-care status of patients. *Archives of Physical Medicine and Rehabilitation, 46*, 689–687.

Shah, S., Vanclay, F., & Cooper, B. (1989). Improving the sensitivity of the Barthel index for stroke rehabilitation. *Journal of Clinical Epidemiology, 42*, 703–709.

Sheldon, M.P. (1935). A physical achievement record for use with crippled children. *Journal of Health and Physical Education, 6*, 30–31, 60.

Shinar, D., Gross, C.R., Bronstein, K.S., et al. (1987). Reliability of the activities of daily living scale and its use in telephone interview. *Archives of Physical Medicine and Rehabilitation, 61*, 723–728.

Spitzer, W.O. (1987). State of science 1986: Quality of life and functional status as target variables for research. *Journal of Chronic Diseases, 40*, 465–471.

Sullivan, M., Karlsson, J., Bengtsson, C., et al. (1994). Health related quality of life in Swedish populations: Validation of the SF-36 Health Survey. *Quality of Life Research, 3*, 95.

Tennant, A., Geddes, J.M.L., & Chamberlain, M.A. (1996). The Barthel index: An ordinal score or interval level measure? *Clinical Rehabilitation, 10*(4), 301–308.

Turner-Stokes, L., Nyein, K., Turner-Stokes, T., & Gatehouse, C. (1999). Development and evaluation of the UK FIM+FAM. *Clinical Rehabilitation, 13*, 277–287.

Turner-Stokes, L., & Turner-Stokes, T. (1997). The use of standardised outcome measures in rehabilitation centres in the UK. *Clinical Rehabilitation, 11*(4), 306–313.

UK-TIA Study Group. (1988). The UK-TIA aspirin trial: Interim results. *British Medical Journal, 296*, 316–320.

Van Swieten, J.C., Koudstaal, P.J., Visser, M.C., et al. (1988). Interobserver agreement for the assessment of handicap in stroke patients. *Stroke, 19*, 604–607.

Vreede, C.F. (1988). The need for a better definition of ADL. *International Journal of Rehabilitation Research, 11*, 29–35.

Wade, D.T. (1992). *Measurement in neurological rehabilitation*. Oxford: Oxford University Press.

Wade, D.T., & Collin, C. (1988). The Barthel ADL index: A standard measure of disability? *International Disability Studies, 10*, 64–67.

Wade, D.T., & Langton Hewer, R. (1987). Functional abilities after stroke: Measurement, natural history and prognosis. *Journal of Neurology, Neurosurgery and Psychiatry, 50*, 177–182.

Wade, D.T., Wood, V.A., & Langton Hewer, R. (1985). Recovery after stroke—the first three months. *Journal of Neurology, Neurosurgery and Psychiatry, 48*, 7–13.

Ware, J.E., Kosinski, M., & Keller, S.D. (1995). *SF-12: How to score the SF-12 physical and mental health summary scales*. Boston: The Health Institute, New England Medical Centre.

Ware, J.E., & Sherbourne, C.D. (1992). The MOS 36-item Short Form Health Survey (SF-36): Conceptual framework and item selection. *Medical Care, 30*, 473–483.

World Health Organization. (1980). *ICIDH: International classification of impairments, disabilities and handicaps*. Geneva: World Health Organization.

World Health Organization. (1997). *ICIDH-2: International classification of impairments, activities and participation: A manual of dimensions of disablement and functioning (Beta-1 draft for field trials)*. Geneva: World Health Organization.

Wylie, C.M. (1967). Measuring end results of rehabilitation of patients with stroke. *Public Health Reports, 82*, 893–898.

6. Ethical implications of disablement

Michael Saunders

INTRODUCTION

Practical philosophy concerns a fundamental question that is relevant to the ethics of disability. What is the best or right way for people to live as individuals or in community? Ethics or moral philosophy is concerned traditionally with the behaviour of individuals, whereas political philosophy is involved with the best way of organising society. Both aspects impinge on the everyday life of the disabled person. Since the Enlightenment moral philosophy has become fragmented and emotivism has emerged as a dominant feature in personal morality (Macintyre, 1985). A similar situation prevails with theories of justice and the rationality that underpins them (Macintyre, 1988). This presents serious difficulty when debating ethical aspects of health care; agreement or disagreement may be disconnected from any common framework.

With these limitations in mind this chapter explores some general concepts relating to the ethics of disability and rehabilitation and examines briefly illustrative issues that arise in the day-to-day lives of people affected by neurological disease.

CONCEPTS AND PRINCIPLES

Non-maleficence and beneficence

The distinction between these two principles is blurred (Frankena, 1973). However it is possible to distinguish them. Non-maleficence is the duty to avoid doing harm. Beneficence is the duty to prevent harm, to remove evil and to promote or do good (Beauchamp & Childress, 1983). Non-maleficence is at the heart of health-care delivery but there may be considerable disagreement about harms and benefits in particular situations. An example of this is the issue of truth telling. Some physicians avoid revealing diagnoses such as multiple sclerosis at an early stage (Elian & Dean, 1985) on the grounds that the patient will be asked to carry a burden that will increase distress and foreboding when there is minimal disability. Although such a decision is paternalistic and denies the patient full autonomy, it may be regarded as avoiding inflicting an unnecessary harm, which upholds the principle of non-maleficence. Truth telling in these circumstances is judged to be harmful. The alternative view is that, unless the patient indicates that he or she does not want to be told what is wrong, his or her autonomy should be respected and the harm done in withholding information is greater than that done by truth telling in the long term. It could be argued that individual examples might not support the principle of truth telling but such outcomes are not known in advance and are not a convincing argument for a denial of autonomy.

It is clear that philosophical medical ethics does not provide simple agreed answers to problems. People rank principles in different orders and apart from an unadorned utilitarianism there is no simple route through the complexities of moral dilemmas. What can be achieved is informed dialogue and an exposure of the assumptions on which practice is based.

Personhood

A concept much discussed recently is the nature of personhood (Gillett, 1987; Harre, 1987; Harris, 1985). This has particular relevance to those with brain diseases as in medical ethics the discussion has centred around the presence or absence of specific cerebral criteria (Glover, 1987; Lockwood, 1985). The practical outcome of regarding personhood in this way is that it provides a structure for treating certain categories of humanity as less than people and this can be used as a means to justify destructive acts (Harris, 1985).

On the surface it would seem that those with physical disability and an intact brain escape the issues surrounding the concept of personhood but reflection indicates that this is not the case. Many people with disabilities are regarded as impaired mentally whatever evidence there is to the contrary. An obvious example is those with cerebral palsy who are unable to communicate freely; but the problem is not restricted to this group. There is a general tendency to regard anyone with a disability as globally impaired and this leads to paternalism, ignoring the individual's right to exercise autonomy and having a limited perspective on his or her potential. The most sinister outcome of regarding disabled people as less than persons is neglect.

The concept of personhood founders on boundary definitions and is an unsatisfactory basis for caring (Warnock, 1987). The essential of good health care is that an individual matters.

Paternalism

Benign paternalism is at the heart of a great deal of medical practice (Faulder, 1985). People with physical disabilities are at risk of being ignored and cared for in a beneficent but paternalistic manner. Remarkably little notice is taken of disabled people when it comes to planning clinical services and those designated as expert often have difficulty in consulting a representative body of opinion with personal experience of disability. The argument in favour of some form of soft paternalism centres around the view that the skilled health-care professional has a level of expertise that puts him or her in a position of knowledge which the uninformed cannot hope to achieve; there is a perspective that can be acquired only after years of specialised training and experience. On the other hand the disabled person has an individual knowledge of what disability means in daily living. There is no substitute for this. Only a mutual exchange of knowledge and experience with each group respecting the "expertise" of the other will lead to satisfactory decision making.

Freedom and autonomy

Disability involves loss of freedom to do what one wants. The loss varies but the options available decrease as disability progresses. One purpose of rehabilitation is to restore freedom to carry out intentions but in many instances there is inevitably a dependence on others, which is restrictive.

The disabled person may be unable to walk, travel unaccompanied, work, or live at home independently. There is an impaired capacity to shape one's life and even the simplest activities may be dependent on the assistance of others.

Freedom and autonomy are linked (Beauchamp & Childress, 1983), but in the context of disability medicine it is worth separating them. Autonomy is a concept which requires the presence of adequate intellectual capacities to make an informed decision. Thus, someone with serious mental illness may be unable to come to a conclusion about the risks and benefits of any proposed treatment. Autonomy is impaired in people with mental illness, severe organic brain disease and in children. One cannot make an autonomous decision without adequate information being made available and disabled people are at risk of being excluded from decision-making processes regardless of their intellectual capacities.

Loss of freedom often has political connotations but impaired freedom affects everyone to some extent; those with a severe disability are restricted in a specific way. A disabled person may be able to come to a decision about what he or she wants to do, but physical limitation and the attitudes of individuals and society may restrict the freedom to enact the decision. A school leaver may find that job opportunities are restricted and the restriction unrelated to the capacity to perform the job. Loss of freedom in the context of disablement has at least three elements: inevitable restriction resulting from physical disease; loss of physical independence, which is soluble with help; and impaired freedom imposed by individuals and society. Rehabilitation is concerned with overcoming the second and third factors.

Loss of freedom and autonomy raise important issues concerning the rights of the disabled. What rights has a disabled person to expect assistance in restoring freedom and value to life?

Rights and duties

The concept of rights is associated with the related concepts of duties and obligations. People talk of all sorts of rights but it is important to enquire whether the concept has much relevance if the right is not enforced in law. One may argue that a foetus has a right to life but unless that right is protected in some way it is likely to be violated. In a humane society there is likely to be some agreement about basic rights although they may conflict with one another. There is a general right to life, although this is by no means absolute and may be violated when individual and communal interests conflict with it.

Most would agree that there is a right to food and shelter and that those disadvantaged through no fault of their own should receive some form of special provision to facilitate their well-being. On the other hand in many societies stress is placed on the freedom of the individual and this may be in conflict with obligations to provide for the disadvantaged. It may be objected that the funding of services for the disabled from personal taxation is in conflict with individual liberty and that the provision of care should be left to acts of charity rather than State legislation. An individual may feel some sense of duty and obligation to those near at hand but have no such response at a state or international level. The limits of duty and individual freedom lead to a variety of solutions to the provision of facilities for people with disabilities embodied in theories of justice (Brown, 1986).

Justice

Justice is an integral part of social morality. When we regard something as just we consider it right in a particular kind of way. In the case of those with severe physical disability we may think it important that special measures should be taken to provide them with adequate health care and financial grants to mitigate loss of earning capacity and the increased cost of a disabled existence.

We often contrast justice with generosity or charity. Justice is linked to the concept of fairness. Those who are disadvantaged or handicapped are entitled to particular treatment because in most societies it would be accepted that when this has happened randomly without personal fault resources should be made available to provide a reasonable quality of life. There may be disagreement as to whether special provisions should be means tested, and the basic level of provision may vary enormously.

It is difficult to judge the various theories of justice without some concept of what the good life is. If one can agree the nature of the basic human goods, any worthwhile theory of justice needs to have the aim of making them available to all even if that involves depriving others of non-essential goods. This assumes that the acquisition of the basic goods for all is equally important for the advantaged as for the deprived; one cannot have a truly good life in the presence of widespread deprivation.

Conclusion

The problem of how to organise a society that takes into account the burdens and benefits of life remains an unsolved challenge. We can distribute according to need, merit, or desert, or equally; whichever theory we work with we tend to run into a conflict of principles. One way forward is to identify the basic goods that are the framework of a satisfactory human life. Obvious candidates are: pleasure, work, rest and play, social relationships, and aesthetic experience. These are goods beyond the basic needs of food and shelter but form the goal that should be at the heart of all care for the disabled.

SOME PRACTICAL PROBLEMS

The principles discussed briefly have practical implications across the whole range of disability medicine. What follows is illustrative of some of the practical issues in everyday life.

Selection for treatment

Clinical practice involves inevitably decisions which may appear unjust to the disabled person. There are relatively few specialised neurological rehabilitation units and they are unequally distributed within countries and across the world. Those who are involved in disability medicine have to be realistic and it helps if those to whom they seek to provide a service can share in that realism; a good deal of anguish can be avoided if adequate communication takes place, paternalism is reduced, and the client is part of the decision-making process. The basic criteria for intervention at in-patient or out-patient level need to be related to whether the therapist can assist the promotion of the elements of the good life referred to earlier. Because the goods are not directly, in many instances, related to acts of health-care intervention one needs to question in what way treatment or assessment will enhance human well-being. The contact of patient and therapist may have social and psychological benefits that encourage acceptance for treatment for reasons unconnected with the specific therapeutic activity. Although understandable this involves role confusion. The doctor and therapist have particular skills and once they take on a broader and unstructured social role they impair the effectiveness of their prime function. Acceptance for specific therapeutic programmes has to be related to what can be achieved realistically and this has to be discussed with client and family.

The problem of limited resources raises the principle of justice. The just basis of the good life is that all should have an equal opportunity of sharing it and the disabled require such provision that maximises this possibility. The health-care worker who has to choose between one client or another is involved in an ethical dilemma. One can enter into complicated analyses of individual circumstances and make judgements using a variety of principles but the most just procedure is to toss a coin given that both people would benefit equally or operate on a first come first served policy. Within a cash-limited framework, rationing in health care is inevitable.

The rights of the carer

The disabled person and the carer have equal rights to the good life. Caring for a severely disabled person is productive of chronic stress and the carer may have given up work, friends, and lovers and many of the pleasures that make life worth living. It may be argued that to give oneself unconditionally for love of another person is one of the highest ends of humanity. This is unrealistic as most people under the strain of a prolonged caring role, if not supported, suffer a variety of physical and psychological problems.

The fundamental question is the extent of the duty of a relative or close friend towards a disabled person. Although there may be a duty to care for a sick relative there is no duty to undertake a responsibility that is self destructive as this undermines the concept that everyone should have an opportunity to enjoy the goods of life. Unfortunately in most societies there is considerable pressure put on relatives to care, often over long periods of time, without significant aid or respite. Such circumstances may reduce the willingness of relatives to care for family members, leading to anger and conflict with health-care workers and personal guilt and confusion. These situations can be mitigated if there is a level of communal support that recognises the carer's need to pursue some individual goals without recrimination.

Consent for therapeutic trials

Recent years have been associated with vigorous debate concerning consent procedures for therapeutic research (King, 1986; Silverman, 1989). People with severe disability are usually eager to avail themselves of opportunities to enter clinical trials. They are a vulnerable group open to manipulation and if individual autonomy is impaired relatives may be equally keen to include their loved ones in trials. Therapeutic trials should be conducted with adequate consent procedures and this requires that a neutral informed party should seek the consent, that there should be no pressure of any kind, and that ample time for reflection should be allowed. It is impossible for an autonomous decision to be obtained in certain circumstances, such as progressive dementia and severe learning difficulties.

The connections between autonomy, beneficence, and informed consent in such circumstances has been discussed by Shatz (1986) and Thomasma (1984). In trial situations it is debatable whether anyone else can act for the patient. This is a different circumstance to the giving of the best available care to an incompetent patient, although this situation contains problems related to autonomy as well (Ekman & Norberg, 1988). In certain situations a person might wish to issue a directive for someone to act on their behalf prior to their autonomy becoming impaired, but in the complex area of clinical trials no directive could be adequate. It is an uncomfortable fact that a rigid policy on consent would reduce the number of patients available in areas such as dementia research unless the principle of utility is ranked above that of individual autonomy.

Behaviour modification

Behaviour modification is used because it is claimed that it works. In the context of disability neurology it may be claimed justifiably that nothing else does and that these two elements alone are sufficient to provide a moral reason for the treatment. This is the view taken by Giles and Fussey (1988), who consider that those who object on philosophical grounds should demonstrate that there are alternative effective methods for improving quality of life.

The ethical problems are summarised in a statement by Mechanic (1981), which draws attention to the lack of consensus concerning the use of coercive therapies to stimulate and maintain "appropriate functioning". He suggests practices vary a good deal from one context to another, depending on the values and commitments of those involved. However, aversion techniques, "token economies", and other forms of behaviour control raise questions concerning the limits of treatment methods.

Behaviour control involves the use of power (London, 1969), but its particular difficulty is the diminution of the concept of "the whole person"; it is problems not people that are at issue and this leads to the mechanisation of humans. The therapist can be seen as a social reinforcement machine (Krasner, 1962). The picture is created of manipulation regardless of the person's will or by-passing the will to achieve specified ends (Bandura, 1975). The fact that behaviour techniques are efficient is beside the point; one does need to ask whether such procedures without consent from the subject can be justified. The therapist is sometimes seen as a "mole" working for society and using techniques that are disciplinary or dependent on reward incentives (Karasu, 1981).

Because there are two incompatible ethical views at issue there will never be agreement concerning this matter. The utilitarian will point to the clear advantages of more acceptable social behaviour that makes life easier for everyone. Those who are deontologists and hold individual autonomy to be of supreme importance will not accept the end as worthwhile if it involves violating human dignity. Practitioners will want to affirm that they are seeking to restore dignity and that their motives are directed entirely towards the welfare of their client.

Terminal care decisions

Profound disability incompatible with any recognisable quality of life raises ethical questions about letting people die or carrying out active euthanasia (Gillett, 1988; Gillon, 1988; Miller, 1987). Those in persistent vegetative states from head injury, the severely demented, and anyone with a very severe physical disability may provoke debate about the value of continued life and the proposal that death is to be preferred to living. How we react initially to these situations depends on our personal fiduciary framework. An absolute adherence to the sanctity of life principle would not allow positive acts intended to terminate life, but is compatible with a policy of non-interference and the administration of treatment to relieve suffering that might also shorten life.

People in a vegetative state may be kept alive for months or years. It is difficult to avoid the conclusion that they would be better off dead yet it is far from clear what ought to be done. Those who use specific criteria to establish personhood may conclude that since an individual is no longer a person and cannot value life, every advantage is to be gained by withdrawal of supportive treatment. There would appear to be no rational reason for relatives to object and the act could be interpreted as beneficent as the state of death is to be preferred to life. One objection to this is that the patient cannot exercise autonomy and that no decision can be made without personal consent. One way round this is the use of a "living will" to convey the wishes of the patient in advance of any debilitating illness that will destroy autonomy. However such wills have proved difficult to enforce, although they provide a potential way forward in a difficult area of management (Greaves, 1989). The essential feature of a living will is that a directive with respect to future management is given while the patient is still fully competent. The author was involved in a case of someone with severe dementia where the husband insisted on all treatment being given including courses of antibiotics when all those involved in care were convinced that the patient should be allowed to die. The wishes of the patient were unknown. In such a situation a living will might have been of considerable value in management.

Decisions concerning terminal care are associated inevitably with emotional responses from all involved. They focus attention on the fact that feelings cannot be removed or educated out of ethics. Many of the paradigm shifts that occur in individual responses to ethical issues are determined by emotional factors rather than rational consideration of evidence. It is essential to bear this in mind when approaching the ethical aspects of disability neurology.

REFERENCES

Bandura, A. (1975). The ethics and social purpose of behaviour modification. In C.M. Franks & G.T. Wilson (Eds.), *Annual review of behaviour therapy and practice* (Vol. 3, pp. 13–20). New York: Brunner/Mazel.

Beauchamp, T.L., & Childress, J.E. (1989). *Principles of biomedical ethics*. (3rd ed.). New York: Oxford University Press.

Brown, A. (1986). *Modern political philosophy: Theories of the just society*. London: Penguin.

Ekman, S.L., & Norberg, A. (1988). The autonomy of demented patients: Interviews with caregivers. *Journal of Medical Ethics, 14*, 184–187.

Elian, M., & Dean, G. (1985). To tell or not to tell the diagnosis of multiple sclerosis. *Lancet, 2*, 27–28.

Faulder, C. (1985). *Whose body is it? The troubling issue of informed consent*. London: Virago Press.

Frankena, W.K. (1973). *Ethics* (2nd ed.). Englewood Cliffs, NJ: Prentice-Hall.

Giles, G.M., & Fussey, I. (1988). Models of brain injury rehabilitation from theory to practice. In I. Fussey & G.M. Giles (Eds.), *Rehabilitation of the severely brain-injured adult* (p. 28). London: Croom Helm.

Gillett, G. (1987). Reasoning about persons. In A.R. Peacocke & G. Gillett (Eds.), *Persons and personality* (pp. 75–98). Oxford, UK: Basil Blackwell.

Gillett, G. (1988). Euthanasia: Letting die and the pause. *Journal of Medical Ethics, 14*, 61–68.

Gillon, R. (1988). Editorial. Medical treatment, medical research and informed consent. *Journal of Medical Ethics, 15*, 3–5.

Glover, J. (1987). *Causing death and saving lives*. Harmondsworth, UK: Penguin.

Greaves, D. (1989). The future prospects for living wills. *Journal of Medical Ethics, 15*, 179–182.

Harre, R. (1987). Persons and selves. In A.R. Peacocke & G. Gillett (Eds.), *Persons and personality* (pp. 99–115). Oxford, UK: Basil Blackwell.

Harris, J. (1985). *The value of life: An introduction to Medical Ethics*. London: Routledge, Kegan & Paul.

Karasu, T. (1981). Ethical aspects of psychotherapy. In S. Bloch & P. Chodoff (Eds.), *Psychiatric ethics* (pp. 100–102). Oxford, UK: Oxford University Press.

King, J. (1986). *Informed consent* [Institute of Medical Ethics bulletin, Suppl. 3]. London: IME Publications.

Krasner, L. (1962). The therapist as social reinforcement machine. In H. Strupp & L. Luborsky (Eds.), *Research in psychotherapy* (Vol. 2, pp. 61–94). Washington, DC: American Psychological Association.

Lockwood, M. (1985). When does life begin? In M. Lockwood (Ed.), *Moral dilemmas in medicine* (pp. 9–31). Oxford, UK: Oxford University Press.

London, P. (1969). *Behaviour control*. New York: Harper & Row.

MacIntyre, A. (1985). *After virtue—a study in moral theory* (2nd ed.) London: Duckworth.

MacIntyre, A. (1988). *Whose justice? Which rationality?* London: Duckworth.

Mechanic, D. (1981). The social dimension. In S. Bloch & P. Chodoff (Eds.), *Psychiatric ethics*. Oxford, UK: Oxford University Press.

Miller, P.J. (1987). Death with dignity and the right to die: Sometimes doctors have a duty to hasten death. *Journal of Medical Ethics, 13*, 81–85.

Shatz, D. (1986). Autonomy, beneficence and informed consent: Rethinking the connections. *Cancer Investigations, 4*, 257–269.

Silverman, W.A. (1989). The myth of informed consent: In daily practice and clinical trials. *Journal of Medical Ethics, 15*, 6–11.

Thomasma, D.C. (1984) Freedom, dependency and the care of the very old. *Journal of the American Geriatric Society, 32*, 906–914.

Warnock, M. (1987). Do human cells have rights? *Bioethics, 1*, 1–14.

Mechanisms of recovery

7. Mechanisms of cellular damage and recovery

Andrew J. Larner   Michael V. Sofroniew

... the functional specialization of the brain imposed upon the neurones two great lacunae; proliferative inability and irreversibility of intraprotoplasmic differentiation. It is for this reason that, once the development has ended, the fonts of regeneration of the axons and dendrites dried up irrevocably. In adult centres the nerve paths are something fixed, ended, immutable. Everything may die, nothing may regenerate.

It is for the science of the future to change, if possible, this harsh decree. Inspired with high ideals, it must work to impede or moderate the gradual decay of the neurones, to overcome the almost invincible rigidity of their connections, and to re-establish normal nerve paths, when disease has severed centres that were intimately associated.

—S.R. Cajal, 1928

INTRODUCTION

150 years ago, Dax and Broca provided the first unequivocal evidence that loss of a higher function, language, could be ascribed to damage to a specific brain region. Since that time it has become clear that all forms of neurological or psychiatric dysfunction have cellular and molecular substrates. Cajal was among the first to recognise the importance of minimising cellular degeneration and re-establishing cellular functions after injury or disease because he had correctly surmised that interactions between cells formed the basis of all functions performed by the central nervous system (CNS). As the goals he laid down 70 years ago are slowly realised, rehabilitation after neurological injury or disease will increasingly be influenced by efforts to minimise cellular dysfunction and promote cellular recovery.

SUBSTRATES OF DYSFUNCTION IN THE NERVOUS SYSTEM

Most forms of neurological or psychiatric dysfunction can now be associated with specific disruptions of structural integrity or specific disturbances in chemical processes localised to defined regions in the CNS. At the cellular level, structural degeneration capable of causing neurological dysfunction can involve both neurones and glia. The types of changes that can affect neurones include outright neuronal cell death, neuronal atrophy (e.g., shrinkage of the cell body and dendrites, retraction of processes, and loss of synapses), subcellular abnormalities (e.g., neurofibrillary tangles), and aberrant growth (e.g., hypertrophy

of the cell body and dendrites, growth of inappropriate or dystrophic neurites, and formation of neuritic plaques). Glial cell changes include cell loss, demyelination, gliosis, and glial scarring. Molecular disturbances that can lead to CNS malfunction in the absence of obvious structural abnormalities are less well characterised, but include metabolic disturbances, dysfunction of transmitter associated enzymes, and effects mediated via specific receptors either by exposure to exogenous ligands such as drugs or other environmentally derived substances, or by exposure to inappropriate levels of endogenous ligands. It is not known whether prolonged dysfunction of this type can occur in the absence of eventual structural changes. Here we will focus on events that lead to detectable degenerative changes in neural tissues.

Understanding the basis of CNS dysfunction at the cellular level is complicated by the likelihood that clinical symptoms associated with a particular condition are due to a mixture of disturbances occurring in several regions in the CNS. Thus, the identification of a single form of cellular dysfunction usually cannot be equated with an understanding of the disease mechanism. Moreover, the degree of cellular change required to cause clinically apparent CNS dysfunction is generally uncertain because the CNS shows a remarkable ability to retain complex function in the face of substantial and irreversible tissue damage. For example, it has been estimated that over 80% of the striatal dopamine innervation from the substantia nigra must be lost before the symptoms of Parkinson's disease begin to manifest themselves (Zigmond, Abercrombie, Berger, Grace, & Stricker, 1990). The ability to maintain function despite structural damage is probably due to a certain amount of redundancy of function in CNS organisation (Glassman, 1987), as well as a considerable capacity for plasticity in the injured adult CNS, both in the form of reorganisation of local and afferent cellular constituents (Isacson & Sofroniew, 1992; Kolb, 1995), and the ability of certain nerve cells to compensate for the functions of damaged counterparts (Chollet et al., 1991).

Recovery without regeneration

Useful if incomplete recovery of neurological function after brain injury is commonly observed in clinical practice, for example speech, swallowing, or limb function after an ischaemic cerebrovascular event. In view of the limited scope for axonal regeneration within the CNS, it seems unlikely that this is the mechanism underpinning such recovery, and this has led to the concept of "functional regeneration" or "recovery without regeneration", even though anatomical changes may be relevant to these phenomena (Boyeson, Jones, & Harmon, 1994). It seems that at least three mechanisms may be responsible for this "neuroplasticity", as revealed by functional studies using positron emission tomography (PET) scanning and transcranial magnetic stimulation (TCMS): Undamaged cortical regions may "take over" the lost functions, perhaps reflecting the redundancy of CNS circuitry (Glassman, 1987); existing but functionally inactive neuroanatomical pathways may be unmasked or uncovered through loss of the inhibitory effects of interneurones; or there may be sprouting of fibres from surviving neurones to form new synapses (Lee & van Donkelaar, 1995). Evidence for the uncovering of silent or accessory pathways has come from PET studies: Weiler, Ramsay, Wise, Friston, and Frackowiak (1993) showed that, following a capsular infarct, recovery of function was associated with activation of undamaged ipsilateral and contralateral motor pathways, with considerable interindividual variation. A doubling in size of the cortical representation of the pharyngeal musculature in the undamaged hemisphere, as shown by TCMS, has been demonstrated during recovery from post-stroke dysphagia (Hamdy et al., 1996). The somatotopic and columnar organisation of the cerebral cortex may favour these mechanisms of reorganisation. Clearly such observations may have implications for appropriate therapeutic interventions following brain injury.

In view of the absence of spontaneous repair of the damaged nervous system, exploiting and maximising the capacity for plasticity in the adult CNS will form an important part of attempts to influence positively the cellular mechanisms that contribute to rehabilitation after clinical dysfunction of the CNS. It will also be important to identify and counteract the degenerative processes that occur early in disease or after injury, as well as to develop ways of repairing dysfunctional neuronal connections by replacing lost nerve cells and/or facilitating the regrowth of axonal connections. There has long been a debate about the use of steroids in the acute phase of CNS injury to minimise damage and hasten recovery, but their place remains uncertain (Alderson & Roberts, 1997) and there are experimental data suggesting that their effects may be deleterious (Chan et al., 1996; Goodman, Bruce, Cheng, & Mattson, 1996).

MECHANISMS OF NEURAL DAMAGE

A number of intracellular metabolic pathways potentially detrimental to neuronal integrity have been described. Experimental work regarding these pathways will be briefly reviewed, followed by evidence implicating them in particular neurological diseases. Especial reference will be made to ischaemic-hypoxic brain injury, multiple sclerosis (MS), and to a number of neurodegenerative diseases including Alzheimer's disease (AD),

Parkinson's disease (PD), Huntington's disease (HD), and motor neurone disease (MND), although other conditions will be mentioned where they are thought to be illustrative of particular pathogenetic mechanisms. These observations form a prelude to consideration of rational therapeutic approaches to neurological disease aimed at preventing neuronal dysfunction and death, and hastening cellular recovery.

Endogenous substances

Glutamate excitotoxicity. Glutamate is the principal excitatory neurotransmitter in brain and spinal cord. It acts through two major receptor subclasses, namely metabotropic (mGluR, coupled to G proteins, leading to modulation of intracellular second messengers) and ionotropic (iGluR, coupled to membrane ion channels). Of the ionotropic glutamate receptors, a variety of subtypes have been described according to the differing pharmacological specificity of their preferred agonists, namely N-methyl-D-aspartate (NMDA); α-amino-3-hydroxy-5-methyl-4-isoxazole propionate (AMPA), or quisqualate; and kainate (KA). The cloning of glutamate receptor genes has revealed multiple functional receptor subunits from each family (Hollmann & Heinemann, 1994).

The NMDA receptor is a ligand-gated ion channel permeable to both Na^+ and Ca^{2+} ions that is further regulated by Mg^{2+} ions in a voltage dependent manner; only after a basal level of depolarisation is reached do Mg^{2+} ions leave the channel and allow passage of Ca^{2+} ions. NMDA receptor function is liable to modulation by various agents: Glycine is an allosteric activator; zinc inhibits receptor-gated ion fluxes; and there is also a redox modulatory site(s) which down-regulates activity: Nitric oxide (NO^+) can act at this site to exert a neuroprotective effect.

NMDA channels have a high Ca^{2+}/Na^+ permeability but rather slow kinetics whereas AMPA receptors have fast kinetics but, usually, a much lower permeability to Ca^{2+}. However, this latter property may be modified. Some AMPA and kainate receptors which lack a single positively charged amino acid residue in the channel structure have a high permeability to Ca^{2+}. Four genes encoding AMPA preferring subunits have been described (GluR1–GluR4); absence of GluR2 RNA transcripts results in the AMPA channel having high Ca^{2+} permeability. Some neurones, particularly GABAergic inhibitory neurones, possess large numbers of such Ca^{2+} permeable AMPA channels and may therefore be particularly vulnerable to damage induced by AMPA receptor activation. Moreover, ischaemic insults have been reported to reduce GluR2 expression in hippocampal neurones, leading to increased vulnerability to AMPA receptor-mediated Ca^{2+} toxicity (Pellegrini-Giampietro, Zukin, Bennett, Cho, & Pulsinelli, 1992).

Usually neurones are only briefly exposed to glutamate in the course of excitatory neurotransmission. However, under certain pathological conditions, reduced cellular uptake and increased efflux can lead to excessive levels of extracellular glutamate which causes excessive stimulation of iGluR with consequent deleterious effects on neurones. The toxic effects on CNS neurones of excessive exposure to glutamate or related amino acids was first noted by Lucas and Newhouse (1957) and Olney and Sharpe (1969), and Olney labelled this process "excitotoxicity". Different glutamate receptor subtypes do not contribute equally to excitotoxicity, two main patterns of which have been observed (Choi, 1997): rapidly triggered, induced by brief stimulation of NMDA receptors; and slow triggered, following prolonged stimulation of AMPA/kainate receptors. The former is critically dependent on the presence of extracellular Ca^{2+}, and therefore seems dependent on Ca^{2+} influx through the NMDA receptor-gated ion channel. "Slow triggered" excitotoxicity may also be related to Ca^{2+} influx, either directly through GluR2-deficient AMPA channels or, probably more importantly, indirectly through voltage-gated Ca^{2+} channels activated by Na^+ influx and membrane depolarisation and/or reverse operation of the Na^+/Ca^{2+} exchanger. Ca^{2+} ions entering through NMDA and AMPA/KA channels activate various intracellular enzymes and effector mechanisms, and may trigger a cascade of deleterious events (as discussed in greater detail later; Meldrum & Garthwaite, 1990). These various mechanisms have implications for therapeutic manipulation of iGluR function.

mGluRs are currently not thought to mediate excitotoxic injury, but may be able to modify it (Bruno, Copani, Battaglia, Casabona, & Nicoletti, 1997), with some subtypes facilitating and others attenuating NMDA receptor mediated toxicity. Selective mGluR agonists may therefore find a role as neuroprotective agents.

Astrocytes take up extracellular glutamate and convert it to glutamine; this latter is then recycled to neurones for further use. This cycle is energy dependent and impeded in situations of energy failure. The importance of this function of astrocytes as a sink for the uptake of excess glutamate is demonstrated by the observation of neurotoxicity at lower concentrations of glutamate in neuronal cultures devoid of glia (Rosenberg & Aizenman, 1989). In addition, experimental disruption of astrocyte glutamate uptake, by genetic deletion of glutamate transporters, increases neuronal vulnerability to excitotoxic death (Rothstein et al., 1996; Tanaka et al., 1997). Glial cell glutamate receptors may also initiate Ca^{2+}-dependent gene transcription and regulate glial proliferation and differentiation (Steinhauser & Gallo, 1996).

Excitotoxicity may mediate, at least in part, a wide variety of acute neurological disorders (Lipton & Rosenberg, 1994), such as hypoxia/ischaemia, hypoglycaemia, trauma, and epilepsy (especially status epilepticus). It has also been implicated in chronic neurodegenerative disorders such as MND, HD, human immunodeficiency virus (HIV)-associated dementia, and neuropathic pain. In hypoxic/ischaemic brain injury, there is impairment of neuronal ATP production and a failure of cellular Na^+/K^+-ATPases with resultant loss of transmembrane ionic gradients, depolarisation of neurones, and increased glutamate release (Benveniste, Drejer, Schousboe, & Diemer, 1984). Failure of the astrocyte glutamate recycler may also contribute to elevated glutamate levels. The pathology of hypoxic and excitotoxic injury is similar, and excitatory pathway deafferentation can reduce hypoxic neuronal injury (Siesjo, 1991). Moreover, many studies have shown that laboratory models of hypoxic-ischaemic neuronal death can be attenuated by drugs which block excitotoxicity.

Kainic acid is a potent limbic convulsant, administration of which to rats produces lesions similar to those seen in human mesial temporal sclerosis, the commonest neuropathological substrate of temporal lobe seizures, hence affording a useful model system for the study of this condition (Nadler, 1981). Human temporal lobe tissue, surgically resected for the treatment of intractable epilepsy, has been reported in some studies to contain increased autoradiographic density of KA and NMDA receptors in certain subregions (Geddes et al., 1990; McDonald et al., 1991), suggesting that enhanced excitatory amino acid neurotransmission occurs in these areas, although the precise correlation of structure with function remains uncertain.

The neurotoxicity of gp120, an envelope glycoprotein of HIV, may be exerted through activation of neuronal NMDA receptors, and in HIV-associated dementia increased levels of the NMDA receptor agonist quinolinic acid have been found (Heyes et al., 1991), although this finding is not specific to HIV-associated dementia. Putative environmental neurotoxins causing motor neurone diseases such as neurolathyrism and amyotrophic lateral sclerosis-parkinsonism-dementia complex (ALS-PD) of Guam (e.g., BOAA, BMAA; discussed later) may operate through excitotoxic mechanisms; selective loss of motor neurones in MND itself may also result from excitotoxic mechanisms (Shaw, 1994). Glutamate toxicity may contribute to the deleterious effects of other neurotoxins, such as amyloid β-peptide in AD (Koh, Yang, & Cotman, 1990; Mattson et al., 1992).

Autoimmunity to glutamate receptors has been implicated in the pathophysiology of a number of progressive degenerative CNS conditions. For example, autoantibodies to GluR3 have been identified in some patients with Rasmussen's syndrome of chronic encephalitis and intractable epilepsy, and have been used to create an animal model of this condition (Rogers et al., 1994). Autoantibodies to other GluRs have been described in a subset of paraneoplastic degenerations and olivopontocerebellar degeneration. It is postulated that an autoimmune GluR-mediated excitotoxic mechanism produces the observed pathology, but definitive evidence is currently lacking and it remains possible that the autoantibodies are epiphenomenal.

Toxicity of other neurotransmitters and neuromodulators. Overactivation of transmitter pathways other than glutamate can promote neuronal injury, possibly through pathways convergent with those mediating glutamate-induced damage. For example, exposure to catecholamines prior to an ischaemic insult augments necrotic neuronal death, possibly by producing hyperglycaemia and/or antagonising the effects of insulin. In contrast, post-ischaemic exposure of neurones to catecholamines decreases necrotic death (Chan et al., 1996). Hyperactivity of mutant acetylcholine receptor (AChR) channels can cause neuronal degeneration in nematodes (Treinin & Chalfie, 1995); similarly, in the congenital human condition of slow-channel myasthenic syndrome, in which mutant AChRs show prolonged channel opening times, calcium-mediated degeneration of post-synaptic mitochondria and nuclei is observed (Gomez et al., 1997). This condition is the prototypic hereditary excitotoxic disorder: Sustained AChR ion channel activation leads to post-synaptic accumulation of cytosolic Ca^{2+}. Cholinergic agonists have been reported to enhance the toxicity of the parkinsonian neurotoxin MPTP, perhaps by upregulating dopamine metabolism (Hadjiconstantinou, Hubble, Wemlinger, & Neff, 1994).

Amphetamines such as "Ecstasy" (3,4-methylenedioxymethamphetamine, MDMA), used as a drug of abuse, can cause acute toxicity through release of the brain neurotransmitter serotonin (5-hydroxytryptamine, 5HT), manifesting clinically as hyperpyrexia and behavioural excitation. Long-term destruction of serotoninergic axons, perhaps due to free radical release and oxidative stress, may also occur; this may be modulated through increased dopamine release secondary to 5HT release. There is a concern that this neurodegenerative process may in the future lead to major depression in regular users of "Ecstasy" (Green & Goodwin, 1996). The neurotransmitter nitric oxide (NO) may also exert deleterious effects on neurones in certain circumstances (discussed later).

The hippocampus contains high levels of zinc ions (Zn^{2+}) which are released from excitatory synapses and bind to and modulate activity at postsynaptic glutamate receptors; excessive levels of Zn^{2+} are highly toxic to hippocampal neurones both *in vitro* and *in vivo*. Zn^{2+} may act by entering neurones via NMDA receptors which they inhibit. Zn^{2+} has been reported to promote aggregation of amyloid β-peptide and may exacerbate cognitive impairment in AD (Bush et al., 1994). However, other studies have suggested that AD may be associated with Zn^{2+} deficiency, possibly dietary in origin, and that this may contribute to the formation of neurofibrillary tangles. Hence, there is currently no consensus about the precise role of Zn^{2+} in the pathogenesis of AD, nor its appropriate manipulation for therapeutic purposes (Nachev & Larner, 1996).

Swollen astrocytes release large amounts of the inhibitory neuromodulator taurine, which could affect neuronal excitability and thereby contribute to neuronal dysfunction in pathological situations associated with astrocyte swelling (Kimelberg, Goderie, Higman, Pang, & Waniewski, 1990).

Glucocorticoids increase neuronal vulnerability to excitotoxicity, oxidative injury, and amyloid β-peptide (Aβ) toxicity (Goodman et al., 1996), observations of possible relevance to the pathogenesis of AD. Hippocampal neurones are particularly susceptible to glucocorticoid induced damage, perhaps due to failure of energy production (reduced glucose uptake), impaired neuronal defence mechanisms, and/or reduced availability of neurotrophic stimuli (Chan et al., 1996). Other hormones may also augment experimental necrotic neuronal death, such as corticotropin-releasing factor and thyroid hormone, whereas insulin and oestrogen are protective (Chan et al., 1996). The latter observation is of particular note in view of the postulated protective effect of postmenopausal oestrogens on the development of AD (Henderson, 1997).

Calcium. Excessive intracellular Ca^{2+} ion concentration ($[Ca^{2+}]_i$) may contribute to the overstimulation of normal cellular processes, such as enzyme activation, and lead to neuronal damage and death in a variety of disease processes (Meldrum & Garthwaite, 1990; Siesjo, 1991). Ca^{2+} triggers a cascade of biochemical reactions that may be detrimental to cellular integrity, encompassing activation of lipolysis with cell membrane damage, altered protein phosphorylation, proteolysis, increased production of reactive oxygen species (for example by activation of nitric oxide synthases), and disassembly of microtubules, leading to apoptotic or necrotic cell death (Siesjo, 1991).

There are two potential sources for increased intracellular calcium: release from intracellular stores, or influx from the extracellular environment where ambient $[Ca^{2+}]$ is on average ten thousand fold higher than in the intracellular compartment. Ca^{2+} influx from the extracellular environment may itself activate intracellular calcium release, a process termed calcium-induced calcium release (CICR). A number of pathways for entry of extracellular Ca^{2+} are known, including voltage-gated (or voltage-sensitive) calcium channels (of which L, N, P, Q, and T subtypes are described), ligand-gated calcium channels (including the NMDA and AMPA excitatory amino acid receptors), and stretch channels "activated" by loss of membrane integrity.

Ca^{2+}-induced lipase and phospholipase activation leads to increased production of free fatty acids and lysophospholipids which are potentially toxic. Activation of phospholipase C leads to the release of arachidonic acid, a substrate for cyclo-oxygenase and lipo-oxygenase enzymes, reactions which lead to the formation of free radicals, particularly superoxide. These reactions may cause sustained membrane dysfunction due to changes in ion channels and receptor activity. Likewise, Ca^{2+}-mediated changes in the activity of enzymes which control the phosphorylation state of proteins such as protein kinases and phosphatases can affect not only ion channel and receptor activity but also gene transcription and translation which may activate intrinsic cell death programmes (apoptosis).

Increased $[Ca^{2+}]_i$ may activate proteolytic enzymes which degrade cytoskeletal proteins. Consequences of microtubule dysfunction include plasma membrane blebbing and impaired cytoplasmic and axonal transport. These changes may be critical factors in promoting neuronal dysfunction and death.

Mitochondria may have an important role in buffering excessive intracellular changes in $[Ca^{2+}]$, but their capacity to do this is both ATP dependent and finite. Excessive mitochondrial Ca^{2+} uptake leads to increased mitochondrial membrane permeability, possibly through phospholipase activation and membrane lipid breakdown, with consequent release of Ca^{2+}, acidosis, generation of reactive oxygen species, and reduced energy production. An autocatalytic process may thus be activated leading to energy failure and irreversible neuronal damage. This failure of mitochondrial function may explain delayed neuronal death after transient metabolic insults and possibly may contribute to "slow triggered" excitotoxicity.

Influx of extracellular Ca^{2+} may follow various pathological stimuli, for example ischaemia, or exposure to neurotoxic peptides, both of which may cause activation of excitatory amino acid receptors. In ischaemia, early and delayed increases in $[Ca^{2+}]_i$ are observed; the former may be relevant to the triggering of the neurotoxic cascades mentioned earlier; the decline in $[Ca^{2+}]_i$ presumably reflects the activation of various cellular buffering, sequestration, and extrusion mechanisms. The larger secondary $[Ca^{2+}]_i$ rise reflects a failure to adapt, perhaps concurrent with mitochondrial failure, and is coincident with cell death when membrane integrity is lost.

The HIV coat protein gp120 has been shown to increase $[Ca^{2+}]_i$ in rat retinal ganglion cells (Dreyer, Kaiser, Offerman, & Lipton, 1990), an activity which may be relevant to the neurodegenerative effects of HIV. Aβ peptides destabilise $[Ca^{2+}]_i$ (Joseph & Han, 1992; Mattson et al., 1992), an effect that may render neurones more susceptible to excitotoxic insult (Mattson et al., 1992). Ca^{2+}-mediated damage to oligodendrocytes may play a role in the process of demyelination in multiple sclerosis (Scolding, Morgan, Campbell, & Compston, 1992). Many of these effects can be blocked or abrogated with calcium channel antagonists of varying specificity.

Nitric oxide. Since its first identification as the "endothelium-derived relaxing factor", the ubiquity and physiological importance of nitric oxide (NO) as a neurotransmitter have been increasingly recognised. Roles have been defined in blood pressure regulation (as a potent vasodilator), inflammation, and cytotoxicity (bacteria may be killed following NO production by macrophages). A role in the pathogenesis of certain neurological diseases has also been suspected (Dawson & Snyder, 1994; Moncada, Palmer, & Higgs, 1991).

NO is a short-lived free radical gas. It may exist as a number of different species (NO^+, $NO\bullet$, NO^-) which participate in different chemical reactions with sometimes diametrically opposed effects on neuronal survival. Hence $NO\bullet$ reacts with superoxide anion to form the highly toxic peroxynitrite ($ONOO^-$), whereas NO^+ modulates the NMDA receptor with neuroprotective effects. Nitric oxide synthase (NOS) catalyses the reaction between the amino acid L-arginine and molecular oxygen which produces NO. Three NOS isoforms exist: The constitutively expressed neuronal (nNOS) and endothelial (eNOS) forms, and an inducible form (iNOS), all encoded by separate genes on different chromosomes. The different sources of NO may have differing effects on neuronal integrity.

Although essential to a variety of physiological functions, excess NO can exert deleterious effects via a number of mechanisms. For example, it may impair mitochondrial function by inhibiting enzymes such as complexes I and II of the electron transport chain. The formation of $ONOO^-$ may be the major pathway through which cell death is mediated (Beckman, 1997), since, unlike the free radical superoxide and hydroxyl ions, peroxynitrite is relatively stable and able to diffuse over several cell diameters. The balance between physiological and pathological NO effects may depend upon the redox state of the cell: Under oxidising conditions, NO may reduce excitatory neurotransmission, whereas in reducing conditions $ONOO^-$ formation may be favoured.

These oxidants may damage DNA, mediate NMDA toxicity, and initiate programmed cell death. Cortical cultures exposed to NO donors have shown delayed neuronal death with apoptotic features, which may be attenuated by superoxide dismutase and catalase, probably by reducing formation of peroxynitrite (Bonfoco, Kraine, Ancarcrona, Nicotera, & Lipton, 1995). Since mutations in the gene encoding copper-zinc superoxide dismutase have been linked to familial MND (Rosen et al., 1993), it is possible that peroxynitrite may play a role in the selective death of motor neurones seen in this condition. NO can induce microfilament and microtubule disruption in cells, and cytoskeletal accumulations are seen in motor neurones in MND (Beckman, 1997); however, other explanations of the effects of SOD mutations are available, as discussed later. With regard to other neurological diseases, it has been reported that iNOS is increased in the plaques of multiple sclerosis, predominantly in astrocytes; that NO can induce the necrosis of oligodendrocytes *in vitro* (Mitrovic et al., 1995); and that NO donors can induce conduction block in axons, particularly if they are already partly demyelinated (Redford, Kapoor, & Smith, 1997).

Further information about the roles of NO has been derived from observations on NOS knockout animals and the use of NOS inhibitors. Transgenic mice lacking the gene for nNOS have smaller infarcts following middle cerebral artery occlusion (a model of global ischaemia; Huang et al., 1994), whereas deficiency of eNOS results in larger infarcts (Huang et al., 1996). These results suggest that neuronally derived NO is detrimental during ischaemia, whereas NO from the endothelium is protective. iNOS knockouts have a delayed reduction in susceptibility to cerebral ischaemia, suggesting that iNOS expression contributes to brain damage in the post-ischaemic period (Iadecola, Zhang, Casey, Nagayama, & Ross, 1997). Hence, selective nNOS and iNOS inhibition might be of possible therapeutic benefit in cerebral ischaemia. In humans, NOS inhibition with N^G monomethyl L-arginine results in a pronounced decrease in resting cerebral blood flow but does not inhibit the hyperaemic response to hypercapnia; it is thought that NO inhibition may therefore be neuroprotective in acute stroke but that the fall in cerebral blood flow induced by non-selective inhibitors may be potentially deleterious (White, Deane, Vallance, & Markus, 1998).

Reactive oxygen species. The central nervous system is peculiarly vulnerable to oxidative injury. It has a high consumption of oxygen and is rich in oxidisable substances such as polyunsaturated fatty acids and catecholamines; moreover, certain areas have high concentrations of iron, which can catalyse the production of free radicals; yet it is relatively deficient in antioxidative defence capacities, such as the enzymes catalase and glutathione peroxidase. Hence, this is an environment with considerable potential for the formation of reactive oxygen species, including free radicals. These latter are chemical species possessing an unpaired electron, chemically a highly unstable state, and having the ability to donate or accept an electron to complete their molecular orbitals. Hence, they are able to propagate and take part in chain reactions that may contribute to tissue damage and the mediation of neurodegeneration in ischaemia and other conditions (Halliwell, 1992; Simonian & Coyle, 1996).

The oxygen molecule is a potentially powerful oxidising agent with two unpaired electrons, and acceptance of a single electron will form the free radical superoxide, O_2^-. All aerobic cells contain superoxide dismutases (SODs), enzymes that specifically scavenge O_2^- to convert it to hydrogen peroxide (H_2O_2), strongly suggesting that superoxide radicals represent a major source of potential oxidative toxicity to cells. When H_2O_2 comes into contact with reduced forms of certain metal ions, such as iron or copper (the Fenton reaction), or interacts with superoxide, it decomposes into the exceptionally reactive and toxic hydroxyl radical ($\cdot OH$). The hydroxyl radical reacts at great speed with almost every molecule found in living cells. The roles of NO and peroxynitrite ($ONOO^-$) have already been mentioned. All these molecules (the free radicals O_2^-, $\cdot OH$, NO, and the non-radicals H_2O_2 and $ONOO^-$) contribute to cellular redox state.

These species are shortlived and hence can usually only be studied indirectly, for example through trapping procedures, such as spin trapping and salicylate trapping. Alternatively, the consequences of oxidative damage may be observed; reactive oxygen species can produce changes in lipids, proteins, and nucleic acids. As a consequence of lipid peroxidation, there is a gradual loss of membrane integrity: Membrane fluidity is reduced, resting membrane potential falls, and membrane permeability to Ca^{2+} may increase, eventually resulting in cytotoxicity. Nitrotyrosine is a stable product of $ONOO^-$ attack on proteins; $ONOO^-$ also inhibits complexes II and IV of the mitochondrial electron transport chain. Protein carbonyl groups are also markers of oxidative protein damage. Reactive oxygen species can cause strand breakage and base modification in DNA, activities that may trigger either necrosis or apoptosis (Halliwell, 1992; Simonian & Coyle, 1996).

There are multiple intracellular pathways by which reactive oxygen species are generated, but the primary source is as a by-product of oxygen metabolism in mitochondria: complex I and complex II of the electron transport chain form superoxide, which is dismutated by manganese superoxide dismutase (MnSOD) to H_2O_2. Uncoupling of mitochondrial respiration, for example in acidosis, can enhance the production of reactive oxygen species. Disease-specific and neuroanatomically selective mitochondrial dysfunction has been reported in PD (see later), and the mitochondrial toxin 3-NP has been reported to produce a picture similar to HD in the striatum (Portera-Cailliau, Hedreen, Price, & Koliatsos, 1995). Overexpression of the mitochondria-localised MnSOD in both cell lines and transgenic animals has been shown to attenuate the accumulation of peroxynitrite and prevent apoptosis (Keller et al., 1998).

Various enzymes can also be a source of reactive oxygen species, particularly mixed function oxidases, including lipo-oxygenases and cyclo-oxygenases, monoamine oxidase (MAO), the P450 system, and xanthine oxidase. These enzymes may be of varying significance for the induction of oxidative stress in the brain: For example, the restricted distribution of xanthine oxidase to the brain endothelium suggests it may be of little pathological significance. Since hypoxia/ischaemia leads to increased levels of free arachidonic acid in the brain

(Bazan, 1970), lipo-oxygenases and cyclo-oxygenases may be an important source of oxidative stress in this situation. Activated leucocytes are able to produce large amounts of superoxide, for example when phagocytosing bacteria, and their presence in certain brain disorders may be of pathological significance.

SOD enzymes form the major defence system against the O_2^- formed in aerobic cells, while most H_2O_2 formed is disposed of by glutathione peroxidase. Catalase, glutathione, vitamins A, C, and E, and DNA repair enzymes also contribute to cellular antioxidant defence capacity. None the less, these agents may be overwhelmed during certain pathological situations when multiple pathways generating reactive oxygen species may be activated. For example, in ischaemia and/or reperfusion injury, NMDA receptor activation leads to increased activity of the enzyme phopholipase A_2, and hence increased breakdown of membrane phospholipids with release of arachidonic acid which is a substrate for cyclo-oxygenases and lipo-oxygenases. Concurrently, a fall in the levels of ATP leads to formation of adenosine and its metabolites inosine and hypoxanthine, the latter being a substrate for xanthine oxidase with formation of superoxide. During reperfusion, a burst of enhanced oxidative metabolism may have deleterious effects on biochemical integrity.

Free radicals and reactive oxygen species have been implicated in the pathogenesis of a number of other neurological disorders, particularly neurodegenerative disorders (Simonian & Coyle, 1996). As previously mentioned, familial MND has been linked to mutations in the gene encoding copper-zinc superoxide dismutase (Rosen et al., 1993), suggesting increased availability of superoxide anions, which are injurious to motor neurones in *in vitro* model systems. Although at first sight it would seem that this results from loss of SOD enzyme function, the mutations described affect the backbone of the enzyme rather than the active site and it is possible that they may in fact result in gain of function, perhaps copper or zinc toxicity, or increased peroxynitrite attack on neurofilament proteins. In PD, a number of experimental observations suggest a pathogenetic role for oxidative stress: Dopamine metabolism results in generation of reactive oxygen species, specifically H_2O_2, through the activity of tyrosine hydroxylase and MAO-B. Moreover, there is an increased concentration of iron in the basal ganglia (Dexter et al., 1987) which may enhance conversion of H_2O_2 to $\cdot OH$ by the Fenton reaction. Glutathione levels are low in the basal ganglia, which may promote, or be a consequence of, oxidative stress. Mitochondrial dysfunction (complex I deficiency) specific to the substantia nigra (Mann et al., 1992) has also been documented in PD, and this may further contribute to oxidative stress. It seems likely that an interaction between an underlying genetic susceptibility and exposure to some kind of environmental toxin may be the trigger for this disease process. Amyloid β-peptides, which are thought to be important in the pathogenesis of AD, have been observed to exert their damaging effects through the generation of reactive oxygen species such as hydrogen peroxide (Behl, Davis, Lesley, & Schubert, 1994). Free radical peptides have been detected in aqueous solutions of $A\beta$ (Butterfield, Hensley,

Harris, Mattson, & Carney, 1994), and evidence for increased oxidative damage in AD brains has been presented (e.g., Lyras, Cairns, Jenner, Jenner & Halliwell, 1997; Mecocci, MacGarvey, & Beal, 1994). Clearly, these observations may have therapeutic implications for neurodegenerative disorders.

Abnormal protein isoforms. Abnormal isoforms of cellular proteins, formed by aberrant folding to produce structures rich in β-sheet conformation, have been implicated in a number of neurological disease processes. Examples include prion proteins in transmissible spongiform encephalopathies such as scrapie and Creutzfeldt-Jakob disease (CJD; Pan et al., 1993; Smith & Clarke, 1997), and amyloid β-peptide in AD (Barrow & Zagorski, 1991; Busciglio et al., 1993); both proteins aggregate to form plaques. Further possible examples of aberrant folding due to β-sheet formation have recently been reported (Lansbury, 1997), including the polyglutamine tail of the huntingtin protein in HD (Scherzinger et al., 1997). The Contersi kindred of autosomal dominant PD has been linked to a substitution mutation in the gene encoding α-synuclein (labelled PD1) in a region which disrupts α-helix to form β-sheet; it is possible that self-aggregation of the mutant protein might be the result (Polymeropoulos et al., 1997). Despite the fact that a number of other autosomal dominant PD kindreds have not been found to show genetic linkage to PD1 nor to harbour mutations in the α-synuclein gene (Farrer et al., 1998; Vaughan et al., 1998), α-synuclein immunohistochemistry has shown this protein to be the major filamentous component of Lewy bodies in both PD and dementia with Lewy bodies (DLB; Spillantini, Crowther, Jakes, Hasegawa, & Goedert, 1998).

In prion disease, the profound effects on disease phenotype exerted by polymorphism at the prion protein codon 129 may result from an effect on protein folding. In AD, the β-sheet structure of amyloid β-peptide is critical, favouring aggregation and the formation of fibrils, which harbour neurotoxic activity (Jarrett, Berger, & Lansbury, 1993; Pike, Burdick, Walencewicz, Glabe, & Cotman, 1993).

It is possible that post-translational structural change of cellular proteins may be a common pathogenetic motif, not only in neurodegeneration but also in a variety of other conditions which may be labelled as "conformational disorders" (Carrell & Lomas, 1997), including neoplasia (e.g., p53 related oncogenesis; Milner & Medcalf, 1991). The mechanism by which these abnormal proteins exert deleterious effects on neurones is not always clear: Loss of function, gain of toxicity, or both, are possible in both AD and prion disease. However, such observations do imply that prevention, or even reversal, of abnormal protein folding could be of therapeutic relevance (Lansbury, 1997).

Growth factors and cytokines

Many growth factors and cytokines are now recognised as being present in the adult CNS with a variety of effects on neurones. They can increase neuronal size, increase terminal branches and regulate transmitter phenotype, and many growth factors can also exert "protective" effects against a variety of insults, including physical injury, hypoxia, glutamate excitotoxicity, and other forms of toxicity, including reactive oxygen species (Dugan, Creedon, Johnson, & Holtzman, 1997; Grimes, Zhou, Li, Holtzman, & Mobley, 1993; Lam et al., 1998; Lucidi-Phillipi & Gage, 1993; Mattson, Cheng, & Smith-Swintosky, 1993; Persson, 1993; Sofroniew, 1996; Sofroniew et al., 1993; Svendsen & Sofroniew, 1995).

The consequences of dysfunction of cytokines and growth factors are incompletely understood. Cytokines may contribute to neurological dysfunction by inducing neurophysiological and pathological changes, as for example in multiple sclerosis, and possibly other CNS inflammatory disorders. The effects of cytokines may interact with other mechanisms, for example interleukin-1β may exacerbate excitotoxic cortical neuronal damage secondary to activation of AMPA receptors, and interleukin-1 receptor antagonists may inhibit such damage (Lawrence, Allan, & Rothwell, 1998). Disruption of constitutive growth factor signalling may also underlie certain forms of neuronal atrophy and dysfunction, as discussed later.

Environmental toxins

A number of examples of neurological disease occurring after the ingestion of toxins, either naturally occurring or synthetic, have been reported. Although the exact pathogenesis of some of these diseases remains to be fully elucidated, it is clear that specific toxins can exert profoundly deleterious effects on neuronal structure and function. Whether similar mechanisms might be applicable to the common neurological disorders such as AD, PD, and MND remains to be determined.

A number of disorders affecting primarily motor neurones have been ascribed to the consumption of environmental toxins of plant origin (Nunn, 1994). Neurolathyrism is an irreversible non-progressive spastic paraparesis caused by consumption of the chickling pea, *Lathyrus sativus*, and is endemic in Ethiopia, India, Bangladesh, Nepal, and China where this legume is grown as a food staple (Tekle-Haimanot, 1996). The active principal is believed to be a non-protein amino acid, β-N-oxalyl-α, β-diaminopropionic acid (β-ODAP; synonym, β-oxalyl-amino-L-alanine, BOAA), acute administration of which to experimental animals produces a neuropathological picture similar to that seen with excitotoxins acting at non-NMDA receptors. However, the pathology of neurolathyrism is much more selective, seeming to affect motor neurones only, and a non-excitotoxic mechanism of action remains a possibility. Furthermore, the precise role of β-ODAP in human neurolathyrism remains unclear, since attempts to model the disease by chronic oral administration of *L. sativus* or purified β-ODAP to macaques produced clinical signs that reversed after toxin withdrawal (Hugon et al., 1988), unlike the human situation.

Consumption of insufficiently processed roots of cassava (*Manihot esculenta*) in rural African communities can lead to epidemics of a symmetrical spastic paraparesis, clinically similar to neurolathyrism but for the fact that it usually comes on very acutely after cassava consumption, often in less than 1 hour. The resulting non-progressive syndrome is known as konzo in Zaire (meaning "tied legs") and mantakassa in Mozambique, and outbreaks have also been reported in the Central African Republic and Tanzania (Rosling & Tylleskar, 1996). Inadequate soaking of the starchy root of cassava, a food staple, leads to retention of cyanide, which can inhibit the enzyme cytochrome oxidase, the terminal reaction of the mitochondrial electron transport chain, with cessation of cellular energy metabolism. Concurrent low sulphur intake may also be important in pathogenesis, since this may contribute to impaired detoxification of cyanide (Rosling & Tylleskar, 1996). The reasons for the selectivity of neuronal injury by a toxin that could affect all cells are unclear. Interestingly, reports of high dose chemical cyanide poisoning from various parts of the world have indicated that survivors can develop a parkinsonian syndrome.

A similarly confused picture has emerged regarding the amyotrophic lateral sclerosis-parkinsonism-dementia (ALS-PD) complex seen in the Chamorros people of Guam. Some authors have ascribed this condition to consumption of the seed of the false sago palm, *Cycas circinalis*. A putative neurotoxin isolated therefrom, α-amino-β-methylaminopropionic acid (MeDAP; synonym, β-methylamino-L-alanine, BMAA), produced some motor neurone dysfunction following oral administration to macaques, but not the complete neurological or neuropathological picture seen in the human disease (Spencer et al., 1987). Hence, the role of MeDAP is not certain, nor yet its mechanism of toxicity, which cannot be entirely ascribed to agonism at NMDA receptors, and may also involve the formation of carbamates. The hypothesis that Guamanian ALS-PD has an excitotoxic aetiology now seems untenable in view of the marked differences in disease incidence in villages separated by only a few miles, and a genetic explanation for the clustering of ALS-PD cases is now being investigated. However, the possible role of excitotoxicity in this exotic motor neurone disorder was a major stimulus to the search for such mechanisms in MND and to the evaluation of treatment for MND with excitatory amino acid receptor antagonists.

Poisoning with domoic acid following ingestion of mussels infested with the phytoplankton *Nitzschia pungens* was reported from Canada in 1990, producing a variable syndrome encompassing headaches, loss of short-term memory, seizures, and myoclonus (Perl et al., 1990). An excitotoxic pathogenesis for this syndrome is possible since domoic acid acts at kainate receptors.

An outbreak of a pure parkinsonian syndrome in young people in northern California in the early 1980s was eventually traced to consumption of the synthetic meperidine analogue 1-methyl-4-phenyl-1,2,3,6-tetrahydropyridine (MPTP; Langston, Ballard, Tetrud, & Irwin, 1983). Although a very rare cause of human parkinsonism, this compound has none the less proven useful in developing animal models that resemble idiopathic PD and may shed light upon its aetiopathogenesis (Langston, 1996). MPTP must be converted by glial monoamine oxidase B (MAO-B) to the 1-methyl-4-phenylpyridinium ion (MPP^+) to exert its neurotoxic effect on dopaminergic neurones. MPP^+ is a substrate for the dopamine re-uptake pathway and is therefore concentrated in substantia nigra pars compacta (Sn_{pc}) neurones. Intracellularly, MPP^+ is concentrated in mitochondria where it irreversibly inhibits NADH-CoQ1 reductase (complex I) of the respiratory chain (Mizuno, Suzuki, Sone, & Saitoh, 1988). This effect can be prevented with free radical scavengers such as glutathione, ascorbate, and catalase (Cleeter, Cooper, & Schapira, 1992), suggesting that MPP^+ interacts with complex I to increase free radical production, which further damages complex I.

Common pathways: Energy failure

Of the mechanisms of neuronal injury discussed, several are common to various disease processes, e.g., excitatory amino acid release, increased $[Ca^{2+}]_i$, and production of reactive oxygen species including nitric oxide. Moreover, a similar pathological cascade of events may also be initiated by "energy failure", for example secondary to glucose or oxygen deprivation. This has led to the realisation that disturbances in neuronal energy status, leading to reduced ATP production and Na^+/K^+-ATPase dysfunction, can render neurones more susceptible to pathological processes such as excitotoxicity (Novelli, Reilly, Lysko, & Henneberry, 1988). Inhibition of the mitochondrial electron transport chain, for example by toxins, can also compromise neuronal energy status and this may be relevant to the pathogenesis of a number of neurodegenerative disorders (Beal, Hyman, & Koroshetz, 1993). It has been suggested that the detrimental effects of NO on DNA may activate the DNA repair enzyme poly(ADP-ribose) synthase which consumes large amounts of ATP, thus leading to cellular energy failure. Thus, inability to maintain energy homeostasis may be critical in rendering neurones vulnerable to other non-toxic insults.

Hence, it has been suggested that, individually or collectively, certain events may represent a "final common pathway" for cellular damage and death, all being concomitants of cellular "energy failure". Whether this is true, or whether individual components play greater or lesser roles in specific disease processes remains a subject of ongoing research, but none the less this formulation does suggest that therapeutic interventions aimed at these intermediates, such as excitotoxic amino acid receptor blockade and free radical scavenging, might have widespread applicability. However, because of the multiple parallel toxic processes, monotherapy may be insufficient to produce the desired clinical effects; this may explain why certain of the mechanisms employed to halt or minimise neuronal degeneration have failed in the clinical arena despite favourable results in animal model systems.

Infectious agents

Infectious agents can give rise to many forms of neurodegenerative change that are for the most part well described in textbooks of neuropathology and are beyond the scope of this chapter. Nevertheless two examples that illustrate novel concepts will be considered.

Prion diseases. Prions were originally characterised as proteinaceous infectious particles associated with transmissible neurodegenerative disorders (Prusiner, 1982), a category now known to encompass animal disorders such as scrapie and bovine spongiform encephalopathy (BSE; Bradley, 1997), and human disorders such as CJD, variant CJD (vCJD), Gerstmann–Straussler–Scheinker syndrome (GSS), and kuru (Collinge & Palmer, 1997; Prusiner, 1994). Initially all these diseases were thought to share common neuropathological features, namely spongiform vacuolation affecting any part of the cerebral grey matter, astrocytic proliferation and gliosis, neuronal loss, and variable deposition of amyloid plaques consisting of prion protein (Ironside & Bell, 1997; Prusiner, 1994). However, advances in the knowledge of the molecular basis of these conditions has led to the description of prion diseases without classical spongiform change (Collinge et al., 1990; Gambetti et al., 1993). Hence, the prion disease phenotype is an expanding one.

The transmissibility of these conditions was established by intracerebral inoculation of non-human primates with brain homogenates from individuals affected with CJD and kuru. The "infective agent", or prion, consists of an abnormal isoform, designated PrP^{Sc}, of a host encoded prion protein, PrP^{C}, transcribed from the prion protein gene (*PRNP*) on chromosome 20; hence it is probably better to speak of prion proteins rather than prions. Mutations in *PRNP* have been identified in familial CJD (Owen et al., 1989) and GSS (Hsiao et al., 1989), and transgenic animals expressing an analogous mutation develop spontaneous spongiform change (Hsiao et al., 1990).

There is no difference in the primary structure of PrP^{C} and PrP^{Sc}, and hence the conversion to the abnormal isoform is presumed to be a post-translational conformational event, probably related to protein folding; PrP^{Sc} has considerably more predicted β-sheet structure than PrP^{C} (Pan et al., 1993). Studies in transgenic animals (Prusiner et al., 1990) suggest that PrP^{Sc} can promote the conversion of PrP^{C} to the disease-related isoform leading to an autocatalytic chain reaction resulting in accumulation of progressively more PrP^{Sc}. Hence, it is envisaged that acquired or iatrogenic CJD results from direct inoculation of PrP^{Sc}; in sporadic CJD this conversion occurs spontaneously as a stochastic event; and in inherited CJD there may be direct production of PrP^{Sc}, or mutant PrP^{C} is unstable leading to more rapid conversion to PrP^{Sc}. In keeping with this hypothesis, PrP null mice are resistant to infection with scrapie. Likewise, the variable age of disease onset in inherited prion disease dependent upon codon 129 genotype (earlier in homozygotes; discussed in greater detail later) may also be explicable in terms of protein folding, homozygosity favouring β-sheet formation, and hence formation of the PrP^{Sc} isoform.

The physiological function of PrP^{C} is uncertain. PrP null mice appear to develop and behave normally but electrophysiological studies show impaired $GABA_{A}$-mediated synaptic inhibition in the hippocampus, raising the possibility that loss of PrP^{C}

function as well as gain of PrP^{Sc} toxicity may contribute to neurodegeneration (Collinge et al., 1994).

Human immunodeficiency virus (HIV). HIV infection is associated with a wide variety of neurological disorders, affecting CNS, PNS, and muscle (Price, 1996). Although these syndromes may occur at any time during the course of the disease, neurological morbidity and mortality occur mainly after the onset of profound immunodeficiency. These disorders may be related to opportunistic processes (e.g., infection, lymphoma) of the nervous system, or as a direct or indirect consequence of HIV infection (Glass & Johnson, 1996; Price, 1996). Pathological features may be inflammatory, demyelinating, or degenerative; however, there is a poor correlation between severity of neuropathological change and extent of neurological symptoms.

HIV is a neurotropic virus; it enters the nervous system at an early stage of the incubation period and is found there in the majority of patients dying of AIDS. The route of entry is still unclear; although astrocytes and neurones can be infected *in vitro*, it is likely that cells of the macrophage lineage are important for HIV penetration into the CNS and are the predominant cells productively infected.

A number of mechanisms have been postulated to account for the neurovirulence of HIV (Glass & Johnson, 1996). Direct toxicity of gp120, the envelope glycoprotein of HIV, which acts as a ligand for the lymphocyte CD4 receptor during infection, has been suggested on the basis of both culture and animal models. Picomolar amounts of gp120 can produce increased $[Ca^{2+}]_i$ in rat retinal ganglion cells, and this can be blocked by calcium channel antagonists (Dreyer et al., 1990). gp120-mediated calcium entry may involve the activation of neuronal NMDA receptors, suggesting an excitotoxic mechanism (Lipton & Rosenberg, 1994). Secretion of diffusible toxins by infected macrophages has been intensively studied but no firm conclusions reached, one candidate neurotoxin of macrophage origin is quinolinic acid which is an excitotoxin at the NMDA receptor (Heyes et al., 1991). However, increased CSF concentrations of quinolinic acid are not specific to AIDS, suggesting that this is a marker, rather than a mediator, of disease. Certainly macrophages and microglia are the source of various proinflammatory cytokines, such as tumour necrosis factor-α, interleukins 1β and 6, which are known to be elevated in response to HIV infection and which could produce a milieu conducive to further HIV replication and progressive immunosuppression.

Increasing knowledge of the pathogenetic mechanisms of HIV-related neurological diseases will increase the number of potential therapeutic targets in this situation. Thus, although treatment with zidovudine to block or slow viral replication has been reported to reverse or improve HIV-associated dementia, infection of the nervous system is unlikely to be the sole determinant of this syndrome.

Genetic predisposition

Many genes that are deterministic for human neurological disease have now been identified, although such identification has not always immediately elucidated the underlying pathogenetic mechanisms (e.g., huntingtin in HD, other trinucleotide repeat disorders; Paulson & Fishbeck, 1996). In addition, genes that are non-deterministic but that render individuals possessing them more vulnerable to certain neurological disease processes have also been described. Two examples may be given, in the context of prion disease and AD.

In iatrogenic CJD, an increased frequency of homozygosity for valine or methionine at codon 129 of the prion protein gene has been documented (Billette de Villemeur et al., 1996; Collinge, Palmer, & Dryden, 1991), a finding subsequently confirmed for sporadic CJD (Palmer, Dryden, Hughes, & Collinge, 1991). All cases of vCJD to date have occurred in individuals homozygous for methionine at codon 129. In addition, heterozygosity at codon 129 can delay disease onset in inherited CJD for 1–2 decades in comparison to homozygotes (Baker et al., 1991). Fatal familial insomnia (FFI), an inherited prion disorder, is linked to a substitution mutation at codon 178 of the prion protein gene (asparagine for aspartic acid); the same mutation is found in some cases of inherited CJD. However, in FFI, codon 129 always specifies methionine in the mutant allele in affected subjects, i.e., FFI is linked to the 129Met/178Asn haplotype, whereas 129Val/178Asn segregates with CJD (Goldfarb et al., 1992). Clearly, the codon 129 polymorphism can have profound effects on the expression of prion disease phenotype and age of disease onset, possibly due to a mechanism related to protein folding (see earlier).

In familial AD, linkage to a marker on chromosome 19 led to the recognition of the apolipoprotein E (ApoE) genotype as a significant risk factor for the development of familial AD, a finding subsequently extended to late-onset sporadic AD (Saunders et al., 1993). Specifically, possession of the $\varepsilon 4\varepsilon 4$ genotype increases the risk of developing AD by eight-fold compared to the commoner $\varepsilon 3\varepsilon 3$ genotype, whereas possession of an $\varepsilon 2$ allele may be protective (Roses, 1996). The exact mechanism by which the $\varepsilon 4$ allele confers this increased risk remains uncertain. One possibility is that it increases brain amyloid β-peptide burden through binding of Aβ to ApoE4 (Polvikoski et al., 1995); a subset of dementia patients with minimal amyloid burden and a high incidence of the $\varepsilon 2$ allele has been reported (Ikeda et al., 1997). Alternative explanations include a destabilising effect of ApoE4 on microtubule binding and hence neuronal cytoskeletal integrity (Strittmatter et al., 1994), and a direct neurotoxic effect confined to ApoE4 (Crutcher, Tolar, Harmony, & Marques, 1997; Nathan et al., 1994). In families with AD due to mutations in the APP gene, ApoE genotype can influence age of disease onset (Hardy, 1995).

ApoE allelism may also influence the phenotypic expression of other neurodegenerative conditions such as prion diseases and MND. It has been suggested that the $\varepsilon 4$ allele is a risk factor for CJD and that $\varepsilon 2$ increases disease duration (Amouyel et al., 1994), although other studies have not confirmed this association. The $\varepsilon 4$ allele is reported to be associated with a bulbar onset of MND, perhaps by influencing the precise pattern of motor neurone loss (Al-Chalabi et al., 1996); in this context, it may be relevant to note that pseudobulbar MND is associated with frontal lobe cognitive dysfunction.

CELLULAR FORMS OF DEGENERATION

Demyelination

Although the aetiology of multiple sclerosis (MS), the commonest of the demyelinating neurological disorders, depends on interactions between genetic and environmental factors, the pathogenesis of the condition is clearly immunologically driven (Scolding, Zajicek, Wood, & Compston, 1994). Blood brain barrier (BBB) disruption, as shown by leakage of gadolinium-DTPA in magnetic resonance imaging (MRI) studies, is one the earliest identifiable events in the development of new inflammatory lesions. The triggers for BBB breakdown are unknown, but may include rather non-specific insults such as viral infection. Influx of T-lymphocytes capable of interacting with antigen(s), as yet undefined, within the brain parenchyma is also an early event which may be cause and/or consequence of enhanced BBB vascular permeability. T cell : myelin antigen interactions, release of cytokines, ingress of complement components through the leaky BBB, and recruitment of microglial cells, all contribute to the amplification of the inflammatory response. The consequence is injury to the oligodendrocyte-myelin complex, possibly mediated by a number of pathways: complement-mediated attack on the oligodendrocyte membrane; destabilisation of oligodendrocyte $[Ca^{2+}]_i$; and cytokine-mediated damage of oligodendroglia. Macrophage-mediated removal of myelin debris and stripping of myelin from axons is then observed. Attempts at remyelination may occur, but these are usually incomplete. The factors that directly damage oligodendroglia also stimulate astrocyte proliferation, hence producing the characteristic scarring manifest as the plaques of MS (Scolding et al., 1994).

The importance of inflammation, rather than demyelination *per se*, in the pathogenesis of acute neuronal dysfunction in MS has become more apparent recently. A correlation between BBB leakage and changes in neurophysiological function of the optic nerve has been demonstrated in optic neuritis (Youl et al., 1991). Recrudescence of previously experienced MS symptoms immediately following administration of the humanised anti-lymphocyte monoclonal antibody CAMPATH-1H (Moreau et al., 1996) is thought to be related to release of inflammatory cytokines and/or NO, since the latter has been shown to cause axonal conduction block in experimental models of demyelinated nerve (Redford et al., 1997). Persisting neurological disability seems to be the result of sustained demyelination of axons and eventually axonal loss (Coles et al., 1999).

Immune dysregulation in HIV disease may play a role in the occurrence of inflammatory demyelinating neuropathies in this condition (Glass & Johnson, 1996).

Retrograde changes after axonal injury

Axotomising injury, resulting from direct axonal transection or indirect tissue reactions to injury, is an important consequence of clinical conditions such as neuronal trauma, compression, and ischaemia. Neurones in the central and peripheral nervous systems show a variety of responses to axotomy, ranging from cell death or severe atrophy without axon regeneration, to full recovery with axon regeneration (Brodal, 1981; Lieberman, 1971; Sofroniew, 1999). Retrograde degenerative changes can occur rapidly, or very gradually over periods of many months. The cellular and molecular mechanisms that underlie the neuronal response to axotomy and determine these differences are not known. In most cases, similar reactions to axotomy are observed amongst neurones that can be grouped together on the basis of topography, function, projection and/or developmental origin. For example, in adults, most motor neurones react similarly to axotomy, as do most cerebellar Purkinje neurones or most retinal ganglion cells. However, these different groups react quite differently to each other: Motor neurones survive axotomy and regenerate (Brodal, 1981); Purkinje cells survive but do not regenerate (Rossi, Jankovski, & Sotelo, 1995); and retinal ganglion cells die (Bray, Villegas-Perez, Vidal-Sanz, Carter, & Aguayo, 1991). The reasons for the similarity in reaction of specific groups of neurones is likely to be related both to common intrinsic properties and to similar extracellular environmental factors. Current hypotheses regarding signals that mediate the neuronal response to axotomy include: the loss or introduction of large molecules that signal via retrograde transport along the axon to the perikaryon; molecules that derive from glial cells around neuronal perikarya; and fast retrograde signals mediated by the influx of ions through membrane damage at the site of axonal injury (Sofroniew, 1999).

Most axotomising injury of clinical significance in the CNS is caused by blunt compression, crush, or shearing forces (Hilton, 1995). After a blunt injury, a core area is likely to suffer irreversible damage caused by direct mechanical axotomy. Neural tissue in a penumbra zone surrounding this core will also be damaged and become oedematous with high levels of extracellular $[K^+]$, glutamate, cytokines, and an inflammatory reaction. Treatment with methylprednisolone and other anti-inflammatory agents such as indomethacin has been reported in some trials to improve clinical outcome significantly, and to reduce the amount of tissue damage and the number of axotomised neurones, apparently by blocking components of the inflammatory response (Bracken et al., 1990; Guth, Zhang, & Roberts, 1994; Naso, Perot, & Cox, 1995; Young, 1993; Young, Kume-Kick, & Constantini, 1994). However, an overview of many trials of the use of steroids in acute CNS injury concluded that their place in treatment remains uncertain (Alderson & Roberts, 1997). None the less, the clinical observations suggest that a component of the inflammatory response can cause delayed "secondary" axotomising injury, resulting in a greater degree of axonal discontinuity than that caused by the original direct physical trauma. Characterising the extent and importance of such secondary axotomy,

and identifying the cellular and molecular events that mediate this reaction, as well as additional ways to block it, represent important areas of future research.

Ageing and degenerative disease

Normal ageing does not inevitably lead to severe neurodegeneration and cognitive decline in humans or laboratory animals. Most cognitive decline in aged humans can be associated with specific diseases, such as AD (Rapp & Amaral, 1992). Laboratory animals can also show age-related variation in cognitive ability due to specific underlying causes (Fischer et al., 1987). Modern anatomical studies using unbiased stereological techniques indicate that there is not substantial neuronal death in normal ageing in animals or humans. Anatomical studies also indicate that some populations of neurones show age-related atrophy, which in part may be due to dysfunction of growth factor signalling (Cooper, Lindholm, & Sofroniew, 1994; Mufson, Conner, & Kordower, 1995; Sofroniew, 1996). Age-related functional changes have also been noted: In some aged rats there is a reduced ability to induce and sustain long-term potentiation (LTP) in the hippocampus, and this reduction correlates significantly with reduced spatial memory (Barnes, 1994).

Atrophy

Neuronal atrophy in the form of shrinkage of the cell body and dendrites, can occur as a result of normal ageing, as well as in degenerative diseases such as AD, and as a consequence of injury (Pearson et al., 1983; Sofroniew, 1996; Sofroniew & Cooper, 1993). The causes underlying neuronal atrophy are not certain, but in some cases may involve dysfunction of target-derived growth factor signalling. Studies in experimental animals show that growth factors are able to increase neuronal size, and that loss of access to target-derived growth factors can cause neuronal atrophy (Gage et al., 1989; Sofroniew, Galletly, Isacson, & Svendsen, 1990). The degree of functional disturbance caused by neuronal atrophy is not certain. However, improved performance in behavioural tests has been correlated with reversal of atrophy of basal forebrain cholinergic neurones after treatment with NGF in aged rats (Fischer et al., 1987). In addition, atrophic neurones are more vulnerable to glutamate-receptor induced excitotoxicity.

Cell death: Apoptosis and necrosis

Apoptosis is a morphological description of a cell undergoing programmed or physiological cell death (Wyllie, Kerr, & Currie, 1980). The features of apoptosis comprise a highly ordered sequence of organelle abnormalities: swelling of the endoplasmic reticulum, vesiculation of the Golgi, followed by nuclear changes and mitochondrial disruption. These latter involve shrinkage of the nucleus, condensation, and fragmentation of chromatin, with or without DNA degradation (internucleosomal DNA fragmentation). This latter process follows release of nuclear endonucleases, which cut the DNA into fragments in multiples of 180–200 base pairs, producing a characteristic "laddering" pattern on gel electrophoresis. Apoptotic cells are swiftly phagocytosed. Such death programmes are constitutive and may be triggered by extracellular signals, for example the withdrawal of growth factors efficiently induces apoptosis in immature neurones.

Apoptosis is often contrasted with necrosis, the features of which include loss of membrane permeability, loss of membrane polarisation and plasma membrane rupture with spillage of cytosolic contents into the environment: This may have a "knock-on" effect, causing damage to adjacent cells, not seen in apoptotic cell death. Nuclear changes include karyolysis and dissolution; there is also organelle swelling, for example disruption of mitochondria with loss of cristae. However, rather than being mutually exclusive events, it is possible that apoptosis and necrosis may simply be different ends of a spectrum, necrosis reflecting the failure to carry out the death programme if a cell is rapidly overwhelmed by adverse stimuli (Bonfoco et al., 1995). Neuronal death following adminstration of kainic acid to the immature rat brain is not uniform, with apoptotic, necrotic, and overlapping morphologies being observed; "apoptotic" DNA laddering can occur simultaneously with morphological evidence of necrosis (Portera-Cailliau, Price, & Martin, 1997a). Furthermore, in the adult brain, the NMDA receptor agonist quinolinate produced a necrotic picture of cell death, whereas non-NMDA receptor agonists produced neuronal death more reminiscent of apoptosis (Portera-Cailliau, Price, & Martin, 1997b). These findings have been interpreted as showing that degree of brain maturity and stimulation of different glutamate receptor subtypes can influence the degenerative phenotype following excitotoxic injury to neurones, independent of the severity of the excitotoxic insult, confirming previous evidence of a morphological continuum or gradient ranging from apoptosis to necrosis (Bonfoco et al., 1995; Portera-Cailliau et al., 1997a,b). Hence, the earlier debate as to whether amyloid β-peptide may exert deleterious effects in AD through the stimulation of apoptotic or necrotic neuronal death may in fact be redundant: Both morphologies have been documented in *in vitro* paradigms (Behl, Davis, Klier, & Schubert 1994; Loo et al., 1993).

It has been known for some time that apoptotic neuronal death is a critical feature in the developmental patterning of the nervous system (Oppenheim, 1991), but its role in the adult brain and in the pathogenesis of neurological disorders is only now becoming clear. It seems likely that alterations in cell survival contribute to the pathogenesis of neurodegenerative disorders, particularly those in which specific sets of neurones are gradually lost, such as AD (LeBlanc, 1997), PD (Mitchell et al., 1994), and MND. However, definitive evidence is currently lacking in all but a few situations. In retinitis pigmentosa, an inherited and selective loss of retinal rod photoreceptors resulting from mutations in various genes, the early stages of photoreceptor degeneration suggest apoptosis as a common pathway (Chang, Hao, & Wong, 1993). Likewise, certain varieties of inherited spinal muscular atrophy, in which there is selective loss of motor neurones within the ventral horn of the spinal cord, have been associated with deletions

in a gene whose normal function is to inhibit apoptosis (Roy et al., 1995). Overexpression of the *bcl*-2 gene, whose product inhibits apoptosis, delays onset of disease in a model of familial MND with an attenuation of spinal cord motor neurone degeneration (Kosic, Jackson-Lewis, de Bilbao, Dubois-Dauphin, & Przedborski, 1997). Apoptosis has been suggested to be a feature of the selective effects of ischaemia, epilepsy, and gp120 toxicity in HIV infection (Charriaut-Marlangue, Aggoun-Zouaoui, Represa, & Ben-Ari, 1996) and may also contribute to loss of dopaminergic striatal projection neurones in PD (Mitchell et al., 1994), possibly accelerated by L-dopa therapy (Ziv et al., 1997). Overexpression of MnSOD has been reported to prevent neuronal apoptosis and reduce ischaemic brain injury, actions concurrent with suppression of $ONOO^-$ production, lipid peroxidation, and mitochondrial dysfunction (Keller et al., 1998). Many apoptosis-modifying compounds have been claimed for clinical use but none has yet proven efficacious (Larner, 2000).

Plaques

Accumulations of proteinaceous material bearing the neuropathological hallmarks of amyloid (i.e., staining with Congo Red and thioflavine T, apple green birefringence in polarised light with Congo Red staining) are found within the brain in a number of neurological conditions; these accumulations are known as plaques and may have a variety of morphologies. In AD, Down's syndrome, dementia pugilistica, and in the normal ageing human brain these plaques have been shown to consist of amyloid β-peptide (Aβ), whereas in prion disorders the peptide is the prion protein (PrP).

Aβ was first characterised from vascular amyloid deposits in AD by Glenner and Wong (1984) and subsequently from plaque amyloid by Masters et al. (1985) as a 39–43 amino acid peptide: The variability in C-terminus, initially thought to be a procedural artefact, is significant. Aβ is derived from a longer amyloid precursor protein (APP), encoded on chromosome 21. The structure of APP is suggestive of a membrane spanning glycoprotein but its exact function remains uncertain; APP knockouts display only minor neuroanatomical, neuropathological, and behavioural anomalies (Müller et al., 1994). Antibodies to Aβ reveal additional and widespread amorphous or diffuse plaques in the AD brain, not stained by Congo Red. These are thought to be the forerunners of the senile plaques containing compact or mature amyloid in which the peptides have aggregated to form insoluble fibrils that take up the Congo Red stain. Plaques seem to consist of Aβ molecules in a dynamic steady state equilibrium of aggregation and disaggregation processes (Cruz et al., 1997). Mature, fibrillar plaques may be surrounded by a halo of dystrophic neuritic processes and hence are sometimes known as neuritic plaques.

Since neuritic plaques may occur in normal ageing (albeit in lesser numbers than in the AD brain), and since extensive diffuse amyloid deposition may occur without cognitive impairment, the significance of amyloid in the causation of the dementing process has been debated; it has been argued that disruption of neuronal integrity is obligatory for cognitive impairments to develop. However, the pivotal role of $A\beta$ in the pathogenesis of AD became apparent when mutations within the APP gene which co-segregated with the disease were described in a small number of families (about 20 worldwide) with autosomal dominant AD (Hardy, 1995). All the APP mutations produce an increase in the synthesis of the longer variants of $A\beta$ (i.e., $A\beta1$–42/43) which have a greater propensity to self-aggregate into β-sheet conformations (Jarrett et al., 1993; Pike et al., 1993). The β-sheet structural motif occurs in a number of abnormal protein isoforms and may be relevant to the pathogenesis of a number of neurological disorders. $A\beta1$–42/43 may therefore be the main pathogenetic culprit in AD (Younkin, 1995): It is deposited first in Down's syndrome (Iwatsubo, Mann, Odaka, Suzuki, & Ihara, 1995) and in transgenic animal models of AD bearing mutant human APP genes (Masliah et al., 1996). Hence, reducing the production of this particular peptide might reduce plaque formation. However, although many neurotoxic activities have been ascribed to $A\beta$ (Iversen et al., 1995) the possibility remains that loss of APP function as well as gain of $A\beta$ toxicity may be important in AD pathogenesis (Larner, 1995c).

In certain of the transmissible spongiform encephalopathies or prion diseases, particularly kuru, Gerstmann–Straussler–Scheinker disease (GSS), and vCJD, amyloid plaques consisting of accumulations of prion protein (PrP) are common. Like $A\beta$ plaques, PrP plaques have a variety of morphologies, and PrP immunohistochemistry reveals a greater number and extent of deposits than are seen using routine histological techniques; diffuse deposits lacking amyloid characteristics may be seen (Hauw et al., 1996). The pathogenetic relevance of these plaques is uncertain, since they are not found in the majority of cases of sporadic CJD; their occurrence may simply reflect a greater tendency for protein aggregation in individuals with codon 129 homozygosity. As in the situation with $A\beta$ and AD, it is possible that loss of a normal function of PrP (for example, in synaptic transmission) may be of greater significance to disease pathogenesis than PrP accumulation (Collinge et al., 1994). Some authors have claimed that neurological symptoms and neuronal death may be transmitted without detectable abnormal prion protein accumulation (Lasmezas et al., 1997).

Accumulations of abnormal proteins without the tinctorial properties of amyloid may also be seen using appropriate immunohistochemistry in HD (Scherzinger et al., 1997) and PD (Spillantini et al., 1998).

Neurofibrillary tangles

Neurofibrillary tangles (NFTs) are argyrophilic intracellular structures composed at the ultrastructural level of paired helical filaments (PHFs). Extracellular or "ghost" tangles are thought to be "tombstones" for dead neurones. NFTs are observed in a variety of neurodegenerative disorders, as well as normal ageing, but in AD their cortical density, especially in temporal neocortex and parahippocampal gyrus, correlates with the severity of cognitive impairment better than senile plaque density (Arriagada, Growdon, Hedley-White, & Hyman, 1992) and their distribution allows the staging of the disease (Braak & Braak,

1991). At the molecular level, PHFs are composed principally of the microtubule-associated protein tau (τ; Wischik et al., 1988) in an abnormally hyperphosphorylated state (Goedert, 1993). In this form, τ is less able to bind to microtubules and this may lead to dysfunction of the cytoskeleton, for example impaired axonal transport, leading to dystrophic neurite formation, neuronal disconnection and eventually neuronal death. The E4 isoform of ApoE may exert its effects through a destabilising effect on microtubule binding and hence on neuronal cytoskeletal integrity (Strittmatter et al., 1994); $A\beta$ may also act as a stimulus to these cytoskeletal changes (Busciglio, Lorenzo, Yeh, & Yankner, 1995; Vickers, 1997). Immunohistochemistry for τ also reveals the dystrophic neurites around senile/mature/neuritic plaques and in a third location, dystrophic neurites scattered throughout the neuropil. These latter structures may be indicative of aberrant neurite growth in AD brain. A hypothetical model, which attempts to draw together the many molecular and cellular factors that interact in the pathogenesis of AD, is presented in Figure 7.1.

Tau positive filamentous lesions are also evident in a number of other neurodegenerative conditions, including Pick's disease, corticobasal degeneration, and frontotemporal dementias with parkinsonism linked to chromosome 17 (FTDP-17). Mutations in the tau gene have recently been identified in FTDP-17, establishing the importance of tau in the neurodegenerative process (Hardy, Duff, Hardy, Perez-Tur, & Hutton, 1998; Spillantini & Goedert, 1998).

Aberrant growth

Altered neuronal morphology with the formation of aberrant and meganeurites is a recognised neuropathological feature of human and animal gangliosidoses, a group of rare conditions characterised by the accumulation within neurones of gangliosides (sialic acid containing glycosphingolipids normally located in the outer leaflets of neuronal cell membranes; Purpura, 1978; Purpura & Baker, 1978). These observations suggested that abnormal neurite growth can lead to neuronal dysfunction as devastating as that caused by neuronal atrophy or death. More recently, the possibility that aberrant neuritic growth may be relevant to the pathogenesis of common neurodegenerative diseases has been suggested. The pathological features of AD include evidence of aberrant neurite growth, manifested as τ-immunopositive dystrophic neurites scattered throughout the neuropil and surrounding mature/senile plaques. The stimuli responsible for this aberrant growth pattern are uncertain, but may include increased expression of neurite growth-promoting factors, reduced expression of neurite growth-inhibitory factors, or changes in the expression of receptors for these classes of molecules (Larner, 1995b). The abnormal cytoskeleton within dystrophic neurites is likely to be dysfunctional, contributing to disordered axonal transport and synaptogenesis, which may in turn lead to neuronal disconnection and death, manifest clinically as dementia. Hence, although dystrophic neurites may reflect an attempted regenerative response to ongoing neuronal

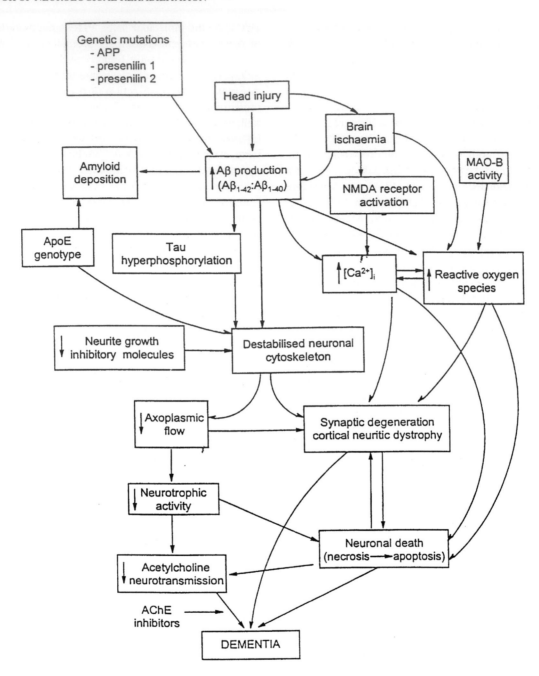

Figure 7.1. Schematic integrating the various molecular and cellular changes implicated in the pathogenesis of Alzheimer's disease. (Reprinted with permission of the editor from *Expert Opinion on Therapeutic Patents*, 1998, *8*, 1753–1759.)

loss, they could also reflect a more primary pathogenetic process, actually contributing to neuronal death. Indeed, since dystrophic neurites are seen, using various immunohistochemical techniques, in many neurodegenerative disorders, this may be a common neuropathological motif underpinning dementia syndromes (Larner, 1997).

Glial cell changes

Since glial cells outnumber neurones by a ratio of approximately 10 : 1 in the vertebrate CNS, it is perhaps to be expected

that they may exert significant effects in pathological processes. Of course, neoplastic glial proliferation is a common cause of tumour formation in the adult CNS, which may cause neuronal dysfunction through local pressure effects, but changes in glial metabolic function may also be of pathogenetic relevance: Hepatic encephalopathy is thought to be primarily a disorder of glial function with secondary neuronal dysfunction. Furthermore, glial dysfunction may contribute to various neurological diseases. Glial swelling is seen in ischaemia, trauma, hypoglycaemia, status epilepticus, hypotonicity, and fulminant hepatic failure, and may be a stimulus for reactive astrocytosis or gliosis, the most characteristic response of the CNS to destructive tissue injury (Norenberg, 1994). Reactive astrocytes show characteristic morphological changes; moreover, they are metabolically active cells, filled with filaments which stain with antibodies to glial fibrillary acidic protein (GFAP) and vimentin. GFAP immunopositivity is widely used as a marker for reactive astrocytosis, and this may be seen in the absence of tissue injury and astrocyte morphological change; for instance, in AD, although astrocyte numbers are increased they show no morphological indications of reactivity (Frederickson, 1992) but none the less there is a generalised increase in GFAP immunopositivity suggestive of generalised glial activation (Delacourte, 1990). Aβ can induce reactive astrocytosis *in vitro*; since glial scars inhibit axonal outgrowth it is thought that this astrocytosis may contribute to the formation of dystrophic neurites around neuritic/senile plaques (Canning et al., 1993), but other possible molecular mediators include S100β, a cytokine that promotes excessive neurite growth, and basic fibroblast growth factor. Up-regulation of many proteins with potent biological activities accompanies reactive astrocytosis (Norenberg, 1994). Astrocytosis is commonly seen in prion diseases, along with spongiosis and plaque formation; this may be accounted for by the fact that PrP causes astrocyte proliferation.

Microglia are cells of the macrophage-monocyte lineage which may have critical roles in the genesis of immune responses within the CNS. They have been suggested as the main culprits in the immunopathogenesis of MS (Sriram & Rodriguez, 1997) and may play a role in HIV-related neurodegeneration (Stanley et al., 1994). Microglia produce cytokines such as interleukin-1, which can provoke astrocytosis. Activated microglia are seen at the periphery of mature AD plaques. This may be in response to the presence of Aβ, which can contribute to microglial activation (Meda et al., 1995), or may reflect active phagocytosis of cellular remnants similar to the removal of apoptotic bodies. This inflammatory component in plaques could be a therapeutic target in AD: There is some evidence that anti-inflammatory therapy may delay the onset of the condition (Breitner et al., 1994).

The metabolic activities of glial cells may have beneficial or detrimental effects on adjacent neurones. For example, they may protect against excitotoxic injury, possibly through the uptake of glutamate and its conversion to glutamine (Rosenberg & Aizenman, 1989; Rothstein et al., 1996; Tanaka et al., 1997). However, glial MAO-B converts MPTP to the dopaminergic neuronal toxin MPP+, which may be relevant to the pathogenesis of PD. iNOS in astrocytes, microglia, and macrophages may contribute to the inflammation in the MS plaque. The different behaviour of adult and neonatal glia in respect of scar formation may be relevant to the loss of CNS regenerative capacity during ontogeny (McKeon, Schreiber, Rudge, & Silver, 1991).

AXONAL GROWTH AND NEURAL REGENERATION

Peripheral nervous system

Following axotomy of a peripheral nerve, axonal regeneration and recovery of function are possible, dependent on a number of factors including species, age, and the nature of the injury. The response to axotomy may be conveniently divided into two processes: The degeneration and clearing of the distal stump, known as Wallerian degeneration, which is crucially dependent on macrophages; and successful axonal regeneration, which seems to be critically dependent upon Schwann cells (Brecknell & Fawcett, 1996; Fawcett & Keynes, 1990; Tonge & Golding, 1993).

Wallerian degeneration. Since the arborisations of a neurone are dependent for their survival on molecules synthesised and transported from the perikaryon, the distal portion of an axon will degenerate if severed from the cell body. Myelin sheaths and axonal debris are phagocytosed and recycled by Schwann cells and macrophages. The latter are recruited to the degenerating distal segment 2–3 days after a lesion, possibly in response to the secretion of chemotactic substances. In the C57BL/Ola mouse mutant, in which macrophage recruitment and Wallerian degeneration do not usually occur, wild-type nerve transplanted into the mutant will undergo normal degeneration, suggesting that the axon is the source of the chemotactic signal (Lunn, Perry, Brown, Rosen, & Gordon, 1989). Once recruited, macrophages play a key role not only in removing debris but also in secreting factors which are mitogenic for Schwann cells (Beuche & Friede, 1984), such as platelet-derived growth factor, transforming growth factor-β, and fibroblast growth factors (Schubert, 1992). The proliferated Schwann cells within the remaining endoneurial tubes form the morphological feature known as the bands of Büngner.

Axonal regeneration. Within a few hours of lesioning, axons within the proximal stump of an injured nerve will form growth cones at the node of Ranvier adjacent to the site of injury (nodal sprouting) or from the terminals of injured axons themselves (terminal sprouting). Axonal elongation through remaining Schwann cell tubes may permit reconstitution of appropriate synaptic contacts (homotypic sprouting) and full restoration of function. Undamaged axons can also sprout collateral branches in response to partial deafferentation, and these collateral sprouts are able to fill vacated synaptic contacts (heterotypic sprouting), thus effectively "reorganising" synaptic circuitry. Such aberrant regeneration may be detrimental, as seen for example following recovery from a Bell's palsy, leading to muscular synkinesis and "crocodile tears". A similar phenomenon may also underpin the reorganisation of CNS circuitry after injury, for example in the hippocampus in temporal lobe epilepsy (Larner, 1995a).

Axonal sprouts enter the distal stump in intimate contact with the Schwann cell basal lamina and Schwann cell membrane. Experimental studies suggest that this targeting is due to the secretion of a neurotrophic activity from the degenerating nerve stump. However, Wallerian degeneration is not absolutely crucial to this process since it may be observed in the C57BL/Ola mouse in which degeneration does not occur (Brown, Perry, Hunt, & Lapper, 1994). A number of molecules may contribute to this activity: Increased secretion and/or transcription of nerve growth factor (NGF), brain-derived neurotrophic factor (BDNF), and ciliary neurotrophic factor (CNTF) has been shown; these agents can exert specific neurotrophic actions on subsets of neurones (sensory, sympathetic, motor), as evidenced by the phenotypic changes in animals in which individual neurotrophin genes or their receptors have been "knocked out" (Snider, 1994). However, their precise role is unclear since antibodies to individual components, such as NGF, do not block successful PNS regeneration. Cell surface and extracellular matrix molecules with adhesive properties may also be important, such as laminin, fibronectin, J1/tenascin, L1 and N-cadherin.

Axonal regeneration can be effectively blocked by glial scar tissue, inflammatory exudates, and infection. The larger the gap between cut nerve ends the less the chance of sprouts finding their appropriate endoneurial tubes and hence regenerating to correct targets; hence crush injuries tend to recover better than sections. However, even if successful axonal elongation occurs, there is no guarantee that effective synaptic contacts will be made.

It is therefore clear that environmental factors are important in determining the success of peripheral nerve regeneration, but intrinsic neuronal factors may also play a role. Accuracy of reinnervation may be better in lower vertebrates: For example, in the neuromuscular system, regeneration with the formation of appropriate connections is seen in adult urodeles, larval anurans, and neonatal rats, whereas aberrant reinnervation is seen in adult mammals and adult anurans (Fawcett & Keynes, 1990; Tonge & Golding, 1993). There may also be differences in the capacities of motor and sensory fibres to regenerate, perhaps due to the persistence or recapitulation of developmental cues for axonal growth (Fawcett & Keynes, 1990). However, these phylogenetic and ontogenetic parameters seem less important in determining the efficacy of regeneration in the PNS than the CNS.

Central nervous system

Unlike the situation in the PNS, spontaneous axonal regrowth with the establishment of appropriate, functional neural connections does not occur after axotomy in the adult mammalian CNS. In contrast, in anamniote poikilothermic non-mammalian vertebrates, such as cyclostomes, fish, urodeles, and anurans, certain CNS pathways, such as the spinal cord and retinotectal tract, are able to undergo structural regeneration with restitution of function; similar phenomena are also observed in embryonic birds and neonatal mammals (Larner, Johnson, & Keynes, 1995). The implication that regenerative properties have been lost during CNS evolution and development begs the question as to the factors responsible for this loss of regenerative capacity in the CNS. Two major areas have been focused on: The CNS environment, and intrinsic properties of CNS neurones themselves (Brecknell & Fawcett, 1996).

Cues in adult CNS environment that may prevent regeneration.   It was recognised in the early years of the twentieth century that whereas axotomised CNS axons demonstrated only abortive spontaneous regeneration, they could none the less grow for short distances into PNS grafts implanted into the CNS (Cajal, 1928; Forsmann, 1900; Tello, 1911). However,

these observations were apparently forgotten and for many years the notion that CNS axons were intrinsically incapable of making the necessary metabolic responses to sustain regeneration held sway. The rediscovery of the PNS graft paradigm showed convincingly, with the aid of modern tract tracing techniques, that extensive CNS axonal regeneration was possible when the appropriate environmental cues were present (David & Aguayo, 1981; Richardson, McGuinness, & Aguayo, 1980). Indeed, CNS axons can regenerate extensive distances through PNS grafts and emerge to make appropriate functional synaptic contacts (Carter, Bray, & Aguayo, 1989, 1994). These studies suggested that the adult mammalian CNS was a constitutively inhibitory environment for axonal growth, as did the inability of dissociated neurones to grow into optic but not sciatic nerves (Schwab & Thoenen, 1985). The cellular and molecular substrates of the inhibitory CNS environment remain subjects of intensive investigation.

Oligodendrocytes and myelin.   Berry (1982) suggested that myelin breakdown products might account for the failure of mammalian CNS regeneration, and a body of evidence has subsequently been forthcoming to indicate that oligodendrocytes and myelin are inhibitory to axonal growth. CNS white matter (rat and human), but not grey matter, is a non-permissive substrate for neuronal cell adhesion and axon elongation (Crutcher & Privitera, 1989; Schwab & Caroni, 1988), and two proteins have been characterised from adult rat CNS myelin, NI35 and NI250, which inhibit axon growth and fibroblast spreading (Caroni & Schwab, 1988). It took more than a decade for the full characterisation of these proteins as No-go (Chen et al., 2000). In the meantime, a monoclonal antibody raised against them (IN-1) was shown to permit the growth of axons in a variety of "non-permissive" situations, e.g., adult rat corticospinal tract fibres through a glial scar (Schnell & Schwab, 1990), acetylcholinesterase-positive septo-hippocampal fibres within the hippocampus following fimbria-fornix lesions (Cadelli & Schwab, 1991), and retinal ganglion cell axons following optic nerve crush (Weibel, Cadelli, & Schwab, 1994). Claims for functional recovery after lesioning and IN-1 application have been made, e.g., recovery of segmental reflexes following spinal cord injury (Bregman et al., 1995) and reaching behaviours after pyramidal tract lesions (Z'Graggen, Metz, Kartje, Thallmair, & Schwab, 1998).

Similar inhibitory molecules have been identified in fish optic nerve myelin (Sivron, Schwab, & Schwartz, 1994), even though this system has long been known to undergo spontaneous regeneration. Differing regenerative capacity has therefore been attributed to differing response to injury, the prompt macrophage and microglial response in fish, but not rat, optic nerve clearing away growth-inhibitory material to produce a temporarily (rather than constitutively) permissive CNS environment for axonal growth (Sivron et al., 1994).

Astrocytes and the glial scar.   CNS injury causes astrocytic proliferation and hypertrophy with the production of a glial scar. Regenerating axons come to a stop when they encounter such a scar and form synapse-like terminals as though their physiological "stop" pathway had been activated (Liuzzi & Lasek, 1987). Although the dense astrocytic scars were initially thought to be a mechanical barrier to regeneration, the morphology of the arrested axon terminals is unlike that of regenerating peripheral axons obstructed by a neuroma (Liuzzi & Lasek, 1987) and therefore it is likely that neurite inhibitors of astrocyte origin are responsible for regenerative failure. A number of chondroitin sulphate proteoglycans derived from adult, but not neonatal, astrocytes have been shown to inhibit neurite growth (Bovolenta, Wandosell, & Nieto-Sampedro, 1993; Levine, 1994; McKeon et al., 1991; Smith-Thomas et al., 1994).

Intrinsic neuronal properties. Although the role of the adult CNS environment in blocking axonal regeneration has received increasing attention in recent years, the role of intrinsic neuronal properties, once held to be the key to CNS regeneration failure, should not be forgotten. This area has attracted less attention, perhaps because of the difficulty in designing experiments to test hypotheses related to intrinsic factors (Fawcett, 1992). However, it seems that neurones at different stages of development, and different neuronal types, have differing regenerative capacities.

Developmental stage. That neuronal age may influence regenerative capacity is suggested by the more vigorous regeneration seen in younger teleosts and urodeles, and embryonic birds and neonatal mammals (Larner et al., 1995). The neural transplantation paradigm has also provided evidence of this: Foetal mesencephalic dopaminergic allografts have replaced adult adrenal autografts for clinical transplantation in Parkinson's disease (see Chapter 9), and in experimental animals neuroblasts are capable of even more extensive axonal regeneration, even along myelinated tracts (Wictorin, Brundin, Sauer, Lindvall, & Bjorklund, 1992). The capacity of foetal neurones to regenerate independently of environmental constraints, including white matter, has now been demonstrated in several model systems (Davies, Field, & Raisman, 1994; Dusart, Airaksinen, & Sotelo, 1997; Li, Field, & Raisman, 1995; Shewan, Berry, & Cohen, 1995). It has been suggested that neuronal maturity is marked by the turning off of a "growth programme", which cannot be reinstituted despite the presence of a permissive microenvironment, perhaps due to developmental regulation of receptors for inhibitory cues.

Neuronal types. There are various examples of the differing efficacy of regeneration of different neuronal types. In cyclostomes, the simplest vertebrates, identified reticulospinal neurones with cell bodies and axons located in similar areas of the nervous system consistently show different regenerative responses after section (Davis & McClellan, 1994), as do frog optic axons and tectal efferent axons encountering similar environments after section by a single diencephalic lesion (Lyon & Stelzner, 1987). Cerebellar axons from the deep nuclei, but not from the cortex, will grow into peripheral nerve grafts inserted into the cerebellum (Dooley & Aguayo, 1982) and GABAergic neurones of the thalamic reticular nucleus extend axons into similar grafts in greater numbers than other thalamic neuronal types (Benfey, Bunger, Videl-Sanz, Bray, & Aguayo, 1985; Morrow,

Campbell, Lieberman, & Anderson, 1993). In addition, injured CNS axons encountering PNS grafts show varying responses dependent upon the distance of the injury from the perikaryon (Richardson, Issa, & Aguayo, 1984).

APPLICATION TO TREATMENT AND RECOVERY

Halting or minimising degeneration

Prevention of excitotoxicity by receptor blockade. Antagonists to both NMDA and AMPA receptors have been shown to be of benefit in experimental paradigms of focal brain ischaemia. For example, the high-affinity use-dependent NMDA non-competitive antagonist MK-801 (dizocilpine) has been shown to be neuroprotective in rodent models of focal ischaemia. Unfortunately, this agent failed to translate to the clinical situation because of toxicity and vacuolation in the cingulate cortex, but other candidates are currently under trial, and it may be that AMPA receptor anatagonists will have more to offer in terms of protecting against the delayed neuronal death in the ischaemic penumbra of an infarct (Buchan et al., 1993).

In epilepsy, some of the newer anticonvulsant agents may act, at least in part, through interactions with glutamate: Felbamate protects against kainic acid induced seizures and may be a competitive antagonist at the glycine-binding modulatory site of the NMDA receptor (it has also been shown to be neuroprotective in focal hypoxic-ischaemic lesions); lamotrigine acts through inhibition of presynaptic glutamate release; and topiramate apparently has antagonistic effects on KA/AMPA receptors.

Various lines of evidence have suggested that primary or secondary excitotoxic mechanisms may contribute to selective neuronal damage in MND (Shaw, 1994), as originally suggested in other motor neurone disorders such as neurolathyrism and ALS-PD of Guam (Nunn, 1994). Hence the rationale for attempting to treat this condition with the glutamate antagonist riluzole; one widely reported trial apparently did show riluzole to be beneficial (Bensimon, Lacomblez, Meininger, & the ALS/Riluzole Study Group, 1994) but a closer analysis of all the various trials of riluzole, including unpublished ones, has been less compelling (Anonymous, 1997). None the less, riluzole has been licensed for the treatment of MND and is now in regular clinical use.

Protection from intracellular calcium overload. Since raised $[Ca^{2+}]_i$ may play an important part in the pathogenesis of many processes injurious to neurones, blockade of calcium entry from the extracellular space may be a viable therapeutic option. The efficacy of excitatory amino acid receptor blockade may derive, at least in part, from an effect on this ligand-gated calcium ion ingress. Blockade of voltage-gated calcium channels is also possible through the availability of specific antagonists, a number of which have been shown to have effects in experimental paradigms and/or clinical neurological disorders. For example, calcium channel antagonists can block the increase in $[Ca^{2+}]_i$ induced in rat retinal ganglion cells by HIV coat protein gp120 (Dreyer et al., 1990), a process which may contribute to HIV neurotoxicity. There is some evidence that the neurotoxic effects of amyloid β-peptide *in vitro* may be partially abrogated by voltage-gated calcium channel antagonists such as nimodipine (Weiss, Pike, & Cotman, 1994) and nifedipine (Larner, 1998); trials of calcium channel antagonists in dementia are ongoing. However, it is in the field of hypoxic-ischaemic brain injury that calcium channel antagonists may have most to offer, particularly the possibility that they might enhance the viability of neurones within the ischaemic penumbra. There is no doubt that nimodipine prevents ischaemic neurological deficits following aneurysmal subarachnoid haemorrhage, and this has prompted a number of studies of nimodipine in ischaemic stroke. Overall, these have failed to show improved patient outcome, but the belief remains that such agents could be helpful in selected patients, for example those with a progressing neurological deficit in the face of haemodynamic stability (Grotta, 1991).

Protection from NO-induced neurotoxicity.   As previously mentioned, the actions of the NO group may be either neuroprotective or neurotoxic, dependent upon redox state; hence, NO and $ONOO^-$ are neurotoxic, whereas NO^+ equivalents are neuroprotective through an action on the NMDA receptor redox modulatory site(s). Appropriate manipulation of NO for therapeutic purposes may therefore be difficult, depending on cellular redox state and origin of NO. Knockout animals suggest that selective inhibition of nNOS and iNOS may be neuroprotective in cerebral ischaemia (Huang et al., 1994; Iadecola et al., 1997), as may scavengers of superoxide anions (which react with NO to produce the highly toxic $ONOO^-$). Neuroprotection may also be facilitated through the transfer of NO^+ equivalents to the redox modulatory site of NMDA receptors, so down-regulating receptor activity.

Although pharmacological manipulation of NO-induced neurotoxicity is currently of little therapeutic utility, this field is likely to become a major growth area in the near future. Recently it has been shown that NGF rapidly suppresses basal as well as NMDA- and AMPA-evoked increases in hippocampal NO synthase activity (Lam et al., 1998), which may partially explain the neuroprotective effects of NGF in models of excitotoxic neurodegeneration.

Protection from reactive oxygen species.   Although neurones have endogenous mechanisms to protect against the effects of reactive oxygen species, including the enzymes superoxide dismutase, catalase, and glutathione peroxidase, these are sometimes overwhelmed during pathological processes, which may lead to neurological dysfunction. The use of exogenous antioxidant enzymes for treatment purposes has proved impractical, for example due to the very short half-life of SOD and its failure to cross the intact BBB. Hence, there has been an ongoing search for exogenous antioxidant agents, which might prove useful in the prevention or treatment of neurological disease. These agents include inhibitors of the formation of reactive oxygen species and antioxidants. In the first category are included inhibitors of xanthine oxidase (e.g., allopurinol), phospholipase (e.g., mepacrine), and of arachidonic acid metabolism

(e.g., indomethacin, piroxicam, flurbiprofen). Although formal clinical trials of such agents have not yet been undertaken, it is of interest that prior treatment with non-steroidal anti-inflammatory agents such as indomethacin has been reported to delay the onset of AD (Breitner et al., 1994). Antioxidant agents include spin trapping agents, α-lipoic acid, the vitamin A precursor β-carotene, vitamin C (ascorbic acid), and vitamin E (the biologically active component of which is α-tocopherol). Certainly vitamin E deficiency can have profound detrimental effects on the nervous system (spinocerebellar syndrome, peripheral neuropathy, dementia; Harding, 1987), although whether these effects are mediated through reactive oxygen species is currently not known. 21-aminosteroids ("lazaroids") are non-glucocorticoid steroids with antioxidant activity through the inhibition of lipid peroxidation, independent of steroid receptor pharmacology.

Routine clinical use of such agents is still awaited, but there are theoretical reasons to believe that they may find a niche. Trials of the 21-aminosteroid tirilazad mesylate (U74006F) in acute neural insults (CNS injury, ischaemia, and subarachnoid haemorrhage) are in progress (Hall, 1997). The neurotoxic effects of Aβ *in vitro* can be partially blocked by agents such as catalase (Behl, Davis, Lesley, & Schubert, 1994), vitamin E (Behl, Davis, Cole, & Schubert, 1992), and *n*-propyl gallate (Behl et al., 1992; Larner, 1998). α-tocopherol, the moiety of vitamin E which can attenuate lipid peroxidation by trapping free radicals, was not found to be helpful in slowing the progression of PD in the DATATOP trial (Parkinson Study Group, 1993), but the question remains as to whether an appropriate dose was used. Deprenyl, an MAO-B inhibitor, certainly delayed functional disability in PD (Parkinson Study Group, 1993), but it is not clear whether this was solely a symptomatic effect or whether it was related to an antioxidant action (decreased reactive oxygen species, such as H_2O_2).

Protection from abnormal protein isoforms.   In AD, the identification of factors which promote the aberrant folding of the Aβ protein and its aggregation into insoluble fibrils may be of great importance in designing therapies to interrupt the pathogenetic cascade and so halt the clinical progression of AD (Larner & Rossor, 1997). Synthetic peptides which prevent β-sheet formation have been reported to block Aβ fibril formation and neurotoxicity (Soto, Kindy, Baumann, & Frangione, 1996). Such a strategy may be applicable not only to other neurological disorders associated with abnormally folded protein isoforms, such as prion diseases (Prout & Larner, 1998), but also to a wide variety of other conditions characterised by post-translational structural change of cellular proteins (Carrell & Lomas, 1997), including neoplasia (e.g., p53 related oncogenesis; Milner & Medcalf, 1991). Recently, transgenic mice bearing mutant APP genes known to be deterministic for AD have been shown to be protected from the development of AD pathology by immunisation with Aβ peptides (Schenk et al., 1999). Clinical trials of Aβ vaccine are now being planned.

Protection from degeneration, and upregulation of function, by growth factors. Growth factors have been demonstrated to protect various neuronal populations from degeneration both *in vitro* and *in vivo*, and following a variety of insults including toxic, traumatic, and ischaemic. The cascade of events mediating the protective effects of growth factors and cytokines appears to involve the activation of receptors that stabilise $[Ca^{2+}]_i$ and/or reduce the generation of free radicals or nitric oxide stimulated by excitotoxic activation of glutamate receptors (Dugan et al., 1997; Mattson, Cheng, & Smith-Swintosky, 1993). Of possible clinical relevance, basic fibroblast growth factor (bFGF) protects hippocampal neurones from $A\beta$-induced increases in $[Ca^{2+}]_i$ (Mattson, Tomaselli, & Rydel, 1993), an effect not seen with NGF. Nevertheless, NGF protects striatal, retinal, and hippocampal neurones from infusions of excitotoxic glutamate agonists or from ischaemic events thought to involve excitotoxiciy (Aloe, 1987; Holtzman, Sheldon, Jaffe, Cheng, & Ferriero, 1996; Schumacher, Short, Hyman, Breakefield, & Isacson, 1991). Gene therapy with glial-cell-line-derived neurotrophic factor (GDNF) can protect dopaminergic cells from neurotoxic insults (Choi-Lundberg et al., 1997). There may be overlap or redundancy of trophic effects: The increased survival of axotomised corticospinal tract neurones observed following treatment with exogenous GDNF requires endogenous BDNF, the latter acting as a paracrine/autocrine survival factor (Giehl Schutte, Mestres, & Yan, 1998).

In addition to having protective effects, growth factors can augment neuronal function by inducing neuronal hypertrophy, increasing gene expression or altering synaptic plasticity, which in some cases appears to lead to enhanced performance in behavioural tests in experimental animals (Fischer et al., 1987; Gage et al., 1989; Garofalo, Ribeiro-Da-Silva, & Cuello, 1992; Sofroniew & Cooper, 1993).

MS therapies. The importance of immunological mechanisms in the pathogenesis of demyelinating lesions in MS (Scolding et al., 1994) has directed attention to immunomodulatory agents as possible treatments for this condition. Interferon (IFN)-β1b has been reported to reduce relapse rate in MS by approximately one-third (IFNB Multiple Sclerosis Study Group, 1993), a finding also observed with IFN-β1a (Jacobs et al., 1996). The latter was also claimed to produce a small but significant delay in the acquisition of disability in relapsing-remitting MS (Jacobs et al., 1996), the first agent for which such a result has been found. These reports, although far from compelling, none the less suggest that IFN-β may be the first therapy to alter the natural history of MS, although trials to assess whether IFN-β slows progression in secondary progressive MS have been contradictory. The exact mechanisms whereby IFN-β exerts its beneficial effects are not currently clear: There is evidence that it has actions on microglia and T-lymphocytes, key players in the pathogenesis of demyelination (Scolding et al., 1994), but antagonism of endogenous IFN-γ by exogenous IFN-β has been suggested to be the critical effect (Hall, Compston, & Scolding, 1997). IFN-β is now in clinical usage, despite major difficulties with the funding of its prescription.

The human monoclonal antibody CAMPATH-1H is a treatment directed at lymphocytes: Infusion produces a profound and long-lasting lymphocytopenia. In MS it has been shown to reduce disease activity (Moreau et al., 1994). Infusion is occasionally associated with an acute but transient recapitulation of neurological dysfunction previously encountered in the course of the individual patient's disease, phenomena associated with the release of cytokines such as interleukin-6, interferon-γ, and tumour necrosis factor-α (Moreau et al., 1996). Concurrent treatment with steroids blocks these effects. These results, along with previous MRI evidence for acute BBB changes (Youl et al., 1991), have suggested the critical role of inflammation in the pathogenesis of acute neurological dysfunction in MS (Coles et al., 1999). Nitric oxide may also contribute to these phenomena since in experimental models it can induce conduction block in axons, more so in previously demyelinated preparations (Redford et al., 1997).

Replacement of cells

The replacement of lost neurones would seem to be a logical therapeutic approach in neurodegenerative disorders in which specific neuronal populations are lost (see Chapter 9). Much experimental work, particularly using experimental paradigms of PD, has been performed, and some of the lessons learned are now being applied in the clinical situation (Chapter 9; Dunnett, Kendall, Watts, & Torres, 1997; Larner, 1995d). Transplantation of neurones may also be feasible in HD (Dunnett et al., 1997). Repair of areas of demyelination through transplantation of oligodendrocyte precursors may also be possible (Groves et al., 1993).

Symptomatic treatment strategies

In the absence of definitive strategies for repair of damaged neural tissue, clinicians have had to rely on symptomatic therapies to maintain or enhance neurological function. This approach has been particularly evident in the field of neurodegenerative diseases, the most salient example being the replacement of the striatal dopamine deficiency in PD with the precursor L-dopa, which is metabolised by remaining nigrostriatal neurones to dopamine. This strategy produces symptomatic benefit in most PD patients. There is a persisting concern that L-dopa itself may be toxic to dopaminergic neurones, for example by increasing oxidative stress or promoting apoptosis (Ziv et al., 1997); although there is no firm evidence for this occurring *in vivo*, the possibility still exists. Dopamine receptor agonists may have neuroprotective effects and there is certainly now a move to introduce them earlier in the clinical course of PD. The belief that selegiline, a monoamine oxidase B inhibitor, might be neuroprotective (Parkinson Disease Study Group, 1993) has waned in recent years, since such an action cannot be disentangled from its unequivocal symptomatic effect; however, it certainly delays the need for L-dopa treatment. A report that combined L-dopa/selegiline treatment increases mortality in early PD (Lees, & the Parkinson's Disease Research Group, 1995) is thought to reflect a statistical rather than a biological effect.

Although many neurotransmitter systems are affected in AD, the greatest loss is in the cholinergic system. This observation has prompted the use of various strategies to improve cholinergic neurotransmission in the AD brain; inhibition of the enzyme acetylcholinesterase (AChE), with agents such as tacrine (Soares & Gershon, 1995) and donepezil (Rogers et al., 1998), has been shown to have beneficial effects in some AD patients. Donepezil, rivastigmine, and galanthamine are now licensed for use in mild to moderate AD in the UK and USA. However, the effects are at best modest, and although other AChE inhibitors are in preparation (Larner & Rossor, 1997) it is unlikely that their effects will be as dramatic as those of levodopa in PD.

Facilitating regeneration, repair, and restitution of function

Peripheral nervous system

Graft materials. The best outcome following peripheral nerve section occurs when the cut ends remain apposed, as in a crush injury, so allowing sprouting axons to enter the same, intact, endoneurial tube as previously occupied. Microsurgical suturing of cut nerve ends aims to achieve a similar result. When direct union is not possible, use of a graft to bridge the gap has been attempted, for example using autologous or heterologous nerve grafts. A variety of materials or "regeneration chambers" have also been fashioned for this purpose (see Brecknell & Fawcett, 1996, for details), some of which have produced encouraging results. In these chambers, regenerating axons are always seen in association with Schwann cells; that they are essential is shown by the fact that inhibition of Schwann cell migration with mitomycin D always leads to a failure of axonal regeneration (Hall, 1986). The observation that muscle basal lamina, a preferred substrate for axonal elongation, could facilitate peripheral nerve repair over long distances (Fawcett & Keynes, 1986) has found clinical application in the repair of lepromatous nerves (Pereira et al., 1991) and in the treatment of painful neuromata (Thomas, Stirrat, Birch, & Glasby, 1994).

Neurotrophic factors. Since neurotrophic factors are essential in sustaining various neuronal populations during development, in the patterning of developing neuronal connections, and are produced by the distal nerve stump during Wallerian degeneration, their use to promote therapeutic PNS regeneration, with or without grafting strategies, would seem logical. Neurotrophic factors have been reported to prevent or ameliorate experimental neuropathies caused by diabetes and the cytotoxic drugs paclitaxel (Taxol) and cisplatin. However, evidence of efficacy in the clinical situation has been slow to emerge (Yuen & Mobley, 1996). A trial of CNTF in MND, predicated on the observation of its ability to prevent programmed motor neurone death in an animal model, had to be stopped because of significant toxicity, the development of neutralising antibodies, and absence of clinical benefit. IGF-1 was reported to decrease the rate of progression of MND in a statistically significant manner but the biological effects were modest. It is possible that combination therapy may produce a more robust response (Yuen & Mobley, 1996). These disappointing clinical outcomes may in part reflect the fact that MND is a poor choice for growth factor therapy, since its pathology is both central and peripheral, and neurotrophic factors do not cross the blood brain barrier if infused peripherally. Peripheral sensory neuropathies of the "dying back" variety may be more appropriate for this approach, as suggested by the aforementioned experimental studies. However, adverse effects may prove dose limiting: Intradermal NGF injections reduce local heat-pain threshold and induce pressure allodynia (Dyck et al., 1997).

Central nervous system

Despite the ongoing advances in understanding the cellular and molecular mechanisms responsible for the failure of CNS regeneration, procedures to abrogate these mechanisms and so facilitate CNS repair and recovery of function in the clinical situation remain disappointingly few. Various options have been explored with partial success, including the transplantation of neurones or the grafting of new substrates for axonal growth into the CNS, provision of neurotrophic factors, neutralisation of growth-inhibitory factors, or combinations of these (Brecknell & Fawcett, 1996; Schwab & Bartholdi, 1996). Transplantation of foetal neurones or neural progenitors into the CNS to replace lost or damaged cell populations has been extensively investigated in experimental paradigms, principally in models of PD but also for HD (see Chapter 9).

Grafting of materials that might provide suitable substrates for CNS axonal regeneration has been attempted with variable success. A variety of materials have been used in addition to peripheral nerve grafts, for example: embryonic hippocampal tissue (Kromer, Bjorklund, & Stenevi, 1981); ensheathing glia from the olfactory bulb (one of the few locations within the CNS where successful axonal regeneration can occur; Ramon-Cueto & Nieto-Sampedro, 1994); embryonic astrocytes (Wunderlich, Stichel, Schroeder, & Muller, 1994); cultured or dissociated Schwann cells (Brook, Lawrence, Shah, & Raisman, 1994; Kromer & Cornbrooks, 1985; Paino, Fernandez-Valle, Bates, & Bunge, 1994; Xu, Chen, Guenard, Kleitman, & Bunge, 1997); microglia (Rabchevsky & Streit, 1997); and fibroblasts modified genetically to express NGF (Kawaja, Rosenberg, Yoshida, & Gage, 1992). Foetal spinal cord segments have been implanted microsurgically to repair spinal cord transections in neonatal mammals (Iwashita, Kawaguchi, & Murata, 1994). Cheng, Cao, and Olson (1996) used multiple intercostal nerve grafts, re-routing of axons from white to grey matter, fibrin glue containing acidic FGF, and compressive wiring of posterior spinal processes, to restore function in adult rats rendered paraplegic by complete cord transections. These animals improved clinically over 6 months with histological evidence of regeneration of the corticospinal tract through the graft area. These results, if confirmed, could signal a major advance in spinal cord repair. Similarly, the report by Rapalino et al. (1998) documented behavioural, electrophysiological, and morphological recovery following implantation of autologous macrophages, pre-exposed *ex vivo* to peripheral nerve segments, with or without acidic FGF, following transection of the adult rat thoracic spinal cord. It is hypothesised that this manipulation acts upstream of the postinjury process, interfering with the immune privileged status of the CNS.

The provision of neurotrophic agents for restitution of CNS function has attracted less attention than for PNS pathologies. There is evidence that atrophy and loss of cholinergic cells in the basal forebrain nuclei in AD results from a failure of axonal transport of NGF from cortical targets (Sofroniew, 1996). Hence, treatment with NGF to the basal forebrain may be a valid symptomatic treatment in AD, and a single clinical case has already been reported. The availability of neurotrophic factors of greater potency and bioavailability may greatly facilitate morphological and functional recovery; examples include the use of GDNF (Tomac et al., 1995) and synthetic immunophilin ligands (Steiner et al., 1997) in animal models of neurodegenerative disorders such as MPTP parkinsonism. NGF, NT-3, and, especially, GDNF, but not BDNF, have been shown to facilitate regrowth of peripheral nerve roots into the dorsal horn of the spinal cord, so overcoming the adult CNS barrier to regeneration (Ramer, Priestley, & McMahon, 2000).

The inhibitory nature of the CNS environment presents a significant obstruction to successful axonal regeneration. Neutralisation of myelin-associated neurite growth inhibitors has been reported to facilitate axonal regeneration in the corticospinal tract (Schnell & Schwab, 1990) and the optic tract (Weibel et al., 1994), and may promote functional recovery (Bregman et al., 1995). The structural and functional recovery detected following treatment of the transected adult rat optic nerve with transglutaminase has also been interpreted in terms of abrogation of growth inhibition by myelin components (Eitan et al., 1994). The role of inhibitory factors in axonal pathfinding and patterning has become increasingly apparent in recent years

(Goodman, 1996) and it is likely that further CNS inhibitory factors remain to be discovered, manipulation of which might facilitate axonal regeneration.

It may be that combinations of all these strategies will be necessary for effective CNS recovery. Provision of growth factors at the time of neural transplantation has been quite extensively investigated in experimental paradigms (Barker, Dunnett, & Fawcett, 1993), and it may be that concurrent provision of molecules to block neurite growth-inhibitory factors to try to overcome the non-permissive CNS milieu could improve the extent of axonal growth from transplanted cells (Larner, 1995d). Combined use of antibodies to myelin-associated neurite growth-inhibitors and neurotrophic factors (neurotrophin-3) produced more extensive regeneration in lesioned rat corticospinal tract than treatment with the former alone (Schnell, Schneider, Kolbeck, Barde, & Schwab, 1994).

Even if the goal of improved CNS axonal regeneration, through the mechanisms described previously, does prove possible, the fine patterning of connections required for learning will remain a problem. Functional electrical stimulation training programmes, as used to reorganise preserved spinal cord circuits, may be necessary to refine the pattern of regenerating synaptic connections (Muir & Steeves, 1997).

CONCLUSION

Although much has been learned in recent years about the mechanisms underpinning neuronal injury and death in a variety of pathological situations, effective therapeutic manipulation to achieve clinically meaningful recovery of neurological function remains elusive. Cajal's (1928) aspirations for "the science of the future" remain valid today. Various experimental approaches suggest that these goals will best be achieved by a combination of approaches, aiming to maximise inherent neuroplasticity and minimise the detrimental effects of neuro-inhibitory factors, as well as to replace cells and growth factors where these have been lost.

REFERENCES

Al-Chalabi, A., Enayat, Z.E., Bakker, M.C., Sham, P.C., Ball, D.M., Shaw, C.E., Lloyd, C.M., Powell, J.F., & Leigh, P.N. (1996). Association of apolipoprotein E ε4 allele with bulbar-onset motor neuron disease. *Lancet, 347*, 159–160.

Alderson, P., & Roberts, I. (1997). Corticosteroids in acute traumatic brain injury: Systematic review of randomised controlled trials. *British Medical Journal, 314*, 1855–1859.

Aloe, L. (1987). Intracerebral pretreatment with nerve growth factor prevents irreversible brain lesions in neonatal rats injected with ibotenic acid. *Biotechnology, 5*, 1085–1086.

Amouyel, P., Vidal, O., Launay, J.M., et al. (1994). The apolipoprotein E alleles as major susceptibility factors for Creutzfeldt-Jakob disease. *Lancet, 344*, 1315–1318.

Anonymous. (1997). Riluzole for amyotrophic lateral sclerosis. *Drug and Therapeutics Bulletin, 35*, 11–12.

Arriagada, P.V., Growdon, J.H., Hedley-White, E.T., & Hyman, B.T. (1992). Neurofibrillary tangles but not senile plaques parallel duration and severity of Alzheimer's disease. *Neurology, 42*, 631–639.

Baker, H.F., Poulter, M., Crow, T.J., Frith, C.D., Lofthouse, R., Ridley, R.M., et al. (1991). Amino acid polymorphism in human prion protein and age at death in inherited prion disease. *Lancet, 337*, 1286.

Barker, R.A., Dunnett, S.B., & Fawcett, J.W. (1993). Neurotrophic factors and neural grafts: A growing field. *Seminars in the Neurosciences, 5*, 431–441.

Barnes, C.A. (1994). Normal aging: Regionally specific changes in hippocampal synaptic transmission. *Trends in Neurosciences, 17*, 13–18.

Barrow, C.J., & Zagorski, M.G. (1991). Solution structures of β peptide and its constituent fragments: Relation to amyloid deposition. *Science, 253*, 179–182.

Bazan, N.G. (1970). Effects of ischemia and electroconvulsive shock on free fatty acid pool in the brain. *Biochimica et Biophysica Acta, 218*, 1–10.

Beal, M.F., Hyman, B.T., & Koroshetz, W. (1993). Do defects in mitochondrial energy metabolism underlie the pathology of neurodegenerative diseases? *Trends in Neurosciences, 16*, 125–131.

Beckman, J. (1997). Nitric oxide, superoxide, and peroxynitrite in CNS injury. In K.M.A. Welch, L.R. Caplan, D.J. Reis, B.K. Siesjo, & B. Weir (Eds.), *Primer on cerebrovascular diseases* (pp. 209–210). San Diego: Academic Press.

Behl, C., Davis, J., Cole, G.M., & Schubert, D. (1992). Vitamin E protects nerve cells from amyloid β protein toxicity. *Biochemistry and Biophysical Research Communications, 186*, 944–950.

Behl, C., Davis, J.B., Klier, F.G., & Schubert, D. (1994). Amyloid β peptide induces necrosis rather than apoptosis. *Brain Research, 645*, 253–264.

Behl, C., Davis, J.B., Lesley, R., & Schubert, D. (1994). Hydrogen peroxide mediates amyloid β protein toxicity. *Cell, 77*, 817–827.

Benfey, M., Bunger, U.R., Videl-Sanz, M., Bray, G.M., & Aguayo, A.J. (1985). Axonal regeneration from GABAergic neurons in the adult rat thalamus. *Journal of Neurocytology, 14*, 279–296.

Bensimon, G., Lacomblez, L., Meininger, V., & the ALS/Riluzole Study Group. (1994). A controlled trial of riluzole in amyotrophic lateral sclerosis. *New England Journal of Medicine, 330*, 585–591.

Benveniste, H., Drejer, J., Schousboe, A., & Diemer, N.H. (1984). Elevation of the extracellular concentrations of glutamate and aspartate in rat hippocampus during transient cerebral ischaemia monitored by intracerebral microdialysis. *Journal of Neurochemistry, 43*, 1369–1374.

Berry, M. (1982). Post-injury myelin-breakdown products inhibit axonal growth: An hypothesis to explain the failure of axonal regeneration in the mammalian central nervous system. *Bibliotheca Anatomica, 23*, 1–11.

Beuche, W., & Friede, R.L. (1984). The role of non-resident cells in Wallerian degeneration. *Journal of Neurocytology, 13*, 767–796.

Billette de Villemeur, T., Deslys, J.-P., Pradel, A., et al. (1996). Creutzfeldt-Jakob disease from contaminated growth hormone extracts in France. *Neurology, 47*, 690–695.

Bonfoco, E., Kraine, D., Ancarcrona, M., Nicotera, P., & Lipton, S.A. (1995). Apoptosis and necrosis: Two distinct events induced respectively by mild and intense insult with NMDA or nitric oxide/superoxide in cortical cell cultures. *Proceedings of the National Academy of Sciences of the United States of America, 91*, 7162–7166.

Bovolenta, P., Wandosell, F., & Nieto-Sampedro, M. (1993). Characterisation of a neurite outgrowth inhibitor expressed after CNS injury. *European Journal of Neuroscience, 5*, 454–465.

Boyeson, M.G., Jones, J.L., & Harmon, R.L. (1994). Sparing of motor function after cortical injury: A new perspective on underlying mechanisms. *Archives of Neurology, 51*, 405–414.

Braak, H., & Braak, E. (1991). Neuropathological stageing [*sic*] of Alzheimer-related changes. *Acta Neuropathologica (Berlin), 82*, 239–259.

Bracken, M.B., Shepard, M.J., Collins, W.F., Holford, T.R., Young, W., Baskin, D.S., et al. (1990). A randomized, controlled trial of methylprednisolone or naloxone in the treatment of acute spinal-cord injury: Results of the second national acute spinal cord injury study. *New England Journal of Medicine, 322*, 1405–1411.

Bradley, R. (1997). Animal prion diseases. In J. Collinge & M.S. Palmer (Eds.), *Prion diseases* (pp. 89–129). Oxford, UK: Oxford University Press.

Bray, G.M., Villegas-Perez, M.P., Vidal-Sanz, M., Carter, D.A., & Aguayo, A.J. (1991). Neuronal and nonneuronal influences on retinal ganglion cell survival, axonal regrowth, and connectivity after axotomy. *Annals of the New York Academy of Sciences, 633*, 214–228.

Brecknell, J.E., & Fawcett, J.W. (1996). Axonal regeneration. *Biological Reviews, 71*, 227–255.

Bregman, B.S., Kunkel-Bagden, E., Schnell, L., Dai, H.N., Gao, D., & Schwab, M.E. (1995). Recovery from spinal cord injury mediated by antibodies to neurite growth inhibitors. *Nature, 378*, 498–501.

Breitner, J.C.S., Gau, B.A., Welsh, K.A., Plassman, B.L., McDonald, W.M., Helms, M.J., & Anthony, J.C. (1994). Inverse association of anti-inflammatory treatments and Alzheimer's disease: Initial results of a co-twin control study. *Neurology, 44*, 227–232.

Brodal, A. (1981). *Neurological anatomy in relation to clinical medicine* (3rd ed.). New York: Oxford University Press.

Brook, G.A., Lawrence, J.M., Shah, B., & Raisman, G. (1994). Extrusion transplantation of Schwann cells into the adult rat thalamus induces directional host axon growth. *Experimental Neurology, 126*, 31–43.

Brown, M.C., Perry, V.H., Hunt, S.P., & Lapper, S.R. (1994). Further studies on motor and sensory nerve regeneration in mice with delayed Wallerian degeneration. *European Journal of Neuroscience, 6*, 420–428.

Bruno, V., Copani, A., Battaglia, G., Casabona, G., & Nicoletti, F. (1997). Metabotropic glutamate receptors as a drug target in brain ischemia. In K.M.A. Welch, L.R. Caplan, D.J. Reis, B.K. Siesjo, & B. Weir (Eds.), *Primer on cerebrovascular diseases* (pp. 199–200). San Diego: Academic Press.

Buchan, A.M., Lesiuk, H., Barnes, K.A., Li, H., Huang, Z.G., Smith, K.E., & Xue, D. (1993). AMPA antagonists: Do they hold more promise for clinical stroke trials than NMDA antagonists? *Stroke, 24*, 148–152.

Busciglio, J., Lorenzo, A., Yeh, J., & Yankner, B.A. (1995). β-amyloid fibrils induce tau phosphorylation and loss of microtubule binding. *Neuron, 14*, 879–888.

Busciglio, J., Yeh, J., & Yankner, B.A. (1993). β-amyloid neurotoxicity in human cortical culture is not mediated by excitotoxins. *Journal of Neurochemistry, 61*, 1563–1568.

Bush, A.I., Pettingell, W.H., Multhaup, G., de Paradis, M., Vonsattel, J.P., Gusella, J.F., Beyreuther, K., Masters, C.L., & Tanzi, R.E. (1994). Rapid induction of Alzheimer Aβ amyloid formation by zinc. *Science, 265*, 1464–1467.

Butterfield, D.A., Hensley, K., Harris, M., Mattson, M., & Carney, J. (1994). β-amyloid peptide free radical fragments initiate synaptosomal lipoperoxidation in a sequence-specific fashion: Implications to Alzheimer's disease. *Biochemistry and Biophysical Research Communications, 200*, 710–715.

Cadelli, D., & Schwab, M.E. (1991). Regeneration of lesioned septohippocampal acetylcholinesterase-positive axons is improved by antibodies against the myelin-associated neurite growth inhibitors NI-35/250. *European Journal of Neuroscience, 3*, 825–832.

Cajal, S.R. (1928). *Degeneration and regeneration of the nervous system.* Oxford, UK: Oxford University Press.

Canning, D.R., McKeon, R.J., DeWitt, D.A., Perry, G., Wujek, J.R., Frederickson, R.C.A., & Silver, J. (1993). Amyloid of Alzheimer's disease induces reactive gliosis that inhibits axonal outgrowth. *Experimental Neurology, 124*, 289–298.

Caroni P., & Schwab, M.E. (1988). Two membrane protein fractions from rat central myelin with inhibitory properties for neurite growth and fibroblast spreading. *Journal of Cell Biology, 106*, 1281–1288.

Carrell, R.W., & Lomas, D.A. (1997). Conformational disease. *Lancet, 350*, 134–138.

Carter, D.A., Bray, G.M., & Aguayo, A.J. (1989). Regenerated retinal ganglion cell axons can form well-differentiated synapses in the superior colliculus of adult hamsters. *Journal of Neuroscience, 9*, 4042–4050.

Carter, D.A., Bray, G.M., & Aguayo, A.J. (1994). Long-term growth and remodelling of regenerated retinocollicular connections in adult hamsters. *Journal of Neuroscience, 14*, 590–598.

Chan, R.S., Huey, E.D., Maecker, H.L., et al. (1996). Endocrine modulators of necrotic neuron death. *Brain Pathology, 6*, 481–491.

Chang, G.-Q., Hao, Y., & Wong, F. (1993). Apoptosis: Final common pathway of photoreceptor death in *rd, rds* and rhodopsin mutant mice. *Neuron, 11*, 595–605.

Charriaut-Marlangue, C., Aggoun-Zouaoui, D., Represa, A., & Ben-Ari, Y. (1996). Apoptotic features of selective neuronal death in ischemia, epilepsy and gp120 toxicity. *Trends in Neurosciences, 19*, 109–114.

Chen, M.S., Huber, A.B., Van den Haar, M.E., et al. (2000). Nogo-A is a myelin-associated neurite outgrowth inhibitor and an antigen for monoclonal antibody IN-1. *Nature, 403*, 434–439.

Cheng, H., Cao, Y., & Olson, L. (1996). Spinal cord repair in adult paraplegic rats: Partial restoration of hind limb function. *Science, 273*, 510–513.

Choi, D.W. (1997). The excitotoxic concept. In K.M.A. Welch, L.R. Caplan, D.J. Reis, B.K. Siesjo, & B. Weir (Eds.), *Primer on cerebrovascular diseases* (pp. 187–190). San Diego: Academic Press.

Choi-Lundberg, D.L., Lin, Q., Chang, Y.-N., et al. (1997). Dopaminergic neurons protected from degeneration by GDNF gene therapy. *Science, 275*, 838–841.

Chollet, F., DiPiero, V., Wise, R.J.S., Brooks, D.J., Dolan, R.J., & Frackowiak, R.S.J. (1991). The functional anatomy of motor recovery after stroke in humans: A study with positron emission tomography. *Annals of Neurology, 29*, 63–71.

Cleeter, M.J.W., Cooper, J.M., & Schapira, A.V.H. (1992). Irreversible inhibition of mitochondrial complex I by 1-methyl-4-phenylpyridinium: Evidence for free radical involvement. *Journal of Neurochemistry, 58*, 786–789.

Coles, A.J., Wing, M.G., Molyneux, P., et al. (1999). Monoclonal antibody treatment exposes three mechanisms underlying the clinical course of multiple sclerosis. *Annals of Neurology, 46*, 296–304.

Collinge, J., Owen, F., Poulter, M., Leach, M., Crow, T.J., Rossor, M.N., et al. (1990). Prion dementia without characteristic pathology. *Lancet, 336*, 7–9.

Collinge, J., & Palmer, M.S. (1997). Human prion diseases. In J. Collinge & M.S. Palmer (Eds.), *Prion diseases* (pp. 18–56). Oxford, UK: Oxford University Press.

Collinge, J., Palmer, M.S., & Dryden, A.J. (1991). Genetic predisposition to iatrogenic Creutzfeldt-Jakob disease. *Lancet, 337,* 1441–1442.

Collinge, J., Whittington, M.A., Sidle, K.C.L., Smith, C.J., Palmer, M.S., Clarke, A.R., & Jeffreys, J.G.R. (1994). Prion protein is necessary for normal synaptic function. *Nature, 370,* 295–297.

Cooper, J.D., Lindholm, D., & Sofroniew, M.V. (1994). Reduced transport of [^{125}I]nerve growth factor by cholinergic neurons and down-regulated TrkA expression in the medial septum of aged rats. *Neuroscience, 62,* 625–629.

Crutcher, K., & Privitera, M. (1989). Axonal regeneration on mature human brain tissue sections in culture. *Annals of Neurology, 26,* 580–583.

Crutcher, K.A., Tolar, M., Harmony, J.A.K., & Marques, M.A. (1997). A new hypothesis for the role of apolipoprotein E in Alzheimer's disease pathology. In K. Iqbal, B. Winblad, T. Nishimura, M. Takeda, & H.M. Wisniewski (Eds.), *Alzheimer's disease: Biology, diagnosis and therapeutics* (pp. 543–552). Chichester, UK: John Wiley.

Cruz, L., Urbanc, B., Buldyrev, S.V., et al. (1997). Aggregation and disaggregation of senile plaques in Alzheimer disease. *Proceedings of the National Academy of Sciences of the United States of America, 94,* 7612–7616.

David, S., & Aguayo, A.J. (1981). Axonal elongation into peripheral nervous system "bridges" after central nervous system injury in adult rats. *Science, 214,* 931–933.

Davies, S.J.A., Field, P.M., & Raisman, G. (1994). Long interfascicular axon growth from embryonic neurons transplanted into adult myelinated tracts. *Journal of Neuroscience, 14,* 1596–1612.

Davis, G.R., Jr., & McClellan, A.D. (1994). Long distance axonal regeneration of identified lamprey reticulospinal neurons. *Experimental Neurology, 127,* 94–105.

Dawson, T.M., & Snyder, S.H. (1994). Gases as biological messengers: Nitric oxide and carbon monoxide in the brain. *Journal of Neuroscience, 14,* 5147–5159.

Delacourte, A. (1990). General and dramatic glial reaction in Alzheimer brains. *Neurology, 40,* 33–37.

Dexter, D.T., Wells, F.R., Agid, Y., Lees, A.J., Jenner, P., & Marsden, C.D. (1987). Increased iron content in post-mortem parkinsonian brain. *Lancet, ii,* 1219–1220.

Dooley, J.T., & Aguayo, A.J. (1982). Axonal elongation from cerebellum into PNS grafts in the adult rat. *Annals of Neurology, 12,* 221.

Dreyer, E.B., Kaiser, P.K., Offermann, J.T., & Lipton, S.A. (1990). HIV-1 coat protein neurotoxicity prevented by calcium channel antagonists. *Science, 248,* 364–367.

Dugan, L.L., Creedon, D.J., Johnson, E.M., & Holtzman, D.M. (1997). Rapid suppression of free radical formation by nerve growth factor involves the mitogen-activated protein kinase pathway. *Proceedings of the National Academy of Sciences of the United States of America, 94,* 4086–4091.

Dunnett, S.B., Kendall, A.L., Watts, C., & Torres, E.M. (1997). Neuronal cell transplantation for Parkinson's and Huntington's diseases. *British Medical Bulletin, 53,* 757–776.

Dusart, I., Airaksinen, M.S., & Sotelo, C. (1997). Purkinje cell survival and axonal regeneration are age dependent: An *in vitro* study. *Journal of Neuroscience, 17,* 3710–3726.

Dyck, P.J., Peroutka, S., Rask, C., et al. (1997). Intradermal recombinant human nerve growth factor induces pressure allodynia and lowered heat pain threshold in humans. *Neurology, 48,* 501–505.

Eitan, S., Solomon, A., Lavie, V., Yoles, E., Hirschberg, D.L., Belkin, M., & Schwartz, M. (1994). Recovery of visual response of injured adult rat optic nerves treated with transglutaminase. *Science, 264,* 1764–1768.

Farrer, M., Gasser, T., Gwinn, K., et al. (1998). Sequencing the α-synuclein gene in a large number of families with Parkinson's disease. *Neurology, 50*(Suppl. 4), A116 (P02.097).

Fawcett, J.W. (1992). Intrinsic neuronal determinants of regeneration. *Trends in Neurosciences, 15,* 5–8.

Fawcett, J.W., & Keynes, R.J. (1986). Muscle basal lamina: A new graft material for peripheral nerve repair. *Journal of Neurosurgery, 65,* 354–363.

Fawcett, J.W., & Keynes, R.J. (1990). Peripheral nerve regeneration. *Annual Review of Neuroscience, 13,* 43–60.

Fischer, W., Wictorin, K., Bjorklund, A., Williams, L.R., Varon, S., & Gage, F.H. (1987). Amelioration of cholinergic neuron atrophy and spatial memory impairment in aged rats by nerve growth factor. *Nature, 329,* 65–68.

Forsmann, J. (1900). Zur Kenntniss des Neurotropismus. *Ziegler's Beitrage zur Pathologischen Anatomie, 27,* 407–430.

Frederickson, R.C.A. (1992). Astroglia in Alzheimer's disease. *Neurobiology of Aging, 13,* 239–253.

Gage, F.H., Batchelor, P., Chen, K.S., Chin, D., Higgins, G.A., Koh, S., Deputy, S., Rosenberg, M.B., Fischer, W., & Bjorklund, A. (1989). NGF receptor reexpression and NGF-mediated cholinergic neuronal hypertrophy in the damaged adult neostriatum. *Neuron, 2,* 1177–1184.

Gambetti, P., Peterson, R., Monari, L., Tabaton, M., Autilio-Gambetti, L., Cortelli, P., et al. (1993). Fatal familial insomnia and the widening spectrum of prion diseases. *British Medical Bulletin, 49,* 980–994.

Garofalo, L., Ribeiro-Da-Silva, A., & Cuello, A.C. (1992). Nerve growth factor-induced synaptogenesis and hypertrophy of cortical cholinergic terminals. *Proceedings of the National Academy of Sciences of the United States of America, 89,* 2639–2643.

Geddes, J.W., Cahan, L.D., Cooper, S.M., Kim, R.C., Choi, B.H., & Cotman, C.W. (1990). Altered distribution of excitatory amino acid receptors in temporal lobe epilepsy. *Experimental Neurology, 108,* 214–220.

Giehl, K.M., Schutte, A., Mestres, P., & Yan, Q. (1998). The survival-promoting effect of glial cell line-derived neurotrophic factor on axotomized corticospinal neurons *in vivo* is mediated by an endogenous brain-derived neurotrophic factor mechanism. *Journal of Neuroscience, 18,* 7351–7360.

Glass, J.D., & Johnson, R.T. (1996). Human immunodeficiency virus and the brain. *Annual Review of Neuroscience, 19,* 1–26.

Glassman, R.B. (1987). An hypothesis about redundancy and reliability in the brains of higher species: Analogies with genes, internal organs and engineering systems. *Neuroscience and Biobehavior, 11,* 275–285.

Glenner, G.G., & Wong, C.W. (1984). Alzheimer's disease: Initial report of the purification and characterization of a novel cerebrovascular amyloid protein. *Biochemistry and Biophysical Research Communications, 120,* 885–890.

Goedert, M. (1993). Tau protein and the neurofibrillary pathology of Alzheimer's disease. *Trends in Neurosciences, 16,* 460–465.

Goldfarb, L.G., Petersen, R.B., Tabaton, M., et al. (1992). Fatal familial insomnia and familial Creutzfeldt-Jakob disease: Disease phenotype determined by a DNA polymorphism. *Science, 258,* 806–808.

Gomez, C.M., Maselli, R., Gundeck, J.E., et al. (1997). Slow-channel transgenic mice: A model of postsynaptic organellar degeneration at the neuromuscular junction. *Journal of Neuroscience, 17,* 4170–4179.

Goodman, C.S. (1996). Mechanisms and molecules that control growth cone guidance. *Annual Review of Neuroscience, 19,* 341–377.

Goodman, Y., Bruce, A.J., Cheng, B., & Mattson, M.P. (1996). Estrogens attenuate and corticosterone exacerbates excitotoxicity, oxidative injury and amyloid β peptide toxicity in hippocampal neurons. *Journal of Neurochemistry, 66,* 1836–1844.

Green, A.R., & Goodwin, G.M. (1996). Ecstasy and neurodegeneration. *British Medical Journal, 312,* 1493–1494.

Grimes, M., Zhou, J., Li, Y., Holtzman, D., & Mobley, W.C. (1993). Neurotrophin signalling in the nervous system. *Seminars in the Neurosciences, 5,* 239–247.

Grotta, J.C. (1991). Clinical aspects of the use of calcium antagonists in cerebrovascular disease. *Clinical Neuropharmacology, 14,* 373–390.

Groves, A.K., Barnett, S.C., Franklin, R.J.M., Crang, A.J., Mayer, M., Blakemore, W.F., & Noble, M. (1993). Repair of demyelinated lesions by transplantation of purified O-2A progenitor cells. *Nature, 362,* 453–455.

Guth, L., Zhang, Z., & Roberts, E. (1994). Key role for pregnenolone in combination therapy that promotes recovery after spinal cord injury. *Proceedings of the National Academy of Sciences of the United States of America, 91,* 12,308–12,312.

Hadjiconstantinou, M., Hubble, J.P., Wemlinger, T.A., & Neff, N.H. (1994). Enhanced MPTP neurotoxicity after treatment with isoflurophate or cholinergic agonists. *Journal of Pharmacology and Experimental Therapeutics, 270,* 639–644.

Hall, E.D. (1997). 21-aminosteroids. In K.M.A. Welch, L.R. Caplan, D.J. Reis, B.K. Siesjo, & B. Weir (Eds.), *Primer on cerebrovascular diseases* (pp. 257–261). San Diego: Academic Press.

Hall, G.L., Compston, A., & Scolding, N.J. (1997). Beta-interferon and multiple sclerosis. *Trends in Neurosciences, 20,* 63–67.

Hall, S.M. (1986). The effect of inhibiting Schwann cell mitosis on the re-innervation of acellular autografts in the peripheral nervous system of the mouse. *Neuropathology and Applied Neurobiology, 12,* 401–414.

Halliwell, B. (1992). Reactive oxygen species and the central nervous system. *Journal of Neurochemistry, 59*, 1609–1623.

Hamdy, S., Aziz, Q., Rothwell, J.C., Singh, K.D., Barlow, J., Hughes, D.G., Tallis, R.C., & Thompson, D.G. (1996). The cortical topography of human swallowing musculature in health and disease. *Nature Medicine, 2*, 1217–1224.

Harding, A.E. (1987). Vitamin E and the nervous system. *CRC Critical Reviews in Neurobiology, 3*, 89–103.

Hardy, J. (1995). Genetics of Alzheimer's disease: Age of onset as a key discriminator of etiology. In D. Dawbarn & S.J. Allen (Eds.), *Neurobiology of Alzheimer's disease* (pp. 77–88). Oxford, UK: Bios Scientific Publishers.

Hardy, J., Duff, K., Hardy, K.G., Perez-Tur, J., & Hutton, M. (1998). Genetic dissection of Alzheimer's disease and related dementias: Amyloid and its relationship to tau. *Nature Neuroscience, 1*, 355–358.

Hauw, J.-J., Sazdovitch, V., Seilhean, D., Camilleri, S., Lazarini, F., Delasnerie-Laupretre, N., & Duyckaerts, C. (1996). The nosology and neuropathology of human conditions related to unconventional infectious agents or prions. *European Journal of Neurology, 3*, 487–499.

Henderson, V.W. (1997). The epidemiology of estrogen replacement therapy and Alzheimer's disease. *Neurology, 48*(Suppl. 7), S27–S35.

Heyes, M.P., Brew, B.J., Martin, A., Price, R.W., Salazar, A.M., et al. (1991). Quinolinic acid in cerebrospinal fluid and serum in HIV-1 infection: Relationship to clinical and neurological status. *Annals of Neurology, 29*, 202–209.

Hilton, G. (1995). Diffuse axonal injury. *Journal of Trauma Nursing, 2*, 7–12.

Hollmann, M., & Heinemann, S. (1994). Cloned glutamate receptors. *Annual Review of Neuroscience, 17*, 31–108.

Holtzman, D.M., Sheldon, R.A., Jaffe, W., Cheng, Y., & Ferriero, D.M. (1996). Nerve growth factor protects the neonatal brain against hypoxic-ischemic injury. *Annals of Neurology, 39*, 114–122.

Hsiao, K., Baker, H.F., Crow, T.J., Poulter, M., Owen, F., Terwilliger, J.D., et al. (1989). Linkage of a prion protein missense variant to Gerstmann–Straussler syndrome. *Nature, 338*, 342–345.

Hsiao, K.K., Scott, M., Foster, D., Groth, D.F., DeArmond, S.J., & Prusiner, S.B. (1990). Spontaneous neurodegeneration in transgenic mice with mutant prion protein. *Science, 250*, 1587–1590.

Huang, Z., Huang, P.L., Ma, J., Meng, W., Ayata, C., Fishman, M.C., & Moskowitz, M.A. (1996). Enlarged infarcts in endothelial nitric oxide synthase knockout mice are attenuated by nitro-L-arginine. *Journal of Cerebral Blood Flow and Metabolism, 16*, 981–987.

Huang, Z., Huang, P.L., Panahian, N., Dalkara, T., Fishman, M.C., & Moskowitz, M.A. (1994). Effects of cerebral ischemia in mice deficient in neuronal nitric oxide synthase. *Science, 265*, 1883–1885.

Hugon, J., Ludolph, A., Roy, D.N., et al. (1988). Studies on the etiology and pathogenesis of motor neurone diseases: II. Clinical and electrophysiologic features of pyramidal dysfunction in macaques fed *Lathyrus sativus* and IDPN. *Neurology, 38*, 435–442.

Iadecola, C., Zhang, F., Casey, R., Nagayama, M., & Ross, M.E. (1997). Delayed reduction of ischemic brain injury and neurological deficits in mice lacking the inducible nitric oxide synthase gene. *Journal of Neuroscience, 17*, 9157–9164.

The IFNB Multiple Sclerosis Study Group. (1993). Interferon beta-1b is effective in relapsing-remitting multiple sclerosis: I. Clinical results of a multicenter, randomized double-blind, placebo-controlled trial. *Neurology, 43*, 655–661.

Ikeda, K., Akayama, H., Sahara, N., et al. (1997). Senile dementia with abundant neurofibrillary tangles without accompanying senile plaques: A subset of senile dementia with high incidence of the APOE ε2 allele. In K. Iqbal, B. Winblad, T. Nishimura, M. Takeda, & H.M. Wisniewski (Eds.), *Alzheimer's disease: Biology, diagnosis and therapeutics* (pp. 257–265). Chichester, UK: John Wiley.

Ironside, J.W., & Bell, J.E. (1997). Pathology of prion diseases. In J. Collinge & M.S. Palmer (Eds.), *Prion diseases* (pp. 57–88). Oxford, UK: Oxford University Press.

Isacson, O., & Sofroniew, M.V. (1992). Neuronal loss or replacement in the injured adult cerebral neocortex induces extensive remodelling of intrinsic and afferent neural systems. *Experimental Neurology, 117*, 151–175.

Iversen, L.L., Mortishire-Smith, R.J., Pollack, S.J., & Shearman, M.S. (1995). The toxicity *in vitro* of β-amyloid protein. *Biochemical Journal, 311*, 1–16.

Iwashita, Y., Kawaguchi, S., & Murata, M. (1994). Restoration of function by replacement of spinal cord segments in the rat. *Nature, 367*, 167–170.

Iwatsubo, T., Mann, D.M., Odaka, A., Suzuki, N., & Ihara, Y. (1995). Amyloid β protein (Aβ) deposition: Aβ42(43) precedes Aβ40 in Down syndrome. *Annals of Neurology, 37*, 294–299.

Jacobs, L.D., Cookfair, D.L., Rudick, R.A., et al. (1996). Intramuscular interferon beta-1a for disease progression in relapsing multiple sclerosis. *Annals of Neurology, 39*, 285–294.

Jarrett, J.T., Berger, E.P., & Lansbury, P.T., Jr. (1993). The carboxy terminus of the β amyloid protein is critical for the seeding of amyloid formation: Implications for the pathogenesis of Alzheimer's disease. *Biochemistry, 32*, 4693–4697.

Joseph, R., & Han, E. (1992). Amyloid β-protein fragment 25–35 causes activation of cytoplasmic calcium in neurons. *Biochemistry and Biophysical Research Communications, 184*, 1441–1447.

Kawaja, M.D., Rosenberg, M.D., Yoshida, K., & Gage, F.H. (1992). Somatic gene transfer of nerve growth factor promotes the survival of axotomised septal neurons and the regeneration of their axons in adult rats. *Journal of Neuroscience, 12*, 2849–2864.

Keller, J.N., Kindy, M.S., Holtsberg, F.W., et al. (1998). Mitochondrial manganese superoxide dismutase prevents neuronal apoptosis and reduces ischemic brain injury: Suppression of peroxynitrite production, lipid peroxidation, and mitochondrial dysfunction. *Journal of Neuroscience, 18*, 687–697.

Kimelberg, H.K., Goderie, S.K., Higman, S., Pang, S., & Waniewski, R.A. (1990). Swelling-induced release of glutamate, aspartate, and taurine from astrocyte cultures. *Journal of Neuroscience, 10*, 1583–1591.

Koh, J.Y., Yang, L.L., & Cotman, C.W. (1990). β-amyloid protein increases the vulnerability of cultured cortical neurons to excitotoxic damage. *Brain Research, 533*, 315–320.

Kolb, B. (1995). *Brain plasticity and behavior*. Mahwah, NJ: Lawrence Erlbaum Associates Inc.

Kosic, V., Jackson-Lewis, V., de Bilbao, F., Dubois-Dauphin, M., & Przedborski, S. (1997). Bcl-2: Prolonging life in a transgenic mouse model of familial amyotrophic lateral sclerosis. *Science, 277*, 559–562.

Kromer, L.F., Bjorklund, A., & Stenevi, U. (1981). Regeneration of the septohippocampal pathways in adult rats is promoted by utilizing embryonic hippocampal implants as bridges. *Brain Research, 210*, 173–200.

Kromer, L.F., & Cornbrooks, C.J. (1985). Transplants of Schwann cell cultures promote axonal regeneration in the adult mammalian brain. *Proceedings of the National Academy of Sciences of the United States of America, 82*, 6330–6334.

Lam, H.H.D., Bhardwaj, A., O'Connell, M.T., Hanley, D.F., Traystman, R.J., & Sofroniew, M.V. (1998). Nerve growth factor rapidly suppresses basal, NMDA-evoked, and AMPA-evoked nitric oxide synthase activity in rat hippocampus *in vivo. Proceedings of the National Academy of Sciences of the United States of America, 95*, 10,926–10,931.

Langston, J.W. (1996). The etiology of Parkinson's disease with emphasis on the MPTP story. *Neurology, 47*(Suppl. 3), S153–S160.

Langston, J.W., Ballard, P., Tetrud, J.W., & Irwin, I. (1983). Chronic parkinsonism in humans due to a product of meperidine analog synthesis. *Science, 219*, 979–980.

Lansbury, P.T. (1997). Structural neurology: Are seeds at the root of neuronal degeneration? *Neuron, 19*, 1151–1154.

Larner, A.J. (1995a). Axonal sprouting and synaptogenesis in temporal lobe epilepsy: Possible pathogenetic and therapeutic roles of neurite growth inhibitory factors. *Seizure, 4*, 249–258.

Larner, A.J. (1995b). The cortical neuritic dystrophy of Alzheimer's disease: Nature, significance, and possible pathogenesis. *Dementia, 6*, 218–224.

Larner, A.J. (1995c). Hypothesis: Physiological and pathological interrelationships of amyloid β peptide and the amyloid precursor protein. *BioEssays, 17*, 819–824.

Larner, A.J. (1995d). *The possible interaction between neural transplants and nerve growth inhibitory factors in Parkinson's disease*. London: Parkinson's Disease Society.

Larner, A.J. (1997). The pathogenesis of Alzheimer disease: An alternative to the amyloid hypothesis. *Journal of Neuropathology and Experimental Neurology, 56*, 214–215.

Larner, A.J. (1998). Intracellular mechanisms of amyloid β-peptide Aβ25–35 induced neurite outgrowth inhibition *in vitro. Alzheimer's Reports, 1*, 55–60.

Larner, A.J. (2000). Neuronal apoptosis as a therapeutic target in neurodegenerative disease. *Expert Opinion on Therapeutic Patents, 10*, 1493–1518.

Larner, A.J., Johnson, A.R., & Keynes, R.J. (1995). Regeneration in the vertebrate central nervous system: Phylogeny, ontogeny, and mechanisms. *Biological Reviews, 70,* 597–619.

Larner, A.J., & Rossor, M.N. (1997). Alzheimer's disease: Towards therapeutic manipulation of the amyloid precursor protein and amyloid β-peptides. *Expert Opinion on Therapeutic Patents, 7,* 1115–1127.

Lasmezas, C.I., Deslys, J.-P., Robain, O., et al. (1997). Transmission of the BSE agent to mice in the absence of detectable abnormal prion protein. *Science, 275,* 402–405.

Lawrence, C.B., Allan, S.M., & Rothwell, N.J. (1998). Interleukin-1β and the interleukin-1 receptor antagonist act in the striatum to modify excitotoxic brain damage in the rat. *European Journal of Neuroscience, 10,* 1188–1195.

LeBlanc, A. (1997). Apoptosis and Alzheimer's disease. In W. Wasco & R.E. Tanzi (Eds.), *Molecular mechanisms of dementia* (pp. 57–71). Totowa, NJ: Humana Press.

Lee, R.G., & van Donkelaar, P. (1995). Mechanisms underlying functional recovery following stroke. *Canadian Journal of Neurological Sciences, 22,* 257–263.

Lees, A.J., & the Parkinson's Disease Research Group of the United Kingdom. (1995). Comparison of therapeutic effects and mortality data of levodopa and levodopa combined with selegiline in patients with early, mild Parkinson's disease. *British Medical Journal, 311,* 1602–1607.

Levine, J.M. (1994). Increased expression of the NG2 chondroitin-sulfate proteoglycan after brain injury. *Journal of Neuroscience, 14,* 4716–4730.

Li, D., Field, P.M., & Raisman, G. (1995). Failure of axon regeneration in postnatal rat entorhinohippocampal slice coculture is due to maturation of the axon, not that of the pathway or target. *European Journal of Neuroscience, 7,* 1164–1171.

Lieberman, A.R. (1971). The axon reaction: A review of the principal features of perikaryal response to axonal injury. *International Review of Neurobiology, 14,* 49–124.

Lipton, S.A., & Rosenberg, P.A. (1994). Excitatory amino acids as a final common pathway for neurologic disorders. *New England Journal of Medicine, 330,* 613–622.

Liuzzi, F.J., & Lasek, R.J. (1987). Astrocytes block axonal regeneration in mammals by activating the physiological stop pathway. *Science, 237,* 642–645.

Loo, D.T., Copani, A., Pike, C.J., Whittemore, E.R., Walencewicz, A.J., & Cotman, C.W. (1993). Apoptosis is induced by β-amyloid in cultured central nervous system neurons. *Proceedings of the National Academy of Sciences of the United States of America, 90,* 7951–7955.

Lucas, D.R., & Newhouse, J.P. (1957). The toxic effect of sodium L-glutamate on the inner layers of the retina. *Archives of Ophthalmology, 58,* 193–201.

Lucidi-Phillipi, C., & Gage, F.H. (1993). Functions and applications of neurotrophic molecules in the adult central nervous system. *Seminars in the Neurosciences, 5,* 269–277.

Lunn, E.R., Perry, V.H., Brown, M.C., Rosen, H., & Gordon, S. (1989). Absence of Wallerian degeneration does not hinder regeneration in peripheral nerve. *European Journal of Neuroscience, 1,* 27–33.

Lyon, M.J., & Stelzner, D.J. (1987). Tests of the regenerative capacity of tectal efferent axons in the frog, *Rana pipiens. Journal of Comparative Neurology, 255,* 511–525.

Lyras, L., Cairns, N.J., Jenner, A., Jenner, P., & Halliwell, B. (1997). An assessment of oxidative damage to proteins, lipids and DNA in brains from patients with Alzheimer's disease. *Journal of Neurochemistry, 68,* 2061–2069.

Mann, V.M., Cooper, J.M., Krige, D., Daniel, S.E., Schapira, A.H.V., & Marsden, C.D. (1992). Brain, skeletal muscle and platelet homogenate mitochondrial function in Parkinson's disease. *Brain, 115,* 333–342.

Masliah, E., Sisk, A., Mallory, M., Mucke, L., Schenk, D., & Games, D. (1996). Comparison of neurodegenerative pathology in transgenic mice overexpressing V717F β-amyloid precursor protein and Alzheimer's disease. *Journal of Neuroscience, 16,* 5795–5811.

Masters, C.L., Simms, G., Weinman, N.A., Multhaup, G., McDonald, B.L., & Beyreuther, K. (1985). Amyloid plaque core protein in Alzheimer's disease and Down syndrome. *Proceedings of the National Academy of Sciences of the United States of America, 82,* 4245–4249.

Mattson, M.P., Cheng, B., Davis, D., Bryant, K., Lieberburg, I., & Rydel, R.E. (1992). β amyloid peptides destabilize calcium homeostasis and render human cortical neurons vulnerable to excitotoxicity. *Journal of Neuroscience, 12,* 376–389.

Mattson, M.P., Cheng, B., & Smith-Swintosky, V.L. (1993). Neurotrophic factor mediated protection from excitotoxicity and disturbances in calcium and free radical metabolism. *Seminars in the Neurosciences, 5,* 295–307.

Mattson, M.P., Tomaselli, K., & Rydel, R.E. (1993). Calcium-destabilizing and neurodegenerative effects of aggregated β-amyloid peptide are attenuated by basic FGF. *Brain Research, 621,* 35–49.

McDonald, J.W., Garofalo, E.A., Hood, T., et al. (1991). Altered excitatory and inhibitory amino acid receptor binding in hippocampus of patients with temporal lobe epilepsy. *Annals of Neurology, 29,* 529–541.

McKeon, R.J., Schreiber, R.C., Rudge, J.S., & Silver, J. (1991). Reduction of neurite outgrowth in a model of glial scarring following CNS injury is correlated with the expression of inhibitory molecules on reactive astrocytes. *Journal of Neuroscience, 11,* 3398–3411.

Mecocci, P., MacGarvey, U., & Beal, M.F. (1994). Oxidative damage to mitochondrial DNA is increased in Alzheimer's disease. *Annals of Neurology, 36,* 747–751.

Meda, L., Cassatella, M.A., Szendrei, G.I., Otvos, L., Baron, P., Villalaba, M., Ferrari, D., & Rossi, F. (1995). Activation of microglial cells by β-amyloid protein and interferon-γ. *Nature, 374,* 647–650.

Meldrum, B., & Garthwaite, J. (1990). Excitatory amino acid neurotoxicity and neurodegenerative disease. *Trends in Pharmacological Sciences, 11,* 379–387.

Milner, J., & Medcalf, E.A. (1991). Cotranslation of activated mutant p53 with wild type drives the wild type p53 protein into the mutant conformation. *Cell, 65,* 765–774.

Mitchell, I.J., Lawson, S., Moser, B., Laidlaw, S.M., Cooper, A.J., Walkinshaw, G., & Waters, C.M. (1994). Glutamate-induced apoptosis results in a loss of striatal neurons in the parkinsonian rat. *Neuroscience, 63,* 1–5.

Mitrovic, B., Ignarro, L.J., Vinters, H.V., Akers, M.-A., Schmid, I., Uittenbogaart, C., & Merrill, J.E. (1995). Nitric oxide induces necrotic but not apoptotic cell death in oligodendrocytes. *Neuroscience, 65,* 531–539.

Mizuno, Y., Suzuki, K., Sone, N., & Saitoh, T. (1988). Inhibition of mitochondrial respiration by MPTP in mouse brain *in vivo. Neuroscience Letters, 91,* 349–353.

Moncada, S., Palmer, R.M.J., & Higgs, E.A. (1991). Nitric oxide: Physiology, pathophysiology and pharmacology. *Pharmacological Reviews, 43,* 109–142.

Moreau, T., Coles, A., Wing, M., Isaacs, J., Hale, G., Waldmann, H., & Compston, A. (1996). Transient increase in symptoms associated with cytokine release in patients with multiple sclerosis. *Brain, 119,* 225–237.

Moreau, T., Thorpe, J., Miller, D., Moseley, I., Hale, G., Waldmann, H., et al. (1994). Preliminary evidence from magnetic resonance imaging for reduction in disease activity after lymphocyte depletion in multiple sclerosis. *Lancet, 344,* 298–301; Erratum, *344,* 486.

Morrow, D.R., Campbell, G., Lieberman, A.R., Anderson, P.N. (1993). Differential regenerative growth of CNS axons into tibial and peroneal nerve grafts in the thalamus of adult rats. *Experimental Neurology, 120,* 60–69.

Mufson, E.J., Conner, J.M., & Kordower, J.H. (1995). Nerve growth factor in Alzheimer's disease: Defective retrograde transport to nucleus basalis. *NeuroReport, 6,* 1063–1066.

Muir, G.D., & Steeves, J.D. (1997). Sensorimotor stimulation to improve locomotor recovery after spinal cord injury. *Trends in Neurosciences, 20,* 72–77.

Müller, U., Cristina, N., Li, Z.-W., Wolfer, D.P., Lipp, H.-P., Rulicke, T., Brandner, S., Aguzzi, A., & Weissmann, C. (1994). Behavioral and anatomical deficits in mice homozygous for a modified β-amyloid precursor protein gene. *Cell, 79,* 755–765.

Nachev, P.C., & Larner, A.J. (1996). Zinc and Alzheimer's disease. *Trace Elements and Electrolytes, 13,* 55–59.

Nadler, J.V. (1981). Kainic acid as a tool for the study of temporal lobe epilepsy. *Life Sciences, 29,* 2031–2042.

Naso, W.B., Perot, P.L.J., & Cox, R.D. (1995). The neuroprotective effect of methylprednisolone in rat spinal hemisection. *Neurosciences Letters, 189,* 176–178.

Nathan, B.P., Bellosta, S., Sanan, D.A., Weisgraber, K.H., Mahley, R.W., Pitas, R.E. (1994). Differential effects of apolipoproteins E3 and E4 on neuronal growth *in vivo. Science, 264,* 850–852.

Norenberg, M.D. (1994). Astrocyte responses to CNS injury. *Journal of Neuropathology and Experimental Neurology, 53,* 213–220.

Novelli, A., Reilly, J.A., Lysko, P.G., & Henneberry, R.C. (1988). Glutamate becomes neurotoxic via the N-methyl-D-aspartate receptor when intracellular energy levels are reduced. *Brain Research, 451,* 205–212.

Nunn, P.B. (1994). Chemical toxins. In A.C. Williams (Ed.), *Motor neuron disease* (pp. 567–586). London: Chapman & Hall.

Olney, J.W., & Sharpe, L.G. (1969). Brain lesions in an infant rhesus monkey treated with monosodium glutamate. *Science, 166,* 386–388.

Oppenheim, R.W. (1991). Cell death during development of the nervous system. *Annual Review of Neuroscience, 14,* 453–501.

Owen, F., Poulter, M., Lofthouse, R., Collinge, J., Crow, T.J., Risby, D., et al. (1989). Insertion in prion protein gene in familial Creutzfeldt-Jakob disease. *Lancet, 1,* 51–52.

Paino, C.L., Fernandez-Valle, C., Bates, M.L., & Bunge, M.B. (1994). Regrowth of axons in lesioned adult rat spinal cord: Promotion by implants of cultured Schwann cells. *Journal of Neurocytology, 23,* 433–452.

Palmer, M.S., Dryden, A.J., Hughes, J.T., & Collinge, J. (1991). Homozygous prion protein genotype predisposes to sporadic Creutzfeldt-Jakob disease. *Nature, 352,* 340–342.

Pan, K.-M., Baldwin, M., Nguyen, J., Gasset, M., Serban, A., Groth, D., Mehlhorn, I., Huang, Z., Fletterick, R.J., Cohen, F.E., & Prusiner, S.B. (1993). Conversion of α-helices into β-sheets features in the formation of the scrapie prion proteins. *Proceedings of the National Academy of Sciences of the United States of America, 90,* 10,962–10,966.

The Parkinson Study Group. (1993). Effects of tocopherol and deprenyl on the progression of disability in early Parkinson's disease. *New England Journal of Medicine, 328,* 176–183.

Paulson, H.L., & Fishbeck, K.H. (1996). Trinucleotide repeats in neurogenetic disorders. *Annual Review of Neuroscience, 19,* 79–107.

Pearson, R.C.A., Sofroniew, M.V., Cuello, A.C., Powell, T.P.S., Eckenstein, F., Esiri, M.M., & Wilcock, G.K. (1983). Persistence of cholinergic neurons in the basal nucleus in a brain with senile dementia of the Alzheimer's type demonstrated by immunohistochemical staining for choline acetyltransferase. *Brain Research, 289,* 375–379.

Pellegrini-Giampietro, D.E., Zukin, R.S., Bennett, M.V.L., Cho, S., & Pulsinelli W.A. (1992). Switch in glutamate receptor subunit gene expression in CA1 subfield of hippocampus following global ischemia in rats. *Proceedings of the National Academy of Sciences of the United States of America, 89,* 10,499–10,503.

Pereira, J.H., Palande, D.D., Subramanian, A., Narayanakumar, T.S., Curtis, J., & Turk, J.L. (1991). Denatured autologous muscle graft in leprosy. *Lancet, 338,* 1239–1240.

Perl, T.M., Bedard, L., Kosatsky, T., et al. (1990). An outbreak of toxic encephalopathy caused by eating mussels contaminated with domoic acid. *New England Journal of Medicine, 322,* 1775–1780.

Persson, H. (1993). Neurotrophin production in the brain. *Seminars in the Neurosciences 5,* 227–237.

Pike, C.J., Burdick, D., Walencewicz, A.J., Glabe, C.G., & Cotman, C.W. (1993). Neurodegeneration induced by β-amyloid peptides *in vitro:* The role of peptide assembly state. *Journal of Neuroscience, 13,* 1676–1687.

Polvikoski, T., Sulkava, R., Haltia, M., Kainulainen, K., Vuorio, A., Verkkoniemi, A., Niinisto, L., Halonen, P., & Kontula, K. (1995). Apolipoprotein E, dementia, and cortical deposition of β-amyloid protein. *New England Journal of Medicine, 333,* 1242–1247.

Polymeropoulos, M.H., Lavedan, C., Leroy, E., et al. (1997). Mutation in the α-synuclein gene identified in families with Parkinson's disease. *Science, 276,* 2045–2047.

Portera-Cailliau, C., Hedreen, J.C., Price, D.L., & Koliatsos, V.E. (1995). Evidence for apoptotic cell death in Huntington disease and excitotoxic animal models. *Journal of Neuroscience, 15,* 3775–3787.

Portera-Cailliau, C., Price, D.L., & Martin, L.J. (1997a). Excitotoxic neuronal death in the immature brain is an apoptosios–necrosis morphological continuum. *Journal of Comparative Neurology, 378,* 70–87.

Portera-Cailliau, C., Price, D.L., & Martin, L.J. (1997b). Non-NMDA and NMDA receptor-mediated excitotoxic neuronal deaths in adult brain are morphologically distinct: Further evidence for an apoptosis–necrosis continuum. *Journal of Comparative Neurology, 378,* 88–104.

Price, R.W. (1996). Neurological complications of HIV infection. *Lancet, 348,* 445–452.

Prout, K.A., & Larner, A.J. (1998). Emerging therapeutic possibilities in prion diseases: Patents 1993–1998. *Expert Opinion on Therapeutic Patents, 8,* 1099–1108.

Prusiner, S.B. (1982). Novel proteinaceous infectious particles cause scrapie. *Science, 215,* 136–144.

Prusiner, S.B. (1994). Prion diseases of humans and animals. *Journal of the Royal College of Physicians of London, 28*(Suppl.), 1–30.

Prusiner, S.B., Scott, M., Foster, D., Pan, K.M., Groth, D., Mirenda, C., et al. (1990). Transgenetic studies implicate interactions between homologous PrP isoforms in scrapie prion replication. *Cell, 63,* 673–686.

Purpura, D.P. (1978). Ectopic dendritic growth in mature pyramidal neurons in human ganglioside storage disease. *Nature, 276,* 520–521.

Purpura, D.P., & Baker, H.J. (1978). Meganeurites and other aberrant processes of neurons in feline GM1-gangliosidoses: A Golgi study. *Brain Research, 143,* 13–26.

Rabchevsky, A.G., & Streit, W.J. (1997). Grafting of cultured microglial cells into the lesioned spinal cord of adult rats enhances neurite outgrowth. *Journal of Neuroscience Research, 47,* 34–48.

Ramer, M.S., Priestley, J.V., & McMahon, S.B. (2000). Functional regeneration of sensory axons into the adult spinal cord. *Nature, 403,* 312–316.

Ramon-Cueto, A., & Nieto-Sampedro, M. (1994). Regeneration into the spinal cord of transected dorsal root axons is promoted by ensheathing glia transplants. *Experimental Neurology, 127,* 232–244.

Rapalino, O., Lazarov-Spiegler, O., Agranov, E., et al. (1998). Implantation of stimulated homologous macrophages results in partial recovery of paraplegic rats. *Nature Medicine, 4,* 814–821.

Rapp, P.R., & Amaral, D.G. (1992). Individual differences in the cognitive and neurobiological consequences of normal aging. *Trends in Neurosciences, 15,* 340–345.

Redford, E.J., Kapoor, R., & Smith, K.J. (1997). Nitric oxide donors reversibly block axonal conduction: Demyelinated axons are especially susceptible. *Brain, 120,* 2149–2158.

Richardson, P.M., Issa, V.M.K., & Aguayo, A.J. (1984). Regeneration of long spinal axons in the rat. *Journal of Neurocytology, 13,* 165–182.

Richardson, P.M., McGuinness, U., & Aguayo, A.J. (1980). Axons from CNS neurones regenerate into PNS grafts. *Nature, 284,* 264–265.

Rogers, S.L., Farlow, M.R., Doody, R.S., Mohs, R., Friedhoff, L.T., and the Donepezil Study Group. (1998). A 24-week, double-blind, placebo-controlled trial of donepezil in patients with Alzheimer's disease. *Neurology, 50,* 136–145.

Rogers, S.W., Andrews, P.I., Gahring, L.C., Whisenand, T., Cauley, K., Crain, B., Hughes, T.E., Heinemann, S.F., & McNamara, J.O. (1994). Autoantibodies to glutamate receptor GluR3 in Rasmussen's encephalitis. *Science, 265,* 648–651.

Rosen, D.R., Siddique, T., Patterson, D., et al. (1993). Mutations in Cu/Zn superoxide dismutase gene are associated with familial amyotrophic lateral sclerosis. *Nature, 364,* 359–362.

Rosenberg, P.A., & Aizenman, E. (1989). Hundred-fold increase in neuronal vulnerability to glutamate toxicity in astrocyte-poor cultures of rat cerebral cortex. *Neuroscience Letters, 103,* 162–168.

Roses, A.D. (1996). Apolipoprotein E alleles as risk factors in Alzheimer's disease. *Annual Review of Medicine, 47,* 387–400.

Rosling, H., & Tylleskar, T. (1996). Konzo. In R.A. Shakir, P.K. Newman, & C.M. Poser (Eds.), *Tropical neurology* (pp. 353–364). London: Saunders.

Rossi, F., Jankovski, A., & Sotelo, C. (1995). Differential regenerative response of Purkinje cell and inferior olivary axons confronted with embryonic grafts: Environmental cues versus intrinsic neuronal determinants. *Journal of Comparative Neurology, 359,* 663–677.

Rothstein, J.D., Dykes-Hoberg, M., Pardo, C.A., et al. (1996). Knockout of glutamate transporters reveals a major role for astroglial transport in excitotoxicity and clearance of glutamate. *Neuron, 16,* 675–686.

Roy, N., Mahadevan, M.S., McLean, M., et al. (1995). The gene for neuronal apoptosis inhibitory protein is partially deleted in individuals with spinal muscular atrophy. *Cell, 80,* 167–178.

Saunders, A.M., Strittmatter, W.J., Schmechel, D., et al. (1993). Association of apolipoprotein E allele ε4 with late-onset familial and sporadic Alzheimer's disease. *Neurology, 43,* 1467–1472.

Schenk, D., Barbour, R., Dunn, W., et al. (1999). Immunization with amyloid-beta attenuates Alzheimer-disease-like pathology in the PDAPP mouse. *Nature, 400,* 173–177.

Scherzinger, E., Lurz, R., Turmaine, M., Mangiarin, L., Hollenbach, B., Hasenbank, R., Bates, G.P., Davies, S.W., Lehrach, H., & Wanker, E.E. (1997). Huntingtin-encoded polyglutamine expansions form amyloid-like protein aggregates *in vitro* and *in vivo*. *Cell, 90,* 549–558.

Schnell, L., Schneider, R., Kolbeck, R., Barde, Y.-A., & Schwab, M.E. (1994). Neurotrophin-3 enhances sprouting of corticospinal tract during development and after adult spinal cord lesion. *Nature, 367,* 170–173.

Schnell, L., & Schwab, M.E. (1990). Axonal regeneration in the rat spinal cord produced by an antibody against myelin-associated neurite growth inhibitors. *Nature, 343,* 269–272.

Schubert, D. (1992). Synergistic interactions between transforming growth factor beta and fibroblast growth factor regulate Schwann cell mitosis. *Journal of Neurobiology, 23,* 143–148.

Schumacher, J.M., Short, M.P., Hyman, B.T., Breakefield, X.O., & Isacson, O. (1991). Intracerebral implantation of nerve growth factor-producing fibroblasts protects striatum against neurotoxic levels of excitatory amino acids. *Neuroscience, 45,* 561–570.

Schwab, M.E., & Bartholdi, D. (1996). Degeneration and regeneration of axons in the lesioned spinal cord. *Physiological Reviews, 76,* 319–370.

Schwab, M.E., & Caroni, P. (1988). Oligodendrocytes and CNS myelin are nonpermissive substrates for neurite growth and fibroblast spreading *in vitro. Journal of Neuroscience, 8,* 2381–2393.

Schwab, M.E., & Thoenen, H. (1985). Dissociated neurons regenerate into sciatic but not optic nerve explants in culture irrespective of neurotrophic factors. *Journal of Neuroscience, 5,* 2415–2423.

Scolding, N.J., Morgan, B.P., Campbell, A.K., & Compston, D.A.S. (1992). The role of calcium in rat oligodendrocyte injury and repair. *Neuroscience Letters, 135,* 95–98.

Scolding, N.J., Zajicek, J.P., Wood, N., & Compston, D.A.S. (1994). The pathogenesis of demyelinating disease. *Progress in Neurobiology, 43,* 143–173.

Shaw, P.J. (1994). Excitotoxicity and motor neurone disease: A review of the evidence. *Journal of the Neurological Sciences, 124*(Suppl.), 6–13.

Shewan, D., Berry, M., & Cohen, J. (1995). Extensive regeneration *in vitro* by early embryonic neurons on immature and adult CNS tissue. *Journal of Neuroscience, 15,* 2057–2062.

Siesjo, B.K. (1991). The role of calcium in cell death. In D.L. Price, H. Thoenen, & A.J. Aguayo (Eds.), *Neurodegenerative disorders: Mechanisms and prospects for therapy* (pp. 35–59). Chichester: Wiley.

Simonian, N.A., & Coyle, J.T. (1996). Oxidative stress in neurodegenerative disease. *Annual Review of Pharmacology and Toxicology, 36,* 83–106.

Sivron, T., Schwab, M.E., & Schwartz, M. (1994). Presence of growth inhibitors in fish optic nerve myelin: Postinjury changes. *Journal of Comparative Neurology, 343,* 237–246.

Smith, C., & Clarke, A.R. (1997). Structural properties of the prion protein. In J. Collinge & M.S. Palmer (Eds.), *Prion diseases* (pp. 177–194). Oxford, UK: Oxford University Press.

Smith-Thomas, L.C., Fok Seang, J., Stevens, J., Du, J.S., Muir, E., Faissner, A., Geller, H.M., Rogers, J.H., & Fawcett, J.W. (1994). An inhibitor of neurite outgrowth produced by astrocytes. *Journal of Cell Science, 107,* 1687–1695.

Snider, W.D. (1994). Functions of the neurotrophins during nervous system development: What the knockouts are teaching us. *Cell, 77,* 627–638.

Soares, J.C., & Gershon, S. (1995). THA—historical aspects, review of pharmacological properties and therapeutic effects. *Dementia, 6,* 225–234.

Sofroniew, M.V. (1996). Nerve growth factor, ageing and Alzheimer's disease. *Alzheimer's Research, 2,* 7–14.

Sofroniew, M.V. (1999). Neuronal responses to axotomy. In M. Tuszynski, J. Kordower, & K. Bankiewicz (Eds.), *CNS regeneration: Basic science and clinical applications* (pp. 3–26). San Diego: Academic Press.

Sofroniew, M.V., & Cooper, J.D. (1993). Neurotrophic mechanisms and neuronal degeneration. *Seminars in the Neurosciences, 5,* 285–294.

Sofroniew, M.V., Cooper, J.D., Svendsen, C.N., Crossman, P., Ip, N.Y., Lindsay, R.M., Zafra, F., & Lindholm, D. (1993). Atrophy but not death of adult septal cholinergic neurons after ablation of target capacity to produce mRNAs for NGF, BDNF and NT3. *Journal of Neuroscience, 13,* 5263–5276.

Sofroniew, M.V., Galletly, N.P., Isacson, O., & Svendsen, C.N. (1990). Survival of adult basal forebrain cholinergic neurons after loss of target neurons. *Science, 247,* 338–342.

Soto, C., Kindy, M.S., Baumann, M., & Frangione, B. (1996). Inhibition of Alzheimer's amyloidosis by peptides that prevent β-sheet conformation. *Biochemistry and Biophysical Research Communications, 226,* 672–680.

Spencer, P.S., Nunn, P.B., Hugon, J., et al. (1987). Linkage of Guam amyotrophic lateral sclerosis-parkinsonism-dementia to a plant excitant neurotoxin. *Science, 237,* 517–522.

Spillantini, M.G., Crowther, R.A., Jakes, R., Hasegawa, M., & Goedert, M. (1998). α-synuclein in filamentous inclusions of Lewy bodies from Parkinson's disease and dementia with Lewy bodies. *Proceedings of the National Academy of Sciences of the United States of America, 95,* 6469–6473.

Spillantini, M.G., & Goedert, M. (1998). Tau protein pathology in neurodegenerative diseases. *Trends in Neurosciences, 21,* 428–433.

Sriram, S., & Rodriguez, M. (1997). Indictment of the microglia as the villain in multiple sclerosis. *Neurology, 48,* 464–470.

Stanley, L.C., Mrak, R.E., Woody, R.C., Perrot, L.J., Zhang, S., Marshak, D.R., Nelson, S.J., & Griffin, W.S.T. (1994). Glial cytokines as neuropathogenic factors in HIV infection: pathogenic similarities to Alzheimer's disease. *Journal of Neuropathology and Experimental Neurology, 53,* 231–238.

Steiner, J.P., Hamilton, G.S., Ross, D.T., et al. (1997). Neurotrophic immunophilin ligands stimulate structural and functional recovery in neurodegenerative animal models. *Proceedings of the National Academy of Sciences of the United States of America, 94,* 2019–2024.

Steinhauser, C., & Gallo, V. (1996). News on glutamate receptors in glial cells. *Trends in Neurosciences, 19,* 339–345.

Strittmatter, W.J., Weisgraber, K.H., Goedert, M., et al. (1994). Hypothesis: Microtubule instability and paired helical filament formation in the Alzheimer disease brain are related to apolipoprotein E genotype. *Experimental Neurology, 125,* 163–171.

Svendsen, C.N., & Sofroniew, M.V. (1995). Do CNS neurons require target-derived neurotrophic support for survival throughout life and aging? *Perspectives in Developmental Neurobiology, 3,* 131–140.

Tanaka, K., Watase, K., Manabe, T., et al. (1997). Epilepsy and exacerbation of brain injury in mice lacking the glutamate transporter GLT-1. *Science, 276,* 1699–1702.

Tekle-Haimanot, R. (1996). Lathyrism. In R.A. Shakir, P.K. Newman, & C.M. Poser (Eds.), *Tropical neurology* (pp. 365–374). London: Saunders.

Tello, F. (1911). La influencia del neurotropismo en la regeneracion de los centros nerviosos. *Trabajos del Laboratorio de Investigaciones Biologicas de la Universidad de Madrid, 9,* 123–159.

Thomas, M., Stirrat, A., Birch, R., & Glasby, M. (1994). Freeze-thawed muscle grafting for painful cutaneous neuromas. *Journal of Bone and Joint Surgery, 76B,* 474–476.

Tomac, A., Lindqvist, E., Lin, L.-F.H., Ogren, S.O., Young, D., Hoffer, B.J., & Olson, L. (1995). Protection and repair of the nigrostriatal dopaminergic system by GDNF *in vivo. Nature, 373,* 335–339.

Tonge, D.A., & Golding, J.P. (1993). Regeneration and repair of the peripheral nervous system. *Seminars in the Neurosciences, 5,* 385–390.

Treinin, M., & Chalfie, M. (1995). A mutated acetylcholine receptor subunit causes neuronal degeneration in *C. elegans. Neuron, 14,* 871–877.

Vaughan, J., Muller-Myhsok, B., Wszolek, Z.K., et al. (1998). Genomic heterogeneity in familial parkinsonism: No linkage to the PD1 locus on chromosome 4q in 11 of 13 families. *Journal of Neurology, Neurosurgery and Psychiatry, 64,* 695–696.

Vickers, J.C. (1997). A cellular mechanism for the neuronal changes underlying Alzheimer's disease. *Neuroscience, 78,* 629–639.

Weibel, D., Cadelli, D., & Schwab, M.E. (1994). Regeneration of lesioned rat optic nerve fibers is improved after neutralization of myelin-associated neurite growth inhibitors. *Brain Research, 642,* 259–266.

Weiller, C., Ramsay, S.C., Wise, R.J.S., Friston, K.J., & Frackowiak, R.S.J. (1993). Individual patterns of functional reorganization in the human cerebral cortex after capsular infarction. *Annals of Neurology, 33,* 181–189.

Weiss, J.H., Pike, C.J., & Cotman, C.W. (1994). Ca^{2+} channel blockers attenuate β-amyloid peptide toxicity to cortical neurons in culture. *Journal of Neurochemistry, 62,* 372–375.

White, R.P., Deane, C., Vallance, P., & Markus, H.S. (1998). Nitric oxide synthase inhibition in humans reduces cerebral blood flow but not the hyperemic response to hypercapnia. *Stroke, 29,* 467–472.

Wictorin, K., Brundin, P., Sauer, H., Lindvall, O., & Bjorklund, A. (1992). Long distance directed axonal growth from human dopaminergic mesencephalic neuroblasts implanted along the nigrostriatal pathway in 6-hydroxydopamine lesioned adult rats. *Journal of Comparative Neurology, 323,* 475–494.

Wischik, C.M., Novak, M., Thogersen, H.C., et al. (1988). Isolation of a fragment of tau derived from the core of the paired helical filaments of Alzheimer's disease. *Proceedings of the National Academy of Sciences of the United States of America, 85,* 4506–4510.

Wunderlich, G., Stichel, C.C., Schroeder, W.O., & Muller, H.W. (1994). Transplants of immature astrocytes promote axonal regeneration in the adult rat brain. *Glia, 10,* 49–58.

Wyllie, A., Kerr, J.F., & Currie, A.R. (1980). Cell death: The significance of apoptosis. *International Review of Cytology, 68,* 251–306.

Xu, X.M., Chen, A., Guenard, V., Kleitman, N., & Bunge, M.B. (1997). Bridging Schwann cell transplants promote axonal regeneration from both the rostral and caudal stumps of transected adult rat spinal cord. *Journal of Neurocytology, 26,* 1–16.

Youl, B.D., Turano, G., Miller, D.H., Towell, A.D., MacManus, D.G., Moore, S.G., et al. (1991). The pathophysiology of acute optic neuritis: An association of gadolinium leakage with clinical and electrophysiological deficits. *Brain, 114,* 2437–2450.

Young, W. (1993). Secondary injury mechanisms in acute spinal cord injury. *Journal of Emergency Medicine, 11*(Suppl. 1), 13–22.

Young, W., Kume-Kick, J., & Constantini, S. (1994). Glucocorticoid therapy of spinal cord injury. *Annals of the New York Academy of Sciences, 743,* 241–263.

Younkin, S.G. (1995). Evidence that Aβ42 is the real culprit in Alzheimer's disease. *Annals of Neurology, 37,* 287–288.

Yuen, E.C., & Mobley, W.C. (1996). Therapeutic potential of neurotrophic factors for neurological disorders. *Annals of Neurology, 40,* 346–354.

Z'Graggen, W.J., Metz, G.A.S., Kartje, G.L., Thallmair, M., & Schwab, M.E. (1998). Functional recovery and enhanced corticofugal plasticity after unilateral pyramidal tract lesion and blockade of myelin-associated neurite growth inhibitors in adult rats. *Journal of Neuroscience, 18,* 4744–4757.

Zigmond, M.J., Abercrombie, E.D., Berger, T.W., Grace, A.A., & Stricker, E.M. (1990). Compensations after lesions of central dopaminergic neurons: Some clinical and basic implications. *Trends in Neurosciences, 13,* 290–296.

Ziv, I., Zilkha-Falb, R., Offen, D., Shirvan, A., Barzilai, A., & Melamed, E. (1997). Levodopa induces apoptosis in cultured neuronal cells—a possible accelerator of nigrostriatal degeneration in Parkinson's disease. *Movement Disorders, 12,* 17–23.

8. Neural plasticity and recovery of function

Leonardo G. Cohen   Mark Hallett

INTRODUCTION

The attention to neurological rehabilitation and the development of terms like neuroplasticity and neurorehabilitation are the expression of a relatively new interest in recovery of function. Before this trend became evident, approximately 10–15 years ago, neuroscience considered the adult central nervous system (CNS) hard-wired and largely unmodifiable. The groundwork for this change was established in the 1950s and 1960s by the advances in understanding of synaptic physiology. Influential landmarks included the finding that nerve growth factor (NGF) is expressed in the adult brain leading to the hypothesis that it might continue to exert trophic effects later in life (Levi-Montalcini & Angeletti, 1968); the demonstration of sprouting in the CNS (Raisman & Field, 1973; Wall & Egger, 1971); and the finding that long-term potentiation (LTP) induced by repetitive stimulation in the hippocampus enhances synaptic transmission (Bliss & Gardner, 1973).

It is now known that the cerebral cortex experiences constant remodelling and these changes are shaped by experience. Representations of skin regions (Donoghue & Sanes, 1988; Donoghue, Suner, & Sanes, 1990; Kalaska & Pomeranz, 1979; Merzenich et al., 1983, 1984; Pons et al., 1991), the cochlea (Robertson & Irvine, 1989), and the retina (Chino, Kaas, Smith, Langston, & Cheng, 1992; Kaas et al., 1990; Wall, 1988; Wall & Kaas, 1986), experience reorganisation after deafferentation. In general, cortical representations near the deafferented region take over the cortical sites deprived of inputs. In the somatosensory system, cortical reorganisation has been detected after interruption and reconnection of peripheral nerves (Wall et al., 1986), after crossing the connections between two peripheral nerves, after fusion of fingers (Allard, Clark, Jenkins, & Merzenich, 1991), after moving islands of skin to new locations across the hand (Merzenich, Recanzone, Jenkins, Allard, & Nudo, 1988), after operant conditioning like discrimination of surface roughness (Guic, Rodriguez, Caviedes, & Merzenich, 1993), maintaining finger contact pressure for several seconds for food reward (Jenkins, Merzenich, Ochs, Allard, & Guic-Robles, 1990), and following experience in discrimination of vibratory frequencies (Recanzone, Jenkins,

Hradek, & Merzenich, 1992; Recanzone, Merzenich, & Jenkins, 1992; Recanzone, Merzenich, Jenkins, Grajski, & Dinse, 1992; Recanzone, Merzenich, & Schreiner, 1992). In the motor system, cortical reorganisation has been detected after nerve transections (Donoghue & Sanes, 1987, 1988; Donoghue et al., 1990; Sanes, Suner, & Donoghue, 1990), modified limb positions (Sanes, Wang, & Donoghue, 1992), repetitive stimulation of the motor cortex (Nudo, Jenkins, & Merzenich, 1990), focal lesions in motor cortex (Nudo, Wise, & SiFuentes, 1995), practice of a small object retrieval task (Nudo, Milliken, Jenkins, & Merzenich, 1996), and training in a target reaching task (Aizawa, Inase, Mushiake, Shima, & Tanji, 1991; Mitz, Godschalk, & Wise, 1991).

Therefore these studies depict an adult mammal cortex that, far from having a static and rigid configuration, has the ability to reorganise and adapt to compensate for injury or changes in the environmental conditions.

SHORT-TERM PLASTICITY

Animal studies have shown that interruption of afferents from the periphery is capable of inducing profound modifications in cortical organisation. Some of these changes start taking place shortly after deafferentation. The mechanism by which a peripheral lesion induces fast changes in cortical representations is called unmasking and it is not based on the establishment of new synaptic contacts, since there is not enough time for them to develop (Calford & Tweedale, 1991a,b; Cusick, Wall, Whiting, & Wiley, 1990). These fast changes are evoked by a variety of manipulations like modifications in stimulation patterns, arousal, injury, and intracortical microstimulation (ICMS) (Garraghty & Kaas, 1992). Intracortical microstimulation, for example, can induce fast reorganisational changes in both motor and somatosensory cortex (Dinse, Recanzone, & Merzenich, 1993; Nudo et al., 1990; Recanzone, Merzenich, & Dinse, 1992; Spengler & Dinse, 1994). Stimulation can result in enlargement of cortical receptive fields or in the number of neurons or cortical area activated by a sensory stimulus. These plastic changes are short lasting. In general, the duration of plastic changes appears to be directly related to the time required to evoke them in stimulation or behavioural paradigms (Elbert, Pantev, Wienbruch, Rockstroh, & Taub, 1995; Pascual-Leone & Torres, 1993). For example, when ICMS was delivered to primary somatosensory cortex for 45 minutes, a several-fold increase of the response area was reported and full recovery took place within approximately 60 minutes. In the motor system, nerve transection also results in fast cortical reorganisational changes in motor outputs (Donoghue et al., 1990). In the visual system, retinal detachment, induction of artificial scotomas and partial retinal lesions result in fast changes in cortical receptive fields (Chino et al., 1992; DeWeerd, Gatlass, Desimone, & Ungerleider, 1995; Schmid, Rosa, & Calford, 1995). In humans, transient deafferentation by regional anaesthesia or ischaemic nerve block (inflation of a blood pressure cuff above systolic blood pressure for 30–60 minutes) leads to an enlargement of motor evoked potentials (MEP) amplitudes to transcranial magnetic stimulation (TMS) recorded from muscles immediately proximal to the ischemic level (Brasil-Neto et al., 1992). The implication of this

finding was that the human motor system is capable of rapid and selective facilitation of motor outputs to muscles immediately above the deafferentation level. In a follow-up experiment, it was demonstrated that the main site where this plasticity takes place is the cerebral cortex (Brasil-Neto et al., 1993). Therefore, the excitability of the cortical representation for regions proximal to the ischaemic level increased as a consequence of the ischaemic block (Figure 8.1).

In agreement with this interpretation, a PET study in subjects undergoing forearm ischaemia showed that regional cerebral blood flow (rCBF) at rest was increased in primary sensorimotor regions bilaterally (Sadato et al., 1995). The human motor cortex then is capable of fast modulation of outputs to specific muscle groups. In the somatosensory system, the cortical representation of fingers (measured by somatosensory magnetic fields evoked by finger stimulation) neighbouring a finger deafferented by local anaesthesia are shifted towards the representation of the deafferented finger (Rossini et al., 1994). This finding suggested that the cortical representations of neighbouring

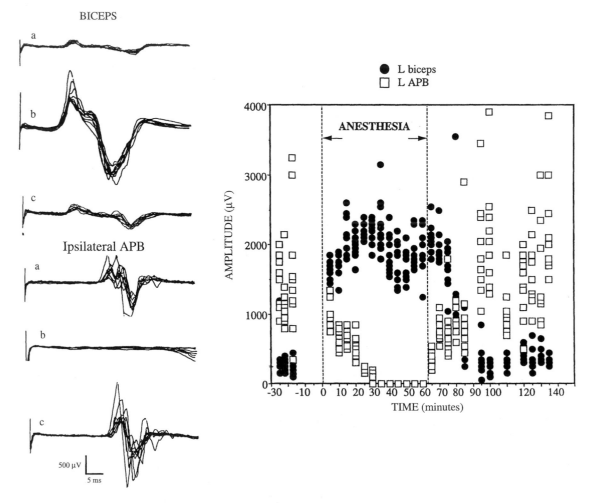

Figure 8.1. Recordings obtained from biceps and abductor pollicis brevis muscles before (a), during (b), and after (c) a Bier block at elbow level in a normal volunteer. The traces on the left show the remarkable increase in biceps MEP amplitudes during the anaesthesia procedure with subsequent return to baseline amplitudes after anaesthesia. Traces from APB show the motor block across the elbow during anaesthesia with subsequent amplitude normalisation. The graph on the right shows the time course of amplitude changes in biceps (filled circles) and APB (squares) MEP (modified from (Brasil-Neto et al., 1992)).

fingers are in permanent competition and that the lack of input from the periphery into one of these representations results in the invasion of the neighbouring representations.

Following the theories of Hebb, ideas were formalised into the Hebbian rules that described mechanisms for change in the central nervous system. Hebbian rules included the concept that temporal coincidence of inputs are an effective way to change synaptic excitability. An elegant set of experiments tested these postulates in the somatosensory system. Animals and human subjects were presented with paired peripheral tactile stimuli geared to improve tactile discriminatory ability. Training for 2 or 6 hours resulted in significant improvement of discriminatory abilities and discrimination thresholds in humans (Dinse, Godde, Spengler, Stauffenberg, & Kraft, 1994). When similar training was used in animals and the somatosensory cortex was mapped, training resulted in overall expansion of the cortical representation of the skin where the stimuli were applied. These findings indicated at least an association between plastic processes and perceptual changes. It remains to be demonstrated if these behavioural improvements are perceptual correlates of plasticity. Hebbian postulates also apply to the human motor system. We have recently demonstrated that progressive improvement in synchronisation of activation of two arm muscles (abductor pollicis brevis and deltoid) result in increased excitability and overlapping of their cortical motor representations (Cohen, Gerloff, Ikoma, & Hallett, 1995). This finding supports the role of synchronicity of motor outputs as a stimulus for cortical reorganisation.

All of the plasticity detected in sensory representations does not necessarily take place in the cerebral cortex. For example, deafferentation induces reorganisation at all levels of the somatosensory pathway (Devor & Wall, 1981; Florence & Kaas, 1995; Garraghty & Kaas, 1991; Millar, Basbaum, & Wall, 1976). Similarly, in the visual system, there are documented changes in the lateral geniculate nucleus after modification of visual inputs (Eysel, 1982). Therefore, plastic changes detected in the cortex can start at subcortical levels and be secondarily relayed to cortical regions.

SKILL ACQUISITION AND MOTOR LEARNING

The previously described examples indicate that short-term plasticity is a feature of the organisation of the animal and human brain. These changes also play a role during the acquisition of motor skills. TMS was used to map cortical representations of muscles involved in learning a unimanual sequence of keypresses on a piano (Pascual-Leone, Nguyet, et al., 1995). Over the course of 5 days, as subjects learned to perform this sequence, the muscle maps corresponding to the hand engaged in the learning task enlarged, whereas the maps corresponding to the same muscle in the other hand or in control subjects did not change. Therefore, acquisition of a motor skill is associated with modulation of the cortical motor outputs to the muscles involved in the task. Another important finding from this study was that

mental practice of the exercise was sufficient to trigger this form of plasticity resulting in both performance improvement and enlargement of motor maps. This result provides a physiological basis for the finding that a combination of mental and physical practice leads to greater improvement in performance than physical practice alone (McBride & Rothstein, 1979; White, Ashton & Lewis, 1979).

If this is the case, one would expect that disuse results in decreased excitability or size of the cortical representations for the unused body part. In fact, Liepert, Tegenthoff, and Malin (1995) found that immobilisation of the ankle resulted in smaller motor maps targeting the immobilised tibialis anterior in comparison to the unaffected leg in a group of human subjects. The reduction in the size of the motor map correlated well with the duration of immobilistion and could be quickly reversed by voluntary muscle contraction.

The acquisition of procedural knowledge depends upon both implicit learning and explicit learning (Squire, 1986). Implicit learning is characterised as an unintentional, non-conscious form of learning recognised by behavioural improvement. Explicit learning integrates conscious recollection of previous experiences (Schacter, 1994; Schacter, Chiu, & Ochsner, 1993). These forms of learning were studied in the process of acquisition of a complex motor sequence as part of a serial reaction time task (SRTT) (Nissen & Bullemer, 1987; Willingham, Nissen, & Bullemer, 1989). Implicit knowledge is associated with a progressive shortening of reaction times (RT) in the absence of conscious recognition of the presence of a stereotyped sequence. Explicit knowledge is acquired when the subject can consciously identify the presence and characteristics of the repeating sequence. A recent report studied the changes in excitability of the human motor cortex in the process of acquisition of implicit and explicit knowledge. During an SRTT task, normal volunteers acquired first implicit and later explicit knowledge of a sequence. TMS mapping in these subjects showed that the cortical representation of muscles involved in the motor task (SRTT) became progressively larger until explicit knowledge was acquired and then returned to baseline levels (Pascual-Leone, Grafman, & Hallett, 1994). Therefore, the progressive improvement in RT during implicit learning correlates with an enlargement in the maps of outputs targeting the muscle involved in the SRTT. This increasing role of the primary motor cortex in implicit learning has also been demonstrated with neuroimaging techniques (Grafton et al., 1992). The fact that the motor maps returned to baseline when the motor sequence was explicitly learned suggests that at that point in time other cortical regions assume more active roles in task performance (Pascual-Leone et al., 1994).

The two studies described, in addition to many others, show that learning a complex motor task is associated with fundamental changes in cortical activity. These flexible changes in cortical organisation during learning, are likely to be important in the acquisition of motor skills and could lead to structural changes as skills become overlearned and automatic (Pascual-Leone et al., 1994). For example, rats that learned new motor skills had a greater number of synapses per neuron than those that simply exercised (Anderson et al., 1994).

LONG-TERM PLASTICITY

With time, more extensive changes take place in sensory and motor systems after deafferentation. For example, cutting the median nerve deprives the hand cortical representation of approximately half of its afferents. Over 3 weeks, the deprived cortex becomes responsive to inputs from the back of the hand (Merzenich et al., 1983). When the input from the entire glabrous hand is interrupted by cutting both median and ulnar nerves, it takes approximately 2 months for the cortex to become responsive to input from the dorsal surface of the hand (Garraghty & Kaas, 1992). The extent of cortical changes described in the experiments of Merzenich and collaborators was approximately 1.5–2 mm. Subsequent work by Pons, Garraghty, and Mishkin (1988) showed that the second somatosensory cortex (SII) undergoes substantial reorganisation after total removal of the hand representation in primary somatosensory cortex. This form of plasticity expanded over more than 5 mm in the cortex, therefore indicating further boundaries than those thought of in the early experiments of Merzenich and Kaas. Moreover, these experiments raised the possibility that the extent of cortical reorganisation after perturbations in the central nervous system is larger than after manipulations to the periphery. Subsequently, cortical reorganisation in the somatosensory system was studied in a group of four macaques after long-term dorsal rhizotomies in the upper limb, a procedure in which sensory nerve roots are severed between the dorsal root ganglion and the entrance in the spinal cord (Pons et al., 1991). The dramatic result was that the whole original cortical representation for the arm became responsive to stimulation from the chin and jaw. Therefore, these experiments extended the potential magnitude of cortical reorganisation to 1.5–2.0 cm or one-third of the entire somatosensory cortex. This degree of reorganisation exceeds the cortical arborisation zones of single axons from the thalamus. Additionally, in normal monkeys, inputs from face and arm do not overlap at brainstem, thalamic or early cortical levels and intrinsic connections in area 3b do not interconnect hand and face regions (Kaas & Pons, 1988). Therefore, new connections must have developed to allow these findings. Later findings indicated that massive reorganisation does not necessarily require many years, but can occur even 1 year after injury (Dykes, Avendaño, & Leclerc, 1995). Some of these plastic changes, for example those detected in the case of nerve section, do revert after nerve regeneration (Wall, Felleman, & Kaas, 1983).

Plasticity after amputations has been demonstrated across species in racoons, rodents, cats, bats, and also in humans. Amputations represent a most dramatic example of deafferentation. In the rat motor system, amputation results in enlargement of the cortical area from where stimulation elicited movements of body parts adjacent to the amputated region and the threshold for eliciting these movements also decreased (Sanes et al., 1990). In humans, plasticity after amputations was demonstrated using TMS (Cohen, Bandinelli, Findlay, & Hallett, 1991; Hall, Flament, Fraser, & Lemon, 1990) (Figure 8.2).

In these studies, TMS recruited a larger percentage of the alpha motoneuron pool for muscles proximal and ipsilateral to the stump than for the same muscles on the intact side (Cohen,

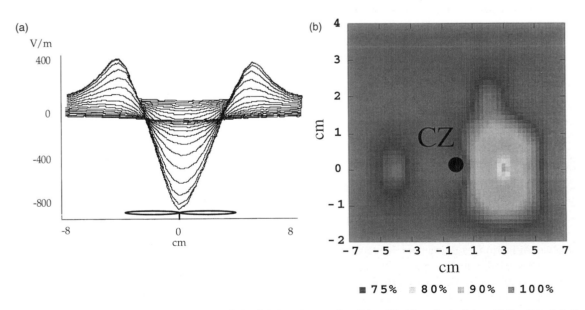

Figure 8.2. (a) Magnitude of the electric field induced in air by a Cadwell 8-shaped magnetic coil (modified from Roth, Cohen, Hallett, Friauf, & Basser, 1990) and (Roth, Saypol, Hallett, & Cohen, 1991). Note that the electric field is larger under the junction of both wings of the coil (showed in the lower part of the figure). (b) View of the top of the head of a patient who suffered a left arm amputation 11 months before testing. The CZ position is located at the midline. The maps on the left and right hemisphere show the minimal intensities of transcranial magnetic stimulation (motor thresholds) necessary to induce small muscle responses in contralateral deltoid (first complete muscle above the stump) when stimulating different scalp positions. Note that the map of outputs targeting the deltoid on the normal arm (right) is much smaller than the map for the left deltoid just above the stump (modified from Cohen, Bandinelli, et al., 1991).

Bandinelli, et al., 1991). These results were later confirmed and expanded using neuroimaging techniques (Kew et al., 1994). The excitability of the alpha motoneuron pool as measured with H reflexes from muscles immediately proximal to the stump (i.e., quadriceps) in patients with lower extremity amputations is similar in the amputee and normal sides (Fuhr et al., 1992). In these patients, transcranial magnetic stimuli recruited a larger percentage of the alpha motoneuron pool in quadriceps ipsilateral to the stump than in the normal side. The absence of changes in the excitability of the alpha motoneuron pool in the process of motor reorganisation targeting muscles proximal to the stump indicates that reorganisation occurs proximal to the alpha motoneuron level. In a follow up study (Cohen et al., 1993) to determine where along the human neuroaxis motor plasticity takes place after amputations, we recorded MEPs from muscles immediately proximal to the stump and from the homonymous contralateral muscles in patients with lower limb amputations. Stimulation was delivered to the motor cortex with a 9 cm diameter magnetic coil (TMS) and electrically (TES) with surface electrodes optimally positioned for stimulation of each muscle. Long descending tracts were stimulated electrically with the cathode at the level of the seventh cervical vertebrae (spinal electrical stimulation, SES). Intensity of stimulation was 120% of motor threshold. Supramaximal muscle responses were elicited by peripheral nerve stimulation. TMS recruited larger MEPs and thresholds for activation were lower from muscles ipsilateral to the stump than from homonymous muscles on the normal side. These differences were not found when stimulating at subcortical levels. These results suggest that a substantial portion of motor reorganisation after amputation occurs intracortically.

One of the hypotheses raised from the studies described earlier is that the cortical representations corresponding to body parts

neighbouring the deafferented representation appear to take over the deafferented region. Other evidence in this direction comes from studies done in patients with cervical (Levy, Amassian, Traad, & Cadwell, 1990) and thoracic (Topka, Cohen, Cole, & Hallett, 1991) spinal cord injury. The investigators used TMS and recorded from muscles immediately proximal to the level of complete spinal cord injury in paraplegic patients. They found that TMS recruited a larger percentage of the alpha motoneuron pool in muscles at rest immediately proximal to the sensory/motor level in patients in comparison to the same muscles in normal controls. These data indicate an enhanced excitability of motor pathways targeting muscles rostral to the level of a spinal cord injury. Interestingly, Topka et al. (1991) reported that this form of plasticity, seen when testing was performed with target muscles at rest, was absent when the same recordings were done under slight activation of target muscles (Figure 8.3).

A similar finding was later reported in patients with amputations (Ridding & Rothwell, 1995) and also during ischaemia (Ridding & Rothwell, 1995; Sadato et al., 1995). That is, the plastic changes described using TMS at rest (Cohen, Bandinelli, et al., 1991; Hall et al., 1990), were absent when the testing was performed under slight muscle facilitation. Two interpretations were offered to explain this phenomenon: one suggesting that under muscle facilitation a ceiling effect operated, by which TMS recruited a similar percentage of the alpha motoneuron pool in normal and plastic muscles, therefore not allowing for further increases in plastic muscles (Topka et al., 1991); the other proposing that since no plasticity is seen when muscles are active, plasticity does not contribute to functional performance of the body part immediately above the lesion (Ridding & Rothwell, 1995) (upper arm–shoulder in

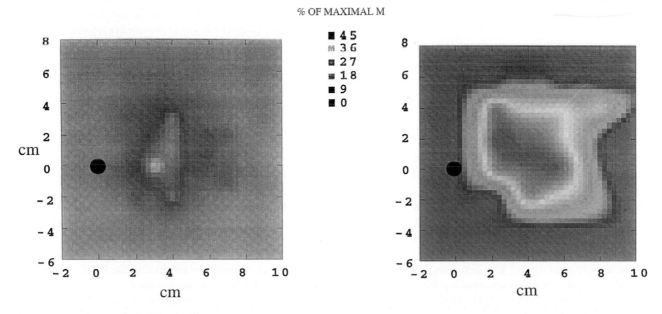

% OF MAXIMAL M

■ 45
▨ 36
▨ 27
▨ 18
■ 9
■ 0

Figure 8.3. Deltoid motor maps showing the largest motor responses in any of 10 normal volunteers (left) and in a patient with quadriplegia (right). Note the remarkable expansion of deltoid motor map in the quadriplegic patient (modified from Hallett et al., 1993).

hand amputations, upper abdominal muscles in thoracic SCI). These different interpretations underline the need for studies specifically designed to determine if plastic changes described in different settings are functionally useful for the individual (Cohen et al., 1997) (see later).

The previously described studies showed that severe lesions involving distal body regions are important triggers of human plasticity. In the motor and sensory strips, the face is represented most laterally, and the hand, arm, and trunk more medially. The foot is represented in the interhemispheric region of the sensorimotor cortex (Penfield & Boldrey, 1937; Woolsey, Erickson, & Gilson, 1979; Woolsey et al., 1952). Diseases involving cranial nerves also lead to cortical reorganisation. For example, studies using TMS and positron emission tomography (PET) showed that patients with Bell's palsy (facial palsy caused by a lesion of the VIIth nerve), had larger cortical representation of the hand (the cortical limb representation neighbouring the face in the medial direction). The hand representation grew in size in part by a lateral expansion into the face representation (Rijntjes et al., 1997). Therefore, the face representation, deprived of output connections to muscles involved in facial movements, became involved in controlling hand movements. This finding highlights another interesting feature of human motor cortical plasticity: It can take place across limb representation boundaries, as has been demonstrated in animals before (Pons et al., 1991).

A particularly important study was done in patients with complete upper limb palsy secondary to traumatic cervical root avulsion. The patients had surgical anastomosis of the intercostal nerve into the musculocutaneous nerve to restore function in biceps brachii and therefore allow arm movements. Over the first 4–6 months after surgery, motor unit discharges were recorded in biceps in association with respiration. One to two years later, motor unit discharges became independent from respiration and more susceptible to voluntary control. In terms of mapping, immediately following the anastomosis, the motor representation of the biceps was located in the region of intercostal muscles. With time and training to control biceps voluntarily, the biceps cortical representation moved laterally towards the cortical regions normally representing the arm (Mano et al., 1995). Therefore, the arm cortical representation recovered control of the biceps muscle through the intercostal nerves. The correlation between improvement in motor control of biceps and topographic remapping strongly suggests that the described cortical reorganisation is functionally useful for controlling the biceps.

The effects of small cortical lesions have been studied in monkeys. Small infarcts in the primary somatosensory cortex lead to cortical reorganisation. The skin regions previously represented in the lesioned cortical site become represented in cortical areas surrounding the lesioned one. Similarly, the receptive fields of cortical regions surrounding the lesioned one experienced reorganisation (Jenkins & Merzenich, 1987). In the motor system, focal lesions in the thumb representation of the motor cortex (Glees & Cole, 1950) resulted in reappearance of the thumb representation in areas surrounding the infarct. There seems to be a differential effect on plasticity depending on the degree to which the affected body part is used following the injury. When the affected body part was heavily used, movements represented in the lesioned cortical site became represented in adjacent cortical areas. In some cases, the hand representation even expanded to cortical regions previously representing elbow and shoulder in intact monkeys (Nudo, Wise, SiFuentes, & Milliken, 1996). In the absence of training, it has been argued that small lesions confined to the representation of one hand result in further loss of hand territory in the adjacent, undamaged cortex in adult squirrel monkeys (Nudo, Wise, et al., 1996). Therefore, when cortical lesions are focal, the neighbouring regions could possibly replace the function of the lesioned one. In addition to M1 plasticity, other cortical regions are also involved in the process of recovery of function. For example, neurons in the supplementary motor area (SMA) are active preceeding movement onset but become much less active when movement becomes overlearned (Aizawa et al., 1991). In cases of focal cortical lesions in the primary motor cortex, it is possible to detect reappearance of activity in SMA neurons, perhaps indicating a contribution of this area to the recovery process.

PERCEPTION AND CORTICAL REORGANISATION

In the last few years different reports have highlighted the importance of the careful evaluation of perceptions as a way to study plasticity. Perhaps the most important work in this area was done in patients with amputations. These patients experience abnormal perceptions called "phantom limb", or, when painful, "phantom pain", felt as originated in the missing limb. They can be elicited spontaneously or by tactile stimulation in the stump areas and they can lead to substantial disability. Ramachandran and collaborators (Ramachandran, 1993; Ramachandran, Stewart, & Rogers-Ramachandran, 1992; Yang et al., 1994), in an interesting series of experiments, reported that in some patients with amputations somatosensory stimulation of the face evoked phantom sensations referred to the missing hand. They called this phenomenon "remapping", and they were able to define maps of the hand on the face of some patients. That is, stimulation of a specific spot on the face consistently induced sensations in one missing finger, while stimulation of another position just 1 or 2 cm away resulted in phantom sensations referred to another finger in the missing hand. These findings were interpreted as indicators that the cortical sites that usually identify and process somatosensory information from the hand, in some amputees, become responsive to stimulation of areas of the face. Therefore, this finding suggested that the expansion of the face representation over the deafferented hand cortical representation carries a behavioural effect, since stimulation of the face now evoke sensations referred to the hand.

An MEG study showed medial displacement of the face cortical somatosensory representation towards the hand representation contralateral to the amputated arm (Flor et al., 1995). This finding also suggested responsivity of the hand sensory representation to inputs from the face and was interpreted as indicating an invasion of the face representation over the deafferented hand somatosensory representation. However, the striking result reported in these experiments was that the extent of this reorganisation correlated very well with the magnitude of phantom pain, therefore establishing a link between pain and plasticity. In this way, the authors hypothesised that phantom pain could be caused by "harmful" plasticity (Birbaumer et al., 1997; Flor et al., 1995). Although plasticity in some cases may be associated with behavioural gain, it is possible that plasticity in other cases like this one results in harmful effects. There are also other abnormalities in patients with traumatic amputations that could underlie painful phantom sensations. For example, in a recent PET study, patients with phantom sensations activated posterior parietal regions more than controls or congenital amputees suggesting a role for this region in phantom pain (Kew et al., 1994).

Another way to explore brain functions in different settings of plasticity is to stimulate cortical representations of regions deafferented by lesions, for example amputations or spinal cord injury, and ask the patients to describe sensations induced by this type of stimulation. We have found that in patients with complete thoracic spinal cord injury, cortical stimulation of regions close to the foot representation (midline) induced sensations in the deafferented legs (Cohen, Topka, Cole, & Hallett, 1991). Similarly, stimulation of cortical representation for the missing limb in patients with amputations induced sensations of movement referred to the missing limb (Cohen, Bandinelli, et al., 1991). Therefore, cortical representations of regions deafferented by complete SCI or amputations can remain related to those body parts for up to several years after the original injury.

HUMAN PLASTICITY AFTER STROKE

Stroke poses an immense challenge to neuroscientists and clinicians. Several factors coalesce to make this one of the most difficult areas of plasticity to study. On one hand, stroke is a common disorder, the third leading cause of death in the United States, and the leading cause of long-term disability among adults with a prevalence of 3,000,000 stroke survivors with varying degrees of residual neurologic impairment. On the other hand, each stroke patient is different from the others and slight differences in lesion location and each patient's pre-existing condition could potentially result in enormous, still unknown changes in plasticity and rehabilitation. In most cases, spontaneous recovery takes place to various degrees in the initial months following the ictal episode. Motor function improves at progressively slower pace over the first year after the episode (Kelly-Hayes et al., 1989) and a useful predictor of outcome appears to be the severity of initial neurologic deficit (Heinemann, Roth, Cichowski, & Bets, 1987). Different mechanisms are likely to participate in the different stages of motor recovery. Recovery in the initial days following the ictal episode could be related with the resolution of oedema or reperfusion of the ischaemic penumbra. But it is also possible that

other areas of the brain, taking over the functions of the lesioned area, contribute to recovery. The neuroanatomical basis for this effect in the motor system could be the existence of corticomotoneuronal connections from various cortical motor areas (Dum & Strick, 1991; He, Dum, & Strick, 1995; Martino & Strick, 1987). At later stages, it is conceivable that sprouting from surviving fibres to establish new synaptic contacts contribute to build the neuroanatomical basis of recovery (Lee & van Donkelaar, 1995).

Studies looking at patients with hemispherectomy, provided an interesting model for the study of the ability of one hemisphere to control movements of the ipsilateral limb. It is a common finding that individuals with hemispherectomy (usually performed as treatment for medically unresponsive seizures) in early age have relatively good control of ipsilateral arm movements, particularly in the proximal segments. Stimulation of the intact hemisphere using TMS in these patients induced prominent motor responses from ipsilateral upper extremity muscles, a finding not seen under similar conditions in normal volunteers (Benecke, Meyer, & Freund, 1991; Cohen, Zeffiro, et al., 1991; Pascual-Leone et al., 1992). These reports suggested that the intact hemisphere is capable of taking over the function of the missing hemisphere, and that this reorganisation could be effective enough to allow moderate degree of motor control. Interestingly, muscles ipsilateral to the intact hemisphere were activated by stimulation of scalp positions anterior and lateral to those activating muscles on the normal side. Similarly, ipsilateral elbow movements were associated with cerebral blood flow increases in an area centred 1.4 cm anterior and lateral to that activated by the same movements on the normal side (Cohen, Zeffiro, et al., 1991). These results indicate that the intact hemisphere developed differentiated cortical representations for the ipsilateral and contralateral arm, a remarkable form of plasticity.

One important report suggesting that the hemisphere ipsilateral to a paretic arm is important for motor recovery was that of Fisher (1992). He described two patients with pure motor hemiplegia recovering from a unilateral subcortical lesion. In the process of recovery, they developed a subsequent motor hemiplegia from a subcortical lesion on the other side. As a consequence, the recovering arm became re-paralysed.

Initial PET studies of patients with capsular strokes who recovered full strength showed increased rCBF in contralateral primary sensorimotor cortex and in the ipsilateral cerebellar hemisphere in association with finger movements of the intact hand. However, when the fingers of the recovered hand were moved, rCBF increased bilaterally in primary sensorimotor cortex, cerebellar hemispheres, insula, inferior parietal, and premotor cortices. The recovered hand, compared with the normal hand, showed increased activation of ipsilateral sensorimotor cortex, insula and inferior parietal cortex, and contralateral cerebellum (Chollet et al., 1991). Increased activation of the hemisphere ipsilateral to a paretic hand was also found by Honda et al. (1997). In a later study on 10 patients with striatocapsular infarcts and good motor recovery, Weiller, Chollet, Friston, Wise, and Frackowiak (1992) found that the earlier finding of increased activation in patients was confirmed in relation to the contralateral cerebellum, the ipsilateral insula and inferior parietal cortex, but not the ipsilateral sensorimotor cortex. Activation was greater than in normal subjects in bilateral insulae, inferior parietal, prefrontal and anterior cingulate cortices, and in the ipsilateral premotor cortex and basal ganglia. Bilateral activation of cerebral structures appeared to be one of the findings associated with motor recovery from striatocapsular strokes. In a different study, the same authors studied the individual patterns of cerebral activation in eight patients compared with the pattern of a group of ten normal subjects. They found an anterior displacement of the hand representation in the contralateral sensorimotor cortex in all patients with lesions of the posterior limb of the internal capsule. Additionally, they found a greater activation than normal in the supplementary motor areas, the insula, the frontal operculum, and the parietal cortex. Motor pathways ipsilateral to the recovered limb were also more activated in the patients than in normal subjects but additional activation of the ipsilateral sensorimotor cortex was only found in the four patients who exhibited associated movements of the unaffected hand when the recovered hand performed the motor task. These associated movements can not be the only reason for ipsilateral activation of primary sensorimotor cortices since more recent fMRI studies have also found this activation in stroke patients in the absence of mirror or associated movements (Cramer et al., 1997; Leifer et al., 1997).

Neurophysiological studies in stroke patients are important because they provide information about the functional role of the cortical area stimulated. That is, if TMS of the sensorimotor cortex ipsilateral to a muscle in the paretic arm induces motor responses in this muscle, it would indicate that there are functionally active corticomotoneuronal connections between the stimulated hemisphere and ipsilateral arm muscles. If so, that hemisphere is likely to participate in motor control of the ipsilateral arm. Some studies have reported findings like this (Caramia, Iani, & Bernardi, 1996; Turton, Wroe, Trepte, Fraser, & Lemon, 1995, 1996), but in the context of poor motor recovery. Therefore, even if present, these reorganisational processes are unlikely to play a functionally relevant role in motor recovery in adult humans.

The situation may be different in children. In addition to the findings reported after hemispherectomy, Carr, Harrison, Evans, and Stephens (1993; see also Maegaki, Maeoka, & Takeshita, 1995) found that when the lesion is prenatal, individual corticomotoneuronal connections in the pyramidal tract may target simultaneously ipsi- and contralateral alphamotoneuron pools.

Many studies now agree that the presence of contralateral motor responses to stimulation of the affected hemisphere after stroke is a good marker for motor recovery (Binkofski et al., 1996; Catano, Houa, Caroyer, Ducarne, & Noel, 1995, 1996; Heald, Bates, Cartlidge, French, & Miller, 1993; Misra & Kalita, 1995; Rapisarda, Bastings, de Noordhout, Pennisi, & Delwaide, 1996; Turton et al., 1996). Combined TMS and PET studies in patients with good motor recovery showed robust activation of the sensorimotor cortex of the affected hemisphere in association with movements of the paretic hand (Wassermann et al., 1996). TMS stimulation of that reorganised cortex rendered relatively small motor responses suggesting a strong effort of the reorganised motor cortex to accomplish a relatively modest motor result. The idea that plastic changes play a role in recovery of motor function is also supported by other studies (Bastings & Good, 1997; Traversa, Cicinelli, Bassi, Rossini, & Bernardi, 1997).

Motor recovery after stroke

Can the information presently available on plasticity associated with use contribute to the design of rationale strategies for recovery of function? One example will be presented here to demonstrate that this is the case.

Monkeys who had severed dorsal roots innervating a single upper extremity stop making use of that limb in the free situation. However, it is possible to influence a monkey to use the deafferented limb by restricting movement of the intact upper extremity and by shaping, a technique in which a desired motor or behavioural objective is approached in small steps, by successive approximations (Taub, 1980; Taub et al., 1993, 1994). On the basis of this observation, it was postulated that the non-use of a single deafferented limb is a learned phenomenon involving a conditioned suppression of movement. It was found that the restraint and shaping appeared to be effective because the primates studied overcame the learned non-use.

On the basis of these experiments, it was then postulated that this approach could be used to treat the motor disability in patients with chronic stroke. It was hypothesised that the motor deficit in many stroke patients can be substantially reduced through the use of techniques designed to overcome the lack of use of the affected arm. Such techniques include prolonged restraint of the unaffected upper extremity and practice in using the affected upper limb. Initial experiments showed that restriction of the unaffected arm in patients with chronic stroke and traumatic-brain-injury may contribute to recovery of motor function in the affected arm (Ostendorf & Wolf, 1981; Wolf, Lecraw, Barton, & Jann, 1989). In a more recent study (Taub, et al. 1994; see also Taub et al., 1993) reported that patients undergoing this type of treatment experienced significant beneficial changes in motor ability in reference to controls. Gains in motor function in the experimental subjects lasted for more than 2 years after the completion of 2 weeks of treatment.

PLASTICITY ACROSS SENSORY MODALITIES

Until this point, we have described models of plasticity within specific sensory or motor modalities. However, deafferentation in one modality can cause marked changes in cortical representations of different sensory modalities (Rauschecker, 1995). For example, it has been postulated that these cross-modal changes are the substrate of the improved sound localisation or tactile abilities of the blind (Kujala et al., 1995). From a theoretical point of view, this postulate raised an interesting question: Can cortical regions ordinarily restricted to processing information from one modality change to process information from a different modality? A recent study demonstrated that this is the case. Sadato et al. (1996) studied regional cerebral blood flow (rCBF) in a group of subjects blind since early infancy and a group of sighted volunteers performing the same tactile discrimination task. They found that performance of this task activated visual primary and association areas in the blind, but not in normal volunteers. These results were interpreted as indicating that cortical areas normally reserved for vision may be activated by other sensory modalities. This view gains further support from the work of others. Non-tactile tasks like auditory stimulation (Kujala et al., 1995; Veraart et al., 1990), haptic mental rotation, and Braille reading (Uhl, Franzen, Podreka, Steiner, & Deecke, 1993) appear to also activate normally visual cortical areas in the blind. The motor cortical representation corresponding to the reading finger of blind subjects proficient in reading Braille is larger than the representation of the same finger in the non-reading hand (Pascual-Leone et al., 1993; Pascual-Leone, Wasserman, Sadato, & Hallett, 1995). Similarly, the somatosensory representation of the reading finger in the blind is larger than the representation of the same finger in the non-reading hand. Animal experiments have also shown that brain regions usually responsible for processing visual information can be activated by auditory or somatosensory stimuli in blind cats as well as in monkeys (Hyvarinen, Carlson, & Hyvarinen, 1981; Rauschecker, 1995). Although these examples focus on visual deprivation, cross-modal plasticity has been also described in other forms of sensory deafferentation. For example, regions in the parietal cortex are activated more strongly by moving visual stimuli in the deaf than in normal controls (Neville, 1990). Whereas in hearing subjects attention to peripheral visual stimuli is associated with ERPs larger in contralateral parietal regions, in the deaf this scalp distribution involves bilateral occipital regions (Neville & Lawson, 1987) suggesting that auditory deprivation since birth has a major effect on the development of the visual system. As a whole these data point to a fascinating mode of brain adaptation.

What is the role of the newly activated areas? For example, in the blind, is the occipital activation described in association with performance of tactile discrimination tasks necessary for adequate tactile performance? Does it play a functionally relevant role in tactile discrimination? To address this question we used repetitive transcranial magnetic stimulation (rTMS) applied over different scalp positions while blind and sighted subjects performed tactile identification of Braille and Roman letters. The hypothesis was that disruption of the reading task by rTMS to specific cortical regions would imply that that region was involved in performing the specific task. We found that in the blind stimulation of occipital regions induced more errors in the reading task than stimulation of any other region or controls. Therefore, occipital areas in the blind are not only activated in association with Braille reading tasks, but they are an essential component of the network involved in Braille reading in the blind. These findings indicate the functional relevance of cross-modal plasticity in the blind (Cohen et al., 1997).

MECHANISMS OF PLASTICITY

Different mechanisms can be active in different forms of adult plasticity. In particular, it is possible to differentiate mechanisms involved in short- and in long-term reorganisation. In the somatosensory system, amputation and denervation result in immediate expansion of cortical receptive fields in primary somatosensory cortex (Byrne & Calford, 1991; Calford & Tweedale, 1988; Metzler & Marks, 1979). These rapid changes have also been seen after directed attention, associative learning, and repetitive stimulation. Disinhibition of previously existing, but masked connections has been postulated as a mechanism mediating short-term changes. This hypothesis was supported by the finding that suppression of GABA-related inhibition with GABA antagonists results in immediate enlargement in receptive fields. GABA-related interneurons appear to be good candidates in both the somatosensory (Dykes, Landry, Metherate, & Hicks, 1984; Garraghty, LaChica, & Kaas, 1991) and in the motor (Jacobs & Donoghue, 1991) cortices. It appears that neighbouring representations coexist in a balance between excitatory and inhibitory influences. GABAergic interneurons from one representation exert inhibitory effects over the neighbouring representations. Deafferentation is likely to result in removal of the inhibitory influences of the deafferented representation over the neighbouring representation, leading to expansion of the latter over the former. In the visual system, GABA has been implicated in plasticity seen after visual deprivations (Jones, 1993). Other mechanisms have been put forward to explain different forms of plasticity. The activation of diffusely projecting brainstem noradrenergic and cholinergic systems have been shown to modulate and enhance cortical responsivity (Kaas & Catani, 1995) and the establishment of correlated activity of pre- and post-synaptic elements (Hebb, 1949) can rapidly strengthen connections in the presence of N-methyl-D-aspartic acid (NMDA) (Bear, Kleinschmidt, & Singer, 1990).

When plastic changes take place over longer time periods, it is possible that new synaptic contacts grow as a consequence of the insult (Kaas, 1994). A likely example of this mechanism is the massive reorganisation reported after long-term dorsal rhizotomy (Pons et al., 1991). In humans, a possible example could be cortical plasticity following stroke or the results reported by Mano et al. (1995; see earlier). However, plasticity seen years after the original lesion can be due to maintenance of processes that took place immediately after deafferentation, and remained active for a long time. This possibility is supported by the recent finding that plastic changes associated with phantom pain in the somatosensory cortex of upper extremity amputees readily disappear soon after brachial plexus blockade (Birbaumer et al., 1997).

Different mechanisms may be involved in different forms of plasticity: NMDA receptors are likely to be involved in these processes since reorganisation of primary somatosensory cortex following peripheral nerve cuts is blocked by injection of NMDA antagonists in monkeys (Garraghty, Muja, & Hoard, 1993). Cholinergic activity is also involved in long-term cortical reorganisation since acetylcholine depression can prevent changes in cortical maps in the adult somatosensory cortex (Juliano et al., 1991; Webster, Hanisch, Dykes, & Biesold, 1991). Glutamate appears to be also involved in cortical plasticity. For example, 8 weeks after cutting the three nerves innervating the hand, glutamate immunoreactivity was unaffected in subcortical regions, but was decreased in the hand representation in SII, suggesting that this may be a prime candidate involved in human cortical plasticity (Conti, Minelli, & Pons, 1996). Glutamate receptors can mediate plastic changes by modulating Ca^{2+} (Anwyl, 1991; Watkins & Collingridge, 1989). Neurotrophins have been also involved in activity-dependent synaptic plasticity. These substances including NGF, BDNF, and neurotrophin-3 (NT-3), are polypeptides important for modification of active synapses and maintenance of connections in the mature CNS (Thoenen et al., 1995). They have been implicated in learning and memory and synaptic plasticity (Lo, Dan, Lo, & Poo, 1995). Whereas NGF is produced by fibroblasts and Schwann cells in the peripheral nervous system, in the CNS NGF and BDNF are primarily produced by neurons. However, mechanical brain injury increases NGF mRNA produced by astrocytes in the area surrounding the lesion (Lindholm, Castren, Kiefer, Zafra, & Thoenen, 1992). Conditions that induce LTP also increase levels of mRNA for BDNF (Castren et al., 1993).

As we have described, a number of mechanisms have been associated with plastic changes in different models. However, little is known about the specific role of each of these mechanisms in human plasticity. Understanding of the mechanisms involved in human plasticity is a necessary step for the design of rational therapeutic approaches to recovery of function.

REFERENCES

Aizawa, H., Inase, M., Mushiake, H., Shima, K., & Tanji, J. (1991). Reorganization of activity in the supplementary motor area associated with motor learning and functional recovery. *Experimental Brain Research, 84,* 668–671.

Allard, T., Clark, S.A., Jenkins, W.M., & Merzenich, M.M. (1991). Reorganization of somatosensory area 3b representations in adult owl monkeys after digital syndactyly. *Journal of Neurophysiology, 66,* 1048–1058.

Anderson, B.J., Li, X., Alcantara, A.A., Isaacs, K.R., Black, J.E., & Greenough, W.T. (1994). Glial hypertrophy is associated with synaptogenesis following motor-skill learning, but not with angiogenesis following exercise. *Glia, 11,* 73–80.

Anwyl, R. (1991). The role of metabotropic receptor in synaptic plasticity. *Trends in Pharmacological Sciences, 12,* 324–326.

Bastings, E.P., & Good, D.C. (1997). Changes in motor cortical representations after stroke: Correlations between clinical observations and magnetic stimulation mapping studies. *Neurology, 48*(Suppl. 2), A414.

Bear, M.F., Kleinschmidt, Q., & Singer, W. (1990). Disruption of experience-dependent synaptic modifications in striate cortex by infusion of an NMDA receptor antagonist. *Journal of Neuroscience, 10,* 909–925.

Benecke, R., Meyer, B.U., & Freund, H.J. (1991). Reorganisation of descending motor pathways in patients after hemispherectomy and severe hemispheric lesions demonstrated by magnetic brain stimulation. *Experimental Brain Research, 83,* 419–426.

Binkofski, F., Seitz, R.J., Arnold, S., Classen, J., Benecke, R., & Freund, H.J. (1996). Thalamic metbolism and corticospinal tract integrity determine motor recovery in stroke. *Annals of Neurology, 39,* 460–470.

Birbaumer, N., Lutzenberger, W., Montoya, P., Larbig, W., Unertl, K., Topfner, S., Grodd, W., Taub, E., & Flor, H. (1997). Effects of regional anesthesia on phantom limb pain are mirrored in changes in cortical reorganization. *Journal of Neuroscience, 17,* 5503–5508.

Bliss, T.V., & Gardner, M.A. (1973). Long-lasting potentiation of synaptic transmission in the dentate area of the unanaesthetized rabbit following stimulation of the perforant path. *Journal of Physiology, 232,* 357–374.

Brasil-Neto, J.P., Cohen, L.G., Pascual-Leone, A., Jabir, F.K., Wall, R.T., & Hallett, M. (1992). Rapid reversible modulation of human motor outputs after transient deafferentation of the forearm: A study with transcranial magnetic stimulation. *Neurology, 42,* 1302–1306.

Brasil-Neto, J.P., Valls-Solé, J., Pascual-Leone, A., Cammarota, A., Amassian, V.E., Cracco, R., Maccabee, P., Cracco, J., Hallett, M., & Cohen, L.G. (1993). Rapid modulation of human cortical motor outputs following ischemic nerve block. *Brain, 116,* 511–525.

Byrne, J.A., & Calford, M.B. (1991). Short-term expansion of receptive fields in rat primary somatosensory cortex after hindpaw digit denervation. *Brain Research, 565,* 218–224.

Calford, M.B., & Tweedale, R. (1988). Immediate and chronic changes in responses of somatosensory cortex in adult flying-fox after digit amputation. *Nature, 332* 446–448.

Calford, M.B., & Tweedale, R. (1991a). Acute changes in cutaneous receptive fields in primary somatosensory cortex after digit denervation in adult flying fox. *Journal of Neurophysiology, 65,* 178–187.

Calford, M.B., & Tweedale, R. (1991b). Immediate expansion of receptive fields of neurons in area 3b of macaque monkeys after digit denervation. *Somatosensory Motor Research, 8,* 249–260.

Caramia, M.D., Iani, C., & Bernardi, G. (1996). Cerebral plasticity after stroke as revealed by ipsilateral responses to magnetic stimulation. *Neuroreport, 7,* 1756–1760.

Carr, L.J., Harrison, L.M., Evans, A.L., & Stephens, J.A. (1993). Patterns of central motor reorganization in hemiplegic cerebral palsy. *Brain, 116,* 1223–1247.

Castren, E., Pitkanen, M., Silvio, J., Parsadanian, A., Lindholm, D., Thoenen, H., & Riekkinen, P.J. (1993). The induction of LTP increases BDNF and NGF mRNA but decreases NT-3 mRNA in the dentate gyrus. *Neuroreport, 4,* 895–898.

Catano, A., Houa, M., Caroyer, J.M., Ducarne, H., & Noel, P. (1995). Magnetic transcranial stimulation in non-haemorrhagic sylvian strokes: Interest of facilitation for early functional prognosis. *Electroencephalography and Clinical Neurophysiology, 97,* 349–354.

Catano, A., Houa, M., Caroyer, J.M., Ducarne, H., & Noel, P. (1996). Magnetic transcranial stimulation in acute stroke: Early excitation threshold and functional prognosis. *Electroencephalography and Clinical Neurophysiology, 101,* 233–239.

Chino, Y.M., Kaas, J.H., Smith, E., Langston, A.L., & Cheng, H. (1992). Rapid reorganization of cortical maps in adult cats following restricted deafferentation in retina. *Vision Research, 32,* 789–796.

Chollet, F., DiPiero, V., Wise, R.J., Brooks, D.J., Dolan, R.J., & Frackowiak, R.S. (1991). The functional anatomy of motor recovery after stroke in humans: A study with positron emission tomography. *Annals of Neurology, 29,* 63–71.

Cohen, L.G., Bandinelli, S., Findlay, T.W., & Hallett, M. (1991). Motor reorganization after upper limb amputation in man. *Brain, 114,* 615–627.

Cohen, L.G., Brasil-Neto, J., Daum, M., Findley, T., Macedo, J., Pascual-Leone, A., & Hallett, M. (1993). Evidence for intracortical plasticity in human motor cortex following amputations. *Society for Neuroscience Abstracts, 19,* 1496.

Cohen, L.G., Celnik, P., Pascual-Leone, A., Corwell, B., Faiz, L., Honda, M., Dambrosia, J., Sadato, N., & Hallett, M. (1997). Functional relevance of cross-modal plasticity in the blind. *Nature, 389,* 180–183.

Cohen, L.G., Gerloff, C., Ikoma, K., & Hallett, M. (1995). Plasticity of motor cortex elicited by training of synchronous movements of hand and shoulder. *Society of Neuroscience Abstracts, 21*(1), 517.

Cohen, L.G., Topka, H., Cole, R.A., & Hallett, M. (1991). Leg paresthesias induced by magnetic brain stimulation in patients with thoracic spinal cord injury. *Neurology*, *41*, 1283–1288.

Cohen, L.G., Zeffiro, T., Bookheimer, S., Wassermann, E.M., Fuhr, P., Matsumoto, J., Toro, C., & Hallett, M. (1991). Reorganization in motor pathways following a large congenital hemispheric lesion: Different motor represention areas for ipsi- and contralateral muscles. *Journal of Physiology*, *438*, 33.

Conti, F., Minelli, A., & Pons, T.P. (1996). Changes in glutamate immunoreactivity in the somatic sensory cortex of adult monkeys induced by nerve cuts. *Journal of Comparative Neurology*, *368*, 503–515.

Cramer, S.C., Nelles, G., Benson, R.R., Kaplan, J.D., Parker, R.A., Kwong, K.K., Kennedy, D.N., Finklestein, S.P., & Rosen, B.R. (1997). Simultaneous measurement of cerebral blood flow and functional MRI signal in the evaluation of stroke recovery mechanisms. *Neurology*, *48*(Suppl. 2), A415.

Cusick, C.G., Wall, J.T., Whiting, J.J., & Wiley, R.G. (1990). Temporal progression of cortical reorganization following nerve injury. *Brain Research*, *537*, 355–358.

Devor, M., & Wall, P. (1981). Effect of peripheral nerve injury on receptive fields of cells in the cat spinal cord. *Journal of Comparative Neurology*, *199*, 277–291.

DeWeerd, P., Gatlass, R., Desimone, R., & Ungerleider, L. (1995). Responses of cells in monkey visual cortex during perceptual filling-in of an artificial scotoma. *Nature*, *377*, 731–734.

Dinse, H.R., Godde, B., Spengler, F., Stauffenberg, B., & Kraft, R. (1994). Hebbian pairing of tactile stimulation: II. Human psychophysics: Changes of tactile spatial and frequency discrimination performance. *Society of Neuroscience Abstracts*, *20*, 1429.

Dinse, H.R., Recanzone, G.H., & Merzenich, M.M. (1993). Alterations in correlated activity parallel ICMS-induced representational plasticity. *Neuroreport*, *5*, 173–176.

Donoghue, J.P., & Sanes, J.N. (1987). Peripheral nerve injury in developing rats reorganizes representation pattern in motor cortex. *Proceedings of the National Academy of Sciences of the United States of America*, *84*, 1123–1126.

Donoghue, J.P., & Sanes, J.N. (1988). Organization of adult motor cortex representation patterns following neonatal forelimb nerve injury in rats. *Journal of Neuroscience*, *8*, 3221–3232.

Donoghue, J.P., Suner, S., & Sanes, J.N. (1990). Dynamic organization of primary motor cortex output to target muscles in adult rats. II. Rapid reorganization following motor nerve lesions. *Experimental Brain Research*, *79*, 492–503.

Dum, R.P., & Strick, P.L. (1991). The origin of corticospinal projections from the premotor areas in the frontal lobe. *Journal of Neuroscience*, *11*, 667–689.

Dykes, R.W., Avendaño, C., & Leclerc, S.S. (1995). Evolution of cortical responsiveness subsequent to multiple forelimb nerve transections: An electrophysiological study in adult cat somatosensory cortex. *Journal of Comparative Neurology*, *354*, 333–344.

Dykes, R.W., Landry, P., Metherate, R., & Hicks, T.P. (1984). Functional role of GABA in cat primary somatosensory cortex: Shaping receptive field of cortical neurons. *Journal of Neurophysiology*, *52*, 1066–1093.

Elbert, T., Pantev, C., Wienbruch, C., Rockstroh, B., & Taub, E. (1995). Increased cortical representation of the fingers of the left hand in string players. *Science*, *270*, 305–370.

Eysel, U.T. (1982). Functional reconnections without new axonal growth in a partially denervated visual relay nucleus. *Nature*, *299*, 442–444.

Fisher, C.M. (1992). Concerning the mechanism of recovery in stroke hemiplegia. *Canadian Journal of the Neurological Sciences*, *19*, 57–63.

Flor, H., Elbert, T., Knecht, S., Wienbruch, C., Pantev, C., Birbaumer, N., Larbig, W., & Taub, E. (1995). Phantom-limb pain as a perceptual correlate of cortical reorganization following arm amputation. *Nature*, *375*, 482–484.

Florence, S.L., & Kaas, J.H. (1995). Large-scale reorganization at multiple levels of the somatosensory pathway follows therapeutic amputation of the hand in monkeys. *Journal of Neuroscience*, *15*, 8083–8095.

Fuhr, P., Cohen, L.G., Dang, N., Findley, T.W., Haghighi, S., Oro, J., & Hallett, M. (1992). Physiological analysis of motor reorganization following lower limb amputation. *Electroencephalography and Clinical Neurophysiology*, *85*, 53–60.

Garraghty, P.E., & Kaas, J.H. (1991). Functional reorganization in adult monkey thalamus after peripheral nerve injury. *Neuroreport*, *2*, 747–750.

Garraghty, P.E., & Kaas, J.H. (1992). Dynamic features of sensory and motor maps. *Current Opinion in Neurobiology*, *2*, 522–527.

Garraghty, P.E., LaChica, E.A., & Kaas, J.H. (1991). Injury-induced reorganization of somatosensory cortex is accompanied by reductions in GABA staining. *Somatosensory Motor Research*, *8*, 347–354.

Garraghty, P.E., Muja, N., & Hoard, R. (1993). NMDA receptor blockade prevents most cortical reorganization after peripheral nerve injury in adult monkeys. *Society of Neuroscience Abstracts*, *19*, 1569.

Glees, P., & Cole, J. (1950). Recovery of skilled motor functions after small repeated lesions of motor cortex in macaque. *Journal of Neurophysiology*, *13*, 137–148.

Grafton, S.T., Mazziotta, J.C., Presty, S., Friston, K.J., Frackowiak, R.S., & Phelps, M.E. (1992). Functional anatomy of human procedural learning determined with regional cerebral blood flow and PET. *Journal of Neuroscience*, *12*, 2542–2548.

Guic, E., Rodriguez, E., Caviedes, P., & Merzenich, M.M. (1993). Use-dependent reorganization of the barrell field in adult rats. *Society of Neuroscience Abstracts*, *19*, 163.

Hall, E.J., Flament, D., Fraser, C., & Lemon, R.N. (1990). Non-invasive brain stimulation reveals reorganized cortical outputs in amputees. *Neuroscience Letters*, *116*, 379–386.

Hallett, M., Cohen, L.G., Pascual-Leone, A., Brasil-Neto, J.P., Wassermann, E.M., & Cammarota, A.N. (1993). Plasticity of the human motor cortex. In A.F. Thilmann, W.Z. Rymer, & D.J. Burke (Eds.), *Spasticity: Mechanisms and management* (pp. 67–81). Berlin: Springer.

He, S.Q., Dum, R.P., & Strick, P.L. (1995). Topographic organization of corticospinal projections from the frontal lobe: Motor areas on the medial surface of the hemisphere. *Journal of Neuroscience*, *15*, 3284–3306.

Heald, A., Bates, D., Cartlidge, N.E., French, J.M., & Miller, S. (1993). Longitudinal study of central motor conduction time following stroke: 2 Central motor conduction measured within 72 h after stroke as a predictor of functional outcome at 12 months. *Brain*, *116*, 1371–1385.

Hebb, D.O. (1949). *Organization of behavior*. New York: J. Wiley.

Heinemann, A.W., Roth, E.J., Cichowski, K., & Bets, H.B. (1987). Multivariate analysis of improvement and outcome following stroke rehabilitation. *Archives of Neurology*, *44*, 1167–1172.

Honda, M., Nagamine, T., Fukuyama, H., Yonekura, Y., Kimura, J., & Shibasaki, H. (1997). Movement-related cortical potentials and regional cerebral blood flow change in patients with stroke after motor recovery. *Journal of the Neurological Sciences*, *146*, 117–126.

Hyvarinen, J., Carlson, S., & Hyvarinen, L. (1981). Early visual deprivation alters modality of neuronal responses in area 19 of monkey cortex. *Neuroscience Letters*, *26*, 239–243.

Jacobs, K.M., & Donoghue, J.P. (1991). Reshaping the cortical motor map by unmasking latent intracortical connections. *Science*, *251*, 944–947.

Jenkins, W.M., & Merzenich, M.M. (1987). Reorganization of neocortical representations after brain injury: A neurophysiological model of the bases of recovery from stroke. *Progress in Brain Research*, *71*, 249–266.

Jenkins, W.M., Merzenich, M.M., Ochs, M.T., Allard, T., & Guic-Robles, E.J. (1990). Functional reorganization of primary somatosensory cortex in adult owl monkeys after behaviorally controlled tactile stimulation. *Journal of Neurophysiology*, *63*, 82–104.

Jones, E.G. (1993). GABAergic neurons and their role in cortical plasticity in primates. *Cerebral Cortex*, *3*, 361–372.

Juliano, S.L., Ma, W., Eslin, D., Juliano, S.L., & Bear, M.F. (1991). Cholinergic depletion prevents expansion of topographic maps in somatosensory cortex, cholinergic manipulation alters stimulus-evoked metabolic activity in cat somatosensory cortex. *Proceedings of the National Academy of Sciences of the United States of America*, *88*, 780–784.

Kaas, J.H. (1994). The reorganization of sensory and motor maps in adult mammals. In M.S. Gazzaniga (Ed.), *The cognitive neurosciences* (pp. 51–71). New York: MIT Press.

Kaas, J.H., & Catania, K.C. (1995). Neurobiology: How cortex reorganizes [news; comment]. *Nature*, *375*, 735–736.

Kaas, J.H., Krubitzer, L.A., Chino, Y.M., Langston, A.L., Polley, E.H., & Blair, N. (1990). Reorganization of retinotopic cortical maps in adult mammals after lesions of the retina. *Science*, *248*, 229–231.

Kaas, J.H., & Pons, T.P. (1988). The somatosensory system of primates. *Comparative Primate Biology*, *4*, 421–468.

Kalaska, J., & Pomeranz, B. (1979). Chronic paw denervation causes an age dependent appearance of novel responses from forearm in "paw cortex" of kittens and adult cats. *Journal of Neurophysiology*, *42*, 618–633.

Kelly-Hayes, M., Wolf, P.A., Kase, C.S., Gresham, G.E., Kannel, W.B., & D'Agostino, R.B. (1989). Time course of functional recovery after stroke: The Framingham Study. *Journal of Neurological Rehabilitation*, *3*, 65–70.

Kew, J.J., Ridding, M.C., Rothwell, J.C., Passingham, R.E., Leigh, P.N., Sooriakumaran, S., Frackowiak, R.S., & Brooks, D.J. (1994). Reorganization of cortical blood flow and transcranial magnetic stimulation maps in human subjects after upper limb amputation. *Journal of Neurophysiology*, 72, 2517–2524.

Kujala, T., Alho, K., Kekoni, J., Hamalainen, H., Reinikainen, K., Salonen, O., Standertskjold, N.C., & Naatanen, R. (1995). Auditory and somatosensory event-related brain potentials in early blind humans. *Experimental Brain Research*, 104, 519–526.

Lee, R.G., & van Donkelaar, P. (1995). Mechanisms underlying functional recovery following stroke. *Canadian Journal of the Neurological Sciences*, 22, 257–263.

Leifer, D., Zhong, J., Fulbright, R.K., Graham, G.D., Prichard, J.W., & Gore, J.C. (1997). Functional MRI reveals changes in brain activation during motor tasks by stroke patients. *Neurology*, 48(Suppl. 2); A415.

Levi-Montalcini, R., & Angeletti, P.U. (1968). Nerve growth factor. *Physiological Reviews*, 48, 534–569.

Levy, W.J., Amassian, V.E., Traad, M., & Cadwell, J. (1990). Focal magnetic coil stimulation reveals motor cortical system reorganized in humans after traumatic quadriplegia. *Brain Research*, 510, 130–134.

Liepert, J., Tegenthoff, M., & Malin, J.P. (1995). Changes of cortical motor area size during immobilization. *Electroencephalography and Clinical Neurophysiology*, 97, 382–386.

Lindholm, D., Castren, E., Kiefer, R., Zafra, F., & Thoenen, H. (1992). Transforming growth factor-beta 1 in the rat brain: Increase after injury and inhibition of astrocyte proliferation. *Journal of Cell Biology*, 117, 395–400.

Lo, D.C., Dan, Y., Lo, Y., & Poo, M.M. (1995). Neurotrophic factors and synaptic plasticity: Plasticity of developing neuromuscular synapses. *Neuron*, 15, 979–981.

Maegaki, Y., Maeoka, Y., & Takeshita, K. (1995). Plasticity of central motor pathways in hemiplegic children with large hemispheric lesions. *Electroencephalography and Clinical Neurophysiology*, 97, S192.

Mano, Y., Nakamuro, T., Tamura, R., Takayanagi, T., Kawanishi, K., Tamai, S., & Mayer, R.F. (1995). Central motor reorganization after anastomosis of the musculocutaneous and intercostal nerves following cervical root avulsion [see comments]. *Annals of Neurology*, 38, 15–20.

Martino, A.M., & Strick, P.L. (1987). Corticospinal projections originate from the arcuate premotor area. *Brain Research*, 404, 307–312.

McBride, E.R., & Rothstein, A.L. (1979). Mental and physical practice and the learning and retention of open and closed skills. *Perceptual and Motor Skills*, 49, 359–365.

Merzenich, M.M., Kaas, J.H., Wall, J.T., Sur, M., Nelson, R.J., & Felleman, D.J. (1983). Progression of change following median nerve section in the cortical representation of the hand in areas 3b and 1 in adult owl and squirrel monkeys. *Neuroscience*, 10, 639–665.

Merzenich, M.M., Nelson, R.J., Stryker, M.P., Cynder, M.S., Shoppmann, A., & Zook, J.M. (1984). Somatosensory cortical map changes following digit amputation in adult monkeys. *Journal of Comparative Neurology*, 224, 591–605.

Merzenich, M.M., Recanzone, G., Jenkins, W.M., Allard, T.T., & Nudo, R.J. (1988). Cortical representational plasticity. In P. Rakic & W. Singer (Eds.), *Neurobiology of neocortex* (pp. 41–67). Bernhard: John Wiley & Sons.

Metzler, J., & Marks, P.S. (1979). Functional changes in cat somatic sensory-motor cortex during short term reversible epidermal blocks. *Brain Research*, 177, 379–383.

Millar, J., Basbaum, A.F., & Wall, P.D. (1976). Restructuring of the somatotopic map and appearance of abnormal neuronal activity in the gracile nucleus after partial deafferentation. *Experimental Neurology*, 50, 658–672.

Misra, U.K., & Kalita, J. (1995). Motor evoked potential changes in ischaemic stroke depend on stroke location. *Journal of Neurological Science*, 134, 67–72.

Mitz, A.R., Godschalk, M., & Wise, S.P. (1991). Learning-dependent neuronal activity in the premotor cortex: Activity during the acquisition of conditional motor associations. *Journal of Neuroscience*, 11, 1855–1872.

Neville, H.J. (1990). Intermodal competition and compensation in development: Evidence from studies of the visual system in congenitally deaf adults. *Annals of the New York Academy of Sciences*, 608, 71–87.

Neville, H.J., & Lawson, D. (1987). Attention to central and peripheral visual space in a movement detection task: An event-related potential and behavioral study: II. Congenitally deaf adults. *Brain Research*, 405, 268–283.

Nissen, M.J., & Bullemer, P. (1987). Attention requirements of learning: Evidence from performance measures. *Cognitive Psychology*, 19, 1–32.

Nudo, R.J., Jenkins, W.M., & Merzenich, M.M. (1990). Repetitive microstimulation alters the cortical representation of movements in adult rats. *Somatosensory and Motor Research*, 7, 463–483.

Nudo, R.J., Milliken, G.W., Jenkins, W.M., & Merzenich, M.M. (1996). Use-dependent alterations of movement representations in primary motor cortex of adult squirrel monkeys. *Journal of Neuroscience*, 16, 785–807.

Nudo, R.J., Wise, B.M., & SiFuentes, F. (1995). Neural substrate for effects of rehabilitation on motor recovery following focal ischemic infarct. *Society of Neuroscience Abstracts*, 21, 517.

Nudo, J.R., Wise, B.M., SiFuentes, F.S., & Milliken, G.W. (1996). Neural substrates for the effects of rehabilitative training on motor recovery after ischemic infarct. *Science*, 272, 1791–1794.

Ostendorf, C.G., & Wolf, S.L. (1981). Effect of forced use of the upper extremity of a hemiplegic patient on changes in function: A single-case design. *Physical Therapy*, 61, 1022–1028.

Pascual-Leone, A., Cammarota, A., Wassermann, E.M., Brasil, N.J., Cohen, L.G., & Hallett, M. (1993). Modulation of motor cortical outputs to the reading hand of braille readers. *Annals of Neurology*, 34, 33–37.

Pascual-Leone, A., Chugani, H.T., Cohen, L.G., Brasil-Neto, J.P., Valls-Solé, J., Wassermann, E.W., Fuhr, P., & Hallett, M. (1992). Reorganization of human motor pathways following hemispherectomy. *Annals of Neurology*, 32, 261.

Pascual-Leone, A., Grafman, J., & Hallett, M. (1994). Modulation of cortical motor output maps during development of implicit and explicit knowledge [see comments]. *Science*, 263, 1287–1289.

Pascual-Leone, A., Nguyet, D., Cohen, L.G., Brasil, N.J., Cammarota, A., & Hallett, M. (1995). Modulation of muscle responses evoked by transcranial magnetic stimulation during the acquisition of new fine motor skills. *Journal of Neurophysiology*, 74, 1037–1045.

Pascual-Leone, A., & Torres, F. (1993). Plasticity of the sensorimotor cortex representation of the reading finger in Braille readers. *Brain*, 116, 39–52.

Pascual-Leone, A., Wassermann, E.M., Sadato, N., & Hallett, M. (1995). The role of reading activity on the modulation of motor cortical outputs to the reading hand in Braille readers. *Annals of Neurology*, 38, 910–915.

Penfield, W., & Boldrey, E. (1937). Somatic motor and sensory representation in the cerebral cortex of man as studied by electrical stimulation. *Brain*, 60, 389–443.

Pons, T.P., Garraghty, P.E., & Mishkin, M. (1988). Lesion-induced plasticity in the second somatosensory cortex of adult macaques. *Proceedings of the National Academy of Sciences of the United States of America*, 85, 5279–5281.

Pons, T.P., Garraghty, P.E., Ommaya, A.K., Kaas, J.H., Taub, E., & Mishkin, M. (1991). Massive cortical reorganization after sensory deafferentation in adult macaques. *Science*, 252, 1857–1860.

Raisman, G., & Field, P.M. (1973). A quantitative investigation of the development of collateral reinnervation after partial deafferentation of the septal nuclei. *Brain Research*, 50, 241–264.

Ramachandran, V.S. (1993). Behavioral and magnetoencephalographic correlates of plasticity in the adult human brain. *Proceedings of the National Academy of Sciences of the United States of America*, 90, 10, 413–420.

Ramachandran, V.S., Stewart, M., & Rogers-Ramachandran, D.C. (1992). Perceptual correlates of massive cortical reorganization. *Neuroreport*, 3, 583–586.

Rapisarda, G., Bastings, E., de Noordhout, A.M., Pennisi, G., & Delwaide, P.J. (1996). Can motor recovery in stroke patients be predicted by early transcranial magnetic stimulation? *Stroke*, 27, 2191–2196.

Rauschecker, J.P. (1995). Compensatory plasticity and sensory substitution in the cerebral cortex. *Trends in Neurosciences*, 18, 36–43.

Recanzone, G.H., Jenkins, W.M., Hradek, G.T., & Merzenich, M.M. (1992). Progressive improvement in discriminative abilities in adult owl monkeys performing a tactile frequency discrimination task. *Journal of Neurophysiology*, 67, 1015–1030.

Recanzone, G.H., Merzenich, M.M., & Dinse, H.R. (1992). Expansion of the cortical representation of a specific skin field in primary somatosensory cortex by intracortical microstimulation. *Cerebral Cortex*, 2, 181–196.

Recanzone, G.H., Merzenich, M.M., & Jenkins, W.M. (1992). Frequency discrimination training engaging a restricted skin surface results in an emergence of a cutaneous response zone in cortical area 3a. *Journal of Neurophysiology*, 67, 1057–1070.

Recanzone, G.H., Merzenich, M.M., Jenkins, W.M., Grajski, K.A., & Dinse, H.R. (1992). Topographic reorganization of the hand representation in cortical area 3b owl monkeys trained in a frequency-discrimination task. *Journal of Neurophysiology*, 67, 1031–1056.

Recanzone, G.H., Merzenich, M.M., & Schreiner, C.E. (1992). Changes in the distributed temporal response properties of SI cortical neurons reflect improvements in performance on a temporally based tactile discrimination task. *Journal of Neurophysiology, 67*, 1071–1091.

Ridding, M.C., & Rothwell, J.C. (1995). Reorganization in human motor cortex. *Canadian Journal of Physiology and Pharmacology, 73*, 218–222.

Rijntjes, M., Tegenthoff, M., Liepert, J., Leonhardt, G., Kotterba, S., Muller, S., Kiebel, S., Malin, J.-P., Diener, H.-C., & Weiller, C. (1997). Cortical reorganization in patients with facial palsy. *Annals of Neurology, 41*, 621–630.

Robertson, D., & Irvine, D.R. (1989). Plasticity of frequency organization in auditory cortex of guinea pigs with partial unilateral deafness. *Journal of Comparative Neurology, 282*, 456–471.

Rossini, P.M., Martino, G., Narici, L., Pasquarelli, A., Peresson, M., Pizzella, V., Tecchio, F., Torrioli, G., & Romani, G.L. (1994). Short-term brain "plasticity" in humans: Transient finger representation changes in sensory cortex somatotopy following ischemic anesthesia. *Brain Research, 642*, 169–177.

Roth, B.J., Cohen, L.G., Hallett, M., Friauf, W., & Basser, P.J. (1990). A theoretical calculation of the electric field induced by magnetic stimulation of a peripheral nerve. *Muscle and Nerve, 13*, 734–741.

Roth, B.J., Saypol, J.M., Hallett, M., & Cohen, L.G. (1991). A theoretical calculation of the electric field induced in the cortex during magnetic stimulation. *Electroencephalography and Clinical Neurophysiology, 81*, 47–56.

Sadato, N., Pascual-Leone, A., Grafman, J., Ibañez, V., Deiber, M.-P., Dold, G., & Hallett, M. (1996). Activation of the primary visual cortex by Braille reading in blind subjects. *Nature, 380*, 526–528.

Sadato, N., Zeffiro, T.A., Campbell, G., Konishi, J., Shibasaki, H., & Hallett, M. (1995). Regional cerebral blood flow changes in motor cortical areas after transient anesthesia of the forearm. *Annals of Neurology, 37*, 74–81.

Sanes, J.N., Suner, S., & Donoghue, J.P. (1990). Dynamic organization of primary motor cortex output to target muscles in adult rats: I. Long-term patterns of reorganization following motor or mixed peripheral nerve lesions. *Experimental Brain Research, 79*, 479–491.

Sanes, J.N., Wang, J., & Donoghue, J.P. (1992). Immediate and delayed changes of rat motor cortical output representation with new forelimb configurations. *Cerebral Cortex, 2*, 141–152.

Schacter, D.L. (1994). Implicit knowledge: New perspectives on unconscious processes. *International Review of Neurobiology, 37*, 271–284.

Schacter, D.L., Chiu, C.Y., & Ochsner, K.N. (1993). Implicit memory. A selective review. *Annual Review of Neuroscience, 16*, 59–82.

Schmid, L.M., Rosa, M.G., & Calford, M.B. (1995). Retinal detachment induces massive immediate reorganization in visual cortex. *Neuroreport, 6*, 1349–1353.

Spengler, F., & Dinse, H.R. (1994). Reversible relocation of representational boundaries of adult rats by intracortical microstimulation. *Neuroreport, 5*, 949–953.

Squire, L.R. (1986). Mechanisms of memory. *Science, 232*, 1612–1619.

Taub, E. (1980). Somatosensory deafferentation research with monkeys: Implications for rehabilitation medicine. In L.P. Ince (Ed.), *Behavioral psychology in rehabilitation medicine: Clinical applications* (pp. 371–401). New York: Williams & Wilkins.

Taub, E., Crago, J.E., Burgio, L.D., Groomes, T.E., Cook, E., DeLuca, S.C., & Miller, N.E. (1994). An operant approach to rehabilitation medicine: Overcoming learned nonuse by shaping. *Journal of the Experimental Analysis of Behavior, 61*, 281–293.

Taub, E., Deluca, S.C., & Crago, J.E. (in press). Effects of motor restriction of an unimpaired upper extremity and training on improving functional tasks and altering brain/behaviors. In J. Toole (Ed.), *Imaging in neurological rehabilitation*. New York: Demos Publications.

Taub, E., Miller, N.E., Novack, T.A., Cook, E., Fleming, W.C., Nepomuceno, C.S., Connell, J.S., & Crago, J.E. (1993). Technique to improve chronic motor deficit after stroke. *Archives of Physical Medicine and Rehabilitation, 74*, 347–354.

Thoenen, H., Korte, M., Carroll, P., Wolf, E., Brem, G., Thoenen, H., & Bonhoeffer, T. (1995). Neurotrophins and neuronal plasticity: Hippocampal long-term potentiation is impaired in mice lacking brain-derived neurotrophic factor. *Science, 270*, 593–598.

Topka, H., Cohen, L.G., Cole, R.A., & Hallett, M. (1991). Reorganization of corticospinal pathways following spinal cord injury. *Neurology, 41*, 1276–1283.

Traversa, R., Cicinelli, P., Bassi, A., Rossini, P.M., & Bernardi, G. (1997). Mapping of motor cortical reorganization after stroke: A brain stimulation study with focal magnetic pulses. *Stroke, 28*, 110–117.

Turton, A., Wroe, S., Trepti, N., Fraser, C., & Lemon, R.N. (1995). Ipsilateral EMG responses to transcranial magnetic stimulation during recovery of arm and hand function after stroke. *Electroencephalography and Clinical Neurophysiology, 97*, S192.

Turton, A., Wroe, S., Trepte, N., Fraser, C., & Lemon, R.N. (1996). Contralateral and ipsilateral EMG responses to transcranial magnetic stimulation during recovery of arm and hand function after stroke. *Electroencephalography and Clinical Neurophysiology, 101*, 316–328.

Uhl, F., Franzen, P., Podreka, I., Steiner, M., & Deecke, L. (1993). Increased regional cerebral blood flow in inferior occipital cortex and cerebellum of early blind humans. *Neuroscience Letters, 150*, 162–164.

Veraart, C., De Volder, A.G., Wanet-Defalque, M.C., Bol, A., Michel, C.H., & Goffinet, A.M. (1990). Glucose utilization in human visual cortex is abnormally elevated in blindness of early onset but decreased in blindness of late onset. *Brain Research, 510*, 115–121.

Wall, J.T. (1988). Development and maintenance of somatotopic maps of the skin: A mosaic hypothesis based on peripheral and central contiguities. *Brain Behavior and Evolution, 31*, 252–268.

Wall, J.T., Felleman, D.J., & Kaas, J.H. (1983). Recovery of normal topography in the somatosensory cortex of monkeys after nerve crush and regeneration. *Science, 221*, 771–773.

Wall, J.T., & Kaas, J.H. (1986). Long-term cortical consequences of reinnervation errors after nerve regeneration in monkeys. *Brain Research, 372*, 400–404.

Wall, J.T., Kaas, J.H., Sur, M., Nelson, R.J., Felleman, D.J., & Merzenich, M.M. (1986). Functional reorganization in somatosensory cortical areas 3b and 1 of adult monkeys after median nerve repair: Possible relationships to sensory recovery in humans. *Journal of Neuroscience, 6*, 218–233.

Wall, P., & Egger, M. (1971). Formation of new connections in adult rat brains after partial denervation. *Nature, 232*, 542–545.

Wassermann, E.M., Chmielowska, J., Gerloff, C., Sadato, N., Mercuri, B., Cohen, L.G., Samii, A., & Hallett, M. (1996). Transcranial magnetic stimulation mapping and PET after good motor recovery from large hemispheric strokes. *Neurology, 46*, A340.

Watkins, J.C., & Collingridge, G.L. (1989). *The NMDA receptor.* Oxford, UK: Oxford University Press.

Webster, H.H., Hanisch, U.K., Dykes, R.W., & Biesold, D. (1991). Basal forebrain lesions with or without reserpine injection inhibit cortical reorganization in rat hindpaw primary somatosensory cortex following sciatic nerve section. *Somatosensory Motor Research, 8*, 327–346.

Weiller, C., Chollet, F., Friston, K.J., Wise, R.J., & Frackowiak, R.S. (1992). Functional reorganization of the brain in recovery from striatocapsular infarction in man. *Annals of Neurology, 31*, 463–472.

White, C.A., Ashton, R., & Lewis, S. (1979). Learning a complex skill: Effect of mental practice, physical practice and imagery ability. *International Journal of Sports Psychology, 10*, 71–78.

Willingham, D.B., Nissen, M.J., & Bullemer, P. (1989). On the development of procedural knowledge. *Journal of Experimental Psychology: Learning Memory, and Cognition, 15*, 1047–1060.

Wolf, S.L., Lecraw, D.E., Barton, L.A., & Jann, B.B. (1989). Forced use of hemiplegic upper extremities to reverse the effect of learned nonuse among chronic stroke and head-injured patients. *Experimental Neurology, 104*, 125–132.

Woolsey, C.N., Erickson, T.C., & Gilson, W.E. (1979). Localization in somatic sensory and motor areas of human cerebral cortex as determined by direct recording of evoked potentials and electrical stimulation. *Journal of Neurosurgery, 51*, 476–506.

Woolsey, C.N., Settlage, P.H., Meyer, D.R., Sencer, W., Hamuy, T.P., & Travis, A.M. (1952). Patterns of localization in precentral and supplementary motor areas and their relation to the concept of a premotor area. *Public Association of Research into Nervous Mental Diseases, 30*, 238–264.

Yang, T.T., Gallen, C.C., Ramachandran, V.S., Cobb, S., Schwartz, B.J., & Bloom, F.E. (1994). Noninvasive detection of cerebral plasticity in adult human somatosensory cortex. *Neuroreport, 5*, 701–704.

9. Neural tissue transplantation

Stephen B. Dunnett

HISTORICAL INTRODUCTION

Transplantation of neural tissues is not new. There is a long tradition in developmental neurobiology of neural grafting in submammalian species, such as for investigation of factors controlling formation of retino-tectal connections in amphibians. Although the use of neural transplantation techniques has only recently become established in mammalian research, even this has a long (albeit sporadic) history.

The first attempts at brain tissue transplantation in mammalian species were attempted a century ago, when Thompson (1890) grafted cortical tissues derived from adult cats into the cortex of adult dogs. Although Thompson concluded on an optimistic note that neural grafting "suggests an interesting field for future research . . . that other experimenters will be rewarded by investigating" (p. 702), this and other studies of the time did not achieve good graft survival.

It was not until a quarter of a century later that Elizabeth Dunn (1917) provided the first convincing evidence of survival of neural grafts in mammals, in a study involving implantation of neocortical tissues into cortical cavities in rats. Even so, only two of nearly sixty transplant operations in this study were viable. Nevertheless, her experimental design was such that she fulfilled by chance two conditions that have subsequently been found to be critical for graft viability: She used embryonic donors and she implanted the tissue into cavities that exposed the ventricular system of the brain.

It took a further half century before the advent of the modern neural transplantation era, commencing in the early 1970s. The intervening decades were scattered with periodic reports of neural tissue grafts surviving in the brains or spinal cords of mammals, in the study of diverse topics including scar formation, immunological competence of the nervous system, tumour growth and neuroendocrine functions (Clemente, 1958; Glees, 1955; Greene & Arnold, 1945; Halasz, Pupp, Uhlarik, & Tima, 1965, Le Gros Clark, 1940, Medawar, 1948). However, these studies did not have a major impact on the neurological science of the time for a variety of reasons: The transplantation techniques were not reliable; the neuroanatomical techniques were not available to characterise adequately the grafts that did survive; and not least because such studies were antithetical to the *Zeitgeist* of the time, formulated most explicitly by Cajal (1928), that all regeneration in the mammalian brain is abortive.

Then, at the turn of the 1970s, two main changes took place. First, Raisman (1969) provided unequivocal evidence in the electron microscope of collateral sprouting in the septum, demonstrating that the adult nervous system can (under at least some conditions) undergo regenerative growth. This study finally overturned the absolutism with which Cajal's dictum was held by his followers. Second, several groups started publishing new models in which viable transplants of neural tissues were achieved reliably and reproducibly (Björklund & Stenevi, 1971; Das & Altman, 1971; Olson & Malmfors, 1970).

CONDITIONS FOR GRAFT VIABILITY

The critical factors for achieving good graft viability were finally specified in detail by Stenevi, Björklund, and Srengaard (1976).

Critical factors

Donor age. In her first demonstration of viable neural grafts, Elizabeth Dunn had employed tissue derived from embryonic donors. This factor has turned out to be crucial. Neural tissues derived from the CNS are viable for transplantation only when taken during limited time windows of embryonic or neonatal development. The precise timing differs for each population of neural cells, and corresponds to the stage around final mitotic division when the fate of the cell is determined and active neuritic outgrowth is just commencing. In practice, the critical time window for each cell population of experimental interest is determined pragmatically (Dunnett & Björklund, 1992; Seiger, 1985).

In recent years there has been an active search for alternative methods to prolong the availability of primary neuronal cells *in vitro*, by hibernation for up to a week in cool storage (Sauer & Brundin, 1991) or by expanding neuronal precursor cells under the action of high concentrations of fibroblast or epidermal growth factors (Gage, Coates, et al., 1995; Svendsen, Clarke, Rosser, & Dunnett, 1996).

Non-CNS tissues. Other sources of tissue for transplantation have less restriction on donor age. Thus, in contrast to CNS tissues, peripheral neuroendocrine tissues will survive transplantation even from adult donors (Freed et al., 1981; Halasz et al., 1965). Tumour tissues grow even more readily (Greene & Arnold, 1945), so that if immortalised cell lines are to be used to supply cells for transplantation then the donor cells must be treated pharmacologically or radiologically in order to render them amitotic (Freed et al., 1990; Kordower, Notter, Yeh, & Gash, 1987) or they may be encapsulated in semipermeable polymer membrane that blocks cell proliferation but still allows secreted molecules to diffuse into the host brain (Hoffman, Breakefield, Short, & Aebischer, 1993; Winn et al., 1994). A third alternative that has recently attracted much interest lies in the prospect of using the new techniques of molecular genetics to design cells for particular transplantation purposes by engineering cells to change their phenotype or to express specific inserted genes (Gage et al., 1987; Horellou et al., 1990; Suhr & Gage, 1993).

Transplantation milieu.   The second critical factor identified by Stenevi et al. (1976) was the need to select a suitable implantation site in the host brain with a rich vascular supply that can provide adequate nourishment of the newly transplanted tissue and its rapid incorporation into the host vascular circulation. A few suitable sites occur naturally, such as the choroid plexus, the ependymal lining of the ventricular system, the choroidal fissure, or the iris in the anterior eye chamber. However, in many situations, it is necessary to implant graft tissues in sites that do not have a rich intrinsic vasculature, so that artificial creation of a suitable site is necessary, either by implanting additional tissues such as iris that will provide a vascular bridge to the target site (Stenevi et al., 1976), or by a delayed cavitation procedure in which a new highly vascularised pial lining reforms over the floor and walls of an artificial cavity (Stenevi, Kromer, Gage, & Björklund, 1985).

The requirement for a specialised enriched vascular supply has diminished in recent years with the advent of transplantation of tissues as dissociated cell suspensions (see later). Nevertheless, the effects of host environment on the survival of transplantation remain of importance, not least because many of the ions, neurochemicals, and free radicals released in response to implantation surgery may have important roles in compromising the viability of implanted neurons (Nakao, 1996).

Additional factors

Other factors may be beneficial to promoting graft viability although are not as critical as the source of donor tissue and the vascular milieu at the implantation site.

Age of host.   It has generally been found that the immature nervous system more readily promotes the survival and incorporation of neural grafts than does the mature host brain (Hallas, Das, & Das, 1980; McLoon & Lund, 1983; Sunde & Zimmer, 1983). Nevertheless, when appropriate transplantation procedures are adopted neural tissues can readily survive and grow in the brains of adult and indeed in very old animals (Gage, Björklund, Stenevi, & Dunnett, 1983).

Target denervation.   Denervation of the host target site may promote the extent of graft-derived ingrowth in some model systems (e.g., Gage & Björklund, 1986) and actually provide a major influence over graft survival in other systems (e.g., Björklund & Stenevi, 1981). It is apparent that the survival of some populations of neuronal cells is dependent on target-derived trophic factors which a lesion may either promote or remove. Nevertheless, neural grafts can survive and grow in the absence of any explicit or implicit disturbance of host neural systems (e.g., Dunnett, Hernandez, Summerfield, Jones, & Arbuthnott, 1988). Thus, there are no general rules relating to the necessity of, or benefit provided by, lesions that cause generalised damage or specific target denervation. Rather, each model situation has to be considered individually.

Trophic factors.   As all developing tissues, the survival, differentiation and growth of neurons and glia in grafts is regulated by their trophic factor environment. For grafts which survive only poorly, explicit delivery of neurotrophic factor molecules can markedly enhance graft survival (Sinclair, Svendsen, Torres, Fawcett, & Dunnett, 1996; Strömberg, Ebendel, Olson, & Hoffer, 1990). One of the major problems of growth factor strategies is however the poor penetration of these molecules into brain. Consequently, a major recent research focus has been developing strategies to engineer neuronal or non-neuronal cells to express growth factor genes (Olson et al., 1990). Engineered cells are then implanted either as trophic grafts to promote the survival or retard progressive lesions (Ernfors et al., 1989; Martínez-Serrano, Fischer, Söderström, Ebendel, & Björklund, 1996), or as co-grafts to promote survival of the primary implant cells (Collier & Springer, 1994; Cunningham, Short, Breakefield, & Bohn, 1994).

Immunological factors.   In contrast to other organs, the brain has long been considered an immunologically privileged site (Medawar, 1948). Although it is now clear that this privilege is only partial (Mason et al., 1986), neural transplantation can readily be achieved between animals of outbred strains that would rapidly reject, e.g., skin grafts. Thus, for all practical purposes, immunological issues do not need to be considered in routine experimental research on neural transplants in standard rodent or monkey colonies. Nevertheless, rejection does take place when extensive major and minor histocompatibility barriers are crossed (Mason et al., 1986), and can be induced by immunological priming (Young, Rao, & Lund, 1989), and so might be a major concern in any clinical application of human transplantation techniques. However, although still at an early stage of research, it appears possible that rejection of neural grafts can be inhibited by a number of strategies, including pharmacological immunosuppression (Brundin, Nilsson, Gage, & Björklund, 1985; Pedersen, Zimmer, & Finsen, 1997), selection of nonimmunogenic neuronal precursor cells prior to transplantation (Bartlett, Rosenfeld, Cheesman, Harrey, & Kerr, 1990), depletion of selective subpopulations of host T lymphocytes mediating the rejection process (Nicholas, Chenelle, Brown, Stefansson, & Arnason, 1990), use of antibodies to mask histocompatibility molecules (Pakzaban, Deacon, Burns,

Dinsmore, & Isacson, 1995), and engineering of donor animals to express species-specific complement regulating factors (Cozzi & White, 1995).

TECHNIQUES OF NEURAL TRANSPLANTATION

Once the critical principles have been identified, a variety of different techniques have been adopted for implantation of neural tissues into the mammalian brain. Rats and mice have been by far the most studied species, and several dozen further studies have recently established that very similar principles apply in primates (human as well as non-human—see Dunnett & Richards, 1990). The present account focuses on the implantation of neural tissues derived from the mammalian CNS and implanted into the brain of adult hosts.

Embryonic donor tissues

Information on the critical developmental time windows for many CNS cell populations is now available. The most systematic data has been derived from the intra-ocular transplantation studies of Olson, Seiger, and colleagues (see Seiger, 1985). In experimental animal studies, embryos of the correct age are routinely obtained from staged pregnant dams and removed by hysterotomy (Dunnett & Björklund, 1992). This need not be a major trauma for the mother, and in the case of primates our mothers routinely recover rapidly and return immediately to their normal breeding cycles. The dissection and handling of different populations of embryonic neural tissues for transplantation is similar to the procedures employed for tissue culture, and many guides are available (e.g., Shahar, de Vellis, Vernadakis, & Haber, 1990).

Implantation of solid tissue pieces

A variety of transplantation procedures have been adopted, depending on the particular experimental issues under investigation (Björklund & Dunnett, 1992). For example, several different strategies for implantation of cortical tissues are illustrated in Figure 9.1. Thus, in each case neocortical tissue is dissected from the brains of late embryonic or neonatal donors (Figure 9.1a). The simplest implantation procedure is to insert a narrow plug of this tissue into the donor cortex (Figure 9.1b; e.g., Smith & Ebner, 1986). This technique only works well for relatively small pieces of donor tissue or immature hosts since the vasculature in the host neocortex is not rich. Better survival of large pieces of embryonic donor tissue in the adult brain can be obtained using a delayed transplantation cavity (Figure 9.1c), as has been employed, for example, for implanting cortical tissues in the prefrontal cortex (Dunnett, Ryan, Levin, Reynolds, & Bunch, 1987; Labbe, Firl, Mufson, & Stein, 1983). The intraocular technique of Olson and Seiger (e.g., Olson, Björklund, & Hoffer, 1984) is illustrated in Figure 9.1d.

Implantation of dissociated cell suspensions

A more flexible transplantation procedure is now also available, based on the implantation of dissociated cell suspensions (Björklund, Stenevi, Schmidt, Dunnett, & Gage, 1983a; Schmidt, Björklund, & Stenevi, 1981). The cell suspension procedure is derived from simplified tissue culture techniques, and involves enzymatic digestion and mechanical dissociation of the cells prior to their stereotaxic injection in small ($2–3\,\mu l$) aliquots into the host brain (Figure 9.1e). Because the cells are dispersed and injected directly into the host parenchyma, they become rapidly incorporated into the host microcapillary network and do not require provision of a specialised implantation site. Consequently, the cell suspension procedure is considerably more flexible than solid graft procedures, since it permits single or multiple graft deposits to be placed at will, and with minimal trauma, throughout the host neuraxis. Nevertheless, there remain experimental situations which favour use of solid grafts, e.g., when the protocol requires the placement of electrodes, drugs or anatomical tracers into visible or clearly delimited transplant tissues.

Implantation of cultured and engineered cells

Increasingly, cells are grown, maintained, and manipulated *in vitro* prior to implantation. One advantage of culturing is to simply prolong the availability of cells for transplantation during which time additional safety and selection procedures may be undertaken. Second, the technology is developing for isolating and proliferating neuronal stem cells in the presence of high concentrations of growth factor (Reynolds & Weiss, 1992) which can allow massive expansion of cells from a small numbers of precursors, to yield differentiated neurons and glia for transplantation in different experimental models of disease (Gage, Ray, & Fisher, 1995; Lundberg, Martinez-Serrano, Cattaneo, McKay, & Björklund, 1997). Third, diverse procedures now exist for engineering both neuronal and non-neuronal cells to express particular gene products or cellular phenotypes (Senut et al., 1995). The goal is to achieve a point where cells can be explicitly designed for transplantation, exhibiting a precisely defined list of phenotypic features and available on demand. Although that stage is clearly a long way off, this field is showing very rapid advances.

Once the cells are identified and made available, they may be implanted either as a dissociated cell suspension. Conversely, in situations where the cells might be expected to be rejected (and so need protection from the host brain) or may proliferate as tumours (and so the host brain itself needs protection from uncontrolled growth of the graft) the cells may be encapsulated in semipermeable polymer tubes prior to implantation of stereotaxic implantation of the capsule either into brain ventricle or the parenchyma (Hoffman et al., 1993; Winn et al., 1994).

ANATOMICAL AND BIOCHEMICAL INDICES OF GROWTH

Examples in the hippocampus

Neural grafts not only survive transplantation to the adult brain, they can reform extensive afferent and efferent connections with

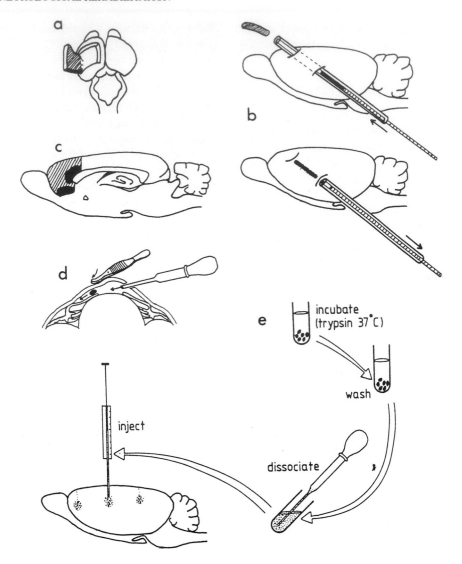

Figure 9.1. Alternative techniques for implanting embryonic cortical tissues into the neocortex. See text for details. (From Dunnett, 1990, with permission from MIT press.)

the host. Such effects have now been demonstrated in many different graft models and neuroanatomical systems. Some of the clearest illustrations of graft growth come from studies in the hippocampal system. The normal hippocampus manifests a precise laminar organisation in terms of the distribution both of pyramidal and granule cells in two interlocked C-shaped tubes, and of a variety of neurotransmitter-specific markers each with its own distinctive laminar pattern. For example, the distribution of cholinergic fibres visualised with the acetylcholinesterase (AChE) enzyme stain is shown in Figure 9.2a. The cholinergic input to the hippocampus originates in the septal nucleus; a lesion of the fimbria-fornix transects the septo-hippocampal fibre bundle and results in a total loss of AChE fibres in the hippocampus. As shown in Figure 9.2b, implantation of embryonic septal suspension into the fimbria-fornix lesioned hippocampus gives rise to an AChE positive fibre reinnervation which re-establishes a laminar pattern within the host hippocampus

that accurately reproduces the fibre distribution of the intact brain.

The capacity of septal grafts to provide a new cholinergic reinnervation of the denervated hippocampus was first demonstrated by using solid septal grafts implanted into fimbria-fornix or posterior cortical cavities (Björklund & Stenevi, 1977), and the same effect has subsequently been confirmed using septal cell suspension grafts (Schmidt et al., 1981).

In fact, the fimbria-fornix lesion transects all subcortical inputs to the hippocampus, including noradrenaline, serotonin, and GABA systems as well as the cholinergic inputs from the septum. Björklund, Stenevi, and Svergaard (1976) therefore compared the effects of implantation of different populations of brainstem monoamine neurones, and found that dopaminergic, noradrenergic and serotonergic grafts would each survive well, and in each case established a new fibre input that was patterned appropriately for the particular population of monoaminergic

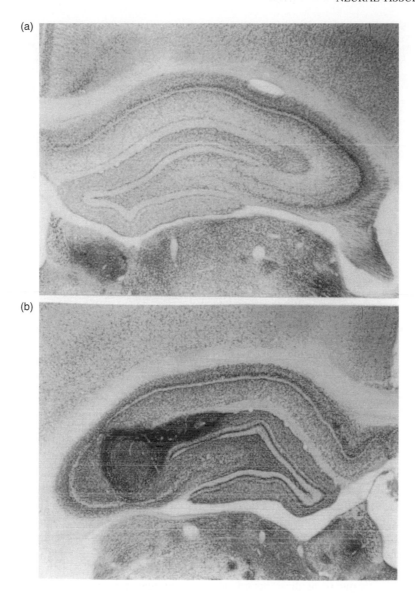

Figure 9.2. Cholinergic innervation of the hippocampus (a) The normal innervation in an intact animal. Note regular laminar input into the hippocampus. (b) Septal graft in the hippocampus of a rat with a fimbria-fornix lesion. The lesion has destroyed the intrinsic innervation, and all cholinergic fibre staining in the hippocampus is derived from the graft. Note that the graft-derived fibres re-establish the normal laminar pattern of innervation. AChE stain.

cells implanted. Several studies have used immunocytochemical visualisation at the ultrastructural level to demonstrate that the graft-derived axons establish morphologically appropriate synaptic contacts with host hippocampal (Clarke, Gage, & Björklund, 1986) and cortical (Clarke & Dunnett, 1986; see Figure 9.3) neurons.

When neural grafts are implanted in the absence of a fimbria-fornix lesion in this model system, fibre growth into the hippocampus is much reduced. Thus, it is necessary to postulate that the lesion-induced denervation of the hippocampus induces release of a variety of trophic and guidance mechanisms that both stimulate regrowth of axons from grafted cells and direct that growth towards the appropriate targets for each individual neurotransmitter-specific population of neurons (Björklund & Stenevi, 1981).

In parallel with these anatomical studies, biochemical indices have also been used to demonstrate the extent of the lesions, to confirm that only limited regeneration takes place spontaneously, and to quantify the extent of regenerative reinnervation derived from different populations of neural transplants. For example, cholinergic reinnervation of the hippocampus by septal grafts has been monitored by quantitation of activity of the marker enzyme choline acetyltransferase which is depleted in excess of 90% by the lesions and restored back to normal levels over 3–6 months following transplantation (Björklund, Stenevi, Schmidt, Dunnett, & Gage, 1983c).

More recently, intracerebral dialysis has been used to demonstrate that the hippocampal reinnervation from septal, locus coeruleus, and raphe grafts is capable of restoring stimulus-dependent acetylcholine, noradrenaline, and serotonin release,

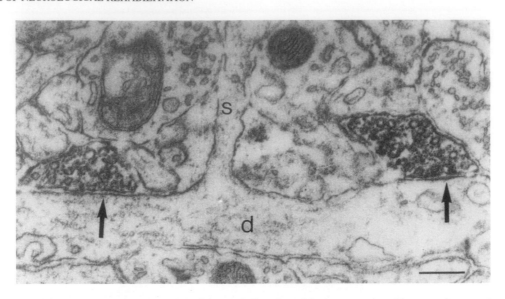

Figure 9.3. Electron micrograph of two cholinergic terminals derived from a cholinergic graft in the neocortex making synaptic connections (arrows) with the dendrite of a host cortical pyramidal neuron. The cholinergic terminals are identified by choline acetyltransferase immunostaining. Abbreviations: d, dendrite; s, spine. Scale bar 250 nm. (From Clarke & Dunnett, 1986, 'Ultrastructural organisation of choline acetyltransferase-immunoreactive fibres innervating the neocortex from embryonic ventral forebrain grafts', *Journal of Comparative Neurology*, *250*, 192–205. Copyright © 1986 Wiley-Liss, Inc. Reprinted by permission of Wiley-Liss Inc., a subsidiary of John Wiley & Sons, Inc.)

respectively, and that the grafts are functionally incorporated into the host neuronal circuitry (Cenci, Nilsson, Kalén, & Björklund, 1993; Leanza, Nilsson, & Björklund, 1993).

Examples in the striatum

A second system that has received considerable attention is the neostriatum. One reason for this interest relates to the fact that several neurodegenerative diseases, notably Parkinson's and Huntington's diseases, which involve loss of identified neural elements within neostriatal circuitries. Indeed, the greatest advances towards development of viable clinical transplantation therapies have been made with regard to these disorders (see later).

Striatal and nigrostriatal lesions. Neurotoxic lesions of the neostriatum can reproduce the critical features of these human neurodegenerative diseases in experimental animals. Thus injection of the toxins 6-hydroxydopamine (6-OHDA) or 1-methyl-4-phenyl-1,2,3,6-tetrahydropyridine (MPTP) in rats or monkeys produces experimental parkinsonism, involving profound degeneration of dopamine neurons of the substantia nigra and loss of the dopaminergic innervation of the neostriatum. Conversely, injection of excitotoxins (e.g., ibotenic or quinolinic acid) or metabolic toxins (e.g., malonate, 3-nitroproprionic acid) into the striatum of rats or monkeys produces experimental chorea, involving profound degeneration of intrinsic neurones of the neostriatum. These two syndromes are each associated with impairments in motor control similar to those observed in the respective human diseases.

Nigral grafts. Dopamine neurones derived from the embryonic substantia nigra survive transplantation to the host neostriatum and provide an extensive dopaminergic reinnervation of the dopamine denervated target areas in rats and monkeys (Björklund, Dunnett, Stenevi, Lewis, & Iversen, 1980; Björklund, Stenevi, Schmidt, Dunnett, & Gage, 1983b; Redmond et al., 1986). As in the cholinergic models in the hippocampus, the dopaminergic axons from nigral grafts establish synaptic connections with the appropriate population of target neurones, i.e., onto the necks of spines of medium spiny neurons in the host striatum (Freund et al., 1985). The reinnervation is incorporated into the host neuronal circuitry: Dopamine release is seen to be appropriately modulated in response to pharmacological or physiological stimuli *in vivo* (Strecker et al., 1987; Zetterström et al., 1986).

Although it is clear that nigral grafts reinnervate the host brain, it remains unclear to what extent these grafts are incorporated into the host circuitry or regulated by ongoing activity in the host brain. There are two possible levels at which the host brain could regulate the grafts. First, electrophysiological studies have indicated that nigral grafts do receive a limited input from a number of neuronal systems that innervate both the nigra and the striatum, including the locus coeruleus, raphe nucleus, and (to a very limited extent) the neocortex (Arbuthnott, Dunnett, & McLeod, 1985). Second, the dopaminergic nerve terminals may come under local regulation from host striatal interneurons. Thus, opiate receptors are seen to be located on graft-derived dopaminergic terminals in the striatum, similar to the normal nigrostriatal innervation, suggesting that dopamine synthesis and release may be under presynaptic control of enkephalinergic striatal interneurons (Sirinathsinghji & Dunnett, 1989).

Nevertheless the grafts are implanted into an "ectopic" location (i.e., into the target site rather than into the normal location of intrinsic nigral dopamine neurons in the ventral mesencephalon) and so it is unlikely that intrastriatal nigral grafts will ever

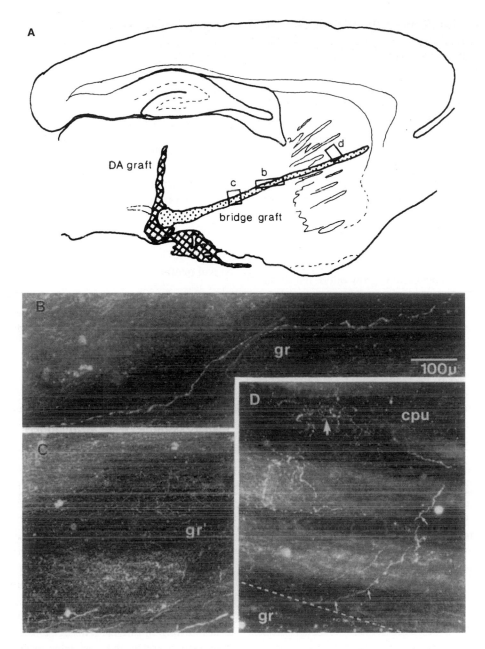

Figure 9.4. A Camera lucida drawing of a nigral graft implanted in the substantia nigra, and a bridge co-graft of striatal tissue implanted obliquely to connect the nigra graft with the distant striatal target. Photomicrographs of boxes marked b, c, d are shown at higher magnification in B, C, and D respectively. B–D Tyrosine hydroxylase stain to show dopamine fibres growing out of the nigral graft along the full length of the bridge graft (gr) and sprouting into the host caudate putamen (cpu). (A from Dunnett et al., 1989, with permission from Springer-Verlag.)

fully restore neuronal circuitries after experimental or neurodegenerative lesions. Nigral grafts can readily be implanted into the vicinity of the host substantia nigra, but in this site the grafted neurons are unable to provide any extensive ingrowth into the host brain (Björklund et al., 1983b). The logical interpretation is that vigorous and directed dopaminergic axon growth is dependent on striatal trophic and guidance factors that are not available in the adult substantia nigra. Accordingly, although they survive, nigral grafts implanted into the nigra show no outgrowth and have no detectable functional effects whatsoever

on the host animal. In order to circumvent this limitation, recent studies have demonstrated the feasibility of making co-grafts (see Figure 9.4): implanting nigral cells into a homotopic nigral site but in combination with a bridge graft of peripheral nerve or target tissues that acts as a substrate to guide and induce extensive dopaminergic axonal growth to distant striatal targets (Aguayo, Björklund, Stenevi, & Carlstedt, 1984; Brecknell et al., 1996; Dunnett, Rogers, & Richards, 1989).

Striatal grafts.   A similar level of anatomical and biochemical analysis has been applied to neostriatal grafts implanted into rats and monkeys with model chorea (Björklund et al., 1994; Hantraye, Riche, Mazière, & Isacson, 1992; Isacson, Brundin, Gage, & Björklund, 1985; Isacson et al., 1987; Isacson, Riche, Hantraye, Sofroniew, & Mazière, 1989). In this case of course the graft tissue is more complex in its internal organisation, but all cell types of the normal striatum (whether defined by immunohistochemical or morphological criteria) are contained within the striatal grafts (Björklund et al., 1994; DiFiglia, Schiff, & Deckel, 1988; Graybiel, Liu, & Dunnett, 1989).

More remarkable has been the demonstration of extensive afferent and efferent connectivity between striatal grafts and the host brain. Thus, all normal afferents to the striatum from neocortex, thalamus, substantia nigra, and raphe are seen to sprout, innervate the grafted striatal tissue, and make synaptic connections with grafted striatal medium spiny neurons (Clarke & Dunnett, 1993; Wictorin & Björklund, 1989; Wictorin et al., 1988). Conversely, efferent connections grow out of the striatal grafts to reach the two major striatal targets, the globus pallidus and substantia nigra pars reticulata (Wictorin, 1992). GABA release, measured by *in vivo* push–pull perfusion, is released by these efferent terminals in the globus pallidus and substantia nigra, and is responsive to pharmacologically induced changes in activity of host afferents to the striatal grafts (Sirinathsinghji, Dunnett, Isacson, Clarke, & Björklund, 1988).

A major difference between the nigral and striatal grafts is that in the latter case the grafts are made homotopically, yet this striatal placement is in close proximity to the first order targets in the globus pallidus. Thus, the capacity of striatal grafts to innervate their normal targets when placed homotopically may reflect a process of growth in a series of small steps from one target to another without requiring trophic or guidance factors to act over long distances at any stage, as would be necessary for nigrostriatal reconstruction with nigral grafts. At least in this one model system, striatal grafts appear to become reciprocally incorporated into the host neural circuitry (Dunnett & Björklund, 1994b).

Other model systems

Since the 1980s many other model systems for neural transplantation have been subject to equally detailed evaluation. These include:

- complex, topographically organised systems such as the somatosensory or visual cortices, retino-tectal connections, or cerebellum
- specific and diffuse regulatory pathways in the spinal cord
- neuroendocrine and other hypothalamic models involving deficiencies of growth hormones, gonadotrophins, circadian rhythmicity, etc
- glial cells, particularly those involved in remyelination and wound repair
- implantation of cells to secrete drugs, trophic factors, or other diffuse release neurochemical systems.

Space does not permit adequate accounts to be given here. Good reviews of these other model systems can be found in the proceedings of several recent symposia, in particular: Björklund & Stenevi, 1985; Dunnett & Björklund, 1994a; Dunnett & Richards, 1990; Gash & Sladek, 1988).

FUNCTIONAL CAPACITY OF NEURAL GRAFTS

In parallel with the demonstration of survival and connectivity of neural grafts, it has been important to ask: "To what extent are the grafts functional?" In particular, it has been of interest to determine the extent to which implanted neurons may functionally replace those lost though genetic deficit, trauma, or neurodegenerative disease, and thereby to repair the damage.

Nigral grafts

The first system to be studied in detail functionally was the 6-OHDA lesioned rat model of parkinsonism. Several distinct features of this model make it ideal for the study of the question of graft viability:

- the neurotoxin 6-OHDA for selective lesion of the nigrostriatal system
- selective pharmacological agents to influence synthesis, storage, release, receptor binding, and re-uptake mechanisms in dopamine neurons
- the availability of catecholamine histofluorescence and sensitive immunohistochemical techniques to visualise the effectiveness of lesions and viability of the grafts
- sensitive biochemical assays to measure dopamine and its metabolites, both post mortem and by *in vivo* dialysis
- simple and sensitive behavioural tests to quantify the effects of unilateral or bilateral nigrostriatal lesions.

Unilateral 6-OHDA lesions of the nigrostriatal bundle induce postural deficits to the side of the lesion. If the animal is activated either by stress or stimulant drugs (e.g., amphetamine), the bias and locomotor activation combine to produce head-to-tail turning in circles. This response (known as "rotation") is easy to quantify and correlates closely with the degree of dopamine depletion induced by the lesion (Dunnett, Hernandez, et al., 1988; Hefti, Melamed, Sahakian, & Wurtman, 1980). Nigral grafts reverse this deficit (see Figure 9.5). This is true whether the grafts are implanted into the lateral ventricle medial to the denervated striatum, as solid pieces into a delayed cavity dorsal to the striatum, or as dissociated cell suspensions directly into the striatum (Björklund et al., 1980; Dunnett, Björklund, Schmidt, Stenevi, & Iversen, 1983a; Perlow et al., 1979). Recovery develops over 2–3 months, which corresponds to the time taken for extensive ingrowth to become established, and the asymptotic level of recovery correlates with the extent of ingrowth determined in post mortem histology or biochemistry (Björklund et al., 1980; Dunnett, Hernandez, et al., 1988; Schmidt, Björklund, Stenevi, Dunnett, & Gage, 1983). Conversely, implants of other (non-dopaminergic) populations of

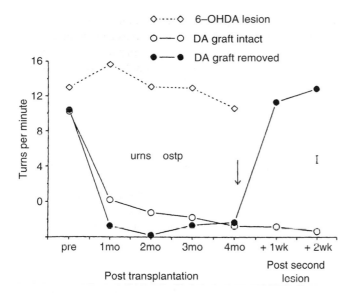

Figure 9.5. Recovery of motor asymmetry following transplantation of nigra grafts. Rats with unilateral 6-OHDA lesions rotate under amphetamine at a rate of 10–12 turns/min (diamonds). Rotation is compensated in rats with nigra grafts 1–2 months after transplantation (open and closed circles). Removal of the graft (arrow) 4 months later results in immediate reinstatement of the initial lesion deficit (filled circles). (Data from Dunnett, Hernandez, et al., 1988.)

embryonic cells have no effects whatsoever on the rotation deficit, which indicates that the recovery induced by nigra grafts is by a specific dopaminergic mechanism (Dunnett, Hernandez, et al., 1988).

Other simple behaviours also recover in this model, such as the contralateral neglect of somatosensory stimuli in rats with unilateral lesions, or the akinesia induced by bilateral lesions (Dunnett et al., 1983a,b). However, other behavioural deficits do not recover. In particular nigral grafts do not restore deficits in complex sensorimotor tests or skilled paw reaching that follow unilateral lesions or the eating and drinking deficits after bilateral lesions (Dunnett et al 1983b; Dunnett, Whishaw, Rogers, & Jones, 1987; Mandel, Brundin, & Björklund, 1990). The most parsimonious interpretation of this difference is that recovery is only achieved on tests that reflect net dopaminergic activation of the neostriatum, but not on tests that are dependent upon patterned nigrostriatal activity. Only in the former case can function be restored by an ectopic graft. It can be hypothesised that recovery on the latter class of tests could only be achieved by grafts that reconstruct the nigrostriatal circuitry (as in the bridge co-graft technique described earlier; see Figure 9.4), but this question awaits experimental investigation.

Striatal grafts

Excitotoxic lesions of the striatum induce deficits on a similar range of tests as do 6-OHDA lesions, although of course through destruction of different cell populations. It might be anticipated a priori that it would be more difficult to restore the extensive cellular destruction of all striatal cell types induced by ibotenic

acid than the loss of a single population of dopamine neurons. In fact the opposite is the case. Striatal grafts reverse not only the rotation deficits in rats with unilateral ibotenic acid lesions, but also the deficits in the control of skilled reaching movements with the contralateral paw (Björklund et al., 1994; Dunnett, Isacson, Sirinathsinghji, Clarke, & Björklund, 1988). A key difference between the striatal and nigral grafts is that the striatal grafts are implanted into a homotopic site and develop a full set of afferent and efferent connections with the host brain, whereas the nigral grafts are implanted into an ectopic site. Thus the behavioural results support the hypothesis, suggested in the previous paragraph, that the degree of recovery is dependent upon the degree to which the graft is fully incorporated into the host neuronal circuitry (Dunnett, 1995).

Cholinergic grafts

Like the dopaminergic innervation of the neostriatum, the cholinergic inputs to the hippocampus and neocortex provide a relatively diffuse regulation of the functional activity in their targets. The hippocampus is of course implicated in more cognitive spatial and memory functions, which have been a major focus of investigation also in the context of neural transplants.

Acetylcholine and fimbria-fornix lesions. The first demonstration that neural grafts could influence learned functions, as opposed to simple maze behaviours, was the demonstration that cholinergic grafts implanted in the hippocampus could ameliorate deficits induced by fimbria-fornix lesions in T-maze alternation learning (Dunnett, Low, Iversen, Stenevi, & Björklund, 1982). Subsequent studies have demonstrated recovery in a variety of other spatial and non-spatial learning tasks including the eight-arm radial maze (Hodges et al., 1991; Hodges, Allen, Sinden, Lantos, & Gray, 1990), the Morris water maze (Hodges et al., 1996; Nilsson, Shapiro, Olton, Gage, & Björklund, 1987; Sinden, Hodges, & Gray, 1995), and operant differential reinforcement of low rates of responding schedules (Dunnett, Martel, Rogers, & Finger, 1990).

Acetylcholine and ageing. One reason for particular interest in the cognitive effects of cholinergic grafts has been the association of decline in this system with the cognitive impairments of ageing and dementia (Bartus, Dean, Beer, & Lippa, 1982; Coyle, Price, & DeLong, 1983). Thus aged rats manifest impairments in spatial learning tasks such as the Morris water maze (Gage, Dunnett, & Björklund, 1984) and in more specific tests of short-term memory, such as operant delayed matching and non-matching tests (Dunnett, Evenden, & Iversen, 1988). Although the aged brain is associated with decline in many different neurotransmitter systems, cholinergic rich grafts implanted into the hippocampus have been demonstrated to ameliorate deficits in both of these particular spatial memory tasks (Dunnett, Badman, Rogers, Everden, & Iversen, 1988; Gage, Björklund, Stenevi, Dunnett, & Kelly, 1984), suggesting that the cholinergic decline is indeed fundamental to this particular functional deficit of old animals.

This does not of course imply that the cholinergic deficit is central to all deficits in old rats. Rather, it has become apparent that ageing is not a unitary process. Heterogeneity of the pattern of symptoms in old animals reflects differences in the profile of underlying neurodegenerative and other physical changes taking place (Gage, Dunnett, & Björklund, 1989). Consequently, cholinergic grafts are effective for spatial memory problems associated with hippocampal dysfunction, whereas different treatments need to be considered for other symptoms manifested by the old animals. For example, passive avoidance deficits in old rats have been found to be responsive to noradrenergic grafts implanted in the hippocampus (Collier, Gash, & Sladek, 1988), whereas some of the old animals' difficulties with motor coordination and balance have benefited both from pharmacological treatment with dopaminergic agonists (Marshall & Berrios, 1979) and from dopaminergic rich transplants into the neostriatum (Gage, Dunnett, Stenevi, & Björklund, 1983).

MECHANISMS OF GRAFT FUNCTION

In the early studies of the functional effects of grafts it was natural to assume that, because the reformation of graft–host connections was observed anatomically, such regrowth provided the basis for functional recovery in the grafted animals. It has since become apparent that this assumption is naive. In fact, with more detailed analysis, it is now clear that grafts can exert functional influences over the behaviour of the host animal by a variety of more or less specific mechanisms (Björklund et al., 1987; Dunnett & Björklund, 1994b):

- non-specific or negative effects of surgery
- acute trophic stimulation of recovery
- chronic diffuse release of neurochemicals (including neurohormones and neurotrophic factors)
- diffuse reinnervation of the host brain
- bridge mechanisms
- reciprocal graft–host reinnervation
- full reconstruction of damaged circuitry.

Several of these mechanisms have been implicit in the preceding description of anatomical integration and functional recovery in grafted animals, but they warrant specification and reconsideration in more detail.

Non-specific effects of surgery

The surgical intervention or graft treatment may induce non-specific disturbance of host function. Such influences are most obvious when they are negative, such as the implantation procedure inducing an additional lesion, or growth of the graft tissue inducing tumour-like compression of the host tissue (e.g., Dunnett & Björklund, 1994b; Ridley, Baker, & Fine, 1988).

Such a mechanism may also be proposed to account for positive effects. For example, caudate lesions were at one stage considered a beneficial therapy for Parkinson's disease (Meyers, 1951), and it has been proposed that (in the light of the grafts

not surviving) the benefits provided by adrenal grafts in the first clinical trials may be due to the cavitations in the caudate nucleus that were made to receive the graft, rather than to the presence of graft tissue *per se*. Along similar lines certain surgical techniques can result in an incomplete ("leaky") blood–brain barrier, which may have the beneficial side-effect of assisting penetration of therapeutic drugs into the brain (Rosenstein, 1987; Rosenstein & Brightman, 1983).

Acute trophic stimulation of recovery

Adrenal medulla grafts have been found to stimulate sprouting of host catecholamine fibres in animals with incomplete nigrostriatal lesions (Bohn, Cupit, Marciano, & Gash, 1987). This is one example of a situation where grafts secrete trophic or other factors that facilitate regenerative and recovery mechanisms in the damaged brain. One way to test for this possibility was suggested by LeVere and LeVere (1985): to lesion the graft once recovery has stabilised. If the mechanism of graft action is an acute stimulation of recovery processes, then graft removal should not effect established recovery. Thus, for example grafts of cortical or hippocampal tissues have been reported to reverse complex learning deficits following aspirative lesions of the cortex or hippocampus respectively (Labbe et al., 1983; Woodruff, Baisden, Whittington, & Benson, 1987). However, in each case recovery appeared to take place more rapidly than could be accounted for by the regrowth of graft–host connectivity. Both groups have subsequently demonstrated that graft removal leaves recovery intact (Stein, 1987; Woodruff, Baisden, & Nonneman, 1990). Consequently, in each case the grafts stimulated recovery but did not provide the critical neural substrate of that recovery.

Chronic diffuse release of neurochemicals

The most widely postulated mechanism for many graft effects is that the grafts provide a reservoir for the diffuse secretion of deficient neurochemicals. This mechanism was early postulated for adrenal medulla grafts following the observation of diffuse increase of catecholamines in the host striatum in the absence of detectable fibre outgrowth from the grafts (Freed et al., 1981, 1983). Functional recovery on apomorphine rotation tests is then readily explained in terms of diffusing catecholamines having the capacity to down-regulate receptor supersensitivity.

A simple diffuse release mechanisms was also considered to be sufficient to achieve recovery on simple neuroendocrine functions. Thus, diffuse release of vasopressin (antidiuretic hormone) or releasing hormone (GnRH) from implanted hypothalamic neurons may make reversal of genetic diuretic or gonadotrophin deficiencies a relatively simple process. Indeed, hypothalamic grafts do reverse the neuroendocrine deficits and re-establish normal sexual development in the hypogonadal mouse (Gibson et al., 1984; Gibson, Silverman, & Silverman, 1990), although the report of functional recovery in the vasopressin-deficient Brattleboro mutant (Gash, Sladek,

& Sladek, 1980) has proved more difficult to replicate. Nevertheless, anatomical analysis of these grafts suggest not that they simply diffuse neurohormones into the brain neuropil, CSF, or circulation, but rather that the grafts regenerate axons that establish precise specialised contacts with the fenestrated capillaries of the median eminence (Silverman, Zimmerman, Kokoris, & Gibson, 1986; Wiegand & Gash, 1987), exactly as in the normal brain.

These observations warn not just that less-specific mechanisms may apply to complex patterns of recovery, but conversely that neural grafts may establish precise, well-organised and appropriate patterns of connection with the host brain even if one believes that a simpler mechanism would suffice.

Nevertheless to the extent that graft effects are mediated by diffuse release mechanisms, this offers powerful new alternatives to the use of foetal tissues for transplantation. Strategies of *in vivo* and *ex vivo* engineering of both neuronal and non-neuronal cells with genes, and alternative polymer and encapsulation delivery devices, all depend upon the transplanted cells exerting their effects via secretion of deficient neurochemicals, neurohormones, or growth factors rather than via explicit repair by replacement of damaged neurons.

Diffuse reinnervation of the host brain

Dopaminergic grafts in the striatum and cholinergic grafts in the hippocampus are the most obvious candidates for diffuse reinnervation mechanisms. As described previously, the systematic pattern of incomplete recovery achieved by such grafts suggests that they do not become fully integrated into the normal neuronal circuitry. Conversely, it has proved more difficult to establish whether axonal reinnervation of their targets is a necessary element in the functional recovery sustained by nigral or cholinergic grafts, or whether they function simply by diffuse release mechanisms.

The strongest argument for the importance of reformation of graft–host connections comes from differences between the efficacy of nigral grafts on the one hand and adrenal grafts or alternative dopamine delivery systems on the other (Dunnett & Björklund, 1994b). Since adrenal grafts are believed to function by diffuse release of deficient catecholamines (Freed et al., 1983; Strömberg, Herrera-Marschitz, Ungerstedt, Ebendal, & Olson, 1985), nigral grafts would be expected to provide a similar pattern of functional recovery if they worked by a similar mechanism. In fact, nigral grafts provide more effective recovery on a broader range of deficits than adrenal grafts or other dopamine-secreting implants (Brown & Dunnett, 1989; Freed, 1983; Lindvall, 1989). Moreover, the pattern of recovery depends on the precise area of striatum that is reinnervated and the extent of recovery correlates highly with the extent of reinnervation of the critical area rather than, e.g., the number of catecholamine-secreting neurons or the size of the grafts (Björklund et al., 1980). These observations all suggest that reinnervation rather than just a diffuse release mechanism is important.

Bridge mechanisms

Bridge mechanisms have already been indicated in the context of promotion of nigrostriatal regrowth over long distances from nigral grafts (see Figure 9.4). More generally, bridge grafts have been used to promote sprouting and regrowth of host axons to distant targets that they would not spontaneously reinnervate.

One type of bridge has taken account of the fact that in the PNS axons will readily regenerate over long distances along peripheral nerves. For example, David and Aguayo (1981) have demonstrated that peripheral nerve grafts can provide an effective substrate for extensive growth of CNS axons when implanted into the CNS. This suggests that the paucity of spontaneous regeneration in the adult mammalian CNS is attributable to the absence of suitable substrates for extensive regenerative growth, rather than to an intrinsic incapacity of CNS neurons for regeneration.

Such observations have stimulated attempts to identify the molecular and cellular substrates that will promote elongation of CNS axons over long distances. For example filters coated with cultures of glial cells can provide a viable surface for growth of callosal axons across the midline in genetically acallosal mice (Smith & Ebner, 1986) or across wound cavities in the CNS (Kromer & Cornbrooks, 1985), and direct intracerebral injections of laminin have been seen to stimulate directed axonal growth from transplanted neurons (Zhou & Azmitia, 1988).

A more complex type of bridge has been investigated in the context of transection of the septo-hippocampal fibres by fimbria-fornix lesions, which have at least three effects on host cholinergic neurons. First, the lesion removes all cholinergic inputs to the dorsal hippocampus and associated behavioural deficits, as described above. Second, the wound cavity causes scarring and an impenetrable barrier to spontaneously regenerating axons. Third, the loss of trophic support by retrograde transport of NGF from the hippocampus leads to atrophy and degeneration of the cholinergic neurons themselves. Embryonic hippocampus implanted into the lesion cavity protects septal neurons from degeneration and promotes axonal growth not only into the hippocampal graft, but also through the graft tissue to reinnervate the host hippocampus (Kromer, Björklund, & Stenevi, 1981). Such grafts can restore normal patterns of electrophysiological theta activity to the host hippocampus (Buzsaki, Gage, Czopf, & Björklund, 1987). Bridge grafts of this type not only provide a substrate for axonal growth, but provide additional targets for ingrowing axons and contain neurons that can grow into the host brain. As such, they contain neuronal elements that become incorporated into a host–graft–host relay of information, rather than simply serving as a passive conduit.

Reciprocal graft–host reinnervation

The striatal tissue grafts described in a previous section establish extensive afferent connections from the host brain and project new axonal connections to appropriate targets in the globus pallidus and even, to a limited extent, the substantia nigra pars reticulata. It is likely that these reciprocal connections are necessary for restitution of function observed in the grafted animals. The striatum is integrally linked into a cortico-striato-pallido-thalamic circuit through which cortical plans of action maintain motor control. Damage of this circuitry results in cognitive as well as motor impairments, which have been reversed by striatal grafts (Björklund et al., 1994; Dunnett, Isacson, et al., 1988). By contrast, no pharmacological treatment has been found to be effective against such deficits, either in experimental chorea or in Huntington's disease, suggesting that diffusely acting pharmacological mechanisms are unlikely to account for the recovery in grafted animals.

A number of other model systems have been described where a relatively precise reformation of connections between graft and host appear to become established (e.g., in the cerebellum; Sotelo & Alvarado-Mallart, 1987), but these have only recently begun to be characterised behaviourally (Triarhou, 1996; Triarhou, Zhang, & Lee, 1996).

Full reconstruction of damaged circuitry

This final category is intended to indicate the ultimate goal of reconstructive neuronal transplantation surgery. Although effective in different contexts, full reconstruction of the CNS in all its complexity is never achieved in any of the graft models so far investigated. Whereas a graft may re-establish afferent and efferent connections with the host, necessary for its functional efficacy, such reconstruction is invariably partial and incomplete—in the precision of internal organisation, in the precise patterns and distribution of afferent connections onto neuronal elements within the grafts, in the extent of fibre outgrowth, and in the routes that efferent axons take to reach distant targets. Moreover, the reformation of some subset of the normal pattern of connectivity does not necessarily apply to all populations of afferent and efferent neurons. Perhaps the most remarkable fact is that neural grafts do exert so many functional effects on the host animal, even though the techniques are so crude and the extent of neuronal reconstruction is so limited.

APPLICATIONS TO NEUROLOGICAL DISEASES

It is now well established that neural tissue transplants can repair some aspects of normal brain function following brain damage in experimental animals. Might similar techniques be applied clinically to repair neurological damage or disease in man? The most detailed functional analyses of the animal models have been conducted in the context of dopamine-denervation models of Parkinson's disease, and parkinsonian patients have been the first candidates for experimental neurosurgical transplantation.

Adrenal grafts

The first operations were conducted using autografts from the patients' own adrenal gland. The chromaffin cells of the adrenal medulla secrete catecholamines, including some dopamine, and because the tissue comes from the patient himself the most difficult ethical and immunological issues surrounding use of foetal CNS tissues are circumvented. The first four operations in 1982–1985 in Sweden involved a stereotactic technique, and did not achieve substantial clinical benefit (Lindvall, 1989) so that the Swedish team have pursued other alternatives (see later).

However, in 1987, a Mexican team published reports of dramatic recovery using an alternative open ventricular transplantation technique (Madrazo et al., 1987). This report stimulated further trials with adrenal autografts in several hundred parkinsonian patients in the following 3 years. The consensus of this world-wide effort is that the open ventricular transplantation approach does achieve detectable clinical improvement in a substantial minority of patients (Goetz et al., 1989, 1990). However, there is little evidence that the adrenal grafts survive even in cases manifesting a reasonable clinical response, so that the mechanisms by which the grafts exert their limited influence in this model is probably non-specific. More critically, the operation is associated with a high rate of complications from the combined surgeries (Bakay, Allen, Apuzzo, Penn, & Tindall, 1990), resulting in levels of morbidity and mortality that many consider unacceptable (Quinn, 1990).

Foetal nigral grafts

The return to the consideration of foetal tissue transplants was based on the fact that evidence in experimental animals suggested a far better functional response could be expected from implantation of the appropriate population of neurons at an appropriate stage of active developmental growth, i.e., use of foetal nigral tissues (Lindvall, 1989). This requires a number of ethical, immunological, and practical issues to be resolved.

Ethical. The use of human foetal donor tissues for transplantation is inevitably controversial and entangled with social, legal, and religious attitudes to the wider issue of abortion. The Swedish Society of Medicine was first to formulate a set of guidelines for the ethical use of foetal tissues, which require at their heart the complete separation of the abortion procedure itself from the use of the tissues in neural transplantation. Great Britain has followed with a similar set of principles advised by a Royal Commission under the chairmanship of Rev. John Polkinghorne (1989), as subsequently interpreted by guidance from the Department of Health. Each country will need to address these issues in terms appropriate for that society.

Age of donor. Experimental studies have indicated that the age of foetal donor tissue is the most critical factor for graft viability. The optimal time window for human foetal dopamine neurons to survive transplantation appears to be at approximately 6–8 weeks of gestation, as established from developmental studies (Freeman et al., 1991) and validated in human nigral xenografts implanted in cyclosporin A immunosuppressed rats (Brundin et al., 1986).

Immunological. As indicated earlier, allografts in outbred strains of rats and monkeys generally survive well, but rejection can be precipitated in allografts and xenografts when sufficient differences at both major and minor histocompatibility loci apply. The degree of immunological tolerance that will apply in transplantation of neural tissues into the brains of unrelated humans remains unknown. On the one hand, a rejection response in the brain could induce major neurological complications; on the other hand immunosuppression therapies themselves have substantial side-effects, in particular nephrotoxicity. The most widely adopted protocol on which most clinical teams have converged is to proceed with adjunct immunosuppression typically with triple cyclosporin-prednisolone-azothioprine for the first 6 months–2 years after implantation, followed by phased withdrawal, apparently with good effect.

Trials in Parkinson's disease. In the 1990s, several hundred cases of implantation of dopamine-rich human foetal grafts in parkinsonian patients were conducted in China, Cuba, Mexico, Poland, Spain, Sweden, UK, France, Canada, and USA. However, only a few dozen of these cases have been assessed rigorously and reported in objective scientific and clinical detail (Olanow, Kordower, & Freeman, 1996). The most convincing cases are from the series first reported by Lindvall et al. (1990) and now followed up beyond 6 years (Lindvall, 1997; Wenning et al., 1997). This longitudinal study provides detailed clinical, neurological, and physiological evaluation over 6 months–1 year preoperatively and then over time following transplantation, and with PET scans of fluoro-dopa incorporation to demonstrate graft viability. Several of these patients have manifested pronounced and sustained recovery in extending the total proportion of "on" time, reductions in disabling drug-induced dyskinesias, and marked improvement in measures of motor coordination, akinesia, and rigidity (but little change in tremor), in particular during "off" phases. Comparable dramatic results have been reported from several other centres (Freeman et al., 1995; Peschanski et al., 1994). In particular, two of the cases from the Tampa series have now come to post mortem, which has confirmed the interpretation that good restitution of the fluorodopa uptake in the PET scans *in vivo* does indeed represent good survival of the nigral grafts rich in dopaminergic neurons (Kordower et al., 1995), as predicted from the rat studies.

The major area requiring further research is the development of procedures to improve the yield of foetal dopamine cells for transplantation. Estimates based on rat-to-rat and human-to-rat grafts suggest that less than 5% of dopamine precursor cells survive transplantation, with the consequence that several donor foetuses are required for each implant operation. In the effective cases described earlier, the ventral mesencephalic cells from four–seven embryos have been implanted into each hemisphere of the patients (Olanow et al., 1996). Further studies are continuing to refine the procedures for dissection, handling, transport, and implantation of human foetal tissues in order to optimise cell viability (Brundin, Björklund, & Lindvall, 1990). In particular a variety of antioxidant treatments have been found to be effective in promoting graft survival (Nakao, Frodl, Duan, Widner, & Brundin, 1994), and the addition of antioxidants to the graft media are now being introduced into the next phase of clinical trials in at least one centre.

Applications in other diseases. Following the clear success of embryonic nigral transplantation in at least a few of the well-studied cases with Parkinson's disease, and based on the success of embryonic striatal grafts to alleviate both motor and cognitive deficits in animals with experimental striatal degeneration, Huntington's disease has been considered as a second potential target for neural transplantation (Peschanski, Cesaro, & Hantraye, 1995). Consequently, several centres have now commenced the first clinical trials of embryonic striatal cell transplantation in Huntington's disease, although at the time of writing (October 1998) these are all at too early a stage for evaluation of outcome.

Second, the success of the encapsulated cell technology in animal has led to the first trials of spinal cord in two conditions: the implantation of adrenal medullary tissues for the treatment of terminal cancer pain, and of baby hamster kidney cell lines engineered to secrete the growth factor CNTF for neuroprotection of motor neurons in rapidly progressing amyotrophic lateral sclerosis (Aebischer et al., 1996; Sagen, Wang, Tresco, & Aebischer, 1993).

Third, rapid advances are being seen in spinal cord transplantation, and the use of neural grafts are likely to be soon applied for prevention of cyst formation as well as for neuronal replacement and for neuroprotection and trophic factor delivery (Bregman, 1994; Cheng, Cao, & Olson, 1996).

CONCLUSIONS

During the 1980s and 1990s neural transplantation has developed through several stages. It started as a series of sporadic and enigmatic observations which had minimal impact. However, the techniques developed as a powerful experimental tool in neurobiology, first for the study of neuronal development, and then applied to experimental studies of neuronal plasticity and functional organisation of the nervous system. Recently, the techniques have started moving out of experimental neurobiology laboratories and into neurosurgical clinics. Neural implants may come to offer radical new treatments for neurodegenerative diseases by reconstructive neurosurgery. Whereas the utility of widespread clinical application remains to be demonstrated, the power of the techniques in experimental neurobiology is established and can be expected to continue contributing to our understanding of the construction and organisation of the nervous system.

REFERENCES

Aebischer, P., Schluep, M., Deglon, N., Joseph, J.M., Hirt, L., Heyd, B., Goddard, M., Hammang, J.P., Zurn, A.D., Kato, A.C., Regli, F., & Baetge, E.E. (1996). Intrathecal delivery of CNTF using encapsulated genetically-modified xenogeneic cells in amyotrophic lateral sclerosis patients. *Nature Medicine*, 2, 696–699.

Aguayo, A.J., Björklund, A., Stenevi, U., & Carlstedt, T. (1984). Fetal mesencephalic neurones survive and extend long axons across PNS grafts inserted into the adult rat neostriatum. *Neuroscience Letters*, 45, 53–58.

Arbuthnott, G.W., Dunnett, S.B., & McLeod, N. (1985). The electrophysiological properties of single units in mesencephalic transplants in rat brain. *Neuroscience Letters*, 57, 205–210.

Bakay, R.A.E., Allen, G.S., Apuzzo, M., Penn, R., & Tindall, G.T. (1990). Preliminary report on adrenal medullary grafting from the American Association of Neurological Surgeons graft project. *Progress in Brain Research*, 82, 603–610.

Bartlett, P.F., Rosenfeld, J., Cheesman, H., Harvey, A.R., & Kerr, R.S.C. (1990). Allograft rejection overcome by immunoselection of neuronal precursor cells. *Progress in Brain Research*, 82, 153–160.

Bartus, R.T., Dean, R.L., Beer, B., & Lippa, A.S. (1982). The cholinergic hypothesis of geriatric memory dysfunction. *Science*, 217, 408–417.

Björklund, A., Campbell, K., Sirinathsinghji, D.J.S., Fricker, R.A., & Dunnett, S.B. (1994). Functional capacity of striatal transplants in the rat Huntington model. In S.B. Dunnett & A. Björklund (Eds.), *Functional neural transplantation* (pp. 157–195). New York: Raven Press.

Björklund, A., & Dunnett, S.B. (1992). Neural transplantation in adult rats. In S.B. Dunnett & A. Björklund (Eds.), *Neural transplantation: A practical approach* (pp. 57–78). Oxford, UK: IRL Press.

Björklund, A., Dunnett, S.B., Stenevi, U., Lewis, M.E., & Iversen, S.D. (1980). Reinnervation of the denervated striatum by substantia nigra transplants: Functional consequences as revealed by pharmacological and sensory motor testing. *Brain Research*, 199, 307–333.

Björklund, A., Lindvall, O., Isacson, O., Brundin, P., Wictorin, K., Strecker, R.E., Clarke, D.J., & Dunnett, S.B. (1987). Mechanisms of action of intracerebral neural implants: Studies on nigral and striatal grafts to the lesioned striatum. *Trends in Neuroscience*, 10, 509–516.

Björklund, A., & Stenevi, U. (1971). Growth of central catecholamine neurons into smooth muscle grafts in the rat mesencephalon. *Brain Research*, 31, 1–20.

Björklund, A., & Stenevi, U. (1977). Reformation of the severed septohippocampal cholinergic pathway in the adult rat by transplanted septal neurons. *Cell and Tissue Research*, 185, 289–302.

Björklund, A., & Stenevi, U. (1981). in vivo evidence for a hippocampal adrenergic neurotrophic factor specifically released on septal deafferentation. *Brain Research*, 229, 403–428.

Björklund, A., & Stenevi, U. (1985). *Neural grafting in the mammalian CNS*. Amsterdam: Elsevier.

Björklund, A., Stenevi, U., Schmidt, R.H., Dunnett, S.B., & Gage, F.H. (1983a). Intracerebral grafting of neuronal cell suspensions: I. Introduction and general methods of preparation. *Acta Physiologica Scandinavica*, 522(Suppl.), 1–7.

Björklund, A., Stenevi, U., Schmidt, R.H., Dunnett, S.B., & Gage, F.H. (1983b). Intracerebral grafting of neuronal cell suspensions: II. Survival and growth of nigral cell suspensions. *Acta Physiologica Scandinavica*, 522(Suppl.), 9–18.

Björklund, A., Stenevi, U., Schmidt, R.H., Dunnett, S.B., & Gage, F.H. (1983c). Intracerebral grafting of neuronal cell suspensions: VII. Recovery of choline acetyltransferase activity and acetylcholine synthesis in the denervated hippocampus reinnervated by septal suspension implants. *Acta Physiologica Scandinavica*, 522(Suppl.), 1–7.

Björklund, A., Stenevi, U., & Svendgaard, N.A. (1976). Growth of transplanted monoaminergic neurones into the adult hippocampus along the perforant path. *Nature*, 262, 787–790.

Bohn, M.C., Cupit, L., Marciano, F., & Gash, D.M. (1987). Adrenal medulla grafts enhance recovery of striatal dopaminergic fibers. *Science*, 237, 913–916.

Brecknell, J.E., Haque, N.S.K., Du, J.-S., Muir, E.M., Hlavin, M.-L., Fawcett, J.W., & Dunnett, S.B. (1996). Functional and anatomical reconstruction of the 6-OHDA lesioned nigrostriatal system of the adult rats by RN22 nigrostriatal bridge grafts. *Neuroscience*, 71, 913–925.

Bregman, B.S. (1994). Recovery of function after spinal cord injury: Transplantation strategies. In S.B. Dunnett & A. Björklund (Eds.), *Functional neural transplantation* (pp. 489–529). New York: Raven Press.

Brown, V.J., & Dunnett, S.B. (1989). Comparison of adrenal and foetal nigral grafts on drug-induced rotation in rats with 6-OHDA lesions. *Experimental Brain Research*, 78, 214–218.

Brundin, P., Björklund, A., & Lindvall, O. (1990). Practical aspects of the use of human fetal brain tissue for intracerebral grafting. *Progress in Brain Research*, 82, 707–714.

Brundin, P., Nilsson, O.G., Gage, F.H., & Björklund, A. (1985). Cyclosporin A increases survival of cross-species intrastriatal grafts of embryonic dopamine-containing neurons. *Experimental Brain Research*, 60, 204–208.

Brundin, P., Nilsson, O.G., Strecker, R.E., Lindvall, O., Åstedt, B., & Björklund, A. (1986). Behavioral effects of human fetal dopamine neurons grafted in a rat model of Parkinson's disease. *Experimental Brain Research*, 65, 235–240.

Buzsaki, G., Gage, F.H., Czopf, J., & Björklund, A. (1987). Restoration of rhythmic slow activity (_) in the subcortically denervated hippocampus by fetal CNS transplants. *Brain Research*, 400, 334–347.

Cajal, S.R. (1928). *Degeneration and regeneration of the nervous system*. London: Oxford University Press.

Cenci, M.A., Nilsson, O.G., Kalén, P., & Björklund, A. (1993). Characterization of in vivo noradrenaline release from superior cervical ganglia or fetal locus coeruleus transplanted to the subcortically deafferented hippocampus in the rat. *Experimental Neurology*, 122, 73–87.

Cheng, H., Cao, Y.H., & Olson, L. (1996). Spinal cord repair in adult paraplegic rats—partial restoration of hind-limb function. *Science*, 273, 510–513.

Clarke, D.J., & Dunnett, S.B. (1986). Ultrastructural organisation of choline acetyltransferase-immunoreactive fibres innervating the neocortex from embryonic ventral forebrain grafts. *Journal of Comparative Neurology*, 250, 192–205.

Clarke, D.J., & Dunnett, S.B. (1993). Synaptic relationships between cortical and dopaminergic inputs and intrinsic GABAergic systems within intrastriatal striatal grafts. *Journal of Chemical Neuroanatomy*, 6, 147–158.

Clarke, D.J., Gage, F.H., & Björklund, A. (1986). Formation of cholinergic synapses by intrahippocampal septal grafts as revealed by choline acetyltransferase immunocytochemistry. *Brain Research*, 369, 151–162.

Clemente, C.D. (1958). The regeneration of peripheral nerves inserted into the cerebral cortex and the healing of cerebral lesions. *Journal of Comparative Neurology*, 109, 123–151.

Collier, T.J., Gash, D.M., & Sladek, J.R. (1988). Transplantation of norepinephrine neurons into aged rats improves performance of a learned task. *Brain Research*, 448, 77–87.

Collier, T.J., & Springer, J.E. (1994). Neural graft augmentation through co-grafting: Implantation of cells as sources of survival and growth factors. *Progress in Neurobiology*, 44, 309–331.

Coyle, J.T., Price, D.L., & DeLong, M.R. (1983). Alzheimer's disease: A disorder of cortical cholinergic innervation. *Science*, 219, 1184–1190.

Cozzi, E., & White, D.J.G. (1995). The generation of transgenic pigs as potential organ donors for humans. *Nature Medicine*, 1, 964–966.

Cunningham, L.A., Short, M.P., Breakefield, X.O., & Bohn, M.C. (1994). Nerve growth factor released by transgenic astrocytes enhances the function of adrenal chromaffin cell grafts in a rat model of Parkinson's disease. *Brain Research*, 658, 219–231.

Das, G.D., & Altman, J. (1971). The fate of transplanted precursors of nerve cells in the cerebellum of young rats. *Science*, 173, 637–638.

David, S., & Aguayo, A.J. (1981). Axonal elongation into peripheral nervous system "bridges" after central nervous system injury in adult rats. *Science*, 214, 931–933.

DiFiglia, M., Schiff, L., & Deckel, A.W. (1988). Neuronal organisation of fetal striatal grafts in kainate- and sham-lesioned rat caudate nucleus: Light and electron microscopic observations. *Journal of Neuroscience*, 8, 1112–1130.

Dunn, E.H. (1917). Primary and secondary findings in a series of attempts to transplant cerebral cortex in the albino rat. *Journal of Comparative Neurology*, 27, 565–582.

Dunnett, S.B. (1990). Neural transplantation in the cerebral cortex. In B. Kolb & R. Tees (Eds.), *Cerebral cortex of the rat*. Cambridge, MA: MIT Press.

Dunnett, S.B. (1995). Functional repair of striatal systems by neural transplants: Evidence for circuit reconstruction. *Behavioural Brain Research*, 66, 133–142.

Dunnett, S.B., Badman, F., Rogers, D.C., Evenden, J.L., & Iversen, S.D. (1988). Cholinergic grafts in the neocortex or hippocampus of aged rats: Reduction of delay-dependent deficits in the delayed non-matching to position task. *Experimental Neurology, 102,* 57–64.

Dunnett, S.B., & Björklund, A. (1992). Staging and dissection of rat embryos. In S.B. Dunnett & A. Björklund (Eds.), *Neural transplantation: A practical approach* (pp. 1–19). Oxford, UK: IRL Press.

Dunnett, S.B., & Björklund, A. (1994a). *Functional neural transplantation.* New York: Raven Press.

Dunnett, S.B., & Björklund, A. (1994b). Mechanisms of function of neural grafts in the injured brain. In S.B. Dunnett & A. Björklund (Eds.), *Functional neural transplantation* (pp. 531–567). New York: Raven Press.

Dunnett, S.B., Björklund, A., Schmidt, R.H., Stenevi, U., & Iversen, S.D. (1983a). Intracerebral grafting of neuronal cell suspensions: IV. Behavioural recovery in rats with unilateral implants of dopamine cell suspensions in different forebrain sites. *Acta Physiologica Scandinavica, 522*(Suppl.), 29–37.

Dunnett, S.B., Björklund, A., Schmidt, R.H., Stenevi, U., & Iversen, S.D. (1983b). Intracerebral grafting of neuronal cell suspensions: V. Behavioural recovery in rats with bilateral 6-OHDA lesions following implantation of nigra cell suspensions. *Acta Physiologica Scandinavica, 522*(Suppl.), 39–47.

Dunnett, S.B., Evenden, J.L., & Iversen, S.D. (1988). Delay-dependent short-term memory impairments in aged rats. *Psychopharmacology, 96,* 174–180.

Dunnett, S.B., Hernandez, T.D., Summerfield, A., Jones, G.H., & Arbuthnott, G. (1988). Graft-derived recovery from 6-OHDA lesions: Specificity of ventral mesencephalic graft tissues. *Experimental Brain Research, 71,* 411–424.

Dunnett, S.B., Isacson, O., Sirinathsinghji, D.J.S., Clarke, D.J., & Björklund, A. (1988). Striatal grafts in rats with unilateral neostriatal lesions: III. Recovery from dopamine-dependent motor asymmetry and deficits in skilled paw reaching. *Neuroscience, 24,* 811–819.

Dunnett, S.B., Low, W.C., Iversen, S.D., Stenevi, U., & Björklund, A. (1982). Septal transplants restore maze learning in rats with fimbria-fornix lesions. *Brain Research, 251,* 335–348.

Dunnett, S.B., Martel, F.L., Rogers, D.C., & Finger, S. (1990). Factors affecting septal graft amelioration of differential reinforcement of low rates DRL and activity deficits after fimbria-fornix lesions. *Restorative Neurology and Neuroscience, 1,* 83–92.

Dunnett, S.B., & Richards, S.-J. (1990). *Neural transplantation: From molecular basis to clinical application. Progress in Brain Research, Volume 82.* Amsterdam: Elsevier.

Dunnett, S.B., Rogers, D.C., & Richards, S.J. (1989). Reconstruction of the nigrostriatal pathway after 6-OHDA lesions by combination of dopamine-rich nigral grafts and nigrostriatal bridge grafts. *Experimental Brain Research, 75,* 523–535.

Dunnett, S.B., Ryan, C.N., Levin, P.D., Reynolds, M., & Bunch, S.T. (1987). Functional consequences of embryonic neocortex transplanted to rats with prefrontal cortex lesions. *Behavioral Neuroscience, 101,* 489–503.

Dunnett, S.B., Whishaw, I.Q., Rogers, D.C., & Jones, G.H. (1987). Dopamine-rich grafts ameliorate whole body motor asymmetry and sensory neglect but not independent skilled limb use in rats with 6-hydroxydopamine lesions. *Brain Research, 415,* 63–78.

Ernfors, P., Ebendal, T., Olson, L., Mouton, P., Strömberg, I., & Persson, H. (1989). A cell line producing recombinant nerve growth factor evokes growth responses in intrinsic and grafted central cholinergic neurons. *Proceedings of the National Academy of Sciences of the United States of America, 86,* 4756–4760.

Freed, W.J. (1983). Functional brain tissue transplantation: Reversal of lesion-induced rotation by intraventricular substantia nigra and adrenal medulla grafts, with a note on intracranial retinal grafts. *Biological Psychiatry, 18,* 1205–1267.

Freed, W.J., Geller, H.M., Poltorak, M., et al. (1990). Genetically altered and defined cell lines for transplantation in animal models of Parkinson's disease. *Progress in Brain Research, 82,* 11–21.

Freed, W.J., Karoum, F., Spoor, E., Morihisa, J.M., Olson, L., & Wyatt, R.J. (1983). Catecholamine-content of intracerebral adrenal medulla grafts. *Brain Research, 269,* 184–189.

Freed, W.J., Morihisa, J.M., Spoor, E., Hoffer, B.J., Olson, L., Seiger, Å., & Wyatt, R.J. (1981). Transplanted adrenal chromaffin cells in rat brain reduce lesion-induced rotational behaviour. *Nature, 292,* 351–352.

Freeman, T.B., Olanow, C.W., Hauser, R.A., Nauert, G.M., Smith, D.A., Borlongan, C.V., Sanberg, P.R., Holt, D.A., Kordower, J.H., Vingerhoets, F.J.G., Snow, B.J., Calne, D.B., & Gauger, L.L. (1995).

Bilateral fetal nigral transplantation into the postcommissural putamen in Parkinson's disease. *Annals of Neurology, 38,* 379–388.

Freeman, T.B., Spence, M.S., Boss, B.D., Spector, D.H., Strecker, R.E., Olanow, C.W., & Kordower, J.H. (1991). Development of dopaminergic neurons in the human substantia nigra. *Experimental Neurology, 113,* 344–355.

Freund, T.F., Bolam, J.P., Björklund, A., Stenevi, U., Dunnett, S.B., Powell, J.F., & Smith, A.D. (1985). Efferent synaptic connections of grafted dopaminergic neurons reinnervating the host neostriatum: A tyrosine hydroxylase immunocytochemical study. *Journal of Neuroscience, 5,* 603–616.

Gage, F.H., & Björklund, A. (1986). Enhanced graft survival in the hippocampus following selective denervation. *Neuroscience, 17,* 89–98.

Gage, F.H., Björklund, A., Stenevi, U., & Dunnett, S.B. (1983). Intracerebral grafting of neuronal cell suspensions: VIII. Survival and growth of implants of nigral and septal cell suspensions in intact brains of aged rats. *Acta Physiologica Scandinavica, 522*(Suppl.), 67–75.

Gage, F.H., Björklund, A., Stenevi, U., Dunnett, S.B., & Kelly, P.A.T. (1984). Intrahippocampal septal grafts ameliorate learning deficits in aged rats. *Science, 225,* 533–536.

Gage, F.H., Coates, P.W., Palmer, T.D., Kuhn, H.G., Fisher, L.J., Suhonen, J.O., Peterson, D.A., Suhr, S.T., & Ray, J. (1995). Survival and differentiation of adult neuronal progenitor cells transplanted to the adult brain. *Proceedings of the National Academy of Sciences of the United States of America, 92,* 11,879–11,883.

Gage, F.H., Dunnett, S.B., & Björklund, A. (1984). Spatial learning and motor deficits in aged rats. *Neurobiology of Aging, 5,* 43–48.

Gage, F.H., Dunnett, S.B., & Björklund, A. (1989). Age-related impairments in spatial memory are independent of those in sensorimotor skills. *Neurobiology of Aging, 10,* 347–352.

Gage, F.H., Dunnett, S.B., Stenevi, U., & Björklund, A. (1983). Aged rats: Recovery of motor impairments by intrastriatal nigral grafts. *Science, 221,* 966–969.

Gage, F.H., Ray, J., & Fisher, L.J. (1995). Isolation, characterization, and use of stem cells from the CNS. *Annual Review of Neuroscience, 18,* 159–192.

Gage, F.H., Wolff, J.A., Rosenberg, M.B., Xu, L., Yee, J.-K., Shults, C., & Friedmann, T. (1987). Grafting genetically modified cells to the brain: Possibilities for the future. *Neuroscience, 23,* 795–807.

Gash, D.M., & Sladek, J.R. (1988). *Transplantation into the mammalian CNS. Progress in Brain Research, Volume 78.* Amsterdam: Elsevier.

Gash, D.M., Sladek, J.R., & Sladek, C.D. (1980). Functional development of grafted vasopressin neurons. *Science, 210,* 1367–1369.

Gibson, M.J., Krieger, D.T., Charlton, H.M., Zimmer, E.A., Silverman, A.J., & Perlow, M.J. (1984). Mating and pregnancy can occur in genetically hypogonadal mice with preoptic area grafts. *Science, 225,* 949–951.

Gibson, M.J., Silverman, R.C., & Silverman, A.J. (1990). Current progress in studies of GnRH cell containing brain grafts in hypogonadal mice. *Progress in Brain Research, 82,* 169–178.

Glees, P. (1955). Studies on cortical regeneration with special reference to central implants. In W.F. Windle (Ed.), *Regeneration in the central nervous system* (pp. 94–111). Springfield, IL: Thomas.

Goetz, C.G., Olanow, C.W., Koller, W.C., et al. (1989). Multicenter study of autologous adrenal medullary transplantation to the corpus striatum in patients with advanced Parkinson's disease. *New England Journal of Medicine, 320,* 337–341.

Goetz, C.G., Stebbins, G.T., Klawans, H.L., Koller, W.C., Grossman, R.G., Bakay, R.A.E., & Penn, R.D. (1990). United Parkinson Foundation neurotransplantation registry. Multicentre US and Canadian data base: Presurgical and 12 month follow-up. *Progress in Brain Research, 82,* 611–617.

Graybiel, A.M., Liu, F.C., & Dunnett, S.B. (1989). Intrastriatal grafts derived from fetal striatal primordia: I. Phenotypy and modular organisation. *Journal of Neuroscience, 9,* 3250–3271.

Greene, H.S.N., & Arnold, H. (1945). The homologous and heterologous transplantation of brain and brain tumours. *Journal of Neurosurgery, 2,* 315–331.

Halasz, B., Pupp, L., Uhlarik, S., & Tima, L. (1965). Further studies of the hormone secretion of the anterior pituitary transplanted into the hypophysiotrophic areas of the rat hypothalamus. *Endocrinology, 77,* 343–355.

Hallas, B.H., Das, G.D., & Das, K.G. (1980). Transplantation of brain tissue in the brain of rat: II. Growth characteristics of neocortical transplants in hosts of different ages. *American Journal of Anatomy, 158,* 147–159.

Hantraye, P., Riche, D., Mazière, M., & Isacson, O. (1992). Intrastriatal transplantation of cross-species fetal striatal cells reduces abnormal movements in a primate model of Huntington disease. *Proceedings of the National Academy of Sciences of the United States of America, 89*, 4187–4191.

Hefti, F., Melamed, E., Sahakian, B.J., & Wurtman, R.J. (1980). Circling behavior in rats with partial, unilateral, nigro-striatal lesions: Effects of amphetamine, apomorphine and DOPA. *Pharmacology, Biochemistry and Behavior, 12*, 185–188.

Hodges, H., Allen, Y.S., Kershaw, T., Lantos, P.L., Gray, J.A., & Sinden, J. (1991). Effects of cholinergic-rich neural grafts on radial maze performance of rats after excitotoxic lesions of the forebrain cholinergic projection system: 1. Amelioration of cognitive deficits by transplants into cortex and hippocampus but not into basal forebrain. *Neuroscience, 45*, 587–607.

Hodges, H., Allen, Y.S., Sinden, J., Lantos, P.L., & Gray, J.A. (1990). Cholinergic-rich transplants alleviate cognitive deficits in lesioned rats, but exacerbate response to cholinergic drugs. *Progress in Brain Research, 82*, 347–358.

Hodges, H., Sowinski, P., Fleming, P., Kershaw, T.R., Sinden, J.D., Meldrum, B.S., & Gray, J.A. (1996). Contrasting effects of fetal CA1 and CA3 hippocampal grafts on deficits in spatial learning and working memory induced by global cerebral ischaemia in rats. *Neuroscience, 72*, 959–988.

Hoffman, D., Breakefield, X.O., Short, M.P., & Aebischer, P. (1993). Transplantation of a polymer-encapsulated cell line genetically engineered to release NGF. *Experimental Neurology, 122*, 100–106.

Horellou, P., Marlier, L., Privat, A., Darchen, F., Scherman, D., Henry, J.-P., & Mallet, J. (1990). Exogenous expression of l-dopa and dopamine in various cell lines following transfer of rat and human tyrosine hydroxylase cDNA: Grafting in an animal model of Parkinson's disease. *Progress in Brain Research, 82*, 23–32.

Isacson, O., Brundin, P., Gage, F.H., & Björklund, A. (1985). Neural grafting in a rat model of Huntington's disease: Progressive neurochemical changes after neostriatal ibotenate lesions and striatal tissue grafting. *Neuroscience, 16*, 799–817.

Isacson, O., Dawbarn, D., Brundin, P., Gage, F.H., Emson, P., & Björklund, A. (1987). Neural grafting in a rat model of Huntington's disease: Striosomal-like organisation of striatal grafts as revealed by immunohistochemistry and receptor autoradiography. *Neuroscience, 22*, 481–497.

Isacson, O., Riche, D., Hantraye, P., Sofroniew, M.V., & Mazière, M. (1989). A primate model of Huntington's disease: Cross-species implantation of striatal precursor cells to the excitotoxically lesioned baboon caudate-putamen. *Experimental Brain Research, 75*, 213–220.

Kordower, J.H., Freeman, T.B., Snow, B.J., Vingerhoets, F.J.G., Mufson, E.J., Sanberg, P.R., Hauser, R.A., Smith, D.A., Nauert, G.M., Perl, D.P., & Olanow, C.W. (1995). Neuropathological evidence of graft survival and striatal reinnervation after the transplantation of fetal mesencephalic tissue in a patient with Parkinson's disease. *New England Journal of Medicine, 332*, 1118–1124.

Kordower, J.H., Notter, M.F.D., Yeh, H.H., & Gash, D.M. (1987). An in vivo and in vitro assessment of differentiated neuroblastoma cells as a source of donor tissue for transplantation. *Annals of the New York Academy of Science, 495*, 606–621.

Kromer, L.F., Björklund, A., & Stenevi, U. (1981). Regeneration of the septohippocampal pathways in adult rats is promoted by utilizing embryonic hippocampal implants as bridges. *Brain Research, 210*, 173–200.

Kromer, L.F., & Cornbrooks, C.J. (1985). Transplants of Schwann cell cultures promote axonal regeneration in the adult mammalian brain. *Proceedings of the National Academy of Science of the USA, 82*, 6330–6334.

Labbe, R., Firl, A., Mufson, E.J., & Stein, D.G. (1983). Fetal brain transplants: reduction of cognitive deficits in rats with frontal cortex lesions. *Science, 221*, 470–472.

Leanza, G., Nilsson, O.G., & Björklund, A. (1993). Functional activity of intrahippocampal septal grafts is regulated by catecholaminergic host afferents as studied by microdialysis of acetylcholine. *Brain Research, 618*, 47–56.

Le Gros Clark, W.E. (1940). Neuronal differentiation in implanted foetal cortical tissues. *Journal of Neurology and Psychiatry, 3*, 263–284.

LeVere, T.E., & LeVere, N.D. (1985). Transplants to the central nervous system as a therapy for brain pathology. *Neurobiological Aging, 6*, 151–152.

Lindvall, O. (1989). Transplantation into the human brain: Present status and future possibilities. *Journal of Neurology, Neurosurgery and Psychiatry* (Special Supplement.), 39–54.

Lindvall, O. (1997). Neural transplantation: Does it work for Parkinson's disease. *NeuroReport, 8*(14), iii–x.

Lindvall, O., Brundin, P., Widner, H., et al. (1990). Grafts of fetal dopamine neurons survive and improve motor function in Parkinson's disease. *Science, 247*, 574–577.

Lundberg, C., Martinez-Serrano, A., Cattaneo, E., McKay R.D.G., & Björklund, A. (1997). Survival, integration, and differentiation of neural stem cell lines after transplantation to the adult rat striatum. *Experimental Neurology, 145*, 342–360.

Madrazo, I., Drucker-Colin, R., Diaz, V., Martinez-Mata, J., Torres, C., & Becerril, J.J. (1987). Open microsurgical autograft of adrenal medulla to the right caudate nucleus in two patients with intractable Parkinson's disease. *New England Journal of Medicine, 316*, 831–834.

Mandel, R.J., Brundin, P., & Björklund, A. (1990). The importance of graft placement and task complexity for transplant induced recovery of simple and complex sensorimotor deficits in dopamine denervated rats. *European Journal of Neuroscience, 2*, 888–894.

Marshall, J.F., & Berrios, N. (1979). Movement disorders of aged rats: Reversal by dopamine receptor stimulation. *Science, 206*, 477–479.

Martínez-Serrano, A., Fischer, W., Söderström, S., Ebendal, T., & Björklund, A. (1996). Long-term functional recovery from age-induced spatial memory impairments by nerve growth factor gene transfer to the rat basal forebrain. *Proceedings of the National Academy of Sciences of the United States of America, 93*, 6355–6360.

Mason, D.W., Charlton, H.M., Jones, A.J., Lavy, C.B.D., Puklavec, M., & Simmonds, S.J. (1986). The fate of allogeneic and xenogeneic neuronal tissue transplanted into the third ventricle of rodents. *Neuroscience, 19*, 685–694.

McLoon, S.C., & Lund, R.D. (1983). Development of fetal retina, tectum and cortex transplanted to the superior colliculus of adult rats. *Journal of Comparative Neurology, 217*, 376–389.

Medawar, P.B. (1948). Immunity to homologous grafted skin: III. Fate of skin homografts transplanted to the brain, to subcutaneous tissue, and to the anterior chamber of the eye. *British Journal of Experimental Pathology, 29*, 58–69.

Meyers, R. (1951). Surgical experiments in the therapy of certain "extrapyramidal" diseases: A current evaluation. *Acta Psychiatrica Neurologica, 67*(Suppl. 13), 1–42.

Nakao, N. (1996). *Protection of striatal and nigral neurons by trophic and antioxidant mechanisms.* Unpublished PhD thesis, University of Lund, Sweden.

Nakao, N., Frodl, E.M., Duan, W.-M., Widner, H., & Brundin, P. (1994). Lazaroids improve the survival of grafted rat embryonic dopamine neurons. *Proceedings of the National Academy of Sciences of the United States of America, 91*, 12,408–12,412.

Nicholas, M.K., Chenelle, A.G., Brown, M.M., Stefansson, K., & Arnason, B.G.W. (1990). Prevention of neural allograft rejection in the mouse following in vivo depletion of L3T4+ but not LYT-2+ T lymphocytes. *Progress in Brain Research, 92*, 161–167.

Nilsson, O.G., Shapiro, M.L., Olton, D.S., Gage, F.H., & Björklund, A. (1987). Spatial learning and memory following fimbria-fornix transection and grafting of fetal septal neurons to the hippocampus. *Experimental Brain Research, 67*, 195–215.

Olanow, C.W., Kordower, J.H., & Freeman, T.B. (1996). Fetal nigral transplantation as a therapy for Parkinson's disease. *Trends in Neurosciences, 19*, 102–109.

Olson, L., Ayer-LeLièvre, C., Ebendal, T., Eriksdotter-Nilsson, M., Ernfors, P., Henschen, A., Hoffer, B.J., Giacobini, M.M.J., Mouton, P., Palmer, M.R., Persson, H., Sara, V., Strömberg, I., & Wetmore, C. (1990). Grafts, growth factors and grafts that make growth factors. *Progress in Brain Research, 82*, 55–66.

Olson, L., Björklund, H., & Hoffer, B.J. (1984). Camera bulbi anterior: New vistas on a classical locus for neural tissue transplantation. In J.R. Sladek & D.M. Gash (Eds.), *Neural transplants: Development and function* (pp. 125–165). New York/London: Plenum Press.

Olson, L., & Malmfors, T. (1970). Growth characteristics of adrenergic nerves in the adult rat. Fluorescence histochemical and 3H-noradrenaline uptake studies using tissue transplantation to the anterior chamber of the eye. *Acta Physiologica Scandinavica, 348*(Suppl.), 1–112.

Pakzaban, P., Deacon, T.W., Burns, L.H., Dinsmore, J., & Isacson, O. (1995). A novel mode of immunoprotection of neural xenotransplants: Masking of donor major histocompatibility complex class I enhances transplant survival in the central nervous system. *Neuroscience, 65*, 983–996.

Pedersen, E.B., Zimmer, J., & Finsen, B. (1997). Triple immunosuppression protects murine intracerebral, hippocampal xenografts in adult rat hosts: Effects on cellular infiltration, major histocompatibility complex antigen induction and blood-brain barrier leakage. *Neuroscience, 78*, 685–701.

Perlow, M.J., Freed, W.J., Hoffer, B.J., Seiger, Å., Olson, L., & Wyatt, R.J. (1979). Brain grafts reduce motor abnormalities produced by destruction of nigrostriatal dopamine system. *Science, 204*, 643–647.

Peschanski, M., Cesaro, P., & Hantraye, P. (1995). Rationale for intrastriatal grafting of striatal neuroblasts in patients with Huntington's disease. *Neuroscience, 68*, 273–285.

Peschanski, M., Defer, G., N'Guyen, J.P., Ricolfi, F., Montfort, J.C., Rémy, P., Geny, C., Samson, Y., Hantraye, P., Jeny, R., Gaston, A., Kéravel, Y., Degos, J.D., & Cesaro, P. (1994). Bilateral motor improvement and alteration of l-dopa effect in two patients with Parkinson's disease following intrastriatal transplantation of foetal ventral mesencephalon. *Brain, 117*, 487–499.

Polkinghorne, J. (1989). *Review of the guidance on the research use of fetuses and fetal material.* London: Her Majesty's Stationery Office.

Quinn, N.P. (1990). The clinical application of cell grafting techniques in patients with Parkinson's disease. *Progress in Brain Research, 82*, 619–625.

Raisman, G. (1969). Neuronal plasticity in the septal nucleus of the adult brain. *Brain Research, 14*, 25–48.

Redmond, D.E., Sladek, J.R., Roth, R.H., Collier, T.J., Elsworth, J.D., Deutsch, A.Y., & Haber, S. (1986). Fetal neuronal grafts in monkeys given methylphenyltetrahydropyridine. *Lancet, i*, 1125–1127.

Reynolds, B.A., & Weiss, S. (1992). Generation of neurons and astrocytes from isolated cells of the adult mammalian central nervous system. *Science, 255*, 1707–1710.

Ridley, R.M., Baker, H.F., & Fine, A. (1988). Transplantation of fetal tissues. *British Medical Journal, 296*, 1469.

Rosenstein, J.M. (1987). Neocortical transplants in the mammalian brain lack a blood-brain barrier to macromolecules. *Science, 235*, 772–724.

Rosenstein, J.M., & Brightman, M.W. (1983). Circumventing the blood-brain barrier with autonomic ganglion transplants. *Science, 221*, 879–881.

Sagen, J., Wang, H., Tresco, P.A., & Aebischer, P. (1993). Transplants of immunologically isolated xenogeneic chromaffin cells provide a long-term source of pain-reducing neuroactive substances. *Journal of Neuroscience, 13*, 2415–2423.

Sauer, H., & Brundin, P. (1991). Effects of cool storage on survival and function of intrastriatal ventral mesencephalic grafts. *Restorative Neurology and Neuroscience, 2*, 123–135.

Schmidt, R.H., Björklund, A., & Stenevi, U. (1981). Intracerebral grafting of dissociated CNS tissue suspensions: A new approach for neuronal transplantation to deep brain sites. *Brain Research, 218*, 347–356.

Schmidt, R.H., Björklund, A., Stenevi, U., Dunnett, S.B., & Gage, F.H. (1983). Intracerebral grafting of neuronal cell suspensions: III. Activity of intrastriatal nigra suspension implants as assessed by measurements of dopamine synthesis and metabolism. *Acta Physiologica Scandinavica, 522*(Suppl.), 19–28.

Seiger, Å. (1985). Preparation of immature central nervous system regions for transplantation. In A. Björklund & U. Stenevi (Eds.), *Neural grafting in the mammalian CNS* (pp. 71–77). Amsterdam: Elsevier.

Senut, M.C., Fisher, L.J., Ray, J., et al. (1995). Somatic gene therapy in the brain. In C. Ricordi (Ed.), *Methods in cell transplantation* (pp. 197–214). New York: R.G. Landes.

Shahar, A., de Vellis, J., Vernadakis, A., & Haber, B. (1990). *A dissection and tissue culture manual of the nervous system.* New York: Alan R. Liss.

Silverman, A.J., Zimmerman, E.A., Kokoris, G.J., & Gibson, M.J. (1986). Ultrastructure of gonadotropin-releasing hormone neuronal structures derived from normal fetal preoptic area and transplanted into hypogonadal mutant (hpg) mice. *Journal of Neuroscience, 6*, 2090–2096.

Sinclair, S.R., Svendsen, C.N., Torres, E.M., Fawcett, J.W., & Dunnett, S.B. (1996). The effects of glial cell line-derived neurotrophic factor (GDNF) on embryonic nigral grafts. *NeuroReport, 7*, 2547–2552.

Sinden, J.D., Hodges, H., & Gray, J.A. (1995). Neural transplantation and recovery of cognitive function. *Behavioral and Brain Sciences, 18*, 10–35.

Sirinathsinghji, D.J.S., & Dunnett, S.B. (1989). Disappearance of the μ-opiate receptor patches in the rat neostriatum following nigrostriatal dopamine lesions and their restoration after implantation of nigral dopamine grafts. *Brain Research, 504*, 115–120.

Sirinathsinghji, D.J.S., Dunnett, S.B., Isacson, O., Clarke, D.J., & Björklund, A. (1988). Striatal grafts in rats with unilateral neostriatal

lesions: II. in vivo monitoring of GABA release in globus pallidus and substantia nigra. *Neuroscience, 24*, 791–801.

Smith, L.M., & Ebner, F.F. (1986). The differentiation of non-neuronal elements in neocortical transplants. In G.D. Das & R.B. Wallace (Eds.), *Neural transplantation and regeneration.* New York: Springer-Verlag.

Sotelo, C., & Alvarado-Mallart, R.M. (1987). Reconstruction of the defective cerebellar circuitry in adult mice Purkinje cell degeneration mutant mice by Purkinje cell replacement through transplantation of solid embryonic implants. *Neuroscience, 20*, 1–22.

Stein, D.G. (1987). Transplant-induced functional recovery without specific neuronal connections. *Progress in Research, American Paralysis Association, 18*, 4–5.

Stenevi, U., Björklund, A., & Svendgaard, N.-A. (1976). Transplantation of central and peripheral monoamine neurons to the adult rat brain: Techniques and conditions for survival. *Brain Research, 114*, 1–20.

Stenevi, U., Kromer, L.F., Gage, F.H., & Björklund, A. (1985). Solid neural grafts in intracerebral transplantation cavities. In A. Björklund & U. Stenevi (Eds.), *Neural grafting in the mammalian CNS* (pp. 41–49). Amsterdam: Elsevier.

Strecker, R.E., Sharp, T., Brundin, P., Zetterström, T., Ungerstedt, U., & Björklund, A. (1987). Autoregulation of dopamine release and metabolism by intrastriatal nigral grafts as revealed by intracerebral dialysis. *Neuroscience, 22*, 169–178.

Strömberg, I., Ebendal, T., Olson, L., & Hoffer, B.J. (1990). Chromaffin grafts: Survival and nerve fiber formation as a function of donor age, nerve growth factor and host sympathetic denervation. *Progress in Brain Research, 82*, 87–94.

Strömberg, I., Herrera-Marschitz, M., Ungerstedt, U., Ebendal, T., & Olson, L. (1985). Chronic implants of chromaffin tissue into the dopamine-denervated striatum: Effects of NGF on graft survival, fiber growth and rotational behavior. *Experimental Brain Research, 60*, 335–349.

Suhr, S.T., & Gage, F.H. (1993). Gene therapy for neurologic disease. *Archives of Neurology, 50*, 1252–1268.

Sunde, N.A., & Zimmer, J. (1983). Cellular, histochemical and connective organisation of the hippocampus and fascia dentata transplanted to different regions of immature and adult rat brains. *Developmental Brain Research, 8*, 165–191.

Svendsen, C.N., Clarke, D.J., Rosser, A.E., & Dunnett, S.B. (1996). Survival and differentiation of rat and human EGF responsive precursor cells following grafting into the lesioned adult CNS. *Experimental Neurology, 137*, 376–388.

Thompson, W.G. (1890). Successful brain grafting. *New York Medical Journal, 51*, 701–702.

Triarhou, L.C. (1996). The cerebellar model of neural grafting: Structural integration and functional recovery. *Brain Research Bulletin, 39*, 127–138.

Triarhou, L.C., Zhang, W., & Lee, W.H. (1996). Amelioration of the behavioral phenotype in genetically ataxic mice through bilateral intracerebellar grafting of fetal Purkinje cells. *Cell Transplantation, 5*, 269–277.

Wenning, G.K., Odin, P., Morrish, P., Rehncrona, S., Widner, H., Brundin, P., Rothwell, J.C., Brown, R., Gustavii, B., Hagell, P., Jahanshahi, M., Sawle, G., Björklund, A., Brooks, D.J., Marsden, C.D., Quinn, N.P., & Lindvall, O. (1997). Short- and long-term survival and function of unilateral intrastriatal dopaminergic grafts in Parkinson's disease. *Annals of Neurology, 42*, 95–107.

Wictorin, K. (1992). Anatomy and connectivity of intrastriatal striatal transplants. *Progress in Neurobiology, 38*, 611–639.

Wictorin, K., & Björklund, A. (1989). Connectivity of striatal grafts implanted into the ibotenic acid lesioned striatum: II. Cortical afferents. *Neuroscience, 30*, 297–311.

Wictorin, K., Isacson, O., Fischer, W., Nothias, F., Peschanski, M., & Björklund, A. (1988). Connectivity of striatal grafts implanted into the ibotenic acid lesioned striatum: I. Subcortical afferents. *Neuroscience, 27*, 547–562.

Wiegand, S.J., & Gash, D.M. (1987). Characteristics of vasculature and neurovascular relations in intraventricular anterior hypothalamic transplants. *Brain Research Bulletin, 20*, 105–124.

Winn, S.R., Hammang, J.P., Emerich, D.F., Lee, A., Palmiter, R.D., & Baetege, E.E. (1994). Polymer-encapsulated cells genetically modified to secrete human nerve growth factor promote the survival of axotomized septal cholinergic neurons. *Proceedings of the National Academy of Sciences of the USA, 91*, 2324–2328.

Woodruff, M.L., Baisden, R.H., & Nonneman, A.J. (1990). Transplantation of fetal hippocampus may prevent or produce behavioral recovery from hippocampal ablation and recovery persists after removal of the transplant. *Progress in Brain Research*, *82*, 367–376.

Woodruff, M.L., Baisden, R.H., Whittington, D.L., & Benson, A.E. (1987). Embryonic hippocampal grafts ameliorate the deficit in DRL acquisition produced by hippocampectomy. *Brain Research*, *408*, 97–117.

Young, M.J., Rao, K., & Lund, R.D. (1989). Integrity of the blood–brain barrier in retinal xenografts is correlated with the immunological status of the host. *Journal of Comparative Neurology*, *283*, 107–117.

Zetterström, T., Brundin, P., Gage, F.H., et al. (1986). in vivo measurement of spontaneous release and metabolism of dopamine from intrastriatal nigral grafts using intracerebral dialysis. *Brain Research*, *362*, 344–349.

Zhou, F.C., & Azmitia, E. (1988). Laminin facilitates and guides fiber growth of transplanted neurons in adult brain. *Journal of Chemical Neuroanatomy*, *1*, 133–146.

10. Learning and skill acquisition

Lorraine L. Pinnington   Christopher D. Ward

Learning can be defined as *the process by which experience brings about relatively permanent changes in behavioural potential* (Anderson, 1995). The French term for rehabilitation, *re-education*, acknowledges the crucial importance of learning in the rehabilitation process. Successful rehabilitation outcomes will depend largely on changes in behaviour continuing outside and beyond the therapeutic period.

Learning is a pervasive aspect of human life and of all nervous systems. An avoidance reaction—for example ducking one's head when walking through a low door—is learned through a simple, reflex-bound process not dissimilar to the type of learning observable in molluscs and other primitive organisms. At the other extreme some human skills—for example playing chess, or translating from one language to another—depend on information processing. Clinical practice embraces the whole spectrum of learning processes between these two extremes.

The best approach to theories of learning is through the experimental paradigms on which they are based. Learning research will be described from four overlapping perspectives in this chapter: (1) Non-associative learning includes relatively primitive behavioural processes, such as habituation, sensitisation, and priming. (2) Associative learning includes classical and operant conditioning and other related paradigms. Most of the evidence for these processes is derived from animal experiments. (3) Studies of memory are centred on the storage, processing, and reuse of information. (4) Skill learning provides a fourth perspective, although to some extent drawing on other learning paradigms. The concept of skill is of fundamental importance. Rehabilitation usually entails the re-acquisition of old skills, the performance of existing skills, and the learning of new ones.

NON-ASSOCIATIVE LEARNING

Habituation and sensitisation

Habituation and sensitisation are two forms of learning in which the behavioural response to a *single* stimulus is shown to change over time. Since only one stimulus is involved, both are categorised as non-associative processes. These have been studied extensively in molluscs and other simple systems (see Kandel, 1976). From a survival point of view it is important that we are

alert and respond to changes in the environment and unexpected events. Thus, the tendency for the head and eyes to turn towards a flashing light will wane (habituate) if the light continues to flash. Similarly, if sitting in a coffee shop, the awareness and recognition of a newly presented pungent odour would override the background aroma of coffee. Sensitisation is the opposite phenomenon to habituation. In some circumstances, an emotional or physical response can be enhanced when a stimulus is repeated. A child may react increasingly violently when an unpleasant but recurring stimulus, such as an injection, is presented on several occasions. In humans, habituation and sensitisation are rarely divorced from other learning mechanisms.

Priming

Priming is another learning phenomenon in which the response to a single stimulus is modified by prior experience. In verbal priming, presentation of a word or "target" has been shown to bias subsequent responses (Schacter, 1985). In a typical priming experiment subjects are exposed to a series of words in such a way that the words cannot be recalled easily or recognised afterwards. They are then asked to complete a series of incomplete words such as "br", "pul", etc. in any way they please. If the target list includes the words "bring", "pulse", etc. subjects are likely to complete the fragments to form these words rather than, say, "brush" or "pulley". Such verbal priming tasks require no explicit effort: The subject is not asked to try to learn the material, and is not required to try to recall anything. Amnesic patients who have severe deficits in explicit learning and recall can often perform well in priming tasks (Warrington & Weiskrantz, 1974; Schacter, 1985). Priming often involves the facilitation of associations with knowledge which existed prior to the test, as when the prime "bread" leads to the more rapid processing of "butter". The duration of measurable priming effects varies according to the paradigm but may be as long as 12 months (Tulving et al., 1991).

Non-associative learning in rehabilitation

Non-associative learning processes such as habituation and sensitisation could play a part in therapeutic procedures which do

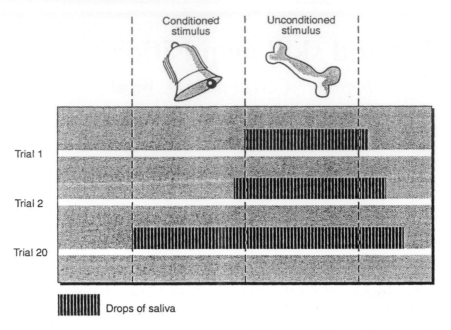

Figure 10.1. Classical conditioning. Effect of successive pairings of an unconditioned stimulus (meat) with a conditioned stimulus (a bell) on the conditioned response (salivation).

not require the patient's active cooperation. The observation that spasticity can be modified for a period of time following muscle stretching (Waters, 1984) suggests a physiological change which might be based on the facilitation of innate reflex patterns. Another application might be the establishment of bowel "habit", which is said to be possible after total cord transection. Repeated stimulation of the rectum by suppositories or other means could sensitise reflex bowel action.

The role of priming in rehabilitation is difficult to evaluate. Verbal priming is often preserved in amnesics (Schacter, 1985), but this does not enable associative learning to occur: The ability to produce the word "bus" after it has been previously primed in some way does not improve the ability to make an association such as "the bus to the station is a number 21". The products of all types of priming are automatic; they may automatically activate pre-existing linkages (e.g., bread to butter, or perhaps bus to driver) but the linkages cannot apparently be used to derive meaning from specific stimuli in the real world. This is why verbal priming and related processes cannot be generalised to produce comparable effects outside the laboratory or therapeutic situation.

ASSOCIATIVE LEARNING

General references for this topic are: Lieberman (1990), Anderson (1995), and Hill (1997).

The two dominant associative learning paradigms are classical (or Pavlovian) and operant (or instrumental) conditioning. Both of these involve the formation of associations between *two or more* stimuli and new connections are formed between one experience and another.

Classical conditioning

A dog normally salivates when it is shown meat, but not when it hears a bell. Pavlov demonstrated in his pioneering work, for which he was awarded the Nobel Prize in 1904, that a dog can be conditioned to salivate in response to the sound of a bell alone, provided the bell is paired repeatedly with the presentation of meat. So-called classical (Pavlovian) conditioning was more influential in the early part of the 20th century than it is today, although the paradigm is still relevant to our understanding of learning processes (Hollis, 1997). The basic elements of a classical conditioning experiment are a reflex (e.g., salivation); a natural stimulus for the reflex (e.g., meat); and an experimental stimulus (e.g., a bell) (Figure 10.1).

In the classical experiment meat, the natural stimulus for the innate reflex of salivation, is called the *unconditioned stimulus* (US).[1] The sound of the bell is an experimental stimulus, termed the *conditioned stimulus* (CS). Salivation induced experimentally by repeated association with the conditioned stimulus is called the *conditioned response* (CR).

Watson and Raynor (1920) were amongst the first to apply Pavlov's principles of classical conditioning to humans. In an ethically dubious experiment involving an 11-month-old infant, they succeeded in inducing fear of a rat by presenting it with the sound of a hammer striking a steel bar.

Effective conditioning depends on the stimuli being associated systematically (Rescorla, 1988). A model proposed by Rescorla and Wagner (1972) shows that many of the phenomena of classical conditioning could be based on a very simple mathematical rule defining "associative strength", the

---

[1] The word unconditioned is a source of confusion: The term Pavlov used should have been translated *unconditional* (McLeish, 1975).

strength of the link between an unconditioned stimulus and a conditioned stimulus. Very subtle effects, for example discriminations between different wavelengths of light stimuli, can be produced. Such effects are seen in simple organisms and are not mediated cognitively.

Extinction.   If the conditioned stimulus is no longer followed by the unconditioned stimulus, the probability of the conditioned response declines and the conditioned response is said to be extinguished. Extinction is not due to the fading away of a memory trace. If the conditioned stimulus is subsequently paired with a novel stimulus, the conditioned response may again be elicited. Such effects can be demonstrated a year or more after training. This and other evidence suggests that extinction involves active inhibition—a form of new learning—rather than passive "forgetting" (see Bouton, 1993).

The everyday relevance of pavlovian conditioning.   Only a limited number of responses can be conditioned experimentally and there is more to life than meat and salivation. How, then, can classical conditioning contribute to everyday learning? One answer to this question is that the innate unconditioned responses (UR) which are subject to Pavlovian conditioning are more numerous than those which are convenient to study and measure in the laboratory. They include a range of behaviours related to feeding, excretion, sex, and escape from danger.

Classical conditioning might explain how we form preferences which have profound effects on behaviour. Aversion to the sound of a dentist's drill can come about, for example, through the formation of a new association between stimuli. Similarly, sexual arousal can become conditioned to previously insignificant stimuli. When a second conditioned stimulus becomes independently capable of inducing a conditioned response *secondary conditioning* is said to have occurred.

Operant conditioning

Operant or instrumental conditioning was first described by B.F. Skinner in the 1930s. Learning through operant conditioning depends on the development of an association between a behaviour and its results. Behaviour can be modified either by rewards or by punishments. Whilst eating chocolate produces pleasant results and is likely to recur, eating soap is usually a once-only event. In behaviourist terminology, behaviours which are closely followed by positive results will be reinforced; behaviours followed by negative effects will diminish.

Operant conditioning experiments are typically carried out on animals such as rats and pigeons. An example is shown in Figure 10.2. Most animal experiments utilise a small range of primary reinforcers, such as food. Secondary reinforcers are stimuli (rewards) which ultimately derive their potency from indirect connections with primary reinforcers. Praise is a form of secondary reinforcement, another classic example being money.

The operant response.   The operant response—e.g., pressing a button—is a "behavioural unit" rather than a precisely stereotyped reflex response of the type induced by Pavlovian

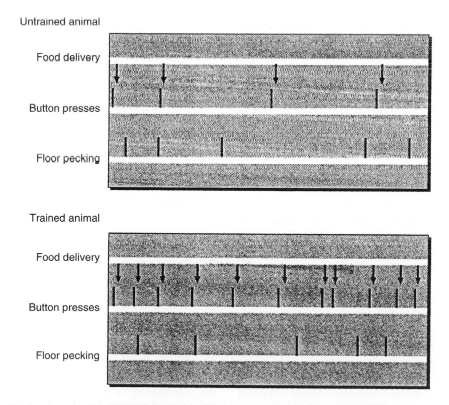

Figure 10.2. An operant conditioning experiment on a pigeon. Effect of successive pairings of a reinforcer (food delivery) on an operant response (button pressing). Another activity—floor pecking—is not reinforced.

conditioning. For example a pigeon can press a button in a number of ways; physiological details such as muscle activation vary from response to response. Similarly, working hard might be the operant response to the secondary reinforcing effect of gaining praise from a manager, but there is a variety of ways of "working hard".

Reinforcement and punishment. If food is provided immediately after a pigeon's beak happens to strike a target button by chance, the same behaviour will be more likely to recur (i.e., will be reinforced). A response is reinforced in one of two ways, both of which are "positive" for the subject: Either the response produces a positive reward (positive reinforcement) or it causes an unpleasant stimulus to cease (negative reinforcement, or escape). Thus, keeping to the speed limit can be positively reinforced by praising drivers publicly, or it can be negatively reinforced by repeated fines for speeding.

Operant conditioning can suppress a target behaviour rather than encouraging a new one. The suppression may be achieved by punishment, as when a patient's aggressive outbursts predictably lead to a period of social isolation. The same effect can be obtained by positive reinforcement of an alternative behaviour which is incompatible with the undesired behaviour (see Chapter 31 on behaviour problems): For example, encouraging a patient's constructive activities through praise or specific rewards might reduce the amount of time available for disruptive behaviour.

Reinforcement cannot begin until the first occasion in which the target behaviour occurs spontaneously, producing a reward. Rather than waiting for this to occur by chance, the experimenter can reinforce intermediate stages—for example when an animal walks towards the button which will produce the reward—so that the target behaviour becomes more probable in successive trials. This technique, termed *shaping by successive approximation*, is sometimes used in human behavioural modification programmes.

Extinction. Extinction of an operant response parallels the extinction of classical conditioning; it occurs when the operant response is no longer reinforced. A temporary increase in the operant response—an extinction burst—may then occur. Thus, the reinforcement for pressing a light switch is illumination of the room, and when the bulb fails to light, a series of rapidly repeated switching movements of the fingers represents an "extinction burst". A patient who throws tantrums may be gaining secondary reinforcement from the attention he receives from staff. If the rehabilitation team resolves to ignore the tantrums, their frequency and severity may initially increase before eventually waning as reinforcement is withheld.

Intermittent reinforcement. Most real-life reinforcers are less reliable than light-bulb illumination: Only a proportion of operant responses are reinforced. Under experimental and therapeutic conditions, responses can be maintained by intermittent reinforcement. Delayed reinforcement halts the extinction process, and maintains the operant response. Thus, obtaining a light on the fifth attempt once again reinforces switching as a response. A patient's disruptive behaviours may gradually be

Table 10.1. The contrast between classical and operant conditioning

	Classical conditioning	Operant conditioning
What properties must the animal/subject have?	• An innate reflex	• Spontaneous behaviour + motivation to seek a reward or to avoid punishment
What features must the environment have?	• A natural stimulus (US) + • An experimental stimulus (CS)	• Reward or punishment results from a specific form of behaviour
What new associations are learned?	• Between an innate response and a new stimulus	• Between a form of behaviour and its result

extinguished by removing a source of reinforcement such as receiving extra attention from staff. A well-meaning visitor who summons a nurse during an outburst will provide intermittent reinforcement and re-establish the behaviour.

Differences between classical and operant conditioning

It is important to stress the contrast between operant and classical conditioning (Table 10.1). To recapitulate: The basic ingredients for classical conditioning are an innate reflex, a natural stimulus, and an experimental stimulus. Responses (such as salivation) are outside the control of the experimenter, being governed by innate factors which determine what unconditioned response is induced by a given unconditioned stimulus, and what conditioned response is induced by a given conditioned stimulus. In operant conditioning, by contrast, the range of possible responses is wider. Responses begin by being random, and become progressively more likely if they are reinforced, or progressively less likely if they are punished.

How does associative learning interact with cognition?

Since both classical and operant conditioning processes can be demonstrated in primitive organisms such as Aplysia (Cook & Carew, 1989), they cannot depend on complex cognition or on consciousness. Radical behaviourists such as Watson (1928) claimed that all human learning is ultimately explicable in terms of conditioning effects. However, human behaviour can hardly ever be uninfluenced by cognitive processes. Even people with severe neurological impairments use knowledge and make choices. Thus even when a task such as dressing is learned through the chaining of a series of subcomponents, there is usually also some evidence of cognitive mediation. General world knowledge (semantic knowledge) is almost always involved—for example in identifying an object as a garment, and a sleeve as a sleeve. Artificial intelligence programmes have shown the importance of such knowledge in seemingly simple tasks (Boden, 1987).

A key characteristic of human behaviour is the feeding-back of data for error correction and this also is difficult (although not impossible) to conceptualise within a conditioning model (Rescorla, 1987). The early behaviourists such as Skinner had little to say about how cognition interacts with conditioning but others such as Tolman incorporated cognitive elements within associative models (see Hill, 1997).

Associative learning in rehabilitation

Despite the shortcomings and misuse of learning theory, it contributes to our understanding of patients and has therapeutic applications. Classical conditioning processes provide a persuasive model (and therapeutic approaches) for emotional disorders such as anxiety and phobic states and the subjective significance of sensory disturbances and pain undoubtedly owe much to learned associations of unconditioned with conditioned stimuli. The concepts of operant conditioning can be used to explain some aspects of many behaviours. For example, disruptive behaviour following brain injury can be interpreted in terms of the reinforcement it provides (see Chapter 38) and a similar account can be given for other behaviour disorders, for example abnormal illness behaviour. A wide variety of symptoms can be shown to be at least partly the result of learning, and should be interpreted in their social and cultural contexts (see Pennebaker, 1982). These insights can be used in the design of programmes to modify behaviour (see Chapter 34).

Conditioning processes exhibit limited degrees of generalisation from the learning situation to other environments. Operant learning brings about progressively finer stimulus discriminations so that the operant response tends to become firmly related to a specific context. The context in which learning occurs is a part of the stimulus array so that the more stereotyped the setting in which conditioning occurs the more limited its applicability. Generalisation of a conditioned response beyond the therapeutic setting requires that learning takes place in more than one environment. For example, a specific therapy department is likely to contain cues which exert stimulus control. At home the patient's responses may be influenced by different features of the environment.

MEMORY: INFORMATION STORAGE AND RETRIEVAL

A general reference for this topic is Baddeley (1997); see also Chapter 31.

Cognitive psychology and neuropsychology are concerned with the processing of *information*. Cognitive research on learning and memory has usually been concerned with information which can be verbalised (declarative memory). Declarative memory can be further subdivided into episodic memory, containing data relating to items or events which are associated with specific contexts; and semantic memory, containing general world knowledge.

Declarative memory data:

- can be stored within defined "spaces" (often in specific brain compartments, sometimes in more distributed forms)
- can often be disrupted by focal brain lesions
- has potentially measurable time courses for acquisition, storage, and processing

- can be stored as representations and expressed in the form of symbols such as words ("declarative" memory)
- is potentially available for conscious cognitive operations.

In cognitive terminology, all other forms of learning are described as "procedural". The learning which occurs in conditioning experiments would be classed as procedural, as would many aspects of the acquisition of motor and non-motor skills (see later). Procedural learning has two important properties which distinguish it from declarative memory. First, the results of procedural learning can be demonstrated physically more easily than they can be expressed in words (for example riding a bicycle); second, procedural learning is less disrupted by focal brain lesions.

Cognitive research makes another important distinction, between explicit and implicit learning. Explicit learning is a conscious, intentional process which can be described verbally. Implicit or incidental learning is information or behaviour which is acquired unconsciously (Schacter et al., 1993). Implicit learning is an everyday experience, as when we "pick up" fragments of a foreign language or new pieces of current jargon. It can be demonstrated in the laboratory in normal subjects, for example by showing/highlighting that they have unwittingly learned to detect grammatical rules used in assembling strings of code (see Berry, 1997).

Many neuropsychological explanations of information learning are closely analogous with the operation of first-generation digital computers in which processing occurs in stages through a series of modules each having limited capacity. Procedural learning can also be described in computer terms, using analogies from more recent technological developments. Software designers use the concept "procedures" as programme segments which in some languages can themselves be remodelled by input data (thus the computer can re-programme itself as a result of "experience"). Modern computer science uses the term "neural nets" to describe systems which progressively adapt themselves to the structure and properties of the "environment" (data from the outside world).

Stages in information storage and retrieval

Iconic and echoic "memory".   There is a general assumption, supported by experimental evidence, that information such as written or spoken words is passed to longer-term stores as sensory traces which decay within 100 ms (Haber & Standing, 1969).

Short-term or immediate memory.   Popular usage refers to memory for recent events (in the last few hours or days) as "short-term" but in experimental psychology this material is regarded as part of the "long-term" store. Short-term memory has a shorter time course. Much evidence supports the general concept of a limited-capacity store within which material is held separately from more permanent traces for a period of a few seconds. Short-term memory requires active neural transmission (Miller & Marlin, 1984). The time course suggests that short-term synaptic plasticity might be involved.

Short-term memory capacity is measured by memory span either for lists of symbols (digits, letters, words) or for non-verbal equivalents. Capacity is normally around seven items. The assumption that short-term memory is separate from long-term memory is supported by the fact that there is a recency effect (increased recall of the last items of lists) for immediate recall, but not for delayed recall. Immediate verbal recall and delayed recall are aided by different cues. Moreover, there is neuropsychological evidence of a double dissociation between short-term and long-term memory impairment (see Baddeley, 1988, 1997).

There is evidence that verbal-based learning tasks interfere with each other more than they do with visual learning. Baddeley's (1988) model of working memory uses the modular approach typical of cognitive psychology. Short-term processing is assumed to occur in several subsystems of which two have been most intensively investigated, an articulatory loop and a visuospatial sketchpad. They are controlled by a central executive based on the model of Shallice (1988) (see Chapter 29 on dysexecutive syndrome). An executive deficit can disrupt both verbal and visuospatial learning.

Long-term memory.   Transfer from temporary to more permanent storage is rapid. Using electroconvulsive shock to induce experimental amnesia in animals shows that transfer to a long-term store can occur within 500 ms (Miller & Marlin, 1984). Whether there is a further period of consolidation of memory traces remains controversial (see Weingartner & Parker, 1984). Long-term traces are resistant to convulsive amnesic agents, suggesting that they are maintained by passive biochemically based storage, rather than continuous neuronal activity (Miller & Marlin, 1984). It is likely that long-term storage involves synaptic modifications: structural changes, or biochemical changes such as occur in long-term synaptic potentiation.

Retrieval.   Data from the long-term store are recovered by a process of retrieval. Retrieval is to some extent automatic, which is why a forgotten name will often "occur" to us spontaneously, whereas a conscious effort to recall it can be counterproductive. Spreading activation models can be used to explain automatic retrieval of either verbal or non-verbal material (Hanson & Burr, 1990).

Factors influencing verbal learning and retrieval

A number of factors influence the extent of information learning. These include:

- attention
- rehearsal strategy
- semantic processing (meaningful learning)
- prior knowledge
- context
- explicit vs implicit (incidental) learning.

Attention and rehearsal strategy.   Attention is a concept which takes different forms in different theoretical systems. In Baddeley's (1988) working memory model selective attention is conceived as the supervisory function of the central executive. Attentional deficits of the type seen with frontal lesions contribute to learning impairments. Attention is also affected by rehearsal strategy. If all the learning is done in one session attention may wander. Distributed practice with interspersed rest periods is often preferable, particularly for long and continuous tasks.

Semantic processing.   Semantic processing, the derivation of *meaning* from a stimulus, has a strong effect on learning. "Depth of processing" influences the degree of retention of material such as word lists (Craik & Lockhart, 1972). Thus, a list of words such as "bus, antelope, virtue..." etc is remembered more easily if processing of the material is meaningful (e.g., "form of transport, wild animal, abstract quality...", etc.) rather than superficial (e.g., "first letter b, first letter a...", etc.).

Prior knowledge.   Semantic processing of the word "antelope" depends on prior knowledge that an antelope is an animal. Prior knowledge greatly affects our ability to learn new information. Thus experienced chess-players are better than novices at retaining chess positions (Simon & Gilmartin, 1973). Since experts have greater prior knowledge than novices they can make greater sense of what they see and can process data more deeply and meaningfully. Professionals sometimes underestimate the extent to which neurological patients are hampered in their learning by factors such as lower level of prior education, limited literacy, or lack of familiarity with the assumptions underlying rehabilitation programmes.

Context.   Information learning is also influenced by the context in which it occurs. This effect has been termed "encoding specificity" (Tulving & Thomson, 1973). Retrieval is facilitated by re-creating the contextual conditions in which learning occurred; this is why if I forget why I have entered a room it is helpful to return to my starting point, which acts as a retrieval cue.

Explicit learning.   Although information can be learned implicitly, without conscious effort, such incidental learning tends to be shallow, and very frequent repetitions may produce little retention. Everyday experience reminds us that information learning is enhanced by effort. Deliberate or explicit learning capitalises on the already mentioned benefits of focused attention and depth of semantic processing. Conscious effort, and therefore motivation, enhances learning (although it has negative effects on retrieval: It is unhelpful to try to remember a name we have forgotten).

Verbal learning in rehabilitation

Cerebral disorders causing impaired information learning are discussed elsewhere in this book and will not be reviewed here (but see Kapur, 1994). Impaired information learning has important consequences in all aspects of rehabilitation, including skill acquisition. For example, speech therapy often involves teaching specific, explicit strategies; occupational therapists often aim to fractionate complex skills into verbally labelled subroutines; and a patient's ability to understand and remember verbal instructions is important in physiotherapy. Acquiring a skill does not depend entirely on information learning but is greatly facilitated by it. Several theories of motor skill learning involve a verbal-motor stage (Adams, 1971; Anderson, 1982; see later).

LEARNING NEW SKILLS

General references on this topic are: Smyth and Wing (1984), Kelso (1982), and Anderson (1995).

The real world presents a never-ending variety of new things to say, new items to remember, new terrains to move across, new movements to accomplish, new social contexts, new intellectual problems to solve. Some aspects of such experiences are unique to specific contexts, but some of what we learn in each activity is available for *transfer* from one context to another, and can bring about changes in the way in which we approach the next similar, but not identical, experience.

The term "skill" is difficult to define. Skills are:

- observable qualities of behaviour
- methods, approaches or procedures, rather than set routines
- acquired, and/or improvable through practice
- adaptable to different environments (i.e., generalisable from one situation to another)
- possessed by different individuals in varying degrees, as a result of learning
- not fully describable in words.

The last listed characteristic—inexpressibility in words—highlights the contribution of non-verbal learning processes to all types of skill (not merely motor skills). Much of the skill someone may demonstrate in tennis, in cooking, or in diplomacy depends on "procedures" rather than on "propositions" (explicit rules) and is the product of what cognitivists call procedural as opposed to episodic learning processes. However, skill-learning is not solely procedural but usually involves a combination of two or more of the learning processes described earlier, and there is still much controversy about the extent to which explicit and episodic learning contributes to implicit learning (e.g., see Neal & Hesketh, 1997 and Berry, 1997).

Motor skill learning

Motor learning is not analogous with verbal learning. Whilst short-term motor memory provides a parallel with short-term information learning the long-term storage of memory for movements and actions poses unique problems.

Memory for basic movements and for movement sequences. A basic movement such as elbow flexion seems a promising starting point for the study of motor learning because a simple movement could perhaps be a building block for more complex actions. Short-term motor memory (STMM) has been studied in terms of variables such as location and distance. In a typical experiment the hand might be moved along a track from a defined starting position to a stop (Smyth, 1984). Such studies have shown how different types of information (including visual cues) might be used to code memories for basic movements.

Stereotyped movement sequences provide another widely used experimental approach, for example in studies of the cerebral localisation of motor memory (e.g., Honda et al., 1998). Studies of single movements and of movement sequences rely on an analogy between motor learning and verbal learning. However, this analogy breaks down when skilled actions rather than basic movements are considered.

Memory for actions.   A motor skill such as pouring fluid from a jug to a cup involves a number of basic movements such as elbow flexion. Based on the verbal learning analogy, one might suppose that information about location and distance for each basic movement in the sequence could be coded in a long-term store, having been transferred there from STMM. However, such a simple model is unlikely to explain human movement because of the novelty problem: Each particular performance has to take account of variations in starting positions, termed initial conditions (see Chapter 11). For example the position of the trunk prior to the action of pouring may vary in relation to the shoulder, as may the upper arm in relation to the trunk. Even a small change in these initial conditions would have a "knock on" effect on each subsequent basic movement in the sequence so that if the action of the arm as a whole were executed by means of a chain of stereotyped basic movements the arm's final position would inevitably miss the target. It is interesting to note that even the response of a simple system such as the long-latency stretch reflex is critically dependent on the physiological and biomechanical context (the initial conditions) in which it is induced (Nashner, 1976; see also Reed, 1982).

Because of the novelty problem, it seems unlikely that motor skills are coded in the brain by means of one-to-one links between muscles and neurons. Defining the starting position of the hand (e.g., for pouring) would require the brain to code the tensions and lengths of a very large number of muscles, or at least the positions of a large number of joints, not just in the arm and shoulder, but also in the spine. Coding all possible starting positions, and all possible movement sequences, would result in information overload. The problem of information overload is reduced if groups of muscles and joints function together in "coordinative structures" or synergies, which operate relatively automatically (Tuller et al., 1982). This view of human motor behaviour has been influenced by the great Soviet physiologist Bernstein (see Whiting, 1984).

The problem of information overload is further reduced if we bear in mind that not all aspects of actions have to be learned. Many routines such as stepping movements can be induced in the spinal cat. It is possible that much of what we call motor learning is the triggering of innate responses and Adams (1984) suggests that a basic repertoire of "instinctive" movement patterns may contribute to the formation of movement sequences. Innate behaviours such as sucking, feeding, etc., are part of the response repertoire of mammals. Kelso (1995) suggests that learning "occurs as a specific modification of already existing behavioural patterns in the direction of the task to be learned". These patterns include some which are expressions of biomechanical constraints, some which are innate reflexes, and some which are acquired behaviours.

One question remains: What kind of neurological processes underlie motor learning? There is abundant evidence that an abstract level of movement coding occurs. For example, a person's handwriting is equally distinctive whether produced in a miniature note-book or on a flip chart, even though very different combinations of muscles are used. Such phenomena suggest that the brain encodes a motor skill in an abstract form, which Schmidt (1982) termed a *schema*. However, it seems likely that no single learning process will adequately explain all aspects of a complex motor skill.

A general theory of skill acquisition

Anderson (1982, 1995) has proposed a theory of skill acquisition which can be applied to non-motor as well as to motor skills. In the *cognitive stage* the learner approaches the task as an explicit problem to be solved. There are often opportunities to break down the major goal into subgoals. For example someone with hemiplegia learning to stand from a sitting position will first learn to adjust the position of the trunk and feet. Similarly, in the cognitive stage of learning to drive the process of starting the engine and getting into first gear must be memorised as a series of discrete stages.

Verbal instructions from a teacher can be crucial at the cognitive stage (Adams, 1971; Anderson, 1982, 1995). It is more efficient (and safer) to tell a new driver which pedal is the brake, rather than waiting for her to discover by trial and error. Similarly, it is helpful to give verbal descriptions in the early stages of recovering sitting balance or learning to use a new walking aid. Later, such facts may play no direct part in executing the skill of driving, standing, or walking.

In the *associative stage* the learner is lumping discrete stages into "condition–action pairs" (one might call them reflexes) of the type: "for the goal of standing up, shift weight forward *and* tuck feet in" or "for the goal of starting the car, turn the ignition-key *and* depress the clutch". The formation of these automatic "production rules" is termed proceduralisation. Procedures lump together subgoals and appear to "cut corners". Finally, in the *autonomous stage*, a series of production rules are amalgamated into a programme which represents the skill (for example standing, or driving). Since the cognitive component at this stage is reduced, the task makes less demands on attention and other tasks can be carried out simultaneously. At this stage skills are accomplished not through the conscious use of learned information but through unconscious application of procedures.

We have seen that motor skills may be encoded as abstract representations of movement termed "schemata" (see earlier). Anderson's more general theory of skill-learning postulates the formation of "productions", a term borrowed from artificial intelligence. Essentially this involves statements of the type "If X . . . then Y". Rules of this type provide a general structure for skills as diverse as parsing a sentence or riding a bicycle.

Factors affecting skill learning

Verbal learning. In the cognitive stage of skill learning, all the factors which promote efficient verbal learning are relevant (see earlier).

Active learning. Much skill learning is procedural (non-verbal), but this does not imply that optimal learning occurs automatically. Active participation enhances procedural learning (Vakil et al., 1998). Skill learning is enhanced by greater engagement in the task. Not all forms of engagement are helpful, however: Conscious (verbal) analysis of performance can be distracting and can impede learning.

Practice. Practice schedules have been studied in many learning situations, including verbal learning (see Baddeley, 1997) and motor skill learning (see Kelso, 1982). The *total time hypothesis* states that the amount of learning achieved is a function of the total time devoted to learning. Another principle is that *distributed practice*—learning in multiple sessions—is preferable to fewer more prolonged practice sessions. Fatigue is one obvious reason for using distributed practice schedules; another is that during a prolonged practice session a particular pattern of response, and of error, may predominate and be perpetuated. A third advantage of distributed practice may be that intervals between practice sessions are used for covert or mental rehearsal. There is growing evidence particularly from research on the acquisition of sporting skill, that active mental rehearsal enhances subsequent performance (Garza & Feltz, 1998).

Context. Learning is facilitated by varying the performance and the context. At a different practice session the context will be different, other types of performance will occur and the resultant learning be more general. The inherent variability of each performance of a motor skill—the changes in initial conditions—may help to explain why motor learning tends to be more robust than information learning: the encoding conditions are less specific.

Feedback: Knowledge of performance and knowledge of results. One prerequisite for improving a motor skill is information about the outcome of each performance, termed knowledge of results (KR). However, knowing that you scored an ace does not in itself improve your tennis serve. KR must be combined in some way with a mechanism for retaining and reproducing good performance and rejecting erroneous trials. Such data will usually be derived firstly from a mental image of the intended movement (feed-forward) and secondly from a memory record of the performance, typically based on visual and proprioceptive feedback. For reasons given in the preceding section on motor learning, these data are likely to be coded in the form of an abstract schema. In motor skills there is a complex relationship between KR and KP (Brisson & Alain, 1997).

The processing of KR is one aspect of motor skill learning which is open to cognitively based experiments since it involves acquiring information and competes with other information-learning for working memory resources (Marteniuk, 1986). The issue of KR is relevant to all skills but the interaction between KR and other learning factors is complex (see Swinnen, 1990; Swinnen et al., 1990; Winstein & Schmidt, 1990).

In non-motor skills KR and KP contribute similarly to learning. KP is derived from a comparison between intentions and a record of performances (for example chess moves which led to a current position).

Positive and negative transfer. In normal learning, specific aspects of one task frequently cause negative effects on related tasks. For example, driving a car whose indicator switch is on the left of the steering column deleteriously affects subsequent driving of a car with the opposite arrangement. In a study of telegraphists, negative transfer was demonstrated when, after learning one letter-symbol code, the telegraphists learned another code. Subsequently, however, performance in the second task benefited from the previous exposure to the original task. The improvement in general aspects of the skill—for example speed of finger or eye movement—represented positive transfer (Siipola & Israel, 1933). The concept of positive and negative transfer applies to all skills.

It is easier to demonstrate that transfer has occurred than to pinpoint precisely what has been transferred during skill learning. Among the candidates as vehicles of transfer are verbal information; other cognitive data such as motor schemata or abstract rules termed "productions"; and conditioned reflexes.

Learning new skills in rehabilitation

Motor skill learning. Learning or relearning a skill such as walking following a hemiplegic stroke is not based purely on memorising a sequence of basic movements such as stepping but is likely to involve the formation of an abstract "schema". An efficient schema must take account of altered biomechanical conditions, for example failure of the hip to flex on the paretic side. Such factors may make pre-existing "coordinative structures" irrelevant or inoperative, and presumably new ones are formed. It therefore seems implausible that motor relearning in rehabilitation consists solely in the revival of memory traces laid down prior to the stroke.

Motor learning takes place against a background of innate, "hard-wired" reactions which can sometimes be exploited but may often be deleterious—for example unselective flexion of the spastic arm.

General aspects of skill acquisition. In rehabilitation, motor learning is just one aspect of the more general problem of skill acquisition, and a number of general learning principles apply both to motor and to non-motor skills. Many lessons can be drawn from the theoretical background of skill acquisition, even though evidence is fragmentary. First, as mentioned earlier, it must be recognised that verbal learning is fundamental to many skills. Preservation of "procedural memory" in experimental tests of brain-injured patients should not disguise this fact. Even

in motor skill acquisition it may be necessary to devise ways of compensating for deficiencies in retaining information which is required especially in the early stages of learning. Therapeutic programmes may need to be prolonged specifically in order to allow basic verbal information required for skill acquisition to "sink in"; or alternatives such as written instructions may be needed.

During rehabilitation the environment for learning tends to be standardised—the same parallel bars, the same bathroom—and the materials for learning are often equally routine: a limited set of words for speech therapy; the same clothes for dressing; etc. But abilities acquired in hospital are often inappropriate to natural conditions. People with severe brain injury tend to have limited ability to generalise from one learning situation to another. Insofar as operant processes contribute to learning, it is important, as we have seen, to vary the context of learning to minimise negative aspects of stimulus control. The same principle applies to the learning of motor skills. For example, transferring from chair to bed should involve more than one bed and chair combination. Alternatively, if learning ability is severely limited and context-specific, it will be necessary to train the patient in the home environment. Therapy assessments should not be limited to the original therapeutic environment. We must ensure that the patient can benefit from speech therapy, carry out self-care tasks, etc., in the outside world.

Negative transfer is an important concept in rehabilitation where learning of one task may have deleterious effects on another. Detection of such interactions requires careful observation and teamwork.

Other negative learning effects must be appreciated. The whole environment provides the patient with the possibility of acquiring undesirable forms of behaviour which are nevertheless, in a sense, highly skilled. These include for example inefficient patterns of gait and the social "skill" of manipulating staff and family.

BIOLOGICAL BASIS OF LEARNING

General references for this topic are: Dudai (1989), Mathies (1989), and Alkon et al. (1991).

Cellular mechanisms of learning

Most evidence suggests that neurologically based learning requires changes in synaptic function (synaptic plasticity). The best understood synaptic changes are those of short duration (seconds or minutes) (Zucker, 1989; Mendell, 1984). Neurons show long-term changes in firing and biochemical properties as a result of stimulation (see Carew & Sahley, 1986). One promising candidate mechanism for human learning is long-term synaptic potentiation (LTP) which is mediated by N-methyl-D-aspartate (NMDA) receptors (see Matthies, 1989; Brown et al., 1988). LTP was first demonstrated following tetanic stimulation of the hippocampus but occurs at other sites (Martinez & Derrick, 1996).

Long-term changes in synaptic transmission may not be based on pre-synaptic firing rates but on enzyme-mediated changes which occur at *selected* post-synaptic sites. Such selection of specific pathways—"neuronal Darwinism"—could be a general property of learning in the central nervous system (Alkon, 1988; Young, 1988).

Anatomy: Where does learning occur?

Processes involved in learning occur at many levels in the central nervous system.

Cerebral hemispheres. Neuropsychological evidence shows that in general verbal learning deficits are associated with left hemisphere lesions, and non-verbal deficits with right hemisphere damage (Newcombe, 1969; Kapur, 1994). The two areas most clearly associated with the amnesic syndrome (see Chapter 28) are the medial temporal lobes and the diencephalon (Squire et al., 1993). There is neuropsychological evidence to suggest that the hippocampus stores event memories, rather than general knowledge (semantic memory) (Eichenbaum, 1997). Focal lesions of the frontal lobes can also impair learning (e.g., Petrides, 1985). In the amnesic syndrome, there may be preservation of implicit, procedural learning (see later, Chapter 28, and Schacter, 1985). Some forms of procedural learning are impaired selectively in Huntington's disease, suggesting that the neostriatum may be implicated (Saint Cyr et al., 1988; Heindel et al., 1989; Knowlton et al., 1996), although not all types of motor learning appear to be affected by striatal damage (Willingham et al., 1996).

Experimental data parallel many of the above clinical findings, with strong evidence for the involvement of the hippocampus in learning (O'Keefe & Nadel, 1978), and evidence implicating associated limbic structures including the amygdala (e.g., Gaffan et al., 1989), and the thalamus (e.g., Canavan et al., 1989). The neostriatum may be involved in specific aspects of cue discrimination and learning (Hikosaka et al., 1989).

Cerebellum and brainstem. Following Marr (1969) there continues to be interest in the role of the cerebellum in motor learning (Raymond et al., 1996; Thach, 1998). In one primitive form of learning, the adaptation of the vestibulo-ocular reflex, intrinsic brainstem neurons have a key role, in conjunction with the cerebellum (Lisberger, 1988; Lisberger & Pavalko, 1988). The cerebellum has also been implicated in classical conditioning of eye blinking (Thompson, 1986; Hesslow et al., 1998).

Spinal cord. Post-tetanic potentiation and habituation are two examples of ways in which the spinal cord can change its responses as a result of stimulation and can therefore be said to "learn". From a clinical point of view, a more interesting intrinsic "learning" ability is shown by spinal cats which regain hind-limb stepping after a period of "training" (Grillner & Dubuc, 1988). Wolpaw and Lee (1989) showed that the H-reflex could be modified by operant conditioning in intact monkeys. The induced change in reflex properties remained following cord transection, implying that a memory "trace" can be stored outside the brain.

The physiological basis of non-associative learning

Simple processes such as sensitisation can be studied readily in simple organisms, and morphological as well as physiological changes can be demonstrated, suggesting facilitation of synaptic transmission (Bailey & Chen, 1989). In higher organisms facilitated transmission through more complex neuronal nets is postulated. "Spreading activation" (Anderson, 1984; Baddeley, 1997) is a mechanism which has been used to explain verbal priming effects (Ratcliff & McKoon, 1981). It is suggested that following the processing of a word at an initial "node", there is a ramification of activation across a network, to involve neighbouring nodes which have previously been associated with the target word. Many such associations would represent semantic links.

The physiological basis for classical and operant conditioning

Classical conditioning. The neurophysiological basis of conditioned eye-blinking has been studied extensively (Thompson, 1988; Hesslow et al., 1998). It is thought that unconditioned and conditioned stimuli converge on the cerebellum. The conditioned response (from the interpositus nuclei) is assumed to inhibit activation of the pathway for the unconditioned stimulus, so that associative strength is controlled by a feed-back process.

Behavioural theorists have often claimed that conditioning reflects a fundamental biological mechanism, if not the sole basis for learning. Their claim gains some support from the fact that both classical and operant conditioning can be demonstrated in lower animals (see Carew & Sahley, 1986). In primitive organisms it is conceivable that conditioning could depend on plastic changes in a small number (perhaps as few as three) neurons, representing the convergence of two inputs on a response-neuron (Alkon, 1988; Alkon et al., 1991).

CONCLUSION

This chapter has outlined a number of experimental perspectives which throw light on learning processes involved in neurological rehabilitation. Further details and clinical examples will be found in relevant chapters elsewhere in the book. An important conclusion to be drawn is that no single theory is adequate for all clinical contexts. The fact that learning occurs at so many levels of the nervous system and in so many forms should increase our respect for the learning which occurs in all patients, even those with the most severe impairments of verbal memory.

REFERENCES

Adams, J.A. (1971). A closed loop theory of motor learning. *Journal of Motor Behavior, 3*, 111–149.

Adams, J.A. (1984). Learning of movement sequences. *Psychological Bulletin, 96*, 3–28.

Alkon, D.L. (1988). Memory traces in the brain: a spatial-temporal model of cell activation. *Science, 239*, 998–1005.

Alkon, D.L., Amaral, D.G., Bear, M.F., Black, J., et al. (1991). Learning and memory. *Brain Research Reviews, 16*, 193–220.

Anderson, J.A. (1982). Acquisition of cognitive skill. *Psychological Review, 89*, 369–406.

Anderson, J.R. (1984). Spreading activation. In J.R. Anderson & S.M. Kosslyn (Eds.), *Tutorials in learning and memory*. San Francisco & New York: W.H. Freeman & Co.

Anderson, J.R. (1995). *Learning and memory: An integrated approach*. New York: John Wiley and Sons.

Baddeley, A. (1988). *Working memory*. Oxford: Oxford University Press.

Baddeley, A. (1997). *Human memory: Theory and practice*. Hove: Psychology Press.

Bailey, C.H., & Chen, M. (1989). Time course of structural changes at identified sensory neuron synapses during long-term sensitization in Aplysia. *Journal of Neuroscience, 9*, 1774–1780.

Berry, D.C. (1997). *How implicit is implicit learning?* Oxford: Oxford University Press.

Boden, M.A. (1987). *Artificial intelligence and natural man*. London: The MIT Press.

Bouton, M.E. (1993). Context, time and memory retrieval in the interference paradigms of Pavlovian learning. *Psychological Bulletin, 114*, 80–99.

Brisson, T.-A., & Alain, C. (1997). A comparison of two references for using knowledge of performance in learning a motor task. *Journal of Motor Behaviour, 29*, 339–350.

Brown, T.H., Chapman, P.F., Kairiss, E.W., & Keenan, C.L. (1988). Long term synaptic potentiation. *Science, 242*, 724–728.

Canavan, A.G., Nixon, P.D., & Passingham, R.E. (1989). Motor learning in monkeys (*Macaca fascicularis*) with lesions of the motor thalamus. *Experimental Brain Research, 77*, 113–126.

Carew, T.J., & Sahley, C.L. (1986). Invertebrate learning and memory: from behaviour to molecules. *Annual Review of Neuroscience, 9*, 435–487.

Cook, D.G., & Carew, T.J. (1989). Operant conditioning of head-waving in Aplysia. III. Cellular analysis of possible reinforcement pathways. *Journal of Neuroscience, 9*, 3115–3122.

Craik, F.I.M., & Lockhart, R.S. (1972). Levels of processing: a framework for memory research. *Journal of Verbal Learning and Verbal Behaviour, 11*, 671–684.

Dudai, Y. (1989). *The neurobiology of memory: Concepts, findings, trends*. Oxford: Oxford University Press.

Eichenbaum, H. (1997). How does the brain organise memories? *Science, 277*, 330–332.

Gaffan, D., Gaffan, E.A., & Harrison, S. (1989). Visual-visual associative learning and reward-association learning in monkeys: the role of the amygdala. *Journal of Neuroscience, 9*, 558–564.

Garza, D.L., & Feltz, D.L. (1998). Effects of selected mental practice on performance, self-efficacy and competition confidence of figure skaters. *Sport Psychologist, 12*, 1–15.

Grillner, S., & Dubuc, R. (1988). Control of locomotion in vertebrates: spinal and supraspinal mechanisms. In S.G. Waxman (Ed.), *Advances in Neurology Vol 47: Functional recovery in neurological disease* (pp. 425–453). New York: Raven Press.

Haber, R.N., & Standing, L.G. (1969). Direct measures of short-term visual storage. *Quarterly Journal of Experimental Psychology, 21*, 43–54.

Hanson, S.J., & Burr, D.J. (1990). What connectionist models learn: learning and representation in connectionist networks. *Behavioral and Brain Science, 13*, 471–489.

Heindel, W.C., Salmon, D.P., Shults, C.W., Walicke, P.A., & Butters, N. (1989). Neuropsychological evidence for multiple memory systems: a comparison of Alzheimer's, Huntington's and Parkinson's disease patients. *Journal of Neuroscience, 9*, 582–587.

Hesslow, G., Yeo, C., Kim, J.J., Krupa, D.J., & Thompson, R.F. (1998). Cerebellum and learning: a complex problem [3]. *Science, 280*, 1817–1819.

Hikosaka, O., Sakamoto, M., & Usui, S. (1989). Functional properties of monkey caudate neurons. III. Activities related to expectation of target and reward. *Journal of Neurophysiology, 61*, 814–832.

Hill, W.F. (1997). *Learning: A survey of psychological interpretations*. New York: Longman.

Hollis, K.L. (1997). Contemporary research on Pavlovian conditioning. *American Psychologist, 52*, 956–965.

Honda, M., Deiber, M.-P., Ibanez, V., Pascual-Leone, A., Zhuang P., & Hallett, M. (1998). Dynamic cortical involvement in implicit and explicit motor sequence learning. *Brain, 121*, 2159–2173.

Kandel, E. (1976). *The cellular basis of behavior: An introduction to behavioral neurobiology*. San Francisco: Freeman.

Kapur, N. (1994). *Memory disorders in clinical practice* (2nd ed.). London: Butterworth Heinemann.

Kelso, J.A.S. (1982). *Human motor behavior*. Hillsdale, NJ: Lawrence Erlbaum Associates Inc.

Kelso, J.A.S. (1995). *Dynamic patterns: The self-organization of brain and behavior*. Cambridge MA: MIT Press.

Knowlton, B.J., Mangels, J.A., & Squire, L.R. (1996). A neostriatal habit learning system in humans. *Science, 273*, 1399–1402.

Lieberman, D. (1990). *Learning: Behavior and cognition*. Belmont: Wadsworth Publishing Co.

Lisberger, S.G. (1988). The neural basis of simple motor skills. *Science, 242*, 728–735.

Lisberger, S.G., & Pavalko, A. (1988). Brainstem neurons in modified pathways for motor learning in the primate vestibular-ocular reflex. *Science, 242*, 771–773.

Marr, D. (1969). A theory of cerebellar cortex. *Journal of Physiology, 202*, 437–470.

Marteniuk, R.G. (1986). Information processes in motor learning: capacity and structural interference effects. *Journal of Motor Behaviour, 18*, 55–75.

Martinez, J.L., & Derrick, B.E. (1996). Long-term potentiation and learning. *Annual Review of Psychology, 47*, 173–203.

Matthies, H. (1989). Neurobiological aspects of learning and memory. *Annual Review of Psychology, 40*, 381–404.

McLeish, J. (1975). *Soviet psychology: history, theory, content*. London: Methuen.

Mendell, L.M. (1984). Modifiability of spinal synapses. *Physiological Reviews, 64*, 260–324.

Miller, R.R., & Marlin, N.A. (1984). The physiology and semantics of consolidation. In H. Weingartner & E.S. Parker (Eds.), *Memory consolidation*. Hillsdale, NJ: Lawrence Erlbaum Associates Inc.

Nashner, L. (1976). Adaptive reflexes controlling the human posture. *Experimental Brain Research, 26*, 59–72.

Neal, A., & Hesketh, B. (1997). What contribution does episodic knowledge make to implicit learning? *Psychonomic Bulletin and Review, 4*, 24–37.

Newcombe, F. (1969). *Missile wounds of the brain*. London: Oxford University Press.

O'Keefe, J.O., & Nadel, L. (1978). *The hippocampus as a cognitive map*. Oxford: Clarendon Press.

Pennebaker, J.W. (1982). *The psychology of symptoms*. New York, Berlin: Springer-Verlag.

Petrides, M. (1985). Deficits on conditional associative learning tasks after frontal- and temporal-lobe lesions in man. *Neuropsychologia, 20*, 249–262.

Ratcliff, R., & McKoon (1981). Does activation really spread? *Psychological Review, 88*, 454–462.

Raymond, J.L., Lisberger, S.G., & Mauk, M.D. (1996). The cerebellum: a neuronal learning machine? *Science, 272*, 1126–1131.

Reed, E.S. (1982). An outline of a theory of action systems. *Journal of Motor Behavior, 14*, 98–134.

Rescorla, R.A. (1987). A Pavlovian analysis of goal-directed behavior. *American Psychologist, 42*, 119–129.

Rescorla, R.A. (1988). Pavlovian conditioning: it's not what you think. *American Psychologist, 43*, 151–161.

Rescorla, R.A., & Wagner, A.R. (1972). A theory of Pavlovian conditioning: variations in the effectiveness of reinforcement and non-reinforcement. In A.H. Black & W.F. Prokasy (Eds.), *Classical conditioning II*. New York: Appleton-Century-Crofts.

Saint Cyr, J.A., Taylor, A.E., & Lang, A.E. (1988). Procedural learning and neostriatal dysfunction in man. *Brain, 111*, 941–959.

Schacter, D.L. (1985). Priming of old and new knowledge in amnesic patients and normal subjects. *Annals of the New York Academy of Sciences, 444*, 41–53.

Schacter, D.L., Chiu, C.-Y.P., & Ochsner, K.N. (1993). Implicit memory: a selective review. *Annual Review of Neuroscience, 16*, 159–182.

Schmidt, R.A. (1982). The schema concept. In J.A.S. Kelso (Ed.), *Human motor behavior*. Hillsdale, NJ: Lawrence Erlbaum Associates Inc.

Shallice, T. (1988). *From neuropsychology to mental structure*. Cambridge: Cambridge University Press.

Siipola, E.M., & Israel, H.E. (1933). Habit-interference as dependent upon stage of training. *American Journal of Psychology, 45*, 205–227.

Simon, D.P., & Gilmartin, K.A. (1973). A simulation of memory for chess problems. *Cognitive Psychology, 5*, 29–46.

Smyth, M.M. (1984). Memory for movements. In M.M. Smyth & A.M. Wing (Eds.), *The psychology of human movement*. London: Academic Press.

Smyth, M.M., & Wing, A.M. (Eds.). (1984). *The psychology of human movement*. London: Academic Press.

Squire, L.R., Knowlton, B., & Musen, G. (1993). The structure and organisation of memory. *Annual Review of Psychology, 44*, 453–495.

Swinnen, S.P. (1990). Interpolated activity during knowledge of results delay. *Journal of Experimental Psychology: Learning Memory and Cognition, 16*, 692–705.

Swinnen, S.P., Schmidt, R.A., Nicholson, D.E., & Shapiro, D.C. (1990). Information feed-back for skill acquisition: instantaneous knowledge of results degrades learning. *Journal of Experimental Psychology: Learning Memory and Cognition, 16*, 706–716.

Thach, W.T. (1998). What is the role of the cerebellum in motor learning and cognition? *Trends in Cognitive Science, 2*, 331–337.

Thompson, R.F. (1986). The neurobiology of learning and memory. *Science, 233*, 941–947.

Thompson, R.F. (1989). A model system approach to memory. In P.R. Solomon, G.R. Goethals, & C.M. Kelley (Eds.), *Memory: Interdisciplinary approaches*. Heidelberg: Springer-Verlag.

Tuller, B., Fitch, H.L., & Turvey, M.T. (1982). The Bernstein perspective II: The concept of muscle linkage or co-ordinative structure. In J.A.S. Kelso (Ed.), *Human motor behavior*. Hillsdale, NJ: Lawrence Erlbaum Associates Inc.

Tulving, E., Hayman, C.A., & Macdonald, C.A. (1991). Long-lasting perceptual priming and semantic learning in amnesia: a case experiment. *Journal of Experimental Psychology: Learning Memory and Cognition, 17*, 595–617.

Tulving, E., & Thomson, D.M. (1973). Encoding specificity and retrieval processes in episodic memory. *Psychological Review, 80*, 352–373.

Vakil, E., Hoffman, Y., & Myzliek, D. (1998). Active versus passive procedural learning in older and younger adults. *Neuropsychological Rehabilitation, 8*, 31–41.

Warrington, E.J., & Weiskrantz, L. (1974). The effect of prior learning on subsequent retention in amnesic patients. *Neuropsychologia, 12*, 419–428.

Waters, R.L. (1984). The enigma of "carry-over". *International Rehabilitation Medicine, 6*, 9–12.

Watson, J.B. (1928). *Behaviorism*. London: Kegan Paul.

Watson, J.B., & Rayner, R. (1920). Conditioned emotional responses. *Journal of Experimental Psychology, 3*, 1–4.

Weingartner, H., & Parker, E.S. (Eds.) (1984). *Memory consolidation*. Hillsdale, NJ: Lawrence Erlbaum Associates Inc.

Whiting, H.T.A. (Ed.) (1984). *Human motor actions: Bernstein reassessed*. Amsterdam: North Holland.

Willingham, D.B., Koroshetz, W.J., & Peterson, E.W. (1996). Motor skills have diverse neural bases: spared and impaired skill acquisition in Huntington's disease. *Neuropsychology, 10*, 315–321.

Winstein, C.J., & Schmidt, R.A. (1990). Reduced frequency of knowledge of results enhances motor learning. *Journal of Experimental Psychology: Learning Memory and Cognition, 16*, 677–691.

Wolpaw, J.R., & Lee, C.L. (1989). Memory traces in primate spinal cord produced by operant conditioning of H-reflex. *Journal of Neurophysiology, 61*, 563–572.

Young, J.Z. (1988). *Philosophy and the brain*. Oxford: Oxford University Press.

Zucker, R.S. (1989). Short-term synaptic plasticity. *Annual Review of Neuroscience, 12*, 13–31.

11. Motor control and learning: Implications for neurological rehabilitation

Theo Mulder   Jacqueline Hochstenbach

INTRODUCTION

Human motor behaviour is characterised by an extreme flexibility. We can pick up a cup with the right hand or with the left hand, while the arm is positioned in all sorts of angles. We can even pick it up by using our feet as the main effector organs. We can walk forward and backward, we can jump, dance, run, shuffle, and produce all sorts of silly walks. We seem to be able to produce an almost infinite stream of movements in order to reach goals in the environment. Motor behaviour can be seen as problem solving. We are forced to find solutions for the problems which appear in the continuously changing environment. These solutions, however, are never static but are always tailored to current requirements. Since the environmental constraints are never the same, the solutions can never be the same. This is an important point since it indicates that motor control cannot be the result of a rigid, hierarchically organised system generating efferent commands to individual muscles and joints on the basis of motor programs stored in some neural warehouse. Control is largely non-hierarchical, self-organising, and driven by multisensory input. Furthermore, the organism never functions *in vacuo*, disconnected from its history and without any knowledge. On the contrary, almost all actions are influenced by knowledge and experience. We have learned how to handle a cup, to ride a bicycle, to write, to play the violin, to dance. Even the simplest actions such as opening a door are influenced by learning. We know, for example, when to push and when to pull on the basis of knowledge derived from experience. Hence, motor processes continuously interact with cognitive and perceptual processes. This interaction between perception, action, and knowledge forms the basis for human motor behaviour and enables us cope with environmental instability.

To describe the organisation of such a system is the first aim of the chapter, to discuss the consequences for neurological rehabilitation forms the second aim. However, we will start with a short historical introduction.

HISTORICAL DEVELOPMENT OF MOTOR CONTROL CONCEPTS

The study of motor control and learning started quite early in the history of experimental psychology. At the end of the nineteenth century Bryan and Harter (1897) studied the fine movements needed for morse code communication, while Woodworth (1899) analysed the characteristics of repetitive, timed movements. The real impetus for motor skills research, however, came from wartime demands for high-speed precision performance. Indeed, optimal performance was critical for surviving in flying, driving, and aiming tasks under combat conditions. The experimental analysis of tracking tasks led to the introduction of formulations from control engineering into the domain of psychology. This resulted in the description of human performances in terms of a closed-loop system (Craik, 1947). A closed-loop system was described as a self-regulating system which has feedback, error detection, and error correction as its key elements. An internal model was hypothesised which specified the desired value for the system; the output of the system was fed back and compared to this specified value for error detection. In 1971 the closed-loop notion was reintroduced by Adams but now under the banner of cognitive psychology and information processing theory. Adams argued that movements were regulated on the basis of two separate memory mechanisms, a *perceptual trace* and a *memory trace*. The perceptual trace acts as an internal model or reference of correctness and is slowly shaped by the feedback from earlier responses. Since the perceptual trace is dependent on sensory information it cannot be responsible for the initiation of movement because at the instant of initiation no response-produced information is available. Therefore a separate mechanism was thought to be responsible for the start of the movement. This mechanism was termed the memory trace.

Adam's theory was elegant, simple, and testable, and represented a clear break with the behaviouristic tradition in experimental psychology. The disadvantage, however, was that the theory could only explain slow and discrete movements.

The closed-loop theory stressed the role of sensory input and argued that without this input the supposed control mechanisms would not operate According to open-loop theorists, on the other hand, control and coordination depended on a central mechanism or motor program containing the information necessary to specify the spatiotemporal aspects of the movement. This standpoint is strongly related to the notion of central pattern generators (CPGs) and is mainly based on studies with deafferented animals showing that, in spite of the absence of feedback, movements could be performed relatively successfully (Taub & Berman, 1968; Nottebohm, 1970; Fentress, 1973). The central approach received a strong impetus from the work of Wilson (1961) who showed that the locust was able to produce rhythmic efferent activity that closely resembled the flight motor pattern even in situations where the nervous system was cut off from all its peripheral input.

Since most of these studies were focused on genetically hard-wired behaviours such as ambulation, grooming, and feeding, the existence of a central repertoire of behaviours was plausible (but see Reed, 1982). However, researchers working on motor skills such as playing music, writing, typing, or painting were sceptical about the notion of purely central control of movement, and there are as yet almost no data showing that human beings can perform complex, sustained movement sequences in an entirely open-loop manner.

Pew in 1974 and shortly afterwards Schmidt (1975) attempted to bridge the gap between the closed-loop and open-loop notions by introducing the concept of a generalised motor program that could regulate a number of movements within the same response category. For example, instead of postulating as many programs as there are ways of throwing a ball, they proposed one *abstract* program governing a class of movements. Pew (1974) described a situation which can clarify this concept. He observed Detroit post-office workers sorting packages. As a package appeared it was examined and then thrown into the correct mailbag (out of a set of 25 mailbags between 5 and 10 feet away). The packages were of many different sizes and shapes. What kind of information was used by the workers? It seemed very implausible that each previous movement and each package weight was retained in a memory store. Pew's idea was that during practice a generalised program had been developed regulating a class of movements. The program would contain prototypical specifications for a class of movements. To tailor such a program to current requirements, parameters would have to be specified. The leading candidates for these parameters are time, force, and direction. After providing the program with parameter values the movement could be initiated. According to this view a horse's trotting can be seen as a single program with invariant sequencing, phasing, and relative force. The horse can trot more quickly or more slowly by applying a movement/speed parameter. One can think of similar examples in which output variability is regulated on the basis of changing a single parameter, e.g., throwing a heavy or a light object. According to Pew and Schmidt, the performer's problem is the determination of adequate parameter specifications by means of which the generalised program can be adapted to the actual requirements. The central program requires feedback, and feedback plays a major role in the development of the (prototypical) program.

These older theoretical notions were all confronted with a serious problem: They were not able to explain the flexibility and adaptability of the human motor system and its capacity to perform totally new movements. In other words, they were not able to solve the "degrees of freedom" problem as discussed first by Bernstein (1967). Bernstein argued that movement can only be efficiently controlled if the nervous system is able to master the enormous number of variables that exist in the muscles, joints, and motor units making up the motor system. Bernstein suggested that muscle-joint systems are constrained to work together as functional units. This type of coordination would decrease the number of degrees of freedom substantially. In an influential paper Turvey (1977) introduced the concept of coordinative structures into the psychology of motor control. He defined a coordinative structure as a set of muscles and joints which are constrained to act together. Compared to the (earlier) motor program approaches more emphasis was placed here on the physical and dynamic features of movement and less emphasis was placed on representations and information processing in the nervous system.

The emphasis on the dynamic aspects of motor control led to experiments in which the self-organising aspects of motor control were explored. In an experiment typical of this approach Kelso, Schoner, Scholz, and Haken (1987) showed that it is easier to oscillate both wrists symmetrically (flexion and extension of the two wrists in phase) than to oscillate them alternately (anti-phase). When the frequency of anti-phase oscillation is increased, it becomes impossible to maintain this type of coordination, and a shift to symmetric oscillation is observed. This phenomenon was explained in terms of a shift between two modes of coordination, comparable for example to the transitions among walk, pace, trot, and gallop observed in quadrupeds as a function of speed. It was further argued that the shift between the modes of coordination arises from the intrinsic properties of the motor control system, so no programming was necessary. This argument was in direct contradiction to the information processing (or computational) approach as discussed above.

In the field of neurological rehabilitation this approach has been applied quite successfully by Wagenaar (1990; Wagenaar & Beek, 1992), who showed that increasing the speed of stroke patients walking on a treadmill improved their gait-pattern in terms of symmetry. Wagenaar (1990) suggested that walking speed *per se* can have a positive influence on the gait pattern of stroke patients.

However, this dynamic approach is not without problems. For example, by focusing almost totally on the self-organising character of control and by rejecting categories such as programs and mental representations, it is difficult (if not impossible) to explain the learning and performance of more complex human motor actions such as writing, drawing, or making music. Besides, the dynamical (or non-linear) approach is largely restricted to the macroscopic level of behaviour. Few attempts have been made to detail the networks that generate the behaviour under study. Nevertheless, the dynamical approach not only opened new vistas of research but also created a breakthrough in traditional thinking on human motor control.

Actions vs reactions

Reed (1982) criticised the classical information processing motor theories as reaction-oriented instead of action-oriented. Reactions are responses directly caused by a certain stimulus; they form the output normally observed in motor laboratories but hardly ever in normal daily behaviour. Even reflexes are not rigid pre-programmed reactions but context-dependent modulations of the output (see Duysens et al., 1990). Reed argued that we should study the human animal in a task-oriented context. We should not focus solely on reactions (e.g., isolated movements) elicited by experimental conditions, but much more on goal-directed actions triggered by ecologically valid stimuli. This perspective is clearly relevant for neurological rehabilitation as we will see later in this chapter. An action differs from a reaction in that it is a complex (non-rigid) answer to some problem in the environment which can never be explained in terms of simple stimulus–response linkages. Actions are undertaken to achieve goals and they are motivated and controlled by these goals. Indeed, in normal life almost no movements take place

without any goal; moving in a "goal-less" vacuum is artificial and makes no sense.

Such an action-oriented approach requires a theoretical framework, whereby motor processes permanently interact with perceptual and cognitive processes. The implication is that pure motor theories cannot exist since they neglect aspects such as attention, motivation, emotion, and memory. These latter determine and colour our motor behaviour to a large extent and determine the large variability of motor responses to the same problems at different times. Hence, what we need is a theory of human motor behaviour which borrows heavily from neuropsychology. It is remarkable that as yet no such theory exists. Most motor theories are formulated against the background of movement science, biomechanics, and/or neurophysiology. By contrast, neuropsychology seems not to be interested in human motor actions and is focused solely or at least primarily on "hardcore" cognition. The fields of motor behaviour and of neuropsychology seem to be separated by tradition. In the model as presented in the following section we attempt to bridge the gap between these two domains.

The organisation of human motor control

Figure 11.1 shows a model of human motor behaviour. The separate parts of the model will be discussed here in a step-like

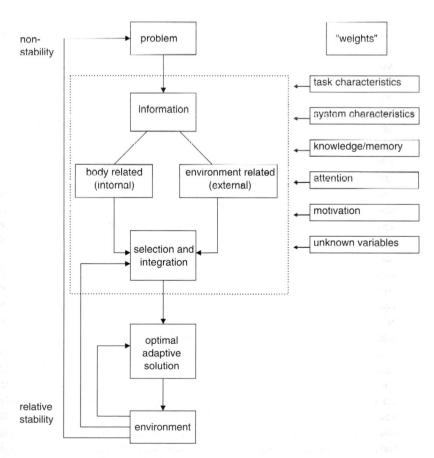

Figure 11.1. The organisation of human motor behaviour.

fashion. Let us start with the non-stable relationship that always exists between the organism and the environment, since the environment is constantly confronting us with new problems that have to be solved. At first sight these problems might seem rather simple (not falling, avoiding hindrances, opening a door, grasping an object), but think for example of the ease with which we can step over an obstacle such as a doorstep. Without changing our speed the foot clears the doorstep by only 2 cm or so. To catch a tennis ball, we have a perceptual-motor decision window of only 14 ms (Anderson et al., 1974). And we can effortlessly combine numerous skilled actions of this sort. We take this all for granted; everything looks so easy for the normal healthy adult. However, when observing a patient with brain damage, we realise the vulnerability of the system and perceive that it is only a short step from the highly skilled, smooth performance of the healthy adult to the impaired motor behaviour of the patient.

Although the environment confronts us with problems, skilled action is never fully constrained by the environment. Indeed, most situations leave room for an almost limitless choice. This means that current sensation is never the sole determinant of the action. Problems suggest *potential* actions based on past experiences and any problem is capable of generating anticipations of what may happen if certain actions are taken.

Hence, our actions are not totally dictated by the environment, and neither are they fully dictated or preprogrammed by the brain on the basis of internal or symbolic representations (see Shaffer, 1992). It is the interaction between the environmental context and the state of the organism which shapes the output. Hence, a fully cognitive approach is as senseless as a fully motor or a fully "environmentalistic" approach.

Information

Humans and other animals are "designed" as biological problem-solving machines that "run" on information. Information is of crucial importance for solving environmental problems. Any sensory system, in fact, can be seen as a control mechanism for regulating behavioural interactions between the sensing organism and its environment. In this chapter the extreme importance of information will be stressed; without information (sensory input) there is no control, no learning, no change, no improvement.

Two basic streams of information are distinguished here: body-related (internal) information and environment-related (external) information. Body-related information refers to all sorts of information produced by the system itself, such as proprioceptive, visceral, or vestibular information. External information refers to all information that can be picked up from the environment, including auditory, olfactory, haptic (positional), and visual information. Vision is the most important source for external information. The perceptual information derived from the optic flow fields informs the observer not only about the layout of the world but also about the observer's own motion. Gibson (1979) showed that much of the critical information for perception appears in the form of temporal patterns

that change continuously. He argued that visual perception is not a static process but an active, "fluid" process. But if perception is an active process then what kind of information do we use while controlling our movements? Lee (1980) showed that an important role is played by a flow parameter, termed *tau*. He described *tau* as the ratio of the distance r which separates any projected point from the center of expansion to the velocity v with which that point is moving. Thus *tau* could specify how long it will be until the performer hits the object, assuming a constant velocity ($tau\ (t) = r(t)/v(t)$). Von Hofsten (1983) showed that even very young children were able to use this innate, "hard-wired" knowledge in order to control their grasping behaviour of moving objects. These and other data on the use of flow-parameters are very interesting since they indicate the existence of neural mechanisms that can select information autonomously, that is to say, without any additional supervisory selection mechanism.

Neisser (1976), in a beautiful essay on "Cognition and Reality", described perception as a constructive process but in a somewhat different way from Gibson. Neisser did not accept that all the information was "in the light" but showed that stored knowledge about the environment was used for perception. He stressed, however, that what is constructed is not a mental image appearing in consciousness where it is admired by an inner man, but anticipations of certain kinds of information (1976, p. 20). These anticipations (or expectations) are the transfer-points where the past affects the future: Information that is known to the organism determines what will be picked up next. Hence, perception is not the pick-up of information by a passive receiver which takes place simply because he/she is equipped with receptors, but the result of a goal-oriented search. This search is as much influenced by cognitive factors as by perceptual factors.

However, the role of vision could be overstated. The knowledge we have of the world results not solely from vision but from a concatenation of information from all sensory modalities. Indeed, most events of ordinary life stimulate more than one sensory system. We see someone walk and hear his footsteps or hear him talk; we experience the effects of our actions not only in terms of vision but also in terms of auditory or tactile sensations. The source of information is less important than the fact that information is available.

Selection and integration: Finding the optimal adaptive solution

The amount of information available from the environment is, in principle, limitless so that we are continuously bombarded by information, not all of it relevant for the act. What sort of information do we attend to and what kind of information do we ignore and why? One would expect that some sort of selection should take place. Indeed, if information is selected from a pool of alternatives there should be some mechanism that "knows" what is relevant and what is not. The latter argument, however, brings us on to very dangerous ground; such an argument tends to suggest the existence of the *homunculus*, the little man in the head knowing everything. That is not, however, what we intend to argue; our claim is that every act is influenced by earlier versions of it and that memory is directly involved in the "selection" of movements. Hence, the selection of information is guided by the goal we want to achieve and by stored knowledge. This is a standpoint closely related to the previously mentioned remarks of Neisser (1976) concerning the anticipatory role of perception. Some stimuli are selected because they possess particular characteristics to which the control structures are receptive. The parameter *tau*, mentioned earlier, is an excellent example of the selection of information without any high-level selection mechanism.

Weighted variables influencing task performance

What is relevant at moment x is not necessarily also relevant at moment y, so even relevance is not a given entity but changes from moment to moment depending on a number of variables. For example, the relevance of food changes depending on the homeostatic state of the organism. For this reason the model we are describing contains a number of variables that can be seen as "weights" determining the solutions reached by the system. The selection and integration of all sensory signals (internal and external) is influenced by fluctuating variables such as: task-characteristics, system-characteristics, knowledge and memory, attention, motivation, emotion, and additional unknown variables. Such variables influence the "decision" to act, whereby the selected action must be seen as the most optimal solution for that particular moment. The same problem at another time or in another context may create another mixture of weights leading to another synthesis and another solution. The weighting of these variables makes the system extremely flexible since each act is a result of a combination of influences which are time- and task-dependent.

Task characteristics. The way in which a response is shaped depends on characteristics such as the degree of complexity, and the importance of the task.

System characteristics. Motor responses are also shaped by system characteristics, i.e., the current state of the organism (healthy or damaged, young or old, strong or weak, fatigued or not).

Knowledge/memory. Organisms possess memory mechanisms by which specific past events can shape current actions. All that we have learned about the environment, about the meaning of objects, or about what is socially acceptable or unacceptable, is cognitive baggage which influences our performance. Without this knowledge every situation and every act would be new. If you pick up a telephone the anticipatory movements towards the receiver are adapted to the function of the apparatus. It will be clear that this is not an emergent characteristic of the receiver but the result of learning and memory. It is therefore remarkable that memory disorders are often seen as totally unrelated to movement disorders (but see Chapter 28).

Attention. Attention is a prerequisite for almost all human actions and is of crucial importance for effective behaviour and survival. We cannot attend to all the information that is available: we listen to what A is saying but ignore B's speaking, we are able to sustain our performances under noisy conditions. Attention, however, should not be seen as a spotlight that is illuminating our dark mental cave. Attention is directly connected to action. It is not possible to attend *in vacuo*: there is always a connection with some sort of action. Attention is like time: We have no sense of empty time, we can only judge the duration of a sensation or an event. It is therefore argued here that the supervisor of attention is not some mystical higher order mechanism, but the act itself: The intention to do something directs the attention.

Attentional mechanisms play a crucial role in the planning and execution of motor actions. In neurological rehabilitation many patients with brain damage suffer from attentional deficits, which interfere with their motor performances.

Motivation. The sensory, perceptual, cognitive, and motor processes are important for actually performing a task, but the decision to initiate and complete the action is regulated by the motivational system. Motivation is, like all cognitive processes, an inferred internal state. According to Kandell et al. (1995) motives serve three functions. First, they have a directing function in that they steer behaviour towards a specific goal. Second, they have an activating function by increasing general alertness and energising the individual to action. Third, they have an organising function, combining individual components into a coherent, goal-oriented behavioural sequence. We know most about basic motives such as hunger, thirst, and desire for safety. These are essentially unlearned and have strong biological roots. Higher-order motives also have their roots in our native endowment, although their development expression are strongly influenced by learning (Gleitman, 1981). A person's motivational state influences both the way he selects and integrates information and the type of action which he selects. In neurological rehabilitation it is important to distinguish organically based impairment of motivation—anergia—from lack of motivation due to psychological mechanisms such as depression or simple indolence (see Lezak, 1995).

Unknown variables. Not all factors that influence behaviour can be identified. Our individual social and learning histories influence our choices. Awareness of oneself psychologically, physically, and in relation to one's surroundings plays a role in determining momentary actions (Lezak, 1995) as does one's genetic make-up and personality. Even momentary chemical fluxes will influence all type of "decisions". These variables, however, are hardly open for observation. They are mentioned here only to stress the multidimensional and dynamic character of action control.

ADAPTATION AND LEARNING

Cognition and action: Some remarks on mental representations

By stressing the role of stored information we implicitly also embrace the concept of mental representations or mental images. It is not, in our view, possible to explain behaviour without the acceptance of some internal model of the external world, how it will be modified by the action, and how the organism will be modified by that action (see Jeannerod, 1997). The digger wasp provides a beautiful example of the use of representations in animals, even in insects (Gallistel, 1985). The digger wasp has a number of nests to attend to, each nest containing a wasp larvum and some paralysed caterpillars put there by the mother for the larvum to feed on. The mother wasp begins her day by inspecting the nests to see which larvum needs more food. The observations made during this survey determine which nest will be provisioned during the rest of the day and the number of caterpillars with which it will be provisioned. It could be shown that the number of caterpillars brought to the nest was entirely determined by the observations the mother made during the morning visit. If the experimenter added caterpillars when the mother was away hunting for more, she persisted in trying to stuff in the number she had decided on initially. If the experimenter removed the caterpillars, she none the less brought only as many as she would have done, had the experimenter left the nest alone (see also Gallistel, 1990).

In human behaviour there are many examples of stored information influencing our behaviour (e.g., a musician playing a memorised melody, or a dancer performing a figure after having observed a model). The interplay between knowledge and action can be observed in almost all daily actions. For example, the stretch and shape of the fingers at the start of reaching movements are determined by the functional characteristics of the object or by the task demands. Take for example a rod which can be held by a precision grip, as in writing, or by a power grip as in hammering; it is the intended activity that determines the type of grip and not the perceived form of the rod *per se* (Jeannerod, 1997, p. 31). Rosenbaum et al. (1990 pp. 322–323) describe a waiter reaching for a glass that has been placed upside down on a table. The waiter reaches for the glass with an underhand posture, that is, with his thumb pointing down. After picking up the glass he turns it over to fill it with water. In principle, the waiter could have reached for the glass with an overhand grip but this would have put him in the awkward position of having to hold the glass with his thumb pointing down during the pouring operation. To avoid ending in this awkward position, the waiter initially grasps the glass in a manner that is relatively uncomfortable. This initial anticipatory movement can only be explained by accepting that the waiter is using knowledge about the observed object in the planning of the action.

Neuropsychological data also support the existence of mental representations and show that the same mechanisms which are used in perceptual recognition are also employed in forming mental representations (Kosslyn, 1990). In an experiment Bisiach and Luzzatti (1978) asked neglect patients to image standing on one side of a familiar plaza and to describe it. Although they were capable of forming a representation, they described only buildings on their right, ignoring buildings on their left. When asked to image standing on the opposite side of the plaza they again mentioned only buildings on their right, which led them to name the buildings they had previously ignored and ignore those they had previously mentioned.

Mental images are also used in learning. Take for example the early stages of rehabilitation where patients have to develop an *image of the act* (Whiting & den Brinker, 1982). For the development of such an image, information (mostly visual) is important. Bamford and Marteniuk (1988) argued that individuals with high spatial ability would be able to integrate perceptual and movement information more easily than those with less spatial ability. This argument was partly based on work by Fleishman and Rich (1963) who showed that subjects with high spatial ability performed more accurately early in learning, whereas subjects with high kinesthetic ability performed better later in learning. From this, Bamford and Marteniuk concluded that early in learning spatio-temporal relationships would be more important, while later in learning kinesthetic information would be used.

The use of mental images can be remarkably effective in (re-)learning skills, and has a number of testable effects on the neuromotor system such as increased muscular strength, increased EMG output, increased speed, and decreased variability. Also altered brain activity and autonomous effects have been reported during mental practice. Decety et al. (1993) studied subjects who where instructed to either actually perform or mentally simulate a leg exercise. Heart rate and respiration rate were measured in both conditions. Heart rate and respiration rate began to increase not only during actual exercise but also in the mental condition where no work was done. There is increasing evidence that movement imagery (mental practice) activates the same brain areas and physiological systems as actually performing a movement (see Sanes & Donoghue, 2000; Papaxanthis et al., 2002). Recently it has been argued that mental practice may play a potential role in neurological rehabilitation (Jackson et al., 2001; Page et al., 2001).

Another important basis for the formation of mental images is observation of another individual's performance. We know that it is surprisingly easy to imitate the observed actions of other people. Watching either a live model or a videorecorded performance activates neurons in the cerebral cortical areas relevant for motor preparation and execution. The same effect is seen during mental rehearsal of the observed action (Jeannerod, 1997, p. 114). Di Pellegrino et al. (1992) showed that neurons in the monkey's premotor cortex not only fire during the execution of a given hand movement but also when the animal is watching another animal or person performing the same movement.

For a social animal such as the human being imitation seems to be a very strong mechanism for shaping behaviour. It is therefore a mechanism of potential value for rehabilitation. It is remarkable to observe how little imitation and observation are exploited in rehabilitation.

Hard-wired knowledge

Although we have stressed the importance of information, memory, and learning, it should be noted that not all motor behaviour has to be learned. Human infants are motorically immature at birth, but they are by no means motionless. They show considerable movement of the face, the head, the limbs, and the trunk, especially when placed in facilitating postures. Thus the behavioural repertoire of a newborn baby does not appear *de novo* at birth but is preceded by a prenatal developmental process. Prechtl (1977, 1986) showed by means of ultrasound that the repertoire of the foetal movements consisted entirely of motor patterns which can also be observed in postnatal life. A further remarkable fact was that the movements were coordinated from the onset. Bruner (1973) described elementary motor patterns used by infants to reach for objects. These patterns were aroused by the sight of an object. Von Hofsten (1982) reported that the antigravity activity of arms and shoulders in babies, although seemingly random, was directed towards the viewed object. Thelen and Fisher (1983) described the kinematics of spontaneous kicking movements in newborns. They found that the temporal and topographic organisation of these movements was striking: The movements were highly rhythmical and showed non-random periodicity. Furthermore, the three involved joints worked in a close temporal and spatial synchrony. The stability of the kicking movements was reflected by the constrained timing of the phase durations. Flexions and extensions were clustered around 300 ms, whereas the activity-bursts detected by surface EMG were remarkably similar. Thelen and Fisher (1983) showed that in early infant movements the joints of the leg were activated not as individual elements, but as a synergy that is highly predictable in space and time.

These and many other studies indicate that much knowledge employed in perceptuomotor activity is available at a very young age. The fact that this knowledge is more or less hardwired does not mean that it is rigid. On the contrary, even the set of infant reflexes are subtly adjusted to the task, are quite variable, and are minutely responsive to the state of the infant.

Adaptability of the human motor system

This chapter stresses the flexibility and adaptability of the human motor system. The capacity to adapt is important in recovery of function and requires further discussion. Adaptability is a crucial property of all animals, even of the lowest ones, and in human beings this flexibility is highly developed. We are continuously adapting our output to the requirements of the environment. There are many examples showing that the adaptive power of humans is impressive. If a blind person who receives no information through the eyes is receiving "visual" information through other modalities, the person reports that he experiences something quite similar to seeing. Bach-y-Rita (1972), for example, showed that when a visual display is converted into a tactile display on a blind person's back, an approaching object can trigger an avoidance reaction. Objects only familiar by palpation can be recognised from the tactile display. That visual impressions can be received from kinaesthetic sensations is a dramatic example of the flexibility of the processes involved in the pick-up of information. These experiments show not only that a categorical distinction exists between sensation and experience but also that

the selected sensory modality is irrelevant: It is the information that counts (see Yates, 1985). Studies of prism adaptation further underscore the fact that sensory input processing is a multimodal process. These studies indicate that a visual image is not derived from the visual system alone, but that it is the result also of a number of non-visual information sources, including corollary discharge of motor neurons, proprioception, and active body motions (Hay, 1968; Held & Freedman, 1963; Welch, 1978).

Yates (1985 p. 269) was therefore correct when he argued that visual adaptation occurs if there is any visual or non-visual source of information that indicates the presence of a non-veridical retinal image. This argument has relevance far beyond the field of vision research. Shifts between input sources are very prominent in motor disorders. For example, some loss in proprioceptive input may be tolerated but when the loss of proprioceptive input exceeds a certain level the system is forced to shift to another control strategy (e.g., visual control or conscious control of movement). This capacity to shift between input sources and output strategies enables the system to keep the output constant and to reach goals even under non-optimal conditions. This is a very important point for neurological rehabilitation since it again indicates the dramatic importance of sensory input. A system deprived from its input sources is not able to function at all.

There is ample evidence that central neural networks change their structure and function as an answer to the elimination of peripheral input. Data on the changes in cortical fields as a result of denervation, disuse and additional use are reviewed in Chapter 8 (see Merzenich & Kaas, 1982; Hall et al., 1990; Hess et al., 1986; Ritter & Schulten, 1986). Further evidence comes from studies of neurochemical changes such as those found in GABA systems (see Hendry & Jones 1988, cited in Marty, da Penha Berzaghi, & Berninger, 1997). Data of this kind provides a structural and neurochemical basis for change and for recovery.

IMPLICATIONS FOR NEUROLOGICAL REHABILITATION

The framework as pictured here has clear implications for neurological rehabilitation. We emphasised earlier the problem-oriented character of motor control and we showed that movement cannot be the result of a hierarchically organised control architecture activating motor programs that contain all information necessary for performing the movements. Movement is the end-result of a flexible system, continuously interacting with the environment; a system where motor, sensory, and cognitive processes interact in order to find the most optimal solution to problems.

We have stressed the importance of input, activity, and adaptation. Without activity there is no input, without input there is no adaptation, and without adaptation survival is impossible. Input, activity and adaptation are therefore the basic ingredients of recovery. One of the basic challenges for neurological rehabilitation is to find alternative input sources when the "normal" ones are no longer accessible. The previously mentioned examples from the work of Bach-y-Rita show clearly how flexible humans are in the use of altered input sources. The use of biofeedback procedures also indicates the capacity of humans to profit from novel forms of sensory input (see Mulder, 1985).

The relearning of motor skills

There are some aspects of motor control and learning that are especially important for rehabilitation. It is important, first, to note that motor learning is not the learning of muscle control, the increase of strength or range of motion, or the mastering of isolated movements. Nor is it the linking-up of individual movements into a chain of motor behaviour. Learning is much more abstract. There are many data underscoring this point, even from the field of animal studies. MacFarlane (1930) showed in a classical study that rats had a high positive transfer to swimming through a maze after learning it by running and vice versa. This is a well-known example of the fact that what is learned is not specific muscle-movement combinations but solutions to problems.

What are the requirements for learning solutions to motor problems and hence the relearning of skills? If we could answer this question we could design the optimal rehabilitation environment. Although we have to admit that a final answer cannot be given, we can describe three important ingredients for optimal learning: (1) optimal sensory information, (2) variability of practice, and (3) similarity between the context of training and the context of application. (See also Mulder, Hochstenbach, & Kamsa, 2002.)

Optimal sensory information. One of the key elements of any interactive situation is the exchange of information. This is also true for any form of therapy in neurological rehabilitation. Information is a *sine qua non* for learning. Without information subjects are severely hindered in mastering novel tasks. This is an important point, particularly in the first stages of the rehabilitation process when, due to neurological damage, the person often can no longer trust his internal information. Failure to provide information will lead to markedly degraded learning, or to no learning at all. The therapist then becomes the most important source of external information. However, since many brain damaged patients suffer from memory disorders, the information offered by the therapist should be unambiguous, concrete, clear, consistent, and brief and should be repeated several times. Offering too much information will lead to the loss of at least part of it.

Variability of practice. Learning always takes place in a context, a person never learns a skill in empty space. Because the environment is continuously changing it is necessary to design the learning situation so that optimal transfer can take place to contexts other than that of the treatment. The transfer of learned information is one of the crucial problems in rehabilitation. Skills which are well practised in a clinical context often deteriorate as the subject attempts to perform them in the home

setting. How can transfer of training be improved? Training or therapy should be variable: the patient should not be exercised under constantly similar conditions but in different learning contexts in order to create a variable stream of input. This is a prerequisite for learning to handle novel situations: the variability of the input during learning determines to a large extent the generalisation value of the training (see Spitzer, 1999). The practical implications are clear. Gait training (e.g., after hemiplegia) should not take place primarily in a physical therapy department under very predictable conditions but should take place under a range of conditions that mimic the environmental constrains (e.g., flat floor, sand, gravel, hindrances, obstacles, noises, dual-tasks).

Similarity between learning context and the context of application. Variability is not enough: The learning context should also be structured in such a way that it contains a large number of elements identical to the transfer situation. The quality of transfer from one learning situation to another depends partly on the ecological validity of the learning situation. An artificial learning situation with almost no variability and only a remote relationship with the actual context of application will lead to very meagre results. The patient will improve but the improvement is more or less conditioned to the treatment context with little transfer to novel situations. In order to improve the generalisation value of the therapy it is important to create a "learning landscape" in which relevant aspects of the outside world can be simulated and in which the therapeutic regime can be tailored to the individual needs of a patient. Against this background the use of virtual environments may be of value for rehabilitation (Stanney, Mourant, & Kennedy, 1998).

Implications for assessment

Our model of motor behaviour and learning stresses the intimate relationship between motor, perceptual, and cognitive processes. The level of the contribution of the individual processes will depend on the novelty and complexity of the task. Tasks such as walking, talking, and reaching are normally performed more or less automatically without noticeable attention or effort. This automaticity enables subjects to perform these tasks simultaneously with other tasks (e.g., walking and talking). In contrast, novices are not able to perform a second task simultaneously without interference, and this is true also of patients relearning skills. At the beginning of a rehabilitation process many tasks are new and a substantial amount of mental effort is necessary to execute them. This is an important point because it implies that by combining tasks the attentional demands of task performance can be established at different stages of a learning or recovery process. If a task is performed less well in combination with a secondary task, then both tasks are thought to require cognitive capacity. During the learning of a skill the dual-task interference effect will decrease. This concept can be exploited in clinical assessment. During recovery a certain amount of re-automatisation should take place and should be reflected in a decreasing dual-task interference across time. This idea has been tested extensively in a series of experiments (Geurts & Mulder, 1994; Geurts et al., 1991, 1992; Mulder & Geurts, 1991, 1993). The experiments clearly showed that dual-task interference could be used as a sensitive measure of automaticity and recovery in rehabilitation. Lundin-Olsson, Nyberg, and Gustafson (1997) showed that geriatric patients who stopped walking when a conversation was started were significantly more prone to falls than patients who continued to walk. The design of an assessment procedure (for balance and gait) in which cognitive, perceptual, and motor processes interact in a number of tasks has been described in Mulder, Nienhuis, and Pauwels (1996); and in Mulder, Zylstra, and Geurts (in press).

CONCLUDING REMARKS

In this chapter we have presented a theory of motor control which is focused on explaining the flexibility of control of human

action. We have described some implications for neurological rehabilitation. Concerning the latter, however, some caution is necessary. First, the implications for learning are almost totally derived from motor learning experiments with healthy young adults and with athletes. Although neurological patients have to learn motor skills they are rarely fit and never healthy. They also have additional cognitive and behavioural problems which can have a severe impact on their learning abilities. Failure to recognise these additional factors may undermine the effectiveness of the therapy. There is a strong case for a much closer relationship between the domains of motor control and learning and neuropsychology. We hope that the present chapter will be read as an argument for such a relationship.

REFERENCES

Adams, J.A. (1971). A closed loop theory of motor learning. *Journal of Motor Behaviour, 3*, 111–150.

Anderson, G.J.K., Sully, D.J., & Sully, H.G. (1974). An operational analysis of one handed catching using high speed photography. *Journal of Motor Behaviour, 6*, 217–226.

Bach-y-Rita, P. (1972). *Brain Mechanisms in Sensory Substitution*. New York: Academic Press.

Bamford, R.B., & Marteniuk, R.G. (1988). Visual feedback, movement learning and the representation of movement. *Human Movement Science, 7*, 1–26.

Bernstein, N. (1967). *The coordination and regulation of movement*. London: Pergamon.

Bisiach, E., & Luzzatti, C. (1978). Unilateral neglect of representational space. *Cortex, 14*, 129–133.

Bruner, J.S. (1973). Organization of early skilled action. *Child Development, 44*, 1–11.

Bryan, W.L., & Harter, N. (1897). Studies in the physiology and psychology of the telegraphic language. *Psychological Review, 6*, 27–53.

Craik, K.J.W. (1947). Theory of the human operator in control systems, I. The operator as an engineering system. *British Journal of Psychology, 38*, 56–61.

Decety, J., Jeannerod, M., Durozard, D., & Baverel, G. (1993). Central activation of autonomic effectors during mental simulation of motor actions. *Journal of Physiology, 461*, 549–563.

Di Pellegrino, G., Fadiga, L., Fogassi, L., Gallese, V., & Rizzolatti, G. (1992). Understanding motor events: a neurophysiological study. *Experimental Brain Research, 91*, 176–180.

Duysens, J., Trippel, M., Horstmann, G.A., & Dietz, V. (1990). Gating and reversal of reflexes in ankle muscles during human walking. *Experimental Brain Research, 82*, 351–358.

Fentress, J.C. (1973). Development of grooming in mice with amputated fore limbs. *Science, 179*, 704–705.

Fleishman, E.A., & Rich, S. (1963). Role of kinesthetic and spatial-visual abilities in perceptual-motor learning. *Journal of Experimental Psychology, 66*, 6–11.

Gallistel, C.R. (1985). Motivation, intention and emotion: goal-directed behaviour from a cognitive-neuroethological perspective. In M. Frese & J. Sabini (Eds.), *Goal-directed Behaviour: the concept of action in psychology* (pp. 48–66). Hillsdale: Lawrence Erlbaum Associates Inc.

Gallistel, C.R. (1990). *The Organization of Learning*. Cambridge, MA: MIT Press.

Geurts, A.C.H., & Mulder, T. (1994). Attention demands in balance recovery from lower limb amputation. *Journal of Motor Behaviour, 26*, 162–171.

Geurts, A.C.H., Mulder, T., Nienhuis, B., & Rijken, R.A.J. (1991). Dual-task assessment of reorganization of postural control in persons with a lower limb amputation. *Archives of Physical Medicine and Rehabilitation, 72*, 1059–1064.

Geurts, A.C.H., Mulder, T., Nienhuis, B., & Rijken, R.A.J. (1992). Postural reorganization following lower limb amputation: possible motor and sensory mechanisms. *Scandinavian Journal of Rehabilitation Medicine, 24*, 83–90.

Gibson, J.J. (1979). *The ecological approach to visual perception*. Boston: Houghton Mifflin.

Gleitman, H. (1981). *Psychology*. New York: Norton & Company.

Hall, E.J., Flament, D., Fraser, C., & Lemon, R.N. (1990). Non-invasive brain stimulation reveals reorganized cortical output in amputees. *Neuroscience Letters, 116*, 379–386.

Hay, J.C. (1968). Visual adaptation to an altered correlation between eye movements and head movement. *Science, 160*, 429–430.

Held, R., & Freedman, S.J. (1963). Plasticity in human sensorimotor control. *Science, 142*, 455–462.

Hess, C.W., Mills, K.R., & Murray, N.M.F. (1986). Magnetic stimulation of the human brain: facilitation of motor responses by voluntary contraction of ipsilateral and contralateral muscles with additional observations on an amputee. *Neuroscience Letters, 71*, 235–240.

Jackson, P.L., Lafleur, M.F., Malouin, F., Richards, C., & Doyon, J. (2001). Potential role of mental practice using motor imagery in neurologic rehabilitation. *Archives of Physical Medicine and Rehabilitation, 82*, 1133–1141.

Jeannerod, M. (1997). *The Cognitive Neuroscience of Action*. Cambridge, MA: Blackwell Publishers.

Kandel, E.R., Schwartz, J.H., & Jessell, T.M. (1995). *Essentials of neurological science and behaviour*. East Norwalk: Appleton & Lange.

Kelso, J.A.S., Schoner, G., Scholz, J.P., & Haken, H. (1987). Phase-locked modes, phase transitions and component oscillators in biological motion. *Physica Scripta, 35*, 79–98.

Kosslyn, S.M. (1990). Mental imagery. In D.N. Osherson, S.M. Kosslyn, & J.M. Hollerbach (Eds.), *Visual Cognition and Action: an invitation to cognitive science*. Cambridge, MA: MIT Press.

Lee, D.N. (1980). The optic flow field: the foundation of vision. *Philosophical Transactions of the Royal Society, London, B290*, 169–179.

Lezak, M.D. (1995). *Neuropsychological Assessment*. New York: Oxford University Press.

Lundin-Olsson, L., Nyberg, L., & Gustafson, Y. (1997). "Stops walking when talking" as a predictor of falls in elderly people. *The Lancet, 349*, 617.

Marty, S., da Penha Berzaghi, M., & Berninger, B. (1997). Neurotrophins and activity-dependent plasticity of cortical interneurons. *Trends in Neurosciences, 5*, 198–202.

MacFarlane, D.A. (1930). The role of kinesthesis in maze learning. *University of California Publications in Psychology, 4*, 277–305.

Merzenich, M.M., & Kaas, J.H. (1982). Reorganization of the mammalian somatosensory cortex following peripheral nerve injury. *Trends in Neurosciences, 5*, 434–436.

Mulder, Th. (1985). *The Learning of Motor Control Following Brain Damage*. Berwyn: Swets & Zeitlinger Publishers.

Mulder, Th., & Geurts, A.C.H. (1991). The assessment of motor functions: preliminaries to a disability-oriented approach. *Human Movement Science, 10*, 565–574.

Mulder, Th., & Geurts, A.C.H. (1993). Recovery of motor skills following nervous system disorders: a behavioural approach. *Bailliere's Clinical Neurology, 2*, 1–13.

Mulder, Th., Hochstenbach, J., & Kamsma, Y.P.T. (2002). What cognitive rehabilitation may learn from motor control theory. In W. Brouwer, E. van Zomeren, I. Berg, A. Bouma, & E. de Haan (Eds). *Cognitive Rehabilitation: a clinical neuropsychological approach* (pp. 255–269). Amsterdam: Boom Publishers.

Mulder, Th., Nienhuis, B., & Pauwels, J. (1996). The assessment of motor recovery: a new look at an old problem. *Journal of Electromyography and Kinesiology, 6*, 137–145.

Mulder, Th., Zijlstra, W., & Geurts (in press). The assessment of motor recovery and decline. *Gait and Posture*.

Neisser, U. (1976). *Cognition and Reality: principles and implications of cognitive psychology*. San Francisco: Freeman Publishers.

Nottebohm, F. (1970). The ontogeny of bird song. *Science, 167*, 950–956.

Page, S.J., Levine, P., Sisto, S.A., & Johnston, M.V. (2001). Mental practice combined with physical practice for upper-limb motor deficit in subacute stroke. *Physical Therapy, 81*, 1455–1462.

Papaxanthis, C., Schieppati, Gentili, R., & Pozzo, T. (2002). Imagined and actual arm movements have similar durations when performed under different conditions of direction and mass. *Experimental Brain Research, 143*, 447–452.

Pew, R.W. (1974). Human perceptual-motor performance. In B.H. Kantowitz (Ed.), *Human Information Processing: tutorials in performance and cognition*. Hillsdale, NJ: Lawrence Erlbaum Associates Inc.

Prechtl, H.F.R. (1977). *The Neurological Examination of the Full-term Newborn Infant*. London: Heinemann.

Prechtl, H.F.R. (1986). Prenatal motor development. In M.G. Wade & H.T.A. Whiting (Eds.), *Motor Development in Children: aspects of coordination and control* (pp. 53–65). Den Haag: Nijhof Publishers.

Reed, E.S. (1982). An outline of a theory of action systems. *Journal of Motor Behaviour, 14*, 98–134.

Ritter, H., & Schulten, K. (1986). On the stationary state of Kohonen's self-organizing sensory mapping. *Biological Cybernetics, 54*, 99–106.

Rosenbaum, D.A., Vaughan, J., Barnes, H.J., Marchak, F., & Slotta, J. (1990). Constraints for action selection: overhand versus underhand grips. In M. Jeannerod (Ed.), *Attention and Performance XIII* (pp. 321–342). Hillsdale, NJ: Lawrence Erlbaum Associates Inc.

Sanes, J.N., & Donoghue, J.P. (2000). Plasticity and primary motor cortex. *Annual Reviews in Neuroscience, 23*, 393–415.

Schmidt, R.A. (1975). A schema theory of discrete motor learning. *Psychological Review, 82*, 225–260.

Shaffer, L.H. (1992). Motor programming and control. In G.E. Stelmach & J. Requin (Eds.), *Tutorials in Motor Behaviour II* (pp. 181–194). Amsterdam: Elsevier Publishers.

Spitzer, M. (1999). *The mind within the net: models of learning, thinking and acting*. Cambridge, MA: MIT-press.

Stanney, K.M., Mourant, R.R., & Kennedy, R.S. (1998). Human factors issues in virtual environments: a review of the literature. *Presence, 7*, 327–351.

Taub, E., & Berman, A.J. (1968). Movement and learning in the absence of sensory feedback. In S.J. Freedman (Ed.), *The neuropsychology of spatially oriented behaviour*. Homewood: Dorsey Press.

Thelen, E., & Fisher, D.M. (1983). The organization of spontaneous leg movements in newborn infants. *Journal of Motor Behaviour, 15*, 353–377.

Turvey, M.T. (1977). Preliminaries to a theory of action with reference to vision. In R. Shaw & J. Bransford (Eds.), *Perceiving, Acting and Knowing: towards an ecological psychology*. Hillsdale, NJ: Lawrence Erlbaum Associates Inc.

Von Hofsten, C. (1982). Eye–hand coordination of the newborn. *Developmental Psychology, 18*, 450–461.

Von Hofsten, C. (1983). Catching skills in infancy. *Journal of Experimental Psychology: Human Perception and Performance, 9*, 75–85.

Wagenaar, R.C. (1990). *Functional Recovery after Stroke*. Amsterdam: Free University Press.

Wagenaar, R.C., & Beek, W.J. (1992). Hemiplegic gait: a kinematic analysis using walking speed as a basis. *Journal of Biomechanics, 25*, 1007–1015.

Welch, R.B. (1978). *Perceptual Modification: adapting to altered sensory environments*. New York: Academic Press.

Whiting, H.T.A., & den Brinker, B. (1982). Image of the act. In J.P. Das, R.E. Mulcahey, & A.E. Wall (Eds.), *Theory and Research in Learning Disabilities*. New York: Plenum Press.

Wilson, D.M. (1961). The central nervous system control of flight in a locust. *Journal of Experimental Biology, 18*, 450–461.

Woodworth, R.S. (1899). The accuracy of voluntary movement. *Psychological Review, 23*, 1–114.

Yates, J. (1985). The content of awareness is a model of the world. *Psychological Review, 92*, 249–284.

Assessment and treatment of functional deficits

Mobility

12. Spasticity

M.P. Barnes

INTRODUCTION

Spasticity is one of the most commonly encountered problems in the field of neurological rehabilitation. It can be the main factor that prevents functional mobility and a major impediment to the rehabilitation process. Untreated spasticity can easily lead to joint contractures which may cause problems in maintaining suitable postures for feeding, communication, and other important aspects of daily living. Muscle spasms can be painful and are one of the predisposing causes to the development of pressure sores.

This chapter will discuss the basic neurophysiology of spasticity and the means by which it can be assessed and monitored. The chapter will then address the management of spasticity, from positioning and handling techniques to the use of neurosurgical and orthopaedic interventions.

NEUROPHYSIOLOGY OF SPASTICITY

Clinically, spasticity occurs in a bewildering variety of different forms that appear to reflect the differing size, location, and age of the lesion in each case. In general terms, spasticity is characterised by inappropriate and excessive activation of skeletal muscle in association with the other features of the upper motor neurone syndrome. It is usually accompanied by impairment of voluntary muscular activation. Such impairment varies from case to case and may involve weakness, slowness in building up to maximal power and in relaxing again, and clumsiness of voluntary movements. The clumsiness usually results from impaired coordination of synergistic agonist muscles and may also involve inappropriate restraint or failure of inhibition of muscles whose action antagonises the intended movement. The range of voluntary movement that can be achieved is sometimes reduced to a small number of stereotyped patterns that may be referred to as "spastic synergies".

Clinically spasticity is classically demonstrated by imposing a passive movement on the limb and inducing involuntary activation of the stretched muscle. The response is usually velocity-dependent, being larger in response to rapid stretch than to slow stretch. However, passive stretch may also induce activation of the shortened muscle (the "Westphal" phenomenon). It may alternatively trigger a "spasm", which is an involuntary and usually self-limiting coactivation of agonist and antagonist muscles of one or more limbs, often involving girdle and trunk muscles anatomically close to the limbs that are worst affected. Spasms are also triggered by cutaneous stimulation and it is often difficult to identify with certainty the stimulus principally responsible for triggering a spasm while passive movements are being attempted.

In extensor muscles, especially in the lower limbs (notably in the quadriceps femoris muscle), a characteristic pattern of response to stretch is often seen, known as the "clasp knife response". When the muscle is stretched progressively from its shortened position, its initial response is the usual velocity-sensitive resistance. Once a certain length is achieved, however, all resistance dies away and the extensor muscle becomes relatively flaccid, only to resume its activation when allowed to shorten. The clasp knife response has not been described in human flexor muscles.

Inappropriate activation occurs not only during voluntary movement and/or passive stretch but may also be present at rest, when the subject attempts to relax.

Finally, there is incontrovertible evidence that the existence of a response to passive stretch does not predict that the same muscle will antagonise a voluntary movement (Duncan & Badke, 1987). In spasticity, the restraint generated by a spastic antagonist during a voluntary movement may be less than, equal to or greater than the resistance it offers to an equivalent passive movement. Moreover, treatment that affects the response to passive stretch may have no effect upon spastic restraint during voluntary movement and vice versa.

It is essential to bear these clinical features in mind when considering the possible neurophysiological basis of spasticity in human subjects. Furthermore, considerable caution should be exercised in extrapolating from experiments that have been undertaken in smaller mammals using acute forms of trauma that differ both in their pathology and in the distribution of the lesions that are responsible for most human cases of spasticity. This section will deal with some basic principles and will not attempt to review in full the literature of this subject, which has been rendered contentious by the eagerness with which physicians and physiotherapists have sought to explain incompletely observed clinical phenomena by partially digested experimental data.

Both animal and human experiments have demonstrated that alpha motor neurones serving skeletal muscle are hyperexcitable in spasticity, and can thus be activated by inputs that would not normally provoke a response. The gamma motor neurones that innervate the intrafusal muscle spindle fibres appear to be activated appropriately for the degree of alpha activation that is taking place. In other words, alpha-gamma linkage is maintained to a degree that is often normal. There remains a possibility that in some cases of spasticity the gamma motor neurones are relatively more excitable than the alpha motor neurones, but this possibility awaits experimental proof in humans (Whitlock, 1990).

Since an input from spindle endings has in most circumstances an excitatory effect upon the alpha motor neurones of the muscle in which the spindle is located, measures that reduce the input along group Ia afferent nerve fibres would be expected to reduce motor neurone activation in spasticity, and generally this appears to hold true. Thus a lack of voluntary activation, blocking the input peripherally with local anaesthetic or neurolytic agents, or potentiating presynaptic inhibition with the drug baclofen, have each been shown to reduce the intensity of muscular activation in response to passive stretch. The action of anti-spastic drugs is briefly indicated below, but it is clear that they act upon the CNS at a number of sites. The net effect of these actions is usually to reduce the excitability of alpha motor neurones to all facilitatory inputs. Electromyographic studies have, however, demonstrated in certain subjects that the voluntary activation of a spastic muscle can be enhanced by anti-spastic medication. It is not clear if this effect is due to disinhibition from the previously more spastic antagonist.

The clasp knife response is best explained on the basis of the effects of an input from secondary spindle endings along group II afferent nerve fibres. Group II afferent activity increases in proportion to the length of the extrafusal muscle fibres and the effects of this input in animal preparations is to inhibit extensor motor neurones and facilitate flexor motor neurones. In the early phases of passive quadriceps muscle stretch, velocity-sensitive primary endings send back a train of excitatory impulses via group Ia afferents to the alpha motor neurone of the quadriceps muscle. While the muscle remains relatively short, little inhibitory input is generated in group II afferents, but as the muscle lengthens this input progressively increases until group II inhibition overrides group Ia facilitation and the "clasp knife" phenomenon occurs (Burke et al., 1971).

Cutaneous stimulation is a potent stimulus of the flexor withdrawal response which is characteristically triggered at low stimulus intensities in spasticity. In subjects whose limbs are prone to coactivation spasms, a stimulus that would normally be expected to reduce a flexor response might produce an extensor response. Measures that reduce the input from cutaneous receptors would be expected to reduce the frequency and intensity of spasms and reduce the excitability of motor neurones. This expectation is borne out in practice by the effect of reducing cutaneous stimulation or blocking cutaneous afferents by local anaesthetic, nerve blocks or cooling of the skins, as described in more detail later.

In animal preparations, sensory pathways in particular tend to show changes in excitability in response to continual or continuous afferent stimulation. This "adaptation" may occur over a period of minutes or hours, a process in which the response in man is not known, but detailed observations in some subjects with spinal cord lesions have demonstrated that prolonged periods of 20–30 minutes stretch of spastic hip adductor muscles may induce a state of reduced excitability in hip adductor and extensor muscles lasting several hours (Odeen, 1981). This mechanism is used in clinical practice by systematic positioning of paralysed limbs or the use of orthoses or serial casting to maintain stretch of a muscle. The effects of such procedures cannot be predicted with certainty in man. In the case of some lesions of the cerebral cortex, in particular, muscular activation can be relatively resistant to such procedures, and damage to the skin and subcutaneous tissue may result from injudicious attempts to overcome powerful and non-adapting muscular spasms by a mechanical restriction in inappropriate cases.

A further example of short- or medium-term adaptation is the response of some spastic subject to continuous electrical stimulation of the dorsal columns of the spinal cord or the superior surface of the cerebellum. In some well-documented subjects, progressive reductions in spasticity have been described over periods of hours or days, the effects tending to subside over a rather faster time course when stimulation ceases. Cerebellar stimulation is thought to activate connections to the reticular formation antidromically. Dorsal column stimulation may act partly through potentiation of presynaptic inhibition of the excitatory Ia afferent input from the limbs (Illis & Sedgwick, 1982).

The known neural circuits are inadequate in themselves to explain the great range and variability of phenomena seen in man under the general rubric of "spasticity". Further insights will depend upon more detailed analysis of clinical phenomena in human subjects linked to better anatomical and physiological localisation of the lesions. This could help guide basic physiological studies designed to explore how the various circuits operate moment to moment, since the demonstration of their existence does not necessarily throw light on how they operate in practice. A further difficulty in man is that the lesions responsible for spasticity have often been present for a long time, so that adaptive changes in connectivity in the nervous system in response to the lesion (some of which changes may be functionally beneficial while others are counterproductive) form part of the overall clinical picture, further complicating our understanding of the pathophysiology.

ASSESSMENT OF SPASTICITY

From the previous discussion it follows that the methods chosen to assess spasticity need to focus clearly on the features of the syndrome that are under study. In clinical studies it is essential to relate the observation to appropriate clinical objectives and not to assume, for example, that a reduction in passive stretch response obtained in subjects lying supine on a couch will necessarily bear any relation to responses to similar passive movements performed in the upright position. Still less may they relate to the patterns of muscular activity seen during voluntary movement. If the objective of the study is to test for improvements in the capacity to make voluntary movements, there is no substitute for measuring the performance of movement itself.

There are particular difficulties measuring spasticity in children because lack of familiarity with the environment, test procedures, or staff involved may have a profound effect upon the pattern and degree of spasticity observed. The influence of systematic variations caused by fatigue, the time course of the doses of drugs, the influence of meals, the presence of a full bowel or bladder, apprehension, or discomfort must be scrupulously controlled if the results of clinical studies are to have much meaning.

Spasticity is usually a chronic or long-term problem and therefore it is important in evaluating treatment to employ prolonged periods of observation and to ensure that the capacity of the nervous system to adapt to an altered input has not in effect reversed any initial benefits that occurred. It is inappropriate to conclude on the basis of a short trial that long-term medication for spasticity can be justified; long-term studies are necessary to do this. Longer term clinical studies have the additional advantage that the predictable complications of spasticity such as contractures can be incorporated into the range of outcome measures.

One of the first clinical scales used to evaluate passive stretch responses was the Ashworth Scale (Ashworth, 1964). The original scale was modified by Bohannon and Smith in 1987 and it is the Modified Ashworth Scale that is now widely used. The reliability of this scale has been confirmed in a number of clinical situations including elbow flexor spasticity (Bohannon & Smith, 1987), knee flexors (Sloan et al., 1992) and plantar flexor spasticity (Allison et al., 1996). However, the Modified Ashworth Scale can be criticised for not being sufficiently precise and is not a particularly useful tool for more detailed and subtle assessment of the effect of anti-spasticity interventions. In an attempt to widen the range of phenomena captured by clinical assessment, Goff (1976) proposed a rather more sophisticated scoring system, but in practice this has proved difficult for different observers to use consistently.

Other tests have been introduced but are often difficult to undertake in the clinical as opposed to the research setting. The Wartenberg Pendulum Test is useful for the quantification of mild spasticity (Bajb & Vodovnik, 1984). The principle mainly applies to the lower limb which is allowed to swing at the knee with the subject seated. Spasticity is measured as the rate of decay of limb oscillation. A relaxation index can be calculated. There are significant changes in the relaxation index within a single Ashworth grade and thus the Pendulum Test is probably

a more sensitive measure of spasticity (Leslie et al., 1992). A number of other mechanical methods have been developed for the quantification of spasticity. Firoozbakhsh and colleagues (1993) have demonstrated the use of an isokinetic dynamometer for quantifying spasticity by measuring the resistance to passive movement. Other authors have demonstrated similar techniques (Shabal et al., 1991; Livesley, 1992). Such techniques are useful but not generally easy to apply in the clinical setting. The same criticism applies to various neurophysiological measurements of spasticity including H reflex parameters and quantification of the tonic vibratory reflex (Dimitrijevic, 1995). Overall the best practical clinical solution is to quantify the disability that is being treated. For example, if anti-spastic measures are being introduced for pain relief then an analgesic scale would be the logical measure. If the aim of treatment is improvement of functional walking then a simple measure such as a timed 10-metre walking test would be an ideal quantification of improvement. In other words the aim of spasticity treatment should be carefully defined and an appropriate functional and practical measure used that can determine whether the aims of treatment have been met.

CLINICAL MANAGEMENT OF SPASTICITY

Spasticity is not a condition that needs treatment in its own right. The purpose and aim of any treatment needs careful definition with the establishment of specific functional goals. There are three potential aims of treatment. First, the improvement of function, often of mobility, but arm function can also be impaired by spasticity. In addition, it may be important to improve posture and the ease with which activities like dressing and washing can be undertaken by those who are paralysed and need personal assistance from other people. The second aim of treatment is the prevention of complications. The most common of these are muscle and joint contractures but occasionally spasticity will need treatment to avoid pressure sores, problems with catheter management and persistent swallowing and inhalation problems when there is marked trunk spasticity and scoliosis. Third, treatment is occasionally required for the alleviation of pain, either from the spasms themselves or more often from their physical consequences.

Conversely, it is not uncommon for an individual to benefit from some degree of spasticity. The extensor "strength" of a relatively rigid and spastic lower limb can be useful in some people for ambulation and particularly for transferring. Inappropriate alleviation of spasticity in these circumstances can lead to a functional reduction in mobility and independence. The other negative effects of treatment, particularly the sedative side effects of anti-spastic medication, also need to be borne in mind. The management of spasticity often depends on finding the right balance between these positive and negative effects. For this reason it is essential to identify the muscles involved and the circumstances in which the spasticity is clinically troublesome before deciding upon treatment.

Treatment of exacerbating factors

There are many external stimuli that can exacerbate and aggravate spasticity. In patients who are comatose, cognitively disturbed, or unable to communicate, and also in those whose touch and pain sensation has been impaired, it is important to look upon spasticity as a problem that may have a variety of underlying exacerbating causes. Common causes include distension or infection of the bladder and bowel, skin irritations such as ingrowing toe nails, pressure sores, and increased sensory stimuli from external causes such as ill-fitting orthotic appliances, catheter leg bags, and even tight clothing or footwear. The presence of potentially treatable and unrelated conditions such as abdominal emergencies and lower limb fractures should not be overlooked, particularly in people who are unable to appreciate pain despite being cognitively intact, for example after spinal cord injury. Attention to the treatment of such noxious stimuli can often lead to improvement in spasticity such that medication and other treatments can be avoided. There is often a complex interaction between inappropriate external stimuli and the effects of spasticity. For example, inappropriate seating or a badly positioned foot rest on a wheelchair can lead to an exacerbation of the spasticity which in turn can lead to discomfort and postural change which leads to a further exacerbation of spasticity and so on. Such vicious circles are best broken by direct treatment of the external cause.

Treatment modalities

This following section outlines a number of treatment modalities for the management of spasticity. These should not be seen as self-contained entities, as the management of spasticity most commonly involves a multimodal and multidisciplinary approach. Proper positioning and seating often needs to be managed in conjunction with adjustment of anti-spastic medication or by use of specific techniques such as motor point injections or localised orthopaedic procedures. The interdisciplinary team approach that underlies the philosophy of this book is just as important in the management of spasticity as it is in the management of other disabilities.

Positioning.   The positioning of the individual with spasticity is vitally important both in the acute situation and in the less mobile patient with established spasticity. In these situations it is essential to prevent a limb from becoming fixed in the position favoured by the pattern of spasticity. This traditionally requires each joint to be put through a full range of movement several times in every 24 hours. It also requires nursing staff and carers not to position the individual so that the spasticity is exacerbated. For example, the supine position that is so commonly adopted in the early stages after stroke or brain injury for the more severely disabled person who spends long periods in bed can exacerbate extensor spasm by facilitation of the tonic labyrinthine supine reflex (Hallenborg, 1990). Similarly, many patients, particularly in the early stages after brain injury, exhibit an asymmetric tonic neck reflex which in supine will encourage a windswept posture. This is a common abnormality characterised by an asymmetric position of the pelvis with one hip assuming a flexed position in abduction and external rotation whilst the other hip assumes an adducted and internally rotated posture. This deformity is a common cause of later orthopaedic problems especially in children where it can lead to subluxation of the hip on the adducted side (Letts et al., 1984).

Some of these problems can be avoided by prone positioning. This position is also helpful in people with marked flexor spasticity as it will induce stretch on the tight hip flexor muscles. However, this is not an absolute rule as some patients can exhibit a tonic labyrinthine prone reflex which will exacerbate flexor spasticity. Periods of prone lying with the hips adducted for 20–30 minutes may suppress spasticity in the legs for up to 6–8 hours, more effectively in some cases than anti-spastic medication. Side lying, sitting, and standing can all be helpful in different circumstances to produce stretch on spastic muscles and to facilitate use of antagonistic muscle groups. Sitting and standing postures are also highly desirable for functional and social reasons. Such postures can sometimes only be maintained by use of special positioning equipment, such as a standing frame. The active involvement of a physiotherapist in the acute ward and in the home situation is often essential in order for the spasticity to be properly evaluated and a realistic schedule of management worked out.

Unfortunately there are few studies that compare the effectiveness of different positioning techniques for the different patterns of spasticity that occur. It is unknown, for example, for how long muscles need to be fully stretched in order to prevent contractures. The Medical Disability Society has published guidelines on the management of traumatic brain injury and suggested that it is reasonable to maintain muscle stretch for 2 hours in every 24 hours (Medical Disability Society, 1988). Bohannon demonstrated the positive effect of tilt table standing for spasticity in an individual with a T12 spinal cord injury and intractable extensor spasms of the lower limbs (Bohannon, 1993). Conversely, Kunkel, and colleagues (1993) failed to demonstrate an effect on spasticity as judged by clinical assessment and H reflex in a cohort of six wheelchair-dependent adult men. However, this study did show a positive psychological effect. Obviously this study, being uncontrolled, was not able to assess the effect of standing on the prevention of contractures. However, most studies have shown a positive effect of prolonged static muscle stretch either by standing or by direct physiotherapy on spasticity (Hale et al., 1995). Overall, there is little doubt that meticulous and regular attention to positioning, standing if possible, and muscle stretch in the early days after traumatic brain injury can prevent the later complication of spasticity which if allowed to develop may have serious consequences of functional recovery.

Seating.   One of the mainstays of management of spasticity in the less mobile patient is the prescription of proper seating. The principles of seating are that the body should be maintained in a balanced, symmetrical, and stable posture and that is both comfortable and maximises function. The seating system should minimise development of inappropriate shear forces and should distribute the body weight over as wide an area as possible in order that the risk of pressure sores can be minimised (Pope et al., 1988; see Chapter 20). It is often appropriate to stabilise the pelvis first without lateral tilt or rotation but with a slight anterior tilt in order that the spine can adopt its normal slight lumbar lordosis, thoracic kyphosis, and cervical lordosis. The hips should generally be maintained at an angle of 90° or slightly more. Cushioning with a slight backward slope facilitates this posture. The knees and ankles should also be maintained at 90°. The maintenance of this posture against opposing spastic forces may require a variety of seating adjustments and supports. These commonly include foot straps, knee blocks, adductor pommels, lumbar supports, lateral trunk supports and head and neck support systems. There are a number of commercially available seating systems (e.g., Chailey Adapta Seat; Mulcahy et al., 1988) that provide fully adaptable and adjustable seating systems that can accommodate a variety of different spastic patterns and joint deformities. If spasticity has produced fixed contracture then personalised seating systems are often required such as moulded seats or adjustable matrix systems (e.g., McQuilton & Johnson, 1981; Trail, 1990).

Physiotherapy. The more mobile patient whose functional gait is impaired by spasticity can benefit from various dynamic approaches from a physiotherapist. The Bobath technique is now widely practised (Bobath, 1978) and there are other schools of thought which favour alternative approaches such as proprioceptive neuromuscular facilitation (Knott & Voss, 1968) and the Brunnstrom technique (Brunnstrom, 1970). These techniques are described further in Chapter 17. There is little evidence that any particular technique is more efficacious than another for the promotion of functional gait or for the management of spasticity (Dickstein, 1986; Palmer et al., 1988). It is thus difficult to evaluate the role of dynamic physiotherapy in the overall management of spasticity and formal prospective controlled studies are urgently needed. Whatever system of therapy is employed, other adjunctive physical therapies can help in the management of spasticity.

It is well documented that the application of cold can inhibit a spastic muscle (Knuttson & Mattsson, 1969; Price et al., 1993). In a later study Knuttson (1970) applied cold bags to spastic muscles for 15–20 minutes and found an increase in the range of movement of an average of 35° in most people. Similar results have been found by other authors (e.g., Kelly, 1969). There is no evidence that the muscle itself is cooled by this technique but reflex inhibition may be induced by cooling of the superficial tissues. The effect on spasticity would seem to be short lived, lasting approximately half an hour after 15–20 minutes of sustained cold application. This technique is thus not a long-term treatment in its own right but is a useful adjunct to active stretching and functional exercises. A more extreme use of cold is treatment in a cooling suit. A whole body cooling garment consisting of a vest and head cap is worn with channels for circulating cooling fluid. The individual wears the suit for around 45 minutes which is sufficient to induce a reduction of around 0.2–0.3°C in core body temperature (Coyle et al., 1996). The practicality of this technique should be questioned.

Heat can also be used for local relaxation of a spastic muscle (Lehmann & Delateur, 1982). Heat can be applied locally to the skin overlying spastic muscles by warm packs or paraffin or can be applied generally as in a hydrotherapy pool. Ultrasound is another method of delivering heat to spastic muscles. Although the application of heat has been shown to reduce spasticity in the short term, the effects are localised and the benefits tend to wear off fairly quickly (Giebler, 1990). The psychological benefits from even the short-term relief of spasticity in very stiff muscles should not be underestimated but in general this technique, like the application of cold, should be seen as only an adjunct to other treatment modalities, enabling limbs to be put through a full range of movement more easily and with less risk of trauma.

Over the last few years there has been increased interest in the use of electrical stimulation in the relief of spasticity. The stimulus is often applied to the skin overlying the antagonist of the spastic muscle on the grounds that this will decrease spasticity by reciprocal inhibition. The stimulation of the skin itself could, of course, effect the response. Stimulation can also be applied to the skin overlying the spastic agonist in an attempt to inhibit or fatigue the muscle. Few formal studies have attempted to disentangle the potentially complex effects that such stimulation might have. There is a wide variety of devices and a bewildering range of regimes for pulse frequency, duration, and stimulus intensity (Giebler, 1990). As an example, Alfieri (1982) found that 10 minutes of stimulation to the finger extensors produced a decrease in spasticity on the Ashworth Scale that lasted from 50 minutes to 3 hours. The range of movement can be improved following this technique although only after a few weeks of daily treatment (Benton et al., 1981). A study by Potisk et al. (1995) further demonstrated the efficacy of transcutaneous electrical nerve stimulation in a study of 20 patients with long-term hemiplegia after stroke. Stimulation was applied over the sural nerve of the affected limb and in 18 out of 20 patients a mild but significant decrease in resistive torques at all frequencies of passive ankle movements was recorded following 20 minutes of TENS application. The decrease in resistive torque was usually accompanied by a decrease in reflex EMG activity and the effect persisted up to 45 minutes after the end of the TENS session. However, the precise role of electrical stimulation in the management of spasticity has yet to be defined. At least 10 years' experience in several centres has failed to demonstrate a convincing effect that cannot be achieved by simpler means but some patients may prefer it to other measures. Other techniques such as electromyographic (EMG) biofeedback (Binder et al., 1981), vibration (Hagbarth & Eklund, 1968), and feedback of tonic stretch reflex (O'Dwyer et al., 1994) have also shown an anti-spastic effect and in some centres are used as adjunctive therapy.

Splinting and casting. A further approach in the management of spasticity and of joint contractures secondary to spasticity has been the use of various forms of splints and casts. There is little doubt that splinting and casting can prevent the formation of contractures in the spastic limb. It is also clear that range of movement in a contracted joint can be improved by the serial application of splints or preferably casts—a new cast being applied every few days as range of movement improves (Feldman, 1990). However, is this purely a mechanical effect or does splinting/casting actually reduce spasticity? There is no clear answer to this question. Mathiowetz et al. (1983) assessed EMG activity in spastic flexor forearm muscles using several different splinting devices and no device at all. EMG activity was not significantly reduced with any of the splints used. Mills (1984) compared EMG activity in forearm muscles in eight subjects in splinted and unsplinted conditions. Again it was found that EMG activity did not differ whether the subject was wearing the splint or not. Some workers (e.g., Brennan, 1959) have documented a reduction in spasticity. Some splints have been specifically designed to reduce spasticity such as the spasticity reduction splint (Snook, 1979) and the MacKinnon splint (MacKinnon et al., 1975). The designers of such splints usually claim reduction in spasticity although with very few exceptions such studies involve very few patients and are uncontrolled.

It is clear that splinting and casting has a role to play in prevention of contractures and an improvement in range of movement of a contracted limb (Ricks & Eilert, 1993; Wallen & MacKay, 1995). However, the role of splints and casts in the management of spasticity *per se* is far from clear. Basic questions such as the most appropriate design and length of time that the splint should be applied have yet to be answered. It is equally unclear whether splints should be static in construction or allow some movement across the relevant joints. If it is accepted that some splints can reduce spasticity then it is further unclear as to whether this effect only occurs whilst the splint is in place or can still be detected after the splint has been removed.

If a spastic limb, however, can be comfortably and safely accommodated in an orthotic device then this might produce functional benefit whether or not spasticity is reduced. A prime example would be the use of an ankle foot orthosis to improve functional gait in a spastic lower limb (see Chapter 20).

Oral medication

Pharmacological management in spasticity is not usually an important component in an overall treatment programme. However, the pharmacological armamentarium includes three or four useful agents despite their limitations from a range of troublesome side effects. Major failings in most reported clinical trials are that the pattern of spasticity is inadequately described, the objectives of treatment are not specified and only short-term rather than medium or long-term outcomes are assessed.

Diazepam. This was the first anti-spastic agent to be used (Kendall, 1964). The effect of diazepam in spasticity is probably mediated by its ability to enhance the action of the inhibiting neurotransmitter GABA (γ-aminobutyric acid). There are surprisingly few double-blind controlled studies of adequate size but such studies that there are (e.g., Wilson & McKechnie, 1966; Corbett et al., 1972) appear to confirm that diazepam is an effective anti-spastic agent, lasting for 6–8 hours after an oral dose, with unacceptable drowsiness and weakness as major side-effects. Other adverse effects, especially in people with cognitive impairment, are aggression and depression. The compound has well known problems on withdrawal. It has a strictly limited usefulness as for most situations there are better and safer alternatives.

Baclofen. Baclofen is a GABA-B receptor agonist but may also have a presynaptic inhibitory effect on the release of excitatory neurotransmitters such as glutamate, aspartate, and substance P. It would appear to act at a spinal cord level by inhibition of polysynaptic spinal reflexes. This may imply that baclofen is more helpful in "spinal cord" spasticity as opposed to spasticity of "cerebral" origin. It is certainly the case that all double-blind studies of baclofen have been conducted in spinal cord conditions and other than a few open trials there is no convincing evidence of efficacy in disorders of cerebral origin (e.g., Hudgson & Weightman, 1971; Duncan et al., 1976; Sawa & Paty, 1979). Baclofen shares with other anti-spastic medication the side-effects of drowsiness, fatigue, and muscle weakness which are usually dose-dependent symptoms. The effect of each dose lasts for 3–5 hours. In practice the dose of baclofen can usually be increased until the desired benefit is achieved or side-effects become unacceptable. However, it may be difficult to identify side-effects in some cases and there are many instances of people with head injury becoming more alert or people with multiple sclerosis becoming stronger in their arms after baclofen is withdrawn even though these had not been identified as side-effects at the time. A reasonably balanced dose is usually in the order of 40–80 mg in divided doses. Occasionally abrupt discontinuation has resulted in severe withdrawal symptoms such as hallucinations and convulsions. Baclofen should be used with caution in people whose renal function is impaired.

Dantrolene sodium. This is a less useful anti-spastic medication. The mode of action is peripheral with a direct effect on skeletal muscle so that all muscles including spastic ones become weaker. It suppresses the release of calcium ions from the sarcoplasmic reticulum with the consequent inhibition of excitation, contraction, and coupling (Young & Delwaide, 1981). It could be postulated that dantrolene should have an anti-spastic effect regardless of the origin of the spasticity and this is now generally accepted to be the case (e.g., Shyatte et al., 1971). Drowsiness, dizziness, weakness, fatigue, and diarrhoea are frequent side-effects. There have been reports of hepatotoxicity although this mainly occurs in long-term and relatively high dosage treatment regimens. Dantrolene should not be used in those whose liver function is known to be impaired. Side-effects can be made less obvious or avoided by slowly increasing treatment starting at 25 mg daily and increasing over several weeks to a maximum of 400 mg daily in divided doses. Liver function should be monitored.

Tizanidine. Tizanidine has been available in some countries for a number of years but has only recently become more broadly available and was only licensed as an anti-spastic agent in the US and UK in 1997. Tizanidine is a imidazoline derivative and principally affects spinal polysynaptic reflexes. This action probably arises from agonistic activities at noradrenergic alpha 2 receptors which results in both direct impairment of excitatory amino acid release from spinal interneurones and the concomitant inhibition of facilitatory coeruleo spinal pathways (Coward, 1994). Tizanidine appears to have similar anti-spastic efficacy to baclofen that seems to induce less clinical weakness at anti-spastic doses and is well tolerated. The drug exhibits a relatively mild side-effect profile including dry mouth, fatigue, and dizziness with very occasionally elevation in liver function tests which tend to improve on dose reduction. It would seem to be a useful and valid alternative to baclofen and dantrium (Young, 1994).

Other anti-spastic agents. There is a range of other anti-spastic agents that have been the subject of further study. However, few agents have been subjected to large-scale controlled trials and few definite conclusions can be drawn regarding their place in clinical practice. These agents include:

- clonidine (Dall et al., 1996)
- L-dopa (Eriksson et al., 1996)
- glycine (Simpson et al., 1995)
- intravenous orphenadrine citrate (Casale et al., 1995)
- subcutaneous bupivacaine (Goodman et al., 1995)
- divalproex (Zachariah et al., 1994)
- L-threonine (Lee & Patterson, 1993)
- cyproheptadine (Nance, 1994)
- tetrahydrocannabinol (Petro & Ellenberger, 1981)
- new selective GABA-B agonists (Froestl et al., 1995).

Nerve blocks

The first description of the use of phenol in the treatment of spasticity was by Kelly and Gautier-Smith (1959). However, this original description was of the intrathecal injection of phenol and it was not until a few years later that Khalili et al. (1964) described the use of phenol for selective peripheral nerve block. Since then the technique has been widely developed and there are now descriptions of chemical neurolysis of most accessible peripheral nerves. The technique is obviously difficult to subject to a controlled clinical trial and most of the reports of the effectiveness of nerve block have been straightforward descriptions of a series of patients. In most instances the effect is immediate and the results are often dramatic (Halpern & Meelhuysen, 1966; Copp et al., 1970; Delateur, 1972). The technique is relatively free from side-effects with the main disadvantage being the need in most cases for repeated injections at 2–6 monthly intervals. However, this may be better for the patient than the need to take regular medication and is less of a disadvantage in potentially recoverable spastic conditions such as post-stroke and post-head injury. The technique has a place in the management of spasticity in its own right. In addition, it is often useful as a procedure before casting or splinting to enable the limb to be manipulated into a more satisfactory position. The technique of phenol peripheral nerve blocks has recently been reviewed both by Barnes (1993), Botte and colleagues (1995), and Bakheit and colleagues (1996).

Technique

Nerve blocks are relatively simple procedures. Details will vary but in principle a needle electrode insulated except at the tip is used as an exploratory electrode. In practice an intravenous cannula may be used provided that the metal introducer is sheathed by a non-conducting plastic cannula. This can then be connected to the cathode of an electrical stimulator and inserted in the vicinity of the nerve. A plate cutaneous electrode is used as the anode and stimulus pulses lasting 0.05 or 0.1 s delivered at approximately 3–5 mA. When a clinically observable rhythmic response is observed a check is made in order to ascertain whether the appropriate muscle group is contracting. The need is then redirected until the current can be reduced to around 0.5 mA while still inducing a clinically detectable response. This implies that the tip of the needle is in close proximity to the nerve and the injection takes place. Normally the contraction will immediately disappear. Some operators will also use EMG recording in order to ensure that the target muscle is contracting. The normal pulse is of 0.1 s duration at about 2–3 Hz. The technique is normally well tolerated although some discomfort is to be expected lasting 15–20 s from the moment of the injection. Local anaesthetic skin infiltration is often appreciated by patients, but deeper infiltration cannot be used as the response to stimulation would be blocked. In particularly anxious patients and children, a brief general anaesthetic (which should not include a muscle-depolarising agent) may be needed.

Most authors use dilute phenol solution between 2% and 6% with an injected volume between 1 and 6 ml. The present authors use 3 ml of 3–4.5% phenol. Nerve blocks with 50% alcohol are possible and there do not appear to be major differences between alcohol and phenol. Nerve blocks with local anaesthetic agents such as a 0.25% solution of bupivacaine are particularly useful to use as a trial temporary block. Such a trial should always be conducted if there is some doubt as to the functional effect of a more definitive phenol or alcohol block. For example, a bupivacaine block to the obturator nerves can be useful to assess whether relief of adductor spasticity produces the desired relief of spastic symptoms or whether the adductor tone was necessary to maintain a functional gait. The duration of action of bupivacaine is approximately 6–8 hours. The duration of the effect of phenol or alcohol blocks is variable and a major determinant is probably the proximity of the needle tip to the nerve at the time of injection. The authors' experience is that if the current needs to be greater than 1 mA with a pulse duration of 0.05 s in order to observe a visible muscle contraction, then the duration of clinical response is likely to be less than satisfactory. Reported durations of clinical response are highly variable but average approximately 2–3 months (Glenn, 1990).

Injection sites

It is normally preferable to perform motor nerve blocks rather than injecting mixed sensory motor nerves with the attendant risk of dysaesthesia. However, it is the general impression that more proximal mixed nerve blocks are more effective and last longer than the more distal motor nerve blocks or motor end point blocks. The latter technique is obviously more time consuming and uncomfortable for the patient as several motor points may need to be identified in each target muscle.

Obturator nerve. The obturator nerve that supplies the adductor muscles is usually found just lateral to the adductor longus tendon using an anterior approach (Felsenthal, 1974). This technique is particularly useful for the management of adductor spasticity and is not normally associated with any dysaesthetic complications as the obturator is largely a motor nerve.

Posterior tibial nerve. This nerve is relatively easily accessible in the popliteal fossa and can be blocked either at the apex of the fossa between the medial and lateral hamstrings or at the popliteal crease slightly lateral to the midline. This is a useful technique that will relieve calf spasticity and will often abolish troublesome clonus or facilitate the fitting of an ankle foot orthosis (Petrillo et al., 1980).

Other lower limb blocks. The sciatic nerve and the femoral nerve can also be blocked but there are higher risks of sensory complications (Keenan, 1987).

Paravertebral block. The paravertebral approach is possible for locating the nerve supply to the iliopsoas (Meelhuysen et al., 1968). Koyama and colleagues have described (Koyama et al., 1992) a phenol block technique for hip flexor muscle spasticity using ultrasonic monitoring. Although such techniques are not without risk, no significant complication was observed in their series of 12 individuals. All subjects showed improvement in hip flexor spasticity with further improvements following additional physiotherapy.

Median and ulnar nerves. These nerves have significant sensory components and injection of the nerve trunk is thus usually undesirable. It is preferable to identify motor points using surface electrical stimulation. The points of maximal response are marked on the skin and then the technique described earlier is employed with the needle being entered at the marked point and moved to determine the point of maximum stimulation. This technique can be useful for wrist and finger flexor spasticity. Intrinsic spasticity in the hand can be helped by phenol injection into the motor branch of the ulnar nerve though this is technically more difficult than other blocks and often requires an open surgical procedure. Adduction deformity of the thumb can be treated by a block of the recurrent motor branch at the median nerve which can normally be found by surface stimulation as it enters the thenar mass (Keenan, 1987).

Musculocutaneous nerve. Musculocutaneous block can be helpful for spasticity at the elbow causing flexion deformity. The nerve can be located percutaneously in the axilla or more distally in the upper arm (Keenan, 1987; Glenn, 1990) or be sectioned surgically.

Shoulder adduction. This problem can be helped by motor point injections into the pectoralis major with identification of motor points using a surface stimulator. The lattissimus dorsi can be injected by percutaneous approach (Glenn, 1990). Hecht (1992) describes a subscapula nerve block which is useful for shoulder spasticity but is also particularly useful for the

alleviation of shoulder pain which is such a frequent problem in people with hemiplegia. Given the frequency with which spasticity occurs, the literature regarding specific nerve blocks is unsatisfactory, surprisingly sparse, and anecdotal. However, as a generalisation, adductor and posterior tibial blocks are usually the most effective and the results of nerve blocks in the upper limb are less satisfactory.

Side-effects

Side-effects will obviously depend on whether a mixed sensory motor nerve is blocked with consequent risk of dysaesthesia or whether the block is confined to motor nerve or motor end points. The most common problem is loss of motor function and if there is any doubt as to the potential functional effects of a nerve block then bupivacaine should be used before a definitive block with phenol or alcohol. The incidence of dysaesthesae is highly variable and reported as 3–32%. Fortunately the complication usually consists of a transient burning sensation lasting for a few days. Occasionally there is more persistent dysaesthetic pain (Khalili & Betts, 1967). Damage to local structures is possible and local pain, oedema, and infection have all been reported.

Botulinum toxin

The injection of botulinum toxin is now an established first line treatment for the management of dystonia, particularly blepharospasm, hemifacial spasm, and spasmodic torticollis (National Institutes of Health, 1991). The mode of action of botulinum toxin is the inhibition of release of acetylcholine into the neuromuscular junction. There are several serotypes of the toxin but currently the most potent is type A which is now commercially purified for clinical use. It is important to note that there are two commercially available products which, while being the same serotype, have different unit doses. The first report of the use of botulinum toxin in spasticity was published in 1989 by Das and Park. In recent years there have been a number of placebo-controlled double-blind studies that have now confirmed the efficacy of botulinum toxin as an antispastic agent. For example, Burbaud and colleagues (Burbaud et al., 1996) conducted a double-blind, placebo-controlled study in 23 hemiparetic individuals with spasticity of ankle plantar flexors and foot invertors. Patients reported a clear, subjective improvement in foot spasticity after botulinum toxin but not after placebo and there were significant changes noted in the Ashworth scale values for ankle extension and inversion and significant improvement in gait velocity. Other studies have confirmed efficacy in the lower (Hesse et al., 1994; Dunne et al., 1995) and upper limbs (Simpson et al., 1996).

The technique is quite simple and involves the intramuscular injection of the botulinum toxin diluted in normal saline. EMG control of the injection is probably not necessary for larger muscles such as the quadriceps, adductors and posterior tibial group. However, EMG control may be necessary in order to identify the muscle in, for example, the forearm compartment. There is no consensus on this point at the moment. The technique appears quite safe and to date there are no serious reported side effects. In a small proportion of individuals resistance can develop, probably secondary to antibody formation, but this seems to happen in only 2–5% of individuals. The technique has now been used in all age groups and may find particular use in the management of spasticity in the cerebral palsied child in order to save repeat orthopaedic procedures such as tendon lengthening over the child's main growing phase (Koman et al., 1993). Interesting experimental work by Cosgrove and Graham (1994) has shown that botulinum toxin A prevents the development of contractures in the hereditary spastic mouse which was used as a model of cerebral palsy in childhood.

The effect of botulinum toxin might be enhanced by physiotherapy after the injection or by electrical stimulation. Work by Hesse and colleagues in Berlin (Hesse et al., 1995) divided patients into two groups, one group having botulinum administered in the soleus, tibialis posterior, and gastrocnemius muscles alone and the secondary group receiving additional repetitive alternating electrical stimulation of the muscles for 30 minutes, six times a day for 3 days following the injection. The combined treatment proved to be more effective with respect to clinical assessment of tone reduction, gait velocity, stride length, stance, and swing symmetry. Animal studies have demonstrated enhanced toxin uptake by electrical stimulation.

Botulinum toxin is now established as a useful treatment in the management of focal spasticity. The main drawback is the cost of the toxin and the inconvenience to the patient as the injection usually wears off at approximately 3 months and the individual will need to re-attend the clinic at these intervals. However, botulinum does offer one of the most useful advances in the management of spasticity in recent years.

Neurosurgical and orthopaedic procedures

Intrathecal injections

There has been increasing interest in recent years in the use of intrathecal infusions of baclofen for the longer term treatment of spasticity. The first techniques involved destruction of the nerve roots by phenol and glycerine injections (Kelly & Gautier-Smith, 1959; Nathan, 1959). This technique alleviated spasticity in many patients with severe and late stage multiple sclerosis but it is now little used both because of the advent of intrathecal baclofen and also because of further experience with phenol peripheral nerve injection techniques. Intrathecal phenol is likely to damage the sacral nerves and should therefore be restricted to those who already have irreversible faecal and urinary incontinence. There is also an increased risk of pressure sores because the abolition of spasms reduces the amount of movement, reduces the frequency with which patients ask to be turned because of discomfort, and may also affect the sympathetic nerve supply to the blood vessels of the skin and subcutaneous tissues. The technique if used at all should be reserved for patients who are already paraplegic and preferably incontinent but who are still troubled by pain from the spasticity. Occasionally the techniques can be justified to aid positioning and to ease nursing and carer

intervention. After the injection it is essential to ensure that turning procedures are undertaken by experienced staff or carers at regular and frequent intervals, whether or not the patient reports discomfort. More accurate nerve localisation with intrathecal nerve stimulation techniques can produce better control of the procedure and may still have a place when there is spasticity in several muscle groups and for patients for whom more complex neurosurgical and orthopaedic procedures are inappropriate (Dimitrijevic, 1990; Iwatsubo et al., 1994).

The use of intrathecal baclofen was first described by Penn and Kroin (1984). The technique has now been refined and involves the implantation of a subcutaneous drug pump to allow programmable intrathecal delivery of baclofen solution via a silastic catheter. Baclofen is administered either in regular boluses or by continuous infusion. The daily dose needs adjustment according to clinical effect and normally ranges from 50 to 1000 μg of baclofen per day. The efficacy of the technique has now been confirmed in a number of controlled studies. Azouvi and colleagues (1996) administered intrathecal baclofen by implantable pump to 80 patients with severe and disabling spinal spasticity with an average follow-up period of 37 months. All individuals showed a significant decrease in tone and spasms. The efficacy tended to remain stable except in cases of mechanical problems of the pump or catheter. There is some risk of pump failure and consequent lack of effect or alternatively the delivery of an overdose of intrathecal baclofen. The latter problem occurred in two cases in this study. Tolerance can occur in some individuals. Other technical problems can relate to catheter movement or infection. The relative expense of the technique should also be borne in mind and perhaps the technique is best reserved for individuals with severe spasticity resistant to non-invasive treatment strategies. An interesting recent study by Dressandt and Conrad (1996) demonstrated lasting reduction of spasticity after ending intrathecal treatment. The spasticity remained absent or markedly reduced after stopping treatment in 7 out of 27 individuals. The reason for this continuing reduction in spasticity is not clear.

Occasionally other compounds can be administered intrathecally including morphine (Struppler et al., 1983) and clonidine (Middleton et al., 1996).

Rhizotomy

Anterior and posterior rhizotomy have been performed for many years for the treatment of severe and resistant spasticity. In recent years the procedures have become more selective and more effective. Sindou has pioneered selective techniques and now usually advocates a microsurgical dorsal route entry zone lesion (DREZ-otomy; Sindou, 1995). The procedure can be used for both upper and lower limbs and Sindou reports consistently good results with minimal morbidity. Sensory diminution is an obvious risk but functional improvements are reported by Sindou in excess of 90% of his patients. This technique should probably be reserved for patients with severe spasticity in whom more conservative measures have failed. A less invasive technique is percutaneous radiofrequency rhizotomy (Kasdon & Lathi, 1984). This is a useful, although not widely practised technique, with minimal risk to sphincter and sexual function—a relatively simple operative procedure with a high rate of efficacy but nevertheless with a small but significant rate of recurrence of spasticity which may require the procedure to be repeated. A useful review of selective posterior lumbo-sacral rhizotomy has recently been published by Peter and Arens (1994). The paper reported the outcome of 30 teenagers and young adults who underwent this procedure for cerebral palsy associated with spasticity. All 30 individuals had satisfactory long-term tone reduction, sitting and standing were improved in about two-thirds, and walking patterns improved in the majority. A few individuals had dysaesthetic sensations in the legs and feet and some had patchy areas of sensory loss. No individual had incontinence.

More invasive and extensive neurosurgical procedures such as chordotomy are now rarely performed.

Spinal cord and cerebellar stimulation

These techniques have been reported to be effective (Illis & Sedgwick, 1982). However, the effects tend to be short lived although some authors have reported satisfactory long-term outcome. Barolat and colleagues (1995) reported positive reduction of spasticity in all 48 spinal cord individuals who underwent an implanted epidural spinal cord stimulation system. Satisfactory response was still found at 24 months. However, the technique is not widely practised and is relatively expensive. There is the additional risks of equipment failure and electrode movement.

A useful review of the role of the neurosurgeon in the management of spasticity has recently been published by Shetter (1996).

Orthopaedic procedures

This section will briefly outline potential orthopaedic procedures in the management of spasticity according to the joints involved. Comprehensive and good quality management of spasticity should prevent the need for operative intervention but patients are often first seen when contractures and joint deformities are established. In these circumstances operations are often justified in order to prevent further complications. Further, surgical repositioning of joints can facilitate proper seating, ease positioning and the application of orthoses. With careful selection and close postoperative supervision quality of life is often improved and in many instances functional mobility can be restored. The surgeon also has a role in the use of procedures such as neurectomy.

Foot and ankle. One of the more common orthopaedic procedures is one of the various Achilles tendon lengthening operations for fixed equinus deformity. Varus deformity is often associated with equinus. Hind-foot varus is normally caused by spasticity of tibialis posterior. Midfoot varus is normally secondary to a tibialis anterior spasticity. Tibialis posterior can be lengthened by a Z-plasty procedure. If anterior tibialis spasticity is a problem then a split anterior tibialis transfer procedure (SPLATT) is normally helpful (Mooney et al., 1976; Tracy, 1976). Often equinovarus deformities need a combination of Achilles tendon lengthening, tibialis posterior lengthening, SPLATT procedure, and sometimes further combined with lengthening of the toe flexors. The latter technique can be used in isolation for toe flexion deformities. Clawing of the toes with hyperextension of the metacarpal phalangeal joints and flexion of the interphalangeal joints can be alleviated by fusion of the proximal interphalangeal joints combined with extensor digitorum longus and extensor digitorum brevis tenotomies. If the great toe is involved the tendon of extensor hallux longus can also be lengthened.

Knee. The most common problem is a spastic knee flexion deformity, often associated with a hip flexion deformity. If spasticity cannot be overcome by passive stretching or by serial casting then operative intervention may be necessary. The hamstrings can be lengthened although some surgeons prefer hamstrings tenotomy and transposition even in ambulatory patients. This procedure involves suturing the biceps femoris, sartorius, semitendinosus, and semimembranosus tendons to the quadriceps. Occasionally there is a marked difference in spasticity between the medial and lateral hamstrings and more limited operations are possible (Lusskin & Grynbaum, 1988). Occasionally there is extensor deformity of the knee in which case rectus femoris and vastus intermedius muscle can be released without affecting knee stability. After most procedures plaster casts are applied for 2–3 weeks before ambulation begins.

Hip. Hip adduction is a common problem but one which is often relieved by relatively simple obturator phenol nerve blocks. If necessary obturator neurectomy or adductor tenotomies can be carried out.

Severe hip flexion is often a problem associated with knee flexion deformities. Iliopsoas recession or iliopsoas tenotomy can both be performed.

Upper limb. Surgery in the upper limb for spastic conditions is generally less successful than those in the leg. One of the more common problems is elbow flexion which can be treated by neurectomy of the musculocutaneous nerve or open phenol block. Tenotomy or lengthening of the biceps and/or brachioradialis can also be helpful (Keenan et al., 1996).

Flexion deformity of the wrists and fingers can be helped by selective tendon lengthenings. For example, isolated wrist flexor spasticity can be treated by wrist fusion and lengthening of the flexor carpi ulnaris and flexor carpi radialis tendons. Isolated thumb-in-palm deformities can be corrected by flexor pollicis longus being transferred to the radial side of the thumb (Smith, 1982). Shoulder surgery is difficult but such procedures such as tenotomy of the pectoralis major, subscapularis, and latissimus dorsi for severe internal rotation of the shoulder are possible.

There are a large number of different surgical techniques which cannot be discussed within the confines of this chapter. For a more comprehensive review the reader is referred to Craig and Zimbler (1990).

CONCLUSION

This brief review of the neurophysiology, assessment, and treatment of spasticity gives some indication of the complexity of the subject. The need for careful evaluation of spasticity and careful definition of the goals for treatment are paramount requirements. The importance of teamwork with input from physiotherapist, orthotist, rehabilitation physician, and orthopaedic surgeon cannot be overemphasised.

REFERENCES

Alfieri, V. (1982). Electrical treatment of spasticity. *Scand. J. Rehabil. Med.*, *14*, 177–182.

Allison, S.C., Abraham, L.D., & Petersen, C.L. (1996). Reliability of the Modified Ashworth Scale in the assessment of plantar flexor muscle spasticity in patients with traumatic brain injury. *Int. J. Rehab. Res.*, *19*, 67–78.

Ashworth, B. (1964). Preliminary trial of corifoprodol in multiple sclemis. *Practioner*, *162*, 540.

Azouvi, P., Mane, M., Thiebaut, J.B., et al. (1996). Intrathecal baclofen administration for control of severe spinal spasticity: functional improvement and long term follow-up. *Arch. Phys. Med. Rehabil.*, *77*, 35–39.

Bajb, T., & Vodovnik, L. (1984). Pendulum testing for spasticity. *J. Biomed. Eng.*, *6*, 9–16.

Bakheit, A.M.O., Badwan, D.A.H., & McLellan, D.L. (1996). The effectiveness of chemical neurolysis in the treatment of lower limb muscle spasticity. *Clin. Rehab.*, *10*, 40–43.

Barnes, M.P. (1993). The local treatment of spasticity. *Bailliere's Clinical Neurology*, *2*, 55–71.

Barolat, G., Singh-Sahli, K., & Staas, W.E. (1995). Epidural spinal cord stimulation in the management of spasms in spinal cord injury: a prospective study. *Stererotactic & Functional Neurosurgery*, *64*, 153–164.

Benton, L.S., Baker, L.C., Bowman, B.R., & Waters, R.L. (1981). *Functional electrical stimulation: A practical clinical guide* (2nd Ed.). California: Professional Staff Association of the Ranchos Los Amigos Hospital.

Binder, S.A., Moll, C.B., & Wolf, S.L. (1981). Evaluation of electromyographic biofeedback as an adjunctive therapeutic exercise treating the lower extremities of hemiplegic patients. *Physical Therapy*, *61*, 886–893.

Bobath, B. (1978). *Adult hemiplegia: evaluation and treatment*. London: Spottiswoode Ballantyre.

Bohannon, R.W. (1993). Tilt table standing for reducing spasticity after spinal cord injury. *Arch. Phys. Med. Rehabil.*, *74*, 1121–1122.

Bohannon, R.W., & Smith, M.B. (1987). Inter-rater reliability of a Modified Ashworth Scale of muscle spasticity. *Physical Therapy*, *67*, 206–207.

Botte, M.J., Abrams, R.A., & Bodine-Fowler, S.C. (1995). The treatment of acquired muscle spasticity using phenol peripheral nerve blocks. *Orthopaedics*, *18*, 151–159.

Brennan, B.J. (1959). Response to stretch of hypertonic muscle groups in hemiplegia. *BMJ*, *1*, 1504–1509.

Brunnstrom, S. (1970). *Movement, therapy and hemiplegia: A neurophysiological approach*. New York: Harper & Row.

Burbaud, P., Wiart, L., Dubos, J.L., et al. (1996). A randomised, double-blind, placebo-controlled trial of botulinum toxin in the treatment of a spastic foot in hemiparetic patients. *J. Neurol., Neurosurg. & Psychiatry*, *61*, 265–269.

Burke, D., Andrews, C., & Ashly, P. (1971). Autogenic effects of static muscle stretch in spastic man. *Arch. Neurol.*, *25*, 367–372.

Casale, R., Glynn, C.J., & Buonocore, M. (1995). Reduction of spastic hypertonia in patients with spinal cord injury: a double-blind comparison of intravenous orphenadrine citrate and placebo. *Arch. Phys. Med. Rehabil.*, *76*, 660–665.

Copp, E.P., Harris, R., & Keenan, J. (1970). Peripheral nerve block and motor point block with phenol in the management of spasticity. *Proceedings of the Royal Society of Medicine*, *63*, 937–938.

Corbett, M., Frankal, H.L., & Micalis, L. (1972). A double-blind cross-over trial of Valium in the treatment of spasticity. *Paraplegia*, *10*, 19–22.

Cosgrove, A.P., & Graham, H.K. (1994). Botulinum toxin A prevents the development of contractures in the hereditary spastic mouse. *Develop. Med. Child. Neurol.*, *36*, 379–385.

Coward, D.M. (1994). Tizanidine: neuropharmacology and mechanism of action. *Neurology*, *44*(suppl. 9), S6–11.

Coyle, P.K., Krupp, L.B., & Doscher, C., et al. (1996). Clinical and immunological effects of cooling in multiple sclerosis. *J. Neurologic. Rehabil.*, *10*, 9–15.

Craig, C.L., & Zimbler, S. (1990). Orthopaedic procedures. In M.B. Glenn & J. Whyte (Eds.), *The practical management of spasticity in children and adults*. Philadelphia: Lea & Febiger.

Dall, J.T., Harmon, R.L., & Quinn, C.M. (1996). The use of Clonidine for the treatment of spasticity arising from various forms of brain injury: a case series. *Br. Inj.*, *10*, 453–458.

Das, T.K., & Park, D.M. (1989). Effect of treatment with botulinum toxin on spasticity. *Postgraduate Med. J.*, *65*, 208–210.

Delateur, B.J. (1972). A new technique of intramuscular phenol neurolysis. *Arch. Phys. Med. Rehabil.*, *53*, 179–185.

Dickstein, R. (1986). Stroke rehabilitation—three exercise therapy approaches. *Physical Therapy*, *66*, 1233–1238.

Dimitrijevic, M.R. (1990). Spasticity. *Curr. Opin. Neurol. Neurosurg.*, *3*, 742–745.

Dimitrijevic, M.R. (1995). Evaluation and treatment of spasticity. *J. Neurologic. Rehab.*, *9*, 97–110.

Dressandt, J., & Conrad, B. (1996). Lasting reduction of severe spasticity after ending chronic treatment with intrathecal baclofen. *J. Neurol., Neurosurg. & Psychiatry*, *60*, 168–173.

Duncan, G.W., Shahani, B.T., & Young, R.R. (1976). An evaluation of baclofen treatment for certain symptoms in patients with spinal cord lesions. *Neurology*, *26*, 441–446.

Duncan, P.W., & Badke, M.B. (1987). Determinants of abnormal motor control. In P.W. Duncan & M.B. Badke (Eds.), *Stroke rehabilitation: the recovery of motor control*. Chicago: Year Book Medical Publishers.

Dunne, J.W., Heye, N., & Dunne, S.L. (1995). Treatment of chronic limb spasticity with botulinum toxin A. *J. Neurol., Neurosurg. & Psychiatry*, *58*(2), 232–235.

Eriksson, J., Olausson, B., & Jankowska, E. (1996). Anti-spastic effects of L-dopa. *Experi. Br. Res.*, *111*, 296–304.

Feldman, P.A. (1990). Upper extremity casting and splinting. In M.B. Glenn & J. Whyte (Eds.), *The practical management of spasticity in children and adults* (pp. 149–166). Philadelphia: Lea & Febiger.

Felsenthal, G. (1974). Nerve blocks in the lower extremities: anatomic considerations. *Arch. Phys. Medicine Rehabil.*, *55*, 504–507.

Firoozbakhsh, K.K., Kunkel, C.F., Scremin, A.M., & Moneim, M.S. (1993). Isokinetic dynamometric technique for spasticity assessment. *Am. J. Phys. Med. Rehabil.*, *72*, 379–385.

Froestl, W., Mickle, S.J., Hall, R.G., et al. (1995). Phosphinic acid analogues of GABA 1: new potent and selective GABA-B agonists. *J. Medicinal Chem.*, *38*, 3297–3312.

Giebler, K.B. (1990). Physical modalities. In M.B. Glenn & J. Whyte (Eds.), *The practical management of spasticity in children and adults* (pp. 118–148). Philadelphia: Lea & Febiger.

Glenn, M.B. (1990). Nerve blocks. In M.B. Glenn & J. Whyte (Eds.), *The practical management of spasticity in children and adults*. Philadelphia: Lea & Febiger.

Goff, B. (1976). Grading of spasticity and its effect on voluntary movement. *Physiotherapy*, *62*, 358–360.

Goodman, B.S., Jann, B.B., Haddox, J.D., & Denson, D. (1995). Subcutaneous bupivacaine for treatment of spasticity: a case report. *Arch. Phys. Med. Rehabil.*, *76*, 202–204.

Hagbarth, K., & Eklund, G. (1968). The effects of muscle vibration in spasticity, rigidity and cerebellar disorders. *J. Neurol., Neurosurg. & Psychiatry*, *31*, 207–213.

Hale, L.A., Fritz, V.U., & Goodman, M. (1995). Prolonged static muscle stretch reduces spasticity. *S. African J. Physio.*, *51*, 3–6.

Hallenborg, S.C. (1990). Positioning. In M.B. Glenn & J. Whyte (Eds.), *The practical management of spasticity in children and adults* (pp. 97–117). Philadelphia: Lea & Febiger.

Halpern, D., & Meelhuysen, F.E. (1966). Phenol motor point block in the management of muscular hypertonia. *Arch. Phys. Med. Rehabil.*, *47*, 659–664.

Hecht, J.S. (1992). Sub-scapular nerve block in the painful hemiplegic shoulder. *Arch. Phys. Med. Rehabil.*, *73*, 1036–1039.

Hesse, S., Jahnke, M.T., Luecke, D., & Mauritz, K.-H. (1995). Short term electrical stimulation enhances the effectiveness of botulinum toxin in the treatment of lower limb spasticity in hemiparetic patients. *Neuro. Sci. Letters*, *201*, 37–40.

Hesse, S., Lucke, D., Malezic, M., Bertelt, C., et al. (1994). Botulinum toxin treatment for lower limb extensor spasticity in chronic hemiparetic patients. *J. Neurol., Neurosurg. & Psychiatry*, *57*(1), 1321–1324.

Hudgson, P., & Weightman, D. (1971). Baclofen and the treatment of spasticity. *BMJ*, *4*, 15–17.

Illis, L.S., & Sedgwick, E.M. (1982). Stimulation procedures. In L.S. Illis, E.M. Sedgwick, & H.J. Glanville (Eds.), *Rehabilitation of the neurological patient*. Oxford: Blackwell Science.

Iwatsubo, E., Okada, E., & Takehara, T. (1994). Selective intrathecal phenol block to improve activities of daily living in patients with spastic quadriplegia. A preliminary report. *Paraplegia*, *32*, 489–492.

Kasdon, D.L., & Lathi, E.S. (1984). A prospective study of radiofrequency rhizotomy in the treatment of post-traumatic spasticity. *Neurosurgery*, *15*, 526–529.

Keenan, M.A.E. (1987). The orthopaedic management of spasticity. *J. Head. Trauma Rehabil.*, *2*, 62–71.

Keenan, M.A., Ahearn, R., Lazarus, M., & Perry, J. (1996). Selective release of spastic elbow flexors in the patient with brain injury. *J. Head. Trauma. Rehabil.*, *11*, 57–68.

Kelly, M. (1969). Effectiveness of a cryotherapy technique in spasticity. *Physical Therapy*, *49*, 349–353.

Kelly, R.E., & Gautier-Smith, P.C. (1959). Intrathecal phenol in the treatment of reflex spasms and spasticity. *Lancet*, *ii*, 1102–1105.

Kendall, H.P. (1964). The use of diazepam in hemiplegia. *Annals of Physical Medicine*, *7*, 225–228.

Khalili, A.A., & Betts, H.B. (1967). Peripheral nerve block with phenol in the management of spasticity: indications and complications. *J. Am. Med. Assoc.*, *200*, 1155–1157.

Khalili, A.A., Harmel, M.H., Forster, S., & Benton, J.G. (1964). Management of spasticity by selective peripheral nerve block with dilute phenol solutions in clinical rehabilitation. *Arch. Phys. Med. Rehabil.*, *45*, 513–519.

Knott, M., & Voss, D.E. (1968). *Proprioceptive neuromuscular facilitation: Patterns and techniques*. New York: Harper & Row.

Knuttson, E. (1970). Topical cryotherapy and spasticity. *Scand. J. Rehabil. Med.*, *2*, 159–163.

Knuttson, E., & Mattsson, E. (1969). Effects of local cooling on mono-synaptic reflexes in man. *Scand. J. Rehabil. Med.*, *1*, 126–132.

Koman, A.L., Mooney, J.F., Smith, B., Goodman, A., & Mulvaney, T. (1993). Management of cerebral palsy with botulinum A toxin: preliminary investigation. *J. Paediat. Ortho.*, *13*, 489–495.

Koyama, H., Murakami, K., Suziki, T., & Suzaki, K. (1992). Phenol block for hip flexor muscle spasticity under ultrasonic monitoring. *Arch. Phys. Med. Rehabil.*, *73*, 1040–1043.

Kunkel, C.F., Scremin, A.M., Erica, E.B., et al. (1993). The effect of standing on spasticity contracture and osteoporosis in paralysed males. *Arch. Phys. Med. Rehabil.*, *74*, 73–78.

Lee, A., & Patterson, V. (1993). A double blind study of L-threonine in patients with spinal spasticity. *Acta Neurol. Scand.*, *88*, 334–338.

Lehmann, J.F., & Delateur, B.J. (1982). Therapeutic heat. In J.F. Lehmann (Ed.), *Therapeutic heat and cold* (3rd Ed.). Baltimore: Williams & Wilkins.

Leslie, G.C., Muir, C., Part, N.J., & Roberts, R.C. (1992). A comparison of the assessment of spasticity by the Wartenberg Pendulum Test and the Ashworth Grading Scale in patients with multiple sclerosis. *Clin. Rehab.*, *6*, 41–48.

Letts, M., Shapiro, L., Mulden, K., & Klasen, O. (1984). The windblown hip syndrome in total body cerebral palsy. *J. Paediatrics*, *4*, 55–62.

Livesley, E. (1992). The intra-observer reliability of the hand held myometer in the measurement of isotonic muscle strength in chronic spasticity. *Physiotherapy*, *78*, 918–921.

Lusskin, R., & Grynbaum, B.B. (1988). Spasticity and spastic deformities. In J. Goodgold (Ed.), *Rehabilitation medicine*. St Louis: C.V. Mosby.

MacKinnon, J., Sanderson, E., & Buchannen, J. (1975). The MacKinnon splint—a functional hand splint. *Can. J. Occ. Therapy*, *42*, 157–158.

Mathiowetz, V., Bolding, D., & Trombly, C. (1983). Immediate effects of positioning devices on the normal and spastic hand measured by electromyography. *Am. J. Occ. Therapy*, *37*, 247–254.

McQuilton, G., & Johnson, G.R. (1981). Cost effective moulded seating for the handicapped child. *Prosthetics & Orthotics International*, *5*, 37–41.

Medical Disability Society (1988). *The management of traumatic brain injury*. London: Development Trust for the Young Disabled.

Meelhuysen, F.E., Halpern, D., & Quast, J. (1968). Treatment of flexor spasticity of the hip by paravertebral lumbar spinal nerve block. *Arch. Phys. Med. Rehabil.*, *49*, 36–41.

Middleton, J.W., Siddall, P.J., & Walker, S. (1996). Intrathecal Clonidine and baclofen in the management of spasticity in neuropathic pain following spinal cord injury: a case study. *Arch. Phys. Med. Rehabil.*, *77*, 824–826.

Mills, V. (1984). Electromyographic results of inhibitory splinting. *Physical Therapy*, *64*, 190–193.

Mooney, V., Perry, J., & Nickel, V. (1976). Surgical and non-surgical orthopaedic care of stroke. *J. Bone Joint Surg.*, *49a*, 989–994.

Mulcahy, C.M., et al. (1988). Adaptive seating for motor handicap: problems, a solution, assessment and prescription. *Br. J. Occ. Th.*, *51*, 347–352.

Nance, P.W. (1994). A comparison of Clonidine, Cyproheptadine and Baclofen in spastic spinal cord injured patients. *J. Am. Para. Soc.*, *17*, 150–156.

Nathan, P.W. (1959). Intrathecal phenol to relieve spasticity in paraplegia. *Lancet*, *ii*, 1099–1102.

National Institutes of Health. (1991). Consensus development statement. Clinical use of botulinum toxin A. *Arch. Neurol.*, *48*, 1294–1297.

Odeen, I. (1981). Reduction of muscular hypertonus by long term muscle stretch. *Scan. J. Rehab. Med.*, *13*, 93–99.

O'Dwyer, N., Nielson, P., & Nash, J. (1994). Reduction of spasticity in cerebral palsy using feedback of the tonic stretch reflex: a controlled study. *Develop. Med. & Child Neurol.*, *36*, 770–786.

Palmer, F.C., Shapiro, B.K., & Wachtel, R.C. (1988). The effects of physical therapy on cerebral palsy. *N. Eng. J. Med.*, *313*, 803–808.

Penn, R.D., & Kroin, J.S. (1984). Intrathecal baclofen alleviates spinal cord spasticity. *Lancet*, *i*, 1078.

Peter, J.C., & Arens, J.L. (1994). Selective posterior lumbo-sacral rhizotomy in teenagers and young adults with spastic cerebral palsy. *Br. J. Neurosurg.*, *8*, 135–139.

Petrillo, C.R., Chu, D.S., & Davis, S.W. (1980). Phenol block of the tibial nerve in the hemi-plegic patient. *Orthopedics*, *3*, 871–874.

Petro, D.J., & Ellenberger, C. (1981). Treatment of human spasticity with Delta-9-Tetrahydrocannabinol. *J. Clin. Pharma.*, *21*, 413s–416s.

Pope, P.M., Booth, E., & Gosling, G. (1988). The development of alternative seating and mobility systems. *Physiotherapy Practice*, *4*, 78–93.

Potisk, K.P., Gregoric, M., & Vodovnik, L. (1995). Effects of transcutaneous electric nerve stimulation (TENS) on spasticity in patients with hemiplegia. *Scan. J. Rehab. Med.*, *27*, 169–174.

Price, R., Lehmann, J.F., & Boswell-Bessette, S., et al. (1993). The influence of cryotherapy on spasticity of the human ankle. *Arch. Phys. Med. Rehabil.*, *74*, 300–304.

Ricks, N.R., & Eilert, R.E. (1993). The effects of inhibitory casts and orthoses on bony alignment of foot and ankle during weight bearing in children with spasticity. *Develop. Med. Child. Neurol.*, *35*, 11–16.

Sawa, G.M., & Paty, D.W. (1979). The use of baclofen in the treatment of spasticity in multiple sclerosis. *Can. J. Neurol. Sci.*, *6*, 351–354.

Shabal, C., Schwid, H., & Jacobson, L. (1991). The dynamic flexometer. An instrument for the objective evaluation of spasticity. *Anaesthesiology*, *74*, 609–612.

Shetter, A.G. (1996). The neurosurgical treatment of spasticity. *Neurosurg. Quarterly*, *6*, 194–207.

Shyatte, S.B., Birdsong, J.H., & Bergman, B.A. (1971). The effects of dantrolene sodium on spasticity and motor performance in hemi-plegia. *Southern Medical Journal*, *64*, 180–185.

Simpson, D.M., Alexander, D.N., & O'Brien, C.F., et al. (1996). Botulinum toxin type A in the treatment of upper extremity spasticity: a randomised, double-blind, placebo-controlled trial. *Neurologia*, *46*, 1306–1310.

Simpson, R.K., Gondo, M., Robertson, C.S., & Goodman, J.C. (1995). The influence of Glycine and related compounds on spinal cord injury induced spasticity. *Neuro. Chem. Res.*, *20*, 1203–1210.

Sindou, M. (1995). Microsurgical DREZ-otomy (MDT) for pain, spasticity and hyperactive bladder: a 20 year experience. *Acta Neurochirurgica*, *137*, 1–5.

Sloan, R.L., Sinclair, E., Thompson, S., Taylor, S., et al. (1992). Inter-rater reliability of the Modified Ashworth Scale for spasticity in hemiplegic patients. *Int. J. Rehab. Res.*, *15*, 158–161.

Smith, R.J. (1982). Flexor pollicis longus abductor plasty for spastic thumb-in-palm deformity. *J. Hand. Surg.*, *7*, 327–331.

Snook, J. (1979). Spasticity reduction splint. *Am. J. Occ. Therapy*, *33*, 638–651.

Struppler, A., Burgmayer, B., Ochs, G., & Pfeiffer, H.G. (1983). The effect of epidural application of opioids on spasticity of spinal origin. *Life Science*, *33*(suppl. 1), 607–610.

Tracy, W.H. (1976). Operative treatment of the plantar flexed inverted foot in adult hemiplegia. *J. Bone & Joint Surg.*, *58a*, 1142–1148.

Trail, I.A. (1990). The Matrix Seating System. *J. Bone Joint Surg.*, *72*, 666–669.

Wallen, M., & MacKay, S. (1995). An evaluation of a soft splint in the acute management of elbow hypertonicity. *Occ. Th. J. Res.*, *15*, 3–16.

Whitlock, J.A. (1990). Neurophysiology of spasticity. In M.B. Glenn & J. Whyte (Eds.), *The practical management of spasticity in children and adults* (pp. 8–33). Philadelphia: Lea & Febiger.

Wilson, L.S., & McKechnie, A.A. (1966). Oral diazepam and the treatment of spasticity in paraplegia. A double-blind trial and subsequent impressions. *Scottish Medical Journal*, *11*, 46–51.

Young, R.R. (1994). Role of Tizanidine in the treatment of spasticity. *Neurology*, *44*(suppl. 9), S1–80.

Young, R.R., & Delwaide, P.J. (1981). Spasticity. *New England Journal of Medicine*, *304*, 28–33, 96–99.

Zachariah, S.B., Borges, E.F., & Varghese, R., et al. (1994). Positive response to oral divalproex sodium (Depakote) in patients with spasticity and pain. *Am. J. Med. Sci.*, *308*, 38–40.

13. Tremor and ataxia

Richard J. Hardie   John C. Rothwell

INTRODUCTION

Tremor and ataxia may each vary between the extremes of severity from being barely perceptible to causing gross disability. In general, both interfere with fine control of any motor activity and thus may impair speech, limb functions, posture, stance, and gait. Although they may coexist, this is unusual and thus tremor and ataxia will be discussed separately.

Accurate diagnosis is an essential prerequisite to correct management. Although space does not permit detailed consideration of the investigation of a person with either tremor or ataxia, it is necessary first to consider the wide range of differential diagnoses in each condition. It should be recognised that more than one underlying cause may be found in a single subject, who may be predisposed by a particular underlying neurological disorder to other problems. For example, someone with cerebellar disease is typically very sensitive to drug-induced ataxia, and the diagnosis of hyperthyroidism is easily overlooked in those with pre-existing tremor.

TREMOR

Behavioural definitions

Tremor is defined as rhythmical involuntary oscillation of any body part. Tremor is classified according to the part of the body affected and also the conditions under which it is best observed (Deuschl et al., 1998b). Two basic types of tremor are recognised:

(1) *Rest* tremor occurs when the body part is fully supported and the patient relaxed. For example, the resting component of head tremor is observed with the patient lying supine and the head supported by pillows; resting tremor of the hand is observed with the patient seated and the hands fully supported and relaxed in the lap.

(2) *Action* tremor occurs during any type of voluntary movement. Various types of action tremor are recognised:

(a) *Postural* tremor occurs during active maintenance of a static posture against the force of gravity. In the arms, this is best observed by asking the patient to hold the hands prone in front of the nose with the elbows abducted.

(b) *Kinetic* tremor occurs during a movement. In the finger-nose test, this component is seen during the middle part of the transit phase.

(c) *Intention* tremor occurs in visually guided pointing movements as the target is approached. In the finger-nose test this corresponds to the terminal 25% of the task.

(d) Some patients have a *task-specific* action tremor that appears or becomes exaggerated during particular activities. Occupational tremors (e.g., in golfers or musicians) and primary writing tremor are examples in this category.

The frequency of a tremor is also a useful criterion in classification. In general the higher the frequency of tremor, the smaller its amplitude. Tremors with a frequency of <4 Hz are classified as low frequency; 4–7 Hz as medium frequency; >7 Hz as high frequency. Most rest tremors have a medium frequency, whilst most action tremors have a medium/high frequency.

Mechanisms of tremor

All parts of the body have a natural "resonant frequency" at which they will oscillate transiently if tapped briskly. This frequency depends on the mass of the part concerned, and the stiffness and viscosity of the joints to which it is attached. During postural maintenance, the fingers have a natural frequency of around 12 Hz, whereas that of the wrist is 4–6 Hz. As muscles become more active, joint stiffness increases and the natural frequency rises.

A small amplitude physiological tremor occurs in all normal subjects during active maintenance of a posture. Two main factors contribute to it. First, the contraction of those muscles supporting the limb may be incompletely fused, allowing tiny fluctuations to act as "forcing inputs" that tend to make the part oscillate at its natural frequency. Thus when the upper limbs are outstretched, the fingers oscillate at 10–12 Hz whilst the forearm oscillates at around 5 Hz. A second type of "forcing input" is the arterial pulse, or ballistocardiogram, which again tends to support oscillation at the natural frequency of the limb. The important point to note is that these forcing inputs do not need to occur at the same frequency as the tremor itself. One force pulse starts the finger oscillating at its natural frequency. The oscillations go on for one or two cycles and then die away. If another pulse comes along, the tremor is sustained a little longer, and so on.

The only pathological tremor resulting from abnormalities in these mechanisms is that of hyperthyroidism, in which the contraction time of the motor units in muscle is reduced. This means that muscle contraction tends to be less completely fused than normal. The "forcing inputs" are increased and tremor amplitude increases.

All other pathological tremors differ from physiological tremor in that active muscle forces are applied to the limb at the same frequency as the tremor itself. The electromyogram (EMG) does not show a normal, continuous interference pattern, but is broken up into pulses that activate the muscles intermittently, causing the body part to oscillate at any frequency. The physiological mechanisms responsible for the intermittent activation of muscle in different types of tremor are not completely understood. At least two different processes are involved. In some circumstances the stretch reflex itself might cause a limb to oscillate. Because of time delays in the feedback loop, stretch reflex recruitment of muscle force can sometimes arrive too late to oppose the original stretch of muscle, and actually cause the limb to overshoot its original position. This can generate reflexes in the antagonist muscles, which again arrive too late, and tend to reinforce the oscillation, etc. Such a mechanism is probably important in producing the exaggerated physiological tremor seen during fatiguing muscle contractions. It is not thought to be important in normal physiological tremor.

A second process suggests the existence of a "central nervous oscillator". In some conditions circuits of neurones in the brain may begin to oscillate spontaneously, and if in the motor system, they can theoretically drive the intermittent muscle contractions responsible for tremor. Possible circuits involve the connections between thalamus and cortex, and between the inferior olive and cerebellum. These may be influenced by inputs from nuclei in the basal ganglia. However, remarkably little is known at present about why such oscillations occur, and what processes might trigger them. Frequency analysis techniques sometimes reveal the presence of central oscillator tremor even in control subjects, indicating that it may have a role in normal movement control.

When regular EMG bursts in pathological tremors alternate in agonist and antagonist muscles, it is easy to understand how the tremor is generated. Often, however, the bursts happen simultaneously in both. In this case, movement only occurs because activity in one set of muscles is larger than in the other and the amplitude will be smaller than that seen in alternating tremor. Tremor can switch between alternating and co-contracting types even in the same individual at different times of day and there seems to be no diagnostic value in the distinction.

Common clinical tremors

Essential tremor is the most common movement disorder (Louis, Ottman, & Hauser, 1998) (Table 13.1). It is far more common, perhaps 10–20 times more, than Parkinson's disease, for which it is often mistaken clinically. Typically it consists of a bilateral postural and/or kinetic tremor of the hands and forearms that is visible and persistent. Tremor of the voice, head, or legs is less common. Rest tremor can occur, but in most cases will disappear if the subject is at complete rest. Most cases are familial and inherited on an autosomal dominant basis, with the first symptoms usually appearing in teenage years. A study of positively identified cases of hereditary essential tremor (Bain et al., 1994) indicated that most patients experience substantial social and functional disability; 85% reported some degree of social handicap, and 25% had been forced to change their job because of the tremor.

In the past, task-specific tremors were often thought to be variants of essential tremor, but it is preferable to consider them

Table 13.1. The causes of tremor

Rest tremor
  Parkinsonism
  Midbrain tremor ("rubral" tremor)
  Wilson's disease
  Essential tremor

Postural tremor
  Enhanced physiological tremor
    anxiety, fever, fatigue, hypoglycaemia,
     hyperthyroidism, phaeochromocytoma
    drug intoxication:
      sympathomimetics: salbutamol, ephedrine
      xanthines: caffeine, theophylline
      anti-convulsants
      lithium, lead, mercury
      major tranquillisers, antidepressants
      steroids
    drug withdrawal:
      alcohol, barbiturates, benzodiazepines, opiates
  Essential tremor
  Postural tremor of Parkinson's disease
  Midbrain tremor
  Cerebellar disease
  Peripheral neuropathy
  Hereditary motor and sensory neuropathy (HMSN)
  Paraproteinaemic
  Syphilis

Kinetic tremor
  Multiple sclerosis
  Cerebellar and spinocerebellar degenerations
  Traumatic brain injury
  Posterior fossa tumours, strokes
  Wilson's disease
  Midbrain tremor
  Drugs:
    alcohol
    anti-convulsants
    lithium

Psychogenic tremor

Other involuntary rhythmical movements
  Clonus
  Rhythmic myoclonus
  Dystonic tremor

as a separate class. The commonest form is primary writing tremor (Pahwa, 1995) in which oscillations of the hand occur only during the act of writing. The amplitude of the tremor can be quite large and cause difficulties in identification of patients' signatures. Occupational tremors fall into this group.

A special form of task-specific tremor is orthostatic tremor (Thompson, 1995). This occurs mainly in leg muscles during quiet stance, and disappears during sitting or walking. Patients complain of a feeling of unsteadiness when standing still, and have to walk to obtain relief. Its frequency is much higher than any other form of tremor, usually reaching about 16 Hz, so that the muscle contractions are partially fused. Therefore the visible movement of the leg can be quite small, and this form of tremor is best diagnosed physiologically by recording the frequency of EMG bursts in leg muscles.

Parkinson's disease is the second most common cause of tremor after essential tremor and affects about 70% of all patients with the condition. Rest tremor is characteristic with a low/medium frequency "pill-rolling" tremor of the thumb, fingers, and wrist. In most cases, tremor also occurs on action, and such parkinsonian action tremor may even have a slightly higher frequency than that observed at rest. Parkinsonian tremor is discussed in more detail in Chapter 38.

Disorders of the cerebellum and/or its connections (e.g., alcohol intoxication, spino-cerebellar degeneration, post-traumatic brain injury, or multiple sclerosis) cause a characteristic intention tremor that increases in magnitude as the patient's hand approaches a visual target. Kinetic and postural tremor also occur (Brown et al., 1998), but not resting tremor. In some cases tremor amplitude can be very large, and interfere with or even prevent feeding and dressing. Selective lesions of the cerebellar vermis itself are associated with mainly axial and head tremor.

Tremor may develop after trauma through a combination of mechanisms, whether as a result of diffuse brain injury or direct injury to a limb (Biary et al., 1989). Rubral or midbrain tremor is rare, and may occur following lesions in several locations involving cerebellum, thalamus, and brainstem (Remy et al., 1995). It is usually of a rather slow frequency, often not as rhythmical as other tremors and occurs at rest as well as on posture.

Psychogenic tremors, although not often reported, may follow trivial head injury or other events. Their positive diagnosis is difficult but the following criteria are suggestive: (1) sudden onset; (2) unusual combination of rest and action tremor; (3) decrease in amplitude and variation in frequency during distraction; (4) increased co-contraction during passive manipulation of the joint by an examiner; (5) paradoxical increase in tremor amplitude when the limb is loaded with extra weight (Koller et al., 1989; Deuschl et al., 1998b).

For completeness, several other involuntary movements that may be mistaken for tremor have been included in Table 13.1. *Clonus* is the well-known rhythmical movement at about 6 Hz provoked by passive stretch of a muscle. It is not usually classified as a tremor because it is seldom sustained but it may persist in normal fatigued muscles or in spasticity for minutes or even hours. *Myoclonus* refers to single brief muscle jerks which

normally occur spontaneously or in response to exteroceptive stimuli such as touch or startle. However, rhythmic myoclonus can also occur. Clinically the movements are usually more jerky than the sinusoidal motion seen in tremor, but the difference can be difficult to spot. If the jerks are bilateral, occur at rest (and even during sleep) and affect only muscles innervated by a single or neighbouring segments of spinal cord, then it is likely that there is some structural pathology in the spinal cord. If the movements occur in distal muscles and only during voluntary activity, then the myoclonus may arise in the cerebral cortex ("cortical tremor"). The "flap" of the outstretched arms in hepatic and renal failure may be mistaken for a tremor but is actually a form of (negative) myoclonus known as *asterixis*, in which the jerks are caused by sudden lapses in muscle activity. Similarly, although *dystonia* is characteristically manifested as sustained twisting postures, both focal and generalised dystonias may be associated with jerky tremor of the affected body part assumed to be caused by the same underlying mechanism.

Assessment

Because diverse factors influence its severity, clinical assessment of tremor is notoriously unreliable. Intermittent tremor of normally low amplitude may suddenly become severe and continuous during the stress of a medical consultation. In the past, computerised accelerometry in one or more axes has been used to measure objectively the amount of movement in a tremulous limb. It is a simple technique, readily acceptable to most patients, and can give estimates of both the amplitude of the tremor as well as its frequency. However, experience has shown that such instrumental recording methods often do not correlate well with self-ratings of disability. One reason for this is that, even with more than one accelerometer, it is difficult to capture the complex behaviour of a trembling limb. Infrequent intermittent large amplitude displacements may be more disabling than the averaged tremor amplitude or its frequency.

Simple functional rating scales seem to provide the best assessment of tremor, and have been described in detail by Bain and Findley (1993). In brief, the authors recommend a combination of clinical rating and performance of simple tasks. They stress the importance of examining each part of the body separately, and during different types of task. They also provide rating scales for assessment of spirography (the ability to draw on paper a spiral of at least four successive turns) and of handwriting. Finally they recommend a simple volumetric measure: the amount of liquid remaining in a full 100 ml beaker of water after 60 s. All of these results correlate well between themselves and with self-assessment disability rating scales (Atchison et al., 1993). They presently form the most practical method of assessing tremor, although more comprehensive diagnostic screening methods have been described for genetic studies of essential tremor (Louis, Ford, & Bismuth, 1998).

Other instruments that are not specific to tremor should be considered as well, but are likely to be susceptible to other confounding factors. For example, Hariz et al. (1998) reported the results of using an occupational therapy tool called Assessment of Motor and Process Skills (AMPS) about 1 year following neurosurgical implantation of electrodes to provide chronic thalamic stimulation. In a group of 13 patients with disabling essential tremor or Parkinson's disease, AMPS was used to evaluate performance of two standardised domestic tasks with the stimulator turned off and two with it turned on in each subject. The assessments took between 1 and 2 hours to complete, and were affected by coexisting conditions such as visual impairment and painful arthritis. Improvement was much more likely in patients having undergone surgery for tremor of their dominant hand.

Management

The ideal management of any symptomatic tremor should be directed towards the underlying cause. Accurate diagnosis is therefore essential and in all cases alcohol and drug intake should be reviewed for causative or exacerbating agents (see Table 13.1). Certain tremors such as those associated with hyperthyroidism, Wilson's disease, and drug intoxication are totally reversible and should always be specifically excluded.

All tremors are exacerbated by anxiety and improve with deep relaxation, hypnosis, and sleep. Minor tranquillisers and sedative drugs, including small doses of alcohol, have a non-specific mild beneficial effect. Certain tremors are action-specific or highly posture-dependent, and it is often worth exploring these vagaries in case adaptive strategies can be taught. The specific management of irreversible disabling tremor is mainly pharmacological and depends upon the underlying cause.

Rest tremor is the predominant symptom in at least a third of cases of Parkinson's disease and often causes great distress and disability. Although traditionally it was taught that tremor did not respond to L-dopa, many patients derive relief of this as well as of the other cardinal features of the disease when receiving adequate dosage (Koller, 1986). The same is true of dopamine receptor agonists. Anti-cholinergic drugs provide small and variable improvements but may be very beneficial in individual cases.

Essential tremor is the commonest cause of disabling postural tremor although postural tremors of any cause usually respond to β-adrenoceptor antagonists such as propranolol 160–320 mg daily, given as a single dose of a long-acting formulation to improve compliance (Cleeves & Findley, 1988). Primidone, phenobarbitone, or medicinal doses of alcohol are effective oral alternatives, and sometimes intramuscular injections of botulinum toxin may be considered (Ondo & Jankovic, 1996).

Drug treatment for action tremor associated with ataxia has been largely unrewarding (Manyam, 1986; Trouillas, 1993) because of resultant drowsiness and lack of convincing benefit, perhaps related to coexisting ataxia in the majority of cases. If tolerated, clonazepam or carbamazepine are occasionally helpful. Since some cases of midbrain tremor may be caused by interruption of dopaminergic input to the striatum, levodopa may be worth trying (Remy et al., 1995).

Weighting limbs with heavy bracelets or shoes is known to damp intention tremor (Langton Hewer et al., 1972; Morgan et al., 1975) but accentuates fatigue and is neither practical nor acceptable for many sufferers. Limited success has been reported with elbow orthoses that increase resistance to movement and thus make feeding easier but they are unacceptable for long-term wear, and adequate fixation of proximal joints, e.g., by providing a raised table or armrests for elbow support, may achieve similar results. Tremor amplitude can also be reduced by encouraging the patient to execute a goal-movement from memory without visual guidance (Sanes et al., 1988) and rehabilitation techniques based on these observations might prove more beneficial.

In rare selected cases with predominantly unilateral tremor causing severe disability and resistant to other therapy, stereotactic thalamotomy may be considered (Koller & Hristova, 1996). Lesions of the ventro-intermediate (V_{im}) nucleus alleviate most forms of tremor, including parkinsonian, cerebellar, and essential forms, with no noticeable deterioration in control of other movements. Unilateral lesions placed by an experienced surgeon are often highly effective but obviously cause irreversible damage, and bilateral lesions carry a significant risk of producing speech deficits and mental changes. Experience in stereotactic treatment of the tremor in multiple sclerosis is limited, with variable but promising results (Haddow et al., 1997; Alushi et al., 2001).

A further development has been the stereotactic implantation of stimulating electrodes into the same area of thalamus. Despite the adjective, stimulating actually produces inhibition of activity around the electrode contacts, which disappears when the stimulator is switched off, effectively causing a reversible lesion. The advantage is that the stimulation parameters can be adjusted after implantation to produce the most effective tremor relief. Increasing the intensity or frequency of stimulation is equivalent to increasing the size of the functional "lesion". Bilateral chronic thalamic stimulation is also reversible and appears to be much safer than bilateral thalamotomy (Benabid et al., 1996; Hubble et al., 1997), but the electrodes and stimulator are expensive and long-term experience is lacking. In some centres a compromise is reached by performing an initial stereotactic lesion, and then implanting a contralateral stimulator later if necessary. Finally, the most recent research has identified a second possible target to alleviate tremor in Parkinson's disease. Chronic stimulation of the subthalamic nucleus appears to be an effective way of treating late stage Parkinson's disease. Stimulation here reduces akinesia, rigidity and tremor. Thus, even if a patient presents with tremor, it may be best to place the stimulator in this region, rather than the thalamus. As the disease progresses, it will be possible to continue stimulation at the same site and treat other symptoms of the disease (Benabid et al., 2001).

ATAXIA

Definition

Ataxia is a crude term indicating poor coordination of movement. It is particularly apparent when many groups of muscles are involved and comprises a variety of abnormalities of movement including:

(1) Difficulty halting a movement at a specified end point—*dysmetria*.
(2) Inappropriate timing of activity in proximal and distal or agonist and antagonist muscles during natural movement—*dyssynergia*, leading to decomposition of smooth movement.
(3) Slow, awkward performance of rapid alternating movements—*dysdiadochokinesis*.
(4) *Intention tremor*—also often present.

Mechanisms of ataxia

Ataxia affects all movements from the very simplest to the most complex. However, in all cases the basic fault seems to be that corrective pulses of muscle force, which normally ensure a smooth point-to-point movement, are the wrong size and/or occur at the wrong time. In a single-joint task, such as rapid flexion of the wrist through a certain angle, the antagonist extensor muscle must be activated at the correct time to halt the wrist at the appropriate angle. The size of the antagonist burst has to be adjusted, being larger for high loads and fast movements, but the right muscle is often activated later than necessary in ataxic patients, and the wrist overshoots its target (*hypermetria*).

The same is true of more complex movements. Consider a pointing movement, such as the finger-nose test. Normal subjects may be consciously aware only of the motion of the fingertip, perhaps sensing that it is produced by the biceps and forearm muscles. However, many more muscles are involved, many of which correct for the unwanted forces that result from the prime movement. If the arm starts from an outstretched supinated position, then flexion at the elbow will tend to cause the wrist to extend passively. This is prevented by activation of wrist flexor muscles. Similarly, when the finger reaches the nose, triceps may stop the elbow flexion, but unless the wrist and finger extensors are also activated, the wrist will flex and the finger will hit the nose.

These additional muscle contractions are said to compensate for "interaction torques" between limb joints, and the faster the limb moves, the more they are needed. The important point is that, like the antagonist activation in rapid single-joint tasks, they are not reflex corrections but thought to be centrally programmed, perhaps calculated before the movement itself begins. The timing and amplitude of this activity depends on the speed of movement and the mechanical properties of the limb (e.g. whether or not it is moving freely or carrying extra weight). Since it receives a massive afferent input from the limbs, together with a copy of the efferent motor command sent from the motor cortex to muscle, the cerebellum is believed to calculate the corrective forces needed to ensure smooth movement. EMG recordings during movement suggest that ataxia occurs because these phasic corrective pulses of activity are the wrong size and start at the wrong time, resulting in dyssynergia and decomposition of movement.

Causes

Ataxia is typically associated with lesions of the cerebellum and its brainstem connections from any cause. Damage to the vermis and other midline structures produces an ataxic gait with a wide base, marked postural instability, and a tendency to fall. Stance and posture of the head and trunk are abnormal and axial tremor (titubation) may occur. Disease of the lateral zone affecting the cerebellar hemisphere and dentate nucleus results in ipsilateral limb ataxia. Dysarthria and abnormalities of smooth pursuit and saccadic eye movements are common to both midline and laterally placed lesions. As already mentioned in relation to intention tremor, certain drugs such as alcohol and phenytoin may impair global cerebellar function both acutely and after more chronic exposure. A deficiency of serotonin has been proposed as the neurochemical defect causing ataxia in degenerative cerebellar disorders (see later).

Normal cerebellar function is critically dependent upon its afferent inputs, particularly proprioceptive. Thus damage to large type Ia sensory fibres in a demyelinating neuropathy or to the dorsal columns of the spinal cord can result in almost identical disturbances of coordination termed sensory ataxia. Some inflammatory polyneuropathies and deficiencies of vitamins E and B12 are treatable, and hence important, examples of this syndrome. Acute bilateral or unilateral loss of vestibular function results in severe disorders of posture and gait in association with vertigo, but fortunately compensatory changes soon take place centrally.

Assessment

Because ataxia is not a pure concept, objective assessment is very difficult. Indeed the validity of a diagnosis of the presence of ataxia is largely a subjective judgement on the part of the examiner and it may be impossible to evaluate clinically the relative severity of two types of motor impairment in combination. Assessment methods are broadly similar to those already discussed for tremor, and share similar drawbacks. Some variability can be eliminated by testing under uniform conditions at consistent times of the day. The crudest measure is an attempt to grade each limb or task on a simple semi-quantitative (but non-linear) scale from absent through mild and moderate to severe. For example, Nobile-Orazio et al. (1988) used an unvalidated 6-point scale to rate sensory ataxia during standing and walking when treating patients with neuropathy associated with paraproteinaemia (see Table 13.2).

One of the commonest causes of cerebellar dysfunction is multiple sclerosis, and the Kurtzke "expanded disability status" scale (EDSS) is based on clinical grading scales of various neurological impairments, including cerebellar and brainstem function (Table 13.2), which correlate roughly with disease severity (Kurtzke, 1983). Unfortunately its inter-rater reliability is also not high (Amato et al., 1988), the terminology is not consistent with the WHO classification of impairment, disability and handicap, and there are other flaws which seriously limit its usefulness (Willoughby & Paty, 1988; Rudick et al., 1996).

Table 13.2. Ordinal rating scales of ataxia

1. Two functional systems in the Kurtzke Expanded Disability Status Scale (EDSS; 1983)
   Cerebellar functions
     0. Normal
     1. Abnormal signs without disability
     2. Mild ataxia
     3. Moderate truncal or limb ataxia
     4. Severe ataxia, all limbs
     5. Unable to perform coordinated movements due to ataxia
     V = Unknown
     X = Is used throughout after each number when weakness (grade 3 or more on pyramidal functions) interferes with testing
   Brainstem functions
     0. Normal
     1. Signs only
     2. Moderate nystagmus or other mild disability
     3. Severe nystagmus, marked extra-ocular weakness, or moderate disability of other cranial nerves
     4. Marked dysarthria or other marked disability
     5. Inability to swallow or speak
     V = Unknown

2. Ataxia score (Nobile-Orazio et al., 1988)
     0. Normal—stand on one foot with eyes closed
     1. Stand/walk normally with eyes closed
     2. Stand/walk with minor swaying with eyes closed, but normally with eyes open
     3. Stand/walk with some swaying with eyes open
     4. Stand/walk on a large base with eyes open
     5. Standing/walking impossible without support

Interval methods were subsequently developed by, for example, Notermans et al. (1994), who quantified upper and lower limb tapping tests, the finger-nose test, and Romberg's testing in patients with cerebellar and sensory ataxia, and showed that these tests of impairment were sensitive to change over time. Subsequently Trouillas, Takayanagi et al. (1997) have published a 100-point ordinal battery ataxia rating scale for posture and gait, limb movement, speech and eye movements, which remains to be validated.

The measurement of postural sway standing on a force platform with strain gauges at each corner, a technique known as quantitative posturography, can be helpful in following the course of midline cerebellar disturbances, although interestingly those with pure lesions of the cerebellar hemispheres cannot be distinguished from normals by this technique alone (Diener & Dichgans, 1996). Detailed analysis of gait in a fully equipped gait laboratory requires expert interpretation, and is beyond the scope of this chapter.

Accurate recordings of limb movement can be made simply using a video-camera or more quantitatively using computerised goniometry, tracking methods, or kinematic techniques to measure trajectory and velocity, supplemented by accelerometry or recordings of bioelectrical activity by EMG or microneurography. Unfortunately reliability is compromised because of the marked influence of fatigue and emotional stress upon performance and results often correlate poorly with a person's functional disability. For example, Fillyaw et al. (1989) found that 10 of 11 quantitative measures of ataxia had poor reliability because subjects had difficulty performing standard and reproducible test movements in both time and space. These authors included electro-oculography, hand and foot accelerometry, tracing sine and square wave lines on graph paper or a computer screen, etc., but found that only a timed syllable repetition test of dysarthria was acceptably reliable. Hence it is essential to include symptom self-rating scales and general assessments of simple motor tasks and activities of daily living in any ataxia test battery (Rudick et al., 1996; Shumway-Cook et al., 1996).

Management

In striking contrast to other motor impairments such as weakness and spasticity, there exists very little published evidence concerning the best management of disability resulting from ataxia. This may be partly because ataxia is often associated with progressive degenerative disease and it is seldom possible to influence the underlying cause. Prospects for improvement are greater if the impairment is of acute onset and/or secondary for example to hydrocephalus, stroke, acute infection, or trauma. Ataxia secondary to peripheral vestibular lesions causing vertigo usually recovers spontaneously, has been well reviewed by Shumway-Cook et al. (1996) and will not be considered further.

Exposure to alcohol and phenytoin should probably be minimised, and trials of thiamine and gluten-free diet may be worth considering. Exceptionally, plasma exchange, iv gamma globulin, or other immunotherapy may improve the underlying disease process in conditions such as Miller-Fisher syndrome or paraneoplastic cerebellar degeneration, although the latter still has a very poor prognosis. Attempts at specific pharmacotherapy have been unrewarding despite theoretical bases for clinical trials with agents such as choline and lecithin, physostigmine, valproate, and thyrotrophin-releasing hormone (TRH) (Manyam, 1986; Trouillas, 1993). The benefits of serotonin agonists such as L-5-hydroxy-tryptophan and buspirone offer more promise but remain unimpressive (Trouillas et al., 1995; Wessel et al., 1995; Trouillas, Xie, et al., 1997).

Eventually in most cases of chronic progressive ataxia, it becomes necessary to accept functional limitations and adopt compensatory strategies including the use of aids and appliances. However, the timing of such interventions can be critical, such as the decision when to provide a wheelchair for a person with moderate gait ataxia. Particularly when accompanied by severe intention tremor, weighting the limbs can be helpful (Langton Hewer et al., 1972; Morgan et al., 1975; Morice et al., 1990) and other mechanical measures can be tried to help, for example, feeding (Michaelis 1993). As for tremor, there has been a resurgence of interest in thalamic electrostimulation via surgically implanted electrodes, but experience is so far very limited (Benabid et al., 1996; Nguyen et al., 1996).

Because of frustration, there is a real danger that sufferers from chronic ataxia become unnecessarily inactive and dependent, so just preventing disuse may be helpful as well as general endurance training, which Fillyaw and Ades (1989) reported to be beneficial in patients with Friedreich's ataxia. In addition formal retraining can be rewarding. The remarkable balancing skills of gymnasts and steeplejacks demonstrate that congenital human postural reflexes are not perfect but can be adjusted to higher performance by training. Rapid reductions in the postural sway induced by certain manoeuvres can be achieved within a few days by a daily hour of balance training on foam rubber with head extension and closed eyes, and early response to such treatment could be used to select patients with acquired ataxia for more prolonged rehabilitation (Brandt et al., 1981, 1986).

Various techniques are employed by therapists using the following strategies:

(1) Encouraging the use of visual, kinaesthetic, and conscious voluntary pathways to compensate.
(2) Emphasis on adequate experience of movement with stimulation of balance and righting reactions.
(3) Repeated practice of exercises of increasing complexity over a prolonged time, thereby reinforcing experience-dependent plasticity of cerebellar neuronal networks.
(4) Avoidance of fatigue and redevelopment of self-confidence to prevent the breakdown of compensation under stress.
(5) Measures to reduce action tremor discussed earlier.

In the upper limbs, simple flexion-extension movements are usually practised before graduating to exercises against resistance and later introducing more complex and accurate actions. Other exercises that involve balancing and foot placement using a gym ball or whilst walking or standing, perhaps using mirrors to improve body awareness, may help lower limb ataxia. Frenkel's exercises, first described over 60 years ago, are often mentioned in therapy textbooks. They prescribe the performance of precise rhythmical movements repeatedly and with intense concentration aided initially by the patient counting aloud, and can be used for upper and lower limbs or for re-educating specific functions. The use of EMG audio-visual feedback has also been advocated.

Balliet et al. (1987) described ambulation re-education in a series of five patients with cerebellar damage, mostly following trauma. They used three increasingly demanding stages of ambulation starting with reciprocal sequencing of lower limb stepping movements whilst seated, progressing to independent standing and balancing first static and then on a rocker board, and finally walking using methods that progressively reduced the use of walking aids requiring upper limb weight-bearing, which they believed to be important.

Brandt et al. (1981) recommended that "clinicians should treat ataxia by exposing patients to stimulus situations producing increasing body instability in order to facilitate sensorimotor rearrangement". Unfortunately success probably depends upon intact sensory input and the ability to relearn motor coordination, and spino-cerebellar syndromes are often resistant, especially if there is a coexistent neuropathy. The ultimate prognosis for other degenerative ataxias is equally poor. Despite much greater interest in rehabilitation generally since the 1980s, however, there is little scientific information about the indications for and effectiveness of individual approaches to ataxia, most of which have never been formally evaluated and are handed down to successive generations as therapists' folklore without critical evaluation. In one of the rare exceptions, a difficult but careful attempt was made to compare the effects of eight daily occupational and physiotherapy treatment sessions in ataxic multiple sclerosis subjects delivered in an in-patient rehabilitation unit against a smaller non-randomised control group (Jones et al., 1996). These authors concluded that, not unexpectedly, intervention was not followed by any significant change in cerebellar impairments but that worthwhile reductions in disability were achieved.

CONCLUSION

Instrumental techniques are now readily available to provide accurate and sensitive objective measurements of both tremor and ataxia. Unfortunately reliability is poor because of variations in performance related to emotional stress and fatigue, and to spontaneous fluctuations in the underlying condition, for example in multiple sclerosis and Parkinson's disease, and often no clear functional correlation can be found. Additional difficulties are posed by the presence of multiple motor impairments and often a progressive disease process, where improvement may be best measured as a slowing down of the natural rate of deterioration.

The rehabilitation of those people with chronic neurological disorders causing predominantly tremor or ataxia has for too long been utterly nihilistic. It is to be hoped that recent advances in technology and greater understanding of research methodology can be combined with improved collaboration between physicians, therapists, and scientists to bring about advances in the near future.

REFERENCES

Alushi, S.H., Aziz, T.Z., Glickman, S., Jahanshabi, M., Stein, J.F., & Bain, P.G. (2001). Stereotactic lesional surgery for the treatment of tremor in multiple sclerosis: a prospective, case-controlled study. *Brain*, *124*, 1576–1589.

Amato, M.P., Fratiglioni, L., Groppi, C., Siracusa, G., & Amaducci, L. (1988). Interrater reliability in assessing functional systems and disability on the Kurtzke scale in multiple sclerosis. *Archives of Neurology*, *45*, 746–748.

Atchison, P., Bain, P.G., & Findley, L.J. (1993). Assessing tremor severity. *Journal of Neurology, Neurosurgery and Psychiatry*, *56*, 868–873.

Bain, P.G., & Findley, L.J. (1993) *Assessing tremor severity*. London: Smith Gordon.

Bain, P.G., Findley, L.J., Thompson, P.D., Gresty, M., Rothwell, J.C., Harding, A.E., & Marsden, C.D. (1994). A study of hereditary essential tremor. *Brain*, *117*, 805–824.

Balliet, R., Harbst, K.B., Kim, O., & Stewart, R.V. (1987). Retraining of functional gait through the reduction of upper extremity weight-bearing in chronic cerebellar ataxia. *International Rehabilitation Medicine*, *8*, 148–153.

Benabid, A.L., Koudsie, A., Benazzouz, A., Piallet, B., Krack, P., Limousin-Dowsey, P., Lebas, J.F., & Pollak, P. (2001). Deep brain stimulation for Parkinson's disease. *Adv. Neurol.*, *86*, 405–412.

Benabid, A.L., Pollak, P., Gao, D., et al. (1996). Chronic electrical stimulation of the ventralis intermedius nucleus of the thalamus as a treatment of movement disorders. *Journal of Neurosurgery*, *84*, 203–214.

Biary, N., Cleeves, L., Findley, L.J., & Koller, W. (1989). Post-traumatic tremor. *Neurology, 39,* 103–106.

Brandt, T., Buchele, W., & Krafczyk, S. (1986). Training effects on experimental postural instability: a model for clinical ataxia therapy. In W. Bles & T. Brandt (Eds.), *Disorders of posture and gait* (pp. 353–365). Amsterdam: Elsevier.

Brandt, T., Krafczyk, S., & Malsbenden, I. (1981). Postural imbalance with head extension: improvement by training as a model for ataxia therapy. *Annals of the New York Academy of Sciences, 374,* 636–649.

Brown, P., Rothwell, J.C., Stevens, J.M., Lees, A.J., & Marsden, C.D. (1998). Cerebellar axial postural tremor. *Movement Disorders, 12,* 977–984.

Cleeves, L., & Findley, L.J. (1988). Propranolol and propranolol-LA in essential tremor: a double blind comparative study. *Journal of Neurology, Neurosurgery and Psychiatry, 51,* 379–384.

Deuschl, G., Bain, P., Brin, M., et al. (1998b). Consensus statement of the Movement Disorder Society on tremor. *Movement Disorders, 13*(Suppl. 3): 2–23.

Deuschl, G., Köster, B., Lücking, C.H., & Scheidt, C. (1998a). Diagnostic and pathophysiological aspects of psychogenic tremors. *Movement Disorders 13,* 294–302.

Diener, H.C., & Dichgans, J. (1996). Cerebellar and spinocerebellar gait disorders. In A.M. Bronstein, T. Brandt, & M.H. Woollacott (Eds.), *Clinical disorders of balance, posture and gait* (pp. 147–155). London: Arnold.

Fillyaw, M.J., & Ades, P.A. (1989). Endurance exercise training in Friedreich ataxia. *Archives of Physical Medicine and Rehabilitation, 70,* 786–788.

Fillyaw, M.J., Badger, G.J., Bradley, W.G., et al. (1989). Quantitative measures of neurological function in chronic neuromuscular diseases and ataxia. *Journal of Neurological Sciences, 92,* 17–36.

Haddow, L.J., Mumford, C., & Whittle, I.R. (1997). Stereotactic treatment of tremor due to multiple sclerosis. *Neurosurgery Quarterly, 7,* 23–34.

Hariz, G.-M., Bergenheim, A.T., Hariz, M.I., & Lindberg, M. (1998). Assessment of ability/disability in patients treated with chronic thalamic stimulation for tremor. *Movement Disorders, 13,* 78–83.

Hubble, J.P., Busenbark, K.L., Wilkinson, S., Pahwa, R., Paulson, G.W., Lyons, K., & Koller, W.C. (1997). Effects of thalamic deep brain stimulation based on tremor type and diagnosis. *Movement Disorders, 12,* 337–341.

Jones, L., Lewis, Y., Harrison, J., & Wiles, C.M. (1996). The effectiveness of occupational therapy and physiotherapy in multiple sclerosis patients with ataxia of the upper limb and trunk. *Clinical Rehabilitation, 10,* 277–282.

Koller, W.C. (1986). Pharmacologic treatment of parkinsonian tremor. *Archives of Neurology, 43,* 126–127.

Koller, W., & Hristova, A. (1996). Efficacy and safety of stereotactic surgical treatment of tremor disorders. *European Journal of Neurology, 3,* 507–514.

Koller, W., Lang, A., & Vetere-Overfield, B., et al. (1989). Psychogenic tremors. *Neurology, 39,* 1094–1099.

Kurtzke, J.F. (1983). Rating neurologic impairment in multiple sclerosis: an expanded disability status scale (EDSS). *Neurology, 33,* 1444–1452.

Langton Hewer, R., Cooper, R., & Morgan, M.H. (1972). An investigation into the value of treating intention tremor by weighting the affected limb. *Brain, 95,* 579–590.

Louis, E.D., Ford, B., & Bismuth, B. (1998). Reliability between two observers using a protocol for diagnosing essential tremor. *Movement Disorders 13,* 287–293.

Louis, E.D., Ottman, R., & Hauser, W.A. (1998). How common is the most common adult movement disorder? Estimates of the prevalence of essential tremor throughout the world. *Movement Disorders, 13,* 5–10.

Manyam, B.V. (1986). Recent advances in the treatment of cerebellar ataxias. *Clinical Neuropharmacology, 9,* 508–516.

Michaelis, J. (1993). Mechanical methods of controlling ataxia. In C.D. Ward (Ed.), *Rehabilitation of motor disorders* (pp. 121–139). London: Bailliere Tindall.

Morgan, M.H., Langton Hewer, R., & Cooper, R. (1975). Application of an objective method of assessing intention tremor—a further study on the use of weights to reduce intention tremor. *Journal of Neurology, Neurosurgery and Psychiatry, 38,* 259–264.

Morice, B.-L., Becker, W.J., Hoffer, J.A., & Lee, R.G. (1990). Manual tracking performance in patients with cerebellar incoordination: effects of mechanical loading. *Canadian Journal of Neurological Sciences, 17,* 275–285.

Nguyen, J.P., Feve, A., & Keravel, Y. (1996). Is electrostimulation preferable to surgery for upper limb ataxia? *Current Opinions in Neurology, 9,* 445–450.

Nobile-Orazio, E., Baldini, L., Barbieri, S., et al. (1988). Treatment of patients with neuropathy and anti-MAG IgM M-proteins. *Annals of Neurology, 24,* 93–97.

Notermans, N.C., van Dijk, G.W., van der Graaf, Y., et al. (1994). Measuring ataxia: quantification based on the standard neurological examination. *Journal of Neurology, Neurosurgery and Psychiatry, 57,* 22–26.

Ondo, W., & Jankovic, J. (1996). Essential tremor treatment options. *CNS Drugs, 6,* 178–191.

Pahwa, R. (1995). Primary writing tremor. In L.J. Findley & W.C. Koller (Eds.), *Handbook of tremor disorders* (pp. 401–404). New York: Dekker.

Remy, P., de Recondo, A., Defer, G., et al. (1995). Peduncular "rubral" tremor and dopaminergic denervation: a PET study. *Neurology 45,* 472–477.

Rudick, R., Antel, J., Confavreaux, C., et al. (1996). Clinical outcomes assessment in multiple sclerosis. *Annals of Neurology, 40,* 469–479.

Sanes, J.N., LeWitt, P.A., & Mauritz, K.-H. (1988). Visual and mechanical control of postural and kinetic tremor in cerebellar system disorders. *Journal of Neurology, Neurosurgery and Psychiatry, 51,* 934–943.

Shumway-Cook, A., Horak, F.B., Yardley, L., & Bronstein, A.M. (1996). Rehabilitation of balance disorders in the patient with vestibular pathology. In A.M. Bronstein, T. Brandt, & M.H. Woollacott (Eds.), *Clinical disorders of balance, posture and gait* (pp. 211–235). London: Arnold.

Thompson, P.D. (1995). Primary orthostatic tremor. In L.J. Findley & W.C. Koller (Eds.), *Handbook of tremor disorders* (pp. 387–399). New York: Dekker.

Trouillas, P. (1993). Theoretical basis and proposals for neuropharmacology of cerebellar ataxia. *Revue Neurologique, 149,* 637–646.

Trouillas, P., Serratrice, G., Laplane, D., et al. (1995). Levorotatory form of 5-hydroxytryptophan in Friedreich's ataxia: results of a double-blind drug-placebo cooperative study. *Archives of Neurology, 52,* 456–460.

Trouillas, P., Takayanagi, T., Hallett, M., et al. (1997). International cooperative ataxia rating scale for pharmacological assessment of the cerebellar syndrome. *Journal of the Neurological Sciences, 145,* 205–211.

Trouillas, P., Xie, J., Adeleine, P., et al. (1997). Buspirone, a 5-hydroxytryptophan$_{1a}$ agonist, is active in cerebellar ataxia: results of a double-blind drug-placebo study in patients with cerebellar cortical atrophy. *Archives of Neurology, 54,* 749–752.

Wessel, K., Hermsdorfer, J., Deger, K., et al. (1995). Double-blind crossover study with levorotatory form of hydroxytryptophan in patients with degenerative cerebellar diseases. *Archives of Neurology, 52,* 451–455.

Willoughby, E.W., & Paty, D.W. (1988). Scales for rating impairment in multiple sclerosis: a critique. *Neurology, 38,* 1793–1798.

14. Physical therapies

Sue Edwards   Sue Mawson   Richard J. Greenwood

INTRODUCTION

The treatment of patients with neurological disease by means of exercise and the application of heat is as old as medicine itself (Venzmer, 1972). Present treatment and management of these patients' physical disabilities involves, in conjunction with other disciplines, a specialist area of practice within physiotherapy which is particularly focused on the re-training of motor skills. In this chapter some of the most frequently used techniques and approaches are described. They are directed toward maintaining and regaining selective movement by reducing the effects of abnormal tone and contracture, developing coordination and control, and, if possible, increasing strength and endurance.

The continued prescription, worldwide, of physiotherapy, and observations from clinical practice, suggest that it is of value in assisting patients with neurological disability to move and function more effectively. Objective confirmation of the effectiveness of physiotherapy treatment in a particular clinical context, let alone a demonstration that one physiotherapy technique or approach is more effective than another, is more difficult, as it is in many areas of rehabilitation. In general it is probably important to focus initially on outcome at the level of impairment, including physiological measures, when exploring benefit of dose or type of physical therapy. Even if a treatment reduces impairment it is often much more difficult to show benefit at other outcome levels, if only because noise introduced at these other levels by cognitive and environmental factors demands much higher numbers in group studies than can practically be recruited. Thus, studies that rely on a global disability (activity) measure, for example the Barthel Index (BI; Mahoney and Barthel, 1965), as a main outcome measure (e.g., Dickstein et al., 1986) may show no effect, miss effects on impairment, and conclude that the treatment studied is ineffective. Of course, if reduction in impairment and/or focal disability is not accompanied by parallel benefit at other outcome levels, then incorporation of that treatment into a rehabilitation programme may fail because of organisational and resource-related issues, but this can reasonably be addressed secondarily.

The majority of group studies of rehabilitation in patients with neurological disease have recruited patients early or late after stroke, and examined the effectiveness of various, largely multidisciplinary, in-patient, out-patient, or community programmes. Briefly, in-patient stroke units reduce death and dependency (Stroke Unit Triallist's Collaboration, 1997a), even long term (Indredavik et al., 1997), and early discharge and outreach programmes (e.g., Rodgers et al., 1997; Rudd et al., 1997) produce gains equivalent to traditional practice even at the level of disability without increasing resource utilisation (see Chapter 36). Early in recovery, during in-patient treatment, how particular therapies contribute and which elements of these programmes produce these benefits, apart from organised rather than disorganised care (Stroke Unit Triallist's Collaboration, 1997b), has remained elusive and the contribution of physiotherapy ill-defined. Recently, Kwakkel and colleagues (1998) randomised 101 patients within 14 days of a middle cerebral artery infarct to one of three treatment conditions, a control condition comprising inflatable pressure splinting of the affected arm and leg, or additional physiotherapy to either the arm or the leg. All patients received 30 minutes of physiotherapy a day and 1.5 hours of training in activities of daily living (ADL) a week, supplemented by one additional experimental condition applied for 30 minutes 5 times a week for 20 weeks. Those patients receiving additional physiotherapy treatment to the leg showed significant improvements not only in postural control, gait, and visuospecial perception, but also in measures of upper limbs function, ADL, and physical health.

Later after onset, Wade et al. (1992) showed that 3 months of physiotherapy alone four times a week more than 1 year after stroke significantly increased walking speed, which deteriorated without treatment, but not global measures of disability. Interestingly, and by contrast, 4 weeks of a daily multidisciplinary out-patient programme in 40 stroke patients more than 1 year post-stroke, using a pre-treatment base-line and non-validated measures of impairment and personal, domestic, and extended ADL, resulted in significant gains in both impairment and disability (activity) measures, retained during a 3-month follow-up period (Tangeman et al., 1990). Similarly Dam et al. (1993) showed that impairment (Hemiplegic Stroke Scale) and disability (BI) improved over a 1- to 2-year period in 51 patients unable to walk at 3 months post-stroke with at least seven periods of a daily multidisciplinary programme for 1–3 months at a time, and 74% of patients became able to walk without assistance at the end of the study. Studies of this sort begin to examine the vexed questions of how, to whom, how frequently and for how long physiotherapy should be given during the 1–2 years after stroke when improvements, with out-patient rehabilitation, can be demonstrated (e.g., Smith et al., 1981), and whether it should be given in isolation or in the context of a multidisciplinary input. The resource implications of any recommendations that might be made remain, not surprisingly, to be explored.

There has been some exploration of the types of physical therapies that may or may not be effective after stroke. Group studies comparing the efficacy of different physiotherapy handling methods after stroke have not shown a difference in outcome, but have been flawed by small sample sizes, short periods of treatment and follow-up, relatively insensitive or inappropriate outcome rating scales, and lack of information about what was done in the name of the method used. Thus, outcomes measured were similar in groups exposed prospectively to: "proprioceptive neuromuscular facilitation", derived from techniques described by Knott and Voss, versus "traditional" techniques (Logigian et al., 1983); "traditional" exercises and functional activities, versus "proprioceptive neuromuscular facilitation techniques" derived from Knott, versus the Bobath approach (Dickstein et al., 1986); traditional exercises versus Bobath (Lord and Hall, 1986); the Bobath approach versus biofeedback plus physical therapy (Basmajian et al., 1987); and Bobath versus Brunnstrom (Wagenaar et al., 1990).

By contrast, more recently many studies of task or modality specific physical therapies have been shown to be effective, generally at the level of the impairment or focal disability treated, for example gait or arm function, rather than at the level of global disability. For example, treadmill training improves gait, compared with conventional physiotherapy, but not other motor abilities (Hesse et al., 1995). This is most effective, in patients 2–3 months post stroke, when the body weight is up to 40% supported rather than not supported (Visintin et al., 1998). Increased practice of arm and hand movements (Sunderland et al., 1992; Butefisch et al., 1995), sometimes involving restraint of the normal arm (Wolf et al., 1989; Taub et al., 1993), produces significant improvement in hand movement and function. Afferent electrical stimulation of the upper limb improves voluntary range of wrist movements using mesh glove stimulation of the hand (Dimitrijevic et al., 1996; Fugl-Meyer, 1975) but not Barthel scores using low frequency (1.7 Hz) transcutaneous electrical nerve stimulation (TENS; Sonde et al., 1998); and, apparently, the BI as well as spasticity scores using high frequency (100 Hz) TENS (Tekeoolu et al., 1998). Lastly, the Johnstone (1987) handling technique applied to the upper limb daily over 6 weeks early after stroke in 100 patients randomised to treatment or control (attention only) improved Fugl-Meyer et al. (1975) impairment scores but not measures of focal (Action Research Arm test; Lyle, 1981) or global (BI) disability (Feys et al., 1998).

A rationale for findings of this sort is provided by studies in normal or lesioned animals and man of neural plasticity at hemisphere and spinal levels (Dobkin, 1998; Chapter 8). These show that the presence or absence of either motor training or sensory stimulation expand or reduce central neural representations of a movement or a body part. This plasticity may be restitutional, involving motor cortex adjacent to a lesion; substitutional, involving parallel motor pathways; or adaptive, recruiting attentional mechanisms via dorsolateral prefrontal cortex (Weiller, 1995). Exactly how physical treatment modalities can facilitate these changes, perhaps with pharmacological, particularly noradrenergic (Walker Batson et al., 1995; Grade et al., 1998), assistance, remains an exciting and expanding area of research.

PHYSIOTHERAPY APPROACHES

The evolution of manual handling techniques has reflected changing ideas about neural recovery, the neurophysiological control of posture and movement, and the nature of skill learning. Conventional physical treatment for people with neurological impairment prior to the 1950s usually involved massage, passive and active movements, and exercises, using pulleys, suspensions and weights, heat, and various forms of electrotherapy for the affected limbs. There was an emphasis on rapid reacquisition of function by any means, compensation for deficits by more *efficient* use of the unaffected parts of the body, for example by aids or rails, and muscle strengthening of the unaffected side, encouraged by the results of treatment after polio and the idea that central neural damage was irreversible.

During the 1940s and 1950s concern grew about the limitations of this type of rehabilitation and the development in the longer term of fixed deformity of the affected side. A number of new handling techniques were developed, focusing on the quality of movement of the *affected* parts, and the extent to which it approximated to normal movement. Using ideas largely derived from Sherrington (1931, 1906), these practitioners, most notably Bobath (1985, 1990), emphasised how, after damage to higher centres, released tonic and phasic spinal and supraspinal postural reflexes inhibit normal movement. Attention was drawn to the tonic local, segmental, and general static ("attitudinal") reactions of Magnus (1926), which comprised positive and negative support reactions, the crossed extension reflex, and the tonic neck and labyrinthine reactions. In hemiplegic and quadriplegic man these had been described by Riddoch and Buzzard (1921) as "association" reactions, upon which the influence of tonic neck and labyrinthine reactions was described by Walshe (1923). At the same time the way in which phasic righting and equilibrium reactions—described by, amongst others, Magnus (1924, 1926), Schaltenbrand (1928), and Rademaker (1935)—underpinned normal movement was highlighted. It was proposed that attitudinal reactions produced abnormal movements and contractures and inhibited normal movements, and that the facilitation of equilibrium reactions via peripheral and central afferent input, plus the practice of righting reactions seen in developmentally early actions—for example, rolling over and crawling—would improve balance and normal movements, which would then transfer to functional tasks. These "neurodevelopmental" or "neurophysiological" techniques developed largely in relation to the treatment and management of children with cerebral palsy and adults with hemiplegia after stroke. All the approaches were subsequently used for patients with a wide range of conditions causing neurological dysfunction in both children and adults, often developed, extended, and refined by their originators and by others. Latterly, the description of both afferent- and activity-dependent modification of synaptic function at many levels in the nervous system has encouraged the belief that manipulation of the neural environment by both handling techniques and training will result in adaptive neural reorganisation.

Further change has resulted from ideas derived from biomechanical analysis of normal and abnormal movement, the principals of motor learning and skill acquisition, and more recent neurophysiological investigations of motor control and postural mechanisms. A major shift to the task orientated "motor relearning" approaches resulted from emphasis on the practice of goal-orientated functional tasks, and thus the importance of perceptual, cognitive, and behavioural factors to performance; confirmation that weakness as well as loss of control and coordination contributes significantly to deficit in hemiparesis (Sunderland et al., 1992; Bohannon & Andrews, 1990); and demonstration that repetitive exercise, for example of the hand (Butefisch et al., 1995), improves muscle strength and limb function without obviously increasing muscle tone. Relearning of normal movements, for example reaching, standing up, walking, and so on, should therefore be task and context specific, rather than solely the result of carry-over of therapeutic exercise into normal movement (see Carr & Shepherd, 1989, 1998; Mulder, 1991; Chapter 11): Practice of a task may itself improve function, for example standing from sitting after a 2-week training period of reaching whilst seated in chronic stroke patients (Dean & Shepherd, 1997), and may be useful even if tone and movement have not previously been normalised.

Bobath

Bobath developed her approach empirically during the 1950s, largely as a result of observations in children with cerebral palsy. Her work has influenced physiotherapy practice worldwide, and formed the basis of other techniques. It is at present the most widely used approach in Britain for the treatment of both adults and children with neurological disablement.

The principles and techniques of treatment were originally based on the view (Bobath, 1985) that the release of tonic postural reflexes interferes with the dynamic control of normal posture and movement. Handling techniques were largely directed toward inhibiting abnormal movement patterns, often by passive positioning. More recently (Bobath, 1990), therapists have adopted more active techniques aimed at modifying afferent input in order to change postural tone and facilitate three stages in relearning normal movement. These are the ability to adapt postural tone during movement, to produce normal automatic activity in response to a perturbation, and to programme normal voluntary activity.

Treatment centres upon the handling of a movement around "key points of control" at the head and spine, shoulder and pelvic girdles, and distally the feet and hands, from which postural tone can be altered in the context of gravity, the base of support and a defined motor goal. Volitional activity on the part of the patient is requested only against the background of normal automatic postural activity. The choice of treatment position is influenced by the pathological distribution of postural tone and static patterning, the relationship between gravity and the base of support, the available range of movement and function in a particular position, and the goal to be achieved. There are no defined Bobath "exercises" and the choice of speed, range, and pattern of movement at any one time is considered on an individual basis. Treatment cannot be predictable, stereotyped, or repetitive, as it must continuously adapt to the individual's responses. Most recently, "specific inhibitory mobilisations" (SIMS) of affected muscle groups, to reverse both the neural and soft tissue components of high tone, have been advocated as a key component of treatment by the British Adult Bobath Tutor Association, and take into account the increase in connective tissue that occurs in shortened and immobilised muscle (see Williams et al., 1988).

Proprioceptive neuromuscular facilitation (PNF)

This approach was developed by Kabat and Knott (1954) at the Kaiser Foundation in Vallejo, California. It had an influence on practice worldwide and like others has been developed and refined over time at Vallejo and elsewhere. The handling techniques, described by Voss (1967) and Voss et al. (1985), used active and passive movements and afferent input to "bring about maximal excitation of the available anterior horn cells" (Kabatt, 1952, p. 522). Kabat (1952) extrapolated from classical experiments by Mott and Sherrington (1895) who reported that unilateral limb deafferentation resulted in complete loss of voluntary but not automatic movement, demonstrating the effectiveness of central programming. Actively resisted muscle contraction, during resistive exercises, was intended to stimulate "afferent proprioceptive discharges in the central nervous system, which greatly increase excitation at motor centres and thereby excite many additional motor units" (Kabat & Knott, 1953, p. 54). Diagonal and spiral patterns of active and passive movement were described, since many muscles pull in a spiral direction in the long axis of the limb, and stretch reflexes were superimposed on these patterns to increase muscle activity; a quick stretch at the lengthened range of a movement pattern was given to produce a contraction followed by relaxation. The therapist applies manual pressure to encourage movements which have a purpose, using both isotonic and isometric active muscle contractions, and traction, and approximation of joint surfaces, to stimulate postural reflexes.

Rood

Rood's approach to treatment developed at the University of Southern California in Los Angeles. Her method is clearly described by Goff (1969), and emphasised the use of afferent input of all sorts to produce movement and postural reactions in the absence of voluntary control. A "developmental sequence" of movements is elicited in turn, initially mass patterns of flexion and extension in supine and side-lying. Then stability of the head, trunk, and proximal limb joints is trained by using prone positions. This is followed by mobility and weight-bearing, by, for example, weight shifting from one forearm to the other in prone-lying, and skilled movements are then introduced. Afferent input is emphasised, using stretch, "bone-pounding", pressure, skin stimulation by different means, including brushing either with fingertips or a small brush, and cold stimulation with ice.

Brunnstrom

Brunnstrom's approach, developed in the 1950s at the Bellevue Medical Center in New York, used association reactions (Riddoch & Buzzard, 1921) and the influence of tonic neck and labyrinthine reflexes (Walshe, 1923) "as the basis of training patients with hemiplegia . . . reflex elicitation of the motion synergy would be employed until the patient had 'captured' the reflex, then a conditioning of the reflex would be attempted" (Brunnstrom, 1956, p. 227). Other sensory "cues" were also used "in developing co-ordinated movement" including stroking, tapping or slapping of muscles, and resistance to movement of the affected or unaffected side (Perry, 1967).

Reynolds et al. (1957) and Brunnstrom (1964, 1965, 1966) provided detailed descriptions of the limb movements seen during recovery from stroke, each patient following a similar pattern of motor recovery. Depending on the stage of recovery, patterns of reflex training were advised, to help the patient to progress from "subcortical to cortical control of muscle function". Perry (1967, p. 790) describes four stages of Brunnstrom's approach: first, "elicitation of major synergies on a reflex level"; then "an attempt is made to establish voluntary control of the synergies"; the third phase is "to try to break away from the synergies by mixing components from antagonistic synergies"; then an attempt is made to elicit voluntary hand and finger functions. Thus this technique encourages association reactions in contrast to the Bobath approach which regards them as unwanted and pathological manifestations of spasticity which the therapist should inhibit.

The motor relearning programme

This technique was developed in Australia by Carr and Shepherd (1989, 1998) in response to their clinical and teaching experience and an extensive review of the literature in the movement and the behavioural sciences. It is used particularly in the treatment of stroke. The programme is aimed at seven motor skills: orofacial function, upper limb function, motor tasks performed when sitting or standing, standing up and sitting down, and walking. These are regarded as the essential motor tasks of daily life. The programme is more prescriptive in nature than the Bobath approach on the basis that in spite of some individual differences we all have the same basic requirements and use similar methods to acquire motor skills.

Treatment involves four components: analysis of the task, practice of the missing components, practice of the task, and transference of training. The key is seen to be cognitive relearning as opposed to manual facilitation of motor skills. Little significance is given to the effects of afferent input and spasticity on selective movement. Abnormal postures are seen as largely the result of changes in soft tissues and the resting length of shortened muscle, and abnormal patterns of movement the result of functional adaptation of motor performance in the presence of muscle imbalance and weakness. This remains a point of particular controversy between advocates of different approaches. The programme is therefore directed towards the repeated practice of specific motor tasks. It concentrates on the retraining of controlled muscle action necessary for the performance of specific components of a task; for example, the practice of controlled wrist extension as part of the pattern of grasping. Emphasis is also placed upon feedback and great attention is given to detailed verbal explanation of the task to the patient prior to performance. This is followed up with immediate verbal, visual, or manual feedback. There is little mention of treatment strategies for those patients in whom cognitive or behavioural difficulties prevent their participation in the analysis of their own performance, although the authors maintain that the use of this programme "appears to prevent the entrenchment of perceptual problems in many patients".

Conductive education

In the 1950s Peto founded the Institute for Conductive Education of the Motor Disabled in Budapest and developed a new method of teaching or training which he called conductive education. Its aim was to deal with all the problems of the motor disabled, in particular children with cerebral palsy. Peto emphasised that the functional development of these children was in many cases prevented by a "dysfunctional" personality resulting from failure, due to physical disablement, conditional passivity, and dependence. He was dissatisfied with the interprofessional conflicts seen in those dealing with the children, and he felt "fragmentation and confusion were the worst enemies of children with cerebral palsy" (Cotton & Kinsman, 1983, p. 15). A new professional, a conductor, who trained for 4 years so as to be able to deal with all problems of patients with neurological deficits, was thus introduced. Peto emphasised that rehabilitation of "dysfunctionals" is an educational task rather than a therapeutic one, hence the term conductive education.

Conductive education thus represents a particular rehabilitation, habilitation, training programme, rather than a physiotherapy handling technique; its particular emphasis on motor disabilities is derived from the characteristics of the society in which it developed, where independent mobility, at least indoors, is a prerequisite for schooling. Like all rehabilitation programmes it has its own entry and exclusion criteria. Entry to the programme is dependent upon level of learning ability; profound mental handicap, uncontrolled epilepsy, and deteriorating neurology preclude acceptance.

The system Peto devised differed from others in that it was a totally integrated system. The operator of the system, the conductor, is concerned with teaching "dysfunctionals" to become "orthofunctionals" by developing their adaptive and learning abilities. Peto has compared the methods of his conductors with those of a conductor of an orchestra, each aiming to evoke repeated sequences or harmonious movement, the players "in tune" with the conductor (Cotton & Kinsman, 1983). There is an emphasis on group work to learn and develop effective interpersonal relationships, groups comprising children with similar abilities rather than children with similar patterns of cerebral palsy. Groups are used to develop initiative, drive, motivation, and learning, and facilitate the process of learning a new skill by emphasis upon repetition and reinforcement. With a "task series", which is worked out for each person and discarded when redundant for new ones, small steps build up to a common group goal, routes to which may vary individually. The changing ("rhythmical intention") which accompanies the movement is an integral part of the learning; while performing or attempting to perform the appropriate movement the person chants rhythmically, for example, "I clasp my hands", "I lift my arms up", etc.

A number of centres in the UK have based their approach on these methods. Cotton (1994), for example has been using an adapted form for many years with children with cerebral palsy, and its use in adults after stroke has been described by Kinsman (1989). Claims are made that the centre for Conductive Education in Budapest can produce "cures", and enable children to function at a near-normal level whereas without it they would have remained helpless. Whilst this may be so, such claims are made in the context of a selection process for "children mainly of good cognitive potential with fairly modest motor disorder" (Robinson et al., 1989, p. 1148), and the absence of studies comparing the effectiveness of Peto's training programme with others of similar intensity, perhaps combined with carefully planned surgical intervention (Patrick, 1989). At the least, however, as Robinson et al. (1989) emphasised, it seems probable that the integrated methods of working evolved in Budapest have lessons for multidisciplinary programmes, whether treating children or adults.

A clinical overview

In clinical practice in the UK, physiotherapists often have a more eclectic approach, and use various aspects of the different approaches described above, with useful function as the final goal. This recognises that while quality of movement is imperative, restoration of normal movement is often an unattainable goal, and intervention requires a balance between re-education of *more* normal movement patterns, and acceptance, and indeed promotion, of the compensation needed to achieve the best function possible (Edwards, 1998). Treatments focus on the management of the neural aspects of abnormal muscle tone, usually manifest as "spastic hypertonus" and the spastic dystonias, prevention of muscle shortening, and maintenance of muscle and joint range of movement, subsequently task-oriented skills, and sometimes muscle strengthening and fitness programmes. There is particular emphasis on the prevention of secondary physical complications and facilitation of mobility, particularly of transfers and walking, by physical handling methods, and rather less involvement with the cognitive aspects of motor relearning. This may reflect focus in the UK NHS on in-patient treatment and relative lack of funding for out-patient programmes after neurological damage.

Various handling and positioning techniques are designed to prevent progressively asymmetrical postures of the trunk and limbs developing as the patient is "sandwiched" between gravity and the supporting surface, a process which may eventually produce trunk flexion and scoliosis, rotation of the pelvis, and windswept legs with flexion at the knees (Pope, 1992). Increased tone in patients who initially have low tone after brain or spinal cord injury should not usually result in reduced range of movement if adequate and effective physiotherapy, in terms of positioning, passive/active movement, and splinting as necessary, is provided. By contrast, patients with traumatic brain injury often demonstrate hypertonia within the first 24–48 hours after injury. Clearly this is a different phenomenon to the slowly evolving tone following cerebral or spinal shock and requires a different approach to management. These patients may have such severe "total body" hypertonus that attempts by the physiotherapist to take a limb through its full range of movement is likely to prove singularly unsuccessful and possibly dangerous, producing, for example, microtears of muscle, which may contribute to heterotopic ossification (Ada et al., 1990). In these patients, positioning techniques to support body posture in lying, sitting, and standing are particularly useful (Pope, 1992).

To prevent hypertonus becoming a major factor contributing to loss of function, tone is reduced by specific mobilisation of affected muscle groups to enable more selective movement of body parts. Muscle and joint range of movement will be simultaneously preserved. Where possible, the patient is encouraged to be an active participant in treatment sessions. Movement of the limbs also depends upon adequate proximal control and stability. Postural adjustments which normal accompany active, volitional movements of the limbs may be impaired if motor function is abnormal. For example, when a patient reaches forward in sitting, movement is dependent upon appropriate activity of the pelvis and the trunk to enable effective movement of the arms. Physiotherapy must therefore ensure that these accompanying movements are attainable and that limb movements are not carried out on a background of inappropriate muscle activity. Mobilisation of the trunk, head, and shoulder and pelvic girdles, either on a couch (Figure 14.1), or using a gymnastic ball (Lewis, 1989), may be used as a means of modulating proximal muscle tone and length and facilitating normal postural responses.

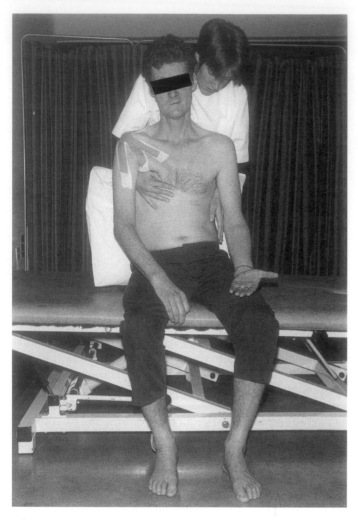

Figure 14.1. Trunk mobilisation to improve proximal symmetry and alignment, and facilitate normal postural responses.

Postural tone can also be reduced by appropriate positioning in lying, sitting, or standing. Generally speaking, in normal subjects, a large base of support, such as that provided by a supportive bed, is conducive to relaxation and therefore low postural tone. Conversely, when an individual stands on one leg, with a very small base of support, postural tone is considerably higher. Working on this principle, patients with low tone need greater stimulation up against gravity to increase their tone, and those with hypertonia require a larger base of support to fixate the central body mass and reduce tone. Knowledge of the normal alignment of body parts and the effect of various positions on tone allows the therapist to select the most suitable positions for treatment of the patient as the medical condition allows. Optimal positioning of patients during a 24-hour period of rest and activity, both to reduce tone and to optimise function, for example feeding, is particularly challenging to the organisation of multidisciplinary teamwork.

Often the patient with hypertonus is unable to accept and accommodate to the supporting surface, and the supine or prone positions in lying are unstable and encourage trunk extension or

flexion respectively. Modified positions, resulting, for example, from the use of a wedge when prone, a T-roll when supine, or a roll between the legs in side lying, may be needed to effect and maintain reduction in tone. In sitting, balance and stability are necessary to prevent established spastic dystonia and enable the generation of normal limb movements. Sometimes this is only achieved by the provision of special seating systems (Pope, 1996).

Standing is advocated as a means of stimulating anti-gravity activity to prevent flexed trunk and limb postures, and utilises gravity to stretch soft tissues and maintain muscle and joint range of movement. Its benefits are illustrated by case studies after head (Richardson, 1991) and spinal (Bohannon, 1993) injury, but none were found by Kunkel et al. (1993) very late (10–30 years) after spinal injury. Various standing aids exist, including the tilt table, standing frames of various types, and standing wheelchairs. The patient may also be supported in standing between two or possibly more physiotherapists or assistants; this is considered a more dynamic intervention. For many years the Oswestry standing frame (Figure 14.2) has been used as the most cost-effective and supportive means of standing dependent patients. This frame was originally designed by and built for paraplegic patients who were able to lift themselves into standing. Its use to stand the more dependent patients after many types of neurological insult has become relatively common practice in the UK, either in treatment, or, long term, as a means of preventing flexor tone and contractures, and maintaining joint range of movement, by daily standing of patients who are otherwise wheelchair bound; as Thornton and Kilbride (1998) point out, there is no good evidence to support its use in these circumstances. However, new legislation, designed to prevent injury to therapists when lifting patients into the frame, may result in increased use of a standing frame with a motorised lifter, as it has the use of hoists by nurses on the ward when transferring patients. The risk that legislation will result in an inappropriate increase in treatment done to, rather than with, the patient, must be avoided.

Splinting may be a useful adjunct to positioning and assisted or passive joint range of movement, either to prevent muscle shortening and the development of contractures, or to reverse established contractures of moderate severity (Moseley, 1997). The various types of splints and orthoses available are described and illustrated in Chapter 16 and by Edwards and Charlton (1996). Sometimes their use is also facilitated by intramuscular injection of botulinum toxin if there is a significant neural component to limited joint range of movement (Edwards, 1998). Prophylactic splinting is more commonly used in neurosurgical patients, especially after head injury, to prevent plantar flexion contractures at the ankles by plaster boots (Connine et al., 1990) or to prevent flexion contractures at the knees and elbows by plaster cylinders of backslabs. Serial splinting every 7–10 days, or drop out casting, enabling knee or elbow extension but not flexion, are used to reverse moderately severe contractures not requiring surgical reversal. Surgery may be necessary if the contracture is severe or if there is a blocked feel, which is

Control of tone and reversal of soft tissue shortening enable the practice of more normal movement, using reciprocal activity, rather than co-contraction, of agonist and antagonist prime movers, synergists and proximal fixating muscles, and the adaptive use of effort. It then becomes possible to retrain motor skills and balance, strengthen weakened muscle groups, or increase levels of aerobic fitness (Potempa et al., 1995), without persistent increases in tone or abnormal posturing, but with measurable functional gains.

ADJUNCTIVE TREATMENTS

Repetitive exercises

The idea that practice can induce functional neural circuits by long-term potentiation (Dobkin, 1998), is likely to encourage further interest in trials of repetitive exercise. Various ways in which repetitive exercise programmes might contribute to functional gains have been studied. Perhaps of most interest over the last 10 years have been the results of treadmill training of gait, initially after spinal injury, stimulated by studies of gait retraining in spinal animals (Muir & Steeves, 1997), and subsequently after a stroke, when treadmill training consistently improves walking speed and endurance (e.g., Hesse et al., 1995; Visintin et al., 1998), particularly with partial body weight support, compared with conventional (Bobath) physiotherapy. Other treatments producing improvement versus a control condition include repetitive wrist and hand exercises (Butefisch et al., 1995), forced use of the affected upper limb whilst the unaffected arm is immobilised, improving writing, feeding, and grooming (Taub et al., 1993), quadriceps muscle strength training to improve gait speed and the extent of daily activities (Sharp & Brouwer, 1997), aerobic training to improve fitness (Potempa et al., 1995), training in reaching whilst seated to improve standing from sitting (Dean & Shepherd, 1997), or a home exercise programme designed to improve strength, balance, and endurance during 24 sessions over 8 weeks (Duncan et al., 1998). Clearly, this is an area in which robotic assistance of physical therapies may find a place (Aisen et al., 1997; Krebs et al., 1998).

Electromyographic (EMG) biofeedback

Biofeedback has been used as an adjunct to the retraining of disordered movement or balance in a variety of neurological disorders (Marzuk, 1985), and has also been used to control autonomic functions including blood pressure (Basmajian, 1981). Therapists frequently provide feedback of information to patients about their motor performance in relation to goals of treatment; the feedback is usually visual, sensory, or auditory. Biofeedback uses other methods to transduce biological information—usually EMG activity but also joint angle or posture—into appropriate sensory cues to emphasise motor control. It takes advantage of the fact that electronic feedback of quantifiable visual or auditory information is continuous, undisrupted, faster, and more accurate than any verbal instruction given by the therapist (Wolf, 1978). This information, and the

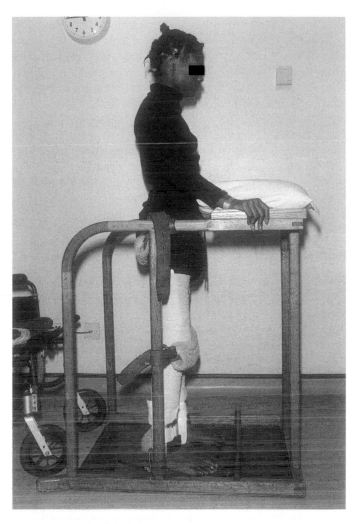

Figure 14.2. Standing in an Oswestry standing frame with backslabs to maintain muscle and joint range of movement, and, by stabilising the lower limbs, facilitate more effective trunk control.

sometimes due to para-articular heterotopic ossification, when attempting to reverse the contracture by handling. The splinting guidelines produced in 1998 by the Association of Chartered Physiotherapists Interested in Neurology (ACPIN) provide useful information and recommendations for the effective use of splints. Before splinting one should consider:

- the purpose of the splint. Is it to maintain range of movement, regain range of movement, or address the problems of muscle imbalance?
- whether the patient is able to accommodate to the splint, or whether it serves as a resistance against which the patient's spasticity is exacerbated
- that the advantages of maintaining muscle and joint range outweigh the atrophic effect on immobilised muscle
- that the use of a splint distally has a positive effect on proximal control, and that hypertonus is not "shunted" to the more proximal muscles.

motivation resulting from the use of the technique (Wissel et al., 1989), are thought to produce its effects, and mental impairment may, or interestingly may not (Balliet et al, 1986), limit its use.

Its clinical use to facilitate voluntary control of disordered movement was first alluded to by Mimms (1956) and described by Marinacci and Horande (1960) in patients with upper and lower motor neuron dysfunction. Soon afterwards Harrison and Mortensen (1962) and Basmajian (1963) described the fine voluntary control of the firing of single motor units in normal subjects. Later, Middaugh and her colleagues provided confirmation that the information and/or reinforcement provided by biofeedback itself, rather than some other factor in the procedure—for example, more stringent goal setting—was responsible for the increase in EMG activity seen in normal (Middaugh et al., 1982) or paretic (Middaugh & Miller, 1980) subjects.

However, as is illustrated by a meta-analysis by Moreland et al. (1998) of trials of EMG biofeedback to improve lower limb function after stroke, whilst increase in ankle dorsiflexion muscle strength or joint range of movement occurs, it has been more difficult to demonstrate convincingly that this is accompanied by worthwhile functional gains. For example, in chronic stroke patients gait kinemetics but not step length or gait velocity improved in eight patients compared with controls over 30 sessions of biofeedback of anterior tibial surface EMG at rest and during walking (Intiso et al., 1994). Wolf and Binder-Macleod (1983a) found that active range of knee flexion and ankle dorsiflexion increased significantly in seven patients treated with EMG biofeedback aimed at reducing co-contraction in leg muscles initially in supine and subsequently in sitting, standing, and walking during 60 sessions over 3 months, compared with six controls receiving no treatment, sixteen patients receiving biofeedback to the involved arm, and eight receiving general relaxation training; walking speed showed no significant benefit, but the provision of walking aids decreased significantly in the treated group. The same authors (Wolf & Binder-Macleod, 1983b) also showed that EMG biofeedback training of the involved arm in 22 chronic patients improved EMG parameters and active range of movement compared with nine controls (no treatment) but only in the five treated patients with some initial voluntary finger extension were functional gains observed. Modest gains in movement though not a function of the upper limb were reported by Inglis et al. (1984) in 30 chronic stroke patients randomised to physiotherapy plus EMG biofeedback, which was aimed at reducing co-contraction and increasing strength, or physiotherapy alone.

There is still potential to explore biofeedback during a functional rather than non-functional movement, when the need for carry-over from the "feedback" to the functional movement is minimised (Winstein et al., 1989), and particularly to examine which component of a functional movement is best fed back. Colborne et al. (1993), for example, found that gait velocity and stride length significantly increased when feedback focused on achieving normal soleus EMG and ankle angle during the early and late stance phase of walking. Dursun et al. (1996) found that

after angular biofeedback training of sitting balance 3 months post-stroke, 75% of the treated group achieved sitting balance after 10 days of treatment compared with only 12% of the control group, and in ambulating patients, length of stay in rehabilitation was significantly shorter in the biofeedback (9.5 weeks) than in the control (13.8 weeks) patients, both groups receiving "conventional", but not, however, "neurophysiological", physiotherapy. If functional benefits can be demonstrated, then the cost effectiveness of biofeedback training, which can be carried out by the subject without a therapist present—an aspect emphasised by Basmajian et al. (1987) and by Bertoti and Gross (1988) in the context of postural training of children with cerebral palsy—may become apparent.

Functional electrical stimulation (FES)

Neuromuscular electrical stimulation to produce movement, as opposed to continence or sexual function or to reduce pain, involuntary movements, or seizures, has been employed during the last 30 years to improve or replace function. Electrical stimulation to produce standing in paraplegics was first reported by Kantrowitz in 1960 and to facilitate gait after stroke by Liberson et al. in 1961, in which context the term functional electrical stimulation (FES) was first used by Moe and Post in 1962. There had been an upsurge of interest in the last 20 years in the use of FES, particularly in patients with spinal injury following the report by Brindley et al. (1979) of its use to produce gait, and the subject is addressed in detail in Chapter 18.

FES has been used following stroke in some centres for the last 30 years, usually to improve ankle dorsiflexion during the swing phase of walking by peroneal nerve stimulation at heel-off, sometimes for many years in individual patients (Waters et al., 1985). Gait velocity may increase, especially if FES is combined with biofeedback (Cozean et al., 1988). Additional stimulation of more proximal leg muscles, to produce hip abduction and extension and knee flexion and extension, may be more effective in functional terms (Waters et al., 1988). FES of upper limb muscles is normally used as a form of active repetitive excercise, either applied passively or initiated voluntarily by EMG from the target muscle (Hansen, 1979). It has been used to reduce shoulder subluxation (Baker & Parker, 1986; Faghri et al., 1994) or, more commonly, to increase wrist and finger extension, and thus hand opening before grasping (Merletti et al., 1975). As well as increasing muscle strength, a reduction of spasticity in both upper and lower limb antagonist muscles after stimulation is reported (e.g., Alfieri, 1982; Pease, 1998; Weingarden et al., 1998). These techniques have not yet found a general clinical application after brain injury in the UK. To date, using prospective randomised and controlled methodology, gait speed and effort have been shown to increase and decrease respectively by about 20% (Granat et al., 1996; Burridge et al., 1997): In the arm, motor recovery but not self care (Chae et al., 1998), and both motor recovery and self care (Francisco et al., 1998), have improved with passively applied and voluntarily triggered FES respectively.

Afferent stimulation

Manipulation of peripheral afferent input in animals and man is well recognised to induce a reorganisation of the cortical representation of movement (Lee & van Donkelaar, 1995). Whether afferent stimulation plays a part in the benefits seen following neuromuscular stimulation is not known (Francisco et al., 1998): no studies have compared the effects of afferent stimulation alone with neuromuscular stimulation.

Acupuncture (Johansson et al., 1993: Hu et al., 1993) and low frequency (Sonde et al., 1998) or high frequency (Tekeoolu et al., 1998) TENS have been reported to improve not only motor function but also disability measures in prospective randomised trials, controlled by no or sham treatment. Electrical stimulation of the hand with a wire mesh glove has been reported to change elbow flexor and wrist extensor EMG characteristics, and improve voluntary wrist extension, in a case series of chronic stroke patients (Dimitrijevic et al., 1996). Other afferent stimuli studied included rhythmic auditory stimulation, which was found to increase gait velocity and stride length using single blind, prospective randomised methodology (Thaut et al., 1997), and rhythmic auditory and visual pacing during EMG biofeedback which improved gait speed (Mandel et al., 1990).

In the context of sensory impairment, after stroke sensory retraining can improve sensory performance (Yekutiel & Guttman, 1993; Carey et al., 1993) but it's effect on function has not yet been properly examined. After peripheral de-afferentation, cognitive strategies utilising other information, possibly including the imagination of movement, are postulated to generate functional movement (Cole, 1998). These mechanisms as well as repetitive exercises, presumably contribute to the generation of movement in "constraint-induced movement therapy", when constraining the unaffected arm after stroke improves function of the weaker arm (Miltner et al., 1999; Taub et al., 1993), a technique derived from experiments in monkeys in which non-use of an arm de-afferented by dorsal rhizotomy was reversed by constraint of the normal arm (Taub, 1977).

CONCLUSION

It has therefore been possible over the last 15 years to demonstrate the effectiveness, at various levels of disablement, of many physical therapies in the context of a variety of neurological insults, most commonly stroke. In the UK, techniques tend to address modification of tone and control by handling, and the use of adjunctive techniques to improve movement and fitness is minimal. Recently, Lincoln et al. (1999) were unable to show that 10 hours of additional Bobath-based physiotherapy early after stroke improved arm function. Since studies of other interventions have shown benefit, this negative result emphasises the need now to explore the prescription of different physical therapies of known efficacy for different severities and types of impairment at different times after neurological damage. This will begin to make possible evidence-based prescription of particular physical therapies in given clinical circumstances and contribute to the development of the restorative neurosciences.

REFERENCES

Ada, L., Canning, C., & Paratz, J. (1990). Care of the unconscious head-injured patient. In L. Ada & C. Canning (Eds.), *Key issues in neurological physiotherapy: Physiotherapy foundations for practice* (pp. 246–286). Oxford: Butterworth, Heinemann.

Aisen, M.L., Krebs, H.I., McDowell, F., Hogan, N., & Volpe, B.T. (1997). Effect of robot assisted therapy and rehabilitative training on motor recovery following stroke. *Archives of Neurology, 54*, 443–446.

Alfieri, V. (1982). Electrical treatment of spasticity. *Scandinavian Journal of Rehabilitation Medicine, 14*, 177–182.

Association of Chartered Physiotherapists Interested in Neurology (ACPIN) (1998). *Clinical practice guidelines on splinting adults with neurological dysfunction.* London: Chartered Society of Physiotherapy.

Baker, L.L., & Parker, K. (1986). Neuromuscular electrical stimulation of the muscle surrounding the shoulder. *Physical Therapy, 66*, 1930–1937.

Balliet, R., Levy, B., & Blood, K.M.T. (1986). Upper extremity sensory feedback therapy in chronic cerebrovascular accident patients with impaired expressive aphasia and auditory comprehension. *Archives of Physical Medicine and Rehabilitation, 67*, 304–310.

Basmajian, J.V. (1963). Control and training of individual motor units. *Science, 141*, 440–441.

Basmajian, J.V. (1981). Biofeedback in rehabilitation: a review of principles and practices. *Archives of Physical Medicine and Rehabilitation, 62*, 469–475.

Basmajian, J.V., Gowland, C.A., Finlayson, A.J., et al. (1987). Stroke treatment: comparison of integrated behavioural-physical therapy vs traditional physical therapy programmes. *Archives of Physical Medicine and Rehabilitation, 68*, 267–272.

Bertoti, D.B., & Gross, A.L. (1988). Evaluation of biofeedback seat insert for improving active sitting posture with cerebral palsy: a clinical report. *Physical Therapy, 68*, 1109–1113.

Bobath, B. (1985). *Abnormal postural reflex activity caused by brain lesions* (3rd ed.). London: Heinemann.

Bobath, B. (1990) *Adult hemiplegia: Evaluation and treatment* (3rd Ed.). London: Heinemann.

Bohannon, R.W (1993). Tilt table standing for reducing spasticity after spinal cord injury. *Archives of Physical Medicine and Rehabilitation, 74*, 1121–1122.

Bohannon, R.W., & Andrews, A.W. (1990). Correlation of knee extensor muscle torque and spasticity with gait speed in patients with stroke. *Archives of Physical Medicine and Rehabilitation, 71*, 330–333

Brindley, G.S., Polkey, C.E., & Rushton, D.N. (1979). Electrical splinting of the knee in paraplegia. *Paraplegia, 16*, 428–435.

Brunnstrom, S. (1956). Associated reactions of the upper extremity in adult patients with hemiplegia. An approach to training. *Physical Therapy Review, 36*, 225–236.

Brunnstrom, S. (1964). Recording gait patterns of adult hemiplegic patients. *Physical Therapy, 44*, 11–18.

Brunnstrom, S. (1965). Walking preparation for adult patients with hemiplegia. *Physical Therapy, 45*, 17–32.

Brunnstrom, S. (1966). Motor testing procedures in hemiplegia, based on sequential recovery stages. *Physical Therapy, 46*, 357–375.

Burridge, J.H., Taylor, P.N., Hagen, S.A., Wood, D.E., & Swaine, I.D. (1997). The effects of common peroneal stimulation on the effort and speed of walking: a randomised control trial with chronic hemiplegic patients. *Clinical Rehabilitation, 11*, 201–210.

Butefisch, C., Hummelsheim, H., Denzler, P., & Mauritz, K.-H. (1995). Repetitive training of isolated movements improves the outcome of motor rehabilitation of the centrally paretic hand. *Journal of the Neurological Sciences, 130*, 59–98.

Carey, L.M., Matyas, T.A., & Oke, L.E. (1993). Sensory loss in stroke patients: effective training of tactile and proprioceptive discrimination. *Archives of Physical Medicine and Rehabilitation, 74*, 602–611.

Carr, J.H., & Shepherd, R.B. (1989). A motor learning model for stroke rehabilitation. *Physiotherapy*, 75, 372–380.

Carr, J.H., & Shepherd, R.B. (1998). *Neurological rehabilitation—optimising motor performance*. Oxford: Butterworth-Heinemann.

Chae, J., Bethoux, F., Bohinc, Tt., Dobos, L., Davis, T., & Friedl, A. (1998). Neuromuscular stimulation for upper extremity motor and functional recovery in acute hemiplegia. *Stroke*, 29, 975–979.

Colborne, G.R., Olney, S.Y., & Griffin, M.P. (1993). Feedback of ankle joint angle and soleus electromyography in the rehabilitation of hemiplegic gait. *Archives of Physical Medicine Rehabilitation*, 74, 1100–1106.

Cole, J. (1998). Rehabilitation after sensory neuronopathy syndrome. *Journal of the Royal Society of Medicine*, 91, 30–32.

Conine, T.A., Sullivan, T., Mackie, T., & Goodman, M. (1990). Effect of serial casting for the prevention of equinus in patients with acute head injury. *Archives of Physical Medicine and Rehabilitation*, 71, 310–312.

Cotton, E. (1994). The Petö system in England. The first twenty-five years. In A. Russell, & E. Cotton (Eds), *The Petö system and its evolution in Britain. Philosophy, principles and practice* (pp. 35–48). London: Acorn Foundation Publications.

Cotton, E., & Kinsman, R. (1983). *Conductive education and adult hemiplegia*. Edinburgh: Churchill Livingstone.

Cozean, C.D., Pease, W.S., & Hubbell, S.L. (1988). Biofeedback and functional electric stimulation in stroke rehabilitation. *Archives of Physical Medicine and Rehabilitation*, 69, 401–405.

Dam, M., Tonin, P., Casson, S., et al. (1993). The effects of long-term rehabilitation therapy on post-stroke patients. *Stroke*, 24, 1186–1191.

Dean, C.M., & Shepherd, R.B. (1997). Task-related training improves performance of seated reaching tasks after stroke: a randomised trial. *Stroke*, 28, 722–728.

Dickstein, R., Hocherman, S., Pillar, T., & Shaham, R. (1986). Stroke rehabilitation: three exercise therapy approaches. *Physical Therapy*, 66, 1233–1238.

Dimitrejvic, M.M., Stokic, D.S., Wawro, A.W., & Woun, C.-C. (1996). Modification of motor control of wrist extension by mesh-glove electrical afferent stimulation in stroke patients. *Archives of Physical Medicine and Rehabilitation*, 77, 252–258.

Dobkin, B.H. (1998). Activity-dependent learning contributes to motor recovery. *Annals of Neurology*, 44, 158–160.

Duncan, P., Richards, L., Wallace, D., Stoker-Yates, J., Pohl, P., Luchies, C., Ogle, A., & Studenski, S. (1998). A randomised, controlled pilot study of a home based exercise programme for individuals with mild and moderate stroke. *Stroke*, 29, 2055–2060.

Dursun, E., Hamamci, N., Donmez, S., Tuzunalp, O., & Cakci, A. (1996). Angular biofeedback device for sitting balance of stroke patients. *Stroke*, 27, 1354–1357.

Edwards, S. (1998). Physiotherapy management of established spasticity. In G. Sheean (Ed.), *Spasticity rehabilitation* (pp. 71–89). London: Churchill Livingstone.

Edwards, S., & Charlton, P. (1996). Splinting and the use of orthoses in the management of patients with neurological disorders. In S. Edwards (Ed.), *Neurological physiotherapy: A problem-solving approach* (pp. 161–188). London: Churchill Livingstone.

Faghri, P., Rodgers, M., Glaser, R., Bors, J., Ho, C., & Akuthota, P. (1994). The effects of functional electrical stimulation on shoulder subluxation, arm function recovery, and shoulder pain in hemiplegic stroke patients. *Archives of Physical Medicine and Rehabilitation*, 75, 73–79.

Feys, H.M., DeWeedt, W.J., Selz, B.E., Cox Steck, G.A., Spichiger, R., Vereeck, L.E., Putman, K.D., & Van Hoydonck, G.A. (1998). Effect of a therapeutic intervention for the hemiplegic upper limb in the acute phase after stroke: a single-blind, randomised, controlled multicenter trial. *Stroke*, 29, 785–792.

Francisco, G., Chae, J., Chawla, H., Kirshblum, S., Zorowitz, R., Lewis, G., & Pang, S. (1998). Electromyogram-triggered neuromuscular stimulation for improving arm function of acute stroke survivors: a randomised pilot study. *Archives of Physical Medicine and Rehabilitation*, 79, 570–579.

Fugl-Meyer, A.R., Jaask, O.L., Leyman, I., Olsson, S., & Steglind, S. (1975). The post-stroke hemiplegic patient. 1: a method for evaluation of physical performance. *Scandinavian Journal of Rehabilitation Medicine*, 7, 13–31.

Goff, B. (1969). Appropriate afferent stimulation. *Physiotherapy*, 51, 9–11.

Grade, C., Redford, B., Chrostowski, J., Toussaint, L., & Blackwell, B. (1998). Methylphenidate in early post stroke recovery: a double-blind placebo-controlled study. *Archives of Physical Medicine and Rehabilitation*, 79, 1047–1050.

Granat, M.H., Maxwell, D.J., Ferguson, A.C.B., Kennedy, R.L., & Barbanel, J.C. (1996). Peroneal stimulator: evaluation for the correction of spastic drop foot in hemiplegia. *Archives of Physical Medicine and Rehabilitation*, 77, 19–24.

Hansen, G. (1979). EMG-controlled functional electrical stimulation of the paretic hand. *Scandinavian Journal of Rehabilitation Medicine*, 11, 189–193.

Harrison, V.F., & Mortensen, O.A. (1962). Identification and voluntary control of single motor unit activity in the tibialis anterior muscle. *Anatomy Record*, 144, 109–116.

Hesse, S., Bertelt, C., Jahnke, M.T., Schaffrin, A., Baake, P., Malezic, M., & Mauritz, K.H. (1995). Treadmill training with body weight support compared with physiotherapy in non-ambulatory hemiparetic subjects. *Stroke*, 26, 976–981.

Hu, H.-H., Chung, C., Liu, T.J., Chen, R.C., Chen, C.-H., Chou, P., Huang, W.-S., Lin, J.C.T., & Tsuei, J.J. (1993). A randomised controlled trial on the treatment for acute partial ischaemic stroke with acupuncture. *Neuroepidemiology*, 12, 106–113.

Indredavik, B., Slordahl, S.A., Bakke, F., Rokseth, R., & Haheim, L.L. (1997). Stroke unit treatment: long-term effects. *Stroke*, 28, 1861–1866.

Inglis, J., Donald, M.W., Monga, T.N., et al. (1984). Electromyographic biofeedback and physical therapy of the hemiplegic upper limb. *Archives of Physical Medicine and Rehabilitation*, 65, 755–759.

Intiso, D., Santilli, V., Grasso, M.V., Rossi, R., & Caruso, I. (1994). Rehabilitation of walking with electromyographic biofeedback in foot drop after stroke. *Stroke*, 25, 1189–1192.

Johansson, K., Lingran, I., Widner, H., Wiklund, I., & Johansson, B.B. (1993). Can sensory stimulation improve the functional outcome in stroke patients? *Neurology*, 43, 2189–2192.

Johnstone, M. (1987). *Restoration of motor function in the stroke patient: A physiotherapist's approach*. Edinburgh: Churchill Livingstone.

Kabat, H. (1952). Studies on neuromuscular dysfunction. XV. The role of central facilitation in restoration of motor function in paralysis. *Archives of Physical Medicine and Rehabilitation*, 33, 521–533.

Kabat, H., & Knott, M. (1953). Proprioceptive facilitation techniques for treatment of paralysis. *Physical Therapy Reviews*, 33, 53–64.

Kabat, H., & Knott, M. (1954). Proprioceptive facilitation therapy for paralysis. *Archives of Physical Medicine and Rehabilitation*, 40, 171–176.

Kantrowitz, A. (1960). *Electronic physiologic aids: A report of the Maimonides Hospital, Brooklyn* (pp. 4–5). New York: Maimonides Hospital.

Kinsman, R. (1989). A conductive education approach to stroke patients at Barnet General Hospital. *Physiotherapy*, 75, 418–421.

Krebs, H.I., Hogan, N., Aisen, M.L., & Volpe, B.T. (1998). Robot-aided neurorehabilitation. *HEET Rehabilitation Engineering*, 6, 75–87.

Kunkel, C.F., Scremin, E., Eisenberg, B., Garcia, J.F., Roberts, S., & Martinez, S. (1993). Effect of "standing" on spasticity, contracture, and osteoporosis in paralysed males. *Archives of Physical Medicine and Rehabilitation*, 74, 73–78.

Kwakkel, G., Wagenaar, R.C., Twisk, J.W.R., Lankhorst, G.J., & Koetsier, J.C. (1998) Effects of intensity of lower and upper extremity training after a primary middle cerebral artery stroke: a randomised clinical trial. In G. Kwakell (Ed.), *Dynamics in functional recovery after stroke*. PhD thesis, Amsterdam: Vrije University.

Lee, R.G., & van Donkelaar, P. (1995). Mechanisms underlying functional recovery following stroke. *Canadian Journal of Neurological Sciences*, 22, 257–263.

Lewis, Y. (1989). The use of the gymnastic ball in adult hemiplegia. *Physiotherapy*, 75(7): 421–424.

Liberson, W. T., Holmquest, H.J., Scott, D., & Dow, M. (1961). Functional electrotherapy: stimulation of the peroneal nerve synchronised with the swing phase of the gait of hemiplegic patients. *Archives of Physical Medicine and Rehabilitation*, 42, 101–105.

Lincoln, N.B., Parry, R.H., & Vass, C.D. (1999). Randomised, controlled trial to evaluate increased intensity of physiotherapy treatment of arm function after stroke. *Stroke*, 30, 573–579.

Logigian, M.K., Samuels, M.A., & Falconer, J. (1983). Clinical exercise trial for stroke patients. *Archives of Physical Medicine and Rehabilitation*, 64, 364–367.

Lord, J., & Hall, L. (1986). Neuromuscular re-education versus traditional programs for stroke rehabilitation. *Archives of Physical Medicine and Rehabilitation*, 67, 88–91.

Lyle, R.C. (1981). A performance test for assessment of upper limb function in physical rehabilitation treatment and research. *International Journal of Rehabilitation Research*, 4, 483–492.

Magnus, R. (1924). *Korperstellung*. Berlin: Springer.

Magnus, R. (1926). Some results of studies in the physiology of posture. *Lancet*, ii, 531–536, 585–588.

Mahoney, R.I., & Barthel, D.W. (1965). Functional evaluation: the Barthel Index. *Maryland State Medical Journal*, 14, 61–65.

Mandel, A.R., Nymark, J.R., Balmer, S.J., Grinnell, D.M., & O'Riain, M.D. (1990). Electromyographic versus rhythmic positional biofeedback in computerised gait retraining with stroke patients. *Archives of Physical Medicine and Rehabilitation*, 71, 649–654.

Marinacci, A.A., & Horande, M. (1960). Electromyogram in neuromuscular re-education. *Bulletin of the Los Angeles Neurological Societies*, 25, 57–71.

Marzuk, P.M. (1985). Biofeedback for neuromuscular disorders. *Annals of Internal Medicine*, 102, 854–858.

Merletti, R., Acimovic, R., Grobelnik, S., & Cvilak, G. (1975). Electrophysiological orthosis for the upper extremity in hemiplegia: feasibility study. *Archives of Physical Medicine and Rehabilitation*, 56, 507–513.

Middaugh, S.J., & Miller, M.C. (1980). Electromyographic feedback: effect on voluntary muscle contractions in paretic subjects. *Archives of Physical Medicine and Rehabilitation*, 61, 24–29.

Middaugh, S.J., Miller, M.C., Foster, G., & Ferdon, M.R. (1982). Electromyographic feedback: effects on voluntary muscle contractions in normal subjects. *Archives of Physical Medicine*, 63, 254–260.

Miltner, W.H.R., Bauder, H., Sommer, M., Dettmers, C., & Taub, E. (1999). Effects of constraint-induced movement therapy on patients with chronic motor deficits after stroke: a replication. *Stroke*, 30, 586–592.

Mimms, H.W. (1956). Electromyography in clinical practice. *Southern Medical Journal*, 49, 804–806.

Moe, J.H., & Post, H.W. (1962). Functional electrical stimulation for ambulation in hemiplegia. *Lancet*, 82, 285–288.

Moreland, J.D., Thomson, M.A., & Fuoco, A.R. (1998). Electromyographic feedback to improve lower extremity function after stroke; a meta-analysis. *Archives of Physical Medicine and Rehabilitation*, 79, 134–140.

Moseley, A.M. (1997). The effect of casting combined with stretching on passive ankle dorsiflexion in adults with traumatic head injury. *Physical Therapy*, 77, 240–247.

Mott, F.W., & Sherrington, C.S. (1895). Experiments upon the influence of sensory nerves upon movement and nutrition of the limb. *Proceedings of the Royal Society*, 57, 481–488.

Muir, G.D., & Steeves, J.D. (1997). Sensory motor stimulation to improve locomotor recovery after spinal cord injuries. *Trends in Neurosciences*, 20, 72–77.

Mulder, T. (1991). A process-orientated model of human motor behaviour: toward a theory-based rehabilitation approach. *Physical Therapy*, 71, 157–164.

Patrick, J. (1989). Cerebral diplegia: improvements in walking. *British Medical Journal*, 299, 1115–1116.

Pease, W.S. (1998). Therapeutic electrical stimulation for spasticity: quantitative gait analysis. *American Journal of Physical Medicine and Rehabilitation*, 77, 351–355.

Perry, C.E. (1967). Principles and techniques of the Brunnstrom approach to the treatment of hemiplegia. *American Journal of Physical Medicine*, 46(1): 789–811.

Pope, P.M. (1992). Management of the physical condition in patients with chronic and severe neurological pathologies. *Physiotherapy*, 78, 896–903.

Pope, P.M. (1996). Postural management and special seating. In S. Edwards (Ed.), *Neurological physiotherapies: A problem-solving approach* (pp. 135–160). London: Churchill Livingstone.

Potempa, K., Lopez, M., Braun, L.T., Szidon, J.P., Fogg, L., & Tinknell, T. (1995). Physiological outcomes of aerobic exercise training with hemiparetic stroke patients. *Stroke*, 26, 101–105.

Rademaker, G.G.J. (1935). *Reactions labyrinthiques et equilibre. L'Ataxie labyrinthique*. Paris: Masson.

Reynolds, G., Archibald, K.C., Brunnstrom, S., & Thompson, N. (1957). Preliminary report on neuromuscular function testing of the extremity in adult hemiplegic patients. *Archives of Physical Medicine and Rehabilitation*, 39, 303–310.

Richardson, D.L.A. (1991). The use of the tilt table to effect passive tendon achilles stretch in a patient with head injury. *Physiotherapy Theory and Practice*, 7, 45–60.

Riddoch, G., & Buzzard, E.F. (1921). Reflex movements and postural reactions in quadriplegia and hemiplegia, with special reference to those of the upper limb. *Brain*, 44, 397–489.

Robinson, R.O., McCarthy, G.T., & Little, T.M. (1989). Conductive education at the Peto Institute, Budapest. *British Medical Journal*, 299, 1145–1149.

Rodgers, H., Soutter, J., Kaiser, W., Pearson, P., Dobson, R., Skilbeck, C., & Bond, J. (1997). Early supported hospital discharge following acute stroke: pilot study results. *Clinical Rehabilitation*, 11, 287–288.

Rudd, A.G., Wolfe, C.D., Tilling, K., & Beech, R. (1997). Randomised controlled trial to evaluate early discharge scheme for patients with stroke. *British Medical Journal*, 315, 1039–1044.

Schaltenbrand, G. (1928). The development of human motility and motor disturbances. *Archives of Neurology and Psychiatry*, 20, 720–730.

Sharp, S.A., & Brouwer, B.J. (1997). Isokinetic strength training of the hemiparetic knee: effects on function and spasticity. *Archives of Physical Medicine and Rehabilitation*, 48, 1231–1236.

Sherrington, C. (1906). *The integrative action of the nervous systems*. New Haven: University Press.

Sherrington, C.S. (1931). Reflex inhibition as a factor in the co-ordination of movement and postures. *Quarterly Journal of Experimental Physiology*, 6, 251–259.

Smith, D.S., Goldenberg, E., Ashburn, A., Kinsella, G., Sheikh, K., Brennan, P.J., Meade, T.W., Zutschi, D.W., Perry, J.D., & Reeback, J.S. (1981). Remedial therapy after stroke: a randomised controlled study. *British Medical Journal*, 282, 517–520.

Sonde, R.P.T., Gip, C., Fernaeu, S.S.E., Nilsson, C.G., & Viitanen, M. (1998). Stimulation with low frequency (1.7 Hz) transcutaneous electrical nerve stimulation (low-tens) increases motor function of the post-stroke paretic arm. *Scandinavian Journal of Rehabilitation Medicine*, 30, 95–99.

Stroke Unit Trialist's Collaboration. (1997a). Collaborative systematic review of the randomised trials of organised in-patient (stroke unit) care after stroke. *British Medical Journal*, 314, 1151–1158.

Stroke Unit Trialist's Collaboration. (1997b). How do stroke units improve patient outcome? A collaborative systematic review of the randomised trials. *Stroke*, 28, 2139–2144.

Sunderland, A., Tinson, D.J., Bradley, E.L., Fletcher, D., Langton Hewer, R., & Wade, D.T. (1992). Enhanced physical therapy improves the recovery on arm function after stroke: a randomised control trial. *Journal of Neurology, Neurosurgery and Psychiatry*, 55, 530–535.

Tangeman, P.T., Banaitis, D.A., & Williams, A.K. (1990). Rehabilitation of chronic stroke patients: changes in functional performance. *Archives of Physical Medicine and Rehabilitation*, 71, 876–880.

Taub, E. (1977). Movement in nonhuman primates deprived of somatosensory feedback. *Exercise and Sports Science Review*, 4, 335–374.

Taub, E., Miller, N.E., Novack, T.A., Cook, E.W., Fleming, W.C., Nepumucerio, S.C., Conell, J.S., & Crago, J.E. (1993). Technique to improve chronic motor deficit after stroke. *Archives of Physical Medicine and Rehabilitation*, 74, 347–354.

Tekeoolu, Y., Adak, B., & Goksoy, T (1998). Effect of transcutaneous electrical nerve stimulation (TENS) on Barthel activities of daily living (ADL) Index following stroke. *Clinical Rehabilitation*, 12, 277–280.

Thaut, M.H., McIntosh, G.C., & Rice, R.R. (1997). Rhythmic facilitation of gait training in hemiparetic stroke rehabilitation. *Journal of Neurological Sciences*, 151, 207–212.

Thornton, H., & Kilbride, C. (1998). Physical management of abnormal tone and movement. In Stokes M. (Ed.), *Neurological physiotherapy* (pp. 313–325). Philadelphia: Mosby.

Venzmer, G. (1972). *Five thousand years of medicine*. London: Macmillan.

Visintin, M., Barbeau, H., Korner-Bitensky, N., & Mayo, N.E. (1998). A new approach to retrain gait in stroke patients through body weight support and treadmill stimulation. *Stroke*, 29, 1122–1128.

Voss, D.E. (1967). Proprioceptive neuromuscular facilitation. *American Journal of Physical Medicine*, 46, 838–898.

Voss, D.E., Ionta, M.K., & Myers, B.J. (1985). *Proprioceptive neuromuscular facilitation patterns and techniques* (3rd Ed.). Philadelphia: Harper Row.

Wade, D.T., Collen, F.M., Robb, G.F., & Warlow, C.P. (1992). Physiotherapy intervention late after stroke and mobility. *British Medical Journal*, 304, 609–613.

Wagenaar, R.C., Meijer, O.G., Wieringen, P.C.W., et al. (1990). The functional recovery of stroke: a comparison between neurodevelopmental treatment and the Brunnstrom method. *Scandinavian Journal of Rehabilitation Medicine*, 22, 1–8.

Walker-Batson, D., Smith, P., Kurtis, S., Unwin, H., & Greenlee, R.G. (1995) Amphetamine paired with physical therapy accelerates motor recovery following stroke: further evidence. *Stroke*, *26*, 2254–2259.

Walshe, F.M.R. (1923). On certain tonic reflexes in hemiplegia with special reference to the so called "associated movements". *Brain*, *46*, 1–37.

Waters, R.L., Campbell, J.M., & Nakai, R. (1988). Therapeutic electrical stimulation of the lower limb by epimyseal electrodes. *Clinical Orthopaedics and Related Research*, *233*, 44–52.

Waters, R.L., McNeal, D.R., Faloon, W., & Clifford, B. (1985). Functional electrical stimulation of the peroneal nerve for hemiplegia. *Journal of Bone and Joint Surgery*, *67-A*, 792–793.

Weiller, C. (1995). Recovery from motor stroke: human positron emission tomography studies. *Cerebrovascular Diseases*, *5*, 282–291.

Weingarden, H.P., Zeilig, G., Heruti, R., Shemesh, H.Y., Ohry, A., Dar, A., Katz, D., Nathan, R., & Smith, A. (1998). Hybrid functional electrical stimulation orthosis system for the upper limb. *American Journal of Physical Medicine and Rehabilitation*, *77*, 276–281.

Williams, P.E., Catanese, T., Lucey, E.G., & Goldspink, G. (1988). The importance of contractile activity in the prevention of connective tissue accumulation in muscle. *Journal of Anatomy*, *158*, 169–114.

Winstein, C.J., Gardener, E.R., McNeal, D.R., et al. (1989). Standing balance training: effect on balance and locomotion on hemiparetic adults. *Archives of Physical Medicine and Rehabilitation*, *70*, 755–762.

Wissel, J., Ebersback, G., Gutjahr, L., & Dahlke, F. (1989). Treating chronic hemiparesis with modified biofeedback. *Archives of Physical Medicine and Rehabilitation*, *70*, 612–617.

Wolf, S.L. (1978). Essential considerations in the use of EMG biofeedback. *Physical Therapy*, *58*, 25–31.

Wolf, S.L., & Binder-Macleod, S.A. (1983a). Electromyographic biofeedback applications to the hemiplegic patient: changes in lower extremity neuromuscular and functional status. *Physical Therapy*, *63*, 1404–1413.

Wolf, S.L., & Binder-Macleod, S.A. (1983b). Electromyographic biofeedback applications to the hemiplegic patient: changes in upper extremity neuromuscular and functional status. *Physical Therapy*, *63*, 1393–1403.

Wolf, S.L., Lecraw, D.E., Barton, L.A., & Jann, B.B. (1989). Forced use of hemiplegic upper extremities to reverse the effect of learned non-use among chronic stroke and head injured patients. *Experimental Neurology*, *104*, 125–132.

Yekutiel, M., & Guttman, E. (1993). A controlled trial of the retraining of the sensory function of the hand in stroke patients. *Journal of Neurology, Neurosurgery, and Psychiatry*, *56*, 241–244.

15. Physical consequences of neurological disablement

Gavin Yamey   Richard J. Greenwood

INTRODUCTION

The process of rehabilitation facilitates both recovery following a single pathological insult, and longer term management of disablement over months or years. In both cases, an important consequence of the process is the prevention of secondary deterioration and disability. In the context of neurological disease, secondary deterioration may be a consequence of a primary feature of the disorder—for example, the contractures following spastic hypertonus or aspiration pneumonia following dysphagia. Other complications may result from immobility alone, such as pressure sores and osteoporosis, or from medical treatment, such as the extrapyramidal side effects of neuroleptic medication or the gum hypertrophy due to phenytoin. Whatever the cause, the whole rehabilitation team must be sensitive to the prevention of further damage, since most of these secondary conditions are difficult or impossible to correct once established. This chapter emphasises the adverse consequences of immobility and the growing recognition of the role of exercise in counteracting the secondary effects of chronic neurological disability.

THE CONSEQUENCES OF IMMOBILITY

Since the time of Hippocrates in 400 BC, bed rest and immobilisation have been used in the management of trauma and acute illness, particularly in the treatment of limb injury or disease (Bick, 1948). However, the side-effects of bed rest, even in the short term, are often underestimated. For example, Krolner and Toft (1983) showed that patients aged 18–60 subjected to a mean of 27 days of "therapeutic" bed rest for lumbar disc disease averaged a 0.9% loss of bone mineral content per week. Clearly the effects of long-term inactivity may produce major problems for the chronically disabled person and warrant early mobilisation even in conditions where bed rest is thought to be essential. The data describing tissue changes secondary to immobility are derived from either studies designed to explore and counteract the effects of weightlessness during space flight or from studies of experimental limb immobilisation.

Central nervous system

The effects of the sensory deprivation of recumbency and immobilisation on behaviour and cognition are well described (Zubeck et al., 1969). Twenty nine percent of healthy people placed in a simulated hospital room developed subjective sensory distortions after 2.5 hours (Downs, 1974). After 20 days of bed rest, healthy subjects show a deterioration in their mental health according to a self-rating depression scale and the General Health Questionnaire (Ishizaki et al., 1994). These effects should not be forgotten in hospitalised, bed-bound, or paralysed patients in whom decreased kinaesthetic, visual, auditory, tactile, and social stimulation may combine to produce disorientation, confusion, delusions, and hallucinations (Leiderman et al., 1958). The loss of sleep that may occur as a result, as well as that due to the noise on the ward, may in turn affect the social, emotional, behavioural, and physical functioning of patients.

Sleep disorders are well described in patients with chronic disease and disability. They are a risk factor for the prevalence and future emergence of cardiovascular and gastrointestinal disorders and can compromise quality of life (Shapiro & Devins, 1993). Patients with Parkinson's disease report poor quality nocturnal sleep related to the cumulative effects of motor abnormalities, neurochemical changes, mood disorders, drugs, and dementia (Culebras, 1992). Stroke patients with shoulder pain show significantly more sleep disturbance than those without pain, leading to fatigue and social isolation (Küçükdeveci et al., 1996). Initial and intermittent nocturnal disturbances, influenced by both physical and psychological factors, were found amongst boys with Duchenne muscular dystrophy (Bazelmans & Mulder, 1992). The effects of sleep deprivation, reviewed by Parkes (1985), are principally to interfere with memory and learning, to the extent that symptoms of a dementia may occur, reversible by sleep (Kelly & Feigenbaum, 1982). Sleep abnormality may impair motor control, and sleep benefit on motor control in Parkinson's disease is well recognised. Poor sleep is therefore likely to have a negative impact on physical and functional abilities, and adequate sleep is essential for the training involved in a rehabilitation programme. The tissue renewal that occurs during sleep (Oswald, 1987) may also be of importance to recovery from trauma or the healing of pressure sores. Attention should be paid to reducing noise on the ward at night, and addressing other causes of sleep disturbance including pain and depression.

Muscles and inactivity

Bed rest produces profound changes in muscle structure and function within 7 days, including a 2–5% increase in fat volume (Shangraw et al., 1988) and a 3% loss of muscle volume (Ferrando et al., 1995). The loss of muscle bulk takes several days of remobilisation before it begins to increase (LeBlanc et al., 1987). Convertino et al. (1989) showed that the decrease in the cross-sectional area of the leg during 30 days of bed rest was largely due to decrease in the muscle compartment. They felt that this contributed to the associated orthostatic hypotension (see later). Immobilisation leads to loss of muscle strength, most dramatically during the first week (Appell, 1990). Suzuki et al. (1994), in their study of sedentary voluntary students subjected to 10–20 days bed rest, found a reduction in isometric muscle strength as well as a loss of muscle mass measured by dual energy X-ray absorptiometry. The rate of changes of strength did not correlate to the corresponding changes in mass, and they concluded that the decrease in muscle strength may also be due to reduction of neuromuscular function. At the cellular level, structural changes after immobilisation include mitochondrial swelling, myofibrillar disorganisation (Kauhanen et al., 1993), and capillary wall fenestration (Oki et al., 1995). The loss of body protein associated with inactivity is predominantly due to a decrease in muscle protein synthesis (Ferrando et al., 1996).

The muscle groups are not all equally affected by bed rest. For instance, Le Blanc et al. (1988) found in a study of 10 healthy men on 5 weeks of bed rest that the muscle *area* of the plantar flexors (gastrocnemius and soleus) decreased by 12%, whilst that of the dorsiflexors did not decrease significantly. Similarly the muscle *strength* of the plantar flexors was decreased by 26% whilst there was no significant decrease in the strength of the dorsiflexors. Gogia et al. (1988) also showed that inactivity produces greater decrement in antigravity muscle strength: After 5 weeks of bed rest the torque in soleus was decreased by 24%, in gastrocnemius by 26%, in ankle dorsiflexors and knee flexors by only 8%, and in knee extensors by 19%. Disuse muscle atrophy does not therefore contribute significantly to foot drop, a clinical complication of prolonged bed rest.

The secondary effects of bed rest and immobility on muscle can be counteracted to some extent by exercise training. Ellis et al. (1993) measured muscle thickness in 19 bed-rested men subjected to isotonic (cycle ergometer) and isokinetic (torque ergometer) lower extremity exercise training, and no exercise training. Rectus femoris thickness was unchanged in the two exercise groups, but decreased by 10% in the no exercise group, whilst vastus intermedius thickness was unchanged in the isotonic exercise group but decreased by 12–16% in the isokinetic and no exercise groups. Measures of muscular strength and endurance can also be maintained or even increased during bed rest by exercise (Greenleaf et al., 1994). Ferrando et al. (1997)

found that leg resistance exercise every other day during bed rest prevents a reduction in muscle protein synthesis.

Cardiovascular system

Takenaka et al. (1994) assessed cardiovascular function in 14 healthy subjects before and after 20 days of bed rest, using echocardiography and vascular ultrasound of the common carotid artery, abdominal aorta, and femoral artery. After bed rest, heart rate increased whilst there were significant decreases in left ventricular diastolic dimension, systolic blood pressure, cardiac output, abdominal aortic, and femoral artery flow. Chronically bedridden elderly people have smaller ventricular and atrial dimensions, and lower stroke and cardiac indices than age- and sex-matched controls whose activities are unrestricted (Katsume et al., 1992). Maximal oxygen uptake (VO2max), a measure of aerobic fitness, is reduced by bed rest. The magnitude of this reduction is dependent upon duration of bed rest and the initial level of aerobic fitness (Convertino, 1997). Despite the elevation in heart rate, reduction in VO2max results primarily from decreased stroke volume and cardiac output. The deterioration of aerobic fitness due to bed rest causes aerobic tasks, such as walking, to become tiring and the individual complains of fatigue. This may impede active rehabilitation of patients with chronic neurological disability who also demonstrate impaired levels of aerobic fitness (see later).

Orthostatic hypotension. Bed rest is associated with orthostatic hypotension (Greenleaf et al., 1989; Harper & Lyles, 1988) with the clinical consequence of the presyncopal state or syncope. The causes are not fully understood and several possible mechanisms seem to be involved. This effect may complicate a variety of neurological disorders which themselves affect autonomic control of blood pressure at various points.

Sandler et al. (1988) found that the cardiovascular deconditioning associated with recumbent bed rest involved factors other than simple loss of blood volume, and required 3 weeks or longer of ambulation to resolve. A loss of blood volume does occur within the first few days of bed rest (Fortney et al., 1988), an effect less marked in women than men due to their higher oestrogen levels (Fortney et al., 1994), and this contributes to the impaired orthostatic and exercise tolerance seen on ambulation. Other factors include attenuated autonomic reflex control of the cardiovascular system and alterations in peripheral vascular reactivity. Convertino et al. (1990) found impaired vagally mediated carotid baroreceptor reflexes in 11 healthy men subjected to 30 days of bed rest. There was no significant correlation between reductions of plasma volume and changes of baroreflex responses. Billman et al. (1982) showed that prolonged recumbency in primates impairs the baroreceptor control of heart rate, although at what level the reflex was affected was unclear. The effect on baroreceptor control of peripheral vascular resistance remains uncertain.

Increased venous compliance and peripheral pooling have also been suggested as contributory mechanisms. Buckey et al. (1988) argue that, since the deep veins of the leg have little sympathetic innervation or vascular smooth muscle, their compliance may be related to the properties of the surrounding skeletal muscle. They measured the deep venous volume during progressive venous occlusion using magnetic resonance scanning and showed that a large fraction of the calf volume change during venous occlusion was attributable to filling of the deep venous spaces. They therefore argued that the changes in skeletal muscle described earlier allowed for an increase in peripheral pooling on standing and contributed to orthostatic intolerance after bed rest. However, Melchior and Fortney (1993) used venous occlusion plethysmography to evaluate leg compliance in ten men subjected to 13 days bed rest. Orthostatic tolerance was similar in five patients and reduced in the other five after bed rest, but neither group showed any significant change in leg compliance. They concluded that mechanisms other than increased leg compliance have to be taken into account to explain the orthostatic intolerance.

These findings stress the importance of the avoidance of bed rest and immobility, and especially recumbency, in the management of patients with postural hypotension. Head up tilt at night is now a well-established first line of treatment in any patient with autonomic failure (Bannister & Mathias, 1993). Pharmacological therapies aim to increase intravascular volume with high sodium intake and mineralocorticoids (e.g., fludrocortisone), or increase vascular resistance by stimulating alpha or blocking beta vascular receptors (Lathers & Charles, 1994). In a 30-day head-down bed rest project, neither isotonic cycle ergometer exercise nor intermittent resistive isokinetic exercise prevented orthostatic intolerance (Greenleaf, 1997). This exercise training did however prevent other aspects of the cardiovascular deconditioning associated with bed rest, including loss of plasma and red cell volume. The performance of isometric exercises, to reduce peripheral pooling, during postural "retraining" by tilt-table conditioning, may be helpful (Hoeldtke et al., 1988), just as toe standing during passive head up tilt may prevent syncope in otherwise normal individuals (Mayerson & Burch, 1940).

Thrombo-embolic disease. Although platelet reactivity is stimulated by immobilisation (Buczynski et al., 1991), bed rest alone does not appear to be a potent cause of deep venous thrombosis (DVT). Rosenfeld et al. (1994) studied 12 non-smoking healthy volunteers who were kept supine for 36 hours, and found no increase in haemostatic function. In fact the changes in fibrinolytic proteins were more suggestive of enhanced fibrinolysis, perhaps representing a protective mechanism to counter the effects of stasis from bed rest. Of Virchow's triad of stasis, vessel wall injury and hypercoagulation, the combination of stasis and hypercoagulability that exists in the context of myocardial infarction (Murray et al., 1970), stroke (Lane et al., 1983), spinal cord injury (Rossi et al., 1980), and surgery (Collins et al., 1988), appears to be the most effective trigger for thrombogenesis (Thomas, 1985). The incidence of DVT in the paralysed leg after stroke is over 50%, compared to 10% in the normal leg (Warlow et al., 1976). It develops in about 40–50% of patients with acute spinal cord injury, the greatest risk being within the first 2 weeks when the incidence of symptomatic DVT and

pulmonary embolism (PE) may be as high as 14.5 and 4.6% respectively (Waring & Karunas, 1991). Pulmonary embolism is nearly 50 times more likely to occur in a patient after spinal cord injury than in an age-matched control cohort in the general population (DeVivo et al., 1993).

The difficulty in diagnosing DVT clinically is well recognised, and indeed there may be no findings on physical examination (Hall et al., 1977). In 76 legs paralysed by stroke, Warlow et al. (1976) found only 24 thromboses clinically, but 40 using 125 I-labelled fibrinogen uptake scanning. This may partly account for the small number of patients (4%, with PE in 3%) developing thromboses during rehabilitation after severe head injury (Kalisky et al., 1985). Only 13% were found after spinal cord injury using clinical examination (Walsh & Tribe, 1965/1966); detection in spinal patients using 125 I-labelled fibrinogen uptake scanning increases to about 50% (Merli et al., 1988). Compression ultrasound is now widely used for the diagnostic management of patients with clinically suspected DVT (Lensing et al., 1993). It is highly sensitive for proximal DVT, but much less so for DVT confined to calf veins (Kearon et al., 1998). Since a large calf DVT may quickly extend to more proximal veins and then embolise, repeat ultrasonography is recommended at 1 week to safely exclude DVT in patients with a normal scan at presentation (Cogo et al., 1998). Measurement of D-dimer, a fragment specific to the degradation of fibrin, may prove to be a useful diagnostic adjunct (Bernardi et al., 1998).

Many studies have investigated the prevention of thromboembolism during relatively brief periods of immobilisation. There is good evidence that unfractionated heparin prevents DVT after surgery (Kakkar et al., 1982). The new low molecular weight heparins appear to provide even better surgical prophylaxis, and they have a number of advantages over unfractionated heparin including less risk of causing bleeding and a lower incidence of associated thrombocytopaenia (Weitz, 1997). In 192 patients requiring bed rest for 3 days or more due to pulmonary disease, Ibarra-Perez et al. (1988) found that graded compression stockings, subcutaneous heparin, or oral aspirin were significantly more effective in preventing thrombosis compared with a control group or treatment with elastic bandages. However, there were haemorrhagic complications in some of those on heparin or aspirin.

After stroke, there is still no general consensus about DVT prevention. Elasticated stockings are under trial and intermittent pneumatic compression has been reported to be ineffective (Prasad et al., 1982). In a study of 68 patients with spontaneous intracerebral haemorrhage, early low dose heparin significantly lowered the incidence of PE without an associated increase in rebleeding (Boeer et al., 1991). There is good evidence that subcutaneous heparin provides useful thrombo-embolic prophylaxis in ischaemic stroke, although full anticoagulation by intravenous heparin or oral warfarin risks haemorrhagic complications. McCarthy and Turner (1986) found that the incidence of DVT in acute stroke patients fell from 73% in 161 prospectively randomised controls to 22% in 144 patients treated with subcutaneous unfractionated calcium heparin. Several studies of ischaemic stroke patients have addressed the role of low molecular weight heparins. In a randomised trial, low molecular weight heparin was better than placebo in reducing the incidence of DVT and it did not increase the incidence of bleeding (Prins et al., 1989). In another study, there was no difference in the rates of thrombosis between patients receiving once daily low molecular weight heparin and those receiving placebo, but the dose of heparin used was very low (Sandset et al., 1990). Finally, danaparoid sodium was superior to low dose unfractionated heparin in reducing the incidence of DVT (Turpie et al., 1991). On the basis of these data, low molecular weight heparins appear to provide the best prophylaxis for stroke patients (Weitz, 1997).

In acute spinal cord injury, external pneumatic compression boots and rotating beds are helpful in preventing thromboembolism (Becker et al., 1987) but pharmacological management is of additional benefit. Over a period of a month, within 2 weeks of spinal injury Merli et al. (1988) found prospectively in 66 patients that 5000 units of heparin 8-hourly with or without dihydroergotamine was no better than placebo controls in preventing DVT, whilst electrical stimulation plus low dose heparin significantly reduced the incidence of DVT. Recent studies have shown the benefit of low molecular weight heparins in preventing DVT in spinal patients (Green et al., 1994; Harris et al., 1996). Their use for 12 weeks in combination with external pneumatic compression affords useful prophylaxis (Green, 1994).

Recommendations for the prevention of DVT in chronically disabled patients are more difficult. The hypercoagulability seen after acute illness and immobility diminishes with time such that, for example, 4 weeks after stroke, blood coagulation systems return to normal (Lane et al., 1983). The risk of thrombosis in chronic disability may therefore be fairly low despite immobility; hence the small number of thromboses occurring in severely head-injured patients in rehabilitation (Kalisky et al., 1985) although, as mentioned, their diagnosis of DVT was on clinical rather than radiological grounds. A reasonable policy in these patients might therefore be to avoid thromboembolism prophylaxis unless an intercurrent event—for example, sepsis or surgery—causes superimposition of a hypercoagulable state upon the pre-existing immobility. In this case subcutaneous heparin, most conveniently given as a once daily low molecular weight preparation, should be instituted for an appropriate time.

In a rehabilitation setting, once a DVT has occurred in a patient, there is often reluctance to proceed in mobilising the patient for fear of causing embolism. There are few studies of the effect of mobilising the affected lower extremity. Kiser and Stefans (1997) conducted a retrospective case-controlled study over a 4.5 year period to detect any change in the rate of PE occurrence dependent on time to mobilisation in patients diagnosed with a DVT in a rehabilitation hospital. DVT was diagnosed by Doppler ultrasound or venogram, and PE by ventilation/perfusion scan. One hundred and twenty one patients had a DVT without subsequent PE and a mean time of 123.2 hours until mobilisation. Six patients had a subsequent PE and a mean time of 48.3 hours until mobilisation. The authors recommend

that once a DVT is diagnosed, it is prudent to keep the affected limb immobilised for at least 48–72 hours while the patient is being anticoagulated.

Respiratory changes

There is good evidence that position in bed affects arterial oxygen tensions in the presence or absence of lung disease. When one lung is diseased, lateral positioning with the diseased, or smaller left, lung down impairs PaO_2 values more than lateral positioning with the healthy lung down; when both lungs are diseased, lying on the right side results in higher PaO_2 values than when lying on the left (Zack et al., 1974). In the absence of lung disease in the supine position as opposed to standing, abdominal muscle breathing predominates over rib cage breathing, which halves its contribution to the tidal volume (Druz & Sharp, 1981). This impairs coughing, which depends predominantly on rib cage movement; in addition, the diaphragm moves cephalad, reducing thoracic size and causing a decrease in functional residual capacity which may be exceeded by closing volume, especially in middle-aged and elderly subjects. Atelectasis results and, with pooling of secretions, predisposes to infection (Harper & Lyles, 1988). Prolonged immobility also impairs the normal mucociliary escalator and may cause an increase in extravascular lung water, two additional factors in the development of pneumonia (Sahn, 1991). In elderly subjects, adopting the supine position leads to a fall in PaO_2 of 8 mm Hg (Ward et al., 1966), which may be sufficient to produce symptoms such as confusion in a person at the threshold of pulmonary insufficiency (Creditor, 1993). It may also contribute to the occurrence of syncope in patients who are already sensitised by vasomotor instability.

Continuous lateral rotational therapy (CLRT) should theoretically reverse the respiratory changes associated with immobility. Three prospective, randomised studies evaluating patients with acute head trauma, stroke, orthopaedic injuries requiring traction, and blunt chest trauma all showed a decreased incidence of pneumonia with CLRT compared with those treated in a conventional bed and turned every 2 hours by the nursing staff (Kelley et al., 1987; Gentilello et al., 1988; Fink et al., 1990). A fourth study performed in a medical intensive care unit with a heterogeneous group of patients did not show a difference in incidence of nosocomial pneumonia between treatment in CLRT and a conventional bed, but it did show a decreased length of stay for patients with pneumonia treated with CLRT (Summer et al., 1989). It appears that if CLRT is to be effective, it needs to be instituted early, but the length of time that it should be used for is unknown (Sahn, 1991).

Silent aspiration is another problem in immobile patients, and risks respiratory infection. Meguro et al. (1992) studied elderly bed-bound nursing home patients who suffered mainly from cerebral infarction and dementia. They cleaned patients' mouths with povidone iodine and kept them in a sitting position for 2 hours after each meal to restrict respiratory bacterial infection and to prevent aspiration of gastric juices, respectively.

During the treatment for 103 days, the number of febrile days was significantly decreased in the treatment group compared with the control group, probably due to minimising respiratory infections.

Renal function

The effect of posture on renal function is poorly understood. Guite et al. (1988) found that in old people, in whom there is loss of the normal urinary circadian rhythm, bed rest over 3 days produced no difference between the day and night excretion of water, sodium, potassium, urea, or creatinine, but sitting up in a chair for 8 hours a day produced a negative day–night excretion of water, sodium, urea, and creatinine but not of potassium. They concluded that sitting upright out of bed during the day may contribute to the nocturia and nocturnal incontinence seen in elderly people. A reversal of the normal circadian rhythm may also be seen in younger patients after head injury (Payne & de Wardener, 1958), but whether this is influenced by recumbency or might contribute to nocturnal incontinence in younger patients with neurological disability is unexplored.

Immobilisation of rats leads to a 50% increase in urinary bladder fresh weight compared to controls (Anderson et al., 1990). This increase is not due to tissue oedema, but is accompanied by epithelial hyperplasia. Total urine volume is unchanged, but there is a decrease in frequency of voiding and a doubling of the mean urine weight per voiding. It is postulated that bladder distension from the increased volume per voiding leads to a rapidly induced increase in bladder tissue growth.

Prolonged bed rest increases the risk of developing renal stones. In normal subjects on 5 weeks of bed rest, urinary saturation with calcium oxalate and phosphate increases (Hwang et al., 1988). The excretion of magnesium and citrate, both inhibitors of stone formation, does not change significantly, increasing the risk of forming calcium-containing renal stones. These changes are not reversed by seated exercise (Zorbas et al., 1988). Stone formation has been described principally in children and young adults in the context of the poliomyelitis epidemic in the 1950s, spinal injury, and immobilisation after skeletal fracture. Hydration and ambulation as soon as possible reduces this complication of immobiliation; the use of calcitonin to prevent bone resorption, and thus hypercalcuria, may require consideration if ambulation is not possible (Rosen et al., 1978; Musselman & Kay, 1985).

Metabolic changes

Bed rest for 7 days increases endogenous insulin secretion (Shangraw et al., 1988) and the glucose-stimulated insulin response, at least partly due to beta cell adaptation, although insulin secretion does not increase adequately compared with the increase in peripheral insulin resistance induced by bed rest (Mikines et al., 1989). By measuring the effect of insulin on glucose uptake rates in the whole body and the leg before and after bed rest, Mikines et al. (1991) showed that bed rest decreases whole body insulin action, a fact that is explained by decreased insulin action in inactive muscle. In addition to impaired carbohydrate metabolism, bed rest alters the processing of lipids, with changes including a reduction in apolipoprotein A1 and HDL-2 cholesterol and an increase in HDL-3 cholesterol (Yanagibori et al., 1994). During 20 days of bed rest in 14 healthy people, basal metabolic rate was reset at a decreased level during the first 10 days with no relationship to the dietary energy intake or to body temperature (Haruna et al., 1994). No further change occurred during the next 10 days.

Bed rest increases faecal and urinary zinc excretion, leading to decreased zinc balance, whilst copper balance is unchanged (Krebs et al., 1993). Nitrogen excretion is also increased. Fluoride supplementation increases the zinc and nitrogen balance and increases bone formation (Krebs et al., 1988), offering one potential method of preventing osteoporosis during prolonged bed rest. Negative calcium balance is another consequence of bed rest, manifested in elevated urine and faecal calcium (LeBlanc et al., 1995). In patients with complete spinal cord injury, nitrogen and calcium excretion rise to levels exceeding those predicted by immobilisation alone (Kearns et al., 1992).

Immune system

Schmitt et al. (1996) found that 4 weeks of bed rest in six subjects led to a significant decrease in interleukin-2 (IL-2) secretion from T lymphocytes. They also studied two subjects over 113 days, both of whom showed decreased IL-2 receptor expression in peripheral blood mononuclear cells, although only one showed a decrease in IL-2 production. Under the same conditions, IL-1 production was increased in both subjects. Increased IL-1 production could contribute to the bone mineral loss encountered during bed rest, whilst decreased IL-2 secretion could play a role in the appearance of infectious diseases often seen in immobile patients.

Osteoporosis

Mechanical forces are important in maintaining bone mass, and immobilisation is associated with loss of bone mass, osteopaenia, and osteoporosis with an increased risk of fractures (Uebelhart et al., 1995). Permanently impaired mobility leads to a four- to five-fold risk of hip fracture (Wickham et al., 1989; Boyce & Vessey, 1988). Histomorphometric and biochemical analysis have shown that immobilisation leads to an uncoupling between bone formation and resorption, with a marked increase in resorption parameters such as the fasting urinary hydroxyproline/creatinine ratio (van der Wiel et al., 1991). Healthy bed-rested subjects show an increase in the number of osteoclasts in trabecular bone (Chappard et al., 1991). In acute spinal cord injury the main finding soon after onset is decreased osteoblastic activity associated with a marked increase in bone degradation. This can result in the development of a rapid and severe osteoporosis only seen in the paralysed part of the body, and the biosynthesis of a structurally modified bone matrix which is unable to sustain normal mechanical stress. In this situation, the risk of lower extremity fractures is dramatically increased (Ingram et al., 1989). There is also an increased rate of collagen synthesis but a greater increase in collagen degradation (Claus-Walker, 1980; Rodriguez et al., 1989), which further predisposes the patient to osteoporosis. The excretion of galactosyl hydroxylysine, a breakdown product of bone collagen, increases after injury, reaches a peak between 3 and 6 months, and then gradually declines to reach normal ranges by 1 year after injury (Rodriguez et al., 1989).

Intense physical training has been shown to increase bone mineral content and cortical area (Margulies et al., 1986; Woo et al., 1981) and exercise is generally regarded as being important in preventing osteoporosis (e.g., Wickham et al., 1989; Law et al., 1991; Royal College of Physicians Working Party, 1991). However, in healthy young men, exercise without weight-bearing (e.g., 4 hours of cycling on a bicycle ergometer when sitting or supine) does not counteract the loss of bone seen during bed rest, whereas quiet standing for 3 of 24 hours does (Issekutz et al., 1966; Schoutens et al., 1989). Hormone replacement, the avoidance of smoking and dietary calcium intake appear to be of secondary importance to the level of weight-bearing physical activity in the prevention of osteoporotic hip fracture (Law et al., 1991). The importance of weight-bearing exercise, or even of passive standing in a standing frame or tilt-table, to prevent osteoporosis in the context of neurological disablement would thus seem clear.

Immobilisation hypercalcaemia

Immobilisation hypercalcaemia, first described by Albright in 1941, is an uncommon but important condition associated with both osteoporosis and nephrolithiasis. It is most commonly seen in children and adolescents, particularly in those with higher neurological levels of injury, complete injuries, and prolonged immobilisation (Lawrence et al., 1973; Tori & Hill, 1978; Maynard, 1986). The aetiology remains unclear, but it is thought to result from normal levels of parathyroid hormone acting with increased activity in the abnormal environment of immobilised bone. Gallacher et al. (1990) found an association with sepsis and postulated that cytokine release may be a factor. Failure of conventional therapy (vigorous hydration, diuretics, prednisolone) warrants a trial of newer agents, which include calcitonin (Kaul & Sockalosky, 1995), etidronate, and pamidronate (Gallacher et al., 1990).

EXERCISE TRAINING

Individuals who lead a sedentary lifestyle develop reduced levels of cardiorespiratory fitness (Seigel et al., 1970) because the maintenance of aerobic fitness depends upon the continuing stimulus of physical activity on cardiorespiratory function and the oxygen-carrying capacity of the blood. The immobility of bed rest in normal healthy subjects produces profound changes in aerobic capacity, fitness, and endurance (Convertino, 1997), and these changes are also seen in chronic neurological disability resulting from stroke (Potempa et al., 1995), multiple sclerosis (Petajan et al., 1996), or head injury (Jankowski & Sullivan,

1990). They are likely to contribute to the reduction of functional performance, mood, and quality of life that result from illness, and the fatiguability and reduced work tolerance may impair patients' participation in rehabilitation (Sullivan et al., 1990).

An aerobic exercise training programme has been shown to improve cardiorespiratory fitness and aerobic capacity in such individuals (Santiago et al., 1993). Exercise needs to be performed for a minimum of 20 minutes three times a week working at a level of about 70–80% of the maximum heart rate to produce an improvement in cardiorespiratory function. There may be other benefits, including improvement in insulin sensitivity and in lipid profiles in the blood, a general sense of well-being and a greater level of functional independence seen in, for example, the 12 subjects with post polio syndrome subjected to 6 weeks of a high-intensity resistance exercise programme (Einarsson, 1991). Other aspects of the deconditioning syndrome associated with immobility can be manipulated by exercise training, including the maintenance of plasma and red cell volumes and of a positive water balance (Greenleaf, 1997). Aerobic training leads to improved aerobic capacity, muscle strength, and daily functional activities in patients with spinal cord injury (Pentland, 1993) and multiple sclerosis (Petajan et al., 1996). More than 6 months post stroke, Potempa et al. (1995) showed that cycle ergometer training for 10 weeks produced significant improvements in maximal oxygen consumption, workload, and exercise time. After head injury, aerobic training improves fitness prospectively (Jankowski & Sullivan, 1990; Hunter et al., 1990; Wolman et al., 1994); in a retrospective study it was associated with improved mood and aspects of health status without changing measures of disability and handicap (Gordon et al., 1998).

The exact methods of exercise appropriate to each patient largely remain to be defined. For example, treadmill or bicycle exercising is probably preferred to stair climbing in obese subjects (Hunter et al., 1990). Some neurological patients may be unable to perform continuous repetitive movements of either the arms or legs, and arm cranking or wheelchair ergometry (Martel et al., 1991) or an exercise bicycle with a facility to work either the unaffected upper and/or lower limbs may be required. If there is preservation of upper limb function in patients with paraplegia, then they may be able to participate in activities such as callisthenics, weight-training, and swimming, aimed at augmenting upper body strength (Davis & Glaser, 1990). However, the muscle mass available to be trained is unlikely to be sufficient to lead to any improvement in cardiovascular fitness, most of the potential benefit being in the fostering of independent wheelchair propulsion and self-care activities (Hoffman, 1986). In other patients the nature of their disability may completely preclude the sustained exercise required to obtain fitness; alternatively, it may be possible to exercise the affected limbs but there is at least a theoretical risk of increasing spasticity, and thus decreasing function of the limbs.

Functional electrical stimulation (FES), in which tetanic muscular contractions of controlled intensity are evoked in paralysed muscles, can be used to induce isometric resistance exercise or to effect leg cycling with a cycle ergometer (Davis & Glaser,

1990). FES-induced cycle ergometry increases left ventricular mass in quadriplegics (Nash et al., 1991), and may reduce bone demineralisation. Complications of the technique include aggravation of muscle spasms, overheating due to disturbed thermoregulation and dangerous changes in blood pressure. Further research is needed to assess its suitability as an effective form of exercise.

PRESSURE SORES

Pressure sores, first described in Egyptian mummies (Thomson-Rowling, 1961), are defined as localised areas of tissue damage resulting either from direct pressure on the skin causing pressure ischaemia or from shearing forces causing mechanical stress to the tissues (Vohra & McCollum, 1994). Almost all pressure sores start during a period of acute illness or trauma (Bliss, 1998). A national survey of pressure sores revealed an in-patient prevalence of 6.7% (David et al., 1985), although in individual units this may reach 66% (Livesley, 1987). Elderly people are particularly susceptible, with 70% of all pressure sores occurring in patients aged over 70 years (Young & Dobrzanski, 1992). In younger patients there is usually an underlying neurological disorder, particularly multiple sclerosis, cerebral palsy, and spinal cord lesions. Sores develop in approximately 25% of wheelchair users (Barbenel, 1991). The most common sites are the sacrum (43%), greater trochanter (12%), heel (11%), ischial tuberosities (5%), and lateral malleolus (6%) (Petersen, 1976) (Figure 15.1). The development of pressure sores is a complex process, and it is usual to consider the causative factors as extrinsic or intrinsic (Clarke, 1997). The classification system of the National Pressure Ulcer Advisory Panel (1989) of the USA is now widely accepted as a standard (Table 15.1).

Causative factors: extrinsic.   Pressure over bony prominences might be expected to be the main extrinsic cause of pressure sores, but this is only part of the story. It is impossible to apply uniaxial pressure to tissue without producing tissue deformation, distortion, or shear forces (Bader, 1990). It is this deformation which produces distortion of the cross-section of the capillaries, which in turn decreases the blood flow. Tissue deforms under its own weight at rest in a gravitational field unless immersed in a liquid of the same density as the tissue. Thus a deep sea diver can spend up to 2 or 3 hours with a pressure of up to 2025 mmHg on the skin and yet does not develop pressure

sores, probably because there is no deformation of the tissue (Neumark et al., 1981).

Pressure is, however, one of the most important causative factors. In ordinary circumstances, when sitting or in bed, pressure on the skin may be as high as 150 mmHg (Lindan et al., 1965), whilst the capillary pressure is only about 12–33 mmHg (Houle, 1969; Siegel et al., 1973), and may be reduced further in debilitated patients. About 70–80% of externally applied pressure reaches the subcutaneous tissues (Kosiak, 1961), but a bony prominence pressure may be three to five times higher internally than at the skin surface (Le et al., 1984). This explains the observation that deep sores start near the bone. Very low external pressures are capable of decreasing capillary blood flow: Localised pressure of about 10 mmHg reduces forearm skin blood flow in normals to about one-third of the non-load value (Holloway et al., 1976). The greater the pressure, the less time is needed for tissue necrosis due to impaired capillary perfusion. Normal fit people adjust their posture to avoid sustained pressure. Measurement over the bony prominences of 980 seated subjects showed a tolerance curve with an inverse relation between pressure and duration (Barbenel, 1991). The threshold for pressure in healthy humans has been established to be 60 mmHg for 1 hour before tissue damage occurs. Intermittent relief of pressures as high as 240 mmHg may prevent ischaemic damage (Brooks & Duncan, 1940). Constant application of 70 mmHg for 2 hours or more produces irreversible change (Dinsdale, 1974), but this period may be very much less in illness. The high prevalence of pressure sores in tissue over the sacrum is associated with higher deep tissue pressure and lower deep microvascular flows at a given local skin pressure, as measured by laser Doppler fluxmetry (Schubert & Fagrell, 1989). In addition to the effect of pressure causing capillary occlusion, it can also impair the lymphatic drainage of the subcutaneous tissues (Barbenel, 1991).

Shear forces (Lowthian, 1970; Cochrane & Slater, 1973; Dinsdale, 1974; Stark, 1977), friction (Naylor, 1955; Sulzberger et al., 1966; Dinsdale, 1974), and abrasions are also important extrinsic factors. Shear can decrease by 50% the amount of pressure needed to cause a pressure sore (Reichel, 1958). Shearing pressures depend on one area of the skin being fixed whilst movement of the underlying tissues takes place. For instance, with the sacral skin area fixed, the shearing forces in the deep part of the superficial fascia lead to stretching and distortion of the blood vessels, and thus thrombosis, ischaemia, and necrosis (Reichel, 1958). In this case the ulceration starts below the surface of the skin. Shear is important when heavily dependent patients have to be transferred from bed to chair, chair to commode, or back into bed, and when patients are badly positioned so that they slip down the chair or bed. Patients more often develop sores when the head of the bed is raised (Reichel, 1958). Friction also occurs when the skin moves across a surface, such as when a patient is pulled across a bed. This results in damage to the stratum corneum, which may produce superficial ulceration (Allman, 1989). The posture adopted by wheelchair users may also affect shear force at the body–seat interface. For example, full body tilt to approximately 25 degrees reduces the

Table 15.1. Classification of pressure sores (National Pressure Ulcer Advisory Panel, 1989)

Stage I	Non-blanchable erythema of the intact skin. This is a red or violaceous area that does not blanch when pressed, indicating that blood has escaped from capillaries into the interstitial tissues.
Stage II	Partial thickness skin loss. The skin surface is broken resulting in an abrasion or shallow crater.
Stage III	Full thickness skin loss and extension into subcutaneous fat but not through underlying fascia.
Stage IV	Extensive destruction involving damage to muscle, bone, or tendon.

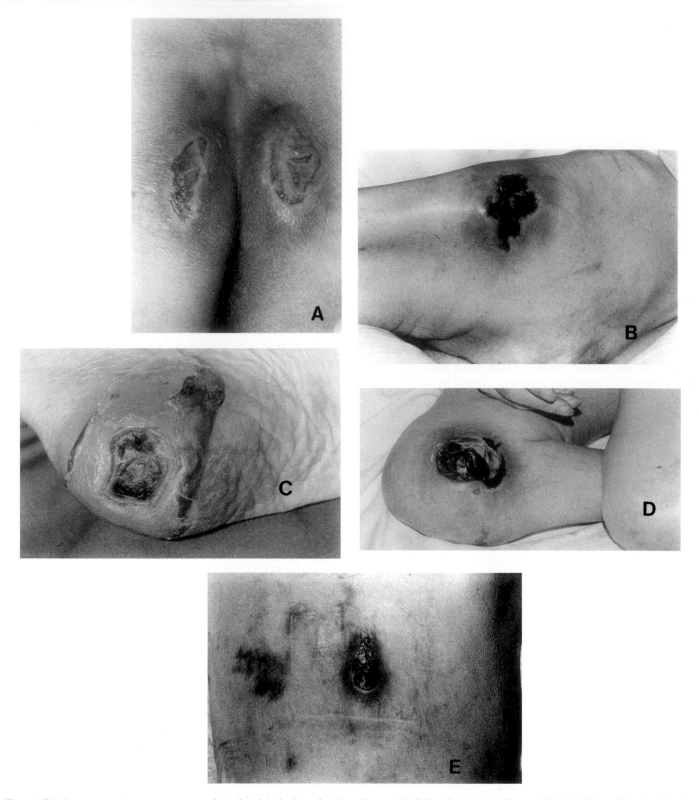

Figure 15.1. Pressure sores may occur at many sites other than the buttocks (A) and sacrum, including the greater trochanter (B), heel (C), medial epicondyle (D), and thoracic spine (E).

surface shear force to near zero, whilst a backrest-only recline of 20 degrees causes a 25% increase in this force (Hobson, 1992). Maintaining the knees at a right angle is also important: Colin (1997) showed that ischial transcutaneous oxygen tensions measured in 20 spinal cord injured patients were reduced from 28.3 ± 23.9 to 21.7 ± 21.3 mmHg by raising the wheelchair foot rest 8 cm.

Causative factors: intrinsic. Acute illness is the most important precipitating factor causing tissue necrosis due to pressure (Bliss, 1998). Healthy patients, even if they are very immobile, rarely develop pressure sores. Acute sepsis or trauma impairs capillary vasodilatation and reactive hyperaemia, thus reducing the ability of the tissues to withstand pressure ischaemia. Pressure injuries due to peripheral circulatory failure are part of multi-organ failure in acute illness. They most commonly affect susceptible individuals in whom the microcirculation is abnormal due to vascular or neurological disease, diabetes, age, or chronic illness. Failure of the peripheral circulation is exacerbated by oxygen desaturation and hypotension which increase the effects of tissue deformability due to pressure (Bader, 1990).

Older patients are more susceptible to pressure sores due to changes in ageing skin, loss of subcutaneous tissue, reduced pain perception, decreased cell mediated immunity and slower wound healing (Levine et al., 1989). As skin ages it shows diminished elasticity, attenuated microvasculature, and a slowing down in collagen synthesis reducing the collagen-elastin matrix in the dermis. All of these factors increase the effect of pressure and shear stress in creating pressure necrosis. Bennett et al. (1981) found that blood flow over the ischial tuberosities was occluded in none of the healthy young males tested under a pressure of 120 mmHg, whereas occlusion occurred with pressures as low as 20 mmHg in elderly men.

Any cause of immobility, including psychiatric or neurological disease, excessive sedation, pain, and hip fracture, increases the risk of pressure sores (Levine & Simpson, 1989; Low, 1990). In neurological disease, the nature of the underlying disorder may be important. Patients with multiple sclerosis are at high risk due in part to their sensory deficits, incontinence, cognitive impairment, and abnormalities of autonomic control of the microvasculature. Elderly stroke patients are another high risk group, especially as sensation over the pressure areas may be impaired (Berlowitz & Wilking, 1989). By contrast, patients with motor neurone disease have a low incidence of pressure sores, even in the terminal stages (Furukawa & Toyokura, 1976), probably due to their lack of sensory, or autonomic involvement. Watanabe et al. (1987) speculate that an amorphous, fine granular material on electron microscopy in the ground substance of the dermis may act to absorb pressure, thereby preventing occlusion of the blood vessels. In spinal cord injury, there is growing evidence that the high susceptibility to pressure sores is due to the interactive effects of prolonged immobilisation and injury-related autonomic dysfunction associated with reduced tissue perfusion. Paraplegic patients with flaccid paralysis and impairment of spinal reflexes have been shown to have

higher incidences of pressure sores than less mobile quadriplegic patients with spastic paralysis and intact reflexes (Constantian & Jackson, 1980). The risk of pressure sore development increases with the length of time immobilised (Exton-Smith & Sherwin, 1961; Curry & Casady, 1992). To determine whether tissue oxygenation at the sacrum is reduced in spinal cord injury, Mawson et al. (1993a) compared transcutaneous oxygen tension levels in 21 injured subjects and 11 able-bodied controls. Oxygen tension levels were significantly lower in the spinal cord injured group, in whom there was also an association between the presence of a pressure sore and low transcutaneous oxygen tension. The increased degradation of skin collagen in these patients—reflected by a raised urinary excretion of glucosylgalactosyl hydroxylysine, a breakdown product of skin rather than bone collagen—increases the risk of pressure sores (Rodriguez et al., 1989).

The association between the protein depletion of malnutrition (Bergstrom & Braden, 1992), and hypoalbuminaemia and pressure sores (Berlowitz & Wilking, 1989), may be because malnourished patients are more likely to develop multi-organ failure including peripheral circulatory failure with acute sepsis or trauma. However it may be more important to the healing than the cause of sores. In the presence of pressure sores, institutionalised patients with multiple sclerosis have increased requirements for specific nutrients including zinc and iron (Williams et al., 1988). The presence of an isolated anaemia, and thus the need for transfusion, seems relatively unimportant to wound healing, which may be normal even with haematocrits as low as 20% (Zederfeldt, 1957; Trueblood et al., 1969; Jensen et al., 1986). Chronic inflammation and infection due to the pressure sore itself may aggravate hypoproteinaemia and anaemia. This pressure sore anaemia is often resistant to treatment with iron and red cell transfusion, but responds to recombinant human erythropoietin (Turba et al., 1992).

Thin patients with reduced body weight develop higher pressures over bony prominences than do average weight or obese people (Garber & Krouskop, 1982). On the other hand, obese people also develop sores. This may be partly because the poorer blood supply to fat makes it vulnerable to damage from external forces, but more important is the wide spread capillary distortion which occurs in fatty tissues which are rendered soft and flabby by dehydration or hypotension in acute illness. In the obese patient the sore is therefore more likely to be a result of shearing forces, though superficial ulceration is also seen where moisture accumulates in skin folds producing maceration.

Several other intrinsic factors are likely to play a part in pressure sore development. Skin maceration follows contamination by urine, faeces, and food spillage (Low, 1990), and hence incontinent patients are at risk of sores (Moolten, 1972), particularly in the pelvic area (Lowthian, 1976; Reuler & Cooney, 1981). A rise in skin temperature increases the metabolic rate (Brown & Brenglemann, 1965) which may further compromise the tissues, especially in the presence of anoxia. Cushions and mattresses are designed to retain heat, raising skin temperature and exacerbating ischaemia, an effect which may persist for over an hour after relief from pressure (Finestone et al., 1991). Hypotension from any cause is a risk factor—the pressure needed to occlude capillary blood flow in tissues over the bony prominences is lower in hypotension. This is shown by the correlation between a low resting skin blood cell flux on laser Doppler fluxmetry and low mean blood pressures (Schubert, 1991). Other factors contributing to skin ulceration include cardiovascular and peripheral vascular disease, lung disease, anaemia, lymphopaenia, oedema, contractures, diabetes mellitus, and smoking (Allman et al., 1995; Niazi et al., 1997).

Complications. Pressure sores may be complicated by infection, dehydration, electrolyte imbalance, and malnutrition (Berlowitz & Wilking, 1989). Sepsis due to pressure sores exacerbates peripheral circulatory failure and carries a significant mortality (Allman et al., 1986). The presence of pressure sores in spinal cord injured patients increases the reduction in serum 25(OH)-vitamin D seen in this group (Zhou et al., 1993). Pressure sore carcinoma is a late, rare event with a high metastatic rate and a very poor prognosis (Dumurgier et al., 1991). Histology shows squamous cells, and treatment is usually with surgery and adjuvant radiotherapy. Renal amyloid, which once caused 10–20% of deaths late after spinal injury complicated by chronic pressure sores (Baker et al., 1984), is now seldom seen.

Prevention. A working knowledge of these extrinsic and intrinsic risk factors should be made available to all members of a multidisciplinary team, and the importance of illness precipitating tissue injury emphasised. The need for increased bed rest and local measures to relieve pressure, such as an alternating pressure mattress overlay (Gebhardt et al., 1996) from the moment of onset of acute illness or trauma, including a pressure sore itself, surgery, or invasive investigations, needs to be emphasised to carers and patients. Enhanced pressure relief should be continued until the wound is healed and/or the patient has regained his normal state of health and mobility.

More chronic pressure care in healthy wheelchair bound patients may be more usefully carried out by a single individual, whose appointment highlights the need to prevent sores in a given population (Dowding, 1983) and who can provide patient/carer education. Garber et al. (1996) found that spinal cord injured individuals who wait longer to come to a clinic present with more severe sores, and they suggest that educational programmes should emphasise immediate visits to a physician on detecting a pressure sore. The establishment of a specific pressure clinic, measuring interface pressures and using thermography to assess blood flow to the skin, led to a reduction of over 50% in the incidence of and admission rates due to sores in a spinal unit (Dover et al., 1992). Prevention can be assisted by assessing the knowledge and caring of caregivers, and intervening where appropriate (Olshansky, 1994). A staff educational programme reduced the incidence of pressure sores in elderly hospitalised patients by as much as 65% (Moody et al., 1988). High risk patients can be identified using a number of established rating scales (e.g., Barrett, 1988), and a new scale has been described for spinal patients which shows a significant improvement in quantifying risk (Salzberg et al., 1996). Kiernan

(1998) argues that risk management should go beyond the use of a scale to include systems of risk-related reporting and the appropriate implementation of effective interventions. Rowe and Barer (1995) describe a successful regional specialty policy for pressure sores.

Important general measures in preventing pressure sores include proper positioning, good lifting technique to prevent patients being dragged, frequent weight shifts, care of body fluids, and frequent skin inspections. Particulate matter in the bed predisposes to skin breakdown and should be removed. The prone position has larger low-pressure areas and smaller high-pressure areas (Lindan et al., 1965) and should be encouraged at night (Vohra & McCollum, 1994). Shearing forces are reduced by avoiding raising the head of the bed, proper seating, and the use of sheep skin, which also effectively absorbs moisture (Denne, 1979). The appropriate treatment of spastic hypertonus (see Chapter 12) and contractures may be required to prevent the exposure of bony prominences to excessive pressure. In spinal cord injured patients, pressure sore recurrence rates are higher in those who smoke or who have uncontrolled diabetes or cardiovascular disease (Niazi et al., 1997), all of which are amenable to intervention (Viehbeck et al., 1995).

The complete relief of pressure, especially over bony prominences, at short intervals of less than 2 hours, is crucial. This is often accomplished by manual turning. Alternatively, a variety of pressure reducing and relieving devices and systems have become available. These include mattress overlays using foam, sheepskin, gel, and air products. Of the pressure relieving beds, fluidising systems are the most consistent at reducing pressure over the bony high points (Allman et al., 1987; Wild, 1991). A recent study in an intensive care setting demonstrated the clinical utility and cost-effectiveness of low air loss beds in the prevention of sores (Inman et al., 1993). In spinal patients undergoing surgery for sacral pressure sores, the use of a ROHO air mattress post-operatively led to a huge reduction in recurrence rate (Kato et al., 1998). In this same group of patients, airfilled wheelchair cushions reduce pressures at the ischial tuberosities (Bar, 1991), whilst armrests can significantly reduce seat forces by carrying some of the body weight (Gilsdorf et al., 1991). Contoured cushions are more effective than flat foam cushions in reducing interface pressure (Brienza & Karg, 1998). The insertion of carbon fibre pads into the sites of previously closed pressure sores or threatened sores achieves soft tissue augmentation and reduces the liability to sore development (Minns & Sutton, 1991). Functional electrical stimulation prevents pressure sores in paraplegic patients by increasing cutaneous blood flow and inducing shape changes in the buttocks (Levine et al., 1990; Ferguson et al., 1992; Mawson et al., 1993b).

Treatment. Local treatment for sores confined to the dermis or subcutaneous fat may be confined to surgical or biochemical wound debridement to promote granulation, and the frequent application of a variety of topical dressings and agents, all of which themselves promote turning and the relief of pressure. A wide variety of such applications is marketed, usually with little evidence of efficacy (Knight, 1988). Maggot therapy is enjoying a rennaissance, backed up by clinical trials (Sherman et al., 1995). Pressure sore healing may also be promoted by non-thermal pulsed electromagnetic energy (Salzberg et al., 1995), ultrasound and ultraviolet-C (Nussbaum et al., 1994). Co-existent infection with methicillin resistant Staphylococcus aureus, present in 2% of pressure sores after spinal cord injury, is best treated with povidine-iodine preparations (Michel & Zach, 1997). More extensive or deeper sores, especially those accompanied by sepsis and osteomyelitis, will often require surgical intervention to excise the ulcer, bony prominences, or infected bone, and resurface the defect by skin grafting or the use of a myocutaneous flap (Kuhn et al., 1992). The initial results with muscle flaps are good, but there is a high recurrence rate of pressure necrosis (Disa et al., 1992). Thigh flap procedures may be complicated by heterotopic ossification (Rubayi et al., 1992). There is evidence that non-healing after a myocutaneous flap procedure may be reversed by the application of a range of motion programme that applies tension (Goldstein et al., 1996). Recalcitrant ischial and trochanteric pressure sores in spinal patients may be amenable to the use of a rectus abdominus myocutaneous flap (Kierney et al., 1998). Occasionally amputation or even hemicorporectomy may be required. Magnetic resonance imaging is helpful in determining the depth and extent of soft tissue involvement underlying pressure sores, including underlying fluid collections, heterotopic bone, and adjacent bone marrow oedema, and it is therefore useful in planning proper therapy (Hencey et al., 1996). For a more extensive discussion of these topics than is possible here, the reader is referred elsewhere (e.g., Lee, 1997).

NUTRITION

Neurological disorders frequently result in problems of nutrition for a variety of reasons including disordered swallowing, physical difficulties with feeding, cognitive or behavioural disturbances, autonomic disturbances, or increased nutritional demands. Some of the nutritional problems may be a result of the neurological disorder whilst others are a consequence of drug therapy or insufficient attendant time. Changes in mental state, particularly after traumatic brain injury and stroke, may alter patients' ability to remember how to eat (apraxia) and may interfere with their response to feelings of hunger, which may also contribute to poor nutritional status (Consultant Dietitians in Health Care Facilities 1994). Malnutrition is under-recognised in neurological patients: Newmark et al. (1981) found evidence of malnutrition in 56% of patients undergoing neurological rehabilitation for stroke, spinal cord injury, degenerative neurological disease, and peripheral neuropathy.

Whilst the incidence of dysphagia soon after acute stroke is high (see Chapter 25) and there may be early difficulties due to aspiration and poor fluid intake, in the majority of patients the swallowing problems resolve within 2 weeks (Gordon et al., 1987), and the implications for nutrition are minor. Persistence of dysphagia after brain stem or bilateral hemisphere damage—for example after head injury (Weinstein, 1983)—and

its development in the course of motor neurone disease or Parkinson's disease may, however, have significant nutritional consequences. Sitzmann (1990) found that in patients admitted with dysphagia due to neurological dysfunction, 80% showed dysphagia-induced starvation as evidenced by weight loss and abnormal anthropometric examination, and over 70% showed visceral protein depletion. Such patients require nutritional support, either through adopting a special dysphagia diet (Pardoe, 1993), or through alternative methods of feeding (see later).

Nutritional requirements may be normal—for example, in the profoundly impaired, non-ambulatory, institutionalised youths studied by Van Calcar et al. (1989)—with only zinc and calcium needs being decreased. By contrast, the nutritional demands of Huntington's disease patients are increased, for reasons that are unclear (Sandberg et al., 1981). Traumatic brain injury leads to an immediate profound increase in protein and calorie catabolic rate (Rapp et al., 1983; Clifton et al., 1986; Gaddisseux et al., 1984), with an increase in mean nitrogen excretion and a negative nitrogen balance (Bruder et al., 1991). This may explain why many patients are so emaciated on transfer to rehabilitation. Resting metabolic expenditure may be 250% of normal, and patients may require 4500 kcal per 24 hours and protein replacements of 2.2 g/kg/day to maintain positive nitrogen balance (Clifton et al., 1986; Twyman et al., 1985). In the first 72 hours after injury, every effort should be made to provide aggressive nutritional support (Twyman, 1997). This may best be provided by total parenteral nutrition (TPN), particularly when there is persisting paralytic ileus or gastrointestinal intolerance to a degree precluding enteral feeding. The increased mean energy expenditure persists for several weeks after the injury: Bruder et al. (1991) found that the energy expenditure of unsedated, spontaneously breathing, severely brain-injured patients was still elevated at 18 days. Whilst these increased requirements seem to be related to severity of the brain damage, this does not seem to be linear. Robertson et al. (1984) found that those with a Glasgow Coma Scale (GCS) of 4–5 had the highest energy expenditure, those with a GCS of 6–7 had the lowest whilst those with a GCS of 8 or more had an intermediate expenditure. Sometimes energy requirements increased during neurological improvement over the 28-day study period. High energy expenditure is associated with abnormal motor activity, including muscle rigidity, motor tremor, and decerebrate or decorticate posture (Fruin et al., 1986).

There is now compelling evidence that malnourishment in rehabilitation patients significantly impairs outcome. Finestone et al. (1995, 1996) studied 49 consecutive stroke patients and found that 49% were malnourished on admission to a rehabilitation unit. Malnourishment was associated with both prolonged length of stay and worse functional outcome as measured by the Modified Barthel Index. In another study of stroke patients, malnourished patients showed a higher incidence of sepsis and pressure sores, a lower Barthel Index at 30 days, and a greater risk of mortality (Davalos et al., 1996). Hypoalbuminaemia is a predictor of prolonged length of stay in spinal injured (Burr et al., 1993) and elderly stroke rehabilitation patients (Aptaker et al., 1994). Furthermore, proper nutritional support can assist recovery. In their study of patients with severe head injury, Young et al. (1987) found a quicker early recovery in GCS scores and better Glasgow Outcome Scale scores at 3 months in 23 patients prospectively randomised in the acute stage to TPN compared with 28 patients randomised to enteral nutrition. The latter form of nutrition may have been inadequate in providing protein and energy intake due to impaired gastric emptying (Ott et al., 1991). There is even evidence that nutritional support given late in the rehabilitation process may be beneficial. In dysphagic stroke patients with recurrent aspiration pneumonia and/or nasogastric tube displacement, whose recovery was poor at 4–6 months, the initiation of gastrostomy feeding improved weight, albumin, and response to physiotherapy (Allison et al., 1992).

Maintenance of good nutritional status can be difficult in the long term. Oral feeding can be extremely slow and hazardous. For instance, Gisel and Patrick (1988) found that children with cerebral palsy took up to 12 times longer to chew and swallow pureed food, and up to 15 times longer for solid food, than did normal children. They also noted that prolonged meal times did not compensate for the severity of the feeding impairment. Nasogastric tube insertion is the traditional route of enteral feeding, but it is slow—taking about 3 hours a day of attendant time to achieve good levels of nutrition—aesthetically unpleasing, and easily displaced, especially by confused patients. It may cause inhibition of oral feeding, aspiration, oesophageal ulceration, and sinusitis. These complications are not reduced by transpyloric passage of the tube (Spain et al., 1995). In a study comparing nasogastric and gastrostomy feeding after acute dysphagic stroke, patients fed via the nasogastric route received a significantly smaller proportion of their prescribed feed and were less well nourished at 6 weeks (Norton et al., 1996). In addition there can be difficulties in ensuring that the nasogastric tube is correctly positioned in the stomach (Biggart et al., 1987), and clinical tests to determine correct placement can be unreliable unless the procedure is carried out by an experienced practitioner. Gordon (1981) has suggested that misplacement is rare provided there is at least 50 cm of tube length past the nostril, there is no evidence of coiling on visual inspection of the oropharynx or by palpation, that air insufflation through the tube can be carried out without resistance, that auscultation of the abdomen during insufflation demonstrates bubbling, that water infused through the tube passes without difficulty, and that some of it can be retrieved through the tube. It is essential that these tests are used in the set order.

Because of these difficulties, there has been great interest in gastrostomy feeding, especially using fine-bore percutaneous endoscopic gastrostomy (PEG) tube insertion. With this method of feeding most patients maintain or regain their weight (Wicks et al., 1992) and there is good acceptance by patient and family (Llaneza et al., 1988). This method is generally more acceptable and has fewer complications than surgical gastrostomy (Himal & Schumacher, 1987; Grant, 1988; Ho et al., 1988; Wollman et al., 1995). Peters & Westaby (1994) report a rate of only 1–4% for

major complications. There is a lower incidence of aspiration, bleeding, pneumonia, wound infection, complications requiring surgical intervention, and mortality than surgical gastrostomy. There is a high success rate of PEG placement: Larson et al. (1987) in a study of 314 consecutive PEG procedures were able to place the tube in 95% of cases. The reasons for the failures were either medical complications such as cancer at the potential site of gastrostomy placement, aspiration or laryngospasm during the procedure, or inability to oppose the anterior gastric wall to the abdominal wall or to get the gastrostomy tube into the stomach. They had an overall procedure-related complication rate of 3% and a mortality rate of 1%. The major complications included gastric perforation (all recovered eventually), gastric bleeding, or haematoma formation. One of the major advantages of PEG is that if the patient recovers the ability to swallow, the tube can be easily removed without a permanent gastrocutaneous fistula developing and without the need for surgical correction.

Recent studies have confirmed the suitability of PEG feeding for patients undergoing neurological rehabilitation. Fertl et al. (1998) reviewed 28 patients fed by PEG on a neurorehabilitation unit and found no life-threatening complications during a total observation period of 5172 days. Minor complications were observed in 12 patients in the first 2 weeks after insertion and in 5 patients thereafter, and the nutritional status stabilised in all subjects. Annoni et al. (1998) report the cases of six patients with severe chronic neurological disability and swallowing difficulties due to traumatic brain injury, anoxia and multiple sclerosis. Nutritional supplementation via PEG led to a decrease in intercurrent medical complications, especially pressure sores, and in some patients there was an improvement in oropharyngeal and psychomotor functions. The advantages of PEG over nasogastric feeding on oropharyngeal function may be related to the absence of pharyngeal irritation, and its role in overall recovery could be due to an increase in social activities, a reduction in intercurrent infection, a better rehabilitation schedule and a long-term effect on brain function due to better nutritional support. PEG is a safe, comfortable and easily managed method of nutritional support in patients with spinal cord injury (Frost et al., 1995) and severe cerebral injury (Akkersdijk et al., 1998).

Some authors have challenged the vogue for endoscopic placement of gastrostomies, arguing that percutaneous, radiologically guided gastrostomy is safer, simpler, and cheaper to perform (Bodley & Banerjee, 1995; Wollman et al., 1995; Murphy et al., 1996). An analysis of 5752 gastrostomies and a review of the literature involving a further 5680 cases concluded that the percutaneous radiological method is significantly safer and more successful than the endoscopic route (Wollman et al., 1995). The success rate of the radiological method is 99.2% and it has a lower complication rate than endoscopic gastrostomy (Murphy et al., 1996). It requires minimal sedation and is therefore more suitable for patients who are prone to aspiration. Visualisation of the colon radiologically during the procedure reduces the risk of causing inadvertent colonic perforation when it is interposed between the stomach and anterior abdominal wall. Infection at the tube site is less common with the radiological method as the tube is introduced through the surgically scrubbed anterior abdominal wall rather than the contaminated oral cavity (Nemcek & Vogelzang, 1994).

With enteral feeding there is the opportunity to feed either continually or intermittently (bolus feeding). Nutrient absorption and protein balance are the same in each method (Heymsfield et al., 1987). The advantages of bolus feeding (Perkins, 1985) are that it allows other medication to be given enterally without the problems of reaction with the feed (see later), greater mobility of the patient, and easier aspiration of gastric contents to determine absorption of the food. It is cheaper than an enteral pump and more physiological since it stimulates the normal feeding pattern. Bolus feeding at a high infusion rate over 8–16 hours per day may be helpful in the transition from enteral feeding to oral diet, with enteral feeds given at night and oral diet ingested during the day (Ideno, 1993). The disadvantages, compared to continuous feeding, are that it is labour intensive and may be associated with delayed gastric emptying and increased risk of aspiration pneumonia; initial energy and protein intakes are reduced because of the need for low initial concentration and rate of feeding, correct volume delivery is not as reliable, and it is more often associated with bloating and diarrhoea. The advantage of continuous feeding is that it gives a greater opportunity to maintain a good intake of food which might be more difficult with bolus feeding. There is some empirical evidence (Parathyras & Kassak, 1983) that aspiration into the lungs is less common with continuous feeding than with the bolus method. In the latter, elevating the head to over 30 degrees during feeding and for at least 1 hour after may reduce the aspiration risk.

Enteral feeding intolerance sometimes accompanied by aspiration may occur. An ileus, predominantly involving the stomach and colon (Silen & Skillman, 1976), may make it necessary to site the tube in the duodenum to maintain a good nutritional intake. Gastroparesis, seen in patients after severe traumatic brain injury, can be treated with the novel prokinetic agent cisapride (Altmayer et al., 1996). The superior mesenteric artery syndrome, resulting from compression of the duodenum by the superior mesenteric artery against the aorta, has also been reported after severe brain injury (Pedoto et al., 1995); risk factors include acute weight loss, prolonged recumbency, and spasticity. After gastric decompression, symptoms often resolve, allowing weight gain. Diarrhoea may be due to hyperosmolality of the feed, concomitant antibiotics, a high fat intake, or a low vitamin A content of the feed (Gottschlich et al., 1988).

One difficulty of enteral feeding, often unrecognised, is the effect of the enteral product on absorption of certain drugs, especially when they are mixed with the enteral feed. This has been studied by Holtz et al. (1987) who found that theophylline increased the osmolality of the feed, there was a wide variation in phenytoin blood levels when the drug was added to the feed (corrected by using the injectable form), and methyldopa concentrations decreased by about a quarter over a 12 hour infusion time. It was therefore recommended that theophylline, phenytoin suspension and methyldopa are not added to nutritional feeds. Carbamazepine in the enteral feed produces lower trough and maximum serum concentrations when compared with a single dose administered orally after an overnight fast (Bass et al., 1989). Clamping the gastrostomy tube for 1 hour after giving a dose of phenytoin results in significantly higher serum levels of the drug than in patients given phenytoin with no interruption to their feeding (Faraji & Yu, 1998). Altmann and Cutie (1984) have studied in great detail the compatibility of certain pharmacological agents with enteral feeds. They found that a wide range of drugs were incompatible with some feeding preparations, including cough and cold remedies (Dimotane elixir, Sudafed syrup), antipsychotic agents (thioridazine), urinary tract antibacterial agents (mandelamine), and iron and potassium chloride.

There is often much pressure from the family to feed the patient orally even when there is an obvious swallowing disorder present. It can be difficult to decide whether oral feeding would be safe. Many clinicians equate the presence of a gag reflex in a patient with the ability to swallow, but its absence does not predict swallowing dysfunction or aspiration risk (Homer & Massey, 1988; Bleach, 1993; Smithard et al., 1994; Smithard, 1996). The recently validated 50 ml bedside drinking test (Gottlieb et al., 1996) has a role as a screening test in the evaluation of swallowing, but it does not detect silent aspiration (Smithard, 1995). Even bedside tests may be difficult to perform in patients with disordered mentation or communication; for example, half of the institutionalised elderly patients studied by Siebens et al. (1986) were unable to cooperate in such tests. Aspiration after a stroke is predicted by the absence of subjective complaints of swallowing difficulties, bilateral neurological signs, a weak cough, and dysphonia (Homer & Massey, 1988). Videofluoroscopy is generally regarded as an important—some would say essential—tool in the assessment of swallowing disorders. Its disadvantages include the need to transport the patient to an abnormal environment, where they may be tired if the journey is long, and where they are expected to swallow in unusual circumstances a substance which may bear little relationship to normal food. For this reason some practitioners believe that a clinical assessment by a speech and language therapist is of more value. However, when Splaingard et al. (1988) compared videofluoroscopy with bedside clinical evaluations by speech pathologists they found that the bedside evaluation alone underestimated the frequency of aspiration as seen on videofluoroscopy. It seems therefore that the ideal is a combination of the two, with the speech and language therapist using information from the videofluoroscopy to make appropriate recommendations (Logemann, 1993).

There are inherent ethical dilemmas in the enteral feeding of patients with degenerating conditions such as Huntington's disease and motor neurone disease (MND). It is important to decide whether any deterioration might be due to poor nutrition rather than the progression of the neurological disorder. There are some (Newrick & Hewer, 1984) who argue that enteral feeding prolongs distress, whilst others (Norris et al., 1985; Vellodi, 1989; Mazzini et al., 1995) feel that it improves the quality of life. Mazzini et al. (1995) studied 31 patients with MND and bulbar palsy who agreed to PEG feeding, and compared them to a control group of 35 patients who declined PEG. Mortality did not differ significantly between the two groups during the first 6 months of observation, after which it was lower in the PEG group. The body mass index improved in the PEG group and deteriorated in the control group. The authors concluded that PEG can improve survival and enhance quality of life, with greater integration into family and social life. Many patients with MND and bulbar palsy have marked cachexia but good mobility (Gawel et al., 1983), and it has been suggested (Gawel et al., 1989) that the progressive weakness in these patients may in part be due to the effect of malnutrition rather than the disease process. There is a high acceptance of and compliance with PEG feeding in patients with MND (Mathus-Vliegen et al., 1994). Gastrostomy feeding in Huntington's disease may also have a marked effect on the chorea and general comfort of the patient.

CONSTIPATION

Bowel frequency in a normal population can range from three times a day to three times a week (Connell et al., 1965). Hard impacted faeces may be present but this may not prevent daily bowel action in the form of spurious diarrhoea. Immobility or a lack of physical exercise are widely referred to in the literature as causing constipation (Donald et al., 1985; Read & Timms, 1986). However, one study of aerobic exercise in young healthy individuals showed no overall change in transit time or bowel habit (Bingham & Cummings, 1989), whilst another showed an increase in mouth to caecum transit time with exercise (Meshkinpour et al., 1989). In men between the ages of 52 and 69 years, strength training accelerates whole bowel transit time by 56% (Koffler et al., 1992). Brocklehurst and Kahn (1960) found that elderly neurologically disabled bedfast patients had prolonged bowel transit times compared with elderly, mobile non-institutionalised people. Recent studies have examined transit times in young people with neurological disability. In spinal cord injury, there is a prolonged colonic transit time (De Looze, De Muynck et al., 1998), and this is not just restricted to the rectosigmoid region but involves the entire colon (Keshavarzian et al., 1995). Treating constipation in this group may therefore require both prokinetic agents as well as local rectal manoeuvres. Large bowel transit studies in patients with multiple sclerosis also show an abnormally slow transit (Waldron et al., 1993).

Constipation is particularly a problem in the spinal cord injured patient, with a prevalence of 42% among 221 long-term survivors (Menter et al., 1997) and 58% in a study of 90 patients with a complete injury above L2 (De Looze, Van Leere et al., 1998). Longo et al. (1989) point out that since the small bowel is innervated by the parasympathetic fibres in the vagus and the sympathetic fibres from the lower sixth thoracic vertebrae, it may therefore function normally. However, the large bowel is innervated by the parasympathetic fibres from the sacral plexus and sympathetic fibres from the lumbar spinal column. In high cord lesions there is likely to be a decrease in colonic motility,

whereas in low cord lesions there is a lack of inhibition of the colonic sphincter activity thereby increasing left colonic transit time and producing constipation.

Disturbance of anorectal physiology is another important cause of constipation in the neurologically disabled. Defecography in patients with multiple sclerosis demonstrates rectal outlet obstruction and failure of the puborectalis and anal sphincter to relax (Gill et al., 1994). Paradoxical puborectalis contraction is common in constipated patients with MS (Chia, Gill et al., 1996), and may be a feature of the disturbed voluntary sphincter control mechanism. Patients with stroke and constipation show a different pattern of anorectal physiology to those with chronic constipation of unknown aetiology (Ho & Goh, 1995).

Hence some of the constipation in an individual patient may be due to neurological damage, particularly in spinal cord injury or myelomeningocele (Lozes, 1988), while other factors include inactivity, and the effect of medications commonly used in neurological disorders, such as antidepressants, muscle relaxants, anticholinergics, and opiate analgesics. Low dietary fibre and poor fluid intake may be contributory. Management (Bateman, 1991) includes the maintenance of proper faecal consistency and, in spinal patients, the development of reflex emptying of the rectum and sigmoid colon. Adequate hydration and roughage are important and the use of faecal moistening or bulk-producing agents may be helpful. Fibre supplementation of elderly rehabilitation patients reduces the need for prescribing other bowel agents (Gibson et al., 1995), and the use of a fibre-fortified enteral feed rather than a standard feed improves stool consistency in immobile tube-fed patients (Grant et al., 1994). However, a high fibre diet did not improve large bowel function in spinal patients (Cameron et al., 1996). The use of cisapride can lead to a subjective improvement in constipation in spinal patients (Longo et al., 1995), and it may increase left-sided colonic transit time (Geders et al., 1995). An implanted anterior sacral nerve root stimulator can significantly improve constipation in patients with spinal cord injury (MacDonagh et al., 1990; Binnie et al., 1991; Chia, Lee et al., 1996), allowing complete unassisted defaecation and improving quality of life. Postprandial defaecation makes use of the gastro-colic reflex and stimulation of the anal canal digitally and by a suppository increases local reflex activity. Abdominal massage may then be used to increase intra-abdominal pressure (Holey & Lawler, 1995). A combined programme of exercise and abdominal massage on a continuing care unit led to a significant increase in the number of bowel motions, with a reduction in enema requirement and in episodes of faecal incontinence (Resende et al., 1993). Faecal impaction in patients with a neuropathic bowel can be treated with pulsed irrigation evacuation (Puet et al., 1997).

HETEROTOPIC OSSIFICATION

Neurogenic para-articular heterotopic ossification (HO) involves the formation of extraskeletal new lamella bone about a normal joint. It occurs mainly around large proximal limb joints

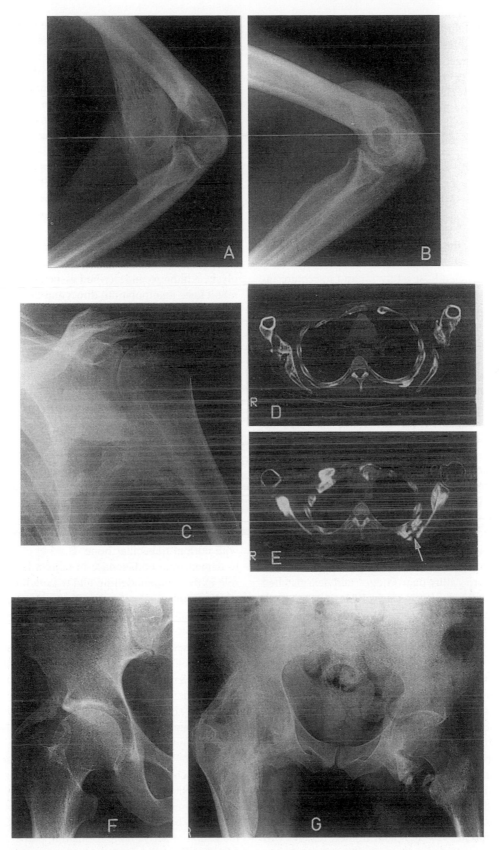

Figure 15.2. HO formation at the flexor (A) and extensor (B) aspects of the elbow, between the scapula and the humerus (C, D) and scapula and chest wall (E), and of varying degrees of severity at the hip (F, G). (Reproduced with the permission from Greenwood et al., 1989.)

(Figure 15.2), although there are recent reports of HO in unusual locations such as the extensor tendons of the hand affecting the metacarpophalangeal and interphalangeal joints (Spencer, 1991; Meythaler et al., 1992). It is usually found following traumatic spinal cord injury (Venier & Ditunno, 1971; Stover, 1987; Garland & Orwin, 1989; Lal et al., 1989; Bravo-Payno et al., 1992) or head injury (Garland et al., 1982; Ritter, 1987; Rogers, 1988; Greenwood et al., 1989; Hurvitz et al., 1992). It is also seen in the context of hip fracture after stroke (White, 1987). It occurs much less frequently (Garland, 1988) after non-traumatic neurological lesions such as encephalitis (An et al., 1987), the cerebral complications of AIDS (Drane & Tipler, 1987), cerebral cysticercosis (Spencer & Ganpath, 1988), cerebral anoxia or subarachnoid haemorrhage (Greenwood et al., 1989), and stroke (Hajek, 1987). Studies in the US, Israel, the UK, and elsewhere have shown that after head injury the incidence of HO is about 10–20% in patients sufficiently severely injured to require in-patient rehabilitation, and up to 80% in patients unconscious for more than 1 month (Mielants et al., 1975; Garland et al., 1980; Sazbon et al., 1981). After spinal injury there is an incidence of up to 53% (Wharton & Morgan, 1970; Venier & Ditunno, 1971). It has been previously under-recognised in children: in a 3 year prospective study in a paediatric brain injury rehabilitation unit, Citta-Pietrolungo et al. (1992) found HO in 25 of 111 cases (22.5%). Whilst HO is common in these contexts, it only occasionally results in ankylosis and consequent major disability, and major surgical intervention is not often required.

The pathogenesis of HO remains obscure and it is still not known what causes the inducible or determined progenitor cells of connective tissue to begin forming heterotopic bone (Smith, 1987). In their blind, prospective study of the effect of sera from patients with spinal cord and head injuries on osteoblast proliferation, Renfree et al. (1994) failed to show evidence of a humoral mechanism in the initiation of HO. The observation that fractured long bones in head-injured patients heal more quickly and make more callus than in age- and sex-matched controls (Perkins & Skirving, 1987) also remains unexplained. Immobility is clearly implicated—none of the 63% of Orzel and Rudd's (1985) spinal injury patients who developed HO did so above the site of the lesion. Tsur et al. (1996) found peri-articular HO in 26 out of 48 brain injured patients who had recovered consciousness at least 1 month after the accident; new bone formation was closely correlated with pathological movement (paresis or plegia), but there was only a borderline correlation with hypertonus and no correlation with hypotonus or with associated fractures. There is no clear evidence that neglect, infection, spasticity, or autonomic dysfunction play a major role, as bone forms in patients in the absence of pressure sores and in flaccid limbs, and no series has noted sympathetic dystrophy in affected limbs. However, Lal et al. (1989) found that when advancing age, a complete lesion, pressure sore, and spasticity were all present, 92% of spinal-injured patients had HO. HO in this group occurs more often in male patients than in female, most frequently in the 20–30-year-old age group, and it is more common after injuries of the lower cervical or thoracic spine than those of the lumbar spine (Wittenberg et al., 1992). Snoecx et al. (1995) subjected paraplegic patients with subacute limitation of hip joint mobility to serial sonographic examinations and found four with evidence of muscle rupture; all four developed sonographic and radiographic evidence of HO, suggesting a possible traumatic origin for HO around the hip. This is supported by animal experiments implicating the microtrauma and para-articular haemorrhage that result from vigorous manipulation (Izumi, 1983). Ultrasound examination of HO around joints in spinal patients provides supportive evidence of microtrauma in aetiology (Bodley et al., 1993). Clearly, most patients who receive physiotherapy and general nursing care are likely to sustain paraarticular microtrauma, and why this should lead to ossification in one patient and not in another remains uncertain. Bethoux et al. (1995) report the development of HO around the left hip in a patient with left upper and lower limb rhabdomyolysis, a hitherto undescribed association. In an experiment on rabbit knee manipulation, direct and extensive contact between bone and muscle was essential for the formation of experimental heterotopic bone (Michelsson et al., 1994). New animal models of HO are currently in development, including transgenic mice and transformed human cell lines injected into animal muscle (O'Connor, 1998), but a genetic predisposition has not been confirmed (Garland et al., 1984).

The histology and biochemical analysis of heterotopic bone has recently been elucidated. Using cell culture techniques, Kaysinger et al. (1997) compared osteogenic cells from HO with trabecular osteoblasts isolated from the same patient. HO-derived cells were shown to produce osteocalcin, Type 1 collagen, and alkaline phosphatase. They had increased rates of collagen synthesis, alkaline phosphatase activity and cell proliferation compared with normal osteoblasts, and tissue from HO sites showed a greater concentration of osteocytes compared with normal trabecular bone. Bord et al. (1996) were the first to demonstrate collagenase in human bone, and suggested its role in the bone modelling and remodelling of HO. In samples of HO from spinal patients, Chantraine et al. (1995) confirmed biochemically that HO is a newly formed bone with a high rate of turnover.

The onset of HO is usually 1–4 months after injury, about 20 days being the earliest recorded, whilst mature bone is seen after 12–18 months. Early clinical signs include decreased range of movement (Garland & Orwin, 1989), acute leg swelling (Stover et al., 1976; Pidcock, 1987), fever (Stover et al., 1976; Tow & Kong, 1995), and pain (Hajek, 1987). Biochemical markers of early HO are increased erythrocyte sedimentation rate (Bayley, 1979) and increased urinary excretion of prostaglandin E2 (Schurch et al., 1997). Persistent elevation of alkaline phosphatase (Nicholas, 1973; Mital et al., 1987, Garland & Orwin, 1989) and urinary galactosyl hydroxylysine (Rodriguez et al., 1989) may be noted later. Alkaline phosphatase levels are a good indication of active bone formation, particularly in conjunction with levels of inorganic phosphorus (Kim et al., 1990), and the level correlates well with the amount of HO (Kjaersgaard-Andersen et al., 1988). However, normal values do not rule out active HO (Hardy & Dickson, 1963; Furman et al., 1970; Orzel & Rudd, 1985; Stover, 1986; Garland & Orwin, 1989). Both ultrasound (Bodley et al., 1993; Cassar-Pullicino et al., 1993) and radioisotope bone scanning (Banovac & Gonzalez, 1997) are useful in early diagnosis, whilst X-rays may not show evidence of early calcification until 7–10 days after the clinical signs appear (Stover et al., 1976). Sobus, Alexander, and Harcke (1993) advocate total bone scanning for all children with traumatic brain or spinal cord injuries on entry to a rehabilitation programme, to detect HO and musculoskeletal trauma not recognised during acute care.

The natural history of HO is one of progression, though it may remain static for some considerable time and a degree of resorption may occur (Spencer & Missen, 1989). Sferopoulos and Anagnostopoulos (1997) report the case of a 3-year-old with traumatic brain injury who developed HO around her right hip joint, causing pain and reduced range of movement; 1 year after injury the HO had resolved spontaneously. Apart from limiting movement about a joint, HO can cause nerve entrapment (Vorenkamp & Nelson, 1987; Keenan, Kauffman et al., 1988) and neurovascular compression (Colachis et al., 1993). Development of HO at the elbow can cause bilateral ulnar nerve palsy (Cope, 1990; Chua et al., 1997). There is an association between HO and DVT in patients with spinal cord injury (Colachis & Clinchot, 1993) and traumatic brain injury (Sobus, Sherman, & Alexander, 1993), perhaps because expanding heterotopic bone leads to venous compression. HO is associated with persistent hypercoagulation long after neurological injury has occurred (Perkash et al., 1993).

Ideally HO should be prevented because, once present, treatment does not always lead to functional recovery. Clearly, periarticular trauma by prostheses (Figure 15.3), injections, or infection should be minimised (Rogers, 1988). Pharmacological prevention of HO remains controversial. The successful use of drugs, such as indomethacin, ibuprofen, and diphosphonates, or local irradiation (e.g., Coventry & Scanlon, 1981; Thomas & Amstutz, 1985; Evarts et al., 1987; Schmidt et al., 1988; Sodemann et al., 1988; Kantorowitz & Muff, 1998; Dorn et al., 1998; Persson et al., 1998) in the prevention of HO associated with orthopaedic surgery is not necessarily applicable to the HO found in neurological disorders. Even following orthopaedic surgery the effects of these adjunctive therapies may be short-lived. Thomas and Amstutz (1987) investigated the effect of diphosphonates in patients undergoing hip arthroplasty for arthritis. They found that the incidence of HO was as high in the treated group as in the placebo-treated group, and felt that this was because although diphosphonates inhibit the growth of hydroxyapatite crystals, they have no inhibitory effect on osteoid matrix formation, and mineralisation continues once the therapy is discontinued. Indomethacin (Ritter & Sieber, 1985; Ritter, 1987), ibuprofen (Elmstedt et al., 1985), and low dose irradiation (McAuliffe & Wolfson, 1997) have been shown to prevent recurrence when the HO associated with head injury is removed surgically. Salicylates may also be a useful adjunct

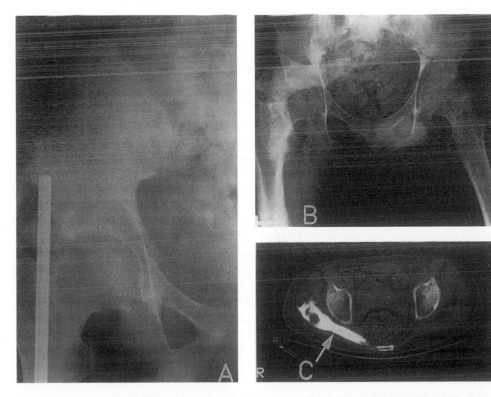

Figure 15.3. A malpositioned femoral nail (A) resulted in HO formation (B, C) between the femoral head and sacrum, preventing hip flexion and thus standing from sitting. (Reproduced with permission from Greenwood et al., 1989.)

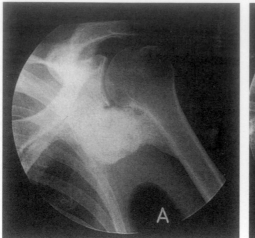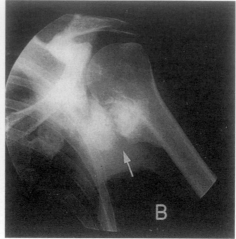

Figure 15.4. Severe HO at the shoulder (A), causing significant limitation of movement. Its fracture (B) during rehabilitation made operation unnecessary. (Reproduced with permission from Greenwood et al., 1989.)

to surgery of HO in spinal injured patients (Stover et al., 1976; Subbarao et al., 1987; Spielman et al., 1983). In this same group, anticoagulation with warfarin prevents HO, possibly because osteocalcin is produced by a vitamin K-dependent carboxylation (Buschbacher et al., 1992).

The physical management of established HO includes range-of-movement exercises (Figure 15.4) near here and progressive stretching followed by serial splinting. Rogers (1988) suggests that modalities such as ice, moist heat, and ultrasound are useful when starting such exercises. These techniques may be combined with surgery, which is required infrequently. Since surgery may also contribute to the development of HO there is some reservation amongst many surgeons to operate. Preoperative selection is the key to achieving satisfactory results. In one series (Moore, 1993), 17 patients with traumatic brain injury had periarticular HO resected in 20 joints (13 hips and 7 elbows) for joint ankylosis. At follow up, which averaged 23 months, 17 of the 20 resected joints had maintained functional range of motion. Meiners et al. (1997) selected spinal patients with HO for surgical resection on the basis of seating problems, loss of function, pressure sores, and pain, and recurrence occurred in only 3 out of 29. The previously held view that there should be a delay between injury and excision, to allow for maturation of heterotopic bone and thus to lessen the likelihood of recurrence, is now being challenged (Frischhut et al., 1993; McAuliffe & Wolfson, 1997). Complications of surgery include infection, haemorrhage, fractures, and recurrence (Garland & Orwin, 1989; Stover et al., 1991). The consequences of recurrence may be minimised pharmacologically and by physical therapy. For example, Spencer and Missen (1989) report an 8-year-old boy in whom complete excision of a massive area of HO produced rapid improvement in clinical features but by 2 weeks the mass had recurred and was even more extensive. However, with conservative treatment he remained free of pain and there was progressive resorption and remodelling of the heterotopic bone. Other treatment modalities for established HO include low

dose radiotherapy (Schaeffer & Sosner, 1995) and intravenous etidronate (Banovac et al., 1993, 1997).

CONTRACTURES

A contracture is said to be present when passive range of motion about a joint is impaired as a result of changes in muscle, joint or soft tissues. In neurological disease, contractures are usually the result of muscle and soft tissue changes following immobilisation of a joint due to inactivity, paralysis, or active muscle contraction, usually caused by spasticity but sometimes rigidity, dystonia, or even a conversion syndrome. Immobility causes joint adhesions and biochemical changes in periarticular collagen, with increased collagen cross-linking and decreased lubricating glycosaminoglycans (Akeson et al., 1987). Trudel et al. (1998) have developed an animal model of joint contracture involving immobilisation of the rat knee; the proliferative changes in the posterior aspect of the knee joint suggest local mediation of connective tissue proliferation in the contracture process. In shortened muscle compliance reduces, connective tissue increases, and sarcomere numbers decrease by up to 40%, over days if shortening results from active muscle contraction (O'Dwyer et al., 1989).

The pattern of contracture varies for different disorders. In cerebral palsy, the contractures are usually in flexion and adduction at the hips and flexion of the knees, and plantarflexion and varus at the ankles; occasionally extension contractures of the hip and knee develop and dorsiflexion and valgus contractures are found at the ankle (Hoffer et al., 1987). After craniocerebral trauma Yarkony and Sahgal (1987) found that contractures occurred in 84% of their patients, all of whom needed in-patient rehabilitation, and the number of contractures increased with coma duration. The joints most affected were the hips (81%), shoulders (76%), ankles (76%), and elbows (44%). Contractures of pelvic and trunk muscles are often forgotten; jaw closure muscles may also be involved. After stroke, contractures at shoulder, elbow, hip, knee, and ankle are recognised but are seldom severe, other postural consequences of spastic hypertonus being more relevant functionally. In children with spinal cord injuries, those with spastic injury develop hip flexion and adduction contractures, whilst those with flaccid injury mirror the "flail" hips of myelomeningocele (Rink & Miller, 1990). Contractures may develop over long periods of time. For instance, in children after head injury Blasier and Letts (1989) found that the average time to permanent foot deformity was 11 months, for scoliosis 22 months and for hamstring contractures an average of 37 months. This may result in late deterioration in gait or sitting posture after stroke or head trauma, and so preventative measures may have to be applied long term. Dalyan et al. (1998) recently studied contractures in the context of acute spinal cord injury, and found a significant association with pressure sores, spasticity, and co-existent head injury. Other associations were with HO, extremity fracture, peripheral nerve injury, and reflex sympathetic dystrophy.

Considerable functional disadvantage may result from these contractures (Perry, 1987). In 222 disabled elderly residents in continuing care in Scotland, those with upper limb contractures were nearly twice as likely to be unable to feed themselves as those without contractures (Yip et al., 1996). The presence of at least one lower limb contracture was significantly associated with reduced mobility. Souren et al. (1995) studied 161 patients with a clinical diagnosis of Alzheimer's disease, and found that the prevalence of contractures correlated highly with degree of functional impairment. Contracture of hip flexors reduces extension during the stance phase of walking, shortening stride, and encouraging toe-walking with knee flexion, whilst if severe the trunk may require support by a crutch if standing is to occur. Adductor contractures impede gait and maintenance of perineal hygiene. Knee flexion contractures promote the formation of pressure sores and increase work required in leg extensors during walking, reducing endurance or even preventing standing. If severe, they can impede transfers and turning in bed. Plantarflexion contractures at the ankle encourage knee hyperextension to achieve heel strike and place abnormal stresses upon the forefoot, knee, and low back, which may become painful. If severe, weight-bearing in a standing frame or during transfers is prevented. Extension contracture at the hip prevents hip flexion prior to standing and, if severe at the hip or knee, prevents wheelchair mobility and car transfers. In the upper limb, residual contracture at any joint may limit arm and hand function if there is later return of movement, such as after severe head injury. In an immobile limb, severe flexion contracture of the elbow or wrist may interfere with dressing and cosmesis, and of the fingers with hand hygiene. In patients with quadriplegia at the sixth cervical level, development of a flexion contracture at the elbow of 25 degrees or more can result in loss of independent transfers and mobility in bed (Grover et al., 1996). This would effectively render the patient as dependent as one who has quadriplegia at the fifth cervical level. In a survey of patients with spinal muscular atrophy and congenital myopathy, elbow flexion contractures were common and were perceived by many to be associated with loss of daily function and discomfort (Willig et al., 1995).

Prevention of contractures involves proper positioning (Figure 15.5), handling, and passive standing and range of motion exercises. Whilst 2 hours per day of passive exercises may prevent most contracture, particularly in flaccid limbs, sometimes 6 hours per day is required for prevention in spastic limbs (Tardieu et al., 1988). Spasticity may be so severe that passive movements may have little impact upon joint position, particularly in decerebrate or decorticate patients after severe head injury. In this situation serial splinting may be useful acutely to prevent equinus (Conine et al., 1990) and other limb deformities (Booth et al., 1983). Oral antispasmodic medication is of little use, whilst nerve or neuromuscular junction blockade may be of some help to prevent contractures forming at the elbow, hand, hip, knee, and ankle. Phenol nerve blocks are particularly useful in the early period of acquired spasticity following traumatic brain and spinal cord injury, allowing passive limb mobilisation to prevent contracture formation (Botte et al., 1995).

Once formed, low loads applied for long periods appear more effective in reversing contractures than high loads for short periods (Kottke et al., 1966); this is also true when elongating rat-tail tendon (Warren et al., 1976). Clinically this is applied by means of the Dynasplint (Mackay-Lyons, 1989), soft night (Anderson et al., 1988), or serial plaster splints, or adjustable plastic orthoses (Collins et al., 1985). However, in their study of nursing home residents with knee flexion contractures of greater than 10 degrees, Steffen and Mollinger (1995) found no difference in treatment outcome between low-load prolonged stretch using a splint and traditional passive range of movement exercises. Serial casting is now well established as a method of reducing contractures (Zander & Healy, 1992; Hill, 1994), and it may impact on the modulation of reflex activity of a spastic limb through unexplained physiological mechanisms (Phillips & Audet, 1990). The longer the cast is worn, the greater the increase in range of movement, perhaps through inducing basic alterations in connective tissue and muscle physiology (Flowers & LaStayo, 1994). Peripheral nerve blocks have an adjunctive role in treatment, and can be used prior to applying serial casts to allow improved position of the limb and better cast tolerance (Bell, 1995). Intramuscular botulinum toxin injection can reduce muscle tone and improve active and passive range of motion in non-fixed contractures (Calderon-Gonzalez et al., 1994; Mall et al., 1997). Electrical stimulation leads to temporary improvements in contractures at the wrist in post-stroke hemiplegia (Pandyan et al., 1997).

Surgical release of contractures in functioning and non-functioning limbs is extensively described in the orthopaedic literature in cerebral palsy (Bleck, 1990), and in adults with acquired neurological disease (Ough et al., 1981; Garland & Keenan, 1983; Roper, 1987; Keenan, Ure et al., 1988; Warner, 1990). In the latter group, the most useful releases in the upper limb are of the elbow, wrist, and finger flexors; in the lower limb, hip adductor, and hamstrings release may be useful, and Achilles

Lying on the good side

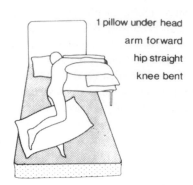

1 pillow under head

arm forward

hip straight

knee bent

Lying on the affected side

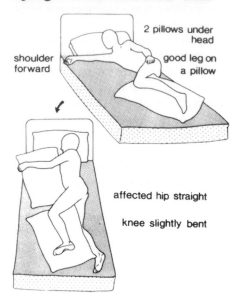

2 pillows under head

shoulder forward

good leg on a pillow

affected hip straight

knee slightly bent

Supine lying

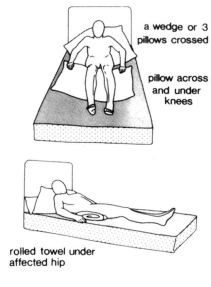

a wedge or 3 pillows crossed

pillow across and under knees

rolled towel under affected hip

Sitting

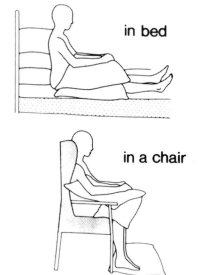

in bed

in a chair

Figure 15.5. Positions to adopt during the early care of patients after stroke or head injury to protect joints, maintain the length of soft tissue structures, prevent shoulder and/or hip pain and to inhibit the development of spastic patterning. The usual position of half-lying against a backrest, and the flexion contractures of the spine and hips that result, is avoided. If available, foam rolls are preferable to pillows as they deform less under pressure.

In *side-lying* the number of pillows under the head is varied to ensure a neutral alignment of the neck or slight side-flexion towards the unaffected side. The affected shoulder girdle is always in a protracted position with the arm extended and the hand supported. The hip of the affected limb is kept in a neutral position to prevent the development of flexion contractures. The foot must always be supported to prevent the foot resting in an inverted position.

Supine lying is only used when it cannot be avoided. A wedge of pillows behind the head and shoulder girdles ensures a neutral alignment of the head and neck with protraction of the shoulder girdles, inhibiting spastic retraction of the upper limb. A rolled up towel placed under the hip ensures neutral alignment of the pelvis and limits the outward rotation of the hip which can lead to pressure on the lateral malleolus. A pillow under the knees is used *only* in the presence of severe spastic extension to break up the extensor pattern.

Sitting up in bed should be avoided when possible. If essential, pillows rather than the back rest should be used to prevent the patient sliding down the bed into half-lying posture. In bed or a chair the patient's bottom should be placed as near to the back support as possible to achieve an upright trunk posture. The upper limb is supported by placing a pillow across the chest high in the axilla. This produces a more symmetrical posture than only a pillow under one arm. (Courtesy Ms C. Cornall & A. Holland.)

tendon lengthening may need to be combined with a split tibialis anterior tendon transfer and toe flexor releases. Improvement in range of motion occurring immediately after surgical release of contractures will almost always decrease to some extent over the first few months (Weiss & Sachar, 1994), although factors causing postoperative recurrence are unclear. Age, preoperative ability, and postoperative immobilisation are not correlated with the occurrence of knee contractures after distal hamstring release in patients with cerebral palsy (Dhawlikar et al., 1992). A temporary stabilising plaster may be worn for some weeks postoperatively, followed by an orthosis or continued physiotherapy for up to 6 months to prevent recurrence. In patients with spastic cerebral palsy, in whom surgery is being considered for lower extremity contractures, intrathecal baclofen infusion may reduce the need for surgery (Gerszten et al., 1998). Pinzur (1996) describes five patients with voluntary hand control complicated by severe flexion contracture after brain injury, whose deformities were beyond the scope of correction with soft tissue release. Four achieved meaningful gains in grasp-release of the hand after carpectomy and radio-carpal or radio-metacarpal fusion.

SHOULDER PAIN

Shoulder weakness of any cause may be complicated by local pain. After stroke, shoulder pain occurs in up to 70% of patients at some time during the first year post-stroke (Van Ouwenaller et al., 1986); up to 25% of patients also develop the shoulder-hand syndrome (Tepperman et al., 1984; Van Ouwenaller et al., 1986). The incidence of pain is related to the severity of the stroke (Sodring, 1980). After controlling for other indicators of stroke severity, Roy et al. (1995) found that shoulder pain on movement was the most important predictor of poor recovery of arm power and function, and an important contributor to length of stay in hospital. Hemiplegic shoulder pain is associated with poor recovery of activities of daily living, and lower rates of disharge home (Roy et al., 1994). It causes significant sleep disturbance and is associated with less general well-being and higher rates of depression and anxiety (Küçükdeveci et al., 1996).

The pathology of the joint is poorly documented in neurological patients. In idiopathic cases an inflammatory adhesive capsulitis develops (Neviaser, 1945; Lundberg, 1969) and this is presumably present in neurological patients in whom arthrography demonstrates adhesive changes (Hakuno et al., 1984). Experimental immobilisation of the glenohumeral joint in beagle dogs leads to a progressive restriction in range of motion and an increase in intraarticular pressure (Schollmeier et al., 1994). Morphologically, the capsule and the subcapsular bursa show focal adhesions. Other animal experiments have shown that immobilisation leads to a depletion of proteoglycans in the cartilage of joint surfaces, which is not completely restored by remobilisation (Jortikka et al., 1997), and a rise in plasma hyaluronan (Konttinen et al., 1991). An accumulation of hyaluronan

could be deleterious for joint tissues through its stimulation of interleukin-1 (catabolin) synthesis and secretion.

The sequence of events leading to shoulder pain in neurological patients is still debated. Immobilisation of the shoulder alone—for example, by splinting—is not a cause. Weakness of the joint may lead to trauma of the joint mechanism, causing a capsulitis, the consequences of which are further worsened by immobility. Some (Fitzgerald-Finch & Gibson, 1975; Van Ouwenaller et al., 1986; Roy et al., 1994) have found that anteroinferior subluxation is associated with shoulder pain, whilst others (Bohannon, 1988) have not, and subluxation may be painless (Miglietta et al., 1959). Rotator cuff tears have been reported by some (Najenson et al., 1971) but not by others (Hakuno et al., 1984). These findings may indicate that various forms of trauma may trigger the capsulitis. There are also associations with reduced external rotation of the shoulder (Bohannon, 1988) and reflex sympathetic dystrophy (Swann, 1954; Roy et al., 1994). Poulin de Courval et al. (1990) were unable to show an association of neglect with pain, although pain was more frequent after right than left hemisphere stroke. Some authors have found an association with spastic hypertonus (Shahani et al., 1981; Anderson, 1985; Brudny, 1985), possibly because this prevents normal movement during abduction of the glenohumeral joint, when the scapula rotates upwards and the humeral head is depressed and rotates externally. Thus inexpert and vigorous attempts to move the arm traumatise the joint and cause pain and subsequently capsulitis.

It is thus widely held that the painful shoulder in neurological patients is the result of mishandling and is preventable by proper positioning, support, and mobilisation. Use of a sling to treat glenohumeral subluxation is controversial and may not be effective (Varghese, 1981); a more recent orthosis, the Functional Shoulder Orthosis (Brudny, 1983) seems to offer little advantage over a sling (Roy & Blamire, 1989). The place of lapboards and armrests remains to be established, as does that of oral medications, local injections, manipulations under anaesthesia, or open operation (Irvine & Strouthidis, 1978; Irwin-Carruthers & Runnals, 1980; Griffin & Reddin, 1981; Smith et al., 1982). Attention to adequate shoulder pain management in stroke patients may help reduce the high dependency on benzodiazepines seen in some rehabilitation settings (Küçükdeveci et al., 1996).

DENTAL PROBLEMS

There is a high prevalence of intra-oral pathology in the neurologically disabled, affecting both the hard tissues, such as dental caries or malocclusion of the teeth, and soft tissues, including ulcers, candida, and xerostomia. This may be due to the local effects of the neurological disorder, leading to impaired swallow, retention of food and saliva and oropharyngeal motor problems. In addition, an individual may not be physically able to perform oral hygiene, demonstrated by the higher incidence of dental plaque and gingivitis in quadriplegic compared to hemiplegic patients (Lancashire et al., 1997). Poor dexterity correlates with poor oral hygiene (Felder et al., 1994), and dexterity tests can help to identify patients unable to perform adequate oral self care. Carers may find it difficult to gain access to the teeth for adequate cleansing, restricted by factors such as involuntary movements, and cognitive and behavioural disturbance, so that food may lie in the mouth for prolonged periods. This has been highlighted by the high incidence of dental caries seen in neurologically disabled children requiring medications that contain a high level of sugar (Kenny & Somaya, 1989). Even when swallowing and chewing is normal, high sugar diets predispose to an acidic plaque pH, which is associated with dental caries (Sgan-Cohen et al., 1988). It may be difficult to access dental treatment, through physical disability, cognitive disturbance, financial constraints, or the lack of appropriate dental services.

A number of dental problems arise in stroke patients. Selley (1977) has pointed out that the edentulous stroke patient often complains that their dentures will not fit. The reasons for this include the loss of muscular control, imbalance of muscular forces, and the loss of palatal fat. Modifications to the dentures at this stage are important if nutrition, as well as the aesthetic appearance of the patient, are to be improved. Food may accumulate in the buccal cavity on the hemiplegic side. One solution to this may be to fill the buccal sulcus by adding acrylic resin to the lower dentures, which can be removed when the patient recovers.

In cerebral palsy, bruxism is twice as frequent as in normal individuals (Rosenbaum et al., 1966) and chewing and swallowing disorders contribute to poor oral hygiene. Mouth care is complicated by the high prevalence of malocclusion of the teeth (Rosenstein, 1978; Oreland et al., 1987), which is more likely to be present when there is associated cognitive impairment than in primarily physical disability (Oreland et al., 1989).

Some of the problems of mouth care are related to medication. Probably the best known is the gum hypertrophy associated with phenytoin, though Grant et al. (1988) point out that since only 1% of patients on phenytoin develop severe swelling, gum hypertrophy *per se* should not deter a physician from using phenytoin in the treatment of epilepsy. There are, however, more compelling reasons for using other anticonvuls-

ants (see Chapter 37). Other dental and oral clinical features associated with drugs (Somerman, 1987) include sialorrhoea (cholinomimetics, anticholinesterases, acetylcholine precursors), sublingual irritation (ergot alkaloids), xerostomia (L-dopa, anticholinergics, and tricyclic antidepressants), and oral ulceration and candida (steroids). Xerostomia affects the ability to chew and start a swallow, and leads to avoidance of certain foods which may contribute to undernutrition (Loesche et al., 1995).

Diagnosis of dental problems may be delayed due to communication difficulties, lack of awareness of oral disease among carers and the lack and difficulty of performing regular examination. The maintenance of oral hygiene is essential, and chlorhexidine mouth rinse has been shown to be an effective antiplaque agent (Roberts & Addy, 1981; Gazi, 1988; Yanover et al., 1988). Xerostomia can be managed with saliva substitutes, and changing xerogenic drugs if possible and oral candida can be cleared with the application of regular nystatin suspension. Chronic drooling in patients with cerebral palsy and related neurodevelopmental disabilities can be controlled with oral glycopyrrolate (Blasco & Stansbury, 1996). Hard tissue pathology may require fillings, scaling, extraction, or prosthetics. The benefits of treatment include the prevention of local complications such as pain, sepsis, ulceration, and halitosis, as well as systemic problems such as malnutrition and aspiration pneumonia. These should be weighed against the risks, including discomfort, sepsis, haemorrhage, and the risks of general anaesthesia if required. Antibiotic prophylaxis may be required during dentistry in patients at risk of endocarditis or with ventricular shunts, and appropriate precautions may be needed in patients on anticoagulants or steroids. Specialist advice and treatment can often be provided by special needs dentists.

ACKNOWLEDGMENTS

We would like to thank Dr Martin Vernon for help with the section on dental problems, and Dr Mary Bliss for her contribution to the section on pressure sores.

REFERENCES

Akeson, W.H., Amiel, D., Abel, M.F., et al. (1987). Effects of immobilisation on joints. *Clinical Orthopaedics, 219*, 28–37.

Akkersdijk, W.L., Roukema, J.A., & van der Werken, C. (1998). Percutaneous endoscopic gastrostomy for patients with severe cerebral injury. *Injury, 29*(1), 11–14.

Albright, F., Burnett, C. H., Cope, O., Parson, W. (1941). Acute atrophy of bone (osteoporosis) simulating hyperparathyroidism. *Journal of Clinical Endocrinology & Metabolism, 1*, 711–716.

Allison, M.C., Morris, A.J., Park, R.H.R., & Mills, P.R. (1992). Percutaneous endoscopic gastrostomy tube feeding may improve outcome of late rehabilitation following stroke. *Journal of the Royal Society of Medicine, 85*, 147–149.

Allman, R.M. (1989). Pressure sores in the elderly. *New England Journal of Medicine, 320*, 850–853.

Allman, R.M., Laprade, C.A., Noel, L.B., et al. (1986). Pressure sores among hospitalized patients. *Annals of Internal Medicine, 105*, 337–342.

Allman, R.M., Walker, J.M., Hart, M.K., et al. (1987). Air-fluidized beds or conventional therapy for pressure sores: a randomized trial. *Annals of Internal Medicine, 107*, 641–648.

Allman, R.M., Goode, P.S., Patrick, M.M., Burst, N., & Bartolucci, A.A. (1995). Pressure ulcer risk factors among hospitalized patients with activity limitation. *Journal of the American Medical Association, 273*(11), 865–870.

Altman, E., & Cutie, A.J. (1984). Compatibility of enteral products with commonly employed drug additives. *Nutritional Support Services, 12*, 8–17.

Altmayer, T., O'Dell, M.W., Jones, M., Martin, V., & Hawkins, H.H. (1996). Cisapride as a treatment for gastroparesis in traumatic brain injury. *Archives of Physical Medicine and Rehabilitation, 77*(10), 1093–1094.

An, H.S., Ebraheim, N., Kim, K., et al. (1987). Heterotopic ossification and pseudoarthrosis in the shoulder following encephalitis: a case report and review of the literature. *Clinical Orthopaedics, 219*, 291–298.

Anderson, J.P., Snow, B., Dory, F.J., & Kabo, J.M. (1988). Efficacy of soft splints in reducing severe knee-flexion contractures. *Developmental Medicine and Child Neurology, 30*, 502–508.

Anderson, L.T. (1985). Shoulder pain in hemiplegia. *American Journal of Occupational Therapy*, 39, 11–19.

Anderson, R.L., Lefever, F.R., Francis, W.R., & Maurer, J.K. (1990). Urinary and bladder responses to immobilization in male rats. *Food and Chemical Toxicology* 28(8), 543–545.

Annoni, J.M., Vuagnat, H., Frischknecht, R., & Uebelhart, D. (1998). Percutaneous endoscopic gastrostomy in neurological rehabilitation: a report of six cases. *Disability and Rehabilitation: An International Multidisciplinary Journal*, 20(8), 308–314.

Appell, H.J. (1990). Muscular atrophy following immobilisation: a review. *Sports Medicine*, 10(1), 42–58.

Aptaker, R.L., Roth, E.J., Reichhardt, G., Duerden, M.E., & Levy, C.E. (1994). Serum albumin level as a predictor of geriatric stroke rehabilitation outcome. *Archives of Physical Medicine and Rehabilitation*, 75, 80–84.

Bader, D.L. (1990). Effects of compressive loading regimes on tissue viability. In D.L. Bader (Ed.), *Pressure sores—clinical practice and scientific approach* (pp. 191–201). London: Macmillan.

Baker, J.H.E, Silver, J.R., & Tudway, A.J.C. (1984). Late complications of pressure sores. *Care—Science and Practice*, 3, 56–59.

Bannister, R., & Mathias, C. (Eds.) (1993). *Autonomic failure: a textbook of clinical disorders of the autonomic nervous system* (3rd Ed.). Oxford University Press, Oxford.

Banovac, K., & Gonzalez, F. (1997). Evaluation and management of heterotopic ossification in patients with spinal cord injury. *Spinal Cord*, 35(3), 158–162.

Banovac, K., Gonzalez, F., Wade, N., & Bowker, J.D. (1993). Intravenous disodium etidronate therapy in spinal cord injury patients. *Paraplegia*, 31, 660–666.

Bar, C.A. (1991). Evaluation of cushions using dynamic pressure measurement. *Prosthetics and Orthotics International*, 15, 232–240.

Barbanel, J.C. (1991). Pressure management. *Prosthetics and Orthotics International*, 15, 225–231.

Barrett, E. (1988). A review of risk assessment methods. *Care—Science and Practice*, 6, 49–52.

Bass, J., Miles, M.V., Tennison, M.B., et al. (1989). Effects of enteral tube feeding on the absorption and pharmacokinetic profile of carbamazepine suspension. *Epilepsia*, 30, 364–369.

Bateman, D.N. (1991). Management of constipation. *Prescribers Journal*, 31, 7–15.

Bayley, S.J. (1979). Funnybones: a review of the problem of heterotopic bone formation. *Orthopaedic Review*, 3, 113–120.

Bazelmans, E., & Mulder, T. (1992). Restless nights: nocturnal disturbances in families with a boy suffering from Duchenne muscular dystrophy. *Journal of Rehabilitation Science*, 5, 52–55.

Becker, D., Gonzalez, M., Gentil, A., et al. (1987). Prevention of deep vein thrombosis in patients with acute spinal cord injuries: use of rotating treatment tables. *Neurosurgery*, 20, 675–677.

Bell, K. (1995). The use of neurolytic blocks for the management of spasticity. *Physical Medicine and Rehabilitation Clinics of North America*, 6, 885.

Bennett, J.S., Brereton, W.D., Cochrane, I.W., & Lyttle, D. (1987). Continuous passive motion device for hand rehabilitation. *Archives of Physical Medicine and Rehabilitation*, 68, 248–250.

Bennett, L., Kavner, D., Lee, B.Y., et al. (1981). Skin blood flow in seated geriatric patients. *Archives of Physical Medicine and Rehabilitation*, 62, 392–398.

Bergstrom, N., & Braden, B.J. (1992). A prospective study of pressure sore risk among the institutionalised elderly. *Journal of the American Geriatrics Society*, 40, 747–758.

Berlowitz, D.R., & Wilking, S.V.B. (1989). Risk factors for pressure sores: a comparison of cross-sectional and cohort-derived data. *Journal of the American Geriatrics Society*, 37, 1043–1050.

Bernardi, E., Prandoni, P., Lensing, A.W.A., et al. (1998). D-dimer testing as an adjunct to ultrasonography in patients with clinically suspected deep vein thrombosis: prospective cohort study. *British Medical Journal*, 317, 1037–1040.

Bethoux, F., Calmels, P., Aigoin, J.L., et al. (1995). Heterotopic ossification and rhabdomyolysis. *Paraplegia*, 33(3), 164–166.

Bick, E.M. (1948). *Source book of orthopaedics*. Williams and Wilkins; Baltimore.

Biggart, M., McQuillan, P.J., Choudry, A.K., & Nickalls, R.W. (1987). Dangers of placement of narrow bore gastric feeding tubes. *Annals of the Royal College of Surgeons of England*, 69, 119–121.

Billman, G.E., Dickey, D.T., Sandler, H., & Stone, H.L. (1982). Effects of horizontal body casting on the baroreceptor reflex control of heart rate. *Journal of Applied Physiology*, 52, 1552–1556.

Bingham, S.A., & Cummings, J.H. (1989). Effect of exercise and physical fitness on large intestinal function. *Gastroenterology*, 97, 1389–1399.

Binnie, N.R., Smith, A.N., Creasey, G.H., & Edmond, P. (1991). Constipation associated with chronic spinal cord injury: the effect of pelvic parasympathetic stimulation by the Brindley stimulator. *Paraplegia*, 29(7), 463–469.

Blasco, P.A., & Stansbury, J.C. (1996). Glycopyrrolate treatment of chronic drooling. *Archives of Pediatrics and Adolescent Medicine*, 150(9), 932–935.

Blasier, D., & Letts, R.M. (1989). Paediatric update no. 7: The orthopaedic manifestations of head injury in children. *Orthopaedic Review*, 18, 350–358.

Bleach, N. (1993). The gag reflex and aspiration: a retrospective analysis of 120 patients assessed by videofluoroscopy. *Clinical Otolaryngology*, 18, 303–307.

Bleck, E.E. (1990). Management of the lower extremities in children who have cerebral palsy. *Journal of Bone and Joint Surgery*, 72A, 140–144.

Bliss, M.R. (1998). Pressure injuries. *Hospital Medicine*, 59, 841–844.

Bodley, R., & Banerjee, S. (1995). Radiological percutaneous gastrostomy placement for enteral feeding. *Paraplegia*, 33(3), 153–155.

Bodley, R., Jamous, A., & Short, D. (1993). Ultrasound in the early diagnosis of heterotopic ossification in patients with spinal injuries. *Paraplegia*, 31(8), 500–506.

Boeer, A., Voth, E., Henze, T., & Prange, H.W. (1991). Early heparin therapy in patients with spontaneous intracerebral haemorrhage. *Journal of Neurology, Neurosurgery and Psychiatry*, 54(5), 466–467.

Bohannon, R.W. (1988). Relationship between shoulder pain and selected variables in patients with hemiplegia. *Clinical Rehabilitation*, 2, 111–117.

Booth, B.J., Doyle, M., & Montgomery, J. (1983). Serial casting for the management of spasticity in the head injured adult. *Physical Therapy*, 12, 1960–1966.

Bord, S., Horner, A., Hembry, R.M., Reynolds, J.J., & Compston, J.E. (1996). Production of collagenase by human osteoblasts and osteoclasts in vivo. *Bone*, 19(1), 35–40.

Botte, M.J., Abrams, R.A., & Bodine-Fowler, S.C. (1995). Treatment of acquired muscle spasticity using phenol peripheral nerve blocks. *Orthopedics*, 18(2), 151–159.

Boyce, W.J., & Vessey, M.P. (1988). Habitual physical inertia and other factors in relation to risk of fracture of the proximal femur. *Age and Ageing*, 17, 319–327.

Bravo-Payno, P., Esclarin, A., Arzoz, T., Arroyo, O., & Labarta, C. (1992). Incidence and risk factors in the appearance of heterotopic ossification in spinal cord injury. *Paraplegia*, 30(10), 740–745.

Brienza, D.M., & Karg, P.E. (1998). Seat cushion optimization: a comparison of interface pressure and tissue stiffness characteristics for spinal cord injured and elderly patients. *Archives of Physical Medicine and Rehabilitation*, 79(4), 388–394.

Brocklehurst, J.C., & Khan, Y. (1969). A study of faecal stasis in old age and the use of dorbanex in its prevention. *Gerontologia Clinica*, 11, 293–300.

Brooks, B., & Duncan, G.W. (1940). Effects of pressure in tissues. *Archives of Surgery*, 40, 696–709.

Brown, A.C., & Brenglemann, G. (1965). Energy metabolism. In R.C. Ruch & H.D. Patton (Eds.), *Physiology and biophysics* (pp. 1030–1079). Philadelphia: W.B. Saunders.

Bruder, N., Dumont, J.C., & Francois, G. (1991). Evolution of energy expenditure and nitrogen excretion in severe head-injured patients. *Critical Care Medicine*, 19(1), 43–48.

Brudny, J. (1983). *Functional shoulder orthosis for reduction of shoulder subluxation and for retraining of the hemiparetic limbs*. Camp International Inc, Jackson, Michigan.

Brudny, J. (1985). New orthosis for treatment of hemiplegic shoulder subluxation. *Orthotics and Prosthetics*, 39, 14–20.

Buckey, J.C., Peshock, R.M., & Blomqvist, C.G. (1988). Deep venous contribution to hydrostatic blood volume change in the human leg. *American Journal of Cardiology*, 62, 499–453.

Buczynski, A., Kedziora, J., Wachowicz, B., & Zolynski, K. (1991). Effect of bed rest on the adenine nucleotides concentration in human blood platelets. *Journal of Physiology and Pharmacology*, 42(4), 389–395.

Burr, R.G., Clift-Peace, L., & Nuseibeh, I. (1993). Haemoglobin and albumin as predictors of length of stay of spinal injured patients in a rehabilitation centre. *Paraplegia*, *31*(7), 473–478.

Buschbacher, R., McKinley, W., Buschbacher, L., Devaney, C.W., & Coplin, B. (1992). Warfarin in prevention of heterotopic ossification. *American Journal of Physical Medicine and Rehabilitation*, 71(2), 86–91.

Calderon-Gonzalez, R., Calderon-Sepulveda, R., & Rincon-Reyes, M. (1994). Botulinum toxin A in management of cerebral palsy. *Paediatric Neurology*, *10*, 284.

Cameron, K.J., Nyulasi, I.B., Collier, G.R., & Brown, D.J. (1996). Assessment of the effect of increased dietary fibre intake on bowel function in patients with spinal cord injury. *Spinal Cord*, *34*(5), 277–283.

Cassar-Pullicino, V.N., McClelland, M., Badwan, D.A., et al. (1993). Sonographic diagnosis of heterotopic bone formation in spinal injury patients. *Paraplegia*, *31*(1), 40–50.

Chantraine, A., Nusgens, B., & Lapiere, C.M. (1995). Biochemical analysis of heterotopic ossification in spinal cord injury patients. *Paraplegia*, *33*(7), 398–401.

Chappard, D., Petitjean, M., Alexandre, C., et al. (1991). Cortical osteoclasts are less sensitive to etidronate than trabecular osteoclasts. *Journal of Bone and Mineral Research*, *6*(7), 673–680.

Chia, Y.W., Gill, K.P., Jameson, J.S., Forti, A.D., Henry, M.M., Swash, M., & Shorvon, P.J. (1996). Paradoxical puborectalis contraction is a feature of constipation in patients with multiple sclerosis. *Journal of Neurology, Neurosurgery and Psychiatry*, *60*(1), 31–35.

Chia, Y.W., Lee, T.K., Kour, N.W., Tung, K.H., & Tan, E.S. (1996). Microchip implants on the anterior sacral roots in patients with spinal trauma: does it improve bowel function? *Diseases of the Colon and Rectum*, *39*(6), 690–694.

Chua, H.C., Tan, C.B., & Tija, H. (1997). A case of bilateral ulnar nerve palsy in a patient with traumatic brain injury and heterotopic ossification. *Singapore Medical Journal*, *38*(10), 447–448.

Citta-Pietrolungo, T.J., Alexander, M.A., & Steg, N.L. (1992). Early detection of heterotopic ossification in young patients with traumatic brain injury. *Archives of Physical Medicine and Rehabilitation*, *73*(3), 258–262.

Clarke, G. (1997). The problem of pressure sores and how to treat them. *British Journal of Therapy and Rehabilitation*, *4*(11), 589–595.

Claus-Walker, J. (1980). Clinical implications of disturbance in calcium and collagen metabolism in quadriplegia. *International Journal of Rehabilitation Research*, *3*, 540–541.

Clifton, G.L., Robertson, C.S., & Grossman, R.G., et al. (1984). The metabolic response to severe head injury. *Journal of Neurosurgery*, *60*, 687–695.

Clifton, G.L., Robertson, C.S., & Sung, C.C. (1986). Assessment of nutritional requirements of head-injured patients. *Journal of Neurosurgery*, *64*, 895–901.

Cochrane, G.V., & Slater, G. (1973). Experimental evaluation of wheelchair cushions. *Bulletin of Prosthetics Research*, *10*(19), 29061.

Cogo, A., Lensing, A.W.A, Koopman, M.M.W., et al. (1998). Compression ultrasound for diagnostic management for patients with clinically suspected venous thrombosis. *British Medical Journal*, *316*, 17–20.

Colachis, S.C., & Clinchot, D.M. (1993). The association between deep venous thrombosis and heterotopic ossification in patients with acute traumatic spinal cord injury. *Paraplegia*, *31*(8), 507–512.

Colachis, S.C., Clinchot, D.M., & Venesy, D. (1993). Neurovascular complications of heterotopic ossification following spinal cord injury. *Paraplegia*, *31*(1), 51–57.

Colin, D. (1997). Changes in ischial transcutaneous oxygen tension in spinal cord injured patients according to the position of the wheelchair footrest. *Journal of Wound Care*, *6*(Suppl), 8.

Collins, K., Oswald, P., Burger, G., & Nolden, J. (1985). Customised adjustable orthoses: their use in spasticity. *Archives of Physical Medicine and Rehabilitation* 66, 397–398.

Collins, R., Scrimgeour, A., Yusuf, S., & Peto, R. (1988). Reduction in fatal pulmonary embolism and venous thrombosis by perioperative administration of subcutaneous heparin. *New England Journal of Medicine*, *318*, 1162–1173.

Conine, T.A., Sullivan, T., Mackie, T., & Goodman, M. (1990). Effect of serial casting for the prevention of equinus in patients with acute head injury. *Archives of Physical Medicine and Rehabilitation*, *71*, 310–312.

Connell, A.M., Hilton, C., Irvin, G., et al. (1965). Variations in bowel habit in two populations. *British Medical Journal*, *2*, 1095–1099.

Constantian, M.B., & Jackson, H.S. (1980). Factors affecting pressure ulcer development. In M.B. Constantian (Ed.), *Pressure ulcers: principles and techniques of management* (pp. 143–148). Boston: Little Brown.

Consultant Dietitians in Health Care Facilities/American Dietetic Association (1994). *Mental status, nutrition care for specific diseases: practical interventions for the caregivers of the eating-disabled older adult*. American Dietetic Association, Chicago, pp. 109–122, 147–172.

Convertino, V.A. (1997). Cardiovascular consequences of bed rest: effect on maximal oxygen uptake. *Medicine and Science in Sports and Exercise*, *29*(2), 191–196.

Convertino, V.A., Doerr, D.F., Eckberg, D.L., et al. (1990). Head-down bed rest impairs vagal baroreflex responses and provokes orthostatic hypotension. *Journal of Applied Physiology*, *68*(4), 1458–1464.

Convertino, V.A., Doerr, D.F., & Stein, S.L. (1989). Changes in size and compliance of the calf after 30 days of simulated microgravity. *Journal of Applied Physiology*, *66*, 1509–1512.

Cope, R. (1990). Heterotopic ossification. *Southern Medical Journal*, *83*(9), 1058–1064.

Coventry, M.B., & Scanlon, P.W. (1981). The use of radiation to discourage ectopic bone. *Journal of Bone and Joint Surgery (America)* 63, 201–208.

Creditor, M.C. (1993). Hazards of hospitalization of the elderly. *Annals of Internal Medicine*, *118*(3), 219–223.

Culebras, A. (1992). Neuroanatomic and neurological correlates of sleep disturbances. *Neurology*, *42*(Suppl 6): 19–27.

Curry, K., & Casady, L. (1992). The relationship between extended periods of immobility and decubitus ulcer formation in the acutely spinal-cord injured individual. *Journal of Neuroscience Nursing*, *24*(4), 185–189.

Dalyan, M., Sherman, A., & Cardenas, D.D. (1998). Factors associated with contractures in acute spinal cord injury. *Spinal Cord*, *36*, 405–408.

Davalos, A., Ricart, W., Gonzalez-Huix, F., et al. (1996). Effect of malnutrition after acute stroke on clinical outcome. *Stroke*, *27*(6), 1028–1032.

David, J.A., Chapman, E.J., Chapman, R.G., & Locket, B. (1985). A survey of prescribed nursing treatments for patients with established pressure sores. *Care—Science and Practice*, *1*, 18–20.

Davis, G., & Glaser, R. (1990). Cardiorespiratory fitness following spinal cord injury. In L. Ada & C. Canning (Eds.) *Key issues in neurological physiotherapy* (pp. 155–196). London: Heinemann Medical.

De Looze, D.A., De Muynck, M.C., Van Laere, M., De Vos, M.M., & Elewaut, A.G. (1998). Pelvic floor function in patients with clinically complete spinal cord injury and its relation to constipation. *Diseases of the Colon and Rectum 41*(6), 778–786.

De Looze, D.A., Van Laere, M., De Muynck, M.C., Beke, R., & Elewaut, A.G. (1998). Constipation and other chronic gastrointestinal problems in spinal cord injury patients. *Spinal Cord*, *36*(1), 63–66.

Denne, W.A. (1979). An objective assessment of the sheepskins used for decubitus sore prophylaxis. *Rheumatology and Rehabilitation*, *18*, 23–29.

DeVivo, M., Black, K., & Stover, S. (1993). Causes of death during the first 12 years after spinal cord injury. *Archives of Physical Medicine and Rehabilitation 74*, 1208–1210.

Dhawlikar, S., Root, L., & Mann, R. (1992). Distal lengthening of the hamstrings in patients who have cerebral palsy. Long-term retrospective analysis. *Journal of Bone and Joint Surgery (American)*, *74*, 1385.

Dinsdale, S.M. (1974). Decubitus ulcers: role of pressure and friction in causation. *Archives of Physical Medicine and Rehabilitation*, *55*, 147–152.

Disa, J.J., Carlton, J.M., & Goldberg, N.H. (1992). Efficacy of operative cure in pressure sore patients. *Plastic and Reconstructive Surgery*, *89*, 272–278.

Donald, I.P., Smith, R.J., Cruikshank, J.G., Elton, R.A., & Stoddart, M.E. (1985). A study of constipation in the elderly living at home. *Gerontology*, *31*, 112–118.

Dorn, U., Grethen, C., Effenberger, H., et al. (1998). Indomethacin for prevention of heterotopic ossification after hip arthroplasty: a randomized comparison between 4 and 8 days of treatment. *Acta Orthopaedica Scandinavica*, *69*(2), 107–110.

Dover, H., Pickard, W., Swain, I., & Grundy, D. (1992). The effectiveness of a pressure clinic in preventing pressure sores. *Paraplegia*, *30*(4), 267–272.

Dowding, C. (1983). Tissue viability nurse, a new post. *Nursing Times*, *79*, 61–64.

Downs, F.S. (1974). Bed rest and sensory disturbances. *American Journal of Nursing*, *74*, 434–438.

Drane, W.E., & Tipler, B.M. (1987). Heterotopic ossification (myositis ossificans) in acquired immune deficiency syndrome: detection by gallium scintigraphy. *Clinical Nuclear Medicine*, *12*, 433–435.

Druz, W.S., & Sharp, J.T. (1981). Activity of respiratory muscles in upright and recumbent humans. *Journal of Applied Physiology, 51,* 1552–1561.

Dumurgier, C., Pujol, G., Chevalley, J., et al. (1991). Pressure sore carcinoma: a late but fulminant complication of pressure sores in spinal cord injury patients: case reports. *Paraplegia, 29*(6), 390–395.

Einarsson, G. (1991). Muscle conditioning in late poliomyelitis. *Archives of Physical Medicine and Rehabilitation, 72,* 11–14.

Ellis, S., Kirby, L.C., & Greenleaf, J.E. (1993). Lower extremity muscle thickness during 30-day 6 degrees head-down bed rest with isotonic and isokinetic exercise training. *Aviation Space and Environmental Medicine, 64*(11), 1011–1015.

Elmstedt, E., Londholm, T.S., Nilsson, O.S., & Tornkvist, H. (1985). Effect of ibuprofen on heterotopic ossification after hip replacement. *Acta Orthopaedica Scandinavica, 56,* 25–27.

Evarts, C.M., Ayers, D.C., & Puzas, J.E. (1987). Prevention of heterotopic bone formation in high risk patients by postoperative irradiation. In *Hip: Proceedings of the Hip Society* (pp. 70–83). Philadelphia: J.B. Lippincott.

Exton-Smith, A.N., & Sherwin, R.W. (1961). The prevention of pressure sores. Significance of spontaneous bodily movements. *Lancet, ii,* 1124–1126.

Faraji, B., & Yu, P.P. (1998). Serum phenytoin levels of patients on gastrostomy tube feeding. *Journal of Neuroscience Nursing, 30*(1), 55–59.

Felder, R., James, K., Brown, C., Lemon, S., & Reveal, M. (1994). Dexterity testing as a predictor of oral care ability. *Journal of the American Geriatrics Society, 42*(10), 1081–1086.

Ferguson, A.C., Keating, J.F., Delargy, M.A., & Andrews, B.J. (1992). Reduction of seating pressure using FES in patients with spinal cord injury: a preliminary report. *Paraplegia, 30*(7), 474–478.

Ferrando, A.A., Lane, H.W., Stuart, C.A., et al. (1996). Prolonged bed rest decreases skeletal muscle and whole body protein synthesis. *American Journal of Physiology, 270*(4, Pt 1), E627–633.

Ferrando, A.A., Tipton, K.D., Bamman, M.M., & Wolfe, R.R. (1997). Resistance exercise maintains skeletal muscle protein synthesis during bed rest. *Journal of Applied Physiology, 82*(3), 807–810.

Ferrando, A.A., Stuart, C.A., Brunder, D.G., & Hillman, G.R. (1995). Magnetic resonance imaging quantitation of changes in muscle volume during 7 days of strict bed rest. *Aviation Space and Environmental Medicine, 66*(10), 976–981.

Fertl, E., Steinhoff, N., Scholl, R., et al. (1998). Transient and long-term feeding by means of percutaneous endoscopic gastrostomy in neurological rehabilitation. *European Neurology, 40*(1), 27–30.

Finestone, H.M., Green-Finestone, L.S., Wilson, E.S., & Teasell, R.W. (1995). Malnutrition in stroke patients on the rehabilitation service and at follow-up: prevalence and predictors. *Archives of Physical Medicine and Rehabilitation, 76*(4), 310–316.

Finestone, H.M., Green-Finestone, L.S., Wilson, E.S., & Teasell, R.W. (1996). Prolonged length of stay and reduced functional improvement rate in malnourished stroke rehabilitation patients. *Archives of Physical Medicine and Rehabilitation, 77*(4), 340–345.

Finestone, H.M., Levine, S.P., Carlson, G.A., et al. (1991). Erythema and skin temperature following continuous sitting in spinal cord individuals. *Journal of Rehabilitation Research and Development, 28,* 27–32.

Fink, M.P., Helsmoortel, C.M., Stein, K.L., Lee, P.C., & Cohn, S.M. (1990). The efficacy of an oscillating bed in the prevention of lower respiratory tract infection in critically ill victims of blunt trauma: a prospective study. *Chest, 97,* 132–137.

Fitzgerald-Finch, O.P., & Gibson, I.I.J.K. (1975). Subluxation of the shoulder in hemiplegia. *Age and Ageing, 4,* 16–18.

Flowers, K., & LaStayo, P. (1994). Effect of total end range time on improving passive range of motion. *Journal of Hand Therapy, 7,* 150.

Fortney, S.M., Beckett, W.S., Carpenter, A.J., et al. (1988). Changes in plasma volume during bed rest: effects of menstrual cycle and oestrogen administration. *Journal of Applied Physiology, 65,* 525–533.

Fortney, S.M., Turner, C., Steinmann, L., et al. (1994). Blood volume responses of men and women to bed rest. *Journal of Clinical Pharmacology, 34*(5), 434–439.

Frischhut, B., Stockhammer, G., Saltuari, L., Kadletz, R., & Bramanti, P. (1993). Early removal of periarticular ossifications in patients with head injury. *Acta Neurologica, 15*(2), 114–122.

Frost, R.A., Rivers, H., Tromans, A.M., & Grundy, D.J. (1995). The role of percutaneous endoscopic gastrostomy in spinal cord injured patients. *Paraplegia, 33*(7), 416–418.

Fruin, A.H., Taylon, C., & Pettis, M.S. (1986). Caloric requirements in patients with severe head injuries. *Surgical Neurology, 25,* 25–28.

Furman, R., Nicholas, J.J., & Jivoff, L. (1970). Elevation of the serum alkaline phosphatase coincident with ectopic-bone formation in paraplegic patients. *Journal of Bone and Joint Surgery (America), 52,* 1131–1133.

Furukawa, T., & Toyokura, Y. (1976). Amyotrophic lateral sclerosis and bed sores. *Lancet, i,* 862.

Gaddisseux, P., Ward, J.D., Young, H.F., & Becker, D. (1984). Nutrition and the neurosurgery patient. *Journal of Neurosurgery, 60,* 219–232.

Gallacher, S.J., Ralston, S.H., Dryburgh, F.J., et al. (1990). Immobilisation—related hyper calcaemia—a possible novel mechanisam and response to pamidronate. *Postgraduate Medical Journal, 66*(781), 918–922.

Garber, S.L., & Krouskop, T.A. (1982). Body build and its relationship to pressure distribution in the seated wheelchair patient. *Archives of Physical Medicine and Rehabilitation, 63,* 17–20.

Garber, S.L., Rintala, D.H., Rossi, C.D., Hart, K.A., & Fuhrer, M.J. (1996). Reported pressure ulcer prevention and management techniques by persons with spinal cord injury. *Archives of Physical Medicine and Rehabilitation, 77*(8), 744–749.

Garland, D.E. (1988). Clinical observations on fractures and heterotopic ossification in the spinal cord and traumatic brain injured populations. *Clinical Orthopaedics, 233,* 86–101.

Garland, D.E., Alday, B., & Venos, K.G. (1984). Heterotopic ossification and HLA antigens. *Archives of Physical Medicine and Rehabilitation, 65,* 531–532.

Garland, D.E., Blum, C.E., & Walter, R.L. (1980). Periarticular heterotopic ossification in head injured adults, incidence and location. *Journal of Bone and Joint Surgery, 62,* 1143–1146.

Garland, D.E., & Keenan, M.E. (1983). Orthopaedic strategies in the management of the adult head-injured patient. *Physical Therapy, 63,* 2004–2009.

Garland, D.E., & Orwin, J.F. (1989). Resection of heterotopic ossification in patients with spinal cord injuries. *Clinical Orthopaedics, 242,* 169–176.

Garland, D.E., Razza, B.E., & Waters, R.L. (1982). Forceful joint manipulation in head injured adults with heterotopic ossification. *Clinical Orthopaedics, 169,* 133–138.

Gawel, M.J., Somerville, J., & Beggs, C. (1989). Motor neurone disease: the aggressive approach. *Clinical Rehabilitation, 3,* 309–312.

Gawel, M.J., Zaiwaller, Z., Capildeo, R., & Rose, C.F. (1983). Antecedent events in motor neurone disease. *Journal of Neurology, Neurosurgery and Psychiatry, 46,* 1014–1045.

Gazi, M.I. (1988). Photographic assessment of the antiplaque properties of sanguinarine and chlorhexidine. *Journal of Clinical Peridontology, 15,* 106–109.

Gebhardt, K.S., Bliss, M.R., Winwright, P.L., & Thomas, J.M. (1996). Pressure relieving supports in an ICU. *Journal of Wound Care, 5,* 116–121.

Geders, J.M., Gaing, A., Bauman, W.A., & Korsten, M.A. (1995). The effect of cisapride on segmental colonic transit time in patients with spinal cord injury. *American Journal of Gastroenterology, 90*(2), 285–289.

Gentilello, L., Thompson, D.A., Tonnesen, A.S., et al. (1988). Effect of a rotating bed on the incidence of pulmonary complications in critically ill patients. *Critical Care Medicine, 16,* 783–786.

Gerszten, P.C., Albright, A.L., & Johnstone, G.F. (1998). Intrathecal baclofen infusion and subsequent orthopedic surgery in patients with spastic cerebral palsy. *Journal of Neurosurgery, 88*(6), 1009–1013.

Gibson, C.J., Opalka, P.C., Moore, C.A., Brady, R.S., & Mion, L.C. (1995). Effectiveness of bran supplement on the bowel management of elderly rehabilitation patients. *Journal of Gerontological Nursing, 21*(10), 21–30.

Gill, K.P., Chia, Y.W., Henry, M.M., & Shorvon, P.J. (1994). Defecography in multiple sclerosis patients with severe constipation. *Radiology, 191*(2), 553–556.

Gilsdorf, P., Patterson, R., & Fisher, S. (1991). Thirty-minute continuous force measurements with different support surfaces in the spinal cord injured and able-bodied. *Journal of Rehabilitation Research and Development, 28*(4), 33–38.

Gisel, E.G., & Patrick, J. (1988). Identification of children with cerebral palsy unable to maintain a normal nutritional state. *Lancet, i,* 283–286.

Gogia, P., Schneider, V.S., LeBlanc, A.D., et al. (1988). Bed rest effect on extremity muscle torque in healthy men. *Archives of Physical Medicine and Rehabilitation, 69,* 1030–1032.

Goldstein, B., Sanders, J.E., & Benson, B. (1996). Pressure ulcers in SCI: does tension stimulate wound healing? *American Journal of Physical Medicine and Rehabilitation, 75*(2), 130–133.

Gordon Jr, A.M. (1981). Enteral nutritional support: guidelines for feeding tube selection and placement. *Postgraduate Medicine*, *70*, 155–162.

Gordon, C., Hewer, R.L., & Wade, D.T. (1987). Dysphagia in acute stroke. *British Medical Journal*, *295*, 411–414.

Gordon, W.A., Sliwinski, M., Echo, J., et al. (1998). The benefits of exercise in individuals with traumatic brain injury: a retrospective study. *Journal of Head Trauma Rehabilitation*, *13*(4), 58–67.

Gottlieb, D., Kipnis, M., Sister, E., Vardi, Y., & Brill, S. (1996). Validation of the 50 ML^3 drinking test for evaluation of post-stroke dysphagia. *Disability and Rehabilitation: An International Multidisciplinary Journal*, *18*(10), 529–532.

Gottschlich, M.M., Warden, G.D., Michel, M., et al. (1988). Diarrhea in tube-fed burn patients: incidence, etiology, nutritional impact and prevention. *Journal of Parenteral and Enteral Nutrition*, *12*, 338–345.

Grant, J.P. (1988). Comparison of percutaneous endoscopic gastrostomy with Stamm gastrostomy. *Annals of Surgery*, *207*, 598–603.

Grant, L.P., Wanger, L.I., & Neill, K.M. (1994). Fiber-fortified feedings in immobile patients. *Clinical Nursing Research*, *3*(2), 166–172.

Grant, R.H., Parsonage, M.J., & Barot, M.H. (1988). Phenytoin-induced gum hypertrophy in patients with epilepsy. *Current Medical Research Opinion*, *10*, 652–655.

Green, D. (1994). Prophylaxis of thromboembolism in spinal cord injured patients, *Chest*, *102*(Suppl A), 6495–6515.

Green, D., Chen, D., Chmiel, J.S., et al. (1994). Prevention of thromboembolism in spinal cord injury: role of low molecular weight heparin. *Archives of Physical Medicine and Rehabilitation*, *75*, 290–292.

Greenleaf, J.E. (1997). Intensive exercise training during bed rest attenuates deconditioning. *Medicine and Science in Sports and Exercise*, *29*(2), 207–215.

Greenleaf, J.E., Bernauer, E.M., Ertl, A.C., Bulbulian, R., & Bond, M. (1994). Isokinetic strength and endurance during 30-day 6 degrees head-down bed rest with isotonic and isokinetic exercise training. *Aviation Space and Environmental Medicine*, *65*(1), 45–50.

Greenleaf, J.E., Wade, C.E., & Leftheriotis, G. (1989). Orthostatic responses following 30-day bed rest deconditioning with isotonic and isokinetic exercise training. *Aviation Space and Environmental Medicine*, *60*, 537–542.

Greenwood, R., Luder, R., & Gilchrist, E. (1989). Neurogenic para-articular heterotopic ossification: a retrospective survey of 48 cases occurring after brain damage. *Clinical Rehabilitation*, *3*, 281–287.

Griffin, J., & Reddin, D. (1981). Shoulder pain in patients with hemiplegia. *Physical Therapy*, *61*, 1041–1045.

Grover, J., Gellman, H., & Waters, R.L. (1996). The effect of a flexion contracture of the elbow on the ability to transfer in patients who have quadriplegia at the sixth cervical level. *Journal of Bone and Joint surgery (American)*, *78*(9), 1397–1400.

Guite, H.F., Bliss, M.R., Mainwaring-Burton, R.W., et al. (1988). Hypothesis: posture is one of the determinants of the circadian rhythm of urine flow and electrolyte excretion in elderly female patients. *Age and Ageing*, *17*, 241–248.

Hajek, V.E. (1987). Heterotopic ossification in hemiplegia following stroke. *Archives of Physical Medicine and Rehabilitation*, *68*, 313–314.

Hakuno, A., Sashika, H., Ohkawa, T., & Itoh, R. (1984). Arthrographic findings in hemiplegic shoulders. *Archives of Physical Medicine and Rehabilitation*, *65*, 706–711.

Hall, R., Hirsch, J., Sackett, D.L., et al. (1977). Combined use of leg scanning and impedance plethysmography in suspected deep venous thrombosis: an alternative to venography. *New England Journal of Medicine*, *296*, 1497–1500.

Hardy, A.G., & Dickson, J.W. (1963). Pathologic ossification in traumatic paraplegia. *Journal of Bone and Joint Surgery (British)* *45*, 76–80.

Harper, C.M., & Lyles, Y.M. (1988). Physiology and complications of bed rest. *Journal of the American Geriatrics Society*, *36*, 1047–1054.

Harris, S., Chen, D., & Green, D. (1996). Enoxaparin for thromboembolism prophylaxis in spinal injury. *American Journal of Physical Medicine and Rehabilitation*, *75*, 326–327.

Haruna, Y., Suzuki, Y., Kawakubo, K., Yanagibori, R., & Gunji, A. (1994). Decrement in basal metabolism during 20-days bed rest. *Acta Physiologica Scandinavica Supplementum*, *616*, 43–49.

Hencey, J.Y., Vermess, M., van Geertruyden, H.H., Binard, J.E., & Manchepalli, S. (1996). Magnetic resonance imaging examinations of gluteal decubitus ulcers in spinal cord injury patients. *Journal of Spinal Cord Medicine*, *19*(1), 5–8.

Heymsfield, S.B., Casper, K., & Grossman, G.D. (1987). Bioenergetic and metabolic response to continuous v intermittent nasogastric feeding. *Metabolism*, *36*, 570–575.

Hill, J. (1994). The effects of casting on upper extremity motor disorders after brain injury. *American Journal of Occupational Therapy*, *48*, 219.

Himal, H.S., & Schumacher, S. (1987). Endoscopic vs surgical gastrostomy for enteral feeding. *Surgical Endoscopist*, *1*, 33–35.

Ho, C.S., Yee, A.C., & McPherson, R. (1988). Complications of surgical percutaneous nonendoscopic gastrostomy: review of 233 patients. *Gastroenterology*, *95*, 1206–1210.

Ho, Y.H., & Goh, H.S. (1995). Anorectal physiological parameters in chronic constipation of unknown aetiology (primary) and of cerebrovascular accidents—a preliminary report. *Annals of the Academy of Medicine, Singapore*, *24*(3), 376–378.

Hobson, D.A. (1992). Comparative effects of posture on pressure and shear at the body-seat interface. *Journal of Rehabilitation Research and Development*, *29*(4), 21–31.

Hoeldtke, R.D., Cavanaugh, S.T., & Hughes, J.D. (1988). Treatment of orthostatic hypotension: interaction of pressor drugs and tilt table conditioning. *Archives of Physical Medicine and Rehabilitation*, *69*, 895–898.

Hoffer, M.M., Knoebel, R.T., & Roberts, R. (1987). Contractures in cerebral palsy. *Clinical Orthopaedics*, *219*, 70–77.

Hoffman, M.D. (1986). Cardiorespiratory fitness and training in quadriplegics and paraplegics. *Sports Medicine*, *3*, 312–330.

Holey, L.A., & Lawler, H. (1995). The effects of classical massage and connective tissue manipulation on bowel function. *British Journal of Therapy and Rehabilitation*, *2*(11), 627–631.

Holloway, G.A., Daly, C.H., Kennedy, D., & Chimoskey, J. (1976). Effects of external pressure loading on human skin blood flow measured by 133Xe clearance. *Journal of Applied Physiology*, *40*, 597–600.

Holtz, L., Milton, J., & Struek, J.K. (1987). Compatability of medications with enteral feedings. *Journal of Parenteral and Enteral Nutrition*, *11*, 183–186.

Homer, J., & Massey, E.W. (1988). Silent aspiration following stroke. *Neurology*, *38*, 317–319.

Houle, R.J. (1969). Evaluation of seat devices designed to prevent ischaemic ulcers in paraplegic patients. *Archives of Physical Medicine and Rehabilitation*, *50*, 587–594.

Hunter, M., Tomberlin, J., Kirkikis, C., & Kuna, S.T. (1990). Progressive exercise testing in closed head injured subjects: comparison of exercise apparatus in assessment of a physical conditioning program. *Physical Therapy*, *70*(6), 363–371.

Hurvitz, E.A., Mandac, B.R., Davidoff, G., Johnson, J.H., & Nelson, V.S. (1992). Risk factors for heterotopic ossification in children and adolescents with severe traumatic brain injury. *Archives of Physical Medicine and Rehabilitation*, *73*(5), 459–462.

Hwang, T.I., Hill, K., Schneider, V., & Pak, C.Y. (1988). Effect of prolonged bed rest on the propensity for renal stone formation. *Journal of Clinical Endocrinology and Metabolism*, *66*, 109–112.

Ibarra-Perez, C., Lau-Cortes, E., Colmenero-Zubiate, S., et al. (1988). Prevalence and prevention of deep vein thrombosis of the lower extremities in high risk pulmonary patients. *Angiology*, *39*, 505–513.

Ideno, K.T. (1993). Enteral nutrition. In M.M. Gottschlich, L.E. Matarese & E.P. Shronts (Eds.), *Nutrition support dietetics-core curriculum* (pp. 71–103). American Society for Parenteral and Enteral Nutrition, Silver Springs, M D.

Ingram, R.R., Suman, R.K., & Freeman, P.A. (1989). Lower limb fractures in the chronic spinal cord injured patients. *Paraplegia*, *28*, 133–139.

Inman, K.J., Sibbald, W.J., Rutledge, F.S., & Clark, B.J. (1993). Clinical utility and cost-effectiveness of an air suspension bed in the prevention of pressure ulcers. *Journal of the American Medical Association*, *269*, 1139–1143.

Irvine, R.E., & Strouthidis, T.M. (1978). Stiff shoulder after a stroke. *British Medical Journal*, *i*, 1622.

Irwin-Carruthers, S., & Runnals, M.J. (1980). Painful shoulder in hemiplegia—prevention and treatment. *South African Journal of Physiotherapy*, *36*, 18–23.

Ishizaki, Y., Fukuoka, H., Katsura, T., Nishimura, Y., Kiriyama, M., Higurashi, M., Suzuki, Y., Kawakubo, K., & Gunji, A. (1994). Psychological effects of bed rest in young healthy subjects. *Acta Physiologica Scandinavica Supplementum*, *616*, 83–87.

Issekutz, B., Blizzard, J.J., Birkhead, N.C., & Rodahl, K. (1966). Effect of prolonged bed rest in urinary calcium output. *Journal of Applied Physiology*, *21*, 1013–1020.

Izumi, K. (1983). Study of ectopic bone formation in experimental spinal cord injured rabbits. *Paraplegia*, *21*, 351–363.

Jankowski, L.W., & Sullivan, S.J. (1990). Aerobic and neuromuscular training: effect on the capacity, efficiency, and fatiguability of patients with traumatic brain injuries. *Archives of Physical Medicine and Rehabilitation*, *71*, 500–504.

Jensen, J.A., Goodson III, W.H., Vasconez, L.O., & Hunt, T.K. (1986). Wound healing in anaemia. *Western Journal of Medicine*, *144*, 465–467.

Jortikka, M.O., Inkinen, R.I., Tammi, M.I., et al. (1997). Immobilisation causes longlasting matrix changes in both the immobilised and contralateral joint cartilage. *Annals of the Rheumatic Diseases*, *56*(4), 255–261.

Kakkar, V.V., Djazacri, B., Fox, J., et al. (1982). Low molecular weight heparin and prevention of post-operative deep vein thrombosis. *British Medical Journal*, *284*, 375–379.

Kalisky, Z., Morrison, D.P., Meyers, C.A., & Von Laufen, A. (1985). Medical problems encountered during rehabilitation of patients with head injury. *Archives of Physical Medicine and Rehabilitation*, *66*, 25–29.

Kantorowitz, D.A., & Muff, N.S. (1998). Preoperative vs. postoperative radiation prophylaxis of heterotopic ossification: a rural community hospital's experience. *International Journal of Radiation Oncology, Biology, Physics* *40*(1), 171–176.

Kato, H., Inoue, T., & Torii, S. (1998). A new postoperative management scheme for preventing sacral pressure sores in patients with spinal cord injuries. *Annals of Plastic Surgery*, *40*(1), 39–43.

Katsume, H., Furukawa, K., Azuma, A., et al. (1992). Disuse atrophy of the left ventricle in chronically bedridden elderly people. *Japanese Circulation Journal*, *56*(3), 201–206.

Kauhanen, S., Leivo, I., & Michelsson, J.E. (1993). Early muscle changes after immobilisation: an experimental study on muscle damage. *Clinical Orthopaedics and Related Research*, *297*, 44–50.

Kaul, S., & Sockalosby, J.J. (1995). Human synthetic calcitonin therapy for hypercalcaemia of immobilization. *Journal of Paediatrics*, *126*(5, Pt 1), 825–827.

Kaysinger, K.K., Ramp, W.K., Lang, G.J., & Gruber, H.E. (1997). Comparison of human osteoblasts and osteogenic cells from heterotopic bone. *Clinical Orthopaedics and Related Research*, *342*, 181–191.

Kearon, C., Julian, J.A., Newman, T.E., & Ginsberg, J.S. (1998). Noninvasive diagnosis of deep vein thrombosis. *Annals of Internal Medicine*, *128*, 663–677.

Kearns, P.J., Thompson, J.D., Werner, P.C., et al. (1992). Nutritional and metabolic response to acute spinal-cord injury. *Journal of Parenteral and Enteral Nutrition*, *16*(1), 11–15.

Keenan, M.A., Kauffman, D.I., Garland, D.E., & Smith, C. (1988). Late ulnar neuropathy in the brain injured adult. *Journal of Hand Surgery of America*, *13*, 120–140.

Keenan, M.E., Ure, K., Smith, C.W., & Jordan, C. (1988). Hamstring release for knee flexion contracture in spastic adults. *Clinical Orthopaedics*, *236*, 221–226.

Kelley, R.E., Vibulsresth, S., Bell, L., & Duncan, R.C. (1987). Evaluation of kinetic therapy in the prevention of complications of prolonged bed rest secondary to stroke. *Stroke*, *18*, 638–642.

Kelly, J., & Feigenbaum, L.Z. (1982). Another cause of reversible dementia: sleep deprivation due to prostatism. *Journal of the American Geriatrics Society*, *30*, 645–646.

Kenny, D.J., & Somaya, P. (1989). Sugar load of oral liquid medication on chronically ill children. *Canadian Dental Association Journal*, *55*, 43–46.

Keshavarzian, A., Barnes, W.E., Bruninga, K., et al. (1995). Delayed colonic transit in spinal cord-injured patients measured by indium-111 Amberlite scintigraphy. *American Journal of Gastroenterology*, *90*(8), 1295–1300.

Kiernan, M. (1998). Pressure sores: adopting the principles of risk management. *British Journal of Therapy and Rehabilitation*, *5*(8), 402–405.

Kierney, P.C., Cardenas, D.D., Engrav, L.H., Grant, J.H., & Rand, R.P. (1998). Limb-salvage in reconstruction of recalcitrant pressure sores using the inferiorly based rectus abdominis myocutaneous flap. *Plastic and Reconstructive Surgery* *102*(1), 111–116.

Kim, S.W., Charter, R.A., Chai, C.J., Kim, S.K., & Kim, E.S. (1990). Serum alkaline phosphatase and inorganic phosphorus values in spinal cord injury patients with heterotopic ossification. *Paraplegia*, *28*(7), 441–447.

Kiser, T.S., & Stefans, V.A. (1997). Pulmonary embolism in rehabilitation patients: relation to time before return to physical therapy after diagnosis of deep vein thrombosis. *Archives of Physical Medicine and Rehabilitation*, *78*(9), 942–945.

Kjaersgaard-Andersen, P., Pedersen, P., Kristensen, S.S., et al. (1988). Serum alkaline phosphatase as an indicator of heterotopic bone formation following total hip arthroplasty. *Clinical Orthopaedics*, *234*, 102–109.

Knight, A.L. (1988). Medical management of pressure sores. *Journal of Family Practice*, *27*, 95–100.

Koffler, K.H., Menkes, A., Redmond, R.A., et al. (1992). Strength training accelerates gastrointestinal transit in middle-aged and older men. *Medicine and Science in Sports and Exercise*, *24*, 415–419.

Konttinen, Y.T., Michelsson, J.E., Gronblad, M., et al. (1991). Plasma hyaluronan levels in rabbit immobilization osteoarthritis: effect of remobilization. *Scandinavian Journal of Rheumatology*, *20*(6), 392–396.

Kosiak, M. (1961). Etiology of decubitus ulcers. *Archives of Physical Medicine and Rehabilitation*, *42*, 19–29.

Kottke, F.J., Pauley, D.L., & Ptak, R.A. (1966). The rationale for prolonged stretching for correction of shortening of connective tissue. *Archives of Physical Medicine and Rehabilitation*, *47*, 345–352.

Krebs, J.M., Schneider, V.S., & LeBlanc, A.D. (1988). Zinc, copper and nitrogen balances during bed rest and fluoride supplementation in healthy adult males. *American Journal of Clinical Nutrition*, *47*, 509–514.

Krebs, J.M., Schneider, V.S., Leblanc, et al. (1993). Zinc and copper balances in healthy adult males during and after 17 wks of bed rest. *American Journal of Clinical Nutrition*, *58*(6), 897–901.

Krolner, B., & Toft, B. (1983). Vertebral bone loss: an unheeded side effect of therapeutic bed rest. *Clinical Science*, *64*, 537–540.

Küçükdeveci, A., Tennant, A., Hardo, P., & Chamberlain, M.A. (1996). Sleep problems in stroke patients: relationship with shoulder pain. *Clinical Rehabilitation*, *10*, 166–172.

Kuhn, W., Luscher, N.J., de Roche, R., Krupp, S., & Zach, G.A. (1992). The neurosensory musculocutaneous tensor fasciae latae flap: long term results. *Paraplegia*, *30*, 396–400.

Lal, S., Hamilton, B.B., Keinemann, A., & Betts, H.B. (1989). Risk factors for heterotopic ossification in spinal cord injury. *Archives of Physical Medicine and Rehabilitation*, *70*, 387–390.

Lancashire, P., Janzen, J., Zach, G.A., & Addy, M. (1997). The oral hygiene and gingival health of paraplegic patients—a cross-sectional survey. *Journal of Clinical Periodontology*, *24*(3), 198–200.

Lane, D.A., Wolff, S., Ireland, H., et al. (1983). Activation of coagulation and fibrinolytic systems following stroke. *British Journal of Haematology*, *53*, 655–658.

Larson, D.E., Burton, D.D., Schroeder, K.W., & DiMagno, E.P. (1987). Percutaneous endoscopic gastrostomy: indications, success, complications, and mortality in 314 consecutive patients. *Gastroenterology*, *93*, 48–52.

Lathers, C.M., & Charles, J.B. (1994). Orthostatic hypotension in patients, bed rest subjects, and astronauts. *Journal of Clinical Pharmacology*, *34*(5), 403–417.

Law, M.R., Wald, N.J., & Meade, T.W. (1991). Strategies for prevention of osteoporosis and hip fracture. *British Medical Journal*, *303*, 453–459.

Lawrence, G.D., Loeffler, R.G., Martin, L.G., & Connort, D. (1973). Immobilisation hypercalcaemia. *Journal of Bone and Joint Surgery 55-A*, 87–94.

Le, K.M., Madsen, B.L., Barth, P.W., et al. (1984). An in-depth look at pressure sores using monolithic silicon pressure sensors. *Plastic and Reconstructive Surgery*, *74*, 745–754.

LeBlanc, A., Evans, H., Schonfeld, E., et al. (1987). Changes in nuclear magnetic resonance (T2) relaxation of limb tissue with bed rest. *Magnetic Resonance Medicine*, *4*, 487–492.

LeBlanc, A., Gogia, P., Schneider, V., et al. (1988). Calf muscle area and strength changes after 5 weeks horizontal bed rest. *American Journal of Sports Medicine*, *16*, 624–629.

LeBlanc, A., Schneider, V., Spector, E., et al. (1995). Calcium absorption, endogenous excretion, and endocrine changes during and after long-term bed rest. *Bone 16*(4, Suppl), 301S–304S.

Lee, B.Y., (Ed.), (1997). *Surgical management: Cutaneous ulcers and pressure sores*. London: Chapman & Hall.

Leiderman, H., Mendelson, J.H., Wexler, D., & Solomon, P. (1958). Sensory deprivation. *Archives of Internal Medicine*, *101*, 389–396.

Lensing, A.W.A., Hirsh, J., & Büller, H.R. (1993). Diagnosis of venous thrombosis. In R.W. Colman, J. Hirsh, V.J. Marder, & E.W. Salzman, (Eds.) *Haemostasis and thrombosis: basic principles and clinical practice* (3rd Ed.) (pp. 1297–1321). Philadelphia: J.B. Lippincott.

Levine, J.M., Simpson, M., & McDonald, R.J. (1989). Pressure sores: a plan for primary care prevention. *Geriatrics, 44*, 75–90.

Levine, S.P., Kett, R.L., Cederna, P.S., & Brooks, S.V. (1990). Electric muscle stimulation for pressure sore prevention: tissue shape variation. *Archives of Physical Medicine and Rehabilitation, 71*, 210–215.

Lindan, O., Greenway, R.M., & Piozza, J.M. (1965). Pressure distribution on the surface of the human body: I. Evaluation in lying and sitting positions using a "bed of springs and nails". *Archives of Physical Medicine and Rehabilitation, 46*, 378–385.

Livesley, B. (1987). An expensive epidemic. *Nursing Times, 83*(6), 79.

Llaneza, P.P., Menendez, A.M., Roberts, R., & Dunn, G.D. (1988). Percutaneous endoscopic gastrostomy: clinical experience and follow up. *Southern Medical Journal, 81*, 321–324.

Loesche, W.J., Bromberg, J., Terpenning, M.S., et al. (1995). Xerostomia, xerogenic medications and food avoidances in selected geriatric groups. *Journal of the American Geriatrics Society, 43*(4), 401–407.

Logemann, J.A. (1993). *A manual for the videofluoroscopic evaluation of swallowing* (2nd Ed.) Pro-Ed, Austin, TX.

Longo, W.E., Ballantyne, G.H., & Modlin, I.M. (1989). The colon, anorectum and spinal cord patient: a review of the functional alterations of the denervated hindgut. *Disorders of the Colon and Rectum, 32*, 261–267.

Longo, W.E., Woolsey, R.M., Vernava, A.M., et al. (1995). Cisapride for constipation in spinal cord injured patients: a preliminary report. *Journal of Spinal Cord Medicine, 18*(4), 240–244.

Low, A.W. (1990). Prevention of pressure sores in patients with cancer. *Oncology Nursing Forum, 17*, 179–184.

Lowthian, P.T. (1970). Bed sores—the missing link. *Nursing Times, 66*, 1454–1458.

Lowthian, P.T. (1976). Pressure sores: practical prophylaxis. *Nursing Times, 72*, 295–298.

Lozes, M.H. (1988). Bladder and bowel management for children with myelomeningocele. *Infants and Young Children, 1*, 52–62.

Lundberg, B. (1969). The frozen shoulder. *Acta Orthopaedica Scandinavica, 119*(Suppl).

MacDonagh, R.P., Sun, W.M., Smallwood, R., Forster, D., & Read, N.W. (1990). Control of defecation in patients with spinal injuries by stimulation of sacral anterior nerve roots. *British Medical Journal, 300*(6738), 1494–1497.

Mackay-Lyons, M. (1989). Low-load, prolonged stretch in treatment of elbow flexion contractures secondary to head trauma: a case report. *Physical Therapy, 69*, 292–296.

Mall, V., Heinen, F., Linder, M., Philipsen, A., & Korinthenberg, R. (1997). Treatment of cerebral palsy with botulinum toxin A: functional benefit and reduction of disability. Three case reports. *Pediatric Rehabilitation, 1*(4), 235–237.

Margulies, J.Y., Simkin, A., Leichter, I., et al. (1986). Effect of intense physical activity on the bone—mineral content in the lower limbs in young adults. *Journal of Bone and Joint Surgery (American) 68*, 1090–1093.

Martel, G., Norean, L., & Jobin, J. (1991). Physiological responses to maximal exercise on arm cranking and wheelchair ergometer with paraplegics. *Paraplegics, 29*, 447–456.

Mathus-Vliegen, L.M.H., Louwerse, L.S., Meskus, M.P., Tytgat, G.N.J., & Vianney, D.E. Jong (1994). Percutaneous endoscopic gastrostomy in patients with amyotrophic lateral sclerosis and impaired pulmonary function. *Gastrointestinal Endoscopy, 40*, 463–469.

Mawson, A.R., Siddiqui, F.H., & Biundo Jr, J.J. (1993b). Enhancing host resistance to pressure ulcers: a new approach to prevention. *Preventive Medicine, 22*(3), 433–450.

Mawson, A.R., Siddiqui, F.H., Connolly, B.J., et al. (1993a). Sacral transcutaneous oxygen tension levels in the spinal cord injured: risk factors for pressure ulcers? *Archives of Physical Medicine and Rehabilitation, 74*(7), 745–751.

Mayerson, H.S., & Burch, C.E. (1940). Relationship of tissue (subcutaneous and intramuscular) and venous pressure to syncope induced in man by gravity. *American Journal of Physiology, 128*, 258–269.

Maynard, F.M. (1986). Immobilization hypercalcaemia following spinal cord injury. *Archives of Physical Medicine and Rehabilitation, 67*, 41–44.

Mazzini, L., Corra, T., Zaccala, M., et al. (1995). Percutaneous endoscopic gastrostomy and enteral nutrition in amyotropic lateral sclerosis. *Journal of Neurology, 242*(10), 695–698.

McAuliffe, J.A., & Wolfson, A.H. (1997). Early excision of heterotopic ossification about the elbow followed by radiation therapy. *Journal of Bone and Joint Surgery (America), 79*(5), 749–755.

McCarthy, S.T., & Turner, J. (1986). Low-dose subcutaneous heparin in the prevention of deep-vein thrombosis and pulmonary emboli following acute stroke. *Age and Ageing, 15*, 84–88.

Meguro, K., Yamagauchi, S., Doi, C., et al. (1992). Prevention of respiratory infections in elderly bed-bound nursing home patients. *Tohoku Journal of Experimental Medicine, 167*(2), 135–142.

Meiners, T., Abel, R., Bohm, V., & Gerner, H.J. (1997). Resection of heterotopic ossification of the hip in spinal cord injured patients. *Spinal Cord, 35*(7), 443–445.

Melchior, F.M., & Fortney, S.M. (1993). Orthostatic intolerance during a 13-day bed rest does not result from increased leg compliance. *Journal of Applied Physiology, 74*(1), 286–292.

Menter, R., Weitzenkamp, D., Cooper, D., et al. (1997). Bowel management outcomes in individuals with long-term spinal cord injuries. *Spinal Cord, 35*(9), 608–612.

Merli, G.J., Herbison, G., Weitz, H.H., et al. (1988). Comparison of low dose heparin, low dose heparin plus dihydroergotamine, low dose heparin plus electrical stimulation, and placebo as prophylaxis for deep vein thrombosis in acute spinal cord injury. *Paraplegia, 26*, 124–125.

Meshkinpour, H., Kemp, C., & Fairshter, R. (1989). Effect of aerobic exercise on mouth-to-caecum transit time. *Gastroenterology, 96*, 938–941.

Meythaler, J.M., Tuel, S.M., Cross, L.L., & Mathew, M.M. (1992). Heterotopic ossification of the extensor tendons in the hand associated with traumatic spinal cord injury. *Journal of the American Paraplegia Society, 15*(4), 229–231.

Michel, D., & Zach, G.A. (1997). Antiseptic efficacy of disinfecting solutions in suspension test in vitro against methicillin-resistant Staphylococcus aureus, Pseudomonas aeruginosa and Escherichia coli in pressure sore wounds after spinal cord injury. *Dermatology, 195*(Suppl 2), 36–41.

Michelsson, J.E., Pettila, M., Valtakari, T., Leivo, I., & Aho, H.J. (1994). Isolation of bone from muscles prevents the development of experimental callus-like heterotopic bone: a study of the interaction of bone and muscle in new bone formation. *Clinical Orthopaedics and Related Research, 302*, 266–272.

Mielants, H., Vanhove, E., deNeels, J., & Veys, E. (1975). Clinical survey of, and pathogenic approach to, para-articular ossification in long term coma. *Acta Orthopaedica Scandinavica, 46*, 190–198.

Miglietta, O., Lewithan, A., & Rogoff, J.B. (1959). Subluxation of the shoulder in hemiplegic patients. *New York State Journal of Medicine, 59*, 457–460.

Mikines, K.J., Dela, F., Tronier, B., & Galbo, H. (1989). Effect of seven days of bed rest on dose-response relation between plasma glucose and insulin secretion. *American Journal of Physiology, 257*, E43–48.

Mikines, K.J., Richter, E.A., Dela, F., & Galbo, H. (1991). Seven days of bed rest decrease insulin action on glucose uptake in leg and whole body. *Journal of Applied Physiology, 70*(3), 1245–1254.

Minns, R.J., & Sutton, R.A. (1991). Carbon fibre pad insertion as a method of achieving soft tissue augmentation in order to reduce the liability to pressure sore development in the spinal injury patient. *British Journal of Plastic Surgery, 44*(8), 615–618.

Mital, M.A., Garber, J.E., & Stinson, J.T. (1987). Ectopic bone formation in children and adolescents with head injuries: its management. *Journal of Pediatric Orthopedics, 7*, 83–90.

Moody, B.L., Fanale, J.E., Thompson, M., et al. (1988). Impact of staff education on pressure sore development in elderly hospitalized patients. *Archives of Internal Medicine, 148*, 2241–2243.

Moolten, S.E. (1972). Bedsores in chronically ill patients. *Archives of Physical Medicine and Rehabilitation, 53*, 430–438.

Moore, T.J. (1993). Functional outcome following surgical excision of heterotopic ossification in patients with traumatic brain injury. *Journal of Orthopaedic Trauma, 7*(1), 11–14.

Murphy, B.L., Sidhu, P.S., & Greene, R.E. (1996). Radiological placement of the gastrostomy tube should be the preferred method. *British Medical Journal, 312* (7036), 972–973.

Murray, T.S., Cox, F.C., Lorimer, A.R., & Lawrie, T.D.V. (1970). Leg-vein thrombosis following myocardial infarction. *Lancet ii*, 792–793.

Musselman, P.W., & Kay, R. (1985). Urinary tract stones in immobilised children. *Cleveland Clinic Quarterly, 52*, 11–13.

Najenson, T., Yachbovich, E., & Pikiekni, S.S. (1971). Rotator cuff injury in shoulder joints of hemiplegic patients. *Scandinavian Journal of Rehabilitation Medicine, 3*, 131–137.

Nash, M.S., Bilsker, S., Marcillo, A.E., et al. (1991). Reversal of adaptive left ventricular atrophy following electrically-stimulated exercise training in human tetraplegics. *Paraplegia, 29*, 590–599.

National Pressure Ulcer Advisory Panel (1989). Pressure ulcers prevalence, cost and risk assessment: consensus development conference statement. *Decubitus, 2*, 24.

Naylor, P.F.D. (1955). Experimental friction blisters. *British Journal of Dermatology, 67*, 327–342.

Nemcek, A.A., & Vogelzang, R.L. (1994). Angiography and interventional radiology. In R.M. Gore, M.S. Levine, & I. Laufer (Eds.), *Textbook of Gastrointestinal Radiology* (pp. 336–340). Philadelphia: W.B. Saunders.

Neumark, O.W. (1981). Deformities, not pressure, is the cause of pressure sores. *Care—Science and Practice, 1*, 41–45.

Neviaser, J.S. (1945). Adhesive capsulitis of the shoulder. *Journal of Bone and Joint Surgery, 27*, 211–222.

Newmark, S.R., Sublett, D., Block, J., & Geller, R. (1981). Nutritional assessment in a rehabilitation unit. *Archives of Physical Medicine and Rehabilitation, 62*, 279–282.

Newrick, P.G., & Hewer, R.L. (1984). Motor neurone disease: can we do better—a study of 42 patients. *British Medical Journal, 289*, 539–542.

Niazi, Z.B., Salzberg, C.A., Byrne, D.W., & Viehbeck, M. (1997). Recurrence of initial pressure ulcer in persons with spinal cord injuries. *Advances in Wound Care 10*(3), 38–42.

Nicholas, J.J. (1973). Ectopic bone formation in patients with spinal cord injury. *Archives of Physical Medicine and Rehabilitation, 54*, 354–359.

Norris, P.H., Smith, R.A., & Denys, E.H. (1985). Motor neurone disease: towards better care. *British Medical Journal, 291*, 259–262.

Norton, B., Homer-Ward, M., Donnelly, M.T., Long, R.G., & Holmes, G.K. (1996). A randomised prospective comparison of percutaneous endoscopic gastrostomy and nasogastric tube feeding after acute dysphagic stroke. *British Medical Journal, 312*(7022), 13–16.

Norton, D., McLaren, R., & Exton-Smith, A.M. (1975). *An investigation of geriatric nursing problems in hospital*. Edinburgh: Churchill Livingstone.

Nussbaum, E.L., Biemann, I., & Mustard, B. (1994). Comparison of ultrasound/ultraviolet-C and laser for treatment of pressure ulcers in patients with spinal cord injury. *Physical Therapy, 74*(9), 812–823.

O'Connor, J.P. (1998). Animal models of heterotopic ossification. *Clinical Orthopaedics and Related Research, 346*, 71–80.

O'Dwyer, N.J., Neilson, P.D., & Nash, J. (1989). Mechanisms of muscle growth related to muscle contracture in cerebral palsy. *Developmental Medicine and Child Neurology, 31*, 543–547.

Oki, S., Desaki, J., Matsuda, Y., Okumura, H., & Shibata, T. (1995). Capillaries with fenestrae in the rat soleus muscle after experimental limb immobilization. *Journal of Electron Microscopy, 44*(5), 307–310.

Olshansky, K. (1994). Essay on knowledge, caring and psychological factors in prevention and treatment of pressure ulcers. *Advances in Wound Care, 7*(3), 64–68.

Oreland, A., Heijbel, J., & Jagell, S. (1987). Malocclusion in physically and/or mentally handicapped children. *Swedish Dental Journal, 11*, 103–119.

Oreland, A., Heijbel, J., Jagell, S., & Persson, M. (1989). Oral function in the physically handicapped with or without severe mental retardation. *Journal of Dentistry for Children, 56*, 17–25.

Orzel, J.A., & Rudd, T.G. (1985). Heterotopic bone formation: clinical laboratory and imaging correlation. *Journal of Nuclear Medicine, 26*, 125–132.

Oswald, I. (1987). Sleep helps tissue renewal. *Clinical Rehabilitation, 1*, 239–241.

Ott, L., Young, B., Phillips, R., McClain, C., et al. (1991). Altered gastric emptying in the head-injured patient: relationship to feeding intolerance. *Journal of Neurosurgery, 74*, 738–742.

Ough, J.L., Garland, D.E., Jordan, C., & Waters, R.L. (1981). Treatment of spastic joint contractures in mentally disabled adults. *Orthopedic Clinics of North America, 12*, 143–151.

Pandyan, A.D., Granat, M.H., & Stott, D.J. (1997). Effects of electrical stimulation on flexion contractures in the hemiplegic wrist. *Clinical Rehabilitation, 11*(2), 123–130.

Parathyras, A.J., & Kassak, L.A. (1983). Tolerance, nutritional adequacy, and cost-effectiveness in continuing drip versus bolus and/or intermittent feeding techniques. *Nutritional Support Services, 40*, 56–57.

Pardoe, E.M. (1993). Development of a multistage diet for dysphagia. *Journal of the American Dietetic Association, 93*, 568–571.

Parkes, J.D. (1985). *Sleep and its disorders*. W.B. Saunders, London.

Payne, R.W., & de Wardener, H.E. (1958). Reversal of urinary diurnal rhythm following head injury. *Lancet, i*, 1098–1101.

Pedoto, M.J., O'Dell, M.W., Thrun, M., & Hollifield, D. (1995). Superior mesenteric artery syndrome in traumatic brain injury: two cases. *Archives of Physical Medicine and Rehabilitation, 76*(9), 871–875.

Pentland, B. (1993). Rehabilitation: quadriplegia and cardiorespiratory fitness. *Lancet, 341*, 413–414.

Perkash, A., Sullivan, G., Toth, L., et al. (1993). Persistent hypercoagulation associated with heterotopic ossification in patients with spinal cord injury long after injury has occurred. *Paraplegia, 31*(10), 653–659.

Perkins, M.R. (1985). Bolus enteral feeding. *Journal of Food and Nutrition, 42*, 195–196.

Perkins, R., & Skirving, A.P. (1987). Callus formation and the rate of healing of femoral fractures in patients with head injuries. *Journal of Bone and Joint Surgery (British) 69*, 521–524.

Perry, J. (1987). Contractures: a historical perspective. *Clinical Orthopaedics 219*, 8–14.

Persson, P.E., Sodemann, B., & Nilsson, O.S. (1998). Preventive effects of ibuprofen on periarticular heterotopic ossification after total hip arthroplasty: a randomized double-blind prospective study of treatment time. *Acta Orthopaedica Scandinavica, 69*(2), 111–115.

Petajan, J.H., Gappmaier, E., White, A.T., et al. (1996). Impact of aerobic training on fitness and quality of life in multiple sclerosis. *Annals of Neurology, 39*, 432–441.

Peters, R.A., & Westaby, D. (1994) Percutaneous endoscopic gastrostomy—indications, timing and complications of the technique. *British Journal of Intensive Care, 3*, 88–95.

Petersen, N.C. (1976). The development of pressure sores during hospitalisation. In R.M. Kenedi, J.M. Cowden, & Scales, J.T. (Eds.), *Bed sore biomechanics* (pp. 219–224). London: Macmillan.

Phillips, W., & Audet, M. (1990). Use of serial casting in the management of knee joint contractures in an adolescent with cerebral palsy. *Physical Therapy, 70*, 521.

Pidcock, F.S. (1987). Heterotopic ossification presenting as acute leg swelling in a comatose adolescent. *Clinical Pediatrics, 26*, 541–543.

Pinzur, M.S. (1996). Carpectomy and fusion in adult acquired hand spasticity. *Orthopedics, 19*(8), 675–677.

Potempa, K., Lopez, M., Braun, L.T., et al. (1995). Physiological outcomes of aerobic exercise training in hemiparetic stroke patients. *Stroke, 26*, 101–105.

Poulin de Courval, L., Barsanskas, A., Berenbaum, B., et al. (1990). Painful shoulder in the hemiplegic and unilateral neglect. *Archives of Physical Medicine and Rehabilitation, 71*, 673–676.

Prasad, K., Banerjee, K., & Howard, K. (1982). Incidence of deep vein thrombosis and the effect of pneumatic compression on the calf in elderly hemiplegics. *Age and Ageing, 11*, 42–44.

Prins, M.H., Gelsema, R., Sing, A.K., et al. (1989). Prophylaxis of deep venous thrombosis with a low-molecular weight heparin (Kabi (2165)/Fragmin) in stroke patients. *Haemostasis, 19*, 245–250.

Puet, T.A., Jackson, H., & Amy, S. (1997). Use of pulsed irrigation evacuation in the management of the neuropathic bowel. *Spinal Cord, 35*(10), 694–699.

Rapp, R.P., Young, A.B., Ywyman, D.L., et al. (1983). The favourable effect of early parenteral feeding on survival in head injured patients. *Journal of Neurosurgery, 58*, 906–912.

Read, N.W., & Timms, J.M. (1986). Defecation and the pathophysiology of constipation. *Clinical Gastroenterology, 15*, 937–965.

Reichel, S.M. (1958). Shearing force as a factor in decubitus ulcer in paraplegics. *Journal of the American Medical Association, 166*, 762–763.

Renfree, K.J., Banovac, K., Hornicek, F.J., et al. (1994). Evaluation of serum osteoblast mitogenic activity in spinal cord and head injury patients with acute heterotopic ossification. *Spine, 19*(7), 740–746.

Resende, T.L., Brocklehurst, J.C., & O'Neill, P.A. (1993). A pilot study on the effect of exercise and abdominal massage on bowel habit in continuing care patients. *Clinical Rehabilitation, 7*, 204–209.

Reuler, J., & Cooney, T. (1981). The pressure sore: pathophysiology and principles of management. *Annals of Internal Medicine, 94*, 661–666.

Rink, P., & Miller, F. (1990). Hip instability in spinal cord injury patients. *Journal of Pediatric Orthopedics, 10*(5), 583–587.

Ritter, M.A. (1987). Indomethacin: an adjunct to surgical excision of immature heterotopic bone formation in a patient with a severe head injury: a case report. *Orthopaedics, 10*, 1379–1381.

Ritter, M.A., & Sieber, J.M. (1985). Prophylactic indomethacin for the prevention of heterotopic bone formation following total hip arthroplasty. *Clinical Orthopaedics and Related Research, 196*, 217–225.

Roberts, W.R., & Addy, M. (1981). Comparison of the in-vivo and in-vitro antibacterial properties of antiseptic mouthrinse containing chlorhexidine, alexidine, cetylpyridinum chloride and hexetidine. *Journal of Clinical Peridontology*, *8*, 295–310.

Robertson, C.B., Clifton, G.L., & Grossman, R.G. (1984). Oxygen utilisation and cardiovascular function in head injured patients. *Neurosurgery*, *15*, 307–314.

Rodriguez, G.P., Claus-Walker, J., Kent, C., & Garza, H.M. (1989). Collagen metabolite excretion as a predictor of bone- and skin-related complications in spinal injury. *Archives of Physical Medicine and Rehabilitation*, *70*, 442–444.

Rogers, R.C. (1988). Heterotopic calcification in severe head injury: a preventive programme. *Brain Injury*, *2*, 169–173.

Roper, B.A. (1987). The orthopaedic management of the stroke patient. *Clinical Orthopaedics*, *219*, 78–86.

Rosen, J.F., Wolin, D.A., & Finberg, L. (1978). Immobilisation hypercalcaemia after single limb fractures in children and adolescents. *American Journal of Diseases of Children*, *132*, 560–564.

Rosenbaum, C.H., McDonald, R.E., & Lewitt, E.E. (1966). Occlusion of cerebral palsied children. *Journal of Dental Research*, *45*, 1696–1700.

Rosenfeld, B.A., Faraday, N., Campbell, D., Sakima, N., & Bell, W. (1994). The effects of bedrest on circadian changes in haemostasis. *Thrombosis and Haemostasis* *72*(2), 281–284.

Rossi, E., Green, D., Rosen, J., et al. (1980). Sequential changes in factor VIII and platelets preceding deep vein thrombosis in patients with spinal cord injury. *British Journal of Haematology*, *45*, 143–151.

Rowe, J., & Barer, D. (1995). A regional specialty policy for pressure sores. *Clinical Rehabilitation*, *9*, 262–266.

Roy, C.W., & Blamire, J.G. (1989). The functional shoulder orthosis in hemiplegic shoulder subluxation: a pilot study. *Clinical Rehabilitation*, *3*, 107–109.

Roy, C.W., Sands, M.R., & Hill, L.D. (1994). Shoulder pain in acutely admitted hemiplegics. *Clinical Rehabilitation*, *8*, 334–340.

Roy, C.W., Sands, M.R., Hill, L.D., et al. (1995). The effect of shoulder pain on outcome of acute hemiplegia. *Clinical Rehabilitation*, *9*, 21–27.

Royal College of Physicians Working Party (1991). Medical aspects of exercise. *Journal of the Royal College of Physicians of London*, *25*(3), 193–196.

Rubayi, S., Ambe, M.K., Garland, D.E., & Capen, D. (1992). Heterotopic ossification as a complication of the staged total thigh muscles flap in spinal cord injury patients. *Annals of Plastic Surgery*, *29*(1), 41–46.

Sahn, S.A. (1991). Continuous lateral rotational therapy and nosocomial pneumonia. *Chest*, *99*(5), 1263–1267.

Salzberg, C.A., Byrne, D.W., Cayten, C.G., et al. (1996). A new pressure ulcer risk assessment scale for individuals with spinal cord injury. *American Journal of Physical Medicine and Rehabilitation*, *75*(2), 96–104.

Salzberg, C.A., Cooper-Vastola, S.A., Perez, F., et al. (1995). The effects of non-thermal pulsed electromagnetic energy on wound healing of pressure ulcers in spinal cord-injured patients: a randomized, double-blind study. *Ostomy Wound Management*, *41*(3), 42–48.

Sandberg, P.R., Fibiger, H.C., & Mark, R.F. (1981). Body weight and dietary factors in Huntington's disease patients compared with matched controls. *Medical Journal of Australia*, *1*, 407–409.

Sandler, H., Popp, R.L., & Harrison, D.C. (1988). The haemodynamic effects of repeated bed rest exposure. *Aviation Space and Environmental Medicine*, *59*, 1047–1054.

Sandset, P.M., Dahl, T., Stiris, M., et al. (1990). A double-blind and randomized placebo-controlled trial of low molecular weight heparin once daily to prevent deep-vein thrombosis in acute ischaemic stroke. *Seminars in Thrombosis and Haemostasis*, *16*(Suppl), 25–33.

Santiago, M.C., Coyle, C.P., & Kinney, W.B. (1993). Aerobic exercise effects on individuals with physical disabilities. *Archives of Physical Medicine and Rehabilitation*, *74*(11), 1192–1198.

Sazbon, L., Najenson, T., Tartakovsky, M., et al. (1981). Widespread periarticular new bone formation in long-term comatose patients. *Journal of Bone and Joint Surgery (American)* *63*, 120–125.

Schaeffer, M.A., & Sosner, J. (1995). Heterotopic ossification: treatment of established bone with radiation therapy. *Archives of Physical Medicine and Rehabilitation*, *76*(3), 284–286.

Schmidt, S.A., Kjaersgaard-Andersen, P., Pedersen, N.W., et al. (1988). The use of indomethacin to prevent the formation of heterotopic bone after total hip replacement: a randomised double-blind controlled trial. *Journal of Bone and Joint Surgery (American)* *70*, 834–838.

Schmitt, D.A., Schaffar, L., Taylor, G.R., et al. (1996). Use of bed rest and head-down tilt to stimulate spaceflight-induced immune system changes. *Journal of Interferon and Cytokine Research*, *16*(2), 151–157.

Schollmeier, G., Uhthoff, H.K., Sarkar, K., & Fukuhara, K. (1994). Effects of immobilization on the capsule of the canine glenohumeral joint: a structural functional study. *Clinical Orthopaedics and Related Research*, *304*, 37–42.

Schoutens, A., Laurent, E., & Poortmans, J.R. (1989). Effects of inactivity and exercise on bone. *Sports Medicine*, *7*, 71–81.

Schubert, B. (1991). Hypotension as a risk factor for the development of pressure sores in elderly subjects. *Age and Ageing*, *20*, 255–261.

Schubert, V., & Fagrell, B. (1989). Local skin pressure and its effects on skin microcirculation as evaluated by laser-Doppler fluxmetry. *Clinical Physiology*, *9*, 535–545.

Schurch, B., Capaul, M., Vallotton, M.B., & Rossier, A.B. (1997). Prostaglandin E2 measurements: their value in the early diagnosis of heterotopic ossification in spinal cord injury patients. *Archives of Physical Medicine and Rehabilitation*, *78*(7), 687–691.

Seigel, W., Blomquist, G., & Mitchell, J.H. (1970). Effects of a quantitated physical training programme on middle-aged sedentary men. *Circulation*, *41*, 19.

Selley, W.G. (1977). Dental help for stroke patients. *British Dental Journal*, *143*, 409–412.

Sferopoulos, N.K., & Anagnostopoulos, D. (1997). Ectopic bone formation in a child with a head injury: complete regression after immobilisation. *International Orthopaedics*, *21*(6), 412–414.

Sgan-Cohen, H.D., Newbrun, E., Huber, R., et al. (1988). The effect of previous diet on plaque pH response to different foods. *Journal of Dental Research*, *67*, 1434–1437.

Shahani, B.T., Kelly, E.B., & Glaser, S. (1981). Hemiplegic shoulder subluxation. *Archives of Physical Medicine and Rehabilitation*, *63*, 519.

Shangraw, R.E., Stuart, C.A., Prince, M.J., et al. (1988). Insulin responsiveness of protein metabolism in vivo following bedrest in humans. *American Journal of Physiology*, *255*(4, Pt 1), E548–558.

Shapiro, C.M., & Devins, G.M. (1993). Sleep problems in patients with medical illness. *British Medical Journal*, *306*, 1532–1535.

Sherman, R.A., Wyle, F., & Vulpe, M. (1995). Maggot therapy for treating pressure ulcers in spinal cord injury patients. *Journal of Spinal Cord Medicine*, *18*(2), 71–74.

Siebens, H., Trup, E., Sonies, A. et al. (1986). Correlates and consequences of eating dependency in institutionalised elderly. *Journal of the American Geriatric Society*, *34*, 192–198.

Siegel, R.J., Vistnes, L.M., & Laub, D.R. (1973). Use of water beds in the prevention of pressure sores. *Journal of Plastic and Reconstructive Surgery*, *47*, 31–37.

Silen, W., & Skillman, J.J. (1976). Gastrointestinal responses to injury and infection. *Surgical Clinics of North America*, *56*(4), 945–952.

Sitzmann, J.V. (1990). Nutritional support of the dysphagic patient: methods, risks, and complications of therapy. *Journal of Parenteral and Enteral Nutrition*, *14*, 60–63.

Smith, R. (1987). Editorial. Head injury, fracture healing and callus. *Journal of Bone and Joint Surgery*, *69B*, 518–520.

Smith, R.G., Cruikshank, J.G., Dunbar, S., & Akhtar, A.J. (1982). Malalignment of the shoulder after stroke. *British Medical Journal*, *284*, 1224–1226.

Smithard, D. (1995). Dysphagia assessment after acute stroke. *Hospital Update*, Dec, 555–561.

Smithard, D.G. (1996). Gag reflex has no role in ability to swallow. *British Medical Journal*, *312*(7036), 9.

Smithard, D.G., England, R., Renwick, D.S., et al. (1994). Aspiration following acute stroke: incidence and diagnosis. *Cerebrovascular Diseases*, *4*(Suppl 1), 52.

Snoecx, M., De Muynck, M., & Van Laere, M. (1995). Association between muscle trauma and heterotopic ossification in spinal cord injured patients: reflections on their casual relationship and the diagnostic value of ultrasonography. *Paraplegia*, *33*(8), 464–468.

Sobus, K.M., Alexander, M.A., & Harcke, H.T. (1993). Undetected musculoskeletal trauma in children with traumatic brain injury or spinal cord injury. *Archives of Physical Medicine and Rehabilitation*, *74*(9), 902–904.

Sobus, K.M., Sherman, N., & Alexander, M.A. (1993). Coexistence of deep venous thrombosis and heterotopic ossification in the pediatric patient. *Archives of Physical Medicine and Rehabilitation*, *74*(5), 547–551.

Sodemann, B., Persson, P.E., & Nilsson, O.S. (1988). Prevention of periarticular heterotopic ossification following total hip arthroplasty: clinical experience with indomethacin and ibuprofen. *Archives of Orthopaedic and Traumatic Surgery, 107*, 329–333.

Sodring, K.M. (1980). Upper extremity orthosis for stroke patients. *International Journal of Rehabilitation Research, 3*, 33–38.

Somerman, M.J. (1987). Dental implications of pharmacological management of the Alzheimer's patient. *Gerodontology, 6*, 59–66.

Souren, L.E., Franssen, E.H., & Resiberg, B. (1995). Contractures and loss of function in patients with Alzheimer's disease. *Journal of the American Geriatrics Society, 43*(6), 650–655.

Spain, D.A., DeWeese, R.C., Reynolds, M.A., & Richardson, J.D. (1995). Transpyloric passage of feeding tubes in patients with head injuries does not decrease complications. *Journal of Trauma, 39*(6), 1100–1102.

Spencer, J.D., & Missen, G.A. (1989). Pseudomalignant heterotopic ossification ("myositis ossificans"): recurrence after excision with subsequent resorption. *Journal of Bone and Joint Surgery (British), 71*, 317–319.

Spencer, R.F. (1991). Heterotopic ossification in a finger following head injury. *Journal of Hand Surgery (British), 16*(2), 217–218.

Spencer, R.F., & Ganpath, V. (1988). Heterotopic bone formation following cerebral cysticercosis: a case report. *South African Medical Journal, 74*, 35–36.

Spielman, G., Gennarelli, T., & Rogers, R.C. (1983). Disodium etidronate: its role in preventing heterotopic ossification in severe head injury. *Archives of Physical Medicine and Rehabilitation, 64*, 539–542.

Splaingard, M.L., Hutchins, B., Sulton, L.D., & Chaudhuri, G. (1988). Aspiration in rehabilitation patients: videofluoroscopy vs bedside clinical assessment. *Archives of Physical Medicine and Rehabilitation, 69*, 637–640.

Stark, H.L. (1977). Directional variations in the extensibility of human skin. *British Journal of Plastic Surgery, 30*, 105–114.

Steffen, T.M., & Mollinger, L.A. (1995). Low-load, prolonged stretch in the treatment of knee flexion contractures in nursing home residents. *Physical Therapy 75*(10), 886–895.

Stover, S.L. (1986). Heterotopic ossification after spinal cord injury. In R.F. Bloch & M. Basbaum (Eds.) *Management of spinal cord injuries* (pp. 284–301). Baltimore: Williams & Wilkins.

Stover, S.L. (1987). Arthritis related interests in spinal cord injury. *Journal of Rheumatology, 14*(Suppl 15), 82–89.

Stover, S.L., Hahn, H.R., & Miller III, J.M. (1976). Disodium etidronate in the prevention of heterotopic ossification following spinal cord injury (preliminary report). *Paraplegia, 14*, 146–156.

Stover, S.L., Niemann, K.M., & Tulloss, J.R. (1991). Experience with surgical rejection of heterotopic bone in spinal cord injury patients. *Clinical Orthopaedics and Related Research, 263*, 71–77.

Subbarao, J.V., Nemchausky, B.A., & Gratzer, M. (1987). Resection of heterotopic ossification and Didronel therapy—regaining wheelchair independence in the spinal cord injured patient. *Journal of the American Paraplegic Society, 10*, 3–7.

Sullivan, S.J., Richer, E., & Laurent, F. (1990). The role of and possibilities for physical conditioning programmes in the rehabilitation of traumatically brain-injured persons. *Brain Injury, 4*(4), 407–414.

Sulzberger, M.B., Cortese, T.A., Fishman, L., et al. (1966). Studies on blisters produced by friction: results of linear rubbing and twisting techniques. *Journal of Investigational Dermatology, 47*, 456–465.

Summer, W.R., Curry, P., Haponik, E.F., et al. (1989). Continuous mechanical turning of ICU patients shortens length of stay in some diagnostic-related groups. *Journal of Critical Care, 4*, 45–53.

Suzuki, Y., Murakami, T., Haruna, Y., et al. (1994). Effects of 10 and 20 days bed rest on leg muscle mass and strength in young subjects. *Acta Physiologica Scandinavica Supplementum, 616*, 5–18.

Swann, D.M. (1954). Shoulder-hand syndrome following hemiplegia. *Neurology, 4*, 480–482.

Takenaka, K., Suzuki, Y., Kawakubo, K., et al. (1994). Cardiovascular effects of 20 days bed rest in healthy young subjects. *Acta Physiologica Scandinavica Supplementum, 616*, 59–63.

Tardieu, C., Lespargot, A., Tabary, C., & Bret, M.D. (1988). For how long must the soleus muscle be stretched each day to prevent contracture? *Developmental Medicine and Child Neurology, 30*, 3–10.

Tepperman, P.S., Greyson, N.D., Hilbert, L., et al. (1984). Reflex sympathetic dystrophy in hemiplegia. *Archives of Physical Medicine and Rehabilitation, 65*, 442–447.

Thomas, B.J., & Amstutz, H.C. (1985). Results of administration of diphosphonate for prevention of heterotopic ossification after total hip arthroplasty. *Journal of Bone and Joint Surgery (American), 67*, 400–403.

Thomas, B.J., & Amstutz, H.C. (1987). Prevention of heterotopic bone formation: clinical experience with diphosphonates, In *Hip: Proceedings of the Hip Society* (pp. 59–69). Philadelphia: J.B. Lippincott.

Thomas, D.P. (1985). Venous thrombogenesis. *Annual Review of Medicine, 35*, 39–50.

Thomson-Rowling, J. (1961). Pathological change in mummies. *Proceedings of the Royal Society of Medicine, 54*, 409–415.

Tori, J.A., & Hill, L.L. (1978). Hypercalcaemia in children with spinal cord injury. *Archives of Physical Medicine and Rehabilitation, 59*, 443–447.

Tow, A.P., & Kong, K.H. (1995). Prolonged fever and heterotopic ossification in a C4 tetraplegic patient: case report. *Paraplegia, 33*(3), 170–174.

Trudel, G., Jabi, M., & Uhthoff, H.K. (1998). Intraarticular tissue proliferation after immobility: methods of assessment and preliminary results in rat knee joints. *Journal of Rheumatology, 25*(5), 945–950.

Trueblood, H.W., Nelsen, T.S., & Oberhelman Jr, H.A. (1969). The effect of anaemia and iron deficiency on wound healing. *Archives of Surgery, 99*, 113–116.

Tsur, A., Sazbon, L., & Lotem, M. (1996). Relationship between muscular tone, movement and periarticular new bone formation in post coma-unaware (PC-U) patients. *Brain Injury, 10*(4), 259–262.

Turba, R.M., Lewis, V.L., & Green, D. (1992). Pressure sore anaemia: response to erythropoietin. *Archives of Physical Medicine and Rehabilitation, 73*, 498–500.

Turpie, A.G.G, Levine, M.N., Powers, P., et al. (1991). A double blind randomized trial of ORG 10172 low molecular weight heparinoid versus unfractionated heparin in the prevention of deep vein thrombosis in patients with thrombotic stroke. *Thrombosis and Haemostasis, 65*, 753.

Twyman, D. (1997). Nutritional management of the critically ill neurologic patient. *Critical Care Clinics, 13*(1), 39–49.

Twyman, D.L., Young, A.B., Ott, L., et al. (1985). High protein enteral feedings: a means of achieving positive nitrogen balance in head injured patients. *Journal of Parenteral and Enteral Nutrition, 9*, 679–684.

Uebelhart, D., Demiaux-Domenech, B., Roth, M., & Chantraine, A. (1995). Bone metabolism in spinal cord injured individuals and in others who have prolonged immobilisation: a review. *Paraplegia, 33*(11), 669–673.

Van Calcar, S.C., Liebl, B.H., Fischer, M.H., & Marlett, J.A. (1989). Long term nutritional status in an enterally nourished institutionalized population. *American Journal of Clinical Nutrition, 50*, 381–390.

van der Wiel, H.E., Lips, P., Nauta, J., et al. (1991). Biochemical parameters of bone turnover during ten days of bed rest and subsequent mobilization. *Bone and Mineral, 13*(2), 123–129.

Van Ouwenaller, C., Laplace, P.M., & Chantraine, A. (1986). Painful shoulder in hemiplegia. *Archives of Physical Medicine and Rehabilitation, 67*, 23–26.

Varghese, G. (1981). Shoulder complications in hemiplegia. *Journal of the Kansas Medical Society, 82*, 451–453.

Vellodi, C. (1989). Motor neurone disease: the controversy. *Clinical Rehabilitation, 3*, 313–316.

Venier, L.H., & Ditunno Jr, J.F. (1971). Heterotopic ossification in the paraplegic patient. *Archives of Physical Medicine and Rehabilitation, 52*, 475–479.

Viehbeck, M., McGlynn, & Harris, S. (1995). Pressure ulcers and wound healing: educating the spinal cord injured individual on the effects of cigarette smoking. *SCI (Spinal Cord Injury) Nursing, 12*(3), 73–76.

Vohra, R.K., & McCollum, C.N. (1994). Pressure sores. *British Medical Journal, 309*, 853–857.

Vorenkamp, S.E., & Nelson, T.L. (1987). Ulnar nerve entrapment due to heterotopic bone formation after a severe burn. *Journal of Hand Surgery, 12*, 378–380.

Waldron, D.J., Horgan, P.G., Patel, F.R., Maguire, R., & Given, H.F. (1993). Multiple sclerosis: assessment of colonic and anorectal function in the presence of faecal incontinence. *International Journal of Colorectal Disease, 8*(4), 220–224.

Walsh, J.J., & Tribe, C. (1965/1966). Phlebothrombosis and pulmonary embolism in paraplegia. *Paraplegia, 3*, 209–213.

Ward, R.J., Tolas, A.G., Benveniste, R.J., Hansen, J.M., & Donnica, J. (1966). Effect of posture on normal arterial blood gas tensions in the aged. *Geriatrics, 21*, 139–143.

Waring, W.P., & Karunas, R.S. (1991). Acute spinal cord injuries and the incidence of clinically occurring thromboembolic disease. *Paraplegia, 29*, 8–16.

Warlow, C., Ogston, E., & Douglas, A.S. (1976). Deep vein thrombosis of the legs after stroke. *British Medical Journal, 1*, 1178–1183.

Warner, J.J.P. (1990). The Judet quadricepsplasty for management of severe posttraumatic extension contracture of the knee. *Clinical Orthopaedics, 256,* 169–173.

Warren, C.G., Lehmann, J.F., & Koblanski, J.N. (1976). Heat and stretch procedures: an evaluation using rat tail tendon. *Archives of Physical Medicine and Rehabilitation, 77,* 122–126.

Watanabe, S., Yamada, K., Ono, S., & Ishibashi, Y. (1987). Skin changes in patients with amyotrophic lateral sclerosis: light and electron microscopic observations. *Journal of the American Academy of Dermatology, 17,* 1006–1012.

Weinstein, C.J. (1983). Neurogenic dysphagia: frequency, progression and outcome in adults following head injury. *Physical Therapy, 63,* 1992–1996.

Weiss, A., & Sachar, K. (1994). Soft tissue contractures about the elbow. *Hand Clinics, 10,* 439.

Weitz, J.I. (1997). Low-molecular-weight heparins. *New England Journal of Medicine, 337*(10), 688–698.

Wharton, G.W., & Morgan, T.H. (1970). Ankylosis in the paralyzed patients. *Journal of Bone and Joint Surgery (American), 52,* 105–112.

White, H.C. (1987). Heterotopic ossification in post-stroke hip fracture: a case report. *Journal of the American Geriatrics Society, 35,* 688–691.

Wickham, C.A., Walsh, K., Cooper, C., et al. (1989). Dietary calcium, physical activity, and risk of hip fracture: a prospective study. *British Medical Journal, 299,* 889–892.

Wicks, C., Gimson, A., Vlavianos, P., et al. (1992). An assessment of the percutaneous endoscopic gastrostomy (PEG) feeding tube as part of an integrated approach to enteral feeding. *Gut, 33,* 613–616.

Wild, D. (1991). Body pressures and bed surfaces. *Nursing Standard, 5,* 23–27.

Williams, C.M., Jones, C.M., & McKay, E.C. (1988). Iron and zinc status in multiple sclerosis patients with pressure sores. *European Journal of Clinical Nutrition, 42,* 335–345.

Willig, T.N., Bach, J.R., Rouffet, M.J., Krivickas, L.S., & Maquet, C. (1995). Correlation of flexion contractures with upper extremity function and pain for spinal muscular atrophy and congenital myopathy patients. *American Journal of Physical Medicine and Rehabilitation, 74*(1), 33–38.

Wittenberg, R.H., Peschke, U., & Botel, U. (1992). Heterotopic ossification after spinal cord injury: epidemiology and risk factors. *Journal of Bone and Joint Surgery, 74*(2), 215–218.

Wollman, B., D'Agostino, H.B., Walus-Wigle, J.R., Easter, D.W., & Beale, A. (1995). Radiologic, endoscopic, and surgical gastrostomy: An institutional evaluation and meta-analysis of the literature. *Radiology, 197,* 699–704.

Wolman, R.L., Cornall, C., Fulcher, K., & Greenwood, R. (1994). Aerobic training in brain-injured patients. *Clinical Rehabilitation, 8,* 253–257.

Woo, S.L.Y, Kuei, S.C., Amiel, D., et al. (1981). The effect of prolonged physical training on the properties of long bones: a study of Wolff's law. *Journal of Bone and Joint Surgery (American), 63,* 780–787.

Yanagibori, R., Suzuki, Y., Kawakubo, K., Makita, Y., & Gunji, A. (1994). Carbohydrate and lipid metabolism after 20 days of bed rest. *Acta Physiologica Scandinavica Supplementum, 616,* 51–57.

Yanover, L., Banting, D., Grainger, R., & Sandhu, H. (1988). Effect of a daily 0.2% chlorhexidine rinse on the oral health of an institutionalised elderly population. *Canadian Dental Association Journal, 54,* 595–598.

Yarkony, G.M., & Sahgal, V. (1987). Contractures: a major complication of craniocerebral trauma. *Clinical Orthopaedics, 219,* 93–96.

Yip, B., Stewart, D.A., & Roberts, M.A. (1996). The prevalence of joint contractures in residents in NHS continuing care. *Health Bulletin, 54*(4), 338–343.

Young, B., Ott, L., Twyman, D., et al. (1987). The effect of nutritional support on outcome from severe head injury. *Journal of Neurosurgery, 67,* 668–676.

Young, J.B., & Dobrzanski, S. (1992). Pressure sores: epidemiology and current management concepts. *Drugs and Ageing, 2,* 42–57.

Zack, M.B., Pontoppidian, H., & Kazemi, H. (1974). The effect of lateral positions on gas exchange in pulmonary disease. *American Review of Respiratory Disease, 110,* 49–55.

Zander, C., & Healy, N. (1992). Elbow flexion contractures treated with serial casts and conservative therapy. *Journal of Hand Surgery, 17,* 694.

Zederfeldt, B. (1957). Studies on wound healing and trauma. *Acta Chirgurica Scandinavica, 224*(Suppl), 1–85.

Zhou, X.J., Vaziri, N.D., Segal, J.L., et al. (1993). Effects of chronic spinal cord injury and pressure ulcer on 25(OH)-vitamin D levels. *Journal of the American Paraplegia Society, 16*(1), 9–13.

Zorbas, Y.G., Andreyev, V.G., & Popescu, L.B. (1988). Fluid-electrolyte metabolism and renal function in men under hypokinesia and physical exercise. *International Urology and Nephrology, 20,* 215–223.

Zubeck, J.P., Bayer, L., Milstein, S., & Shephard, J.M. (1969). Behavioural and physiological changes during prolonged immobilisation plus perceptual deprivation. *Journal of Abnormal Psychology, 74,* 230–236.

16. Biomechanics and rehabilitation engineering

Garth R. Johnson

INTRODUCTION

Relevance and contributions of engineering

In the field of rehabilitation, the skills of the engineer, both practical and theoretical, make possible the development and design of new devices and measurement techniques. In particular, the ability to understand a technical problem in terms of a theoretical *model* allows the engineer to propose entirely original solutions. In some circumstances, this may lead to a new approach to measurement while, in others, it may permit the design and development of novel equipment. Engineers are perhaps most commonly considered as people who make things and this is no less true in rehabilitation engineering where there is an ever-increasing demand for new types of equipment. This chapter will examine these various skills and identify some of the major contributions to rehabilitation. In the final section, some of the possible applications of new technologies will be identified.

BASIC MECHANICS AND MODELLING

Laws of mechanics and their application to the modelling of human joints

Virtually all of the techniques discussed here are dependent upon the understanding and application of a few basic laws of mechanics and, in particular, Newton's Laws of Motion. These are described well in a number of textbooks (e.g., Whittle, 1996) and so will not be covered here.

From the viewpoint of the engineer, a human joint can be considered as an engineering bearing connecting a pair of rigid structures. A joint has surfaces of geometry required to permit particular movements and ligaments which may both carry forces and control movement. The movement and application of forces at the joint is provided by muscles which may be considered as mechanical actuators, which are, of course, controlled from the brain by nerves. Each of these elements and, therefore, their assembly can be represented by a mathematical model which describes their behaviour under known conditions.

Muscle

Muscle is, of course, the element of major importance in neurological rehabilitation and the mathematical modelling of muscle has been central to much biomechanically oriented research concerned with neurological disability. Its force production characteristics, which are dependent upon length and rate of shortening, have been studied by Hill (1938), Huxley (1957), and others, and are shown graphically in Figure 16.1. Since these models simulate only the force production properties of muscle, models to simulate voluntary movement must include further and more complex models taking into account the information processing aspects of the nervous control system. A discussion of the resulting mathematical models is outside the scope of this text, but it is useful to identify their clinical applications.

Real joints, muscles, and tendons

Movement and the application of force at a limb is the result of the control of muscle, the production of force and the transmission of force to the limb segment. This means that other biomechanical models must be developed in order to predict the limb and joint forces. In this situation, in addition to the muscle parameters discussed earlier, we must now have information on the length of the tendon, its point of attachment to the bone and the geometry and kinematics of the joint. An example is the simplified model of the muscle acting on the scapula shown in Figure 16.2. This model, which includes only one muscle, allows immediate interpretation of the winging of the scapula which occurs with abduction of the shoulder but does not include information on either force generation or aspects of voluntary control. However, in some cases it may be possible to incorporate the muscle models described earlier into a biomechanical model of this kind.

Modelling of the behaviour of a complete limb and its joints must involve a higher order of complexity still because even a single one degree of freedom joint (e.g., the elbow) is invariably controlled by more than one muscle. Similarly, many muscles cross more than one joint, entailing analysis of several joints together, and making it necessary to estimate

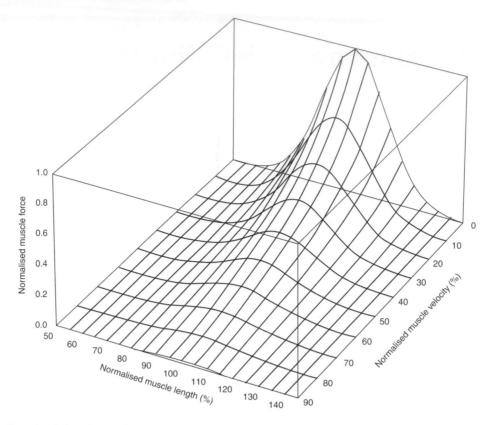

Figure 16.1. Three-dimensional chart showing the relationship between the force that can be developed by a muscle, its rate of shortening, and its length.

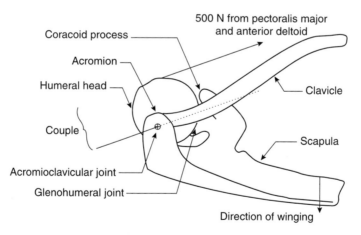

Figure 16.2. A simple biomechanical model of the muscles of the scapula illustrating how, in the absence of stabilising muscles, the anterior fibres of deltoid can lead to winging of the scapula during abduction. (This material has been reproduced from the *Proceedings of the Institution of Mechanical Engineers*, Part H, 1995, Vol 209, pp. 215–223, Figure 2, titled "Winging of the scapula: The underlying biomechanics and an orthotic solution" by Johnson, G. R. et al. by permission of the Council of the Institution of Mechanical Engineers.)

how force is shared by the muscles taking part in a particular activity. While this aspect of biomechanics, involving the study of multiple muscle systems, is the subject of much research and is too complex to discuss here, the clinician should be aware of the potentially complex interactions between muscles and their associated joints. This can become particularly significant when considering the deformities arising from

spasticity or contractures (e.g., the upper limb in a patient after stroke). Similarly, understanding these mechanisms is the key to the successful use of the muscle transfer techniques sometimes used, for instance, to improve the gait of children with cerebral palsy (Gage, 1991) or when developing an orthotic approach to correction of the winging scapula (Barnett et al., 1995).

MEASUREMENT

The need for outcome measurement in neurological rehabilitation is, of course, well established (Wade, 1992), and the majority of the measurement is based on validated questionnaire-based techniques. However, several physical measurements, which can frequently provide the clinician with useful and reliable information, have been developed by bioengineers. Some of the major applications are discussed in this section.

Motion

Goniometry.   Probably the most straightforward measurement to be made is that of joint angle or position which may be of use when assessing fixed deformities such as contractures where it is important to monitor rehabilitation progress. However, dynamic measurements have greatest potential in monitoring rehabilitation. These may be either of ranges of lower limb motion during gait or else of the upper limb when following progress, for instance, after stroke.

Instruments for these measurements (goniometers) are readily available either for static measurement (simple protractor instruments) or for dynamic measurement where new designs of electrogoniometer are now being used. An interesting example is the flexible electrogoniometer, first described by Nicol (1987), in which a flexible strain gauged strip is used as the measuring element. It can be shown that this device, which can measure movement in two perpendicular planes, provides accurate measurements without the need for alignment with respect to joint centres of rotation. These goniometers can be used in conjunction with a simple hand-held digital display or with a lightweight data logger which can be interfaced to a computer after data collection. The data collection may be for a short period to evaluate a gait pattern or for a 24 hour period if it is required to study levels of activity.

Movement in three dimensions.   While the goniometers described previously can measure limb movements in two planes they cannot completely describe the three-dimensional movements, for instance, of the upper limb when performing ADL tasks, or of the back. The author's group have examined this requirement and demonstrated the use of electromagnetic movement sensors to measure three-dimensional movements at the shoulder complex and, more recently, using a palpation technique to determine the three-dimensional position of the scapula. This technique is now being used to make measurements of shoulder posture in patients after stroke. Typical results are shown in Figure 16.3.

Three-dimensional movements can also be measured using multiple camera systems such as VICON or Kinemetrix in which mathematical processing allows the construction of a three-dimensional image from combinations of two or more two-dimensional camera views. These methods are commonly used in gait analysis but have also been demonstrated in studies of the upper limb. However, unless they already form part of a clinical gait analysis facility, they are likely to be prohibitively costly.

Neurological tremor.   While the measurement of tremor is an extension of the measurement of other movements, different

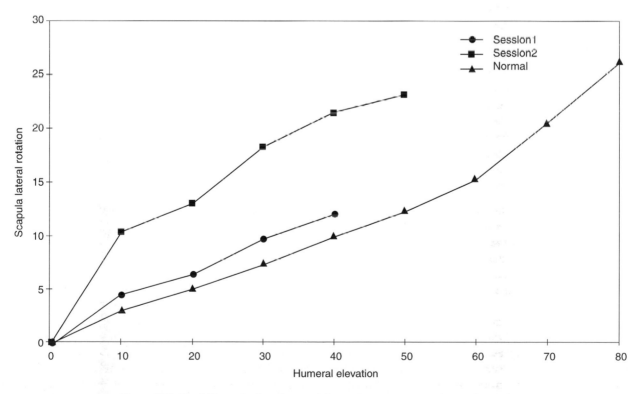

Figure 16.3. Graph illustrating how the scapulohumeral movements may change after stroke.

techniques are appropriate. This arises from the fact that it commonly entails the study of the joints of a single (upper) limb and is concerned with the study of oscillatory motion. It is normal to use accelerometers to measure this relatively low frequency vibration.

Forces

As well as measuring movements, there can frequently be a need to measure forces also. This may be required in the assessment of strength, spasticity, or in more sophisticated studies of gait. Force can be measured by a variety of *transducers* which produce electrical outputs that are normally linearly related to applied force. The simplest force measurement device is, of course, the spring balance which can be used in the assessment of limb strength. However, the need for compactness and reliability has led to the widespread use of electronic systems. Probably the most common method of producing a force transducer is by the application of strain gauges to a structural component (for instance a ring) having known mechanical properties. Then, using suitable electronics, it is possible to achieve an electrical output for display by a digital display, in either data storage or graphical form. Other systems make use of *piezoelectric* materials in which an electrical charge is produced in proportion to applied force.

Many clinical applications of these transducers have been demonstrated. In the form of a "myometer" (a single axis force transducer for the measurement of limb forces produced by muscle), techniques have been developed for the assessment of spasticity (Duckworth & Jordan, 1995) as well as for strength measurement.

Measurement of pressure.   Pressure is defined as force per unit area (in engineering terms this is the same as stress) and is an important clinical variable, particularly in the study of loaded interfaces, for instance under the foot. In the assessment of foot deformities, there has been the development of the pedobarograph which can measure the static pressure distribution under the foot while standing. While this has been used predominantly in the study of orthopaedic foot disorders, similar techniques have been used to assess load distribution under the foot of patients after stroke. However, perhaps the most interesting development from the technical point of view has been that of the dynamic foot pressure transducer for use in the shoe. The output from such a device is shown in Figure 16.4. Similar systems have also been developed for the measurement of pressures during lying and sitting to allow the assessment of seating systems and to minimise problems of pressure sores and to assist in the design of seating systems.

GAIT MECHANICS AND GAIT ANALYSIS

While neurological disability can affect the upper and lower limbs equally, it is probably the lower limb which has received the greater attention from the bioengineer. This has arisen because of the dominant importance of mobility as a

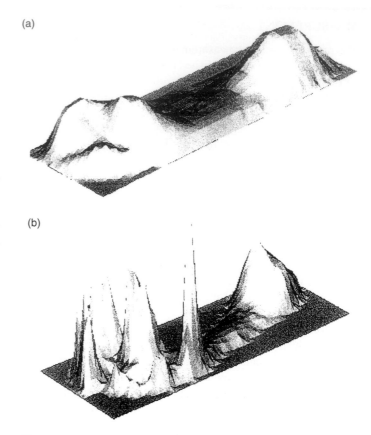

Figure 16.4. Graphical display of pressure under the foot during walking for: (a) normal subject and (b) patient with diabetic neuropathy (courtesy of Dr M. Shorten, Teleport Inc).

rehabilitation goal. The basic principles of the mechanics of walking are well understood and are summarised in Figure 16.5.

The force platform and video vector display

In some applications, particularly in gait analysis, there arises a need to measure forces and moments in three dimensions. This can be achieved by using combinations of the transducers described earlier attached to a rigid plate, which is usually mounted in the floor. Such a *force plate* is available and is in use in gait analysis centres around the world. This device normally allows the calculation of forces in three directions as well as the moments about the same three axes.

When describing the basic mechanics of gait, it has been shown that the muscle actions at the major joints are related to the force actions (in particular, the moments) at the ground described by the magnitude, point of application, and direction of the ground reaction force vector. Thus, it is possible to identify joints that are subject to large moments by examination of the relationship between the ground reaction force vector and the centre of rotation of the joint being considered. The value of this method of display is shown in Figure 16.6, when assessing the benefits of an ankle foot orthosis supplied to a child with cerebral palsy. The ability to make these measurements in the clinical setting has provided the facility to "tune" ankle foot orthoses (Butler et al., 1992).

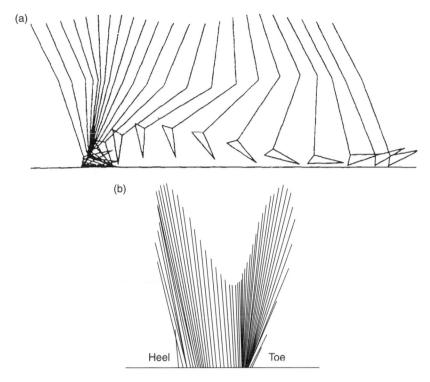

Figure 16.5. Diagrams illustrating (a) the kinematics of the leg during normal walking, and (b) the force acting on the foot during the stance phase of normal walking. (From Whittle, M.W. (1996) *Gait analysis—an introduction* 2nd edition. Reprinted by permission of Elsevier Science Limited.)

Figure 16.6. Video vector display of the ground reaction vector during gait in a patient illustrating the malalignment of the vector and the changes achieved by an ankle foot orthosis. This shows the classic barefoot midstance with anterior excursion of the ground reaction vector. (1) An afo fails to control this (2), but with wedging to the heel the ground reaction vector alignment at midstance is normalised (3). (Courtesy of Orthotics Research and Locomotor Assessment Unit, Robert Jones and Agnes Hospital, Oswestry, SALOP.)

MANUFACTURE AND DESIGN

It is not possible, in a text of this kind, to describe all of the relevant equipment designed by engineers. Therefore, this section will concentrate on orthoses which are relevant to neurological disability and to some new applications of advanced technology.

Orthoses

Orthoses probably represent the greatest biomechanical contribution to the field of neurological disability. The ankle foot orthosis (AFO) has already been referred to when discussing gait analysis. It is, perhaps, a perfect example of how a simple device having the correct properties and design can make a profound

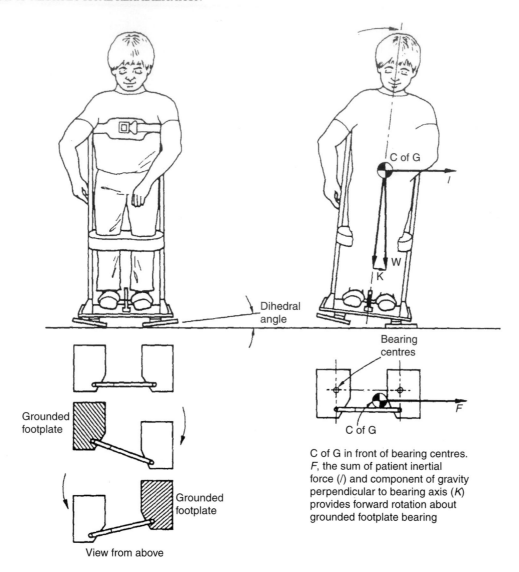

Dihedral angle

Grounded footplate

Grounded footplate

View from above

Bearing centres

C of G

C of G in front of bearing centres. *F*, the sum of patient inertial force (*I*) and component of gravity perpendicular to bearing axis (*K*) provides forward rotation about grounded footplate bearing

Figure 16.7. The mechanical principles of the swivel walker. (From Bowker, P., Bader, D.L., Pratt, D.J., Condie, D.N., & Wallace, W.A. eds *Biomechanical basis of orthotic prescription*. Reprinted by permission of Elsevier Science Limited.)

contribution. It is appropriate here to describe other devices based upon the same fundamentals of mechanics. The swivel walker, first demonstrated by Hall in 1962, provides a child with mobility through the application of appropriate forces and movements. The principles of its use are shown in Figure 16.7.

Other devices used, for instance by children with spina bifida, are the reciprocating gait orthosis (RGO; Douglas et al., 1983) and hip guidance orthosis (HGO; Rose, 1979). While relying on slightly different principles, both of these devices allow reciprocal ambulation using upper limb forces (applied by latissimus dorsi) applied to the ground by crutches. In the case of the RGO, reciprocation is achieved by the action of cables which connect the hip articulations. In the HGO, the forward swing of the limb is produced by gravity while sufficient ground clearance is achieved by the action of the crutch and the stiffness of the orthotic structure. This is illustrated in Figure 16.8. While the prescription criteria differentiating between these two

devices are not yet clear, energy efficient ambulation has been demonstrated for both.

Upper limb orthoses

While upper limb orthoses are used rather less than those for the lower limb, there are two important applications to be mentioned here:

Flexor hinge/powered orthosis for the hand.   This device, in its simplest form, allows the use of wrist extension strength to produce a pinch grip. It is, therefore, particularly useful for patients who have spinal cord injury at a level which paralyses the flexors muscles but not the extensors. For people with more severe impairments, a powered version using a gas operated "artificial muscle" may be used.

Upper limb orthosis after brachial plexus injury.   Patients with brachial plexus lesions (see Chapter 47) typically present

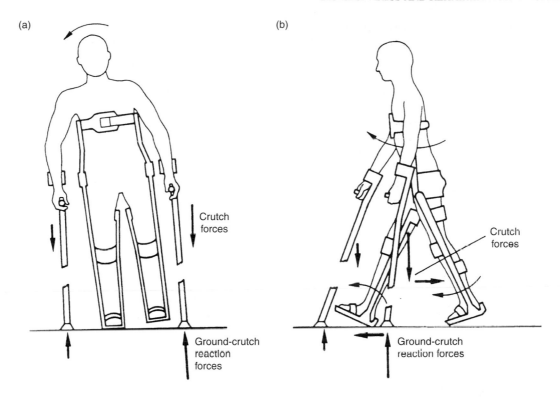

Figure 16.8. The mechanical principles of the hip guidance orthosis (HGO). (a) Patient clearing swing leg by using a crutch to tilt himself sideways. (b) Swing leg moving from extension to flexion under the influence of gravity and patient using latissimus dorsi to produce crutch forces to drive stance leg into extension. (Curved arrows indicate direction of rotation of body segments, straight arrows show vertical and horizontal crutch force vectors.) (From Bowker, P., Bader, D.L., Pratt, D.J., Condie, D.N., & Wallace, W.A. eds *Biomechanical basis of orthotic prescription*. Butterworth, London, p. 179.)

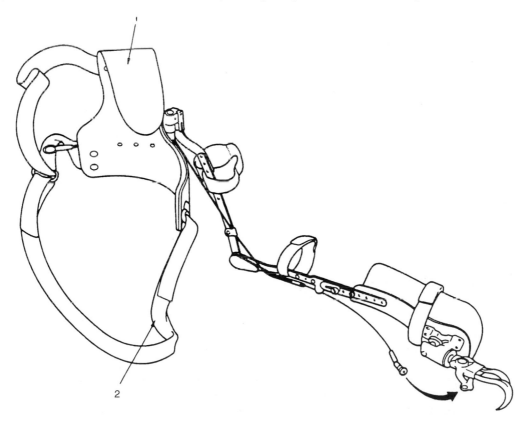

Figure 16.9. Stanmore orthosis. (From Bowker, P., Bader, D.L., Pratt, D.J., Condie, D.N., & Wallace, W.A. eds *Biomechanical basis of orthotic prescription*. Butterworth, London, p. 209.)

with a flail arm caused by combined denervation of the wrist extensors, elbow flexors, and forearm supinators. The shoulder muscles innervated by the brachial plexus are also commonly involved. This results in inferior displacement of the shoulder with the arm hanging limp against the trunk in a position of internal rotation and pronation. A number of orthoses have been developed to deal with this problem and one of them, the Stanmore orthosis, is shown in Figure 16.9. This orthosis does not provide stabilisation of the shoulder but can allow stabilisation of the elbow by a ratchet device so that the arm may be "thrown" into a convenient position. The weight of the arm and orthosis is supported by a suitable shoulder/trunk harness. If required, a suitable hook or other terminating device can be fitted and operated by the opposite shoulder through a flexible cable.

THE FUTURE

Future developments in rehabilitation engineering will result from the developments in materials and in control and computing technology. Perhaps one of the most exciting areas is that of mechatronics and robotics, which are making possible new robotic devices for people with severe disabilities. While there are currently only two robots available commercially, and only a small number in use at the time of writing, it seems certain that the field will develop over the coming years. Currently, the major obstacle to use of these devices concerns the problems of control. A useful robot must have several degrees of freedom and so must be controlled through several input channels. However, many potential users cannot provide these inputs because of their severe disability. However, the rapid development of speech-controlled systems may reduce these obstacles in the future. This is a major field for future research.

Another new field is that of virtual reality in which virtual environments can be produced entirely by software and appropriate vision systems. Potentially this technology has exciting applications in training (Grealy et al., 1999), in the assessment of disability, and in allowing people with severe disabilities to control sophisticated devices (Rose et al., 1996).

REFERENCES

Barnett, N.D., Mander, M., Peacock, J.C., Bushby, K., Gardner-Medwin, D., & Johnson, G.R. (1995). Winging of the scapula: the underlying biomechanics and an orthotic solution. *J. Eng. Med, Proc. I. Mech. E., Part H, 209*, 215–223.

Butler, P.B., Thompson, N., & Major, R.E. (1992). Improvements in walking performance of children with cerebral palsy: preliminary results. *Dev. Med. Child Neurol., 34*, 567–576.

Douglas, R., Larson, P., D'Ambrosia, R., et al. (1983). The LSU reciprocating brace orthosis. *Orthopaedics, 6*, 834–839.

Duckworth, S., & Jordan, N. (1995). Peripheral nerve blockade with phenol in spasticity—a myometric and functional assessment. *Abstract J. Neurol., Neurosurg., Psych., 59*, 214.

Gage, J.R. (1991). *Gait analysis in cerebral palsy*. London: MacKeith Press.

Grealy, M.A., Johnson, D.J., & Rushton, S.K. (1999). Improving cognitive function following brain injury: the use of exercise and virtual reality. *Ann. Phys. Med. Rehab., 80*, 661–667.

Hall, C.B. (1962). Ambulation of congenital bilateral lower extremity amelias and/or phocomelias. *Inter. Clin. Inform. Bull., 1*, 34.

Hill, A.V. (1938). The heat of shortening and the dynamic constants of muscle. *Proc. Roy. Soc. [Biol.], 126*, 136–195.

Huxley, A.F. (1957). Muscle structure and theories of contraction. *Prog. Biophys., 7*, 255–318.

Nicol, A.C. (1987). Measurement of joint motion. *Clin. Rehabil., 3*, 1–9.

Rose, F.D., Attree, E.A. & Johnson, D.A. (1996). Virtual reality: an assistive tool in neurological rehabilitation. *Curr. Opin. Neurol., 9*, 461–467.

Rose, G.K. (1979). The principles and practice of hip guidance articulations. *Prosthet. Orthot. Int., 3*, 37–43.

Wade, D.T. (1992). *Measurement in neurological rehabilitation*. Oxford University Press.

Whittle, M.W. (1996). *Gait analysis—an introduction* 2nd edition. Butterworth Heinemann, Oxford.

17. Assistive technology: Mobility aids, environmental control systems, and communication aids

N.C.M. Fyfe   E.J.W. McClemont   L.E. Panton   L.J. Sandles

INTRODUCTION

The ability to mobilise whether by foot, wheelchair, car, or public transport system is fundamental to the fulfilment of many functional activities and thus to participation in society. To limit a person's mobility is to confine them to a life within their home environment with a high level of dependency. The main focus of many patients' attention following trauma or the main concern of patients whose condition is progressing is the restoration or maintenance of mobility, as the consequences of immobility are all too apparent. The value placed upon mobility is high. The integration of people with disabilities into society is dependent upon many factors one of which is the ability to move freely within that society using whatever method of mobility is appropriate and to have access to the same opportunities as everyone else. This subject area envelopes many far reaching issues and relates to environmental and attitudinal barriers, corporate and governmental policy, and the availability and allocation of resources as well as the actual aids to mobility available to people. The first aim of this chapter is to consider ways in which the ability to mobilise can be enhanced for patients whose mobility has been impaired by a neurological condition. The assessment for and prescription of wheelchairs powered and non-powered—is reviewed in outline. Thereafter the assistance available to disabled individuals who wish to continue driving their own cars is also discussed.

There remain those patients whose condition has deteriorated to such an extent that mobility is impossible even within the confines of their own homes. Here it is not just the ability to move around that has been lost but also the ability to perform relatively mundane, yet often for the individual, crucially important activities of daily living. The harnessing of modern electronic and microprocessor technology in the development of Environmental Control Systems (ECS) can confer on the most severely disabled considerably lessened dependence on carers. We consider the ways in which equipment of various levels of sophistication can achieve this.

The category of the neurologically impaired for whom ECS may be appropriate may frequently show coexistent difficulties with communication and the third aim of this chapter is to consider the ways in which technology may make a beneficial contribution.

These three areas—mobility, control over the environment, and communication—although treated separately here are, of course, interactive in individuals with complex neurological disability. Each area requires evaluation by appropriate experts acting cooperatively so that through the interdisciplinary network, an holistic solution may eventually be reached.

WHEELCHAIRS AND WHEELCHAIR SEATING

Progress in technology and design has, over recent years, led to a vast improvement in the performance of wheelchairs.

Several factors have played a role, the use of new materials such as titanium, plastics, and carbon fibre, the implementation of safety parameters, more rigorous laboratory testing and evaluation, and a concern for aesthetics (Dollfus, 1990). The aim of this section is to introduce some of the principles involved in the selection of wheelchairs. It is not seen as a comprehensive guide to wheelchair assessments as the detail necessary to cover this topic is too great for inclusion in this format. Further details on wheelchair hardware and assessment are available elsewhere (Cochrane, 1993; Marks, 1997). The choice of wheelchair has never been larger.

The use of a wheelchair is considered to facilitate mobility when:

(1) a patient does not have the functional capacity to ambulate
(2) the time or effort involved in ambulation is prohibitive to other aspects of function
(3) the patient is dependent in terms of mobility and a chair is indicated to assist a carer in moving a patient from one place to another.

The decision to introduce a wheelchair into a patient's life is usually taken by a clinician or therapist involved closely in the management of the patient. The person taking this decision is not necessarily the person who prescribes the specific wheelchair as a referral to a specialist clinic may be indicated. Patients with neurological conditions frequently have special needs in relation to wheelchair assessment that are dealt with on a regular basis by specialists whose level of expertise is thereby enhanced. The team encountered in this specialist area usually comprises:

- physician
- therapist—occupational or physio
- rehabilitation engineer
- orthotist.

The role of the first two is to set prescriptive objectives in the light of their knowledge of the patient, his or her clinical condition, and his or her disability in terms of the type of chair, seating, accommodation of deformity, postural support, pressure care, and lifestyle. The rehabilitation engineer is responsible for the specification of modifications and adaptations, such as specialist controls for powered wheelchairs. The orthotist is responsible for the fabrication of inserts such as moulded seats. Such teams now exist (usually multiply) in all National Health Service Regions in the UK. All NHS Districts have a wheelchair service catering for the less specialist requirements.

Clients who opt to purchase chairs privately rarely have access to such expertise. In some areas Disabled Living Centres exist, where therapists provide information and advice and demonstrate assistive equipment, including wheelchairs. Access to such a resource centre will enable a patient to gain advice otherwise unavailable in the private sector. Once opting to purchase privately, the accommodation of specialist needs, such as those of seating or switching, becomes more difficult as companies offer such services rarely and they tend to be costly.

The extent of public provision of wheelchairs varies considerably from country to country. In some countries there are no restrictions upon the chair which can be prescribed by the clinician while in others (including the UK) the state provides a limited range free of charge and anything outside of that range must be funded, in whole or part, by the patient. Chairs required for use in an employment situation can sometimes be supplied via Governmental departments of employment. If clients purchase chairs privately they must be made aware of the ongoing costs of maintaining the chair, especially in the case of powered chairs and the extra cost of purchasing specialised cushions if required.

For some the transition to a wheelchair may be a matter of rapid change, or it may mark a period of gradual deterioration and for others it will be the only method of mobility they have known. Many patients may have difficulty in accepting this transition and may prefer to battle on against increasing adversity. Some patients may resort to wheelchair use too early and may accordingly suffer accelerated loss of remaining faculties. Patients should be taught to regard their wheelchair as a symbol of mobility rather than as a mark of increasing disability. At whatever point a wheelchair is introduced into a person's life, the clinician must not underestimate the adjustments the patient is having to go through physically, psychologically, and socially. The assessment of a client for a wheelchair must be an holistic assessment which covers not only the patient's clinical condition but also their functional requirements, the psychological

and social factors entailed in being a wheelchair user, and any environmental considerations that may influence the choice of a chair. While from an objective point of view these factors may be apparent, subjectively the changes in body image, level of functioning, and the inescapable symbolism of a wheelchair as a sign of disability that is restrictive in terms of coping with environmental barriers are all too apparent for the patient. Time and counselling may be required to assist the patient in making this transition. The skills and confidence required to use a wheelchair should also not be underestimated. Although using a wheelchair in a hospital environment seems relatively trouble free, coping with roads, traffic, kerbs, and other such environmental hazards, including extremes of weather, is totally different. All of these considerations indicate that careful assessment is necessary if a wheelchair is to contribute positively to a person's lifestyle and functional ability and that training is needed to ensure patients are able to maximise their independence when using a wheelchair.

Method of propulsion

Once the decision to recommend a wheelchair has been made, the first factor to identify is the method of propulsion to be used. Wheelchairs can be categorised as follows:

- self-propelling wheelchairs
- powered wheelchairs
- attendant controlled—manual or powered.

Self-propelling wheelchairs. These chairs are indicated when a patient has the upper limb function and trunk control to propel themselves without assistance. Within this category of chairs there is a variation in design ranging from standard wheelchairs to lightweight chairs. There is also a variation in the method of propulsion. The majority of wheelchair users will propel with the use of both arms. Hemiplegic patients may use a one-arm drive chair. These chairs are propelled either by the use of two propelling rims being placed on one wheel and connecting the two axles, or by the use of a pump action lever that both propels and steers the chair. One-arm drive chairs may cause a deterioration in posture or an increase in spasticity.

The provision of lightweight chairs enables a wheelchair user to maximise their functional ability, expending less energy in propulsion and utilising the design and balance of the chair to enable independent mobility in a variety of environments.

Lightweight chairs are made commonly of titanium, magnesium, or aluminum alloys. Their frames are either folding or rigid. A rigid frame is used for sport. The wheels on lightweight chairs are usually quick release, allowing them to be removed for ease of transportation and to minimise the weight of the chair when it is lifted into a car. The upholstery is usually nylon which does not sag and hammock as much as plastic, is not as sticky, and can usually be tightened and adjusted if it stretches a little. These chairs are frequently made to measure and the balance of the chair can be adjusted, by the positioning of the rear wheels, to suit the needs of the individual. The wheels on some lightweight chairs are cambered to provide both lateral and directional stability and economy of arm movement when propelling. These factors enable some patients to cope independently, once they have developed skill with kerbs and some of the other environmental barriers encountered frequently. These chairs are also used frequently to pursue sporting hobbies. The economy of effort with which these chairs can be propelled, their lightness for transportation, and their higher performance makes these the chairs of choice for many patients with neurological conditions, providing the funding is available to obtain the chair (Fyfe & Wood, 1990). An added bonus for many patients is that lightweight chairs are usually more aesthetic as they come in a wide range of colours and generally give a more stylish appearance.

Powered wheelchairs.   If a patient does not have the upper limb function and trunk control to propel themselves, a powered chair may be indicated. The power is derived from a battery that is an integral component of the chair and is rechargeable. The chair is controlled by a switch positioned according to the patient's need. This control can be operated by a wide range of functional movements, including hand, foot, head, chin, and mouth control, and can be sensitive for patients with minimal strength or adjusted and positioned to minimise the effects of poor coordination, tremor, or ataxia. Outdoor powered chairs are usually fitted with kerb climbers to enable the user to cope with up to 4 or 5 inch kerbs independently.

Powered chairs vary considerably in their potential, some are purely for use inside, others will cope with indoor and outdoor use and the larger more powerful chairs are designed primarily for outdoor use and can cope with a wider variety of surfaces and gradients and travel a longer distance.

Powered wheelchairs are more difficult to transport, primarily because of their weight. Some of them can be dismantled into smaller components to make transportation more easier. Some patients will choose to purchase a vehicle in which the chair can be easily transported, either a car into which the patient can drive the chair, via a ramp at the back, and travel in the chair, or an estate car which enables the chair to be driven into the boot by a carer with the aid of portable ramps.

Attendant-controlled wheelchairs.   If a patient does not have the functional ability to control a wheelchair by the above methods an attendant-controlled chair may be indicated to enable a carer to move a patient easily. Attendant-controlled chairs can be manual or powered depending upon the ability of the carer.

Chairs with specialist functions

These chairs fall primarily into the category of powered chairs as many of them utilise a power source to perform specific functions. They include chairs such as Levo Chairs which have the ability to bring a person from a seated position into a vertical position, providing an upright position of function or therapeutic stretch and exercise. Other chairs have seat-elevating units which enable the user to reach up onto shelves or lower down to ground level. A chair like the Mobility 2000 offers the option to climb a flight of stairs as well as perform the other standard functions of a powered chair.

Assessment

Through identification of the method of propulsion, the range of chairs to be considered can be significantly narrowed down and more specific factors relating to the patients seating, positioning, and environmental needs can be identified:

- seating
- positioning
- cushions
- transfers
- environment.

The key consideration for any wheelchair assessment are summarised in Figure 17.1.

Seating.   The wheelchair should be of the right dimensions to enable the user to be seated correctly ensuring that the base from which they are going to function is one that is stable, promotes a symmetrical position, and will maximise their functional ability. When patients are fitted into standard wheelchairs the resulting imbalance of anthropometric measurements is often all too apparent (Nitz & Bullock, 1983). The dimensions of the chair should be considered in relation to: seat height, width, and depth; position and type of armrests, footrest, and backrest; and position of wheels. The height, width, and depth of the seat are fundamental to providing a functional seating position, minimising areas of high pressure, accommodating additional postural support, providing comfort, and preventing deformity.

The seat width should comfortably accommodate the width of a person's hips and also allow for outdoor clothing. Patients using lightweight wheelchairs tend to have closer fitting chairs as they are tailor-made. The depth of the seat should be slightly less than the distance from the sacrum to the back of the knee to ensure that the seat canvas does not dig into the knees. A canvas that is too short will increase pressure on the thighs.

The seat height should accommodate the use of a cushion and should be greater than the measurement from the back of the knee to the heel. This enables correct positioning on footrests while allowing ground clearance. The material used for the seat sling may make some chairs more prone to seat sag than others. If the sling becomes stretched the base from which the patient is functioning will become less stable and more uncomfortable with an increase in shear forces.

The distance from the seat to the footrest should be the same as the measurement from the back of the knee to the heel when the knees are at right angles to the hips, plus an allowance for the thickness of the cushion being used in conjunction with the chair. It is sometimes necessary to adapt the footrest to accommodate restricted knee flexion or spasticity. The correct height of footrests is essential to allow access under tables and work surfaces. Some patients may require elevating leg rests to accommodate limited knee or hip flexion or provide a position of rest.

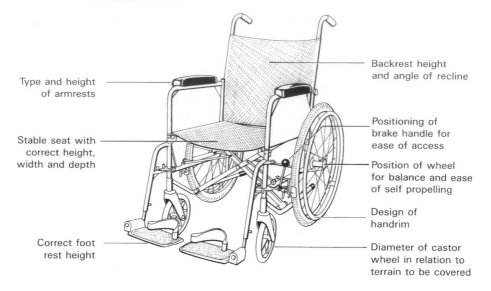

Type and height
of armrests

Stable seat with
correct height,
width and depth

Correct foot
rest height

Backrest height
and angle of recline

Positioning of
brake handle for
ease of access

Position of wheel
for balance and ease
of self propelling

Design of
handrim

Diameter of castor
wheel in relation to
terrain to be covered

Figure 17.1. The main areas to be considered when carrying out a wheelchair assessment.

The addition of these do, however, increase greatly the overall length of the chair.

The type of armrest will differ according to the patient's needs. An active wheelchair user with good trunk control may not use armrests as they may be felt to impede propulsion and a sideways transfer. Patients with poor trunk control or who transfers forwards will use the armrests to provide stability during sitting or transfers. Desk style armrests allow access to a table providing a better functional position. The height of armrests should enable the elbows to be rested at right angles to the shoulder. Many armrests are removable to assist with transfers.

The height of backrests will vary according to the patient's needs. They can be minimal for a person with trunk stability or fully extended for a person with poor trunk and head control. The position of the backrest must be considered. Patients who are spending a long time in their chairs and suffer from fatigue or poor trunk and head control may benefit from the provision of a reclining backrest to provide a change of position. Reclining backrests are provided in conjunction with elevating leg rests to provide a comfortable seating position and head support to enable the patient to see in front of themselves. The backrests of most wheelchairs have the ability to fold, assisting in both transportation and assisted transfers.

Positioning. The aim of positioning someone in a wheelchair is to achieve, as far as possible, a symmetrical posture with pressure evenly distributed. Patients with neurological conditions may require additions to the standard seat to help maintain a seating posture, minimise the effects of spasticity, ataxia, poor trunk control or deformity, and alleviate pressure on the sacral area. Specific supports can be provided for the head and trunk, aiming to provide lateral support and maintain the patient in a mid-line position.

Spastic patterns can be controlled by additions such as pommels, knee blocks, and foot straps or wedged cushions. Specialist chairs have been designed to provide flexibility in

Figure 17.2. Highly adjustable mobile seating allows either correction or accommodation of deformities while maintaining sitting posture.

positioning to enable therapists to control spasticity and obtain an optimal seating position for clients with profound seating problems (Figure 17.2).

The sitting posture of some patients may be so compromised that custom-made seats may be needed to insert into the wheelchair to obtain a seated position. These seats are made on an individual basis enabling the patient to be positioned in the optimal position to accommodate deformity and minimise spasticity. The main types are seat "moulds" (McQuilton & Johnson, 1981) made from polypropylene, formed around a plaster cast taken while the patient is held in the correct position, and the Matrix seat (Trail, 1990), which is a modular system constructed from adjustable interlocking units. These systems permit not only the possible accommodation of a fixed deformity but also the positioning of spine and limb so as to enhance function and prevent the development of deformity. When prescribing a bespoke seating insert for a patient, thought should also be given to the method of transfer and pressure relief as problems can be experienced in these areas.

Cushions.   Many patients with neurological conditions will require more than a standard foam wheelchair cushion. The need to assess for cushions is vitally important in the overall assessment for a wheelchair. A cushion is an integral component of the chair and it will effect the dimensions and seating position of a patient in the chair. The British standard specification for folding wheelchairs (BS 5568) assumes that a cushion will be supplied with each wheelchair. Despite this fact many patients are found to be sitting on the canvas sling. If the cushion is provided after the initial wheelchair assessment the dimensions will be altered and may no longer be correct. Cushions are primarily provided for the seat of the chair but may also be used to provide pressure, relief, or comfort for a patient's back and in some cases to alleviate pressure from the prominent spine of a person with scoliosis, kyphosis, or spina bifida.

A wheelchair cushion provides a platform from which to function, improves posture, provides comfort, and reduces the transmission of shock on uneven ground. It contributes to the prevention of pressure sores which are the combined result of pressure and shear force, humidity over the contact area, sensory changes, inability to adjust one's own seating position, and decrease in nutritional status (Jay, 1984).

A wide range of cushions are currently available. The cushion prescribed will depend upon the needs of each patient. Some patients will manage well with a foam cushion whereas others will need a much lighter degree of pressure relief to be provided and therefore need a cushion like a Roho cushion, which is air filled, adjustable in terms of pressure, and can be made to individual requirements. The more common cushions comprise foam, air, gel, water, silicone polystyrene pellets, or a combination of these. Further detail on cushions and pressure care for wheelchair users is beyond the scope of this text but may be found elsewhere (Fenwick, 1977; Tuttiett, 1989) (Figure 17.3).

Transfers.   The way in which a patient transfers should be considered during assessment to ensure that the chair does not impede transfer in any way. Transfers are carried out either independently or assisted and can be forwards, sideways, or for some patients backwards. The ability to move armrests, footrests, and the angle and the height of the seat in relative to the surface onto which the person is transferring are some factors that will influence ease of transfer.

Environment.   The environment in which the chair is to be used can be influential in the choice of chair. The ability to cope with carpets and uneven surfaces, to negotiate doorways, manoeuvre in a room, position for transfer and gain access to work surfaces should be considered along with the need to transport the chair from one environment to another and the way in which this will be done.

The independence of a person with muscle weakness may be compromised by the provision of a chair which they are unable to lift in and out of a car, thus always needing to seek assistance. A single wheelchair is frequently required to cope with a variety of environments and this should be borne in mind when carrying out the assessment. Alterations and adaptations to the internal home environment may be necessary to allow optimal use of the wheelchair.

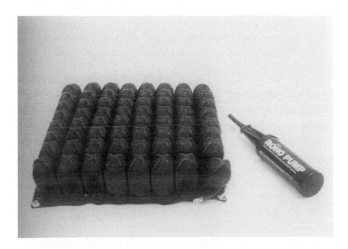 

Figure 17.3. Example of air flotation (left) and gel-foam (right) cushions.

Summary

The previous paragraphs provide an introduction to some of the main factors involved in the selection of a wheelchair. A detailed comprehensive assessment must be carried out by a person who has knowledge not only of the patient and their needs but also of the range of options available in terms of wheelchairs and accessories. The progressive nature of many neurological conditions necessitates the review of wheelchair needs. This factor should be taken into account during the initial assessment as the adaptability of some chairs is greater than others. Sometimes forgotten is that training in wheelchair use, propelling, manoeuvring, kerb-climbing, etc. may well be required to maximise the benefit from the chair selected. Equally important is the need for regular maintenance without which wheelchair performance may be expected to deteriorate (Mulley, 1989).

DRIVING IN REHABILITATION

The car has an important role in providing mobility to places of employment and social activities. In the developed world, driving is almost regarded as another activity of daily living. Driving is a skill that requires coordinated sensory and motor activity in a dangerous environment using expensive equipment. It is therefore essential that all drivers, both ablebodied and disabled, should be able to show that they are capable of driving in all sorts of driving conditions and also that they are physically capable of controlling the car.

For a person with a physical disability which is not a result of brain damage, it is important that if they wish to return, or to continue driving that they are advised on the type of controls and adaptations they can use if they are to drive safely. An assessment of physical ability in relation to car use needs to be carried out. There are a number of vehicle conversion specialists in Europe. A wealth of adaptations are available ranging from push–pull hand controls which can be fitted to an automatic vehicle for a driver who is not able to operate foot pedals, to ultra light powered steering and vacuum braking systems using a joy stick control (Kuppers, 1986) (Figures 17.4 and 17.5). Consideration also needs to be given to transferring into and out of the vehicle and if appropriate, to stowage of a wheelchair. Here it should be noted that when choosing a wheelchair, the weight and ability of the person to fold the chair should be taken into consideration if they are going to lift their chair into the car. If it is not possible for the driver to lift the wheelchair into the car independently then hoisting devices may be recommended, either to pull the wheelchair into the car or to place the wheelchair on top of the car. Because of the increasing number of adaptations available for a car user, it is important that an accurate physical assessment is carried out and that the driver is then advised accordingly.

Where brain damage has occurred a more detailed assessment including cognitive skills is required. A full assessment for a driver looking at driving ability and also the need for any car adaptation is described next.

Figure 17.4. A rotating car seat may assist transfers into and out of the vehicle.

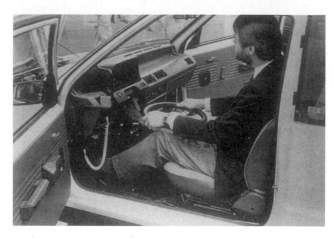

Figure 17.5. For a person with proximal weakness, a horizontal steering wheel with power steering.

There is increasing interest in the development of driving assessment centres and a number of centres in Britain are members of the Forum of Driving Assessment Centres in the United Kingdom. The aim of this forum is to share the experience of members in assessing and advising disabled people with regard to driving and other mobility problems and to develop policies and to promote research in this area.

The professionals involved in the driving assessment team may vary, depending on the resources of a particular unit, but the following people may be involved:

- medical consultant
- physiotherapist
- occupational therapist
- psychologist
- driving instructor
- orthotist.

A driving instructor is required to give driving education to people who have never driven, or to newly disabled persons who need to acquire skills with adapted cars. It is important that if successful training is to be provided, that driving instructors are available who can undertake this specialised form of instruction

(Beynon, 1987). A driving instructor working from a rehabilitation centre would be able to consult staff and discuss any practical difficulties a patient may have with driving and could play an important role in the training of personal mobility. The need for specialised driving tuition involving therapists, driving instructors, and manufacturers has been recognised through organisations such as ADED (Association of Driving Educators for the Disabled) in the USA and ADEPD (Association of Driving Educators for People with Disabilities) in Britain.

Medical assessment

Ordinary driving licences in Great Britain are issued by the Driver Vehicle and Licensing Agency (DVLA) in Swansea. The onus is on the individual to notify the Driver's Medical Branch as soon as he/she becomes aware that his/her medical condition is likely to affect safe driving either now or in the future.

Failure to notify condition to DVLA may adversely affect the motor insurance position of the driver. Doctors have the responsibility for advising patients that they have a medical condition which may interfere with fitness to drive. Detailed guidelines on the medical aspects of fitness to drive are published and regularly updated by the DVLA, whose medical advisers can also be consulted by telephone (01792 783686).

Disabilities likely to render the driving of the vehicle a source of danger to the public are referred to by British law as "relevant disabilities". The term relevant disabilities also includes epilepsy, liability to sudden attacks of disabling giddiness or fainting, severe abnormality (in Scottish terminology, mental deficiency such that the person is incapable of living an independent life or of guarding himself against serious exploitation), and inability to meet the prescribed eyesight requirements. Epilepsy is a relevant disability which is compatible with holding an ordinary driving licence under certain conditions that mainly relate to a stipulated period free from attacks. The risk that epilepsy may begin after a head injury or craniotomy may constitute a prospective disability (Jennett, 1983; Harvey & Hopkins, 1983). The number of accidents due to epilepsy is difficult to determine, but studies have indicated that a driver with epilepsy is up to twice as likely to have an accident as a non-epileptic driver (Raffle, 1985). In Britain it is up to the driver himself to declare any epilepsy to the DVLA. In several American states, the physician is now required by law to inform the authorities if a patient has a tendency to epilepsy.

The relevant disability termed "likely to be a source of danger to the public" can pose problems when determining fitness to drive. By including a detailed physical and psychological assessment, it may be possible to gain a more precise picture of a person's driving ability.

Visual assessment

Tests for visual acuity, field of vision and evidence of diplopia are essential when assessing driving ability. In the UK a driver is required by law to inform the licensing centre of any visual impairment likely to affect the safety of his driving. In the UK the standard of visual acuity required for drivers is the ability to read a clean car number plate with figures $3\frac{1}{2}''$ high at 25 yards in bright daylight and with spectacles if worn.

An adequate field of vision is a necessary requirement. Hemianopia may cause driving difficulties. A complete hemianopia is a bar to driving. Diplopia may affect driving ability but if symptoms can be controlled by drugs, e.g., for myasthenia, driving may be permissible. If diplopia is not controlled by treatment then driving should not be allowed. Oscillopsia and severe defects of conjugate eye movements in lateral directions may also interfere with driving performance (Raffle, 1985).

Physical assessment

A physical assessment would take the following into consideration:

(1) mobility
(2) muscle power
(3) range of movement
(4) proprioceptive and sensory impairment
(5) transfer ability
(6) seating position and support
(7) reaction times
(8) steering ability
(9) accelerator and brake control
(10) gear changing ability
(11) use of secondary controls
(12) wheelchair stowage (if applicable)
(13) in-car testing on a test track or public road.

A static car simulator can be useful in assessing brake strength and brake reaction times, steering strength and seating positions prior to a test in a car "on the road" (Figure 17.6). Determining driving ability in relation to looking skill, lane position skill, speed skill, coordination of visual scans, interacting with the same directional traffic, and maintaining safety space is difficult to do from a standard clinical assessment. As yet, a test battery to determine a driver's ability to carry out tasks has not proved to be reliable. Specific problems encountered by stroke patients have been identified as entering and leaving motorways and handling traffic at roundabouts. On private roads, these patients were relatively unaware of other vehicles, exhibited difficulty in reversing, had difficulty in doing two things at once in an emergency and had difficulty in placing their car accurately on the road (Wilson & Smith, 1983).

Psychological assessment

Concentration, reasoning skills, decision making skills and perceptual and spatial ability have implications for driving (Simms, 1985). It is important that these cognitive skills are considered during all parts of the driving assessment by other members of the assessment team. It is particularly relevant for example, if a

Figure 17.6. A static test unit is used for assessing brake reaction times, brake pressure readings, and steering ability.

driving instructor is likely to take a patient out onto the public road, that he or she is made aware of any potential dangers. Both psychometric and performance tasks together have proved to be valid predictors of driving (Gouvier et al., 1989).

Financial consideration

Adapting a car can be an expensive venture. Statutory provision varies throughout Europe. For example, in Denmark financial support to buy a car may be granted when an important and continuous reduction of the ability of function is found which makes it difficult to travel, or difficult to get/keep a job without having a car. In Britain, Disability Living Allowance is granted to people who are unable or virtually unable to walk. This may be enough to help them to buy a standard vehicle but if expensive adaptations are required, the driver may not be able to afford to adapt his car.

If driving is to be considered as an important functional activity which can be improved with rehabilitation, then the retaining or training of driving skills should be considered. Driving and training programmes have been developed, the results of which have indicated that perceptual skills may improve after training and that training was also associated with improved driving performance. Sivak et al. (1984) asked what are the long-term benefits of perceptual training in relation to brain damaged drivers? Their results indicated that perceptual skills improved following such training and that the training was associated with improved driving performance and, moreover the degree of improvement in driving performance was directly related to the degree of improvement of perceptual skills.

Van Zomeren et al. (1987) suggested that new techniques could be developed to enable more valid statements about the skills needed for safe traffic participation. These assessment techniques should emphasise the higher cognitive levels in driving at the tactical and strategic levels. At the moment, driver training programmes in rehabilitation focus mainly on the operational levels, with emphasis on handling the car, use of controls

and mirrors, and technical adaptation of the vehicle. There is clearly great scope for further research in the field of driving, especially for drivers with brain damage.

In a society which demands flexibility and mobility from every employee, the car has assumed a very important role. It is particularly important as a means of integrating people with disabilities back into employment and social activities which is the main aim of rehabilitation.

ENVIRONMENTAL CONTROL SYSTEMS

The field of Environmental Controls is one example of many areas in which modern technology has a tremendous potential to benefit disabled people. Since the original system, POSSUM (Patient Operated Selector Mechanism) was produced in the early 1950s for survivors of the poliomyelitis epidemic, increasingly sophisticated control systems have become available with advances in fields such as microelectronics. Application varies from simple installations covering control of front-door security and a few appliances such as television and radio, to more sophisticated needs to facilitate ongoing employment or study. Integration of Environmental Controls and other essentials, such as communication aids and electric wheelchair control is now essential for the more severely disabled user. More sophisticated systems will be required to allow effective access to the range of services becoming available from developments such as cable television and interactive CD-ROM, which have great potential for the disabled user.

Although 2% of the adult population in Britain is estimated to have a disability leading to some problems of daily living, commonly used rehabilitation assessment and outcome measures such as Barthel and the Nottingham ADL generally focus on major problems such as mobility, washing, dressing, and toileting. There is, therefore, a paucity of data on the numbers of the most disabled people in the community who would benefit from assistive technology. All too commonly there is also a corresponding lack of awareness amongst professionals of the potential benefits in independence, gain in dignity, and reduction in the burden of care which can be achieved by providing a severely disabled person with an appropriate Environmental Controls System.

Until 1993, systems were provided via the UK Departments of Health, with centralised funding and a cumbersome bureaucratic procedure. Medical Assessors who authorised eligibility had little or no training, and were often isolated from other professionals involved in provision of services to the individual. No feedback or audit of effectiveness of equipment was carried out on a routine basis. Some clients used only one or two functions on a complex system: Others had extensive needs which were unmet.

Devolution of the budget to regional or district level and the accompanying growth of rehabilitation services in Britain in recent years has led to major changes in the provision of assistive technology. Medical assessment continues to be essential to establish eligibility, but criteria are applied less rigidly and a more flexible view of prognosis is possible. Rapid deterioration (as in motor neurone disease) or fluctuating levels of disability are recognised and the potential for independence is a key consideration. A holistic view of the disability enables other issues such as wheelchair prescription, drug therapy, or care package to be reassessed as well as the potential benefit to be gained from the prescription of an Environmental Control System. Close collaboration with rehabilitation engineers, occupational therapists, and speech and language therapists over the configuration of the system is now becoming the rule rather than the exception. Increased awareness of the benefits of technology are occurring in both the professional and disabled population, leading to a steady rise in the numbers of users. Innovative service developments, such as local emergency back-up services or simple next-day trolley installations are being created in response to perception of need. Environmental Control Services are now an integral, rather than isolated, part of Rehabilitation Medicine Services for disabled people.

Choosing the appropriate system for the individual requires a careful evaluation of all physical, cognitive, functional, and social problems. Some needs may be simply met, such as provision of a combined infra-red handset for home entertainment equipment. Social Services Departments have an obligation (under the terms of the Chronically Sick and Disabled Persons Act 1970) to provide individual pieces of equipment to enable disabled persons to control aspects of their environment, such as door-entry, phone alarm, or intercom systems. These are easy to install and generally operated by a button within the person's reach.

A more complex system, addressing issues of home security, communication via intercom or telephone, and appliance control, will be a permanent installation involving additional wiring, modifications to door locks and repositioning of equipment. It may cost between £3000 and £6000. It is essential that the final design of the system has user and family acceptability and addresses all the needs identified at assessment. The initial assessment by medical and other professionals should identify the type of system appropriate for the user's needs and abilities, but the final design involves detailed work done in the user's home with a technician from the Environmental Controls Contractor and supported by relevant members of the multidisciplinary team.

System characteristics

There are three distinct components of a system.

(1) The *selection unit*, or "nerve centre" of the system is generally a scanning indicator system in which an array of lights is used to indicate each function in turn (Figure 17.7). Synthetic speech annunciation of the scan position or illuminated symbol positions can also be used to facilitate use where intellectual or visual difficulties exist or enable operation in bed at night. The rate of scanning can be adjusted to suit the ability of the operator.

(2) Choice of appropriate *user switch* is of fundamental importance to a successful system operation. Simple lever switches can be used if there is sufficient fine motor control by either hand or foot, but careful positioning is required to ensure that it is within reach of the user at all times and not affected by spasm or a slip from normal posture. Neither the switch nor its movements should provide a hazard to the user. Freedom of movement can be provided by wireless connections to the selection unit. Some less disabled users can operate built-in switches or buttons for a more rapid and direct selection of functions, others may need to rely on utilising chin, suck-puff, or eye

Figure 17.7. A typical environmental control selection unit.

Table 17.1. Types of switch

- Lever switches—hand or foot where fine motor control is sufficient
- Chin/headrest switch—in high tetraplegia
- Suck/puff—where head movement restricted but lips can be sealed
- Pressure pad—an alternative for use in bed
- Specialised inputs (eye movement/sound)—very severe disability

movement. A second switch mechanism may be required for effective operation from bed (Table 17.1).

Deterioration in condition, intercurrent illness or even movement of equipment by well-meaning carers can all render a system non-operational. Regular review of the installation and knowledge of how to address these problems must be readily available to all involved professionals, carers as well as users, if systems are to be effective.

(3) *Appliance control* from the selection box is generally considered in three areas: security, communication, and equipment operation. Electronically operated door-entry locks combined with an entry-phone or a security camera are generally a high priority in most system designs. An alarm system, accessible throughout home and garden is often essential as is entry to the nurse or warden call systems in residential settings. Powered wheelchair users require facilities for independent access to their home with door opener/closers.

Control over telephone operation can greatly alleviate the social isolation experienced by many disabled people. A directory of pre-stored numbers and a carefully sited remote control loud-speaking telephone can put users on an equal footing with the rest of society. Where speech is seriously impaired the system can perform as, or be used with, a synthetic speech communication aid.

Appliance control requirements commonly include home entertainment equipment, including television, videos, satellite and cable systems, and music centres, much of which have standard infra-red control and therefore require no modification. A more sophisticated system may also include motorised bed, chair control, or computer access. Careful evaluation of the most appropriate technological solution is then required, as the expectations of the individual may be difficult or impossible to meet.

Assistive technology is now beginning to benefit from recent overall expansion of rehabilitation services and much has been done to educate and inform local professionals about the potential benefit of equipment to their most disabled clients as well as how to access the service. Cost effectiveness needs to be demonstrated by outcome, audit, and quality control of service provision.

Developments in this field are rapid and the new systems of recent years have brought both mobility and family integration to the disabled user. The growth of service developments in the rehabilitation arena has paralleled this change and the benefits to the user are just beginning to emerge. The size of the market and commercial pressures may well limit future equipment developments unless awareness of the benefits of assistive technology continues to be stressed. People with physical disabilities demand the improvement in the quality of life that technology can bring.

COMMUNICATION AIDS

People with impaired speech who would benefit from using a communication aid are those who would otherwise find that their communication, their lifestyles, their opportunities, and independence are severely restricted (Huer & Lloyd, 1990).

An important function of the speech and language therapist in communication aid assessment and intervention is to consider the options of enabling, augmenting, amplifying, or otherwise improving the intelligibility of speech. Intelligibility can also be improved, without altering the acoustics of speech, by increasing the listener's ability to predict the content of speech. This can be achieved by "cueing in" the listener to the topic of conversation, for example by indicating a topic-related picture. A similar effect can be achieved by pointing to the initial letters of words, thus increasing the predictability of individual words and with each word of the complete utterance. Indicating initial letters can have other beneficial effects. It can reduce speech rate to a speed at which it is more intelligible or which enables more precise articulation, better timing of breathing with phonation and other features of more intelligible speech. These approaches are outlined clearly by Yorkston and Garrett (1997).

"Standard" and "special" communication aids

"Standard" aid components are those techniques and aids that are also used routinely by the general population to supplement speech. They include gestures, facial expression, typing, writing, drawing maps and diagrams, tracing the shapes of letters in the air, or the palm of the hand or other convenient surface. These standard components can also be used in special ways to overcome a communication problem due to severe speech impairment. For example, Garrett et al. (1989) describe an adult with Broca's aphasia who was able to indicate preferred topics, provide biographical details, and exert some control over the pace and turns of a conversation by using:

- a personal organiser notebook with pre-printed messages, maps, pictures, etc.
- a portable computer with stored messages and/or for typing new messages.

"Special" aid components are those techniques and aids that have been developed or refined specifically for use by people with severe speech impairments. They include special gestures, signing, graphic symbols, personal speech aids, communication aids, and special selection techniques. Recently a wider range of portable, speech output, microprocessor-based dedicated communication aids and customised systems of re-packaged hardware plus specialist software have become commercially available.

Dedicated communication aids and customised systems are normally designed with a specific "user profile" in mind.

- Some are designed for use by people who have severe physical disabilities.
- Some have been designed to help when users, or people close to them, have poor sight or hearing, whereas good sight or hearing are needed to use some others.
- Some are for users who have good spelling or typing skills, and partners who can read.
- Some have a display of special picture symbols which have to be taught and learned, and can sometimes be more efficient than spelling or pointing to words. Some people will have difficulties with the written word, but have retained the ability to use pictures.

What is the "right" communication aid?

The right aid is the one that, with the right training, will give the best possible results for the user.

A communication aid may be someone's:

- only means of communication
- primary means of communication with strangers
- "back up" for speech when talking to familiar people.

The right aid for one person might be a "high-tech" voice output communication aid. For another person it might be a notepad and pencil. For another it might be a picture chart.

Some important questions are:

- What does the user want to achieve?
- How quickly do they need to see results?
- How happy do they feel about using the equipment?
- What is the relative priority, for the user, of improving communication?
- What are the levels of enthusiasm, emotional support, and practical training available from family, carers, professionals, etc.?
- How reliable are the equipment and "after sales" services?

What skills and abilities are needed?

The most useful combination of equipment, skills, techniques, and strategies:

- depends on the equipment and how it is going to be used
- varies from one situation to another
- will usually change over time.

Some users need help to achieve their full communicative potential. If the skills of familiar communication partners are critical to success then "Communication Facilitator Training" may help. Other users can take more responsibility for assisting communication partners. Whenever feasible, "user training" should include strategies for dealing with unfamiliar people and situations and conversational control skills.

Features of communication aids

It is useful to consider the ways in which communication aids vary. It is these features that we will be matching to the aims, skills, abilities, and preferences of the user.

Method of access

Cook (1985) separates and describes two aspects of access to communication aids: the physical selection method and the cognitive selection method.

Physical selection. Physical selection occurs at the human–machine interface, which may be represented by a single switch, an array of switches, a keyboard or a display of pictures on a "low-tech" communication board. The user needs to make a movement, or produce a change in muscle potential, to operate or activate the interface. Selection may be by physical contact with, or proximity to, the interface. Alternatively, an electronic selection method might be used, e.g., laser-pointer to indicate a location on an array, an infra-red transmitter-receiver unit to activate a switch, or a "mouse" system that interprets relative positions as "pointing".

Cognitive selection. The main cognitive selection methods are: direct selection, scanning, and encoding. Direct selection is one of the quickest ways to operate an aid and should be used whenever possible. Examples of direct selection are hitting a single "talking switch", using a head-mounted laser-pointer to point to line drawing on a communication chart, or typing on a conventional typewriter.

The scanning method is slower than direct selection. Options are presented in sequence until (possibly) the target message is proffered for selection, for example by a head movement to indicate "yes". Device-dependent timing of switch activation and/or release can be rendered impossible or difficult by neurological damage, resulting in intention-related spasms or "freezing". If this is the case then a scan mode where the user sets the pace and determines the time frame for activation might be preferable. This is most easily and efficiently achieved if the user can manage two switches—one to step through the options and the other as a "fire-button" to select when on target.

The physical demands of an encoding system are usually less than direct selection but more than scanning. The cognitive demands are usually greater than both and there are many widely different types of encoding systems. Activation of a Morse key does not require great strength or range of movement but repeated activations are needed to encode most characters and the codes must be learnt.

Choice of access method. The choice of an access method depends on the client's physical and cognitive abilities. There is a trade-off between cognitive load and physical effort between scanning and direct selection: Scanning requires the user to learn how the scan operates but may require minimal physical effort to activate the switch. In contrast direct selection is easier cognitively, but requires greater range and control of movement.

Vocabulary content and organisation

This is not an issue for aids with alphanumeric displays and no memory for messages, e.g., alphabet boards, "talking typewriters"—they are "content free". In all other cases vocabulary content should be matched to the user's needs, age, developmental or rehabilitation stage and progress, gender, environment, personal circumstance, interests, and communication style. These are best identified by the user and those who know him or her well. There are several commercially available "vocabulary packages" that can be "personalised" for individual users.

The organisation and representation of vocabulary items affect the user's ability to access the vocabulary available. The vocabulary items output by the device impact both on communication partners and on the user herself. If these are whole messages then the user's "communication style" is constrained by the device to production of pre-programmed messages. However, this may represent the user's full potential when assisted by the communication aid. If the vocabulary items outputted are single words then a range of "communication styles" is possible, involving more of less "co-construction" of messages by communication partners. The larger the set of "single word" vocabulary items the more important it is to distinguish between what the aid can "say" and what the user can "say" with the aid. The latter depends on competent use and "communication style".

Acceleration features

Several communication aids have facilities that are designed to accelerate the speed of communication. It is by no means proven that these are successful and some "rate acceleration" features may slow some users down (Millar & Nisbet, 1992).

(1) Abbreviation expansion: The client stores text under a very short code of letters, numbers or, a combination, which gives quick retrieval e.g., HH = "Hello, how are you?"
(2) Word prediction—where text is used, some aids have the optional facility whereby when you enter an initial letter of a word, a number of the most likely "next" words appear on a screen. If the user chooses an item from this "prediction list" the word and following space are normally generated. Word prediction can be content sensitive, and can be based on frequency and/or recency of use. The least efficient systems are based solely on frequency of use and those using recency and contextual cues are to be preferred.
(3) Memory key—some aids have a memory key, which when selected in conjunction with a letter or number retrieves a pre-stored message.
(4) Predictive selection—these are "cueing" systems to direct the users attention to those locations in which messages are stored by highlighting "live" cells or blanking out "empty" cells. If the system also "skips" empty cells when in scanning mode this also speeds up presentation of "live" locations for selection.

Method of output

"Messages" can be outputted by sound (e.g., a buzzer, pre-recorded dog barking), speech transient visual display, print, or electronic media.

Visual. Some aids require the communication partner to observe the word or message being built up (e.g., alphabet board, or symbol board) and to "co-construct" the communication. Other aids display the completed or retrieved message on a screen. The type, size, capacity, and position of visual message screens vary. Some can be difficult to read unless lighting conditions are just right and most cannot cope with direct sunlight out of doors. Some aids can produce a hard copy of the message.

Acoustic. It is now almost inconceivable that a new type of communication aid would be marketed without the option of speech output. The voice may either be digital (recorded) or synthesised speech and some aids support both. The quality of the digital sound varies and digital recording takes up a great deal more computer memory than synthesised speech. Some aids have the facility to choose between higher quality digital recordings of shorter duration and lower quality digital recordings of longer duration.

Memory capabilities

The storage capacity or memory within aids varies tremendously. Some devices come in different versions with different amounts of memory and the option to add extra memory if needed. With some aids, it is possible to back up the memory on disc, normally on PC, Apple Mac computer or a dedicated disc drive. It is recommended that this is done whenever possible.

Portability

Communication aids also vary tremendously in size and weight. At one extreme there are very portable aids that can easily be carried by an ambulant child. Others are more correctly described as "transportable" and most suit being mounted on a wheelchair tray or walking frame. Some even include some environmental and/or wheelchair control functions that assist independent mobility and other activities as well as communication. A few are static, due to size and weight, or because they are mains powered. However, the aim is generally to find the most portable aid to meet the client's needs as anything less may interfere with other activities or access.

Acceptability

Communication aids vary in the material they are made of, size, colour, and shape. These all influence how aesthetically pleasing and acceptable the client may find them. This is an especially important consideration for adults with an acquired disorder of sudden onset. These clients may be finding it difficult enough to come to terms with their disability without the extra unnecessary distress of being confronted with equipment that is both obvious and ugly.

It is worth noting that the communication aid of choice for many literate users is a Light Writer, even when another aid might offer a more favourable constellation of features. The Light Writer has won several awards, including one from the Design Council, was designed by a communication aid user, and is among those aids that look least like aids and more like a robust and attractive "executive toy".

Integration

Some communication aids go beyond being aids to augment conversation. They can give access to environmental controls, electric wheelchairs, and computers.

Cost

The cost of the communication aid and its peripherals can vary. The total "product package" can also vary. For example, the purchase price of the aid may include training in its operation, warranty, insurance, back-up support, resource materials, updates of hardware, and consumables. A "cheaper" equivalent does not necessarily represent better value for money and it may well be worth paying a little extra if it will guarantee that the user is provided with a replacement if their own aid is stolen or needs to go for repair. Most reputable UK suppliers are able to offer a replacement within 24 hours.

REFERENCES

Beynon, C.J. (1987). Teaching the driving instructors. *International Disability Studies, 9*(4), 182–183.

Cochrane, G. (Ed.) (1993). *Equipment for disabled people—wheelchairs.* Oxford: The Disability Information Trust.

Cook, A. (1985). General concepts. In J.G. Webster, A.M. Cook, W.J. Thompkins, & G.C. Vanderheiden (Eds.), *Electronic devices for rehabilitation.* London: Chapman & Hall.

Dollfus, I.P. (1990). Functional evaluation and the user's perspective. In R. Ronchi & A. Audrich (Eds.), *Wheelchair testing in Europe: Commission of the European Communities.* Milan: Edizioni pro Juventute.

Fenwick, D. (1977). *Wheelchairs and their users.* London: HMSO, Office of Population Censuses and Surveys.

Fyfe, N.C.M., & Wood, J. (1990). The choice of self-propelling wheel-chairs for spinal patients. *Clinical Rehabilitation, 4,* 51–56.

Garrett, K., Beukelman, D., & Low-Morrow, D. (1989). A comprehensive augmentative communication system for an adult with Broca's aphasia. *Augmentative and Alternative Communication, 5*(1): 55–64.

Gouvier, W.D., Maxfield, M.W., Schweitzer, J.R., et al. (1989). Psychometric prediction of driving performance among the disabled. *Archives of Physical Medicine and Rehabilitation, 70,* 745–750.

Harvey, P., & Hopkins, A. (1983). Views of British neurologists on epilepsy after head trauma and fitness to drive. *Lancet i:* 401–402.

Huer, M. & Lloyd, L. (1990). AAC user's perspectives on augmentative and alternative communication. *Augmentative and Alternative Communication, 6*(4), 220–230.

Jay, P.E. (1984). *Choosing the best wheelchair cushion for your needs, your chair and your lifestyle.* London: Royal Association for Disability and Rehabilitation.

Jennett, R. (1983). Anticonvulsant drugs and advice about driving after head injury and intracranial surgery. *British Medical Journal, 286,* 627–628.

Kuppers, H.J. (1986). *Proceedings of workshop on the Adaptation of Cars for Paralysed Persons.* Heidelberg: Commission of the European Communities.

Marks, L. (1997). Wheelchairs. In C.J. Goodwill, M.A. Chamberlain, & C. Evans (Eds.), *The rehabilitation of the physically disabled adult* (pp. 615–631) (2nd Ed.). Cheltenham: Stanley Thomas.

McQuilton, G., & Johnson, G.R. (1981). Cost effective moulded seating for the handicapped child. *Prosthet. Orthot. International, 5:* 37–41.

Millar, S., & Nisbet, P. (1992). *Accelerated writing for people with disabilities: An evaluation of a range of predictive systems currently available for widely used computers, incorporating comparisons with other specialised systems for communication.* Edinburgh: Call Centre and Scottish Office.

Mulley, G.P. (1989). Standards of wheelchairs. *British Medical Journal, 298,* 1198–1199.

Nitz, J.C., & Bullock, M. (1983). Wheelchair design for people with neuromuscular disability. *Australian Journal of Physiotherapy, 29*(2): 43–47.

Raffle, A. (1985). *Medical aspects of fitness to drive, a guide for medical practitioners* (4th Ed.). London: Medical Commission on Accident Prevention.

Simms, B. (1985). The assessment of the disabled for driving: a preliminary report. *International Rehabilitation Medicine, 7,* 187–192.

Sivak, M., Hill, C.S., & Henson, D.L., et al. (1984). Improved driving performance following perceptual training in persons with brain damage. *Archives of Physical Medicine and Rehabilitation, 65,* 163–167.

Trail, I.A. (1990). The matrix seating system. *Journal of Bone Joint Surgery, 72*(4), 666–669.

Tuttiett, S. (1989). *Dept. of Health Disability Equipment Assessment Programme: Wheelchair cushions summary report* (2nd Ed.). Heywood: Dept. of Health Store.

Van Zomeren, A.M., Brouwer, W.H., & Minderhoud, J.M. (1987). Acquired brain damage and driving: a review. *Archives of Physical Medicine and Rehabilitation, 68,* 697–705.

Wilson, T., & Smith, T. (1983). Driving after a stroke. *International Rehabilitation Medicine, 5:* 170–177.

Yorkston, K.M., & Garrett, K.L. (1997). Assistive communication technology for elders with motor speech disability. In R. Lubinski & D.J. Higginbotham (Eds.). *Communication technologies for the elderly: vision, hearing and speech* (pp. 235–261). London: Singular Publishing Ltd.

FURTHER READING

Barnes, M.P. (1994). Switching devices and independence of disabled people. *British Medical Journal, 309,* 1181–1182.

British Society of Rehabilitation Medicine (1994). *Prescription for independence: a working party report of the BSRM Environmental Control Special Interest Group.* London: British Society of Rehabilitation Medicine.

Dambrough, A., & Kinrade, D. (1988). *Motoring and mobility for disabled people.* London: Royal Association for Disability and Rehabilitation.

Department of Health. (1995). *Environmental control systems: An evaluation—disability equipment assessment.* London: HMSO.

Panton, L. (1987). Speech, language, cognitive and physical assessment for communication aids. In P. Enderby (Ed.), *Assistive communication aids for the speech impaired* (pp. 12–26). Edinburgh: Churchill Livingstone.

Royal College of Physicians of London. (1995). *The provision of wheelchair and special seating: guidance for purchasers and providers.* London: Royal College of Physicians.

Welling, D., & Unsworth, J. (1997). Environmental control systems for people with a disability: an update. *British Medical Journal, 315:* 409–412.

18. Functional neurostimulation in rehabilitation

D.N. Rushton

REHABILITATION AND NEUROSTIMULATION

Adaptation and substitution in disability

All the activities of daily living require neural control for their performance. Most of the factors that lend quality to life require preserved neural function. The nervous system is vulnerable to injury, and has limited powers of recovery. For these reasons, a large proportion of human disabilities, and an even larger proportion of severe and complex disabilities, are caused by disorders of neurological function. The most complex of bodily functions occur in the central nervous system (CNS), where powers of *biological* regeneration following disease or injury are smallest. However, powers of *functional* recovery (by adaptation and substitution) mainly reside in the CNS, which is therefore rightly the main target of rehabilitation effort. Only when adaptation and functional substitution fail or decompensate do we need to think of external aids. Substitutive aids such as wheelchairs and orthoses perform well in restoring some functions, but poorly in others. Where mechanical substitutive aids perform poorly, functional neuroelectrical stimulation (FES) may sometimes do better, by providing a neurally mediated functional substitution. Functional neurostimulation differs in the time domain from all other forms of medical or surgical treatment. Because the medium is electrical, its effect on impaired neural functions can be regulated so as to respond rapidly to change in wishes and activities. Neuroprostheses therefore have a unique potential for substituting artificial for impaired natural neurological functions, even though at the present stage of development they may do so only crudely. In the clinical context, neurostimulation can be broadly divided into three kinds, according to purpose: diagnostic, therapeutic, and functional.

Diagnostic stimulation. Diagnostic nerve and brain stimulation using the electrical and electromagnetic techniques developed in clinical neurophysiology has a role in the world of FES, as an aid to patient assessment and selection. For example, it is often important to assess such features as motor point location, the presence of denervation or neuropathic changes, the conductivity of central and peripheral pathways, and the activity of reflexes, before making decisions about FES.

Therapeutic stimulation. Therapeutic electrical stimulation (TES) is undertaken to provide clinical benefit; it is a form of treatment, and is therefore usually carried out under clinical supervision. The benefits from TES may include for example improved muscle tone, bulk and strength, reduced spasticity, improved limb blood flow, or a reduction in disuse osteoporosis (Swain, 1992). The abbreviation TES is used here to maintain a distinction from transcutaneous nerve stimulation (TNS, or TENS), which is a form of therapeutic sensory stimulation, mainly used for pain relief (Frampton, 1996).

Functional stimulation. FES aims to generate movements or functions which mimic normal functions. It is therefore necessary for it to be under the subject's control, and to be available when required at home and elsewhere, rather than being applied in a time and place for "treatment". There may often be a requirement that the system be supported indefinitely. For these reasons the techniques of FES are different from those of TES. FES equipment must be portable, rugged, reliable, easy to use, and easy to control.

Neuroprostheses

Effective FES requires the safe delivery of correct stimulation currents to the right tissues. This calls for detailed attention to the design of stimulating circuits and electrodes. The devices that result, which may be external, implanted, or a combination of both, are termed *neuroprostheses*. Neuroprostheses can be divided into three broad groups: those that substitute for lost sensory functions ("sensory prostheses"); those that substitute for lost motor functions ("motor prostheses"); and those that regulate deranged sensory or motor functions ("neuromodulators"). The neuroprostheses considered here work by electrical stimulation of sensory or motor nerve structures, but there are some which work by timed drug delivery, and they are akin to other drug delivery devices.

Neuroprostheses and rehabilitation goals. The rehabilitation process aims to minimise the impact of impairments, to minimise disability and handicap, and to prevent predictable complications. But there are limits dictated by the impairment; for example, a totally deaf person cannot use the telephone, however good their signing or lipreading may be. A neuroprosthesis, by substituting a function, may enable rehabilitation to move on to a different plane and continue there. It does not substitute for the rehabilitation process. The impact and implications of the neuroprosthetic device can therefore go well beyond the specific function being replaced; and patients, carers, and professionals should be prepared for these effects and consequences.

The role of the rehabilitation method.   The neuroprosthetic devices and applications available were developed by different specialist teams, often with deep but narrow technical and clinical interests. Nevertheless, it has always been found that excellent patient selection is crucial to success. There are several reasons for this. First, many devices are surgically implanted. It is obviously essential to have a clear agreement of the functional goals before surgery. There is no place for a "try it and see" approach (although planned trials of therapy, discussed later, are valuable). Second, most devices offer at best a crude approximation to normal function, and patients need to know this, and understand the limited goals it may imply. Third, many devices require a long period of postoperative testing and training, and some fully rehabilitated patients may not understand how this can require them to alter their established pattern of life. The specialist implanting team may not have a detailed understanding of the social, cultural, functional and economic contexts of the individuals who are to use the devices. Rehabilitation expertise can be used to provide much of this context. This requires that rehabilitation professionals be conversant with the current state of development, success, value, and limitations of the principal devices. They are likely to be one of the first points of enquiry for interested disabled people and their relatives, who wish to know how their health, function, and quality of life could be improved by an appropriate choice of assistive technology.

Trials of therapy.   For some devices, a therapeutic trial lasting for a few days or weeks may be essential in reaching a decision on implanting a permanent device. A percutaneous cannula can be used for infusing intrathecal baclofen (Teddy, 1995) or morphine in patients with severe spasticity or pain. A percutaneous epidural electrode can be used for trial stimulation of the cord for pain (North et al., 1993), or of the cauda equina for treatment of reflex incontinence by neuromodulation (Thon et al., 1991). If the trial is successful, the device can subsequently be replaced by a permanent totally implanted system.

Improving the quality of life.   Like any other device or system, a neuroprosthesis which restores a function at the cost of excessive time consumption, inconvenience, discomfort, or poor cosmesis does not improve the overall quality of life, will not be successful, and will not continue to be used. However, some devices offer a long-term functional gain, while requiring a lot of cooperation and user involvement in training and testing before reaching their full potential. These devices in particular call for a high level of understanding and participation in decision-making in users and carers. A rehabilitation-centred assessment and explanation will enable the potential functional gains to be set in the context of the user's overall lifestyle.

Health gains.   There are some examples of neuroprostheses which may result in a gain of health, as well as function. For example, bladder control by sacral anterior root stimulator implant (SARSI) gives good voiding without the use of a catheter, and has been shown to result in a marked reduction in the incidence of urinary tract infections and their complications (van Kerrebroeck et al., 1997). Phrenic pacers may improve the survival of high quadriplegics who use them, although their main impact is on the quality of life (Potter, 1995). It seems possible that lower limb FNS may reduce bone mineral loss and osteoporosis, improve limb blood flow and gluteal muscle bulk, and discourage sacral and ischial pressure sores (Swain, 1992); though the full evidence is not yet available.

Regulatory framework

Until recently there was little regulation applied to active implantables, although there were national standards. There are now increasingly detailed and stringent governmental and international regulatory systems which have been developed to ensure that clinical devices are safe and effective (European Community, 1990). Procedures are now comparable with (though different from) the procedures required for marketing approval of a new drug. However, large-scale clinical trials are often not practicable. Devices often have to be evaluated initially on the basis of small numbers.

Costs of neuroprostheses

The initial costs of treating a patient using a neuroprosthesis are high, and for implantable devices they may be very high. The purchase cost of an implantable system may range from about £3000 up to £25,000 or more. The NHS cost of surgical implantation may be several thousand pounds, depending on the length of stay required. There may be an intensive postimplantation testing and training programme, which is expensive in professional time. Any person with an active implanted device must continue to be supported for the lifetime of the device, including any repairs or replacement. The cost of this commitment should be budgeted for. For these reasons it is inevitable, and probably desirable, that the implementation of neuroprosthesis programmes should take place within a small number of designated specialist centres in the UK. In order for such specialist centres to function properly, it is essential that the appropriate patients are referred to them, and that suitable patients gain equitable access, even though they may live far from such a centre. It is therefore right that members of the local rehabilitation team should be familiar with the general indications, contra-indications, health and functional benefits, maintenance requirements and complication or failure rates for neuroprostheses that are in clinical use in the NHS today. It is the responsibility of specialist teams to be able to give a clear account of these in the appropriate publications, so that non-specialists can keep up to date. Technical accounts should be balanced by reports which give a critical evaluation of patient impact, outcome and complications, costs and cost–benefits, and potential future developments.

Table 18.1. Popularity of different implanted "neuroprostheses" (modified from BSRM, 1997)

Number	Extent of use	Devices
$>10^6$	In use in most countries, many centres	Cardiac pacemakers
10^3-10^4	In use in several countries, specialised centres	Spinal "dorsal column" stimulators Phrenic stimulators Cochlear stimulators Intrathecal baclofen or morphine pumps Bladder controllers
10^2-10^3	Establishing a clinical role, used at more than one centre	Cerebellar stimulators (spasticity) Peroneal braces Activated gracilis slings Upper limb stimulators
10^1-10^2	New, complex, or unproven devices	Lower limb stimulators Cerebellar stimulators (epilepsy) Visual cortex stimulators Deep brain stimulators Cavernosal drug pumps Latissimus cardiac assist Vagus stimulators (epilepsy)

Numbers. The numbers of neuroprostheses of different types implanted worldwide are summarised in Table 18.1. There are several factors that contribute to this very wide range, besides clinical success rate. They include the stage of the device in its development cycle, the complexity and expense of the device, surgical complexity, the size of the team required, the population of suitable patients, training and follow-up requirements, complication and failure rate, and the importance of its benefit. For example, the number of high quadriplegics per year who are physically suitable for a phrenic pacer is not very large, but a large proportion of them could probably gain an improved quality of life from its use. On the other hand, the number of fit paraplegics is large, but many of them are either physically unsuitable for lower limb FES for standing (e.g., because of excess spasticity or contractures), or else their inclination and lifestyle do not lead them to desire the (currently quite small) functional benefits to be obtained, bearing in mind the large devotion to muscle training that is needed to enable durable paraplegic standing using FES. Again, a large proportion of people with a complete spinal cord injury can gain quality of life from use of an implanted bladder controller, because many people are dissatisfied with the alternatives, and appreciate the catheter-free good voiding with reliable continence which this device affords. For all neuroprostheses the current market penetration is low, and potential numbers are much larger than actual numbers. Many devices and applications however are still in the investigational stage, where quality of study is of high importance, and in many cases addressing the scale of the need is not yet the current task.

User-centred assessments for neuroprostheses

These considerations suggest that there are two assessments that need to be made: the rehabilitation assessment, and the technical assessment. The user must be fully informed about the relevant features of the device under consideration, and what they will mean. This process should normally take the form of a dialogue between user and rehabilitation team. Any resulting referral to a specialist centre will then be informed as to the user's needs, aspirations, and concerns, as well as taking account of likely technical questions. The detailed technical assessment will properly be done by the specialist centre, and its form may be dictated in part by research protocols (if the device is in the development phase), or by clinical criteria (if the device is in service). It should be accepted that the user is likely to receive fuller details and a somewhat different perspective at this stage, and will probably benefit from the opportunity of discussion with other users, if this had not been possible earlier. After the technical assessment there may therefore need to be a "cooling-off" period at home, during which time it is emphasised that the user is of course free to withdraw, or ask for a delay or extra information.

The decision to implant an active device implies a lifelong commitment to support if necessary, just as there is for a cardiac pacemaker. However, the neuroprosthesis differs from the cardiac pacemaker in that the main gain resulting is functional rather than medical. This is another reason why all decisions should be collective and patient centred, being based on an informed dialogue with the user in their appropriate social context, rather than being medically centred based on a narrow analysis of the patient's best clinical interests. This suggests that there needs to be careful consideration of the ethics of clinical decisions regarding neuroprostheses.

Expert centres

Networks and pockets of expertise and experience exist in the UK for most of the available neuroprostheses (BSRM, 1997). For new devices and procedures it is important that the initial experience should be concentrated, so as to build up a body of expertise and avoid reduplication of effort and errors. The necessary expertise will be multidisciplinary, involving bioengineers, nurses, and therapists, as well as doctors. For established devices, the appropriate location and number of centres will depend on the type of device, and the number of devices in circulation. A regional structure may be considered to be preferable to a national referral service, as it can provide a more accessible service. This is particularly so because the need for access to technical expertise will be lifelong, and not limited to one or two episodes. It would seem undesirable for clinicians to become occasional implanters of neuroprostheses, or to undertake ongoing support of people with neuroprostheses if they do not have the necessary therapy and engineering support. Commercial implant service companies are now becoming established in the UK, but the responsibility for the clinical support should properly remain an NHS function.

Cost implications for the NHS

The value of a neuroprosthesis is usually considered in terms of capability, functional independence, health, and quality of life. In the long run, an increase in ability and independence for a disabled person is also likely to result in a net saving to the health and social services. The problem is that the initial and continuing costs are quite high, and they are all clearly perceived in the current year's budget of the service concerned. On the other hand, the savings are longer term and harder to evaluate, being spread through budgets in the healthcare, social services, housing, and employment sectors. For many devices the appropriate health economic studies have not been done, though for some they have; and the sums concerned may not be small. For the phrenic pacer, a leading US manufacturer claims a saving over ventilator-dependence costs, in individual patients, of "over \$1000/month, every month for decades" (Dobelle et al., 1994). Less startlingly, a European health economic study has assessed that bladder control using the sacral anterior root stimulator took some 8 years to save enough to pay for its installation, though it also pointed out that this equation ignored the improvement in the quality of life in the meantime (Wielink et al., 1997).

Future developments

Unlike many other electronic devices, active medical implants are not likely to become cheaper in the foreseeable future. Reasons for this include the high cost of meeting the regulatory framework; the costs to the manufacturers and suppliers of insurance against potential claims for injury; the high level of support required (it is common for manufacturers to send an expert to assist with surgical procedures); and the high cost of the necessary lifetime support. Even the most successful devices are not produced in huge numbers. All devices are subject to constant development and improvement, and the support system has to be capable of servicing all the devices still in use. For any device a projection of likely future costs must take account of the present rate of increase, the size of the target population, the expected lifetime of the average recipient, the initial and annual unit costs, and the cost of maintaining an adequate clinical structure to deal with the load.

What a doctor needs to do before referring

If a disabled person or their attendant feels that the existing method of managing a disability is unsatisfactory, then the first obligation of the medical team is to ensure that the method is being used as effectively as possible. If after this review the arrangement is still seen as being unsatisfactory, then there needs to be a full discussion of the range of alternative options available. If a neuroprosthesis is one of them, and the patient is clinically suitable, then the next question is whether patient and professionals agree that there is a potential for functional gain and an improved quality of life from using an implant, that will not be provided by existing methods. This functional gain should be sufficient to outweigh the inconvenience and risk of surgery, the task of managing the implant and ancillary equipment, and dealing with any complications and repairs that may arise during the remainder of the patient's lifetime. It is important not to refer patients who are obviously unsuitable, because they will be needlessly disappointed. It is perhaps even more important not to withhold patients who are obviously suitable, in need, and willing to benefit.

MOTOR STIMULATOR DEVICES

Phrenic stimulators

Applications. Phrenic pacing for ventilatory assistance is now a successful and standard form of treatment which has been applied in several thousand patients ("Phrenic Nerve", 1990). It is possible to stimulate the phrenic nerves transcutaneously in the neck, and electrical or magnetic (Simolowski et al., 1989) stimulation of the phrenic nerves is used as a test of their viability, before deciding on surgery. Reliable and comfortable stimulation adequate for respiration however requires implanted electrodes, and a system of this sort was first reported by Glenn and co-workers (Judson & Glenn, 1968). The diaphragm is a purely inspiratory muscle, so expiration is passive, and the stimulator cannot generate a cough. Stimulation is cyclical, with a train of stimulation pulses of increasing strength being followed by a pause for expiration. Present devices comprise a passive radiofrequency (RF) linked receiver controlled by an external pulse generator and transmitter system, which controls the pattern of activation.

Patient selection. Phrenic nerve stimulators are used in two main groups of patient: those with a high spinal cord injury (SCI), and those with central alveolar hypoventilation (CAH). Patients with CAH usually breathe adequately when awake, but are liable to stop breathing when asleep. They usually require phrenic pacing only while asleep. CAH is commonly congenital ("Ondine's curse"), but it can be acquired, in patients with brainstem lesions or CO_2 insensitivity. Patients with CAH usually have normal phrenic function. However, it is essential to ensure that they do not develop upper airway obstruction during sleep, as phrenic pacing will tend to make this worse, not better. Patients with high SCI may require ventilation 24 hours a day. Their diaphragm becomes fatiguable because of disuse during the period between injury and implantation, so it requires training.

Testing and training. In patients with high spinal injury the phrenic nucleus may be wholly or partially destroyed, since the phrenic nucleus is located around C4. If the nucleus is substantially intact and the diaphragm excitable the patient is likely to be suitable. However, there may be disuse atrophy and abnormal fatiguability of the diaphragm muscle. A normal phrenic nerve when adequately stimulated in the neck (surface electrical or magnetic stimulation can be used for the test) can make the diaphragm descend by 10 cm, as seen on fluoroscopy, and can raise intra-abdominal pressure by 100 cm H_2O. If the figures are less than half of these, phrenic pacing should be approached with caution. However, disuse atrophy and fatiguability (unlike excessive denervation) can be successfully treated using a progressive programme of training stimulation (Glenn et al., 1984).

Technical variations. In adults, stimulating only one phrenic nerve may give an adequate tidal volume, though the lungs of course are then ventilated unequally. In children, the mediastinum is more mobile, and unilateral stimulation is useless (Potter, 1995). Even in adults, bilateral stimulation gives more than twice the tidal volume achieved with unilateral stimulation.

In a few patients with phrenic denervation occurring as a result of their spinal lesion, an intercostal nerve has been successfully grafted onto the phrenic nerve, and the graft subsequently activated using a phrenic pacer (Krieger, 1994).

Results in SCI. Even the untrained tetraplegic patient may quickly be enabled to spend several hours a day away from the ventilator. In one series (Glenn et al., 1986), only 6% of 81 implants failed to achieve a useful result in tetraplegia. Of the successful implants, half were in use for a large part of the waking hours, while half were maintaining adequate ventilation for substantially the whole 24-hour day. Phrenic stimulation gives a worthwhile improvement in the quality of life for patients with high cord injury. Attachment to the ventilator can be dispensed with, although it is usually considered advisable to keep one available in the house at all times, in case of a failure in the implant or driver. Similarly, the question of tracheostomy closure is controversial; patients often wish to breathe more normally, but many doctors think it safer to keep the tracheostomy available in case of emergency. It is not entirely clear whether the life expectancy of patients with high cord lesions is improved with phrenic pacing; the main impact is on the quality of life.

Results in CAH. In patients with CAH, the diaphragm does not usually require any training, as it has not been out of use. Also, CAH patients usually require pacing only at night. They may or may not have neurological disabilities other than CAH (depending on the cause of the CAH); if they do not, they have a long life expectancy in comparison with the high SCI group.

Bladder controllers

Electrical stimulation of nerves or nerve roots associated with the bladder can have two main purposes: to restore continence, or to achieve efficient voiding. Continence may be promoted either by activating the sphincter mechanism, or by inhibiting the detrusor reflex. Efficient voiding may be achieved by activating the detrusor reflex, or by activating the detrusor innervation directly.

Devices whose main aim is to restore voiding

In the past, stimulators have been described which aimed to restore voiding by stimulation of the conus medullaris (Nashold et al., 1972; Sarramon et al., 1979), the sacral anterior roots (Brindley, 1977; Brindley et al., 1982, 1986), the sacral nerves (Habib, 1967), or the detrusor muscle (Bradley et al., 1962; Halverstadt & Parry, 1975). The stimulators of the conus are designed to trigger reflex detrusor contractions, while the others all aim to stimulate the parasympathetic outflow to detrusor

directly. For a number of practical reasons, the successful approach has proved to be by stimulation of the sacral anterior roots using an implanted stimulator (SARSI; Brindley, 1994).

Sacral anterior root stimulators. At this site, the motor fibres to the detrusor muscle are compactly arranged, so they can be stimulated easily. The motor fibres are largely segregated from the sensory fibres, so that stimulation of the latter can be avoided, and they can be cut if deafferentation is required (see deafferentation, next). Electrode movement and the risk of electrode or cable fracture is minimised, the electrodes being far from the mobile bladder itself. The main problem is that the preganglionic parasympathetic fibres to detrusor run in the roots together with the somatic motor fibres to the striated urethral sphincter. The sphincteromotor fibres are larger and of lower threshold than the parasympathetic motor fibres, so that stimulation of the whole root causes sphincter closure as well as detrusor contraction. The resulting obstruction of voiding, which is highly undesirable, can be prevented by using one of several special techniques (see stimulation dyssynergia, later).

Sacral deafferentation. This is usually done at the S2–S4 levels, at the same time as the implantation of the stimulator. The benefits that result are abolition of reflex incontinence, increase in functional bladder capacity, improvement in bladder compliance, a great reduction in active detrusor–sphincter dyssynergia, and (in patients with lesions above T6) abolition of bladder- or bowel-induced autonomic dysreflexia. Without sacral deafferentation, the main benefits of SARSI, such as continence and good voiding, are often not achieved (Brindley et al., 1986; Brindley & Rushton, 1990).

Stimulation dyssynergia. The most commonly used method of overcoming striated sphincter closure is by stimulating in a pattern of alternating bursts and gaps, with each cycle lasting for a few seconds. The timing is adjusted to take advantage of the longer time course of the contraction and relaxation of detrusor smooth muscle, when compared with the striated sphincter. The gaps in stimulation, and hence the period of sphincter relaxation, are timed to coincide with the peak of detrusor pressure. Urinary voiding occurs during the gaps in stimulation. The speed of detrusor smooth muscle contraction varies somewhat between individuals, and the cycle length is adjusted accordingly. The other stimulus parameters are adjusted so that voiding occurs at acceptable pressures.

Other methods which have been used for overcoming stimulation dyssynergia have been less successful to date; they include anodal block of the large sphincteromotor fibres (Brindley & Craggs, 1980) (which has promise, but requires more complex equipment); pre-fatigue of sphincter by high-frequency stimulation (which is not very effective by itself, but can be a useful supplement); Wedensky block (Baratta et al., 1989); and pudendal neurectomy (which significantly reduces continence).

Patient selection. There are three main criteria which have to be satisfied before an individual can be considered suitable for SARSI. First, the bladder dysfunction should be associated with a spinal cord lesion, which is usually but not always complete. If the lesion is incomplete and there is preserved pelvic pain sensibility, then special precautions have to be taken to ensure that stimulation will not be painful.

Second, there must be good evidence that the bladder is responsive to sacral root stimulation. In patients with a cauda equina lesion, the bladder is usually unresponsive. If the bladder is shown on urodynamic testing to be sufficiently reflexly active, this is good enough. Otherwise, one can seek an adequate detrusor response to transrectal or transforaminal electrical stimulation of the sacral nerves during urodynamic testing.

Third, the patient must be dissatisfied with their existing method of bladder management. There are various reasons why they may be dissatisfied. If they void by spinal reflex, then they are likely also to have reflex incontinence. In men, this can be managed by using a condom urinal, but reflex incontinence is a strong reason for women to desire SARSI. In both sexes, reflex voiding is usually incomplete and persistent or recurrent urinary infection is common. Some patients who void by intermittent self-catheterisation also suffer from reflex incontinence between voidings, in spite of anticholinergic medication. They often wish to change to SARSI for this reason.

Benefits to be expected. The most obvious benefits are restoration of continence and the ability to empty the bladder at will. However, there are a number of other benefits to bladder function. The functional bladder capacity is increased, partly because sacral deafferentation improves the actual capacity and compliance of the bladder, but also because the residual volume is reduced. Any ureteric reflux and upper tract dilatation is usually prevented, cured, or reduced, so that renal function is preserved or improved. The frequency of urinary tract infections is reduced, largely as a result of the improved residual volume. Active detrusor–sphincter dyssynergia is abolished or reduced by sacral deafferentation, so that voiding pressure and pattern are normalised.

There are also some benefits to be found outside bladder function. In many patients, sacral root stimulation in an appropriate pattern can drive defaecation, or assist manual evacuation of faeces. In more than half of male patients, sacral root stimulation can give sustained penile erection. Sacral deafferentation reduces the incidence of episodes of autonomic dysreflexia in patients with high spinal cord lesions.

Disadvantages of SARSI. Many of these benefits only occur because of sacral deafferentation. The SARSI itself simply allows the deafferented bladder to be emptied at will, without a catheter. For the benefits to be seen in full, the deafferentation must be thorough (i.e., S2–S4, bilaterally). Some functions, particularly genital sensation and reflex erection or ejaculation, are thereby lost. Loss of genital sensation is significant only in patients with incomplete lesions who happen to have genital sensory preservation. In those who do, it may be a good reason for refusing SARSI, or accepting incomplete deafferentation. For example, if the sensory preservation is unilateral, then the insensate side can be deafferented. Reflex erection occurs to some extent in a majority of spinal men, although it is not usually well sustained. It will usually be abolished by deafferentation. Whether to exchange this for the probability (but not certainty)

of well-sustained stimulator-evoked erections can be a difficult decision. Reflex ejaculation occurs in only about 10% of spinal men, and when present it is abolished by sacral deafferentation. However, semen can be obtained for purposes of fertility by a variety of other means.

Devices whose main aim is to restore continence

Reflex incontinence can often be abolished by weak stimulation of the sacral nerves or roots, at a strength which is sufficient to activate the large myelinated fibres, but insufficient to activate the parasympathetic outflow to detrusor (Thon et al., 1991). This may work in part by activating the striated sphincter of the urethra, but also, and probably more importantly, there is a central or reflex effect which reduces or abolishes the abnormal voiding reflex. Stimulation of this sort can be achieved by putting an electrode in the sacral hiatus, so the surgical procedure is much simpler than the procedure required for insertion of a SARSI with sacral deafferentation. It is more like that required for a "dorsal column" stimulator, and the purpose is a form of neuromodulation. The patient group here is quite different from the patient group for whom SARSI is appropriate. These are patients who can initiate a normal voiding contraction, so that they have no difficulty voiding, but who have intractable reflex incontinence. Some of these people have no identifiable neurological lesion (their abnormal detrusor activity is called "detrusor instability"), while some do have neurological disease (they are said to have "detrusor hyperreflexia"); but in both cases it is presumed that the extra impulse traffic in the large sacral sensory nerve fibres is responsible for the benefit. Whether this is acting at spinal or supraspinal level, or both, is uncertain.

It is possible that neuromodulation methods may also in the future be developed for use in conjunction with the SARSI. If successful, this would enable good voiding and continence in paraplegia without requiring dorsal root section. An alternative method for modifying sensory nerve activity in reflex incontinence may be the use of intravesical capsaicin.

Upper limb stimulators

Applications. There is scope for using FES to restore some hand grasp functions in suitable patients with circumscribed lesions at C5/6 level. Voluntary control of the shoulder and of elbow flexion movements is preserved in this group, often with wrist extension as well, so they can position the arm appropriately. Because both arms are usually similarly disabled, they have much to gain from an implanted stimulator which restores grasps to one hand. Patients with hemiplegia would seem to have less to gain from restoring a limited range of grasp functions to the affected hand, if they already have one normal hand.

Patient selection. It is essential to confirm that the patient is physically suitable for neurostimulation, and that it will in fact increase independence in ways that the patient desires. If the muscles innervated from the C7, C8, and T1 segments of the cord are denervated, then neurostimulation has nothing to offer.

Denervation occurs if a long segment of the cord is infarcted, or if the nerve roots in the lower brachial plexus were avulsed or destroyed at the time of injury. Excitability of the forearm muscles is easily tested by surface stimulation at the motor points. It is possible in this way to estimate the potential for function of any partially denervated muscles. Even when the cord lesion is very short, some muscles whose motor neurones are at that level will be partially denervated. If the remainder of the colony is above the lesion, the muscle will be weak but under voluntary control; if below, it will not be under voluntary control, but will be partially excitable. Also, the arm should be free from serious contractures, the patient must be fully wheelchair rehabilitated, have a good wheelchair posture, and be without uncontrolled spasticity or spasms.

Apart from all these physical considerations, the patient and the team must be clear about the goals in terms of increased independence in the activities of daily living. The expectations of the team, the patient, and the carers must be analysed in sufficient detail to ensure they are realistic.

Clinical systems. Upper limb neurostimulation is available using surface stimulation systems, and implanted systems. There is a commercially available surface stimulation system (the Ness Hand-Master) which is mounted in an orthosis. It is designed to be easy for the patient to don and doff unaided, and provides a switch-controlled grasp and release function. The Bionic Glove (Prochazka et al., 1997) is also commercially available.

Surface and implanted methods can be used in the same patient, in a way that has been explored most thoroughly by the Cleveland group (Peckham et al., 1993). For example, surface stimulation can establish that the patient is suitable; while fine percutaneous leads can be used if necessary for a matter of weeks or months to train the muscles and establish exactly what the functional gains are likely to be. Later, an implanted multichannel stimulator can be installed which is tailored to the individual's needs, and where the performance can be accurately predicted. These systems are applied to one arm only. They are applicable in patients who do not have the potential for tendon transfer to enable grasp.

Just as much effort has gone into the development of appropriate control systems, as into the stimulator system itself. Obviously, the possibilities for manual control are limited. However, a patient with control of shoulder movements and elbow flexion can control a wheelchair-mounted joystick, using the unstimulated hand, giving two dimensions of control of the stimulated hand (Perkins et al., 1994). This is sufficient to enable two grasp-release patterns, usually lateral prehension (key-grip) and palmar prehension (grasp), and their corresponding release movements.

However, there are obvious disadvantages to using wheelchair-mounted equipment. The Cleveland control method is the shoulder-mounted transducer, which can be worn under the clothing. Most C5/6 tetraplegics have normal sensorimotor function around the shoulder joint, and the shoulder has sufficient degrees of freedom to allow control of two grasps and

switching between control states. Three control states are probably the minimum, and they can be summarised as "Implement proportional control", "Maintain existing settings", and "Off". The user needs to be able to recalibrate the system during use, whenever necessary.

Other control systems which have received some attention include myoelectric control, voice control, and wrist control, using preserved voluntary wrist extension on the stimulated side. A special case of myoelectric control, the "muscle amplifier", used in conjunction with surface stimulation systems, senses small voluntary emg potentials in a paretic muscle, and uses them as the control signal for graded electrical stimulation of the same muscle. The signal processing circuit has to be capable of filtering out the stimulus artefact and stimulus-evoked emg, both of which are much larger than the control signal (Hollander et al., 1987).

Supplementary procedures. At present, neurostimulation offers relatively few stimulation channels, and therefore a limited number of grasps. In these circumstances, there are benefits to be gained by limiting some of the unused degrees of freedom in the hand, so as to provide improved control and stability. Adjunctive procedures of this sort include tethering the long flexor tendons of the fingers, so that the fingers move in line, or arthrodesis of the interphalangeal joint of the thumb, to stabilise the posture of the thumb. Tendon transfers can extend the range of movements that are under voluntary control, as for example transfer of biceps, or the posterior part of deltoid, to provide elbow extension; or transfer of brachioradialis so that it gives some wrist extension (Freehafer et al., 1988).

Lower limb stimulators for paraplegic standing and stepping

Standing. Kantrowitz demonstrated paraplegic standing in 1963, using surface stimulation of the quadriceps femoris muscles. Balance was maintained using elbow crutches, or a frame. Several problems have to be overcome in order to turn this kind of demonstration into a useful system. First, muscle training for fatigue-resistance is required. Even then, the endurance of continuously stimulated quadriceps muscles is limited. Second, the hips must be stabilised in extension. This is most commonly done by stimulating gluteus maximus as well. Third, control mechanisms must be introduced which allow safe stand-up and sit-down transitions (Kralj et al., 1983).

Muscle fatigue. Fatigue is a particularly serious problem in lower limb FES, because it can result in falls and possible injury. There are several tactics for avoiding and overcoming fatigue. One is to tailor the stimulation parameters to minimise the amount of muscle activation. The stimulus frequency can be reduced until the contraction starts to become significantly unfused. The strength or frequency of stimulation can be controlled by (for example) knee-angle sensors, providing a closed-loop control system which minimises the stimulus strength, and matches it to the requirement. There is some evidence that irregular stimulus trains (in particular, with initial pulse doublets) may enable a muscle to give more work for less fatigue (Kwende et al., 1995). If intramuscular pressure is prevented from rising above the perfusion pressure, fatigue is delayed. Muscles are trained in order to convert many of the fibres to fatigue-resistant types. This is a process that may require many weeks, because there are changes in the structural contractile proteins, as well as an increase in the capillary network density and a metabolic change from the glycolytic to the oxidative pathway (Salmons & Henriksson, 1981).

Another tactic for delaying muscle fatigue is to adopt postures which minimise the need for muscle activity, or rotate the duty between different muscle groups, so as to delay fatigue. The knee is stable in extension if the ground reaction vector (GRV) is in front of the knee joint. The hip is stable in full extension if the GRV is behind the hip joint. Therefore, a position commonly (but inelegantly) adopted by paraplegics when standing is the "C" posture, so called because their axis is lordotic, so as to resemble the shape of a shallow "C" (if facing to the left of the observer). However, bringing the GRV in front of the knee requires that the weight be carried through the forefoot. This requires that the ankle plantarflexors be active. When it is time to rest the plantarflexors, the weight moves back towards the heel and the GRV moves back, so that the quadriceps femoris must be activated in order to maintain stable knee extension. Alternating quadriceps and calf muscle activation (so-called "posture-switching") is a normal tactic for fatigue-saving in intact people, as well as being used in FES standing in paraplegia. It also follows that the position of the GRV in relation to the knee joint can be used as the controlling variable for quadriceps stimulation, because the knee will remain locked in extension so long as the GRV is in front of the knee joint. As the GRV approaches the knee joint, incipient knee unlocking can be predicted, and quadriceps stimulation switched on. The GRV can be kept forward either by activation of the calf muscles, or by a special design of ankle-foot orthosis (AFO), called the floor reaction orthosis (FRO) (Andrews et al., 1988), which also contains sensors. In effect, the sensors in the FRO detect the extension moment at the knee. While it is above a threshold level, the quadriceps stimulation is reduced or turned off. When it falls, stimulation is started. This is an example of a *hybrid system*, which is a system employing both FES and orthotic components.

Stepping. From quiet stance, stepping can be initiated by first transferring weight onto the stance leg, and moving the centre of gravity forward. This is done through trunk and upper limb control. Then the swing leg must be brought forward, through a sequence of hip and knee flexion, followed by knee extension and ankle dorsiflexion. This can be achieved using surface FES, by activating the flexor withdrawal reflex on the swing side (Kralj & Bajd, 1989). The flexor withdrawal response can be conveniently evoked by strong stimulation of the common peroneal nerve, which results in ipsilateral hip and knee flexion, and ankle dorsiflexion. The method is severely limited, however, by the long latency and habituation of this nociceptive reflex in spinal man. Habituation can sometimes be temporarily

reversed by a dishabituating stimulus (Granat et al., 1991), but the method does not allow for a well-controlled or dynamic gait, and the speed of progression is slow. Besides the long latency of the response, the premature ankle dorsiflexion prevents the plantarflexor push-off at the end of stance, which is needed for a dynamic gait. Stepping at a reasonable velocity can be achieved in patients with percutaneous systems where the flexor muscles are accessed as well as the extensors (Marsolais & Kobetic, 1986). The metabolic requirement is less heavy than for swing-through gait, as much of the body weight is carried through the stance leg, and less through the shoulder girdle. However, control of percutaneous systems to date has been by open-loop triggered-programme, so adequate allowance cannot be made for muscle fatigue or unexpected perturbations. For this reason, the system is only considered safe for use in the laboratory.

Swing-through. In three-point swing-through or swing-to gait, the crutches are brought forward together and placed on the ground ahead, while the legs are maintained in extension, using calipers or quadriceps stimulation (Brindley et al., 1979). Then the whole weight is taken through the crutches, and the legs are swung forward together. Swing-through can give a dynamic and high speed gait, because the leg length is in effect extended to the axillae. However, the energy cost is very high (Heller & Andrews, 1989), because the shoulder girdle has to take the whole weight during the swing phase, as well as providing the energy for progression, and the FES of the lower limb extensors, which merely provides support, uses further energy. It is therefore tiring, and cannot be maintained for long.

Hybrid systems. There are two main reasons why FES is often combined with orthotic components to form so-called hybrid systems. First, orthoses can help to maintain posture without unnecessary fatiguing muscle stimulation, the FES then being used to produce movements, rather than being wasted in opposing gravity. Second, braces can help to control joints whose muscles are relatively inaccessible to FES. The FRO, described previously, serves mainly the first purpose.

Orthoses which control hip motion such as the reciprocating gait orthosis (RGO) or hip guidance orthosis (HGO) types, are among those which serve mainly the second purpose. The RGO and HGO work on different principles. In the RGO the hip joints are mechanically reciprocally linked in flexion–extension using Bowden cables (Douglas et al., 1983). The HGO (Parawalker type) restrains the hips to move in the flexion–extension plane using a low-friction hinge joint, but does not force the limbs to reciprocate (Butler & Major, 1987). The RGO may be used in a hybrid system in conjunction with surface FES (Hirokawa et al., 1996); the RGO provides support and the FES provides movement, enabling a relatively low-energy gait pattern.

Implanted stimulators. Implanted electrodes offer access to muscles which cannot be reached using surface electrodes, as well as the potential for increased numbers of channels, and greatly reduced stimulus currents. All of these features are of the greatest importance for lower limb control in paraplegia.

A few small patient series have been published reporting results using implanted devices of different types. These include many-channel percutaneous intramuscular coiled wire electrodes (Marsolais & Kobetic, 1988), few-channel motor nerve-cuff systems (McNeal et al., 1977, 1987; Brindley et al., 1979), many-channel mixed-type motor nerve electrode systems (Rushton, 1990), and many-channel lumbo-sacral motor nerve root electrode systems (Rushton et al., 1997). None of these implant systems has yet reached the stage of large-scale trials, or regular usage outside the laboratory. This may be attributable to immaturity in the control systems used, rather than unreliability in the implant stimulator system itself. Multichannel multiplexed stimulator implants, designed to meet the requirements of lower limb FES, are available (Donaldson, 1990; Donaldson et al., 1995). Injectable microstimulator implants, placed near nerves and individually addressable by code, are being developed (Loeb et al., 1991), though they have not yet reached the stage of human implantation.

Peroneal brace stimulators

Foot-drop. Foot-drop is often a gait-limiting factor in patients with stroke or incomplete spinal cord injury. The toe catches the ground in early swing phase, and slaps the ground following heel-strike, often with inversion as well. The hip and knee are excessively flexed during the swing phase to compensate, and if this is not possible because of more proximal weakness, the leg is circumducted. Foot-drop may be relieved using an ankle-foot orthosis, or by FES. A rigid toe-raising orthosis does not allow active plantarflexion, so that there is no push-off, and the stride length and walking speed are reduced. These problems can be addressed using a peroneal brace stimulator.

Surface stimulation. The branches of the common peroneal nerve are easily stimulated near the fibular head, and large series of patients have been reported using surface stimulation (Acimovic et al., 1987). The main difficulties are in achieving and maintaining correct electrode location to give a balanced dorsiflexion, and in obtaining reliability in the electrode leads, and particularly in the heel-switch. They are often eventually rejected by patients, as being too cumbersome or difficult to adjust. On the other hand, it is often found that voluntary dorsiflexion power improves after several months of using the peroneal brace, even in patients whose foot-drop had been present for long periods, so the device may be discarded for this reason also (Karsznia et al., 1990; Burridge et al., 1997).

Implanted devices. Implanted stimulators could potentially solve the problem of maintaining a stable and accurate electrode location (Kljajic et al., 1992). A two-channel implant, activating the tibialis anterior and peronei separately, may be the way to achieve balanced dorsiflexion (Holsheimer et al., 1993). However, published series of implanted devices are still much smaller than for surface stimulation. In the series of Kljajic et al. there were 35 patients, of whom 22 continued to use their devices in the long term. Of the remainder, one had recovered active dorsiflexion, three had died, one had undergone amputation

for unrelated reasons, three had a poor foot posture, four had unpleasant sensations as a result of stimulation, and one was lost to follow-up.

Future developments. There will continue to be scope for further development of surface stimulation systems, perhaps with a self-adjusting electrode system which optimises the current distribution for foot posture, and a sensor which is more reliable and preferably positioned more proximally, than the conventional heel-strike sensor. We also need to know how, and under what conditions, the peroneal brace can "cure" established footdrop in stroke, as it sometimes seems to do.

Stimulators for ano-rectal incontinence

Activated gracilis slings. There are several common causes of insufficiency of the anal sphincter, including mechanical tear (usually obstetric injury, or following anal surgery), myopathy, autonomic neuropathy, or pudendal neuropathy. Pudendal neuropathy is thought often to be a self-sustaining traction neuropathy associated with excessive pelvic descent, either precipitated acutely during childbirth (Snooks et al., 1984), or an episode of rectal prolapse, or chronically by straining at stool (Parks et al., 1977). Loss of rectal sensation, and hence of an adequate call to stool, may be associated with some of these, and also occurs most obviously in spinal cord lesions. However, anal sphincter tone is usually present in paraplegia. Therefore, the problem in paraplegia is much more one of bowel training and avoiding constipation, than of faecal incontinence due to sphincteric weakness.

Moderate degrees of sphincteric insufficiency can often be successfully treated medically, or by physiotherapy, muscle training or biofeedback. More severe degrees are treated surgically, particularly where a torn sphincter can be repaired. In patients with pudendal nerve damage the conventional procedure of pelvic floor repair attempts to restore the normal ano-rectal angle and facilitate the action of pubo-rectalis. Although the early results of post anal repair surgery are good, in the longer term ano-rectal incontinence often recurs (Browning & Parks, 1983), and the progress of the pudendal neuropathy may even be accelerated (Keighley & Fielding, 1983).

In patients with severely denervated anal sphincters attempts have been made to develop an active neosphincter system using FES. Pedicles of gluteal or gracilis muscle were wrapped around the anal canal in various ways, and activated voluntarily at the call to stool. Results were variable, and consistent success was not really achieved until the neuromuscular graft was combined with electrical training and activation of the neosphincter using an implanted stimulator (Baeten et al., 1991; Williams et al., 1991; Abercrombie & Williams, 1995). Chronic stimulation schedules are used, which facilitate increased capillary density, and conversion to Type 1 (slow-twitch, oxidative metabolism, fatigue-resistant) fibres. In the case of gracilis, which has a segmental blood supply, special precautions are also required to ensure maintenance of an adequate blood supply to the whole transplanted muscle (Patel et al., 1991).

SENSORY STIMULATOR DEVICES

Cutaneous sensation

Subcutaneous stimulator electrodes give a useful signal indicating that the NeuroControl Freehand stimulator is activated, as noted earlier. A small number of patients have been given implanted stimulators of the visual cortex, either using cortical surface electrodes or intracortical semi-micro electrodes. However, these devices have not reached clinical application. The only complex implantable sensory prosthesis in clinical use now is the cochlear stimulator.

Cochlear stimulators

History. Potentially useful auditory sensations were demonstrated to result from cochlear stimulation by an implanted electrode in a totally deaf subject very early in the history of neuroprostheses (Djourno & Eyries, 1957). A decade later Simmons (1966) implanted an array of electrodes, and demonstrated that (for similar stimulus patterns) perceived pitch varied with the location of the electrode within the cochlear spiral, as the electrophysiological evidence would have predicted. The perceived pitch was also found to vary with the stimulus frequency, and there was for some years controversy about the advantages of single- versus multi-channel cochlear implants. This could only be resolved by careful study of the auditory test performance of significant numbers of patients with the different implant types. Most devices used intracochlear electrodes, but useful results could also be obtained by placing the electrode in an extracochlear position, near the round window (Douek et al., 1977). It was felt that the relative technical simplicity of this approach might compensate for poorer performance. However, as techniques for intracochlear implantation of multichannel electrode arrays have developed, the success rates have become high. Multichannel intracochlear electrodes were found to give a much higher performance on hearing tests (Eddington, 1983); so this approach has become standard. Early multichannel devices often comprised a small array of simple radiofrequency receivers, each with an output capacitor to ensure charge balance, and an output series resistor to prevent excessive stimulation current. Recent models are multiplexed, and digitally controlled. The electrodes are arranged along a flexible thin mount, pre-curved to approximate to the curvature of the cochlea.

Patient selection. Careful patient selection and preoperative testing is essential, to ensure that the patient is physically and psychologically suitable for a cochlear stimulator, and that they will be capable of learning to take useful advantage of the distorted sounds they will hear while using it. Patients should be profoundly deaf, with a pure tone audiogram showing more than 100 dB of hearing loss throughout most of the frequency spectrum. Adults should be postlingually deaf, so that they will be able to make use of speech sensations. A knowledge of spoken language is often not retained by children who become deaf before the age of 7 years. Good lipreading skills are not a contraindication to cochlear stimulation. It is a valuable addition even

to an excellent lip-reader, and may enable them to carry on telephone conversations. It is usual to evaluate the response to electrical stimulation in the promontory area, before proceeding to surgery. A positive (low-threshold hearing) response to promontory stimulation is encouraging. However, a negative promontory test does not exclude a subsequent good result from a cochlear implant.

External equipment. External equipment must be small, light and unobtrusive, in order to be acceptable to patients in the long run. It comprises a microphone, signal processor, radiofrequency transmitter, and battery pack. The battery pack must last at least for a whole day before needing recharging. The signal processor must be capable of adjustment to suit the needs of the individual.

Adjusting the device. Preoperative assessments give the team knowledge of what the patient can do, and wishes to achieve. Postoperative testing starts by measuring the threshold and maximal stimulus strengths for each channel, so that the device will work within the acceptable dynamic range of loudness. Pitch discrimination, speech perception, lipreading, and voice quality are all the subject of training in the postoperative period. There are now sets of test material which have been standardised for use with cochlear stimulation patients. A cochlear implantation service is now established within the NHS (O'Donoghue, 1996).

NEUROMODULATOR DEVICES

These are distinct from FES devices, but they are briefly reviewed here because many of the methods and considerations are similar to those found in neuroprostheses. The use of the term *neuromodulation* in this context is controversial, because it is a term which is already used in neurosciences, with a different meaning.

Sensory gating

The idea that stimulation of large sensory fibres in peripheral nerves or in the spinal cord might relieve pain was made respectable by the publication of the "gate control" theory of pain (Melzack & Wall, 1965). In this theory, the interplay of impulses in large and small fibres at a gating site (in the substantia gelatinosa of the dorsal horn) tended to open or close pain pathways. Conventional weak brief-pulse electrical stimulation selectively activates large fibres, so the obvious way to change the balance of activity in favour of large fibres was by electrical stimulation. Peripheral stimulation (of affected skin areas, or of sensory nerves) or central stimulation (of the spinal cord and associated structures) were both found to be effective; they have since evolved rather different areas of usage, which will be considered separately.

Sensory nerve stimulators

Transcutaneous electrical nerve stimulation ("TENS") can provide worthwhile pain relief in many clinical situations where there is severe neuropathic pain, such as causalgia, brachial plexus injury (Wynn Parry et al., 1987), or low back pain (Long, 1976) in which surgery is either inappropriate or has failed. The system is battery powered, portable, and harmless, and the position of the electrodes can be adjusted by trial and error, or by using published diagrams, to give the greatest pain relief. Clinicians need to ensure that there has been an adequate trial of stimulus strength, electrode location, and duration of stimulation, before deciding that TENS is a failure in any patient. Occasionally, implanted peripheral nerve stimulators have been used for pain relief, for example in causalgia, but the added risk and the surgery required are seldom thought to be worthwhile.

Spinal cord stimulators

Spinal cord stimulation ("SCS") has been used in treatment of back pain following failed surgery, and in neuropathic pain, pain from angina and circulatory insufficiency, malignancy, and other indications. It requires implanted electrodes, because of the depth of the cord. When first introduced, the technique was called dorsal column stimulation, but it is now recognised that other structures may be stimulated as well as the dorsal columns. As with TENS, pain relief is usually best when the evoked paraesthesiae are referred to the whole of the painful area. Spinal cord stimulation can thus cope with pain in a whole leg, both legs, or in the perineum, areas for which pain relief using TENS may be inadequate or difficult to achieve. It is usually considered to be indicated in patients with severe disabling localised neuropathic pain, whose life expectancy is good, and whose pain is not relieved by non-narcotic analgesics. It may be necessary to assess the response to stimulation before implanting a permanent system. Pain is hard to assess objectively, and patient selection for procedures such as spinal cord stimulation is difficult. Significant psychiatric illness, opiate addiction or secondary gain are often thought to be contra-indications. Some surgeons prefer a formal trial of SCS using a percutaneous lead for a few days, before embarking on a permanent implant. However, even this cannot necessarily predict the amount of long-term pain relief to be expected. Some authors have emphasised the value of even partial pain relief (Koeze, 1995). It is similarly difficult to evaluate the results, but the same author in his review concluded that in most series where "reasonable" selection criteria were used, 50% of implanted patients would achieve a better than 50% relief of their pain.

Cerebellar stimulators

Cerebellar stimulation ("CS") using an implanted array of electrodes on the dorsal surface of the cerebellum was introduced by Cooper (1973, 1974). The rationale was that neurophysiological studies had shown that the output of the cerebellar cortex was wholly inhibitory. Cooper used CS in the treatment of intractable epilepsy, and of severe spasticity particularly in association with cerebral palsy. His group developed methods for "tuning" the stimulation for greatest effect (Cooper & Upton, 1978), and reported good results in quite large series.

However, other centres, often in much smaller series, could not replicate the results in epilepsy, and one controlled trial (Wright et al., 1984), using effective versus dummy stimulation, failed to show any objective benefit from the active treatment, even though 11 of the 12 patients were convinced it was beneficial to them. This is much higher than an expected placebo rate of benefit, and it may be that short-term changes in fit frequency do not tell the whole story. Although not currently fashionable, cerebellar stimulation for epilepsy and spasticity in cerebral palsy is still performed with reported success at some centres (Davis, 2000).

Cerebellar stimulation for spasticity is easier to judge than its effect on fit frequency, and may be of significant functional benefit, particularly in children with severe spasticity associated with cerebral palsy (Sutcliffe, personal communication).

Deep brain stimulators

Deep brain stimulation (DBS) tends to be a treatment of last resort for pain (Gybels & Kuypers, 1990; Kumar et al., 1990) or tremor (Lyons et al., 1998). A variety of different sites have been favoured, and it has often been used in patients whose life expectancy is short. The theory is usually that opioid-releasing pathways will be activated, and electrodes are placed stereotaxically in the periaqueductal grey matter, periventricular grey matter, or the thalamic centrum medianum. There have been no well-controlled trials of DBS, and results have been variable, though impressive in some hands (Young, 1990).

Vagus stimulators

Stimulation of the vagus nerve, like the cerebellum, has been found to have widespread inhibitory effects in the brain (Rutecki, 1990). It can inhibit experimental seizures, and trials in several centres have shown significant improvements in patients with intractable epilepsy. Unlike cerebellar stimulation, "double-blind" trial of effective and dummy vagal stimulation, or stimulation at different current levels, has demonstrated a therapeutic effect which is claimed to be dose-related (Holder et al., 1992). However, vagal stimulation causes several easily perceived side-effects, particularly at the onset of a stimulus train. The patient is therefore unlikely to be blind to the stimulus conditions, so that a controlled trial of such treatment will be difficult. In this respect, objective assessment of vagus stimulators is more difficult than for cerebellar stimulators, whose effect is usually imperceptible to the patient.

REFERENCES

Abercrombie, J.F., & Williams, N.S. (1995). Development of an electrically-stimulated skeletal muscle neoanal sphincter. In G.S. Brindley & D.N. Rushton (Eds.), *Baillière's clinical neurology 4.1: Neuroprostheses* (pp. 21–34). London: Baillière Tindall.

Acimovic, R., Gros, N., & Malezic, M. (1987). A comparative study of the functionality of the second generation of peroneal stimulators. In

Proceedings of the 10th Annual Conference on Rehabilitation Technology, San Jose (pp. 621–623). Association for the Advancement of Rehabilitation Technology.

Andrews, B.J., Baxendale, R.H., Barnett, R., et al. (1988). Hybrid FES orthosis incorporating closed loop control and sensory feedback. *Journal of Biomedical Engineering, 10,* 189–195.

Baeten, C.G.M.I, Konsten, J., Spaans, F., et al. (1991). Dynamic graciloplasty for treatment of faecal incontinence. *Lancet, 338,* 1163–1165.

Baratta, R., Ichie, M., Hwang, S., & Solomonow, M. (1989). Method for studying muscle properties under orderly stimulated motor units with tripolar nerve cuff electrodes. *J. Biomed. Eng., 11,* 141–147.

Bradley, W.E., Wittmers, L.E., Chou, S.N., & French, S.A. (1962). Use of a radio transmitter receiver unit for the treatment of neurogenic bladder: a preliminary report. *J. Neurosurg., 19,* 782–786.

Brindley, G.S. (1977). An implant to empty the bladder or close the urethra. *Journal of Neurology, Neurosurgery and Psychiatry, 40,* 358–369.

Brindley, G.S. (1994). The first 500 patients with sacral anterior root stimulator implants; general description. *Paraplegia, 32,* 795–805.

Brindley, G.S., & Craggs, M.D. (1980). A technique for anodally blocking large nerve fibres through chronically implanted electrodes. *Journal of Neurology, Neurosurgery and Psychiatry, 43,* 1083–1090.

Brindley, G.S., Polkey, C.E., & Rushton, D.N. (1979). Electrical splinting of the knee in paraplegia. *Paraplegia, 16,* 428–435.

Brindley, G.S., Polkey, C.E., & Rushton, D.N. (1982). Sacral anterior root stimulation for bladder control in paraplegia. *Paraplegia, 20,* 365–381.

Brindley, G.S., Polkey, C.E., Rushton, D.N., & Cardozo, L.D. (1986). Sacral anterior root stimulators for bladder control in paraplegia: the first 50 cases. *Journal of Neurology, Neurosurgery and Psychiatry, 49,* 1104–1114.

Brindley, G.S., & Rushton, D.N. (1990). Long-term follow-up of patients with sacral anterior root stimulator implants. *Paraplegia, 28,* 469–475.

British Society of Rehabilitation Medicine. (1997). *Report on Neuroprostheses.* BSRM/Royal College of Physicians, London.

Browning, G.G.P., & Parks, A.G. (1983). Post anal repair for neuropathic faecal incontinence: correlation of clinical result and anal canal pressures. *British Journal of Surgery, 70,* 101–104.

Burridge, J., Taylor, P., Hagan, S., & Swain, I. (1997). Experience of clinical use of the Odstock Dropped Foot Stimulator. *Artificial Organs, 21,* 254–260.

Butler, P.B., & Major, R.E. (1987). The ParaWalker: a rational approach to the provision of reciprocal ambulation for paraplegic patients. *Physiotherapy, 73,* 393–397.

Cooper, I.S. (1973). Effect of chronic stimulation of anterior cerebellum on neurological disease. *Lancet, 1,* 206.

Cooper, I.S. (1974). *The cerebellum, epilepsy and behaviour.* New York: Plenum.

Cooper, I.S., & Upton, A.R.M. (1978). Effects of cerebellar stimulation on epilepsy, the EEG and cerebral palsy in man. *Electroencephalography and Clinical Neurophysiology, 34*(Suppl.), 349–354.

Davis, R. (2000). Cerebellular stimulation for cerebral palsy spasticity, function and seizures. *Arch. Med. Res., 31,* 290–299.

Djourno, A., & Eyries, C. (1957). Prothèse auditive par excitation électrique à distance du nerf sensoriel à l'aide d'un bobinage inclus à demeure. *Presse Médicale, 65,* 1417–1423.

Dobelle, W.H., D'Angelo, M.S., Goetz, B.F., et al. (1994). 200 cases with a new breathing pacemaker dispels myths about diaphragm pacing. *Trans. Amer. Soc. Artific. Internal Ortg., 40(3),* M244–252.

Donaldson, N., & de, N. (1990). A new multiplexed stimulator for FNS. In D.B. Popovic (Ed.), *Advances in the external control of the human extremities, X* (pp. 345–358). Belgrade, Nauka.

Donaldson, N., de, N., Perkins, T.A., & Worley, A.C.M. (1995). Lumbar root stimulation for restoring leg function. Methods: stimulator and measurement of muscle actions. In *Proceedings, 5th Vienna International Workshop on Functional Electrostimulation* (pp. 323–326). University of Vienna.

Douek, E.E., Fourcin, A.J., Moore, B.C.J., & Clark, G.P. (1977). A new approach to the cochlear implant. *Proceedings of the Royal Society of Medicine, 70,* 379.

Douglas, R, Larson, P.F., D'Ambrosia, R., et al. (1983). LSU Reciprocating Gait Orthosis. *Orthopaedics, 6,* 834–838.

Eddington, D.K. (1983). Speech recognition in deaf subjects with multichannel intracochlear electrodes. *Annals of the New York Academy of Sciences, 405,* 241–258.

European Community. (1990). Council Directive of 20th June 1990 on the approximation of the laws of Member States relating to active implantable medical devices (90/385/EEC). *Official Journal of the European Communities, 189,* 17–35.

Frampton, V. (1996). Transcutaneous electrical nerve stimulation (TENS). In S. Kitchen & S. Bazia (Eds.), *Clayton's Electrotherapy* (pp. 287–305) (10th Ed.). London: WB Saunders.

Freehafer, A.A., Peckham, P.H., & Keith, M.W. (1988). New concepts on treatment of the upper limb in the tetraplegic: surgical restoration and functional neuromuscular stimulation. *Hand Clinics, 4,* 563–574.

Glenn, W.W.L., Hogan, J.F., Loke, J.S.O., et al. (1984). Ventilatory support by pacing the conditioned diaphragm in quadriplegia. *New England Journal of Medicine, 310,* 1150–1152.

Glenn, W.W.L., Phelps, M.L., Elefteriades, J.A., et al. (1986). Twenty years experience in phrenic nerve stimulation to pace the diaphragm. *PACE, 9,* 780–784.

Granat, M.J., Nicol, D.J., Baxendale, R.H., & Andrews, B.J. (1991). Dishabituation of the flexion reflex in spinal cord injured man and its application in the restoration of gait. *Brain Research, 559,* 344–346.

Gybels, J., & Kupers, R. (1990). Deep brain stimulation in the treatment of chronic pain in man: where and why? *Neurophysiologie Clinique, 20,* 389–398.

Habib, H.N. (1967). Experience and recent contributions in sacral nerve stimulation for voiding in both human and animal. *British Journal of Urology, 39,* 73–83.

Halverstadt, D.B., & Parry, W.L. (1975). Electronic stimulation of the human bladder: nine years later. *Journal of Urology, 13,* 341–344.

Heller, B.W., & Andrews, B.J. (1989). An analysis of swinging gaits and their synthesis using FES. In *Proceedings of the 3rd Vienna International Workshop on FES* (pp. 77–80). University of Vienna.

Hirokawa, S., Solomonow, M., Baratta, R., & D'Ambrosia, R. (1996). Energy expenditure and fatiguability in paraplegic ambulation using reciprocating gait orthosis and electric stimulation. *Disability and Rehabilitation, 18,* 115–122.

Holder, L.K., Wernicke, J.F., & Tarver, W.B. (1992). Treatment of refractory partial seizures: preliminary results of a controlled study. *Pacing and Clinical Electrophysiology, 15*(Pt II), 1557–1569.

Hollander, H.-J., Huber, M., & Vossius, G. (1987). An EMG controlled multichannel stimulator. In *Advances in External Control of Human Extremities, IX* (pp. 291–295), Belgrade: Yugoslav Committee for Electronics and Automation.

Holsheimer, J., Bulstra, G., Verloop, A.J., et al. (1993). Implantable dual channel peroneal nerve stimulator. In R. Jaeger & T. Bajd (Eds.), *Proceedings of the Ljubljana FES Conference* (pp. 42–44). Kocevje: Slovenian Society of Medical and Biological Engineering.

Judson, J.P., & Glenn, W.W.L. (1968). Radiofrequency electrophrenic respiration: long term application to a patient with primary hypoventilation. *Journal of the American Medical Association, 203,* 1033–1037.

Kantrowitz, A. (1963). Electronic physiologic aids. Report of the Maimonides Hospital of Brooklyn.

Karsznia, A., Dillner, S., Ebefors, I., & Lundmark, P. (1990). Why do patients use or reject a peroneal muscle stimulator? In D.B. Popovic (Ed.), *Advances in the External Control of the Human Extremities, X* (pp. 251–260). Belgrade, Nauka.

Keighley, M.R.B., & Fielding, J.W.L. (1983). Management of faecal incontinence and results of surgical treatment. *British Journal of Surgery, 70,* 463–468.

Kljajic, M., Malezic, M., Acimovic, R., et al. (1992). Gait evaluation in hemiparetic patients using subcutaneous peroneal electrical stimulation. *Scandinavian Journal of Rehabilitation Medicine, 24,* 121–126.

Koeze, T.H. (1995). Neuromodulation for pain and epilepsy. In G.S. Brindley & D.N. Rushton (Eds.), *Baillières clinical neurology 4.1: Neuroprostheses* (pp. 167–183). London: Baillière Tindall.

Kralj, A., & Bajd, T. (1989). *Functional electrical stimulation: Standing and walking after spinal injury.* Boca Raton USA: CRC Press Inc.

Kralj, A., Bajd, T., Turk, R., Krajnik, J., & Benko, H. (1983). Gait restoration in paraplegic patients: a feasibility demonstration using multichannel surface electrode FES. *Journal of Rehabilitation Research and Development, 20,* 3–19.

Krieger, A.J. (1994). Electrophrenic respiration after intercostal to phrenic nerve anastomosis in a patient with anterior spinal artery syndrome: technical case report. *Neurosurgery, 35,* 760–763.

Kumar, K., Wyart, G.M., & Nath, R. (1990). Deep brain stimulation for control of intractable pain in humans, present and future: a ten year follow-up. *Neurosurgery, 26*, 774–781.

Kwende, M.M.N., Jarvis, J.C., & Salmons, S. (1995). The input-output relationships of skeletal muscle. *Proceedings of the Royal Society of London (B), 261*, 193–201.

Loeb, G.E., Zamin, C.J., Schulman, J.H., & Troyk, P.R. (1991). Injectable microstimulator for functional electrical stimulation. *Medical and Biological Engineering and Computing, 29*, NS13–NS19.

Long, D.M. (1976). Use of peripheral and spinal cord stimulation in the relief of chronic pain. *Advances in Pain Research and Therapy, 1*, 395–403.

Lyons, K.E., Pahwa, R., Busenbask, K.L., Troster, A.I., Wilkinson, S., & Koller, W.L. (1998). Improvements in daily functioning after deep brain stimulation of the thalamus for intractable tremor. *Movement Disorders, 13*, 690–692.

Marsolais, E.B., & Kobetic, R. (1986). Implantation techniques and experience with percutaneous intramuscular electrodes in the lower extremities. *Rehabilitation Research and Development, 23*, 1–8.

Marsolais, E.B., & Kobetic, R. (1988). Development of a practical electrical stimulation system for restoring gait in paralysed patients. *Clinical Orthopedics, 233*, 64–74.

McNeal, D.R., Baker, L.L., & Symons, J. (1987). Recruitment characteristics of nerve cuff electrodes and their implications for stimulator design. In D. Popovic (Ed.) *Advances in External Control of Human Extremities, IX* (pp. 15–25). Belgrade: Yugoslav Committee for Electronics and Automation.

McNeal, D.R., Waters, R., & Reswick, J. (1977). Experience with implanted electrodes. *Neurosurgery, 1*, 228–229.

Melzack, R., & Wall, P. (1965). Pain mechanisms: a new theory. *Science, 150*, 971–979.

Nashold, B.S., Friedman, H., Glenn, J.F., et al. (1972). Electromicturition in paraplegia. *Arch Surg, 104*, 195–202.

North, R.B., Kidd, D.H., Zahurak, M., et al. (1993). Spinal cord stimulation for chronic intractable pain: experience over two decades. *Neurosurgery, 32*, 384–395.

O'Donoghue, G. (1996). Purchasing and providing cochlear implantation services. *Health Trends, 28*, 106–110.

Parks, A.G., Swash, M., & Urich, H. (1977). Sphincter denervation in anorectal incontinence and rectal prolapse. *Gut, 18*, 656–665.

Patel, J., Shanahan, D., Riches, D.J., et al. (1991). The arterial anatomy and surgical relevance of the human gracilis muscle. *Journal of Anatomy, 176*, 270–272.

Peckham, P.H., Kilgore, K.L., Keith, M.W., et al. (1993). An implanted neuroprosthesis for restoration of grasp and release. In R. Jaeger & T. Bajd (Eds.), *Proceedings of the Ljubljana FES Conference* (pp. 199–202). Slovenian Society of Medical and Biological Engineering Ljubljana.

Perkins, T.A., Brindley, G.S., Donaldson, N., de, N., et al. (1994). Implant provision of key, pinch and power grips in a C6 tetraplegic. *Medical and Biological Engineering and Computing, 32*, 367–372.

Phrenic nerve pacing in quadriplegia. (1990). *The Lancet, 2*, 88–90.

Potter, D. (1995). Neuroprostheses for ventilatory support. In G.S. Brindley & DN Rushton (Eds.), *Baillière's clinical neurology 4.1: Neuroprostheses* (pp. 77–94). London: Baillière Tindall.

Prochazka, A., Gauthier, M., Wieler, M., & Kenwell, Z. (1997). The Bionic Glove: an electrical stimulator garment that provides controlled grasp and hand opening in quadriplegia. *Arch. Phys. Med. Rehabil., 78*, 608–614.

Rushton, D.N. (1990). Choice of nerves or roots for multichannel leg controller implant. In D.B. Popovic (Ed.), *Advances in external control of the human extremities, X* (pp. 99–108). Belgrade, Nauka.

Rushton, D.N., Donaldson, N., de, N., Barr, F.M.D., Harper, V.J., Perkins, T.A., Taylor, P.N., & Tromans, A.M. (1997). Lumbar root stimulation for restoring leg function: results in paraplegia. *Artificial Organs, 21*, 180–182.

Rutecki, P. (1990). Anatomical, physiological and theoretical basis for the antiepileptic effect of vagus nerve stimulation. *Epilepsia, 31*(Suppl.2), S1–S6.

Salmons, S., & Henriksson, J. (1981). The adaptive response of skeletal muscle to increased use. *Muscle and Nerve, 10*, 94–105.

Sarramon, J.P., Lazathes, Y., Sedan, R., et al. (1979). Neurostimulation médullaire dans les vessies neurogènes centrales. *Acta Urologe Belgique, 47*, 129–138.

Simmons, F.B. (1966). Electrical stimulation of the auditory nerve in man. *Archives of Otolaryngology, 84*, 2–54.

Simolowski, T., Fleury, B., Launois, S., et al. (1989). Cervical magnetic stimulation: a painless method for bilateral phrenic nerve stimulation in conscious humans. *Journal of Applied Physiology, 67*, 1311–1318.

Snooks, S.J., Setchell, M., Swash, M., & Henry, M.M. (1984). Injury to innervation of the pelvic floor sphincter musculature in childbirth. *Lancet, 2*, 546–550.

Swain, I.D. (1992). Conditioning of skeletal muscle by long-term functional electrical stimulation—implications for the development of practical systems. In L.S. Illis (Ed.), *Spinal cord dysfunction III: Functional stimulation* (pp. 75–205). Oxford, OUP.

Teddy, P.J. (1995). Implants for spasticity. In G.S. Brindley & D.N. Rushton (Eds.), *Baillières Clinical Neurology 4.1: Neuroprostheses* (pp. 95–114). London: Baillière Tindall: London.

Thon, W.F., Baskin, L.S., Jonas, U., Tanagho, E.A., & Schmidt, R.A. (1991). Neuromodulation of voiding dysfunction and pelvic pain. *World J. Urology, 9*, 138–141.

van Kerrebroeck, P.E.V., Aa, H.E., van der, Bosch, J.L.H.R., Koldewijn, E.L., Vorsteveld, J.H.C., & Debruyne, F.M.J. (1997). Sacral rhizotomies and electrical bladder stimulation in spinal cord injury. 1: Clinical and urodynamic analysis. *European Urology, 31*, 263–271.

Wielink, G., Essink-Bot, M.L., van Kerrebroeck, P.E.V., & Rutten, F.F.H. (1997). Sacral rhizotomies and electrical bladder stimulation in spinal cord injury. 2: Cost-effectiveness and quality of life analysis. *European Urology, 31*, 441–446.

Williams, N.S., Patel, J., George, B.D., et al. (1991). Development of an electrically stimulated neoanal sphincter. *Lancet, 338*, 1166–1169.

Wright, G.D., McLellan, D.L., & Brice, J.G. (1984). A double-blind trial of chronic cerebellar stimulation in twelve patients with severe epilepsy. *Journal of Neurology, Neurosurgery and Psychiatry, 47*, 769–774.

Wynn Parry, C.B., Frampton, V., & Monteith, A. (1987). Rehabilitation of patients following traction lesion of the brachial plexus. In J.K. Terzis (Ed.), *Microreconstruction of nerve injuries*. Philadelphia: WB Saunders.

Young, R.F. (1990). Brain stimulation. *Neurosurgery Clinics of North America, 1*, 865–879.

PART B
Other physical disability

19. Pain relief in neurological rehabilitation

Douglas Justins   Malcolm Paes (deceased)   Philip Richardson

INTRODUCTION

In this chapter the working definition of pain is that formulated by the International Association for the Study of Pain (Merskey & Bogduk, 1994), which states that pain is: (1) an unpleasant sensory and emotional experience associated with actual or potential tissue damage; or (2) described in terms of such damage. Pain is always subjective and it is always unpleasant, so that some abnormal sensory experiences that resemble pain but are not unpleasant fall outside this definition. Many patients report pain in the absence of tissue damage or any identifiable pathophysiology. This often happens for psychological reasons but there is no way to distinguish their experience from that due to tissue damage and their complaint should be accepted as pain. The following definitions are taken from the *Classification of chronic pain*, published by the International Association for the Study of Pain (Merskey & Bogduk, 1994), and they explain some of the terms used throughout this chapter:

- *allodynia*: pain due to a stimulus that does not normally provoke pain
- *dysaesthesia*: an unpleasant abnormal sensation, whether spontaneous or evoked
- *hyperalgesia*: an increased reponse to a stimulus that is normally painful
- *hyperaesthesia*: an increased sensitivity to stimulation
- *hyperpathia*: a painful syndrome characterised by an increased reaction to a stimulus, especially a repetitive stimulus, as well as an increased threshold
- *paraesthesia*: an abnormal sensation, whether abnormal or provoked.

In patients with neurological disease, pain can be generated directly by the disordered or damaged nervous system (neuropathic pain) or can occur as a secondary phenomenon caused by a non-neurological source of continuing noxious stimulation in the periphery, such as joint contracture, bladder disease, or pressure ulcers (nociceptive pain). Psychological factors can play an important role in generating or magnifying pain in these patients even when other identifiable neurological or peripheral causes exist (psychogenic pain). Pain can be used to communicate distress and disability. Psychosocial problems are common in patients referred with physical ailments to rehabilitation units. The patient exhibits low morale, poor coping ability, and abnormal or inappropriate behaviour (Roy et al., 1988). Pain can also be a symptom of some unrelated pathological process and the neurological abnormality could obscure the presentation of the new illness. Various treatments, particularly neurosurgery, can also cause painful side-effects. The assessment and management of complex neurological pain problems is a challenge for the individual clinician. A multidisciplinary approach is often desirable and this might utilise: neurologist, neurosurgeon, orthopaedic surgeon, anaesthetists specialising in chronic pain, rehabilitation specialist, physiotherapist, occupational therapist, clinical psychologist, nurse therapist, acupuncturist, and social worker. The traditional medical model of treatment using a sole practitioner is inappropriate for most patients with chronic pain.

PATHOPHYSIOLOGY AND PHARMACOLOGY OF NEUROPATHIC PAIN

The nociceptive transmission pathways are not fixed and inflexible but instead exhibit considerable degrees of functional and structural plasticity following damage or injury (McQuay & Dickenson, 1990). The time course of these changes ranges from seconds to weeks, so that the clinical picture can vary with time. Pain and cutaneous hypersensitivity (secondary hyperalgesia) frequently spread far beyond the area of initial injury and pain will occur at a time when there is no longer any evidence of any ongoing tissue damage, perhaps days, weeks, or even months after injury. Peripheral neural lesions induce neurophysiological changes in the central nervous system (CNS) and lesions of the CNS can manifest as abnormalities in the periphery, so that therapies that are targeted at a single site often prove to be inadequate.

The pathophysiology of neuropathic pain is beginning to be understood (Bennett, 1990; Meyer et al., 1994). The transmission of acute pain involves activation of sensory receptors on peripheral C-fibres, the nociceptors. However, once tissue damage and inflammation occurs, the action of neurochemicals such as prostanoids, bradykinins, and 5HT on their excitatory receptors plays a major role in sensitisation and activation of C-fibres. Other factors such as nerve growth factor (NGF) and cytokines are also important at the peripheral level. C-fibres have unique sodium channels and some such fibres are "sleeping", in that they do not respond to natural stimuli until after inflammation. The former channels can become important channels for drugs (Dickenson, 1995). Neuropathic pain states can be generated in the peripheral sensory neurones by events that are independent of nociceptors. Clustering of sodium channels around areas of nerve damage sets up ectopic activity that can spread to ganglion cells. Sympathetic activity can facilitate these events. It is for these reasons that membrane stabilisers and agents acting on the sympathetic nervous system have a place in the control of neuropathic pain. The arrival of afferent sensory information in the dorsal horn of the spinal cord adds further complexity to the study of pain and analgesia because receptors found elsewhere in the CNS are also present in the spinal cord where the C-fibres terminate. Normal nociceptive transmission is accomplished by small afferent axons that enter the dorsal horn via the lateral aspect of the dorsal root entry zone. An appreciable number of unmyelinated afferent fibres can exist within the ventral roots. Most nociceptive fibres synapse in the superficial dorsal horn laminae I and II, but some of the myelinated fibres terminate in lamina V.

The neuroactive substances in primary afferents include the excitatory amino acids aspartate and glutamate and a large number of peptides including somatostatin, vasoactive intestinal peptide, cholecystokinin, calcitonin gene-related peptide (CGRP), tachykinins such as substance P, and endogenous opioids such as dynorphins A and B, leu-enkephalin and beta endorphin. Any one afferent fibre can contain more than one releasable neurotransmitter. Interactions between peptides and excitatory amino acids (EAA) are critical for setting the level of nociceptive transmission from the spinal cord to the brain. Activation of the N-methyl-D-aspartate (NMDA) receptor underlines wind-up whereby the baseline response is amplified and prolonged even though the peripheral input remains the same. This increased responsivity of the dorsal horn neurones is probably the basis for the central hypersensitivity found in many neuropathic pains. The NMDA receptor plays a key role in persistent inflammatory and neuropathic pains, in which it is critical for both the induction and maintenance of the enhanced pain state. Antagonists at multiple sites on the NMDA receptor complex, including drugs such as ketamine, dextromethorphan, and memantine, have been shown not only to be effective in animal models but also in humans. Both volunteer and clinical studies support the ideas that have come from basic research, namely that the NMDA receptor appears to underlie the hyperalgesia and allodynia seen in inflammatory, postoperative, and neuropathic pains. Higher doses of opioids are required to control the enhanced levels of firing that the NMDA receptor activation produces compared to acute pains. Spinal generation of prostanoids also occurs after NMDA receptor activation, almost certainly enhancing central sensitisation. Induction of the immediate early

gene, *C-fos*, in spinal neurones is rapid and, as it relates to the intensity of stimulus, can be used as a marker of activity. However, it can be used only as a monitor of induction, and not maintenance, of this activity. The effects of the brief afferent input upon *C-fos* can induce long lasting changes. This can initiate changes in processes such as neuropeptide production (Aldskogius et al., 1985; Devor, 1991; Wall, 1991).

Central inhibitory systems

There are many more neuroactive substances within the dorsal horn, including the inhibitory amino acids gamma aminobutyric acid (GABA) and glycine. Tonic GABAa and GABAb receptor controls are important in controlling acute, inflammatory, and neuropathic pain states. The former receptor appears to prevent low-threshold inputs from triggering nociception. GABA levels are reduced after nerve damage yet increased in the presence of inflammation. The roles of the mu, delta, and kappa opioid receptors have been established. Most clinically used drugs act on the mu and delta receptors, and might provide a target for opioids with fewer side-effects than morphine. The endogenous opioid peptides, the enkephalins, have clear controlling influences on the spinal transmission of pain, whereas the dynorphins have complex actions. Until recently there have been three receptors for the opioids—mu, delta, and kappa—but a fourth receptor, the orphan receptor, has recently been characterised. Morphine acts on the mu receptor, and so do most clinically used opioid drugs. The best described central sites of action of morphine are at spinal and brainstem/midbrain loci. There will certainly be actions at the highest centres of the brain but these are poorly understood. The spinal actions of opioids and their mechanisms of analgesia involve: (1) reduced transmitter release from the nociceptive C-fibres so that spinal neurones are less excited by incoming painful messages; and (2) postsynaptic inhibition of neurones conveying information from the spinal cord to the brain. This dual action of opioids can result in total block of sensory inputs as they arrive in the spinal cord. Some opioids such as methadone and ketobemidone might have additional NMDA blocking actions and so could be valuable in cases where morphine effectiveness is reduced, as in neuropathic pain.

A number of pathological factors can influence the degree of opioid analgesia; these are relevant to nerve injury and hence are relevant for patients in pain undergoing neurological rehabilitation. Nerve damage can cause a loss of opioid receptors, which would be expected to contribute to a reduction in opioid sensitivity. One well-established example is the reduction in spinal opioid receptor number seen after nerve section, and this could be an explanation of the poor opioid sensitivity of postamputation pains. Less severe damage can increase the spinal or supraspinal levels of the non-opioid peptides (e.g. cholecystokinin; CCK), which act as negative influences on opioid actions. There is now evidence that this has physiological relevance and that the levels of CCK in the cord can determine the potency of morphine. The cell body is initially alerted to any peripheral tissue or axonal damage by the intense afferent discharge but alterations in chemical transport are mainly responsible for the long-term changes. The dorsal horn exhibits both structural and functional plasticity, resulting in abnormal somatosensory processing. There is a mismatch of afferent input and perceived sensation so that normally innocuous stimuli can be projected onto second-order neurones that usually respond only to nociceptive input, and the previously innocuous stimuli begin to be perceived as pain. There is thus an increased sensitivity of the sensory system and a change in the response properties of the dorsal horn neurones. The pattern of reflex sympathetic response is also altered and can influence the clinical picture in some chronic pain states, as is described below.

ASSESSMENT AND EVALUATION OF PAIN IN NEUROLOGICAL PATIENTS

Neuropathic pain, which is associated with nerve damage, can be distinguished from nociceptive pain, which follows tissue injury or inflammation, by clinical features whose origins lie in the pathophysiological changes considered in the previous section. Fields (1987) lists the following clinical features of neuropathic pain:

(1) Pain occurs in the absence of a detectable tissue damaging process.
(2) There are abnormal or unfamiliar unpleasant sensations, frequently described as burning or electrical in nature.
(3) There is a delay in onset after the precipitating injury.
(4) Pain is felt in a region of sensory deficit.
(5) Symptoms can occur as paroxysmal, brief, shooting pains or as stabbing pains.
(6) Normally innocuous stimuli are painful.
(7) There is pronounced summation and after-reaction with repetitive stimuli.

The assessment and evaluation of the neurological patient with persistent pain should aim to identify the various components of the pain, including the nociceptive, neuropathic, psychological, and behavioural elements. A specific pain history should include a detailed description of the present pain, medication consumption, previous pain problems, and past medical history, and should be followed by a full examination. An assessment must be made of the degree of distress and disability induced by the pain at work, socially, and at home. Physical performance and pain behaviours should be recorded. The latter could consist of speech content, tone of voice, gestures, postures, facial grimacing, gait, and use of physical aids. These can all serve to convey pain and suffering to the onlooker. Psychosocial assessment should reveal the patient's cognitions about the pain, the coping skills employed in dealing with it, and an estimate of self-efficacy (Waddell et al., 1984). Spouse and family must also be included in this evaluation. Assessment can be made by the use of questionnaires such as the Sickness Impact Profile, which is a functional assessment (Follick et al., 1985); the Coping Strategies Questionnaire (Rosentiel & Keefe, 1983), which

is widely used in chronic pain populations; the Beck Depression Inventory (Beck et al., 1961), which assesses depressed mood severity; and the Pain Self-Efficacy Questionnaire (Nicholas, 1989), which assesses the patient's confidence in activity despite pain. All this information should be documented so as to form a baseline prior to instituting treatment.

PAIN MANAGEMENT IN SPECIFIC NEUROLOGICAL CONDITIONS

Pain from peripheral structures

Peripheral neuropathy.   Pain is not an inevitable consequence of peripheral neuropathy. The incidence varies widely and there is apparently no consistent pathophysiological pattern. The suggestion that loss of central inhibition following destruction of myelinated afferents can account for pain in peripheral neuropathy is not supported by findings in Friedreich's ataxia or in uraemia, which predominantly affect large fibres yet are rarely associated with pain. Small fibres are mainly affected in diabetic neuropathy and Fabry's disease and yet these conditions are frequently painful (Scadding, 1989; Thomas, 1982). Typical symptoms are constant burning pain with paroxysms of sharp lancinating pain. Sensory disturbances include allodynia and hyperalgesia. In polyneuropathy the nature of the pain can be similar but the distribution is more generalised than in mononeuropathy. Anticonvulsants such as carbamazepine and phenytoin, as well as antidepressants such as amitriptyline and desipramine, form the mainstay of treatment (Brown & Ashbury, 1984; Max et al., 1992). Somatic or sympathetic blocks can work occasionally. There have been several promising reports of the use of other sodium channel blockers such as mexiletene (Dejgard, et al., 1988; Stracke, 1992) and lamotrigine (Vadi & Hamann, 1998) in treating painful diabetic neuropathy. Intravenous lidocaine was reported as beneficial by Kastrup et al. (1987). Acupuncture and transcutaneous electrical nerve stimulation (TENS) are used on an empirical basis.

Muscle disorders.   Muscle pain and cramps of neurogenic origin can occur in conditions such as motor neurone disease (Newrick & Langton Hewer, 1984), multiple sclerosis, and following spinal cord damage. Muscle pain can be a presenting feature of motor neurone disease (Mills & Edwards, 1983). Painful cramps can also occur as an incidental event in any neurological illness. Muscle aches and pains can result from lack of fitness or be a symptom of depression. Widespread musculoskeletal pain can fit in the patterns of myofascial pain or fibromyalgia (Simons & Travell, 1989). A wide range of treatments has been suggested for muscle pains (Mills et al., 1989). Simple physical measures such as massage, heat, cooling, and ultrasound and vibration should be tried first. Favourable results have been reported with TENS, especially with severe muscle cramps (Mills et al., 1982) and acupuncture (McDonald, 1980). Relaxation techniques and even hypnosis might be useful in selected patients. Exercises in patients to improve fitness can produce substantial improvements in those who are unfit. Medication is frequently prescribed for intractable cases and potential drugs include non-steroidal anti-inflammatory drugs, benzo-diazepines, baclofen, dantrolene, antidepressants, verapamil, and quinine (Mills et al., 1989).

Restless legs syndrome. This syndrome describes an unpleasant creeping sensation that patients experience deep in the legs, usually in the evening when resting. The discomfort is often relieved by movement or walking (Ekbom, 1960). Gibbs and Lee (1986) have suggested diagnostic criteria for this syndrome. Neurological conditions that are associated with this syndrome include poliomyelitis, Parkinson's disease, and some peripheral neuropathies, e.g. avitaminosis and diabetes. A wide range of medication has been prescribed for this condition (Clough, 1987). Carbamazepine, clonazepam, and clonidine have shown satisfactory results in controlled studies but dopam-inergic agents, e.g. levodopa and pergolide, and opioids have also been used successfully (Grandjean, 1997).

Pain and the sympathetic nervous system

In the English language alone there are over 30 descriptive labels for painful conditions in which sympathetic activity is claimed to be abnormal. The sympathetic nervous system has an important role in generation and maintenance of chronic pain states (Jänig & Stanton-Hicks, 1996). Nerve damage and even minor trauma can lead to a disturbance in sympathetic activity, which can then lead to a sustained group of conditions now termed complex regional pain syndrome (CRPS) types I and II, replacing the previously popular terms "reflex sympathetic dystrophy" and "causalgia", respectively (Merskey & Bogduk, 1994). There was dissatisfaction with the term "reflex sympathetic dystrophy" because not all the cases seemed to have sympathetically mediated pain (SMP) and they were thus described as having sympathetically independent pain (SIP). Additionally, not all had dystrophic features.

Complex regional pain syndrome type I. This is a syndrome that usually develops after an initiating noxious event, is not limited to the distribution of a single peripheral nerve, and is apparently disproportionate to the inciting event. It is associated at some point with evidence of oedema, changes in skin blood flow, abnormal sudomotor activity in the region of pain, or allodynia or hyperalgesia.

Pain usually follows mild trauma and is not associated with significant nerve injury. It can follow fracture, soft tissue lesion, immobilisation, or medical events such as myocardial infarction or stroke. The onset of symptoms usually occurs within a month of the inciting event. The pain is frequently described as burning and continuous and exacerbated by movement, continuous stimulation, or stress. The intensity of pain varies over time and the clinical features described above can be present to varying extents. Symptoms and signs can spread proximally or involve other extremities. Impairment of motor function is frequently seen and can include weakness, tremor, and, in rare cases, dystonia. Atrophy of the nails and skin, alterations in hair growth, and loss of joint mobility can develop, with guarding of the affected part. Affective symptoms can then accompany the disorder secondary to the pain and disability.

Complex regional pain syndrome type II. The presence of continuing pain, allodynia, or hyperalgesia after a nerve injury is not necessarily limited to the distribution of the injured nerve. The onset usually occurs after partial nerve injury, but could be delayed for months. The pain is often described as burning and is exacerbated by light touch, stress, temperature change, or movement of the involved limb. As with type I, oedema might be a feature and there could be vasomotor and sudomotor changes, as well as impairment of motor function.

Laboratory findings

Non-contact measurement of skin temperature indicates a side-to-side asymmetry of more than one degree centigrade (1° C). Because of the unstable nature of the condition, several measurements at different times are recommended. Testing of sudomotor function, both at rest and when provoked, indicates side-to-side asymmetry. The bone uptake phase with three-phase bone scan reveals a characteristic uptake pattern of periarticular uptake. Radiographic uptake can detect patchy demineralisation of bone. However, data are not available for the specificity or sensitivity of any of the above tests and they are intended to estimate the degree of autonomic and somatic dysfunction (Jänig & Stanton-Hicks, 1996).

Mechanisms of dysfunction

Basic studies have demonstrated that several changes involving the sympathetic nervous system might be responsible for the development of these features. Inflammation can result in the sensitisation of primary nociceptive afferent fibres by prostanoids that are released from sympathetic fibres (Levine et al., 1993). Following nerve injury, sympathetic stimulation can excite primary afferent fibres via an action at alpha adrenoreceptors; there is also innervation of dorsal root ganglia by sympathetic root terminals. This means that activity in the sympathetic efferent fibres can lead to abnormal activation or responsiveness of the primary afferent fibres. When sympathetic involvement is suspected, then aggressive therapy initiated as early as possible would seem to provide the best chance for these patients. Even when a sympathetically mediated pain is identified, a successful outcome is not inevitable and some cases remain intractable despite every therapeutic endeavour. Sympathetic nerve blocks and various forms of physiotherapy form the cornerstones of most treatment programmes (Schutzer et al., 1984). Transcutaneous electrical nerve stimulation is commonly used. A wide range of medications has been suggested for management of CRPS types I and II and these include antidepressants, anticonvulsants, anxiolytics, narcotic analgesics, non-steroidal anti-inflammatory drugs, corticosteroids, local anaesthetics, vasodilators, and sympathetic blocking agents. The newer anticonvulsant gabapentin, which has a low efficacy-to-toxicity ratio and reduced side-effects has been reported as effective in five patients. Most of the reports in the literature are not based on randomised, double-blind, controlled trials, and therefore do not carry a strong weight of evidence.

Sympathetic nerve blockade

The sympathetic nervous system has been the target of pain relieving techniques since the early part of the twentieth century when, for example, stellate ganglion blocks were recommended following stroke and coeliac plexus block was recommended for tabetic crises. Because the pathophysiology of many chronic neurological pains remains poorly understood, it is difficult to suggest why or how sympathetic blockade helps some of these conditions. The mechanism might involve the interruption of afferent nociceptive pathways that are carried along with autonomic nerve fibres, or it could be more complex and be linked to interruption of sympathetic efferent fibres and the disruption of reflex control systems so that peripheral somatosensory processing is altered. Sympathetic blocks distal to the site of injury can produce relief of pain even when sympathetic abnormality is not evident (Loh & Nathan, 1978).

Diagnostic procedures

A diagnostic block must be a pure selective sympathetic block without any accompanying somatic blockade, and this can be achieved only with precise interruption of the sympathetic chain. An image intensifier is mandatory to confirm needle position and solution spread. Objective signs of sympathetic block must be identified afterwards using skin temperature, skin conduction response, or tests of sweat production. False positive results might be caused by spread of solution onto somatic sensory nerves, systemic effects of local anaesthetic absorbed from the injection site, or the placebo response. False negative results can follow an incomplete block or inappropriate assessment.

Therapeutic procedures

Sympathetic blocks have been shown to be superior to conservative therapy in a series of CRPS patients (Wang et al., 1985). There are no guidelines as to the indications for different techniques and many questions remain unanswered. Generally, a series of sympathetic blocks is performed and continued until only minimal discomfort persists, although the optimal frequency and duration of treatment has not been established. Intravenous regional blocks using local anaesthetic and guanethidine or bretylium can be used for both the upper and lower limb. In the upper limb, stellate ganglion and brachial plexus blocks have been used and in the lower limb lumbar sympathetic or epidural blocks have been tried. Unfortunately, most of the studies utilising sympathetic block techniques do not meet the requirement of being prospective, randomised, double-blind, controlled studies but nevertheless these procedures continue to be used. In a systematic review of randomised controlled trials of intravenous sympathetic blocks, Jadad et al. (1995) found that none

of the four guanethidine trials showed significant effect. Two reports, one using bretylium the other using ketanserin, showed some advantage over control. However, this systematic review has been criticised on the grounds that the numbers included in the individual trials were small and thus the conclusion that the use of guanethidine in intravenous regional anaesthesia could not be supported is still subject to scrutiny. The carrier agent, tourniquet pressure, and the ischaemic period might be some of the factors involved in analgesic efficacy (Glynn et al., 1981; Loh et al., 1980; McKain et al., 1983).

Stimulation analgesia. The reported success of TENS in the management of CRPS varies widely. Wilder et al. (1992) reported benefit in 50% of children in an uncontrolled study. As this therapy is non-invasive and has no side-effects apart from occasional irritation from the electrode pads, a trial of treatment is worth considering. In a small proportion of patients stimulation using a TENS machine can aggravate the pain.

Spinal cord stimulation is being used increasingly for pain management as newer technology allows a more widespread and flexible pattern of stimulation. Theories for the efficacy of this treatment suggest antidromic inhibition of spinothalamic tract neurones that are activated by small fibre afferents (Chandler et al., 1993). Law (1992) reported 80% success of spinal cord stimulation in 79 cases of CRPS. However, four of the 79 patients had neurological sequelae postulated as due to spinal artery spasm due to the greater vascular reactivity of such patients.

Psychological management. This will be considered in greater detail in the final section of this chapter. Patients with longstanding CRPS often require cognitive and behavioural therapy to break the pattern of disuse and fear of pain. Behavioural responses are particularly important in patients with CRPS, as immobilisation and overprotection of the affected limb can produce or exacerbate demineralisation, vasomotor changes, oedema, and trophic changes. Wilder et al. (1992) used cognitive behavioural management in the treatment of 70 children with CRPS in conjunction with TENS and physical therapy. Fifty per cent of patients reported beneficial effect from this combined approach.

Central pain syndromes

Central poststroke pain (CPSP) used to be known as "thalamic syndrome". Early postmortem studies showed that many cases had extrathalamic lesions and modern imaging methods have confirmed this. CPSP affects between 2 and 6% of stroke patients. There is an annual incidence of between 2000 and 6000 cases in the UK. Most patients with CPSP appear to be younger than the general stroke patient and appear to have a relatively mild motor affliction. True CPSP, characterised by a partial or total deficit for thermal or sharpness sensations, can also follow any disease process that causes damage to the CNS, and this includes tumours, trauma, multiple sclerosis, arteriovenous malformations, and neurosurgery. The onset of pain can be immediate or delayed many months. Most patients experience more than one type of pain but a burning sensation is common to all. A wide range of factors including movement, touch, cold, and emotion typically aggravates the pain. Distraction, hobbies, work, occupational therapy, physiotherapy, and psychological methods can all play a vital role in minimising the impact on the patient of this terrible pain. It is best treated therapeutically with adrenergically active antidepressants. If these do not work then mexiletine can be added in suitable cases (Bowsher, 1995). Naloxone infusions have been tried and a few patients have been reported as having benefited (McQuay, 1988). Intravenous lidocaine infusions have been suggested by Boas et al. (1982) and both sympathetic and intravenous regional blockade have produced variable results (Loh et al., 1981). Recent studies suggest that stimulation of the motor cortex or spinal cord by implanted electrodes could help some patients who are resistant to medical treatment (Herregodts et al., 1995; Peyron et al., 1995).

Evaluation of specific therapies used in pain management

The literature abounds with opinions and isolated case reports praising particular therapies, but hard scientific evidence in the form of randomised, double-blind, controlled trials are sadly lacking. In cases where pain control is impossible, therapy should be directed at lessening the disability and distress produced by pain and this rehabilitation is best achieved in the form of pain management programmes, as mentioned earlier.

Physical therapy and exercise

In most neurological conditions, physical therapy plays an important role in overcoming the disuse and disability induced by the pain and in increasing the patient's confidence. This is further enhanced by input from the occupational therapist, who will advise about setting realistic, achievable goals to promote personal esteem, and will introduce the concept of pacing activities to prevent the perpetuation of the underactivity/overactivity cycle that is so common in this group of patients. The evidence from back pain studies suggests, however, that on rigorous outcome measures, physiotherapy and other forms of manipulation therapy have limited success. Such analyses did not look at any measure of quality of life. If physical therapy does make the patient feel any better, and as it is cheap, then it is a decision for the third-party payer as to whether these physiotherapy manoeuvres should be offered (Anderson et al., 1992; van Tulder et al., 1997).

Stimulation-induced analgesia

The first recorded use of electrical stimulation was in ancient Greece, where the electrical torpedo fish was used to treat the pain of arthritis and headache (Woolf, 1989). The modern use of TENS was derived from the gate control theory, which predicted that the stimulation of large myelinated afferents would act in the dorsal horn to inhibit transmission in small unmyelinated primary afferent nociceptive fibres (Melzack & Wall, 1965).

Stimulation had also been applied to other parts of the nociceptive pathway including peripheral nerves, spinal cord, and deep brain areas such as the periaqueductal grey, periventricular areas as well as the motor cortex (supra). TENS has been used successfully in peripheral nerve injury (Bates & Nathan, 1980), spinal cord injury (Richardson et al., 1980) and other conditions but there are reports of failure in many forms of peripheral neuropathy, neuralgia in spinal cord injury and in central poststroke pain (Woolf, 1989). What seems certain is that attention to detail makes a considerable difference to the efficacy of TENS treatment in chronic pain (Johnson et al., 1992), and patients need to be told that the machine should be connected for at least an hour at a time and over several days. Instruction should be given about where to connect the electrodes, how to put them on, and how to manipulate the stimulus to best effect.

Acupuncture is another treatment with few side-effects and, although it is not effective for all patients, a trial is worthwhile. Three systematic reviews in chronic non-malignant pain show an unfortunately short-lived effect in clinical practice at 3 days (McQuay & Moore, 1998).

Spinal cord stimulation (SCS) can be performed via electrodes inserted percutaneously or placed surgically by a surgeon via a laminectomy. A trial with percutaneous electrodes should precede any form of implantation. As these devices are very expensive, the patients must be selected with the utmost care and the decision to perform an implantation should be made using stringent selection criteria. The following are claimed to be good indications for SCS: pain caused by peripheral nerve lesions following entrapment, accidental trauma or incisions for common surgical interventions (inguinal nerves), knee surgery (infrapatellar nerve), vein stripping (saphenous nerve), and mastectomy (costobrachial nerve). Stump pain after amputation generally responds better than phantom limb pain. Other indications are: post-herpetic neuralgia with sparing of sensory function, postradiation plexopathy, and polyneuropathies (e.g. diabetic), provided there is preservation of some large fibre function. Chronic cervical and lumbosacral radiculopathy due to lesions caused by compression, ischaemia, surgical intervention, accidental trauma or arachnoiditis might also benefit. Pain due to cervical or lumbosacral root avulsion, or syringomyelia, is not alleviated by SCS. Turner et al. (1995) published a systematic review of the use of SCS in lower back pain and concluded that, of the studies that performed a 1-year follow-up, the mean success rate was 62% as defined by having at least 50% pain relief. However, the evidence on SCS is limited and is likely to be biased due to lack of randomisation and blinding, and because the studies have been conducted by enthusiasts.

Peripheral nerve stimulation. There is evidence that peripheral nerve stimulation (PNS) can relieve certain forms of neuropathic pain in the territory of a single sensory or mixed nerve. Consequently, CRPS type II might be a good indication. A favourable response to appropriate screening tests is mandatory and these include a preoperative percutaneous stimulation of the involved nerve; a peroperative trial stimulation to determine the distribution of paraesthesia and, when a preoperative trial stimulation cannot be performed, a postoperative trial prior to implanting the stimulating device.

Neural blockade. The use of peripheral nerve blocks in chronic pain often ignores the fact that the pathophysiological changes are centrally located within the spinal cord or brain. Local anaesthetic somatic nerve blocks can produce transient relief but neuroablative techniques using cryotherapy, radiofrequency, or neurolytic solutions rarely result in sustained relief. These procedures are non-selective and destroy all peripheral sensory and motor nerves, resulting in a high incidence of side-effects. Pain can then return because of the plasticity of the CNS, and can be even more difficult to treat. In cancer pain there is perhaps a justification for these procedures if the life expectancy is less than 3 months or where alternative drug treatment proves difficult.

Neurosurgery

The work of Noordenbos and Wall (1981) questions the wisdom of ever cutting a peripheral nerve. However, Campbell et al. (1988) and others state that peripheral neural repair can relieve pain and hyperalgesia following peripheral nerve damage, even though central changes persist (Gilliatt & Harrison, 1984)

Anterolateral cordotomy. Sindou and Daher (1988) examined reports on 455 patients. The best results were obtained in pain related to lower spinal cord or cauda equina injuries, and in painful amputation stumps or phantom limbs. There is a significant morbidity and mortality attached to these procedures, whether percutaneous or open, and often the pain relief is not long lasting despite initial good effect.

Cordectomy. First performed in 1949 for pain associated with complete paralysis due to tumour or trauma. Jefferson (1983) found cordectomy very effective in relieving pain due to traumatic lesions of the spine below T10, especially when the pain was episodic and located in the anterior thigh and knees. He concluded that cordectomy should be considered in treating pain after spinal cord injury, particularly when the lesion is at the level of the conus medullaris. Other authors state that long-term relief is unlikely and that the operations can produce worsening of pain and dysaesthesia (Beric et al., 1988).

Dorsal root entry zone lesions. Lesioning of the dorsal root entry zone can relieve spontaneous burning aching or throbbing pains and hyperalgesia. Good results are claimed for spinal cord lesions in which pain is experienced at or below the level of the lesion (Friedman & Nashold, 1986) and when pain is associated with spasticity (Sindou & Jeanmonod, 1989). This therapy might be considered for brachial plexus avulsion injuries (Samii & Moringlane, 1984). Whatever the indication, there is significant incidence of side-effects and relief is often short lived (Nashold, 1988; Sindou & Daher, 1988).

Extralemniscal myelotomy. Gildenberg and Hirschberg (1984) report good results in 18 patients with neuropathic pain.

Medication

Conventional medication should be tried first, starting with paracetamol and non-steroidal anti-inflammatory drugs, before considering the use of weak or strong opioids. Failure of one drug from a particular class suggests that trial of other drugs of similar strength is unlikely to be helpful; it is better to progress to a stronger drug. A wide range of other drugs is effective in certain chronic pain syndromes and for drugs such as the anticonvulsants, antidepressants, local anaesthetics, and corticosteroids there are reasonable explanations as to why the drugs are active in neuropathic pain. These drugs should be employed early, either alone or in combination with other analgesics, in many neuropathic pains.

Conventional analgesics. Neuropathic pain is notoriously resistant to treatment with conventional analgesics. Peripherally acting non-steroidal anti-inflammatory drugs are rarely effective. The opioids act more centrally but neuropathic pains are often opioid resistant. Workers have demonstrated a lack of response with any type of deafferentation pain (Mazars & Choppy, 1983; Tasker et al., 1983). Arner and Arner (1985) showed that neuropathic pain did not respond well to epidural opioids.

Opioids for chronic non-malignant pain. If a patient has an opioid-sensitive pain that is otherwise intractable then long-term opioid administration should be considered despite the risk of dependence and tolerance. Tolerance (the need to take ever-increasing doses to achieve the same therapeutic effect) is rarely a problem once an optimal dose has been found (Melzack, 1988). Physical dependence can develop with long-term administration but withdrawal is generally not difficult. Psychological dependence is very rare in patients taking opioids for chronic pain and should not be confused with either tolerance or physical dependence (Medina & Diamond, 1977; Portenoy & Foley, 1986; Porter & Jick, 1989). Problems arise when an opioid is prescribed for an opioid-insensitive pain or for a pain with a strong psychological component. Inappropriate opioid consumption, particularly of drugs such as codeine, dihydrocodeine, or dextropropoxyphene, occurs commonly and drug withdrawal is a component of many chronic pain management programmes (Buckley et al., 1986). Partial opioid agonists such as buprenorphine find occasional advocates but effects are unpredictable in many cases and side-effects such as nausea, sedation, dizziness, and psychomimetic disturbances are common.

Steroids. Devor et al. (1985) showed that local application of steroids to experimental neuromas produced a profound and long-lasting suppression of spontaneous and evoked hyperexcitability. Local injection of steroid into trigger points is sometimes useful. Oral dexamethasone is the drug of choice in nerve compression pains due to cancer (Hanks et al., 1983).

Anticonvulsants. The abnormal repetitive ectopic discharges induced in experimentally demyelinated axons are damped down by anticonvulsants (Burchiel, 1980; McLean & McDonald, 1986). These drugs have membrane-stabilising activities. Anticonvulsants have been used in pain management since the 1960s. The clinical impression is that they are useful for neuropathic pain, especially where the pain is lancinating or burning. Carbamazepine is the drug of choice for trigeminal neuralgia, for which it is licensed in the UK. Phenytoin is also licensed as second-line to carbamazepine when the latter is ineffective or there are unacceptable side-effects; oxcarbazepine can also be effective. When anticonvulsants are used as adjuvant drugs in pain syndromes, sodium valproate is often preferred to carbamazepine because it is better tolerated. Lamotrigine is a relatively new sodium channel blocker that reduces the amount of transmitter substance released at glutaminergic synapses. Anecdotal case reports have been published of its use in neuropathic pain refractory to other standard treatments (Vadi & Hamann, 1998). Gabapentin is another anticonvulsant drug licensed for the treatment of chronic pain that does not cause sedation, one of the major drawbacks of anticonvulsant use. Reports of its use in chronic neuropathic pain are promising (Backonja et al., 1998; Rowbotham et al., 1998) and it has been claimed to be particularly useful in the treatment of complex regional pain syndromes (Mellick et al., 1995).

The precise mechanism of action of these drugs remains uncertain. The two standard explanations are enhanced GABA inhibition (valproate and clonazepam) or a stabilising effect on neuronal cell membranes; a third possibility is action via NMDA receptor sites. Anticonvulsant use is not without risk: serious side-effects including death have been reported from haematological reactions. The most common adverse effects are impaired mental or motor function, which can limit clinical use, especially in the elderly. In a systematic review of 20 randomised, controlled trials of carbamazepine in trigeminal neuralgia, relative effectiveness was demonstrated compared with placebo, although significant side-effects did occur (McQuay & Moore, 1998). Although anticonvulsants are widely used in chronic pain there are suprisingly few randomised, controlled studies to show analgesic effectiveness, and no randomised, controlled trials have compared different anticonvulsants. The usual decision is between antidepressants and anticonvulsants as first-line treatment and the existing evidence favours the antidepressants.

Antidepressants. Tricyclic antidepressants inhibit noradrenaline and serotonin uptake in the brainstem. These monoamines act as neurotransmitters in the inhibitory control systems, particularly in the bulbospinal system (Butler, 1984). Anticholinergic and anticonvulsant activity have also been suggested as analgesic actions of these drugs. Antidepressants are powerful local anaesthetics and it is possible that this contributes to their analgesic effect in cases of nerve damage (Feinmann, 1985; Sandyk et al., 1986). It has recently been shown that amitriptyline inhibits central NMDA receptors, which are important in mediating central excitability associated with chronic pain. The effect occurs at lower doses and plasma concentrations than are required for antidepressant action (McQuay, 1988). Many of the studies of antidepressants in neuropathic pain are open case reports. Interpreting these open studies is difficult because of the different drugs and doses used and because of the concurrent use of other drugs. In a systematic review of antidepressants in neuropathic pain, McQuay et al. (1996) concluded that, compared with placebo, of every 100 patients with neuropathic pain who are given antidepressants, 30 will achieve more than 50% pain relief, 30 will receive minor adverse effects, and 4 will have

to stop treatment because of major adverse effects. Within this overall pattern, selective serotonin reuptake inhibitors (SSRIs) were less effective in two reports than the older tricyclic antidepressants. There were insufficient data to say whether SSRIs caused fewer minor adverse effects but the rate of major adverse effects is half that seen with the tricyclics. Although controversy has continued as to whether the analgesic effect of the antidepressants is separable from the effect of the antidepressant on mood, many of the case reports showed analgesic benefit without significant effects on mood. Comparisons of antidepressants in trials have not shown any significant difference between them, but they were significantly more effective than benzodiazepines, and paroxetine and mianserin were less effective than imipramine. There is evidence that the tricyclics potentiate opioid-produced analgesia in both acute and chronic pain (Levine et al., 1986; Ventafridda et al., 1987).

Systemic local anaesthetic-type drugs in chronic pain. Neuromas can be formed after peripheral nerve injury. Both the neuroma and the dorsal root ganglion display spontaneous activity and increased sensitivity to chemical and mechanical stimuli (Wall & Gutnick, 1974). In experimental models of nerve injury, systemic sodium channel blockers like lidocaine and mexiletine silence spontaneous activity of neuroma and dorsal root ganglion and reduce their mechanosensitivity at concentrations that do not block nerve conduction. Low doses of lidocaine can block glutamate-evoked activity in the dorsal horn of the spinal cord. Lidocaine and related anaesthetic-type drugs that block sodium channels have therefore been used to relieve clinical pain (Bach et al., 1990). In a systematic review of 17 studies using lidocaine, mexiletine, and tocainamide, all intravenous lidocaine studies showed significant pain relief over placebo (McQuay & Moore, 1998). Oral mexiletine showed efficacy over placebo in all three studies due to peripheral nerve injury but no effect in central pain. Allodynia in pain due to peripheral nerve injury was relieved by intravenous lidocaine, as was dysaesthesia due to diabetic neuropathy, in which oral mexiletine was also effective. Intravenous lidocaine showed some efficacy in fibromyalgia but had no effect in all three studies in cancer pain. The long-term analgesic effects were not studied and only two studies showed that the pain relief could last several days. It is not known if subsequent infusions provide longer-lasting relief but in any case this is hardly practical in any but intensive care patients with continuous ECG monitoring. Additionally, it is not known if there are patients who benefit from lidocaine who do not benefit from mexiletine; however, there seems little point in using lidocaine to predict mexiletine response if this can be done by mexiletine alone! The best documented effective dose of intravenous lidocaine was 5 mg/kg, which was well tolerated over 30 minutes. Mexiletine (225–750 mg) caused minor adverse effects that were dose related; tocainamide should not be used because of toxicity; flecainide is a similar drug that has been tried but its use is anecdotal (Chong et al., 1997) and should be considered only when more accepted antidepressants and anticonvulsants have failed.

Other agents. Clonidine and other alpha-2-agonists have analgesic effects both in nociceptive and neuropathic pain (Eisenach et al., 1995). They extend the duration of local anaesthetic effect and have a synergistic effect with opioids. Their effect is limited by the adverse effects of sedation and hypotension. In neuropathic pain, single doses of clonidine were effective in postherpetic neuralgia (Max et al., 1988). The GABA receptor antagonist, baclofen, is used orally (Duncan et al., 1976) and by intrathecal pump to treat the painful spasms of cerebral palsy and in other conditions where muscle spasm plays a significant role in generating pain. Ketamine and dextromethorphan, both drugs with NMDA antagonist action, are also being used with variable effect in severe neuropathic pain. Capsaicin is an alkaloid derived from chillies, which first entered western European medical knowledge after Columbus's voyage to the New World in 1494. There is evidence that it can deplete substance P in local sensory terminals. Substance P is associated with the initiation and transmission of afferent pain stimuli. Studies have been difficult to blind adequately because of the irritant effect of the agent but, nevertheless, it has been found to be useful in diabetic neuropathy in a systematic review of 4 trials involving 144 patients treated with capsaicin and 165 with placebo. Thus, for every 4 patients treated with capsaicin, 1 would have pain relieved from diabetic neuropathy who would not have had if they had been treated with placebo (McQuay & Moore, 1998).

PSYCHOLOGICAL METHODS IN THE REHABILITATION OF CHRONIC PAIN PATIENTS

Psychological approaches to the rehabilitation of chronic patients have become increasingly common (Wall & Melzack, 1989). Originally such methods were considered to be only of relevance to pain-related disorders of presumed psychogenic origin but it is now recognised that a psychological approach can be beneficial even in conditions with early discernible organic pathology (Pearce & Richardson, 1987). It seems likely that two principal factors have contributed to the broadening of the psychological perspective. First, contemporary theories of pain have come to acknowledge the important influence of the patient's psychological functioning on his or her perception of pain (Wall, 1985). Second, the limited success of physically based treatment methods has led to the search for alternative and/or supplementary treatment approaches to the rehabilitation of patients suffering from pain problems.

Psychological factors that have been claimed to influence the perception of pain include the following: mood, personality, attention and other perceptual processes, expectations and the placebo response, reinforcement contingencies, observational learning, various social and ethnocultural factors, the therapist/patient relationship, predictability and perceived control of the painful stimulus, and anxiety (Pearce, 1986). The quality of available evidence linking the above factors with experienced pain and pain behaviour is variable. Moreover, the relevant psychological mechanisms are poorly delineated. For example, the demonstration of the placebo effect on pain has been widely documented (White et al., 1985). The specific psychological processes associated with its occurrence remain unclear (Richardson, 1989). Anxiety provides a further example of a widely cited influence on pain perception (Wardle, 1985). Despite this, much of the clinical evidence linking pain and anxiety raises unanswered questions over causality (Craig, 1989) and the measures used to assess pain and anxiety are often confounded (Gross & Collins, 1981).

Despite the uncertainties surrounding the issues relating to the psychological influences on pain perception there is ample evidence for the benefits of the psychological approach to the management of chronic pain (Pearce & Richardson, 1987). A variety of different methods has been described. These include relaxation, hypnosis, stress management, operant methods in which the behaviour in response to pain can be modified by principles of learning, and cognitive–behavioural therapy. Whereas any of these can be employed separately, the most common basis for their application appears to be in the context of a multidisciplinary approach. This approach is founded upon the idea that pain is a multidimensional phenomenon (Fordyce, 1976; Karoly, 1985). Nociceptive, sensory, affective, cognitive, and behavioural components of pain are viewed as semi-independent components, each of which has to be addressed separately during the pain management programme. The staff employed on such programmes are therefore likely to reflect a diversity of health-care professionals, including clinical psychology, physiotherapy, occupational therapy, nursing, and medicine. The typical psychological elements of such programmes are described below.

Assessment. Psychological methods of rehabilitation of the pain patient are typically based upon an initial psychological assessment. This will involve quantitative (e.g. intensity) and qualitative (e.g. pain-type) aspects of the pain itself, as well as pain-related cognitions (coping strategies, self-efficacy), pain behaviour (complaints, help-seeking, avoidance, grimacing), the wearing of aids (e.g. neck collars), and mood (e.g. depression, anxiety). A variety of methods are available for assessing pain intensity, including verbal rating (e.g. none, mild, moderate, severe) and the visual analogue scale of a 10 cm line drawn from 0 to 10 along which patients rate their pain.

Different methods are useful for different purposes. For monitoring change from a rehabilitation programme it appears that the 0–100 numerical rating scale and the visual analogue scale provide the most sensitive and reliable indices (Jensen et al., 1986). The best known and most widely used measure of the quality of pain experience is the McGill Pain Questionnaire (Melzack, 1975). This invites patients to endorse a number of adjectives that might be descriptive of their pain (burning, stabbing, penetrating, etc.) and provides an index of overall pain intensity as well as separate scores on the sensory, affective, and evaluative dimensions of pain. Its psychometric properties are known to be excellent (Byrne et al., 1982; Prieto et al., 1980).

Various methods exist for assessing pain-related cognitions. These include the Coping Strategies Questionnaire (Rosenstiel & Keefe, 1983), the Pain Self-Efficacy Questionnaire (Nicholas, 1989), and the Pain Locus of Control Questionnaire (Main, 1988). Although the content of the measures overlap to some extent, each assesses a slightly different aspect of patients' thoughts about their pain and it is as yet uncertain what the relative merits of each measure will prove to be. Nevertheless, there is good evidence that patients who consistently employ negative cognitions (e.g. catastrophising and feelings of hopelessness) report higher pain levels than those who employ more "positive" coping strategies (Boston et al., 1990; Rosenstiel & Keefe, 1983). Several rating scales have been developed to record pain behaviours. These can be completed by the patients themselves or by an observer (Phillips & Hunter, 1981; Richards et al., 1982; Main & Waddell, 1987). In addition, more generalised measures exist to record the overall impact of the pain problem on the patient's lifestyle. The Sickness Impact Profile is perhaps the best known and most widely used of these (Bergner et al., 1981). It consists of 126 self- or interviewer-rated items covering several broad areas of functioning (e.g. work, mobility, leisure pursuits) and yields a single index of illness-related dysfunction. Numerous self-rating inventories and checklists are available for the assessment of mood. In view of the extensive prevalence of depression in chronic pain patients, a measure such as Beck's Depression Inventory (Beck et al., 1961) is likely to provide a useful basis for monitoring changes in depressed mood over the course of a rehabilitation programme. The above measures, along with a physical assessment identifying areas of good and poor physical functioning, can provide a basis for identifying problems that need to be addressed in a rehabilitation programme and for monitoring change as a result of the programme itself.

Psychological methods of pain management

Psychological methods of pain management generally focus on producing change to: (1) physiological processes presumed to underlie the pain (e.g. relaxation); (2) cognitive processes associated with the perception of pain and its impact on the patient's life (e.g. cognitive therapy, stress management); or (3) behavioural manifestations of pain (e.g. operant conditioning, goal setting, activity scheduling, or pacing). Relaxation training can take many forms involving either muscle relaxation procedures or the use of mental imagery to induce a relaxed state of mind (Benson et al., 1977). The choice of method is likely to depend on the capacities and limitations of the individual patient as well as on the nature and location of the pain. Muscle relaxation techniques have been extensively researched and there is reasonable evidence for their effectiveness in reducing pain-related distress and pain intensity itself both in acute and chronic pain conditions (Benson et al., 1989; Weinman & Johnson, 1989). Cognitive approaches to pain management fall into two broad categories: those that alter the perception of pain directly and

those that address the patient's thoughts about pain and its impact on his or her life. Various direct cognitive manipulations have been described, based largely on findings from laboratory studies of experimentally induced pain (Turk & Genest, 1979). These generally involve teaching the patient to divert attention away from the painful area or, conversely, to focus on the painful sensations but to think of them in another way. In the laboratory both kinds of method appear to have pain-reducing effects (Turk & Genest, 1979) although their relevance has been less clearly established with chronic pain (Fernandez & Turk, 1989). The second group of techniques focuses on teaching patients to avoid unhelpful or maladaptive ways of thinking about their pain (e.g. catastrophising) and to replace these with more adaptive cognitions (e.g. self-reassuring statements). There is reasonably good evidence for the benefits of these methods for patients suffering from chronic pain (Rosenstiel & Keefe, 1983) although it could be that methods targeting the reduction of negative cognitions have a greater impact than those that aim to increase positive ones.

Most rehabilitation programmes have behavioural change as one of the principal aims and behaviourally based pain management techniques have special relevance to the problems of chronic pain. Since the introduction of operant methodology by Fordyce in the 1970s (Fordyce, 1976), the majority of pain management programmes have included at least some of the components of a behavioural approach. These include direct contingency management, in which pain behaviours are unreinforced while "well behaviours" (e.g. increased activity) are actively encouraged and rewarded; goal setting, in which patients are encouraged to identify realistic targets for behavioural change; and activity scheduling, in which the patients pace themselves on a graded programme of activity working towards the achievement of their individual goals. The reduction of analgesic and psychotrophic medication is a common target for such behavioural intervention because chronic pain patients frequently develop excessive requirements for medication while at the same time complaining of its ineffectiveness (Pither & Nicholas, 1991). The success of these methods in reducing pain behaviours and increasing activities is well documented (Kerns et al., 1986; Turner & Clancy, 1988).

Research suggests that non-medical treatments for chronic pain produce significant improvements in mood and symptoms associated with the pain without noticeable changes in pain intensity (Keefe, 1982; Linton, 1982, 1986). Few satisfactory functional measures are available and follow-up assessments rely overmuch on global measures and cover a short period in relation to the chronicity of pain. The inclusion of satisfactory functional measures and of follow-up of at least 1 year after treatment are still not standard in many pain management programmes (Williams, 1993). Such programmes exist as outpatient and, more rarely, inpatient programmes. The latter are more expensive to run but are more convenient for disabled patients to attend, especially if they have to travel long distance to reach the hospital. In a study comparing the two groups of patients, both inpatient and outpatient groups exhibited benefit compared with waiting list controls for up to 1 year of follow-up, but the results favoured inpatient programmes (Williams et al., 1996):

- For every three patients treated as inpatients rather than outpatients, one patient fewer was taking analgesic or psychotropic drugs.
- For every four patients treated as inpatients rather than outpatients, one patient fewer sought additional medical advice in the year following treatment.
- For every five patients treated as inpatients rather than outpatients, one patient more had his or her 10-minute walking distance improved by more than 50%.
- For every six patients treated as inpatients rather than outpatients, one patient fewer was depressed.

In a systematic review of published randomised, controlled trials of psychological treatments for chronic pain looking at the effectiveness of cognitive–behavioural treatment compared to either no treatment or "active" treatment (e.g. just physiotherapy or attending educational lectures), Morley et al. (1999) found that psychological treatments were effective compared to waiting list controls. When the comparison was made with active control groups then the effect of treatment on pain experience, positive coping, and abnormal pain behaviour remained significant. A report of a working party of the Pain Society (1997) recommended that a pain management programme should include physical reconditioning and posture retraining, relaxation, education about pain and pain management, medication review and advice, psychological assessment and intervention, and finally a graded return to activities of daily living. Optional interventions include work with families, vocational and educational guidance, welfare advice, and liaison with other agencies as necessary. The report went on to suggest as a minimum requirement a physician, psychologist, and physiotherapist for a pain management programme, but ideally a nurse and occupational therapist as well.

The achievement of long-lasting change remains the greatest challenge in all these treatment strategies, especially in the face of pressures from home and work, but it is important that in dealing with these complex rehabilitation problems the approach remains interdisciplinary.

REFERENCES

Aldskogius H, Arvidsson J, Grant G (1985) The reaction of primary sensory neurones to peripheral nerve injury with particular emphasis on transganglionic changes. *Brain Research Review* 10: 27–46

Anderson R, Meeker WC, Wirick BE, Mootz RD, Kirk DH, Adams A (1992) A metanalysis of clinical trials of spinal manipulation. *Journal of Manipulative and Physiological Therapeutics* 85: 267–268

Arner S, Arner B (1985) Differential effects of epidural morphine in the treatment of cancer related pain. *Acta Anaesthesiologica Scandinavica* 29: 32–36

Bach FW, Jensen TS, Kastrup J et al. (1990) The effect of intravenous lidocaine on nociceptive processing in diabetic neuropathy. *Pain* 40: 29–34

Backonja M, Beydown A, Edwards KR et al. (1998) Gabapentin for the symptomatic treatment of painful neuropathy in patients with diabetes mellitus; a randomised controlled trial. *JAMA* 280: 1831–1836

Bates JAV, Nathan PW (1980) Transcutaneous electrical nerve stimulation for chronic pain. *Anesthesia* 35: 817–822

Beck AT, Ward CH, Mendelsohn M et al. (1961) An inventory for measuring depression. *Archives of General Psychiatry* 4: 561–571

Bennett G (1990) Experimental models of painful peripheral neuropathies. *News in Physiological Sciences* 5: 128–133

Benson H, Greenwood M, Klemchuk H (1977) The relaxation response: Psychophysiologic aspects and clinical applications. In Lipowski ZJ, Lipsitt DR, Whybrow PC (eds) *Psychosomatic medicine: Current trends and clinical applications*. New York: Oxford University Press, pp 377–388

Benson H, Pomeranz B, Kutz I (1989) The relaxation response and pain. In Wall P, Melzack R (eds) *A Textbook of Pain*, 2nd edn. Edinburgh: Churchill Livingstone, pp 817–822

Bergner M, Bobbitt RA, Carter WB, Gilson BS (1981) The sickness impact profile: Development and final revision of a health status measure. *Medical Care* 19: 787–805

Beric A, Dimitrijevic MR, Lindblom U (1988) Central dysesthesia syndrome in spinal cord injury patients. *Pain* 34: 109–116

Boas RA, Covino RB, Shahnarian A (1982) Analgesic responses to iv lignocaine. *British Journal of Anesthesia* 54: 501–505

Boston K, Pearce SA, Richardson PH (1990) The pain cognitions questionnaire. *Journal of Psychosomatic Research* 34: 103–109

Bowsher D (1995) The management of central post stroke pain. *Postgraduate Medical Journal* 840: 598–604

Brown MJ, Ashbury AK (1984) Diabetic neuropathy. *Annals of Neurology* 15: 2

Buckley FP, Sizemore WA, Charlton JE (1986) Medication management in patients with chronic non-malignant pain. A review of the use of a drug withdrawal protocol. *Pain* 26: 153–165

Burchiel KJ (1980) Abnormal impulse generation in focally demyelinated trigeminal roots. *Journal of Neurosurgery* 53: 674–683

Butler SH (1984) Present status of tricyclic antidepressants in chronic pain therapy. In Benedetti C, Chapman C, Morrica G (eds) *Advances in pain research and therapy*. New York: Raven Press, pp 173–197

Byrne M, Troy A, Bradley LA et al. (1982) Cross-validation of the factor structure of the McGill Pain Questionnaire. *Pain* 13: 193–201

Campbell JN, Raja SN, Meyer RA (1988) Painful sequelae of nerve injury. In Dubner R, Gebhart GF, Bond MR (eds) *Proceedings of the Vth World Congress on Pain*. Amsterdam: Elsevier, pp 135–143

Chandler MJ, Brennan TJ, Garrison DW, Kim KS, Schwrz PT, Foreman RD (1993) A mechanism of cardiac pain suppression by spinal cord stimulation: Implications for patients with angina pectoris. *European Heart Journal* 14: 96–105

Chong SF, Bretscher ME, Maillard JA (1997) Pilot study evaluating local anesthetics administered systemically for treatment of pain in patients with advanced cancer. *Journal of Pain and Symptom Management* 13: 112–117

Clough C (1987) Restless legs syndrome. *British Medical Journal* 294: 262–263

Craig KD (1989) Emotional aspects of pain. In Wall P, Melzack R (eds) *A Textbook of Pain*, 2nd edn. Edinburgh: Churchill Livingstone, pp 220–230

Dejgard A, Petersen P, Kastrup J (1988) Mexiletine for the treatment of chronic painful diabetic neuropathy. *Lancet* i: 9–11

Devor M (1991) Neuropathic pain and injured nerve: Peripheral mechanisms. *British Medical Bulletin* 47: 619–630

Devor M, Govrin-Lippmann R, Raber P (1985) Corticosteroids suppress ectopic neural discharge originating in experimental neuromas. *Pain* 27: 127–137

Dickenson AH (1995) Spinal cord pharmacology of pain. *British Journal of Anaesthesia* 75: 193–200

Duncan GW, Shahani BT, Young RR (1976) An evaluation of baclofen treatment for certain symptoms in patients with spinal cord lesions: A double blind cross-over study. *Neurology* 26: 441–446

Eisenach JC, Dupen S, Dubois M et al. (1995) Epidural clonidine analgesia for intractable cancer pain. *Pain* 61: 391–399

Ekbom KA (1960) Restless legs syndrome. *Neurology* 10: 868–873

Ekbom KA (1977) Carbamazepine in the treatment of tabetic lightning pains. *Archives of Neurology 26*: 374–378

Feinmann C (1985) Pain relief by antidepressants: Possible modes of action. *Pain 73*: 1–8

Fernandez E, Turk DC (1989) The utility of cognitive coping strategies for altering pain perception: A meta-analysis. *Pain 38*: 173–135

Fields HL (1987) *Pain*. New York: McGraw Hill, p 134

Follick MJ, Smith TW, Ahern DK (1985) The sickness impact profile: A global measure of disability in chronic low back pain. *Pain 21*: 67–76

Fordyce WE (1976) *Behavioral methods for chronic pain and illness*. St Louis: CV Mosby

Friedman AHM, Nashold BS (1986) DREZ lesions for relief of pain related to spinal cord injury. *Journal of Neurosurgery 65*: 456–469

Gibbs WRG, Lee AJ (1986) The restless legs syndrome. *Postgraduate Medical Journal 62*: 329–333

Gildenberg PL, Hirschberg RM (1984) Limited myelotomy for the treatment of intractable cancer pain. *Journal of Neurology, Neurosurgery and Psychiatry 47*: 94–96

Gilliat RW, Harrison MJG (1984) Nerve compression and entrapment. In Ashberg AK, Gilliat RW (eds) *Peripheral nerve disorders*. London: Butterworths, pp 243–286

Glynn CJ, Basedow RW, Walsh JA (1981) Pain relief following postganglionic sympathetic blockade with iv guanethidine. *British Journal of Anaesthesia 53*: 1297–1302

Grandjean P (1997) Restless legs syndrome. *Schweizerische Rundschau fur Medizin Praxis 86*(18): 732–736

Gross RT, Collins FI (1981) On the relationship between anxiety and pain: A methodological confounding. *Clinical Psychological Review 1*: 375–386

Hanks GW, Trueman T, Twycross RG (1983) Corticosteroids in terminal cancer – a prospective analysis of current practice. *Postgraduate Medical Journal 59*: 702–706

Herregodts P, Stadnik T, De Ridder F, D'Haens J (1995) Cortical stimulation for central neuropathic pain: 3D surface MRI for easy determination of the motor cortex. In Meyerson BA, Ostertag (eds) *Advances in stereotactic and functional neurosurgery volume 11*. Vienna: Springer-Verlag, pp 132–135

Jadad AR, Carroll D, Glynn CJ, McQuay HJ (1995) Intravenous regional sympathetic blockade for pain relief in reflex sympathetic dystrophy: A systematic review and a randomised double-blind crossover study. *Journal of Pain and Symptom Management 10*: 13–20

Jänig W, Stanton-Hicks M (eds) (1996) *Reflex sympathetic dystrophy: A reappraisal*. Seattle: IASP Press

Jefferson A (1983) Cordectomy for intractable pain in paraplegia. In Lipton S, Miles J (eds) *Persistent pain: Modern methods of treatment*. London: Grune and Stratton, vol 4: p 115

Jensen MP, Karoly P, Braver S (1986) The measurement of clinical pain intensity. *Pain 27*: 117–126

Johnson MI, Ashton CH, Thomson JW (1992) Long term use of TENS at Newcastle Pain Relief Clinic. *Journal of the Royal Society of Medicine 85*: 267–268

Karoly P (1985) The logic and character of assessment in health psychology: Perspectives and possibilities. In Karoly P (ed) *Measurement strategies in health psychology*. New York: John Wiley, pp 3–45

Kastrup J, Petersen P, Dejgard A et al. (1987) Intravenous lidocaine infusion: A new treatment of chronic painful diabetic neuropathy. *Pain 28*: 69–75

Keefe FJ (1982) Behavioural assessment and treatment of chronic pain: Current status and future directions. *Journal of Consulting & Clinical Psychology 50*(6): 896–911

Kerns RD, Turk DC, Holzman AD, Rudy TE (1986) Comparison of cognitive–behavioral and behavioral approaches to the outpatient treatment of chronic pain. *Clinical Journal of Pain 1*: 195–203

Law JD (1992) Clinical and technical results from spinal cord stimulation for chronic pain of diverse pathophysiologies. *Stereotactic and Functional Neurosurgery 59*: 21–24

Levine JD, Gordon NC, Smith R, McBryde R (1986) Desipramine enhances opiate postoperative analgesia. *Pain 27*: 45–49

Levine JD, Fields HL, Basbaum AI (1993) Peptides and the primary afferent nociceptor. *Journal of Neuroscience 13*: 2273

Linton SJ (1982) A critical review of behavioural treatments for chronic benign pain other than headache. *British Journal of Clinical Psychology 21*(4): 321–337

Linton SJ (1986) Behavioural remediation of pain: A status report. *Pain 24*(2): 125–141

Loh L, Nathan W (1978) Painful peripheral states and sympathetic blocks. *Journal of Neurology, Neurosurgery and Psychiatry 41*: 664–671

Loh L, Nathan PW, Schott GD et al. (1980) Effects of regional guanethidine infusion in certain painful states. *Journal of Neurology, Neurosurgery, and Psychiatry 43*: 446–451

Loh L, Nathan PW, Schott GD, Wilson PG (1981) Pain due to lesions of central nervous system removed by sympathetic block. *British Medical Journal 282*: 1026–1028

McDonald AJRI (1980) Abnormal tender muscle regions and associated painful movements. *Pain 8*: 179–205

McKain CW, Urban BJ, Goldner JL (1983) The effects of intravenous guanethidine and reserpine. *Journal of Bone and Joint Surgery 65*: 808–811

McLean MJ, McDonald RI (1986) Carbamazepine and 10,11-epoxycarbamazepine produce use- and voltage-dependent limitation of rapidly firing action potentials of mouse central neurones in cell culture. *Journal of Pharmacology and Experimental Therapeutics 238*: 727–738

McQuay HJ (1988) Pharmacological treatment of neuralgic and neuropathic pain. *Cancer Surveys 7*: 141–159

McQuay H, Moore A (1998) An evidence-based resource for pain relief. Oxford: Oxford University Press

McQuay HJ, Dickenson AH (1990) Implications of nervous system plasticity for pain management. *Anaesthesia 45*: 101–102

McQuay H, Tramer M, Nye B, Carroll D, Wiffen P, Moore RA (1996) A systematic review of antidepressants in neuropathic pain. *Pain 68*: 217–227

Main CJ (1988) *Pain locus of control questionnaire: Recent developments*. Paper presented at the joint meeting of the Canadian and American Pain Societies, Toronto, 11 November 1988

Main CJ, Waddell G (1987) Psychometric construction and validity of the Pilowsky Illness Behaviour Questionnaire. *Pain 28*: 13–25

Max M, Scafer S, Culnane M, Dubner R, Gracely R (1988) Association of pain relief with drug side-effects in post-herpetic neuralgia: A single dose study of clonidine, codeine and ibuprofen and placebo. *Clinical Pharmacology and Therapeutics 43*: 363–371

Max MB, Lynch SA, Muir J et al. (1992) Effects of desipramine, amitriptyline and fluoxetine on pain in diabetic neuropathy. *New England Journal of Medicine 326*: 1250

Mazars GJ, Choppy JM (1983) Reevaluation of the deafferentation pain syndrome. In Bonica JJ, Lindblom U, Iggo A (eds) *Advances in pain research and therapy*. New York: Raven Press, pp 769–773

Medina JL, Diamond S (1977) Drug dependence in patients with chronic headache. *Headache 17*: 12–14

Melzack R (1975) The McGill Pain Questionnaire: Major properties and scoring methods. *Pain 1*: 275–299

Melzack R (1988) The tragedy of needless pain: A call for social action. In Dubner R, Gebhart GF, Bond MR (eds) *Proceedings of the Vth Congress on Pain*. Amsterdam: Elsevier, p 4

Melzack R, Wall PD (1965) Pain mechanisms: A new theory. *Science 150*: 971–979

Mellick GA, Mellick LB (1995) Gabapentin in the management of reflex sympathetic dystrophy. *Journal of Pain and Symptom Management 10*: 265–266

Merskey H, Bogduk N (1994) *Classification of chronic pain: Description of chronic pain syndromes and definitions of pain terms*, 2nd edn. Seattle: IASP Press

Meyer RA, Campbell JW, Raja SN (1994) Peripheral neural mechanisms of nociception. In Wall PD, Melzack R (eds) *Textbook of Pain*, 3rd edn. Edinburgh: Churchill Livingstone, pp 13–44

Mills KR, Edwards RHT (1983) Investigative strategies for muscle pain. *Journal of the Neurological Sciences 58*: 73–88

Mills KR, Newham DJ, Edwards RHT (1982) Severe muscle cramps relieved by transcutaneous nerve stimulation. *Journal of Neurology, Neurosurgery and Psychiatry 45*: 539–542

Mills KR, Newham DJ, Edwards RHT (1989) Muscle pain. In Wall PD, Melzack R (eds) *Textbook of pain*, 2nd edn. Edinburgh: Churchill Livingstone, pp 420–432

Morley S, Eccleston C, Williams A (1999) Systematic review and meta-analysis of randomised controlled trials of cognitive behaviour therapy and behaviour therapy for chronic pain in adults, excluding headache. *Pain 80*: 1–13

Nashold Jr BS (1988) Neurosurgical techniques of the dorsal root entry zone operation. *Applied Neurophysiology 51*: 136–145

Newrick PG, Langton Hewer R (1984) Motor neurone disease: Can we do better? A study of 42 patients. *British Medical Journal 289*: 539–542

Nicholas MK (1989) *Self-efficacy and chronic pain*. Paper presented at the British Psychological Society Annual Conference, St Andrews, April 1989

Pearce SA (1986) Chronic pain: A biobehavioural perspective. In Christie MJ, Mellett PG (eds) *The psychosomatic approach: Contemporary practice of whole-person care*. Chichester: John Wiley, pp 217–237

Pearce SA, Richardson PH (1987) Chronic pain: Treatment. In Lindsay S, Powell G (eds) *A handbook of clinical adult psychology*. Aldershot: Gower, pp 579–594

Peyron R, Garcia-Larrea L, Deiber MP, Cinotti L, Convers L, Conver P, Sindou M, Mauguiete F, Laurent B (1995) Electrical stimulation of precentral cortical area in the treatment of central pain: Electrophysiological and PET study. *Pain 62(3)*: 275–286

Phillips C, Hunter M (1981) Pain behaviour in headache sufferers. *Behaviour Analysis and Modification 4*: 257–266

Pither C, Nicholas MK (1991) The identification of the iatrogenic factors in chronic pain syndromes: Abnormal treatment behaviours? In Bond MR, Charlton JE, Woolf CJ (eds) *Proceedings of the VIth World Congress on Pain*. Amsterdam: Elsevier, pp 429–434

Portenoy RK, Foley KM (1986) Chronic use of opioid analgesics in non-malignant pain: Report of 38 cases. *Pain 25*: 171–186

Porter J, Jick H (1980) Addiction rate in patients treated with narcotics. *New England Journal of Medicine 302*: 123

Prieto EJ, Hopson L, Bradley LA et al. (1980) The language of low back pain: Factor structure of the McGill Pain Questionnaire. *Pain 8*: 11–19

Report of a Working Party of the Pain Society (1997) *Desirable characteristics for pain management programmes*. London: The Pain Society

Richards JS, Nepomuceno C, Riles M, Suer Z (1982) Assessing pain behaviour: The UAB Pain Behaviour Scale. *Pain 14*: 393–398

Richardson PH (1989) Placebos: Their effectiveness and modes of action. In Broome A (ed) *Health psychology: Processes and application*. London: Chapman and Hall, pp 34–56

Richardson RR, Meyer PR, Cerullo LJ (1980) Neurostimulation in the modulation of intractable paraplegic and traumatic neuroma pains. *Pain 8*: 75–84

Rosenstiel AK, Keefe FJ (1983) The use of coping strategies in chronic low back pain patients: Relationship of patient characteristics to current adjustment. *Pain 17*: 33–44

Rowbotham M, Harden N, Stacey B et al. (1998) Gabapentin for the treatment of postherpetic neuralgia: A randomised controlled trial. *JAMA 280*: 1837–1842

Roy CW, Arthurs Y, Hunter J et al. (1988) Works of a rehabilitation medicine service. *British Medical Journal 297*: 601–604

Samii M, Moringlane JR (1984) Thermocoagulation of the dorsal root entry zone for the treatment of intractable pain. *Neurosurgery 15*: 953–955

Sandyk R, Iacono RP, Linford J (1986) Cholinergic mechanisms of pain relief by antidepressants. *Pain 26*: 133–134

Scadding JW (1989) Peripheral neuropathies. In Wall PD, Melzack R (eds) *Textbook of pain*, 2nd edn. Edinburgh: Churchill Livingstone, pp 522–531

Schutzer SF, Gossling HR, Connecticut F (1984) The treatment of reflex sympathetic dystrophy syndrome. *Journal of Bone and Joint Surgery 66(4)*: 625–629

Simons DG, Travell JG (1989) Myofascial pain syndromes. In Wall PD, Melzack R (eds) *Textbook of pain*, 2nd edn. Edinburgh: Churchill Livingstone, pp 368–385

Sindou M, Daher A (1988) Spinal cord ablation procedures for pain. In Dubner R, Gebhart GF, Bond MR (eds) *Proceedings of Vth World Congress on Pain*. Amsterdam: Elsevier, pp 477–495

Sindou M, Jeanmonod D (1989) Microsurgical DREZ-otomy for the treatment of spasticity and pain in the lower limbs. *Neurosurgery 24*: 655–670

Straeke H, Meyer UE, Schumacher HE, Federlin K (1992) Mexiletine in the treatment of diabetic neuropathy. *Diabetes Care 15*: 1550–1555

Tasker RR, Tsuda T, Hawrylyshyn P (1983) Clinical neurophysiological investigation of deafferentation pain. In Bonica JJ, Linblom U, Iggo A (eds) *Advances in pain research and therapy*. New York: Raven Press, vol 5, pp 713–738

Thomas PK (1982) Pain in peripheral neuropathy: Clinical and morphological aspects. In Culp WJ, Ochoa J (eds) *Abnormal nerves and muscles as impulse generators*. Oxford: Oxford University Press, pp 552–587

Turk DC, Genest M (1979) Regulation of pain: The application of cognitive and behavioral techniques for prevention and remediation. In Kendall PC, Hollon SD (eds) *Cognitive-behavioral interventions: Theory, research and procedure*. New York: Academic Press, pp 287–318

Turner J, Clancy S (1988) Comparison of operant behavioral and cognitive behavioral group treatment for chronic low back pain. *Journal of Consulting and Clinical Psychology 56*: 261–266

Turner JA, Loeser JD, Bell KG (1995) Spinal cord stimulation for chronic low back pain: A systematic synthesis. *Neurosurgery 37*: 1088–1096

Vadi PP, Hamann W (1998) The use of lamotrigine in neuropathic pain. *Anaesthesia 53(8)*: 808–809

van Tulder MW, Koes BW, Bouter LM (1997) Conservative treatment of acute and chronic nonspecific low back pain. *Spine 22*: 2128–2156

Ventafridda V, Ridamonti C, DeConno F et al. (1987) Antidepressants increase bioavailability of morphine in cancer patients. *Lancet 1*: 1204

Waddell G, Bircher M, Finlayson D, Main CJ (1984) Symptoms and signs: Physical disease or illness behaviour? *British Medical Journal 289*: 739–741

Wall PD (1985) Future trends in pain research. *Philosophical Transactions of the Royal Society of London Series B308*: 393–401

Wall PD (1991) Neuropathic pain and injured nerve: Central mechanisms. *British Medical Bulletin 47*: 631–643

Wall PD, Gutnick M (1974) Properties of afferent nerve impulses originating from a neuroma. *Nature 248*: 740–743

Wall P, Melzack R (eds) (1989) *A textbook of pain*, 2nd edn. Edinburgh: Churchill Livingstone

Wang JK, Johnson KA, Ilstrup DM (1985) Sympathetic blocks for reflex sympathetic dystrophy. *Pain 23*: 13–17

Wardle J (1983) Psychological management of anxiety and pain during dental treatment. *Journal of Psychosomatic Research 27(5)*: 399–402

Weinman J, Johnston M (1989) Stressful medical procedures: An analysis of the effects of psychological interventions and of the stressfulness of the procedures. In Maes S, Detares P, Sarason IG, Spielberger CD (eds) *Proceedings of the First International Expert Conference on Health Psychology*. Chichester: John Wiley

White L, Tursky B, Schwarz GE (eds) (1985) *Placebo: Theory research and mechanisms*. New York: Guilford Press

Wilder RT, Berde CB, Wolohan M, Vieyra MA, Masek BJ, Micheli L-J (1992) Reflex sympathetic dystrophy in children. *Journal of Bone and Joint Surgery 6*: 910–919

Williams AC de C (1993) In-patient management of chronic pain. In Hodes M, Moorey S (eds) *Psychological treatment in disease and illness*. London: Gaskell and the Society for Psychosomatic Research

Williams AC de C, Richardson PH, Nicholas MK et al. (1996) Inpatient vs. outpatient pain management: Results of a randomised controlled trial. *Pain 66*: 13–22

Woolf CJ (1989) Segmental afferent fibre-induced analgesia: Transcutaneous electrical nerve stimulation (TENS) and vibration. In Wall PD, Melzack R (eds) *Textbook of pain*, 2nd edn. Edinburgh: Churchill Livingstone, pp 884–896

Working Party of the Pain Society (1997) *Desirable characteristics for pain management programmes*. London: The Pain Society

20. Special senses

Alidz Pambakian   Christopher Kennard   Arnold J. Wilkins

INTRODUCTION

Within neurology, the typical approach to rehabilitation begins with establishing a diagnosis and broadens to consider the implications for treatment and management. The approach within neuropsychology, is different, and typically begins with the measurement of cognitive function and dysfunction. In this chapter we seek to integrate both approaches and to add a third, namely an analysis of the processing requirements of every-day tasks and the practical approach to relearning found in occupational therapy. We concentrate on olfaction, vestibular function, and vision. We consider diagnosis and management, and describe various simple rehabilitative techniques.

OLFACTION AND TASTE

The olfactory system plays a limited, although important, role in daily life. The sense of smell warns us of the presence of toxins, such as spoiled food, leaking natural gas, polluted air, and smoke, and its loss places an individual at potential risk. Olfaction is served by two chemosensory systems in the nose: the free nerve endings of the trigeminal nerve and the sensory receptors of the olfactory system. Concentrated pungent smells stimulate the trigeminal nerve endings and cause irritation, whereas more subtle odours are distinguished by the olfactory receptors. Therefore, in the presence of complete anosmia, nasal irritation can be preserved even though odours cannot be discriminated. The olfactory organs have a unique property in the mammalian nervous system that is particularly relevant to restorative neurology: this is the capacity of bipolar olfactory receptor cell neurones to regenerate continuously throughout adult life (Graziadei, 1973). This fact might explain the phenomenon, in some individuals, of the delayed return of olfactory function, over a period of several months, following viral infections or head injuries. However, we know of no proven rehabilitative techniques that can be offered to anosmic patient, or means whereby this spontaneous regeneration of olfactory neurones can be facilitated.

When dealing with patients who have lost their sense of smell it is important to establish a specific diagnosis for the deficit, because some local diseases of the nasal passages, such as polyps, are amenable to treatment. The ability to smell can be affected in various ways by different disease entities. Anosmia refers to a complete loss of the sense of smell, whereas hypo- and hyperosmia imply a reduced or increased ability. In parosmia/dysosmia, smells are distorted. Patients with anosmia usually complain of taste disturbances as well, because the appreciation of the flavour of food and drink depends to a large extent on their aroma. The taste receptors are predominantly responsible for the four primary taste sensations—namely salty, sweet, bitter, and sour. More complex flavours are combinations of olfactory and gustatory sensations.

The causes of olfactory distortion or loss arise from a variety of disorders, which include mechanical obstruction to the nasal airways, intranasal pathology such as rhinitis or sinusitis, environmental or industrial pollutants, cigarette smoking, dental procedures, radiation therapy, drugs (including drugs of abuse), and ageing. Olfactory hallucinations occur in various neurological disorders such as Alzheimer's disease, uncinate seizures, and Korsakoff's psychosis (Doty, 1979). They are also seen in depression, schizophrenia, and alcohol withdrawal. Head trauma is probably the most common cause of anosmia presenting to rehabilitation neurologists. It has been estimated that the overall incidence is around 7%, although with severe injuries this figure is undoubtedly higher (30–80%; Summer, 1976). Although head trauma is usually considered to produce shearing of the fine nerve filaments as they pass through the cribriform plate to the olfactory bulb, there might also be central effects. Experimentally, degeneration of the olfactory epithelium has been demonstrated without transection of the olfactory nerve in cases of intracranial haemorrhage (Nakashima et al., 1984). Apart from trauma, anosmia is rarely caused by intracranial pathologies.

Assessment and management

The standard method of testing olfaction is by means of a series of bottles containing different odiferous substances, e.g. coffee, rose water. The patient is asked to sniff each in turn, specifying whether or not any smell can be detected and, if so, identifying its origin. It is customary to allow the use of both nostrils, although lateral asymmetries in olfaction have been demonstrated (Pendse, 1987). In recent years a number of workers have developed methods of quantitative assessment. These are largely based on psychophysical procedures to determine the absolute level of an odorant that a patient can detect. Performed in conjunction with methods to determine the degree to which qualitative olfactory sensations are present—for example, the 40-item microencapsulated (scratch 'n' sniff) smell test (Doty et al., 1984)—these techniques could in the future be of great value in monitoring the efficiency of any interventions or treatments. At present, however, with the exception of problems caused by mechanical obstruction of the nose, proven treatments are not available. Although zinc and vitamin therapies have been advocated, there is no convincing evidence for their efficacy.

As was discussed earlier, complete anosmia places an individual at potential risk from inhaling noxious fumes, etc. Sensible precautionary advice should therefore be offered. For example, use of domestic smoke and gas detectors would be prudent, as would the provision of adequate ventilation in enclosed areas in which toxic solvents are being used.

Table 20.1. Differential diagnosis of vestibular disorders

Category of lesion	Differential diagnosis
Peripheral vestibular lesions (vestibular nerve and labyrinth)	Benign paroxysmal positional vertigo Vestibular neuritis Ménière's disease Perilymph fistula Vestibular paroxysmal (disabling positional vertigo) Post-traumatic vertigo Drug toxicity
Central lesions (vestibular portion of VIII cranial nerve, brainstem vestibular nuclei and their central connections)	Brainstem ischaemia/infarction Demyelination Paraneoplastic syndromes Cerebellopontine angle tumours Cranial neuropathies Vestibular epilepsy Basilar artery migraine Spinocerebellar degeneration
Systemic disorders	Hypotension Cardiac lesions Diabetes Infections Hypothyroidism Blood dyscrasias Granulomatous disorders Psychogenic disorders

THE VESTIBULAR SYSTEM

Irrespective of the underlying cause, all patients with vestibular dysfunction share the common symptom of vertigo. Vertigo is the hallucination of movement, the erroneous perception of motion of either the sufferer or his or her environment. However, the description of the sensation of dizziness varies considerably among its sufferers. The management of patients with vestibular dysfunction is often complicated by the fact that vertigo can also be due to a wide range of different pathological processes involving the ears, eyes, central nervous system (CNS), cardiovascular and endocrine systems, and psychiatric diseases.

Differential diagnosis

The differential diagnosis of vestibular disorders falls broadly into three categories (Table 20.1):

(1) peripheral vestibular lesions
(2) central lesions
(3) systemic disorders.

Detailed consideration of the differential diagnosis of vestibular disorders (Baloh & Honrubia, 1990) is beyond the scope of this chapter. Rather, in this section the relevant vestibular physiology, the methods of testing, and compensation mechanisms will be reviewed briefly to provide a basis for management and rehabilitation of patients with these symptoms.

Pathophysiology

The vestibular apparatus consists of five sensory organs within each labyrinth: two otoliths, which transduce linear acceleration

due to gravity, and the three semicircular canals, which transduce angular acceleration due to head rotation. These vestibular inputs are integrated with other sensory, visual, and proprioceptive information in the CNS to produce a motor outflow that maintains the equilibrium of the eyes, head, and body. This is best observed by evaluation of the vestibulo-ocular reflex (VOR) and the vestibulospinal reflex. Disturbance of the semicircular canals can result in a mismatch between the inputs from these three end organs when the head is turning. This is interpreted by the brain as a sensation of rotation of the body or of the environment and might be manifest as nystagmus and the symptom of oscillopsia; the latter being due to the failure of the VOR to compensate for head rotation. Similarly, disturbances of the otolith organs give rise to a sensation of tilt and a feeling that the body is moving through the environment.

The other symptoms and signs that accompany vertigo depend primarily on their cause. It is essential to try to exclude non-vestibular causes by taking a careful history and by physical examination, as this determines the appropriate treatment. Apart from the sensation of vertigo, patients with vestibular disturbance also experience a combination of symptoms including ocular motor (nystagmus), postural (ataxia), and vegetative (nausea) phenomena. As mentioned earlier, nystagmus results from the brain receiving conflicting sensory information in the VOR. Vestibular ataxia results from interference with vestibulospinal conduction. Vegetative symptoms of nausea, vomiting, and prostration are usually more marked with peripheral rather than central lesions, and are due to triggering of the medullary vomiting centre. As will be seen later, it is important to separate these classes of symptoms when considering the rehabilitation of such patients.

Investigations

Non-specific tests

Patients with vertigo, under investigation for vestibular disorders, should be screened for systemic illnesses with a battery of baseline tests including: full blood count; urea, electrolytes, and glucose; liver function and thyroid function. Further consideration should be given to excluding blood dyscrasias and immune conditions and the need for cardiac investigations, including electrocardiography and 24-hour monitoring of heart rhythm and blood pressure.

Vestibular function tests

Unfortunately, the tests currently available for evaluating vestibular function are very limited. Both caloric stimulation and rotating tests stimulate only the horizontal semicircular canals, leaving the two other canals and otolith organs untested. Moreover, both tests have inherent limitations.

Caloric tests. In the caloric test the stimulus is imprecise and mimics only the low-frequency components of natural head motions.

Rotational tests. Rotational tests are more precise and capable of testing a wide range of frequencies. However, they always stimulate both labyrinths simultaneously and are unable to detect unilateral peripheral vestibular lesions reliably.

Vestibulospinal reflexes

Until relatively recently, testing of vestibulospinal reflexes consisted of simple clinical tests such as the Rhomberg test. More sophisticated quantitative measures of these reflexes using posturography are now available, although the precise role of these measures in the evaluation of vestibular function has not been adequately defined (Black et al., 1983). However, a combination of various tests evaluating VOR and vestibulospinal reflexes should provide not only improved diagnostic sensitivity to vestibular lesions but also an important quantitative monitor of the effects of treatment (Wall & Black, 1983).

Compensatory mechanisms

The CNS has a number of different adaptive mechanisms to cope with disturbances of vestibular tone, as exemplified by the gradual cessation of spontaneous vestibular nystagmus (Igarashi, 1984). Other compensatory mechanisms include the substitution of alternative reflexes using other sensory inputs. An example of the latter in patients with complete vestibular failure is the development of compensatory eye movements in response to head and body motion, produced by proprioceptive and visual inputs alone (Kasai & Zee, 1978). These two mechanisms—modulation of vestibular tone and substitution of alternative sensory inputs to re-adjust vestibulo-ocular and vestibulospinal reflexes—are essential for the satisfactory rehabilitation of patients with vestibular lesions. If, for any reason,

other CNS structures concerned with vestibular compensation, for example, the cerebellum, vestibular commissure, reticular formation, and spinal cord, are damaged along with the vestibular system, severe disability, vertigo, and irritability can ensue (Pfaltz, 1983; Rudge & Chambers, 1982). A similar impediment to satisfactory compensation exists if the alternative sensory inputs are impaired, for example, reduced vision due to cataracts or impaired proprioception due to a peripheral neuropathy (Drachman & Hart, 1972).

There is evidence from animal experiments that compensation for acute vestibular lesions is delayed and even limited in amount by a period of immobilisation (Lacour & Xerri, 1981; Pfaltz, 1983; Precht, 1983). Although these studies measured vestibulospinal responses and not VOR, the implication is that patients with acute vestibular lesions should be mobilised at the earliest possible stage after the insult, when the vegetative symptoms are at their maximum. An important aim of therapy in the early stages is, therefore, to suppress these vegetative symptoms with drugs that do not have an effect on the compensatory mechanisms. At the same time, physical treatment must be aimed towards promoting rehabilitation of both VOR and vestibulospinal function. This necessitates the production of sensory conflicts. The conflicts can be within the vestibular apparatus or intersensory (between vision, proprioception, and vestibular inputs) to signal the need for, and direction of, adaptive change.

Pharmacological therapy for vertigo and vegetative symptoms

Although a variety of drugs is used in the management of dizzy patients, these drugs might, in fact, have a deleterious effect. Most drugs used for vertigo are loosely termed vestibular suppressants, but their mechanism of action is largely unknown. It is important to remember that vestibular suppressant drugs, although relieving the vegetative symptoms of nausea and vomiting, can retard the central compensation of an acquired vestibular tone imbalance, thereby limiting the ultimate degree of compensation reached (Zee, 1988). There are only three clear indications for the use of drugs in symptomatic relief of nausea and vertigo (Brandt, 1986):

(1) acute peripheral vestibulopathy (Ménières disease, vestibular neuritis)
(2) acute brainstem or archicerebellar lesions near the vestibular nuclei
(3) prevention of motion sickness.

These drugs should not be given for longer than nausea lasts and certainly should not be prescribed for patients with chronic dizziness or benign paroxysmal postural vertigo.

The vegetative symptoms are best treated with antihistamine drugs such as dimenhydrinate (Dramamine) 50 mg every 6 h, or the anticholinergic, scopolamine, 0.45–0.5 mg every 6 h, which can either be given parenterally or transdermally. Alternatives include the antihistamines promethazine hydrochloride (Phenergan), cyclizine (Marezine), or cinnarizine

(Stugeron), as well as phenothiazines like prochlorperazine (Compazine) and triethylperazine (Torecan).

Physical therapy

Vestibular exercises. As mentioned earlier one of the paradoxes relating to vestibular rehabilitation is the need to encourage affected patients to utilise their vestibular system. This activity can itself induce those unpleasant vegetative symptoms the patient is trying to avoid. The aim is either to promote central habituation or to encourage the readjustment of vestibulo-ocular and vestibulospinal reflexes. A formal programme of physical therapy should be instituted as soon as possible in patients with acute vestibular insults and in those with chronic symptoms of vestibular dysfunction. Unfortunately, there are no satisfactory controlled clinical trials of vestibular exercises in the long-term rehabilitation of such patients, although there are very good theoretical reasons why such exercises should be helpful. Anecdotal reports suggest that their effect is substantial and surprisingly rapid.

Vestibular exercises are governed by two basic principles:

(1) Patients must be exposed increasingly often to stimuli that stress the mechanisms of postural stabilisation just beyond their capacity to produce an appropriate response.
(2) Patients must be encouraged to develop alternative patterns of motor responses that can augment or supplement their inadequate vestibular control (Zee, 1985).

In the classic Cawthorne–Cooksey (Cawthorne, 1944) exercises, patients are instructed to move their eyes around in the sitting position, before progressing to more vigorous exercises while standing. These exercises are designed to increase visual input in relation to head movement. Subsequently, exercises are done with the eyes closed to increase proprioceptive input. Ultimately, ball games are played to complete the necessary vestibular adaptation. Similar exercises, modified in the light of current knowledge of vestibular physiology, are described by Zee (1985), and consist of eye, head, and body movements designed to provoke sensory mismatch. They include exercises involving voluntary eye movements to improve visual tracking, exercises to improve gaze stability during head rotations by recalibrating the VOR, active head movements to improve capacity for visual modulation of vestibular responses, and finally active body movement exercises to improve vestibulospinal regulation.

Specific physical therapy for benign paroxysmal postural vertigo. A specific physical therapy has been devised for benign paroxysmal postural vertigo (BPPV), a condition that not infrequently occurs following head injury, although it can occur spontaneously (Brandt & Daroff, 1980; Brandt et al., 1994). This requires the patient to repeatedly tilt laterally, first to one side and then the other, whilst sitting on the edge of the bed, so inducing the vertigo, and each time waiting for the symptoms to subside. The entire sequence is repeated 15–20 times and performed at least three times daily. Within 1–2 weeks the symptoms have usually resolved.

Modifications of these manoeuvres include Sermont and Epley's liberatory manoeuvres, which are illustrated in Figs 20.1 and 20.2. The pathogenesis of BPPV involves debris in the endolymph congealing to form a plug that is heavier than endolymph itself. This will migrate to the most dependent part of the semicircular canal as its orientation changes with movements of the head. As it moves around, the plug exerts push or pull forces on the cupula, which precipitate a BPPV attack. The described manoeuvres aim to steer the debris from the semicircular canals and release it into the utricular cavity, where it no longer causes symptoms.

Physical aids

Aids, such as neck collars, are available to stabilise patients' heads and thereby improve their postural stability. However, their benefit is not long-lasting and they can interfere with the process of vestibular rehabilitation by providing additional sensory feedback.

The role of surgery

Surgery is an option for the treatment of chronic peripheral vestibular dysfunction in conditions such as Ménière's disease. It involves destruction of the peripheral labyrinth or selective section of the vestibular nerve to alleviate the vertigo without causing permanent deafness.

Management of oscillopsia

Disturbance of either the peripheral or central vestibular pathways can give rise to oscillopsia—an illusion of movement of the seen world. This is due to excessive slip of the images of stationary objects upon the retina that, if greater than $4°/s$, can lead to a reduction in visual acuity. The two most common situations in which oscillopsia occurs are:

(1) during head movement when there is a hypoactive, or, more rarely, hyperactive VOR
(2) when there are spontaneous oscillations of the eye, e.g. nystagmus.

In a group of patients with nystagmus of similar amplitude, some complain of oscillopsia and some do not, indicating that there must be certain mechanisms available for dealing with the excessive retinal slip. These could include changes in perceptual thresholds for motor detection or partial use of an extraretinal signal to maintain some space constancy. Examples of mechanisms that deal with increased retinal slip due to reduced VOR that occurs in vestibular disturbances include potentiation of the cervico-ocular reflex, perceptual adaptation, and pre-programming of compensatory slow eye movements in anticipation of head movement (Bronstein & Hood, 1986; Kasai & Zee, 1978).

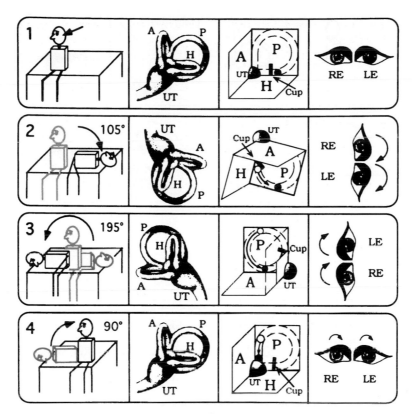

Figure 20.1. Schematic drawing of the Sermont liberatory manoeuvre in a patient with typical BPPV of the left ear. Boxes from left to right: position of body and head; position of labyrinth in space; position and movement of the clot in the posterior canal and resulting cupula deflection; direction of the rotatory nystagmus. The clot is depicted as an open circle within the canal: a black circle represents the final resting position of the clot. **1** In the sitting position, the head is turned horizontally 45° to the unaffected ear. The clot, which is heavier than endolymph, settles at the base of the left posterior semicircular canal. **2** The patient is tilted approximately 105° towards the left (affected) ear. The head position change, relative to gravity, causes the clot to gravitate to the lowermost part of the canal and the cupula to deflect downwards, inducing BPVV with rotatory nystagmus beating towards the undermost ear. The patient maintains this position for 3 minutes. **3** The patient is turned approximately 195°, with the nose down, causing the clot to move towards the exit of the canal. The endolymphatic flow again deflects the cupula such that the nystagmus beats towards the left ear, now uppermost. The patient remains in this position for 3 minutes. **4** The patient is slowly moved to the sitting position; this causes the clot to enter the utricular cavity. Abbreviations: A, anterior semicircular canal; cup, cupula; H, horizontal semicircular canal; LE, left eye; P, posterior semicircular canal; RE, right eye; UT, utricular cavity. From Brandt, T., Steddin, S., Daroff, R.B. (1994) Therapy for benign paroxysmal positional vertigo, revisited. *Neurology, 44*: 796–800. Copyright Lippincott, Williams & Wilkins.

Treatment measures do not need to stop the nystagmus completely to abolish oscillopsia. In patients with downbeat nystagmus, for example, it has been shown that the magnitude of the oscillopsia was, on average, only 37% of the magnitude of the nystagmus (Wist et al., 1983). Several different methods have been devised to stop acquired nystagmus. Various drugs have been tried, the most successful being baclofen (a GABAB agonist) 5–10 mg tds for periodic alternating nystagmus (Halmagyi et al., 1980) and, more recently, clonazepam (a GABAA agonist) 0.5–1 mg tds for downbeat, see-saw, or circular nystagmus (Currie & Matuso, 1986). Gabapentin, up to 900 mg/day, has a more complicated effect on the synthesis and metabolism of GABA and is particularly useful in the treatment of acquired pendular nystagmus (Averbuch-Heller et al., 1997). Other useful treatment options reported to have different degrees of success in treating various forms of nystagmus include anticholinergic drugs like bipcriden or scopolamine, alcohol 1.2 g/kg body weight, 5-hydroxytryptophan 0.5–1 g daily, glutamate antagonists like memantine 15–60 mg daily, and trihexyphenidyl in high doses.

A variety of optical devices can also reduce the oscillopsia in patients with nystagmus. Of particular interest is the use of a routine spectacle lens together with a highly negative contact lens to artificially stabilise the image on the retina (Leigh et al., 1988; Rushton & Cox, 1987).

VISION

Neurological disorders can lead to loss of acuity and to more complex perceptual abnormalities present in agnosias, achromatopsias, and dyslexias, etc., some of which can be very subtle. This section discusses neurological rather than orthoptic or ophthalmic rehabilitation (Lundervold et al., 1987). Rehabilitation of visual neglect is discussed elsewhere in this volume (Chapter 30).

An understanding of the various visual complaints of patients with brain disorders requires a knowledge of normal visual processing, the complex ways in which it can be disturbed and the methods by which such disturbance can be assessed. All too often, a patient's visual complaints are dismissed because

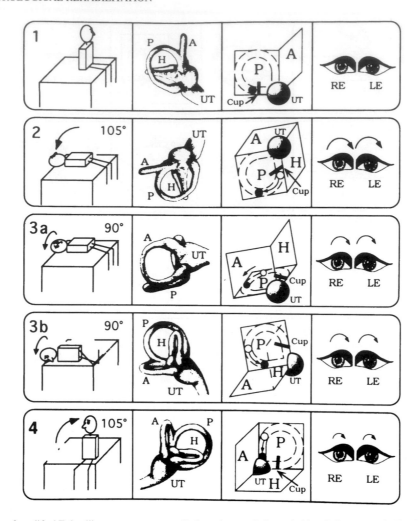

Figure 20.2. Schematic drawing of modified Epley liberatory manoeuvre. Patient characteristics and abbreviations are as in Fig. 20.1. **1** In the sitting position, the head is turned horizontally 45° to the affected (left) ear. **2** The patient is tilted approximately 105° backwards into a slight head-hanging position, causing the clot to move in the canal, deflecting the cupula downwards and inducing the BPPV attack. The patient remains in this position for 3 minutes. **3a** The head is turned 90° to the unaffected ear, now undermost, and **3b** the head and trunk continue turning another 90° to the right, causing the clot to move towards the exit of the canal. The patient remains in this position for 3 minutes. The positioning nystagmus beating towards the affected uppermost ear in positions 3a and 3b indicates effective therapy. **4** The patient is moved to the sitting position. From Brandt, T., Steddin, S., Daroff, R.B. (1994) Therapy for benign paroxysmal positional vertigo, revisited. *Neurology, 44*: 796–800. Copyright Lippincott, Williams & Wilkins.

Snellen acuity is normal and the visual fields to confrontation are full. It is important to make a detailed visual assessment in all patients entering a neurological rehabilitation programme, not only those complaining of a visual difficulty, because poor progress can often result from an undetected visual disturbance. With this in mind, this section begins with a brief account of normal visual processing and methods of assessment, and then surveys the range of visual complaints and the practical measures that can be used to improve function.

Visual pathways and processing

The visual pathways can be thought of as a series of separate but parallel pathways that relay different types of visual information to areas of the brain primarily concerned with separate aspects of visual processing. The direct retinofugal projection separates into two main divisions: the majority of fibres passing to the lateral geniculate nucleus (LGN) and others projecting to the superior colliculus (SC). Although the SC is often said to be concerned only with eye movements, its possible role in providing residual vision in some patients with lesions of their primary visual cortex will be discussed later. The visual pathway to the LGN, and from there to the cortex, is itself subdivided into two functionally and anatomically distinct divisions: the magnocellular and parvocellular systems, which remain largely segregated at the visual cortex. These two systems appear to handle different types of visual information. The magno system has a higher sensitivity to brightness contrast, faster response times, and lower acuity. These are ideal characteristics for a pathway selective for movement detection and stereoscopic depth perception. From the striate cortex it projects to visual area 5 (V5), which in man lies at the temporo-occipitoparietal junction of the extrastriate visual cortex. This system is largely concerned with spatial, or "where", aspects of perception. The parvo system is concerned with colour, form, and shape, or "what" discrimination. It projects to V4, an area primarily concerned with colour vision, which in man lies in the lingual and fusiform gyrus on the inferior aspect of the occipital lobe. Although this functional segregation can help explain selective visual disturbances in patients with brain lesions, the above description is grossly oversimplified and there are widespread and complex interconnections between both systems (Walker, 1989).

Methods of assessment

As already mentioned, it is essential to document visual function adequately in all patients before a programme of rehabilitation is instituted. The standard test of visual acuity uses the Snellen letter chart. In some brain-damaged patients with speech or cognitive impairment, the "tumbling E" test, in which the subject has to identify the orientation of a series of Es drawn in diminishing size, is preferred. Both near and distant acuity should be tested. Some patients with damage to cortical visual areas exhibit visual crowding to such an extent that a visual acuity of 6/60 can be recorded using the conventional chart, but this could be nearly normal if the acuity for single letters is tested (Wilkins et al., 1989). Unfortunately, because of the high contrast of the letters, patients with difficulties at low contrast will perform normally using this test. In recent years, various methods from visual psychophysics have been applied to patients with visual disturbances. The assessment of sensitivity to grating patterns with low contrast has been shown to reveal abnormalities in patients with normal Snellen acuity. For example, after damage to the visual cortex or an episode of optic neuritis, contrast sensitivity will often be reduced, particularly at grating frequencies close to 4 cycles/degree. Various systems for assessing contrast sensitivity have become available, the cheapest of which is the Cambridge gratings, a test that has received extensive clinical evaluation (Wilkins et al., 1988). A quicker test based on large letters that decrease in contrast (Pelli et al., 1988) is also available. The more widely used VisTech chart has been criticised as insensitive (Pelli et al., 1988).

Computerised perimetry is becoming increasingly available. It has advantages over manual perimetry in that it eliminates the operator's testing errors, provides the results in numerical form, and might be superior to routine manual perimetry for the detection and follow-up of small and shallow visual field defects. However, the testing procedure can be lengthy and patients who fatigue rapidly or who are inattentive could give unreliable data. The Amsler grid is quick and handy for exploration of the 10° area surrounding the fixation point, but the phenomenon of contour completion could mask subtle deficits.

It is also important to assess colour vision in patients with possible visual disturbances. A variety of pseudoisochromatic plates are available but the most commonly used, the Ishihara, does not include a measure of tritanopia, and might be subject to subtle masking phenomena due to the high contrast of the elements. The City University Colour Vision Test is inexpensive and provides a rapid assessment that is sensitive to tritanopia and which avoids the complex perceptual demands of the Ishihara. In clinical practice it can sometimes be less sensitive than the Ishihara to the more common forms of colour vision deficit.

It is always important to distinguish between disorders resulting from impaired perception as opposed to those that reflect the patient's inability to respond adequately. For example, difficulties in colour naming could reflect a word-finding difficulty or a visual–verbal disconnection syndrome rather than impaired colour perception.

Although the measurement of visual evoked potentials (VEP) is widely available and useful in the assessment of patients with lesions of the anterior visual pathways, it is of limited use in the assessment of brain-damaged patients who complain of visual disturbances. However, when applied in relation to specific visual problems it can provide useful results. An excellent example is in patients complaining of blurred or "foggy" vision or fluctuation after prolonged inspection of a visual stimulus. Although the patients have normal pupillary responses, visual acuity, accommodation, and convergence, their pattern VEP can show marked attenuation of P100 amplitudes with prolonged stimulation (Zihl & Schmid, 1989).

Finally, although accommodative ability is not part of the routine visual assessment, blurring of vision when looking at near-objects can be due to impaired accommodation. It is a common complaint following head trauma, but often for reasons that have little to do with accommodation.

Training procedures

It has been known for some time that there can be some recovery of function following lesions of the geniculostriate pathway (Poppelreuter, 1917; Riddoch, 1917; Holmes, 1918). The extent of recovery depends on the underlying aetiology of the lesion. Following vascular infarction there can be some initial recovery within 7–14 days but subsequently there is a poor prognosis for further recovery (Gloning et al., 1962; Haerer, 1973). Trauma (in the literature mostly due to gunshot wounds) is often followed by considerable recovery (Hine, 1918; Teuber et al., 1960).

Although several studies of natural recovery have been carried out, systematic attempts to restore visual function after occipital lobe lesions have rarely been reported. Poppelreuter (1917) trained hemianopic patients (mainly in reading) and found a markedly improved reading performance. Using similar training techniques, Preobrazhenskaya (cited by Luria, 1963) reported an enlargement of the perifoveal visual field, again resulting in improved reading performance.

In experiments in non-human primates it has been shown that systematic saccadic training after striate cortex lesions resulted in the restoration of detection and localisation of light stimuli (Mohler & Wurtz, 1977). This was dependent on the function of the superior colliculus, which is also thought by some to be the explanation for "blindsight" or residual vision in man after similar lesions (see Weiskrantz, 1987, for a review). In analogues of these animal experiments in man, Zihl and Von Cramon (1979, 1985) used either psychophysical methods of light threshold detection or saccadic training in which patients with homonymous visual field defects were forced to make saccadic eye movements to light targets presented briefly in the perimetrically blind regions. This systematic treatment led, in the majority of their 55 patients, to an enlargement of the visual field, an improvement that could not be attributed to spontaneous recovery. However, the effect was seen mainly in patients with visual scotomas that did not have a sharp edge. Patients with a homonymous hemianopia or quadrantanopia, usually due to vascular infarction, in which there was a sharp demarcation between the blind and seeing field, showed no return of visual field (Balliet et al., 1985). As sharply demarcated visual fields are the most common type seen in clinical practice, it seems unlikely that restoration of vision is a prospect for most patients. Saccadic training might nevertheless be of value. Zihl and Von Cramon found that, symptomatically, many of the patients reported improvement in their reading performance and in their avoidance of obstacles. There was also an objective improvement in reading performance, although this was probably the result of improved eye movement strategies.

It has been shown that hemianopic patients can develop new eye and head movement strategies to compensate for their field loss (Gassel & Williams, 1966; Meienberg et al., 1981; Zangemeister et al., 1982). We have noted that compensatory movements of the head can sometimes have greater effect if the patient is instructed to glance at the tip of the nose as the head is turned so that the gaze follows the direction of head rotation rather than remaining directed at a point in space as a result of the VOR.

Many patients with hemianopia fail to make saccades into the blind field, and this might perhaps underlie some forms of neglect. Zihl (1988) has shown that, with training, the number of such saccades can be increased. The training methods zihl uses require sophisticated equipment and cannot be undertaken at home. An alternative simple technique that has yet to be evaluated is to adhere a small spot of day-glow material onto the lenses of a pair of spectacles, the material positioned within the blind field. The patient is instructed to practise making saccades that bring the spot into view. Such saccades must necessarily be made towards the blind field because head movements are ineffectual.

Adaptive strategies

Overcoming the effects of crowding.   The visual scene usually contains many contours that are quite irrelevant for the purposes of the task at hand. The presence of this irrelevant information serves to make visual computation unnecessarily complex, even in people with normal vision, but particularly after damage to cortical visual areas when, as mentioned earlier, the effects of the crowding can be extreme.

There are many ways in which the visual scene can be purged of unnecessary clutter. Unnecessary objects can be removed from the observer's visual field, particularly those that can easily be confused with the relevant objects. For example, when counting money in a purse it might be helpful to remove each coin in turn and place it in one of a few piles, rather than to empty the entire contents onto a surface, necessitating the location and discrimination of similar objects.

The patient might find that objects are more clearly seen when viewed monocularly through a tube, or through the hole between the fingers and palm formed when a hand is held in a fist and the fingers are relaxed. Although the improvement in clarity can provide an index of the extent to which crowding is impairing vision, such a technique is of limited practical use, because the aperture itself has to be directed appropriately, using visual cues.

The ability to read text can sometimes be greatly improved when the lines above and below those being read are masked. The mask can be a simple sheet of card with a "letter box" aperture sufficient to reveal no more than three lines. Such a mask is effective in cases of headache from reading and in reading epilepsy (Wilkins & Nimmo-Smith, 1987). It is often helpful to increase the size of the text in the aperture of the mask. A bar magnifier can be used, and the upper and lower sides flanked so as to mask the surrounding text.

The clarity of the text can be further improved by masking the text so as to reveal only a few letters at a time, but such masks cease to be practical aids because of the difficulty in following the line of text. Zihl (1988) has recently presented isolated lines of text on a computer screen that move to the left past the observer's gaze. Patients with a visual loss in the right hemifield practise keeping the eyes positioned at the left-hand extreme of the left-most word; patients with a left hemianopia practise keeping the eyes on the right-hand extreme of the left-most word. The speed at which the line moves to the left is increased progressively, as practice makes perfect. Zihl reports considerable improvement in reading speed, and the transfer of training to normal text.

Sometimes a patient might be able to write but then be unable to read the writing. One such patient discovered for herself that if she wrote on an overhead projector she could read her writing from the surface of the projector. This was presumably because the brightness of the surface was so much greater than that of the surroundings that the number of visible contours in the visual field was substantially reduced, thereby reducing the effects of crowding. She was given a simple box that contained a bulb and had the uppermost side made of opaque plastic. She used it for writing letters, holding the paper against the screen (Wilkins et al., 1989).

The ease with which objects can be perceived can be increased not only by removing unnecessary and confusing contours but also by increasing the conspicuity of those relevant for the task. There are many ways in which this can be done, based on changes in brightness or colour contrast. Patients might find it helpful to select cups with white interiors and coloured exteriors. As the cups are filled, the white interior decreases in visible extent, providing a conspicuous cue as to how full the cup has become.

Patients with hemiplegia often drag the foot on the affected side, catching it on the legs of beds and tables. It can be helpful for the patients to wear white or brightly coloured socks and contrasting trousers, so that the foot is made more conspicuous. (Vision can be one of the few remaining sources of information that patients have as to the position of their limbs.)

The conspicuity of an object depends not only on brightness contrast but also on its colour. Indeed, colour can be one of the most salient features that discriminate objects from their background. The perception of colour is subserved by brain structures different from those that contribute to the perception of form, and can be preserved when form perception is almost completely lost. In such cases, a coloured object can be located on a background of different colour without any knowledge as to the nature of the object.

Even when the loss of form vision is less catastrophic, the appropriate use of cues from colour can greatly facilitate the performance of everyday tasks. Marking objects such as the knobs on cookers and other kitchen appliances with colours different from the colour of the surround can greatly facilitate the visual task of locating the appropriate object. Coloured adhesive labels are often useful for this purpose. The colours should not only differ from the surround in which they are placed, they should have a semantic code, such as red for "danger", etc., and it might therefore be necessary to change the colour of the background to keep the semantic code consistent from one context to another. For related techniques that improve visual tasks around the home see Cristarella (1977).

Cues to distance and position. The appreciation of distance relies on many cues but, in common with most other aspects of vision, it is dependent upon a segregation of contours. A patient with visual disorientation was unable to walk around her hospital surroundings because her immediate appreciation of distance had been lost. Moving objects appeared to loom towards her, affecting balance. We provided a simple cue that enabled her to categorise objects as "distant" and "close enough to worry about". We suggested that the patient look down her nose turning her head to one side and half closing an eye to make the tip of her nose more visible. When the contour between objects and the floor was nearer to her than the image of the tip of her nose it was time to take evasive action. This cue enabled her to avoid objects and rapidly gave her confidence to move around.

Colour imperception. The role of colour in form perception is rarely appreciated, except by those unlucky enough to lose colour vision. Many things are colour coded and some are distinguishable only on the basis of their colour. The loss of blue-cone function is particularly disabling because many natural objects can no longer be discriminated. Sometimes tinted glasses can help increase the contrast of certain objects, for example enabling gold and silver coins to be distinguished, or blue flowers to be seen amongst green foliage.

It can be very difficult for patients with colour deficiency to determine the colours of objects on the basis of the lightness of the objects when viewed through coloured filters. The anomalous colour perception can interfere with the perception of relative brightness.

Asthenopia

Many patients describe visual discomfort following posterior cerebral lesions. They become sensitive to glare, to flicker, and to dazzling patterns. Some of this discomfort has been attributed to disorders of light or dark adaptation (see Best, 1917; Potzl, 1928; Teuber et al., 1960; Ullrich, 1943). Zihl (1988) demonstrated an impairment of light or dark adaptation in 64% of stroke patients who complained of dazzle, or who said they now needed more light for reading. Some patients describe a transitory instability of sight: the contours of objects appear sharp and clear for a short time and then become blurred, sometimes disappearing. The visual impairment has been termed "cerebral asthenopia" by Potzl (1928) and "increased optical fatiguability" by Gloning et al. (1962). The prevalence can be greater after closed head injury than after vascular lesions, although unilateral or bilateral lesions can be responsible.

Many patients with migraine complain of "glare" and uncomfortable perceptual distortions upon viewing patterns that are capable of eliciting seizures in patients with light-sensitive epilepsy (Marcus & Soso, 1989; Wilkins et al., 1984). The mechanisms of light sensitivity in migraine can resemble those of certain types of cerebral asthenopia and the mechanisms are probably central in origin. Some patients with a sensitivity to patterns (of which text can be one example) find relief from coloured glasses, although the mechanisms are poorly understood and the choice of tint is a matter of individual preference. For example, a patient who complained of discomfort after recovering from cortical blindness found a blue tint improved the clarity of her vision. Blue was one of the colours that she saw earliest during the period of her recovery from blindness. Following a severe head injury, another patient became prone to headaches when reading and found some relief from a green tint. A patient with post-traumatic photosensitive epilepsy reported a rose tint helpful in preventing "dizzy spells". The symptoms of cerebral asthenopia closely resemble those reported by certain children with reading difficulty. In a controlled trial, Wilkins et al. (1994) showed that a reduction in headache could result from wearing tinted glasses, provided the colour was chosen with precision to suit the individual: suboptimal colours differing by six just-noticeable differences were less effective under double-masked conditions.

It is not uncommon for patients to experience difficulty watching television following cerebral lesions involving the posterior areas. The flickering picture places an extra demand on the mechanisms that control eye movements, so much so that the eye movements of normal observers are disrupted (Neary & Wilkins, 1989; Wilkins, 1986, 1995). Some LCD portable television sets have "thin film transistor" circuits in each picture element to hold the picture from one scan of the screen to the next; as a result, the picture does not flicker. These sets can help patients with ocular motor difficulties and those who complain of asthenopia, although at present they have very small screens.

Electrical stimulation as therapy

Consideration of therapeutic techniques would not be complete without a mention of electrical stimulation. Although electrical point stimulation of the visual cortex in patients with blindness has been a goal for many years—since the initial studies in the 1960s (Brindley et al., 1969)—progress has been very slow and this method is unlikely to offer any practical benefits for many years to come. However, electrical stimulation of the optic nerve, either by electrodes placed on the surface or percutaneously over the closed eyelid, has been reported to benefit patients with impaired vision from a variety of different optic neuropathies (Bechtereva et al., 1985). Although the studies so far are uncontrolled, they do offer a potentially useful therapy (A. Shandurina, personal communication, 1985).

THE TASK-BASED APPROACH: SOME GENERAL PRINCIPLES

This chapter has concentrated initially on the primary sensory pathways in the traditional way. Such an approach is useful for the diagnosis of a disorder and for the assessment of consequent dysfunction. As has been shown, however, the rehabilitation of patients requires a completely different approach. This approach considers the patients' ability to function in their environment and to perform everyday tasks. Such tasks require a range of sensory and cognitive processes and can be undertaken in a variety of ways. The sensory or cognitive deficits revealed by a neuropsychological examination, no matter how extensive, can

therefore provide only a rough guide as to the likely ability to perform everyday tasks. The task of driving is a case in point. For a review of the role of vision in driving see Strano (1989).

Because everyday tasks are habitual they comprise overlearned components that, prior to injury, were undertaken completely automatically in a smooth sequence. After injury there can be a tendency to attempt to continue to perform the tasks in the same automatic way, using processes that are now impaired, and the attempt can end in a demoralising failure. The tendency to use overlearned and impaired automatic processing needs to be combated by breaking the task down into simple components, each sufficiently novel that it avoids triggering the automatic sequence. For example, consider the everyday task of dialling a telephone number. The task tends to be performed automatically (and erroneously) by patients with field defects, no matter whether the dial is rotary or pushbutton. It is sometimes sufficient to interrupt the automatic sequence of action by instructing patients to check that the desired digit is covered by the finger and disappears from view before the dialling movement is made (Wilkins et al., 1989). Such a check provides feedback and elaborates visuospatial aspects of the task with verbal processing.

In summary, rehabilitation can often involve the relearning of everyday tasks. The relearning might necessitate the restructuring of the tasks, breaking them into novel components. These components need to be designed by the therapist: (1) so that they interrupt the automatic sequence of earlier behaviour; (2) so that each component can be practised separately; (3) so that each provides its own form of feedback, indicating to the patient when it has been successfully completed; and (4) so that each takes advantage of the patient's residual abilities, using, as far as possible, cognitive components that involve undamaged brain areas.

REFERENCES

Averbuch-Heller L, Tusa RJ, Fuhry L et al. (1997) A double blind controlled study of gabapentin and baclofen as treatment for acquired pendular nystagmus. *Annals of Neurology 41*: 8188–8825

Balliet R, Blood KMT, Bach-y-Rita P (1985) Visual field rehabilitation in the cortically blind. *Journal of Neurology, Neurosurgery and Psychiatry 48*: 1113–1124

Baloh RW, Honrubia V (1990) *Clinical neurophysiology of the vestibular system*. FA Davis, Philadelphia

Bechtereva NP, Shandurina AN, Khilko VA et al. (1985) Clinical and physiological basis for a new method underlying rehabilitation of the damaged visual nerve function by direct electrical stimulation. *International Journal of Psychophysiology 2*: 257–272

Best F (1917) Hemianopsie und Seelenblindheit. *Von Graefes Archiv für Ophthalmologie 93*: 49–150

Black FO, Wall C, Nashner LM (1983) Effects of visual and support surface orientation references upon postural control in vestibular deficient subjects. *Acta Oto-Laryngologica 95*: 199–210

Brandt T (1986) Episodic vertigo. In: Rakel RE (ed) *Conn's current therapy*. WB Saunders, Philadelphia, pp 723–728

Brandt T, Daroff RB (1980) Physical therapy for benign paroxysmal positional vertigo. *Archives of Otolaryngology 106*: 484–485

Brandt T, Steddin S, Daroff RB (1994) Therapy for benign paroxysmal positional vertigo, revisited. *Neurology 44*: 796–800

Brindley GS, Gautier-Smith PC, Lewin W (1969) Cortical blindness and the functions of the non-geniculate fibres of the optic tracts. *Journal of Neurology, Neurosurgery and Psychiatry 32*: 259–264

Bronstein AM, Hood JD (1986) The cervico-ocular reflex in normal subjects and patients with absent vestibular function. *Brain Research 373*: 399–408

Cawthorne T (1944) The physiologic basis for head exercises. *Journal of the Chartered Society of Physiotherapists* 106–107

Cristarella MC (1977) Visual functions of the elderly. *American Journal of Occupational Therapy 31*(7): 432–440

Currie JN, Matuso V (1986) The use of clonazepam in the treatment of nystagmus-induced oscillopsia. *Ophthalmology 93*: 924–932

Doty RL (1979) A review of olfactory dysfunctions in man. *American Journal of Otolaryngology 1*: 57–79

Doty RL, Sharman P, Darn M (1984) Development of the University of Pennsylvania Smell Identification Test: A standard microencapsulated test of olfactory function. *Physiological Behaviour 32*: 489–502

Drachman DA, Hart CV (1972) An approach to the dizzy patient. *Neurology (Minneapolis) 22*: 323–334

Gassel MM, Williams D (1963) Visual function in patients with homonymous hemianopia. Part II. Oculomotor mechanisms. *Brain 86*: 1–36

Gloning I, Gloning K, Tschabitscher H (1962) Die occipitale Blindleit auf vascularer Basis. *Graefe's Archive for Clinical and Experimental Ophthalmology 165*: 138–177

Graziadei PPC (1973) The ultrastructure of vertebrate olfactory mucosa. In: Friedmann I (ed) *The ultrastructure of sensory organs*. Elsevier, Oxford, pp 267–305

Haerer AF (1973) Visual field defects and the prognosis of stroke. *Stroke 4*: 163–168

Halmagyi GM, Rudge P, Gresty MA et al. (1980) Treatment of periodic alternating nystagmus. *Annals of Neurology 8*: 609–611

Hine ML (1918) The recovery of fields of vision in concussion injuries of the occipital cortex. *British Journal of Ophthalmology 2*: 12–25

Holmes G (1918) Disturbances of vision by cerebral lesions. *British Journal of Ophthalmology 2*: 353–384

Igarashi M (1984) Vestibular compensation: An overview. *Acta Oto-Laryngologica 406* (suppl): 78–82

Kasai T, Zee DS (1978) Eye–head coordination in labyrinthine-defective human beings. *Brain Research 144*: 123–141

Lacour M, Xerri C (1981) Vestibular compensation: New perspectives. In: Flohr H, Precht W (eds) *Lesion-induced neuronal plasticity in sensorimotor systems*. Springer-Verlag, Berlin, pp 240–253

Leigh RJ, Rushton DN, Thurston SE et al. (1988) Effects of retinal image stabilisation in acquired nystagmus due to neurologic disease. *Neurology 38*: 122–127

Lundervold D, Lwein LM, Irvin LK (1987) Rehabilitation of visual impairments: A critical review. *Clinical Psychology Review: 7*(2) 169–185

Luria AR (1963) *Restoration of function after brain injury*. Pergamon Press, Oxford

Marcus DA, Soso MJ (1989) Migraine and stripe-induced visual discomfort. *Archives of Neurology 46*: 1129–1132

Meienberg O, Zangemeister WH, Rosenberg M et al. (1981) Saccadic eye movement strategies in patients with homonymous hemianopia. *Annals of Neurology 9*: 537–544

Mohler CW, Wurtz RH (1977) Role of striate cortex and superior colliculus in the visual guidance of saccadic eye movements in monkeys. *Journal of Neurophysiology 40*: 74–94

Nakashima T, Kimmelman CP, Snow Jr JB (1984) Effect of olfactory nerve section and haemorrhage on the olfactory neuroepithelium. *Surgical Forum 35*: 562–564

Neary C, Wilkins AJ (1989) Effects of phosphor persistence on perception and the control of eye movements. *Perception 18*: 275–264

Pelli DG, Robson JG, Wilkins AJ (1988) The design of a new letter chart for measuring contrast sensitivity. *Clinical Vision Sciences 2*(3): 187–199

Pendse SG (1987) Hemispheric asymmetry in olfaction on a category judgment task. *Perceptual and Motor Skills 64*(2): 495–498

Pfaltz CR (1983) Vestibular compensation: Physiological and clinical aspects. *Acta Oto-Laryngologica 95*: 402–406

Poppelreuter W (1917) *Die Psychischen Schadigungen durch Kopfschreb im Krege 1914–16, Bard 1: Die Storrugen der Niedern und Hoheren Sehleisturgen durch Verletzugen der Okzipitalhirs*. L Voss, Leipzig

Potzl O (1928) *Die Aphasielehre vom Standpunkte der klinischen Psychiatrie. Erster Bank: Die optisch-agnotischen Storungen*. Deuticke, Leipzig

Precht W (1983) Neurophysiological and diagnostic aspects of vestibular compensation. *Advances in Otolaryngology 30*: 319–329

Riddoch G (1917) Dissociation of visual perceptions due to occipital injuries with especial reference to appreciation of movement. *Brain 40*: 15–57

Rudge P, Chambers BR (1982) Physiological basis for enduring vestibular symptoms. *Journal of Neurology, Neurosurgery and Psychiatry 45*: 126–130

Rushton DN, Cox N (1987) A new optical treatment for oscillopsia. *Journal of Neurology, Neurosurgery and Psychiatry 50*: 411–415

Strano CM (1989) Effects of visual deficits on ability to drive in traumatically brain-injured population. *Journal of Head Trauma Rehabilitation 4*(2): 35–43

Summer D (1976) Disturbances of the senses of smell and taste after head injuries. In: Vinken PJ, Bruyn GW (eds) *Handbook of clinical neurology, injuries of the brain and skull, Part 11*. Elsevier, New York, pp 1–25

Teuber HL, Battersby WS, Bender MB (1960) *Visual field defects after penetrating missile wounds of the brain*. Harvard University Press, Cambridge, MA

Ullrich N (1943) *Adaptationsstörungen bei Sehhirn-Verietzten. Deutsche Zeitschrift für Nervenheilkunde 155*: 1–31

Walker KF (1989) Clinically relevant features of the visual system. *Journal of Head Trauma Rehabilitation 4*(2): 1–8

Wall C, Black FO (1983) Postural stability and rotational tests: Their effectiveness for screening dizzy patients. *Acta Oto-Laryngologica 95*: 235–246

Weiskrantz L (1987) *Blindsight: A case study and implications*. Clarendon Press, Oxford

Wilkins A (1986) Intermittent illumination from visual display units and fluorescent lighting affects movements of the eye across text. *Human Factors 28*: 75–81

Wilkins AJ, Nimmo-Smith MI (1987) The clarity and comfort of printed text. *Ergonomics 30*(12): 1705–1720

Wilkins AJ, Nimmo-Smith MI, Tait A et al. (1984) A neurological basis for visual discomfort. *Brain 107*: 989–1017

Wilkins A, Della Sala S, Somazzi L, Nimmo-Smith IM (1988) Age-related norms for the Cambridge low contrast gratings, including details concerning their design and use. *Clinical Vision Sciences 2*(3). 201–212

Wilkins AJ, Plant G, Huddy A (1989) Neuropsychological principles applied to rehabilitation of a stroke patient. *Lancet i*: 54

Wilkins AJ, Evans BJW, Brown JA, Busby AE, Wingfield AE, Jeanes RJ, Bald J (1994) Double-masked placebo-controlled trial of precision spectral filters in children who use coloured overlays. *Ophthalmic and Physiological Optics 14*(4): 365–370

Wilkins AJ (1995). *Visual stress*. Oxford University Press, Oxford

Wist ER, Brandt T, Krafczyk S (1983) Oscillopsia and retinal slip. *Brain 106*: 153–68

Zangemeister WM, Meienberg O, Stark L, Hoyt WF (1982) Eye–head coordination in homonymous hemianopia. *Journal of Neurology 226*: 243–254

Zee DS (1985) Vertigo. In: Johnson RT (ed) *Current therapy in neurologic disease 1985–1986*. Decker, Philadelphia, pp 8–13

Zee DS (1988) The management of patients with vestibular disorders. In: Barber HO, Sharpe JA (eds) *Vestibular disorders*. Year Book Medical Publishers, Chicago, pp 254–274

Zihl J (1988) Sehen. In: Von Cramon D, Zihl J (eds) *Neuropsychologische Rehabilitation*. Springer, Berlin, pp 105–131

Zihl J, Schmid C (1989) Use of visual evoked responses in evaluation of visual blurring in brain damaged patients. *Electroencephalography and Clinical Neurophysiology 24*: 394–398

Zihl J, Von Cramon D (1979) Restoration of visual function in patients with cerebral blindness. *Journal of Neurology, Neurosurgery and Psychiatry 42*: 312–322

Zihl J, Von Cramon D (1985) Visual field recovery from scotoma in patients with postgeniculate damage. *Brain 108*: 335–365

21. Neurogenic bladder dysfunction and its management

Iqbal F. Hussain   Collette Haslam   Clare J. Fowler

INTRODUCTION

Many patients with neurological disease present with bladder symptoms. This is not surprising as the neural pathways that control the bladder pass from the cerebral cortex through the pons and down the entire length of the spinal cord. For many neurological patients, urinary incontinence can be their most troublesome symptom, but it is one that is most amenable to management by simple medical means. Possible urinary problems include urinary retention, incomplete bladder emptying, detrusor hyper-reflexia, detrusor–sphincter dyssynergia, and recurrent urinary tract infections leading to renal failure.

There are two principal aims in the management of bladder dysfunction in neurological patients. The first is to relieve symptoms, of which the most disabling is urinary incontinence, which is often associated with frequency and urgency. The second is to minimise the risk of renal damage. This is a potential problem where there is sustained high pressure within the system, but it can also result from the severe recurrent urinary infections that complicate urinary stasis. Renal impairment is an important potential complication of traumatic or congenital spinal cord dysfunction but is fortunately rare in progressive neurological disease. In most cases, management is by clean intermittent self-catheterisation and medication to inhibit detrusor contractility. Surgery is usually reserved for those who do not have a progressive disease or those in whom these first line measures fail.

NEURAL CONTROL OF THE BLADDER

Innervation of the bladder and urethra

Continence requires voluntary control of micturition. The bladder and urethra are innervated by sympathetic, parasympathetic, and somatic efferents and afferents. Under the control of the central nervous system (CNS), both at spinal and brainstem levels, these pathways are coordinated to ensure proper function of the detrusor–sphincter mechanism.

Central connections

There are complex interrelationships between the CNS and the lower urinary tract. Until recently, evidence for some of these pathways was available only from experiments with cats (Gjone, 1966; Gjone & Setekleiv, 1963). These experiments identified areas in the cerebral cortex—the superior frontal and anterior cingulate gyri of the frontal lobe, the anterior vermis in the cerebellum and within the subcortical areas, the thalamus, the basal ganglia, the limbic system, and the hypothalamus, from all of which there are descending pathways to the periaqueductal grey (PAG) (Holstege, 1995; Noto et al., 1991). The recent PET study of human micturition shows a similar central organisation in man (Blok et al., 1997).

Pontine micturition centre. The pontine micturition centre (PMC) coordinates micturition by a spinal–bulbar–spinal reflex or long loop reflex. From cat experiments, de Groat has proposed that the pontine micturition centre is the "switch point" at which trans-spinal–bulbar reflexes are switched between the neural mechanisms required for either bladder storage or voiding (de Groat, 1990). According to this model, the PMC acts as an integration centre that regulates spinal reflexes and receives modulatory input from other areas of the brain. The PMC has direct projections to Onuf's nucleus in the sacral cord (Holstege et al., 1979, 1986).

After studying human patients with lesions in the brain and spinal cord, Blaivas (1982) suggested that the coordination between the bladder and the urethral sphincter takes place in the pons. Manente et al. (1996) showed that, in humans, bilateral pontine lesions were required to cause voiding dysfunction. PET scan of the human brain can show areas with increased regional cerebral blood flow (rCBF). Blok et al. (1997) used this technique to demonstrate that micturition in humans seem to be organised in the brainstem, not dissimilar to the cat. The human volunteers, who were unable to void during PET scanning, had increased rCBF in the ventral pontine tegmentum. This corresponds to the "L-region" in cats, which projects to Onuf's nucleus and cause urethral sphincter contraction (Blok et al., 1997).

Structure of the detrusor and sphincter muscles

Three distinct layers of smooth muscle make up the detrusor. Although these are often described as being orientated into an outer longitudinal, a middle circular, and an inner longitudinal layer, there is considerable interchange of fibres in all the layers. This interchange allows the detrusor to contract as a syncytial mass to expel urine from the bladder effectively. There is an extensive parasympathetic innervation of the detrusor that is reflected in the abundance of acetyl cholinesterase positive staining in all areas of the detrusor (Ek et al., 1977). The bladder neck is a modified region where the smooth muscle bundles lie obliquely and are quite distinct from the rest of the detrusor. In the male, this region is important in preventing retrograde ejaculation but in neither sex is there thought to be any significant contribution to maintain continence.

The external sphincter or rhabdosphincter urethrae is composed of striated muscle fibres found within the wall of the urethra just distal to the prostate in a man and along most of the length of the urethra in women (Dixon & Gosling, 1987). The striated muscle of the sphincter is quite separate from the pelvic floor and is composed mainly of small-diameter muscle fibres. These are rich in acid-stable myosin and ATPase and possess numerous mitochondria, they are therefore classified as slow twitch fibres and it is these that contribute to urethral closure at rest. Electromyography (EMG) of this muscle reveals a constant tonic discharge that ceases when the sphincter relaxes as micturition starts (Tanago & Miller, 1970).

PHYSIOLOGY OF NORMAL CONTINENCE

Storage of urine

Physiological bladder filling occurs at a rate of 0.5–5 ml per minute. Under these conditions intravesical pressure does not rise because there is both an inhibition of detrusor activity and active compliance of the bladder. Uvelius and Gabella (1980) showed that the detrusor muscle bundles undergo reorganisation and elongation up to four times their minimal resting length during filling. Bladder distension activates mechanoreceptor (stretch receptors) in the bladder wall, which run with the parasympathetic nerves in the pelvic plexus to the spinal cord at the level of S2–S4. Inhibition of detrusor motor activity requires intact pathways between the pontine micturition centre and the sacral cord. The mechanism of active bladder compliance is rather less clear but it is also a process requiring intact innervation, because it is lost if the sacral root S2–S4 is damaged.

In addition to accommodation, continence during filling is dependent on the combined passive and active effect of the urethra's smooth and striated muscle components of the urethra on its elastic content and on its blood supply. This is aided by the close apposition of the urothelial lining. By these means, the urothelial pressure remains higher than the intravesical pressure and urine does not flow. It is interesting that although the bladder neck is usually closed in males, continence is maintained even after the bladder neck mechanism has been destroyed. Studies show that up to 50% of continent women will have open bladder necks (Versi et al., 1986).

During normal physiological bladder filling, afferent impulses ascend to the cerebral cortex but remain at a subconscious level. Conscious appreciation of bladder filling usually occurs when the bladder has been filled to 200–250 ml, or half its functional capacity. In physiological conditions there is a set volume threshold for micturition, which is determined by age and sex, but this threshold can be changed by psychogenic factors. Although the first sensation of bladder filling is easy to suppress, as the bladder continues to fill the desire to void becomes stronger, until eventually it becomes all pervasive. In spite of cortical suppression of detrusor activity and voluntary pelvic floor contraction, if a suitable time, site, and posture for micturition is not found it no longer becomes possible to suppress the pontine micturition centre and maintain continence.

Voiding of urine

Although the normal mechanism of voluntary voiding has not been fully elucidated, it is known, from radiological and electromyographical studies, that the pelvic floor musculature relaxes early in the process. At, or very soon after, there is simultaneous relaxation of the intrinsic striated muscle, causing a marked fall in intraurethral pressure. This precedes any rise in intravesical pressure. Complete bladder emptying depends upon reflexes that inhibit sphincter activity and sustain detrusor contraction throughout the voiding cycle.

PATHOPHYSIOLOGICAL CONSEQUENCES OF NEUROLOGICAL LESIONS

Disorders of bladder function could be expected as a consequence of neurological damage at many different levels of the nervous system. There are various different ways of classifying voiding dysfunction (Fowler, 1996a; Staskin, 1991). These classifications include the Bors/Cormarr classification, the Hald–Bradley classification, the Bradley classification, the Lapides classification, classification based on urodynamic findings, and the International Continence Society classification. Of the systems of classification, that proposed by Bradley allows a concise description of the principal pathological lesions affecting the nervous control of bladder function because it is based on neuroanatomical and neurophysiological criteria (Fig. 21.1).

Suprapontine lesion

These lesions are classically seen in conditions such as intracranial neoplasms, trauma, encephalitis, cerebrovascular disease, and neurodegenerative disease such as Alzheimer's or idiopathic Parkinson's disease. The neural connections between the medial frontal cortex, thalamus, parietal cortex, cerebellum, basal ganglia, amygdaloid nucleus, and the pontine mesencephalic reticular formation can be involved. The corticopontine pathway is inhibitory to detrusor contractility and therefore

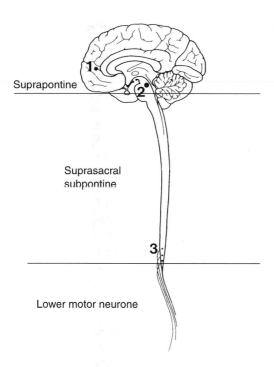

Figure 21.1. Levels of neurological lesions.

suprapontine lesions affecting this pathway would be expected to produce detrusor hyper-reflexia, but with preservation of sphincter–detrusor coordination.

Suprasacral lesion

The two most common lesions of this pathway are multiple sclerosis and spinal cord trauma. Spinal cord damage can occur following fracture dislocation, extradural or subdural haematoma, protrusion and prolapse of intravertebral discs, or neoplastic lesions causing cord compression or ischaemia. The pontine micturition centre provides motor innervation to the detrusor muscle via the pudendal nerve (Onuf's) nuclei in the sacral spinal cord, as well as receiving afferent innervation. Therefore, lesions of the spinal cord between the pontine micturition centre and the sacral spinal cord interrupt the pathways that inhibit detrusor contraction and coordinate sphincter–detrusor function. Patients with suprasacral lesions can therefore have any of the following:

Hyper-reflexic bladder.   As with suprapontine lesions, loss of the normal inhibitory mechanism results in a hyper-reflexic bladder. There is an involuntary pressure rise during filling cystometry (Fig. 21.2).

Detrusor–sphincter dyssynergia.   Instead of the normally coordinated relaxation of the sphincter that precedes detrusor contraction, there can be a simultaneous contraction of the sphincter and the detrusor muscle. The failure of the sphincter to relax appropriately obstructs voiding so that high intravesical pressures can develop, sometimes leading to upper tract dilatation and renal failure. Urine escapes from the bladder only if the

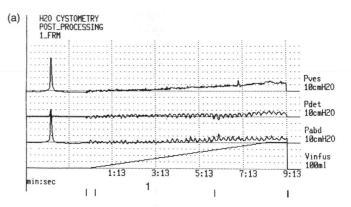

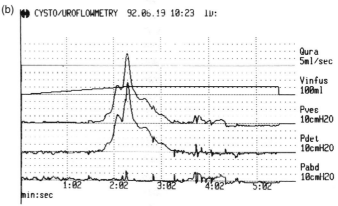

Figure 21.2. Filling cystometry. (a) In a healthy subject. Detrusor pressure, Pdet, is derived by subtracting the abdominal pressure, Pabd, from the intravesical pressure, Pves (Pdet = Pves − Pabd). The filling rate, Vinfus, was 50 ml/min. The detrusor pressure remained unchanged during filling to 450 ml. (b) In a woman with multiple sclerosis showing detrusor hyper-reflexia. After filling to 100 ml there was a detrusor contraction that resulted in a pressure rise of 90 cm H_2O.

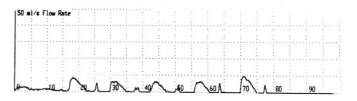

Figure 21.3. Uroflowmetry in a patient with multiple sclerosis. The interrupted flow of urine is characteristic of detrusor–sphincter dyssynergia.

detrusor contraction outlasts the contraction of the sphincter, so that urinary flow is in interrupted bursts (Fig. 21.3).

Poorly sustained detrusor contractions.   The hyper-reflexic contractions are often poorly sustained such that the bladder empties incompletely. This, combined to some degree with the dyssynergia, leads to an abnormally increased postmicturition residual volume.

Increased postmicturition residual volume.   A hyper-reflexic bladder with a large residual volume requires little further filling to trigger bladder contraction. The patient has urinary frequency, often associated with incontinence. Poor bladder emptying is most easily treated if the patient or carer can perform intermittent self-catheterisation and a major effort

Table 21.1.   Underlying pathophysiological causes of symptoms

Urgency and frequency	Urinary retention	Urinary incontinence
Detrusor hyper-reflexia	Detrusor–sphincter dyssynergia	Detrusor hyper-reflexia
Detrusor instability	Failure to initiate micturition reflex	Detrusor instability
Urological causes	Impaired detrusor contraction	"Stress" incontinence
urinary tract infection	Impaired sphincter relaxation	Urological causes
intravesical calculi	Urological causes	chronic retention with overflow
intravesical neoplasia	outflow tract obstruction	postoperative sphincter damage

in management should be directed at recognising the presence of this disorder.

Subsacral lesion.   Damage to the sacral roots S2–S4, either within the spinal canal or extradurally, results in a lower motor neurone defect of bladder function with corresponding loss of bladder sensation. Lesions causing these symptoms are characteristic of damage to the cauda equina (see http://www.caudaequina.com). Damage can be due to spinal cord trauma, intervertebral disc protrusion, neural tube defects, or neoplasms causing pressure symptoms. Voluntary initiation of micturition is lost and, because the neural mechanisms for driving detrusor contraction are absent, the bladder becomes atonic. Bladder compliance on filling is also lost because this is an active process that depends upon an intact nervous supply. Sensation of bladder stretch is impaired but some awareness of pain can still be present, possibly due to the afferent information conveyed in the sympathetic nervous system passing via the hypogastric nerve to the thoracolumbar region.

Denervation of the striated muscle of the sphincter impairs the closure mechanism but the elastic tissues of the bladder neck can permit some degree of continence provided bladder volumes remain small. The mechanisms for maintaining continence during sudden rise in intra-abdominal and hence intravesical pressure is lost, so that stress incontinence is likely. Stress incontinence, which is common in women after childbirth injuries, is an unusual complaint in men and if it occurs it is most likely due to a lower motor neurone injury to the innervation of the sphincter.

Pelvic plexus lesion.   Pelvic plexus injury, iatrogenic damage following pelvic surgery, and small fibre neuropathies such as diabetes mellitus can also produce marked disturbances of the bladder through loss of sensorimotor and autonomic control.

SYMPTOMS OF BLADDER DYSFUNCTION

Urgency and frequency

Although detrusor hyper-reflexia can be the underlying cause of urinary frequency, urinary urgency, and urge incontinence, this has little neurological localising value because detrusor hyper-reflexia can arise from damage to controlling pathways at either the suprapontine or suprasacral level. Any involuntary detrusor contraction on bladder filling during cystometry is called "bladder instability". When a specific neurogenic cause has been recognised for the bladder instability, the term "hyper-reflexia"

is used. Any lesion that disturbs the normal inhibitory neural control of the PMC can give rise to a hyper-reflexic bladder.

Urinary retention

Urinary retention can be the result of various different underlying pathophysiological states (Table 21.1). In men it is essential to exclude outflow tract obstruction due to urological causes such as benign prostatic hypertrophy or a urethral stricture. Benign prostatic hypertrophy is ubiquitous in the elderly male population and urethral strictures can occur at any age, but are particularly common following urethral instrumentation and prostatic surgery. Once urological causes are excluded, detrusor–sphincter dyssynergia, impaired detrusor contraction, failure to initiate the micturition reflex, or impaired sphincter relaxation can all cause some degree of urinary retention.

Detrusor–sphincter dyssynergia is an involuntary detrusor contraction without simultaneous relaxation of the external urethral sphincter. It is due to a lesion of the suprasacral, subpontine spinal cord. In these patients, the accompanying detrusor hyper-reflexia frequently dominates the clinical picture above and beyond the variable degrees of urinary retention from detrusor–sphincter dyssynergia.

Urinary retention can also result from impaired detrusor contraction as occurs with a lower motor neurone type of lesion. Some degree of sphincter function can be preserved if the sympathetic innervation (from the lumbar spinal cord) remains intact.

Urinary retention in young women as an isolated symptom can result from myotonic-like activity localised to the striated muscle of the urethral sphincter, the disorder being frequently associated with polycystic ovaries (Fowler et al., 1988). In this condition there is thought to be a primary failure of sphincter relaxation, which explains the absence of neurological features. The EMG findings from the urethral sphincter shows myotonia-like activity consisting of complex repetitive discharges together with decelerating bursts.

Finally, retention can result from a failure to initiate a micturition reflex, as can occur with some lesions of the CNS. Although a minority of frontal lesions produce retention (Andrew & Nathan, 1964), lesions of the pons are particularly liable to do so (Ueki, 1960).

Urinary incontinence

Urinary incontinence can result from detrusor hyper-reflexia in suprapontine and suprasacral lesions. It is then typically associated with urinary frequency and urgency. Lower motor neurone lesions are associated with sphincter weakness that can be manifested as stress incontinence and with failure of detrusor contractility leading to chronic retention with overflow incontinence. These have to be differentiated from the common condition of genuine stress incontinence in which a weak sphincter fails to produce a sufficient pressure to prevent urine leakage during a sudden rise in intra-abdominal pressure as occurs on coughing or sneezing.

INVESTIGATIONS

The bladder has often been described as "an unreliable witness". This does not preclude taking a detailed history and full clinical examination. However, the management of uro-neurological disorders often rests on the results of investigations. There is some disparity between the views of urologists and neurologists as to the appropriate minimum investigations (Fowler, 1996b; Fowler et al., 1992a). Investigations might include an analysis of the urine, measurement of residual urine, urine flow test, filling and voiding cystometry, urethroscopy, radiological investigations such as an intravenous urography or micturition cystourography, and neurophysiological examination of the pelvic floor.

For the neurologist, a midstream urine (MSU), together with a flow and residual, can be sufficient to manage the patient. In contrast, urologists may want to visualise the anatomy of the urogenital tract. The anatomy, together with physiological bladder function tests, such as filling and voiding cystometry, is particularly useful if surgical intervention is planned. History and examination combined with some of the above investigations will usually be sufficient to exclude a non-neurological cause for the patient's symptoms, particularly in elderly men where prostatic disease might complicate the issue.

The assessment of neurological bladder dysfunction needs to answer two important questions. First, is there a failure of bladder emptying? Second, is there detrusor hyper-reflexia? Once these questions have been answered by the simplest, least invasive means available, the results of further urodynamic and neurophysiological tests are unlikely to add much that will influence management.

Assessment of the upper urinary tract

In progressive neurological disease, problems of the upper urinary tract are uncommon. However, life-threatening renal failure can complicate patients with spinal trauma or with congenital neurological lesions such as spina bifida. If the initial intravenous urogram (IVU) and a serum creatinine are normal, follow-up can reasonably be confined to routine biochemical tests and ultrasound studies to detect upper tract dilatation along with an examination of the urine for infection. Hydronephrosis seen on an initial assessment IVU is likely to be due to intravesical obstruction, especially where there is a large residual urine on the postmicturition film or there is hypertrophic bladder wall, sacculations, and diverticulae. A measurement of glomerular filtration rate and a $99\,m^{TC}$-DMSA (dimercaptosuccinic acid) renogram at this stage will provide a valuable baseline measure of total and differential renal function. Where there is already evidence of renal impairment, the degree of recovery to be expected can be assessed by repeating these investigations after a suitable period of catheter drainage.

Assessment of bladder emptying

Assessment of bladder emptying is fundamental to the management of the neurogenic bladder. This can be done by urethral catheterisation or an approximation of the residual urinary volume can be computed from an ultrasound scan of the postmicturition bladder. Ultrasound machines can allow the outline of the bladder to be traced with a light pen, from which the urinary volume is computed. A residual urinary volume greater than 100 ml is considered to be significant. When ultrasound is not available, the postmicturition film of an IVU series can give imprecise but useful information.

Detection of detrusor hyper-reflexia

If there is a need to confirm a hyper-reflexic bladder (which can often be predicted from the history), filling cystometry can be performed. The procedure requires passage of a small rectal pressure line with which to monitor intra-abdominal pressure. The bladder is catheterised and the intravesical pressure is measured using a similar intravesical pressure line. The catheter allows sterile water to be instilled into the urinary bladder. Detrusor pressure is derived by subtracting intra-abdominal pressure from the intravesical pressure.

A normal bladder will accommodate even unphysiologically high rates of bladder filling (50 ml per minute) without a rise in pressure, until voiding is imminent. In a hyper-reflexic bladder, the pressure trace is characterised by spontaneous rises as the detrusor contracts in response to filling. These are involuntary and might be accompanied by incontinence. If a radio-opaque fluid is used to fill the bladder during filling cystometry the changing morphology of the bladder can be monitored by fluoroscopy and correlated with any pressure changes that occur (by video cystography). Important information obtained from a filling cystometry investigation includes detrusor instability or hyper-reflexia, bladder compliance, bladder sensation, bladder hypersensitivity, and urinary leakage.

Voiding cystometry monitors intravesical pressure while a urinary flow test is being performed. Bladder outlet obstruction can be inferred from a trace that shows low urinary flow with high detrusor pressure. Detrusor–sphincter dyssynergia causes sphincter spasms that result in an intermittent pattern of urinary flow with intravesical pressure rising as the flow stops and falling as flow restarts. This could be associated with ureteric reflux and incomplete bladder emptying.

Detection of detrusor–sphincter dyssynergia

Urethral or anal sphincter EMG can be recorded simultaneously with filling and voiding urodynamic assessment. Continence is maintained by the striated urethral sphincter. This muscle is tonically active, maintaining a higher intraurethral than intravesical pressure. When voiding starts, the sphincter becomes electrically silent and relaxes, remaining so throughout the void. Detrusor–sphincter dyssynergia can be diagnosed by showing high detrusor pressure with a low urinary flow rate and electrical activity in the external urethral sphincter. If bladder outflow obstruction is due to bladder neck hypertrophy or prostatic enlargement, then synchronous EMG and pressure flow traces will show a high detrusor pressure, a low urinary flow rate with an electrically silent external urethral sphincter.

MANAGEMENT

Non-surgical management

Management of impaired bladder emptying

Stimulating detrusor contractions. Some patients, especially those with acquired cord lesions can induce a useful "reflex" detrusor contraction by suprapubic tapping or by perianal stimulation, and occasionally the external urethral sphincter can be made to relax by similar means. These measures can form part of a comprehensive bladder retraining, which can be of value in some patients with spinal injury.

External compression and abdominal straining. Manual expression of urine from the bladder by suprapubic pressure (Credés manoeuvre) can raise intravesical pressure to over 50 cm of water and help empty the bladder. Many spinal units find it ineffective and there is a theoretical risk of inducing upper tract renal damage (J. Shah, personal communication). For most patients, some mechanical means of bladder drainage inevitably becomes necessary.

Clean, intermittent self-catheterisation. Intermittent catheterisation was first proposed as an alternative to long-term indwelling urethral catheters or suprapubic catheters in patients with spinal injuries (Guttman & Frankel, 1966). Initially, it was performed as a completely aseptic procedure by technical staff. Lapides and associates reported "tremendous improvement" in all abnormal parameters for bladder function, particularly infections, using a clean but non-sterile technique (Lapides et al., 1972, 1974). These findings led to the popularisation of clean but non-sterile intermittent self-catheterisation. Indeed, the method has been successfully used by children (Hannigan, 1979), the elderly (Whitelaw et al., 1987), and in neurological patients (Webb et al., 1990).

Clean, intermittent self-catheterisation is performed by the patient or carer one or more times every 24 h. Using the clean technique, a 10F or 12F plastic catheter is introduced into the bladder. Patients are usually taught the method by nurse specialists or continence advisors. It can be more difficult for females to learn to self-catheterise but they can often be helped by using a mirror or trying a different position. Success is dependent upon motivation and adequate manual dexterity. Our experience is that patients capable of writing and feeding themselves will be able to cope with the technique. Interestingly, good eyesight is not an essential requirement. There is considerable benefit in introducing the prospective candidate to someone who is already using the technique successfully.

Those who are suitable to learn the technique are patients with a good-capacity bladder and well-innervated sphincter, who are able to retain reasonable volumes (over 100 ml) inbetween catheterisation. An unstable bladder might not fulfil these criteria, although simultaneous drug treatment can lessen bladder contractility and improve storage capacity. The anxiety that serious bladder infection would be introduced by this procedure seems not to have been realised. Indeed, patients who would otherwise get recurrent infections from stagnant urine report fewer episodes of urinary tract infections. Asymptomatic bacteriuria in these patients is not thought to be harmful and does not usually require antibiotic treatment.

Indwelling urethral catheter. The presence of concomitant disabilities often precludes intermittent self-catheterisation. Consequently, many patients with advanced or progressive neurological disease will require an indwelling urethral catheter. Leakage and by-passing can be a problem, especially with uninhibited detrusor contractions. Futile attempts to overcome this by increasing the size of the catheter and its balloon can aggravate the problem. Not only does a larger volume in the catheter balloon increase detrusor irritability, but a larger catheter can cause the urethra to become more patulous until even the largest balloon is expelled. A trial of drugs to suppress detrusor activity seems logical but often proves disappointing in these circumstances. Biologically inert silastic catheter of appropriate sizes 12–14F in an adult (retained with a 5 ml balloon) should be changed every 3 months, or more frequently if encrustation and debris formation is a particular problem.

Suprapubic catheter. For long-term use, the preferred means of urinary drainage is by suprapubic rather than urethral catheterisation. The main complications are urinary leakage, by-passing, and blockage of the catheter due to encrustation and stone formation. All this will inevitably lead to urinary tract infections. Suppression of infection with antibiotics and antiseptic washouts is likely to be incomplete and occasional cystoscopy and endoscopic stone removal might become necessary. If problems of infection, leakage, catheter expulsion, or stone formation occur, referral to a urologist is appropriate.

"Queen Square bladder stimulator". The neurogenic bladder can sometimes be made to empty by using a vibrator on the abdominal wall between the umbilicus and the symphysis pubis (Nathan, 1977). In a recent study from our hospital, the battery-operated bladder stimulator produced symptomatic benefit in 70% of the study patients (Dasgupta et al., 1997). Twenty-nine of the 36 patients in the study had multiple sclerosis—none had traumatic spinal cord injury. The postmicturition urinary residuals were reduced from 175 ± 78 ml to 68 ± 32 ml. The device was less successful in patients with residuals above 400 ml, suprapubic sensory deficit, and Kurtzke pyramidal function scores greater than 3.

Management of detrusor hyperreflexia

Bladder retraining (bladder drill). Bladder drill is rarely effective in patients with an established neurological disease. However, patients with mild symptoms of urinary urgency and frequency following head injury, encephalitis, and frontal lobe damage can benefit by following simple measures to change their bladder behaviour. The method relies on a regime of timed voiding (every 2–4 h) and bladder drill with increasing voiding intervals to decrease the sensitivity of mechanoreceptors in the bladder wall (Jarvis, 1981). To be successful, it demands a high degree of patient compliance as well as expert supervision.

Oral medication. Many pharmacological agents have been used to attempt to reduce bladder hyper-reflexia. The most effective to date have been those with predominantly anticholinergic properties:

- oxybutynin
- tolterodine
- flavoxate
- propantheline
- imipramine
- amitriptyline.

Imipramine, although usually taken as an antidepressant, has marked anticholinergic properties that might be of benefit in the treatment of bladder hyper-reflexia. Oxybutynin is both a potent anticholinergic with a high affinity for muscarinic receptors in human bladder tissue as well as a smooth muscle relaxant. The drug is moderately effective in lessening hyper-reflexic contractions but dosage is limited by unwanted anticholinergic side-effects. A dry mouth and constipation are the most frequent complaints. Newer drugs such as tolterodine have better side-effect profiles.

Alpha-blockers such as phenoxybenzamine might be expected to improve bladder emptying in those patients in whom there is a failure of relaxation of the detrusor in the region of the bladder neck. In practice, bladder outflow obstruction in neurological disease is likely to be due to a failure of relaxation of the urethral rhabdosphincter and poorly sustained detrusor contractions. Therefore, phenoxybenzamine and the neural alpha-blockers such as prazosin, indoramine, alfuzosin, are unlikely to be very helpful.

Intravesical capsaicin. It is thought that, following neurological damage and interruption of the spinobulbospinal pathways, detrusor hyper-reflexia can result from a new emergent spinal reflex, the afferent limb of which is mediated by small unmyelinated C fibres (de Groat, 1990; de Groat et al., 1990). Capsaicin (an extract of hot chilli peppers) is a neurotoxin that activates a vanilloid receptor on C afferent fibres (Szallasi et al., 1993), resulting in long-lasting functional changes and structural damage. Intravesical capsaicin treatment for detrusor hyper-reflexia was first used at The National Hospital for Neurology

and Neurosurgery in 1990 and the preliminary findings reported in the *Lancet* (Fowler et al., 1992a). The response from 100 ml of a 1–2 mmol/l of intravesical capsaicin for 30 min is biphasic. Symptoms usually deteriorate for up to 2 weeks followed by an increase in bladder capacity and a fall in maximum detrusor pressure. Recent studies have shown a reduction in the nerve densities from detrusor biopsies after capsaicin treatment (Dasgupta et al., 1996). Up to 70% of patients with detrusor hyper-reflexia show a beneficial response but the effectiveness is related to the patient's overall neurological condition (Fowler et al., 1994).

SURGICAL MANAGEMENT

The indications for surgical management of neurogenic bladder dysfunction remain relatively restricted. Understandably, there is a reluctance to submit patients with progressive neurological disease to surgery but the situation is quite different in younger patients with a congenital neurological disorder (such as spina bifida) or those with spinal injuries. Surgery is carried out for three principal reasons: (1) to alter urethral resistance; (2) to reduce involuntary hyper-reflexic detrusor contractions; and (3) for the management of persistent incontinence.

Surgery for altering urethral resistance. In most cases, urethral sphincter resistance has to be increased surgically to maintain urinary continence. The options available to achieve this will include injection of Teflon or GAX collagen, endoscopic bladder neck suspension as described by Stamie, Burch colposuspension, or urethral sling procedures. Where intermittent self-catheterisation is not possible, the male patient with neurogenic urinary retention might benefit from sphincter ablation. The recent development of indwelling endourethral stents and artificial urinary sphincters (Singh & Thomas, 1996) holds the promise of a non-destructive means of obtaining free bladder drainage in such patients.

Surgery for reducing detrusor hyper-reflexia. Surgery is only indicated for detrusor hyper-reflexia when medical and non-surgical management has failed. Endoscopic measures such as subtrigonal phenol injection (Rosenbaum et al., 1990), cystodistention (Pengelly et al., 1980), or bladder transection (Parsons, 1988) are either largely discredited or at best of short-term benefit. The method of choice is the clam ileocystoplasty (Bramble, 1982, 1990; Lewis et al., 1990). Following suitable bowel preparation, a segment of ileum is laid into the wall of the bivalved bladder to augment its capacity and to absorb the rises in intravesical pressure caused by hyper-reflexic contractions (Fig. 21.4). Urodynamic studies following clam ileocystoplasty have shown absence of contractions during filling, and this procedure is successful in relieving symptoms in most patients. Voiding dysfunction following this surgery necessitates 15% of patients to perform clean intermittent self-catheterisation. Possible complications include urinary tract infections and excessive production of mucus. Reabsorption of urinary constituents from cystoplasties is well recognised but is rarely a clinical problem. There are also concerns about the

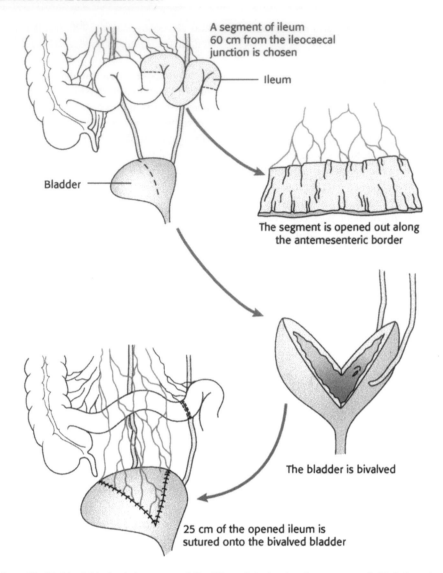

A segment of ileum
60 cm from the ileocaecal
junction is chosen

Ileum

Bladder

The segment is opened out along
the antemesenteric border

The bladder is bivalved

25 cm of the opened ileum is
sutured onto the bivalved bladder

Figure 21.4. Clam ileocystoplasty. The bladder is bivalved. A segment of distal ileum is isolated on its mesentery, divided along the antimesenteric border and the patch sutured along the edges of the divided bladder. Reproduced by kind permission of Health Press Ltd from *Fast Facts – Continence*, by P. J. R. Shah.

development of malignancies in the bowel segment and data from long-term follow-up is awaited.

Surgery for persistent incontinence. Permanent urinary diversion can be indicated as a last resort when other attempts to manage the problem have failed. There are two groups of urinary diversions, the non-continent and the continent. The most widely used technique for supravesical diversion is the ileal conduit described by Bricker (1950). In this procedure, a segment of distal ileum is brought out to the anterior abdominal wall as a stoma and the ureters are implanted to the proximal end of the conduit. Long-term complications of this technique include ascending urinary infections leading to chronic pyelonephritis and formation of upper tract calculi. Also, because the conduit will continue to undergo peristalsis, high pressures can be generated, leading to deterioration in renal function. One significant disadvantage of the conduit is that patients dislike having an ileostomy and a bag collecting urine. This led to the desire

to create a low-pressure, non-refluxing urine reservoir with a continent stoma. In the Mitrofanoff procedure, the appendix, ureter, bowel, or even the vas deferens can be used as such a catheterisable stoma. These are complex procedures but, in carefully selected patients, can be very effective.

A CONTINENCE SERVICE

Continence services throughout the United Kingdom vary greatly, even within Trusts in the same area. Some continence services have access to clinical nurse specialists/continence advisors, consultant support, and urodynamic investigation, whereas other areas do not, and incontinence is regarded as an exclusively nursing management problem (Wells, 1994).

In 1993, the Association for Continence Advice (ACA) published its *Guidelines for continence care*. These guidelines were formulated to help continence services develop improved

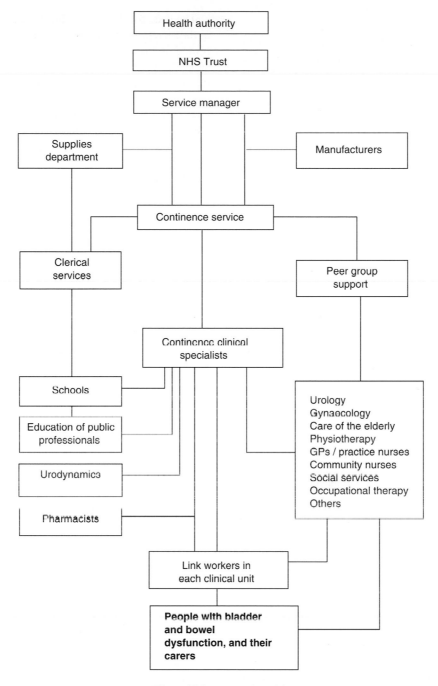

Figure 21.5. A network model.

services and raise standards throughout the country. The ACA identified six points of importance in this area:

(1) assessment
(2) treatment
(3) continence services
(4) provision of continence products
(5) professional education
(6) information.

The guidelines for continence services state that, "services should not be delivered on an *ad hoc* reactive basis, but should be planned to meet the needs of the total population". This is why it might be more prudent to plan a network model and multidisciplinary approach to ensure correct patient management. Figure 21.5 shows a model that is based on one developed by the ACA in 1993.

In 1995 a multidisciplinary working party of the Royal College of Physicians recommended that a continence service should have:

(1) A defined method of entry for patients referred by general practitioners, nurse, hospital staff, and patients themselves.
(2) Access to appropriate diagnostic facilities, including urodynamic and anorectal investigations.
(3) Access to medical and surgical consultants with a special interest in incontinence.
(4) Integration of incontinence services for children with other paediatric services.
(5) A process by which attention is given to the wishes of the patients and carers.
(6) Access to nurses and physiotherapists with special training in treating modalities for incontinence.
(7) A role for one or more specialist continence advisors in the education of the public in continence maintenance.
(8) A policy concerning the purchasing and supply of containment materials and equipment in the community, in residential and nursing homes and in hospitals.
(9) A well-defined audit and quality assurance system.

Unfortunately, many services do not achieve all these aims.

Continence advisor/clinical nurse specialist

Although all aspects of a service are equally important if an efficient system is required, it is often thought that the role of the nurse continence advisor is seen as a focal point both for patients and for the multidisciplinary team. In some areas, however, the continence advisor is a physiotherapist who specialises in pelvic floor problems. The role of the continence advisor has become a critical part of any continence service, with this person often leading the service. The number of specialist continence nurses rose significantly in the last twenty years of the twentieth century; in 1981 there were 17 continence advisors; by 2000 there were over 450.

The need for this role to develop has been seen as a necessity, as the recognition of the increase in the prevalence of continence problems has been acknowledged. With more public awareness and willingness of the general public to talk about incontinence, this number can only increase. The role of the continence advisor has four main components: clinical, educational, managerial, and research. These components have developed in depth over the years, from the so-called "pad nurse", who simply supplied incontinence pads, to continence advisors with large caseloads and their own clinics carrying out assessments, investigations, and treatments. Education has a large remit, be it information, advice, or research, and aspects of these are invaluable to patients, carers, and the multidisciplinary team alike. In her study into the role of the continence advisor, Rhodes (1994) found that educational and training activities had been successful in effecting change in nursing practice. The managerial structure can vary greatly from area to area, from hospital to community, and it is therefore very difficult to define the managerial role of an advisor. However, it has been shown that a nurse-led continence promotion service improved management, increased levels of awareness, and resulted in resource saving, also increasing patient accessibility to the service offered (McGhee et al., 1997).

In a climate where primary care and finance are often foremost, consideration should be given to a comment by Rhodes, "The post of continence advisor acts as a marker of the importance of continence issues to employees and purchasers".

Hopefully, acknowledging that continence problems can be managed successfully, with understanding and compassion, will encourage people to use the continence services and continence specialist and so benefit from a holistic approach to their specific continence problems.

REFERENCES

ACA (1993) *Guidelines for continence care.* London: Association for Continence Advice.
Andrew, J., Nathan, P.W. (1964) Lesions of the anterior frontal lobes and disturbances of micturition and defaecation. *Brain 87:* 233–262
Blaivas, J.G. (1982) The neurophysiology of micturition: A clinical study of 550 patients. *J. Urol. 127:* 958–963
Blok, B.F.M., Willemsen, A.T.M., Holstege, G. (1997) A PET study on brain control of micturition in humans. *Brain 120:* 111–121
Bramble, F.J. (1982) The treatment of adult enuresis and urge incontinence by enterocystoplasty. *Br. J. Urol. 54*(6): 693–696
Bramble, F.J. (1990) The clam cystoplasty. *Br. J. Urol. 66*(4): 337–341
Bricker, E.M. (1950) Bladder substitution after pelvic evisceration. *Surg. Clin. North Am. 30:* 1511–1521
Dasgupta, P., Chandiramani, V.A., Fowler, C.J., Ycol. J. (1996) Intravesical capsaicin. Its effects on nerve sensitivities in human urinary bladder. *Neurourol. Urodynam, 15:* 373–374
Dasgupta, P., Haslam, C., Goodwin, R., Fowler, C.J. (1997) The "Queen Square bladder stimulator": A device for assisting emptying of the neurogenic bladder. *Br. J. Urol. 80:* 234–237
de Groat, W.C. (1990) Central neural control of the lower urinary tract. In: Bock, G., Whelan, J. (eds.) *Neurobiology of Incontinence,* pp. 27–56. Chichester: John Wiley

de Groat, W.C., Kawatani, M., Hisamitsu, T., Cheng, C.L., Ma, C.P., Thor, K., Steers, W. (1990) Mechanism underlying the recovery of urinary bladder function following spinal cord injury. *J. Auton. Nerv. Syst. 30:* S71–S78
Dixon, J., Gosling, J. (1987) Structure and innervation in the human. In: Torrens, M., Morrison, J.F.B. (eds.) *The Physiology of the Lower Urinary Tract,* pp. 2–23. London: Springer-Verlag
Ek, A., Alm, P., Andersson, K.E., Persson, C.G.A. (1977) Adrenergic and cholinergic nerves of the human urethra and urinary bladder. A histochemical study. *Acta Physiol. Scand. 99*(3): 345–352
Fowler, C.J. (1996a) Classification and investigation of neurovesical dysfunction. In: Whitfield, H., Hendry, W., Kirby, R., Duckett, J. (eds.) *The Textbook of Genito-urinary Surgery,* 2nd edn. London: Blackwell Science
Fowler, C.J. (1996b) Investigation of the neurogenic bladder. *J. Neurol. Neurosurg. Psychiatry 60:* 6–13
Fowler, C.J., Christmas, T.J., Chapple, C.R. (1988) Abnormal electromyographic activity of the urethral sphincter, voiding dysfunction and polycystic ovaries: a new syndrome. *Br. Med. J. 297:* 1436–1438
Fowler, C.J., Jewkes, D., McDonald, W.I., Lynn, B., de Groat, W.C. (1992a) Intravesical capsaicin for neurogenic bladder dysfunction. *Lancet 339:* 1239
Fowler, C.J., van Kerrebroeck, P.E., Nordenbo, A., Van Poppel, H. (1992b) Treatment of lower urinary tract dysfunction in patients with multiple sclerosis. *J. Neurol. Neurosurg. Psychiatry 55:* 986–989
Fowler, C.J., Beck, R.O., Gerrard, S., Betts, C.D., Fowler, C.G. (1994) Intravesical capsaicin for the treatment of detrusor hyperreflexia. *J. Neurol. Neurosurg. Psychiatry 57:* 169–173

Gjone, R. (1966) Excitatory and inhibitory bladder responses to stimulation of 'limbic' diencephalic and mesencephalic structures in the cat. *Acta Physiol. Scand. 66*: 91–102

Gjone, R., Setekleiv, J. (1963) Excitatory and inhibitory bladder responses to stimulation of the cerebral cortex in the cat. *Acta Physiol. Scand. 59*: 337–348

Guttman, L., Frankel, H. (1966) The value of intermittent catheterisation in the management of traumatic paraplegia and tetraplegia. *Paraplegia. 4*: 63–84

Hannigan, K.F. (1979) Teaching intermittent self catheterisation to young children with myelodysplasia. *Development Medicine and Child Neurology 21*: 365–368

Holstege, G. (1995) The basic, somatic and emotional components of the motor system in mammals. In: Paxinos, G. (ed.) *The Rat Nervous System*, 2nd edn. pp. 137–154. San Diego: Academic Press

Holstege, G., Kuypers, H.G.J.M., Boer, R.C. (1979) Anatomical evidence for direct brain stem projections to the somatic motoneuronal cell groups and autonomic preganglionic cell groups in cat spinal cord. *Brain Res. 171*: 329–333

Holstege, G., Griffiths, D., de Wall, H., Dalm, E. (1986) Anatomical and physiological observations on supraspinal control of bladder and urethral sphincter muscles in the cat. *J. Comp. Neurol. 250*: 449–461

Jarvis, G.J. (1981) A controlled trial of bladder drill and drug therapy in the management of detrusor instability. *Br. J. Urol. 53*(6): 565–566

Lapides, J., Diokno, A.C., Siber, S.J., Rowe, B.S. (1972) Clean intermittent self catheterisation in the treatment of urinary tract disease. *J. Urol. 197*: 458–461

Lapides, J., Diokno, A.C., Lowe, B.S., Kalish, M.D. (1974) Followup on unsterile, intermittent self-catheterisation. *J. Urol. 111*: 184–187

Lewis, D.K., Morgan, J.R., Weston, P.M.T., Stephenson, T.P. (1990) The 'clam': Indications and complications. *Br. J. Urol. 65*(5): 488–491

Manente, G., Melchionda, D., Uncini, A. (1996) Urinary retention in bilateral pontine tumour: Evidence for a pontine micturition centre in humans. *J. Neurol. Neurosurg. Psychiatry 61*: 528–536

McGhee, M., O'Neill, K., Major, K., Twaddle, S. (1997) Evaluation of a nurse led continence service in the south west of Glasgow, Scotland. *J. Adv. Nurs. 26*(4): 723–728

Nathan, P. (1977) Emptying the paralysed bladder. *Lancet i*: 377

Noto, H., Roppolo, J.R., Steers, W.D., de Groat, W.C. (1991) Electrophysiological analysis of the ascending and descending components of the micturition reflex pathway in the rat. *Brain Res. 549*: 95–105

Parsons, K.F. (1988) Bladder transection. In: Gingell, C., Abrams, P. (eds.) *Controversies and Innovations in Urological Surgery*, pp. 229–234. London: Springer-Verlag

Pengelly, A.W., Stephenson, T.P., Milroy, E.J.G. (1980) Results of prolonged bladder distension as treatment for detrusor instability. *Br. J. Urol. 52*(6): 243–245

Rhodes, P. (1994) Continence advisers role in education. *Nursing Standard 8*(30): 47–53

Rosenbaum, T.P., Shah, P.J.R., Worth, P.H.L. (1990) Trans-trigonal phenolfailed the test of time. *Br. J. Urol. 66*(2): 164–169

Singh, G., Thomas, D.G. (1996) Artificial urinary sphincter in patients with neurogenic bladder dysfunction. *Br. J. Urol. 77*(2): 252–255

Staskin, D.R. (1991) The classification of voiding dysfunction. In: Krane, R.J., Siroky, M.B. (eds.) *Clinical Neurology*, 2nd edn. pp. 411–424. Boston: Little, Brown

Szallasi, A., Conte, B., Goso, C., Blumberg, H., Manzini, S. (1993) Characterisation of a peripheral vanilloid (capsaicin) receptor in the urinary bladder of the rat. *Life Sci. 52*(20): PL221–226

Tanago, E.A., Miller, E.R. (1970) The initiation of voiding. *Br. J. Urol. 42*: 175–183

Ueki, K. (1960) Disturbances of micturition observed in some patients with brain tumour. *Neurologia 2*(1–2): 25–33

Uvelius, B., Gabella, G. (1980) Relation between cell length and force production in urinary bladder smooth muscle. *Acta Physiol. Scand. 110*(4): 357–365

Versi, E., Cardozo, L.D., Studd, J.W.W., Brincat, M., O'Dowd, T.M., Cooper, D.J. (1986) Internal urethral sphincter in maintenance of female continence. *Br. Med. J. 292*: 166–267

Webb, R.J., Lawson, A.L., Neal, D.E. (1990) Clean intermittent self catheterisation in 172 adults. *Br. J. Urol. 65*(1): 20–23

Wells, M. (1994) Achieving good care. *Nursing Times 90*(43): 68

Whitelaw, S., Hammonds, J.C., Tregallis, R. (1987) Clean intermittent self catheterisation in the elderly. *Br. J. Urol. 60*: 125–127

22. Sex and relationships in neurological disability

Barbara J. Chandler

INTRODUCTION

At the time of conception, sex can be defined in terms of the genetic make-up of the individual. As the embryo develops, male and female characteristics emerge in terms of anatomy, physiology, and the endocrine system. At birth, the distinct anatomical characteristics allow a gender to be assigned. In the vast majority of individuals this will be the gender that they assume as they develop postnatally. Awareness of gender develops as the infant grows into childhood and subsequently enters adolescence. The influence of psychosocial factors becomes stronger throughout this transition. Bancroft (1989) describes three strands of sexual development,

(1) sexual differentiation, which begins *in utero*, and the development of gender identity
(2) sexual responsiveness
(3) the capacity for intimate dyadic relationships.

During adolescence these strands become integrated to form the mature adult. Ideally, the sexually mature adult should feel confident about his or her sexuality and be able to form an intimate dyadic relationship in which he or she can respond sexually to give and receive pleasure and strengthen the relationship for mutual support and love. Throughout this development, which can be considered as a life-long process, stresses can occur that challenge the developmental strands. The stresses include psychosocial changes, peer group influences, and illness. The stress can lead to a strengthening of the individual or to a dysfunctional situation affecting the individual, his or her partner, and their relationship.

Sexual expression is dependent upon functioning anatomical and physiological systems. Cognitive processes are essential to monitor the response of self and that of the partner; it is a truly psychosomatic process (Annon, 1976). The extent to which individuals are able to allow expression of their sexuality is also influenced by the social context, past experience, expectations, prevailing attitudes, and confidence within a relationship. The multitude of parameters influencing sexual expression make it a difficult phenomenon to study. Another complicating factor for research is the difficulty of establishing norms. With regard to the physiological responses, this has now been achieved and has helped in the understanding of some dysfunctions. What is the norm with regard to overall sexual responsiveness within the dyadic relationship is probably unique to each couple, but their perception of the norm can enhance or detract from their sex life, depending on whether the reality of their experience is in accordance with their expectations. In summary, the complex interactions of physiological, psychological, and social functioning that result in a sexual relationship are vulnerable to insult and problems are common.

THE SEXUAL RESPONSE

The work of Masters and Johnson in the 1960s for the first time gave a detailed account of the physiological processes involved in the sexual response (Masters & Johnson, 1966). Their studies highlighted the marked similarity of response between males and females. Any division of the sexual response is somewhat arbitrary as it is a continuous process, but the working definition proposed by Masters and Johnson continues to be very useful in understanding many disorders of sexual function and planning treatment regimes. They divided the response cycle into four phases: excitement, plateau, orgasm, and resolution. The psychological and physiological responses occur in sequence, but the cycle does not have to be completed for sex to be a fulfilling experience (Stanley, 1981a); this is an important therapeutic concept.

Peripheral changes during sexual activity

Through their laboratory work, Masters and Johnson demonstrated the occurrence of changes in heart rate, blood pressure, respiratory rate, skin colour, and muscle tone during sexual activity. The cardiovascular changes often cause anxiety for individuals wishing to return to sexual activity following myocardial infarction or the diagnosis of ischaemic heart disease. The changes recorded by Masters and Johnson were marked. The heart rate increased to 100–175 beats per minute during the plateau phase and to 110–180 beats per minute during the orgasmic phase. In males, systolic blood pressure rose by 40–100 mm Hg and diastolic pressure by 20–50 mm Hg; the increase was slightly less marked in females. It is possible that the added stress or excitement of the laboratory situation could have contributed to an artificial elevation of values (Bancroft, 1989). More recent research suggests that cardiac changes during sex with an established partner are of modest severity and are similar to the changes that occur on climbing two flights of stairs (Larson et al., 1980; Nemec et al., 1976). This allows information about sexual activity to be given to patients as part of the standard cardiac rehabilitation programme.

The common sexual dysfunctions can be categorised according to the phase of the sexual response cycle in which they occur. For example, vaginismus, dyspareunia, and erectile dysfunction represent dysfunctions within the excitement phase. Within the orgasmic phase there might be problems with ejaculation, most commonly premature ejaculation, but delayed orgasm and ejaculation is not uncommonly seen often as a side-effect of certain antidepressants, for example the SSRI group. Classifying the dysfunctions in this way is only a small part of the diagnostic process, which involves a close analysis of aetiological factors.

The place of the nervous system in the sexual response

Peripheral and autonomic nervous system. The genitalia are richly supplied with sensory nerve endings, which travel in the pudendal nerve to sacral segments S2, S3, and S4. Both arms of the autonomic nervous system are involved in the sexual response. The sympathetic nerves come from the thoracic and upper lumbar rami and the parasympathetic supply from the sacral outflow, S2, S3, and S4. A simplistic summary is that the parasympathetic supply results in vasocongestion and erection and the sympathetic supply is responsible for ejaculation. However, there is evidence that the sympathetic nervous system is also involved in erection both from animal work and studies of men with spinal cord injuries. There is a more complex interplay of the nervous system and the neurotransmitters than has been hitherto thought; it is beyond the scope of this chapter to consider this further (Bancroft, 1989; Lundberg, 1999; Beck, 1999).

Erection of the penis is paralleled in the female by analogous changes due to vasocongestion resulting in engorgement of the clitoris and uterus. The uterus increases in size and rises in the pelvis, pulling the cervix out of the way of the thrusting penis. The upper two-thirds of the vagina balloon and the vagina becomes lubricated by a transudate. If vaginal entry is attempted without these changes of the excitement phase having occurred, discomfort or pain can be experienced.

Central nervous system (CNS). The control of sexual expression and sexual desire lies in the CNS. Sexual desire represents a complex interaction between neurophysiological responses, cognitive processes, mood, and indeed social context or environment. Bancroft (1989) describes a state of central arousability that determines the individuals' capacity for reacting to an appropriate stimulus with a sexual response. A complex interplay of neurotransmitters and the endocrine system affects both sexual desire and sexual response. Changes in sexual interest can present as a problem if the individual is concerned about the changes or if his or her partner expresses concern. Lack of sexual interest is a not uncommon dysfunction in women presenting to a sexual problem clinic (Bancroft & Coles, 1976; Warner & Bancroft, 1987). It can be unmasked by the restoration of function in one partner. For example, a man with erectile dysfuncion might report how supportive and understanding his partner has been. However, restoration of his potency can force the couple to recognise that the partner has reduced sexual interest. This can lead to quite serious relationship problems if help is not available.

THE DYADIC RELATIONSHIP

Other than in masturbation and fantasy, sexual expression occurs within a relationship (Neumann, 1979). The couple has been described as the true unit of sexual experience (Frank et al., 1978). The fullness of expression therefore depends upon the functioning of that relationship, which can be influenced by many internal and external factors. Most importantly, the relationship is dependent upon its two component parts and they in turn are influenced by the relationship.

Sexual expression is one means of communication within the dyadic relationship, but it cannot survive as the only form of intimate communication. Love, acceptance, and trust can be demonstrated through sexual contact but sexual expression also demands vulnerability. If only one partner accepts that vulnerability, sexual contact can allow dominance anger and jealousy to be expressed by the other partner, with very damaging consequences for the relationship. Such a couple will need help to identify how they are using sex to communicate negative emotions. Help can then be offered to allow the couple to develop their communication skills and take the expression of damaging emotions away from their sex life.

The complex interplay of sexual experience and the functioning of the dyadic relationship was illustrated in a study of American couples. One hundred volunteers from various predominantly middle-class groups and whose marriages were "working" were studied. In 5–10% of cases it became apparent that one partner who thought the marriage was working was not aware of the marital distress experienced by the spouse. This illustrated one of the many types of communication problem that can develop within relationships. Of equal interest was the finding that 40% of the men reported some sexual dysfunction (e.g. erectile or ejaculatory problems) and 50% some sexual difficulty (e.g. difficulty relaxing, being attracted to someone else). Amongst the female partners, 63% described some dysfunction (e.g. arousal or orgasmic problems) and 77% some difficulties. The authors advise caution in interpreting the results because this was a self-selected group and the evidence is based on self-reports. Nevertheless, there is a high level of dysfunction within these otherwise functioning relationships (Frank et al., 1978).

THE IMPACT OF NEUROLOGICAL DISABILITY ON SEX AND RELATIONSHIPS

Within the context of neurological disease and disability, sexual and relationship dysfunction as a result of all the factors that operate for the population at large, plus the impact of acquired impairment of anatomy, physiology, and cognition, is common. Many of the dysfunctional situations are amenable to treatment but, as Ducharme comments, "a substantial number of patients fail to resume an active sex life owing to fear, misinformation or problems of adjustment" (Ducharme, 1994).

It appears that sexual activity decreases after the onset of disability (Humphrey, 1985; Szasz, 1991). The reasons for this are many and varied and include physical difficulties, pain, anxiety, depression, fatigue, side-effects of medication, disruption to normal lifestyle, aversion, and role change (Rosenbaum & Najenson, 1976; Rolland, 1994; Szasz, 1991). Some of these reasons can apply equally to the non-disabled partner, who must therefore be given due consideration during the assessment and treatment of dysfunctions. When a client presents with a sexual or relationship problem three distinct parameters must be considered:

(1) the individual
(2) the partner
(3) the relationship.

The aetiology of the dysfunction can reside chiefly in one area but it will certainly impact upon the others. Alternatively, it could be part of the complex interplay referred to above. A single cause of sexual dysfunction is rare (Halvorsen & Metz, 1991, 1992). Individuals who are not in a relationship can also have anxieties about their sexuality and sexual functioning that require help.

The partner with the disability

Neurological disease and disability can affect cognition, behaviour, and emotional responsiveness in addition to physical functioning. These changes have major implications for the functioning of the dyadic relationship and sexual responsiveness. Fear, expectations, mood, past experience, and prevailing attitudes will also impact upon the individual's ability to respond sexually.

Physical functioning. Sexual dysfunction can occur as the presenting symptom of a neurological disease, for example, multisystem atrophy. This condition can have profoundly damaging effects upon the autonomic nervous system, such that erectile dysfunction is very common. Sexual problems can develop during the course of a disease such as diabetes mellitus, in which vascular pathology and neuropathic processes contribute to the dyfunction. Another example is multiple sclerosis, in which central demyelination interferes with the peripheral sexual response. A traumatic event such as spinal cord injury can result in immediate sexual dysfunction along with a global loss of neurological function below the level of the lesion. In any of these case scenarios, sexual dysfunction can cause distress, anxiety, a sense of failure, or a feeling of lost manhood or femininity.

Fear. This can be experienced by the individual with disability or the partner. There might be fear of pain either due to the disabling condition (Blake et al., 1987) or due to problems in the sexual response cycle causing dyspareunia. There could be fear of triggering a catastrophic event after a myocardial infarction or subarachnoid haemorrhage (Seidl et al., 1991). Sexual dysfunctions commonly cause anxiety, which further exacerbates the problem (Kaplan, 1974). For example, a man could experience erectile dysfunction on one occasion, which results in anxiety on the next occasion he makes love, leading to a further episode of dysfunction. He then enters a vicious circle of failure promoting further failure. The fears can relate to aspects of physical functioning such as continence, spasticity, excess salivation, and so on. There could be imagined or genuine fears for the relationship. The level of fear can be influenced by the individual's mood, ability to communicate his or her fears with their partner, and by the information that is available to the couple from health-care professionals.

Expectations. A not uncommon source of distress is unrealistic expectations. After a prolonged period in a hospital or rehabilitation unit, the individual will look forward to returning home, to the re-establishment of the intimate dyadic relationship with the partner, and to the resumption of their sex life. However, a period of adjustment on the part of both the individual and the partner might be necessary before they can express and enjoy the same degree of intimacy as they had prior to the hospitalisation. Unless couples anticipate this or have the opportunity to discuss it, great distress can occur, with accompanying accusations of lack of love and understanding.

Mood. Depression and anxiety are recognised as potent aetiological factors in sexual dysfunctions (Kaplan, 1974). Anxiety is also recognised as a very common factor contributing to the persistence and exacerbation of certain dysfunctions. Reducing anxiety therefore plays a major role in sex therapy (Kaplan, 1974; Masters & Johnson, 1966).

Past experience. Studies have shown that one of the positive prognostic factors for resuming a satisfactory sex life after a major insult (acquired disease or injury) is the quality of the sex life prior to the event (Bancroft, 1993; Bowers et al., 1971; Miller et al., 1981). In helping people with sex and relationship problems, it is essential to establish how they functioned in these areas prior to the traumatic event. However, paradoxically, those relationships formed prior to the onset of disease or trauma can be more adversely affected than those formed subsequently because of the number of adjustments that must be made (Abrams, 1981; Halvorsen & Metz, 1991).

In the past, there might be hitherto undisclosed traumas such as sexual abuse, rape, or a traumatic childhood, which affect the ability of the individual to form an intimate relationship and respond sexually (Cotgrove & Kolvin, 1996). These aspects of the history have to be acknowledged and might require therapy before the issues around the acquired disability can be examined and dealt with.

Attitude.   Wendy Greengross (1976) highlights the paradox of living in an almost totally sex-orientated world that feels uncomfortable about people with handicaps also enjoying sexual intimacy. Negative attitudes towards sexual development and expression can be very damaging. Goffman (1963) talks of the restriction of life chances resulting from the stigma of impairment, and this is well illustrated by the experience of many people in seeking help for sexual problems. There is still a prevalent attitude that people with disabilities do not have sexual feelings and should not attempt a sexual relationship (Becker & Abel, 1983; Litvinoff, 1992). For adolescents, a clear message that forming a sexual relationship will not be possible might have been imparted from childhood (Castree, 1979; Greengross, 1976). This will affect their expectations and impact on their outlook with regard to forming close dyadic relationships. Kreuter et al. (1994) comment that the sexual expression of persons with spinal cord injury can be affected not only by their particular physical condition but also by the attitudes of society and of their partners toward the disability. This can be generalised to many types of disability.

Examples of specific diseases and disabilities

Sexuality is common to all people, whatever their level of physical and cognitive functioning. Many of the aspects of sexuality discussed in this chapter are pertinent whatever the aetiology of the neurological disability. The specific conditions discussed below illustrate the effect of damaged physical, cognitive, and behavioural functioning on both sex life and intimate relationships.

Multiple sclerosis (MS).   Disturbance of sexual functioning is common in MS. For example, a postal survey amongst members of an MS group in Helsinki ($n = 302$, replies obtained from 249 individuals) revealed that 91% of the male respondents had experienced a change in their sex lives; 64% of these men described their sex life as unsatisfactory or inactive. In the same study, 72% of women reported a change in their sex life, with 39% experiencing an unsatisfactory or inactive sex life. For men, the most common problem was erectile dysfunction and for woman orgasmic dysfunction. Other problems highlighted were muscle weakness, spasticity, loss of libido, and, in the male group, "frigidity" of the partner, illustrating the impact of disability upon the non-disabled partner (Lilius et al., 1976). In a study of sexual functioning amongst women with advanced MS the most common dysfunction was a decrease in sexual desire, which was present in 28 of the 47 participants in the study (Hulter & Lundberg, 1995).

Sexual dysfunction correlates positively with the presence of other disabilities resulting from demyelination, in particular, bladder and bowel symptoms, sensory disturbance of the genitalia, weakness of the pelvic floor, and also spasticity (Hulter & Lundberg, 1995; Valleroy & Kraft, 1984; Vas, 1969). Psychological factors also play a major role in the aetiology of

sexual dysfunction in this group of patients (Bourdette, 1991; Valleroy & Kraft, 1984).

Although at least 50% of people with MS might experience a change in their sex lives, not all are concerned about this and therefore not all will require help. Szasz (1984a) estimates that a minimum of 1 in 4 people with MS will require help. From the perspective of understanding the aetiology of dysfunction, there is a lot to be learned from examining the coping strategies of those individuals and couples who adjust to alterations in their sexual relationship.

Traumatic brain injury (TBI).   Traumatic brain injury is well recognised as causing profound and often destructive effects upon the family and social network (Lezak, 1978, 1988). Increased depression and anxiety in the partner is common and can persist (McKinlay et al., 1981; Oddy et al., 1978; Rosenbaum & Najenson, 1976). Sexual problems following injury are also common, although there is no consistent pattern of sexual dysfunction (Elliott & Beiver, 1996; Garden, 1991). The dysfunctions can result from factors within the individual, within the partner, or within the relationship. Reduced sexual desire and reduced frequency of intercourse can occur. The reasons for this can include fatigue, depression, anxiety, low motivation, lack of a partner, and, in a small number, reduced levels of testosterone (Clark et al., 1988; Elliott & Biever, 1996).

In a study of people who had been admitted to hospital for a minimum of 24 h after a closed head injury over a 15-year period, 50% of the males had scores in the dysfunctional range of a standardised assessment tool of sexual functioning (the Golombok Rust Inventory of Sexual Satisfaction, developed by Rust & Golombok, 1986). The researchers also found that time since injury correlated positively with male sexual dissatisfaction. In the female partners, time since injury correlated with non-communication. Sexual dysfunctions therefore do not appear to resolve with time. The authors comment that early psychological intervention could prevent the deterioration that was evident over time in this study (O'Carroll et al., 1991).

Increased sexual drive can present as a problem following traumatic brain injury, albeit in a smaller proportion of individuals. Patients who present as more sexually demanding postinjury are more likely to have frontal lobe damage (Elliott & Biever, 1996; Sandel et al., 1996). Increased demands might be placed on the partner. There might be inappropriate comments or physical contact with friends, family, or professionals. This can cause great distress, and result in alienation from friends and family. From the perspective of the health-care professional it can lead to the label of a "behaviour problem". It is very important that the brain-injured individual is helped to understand and relearn those aspects of behaviour that are acceptable and those that are not (Strauss, 1991). Partners must be able to raise questions with professionals, such as should they acquiesce with all demands and will saying "No" harm the injured partner?

There is little privacy within a hospital or rehabilitation unit. Masturbation can quickly be labelled a behavioural problem when in fact the individual simply needs to be given the opportunity to have some privacy. Neurological trauma often results in long periods within an institution, whether hospital or rehabilitation centre. Many of the patients are young and therefore at a stage of high interest in sex. Older patients might have been in long-term relationships and perhaps never have had a long period of separation before. Masturbation and fantasy might have played an important role in an individual's sex life prior to injury and can remain important strategies while in hospital or form a new means of dealing with sexual interest and energy while the person is away from his or her partner (Lidster & Horsburgh, 1994). Patients who are masturbating in inappropriate circumstances should be offered privacy in a manner that acknowledges that what they are doing is not abnormal, but requires privacy. A message of "don't do that, it is dirty and perverted" can make patients feel dirty and might further lower an already low self-esteem. Alternatively, it might fuel a behaviour that can be used to manipulate staff by gaining attention. Increased sexual behaviour can make patients very vulnerable, particularly women. It is important to consider safety issues such as sexual abuse, sexually transmitted disease, and pregnancy. Ducharme (1994) comments that much of the attention given to helping with sexuality after head injury has been directed at managing unwanted sexual activity rather than rehabilitating the individual's sex life (Ducharme, 1994).

Parkinson's disease (PD).   Changes in sexual functioning have been observed amongst patients with PD. The cause of the changes is, as one might expect, multifactorial. The onset of a chronic disease, the resultant psychosocial changes, altered mobility, altered self-image, altered role of the partner, drugs, and associated conditions such as depression can all contribute. A study of couples attending a Parkinson's Disease Society residential weekend (the participants were 23 male patients, 11 female patients, 11 male spouse and 27 female spouses) found that over half the male patients and their spouses indicated likely sexual dysfunction as measured by the Golombok Rust Inventory of Sexual Satisfaction (referred to earlier). Over one-third of the female patients indicated a possible problem, although none of their male spouses scored in the problem area. In examining relationship satisfaction, slightly less than half the male patients and slightly over half the female spouses indicated likely marital dissatisfaction, whereas few of the female patients and their spouses scored in the dissatisfaction range (Brown et al., 1990). The discrepancy between male and female perceptions has been evident in other studies (Frank et al., 1978; Hulter & Lundberg, 1995; Rust et al., 1988b). Hypersexuality was not specifically assessed but five female spouses reported excessive demands from their male partners. Whether this was hypersexuality in the male or reduced desire in the woman could not be assessed in this study (Brown et al., 1990).

A study of 25 young people with PD (age range 36–56 years) found a particularly high incidence of an altered sex life in women; 70% of the women described reduced libido, compared with 20% of men. The main conclusion of this study was that health-care professionals should be more aware of the potential for altered sex lives in patients with Parkinson's disease

and be able to discuss this with patients (Wermuth & Stenager, 1995).

There have been a number of reports of increased sexual behaviour amongst PD patients following treatment with L-dopa (Goodwin, 1971; Weinman & Ruskin, 1994). The role of neurotransmitters in human sexuality is complex. Dopaminergic transmission is undoubtedly important as a direct neurotransmitter and through its control of prolactin levels. However, the effect of dopaminergic agents on the sexual drive of PD patients is not consistent. On closer examination of the study results, the heightened sex drive might not be a simple direct drug effect. L-dopa causes an improvement in well-being and this could be sufficient to effect a restoration of sexual interest (Goodwin, 1971). A study of 19 PD patients on L-dopa found three patterns of altered sexual functioning on treatment. One group experienced a general improvement, which included a slight improvement in their sex life depending on age, previous sex life, and availability of a partner. The second pattern was of a specific stimulation of sex drive. This occurred in three men and was transient, despite continuation of the drug. The third pattern was the development of sexual disinhibition in patients who developed an "acute brain syndrome" on treatment (Bowers et al., 1971). Whatever the pattern of altered sexual drive, it could potentially be the source of much distress with the individual and his or her family. Availability of confidential help is therefore important. There are individual case reports of abuse of dopaminergic agents and hypersexuality. For example, with levodopa (Weinman & Ruskin, 1994) and apomorphine (a case treated by the author).

Spinal injury.   Because of the disruption to the functioning of the neural mechanisms responsible for the somatic response to sexual stimulation or interest, spinal cord injury can have a marked effect on sexual functioning. It does not affect sexual drive or interest *per se*, although associated conditions such as depression, psychosocial stress, relationship difficulties, and many of the factors discussed above can influence sexual functioning. The majority of patients who sustain spinal cord injury spend a lengthy period in hospital. During this time they will undergo many sensitive procedures dealing with parts of their body that, under normal circumstances, would be viewed as private or personal. In particular, the genitalia, which previously would have responded to erotic stimuli, now become part of bladder regimes and hygiene programmes. A number of authors talk about the individual with disability being viewed as asexual and progression towards this might begin in hospital (Greengross, 1976; Litvinoff, 1992). In an information sheet about sexuality produced by the Spinal Cord Injury Association the concept of individuals "reclaiming their body" is discussed (Hooper, 1992). This implies taking control and, although help might still be required to undertake some procedures such as catheter changes, the individual is encouraged to take charge of how and when such procedures occur. This is an important concept for the re-establishment of self-esteem, sexuality, and, ultimately, the individual's sex life. Included in this concept is the question of how big a role should a partner play in the caring process? Is dealing with catheters and bowels compatible with being a sexual partner? For some the two roles can be compatible, for others not, in which case help from outside agencies such as care assistants will be essential to facilitate the re-establishment of the dyadic relationship. This applies to many other groups of patients who spend lengthy periods in hospital and who will continue to need care on discharge.

Spinal cord injury is more common amongst men than women and more studies of sexual function in men have been carried out. Erectile and ejaculatory function in the male are determined by the level and completeness of the lesion. From the physiological perspective, sexual dysfunction in women with spinal cord injury is similar to that in men, with the effect on vaginal lubrication and orgasm also depending upon the level and completeness of the lesion (Berard, 1989). Erectile capability can be considered in two parts: (1) reflex erections; (2) psychogenic erections. Amongst patients with complete lesions, reflex erectile capability is more likely to be preserved in high upper motor neurone lesions. The incidence ranges from 100% erectile capability in cervical groups to no erectile capability in some patients with lower thoracic lesions, particularly if they were of lower motor neurone type (Bors & Comarr, 1960; Higgins, 1979). Psychogenic erections are more likely to be preserved in incomplete lesions. In a small proportion of patients, psychogenic erections can be preserved in the absence of reflex erections. This suggests the possibility of a different mechanism of erection, and this is borne out by animal work (Bancroft, 1989; Bors & Comarr, 1960; Higgins, 1979).

Ejaculatory ability is more susceptible to damage in spinal injury. Again, capability is correlated with the completeness and level of the injury. The incidence of ejaculation varies from 0% to 4% in patients with complete upper motor neurone lesions to 32% in incomplete upper motor neurone lesions and 70% in incomplete lower motor neurone lesions (Bors & Comarr, 1960; Higgins, 1979). In patients with complete lesions above T6, autonomic dysreflexia can be triggered if ejaculation is achieved (see Chapter 44). Patients are taught how to manage this condition as part of their general postspinal-cord-injury education programme. The advice in this situation is to stop, check that there is no other trigger such as a full bladder, sit up, and obtain help if the headache that accompanies autonomic dysreflexia persists. Just prior to ejaculation, individuals might notice an increase in spasticity with a marked reduction in tone postejaculation, which can persist for several hours (Bors & Comarr, 1960).

Fertility is reduced in the male postspinal injury. It is important that this is discussed early in the rehabilitation process so that questions about subsequent fertility can be addressed or returned to at a later date if the patient so wishes. Optimum bladder management is important to maintain sperm quality (Rutkowski et al., 1995). For women, there might be an interruption of the menstrual cycle immediately postinjury, but this returns to normal with time. With the return to an active sex life there is a risk of pregnancy, even if the menstrual cycle does not appear to have been fully re-established. Contraceptive advice should therefore be available. Spinal injury is not a contraindication to pregnancy and fertility is largely unaffected in women. Antenatal care is best provided through a department with experience of providing obstetric care to women with spinal cord injuries or with close liaison between the spinal injury unit and obstetric team. There is some increased risk of pressure sores and urinary tract infection during pregnancy and a risk of autonomic dysreflexia in those with lesions above T6 (McCuniff & Dewan, 1984; Robertson & Guttman, 1963). However, with appropriate care, pregnancy can be managed successfully.

Despite the major disruption of normal physiological function following spinal cord injury, individuals can establish fulfilling sex lives with their partners (Kreuter et al., 1994; Harrison et al., 1995). Because of the altered sensory perception below the level of the lesion, spinal-cord-injured patients can find that other areas of their body become sensitive to erotic stimuli. Individuals and their partners need to explore and communicate to re-establish their sex life. The importance of offering information to patients after injury and giving permission to discuss sex is emphasised by many authors (Cole et al., 1973; Courtois et al., 1995; Ide & Ogata, 1995). Newly injured spinal-injury patients have indicated that one of their early concerns was in sexual functioning. Evidence suggests that the outcome is better if sex is approached early rather than late in the rehabilitation process. "A critical factor . . . is the early acknowledgement to the patient and family that sex related problems occur as a consequence of most spinal cord injuries" (Miller et al., 1981).

The non-disabled partner

Masters and Johnson (1966) observed that there is no such thing as an uninvolved partner. Yet it is easy to forget about the partner as an equal in the dyadic relationship during the process of rehabilitation of the neurologically disabled individual. The emotions that the partner can experience in response to the disability have been listed as fear, anxiety, pity, shame, anger, helplessness, hopelessness, loneliness, depression, worry, and sadness (Hartman et al., 1983). To these can be added resentment, guilt, confusion, and, at times, despair. While struggling through this turmoil of emotions the partner must face the expectations of the community to nurture, understand, and care for the disabled individual (Hartman et al., 1983). These feelings and cognitions can have a detrimental effect both on the physiological and psychological processes of sexual expression and the functioning of the relationship.

As part of the rehabilitation process, the partner might be drawn into a caring and supportive role that can generate feelings of confusion regarding how he or she functions as a sexual partner. Alternatively, the partner might be excluded from the rehabilitation process and be left feeling alone and forgotten (Neumann, 1979). Professionals in rehabilitation have to guard against making assumptions about the degree and nature of involvement that relatives would like in the rehabilitation and caring process.

A common complaint from the partner of a brain-injured person is "he/she is not the person I knew before". After brain injury, this is not the person he or she chose as their sexual partner, the person with whom they wished to spend the rest of their lives, and with whom they could lower their defences and become vulnerable within the act of making love. Such thoughts can progress to feelings of aversion, which can in turn trigger feelings of guilt as well as contributing to the high frequency of anxiety and depression amongst partners. Changes in the behavioural aspects of functioning are the most damaging to interpersonal relationships (Liss & Willer, 1990; McKinlay et al., 1981; O'Carroll et al., 1991; Oddy et al., 1978; Rosenbaum & Najenson, 1976). In a study of the wives of soldiers injured during military service, it was found that there was a marked reduction in sexual activity amongst those couples where the husband had sustained a spinal or brain injury compared with non-disabled couples. In the case of those with spinal injury this was because of the altered physiology but, where the husband had a brain injury, wives reported a feeling of dislike towards physical contact with their husbands (Rosenbaum & Najenson, 1976).

If the needs of the partner are not taken into account then treatment of sexual dysfunction in the disabled individual can fail. For example, a patient with erectile dysfunction can be treated and potency restored. But if his partner is unable to respond to him sexually because of the problems discussed above, then the treatment has failed, because it has not restored the individual's sex life with his partner. Indeed, as Vermote and Peuskins (1996) describe, this scenario could challenge the "brittle equilibrium" based on nursing that now holds the relationship together. The only way to move forward in this setting is to focus on the issues for each partner and the relationship, if they are willing to do this.

The relationship

Sexual expression within an intimate relationship represents an important declaration of commitment and trust. Dysfunctions can occur independently or alongside each other, and can also represent a complex interaction with cause and effect operating in both directions (Hartman, 1980; Hopper & Dryden, 1991; Kaplan, 1974; Sager, 1976). Similar negative emotions occur in couples seeking help for sexual difficulties and those seeking relationship therapy, and these differ significantly from couples not experiencing these problems (Zimmer, 1983). Zimmer (1987), in a fascinating experimental study, found that offering couples marital therapy prior to sex therapy resulted in a more pronounced and persistent sexual improvement, as well as in a better marital adjustment. In addition, although sexual dissatisfaction decreased after marital therapy, little generalisation was found from treatment of the sexual symptoms to marital satisfaction. From a treatment or management viewpoint, it was emphasised that clinicians should evaluate the functioning of the relationship at the start of therapy.

Many stresses exist to challenge the dyadic relationship, such as financial insecurity, unemployment, and concerns about children. Disability can be a confounding factor when eliciting the main area of concern. One study amongst people with MS found

that of those participants who felt their relationship had deteriorated over the years all attributed the change to the disease, whereas those whose relationships had fluctuated attributed this to general stressful events rather than to the MS (Rodgers & Calder, 1990). Financial worries and unemployment are recognised as posing major threats to the stability of relationships amongst people with disability and are, of course, associated with the presence of disability (Abrams, 1981; Martin & White, 1988; Szasz et al., 1984b; Townsend et al., 1988).

The acquisition of disability impacts upon a relationship in a number of ways. The balance of power can be disturbed. The most commonly occurring scenario is where the male partner is the principal wage earner and the female partner runs the home and plays the major role in child-rearing. If the male partner becomes disabled and unable to work, the following changes can occur: He is now at home and must explore what tasks he can undertake within the home or look to recreational pursuits, attendance at a day centre, etc; he intrudes on his partner's daily routine and accepted tasks; his partner must now decide whether to pursue a principal caring role or return to work—either way, her lifestyle and previous commitments undergo significant change; financially, the couple will be less well off and this financial strain can further compromise the already challenged relationship. The dynamics of the relationship have been turned upside down and this can trigger feelings of resentment, isolation, loneliness, anger, bereavement, and sadness.

A change in lifestyle for one partner can highlight problems that have existed within the relationship for some time. A couple who have led independent lives with little communication will suddenly be forced to spend a considerable amount of time together. Previously, one partner might have questioned whether or not the relationship should continue. However, with joint investment in a house, commitment to children, and independent interests, the advantages of staying together might have outweighed those of leaving, and each partner maintained free choice. With one partner disabled, this delicate and vulnerable situation is challenged. Social and family pressures can exist to encourage the partners to stay together, as the able-bodied member is now needed in a caring role. The dynamics of the rather shaky relationship have now changed to carer and cared for. One partner, or the couple, might present with sexual problems but these cannot be resolved without first addressing the much greater issues and the prognosis for restoring an enjoyable sex life in this case setting is often poor.

The dyadic relationship is an important institution in the management of disability. Dysfunction within the relationship can cause considerable emotional distress and can contribute to psychiatric and physical illness and many practical difficulties. Some relationships are known to be more at risk than others, in particular those where one partner has a progressive condition (Halvorsen & Metz, 1992), where the relationship was formed prior to the onset of the disability (De Loach & Greer, 1981), and where there is sexual dysfunction (Chandler & Brown, 1998). Indeed, Chandler and Brown concluded from their study of 70 people with neurological disability that any service designed to address sexual problems should also address relationship issues.

Different perceptions of men and women

A study by Frank et al. (1978) found no significant difference between wives' perceptions of their husbands' dysfunction and the husbands' reported dysfunction. However, the husbands tended to underestimate the occurrence of sexual dysfunction in their wives. For example, 33% of women had difficulty maintaining excitement but only 15% of their partners thought they had this problem ($p < .01$). A similar discrepancy was seen in Brown's study of Parkinson's disease patients (Brown et al., 1990).

It appears that women take part in sexual activity not always because they wish to, and this can reflect a difficulty in communication within the relationship. In a study of women with advanced MS, when asked how frequently they would have liked to have intercourse 13 of the 47 said they would have preferred not to have intercourse at all (Hulter & Lundberg, 1995).

Individuals without a sexual partner

People can present for sexual help when they are not in a current relationship. There might be concern about forming a relationship, masturbation, or the possibility of sexual dysfunction. Individuals might wish to discuss how they could overcome sexual difficulties, should they occur in a relationship. There could be practical concerns about meeting people, particularly if mobility is compromised. There might be anger, sadness, or resentment about the break-up of a relationship. The role of the disability in the failed relationship might need exploration. Low self-esteem is a frequently expressed phenomenon when there has been a failed relationship and a disability can exacerbate this. Therapy exploring an individual's concept of sexual expression and sexuality can be helpful and this can be done successfully either on a one-to-one basis or in a group setting (Zilbergeld, 1975).

Adolescents with physical disabilities

Adolescence is a time of exploration. The individual experiences changes in body habitus and changes in emotions and interests. Peer group pressure to conform can be very strong. With regard to sexuality, there are clear messages from the media that those who find long-lasting love and romance are athletic and beautiful, with not a wheelchair or blemish in sight. Many other myths about the human sex life contribute to a significant number of the sexual problems, which occur throughout adult life. Adolescence is an appropriate time to dispel these myths. For example that:

- The size of the penis and the tightness of the vagina determine the amount of pleasure a couple will experience when making love.
- Physical contact must always lead to sexual expression.

- Sexual activity should always involve sexual intercourse.
- Sexual activity involves a fixed path, which should always end in earth-moving simultaneous orgasm.
- A man cannot be in love and fail to get an erection with his partner.
- Men should know instinctively how to be sexually competent.
- Sex must be natural and spontaneous.
- "Handicapped people have no sexual needs or desires . . . or have perverted or excessive sexual desires."

There are many more myths, all of which can lead to unrealistic expectations and a cycle of failure (Cole et al. 1973; Giurguis, 1991; Spence, 1991; Stanley, 1981b; Zilbergeld, 1978). Sex education is extremely important and should be available not only through childhood but in adult life as well (Morgan et al., 1995). Programmes of sex education have to be flexible enough to allow young people to raise specific concerns. Expert advice might be needed about relationships, practical aspects of making love, contraception, continence, and genetic counselling. An important issue to discuss in the context of sex education is the possibility of abuse and how to deal with the threat of abuse (Morgan et al., 1995). Some health-care professionals might have difficulty in discussing these issues, and this reflects a lack of training in dealing with this area of life (Sawyer, 1996). This can result in further problems for the patient (Cole et al., 1973): "In some cases the physician's personal anxieties regarding sexuality make him virtually inaccessible to the patient who wishes to seek advice on this subject. The subtly rebuffed patient cannot distinguish between the physician's discomfort and the appropriateness of his sexually oriented questions or needs".

MANAGEMENT OF SEX AND RELATIONSHIP DYSFUNCTIONS WITHIN NEUROLOGICAL REHABILITATION

There is no doubt that sex and relationship problems occur, that they are common, and that they respond to treatment. Such frequently occurring dysfunction in any other area of health care would indicate an urgent need for assessment and treatment facilities, and perhaps a screening programme as well. Why not for this area of dysfunction? The apparent reticence in addressing these needs stems from a number of concerns:

1. Do patients want to discuss sex and relationship issues. Will they see questions on these subjects as an unnecessary intrusion into their private lives? Many authors have formed the opinion that health-care professionals should be proactive in offering information and help (Cole et al., 1973; Miller et al., 1981; Szasz, 1991). Patients might be too shy to approach health-care personnel about sexual problems for fear of such questions being seen as inappropriate. There is often a great sense of relief when they understand that this area of life can be discussed. The individual might not have any specific concerns at that time but, having been given permission to discuss sex, they might contact the professional at a later date.

Questions about sexual functioning can be included in a general rehabilitation history. Patients who do not wish to talk about their sex life can easily move on to the next issue to be discussed. Szasz (1991) identifies some useful screening questions such as, "Have you any sexual concerns?" or "Many people with your disability report difficulties with some aspect of their sexual lives. What have been your experiences?" The enquiry and the implicit permission to discuss sexual issues can in itself be therapeutic (Annon, 1976; Szasz et al., 1984b). Particular circumstances can cause the patient anxiety. For example, a patient without a partner might be worried about how to start exploring his or her sexuality (Beckers & Abel, 1983). By giving permission to discuss sex, the clinician can facilitate the patient in voicing their concerns.

2. Whose role is it to address these issues?   Within rehabilitation, patients have contact with a wide range of professionals from different disciplines. An individual might establish a particularly trusting relationship with one member of the team. This team member might be the person to whom the patient will first confide their sexual difficulties. Many problems can be dealt with by giving the patient an opportunity to voice concerns, and they do not all require expert counselling or therapy. Sufficient familiarity with sex and relationship issues to allow the professional to feel comfortable when a patient presents a problem is, therefore, necessary to achieve the goal of holistic care within rehabilitation. For more complex issues there must be a system of referral to someone experienced in sexual counselling or therapy. The PLISSIT model (which is discussed later) of approaching sex and relationship problems allows flexibility depending on the skill and experience of the professional concerned.

3. Is it a health issue?   Sexuality is part of health. The effects of disease and disability upon sexual functioning were illustrated earlier. Sexual and relationship dysfunction can be secondary to, or a contributor to, other disease processes. Sexuality therefore has to be considered as part of the overall management of the patient. Problems in sexual and indeed relationship functioning can be investigated, an aetiology determined, and treatment planned as with other aspects of health care.

4. Is it a rehabilitation issue?   Services are already in existence for the general population to assess and treat sexual and relationship problems, e.g. Relate (see the list of useful addresses at the end of this chapter), professionals trained in psychosexual medicine, and trained sex therapists. People with disabilities are welcome to access any of these services. However, these therapists might not have the level of expertise necessary to deal with the specific issues generated by neurological disability. It is well recognised that the aetiology of many dysfunctions is multifactorial (Bancroft, 1993; Brown et al., 1990). A large number of the factors that can trigger dysfunction in the disabled population act in the population at large but there is an equally large number of factors specific to those with neurological disability. It is therefore appropriate that the individual or couple talk to someone who understands the nature of neurological disease and disability. The need for understanding of specific conditions

such as spasticity, pain, and the psychosocial impact of disability is illustrated in the examples of the problems encountered by specific patient groups given above.

SPOD is a national organisation that aims to help the sexual problems of people with disabilities (see list of useful addresses). It is London based and produces literature and runs a telephone help-line. The organisation has given help to a very large number of clients over the years. It does not, however, obviate the need for a local service that patients can access face to face.

5. The professional might be reticent to discuss such a sensitive issue for fear of causing offence or distress.   Professionals might have their own fears and embarrassment about sexuality. Lack of training in sexual medicine and how to deal with relationship issues contribute to the difficulties that professionals face (Finger et al., 1992; Sawyer, 1996; Weston, 1993).

P-LI-SS-IT

The P-LI-SS-IT model (Annon, 1976) of approaching both sex and relationship problems can be applied within the context of neurological rehabilitation. It has been described as a hierarchical model, with the depth of interaction depending upon the skill and experience of the professional concerned (Annon, 1976; Dupont, 1995; Seidl et al., 1991). The key to approaching problems of sexual functioning and relationship conflict is for the professional to develop a trusting and permission-giving rapport with the patient. Counselling skills encompassing empathy, and unconditional positive regard can be used to good effect in this context.

P: Permission.   Giving patients permission to discuss sexual problems can involve simply creating a trusting and confidential relationship in which patients can express their concerns. A number of authors suggest that the professional should initiate discussion. They explain that patients who have experienced a major illness, operation, or acquisition of disability are often hoping to be asked whether they have concerns about sex but are too reticent to initiate the discussion (Weston, 1993; Young, 1984).

Individuals can sort out their difficulties by discussing them with a professional who will listen. They might need "permission" to explore a different pattern of sex life. Changing the time at which they make love to accommodate the fatigue of neurological conditions can require a lot of readjustment at a stage when many other aspects of life are undergoing change. One partner, often the female, might seek "permission" to initiate love making in the relationship where the male partner always took the lead previously. Other individuals or couples might wish to discuss oral sex, masturbation, or the use of aids to sexual pleasure. An individual might seek permission to decline sexual activity if his or her partner has become too demanding. The professional, although acknowledging his or her own beliefs and value systems, must remain open and non-judgemental so as to listen and advise where necessary.

LI: Limited information.   Giving information to patients and their partners can address concerns or give reassurance that can restore confidence in their sex life. Stanley (1987) lists ignorance, cultural taboos and myths, poor communication skills, and unrealistic expectations as some of the causes of sexual problems. It is important to ascertain from the individual or couple exactly what their concerns are and what these concerns are based upon. There might be myths about sexual functioning that are deeply ingrained from childhood; there might be ignorance about the newly acquired disability and whether it is safe to have sex. Information could have been misinterpreted in the past, leading to further false beliefs and distress. An explanation of the reasons for altered physical functioning or behaviour change can prevent misinterpretation by the other partner. It can also be helpful to discuss the types of treatment available for specific dysfunctions and to give patients the opportunity to decide whether they wish to pursue a particular treatment option or deal with their dysfunction in a different way.

SS: Specific suggestions.   Following the establishment of a full history, often supported by an examination and possibly laboratory tests, suggestions can be offered about treatment. This could include drugs, counselling, behavioural therapy, or offering more specific information. Referral to another agency such as Relate (see list of useful addresses); Clinical psychology or Urology could be indicated at this stage.

IT: Intensive therapy.   At this stage, skilled treatment with a trained sex therapist is indicated. The number of patients requiring help at this level of the P-LI-SS-IT model is small.

TREATMENT

The approach when offering help to patients with sexual difficulties is very similar to that taken when dealing with other issues. As part of taking the history, it is essential to ascertain the goals patients have for their sex life. It is as important in this, as in any other aspect of health care, that assumptions are not made about an individual. Arriving at the wrong conclusion about what information a patient actually wants can be distressing and damaging (Young, 1984). Patients might need to mourn the loss of their previous sex life before they can look at new means of sexual expression given their disability (Becker & Abel, 1983). Help can be required to assist the grieving process. There could be other emotions concerned with the disability, which need to be acknowledged either before or along-side the treatment programme for the sexual dysfunction.

The examination of the patient with a sexual dysfunction can be a therapeutic as well as an investigative procedure. This is emphasised by the Institute of Psychosexual Medicine, in its training programme for clinicians. During an examination, patients can give a clear indication about how they feel about their body. They might be ashamed or indicate the distress that the changes of disability have produced. Comments about whether or not parts of the body are too big, too small, or "not right" can offer insight into the patient's true concerns. For women, the genital area is largely hidden from view and there are often misconceptions about the genitalia. It can be very helpful to allow a woman to examine her vagina and use a mirror to see her perineum. Again, it is important not to make assumptions, so that even if a woman has successfully used intermittent self-catheterisation since childhood she might still have little knowledge of her genital area in relation to sex. Non-consummation of relationships because of ignorance still occurs.

EXAMPLES OF SPECIFIC DYSFUNCTIONS AND PROBLEMS

Erectile dysfunction

Impotence, "the persistent failure to develop erections of sufficient rigidity for penetrative sexual intercourse" (Kirby, 1994) is common. At the age of 40 years, 2% of men can experience this and, by the age of 65 years, 25–30% of men experience impotence (Kirby, 1994). It is a frequently occurring problem amongst people with neurological disability, especially those with spinal cord injury, MS, and rarer conditions such as multisystem atrophy.

Treatment of erectile dysfunction can be divided into groups, depending to some extent on the underlying cause:

Drugs.   The intracavernosal injection of drugs, such as phenoxybenzamine or papaverine, to produce an erection was established some years ago (Brindley, 1986a,b). The pharmacological effect of these substances is to produce a dilatation of the arterioles resulting in an influx of blood into the cavernosal tissue, so producing an erection. Patients with a neurological cause to their sexual dysfunction were noted to be particularly sensitive to papaverine. Although widely used, the early drugs (papaverine and phentolamine) were never licensed for use. Prostaglandin E1 (Alprostadil) has now been licensed for use in the treatment of erectile dysfunction and, although expensive, was the drug of first choice until the more recent addition of an effective oral medication. Patients or their partners can be taught the technique of intacavernosal injection. The main side-effect, particularly with the older drugs, was a prolonged erection and patients must be warned that if the erection has not subsided in 4 h it will require formal detumescence. With Alprostadil, this is a much less common complication. Alprostadil can also be given by the simpler urethral route (Nathan et al., 1997), a mode of administration that requires less manual dexterity but is less effective in some patients, particularly those who regularly manage their bladder by clean intermittent self-catheterisation. In 1998, Sildenafil the first oral treatment of erectile dysfunction, was licensed for use in the United Kingdom. It appears to be effective and has a low incidence of side-effects, but is absolutely contraindicated in patients on nitrate therapy (Boolell et al., 1996; *Drugs and Therapeutics Bulletin*, 1998; Goldstein et al., 1998). Concern about the potential cost of treating erectile failure has resulted in a great deal of debate and controversy about the National Health Service provision of such treatments. Patients with certain specified diagnoses are entitled to receive NHS treatment; these include MS, spinal injury and Parkinson's syndromes. Patients with erectile failure due to factors other than those on the list, including psychogenic causes, can obtain a private prescription from their GP. Drugs can be a valuable adjunct to the treatment of psychogenic erectile dysfunction (Williams et al., 1987). The restoration of potency reduces the anxiety about performance and can allow normal erectile function to recover. It is essential that drugs form only part of the treatment. Counselling, to a lesser or greater extent, is important for all those embarking on drug treatment. It is also very important that the partner is happy about the treatment because, if not, although the pharmacological and physiological response might be achieved the ultimate goal of a restored sex life might not occur. Drugs will assist potency but will not by themselves solve a relationship dysfunction.

Mechanical treatment.   The vacuum device allows an erection to be achieved by creating a mechanical vacuum around the penis, which encourages venous blood to pool in the penis. The erection is then held in place by a ring, which must be removed after intercourse. This has the advantage of not involving drugs, but is considered rather bulky and intrusive by some couples.

Penile prostheses.   The original prosthesis was a semi-rigid silastic rod, which gave a permanent erection. More sophisticated models are now available that allow the erection to be created when required and then deflated. It is essential that careful counselling is undertaken prior to accepting a patient for surgery. This very major step implies that the professionals involved accept the view that good sex requires an erect penis and that erectile function can be equated with masculinity and potency (Bancroft, 1989). A very small proportion of patients opt for this treatment.

Other methods.   Counselling (either individual or couples counselling), psychosexual medicine, and cognitive behavioural therapy are all valuable alternative or complementary treatments. Patients with neurological conditions often require a combination of physical and psychological treatment.

An effective approach to treatment is to present the individual or, ideally, the couple with the available options, giving written as well as verbal information, and then arrange to see them again after they have had the opportunity to discuss the options at home.

Pain and spasticity

Perineal dysaesthesia can be a distressing cause of superficial dyspareunia, particularly in women. It responds well with treatment for neurogenic pain, such as amitriptyline or carbamazepine. Whenever a woman presents with dyspareunia she must be examined to exclude other causes of the symptoms and, if there is doubt about possible pelvic pathology, referral for a gynaecology opinion is indicated. Because of the focus of health-care professionals on the disability, it is easy to overlook the standard screening tests that are recommended for women. This presents a good opportunity to check that cervical smear tests are up to date and that the woman knows how to undertake breast self-examination.

Spasticity of the lower limbs can cause problems with sexual intercourse. Treatment with either drugs or injection of specific muscle groups, such as the adductors, with botulinum toxin can improve this considerably.

Anxiety

As discussed earlier, performance anxiety commonly accompanies sexual problems. Masters and Johnson (1966) established a technique for reducing anxiety in sexual expression, and this sensate focus programme is now widely used to good effect in many settings. It has been adapted from the original description, which was very time consuming and intensive, and can be undertaken from an out-patient setting. It is a valuable adjunct to treatment even when the diagnosis has been of an organic problem, e.g. erectile failure due to spinal cord injury where the first-line of treatment might be intracavernosal injection.

Couples require time and guidance to allow them to enjoy their sex life again without anxiety. At the heart of the sensate focus programme is communication. Couples have to talk and listen to each other. They must monitor their own feelings throughout the programme and each individual must communicate their likes and dislikes to his or her partner. Avoidance of the spectator role is emphasised. Anxiety is diffused by setting strict boundaries in the love making over which each partner must not stray. The couple meet with the therapist or clinician at regular intervals and, depending on their progress with regard to diffusing anxiety, they are permitted to move further through the sexual response cycle. If anxiety surfaces at any stage they move back to a previous stage. At all stages they must communicate and, if anxiety returns, they move back down again. This programme, with its emphasis on communication, can help in relationship problems and can also be helpful where penetrative sex is not a possibility and new means of sexual fulfilment must be found. More details of the sensate focus programme can be found in texts such as Bancroft's *Human sexuality and its problems.*

A valuable concept in therapy is that of the ladder (Stanley, 1981a). Each individual has his or her own sexual response ladder, which stretches from no sexual thoughts at the lowest point to orgasm and resolution at the top. Individuals can climb as far as they wish up the ladder in sexual expression and they do not have to "aim for the top". Individuals also do not have to arrive at the same points of the sexual response cycle or the same rung of the ladder at the same time.

Lack of communication

Lack of communication often lies at the heart of relationship dysfunction. Hidden emotions such as fear, resentment, and anger can obstruct the functioning of the dyad. Using the P-LI-SS-IT model, and giving the couple permission to voice their concerns, can be of great benefit. Where the problems are deeply rooted, referral to a couple's counsellor might be required. The rehabilitation professional is ideally placed to help the couple explore how the disability has impacted on the functioning of their relationship and to look at practical ways in which help might alleviate some of the stressful factors.

FERTILITY

No discussion of sexuality is complete without consideration of the possible outcome of sexual activity. It is easy to forget that, once sex is resumed, there is a chance of pregnancy. If the couple are planning pregnancy they might require information about fertility and methods of assisted conception, especially in the case of a man with spinal cord disease or spinal cord injury. For women with spinal cord injury and other neurological conditions fertility might be unimpaired but the pregnancy could create some practical difficulties. Although these can be overcome, it is helpful if the individual can be prepared for them. Women who walk with some difficulty might prefer to use a chair in the later stages of pregnancy and in the early postpartum period. Fatigue, which is so common after traumatic brain injury or in MS, will be exacerbated by the demands of a young baby. With forward planning extra help can be organised. Having recognised and prepared for this, there is no sense of failure when it happens.

CONTRACEPTION

Patients should be encouraged to discuss issues of contraception or fertility with either their GP or Family Planning Clinic (FPC). Some methods, such as the IUCD, are contraindicated in paraplegia because of the lack of abdominal sensation should a problem arise. Some oral contraceptives are contraindicated where there is a risk of thromboembolism. Reduced manual dexterity might preclude the use of barrier methods such as the diaphragm or condoms. If the patient is willing, liaison with, for example the FPC not only allows the rehabilitation issues to be discussed but also enables a pooling of information and resources. An excellent review of contraception has been written by John Guillebaud (1999).

SUMMARY

Sex is a fundamental part of every individual. It is given its most intense expression within the dyadic relationship. The complexity of this system is such that it is subject to physical, psychological, and social stresses that can cause a major disruption of function. Sex is recognised as something intensely personal and there are many myths surrounding sexual expression. There is implicit pressure to achieve a norm of sexual expression, which might be inappropriate for an individual who has experienced major change such as the acquisition of disability. The so-called norms that are being aimed at could well be part of the myths generated by the media and peer group.

It is recognised that the marital dyad might constitute "the most important social context within which the psychological aspects of chronic illness are managed" (Rodgers & Calder, 1990). Accepting this fact emphasises the importance of supporting couples through the changes in their relationship that are an inevitable accompaniment to the acquisition of disease or disability. Sager (1976) states that, "The goal of marital therapy . . . is not simply or necessarily to make the relationship work but to foster the growth of two individuals by harnessing the forces within the marital system and directing them towards constructive ends". Sex and relationship therapy should, therefore, be part of the holistic care within neurological rehabilitation.

REFERENCES

Abrams KS (1981) The impact on marriages of adult onset paraplegia. *Paraplegia 19*: 253–259

Annon JS (1976) *The behavioural treatment of sexual problems: brief therapy*. Harper and Row, New York

Bancroft J (1989) *Human sexuality and its problems*. Churchill Livingstone, Edinburgh

Bancroft J (1993) Impact of environment, stress, occupational, and other hazards on sexuality and sexual behavior. *Environmental Health Perspectives Supplements 101*(suppl 2): 101–107

Bancroft J, Coles L (1976) Three years' experience in a sexual problem clinic. *British Medical Journal 1*: 1575–1577

Beck RO (1999) Physiology of male sexual function and dysfunction in neurologic disease. In *Neurology of bladder, bowel and sexual dysfunction* (Ed Fowler CJ), Chapter 5. Butterworth Heinemann, New York

Becker JB, Abel GG (1983) Sex and disability: Treatment issues. *Behavioural Medicine Update 4*(4): 15–20

Berard EJJ (1989) The sexuality of spinal cord injured women: Physiology and pathophysiology. A review. *Paraplegia 27*: 99–112

Blake DJ, Maisiak R, Alarcon GS, Holley HL, Brown S (1987) Sexual quality of life of patients with arthritis compared to arthritis free controls. *Journal of Rheumatology 14*: 570–575

Boolell M, Gepi-Attee S, Gingell JC, Allen MJ (1996) Sildenafil, a novel effective oral therapy for male erectile dysfunction. *British Journal of Urology 78*: 257–261

Bors E, Comarr AE (1960) Neurological disturbances of sexual function with special reference to 529 patients with spinal cord injury. *Urological Survey 10*: 191–222

Bourdette DN (1991) Bladder, bowels and sexual dysfunction in multiple sclerosis. In *Multiple sclerosis: Current status of research and treatment* (Eds Herndon RM, Seil FJ), Chapter 14. Demos Publications, New York

Bowers MB, Woert MV, Davis L (1971) Sexual behaviour during L-dopa treatment for Parkinsonism. *American Journal of Psychiatry 127*: 1691–1693

Brindley GS (1986a) Maintenance treatment of erectile impotence by cavernosal unstriated muscle relaxant injection. *British Journal of Psychiatry 149*: 210–215

Brindley GS (1986b) Pilot experiments on the actions of drugs injected into the human corpus cavernosus penis. *British Journal Pharmacology 87*: 495–500

Brown RG, Jahanshahi M, Quinn N, Marsden CD (1990) Sexual function in patients with Parkinson's disease and their partners. *Journal of Neurological and Neurosurgical Psychiatry 53*: 480–486

Castree BJ (1979) *A study of young people with spina bifida*. Thesis, University of Newcastle upon Tyne

Chandler BJ, Brown S (1998) Sex and relationship dysfunction in neurological disability. *Journal of Neurological and Neurosurgical Psychiatry 65*: 877–880

Clark JDA, Raggett PR, Edwards OM (1988) Hypothalamic hypgonadism following major head injury. *Clinical Endocrinology 29*: 153–165

Cole TM, Chilgren R, Rosenberg P (1973) A new programme of sex education and counselling for spinal cord injured adults and health care professionals. *Paraplegia 11*: 111–124

Cotgrove AJ, Kolvin I (1996) Child sexual abuse. *Hospital Update 22*: 401–406

Courtois FJ, Charvier KF, Leriche A, Raymond DP, Eyssette M (1995) Clinical approach to erectile dysfunction in spinal cord injured men. A review of clinical and experimental data. *Paraplegia 33*: 628–635

De Loach C, Greer BG (1981) *Adjustment to severe physical disability: A metamorphosis.* McGraw Hill, New York

Drugs and Therapeutics Bulletin (1998) Sildenafil for erectile dysfunction. *Drugs and Therapeutics Bulletin 36*: (11): 81–84

Ducharme S (1994) Providing sexuality services in head injury rehabilitation centres: Issues in staff training. *International Journal of Adolescent Medicine & Health 7*: 179–191

Dupont S (1995) Multiple sclerosis and sexual functioning – a review. *Clinical Rehabilitation 9*: 135–141

Elliott ML, Biever LS (1996) Head injury and sexual dysfunction. *Brain Injury 10*: 703–717

Finger WW, Hall ES, Peterson FL (1992) Education in sexuality for nurses. *Sexuality and Disability 10*: 81–89

Frank E, Anderson C, Rubenstein D (1978) Frequency of sexual dysfunction in 'normal' couples. *New England Journal of Medicine 299*: 111–115

Garden FH (1991) Incidence of sexual dysfunction in neurologic disability. *Sexuality and Disability 9*: 39–47

Goffman E (1963) *Stigma.* Penguin Books, Middlesex

Goldstein I, Lue TF, Padma-Nathan H, Rosen RC, Steers WD, Wicker PA (1998) Oral sildenafil in the treatment of erectile dysfunction. *New England Journal of Medicine 338*: 1397–1404

Goodwin FK (1971) Behavioural effects of L-dopa in man. *Seminars in Psychiatry 3*(4): 477–491

Greengross W (1976) *Entitled to love.* National Fund for Research into Crippling Diseases, Mallaby Press, London

Guillebaud J (1999) *Contraception, your questions answered.* Elsevier Health Sciences, New York

Guirgius W (1991) Sex therapy with couples. In *Couple therapy. A handbook* (Eds Hooper D, Dryden W), pp. 138–164. Open University Press, Buckingham

Halvorsen JG, Metz ME (1991) Sexual dysfunction, part 1: Classification, aetiology and pathogenesis. *Journal of the Applied Board of Family Practice 5*: B51–61

Halvorsen JG, Metz ME (1992) Sexual dysfunction, part 2: Diagnosis, management and prognosis. *Journal of the Applied Board of Family Practice 5*(2): 177–192

Harrison J, Glass CA, Owens RG, Soni BM (1995) Factors associated with sexual functioning in women following spinal cord injury. *Paraplegia 33*: 687–692

Hartman LM (1980) The interface between sexual dysfunction and marital conflict. *American Journal of Psychiatry 137*: 576–579

Hartman C, MacIntosh B, Englehardt B (1983) The neglected and forgotten sexual partner of the physically disabled. *Social Work 28*: 370–374

Higgins GE (1979) Sexual response in spinal cord injured adults: A review. *Archives of Sexual Behaviour 8*: 173–196

Hooper M (1992) *Spinal cord injured men and sexuality.* Spinal Injuries Association, London

Hooper D, Dryden W (1991) *Couple therapy. A handbook.* Open University Press, Buckingham

Hulter BM, Lundberg PO (1995) Sexual function in women with advanced MS. *Journal of Neurological Neurosurgical Psychiatry 83*: 83–86

Humphrey M (1985) Sexual consequences of cerebral vascular accident. *Journal of the Royal Society of Medicine 78*: 338–390

Ide M, Ogata H (1995) Sexual activities and concerns in persons with spinal cord injuries. *Paraplegia 33*: 334–337

Kaplan HS (1974) *The new sex therapy.* Ballière Tindall, London

Kirby RS (1994) Impotence: Diagnosis and management of male erectile dysfunction. *British Medical Journal 308*: 957–961

Kreuter M, Sullivan M, Siosteen A (1994) Sexual adjustment after spinal cord injury (SCI) focusing on partner experiences. *Paraplegia 32*: 225–235

Larson JL, McNaughton MW, Wrad Kennedy W, Mansfield LW (1980) Heart rate and blood pressure responses to sexual activity and a stair climbing test. *Heart and Lung 9*: 1025–1030

Lezak MD (1978) Living with the characterologically altered brain injured patient. *Journal of Clinical Psychiatry 39*: 592–599

Lezak MD (1988) Brain damage is a family affair. *Journal of Clinical and Experimental Neuropsychology 10*: 111–123

Lidster CA, Horsburgh ME (1994) Masturbation – beyond myth and taboo. *Nursing Forum 29*: 18–27

Lilius HG, Valtonen EJ, Wikstrom J (1976) Sexual problems in patients suffering from multiple sclerosis. *Journal of Chronic Diseases 29*: 643–647

Liss M, Willer B (1990) Traumatic brain injury and marital relationships: A literaure review. *International Journal of Rehabilitation Research 13*: 309–320

Litvinoff S (1992) *The Relate guide to sex in loving relationships.* Vermillion, London

Lundberg PO (1999) Physiology of female sexual function and effect of neurologic disease. In *Neurology of bladder, bowel and sexual dysfunction* (Ed Fowler CJ), chapter 4. Butterworth Heinemann, New York

Martin J, White A (1988) The financial circumstances of disabled adults living in private households. *OPCS surveys of disability on Great Britain.* HMSO, London

Masters WH, Johnson VE (1966) *Human sexual response.* J & A Churchill, London

McCunniff DE, Dewan D (1984) Pregnancy after spinal cord injury. *Obstetrics and Gynaecology 63*: 757

McKinlay WW, Brooks DN, Bond MR, Martinage DP, Marshall MM (1981) The short term outcome of severe blunt head injury as reported by relatives of the injured persons. *Journal of Neurological and Neurosurgical Psychiatry 44*: 527–533

Miller S, Szasz G, Anderson L (1981) Sexual health care clinician in an acute spinal cord injury unit. *Archives of Physical and Mental Rehabilitation 62*: 315–320

Morgan DJR, Blackburn M, Bax M (1995) Adults with spina bifida and/or hydrocephalus. *Postgraduate Medical Journal 71*: 17–21

Nathan HP, Hellstrom WJG, Kaiser FE, Labasky RF, Lue TF, Nolten WE, Norwood PC, Peterson CA, Shabsigh R, Tam PY, Place VA, Gesundheit N (1997) Treatment of men with erectile dysfunction with transurethral alprostadil. *New England Journal Medical 336*, 1–7

Nemec ED, Mansfield L, Ward Kennedy J (1976) Heart rate and blood pressure responses during sexual activity in normal males. *American Heart Journal 92*: 274–277

Neumann RJ (1979) The forgotten other: Women partners of spinal cord injured men, a preliminary report. *Sexuality and Disability 2*(4): 287–292

O'Carroll RE, Woodrow J, Marouns F (1991) Psychosexual and psychosocial sequelae of closed head injury. *Brain Injury 5*: 303–313

Oddy M, Humphrey M, Uttley D (1978) Stresses upon the relatives of head injured patients. *British Journal Psychiatry 133*: 507–513

Robertson DNS, Guttmann L (1963) The paraplegic patient in pregnancy and labour. *Proceedings of the Royal Society of Medicine 56*: 381–387

Rodgers J, Calder P (1990) Marital adjustment: A valuable resource for the emotional health of individuals with multiple sclerosis. *Rehabilitation Counselling Bulletin 34*: 24–32

Rolland JS (1994) In sickness and in health: The impact of illness on couples' relationships. *Journal of Marital and Family Therapy 20*: 327–347

Rosenbaum M, Najenson T (1976) Changes in life patterns and symptoms of low mood as reported by wives of severely brain injured soldiers. *Journal of Consulting and Clinical Psychology 44*(6): 881–888

Rust J, Golombok S (1986) *The Golombok rust inventory of sexual satisfaction.* NFER Nelson, Windsor

Rust J, Bennun I, Crowe M, Golombok S (1988a) *The Golombok rust inventory of marital state.* NFER-Nelson, Windsor

Rust J, Golombok S, Collier J (1988b) Marital problems and sexual dysfunction: How are they related? *British Journal of Psychiatry 152*: 629–631

Rutkowski SB, Middleton JW, Truman G, Hagen DL, Ryan JP (1995) The influence of bladder mangement on fertility in spinal cord injured males. *Paraplegia 33*: 263–266

Sager CJ (1976) The role of sex therapy in marital therapy. *American Journal of Psychiatry 133*: 555–558

Sandel ME, Williams KS, Dellapietra L, Derogatis LR (1996) Sexual functioning following traumatic brain injury. *Brain Injury 10*: 719–728

Sawyer SM (1996) Reproductive and sexual health in adolescents with cystic fibrosis. *British Medical Journal 313*: 1095–1096

Seidl A, Bullough B, Haughey B, Scherer Y, Rhodes M, Brown G (1991) Understanding the effects of a myocardial infarction on sexual functioning: A basis for sexual counselling. *Rehabilitation Nursing 16*: 255–263

Spence SH (1991) *Psychosexual therapy: A cognitive behavioural approach.* Chapman and Hall, London

Stanley E (1981a) Dealing with fear of failure. *British Medical Journal 282*: 1281–1283

Stanley E (1981b). Non organic causes of sexual problems. *British Medical Journal 282*: 1042–1044

Stanley E (1987) Psychosexual problems. *British Medical Journal 294*: 39–42

Strauss D (1991) Biopsychosocial issues in sexuality with the neurologically impaired patient. *Sexuality and Disability 9*: 49–67

Szasz G (1991) Sex and disability are not mutually exclusive. Evaluation and management. *The Western Journal of Medicine 154*: 560–563

Szasz G, Paty D, Lawton-Speert S, Eisen K (1984a) A sexual function scale in multiple sclerosis. *Acta Neurologica Scandinavica 101*: 37–43

Szasz G, Paty D, Maurice WL (1984b) Sexual dysfunctions in multiple sclerosis. *Annals New York Acadamy of Sciences 436*: 443–452

Townsend P, Phillimore P, Beattie A (1988) *Health and deprivation: Inequality and the north.* Croom Helm, London

Valleroy ML, Kraft GH (1984) Sexual dysfunction in multiple sclerosis. *Archives of Physical and Mental Rehabilitation 65*: 125–128

Vas CJ (1969) Sexual impotence and some autonomic disturbance in men with multiple sclerosis. *Acta Neurologica Scandinavica 45*: 166–183

Vermote R, Peuskins J (1996) Sexual and micturition problems in multiple sclerosis patients: Psychological issues. *Sexuality and Disability 14*: 73–82

Warner P, Bancroft J (and members of the Edinburgh Human Sexuality Group) (1987) A regional clinical service for sexual problems: A 3-year study. *Sexual and Marital Therapy 2*: 115–126

Weinman E, Ruskin PE (1994) Levodopa dependence and hypersexuality in an older Parkinson's disease patient. *American Journal of Geriatric Psychiatry 3*: 81–83

Wermuth L, Stenager E (1995) Sexual problems in young patients with Parkinson's disease. *Acta Neurologica Scandinavica 91*: 453–455

Weston A (1993) Challenging assumptions. *Nursing Times 89*: 26–31

Williams G, Mulcahy MJ, Kiely EA (1987) Impotence: Treatment by autoinjection of vasoactive drugs. *British Medical Journal 295*: 595–596

Young EW (1984) Patients' plea: Tell us about our sexuality. *Journal of Sex Education and Therapy 10*: 53–56

Zilbergeld B (1975) Group treatment of sexual dysfunction in men without partners. *Journal of Sex and Marital Therapy 1*: 204–214

Zilbergeld B (1978) *Men and sex.* Fontana, London

Zimmer D (1983) Interaction patterns and communication skills in sexually distressed, and normal couples: Two experimental studies. *Journal of Sexual and Marital Therapy 9*: 251–265

Zimmer D (1987) Does marital therapy enhance the effectiveness of treatment for sexual dysfunction? *Journal of Sexual and Marital Therapy 13*: 193–209

USEFUL ADDRESSES

Institute of Psychosexual Medicine, 11, Chandos Street, Cavendish Square, London, WIM 9DE

Relate External Training Services, Herbert Gray College, Little Church Treet, Rugby, CV21 3AP

SPOD. The Association to Aid the Sexual and Personal Relationships of People with a Disability, 286 Camden Road, London N7 0BJ

23. Neurogenic respiratory failure

R. S. Howard   D. El Kabir   A. J. Williams

INTRODUCTION

Respiratory insufficiency is the inability to maintain adequate ventilation to match acid–base status and oxygenation to metabolic requirements. The initial abnormality is often intermittent nocturnal hypoventilation leading to hypercapnia and hypoxia, this eventually persists when the patient is awake and symptoms can develop concurrently. Respiratory failure is defined as arterial partial pressure of oxygen in the arteries (P_aO_2) of less than 8.0 kPa (60 mmHg) and/or arterial partial pressure of carbon dioxide in the arteries (P_aCO_2) of greater than 6.7 kPa (50 mmHg) (Sykes et al., 1976). Respiratory insufficiency can develop during the course of many neurological disorders. It occurs most commonly as a consequence of neuromuscular weakness but can also accompany disturbances of brainstem function or interruption of descending respiratory pathways. Respiratory failure can occur during the course of acute and potentially treatable or self-limiting disorders (e.g. Guillain–Barré syndrome, myasthenia gravis, polymyositis), following an acute insult resulting in permanent disability (e.g. spinal cord injury), or due to progressive disease (e.g. muscular dystrophy, motor neurone disease). In a number of apparently stable disorders (e.g. poliomyelitis), late deterioration can lead to the development of respiratory failure many years after the acute illness (Howard et al., 1988).

It is important to recognise patients at risk of respiratory failure because providing appropriate support reduces morbidity and mortality, allowing survival for prolonged periods with or without respiratory support (Douglas et al., 1983; O'Donohue et al., 1976). The decision to assist ventilation in acute neurological disorders is usually straightforward. However, more difficult issues are raised in progressive neuromuscular disease, particularly if associated with bulbar weakness. In this situation an accurate diagnosis and prognosis is essential to determine the aims and type of ventilatory support. For example, non-invasive support in motor neurone disease can alleviate distressing symptoms of breathlessness and orthopnoea without preventing the development of aspiration and bronchopneumonia, whereas ventilation via a cuffed tracheostomy will protect the airway and might prolong survival inappropriately in the face of severe or total paralysis. The ethical considerations in providing ventilatory support in progressive neuromuscular disease are complex and depend on detailed individual assessment and discussion with the patient and the family.

PATHOPHYSIOLOGY

Adequate ventilation is dependent on the balance between ventilatory load, capacity, and drive. For ventilatory failure to occur, either the load placed on the respiratory system must exceed the capacity to accommodate this or the ventilatory drive must be inadequate. In normal individuals there is considerable respiratory reserve, but the balance can be more precarious among patients with neuromuscular disease. During sleep, there are changes in central drive and responsiveness, respiratory muscle function, and airway tone, and hence sleep-disordered breathing is often the initial abnormality of ventilation in neuromuscular patients. Respiratory muscle weakness, bulbar failure, or disturbance of the automatic control of respiration exacerbate nocturnal hypoventilation and can precipitate respiratory failure (Howard & Newsom Davis, 1991; Laroche et al., 1989; Plum, 1970). Sleep remains the critical period for respiratory compromise and sudden death (Phillipson & Bowes, 1986).

Respiratory muscles

The relative contribution made by respiratory muscle weakness to neurogenic respiratory failure, and the pattern of respiratory muscle involvement, varies between acute and chronic neuromuscular diseases and also according to the particular disease. For example, in acute neuromuscular disease, or those characterised by recurrent attacks such as myaesthenia gravis, muscle weakness is the principal cause of the respiratory problems (De Troyer et al., 1980). Among the chronic neuromuscular diseases, certain conditions such as motor neurone disease and acid maltase deficiency appear to preferentially affect the diaphragm (Howard et al., 1989; Mulvey et al., 1993; Rosenow & Engel, 1978). Adequate ventilation during rapid eye movement (REM) sleep is entirely dependent on diaphragm function and hypoventilation during REM sleep is inevitable if the diaphragm is paralysed (Phillipson & Bowes, 1986). In other diseases such as Duchenne muscular dystrophy and myotonic dystrophy, expiratory muscle weakness develops before inspiratory muscle weakness (Gillam et al., 1964; Inkley et al., 1974) leading to impaired cough and risk of aspiration and pneumonia.

Longstanding respiratory muscle weakness can itself lead to secondary problems such as scoliosis (Bergofsky et al., 1959) and widespread atelectasis leading to reduced cheat wall and lung compliance, recurrent infections, and ventilation perfusion imbalance. These factors increase the ventilatory load and therefore patients with weak respiratory muscles working against poorly compliant structures are working closer to their fatigue threshold (Moxham, 1990). Any additional load on the system such as a respiratory tract infection, aspiration pneumonitis, airways obstruction, or abdominal distension will further upset the load-capacity balance and could precipitate respiratory failure (Kreitzer et al., 1978; Smith et al., 1987). Other factors that can affect the load-capacity balance include obesity, anaesthesia, sedative drugs, surgery, and general medical disorders (Howard et al., 1988).

Central control

Hypoventilation and apnoeic periods during sleep, or a variable pattern of tidal volume or frequency, suggest impaired automatic control of ventilation (Howard & Newsom Davis, 1991; Plum, 1970). Failure of the automatic system is associated with acute bulbar lesions (Baker et al., 1950) and the combination of an impaired swallowing mechanism, reduced vital capacity, and reduced or absent cough reflex all increase the risk of aspiration pneumonia.

Sleep apnoea and alveolar hypoventilation

Periodic apnoea is conventionally divided into obstructive and central types. In obstructive apnoea there is upper airway obstruction despite normal movement of the intercostals and diaphragm. In central apnoea all respiratory phased movements are absent (Douglas, 1984). Alveolar hypoventilation is characterised by a reduced ventilatory response to CO_2 and consequent CO_2 retention in the absence of primary pulmonary disease. There is progressive reduction in the tidal volume and reduced hypoxic and hypercapnic drive, which can culminate in central apnoea. These effects occur primarily during sleep but hypercapnia can persist when awake, with the development of respiratory failure (Phillipson & Bowes, 1986). Nocturnal alveolar hypoventilation might be due to a central lesion of the automatic pathway or respiratory muscle weakness. Most causes of severe diaphragm weakness will lead to alveolar hypoventilation during REM sleep culminating in hypercapnia and secondary depression of hypercapnic ventilatory drive (Newsom Davis et al., 1976). Coexisting obstructive sleep apnoea (OSA) will lead to a greater degree of nocturnal hypoventilation than expected in patients with neuromuscular disease and might be secondary to bulbar dysfunction in some. There is some evidence for OSA predating nocturnal hypoventilation in some patients (Khan & Heckmatt, 1994), whereas in others upper airways obstruction can coexist with central hypoventilation.

CLINICAL FEATURES OF RESPIRATORY INSUFFICIENCY AND FAILURE

Symptomatology

Respiratory insufficiency can develop insidiously and present few symptoms, particularly in the context of a patient whose mobility might be compromised. Hypercapnia commonly first occurs during sleep and is usually asymptomatic but, when severe, can lead to morning headache, daytime hypersomnolence, impaired intellectual function, and depression or irritability. The symptoms of obstructive sleep apnoea are similar but the patient or their partner often complains of snoring, choking, abnormal sleep movements, and disturbed sleep with distressing dreams.

Severe generalised respiratory muscle weakness leads to breathlessness and tachypnoea. Patients with significant diaphragm weakness are often first aware of breathlessness sitting or standing in water or whilst carrying large objects, due to the upwards displacement of abdominal contents. Orthopnoea is a characteristic feature and patients often report that lying down produces backache, claustrophobia, or panic attacks. Nocturnal orthopnoea can mimic paroxysmal nocturnal dyspnoea. Eventually, ventilatory failure and cor pulmonale develop.

Clinical signs

Clinical signs are often absent in the early stages and can easily be missed. Bulbar dysfunction is revealed by clinical signs of lesions of the IXth and Xth cranial nerves including loss of posterior pharyngeal wall sensation, reduced palatal movement and pharyngeal reflex, poor cough, impaired speech, and ineffective swallowing (Howard & Newsom Davis, 1991). However, clinical signs of bulbar dysfunction are not always a good guide to the development of aspiration (Linden & Siebens, 1983; Splaingard et al., 1988). Obesity is often present in patients with obstructive sleep apnoea.

Only when diaphragm strength is reduced to about a quarter of normal is the characteristic feature of abdominal paradox present. This describes the paradoxical inwards motion of the anterior abdominal wall on inspiration and might be more obvious with the patient supine during a sniff manoeuvre (Laroche et al., 1988). There could be an increase in accessory muscle activity. In the upright position, active expiratory recruitment of the abdominal muscles might be present, allowing gravity-assisted "passive" descent of the diaphragm during inspiration, which can mask abdominal paradox (Gibson, 1989).

As the condition progresses there might be an unexplained tachycardia, an accentuated second heart sound over the pulmonary valve area, and signs of polycythaemia. Eventually, the full picture of respiratory failure is present. This can lead to inappropriate treatment if the neurological aetiology is not appreciated. Sudden unexpected death might then occur (Stradling & Phillipson, 1986).

INVESTIGATIONS

In progressive neuromuscular disease, forced vital capacity (FVC) falls because of both respiratory muscle weakness and/or fatigue and reduced chest compliance (De Troyer et al., 1980; Estenne et al., 1983; Seresier et al., 1982) due to microatelectasis (Gibson et al., 1977) and restriction of chest wall movement (Caro & DuBois, 1961). Other pulmonary function tests can be misleading; If the FVC is low the forced expiratory volume in the first second (FEV_1) becomes meaningless and apparent volume-dependent airways collapse can reflect lack of effort due to neuromuscular weakness. Diaphragm weakness is associated with a marked fall in FVC when sitting or lying (Loh et al., 1977), although this must be greater than 25% to be unequivocably abnormal (Allen, 1989). A normal supine FVC is valuable in excluding clinically relevant inspiratory muscle weakness. Regular measurements of FVC (both erect and supine) allow assessment of the extent and progression of respiratory muscle weakness, however, it should be noted that FVC measurements depend on effort and cooperation by the patient and, furthermore, are not specific for the detection of respiratory muscle weakness.

Chest radiographs can show unilateral or bilateral elevated hemidiaphragms, aspiration pneumonitis, or bronchopneumonia. However, the radiograph can be entirely normal, even with substantial bilateral diaphragm weakness. Fluoroscopic screening performed when supine might show paradoxical upwards movement of the paralysed diaphragm during inspiration or sniff. Ultrasound can be used to semiquantitatively assess hemidiaphragm function, and has the advantage of avoiding irradiation (Houston et al., 1994)

Waking arterial blood gas tensions are often virtually normal during the early stages of neurological respiratory insufficiency, even when significant nocturnal hypoventilation is occurring. P_aO_2 might be slightly reduced, leading to the erroneous suspicion of intrinsic lung disease. As the condition progresses, daytime P_aCO_2 becomes elevated. Arterial gas tension monitoring by indwelling arterial catheter provides definitive evidence of nocturnal hypoventilation but is highly invasive and can be performed only in a specialised unit. Surface P_aCO_2 electrodes can produce misleading results when used overnight because of the changes in skin temperature and blood flow that occur during sleep. Nocturnal oximetry can be helpful but its role is limited because desaturation is a late feature of progressive nocturnal hypoventilation. Oximetry, however, remains a useful screening test detect periodic sleep apnoea. Detailed analysis of the mechanisms of sleep-induced respiratory failure require full polysomnography (Bye et al., 1990).

When the lung is normal, transpulmonary pressure is low and static mouth occlusion pressure reflects pleural pressure, thus providing a useful non-invasive method of measuring global inspiratory and expiratory muscle strength (Black & Hyatt, 1969, 1971). Portable, inexpensive mouth pressure meters facilitate measurement of the MIP (maximum inspiratory pressure) and MEP (maximum expiratory pressure) at the bedside or in clinic (Hamnegard et al., 1994). As with FVC, a high MIP and MEP exclude significant respiratory muscle weakness, but are also volitional tests and low recorded values due to poor technique or submaximal effort are relatively common. The maximum pressure measured nasally during maximal sniff (sniff nasal pressure, SNIP) provides a close reflection of oesophageal pressure and hence gives an additional measure of global inpiratory muscle strength (Hertier et al., 1994). This technique has the advantage that the maximal sniff is a relatively easy manoeuvre to perform and falsely low results are therefore less common than for the MIP measurement. The SNIP provides a useful complementary test to the MIP in assessing global inspiratory muscle strength and portable sniff meters have also been developed (Hamnegard et al., 1995).

To assess diaphragm function more specifically, the transdiaphragmatic pressure can be determined from the electronic subtraction of the oesophageal pressure from the gastric pressure using a pair of balloon-tipped catheters passed nasogastrically under topical anaesthesia. Thus, the transdiaphragmatic pressure during maximal sniff can be recorded (sniff Pdi; Miller et al., 1985) in addition to the sniff oesophageal pressure (sniff Poes), which provides information about global inspiratory muscle strength. These tests are the most reliable non-volitional tests of inspiratory muscle function currently available. More precise and reproducible measurements of diaphragm strength can be obtained using non-volitional tests. The discharge of a magnetic coil placed either on the side or at the back of the neck will induce current to flow within one or both phrenic nerves respectively, causing the diaphragm to contract (Similowski et al., 1989). The twitch transdiaphragmatic pressure (Tw Pdi) can then be recorded using the balloon system mentioned above. Supramaximal bilateral phrenic nerve stimulation can be achieved either by a circular coil placed over the cervical phrenic nerve roots (Wragg et al., 1994) or by using a bilateral anterior approach, for example to study patients in the intensive care unit (ICU) (Mills et al., 1994a). Furthermore, each hemidiaphragm can be assessed separately by unilateral anterior phrenic nerve stimulation using a figure-of-eight coil (Mills et al., 1994b). Electrical stimulation of the phrenic nerves in the neck can also be used to measure the Tw Pdi (Mier et al., 1987) as well as the phrenic nerve conduction time (Newsom Davis, 1967) and provides a useful guide to phrenic nerve involvement in neuropathies or damage following neck or cardiothoracic surgery.

Needle electromyography (EMG) from the diaphragm is safe, causes little discomfort, and provides good recording of diaphragm activity. In particular the spontaneous breathing pattern and the appearance and firing pattern of the motor units can be observed. Spontaneous activity, myotonia, polyphasic motor units, and recruitment can be shown (Bolton et al., 1992; Misra et al., 1995).

CLINICAL DISORDERS

Abnormalities of the respiratory rhythm leading to insufficiency can be caused by neurological lesions at any site on the pathway

Table 23.1. Cases referred to the Lane Fox Respiratory Unit between 1969 and 1997 with a primarily neurological cause for respiratory insufficiency

Neurological cause	Number of cases
Poliomyelitis	831
Myopathies	
Dystrophies	
Duchenne	12
limb girdle	10
fascioscapulohumoral	5
scapuloperoneal	1
unknown	4
Congenital	
nemaline	2
Emery Dryfuss	1
others	4
Metabolic	
acid maltase	6
mitochondrial	1
Inflammatory	
polymyositis	1
systemic lupus erythematosus	3
others	2
Myotonia	
dystrophica myotonica	13
Neuropathies	
Guillain–Barré syndrome	13
Hereditary motor sensory	9
Friedreich's ataxia	3
IgM paraproteinaemia	1
Neuralgic amyotrophy	2
Spinal muscular atrophy	10
Motor neurone disease	17
Myasthenia gravis	5
Multiple sclerosis	3
Postencephalitic	9
Multisystem atrophy	2
Chest wall defects	10
Others	15
Brainstem/spinal cord lesions	
Trauma	6
Birth injury/malformations	17
Vascular	8
Tumour	6
Syringomyelia	2
Progressive cerebellar degeneration	1
Total 1035 Patients	

from the cortex to muscle or due to more diffuse degenerative and infective disease (Howard, 1990). Table 23.1 summarises the cause of respiratory insufficiency in 1035 consecutive patients referred to the Lane Fox Respiratory Unit between 1969 and 1997 with neurological disorders. This series reflects a specialist interest in long-term and domiciliary respiratory support, and under-represents the incidence of respiratory failure due to spinal injuries and acute neurological disorders.

MANAGEMENT

For the efficient management of respiratory failure in these diseases it is essential to anticipate or recognise at an early stage the critical warning signs. The development of augmented alveolar ventilation by non-invasive techniques now forms the mainstay of treatment. The criteria for intervention remain those of symptoms of excessive daytime sleepiness, morning headaches, and cognitive impairment in the presence of sleep-disordered breathing. The following should be considered risk factors for developing acute respiratory failure in patients with neuromuscular diseases:

(1) The development of diaphragmatic weakness. This can be evident in the clinical signs of respiratory paradox or standing-to-supine fall in vital capacity of greater than 25%, or in the development of low inspiratory pressures or other measurements of respiratory muscle strength.
(2) An independent association has been found in a vital capacity that is less than 30% predicted.
(3) An accelerated decline in vital capacity. These might or might not be related to alterations in respiratory pressures as measured at the mouth, i.e. maximum inspiratory and maximum expiratory. Although these are inherently quite variable and poorly predictive, they can be useful as a way of following patients. It has been said that the maximum inspiratory pressure of <30% predicted or a maximum expiratory of <70 cmH$_2$O are indicative of the development of respiratory failure. In addition, weakness of the expiratory muscles with the development of a poor cough can predispose to respiratory tract infections and, as an independent issue, an associated scoliosis that also is associated with impaired respiratory defence against infection.

In choosing the optimal method of management for an individual, it is essential to consider not only the level of assistance needed but also its possible duration. If long term, it is important to consider how to minimise interference with normal life. This is particularly so if respiratory assistance is to continue after the patient's discharge from hospital. The practicality of home respiratory assistance depends on the:

(1) severity of associated non-respiratory disability
(2) availability of family support or suitable helpers
(3) home living conditions.

Methods of assisted ventilation

Airway management

Bulbar and respiratory failure are different conditions, although they can often coexist in neuromuscular disease and management of each must be modified accordingly. Bulbar weakness by itself might not require intervention provided a strong cough reflex and normal FVC are preserved. Patients can compensate by careful selection of food, slow mastication without simultaneous speech, and cautious or repeated deglutition to clear a single mouthful. Complete or severe bulbar paralysis, particularly of sudden onset, always necessitates rapid intervention if a fatal outcome is to be avoided.

Tracheostomy.   There are four indications for tracheostomy:

(1) To bypass an obstruction in the air passages above the level of the trachea.
(2) To separate the food and air passages when the patient is unable to do so.
(3) To allow repeated aspirations of secretions when the cough is inadequate for long periods.
(4) To provide a route for long-term, continuous artificial respiration by intermittent positive pressure.

The operation should be performed as an elective procedure under general anaesthesia with a cuffed endotracheal tube in place. Emergency tracheostomy under local anaesthetic is justified only if no anaesthetist is available or if it has proved impossible to pass an endotracheal tube. Tracheostomy carries its own complications, both immediate and delayed. Most are avoidable with careful anaesthesia, surgery, and long-term management. It should be regarded as a major procedure and not left to inexperienced staff. Whatever the need for tracheostomy, a cuffed tracheostomy tube should be used initially to prevent aspiration of blood from the wound. However, the presence of a cuff increases the incidence and range of potential complications. It also prevents swallowing for at least the first few days. Indications (2) and (4) above are the only ones that necessitate longer-term use of a cuffed tube, which should otherwise be changed for a non-cuffed tube at the earliest possible moment.

Non-mechanical respiratory support

Glossopharyngeal (frog) breathing.   This uses the mouth and pharynx to inflate the passive chest (Ardran et al., 1959; Dail et al., 1955; Feigelson et al., 1956). Serial incremental inflation of the lungs is produced by gulping air into the oropharynx, closing the mouth and soft palate, opening the larynx, and forcing the air from the pharynx to the trachea. The vocal cords are then closed and the process repeated. By learning this method, patients can often take a deep breath three or four times the amount of their vital capacity. This technique greatly assists coughing and maintains mobility of the costovertebral and sternocostal joints. It is a useful adjunct to breathing in poliomyelitis and many patients can manage for long periods of the day by glossopharyngeal breathing alone (Howard et al., 1988).

Pharmacological.   Centrally acting drugs such as doxapram and aminophylline are of no value in neuromuscular disorders. Although theoretically analeptic, the tricyclic agent protriptyline has a limited role. Respiratory irregularities leading to desaturation and hypercarbia occur mainly during REM sleep, the duration of which is reduced by this drug. Side-effects, including constipation and male impotence, limit its use (Simonds et al., 1986).

Continuous positive airway pressure (CPAP).   This is not strictly a method of artificial ventilation. The technique is mentioned, however, because it is valuable in the management of obstructive and central sleep apnoea, for which it has largely replaced tracheostomy. Continuous air pressure from a blower is applied to the nose maintaining a minimum pressure of 5–15 cmH$_2$O throughout the respiratory cycle. It apparently works by maintaining continuous patency of the upper air passages (Issa & Sullivan, 1986).

Diaphragm pacing

The embryological development of the diaphragm results in its anatomically remote innervation via the phrenic nerve. This long nerve is both vulnerable during cardiothoracic surgery and accessible for therapeutic manoeuvres in the neck. These have included crushing it to reduce cavitation in pulmonary tuberculosis and stimulating it to cause diaphragmatic contractions and thus assist respiration (Glenn et al., 1986). To achieve this both the phrenic nerve and the diaphragm must be intact. Originally it was hoped that it might be of use in treating brainstem lesions and idiopathic central hypoventilation. In practice its use is limited to spinal cord injury above C3, but early hopes for the technique have not been fulfilled. Repeated surgery for insertion of radiocontrolled stimulators is needed. The nerves become refractory even if stimulated alternately. Tracheostomy is still necessary and the apparatus is expensive (Moxham & Potter, 1988).

Non-invasive assisted ventilation (without an endotracheal or tracheostomy tube) encompasses three distinct modalities: (1) negative pressure ventilation such as the iron lung or cuirass; (2) body ventilators such as the rocking bed; and (3) positive pressure ventilators.

Negative pressure ventilation

The basic device operating in this way is the iron lung (tank or cabinet respirator) (Drinker & McKhann, 1986). Despite its size and antiquity, it is still occasionally used today. In principle, it consists of an opening chamber in which the whole body is placed, with only the head protruding. An airtight collar fits around the neck and the chamber is intermittently evacuated by a large bellows, causing air to pass in and out of the lungs. It is particularly useful during acute illnesses and after surgery in patients with moderate respiratory dependence (Patrick et al., 1990; Sawicka et al., 1986; Simmonds et al., 1988), but some patients continue to use the iron lung for nocturnal ventilatory support. Current iron lungs range from the Khelleher rotating tank for postural drainage (Figs 23.1, 23.2) (Kelleher, 1961) to a simple, small tank specifically designed for home use (Figs 23.3, 23.4).

The cuirass shell (Fig 23.5) and Tunnicliffe jacket (Spalding & Opie, 1958) operate on the same principle as the iron lung but are relatively portable, although less efficient. Both are unsuitable for patients with sensory as well as motor disturbances (e.g. spinal cord injury) because they cause pressure sores. The cuirass is a dome-shaped shell with a padded edge applied to the chest wall anteriorly just below the clavicles, laterally in the posterior axillary line, and inferiorly just above the iliac crests curving down medially to rest on the symphysis pubis. It often

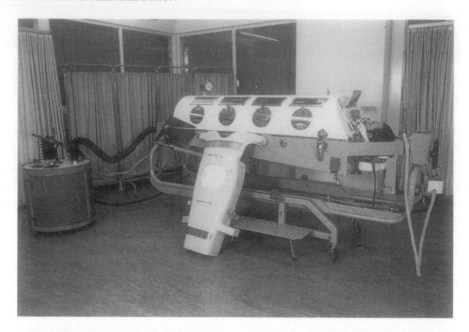

Figure 23.1. The Kelleher rotating iron lung showing the small bellows for synchronised positive pressure on top of the main negative pressure bellows connected via long hose to mouthpiece above the patient's head and the shell (resting against side of cabinet) for holding the patient when the iron lung is rotated.

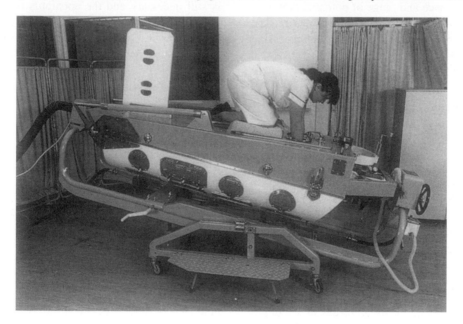

Figure 23.2. The Kelleher iron lung in fully rotated and Trendelenburg position for physiotherapy. Note the removable section of the mattress and the base in the slot to prevent return to normal position without replacement.

has to be made to measure. The Tunnicliffe jacket envelopes the trunk and upper arms and is tight around the neck and hips. The central part of the jacket is held away from the trunk by a frame. It is more efficient than the cuirass but cumbersome to put on. The air-filled central section of both devices is connected to a pump and rhythmically evacuated to produce inspiration.

The pneumobelt is an inflatable corset applied to the abdomen and lower chest. When rhythmically inflated it augments expiration. It can be of value in patients with paralysis of both diaphragm and abdominal wall who need assistance by day when

sitting. The weight of the abdominal contents otherwise prevents adequate exhalation.

Rocking bed

The idea that breathing could be assisted by rocking a patient head up and head down first occurred to Eve (1932), who used the family rocking chair when trying to help a diphtheritic child. He adapted it for resuscitation and for many years it was known as Eve's rocking method. A mechanical rocking

Figure 23.3. The St Thomas's transportable iron lung for home use. A removable pump unit is contained in the base and the mattress section of the cabinet is low enough for transfers to a wheelchair.

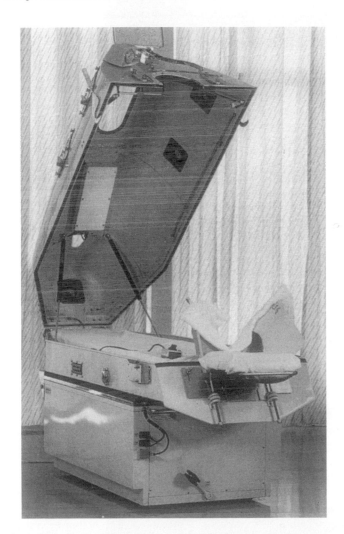

Figure 23.4. The St Thomas's iron lung open. Handles for self-release are visible in the cabinet lid.

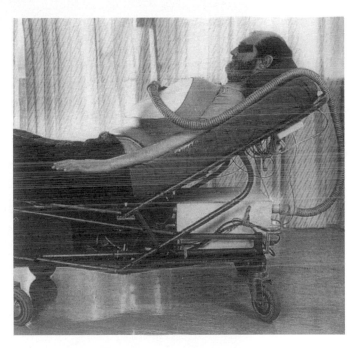

Figure 23.5. Cuirass shell user on a mobile trolley with evacuating pump (Monaghan 170 C) beneath.

bed was described by Schuster and Fischer-Williams (1953) and the technique has remained popular and effective in patients whose respiratory weakness is predominantly diaphragmatic (Trend et al., 1985). It is the only method of respiratory assistance that leaves the patient completely unconnected to apparatus (Figs 23.6, 23.7, 23.8). Although diaphragmatic weakness commonly involves the crura, it is unusual for rocking bed users to experience reflux. Disadvantages include non-portability and engineering problems in achieving a smooth motion (Chalmers et al., 1994).

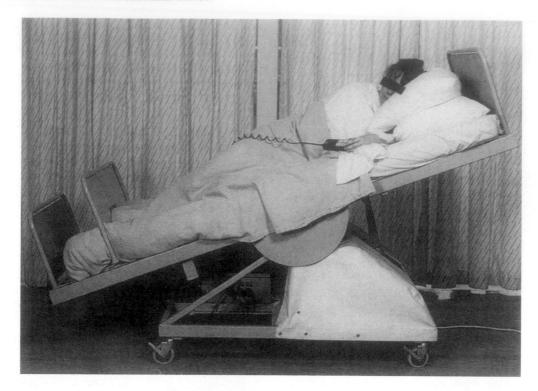

Figure 23.6. Rocking bed, inspiratory position.

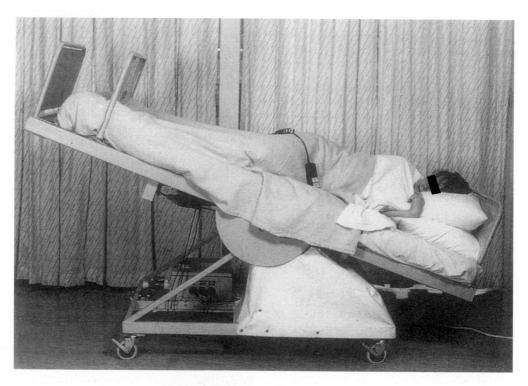

Figure 23.7. Rocking bed, expiratory position.

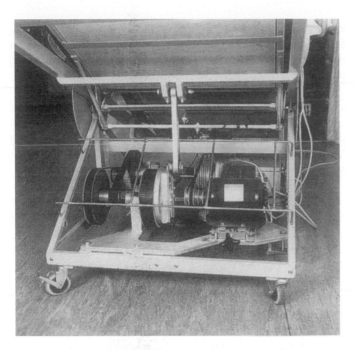

Figure 23.8. Rocking bed mechanism, showing multiple pulley system to ensure smooth motion of bed.

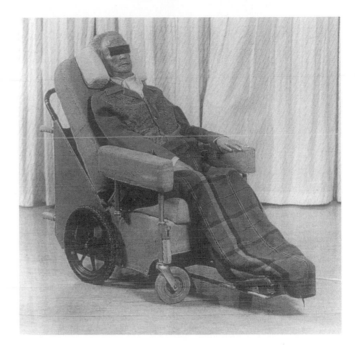

Figure 23.9. Totally paralysed patient receiving continuous artificial ventilation via tracheostomy in a Cavendish combined wheelchair ventilator. The ventilator tubes are just visible emerging from the chair, and are otherwise concealed by clothing.

Intermittent positive pressure ventilation

This is the most efficient method of artificial ventilation and is usually called intermittent positive pressure ventilation (IPPV). For continuous use (greater than 16 hours a day), a connection to the trachea via cuffed endotracheal tube or directly by tracheostomy is required. For such long-term use, positive pressure is generated by machines of two principal types.

1. Machines delivering a preset volume per breath (volume cycled). These maintain a constant respiratory minute volume (RMV) despite changes in airway resistance or compliance, which, in acutely ill patients, can vary greatly over short periods. They are leak sensitive, as a leak causes an immediate fall in alveolar ventilation. They therefore necessitate a cuffed tube and speech is prevented. They can be set to deliver a constant respiratory minute volume or, more usually, to respond to respiratory efforts as well (assist control ventilation). Volume ventilation is particularly indicated when the compliance of the respiratory system is reduced, as might occur in severe restrictive lung disease or, more importantly, when the compliance is variable, as occurs in children, and mandated alveolar ventilation is required.

2. Machines delivering a predetermined pressure (pressure or pressure/time cycled). The RMV delivered will vary with changes in airway resistance or compliance and this type is therefore less suitable for patients with severe pulmonary pathology. Assisted ventilation in the intensive care unit is now much more commonly provided in this form as so-called pressure support ventilation. The advantages lie in the ability for the patient to vary tidal volume on a breath-to-breath basis. They are leak compensating so can be used with a non-cuffed tracheostomy tube, permitting intermittent speech during the inspiratory stroke of

the ventilator. They are particularly suitable for long-term use in neurological disease and can be simply and reliably constructed, making them suitable for home use. For this purpose, the East Radcliffe ventilators (Russell et al., 1956), although old fashioned, have never been bettered. A simple version of the East Radcliffe ventilator has been incorporated into a comfortable wheelchair containing complete suction and, if necessary, humidification equipment, all of which can be either mains or battery powered. It is self-contained and known as the Cavendish Chair (Figs 23.9, 23.10, 23.11). It is ideal for severely paralysed patients.

These ventilators are often used to deliver the positive pressure through nasal masks (Fig. 23.12), so-called "nasal or mouthpiece intermittent positive pressure ventilation" (NIPPV; Alba et al., 1981). The successful application of this mode of ventilation is discussed below. These methods require a machine able to deliver a large stroke volume (up to 2 litres), because a considerable proportion of the delivered air is lost through whichever facial orifice is not receiving the machine's input. The technique cannot be used continuously. Both the nasal mask and mouthpiece are obtrusive by day and prevent eating and drinking, and the nasal masks cause pressure sores if used continuously. Some subjects find a mask over the nose claustrophobic and liable to cause drying of the upper air passages. Others complain of sialorrhoea or aerogastria. Obtaining a suitable lightweight, well-fitting nose mask can be difficult, as can use during nasal congestion or other nasal pathology. Within these limitations, NIPPV is now the most popular method of nocturnal respiratory assistance.

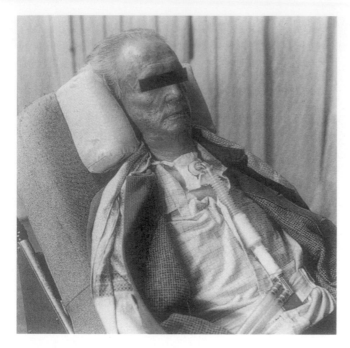

Figure 23.10. Cavendish wheelchair respirator with the patient's outer clothing removed to show the secure screw connection to the tracheostomy tube and the waist belt securing the ventilator tubes, which therefore move with the patient during adjustments to position in the chair and cannot pull on the tracheostomy tube.

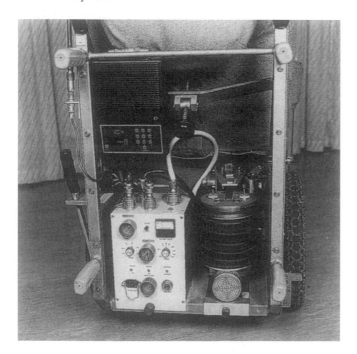

Figure 23.11. Rear of the Cavendish chair (cover removed) showing the telemetry patient call system, the solenoid-powered silent bellows, the electronic control unit and the mains socket for battery charging and automatic mains operation when convenient.

Success of non-invasive ventilation

In the early 1980s nocturnal use of negative pressure ventilators was associated with sustained improvement in daytime gas exchange and symptoms of hypoventilation in patients with respiratory failure due to neuromuscular disease, as well as chest wall deformities and central hypoventilation. More recently, similar studies using the nasal mask have appeared confirming the earlier findings (Bye et al., 1990). These studies have consistently demonstrated the use of non-invasive ventilation for as little as 6–8 h nightly lowers the daytime P_aCO_2, raises daytime P_aO_2 and eliminates symptoms of morning headache and hyposomnolence (Ellis et al., 1987; Khan & Heckmatt, 1994; Schneerson, 1996; Smith et al., 1991; Steljes et al., 1990).

The success of intermittent non-invasive ventilation (usually nocturnal) in large part lies with the acceptibility of the device to the patient. The choice of ventilator is less important than that of the interface. The time spent accommodating the patient to the relevant mask is well spent. These masks can be applied around the nose with a pneumatic seal produced by positive pressure. They can also be introduced into the nares in the form of nasal pillows, or applied at the nares in the form of a nasal sling. Having more than one form of mask available is an advantage, although adds to the cost. It is convenient to accommodate the patient to the idea of assisted ventilation during a diurnal waking trial. This will establish not only the comfort but also the level of pressure required to maintain adequate ventilation. During the initial nocturnal trials, ventilation can be reasonably monitored by nocturnal oxygen saturation to identify periods of underventilation. Monitoring of this, and of the patient's symptoms, is a sufficient guide to the adequacy of ventilatory assistance.

After the stabilisation on nocturnal ventilation, problems frequently arise relating to nasal stuffiness, which is managed by humidification or a trial of nasal steroids or nasal ipratropium. It is usually possible to overcome these reactions, although very occasionally a period of rest off the ventilator is indicated. We have found it particularly useful at these times to consider other modes of ventilation, including the cuirass and iron lung, and even the rocking bed.

How does intermittent non-invasive ventilation work?

Hill has proposed three theories to explain how as little as 4–6 h of nightly non-invasive ventilation improves daytime symptoms and gas exchange (Hill, 1993). These hypotheses are:

(1) The intermittent rest of the fatigued muscles restores function leading to improved daytime gas exchange and symptoms (Laroche et al., 1989; Moxham, 1990).
(2) Intermittent ventilatory assistance improves daytime gas exchange by increasing lung compliance (Estenne et al., 1983; Gibson et al., 1977).
(3) Respiratory control is blunted during the development of chronic respiratory failure and can be restored by nocturnal non-invasive ventilation.

In more recent studies, Hill and co-workers (1993) withdrew nocturnal ventilation for a week from patients with neuromuscular disease whose respiratory failure had been stabilised by nocturnal ventilation for at least 6 months. During the

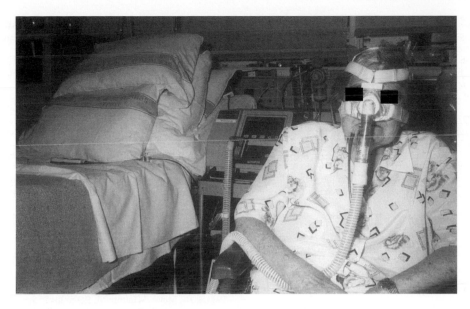

Figure 23.12. Nasal positive pressure ventilator.

non-ventilated phase, nocturnal hypoventilation worsened and symptoms recurred, but vital capacity and the respiratory muscle strength did not change. This suggests that variation of nocturnal hypoventilation with the resetting of the respiratory sensitive CO_2 is the most important of the three mechanisms.

Domiciliary ventilation

Many patients dependent on long-term mechanical ventilation have been well maintained in the home environment (Branthwaite, 1989; Loh, 1983; Sawicka et al., 1988). Such domiciliary ventilation requires detailed initial assessment and meticulous attention to the availability of home care, equipment maintenance, and hospital access. Suitability for domiciliary support is determined by a number of factors, including the degree of respiratory dependence, the associated non-respiratory

disability, and the family back-up. It is necessary to provide the patients and their families with detailed education in the techniques and equipment, the necessary aids (e.g. hoists, suction and communication aids), back-up ventilator and power support, regular medical review (including annual influenza vaccination), and instant access to hospital for servicing and at the earliest indication of intercurrent infection. Equipment maintenance is provided by most manufacturers but in larger units it is cost effective to have technicians available and a store of replacement machines. Thus domiciliary support should be provided and organised by regional centres with appropriate arrangements for funding the cost of the equipment and its maintenance and supervision (Branthwaite, 1989, 1991). Domiciliary ventilatory support is well tolerated by patients and their families and can provide an acceptable and cost-effective alternative to prolonged hospitalisation.

REFERENCES

Alba A, Kahn A, Lee N (1981) Mouth intermittent positive pressure for sleep. *Rehabilitation Gazette 24*: 47

Allen S, Hunt B, Green M (1989) Fall in vital capacity with posture. *British Journal of Diseases of the Chest 79*: 267

Ardran GM, Kelleher WH, Kemp FH (1959) Cineradiographic studies of glossopharyngeal breathing. *British Journal of Radiology 254*: 611

Baker AB, Matzke HA, Brown JR (1950) Poliomyelitis; III Bulbar poliomyelitis. A study of medullary function. *Archives of Neurology and Psychiatry 63*: 257

Bergofsky EH, Turino GM, Fishman AP (1959) Cardiorespiratory failure in kyphoscoliosis. *Medicine 38*: 263

Black LF, Hyatt RE (1969) Maximal respiratory pressures: Normal values and relationship to age and sex. *American Review of Respiratory Diseases 99*: 696

Black LF, Hyatt RE (1971) Maximal static respiratory pressures in generalized neuromuscular disease. *American Review of Respiratory Diseases 103*: 641

Bolton CF, Grand'Maison F, Parkes A, Shukrum M (1992) Needle electromyography of the diaphragm. *Muscle & Nerve 15*: 678

Branthwaite MA (1989) Mechanical ventilation at home. *British Medical Journal 298*: 1409

Branthwaite MA (1991) Non-invasive and domiciliary ventilation: Positive pressure techniques. *Thorax 46*: 208

Bye PTP, Ellis ER, Issa FG, Donnelly PM, Sullivan CE (1990) Respiratory failure and sleep in neuromuscular disease. *Thorax 45*: 241

Caro CG, DuBois AB (1961) Pulmonary function in kyphoscoliosis. *Thorax 16*: 282

Chalmers RM, Howard RS, Wiles CM, Spencer GT (1994) Use of the rocking bed in the treatment of neurogenic respiratory insufficiency. *Quarterly Journal of Medicine 87*: 423

Dail CW, Affeldt JE, Collier CR (1955) Clinical aspects of glossopharyngeal breathing. *Journal of the American Medical Association 158*: 445

De Troyer A, Borenstein S, Cordier R (1980) Analysis of lung volume restriction in patients with respiratory muscle weakness. *Thorax 35*: 603

Douglas JG, Fergusson RJ, Crompton GK, Grant IWB (1983) Artificial ventilation for neurological disease; retrospective analysis 1972–1981. *British Medical Journal 286*: 1943

Douglas NJ (1984) Control of breathing during sleep. *Clinical Science 67*: 465

Drinker PA, McKhann LF (1986) The iron lung. First practical means of respiratory support. *Journal of the American Medical Association 225*: 1476

Ellis ER, Bye PTB, Bruderer JW, Sullivan CE (1987) Treatment of respiratory failure during sleep in patients with neuromuscular disease. *American Review of Respiratory Disease 135*: 148–152

Estenne M, Heilporn A, Delhez L, Yernault JC, De Troyer A (1983) Chest wall stiffness in patients with chronic respiratory muscle weakness. *American Review of Respiratory Disease 128*: 1002

Eve FC (1932) Activation of the inert diaphragm by a gravity method. *Lancet ii*: 995

Feigelson CI, Dickinson DG, Talner NS, Wilson JL (1956) Glossopharyngeal breathing as an aid to coughing mechanism in the patient with chronic poliomyelitis in a respirator. *New England Journal of Medicine 254*: 611

Gibson G (1989) Diaphragmatic paresis: Pathophysiology, clinical features and investigation. *Thorax 44*: 960

Gibson GJ, Pride NB, Newsom Davis J, Loh L (1977) Pulmonary mechanics in patients with respiratory muscle weakness. *American Review of Respiratory Disease 115*: 389

Gillam PMS, Heaf PJD, Kaufman L, Lucas BGB (1964) Respiration in dystrophia myotonica. *Thorax 19*: 112

Glenn WWL, Phelps ML, Elefteriades JA, Dentz B, Hogan JF (1986) Twenty years experience in phrenic nerve stimulation to pace the diaphragm. *Pace 9*: 780

Hamnegard C-H, Wragg S, Kyroussis D, Aquilina R, Moxham J, Green M (1994) Portable measurement of maximal mouth pressures. *European Respiratory Journal 7*: 398

Hamnegard C-H, Wragg S, Kyroussis D, Mills GH, Polkey MI, Moxham J, Green M (1995) Sniff nasal pressure measured with a portable meter. *American Journal of Respiratory and Critical Care Medicine 151*: A415

Hertier F, Rahm F, Pasche P, Fitting J-W (1994) A non-invasive assessment of inspiratory muscle strength. *American Journal of Respiratory and Critical Care Medicine 150*: 1678

Hill NS (1993) Noninvasive ventilation: Does it work, for whom, and how? *American Review of Respiratory Disease 147*: 1050–1055

Houston JG, Angus RM, Cowan MD, McMillan NC, Thomson NC (1994) Ultrasound assessment of normal hemidiaphragmatic movement: Relation to inspiratory volume. *Thorax 49*: 500

Howard RS (1990) Respiratory complications of neurological disease. *Current Medical Literature (Neurology) 6*: 67

Howard RS, Newsom-Davis J (1991) The neural control of respiratory function. In *Neurosurgery: The scientific basis of clinical practice*, 2nd edn. Eds Crockard HA, Hayward R, Hoff JT. Blackwell Scientific Publications, Oxford, pp 318–333

Howard RS, Wiles CM, Spencer GT (1988) The late sequelae of poliomyelitis. *Quarterly Journal of Medicine 251*: 219

Howard RS, Wiles CM, Loh L (1989) Respiratory complications and their management in motor neurone disease. *Brain 112*: 1150

Inkley SR, Oldenburg FC, Vignos PJ (1974) Pulmonary function in Duchenne muscular dystrophy related to stage of disease. *American Journal of Medicine 56*: 297

Issa FG, Sullivan CE (1986) Reversal of central sleep apnoea using nasal CPAP. *Chest 90*: 165

Kelleher WH (1961) A new pattern of iron lung for the prevention and treatment of airway complications in paralytic disease. *Lancet ii*: 1113

Khan Y, Heckmatt JZ (1994) Obstructive apneas in Duchenne muscular dystrophy. *Thorax 49*: 157–161

Kreitzer SM, Saunders NA, Tyler HR, Ingram RH (1978) Respiratory function in amyotrophic lateral sclerosis. *American Review of Respiratory Disease 117*: 443

Laroche CM, Carroll N, Moxham J, Green M (1988) Clinical significance of severe isolated diaphragm weakness. *American Review of Respiratory Disease 147*: 1050

Laroche CM, Moxham J, Green M (1989) Respiratory muscle weakness and fatigue. *Quarterly Journal of Medicine 71*: 373

Linden P, Siebens AA (1983) Dysphagia: Predicting laryngeal penetration. *Archives of Physical Medicine and Rehabilitation 64*: 281

Loh L (1983) Home ventilation. *Anaesthesia 38*: 621

Loh L, Goldman M, Newsom Davis J (1977) The assessment of diaphragm function. *Medicine (Baltimore) 56*: 165

Mier A, Brophy C, Moxham J, Green M (1987) Phrenic nerve stimulation in normal subjects and in patients with diaphragmatic weakness. *Thorax 42*: 885

Miller JM, Moxham J, Green M (1985) The maximal sniff in the assessment of diaphragm function in man. *Clinical Science 69*: 91

Mills GH, Kyroussis D, Hamnegard CH, Polkey MI, Green M, Moxham J (1994a) Bilateral magnetic stimulation of the phrenic nerves using an anterior approach. *Thorax 49*: 1058P

Mills GH, Kyroussis D, Hamnegard CH, Wragg S, Moxham J, Green M (1994b) Unilateral magnetic phrenic nerve stimulation in unilateral diaphragm paresis. *Thorax 49*: 1058–1059P

Misra VP, Howard RS, Youl BD (1995) Neurophysiological examination of respiratory muscle function in myotonic disorders. *Journal of Neurology, Neurosurgery and Psychiatry 59*: 216(A)

Moxham J (1990) Respiratory muscle fatigue: mechanisms, evaluation and therapy. *British Journal of Anaesthetics 65*: 45

Moxham J, Potter D (1988) Diaphragm pacing. *Thorax 43*: 161

Mulvey DA, Aquilina RJ, Eliot MW, Moxham J, Green M (1993) Diaphragmatic dysfunction in neuralgic amyotrophy: An electrophysiologic examination of 16 patients presenting with dyspnoea. *American Review of Respiratory Disease 147*: 66

Newsom Davis J (1967) Phrenic nerve conduction in man. *Journal of Neurology, Neurosurgery and Psychiatry 30*: 420

Newsom Davis J, Goldman M, Loh L, Casson, M (1976) Diaphragmatic function and alveolar hypoventilation. *Quarterly Journal of Medicine 45*: 87

O'Donohue WJ, Baker JP, Bell GM, Muren O, Parker CL, Patterson JL (1976) Respiratory failure in neuromuscular disease. Management in a respiratory intensive care unit. *Journal of the American Medical Association 235*: 733

Patrick JA, Meyer-Whitting M, Reynolds F, Spencer GT (1990) Perioperative care in restrictive respiratory disease. *Anaesthesia 45*: 390

Phillipson EA, Bowes G (1986) Control of breathing during sleep. In *Handbook of physiology, the respiratory system, vol. II*. Ed. Fishman AP. American Physiological Society, Bethesda, MD, p. 649

Plum E (1970) Neurological integration of behavioural and metabolic control of breathing. In *Breathing: Hering–Breuer Centenary Symposium*. Ed. Parker, R. Churchill Livingstone, London, p. 314

Rosenow EC III, Engel AG (1978) Acid maltase deficiency in adults presenting as respiratory failure. *American Journal of Medicine 64*: 485

Russell WR, Schuster E, Smith AC, Spalding JMK (1956) Radcliffe respiration pumps *Lancet i*: 539

Sawicka EH, Spencer GT, Branthwaite MA (1986) Management of respiratory failure complicating pregnancy in severe kyphoscoliosis: A new use for an old technique. *British Journal of Diseases of the Chest 80*: 191

Sawicka EH, Loh L, Branthwaite MA (1988) Domiciliary ventilatory support: An analysis of outcome. *Thorax 43*: 31

Schuster E, Fischer-Williams M (1953) A rocking bed for poliomyelitis. *Lancet ii*: 1074

Seresier DE, Mastaglia FL, Gibson GJ (1982) Respiratory muscle function and ventilatory control. I. In patients with motor neurone disease; II. In patients with myotonic dystrophy. *Quarterly Journal of Medicine 202*: 205

Shneerson JM (1996) Is chronic respiratory failure in neuromuscular diseases worth treating? *Journal of Neurology, Neurosurgery and Psychiatry 61*: 1–3

Similowski T, Fleury B, Launois S, Cathala HP, Bouche P, Derenne JP (1989) Cervical magnetic stimulation: A new painless method for bilateral phrenic nerve stimulation in conscious humans. *Journal of Applied Physiology 67*: 1311–1318

Simonds AK, Parker RA, Branthwaite MA (1986) Effects of protriptyline on sleep related disturbances of breathing in restrictive chest wall disease. *Thorax 41*: 586

Simonds AK, Sawicka EH, Carroll N, Branthwaite MA (1988) Use of negative pressure ventilation to facilitate the return of spontaneous ventilation. *Anaesthesia 43*: 216

Smith PEM, Calverley PMA, Edwards RHT, Evans GA, Campbell EJM (1987) Practical problems in the respiratory care of patients with muscular dystrophy. *New England Journal of Medicine 316*: 1197

Smith PEM, Edwards RHT, Calverley PMA (1991) Mechanisms of sleep disordered breathing in chronic neuromuscular disease: Implications for management. *Quarterly Journal of Medicine 81*: 961–973

Spalding JMK, Opie L (1958) Artificial respiration with the Tunnicliffe breathing jacket. *Lancet i*: 613

Splaingard ML, Hutchins B, Sulton LD, Chaudhuri G (1988) Aspiration in rehabilitation patients: Videofluoroscopy vs bedside clinical assessment. *Archives of Physical Medicine and Rehabilitation 69*: 637

Steljes DG, Kryger MH, Kirk BW et al. (1990) Sleep in post-polio syndrome. *Chest 81*: 133–140.

Stradling JR, Philipson EA (1986) Breathing disorders during sleep. *Quarterly Journal of Medicine 225*: 3

Sykes MK, McNicol MW, Campbell EJM (1976). Introduction. In *Respiratory failure*. Eds Sykes MK, McNicol MW, Campbell EJM. Blackwell Scientific Publications, Oxford, p. xi

Trend P StJ, Wiles CM, Spencer GT, Morgan-Hughes JA, Lake BD, Patrick AD (1985) Acid maltase deficiency in adults. *Brain 108*: 845

Wragg S, Hamnegard CH, Kyroussis D, Mills G, Green M, Moxham J (1994) Assessment of diaphragm strength in patients using cervical magnetic stimulation. *American Journal of Respiratory and Critical Care Medicine 149*: A130

24. Chronic fatigue

Simon Wessely   Trudie Chalder

WHAT IS FATIGUE?

There are few statements to rival "Doctor, I feel tired all the time" in their ability to frustrate the neurologist. Fatigue is vague, imprecise, and difficult to measure. In theory it can be a symptom of most of the contents of the Oxford Textbooks of Medicine and Psychiatry, but in practice it is often unexplained. It is also common, and can be incapacitating. Most neurologists will admit to having little idea of how to manage patients once the usual tests have proven negative, as they so often do. This chapter will begin by describing the nature of chronic fatigue, and will then turn to the management of the chronically fatigued patient in neurological practice.

In neurophysiological terms, fatigue is the failure to sustain force or power output, in contrast to weakness, which is the failure to generate force (Edwards, 1981). As such, fatigue can be measured objectively. In neuropsychology, fatigue can refer to time-related decrements in the ability to perform mental tasks, and can also be measured, although such measures are influenced by other factors such as motivation, attention, and arousal. However, fatigue is also a subjective sensation, experienced by patients, inaccessible to objective measurement (Muscio, 1921; Wessely et al., 1998). Patients use a variety of terms to describe this elusive but unpleasant feeling, such as tiredness, weariness, and exhaustion. It also merges into the experience of muscle pain. Overall, the distinctions between fatigue, weakness, and pain, which are so vital for the neurologist or neurophysiologist, are in practice less important for the patient.

WHAT IS CHRONIC FATIGUE SYNDROME?

Chronic fatigue is as old as medicine itself. During the Victorian era, patients with chronic fatigue made up a substantial part of neurological practice, where they usually carried the label of "neurasthenia". The history of neurasthenia is outside the scope of this chapter (see Shorter, 1992; Wessely, 1994), but it occupies a key place in the history of neurology. Indeed, those interested not only in the history of their discipline but also in the wider subject of the often troubled relations between patients and doctors, and the way in which the treatments of chronic fatigue remain subject to fashion, would probably enjoy reading more on this subject.

During the 1980s there was a very welcome revival of interest in the subject of chronic fatigue, and in the patients who suffer from it. This was heralded in the United Kingdom by the extensive publicity awarded a "new" illness, myalgic encephalomyelitis (ME). In fact, the condition was neither new nor an encephalomyelitis, but nevertheless it caught the public imagination. It also caught the profession unprepared and it was some time before doctors woke up to this problem. However, since the 1990s we have seen a steady progress in terms of our recognition of, understanding of, and management of the condition. We now recognise that "ME" was an inappropriate label, and it has been replaced by the term "chronic fatigue syndrome" (CFS), a label that is short and accurate.

CFS is defined operationally. The criteria include patients who complain of chronic physical and mental fatigue as well as other symptoms such as muscle pain with no identifiable organic disease, and marked physical disability (Fukuda, 1994; Sharpe et al., 1991). The symptoms should be present for 6 months or more and patients suffering from physical diseases known to produce fatigue should be excluded. Patients with depression and anxiety are not excluded but the presence of a major mental illness such as schizophrenia would be considered an exclusion criterion.

THE SCOPE OF THE PROBLEM

Chronic fatigue is common in the community—between 20 and 30% of people will answer positively to a question "do you feel tired all the time?" It is common in general practice. Between 10 and 20% of attendees will complain of chronic fatigue, and for 5 to 10% it will be the principal complaint. It is common in general medicine: 8% of those attending an American internal medicine clinic did so with a new complaint of fatigue (Kroenke & Mangelsdorff, 1989); 5% of those seeing British neurologists were recorded as having "giddiness, fatigue", over and above those with recognised psychiatric problems (Hopkins et al., 1989).

There is no disagreement that patients with chronic fatigue are common in all medical settings, but what about chronic fatigue syndrome? Initial reports suggested the condition might be unusual. However, all of these were based on specialist samples and/or key informants and, as such, subject to considerable selection and information biases (Wessely, 1995). More recent studies using systematic case ascertainment have shown considerably higher prevalences. At present it appears that about 0.2–0.5% of primary care attenders fulfil criteria for CFS, even if the majority do not use terms like CFS or ME to describe their illness (Wessely et al., 1997).

Whatever names are given to these conditions, and whatever criteria are used for diagnosis, one thing seems clear. These patients are characterised by very high rates of symptoms, distress, and disability. As many are young adults rendered incapable of work because of their illness, the personal, social, and economic impact of the syndrome is very high (Buchwald et al., 1996; Henriksson & Burckhardt, 1996; Schweitzer et al., 1995; Wessely et al., 1997).

MUSCLE PATHOLOGY AND BIOCHEMISTRY

Because patients with chronic fatigue and CFS can be so limited in terms of physical activity, and because they also frequently complain of pain in their muscles, many investigators have been interested in the subject of possible neuromuscular dysfunction. Unlike the central nervous system (CNS) and, perhaps, the psyche, it is relatively easy to obtain samples of peripheral muscle for investigation. In consequence there is a large literature on the topic of muscle structure and function in CFS.

Is there a disorder of muscle structure?

There were several early reports of histological abnormalities in patients with CFS. Later work suggested these were mild and non-specific (Byrne & Trounce, 1987; Preedy et al., 1993). Edwards and colleagues found a range of changes in 81% of muscle biopsies from patients with CFS (Edwards et al., 1993). These included degenerative and regenerative changes, mitochondrial hyperplasia, increased single fibre electromyographic activity, and others. However, one-third of those from normal controls were similarly abnormal—the range of abnormalities resembling those of the cases. Edwards et al. concluded that there are no consistent changes in fibre size. Connolly and co-workers, in a study that deserves to be better known, found that in patients with typical symptoms of CFS, both with and without an apparent viral trigger, muscle biopsy and electrophysiology were essentially normal (Connolly et al., 1993). However, in a third group of patients with prominent symptoms of myalgia but no symptoms of mental fatigue and fatigability, muscle biopsy abnormalities, albeit non-specific, were noted. The authors noted that this group made up only 2% of those referred to the clinician concerned, who specialises in chronic fatigue.

A similar story comes from the literature on fibromyalgia, a disorder that some feel is synonymous with CFS, and certainly shows considerable overlap. After a series of studies reporting various abnormalities, none have withstood the introduction of better blinded methodologies (Wortmann, 1994; Yunus et al., 1989). The most recent reviews now assume that the frequency of type I and type II fibres is normal (Henriksson et al., 1993). Rather than a global disorder of muscle histology, some samples of muscle tissue show areas of muscle microtrauma. This is a normal finding, the changes in fibromyalgia being quantitative rather than qualitative (Jacobsen et al., 1991b).

Is CFS a metabolic disorder?

No evidence has been found of an inflammatory response consistent with myositis. There is no evidence of increases in serum levels of skeletal muscle enzymes, such as creatine kinase, a sensitive indicator of muscle damage. Extensive biochemical studies have shown no evidence of abnormalities in mitochondrial or glycolytic enzymes (Byrne & Trounce, 1987). Overall, there is no evidence of widespread muscle cell damage when investigated by traditional histological methods (Jamal & Miller, 1991).

Modern techniques now permit dynamic measures of muscle biochemistry in response to exercise. An early single case report raised the possibility that symptoms could be the result of a metabolic myopathy (Arnold et al., 1984). Conventional neurological examination was normal but a muscle biopsy revealed scattered necrotic fibres and type II fibre predominance. Using ^{31}P nuclear magnetic resonance spectroscopy as a non-invasive way of measuring intracellular muscle fibre pH and changes in intermediary metabolites, the researchers demonstrated early and severe acidification following prolonged ischaemic exercise. The conclusion was that the basis of the patient's fatigue was abnormal lactic acid accumulation as a result of excessive glycolytic activity. A subsequent larger study failed to replicate the original *Lancet* report, instead finding a tendency to slow recovery, as predicted, but no excess acidification and no accumulation of inorganic phosphate (Kent-Braun et al., 1993). These researchers, and two other groups, have failed to find any evidence of early acidosis or evidence of a metabolic myopathy in CFS (Miller et al., 1996; Sisto et al., 1996; Wong et al., 1992). Normal biochemical and metabolic responses to exercise have also been found in fibromyalgia—a global alteration in energy metabolism is not thought to contribute to that condition either (Jacobsen et al., 1992; Wortmann, 1994).

Lactate responses to exercise provide another, simpler, method of assessing muscle metabolism. Researchers in Liverpool reported that lactate response to exercise in CFS is either normal or mildly increased compared to controls, but only towards the end of the test (Riley et al., 1990; Wagenmakers et al., 1988). Researchers at Charing Cross Hospital have found a subgroup with an abnormal lactate response to submaximal exercise (Lane et al., 1995). This group was less likely to have overt psychiatric disorder than those with normal lactate responses. Lane et al. concluded that exercise intolerance might result from several different processes—psychiatric disorder, deconditioning, and impaired anaerobic metabolism.

There have also been claims of deficits in mitochondrial numbers, structure, and function. A group working in Glasgow reported that 35 out of 50 electron microscopic examinations revealed considerable structural abnormalities in the mitochondria (Behan et al., 1991), as did an Italian group, albeit in a smaller sample (Vecchiet et al., 1996). This would be compatible with the demonstration of reduced oxidative metabolism in CFS (McCully et al., 1996b), but there remain objections to such a hypothesis. First, the frequent finding of normal physiological performance is incompatible with claims of a mitochondrial myopathy (Barnes et al., 1993). Second, the potential role of inactivity must be considered. Edwards and his team demonstrated impaired mitochondrial function in a series of patients with unexplained muscle pain, labelled at that time as effort syndrome but probably equally well described as CFS. Activity levels have a significant effect on mitochondrial enzyme activity (Brierley et al., 1996), so reductions in enzyme activity could be secondary to reduced muscle use (Brierley et al., 1996; Edwards et al., 1993) as could the finding of reduced muscle oxidative metabolism (McCully et al., 1996b). Third, a blinded study found no difference in the prevalence of mitochondrial abnormalities between cases and controls (Plioplys & Plioplys, 1995).

The suggestion that fatigue in CFS was the result of a myopathy has therefore not found widespread acceptance. It seems unlikely that any specific metabolic abnormality underlies fatigue in this syndrome, although abnormalities might be present in a minority of patients (Barnes et al., 1993).

Total RNA and total protein per cell has been shown to be reduced in muscle biopsies of CFS patients (Edwards et al., 1991). In vivo studies of whole body protein synthesis and quadriceps muscle protein synthesis were investigated using radiolabelled isotopes (Preedy et al., 1993), and significant decreases were found in CFS cases: muscle RNA and protein synthesis were decreased (Preedy et al., 1993). These results confirm a reduced capacity for protein synthesis. One possibility is that persistent infection interferes with the balance of protein synthesis and degradation, as found in acute sepsis (Baracos et al., 1983). Alternatively, these findings are another result of inactivity—profound decreases in muscle protein synthesis and muscle RNA activity were observed in normal men with 1 month unilateral leg immobilisation after tibial fracture (Gibson et al., 1987).

In conclusion, a variety of abnormalities of muscle structure and function have been noted in CFS and fibromyalgia. Many represent normal variations, albeit at increased frequency. Specific abnormalities are found less frequently and are a conflicting mixture of atrophy and hypertrophy of different fibre groups. No consensus exists as to their meaning. There is little to suggest a primary metabolic problem. The most recent commentators have concluded that both CFS and fibromyalgia are unlikely in the most part to be a primary muscle disorder, and that impaired muscle function and pain are secondary phenomena (Bennett & Jacobsen, 1994; Geel, 1994).

NEUROPHYSIOLOGY AND NEUROMUSCULAR FUNCTION

Structural or biochemical deficits in the muscle appear unlikely to explain fatigue in CFS. What then is the physiological basis for fatigue in the condition? This question baffled investigators into neurasthenia, and remains a source of contention today. A useful conceptual framework is that of Richard Edwards, who divided fatigue into peripheral elements (caused by a failure at or beyond the neuromuscular junction) and central fatigue (caused by a failure of neural drive, reflected in an inability to sustain the necessary motor unit firing) (Edwards, 1981). Central fatigue might reflect deficits in the organisation, integration, and initiation of motor activity (see Chapter 3). Like so much else, this is not a new concept—something similar was proposed over a hundred years ago by Vivian Poore, physician at Charing Cross Hospital (Poore, 1875). Loss of power was a feature of local fatigue, but general fatigue has both physical and mental symptoms. Some people assume that central fatigue is a euphemism for abnormal motivation, but this is erroneous.

Is neuromuscular function abnormal?

Several studies have looked at muscle strength and performance in CFS. Stokes et al. (1988) examined 30 patients with excessive fatigue, present for between 1 and 19 years, and associated with severe morbidity and functional impairment. They were compared with normal controls. Maximum isometric force, assessed in the quadriceps, was normal for all the males. Half of the female cases failed to achieve maximum force but showed increases in force when twitches induced by electrical stimulation of the muscle were interpolated. This shows that the failure of force was not due to a peripheral mechanism but to a reduction of central drive. This was not found in males. The Liverpool group also studied adductor pollicis brevis fatigability during arterial occlusion using a sphygmomanometer (Stokes et al., 1988). No significant differences emerged between cases and controls, nor were abnormalities found in maximal relaxation or the length of time for aerobic recovery.

From Australia, Andrew Lloyd, in collaboration with Simon Gandevia, reported two studies of neuromuscular function in CFS. In the first (Lloyd et al., 1988) they studied endurance assessed by measurements of repeated maximal isometric contractions of elbow flexors. Maximum isometric strength was normal. Later they studied repetitive, submaximal exercise, which more closely approximates to the normal demands made on muscles in real life (Lloyd et al., 1991). Maximal voluntary isometric strength was again normal, as were twitch interpolation studies, suggesting that there was no peripheral component to fatigue and that central activation was also complete. Gandevia's group report similar findings in fibromyalgia (Miller et al., 1996). The decline in force produced by submaximal isometric exercise was also normal, which was also noted in fibromyalgia. Fatigue index, a measure of the ratio of muscle endurance and maximal voluntary contraction, was reported as normal in CFS, in contrast to multiple sclerosis (Djaldetti et al., 1996).

One group reports a slowed acceleration of heart rate in response to exercise, which would not be compatible with deconditioning (Montague et al., 1989). However, the Liverpool group found that CFS patients had significantly higher heart rates at submaximal exercise (Riley et al., 1990), and a third group reports entirely normal responses (Sisto et al., 1996).

Is CFS characterised by delayed fatigue?

Ramsay, who was almost single handedly responsible for the revival of interest in chronic fatigue in the United Kingdom, always argued that the characteristic fatigue in CFS was its delayed nature, "this phenomenon of muscle fatigability is the dominant and most persistent feature of the disease and in my opinion a diagnosis should not be made without it. Restoration of muscle power after exertion can take three to five days or more" (Ramsay, 1986). Similar claims were made for neurasthenia (Wessely, 1994). However, this has largely not been confirmed. The Australian group concluded that, "the prominent subjective complaints of muscle fatigue in these patients contrasted with the relatively normal behaviour of their muscles during a controlled test" (Lloyd et al., 1988). They later wondered if the prominent complaints of increased symptoms after exercise were related to excessive production of cytokines in response to exercise, but they were not (Lloyd et al., 1994). Workers from the Liverpool group also studied delayed fatigue (Gibson et al., 1993). Chronically fatigued patients were exercised to exhaustion using cycle ergometry. They were restudied at 24 and 48 h later. Both patients and controls demonstrated fatigability following maximal exercise. However, the rate of recovery of force was identical between the two groups, despite the fact that the patient group continued to complain of persistent weakness and fatigability even at 48 h after exercise. An American study (McCully et al., 1996a) retested subjects 48 h after a single bout of strenuous exercise. Only one out of 15 subjects was unable to repeat the exercise test, and no differences in metabolic responses were noted. The same group went on to report that exercise caused a substantial increase in symptoms in only one patient, whereas for the majority subjective recordings of vigour and fatigue showed only minor changes (Sisto et al., 1996).

In general, laboratory studies have failed to reveal evidence that exercise is associated either with an abnormal deterioration in performance, and/or evidence of "relapse" (McCully et al., 1996a and b). This is in sharp contrast to the anecdotal reports of sufferers. The differences could relate to the particular setting of the investigation, and the fact that controlled studies in laboratory conditions with trained investigators fail to activate the particular cognitive responses to exercise that occur in the natural setting. Rutherford and White studied a group of subjects with persistent fatigue after proven Epstein–Barr infection— a unique group of subjects with definite postinfectious fatigue (Rutherford & White, 1991). The pattern of results was similar to those observed by Lloyd and his colleagues, and the conclusions identical: that, "neither poor motivation nor muscle contractile failure is important in the pathogenesis of fatigue" (Lloyd et al., 1991).

Nerve conduction studies and CFS

There is agreement that conventional neurophysiological studies provide no evidence for abnormalities in the structure and function of motor units (Jamal & Miller, 1991). There is less agreement about the results of more sophisticated electrophysiological investigations, in particular single fibre electromyography (SF-EMG). Experienced investigators in Glasgow reported abnormal jitter values in 75% of a selected sample (Jamal & Miller, 1991). However, impulse blocking, a feature of deficits in neuromuscular transmission, did not occur. Others have argued that abnormal jitter alone cannot be related to fatigability (Lloyd et al., 1988; Stokes et al., 1988), because there was no evidence of impulse blocking, which alone would indicate failure of the neuromuscular junction. Attempts at replication have been unsuccessful (Kent-Braun et al., 1993; Nix, 1994; Roberts & Byrne, 1994).

CFS and the perception of effort

Neurophysiological and neuromuscular research has not shown any compelling evidence of a primary muscle disorder in CFS. But if this is the case, why are so many CFS patients so limited in terms of exercise tolerance? One theory is of a disorder of perception—that CFS patients rate themselves as subjectively more fatigued than the results of objective tests would indicate, and thus cease work at an earlier stage than indicated by the state of their muscles. Several investigators have studied the differences between perceived measures of work rate and exercise tolerance, and actual measures. Workers from Liverpool looked at exercise tolerance and perceived exertion using cycle ergometry (Gibson et al., 1993). They found that, despite subjective evidence that maximum exercise had been achieved, this was not corroborated by the physiological findings. Riley and colleagues (1990) also noted that ratings of perceived exertion differed between cases and both normal controls and those with irritable bowel syndrome (IBS). Similar findings have been noted in fibromyalgia (Mengshoel et al., 1995; Miller et al., 1996; Norregaard et al., 1994). CFS patients tended to over-rate both their premorbid exercise tolerance and their desired exercise tolerance, compared to both normal and IBS controls. Only the Australian group, using the same rating scale, was unable to confirm differences in perceived exertion (Lloyd et al., 1991). There is thus some evidence suggesting a dissociation between subjective experience of muscle fatigability and objective evidence, perhaps allied to a tendency to symptom monitoring.

To summarise, some CFS patients have normal exercise responses, both physiologically and metabolically. Others have reduced endurance and an increase in the metabolic products of exercise. Yet others have a reduced exercise capacity, associated with a reduced heart rate. No single abnormality or explanation can link all these findings. Overall, the two most likely explanations are that many CFS patients have a completely normal exercise capacity, whereas others have a reduced capacity secondary to physical deconditioning. A third group of patients fails to exercise to their apparent capacity, but whether or not this represents a reluctance to do so (because, for example, of a fear of pain, exhaustion, and relapse) or an inability to do so because of a reduced central drive, is unclear.

MENTAL FATIGUE AND FATIGABILITY

One reason for caution in accepting a primary neuromuscular cause is the clinical observation that, in many patients, pain occurs at rest or immediately after waking up. Such myalgia cannot be accounted for by any known mechanism of muscle function. Similarly, fatigue after mental exertion, a characteristic of CFS, cannot be explained by a muscle defect either (Wessely & Powell, 1989).

Fatigue in CFS is mediated by central rather than peripheral mechanisms, although the nature of these mechanisms remains obscure. Possibilities include aberration in circulatory regulation during exercise, as noted in neurocirculatory asthenia (Mantysaari et al., 1988), the effects of inactivity on performance, and centrally mediated disorders of perception and mood disorder. It is unlikely to represent abnormal muscle physiology at the level of the muscle, motor cortex, or motor neurones responsible for voluntary muscle activation (McComas et al., 1995). Poor motivation is likely to be an explanation for only a small number of cases (Miller et al., 1996).

Overall, CFS is not a neuromuscular disorder. There is probably a subgroup in whom primary neuromuscular mechanisms for abnormal fatigability do exist, but this will be a small minority of subjects. At present, we would consider alternative neuromuscular diagnoses and/or mechanisms mainly in subjects presenting with symptoms such as fatigue and myalgia that are clearly exercise related, do not occur at rest, and are not accompanied by any particular symptoms of mental fatigability (Connolly et al., 1993).

PSYCHIATRY AND CHRONIC FATIGUE

Prevalence of psychiatric disorder

Numerous studies have been published concerning the role of psychiatric disorder in adults with CFS, of which at least 11 use direct interviews (see Wessely et al., 1998). A variety of instruments and operational criteria have been used, but the results are surprisingly consistent. Approximately half of those seen in specialist care with a diagnosis of one or other form of CFS fulfil criteria for affective disorder, even with fatigue removed from the criteria for mood disorder. The majority of studies find that a further quarter fulfil criteria for other psychiatric disorders, chief amongst which are anxiety and somatisation disorders. Nearly all also agree that between one-quarter and one-third do not fulfil any criteria.

Affective disorder is thus linked with CFS, but the association is not a simple one. First, the pattern of mood disorder is not always that with which psychiatrists are most familiar. The atypical depressive disorders (in which there is increased sleep and appetite rather than the more customary decrease) might be more relevant. Assessing the phenomenology of depressive illness in CFS subjects is not always straightforward—difficulties can arise in distinguishing anhedonia, which is the loss of pleasure and is central to the concept of depression, from an inability to perform previously enjoyable activities.

Anxiety disorders are also common, but often overlooked, partly because of the difficulties in determining whether avoidance is related to phobic processes or neuromuscular weakness. Hyperventilation can play an important role in some patients. There have been claims that hyperventilation was found in all CFS patients but, like all unitary explanations of CFS, this has not been confirmed (Saisch et al., 1994).

Somatisation disorder presents another difficult problem. Patients with long histories of multiple somatic symptoms, stretching back to adolescence, are common in CFS clinics, as they are across general medicine. They can have previous episodes of unexplained abdominal pain, food allergies, chemical sensitivities, unresolved gynaecological problems, funny turns, and so on. Some fulfil criteria for somatisation disorder (Briquet's syndrome).

To a certain extent, this overlap between CFS and somatisation disorder (SD) is predictable, as the definitions of both CFS and SD require multiple symptoms (Johnson et al., 1996a); indeed the multiple symptom criteria for CFS actively select for SD. When another group of researchers excluded those symptoms common to the definitions of CFS and SD, the prevalence of SD fell but was still substantially elevated at 20% (Katon et al., 1991). A more relevant observation could be that the greater the number of somatic symptoms, the greater the probability of psychiatric disorder—hence the greater the somatic distress, the more assiduously should the neurologist be aware of the probability of psychiatric disorder.

These, and other, observations serve to dispel the idea, prevalent in some quarters, that there is a wide group of disorders that fall under the term "CFS", which is predominantly psychosocial, and a core called "ME", which is more severe, has a characteristic pattern of fatigability, and is primarily of organic origin. In fact the converse is true. There is no evidence that mild forms of CFS are primarily psychological and severe forms are more likely to be organic in origin. Instead, that group within CFS with more symptoms, profounder fatigability, greater disability, and longer illness duration is the subset with the strongest associations with psychological disorder (see Anon., 1996; Wessely et al., 1998).

Explanations

If psychiatric disorders are common, what are the possible explanations? One is artefactual—the criteria used to diagnose common psychological disorders overlap with those for the

Table 24.1. Current psychiatric disorder in CFS compared with medical controls

Author(s)	Control group	% psychiatric disorder: CFS	% psychiatric disorder: controls	Relative risk of psychiatric disorder in CFS compared with controls
Wessely and Powell (1989)	Neuromuscular	72	36	2.0
Katon et al. (1991)	Rheumatoid arthritis	45	6	7.5
Wood et al. (1991)	Myopathy	41	12.5	3.3
Pepper et al. (1993)	Multiple sclerosis	23	8	2.9
Fischler et al. (1997)	ENT/dermatology	77	50	3.4
Lynch (1997)	Diabetes	81	28	2.9
Johnson et al. (1996b,c)	Multiple sclerosis	45	16	2.8

diagnosis of CFS. High rates of psychiatric disorders in CFS are thus inevitable, and do not themselves imply causality. As Kendell has written in the context of CFS, "the statement that someone has a depressive illness is merely a statement about their symptoms. It has no causal implications" (Kendell, 1991).

The next explanation is that these are simply misdiagnosed cases of depression and anxiety. This must be true for some, and there are many subjects for whom the standard psychiatric classification, explanations, and treatments are adequate to the situation. In its severe form, the symptoms of CFS and those of major depression are hard to distinguish, and it is also known that depressive disorder alone is associated with severe functional impairment.

However, this unitary explanation flounders on the reasons outlined in the previous paragraph because, with the occasional exception, it implies an implicit hierarchy of symptomatic classification. It also ignores the fact that in many there is insufficient to justify a psychiatric diagnosis.

Could the observed psychological disorder simply be a reaction to physical illness? This explanation is the least appealing, first because there is as yet no definitive evidence of a clear-cut physical pathology, and second because studies that use medical controls find rates of psychiatric disorder in the CFS cases that are invariably in excess of those in the control, often substantially so (Table 24.1). Alternatively, could it be due to selection bias? Again, this is unlikely, because a similar proportion seen in primary care with chronic fatigue or CFS also fulfil criteria for psychiatric disorder (Wessely et al., 1997), although in other ways the samples are different.

The final explanation suggests that CFS and psychiatric disorder arises from a common pathology. This argument must therefore involve some common neurobiological dysfunction.

THE NEUROPSYCHIATRY AND NEUROPSYCHOLOGY OF CHRONIC FATIGUE

Models linking CFS with muscular dysfunction no longer find much favour. This interest has largely been transferred to studies of possible central nervous or neuroendocrine disorders. This is a welcome development because, unlike muscular studies, this paradigm is closer to the clinical features of the condition.

The first line of evidence comes from studies of neuroendocrine function. Several lines of inquiry have centred on neuroendocrine aspects of CFS. First, there is the relationship between mood disorder, with its well-documented abnormalities in neuroendocrine function. Second, some have pointed out the similarities between CFS and glucocorticoid deficiency. Severe fatigue (including postexertional fatigue), myalgia, arthralgia, and mood and sleep disturbances occur in both. Abnormalities of the hypothalamic–pituitary adrenal axis (HPA) have recently been described in a series of 30 patients with CFS compared to 72 normal controls (Demitrack et al., 1991). The patients had lower urinary excretion rates of free cortisol and reduced evening plasma cortisol concentrates in conjunction with an elevated plasma adrenocorticotrophic hormone (ACTH). The adrenal cortex was hypersensitive to low doses of ACTH, with a blunted ceiling response. ACTH responses to cortisol releasing hormone (CRH) were attenuated, despite low ambient cortisol levels (which therefore cannot be exerting an inhibitory feedback effect). The impaired HPA function cannot be due to primary adrenal insufficiency because ACTH responsiveness is preserved, and pituitary insufficiency is unlikely because of the elevated ACTH concentrations: the findings are thus most compatible with impaired function at the level of the hypothalamus, which is compromising CRH synthesis/secretion. Meanwhile, in the related condition of fibromyalgia, Crofford and colleagues (1994) also reported low 24-h urinary cortisol, but a different pattern of response to CRH challenge.

It can thus be argued that, in a subgroup of CFS (those without evidence of major depression), a pattern can be discerned of an underactive HPA system, which should be contrasted with the overactive pattern characteristic of severe depression. Indeed, one can speculate that CFS and depression lie along a continuum of serotonin activity in the CNS, reflected in differing patterns of HPA activity, and finally in differing patterns of exhaustion versus agitation, insomnia versus hypersomnia, and so on. Furthermore, as a recent study was able to reproduce the neuroendocrine profile of CFS in a group of healthy nightshift workers, the possibility that such changes are the consequences, and not the causes, of the pattern of symptoms found in CFS remains very much open (Leese et al., 1996).

Another role for neuroendocrine studies is to gain information on central neurotransmitter function—the "window on the brain" paradigm. Studies using agents that act at the 5-hydroxytryptamine (5-HT) receptor have shown that 5-HT neurotransmission is increased relative to not only normal, but also depressed, controls (Bakheit et al., 1992; Sharpe et al., 1997b). Cleare and colleagues (1995) measured the prolactin response to D-fenfluramine, a selective 5-HT-releasing agent. The prolactin response was highest in the CFS patients, lowest in the depressed subjects (as expected), and intermediate in the controls (Cleare et al., 1995). The tentative conclusion is that those CFS patients without concurrent depression show evidence of reduced HPA axis activity and increased 5-HT function, the mirror image of major depression. This might either explain (or be the result of) the clinical observation that CFS is characterised by hypersomnia and preserved appetite, in contrast to classic major depression.

The next piece in the jigsaw is provided by neuropsychological studies. To date, there have been at least twenty studies of varying degrees of methodological sophistication. There is no doubt that patients experience substantial complaints of cognitive dysfunction. Pierre Janet recognised the same when he wrote that, "Tiredness and a horrible sense of fatigue is caused in psychasthenics by the least sense of physical or psychological effort. Fatigue rapidly affects sensations and perceptions, intellect and movement" (Janet, 1919). Modern neuropsychological testing has revealed few further insights beyond his observations.

With regards to global intellectual functioning, research to date is unequivocal. There is no decline or primary deficit in intellectual functioning (Moss-Morris et al., 1996; Wearden & Appleby, 1996). Similarly, there is no evidence of sensory or perceptual impairments in CFS (Prasher et al., 1990). What seems to be emerging is a picture of a mismatch between the subject's own perception of cognitive disturbance and the level of actual decrements in performance determined on testing (Schmaling et al., 1994). Although selective attention appears impaired (Joyce et al., 1996), formal deficits in memory appear increasingly unlikely. The complaints of poor memory and concentration are most likely to be related to the same processes observed in mood disorder, but the problems of selective attention are less likely to be the result of depression. Patients with CFS might have a bias for processing somatic or fatigue-related information and increased attention to bodily sensations could well affect attentional processes. However, higher cognitive functioning, such as planning, organising, problem-solving, and conceptualisation, do not appear to be affected.

Perhaps the best publicised, but the least researched, area is that of neuroimaging. Studies using magnetic resonance techniques have concentrated on the appearance of punctate foci of high signal intensity (so-called "unexplained bright objects" (UBOs)). These have either been substantially increased, moderately increased, or not increased at all compared to controls (Cope & David, 1996; Greco et al., 1997).

It is also too early to judge the results of functional neuroimaging studies. There are at least six published studies using functional neuroimaging techniques such as single photon emission tomography (SPET) in CFS. None is without problems (Cope & David, 1996). In one study (Schwartz et al., 1994) a substantially increased number of defects was seen in CFS subjects than in normal controls. However, there was no difference in the number or situation of defects between CFS and depressed controls, all being confined to the frontal and temporal lobes. There were, however, differences in the patterns of radionucleotide uptake between depression and CFS. Another study found that brainstem perfusion was significantly reduced in CFS subjects compared to controls, with depressed patients showing intermediate values (Costa et al., 1995). However, other groups do not report brainstem perfusion values because of the technical difficulties of imaging this small structure. Any interpretation of this finding must await its independent replication. It is, however, most unlikely that this will be a test for "ME", as so frequently claimed by the media. Instead a more accurate statement of the current evidence of neuroimaging in the investigation of CFS is that, "findings are neither sufficiently sensitive nor specific to allow its use as a diagnostic tool, although it may have a role in understanding the pathophysiology of the disease" (Patterson et al., 1995).

BELIEFS, BEHAVIOURS AND CHRONIC FATIGUE

We now move away from either a medical or a psychiatric perspective on chronic fatigue and its syndromes. The reason is that, to date, although there has been considerable activity and ingenuity looking for the "cause" of CFS, this has not led to any startling revelations. True, certain factors have been shown to convey a higher risk of subsequent CFS, such as infection by the Epstein–Barr virus or episodes of viral meningitis (White, 1997). In their place, we consider what happens to patients after they develop symptoms, regardless of their original cause.

The effects of inactivity.   All of us know that rest is appropriate in the initial stages of a viral infection, and can indeed have a protective function. However, the prolonged rest and extreme inactivity that is common in CFS (reinforced by the advice given to sufferers) is less helpful. Rest relieves fatigue in the short term but, in the longer term, it reduces activity tolerance and has profound effects on cardiovascular and neuromuscular function, as well as thermoregulation (see Sharpe et al., 1992). Inactivity not only increases the sensation of fatigue on exertion but also reduces the desire to undertake activity (Zorbas & Matveyev, 1986). With the passage of time, more symptoms and greater fatigue will continue to occur at progressively lower levels of exertion. Inactivity therefore sustains symptoms, and increases sensitivity to them.

Why do so many patients adopt rest as the key strategy to reduce symptoms? It is important to realise that this strategy has been adopted for good reasons. First, many patients have been advised this is the best method to reduce symptoms and prevent permanent disability—one self-help book promotes something called "aggressive rest therapy" as the best management for CFS (Feiden, 1990). Fortunately, such nihilistic advice is now less frequently encountered, linked to increased recognition of the deleterious effects of total rest (Anon., 1994). Nevertheless, media reports on the subject continue to give firm advice to reduce activity in response in symptoms on a bad day, advice for which empirical evidence remains lacking. The second reason is that patients have found from their own experience that rest works—it reduces aversive symptoms such as muscle pain. However, this short-term benefit comes with a long-term cost. Finally, most patients have found that the opposite of rest—exercise—increases symptoms.

Inconsistent activity. Not every CFS sufferer is profoundly inactive, many strive to keep going and, to this end, adopt a "boom and bust" pattern, as do fibromyalgia patients (Nielsen et al., 1992). Typically, excessive or prolonged rest is followed by a burst of activity, which, compared to the preceding level of inactivity, is often "too much, too soon". This pattern can be reinforced by the sense of frustration often encountered in sufferers, and perhaps also by pre-existing personality and lifestyle factors, such as perfectionism and high level of physical fitness. In practice, many patients have attempted sudden increases in activity and find that they culminate in exhaustion, for which the inevitable response is further rest. This "stop–start" pattern means that although extremes of disability are often avoided, sufferers are unable to build up a sustained level of recovery. This pattern often leads to the characteristic complaint of CFS sufferers—that any activity must be "paid for" later by further pain and fatigue. Delayed fatigue and myalgia are well-recognised physiological phenomena that occur between 24 and 48 h after any exertion in excess of a person's current (and not previous) fitness (Anon., 1987). The mechanism is due to the appearance of eccentric muscle contractions leading to local muscle microtrauma in muscles subjected to excess work, occurring in anyone undertaking exertion after a period of inactivity (Klug et al., 1989; Newham, 1988). This is an attractive hypothesis for the delayed fatigue and myalgia reported as characteristic of CFS, although local muscle microtrauma cannot fully explain the generalised and diffuse myalgia often reported.

Illness beliefs and fears about symptoms. Beliefs and fears can influence disability, mood, and behaviour in any illness. In CFS, unhelpful illness beliefs include fear that any activity that causes an increase in fatigue is damaging or impossible; that "doing too much" causes permanent muscle damage; and that CFS is irreversible or untreatable. Such catastrophic beliefs are both common in CFS patients and are related to disability (Petrie et al., 1995). In the initial stages of CFS, such beliefs can fuel avoidance of activity and are often powerfully reinforced by each successive aversive experience of activity-related fatigue, leading to increasing restrictions. Using avoidant strategies to cope with chronic fatigue was associated with worse disability (Antoni et al., 1994; Ray et al., 1995). A Dutch study reported a relationship between attributing fatigue to a physical cause and lack of physical activity, and between lack of physical activity and severity of fatigue, implying that in CFS it is the specific illness beliefs that determine the pattern of behavioural avoidance and contribute to the experience of fatigue. Such a pattern was not found in controls with multiple sclerosis (Vercoulen et al., 1996b).

Symptom focusing. Increased symptom focusing is also noted in CFS (Ray et al., 1995; Vercoulen et al., 1996b). Concern about the meaning and significance of symptoms

(which are often interpreted as "warning signals") is heightened by the unpredictable nature of CFS. Increased concern leads to heightened awareness, selective attention, and "body watching", which can then intensify both the experience and perceived frequency of symptoms, thereby confirming illness beliefs and reinforcing illness behaviour.

Emotional consequences. For some CFS patients, depression is the primary cause of ill health, but for others depression can arise during the illness, together with anxiety, frustration, and simple boredom. Of whatever cause, depression and anxiety are strongly associated with fatigue and muscle pain, impaired memory and concentration, and reduced activity. It has also been suggested that the aversive and apparently uncontrollable symptoms of fatigue and myalgia engender a state of "learned helplessness", which can trigger or exacerbate mood disorder.

CLINICAL ASSESSMENT

Fatigue is a symptom of many illnesses, both medical and psychiatric. It is essential that an appropriate history is taken and basic investigations are carried out in every patient. Table 24.2 is a reasonable compromise between under- and overinvestigation, based on systematic research (Kroenke et al., 1988; Lane et al., 1990; Ridsdale et al., 1993; Valdini et al., 1989) supplemented by clinical experience (Anfinson, 1995). The yield of conventional investigations is low—the highest number of alternative diagnoses found after further investigation is 5% (Swanink et al., 1995), and most are lower. Reports from specialist settings have shown statistically increased rates of abnormal results on tests for parameters such as antinuclear factor, immune complexes, cholesterol, immunoglobulin subsets, and so on. These are encountered only in a minority, and are rarely substantial (Bates et al., 1995). Their significance is for researchers rather than clinicians. Routine testing for such variables is not indicated. There is currently no diagnostic test or pattern of tests that can assist in the diagnosis of CFS. It is our policy only to carry out further investigations if the history is unusual (pronounced weight loss, foreign travel), the pattern of symptoms atypical (no mental fatigue or fatigability) or if any abnormalities are found on physical examination or basic investigations (Sharpe et al., 1997b).

Table 24.2. Recommended investigations

Status	Recommended investigations
All patients	Full blood count, erythrocyte sedimentation rate or C-reactive protein, urea and electrolytes, thyroid function tests, urine for protein and sugar
Can be helpful	Epstein–Barr serology, chest X-ray, rheumatoid factor, antinuclear factor, serological testing for cytomegalovirus, Q fever, toxoplasmosis or HIV
Not helpful	Enteroviral serology (including VP-1), neuroimaging

HOW TO MANAGE CFS

It is a truism to state that it is only possible to manage a patient when both doctor and patient have constructed a therapeutic alliance, and are "on the same side". There are probably few examples where this is more important than CFS, but there are also several factors in CFS that can make this task less than easy (Sharpe et al., 1997b).

Establishing a therapeutic relationship is the first task facing the clinician. One of the main causes of difficulty is conflict between the doctor and patient in their beliefs about the nature and cause of the illness. The majority of patients seen in specialist clinics typically believe that their symptoms are the result of an organic disease process and resent any suggestion that they are psychological in origin or psychiatric in nature. Many doctors believe the converse.

Such illness beliefs are not merely abstractions but can be associated with strong emotion. The reasons for this emotion can be discerned from the views expressed by both patient literature and individual patients. The literature is replete with statements by patients such as "CFS is a real illness—it is not psychiatric" and "CFS is a genuine physical disorder and not a psychiatric problem". Individuals explain that a psychiatric label implies not only that the symptoms are unreal but also that they are at fault for developing them. Consequently, any suggestion by the clinician that the patient's symptoms are psychiatric is almost certain to be perceived as a personal attack, lead to anger and irretrievably damage the relationship (see Butler & Rollnick, 1996; Cooper, 1997; Wessely, 1998).

The patient might not be the only one with idiosyncratic beliefs about the illness. Physicians' beliefs and attitudes are also important in determining whether a positive relationship is established. Some physicians appear to believe that somatic symptoms in the absence of demonstrable disease are imaginary and dismiss them as not deserving their attention. Even if the assessing clinician is sympathetic, the patient's behaviour can be influenced by previous encounters with others who were not.

We believe that the most effective way of avoiding such difficulties is for the physician to enquire into the patient's beliefs and to treat them with respect. It is also important that the physician avoids the tendency automatically to translate somatic complaints into psychiatric jargon or to imply that these complaints are psychogenic in origin. Our research shows that to have a successful outcome it is not necessary for the patient to alter any of his or her beliefs about the nature of the illness, what it is called, or what it is due to. Instead, a positive outcome requires only a shift in beliefs about the most appropriate management, and in particular the merits of rest and exercise (Deale et al., 1998).

This acceptance of the patient is combined with empathy for his or her predicament, which is often not only one of distress and disability but also of disbelief. We routinely ask if the patient has ever experienced "illness disconfirmation" from others, including professionals, in order to permit them to ventilate previous dissatisfaction. We also emphasise how difficult it must be to face directly the limits of medicine, "it must have been difficult for you, since no one has given an adequate explanation, for your illness let alone an effective treatment" or "no doubt you have received many conflicting messages from other doctors about what is wrong". It is our experience that this combination of open-mindedness, empathy, and awareness of the difficulties the patient is likely to have experienced makes it possible to establish a therapeutic alliance in most cases (Sharpe et al., 1997b).

Some neurologists wonder whether they should confirm or refute the diagnosis of CFS. We believe that a firm diagnosis of CFS has a place in neurological practice (although we see no place for the outdated and misleading term myalgic encephalomyelitis). Patients need a convincing label to make sense of their illness and to organise their dealings with family and work. Not to give a diagnosis leaves them isolated and with a sense of disconfirmation (Ware, 1992). Not to give them a diagnosis, or to give a diagnosis that is unacceptable to the patient, leads to a "contest of diagnosis" (Hadler, 1996) from which neither side will emerge the winner.

We believe that the making of a positive diagnosis of CFS has a place in clinical practice, providing that it is used in a constructive fashion. This means that the aetiological neutrality and purely descriptive nature of the diagnosis is emphasised. The meaning that the diagnosis carries for the individual patient should be explored so that inaccurate and unhelpful ideas can be corrected. However, just as it is unacceptable to say to the patient "there is no such thing as CFS" or "there is nothing wrong with you", it is equally unacceptable, and verging on unethical, to say "yes, you have CFS, and there is nothing that can be done for you" (Wessely, 1998).

HOW TO NEGOTIATE GRADED ACTIVITY NOT EXERCISE

The inescapable conclusion of the literature is to promote interventions that either discourage avoidance of activity or enhance perceived control of symptoms (Anon., 1996; Ray et al., 1997; Vercoulen et al., 1997). One obvious approach involves increasing activity. Hence telling CFS patients to do more seem eminently sensible in the light of the evidence of normal neuromuscular function and the adverse effects of doing little. It is also a mistake. No doubt many clinicians who have offered such advice in good faith have been surprised by the intensity of the reaction from the patient.

There are two reasons for this. First, as outlined above, many will already have tried this and found it increased their symptoms. Second, telling someone to do more implies they have previously not being doing enough, and comes close to suggesting they are not trying hard enough. The patient's own expectation is that he or she will be able to do more when symptoms decrease, but by the time people have reached a specialist neurological clinic the chances of this happening are increasingly remote (Joyce et al., 1997). Yet without some form of increase in activity, few will ever get better. How can this be managed?

We suggest that the key lies in these areas. First, what is needed is not exercise but activity: we do not believe that disability in CFS can be explained with a simple physiological model. Second, what is needed is not increased activity, at least not at first, but consistent activity.

The first aim of treatment is therefore to regularise activity levels, often using a diary. Fluctuations in activity must be avoided. It might be necessary to actually reduce activity at first, both in the interests of avoiding activity fluctuations and of gaining patient trust. This breaks the cycle of exercise leading to exhaustion, thus reinforcing catastrophic thinking and demoralisation, which in turn leads to days of inactivity as the patient attempts to recover. Second, this strategy reduces the defensive hostility that almost inevitably follows any suggestion, no matter how subtly put, that the patient is not doing enough.

THE EFFICACY OF THERAPY

We will review the evidence for the efficacy of exercise therapy, followed by that for cognitive behaviour therapy (CBT).

Exercise therapy

Does exercise work in CFS? Until recently most evidence to address this question came from fibromyalgia. To date, four randomised trials of exercise have been reported in fibromyalgia patients. The overall effects are beneficial and, equally importantly, exercise does not seem to cause harm in these trials. What about exercise in CFS?

The first major trial of graded exercise was carried out by Kathy Fulcher and Peter White (1997) at St Bartholomew's Hospital in 66 non-depressed patients diagnosed according to the Oxford criteria. Patients were randomised to participate either in aerobic exercises or flexibility training. Aerobic exercise was postulated to be the active ingredient in this trial, with flexibility training forming a control group. Subjects were seen once weekly over the 12-week programme and told to exercise at least 5 days per week, building up their level of activity by 1–2-minute increments each week until they were exercising for 30 minutes per day, at which point exercise intensity was increased up to a maximum of 60% VO_2 max. Flexibility training consisted of stretching and relaxation exercises, which the subjects were encouraged to do at home as well. The main outcome was change on a clinical global impression scale.

The results of this trial were impressive: 55% of those who completed aerobic training reported feeling much better or very much better, as opposed to 27% of the comparison group. One patient in each group felt worse at the end of treatment. As a group, those on the aerobic treatment had a significantly better outcome in terms of physical fatigue, global ratings of health on the SF-36, and better physical functioning on the SF-36. The investigators allowed those given flexibility training to cross over to aerobic training following the end of the trial, and they were also able to show significant improvements in this group. It is worth noting that self-rated improvement was not correlated with

improvements in VO_2 max, confirming that subjective fatigue is not synonymous with exercise capacity.

A key finding in this study is that objective measures of physical fitness were not associated with outcome, that is, that clinical improvement was not related to improving physical fitness. It is more plausible that the benefits were linked to confidence, predictability, and overcoming avoidance. We have interpreted this as evidence that disability is more related to behavioural avoidance and confidence than simple physical fitness.

Similar results have been reported by a group in Manchester (Wearden et al., 1998). CFS patients were randomised to receive fluoxetine, or placebo and exercise, or no exercise. The exercise group was instructed to do graded exercise for 20 minutes three times a week up to 75% of VO_2 max. Problems were encountered with compliance, perhaps because no attempt was made to address illness beliefs, and in particular to challenge catastrophic interpretations of exercise-related symptoms ("I am going to have a relapse if I do any more"). None the less, exercise produced a significant improvement in fatigue, functional work capacity, and health perception, even on the intention to treat analysis.

There remain significant questions about the acceptability of exercise. In the St Bartholomew's study, patients were seen at the National Sports centre, and might have implicitly already accepted an exercise model before randomisation. In the Manchester study, problems were encountered with drop-out and treatment compliance. We argue that a large proportion of patients with CFS require more than simply the experience of gradual exercise programmes to persuade them that exercise can be beneficial.

Cognitive behaviour therapy

Cognitive behaviour therapy (CBT) differs from exercise in two important areas. First, targets are chosen on behavioural grounds, and involve the resumption of activities that are currently avoided, rather than achieving ergonomic goals. Second, CBT involves some explicit discussion and possibly challenging of the patient's beliefs about activity, exercise, and symptoms before any activities are attempted. Does CBT work in CFS?

In the first edition of this text we were able to quote only one uncontrolled evaluation (Butler et al., 1991), which, although demonstrating clinically meaningful improvements in some, also showed problems with recruitment and acceptability. Since then much has changed.

We now know that the benefits of treatment are maintained at 4 years (Bonner et al., 1994), and that spontaneous improvement in this severe group is unlikely without treatment (Bonner et al., 1994; Joyce et al., 1997). Problems of recruitment and acceptability have been largely overcome by more attention to engagement, a greater realisation of the potency of the patient's own catastrophic beliefs, and, most important of all, a realisation of the need to ensure consistency of activity before attempting any graded increases.

Nevertheless, the first randomised controlled trial of CBT demonstrated no appreciable benefits over standard care

(Lloyd et al., 1993). There were several reasons for this result. The first was that standard care, as practised by the group, was itself successful, perhaps because the Australian group has produced convincing evidence that neuromuscular function in CFS was normal (as discussed earlier). The second was that the duration of treatment (six sessions) might be considered rather short for a chronic illness. The third might be because the treatment rationale was compromised by being included with randomised trial of an active immunotherapy, which might contradict what we regard as the key message—that whatever started your illness (a virus, an immunological disturbance, and so on) is not now responsible for current disability.

Michael Sharpe and his Oxford colleagues reported an unequivocally successful trial of CBT with a strong cognitive flavour (Sharpe et al., 1996). The comparison was normal care by the patient's general practitioner. CBT consisted of an assessment of the patient and an individualised cognitive formulation of his or her symptoms, accompanied by explanation and education. The therapy involved behavioural experiments, collaborative re-evaluation of thoughts and beliefs inhibiting return to normal functioning, and problem-solving activities. The active treatment was successful, in terms of functional impairment, exercise tolerance, and fatigue, but not until 6 months after the end of treatment. Although the CBT group showed an advantage in terms of Karnofsky score, these were not significant until 12 months, when 73% of those treated had improved satisfactorily compared with 27% on standard care. Other measures, such as metres walked, days in bed per week, subjective assessment of effect of illness, and fatigue severity showed a significant advantage for CBT at 5 and 8 months.

At King's College Hospital in London we have replicated Sharpe's results. We randomised 60 patients with CFS to received either CBT or relaxation (Deale et al., 1997). CBT was given over 13 sessions at weekly–fortnightly intervals. The model of CBT was similar to that used in Sharpe's study, although the emphasis was more behavioural, involving earlier activity scheduling. The first three sessions aimed at engaging the patient and explaining the treatment rationale. At the fourth session a schedule of activities was prescribed. The activity scheduling continued, and cognitive strategies were introduced gradually, to address fears about symptoms, perfectionism, and performance expectations. Relaxation involved progressive muscle relaxation and visualisation. The study reported a good outcome in 63% of those treated with CBT as opposed to 17% with relaxation, a highly statistically significant result. CBT showed a particular benefit for measures of fatigue and disability, whereas it did not have a significant effect on depression.

The differences between the Australian and British studies relate to the different models of illness used—those that involved some form of gradual return to activity combined with some form of cognitive reattribution were successful, whereas those that did not offer adequate alternative explanations for symptom maintenance, or address illness and symptoms beliefs, were less successful (Moss-Morris, 1997).

Cognitive behaviour therapy requires skilled personnel, who are likely to be available in only a few specialist centres. However, elements of CBT, most particular activity management, sleep hygiene, planned rest, graded activity, education, and looking for alternative explanations, are now routinely incorporated into many standard programmes. Self-help guides are now being developed—a recent randomised controlled trial of such a guide was effective in a primary care setting (Chalder et al., 1997).

PHARMACOLOGICAL MANAGEMENT OF CFS

At present, if we adhered rigorously to the principles of evidence-based medicine, this section would be short indeed. We recently reviewed all the evidence from well conducted clinical trials and concluded that there was insufficient evidence to recommend any drug management in the condition (Wessely et al., 1998).

However, we feel we should expand on this a little, as in practice many drug interventions are used and it is an unusual patient who has not tried some pharmacological therapy, either conventional or alternative. Some are based on specific disease models, such as attempts to remove a persistent virus, remedy an immune deficiency, or treat a depressive disorder. Others are drawn from more alternative and cultural models of the illness, such as dietary modifications. Three areas deserve more comment.

First, there is no evidence that attempts to treat viral persistence can be justified (Straus et al., 1988). Unless and until any evidence confirming that viral persistence is an important determinant of illness or disability, and the current evidence is firmly against such a model, these interventions cannot be justified in terms of efficacy, cost, or risk of side-effects.

Second, there is no current justification for an attempt to modify immune function. It is true that there are numerous studies finding evidence of deviations from the immunological norm in CFS patients—either in numbers or function of immune cells, or levels of one or more cytokines. However, the evidence is far from consistent and no specific pattern has emerged. The observed abnormalities are generally minor, and little effort has been made to address the role of important confounders such as mood, medication, or inactivity. Although some commentators see CFS as a primary immune disturbance, others view the immune perturbations as secondary to an as yet unidentified persistent viral agent, whereas yet others feel that confounders, such as mood or relative hypocortisolaemia, can account for the changes. So far, none has been shown to have clinical or prognostic significance (Peakman et al., 1997).

It is hence not surprising that randomised controlled trials of immunological interventions have been unsatisfactory. For example, two early trials of intravenous immunoglobulins gave opposing results (Lloyd et al., 1990; Petersen et al., 1990), leading editorialists at the time to conclude that the side-effects of the active treatment (which might also have led to unblinding) did not justify any benefit. The Australian group who reported the positive trial commendably attempted to repeat their findings, and to look for evidence of a dose–response relationship. They found neither (Vollmer-Conna et al., 1997). At present, the sole support for immunotherapy lies with a single trial in adolescents (Rowe, 1997). Given the lack of evidence for any relevant immune deficiency in subjects, these approaches cannot be recommended.

The third area in which hopes are frequently expressed for a pharmacological treatment for CFS are the antidepressants. The intellectual justification for their use is reasonably sound, at least in some patients, because even if one views CFS as a solely physical illness (and one hopes that the readers of this volume will take a more balanced view), antidepressants are still indicated in the presence of mood disorder. However, the first properly conducted trial of antidepressants was resoundingly negative (Vercoulen et al., 1996a). It might be that the choice of agent, fluoxetine (a serotonin re-uptake inhibitor) was wrong, or that the sample was too chronic to expect any simple benefit.

Thus, uncertainty continues to exist at present on the appropriate role for antidepressants in CFS. We suggest that, given the overwhelming evidence for the efficacy of antidepressants in the presence of mood disorder, irrespective of aetiology, they continue to be used when clinicians feel that low mood is contributing to symptoms or disability.

CONCLUSION

Since the first edition of this text was published in 1993, substantial progress has been made in our understanding and treatment of chronic fatigue and its syndromes. There is a greater understanding of its epidemiology and personal impact. There has been a shift away from the search for a single "cause" to an endorsement of more complex multifactorial models. In general, less attention is being paid to neuromuscular dysfunction and more to the role of the CNS as a final common pathway for symptoms. There is increased emphasis on the role of rehabilitation, even in the absence of a full understanding of aetiology. Those sceptical of the role or utility of rehabilitation in this group of patients can now be shown consistent evidence from well-conducted clinical trials. Most of all, chronic fatigue and its syndromes are gradually become less controversial, less in the public eye, and instead accepted as part and parcel of mainstream clinical practice.

REFERENCES

Anfinson T (1995) Diagnostic assessment of chronic fatigue syndrome. In: Stoudemire A, Fogel B (Eds) *Medical–psychiatric practice*. Washington DC, American Psychiatric Press, pp. 215–256

Anon. (1987) Aching muscles after exercise. *Lancet ii*: 1123–1125

Anon. (1994) Report from the National Task Force on Chronic Fatigue Syndrome (CFS), *Post Viral Fatigue Syndrome (PVFS), Myalgic Encephalomyelitis (ME)*. Bristol, Westcare

Anon. (1996) *Chronic fatigue syndrome: Report of a committee of the Royal Colleges of Physicians, Psychiatrists and General Practitioners*. London: Royal Colleges of Physicians

Antoni M, Brickman A, Lutgendorf S et al. (1994) Psychosocial correlates of illness burden in chronic fatigue syndrome. *Clin Infect Dis 18*(suppl. 1): S73–78

Arnold D, Bore P, Radda G, Styles P, Taylor D (1984) Excessive intracellular acidosis of skeletal muscle on exercise in a patient with a post-viral exhaustion/fatigue syndrome. A 31P nuclear magnetic resonance study. *Lancet 1*: 1367–1369

Bakheit A, Behan P, Dinan T, Gray C, O'Keane V (1992) Possible upregulation of hypothalamic 5-hydroxytryptamine receptors in patients with postviral fatigue syndrome. *Br Med J 304*: 1010–1012

Baracos V, Rodemann HP, Dinarello CA, Goldberg AL (1983) Stimulation of muscle protein degradation and prostaglandin E2 release by leukocytic pyrogen (interleukin-1). A mechanism for the increased degradation of muscle proteins during fever. *N Engl J Med 308*: 553–558

Barnes P, Taylor D, Kemp G, Radda G (1993) Skeletal muscle bioenergetics in the chronic fatigue syndrome. *J Neurol Neurosurg Psychiatry 56*: 679–683

Bates D, Buchwald D, Lee J et al. (1995) Clinical laboratory test findings in patients with chronic fatigue syndrome. *Arch Intern Med 155*: 97–103

Behan W, More I, Behan P (1991) Mitochondrial abnormalities in the post-viral fatigue syndrome. *Acta Neuropathologica 83*: 61–65

Bennett R, Jacobsen S (1994) Muscle function and origin of pain in fibromyalgia. *Baillieres Clin Rheumatol 8*: 721–746.

Bonner D, Butler S, Chalder T, Ron M, Wessely S (1994) A follow up study of chronic fatigue syndrome. *J Neurol Neurosurg Psychiatry 57*: 617–621

Brierley E, Johnson M, James O, Turnbull D (1996) Effects of physical activity and age on mitochondrial function. *Quart J Med 89*: 251–258

Buchwald D, Pearlman T, Umali J, Schmaling K, Katon W (1996) Functional status in patients with chronic fatigue syndrome, other fatiguing illnesses, and healthy controls. *Am J Med 171*: 364–370

Butler C, Rollnick S (1996) Missing the meaning and provoking resistance: A case of myalgic encephalomyelitis. *Family Practice 13*: 106–109

Butler S, Chalder T, Ron M, Wessely S (1991) Cognitive behaviour therapy in chronic fatigue syndrome. *J Neurol Neurosurg Psychiatry 54*: 153–158

Byrne E, Trounce I (1987) Chronic fatigue and myalgia syndrome: Mitochondrial and glycolytic studies in skeletal muscle. *J Neurol Neurosurg Psychiatry 50*: 743–746

Chalder T, Wallace P, Wessely S (1997) Self-help treatment of chronic fatigue in the community: A randomised controlled trial. *Br J Health Psychol 2*: 189–197

Cleare A, Bearn J, Allain T et al. (1995) Contrasting neuroendocrine responses in depression and chronic fatigue syndrome. *J Affect Disord 35*: 283–289

Connolly S, Smith D, Doyle D, Fowler C (1993) Chronic fatigue: Electromyographic and neuropathological evaluation. *J Neurol 240*: 435–438

Cooper L (1997) Myalgic encephalomyelitis and the medical encounter. *Sociol Health Illness 19*: 17–37

Cope H, David A (1996) Neuroimaging in chronic fatigue syndrome. *J Neurol Neurosurg Psychiatry 60*: 471–473

Costa D, Tannock C, Brostoff J (1995) Brainstem perfusion is impaired in patients with myalgic encephalomyelitis/chronic fatigue syndrome. *Quart J Med 88*: 767–773

Crofford L, Pillemer S, Kalogeras K et al. (1994) Hypothalamic–pituitary–adrenal axis perturbations in patients with fibromyalgia. *Arth Rheumat 37*: 1583–1592

Deale A, Chalder T, Marks I, Wessely S (1997) A randomised controlled trial of cognitive behaviour versus relaxation therapy for chronic fatigue syndrome. *Am J Psych 154*: 408–414

Deale A, Chalder T, Wessely S (1998) Illness beliefs and outcome in chronic fatigue syndrome: Is change in causal attribution necessary for clinical improvement? *J Psychosom Res 45*: 77–83

Demitrack M, Dale J, Straus S et al. (1991) Evidence for impaired activation of the hypothalamic–pituitary–adrenal axis in patients with chronic fatigue syndrome. *J Clin End Metab 73*: 1224–1234

Djaldetti R, Ziv I, Achiron A, Melamed E (1996) Fatigue in multiple sclerosis compared with chronic fatigue syndrome. *Neurology 46*: 632–635

Edwards R (1981) *Human muscle function and fatigue. Human muscle fatigue: Physiological mechanisms*. London, Pitman Medical, pp. 1–18

Edwards R, Gibson H, Clague J, Helliwell T (1993) Muscle physiology and histopathology in chronic fatigue syndrome. In: Kleinman A, Straus S (Eds) *Chronic fatigue syndrome*. Chichester, John Wiley, pp. 101–131

Edwards R, Newham D et al. (1991) Muscle biochemistry and pathophysiology in postviral fatigue syndrome. *British Medical Bulletin 47*: 826–837.

Feiden K (1990) *Hope and help for chronic fatigue syndrome: The official guide of the CFS/CFIDS network*. New York, Prentice Hall

Fukuda K, Straus S, Hickie I, Sharpe M, Dobbins J, Komaroff A (1994) The chronic fatigue syndrome: A comprehensive approach to its definition and study. *Ann Int Med 121*: 953–959

Fulcher K, White P (1997) Randomised controlled trial of graded exercise in patients with chronic fatigue syndrome. *Br Med J 314*: 1647–1652

Geel SE (1994) The fibromyalgia syndrome: Musculoskeletal pathophysiology. *Seminars in Arthritis and Rheumatism 23*: 347–353

Gibson JN, Halliday D, Morrison WL et al. (1987) Decrease in human quadriceps muscle protein turnover consequent upon leg immobilization. *Clin Sci 72*: 503–509

Gibson H, Carroll N, Clague J, Edwards R (1993) Exercise performance and fatiguability in patients with chronic fatigue syndrome. *J Neurol Neurosurg Psychiatry 156*: 993–998

Greco A, Tannock C, Brostoff J, Costa D (1997) Brain MR in chronic fatigue syndrome. *Am J Neuroradiol 18*: 1265–1269

Hadler NM (1996) If you have to prove you are ill, you can't get well. The object lesson of fibromyalgia. *Spine 21*: 2397–2400

Henriksson K, Bengtsson A, Lindman R, Thornell L (1993) Morphological changes in muscle in fibromyalgia and chronic shoulder myalgia. In: Vaeroy H, Merskey H (Eds) *Progress in fibromyalgia and myofascial pain*. Amsterdam, Elsevier, pp. 61–73

Henriksson C, Burckhardt C (1996) Impact of fibromyalgia on everyday life. A study of women in the USA and Sweden. *Disabil Rehabil 18*: 241–248

Hopkins A, Menken M, DeFriese G (1989) A record of patient encounters in neurological practice in the United Kingdom. *J Neurol Neurosurg Psychiatry 52*: 436–438

Jacobsen S, Bartels EM, Danneskiold Samsoe B (1991a) Single cell morphology of muscle in patients with chronic muscle pain. *Scand J Rheumatol 20*: 336–343

Jacobsen S, Wildschiodtz G, Danneskiold Samsoe B (1991b) Isokinetic and isometric muscle strength combined with transcutaneous electrical muscle stimulation in primary fibromyalgia syndrome. *J Rheumatol 18*: 1390–1393

Jacobsen S, Jensen KE, Thomsen C, Danneskiold Samsoe B, Henriksen O (1992) 31P magnetic resonance spectroscopy of skeletal muscle in patients with fibromyalgia. *J Rheumatol 19*: 1600–1603

Jamal G, Miller R (1991) Neurophysiology of postviral fatigue syndrome. *Br Med Bull 47*: 815–825

Janet P (1919) *Les obsessions et la psychasthénie, vol 1*. Paris, Alcan

Johnson S, DeLuca J, Natelson B (1996a) Assessing somatization disorder in the chronic fatigue syndrome. *Psychosom Med 58*: 50–57

Johnson S, DeLuca J, Natelson B (1996b) Depression in fatiguing illness: Comparing patients with chronic fatigue syndrome, multiple sclerosis and depression. *J Affect Disord 38*: 21–30

Johnson S, DeLuca J, Natelson B (1996c) Personality dimensions in the chronic fatigue syndrome: A comparison with multiple sclerosis and depression. *J Psych Res 30*: 9–20

Joyce E, Blumenthal S, Wessely S (1996) Memory, attention and executive function in chronic fatigue syndrome. *J Neurol Neurosurg Psychiatry 60*: 495–503

Joyce J, Hotopf M, Wessely S (1997) The prognosis of chronic fatigue and chronic fatigue syndrome: A systematic review. *Quart J Med 90*: 223–233

Katon W, Buchwald D, Simon G, Russo J, Mease P (1991) Psychiatric illness in patients with chronic fatigue and rheumatoid arthritis. *J Gen Intern Med 6*: 277–285

Kendell R (1991) Chronic fatigue, viruses and depression. *Lancet 337*: 160–162

Kent-Braun J, Sharma K, Weiner M, Massie B, Miller R (1993) Central basis of muscle fatigue in chronic fatigue syndrome. *Neurology 43*: 125–131

Klug G, McAuley E, Clark S (1989) Factors influencing the development and maintenance of aerobic fitness: Lessons applicable to the fibrositis syndrome. *J Rheumatol 16*(suppl. 19): 30–39

Kroenke K, Mangelsdorff D (1989) Common symptoms in ambulatory care: Incidence, evaluation, therapy and outcome. *Am J Med 86*: 262–266

Kroenke K, Wood D, Mangelsdorff D, Meier N, Powell J (1988) Chronic fatigue in primary care: Prevalence, patient characteristics and outcome. *J Am Med Assoc 260*: 929–934

Lane T, Matthews D, Manu P (1990) The low yield of physical examinations and laboratory investigations of patients with chronic fatigue. *Am J Med Sci 299*: 313–318

Lane R, Burgess A, Flint J, Riccio M, Archard L (1995) Exercise responses and psychiatric disorder in chronic fatigue syndrome. *Br Med J 311*: 544–545

Leese G, Chattington P, Fraser W, Vora J, Edwards R, Williams G (1996) Short-term night-shift working mimics the pituitary–adrenocortical dysfunction of chronic fatigue syndrome. *J Clin Endocrinol and Metab 81*: 1867–1870

Lloyd A, Hales J, Gandevia S (1988) Muscle strength, endurance and recovery in the postinfection fatigue syndrome. *J Neurol Neurosurg Psychiatry 51*: 1316–1322

Lloyd A, Hickie I, Wakefield D (1990) A double blind placebo-controlled trial of intravenous immunoglobulin therapy in patients with chronic fatigue syndrome. *Am J Med 89*: 561–567

Lloyd A, Gandevia S, Hales J (1991) Muscle performance, voluntary activation, twitch properties and perceived effort in normal subjects and patients with the chronic fatigue syndrome. *Brain 114*: 85–98

Lloyd A, Hickie I, Brockman A et al. (1993) Immunologic and psychological therapy for patients with chronic fatigue syndrome. *Am J Med 94*: 197–203

Lloyd A, Gandevia S, Brockman A, Hales J, Wakefield D (1994) Cytokine production and fatigue in patients with chronic fatigue syndrome and healthy controls in response to exercise. *Clin Infect Dis 18*(suppl. 1): S142–146

Lynch S (1997) *The nature of fatigue in the chronic fatigue syndrome: A longitudinal study*. PhD thesis, University of London

Mantysaari MJ, Antila KJ et al. (1988) Blood pressure reactivity in patients with neurocirculatory asthenia. *Am J Hypertens 1* 132–139

McComas A, Miller R, Gandevia S (1995) Fatigue brought on by malfunction of the central and peripheral nervous systems. In: Gandevia S (ed) *Fatigue*. New York, Plenum Press, pp. 495–512

McCully K, Sisto S, Natelson B (1996a) Use of exercise for treatment of chronic fatigue syndrome. *Sports Medicine 21*: 35–48

McCully K, Natelson B, Iotti S, Sisto S, Leight J (1996b) Reduced oxidative muscle metabolism in chronic fatigue syndrome. *Muscle and Nerve 19*: 621–625

Mengshoel A, Vollestad N, Forre O (1995) Pain and fatigue induced by exercise in fibromyalgia patients and sedentary healthy subjects. *Clin Exp Rheumatol 13*: 477–482

Miller T, Allen G, Gandevia S (1996) Muscle force, perceived effort, and voluntary activation of the elbow flexors assessed with sensitive twitch interpolation in fibromyalgia. *J Rheumatol 23*: 1621–1627

Montague T, Marrie T, Klassen G, Bewick D, Horacek B (1989) Cardiac function at rest and with exercise in the chronic fatigue syndrome. *Chest 95*: 779–784

Moss-Morris R (1997) The role of illness cognitions and coping in the aetiology and maintenance of the chronic fatigue syndrome (CFS). In: Weinman J, Petrie K (Eds) *Perceptions of health and illness: Current research and applications*. Reading, Harwood Academic Publishers

Moss-Morris R, Petrie K, Large R, Kydd R (1996) Neuropsychological deficits in chronic fatigue syndrome: artifact or reality? *J Neurol Neurosurg Psychiatry 60*: 474–477

Muscio D (1921) Is a fatigue test possible? *British Journal of Psychology 12*: 31–46

Newham D (1988) The consequences of eccentric contractions and their relationship to delayed onset muscle pain. *Eur J Appl Physiol 57*: 353–359

Nielsen W, Walker C, McCain G (1992) Cognitive behavioral treatment of fibromyalgia syndrome. *J Rheumatol 19*: 98–103

Nix W (1994) Normal neuromuscular transmission and "central" muscle fatigue in chronic fatigue patients. *International Conference on Chronic Fatigue Syndrome, May 18th–20th 1994, Dublin*.

Norregaard J, Bulow P, Danneskiold-Samsoe B (1994) Muscle strength, voluntary activation, twitch properties, and endurance in patients with fibromyalgia. *J Neurol Neurosurg Psychiatry 57*: 1106–1111

Patterson J, Aitchinson F, Wyper D, Hadley D, Majeed T, Behan P (1995) SPECT brain imaging in chronic fatigue syndrome. *Revista di Immunologia ed immunofarmacologia 15*: 53–58

Peakman M, Deale A, Field R, Mahalingam M, Wessely S (1997) Clinical improvement in chronic fatigue syndrome is not associated with lymphocyte subsets of function or activation. *Clin Immun Immunopath 82*: 83–91

Pepper C, Krupp L, Friedberg F, Doscher C, Coyle P (1993) A comparison of neuropsychiatric characteristics in chronic fatigue syndrome, multiple sclerosis and major depression. *J Neuropsych Clin Neurosci 5*: 200–205

Petersen P, Shepard J, Macres M (1990) A controlled trial of intravenous immunogloublin G in chronic fatigue syndrome. *Am J Med 89*: 554–560

Petrie K, Moss-Morris R, Weinman J (1995) The impact of catastrophic beliefs on functioning in chronic fatigue syndrome. *J Psychosom Res 39*: 31–37

Plioplys A, Plioplys S (1995) Electron-microscopic investigation of muscle mitochondria in chronic fatigue syndrome. *Neuropsychobiology 32*: 175–181

Poore G (1875) On fatigue. *Lancet i*: 163–164

Prasher P, Smith A, Findley L (1990) Sensory and cognitive event-related potentials in myalgic encephalomyelitis. *J Neurol Neurosurg Psychiatry 53*: 247–253

Preedy V, Smith D, Salisbury J, Peters T (1993) Biochemical and muscle studies in patients with acute onset post-viral fatigue syndrome. *J Clin Path 46*: 722–726

Ramsay M (1986) *Postviral fatigue syndrome: The saga of royal free disease.* London, Gower Medical

Ray C, Jeffries S, Weir W (1995) Coping with chronic fatigue syndrome: Illness responses and their relationship with fatigue, functional impairment and emotional status. *Psychol Med 25*: 937–945

Ray C, Jefferies S, Weir W (1997) Coping and other predictors of outcome in chronic fatigue syndrome: A 1-year follow-up. *J Psychosom Res 43*: 405–415

Ridsdale L, Evans A, Jerrett W, Mandalia S, Osler K, Vora H (1993) Patients with fatigue in general practice: A prospective study. *Br Med J 307*: 103–106

Riley M, O'Brien C, McCluskey D, Bell N, Nicholls D (1990) Aerobic work capacity in patients with chronic fatigue syndrome. *Br Med J 301*: 953–956

Roberts L, Byrne E (1994) Single fibre EMG studies in chronic fatigue syndrome: A reappraisal. *J Neurol Neurosurg Psychiatry 57*: 375–376

Rowe K (1997) Double-blind randomized controlled trial to assess the efficacy of intravenous gammaglobulin for the management of chronic fatigue syndrome in adolescents. *J Psych Res 31*: 133–147

Rutherford O, White P (1991) Human quadriceps strength and fatigability in patients with post-viral fatigue. *J Neurol Neurosurg Psychiatry 54*: 961–964

Saisch S, Deale A, Gardner W, Wessely S (1994) Hyperventilation and chronic fatigue syndrome. *Quart J Med 87*: 63–67

Schmaling K, DiClementi J, Cullum M, Jones J (1994) Cognitive functioning in chronic fatigue syndrome and depression: A preliminary comparison. *Psychosom Med 56*: 383–388

Schwartz R, Komaroff A, Garada B et al. (1994) SPECT imaging of the brain: Comparison of findings in patients with chronic fatigue syndrome, AIDS dementia complex, and major unipolar depression. *Am J Roentgenology 162*: 943–951

Schweitzer R, Kelly B, Foran A, Terry D, Whiting J (1995) Quality of life in chronic fatigue syndrome. *Soc Sci Med 41*: 1367–1372

Sharpe M, Bass C (1992) Pathophysiological mechanisms in somatization. *Int Rev Psych 4*: 81–97

Sharpe M, Archard L, Banatvala J et al. (1991) Chronic fatigue syndrome: Guidelines for research. *J R Soc Med 84*: 118–121

Sharpe M, Hawton K, Seagroatt V, Pasvol G. (1992) Follow up of patients with fatigue presenting to an infectious diseases clinic. *Br Med J 302*: 347–352

Sharpe M, Hawton K, Simkin S et al. (1996) Cognitive behaviour therapy for chronic fatigue syndrome: A randomized controlled trial. *Br Med J 312*: 22–26

Sharpe M, Hawton K, Clements A, Cowen P (1997a) Increased brain serotonin function in men with chronic fatigue syndrome. *Br Med J 315*: 164–165

Sharpe M, Chalder T, Palmer I, Wessely S (1997b) Chronic fatigue syndrome: A practical guide to assessment and management. *Gen Hosp Psych 19*: 195–199

Shorter E (1992) *From paralysis to fatigue: A history of psychosomatic illness in the modern era.* New York, Free Press

Sisto S, MaManca J, Cordero D et al. (1996) Metabolic and cardiovascular effects of a progressive exercise test in patients with chronic fatigue syndrome. *Am J Med 100*: 634–640

Stokes M, Cooper R, Edwards R (1988) Normal strength and fatigability in patients with effort syndrome. *Br Med J 297*: 1014–1018

Straus S, Dale J, Tobi M et al. (1988) Acyclovir treatment of the chronic fatigue syndrome: Lack of efficacy in a placebo-controlled trial. *N Engl J Med 319*: 1692–1698

Swanink C, Vercoulen J, Bleijenberg G, Fennis J, Galama J, Van Der Meer J (1995) Chronic fatigue syndrome: A clinical and laboratory study with a well matched control group. *J Intern Med 237*: 499–506

Valdini A, Steinhardt S, Feldman E (1989) Usefulness of a standard battery of laboratory tests in investigating chronic fatigue in adults. *Family Practice 6*: 286–291

Vecchiet L, Montanari G, Pizzigallo E et al. (1996) Sensory characterization of somatic parietal tissues in humans with chronic fatigue syndrome. *Neuroscience Letters 208*: 117–120

Vercoulen J, Swanink C, Zitman F et al. (1996a) Fluoxetine in chronic fatigue syndrome; a randomized, double-blind, placebo-controlled study. *Lancet 347*: 858–861

Vercoulen J, Hommes O, Swanink C et al. (1996b) The measurement of fatigue in patients with multiple sclerosis: A multi-dimensional comparison with patients with chronic fatigue syndrome and healthy subjects. *Arch Neurol 46*: 632–635

Vercoulen J, Bazelmans E, Swanink C et al. (1997) Physical activity in chronic fatigue syndrome: Assessment and its role in fatigue. *J Psych Res 31*: 661–673

Vollmer-Conna U, Hickie I, Hadzi-Pavlovic D et al. (1997) Intravenous immunoglobulin is ineffective in the treatment of patients with chronic fatigue syndrome. *Am J Med 103*: 38–43

Wagenmakers A, Coakley J, Edwards R (1988) The metabolic consequences of reduced habitual activities in patients with muscle pain and disease. *Ergonomics 31*: 1519–1527

Ware N (1992) Suffering and the social construction of illness: The delegitimisation of illness experience in chronic fatigue syndrome. *Medical Anthropology Quarterly 6*: 347–361

Wearden A, Appleby L (1996) Research on cognitive complaints and cognitive functioning in patients with chronic fatigue syndrome (CFS): What conclusions can we draw? *J Psychosom Res 41*: 197–211

Wearden A, Morris R, Mullis R et al. (1998) A double-blind, placebo controlled treatment trial of fluoxetine and a graded exercise programme for chronic fatigue syndrome. *British Journal of Psychiatry 172*: 485–490

Wessely S (1994) The history of chronic fatigue syndrome. In: Straus S (ed) *Chronic fatigue syndrome.* New York, Mark Dekker, pp. 41–82

Wessely S (1995) The epidemiology of chronic fatigue syndrome. *Epidemiol Rev 17*: 139–151

Wessely S (1999) To tell or not to tell: The problem of medically unexplained symptoms. In: Zeman A, Emanuel L (Eds) *Ethical dilemnas in neurology.* London, WB Saunders, pp. 41–53

Wessely S, Powell R (1989) Fatigue syndromes: A comparison of chronic 'postviral' fatigue with neuromuscular and affective disorder. *J Neurol Neurosurg Psychiatry 52*: 940–948

Wessely S, Chalder T, Hirsch S, Wallace P, Wright D (1997) The prevalence and morbidity of chronic fatigue and chronic fatigue syndrome: A prospective primary care study. *Am J Pub Health 87*: 1449–1455

Wessely S, Hotopf M, Sharpe M (1998) *Chronic fatigue and its syndromes.* Oxford, Oxford University Press

White P (1997) The relationship between infection and fatigue. *J Psychosom Res 43*: 346–350

Wood G, Bentall R et al. (1991) A comparative psychiatric assessment of patients with chronic fatigue syndrome and muscle disease. *Psychological Medicine 21*: 619–628

Wong R, Lopaschuk G, Zhu G et al. (1992) Skeletal muscle metabolism in the chronic fatigue syndrome. *In vivo* assessment by 31P nuclear magnetic resonance spectroscopy. *Chest 102*: 1716–1722

Wortmann R (1994) Searching for the cause of fibromyalgia: Is there a defect in energy metabolism? *Arth Rheumat 37*: 790–793

Yunus MB, Kalyan Raman UP, Masi AT, Aldag JC (1989) Electron microscopic studies of muscle biopsy in primary fibromyalgia syndrome: A controlled and blinded study. *J Rheumatol 16*: 97–101

Zorbas Y, Matveyev I (1986) Man's desirability in performing physical exercises under hypokinesia. *Int J Rehabil 9*: 170–174

25. The assessment and management of swallowing disorders

Jane Whitaker   Alison Dunnachie   Tom Hughes

INTRODUCTION

Swallowing is a complex process that relies on the effective coordination of numerous neurological, anatomical, and physiological interactions. This chapter first outlines the anatomy and physiology of swallowing and then describes the clinical assessment, further investigation, and management of dysphagia and of associated nutritional problems.

An awake adult swallows about once per minute (1000 times daily) irrespective of eating. This high rate of swallowing is required because 1000–1500 ml saliva is produced daily: the basal rate of secretion is 0.3–0.4 ml/min, rising to 2 ml/min during chewing (Dodds et al., 1973; Helm et al., 1982). During these hundreds of swallowing acts, food, fluid, or saliva rarely enter the laryngeal vestibule or penetrate the trachea.

Swallowing is essential to maintain nutrition and to deal with saliva. Swallowing can give intense pleasure when associated with taste and with the satiation of hunger and thirst. Swallowing disorders can, however, cause profound misery and can lead to biological sequelae such as malnutrition, recurrent chest infections, aspiration pneumonia, and airway obstruction.

The patient with swallowing problems often traverses clinical specialties. Inadequate communication between clinical disciplines and a lack of mutual understanding of terminology, diagnostic data, and methodology severely hamper the problem-solving process. Clinical specialists often have differing priorities: for example, a surgeon might see his or her role as removing a tumour and perhaps pays little attention to the functional consequences of surgery. These problems often leave the dysphagic patient in a no-man's land of clinical indecision and inadequate management. In the authors' experience it is not uncommon for patients to languish for weeks and even months on acute medical and surgical wards because simple diagnostic procedures to determine the nature of the swallowing problems have either not been carried out or else have been misunderstood. As a result, appropriate interventions are frequently delayed.

The speech–language therapist and the dietitian will often regard a successful outcome as one that compensates for impaired swallowing, whether neurological or non-neurological in aetiology. Their roles are to determine if patients have adequate swallowing ability to maintain sufficient and safe oral food and fluids for their nutritional needs.

Successful management requires a team approach, entailing coordination of local resources and skills and evaluation of outcomes. The ideal core team has been widely recognised to include a dietitian, a speech–language therapist, a nurse, and a physician, as well as the patient and family. Radiologists often contribute to assessment, and effective management will often require other professionals such as occupational therapists and physiotherapists.

Ethical dilemmas (see Chapter 6) cause great concern. For example, should different categories of patient, such as those with progressive neurological disease, those with severe learning difficulties, or very elderly people, be fed artificially? The argument often revolves around resources and quality of life issues but the underlying dilemma lies with individual moral judgements.

INCIDENCE AND PREVALENCE OF SWALLOWING DISORDERS

During the 1990s there was a growing interest in swallowing disorders and their management. Research literature, as well as the experience of specialist swallowing clinics in both the US and the UK have increased our awareness of the magnitude of the clinical problem (Massey & Shaker, 1997). Despite these advances there is still insufficient information on the incidence and prevalence of swallowing disorders in the population to enable services to be planned and developed. Even in the more common conditions such as stroke, head injury, Parkinson's disease, motor neurone disease (MND), and multiple sclerosis (MS), estimates for dysphagia vary widely (Park & O'Neill, 1994).

It is possible to make some predictions about future need by analysing data from the British Artificial Nutrition Survey (Elia et al., 1997), which estimated that more than 10,000 patients were on home enteral tube feeding (HETF), with numbers increasing by 20–25% per annum. These figures include patients feeding via nasogastric (NG) tubes, although the majority of adults had gastrostomies. Indications for the use of HETF in

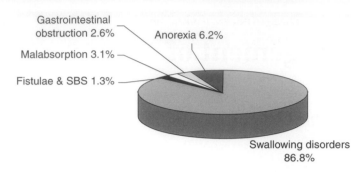

Figure 25.1. Indications for home enteral tube feeding (from Elia et al., 1997 with permission from The British Association for Parenteral and Enteral Nutrition (BAPEN)).

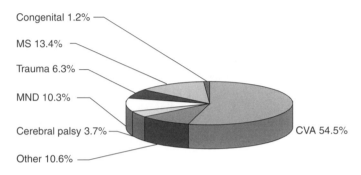

Figure 25.2. Neurological disorders and home enteral nutrition (from Elia et al., 1997 with permission from The British Association for Parenteral and Enteral Nutrition (BAPEN)).

adults are shown in Fig. 25.1. Neurological causes of dysphagia identified in the BANS survey are shown in Fig. 25.2.

The BANS survey identifies the more severe cases of dysphagia that need artificial feeding, but not those needing modified diets and nutritional supplements or those with unidentified dysphagia. As we enter a new century our goals must be to:

(1) identify all groups of patients predisposed to swallowing disorders
(2) determine which patients would benefit from early intervention
(3) clarify what resources are needed to manage long-term swallowing disorders.

ANATOMY AND PHYSIOLOGY OF SWALLOWING

Accurate diagnosis and management of neurogenic dysphagia must begin with an understanding of the relevant neuroanatomy and physiology. This chapter describes the normal physiological swallowing process; a further description of the functional controls of deglutition are described by Miller et al. (1997). Swallowing impairment can result from a variety of biomechanical or physiological changes to deglutition mechanisms. The stages of swallowing can be used as a clinical assessment tool to identify symptoms at each stage.

The normal swallowing process can be divided into four stages (Fig. 25.3): (1) oral preparatory; (2) oral; (3) pharyngeal; and (4) oesophageal (Donner & Bosma, 1985; Logemann, 1983).

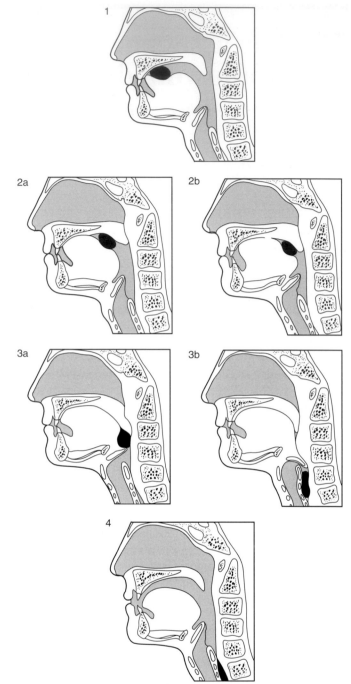

Figure 25.3. The four stages of swallowing. (1) The oral preparatory stage; (2a,b) the oral stage; (3a,b) the pharyngeal stage; (4) the oesophageal stage.

Preparatory and oral stage

The preparatory and oral stage of deglutition, in which food is formed into a bolus by biting and chewing, is under voluntary control. Mastication is a complex process, food is placed in the mouth and positioned by the tongue on the occlusal surfaces of the teeth. The mandible deviates and moves to the preferred chewing side. Sensory receptors in the teeth determine food viscosity and transarticular pressure (Ahlgren, 1967; Hylander &

Crompton, 1986). The food is crushed on the teeth surfaces. During this grinding phase the maxillary and mandible molars slide across each other in a constant cyclic pattern. Saliva is mixed with food and binds food particles into a cohesive bolus, it also lubricates the hard and soft tissue of the oral cavity. Sensory receptors in the lips, teeth, and tongue are responsible for detecting temperature and taste.

Oral stage

The oral stage, which lasts 0.7–1.2 s, accomplishes the voluntary transfer of food and fluid from the oral cavity into the pharynx. During the oral stage, the tongue elevates, contacts with the hard palate and forms a negative seal between the lateral edges of the tongue and the upper teeth. The food bolus or fluid is propelled backwards in a peristaltic movement into the pharynx. Entry into the pharynx coincides with elevation of the soft palate against the posterior pharyngeal wall—this motion permits the bolus to leave the mouth and seals off the nasopharynx from regurgitation.

Pharyngeal stage

This stage can be voluntarily initiated, but proceeds reflexly. The pharyngeal stage begins as food, fluid, or saliva pass the anterior faucial arches. The following events occur concurrently:

(1) The back of the tongue contacts with the posterior pharyngeal wall.
(2) The velopharynx closes to prevent food or fluid refluxing down the nose.
(3) There is superior and anterior movement of the larynx—this movement widens the pharynx for the passage of the bolus, it also opens the cricopharyngeal sphincter (the upper oesophageal sphincter) by means of traction (Sasaki & Isaacson, 1988).

The main processes that prevent aspiration of material into the larynx during the pharyngeal stage are: (1) contraction of the intrinsic laryngeal muscles, initiating false and true vocal cord closure; and (2) the downwards and dorsal movement of the epiglottis to cover the laryngeal additus. Swallows occur more frequently during the expiratory phase of respiration and include an apnoeic event, which lasts between 0.3 and 2.5 s (Clark, 1920; Miller & Sherrington, 1915; Selley et al., 1994; Smith et al., 1989).

Oesophageal stage

The oesophageal stage of the swallow begins as the bolus passes through the relaxed upper oesophageal sphincter/cricopharyngeus muscle and enters the lumen of the oesophagus. The bolus passes along the tube and leaves the oesophagus to enter the stomach through the relaxed gastro-oesophageal/cardiac sphincter. Sensation and motility are served by the vagus nerve.

Pressure changes during deglutition

Another useful way of describing deglutition is as a single pressure-driven event. The alimentary tract from the lips to the upper oesophageal sphincter forms one continuous tube. Along its route there are four valves:

(1) the lips
(2) velopharyngeal port
(3) larynx
(4) cricopharyngeus.

The lips close during swallowing, there is tension in the buccal muscles, closure of the velopharyngeal port, and closure of the true and false vocal cords. The piston-like movement of the tongue and contraction of the pharyngeal muscles results in an increase of pressure in the tube, acting to clear the bolus as it passes through the hypopharynx. As the cricopharyngeus opens there is a pressure differential that draws the bolus into the oesophagus. McConnel et al. (1988) liken this process to an oropharyngeal suction pump. The pressure behind the tongue pushes the bolus through the pharynx and the opening of the cricopharyngeus sucks it into the oesophagus.

CLINICAL FEATURES OF DYSPHAGIA IN DIFFERENT NEUROLOGICAL DISEASES

Overview

The factors listed in Table 25.1, particularly the behavioural deficits, highlight the need to maintain a telescopic, rather than a microscopic, perspective of the purely neurological aspects of swallowing problems. The presence of abnormal posture, poor respiratory function, a tracheostomy, cognitive dysfunction, and reduced appetite can contribute more to failure of, or complications of, attempts at oral feeding than abnormal bulbar function *per se*. In this regard, the term "failure of oral feeding" is more helpful than "dysphagia" because it encourages the holistic view required to make sense of the relationship between disorders of swallowing and disorders of successful oral sustenance. However, there are important differences in the neurology of swallowing disorders, an appreciation of which helps structure a discussion of management and prognosis.

The main reason for disorders of swallowing posing such a threat to patients with neurological disease relates to the common aerodigestive tract. Both food and air pass through the pharynx but then have to be steered to either the oesophagus or larynx. Even minor abnormalities of this process can produce dramatic symptoms and serious, potentially life-threatening, complications as listed in Tables 25.2 and 25.3. The intricate system described in the introduction is designed to close the airway, cease respiration, and move the bolus from mouth to pharynx to oesophagus, without breaching the airway defences. It is very susceptible to changes in the speed, amplitude, strength, and timing of movement of the face, larynx, lips, tongue, palate, and pharynx. Before considering individual diseases, there are

Table 25.1. Signs associated with dysphagia and risk of aspiration

Behavioural deficits
- decreased alertness
- cognitive dysfunction
- other behavioural deficits: playing with food, inappropriate size of bites, talking or emotional liability while trying to swallow

Observations during or after feeding
- difficulty initiating swallow
- difficulty managing oral secretions
- prolonged meal time, frequently washes food down with liquid
- compensatory head and neck movements
- laborious chewing, repetitive swallowing, choking
- leakage of food/fluid or saliva from tracheostomy site
- difficulty breathing during or after eating

Other signs of impaired oropharyngeal dysfunction
- motor speech disorder (dysarthria)
- saliva pooling in oral cavity or drooling
- wet, hoarse voice
- abnormal reflexes, dystonia, dyskinesia, facial asymmetry or weakness
- tongue wasting or fasciculations
- leakage of food/fluids from lips, pocketing of food in oral cavity
- frequent throat clearing
- need for frequent suction
- weight loss

Table 25.2. Symptoms associated with dysphagia and risk of aspiration

Changes in approach to food
- avoidance or embarrassment when eating in company
- avoidance of foods of specific consistency

Symptoms experienced during meals
- prolonged meal time, frequently washes food down with liquid
- compensatory head and neck movements
- laborious chewing, repetitive swallowing
- cough, choking, spluttering when eating or drinking
- difficulty initiating swallow
- sensation of food sticking in throat or chest
- reflux or regurgitation of food or fluid
- difficulty breathing
- fear/anxiety of choking while eating
- pain when swallowing
- leakage of food/fluid or saliva from tracheostomy site

Symptoms reported during/after meals
- weight loss
- increased throat clearing
- postprandial wheezing/bronchospasm

Table 25.3. Clinical effects of malnutrition

Loss of weight
Loss of muscle tissue and tone
Oedema
Skin breakdown
Impaired immunity
Increased susceptibility to infection
Poor wound healing
Anorexia
Depression, lethargy
Increased toxicity of some drugs
Increased duration of hospitalisation
Increased mortality

some useful generalisations and distinctions, which inform a discussion of the many different types of dysphagia.

In supranuclear disease, that is, diseases affecting the descending corticobulbar fibres, the lower motor neurone circuitry is intact and the larynx, tongue, and pharynx are not denervated. The voluntary control of bulbar function and movement is impaired but reflex function is relatively preserved and might be exaggerated by loss of descending inhibition. At its simplest, this will lead to a loss of fine control of the bolus in the mouth, disrupt the control and rhythm of chewing, and lead to chaotic and untimely presentation of the bolus to the pharynx. However, a crude untailored swallow, consisting of laryngeal elevation and closure with associated opening of the upper oesophageal sphincter, is still possible and can occur in response to stimulation by the bolus of laryngeal and oropharyngeal receptors.

This laryngeal closure and movement can be thought of as a protective upper airway reflex, which complements coughing and gagging. These promote the egress of the bolus from pharynx to mouth whereas reflex laryngeal closure and movement, the crucial component of the oropharyngeal suction pump (McConnel et al., 1988), pull the bolus downwards into the oesophagus.

This contrasts with nuclear or infranuclear lesions, which lead to denervation of the involved structures. This is of particular importance in relation to the larynx and the suprahyoid musculature. Lesions of the recurrent laryngeal or vagus nerve cause paralysis of the true and false vocal cords, arytenoids, and epiglottis on one side and voluntarily or reflexly the larynx cannot close, and apposition of the true cords is impossible. Thus phonation is impossible and reflex closure of the larynx during swallowing cannot occur, making aspiration inevitable. Ineffective coughing, also due to the vocal cord paresis, compounds the situation. If the anterior and posterior suprahyoid musculature is severed from its points of insertion or denervated, the hyoid and larynx cannot be elevated and the subject cannot swallow because the upper oesophageal sphincter cannot be opened.

The control of respiration around the deglutition apnoea is another process susceptible to disruption by neurological disease (Selley et al., 1994). As mentioned earlier, the deglutition apnoea is usually preceded by and followed by expiration. This promotes the egress of bolus remnants around the laryngeal vestibule back into the pharynx and pyriform fossae. If this pattern of respiration around the deglutition apnoea is abnormal there is a risk of inhalation, even when other aspects of bulbar function are unaffected.

Swallowing and feeding disorders occur with such regularity in some diseases that they merit more detailed discussion.

Cerebrovascular disease

Hemispheric stroke. Strokes involving the cerebral cortex or the internal capsule/basal ganglia typically produce weakness and impaired fine movement with or without sensory loss. The bulbar structures retain their lower motor neurone innervation but lose the fine control required to prepare the bolus adequately. In most cases the swallowing function recovers within 2 weeks.

In severe cerebrovascular disease with multiple strokes involving extensive areas of the deep white matter, or the inferior frontal lobes bilaterally, a supranuclear paralysis (pseudobulbar palsy) can result and only crude reflex swallowing (and coughing) is preserved, but chewing and bolus preparation are grossly abnormal. Typically, this is associated with a severe dysarthria and dysphonia.

In some cortical strokes there might be a prominent apraxia of the lips and tongue and this can cause severe difficulties with oral preparation of the bolus but, once initiated, a crude swallow, good enough to move the bolus on and reduce its threat to the airway, is still possible.

Brainstem strokes.   Brainstem strokes are traditionally associated with severe dysphagia but in practice this is not true in all cases. Medial medullary syndrome, which causes unilateral paralysis of the tongue and a contralateral hemiparesis, causes a mild dysarthria and a mild dysphagia but laryngeal closure and elevation is preserved and oral feeding is not significantly disrupted.

However, lateral medullary syndrome causes a profound dysphagia and dysphonia due to infarction of the nucleus ambiguus, which contains the cell bodies of the nerves innervating the larynx, palate, and pharynx. Although there is asymmetry and weakness of the palatal and pharyngeal movements, the failure of the larynx to close adequately, due to unilateral denervation, allows the bolus to pass freely into the airway, causing profound distress and potentially severe respiratory complications. Oral preparation is reasonably preserved, as is elevation of the hyoid and larynx, but the failure of laryngeal closure unhinges the whole process. As mentioned earlier, the situation is compounded by impaired coughing. Furthermore, the accompanying nausea, vertigo, pain, and inappetence can contribute as much or more to the failure of oral feeding as the laryngeal paresis.

This small selection of different strokes syndromes highlights the shortcomings of considering dysphagia after stroke as a homogenous problem. Not only is the neurology of the swallowing dysfunction clearly different depending on the site of the lesion, but the relative contribution of it to the failure of oral nutrition and hydration also varies considerably.

Extrapyramidal diseases

As a rule, these diseases affect the speed, initiation, and amplitude of movement but do not cause lower motor disease and are not associated with weakness. In the limbs, rigidity and tremor are often prominent but these impairments are less easily appreciated in the bulbar region. In clinical practice the disorders of kinesis impair the preparation of the bolus and the transfer of the bolus through the mouth; a reduced rate of swallowing coupled with the typical posture (forward flexion) also lead to troublesome drooling. A number of radiological studies have suggested that hold-up of the bolus at the upper oesophageal sphincter is due to cricopharyngeal spasm. The known impairments in extrapyramidal disease make it more likely that a reduced amplitude of anterior and superior laryngeal movement produces this radiological appearance.

The syndromes that mimic Parkinson's disease are characterised by the same disorders of kinesis as idiopathic Parkinson's diseases but can be complicated by additional relevant problems, which can lead to a failure of oral feeding at an earlier stage. Multisystem atrophy is an illustrative example. Against a backcloth of parkinsonism, these patients can develop a cranial dystonia—a disproportionate antecollis or an oromandibular dystonia—or a vocal cord palsy. Although cranial dystonias do not usually preclude oral feeding they can do so when occurring in combination with parkinsonism. The cord palsy does not preclude oral feeding because it is selective for the abductors and therefore does not affect laryngeal closure; however, if a tracheostomy is required this can tether the laryngeal movements and in this way impair opening of the upper oesophageal sphincter.

Motor neurone disease

This disease can affect lower motor neurones and upper motor neurones; in practice most patients have some evidence of involvement of both at some time during the course of the illness.

In the upper motor neurone form, corticobulbar fibre degeneration leads to a loss of fine motor control of the face, lips, tongue, and palate, with slowing of movement and marked impairment of bolus preparation and oral control. The bulbar reflexes are usually preserved and can be exaggerated; some patients find it difficult not to gag when brushing their teeth. Coughing in response to trivial stimulation of the larynx and pharynx is dramatic in some patients and bouts of severe coughing, sometimes with upper airway obstruction, have been attributed to an exaggerated glottic closure reflex in the absence of good evidence of bolus obstruction. The associated speech disorder reflects the slowing of tongue movements and bulbar presentations are often associated with emotional lability.

As the disease advances, the patient becomes anarthric and aphonic with a complete loss of voluntary control. However, the preservation of reflex coughing and reflex untailored swallowing protects the airway and might explain why patients with such limited voluntary control do not succumb earlier.

In lower motor neurone forms of the disease the tongue and face can be wasted and fasciculating at an early stage of the disease but the preservation of speed of movement tends not to disrupt oral control—and speech—until the weakness becomes quite profound. Kennedy's syndrome is an excellent example of this. It involves only lower motor neurones and often patients have a profound weakness of the face and tongue with obvious wasting and fasciculation but yet their articulation is relatively preserved. Weakness of the suprahyoid musculature can cause incomplete opening of, and premature closure of, the upper oesophageal sphincter.

Lower cranial nerve palsies

Qualitative cranial nerve palsies, if unilateral, have predictable effects on swallowing. The reason for vagal nerve lesions disrupting swallowing so much more than hypoglossal nerve lesions was discussed earlier. Recurrent laryngeal nerve palsies have a similar effect on swallowing despite sparing the pharynx and palate, highlighting the importance of the larynx.

Although the fifth and seventh nerves are heavily involved in preparation of the bolus and opening of the upper oesophageal sphincter, unilateral lesions rarely lead to failure of oral feeding. Bilateral facial nerve palsies have a more pronounced effect and make manipulation and retention of the bolus in the mouth difficult due to pocketing of bolus particles, even with normal tongue movements.

Myasthenia gravis

This is an autoimmune disease affecting the neuromuscular junction and leading to weakness. It is a useful illustrative example of how muscle disease can affect swallowing. It has a predeliction for the musculature of the head and neck and the proximal limbs. It typically involves the eyes and can be associated with severe swallowing problems. Jaw weakness is often profound and the hanging jaw makes chewing and oral preparation of the bolus quite impossible; the same problem unhinges articulation. The tongue, palate, pharynx, face, and the suprahyoid musculature can all be affected and weakness of the neck extensors can affect head posture. Typically, the disease exhibits fatiguability and chewing can be impossible later in the day. The prognosis has improved considerably since the introduction of effective immunosupression and the potential for a prompt response to treatment should influence decision-making about methods of feeding, particularly the need for a percutaneous endoscopic gastrostomy.

Iatrogenic causes

In clinical practice, particularly in severely disabled adults, iatrogenic problems can worsen function or become the main cause of dysphagia in susceptible patients.

Tracheostomies.   The importance of the movements of the larynx in relation to opening of the upper oesophageal sphincter was emphasised earlier. The corollary is that anything that impedes this movement can have a profound effect on swallowing, particularly in subjects who have other problems. Mechanical causes include large goitres, particularly if there is retrosternal extension, fibrosis, or infiltration of the suprahyoid musculature and tracheostomies. In some cases extensive scar tissue over a tracheostomy site can have the same effect.

In practice, this can lead to situations where a tracheostomy is used mainly to allow tracheal toilet but its presence reduces the patient's ability to use swallowing as a method of clearing secretions. In addition, coughing, although still effective for tracheal secretions, is less effective for oropharyngeal clearance.

Drugs.   The ability of anticholinergic drugs to dry-up secretions, impede oesophageal peristalsis, and cause confusion, particularly in the elderly, means that swallowing problems can be precipitated in susceptible patients. Major tranquillisers affect swallowing in different ways according to the duration of treatment. In the early stages they can induce an acute oromandibular dystonia, after a few weeks or months of treatment

bulbar parkinsonism, and after years a chronic tardive dystonia involving the lips and jaw. All of these side-effects can alter oral intake.

Botulinum toxin.   The use of this drug is increasing for a number of different neurological conditions and, when used for torticollis, dysphagia is a well recognised side-effect. The site of the injections can affect the severity of the swallowing problem. Spread of the toxin to the pharyngeal musculature is one possible mechanism. In those who need nasogastric feeding after injection, the involvement of the suprahyoid musculature, which is in close anatomical proximity to the sternomastoids, is a more convincing explanation; bilateral weakness could produce severe dysphagia due to defective upper oesophageal sphincter opening.

CLINICAL ASSESSMENT AND INVESTIGATION OF DYSPHAGIA

Clinical assessment is an essential basis for management, establishing the adequacy and safety of oral feeding regimes. The clinical case history together with the physical examination should establish a cause for the dysphagia and/or the requirement for prognosis.

Clinical assessment is multidisciplinary and includes: (1) the case history, along with information gathered not only from the patient but also from medical notes and interviews with relatives and carers; (2) physical examination; (3) bedside or clinic assessment of swallowing function; (4) assessment of nutritional status; and (5) standardised screening protocols incorporating key elements of the above.

Clinical history

Dysphagia most often occurs against a background of multiple medical problems and complications. Dysphagia can be one of the first symptoms of an undiagnosed or newly emerging neurological disease such as motor neurone disease, myasthenia gravis, or Parkinson's disease. However, patients often ignore dysphagic symptoms such as those listed in Table 25.2 (p. 344) perhaps regarding them merely as age-related problems.

In the acute in-patient population, latent dysphagia can surface following general anaesthesia and surgery. Chronic, untreated dysphagia in elderly people can also come to the fore following admission for an unrelated problem. It is not uncommon for a patient with fractured neck of femur to be discharged on home enteral tube feeding at the insistence of hospital staff. All too often the dysphagia is attributed to some acute disorder following intubation or surgery, whereas systematic enquiry would have established evidence of previous dysphagia requiring appropriate management.

Physical examination and observation

Some of the most important signs suggesting dysphagia and risk of aspiration are shown in Table 25.1 (p. 344).

Consciousness, cognition, and swallowing behaviour. The physical examination includes the patient's level of alertness, cognitive function, and ability to cope with the external environment. Non-compliance with treatment could be due to cognitive impairment, or to reduced level of consciousness or delirium associated with cerebral pathology. Cognitive impairments that affect swallowing include deficits in attention, executive function, praxis, language, and perception. Drowsy or inattentive patients are likely to inhale food or fluid fed to them by care staff. They might sleep through or ignore food or fluid if they are not helped.

Disturbances to motor and sensory processing can also affect the patient's ability to cope with oral feeding. Difficulties can range from patients being unable to see or recognise food to being incapable of coordinating the necessary hand and mouth movements to eat or drink. Inability to cut food up to manageable mouthfuls or to hold a cup can cause or exacerbate swallowing problems as patients struggle with food particles or volumes of fluid that are too large to swallow safely.

Cranial nerves. It is important to assess the cranial nerves, especially the fifth (trigeminal), seventh (facial), ninth (glossopharyngeal), tenth (vagus), and twelfth (hypoglossal).

Oral cavity and tongue. The condition of the mouth and teeth and the fit of dentures influence the patient's ability to chew and swallow. Examination sets out to eliminate:

(1) trauma, infection or structural abnormality
(2) impaired secretion of salivary glands
(3) decayed or inadequate dentition or poorly fitting dentures.

Functional swallow. No assessment of oropharyngeal function is complete without an evaluation of oral feeding function. The risks of this assessment can be minimised by following some basic procedures. The patient must be alert and seated in a position where the head cannot be tilted backwards. The trunk and the head need to be as symmetrical as possible. The patient needs to be offered at least two different consistencies: (1) a thick smooth consistency, such as custard or yoghurt; and (2) water. The patient should be encouraged to take sips of fluid and teaspoons of the "pudding". The examiner should note if the larynx rises to indicate a swallow or if there are any clinical signs of swallowing dysfunction such as coughing, spluttering, respiratory distress, or wet hoarse voice during the trial. Some patients might be silent aspirators, no overt signs such as a reflexive cough occurring as material enters the laryngeal vestibule (Linden & Sibens, 1983). Where possible, note the quality of the patient's voice before and after the ingestion of food and fluid: a wet, hoarse voice together with an impaired pharyngeal reflex strongly suggests laryngeal aspiration.

Diagnostic testing of deglutition

The range of diagnostic tests to evaluate disorders of deglutition increased during the 1990s (Brown & Sonies, 1997). However, access to specialised tests is limited in most general hospitals and videofluroscopic swallowing examination (VFE) still remains the gold standard. This routinely used procedure elucidates both the anatomy and the dynamics of swallowing and is a useful rehabilitation tool.

Videofluroscopic swallowing examination (VFE). The VFE provides an extensive assessment of swallowing function during all stages of the swallowing process. It is carried out on an alert patient who is either in a standing or sitting position. Small amounts of barium liquids or coated foods are given to the patient to assess the ability to tolerate food intake. In our clinic we routinely use four different consistencies: barium liquid, barium mixed with yoghurt (paste), barium cookie (prepared by our diet kitchen), and barium liquid with marshmallow.

During the VFE, the speech and language therapist or radiologist will try various manoeuvres to improve the patient's swallowing function (see Management of swallowing impairment, p. 351). Successful compensatory techniques will be included in the dysphagia rehabilitation programme and extended to mealtimes.

Penetration and aspiration

Abnormal swallowing during the oral and pharyngeal stages can cause misdirection of food and fluids into the airway (larynx, trachea, bronchi). This misdirection, known as penetration if it enters the laryngeal vestibule or aspiration if material passes through the true vocal cords into the trachea and beyond, can cause varying degrees of respiratory discomfort or deterioration. The extent to which aspirated material contributes to morbidity and mortality depends on the nature of the aspirate, the amount and frequency of aspiration and the patient's immune system (Bartlett & Corbach, 1975; Feinberg et al., 1990). Patients who are chronically debilitated as a result of airway disease are less likely to cope with even small amounts of material entering the airway.

Conditions that increase the risk of aspiration include depressed consciousness, feeding fluids with a syringe, feeding patients in a recumbent position, and intubation of the trachea.

Tracheal or endotracheal intubation. Clinicians must be aware of standard procedures for assessing swallowing function in intubated patients. Laryngeal complications of intubation can be short or long term. Any damage to vocal cord competence can adversely affect the ability to swallow safely. Complications associated with endotracheal intubation and causing swallowing problems include:

(1) trauma to oral structures, pharynx, and larynx, causing temporary pain or discomfort
(2) trauma to vocal cords secondary to cuff overinflation causing more permanent damage
(3) vocal cord oedema.

Patients with endotracheal tubes *in situ* must be fed artificially. It is all too common to see that this general dictat is not adhered to, with the result that many patients suffer from avoidable aspiration pneumonia and associated malnutrition problems. Hospitals should ensure that standard policies are in place for managing nutrition in patients whose swallowing is altered through artificial airway management.

Standardised screening protocols

Standardised screening tests are now used routinely in some hospitals. Figure 25.4 shows examples of dysphagia screening and

management protocols produced by the Scottish Intercollegiate Guidelines Network (SIGN).

ASSESSMENT OF NUTRITION

Assessment of nutritional status

There is no single definitive measure of nutritional status. A combination of anthropometric, biochemical, clinical and dietary

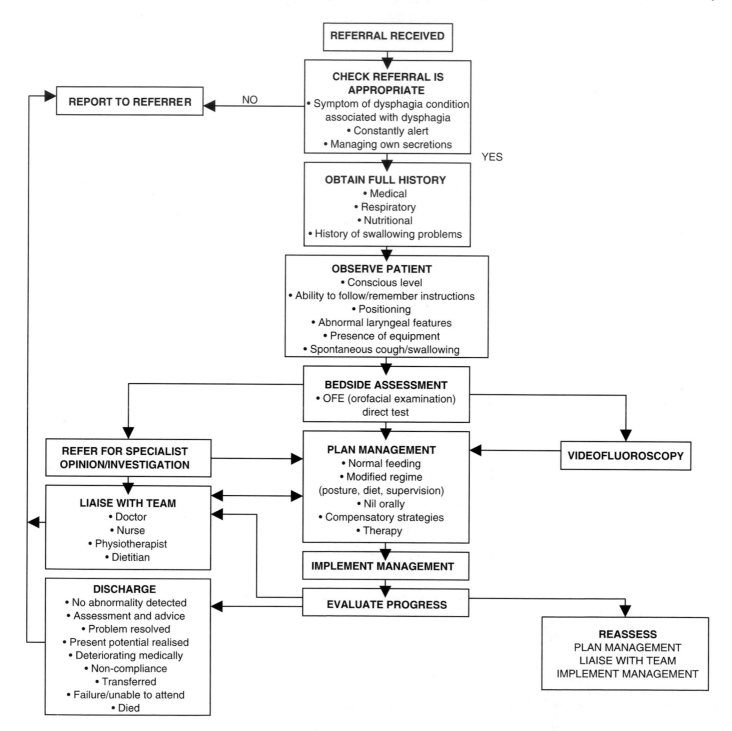

Figure 25.4. Continued.

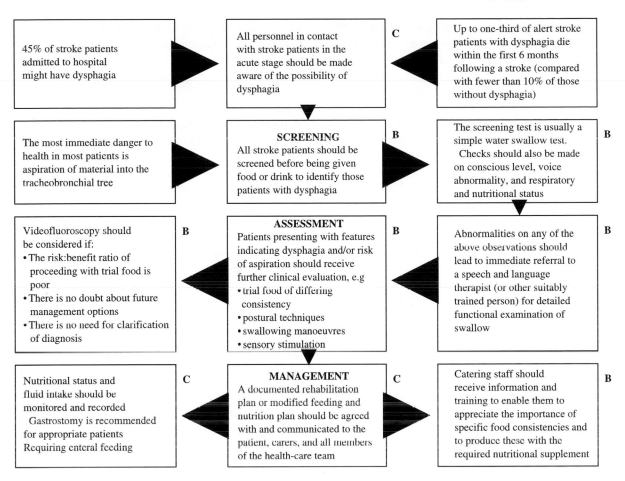

Figure 25.4. Examples of dysphagia protocols and patient-specific reminders that can serve as the basis for development of local protocols. (a) Dysphagia care model from the Western General Hospital, Edinburgh; (b) guideline derived from the National Clinical Guideline recommended for use in patients after stroke by the Scottish Intercollegiate Guidelines Network (SIGN) (A, B, C, refer to the grade of recommendation).

evaluations is essential to assess the clinical picture. Two key factors in this assessment are weight history and diet history.

Weight history. The overall clinical effects of malnutrition are far reaching (Table 25.3, p. 344). Rapid weight loss increases morbidity and mortality. Illness-related weight loss of more than 10% is associated with impaired muscle strength and respiratory function and reduced resistance to infection as well as affecting mental function (BAPEN, 1996). Weight loss of more than 35% is life threatening on nutritional grounds alone (Allison, 1992).

The importance of closely monitoring weight changes in patients with dysphagia, to identify undernutrition early and to take the necessary action, cannot be overemphasised. Dysphagic patients should be weighed regularly, to ensure that a body mass index (BMI) within the ideal range for height is achieved and maintained. Correctly calibrated scales must be available in all wards and clinics. Digital versions provide the most accurate readout and sitting scales are often easier for patients with neurological disorders to use. The presence of clothes and/or shoes must also be consistent to ensure accurate comparison with previous weights. Weight can also be affected by oedema and/or dehydration. A stadiometer, to measure height, should also be available to allow calculation of BMI.

If a patient cannot be weighed, or if weight is unreliable, alternative methods should be used, e.g. mid–upper arm circumference, mid-arm muscle circumference, or triceps skinfold thickness. Despite limitations such as poor inter-rater reliability, these methods are particularly helpful in unconscious or ventilated patients where a true body weight might be impossible to obtain for some time. Correct techniques must be learned and used consistently, preferably with the same observer making successive measurements.

Diet history. The diet history provides essential information for the assessment of nutritional status for the planning of management strategies. Some patients are unable to identify specific problems when asked about their swallowing difficulties, as their own self-imposed dietary modifications have become their "normal" pattern over time. However, by taking a careful diet history, changes in meal pattern and eating habits can become apparent. These can include switching to a softer diet and avoiding certain foods; taking fluid items only, e.g. soups, milk, tea; taking longer to complete meals or leaving food unfinished; and avoiding social contact when eating.

For all patients with suspected swallowing difficulties, a daily record of all food and fluid intake should be kept. Textures and consistencies that cause problems can then be identified. The record also provides information about volumes consumed and about the intake of protein, energy, vitamins, and minerals.

Blood tests can be used to augment general indicators of nutritional status but do not accurately reflect nutritional status in isolation. A low serum albumin level can simply indicate that the patient is acutely ill. Other serum proteins, e.g. C-reactive protein and pre-albumin, can be more helpful but there is no absolute measure. Routine measurement of key vitamins and trace elements, e.g. vitamin B12, thiamin, zinc, copper, iron, and selenium, is also recommended, as supplementation might be required.

Nutrition assessment tools. The implementation of formal protocols for nutritional assessment is recommended as a minimum standard to aid early identification of nutritionally compromised patients (BAPEN, 1996). Many studies have shown the incidence of significant malnutrition in hospital in-patients to be between 10 and 40% of all admissions, depending on the group studied (Lennard-Jones, 1992; McWhirter & Pennington, 1994). Patients exhibiting any signs or symptoms of dysphagia are potentially at high risk of malnutrition and subsequent complications. Nutritional assessment should be carried out on admission and at regular intervals, with the results documented, to allow appropriate action to be taken.

Assessment of nutritional requirements

When the patient's weight is known, approximate energy and protein requirements can be assessed by using a predictive formula (Schofield et al., 1985). This enables approximate calculation of the patient's basal metabolic rate (BMR), taking account of stress factors including infection, pyrexia, impaired mobility, and ventilatory support. Such assessment methods are not precise, especially if an accurate weight is not available, and must be used with caution but, combined with clinical judgement, they provide a starting point for appropriate nutritional intervention.

Indirect calorimetry allows measurement of resting energy expenditure, but this method is not routinely available on most units. There is evidence to suggest that standard predictive formulae are less satisfactory in assessing nutritional requirements in traumatic brain injury, because energy expenditure and nitrogen balance are influenced by the nature and severity of the injury, by the length of time postinjury, and by the effects of treatment such as ventilatory support, paralysis, sedation, and medication (Clifton et al., 1986; Sunderland & Heilbrun, 1992; Weekes & Elia, 1996). However, in the absence of indirect calorimetry, predictive equations continue to provide useful guidance to estimate requirements.

INITIAL MEASURES TO IMPROVE NUTRITION

Following assessment of swallow function by the speech–language therapist, an appropriate diet plan should be agreed in conjunction with the patient, dietitian, and nursing staff. This might entail modifications to the oral diet or the feeding regime, with or without nutritional supplements.

Modifying the oral diet

For those patients able to sustain oral nutrition, the texture, consistency, and temperature of the diet require particular attention. Modification of food and fluids to consistencies that facilitate 'safe' swallowing are probably the most commonly used management technique in dysphagia rehabilitation. Solid foods that require mastication and precise oral motor and sensory control are often eliminated from the diet during the rehabilitation process and replaced with puréed foods or a soft diet. Patients with either progressive or recovering conditions often learn which foods and recipes they can manage safely and will introduce a range of textures and consistencies into their diet. The implementation of multistage diets devised to suit varying levels of dysphagia has become commonplace in many units. This type of regimen aims to provide the patient with the widest choice of foods that can be consumed safely, following assessment of the degree of swallowing impairment (Martin, 1991; Pardoe 1993). Table 25.4 shows five dietary stages, from the easiest to the most difficult swallowing consistencies.

Many patients with dysphagia, notably those with stroke, have difficulty swallowing liquids safely (Larsen, 1973; Linden & Siebens, 1983; Logemann, 1983). This is due to limited control of the oral bolus or delay initiating a swallow. Thickened fluids are often essential to maintain hydration in patients unable to tolerate thin fluids safely, without aspiration. Thin liquids are the most difficult to control in the mouth and can easily spill

Table 25.4. Modifications to food and fluid consistency

Solid foods
Five categories of food, that which range from easiest to most difficult to swallow:

Stage 1   All puréed food, smooth hot cereals, strained soups thickened to puréed consistency, creamed cottage cheese, smooth yoghurt, and puddings

Stage 2   All foods in previous stages plus soft moist whole foods such as pancakes; finely chopped tender meats, fish and eggs bound with thick dressing; soft cheeses; noodles and pasta; tender cooked leafy greens; sliced ripe banana; soft breads; soft, moist cakes

Stage 3   All foods in previous stages plus eggs any style, tender ground meats bound with thick sauce, soft fish, whole soft vegetables, drained canned fruits

Stage 4   All foods in previous stages plus foods with solids and liquids together (e.g. vegetable soup), all whole foods except hard and particulate foods such as dry breads, tough meat, corn, rice, apples

Stage 5   Regular diet

Liquids
Two categories that are unrelated in ease of swallowing:

(1) Thin: water, all juices, other clear liquids

(2) Thick: all other liquids including milk, any juice not classified as thin liquid

Thickened liquids
Liquids thickened with starch to puréed consistency for those who cannot tolerate any other liquids

over past the larynx, frequently without detection. Several commercial thickening products are now available on prescription to be added to fluids such as milk, juice, tea, coffee, soups, and soft drinks until a safe, manageable consistency is achieved. Some can also be incorporated into more solid foods to achieve a suitable smooth texture.

Appearance and presentation of modified texture diets must not be overlooked in the search for a safe consistency. Being able to distinguish between individual flavours, and recognising familiar foods by sight and taste, even when the texture has been altered, will contribute significantly to improving nutritional intake. An unrecognisable puréed meal that is unattractively presented will do nothing to stimulate the appetite and might deter the patient from even trying to eat. Associations made with "baby food" must be avoided and care given to establishing a meal pattern, incorporating favourite foods, which can be enjoyed rather than simply tolerated. Even in situations when oral intake is safe and a diet of modified texture is well-tolerated, the content and volume of the nutritional intake must be monitored. The diet must be sufficient to meet energy requirements. Just because a patient can physically eat a soft or puréed diet, does not mean that he or she will consistently consume sufficient quantity on a daily basis to meet nutritional requirements. Puréed foods can be particularly low in energy unless energy-dense liquids are used to achieve the correct consistency.

Nutritional supplements

Appropriate nutritional supplements must be considered as soon as there is evidence that dietary intake alone is insufficient. There is now an extensive range of oral nutritional supplements available in milk-based and non-milk-based versions, as well as "dessert"-type products that are ideal in texture for many dysphagic patients. These supplements are generally protein- and energy-dense and prescribable in a variety of flavours. High-energy snacks, meals, and drinks can also be devised without using specialist products and referral to a dietitian is advised to provide a specific regimen tailored to meet individual needs.

Factors such as fatigue, muscle weakness, and poor appetite can easily interfere with food intake. These problems can become particularly apparent as the day progresses, with a better dietary intake during the earlier part of the day and deteriorating towards evening, with the last meal of the day proving to be the most difficult, and often missed altogether. This is frequently a problem for patients with multiple sclerosis. In such cases, artificial feeding methods can sometimes be avoided by offering the patient five or six small meals/supplements daily (Feinberg et al., 1990).

MANAGEMENT OF SWALLOWING IMPAIRMENT

Compensatory strategies to facilitate a safe swallow include indirect and direct therapeutic interventions.

Direct therapy to facilitate safe swallowing

Postural changes and swallowing manoeuvres. Postural changes and swallowing manoeuvres alter the anatomical and physiological relationship of the structures of swallowing (Horner et al., 1988). Logemann (1989, 1993) reported that in 80% of patients who aspirated while swallowing liquids during any stage of the swallowing cycle, the use of a compensatory posture eliminated aspiration on at least one size of bolus, and in 33% postural changes eliminated aspiration on all boluses of thin fluid. These postural and swallowing manoeuvres require the patient to be able to follow instructions and are not suitable for patients with significant language or cognitive problems. Some of the manoeuvres, such as those involved with laryngeal closure and the Mendelsohn's manoeuvre, require sustained physical effort and are not appropriate for patients who tire easily or who experience muscle fatigue.

It is important to verify that compensatory techniques deemed successful in the videofluoroscopy clinic can be extended to the mealtime situation and maintained for the duration of the meal. The patient might need nutritional support dovetailed with oral feeding until compensatory techniques have been fully established.

Procedures to improve oral sensory function. Techniques to restore oral sensory awareness are used when delayed onset of swallowing is due either to oral dyspraxia or to delay in initiating the pharyngeal stage of the swallow. These techniques include:

(1) thermal stimulation to the anterior faucal arch
(2) offering foods that taste sour or tart
(3) offering cold food and fluids
(4) encouraging self-feeding so that hand–mouth movements provide additional sensory input and prepare the patient for swallowing
(5) increasing the pressure of the spoon on the tongue when presenting the food

Medication. There are few reported studies on the use of medication to improve oropharyngeal dysfunction. Levodopa formulations have been reported to improve swallowing function in Parkinson's disease (Bushman et al., 1989; Robbins et al., 1984). Medical treatment for myasthenia gravis also improves swallowing function.

Surgical procedures. Cricopharyngeal myotomy has been used in patients who have an isolated relaxation failure of the cricopharyngeus muscle or upper oesophageal sphincter. Careful clinical assessment is needed before this type of procedure is carried out to ensure that there is no failure in other phases of the oropharyngeal swallow. In addition, invasive procedures have been used for laryngeal or glottic incompetence secondary to vocal cord palsy. These procedures aim to improve glottic closure through thyroplasty, or by injection of fat, collagen, or Teflon into the affected cord (Benninger et al., 1994).

Indirect therapy to facilitate safe swallowing

Adaption to food and fluid consistencies. As described earlier, current practice is to thicken drinks to facilitate safe swallowing in those who are dysphagic for liquids (Pennington & Krutsch, 1990). Several studies (Jacobs et al., 1990; Kahrilis & Logemann, 1993) have demonstrated the following effects of increased viscosity on the swallow mechanism in healthy subjects and stroke patients:

(1) longer oropharyngeal transit times
(2) extended cricopharyngeus or upper oesophageal opening
(3) increase in the forces required to swallow, i.e. tongue driving force is increased significantly as the fluid viscosity increases.

By increasing fluid viscosity, muscular forces used in the swallow mechanism will also increase and help reduce episodes of coughing and laryngeal aspiration (Goulding, 1988).

ARTIFICIAL NUTRITIONAL SUPPORT

Enteral non-oral feeding

When oral nutrition is contraindicated or inadequate to meet requirements, a suitable method of non-oral feeding must be introduced. Figure 25.5 (Park & O'Neill, 1994) gives a summary of the options available for nutritional support once a clinical assessment has been made. The two non-oral routes used most frequently are nasogastric and gastrostomy feeding.

Nasogastric (NG) feeding. NG feeding tends to remain the first choice for non-oral feeding because it is the quickest to initiate. The development of highly durable polyurethane fine-bore tubes has improved comfort as well as extending the length of time tubes can remain *in situ*. The NG route is also useful for short-term, "top-up" feeding, e.g. over night to supplement an inadequate oral intake without interfering with whatever oral intake can be tolerated by day. However, there are well-documented problems related to NG feeding and growing evidence that percutaneous endoscopic gastrostomy (PEG) for nutritional support improves patient outcome and reduces mortality (Norton et al., 1996; Park et al., 1992).

Confused and cognitively impaired patients frequently remove their NG tubes. Reintubation is upsetting for the patient, can cause nasal trauma, and is costly in terms of nursing time and the need for repeat radiography. Other disadvantages include tubes blocking or becoming displaced, which delays feed administration. Moreover, the NG tube might further impair a defective swallow and impede retraining of speech and swallowing (Pennington & Krutsch, 1990).

Percutaneous endoscopic gastrostomy. In recent years percutaneous endoscopic gastrostomy (PEG) (see Chapter 15) has gained acceptance as a quicker, safer alternative to surgical gastrostomy. With a shorter procedure time and avoiding the need for general anaesthesia, it is a more appropriate alternative for disabled or frail patients. Other advantages include improved patient tolerance and less risk of tubes blocking or dislodging. Studies have shown that a significant advantage of PEG feeding is that patients receive a far greater proportion of their prescribed feed than via the nasogastric route, and gain significantly more weight after 7 days of feeding (Park et al., 1992).

In a controlled comparison of patients fed with or without a PEG tube, Norton et al. (1996) found that the PEG group had increased serum albumin, significantly reduced mortality at

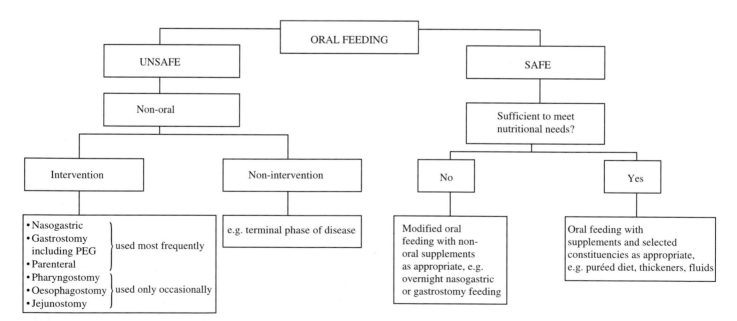

Figure 25.5. Algorithm summarising the decisions that have to be made about nutritional management following bedside and/or radiographic assessment (adapted from Park & O'Neill, 1994).

6 weeks, and fewer treatment failures. Compared with NG tubes, the positioning of PEG tubes is aesthetically more acceptable to patients, more comfortable, less obtrusive, and less likely to interfere with rehabilitation. Bolus feeds are also easier to administer. PEG feeding is recommended as the most effective route when enteral nutritional support is required for more than 4–6 weeks, with nasogastric feeding recommended for no longer than 2 weeks.

PEG tubes can be positioned under radiological guidance when the endoscopic route is contraindicated, for example following oesophageal trauma or obstruction. In a study evaluating the effectiveness and safety of different methods of forming gastrostomies, Wollman et al. (1995) found a higher rate of successful tube placements when a radiological rather than endoscopic method was used. Surgical gastrostomy had the highest total complication rate (29%) compared with 13.3% for radiological gastrostomy and 15.4% for PEG. PEG had the lowest minor complication rate (5.9%) but radiological gastrostomy had fewer tube-related complications than did PEG with rates of 12.1% and 16.0% respectively. Thirty-day procedure-related mortality rates were highest for surgery (2.5%) versus 0.3% for radiological gastrostomy and 0.53% for PEG.

Other enteral routes.   In some neurological conditions, regurgitation and possible aspiration of the feed from the stomach is a potential risk. Enteral feeding beyond the pyloric sphincter can be used to eliminate reflux. Several studies have confirmed that gastrostomy feeding does not protect against aspiration pneumonia (Olson et al., 1993; Park et al., 1992). Post-pyloric feeding can be delivered via nasoduodenal or nasojejunal tube but placement can be difficult and, as in NG feeding, tube displacement is a common complication. A comparative study of percutaneous gastrostomy (PG) tubes versus percutaneous gastrojejunostomy (PGJ) tubes (Olson et al., 1993), did not support a causal relationship between PG placement and gastroesophageal reflux. It was concluded that the more costly PGJ tube is unnecessary if there is no evidence of reflux but is potentially beneficial when there is demonstrable reflux. Jejunal feeding can also be administered via needle–catheter jejunostomy but this entails a surgical procedure.

Other enteral routes are less commonly used but might be considered depending upon the patient's diagnosis and available access. An orogastric or pharyngeal tube might be required to initiate feeding in the case of head trauma, especially basal skull fractures and/or facial injuries, where passage of a nasogastric tube is contraindicated. This must be used only in the short term, as tubes can be dislodged or bitten through and a PEG tube should be placed as soon as possible.

Administration of tube feeds.   Tube feeds are usually administered either by continuous pump delivery or by bolus feeds. Both methods have advantages and disadvantages, and the choice depends on the patient's and carers' individual needs. If continuous pump feeding is used, the feed should be initiated at a slow rate such as 50 ml/h, and increased gradually according to patient tolerance until the desired volume is reached. Patients who have had no enteral intake for several days might need to start the feed at a slower rate. The feed should ideally be discontinued for a period of about 6 h each day to lessen the chances of aspiration from regurgitation, which is more likely to occur with continuous pump feeding (Jacobs et al., 1990). Overnight feeding via pump delivery is a useful way to supplement an inadequate oral intake. The continuous pump method is not recommended for very restless or confused patients, who have a high risk of self-extubation.

Bolus feeding involves the delivery of a specified amount or bolus of feed given at set intervals throughout the day. This method has the advantage that the patient is free to be more mobile, not being connected to a pump for lengthy periods. Boluses should be initiated at 1–2-hourly intervals until tolerance is established but, as the volume of feed is increased, a 4–6-hourly regimen can normally be implemented. Many ambulatory patients, especially those in the rehabilitation phase, can tolerate boluses of 200–400 ml at a time, often requiring only 3–4 feeds per day. A pump can be used to deliver larger boluses, e.g. over 30 min to 1 h. Bolus feeding regimens have more significant implications for the amount of nursing time required, especially if needed 2-hourly. When an NG tube is being used for bolus feeding of a confused patient who is liable to self-extubate, it might be necessary to pass the NG tube prior to each bolus being given. In this situation, placement of a PEG tube would be strongly recommended. Bolus feeds given via the PEG route are particularly successful for home tube-fed patients who are simply supplementing an unreliable or inadequate oral intake because of the degree of flexibility provided and the aesthetic advantages. All tube feeds should be combined with sufficient water flushes to prevent the tube blocking. This is especially important after liquid medications have been given down the tube. Crushed tablets or powders should never be given via a feeding tube.

Intolerance to tube feeding.   The most common symptoms that indicate poor tolerance of a feeding regimen are diarrhoea, steatorrhoea, abdominal pain distension, gastric reflux, and vomiting. The presence of such symptoms should not automatically be assumed to be feed related, especially if the patient has been receiving the feed for some time without problems. However, rate, volume, temperature, and feed composition can be important contributing factors. Depending on the nature of the problem, the solution might be to decrease the rate of feeding temporarily, or to include adequate rest periods within the regimen. If the required volume of feed is poorly tolerated, it might be possible to change to a more nutrient-dense formula delivered at a slower rate. Additional fluids could be needed to compensate.

Feeds should always be administered at room temperature, not taken straight from a refrigerator. In some situations, using a fibre-containing enteral feed can help improve gastrointestinal tolerance and bowel function (Shankardass et al., 1990). If intolerance to the fat content or whole protein content of the feed is suspected, modified fat feeds and semi-elemental or elemental formulae can provide suitable alternatives.

Parenteral nutrition

Parenteral feeding should not be considered unless there is severe gastrointestinal dysfunction or obstruction. It carries a higher risk of infection and metabolic complications and should only be contemplated when all enteral feeding options have been exhausted. A period of gastrointestinal deprivation can lead to a breakdown of bacterial defence systems in the gut (Shikora & Ogawa, 1996), so if the gut is functioning it should be used. Even in situations where parenteral nutrition is indicated, a small amount of enteral feeding should be introduced as early as possible to maintain gut integrity.

Dove-tailing oral intake with artificial feeding. There can be considerable physical as well as psychological benefits for the patient if a combination of non-oral and oral nutrition can be delivered. Supplementing a non-oral regimen with small quantities of food of a safe consistency can help to achieve an enhanced energy intake with subsequent improvements in weight gain, compared with patients who transfer from completely non-oral to oral intake without a gradual transition phase. Patients do better on a combination of oral and non-oral nutrition than on non-oral feeding alone.

REFERENCES

Ahlgren J (1967) Kinesiology of the mandible. *Acta Odontologica Scandinavica 25*: 593–611

Allison SP (1992) Uses and limitations of nutritional support. *Clinical Nutrition 11*: 319–330

BAPEN (1996) *Standards and Guidelines for Nutritional Support of Patients in Hospital*. A Report by a Working Party of the British Association for Parenteral and Enteral Nutrition. BAPEN, Maidenhead

Bartlett JG, Corbach SL (1975) The triple threat of aspiration pneumonia. *Chest 91*: 901–909

Benninger MS, Crumley RL, Ford CN, Gould WJ, Hanson DG, Ossoff RH, Sataloff RT (1994) Evaluation and treatment of the unilateral paralyzed vocal fold. *Archives of Otolaryngology—Head and Neck Surgery 111*: 495–508

Brown BP, Sonies BC (1997) Diagnostic methods to evaluate swallowing other than barium contrast. In: A Perlman, K Schulze-Delrieu (Eds) *Deglutition and its disorders*. Singular Publishing Group, Inc., San Diego

Bushmann M, Dobmeyer SM, Leeker L, Perlmutter JS (1989) Swallowing abnormalities and their response to treatment in Parkinson's disease. *Neurology 39*: 1309–1314

Clark GA (1920) Deglutition apnea. *Proceedings of the Physiological Society*: 54–59

Clifton GL, Robertson CS, Choi SC (1986) Assessment of nutritional requirements of head-injured patients. *Journal of Neurosurgery 64*: 895–901

Dodds WJ, Hogan WJ, Reid DD, Stuart ET, Andorfer RC (1973) A comparison between primary esophageal peristalsis following wet and dry swallows. *Journal of Applied Psychology 35*: 851–857

Donner MW, Bosma J (1985) Anatomy and physiology of the pharynx. *Gastrointestinal Radiology 10*: 212

Elia M et al. (1997) *Annual Report of the British Artificial Nutrition Survey*. BAPEN, Maidenhead

Feinberg MJ, Knebl J, Tully J, Segall L (1990) Aspiration and the elderly. *Dysphagia 5*: 61–71

Goulding R (1988) *A study to evaluate the use of the Holownia and Jouallt Viscometer in the dietary management of stroke patients*. MSc dissertation. University of Southampton, Faculty of Medicine, Health and Biological Sciences

Helm JF, Dodds WJ, Hogan WJ, Soergel KH, Egide MS, Wood CM (1982) Acid neutralizing capacity of human saliva. *Gastroenterology 83*: 69–74

Horner J, Massey EW, Riski JE, Lathrop D, Chase KN (1988) Aspiration following stroke: Clinical correlates and outcome. *Neurology 38*: 1359–1362

Hylander WL, Crompton AW (1986) Jaw movements and patterns of mandibular bone strain during mastication in the monkey macacci fascicularis. *Archives of Oral Biology 31*: 841–848

Jacobs S, Chang RWS, Lee B, Bartlett FW (1990) Continuous enteral feeding: A major cause of pneumonia among ventilated intensive care unit patients. *Journal of Parenteral and Enteral Nutrition 14*: 353–356

Larsen GL (1973) Conservative management for incomplete dysphagia paralytica. *Archives of Physical Medicine and Rehabilitation 54*: 180–185

Lennard Jones JE (1992) (Ed) *A positive approach to nutrition as treatment*. King's Fund Centre, London

Linden P, Siebens AA (1983) Predicting laryngeal penetration. *Archives of Physical Medicine and Rehabilitation 64*: 281–283

Logemann JA (1983) *Evaluation and treatment of swallowing disorders*. College Hill Press, San Diego.

Logemann JA (1989) Swallowing disorders and rehabilitation. *Journal of Head Trauma Rehabilitation 4*(4): 24–33

Logemann JA (1993) The dysphagia diagnostic trail. *Clinics in Communication Disorders 3*(4): 1–10

Martin AW (1991) Dietary management of swallowing disorders. *Dysphagia 6*: 129–134

Massey T, Shaker R (1997) Introduction to the field of deglutition and deglutition disorders. In: A Perlman, K Schulze-Delrieu (Eds) *Deglutition and its disorders*, Singular Publishing Group, Inc., San Diego

McConnel FMS, Cerenko D, Jackson RT, Griffin TN (1988) Timing of major events of the pharyngeal swallowing. *Archives of Otolaryngology—head and neck surgery 114*: 1413–1418

McWhirter JP, Pennington CR (1994) Incidence and recognition of malnutrition in hospital. *British Medical Journal 308*: 945–948

Miller A, Bieger D, Conklin JL (1997) Functional controls of deglutition. In: A Perlman, K Schulze-Delrieu (Eds) *Deglutition and its disorders*. pp. 43–97, Singular Publishing Group, Inc., San Diego

Miller FR, Sherrington CS (1915) Observations on the bucco-pharyngeal stage of reflex deglutition in the cat. *Experimental Physiology and Cognate Medical Sciences 9*: 147–186

Norton B, Homer-Ward M, Donnelly MT, Long RG, Holmes GKT (1996) A randomised prospective comparison of percutaneous endoscopic gastrostomy and nasogastric tube feeding after acute dysphagic stroke. *British Medical Journal 312*: 13–16

Olson DL, Krubsack AJ, Stewart ET (1993) Percutaneous enteral alimentation: Gastrostomy versus gastrojejunostomy. *Radiology 187*: 105–108

Pardoe EM (1993) Development of a multistage diet for dysphagia. *Journal of the American Dietetic Association 93*(5): 568–571

Park C, O'Neill PA (1994) Management of neurological dysphagia. *Clinical Rehabilitation 8*: 166–174

Park RHR, Allison MC, Lang J, Spence E, Morris AJ, Danesh BJZ, Russell RI, Mills PR (1992) Randomised comparison of percutaneous endoscopic gastrostomy and nasogastric tube feeding in patients with persisting neurological dysphagia. *British Medical Journal 304*: 1406–1409

Pennington GR, Krutsch JA (1990) Swallowing disorders: Assessment and rehabilitation. *British Journal of Hospital Medicine 44*: 17–22

Robbins J, Webb W, Kirchner H (1984) Effects of Sinemet on speech and swallowing in Parkinsonism. Paper presented at the *Annual Convention of the American Speech and Hearing Association*, San Francisco

Sasaki CT, Isaacson G (1988) Functional anatomy of the larynx. *Otolaryngologic Clinics of North America 21*: 595–612

Schofield WN, Schofield C, James WPT (1985) Basal metabolic rate – review and prediction, together with annotated bibliography of source material. *Human Nutrition: Clinical Nutrition 39C*(suppl. 1): 5–96

Selley WG, Ellis RE, Flack FC, Bayliss CR, Pearce VR (1994) The synchronization of respiration and swallowing. *Dysphagia 9*(3): 162–167

Shankardass K, Chuchmach S, Chelswick K, Stefanovich C, Spurr S, Brooks J, Tsai M, Saibil FG, Cohen LB, Edington JD (1990) Bowel function of long-term tube-fed patients consuming formulae with and without dietary fiber. *Journal of Parenteral and Enteral Nutrition 14*: 508–512

Shikora AS, Ogawa AM (1996) Enteral nutrition and the critically ill. *Postgraduate Medical Journal 72*: 395–402

Smith J, Wolkove N, Colacone A, Kineisman, H (1989) Coordination of eating, drinking, and breathing in adults. *Chest 96*: 578–582

Sunderland PM, Heilbrun MP (1992) Estimating energy expenditure in traumatic brain injury: Comparison of indirect calorimetry with predictive formulas. *Neurosurgery 31*(2): 246–253

Weekes E, Elia M (1996) Observations on the patterns of 24-hour energy expenditure changes in body composition and gastric emptying in head-injured patients receiving nasogastric tube feeding. *Journal of Parenteral and Enteral Nutrition 20*: 31–37

Wollman B, D'Agostino HB, Walus-Wigle JR, Easter DW, Beale A (1995) Radiologic, endoscopic, and surgical gastrostomy: An institutional evaluation and meta-analysis of the literature. *Radiology 197*: 699–704

26. Dysarthria

Pamela Enderby

INTRODUCTION

Dysarthria is the speech disorder resulting from disturbance of neuromuscular control. Impairments can be due to central or peripheral nervous system damage, resulting in weakness, slowing, incoordination, or altered muscle tone, and leading to changes in the characteristics of the speech produced.

The term "dysarthria" was originally applied to disorders of articulation. The terms "dysarthraphonia" and "dysarthria–pneumophonia" identify combinations of deviant articulation, respiration, and phonation, but these terms are rarely used (Peacher, 1950). The interdependence of the various speech systems is such that it is more useful to consider the entire speech mechanism as essentially a unitary system. When the function of that system is disrupted at any point, the function of more than one part is highly likely to be affected, even though the effects might not be readily perceived in the speech signal. Hence, "dysarthria" has become an inclusive term to encompass "coexisting motor disorders of respiration, phonation, articulation, resonance and prosody" (Darley et al., 1975), including isolated single process impairments such as cranial nerve XII paresis, an isolated palatopharyngeal incompetence of neurological origin, or an isolated dysphonia due to unilateral or bilateral vocal fold paresis. The term "anarthria" describes a person who is unable to speak because of a severe neuromuscular disorder preventing vocalisation and articulation. This term is rarely used and I concur with Hardy (1967) and Netsell (1986), who state that the term "dysarthria" should be used as a generally encompassing term, despite this being semantically incorrect.

It is important to recognise that a dysarthric condition can exist in conjunction with other types of communication disorder, particularly dyspraxia and dysphasia. Furthermore, many people with dysarthria will simplify their language structure and articulation, thus reducing the stress on the system in order to express themselves with greater ease. This language change should be seen as a secondary rather than a primary consequence of the dysarthria.

NEUROMUSCULAR BASIS OF SPEECH MOTOR CONTROL

Speech production is a highly developed motor skill that takes many years to acquire and continues to modify and adapt even up to the early teenage years. It involves the production of a sequence of movements that are controlled by several regions of the nervous system and, given its extreme complexity, the speech production process is usefully conceptualised in terms of different physical levels. In addition to central nervous system (CNS) involvement, the physical structures involved must be considered. These include not only the most obvious, such as the larynx, the tongue and the pharynx, the velopharynx, the jaw, and lips, but also the rib cage, the diaphragm, and the abdominal muscles. Impairments in any of these can produce abnormalities in speech production. Aerodynamic features are also important, including oral, nasal, and glottal airflow. Intraoral air pressure affects the ability to produce certain phonemes and subglottal air pressure affects phonation (Netsell, 1986).

According to Paillard (1983), motor planning involves selection of an appropriate movement strategy in the light of intended goals and prevailing physical conditions. Intended goals for speech can be thought of as words and phrases and thus, in planning a speech utterance, such units can be represented or coded as spatial, aerodynamic, or acoustic targets. A general strategy for the achievement of such targets would be part of the speech motor plan. In order for this plan to be enacted there has to be a motor programming stage that entails provisional specifications of precisely how the motor plan is to be achieved: for example, which muscles contract and at what time. It is probable that this programming stage also involves sensory aspects so that when the movement is initiated the programming can change according to the sensory feedback received (Tohgi et al., 1996).

Through the course of this execution process, the discharge of motor neurones is influenced by numerous motor and sensory pathways. Thus, the neural correlates of motor planning, programming, and execution are likely to vary with the type of movement and the degree of learning and with any impediments—physical or emotional.

Although the nature of these processes is not well understood, advances in clinical neurophysiology have increased our understanding of physiological aspects of dysarthria since the 1980s (Abbs & Cole, 1982).

The cerebral cortex is recognised as the major structure of speech processing (Abbs & Cole, 1982). Abbs and Welt (1985) suggest that multiple representations of muscles in cortical area 4 might provide a partial basis for the control of diverse speech gestures in a single structure, for example, lip movement for rounding and closure. It has been found that primary motor cortex activity is well correlated with muscle force changes in learned movements (Hoffman & Luschei, 1980). This would suggest that the motor cortex is an important site for sensory motor integration immediately prior to the involvement of the lower motor neurones.

Further integration takes place in the cerebellum, which has long been recognised as a centre that is specialised for movement control, and one that no doubt plays a large role in the coordination of speech production. The two distinct corticocerebellar pathways that seem to be important in the regulation of output of speech are discussed by Neilson and O'Dwyer (1984), who conclude that the characteristics of these pathways support the general view that the intermediate cerebellum utilises sensory input to effect rapid modifications of cortical motor output during movement execution.

The distinctive characteristics of dysarthric speech associated with basal ganglia disease suggest that this collection of subcortical nuclei plays a very specialised role in speech motor control. In general, the basal ganglia are seen to be important in the planning and programming of learned movements, which might involve setting kinematic parameters such as the direction and amplitude of movements.

The existence of different types of motor units, which act as an interface between the nervous system, and the mechanical systems, is an important concept in motor physiology (Burke & Edgerton, 1975) and has direct application in the assessment and treatment of dysarthria. The variety of properties of each motor unit is utilised in different muscle systems to achieve unique functions (Clamman, 1981). Netsell (1986) has suggested that the muscles used in speech production tend to have motor units with properties that are intermediate between those for the eyes and for the limbs. For example, there is considerable variability in the motor neurones in the lip muscles. It is evident that further research is needed.

The contribution of sensory feedback to speech motor control has attracted more attention recently (Barlow & Netsell, 1989). The temporary dysarthria experienced by patients who have received local anaesthesia for dental or oral surgery demonstrates some similarities to other pathologies. It is important to recognise the role not only of proprioception and touch, but also of auditory receptors and receptors detecting subglottal, glottal, and intraoral air pressure during speech. McClean (1987) calls

for continued research in this area and points out that recent discussions about the neural mechanisms underlying dysarthria have emphasised the potential significance of abnormal processing of sensory information. Neilson and O'Dwyer (1984) suggest that a major contribution to the disordered movement processes associated with cerebral palsy speech comes from sensory deficits caused by congenital deformity of the neural pathways projecting over the ventral thalamic nuclei. The separation of the oral motor and oral sensory systems is clearly not as straightforward as previously suggested.

DIFFERENTIAL CHARACTERISTICS OF THE DYSARTHRIAS

Dysarthria is present in approximately one-third of all patients with traumatic brain injuries (Sarno et al., 1986). Dysarthria also affects a high percentage of those with pre- and perinatal neural damage; estimates of the prevalence of dysarthria among those with degenerative neurological diseases such as multiple sclerosis, Parkinson's disease and motor neurone disease have varied from 19 to 100% (Darley, 1978; Darley et al., 1972; Logeman & Fisher, 1981).

Descriptions in medical textbooks suggest that characteristic speech patterns can be of assistance in medical diagnosis (Chusid, 1979; Merritt, 1969). A body of literature in the field of speech pathology describes speech disorders characteristic of specific conditions such as multiple sclerosis, Parkinson's disease, motor neurone disease, cerebellar disease, cerebral vascular disease, and cerebral palsy. Darley et al. (1975) hypothesised that analysis of the sound patterns of dysarthria can lead to identification of clusters of features that "reflect impairment of function of portions of central nervous system". However, problems arise with regard to the diagnosis of dysarthria types that are not "pure forms". Among the best-known classification systems is that used in the Mayo Clinic Study (Darley et al., 1975). It has similarities to the Frenchay scheme (Enderby, 1983). Both studies rated the systems commonly associated with dysarthria according to the underlying pathology. The studies agree that spastic dysarthria caused by upper motor neurone lesions produces imprecise articulation, reduced rate of speech, hypernasality, abnormal prosody, reduced alternating speech movement, and reduced intelligibility. This contrasts with flaccid dysarthria caused by lower motor neurone lesions; these patients tend to have difficulty with swallowing and dribbling, marked hypernasality, and a tendency to speak in short phrases supported by shallow respiration. This speech is slow, volume is unvarying, and articulation can be weak and unformed. Disorders of the cerebellum can affect speech in a number of ways. One obvious pattern is ataxic dysarthria, which demonstrates hyperactivity of the muscles of articulation with irregular alternating movements, slowed rate, and poor control over excessive volume of speech. Less readily recognised is cerebellar mutism, which most often occurs after the removal of cerebellar tumour. Several studies now implicate the cerebellum in cognitive as well as motor aspects of speech disorders (Gordon, 1996).

Patients with extrapyramidal dysarthria show monotonous pitch, reduced tonal stress, reduction of lip movements, poor alternating movements, weak phonation, and an increased speaking rate (Hammen & Yorkston, 1996).

ASSESSMENT

Until recently, the assessment of dysarthria by speech and language therapists was unstandardised and depended upon the experience and interest of the therapist. However, a study of 100 speech and language therapists indicated that most found a systematic approach helpful with regard to diagnostic classification. The majority of speech and language therapists felt that, with experience, they were able to perceive the features related to differential diagnosis without using a formal structured approach (Simmons & Mayo, 1997). But it must be remembered that it is not unusual for patients to have dysarthrias related to more than one impaired system, and detailed assessment does assist with these more complex cases. McNeil and Kennedy (1984) list the following reasons for assessing a dysarthric speaker:

(1) to detect or confirm a suspected problem
(2) to establish a differential diagnosis
(3) to classify a specified disorder group
(4) to determine a site of lesion or disease process
(5) to specify the degree of the severity of the involvement
(6) to establish a prognosis
(7) to specify more precisely the treatment focus
(8) to establish criteria for treatment termination
(9) to measure any change.

From a therapeutic point of view it is important to add to this list the necessity to be able to determine the retained abilities of the patient, so that treatment programmes incorporate methods of articulatory compensation.

Methods of assessing dysarthria for research purposes are often impractical in the clinic; they tend to provide detailed information on one aspect of speech (e.g. volume of breath or power of particular muscles used in articulation), leaving the investigator uninformed about the remaining features. Research methods include electromyographic studies (Tuller et al., 1979), assessment of muscular strength (Dworkin & Culaata, 1980), spectrographic analysis (Kent & Netsell, 1975), other neurophysiological examinations (Netsell et al., 1989), and panel judgements (Berry et al., 1974; Darley et al., 1975).

Descriptive assessments are simple, economical, and practical, but are frequently unreliable and lack sensitivity and quantification. Several formal procedures are commonly used by clinicians for detailing dysarthria, two of which are standardised.

1. Dysarthria profile (Robertson, 1982). The areas covered by this assessment are voice, respiration, articulation, prosody, rate, intelligibility, reflexes, and diadochokinesis. The results of the assessment are demonstrated on the profile, which covers four A4 sheets. It is a useful procedure for assisting the planning treatment given by speech and language therapists.

2. Test of intelligibility for dysarthria (Yorkston & Beukelman, 1980). This test provides a standardised method of assessing the clarity of dysarthric speech. The test is easy to use and reliable, but is lengthy and does not cover aspects of dysarthria other than clarity. Although intelligibility of speech is probably the most important functional aspect, and is obviously related to the degree of disability and handicap, one must consider how intelligibility scores can be changed depending upon the speaker's tasks, the transmission system, and the judge's experience. Considerable work has been done on factors affecting intelligibility. It is clear that, whereas improving intelligibility would be a goal in the therapy, each clinician must be aware of the various ways in which this can be improved. Thus, intelligibility can be improved with no change in the underlying neurological system. Therefore, it is important to consider other factors in addition to intelligibility.

3. The Frenchay dysarthria assessment (Enderby, 1983). This standardised test is divided into subsets for associated reflexes, respiration, lips, jaw, palate, laryngeal, tongue, and intelligibility. It also assesses the speaking rate, sensation, and other influencing factors. Predictive data and scoring profiles show mean and standard deviations of specific dysarthrias and a computer program enables the user to compare given scores with those of a research group, which helps with categorisation of the dysarthric systems.

4. Computerised assessment of intelligibility. Several developments suggest that a more reliable method of objectively transcribing speech characteristics will soon be available using PC-based methods of analysis. One such approach compared PC-based intelligibility ratings of dysarthric speakers (101 patients, 16 normal speakers) with 45 transcribers. The analysis showed that the Munich Intelligibility Profile was both reliable and a valid instrument. It is likely that more will be seen of this approach to the assessment of speech disorders and the analysis of the degree of deviation from norms in the near future (Ziegler & Hartmann, 1993).

SPEECH AND LANGUAGE THERAPY

Most patients with dysarthria, including those with static and progressive disorders, would benefit from speech therapy. There are many ways of compensating, facilitating, and improving communication, but these are not always obvious.

Despite being the most common of the acquired speech disorders, dysarthria has attracted relatively little attention in the literature regarding treatment and the efficacy of treatment. This might be due to the fact that dysarthria is frequently associated with either severe brain damage or with progressive neurological disease and there has, in the past, been a negative attitude to the role of therapy in these areas. Attitudes are changing, however, and doctors and therapists are more aware of the broad nature of rehabilitation in this context.

All speech therapy for dysarthric patients is dependent on a full assessment of intact as well as impaired aspects of speech. The therapist might decide to work on the intact aspects and use methods to facilitate intelligibility, or to work on impaired functions to promote restoration (Fukusako et al., 1989; Netsell, 1991).

In the former approach, the therapist might develop exaggerated phrasing, intonation, pacing or lip movements, which will assist the listener by giving more clues to the message. Restorative therapy might concentrate on improving control of respiration, the signalling of voiced and voiceless sounds, the accuracy of plosion rather than friction in articulation, and developing strength, accuracy, and speed of the muscles involved in speech. Frequently, both methods are pursued in therapy and both are dependent on the patient improving his or her speech awareness, auditory discrimination, and speech monitoring.

Dysarthria therapy usually follows a hierarchical programme, starting with work on respiration; phonation, including initiating, sustaining, and projecting the voice; resonance, including appropriate use of nasal and oral emission; and then the development of movements of the facial musculature. It is important that this underlies any work on articulation. However, work is not complete until the patient can use these skills with a degree of consistency and confidence in less familiar settings.

Earlier in the chapter it was stressed that speech is a highly integrated system and, therefore, it is not surprising that one area of dysfunction can have an effect upon other areas, which, although not impaired, might not be able to function normally as a result of secondary effects. For example, the person with palatal palsy, resulting in nasal emission and hypernasality, might also be unable to produce crisp plosion for bilabial consonants such as "p" and "b" because there is insufficient air pressure in the mouth. This could be in the absence of any involvement of the lips. This example highlights the importance of detailed evaluation because it is clear that, in this case, manipulation of the velopharyngeal dysfunction would improve the ability to produce bilabial sounds whereas work on bilabial sounds on their own would have no effect.

The majority of patients with dysarthria have a chronic underlying motor impairment and "normal speech is rarely a realistic goal" (Yorkston & Beukelman, 1987). The clinician should find realistic treatment goals for those with both progressive and static disorders. For example, those patients who are severely impaired and have a static or deteriorating medical condition should be assessed for a communication aid to improve their functional interaction. Alternative communication systems do not preclude the use of residual oral speech. Many patients, even with severe dysarthria, can be encouraged to express verbal indications of affirmative and negative, humour, emotions, questioning, etc. These facial and verbal accompaniments to non-verbal methods of communication personalise messages and can reduce frustration by ensuring that the patient is fully involved in the message that he or she is sending.

The term "compensated intelligibility" used by Rosenbek and La Pointe (1985) describes the goal of speech therapy for many patients with moderate dysarthria, who might have static or possibly improving neurological conditions. There are many ways in which message sending can be improved. Interestingly, the therapist is often teaching the patient abnormal ways of communicating in order to achieve a successful communication; one might have to sacrifice quality for intelligibility. Thus, the patient can be encouraged to speak at a very abnormal speaking rate, or to use phrasing techniques that will facilitate clarity (Crow & Enderby, 1989). Therapy concentrates on the quality of spoken output with patients with mild dysarthria. These patients might already be able to send their message quite intelligibly but find it embarrassing and frustrating that their speech is abnormal. Prosthetic management, postural changes, language structuring, and attention to non-verbal behaviour can all be used to assist the patient to maximise potential.

EFFICACY OF SPEECH AND LANGUAGE THERAPY

A review of literature related to the efficacy of speech and language therapy with dysarthria found few texts detailing therapeutic approaches with sufficient detail to ensure that they could be appropriately replicated. However, the few that are available have made up in quality for what is lacking in quantity. Shortcomings in evidence of the efficacy of speech and language therapy for dysarthria relate to the inadequate development of outcome measures. For example, many studies use specific speech analysis techniques, such as spectroanalysis, whereas other features of the speech, for example fluency, are not reported. Research into the efficacy of speech and language therapy for dysarthria is hampered by the lack of standardised methods of assessing the overall effects of the disorder and the majority of the efficacy studies lack sufficient detail regarding the aetiology of the dysarthria to make them sufficiently useful. The author has not come across any studies that have looked at the effects of dysarthria in a more general way, for example the psychosocial effects of the impairment and the value of speech and language therapy in improving the quality of life (Enderby & Emerson, 1995).

It is interesting that many patients who are dysarthric but remain intelligible do not get referred to speech therapy as this impairment is frequently viewed as cosmetic. However, many studies have shown the negative effect of speech impairment on the social lives of people and there is no doubt that this impairment can lead to quite marked handicap unless it is treated appropriately.

COMMUNICATION AIDS

Some patients who have difficulty in making themselves understood benefit from communication aids. These can make existing speech more intelligible (e.g. an amplifier), or can replace speech so that a person is able to communicate via the aid (e.g. a notebook computer). However, all communication aids require a degree of language ability and therefore they are mainly used by people with speech disability but with some retained language and cognitive processes.

There has been a rapid expansion in the range of communication aids available and it is important that the patient is thoroughly assessed so that the correct equipment is given. The speech and language therapist has to assess the language abilities, the physical abilities, eyesight, hearing, and other psychological factors before deciding which would be the most appropriate aid to introduce. In addition to the abilities and needs of the patient, it is important that the therapist considers the patient's environment. For example, it would be inadvisable to provide an aid with a synthesised voice to a patient living at home with a carer with marked hearing problems. Furthermore, the supply of appropriate equipment is not sufficient on its own. It is essential that patients and relatives are taught how to use the equipment in a useful and functional manner (Easton, 1987).

Aids can be categorised according to the method of input. There are three groups of aids: direct select, scanning, and encoding. Some aids offer more than one inputting system.

Direct select

In direct select techniques, the desired choice is directly indicated by the user (Vanderheiden & Lloyd, 1986). This can involve any part of the body that is able to make an indication of a symbol.

The upper body is used when possible, for example a finger, elbow, chin, fist, or eye. If these are ruled out then the lower body (e.g. the foot) can be chosen. Simple appliances that might aid this indication, such as head sticks, mouth sticks, or hand sticks might need to be considered. If direct selection is a possibility, then this method is preferred to others because of its simplicity and speed. However, it does require accuracy and a reasonable range of movement. Another advantage of this method is its wide range of application. Moderately intelligible dysarthric patients can use an alphabet board and point to the first letter of each word as they say it, or spell out a whole word in noisy situations.

Aids using conventional keyboards, such as computers, can be appropriate but some aids are made specifically for the disabled person and use the direct select technique. Examples of these are the Canon Communicator, which is a small, hand-held method of typing one's communication, or the Lightwriter, which has an LED, voice output, and printed output options.

Scanning

This method of indication would be chosen for severely speech-impaired individuals who are grossly physically impaired. It is a relatively slow method and is cognitively more complex than direct select. Methods of scanning include any technique in which the selections are offered to the user by a person or a display. The user might respond by signalling when he or she sees the correct choice presented. The simpler scanning method is for the carer to go through a series of yes/no questions, the individual using a prepared signal to indicate the required item.

Linear scanning involves each item being indicated in sequence by the listener or by the aid automatically and the patient indicating when the chosen symbol is reached. Items can be displayed on a simple communication chart, or on a clockface with an indicator. In group item scanning, the letter, words, or symbols are placed in rows or groups. The individual is encouraged to scan along rows and to indicate when the appropriate column is reached. The column is then scanned in turn to reach the correct item. This reduces the length of time required to reach the appropriate symbol, but it is still a slow method.

Encoding

This technique is cognitively sophisticated but is very useful for individuals who want to use a large vocabulary even though they have limited movement. Encoding can be described as a method by which individuals make their choice from a pattern or code of symbols that, when deciphered, indicates a whole message. The code needs to be either memorised or set out on separate cards for reference: morse code provides an example, where sequences of dots and dashes when decoded represent traditional orthography. One simple encoding method is to have on one card a list of commonly used phrases, with each of these being numbered, and on another card the numbers of the phrases. It is then possible for the individual to indicate, by an arranged method, the number that corresponds to the appropriate phrase. Encoding can be combined with direct selection or with scanning in order to indicate messages.

Communication aids now offer greater flexibility than ever because of the improvements in computer technology. Some incorporate predictive software, which allows a patient to key in a code or a couple of letters and the computer then predicts which word, phrase, or sentence is required. Others incorporate tree structures, allowing patients to develop shorthand routes to accessing the vocabulary they require. These approaches are necessary as one of the great difficulties with communication aids is the slow speed of communication. Most communication aids can now be tailored to the particular needs of an individual client, incorporating his or her own preferences, personal vocabularies, and other idiosyncrasies. However, the skills required by therapists are being stretched because they need to become more versatile in their use of technology so that they can bridge the gap between what is available and ensuring that patients can be trained to use these aids adequately.

When using communication aids it is important to consider that communication is not seen as a one-way process. Patients using communication aids will have to learn different techniques of communication, as will the listeners. Otherwise, patients will be limited to sending fairly arid messages of needs and wants, rather than being able to express themselves more broadly.

CONCLUSION

Dysarthria is a fascinating area that challenges neurophysiologists, offers information to diagnosticians, and demands particular and inventive therapy to give many the opportunity of assisting persons thus impaired to improve the quality of their lives.

REFERENCES

Abbs JH, Cole KL (1982) Consideration of bulbar and suprabulbar afferent influences upon speech motor coordination programming. In: Grillner S, Linblom B, Lubker J, Persoon A (Eds) *Speech motor control.* Pergamon Press, Oxford

Abbs J, Welt C (1985) Structure and function of the lateral precentral cortex: Significance for speech motor control. In: Daniloff R (Ed) *Speech science: Recent advances.* College-Hill Press, San Diego

Barlow SM, Netsell R (1989) Clinical neurophysiology for individuals with dysarthria. In: Yorkston KM, Beukelman DR (Eds) *Recent advances in clinical dysarthria.* College-Hill Press, Boston

Berry W, Darley FC, Aronson AE, Goldstein N (1974) Dysarthria in Wilson's disease. *Journal of Speech and Hearing Research 17*(2): 167–183

Burke R, Edgerton V (1975) Motor unit properties and selected involvement in movement. In: Wilmore J, Keogh J (Eds) *Exercise and sports sciences reviews*, vol. 3. Academic Press, New York

Chusid J (1979) *Correlative neurology and functional neurology.* Lang Medical, California

Clamman HP (1981) Motor units and their activity during movement. In: Towe A, Luschei E (Eds) *Handbook of neurobiology: Motor co-ordination.* Plenum Press, New York

Crow E, Enderby P (1989) The effects of an alphabet chart on the speaking rate and intelligibility of speakers with dysarthria. In: Yorkston KM, Beukelman DR (Eds) *Recent advances in clinical dysarthria.* College-Hill Press, Boston

Darley FL (1978) Differential diagnosis of acquired motor speech disorders. In: Darley FL, Spriestersbach DC (Eds) *Disgnostic methods in speech pathology*, 2nd edn. Harper and Row, New York

Darley FL, Brown JR, Goldstein NP (1972) Dysarthria in multiple sclerosis. *Journal of Speech and Hearing Research 15*: 229–245

Darley FL, Aronson AE, Brown JR (1975) *Motor speech disorders.* WB Saunders, Philadelphia

Dworkin JP, Culatta RA (1980) Tongue strength: Is relationship to tongue trusting, open bite, and articulatory proficiency. *Journal of Speech and Hearing Disorders XLV*: 277–282

Easton J (1987) Developing effective communication in aid users. In: Enderby P (Ed) *Assistive communication aids for the speech impaired.* Churchill Livingstone, Edinburgh

Enderby P (1983) *Frenchay dysarthria assessment.* College-Hill Press, San Diego

Enderby P, Emerson J (1995) *Does speech and language therapy work? A review of the literature.* Whurr Publishers, London

Fukusako Y, Endo K, Konno K, Hasegawa K, Tatsumi I, Masaki S, Kawamura M, Shiota J, Hirose H (1989) Changes in speech of spastic dysarthric patients after treatment based on perceptual analysis. *Annual Bulletin RILP 23*: 119–140.

Gordon N (1996) Speech, language and the cerebellum. *European Journal of Disorders of Communication 31*(4): 359–367.

Hammen VL, Yorkston KM (1996) Speech and pause characteristics following speech rate reduction in hypokinetic dysarthria. *Journal of Communication Disorders 29*(6): 429–445

Hardy JC (1967) Physiological research in dysarthria. *Cortex 3*: 128–156

Hoffman D, Luschei E (1980) Responses of monkey precentral cortical cells during controlled jaw bite tasks. *Journal of Neurophysiology 44*: 333–348

Kent R, Netsell R (1975) A case study of an ataxic dysarthric – cineradiographic and spectrographic observations. *Journal of Speech and Hearing Disorders 40*(part 1): 115–134

Logemann JA, and Fisher HB (1981) Vocal tract control in Parkinson's disease: Phonetic feature analysis of mis-articulations. *Journal of Speech and Hearing Disorders 46*(4): 248–352

McClean MD (1987) Neuromotor aspects of speech production and dysarthria. In: Yorkston KM, Beukelman DR, Bell KR (Eds) *Clinical management of dysarthric speakers.* Taylor & Francis, London

McNeil MR, Kennedy JG (1984) Measuring the effects of treatment for dysarthria: Knowing when to change or terminate. *Seminars in Speech and Language 5*(4): 337–358

Merritt H (1969) *A textbook of neurology.* Lea & Febiger, Philadelphia

Neilson P, O'Dwyer N (1984) Reproducibility and variability of speech muscle activity in athetoid dysarthria of cerebral palsy. *Journal of Speech and Hearing Research 27*: 502–517

Netsell R (1986) *A neurobiologic view of speech production and the dysarthrias.* College Hill Press, San Diego

Netsell R (1991) *A neurobiologic view of speech production and the dysarthrias.* Singular Publications, San Diego

Netsell R, Lotz WK, Barlow SM (1989) A speech physiology examination for individuals with dysarthria. In: Yorkston KM, Beukelman DR (Eds) *Recent advances in clinical dysarthria.* Singular Publications, Boston

Paillard J (1983) Introductory lecture: The functional labelling of neural codes. In: Massion J, Paillard J, Schultz W, Weisendanger M (Eds) *Neural coding of motor performance.* Springer-Verlag, Berlin, pp. 1–19

Peacher WG (1950) The aetiology and differential diagnosis of dysarthria. *Journal of Speech and Hearing Disorders 15*: 252–265

Robertson S (1982) *Dysarthria profile.* Available from Department of Speech Therapy, Manchester Metropolitan University, Manchester, M13 0JA

Rosenbek JC, La Pointe LL (1985) *The dysarthrias: Description, diagnosis and treatment.* In: Johns DF (Ed) Clinical management of neurogenic disorders. Little Brown, Boston

Sarno MT, Buonagura A, Levita E (1986) Characteristics of verbal impairment in closed head injured patients. *Archives of Physical Medicine & Rehabilitation 52*: 73–78

Simmons KC, Mayo R (1997) The use of the Mayo Clinic system for differential diagnosis of dysarthria. *Journal of Communication Disorders 30*(2): 117–132

Tohgi H, Takahashi S, Takahashi H, Tamura K, Yonezawa H (1996) The side and somatotopical location of single small infarcts in the corona radiata and pontine base in relation to contralateral limb pareses and dysarthria. *Eur-neurol 36*(6): 338–342

Tuller N, Harris K, Gross B (1979) Electro-myographic studies of the jaw muscles during speech. *Haskins Laboratories–Status Report SR 59/60*: 83–102

Vanderheiden G, Lloyd L (1986) Communication systems and their components. In: Blackmore S (Ed) *Augmentative communication: An introduction.* American Speech, Language and Hearing Association, Rockville, MD

Yorkston KM, Beukelman DR (1987) *Clinical management of dysarthric speakers.* Taylor & Francis, Boston

Ziegler W, Hartmann E (1993) The Münich Intelligibility Profile (MVP): Reliability and validity. *Nervenarzt 64*(10): 653–658

PART C
Cognitive function

27. Therapy for the language impairment in aphasia

Sally Byng   Eirian Jones

INTRODUCTION

This chapter describes a means of providing and evaluating therapy for the language impairment in aphasia. To do this, we first provide a brief overview of the issues involved in evaluating aphasia therapy, outlining some of the hazards encountered. We go on to set the context for undertaking work on the language impairment by describing how therapy addressing specific aspects of the language difficulties fits into a framework of goals for intervention when dealing with the impact of aphasia.

In discussing therapy for specific language impairments, we will outline a theoretical framework for interpreting the nature of the language impairment and then provide some exemplars of therapies for specific language impairments, together with the use of single case methodologies to evaluate the impact of the intervention on language. We will finish by discussing briefly the nature of the evidence for the effectiveness of interventions for people with aphasia.

BACKGROUND TO THE STUDY OF THE EFFECTIVENESS OF APHASIA THERAPY

Recent years have seen a major emphasis in health-care delivery to provide evidence-based intervention, with a call to have a research-led National Health Service (Department of Health, 1993). The need to provide evidence for the effectiveness of health-care interventions has placed pressure on all health-care professionals to both deliver and act on that evidence. In theory, we should be able to describe the effects of an intervention and evaluate its cost-effectiveness. This is a complex enterprise. It calls into question whose evidence counts—that of the provider of the intervention or that of the recipient—what we consider to be evidence (Greenhalgh, 1999), how we define an intervention, and whether we perceive the effects of the intervention to be worth paying for (International Stroke Trial Collaborative Group, 1997).

This enterprise has been accompanied by much debate about methodologies for determining effectiveness—what is the most robust and convincing method of obtaining evidence: double-blind, randomised controlled trials, single case studies, quantitative or qualitatively obtained results, with many polarised positions being taken. Increasingly there is a suggestion that unless the view of the recipient of the intervention is included as part of the evidence—even in a randomised controlled trial—the findings are not valid (Swales, 1998). These debates are calling into question the very nature of science and asking profound questions about the purpose of health-care intervention and who defines that purpose.

In some respects, these debates are nothing new to speech and language therapists providing services to people with aphasia following neurological damage. The effectiveness or otherwise of aphasia therapy has been called into question for nearly three decades now (Lincoln et al., 1984), with a corresponding impact on aphasia therapy services and therapists (Byng, 1993, 1998). These studies included randomised, controlled trials (RCTs) and large group studies. Some early studies investigated the effects of speech and language therapy provision and concluded quite baldly that it was ineffective (Lincoln et al., 1984).

There is, however, a twofold problem with most of these studies (Howard, 1986; Pring, 1986):

(1) They make an assumption about the purpose and composition of therapy for aphasia. It seemed to be assumed that the purpose of the therapy was only to modify in some global fashion the language and communication system of the aphasic person, so that was what was measured. Other aspects of providing therapy and support to people with aphasia were not usually taken into account. In most cases the intervention was expected to consist of one-to-one therapy involving some kind of language exercises.

(2) Neither the therapy interventions nor the population being studied were described fully. For example, it was seen to be sufficient to describe the aphasic people who received the therapy only in terms of the broad aphasia syndrome to which they could be classified. We will discuss this issue in more detail later.

The interventions were not detailed, so that even had the studies had a positive outcome, other therapists could not have replicated them. A corollary would be to evaluate a drug without specifying its chemical content or to whom it should be given.

This kind of study would probably not be given ethical permission now. As Black (1996) points out, non-drug therapies do not lend themselves to evaluation by RCTs because of the problem in defining the intervention:

The results of drug trials can, in the main, be generalised to other doctors and settings. In contrast, the outcome of activities such as surgery, physiotherapy, psychotherapy and community nursing may be highly dependent on the characteristics of the provider, setting and patients. As a consequence, unless care is taken in the design and conduct of a randomised trial, the results may not be generalisable. (Black, 1996, p. 1216).

Nevertheless the studies led to conclusions such as "Our study indicates that speech therapy did not improve language abilities more than was achieved by spontaneous recovery . . . [our results] suggest that one aspect of the speech therapy service for aphasia patients—namely, individual treatment—is effective" (Lincoln et al., 1984). This particular study has had a profound effect on the perception of a wide variety of health-care personnel: namely that speech and language therapy for people with aphasia after stroke is ineffective. The stimulus that the impact of this study had on speech and language therapists cannot be underestimated. It spawned a whole new movement in therapy—to ensure that our understanding of the impairment in aphasia was improved and, correspondingly, that therapies also improved, so that we could establish whether, indeed, it was the case that all therapy for people with aphasia was ineffective (Byng, 1993).

In this chapter we will examine how we might think about establishing appropriate areas for remediation. We will then go on to illustrate some specific therapies for some specific aspects of the effects of aphasia, demonstrating how the effectiveness of those therapies can be established.

THE CONTEXT FOR LANGUAGE THERAPY: THE IMPACTS OF APHASIA

We suggested that assumptions that therapy focused almost solely on improving the language impairment were made in the early studies of the efficacy of aphasia therapy. Does this view of aphasia therapy match what therapists provide or, more importantly, what people with aphasia want? Until recently there has not been much evidence from people with aphasia themselves, and rehabilitation has often been determined by what the professional or the service can provide. A recent qualitative study, which involved talking to people with aphasia 5 or more years after the onset of aphasia (Parr, Byng, & Gilpin, 1997), suggested that the preoccupations of people with aphasia themselves had been rather different from those of the health and social care professionals providing services. They certainly included issues to do with enhancing language and communication skills, but also included a range of other issues, as set out in Table 27.1 (taken from Byng, Pound, & Parr, 2000). These concerns cannot be separated from those of addressing the language and communication impairment: none of these issues exists in isolation from a range of other issues. The impairment in language affects the

Table 27.1. A summary of the psychosocial impacts of living with aphasia

Effects on lifestyle	Effects on person	Effects on others in the immediate social context
Employment	Psychological effects	Identity
Education	Identity	Relationships
Leisure	Self-esteem and stigma	Psychological effects
Finances	Relationships	Role changes
Social networks	Role changes	
Social inclusion		

role you can play in society and in the immediate social context. This is illustrated vividly by an aphasic man, PG, who expressed to Elman and Bernstein-Ellis (1995) how he felt about the current status of his language and communication skills:

PG was frustrated that a previous facility had terminated therapy because the severity of his aphasia no longer affected "basic" communicative skills. PG literally shouted to us, "I am *not* functional!" This retired dentist told us that he could no longer maintain his premorbid role as the joke teller, debater, or group discussant at social or business functions. He pleaded with us to enrol him in our research project so that he could have a chance to regain his personality.

Elman and Bernstein-Ellis point out that ". . . although they [aphasic people] are judged functional given a 'basic skills' definition, they are not functional in everyday life."

This underlines the limitations of providing therapy only for one aspect of the impact of aphasia. It emphasises the interrelatedness and interdependency of what have traditionally been regarded as the "psychosocial" issues following aphasia and the language and communication skills. Byng et al. (2000) point out that:

An equilibrium has to be achieved in intervention between working to enhance communication skills—by working directly on the impairment and on strategies to use skills most effectively—and working on achieving a satisfactory sense of identity, making appropriate and acceptable lifestyle choices. Intervention which focuses on only one side of this equation is not going to be satisfying for the aphasic person or for the therapist; the inter-relatedness and interdependency of communication skills and identity is critical.

A framework for intervention in aphasia is proposed (see Fig. 27.1), which demonstrates the interrelatedness of all the goals of intervention required for working with someone with aphasia, if the overall goal of achieving healthy living with aphasia is to be achieved. "Healthy" here is interpreted broadly as mental, intellectual and physical health combined. The framework demonstrates that providing therapy after aphasia needs to comprise more than just working on impaired language.

This framework contains six major foci of intervention, one of which is to enhance communication and language. The remainder of this chapter will be concerned with elaborating a means of evaluating the effectiveness of *one* means of enhancing communication—that of working directly on the language impairment. This chapter will not consider the other goals of

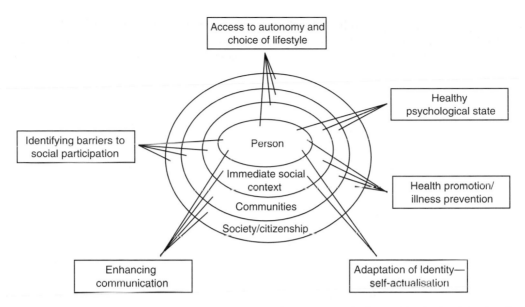

Figure 27.1. A framework for intervention in aphasia to meet the overarching goal of promoting healthy living with aphasia. (Taken from Byng, Pound, & Parr, 2000 with permission from Whurr Publishers.)

intervention, as it is concerned only with working on the language impairment. We shall first of all discuss what the goal of enhancing communication represents.

Enhancing communication

This goal represents that which perhaps has been most familiar to speech and language therapists. The aim of this goal could perhaps be stated as "achieving maximum potential for communication by enhancing both the communication skills of the aphasic person *and* the skills of those with whom they communicate". There is an implicit understanding that "communication" here represents both interaction and transaction (Simmons, 1993); that is, that therapy needs not just to enable the aphasic person to transmit information but also to engage with other people in the exchange of ideas, thoughts and opinions that represent a reflection of who they are. In this way, enhancing communication also serves to facilitate expression of identity.

A variety of means of achieving enhanced communication can be employed and the following categories represent some of the programmes which might be implemented:

(1) Impairment-based therapies. The impairment itself may be directly addressed. This is where the bulk of the research in aphasia has been carried out. Addressing the impairment directly includes therapies that aim to change or modify aspects of the impaired language. It is this aspect of intervention that will be addressed in this chapter. The theoretical approach underlying these therapies can vary.

(2) Communication strategies. The development of strategies to find a way round the language impairments, rather than tackling them head on, has been well defined by aphasiologists since the 1980s (Aten, Caligiuri, & Holland, 1982; Davis & Wilcox, 1985; Holland, 1991; Lesser & Algar, 1995).

This kind of work aims to circumvent the language impairment and to supplement the means of communication to be employed and stems from the observation that aphasic people are better communicators than talkers (Holland, 1991).

(3) Conversation partners. This (Kagan, 1998; Kagan & Gailey, 1993; Lyon et al., 1997) represents a newer concept and focuses on providing individuals with opportunities for genuine adult conversation and interaction by emphasising less the use of independent communication strategies by the aphasic partner in a conversation, but more what the participants in a conversation achieve interdependently (Kagan, 1998). The onus on changing communication skills is not all on the individuals with aphasia, but also on the persons with whom they are communicating to adapt and modify their style of communication to include and support the aphasic person, revealing his or her communicative competence (Kagan, 1995).

(4) Enhancing the communication skills of caregivers and others in the immediate social environment. Caregivers are not necessarily the communication partners referred to by Kagan and others above. However, the principle underlying the need for spouses, partners, residential care staff, family members and friends to change their communication skills to accommodate the aphasic person remains the same: the communicative competence of the aphasic person cannot be revealed without the non-aphasic partner supporting his or her attempts to communicate.

These four examples of means of enhancing communication serve as illustrations of interventions that aim to address more or less directly the communication difficulties caused by the aphasia. There are many examples of each kind, and other categories that have not been included: the ideas here serve merely as examples of the kinds of interventions commonly used to address the aim of enhancing communication. However, the literature on aphasia therapy contains predominantly studies that either analyse the language impairment or evaluate therapies for it.

At the beginning of this chapter we suggested that the studies that have evaluated the effectiveness of therapy have often been problematic, both in their conception and their design. This has caused problems for the interpretation of the studies, problems which have not always been understood by receivers of the research. The range of goals of therapy intervention, and the range of possible approaches even to the one goal of enhancing communication, demonstrate why some of the studies of the effectiveness of therapy were poorly designed when the interventions being implemented were not described in any way.

The remainder of this chapter will provide examples of how therapies targeting the language impairment have been implemented, to provide both a sound rationale for the intervention and an account of the evaluation of the intervention. The theoretical basis of one type of language impairment therapy study will be described, based on a language processing account of the impairment, together with a rationale for its development. Some of the methodological issues in trying to establish the effects of therapy for the language impairment will be discussed, followed by three case studies that exemplify some of the principles of doing therapy within this theoretical approach, at the same time illustrating how the effectiveness of the therapies can be established.

INTERPRETING ACQUIRED LANGUAGE IMPAIRMENTS

The 1990s witnessed a major change in the methods for assessing and analysing the language impairment in aphasia, especially in the UK, where the cognitive neuropsychological approach to analysing language impairment has become predominant. Traditionally there had been a greater interest in assigning people with aphasia to syndromes, so that the focus of assessment became to determine to which syndrome the pattern of someone's language impairment indicated they belonged.

Aphasia syndromes re-evaluated

When Broca (1861) discovered cerebral dominance for language, aphasia became a focus of interest for those concerned with mapping brain function onto anatomical localisation. As a result, a range of classification systems has been devised that assign aphasic people to syndrome groups suggestive of damage in a particular area of the brain. Today, the most widely acknowledged system of classification is based on the neoclassical division (Howard & Hatfield, 1987) of people with aphasia into two groups: (1) non-fluent aphasia corresponding to damage in the anterior part of the brain; and (2) fluent aphasia with damage in the posterior part. Investigations of aphasia frequently use the classification system provided by the Boston Diagnostic Aphasic Examination (BDAE; Goodglass & Kaplan, 1972, 1983). The system identifies three non-fluent aphasias—Broca's, transcortical motor aphasia, and global aphasia—and three fluent

aphasias—Wernicke's, transcortical sensory aphasia, and conduction aphasia. Anomic aphasia is considered to be in the latter grouping but there is some debate about the locus of the lesion.

We do not intend to discuss the validity of the classification systems that are available, but rather to suggest that the application of such systems does not assist us to understand the nature of the language impairment and thereby to make decisions about the type of therapy that would be appropriate. In fairness, none of the classification systems was designed to reveal the underlying nature of the language pathology. In general, they were designed to aid "the diagnosis of the presence and type of aphasic syndrome, leading to inferences concerning cerebral localisation" (Goodglass & Kaplan, 1983, p. 1).

All the classification systems aim to cluster people with aphasia into syndrome groups based on the presenting symptomatology—an assessment of what the person with aphasia can or cannot do across all language modalities. Such clustering precludes the question why such symptoms might arise and assumes homogeneity of the underlying cause of the presenting symptoms. Is this assumption valid? Do people with aphasia with the same surface symptoms have the same underlying language impairment? Much of the research in aphasiology and in cognitive neuropsychology more generally since the 1980s has demonstrated that this can no longer be said to be true (Berndt, 1991; Howard & Orchard-Lisle, 1984; Kay & Ellis, 1987; Nickels & Best, 1996).

One of the arguments commonly used in favour of classifying types of aphasia is that it allows comparisons to be made between one person or one group of people with aphasia and another, but if such comparisons are based on groupings that are actually heterogeneous, then the validity of data based on such groupings is called into question (Byng et al., 1989). Furthermore, we begin to see why applying the same therapy to all members of a "group" might not result in successful outcome.

In the next section we describe an approach to evolving coherent theories of language processing and how these can be applied to assist the interpretation of impaired language processing.

Understanding aphasia using a cognitive neuropsychological approach

The development of this approach to aphasia has come through the application of information-processing theory developed in laboratory experiments with non-brain damaged subjects, independently from measuring neuropsychological data. The first application of this approach was made by Marshall and Newcombe (1966, 1973) in their studies of people with acquired dyslexia. They observed two distinct patterns of reading error in two people whom they were studying and realised that these patterns corresponded directly to an explanation derived from current models of word reading in normal subjects. Since then, a plethora of studies has been produced which exemplify this approach: the detailed "unpacking" of a language impairment in terms of which components of the language-processing system are affected. This kind of approach to interpreting

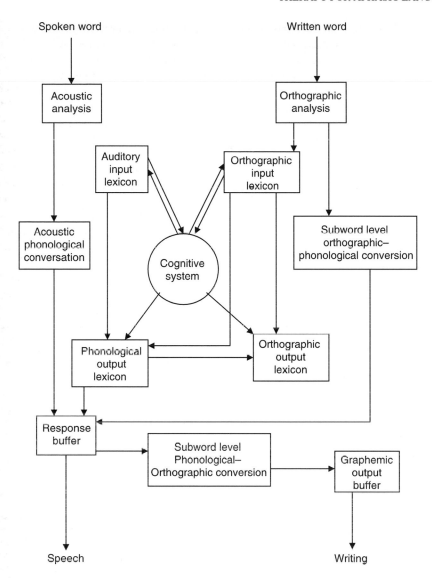

Figure 27.2. An information-processing model of the language system. The auditory input lexicon recognises spoken words and the orthographic input lexicon recognises written words. The phonological output lexicon specifies the phonological and articulatory forms of words and the orthographic output lexicon specifies the spelling. The subword level procedures (acoustic–phonological conversion, subword level orthographic–phonological conversion and subword level phonological–orthographic conversion) permit processing of novel material, non-words, and words, by sublexical processes. (Reproduced with permission from Patterson & Shewell, 1987.)

acquired cognitive impairments has become known as cognitive neuropsychology.

The aims of cognitive neuropsychology are threefold. First, the ability of existing models of cognitive processes to explain cognitive impairments can be established, thereby providing a means of evaluating the robustness of the model. Second, the models can provide theoretically motivated explanations of what has gone wrong in an impaired cognitive processing system, and third, these explanations can be used to devise rational therapeutic procedures, based on a theoretical analysis of the nature of the impairment to be treated.

One of the tenets of this discipline is that cognitive skills are modular, which means that, in relation to language, the language-processing system is made up of a number of relatively independent subsystems, each of which is responsible for a particular linguistic processing task, such as identifying letters, producing spoken or written words or accessing semantic representations. A typical language-processing model is that of Patterson and Shewell (1987), illustrated in Fig. 27.2. It is assumed that each of these subsystems can be independently impaired, giving rise to specific language-processing problems of the kind seen in aphasia. Much work in cognitive neuropsychology has been aimed at examining these component subsystems and their interactions.

In these types of models, the boxes have two functions: first, they are stores of information, such as how a word is pronounced or what it means; second, they contain methods of finding that information within the store. The arrows represent communication between the boxes. As a consequence of brain damage, transmission, access and storage can each be impaired.

Another feature of these models is that they are based upon basic psycholinguistic distinctions, for example between the processing of familiar and novel words, of frequent and infrequent words, of regular and irregular words or of concrete and abstract words. Experiments in psychology have shown the effect that these distinctions have on language processing in people without language impairment, and there is evidence that these variables also affect the performance of aphasic people.

Instead of classifying a person's language impairment within a syndrome, the impairments and retained abilities observed are related to and accounted for only within a particular language-processing model. The purpose of assessment is then to establish which processes are problematic and which remain unimpaired. It is now clear why people presenting with similar symptoms, or classified as having the same syndrome, rarely constitute a homogeneous group and therefore are unlikely to respond to the same therapy: the same surface symptom, e.g. difficulty in naming, could have a variety of different underlying causes, from impairment to the cognitive system, to a problem in the phonological output buffer, the response buffer, or to any of the connections between them. These different types of impairment might all require a different type of therapy procedure.

In the next section we exemplify this approach by describing a number of therapy studies demonstrating how the impairment was diagnosed, what therapy was implemented and why, and how it was evaluated.

THREE THERAPY STUDIES ADDRESSING THE LANGUAGE IMPAIRMENT

Therapy for a semantic and phonological impairment

PC (Jones, 1989) was 51 years old when, in April 1988, he suffered a severe infarction of the right middle cerebral artery, leaving him with a temporary, mild left hemiparesis and a severe fluent aphasia. He was predominantly right handed but had shown some degree of ambidexterity.

Initially, PC presented with the kind of symptoms usually associated with a Wernicke-type aphasia, characterised by poor auditory comprehension, empty or neologistic spoken output, poor repetition skills and inability to use written output. Observation of his language behaviour led to the formation of a number of hypotheses about the various factors contributing to his problems. These hypotheses were tested using a number of assessments based on a language-processing approach. The results suggested that PC had a specific difficulty in accessing an intact semantic system via the auditory processing route (see Fig. 27.2). This auditory input problem was shown to arise because of difficulty in acoustic analysis of the incoming signal, evidenced by his severe difficulty in judging whether two spoken words were the same or different. However, unlike the case of a word-deaf person, under specific circumstances PC was able to use cues from the orthography and from the linguistic context to provide some top-down processing to assist his processing of auditorily presented material. He also had severe naming problems, being unable to name any pictures either orally or in writing, and was unable to make use of any cues to assist his naming. A hypothesis was made that his difficulties in production of spoken and written language arose for two reasons: first, because the semantic representations used to address representations in the phonological output system were insufficiently specified; and second, because of an additional problem in accessing the phonological output system.

A decision was made to focus therapy initially on his impairments in spoken language; although his auditory input impairment was severe, his greatest frustration lay in his inability to speak. The second stage of therapy would then deal with his auditory input impairments. The first therapy programme devised commenced 10 weeks post-onset and was based on the rationale that failure to access adequate semantic information for phonological selection underpinned PC's output problems. The programme was designed to use in-depth semantic judgement tasks to enhance access to semantic representation. Although the aim of the programme was to increase output, it should be noted that the therapy tasks themselves involved little spoken output. A hypothesis was also made that if the semantic system itself was being enhanced then there should be improvement in untreated items and therefore in spontaneous spoken and written naming, even though the therapy does not involve any writing. However, because all the therapy materials would involve the visual modality only, there should not be any improvement in auditory input processing.

When the programme of therapy began, PC was a few weeks post-injury and likely to be still recovering spontaneously. To determine whether any improvements could be attributed to the therapy, a crossover-treatment design was used. That is, baselines were taken before the first therapy programme commenced both on picture naming ability, using simple, single-syllable words, which should improve after the therapy, and also on auditory input tasks, which should not improve. After the first therapy, a retest was carried out involving all the tasks tested pre-therapy. Then the second therapy programme for auditory input began and, at the end of that therapy programme, all tasks were again retested. In this way PC acted as his own control. As a further test of the effects of the therapy, half of the stimuli used in the baseline testing for picture naming were used in the therapy programme and half remained untreated. In this way, effects on treated versus untreated items could be investigated.

The results of the first 20 weeks, shown in Fig. 27.3, illustrate the improvements PC made after 10 weeks of thrice weekly, hour-long therapy sessions. Remember that the therapy did not specifically require him to name pictures, but rather to process semantic information more accurately. PC could now name not only some of the stimuli used in the therapy but also untreated pictures, and the quality of his error responses changed from no response to target names containing one literal paraphasia, e.g. "dut" for "duck". In effect, most of his naming attempts are now readily interpretable, and therefore much more communicative. In fact, with a less stringent criterion for "correctness" his naming of the items presented could be considered to have improved to 100%. Improvement in written naming is also

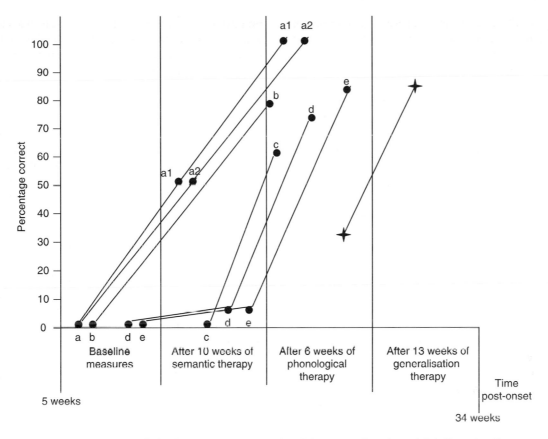

Figure 27.3. PC: results of a cross-over treatment design for treatment of a semantic deficit and an auditory input deficit. Key to baseline measures (taken twice): Semantic therapy related to semantic deficit: a, oral picture naming (a1, untreated items; a2, untreated items); b, written picture naming (untreated items). Phonological therapy related to auditory input deficit: c, non-word oral reading; d, repetition; e, same–different matching, X–X, multisyllabic naming test; o, complex repetition test.

evident. All these areas should have shown change, according to the hypotheses made prior to the commencement of therapy. No improvement in auditory input tasks, which were unrelated to the therapy, was found. PC's wife also reported at this time that his spontaneous speech was less "empty".

At this stage, the focus of therapy changed to address the problem PC was having in acoustic analysis, which at this point remained as severe as it had been when originally assessed. This new programme was intended to enhance phonological segmentation of incoming stimuli. A hypothesis was made that if phonological segmentation skills improved, this should improve not only acoustic analysis tasks but also repetition skills, and as the task also incorporated some grapheme–phoneme conversion, oral reading of unfamiliar words or non-words, which have to be read aloud via some kind of grapheme–phoneme conversion, should also improve.

A 6-week, thrice weekly programme of phonological therapy was then instituted, and at the end of this period acoustic analysis skills were reassessed, as was oral reading of unfamiliar words and non-words, and repetition. Figure 27.3 also represents the results of the second phase of treatment. PC improved in his ability to carry out acoustic analysis and repetition from 6% correct in both tasks to 86% in acoustic analysis and 74% in repetition. Oral reading of non-words improved from 0% to 62.5%

correct. Picture naming performance on the test used previously reached 100% correct. At this stage PC was also assessed using a more complex oral naming task, which included stimuli of more than one syllable, a task that he had been unable to do previously. Performance on this task is also shown in Fig. 27.3, but the score of 33% correct does not reveal that the majority of errors related to items of more than two syllables, i.e. the more phonological information to be accessed, the further "off target" he became.

After these two programmes, therapy became more eclectic, to increase generalisation of these improved skills to a variety of communication settings, and PC continued to show improvement in all language parameters. On the multisyllabic naming test PC achieved a score of 84% correct and in a further, more complex, repetition test he achieved 73% correct. These results show an increasing improvement in both naming and in acoustic analysis, and this improvement generalised into spontaneous output. Therapy also included a considerable amount of counselling for PC and his family in coping with the effects of the aphasia. Fifteen months after the onset of his cardiovascular accident, PC was able to recommence his business interests.

This case exemplifies the use of two very specific therapy programmes for two different aspects of aphasia. The design of the therapy study facilitated monitoring the specific effects of the therapy and ruled out spontaneous recovery as a contributing factor in the improvement measured.

Therapy for a sentence-processing deficit

BB (Jones, 1986) was 41 years old when he suffered a left cerebral embolus resulting in a right hemiplegia and a severe Broca-type aphasia. CT scans showed extensive damage to the territory of the left middle cerebral artery implicating the frontal, temporal and parietal lobes and extending vertically to a depth of 6mm. His language abilities were characteristic of agrammatic Broca's aphasia.

Over the next 3 years BB received intensive speech therapy and, for a further 3 years, daily volunteer input. The study to be reported here was carried out 6 years after the cerebrovascular accident, when he first became known to one of us (EJ). At that time, auditory comprehensive abilities were "functional" but he was still reliant upon the presence of pragmatic and contextual cues. Reading comprehension had also improved for simpler material. Spoken language had remained virtually unchanged over the 3 years since formal speech therapy had ended and was limited to the use of single nouns in the presence of a severe word-finding deficit. Spontaneous writing was at the single word level. The burden of communication lay largely with the listener.

Observations of his performance led to the hypothesis that BB's inability to produce anything beyond the single word level stemmed from a specific deficit in processing verbs, which disrupted the mapping of the meaning relations onto the syntactic representations (Jackendoff, 1972; Jones, 1984; Marshall, 1995; Schwartz et al., 1985). From the study of normal errors in language production, Garrett (1982) proposed a model that comprises two levels in sentence production—the functional level and the positional level. Simplistically, the functional level allows for planning "who-does-what-to-whom" in the projected sentence. An inability to access verb information, the hypothesised deficit for BB, would result in an inability to formulate such planning frames and thereby severely reduce sentence production. It was hypothesised that the previous therapy had focused not on this level of sentence production but on a later level, that of positional planning of elements within sentence. This type of therapy could be considered to be typical of the "traditional" approach to agrammatic aphasia, possibly appropriate for some people but not for those like BB, where the deficit lay at an earlier stage of sentence production.

A number of tasks were given to BB, the results of which confirmed the hypothesis that BB's deficit lay in mapping the meaning, or thematic, roles encoded by the verb onto the syntactic structure. These tasks included measurement of his ability to produce structured sentences in both constrained and less constrained production tasks, and a number of sentence comprehension tasks.

A therapy programme was devised which aimed to improve BB's deficit in mapping thematic roles onto syntactic structure. A full description of this can be found in Jones (1986). A hypothesis was made that this programme should not only bring about improvements in specific tests, but should also generalise to improved spontaneous production. The programme used only input tasks rather than working on production, as it was considered that the mapping of meaning relations is a skill common to both comprehension and production of language (Schwartz et al., 1985): thus, by improving input skills output skills should improve correspondingly. The therapy took the form of asking BB to make judgements about the relationship of various parts of the sentence to the verb, and entailed using questions with words such as "who", "what", "where", in order to underline and mark the relationship.

Table 27.2 shows the progression of BB's sentence production abilities during the course of the therapy, from his output at the start of therapy to his output 9 months later. His sentence comprehension skills improved from chance performance to a performance from 75% to 90% correct, depending on the task requirements. At the time of the last samples illustrated here, the improvements were evident in his spontaneous speech outside the clinic, and, in addition, he was initiating conversation and implementing sentence structure frequently. The sentence comprehension and construction tasks on which BB had performed at chance prior to therapy now showed improvement to well above chance performance. Although in this case no specific control

Table 27.2. BB: speech samples obtained during the course of therapy

Pretherapy—6 years post-onset
Description of the "cookie theft" picture from the BDAE:
Girl, boy . . . eh . . . don't know . . . um . . . water . . . don't know (Therapist, "Can you tell me anything about this?"—points to mother) . . . um . . . man . . . no . . . woman . . . window . . . oh . . . eh . . . /k/ . . . /k/ . . . tea . . . eh . . . don't know.

Description of premorbid occupation:
eh . . . eh . . . oh . . . no . . . um . . . eh . . . don't know . . . no . . . eh . . . potatoes . . . um . . . no.

3 months into therapy
Description of the "cookie theft" picture from the BDAE:
Girl and boy and woman . . . and . . . /kikiz/ . . . kikiz/ (target = cookies) . . . and near the . . . eh . . . no . . . near the . . . don't know . . . no . . . and . . . eh . . . woman . . . drying the washing up. Filled the water . . . /s/ . . . falling to the floor. The window is open and flowers and trees and . . . footpath . . . the . . . no . . . oh . . . no . . . yes all right. Girl wants one.

Description of premorbid occupation:
eh . . . eh . . . sold . . . potatoes . . . um . . . drive . . . van . . . to . . . Cambridge . . . restaurant . . . chips . . . no . . . um . . . don't know . . . sorry . . . pack the van . . . and . . . no . . . um . . . don't know.

9 months into therapy
Description of the "cookie theft" picture from the BDAE:
The woman is washing up . . . and water is flowing all over the bowl . . . on concrete floor and the boy is reaching for cookies and the stool falling down. And the girl is reaching for the cookies. The window is open and through the window . . . see trees and the grass . . . and trees and the pebbles. And the two cups on top of the . . . table and the . . . one bowl is . . . there.

Description of premorbid occupation:
I have a van and drove to the . . . Cambridge and chips in the restaurant . . . shop . . . sold . . . chips. I was a vegetable salesman. (BB then volunteered the following information about his cardiovascular accident) I was in bed in October 1978. Well . . . I don't know! . . . Woke up and I was lifeless. I was in bed at home. Drove to Cambridge . . . sold chips . . . then we went through to the hospital. (Therapist: "What happened there?") Don't know . . . upstairs . . . lie down on the bed . . . arm, leg and couldn't talk!

measures were taken to establish experimentally that spontaneous recovery or non-specific factors were not contributing to the improvement, given the length of time post-onset of aphasia that this therapy was instituted, and the intensive amount of speech therapy previously provided, we consider that these results are convincing of themselves.

This study exemplifies the hazards of basing therapy solely on the outcome of assessments that describe only surface symptomatology. It demonstrates that, to provide effective language therapy, we need to understand the underlying nature of the impairment. Therapy techniques that merely note the omission of structures or types of lexical items, and then attempt to "re-teach" them, are attempting to build without providing foundations.

Replication of therapy for a sentence-processing impairment

A therapy programme for an aphasic person, JG, with a similar impairment to that of BB, was described (Byng, 1988), with a proviso that one of the most important aspects of carrying out single case studies of therapy is that the therapy should be replicated with another, similarly impaired, person. Nickels et al. (1991) describe just such an attempt to replicate the therapy that had been successful with JG with another person, AER.

Both JG and AER could be described as agrammatic Broca's aphasics with very limited spontaneous speech, more severe in AER's case than in JG's. AER could barely utter a single word in spontaneous conversation and relied on answering yes or no in response to questions in order to "converse". At the time that therapy was instituted JG was 60 years old and had been aphasic for 5 years and AER was 68 years old and had been aphasic for 3 years. They had both had cerebrovascular accidents involving the left hemisphere. JG had been a groundsman and AER a recently retired building surveyor prior to the cerebrovascular accident. Both aphasic people had had a considerable amount of speech therapy prior to these studies, and both had just been discharged at the time this therapy had begun.

In doing the replication, the same pretherapy assessment was carried out with AER as had been used with JG, using test procedures based on an information processing rationale. It was ascertained that both aphasic people had similar types and degrees of underlying impairment in the process that maps sentence form and sentence meaning—the same hypothesis underlying the therapy for BB.

The therapy procedure that had been followed with JG was implemented with AER. A full description of this can be found in Nickels et al. (1991) and Byng (1992). The therapy aimed to make explicit the relationship between the thematic roles, which are part of the lexical representation of the verb, and their relative position in syntactic structure, using agentive verbs in simple active sentences, just as in the case of BB above. However, the means of doing this was different from that used with BB; in this case the therapy programme consisted of a two-stage process. The first stage involved a sentence-ordering task

Table 27.3a. JG and AER: an analysis of the structural quality of spoken language pre and post therapy: proportion of each utterance type produced

	JG Pre	JG Post	AER Pre	AER Post	Non-aphasic control
Single words/phrases e.g. bad Cinderella and sisters	0.54	0.15*	0.53	0.12*	0
Noun phrase plus be e.g. Cinderella is	0	0	0.32	0.09*	0
Verbs with one argument e.g. Cinderella is mopping	0.25	0.27	0.03	0.06	0.14
Verbs with two arguments e.g. shoes are perfect the man is riding a horse and carriage	0.19	0.58*	0.09	0.59*	0.51
Two phrases without a verb e.g. Cinderella and two sisters ball	0.04	0.12	0.01	0.09	0
Embedded sentences	0.02	0	0	0	0.33

*significance at $p < 0.001$

Table 27.3b. JG and AER: performance on aspects of language production remaining untreated

	JG Pre	JG Post	AER Pre	AER Post	Control subject
Production of grammatical words	0.40	0.37	0.35	0.36	0.6
Use of obligatory determiners	0.30	0.50	0.50	0.57	1.00
Ratio of nouns:pronouns	4.40	4.80	16.0	18.0	2.00

in relation to pairs of pictures that contrasted the agent, the verb or the theme of the sentence. This technique of contrasting pairs of pictures was used to draw their attention to the relationship between the thematic role of a phrase in the sentence and the position of that phrase within the sentence. Colour cues were used to assist in ordering the elements of the sentence. The second stage involved production of sentences in response to pictures, including photographs of the person and his family and pictures from the newspaper. These were used to assist JG and AER in relating the techniques being learnt to their own daily lives. In this stage of the therapy they were learning how to modify their own production to assist them in structuring utterances rather than producing single words.

Table 27.3a presents the results of the therapy for both JG and AER. Using a method of analysing sentence structure (Byng & Black, 1989) in production, we can see that the structural quality of each person's sentence production has changed significantly. Both people also showed evidence of transfer of this ability to situations outside therapy. For example, AER, in spontaneous conversation, produced utterances such as "Susan come here and take us Brenda's", "but two months you go", "you making me shake up". The control subject, matched for age and educational background to JG and AER, is included to give a context for the structural quality of their sentence production. Table 27.3b illustrates that the gains they have made in language production are specific to improved structural quality. Neither person has made gains in aspects of production such as use of obligatory determiners or production of grammatical words (Saffran et al.,

1989), which are hypothesised to be determined by a later stage in the production process than the therapy focused upon. Both people made statistically significant improvements in comprehending sentences corresponding to the type of sentences used in therapy.

THE NATURE OF EVIDENCE: EVALUATING THE EFFECTIVENESS OF THERAPY FOR APHASIA

The effectiveness or otherwise of therapy for aphasia has been a topic of much debate over the last several decades, much of that debate being fuelled by an adherence to "belief systems" (Holland & Wertz, 1988). We have demonstrated in the first part of this chapter that there is no such as thing as some kind of unitary "therapy for aphasia". People learning to live with aphasia have a wide variety of concerns, only some of which relate to enhancing their impaired language and communication. When we are evaluating the effectiveness of intervention we have to specify what that intervention was targeting and measure it appropriately:

Outcome measures must relate directly to the expected changes as a consequence of an intervention. Thus, outcome of contact has to be related to stated goals, which have generally not been formulated with the precision necessary to permit evaluation. Often outcome measures have related to only one aspect of care, leading to false impressions of treatment and lack of credibility in the eyes of clinicians (Enderby, 1992, p. 61).

For example, if the ultimate aim of intervention was to reduce social isolation, through increasing the communication skills of communication partners (amongst other things), then evaluating changes to the partners' communication skills will be critical, as well as using relevant measures of changes in social isolation.

In the second part of this chapter we have demonstrated how theoretically motivated intervention for specific language impairments can bring about change in language processing abilities, even at some considerable time post-onset of stroke. The approach to language therapy we have illustrated is a way forward in the development of theoretically motivated therapy for the language impairment in aphasia. We have demonstrated that, with a clear analysis of the nature of the language impairment, therapy can be targeted more specifically at the core problems that are affecting a person's language-processing abilities. However, a precursor to carrying out therapy in this fashion is the necessity of good theoretical models from which to work to develop more accurate diagnoses and hypotheses about the language impairment. In practice, clinicians are sometimes hampered by the lack of specificity of the models that are most readily applicable to neuropsychological data. New models are under constant development and investigation by researchers in a range of disciplines related to the cognitive sciences, but their application to and explanation of routine clinical data is not always readily accessible.

An important benefit of using models as a means of interpreting the language impairment is that predictions can be made about those aspects of language processing that should be affected by the therapy and those aspects which should not. For example, we showed that, in the case of PC, the hypothesis held good that therapy for his impaired semantic system should affect both spoken and written naming, because both are addressed by the same semantic system. In addition it was predicted that his auditory-processing impairments would not be affected by the therapy, as it should not have had effects earlier in the system. Again, this prediction was correct. In this way, clear, specific effects of therapy can be monitored, by providing a theoretically motivated way of determining language functions that can be used as controls for the aspects of the language impairment undergoing therapy. It also provides an additional test of the validity of the cognitive model: if, after therapy, functions of the language system, unrelated to the function being treated, are shown to improve—even though therapy was not directed at those functions—evidence is provided which merits a reconsideration of the architecture of the model. In this way therapy studies can be used to address theoretical issues.

It is important to understand that these models do not provide a theory of therapy: they do not specify which therapies should be used, nor how they should be applied; rather, they make clearer the nature of the impairment that requires therapy. The type of therapies provided within this framework are not necessarily different from those in the repertoire of most speech and language therapists. What is different in the therapy that we have described is the way that it involves making explicit to the person the nature of the language impairment and providing a conscious procedure to apply to overcome the impairment. However, we still understand little about the nature of the interactions in therapy between the therapist, the person, and the task, which bring about change in language-processing ability (Byng & Black, 1996). One of the main challenges for aphasia therapists in providing language therapy is to understand and document exactly what kind of changes in language processing the therapy is intended to bring about, and, importantly, how that change is being achieved.

These kinds of cognitive neuropsychological single case studies have been important for developing clinical practice in speech and language therapy in aphasia in the UK. Aphasia therapists have found the methods employed in these studies sufficiently compelling that cognitive neuropsychological methods are now widely used, widely taught in education of speech and language therapists, and have probably become the mainstream method of analysis of language impairment used in speech and language therapy in the UK. Wade (1992), in advice on purchasing stroke care, described the evidence-base for many medical and surgical interventions in stroke as being based not on hard evidence but on "good reason to believe" (on the part of doctors and surgeons) that the interventions are effective. It seems that, for aphasia therapists, the "hard" evidence of single case research studies, and their own experience has given them "good reason to believe" also that this is a principled basis on which to provide effective therapy for the language impairment.

However, the evidence from single case studies is not widely accepted within the evidence-based health-care movement.

Unfortunately for aphasiology (and for recipients of aphasia services), the prevailing ideology about evidence does not permit the use of single case methods, and so the results of such studies are not taken seriously. The problem for aphasiology is that the randomised controlled trial has become the gold standard for providing evidence of effectiveness. It is not, however, a methodology that suits this population of people easily because of: (1) the heterogeneity amongst people even with the same surface symptomatology; (2) the lack of specificity in the interventions provided in the studies published to date; and (3) the breadth of interventions that need to be provided to provide "therapy for aphasia", as we have demonstrated.

Randomised controlled trials that sought to investigate the effectiveness of specific types of therapy interventions might, in theory, be possible to carry out, provided that the following criteria are met (Howard, 1986), in addition to the criteria suggested by Black (1996):

- The people with aphasia should be assigned at random to two groups.
- The therapy must be continued for a reasonable period of time.
- The therapy itself must be explicitly described, not only so that it can be replicated, but also so that the therapy procedure can be carefully evaluated itself.
- The group needs to be large enough to find therapy effects when these might not be measured in all people (Howard & Hatfield, 1987).
- The assessment used must be sensitive enough and appropriate to measure the kind of change that can be observed after the therapy.

To date, no studies have been carried out which meet these criteria even remotely. One way to do this would be to organise a multicentre study, but this could pose problems in standardising the administration of the therapy. As methods of specifying the nature of interventions for language therapies become more developed (e.g. Horton & Byng, 2000) ultimately large-scale systematic trials of therapy might be more feasible. At our current state of knowledge, large group studies have proved premature, uninformative, and misleading. Increasingly, replications of single case studies are being published, providing somewhat more substantial evidence (e.g. Byng, 1988; Byng, Nickels, & Black, 1994; de Partz, 1986; Greenwood, 1999;

Le Dorze et al., 1995; Marshall, 1995, 1999; Nickels et al., 1992; Schwartz et al., 1994; Swinburn, 1999).

The argument made by aphasiologists (Howard, 1986; Pring, 1986) is that single case methods do suit the development of practice in aphasia therapy particularly well, and should be considered as a legitimate contributor to the battery of methods contributing to evidence-based health care. The methods used in the published single case studies have usually been very rigorously and experimentally applied, meeting the demands of Black (1996, p. 1215) "Researchers should be united in their quest for scientific rigour in evaluation, regardless of the method used." Black continues:

The widely held view that experimental methods (randomised-controlled trials) are the 'gold standard' for evaluation has led to the denigration of non-experimental methods, to the extent that research funding bodies and journal editors automatically reject them. I suggest that such attitudes limit our potential to evaluate health care and hence to improve the scientific basis of how to treat individuals and organise services. (Black, 1996, P. 1215)

It has to be acknowledged that single case studies do not, by themselves, provide convincing evidence of speech and language therapy services to aphasic people, but they do inform our knowledge of "how to treat individuals" and provide a basis for further evaluation. Service development initiatives need different forms of evaluation again. Speech and language therapists, like many other health-care professionals, are striving to match methodologies for evaluation to types of intervention to ensure that the demands set out by Enderby (cited earlier) are met convincingly. These will include quantitative, qualitative, ethnographic, observational, experimental, single case study and randomised controlled trial methodologies, amongst others (e.g. Long, 1992; Pope & Mays, 1995). As Wertz (1995, p. 331) suggests: "It is essential that one utilise a design that is appropriate for his or her research question. More importantly we should avoid insisting on only one design to the exclusion of the other. Controversy does not demean us. Scientific McCarthyism does."

Naylor (1995) draws attention to the limitations of relying on one type of methodology for evaluating health care: "a huge amount of the output [of the Cochrane Collaboration] will be inconclusive and will augment the grey zones of practice until a new generation of research is completed". The new generation of research does now seem to be upon us, with research funding bodies taking a much broader view about appropriate methodologies. Nowhere is this more welcome than in evaluating the impact of therapy with people with aphasia.

REFERENCES

Aten J, Caligiuri, M & Holland A (1982) The efficacy of functional communication therapy for chronic aphasic patients. *Journal of Speech and Hearing Disorders, 47*, 93–96.

Berndt RS (1991) Sentence processing in aphasia. In MT Sarno (Ed.), *Acquired Aphasia*, 2nd edn. London: Academic Press, pp. 223–270.

Black N (1996) Why we need observational studies to evaluate the effectiveness of health care. *British Medical Journal, 3*(12), 1215–1218.

Broca P (1861) Perte de la parole. *Bulletin de la Societe d'Anthropologie de Paris, 2*, 219–237.

Byng S (1988) Sentence processing deficits: theory and therapy. *Cognitive Neuropsychology, 5*, 629–676.

Byng S (1992) Testing the tried: Replicating therapy for sentence processing deficits in agrammatism. *Clinics in Communication Disorders: Approaches to the Treatment of Aphasia, 1*(4), 34–42.

Byng S (1993) Hypothesis testing and aphasia therapy. In A Holland & M Forbes (Eds.), *World Perspectives on Aphasia*. California: Singular Publishing Group Inc.

Byng S (1998) *Perceptions of aphasia therapy: Creating sustainable therapy services in partnership with aphasic people.* Clinical Aphasiology Conference, Asheville, North Carolina.

Byng S & Black M (1989) Some aspects of sentence production in aphasia. *Aphasiology, 3*(3), 241–263.

Byng S, Kay J, Edmundson A, & Scott C (1989) Aphasia tests reconsidered. *Aphasiology, 4*(1), 67–91.

Byng S, Nickels L, & Black M (1994) Replicating therapy for mapping deficits in agrammatism: remapping the deficit? *Aphasiology, 8*(4), 315–341.

Byng S & Black M (1996) What makes a therapy? Some parameters of therapeutic intervention in aphasia. *European Journal of Disorders of Communication, 30,* 303–316.

Byng S, Pound C, & Parr S (2000) Living with aphasia: A framework for therapy interventions. In I Papathanasiou (Ed.), *Acquired Neurological Communication Disorders: A Clinical Perspective.* London: Whurr Publishers.

Davis GA & Wilcox MJ (1985) *Adult Aphasia Rehabilitation: Applied Pragmatics.* Windsor: NFER-Nelson.

De Partz MP (1986) Re-education of a deep dyslexic patient: Rationale of the method and results. *Cognitive Neuropsychology, 3,* 149–177.

Department of Health (1993) *Research for Health.* London: Department of Health.

Elman R & Bernstein-Ellis E (1995) What is functional? *American Journal of Speech Language Pathology, 4,* 115–117.

Enderby P (1992) Outcome measures in speech therapy: Impairment, disability, handicap and distress. *Health Trends, 24*(2), 62–64.

Garrett M (1982) Production of speech: Observations from normal and pathological language use. In AW Ellis (Ed.), *Normality and Pathology in Cognitive Functions.* London: Academic Press.

Goodglass H & Kaplan E (1972) *Assessment of aphasia and related disorders.* Philadelphia: Lea & Febiger.

Goodglass H & Kaplan E (1983) *Assessment of aphasia and related disorders,* 2nd edn. Philadelphia: Lea & Febiger.

Greenhalgh T (1999) Narratives in medicine. British Medical Journal, 318, 323–325.

Greenwood A (1999) Early stages in treating a person with non-fluent aphasia. In S Byng, K Swinburn, & C Pound (Eds.), *The Aphasia Therapy File.* Hove, UK: Psychology Press.

Holland A (1991) Pragmatic aspects of intervention in aphasia. *Journal of Neurolinguistics, 6,* 197–211.

Holland AL & Wertz RT (1988) Measuring aphasia treatment effects: Large-group, small-group and single-subject studies. In F Plum (Ed.), *Language, Communication and the Brain.* New York: Raven Press.

Horton S & Byng S (2000) Examining interaction in language therapy. *International Journal of Language and Communication Disorders, 35,* 355–375.

Howard D (1986) Beyond randomised controlled trials; the case for effective case studies of the effects of treatment in aphasia. *British Journal of Disorders of Communication, 21,* 89–102.

Howard D & Hatfield FM (1987) *Aphasia Therapy: Historical and Contemporary Issues.* London: Lawrence Erlbaum Associates Ltd.

Howard D & Orchard-Lisle V (1984) On the origins of semantic errors in naming: Evidence from the case of a global aphasic. *Cognitive Neuropsychology, 2,* 163–190.

International Stroke Trial Collaborative Group (1997) The international stroke trial: A randomised trial of aspirin, subcutaneous heparin, both or neither among 19,436 patients with acute, presumed ischemic stroke. *Lancet, 349*: 1569–1581.

Jackendoff R (1972) *Semantic Interpretation in Generative Grammar.* Cambridge, MA: MIT Press.

Jones EV (1984) Word order processing in aphasia: Effect of verb semantics. In FC Rose (Ed.), *Recent Advances in Neurology, 42: Progress in aphasiology.* New York: Raven Press.

Jones EV (1986) Building the foundations for sentence production in a non-fluent aphasic. *British Journal of Disorders of Communication, 21,* 63–82.

Jones EV (1989) A year in the life of PC and EVJ. *Proceedings of Advances in Aphasia Therapy in the Clinical Setting.* London: British Aphasiology Society.

Kagan A (1995) Revealing the competence of aphasic adults through conversation: A challenge to health professionals. *Topics in Stroke Rehabilitation, 2*(1), 15–28.

Kaga A (1998) Supported conversation for adults with aphasia: Methods and resources for training conversation partners. *Aphasiology, 12,* 816–830.

Kagan A & Gailey G (1993) Functional is not enough: Training conversation partners for aphasic adults. In A Holland and M Forbes (Eds.), *Aphasia Treatment: World Perspectives.* San Diego, CA: Singular Press.

Kay J & Ellis AW (1987) A cognitive neuropsychological case study of anomia: Implications for psychological models of word retrieval. *Brain, 110,* 613–629.

Le Dorze G & Brassard C (1995) A description of the consequences of aphasia on aphasic persons and their relatives and friends, based on the WHO model of chronic diseases. *Aphasiology, 9*(3), 239–255.

Lesser R & Algar L (1995) Towards combining the cognitive neuropsychological and the pragmatic in aphasia therapy. *Neuropsychological Rehabilitation, 5*(1/2), 67–92.

Lincoln NB, McGuirk E, Mulley GP et al. (1984) Effectiveness of speech therapy for aphasic stroke patients: A randomised controlled trial. *Lancet i,* 1197–1200.

Long A (1992) Assessing health and social outcomes. In J Popay & G Williams (Eds.), *Researching the People's Health.* London: Routledge.

Lyon J, Cariski D, Keisler L, Rosenbek J, Levine R, Kumpula J, Ryff C, Coyne S & Levine J (1997) Communication partners: Enhancing participation in life and communication for adults with aphasia in natural settings. *Aphasiology, 11,* 693–708.

Marshall J (1995) The mapping hypothesis and aphasia therapy. *Aphasiology, 9*(6), 517–539.

Marshall J (1999) Doing something about a verb impairment: Two therapy approaches. In S Byng, K Swinburn, & C Pound (Eds.), *The Aphasia Therapy File.* Hove, UK: Psychology Press.

Marshall JC & Newcombe F (1966) Syntactic and semantic errors in paralexia. *Neuropsychologia, 4,* 169–176.

Marshall JC & Newcombe F (1973) Patterns of paralexia. *Journal of Psycholinguistic Research, 2,* 175–199.

Naylor D (1995) Evidence based medicine in its place (Editorial). *Lancet, 346,* 785.

Nickels L & Best W (1996) Therapy for naming disorders (part 1): Principles, puzzles and progress. *Aphasiology, 10,* 21–47.

Nickels L, Byng S, & Black M (1991) Sentence processing deficits: A replication of therapy. *British Journal of Disorders of Communication, 26,* 175–199.

Parr S, Byng S, & Gilpin S (1997) *Talking about Aphasia: Living with Loss of Language after Stroke.* Buckingham: Open University Press.

Patterson KE, Shewell C (1987) Speak and spell: Dissociations and word class effects. In M Coltheart, G Sartori, & R Job (Eds.), *The Cognitive Neuropsychology of Language.* London: Lawrence Erlbaum Associates Ltd.

Pope C & Mays N (1995) Reaching the parts other methods cannot reach: An introduction to qualitative methods in health and health services research. *British Medical Journal, 311,* 42–45.

Pring T (1986) Evaluating the effects of speech therapy for aphasics and volunteers: Developing the single case methodology. *British Journal of Disorders of Communication, 21,* 103–115.

Saffran E, Berndt R, & Schwartz M (1989) The quantitative analysis of agrammatic production: Procedure and data. *Brain and Language, 37,* 440–479.

Schwartz MF, Linebarger M, & Saffran EM (1985) The status of the syntactic theory of agrammatism. In ML Kean (Ed.), *Agrammatism.* New York: Academic Press.

Schwartz MF, Saffran EM, Fink R, Myers JL & Martin N (1994) Mapping therapy: A treatment programme for aphasia. *Aphasiology, 8*(1), 19–54.

Simmons N (1993) *An Ethnographic Investigation of Compensatory Strategies in Aphasia.* Dissertation, Louisiana State University and Agricultural and Mechanical College.

Swales J (1998) *Consumer involvement in health research: The researchers perspective.* Keynote lecture at NHS Executive Conference, "Research: What's in it for me?"

Swinburn K (1999) An informal example of a successful therapy for a sentence processing deficit. In S Byng, K Swinburn, & C Pound (Eds.), *The Aphasia Therapy File.* Hove, UK: Psychology Press.

Wade D (1992) *Epidemiologically Based Needs Assessment.* Leeds: NHS Management Executive.

Wertz RT (1995) Efficacy. In C Code & D Muller (1995) *Treatment of Aphasia: From Theory to Practice.* London: Whurr Publishers Ltd.

28. Rehabilitation of memory disorders

Barbara A. Wilson   Linda Clare

INTRODUCTION

Although all of us experience memory failures at some time or another, these slips of memory do not cause severe disruption to our daily lives. Most of us can still function adequately at work, engage in conversation, and remember the gist of the programme we saw on television last night while accepting as normal the forgetting of certain details. After all, nobody remembers *everything*. For some people, however, their memory failure is of such a proportion that the effects can be devastating.

Imagine waking up and not being able to remember what you did yesterday. Imagine living in a time vacuum where there is no past to anchor the present and no future to anticipate. Such is the fate of many people suffering from organic amnesia. Although amnesia means literally "an absence of memory", in practice, people with organic amnesia do not have a total loss of memory. They remember who they are, they remember how to talk and how to read, and they usually remember how to do things they learned before the onset of their memory loss, such as how to swim, ride a bike, or play the piano. Unfortunately, they have great difficulty in learning new skills or information, experience problems when trying to remember ongoing events, and usually have a memory gap for the few days, weeks, months, or even years before becoming ill.

People with organic memory problems whose other cognitive skills remain unimpaired are considered to have a pure amnesic syndrome. These cases are less common in comparison with those where memory is only one of several cognitive impairments, such as word-finding difficulties, attention problems, and slowed thinking or processing of information. People suffering from these more generalised cognitive impairments are likely to be described as suffering from memory impairment rather than amnesia.

Memory problems are common following brain injury. They are among the most handicapping of cognitive deficits, often preventing return to work or independent living. Although severe memory impairment is usually extremely distressing for family members and carers, these feelings of distress are not always shared by the actual person with the impairment. Usually, lack of concern on the patient's part is associated with the poor insight that can follow from the original injury (Prigatano, 1995). Not surprisingly, those with greater awareness of their difficulties are typically distressed and/or depressed; for example, Kopelman and Crawford (1996) found evidence of depression in over 40% of 200 consecutive referrals to a memory clinic.

Memory-impaired people can feel that other people regard them as stupid or mentally unstable, or they can worry that they are going crazy. Some memory-impaired people report that their life is like a dream. Others, aware that they might have repeated the same story over and over again, become very withdrawn and socially isolated because of their reluctance to bore and irritate their families and friends. People with memory impairments are also frustrated by frequent and sometimes humiliating failures and constant misunderstandings. Memory problems can be exhausting, both for the memory-impaired person and for the relatives, because of the efforts required to cope with daily living and the compensatory behaviour necessary to get through each day.

In this chapter we shall consider how these problems might be better understood and what possibilities exist for helping people with memory impairments and their families.

CONCEPTUALISING MEMORY DISORDERS

Memory is a complex function consisting of a number of component processes, and impairments of memory can range from the global, affecting most aspects, to the very specific and selective. Careful neuropsychological assessment of all aspects of memory is, therefore, an essential precursor to the development of plans for rehabilitation. This makes it possible to see which aspects of memory are affected and which are relatively spared, and thus to identify both strengths and needs. Key dimensions of memory that can be explored in the assessment process are outlined below, and Table 28.1 lists some of the neuropsychological tests that can be used to assess different aspects of memory. Dimensions of memory that should be considered include the following:

(1) **Different time spans**

Separate systems process information acquired very recently and information acquired some time before, and

Table 28.1. Standardised tests for assessment of memory

Memory function	Subsystem	Tests used for assessment
Immediate/working memory	Phonological	Wechsler Memory Scale-Revised (WMS-R) digit span (Wechsler, 1987)
	Visuospatial	Visual Patterns Test (Della Sala, Gray, Baddeley, & Wilson, 1997) WMS-R visual memory span (Wechsler, 1987)
Long-term memory	Episodic	Doors and People (Baddeley, Emslie & Nimmo-Smith, 1994) WMS-R logical memory (Wechsler, 1987) WMS-R visual reproduction (Wechsler, 1987) Recognition Memory Test (Warrington, 1984)
	Semantic	Speed and Capacity of Language Processing (Baddeley, Emslie, & Nimmo-Smith, 1992) Pyramids and Palm Trees (Howard & Patterson, 1992)
	Procedural	Mirror Tracing Task (Wilson, Green, Teasdale et al., 1996)
Prospective memory		Rivermead Behavioural Memory Test (Wilson, Cockburn, & Baddeley, 1985)
Explicit versus implicit	Explicit	WMS-R paired associate learning (Wechsler, 1987) Rivermead Behavioural Memory Test (Wilson, Cockburn, & Baddeley, 1985)
	Implicit	Stem Completion (Baddeley & Wilson, 1994) Perceptual and Auditory Priming (Wilson, Green, Teasdale et al., 1996)
Retrograde memory		Autobiographical Memory Interview (Kopelman, Wilson, & Baddeley, 1989) Remote Memory Battery (Beatty, Goodkin, Monson et al., 1988)

these can be selectively impaired. Assessment should therefore cover:

(a) *Immediate or working memory*—memory for information from the previous few seconds. Working memory is further subdivided into three component systems, a phonological system for auditory information, a visuospatial system for visual information, and a controlling central executive system.

(b) *Long-term memory*:
  (i) *delayed*—memory for events that happened or information that was presented in the previous few minutes
  (ii) *recent*—memory for events that happened or information that was presented in the previous few days or weeks
  (iii) *remote*—memory for events that happened or information collected several years previously.

(c) *Prospective memory*—memory for things that need to be done in the future.

(2) **Differing types of information**
Different kinds of knowledge are represented differently in the brain and can be selectively impaired. Assessment will need to cover:
  (a) *Semantic memory*—memory for factual knowledge.
  (b) *Episodic memory*—memory for events and autobiographical memory.
  (c) *Procedural memory*—memory for skills and practical procedures. This is often relatively preserved in comparison to episodic and semantic memory.

(3) **Information in different forms**
The key distinction here is between *verbal memory*—memory for information in the form of words, whether written or spoken—and *visual memory*, which is memory for things that have to be remembered in visual form. Some people with memory impairments will perform significantly better with one or other form of information.

(4) **The stages of remembering**
Remembering involves the stages of encoding, storage and retrieval of information. Problems can arise at one or more of these stages, and the pattern of difficulty shown by any given individual would have important implications for the rehabilitation process.

(5) **The kind of remembering needed**
Information might need to be recalled, that is, retrieved from memory without specific external guidance to structure the remembering process, or simply recognised as familiar and distinguished from other, unfamiliar items.

(6) **The degree of conscious awareness of the learning process**
Learning can take place with and without conscious awareness. Learning of which one is consciously aware is termed explicit, whereas learning of which one is not consciously aware is termed implicit. Examples of implicit learning include conditioning or priming. Some people with impairments of explicit memory nevertheless show preserved implicit memory, and this can be important when considering the approach to use in rehabilitation.

(7) **Old and new learning**
Where disorders have a clear onset, it is possible to draw a distinction between memories that were laid down before the injury or illness, and memories for events and information from the period since the injury or illness. The term retrograde memory refers to old learning, or memories from before the brain injury. The term anterograde memory refers to new learning, or memories acquired since the injury.

A comprehensive theoretical overview of memory functioning is provided by Baddeley (1990, 1992). Memory disorders are addressed from a number of perspectives in Baddeley, Wilson, and Watts (1995) and Kapur (1988).

More detailed information on neuropsychological assessment of memory can be found in Howieson and Lezak (1995), Lezak (1995), Mayes (1995), and Wilson (1996). Lincoln and Brooks

(1992) provide a rehabilitation-oriented overview of memory assessment.

Brain-injured clients might well have multiple cognitive problems that will need to be tackled in rehabilitation. People with a pure amnesic syndrome are relatively rare, and most clients will present with attentional deficits, word-finding problems or executive difficulties of planning and organisation. Memory problems can be secondary to other cognitive deficits; alternatively, both might be present but separate from each other. Detailed neuropsychological assessment of a range of functions, in addition to memory, will usually be necessary to obtain an accurate picture of a person's cognitive strengths and weaknesses before a coherent and sensible memory therapy programme can be designed.

Information from detailed neuropsychological assessment needs to be supplemented with a behavioural assessment aimed at defining the everyday problems to be targeted for treatment. This might involve, for example, asking relatives to complete a daily memory diary to record the everyday problems encountered. Wilson (1999) describes how a memory diary was used to obtain information about which everyday problems to target in treatment. Relatives were given a memory diary consisting of a daily checklist with 30 questions that had to be completed each day for 3 weeks. Questions covered a variety of everyday topics including getting lost, forgetting details, difficulty in learning new information, and so on. It is also useful to establish which compensatory aids and strategies are currently being used, as it might be possible to focus on improving the efficiency of these during treatment.

HELPING PEOPLE WITH MEMORY PROBLEMS

Although some recovery of memory functioning can be expected during the early stages following head injury and other non-progressive brain injury, memory-impaired people and their families should not be led to believe that significant improvement can occur once the period of natural recovery is over. This does not mean, however, that nothing can be done to help. Not only can people be taught to avoid problems, compensate for their difficulties and learn more efficiently, their distress can be reduced and their awareness and understanding can be increased. In the following sections we will consider a number of aspects of the rehabilitation process: providing information, making environmental adaptations, using external memory aids and internal mnemonic strategies, and facilitating new learning.

Providing information

One simple therapeutic strategy is to listen to what families have to say and provide information or explanations. Families commonly ask why it is that their memory-impaired relative can remember what happened 20 years earlier but cannot remember what happened an hour before, or variations on that theme. Sometimes simple explanations, such as the fact that old memories are stored differently in the brain, will be appropriate.

Some relatives will require a fairly detailed anatomical or biochemical explanation, and in such cases the therapist should be sufficiently knowledgeable and confident to be able to provide such an explanation. Simply being reassured that their relative displays a typical pattern found in most memory-impaired people can also reduce relatives' anxiety.

Written information is appreciated by many families. *Memory problems after head injury* (Wilson, 1989) written for the National Head Injuries Association, *Managing your memory* (Kapur, 1991) a self-help manual for improving memory skills and *Coping with memory problems* (Clare & Wilson, 1997) are all useful booklets to have available for patients and relatives. A useful reference on the topic of self-help and support groups for memory-impaired people and their carers is Wearing (1992).

Environmental adaptations

One effective way of helping people with memory problems is to adapt their surroundings so that they have less need to rely on their memory. It is possible to modify or restructure environments to enable people to cope with the demands of daily living without relying on memory systems that have ceased to function sufficiently adequately to meet those demands.

Some designers have recognised that the correct use of any object should be so obvious that users will find it almost impossible to make an error (e.g. Norman, 1988). Norman's ideas can be extended to help people with organic memory impairment. For example, clients can be provided with kettles, cookers and electric lights that turn themselves off after a certain interval, thereby avoiding dangers for those who are very forgetful. Many memory-impaired people forget where domestic items are kept in the home and frequently cannot remember which room is which in their own house. Labelling cupboards and doors is an effective way of making the environment more manageable. Even directions within the house can be hard to follow for some memory-impaired people so signposts appropriately positioned, or even arrows directing people from, for instance, the dining room to the garden can be of help.

Positioning objects so they cannot be missed is also worth trying. For example, clipping a notebook to a waist-belt or using a neck cord for spectacles will help to prevent people from leaving them in some place soon forgotten. It might be possible to reduce or eliminate repetitive behaviour by identifying and eliminating environmental situations or verbal questions that trigger repetitions.

As in many other areas, the growth in new technology is benefiting memory rehabilitation in several ways. "Smart" houses employ computers and video cameras to monitor and control the living environments of people with dementia; two such houses have been set up in Norway (G. Slaven, personal communication, 1996). The aim is to use and perhaps modify new technology in order to increase independence and activity, and thus the quality of life, of confused elderly people. If success is achieved with the elderly population, then it is possible that "smart" houses will be adapted to suit the needs of other groups with cognitive impairments. The design requirements could open up fruitful dialogue between psychologists, engineers, architects, and computer programmers.

The environmental adaptation model argues for avoidance of problems that arise because of memory impairment. Gross and Schutz (1986) called this the environmental control model, the origins of which can be found within the discipline of behaviour modification. Environmental adaptation can be a very rapid and effective way of eradicating or reducing undesirable behaviours, but this is not always possible to achieve. There is also an ethical argument against a methodology that might involve undue restriction to a point where, let us say, the environment is made so restrictive that no demands are made upon memory at all, and the memory-impaired person is never required to exercise his or her powers of memory, however much they may be weakened. Like many psychiatric and psychological methods of management, environmental control is open to abuse. Nevertheless, there is little doubt that for many severely intellectually impaired people, environmental control is their best chance of obtaining some degree of independence.

External memory aids

It is sometimes worth considering an alternative means to a final goal in much the same way that Luria did with his principle of functional adaptation (Luria, 1963), or Zangwill with his principle of compensation (Zangwill, 1947). In memory rehabilitation such compensation is often achieved through the use of external memory aids such as notebooks, lists, diaries, tape recorders, and so forth. Most people use external memory aids and these are, perhaps, the most useful strategy for people with organic memory impairment. Using an external memory aid can be as simple as putting a notebook by the phone so that any messages can be written down straight away, or making a list of "things to do today". Some patients develop complex systems involving regular use of a number of aids in order to maximise their independence (Wilson & Hughes, 1997). People with memory impairments will usually require training in the use of new memory aids. It is not enough simply to provide a memory aid and expect it to be used appropriately, and patience and ingenuity are required when teaching their use. Kime, Lamb, and Wilson (1996), and Sohlberg and Mateer (1989) describe ways of teaching the use of aids.

Some patients resist using such aids because they feel that it is cheating, or that any natural recovery will be slowed down by reliance upon them. These feelings should be discouraged as it is normal to use compensatory aids and there is neither evidence nor reason to believe their use will slow recovery. As noted above, a bigger problem is the difficulty memory-impaired people have in remembering to use their aids efficiently or even at all. Wilson (1991) found that memory-impaired people were far more likely to be using compensatory aids 5 to 10 years post-rehabilitation than they were during or at the end of rehabilitation, despite the fact that much of their rehabilitation emphasised the use of such aids. Furthermore, those patients

using six or more aids or strategies were significantly more likely to be independent than those using five or less. The numbers of people using each kind of compensation can be found in Wilson (1995). The most popular was writing notes and the least popular was tying a knot in one's handkerchief (analogous to the American custom of tying a string around one's finger).

Developing technology offers new possibilities. A simple and portable paging system designed in California by an engineer father of a head-injured son working together with a neuropsychologist is proving to be an effective tool in memory rehabilitation. Known as NeuroPage, it uses a computer linked by a modem and telephone to a paging company. The scheduling of reminders or cues for each individual is entered into the computer and from then on no further human interaction is necessary (Hersh & Treadgold, 1994). On the appropriate date and time NeuroPage automatically transmits the reminder information to the paging company, which transmits the message to the individual's pager.

A major advantage of NeuroPage is that the system avoids many of the difficulties faced by memory-impaired people when they attempt to use a compensatory aid or strategy. Obviously, using aids or strategies involves exercising memory, so the very people who need them most have the greatest difficulty in managing their complexities. Memory-impaired people can forget to make use of their aids, or find that programming them is too difficult; they might use them unsystematically, or might even be embarrassed by having to refer to them in public. In contrast, NeuroPage is controlled by one large button, which is easy to press even for those with motor difficulties. It is highly portable and has an audible or vibratory alarm depending on the user's preference. It has an accompanying explanatory message and, like other pagers, is viewed as a prestigious possession rather than an embarrassment.

NeuroPage was evaluated in a recent study with 15 brain-injured people whose memory difficulties followed head injury, stroke or tumour (Wilson, Evans, Emslie, & Malinek, 1997). Using an ABA design whereby the first A phase was the treatment period, and the second A phase was the post-treatment baseline period, it was demonstrated that all 15 patients benefited significantly from using NeuroPage. The average number of problems tackled for the group as a whole was 3.86, with a range of 1 to 7, and a mode of 4. Typical reminders included, "Take your medication", "Today is ——", "Make sure you have your spectacles", and "Check your diary". Results from the study can be seen in Fig. 28.1.

The mean percentage success rate for completing tasks in the first baseline period, for the group as a whole, was 37.08; whereas in the treatment phase this rose to 85.56. Using an odds ratio test (Everitt, 1995), which takes into account different underlying success rates for each target and calculates an average improvement factor, it was found that each participant showed a significant improvement, although there were considerable individual differences. Some participants maintained this improvement when the pager was withdrawn, suggesting that they had learned to carry out the prompted tasks, while others

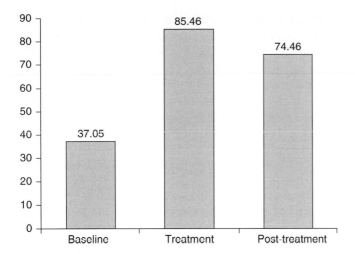

Figure 28.1. Results for 15 memory-impaired people using NeuroPage.

remained dependent on reminders to help them complete the tasks.

Another developing area for new technology is in the use of computers as "interactive task guidance systems" (Kirsch, Levine, Fallon-Krueger, & Jaros, 1987) where they are used to provide a set of cues to guide patients through sequential steps of an everyday task such as cooking or cleaning. The computer acts as a compensatory device, providing step-by-step instructions. Little knowledge of computer operations is needed by the subject. One example is provided by Bergman and Kemmerer (1991), who describe how a 54-year-old woman with a number of cognitive problems learned to use a computerised task guidance system.

Despite general agreement that a compensatory approach is probably the most effective one to adopt, there is uncertainty about why some people use external aids efficiently and others do not. Wilson and Watson (1996) have described a theoretical framework influenced by the work of Bäckman and Dixon (1992), which proposed four stages in the development of compensatory behaviour: (1) origins; (2) forms; (3) mechanisms; and (4) consequences, and discussed how these steps might apply to brain-injured people with memory problems trying to compensate for their difficulties. Using data from a long-term follow-up study, Wilson and Watson went on to show that age, severity of memory impairment, and additional cognitive deficits are important variables in predicting independence and use of compensations several years post-rehabilitation. Current research in Cambridge and Ely is attempting to confirm or disconfirm these predictions.

Facilitating new learning

Although external aids and environmental adaptations can be of great assistance to the memory-impaired person, it is unlikely that they will provide enough support to cover all the demands of daily living. Memory-impaired people need to learn new

information on certain occasions. There are a number of methods that can help to facilitate this process, including the use of internal mnemonic strategies, expanding rehearsal and errorless learning.

Mnemonics are systems that enable people to organise, store and retrieve information more efficiently. Some people use the term "mnemonics" to refer to anything that helps people remember, including external aids. In memory rehabilitation, however, the term is used for methods involving mental manipulation of material. For example, in order to remember how many days there are in each month most people use a system of mnemonics. In the United Kingdom and much of the United States of America people recite a rhyme, "Thirty days hath September..." In other parts of the world people use their knuckles to refer to "long" months and the dips between the knuckles to refer to the "short" months. Mnemonics are often employed to learn the names of cranial nerves, notes of music, colours of the rainbow, and other ordered material.

Simple visual mnemonics can sometimes help memory-impaired people to remember names. It is usually best for the therapist or carer to devise the mnemonic and teach it to the person who has a memory problem, as it is often difficult for memory-impaired people to devise their own mnemonics. Brain-injured people also find it extremely difficult to use mnemonics spontaneously, and are unlikely to apply this strategy themselves in novel situations. The real value of mnemonics is that they are useful for teaching memory-impaired people new information, and they almost invariably lead to faster learning than rote rehearsal. See Wilson (1987) and Moffat (1989) for further discussion of mnemonics in memory rehabilitation, and West (1995) for the use of these strategies in people with age-related memory impairment.

Wilson (1987) evaluated the use of visual imagery mnemonics in teaching names to people with amnesia and demonstrated that this strategy is virtually always superior to rote repetition. Thoene and Glisky (1995) also found visual imagery superior to other methods for teaching people's names to amnesic people.

More recently, Clare et al. were able to teach a 74-year-old man in the early stages of Alzheimer's disease the names of fellow members of a social club (Clare, Wilson, Breen, & Hodges, 1999). They used a combination of strategies, including finding a distinctive feature of the face together with backward chaining and expanding rehearsal, in which the information to be remembered is first presented, then tested immediately, tested again after a very brief delay, tested again after a slightly longer delay and so on. This is a form of distributed practice described in the introduction and is a fairly powerful learning strategy in memory rehabilitation (Baddeley & Longman, 1978; Lorge, 1930). The method of expanding rehearsal owes much to the work of Landauer and Bjork (1978). Clare et al.'s patient learned the names of the club members using photographs in his memory therapy sessions, and demonstrated generalisation by greeting people by name at the club. The results can be seen in Fig. 28.2.

Certain strategies from the field of study techniques (e.g. Robinson, 1970), and learning disability (e.g. Yule & Carr,

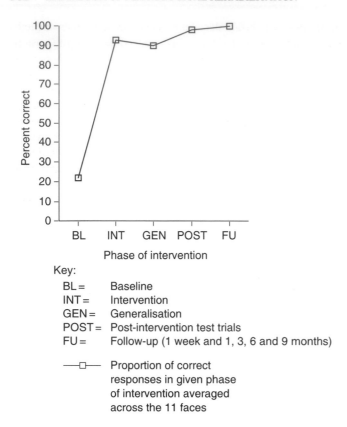

Figure 28.2. Errorless learning of face–name associations in a man with Alzheimer's disease.

Key:
BL = Baseline
INT = Intervention
GEN = Generalisation
POST = Post-intervention test trials
FU = Follow-up (1 week and 1, 3, 6 and 9 months)

—□— Proportion of correct responses in given phase of intervention averaged across the 11 faces

1987) have been used in neuropsychological rehabilitation (Wilson, 1991), and work along these lines continues to be applied in the search for improved methods of learning. One series of potentially important studies in recent years has involved errorless learning. This is a method for teaching new skills to people with learning difficulties (Jones & Eayrs, 1992; Sidman & Stoddard, 1967), but until quite recently its principles have not been applied to any great extent to neurologically impaired adults. As the name implies, errorless learning involves learning without errors or mistakes. Most of us can learn or benefit from our errors because we can remember and thus avoid them in our future efforts to learn. However, people without episodic memory cannot remember their mistakes, so fail to correct them. Furthermore, the very fact of engaging in a behaviour can strengthen or reinforce it even though that behaviour is errorful. Consequently, for someone with a severe memory impairment, it makes sense to ensure that any behaviour that is going to be reinforced is correct rather than incorrect.

Work on errorless learning in memory-impaired adults has been influenced by studies of implicit learning from the field of cognitive neuropsychology, as well as the earlier studies from the field of learning disability. There have been numerous studies showing that amnesic patients can learn some things normally or nearly normally, even though they might have no conscious recollection of learning anything at all (Brooks & Baddeley, 1976; Glisky & Schacter, 1987; Graf & Schacter, 1985). Glisky

and Schacter tried to use the implicit learning abilities of people with amnesia to teach them computer technology, and although some success was achieved this was at considerable expense of time and effort. These attempts, and others that try to build on the relatively intact skills of memory-impaired people, have, on the whole, been disappointing. One reason for failures and anomalies could be that implicit learning is poor at eliminating errors. Error elimination is a function of explicit not implicit memory and, consequently, when people are forced to rely upon implicit memory (as amnesic patients are) the subsequent trial-and-error learning becomes a slow and laborious procedure.

In 1994 Baddeley and Wilson published the first known study demonstrating that amnesic patients learn better when they are prevented from making mistakes during the learning process. This was an experimental study in which a stem completion task was used to teach lists of words to severely memory-impaired people. Each of the 16 amnesic patients in the study showed better learning when they were prevented from making mistakes, that is, prevented from guessing, than when they were forced to guess, that is, forced to make errors. The conclusions to this study were: (1) errorless learning appears to be superior to trial-and-error learning; (2) the effect is greater for amnesic patients than it is for controls; and (3) amnesic patients show less forgetting with errorless learning. Since then we have conducted several single case studies with memory-impaired patients, comparing errorful and errorless learning for teaching practical, everyday information (Wilson, Baddeley, Evans, & Shiel, 1994). In the majority of cases, errorless learning proved to be superior to trial-and-error learning. Squires, Hunkin, and Parkin (1996), and Wilson and Evans (1996) report further studies. The latter paper also discusses some of the potential problems connected with errorless learning.

Results from recent work (Evans, Wilson, Schuri et al., 2000) involving ten errorless learning experiments suggests that tasks and situations that depend upon implicit memory (such as stem completion or retrieving a name from a first letter cue) are more likely to benefit from errorless learning methods than tasks requiring explicit recall of new situations. Nevertheless, Wilson et al. (1994) demonstrated new explicit learning in a memory-impaired, head-injured patient. Clare et al. (submitted), mentioned above, also demonstrated explicit learning in a man with Alzheimer's disease.

THE WIDER CONTEXT

Alongside the use of specific strategies targeted at overcoming problems arising from memory impairment, it is essential to consider the person in context and to bear in mind all the various factors that could influence treatment outcome. Personality, awareness, motivation, anxiety, depression, and social isolation can all affect the manifestations of memory problems in everyday life, the response to the problems, the compensations employed and the final outcome, and may need to be targeted in treatment (Prigatano, 1995).

Memory-impaired people often experience high levels of anxiety. For example, Evans and Wilson (1992) found anxiety common in attenders at a weekly memory group. It might therefore be necessary to explore ways of helping the person to feel less anxious so that he or she can obtain the maximum benefit from attempts at rehabilitation.

Relaxation therapy can be useful in reducing anxiety. Even if memory problems are severe enough to prevent the person remembering the therapy, the beneficial effects of the relaxation are likely to remain. Relaxation audio cassette tapes can be bought or made for each patient, thus avoiding the need to remember the exercises. However, if tense-and-release exercises (Bernstein & Borkovec, 1973) are employed for relaxation, therapists need to be cautious when using these with some brain-injured patients, particularly those with motor difficulties. Tensing muscles can cause a spasm or increase spasticity. It is best to discuss the desirability of the tense-and-release exercises with a physiotherapist treating the patient or, alternatively, look for another form of relaxation, such as that recommended by Ost (1987) or those described by Clark (1989).

Social isolation is another common feature among memory-impaired people, as noted above (Talbot, 1989; Wearing, 1992; Wilson, 1991). The person's social network often falls away because he or she forgets visits and conversations, might not be able to go out alone without getting lost, and might engage in inappropriate behaviour. One way to deal with social isolation is to run memory groups. Wilson and Moffat (1992) describe various kinds of groups for patients; Moffat (1989) reports on a relatives' memory group for people with dementia and Wearing (1992) provides suggestions on setting up self-help groups.

Evans and Wilson (1992) point out not only the social value of memory groups but also the reduction in anxiety that can follow attendance at a group. Indeed, the main value of such groups appears to lie in reducing the emotional sequelae resulting from memory impairment. Psychotherapy groups can achieve the same ends and guidelines for these groups can be found in Jackson and Gouvier (1992).

IMPLEMENTING MEMORY REHABILITATION

The rehabilitation process should ideally begin in the early stages of recovery from the acute phase of the illness or injury, and can extend over a considerable period of time. The rehabilitation needs of individuals will differ depending on the severity of the memory impairment, the extent of other deficits, and the length of time that has elapsed since the illness or injury. The preferences of the individual and his or her relatives, the individual's circumstances, the kinds of goals the individual wishes to attain, and the resources available will also play a part in determining the nature of any plans for rehabilitation.

Rehabilitation should not necessarily be seen as restricted to the months or years immediately following the onset of the memory disorder, as individuals can sometimes benefit considerably from a period of intervention arranged many years after the original injury, perhaps in response to changing needs or circumstances. Equally, the process of rehabilitation should not be seen as restricted to the intervention of professionals. Rehabilitation is best viewed as a partnership between the memory-impaired individual, his or her relatives, and the professionals involved, especially as the strategies learned will certainly need to be carried over into everyday life and adapted to meet new demands as time progresses, and much of this will be effected by the individual and family.

Rehabilitation interventions can be implemented in a variety of settings. These include on the one hand specialist centres such as in-patient wards and residential or non-residential rehabilitation units, and on the other the memory-impaired person's everyday environment.

CONCLUSION

Although restoration of memory functioning is unlikely to occur, there is a considerable amount that can be done to enable memory-impaired people and their relatives to come to terms with their difficulties and surmount a number of them by using various strategies and aids.

Environmental modifications can be of considerable help to people whose memory functioning is impaired and new technology has an increasingly important role to play in future management of memory problems. Successful use of external memory aids is possible through carefully structured teaching, particularly with people who are younger, have less severe memory problems, or who have fewer additional cognitive impairments. Others might need more intensive therapy or rehabilitation to ensure efficient usage.

Internal strategies such as mnemonics and rehearsal techniques can be employed to teach new information, and although they almost always lead to faster learning than rote repetition, it must be recognised that most memory-impaired people will be unable to use mnemonics spontaneously. Instead, relatives, carers and therapists will have to employ mnemonics to encourage learning among memory-impaired people.

Errorless learning can in some circumstances be more effective than trial-and-error learning for memory-impaired people. This is because, in order to benefit from our mistakes we need to be able to remember them, and this is something that most memory-impaired people will not be able to do.

In addition to poor memory, many brain-injured people will have other cognitive problems that will need to be addressed. The emotional sequelae of memory impairment, such as anxiety, depression, and loneliness, need to be reduced by providing written information, counselling, anxiety management techniques, and treatment in memory or psychotherapy groups.

Although we probably cannot restore lost memory functioning, we can indeed help people to bypass problems and compensate for their difficulties. We can help them learn more efficiently and we can reduce the effects of their problems in their daily lives. We must also work to foster a greater understanding of what it means to have severe organic memory impairment and a greater willingness to ensure that resources are available for rehabilitation.

REFERENCES

Bäckman, L. and Dixon, R.A. (1992). Psychological compensation: A theoretical framework. *Psychological Bulletin, 112*, 259–283.

Baddeley, A.D. (1990). *Human memory: Theory and practice*. London: Lawrence Erlbaum Associates.

Baddeley, A.D. (1992). Working memory: The interface between memory and cognition. *Journal of Cognitive Neuroscience, 4*, 281–288.

Baddeley, A.D., Emslie, H. and Nimmo-Smith, I. (1992). *The Speed and Capacity of Language Processing (SCOLP) Test*. Bury St Edmunds, Suffolk: Thames Valley Test Company.

Baddeley, A.D., Emslie, H. and Nimmo-Smith, I. (1994). *Doors and people: A test of visual and verbal recall and recognition*. Bury St. Edmunds, Suffolk: Thames Valley Test Company.

Baddeley, A.D. and Longman, D.J.A. (1978). The influence of length and frequency on training sessions on the rate of learning to type. *Ergonomics, 21*, 627–635.

Baddeley, A.D. and Wilson, B.A. (1994). When implicit learning fails: Amnesia and the problem of error elimination. *Neuropsychologia 32*, 53–68.

Baddeley, A.D., Wilson, B.A. and Watts, F.N. (Eds.) (1995). *Handbook of memory disorders*. Chichester: John Wiley.

Beatty, W.W., Goodkin, D.E., Monson, N. et al. (1988). Anterograde and retrograde amnesia in patients with chronic progressive multiple sclerosis. *Archives of Neurology, 45*, 611–619.

Bergman, M.M. and Kemmerer, A.G. (1991). Computer-enhanced self sufficiency: Part 2. Uses and subjective benefits of a text writer for an individual with traumatic brain injury. *Neuropsychology, 5*, 25–28.

Bernstein, D.A. and Borkovec, T.D. (1973). *Progressive relaxation training*. Champaign, IL: Illinois Research Press.

Brooks, D.N. and Baddeley, A. (1976). What can amnesic patients learn? *Neuropsychologia, 14*, 111–122.

Clare, L., and Wilson, B.A. (1997). *Coping with memory problems: A practical guide for people with memory impairments, relatives, friends and carers*. Bury St Edmunds, Suffolk: Thames Valley Test Company.

Clare, L., Wilson, B.A., Breen, E.K. and Hodges, J.R. (1999). Errorless learning of face–name associations in early Alzheimer's disease. *Neurocase, 5*, 37–46.

Clark, D.M. (1989). Anxiety states: Panic and generalised anxiety. In K. Hawton, P.M. Salkovskis, J. Kirk and D.M. Clark (Eds.), *Cognitive behaviour therapy for psychiatric problems: A practical guide*. Oxford: Oxford Medical Publications.

Della Sala, S., Gray, C., Baddeley, A.D. and Wilson, L. (1997). *Visual Patterns Test*. Bury St Edmunds, Suffolk: Thames Valley Test Company.

Evans, J.J. and Wilson, B.A. (1992). A memory group for individuals with brain injury. *Clinical Rehabilitation, 6*, 75–81.

Evans, J.J., Wilson, B.A., Schuri, U., Baddeley, A.D., Canavan, T., Laaksonen, R., Bruna, O., Lorenzi, L., Della Sala, S. Andrade, J., Green, R. and Taussik, I. (2000). A comparison of "errorless" and "trial and error" learning methods for teaching individuals with acquired memory deficits. *Neuropsychological Rehabilitation, 10*, 67–101.

Everitt, B. (1995). *Cambridge dictionary of statistics in the medical sciences*. Cambridge: Cambridge University Press.

Glisky, E.L. and Schacter, D.L. (1987). Acquisition of domain-specific knowledge in organic amnesia: Training for computer-related work. *Neuropsychologia, 25*, 893–906.

Graf, P. and Schacter, D.L. (1985). Implicit and explicit memory for new associations in normal and amnesic subjects. *Journal of Experimental Psychology: Learning, Memory and Cognition, 11*, 501–518.

Gross, Y. and Schutz, L.E. (1986). Intervention models in neuropsychology. In B. Uzzell and Y. Gross (Eds.), *Clinical neuropsychology of intervention* (pp. 179–205). Boston: Martinus Nijhoff.

Hersh, N. and Treadgold, L. (1994). NeuroPage: The rehabilitation of memory dysfunction by prosthetic memory and cueing. *NeuroRehabilitation, 4*, 187–197.

Howard, D. and Patterson, K. (1992). *Pyramids and palm trees*. Bury St Edmunds, Suffolk: Thames Valley Test Company.

Howieson, D.B. and Lezak, M.D. (1995). Separating memory from other cognitive problems. In A.D. Baddeley, B.A. Wilson and F.N., Watts (Eds.), *Handbook of memory disorders* (pp. 411–426). Chichester: John Wiley.

Jackson, W.T. and Gouvier, W.D. (1992). Group psychotherapy with brain-damaged adults and their families. In C.J. Long and L.K. Ross (Eds.), *Handbook of head trauma: Acute care to recovery* (pp. 309–327). New York: Plenum Press.

Jones, R.S.P. and Eayrs, C.B. (1992). The use of errorless learning procedures in teaching people with a learning disability. *Mental Handicap Research, 5*, 304–312.

Kapur, N. (1988). *Memory disorders in clinical practice*. London: Butterworths.

Kapur, N. (1991). *Managing your memory. A self help memory manual for improving everyday memory skills*. Available from the author at the Wessex Neurological Centre, Southampton General Hospital, Southampton.

Kime, S.K., Lamb, D.G. and Wilson, B.A. (1996). Use of a comprehensive program of external cuing to enhance procedural memory in a patient with dense amnesia. *Brain Injury, 10*, 17–25.

Kirsch, N.L., Levine, S.P., Fallon-Krueger, M. and Jaros, L.A. (1987). The microcomputer as an "orthotic" device for patients with cognitive deficits. *Journal of Head Trauma Rehabilitation, 2*, 77–86.

Kopelman, M. and Crawford, S. (1996). Not all memory clinics are dementia clinics. *Neuropsychological Rehabilitation, 6*, 187–202.

Kopelman, M., Wilson, B.A. and Baddeley, A.D. (1989). *The autobiographical memory interviews*. Bury St Edmunds: Thames Valley Test Company.

Landauer, T.K. and Bjork, R.A. (1978). Optimum rehearsal patterns and name learning. In M.M. Gruneberg, P.E. Morris and R.N. Sykes (Eds.), *Practical aspects of memory* (pp. 625–632). London: Academic Press.

Lezak, M.D. (1995). *Neuropsychological assessment, 3rd edition*. New York: Oxford University Press.

Lincoln, N.B. and Brooks, N. (1992). Assessment for rehabilitation. In B.A. Wilson and N. Moffat (Eds.), *Clinical management of memory problems, 2nd edition* (pp. 32–58). London: Chapman and Hall.

Lorge, I. (1930). Influence of regularly interpolated time intervals upon subsequent learning. Quoted in H.H. Johnson and R.L. Solo (1971). *An introduction to experimental design in psychology: A case approach* (pp. 7–8). New York: Harper and Row.

Luria, A.R. (1963). *Recovery of function after brain injury*. New York: Macmillan.

Mayes, A.R. (1995). The assessment of memory disorders. In A.D. Baddeley, B.A. Wilson and F.N. Watts (Eds.), *Handbook of memory disorders* (pp. 367–391). Chichester: John Wiley.

Moffat, N. (1989). Home based cognitive rehabilitation with the elderly. In L.W. Poon, D.C. Rubin and B.A. Wilson (Eds.), Everyday cognition in adulthood and later life (pp. 659–680). Cambridge: Cambridge University Press.

Norman, D.A. (1988) *The psychology of everyday things*. New York: Basic Books.

Ost, L.G. (1987). Applied relaxation: Description of a coping technique and review of controlled studies. *Behaviour Research and Therapy, 25*, 397–410.

Prigatano, G.P. (1995). Personality and social aspects of memory rehabilitation. In A.D. Baddeley, B.A. Wilson and F.N. Watts (Eds.), *Handbook of memory disorders* (pp. 603–614). Chichester: John Wiley.

Robinson, F.P. (1970). *Effective study*. New York: Harper and Row.

Sidman, M. and Stoddard, L.T. (1967). The effectiveness of fading in programming simultaneous form discrimination for retarded children. *Journal of Experimental Analysis of Behavior, 10*, 3–15.

Sohlberg, M.M. and Mateer, C. (1989). Training use of compensatory memory books: A three-stage behavioural approach. *Journal of Clinical and Experimental Neuropsychology, 11*, 871–891.

Squires, E.J., Hunkin, N.M. and Parkin, A.J. (1996). Memory notebook training in a case of severe amnesia: Generalising from paired associate learning to real life. *Neuropsychological Rehabilitation, 6*, 55–65.

Talbott, R. (1989). The brain-injured person and the family. In R.L. Wood and P. Eames (Eds.), *Models of brain injury rehabilitation* (pp. 3–16). London: Chapman and Hall.

Thoene, A.I.T. and Glisky, E.L. (1995). Learning of name–face associations in memory-impaired patients: A comparison of different training procedures. *Journal of the International Neuropsychological Society, 1*, 29–38.

Warrington, E.K. (1984). *The Recognition Memory Test*. Windsor: NFER-Nelson.

Wechsler, D. (1987). *The Wechsler Memory Scale – Revised*. San Antonio, TX: The Psychological Corporation.

Wearing, D. (1992). Self help groups. In B.A. Wilson and N. Moffat (Eds.), *Clinical management of memory problems, 2nd edition* (pp. 271–301). London: Chapman and Hall.

West, R.L. (1995). Compensatory strategies for age-associated memory impairment. In A.D. Baddeley, B.A. Wilson and F.N. Watts (Eds.), *Handbook of memory disorders* (pp. 481–500). Chichester: John Wiley.

Wilson, B.A. (1987). *Rehabilitation of memory*. New York: Guilford Press.

Wilson, B.A. (1989). *Memory problems after head injury*. Nottingham: National Head Injuries Association.

Wilson, B.A. (1991). Long term prognosis of patients with severe memory disorders. *Neuropsychological Rehabilitation, 1*, 117–134.

Wilson, B.A. (1995). Memory rehabilitation: Compensating for memory problems. In R.A. Dixon and L. Bäckman (Eds.), *Compensating for psychological deficits and declines: Managing losses and promoting gains* (pp. 171–190). Mahwah, NJ: Lawrence Erlbaum Associates, Inc.

Wilson, B.A. (1996). Assessment of memory. In L. Harding and J.R. Beech (Eds.), *Assessment in neuropsychology* (pp. 135–151). London: Routledge.

Wilson, B.A. (1999). *Case studies in neuropsychological rehabilitation*. New York: Oxford University Press.

Wilson, B.A., Baddeley, A.D., Evans, J.J. and Shiel, A. (1994). Errorless learning in the rehabilitation of memory-impaired people. *Neuropsychological Rehabilitation, 4*, 307–326.

Wilson, B.A., Cockburn, J. and Baddeley, A.D. (1985). *The Rivermead Behavioural Memory Test*. Bury St Edmunds, Suffolk: Thames Valley Test Company.

Wilson, B.A. and Evans, J.J. (1996). Error free learning in the rehabilitation of individuals with memory impairments. *Journal of Head Trauma Rehabilitation, 11*, 54–64.

Wilson, B.A., Evans, J.J., Emslie, H. and Malinek, V. (1999). Evaluation of NeuroPage: A new memory aid. *Journal of Neurology, Neurosurgery, and Psychiatry, 63*, 113–115.

Wilson, B.A., Green, R., Teasdale, T., Beckers, K., Della Sala, S., Kaschel R., Schuri, U., Van der Linden, M. and Weber, E. (1996). Implicit learning in amnesic subjects: A comparison with a large group of normal control subjects. *The Clinical Neuropsychologist, 10*, 279–292.

Wilson, B.A., J.C. and Hughes, E. (1997). Coping with amnesia: The natural history of a compensatory memory system. *Neuropsychological Rehabilitation, 7*, 43–56.

Wilson, B.A. and Moffat, N. (1992). The development of group memory therapy. In B.A. Wilson and N. Moffat (Eds.), *Clinical management of memory problems, 2nd edition* (pp. 243–273). London: Chapman and Hall.

Wilson, B.A. and Watson, P.C. (1996). A practical framework for understanding compensatory behaviour in people with organic memory impairment. *Memory, 4*, 465–486.

Yule, W. and Carr, J. (Eds.) (1987). *Behaviour modification for people with mental handicaps*. London: Croom Helm.

Zangwill, O.L. (1947). Psychological aspects of rehabilitation in cases of brain injury. *British Journal of Psychology, 37*, 60–69.

29. Assessment and rehabilitation of the dysexecutive syndrome

Nick Alderman   Paul W. Burgess

INTRODUCTION

In this chapter, our aim is to introduce the reader to the concept of the dysexecutive syndrome, and to briefly summarise some of the issues relating to its assessment and rehabilitation.

WHAT IS THE "DYSEXECUTIVE SYNDROME"?

The term "dysexecutive syndrome" (DES) refers to a cluster of symptoms that people can show following damage to the cognitive processes that are supported by (primarily) frontal lobe brain structures. People with such damage often experience one or more of a wide range of difficulties in everyday life. These can include problems with abstract reasoning, making decisions, and showing good judgement; difficulties in maintaining attention; inappropriate social behaviour; difficulties in devising and following plans; and difficulties with situations involving some forms of memory, e.g. remembering to carry out intended actions at a future time (for review, see books by Levin, Eisenberg, & Benton, 1991; Stuss & Benson, 1986; Shallice, 1988). A more comprehensive list of the most common deficits reported in the literature is shown in Table 29.1, which takes as a starting point the influential reviews of Stuss and Benson (1984, 1986). Historically, these symptoms have been referred to as the "frontal lobe syndrome".

However, in recent years many authors have expressed dissatisfaction with the validity of this syndrome as a concept. For example, Stuss and Benson (1984, p. 3) state that "... the term frontal lobe syndrome is used to refer to an amorphous, varied group of deficits, resulting from diverse aetiologies, different locations, and variable extents of abnormalities".

Similarly, Bigler (1990, p. 436) states that these deficits "... typically accompany frontal, frontal and temporal, or generalised cerebral damage". This assertion reflects the experience of clinical practice, where deficits normally thought to be attributable to injury to the frontal lobes can sometimes be found in the absence of reliable indicators of damage in those brain structures, or that in the case of generalised, diffuse damage, these deficits cannot clearly be attributed to them alone. Recent advances in functional imaging have helped to emphasise how

Table 29.1. Characteristics of the dysexecutive syndrome

DEX item number[1]	Problem being rated
1	Abstract thinking problems
2	Impulsivity
3	Confabulation
4	Planning problems
5	Euphoria
6	Temporal sequencing problems
7	Lack of insight and social awareness
8	Apathy and lack of drive
9	Disinhibition
10	Disturbed impulse control
11	Shallowing of affective responses
12	Aggression
13	Lack of concern
14	Perseveration
15	Restlessness/hyperkinesis
16	Inability to inhibit responses
17	Knowledge-response dissociation
18	Distractibility
19	Loss of decision-making ability
20	Unconcern for social rules

[1] Refers to the question number in the DEX questionnaire that measures this problem (see text).

the different brain areas work together as a system in the performance of all but the very simplest of tasks, which might provide a resolution to this apparent conflict and inevitably questions the conceptual validity of the "frontal lobe" syndrome. Indeed, Baddeley (1986) and Baddeley and Wilson (1988), have argued that to base the concept of this syndrome on localisation alone is misleading. These authors remind us that deficits associated with damage to other brain structures are not classified according to location, but instead by function. For example, in the case of memory impairment we do not refer to a "temporal lobe syndrome"; instead, we describe the nature of the problem with remembering or learning. Similarly, problems with language, perception, and other disorders are classified using functional criteria, not localisation to specific neuroanatomical structures. Baddeley and Wilson argue that a functional definition should also be sought regarding the types of deficit that can arise following damage to the frontal lobes, hence their proposal of the term "dysexecutive syndrome".

A further advantage of such an approach is to reduce the emphasis on attempting to ascribe deficits to definitive brain sites, whilst highlighting that it is problems with function that should form the basis of most clinical activity, particularly when conducted within a rehabilitation environment.

Some of the deficits attributed to frontal lobe damage are seen more frequently than others. One of the earliest accounts of this "core" group of functional deficits was provided by Rylander (1939, p. 22), who described them as comprising "... disturbed attention, increased distractibility, a difficulty in grasping the whole of a complicated state of affairs ... well able to work along routine lines (but) cannot learn to master new types of task". Observations of similar functional deficits, which include these elements, continue to be made today (see for example: Alderman & Ward, 1991; Burke, Zencius, Wesolowski, & Doubleday, 1991; McCarthy & Warrington, 1990).

These brain processes appear to be those that are primarily concerned with higher level cognitive functioning, principally the ability to engage in independent, goal-seeking behaviour. Thus Lezak (1983) conceptualises them as the ability to formulate goals, develop plans, execute those plans, and to effectively monitor and regulate consequent goal-directed behaviour. The inability to effectively direct and regulate behaviour often interferes severely with independent functioning and drives a number of secondary deficits, including emotional lability, irritability, apathy, carelessness, and inappropriate social behaviour.

An important advantage of a syndrome based on a pattern of observable, functional deficits is that this facilitates the development of cognitive models that attempt to account for behavioural manifestations of the underlying organic damage. These can then in turn be used to aid clinicians in conceptualising the root of an observed deficit, and employed in an effort to derive and drive treatment (for example see: Burgess & Alderman, 1990; Alderman, 1996; Alderman, Fry, & Youngson, 1995).

In this area, the models proposed by Shallice (1982) and Baddeley (1986) are particularly relevant. Shallice (1982) argues that the pattern of functional deficits are essentially attributable to an impairment in attentional control mechanisms. Baddeley (1986) identified the supervisory system proposed by Shallice with the central executive component of his own model of working memory. Both models attempt to account for these problems in terms of a breakdown in the allocation of attentional controls which exercise important executive functions.

Many of the functional problems Rylander and others have described in the literature are believed to be secondary to the problems inflicted on the executive system by this breakdown in attentional control resulting in poor monitoring of one's own performance and of changes in the environment with consequent problems in obtaining and utilising feedback, and secondary memory problems (Alderman, 1996). As a result, individuals with the dysexecutive syndrome can present as impulsive, distractible, unresponsive to cues from others, and behave inappropriately in social situations.

Finally, the presence of a dysexecutive syndrome should be differentiated from any general blunting or impairment of cognitive functioning *per se*. In cases of generalised impairment, such as might follow severe, diffuse traumatic brain injury, problems of executive functioning will be observed alongside those in other functional domains, for example, memory. However, a specific diagnosis of dysexecutive syndrome will be especially indicated when the degree of executive impairment is disproportionate to any other cognitive problems. This is most striking when it is observed in individuals whose general level of cognitive functioning appears intact in highly structured, predictable environments, or in situations that are entirely routine to them. However, when placed in novel situations, the dissociation between their apparently preserved level of overall functioning and the observation of their chaotic response attributable to executive impairment, is significant (Shallice & Burgess, 1991).

ASSESSMENT OF THE DYSEXECUTIVE SYNDROME

A number of tools are available for the clinician to determine the presence of the dysexecutive syndrome, its principal characteristics, the functional problems they cause, and their severity. These comprise: the clinical interview; assessment through questionnaire administration; neuropsychological tests; and behavioural and functional assessment.

The clinical interview

A very real potential barrier to accurate assessment to determine the presence and severity of the dysexecutive syndrome is that imposed by the nature of the clinical interview itself. This form of assessment is, by process, very structured in nature. The trained clinician will usually take the interviewee through a series of questions; when responses are unclear, prompts will be given to aid elicitation of the information being sought. Under these conditions, the behaviour of the interviewee will not necessarily give the clinician the impression that any problems are evident. Indeed, the clinician could come away with the view that the person just assessed is quite unimpaired.

The use of open-ended questions, such as "... do you have any problems following your accident?" might not be helpful in assessing executive problems. After noting the response to such a question, the interviewer should then progress to ask much more specific questions. Particular emphasis should be placed on asking the interviewee how well he or she copes in novel situations, and to encourage the interviewee to compare this to his or her perception of behaviour and functioning in routine situations.

A difficulty for this approach, however, is that it is known that problems with reduced insight, especially after severe brain injury, are frequently present (Sazbon & Groswasser, 1991; Wood, 1988). When this is the case, acknowledgement of difficulties by the interviewee might not be forthcoming, and estimates of their severity, or impact on everyday functioning, can be underestimated. It is not uncommon for some individuals with a dysexecutive syndrome to deny a particular difficulty, but to go on to say that a close relative or friend does acknowledge its presence, and that the interviewer should talk to them about it.

In any case, it is absolutely essential that somebody who knows the individual well is also interviewed and asked for his or her observations concerning the interviewee, particularly with reference to how well the interviewee functions in novel situations. This information is particularly helpful if the person knew the interviewee prior to the event in which neurological damage was acquired. Comparison of the two sets of information will facilitate some general impression regarding preservation of insight. However, when this comparison is characterised by differing perceptions of ability, where the interviewee states there is little or nothing wrong, but where the person who knows him or her well indicates difficulties with all but the most routine of activities, the presence of a dysexecutive syndrome may well be suspected.

Questionnaire administration

Although useful qualitative information can be gleaned through a clinical interview, information regarding specific aspects of executive functioning, particularly when the interviewee lacks insight, can be difficult to obtain.

An additional method for assessing the presence of dysexecutive symptoms is to use a questionnaire. One of the most easily available is the Dysexecutive Questionnaire (DEX) originally reported by Burgess et al. (1996). The DEX is a 20-item questionnaire that prompts respondents to rate a variety of potential functional problems using a 5-point Likert scale. Each item takes the form of a brief statement. A higher rating indicates that the respondent perceives the problem described in any statement as being more frequent or severe. The items are based on the work of Stuss and Benson (1986) and sample four broad areas of change or difficulty attributable to the dysexecutive syndrome: emotional or personality changes; motivational changes; behavioural changes; and cognitive changes. Examples include "I act without thinking, doing the first thing that comes to mind" (measuring "impulsivity") and "I lose my temper at the slightest thing" (measuring "aggression"). The characteristics that each statement attempt to measure are functional problems impacting on everyday life: some of these might be driven by the specific difficulties in attentional controls that are central to a diagnosis of dysexecutive syndrome, which are presented in Table 29.1.

As well as the individual suspected of having a dysexecutive syndrome completing the DEX, at least one other person who knows the individual well should also complete it regarding the former. Where possible, it can be helpful to have a number of people who know the individual, for example several members of the multidisciplinary team involved in the rehabilitation of that person, rate the individual. The mean rating for each item can then be compared with that made by the individual.

Wilson et al. (1996) found that the ratings of their problems made by people with acquired neurological damage differed significantly from those made regarding them by others who knew them well. The mean rating made by a moderately sized group of neurologically damaged people was 27.21 (SD = 14.5),

whereas the carers' ratings of the patients' problems were somewhat higher at 32.85 (SD = 15.9) (see Burgess et al., 1998). These results suggest that, as a whole, the neurologically damaged group tended to underestimate the extent of their problems, suggesting that lack of insight into dysexecutive impairments is not unusual in the general neurological population.

The lesson from this study is that, in the assessment of the individual suspected of presenting with a dysexecutive syndrome, it would appear prudent to use the opinions of people who know that person well in estimating the overall level of functional impairment because of these difficulties with reduced insight.

Using the DEX, Burgess et al. (1998) have used the discrepancy between the patient's overall score and that of the sum of ratings made by the person as an indication of the person's degree of insight. It is equally important, however, to compare the responses to individual items in order to profile each symptom individually, since, as the following case shows, there can be considerable differences in degree of insight for different problems.

Lack of insight: Case BR. Data concerns BR, a 23-year-old male, who had sustained a severe traumatic brain injury as a result of a road traffic accident some 3 years earlier. Initial CT scan demonstrated generalised swelling, and a later one showed just the presence of bilateral contusions. Postinjury recovery was characterised by the presence of a severe dysexecutive syndrome.

On interview, BR's level of insight regarding the presence of any sustained problems arising as a result of his brain injury was poor. His general response to questioning was that he had "...no problems".

Unfortunately, in reality BR was no longer able to live independently. He had to disengage from the programme of higher education in which he had been participating prior to the accident. His behaviour and social judgement were particular problems and BR's parents could not manage him at home. Although attempts were made to engage him in rehabilitation in two specialist units previously, these had to be discontinued because of his abusive and aggressive behaviour. As a result, BR was admitted to the Kemsley Division of St Andrew's Hospital, Northampton—a unit that specialises in the rehabilitation of difficult-to-manage brain-damaged people.

As part of an assessment of his dysexecutive syndrome, which was thought to drive many of the problems that led to his exclusion from other rehabilitation units, BR completed the DEX. In addition, two members of the multidisciplinary team working with him also made ratings about BR using the DEX: the mean rating for each item was consequently used for comparison purposes.

Whereas the sum of ratings made by BR regarding himself totalled 26/80 (where a higher figure indicates greater problems), those made by staff working closely with him was double this figure, at 53/80. This comparison suggested BR's overall level of insight into the difficulties caused by his dysexecutive syndrome was poor.

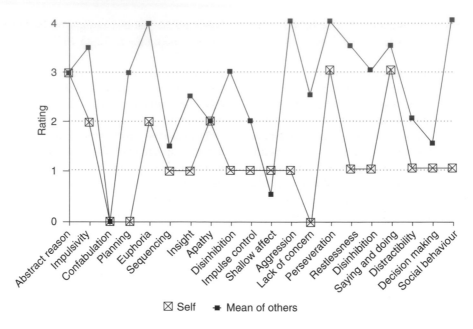

Figure 29.1. Comparison of DEX ratings made by BR with the mean ratings made by two members of staff.

Figure 29.1 compares the ratings for each of the 20 individual items. It is clear that BR was underestimating his level of impairment regarding each of the difficulties described. Particularly striking was his perception of his temper control. In response to the statement "I lose my temper at the slightest thing", BR rated himself at 1 on the 5-point scale ("occasionally a problem"). In comparison, both staff gave him the top rating for this item ("very often a problem").

The validity of this discrepancy between staff and BR is confirmed in Fig. 29.2, which presents the results of a 5-hour time-sample of his behaviour during the first few weeks of admission (see Wood, 1987, for an overview of time-sampling methodology).

The observations were collected by dividing half the time available to include formal rehabilitation sessions where the degree of overt structure in the environment is high, the remainder at other times when structure, although present, is reduced. Observations are collected routinely in this way to determine what effect, if any, the increased level of expectations present during formal rehabilitation sessions has on behaviour.

It can clearly be seen in Fig. 29.2 that the behavioural manifestations of BR's dysexecutive syndrome were evident by the high frequency of blunted social behaviour, especially that of his verbal abuse.

Use of the DEX in this way will not only facilitate specific assessment regarding insight, and the range and severity of problems arising from the dysexecutive syndrome, but will also help in formulating goals for treatment.

Neuropsychological tests

Administration of neuropsychological tests can also be useful in arriving at a diagnosis of the dysexecutive syndrome and in

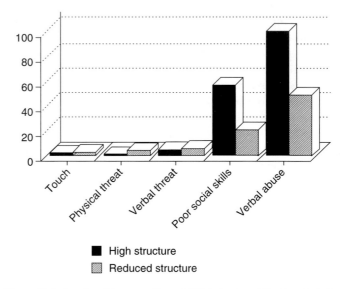

Figure 29.2. Results of time-sampling of BR's behaviour following admission to hospital. Data represents cumulative recordings collected during 30 minute observation periods. Half of the total observations were made during formal rehabilitation sessions (high structure), the remainder at other times (reduced structure).

measuring its severity. These can be especially useful, as it is not uncommon in the clinical situation for someone who knows the person well to be unavailable, or biased in his or her reporting. The objectivity of a family member can also be questioned when the assessment is being carried out for medicolegal purposes. Tests, on the other hand, should be standardised, validated, and reliable. When this is the case, and they are administered by a clinician who is qualified to use them, the objectivity of the results generated is more robust.

Impaired performance relative to neurologically healthy control subjects on specific tests has been claimed to demonstrate difficulties secondary to frontal lobe damage.

Unfortunately, as we have already noted, results of neuropsychological testing might not always reflect well the types of functional difficulties people with acquired brain injury can show. People with dysexecutive problems can show gross impairment in the ability of an individual to perform everyday tasks, other than those that are very routine (e.g. Penfield & Evans, 1935). However, despite these marked impairments in everyday life, performance on traditional neuropsychological tests might suggest that only very minor cognitive changes have occurred. For example, Eslinger and Damasio (1985) reported a now well-known case in which there was a considerable dissociation between intact performance on neuropsychological tests, including those reported to be sensitive to frontal lobe damage, and great difficulties in organising and executing simple everyday tasks (see also cases reported by Duncan et al., 1995; Goldstein et al., 1993).

Shallice and Burgess (1991) have argued that there are three reasons for these discrepancies, which all involve differences between the demands of frontal tests and those found in everyday life. First, in existing frontal lobe tests there is typically only one explicit problem that needs to be undertaken at any one time. Second, the tests, or trials within them, tend to be very short in duration. Finally, there is usually a continual flow of interaction between the examiner and the subject: this strongly facilitates task initiation and clearly stresses to the individual being tested whether he or she is succeeding or not. Shallice and Burgess (1991) suggest that many real-life situations do not share these features, and so the formal tests are not measuring well the cognitive processes that are damaged in these people.

In particular, in the formal testing situation individuals are not required to organise or plan behaviour over lengthy periods, or to set priorities when faced with competing tasks. Nor are they often required to activate an intention after a delay (known as "prospective memory"). This failure of many traditional tests to capture executive skills that clearly feature as major components in everyday functional tasks can thus account for the discrepancy that can sometimes be seen between task performance and capability in everyday life.

Consequently, Shallice and Burgess devised two new assessment procedures whose purpose was to quantify deficits in executive functioning in the assessment situation that paralleled the difficulties such deficits caused individuals in everyday situations: those involving solving competing goals over longer periods of time, and with minimum interaction with the examiner.

One of these tasks, the Multiple Errands Test, required the subject to perform a number of "real life" tasks, without breaking certain rules and constraints, within a shopping centre. The other procedure, the Six Elements Test, aimed to make similar demands on high-level executive skills, but was administered within the confines of a standard hospital office.

The validity of both these procedures was demonstrated with three neurologically impaired subjects. All of these had current WAIS Full Scale IQs within the "superior" range, and all performed normally, or near normally, on a wide range of cognitive tests, including those believed to be sensitive to the effects of frontal lobe damage. However, their unremarkable performance on these latter measures was not paralleled in everyday life, where they had great difficulty in mastering complex non-routine tasks. However, their performance on both the Multiple Errands Test and the Six Elements Test was impaired in comparison to neurologically healthy controls, which was argued to be evidence that many traditional tests of executive function were structured in such a way that they did not tap many cognitive processes that are important in everyday life, such as goal-setting and prospective memory (i.e. remembering to do something at a future time).

More recently, Wilson et al. (1996) have published a test battery called the BADS (Behavioural Assessment of the Dysexecutive Syndrome). This builds directly on the work of Shallice and Burgess. However, it was designed to be used with subjects of average to below average ability, and a battery approach was used to enable the rich nature of executive problems to be better captured.

This battery consists of six subtests. As far as possible, they were designed to emphasise the points made by Shallice and Burgess regarding test design so that they would reflect difficulties with executive functioning. Each subtest is scored from 0 to 4, and these are summed to give a battery score out of 24.

Performance norms were collected by administering the BADS to 78 subjects who presented with a variety of neurologically acquired disorders, and 216 healthy control subjects. A table that categorises performance on the test from "impaired" to "superior" is provided, based on the performance of the control group.

The test discriminates reliably between those subjects with and those without neurological damage. For example, whereas only 5% of control subjects achieved a profile score of 12/24 or less, 36% of the neurologically damaged people tested obtained scores within this range.

However, the more important aspect of the test is how scores on the BADS relate to problems in everyday life. As part of the validation of the test battery, Wilson et al. (see Wilson et al., 1997a) investigated the correlations between relatives' (or carers') ratings of patients' problems in everyday life using the DEX (described above), and their performance on the BADS. They found high correlations between the two measures, suggesting that poor performance on the BADS is associated with everyday dysexecutive problems. Furthermore, when entered into a multiple regression analysis alongside results from other traditional tests of executive function, estimates of intellectual functioning, and age, the BADS proved to be the best predictor of others' ratings on the DEX.

Behavioural and functional assessment

The nature of the dysexecutive syndrome is such that the difficulties experienced by the person presenting with it are best seen outside very tightly constrained situations (i.e. where there are many possible responses or behaviour that one might use, and where the most optimal response or strategy is not obvious). Ideally, the person being assessed should be tested outside the artificial environment of the hospital or examination room, within a naturalistic setting in which the impact of the executive problems on everyday functioning can be observed. Typically, this approach involves placing individuals into controlled situations in which specific variables are manipulated and responses noted. Hypotheses regarding the reasons for behaviour are then formulated and tested, with the aim of "... identification and measurement of meaningful response units and their controlling variables (both environmental and organismic) for the purposes of understanding and altering human behaviour" (Nelson & Hayes, 1981, p. 3). Hart and Jacobs (1993) note that functional assessment procedures "... are generally not standardised or normed to populations" but emphasise that they could have an intimate relationship with neuropsychological tests.

However, as functional difficulties attributable to the dysexecutive syndrome are sometimes most noticeable in the context of everyday environments and situations, and not in the somewhat artificial conditions of a formal neuropsychological examination, there might be potential advantages in using such an approach. Indeed, a number of practitioners have advocated that the area of behavioural assessment is of special relevance given the difficulties imposed by neurological damage on other forms of appraisal (see, for example, Davis, Turner, Rolider, & Cartwright, 1994; Treadwell & Page, 1996; von Cramon & von Cramon, 1994; Wood, 1987).

The Multiple Errands Test (MET, see above) described by Shallice and Burgess (1991) would perhaps meet the requirements for such a task. It will be recalled that the MET required the subject to perform a number of "real life" tasks, without breaking a set of rules, within a shopping area. Although the individual tasks themselves were simple (e.g. "buy a loaf of bread"), the rules served to increase the planning, monitoring, and prospective memory demand of the task, thereby highlighting any difficulties the patients might have in these areas of cognition. Specifically, the achievement of multiple and competing subgoals was required; the test was longer in duration than existing psychometric tests; and there was minimal interaction between the examiner and the subject. A small group of nine neurologically healthy control subjects were tested for comparison purposes and a scoring system was devised and errors calculated as constituting task failures, rule breaks, interpretation failures, and inefficiencies. Performance of each of the three neurologically damaged subjects was impaired relative to that of the normal controls, despite the former's normal, or near normal, performance on existing cognitive tests (the BADS had not been developed at this time).

The Shallice and Burgess version of the MET was developed for people of very high intellectual capacity. Alderman et al. (in press) have developed a version of the MET to use with subjects of average or less ability (as determined by performance on tests

of general intellectual functioning). The potential advantages of a formalised functional assessment of this type are numerous:

(1) Participation in the MET affords the clinician direct observation of executive functioning in the context of an actual everyday task.
(2) Taking the testing environment out of the potentially artificial context of the office and into a "real life" context can elicit behaviours from the subject that would not otherwise be seen.
(3) The shopping centre constitutes a naturalistic environment complete with the type of real distractions that occur naturally.
(4) Some subjects find formal assessment situations somewhat intimidating: by contrast, the nature of the tasks undertaken in the MET make sense to most people, making testing more acceptable and tolerable.
(5) As the examiner follows the subject at a discreet distance, there is less overt dependence on them.
(6) The procedure allows the clinician opportunities to observe any compensatory strategies used by the subject. As the test is conducted within a naturalistic environment, real events occur that have to be dealt with by the subject he or she is to succeed with the goals they are pursuing. For example, how does the subject respond when another checkout in the supermarket is opened? Does he or she join that shorter queue or stay in the original one?
(7) The test gives the opportunity to observe social and other functional skills. Although a subject might behave appropriately in the formal situation of the office, this might not be the case in other environments. For example, does the individual wait patiently for a shop assistant to finish speaking with a customer before requesting directions to the library? Alderman and colleagues have noted a significant difference with some of their patients between social behaviour observed during formal testing, and that at the shopping centre. It is for this reason that a separate category of errors has been added to those previously made by Shallice and Burgess, that of "social rule breaks" (Shallice and Burgess did not distinguish between task rule breaks and social ones).

At the time of writing this chapter the study subsequently reported by Alderman et al. (in press) was ongoing, over 30 neurologically damaged subjects had been assessed using this simplified version of the MET (in the completed study, 46 subjects with acquired neurological damage and 50 healthy controls had been tested). The procedure has been generally well accepted by these people, many of whom acknowledge that it has relevance to the types of everyday problem they experience. Analysis of data showed that performance on this test correlates well with the BADS.

Equally as instructive, however, was the assessment of neurologically healthy controls on this test. Analysis of data raised some interesting points. For example, gender and measures of general intelligence are not good predictors of the number of

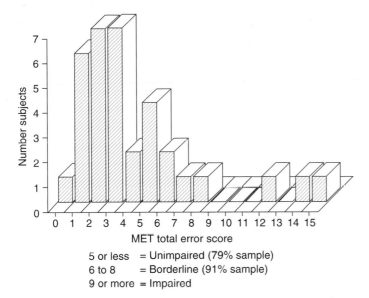

5 or less   = Unimpaired (79% sample)
6 to 8   = Borderline (91% sample)
9 or more   = Impaired

Figure 29.3. Distribution of error scores made by neurologically healthy control subjects on a simplified version of the Multiple Errands Test ($n = 34$).

errors made. Interestingly, familiarity with the shopping centre is also not associated with performance. In fact, other than age, the only variable that is a good predictor of performance is the number of times the control subjects ask for help: more requests for help are generally associated with a higher error score. The range of errors made by healthy controls is also wide: the distribution of errors made by the first 34 control subjects tested at the time this chapter was written is shown in Fig. 29.3. The variability in performance observed amongst controls has been confirmed within the larger group subsequently reported by Alderman et al. (in press).

It can be seen that whereas approximately 80% of normal control subjects make 5 errors or less, a significant minority achieved very poor scores, the highest being 15, despite "average" IQ! This serves to remind us that our understanding of test procedures designed specifically to examine high level executive disorders are still in their infancy: this pattern of scores (i.e. long "tails" in the distribution of performance) is not uncommon for tests of executive function. The reasons for this are not fully understood as yet, but one important factor is probably related to the nature of many executive tasks: often they do not consist of a number of discrete trials where failure on one trial has little or no consequence for performance on the next. Instead, a crucial component of many executive tasks is that failure at one stage has consequences for performance at a later stage (e.g. in the MET task, if one does not carefully study the task rules at the beginning, and form a reasonable initial plan of action, one is likely to run into trouble at a future time—say, by running out of money). These failures will tend to "snowball", possibly creating a rather elongated distribution of performance (see Burgess (1997) for a full discussion of possible explanations). In practice, this means that there will often be a few individuals in the "normal" population who are markedly poorer than their peers if traditional percentile marking systems are considered alone.

It is also becoming increasingly clear that, within neurologically healthy individuals, measures of general intellectual ability do not necessarily equate closely with the level of executive functioning (see Burgess (1997) for further discussion of these points).

Assessment using neuropsychological tests

As outlined previously, the dysexecutive impairments in everyday life need not co-occur. Similarly, impairments on formal tests of executive function can vary: failure on one test should not necessarily be taken as suggesting that another test will be failed. Recent evidence from functional imaging studies (e.g. Bench et al., 1993) is confirming what was suspected from lesion studies: that the frontal lobes do not work as one single "central executive". Thus different lesion sites within the frontal lobes will have differing correlates in impairment profile.

These findings have implications for the strategy of formal neuropsychological assessment one could adopt. If one wishes to use a set of measures that are reasonably "pure" in the functions they assess, one should probably give many of them. Alternatively, one might give fewer tests that putatively measure more than one function. There are dangers with both approaches. With the first one might not give the particular test that taps the impaired function. The second approach has a different danger: this is that if the test measures, say, four or five different executive processes and only one of them is impaired, the degree of deficit demonstrated on the test will be small. Both approaches are conservative for detecting patients' problems: while a clear impairment on a test is quite instructive, relatively little can be concluded from the lack of such finding (unless, perhaps, the assessment was very substantial), which should be borne in mind by clinicians who are asked to assess the presence of dysexecutive problems.

A further problem for the neuropsychologist is that the extent and nature of the fractionation of the executive (frontal lobe) processes is not known. Nor are the exact demands of many executive tasks well understood, with recent evidence suggesting that many tasks are not failed for the reasons previously supposed (Delis et al., 1992; Della Malva et al., 1993; Goel & Grafman, 1995; Karnath, Wallesch, & Zimmerman, 1991).

Some guidance is perhaps given, however, by recent findings of Burgess et al. (1998). A factor analysis of the DEX questionnaire revealed five factors, the first three of which related to cognitive aspects of the dysexecutive syndrome (inhibition, intentionality, and executive memory) with the second two relating to the personality and emotional aspects (positive and negative affect). It was found that performance on a range of traditional neuropsychological tests of executive function (e.g. verbal fluency, cognitive estimates, trail-making, Six Element Test) correlated significantly with the factor scores for factor one ("inhibition") in a group of 92 mixed aetiology (mainly head injury) patients. Thus it would seem that whatever leads to the behavioural manifestations of disinhibition in everyday life also disrupts performance on many formal executive tests.

For factor two, however ("intentionality"—which covered deficits in planning and maintaining an intention) the executive test performance correlates were much more specific: only performance on the Six Element Test was significantly correlated with these factor scores. Furthermore, for factor three ("executive memory"—which included problems such as confabulation) only the performances on the modified Wisconsin Card Sorting Test (WCST) and verbal fluency were related to this factor. These results seem to indicate that different executive tasks reflect different competencies in everyday life: Someone who is poor at, say, the WCST might not present with the same problems in everyday life as someone who fails (for instance) the Six Element Test (SET). Furthermore, they would seem to indicate that some tests can be failed for more than one reason.

This contention is given more direct support by two recent studies carried out by Burgess and Shallice (1996a,b). The primary purpose of the first study was to examine the relationship between deficits in initiation and response suppression in patients with frontal lobe lesions using the Hayling Sentence Completion Test (Burgess & Shallice, 1996b, 1997). In the first part of this test ("initiation") the participant is presented with a series of sentences that have the last word omitted, and is asked to provide a word that completes the sentence. In each case, what this last word might be is strongly used by the sentence frame. In the second part of the test ("response suppression" condition) the patient is required to produce a word that *does not* fit at the end of the sentence. A response that reasonably completed the sentence received an error score of 3, a word semantically related to a word in the sentence received an error score of 1, and an unrelated word a score of 0.

Patients who satisfied a number of criteria, including having a lesion (predominantly primary tumours) involving no more than two lobes, were tested. Patients whose lesions involved the frontal lobes (anterior group) and those with purely posterior lesions were closely matched for age, NART IQ and WAIS FSIQ, and a matched control group ($n = 20$) was also tested.

There were two main findings. First, the anterior group showed significantly longer response latencies on straightforward completion than either the controls ($p < .002$) or the posterior group ($p < .05$), although the posteriors did not differ significantly from the controls. The second finding was that in the second part of the test ("response suppression"), patients with anterior lesions had a much higher average error score than either the posterior group or the controls. In other words, the anterior group found it much more difficult not to produce the triggered response than did the other groups.

However, although the anterior group as a whole showed both initiation and response suppression deficits, these did not necessarily co-occur in any one patient and the overall correlation between the sections of the test was .19, which is not significantly different from zero.

From the point of view of the present argument, however, an interesting observation was made about the way in which the participants performed the Hayling Test. It was noted that they often used a strategy to generate anomalous words. For

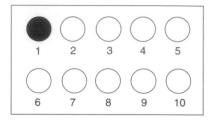

Figure 29.4. Brixton Test Stimulus—position one (Burgess & Shallice, 1997).

instance, the most common was to look around the testing room and name objects within view. Examination of the patients' responses showed that the anterior group showed less evidence of having used such a strategy. Moreover strategy use and sentence completion (e.g. task failure) were highly, and inversely, related. It was argued that in this task response suppression and strategy use stand in a mutual causal relationship: a patient will require some response suppression abilities in order to utilise a strategy. However, inability to formulate a strategy will result in a greater load upon response suppression abilities. In this way it seems possible that deficits on the Hayling Test may occur for more than one reason.

A further study (Burgess & Shallice, 1996a) suggests that these kinds of complex dynamics are not uncommon in tests of executive function (indeed, Burgess (1997) argues that they could be characteristic of them). This study used a task called the Brixton Test, which was administered to a group of patients with similar characteristics to the study just described. This test (see Burgess & Shallice, 1997) consists of a series of plates similar to those shown in Fig. 29.4. On each plate, one of the 10 positions is filled, but the position of the filled circle changes with each trial. The changes in position are governed by a series of simple rules (e.g. +1 or −1), which change without warning, and the participant is given the task of predicting the filled position on each subsequent trial. Thus, if the filled position has previously followed the sequence 1, 2, 3, the participant is required to say that the filled circle on the next plate will be at position 4 (+1 rule).

In accordance with previous findings (Cicerone, Lazar, & Shapiro, 1983; Milner, 1963; Nelson, 1976), the patients with frontal lobe lesions (anteriors) were significantly poorer at set attainment (e.g. performance on the test overall) than the posterior group or the controls. However, when the nature of the anterior group's responses was analysed, they did not show a tendency to perseverate—the traditional explanation of frontal patients' failures on set attainment tasks—instead, they showed an abnormally high incidence of bizarre responses (i.e. answers for which no apparent rationale could be discovered, and which normal individuals did not make). They also showed an exaggerated tendency to abandon a correct rule once it has been obtained. Thus again, results from close examination of patients' performance reveal more than one possible failure type.

To summarise, one might say that while there are now a number of formal executive tasks of which failure has fairly consistently been associated with frontal lobe dysfunction, the implications of such findings for behaviour in the real world are less well understood, although the early evidence is encouraging.

Abandoning the concept of a unitary "frontal lobe" central executive, together with evidence of multiple causes of failure on executive tasks, leaves the practising neuropsychologist in a difficult position as regards choice of assessment tool. Until further evidence is available, it would seem sensible to administer as wide a range of tasks as is reasonable (in addition to, of course, choosing the most psychometrically sound) and to be cautious in one's conclusions—particularly when no deficit is detected. It is obvious good practice to not rely solely upon psychometric data in one's assessment, just as the entire absence of formal testing would in most cases (and with no good reason) be unwise.

REHABILITATION OF THE DYSEXECUTIVE SYNDROME

Specific approaches concerned with rehabilition of the dysexecutive syndrome, or the executive functions, have been reported in the literature for over a decade. However, as the functional problems driven by this are multidimensional, there is no single approach regarding rehabilitation. Interventions reported in the literature are influenced by a number of variables. Some are clearly driven by cognitive models of executive functioning (see, for example, Burgess & Alderman, 1990; Sohlberg, Mateer, & Stuss, 1993). Others attempt to alleviate problems through circumventing underlying executive impairment, often by training people to use external aids that act as cueing systems (see, for example, Burke, Zencius, Wesolowski, & Doubleday, 1991; Zec, Parks, Gambach, & Vicari, 1992). Further approaches adopt a process-oriented approach to rehabilitation in which the goal is to stimulate recovery of cognitive functioning and promote reorganisation of cortical function (see Sohlberg, Mateer, & Stuss (1993) for a review of this work).

As the functional problems driven by the dysexecutive syndrome are multidimensional, interventions will be differentiated from each other in terms of what deficit or problem they are attempting to change. For example, Stuss and Benson (1986) describe these functional problems in terms of difficulties with anticipation, goal selection, planning, organisation, initiation, execution, and self-regulation of goal directed activity. Accordingly, interventions can be designed to modify one or a subset of these problems. Alternatively, problems highlighted through use of the DEX (Wilson et al., 1996) can form the basis of an intervention. It will be recalled from earlier that Burgess and his colleagues found that the DEX, and therefore the dysexecutive syndrome, fractionates into a number of distinct factors (inhibition, intentionality, executive memory, positive and negative affect). Conceptualising difficulties attributable to impaired executive functioning in this way could lead to a different categorisation of interventions than those offered to date (Burgess et al., 1998).

The therapeutic milieu approach

One distinction apparent in the literature is the categorisation of treatment techniques as either being concerned with attempting to manage specific components of executive functioning, for example, remediation of planning deficits, and those that attempt to rehabilitate these functions as a whole through involvement in a therapeutic milieu. Von Cramon and Matthes-von Cramon (1994) point out that most people with dysexecutive syndrome present with both cognitive and behavioural difficulties that are best treated through "holistic" rehabilitation that incorporates cognitive retraining and psychotherapeutic techniques. Successful outcomes have been reported in response to such multidimensional programmes, most notably from within North America (Ben-Yishay & Diller, 1978, 1983; Ben-Yishay, Rattock, & Lakin, 1985; Prigitano, 1986; Scherzer, 1986).

Unfortunately, there appear to be a number of limiting variables that place some restrictions on who is able, and who is not able, to participate in such programmes.

One of these limiting variables is the length of time required for treatment. Von Cramon and Matthes-von Cramon (1994) claim that most holistic rehabilitation programmes require the individual to participate for up to 2 years. However, these authors designed a problem-solving programme of 6 weeks duration, and reported good outcome (von Cramon & Matthes-von Cramon, 1992).

Regardless of the duration of the programme, the characteristics required of the participants in order that they can benefit from treatment appear to be particularly demanding and therefore self-selecting. For example, to be eligible to participate in the programme reported by von Cramon and Matthes-von Cramon (1992), individuals must be able to concentrate for at least 20 minutes, have insight into the nature of their problems, be motivated and free from significant behavioural problems that would inhibit group therapy, be able to think in abstract terms, have no significant memory impairment, no visuoperceptual deficits or major language disorders. Unfortunately, it is hard to imagine that such criteria will not exclude a significant proportion of potential participants.

Modification of the environment

For people whose cognitive and/or behavioural disabilities deny them access to the therapeutic milieu approach, it would appear that, at present, participation in programmes that are very focused in their objectives constitutes the major rehabilitation route.

Some of these attempt to alleviate problems caused by the dysexecutive syndrome by circumventing the executive system, or by providing external aids for individuals to use to subsume the function that has become impaired. Some of these strategies can be particularly effective for individuals whose executive dysfunction is very impaired, and for whom the ability to initiate routine behaviour has been lost. For example, Sohlberg, Mateer, and Stuss (1993) describe how modification of the environment can be used to help in this respect by employing visual prompts (such as labels) and verbal prompts (including audiotaped "action messages"). Modification of the environment can also include the use of trained facilitators, who can direct the action of the individual and act as a kind of "substitute frontal lobe". In this respect, education of carers is paramount. Such provision can also be usefully employed with people who are participating in programmes that aim to return them to some form of useful, productive employment, via a "job coach", where problems with executive functioning are acknowledged to play a significant role in determining outcome (for example, see Brantner, 1992).

Behavioural retraining of specific action sequences

Attempts to reteach previously automatic behaviour that has become lost have also been reported, and are best pursued using a behaviour modification approach (for example, see Fussey & Giles, 1988; Wood, 1987). First, a task analysis is undertaken regarding the behaviour to be retrained: this might most frequently concern activities of daily living, including personal hygiene skills. Following this, the behaviour is broken down into a discrete number of steps, or task-parts. The individual is subsequently requested to engage in the behaviour (for example, to wash and dress). When no action is forthcoming, or when the sequence of the task-parts is deviated from, staff intervene and prompt the individual to engage in the appropriate behaviour. The number of "independents" (task-parts carried out without the necessity of staff intervention) and prompts given are recorded. Training sessions should take place frequently and regularly to facilitate learning; in the case of hygiene skills this would be daily. When behavioural problems coexist it will be necessary to introduce additional strategies to manage these (for example, see Alderman & Knight, 1997). Successful learning will be indicated by a reduction in the number of prompts and an increase in task-parts carried out independently with the passage of time. With regular repetition, these behaviours become overlearned, habitual, and automatic. The ideal conclusion to such training would be that the individual would simply need one prompt to get washed and dressed to initiate a routine that was once again automatic.

Use of external aids to initiate action sequences

In the case of people for whom the basic units of behaviour are reasonably intact, higher level executive impairment can be the chief problem. When this is the case, ongoing behaviour might not be modified appropriately in response to changing conditions, or it could be poorly sequenced, or triggered at inappropriate times or places (Sohlberg, Mateer, & Stuss, 1993).

When this is the case, external cueing systems can be used with great effect to facilitate appropriate initiation and sequencing of automatic behaviours. A good example of this approach has been reported by Burke, Zencius, Wesolowski, and Doubleday (1991) in which improvement to three executive functions was reported, and illustrated through presentation of six individual case studies. The executive functions were: problem-solving (the ability to develop plans and modify them when appropriate); self-initiation (the ability to carry out plans); and self-monitoring/self-regulation (increased ability to monitor

and regulate goal-directed performance). Immediate improvement was brought about through the use of an external aid, in the form of an initiation checklist or through use of a notebook; additional improvement was evident when a facilitator gave regular feedback about behaviour, and when a problem-solving component was introduced following use of the external aids. Data concerning all six case studies reflected significant improvement to those areas of function targeted for treatment. Follow-up data collected following withdrawal of the treatment interventions indicated continued longevity of the gains made.

Other examples of the use of external aids to facilitate initiation of behaviour at appropriate times, with good outcomes, are similarly reported in the literature. For example, Zec, Parks, Gambach, and Vicari (1992) described the use of their "Executive Board System", the heart of which consists of "Job Cards". These break a task into two principal components: command analysis and reinforcement analysis. The information on a card acts to cue and reinforce behaviour, by organising and advertising the discrete tasks that require completion, the steps required, and the consequences of task completion. Furthermore, the method works in such a way to constitute a self-help system.

Another example of this approach has been reported by Sohlberg and Mateer (1989). These authors described a three-phase behavioural approach regarding training in the use of a notebook to improve executive and memory problems. The first phase concerned itself with educating the user about how the system works. Practice in the use of the notebook as an aid to help plan and execute tasks was carried out in the second stage, and generalisation of the system was considered in the third.

Recently, the use of a radio-paging system developed primarily for use with memory impaired people, NeuroPage (Hersh & Treadgold, 1994), has been explored in relation to treatment of dysexecutive impairment. NeuroPage consists of a simple pager, with a screen, which is attached to the belt of the user. It is used in conjunction with a microcomputer system that is linked via a modem to a commercial paging company. Reminders are entered into the microcomputer, and from there sent out to the paging company for transmission on the designated date and time.

Wilson, Evans, Emslie, and Malinek (1997) reported the effectiveness of NeuroPage in a study that involved 15 neurologically damaged people. All had memory problems and some had additional impairment of executive functions. All the subjects benefited from the use of NeuroPage. Before the trial, only 37.05% of tasks requiring action were completed independently across the subject group. Whilst using NeuroPage, this dramatically improved to 84.46%. During the 3-week period immediately following withdrawal of the system, the average number of tasks completed independently across the subject group decreased only marginally, to 74.46%. However, the authors noted that there was considerable variability between subjects regarding sustained improvement in this stage of the trial. For example, some people's performance did not deteriorate at all, whereas others plummeted to baseline levels. The authors argued that particular impairment of executive function was responsible for lack of longevity in these cases. This hypothesis was explored in detail in a case subsequently presented where memory impairment was itself secondary to the presence of a dysexecutive syndrome: use of NeuroPage was again demonstrated to alleviate the problems caused by this (Evans, Emslie, & Wilson, 1998).

Two important advantages of the NeuroPage system are its simplicity and low running costs.

Changing action in response to changes in the environment

"Metacognitive" strategies

Despite their efficacy, the use of external aids (perhaps with the exception of other people acting as facilitators) remains vulnerable to abrupt, unforeseen changes occurring within the environment. Under these conditions, the classic dysexecutive characteristic of failure to modify ongoing action in response to changing circumstances can become evident.

One method to remediate this difficulty can be found through the use of so-called "metacognitive" strategies (Sohlberg, Mateer, & Stuss, 1993). Treatment techniques falling within this category are based around some methods routinely used in cognitive therapy, particularly self-instructional strategies (for examples of this, see Cicerone & Giacino, 1992; Cicerone & Wood, 1987; Sohlberg, Sprunk, & Metzelaar, 1988; von Cramon & Matthes-von Cramon, 1990). For the more impaired patient who lacks the necessary cognitive skills to engage successfully in such training, changing cognitive structures that interact with perception of the environment to guide behaviour can be achieved using combinations of more overt behaviour modification methods (Alderman & Ward, 1991).

Attentional retraining

For the individual who has retained or relearned the basic units of behaviour that together constitute some functional skill, but for whom the ability to initiate or change action in response to fluctuating circumstances is impaired, a further set of interventions can be considered.

It will be recalled from the earlier section of this chapter concerned with definition, that deficits in attentional processes were hypothesised to drive many of the functional problems that characterise the dysexecutive syndrome. In particular, impairment in the central executive component of working memory can lead to inefficiency in the allocation of attentional resources (Baddeley, 1986; Baddeley & Wilson, 1988). Difficulties with attending to two or more sets of stimuli simultaneously can be evident functionally through problems with monitoring one's own performance or changes in the environment. These will result in problems in obtaining and utilising feedback. It is this reduced perception of feedback that has been hypothesised to result in failure to modify behaviour in response to changing circumstances (Alderman, 1996; Alderman, Fry, & Youngson, 1995).

It would therefore seem reasonable to conclude that such individuals might benefit through undertaking appropriate attentional retraining, under the assumption that such training would enhance monitoring skills, or to target monitoring skills directly.

Indeed, specific components of the training programmes described in the literature, including some of those described above, make specific provision for improving attentional skills or self-monitoring ability (for example, see Burke, Zencius, Wesolowski, & Doubleday, 1991; Freeman, Mittenberg, Dicowden, & Bat-Ami, 1992; Lawson & Rice, 1989; Sohlberg, Matter, & Stuss, 1993; Sohlberg, Sprunk, & Metelaar, 1988; von Cramon & Matthes von-Cramon, 1994; Zec, Parks, Gambach, & Vicari, 1992).

The distinction between attentional retraining and improving self-monitoring skills might simply reflect the context in which the therapeutic activity takes place, as the aim with both is ultimately to improve the efficacy of the central executive component of working memory. Attentional retraining is typically undertaken using computer-mediated exercises, with the assumption that improvements evident on these tasks will generalise to other contexts; attempts to improve self-monitoring are usually made directly in the functional situation itself.

One difficulty in assessing the validity of the first approach, that of attentional retraining, is that investigations have reported mixed success. However, Gray, Robertson, Pentland, and Anderson (1992) have attributed this inconsistency to some previous investigators conceptualising attention as a unitary phenomena. Instead, these authors highlight its multidimensional nature, including a component that deals with control and resource allocation. They argue that functional problems arise when attentional resources are not allocated appropriately in complex situations, leading in particular to distractibility and difficulties in dealing with multiple tasks: this is attributed to Baddeley's (1986) concept of a central executive component of working memory. Methodological problems are also highlighted in accounting for interstudy variability regarding efficacy of such training.

Consequently, Gray, Robertson, Pentland, and Anderson (1992) describe a programme in which microcomputer-delivered attentional training tasks were used with a group of seventeen brain-injured people. These tasks were selected as they made demands on a number of attentional processes, including increased alerting, manipulating material in working memory, alternating attention, and dividing attention. Training took place over 14 sessions of 75 minutes each, over 3 to 9 weeks. A matched control group of 14 brain-injured people was also exposed to a range of recreational computing activities over a comparable time period. A range of psychometric tests were administered before and after training to both groups. The group that received the attentional retraining achieved significantly better scores on measures relating to auditory verbal working memory at follow-up. This was not attributable to factors such as IQ, motivation, general stimulation, or spontaneous recovery, with most improvement evident on tests involving storage and manipulation of numerical material in working memory. Furthermore, improvement continued after training stopped.

The authors argue that this was attributable to the attentional strategies acquired during training becoming increasingly automated and integrated into a wider range of behaviours, and that the improvements made represented real-life gains reflecting improvement in working memory.

Improving self-monitoring skills

As indicated earlier, an alternative approach is to attempt to influence attentional skills through improving the ability to self-monitor directly in the functional situation itself. Hartmann, Pickering, and Wilson (1992) demonstrated that people who had sustained traumatic brain injury are likely to experience particular difficulty in dividing attention in order to attend appropriately to two competing stimulus sets. In contrast, normal controls were able to complete a target task as efficiently when this was administered alone, or in conjunction with a second task. The difficulty exhibited by the brain-injured group was attributed to impairment of the central executive component of working memory.

Alderman (1996) argued that individuals with a severe dysexecutive disorder are likely to experience profound difficulty allocating attentional resources to monitor multiple events, to the extent that only one stimulus set at a time can be routinely attended to. When this is the case, individuals will experience difficulties in monitoring changes in the environment, their own behaviour, and internal (physiological) changes. This could be one reason why a characteristic feature of the dysexecutive syndrome is a reduced ability to change behaviour in an adaptive, flexible way, in response to changes in the environment. For example, if a person's attention is solely directed to what he or she is saying, that person will not be able to routinely and simultaneously monitor the response of the individual to whom it is directed. The non-verbal and other cues the latter generate will not be available in the form of feedback, which is normally used to assess the appropriateness of the content of speech. Typically, people are able to simultaneously attend to both their own behaviour and the response of the environment to it: under normal circumstances, perception of positive feedback will lead to a continuation of that behaviour, whereas negative feedback will result in modification of action. This could be one reason why some people who have sustained brain injury tend to "talk over" others and dominate conversation.

Alderman (1996) and Alderman, Fry, and Youngson (1995) argued that this difficulty in attending to more than one stimulus set accounted for some of the poor response to operant approaches shown by people participating in rehabilitation that targets inappropriate behaviour. Indeed, this difficulty both drives the behavioural problem and prevents relearning of appropriate internal controls. As a result, Alderman, Fry, and Youngson (1995) described a programme of self-monitoring training (SMT), which may be appropriate in such cases.

SMT has two specific aims: first, to improve the ability of the individual to attend to multiple events; and second, once this has been established, to reduce the behaviour of concern using an appropriate operant strategy. The latter will be effective only when the ability to attend to multiple events, and in particular, to monitor one's own behaviour and modify it in response to change in the environment, is possible.

These two aims are achieved through participation in the five stages of training involved in SMT. These are briefly as follows:

Stage one—baseline. The therapist first obtains a baseline of the target behaviour.

Stage two—spontaneous self-monitoring. The subject is instructed to monitor the target behaviour whilst conducting some background task over a discrete time period. The subject is given some sort of external counting device to enable him or her to achieve this (for example, a mechanical "clicker", whereby each time a button is pressed, a number display is advanced by one digit). At the same time, the therapist discretely monitors the behaviour using a similar device. At the end of the trial, the therapist compares his or her own recording with that of the subject.

Stage three—prompted self-monitoring. Next, stage two is repeated with one modification: on each occasion the subject engages in the target behaviour and does not record this, the therapist gives one verbal prompt that the subject should do so. The purpose of this stage of the training is to encourage the subject to monitor his or her own behaviour more accurately, and to get into the habit of routinely making a recording whenever it occurs.

Stage four—independent self-monitoring and accuracy reward. Following the use of prompting to encourage more accurate monitoring of behaviour, the purpose of this stage is to withdraw external structure and facilitate self-monitoring by reinforcing accuracy within gross limits. This would usually involve explaining to the subject that reinforcement would be made available at the end of the trial, providing the recording they made was accurate to within 50% of that made by the therapist. During any trial, prompts to record would no longer be given to the subject.

Stage five—independent self-monitoring and reduction of the target behaviour. After successful completion of stage four, the accuracy of the subject to self-monitor and monitor multiple events, should be improved. The aim of the final stage of training is to encourage inhibition of the target behaviour using an appropriate operant strategy. Usually, a differential reinforcement programme will be implemented. This might involve the subject receiving reinforcement at the end of a trial, providing he or she had not engaged in a specified target behaviour no more than a specified number of times. During the trial, the subject continues to use the external counter to monitor behaviour in an effort to keep within the limit that has been set. With success, this target is gradually reduced until the target behaviour is eliminated, or occurs infrequently. Of course, the point is that successful participation in the operant stage of the training is only possible because it has been preceded by improvement in the accuracy of multiple-monitoring skills.

In the original case described by Alderman, Fry, and Youngson (1995), considerable reduction in a very frequent, disruptive

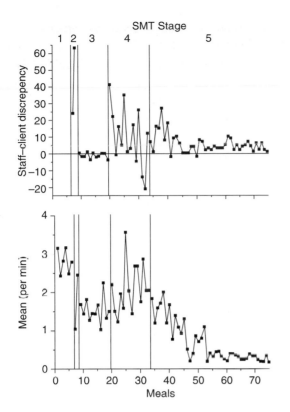

Figure 29.5. Improvement in self-monitoring and reduction in the frequency of requests for food and drink during meals made by HC using SMT.

target behaviour was obtained using SMT. It had not been possible to develop inhibitory control over this behaviour previously using other operant approaches due to a gross impairment in monitoring skills. Furthermore, this improvement was still evident when reassessed some months after the training had been completed.

Improving self-monitoring skills: case HC. An example of the effect of SMT is presented in Fig. 29.5.

The subject, HC, was a 46-year-old male professional who had sustained anoxic brain damage some years previously. Unfortunately, he had acquired a range of physical, cognitive, and functional problems as a result of the damage sustained to his brain. Physically, he presented with a left hemiparesis. In brief, results of neuropsychological assessment were as follows. Performance on the NART-R (Nelson, 1991) estimated his premorbid level of intellectual functioning as lying within the "average" range (estimated WAIS-R FSIQ = 100). In contrast, actual performance on the WAIS-R (Wechsler, 1981) indicated a Full Scale IQ of 84, with a significant discrepancy between Verbal IQ (97) and Performance IQ (68) evident. There was some impairment of memory function. For example, performance on the Rivermead Behavioural Memory Test (Wilson, Cockburn, & Baddeley, 1985) suggested the presence of a "moderate" memory impairment (standard profile score = 14/24). Perceptual and language functions remained unimpaired. However, there was clear evidence of a severe dysexecutive syndrome: performance on the BADS resulted in an age-corrected standardised

score (based on a population mean of 100 with a standard deviation of 15) of 38 (profile score = 6/24: "impaired"), which fell well below the estimate of his general level of cognitive functioning suggested by performance on the WAIS-R.

HC's dysexecutive syndrome was most evident in his behaviour by his complete disregard for social norms and lack of inhibition. He produced very frequent verbalisations that were inappropriate for the context of the situation he was in. For example, during therapy sessions he would maintain a constant, repetitive countdown of the time to go until the next meal. He appeared to be unaware of the impact his behaviour was having on other people. He remained unperceptive of cues from others, both subtle and overt, that demonstrated they found his behaviour irritating and a source of considerable frustration. Functionally, he had enormous difficulty in planning his behaviour. Once he had initiated a plan, he found it almost impossible to modify his action in response to change within the environment.

Observation suggested that HC could only effectively monitor one stimulus set at a time. This was confirmed by his performance on a dual-task experiment where he was required to simultaneously manipulate both visual and verbal information (Alderman, 1996; Baddeley et al., 1986, 1991), where he demonstrated profound impairment.

It was hypothesised that HC's difficulty with multiple monitoring was responsible for much of his inappropriate behaviour. It appeared that he could attend only to his verbal behaviour, and remained simply unaware of the feedback generated from others in the environment concerning the inappropriateness of his conduct.

Behaviour modification programmes that aimed to help HC learn greater inhibitory control over this behaviour were unsuccessful. It was hypothesised that the reason for their lack of success also lay in HC's impaired ability to monitor multiple events (see Alderman (1996) for a discussion regarding this).

HC's behaviour during meal times proved particularly problematic, and a source of frustration and irritation for both staff and other residents within the rehabilitation unit. He would make frequent requests for food and drink, even whilst eating. Consequently, SMT was used to encourage HC to inhibit this behaviour within this situation.

Meals, which tended to last approximately 30 minutes, were divided into two 15-minute trials.

During stage one of SMT, a frequency count of HC's behaviour was maintained: this is shown in the lower half of Fig. 29.5, with an average of 2.8 requests for food and drink made per minute. During stage two, HC was given a counting device and asked at the beginning of each trial to record whenever he made requests for food and drink. At the end of any trial, his recordings were compared with those of the therapist. This data is shown in the top half of Fig. 29.5 in the form of the magnitude of the discrepancy between the two sets of recordings. Absolute agreement between HC and his therapist is indicated by data points on the line running out from 0 on the y-axis. The further the data point is from this line, the poorer HC's monitoring. Figure 29.5

demonstrates his difficulties with self-monitoring, as his average rate of agreement with the therapist was only 8.9%.

It can be seen from Fig. 29.5 that the provision of prompts greatly facilitated increased accuracy in HC's recordings. There was some initial deterioration in his ability to monitor and record his behaviour (as well as engage in it) following the withdrawal of external prompts during stage four. However, as Fig. 29.5 shows, with practice there was a definite trend towards improvement in HC's monitoring skills.

Previously, HC's average rate of agreement with his therapist regarding the frequency of his verbal output was 8.9%: in contrast, during the last stage of SMT, this had increased to 78.9%, with perfect agreement being achieved during three of the trials. The effect of implementing a differential reinforcement programme, which encouraged HC to inhibit his verbal output concerning food and drink was also implemented during the final stage. A cue was placed on the table which reminded him of the target not to exceed. If successful, he earned a reinforcer after the meal, and the target was reduced for the next occasion it was implemented. Figure 29.6 clearly shows the successful reduction in the target behaviour that took place as a result.

It should be noted that HC's data is characteristic in that more efficient multiple-monitoring is by itself insufficient to reduce the target behaviour. However, this must precede attempts to achieve this using operant methods.

Figure 29.6 reflects the longevity of the results obtained during training. It will be recalled that the average frequency of the target behaviour was 2.8 per minute before SMT. One week after it had been withdrawn, the mean rate was 0.66 per minute. This had maintained at follow-up 4 months later, when the mean rate was found to be 0.54 per minute. In our experience this degree of longevity of treatment gains following participation in SMT is characteristic of the training. Our hope is that the gains made are internalised and reflect "real-life" improvements produced by directly influencing the central executive component of working memory.

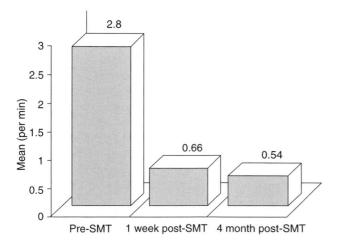

Figure 29.6. Results of time-sampling of verbal requests for food and drink made by HC during meals immediately before SMT, and 1 week and 4 months after it was withdrawn.

Executive strategy training to generalise other cognitive skills

Finally, it should be noted that the rehabilitation of other cognitive functions should not only include training to improve that domain, but executive strategy training to enable those skills to be used outside the training context. For example, Lawson and Rice (1989) argue that the lack of generalisation noted in some studies that had attempted to improve memory function was attributed to the absence of the therapist, who had previously acted as the external executive system for the individual. Use of self-instructional approaches, such as that described by Lawson and Rice, attempt to facilitate the use of skills taught in rehabilitation so that individuals may use them in a spontaneous manner when they are required.

SUMMARY

In this chapter an attempt has been made to summarise some of the main issues regarding assessment and rehabilitation of problems arising from the dysexecutive syndrome.

We hope that we have convinced the reader that the use of the term "frontal lobe syndrome" is no longer valid, whereas that of a dysexecutive syndrome is. Unlike the former term, dysexecutive syndrome captures better the functional problems that can arise following brain injury that are attributable to problems with executive functioning.

Conceptualisation of many of these problems at a cognitive, rather than an organic, level has some advantages. One of these is the construction of cognitive neuropsychological models that attempt to describe how the executive system normally works. Similarly, such models can attempt to account for dysfunction following neurological damage. Although theoretically interesting, a major benefit of such models is to provide clinicians with a rationale for the aetiology of a functional problem that can consequently be used to drive effective treatment interventions.

Similarly, new assessment procedures continue to be developed that will facilitate a broader clinical understanding of how the dysexecutive syndrome can drive many problems in a person's "everyday" life. The dissociation that can occur between apparently intact cognitive functioning and behaviour observed when assessment is conducted within the environment of the office or clinic, and that of grossly impaired ability apparent when circumstances are non-routine, has been especially highlighted and should not be underestimated.

Neuropsychological approaches to the rehabilitation of the dysexecutive syndrome have much to offer. Such approaches are still in their infancy. The challenge is to develop new and innovative treatment programmes whose aim is to teach people skills that generalise into the everyday environment. We look forward to the exciting developments that will undoubtedly occur within the next decade.

ACKNOWLEDGEMENT

Paul Burgess is supported by the Wellcome Trust: Grant number 049241/Z/96/Z/WRE/HA/JAT.

REFERENCES

Alderman, N. (1996). Central executive deficit and response to operant conditioning methods. *Neuropsychological Rehabilitation, 6*, 161–186.

Alderman, N., Burgess, P.W., Knight, C., and Henman, C. (in press). Ecological validity of a simplified version of the Multiple Errands Test. *Journal of the International Neuropsychological Society.*

Alderman, N., Fry, R.K., and Youngson, H.A. (1995). Improvement of self-monitoring skills, reduction of behaviour disturbance and the dysexecutive syndrome: Comparison of response cost and a new programme of self-monitoring training. *Neuropsychological Rehabilitation, 5*, 193–221.

Alderman, N. and Knight, C. (1997). The effectiveness of DRL in the management and treatment of severe behaviour disorders following brain injury, *Brain Injury, 11*, 79–101.

Alderman, N. and Ward, A. (1991). Behavioural treatment of the dysexecutive syndrome: Reduction of repetitive speech using response cost and cognitive overlearning. *Neuropsychological Rehabilitation, 1*, 65–80.

Baddeley, A.D. (1986). *Working memory*. Oxford: Clarendon Press.

Baddeley, A.D., Logie, R., Bresi, S., Della Salla, S., and Spinniler, H. (1986). Dementia and working memory. *Quarterly Journal of Experimental Psychology, 38A*, 603–618.

Baddeley, A.D., Logie, R., Bresi, S., Della Salla, S., and Spinniler, H. (1991). The decline of working memory in Alzheimer's disease. *Brain, 114*, 2521–2542.

Baddeley, A.D., and Wilson, B. (1988). Frontal amnesia and the dysexecutive syndrome. *Brain and Cognition, 7*, 212–230.

Bench, C.J., Frith, C.D., Grasby, P.M., Friston, K.J., Paulesu, E., Fracowiack, R.S.J., and Dolan, R.J. (1993). Investigations of the functional anatomy of attention using the stroop test. *Neuropsychologia, 31*, 907–922.

Ben-Yishay, Y. and Diller, L. (1978). *Working approaches to remediation of cognitive deficits in brain damaged persons*. Rehabilitation Monographs No. 60. New York: New York University Medical Center.

Ben-Yishay, Y. and Diller, L. (1983). Cognitive deficits. In M. Rosenthal (Ed.), *Rehabilitation of the head injured adult*. Philadelphia: F.A. Davis.

Ben-Yishay, Y., Rattock, J., and Lakin, P. (1985). Neuropsychological rehabilitation: Quest for a holistic approach. *Seminars in Neurology, 5*, 252–259.

Bigler, E.D. (1990). *Traumatic brain injury: Mechanisms of damage, assessment, intervention, and outcome* (p. 436). Austin, TX: PRO-ED.

Brantner, C.L. (1992). Job coaching for persons with traumatic brain injuries employed in professional and technical occupations. *Journal of Applied Rehabilitation Counselling, 23*, 3–14.

Burgess, P.W. (1997). Theory and methodology in executive function research. In Rabbitt, P. (Ed.), *Methodology of frontal and executive functions*. Hove, UK: Psychology Press.

Burgess, P.W. and Alderman, N. (1990). Rehabilitation of dyscontrol syndromes following frontal lobe damage: A cognitive neuropsychological approach. In R.Ll. Wood and I. Fussey (Eds.), *Cognitive rehabilitation in perspective*. Basingstoke: Taylor & Francis Ltd.

Burgess, P.W., Alderman, N., Emslie, H., Evans, J.J., and Wilson, B.A. (1996). The Dysexecutive Questionnaire. In Wilson, B.A., Alderman, N., Burgess, P.W., Emslie, H. and Evans, J.J. (Eds.), *Behavioural assessment of the dysexecutive syndrome*. Bury St Edmunds, Suffolk: Thames Valley Test Company.

Burgess, P.W., Alderman, N., Emslie, H., Evans, J.J., and Wilson, B.A. (1998). The ecological validity of tests of executive function. *Journal of the International Neuropsychological Society, 4*, 547–558.

Burgess, P.W. and Shallice, T. (1996a). Bizarre responses, rule detection and frontal lobe lesions. *Cortex, 32*, 241–259.

Burgess, P.W. and Shallice, T. (1996b). Response suppression, initiation and frontal lobe lesions. *Neuropsychologia, 34*, 263–273.

Burgess, P.W. and Shallice, T. (1997). *The Hayling and Brixton Tests*. Bury St. Edmunds, Suffolk: Thames Valley Test Company.

Burke, W.H., Zencius, A.H., Weslowski, M.D., and Doubleday, F. (1991). Improving executive function disorders in brain-injured clients. *Brain Injury, 5*, 241–252.

Cicerone, K.D., Lazar, R.M., and Shapiro, W.R. (1983). Effects of frontal lobe lesions on hypothesis testing during concept formation. *Neuropsychologia, 21*, 513–524.

Cicerone, K.D. and Giacino, J.T. (1992). Remediation of executive function deficits after traumatic brain injury. *Neuropsychological Rehabilitation, 2*, 12–22.

Cicerone, K.D. and Wood, J.C. (1987). Planning disorder after closed head injury: A case study. *Archives of Physical Medicine Rehabilitation, 68*, 111–115.

Davis, J.R., Turner, W., Rolider, A. and Cartwright, T. (1994). Natural and structured baselines in the treatment of aggression following brain injury. *Brain Injury, 8*, 589–597.

Delis, D.C., Squire, L.R. Bihrle, A. and Massman, P. (1992). Componential analysis of problem-solving ability: Performance of patients with frontal lobe damage and amnesic patients on a new sorting test. *Neuropsychologia, 30*, 683–697.

Della Malva, C.L., Stuss, D.T., D'Alton, J., and Willmer, J. (1993). Capture errors and sequencing after frontal brain lesions. *Neuropsychologia, 31*, 363–372.

Duncan, J., Burgess, P.W., and Emslie, H. (1995). Fluid intelligence after frontal lobe lesions. *Neuropsychologia, 33*, 261–268.

Eslinger, P.J. and Damasio, A.R. (1985). Severe disturbance of higher cognition after bilateral frontal lobe ablation: Patient E.V.R. *Neurology, Cleveland, 35*, 1731–1741.

Evans, J.J., Emslie, H., and Wilson, B.A. (1998). External cueing systems in the rehabilitation of executive impairments of action. *Journal of the International Neuropsychology Society, 4*, 399–408.

Freeman, M.R., Mittenberg, W., Dicowden, M., and Bat-Ami, M. (1992). Executive and compensatory memory retraining in traumatic brain injury. *Brain Injury, 6*, 65–70.

Fussey, I. and Giles, G.M. (Eds.) (1988). *Rehabilitation of the severely brain injured adult: A practical approach*. London: Croom Helm.

Goel, V. and Grafman, J. (1995). Are the frontal lobes implicated in "planning" functions? Interpreting data from the Tower of Hanoi. *Neuropsychologia, 33*, 623–642.

Gray, J.M., Robertson, I., Pentland, B., and Anderson, S. (1992). Microcomputer-based attentional retraining after brain damage: A randomised group controlled study. *Neuropsychological Rehabilitation, 2*, 97–115.

Hart, T. and Jacobs, H.E. (1993). Rehabilitation and management of behavioural disturbances following frontal lobe damage. *Journal of Head Trauma Rehabilitation, 8*, 1–12.

Hartmann, A., Pickering, R.M., and Wilson, B.A. (1992). Is there a central executive deficit after severe head injury? *Clinical Rehabilitation, 6*, 133–140.

Hersh, N. and Treadgold, L. (1994). NeuroPage: The rehabilitation of memory dysfunction by prosthetic memory and cueing. *Neurorehabilitation, 4*, 187–197.

Karnath, H.O., Wallesch, C.W., and Zimmerman, P. (1991). Mental planning and anticipatory processes with acute and chronic frontal lobe lesions: A comparison of maze performance in routine and non-routine situations. *Neuropsychologia, 29*, 271–290.

Lawson, M. and Rice, D. (1989). effects of training in use of executive strategies on a verbal memory problem resulting from closed head injury. *Journal of Clinical and Experimental Neuropsychology, 11*, 842–854.

Levin, H.O., Eisenberg, H., and Benton, A. (1991). *Frontal lobe function and dysfunction*. New York: Oxford University Press.

Lezak, M.D. (1983). *Neuropsychological assessment*. Oxford: Oxford University Press.

McCarthy, R.A. and Warrington, E.K. (1990). *Cognitive neuropsychology: a clinical introduction*. London: Academic Press.

Milner, B. (1963). Effects of different brain lesions on card-sorting. *Archives of Neurology, 9*, 90–100.

Nelson, H. (1976). A modified card sorting test sensitive to frontal lobe defects. *Cortex, 12*, 313–324.

Nelson, H. (1991). *National adult reading test* (2nd edition). Windsor, Berkshire: NFER-Nelson.

Nelson, R.O. and Hayes, S.C. (1981). Nature of behavioural assessment. In M. Hersen and A.S. Bellack (Eds.), *Behavioural assessment: A practical handbook* (2nd edition). New York: Pergamon Press.

Penfield, W. and Evans, J. (1935). The frontal lobe in man: A clinical study of maximum removals. *Brain, 58*, 115–133.

Prigitano, G.P. (1986). *Neuropsychological rehabilitation after brain injury*. Baltimore: Johns Hopkins University Press.

Rylander, G. (1939). Personality changes after operation on the frontal lobes. *Acta Psychiatrica Neurologica*, Supplement 30.

Sazbon, L. and Groswasser, Z. (1991). Time-related sequelae of TBI in patients with prolonged post-comatose unawareness (PC-U) state. *Brain Injury, 5*, 3–8.

Scherzer, B.P. (1986). Rehabilitation following severe head trauma: Results of a three year program. *Archives of Physical Medicine and Rehabilitation, 67*, 366–373.

Shallice, T. (1982). Specific impairments of planning. *Philosophical Transactions of the Royal Society of London, B, 298*, 199–209.

Shallice, T. (1988). From neuropsychology to mental structure. New York: Cambridge University Press.

Shallice, T. and Burgess, P.W. (1991). Deficits in strategy application following frontal lobe damage in man. *Brain, 114*, 727–741.

Sohlberg, M.M. and Mateer, C.A. (1989). Training use of compensatory memory books: A three stage behavioural approach. *Journal of Clinical and Experimental Neuropsychology, 11*, 871–891.

Sohlberg, M.M., Mateer, C.A., and Stuss, D.T. (1993). Contemporary approaches to the management of executive control dysfunction. *Journal of Head Trauma Rehabilitation, 8*, 45–58.

Sohlberg, M.M., Sprunk, H., and Metzelaar, K. (1988). Efficacy of an external cueing system in an individual with severe frontal lobe damage. *Cognitive Rehabilitation, 6*, 36–41.

Stuss, D.T. and Benson, D.F. (1984). Neuropsychological studies of the frontal lobes. *Psychological Bulletin*, 95, 3–28.

Stuss, D.T. and Benson, D.F. (1986). *The frontal lobes*. New York: Raven Press.

Treadwell, K. and Page, T.J. (1996). Functional analysis: Identifying the environmental determinants of severe behaviour disorders. *Journal of Head Trauma Rehabilitation, 11*, 62–74.

von Cramon, D.Y. and Matthes-von Cramon, G. (1990). Frontal lobe dysfunction in patients: Therapeutical approaches. In R.Ll. Wood and I. Fussey (Eds.), *Cognitive rehabilitation in perspective*. London: Taylor & Francis.

von Cramon, D.Y. and Matthes-von Cramon, G. (1992). Reflections on the treatment of brain-injured patients suffering from problem-solving disorders. *Neuropsychological Rehabilitation, 2*, 207–229.

von Cramon, D.Y. and Matthes-von Cramon, G. (1994). Back to work with a chronic dysexecutive syndrome? *Neuropsychological Rehabilitation, 4*, 399–417.

Wechsler, D. (1981). *The Wechsler Adult Intelligence Scale–Revised*. San Antonia, TX: The Psychological Corporation.

Wilson, B.A., Alderman, N., Burgess, P.W., and Emslie, H. (1996). *Behavioural assessment of the dysexecutive syndrome*. Bury St. Edmunds, Suffolk: Thames Valley Test Company.

Wilson, B.A., Evans, J.J., Alderman, N., Burgess, P.W., and Emslie, H. (1997a). Behavioural assessment of the dysexecutive syndrome. In P. Rabbitt (Ed.), *Methodology of frontal and executive functions*. Hove, UK: Psychology Press.

Wilson, B.A., Cockburn, J., and Baddeley, A. (1985). *The Rivermead Behavioural Memory Test*. Bury St. Edmunds, Suffolk: Thames Valley Test Company.

Wilson, B.A., Evans, J.J., Emslie, H., and Malinek, V. (1997b). Evaluation of NeuroPage: A new memory aid. *Journal of Neurology, Neurosurgery and Psychiatry, 6*, 113–115.

Wood, R.Ll. (1987). *Brain injury rehabilitation: A neurobehavioural approach*. London: Croom Helm.

Wood, R.Ll. (1988). Management of behaviour disorders in a day treatment setting. *Journal of Head Trauma Rehabilitation, 3*, 53–62.

Zec, R.F., Parks, R.W., Gambach, J., and Vicari, S. (1992). The executive board system: An innovative approach to cognitive-behavioural rehabilitation in patients with traumatic brain injury. In C.J. Long and L.K. Ross (Eds.), *Handbook of head trauma: Acute care to recovery*. New York: Plenum Press.

30. The rehabilitation of visuospatial, visuoperceptual, and apraxic disorders

Ian H. Robertson

INTRODUCTION

The woman fumbling hopelessly with an upside-down cardigan, the man ramming the doorway with the left side of his wheelchair, the person pouring boiling water onto the counter 6 inches away from the teapot: all these people are showing perceptual or praxic deficits of the kind dealt with in this chapter. So is the man who can no longer recognise the faces of his family, the woman who cannot recognise everyday objects until she can touch them, and the woman staring hopelessly at the hairbrush in her hand, not knowing how to carry out the movement necessary for its proper use. Then there is the man who gets lost in the hospital grounds or in his home streets, who cannot navigate from one place to another because he can no longer represent topographical space accurately. There are many more examples of visuospatial, perceptual, and praxic disorders—too numerous to mention in one short chapter.

The capacity to encode and comprehend the visual and spatial environment in all its changing complexity is arguably one of the highest achievements of the human brain. It is also one that can readily be concealed in industrialised societies where so much is governed by language and symbol: one can find one's way to the hospital by street names and road signs in a city; in the Australian desert, the aborigine can navigate by highly developed mental maps and accurate representations of virtually unverbalisable shapes, colours and features—of trees, rocks, and other natural features. Hence visuoperceptual disorders can have less of an impact on survival in Western than in primitive cultures, with the important exception, perhaps, of driving, although this is heavily regulated by symbolic and attentional functions as much as by perceptual ones.

The fact that very much more research has been carried out on the rehabilitation of language disorders than of perceptual and spatial disorders probably reflects the differing cultural needs just mentioned. Previous articles on rehabilitation in this area have tended to focus on perceptual theory much more than on rehabilitation, simply because there has been so little to say about the latter other than what has been based on anecdote and unverifiable clinical experience (see, for instance, the reviews by Delis, Robertson, & Balliet, 1982; Newcombe, 1985; Ratcliff, 1987).

In this chapter, fascinating and important research on theoretical and experimental aspects of visuoperceptual and visuospatial functioning will *not* be covered because it is impossible to do justice to its enormous range and sophistication in a chapter such as this. Rather, the focus will be on those disorders encountered in rehabilitation where systematic attempts have been made to develop and properly evaluate therapeutic strategies. So, for instance, prosopagnosia—impaired face recognition—is not discussed below as there are no known adequate published evaluations of its treatment. This is also the case for disorders such as Balint's syndrome, defective depth perception, and topographical disorientation, to mention just a small number of the huge range of fractionated and dissociable disorders in this complex area.

LOCALISATION AND LATERALISATION

It can no longer be assumed that the dominant cerebral hemisphere is "verbal" and the non-dominant one is "non-verbal". Complex perceptual functions are subserved by both hemispheres. Of course, there are differences in certain perceptual capacities of the two cerebral hemispheres: left visual neglect is more common than right visual neglect, for instance (De Renzi, 1982). Similarly, mental spatial rotation difficulties are more common following right than left brain damage (Ratcliff, 1978). There are literally hundreds of such findings that must be excluded from the main purpose of this chapter. The same can be said for discussion of localisation within hemispheres.

HEMIANOPIA AND QUADRANTANOPIA

Brief mention should be made of visual field defects, although these are not strictly "perceptual" disorders. Homonymous hemianopias might or might not be accompanied by macular sparing. Where the macula is not spared, characteristic errors such as missing the left or right side of small stimuli (e.g. single words) can be apparent.

Compensation for hemianopic deficits tends to be good: Ishiai, Furukawa, and Tsukagoshi (1989), for instance, showed that left hemianopics tended to make more saccades into their blind hemifield than into the intact right hemifield during a line bisection task, whereas hemianopics with neglect made hardly any saccades into their blind hemifield.

Zihl and von Cramon (1979) showed enlargement improvements in contrast sensitivity and increases in size of visual fields following a training procedure with patients with cerebral blindness that involved stimulating the blind areas of the visual field with light stimuli. An attempted replication by Balliet, Blood, and Bach-y-Rita (1985) failed, however, to find the effects reported by Zihl and von Cramon, and the former authors interpreted the latter results as being due to artefacts of the experimental procedure. Hence the question of whether visual fields can be enlarged by stimulation of this kind remains an open one.

Zihl, Krischer, and Meissen (1984) carried out a related training procedure of reading in hemianopics with macular splitting who showed omissions of parts of single words when reading text. Using a graded series of exercises, first with single words, building up to whole sentences, text was moved across a computer screen from right to left and the subjects encouraged to fixate at either the left or right extremities of words, depending on the side of their visual field cut. The authors reported improvements in reading over more than 30 training sessions. Unfortunately, there was no control for spontaneous learning or remission. A partial replication of this study was carried out by Kerkhoff and colleagues (Kerkhoff et al., 1992). More recently, the phenomenon of impaired visual scanning following visual tract lesions has been studied. Of 60 patients with homonymous hemianopia (Zihl, 1995), 24 (40%) showed normal scanning in a visual search task. A further 60% showed abnormal scanning, however, defined by: (1) long search times; (2) short scan paths; and (3) high numbers of fixations during a task involving counting 20 dots presented on a screen. Zihl concluded that normal scanners all had purely visual tract lesions, or primary visual cortex lesions, whereas non-compensating poor scanners (who were poor also on the ipsilesional side of space) tended to have posterior thalamus (pulvinar) and parieto-occipital lesions in addition to visual tract or primary visual cortex lesions.

Zihl then carried out training on 14 of the patients with abnormal scanning, with a resulting normalisation of scanning on the visual search task in 11 out of 14 treated patients. However, the training (subjects were trained to make long saccades to a 1 second target in their blind hemifield in response to an acoustic cue, as well as to search for target shapes in arrays of different objects, varying in number) was on material similar to that tested, and no generalisation was established.

AGNOSIA

Visual agnosia is the inability to recognise objects that cannot be explained by a primary sensory disorder, a deficit of naming, or severe general intellectual impairment Wilson (1990) studied a woman with a visual agnosic disorder who had particular difficulties in naming photographs and line drawings of objects, although she still had problems naming real objects.

Wilson compared several different types of training strategy, the most successful of which was where the patient was simply told the name of a picture that she could not previously identify. This resulted in 100% correct identification of the drawings. This was in contrast to the ineffectiveness of alternative procedures, such as being shown alternative examples of the stimulus, being shown examples of wrong answers that she had given, and no training, which all produced no, or significantly fewer, correct responses. There was, however, no generalisation to other visual representations of the objects whose names had been learned.

APRAXIA

Apraxia refers to a variety of movement disorders that cannot be explained by paralysis, weakness, poor comprehension, or refusal to cooperate. Wilson (1988) reported a case of severe apraxia in a 20-year-old woman who was almost completely apraxic, to the extent of being unable to use a cup, point or carry out equally simple tasks.

Wilson used a shaping/chaining procedure to train two tasks, namely drinking from a cup unaided and pulling a chair into a table, respectively. What was notable about these tasks was the way in which improvements in performance occurred following just one or two sessions where the subject was guided to do the task. For instance, in the drinking task, step five of the task analysis "lift the cup to your mouth" could be achieved at first session only with maximum shaping, that is, the woman's arm was moved through the sequence of actions. For the next three sessions she did this completely alone, with no help whatsoever. Similar patterns obtained in other steps, and the learning seemed to take place in steps rather than in graded sequences. Similarly, step four of the chair task "grasp the chair" required physical prompting at the first session, but immediately on the next trial was done completely alone, and continued to be so for the remainder of the study.

NON-SPECIFIC PERCEPTUAL TRAINING

Taylor, Schaeffer, Blumenthal, and Grisell (1971) compared two types of therapy in two groups of left hemiplegic stroke patients, randomly assigned to two treatments. One group had traditional motor rehabilitation, with extra emphasis placed upon the sensory and cognitive deficits of the patients: for instance, position sense training was carried out, hemianopic patients were given scanning training following a light on a blackboard, apraxic patient were given assembly tasks, and so on. The control group received only standard treatment. At the end of 20 days of treatment, the two groups did not differ on any cognitive or daily activity measures.

A very similar study produced similar results 14 years later. Lincoln, Whiting, Cockburn, and Bhavani (1985) compared 4 weeks of conventional occupational therapy with the same amount of perceptual retraining among a group of stroke and head-injury patients showing perceptual problems. The former group engaged in games, craft work, gardening, and physical activities, whereas the latter engaged in such tasks as stick length sorting, shape recognition games, cylinder sequencing, and a variety of other tasks commonly used in Occupational Therapy departments for perceptual retraining. At the end of treatment, there was no significant difference between the two randomly allocated groups on the level of perceptual functioning.

In a series of four single-case studies (mixed ABAB and multiple baseline designs), Edmans and Lincoln (1989) found virtually no effects of long duration (up to 9 weeks at three 45-minute sessions per week) perceptual training in four patients (three with right cerebrovascular accident (CVA), one with bilateral CVA). The training included scanning training to minimise neglect, cube copying, and other procedures similar to those used in the previous study.

Carter, Caruso, Languirand, and Berard (1980) compared "cognitive skills remediation" among a mixed group of elderly patients, some of whom had suffered strokes and others not. Visual scanning, visual–spatial orientation, short-term memory, verbal learning, and time judgement skills were in the syllabus over 12 30-minute sessions spread over 4 weeks. At post-test, the experiment group was significantly better than the randomly-assigned controls on letter cancellation and on visuospatial performance on a set of tasks similar to the procedures used in training. There was, however, no evidence of wider generalisation, nor a control for the enthusiasm and novelty effect of the experimental treatment. Nor was there blind follow-up.

In a further study, this time of acute stroke patients, Carter, Howard, and O'Neil (1983) compared a random control group of patients with a group of patients who received training in visual scanning, visuospatial, and time judgement skills. Significantly greater improvements on all three types of function was reported for the trained group post-test, although, again, the tests were similar to the tasks trained and no wider generalisation effects were demonstrated, nor were appropriate controls for non-specific effects employed.

Sivak et al. (1984) trained four subjects (two CVA, two head-injured) for 10 hours on a range of commercially available computerised perceptual training programmes. Nine standardised perceptual measures were taken pre- and post-training and a few apparent improvements shown in two of the four subjects. No statistical analysis was carried out, and there was no way of knowing whether the observed changes were due to chance fluctuations (out of 36 repeated tests—9 for each of four subjects—one would expect one or two to be significant by chance). Even if any of the changes were statistically significant, it is not clear that the computer activity caused these changes—test practice effects would be equally plausible. In short, this study tells us nothing about the effectiveness of computerised perceptual training.

In a further study, Sivak et al. (1984) compared pre- and post-performance of a group of eight people with acquired brain damage with a variety of aetiologies on a number of visuoperceptual tests and on driving performance, following general non-computerised perceptual training. Subjects were between 5 and 85 months post-onset, and the authors reported variable improvement on both psychometric and driving performance measures. Lack of a control group here makes this study uninterpretable.

Conclusions from general perceptual training studies

General perceptual training of the type commonly used in Occupational Therapy departments is of unproven effectiveness and is therefore probably inadvisable at the present time, even when this is given reasonably intensively over long periods (see Edmans & Lincoln, 1989). Activities such as shape and colour matching, cube copying, picture arrangement and sequencing, and similar abstract tasks should therefore be abandoned until their utility can be demonstrated.

Valuable therapist time would therefore be better spent in the direct training of functionally relevant skills such as dressing and self-care. The example of Wilson's treatment of apraxia is an example of how effective therapy targeting relevant behaviours can be achieved.

UNILATERAL NEGLECT

One of the earliest studies of attempts to remediate visual neglect was by Lawson (1962), in Aberdeen. He treated two cases of neglect by frequently reminding the patients to "look to the left" while reading, and also to use their fingers to guide their vision while reading. They were also encouraged to find the centre of a book or food-tray by using touch and then to use their finger position as a reference point from which to explore systematically the page or the tray. This important early study was reported informally, but Lawson did note that generalisation to untrained tasks was poor.

The New York studies

It was not for a further 15 years that another study of the rehabilitation of visual neglect appeared, this time in New York at the Rusk Institute of Rehabilitation Medicine. Weinberg et al. (1977) carried out a controlled study of 20 hours of training with 25 patients who had suffered unilateral brain damage following CVA. These were compared with a randomly selected group of 32 patients satisfying similar criteria.

The two groups were reasonably well matched after randomisation, although no data on sex is provided. The subjects were a mean of 10 weeks post-stroke, although the range was considerable. Control subjects received the same normal occupational therapy programme as the experimental subjects, and no attempt was made to control for the non-specific effects of being in a novel treatment programme.

The experimental treatment consisted of a number of tasks designed to "compensate for faulty scanning habits" (Weinberg et al., p. 481). These included use of a "scanning machine", a board over 6 feet wide upon which a light moves on its perimeter, and which the patient must track. Two rows of lights also on the board were used to encourage left head turning in a series of search tasks. The rationale here was to engage patients in a task that was sufficiently compelling to overcome the "pull" to the right. No explicit cognitive strategies are mentioned in this task, except that patients were taught always to look for the target on the left side first.

Also included, however, were a series of tasks that did have a rationale. The first of these was reading and cancellation tasks, where the subjects were provided with a thick red vertical line down the left side of the page, which the patients were taught to use as an "anchor" by always bringing it into vision before beginning the task in hand. This cue is then gradually faded out until the patient is "anchoring left" without its help. Another strategy was to help patients slow down their scanning by requiring them to voice the numbers they were cancelling or to read out the number of the line of prose on which they were currently working. The principle here is that the damaged function is compensated for by those perceptual and motor habits that are trained by the treatment regime. Patients were also trained to read printing that was made especially less dense, and a number of other types of non-verbal material were also used in this way.

Follow-up took place after 4 weeks' training. Tests of arithmetic, copying, cancellation, face-counting, face-matching, motor impersistence, sensory awareness, digit span, object assembly, and picture completion were given. The results were analysed separately for two subgroups of patients, based upon an assessment of the severity of their visual neglect. The "severe" group was selected according to a number of tests, including confrontation testing, and visual cancellation performance— a classification that was found to have some predictive and discriminative validity in a previous study (Diller et al., 1974). The usefulness of this distinction was confirmed in the present study by the different results shown by the two groups. The first, severe group ($n = 14$) showed significantly raised performance on 11 out of 14 tests. On seven of these variables there was at least a 50% improvement in test scores over baseline performance. The control group ($n = 11$) showed such statistically significant improvements on none of the tests. On tests of "primary" functions directly related to neglect (reading, arithmetic, copying), 65% of the severe patients improved on three or more tests, whereas only 11% of the controls showed this performance.

In the mild group, on 5 out of 14 tests the treated group ($n = 11$) showed statistically significant improvements, whereas the control group ($n = 23$) showed such gains in 3 of the tests. Of the treated patients, 55% showed improvements on at least 3 "primary" tests, whereas this was true for only 17% of the controls. No significance tests are reported for this analysis in either of the two subgroups, however, although a signal detection analysis for the combined group is reported, where the untreated group was regarded as "noise" and the treated group as "signal plus noise". The test battery discriminated treated and untreated groups at a high level of statistical confidence.

This study represented an advance in the evaluation of rehabilitation procedures, and had little peer in the subsequent decade, with the exception of a few studies described later. Of course, there are methodological problems, most notably the lack of extended follow-up. Also, the control groups were not subjected to an equally novel experience as the experimental group, nor did they receive equivalent extra occupational therapy time. Furthermore, there was no stratified random sampling according to the severity of neglect, and thus the comparisons within each subcategory must be treated with extreme caution. Nevertheless, as a beginning in the evaluation of such rehabilitation strategies, this is an extremely valuable study.

In a further study, Weinberg et al. (1977) studied a similar group of stroke patients suffering right brain damage. These were randomly allocated to a control and an experimental condition. In this study the control group was given an extra hour of occupational therapy each day to match the extra time given to the treatment group. Of the 53 eligible patients, 30 were allocated randomly to the treatment condition and the remainder to the control condition. The procedures were otherwise similar to those in the previous study, with the exception of the addition of two extra procedures to the treatment condition. The first of these was a task where the patient had to match on a grid upon the back of a manikin, the equivalent point to where he or she was touched by the experimenter on his or her own back. Feedback was given to the subjects as to their accuracy by means of lights, which lit when a correct response was given. In the second task the subjects made estimations of the sizes of different length rods placed in front of them by means of the placement of markers. The rods were presented at times to the left, but also to the centre and to the right. The stimulus rod was each time brought back up to the markers, thus affording the opportunity for comparison and feedback. Of the total of 20 hours of training, 15 hours was devoted to the procedures used in the previous study and 5 hours to the new training procedures just described.

Three more tests were added to the 14 tests in the previous study, namely a line bisection test, a test of estimation of the position of the body midline, and a test of estimation of the width of shoulders and some other simple dimensions. A total of 26 measures were collected, some tests yielding several scores.

At the end of treatment, the groups were reassessed and the subjects classified as showing severe or mild neglect at baseline. The "severe" treatment group ($n = 15$) did not differ significantly pre-test from the controls ($n = 9$), whereas at post-test they were significantly better on 15 out of 26 tests; the tests that showed no difference were digit span, double simultaneous stimulation, and left-sided body and shoulder midline estimation tasks (a total of 11 measures). Among the mild group, the experimentals exceeded controls on only 3 out of 26 scores, and the possibility that these differences were obtained by chance cannot be discounted.

This study partially replicates the previous study and corrects some of its methodological problems, in particular the time devoted to the control group and the direct comparison of scores at follow-up of treatment versus control groups. Nevertheless, it still remains the case that only the treatment group received the novel treatment, and this might have had some effect. The fact that there were no convincing differences among the group makes this latter criticism less powerful, however. Overall, the study replicates the findings of the previous study and suggests that significant treatment effects can only be found with confidence among the severe group. No satisfactory independent analysis of the treated versus untreated mild cases took place in the previous study, and the essential negative findings for this group in the present study suggests that this treatment is not effective with people who show minimal field defects on confrontation testing and relatively few errors on cancellation tasks. The new training strategies had some small effect on body size estimation on the right but not the left side, and the incremental usefulness of this procedure is unclear. What is relatively clear, however, is that scanning training and reading training of the types described above do seem to be effective at producing improvements on tasks with similar stimulus to the training materials. No further generalisation to functional activities was demonstrated.

A third study from the Rusk Institute (Weinberg et al., 1982) specifically excluded obvious neglect patients from groups of right-brain-damaged (RBD) patients who had suffered CVA. The rationale for this was that minimal lateral deviations exist in many RBD patients who have no obvious neglect. Weinberg et al. argued that visuospatial deficits shown by RBD patients could be attributed in large measure to these deflections of attention. They also reported how such people, although able to read faultlessly aloud, often "lost the place" when reading silently and showed poor comprehension of the prose content.

For these reasons, they randomly allocated a group of 35 non-neglecting RBD patients to a treatment ($n = 17$) and a control group ($n = 18$). The treatment group received 20 hours of training whereas the controls received an extra hour of occupational therapy. Training consisted of teaching patients to impose a gross system of spatial coordinates on passages of prose as well as upon dot patterns. They were taught to recall the location of identified words or dots according to these rough spatial coordinates. In addition, subjects were taught to try to create meaningful "Gestalts" of the dot patterns so as to aid recall. Finally, the patients were taught to observe and describe the irregular perimeter of abstract figures, and to do so in a systematic clockwise fashion.

Analysis of covariance on four factors obtained through a principal components analysis showed a significantly better performance of treated versus the untreated group on one of these components—"visual organization and analysis"—comprising scores on cancellation, visual synthesis, Raven's perceptual items from the coloured matrices and embedded figures. Two other tests on this component also loaded on several other components, and are thus not included for discussion here (analysis of covariance for these individual scores revealed no treatment group superiority).

What this study shows, therefore, is generalisation to similar psychometric procedures. No generalisation to reading comprehension could be demonstrated once an analysis of covariance was conducted. Although this study is of theoretical interest, the procedures tested could not be recommended for routine use with this patient group, although it remains to be seen whether they would add to the effectiveness of programmes aimed at rehabilitating severe neglect cases. Young, Collins, and Hren (1983) attempted a partial replication of the first two Weinberg et al. studies in Canada; 27 RBD patients were divided into three groups matched for age, education, degree of neglect, and time post-stroke (approximately 2 months on average). The first group received standard occupational therapy, which included such tasks as teaching figure–ground discrimination. The second received 20 minutes of standard occupational therapy and 40 minutes of cancellation and scanning training identical to the early Weinberg procedures. Group three received the same 40 minutes of training as the previous group plus a further 20 minutes of "block-design training". This latter procedure was developed by Diller et al. (1974) and involves an errorless learning procedure to train subjects to pass the block-design subtest of the Wechsler Adult Intelligence Scale. Young et al. reported apparent generalisation to unrelated tasks—functional and otherwise—as a result of this procedure.

All three groups received 20 hours of therapy. At post-testing, immediately after end of treatment, a linear trend analysis showed that group three was better than group two, and group two better than group one, on letter cancellation, reading, and address copying.

If these results are accepted, then it suggests that block-design training might "potentiate" scanning and cancellation training. Although Diller et al. (1974) did not find that block-design training significantly improved such clear neglect measures as letter cancellation, there was a significant effect on several measures of visuoperceptual organisation. Some generalisation to activities of daily living was also found, and thus this early study, which did not set out specifically to treat neglect, gives results that are compatible with those of Young et al.

There are, however, several problems with this last study. First, matching is a less desirable procedure than randomisation, given the near impossibility of matching on all potentially influential variables. In addition, the authors here do not report baseline test measures other than cancellation, which leads one to doubt that the groups were actually matched pre-treatment on these outcome variables. As no analysis of covariance was performed then, if there were such pretreatment differences, the apparent differences at follow-up could have reflected nothing other than the pre-existing differences

The generalisation problem

Webster et al. (1984) attempted a further partial replication of the New York procedures, this time using a single case design. The three males in the study had all suffered right middle cerebral artery strokes, and all showed both hemianopia and visual neglect on the left.

A multiple-baseline-by-subject design was used, where repeated baseline measures were taken for each subject, and then training commenced in a staggered fashion. Baseline performance on test trials of the scanning procedure used the "scanning machine" developed at the Rusk Institute, in which one measure is the detection of lights on the left and on the right under different conditions; another measure is performance in navigating an "obstacle course" in wheelchairs, based upon the number of collisions with markers on the course.

The training consisted of the basic scanning procedure of the New York studies, although not including the reading and cancellation tasks. In addition, subjects were given an "anchor line" at the far left of the board, and they were prompted to verbalise "anchor left" prior to each trial. As training progressed, the tape used as the anchor stimulus was removed and subjects were encouraged to use their left shoulders or upper arms as anchor points. Next, subjects were trained to scan left using similar methods, but under conditions where their attention was attracted right by a prior far right stimulus.

The subjects were also trained to carry out this procedure when they were moving in their wheelchairs towards the scanning board. Finally, subjects were given training in estimating distances between themselves and various objects, as the researchers had noticed that some collisions were due to defective distance estimation rather than neglect. A total of 25 sessions, each lasting 45 minutes, over 5 weeks, was given.

All three subjects showed an improvement in test performance on the scanning board coincidentally with the onset of training in each case, which is not surprising given the similarity of the training to the testing procedure. In the first two cases, however, improvement in wheelchair navigation occurred in the first or second session following onset of training, although only one of the cases performed in the normal range at follow-up. Furthermore, the main improvement occurred in frontal collisions to the left of the midline. Peripheral collisions, and particularly those out of the peripheral field were not reduced.

In the third case, such an improvement did not occur until the fourth session and thus could not be so readily associated with the training procedure. These improvements were maintained at 1 year follow-up, although of course it is not possible to say that this would not have occurred naturally in any case.

This study is a partial replication of the early studies using a different design, The modifications of the training procedure instituted were useful in so far as they tried to train scanning habits under different conditions, thus making generalisation more likely. One slight caveat, however, is that training was heavily oriented towards wheelchair use, and it would have been interesting to see whether the scanning training generalised to tasks where no training had been given. Also, it is not clear whether testing in each session was done immediately/soon after training. If this was the case, then one cannot be completely confident that this is not a transitory phenomenon as opposed to a lasting one; and, although the maintenance of gains at one year is some solace, as was said earlier it is possible that this could have happened without training.

Gouvier et al. (1984) attempted a replication of the previous study with two patients who also had right middle cerebral artery infarctions and showed left homonymous hemianopia and left visual neglect. The different interventions were staggered so as to examine their separate effects.

The same repeated measures as in the previous study were used, although in case one there was only one baseline measure for the obstacle course and two for the lightboard performance. In case two, the equivalent figures were 0 and 1. For case one the lightboard results were inconclusive, as no obvious trends were apparent and no statistical procedure was carried out. The obstacle course performance showed a drop in head-on collisions only, following stationary scanning and a drop in "glancing" collisions after the addition of mobile scanning (see previous study). At 6 weeks, follow-up errors were apparent only on head-on collisions. In case two, stationary scanning was associated with a significant drop from baseline in scanning errors on the lightboard. This near-perfect performance was maintained throughout the subsequent phases of training. The institution of mobile scanning (in this case including scanning at a variety of different orientations and distances from the board) appeared to reduce head-on and glancing errors, but to increase rear contact errors. The addition of distance estimation (see previous study) was associated with a further drop in the first two categories of errors, although the third category remained at the slightly elevated level. One interesting observation in these cases is that performance in letter cancellation remained unchanged, in spite of improvements on the other measures. This suggests a fairly specific effect of the training, and lends some support to the doubt expressed above about the previous study—that is, that task-specific rather than general skills were being trained.

This is a far less satisfactory study than its predecessors because of the inadequate baseline measures and, in the first case, because each training condition had only one measure reported, allowing no estimation to be made of the stability of the results. The second case does, however, provide a moderately satisfactory replication leading to similar conclusions as for the previous study.

A further study by this group (Gouvier, Bua, Blanton, & Urey, 1987) tended to support the view that the effects of training were much more consistently observed in tasks similar to the training procedure. Taking four men and one woman with similar problems to those in the previous two studies, they carried out three AB and two ABC single case studies, respectively. The A phase was baseline (three measures in each case of the two main target tasks), the B phase was lightboard training (as described in the previous study), and the C phase was cancellation training similar to that carried out by Weinberg's group and described in the first study above. B and C were reversed in one of the three-phase cases. Clear generalisation to lightboard performance was associated, not surprisingly, with lightboard training; noticeable generalisation to letter cancellation was apparent in only two out of four cases. In the case who started with cancellation training, little improvement in lightboard performance was apparent. The third phase of cancellation training added nothing to the performance on either task of one of the three-phase subjects, whereas the onset of lightboard training with the other did improve lightboard performance.

Reading, writing and navigation tasks were given at the end of each phase in four patients—on two occasions for two, on three for one, and on four for the other. In only one subject was consistent improvement on all tasks observed, although the three others all showed improvement on at least one measure.

This study is not just a further replication of the Weinberg procedures. It does point to generalisation difficulties discussed in the discussion of the previous two papers. Nevertheless, some generalisation to dissimilar tasks was observed, although it is unfortunate that a stronger single-case design could not have been used. It also confirms the New York finding as a consistently replicable phenomenon.

Gordon et al. (1985) carried the Rusk Institute work to its logical conclusion by combining all the training programme elements that appeared to have some effect and conducting a controlled trial of the package, this time conducting a 4-month follow-up.

Unfortunately, however, this was not a proper randomisation procedure, with all the subjects in the control group coming from one institution during one 6-month period and all the subjects in the other group coming from a different institution in the same period, although it is not reported over how long a period subjects were collected, and thus how many times the condition was switched, which happened at the end of each 6-month period. This is, however, not a satisfactory procedure because it is not clear that equal numbers of subjects came from each institution; if the numbers were not balanced, then it is perfectly conceivable that one group could have benefited from a therapeutic regime in one institution that fostered compensation for neglect more than the other. Gordon et al. concede that the training procedures developed in earlier studies had to some extent become part of "normal practice" in some therapy departments, and it is probable that some institutions were more active than others in this respect. Hence, a powerful potential contamination of the pseudo-randomisation design exists. Gordon et al. do, however, offer evidence that the experimental ($n = 48$) and control ($n = 29$) subjects were well matched on relevant demographic and clinical data that would influence outcome, such as age, severity of CVA, etc. The two groups were also well-matched on all relevant psychometric tests, but this does not overcome the profound difficulty imposed by the non-random design.

Thirty-five hours of training comprising the procedures described earlier in the Weinberg et al. (1977, 1982) studies was given to the experimental group. The control group participated "in either leisure activities or additional conventional rehabilitation programs during the time allotted for remediation in the experimental group" (Gordon et al., 1985, p. 354). Testing on a wide range of measures similar to those used in previous studies was done at intake, at end of training (at the end of 7 weeks in the case of the control group) and at 4-month follow-up.

At the end of training, the experimental group was significantly better than the control group on cancellation, arithmetic, reading comprehension, line bisection, and on a search task. By 4 months, however, there were no significant differences between the two groups, except that the control group showed significantly less lateral bias on Raven's Coloured Progressive Matrices, and the treatment group reported significantly less anxiety and hostility.

Subsequent scanning-based studies

Robertson, Gray, and McKenzie (1988) studied the effects of computerised training on visual neglect in three cases. The first was a 55-year-old man with a right hemisphere stroke with marked left neglect, who was trained on a computerised scanning task to self-instruct to look left and to engage in systematic scanning of the screen. On three independent target measures—card and word-search, as well as on letter cancellation—he showed little change over a baseline of four testing sessions, whereas over a six-session training period, he showed significant improvements on these tests. No change on two control measures—motor impersistence and visuospatial organisation—was found over the same ten testing sessions.

A second case trained was a 57-year-old woman with a right hemisphere intracerebral haemorrhage who was tested over seven baseline and a further seven training sessions on five target functions (telephone dialling, address copying, letter cancellation, prose reading, and word-list reading) and on three control tests (attentional capacity, visuospatial capacity, and reaction time). Large improvements in the former but not the latter were found coincidentally with the onset of training. The training was a more sophisticated version of the training procedure described in the previous case, with the computer using voice synthesis and visual cues to orient the patient's attention to the left, as well as giving structured exercises in mentally dividing the screen and of systematically scanning it, all carried out via a touch-sensitive screen.

In a third case, a 21-year-old male student suffering from a closed head injury who showed specific neglect dyslexia whereby he misread the left parts of words was subjected to a computerised tachistoscopic training with instructions to refixate attention on words on their left extremity, rather than at their centre. Using the same kind of design as in the previous two cases, improvements in word reading (non-computerised) were found in the absence of improvements in a control measure (visuospatial function).

In the wake of these positive results, Robertson, Gray, Pentland, and Waite (1990) carried out a randomised controlled trial of computerised training with 36 patients suffering unilateral neglect. One group of 20 subjects received a mean of 15.5 (SD 1.8) hours of computerised scanning and attentional training, and a second group of 16 subjects received a mean of 11.4 (SD 5.2) hours of recreational computing selected to minimise scanning and timed attentional tasks.

Training consisted of scanning training of the type described in the second case of the previous study, together with another programme consisting of a range of matching-to-sample tasks of varying complexity, where responses were made on a touch-sensitive screen. Responses would not be accepted by the computer until the subject had touched a red "anchor bar" on the left of the screen, which turned the bar green and unlocked the screen for the response. Care on both programmes was given to give clear feedback about left–right differences and to reinforce reductions in these differences.

For patients who progressed well on the scanning tasks there were also visuospatial reasoning programmes based on block design training with automatically reducing cueing along the lines of the procedures developed by Diller et al. (1974).

Blind follow-up at the end of training and 6-months follow-up revealed no statistically or clinically significant results between groups (which were extremely well matched prior to training) on a wide range of relevant tests. This was not because of large improvements on the part of the control group, as neither group showed dramatic improvements in neglect over 6 months.

Using a multistage design involving scanning and reading training, with intervention phases of a fixed duration of 2 weeks, Wagenaar et al. (1992) assessed the effects of scanning training. Three times in each intervention phase, performance was measured using a computerised visual scanning test, a line bisection test and a letter cancellation test. In addition, wheelchair navigation was also assessed. Four out of the five patients showed a significant effect of visual scanning training on visual scanning behaviour. However, the effect remained restricted to the task on which it was specifically trained. The authors conclude that there was no evidence for any transfer of visual scanning training effects to other functional domains.

Fanthome, Lincoln, Drummond, and Walker (1995) investigated the transfer of training approach using a variety of strategies including scanning. Fourteen patients with visual neglect identified on the Behavioural Inattention Test were involved. All patients received practice on perceptual tasks designed to improve visual neglect for 4 weeks and then results were analysed as single cases using an AB design. Only 3 of the 14 patients who completed the study showed improved perceptual test scores following treatment. The authors concluded that the transfer of training approach did not appear to enhance the recovery of most patients with visual neglect, although those with severe problems showed some improvement. Research in Rome (Antonucci et al. 1995) found that intensive implementation of procedures (24 1-hour treatment sessions over 2 months), combined with optokinetic stimulation, produced significant improvements on several standard outcome tests of hemi-neglect. However, generalisation to situations in daily life at follow up several months later was not demonstrated. Subsequent studies from the Rome group reported that some generalisation was found following intensive scanning training combined with optokinetic stimulation (Paolucci et al., 1996). Also in Italy, Ladavas and colleagues (Ladavas, Menghini, & Umilta, 1994) have reported improvements involving a scanning-based training regime, without clear evidence of generalisation, however.

Conclusions from scanning-based neglect training studies

There is some evidence that visual neglect can be ameliorated by training that attempts to teach scanning habits—verbally regulated—for compensation of left inattention. However, the studies that produced apparent effects were distinguished by the following characteristic: they all contained some training procedures that were targeted at functionally relevant activities, such as reading, writing, or navigating a wheelchair while scanning left. Studies with purely abstract procedures (Robertson, Halligan, & Marshall, 1993) tended to find no generalised effects, the exception being one study by the Rome group (Paolucci et al., 1996).

One is therefore led to conclude that, as is the case for general perceptual programmes, training for neglect should be focused heavily on immediately relevant daily activities rather than at abstract training procedures.

Alternative approaches to rehabilitation of unilateral neglect

Limb activation treatments

Most patients with severe (left) neglect present with a motor paralysis that prevents them using the left hand. As a result, most paper and pencil tests to assess neglect use the right hand, which is primarily under the control of the intact left hemisphere. As we know (from functional imaging studies) that use of the right hand activates the left hemisphere, it might also be the case that use of the right hand could, in fact, be contributing to neglect performance. In other words, left neglect can be regarded as resulting more from the contribution of the intact left hemisphere given impairment to the right hemisphere. On perceptual motor tasks such as line bisection and cancellation, the non-lesioned left hemisphere might be more activated relative to the damaged right hemisphere. In other words, some of neglect performance observed in patients with neglect is no doubt due to the selective involvement of the non-damaged left hemisphere, as it is no longer inhibited by the underactive right hemisphere (Kinsbourne, 1993).

A number of studies have found that limb activation improves unilateral neglect. For instance, when asked to search and cross-out from a complex array of shapes and figures, neglect patients who use their left arm found significantly more targets than patients who use their right arm (Robertson & North, 1992).

One interpretation is that doing something such as moving the left hand on the left side of space draws attention to that side, and consequently this "cueing" procedure helps reduce neglect over and above any hemispheric activation benefit derived from simply using the left hand itself. A study by Halligan, Marshall, and Wade (1990) supported this idea: their patient was asked to bisect lines using the right hand followed by the left hand. There was significantly less neglect when the left hand was used, but this advantage was subsequently abolished when the left hand was positioned on the right side of the line before the patient bisected it. In other words, if attention was first attracted to the right side, the advantage of using the left hand disappeared.

Other studies, however, suggested that beneficial effects occurred when moving the left hand on the left side of space (Robertson & North, 1992) in those patients who have some movement in the left hand. As attention is directed both to the left side of the body and to the left side of external space during such movements, the effect is to produce a more powerful cueing or activation of the brain's representations for that side of space.

Practical implications for rehabilitation.   In describing the scanning training above, we reported how previous studies had often used the paralysed left arm as a "perceptual anchor" for training the patient to scan to the left. If patients can also move the left arm (however small the movement), then one could get the combined effect of placing the left arm at the border of any activity if it is moved partially under voluntary control into position. Several case studies have now shown that improvements in daily life can be obtained by training patients to generate even quite modest movements with the partially paralysed left side of their body when performing everyday activities (Robertson, North, & Geggie, 1992).

This study showed changes in star cancellation between a baseline to a post-training period. Activities of daily living (ADL) ratings showed comparable improvements. This training was done by means of a "neglect alert device", a simple electronic box attached to the patient's trouser belt, with two switches attached to different parts of the left side of the patient's body. The "neglect alert device" was programmed to buzz at certain intervals and, whenever it did, the patient was encouraged to manually press whichever switch was illuminated in order to stop the buzzing. This was done during different activities and therapies, and was simply a means of trying to train the person to activate the left side of the body.

In a study evaluating the "neglect alert device" (Robertson, Hogg, & McMillan, 1998) several functional measures were used, including positioning of the body when walking through a series of corridors and doorways, the extent to which the left side was attended to during hair combing, and the positioning of a series of "buns" on a mock "baking tray". In this last task, devised in Sweden (Tham & Tegnér, 1996), patients are given 16 blocks of wood and are told to position them on a large board so that they are laid out symmetrically, as if they are "buns on a baking tray" to be placed in an oven. Patients with neglect tend to cluster the "buns" to the right-hand side.

Like most clinical tests of neglect, this is a complex perceptuomotor task and impaired performance can be caused by other factors in addition to neglect.

Patient performance on three measures over lengthy baseline, treatment, and follow-up periods were evaluated. All three functional measures improved as a result of training (none of which were carried out during the test sessions). Termination of the use of the neglect alert device coincided with a decline in the improvements in two of the three measures. However, one of the measures—the baking tray test—did maintain improvement despite the cessation of training over a long period, for reasons that are as yet unclear.

Studies by Robertson and North (1994) found that the benefit of activating the left arm was abolished if the two limbs were moved simultaneously. This can be interpreted as a form of "motor extinction", whereby the beneficial cueing or activation effects of the left-hand movements (right hemisphere) were cancelled by the stronger cueing and activation of moving the right hand (left hemisphere). This study, furthermore, has implications for how patients with neglect should be treated in therapy; such patients should preferentially benefit from unilateral activation of their hemiplegic side.

This view is compatible with the results of another study showing that in non-neglecting hemiplegic patients more than a year post-stroke, significant improvements in function of the hemiplegic arm were obtained when the patients were prevented from use of the non-hemiplegic limb for extended periods (Taub et al., 1993). These improvements persisted long after the intervention ended, and suggest that latent activation of the damaged hemisphere might be inhibited by activation of the undamaged hemisphere, again emphasising the value of some degree of unilateral, as opposed to bilateral, activation.

Auditory feedback

Several different types of auditory stimulation have been used in attempts to modify neglect. These vary between studies employing explicit feedback to those that have used different types of music as a way of activating the damaged right hemisphere. The most common form of auditory feedback that has been used to reduce neglect can be seen in most rehabilitation or hospital wards; therapists and nurses remind patients to look left when they fail to find what they are looking for or where they are going to.

This approach has been evaluated more systematically in the case of eye movements. It is a well-established clinical observation that patients with visual neglect tend not to direct their eyes to the visual field contralateral to their stroke. Using eye monitoring equipment, Ishiai et al. (1989) have shown that patients with visual field deficits, unlike patients with neglect, often employ compensatory strategies for looking to their affected side. Although neglect patients often fail spontaneously to move their eyes over to the left, with feedback it might be possible to reduce neglect if they were given information as to where their eyes were looking.

To evaluate whether feedback of eye movements might be a potential treatment strategy, Fanthome et al. (1995) employed a randomised control trial that compared knowledge of eye movements contingent upon auditory feedback. The treatment group ($n = 9$) was seen for over 2 hours a week for 4 weeks. Eye movement detection glasses provided an auditory signal in the form of a continuous bleep as a reminder when patients failed to move their eyes to the left after a fixed interval of 15 seconds. The control group of nine patients received no treatment for their neglect. Comparison of the two groups at 4 weeks, and then at a further 4 weeks, showed no significant difference either in eye movements or neglect performance as measured on the Behavioural Inattention Test (BIT).

Trunk rotation

One aspect of neglect performance that is often taken for granted by therapists and clinicians remains the question of which "reference frame" is involved when describing "left" neglect. In other words—what is neglect "left" of? The midline of the body has been shown to be one of the major frames of reference that determines the relative extent of "left" neglect. Many studies have shown that whether visual stimuli falling to the left or right of the body midline determines whether or not they are detected.

A study by Karnath, Schenkel, and Fischer (1991) in Germany showed, for instance, that simply rotating the trunk 15° to the left could significantly reduce left neglect in a way that neither rotating the eyes nor rotating the head produced. When the trunk is rotated by 15° to the left (while the head and eyes are fixed straight ahead) visual stimuli on the left of the midline defined by the head and eyes are actually located spatially to the right of the midline defined by the rotated body.

More recently, French researchers (Wiart et al., 1997) devised an ingenious method to combine the scanning training methods used by Diller in the New York studies and trunk rotation. They fixed a metal frame to the patient's trunk, and extended a long pointer, fixed to this frame, forward over the patient's head. Patients had then to engage in visual search tasks of the type used by Diller. Instead of using their eyes or fingers, they had to use the movements of the trunk to move the long pointer and to detect and touch targets on a large screen in front of the patient. The results of this study showed significant and long-lasting improvements in unilateral neglect during training, with some evidence of generalisation to functional tasks. This is an example of a very interesting development that combines theoretically important ideas with clinically relevant methods such as scanning training.

Sustained attention training

Sustained attention refers to the ability to maintain alertness in circumstances where there is little change or novelty in the environment. Whereas a loud noise or unexpected visual object draws our attention from the outside (that is, exogenously) we also need the additional capacity to maintain attention (that is, endogenously). We need this capacity when driving along a straight and unchanging road at night, when listening to a long lecture, or reading a long chapter!

The ability to sustain a state of alertness is strongly represented in the right hemisphere, and in particular the right frontal lobe. This has been shown in a study investigating the blood-flow changes that take place when subjects are required to sustain a state of alertness in normal subjects (Pardo, Fox, & Raichle, 1991).

Subjects were asked to count the number of times they were touched on their foot over a 40-second period while their regional cerebral blood flow was charted using (position emission tomography (PET)). Irrespective of which toe was stimulated, the right frontoparietal areas were significantly more activated in this task of sustained attention to parts of the body. A similar finding was obtained when subjects had to look at a computer screen to detect brief reductions in intensity of a central stimulus (Pardo, Fox, & Raichle, 1991).

Posner (1993) argues that the ability to shift attention to the left or right is controlled by a spatial orientation system, partly located in the inferior parietal lobes of the brain. This is one of the areas thought to be impaired in spatial neglect. A second attention system modulates the efficiency with which this spatial orientation system works; this is the right hemisphere sustained attention system, described earlier. Posner argues that the sustained attention system has particularly close links with the neurotransmitter noradrenaline (norepinephrine), and that there is evidence that the noradrenaline pathways are more strongly represented in the right, as compared to the left, hemisphere. Furthermore, the strongest endpoints of this neurotransmitter system lie close to the location of the spatial orientation system. The effects of increasing sustained attention might therefore provide a secondary modulation of the primary orientation system. If this is so, then this modulation could provide yet another approach for reducing neglect that bypasses the problems associated with lack of awareness so characteristic of neglect. An impairment of sustained attention can be manifest in a tendency to easily lose concentration during therapy.

Relatives often comment that the stroke patient "drifts off" and appears not to be listening to them when they are talking to them. Impairments of sustained attention can be assessed using tasks such as the Elevator Counting Task from The Test of Everyday Attention. In this test, patients have to count a series of tones while imagining that they are standing in an elevator, with each tone representing a different floor; the task is to count the number of tones and state the floor at which the elevator eventually arrives.

Could lateralised neglect performance be improved by directing treatment resources to the sustained attention systems? The first evidence in non-neglect patients that suggested this possibility was carried out in Canada by Meichenbaum and Goodman (1971) with impulsive children. Their studies showed that attention could be brought under voluntary control by "self instructional" procedures. The results suggest that it might be possible to train neglect patients who also had sustained attention problems to improve alertness by training them to (self-endogenously) "switch up" their sustained attention system using the types of learned verbal self-instructions used by Meichenbaum and Goodman. If Posner's account is correct, then such training could not only improve sustained attention, but should also improve orientation to the left side of space (given the close connections between the sustained attention and the spatial orientation systems).

A recent study by Robertson et al. (1995) employed this approach with a number of patients suffering from long-standing unilateral neglect. Most patients with severe unilateral neglect also show problems with sustained attention. The procedures involved training subjects to improve their internal, or endogenous control of attention by "talking themselves through it" in a fixed series of stages. The aim of this treatment was to bring attention to task under voluntary verbal control, and thereby reduce distractibility and improve length of concentration.

In the Sustained Attention Training procedure, patients were trained while doing a variety of tasks that did not emphasise lateralised scanning: periodically the patients had their attention drawn to the task by combining a loud noise with an instruction to attend. The patient was then gradually taught to "take over" this alerting procedure, so that eventually it became a self-alerting procedure.

The results of this training with eight patients were very encouraging. Not only were there improvements in sustained attention, but there were also improvements on spatial neglect over and above those expected by natural recovery. One possibility for the success of this treatment is that many patients show greater awareness for problems with sustained attention than they do for similar problems with unilateral neglect. If this is true, then such patients could be more likely to implement the training procedure and to employ it in everyday life.

Training awareness in unilateral neglect

Given the fact that most patients with neglect are typically unaware of the functional implications of their condition, it is hardly surprising that it remains a major predictor of poor outcome following stroke (Gialanella & Mattioli, 1992). Can neglect be reduced by trying to improve awareness of the deficits that result from it?

A study in Sweden investigated this question (Soderback, Bengtsson, Ginsburg, & Ekholm, 1992). Patients were video-taped while engaging in routine household tasks that they considered important and relevant to their lives. They were then shown the videotape recording and the video stopped where the neglect behaviour was most significant. Patients were then led to perceive and interpret the recorded behaviour as indicative of the effects of neglect, and were given strategies for the relearning and remediation of the condition. This preliminary programme requires further evaluation before it can be recommended as an adjunctive form of remediation for neglect.

Another way to improve patients' awareness involves placing the patients' perception from different sense modalities in direct conflict. In one study, patients were required to point to the centre of long metal rods (Robertson, Nico, & Hood, 1997). As with other bisection tasks, patients with unilateral left-sided neglect tended to indicate the centre as located too far to the right of centre. Patients were then given a small number of trials in which they picked up the metal rods on the basis of their visual estimate, and so experienced the conflict between their visual estimate (where they had pointed) and the proprioceptive feedback (the sense of unbalance that they attempted to pick up at this point). As they picked up the metal rods with their thumb and forefinger, patients were permitted to change their grasp, demonstrating

that they were indeed aware that their grip was not central. Patients who received this *brief* feedback (just nine chances to pick up a rod in approximately 2 minutes), showed significantly reduced omissions on cancellation and deviations on bisection tasks up to half an hour later, compared to patients who received no such feedback. By presenting conflicting information within the patient's intact sensory modalities, it might be possible that proprioceptive and kinaesthetic information provide the patients with information that persuades them of the incorrectness of their visual bisection. This approach has to be evaluated clinically, and the short-term improvements in neglect observed might not generalise over a longer period. The principle of utilising other sensory feedback could, however, be worthy of further consideration with a view to developing more clinically effective treatments.

CONCLUSION

Given the complexity of perceptual and praxic processes, and the very limited understanding of how they work which exists, it should come as little surprise to find that therapy that can reliably improve disorders in most of these functions does not yet exist. The "black box" of cognition and perception is as yet opaque, and that is why observable behaviour, and not abstract cognitive processes, must in future be the substance of therapy. Where this approach has been taken, some grounds for very limited therapeutic optimism emerge.

Neglecting patients can learn to scan better during specific tasks such as reading or wheeling a wheelchair. But they do not learn to do so by sitting in front of a computer or by doing abstract puzzles. They do so by learning "on the job", i.e. during the course of reading, pushing the wheelchair, etc. Furthermore, these treatment effects seem to be fairly specific and do not generalise widely to dissimilar situations.

Similarly, at least one apraxic patient was taught to be able to do at least one very important thing: drink from a cup without help. This, again, was done by focusing on the task, and not on a postulated and abstract underlying cognitive system. In a further case of agnosia, simple instruction enabled a patient to recognise pictures (albeit without being able to recognise other pictures of the same object) previously not recognised.

Although it is true that the majority of studies of perceptual retraining have failed to find generalisation beyond the training methods, recent research on the rehabilitation of neglect suggest that theoretically based procedures might produce results that give a greater possibility of generalisation. This is particularly true of unilateral neglect, although firm conclusions about this await the results of properly controlled, randomised-controlled trials.

REFERENCES

Antonucci, G., Guariglia, C., Judica, A., Magnotti, L., Paolucci, S., Pizzamiglio, L., and Zoecolotti, P. (1995). Effectiveness of neglect rehabilitation in a randomised group study. *Journal of Clinical and Experimental Neuropsychology, 17*, 383–389.

Balliet, R., Blood, K., and Bach-y-Rita, P. (1985). Visual field rehabilitation in the cortically blind? *Journal of Neurology, Neurosurgery and Psychiatry, 48*, 1113–1124.

Carter, L., Caruso, J., Languirand, M., and Berard, M. (1980). Cognitive skill remediation in stroke and non-stroke elderly. *Clinical Neuropsychology, 2*, 109–113.

Carter, L., Howard, B., and O'Neill, W. (1983). Effectiveness of cognitive skill remediation in acute stroke patients. *American Journal of Occupational Therapy, 37*, 320–326.

Delis, D., Robertson, L., and Balliet, R. (1982). The breakdown and rehabilitation of visuospatial dysfunction in brain-injured patients. *International Rehabilitation Medicine, 5*, 132–138.

De Renzi, E. (1982). *Disorders of space exploration and cognition.* Chichester: John Wiley.

Diller, L., Ben-Yishay, Y., Gerstman, L., Goodkin, R., Gordon, W., and Weinberg, J. (1974). *Studies in cognition and rehabilitation in hemiplegia.* Rehabilitation Monograph No. 50. New York: New York University Medical Center.

Edmans, J. and Lincoln, N. (1989). Treatment of perceptual deficits after stroke: Four single case studies. *International Disability Studies, 11*, 25–33.

Fanthome, Y., Lincoln, N.B., Drummond, A., and Walker, M.F. (1995). The treatment of visual neglect using feedback of eye movements: A pilot study. *Disability and Rehabilitation, 17*, 413–417.

Gialanella, B. and Mattioli, F. (1992). Anosognosia and extrapersonal neglect as predictors of functional recovery following right hemisphere stroke. *Neuropsychological Rehabilitation, 2*, 169–178.

Gordon, W., Hibbard, M.R., Egelko, S., Diller, L., Shaver, P., Lieberman, A., and Ragnarson, L. (1985). Perceptual remediation in patients with right brain damage: A comprehensive program. *Archives of Physical Medicine and Rehabilitation, 66*, 353–359.

Gouvier, W.D., Bua, B.G., Blanton, P.D., and Urey, J.R. (1987). Behavioural changes following visual scanning training: Observation of five cases. *International Journal of Clinical Neuropsychology, 9*, 74–80.

Gouvier, W.D., Cottam, G., Webster, J., Beissel, G., and Wofford, J. (1984). Behavioural interventions with stroke patients for improving wheelchair navigation. *International Journal of Clinical Neuropsychology, 6*, 186–190.

Halligan, P.W., Marshall, J.C., and Wade, D.T. (1990). Do visual field deficits exacerbate visuo-spatial neglect? *Journal of Neurology, Neurosurgery, and Psychiatry, 53*, 487–491.

Ishiai, S., Furukawa, T., and Tsukagoshi, H. (1989). Visuospatial processes of line bisection and the mechanisms underlying unilateral spatial neglect. *Brain, 112*, 1485–1502.

Karnath, H.O., Schenkel, P., and Fischer, B. (1991). Trunk orientation as the determining factor of the "contra-lateral" deficit in the neglect syndrome and as the physical anchor of the internal representation of body orientation in space. *Brain, 114*, 1997–2014.

Kerkhoff, G., Münßinger, E., Haaf, E., Eberle-Strass, G., and Stogerer, E. (1992). Rehabilitation of homonymous scotomata in patients with postgeniculate damage of the visual system: Saccadic compensation training. *Restorative Neurology and Neuroscience, 4*, 245–254.

Kinsbourne, M. (1993). Orientational bias model of unilateral neglect: Evidence from attentional gradients within hemispace. In I.H. Robertson and J.C. Marshall (Eds.), *Unilateral neglect: Clinical and experimental studies.* Hove, UK: Lawrence Erlbaum Associates Ltd.

Ladavas, E., Menghini, G., and Umilta, C. (1994). A rehabilitation study of hemispatial neglect. *Cognitive Neuropsychology, 11*, 75–95.

Lawson, I.R. (1962). Visual-spatial neglect in lesions of the right cerebral hemisphere. *Neurology, 12*, 23–33.

Lincoln, N.B., Whiting, S.E., Cockburn, J.E., and Bhavani, G. (1985). An evaluation of perceptual retraining. *International Journal of Rehabilitation Medicine, 7*, 99–110.

Meichenbaum, D. and Goodman, J. (1971). Training impulsive children to talk to themselves: A means of developing self-control. *Journal of Abnormal Psychology, 77*, 115–126.

Newcombe, F. (1985). Rehabilitation in clinical neurology: Neuropsychological aspects. In J.A.M. Frederiks (Ed.), *Handbook of clinical neurology, Vol 2 (46): Neurobehavioural disorders* (pp. 609–642). New York: Elsevier Science.

Paolucci, A., Antonucci, G., Guariglia, C., Magnotti, L., Pizzamiglio, L., and Zoccolotti, P. (1996). Facilitatory effect of neglect rehabilitation on the recovery of left hemiplegic stroke patients – a cross-over study. *Journal of Neurology, 243*, 308–314.

Pardo, J.V., Fox, P.T., and Raichle, M.E. (1991). Localisation of a human system for sustained attention by positron emission tomography. *Nature, 349*, 61–64.

Posner, M.I. (1993). Interaction of arousal and selection in the posterior attention network. In A. Baddeley and L. Weiskrantz (Eds.), *Attention: Selection, awareness and control* (pp. 390–405). Oxford: Clarendon Press.

Ratcliff, G. (1978). Spatial thought, mental rotation and the right cerebral hemisphere. *Neuropsychologia, 17*, 49–54.

Ratcliff, G. (1987). Perception and complex visual processes. In M. Meier, A. Benton, and L. Diller (Eds.), *Neuropsychological Rehabilitation* (pp. 242–259). Edinburgh: Churchill Livingstone.

Robertson, I., Gray, J., and McKenzie, S. (1988). Microcomputer-based cognitive rehabilitation of visual neglect: Three multiple baseline single-ease studies. *Brain Injury, 2*, 151–163.

Robertson, I., Gray, J., Pentland, B., and Waite, L. (1990). A randomised controlled trial of computer-based cognitive rehabilitation for unilateral left visual neglect. *Archives of Physical Medicine and Rehabilitation, 71*, 663–668.

Robertson, I.H., Halligan, P.W., and Marshall, J.C. (1993). Prospects for the rehabilitation of unilateral neglect. In I.H. Robertson and J.C. Marshall (Eds.), *Unilateral neglect: Clinical and experimental studies* (pp. 279–292). Hove, UK: Lawrence Erlbaum Associates Ltd.

Robertson, I.H., Hogg, K., and McMillan, T.M. (1998). Rehabilitation unilateral neglect: Improving function by contra-lesional limb activation. *Neuropsychological Rehabilitation, 8*, 19–29.

Robertson, I.H., Nico, D., and Hood, B.M. (1997). Believing what you feel: Using proprioceptive feedback to reduce unilateral neglect. *Neuropsychology, 11*, 53–58.

Robertson, I.H. and North, N. (1992). Spatio-motor cueing in unilateral neglect: The role of hemispace, hand and motor activation. *Neuropsychologia, 30*, 553–563.

Robertson, I.H. and North, N. (1994). One hand is better than two: Motor extinction of left hand advantage in unilateral neglect. *Neuropsychologia 32*, 1–11.

Robertson, I.H., North, N., and Geggie, C. (1992). Spatio-motor cueing in unilateral neglect: Three single case studies of its therapeutic effectiveness. *Journal of Neurology, Neurosurgery and Psychiatry, 55*, 799–805.

Robertson, I.H., Tegnér, R., Tham, K., Lo, A., and Nimmo-Smith, I. (1995). Sustained attention training for unilateral neglect: Theoretical and rehabilitation implications. *Journal of Clinical and Experimental Neuropsychology, 17*, 416–430.

Sivak, M., Hill, C.S., Henson, D.L., Butler, B.P., Silber, S.M., and Olson, P.L. (1984). Improved driving performance following perceptual training in persons with brain damage. *Archives of Physical Medicine and Rehabilitation, 65*, 163–165.

Söderback, I., Bengtsson, I., Ginsburg, E., and Ekholm, J. (1992). Video feedback in occupational therapy: Its effects in patients with neglect syndrome. *Archives of Physical Medicine and Rehabilitation, 73*, 1133–1139.

Taub, E., Miller, N.E., Novack, T.A., Cook, E.W., Fleming, W.C., Nepomuceno, C.S., Connell, J.S., and Crago, J.E. (1993). Technique to improve chronic motor deficit after stroke. *Archives of Physical Medicine and Rehabilitation, 74*, 347–354.

Taylor, M., Schaeffer, J., Blumenthal, F., and Grisell, J. (1971). Perceptual training in patients with left hemiplegia. *Archives of Physical Medicine and Rehabilitation, 52*, 163–169.

Tham, K. and Tegnér, R. (1996). The baking task a test of spatial neglect. *Neuropsychological Rehabilitation, 6*, 19–25.

Wagenaar, R.C., Wieringen, P.C.W.V., Netelenbos, J.B., Meijer, O.G., and Kuik, D.J. (1992). The transfer of scanning training effects in visual attention after stroke: Five single case studies. *Disability and Rehabilitation, 14*, 51–60.

Webster, J., Jones, S., Blanton, P., Gross, R., Beissel, G., and Wofford, J. (1984). Visual scanning training with stroke patients. *Behaviour Therapy, 15*, 129–143.

Weinberg, J., Diller, L., Gordon, W., Gerstman, L., Lieberman, A., Lakin, P., Hodges, G., and Ezrachi, O. (1974). Training sensory awareness and spatial organisation in people with right brain damage. *Archives of Physical Medicine and Rehabilitation, 60*, 491–496.

Weinberg, J., Diller, L., Gordon, W., Gerstman, L., Lieberman, A., Lakin, P., Hodges, G., and Ezrachi, O. (1977). Visual scanning training effect on reading-related tasks in acquired right brain damage. *Archives of Physical Medicine and Rehabilitation, 58*, 479–486.

Weinberg, J., Piasetsky, E., Diller, L., and Gordon, W. (1982). Treating perceptual organisation deficits in non-neglecting RBD stroke patients. *Journal of Clinical Neuropsychology, 4*, 59–75.

Wiart, L., Saint-Come, A., Debelleix, X., Joseph, P.A., Mazaux, J.-M., and Barat, M. (1997). Unilateral neglect syndrome rehabilitation by trunk rotation and scanning training. *Archives of Physical Medicine and Rehabilitation, 78*, 424–429.

Wilson, B.A. (1988). Remediation of apraxia following an anaesthetic accident. In J. West and P. Spinks (Eds.), *Case studies in clinical psychology*. London: John Wright.

Wilson, B.A. (1990). Cognitive rehabilitation for brain injured adults. In B.G. Deelman, R.J. Saan and A.H. van Zomeren (Eds.), *Traumatic brain injury: Clinical, social and rehabilitational aspects* (pp. 121–143). Lisse, Netherlands: Swets & Zeitlinger.

Young, G., Collins, D., and Hren, M. (1983). Effect of pairing scanning training with block design training in the remediation of perceptual

problems in left hemiplegias. *Journal of Clinical Neuropsychology, 5*, 201–212.

Zihl, J. (1995). Visual scanning behaviour in patients with homonymous hemianopia. *Neuropsychologia, 33*, 287–303.

Zihl, J., Krischer, C., and Meissen, R. (1984). Die hemianopische Lesestorung und ihre Behandiung. *Nervenarzt, 55*, 317–323.

Zihl, J. and von Cramon, D. (1979). Restitution of visual function in patients with cerebral blindness. *Journal of Neurology. Neurosurgery and Psychiatry 42*, 312–322.

Personality and behaviour

31. Behaviour problems

Laura H. Goldstein

INTRODUCTION

This chapter will outline the behavioural approach to dealing with behaviour disorders in neurologically damaged patients. The behavioural model fits well within an approach to rehabilitation where the intention is to reduce the impact or consequences of impairments, when the impairments themselves cannot be modified (Haffey & Johnston, 1989). This chapter will set the use of behavioural techniques in the context of residual learning ability found in brain-damaged animals and humans, and will briefly describe the applications of such techniques to adults who have sustained a brain injury. In addition, the practical issues of implementing such techniques will be highlighted.

EXPECTATIONS, MODELS AND LEARNING ABILITY

Psychologically based intervention to deal with behaviour problems focus either on behavioural excesses (behaviours that occur too frequently and can therefore be inappropriate) or behavioural deficits (behaviours that occur less frequently than would be optimal for the individual to achieve independence in social or functional skills) (Wood & Burgess, 1988).

When devising such interventions, a suitable theoretical model must be selected. The selection of an appropriate model to guide rehabilitative interventions should not be an arbitrary process, as the model can influence the therapist's expectations both of treatment outcome and the individual patient's capacity for new learning. Giles and Fussey (1988) reviewed several possible models and finally recommended a learning-theory-based behavioural model.

That learning theory can offer a successful therapeutic model and can incorporate techniques suggested by other models (Burgess & Alderman, 1990; Giles & Fussey, 1988) is not surprising when one considers the robust nature of associative learning (classical and operant conditioning) in the presence of central nervous system (CNS), and particularly neocortical, damage (Goldstein & Oakley, 1985; Oakley 1979a, 1981, 1983a). Associative learning, which underpins learning theory considerations of behaviour, is the process whereby individuals acquire some form of causal relationship between two events occurring in their world (Oakley, 1983b). These sensory or motor events can occur within individuals or in their environment. Where a consistent relationship can be seen to exist between two environmentally originating events, and the second is an important biological stimulus (e.g. food), then the learning of the association between these events is that of Pavlovian or classical conditioning. Operant or instrumental conditioning occurs when individuals correctly learns the association between some action of their own and an environmental consequence, such as the delivery of food or giving of praise to them. Procedures adapted from operant conditioning studies form the majority of behaviour modification interventions.

The suitability of associative-learning-based techniques for neurological rehabilitation is seen in cross-species data, for both animals and humans, with different degrees of neocortical damage. The most forceful evidence that associative learning survives extensive CNS damage comes from studies of this type of learning in rats and rabbits in whom neocortex has been surgically removed (neodecorticated). Thus, classically conditioned responding has been obtained to at least normal if not better than normal levels in rabbits (Oakley & Russell, 1977) and rats (Oakley et al., 1981). Instrumental (operant) learning has also been reported in a variety of testing situations both for neodecorticated rabbits (Oakley & Russell, 1978) and rats (Goldstein & Oakley, 1987; Oakley, 1979a, 1980; Oakley & Russell, 1979). In several of the learning tasks, evidence of an attentional deficit was found. Pretraining programmes, however, facilitated directing the lesioned animals' attention to the salient features of the testing situation, thereby attenuating the differences between the lesioned and control animals on operant tasks (Oakley, 1979b, 1980; Oakley & Russell, 1978).

In addition, support for preserved associative learning despite considerable reduction in the size of the cerebral hemisphere comes from studies of microencephalic animals (Furchtgott et al., 1976; Goldstein & Oakley, 1989; Pereira & Russell, 1981; Rabe & Haddad, 1972; Tamaki & Inouye, 1976; Woods et al., 1974) and humans (Bernal et al., 1975; Jacobson et al., 1973). Evidence also exists of associative learning in human cases of anencephaly or hydranencephaly, in which the cerebral hemispheres are completely or almost entirely absent (Aylward et al., 1978; Berntson et al., 1983; Deiker & Bruno, 1976; Tuber et al., 1980). There has also been much discussion about the importance of consciousness in associative learning and, interestingly, associative learning has been demonstrated even when patients are still in coma (Shiel et al., 1993). Thus there are strong grounds to expect intact associative learning, albeit possibly in the presence of attentional deficits (Van Zomeren et al., 1984) in individuals with extensive neocortical damage. This intact acquisition of associatively mediated responses persists in the presence of higher-order cognitive learning and memory deficits resulting from damage to major forebrain structures (Daum et al., 1989; see also Tate, 1987a) and explains the success of operant techniques with, for example, people with learning disabilities (Goldstein & Oakley, 1985; Yule & Carr, 1987).

LEARNING THEORY APPROACHES TO BEHAVIOUR PROBLEMS

In view of the evidence cited above and other indications that, within the sensory and attentional capacities of the individual, associative learning is spared and in some situations might even be enhanced in the face of reduced cognitive ability (Goldstein, 1986; Goldstein & Oakley, 1985), the relevance of the behavioural approach to intervention can be seen when dealing both with the presence of unwanted behaviours and the absence of desirable self-help skills.

Undesirable behaviours in patients who have suffered traumatic brain damage are often not a direct consequence of the brain damage but have arisen as a means of gaining attention or serving other communication needs (Goldstein & Oakley, 1985; Wood & Eames, 1981). In the early stages following injury—at a time of heightened dependence on others for self-care, and when cognitive processes are functioning below their best recovery level, and also when possibly still in post-traumatic amnesia—patients can be particularly predisposed to acquire maladaptive behaviours via associative learning processes (Goldstein & Oakley, 1985; Tate, 1987a). Other behavioural disorders, particularly those associated with damage to frontal lobe structures, can be explained by the cognitive processes disrupted by the brain injury (Burgess & Alderman, 1990) although they can be maintained through associative learning processes.

Severely brain-injured people form a heterogenous group of people. As Tate (1987b) noted, for some of them, cognitive deficits can persist long after physical recovery is complete, although the converse can also be true and for some people physical and cognitive impairments endure in tandem. For those cases where cognitive functioning remains severely impaired, behaviour modification, as derived originally from animal research, can be more appropriate than interventions that are based exclusively in cognitive psychology because, as Miller (1984) points out, the situation is very similar to that of dealing with individuals who have severe learning disabilities—the main difference between the client populations being the age at which the brain damage was acquired. Cognitive approaches to retraining can be more relevant when cognitive impairments are specific rather than global (Miller, 1984). Tate (1987b) indicates that a common

impairment following acceleration/deceleration head injuries is of new, explicit learning and retrieval, which influence the ways in which rehabilitation programmes can be designed. It has been observed, however, that the use of associative learning procedures with severely cognitively impaired individuals can allow adequate behavioural control to be established to then permit cognitive training programmes to be implemented (Goldstein & Oakley, 1985). Indeed, the principles of a behavioural approach (to be outlined later) can also be applied to cognitive retraining programmes (Wilson, 1987). In addition, the form that a behavioural training approach takes can usefully be influenced by detailed knowledge of cognitive neuropsychology (Alderman & Burgess, 1990). It is clearly important, therefore, to outline a behavioural approach to intervention that is based on learning theory, and to describe some of the available techniques.

Identifying behaviour

As behaviour does not occur in a vacuum, problem behaviours are problems for someone (Yule, 1987). The problems about which carers complain are not necessarily the most important for the client, and thus it will be important to balance the client's and carers' needs when devising intervention programmes.

As indicated, behaviour problems can take the form of behavioural excesses (possibly falling into Eames' (1988) category of active disorders of behaviour) and behavioural deficits. Examples of behaviour excesses and deficits are, respectively, shouting at or hitting staff members whenever asked to participate in a programme, or the inability to complete self-help skills independently. Whichever the target, the behaviour must be described in precise and unambiguous terms, on the basis of what is observable, so that all staff members dealing with the client can identify when the target behaviour occurs. Thus the description must permit complete objectivity of observation, and thereby measurement. It is through the quantification of the behaviour that treatment effectiveness can be evaluated. This is relevant whether a behavioural or other intervention (e.g. psychopharmacological) is undertaken (Jacobs, 1988).

Functional analysis

A behavioural approach to treatment must take into account not only the behaviour but also the context in which it does, or does not, occur, as behavioural management can at times involve modifying the person's environment to bring about change in his or her behaviour. Based as it is on learning theory, the behavioural approach seeks initially to identify what antecedents and consequences of the behaviour increase or decrease the likelihood of the behaviour occurring. That is, behaviour occurs in specifiable settings (physical, social, psychological) and has clear consequences.

There are several frameworks for behavioural or functional analysis. The simplest, the A-B-C framework (Yule 1987), involves the approach implied above, i.e. a systematic investigation into:

A—antecedent or setting events
B—the behaviour, its frequency, duration, etc.
C—the consequences of the behaviour.

Such an approach has been recommended for use with traumatically head-injured adults (Giles & Fussey, 1988; Wood, 1987).

Other complementary frameworks have been described. Gardner (1971) recommended that behaviour analysis should provide details concerning not only the problem behaviour but the interrelationship between problem behaviours. In addition, a reinforcement hierarchy for the individual should be identified, as should his/her behavioural resources. The client's broader environment should be outlined, as should the treatment resources and any aversive control components existing in the person's natural environment. Clients' behavioural assets, as well as behavioural excesses and deficits, must be outlined (Kanfer & Saslow, 1969). This prevents therapists from failing to identify positive qualities in the individual and missing positive behaviours on which further progress can be built (Yule, 1987). Their model also requires clarification of the situation in which the problem behaviour occurs, and a motivational analysis (including a reinforcement hierarchy) for the individual. A developmental analysis is required that details relevant biological, sociological, and behavioural changes in the person's life. The model also permits analysis of the person's self-control, social relationships, and of the interrelationship between the social, cultural, and physical aspects of the person's environment. Other frameworks have also been outlined (Kanfer & Grimm, 1977; Kiernan, 1973; Nelson & Hayes, 1981).

The use of analogue conditions has been an important development (Iwata et al., 1982). Here, the client is exposed to a series of contrived situations where different setting–response–reinforcer relationships can be manipulated. This prevents the clinician from having to wait for the behaviour to occur spontaneously and can accelerate the initial assessment process.

Essentially, all models of functional analysis permit the generation of hypotheses concerning the occurrence of a target behaviour. These hypotheses have treatment implications. Importantly in neurological rehabilitation, functional analysis permits specifically client-centred behaviour analysis and thus helps militate against institution-oriented management practices (Raynes et al., 1979).

Measuring behaviour: observation and recording

Critical both to functional analysis and to the evaluation of treatment effectiveness is accurate observation and recording of behaviour occurrence. Staff need to be highly motivated to record all instances of the target behaviour, so constant feedback as to the usefulness of the data and appreciation of their efforts is valuable within the team. The type of behaviour, when it occurs, and the availability of potential observers will determine in large part the observational method to be used. Murphy (1987)

provides a comprehensive account of methods, their advantages and disadvantages.

Continuous recording. Continuous recording, where the observer records all behaviour exhibited by the individual in a given setting, is rarely practical and it is unlikely that different observers would record identical events. Even using videotapes to enable descriptions of behaviour to be made later is often impractical because of the time-consuming nature of the procedure (Yule, 1987).

It might be more practical to record the frequency of occurrence of the target behaviour. This is known as "event recording" and is a relatively straightforward procedure. As it is likely to be impractical to record over the entire day, it is necessary to select representative periods of time during which to sample behaviour frequency. Care must be taken to ensure that the times chosen do not lead to a bias in the apparent setting condition for the behaviour. In addition, observations must always be made in the same conditions to evaluate the effects of treatment.

Event recording then can be used when the behaviour has been clearly defined. Observations are usually made for representative samples of time during the day, and results are expressed as frequency/unit time, i.e. a rate measure.

With some behaviours, interest might be in the duration of the behaviour, rather than in whether or not it occurs. Of relevance might be the time a person takes to wash, dress, or eat a meal independently. Such recording is called "duration recording" and, although sensitive to change, clear guidelines must be available to indicate the beginning and end of the behaviour being monitored. Problems arise, however, in deciding how to deal with disruptions or interruptions that occur during the behaviour in question.

Interval recording. This requires that the total observation period is divided into time intervals. The observer then notes whether or not the specified behaviour occurs at all in each time period. If one is interested in more than one behaviour, then, providing that each is clearly operationalised and observers well trained, information can be gained as to the sequence of behaviour (Yule, 1987). As, within each time interval, some time is usually allocated for observation and some for recording, interval recording provides only an estimate of frequency and duration of behaviour, because what is recorded is the number of intervals in which the behaviour occurred, however briefly.

Momentary time sampling. This is frequently preferable to interval recording (Murphy & Goodall, 1980). It involves observation of the patient only at the end of a particular specified interval. The length of the interval must be determined by the frequency and duration of the behaviour, but the method does not require continuous observation. On a busy ward, care of other patients can make noticing what a particular person is doing at a specified time quite difficult, but the method has the advantage of not being particularly time-consuming.

Portable microcomputers can also be used for data recording (see Murphy, 1987). These use a real-time base and observers press predetermined keys to indicate the onset (and cessation) of target behaviours. Once the position of the relevant keys has been learnt, observers can devote all their attention to the behaviour, without having to look away for recording purposes. Data analysis can also be automated.

Reliability and validity of measurement

Imperative in all methods of recording behaviour is that observations are accurate and that all members of staff dealing with patients obtain the same results concerning the occurrence of the behaviour; that is, the behaviour recording must be reliable. Different methods exist for computing interobserver reliability (Yule, 1987; Murphy, 1987), and indicate the need to train and retrain observers if sufficient weight is to be placed on observational data alone, concerning treatment outcome. Better still is the use of concurrent, independent measures, all indicating therapeutic effectiveness. Such measures will then have convergent validity. Other useful instruments include self-report measures (questionnaires), rating scales, and checklists. Their use with neurological patients has been discussed by Wilson (1987).

Reinforcement: increasing desirable behaviours

Reinforcement

Functional analysis of a problem behaviour should produce hypotheses about how the behaviour is maintained. In behaviour modification terms, a possible reinforcer is any phenomenon that, when delivered following the occurrence of a behaviour, will increase the probability that the behaviour will be repeated. Examples are primary reinforcers (e.g. food, drink, sexual activity), secondary, or conditioned reinforcers (where a person must learn their values, e.g. tokens, money), social reinforcers (e.g. social praise), and sensory reinforcers (which include activities, e.g. a trip to the cinema).

Behavioural response frequency can also be increased by a negative reinforcer, which is an aversive event or stimulus that, when terminated, increases the frequency of the preceding response. Examples in daily life are of giving attention or sweets to a screaming child who then quietens, or of taking medicine to relieve pain. Whereas negative reinforcement can work as part of a therapeutic intervention used to alter unusually resistant behaviours, ethical considerations imply that the use of aversive stimuli should be avoided wherever possible.

Reinforcement can be delivered on either a continuous or intermittent basis. Continuous reinforcement indicates that a response is reinforced each time it occurs; on intermittent reinforcement schedules some responses are reinforced and others, although the same, are not. Continuous reinforcement has been recommended for use with severely head-injured adults (Wood & Eames, 1981) but it is necessary to fade out continuous reinforcement by using intermittent schedules if behaviour is to become independent of the treatment setting. The use of intermittent reinforcement should ideally result in behaviours that will endure after treatment has ended. Whenever presented, reinforcement should be given contingently upon the occurrence of

the desired behaviour, immediately after it occurs, in a consistent manner, and with great clarity (Hemsley & Carr, 1987). The role of cognitive mediators in associating reinforcement with behavioural change has been addressed by Wood and Burgess (1988).

Developing desirable behaviours: shaping, prompting, fading, chaining, environmental restructuring, and modelling

Skill-building techniques frequently focus on the development of independent daily living skills. A behavioural approach requires the task to be broken down into component elements, with subgoals being set that are within the client's capability. Such specification of task components is known as a "task analysis" and the value of this is seen when considering, for example, how much of the overall task of washing in the morning the client can achieve independently. The techniques to be considered in this section are used to build-up new behaviours, or to reteach previously achievable behaviours taking into account physical limitations. They depend upon a good task analysis of the skill to be taught.

Shaping is used when it is particularly unlikely that the entire desired behaviour would occur spontaneously. It involves the reinforcement of small steps, or increasingly close approximations to the desired behaviour, emitted by the person. As the initial approximation is performed consistently, the person must then emit a response that, according to a task analysis, is even closer to the final, desired response, before reinforcement is delivered. Shaping depends on continuous, accurate observation and reinforcement of the client by the therapist. Fussey (1988) illustrates the use of shaping in teaching a male head-injured patient to sit with others and engage in conversation. Initially, reinforcement (attention, praise, and a tangible reinforcer) was delivered contingent upon his staying in the room with other people. Subsequently, reinforcement was only delivered when he was sitting down, and later only when he was sitting quietly or engaged in socially appropriate conversation.

Prompting has been used to great effect with people with learning disabilities, particularly in training self-help skills and learning generalised imitation skills (Tsoi & Yule, 1987). Prompts are actions by the therapist that help the client emit the desired behaviour, and can help quicken the training process. Prompts are usually verbal (in the form of instructions), gestural (pointing or miming the desired behaviour), or physical (e.g. physically guiding the person's hand through a particular component of the skill). Prompting can be particularly relevant when, for example, poor concentration and memory render it unlikely that a client will initiate spontaneously or complete a behaviour such as drinking (Johnston et al., 1991). In addition, different degrees of physical prompting are possible. Commonly, both verbal and physical prompts are required initially but, after training, the level of prompt can be reduced to only verbal and, finally, none at all. This reduction of levels of prompt is known as "fading". The use of prompts and their fading requires careful judgement by the therapist, because extra prompts will be needed if the desired performance deteriorates. Rosenstein and Price (1994) used audiotaped verbal prompts to pace meal eating in a 36-year-old man with severe cognitive impairment. The use of the taped prompts was faded as the man reached a criterion of taking 15 minutes (rather than his initial 3) to complete his meal, having also been prompted to watch the clock as he ate.

There has been much interest in the use of "errorless learning" with people with learning difficulties and this has been extended to people with acquired brain damage. The importance of enabling the person to succeed during training and, not to have to "unlearn" incorrect responses, can provide a valuable first stage of behavioural training (Tate, 1987b).

In training, one is also enabling the client to complete all the component steps of the desired behaviour in the correct order. There are two approaches to training the person to master the chain of behaviours that comprises the skill—forward or backward chaining. Which is used to some extent depends on the specific skill, although backward chaining is often felt to be most effective, as the person is always reinforced for the completion of the behaviour in question (see Tsoi & Yule (1987) for indications of how this is used).

A desired behaviour can sometimes be more readily emitted if the environment in which the behaviour is to occur is in some way altered. Giles and Clark-Wilson (1988) list materials such as non-slip mats, plate-guards, and wide-handled or angled cutlery, all of which can facilitate independent feeding in the early stages after head injury. Drinking utensils with modified handles can similarly be of use. Over time, and depending upon the ultimate degree of physical impairment, it might be possible, using small sequential changes, to train the person to use normal utensils for eating and drinking. A microswitch-adapted headband and portable radio have been used to reinforce correct head position following severe head injury (Kearney & Fussey, 1991). Walking frames or rollers can be valuable in retraining walking, and the aids can later be discarded (Hooper-Roe, 1988). If fading out the use of these aids proves impossible, then at least the person's quality of life can be improved through their use.

The teaching of desirable behaviours can also be facilitated through modelling by the therapist of the behaviour in question. Imitation of modelled behaviour is a basic means by which new behaviours can be learnt. It occurs readily in normal people and requires good attentional processing (Sarimski, 1982), which might be impaired in severely brain-injured adults (Wood, 1987). Observation of the reinforcement consequences of a model's actions can, however, still offer a process whereby brain-damaged patients can acquire a wide range of desirable skills to replace those that place the person at further disadvantage in a rehabilitation or community setting. The characteristics of the model can be important (Carr, 1987).

Tokens

It might not be convenient, practical, or desirable to deliver a primary reinforcer contingent upon the completion of a targeted response. Indeed, the aim is generally to bring behaviour under the influence of social reinforcement from others. In a rehabilitation setting, this aim might be too ambitious at first and, rather than resort to primary reinforcers, the delivery of which will disrupt on-going activity, some other means must be found to bridge the gap between completion of the behaviour and later reinforcement. One means of achieving this is to use token reinforcement.

Tokens, along with stars, points, or even money, are generalised reinforcers. They have no intrinsic value but can be exchanged, according to a specified exchange rate, for valued edibles, activities, etc. Thus they can be used in skill-building programmes and in programmes designed to decrease undesirable behaviours.

Apart from their delivery causing minimal disruption of on-going behaviour, the use of tokens has other advantages (Carr & Gathercole, 1987). First, they permit the use of a wide range of activities and events as reinforcers that could not be delivered immediately and contingently following the desired behaviour. Second, they maintain their reinforcing properties because they are independent of deprivation states; the client cannot become satiated following their delivery. Third, tokens permit the client to construct a hierarchy of back-up reinforcers, with a different exchange rate for each reinforcer. Fourth, the use of tokens encourages staff to deliver social praise and attention, along with the token, to the individual when the specified behaviour is completed. This ensures the staff maintain positive interaction styles with the clients, and provides the staff with constant reminders as to the progress of clients. Fifth, tokens provide clients with practice in accounting; and, finally, they can be used for groups as well as individuals. It is imperative that staff keep accurate accounts of clients' "earnings" and that token use is appropriately faded. Difficulties with token use must be recognised (Turnbull, 1988).

The successful use of a "token economy" (TE) has been described for groups of severely brain-damaged adults with behaviour disorders (Blackerby, 1988; Eames & Wood, 1985; Wood, 1987; Wood & Eames, 1981). Such TEs incorporate different levels in their structures. When clients enter the first level, tokens are delivered on a frequent basis for cooperative behaviour and task achievements in therapy sessions. After consistent high earnings, higher levels of the TE are entered where more stringent targets are set for appropriate behaviour, which must occur over longer time periods if tokens are to be earned. These levels provide incentives for the clients to achieve more desirable back-up reinforcers. The TE systems reviewed by Wood (1987) and Blackerby (1988) illustrate the ways in which levels can be established within a TE and how individualised and standard targets can be incorporated. Blackerby stresses the importance of using the TE to improve social functioning as well as daily living skills, if the TE is to produce lasting behaviour change. The effectiveness of the TE in conjunction with other behaviour management techniques has been demonstrated in the type of placement clients are offered following treatment (Eames & Wood, 1985).

Summary

A learning-theory-based approach offers techniques that can be used to build-up or maintain desirable behaviours. In practice, these techniques are often used in combination, and in conjunction, with techniques used to decrease undesirable behaviours.

Decreasing undesirable behaviours

The performance of socially undesirable behaviour by neurologically impaired individuals, as by people with learning disabilities, can lead to disruption and deterioration of family and personal relationships such that institutional care might be necessary (Wood, 1987). In addition, severe behaviour disturbances can reduce the available opportunities for rehabilitation (Tate, 1987a,b). Thus, behavioural disturbances can jeopardise the attainable level of independence for the neurologically damaged individual. Reducing undesirable behaviours is therefore an extremely important aim for a behavioural intervention, and can be achieved by the use of punishment and extinction:

- **Punishment** involves the presentation of an aversive stimulus, or the removal of a positive stimulus contingent upon a behaviour, which decreases the probability of that behaviour recurring.
- **Extinction** is a procedure in which the reinforcer is no longer delivered for a previously reinforced response; ultimately this decreases the probability that the behaviour will recur.

Good practice in behaviour modification requires that whenever an undesirable behaviour is decreased or removed from the person's behavioural repertoire an adaptive, desirable skill is taught in its place. This is because many undesirable behaviours serve particular functions for the individual, which should be elucidated by means of a thorough functional analysis (Murphy & Oliver, 1987).

Punishment

The definition of punishment given in the earlier list indicates that it is to be viewed in terms of an effect on behaviour and, as such, its definition is precisely the opposite of that of reinforcement. As for positive reinforcement, punishment stimuli must be chosen for each individual. The main techniques wherein punishing stimuli can be used will be considered below.

Time-out.   The phrase "time-out" is an abbreviation of "time out from positive reinforcement". Thus, in a setting in which positive reinforcement would be continuously available, reinforcement is not delivered for a short time period, contingent upon the occurrence of the undesirable behaviour. Time-out has been used most often, but not exclusively, when praise or social attention is the reinforcer, and time-out then involves a period of separation from the reinforcing situation (either within the same area or in a separate, predesignated one).

Time-out periods need to be of relatively short duration (i.e. less than 15 minutes). The "time-in" situation needs to be (rather than just assumed to be) reinforcing if the technique is to work. If undesirable behaviour is not to be positively reinforced by the termination of time-out, it might be necessary to specify a contingency whereby the time-out period is ended only after a short period of desirable behaviour has occurred, unless this would result in the individual being in time-out for longer than 30 minutes (Murphy & Oliver, 1987). Wood (1987) described the use of three forms of time-out with brain-injured adults.

(1) Time-out-on-the-spot (TOOTS), similar but not identical to activity time-out (Department of Health and Welsh Office, 1993), involves denying attention to behaviours that are reinforced by attention, such as screaming, complaining, or demanding behaviour, either by continuing with a conversation or activity as if oblivious to the behaviour, or by walking away from the client. Used in this way (e.g. Andrewes, 1989; Youngson & Alderman, 1994) time-out is more akin to extinction than to punishment.

(2) Situational time-out (Wood, 1987), which approximates to room time-out (Department of Health and Welsh Office, 1993) involves the removal of the client either from the activity to another part of the room, or to the corridor outside the room without providing verbal reinforcement to the client. A time-out room can be used when the undesirable behaviour is too dangerous or difficult to deal with *in situ*.

(3) In seclusion time-out the client is placed in a bare room for periods of about 5 minutes; removing the client to the time-out room must be achieved with minimal positive reinforcement for the undesirable behaviour. Alderman et al. (1995) indicate that a locked room can no longer be used in this way as part of a treatment programme in the United Kingdom (Department of Health and Welsh Office, 1993).

Alderman et al. (1995) discuss some of the limitations of time-out that involves removing an individual from the setting in which the undesirable behaviour occurs. These include the fact that this is an intrusive procedure, and that the person could receive social reinforcement from those having to remove him or her from the room. If this is the case then the unwanted behaviour could unwittingly be reinforced as the patient finds an effective way of gaining attention from nursing staff or avoiding a disliked rehabilitation programme, and staff must be alert to these possibilities.

Wood (1987) none the less cites evidence of successful use of the time-out room system for aggression, verbally abusive behaviour, inappropriate sexual behaviour, and inappropriate speech. The use of time-out must be carefully documented and must follow both local ethical committee guidelines and those of relevant government documentation.

Response cost.   An addition or an alternative to a token programme can be the use of response cost. Thus one can deduct, or have the client hand over, a specified number of tokens when an undesirable behaviour occurs. The latter increases the client's active involvement in the programme and can thereby heighten the sense of responsibility for his or her own behaviour (Alderman & Burgess, 1990). In addition, handing over the token(s) can be accompanied by the client verbalising the reason for the token loss. This aspect has been held to be important in the use of response cost with clients with behavioural disorders characteristic of frontal lobe damage (Alderman & Burgess, 1990; Alderman & Ward, 1991). The procedure can, however, evoke protests and further inappropriate behaviour from the clients involved. Rather than structuring the response cost procedure so that the client loses tokens already earned for desirable behaviour, it is sometimes preferable for the undesirable behaviour to result in him or her not earning further tokens (Murphy & Oliver, 1987), although adoption of such a strategy must be governed by the client's ability to comprehend such an approach.

Alderman and Ward (1991) have described the successful use of response cost as part of a programme to reduce undesirable repetitive speech in a female patient following herpes simplex encephalitis. The client was given 50 pence in 1 pence pieces. The coins have to be handed back one at a time after each episode of undesirable behaviour. During the course of the programme the "cost" of a small chocolate bar, which she found highly reinforcing and for which the coins remaining at the end of a designated time might be exchanged if enough were retained, was increased. Greatest control over the behaviour was achieved by combining response cost with what has been termed "cognitive overlearning" (see Alderman & Ward, 1991 for details).

Alderman and Burgess (1994) applied a similarly implemented response cost programme to a 39-year-old man with herpes simplex encephalitis who, in addition to a profound global amnesia, exhibited a range of undesirable behaviours. Use of the token system and time-out-on-the-spot had been ineffective and a programme using differential reinforcement of incompatible behaviour (discussed later) had limited success. Considerably greater control over his inappropriate verbal behaviour was achieved with a response cost programme, with 1 pence coins being lost whenever he sang, shouted, or swore. Money left at the end of a session could be exchanged for cigarettes. Alderman and Burgess (1994) suggested that the initial use of the token economy and time-out were ineffective because of the man's severe amnesia, as he probably could not remember over long enough periods to relate the token or its loss to his behaviour.

Three other variants of response cost have been shown to be effective in reducing disinhibited, verbally abusive, physically aggressive, and attention-seeking behaviour as well as incontinence of urine in cases where TE programmes, accompanied by the use of time-out, have not proved effective in controlling these behaviours (for details see Alderman & Burgess, 1990).

Other contingent aversive stimuli. A variety of punishment techniques has been reported in the field of learning disabilities. These techniques involve the use of stimuli, which the people find aversive, contingent upon the targeted, undesirable behaviour. Unpleasant-tasting or unpleasant-smelling substances, water spray, and contingent electric shock have been used with good effect in reducing undesirable behaviours (Murphy & Oliver, 1987). The use of aromatic ammonia vapour has been shown to reduce spitting frequency, an unpleasant throat-clearing habit, and exaggerated nose-picking in a head-injured adult (Wood, 1987). Slightly less effective was the use of exposure to asafoetida, an aversive-smelling liquid, in maintaining reduced spitting in a 20-year-old man who had suffered two subarachnoid haemorrhages, although he did at least spit into a tissue following treatment (Muir, 1992). It is imperative, however, that such stimuli are combined with other positive skill-building programmes, so that the person does not find him- or herself in a totally punitive environment.

Overcorrection. Overcorrection refers to a combination of procedures that might require the person to produce behaviours that are incompatible with, or that correct, the damage produced by the undesirable behaviour. Use of these techniques has been reported extensively for people with learning disabilities.

"Restitution" involves the client restoring the consequences of his or her inappropriate behaviour; for example, someone who damages property through aggressive behaviour would be required to tidy and clear the area and repair whatever they could. "Positive practice" requires the client to practise appropriate styles of responding and behaving in situations in which undesirable behaviour would normally occur (Foxx & Martin, 1975). These two components have been used in conjunction as part of the successful treatment of nocturnal enuresis in a severely brain-injured man (Papworth, 1989). Wood and Burgess (1988) demonstrated that other procedures—"graduated guidance" (which facilitates the desired behaviour through preventing other behaviours from occurring) and "required relaxation" (where the person is required to spend a predesignated period of time in a quiet state following disruptive behaviour)—can be incorporated into overcorrection. They note that the length of overcorrection sessions needs to take into account clients' level of cooperation, and the nature of the disruptive behaviour. They interpret the use of overcorrection as teaching the individual the response cost of the undesirable behaviour through repeated practice, and presumably restitution.

Satiation. Described by Allyon (see Alderman, 1991) satiation involves the repeated, uninterrupted presentation of a specific reinforcer until it acquires neutral or even aversive properties. Alderman (1991) has demonstrated the effectiveness of such an approach in reducing behaviours that have been acquired through negative reinforcement and as such function to enable the individual to avoid particular situations or activities. Alderman (1991) reduced frequency of shouting in a 24-year-old man by exposing the patient to tape-recordings of his own shouting, encouraging him to engage in a difficult behaviour that was likely to result in him shouting, prompting him to shout for several periods of 2–3 minutes and engaging in behaviours that still required some physical effort for him to achieve and that might result in him shouting.

Extinction

When teaching any new skill, there must be contingent reinforcement of the target behaviour in order to increase the probability of its recurrence. By removing the contingent reinforcement, it is therefore possible to reduce the probability that the behaviour will recur. This is extinction. Importantly, once extinction is begun, there will be a transient but significant increase in the undesirable behaviour (the extinction burst) prior to a decline in its frequency. Thus, in the case of life-threatening behaviour, the risk of an extinction burst might well preclude the use of this technique. It is also more difficult to extinguish a behaviour that has been reinforced on an intermittent schedule than one that has received continuous reinforcement (see Murphy & Oliver, 1987). In addition, it can be difficult to prevent a behaviour receiving reinforcement, if not from therapists then from others in the environment. This intermittent reinforcement can strengthen the behaviour and make it more difficult to extinguish. It might be impractical to withold attention, particularly where damage is being done that renders the environment unsafe; the slow decline in frequency of behaviour (particularly following previously intermittently reinforced behaviour) can also render this technique unpopular. Wood and Burgess (1988) also note that extinction can be ineffective if therapists fail to take into account the attentional capabilities of the client, in particular whether the person is aware of the target behaviour and whether or not it is being rewarded.

Decreasing undesirable behaviours using positive reinforcement

Given that it is important to develop adaptive skills when eliminating maladaptive behaviour, and that different intervention techniques can be combined for any one individual, positive reinforcement should play an important role in programmes that reduce undesirable behaviours. In particular, differential reinforcement of desirable behaviours, which might be incompatible with the targeted undesirable behaviour, can be combined with extinction or response cost techniques.

Differential reinforcement of other behaviours (DRO) involves reinforcement for periods of time free from the target behaviour, irrespective of the nature of the other behaviour. Differential reinforcement of incompatible behaviour (DRI) involves reinforcement of behaviours that are incompatible with the target behaviour. This requires greater specification of behaviours to be reinforced than does DRO. Differential reinforcement of low rates of responding (DRL) can be useful where the target behaviour occurs initially with high frequency (see discussion by Alderman et al., 1995) and where differentially reinforcing only low rates of responding can facilitate the later use of a DRO programme (Deitz, 1977). The value of DRO, DRI, and DRL is that they ensure, through careful programme planning, that the probability of occurrence of adaptive behaviour is increased.

Overall, then, a behavioural approach offers techniques for reducing maladaptive behaviours that can be applied to neurological patients. There has been a move, in general, towards the use of positive procedures, wherever possible; whichever technique is used, however, it is likely that the intervention will be successful only if it follows an adequate functional analysis and therefore from a good understanding of the function of the behaviour for that individual.

Ethical issues

Relevant to the use of all behaviour modification techniques, but particularly to the use of punishment and extinction procedures, are ethical considerations. The technology described above can be misused and constant re-evaluation is required of the focus of behavioural interventions—who benefits as a consequence of such interventions, how treatments should be implemented and monitored, and whether individual rights are being infringed. Legal guidelines concerning consent are of relevance. Local ethics committees provide a valuable means of reviewing treatment programmes, and monitoring ethical standards. The nature of aversive techniques that are adopted requires consideration. When dealing with self-injurious behaviour in people with learning disabilities, the principle of using the least restrictive alternative that achieves the desired result (Murphy & Wilson, 1985) is advocated; such a principle is of equal importance when dealing with neurologically damaged, behaviourally disordered clients (Jacobs, 1988).

Programme planning

Neurologically damaged individuals can receive therapeutic input from a variety of disciplines. How services are organised locally will determine whether there is multidisciplinary teamwork or whether services function in isolation with only sporadic communication between them. Fussey (1988) has suggested that, optimally, a team will work together in a way that facilitates therapists' understanding of how their work can be linked to that of other disciplines. Although this is indeed the ideal situation, in practice it might not happen. Although various frameworks exist for management plans (Peters, et al., 1992; Wilson, 1987; Wood, 1989), key information to be included in all programmes should include the following:

(1) **Long-term goal.** What behaviour should the person be performing, in what situations? How does this relate to the discharge setting?

(2) **Task analysis of the behaviour.** What are the component elements of the behaviour? Is the client able to perform all the components independently?

(3) **Short-term goal.** What is the first step (towards the long-term goal) that the client should be trained to complete successfully? What is the criterion for success for passing on to the next short-term goal?

(4) **Selection of appropriate training technique(s).**

(5) **Who will do the training? Where will it take place and when?**

(6) **Materials necessary for training** (including reinforcers).

(7) **Reinforcement contingency.** How and when should reinforcement be delivered?

(8) **Correction procedures.** How to respond if other problem behaviours occur.

(9) **Recording method.** How is the client's performance documented?

(10) **Date of review of progress** so that the programme can be modified where necessary.

Such planning should follow a thorough functional analysis of the problem behaviour and be accompanied by reliable measurement of the problem behaviour in order to acquire sufficient baseline information against which to evaluate improvement due to therapy.

Evaluation of treatment outcome

Good clinical practice requires systematic evaluation of treatment effects. Wilson (1993), discussing the difficulty of specifying rehabilitation programmes with great precision, indicated that double-blind group treatment trials can be difficult to undertake because of the heterogeneous nature of brain damage and its consequences. She therefore recommends that those working in rehabilitation, whether therapists or scientists, should evaluate individual rehabilitation programmes at the level of the individual, although group studies should be conducted where appropriate. She indicates that it is appropriate to adopt a single case design for such evaluations, and that these are particularly efficient for long-term follow-ups of patients or for individual cases with rare syndromes. Several single case designs are available, each with merits and disadvantages (see Barlow & Hersen, 1984). Although they tend to highlight clinical rather than statistical significance (Wilson, 1987), statistics are available for single subject data analysis. Single case designs permit verification that improvement in behaviour results from the intervention and not from non-specific confounding factors, and they have proved invaluable in showing the effectiveness of behaviour programmes with neurological patients (Wilson, 1987; Wood, 1987).

An important aspect of evaluating the effectiveness of behavioural interventions is the recording of an adequate baseline level of behaviour. Davis et al. (1994) have highlighted the necessity of ensuring that baseline data collection provides an accurate representation of the situation in which the undesirable behaviour can occur. They found that baseline data collection might need to be structured because, left to their own devices, staff had been unwilling to deliver feedback and correct a brain-injured client's self care through fear of aggressive responses by the client. This had produced an underestimate of the level of aggressive behaviour prior to treatment.

PRACTICAL ISSUES IN DEVISING AND IMPLEMENTING BEHAVIOUR MODIFICATION PROGRAMMES

Devising and implementing behaviour modification programmes is not necessarily a straightforward endeavour and a number of key issues will need to be considered.

The acceptance of behavioural interventions for brain-injured individuals has come particularly from the work undertaken on a specialist unit with a high staff : client ratio (Eames & Wood, 1985). In such establishments the members of the multidisciplinary team are all trained and are familiar with the use of behaviour modification techniques. In less specialist centres, however, a less favourable staff : client ratio might be established and there can be less familiarity with the principles and methods to be used.

As noted in the earlier discussion of reinforcement, the contingent and consistent delivery of reinforcement is crucial for success. Staff training in non-specialist centres is therefore a necessary first step in the implementation of programmes (Andrewes, 1989). Explanations of procedures might also need to be given to relatives, whose involvement could be crucial for the generalisation of the programme to a non-institutionalised setting. Peters et al. (1992) indicated that training can take a number of forms. Staff should be trained in general to respond appropriately to maladaptive behaviour that occurs with high intensity and frequency, and this training should be highly practical in nature. In addition, staff should receive training in relation to the implementation of specific intervention programmes, i.e. the person responsible for the programme should train all others who will be involved in its implementation. Jacobs (1988) distinguished between training people to devise programmes and to implement them; training in one of these does not automatically qualify someone to do the other.

Inconsistent application of behavioural principles between staff members can be problematic, and there might be value in employing a specialist nurse with the sole duty of implementing a specific programme with a patient in a setting where such interventions are not usually implemented (see McMillan et al. (1990) and discussions by Johnston et al. (1991) and Muir (1992)). Peters et al. (1992) have recommended joint, interdisciplinary development of programmes to ensure consistency of responses made to patients' behaviour.

Even with some training, staff might find the implementation of one client's programme disruptive for the rest of the ward. Andrewes (1989), for example, found that night staff were not prepared to undertake an extinction programme for a client's screaming because leaving the person to scream disturbed the other patients. In addition, the client's parents, to whom behavioural management principles had also been explained, found it hard to ignore his screaming when he seemed to be in pain. Programmes must therefore be designed with a view to what those implementing them can actually bring themselves to do. Training will also need to be given to staff in the client's post-discharge setting to ensure that treatment gains are not lost.

Tate (1987b) has discussed the importance of understanding the range of deficits—cognitive and behavioural—exhibited by an individual with brain injury. Of additional importance are the clients' and their relatives'/carers' understanding of these difficulties and their willingness to accept behavioural interventions that they might find confrontational and hard-hearted. Tate indicates that unless these issues are considered in each client's case, behavioural interventions can be ineffective. Tate suggests that different issues concerning the development and implementation of behavioural programmes can arise, depending on whether the client has: (1) little significant physical injury but is disorientated and confused; (2) significant physical and cognitive deficits but improves over time; or (3) physical, cognitive, and/or behavioural problems of such severity that they require long-term care.

In all applications of behavioural interventions with brain-damaged individuals, however, care has to be taken to recognise the limitations of the severely injured brain. Initial low levels of performance (Miller, 1980) as well as characteristics of the "dysexecutive syndrome" (Baddeley & Wilson, 1988)—including poor attention (Van Zomeren et al., 1984; Wood, 1987) and poor attentional control, impaired planning ability, poor memory (Wilson, 1987), reduced motivation and drive, as well as disorders of hedonic responsiveness (amongst many adverse consequences of head injury; see Eames, 1988)—are some of the many factors that make the design of a behaviour modification programme challenging for the therapist. They serve, however, to emphasise the need to be aware of the neurological and neuropsychological status and the premorbid history of the individual who is being required to learn (Burgess & Wood, 1990; Eames, 1988; Wood, 1989; Wood & Eames, 1981).

Psychiatric disorders (Bond, 1984; Prigatano et al., 1988; Rose, 1988) can also place limitations on programmes, and might require recourse to yet more specialist services, but the behavioural approach will still offer a clear framework within which to set the relevant goals for neurological rehabilitation. In addition, such techniques can permit establishment of adequate behavioural control on which can be built more cognitively oriented programmes (Alderman & Ward, 1991; Goldstein & Oakley, 1985).

Some additional consideration has been given to identifying those patients for whom behaviour modification is ineffective. Eames (1992), reviewing 167 clients who had been admitted to the Kemsley Unit, observed that 54 might be considered to have a hysterical disorder. In this group there was a tendency for behavioural disorders not to respond to reinforcement; these people demonstrated a lack of response to pleasure or pain that Eames considered to be hedonic unresponsiveness.

Alderman (1996) has also considered the characteristics of patients who had failed to respond to a generalised token economy. He identified the presence of deficient performance on a dual-task experiment as a poor prognostic factor; this poor performance indicated impairment of the central executive component in Baddeley's (1986) working memory model. Alderman used these findings to suggest that patients who are poor at allocating attention between different tasks have

difficulty in monitoring competing activities. This could result in their failing to respond to feedback when they are engaged in some other activity, particularly in a busy and distracting environment. Alderman et al. (1995) have outlined a range of features of time-out, response cost, or self-monitoring training that might influence programme design for individuals whose behaviour disorders are thought to be secondary to impaired self-monitoring ability. On a more general level, Tate (1987b) has urged caution in applying behavioural programmes to patients who are still in post-traumatic amnesia, as there is little documented evidence concerning long-term maintenance of behavioural change in such individuals.

Failure to identify suitable reinforcers for patients will often lead to programme failure. Motivational deficits are increasingly being discussed in patients with traumatic brain injury and pharmacological agents could have an increasing role to play in reducing the abulia that might be present and in increasing sensitivity to reward (Powell et al., 1996).

The manner in which maladaptive behaviours have been acquired and maintained should be considered prior to devising a behavioural programme. Youngson and Alderman (1994) suggested that behaviours that have been acquired through negative reinforcement can be particularly difficult to modify simply using standard positive-reinforcement-based techniques. These tend to be behaviours that result in the avoidance of some activity in which the person does not wish to engage.

In view of the need to demonstrate clinical effectiveness of behavioural (or indeed any other) intervention, adequate data collection must be undertaken throughout the implementation of the programme. Staff need to be aware of the value of single case designs in demonstrating treatment efficacy, but will also need training in data collection methods. Peters et al. (1992) recommended ensuring staff accountability for data collection. Jacobs (1988) stressed the importance of regular reviews of the collected data; apart from making staff appreciate the value of their endeavours, changes in programme implementation can then be made on the basis of the data that has been recorded.

Individuals with brain damage are likely to be poor at generalising skills and thus attempts must be made during training to reduce the level of prompting and frequency of reinforcement, as well as encouraging the practising of the skill in a variety of settings, if gains made during treatment are not to be lost rapidly. Enlisting the help and training of future carers in some of the behavioural methods used in developing and maintaining the necessary skills in the brain-damaged adult can help to limit skill loss following discharge.

EXAMPLES OF THE USE OF A BEHAVIOURAL APPROACH TO THE MODIFICATION OF PROBLEM BEHAVIOUR ASSOCIATED WITH NEUROLOGICAL DAMAGE

Throughout the foregoing discussion, references have been made to the use of behaviour modification techniques with individuals who have suffered traumatic brain injury. Given the robust nature of associative learning in the presence of extensive damage to the mammalian brain, it has been shown that this methodology should offer hope for rehabilitating individuals who have lost skills or acquired undesirable behaviours. There has been considerable development in treatment approaches adopted for individual clients, brought about by an integration of behaviour modification technology and cognitive neuropsychology (Burgess & Alderman, 1990). The application of behavioural techniques in dealing with problem behaviour has already been illustrated, but a few further examples might serve to emphasise the point that, for a group of individuals for whom rehabilitation might otherwise be denied, severe brain injury need not imply therapeutic nihilism.

Behavioural interventions are possible not only in specialist treatment units but also in day-treatment settings (Wood, 1988). Examples include: the use of positive reinforcement to shape correct head posture and thus facilitate attention to, and engagement in, therapeutic activities; the use of prompts (and their subsequent fading) and positive reinforcement to train the correct positioning of a wheelchair to enable a client to reach and use a toilet independently; the use of DRO with token reinforcement to decrease inappropriate sexual contact initiated by a male client towards female staff, and to decrease argumentative and uncooperative behaviour in another young male client. As indicated previously, such interventions are also feasible in a unit with little previous experience of managing severe behavioural problems in brain-damaged adults, provided that a special nurse can be available exclusively to administer the behavioural regime for the particular patient (McMillan et al., 1990).

McMillan et al. (1990) describe the treatment of a young woman who developed severe behaviour problems following herpes simplex encephalitis. Violent behaviour was reduced using DRO and brief restraint in conjunction with carbamazepine and a short trial of lithium carbonate. Once this undesirable behaviour no longer occurred, sexually disinhibited behaviour was decreased in supervised situations by a programme incorporating DRO, verbal punishment, and a form of time-out-on-the-spot. Finally, self-care activities were increased in this woman using chaining and prompting. The outcome was discharge to the family home. Violent and sexually disinhibited behaviour has been modified in a range of other cases using different combinations of tokens, differential reinforcement and time-out (Muir, 1992; Slifer, et al., 1995; Tate, 1987b).

Problems of incontinence can place restrictions on rehabilitation and residential placement opportunities. Papworth (1989) treated nocturnal enuresis in a 42-year-old severely brain-damaged man using, in addition to bladder training and regular night-time awakenings, self-correction with positive practice following incontinence as well as reinforcement for being dry. Fear of incontinence was treated in a 34-year-old head-injured man; this had resulted in him avoiding rehabilitation activities that were important for his re-integration into the community (Youngson & Alderman, 1994). This negatively reinforced behaviour was treated successfully using a combination of graded *in vivo* exposure (to reduce his anxiety) and

differential reinforcement of incompatible behaviour. Interestingly, although this man showed a reduction in the times he requested to go to the toilet or referred to wanting to urinate, his subjective anxiety about incontinence did not decrease.

Inappropriate verbal behaviour can also disrupt rehabilitation. Perseverative behaviour, in the form of frequent requests to use the telephone by a 23-year-old woman with anoxic damage secondary to an attempt at self-hanging, was treated initially by encouraging self-monitoring of the target behaviour and then by extinction (Matthey, 1996), although generalisation to the home setting was problematic. Involuntary oral behaviours (exhalations, vocalisations, facial grimacing, tongue protrusions, and lip smacking) were the target of behaviour programmes for a 53-year-old woman who had suffered a subarachnoid haemorrhage (Hanlon et al., 1993). The woman was cued to perform behaviours that were incompatible with the undesirable behaviours, and improvement was sensitive to the active treatment stages of the programme, although dependent to some extent on the specific behaviour being observed.

In addition, Alderman et al. (1995) found that, in the case of a 21-year-old female who had probably contracted herpes simplex encephalitis, a behavioural programme based on response cost (using tokens) was effective in reducing the frequency of unwanted stereotyped phrases; in addition the patient subsequently began to use more appropriate non-verbal ways of communicating her need for attention from staff. This procedure had been considerably more effective than time-out-on-the-spot, but despite impressive results within the rehabilitation unit there was poor generalisation to other settings. Alderman et al. (1995) therefore devised a self-monitoring programme using a variant of differential reinforcement of low rate behaviour. The patient was taught to monitor the frequency of her utterances (and was prompted to do this where necessary) and was reinforced for accurate self-recording. Finally, she was rewarded for successive reductions in the number of inappropriate vocalisations; it was only this aspect of the programme that led her to reduce her unwanted behaviour.

Behavioural approaches to treatment can also be of value in the acute care rehabilitation setting (Howard, 1988), and can facilitate management of patients with impaired alertness, attention and memory, rapid fatigue, confusion, and disorientation. Environmental restructuring as well as response contingent reinforcement can be of value in such cases. The application of operant-based behavioural treatments in the acute settings has been extended to children with traumatic brain injury (Slifer et al., 1995). Here, maladaptive behaviour that was obstructing neuroimaging investigations and rehabilitation was decreased. The range of potential behavioural interventions is therefore considerable.

CONCLUSIONS

Behaviour problems (excesses or deficits) in neurologically damaged patients can impede rehabilitation, raise the cost of care, and prevent independence. As has been demonstrated, behaviour modification techniques, often derived originally from work with animals, can be effective in reducing unwanted behaviour and developing the expression of appropriate behaviour. Certainly, the capacity for associative learning demonstrated in both animals and humans when there is severe damage or reduction to the cerebral cortex should provide encouragement for anyone contemplating the use of behaviour modification in neurological rehabilitation programmes. Such

techniques require objectivity in defining and measuring behaviour, and permit potentially good continuity of care between different members of the therapeutic team. Much of the work reviewed in this chapter serves to indicate that the presence of severe brain damage, in particular, does not mean that extensive behavioural improvements are unattainable goals. Therapists must be positive in their expectations, even if the ends are achieved through many small steps.

REFERENCES

Alderman N (1991) The treatment of avoidance behaviour following severe brain injury by satiation through negative practice. *Brain Injury, 5*, 77–86.

Alderman N (1996) Central executive deficit and response to operant conditioning methods. *Neuropsychological Rehabilitation, 6*, 161–186.

Alderman N, Burgess PW (1990) Integrating cognition and behaviour: a pragmatic approach to brain injury rehabilitation. In RLl Wood, I Fussey (Eds.), *Cognitive rehabilitation in perspective*. London: Taylor & Francis, pp. 204–208.

Alderman N, Burgess PW (1994) A comparison of treatment methods for behaviour disorder following herpes simplex encephalitis. *Neuropsychological Rehabilitation, 4*, 31–48.

Alderman N, Fry RK, Youngson HA (1995) Improvement of self-monitoring skills, reduction of behaviour disturbance and the dysexecutive syndrome: Comparison of response cost and a new programme of self-monitoring training. *Neuropsychological Rehabilitation, 5*, 193–221.

Alderman N, Ward A (1991) Behavioural treatment of the dysexecutive syndrome: Reduction of repetitive speech using response cost and cognitive overlearning. *Neuropsychological Rehabilitation, 1*, 65–80.

Andrewes D (1989) Management of disruptive behaviour in the brain-damaged patient using selective reinforcement. *Journal of Behaviour Therapy and Experimental Psychiatry, 20*, 261–264.

Aylward GP, Lazzara A, Meyer J (1978) Behavioural and neurological characteristics of a hydrancephalic infant. *Developmental Medicine and Child Neurology, 20*, 211–217.

Baddeley AD (1986) *Working memory*. Oxford: Clarendon Press.

Baddeley AD, Wilson B (1988) Frontal amnesia and the dysexecutive syndrome. *Brain and Cognition, 7*, 212–230.

Barlow DH, Hersen M (1984) *Single case experimental designs. Strategies for studying behaviour change*, 2nd edn. New York: Pergamon.

Bernal G, Jacobson L, Lopez G (1975) Do the effects of behaviour modification programs endure? *Behaviour Research and Therapy, 13*, 61–64.

Berntson G, Tuber DS, Ronca AE, Bachman DS (1983) The decerebrate human: Associative learning. *Experimental Neurology, 81*, 77–88.

Blackerby WF (1988) Practical token economies. *Journal of Head Trauma Rehabilitation, 3*, 33–45.

Bond M (1984) The psychiatry of closed head injury. In N Brooks (Ed.), *Closed head injury. Psychological, social and family consequences*. Oxford: Oxford University Press, pp. 148–178.

Burgess PW, Alderman N (1990) Rehabilitation of dyscontrol syndromes following frontal lobe damage: A cognitive neuropsychological approach. In RLl Wood, I Fussey (Eds.), *Cognitive rehabilitation in perspective*. London: Taylor & Francis, pp. 183–203.

Burgess PW, Wood RLl (1990) Neuropsychology of behaviour disorders following brain injury. In RLl Wood (Ed.), *Neurobehavioural sequelae of traumatic brain injury*. London: Taylor & Francis, pp. 110–133.

Carr J (1987) Imitation. In W Yule, J Car (Eds.), *Behaviour modification for people with mental handicaps*, 2nd edn. London: Croom Helm, pp. 95–101.

Carr J, Gathercole C (1987) The use of tokens with individuals and groups. In W Yule, J Carr (Eds.), *Behaviour modification for people with mental handicaps*, 2nd edn. London: Croom Helm, pp. 47–67.

Daum I, Channon S, Canavan AGM (1989) Classical conditioning in patients with severe memory problems. *Journal of Neurology, Neurosurgery and Psychiatry, 52*, 47–51.

Davis JR, Turner W, Rolider A, Cartwright T (1994) Natural and structured baselines in the treatment of aggression following brain injury. *Brain Injury, 8*, 589–597.

Deiker T, Bruno RD (1976) Sensory reinforcement of eyeblink rate in a decorticate human. *American Journal of Mental Deficiency, 80*, 665–667.

Deitz SM (1977) An analysis of programming schedules in educational settings. *Behaviour Research and Therapy, 15*, 103–111.

Department of Health and Welsh Office (1993) *Code of practice: Mental Health Act 1983*. London: HMSO.

Eames P (1988) Behaviour disorders after severe head injury: Their nature and causes and strategies for management. *Journal of Head Trauma Rehabilitation, 3*, 1–6.

Eames P (1992) Hysteria following brain injury. *Journal of Neurology, Neurosurgery and Psychiatry, 55*, 1046–1053.

Eames P, Wood RLl (1985) Rehabilitation after severe brain injury: A follow-up study of a behaviour modification approach. *Journal of Neurology, Neurosurgery and Psychiatry, 48*, 613–619.

Foxx RM, Martin ED (1975) Treatment of scavenging behaviour by over-correction. *Behaviour Research and Therapy, 13*, 153–162.

Furchtgott E, Jones JR, Tacker RS, Deagle J (1976) Aversive conditioning in prenatally X-irradiated rats. *Physiology and Behaviour, 5*, 571–576.

Fussey I (1988) The application of a behavioural model in rehabilitation. In I Fussey, GM Giles (Eds.) *Rehabilitation of the severely brain-injured adult. A practical approach*. London: Croom Helm, pp. 183–195.

Gardner WI (1971) *Behaviour modification in mental retardation*. London: University of London Press.

Giles GM, Clark-Wilson J (1988) Functional skills training in severe brain injury. In I Fussey, GM Giles (Eds.), *Rehabilitation of the severely brain-injured adult. A practical approach*. London: Croom Helm, pp. 69–101.

Giles, GM, Fussey I (1988) Models of brain injury rehabilitation: From theory to practice. In I Fussey, GM Giles (Eds.), *Rehabilitation of the severely brain-injured adult. A practical approach*. London: Croom Helm, pp. 1–29.

Goldstein LH (1986) Learning theory and behaviour therapy in rehabilitation after head injury. *Second International Headway Conference: Models of Brain Injury Rehabilitation, London*.

Goldstein LH, Oakley DA (1985) Expected and actual behavioural capacity after diffuse reduction in cerebral cortex: A review and suggestions for rehabilitative techniques with the mentally handicapped and head injured. *British Journal of Clinical Psychology, 24*, 13–24.

Goldstein LH, Oakley DA (1987) Visual discrimination in the absence of visual cortex. *Behavioural Brain Research, 24*, 181–193.

Goldstein LH, Oakley DA (1989) Autoshaping in micrencephalic rats. *Behavioural Neuroscience, 103*, 566–573.

Haffey W, Johnston MV (1989) An information system to assess the effectiveness of brain injury rehabilitation. In RLl Wood, P Eames (Eds.), *Models of brain injury rehabilitation*. London: Chapman and Hall, pp. 205–233.

Hanlon R, Clontz B, Thomas M (1993) Management of severe behavioural dyscontrol following subarrachnoid haemorrhage. *Neuropsychological Rehabilitation, 3*, 63–76.

Hemsley R, Carr J (1987) Ways of increasing behaviour: Reinforcement. In W Yule, J Carr (Eds.), *Behaviour modification for people with mental handicaps*. 2nd edn. London: Croom Helm, pp. 28–46.

Hooper-Roe J (1988) Rehabilitation of physical deficits in the post-acute brain-injured: Four case studies. In I Fussey, GW Giles (Eds.), *Rehabilitation of the severely brain-injured adult. A practical approach*. London: Croom Helm, pp. 102–115.

Howard ME (1988) Behaviour management in the acute care rehabilitation setting. *Journal of Head Trauma Rehabilitation, 3*, 14–22.

Iwata BA, Dorsey MF, Slifer KJ (1982) Toward a functional analysis of self injury. *Analysis and Intervention in Developmental Disabilities, 2*, 3–20.

Jacobs HE (1988) Yes, behaviour analysis can help, but do you know how to harness it? *Brain Injury, 2*, 339–346.

Jacobson L, Bernal G, Lopez G (1973) Effects of behavioural training on the function of a profoundly retarded microcephalic teenager with cerebral palsy and without language. *Behaviour Research and Therapy, 11*, 143–145.

Johnston S, Burgess J, McMillan T, Greenwood R (1991) Management of adipsia by a behavioural modification technique. *Journal of Neurology, Neurosurgery and Psychiatry, 54*, 272–274.

Kanfer FM, Grimm LG (1977) Behaviour analysis: Selecting target behaviours in the interview. *Behaviour Modification, 1*, 7–28.

Kanfer FM, Saslow G (1969) Behavioural diagnosis. In CM Franks (Ed.), *Behaviour therapy: Appraisal and status*. New York: McGraw-Hill, pp. 417–444.

Kearney S, Fussey I (1991) The use of adapted leisure materials to reinforce correct head positioning in a brain-injured adult. *Brain Injury, 5*, 295–302.

Kiernan C (1973) Functional analysis. In P Mittler (Ed.), *Assessment for learning in the mentally handicapped*. London: Churchill Livingstone, pp. 263–283.

McMillan TM, Papadopoulas H, Cornwall C, Greenwood RW (1990) Modification of severe behaviour problems following Herpes simplex encephalitis. *Brain Injury, 4*, 399–406.

Matthey S (1996) Modification of perseverative behaviour in an adult with anoxic brain damage. *Brain Injury, 10*, 219–227.

Miller E (1980) The training characteristics of severely head-injured patients: A preliminary study. *Journal of Neurology, Neurosurgery and Psychiatry, 43*, 525–528.

Miller E (1984) *Recovery and management of neuropsychological impairments*. Chichester: John Wiley.

Muir S (1992) Haemorrhagic brain injury: A care study. *Nursing Standard, 6*, 25–28.

Murphy G (1987) Direct observation as an assessment tool in functional analysis and treatment. In J Hogg, NV Raynes (Eds.), *Assessment in mental handicap. A guide to assessment practices, tests and check lists*. London: Croom Helm, pp. 190–238.

Murphy G, Goodall E (1980) Measurement error in direct observations. A comparison of common recording methods. *Behaviour Research and Therapy, 18*, 147–150.

Murphy G, Oliver C (1987) Decreasing undesirable behaviours. In W Yule, J Carr (Eds.), *Behaviour modification for people with mental handicaps*, 2nd edn. London: Croom Helm, pp. 102–142.

Murphy G, Wilson B (Eds.), (1985) *Self-injurious behaviour*. Kidderminster: British Institute of Mental Handicap Publications.

Nelson RO, Hayes SC (1981) Nature of behavioural assessment. In M Hersen, AS Bellack (Eds.), *Behavioural assessment. A practical handbook*. New York: Pergamon, pp. 3–37.

Oakley DA (1979a) Cerebral cortex and adaptive behaviour. In DA Oakley, HC Plotkin (Eds.), *Brain behaviour and evolution*. London: Methuen, pp. 154–180.

Oakley DA (1979b) Instrumental reversal learning and subsequent fixed ratio performance on simple and go/no-go schedules in neodecorticate rabbits. *Physiological Psychology, 7*, 29–42.

Oakley DA (1980) Improved instrumental learning in neodecorticate rats. *Physiology and Behaviour, 24*, 357–366.

Oakley DA (1981) Brain mechanisms of mammalian memory. *British Medical Bulletin, 37*, 175–180.

Oakley DA (1983a) Learning capacity outside neocortex in animals and man: Implications for therapy after brain-injury. In G Davey (Ed.), *Animal models of human behaviour: Conceptual, evolutionary and neurobiological perspectives*. Chichester: John Wiley, pp. 247–266.

Oakley DA (1983b) The varieties of memory: A phylogenetic approach. In A Mayes (Ed.), *Memory in animals and humans*. Wokingham: Van Nostrand-Reinhold, pp. 20–82.

Oakley DA, Russell IS (1977) Subcortical storage of Pavlovian conditioning in the rabbit. *Physiology and Behaviour, 18*, 931–937.

Oakley DA, Russell IS (1978) Manipulandum identification in operant behaviour in neodecorticate rabbits. *Physiology and Behaviour, 21*, 943–950.

Oakley DA, Russell IS (1979) Instrumental learning on fixed ratio and go no-go schedules in neodecorticate rabbits. *Brain Research, 161*, 356–360.

Oakley DA, Eames LC, Jacobs JL et al. (1981) Signal-centred action patterns in rats without neocortex in a pavlovian conditioning situation. *Physiological Psychology, 9*, 135–144.

Papworth MA (1989) The behavioural treatment of nocturnal enuresis in a severely brain-damaged client. *Journal of Behaviour Therapy and Experimental Psychiatry, 20*, 265–268.

Pereira S, Russell IS (1981) Learning in normal and microcephalic rats. In MW Van Hof, G Mohn (Eds.), *Functional recovery from brain damage*. Amsterdam: Elsevier, pp. 131–147.

Peters MD, Gluck M, McCormick M (1992) Behaviour rehabilitation of the challenging client in less restrictive settings. *Brain Injury, 6*, 299–314.

Powell JH, al-Adawi S, Morgan J, Greenwood RJ (1996) Motivational deficits after brain injury: Effects of bromocriptine in 11 patients. *Journal of Neurology, Neurosurgery and Psychiatry, 60*, 416–421.

Prigatano GP, O'Brien KP, Klanoff PS (1988) The clinical management of paranoid delusions in postacute traumatic brain-injured patients. *Journal of Head Trauma Rehabilitation, 3*, 23–32.

Rabe A, Haddad RK (1972) Methylazoxymethanol-induced microcephaly in rats: Behavioural studies. *Federation Proceedings, 31*, 1536–1539.

Raynes NV, Pratt MW, Roses S (1979) *Organisational structure and the care of the mentally retarded*. London: Croom Helm.

Rose MJ (1988) The place of drugs in the management of behaviour disorders after traumatic brain injury. *Journal of Head Trauma Rehabilitation, 3*, 7–13.

Rosenstein LD, Price RF (1994) Shaping a normal rate of eating using audiotaped pacing in conjunction with a token economy. *Neuropsychological Rehabilitation, 4*, 387–398.

Sarimski K (1982) Effects of etiology and cognitive ability on observational learning of retarded children. *International Journal of Rehabilitation Research, 5*, 75–78.

Shiel A, Wilson B, Horn S, Watson M, McLellan L (1993) Can patients in coma following traumatic head injury learn simple tasks? *Neuropsychological Rehabilitation, 3*, 161–175.

Slifer KJ, Cataldo MD, Kurtz PF (1995) Behavioural training during acute brain trauma rehabilitation: An empirical case study. *Brain Injury, 9*, 585–593.

Tamaki Y, Inouye M (1976) Brightness discrimination in a Skinner box in prenatally X-irradiated rats. *Physiology and Behaviour, 16*, 343–348.

Tate RL (1987a) Issues in the management of behaviour disturbance as a consequence of severe head injury. *Scandinavian Journal of Rehabilitation Medicine, 19*, 13–18.

Tate RL (1987b) Behaviour management techniques for organic psychosocial deficit incurred by severe head injury. *Scandinavian Journal of Rehabilitation Medicine, 19*, 19–24.

Tsoi M, Yule W (1987) Building up new behaviours: shaping, promoting and fading. In W Yule, J Carr (Eds.), *Behaviour modification for people with mental handicaps*, 2nd edn. London: Croom Helm, pp. 68–78.

Tuber DS, Berntson GB, Bachman DS, Allen JN (1980) Associative learning in premature hydranencephalic and normal twins. *Science, 210*, 1035–1037.

Turnbull J (1988) Perils (hidden and not so hidden) for the token economy. *Journal of Head Trauma Rehabilitation, 3*, 46–52.

Van Zomeren AH, Brouwer WH, Deelman EG (1984) Attentional deficits: The riddles of selectivity, speed and alertness. In N Brooks (Ed.), *Closed head injury. Psychological, social and family consequences*. Oxford: Oxford University Press, pp. 74–107.

Wilson BA (1987) *Rehabilitation of memory*. New York: Guilford.

Wilson BA (1993) Editorial: How do we know that rehabilitation works? *Neuropsychological Rehabilitation, 3*, 1–4.

Wood RLl (1987) *Brain injury rehabilitation: A neurobehavioural approach*. London: Croom Helm.

Wood RLl (1988) Management of behaviour disorders in a day treatment setting. *Journal of Head Trauma Rehabilitation, 3*, 53–61.

Wood RLl (1989) A salient factors approach to brain injury rehabilitation. In RLl Wood, P Eames (Eds.), *Models of brain injury rehabilitation*. London: Chapman and Hall, pp. 75–99.

Wood RLl, Burgess P (1988) The psychological management of behaviour disorders following brain injury. In I Fussey, GM Giles (Eds.), *Rehabilitation of the severely brain-injured adult. A practical approach*. London: Croom Helm, pp. 43–68.

Wood RLl, Eames P (1981) Application of behaviour modification in the treatment of traumatically head-injured adults. In G Davey (Ed.), *Applications of conditioning theory*. London: Methuen, pp. 81–101.

Woods SC, Lawson R, Haddad RK et al. (1974) Reversal of conditioned aversions in normal and microcephalic rats. *Journal of Comparative and Physiological Psychology, 86*, 531–534.

Wright L (1973) Aversive conditioning of self-induced seizures. *Behaviour Therapy, 4*, 713–721.

Youngson HA, Alderman N (1994) Fear of incontinence and its effects on a community-based rehabilitation programme after severe brain injury: Successful remediation of escape behaviour using behaviour modification. *Brain Injury, 8*, 23–36.

Yule W (1987) Identifying problems: Functional analysis and observation and recording techniques. In W Yule, J Carr (Eds.), *Behaviour modification for people with mental handicaps*, 2nd edn. London: Croom Helm, pp. 8–27.

Yule W, Carr J (Eds.), (1987) *Behaviour modification for people with mental handicap*, 2nd edn. London: Croom Helm.

32. Psychiatry in neurological rehabilitation

Allan House

INTRODUCTION

Psychiatry can be involved in many of the clinical problems which present in neurological rehabilitation. There are sections elsewhere in this book on unexplained physical syndromes, somatisation and abnormal illness behaviour (Chapters 24 and 33), chronic pain (Chapter 19), behaviour problems (Chapter 31) and sexual dysfunction (Chapter 22). Each of these clinical problems merits psychiatric input into what should be a multidisciplinary approach to assessment and treatment. This chapter will concentrate on problems that have a major emotional component and for which psychiatric help is often requested. They fall into five main groups.

COMMON PRESENTING PROBLEMS

Mood disorders

There are four common disturbances of mood which merit psychiatric attention.

Depressive disorders. Depressive disorders are commonly found in the physically ill (see, for example, Robertson & Catona, 1997). They are characterised by a sustained, unpleasant mood variously described as sadness, unhappiness or anhedonia (inability to feel pleasure). There might be behavioural accompaniments (social withdrawal, physical slowing, crying), cognitive accompaniments (ideas of hopelessness, worthlessness, guilt), and what are sometimes called physiological, biological, or vegetative accompaniments (anorexia, weight loss, insomnia, early morning waking, diurnal mood variation, loss of libido).

The importance of the cognitive accompaniments is that there is some evidence that they affect the prognosis of depression. Ideas of hopelessness and low self-esteem are particularly likely to lead to recurrence if the patient is faced with new adversities (Beck et al., 1979). The principal importance of biological symptoms is that they are generally held to predict response to antidepressant medication (Paykel, 1971). Although this is true, anybody who has suffered a major bereavement will know that acute grief can produce all the biological symptoms of depression, so that the use of symptoms to predict treatment response

is no more than a rule of thumb. The importance of the behavioural accompaniments of depressive disorders is that it is they that usually bring the problem to attention and that interfere with the rehabilitation process.

Depressive disorders are classified according to a diagnostic typology such as DSM-IV (American Psychiatric Association, 1994) or ICD-10 (World Health Organization, 1992). They fall into three main groups: (1) *adjustment disorders*, which are temporally linked to a stressor (such as onset or relapse of disease) and tend to resolve with time, usually less than 6 months from onset; (2) *major depression*, which is more severe and often more persistent; and (3) *dysthymia*, which is chronic (often lasting years) and unrelated to environmental stress.

To the practising clinician, the specific diagnostic label attached to depression is less important than whether a depressive state is contributing to impairment of function, and how it might best be treated. For these reasons the continuum view of depression (Kendell, 1969) is the most useful in rehabilitation practice, with the most symptomatic and most functionally impaired being those regarded as most clinically ill.

Anxiety states. Like depression, anxiety is a mood disorder with physiological, behavioural, and cognitive accompaniments. Indeed, anxiety is traditionally identified by its autonomic accompaniments. In recent years there has been a growth of interest in the cognitive elements of anxiety, sometimes called psychic anxiety. So-called anxious or catastrophic thinking can have major effects on the individual's functioning because of predictions made about the consequences of any likely action (see, for example, Hawton et al., 1989). Not surprisingly, anxiety is a common accompaniment of many serious physical diseases (Noyes & Hochn-Saric, 1998). Anxiety associated with neurological disorders is just one example of this general phenomenon.

Anxiety provides another example of the importance in rehabilitation of the behavioural and cognitive accompaniments of mood disorder. The central behavioural accompaniment of anxiety is avoidance of anxiety-provoking stimuli. This might, for example, mean agoraphobia, avoiding physical activity (including, perhaps, sexual activity), or even avoiding human company. It can result from (for example) anxious preoccupation with falling, or with the possibility of recurrent stroke brought on by exertion. If avoidance is extensive there might be no obvious somatic anxiety symptoms, leading to the diagnosis being missed and the patient being designated antisocial or lacking in motivation.

Irritability. British practice tends to neglect the irritable mood state (*Verstimmung*) as part of the normal emotional repertoire, incorporating it instead into depressive states. This is unfortunate because it is important in neurological practice (Galbraith, 1985). When irritability is identified in its own right it becomes equated with aggression, which is a type of behaviour and not a mood state. The rehabilitation importance of irritability is twofold. First, it is frequently associated with intolerance of advice or involvement in physical activities. Second, it makes people hard work to be with and thereby puts them at risk of receiving less professional or family attention that they might otherwise do.

For a fuller review of general psychiatric approaches to states of anxiety and irritability the reader is referred to Snaith (1991).

Emotionalism (emotional lability). It is a particular characteristic of neurological disorders that they lead to disturbances of emotionality, that is, to disturbance in the normal control or expression of emotion.

Poeck (1985) distinguished two syndromes; one he called pathological crying and laughing, and the other emotional lability. Pathological crying and laughing is provoked by non-emotional stimuli; there is no persisting affect that accompanies emotional display and which is appropriate to that display; emotional behaviour is stereotyped (Poeck used the term "automatic sequence"), and emotional expression cannot be controlled. By contrast, emotional lability is provoked by emotionally appropriate stimuli, it is often accompanied by mood change, and it looks like normal crying or laughing. Most authors since Poeck have not maintained this distinction, and the terms are often used interchangeably. For that reason, I have preferred the less specific term "emotionalism" to describe these phenomena.

Disorders of emotionality have traditionally been thought of as psychologically meaningless, and the emotional display as being a direct manifestation of brain pathology. Although that might be true of the more extreme forms of pathological crying and laughing, there is evidence for a wider psychological disturbance in many cases of emotionalism, which suggests that it can arise, or be maintained, by other emotional factors such as disturbed adjustment or coping (Calvert et al., 1998; Eccles et al., 1999).

Indifference and denial

Almost the opposite of emotional disorder, but none the less disabling, is the pathological absence of concern about neurological illness. Its two main manifestations are *emotional indifference* and *denial*.

Emotional indifference. This appears more often as apathy, accompanied by behavioural inertia, than it does as light-heartedness or euphoria. Although it can be associated with denial, the two can occur independently.

Denial. This is a term used to cover a range of phenomena stretching from downplaying of physical difficulties that could have psychological causes (Weinstein, 1991) to complete and explicit verbal denial of the existence of illness—anosognosia (Prigatano & Schacter, 1991).

Poor cooperation or poor adherence to treatment

It is an oversimplification to regard people as being either good or bad compliers; it is more appropriate instead to think of compliance as a continuously distributed variable (Feely & Pullar, 1989; Pullar et al., 1989). It is therefore worth distinguishing poor/partial compliance from marked non-compliance. The factors that contribute to completeness of compliance include the complexity and inconvenience of the regimen, the adequacy with which it is explained and understood by the patient, the degree to which the patient's relatives support and encourage compliance, and the patient's individual psychological characteristics (Meichenbaum & Turk, 1987). It is likely that partial (sloppy) compliance has relatively superficial or social explanations related to the complexity or inconvenience of treatment regimens. Marked non-compliance where, for example, tablets are not taken unless severely supervised or therapy sessions are refused or avoided, is more likely to have psychological reasons. Such reasons include attitudes to doctors and authority figures, negative beliefs about hospitals and the efficacy of treatment, or negative beliefs about personal responsibility for treatment.

Relationship problems

Chronic severe neurological illness poses problems for the patient by virtue of the way it affects personal relationships. The illness, by enforcing inactivity, can affect the amount of time the sufferer spends in the company of others, but the time spent is of lower quality because of the intrusion of practical inconveniences and treatment needs. The whole balance of relationships that were established prior to the illness is likely to be upset by the development of physical, social and financial dependence upon a carer (Lyons et al., 1995; Strain, 1978). Such changes in relationships are part and parcel of the experience of illness and become a psychiatric problem only under certain circumstances. There are three common presentations of such interpersonal problems:

(1) Some aspect of the patient's behaviour is complained of by the family, who present it to rehabilitation staff as a symptom of illness:

> A 53-year-old man was presented by his wife as being miserable, apathetic and unable to care for himself at home. She described him as completely changed since transfrontal resection of a craniopharyngioma. During admission for assessment, the man's mood lifted dramatically and his social skills and interest in self-care improved in parallel. His mood symptoms were not the result of frontal lobe damage, but were a response to his wife's unceasing criticism of his personality and behaviour.

(2) The patient's relationship with rehabilitation staff is affecting progress:

A young man had sustained severe non-dominant hemisphere damage from a penetrating injury. He caused problems by his constant challenging banter with rehabilitation therapists, coupled with sexual innuendo and propositioning female members of staff. He was the "black sheep" in a family ruled by an authoritarian father who viewed his injury as retribution for his disobedience. In that context his behaviour towards staff could be seen as an expression of his need for personal freedom and as a manifestation of his lack of experience in negotiating the limits to social behaviour.

(3) Difficulties between staff and family members usually arise when there is a conflict over the appropriate level of family involvement with the patient. Overinvolved families find it difficult to accept the element of risk-taking that is implicit in finding the highest level of independent function of which the patient is capable. Underinvolved or frankly antagonistic families can covertly resist the assumption that they should assist in the care of a relative for whom they have had little or no affection. In either situation, it can become apparent only late in the day that slow rehabilitation is attributable to differences of opinion between staff and family (see Chapter 2).

Provoked mental illness

In rare but problematic patients, severe mental illness appears to be provoked by the stress of neurological disorder. Examples include schizophrenia and other paranoid states provoked by focal brain lesions, and so-called symptomatic mania. Despite the vigorous arguments of some enthusiasts, there is little good evidence that the specific nature of neuropathology accounts for the emergence of these mental illnesses. As with severe puerperal illness, it is personal or family disposition that is likely to explain the problem. For a full review of the relationship between

severe mental illness and neurological disorder see Lishman (1998).

Occasionally, a patient with a sudden illness such as stroke or traumatic injury, where there has been no time to prepare for subsequent disability, will develop a post-traumatic stress disorder (Sembi et al., 1998).

ASSESSMENT AND DIAGNOSIS

We can consider assessment and diagnosis in two ways. The first involves the use of standardised assessments, either self-report inventories or structured interviews. The second approach involves non-structured or unstandardised assessment where we are seeking qualitative information rather than quantitative data. The clinical use of the standardised assessment is predominantly in screening and perhaps to a lesser extent in monitoring change over time. The principal use of the unstandardised assessment is in characterising a particular individual's problems in sufficient detail to enable a specific intervention to be planned.

Mood rating scales

Patient's self-report measures. The common self-report mood scales are listed in Table 32.1. Although each has its own supporters, these scales have more shared characteristics than differences. They have two main functions: they can be used as first-stage screening procedures in the identification of people with clinically diagnosable mood disorders, or they can be used as severity measures in people who have already been diagnosed as suffering from mood disorder. They are not diagnostic instruments in their own right.

One concern about mood rating scales is that many of them include items that, in the depressed but physically well patient, are an index of severity of depression (insomnia, weight loss, etc.) but that might have another explanation when the patient is physically ill. This problem can be surmounted by raising the

Table 32.1. Self-report mood scales

Scale	No. of items	Content	Comment	Reference
Beck Depression Inventory	21	Depression, affective, cognitive, and somatic items	Widely used in general population and medical patients	Beck et al. (1988)
General Health Questionnaire (GHQ 28)	28	Depression, anxiety, somatic, and social dimensions	Developed as a screening measure	Goldberg & Hillier (1979)
Hospital Anxiety and Depression Scale	14	Anxiety, anhedonia	Developed as a screening measure. Excludes biological symptoms and most cognitive symptoms of depression	Zigmond & Snaith (1983)
Wimbledon Self-report Scale	30	Depression, irritability, anxiety	Excludes somatic items. Developed as a screening measure	Coughlan & Storey (1988)
Wakefield Depression Inventory	12	Depression	Designed to assess severity of depressive illness. Somatic, affective and cognitive items	Snaith et al. (1971)
Zung Self-rating Depression Scale	20	Depression	Designed to assess severity of depressive illness. Somatic, affective, and cognitive items	Zung (1965)
CES-D	21	Depression	Widely used in USA, especially in epidemiological surveys in the community	Roberts & Vernon (1983)

cut-off score when the schedule is used as a screening test in neurological practice (Bridges & Goldberg, 1986). There is no good evidence that mood schedules that exclude somatic items (e.g. the Hospital Anxiety and Depression Scale) have better predictive values than scales with somatic items used with higher cut-off scores. Nor is it proven that they are more sensitive to change in mood symptoms in the physically ill (for reviews of methodological issues in screening the physically ill for mood disorder see Goldberg (1985) and House (1988)).

There are other more telling problems with the use of self-report mood rating scales. The first is that between one-fifth and one-quarter of neurological patients are unable to complete the schedule unassisted. This is a serious drawback because non-completers are more likely to have significant physical or cognitive impairments that are associated with an increased risk of mood disorder (House et al., 1989). Second, certain types of problem are likely to be underreported in a self-report format. In my experience, this is particularly true of morbid apathy and irritability. Third, it is important to remember that psychological problems and emotional disorder are not synonymous with having symptoms of distress. In self-report mood rating scales, patients who are having major problems in coping with illness might deny or down-play symptoms that have an impact on their cooperation with rehabilitation, relationships at home, or social function. There is some evidence that this is a particular problem in elderly people (Feldman et al., 1987).

Interview techniques. The alternative to self-report measures of mood is to interview the patient face to face. The number of questions it is necessary to ask to elicit symptoms of mood disorder is limited and therefore the interview need not be unreasonably time-consuming.

There are simple standardised mental state examinations that can be used by non-psychiatrists (Goldberg et al., 1970; Wing et al., 1974) and there are short check-lists of questions that can be asked routinely of all patients admitted to an in-patient unit (Goldberg et al., 1988).

Attitudes to illness

A major influence on the way that a patient deals with physical illness is his or her understanding of that illness. Systematic research into lay understandings of illness is relatively new, but there is now an influential body of literature describing the content and origins of what has come to be known as the *illness representation*. Illness representations contain a number of elements:

- *identity*—somatic symptoms and illness associated labels
- *cause*—beliefs regarding the cause of the illness
- *time-line*—acute, chronic, or cyclic models of the illness
- *consequences*—immediate and long-term effects of the illness
- *curability and controllability*—the extent to which individuals perceive the illness to be under their control.

The representations patients develop can bear little resemblance to a health-care professional's concept of the illness process, and yet they are likely to be determinants of the patient's level of distress and quality of life; it is important, therefore, to understand something of their origins and influences (for a review, see Petrie & Weinman, 1997). A simple method of characterising an individual's illness representation is provided by the self-report Illness Perception Questionnaire (Weinman et al., 1996).

A number of simple self-report or interview-based assessments can be undertaken with a patient (Hackett & Cassem, 1974; Morrow et al., 1978; Rotter, 1966). The Mental Adjustment to Cancer scale developed for use in breast cancer studies (Watson et al., 1988) can be simply modified to a general form for use with all physically ill subjects, and has been used, for example, in stroke research (Dennis et al., 1997). In psychiatric practice, the mental attitude of hopelessness is now recognised as an important determinant of outcome in treatment particularly for depression. It too can be measured using a self-report scale (Beck et al., 1974).

There are standardised measures for the assessment of attitudes to illness and coping styles in families, but they are unsuitable for routine clinical use by non-specialists. None the less, a family interview can provide striking insights. With an awareness of the types of questions posed by attitudes to illness and hopelessness questionnaires, it is possible to ask those who are likely to become carers for their own approach to the illness. The family session is not simply a forum for asking questions, it is also an occasion to make observations. Nursing staff often notice during visiting times those families where individuals are fussy or overprotective, or alternatively rejecting and avoidant. The family interview simply represents an opportunity to make these qualitative judgements in another and more structured context, where knowledge about and response to illness is the explicit agenda. A very similar approach can be adopted by inviting carers to participate in rehabilitation sessions, bearing in mind that these can be assessment as well as educational sessions.

Cognitive impairment

Intellectual impairment resulting from focal deficits and from global deficits (delirium, dementia) is so common as an accompaniment of neurological disorder that most specialist neurorehabilitation services have access to a neuropsychologist. A number of the schedules used by occupational therapists include extensive assessment of cognitive function. The problem is that specialised neuropsychology assessment is time-consuming, and requires training.

The most widely available simple screening tests at least enable gross impairment to be identified by non-specialists. Examples include the Hodkinson Short Mental Test Score (Hodkinson, 1972) and the CAPE Information/Orientation Subscale (Pattie & Gilleard, 1976). The Mini Mental State Examination has the advantage that, because it is slightly longer, it is more sensitive to change over time (Folstein et al., 1975).

All of these tests are highly language-dependent, but none the less they are useful as simple screens for severe impairment in those who are not dysphasic.

AETIOLOGY—MAKING A PSYCHOSOCIAL FORMULATION

In psychiatric practice, the evaluation of a clinical problem has three main aims. These are: (1) to assess those elements of a situation that amount to stresses; (2) to determine the characteristics of the individual patient, and of his or her immediate social network, that determine the responses made to those stresses; and (3) to use this information as the basis for an explanation of the origin of the patient's current mental state. This process is called making a formulation, and can be roughly divided into an assessment of the psychological and social stresses and responses, and the physical or organic stressors and responses.

Understanding the stresses

Some stresses experienced by the patient are illness related (House & Ebrahim, 1991). The most obvious are those that arise directly from the symptoms of disease, such as incontinence, paralysis, or dysphasia. Obviously, not all illnesses have the same consequences. Some have major effects such as precluding paid employment or the use of public transport; others have less severe consequences, for example a minor difficulty in being understood on the telephone. Illness-related stresses can be understood only by a knowledge of the individual patient and the meaning that he or she gives to the illness (Lipowski, 1970). For example, personal or family experience of illnesses can lead people to have very definite views about their own likely prognosis.

Whereas the presence of a serious neurological illness might be the most striking feature of a patient's life to the doctor, it might not be the most salient to the patient. For example, something like 10% of the general population have experienced a seriously threatening life event or difficulty in the past year. In one study of stroke, one-quarter of the sufferers had experienced a severely threatening life event in the 12 months before the stroke onset (House et al., 1990). Most of these events and difficulties involve illness or death to close friends or family members, major disruptions in relationships, or changes of residence. Clearly, the emotional adjustment to such events is going to get caught up with the individual's style of dealing with their neurological disorder and its treatment (Brown & Harris, 1989).

Stress might not reside in events but in the emotional atmosphere of the patient's social network. *High expressed emotion* refers to the presence of freely expressed but mixed feelings, with hostility and overconcern being expressed towards dependent or unusual behaviour—so-called expressed emotion (Vaughn & Leff, 1976). High levels of expressed emotion provoke tension and unease and make it difficult for the patient to find a settled and satisfactory coping style. Experiences in other clinical situations (such as families with a diabetic member) suggest that expressed emotion is relevant in explaining a number of the difficulties in coping experienced by patients with chronic illness (Minuchin et al., 1978). High expressed emotion could, for example, lie behind aggressive outbursts in brain-damaged patients.

Identifying coping responses

The aims of coping are either *problem-focused*, that is, designed to modify the demands of the situation, or they are *emotion-focused*, that is, designed to modify how one feels about a situation (Lazarus & Folkman, 1984). Broadly speaking, informational and instrumental support help problem-focused coping, whereas emotional support assists emotion-focused coping. Emotion-focused coping generally works well but only transiently. It is best reserved for brief stresses, such as unpleasant medical procedures, or for situations in which nothing can realistically be done to modify the stress.

Normally, people have a repertoire of responses that they make to particular stresses in their lives. The wider their repertoire and the more flexibly they can use it, the greater their chances of success in dealing with life's vicissitudes. There is almost no response that is, in itself, unhealthy; problems tend to arise when a given response is used too exclusively and with too much tenacity. For example, a certain sense of independent assertiveness (fighting spirit) can be a most useful response to illness, but not if it leads to rejection of all sensible offers to help. On the other hand, accepting advice and following instructions can be most desirable as long as it does not become a passive/dependent refusal to take the initiative in one's personal life. Stoicism and down-playing of problems is likely to be more healthy than vehement denial of difficulties. In other words, whereas it can be a most useful exercise to ask oneself what particular coping style an individual has, it is an oversimplification to attempt to produce a typology into which one expects all individuals to fit, and which defines their responses as healthy or not.

In the end, what determines the appropriateness of a patient's response to illness is the outcome in terms of social, psychological, and physical function. It is function, after all, which defines the adaptiveness of any particular type of behaviour.

AETIOLOGY—THE ROLE OF THE NEUROLOGICAL LESION

Most people think of the brain as being the organ of the mind. There is a school of biological psychiatry that argues that, in effect, all psychological disorders are the consequences of specific neurological deficits. In its most developed form the argument goes that specific psychiatric syndromes are associated with specific neurological lesions. One example from the psychiatric literature is the claim that major depression is a specific complication of left frontal stroke (Starkstein & Robinson, 1989). This is overstating the case. None the less, there are certain associations between psychological state and lesion location, which are common encountered and which are buttressed by results from experimental psychology (Tucker, 1981) so that they could be regarded as established at least for day-to-day clinical practice. The four most common associations are with lesions in the non-dominant hemisphere, in the dominant hemisphere, in the frontal lobes, and in subcortical regions.

Damage to the non-dominant hemisphere. Extensive damage to the non-dominant hemisphere appears to be particularly likely to lead to:

(1) Problems of lack of awareness of illness amounting at times to complete denial (anosognosia). This phenomenon is commonly associated with, but not dependent on, the existence of perceptual neglect (Bisiach et al., 1986).
(2) A state of emotional apathy and underarousal.
(3) A state of emotional indifference amounting at times to fatuousness.

The boundaries between these different psychological syndromes are blurred, but between them the picture they represent is a highly characteristic one (Heilman et al., 1985). Their importance is in the effect they have on motivation to rehabilitate, accident-proneness, and social behaviour.

Damage to the dominant hemisphere. The right hemisphere syndrome is usually contrasted with the picture in patients with left (dominant) hemisphere damage. Here, a form of unstable or volatile emotionalism is much more common (Gainotti, 1972). When it is associated with dysphasia it is usually attributed to frustration at difficulty with communication, but not all dysphasics appear aware of their deficits (Lebrun, 1987) and both emotional lability and the catastrophic reaction (Goldstein, 1944) have been associated with dominant hemisphere lesions in the absence of significant speech problems.

Damage to the frontal lobe. Frontal lobe damage has been long recognised to have psychological sequelae and here is no place to review that literature (Struss & Benson, 1984). However, it is worth pointing out that there is really no psychological symptom that is exclusively found in association with damage to the frontal lobes and nowhere else. For that reason, it would be better if the term "frontal lobe syndrome" were not used in a descriptive sense.

Damage to the subcortical regions. Apart from hemisphere damage, subcortical lesions have a reputation for producing psychiatric problems. Albert's original description of subcortical dementia (Albert, 1978) included a comment on mental sluggishness and depressed mood in addition to the reportedly characteristic cognitive changes. The subcortical disorder with the greatest reputation for causing psychiatric problems is Parkinson's disease (Taylor et al., 1986). Some of the reputation this disorder has for causing depression is based on the motor deficits that impair facial and vocal expression of emotion, but even so, Parkinson's disease does appear to be associated with rates of depression higher than can be accounted for simply by age and disability. Whereas in parkinsonism, bradykinesia and impaired speech prosody lead to a false impression of depressed mood, in multiple sclerosis poor control of the facial musculature resulting from pseudobulbar palsy can lead to a false impression of fatuousness and euphoria. It is debatable whether subcortical lesions in multiple sclerosis can lead to genuine euphoria, although hemisphere (especially frontal) lesions might occasionally do so.

PRINCIPLES OF MANAGEMENT FOR THE NON-PSYCHIATRIST

Routine psychiatric assessment

When a patient is admitted to a psychiatric facility, a basic physical assessment is an invariable part of the admission procedure. By contrast, psychiatric assessment following neurological or rehabilitation admission is the exception. At least part of the responsibility for this state of affairs lies with psychiatric education, which still teaches a form of history-taking where an hour to an hour-and-a-half is devoted to an extensive review of the patient's personal and family background and an exhaustive examination of their current mental state. Such an approach does not readily import into general medical practice, and yet alternatives or modifications to it are rarely taught. The problem is that because so few doctors know how to undertake a limited psychiatric assessment, they might fail to undertake any assessment at all:

A man of 38 was referred for assessment of his mood because he was apathetic and doing badly in rehabilitation. He was a bachelor living at home and his father and his father's brother had both died since he was originally admitted to a neurosurgical ward. His father had actually died while visiting the patient. There was no note of this occurrence or of its effect upon the patient in the medical record.

Below is a proposal for a basic psychiatric assessment that should be undertaken on any patient accepted into a neurological rehabilitation programme. The assessment can be undertaken by a non-specialist. The professional training of a member of staff undertaking such an assessment is less important than the fact that this person is interested in psychological issues and has a basically sympathetic interviewing style:

(1) A face-to-face interview with the patient, which covers five main areas:
  (i) the patient's ideas and knowledge about his or her illness and prognosis
  (ii) the impact of illness on the following domains in the patient's life—work, family relationships, social and recreational function, marital relationships, sexual relationships
  (iii) past personal and family experience of serious illness
  (iv) current mood and outlook
  (v) any stresses or worries in the patient's life that are not directly related to the current illness.
  With the exception of the standardised ratings of mood and attitudes to illness, this assessment is probably best thought of as eliciting qualitative rather than quantitative information.

(2) A face-to-face interview with the family. The areas covered should be the same as those covered with the patient. In this context, the family can be defined as broadly or narrowly as thought fit by the patient and the rehabilitation team. As a minimum it will include the main carer, but might reasonably be extended to adult members of a household or other involved relatives or intimates. For routine clinical purposes, standardised measures are not necessary for this exercise. If the interview is used to question and listen to people's concerns and to observe the way in which they interact and deal with the issues raised, then non-specialists can usually gain a shrewd idea of the types of problem likely to arise during rehabilitation.

(3) An evaluation of behaviour during rehabilitation. Observations made about exchanges with visitors and about the interaction between a patient, visitors, and staff are not gossip, but an important part of assessment. Non-psychiatric staff often feel rather awkward about discussing these matters—as if they are betraying confidence or talking behind people's backs. Provided the observations are made in a professional manner and with the patient's best interests in mind, this attitude is mistaken. Misgivings can usually be overcome when it is acknowledged that neglecting insights into family dynamics can actually be to the patient's detriment.

The two interview assessments need take no more than half-an-hour each. The discussion of behaviour during therapy and during visiting need add no more than a few minutes to case review. An hour spent assessing psychiatric status might seem a long time but it is not dangerous and, when set against the cost of an extended rehabilitation effort rendered futile by neglect of psychiatric and family issues, it is extremely cheap. It should be undertaken early in rehabilitation so that identified problems can be dealt with before they prove a block to discharge from hospital or an inhibition to recovery.

Psychological treatments

The single most important component of psychiatric treatment in rehabilitation is the establishment of what could be called a therapeutic milieu. What that means is that the ward environment and the attitude of staff are such that psychological issues can be raised naturally and freely during the course of treatment. One of the major benefits of using mood self-rating scales to screen all rehabilitation patients is that it aids this process. In other words, the specific response to the questionnaire might be less important than the permission it gives to discuss psychological issues at all. Milieu is established not just by staff attitudes but by the physical environment. The interview room is to psychological management what the operating theatre is to surgical care. It is not impossible to function without one but there are drawbacks to using a multipurpose "Sister's" office or a treatment or laundry room for interviewing. The sessions are prone to interruption and the environment does not encourage relaxation and confiding (Bridges & Goldberg, 1984).

The most important intervention—so important that it should be routine—is individual counselling. Psychological care is so integral to rehabilitation that counselling should be delivered by a member of the rehabilitation team. In practice, the person best placed to do it is often a member of the nursing staff. Training courses—for example, organised by the English Nursing Board—are available to develop the necessary expertise. The aim of counselling is not to treat psychiatric disorders; there is no evidence that non-specialist, brief psychosocial interventions are effective as psychiatric treatment (Knapp et al., 2000).

More elaborate forms of talking treatment and psychotherapy are beyond the scope of this chapter. The only absolute contraindications are language deficit too severe to allow verbal communication, and memory deficit so severe that none of the content of sessions is retained. Even quite severely disabled neurological patients are able to benefit from psychotherapy. A number of brief, realistic therapies are applicable in physical illness (D'Zurilla, 1986; Klerman & Weissman, 1993). They include, for example, psychological approaches to improving motivation (Miller & Rollnick, 1991), increasing treatment adherence (Myers & Midence, 1998) and overcoming apathy and inertia (Hogg, 1996).

Family sessions focused on practical problem-solving can be a useful vehicle for identifying tensions and looking at ways of alleviating them (Lezak, 1978; Rogers & Kreutzer, 1984). More comprehensively, family members can be integrated at every stage in rehabilitation, both receiving advice and guidance, and acting where appropriate as co-therapists (Smith & Godfrey, 1995).

Rehabilitation staff often wonder about the value of skills in behaviour therapy. In reality, behaviour therapy can rarely be delivered to patients on any neurological or rehabilitation facility unless the whole environment is geared towards running a behavioural regime (Wood, 1987). Otherwise, the numbers of different staff involved and the constant intrusion of the demands of physical nursing care preclude the application of a consistent programme for an individual patient. This is not to say that, occasionally, for specific problems in individual patients, a behavioural approach cannot be very effective, for example, in training continence. However, it is usually time-consuming and labour-intensive. Badly applied behaviour therapy is worse than useless. For example, there is more to the application of the theory of reinforcement than removing a patient's cigarettes and then getting into an argument about returning them in exchange for good behaviour! By contrast, a grasp of certain basic principles of behavioural assessment can be useful (see Chapter 31), even if the assessment is not used to inform strictly behavioural interventions; for example, keeping diaries of problematic behaviour to look at patterns that give pointers to the antecedents of emotional outbursts or refusal to cooperate with treatment (Martin & Pear, 1988).

Behaviour therapy involves the application of principles derived from conditioning or learning theory to the modification of behaviour. It usually requires the patient to make a direct change in his or her behaviour with the aim, for example, of exposing the patient to a feared stimulus or encouraging competing responses to existing unhelpful habits. Examples include provision of rewards (sweets, cigarettes, staff attention) for desired behaviours, or punishments (time out, withdrawal of attention) for undesirable behaviours. Discussion of the patient's thoughts about the treatment are limited to explaining the rationale for treatment; in severely damaged people, behaviour therapy can be implemented without the patient's conscious awareness of what is being implemented.

Cognitive–behavioural therapy centres around discussion of patients' thoughts and beliefs. Behaviour change is negotiated with them as a means for them to test their beliefs and try new ways of dealing with negative thoughts that are impeding progress. An example might be a graded activity programme negotiated with a person who believed that exercise would bring on another stroke. Discussion of patients' thoughts is central, and so is their active collaboration in treatment; it is therefore unsuitable for severely damaged patients but is preferable for those with minimal cognitive impairment.

Psychotropic medication

Antidepressants can be very effective in treating *depressive disorders* in the medically ill (Series, 1992), even in those with brain damage (Lipsey et al., 1984; Andersen et al., 1994). They are very widely used: perhaps too widely. For example, one study showed that one-third of stroke patients were given an antidepressant at some stage during their in-patient stay (Lim & Ebrahim, 1983). There is a danger that the more widely antidepressants are used, the less vigorously they are pursued in an individual patient. It would be better to focus their use on smaller numbers and then concentrate on pushing the dose to the maximum tolerated.

Which drug to use? The older drugs with established efficacy (e.g. amitriptyline, dosulepin (dothiepin)) can cause problems with sedation and thereby impair mobility, and can occasionally cause confusion, retention of urine, or fits. On the other hand, the so-called side-effects of these tricyclic antidepressants are sometimes paradoxically beneficial. For example, sedation can be used to treat insomnia if the drug is given at night and therefore avoid the use of an additional hypnotic. Anticholinergic effects can be beneficial in treating bladder problems. The newer generation of specific 5-HT uptake inhibitors (e.g. fluvoxamine, fluoxetine) are not troubled by these anticholinergic or sedating problems. In some people they can cause unpleasant states of overarousal and insomnia. Their usefulness in neurological patients remains to be demonstrated and we do not have the benefit of the years of experience in clinical use that surrounds the older drugs.

Emotionalism (emotional lability) apparently responds quite dramatically on occasions to antidepressants (Brown et al., 1999). The response has been described with a number of drugs (tricyclics and selective serotonin reuptake inhibitors (SSRIs)), and individual responses are idiosyncratic, so that one drug can fail whereas another works when substituted. The low dose that is effective in some cases, and the rapidity of response reported, suggests that this is not simply an antidepressant effect (Allman & House, 1990).

A number of drugs have a primarily stimulant effect and might possibly be of benefit in those stares of *apathy*, *inertia* and *under-arousal* that are common sequelae of central nervous system (CNS) lesions. Among them are the monoamine oxidase inhibitor tranylcypromine, the tricyclic protriptyline, and the 5-HT reuptake blockers like fluvoxamine. In some places, psychostimulants such as methylphenidate or dexamfetamine are used (Stoudemire et al., 1991). There is no strong research evidence to support this practice, although clinical experience suggests that in certain cases a therapeutic trial can lead to surprising benefit.

In a field where there is so little established knowledge, it is still possible to be reasonably rational about therapeutic trials. The best approach is to pick one or two drugs with which to become familiar. Two useful older drugs are dosulepin (dothiepin) and lofepramine; if they are unsuccessful or not tolerated, then a specific serotonin reuptake inhibitor can be used as an alternative. A therapeutic trial would involve building up to the full therapeutic dose, and then continuing that dose for 3–4 weeks. If it has proved effective, then the drug can be continued for 6 months before stopping. If it has not proved effective, then it should be withdrawn forthwith and an alternative tried.

Benzodiazepines have all the disadvantages in rehabilitation practice that they have in general and psychiatric practice. The one indication that they might have is in patients where increased muscle tone is a problem. Where sedation is required for *anxiety* or *insomnia* there are other choices, such as low-dose tricyclic antidepressants. A major tranquilliser with relatively little in the way of extrapyramidal side-effects is sulpiride. Where stronger sedation is required, haloperidol is preferable to chlorpromazine because it does not have an alpha-blocking action and does not therefore cause postural hypotension.

CONCLUSION

Psychiatry and psychological care should be an integral part of the rehabilitation effort. If, instead, psychiatric opinions are obtained by intermittent consultation then the process is likely to be haphazard and the clinical care provided will not be comprehensive. The ideal approach is for the rehabilitation team to handle family and psychological issues routinely as part of their assessment, with care plans referring explicitly to these matters. Regularly arranged contact with a liaison psychiatrist with a particular interest in physical illness and rehabilitation is more useful than occasional consultation with a general psychiatrist. If this style of rehabilitation is established then specific psychiatric problems are more likely to be identified and dealt with as part of routine clinical practice, and screening patients suitable for psychiatric treatment or psychiatric referral using standardised measures becomes much less important. Psychotropic medication should be used more sparingly, and basic counselling and family interviewing more liberally, than they are at present.

REFERENCES

Albert M (1978) Subcortical dementia. In R Katzman, R Terry, K Bick (Eds.), *Alzheimer's disease, senile dementia and related conditions*. New York: Raven Press, pp. 173–180.

Allman P, House A (1990) Emotionalism: Clinical features and management. *Geriatric Medicine, 20*, 43–48.

American Psychiatric Association (1994) *Diagnostic and statistical manual for psychiatric disorders (DSM-IV)*. Washington DC: American Psychiatric Association.

Andersen G, Vestergaard K, Lauritzen L (1994) Effective treatment of poststroke depression with the selective serotonin reuptake inhibitor citalopram. *Stroke, 25*, 1099–1104.

Beck A, Weissman A, Lester D (1974) The measurement of pessimism: The hopelessness scale. *Journal of Consulting and Clinical Psychology, 42*, 861–865.

Beck A, Rush A, Shaw B, Emery G (1979) *Cognitive therapy of depression*. New York: Guilford Press.

Beck A, Steer R, Garbin M (1998) Psychometric properties of the Beck Depression inventory: 25 years of evaluation. *Clinical Psychology Review, 8*, 77–100.

Bisiach R, Vallar G, Perani D et al. (1986) Unawareness of disease following lesions of the right hemisphere: Anosognosia for hemiplegia and anosognosia for hemianopia. *Neuropsychologia, 24*, 471–482.

Bridges K, Goldberg D (1984) Psychiatric illness in inpatients with neurological disease: Patient's views on discussion of emotional problems with neurologists. *British Medical Journal, 289*, 656–658.

Bridges K, Goldberg D (1986) The validation of the GHQ-28 and the use of the MMSE in neurological in-patients. *British Journal of Psychiatry, 148*, 548–553.

Brown G, Harris T (1989) *Life events and illness*. New York: Guilford Press.

Brown KW, Sloan R, Pentland B (1999) Fluoxetine as a treatment for post-stroke emotionalism. *Acta Psychiatrica Scandinavica, 98*, 455–458.

Calvert T, Knapp P, House A (1998) Psychological associations with emotionalism after stroke. *Journal of Neurology, Neurosurgery and Psychiatry, 65*, 928–929.

Coughlan A, Storey P (1988) The Wimbledon Self-Report Scale: Emotional and mood appraisal. *Clinical Rehabilitation, 2*, 207–213.

Dennis M, O'Rourke S, Slattery J, Staniforth T, Warlow C (1997) Evaluation of a stroke family care worker. *British Medical Journal, 314*, 1071–1076.

D'Zurilla T (1986) *Problem-solving therapy: A social competence approach to clinical intervention*. New York: Springer.

Eccles S, Knapp P, House A (1999) Psychological adjustment and self-reported coping in stroke survivors with and without emotionalism. *Journal of Neurology, Neurosurgery and Psychiatry, 67*, 125–126.

Feely M, Pullar T (1989) Therapeutic compliance: Myths and misunderstandings. *Geriatric Medicine, 19*, 14–18.

Feldman E, Mayou R, Hawton K et al. (1987) Psychiatric disorder in medical inpatients. *Quarterly Journal of Medicine, 241*, 405–412.

Folstein M, Folstein S, McHugh P (1975) Minimental state—a practical method for grading the cognitive state of patients for the clinician. *Journal of Psychiatric Research, 12*, 189–198.

Gainotti G (1972) Emotional behaviour and hemispheric side of lesion. *Cortex, 8*, 41–55.

Galbraith S (1985) Irritability. *British Medical Journal, 291*, 1668–1669.

Goldberg D (1985) Identifying psychiatric illness among general medical patients. *British Medical Journal, 291*, 161–162.

Goldberg D, Hillier V (1979) A scaled version of the general health questionnaire. *Psychological Medicine, 9*, 139–145.

Goldberg D, Cooper P, Eastwood M et al. (1970) A standardised psychiatric interview for use in community surveys. *British Journal of Preventive and Social Medicine, 24*, 18–23.

Goldberg D, Bridges K, Duncan-Jones P, Grayson D (1988) Detecting anxiety and depression in general medical settings. *British Medical Journal, 297*, 897–900.

Goldstein K (1944) The mental changes due to frontal lobe damage. *Journal of Psychology, 17*, 187–208.

Hackett T, Cassem N (1974) Development of a quantitative rating scale to assess denial. *Journal of Psychosomatic Research, 18*, 93–100.

Hawton K, Salkovskis P, Kirk J, Clark D (1989) *Cognitive therapy of psychiatric disorders*. Oxford: Oxford University Press.

Heilman K, Bowers D, Valenstein E (1985) Emotional disorders associated with neurological diseases. In K Heilman, E Valenstein (Eds.), *Clinical neuropsychology*. Oxford: Oxford University Press.

Hodkinson H (1972) Evaluation of a mental test score for the assessment of mental impairment in the elderly. *Age and Ageing, 1*, 233–238.

Hogg L (1996) Psychological treatments for negative symptoms. In G Haddock, P Slade (Eds.), *Cognitive–behavioural interventions with psychotic disorders*. London: Routledge, pp. 151–170.

House A (1988) Mood disorders in the physically ill: Problems of definition and measurement. *Journal of Psychosomatic Research, 32*, 345–353.

House A, Dennis M, Hawton K, Warlow C (1989) Methods of identifying mood disorders in stroke patients: Experience in the Oxford Community Stroke Project. *Age and Ageing, 18*, 371–379.

House A, Dennis M, Mogridge L et al. (1990) Life events and difficulties preceding stroke. *Journal of Neurology, Neurosurgery and Psychiatry, 53*, 1024–1028.

House A, Ebrahim S (1991) Psychological aspects of physical disease. In C Oppenheimer, R Jacoby (Eds.), *Oxford textbook of psychiatry in the elderly*. Oxford: Oxford University Press, pp. 437–460.

Kendell R (1969) The continuum model of depressive illness. *Proceedings of the Royal Society of Medicine, 62*, 335–339.

Klerman G, Weissman M (1993) *New applications of interpersonal therapy*. Washington DC American Psychiatric Press.

Knapp P, Young J, Forster A, House, A (2000) Non-drug strategies to resolve psycho-social difficulties after stroke: A review. *Age and ageing, 29*, 23–30.

Lazarus R, Folkman S (1984) *Stress, appraisal and coping*. New York: Springer.

Lebrun Y (1987) Anosognosia in aphasics. *Cortex, 23*, 251–263.

Lezak M (1978) Living with the characterologically altered brain injured patient. *Journal of Clinical Psychiatry, 39*, 592–598.

Lim M, Ebrahim S (1983) Depression after stroke: A hospital treatment survey. *Postgraduate Medical Journal, 59*, 489–491.

Lipowski Z (1970) Physical illness: the individual and the coping process. *Psychiatry in Medicine, 1*, 91–102.

Lipsey J, Robinson R, Pearlson G et al. (1984) Nortriptyline treatment of poststroke depression. *Lancet, i*, 297–300.

Lishman AW (1998) *Organic psychiatry*, 3rd edition. London: Blackwell.

Lyons R, Sullivan M, Ritvo P, Coyne J (1995) *Relationships in chronic illness and disability*. London: Sage.

Martin G, Pear J (1988) *Behaviour modification: What it is and how to do it*, 3rd edition. New Jersey: Prentice Hall.

Meichenbaum D, Turk D (1987) *Facilitating treatment adherence: A practitioner's guide*. New York: Plenum.

Miller W, Rollnick S (1991) *Motivational interviewing*. New York: Guilford Press.

Minuchin S, Rosman E, Baker L (1978) *Psychosomatic families*. Cambridge, MA: Harvard University Press.

Morrow G, Chiardo R, Derogatis L (1978) A new scale for assessing patients' psychosocial adjustment to medical illness. *Psychological Medicine, 8*, 605–610.

Myers L, Midence K (1998) *Adherence to treatment in medical conditions*. Amsterdam: Harwood Academic.

Noyes R, Hoehn-Saric R (1998) Anxiety in the medically ill. In R Noyes, R Hoehn-Saric (Eds.), *The anxiety disorders*. Cambridge: Cambridge University Press, pp. 285–334.

Pattie A, Gilleard C (1976) The Clifton Assessment Schedule: A further validation of a psychogeriatric assessment schedule. *British Journal of Psychiatry, 129*, 68–72.

Paykel ES (1971) Depressive typologies and response to amitriptyline. *British Journal of Psychiatry, 119*, 555–564.

Petrie K, Weinman J (1997) *Perceptions of health and illness*. Amsterdam: Harwood Academic.

Poeck K (1985) Pathological laughter and crying. In JA Frederiks (Ed.), *Handbook of clinical neurology: Clinical neuropsychology*. Amsterdam: Elsevier, pp. 219–235.

Prigatanao G, Schacter D (Eds.) (1991) *Awareness of deficit after brain injury: Clinical and theoretical issues*. Oxford: Oxford University Press.

Pullar T, Kumar S, Tindall H, Feely M (1989) Time to stop counting the tablets? *Clinical Pharmacology and Therapeutics, 46*, 163–168.

Roberts RE, Vernon S (1983) The CES-D scale: Its use in a community sample. *American Journal of Psychiatry, 140*, 41–45.

Robertson M, Catona C (1997) *Depression and physical illness*. Chichester: John Wiley.

Rogers P, Kreutzer J (1984) Family crises following head injury: A network intervention strategy. *Journal of Neurosurgical Nursing, 16*, 343–346.

Rotter J (1966) Generalised expectancies for internal versus expectancies for external control of reinforcement. *Psychological Monographs, SO, 90(1)*, 1–28.

Sembi S, Tarrier N, O'Neill P, Burns A, Faragher B (1998) Does post-traumatic stress disorder occur after stroke? A preliminary study. *International Journal of Geriatric Psychiatry, 13(5)*, 315–322.

Series H (1992) Drug treatment of depression in medically ill patients. *Journal of Psychosomatic Research, 36(1)*, 1–16.

Smith LM, Godfrey H (1995) *Family support programs and rehabilitation*. New York: Plenum Press.

Snaith P (1991) *Clinical neurosis*, 2nd edition. Oxford: Oxford Medical Publications.

Snaith P, Ahmed S, Mehta S, Hamiliton M (1971) Assessment of the severity of primary depressive illness. *Psychological Medicine, 1*, 143–149.

Starkstein S, Robinson R (1989) Affective disorders and cerebral vascular disease. *British Journal of Psychiatry, 154*, 170–182.

Stoudemire A, Fogel B, Gulley L (1991) Psychopharmacology in the medically ill. In A Stoudemire, B Fogel (Eds.), *Medical psychiatric practice*, vol. 1. Washington DC: American Psychiatric Press, pp. 29–98.

Strain J (1978) The intrafamilial environment of the chronically ill patient. In J Strain (Ed.), *Psychological interventions in medical practice*. New York: Appleton Century Crofts, pp. 151–171.

Struss DT, Benson D (1984) Neuropsychological studies of the frontal lobes. *Psychological Bulletin, 95*, 3–28.

Taylor A, Saint-Cyr J, Lang A, Kenny F (1986) Parkinson's disease and depression: A critical re-evaluation. *Brain, 109*, 279–292.

Tucker D (1981) Lateral brain function, emotion and conceptualisation. *Psychological Bulletin, 89*, 19–46.

Vaughn C, Leff J (1976) The influence of family and social factors on the course of psychiatric illness. *British Journal of Psychiatry, 129*, 125–137.

Watson M, Greer S, Young J (1988) Development of a questionnaire measure of adjustment to cancer: The MAC scale. *Psychological Medicine, 18*, 203–209.

Weinman J, Petrie K, Moss-Morris R, Horne R (1996) The illness perception questionnaire: A new method for assessing the cognitive representation of illness. *Psychology and Health, 11*, 431–445.

Weinstein E (1991) Anosognosia and denial of illness. In G Prigatanao, D Schacter (Eds.), *Awareness of deficit after brain injury: clinical and theoretical issues*. Oxford: Oxford University Press, pp. 240–249.

Wing J, Cooper J, Sartorius N (1974) *The measurement and classification of psychiatric symptoms*. Cambridge: Cambridge University Press.

Wood RL (1987) *Brain injury rehabilitation: a neurobehavioural approach*. London: Croom Helm.

World Health Organization (1992) *The ICD-10 classification of mental and behavioural disorders*. Geneva: World Health Organization.

Zigmond A, Snaith P (1983) The hospital anxiety and depression scale. *Acta Psychiatrica Scandinavica, 67*, 361–370.

Zung W (1965) A self-rating depression scale. *Archives of General Psychiatry, 12*, 63–70.

33. Psychosomatic disorders

H. Merskey

INTRODUCTION

In this chapter I first explore the understanding we have of the relationship between different types of bodily symptoms that might be provoked by emotional disorders. This leads to consideration of the distinctions between psychophysiological symptoms, conversion symptoms, hypochondriasis, and somatisation. The way in which these different factors contribute to the selection process of medical patients is also taken into account. Some of the common so called psychosomatic symptoms are examined in the light of these considerations and then different rehabilitation procedures are considered.

PSYCHOPHYSIOLOGICAL SYMPTOMS AND CONVERSION SYMPTOMS

The concept of psychosomatic disorders is about as old as medicine, and references can be found to it in early Greek writers such as Erasistratus (Finlayson, 1893) and Galen (Nutton, 1979). The favourite story in both instances has to do with love causing sickness or a change in the pulse rate. Likewise, the whole notion of hysteria seems to have involved concepts of physical change related to emotional stress. Only in the nineteenth century did the distinction emerge between changes in the body that might be a consequence of dysfunction in nerve pathways as a result of emotion, and loss of function in a part that might occur simply—or not so simply—because an individual believed he or she could not use it. Reynolds (1869) gets the credit for the first full statement that symptoms in the body could correspond to the patient's idea. He was supported by the work of Charcot (1889). Freud (Breuer & Freud, 1893–1895) was then able to offer an explanation of hysterical symptoms in terms of conflict and unconscious processes. This notion is now in trouble, because an explosion of false memories, recovered in suggestive therapy, has led to the whole theory of repression being challenged. That theory is essentially anecdotal, and experimental efforts to induce repression have failed, despite serious attempts to do so (Holmes, 1974, 1990). Hence, conversion and dissociative symptoms can be attributed to the patient's thoughts, to motivated forgetting, or to differential attention, but cannot

all be adequately explained any longer on the basis of classical psychodynamic theory (Merskey, 1995).

The twentieth century saw much writing on each of these themes. The experiences of the First World War and the widespread occurrence of paralysis, blindness, deafness, and similar classical hysterical symptoms under stress, and their recovery following the relief of stress, established one set of ideas about the interaction between psychological factors and the physical state. Although the effects of the mind might be far reaching, they were treatable in the instance of these classical hysterical symptoms.

The second aetiology that became established, and was distinguished from hysterical symptoms, was that due to physiological dysfunction. The work of Cannon (1915) had an obvious influence, providing a coherent statement of the way in which biological functions respond to emotional needs. Both fear and effort generate activity in the sympathetic nervous system and the effects of that activity are widespread in the organism. Dunbar (1935) developed these early ideas into an extensive statement implicating a psychological aetiology in the production of a wide variety of physical disorders. From the skin inwards, psychosomatic illness burgeoned: alopecia areata, acne, eczema, lichen planus, warts, migraine and tension headaches, hypertension, epilepsy, torticollis, tics, Costen's syndrome (now known as temporomandibular pain and dysfunction syndrome), rheumatoid arthritis, fibrositis (fibromyalgia), asthma, gastric ulcer, duodenal ulcer, ulcerative colitis, regional ileitis and spastic colon, dysmenorrhoea, labour pains, and many other pains were all attributed to the power of the mind over the body. Accident proneness, obesity, and anorexia nervosa were also included.

The popular concept held that emotion did not merely produce complaints or symptoms, but would change the state of the body after a while. This extreme position has not survived. It is hard now to think of even a single illness with physical changes in which psychogenesis is the primary factor, unless the illness is factitious. The altered view has been well described by Lipowski (1985). He makes it clear that psychosomatic medicine today is concerned with the influence of emotional factors in exacerbating an existing condition, or with the emotional changes that follow from somatic illness. This still leaves plenty of scope for the psychiatrist and the psychologist. Indeed, a few conditions remain in which psychological factors can be considered to be of great importance, such as repeated accidents and the eating disorders.

HYPOCHONDRIASIS AND SOMATISATION

The notion of increased sensitivity to bodily stimulation provides an alternative avenue towards the understanding of many patients. This has been applied particularly to the topic of hypochondriasis (Barsky & Klerman, 1983). It certainly fits many clinical cases of individuals who, either temporarily or permanently, react more than the average to external stimuli or to disease. The theory of the amplification of symptoms has been discussed both by Kellner (1986) and by Pennebaker (1982), and applied with success in a controlled study (Warwick et al., 1996). It involves treating hypochondriacal patients with cognitive behavioural methods, not using reassurance after the first full examination has been undertaken, but rather encouraging activities that distract them from health preoccupation, and denying repeated reassurance. There are indications that this has worked well, at least in the short term, but more evidence is needed before this approach can be taken to have compelling evidence in its favour.

Other very well established ways of looking at hypochondriasis include the recognition that some patients have both a fear of disease and a conviction that they are suffering from a disease. This simple, but profound, summary of the essential features of the more severe hypochondriacal patients arises from the writings of Gillespie (1929) and Pilowsky (1967).

Some have sought to characterise the group of physical complaints that seem to depend most on the mental state of the individuals as "somatising" or "somatoform disorders". This concept has its limitations. It fails to discriminate between the mechanisms of hysteria or conversion symptoms on the one hand, and psychophysiological effects on the other. It tends to blur the distinction between hypochondriasis and symptoms induced by anxiety, and to apply the notion of increased bodily sensitivity too broadly.

The category of somatoform disorders has support in the shape of a classification system of the American Psychiatric Association (APA). This association has published five editions of a system for classifying psychiatric disorders. The third, the Diagnostic and Statistical Manual third edition (DSM-III) (APA, 1980) marked an important departure from previous systems of classification because, although it retained for the most part the categories of the International Classification of Diseases (WHO, 1977) it added specific formal criteria for diagnosing each syndrome or category in the classification. This step itself arose out of a need to improve reliability and agreement between different observers in American psychiatry in particular. It was strikingly successful in certain respects but failed badly with regard to Dissociative Disorders. The tenth revision of the International Classification of Diseases of the World Health Organization (WHO, 1992) has not adopted formal criteria with respect to its psychiatric section but is very close now on most topics to the American system which itself has been revised and updated in the form of DSM-III-R (APA, 1987) and DSM-IV (APA, 1994).

Within DSM-III and DSM-IV a specific subsection has been provided entitled "somatoform disorders". This covers conversion disorders, some forms of pain, hypochondriasis, and also a category labelled "somatisation disorder". The category of somatisation disorder provides a particularly good example of the style of the DSM-IV system.

To make the diagnosis, the following is required:

(1) A history of many physical complaints, beginning before age 30 years, that occur over a period of several years and result in treatment being sought, or in significant impairment in social, occupational, or other important areas of functioning.
(2) Each of the following criteria must have been met:
  (i) four pain symptoms
  (ii) two gastrointestinal symptoms
  (iii) one sexual symptom or reproductive symptom other than pain
  (iv) one pseudoneurological symptom not limited to pain, i.e. one of the typical traditional conversion symptoms or hallucinations.

A residual category of undifferentiated somatoform disorder allows for cases that do not quite meet the above criteria. In other words, a boundary is inserted into what is probably a continuous variable. The procedure can be justified. The categories that the system defines in this way are clearly hard if they meet the full criteria and rather soft if they do not do so. This has a considerable advantage for research studies, and also for defining the extremes of clinical populations. It is still usable within the framework of a clinical system of classification because "rag-bag" categories will accommodate the less stringent criteria. The system actually developed out of earlier efforts to define research diagnostic criteria.

These considerations aside, the system has enabled a group of conditions to be categorised and identified. Unfortunately there are reservations about the quality of this section of DSM-IV compared with other sections. Whereas some of the sections on physical illness affecting the brain, affective illness, and schizophrenia have achieved a great deal of well-deserved approval, the section on somatoform illness still has problems.

Patients with "somatisation" tend to fall into distinct categories when their symptoms are examined (Kirmayer & Robbins, 1991). Thus the use of the term overall, as well as for a specific category, gives currency to the notion of "somatising" disorders without distinguishing the important differences between different forms of bodily complaint. The discussion of the above criteria indicates that anxiety and depressive disorders can provide problems because they too can give rise to many physical complaints, but the criteria themselves do not exclude anxiety and depression. It has become common for patients with multiple physical complaints to be called "somatisers" and this is as bad, in a way, as the old habit of calling similar patients "hysterics". It makes a great deal of difference if patients with somatic complaints can be accurately diagnosed as having anxiety or depression, because treatment is much more effective for the latter conditions.

In summarising this section, we can note that hypochondriacal conditions can be recognised and that they are not necessarily identical with multiple somatic complaints. The principal difference on first assessment lies in the way in which the symptom is treated. Hypochondriacal illnesses that attract this diagnosis usually have a more specific focus on particular symptoms and fears. Somatisation disorder is a more extensive and varied condition that is not necessarily associated with the same concern on the part of the patient as the hypochondriacal states.

SELECTION

Perhaps no discussion of the relationship between psychological factors and physical symptoms can or should avoid the issue of selection bias. The failure to recognise selection bias might well have underlain the erroneous notions of psychosomatic illness that obtained currency from the work of Dunbar and her immediate successors in the 1930s and 1940s in particular. The fundamental error is to assume that the cases that the doctor sees constitute a representative sample of any disorder. Even a general practitioner will see only selected cases of any illness. Illustrations of this abound. Only some people with coryza will bother to go to a doctor concerning their illness. There is a wide range of headaches, and perhaps only 3% of headaches and similar symptoms that are experienced in the population are brought to physicians for consultation (Banks et al., 1975). Some symptoms are picked out for medical attention because the public is aware of their importance, e.g. gripping pain in the left chest radiating into the arm, or sore throat with fever. The public also knows that the doctor can treat these conditions effectively. Other conditions might be a matter of importance to one person and not to another.

Some back stiffness with pain, and even crooked postures—"pain behaviour"—might not prevent the reading or writing of a book, or getting up and down to conduct a physical examination. On the other hand, such a disability in a manual labourer like a bricklayer, who has to engage in regular repetitive bending, stooping, and standing, can be wholly disabling and lead to many more medical consultations. Thus, either for internal psychological reasons or external—and quite practical—social and functional reasons, patients with back pain are liable to be steadily selected prior to their first meeting with a physician.

Pond and Bidwell (1959) provided the outstanding example of this fact in neurological work with a survey of epilepsy in general practice. These authors demonstrated that family practitioners referred patients with epilepsy for consultation twice as often if the patients had a psychological problem as when they did not have one. Although the nature of the organic state was not doubted, the practitioners nevertheless referred their patients to neurologists rather than psychiatrists. Every neurologist in the UK is familiar with the pattern of both patients and doctors seeking "reassurance" through such consultations. However, there are clear and often unrecognised implications in the effects of these tendencies. Most neurologists can be expected to suppose that there is a far larger psychological contribution to epilepsy, or even to the management or aetiology, than is actually the case. Unless they check back with general practice, and with epidemiological studies, it will be hard to get rid of this idea. This is not to say that there might not be psychological precipitants of epileptic seizures; only there is a potential fallacy that might not be recognised most of the time and that has probably been influential in determining clinical attitudes.

It remains true—and a platitude—that appreciation of the psychological state of the patient is important in almost all types of clinical practice. Nevertheless, it is better to understand that those psychological factors can arise from the illness, or can complicate it, rather than to suppose that they are a principal cause of illness because they are seen so frequently in hospital and consultative work.

I propose next to look at some specific issues in which psychosomatic conditions are alleged to be important. The emphasis will be upon diagnosis and aetiology in the first instance because without a sound position in regard to these matters, efforts at rehabilitation will be more difficult.

SPECIFIC TOPICS

Chronic headache

There is a common view that headache can be caused by muscle contraction and that it presents typically with a complaint of a tight band around the head. Such headache is said to be due to emotional causes. The notion is enshrined in the criteria of the *Ad Hoc* Committee for the Classification of Headache (Friedman et al., 1962). The evidence that supported this approach came from several sources. Lewis et al. (1931) showed that if a limb was exercised after a tourniquet had been applied, the limb rapidly became painful. This provided direct support for the idea that tension headache might be due to overcontraction of muscles and failure to remove the waste products of metabolism. Wolff (1948) and Hardy et al. (1952) demonstrated regional headaches related to the distorted action of extraocular muscles, e.g. the response imposed by having to wear prisms in spectacles. These manoeuvres gave evident rise to headache that could be related potentially to muscle contraction.

Two sources of scepticism came to bear on this field. First, quantitative electromyography (EMG) was disappointing in that it failed to demonstrate a meaningful link between the amount of excess muscular activity and anxiety or other psychiatric phenomena in the patients (Merskey, 1989). It was evident that although many patients with so-called tension headache had emotional disturbance, they did not have the matching EMG changes that were supposedly necessary to explain the condition. The leading alternative explanation in the past was hysteria, but there are other considerations now that make that also seem dubious. In particular, significant evidence of a hysterical conversion process is strikingly absent in many of these patients. In recognition of the uncertainty of the present diagnosis of what used to be called tension or muscle contraction headache, the International Headache Society (1988) has recommended the classification of "tension-type headache", which is less conclusive in regard to aetiology.

The so-called whiplash syndrome or cervical sprain injury is another form of headache for which psychological attributions were offered. It is noteworthy that there is now a solid corpus of evidence in favour of the idea that the cervical sprain injury is primarily an organic disease—as indeed the name implies. It used to be said that most patients got better within a few weeks or months. It is well known that this statement is misleading (Porter, 1989). A significant minority of patients persist with symptoms that appear to have an organic basis.

This is discussed further later. There are reasons to believe that many patients recover, but that others, without necessarily looking for monetary compensation, sustain troublesome, protracted neck pain. Those who have collars and wear them for long periods tend to do worse than those who do not. Some features of chronic pain of this type can be explained by the nature of the accident, e.g. severity of the impact or the direction in which the patient's head was turned at the time of injury.

Regional pain syndromes

When muscle contraction failed to be an adequate explanation for painful syndromes in a region of the body it was tempting to utilise the idea of hysteria to explain it. There is a very long history of the attribution of pain syndromes to the mind, or what used to be called "hysteria", dating back to ancient times. Regional syndromes of pain correspond to pain in an area of the body that is clearly identifiable by the patient as a part in which some loss or dysfunction can occur. Certain symptoms became established as signs of regional pain syndromes that were taken to be psychological, in particular sensory disorders that exceeded the boundaries of dermatomes and supposedly inconsistent findings on motor examination, such as "give-way weakness". Perceptive clinicians always recognised that there were some patients who had regional pain syndromes of organic origin (e.g. complex regional pain syndrome – type I) and that give-way weakness might be due to unwillingness to respond to the doctor's instructions because it would hurt to use the part. Nevertheless, the contrast between anyone's idea of a symptom, and complaints that in many cases lacked adequate explanation, led to the idea that regional pain syndromes were often hysterical. Walters (1961) described regional superficial skin sensitivity as one of the signs of "psychogenic" pain, although he wished to avoid the use of the expression "hysterical pain", feeling that it was inappropriate.

A variety of evidence has now accumulated to suggest that regional pain syndromes can have a substantial physical basis. First of all, the traditional signs of hysteria on which reliance has been placed in the past have been shown to be misleading. For example, Slater (1965) demonstrated that as many as 60% of patients with a diagnosis of classical hysteria had physical illness or would develop it. His work was confirmed by Whitlock (1967) and Merskey and Buhrich (1975). Gould et al. (1986) have shown that the specific signs on which reliance has been placed are highly unreliable. They examined a series of 30 patients with acute damage to the brain (29 with acute stroke) for such signs as a history suggestive of hypochondriasis, potential secondary gain, belle indifference, non-anatomical or patchy sensory loss, changing boundaries of hypalgesia, sensory loss that splits at the midline, and give-way weakness. All the patients demonstrated at least one of the above. The mean number of these items per patient was 3.4.

It has been suggested by other authors from Kellgren onwards (Kellgren, 1938, 1949) that there are areas of reference from muscles, ligaments, and joints to other deep tissue and to the overlying skin. Both myotomes and sclerotomes could be recognised in addition to the traditional dermatomes. Although a number of workers (e.g. Travell & Simons, 1983) began to treat such problems by physical methods with some reports of success, little notice seems to have been taken by neurologists of this type of approach, perhaps because of the rather diffuse nature of the symptoms, and because of difficulties in demonstrating adequate reliability on physical examination for individuals who were alleged to have muscle contraction, spasm, or the so-called "taut muscle bands" of Travell and Simons. Nevertheless, a steady series of findings emerged from the early 1970s, which showed that there was considerable plasticity in the organisation of the central nervous system and that receptive fields could vary substantially after injury, so that reliance upon single dermatomes or several dermatomes was strikingly misleading. Wall (1984, 1989) summarised the evidence that the receptive fields of neurones in the dorsal horn can change and extend. Three to four days after deafferentation in the rat, cells that formerly would respond to stimulation only within the usual anatomical area would begin to respond to stimuli from other areas. Stimuli that were formerly ineffective would then excite cells that had expanded their receptive fields to incorporate innervated peripheral structures. Receptive fields themselves also vary substantially after injury in the region. McMahon and Wall (1984) demonstrated that the receptive field of the dorsal horn cell in lamina 1 could be mapped out and would then change substantially if a punctate burn was placed in the adjoining area. The changes occurred about 10–15 minutes after applying the burn. It has even been shown in the cat that a simple train of electrical conditioning stimuli at 1 Hz for 20 seconds applied to the proximal cut end of the gastrocnemius muscle will more than triple the receptive field of a cutaneous afferent neurone, whether it responds to firm mechanical stimulus or to pinch (Cook et al., 1987). It has been pointed out elsewhere (Merskey, 1988) that mechanisms exist in the spinal cord that allow regional pain to develop from a localised disturbance, including subcutaneous changes. In these circumstances it is not possible, or reasonable, to assume that non-anatomical pain automatically reflects the presence of hysteria. It follows that regional pain syndromes might have to be understood in terms other than psychiatric ones, and that they require further exploration physically. Their management is considered in Chapter 19.

Other motor and sensory conversion symptoms

Classical motor and sensory conversion symptoms involve a loss of function rather than pain. A limb will be paralysed; patients will fall down in fits; walking is disturbed; sight, hearing, or memory can fail; regional areas of anaesthesia will appear. If we put aside the last of these symptoms there remain many cases where it seems that overt physical complaints have been precipitated by severe emotional stress. The evidence that was quoted earlier from Slater and others tends to suggest that such symptoms often have an organic basis. There was a previous era in neurological practice when, for good reason, the importance of the mind in producing hysterical symptoms was readily recognised. This was the period immediately following the First World War, which had a great influence upon neurological thinking, even up to the present time. During that war it was established both in the English-speaking countries and in Continental Europe that almost anyone, placed under severe stress, might develop syndromes of shaking, paralysis, and general inability to function, as well as more specific losses of function (Merskey, 1990). This did not require the invocation of a particular aetiology of sexual abuse in childhood. The current stresses were so overwhelming that they were correctly taken to be quite enough to account for some of these apparently physical disturbances. Thus, in the past, conversion symptoms were quite reasonably regarded as having a strong basis in psychological phenomena (Merskey, 1995). Today, by contrast, most conversion symptoms are found in association with neurological disease. The exceptions tend to be among children or in rather unsophisticated societies. These can often be rehabilitated successfully, but what has to be said about rehabilitation has to be adjusted to the particular circumstances of each case.

Medicolegal implications

The foregoing sections have considerable medicolegal implications. If it is the case that the traditional methods of diagnosing hysteria are frequently unreliable in *sensory* conditions, and if, also, such signs as give-way weakness cannot be relied upon, we are forced to reconsider the frequent diagnosis of "psychogenic pain" or conscious exaggeration in individuals who have claims for compensation. Other information also tends towards a new view of the matter.

For many years, this field was strongly influenced by the work of Henry Miller (1961) who, with charismatic vigour, maintained that "compensation neurosis is a state of mind, born out of fear, kept alive by avarice, stimulated by lawyers, and cured by a verdict". Part of this memorable sentence appears to have been provided earlier by Foster Kennedy. It led to an assumption that individuals in whom the stigmata of hysteria were recognised on neurological examination would get better as soon as

they had money in their hand or no prospect of more. This has been proved abundantly wrong. Mendelson (1982) reviewed ten follow-up studies dealing with accident victims and observed that not one had supported Miller. All had found that a significant group of patients continued to suffer from pain or other symptoms long after the question of litigation had been settled. Kelly and Smith (1981) showed not only that many symptoms persisted long after settlement and where there was no continuing financial benefit, but also that others got better before settlement. It is well recognised and unarguable that many patients confronted with uncertainty about their financial status, possible debts that they cannot pay, the prospect of not being able to work adequately again, and disturbances in their self-image that follow from their failure to work, will show emotional changes. Chronic pain also gives rise to emotional changes. The combination of these circumstances will produce considerable distress, which becomes most acute near the time of a trial when there is the risk for the average educated or uneducated person that he or she is going to be questioned about almost any aspect of his or her life by a person who is skilled at—dare one say it—misinterpreting evidence. At least this is how patients see it.

Hence, the condition of having chronic pain and unemployment is stressful, and that of facing a trial in court is likewise disturbing. Patients become worse prior to this ordeal and improve afterwards. Professional people, expert witnesses, and lawyers also are known to experience tension in the circumstances of a trial; the same must apply to the patient whose future hangs, to a great extent, upon the matter. Improvement after trial, therefore, can be expected in respect of some of the stress, but not particularly in regard to pain or ability to work. The follow-up studies have demonstrated this very well.

It should also be noted that there is substantial evidence that individuals who are said to be "grossly neurotic" before trial do not improve after trial either (Tarsh & Royston, 1985). It is said that patients who have claims for compensation are more neurotic or emotionally maladjusted than others. This is not always the case and some authors have found very similar patterns in individuals, in the same clinic, claiming compensation or not claiming compensation (Leavitt et al., 1982; Pelz & Merskey, 1982). A critical evaluation was performed by Melzack et al. (1985), who demonstrated, in patients controlled for employment status, that those with chronic pain who were claiming compensation were not more neurotic than others without such claims.

There is a point of view that the effect of chronic pain is distressing and a cause of psychological illness (Teasell & Merskey, 1997). Selection factors also play a part. Those individuals who are seen in specialised clinics are those in whom problems have persisted and in whom psychological factors might be more prominent. This was considered earlier. This is not to say that malingering cannot occur in any centre and that misrepresentation of symptoms cannot take place, but the common view that "the patient will recover with settlement" is generally a travesty of the real situation.

Lastly, in this section, it is worth pointing to the evolution of ideas in regard to the cervical sprain syndrome (hyperextension–flexion injuries). It has been repeatedly demonstrated that patients with this syndrome who are seen in hospital follow a recognisable course, with initial pain and diffuse aching, which gradually declines, in the muscles of the neck and scalp. The force of injury does not have to be great to produce the syndrome, mainly because of the lack of resistance to overextension of muscles when the head is flung backwards (even sometimes in the presence of a headrest) or to the side. Rear-end impacts at speeds ranging from 8 to 32 km/h are quite capable of producing this effect. There is probably a curvilinear relationship between neck injuries and chronic pain because the more severe collisions led to other complications. The cervical sprain injury has, however, worsened or increased in frequency since the introduction of seatbelts. Not all patients get better (Porter, 1989) and it has long been known that there is a significant pathological basis for the condition, including rupture of muscles and ligaments and even partial tear of cervical disks (Macnab, 1973). Several symptoms that used to be thought of as "psychogenic" arise routinely from the severe physical injury. Thus, the more severe cases demonstrate dizziness, which might be due either to disturbances of the labyrinth or effects upon conduction from the rich network of afferent nerves travelling from the neck to the hindbrain. Such "dizziness" often has a characteristic time course of recovery. Trigger points, muscle spasm, and limitation of movement are all quite consistent and typical in patients with the more severe syndromes. What was formerly dismissed as an attempt at malingering, or at best a nearly conscious psychological illness, has now been recognised to be substantially related to physical injury and anatomicophysiological disturbances (Teasell & Shapiro, 1993).

A recent article (Schrader et al., 1996) has suggested that the whiplash syndrome has "little validity" on the basis of a follow-up of 202 individuals who were involved in rear-end collisions in Lithuania, where compensation for continuing symptoms was not available. This particular study was based upon retrospective recollection 1–3 years later, of pain preceding an accident and upon current pain at the time of investigation. The follow-up also identified 31 individuals who recalled pain at the time of the collision. This study was unfortunate in that, because accidents were followed-up rather than injuries, it lacked adequate power. On the other hand, significant prospective work by Radanov et al. (1991) 6 months after rear-end collisions showed that the only factors predicting pain and psychological symptoms at 6 months were the occurrence of a previous similar injury and the intensity of pain at the time of the index event. Meanwhile, Bogduk and his colleagues in Australia have shown that between half and three-quarters of patients with cervical sprain injury appear to suffer pain because of damage to the cervical zygapophysial joints. This was demonstrated by means of radiologically controlled, double-blind comparisons of the relief of pain from injection in the medial branches of the dorsal rami of the spinal nerves, with short-acting and long-acting analgesics (Lord, Barnley, & Bogduk, 1993). Percutaneous radio frequency neurotomy of these nerves supplying the zygapophysial joints has provided sustained worthwhile relief of pain when administered under double-blind, controlled conditions (Lord et al., 1997).

This is not to say that genuine psychological illness does not occur after injuries. The most common is probably a mild form of post-traumatic stress disorder. Thus, patients who have been involved in mildly frightening or unpleasant injuries, or worse, are liable to have some of the following symptoms. They commonly have disturbed sleep or nightmares about frightening accidents or similar experiences, at least for a few weeks or months; they tend to have increased uneasiness in the vicinity of the place where their accident occurred, and might avoid it altogether; and they might become uneasy either as passengers or drivers in motor vehicles. At times, the uneasiness is most marked if another driver approaches their vehicle from a side street or some other direction at a rather high speed and is apparently not going to stop. These conditions often produce well-marked phobic anxiety in relation to motor vehicles and can be severe enough to constitute a post-traumatic stress disorder. Depression is often associated with the illness, either because the pain is sufficiently troublesome by then or because the anxiety is also a cause of increased concern.

Treatment is available both for the cervical sprain syndrome and for post-traumatic anxiety and is considered elsewhere.

REHABILITATION PROCEDURES

The largest step towards the rehabilitation of psychosomatic symptoms depends upon accurate diagnosis and understanding. In specific instances, a diagnosis of a treatable psychiatric illness, e.g. an endogenous or reactive depression, can lead to appropriate treatment such as medication for those with endogenous patterns of illness, consolation for the bereaved, management of problems in the life of the individual patients with reactive depression, forms of psychotherapy, etc. These routine psychiatric measures can help to resolve the problem in patients who have obvious treatable conditions. Whether or not the illness is readily treatable, understanding the dilemmas and fears of the individual can be as important as the specific psychiatric diagnosis.

With patients who are relatively hypochondriacal and show increased sensitivity to peripheral stimulation, it is important to emphasise that their complaints are believed to be accurate statements. It is not enough in such cases simply to say "there is nothing serious", much less, "there is nothing there". There is a need to convey two firm ideas: first, the symptom is not ominous and, second, it relates to particular ways of thinking or feeling about the body. It has developed because the patient has a characteristic way of reacting to stress or other emotional disorders. Reassurance, which is the staple method of most neurologists and other doctors, can only work adequately in many cases if it is coupled with the extra effort to provide understanding of the way in which symptoms arise. One way of putting the matter to patients goes something like this: "Many people have symptoms which they recognise to be due to their feelings. For example, if they tremble when the latter are upset or if they cry this does not surprise them. Other symptoms cause more difficulty because people are less familiar with them: for example, feeling that the world looks different, or that you are dizzy, may be something that happens because of emotions and may be quite typical for some people, but because it is not the usual type of sadness it is hard for that to be understood".

This sort of approach has to be coupled with an analysis of why the person might be upset. Having established initially that the symptom is present, second, that it is not serious, and, third, that it could be due to a way of feeling, one next has to change the direction of discussion and consider what things are happening in a person's life that might be distressing. In the majority of cases there is usually some very obvious cause. If there is no obvious psychological cause one should always think of the significance of an existing physical illness as a source of distress. This often seems to be overlooked and perhaps unduly played down. Just because a physical illness has been defined and its role is known to the physician, it can be neglected somewhat (if it is not cancer or heart disease) as a cause of distress to the patient. Patients can present additional symptoms, largely because they want the accepted physical problem to be treated with more attention. This is a well-known ploy that gets the patient into difficulty with doctors and usually produces the wrong result. As one patient who developed hysterical fits in addition to epileptic fits put it to me: first she had real fits, then she had fake fits to get more attention, and then she got less attention and was discharged.

Overall, the approach to the rehabilitation of psychological symptoms depends on this simple pattern of establishing knowledge of stresses, recognising their presence, and explaining to the patient that those stresses can exacerbate specific physical complaints.

TREATMENT IN SPECIFIC SITUATIONS

Hypochondriasis

As indicated above, certain situations are relieved by recognising a particular diagnosis. Hypochondriasis arises at times in the context of a well-marked depressive illness or schizophrenia. Sometimes it is part of an organic cerebral condition. In such instances, treatment of the underlying condition, if available, can resolve the main difficulty with the somatic complaint. If the mood state or preoccupation persists, extra attention has to be provided according to the particular issue. In the case of individuals who have somatic symptoms and hypochondriasis, the approach just outlined works fairly well, with one major limitation. There are some patients who, despite all that, are not reassured. The reason is usually that the hypochondriacal complaints are held with a degree of intensity that will not respond to the above measures alone. The management of the more protracted hypochondriacal cases is an issue for psychiatrists and has been considered by Kellner (1986). Psychiatrists treating such patients will tend to recognise that the latter are both frightened of the possibility of illness and convinced that they have it. In

other words they have, as mentioned earlier, both disease phobia and disease conviction. These terms are slightly cumbersome, but sum up very effectively the combination of problems that the severely hypochondriacal patient will present recurringly.

Initial full reassurance followed by cognitive–behavioural therapy (Warwick et al., 1996) is one of the best validated types of treatment that can be applied from this starting point.

Headache

Chronic headache can develop, as mentioned, as a problem-solving symptom aimed at resolving conflict, but that is rarely established. More usually the headache will arise out of one of the common forms of psychiatric illness, either depression or anxiety, or be associated with recognised migraine. In these situations a combination of treatments has to be pursued. Individual psychotherapy is appropriate and important if sufficient material can be established in relation to the patient's problems and adjustment. Interviews with the family, or at least with the spouse, can be highly relevant and helpful. The use of benzodiazepines should be avoided, but amitriptyline is a favourite drug in nearly every case because it has both analgesic and antidepressant effects (Watson et al., 1982). It also has anti-anxiety effects and might have a prophylactic action in migraine. So, overall, it is highly favoured despite its side-effects. In modest dosage these are the anticholinergic side-effects of dry mouth and constipation, and undue weight gain. If patients agree to take amitriptyline the most troublesome adverse effect, long term, tends to be weight gain.

It is worth noting some particular points about the prescription of amitriptyline or other antidepressants. In general, and especially for out-patients, a large dose should not be prescribed initially for problems of the sort under consideration here. A small dose, even as little as 10–20 mg of amitriptyline at first, should be offered to the patient to be taken 2 or 3 hours before retiring with emphasis on the facts that it tends to promote sleep, that it tends to be slow in action, and that it is important to take it well in advance of retiring in order to get an adequate hypnotic effect, and also so that the patient will not be too heavy and sleepy the next day. Many doctors seem to be willing to let their patients take enough amitriptyline to be half-doped for the greater part of their waking hours. This is not popular with the patients and is probably unnecessary. If the dose of amitriptyline is sufficiently tailored to the individual it can be used successfully to improve sleep and to reduce symptoms without imposing a great burden of side-effects throughout the day. Some dryness of the mouth is almost inevitable. Other aspects of the prescription of amitriptyline and its use need not be considered in detail here.

Patients might have to be treated empirically even when no clear psychological or physical cause is apparent. In these circumstances, psychological exploration should be presented as a tentative option and the use of antidepressant/analgesic medication likewise made available in a tentative way. On occasion, offer a choice between a simple non-steroidal anti-inflammatory drug and an antidepressant drug that is low in side-effects (such as very small doses of flupenthixol, e.g. 0.5 mg at breakfast and lunch). Patients soon determine which is more useful to them, or whether both are helpful.

Hysterical symptoms

In the case of a classical motor or sensory conversion symptom, the introduction of psychotropic medication is a distraction and sometimes a hindrance to treatment. As mentioned already, most conversion symptoms are found in association with neurological disease. One of the most important initial approaches to them is to be sure that the patients are not intoxicated with medication such as primidone or diphenylhydantoin, which is capable of producing overt hysterical symptoms if the level of medication rises unduly (Niedermeyer et al., 1970). Additional hysterical fits might well occur in individuals with epilepsy partly because their serum anticonvulsant levels have risen too high. If an excess level of anticonvulsants is found on serum measurement and the dose adjusted, it can be anticipated that at least some cases of hysterical symptoms will clear up satisfactorily. However, they might not change quite as fast as the serum level and a little delay of a few days or a week or two might be required for the situation to revert to a more satisfactory state.

Hysterical symptoms can also be treated by a variety of techniques involving suggestion and relaxation. Hypnosis has been favoured for many generations in the management of patients with hysteria. I do not use hypnosis myself any more, partly because I think it is no more than a pattern of suggestion that depends upon offering misleading information. The patients believe it, it is not wholly misleading if the doctor believes it, and it sometimes works, but there is also reason to believe that those results obtained by hypnosis can also be obtained by other more banal techniques, such as additional interviews, discussion, suggestion, relaxation, and "teaching" the possibility of alteration in symptoms. Thus, for example, a patient who has aphonia can be trained first of all to cough—showing that there is some power—and then to cough with the sound "a" and so forth, producing increasing sounds.

There is no objection to the direct removal of almost all symptoms provided the patient remains under observation. It used to be said that patients with hysteria whose symptoms were removed by strong suggestion were at risk of having to face the conflict that had produced the symptom and were liable to become very depressed and suicidal. One or two cases of suicide were alleged to have occurred as a result of this. Such a complication need not necessarily be a contraindication to treatment by symptom removal if proper treatment is provided. It will be necessary, however, to make sure that there is continuity of contact, that the patient is assured of continuing assistance, and that the patient is kept under observation following the removal of the hysterical symptom. Barham Carter (1949) showed that hysterical symptoms could be removed successfully in the majority of *acute* cases of hysterical conversion. However, such cases are less common in current practice in Britain and North America

and it should be noted that attempts at symptom removal are often less successful in consequence, except in children, who tend to be relatively facile in their development of hysterical symptoms and the removal of them.

Besides looking for evidence of physical predisposition, and cases of conflict, the doctor should also look for evidence of other psychological illness. Occasionally, conversion symptoms develop in patients who have incipient schizophrenia or established depressive illness. Conversion symptoms appearing in individuals in middle age and later, without a prior history of hysteria, are almost all due either to latent organic illness or to a recognisable depressive state.

Other treatments that are open to the psychiatrist to pursue, but which will be unlikely to be utilised directly by the neurologist, include narcoanalysis, with the injection of a sedative medication to promote the flow of thoughts and ideas relative to conflict, and insight psychotherapy. Behaviour therapy has also been used to remove hysterical symptoms. Historically, various manipulations have been employed, including removing patients to environments in which they were prone to symptoms (e.g. Carter, 1853). Yealland (1918) used strong electrical stimulation, which was markedly aversive, to "cure" "shellshocked" soldiers. Various reports have appeared about behaviour therapy and the management of patients with hysteria. Scallett et al. (1976) reviewed 23 such reports on the management of "chronic hysteria", which included patients with conversion symptoms; about two-thirds obtained some improvement. Traditionally, "physiotherapy" has been used as a means of encouraging patients to undertake one type of activity and to discourage them from lying in bed or not using a body part. An understanding approach, combined with suggestions through physiotherapy, is often the staple of neurological efforts to rehabilitate patients with conversion hysteria.

In very intractable cases, behavioural techniques that challenge the patient have been tried. It is suggested to the patient that the original complaint might have been organic but has been followed by a maladaptive response. If the original symptoms were organic, the maladaptive response will be removable by treatment. If not, it has to be regarded as so ingrained that it is incurable. Thus a failure to recover will be evidence of the non-organic nature of the problem (Kraupl-Taylor, 1969; Neeleman & Mann, 1993; Teasell & Shapiro, 1993). This approach involves misleading the patient but it has been found to be very powerful therapeutically.

Overall rehabilitation

Rehabilitation of patients with all these varied conditions can be much facilitated if efforts are made to test for vocational skills, intellectual level, vocational preferences, and attitudes. The work of the psychologist is invaluable here and rehabilitation advice from an appropriate specialist is ideal. To some extent there is an untapped reservoir of ability that still escapes the best efforts of universal education in the sense that individuals do not always seem to achieve the education in their ordinary school years for which we might hope. Subsequent opportunities to engage in retraining can be invaluable for patients whose symptoms are produced by their particular job or whose symptoms make their work intolerable. This is particularly applicable to manual workers. A full-scale investigation of these aspects of any patient with protracted unemployment or dissatisfaction with his or her work is well justified in human terms, and is cost efficient also.

REFERENCES

American Psychiatric Association (1980) *Diagnostic and Statistical Manual, 3rd edition, DSM-III.* Washington DC: American Psychiatric Association.

American Psychiatric Association (1987) *Diagnostic and Statistical Manual (revised edition), DSM-III-R.* Washington DC: American Psychiatric Association.

American Psychiatric Association (1994) *Diagnostic and Statistical Manual DSM-IV.* Washington DC: American Psychiatric Association.

Banks MH, Beresford SHA, Morrell DC et al. (1975) Factors influencing demand for primary medical care in women aged 20–40 years; a preliminary report. *International Journal of Epidemiology, 4,* 189–255.

Barsky AJ, Klerman GL (1983) Overview: Hypochondriasis, bodily complaints, and somatic styles. *American Journal of Psychiatry, 140,* 273–283.

Breuer J, Freud S (1893–1895) *Studies on hysteria.* Reprinted in *Complete psychological works of Freud,* vol. 2 (1955). London: Hogarth Press.

Cannon WB (1915) *Bodily changes in pain, hunger, fear and rage.* New York: Appleton.

Carter AB (1949) The prognosis of certain hysterical symptoms. *British Medical Journal, 1,* 1076–1079.

Carter RB (1853) *On the pathology and treatment of hysteria.* London: Churchill.

Charcot JM [transl. T Savill] (1889) *Clinical lectures on diseases of the nervous system.* London: New Sydenham Society, vol. 111.

Cook AJ, Woolf CJ, Wall PD et al. (1987) Dynamic receptive field plasticity in rat spinal cord dorsal horn following C-primary afferent input. *Nature, 325,* 151–153.

Dunbar HF (1953) Emotions and bodily changes. New York: Columbia.

Finlayson J (1893) Hierophilus and Erasistratus. *Glasgow Medical Journal, 4S XXXIX,* 310–352.

Friedman AP, Finley KE, Graham JR et al. (1962) Classification of headache. Special report of the Ad Hoc Committee. *Archives of Neurology, 6,* 173–176.

Gillespie RD (1929) *Hypochondriasis.* London: Kegan Paul.

Gillespie RD (1942) *Psychological Effects of War on Citizen and Soldier.* New York: WW Norton.

Gould R, Miller BL, Goldberg MA, Benson DF (1986) The validity of hysterical signs and symptoms. *Journal of Nervous and Mental Disorders, 174,* 593–597.

Hardy JD, Wolff HG Goodell H (1952) *Pain Sensations and Reactions.* Baltimore: Williams & Wilkins.

Holmes DS (1974) Investigations of repression: Differential recall of material experimentally or naturally associated with ego threat. *Psychological Bulletin, 81,* 632–653.

Holmes DS (1990) The evidence for repression: An examination of sixty years of research. In JL Singer (Ed.), *Repression and dissociation. Implications for personality theory, psychopathology and health.* Chicago: University of Chicago Press, pp. 85–102.

International Headache Society, Headache Classification Committee (1988) Classification and diagnostic criteria for headache disorders, cranial neuralgias and facial pain. *Cephalalgia, 8* (suppl. 7) 1–96.

Kellgren JH (1938) Observations on referred pain arising from muscle. *Clinical Science, 3,* 175–190.

Kellgren JH (1949) Deep pain sensibility. *Lancet, i,* 943–949.

Kellner R (1986) *Somatization and hypochondriasis.* New York: Praeger.

Kelly R, Smith BN (1981) Post-traumatic syndrome: Another myth discredited. *Journal of the Royal Society of Medicine, 74,* 275–277.

Kirmayer LJ, Robbins J (1991) Three forms of somatization in primary care: Prevalence, co-occurrence and sociodemographic characteristics. *Journal of Nervous and Mental Disease, 179,* 647–655.

Kraepl-Taylor R (1969) Prokaletic measures derived from psycho-analytic technique. *British Journal of Psychiatry, 11* (5): 407–419.

Leavitt F, Carron DC, McNeill TW et al. (1982) Organic status, psychological disturbance, and pain report characteristics in low-back-pain patients on compensation. *Spine, 7,* 398–402.

Lewis T, Pickering GW, Rothschild P (1931) Observations upon muscular pain in intermittent claudication. *Heart, 15,* 359–383.

Lipowski ZJ (1985) *Psychosomatic medicine and liaison psychiatry. Selected papers.* New York: Plenum Press.

Lord S, Barnsley L, Bogduk N (1993) Cervical zygapophyseal joint pain in whiplash. In RW Teasell, AP Shapiro (Eds.), *Cervical flexion extension/whiplash injuries: Spine: State of the Art Reviews,* vol. 7: 355–372. Philadelphia: Hanley & Belfus.

Lord SM, Barnsley L, Wallis BJ, et al. (1997) Percutaneous radio-frequency neurotomy for chronic cervical zygaprophyseal joint pain. *New England Journal of Medicine, 335,* 1721–1726.

Macnab I (1973) The whiplash syndrome. *Clinical Neurosurgery, 20,* 232–241.

McMahon SB, Wall PD (1984) Receptive fields of rat lamina 1 projection cells move to incorporate a nearby region of injury. *Pain, 19,* 235–247.

Melzack R, Katz J, Jeans MJ (1985) The role of compensation in chronic pain: Analysis using a new method of scoring the McGill Pain Questionnaire. *Pain, 23,* 101–112.

Mendelson G (1982) Not "cured by a verdict". Effect of legal settlement on compensation claimants. *Medical Journal of Australia, 3,* 132–134.

Merskey H (1995) *The Analysis of Hysteria,* 2nd edition. London: Gaskell Press.

Merskey H (1988) Regional pain is rarely hysterical. *Archives of Neurology, 45,* 915–918.

Merskey H (1989) Current perspectives: Psychiatry and chronic pain. *Canadian Journal of Psychiatry, 34,* 329–336.

Merskey H (1990) "Shellshock". In GE Berrios, H Freeman (Eds.), *150 years of British psychiatry, 1841–1991.* London: The Royal College of Psychiatrists.

Merskey H, Buhrich N (1975) Hysteria and organic brain disease. *British Journal of Medical Psychology, 48,* 359–366.

Miller HG (1961) Accident neurosis. *British Medical Journal, 1,* 919–925, 992–998.

Neeleman J, Mann H (1993) Treatment of hysterical aphonia with hypnosis and prokaletic therapy. *British Journal of Psychiatry, 163,* 816–819.

Niedermeyer E, Blumer D, Holscher E et al. (1970) Classical hysterical seizures facilitated by anticonvulsant toxicity. *Psychiatrica Clinica, Basel, 3,* 71–84.

Nutton V (1979) Galen: On prognosis. *Corpus medicorum graecorum, 8*(1), 101–105, Akademie-Verlag, Berlin.

Pelz M, Merskey H (1982) A description of the psychological effects of chronic painful lesions. *Pain, 14,* 293–301.

Pennebaker JW (1982) *The psychology of physical symptoms.* New York: Springer-Verlag.

Pilowsky I (1967) Dimensions of hypochondriasis. *British Journal of Psychiatry, 113,* 89–93.

Pond DA, Bidwell BH (1959) A survey of epilepsy in 14 general practices. II. Social and psychological aspects. *Epilepsia, 1,* 285–299.

Porter KM (1989) Neck sprains after car accidents. *British Medical Journal, 289,* 973–974.

Radanov BP, Stefano GD, Schnidrig A et al. (1991) Role of psychosocial stress in recovery from common whiplash. *Lancet, 338,* 712–715.

Reynolds JR (1869) Remarks on paralysis and other disorders of motion and sensation, dependent on idea. *British Medical Journal, 2,* 483–485, Discussion, 378–379.

Scallett A, Cloninger CR, Othmer E (1976) The management of chronic hysteria: A review and double-blind trial of electrosleep and other relaxation methods. *Journal of Nervous and Mental Disorders, 37,* 347–353.

Schrader H, Obelieniene D, Bovim G et al. (1996). Natural evolution of late whiplash syndrome outside the medico-legal context. *Lancet, 247,* 1207–1211.

Slater E (1965) Diagnosis of "hysteria". *British Medical Journal, 1,* 1395–1396.

Tarsh MJ, Royston C (1985) A follow-up study of accident neurosis. *British Journal of Psychiatry, 146,* 18–25.

Teasell RW, Shapiro AP (1993) Cervical flexion extension/whiplash injuries. *Spine: State of the Art Reviews, 7,* 355–372, Philadelphia: Hanley, Belfus.

Teasell RW, Merskey H (1997) Chronic pain and disability in the workplace. *Pain Research & Management, 2*, 177–205.

Travell JS, Simmons DG (1983) *Myofascial pain and dysfunction. The trigger point manual*. Baltimore: Williams & Wilkins.

Wall PD (1984) The dorsal horn. In PD Wall, R Melzack (Eds.), *Textbook of pain, 1st edition*. Edinburgh: Churchill Livingstone, pp. 80–87.

Wall PD (1989) The dorsal horn. In PD Wall, R Melzack (Eds.), *Textbook of pain, 2nd edition*. Edinburgh: Churchill Livingstone, pp. 101–111.

Walters A (1961) Psychogenic regional pain alias hysterical pain. *Brain, 84*, 1–18.

Warwick HMC, Clark DM, Cobb AM et al. (1966). A controlled trial of cognitive–behavioural treatment of hypochondriasis. *British Journal of Psychiatry, 169*, 189–195.

Watson GD, Chandarana PC, Merskey H (1982) Relationships between pain and schizophrenia. *British Journal of Psychiatry, 138*, 33–36.

Whitlock FA (1967) The aetiology of hysteria. *Acta Psychiatrica Scandinavica, 43*, 144–162.

Wolff HG (1948) *Headache and other head pain*. London: Oxford University Press.

World Health Organization (1977) *International Classification of Diseases, 9th revision*. Geneva: World Health Organization.

World Health Organization (1992) *International Classification of Diseases, 10th revision*. Geneva: World Health Organization.

Yealland LR (1918) *Hysterical disorders of warfare*. London: Macmillan.

34. Psychosocial consequences of brain injury

Michael Oddy

INTRODUCTION

The term "psychosocial" encompasses many aspects of recovery from traumatic brain injury and is used inconsistently from one study to another. It includes adjustment to disability, the ability to pursue a normal life, the ability to play a variety of social roles, the ability to maintain social relationships, quality of life, satisfaction with life, and the ability to cope with the practical and emotional demands of life as well as the losses experienced through brain injury. It can also include effects on significant others, such as family members, also potential employers, colleagues, and friends or acquaintances. Although cognitive impairment is not normally considered under the heading "psychosocial", personality changes resulting from brain injury often are. Thus the concept cuts across the World Health Organization (WHO) definitions of impairments, disability and handicap.

The concept of "social adjustment" refers to the extent to which a person is able to perform the various social roles that are considered to constitute normality. These include the role of worker, participant in leisure pursuits, friend, and family member. The extent to which a person continues to play these roles satisfactorily is a measure of that person's social adjustment. It is therefore very close to the WHO (1980) definition of handicap, "a disadvantage for a given individual, resulting from an impairment or disability that limits or prevents the fulfilment of a *role* that is normal (depending on the age, sex and cultural factors) for the individual". The term "quality of life" is now commonly used and considerable work has gone into defining this term in other fields, such as AIDS or cancer research. Less attention has been paid to this concept in brain injury research (Oddy & Alcott, 1996) and no satisfactory definitions or measures exist beyond perhaps simple analogue ratings of life satisfaction. This concept will not therefore be used explicitly in this chapter, although the questions addressed concern the extent to which the nature and quality of the lives of people with the brain injury are altered. What changes take place over time; which aspects of their lives are they more likely to be able to resume and which are more likely to be problematic? What happens to the family; what kinds of stress are they under and at what periods are these worse? What interventions can be made to enhance the ability of people with brain injury to return to a normal life?

The personal or subjective aspects of psychosocial recovery raise questions concerned with the process of emotional adjustment to life after brain injury. How do people with the brain injury adjust to their altered circumstances? What psychological adaptations do they have to make? Why do difficulties occur? What factors differentiate between those who cope well and those who do less well? How can psychological adaptations be assisted?

In this chapter the topic will be addressed by examining: (1) the return of the ability to perform various roles; (2) emotional adjustment following brain injury; and (3) the help the family requires.

RETURN TO WORK AFTER BRAIN INJURY

Estimates of how many people are able to return to work after brain injury vary because of the different methods of selecting the samples. Those studies of unselected samples of all those suffering a head injury have given return rates of 90 or 95% (Rowbotham et al., 1954; Steadman & Graham, 1970). Those studies that have taken a minimal level of severity, frequently a post-traumatic amnesia (PTA) of more than 24 hours, have obtained rates of 80–90% (Carlsson et al., 1968; Fahy et al., 1967; Hpay, 1971; Miller & Stern, 1965). If only those admitted to a specialist service are included, the rates can go down to below 40%, depending on the admission criteria for the service (Wehman et al., 1989).

If one looks at the process of returning to work over time, it can be seen that most people who are to return will have done so 2 years after their injury. In a study of 43 patients who have attended the Wolfson Rehabilitation Centre in Wimbledon, Oddy et al. (1985) found that after 2 years, five patients had returned to their previous level of work and a further four patients had returned to their original capacity after 7 years. Only one person who was not working at all at 2 years was working at 7 years. All those who were working at 2 years were still employed at 7 years, although many had had changes of job. A remarkably similar pattern has been found in two more recent studies. In Australia,

Olver et al. (1996) found that the number employed reduced from 50% at 2 years to 40% at 5 years. Of those unemployed at 2 years, only four were working at 5 years. Johnson (1998) found that of a sample of 64 patients followed up 10 years after injury, only two who had not been back to work within 2 years were working at 10 years. In this study, settlement of compensation claims sometimes led to a deterioration in work status but never directly to an improvement.

For those who returned to work successfully there is often an extended period of moving from job to job before finding one in which they can settle. Thomsen (1984), in her 15-year follow-up, gives an interesting example of this kind. She describes a man who went through 20 jobs in 5 years before finding one as a truck driver; he still held this job 10 years later. A study by Wehman et al. (1989) found that one of the main problems in occupation resettlement is the "consistently changing vocational aspirations" of people with brain injury. This is certainly a frequent problem in clinical practice and commonly takes the form of an unwillingness to accept any alternative to the job held before injury.

A case example: John sustained a head injury at the age of 17. He had previously worked as a car sprayer and was single-minded in his intention to return to this. Eventually, despite many failed attempts at employment rehabilitation centres and more than 3 years after his injury, his mother managed to persuade a local proprietor to give him a trial. This only lasted for a couple of days on two consecutive weeks. The proprietor described a variety of incidents that are typical of the difficulties people with brain injury have. On one occasion, John was asked to touch up three marks on a car door. After a while he reported to the proprietor that he had finished. When his work was checked only one of the marks had been dealt with. This had been done to a satisfactory standard but John had failed to monitor his performance to ensure he had completed his task. On another occasion John got paint thinner in his eye and on another the proprietor found him wandering around at the back of the workshop unable to find his way back in. The final straw was when the proprietor spent all evening looking for a set of car keys to enable a customer to collect his vehicle. In the end he decided to telephone John, who said "Oh yes, I've got them in my pocket". John had known they were there but had not thought to let the proprietor know.

In an intensive study of five individuals using a single case design, Wehman et al. (1989) found that the following problems had to be addressed in helping people to return to work: (1) getting to work on time; (2) transportation arrangements; (3) inappropriate verbal behaviour in the workplace; (4) planning and sequencing work activities; (5) remembering work tasks; and (6) inappropriate sexual behaviour.

It is clear that motor and sensory deficits can prevent a resumption of many occupations, but they do not normally result in a person becoming totally unemployable. Cognitive deficits and personality problems cause difficulties that are much less easy to avoid and can result in the person being unable to work productively in any occupation (Ip et al., 1995; Crepeau & Scherzer, 1993).

Vocational rehabilitation

What can be done to facilitate the return to work of a person suffering from brain injury? Studies in this area over the last decade provide arguably the strongest evidence for the value of rehabilitation. In a series of publications, Wehman and colleagues have suggested that "supported employment programmes" can successfully increase rates of return to work amongst those who have had a brain injury. This approach involves matching the client to job opportunities and time-limited inventions involving a "job coach" or "vocational specialist", primarily at the place of work. The specialist initially spends a considerable amount of time in the workplace with the client. Any problems arising, whether they are skill related, interpersonal, or connected with transport to work are tackled by the vocational specialist from his or her experience and knowledge of brain injury. The vocational specialist's role can include ensuring that the exact skill mix of the job is within the competence of the trainee, playing an advocacy role to ensure that employers and colleagues have an understanding of brain injury, as well as helping the trainee to learn new skills or compensatory strategies. The vocational specialist reduces his or her involvement over time but maintains a definite link with the organisation and trainee. Such an approach involves a considerable investment of time initially but, given the long-term benefits that can be achieved, it can be economically viable. Initial results from such programmes appear promising, with initial success rates of around 70% (Haffrey & Abrahams, 1991; Wehman et al., 1989; West et al., 1990). Such figures are difficult to interpret in the absence of matched, non-intervention comparison groups, or at least detailed descriptions of the nature of the selection criteria. A demonstration that high rates of return can be achieved more than 2 years postinjury would, however, be convincing in the light of the studies by Oddy et al. (1985), Olver et al. (1996), and Johnson (1998), which were discussed earlier.

The supported employment approach differs from alternative methods primarily in terms of the amount of work preparation carried out. More traditional programmes combine a period of preparation in a rehabilitation setting with support when entering employment. The proponents of the supported employment schemes argue that these are equally, if not more, successful than those involving expensive periods of preparation. At present, although the results from the former scheme appear impressive, no direct comparisons with similarly selected client groups are available.

In the UK, a well-constructed vocational rehabilitation programme, "Working Out" formed one of a number of experimental schemes sponsored by the Department of Health. This programme consisted of a preparation phase followed by voluntary work experience and finally competitive work placement. The results of this scheme have not yet been published. An organisation called Rehab UK/Rehab Scotland has also developed schemes to assist with work re-entry after brain entry, thus increasing the opportunities for vocational rehabilitation in the UK.

Work is a fundamental part of most people's lives. Through work, a number of non-financial as well as financial benefits are conferred. These include opportunities for social contact, a time structure, a source of identity, opportunities for activity and for creativity and mastery, and a sense of purpose. For those with a brain injury, a further benefit that cannot be ignored is respite for relatives when the individual is at work. A major goal for rehabilitation is therefore to ensure that there is an opportunity to take part in work or work-related activities. The extent to which rehabilitation aimed at impairment of cognition and personality can enhance employment prospects is as yet unclear and needs to be the subject of further research. However, in the present state of knowledge it seems clear that a return to work needs to be attempted within the first 2 years following injury, and that a phased and expertly supported period is required. As well as direct support to the individual, potential cognitive and behavioural problems need to be explained to employers and colleagues at the workplace. Their support is essential for a successful return.

SOCIAL LIFE

Social life after brain injury is frequently profoundly curtailed. Friends often visit frequently in the immediate aftermath, but in the months that follow gradually drop away and people eventually become extremely socially isolated. Olver et al. (1996) found that this downward trend can continue for several years. Thomsen (1984) found that two-thirds of her sample had no contact outside the close family. Weddell et al. (1980) report a corresponding figure of one-third, although this rose to 50% when only those unable to return to work were considered. Kinsella et al. (1989) found that when young head-injured adults were compared with a matched control group, the primary attachment was much more often to a parent. The person with a brain injury might continue to have some social contacts but these commonly become very superficial. Kinsella found that the availability of a social network was greater if the person was employed and married.

In a 7-year follow-up study of head-injury patients discharged from the Wolfson Rehabilitation Centre, Oddy et al. (1985) found loneliness was a major concern. Sixty per cent had no boy- or girl-friend, and this was commonly mentioned by the patients and their relatives as a major problem.

Social isolation following brain injury is now accepted as a ubiquitous phenomenon in both research studies and clinical practice. It appears to be the cognitive and personality changes in those with the brain injury that are the major underlying factors. Although other variables such as unemployment, lack of finance, and lack of mobility contribute, the changes in the individual with the brain injury (whether dramatic or subtle) lead to the loss or distancing of previous friends and difficulty in making new ones (Morton & Wehman, 1995). Training in social and communication skills has been proposed as a means of tackling this problem (McGann et al., 1997) and group therapy or milieu therapy is important (Ben-Yishay, 1996; Prigatano et al., 1984).

However, social isolation remains a major unresolved problem area for rehabilitation. It is likely that energy needs to be devoted to developing a supportive environment, beyond rehabilitation settings, to supplement retraining of the person with a brain injury (Prigatano, 1986).

Gainotti (1997) has sounded a word of warning about the unitary nature of social isolation following brain injury. He contrasts those with a head injury who become isolated because of their personality and motivational changes with patients with a dysphasia who, Gainotti suggests, tend to avoid social situations because of the difficulties they encounter as a result of their communication disorder. Clearly there are different implications for intervention stemming from this analysis.

LEISURE ACTIVITIES

Little attention has been paid to the extent to which people are able to engage in interesting or enjoyable pursuits following brain injury, despite the fact that additional time often becomes available for such activities as a result of being unable to work. Leisure activities are also important for the role they play in family life. Various studies have pointed to the importance of leisure activities in maintaining marital relationships. For example, West and Merriam (1970) found that mutual involvement in activities outside the home was associated with family cohesiveness. Orthner (1976) suggested that the greater the frequency of joint involvement in leisure activities, the better the communication between spouses. Interestingly, Labi et al. (1980) found that amongst stroke patients who had recovered physically, those who lived alone appeared to be more likely to resume leisure and social activities than those who lived with others. A study of a sample of all those with head injury with a PTA of more than 24 hours (Oddy et al., 1980) found that 12 months after the accident 50% still had fewer leisure pursuits than before their injury. After 2 years the situation was unchanged. Those with fewer leisure activities had longer PTAs but there was no relationship with physical disability. However, those with fewer leisure activities were not rated by their relatives as being more bored; they frequently appeared content to lead a more restricted life. In a study of those who had been through a rehabilitation centre, Weddell et al. (1980) obtained a similar finding with a dearth of interests and leisure activities but without the expected boredom. This does not mean that it is unnecessary to encourage and enable people to take part in activities but it does suggest that a major goal of such recreation activity might be to provide some respite for the family, as this might be the only time when they are able to leave the person with the brain injury.

Sjogren (1981) reported a study of the leisure activities of 51 stroke victims whose mean age was 50. All were married and all were hemiplegic. He found that both the number and frequency of participation in leisure pursuits decreased, and this applied to indoor as well as outdoor activities. Interestingly, few appeared able to change their leisure goals to ones consistent with their disability.

Drummond and Walker (1995) found that an out-patient group intervention specifically designed to increase leisure participation in stroke patients was effective. This randomised control trial found that intervention directed towards increasing independence in activities of daily living alone did not increase participation in leisure activities. On the other hand, those receiving leisure rehabilitation achieved equal levels of independence in self care. They therefore advocate more emphasis on leisure *per se* during rehabilitation.

Relatives who have to provide long-term care for people with brain injury frequently encourage creative activities (Oddy et al., 1985); rehabilitation professionals should do the same. Activities with a concrete end product are fulfilling for all of us and brain-injured people can enjoy more life satisfaction if they are able to participate in such activities. All rehabilitation programmes need to address the issue of leisure time and provide training and compensatory strategies to enable people to resume or take up such activities.

Much can be learned from the resourcefulness of families in finding appropriate leisure pursuits for those with brain injury. However, families also need to be helped to understand the various motivational deficits that commonly occur after brain injury. Arousal, initiation and attention deficits, and the like might be familiar to rehabilitation professionals but they are not familiar to families. A lack of understanding of such concepts might mean that other notions such as "laziness" or "obstinacy" are invoked, which are much more likely to lead to dissent. Indeed, studies of a family coping with a schizophrenic member have found that "negative" or "passive" behaviour problems such as poor motivation are at least as distressing for relatives as more active behaviour changes such as poor temper control (Creer & Wing, 1975). This need not be the case for people with a brain injury, if their families attribute the lack of motivation to the injured brain (Oddy, 1990).

FAMILY RELATIONSHIPS

Studies performed since the 1970s provide strong and consistent evidence that brain injury gives rise to severe and chronic stress in the family. It is also clear from these studies that it is the cognitive and personality changes that families find the most difficult to cope with. What is more, Brooks and McKinlay (1983) found that the influence of personality change on relative's stress or burden increased over time.

From her long experience of working with brain-injured families Lezak (1978) produced a list of what she has found to be the most problematic personality changes (Table 34.1). Kinsella et al. (1991) found that mothers' level of emotional distress was closely related to their reporting a "loss of emotional control" but not to "loss of motivation".

One question that has received considerable attention is whether spouses are more prone to stress than parents. A number of arguments would suggest that it is more difficult for spouses. As they often have to cope alone they are at more of a disadvantage than two parents coping together. The change in the

Table 34.1. Personality changes most likely to create problems for families (from Lezak, 1978, *The Journal of Clinical Psychiatry, 39,* 592–598. Copyright 1978, Physicians Postgraduate Press. Reprinted by permission)

(1)	Impaired social perceptiveness
(2)	Impaired control and self-regulation
(3)	Stimulus-bound behaviour
(4)	Emotional alterations
(5)	Inability to profit from experience

role and dependency relationships is greater and more problematic for the spouse. The whole basis of their relationship will have been a reciprocal one with some form of equality. There is the element of choice inherent in Western marital relationships and spouses might feel that this is not the person with whom they chose to share their life. For parents, the carer/dependant child/parent relationship might be much more readily reinstated. A further aspect of this is that, for the spouse, there is often the loss of their most intimate, confiding, and supporting relationship. For two parents, this has not been lost, but for the spouse, as Lezak (1978) has described, there is no easy way out. "The spouse lives in a social limbo, unable to mourn decently, unable to separate or divorce without recrimination and guilt. Yet his/her opportunities for an intimate, sexual and affectionate relationship are lost."

Despite these arguments, research studies have produced equivocal evidence for a difference in level of stress in spouses and in parents. Several studies have specifically investigated this proposition and found no difference in level of stress (Brooks et al., 1987; Livingston, 1987; Oddy et al., 1978). However, all these studies have looked only at the first year after head injury, when it could be argued that the stress of having to live with the consequences of brain injury, as opposed to the distress of the initial accident or illness, has hardly begun. On the other hand, Kreutzer et al. (1994) found that spouses were significantly more likely to report elevated depression scores than parents. Spouses also reported higher levels of unhealthy family functioning in this study. Tate et al. (1989) and Wood and Yurdakul (1997), amongst others, have found high divorce and separation rates in the 5 or 10 years after head injury. Clearly, there is no measure akin to divorce and separation that can be applied to the relationship between parents and their brain-injured offspring. Indeed, the separation of a brain-injured adult from his or her parents can be seen as an aim of rehabilitation (Eames et al., 1995).

As Brooks (1991) has pointed out, the focus of interest should be the way in which the stresses differ qualitatively rather than quantitatively for spouses and parents.

SEXUAL PROBLEMS

Sexual problems after brain injury are common (McKinlay et al. 1981; Rosenbaum & Najenson, 1976; Sandel et al., 1996). Brain injury can result in either an increase or a decrease in sexual appetite, but usually the latter (Kreutzer & Zasler, 1989). Neurological and physiological problems of sexual function also occur after brain injury. These are the primary topic of another chapter but Kreutzer and Zasler (1989), Garden et al. (1990) and Sandel et al. (1996) indicate high levels of reported difficulties in achieving erections and orgasm. Such difficulties can, of course, be related to relationship difficulties and emotional factors as well as to neurological factors. The increasing effects of low confidence are suggested by Sandel et al. (1996), who found that reported levels of sexual arousal decreased with time since injury.

For the partner, the characteristics that initially attracted them to the person might have been lost. The necessity or demands for sexual intimacy with someone who has lost those characteristics can create a major dilemma (Mauss-Clum & Ryan, 1981). To continue a sexual relationship with someone who is totally dependent frequently gives rise to difficulties. Even relatively minor deficits can lead to subtle but highly significant changes. These include changes to the mutuality and reciprocity of the relationship.

The person can appear completely recovered to outsiders, even professional ones. However, to those who know him or her well, there might be subtle changes that radically alter the person's ability to function independently or to maintain close personal relationships, primarily, it seems, because of difficulties in taking the perspective of the other—being egocentric.

Although such difficulties in a relationship can be difficult to resolve, purely sexual problems can respond well to relatively simple procedures. Elliot and Biever (1996) stress the importance of providing couples with information about sexuality after brain injury and note the positive influence sexual activity can have on the rehabilitation and recovery process. Some useful information and practical advice written for people with a brain injury and their families is contained in a book by Griffiths and Lemburg (1993).

STRESS ON RELATIVES AND STAGE OF RECOVERY

It is clear that the immediate aftermath of the injury or illness is a time of acute distress for the family (Oddy et al., 1978). The pattern thereafter appears to depend upon the rate and level of recovery. For those whose relatives suffer relatively moderate damage, the stress subsides a little but remains at a high level indefinitely. In cases of more severe brain injury there appears to be a pattern of increasing distress, certainly over the first 12 months and often over the years that follow (Brooks, 1991).

In the early stages, families might be fully aware that the death of their relative is a possible outcome. But the alternative is "living" and this is not defined in any more detail. As the possibility of death recedes there is relief, with a tendency to interpret survival as indicating eventual full recovery. Lezak (1986) has identified this as the first of six changes in the evolution of the family's reaction to a brain injured member (Table 34.2). The expectation of a full recovery is often fostered by professional staff. Those involved in the acute medical/surgical care can be unaware of the likely outcome themselves. Even where there are people around who are able and willing to give a realistic picture of what the future might hold, there are others who are likely to offer reassurance rather than accuracy. It is natural for relatives to listen more to what they wish to hear. It might be only months, or even years later that they remember and understand more cautious information. For example, one mother was told "in some ways it would be better if these head injured people died, then you could grieve in public". At the time she thought this was a terrible thing to say; 3 years on she understands exactly what was meant.

As time goes by, the relative still hopes for a full recovery and failure to return to normal can often be interpreted by them as a lack of motivation or cooperation. This is a crucial time because often the patient returns home and relatives fail to receive the information they need. Polinko et al. (1985) suggested that during this stage, empathic listening, reassurance, repetition, and structuring of information are required. This can be difficult to provide because brain injury has such a range of outcomes both in severity and type. However, many consequences are so common (e.g. memory problems, fatigue, irritability) that it is better to prepare the relatives.

Relatives are bound to have difficulty in envisaging the future. Attendance at meetings of organisations such as Headway can help because they can meet relatives and people with a brain

Table 34.2.   Stages in the evolution of family reactions to a brain-damaged member (from Lezak, 1986, ©1986 Springer Publishing Company, Inc., New York 10012, used by permission)

Stage	Time since hospitalisation	Perception of patient	Expectation	Family reaction
I	0–1 to 3 months	A little difficult because of fatigue, inactivity, weakness, etc.	Full recovery by 1 year	Happy
II	1–3 months to 6–9 months	Not cooperating, not motivated, self-centred	Full recovery if patient will try harder	Bewildered, anxious
III	6–9 months to 9–24 months; can continue indefinitely	Irresponsible, self-centred, irritable	Independence if know how to help him	Discouraged, guilty, depressed, going crazy
IV	9 months or later; can continue indefinitely	A different, difficult, childlike person	Little or no change	Depressed, despairing, "trapped"
V	15 months or later; usually time-limited	Difficult, childlike, dependent	Little or no change	Mourning
VI	18–24 months or later	Difficult, childlike, dependent	Little or no change	Reorganisation—emotionally if not physically disengaged

injury at a later stage in recovery. However, many relatives are not ready to face realities in this way. Some never are, feeling that they spend all day facing the problems of brain injury so they do not want to go to meetings concerned with it in the evening. People with a brain injury frequently refuse to go because they do not wish to identify themselves with others with a brain injury.

WHEN A PARENT HAS A HEAD INJURY

Despite the likelihood that brain injury in a parent will have major implications for their children (Urbach, 1989) there is little research in this area.

There are probably two reasons why this question has received so little attention. One is that the epidemiology of brain injury means it is relatively uncommon in the parents of young children, obtaining a reasonably sized sample to study is therefore difficult. Second, the effect on the child is likely to vary with his or her age both at the time of injury and the time of the assessment, as well as with all the other variables that pertain in brain injury studies. However, the likely significance of the problem and the importance for families where it is an issue make it an area of priority for investigation. Thomsen's (1984) finding that all couples who had children were divorced by the 15-year follow up emphasises this importance. Lezak (1978) also remarks upon the need for the well-being of children to be of paramount importance when the non-injured spouse weighs divided loyalties.

Like parents and spouses, children are left in an ambiguous position after head injury. They cannot mourn the loss of a parent, although the parent might have changed completely. They might be directly affected by hierarchical and role changes in the family: from having an authoritative and protective parent they might find their father/mother now behaves in a childish manner, competing for the attention of the other parent; or a placid, affectionate parent might have changed into a self-centred, volatile, and unpredictable person.

Certain hypotheses can be made on the basis of children's responses to other forms of adversity. For example, children who suffer the loss of a parent with whom they had a close relationship, either through death or separation, are at risk of suffering emotional problems such as anxiety or depression. Those brought up in a family environment where conflict is rife could well exhibit behaviour problems themselves. Chronic situations are especially significant in that a child can recover from the effects of adversity if circumstances change and they are subsequently in a more congenial set-up.

The only published study in this area (Pessar et al., 1993) found increased acting out, emotional problems, or poor relationships with the injured parent in most children in the study. Such problems appeared more common where the father had the brain injury. However, depression in both injured and non-injured parents was significantly associated with problems in the children. These findings must be interpreted with caution as this was a small, self-selected group and all the data obtained were through the non-injured parents, asking them to rate changes post-injury. An unpublished study by Francis (1990) found that although the uninjured parents reported adverse changes in their children's behaviour, there were few significant differences on a range of measures between children with a brain-injured parent and matched controls. What *did* emerge was a loss of self-esteem, especially among older children with a brain-injured parent.

Anthony (1974), in a study of children in a somewhat similar position—who had a psychotic parent—found that the vulnerability of children to such pressures was, in part, related to poor communication, impaired emotional contact amongst family members, a lack of regular routine and organisation, and absence of clear plans for the future. All of these seem strikingly familiar as characteristics of the family after a brain injury. One important consideration discussed by Anthony is the extent to which the child becomes "involved in the symptoms". In psychosis, this includes symptoms such as delusions; in brain injury it could also include delusions or simply being the focus of the parents' irritability. Anthony suggested the need for active therapeutic intervention with these "vulnerable children" to improve their self-concept, give opportunities for cathartic expression of feelings, and to reduce the impact of being "involved in such symptoms".

HOW FAMILIES COPE

Many factors influence the extent to which a family copes with the emotional and practical problems resulting from a brain injury. In broad terms, these can be divided into the nature of the patient's condition and the personal resources that the relative has to cope with these.

The ability of the relative to cope depends on a range of considerations of a personal, social, and financial nature. The problems of coping with a relative with brain injury are undoubtedly lessened by financial well-being. The emotional resilience and the practical coping skills that the relative possesses clearly have a major impact, because it is clear that coping is not simply a function of the problems presented. The nature of the relationship to the brain-injured person is a significant variable, as is the extent of social support that the family receives.

The personal resources of individual relatives are clearly important determinants of their ability to cope. However, beyond the somewhat sterile aim of "identifying those at risk" in order to target resources, this avenue too often leads to an explanation for inability to cope rather than a procedure for enhancing coping. However, a number of studies have pursued avenues that suggest means of changing the relative's ability to cope rather than merely documenting it. One approach is to attempt to define the differences between relatives who cope well and those who cope less well. This usually involves investigating the coping strategies employed by a relative. Folkman and Lazarus (1980) have suggested that coping with stress can be seen as a function of two variables: the individual's appraisal of the situation and their ability to deal with the threat. There is thus a cognitive component and a practical skills component. This suggests two major

Table 34.3. Strategies for helping relatives cope

Appraisal of the situation
    literature
    verbal information
    counselling
Ability to deal with threat:
    (1) by reducing the problem, i.e. rehabilitation of the patient
    (2) by enhancing relative's ability to cope, i.e. training the relative in methods of management or rehabilitation
    (3) by giving practical assistance—respite care, etc.
    (4) by altering the relative's emotional response:
        —counselling/psychotherapy
        —stress management
        —emotional support—encourage networks

strategies for helping relatives cope with stress. One involves altering the way they appraise the situation, the other enhancing their ability to deal with the situation. Table 34.3 summarises the different approaches that can be employed to achieve these two aims. Attribution theory suggests ways in which a person's appraisal of the stressful situation will determine their ability to cope. Weiner (1985) describes how different emotional states arise, depending upon how the person appraises the situation. If a person is observed to fail on a task and they are thought to have no control over the outcome, then pity is the usual response. However, this response can turn to anger if the task is conceived to be controllable by the person and the negative outcome affects the observer. It is clear from what relatives say that the person with a brain injury can be attributed with greater power to control certain undesirable aspects of behaviour, such as outbursts of temper or lapses of memory, than he or she in fact possesses. If this attribution is made, relatives are more likely to become upset and angry themselves. If the behaviour is seen as an uncontrollable function of the brain injury, the relatives' ability to cope seems to be greater. Zarit and Zarit (1982) describe a process of encouraging relatives to relabel the troubling behaviour of those suffering from dementia. These authors give the pertinent example of helping relatives to see that memory lapses are not the result of the patient's lack of effort.

One method of changing the way in which relatives appraise the situation is to provide information on the nature of brain injury and its effects. This information can be provided in the form of booklets or verbally; it can be provided by a self-help organisation or be given by professionals involved in the treatment and rehabilitation of the person; it can be given in a didactic fashion or it could be given in the context of counselling, advising, and supporting a relative. Most rehabilitation programmes include this as a fundamental part of their programme (e.g. Prigatano et al., 1986). The ability to deal with threat can be enhanced in two types of way; one is by altering the problem and the other is by altering the relative's response to the problem. The rehabilitation of the person comes under the first heading. However, in addition to this, the relative can be trained to help in the rehabilitation of the person with a brain injury. This has been attempted in a variety of ways. Stroke patients with dysphasia have been given intensive therapy by relatives and other volunteers (Griffiths, 1975) in their homes. Quine

et al. (1988) have used relatives as voluntary helpers in an acute rehabilitation programme. Blosser and De Pompei (1995) have described a process whereby rehabilitation staff help families cope through a process they describe as mentoring. Behavioural management techniques have been taught to relatives. These strategies have had mixed success. The use of behavioural modification techniques can be particularly problematic. The nature of the relationship and the home setting can make it difficult if not impossible for relatives to implement a consistent and structured programme. On the other hand, the close family relationship can be at an advantage in that relatives' approval or withdrawal of approval is a form of social reinforcement that can have much greater salience than those reinforcers available to the professional. There is increasing evidence that behavioural methods work with people who have suffered a brain injury in general (McGlynn, 1990) and in the domestic setting in particular (Pace & Colbert, 1996).

Although it appears to be the behavioural problems that cause the relatives most distress, there is also much to be gained by involving relatives in other aspects of rehabilitation and management such as the improvement of physical function or increasing independence skills. Apart from the obvious gains to the patient, and hence a decrease in dependency, relatives also benefit from having a clear role and feeling that they are contributing in a helpful and constructive fashion. It is advisable to encourage relatives to see their efforts as experiments (Zarit & Zarit, 1982). This avoids disappointment if expectations are too high and goals are not attained.

Helping relatives cope better with their emotional responses is another approach. Once again a variety of methods can be employed. Support groups for relatives run by a professional (Lezak, 1978) can combine the advantages of experienced leadership and direction in an emotionally charged atmosphere with the greater credibility of other relatives. These can be run in a variety of ways. Relatives can be taught methods of stress management, the meetings could focus on providing relatives with information about brain injury, or they might focus on the emotions experienced by relatives. Self-help organisations undoubtedly provide a valuable source of informal emotional support and a system should be devised to ensure that all the relatives are informed about the existence of their local organisations. Professional counselling and psychotherapy can be valuable. This might include a number of foci, such as dealing with loss, the absence of an intimate relationship, living with uncertainty and establishing a viable future. The skills the therapist must bring to bear are wide ranging. He or she must provide information about the patient's condition and prognosis, have the therapeutic skills to help the relatives through their inner turmoil, foster a practical and problem-solving approach while supporting the relative's right to opt out without recrimination or guilt. Formal family therapy has been advocated by some (e.g. Maitz & Sachs, 1995). Examination of the interventions advocated by family therapists reveals that many of the suggestions are very similar to those provided from other approaches. However, family therapy provides a valuable reminder of the importance of roles and "sub-systems" within families, and of the way ramifications of any difficulties experienced can spread through the family in surprising and unexpected ways.

THE INDIVIDUAL'S PSYCHOLOGICAL ADJUSTMENT

To suffer from a brain injury is an immensely disturbing experience. This is often seen most clearly in those suffering less severe damage, such as minor to moderate head injury. Confidence can be profoundly undermined and the person has to adjust to a revised sense of self with altered goals and coping strategies. Such adjustments would be difficult enough for the most competent person but people with a brain injury face these tasks with physical and cognitive deficits that reduce their ability to adapt. Their lost competence and increased dependence on others is continually apparent as they struggle with tasks they would not have thought twice about previously.

Weddell (1987), in a study of stroke patients, found that such patients often feel stigmatised by their disability and are depressed by their dependence on others. Those with mild injury to the brain often show high levels of anxiety as they try to readjust. Those with greater impairment can either recognise the extent of their problems, feel overwhelmed, and succumb to feelings of hopelessness (if not suicidal feelings) or, through their cognitive deficit, be completely unaware of their problems and hence unable to develop compensatory strategies or to benefit from rehabilitation (Prigatano & Altman, 1990). Such a lack of awareness of deficits is very common amongst people with acquired brain damage. Lam et al. (1988) found the readiness to change and participate in rehabilitation was greater in those with more awareness of their deficits. Muller et al. (1983) found that relatives, professionals, and dysphasic patients hold incongruent views regarding their recovery, with the patients being most optimistic and clinicians being the least. Roueche and Fordyce (1983) have stated that the chances for successful adjustment are greatest when patients, family, and staff all view the brain injury from a similar, realistic perspective.

Some form of psychotherapy to assist the patient in this process of adjustment is an essential ingredient for any comprehensive rehabilitation service. Prigatano (1986) has proposed seven goals for psychotherapy for the brain injured. These include enabling the patient to understand what has happened to him or her by the provision of a simple but accurate model, helping the patient consider the implications that the injury has for his or her life and fostering a sense of realistic hope.

Thompson et al. (1989) investigated the efficacy of the cognitive adaptation and social support theories of coping in a group of stroke patients. Both theories were supported, in that patients with a good relationship with their carer were less depressed, as were those who perceived meaning and value in their lives. The psychotherapeutic process can promote adaptation in both these ways. As a setting in which unconditional attention, regard, and respect are communicated it represents a very strong form of social support. This can enhance the patient's feeling of

self-value while providing an opportunity in a gradual and non-threatening way to increase the patient's awareness of his or her deficits. Second, through providing a means of making sense of the situation in which the patient finds him- or herself, psychotherapy can assist the level of cognitive adaptation. It can also provide a setting in which to tackle emotions that the brain-damaged person could fear will become totally out of control. Such a fear is particularly pertinent to the brain injured because diminished emotional control is a common consequence of brain injury.

However, psychotherapy with people with brain injury is not easy. Concrete disorganised and perseverative thinking, together with memory and reasoning problems, are obstacles that cannot be ignored. Such problems can be ameliorated by the therapist imposing clear organisation on the session. Prigatano (1986) suggests that analogies can be very helpful, presumably because they enable abstract concepts to be put across in a concrete way. However, the use of analogy and metaphor has to be approached with care, lest a literal interpretation results in a total misunderstanding. Sessions must often be much briefer than in conventional psychotherapy. This is for a number of reasons: (1) it is easier to preserve the structure and organisation for a brief session; (2) constraints of memory mean that one or two points alone should be covered in the session and, as Prigatano suggests, might need to be gone over time and time again—giving a written summary of these points can also be helpful; (3) with some patients, particularly those who are perseverative or disorganised, it can be difficult for the therapist to maintain the essential degree of attention and positive regard for very long. One means of providing an organised focus to such sessions is to use them to help the patient to consider feedback from other aspects of his or her rehabilitation programme. The provision of objective measures, preferably displayed graphically, is essential for people whose memory and perceptual problems might prevent them from picking up feedback in more informal ways. Such feedback can be looked at objectively in the psychotherapy session, and this process can enhance motivation, where necessary through the medium of formal contracts with the patient.

A further problem occurs when the patient is overwhelmed by the catastrophe that has befallen him or her. Prigatano (1986) suggests that the question "Why has this happened to me?" is asked universally, and given one of two provisional answers. The first is one of self-blame ("I deserved what happened"); the other is to blame others and to insist on their punishment. An interesting study of cancer patients (Gotay, 1985) found that "Why me?" was not universally asked. This author suggests that it might be less threatening and debilitating to one's adjustment to believe there is no particular reason why such a catastrophe befell you, and that it could happen to anyone. It could be that Gotay's patients had passed through the questioning stage and, as Prigatano suggests, had learned to set the questions aside. Bulman and Wortman (1977), in a study of accident victims (not all of whom were brain injured), found that self-blame for the accident was associated with good coping whereas blaming others or the feeling that one could have avoided the accident were predictors of poor coping. These findings point to the importance of exploring these issues in a psychotherapeutic framework.

An interesting attributional analysis of psychological and emotional adjustment following brain injury has guided a series of studies by Moore and Stanbrook (1995). These authors suggest that the use of cognitive/behavioural techniques to target the person's cognitive belief structure can help optimise adjustment by preventing the development and overgeneralisation of negative attributions. A similar approach has been advocated by Godfrey et al. (1996).

SUMMARY

Severe brain injury can affect every aspect of a person's functioning and, as a result, the very nature of that person. This in turn can result in changes in every aspect of the person's life and the lives of those close to them. In recent years, the emphasis of head injury rehabilitation has increasingly been towards addressing the person's ability to function in specific situations rather than attempting to remediate underlying deficits. Such rehabilitation appears to have been very successful in enabling people to live more independently and in assisting people with a brain injury to return to work. There are very few published studies of attempts specifically aimed at enhancing participation in leisure activities and the constructive use of time. This is a very important area, particularly for those unable to return to work, and it deserves more attention.

People with a brain injury frequently experience major problems in their social and family relationships. There is a growing literature in this area, but these problems are highly complex and there are few studies comparing the efficacy of different approaches. Both relatives and the person with the brain injury require considerable help in adjusting to the losses and changes that brain injury inevitably imposes. There is reason to believe that the process of rehabilitation helps people make these adjustments, but there is also a need for on-going availability of professional support and guidance at times of crises.

REFERENCES

Anthony, E. J. (1974). A risk vulnerability intervention model for the children of psychotic parents. In E. J. Anthony & C. Koupernik (Eds.), *The child in his family: Children at psychiatric risk*. New York: John Wiley.

Ben-Yishay, Y. (1996). Reflections on the evolution of the therapeutic milieu concept. *Neuropsychological Rehabilitation, 6*(4), 241–360.

Blosser, J., & De Panpei, R. (1995). Fostering effective family involvement through mentoring. *Journal of Head Trauma Rehabilitation, 10*(2), 46–56.

Brooks, D. N. (1991). The head-injured family. *Journal of Clinical and Experimental Neuropsychology, 13*(1), 155–188.

Brooks, D. N., & McKinlay, W. W. (1983). Personality and behavioural change after severe blunt head injury—a relative's view. *Journal of Neurology, Neurosurgery, and Psychiatry, 46*, 336–344.

Brooks, N., Campsie, L., Symington, C., Beattie, A., Bryden, J., & McKinlay, W. (1987). The effects of severe head injury upon patient and relative within seven years of injury. *Journal of Head Trauma Rehabilitation, 2*, 1–13.

Bulman, R. J., & Wortman, C. B. (1977). Attributions of blame and coping in the real world. *Journal of Personality and Social Psychology, 35*, 351–363.

Carlsson, C.-A., Essen, C. V., & Lofgren, J. (1968). Factors affecting the clinical course of patients with severe head injuries. *Journal of Neurosurgery, 29*, 242–251.

Creer, C., & Wing, J. K. (1975). Living with a schizophrenic patient. *British Journal of Hospital Medicine, 14*, 73–82.

Crepeau, F., & Scherzer, P. (1993). Predictors and indicators of work status after traumatic brain injury: A meta-analysis. *Neuropsychological Rehabilitation, 3*(1), 5–35.

Drummond, A. E. R., & Walker, M. F. (1995). A randomized controlled trial of leisure rehabilitation after stroke. *Clinical Rehabilitation, 9*, 283–290.

Eames, P., Cotterill, T. A., Kneale, T. A., Storrar, A., & Yeomans, P. (1995). Outcome of intensive rehabilitation after severe brain injury: A long-term follow-up study. *Brain Injury, 10*(9), 631–650.

Elliott, M. L., & Biever, L. S. (1996). Head injury and sexual dysfunction. *Brain Injury, 10*(10), 703–717.

Fahy, T. J., Irving, M. H., & Millac, P. (1967). Severe head injuries. *Lancet, 2*, 475–479.

Folkman, S., & Lazarus, R. S. (1980). An analysis of coping in a middle aged community sample. *Journal of Health and Social Behaviour, 21*, 219–239.

Francis, E. (1990). *The impact of parental brain injury on children*. Diploma in Clinical Psychology, Leicester: British Psychological Society.

Gainotti, G. (1997). Emotional, psychological and psychosocial problems of aphasic patients: An introduction. *Aphasiology, 11*(7), 635–650.

Garden, F. H., Bontke, C. F., & Hoffman, M. (1990). Sexual functioning and marital adjustment after traumatic brain injury. *Journal of Head Trauma Rehabilitation, 5*(2), 52–59.

Godfrey, H. P. D., Knight, R. G., & Partridge, F. M. (1996). Emotional adjustment following traumatic brain injury: A stress-appraisal-coping formulation. *Journal of Head Trauma Rehabilitation, 11*(6), 29–40.

Gotay, C. C. (1985). Why me? Attributions and adjustment by cancer patients and their mates at two stages in the disease process. *Social Science and Medicine, 20*(8), 825–831.

Griffith, V. E. (1975). Volunteer scheme for dysphasia and allied problems in stroke patients. *British Medical Journal, 89*, 633–635.

Griffiths, E. R., & Lemberg, S. (1993). *Sexuality and the person with a traumatic brain injury: A guide for families*. Philadelphia: F.A.Davis Company.

Haffey, W. J., & Abrams, D. L. (1991). Employment outcomes for participants in a brain injury work reentry program: Preliminary findings. *Journal of Head Trauma Rehabilitation, 6*(3), 24–34.

Hpay, H. (1971). Psycho-social effects of severe head injury. In *Proceedings of International Symposium on Head Injuries* (pp. 110–119). Edinburgh: Churchill Livingstone.

Ip, R. Y., Dornan, J., & Schentag, C. (1995). Traumatic brain injury: Factors predicting return to work or school. *Brain Injury, 9*(5), 517–532.

Johnson, R. (1998). How do people get back to work after severe head injury? A 10-year follow-up study. *Neuropsychological Rehabilitation, 8*(1), 61–80.

Kinsella, G., Ford, B., & Moran, C. (1989). Survival of social relationships following head injury. *International Disability Studies, 11*, 9–14.

Kinsella, G., Packer, S., & Olver, J. (1991). Maternal reporting of behaviour following very severe blunt head injury. *Journal of Neurology, Neurosurgery, and Psychiatry, 54*, 422–426.

Kreutzer, J. S., Gervasio, A. H., & Camplair, P. S. (1994). Primary caregiver's psychological status and family functioning after traumatic brain injury. *Brain Injury, 8*(3), 197–210.

Kreutzer, J. S., & Zasler, N. D. (1989). Psychosexual consequences of traumatic brain injury: Methodology and preliminary findings. *Brain Injury, 3*(2), 177–186.

Labi, M. L. C., Phillips, T. F., & Gresham, G. E. (1980). Psychosocial disability in physically restored long-term stroke survivors. *Archives of Physical Medicine and Rehabilitation, 61*, 561–565.

Lam, C. S., McMahon, B. T., Priddy, D. A., & Gehred-Schultze, A. (1988). Deficit awareness and treatment performance among traumatic head injury adults. *Brain Injury, 2*(3), 235–242.

Lezak, M. D. (1978). Living with the characterologically altered brain injured patient. *Journal of Clinical Psychiatry, 39*(7), 592–598.

Lezak, M. D. (1986). Psychological implications of traumatic brain damage for the patient's family. *Rehabilitation Psychology, 30*, 241–250.

Livingston, M. G. (1987). Head injury: The relative's response. *Brain Injury, 1*, 33–39.

Maitz, E. A., & Sachs, P. R. (1995). Treating families of individuals with traumatic brain injury from a family systems perspective. *Journal of Head Trauma Rehabilitation, 10*(2), 1–11.

Mauss-Clum, N., & Ryan, M. (1981). Brain injury and the family. *Journal of Neurosurgical Nursing, 16*, 36–44.

McGann, W., Werven, G., & Douglas, M. M. (1997). Social competence and head injury: A practical approach. *Brain Injury, 11*(9), 621–628.

McGlynn, S. M. (1990). Behavioral approaches to neuropsychological rehabilitation. *Psychological Bulletin, 108*, 420–441.

McKinlay, W. W., Brooks, D. N., Bond, M. R., Martinage, D. P., & Marshall, M. M. (1981). The short-term outome of severe blunt head injury as reported by relatives of the injured persons. *Journal of Neurology, Neurosurgery, and Psychiatry, 44*, 527–533.

Miller, H., & Stern, G. (1965). The long-term prognosis of severe head injury. *The Lancet* (30 January), 225–229.

Moore, A. D., & Stambrook, M. (1995). Cognitive moderators of outcome following traumatic brain injury: A conceptual model and implications for rehabilitation. *Brain Injury, 9*(2), 109–130.

Morton, M. V., & Wehman, P. (1995). Psychosocial and emotional sequelae of individuals with traumatic brain injury: A literature review and recommendations. *Brain Injury, 9*(1), 81–92.

Muller, D. J., Code, C., & Mugford, J. (1983). Predicting psychosocial adjustment to aphasia. *British Journal of Disorders of Communication, 18*(1), 23–29.

Oddy, M. (1990). Living with someone else. In *INS Workshop* (pp. 1–18). Innsbruck: International Neuropsychology Society.

Oddy, M., & Alcott, D. (1996). Assessment. In F. D. Rose & D. A. Johnson (Eds.), *Brain injury and after: Towards improved outcome* (pp. 49–72). Chichester: John Wiley.

Oddy, M., Coughlan, T., Tyerman, A., & Jenkins, D. (1985). Social adjustment after closed head injury: A further follow-up seven years after injury. *Journal of Neurology, Neurosurgery, and Psychiatry, 48*, 564–568.

Oddy, M., & Humphrey, M. (1980). Social recovery during the year following severe head injury. *Journal of Neurology, Neurosurgery, and Psychiatry, 43*(9), 798–802.

Oddy, M., Humphrey, M., & Uttley, D. (1978). Stresses upon the relatives of head-injured patients. *British Journal of Psychiatry, 133*, 507–513.

Olver, J. H., Ponsford, J. L., & Curran, C. A. (1996). Outcome following traumatic brain injury: A comparison between 2 and 5 years after injury. *Brain Injury, 10*(11), 841–848.

Orthner, D. (1976). Patterns of leisure and marital interaction. *Journal of Leisure Research, 8*, 98–111.

Pace, G. M., & Colbert, B. (1996). Role of behavior analysis in home and community-based neurological rehabilitation. *Journal of Head Trauma Rehabilitation, 11*(1), 18–26.

Pessar, L. F., Coad, M. L., Linn, R. T., & Willer, B. S. (1993). The effects of parental traumatic brain injury on the behaviour of parents and children. *Brain Injury, 7*(3), 231–240.

Polinko, P. R., Barin, J. J., Leger, D., & Bachman, K. M. (1985). Working with the Family. In M. Ylvisaker (Ed.), *Head injury rehabilitation; children and adults*, (pp. 93–115). Boston: College-Hill Press, Inc.

Prigatano, G., Fordyce, D.J., Zeiner, H.K., Roueche, J.R., Pepping, M., & Wood, B.C. (1984). Neuropsychological rehabilitation after closed head injury in young adults. *Journal of Neurology, Neurosurgery, and Psychiatry, 47*, 505–513.

Prigatano, G. (1986). *Neuropsychological rehabilitation after brain injury.* Baltimore: Johns Hopkins University Press.

Prigatano, G. P., & Altman, I. M. (1990). Impaired awareness of behavioral limitations after traumatic brain injury. *Archives of Physical Medicine and Rehabilitation, 71*, 1058–1064.

Quine, S., Pierce, J. P., & Lyle, D. M. (1988). Relatives as lay-therapists for the severely head-injured. *Brain Injury, 2*(2), 139–149.

Rosenbaum, M., & Najenson, T. (1976). Changes in life patterns and symptoms of low mood as reported by wives of severely brain-injured soldiers. *Journal of Consulting and Clinical Psychology, 44*(6), 881–888.

Roueche, J. R., & Fordyce, D. J. (1983). Perceptions of deficits following brain injury and their impact on psychosocial adjustment. *Cognitive Rehabilitation , 1*, 4–7.

Rowbotham, G. F., Maciver, I. N., Dickson, J., & Bousfield, M. E. (1954). Analysis of 1,400 cases of acute injury to the head. *British Medical Journal*, (March 27), 726–730.

Sandel, M. E., Williams, K. S., Dellapietra, L., & Derogatis, L. R. (1996). Sexual functioning following traumatic brain injury. *Brain Injury, 10*(10), 719–728.

Sjogren, K. (1981). Leisure after stroke. *International Rehabilitation Medicine, 4*, 80–87.

Steadman, J. H., & Graham, J. G. (1970). Head injuries: An analysis and follow-up study. *Proceedings of the Royal Society of Medicine, 63*, 3–8.

Tate, R. L., Lulham, J. M., Broe, G. A., Strettles, B., & Pfaff, A. (1989). Psychosocial outcome for the survivors of severe blunt head injury: The results from a consecutive series of 100 patients. *Journal of Neurology, Neurosurgery, and Psychiatry, 52*, 1128–1134.

Thompson, S. C., Sobolew-Shubin, A., Grahan, M. A., & Janigian, A. S. (1989). Psychosocial adjustment following a stroke. *Social Science and Medicine, 28*(3), 239–247.

Thomsen, I. V. (1984). Late outcome of very severe blunt head trauma: A 10–15 year second follow-up. *Journal of Neurology, Neurosurgery, and Psychiatry, 47*, 260–268.

Urbach, J. R. (1989). The impact of parental head trauma on families with children. *Psychiatric Medicine, 7*(1), 17–36.

Weddell, R. (1987). Social, functional and neuropsychological determinants of the psychiatric symptoms of stroke patients receiving rehabilitation and living at home. *Scandinavian Journal of Rehabilitation Medicine, 19*, 93–98.

Weddell, R., Oddy, M., & Jenkins, D. (1980). Social adjustment after rehabilitation: Two year follow-up of patients with severe head injury. *Psychological Medicine, 10*, 257–263.

Weiner, B. (1985). An attributional theory of achievement motivation and emotion. *Psychological Review, 92*, 548–573.

Wehman, P., West, M., Fry, R., Sherron, P., Groah, C., Kreutzer, J., & Sale, P. (1989). Effect of supported employment on the vocational outcomes of persons with traumatic brain injury. *Journal of Applied Behaviour Analysis, 22*(4), 395–405.

West, M., Fry, R., Pastor, J., Moore, G., Killen, S., Wehman, P., & Stonnington, H. (1990). Helping post acute traumatically brain injured clients return to work: Three case studies. *International Journal of Rehabilitation Research, 13*, 291–298.

West, P. C., & Merriam, L. C. (1970). Outdoor recreation and family cohesiveness: a research approach. *Journal of Leisure and Research, 2*, 251–259.

Wood, R. L., & Yurdakul, L. K. (1997). Change in relationship status following traumatic brain injury. *Brain Injury, 11*(7), 491–502.

World Health Organization (1980). The international classification of impairments, disabilities and handicaps—a manual of classification relating to the consequence of disease. Geneva: WHO.

Zarit, S. H., & Zarit, J. M. (1982). Families under stress: Interventions for caregivers of senile dementia patients. *Psychotherapy: Theory, Research and Practice, 19*(4), 461–470.

Specific disorders

35. Head injury rehabilitation

T. M. McMillan   R. J. Greenwood

INTRODUCTION

The need for specialist rehabilitation services after traumatic brain injury (TBI) continues to emerge and was given especial emphasis during the 1990s, most recently in the UK by the British Society for Rehabilitation Medicine (1998) and in the US with a NIH Consensus Development Conference (1998). The development of interest follows advances in surgical and medical techniques that increase rates of survival (Miller, 1991); increasing awareness of the incidence and prevalence of the condition (Kraus & McArthur, 1996); definition of the physical, cognitive, emotional, and behavioural sequelae; and linkage of these impairments with the nature, time course, and long-term effects on daily routines and family life (Brooks et al., 1987a,b; Oddy et al., 1985; Olver et al., 1996; Thomsen, 1987).

Although awareness of the needs of these patients has gradually attracted greater professional and research interest, the lack and haphazard nature of services (certainly in the UK) after acute neurosurgical care (Brooks et al., 1986; Cockburn & Gatherer, 1988; Gloag, 1985a,b; Greenwood & McMillan, 1993; McMillan et al., 1988; Murphy et al., 1989) has continued (McMillan & Greenwood, 1993; Oddy et al., 1990), despite the attention that has been drawn to the situation in the literature since the middle of the twentieth century (British Psychological Society, 1989; British Society for Rehabilitation Medicine, 1998; Editorial (*Lancet*), 1990; SHHD, 1972; McCorquodale, 1965; Medical Disability Society, 1988; Pearcy, 1956; Royal College of Physicians, 1986; Royal College of Psychiatrists, 1991; Sharp, 1974; Tomlinson, 1943; Tunbridge, 1972).

As younger age groups are over-represented, and because life expectancy is often near normal (Jennett & Teasdale, 1981), the role of rehabilitation is potentially crucial if it can maximise quality of life by reducing disability and handicap and help to minimise costs of hospital and community care. To inform the development of these services in the future, it is important to consider evidence in support of demand, need, and effectiveness of rehabilitation.

EPIDEMIOLOGY

The annual attendance rate of patients with head injury at casualty has been found to be large (1778 per 100,000), but less than one-quarter of these tend to be admitted (Jennett & MacMillan, 1981). Studies in Scotland (Jennett & MacMillan, 1981) and in England and Wales (Field, 1976) suggest that the admission rate is of the order of 270–310 cases per 100,000 of the population per annum. Of those admitted, the majority will have sustained less severe head injury. In one study, a "minor" head injury (Glasgow Coma Score (GCS) of 13–14), was found in 84% of cases, 11% had sustained a "moderate" head injury (GCS 8–12) and 5% a "severe" head injury or worse (GCS 7 or less; Miller & Jones, 1985). Other studies accord with a view that 7% of head injury admissions are severe or worse (Lewin, 1968). On this basis, the incidence of severe head injury would be of the order of 14–16 per 100,000 in the UK, or 35–40 per average health district each year, and moderate head injury about 70–85 per district.

Clearly, such figures are dependent on criteria for classification (see also Jennett, 1996). Using criteria that are perhaps more predictive of longer term disability, a more conservative estimate was suggested by the Medical Disability Society (1988): an annual incidence of severe head injury (coma for 6 hours or more and post-traumatic amnesia (PTA) of 24 hours or more) of 8 per 100,000, and moderate head injury (coma of 15 minutes to 6 hours and PTA less than 24 hours) of about 18 per 100,000. This is more consistent with studies that have included follow-up of patients or measures of long-term handicap such as effects on employment (Bryden, 1989; Johnson & Gleave, 1987; Steadman & Graham, 1970), and with recent hospital discharge rates in the US after TBI of 103 per 100,000 population (Centers for Disease Control (CDC), 1997). Data of this sort appear to reflect a decline in hospitalisation after TBI of up to 50% since the early 1980s, perhaps in part due to injury prevention, but also due to changes in hospital practice and the avoidance of admission after less severe injury (National Center for Health Statistics, 1997).

Risk factors (Kraus & McArthur, 1996) include age and gender, with a well-described peak between the ages of 15 and

24, when there is a 2 or 3 : 1 male : female ratio; up to 50% of patients are intoxicated by alcohol and more than half the injuries are transport related. Additional peaks under the age of 5 and over the age of 75 are most frequently the result of falls, sometimes alcohol-related in the elderly. Other risk factors include previous TBI, particular sports and occupations, and lower socioeconomic status. This sort of information can be used to inform strategies designed to prevent TBI, principally legislative, but also technological and educational.

Prevalence is difficult to determine accurately (Bryden, 1989). Estimated prevalence of severe head injury has been suggested as being 100–150 per 100,000 of the population, or 250–375 per average health district, if considering incidence and life expectancy (Bryden, 1989; Medical Disability Society, 1988). This would suggest that head injury is one of the five most prevalent neurological conditions affecting the central nervous system (CNS), together with migraine, cerebrovascular disease, epilepsy, and Parkinson's disease (see Chapter 1).

OUTCOME MEASURES

Validated outcome measures after TBI are crucial for determination of prevalence and description of the type of problem generated. They are a tool for evaluating services required by TBI, the effectiveness of different treatment programmes (when to recommend them and in what circumstances), and examination of change in outcome. Development and validation of outcome measures for TBI continues. At present there is no consensus on a battery for recording outcome after TBI, in terms of pathology, impairment, activities (disabilities), participation (handicaps) (World Health Organization, 1997), and quality of life in the patient or in terms of burden or impact on the relative or carer. The need for such a battery has been emphasised (Hall, 1997).

Short, global, multidimensional measures are well validated. These are useful in epidemiological studies as ball-park predictors or for evaluating outcomes of acute medical treatments (Clifton et al., 1992). They include the five-point Glasgow Outcome Scale (GOS) (Jennett & Bond, 1975; Jennett et al., 1981), where 1 = death, 2 = persistent vegetative state, 3 = severe disability, 4 = moderate disability (disabled but independent), and 5 = good recovery (although often with residual problems), and the Disability Rating Scale (DRS) (Gouvier et al., 1987; Rappaport et al., 1982), where 30 = death and 0 = no disability. However, such scales are not sensitive enough to record changes in function that might have important cost implications and could be generated by rehabilitation, for example the difference between needing supervision and being independent overnight.

More sensitive measures are needed to detect changes of this kind. These are often unidimensional and applicable to a specific period of rehabilitation or domain of disablement. Often used, but little studied in acute care and rehabilitation, is the eight-point Level of Cognitive Functioning Scale (the Rancho Los Amigos Scale; RLA), which records levels of responsiveness

and their appropriateness (Hagen et al., 1972). Most studied for use during in-patient rehabilitation is the 18-item Functional Independence Measure (FIM) (Guide for the Uniform Data System for Medical Rehabilitation, 1993), which has well-recognised ceiling effects that are not obviously changed by adding more cognitive and psychosocial information, such as the Functional Assessment Measure (FAM) (Hall et al., 1996). The much shorter, and thus much quicker, Barthel Index (BI) of personal and domestic activities of daily living (Mahoney & Barthel, 1965), is widely used after stroke (see Chapter 36), but has not been extensively studied after TBI.

A number of instruments are now available to record function in the community after TBI (Brooks et al., 1997), often at the level of activity (disabilities) and participation (handicaps). These include the Craig Handicap Assessment and Reporting Technique (CHART), originally developed for use after spinal injury (Whiteneck et al., 1992) but recently used in a TBI population (Corrigan et al., 1998), for whom the complexity of some of the questions can cause difficulties; the brief 15-item Community Integration Questionnaire (CIQ) (Willer et al., 1994), which samples "home integration", "social integration", and "productive activities" but might suffer from ceiling effects (Hall et al., 1996); the long 55-item Newcastle Independence Assessment Form—Research (NIAF-R), designed as a global measure of functional independence of people with neurological disablement as in-patients or in the community, and validated after TBI (Semlyen et al., 1996, 1997, 1998); and the 39-item Brain Injury Community Rehabilitation Outcome Scales (BICRO-39 Scales), designed and validated for self-completion by a brain-injured population and their carers to record function pre- and post-injury (Powell et al., 1998). A short measure of quality of life and life satisfaction has not been validated in the TBI population, in which the long 136-item, but not the shorter 68-item (Port et al., 1996) Sickness Impact Profile (SIP) (Bergner et al., 1981) has been used (Klonoff et al., 1986). The easily administered Medical Outcomes Study (MOS), 36-item Short Form Health Status Survey (SF-36) (Ware & Sherbourne, 1992) is well documented in normals, but failed to show a difference when comparing relative burden of disease in TBI (Colantonio, 1998).

PREDICTORS OF LONG-TERM OUTCOME

Being able to predict long-term functional outcome during a patient's rehabilitation is crucial to proactive planning of treatment goals and service provision. Important variables relate to pre-injury characteristics, particularly age, pre-injury disease, substance abuse, injury severity, and social and economic support after injury. There is general agreement that older subjects make fewer functional gains over longer periods, particularly in the context of comorbidities and the absence of family support (Cifu et al., 1996; Reeder et al., 1996; Vollmer et al., 1991). There is no data to date to show that complex radiological, biochemical, or electrophysiological measures of the severity of brain injury are more useful as predictors of survival

(Signorini et al., 1999) or GOS outcome (Jennett et al., 1979), than are clinical measures comprising depth of coma (rated by the GCS score), duration of coma (GCS ≤ 8), pupillary reaction, duration of PTA (measured retrospectively or prospectively) (McMillan, Jongen, & Greenwood, 1996), pre-treatment systemic hypotension (Chestnut et al., 1993), and—possibly—a measurement of systemic injury severity. Some of these descriptors can be confounded by concurrent alcohol intoxication, drug treatments (particularly sedation during ventilation), problems defining emergence from PTA or coma, and failure to standardise the timing of the measurement of coma depth. Whether genetic factors might also prove useful is a topic of ongoing interest (Teasdale et al., 1997b).

These biological measures of damage become less obviously linked to function with increasing time after injury, when psychosocial and economic factors increasingly influence outcome, but they remain important predictors of functional ceilings and can be usefully applied clinically. For example, a PTA of 2 or more weeks predicts neuropsychological deficit long term (Van Zomeren et al., 1985) and a need at least for vocational support, whereas a coma duration of more than 20 days predicts a need at least for supervision in the community (Pazzaglia et al., 1975). However, below that ceiling, given levels of a descriptor might be associated with very varied levels of function long term, simply illustrated by unawareness at 1 month predicting—at 1 year—a moderate GOS score at ceiling, but also being followed by death, the permanent vegetative state, or severe disability (Braakman et al., 1988; Jennett & Braakman, 1990).

In addition to this absence of predictive specificity there has been a failure to describe equivalence between the descriptors. For example, a severe injury rated either by PTA greater than 24 hours (Bishara et al., 1992) or by a GCS of 8 or less after resuscitation (Marshall et al., 1991) is followed at 1 year by 81% and 43% of patients, respectively, achieving GOS of 4 or 5. These difficulties reflect a failure to yet achieve a consensus over the definitions of mild, moderate, and severe TBI. Kibby and Long (1996) describe in detail the difficulties associated with defining mild TBI (Kay et al., 1993). They define it as requiring one of the following: (1) any period of loss of consciousness; (2) any loss of memory for events before or after the event; (3) any alteration in mental state at the time of the event; and (4) focal neurological deficits that might or might not be transient; where the consequences of injury do not exceed: (1) loss of consciousness of 30 minutes; (2) an admission GCS of 13 to 15; and (3) a PTA of 24 hours. This definition obviously encompasses a slightly different group of patients from those recruited in studies using previous definitions, for example with a PTA of less than 60 minutes (Russell, 1932; Russel & Smith, 1964), with coma and PTA of less than 6 and 24 hours, respectively (Medical Disability Society, 1988). Separation of moderate TBI has been made on the basis of an admission GCS of 9–12, and an intracranial lesion or focal neurological deficit (Thurman et al., 1996), whereas severe TBI has been defined as coma for 6 hours or more (Jennett et al., 1979) or GCS of less than 8 during the first 24 hours after injury (Thurman et al., 1996) or PTA greater than 24 hours (Jennett & Teasdale, 1981).

LIFE EXPECTANCY

Knowledge of life expectancy with a given functional outcome after TBI informs not only the planning of rehabilitation at both an individual and group level, but also the generation of financial compensation, itself often an important aspect of service provision.

Three studies provide longitudinal data sets to clarify the issue. Walker et al. (1971) and Roberts (1979) showed that in patients who retain mobility long term after TBI, life expectancy is shortened by only 4 or 5 years at most, more commonly than in the general population by epilepsy, meningitis, accidents and suicide, and pulmonary disease. Recently, Strauss and colleagues (1998) have confirmed these earlier findings, and have also shown that the major factors shortening life expectancy after TBI are immobility and the need for gastrostomy feeding: in the context of "no" mobility and "poor" mobility, life expectancy is found to be 10–15 years and 18–35 years, respectively, depending on age. The extent of mobility and the need for tube feeding have also been shown to be the crucial factors reducing life expectancy in patients with congenital brain injury (Eyman et al., 1996).

Between 30% and 50% of patients vegetative at 1 month die in the first year after injury (Multi-Society Task Force on PVS, 1994), but many patients surviving permanently vegetative for 5 or more years have been described, for example 9 of 24 patients after TBI reported by Minderhoud and Braakman (1985). Survival vegetative for more than 20 years is unusual, although occasional patients surviving more than 30 years have been reported (Multi-Society Task Force on PVS, 1994). This is usually the result of a potentially treatable cause rather than a cause unique to the vegetative state. Whether more protracted survival is related to a level of care over and above a "standard" level, adequate, for example, to prevent pressure sores and maintain nutrition, is unclear.

REHABILITATION PROGRAMMES BY SEVERITY OF INJURY

Minor head injury

This group encompasses 60% to 90% of admitted head injuries (Kraus & McArthur, 1996). Symptoms ("post-concussional") that result are cognitive (memory, attention, and concentration problems), affective (anxiety, depression, and irritability), and somatic (headache, dizziness, fatigue, and sleep disturbance). In the majority of cases symptoms resolve spontaneously over months, but in up to 25% of patients the "post-concussional" syndrome persists at 1 year (Alexander, 1995; Rutherford et al., 1979).

It is known that axonal injury can occur after relatively minor injury—from animal studies (Povlishock et al., 1983), and investigation of neuropathology (Blumbergs et al., 1994; Clarke et al., 1974; Oppenheimer, 1968) and MRI scans (Jenkins et al., 1986, Levin et al., 1992) in man. Impairments of information processing, attention, and reaction time have been found, but are unusual more than 3 months after injury (Gronwall & Wrightson 1974, 1975; Levin et al., 1987b; MacFlynn et al., 1984). They can be cumulative following repeated minor head injury (Gronwall & Wrightson, 1975), and can occur in patients who are not involved in litigation (McMillan & Glucksman, 1987). Somatic complaints such as headache, dizziness, insomnia, and fatigue are well documented, but non-specific, and are reported in some cases over many months and even years (Rimel et al., 1981; Rutherford et al., 1977, 1979). In recent years, the balance of evidence has favoured the view that persisting or late-onset symptoms are unlikely to have an organic cause, but are related to psychological factors such as coping style or frank symptom exaggeration (Karzmark et al., 1995; Marsh, 1995; Newcombe et al., 1994; Schrader et al., 1996; Taylor et al., 1996; Wong et al., 1994). Some continue to favour an organic interpretation for a minority of cases (e.g. Ruff et al., 1994, 1996).

The Medical Disability Society (1988) recommended a multidisciplinary out-patient clinic for the treatment of minor-head-injured patients. This would include a neurologist, a clinical psychologist, and a social worker with other specialist input as required, a model reported as being successful in New Zealand (Wrightson, 1989). In principle, the clinic would deal with medical and psychosocial issues, including assessment, general management issues, difficulty coping with stress, provision of information, and liaison with community facilities required by a small proportion of cases, either screened on the basis of PTA at casualty or by local GPs. Although it would seem that psychological treatments are frequently offered, in the US at least (Mittenberg & Burton, 1994), there are few controlled studies evaluating effectiveness (Alves et al., 1993; Gronwall, 1986; Minderhoud et al., 1980; Relander et al., 1972). Recently, Wade et al. (1997) randomly allocated 1156 consecutive patients attending hospital after head injuries of all severities to early follow-up 7–10 days after injury (postal, telephone, or face to face) or to no follow-up; 48% of patients had no PTA, 72% a PTA of less than 1 hour. No differences in symptom frequency and severity, or changes in daily life, were found between the groups at 6 months follow-up. Wade et al. concluded that evidence in support of the Medical Disability Society recommendation was not found, the implication being that follow-up is not required for *all* minor-head-injury patients, but sub-group analysis suggested benefit in patients with a PTA ≥ 1 hour. A subsequent trial of similar contact versus no contact in 314 patients admitted to hospital after head injury showed benefit in those with a PTA less than 7 days (Wade et al., 1998). Paniak et al. (1998) found that outcome in 111 patients admitted to hospital after mild TBI was similar in two groups randomised to a one-session educational consultation versus more extensive needs-led treatment, confirming the suggestion by Wade's group (King et al., 1997), that contact in this group of patients does not usually have to be too demanding upon resources.

For a more detailed review of recent studies, including those that investigate the possibility of brain injury when there is no loss of consciousness, see McMillan (1997b).

Severe head injury

A flow chart of services appropriate to provision after severe TBI is shown in Figure 35.1.

Acute and early (in-patient) rehabilitation

The effectiveness of rehabilitation for patients who are less than 1 year post-injury remains unproven. Appropriate experimental method, such as randomised allocation of cases to formal rehabilitation or not, is logistically and ethically difficult in practice, and acute (0–1 month) and early (1–12 months) in-patient rehabilitation after severe TBI has not yet been subjected to prospective and randomised trial. This situation contrasts with that seen after stroke (see Chapter 36).

The physical changes that do occur early on can produce easily preventable complications. The early studies of Rusk et al. (1966, 1969) documented 40 pressure sores, 200 joint contractions, 30 frozen shoulders and urinary and respiratory tract complications in 127 patients, 75% of whom were more than 18 months post-injury after an average coma length of 3 weeks. Such a dismal outcome would now be very uncommon in Western Europe and North America and is in itself a testament to the effectiveness of the rehabilitation services that already exist. Other potentially preventable consequences include those resulting from post-traumatic hydrocephalus (Scheffler et al., 1994), cachexia (Clifton, 1986; Deutschman, 1986), periarticular new bone formation (see Chapter 14), infection (particularly of the urinary tract or resulting from aspiration), and post-traumatic epilepsy (discussed later).

The only study examining the effect of integrating rehabilitation into acute care is that of Mackay and colleagues (1992), who retrospectively compared two groups admitted to a rehabilitation unit. Both groups received acute care and one group had additional "formalised" rehabilitation in the acute setting. Reduced coma duration by more than a month on average, shortened rehabilitation stay by more than 3 months on average; better cognitive functioning and higher frequency of discharge to home (94% versus 57%) were reported in the acute rehabilitation group. As it is not widely accepted that rehabilitation can reduce coma duration, or reduce cognitive impairment, there must be some doubt as to whether the two groups were equivalent in terms of severity of injury, even though GCS and other measures on admission were similar.

Other studies—one matching groups retrospectively (Cope & Hall, 1982), the others using multivariate analysis (Cowen et al., 1995; High et al., 1996; Rappaport et al., 1989; Spettell et al., 1991)—have produced results that report benefits of early rehabilitation, at least in terms of total length of hospital and rehabilitation stay and costs. Cope and Hall (1982) retrospectively studied outcome at 2 years in patients transferred to

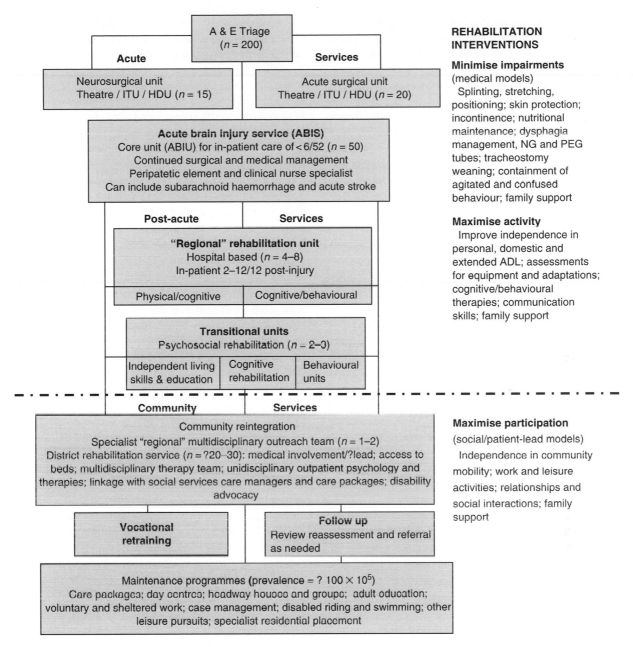

Figure 35.1. Rehabilitation after severe traumatic brain injury (TBI) (n = approximate incidence $\times 10^5$). ADL, actvities of daily living; NG, nasogastric; PEG, percutaneous endoscopic gastroscopy.

early in-patient rehabilitation either before ($n = 16$) or after ($n = 20$) 35 days post-injury. The two groups were matched for severity of injury by duration and depth of coma, although the later admission group had a higher incidence of tracheostomy. The later group received acute/rehabilitation care for twice as long as the earlier group. Functional outcome, as measured by the GOS, DRS and on a seven-point scale of social status, did not differ between groups. These results might merely represent difficulties with matching groups retrospectively for severity of injury. For example, the fact that GCS poorly predicts GOS (e.g. Zafonte et al., 1996), so that after a given GCS score some patients improve more quickly than others,

and the possibility that controlling for GCS scores, CT findings, extremity fractures, aetiology, and age (e.g. Cowen et al., 1995) omits important input variables.

Other studies have examined the functional effectiveness of early in-patient rehabilitation by comparing groups who did or did not receive rehabilitation retrospectively, or examining the question of whether hours in treatment in such an environment relates to outcome. Aronow's (1987) study retrospectively compared 68 patients who received rehabilitation and 61 who did not. Two years post-injury, outcome in the rehabilitation group was as good, and at less cost. However, the control group in this study was less severely injured, PTA $\leq$ 1 month in 74% of control patients versus >4 months in 70% of rehabilitated patients, making interpretation difficult (High et al., 1995). Heinemann et al. (1995) reported data collection prospectively from 140 patients in eight rehabilitation hospitals after TBI between 1990 and 1991 and found no relationship between average hours of daily treatment and FIM outcome, except for psychological treatment and cognitive outcome. Spivack et al. (1992) retrospectively compared hours of treatment with discharge RLA and non-standardised measures of physical and cognitive skills. They found a relationship between high intensity treatment and discharge RLA, but failed to control adequately for confounding variables; in recommending 5–6 hours of treatment per day they make their findings irrelevant in terms of practical provision of services in most NHS early in-patient rehabilitation units in the UK. Blackerby (1990) retrospectively related reduced length of stay after changes in a rehabilitation programme in 149 patients to increased intensity of treatment, but failed to account for other process changes and confounding variables such as severity of injury.

Semlyen et al. (1998) prospectively compared outcome at 2 years in two groups of patients discharged from a neurosurgical unit; 33 to a multidisciplinary specialist rehabilitation unit (HM group) and 18 to a district hospital for non-specialist and often unidisciplinary treatment (OR group). The HM group had a higher proportion of more serious injuries, but 2-year functional outcome measured by BI, FIM, and NIAF-R, was similar in the two groups. Improvement continued after discharge in the HM but not the OR group, although whether this is due to a ceiling effect for the measures used in the OR group is not clear. Carer distress decreased in the HM but not the OR group over time.

Even taking the pessimistic view that acute and early rehabilitation fails to produce a better functional outcome at eventual discharge or long term, the fact that it can optimise the use of expensive in-patient resources, prevent the haphazard delivery of services to this patient group, and generate important organisational changes in service provision, deserves further serious examination.

Late ("post-acute") rehabilitation

This category includes patients who require residential, out-patient, or other community-based rehabilitation. They are medically stable and, for this reason, rehabilitation at this stage need not be conducted by a physician but could be directed by other professionals with appropriate experience, such as clinical psychologists, nurses, social workers, or therapists. A multidisciplinary team approach is considered to be the norm (see Chapter 4).

Transitional living centres are post-acute day or residential units that are designed to bridge a gap between hospital-based facilities and re-entry into the community or home in supervised hostels, and concentrate on functional skills training rather than reducing the severity of impairment. They are relatively widespread in the US but are rare in the UK; length of stay can average 12 months (Boake, 1990). Although the philosophy, procedures, and strategies have been described, there would seem to be relatively few controlled studies of their effectiveness.

Studies have generally focused on evaluation of programmes or services and on specific problem areas. Early work at the Presbyterian Hospital in Oklahoma (Prigatano & Fordyce, 1986; Prigatano et al., 1984) developed a "holistic" approach, working on a combination of cognitive impairment, personality change, and other social and work-related problems. The need for a combined cognitive and psychotherapeutic approach to remediation, within a framework of integrated, interdisciplinary, intense and prolonged rehabilitation, which attacks limited awareness of deficits, was emphasised. Patients were not accepted if they had extremely severe cognitive impairment, no family commitment to the programme, premorbid psychiatric history, or a poor attendance record. Therapeutic input was 6 hours per day, 4 days a week over 6 months (576 hours) with a staff: patient ratio of between 1 or 2 : 1. Eighteen head-injured patients who were on the programme for at least 6 months were compared with 17 others who underwent traditional rehabilitation and who were matched for sex, age, education, and severity of injury. Patients were followed-up after 6–26 months. At follow-up, impairment on selected cognitive tests was better in the rehabilitation programme group (Block Design and Wechsler Memory Scale Quotient) and better in controls on one test (Tactual Performance Test); personality was rated as improved by relatives; performance on the Digit Symbol Substitution Test discriminated between patients who did and did not return to work. Perhaps 60–65% of patients returned to work soon after the end of the programme, at follow-up 50% (nine) remained in employment compared with 36% (six) of controls. As the authors imply, return to work might be too gross a measure of improvement in quality of life; although it is nevertheless a relatively objective measure with which to compare controls at follow-up. The convincingness of the study is marred by the lack of alternative input to the control group; for example, only relatives of patients on the programme attended weekly sessions with staff, and this, together with the fact that patients in this group received additional care, might have positively influenced their appraisal of change.

Ben-Yishay et al. (1987) reported 94 cases also given a "holistic" treatment programme at the Rusk Institute, New York. All patients had received conventional rehabilitation previously and had either returned to work and failed, or had not been able to return to work at all. The programme was divided into three phases. First, "systematic holistic remediation" for 5 hours each day, 4 days per week over 20 weeks (400 hours); remediation was aimed at cognitive impairment, interpersonal communication, social skills, and awareness and acceptance of disability. In the second phase, a detailed treatment plan was created, directed towards possible employment (work placement with guidance and supervision) for 3–9 months, "employability" was then rated. Phase three involved assistance to find work, and this continued during an initial adjustment period, then follow-up at 6-month intervals for up to 3 years, with assessment of progress by relative, patient, and employer. At the end of phase one, 84% of 94 patients were able to return to work and of these 63% were in competitive employment. At 1 year, 78% of 77 were employed, with 57% competitively. At 3 years, 70% of 36 were employed, with 45% in competitive work. It is unfortunate, but perhaps inevitable, that the sample size diminished markedly during follow-up, however, data on the final 36 are reported separately throughout the trial; 94% were initially employed, 89% at 1 year and 78% (50% competitive) at 3 years. Information on drop-outs is not given.

These studies have been criticised because patients were selected for admission, but perhaps it is naive to imagine that intensive input of this kind might be appropriately applied to all patients or that the studies are less convincing because those with high risk of poor outcome (e.g. patients with premorbid serious psychiatric problems) are excluded. Many cognitive–behavioural rehabilitation programmes have been based on the early work by Prigatano, Ben Yishay, and colleagues. The absence of appropriate control groups and of randomised treatment design in their studies is a weakness, but one that, in practice, can be difficult to overcome without ethical objection.

Cope et al. (1991a,b) investigated post-acute (non-hospital) rehabilitation in a single-blind study of 173 of 192 cases consecutively admitted to a rehabilitation system in the western USA; 80% were head injured. The average time since injury was 15 months, although the range was 15 days to 13 years. They investigated pre- and post-treatment residential and work status, and number of hours of attendant care required, and found a significantly positive effect on all of these at 6–24 month follow-up using a telephone interview. In an attempt to circumvent criticism on the grounds of spontaneous change, they reanalysed data on 35 cases who were injured at least 12 months before admission; positive effect was again found at follow-up for work status and attendant care, but not for residential status.

The authors critically appraise their own design, including lack of an adequate control group, that severity of injury was based on functional problems as defined by the DRS rather than acute neurological indices, and that outcome indices were fairly general. In a second paper in the series they go on to assess cost-effectiveness. Based on reduction in attendant care costs, projected annual savings were $41,000 for patients in a severe category (DRS 7–20); this was more than 15 times greater than those in a mild category (DRS 1–3) and would have paid for up to 20 months of treatment in the post-acute facility.

The study by Johnston and Lewis (1991) and Johnston (1991) investigated the effect of participation in community re-entry programmes (which could have included transitional living centres) on independent living and return to work. Eight-two patients from nine facilities were investigated; 80% of these had suffered head injury. Comparison was made between initial assessment and 1 year follow-up information, the latter obtained by telephone interview, usually from a close relative. Attempts were made to exclude effects of spontaneous recovery by determining effect of time since injury on outcome and by re-analysing data on patients admitted more than a year

post-injury (in fact, improvement was not related to time after 6 months post-onset). The number of cases resident in institutions fell from 45% to 7% at follow-up, and community residence increased from 55% to 93%. Prior to admission, 73% received day and night supervision; at follow-up this number fell to 16%. Similarly, positive effects were found for work status. For example, before admission 96% of cases described themselves as not working, compared with 19% at follow-up. In those cases that were care-dependent on admission, significant improvement in self-care, activities of daily living (ADL), and communication was found. Improvement in behaviour and emotional problems was also claimed, although a number of new behaviour problems apparently emerged between discharge and follow-up in half of the cases. Duration of stay and costs per patient averaged 9 months and over $100,000, respectively.

A number of uncontrolled studies on late rehabilitation report improvements in physical and cognitive functioning on questionnaire measures, cognitive testing, improved independence, and work outcome (Do et al., 1988; Malec et al., 1993; Sahgal & Heinemann, 1989; Scherzer, 1986). Although of interest, these studies are limited because changes could be for non-specific reasons such as spontaneous recovery, practice or placebo effect, or due to a component of care rather than showing benefit from the in-patient programme overall. Teasdale et al. (1997b) found that outcome (employment) at 18–60 month follow-up was related to pre-treatment, but not post-treatment, cognitive test scores even though there had been small but significant improvements in these test scores across treatment.

A further Danish study investigated effects of rehabilitation 2–3 years post-injury in head-injury and stroke patients. They reported a reduction in the need for home care and health service usage and improved employment/education post-treatment. At 1 year follow-up only greater time involved in leisure activities compared with pre-treatment had significantly improved (Teasdale et al., 1993). Eames et al. (1995) report improved social outcome in another uncontrolled study and, as in the Danish study, the period between admission and injury was relatively long, reducing the likelihood of spontaneous recovery.

Return to work

The unemployment rate is high in patients who suffer severe head injury. In addition to simple loss of income, this can have devastating effects on self-respect, perceived role within the family, status within the community, and on independence in the broader sense. Brooks et al. (1987a) investigated rate and prediction of return to work in 98 severe head injuries 2–7 years post-injury. Employment rate fell from 86% pre-injury to 29% post-injury. Those who were under 45 years of age and in technical or managerial jobs were more likely to return to work, as were those with fewer persisting behavioural, personality, or cognitive effects. No effects relating to severity or to physical disability were found. This relatively low rate of return to work is consistent with other studies, which report 28% and 19% (McMordie et al., 1990; Stapleton, 1986). Gollaher et al. (1998) found that higher levels of education, being employed pre-injury and lower DRS on discharge from rehabilitation predicted greater likelihood of return to work in 98 cases 1–3 years after injury. Age and GCS did not predict employment outcome; however almost two-thirds of cases had been followed up for 1 year, and later follow-up will be of interest.

A number of American papers have discussed the role of "supported Employment" and job coaching, with given examples of single cases and indication of cost effectiveness. Kreutzer et al. (1988) emphasised four key components of a supported employment programme, namely: (1) job placement; (2) job site training; (3) ongoing client assessment; and (4) job retention and "follow-along". In essence, the client and job are matched, communications between clients, carers, and employer are facilitated, travel arrangements/training is established, and the job itself is analysed to discover potential obstacles and overcome these. There is emphasis on a key element of on-site training by a job coach, who will also act as an advocate on behalf of the client. There are regular assessments of overall performance, punctuality, absenteeism, and general appearance, and this is fed back to the client by the job coach; such assessments also allow ongoing review of training needs of the client. Co-workers would be involved as appropriate. For example, clinical psychologists could carry out a neuropsychological assessment and advise regarding strategies to circumvent problems caused by cognitive impairment. Only eight case examples are described in two papers by Wehman et al. (1989a,b). However, Wehman et al. (1990) provide information on 53 cases. The average age was 23, average duration of unconsciousness was 53 days (range 0–182 days) and average time since injury was 7 years. Before the accident 91% were competitively employed and, before job coaching, 36% were working. The monthly "employment ratio"(number of hours actual work/potential hours of work) was 89% pre-injury and 15% post-injury; 41 cases were placed in competitive employment, and 29 of these were working when the paper was written. The average duration of employment was 10 months, with 12 cases having been employed for 3 months or less and 11 cases for 12 months or more. Weekly hours averaged 31 (range 15–40). Wehman et al. (1990) suggest that brain-injured clients attain "stability and independence" at work after about 20 weeks, and that after 40 weeks little intervention was required (28% of original sample had worked for 10 months or more). At first sight, hours of intervention by the job coach seem relatively high, with an average of 291 hours/case ($8700 per placement). However, the social and economic costs of not having patients return to work must also be considered, and the improvement in the employment ratio (ER) from 36% to 75% (in 19 clients ER = 100%) and trebling of the employment rate seems impressive. Hourly earnings were lower than reported on average before the injury but higher than found before entry to the study. The authors criticise themselves for the absence of a control group. It would also be of interest to provide 2-year follow-up data on the entire population of 53, whether or not job re-entry had been obtained, and to indicate cost-effectiveness in this way.

In a retrospective study, Jellinek and Harvey (1982) examined the rate of employment/further education 3 years after discharge in two cohorts of 43 patients admitted to a rehabilitation unit before or after employment of vocational/educational rehabilitation counsellors. Outcome for spinal and head-injured patients was given separately and, of the latter, none was employed before employment of vocational counsellors, and 78% after their recruitment. The two cohorts are not delineated by key variables such as severity of injury and the staffing of the unit in more general terms is not described (e.g. in some units this role might partly have been adopted by occupational therapists, psychologists, and social workers). More recently, Wall et al. (1998) found that 59% of a group of 38 cases of acquired brain damage were working 18 months after a 10-week community-based work retraining programme (work adjustment training and supported employment), this incidence being *higher* than reported pre-injury (32%).

Finally, a cautionary note. Most follow-up studies on vocational rehabilitation have extended for up to 2 years. However, one study with mean follow-up of 5 years found a *decrease* in work status despite stability of rehabilitation gains on the DRS. The authors suggest a number of explanations for this, including that return to work is often in a reduced capacity, which might not be sufficiently satisfying over the longer term (Ashley et al., 1997).

Coma and the vegetative state

In a retrospective study over 10 years, Bricolo et al. (1980) found that 0.6% (135 cases) of all head-injured patients admitted to a neurosurgical unit remained in "prolonged coma" (defined as coma of more than 2 weeks' duration). They suggested that outcome was better in those aged under 20 years, who have early recovery of vigilance and a short duration in vegetative state.

In another retrospective study, prognostic indicators in 130 cases in the first week after injury included respiratory disturbance, motor reactivity, and "significant extra neural trauma"; after the first month, late epilepsy and hydrocephalus were also found to predict outcome (Sazbon et al., 1991). Fifty-four percent of 134 patients unaware at 1 month subsequently regained awareness, the majority of these within 3 months of injury. Of those who recovered consciousness and survived the first year, 76% returned to live at home. Less than 12% of recovering patients were returned to "gainful employment" with a further 50% in sheltered work (Groswasser & Sazbon, 1990; Sazbon & Groswasser, 1991).

Bricolo et al. (1980) describe prolonged unconsciousness as a "race against time", because, as a general trend, the longer that patients are comatose, the poorer the outcome. In view of this, a number of authors have tried to reduce the duration of unawareness by means of sensory stimulation or drug treatment. These studies have tended to look for effects in terms of change in outcome (e.g. coming out of coma), change in behaviour, or physiological responsiveness (see Wilson & McMillan, 1993 for a review).

Studies in animals suggest that enriched environments can increase brain weight in undamaged adult and neonatally lesioned rats (Ferchmin et al., 1975; Schwartz, 1974; Will & Rosenzweig, 1976). Evidence of change caused by enrichment of sensory input to coma patients or by "coma stimulation" is presently sparse, however (e.g. Le Winn & Dimanescu, 1978), and results are equivocal. Sensory regulation takes the view that too much stimulation is to be avoided as much as too little (Wood, 1991). Results from a pilot study using sensory regulation in 10 patients in vegetative state were promising (Wood et al., 1993). By and large, studies using outcome as the dependent variable have tended to be weakened by limited control groups (see Wilson & McMillan, 1993).

Mitchell et al. (1990) investigated two groups of 12 coma patients, matched for age, sex, surgical intervention, GCS on admission, and type and location of injury. Multisensory stimulation began as soon as the patient was clinically stable (2–12 days) and was given once or twice daily for an hour on each occasion to one group of patients. Average coma duration was shorter in the sensory stimulation group (22 ± 10 days) than in the control group (27 ± 7 days). It is important establish the usefulness of such a procedure, and replication is required.

Some studies using sensory stimulation in vegetative state patients have found no effect (Rader et al., 1989; Hall et al., 1992), others, using single case design, have found limited positive findings immediately after treatment (Wilson et al., 1991, 1992, 1993). Results of drug treatment, generally using dopaminergic stimulation, remains equivocal (Haig & Ruess, 1990; Zafonte et al., 1998). Changes in EEG in response to music have also been found (Aldridge et al., 1990; Sisson, 1990), but not in intracranial pressure during conversation (Johnson et al., 1989). The relevance of the former to outcome is not clear. The finding that behavioural analysis, over time, might predict whether or not patients emerge from PCS is of interest (Wilson et al., 1996). Difficult, aggressive, and even violent behaviour from relatives of patients with prolonged unawareness has been reported and special consideration of their needs in adjusting to the situation is necessary (Stern et al., 1988; Tzidkiahu et al., 1994).

Specific problem areas

Problems can be divided into eight subgroups, although these inevitably overlap.

(i) Long-term physical disablement. These patients are relatively few in number (1 per 100,000), are easily found (Johnson & Gleave, 1987; Lewin, 1968) and tend not to fall through the rehabilitation "net" because of the obvious nature of their impairments: early routine referrals for rehabilitation in district hospitals and neurosurgical units tend to occur only to physiotherapy and not to other rehabilitation professions (Murphy et al., 1989).

Many of the physical therapies used to treat patients after head injury are described elsewhere in this volume (Chapter 14), as is the management of incontinence (Chapter 21), spasticity (Chapter 12), heterotopic ossification and the consequences of immobility (Chapter 15), and dysphagia (Lazarus & Logermann, 1987; Chapter 25), which can result in chronic difficulty in maintaining weight (Cherney & Halper, 1996), in contrast to occasional patients with massive weight gain (foie gras syndrome), which can be accompanied by pituitary endocrine dysfunction of varying degrees.

Early post-injury, physical therapies emphasise the prevention of contractures and the consequences of spasticity. Nociceptive stimuli should be avoided and appropriate positions adopted during recumbency, sitting, or standing in a standing-frame or tilt-table; range-of-motion exercises should be used, and plaster splints and casts applied serially (Coninc et al., 1990), sometimes in combination with peripheral nerve or motor point blocks (Keenan et al., 1990) or intramuscular injections of botulinum toxin type A (Pavesi et al., 1998; Wilson et al., 1997). The judicious proactive use of these techniques on acute wards in the UK is unusual, but could at least reduce the number of tendon lengthening operations required in the longer term, if not total time in rehabilitation for some severely damaged patients. Later post-injury there is more emphasis upon retraining of movement control and coordination, to facilitate functional skills, although in patients with persisting major physical impairment, prevention of the consequences of spasticity remains an important aspect of maintenance treatment (Shaw, 1986). Retraining programmes can include the use of orthoses (Chapter 17) and sometimes neuromuscular electrical stimulation (Zablotney, 1987), particularly to counter spastic equinovarus of the foot, which can also be helped surgically (Keenan, 1984). The fact that, even 6 or 10 years post-injury, short-term intensive mobility retraining, entailing up to 200 hours of exercises, physiotherapy, and outdoor mobility, can, for example, enable a wheelchair-bound subject to walk indoors (Dordel, 1987), emphasises the need for adequate maintenance programmes for patients with residual physical deficits.

It can be helpful for patients to embark upon a fitness programme to reverse the cardiovascular deconditioning that occurs as a result of immobility (Hunter et al., 1990; Jankowski & Sullivan, 1990; see Chapter 17). This detraining effect is only one possible cause of the fatigue of which many patients complain (LaChapelle & Finlayson, 1998), other causes including mood disturbance and disordered sleep, a common but relatively unexplored area of difficulty (Beetar et al., 1996).

(ii) Cognitive impairment. Rehabilitation of cognitive impairment has attracted great interest over the past decade, either by using general programmes or attempts to treat specific impairments such as problem solving, attention, memory, and perception (see Chapters 28, 29 and 30). Intervention needs to account not only for cognitive impairments and use of relatively intact functions, but also for the impact of impairments on day-to-day living. Where possible, strategies should reduce the effects of impairment and maximise use of intact functions. For example, relatively intact procedural learning has been used in patients with declarative memory problems, even if sufficiently severe to engender the label "amnesic" (see Chapter 28).

Experimental method is bedevilled by many of the problems found in research on head injury, including inadequacy of control groups, practice effect, recovery, and difficulty obtaining follow-up (Brooks et al., 1984; McKinlay & Brooks, 1984; Robertson, 1994). Results can lack generalisation from laboratory to everyday situations or can be statistically significant but not have obvious impact on quality of life. Single case methodology can overcome some of these difficulties but must still allow for spontaneous change and non-specific treatment effects. To convince, and result in adoption of techniques for cognitive rehabilitation, case series that report both positive and negative findings are necessary, to allow a clear view of whether a treatment is worthwhile and for which subgroups. Randomised control treatment designs can be difficult to implement but are not impossible if considering the effectiveness of a discrete, specific intervention. Until recently, intervention has largely involved the use of strategies to circumvent everyday problems stemming from impairment. There are signs, however, that impairment of certain cognitive functions, such as some aspects of attentional control, might be remediable to an extent (Robertson et al., 1992, 1998).

Gianutsos (1991), in an insightful overview, likened cognitive rehabilitation to an infant who had yet to come of age and, hopefully, become a valued member of society. She suggests that treatment of cognitive impairment has been widely accepted and has been rapidly adopted, but largely without proven efficacy. She also makes the point that treatment that in itself might or might not be effective can have positive side-effects (such as improving insight) and implies that although the value of such techniques should be assessed, they should not be judged using narrow criteria. A related issue concerns time and cost-effectiveness. Gianutsos cites studies where change in cognitive impairment is expected after 12 weeks (although some studies look for effects after only a few hours), whereas behaviour treatment might not be expected to be effective for up to 6 months. The statistical magnitude of the effect is likely to be less important than the actual impact on daily living; to persuade purchasers to buy a service and therapists to implement a new technique, change in quality of life—in terms of reduced handicap or disability—needs to be clear, and not simply changes that have little obvious practical outcome, might not generalise or be sustained, but which require many hours of treatment.

(iii) Behaviour problems.   It is not uncommon for agitation and restlessness to occur soon after injury (Brooke et al., 1992), when patients are often confused and in PTA. The prevalence of severe behaviour problems post-acutely is, however, small— probably less than 0.3 per 100,000 per annum—nevertheless, they can cause a considerable drain on rehabilitation and financial resources (Greenwood & McMillan, 1993). Both group (Eames & Wood, 1985) and single case studies (Alderman & Knight, 1997; Alderman et al., 1995; Hegel, 1988; Horton & Howe, 1981; Manchester et al., 1997; Wilson, 1989a; Youngson

& Alderman, 1994; Zencius et al., 1990) show that a variety of cognitive and behavioural management techniques can be effective in ameliorating difficult behaviour, and can also improve independent living function and compliance with physical therapy, communication and independent living skills even years after injury (Coelho, 1987; Gajar et al., 1984; Giles & Shore, 1989; Wood, 1987). Such techniques can prove effective on closed units (Eames & Wood, 1985), allowing consistency of approach, and can prevent or reduce inappropriate input from relatives. It has also been shown to be effective in brain-damaged patients in non-specialist units (McMillan et al., 1990; Johnston et al., 1991), although with potential for disruption of staff and other patients. Duration of treatment varies with individual cases but, for severe problems, must be expected to take at least 3–6 months and perhaps considerably longer (see also Chapter 31).

(iv) Personality and emotional problems. Personality change is frequently reported, and is often cited by relatives to be the most difficult persisting change that they have to adjust to. Comments such as "he's not the man I married" or "it's like living with a different person" are not uncommon, particularly after the post-acute phase when rapid and dramatic recovery has ended. Changes might or might not emphasise previous personality traits and include egocentricity, childishness, poor judgement, immediacy, lack of initiation, reduced drive, lethargy, unconcern, disinterest, lack of depth of feeling, irritability, aggressiveness, reduced tact, and increased (or, more commonly) decreased sexual interest. In turn, these changes are associated with marital break-up, social isolation, and unemployment (Brooks et al., 1987a,b; Kreutzer & Zasler, 1989; Oddy et al., 1985; Thomsen, 1987; Zencius et al., 1990; see also Chapter 34).

Research since the mid-1980s has focused on delineation of these emotional and psychosocial effects of head injury, and how they vary in patients and relatives with respect to severity of and time since injury; these studies are reviewed by Oddy (Chapter 34). However, there have been few controlled studies on treatment of specific problems. Ruff and Nieman (1990) randomly allocated 24 cases to cognitive remediation or day treatment and reviewed patient and relative ratings of emotional adjustment after 8 weeks of treatment. They hypothesised that day treatment would ameliorate emotional problems because it addressed these more intensively, whereas cognitive remediation might intensify emotional problems because patients are confronted with neuropsychological impairment, which they might have previously denied. However, no group differences were found, although depressed mood improved generally. The study would have benefited from a non-treatment control group, but in any event the prospect of finding a statistically significant effect with such small numbers is questionable. The incidence of pre-existing psychopathology can be relatively high in head-injured patients (Fahy et al., 1967; Whetsell et al., 1989), and this could be an important factor when considering suitability for intervention, as it might be an indicator of poor prognosis.

In non-psychotic patients, formal psychotherapy has been advocated (Ben-Yishay & Laking, 1989; Forssmann-Falck & Christian, 1989; Prigatano, 1986; Stern & Stern, 1990) but there is little evidence from controlled studies to indicate its effectiveness. A thought-provoking discussion by Gans (1983) raises issues regarding the development of hate in both patients and staff in a rehabilitation setting and reviews possible causes and appropriate and less appropriate means of dealing with this.

(v) Independent living skills.   There have been surprisingly few controlled studies on treatment of dysfunction of everyday living skills following brain injury. Single case studies in herpes simplex encephalitis cases have indicated success for washing and dressing programmes that prompt and chain individual elements of the procedure into an overall effective function (Giles & Morgan, 1989; McMillan et al., 1990). Wood (1987, pp. 94–98) discusses shaping and token economy programmes used with single case design methodology to investigate retraining in dressing and hygiene, and also inappropriate habits (Wood, 1987, pp. 85–91) such as spitting, pushing, and throwing objects. Brotherton et al. (1988) used single case methodology to investigate social skills training in four head-injured patients and they found improvement largely in non-verbal skills such as posture and "self-manipulation" (hand/arm movement unrelated to speech content); these gains tended to be maintained at 1 year. A review by Lloyd and Cuvo (1994) concludes that there is evidence for maintenance of change and generalisation following training of community-relevant social and independent living skills. At a more general level, the concept of transitional living units continues to emerge (see earlier) and, although the idea of an intervening stage between hospital and community, which can concentrate on everyday living skills in a "real-life" environment, has high face validity, there are no evaluative studies.

(vi) Post-traumatic stress disorder (PTSD).   PTSD has been described following road traffic accidents in patients with no brain injury (Fairbank et al., 1981; McCaffrey & Fairbank, 1985). The development of the condition in head-injured cases has been postulated for some time (Davidoff et al., 1988) and described in an early single case report of a patient with post-traumatic amnesia estimated at 6 weeks (McMillan, 1991). Recently, it was argued, that according to the DSM-IV classification (American Psychiatric Association, 1994), PTSD cannot arise *in principle* after closed head injury because the patient has not actually experienced the traumatic event because of loss of consciousness and post-traumatic amnesia (Sbordone & Liter, 1995). This view has been challenged (McMillan, 1996), and there is mounting evidence from single case and group-based studies for the occurrence of PTSD after minor and severe head injury (Bryant & Harvey, 1999; Hickling et al., 1998; Horton & Howe, 1981; King, 1997; Layton & Wardi-Zonna, 1995; McMillan, 1991, 1996; McNeil & Greenwood, 1996; Silver et al., 1997). Studies where evidence for the severity of head injury or for diagnosis of PTSD is not clear are of more limited value, but also support the contention that PTSD can occur after head injury (Ohry et al., 1996; Parker, 1996; Wright, 1996).

The mechanism for the development of PTSD in these cases has been variously postulated as implicit memory (Layton & Wardi-Zonna, 1995), or via the "windows" of experience during PTA in which emotional trauma could occur, or by self-generated imaginings of what happened in the accident, often expressed as nightmares (McMillan, 1996). Evidence for implicit learning during PTA in non-PTSD cases (Ewert et al., 1989; Glisky et al., 1996) and the finding of PTSD in non-head-injury cases who had had no direct experience of the traumatic event (Bledin et al., 1994; Dixon et al., 1993), gives credence to these potential mechanisms.

The condition can be considered to be a normal response to an abnormal experience. It should be distinguished from anxiety and depressive conditions. Cognitive behavioural treatment techniques have been reported to be effective in non-head-injured PTSD cases (see Joseph et al., 1997). There is limited evidence for treatment success in head-injured PTSD cases (McGrath, 1997; McMillan, 1991) and further research is required here. The incidence of PTSD after head injury is probably low, but higher than found in the general population (Hibbard et al., 1998).

(vii) Psychiatric problems.   The incidence of schizophrenia in head-injured patients is above that found in the general population and is commonly 2–4% (Achte et al., 1967, 1969; De Mol, 1987). Some have concluded that the occurrence of schizophrenic-like psychosis after head injury is often related directly to the brain insult (Davison & Bagley, 1969), whereas others have considered that the majority of cases have previously had relevant psychiatric history (De Mol et al., 1987), and yet others have suggested that head injury can trigger a latent tendency towards psychosis (Shapiro, 1939). Diagnosis of a psychotic state should be distinguished from transient acute confusion, agitation, and disorientation of PTA, which is sometimes found together with delusions and hallucinations, to avoid inappropriate labelling, treatment, and placement. Paranoid psychoses, mania, and depression have also been reported after head injury (Achte et al., 1967; Jorge et al., 1993; Saran, 1985; Sarkstein et al., 1990). Major depression and neurotic conditions are most common and can occasionally include severe obsessive compulsive disorders (Hibbard et al., 1998; McKeon et al., 1984). Both early (Achte et al., 1967; Hillbom, 1960) and recent studies (Klonoff & Lage, 1995) suggest that death by suicide is high in head injured people in comparison with general population statistics.

This general area is thoughtfully reviewed by Lishman (1998). For reviews of the effectiveness of drug treatments see Wright et al. (1997).

(viii) Very severe disablement.   Patients who are entirely dependent for all functions and who might have severe communication difficulty in addition to other common sequelae of head injury, require longer-term and slower-stream rehabilitation. It is clear that significant gains in function can be made in some, including discharge to home (Whitlock, 1992). Assessment of cognitive function might need to be tailor-made

for that individual, has to account for likely extraneous biases (McMillan, 1997a), and can be vital in improving quality of life (McMillan & Herbert, 1999), given that life expectancy can span several decades even in the most disabled (Katz et al., 1992; Thadani et al., 1991).

OTHER INTERVENTIONS

Case management

It is clear that severely head-injured patients can suffer from multiple and chronic problems, which are both complex and dynamic. For this reason, therapeutic needs are often wide ranging and, arguably, the outcomes of intervention would derive benefit from coordination. Case management (CM) has been used as a system that attempts to maximise relevant input at the most appropriate time for the patient, preventing the patient from falling through the service "net", and guiding him or her through the maze of services in an organised and optimal sequence (Dixon et al., 1988). Intended results are more rapid recovery, improved quality of life, reduced disability, prevention of secondary deterioration, reduction of carer burden, and lower financial costs overall. Models like this have been used extensively in the US with head-injured patients (Deutsch & Fralish, 1988; Dixon et al., 1988), and in the US and UK with other groups who have complex needs and/or difficulty negotiating the health and social care systems. These have included the mentally handicapped (Audit Commission, 1987), those with mental health problems (Bond et al., 1988; Bush et al., 1990; Holloway, 1991; Marshall, 1996), the elderly (Challis & Davis, 1986; Stuck et al., 1995) and patients after back injury (Leavitt et al., 1972) or myocardial infarction (De Busk et al., 1994).

In the US there are a number of variants of CM after head injury and these can work in concert (Dixon et al., 1988). For example, "external" CMs are often funded by medical insurance companies and their task is to provide quality control, assessment of services, estimate of the length of stay and costs (and have power to regulate the latter), and help to construct discharge plans in liaison with relatives and other professionals. "Internal" CMs (who work within a unit) help to construct the patient treatment plan and act as an information source on the patient, their progress and history, relating this to other professionals and to the purchasers, which are usually insurance companies (Deutsch & Fralish, 1988). The CM role is not envisaged as being the same as that of key worker or social worker (McMillan et al., 1988). Their coordinating role has been described as "reticulist", a networker, or "responsible schemer" who links together the "right people with the right problems", blurring organisational and professional barriers by using the reciprocal nature of power dependence relationships (McKeganey & Hunter, 1986). More specifically, this involves assessment of the patient's needs, planning a service for that individual, linking the patient to services, monitoring progress, and acting as advocate on behalf of the patient with service providers. The way in which such a role can contribute to the setting of mutually agreed goals and the implementation of an action plan to promote the "collaborative

management" of chronic illness (Von Korff et al., 1997) needs emphasis, particularly as this type of "standard" case management has been recommended and adopted as a part of community care in the UK (Department of Health, 1989; Griffith's Report, 1988).

There have been few published studies evaluating effectiveness of CM after TBI. Studies on mental health patients have suggested that "assertive" or "clinical" CM, which includes a range of interventions, can reduce duration and frequency of in-patient care, lower overall costs of care, and increase compliance with medication (Bond et al., 1988; Bush et al., 1990; Mueller & Hopp, 1983), whereas the service brokerage model of "standard" CM is either ineffective (Holloway, 1991; Marshall, 1996) or in need of further exploration (Brugha & Glover, 1998). In the frail elderly, "standard" CM has resulted in: (1) lower costs and increased life expectancy (Challis & Davis, 1986), and delay in the development of disability and nursing home admission (Stuck et al., 1995); (2) effective coronary risk-factor modification after myocardial infarction (De Busk et al., 1994); and (3) in patients with back injuries, CM led to reduced time off work, earlier discharge, and lower costs (Leavitt et al., 1972). The programme change after TBI investigated by Blackerby (1990) included internal case management as well as increase in rehabilitation input from 5 to 8 hours per day in a heterogeneous group of brain-damaged patients, most of whom had suffered head injury. Comparison of outcome before and after implementation of these changes revealed a reduction in duration of inpatient stay of 1.5 months on average after the changes. Measures of changes in disability or quality of care are not reported and, clearly, the changes that were found could not be attributed to case management alone.

A clinical trial of "standard" CM in North London was reported by Greenwood et al. in 1994. Matched hospitals were randomised prospectively to CM or not, and patients, recruited acutely after severe TBI, were followed for 2 years. Practice and process was changed. Contact with, but not time in, rehabilitation was increased in the CM group, but there was no functional or vocational benefit or reduction in carer distress in the CM group compared with controls. The following year Malec et al. (1995) described a medical and vocational case management system intended to decrease the time between all severities of TBI and "successful community re-integration". Outcomes were to be compared against "benchmarks derived from the literature" but no subsequent results have been reported. The role of CM after TBI in the UK remains ill-defined and its effectiveness unproven. The study by Greenwood et al. (1994) could indicate CM's effectiveness at process level (Brugha & Glover, 1998) and, although it is difficult to believe that "assertive" CM is not effective in certain circumstances, what these are remains unclear and in need of further exploration.

Drug treatment

Neurological sequelae. Disordered function of the hypothalamic–pituitary axis, which should be sought particularly after optic chiasmal damage or sella fractures, can cause a spectrum of deficiency states from panhypopituitarism to menstrual irregularity or loss of libido, and indications for replacement are derived from pituitary function tests (Childers et al., 1998; Clark et al., 1988; Edwards & Clark, 1986). Reduced libido and sexual functioning and performance are commonly seen after TBI, rather than hypersexuality (Kreuter et al., 1998; Sandel et al., 1996) they are not usually the result of endocrine deficiency, with occasional exceptions (Su-Ching et al., 1994).

The need for an effective drug treatment for spasticity and the spastic dystonias to prevent contractures after TBI cannot be over-emphasised. Oral medication of cerebral, rather than spinal, spasticity with diazepam, dantrolene Sodium, baclofen, or tizanidine, is unsatisfactory, both because of side-effects and the limited effect upon tone increase. The place of intrathecal baclofen in cerebral spasticity has yet to be defined (Becker et al., 1997; Young, 1989). For individual muscle groups, motorpoint, or percutaneous or open nerve blocks with alcohol or 3–6% phenol (Braun et al., 1973), usually of the musculocutaneous or posterior tibial nerves, are useful, especially if used before contracture occurs, but their use now has largely been supplanted by intramuscular injections of botulinum toxin type-A (Pavesi et al., 1998; Wilson et al., 1997).

Of other physical disorders seen after TBI, treatment of heterotropic ossification is discussed in Chapter 15 . The various involuntary movements that can be seen (see Goetz & Pappert, 1996; Koller et al., 1989) can benefit from drug treatment. Midbrain rubral tremor can respond to L-dopa or anticholinergics (Samie et al., 1990), L-dopa and carbamazepine (Harmon et al., 1991), or propranolol and sodium valproate (Obeso & Narbona, 1983), obviating the need for surgery (Andrew et al., 1982). Reflex action myoclonus can respond to combinations of sodium valproate, primidone, piracetam, and clonazepam (Obeso et al., 1989); hemi-choreoathetosis to sodium valproate (Chandra et al., 1983); kinesigenic choreoathetosis to anticonvulsants (Drake et al., 1986; Richardson et al., 1987); and cerebellar tremor due to multiple sclerosis and stroke to carbamazepine (Sechi et al., 1989). The treatment of hemidystonia is difficult (Pettigrew & Jankovic, 1985) and might require surgery (Andrew et al., 1983).

The effectiveness of prophylactic anticonvulsants, including phenytoin (Young et al., 1983), carbamazepine (Glotzner et al., 1983), and sodium valproate (Temkin et al., 1997), in late post-traumatic epilepsy remains unproven, with the sole exception of the suppression of early epilepsy by phenytoin (Temkin et al., 1990), and there are no studies of the newer anticonvulsants. In all other situations, after acute parenteral administration is no longer required, carbamazepine is usually the drug of first choice, although no studies comparing different anticonvulsants in patients with severe TBI have been done. Prescription is governed (Deutschman & Haines, 1985) first, by the risk of developing late epilepsy—which is known to be particularly high after penetrating head injuries (Salazar et al., 1985), depressed skull fracture, early epilepsy, or an intracranial clot requiring surgery (Jennett, 1975)—as well as CT evidence of

contusion and, to a lesser extent, PTA greater than 24 hours (Annegers et al., 1998), and second, by the known side-effects of current anticonvulsants. Carbamazepine and sodium valproate appear to have the fewest cognitive and behavioural side-effects in epileptic patients, although both can affect motor functions as much as phenytoin, emphasising the need to use minimal effective doses (Duncan et al., 1990), and carbamazepine might have the neurobehavioural benefits noted later.

Various types of headache occur after head injury, more commonly after mild than severe TBI (Kelly, 1988; Packard & Ham, 1994), but little data exist to guide drug treatment. Relander et al. (1972) do not record whether resolution of early post-traumatic headache was a benefit experienced by 82 patients prospectively randomised to active mobilisation and support compared with 96 patients receiving "routine" treatment; the former returned to work on average 18 days post-injury, the latter after 32. The use of antidepressants to treat "late-acquired" post-traumatic headache, which Cartlidge and Shaw (1981) found to be associated with depression, is logical but has never been subject to proper scrutiny (Tyler et al., 1980). Treatment of post-traumatic migraine, including footballers' migraine (Matthews, 1972), and migrainous neuralgia, which occasionally follows head injury, does not differ from treatment of other patients with similar complaints presenting spontaneously.

Neurobehavioural sequelae. The use of drugs to treat affective, cognitive, and behavioural changes after TBI is guided largely by vague notions of post-injury alteration in neurotransmitter function; particularly depletion of catecholamines (reducing arousal and attention), serotonin (producing agitation and aggression), and acetylcholine (impairing memory systems). Evidence comes from studies in non-TBI patients and anecdotal case reports or methodologically inadequate case or group studies. Despite this, it is difficult to dispel the notion that judicious individualised prescription at particular times after injury, in conjunction with appropriate training techniques, might be of significant benefit, because in animals, and even in man, drugs plus training appear to be more effective than drugs or training alone (Feeney, 1997; Feeney et al., 1982; Sutton et al., 1987). This approach has not been adequately tested after TBI but, after stroke, amphetamine and methylphenidate have been found to improve emotional and motor recovery in studies using double-blind, prospective, randomised methodology in small numbers of patients (Grade et al., 1998; Walker-Batson et al., 1995).

Pathological emotions have been helped by amitriptyline in patients with multiple sclerosis (Schiffer et al., 1985), L-dopa after TBI or stroke (Udaka et al., 1984), and fluoxetine after brain injury (Sloan et al., 1992). Depression is sometimes difficult to diagnose in the context of persisting organic deficits (Gans, 1982) but is not uncommon even years after TBI; its aggressive treatment with an antidepressant tolerated by the patient can produce gratifying functional benefit but the choice of drug is dictated, as Gualtieri implies (1988), on little more than "holding a tablet up to the light". Which patients benefit is unclear, and Saran (1985) reported that neither amitriptyline nor phenelzine benefited 10 depressed TBI patients, compared with 12 depressed patients without brain injury who did respond to amitriptyline. The depression in the 10 TBI patients was atypical, lacking vegetative symptoms, and redefinition of some of these problems as resulting from organic disorders of drive, motivation, and hedonic responsiveness, due to a dopaminergic deficit (Wise, 1980) might be more rewarding therapeutically, as might treatment with a newer antidepressant such as fluoxetine.

Severe negative behaviour disorders after brain injury, with patients minimally conscious and with akinetic mutism or lesser degrees of abulia, have apparently improved with dopamine agonists, such as doses of bromocriptine varying from 20 to 100 mg daily (Crismon et al., 1998; Muller & von Cramon, 1994; Powell et al., 1996; Ross & Stewart, 1981), or amantadine (Nickels et al., 1994; Van Reekum et al., 1995; Zafonte et al., 1998). Such treatment has also been shown to reduce visuospatial neglect (Fleet et al., 1986) and speech initiation and fluency (Albert et al., 1988) after stroke. Whether these observations have a common basis in dopaminergic facilitation of executive functions in dorsolateral prefrontal cortex (McDowell et al., 1998) remains to be explored. The use of stimulants, to augment catecholemine availability, has been explored to a limited extent after TBI: Lipper and Tuchman (1976) showed improved concentration and memory using 30 mg of dexamphetamine compared, double-blind, with placebo in a 25-year-old man after severe TBI and similar results have been described using methylphenidate in a single case (Evans et al., 1987) and a group study (Gualtieri & Evans, 1988), but cognitive benefits were not found using double-blind methodology (Speech et al., 1993).

The hope that memory and learning deficits after TBI will improve with cholinergics, including physostigmine, choline, lecithin and tetrahydro-9-amino acridine (Goldberg et al., 1982), nootropics, and vasopressin or ACTH analogues (Van Wimersam et al., 1985) have not yet borne fruit.

Drug treatment of agitated behaviour can be of benefit. Early agitation and combatitiveness, which is associated with low levels of homovanillic and 5-hydroxyindoleacetic acid in the cerebrospinal fluid (Van Woerkom et al., 1977), was more appropriately treated by increasing catecholamine or serotonin receptor activity, with, for example, amitriptyline in 13 of 20 patients (Mysiw et al., 1988), or possibly buspirone (Levine, 1988; Ratey et al., 1992) or trazodone (Rowland et al., 1992), rather than by dopaminergic or alpha-adrenergic blockade with major tranquillisers, which slow or reverse recovery in animals (Feeney et al., 1982; Sutton et al., 1987) although not demonstrably in man (Rao & Woolston, 1989). Other drug side-effects further discourage the use of major tranquillisers after TBI, as they do the benzodiazepines, which can cause impairment of attention and memory (Tinkenberg & Taylor, 1984). Beta-blockade with propranolol to 420 mg per day significantly reduced the maximum intensity and (non-significantly)

the number of agitated episodes using prospective, double-blind, placebo-controlled methodology in 21 patients (Brooke et al., 1992). Later agitation, hypomania, explosive aggression, or episodic temper dyscontrol have improved with amitriptyline in one case (Jackson et al., 1985), possibly with buspirone (Ratey et al., 1992; Stanislav, 1994), sometimes with lithium (Bellus et al., 1996; Glen et al., 1989), with the anticonvulsants sodium valproate (Geracioti, 1994) or carbamazipine (e.g. Lewin & Sumners, 1992; Stewart, 1985), with beta-adrenergic blockade with propanolol in single cases (e.g. Yudofsky, 1981), or with propranolol or pindolol using double-blind, placebo-controlled methodology (Greendyke & Kanter, 1986; Greendyke et al., 1986), with the neuroleptic clozapine when aggressive and agitated behaviours are accompanied by psychotic symptoms (Michals et al., 1993), and with the psychostimulants dexamphetamine or methylphenidate (Max et al., 1995; Mooney & Haas, 1993).

RESOURCE UTILISATION

A number of recent American studies have been concerned to present data on cost as well as on effectiveness of rehabilitation (Cope et al., 1991a,b; Johnston & Keith, 1983; Johnston & Lewis, 1991; Wehman et al., 1989c). In the UK, where neurorehabilitation services have been less well developed, and with increasing emphasis on audit and cost-accounting in the NHS, it is becoming important to determine in what way rehabilitation is effective and when it should be available. In this climate, it becomes important to justify the use of limited resources and to define factors that predict the usefulness of particular rehabilitation programmes. Examples can include age, presence of post-traumatic epilepsy, duration and intensity of rehabilitation, and severity of injury (Armstrong et al., 1990; Blackerby, 1990; Carey et al., 1988; Rao & Woolsten, 1985).

Clearly, "outcome" can be difficult to define, and some find measures such as return to work, or re-entry into the community, insensitive as "quality of life" measures, especially in the more severely disabled patient. Nevertheless, hard and relatively unambiguous data of this kind will be required to persuade purchasers not simply to maintain, but to expand post-acute services for the brain injured. This need will only be met by prospective, randomised, controlled trials comparing outcome in groups of patients randomly assigned to different treatment strategies. The dearth of class 1 evidence of this sort has been emphasised recently (NIH Consensus Development Conference, 1998). However, at the time of going to press, three trials that begin to fill this vacuum are in preparation or have been submitted for publication; one examining intensive treatment in an early in-patient setting and two trialling different methods of post-acute rehabilitation. Hopefully, more will follow so that the evidence-base for rehabilitation after TBI begins to match that already available after stroke (see Chapter 36).

REFERENCES

Achte KA, Hillbom A, Aalberg V (1967). *Post-traumatic psychosis following war brain injuries*. Reports from the Rehabilitation Institute for Brain Injured Veterans, Helsinki: Finland.

Achte KA, Hillbom A, Aalberg V (1969). Psychosis following war brain injuries. *Acta Psychiatr Scand, 45*, 1–18.

Albert ML, Backman DL, Morgan A, Helm-Estabrooks N (1988). Pharmacotherapy for aphasia. *Neurology, 38*, 877–879.

Alderman N, Fry RK, Youngson HA (1995). Improvement of self-monitoring skills, reduction of behaviour disturbance and the dysexecutive syndrome. *Neuropsychol Rehab, 5*, 193–222.

Alderman N, Knight A (1997). The effectiveness of DRL in the management and treatment of severe behaviour disorders following brain injury. *Brain Injury, 11*, 79–101.

Aldridge D, Gustorff D, Hannich H-J (1990). Music therapy allied to coma patients. *J Roy Soc Med, 83*, 345–346.

Alexander MP (1995). Mild traumatic brain injury: Pathophysiology, natural history, and clinical management. *Neurology 45*, 1253–1260.

Alves W, Macchiocchi SN, Barth JT (1993). Post-concussive symptoms after uncomplicated mild head injury. *J Head Trauma Rehab, 8*, 48–59.

American Psychiatric Association (1994). *Diagnostic and Statistical Manual of Mental Disorders*, 4th edition. American Psychiatric Association, Washington DC, pp. 424–429.

Andrew J, Fowler CJ, Harrison MJG (1982). Tremor after head injury and its treatment by stereotaxic surgery. *J Neurol Neurosurg Psychiatry, 45*, 815–819.

Andrew J, Fowler CJ, Harrison MJG (1983). Stereotaxic thalamotomy in 55 cases of dystonia. *Brain, 106*, 981–1000.

Annegers JF, Hauser WA, Coan SP, Rocca WA (1998). A population-based study of seizures after traumatic brain injury. *N Eng J Med, 378*, 20–24.

Armstrong KK, Saghal V, Block R et al. (1990). Rehabilitation outcomes in patients with post traumatic epilepsy. *Arch Phys Med Rehab, 71*, 156–160.

Aronow HU (1987). Rehabilitation effectiveness with severe brain injury: Translating research into policy. *J Head Trauma Rehab, 2*, 24–36.

Artiola I, Fortuny L, Briggs M, Newcombe F et al. (1980). Measuring the duration of post-traumatic amnesia. *J Neurol Neurosurg Psychiatr, 43*, 377–379.

Ashley MJ, Persel CS, Clark MC, Krych DK (1997). Long-term follow up of post-acute traumatic brain injury rehabilitation: A statistical analysis to test for stability and predictability of outcome. *Brain Injury, 11*, 677–690.

Audit Commission (1987). *Community care: developing services for people with a mental handicap. Occasional Paper No. 4*, HMSO, London.

Becker R, Alberti O, Bauer BL (1997). Continuous intra-thecal baclofen infusion in severe spasticity after traumatic or hypoxic brain injury. *J Neurol, 244*, 160–166.

Beetar JT, Guilmette TJ, Sparadco FR (1996). Sleep and pain complaints in symptomatic traumatic brain injury and neurologic populations. *Arch Phys Med Rehab, 77*, 1298–1302.

Bellus SB, Stewart D, Vergo JG, Kost PP, Grace J, Berkstrom SR (1996). The use of lithium in the treatment of aggressive behaviours with two brain-injured individuals in a state psychiatric hospital. *Brain Injury, 10*, 849–860.

Ben-Yishay Y, Lakin P (1989). Structured group treatment for brain-injury survivors. In: Ellis DW and Christensen A-L (Eds.), *Neuropsychological treatment after brain injury*. Kluwer Academic Press, New York, pp. 271–295.

Ben-Yishay Y, Silver S, Paisetsky E, Rattock J (1987). Relationship between employability and vocational outcome after intensive holistic cognitive rehabilitation. *J Head Trauma Rehab, 2*, 35–49.

Bergner M, Bobbit RA, Carter WB, Gilson BS (1981). The Sickness Impact Profile: development and final revision of a health status measure. *Med Care, 8*, 787–805.

Bishara SN, Partridge FM, Godfrey HP, Knight RG (1992). Post-traumatic amnesia and Glasgow Coma Scale related to outcome in survival in a consecutive series of patients with severe closed head injury. *Brain Injury, 6*, 373–380.

Blackerby WF (1990). Intensity of rehabilitation and length of stay. *Brain Injury, 4*, 167–173.

Bledin K (1994). Post traumatic stress disorder "once removed": A case report. *Br J Med Psychol, 67*, 125–129.

Blumbergs PC, Scott G, Manavis J, Wainwright H, Simpson DA, McLean AJ (1994). Staining of amyloid precursor protein to study axonal damage in mild head injury. *Lancet, ii*, 1055–1056.

Boake C (1990). Transitional living centres in head injury rehabilitation. In: JS Kreutzer and P Wehman (Eds.), *Community integration following traumatic brain injury*. Edward Arnold, Sevenoaks, pp. 115–124.

Bond GR, Miller LD, Krumweid RD, Ward RS (1988). Assertive case management in three CMHCs: A controlled study. *Hosp Comm Psychiatry, 39*, 411–418.

Braakman R, Jennett WB, Minderhoud JM (1988). Prognosis of the post-traumatic vegetative state. *Acta Neurochirurgica (Wein), 95*, 49–52.

Braun RM, Hoffer MM, Mooney V, McKeever J, Roper B (1973). Phenol nerve block in the treatment of acquired spastic hemiplegia in the upper limb. *J Bone Joint Surg, 55*, 580–585.

Bricolo A, Turazzi S, Feriotti G (1980). Prolonged post traumatic unconsciousness. *J Neurosurg, 52*, 625–634.

British Psychological Society (1989). Services for young adult patients with acquired brain damage. Working Party Report. British Psychological Society, Leicester.

British Society of Rehabilitation Medicine (1998). *Rehabilitation after traumatic brain injury: A working party report of the British Society or Rehabilitation Medicine*. BSRM, London.

Brooke MA, Questad KA, Patterson DR, Bashak KJ (1992). Agitation and restlessness after closed head injury: A prospective study of 100 consecutive admissions. *Arch Phys Med Rehab, 73*, 320–323.

Brooke MM, Patterson DR, Questad KA, Cardenas D, Farrel-Roberts L (1992). The treatment of agitation during initial hospitalisation after traumatic brain injury. *Arch Phys Med Rehab, 73*, 917–921.

Brooks CA, Gabella B, Hoffman R, Sosin D, Whiteneck G (1997). Traumatic brain injury: designing and implementing a population-based follow-up system. *Arch Phys Med Rehab, 78* (Supp 4): 526–530.

Brooks DN, Deelman BG, van Zomeren AH, van Dongen H, van Harskamp F, Aughton ME (1984). Problems in measuring cognitive recovery after acute brain injury. *J Clin Neuropsychol, 6*, 71–85.

Brooks DN, Campsie LM, Beattie A (1986). Head injury and the rehabilitation profession in the west of scotland. *Health Bulletin (Edin), 44*, 110.

Brooks DN, McKinlay WW, Symington C, Beattie A, Campsie L (1987a). Return to work within the first seven years of severe head injury. *Brain Injury, 1*, 5–19.

Brooks DN, Campsie L, Symington C et al. (1987b). The effects of severe head injury on patient and relative within seven years of injury. *J Head Trauma Rehab, 2*, 1–13.

Brotherton FA, Thomas LL, Wisotzek IE, Milan MA (1988). Social skills training in the rehabilitation of patients with traumatic closed head injury. *Arch Phys Med Rehab, 69*, 827–832.

Brugha T, Glover G (1998). Process and health outcomes: Need for clarity in systematic reviews of case management for severe mental disorders. *Health Trends, 30*, 76–79.

Bryant, RA, Harvey AG (1995). Acute stress response: A comparison of head injured and non-head injured patients. *Psychological Medicine, 25*, 869–873.

Bryden J (1989). How many head injured? The epidemiology of post head injury disability. In: RL Wood, P Eames (Eds.), *Models of brain injury rehabilitation*. Chapman Hall, London.

Bush CT, Langford MW, Rosen P, Gott W (1990). Operation outreach: Intensive care management for severely psychiatrically disabled adults. *Hosp Comm Psychiatry, 41*, 647–649.

Carey RG, Seibert JH, Posarac J (1988). Who makes the most progress in inpatient rehabilitation? An analysis of functional gain. *Arch Phys Med Rehab, 69*, 337–343.

Cartlidge NEF, Shaw DA (1981). *Head injury*. Saunders, Philadephia.

Centers for Disease Control (CDC) (1997). Traumatic brain injury – Colorado, Missouri, Oklahoma and Utah, 1990–1993. *MMWR, 46*, 8–11.

Challis JD, Davis B (1986). *Case management in community care*. Gower, Aldershot.

Chandra V, Spunt AL, Rusinowitz MS (1983). Treatment of post-traumatic choreoathetosis with sodium valproate. *J Neurol Neurosurg Psychiatry, 46*, 963–965.

Cherney LR, Halper AS (1996). Swallowing problems in adults with traumatic brain injury. *Semin Neurol, 16*, 349–353.

Chestnut RM, Marshall LF, Klauber MR, Blunt BA, Baldwin N, Eisenberg HM, Jane JA, Marmarou A, Foulkes MA (1993). The role of secondary brain injury in determining outcome from severe head injury. *J Trauma, 34,* 216–222.

Childers MK, Rupright J, Jones PS, Merveille O (1998). Assessment of neuroendocrine dysfunction following traumatic brain injury. *Brain Injury, 12,* 517–523.

Cifu D, Kreutzer JS, Marwitz JH, Rosenthal M, Englander J, High W (1996). Functional outcomes of older adults with traumatic brain injury: A prospective, multicentre analysis. *Arch Phys Med Rehab, 77,* 883–888.

Clark JDA, Raggatt PR, Edwards OM (1988). Hypothalamic hypogonadism following major head injury. *Clin Endocrinol, 29,* 153–165.

Clarke JM (1974). Distribution of microglial scars in the brain after brain injury. *J Neurol Neurosurg Psychiatry, 34,* 463–474.

Clifton GL, Robertson CS, Choi SG (1986). Assessment of nutritional requirements of head-injured patients. *J Neurosurg, 64,* 895–901.

Clifton GL, Hayes RL, Levin HS et al. (1992). Outcome measures for clinical trials involving traumatically brain-injured patients: Report of a conference. *Neurosurgery, 31,* 975–978.

Cockburn JM, Gatherer A (1988). Facilities for rehabilitation of adults after head injury. *Clin Rehab, 2,* 315–318.

Coelho CA (1987). Sign acquisition and use following traumatic brain injury case report. *Arch Phys Med Rehab, 68,* 229–231.

Colantonio A, Dawson DR, McLellan BA (1998). Head injury in young adults: Long-term outcome. *Arch Phys Med Rehab, 79,* 550–558.

Conine TA, Sullivan T, Mackie T, Goodman M (1990). Effects of serial casting for the prevention of equinovarus inpatients with acute head injury. *Arch Phys Med Rehab, 71,* 310–312.

Cope DN, Hall KM (1982). Head injury rehabilitation: Benefits of early intervention. *Arch Phys Med Rehab, 63,* 433–437.

Cope DN, Cole JR, Hall KM, Barkan H (1991a). Brain injury: Analysis of outcome in a post-acute rehabilitation system. Part 1: General analysis. *Brain Injury, 5,* 111–125.

Cope DN, Cole JR, Hall KM, Barkan H (1991b). Brain injury: Analysis of outcome in a post-acute rehabilitation system. Part 2: Subanalyses. *Brain Injury, 5,* 127–139.

Corrigan JD, Smith-Knapp K, Granger CV (1998) Outcomes in the first 5 years after traumatic brain injury. *Arch Phys Med Rehab, 79,* 298–305.

Cowen TD, Meythaler JM, De Vico MJ, Ivie CS 3rd, Lebow J, Novack TA (1995). Influence of early variables in traumatic brain injury on functional independence measure scores and rehabilitation length of stay and charges. *Arch Phys Med Rehab, 76,* 797–803.

Crismon ML, Childs A, Wilcox RE, Barrow N (1998). The effect of bromocriptine on speech dysfunction in patients with diffuse brain injury (akinetic mutism). *Clin Neuropharmacol, 11,* 462–466.

Davidoff DA, Kessler HR, Laibstain DF, Mark VH (1988). Neurobehavioural sequelae of minor head injury: A consideration of post-concussive syndrome versus post-traumatic stress disorder. *Cognit Rehab, 6,* 8–13.

Davison K, Baggley CR (1969). Schizophrenia-like psychosis associated with organic disorders of the central nervous system. In: RN Herrington (Ed.), *Current problems in neuropsychiatry.* British Journal of Psychiatry, special publication No. 4. Headley Brothers, Ashford, Kent.

De Busk RF, Miller NH, Superko HR et al. (1994). A case-management system for coronary risk factor modification after acute myocardial infarction. *Ann Intern Med, 120,* 721–729.

De Mol J, Violon A, Brihey EJ (1987). Post traumatic psychosis: A retrospective study of 18 cases. *J. Archevio di Psychologia–Neurologia e Psichiatria, 48,* 336–350.

Department of Health (1989). *Caring for people; community care in the next decade and beyond.* HMSO, London (Cm 849).

Deutsch PM, Fralish KB (1988). *Innovations in head injury rehabilitation.* Mathew Bender, Albany, NY, pp. 322–326.

Deutschman CS, Haines SJ. (1985). Anticonvulsant prophylaxis in neurological surgery. *Neurosurgery, 17,* 510–517.

Deutschman CS, Constantinides FN, Raup S (1986). Physiological and metabolic responses to isolated closed head injury. *J Neurosurg, 64,* 89–98.

Dixon P, Goll S, Stanton KM (1988). Case management issues and practices in head injury rehabilitation. *Rehab Counselling Bull, 31,* 325–343.

Dixon P, Rehling G, Schiwach R (1993). Peripheral victims of the Herald of Free Enterprise disaster. *Br J Med Psychol, 66,* 193–202.

Do HK, Sahagian DA, Schuster LC, Sheridan SE (1988). Head trauma rehabilitation: Program evaluation. *Rehab, Nursing, 13,* 71–75.

Dordel HJ (1987). Mobility training following brain trauma – results of intensive individual treatment. *Int J Rehabil Res, 10,* 279–290.

Drake ME, Jackson RD, Miller CA (1986). Paroxysmal choreoathesosis after head injury. *J Neurol Neurosurg Psychiatry, 49,* 837–843.

Duncan JS, Shorvon SD, Trimble MR (1990). Effects of removal of phenytoin, carbamazepine, and valproate on cognitive function. *Epilepsia, 31,* 584–591.

Eames P, Wood R (1985). Rehabilitation after severe brain injury: A follow-up study of a behaviour modification approach. *J Neurol Neurosurg Psychiatry, 48,* 616–619.

Eames P, Cotterill G, Kneale TA, Storrar AL, Yeomans J (1995). Outcome of intensive rehabilitation after severe brain injury: A long term follow-up study. *Brain Injury, 10,* 631–650.

Editorial (1990). Head trauma victims in the UK: undeservedly underserved. *Lancet, 335,* 886–887.

Edwards OM, Clark JDA (1986). Post-traumatic hypopituitarism. *Medicine, 65,* 281–290.

Evans RW, Gualtieri CT, Patterson D (1987). Treatment of chronic closed head injury with psychostimulant drugs: A controlled case study and an appropriate evaluation procedure. *J Nerv Ment Dis, 175,* 106–110.

Ewert J, Levin HS, Watson MG, Kalisky V (1989). Procedural memory during post traumatic amnesia in survivors of closed head injury. *Arch Neurol, 46,* 911–916.

Eyman RK, Strauss D, Grossman HJ (1996). Survival of children with severe developmental disability. *Balliere's Clinical Paediatrics, 4,* 543–556.

Fahy TJ, Irving MH, Millac P (1967). Severe head injuries: A six year follow-up. *Lancet, ii,* 475–479.

Fairbank, JA, DeGood DE, Jenkins CW (1981). Behavioural treatment of a persistent post-traumatic startle response. *J Behav Ther Exp Psychiatry, 12,* 321–324.

Feeney DM (1997). From laboratory to clinic: Noradrenergic enhancement of physical therapy for stroke or trauma patients. *Adv Neurol, 73,* 383–394.

Feeney DM, Gonzalez A, Law WA (1982). Amphetamine, haloperidol, and experience interact to affect rate of recovery after motor cortex injury. *Science, 217,* 855–857.

Ferchmin PA, Bennett EL, Rosenzweig MR (1975). Direct contact with enriched environment is required to alter cerebral weights in rats. *Comp Physiol Psychol, 88,* 360–367.

Field HJ (1976). *Epidemiology of head injuries in England and Wales with particular reference to rehabilitation.* London, HMSO.

Fleet WS, Watson RT, Valerstein E, Heilman KM. (1986). Dopamine agonist therapy for neglect in humans. *Neurology, 36* (suppl), 347.

Forssmann-Falck R, Christian FM (1989). The use of group therapy as a treatment modality for behavioural change following head injury. *Psychol Med, 7,* 43–50.

Gajar A, Schloss PJ, Schloss C, Thompson CK (1984). Effects of feedback and self-monitoring on head trauma youths conversation skills. *J Appl Behav Anal, 17,* 353–358.

Gans JS (1982). Depression diagnosis in a rehabilitation hospital. *Arch Phys Med Rehab, 62,* 386–389.

Gans JS (1983). Hate in the rehabilitation setting. *Arch Phys Med Rehab, 64,* 176–179.

Geracioti TD (1994). Valproic acid treatment of episodic explosiveness related to brain injury. *J Clin Psychiatry, 55,* 416–417.

Gianutsos R (1991). Cognitive rehabilitation: A neuropsychological speciality comes of age. *Brain Injury, 5,* 353–368.

Giles GM, Morgan JH. (1989). Training functional skills following herpes simplex encephalitis: A single case study. *J Clin Exp Neuropsychol, 11,* 311–318.

Giles GM, Shore M (1989). A rapid method for teaching severely brain injured adults how to wash and dress. *Arch Phys Med Rehab, 70,* 156–158.

Glen MB, Wroblewski B, Parziale J, Levine L, Whyte J, Rosenthal M (1989). Lithium Carbonate for aggressive behaviour or affective instability in ten brain-injured patients. *Am J Phys Med Rehab, 68,* 221–226.

Glisky EL, Delaney SM (1996). Implicit memory and new semantic learning in post traumatic amnesia. *J Head Trauma Rehab, 11,* 31–42.

Gloag D (1985a). Services for people with head injury. *Br Med J, 291,* 557–558.

Gloag D (1985b). Rehabilitation after head injury. *Br Med J, 290,* 913–916.

Glotzner FL, Haubitz I, Milter F et al. (1983). Epilepsy prophylaxis with carbamazepine in severe brain injuries. *Neurochirurgia, 26,* 66–79.

Goetz CG, Pappert EJ (1996). Movement disorders: Post-traumatic syndromes. In RW Evans (Ed.), *Neurology and trauma*. Philadelphia, WB Saunders, pp. 569–580.

Goldberg E, Gerstman JL, Mattis S, Hughes JE, Bilder RM, Sirio CA (1982). Effects of cholinergic treatment on post-traumatic anterograde amnesia. *Arch Neurol, 35*, 581.

Gollaher K, High W, Sherer M, Bergloff P, Boake C, Young ME, Ivanhoe C (1998). Prediction of employment outcome one–three years following traumatic brain injury (TBI). *Brain Injury, 12*, 255–263.

Gouvier WD, Blanton PD, LaPorte KK, Nepomuceno C (1987). Reliability and validity of the Disability Rating Scale and the Levels of Cognitive Functioning Scale in monitoring recovery from severe head injury. *Arch Phys Med Rehab, 68*, 94–97.

Grade C, Redford B, Chrostowski J, Toussaint L, Blackwell B (1998). Methylphenidate in early post-stroke recovery: A double-blind, placebo-controlled study. *Arch Phys Med Rehab, 79*, 1047–1050.

Greendyke RM, Kanter DR (1986). Therapeutic effects of pindolol on behavioural disturbances associated with organic brain disease: A double blind study. *J Clin Psychol, 46*, 413–426.

Greendyle RM, Kanter DR, Schuster DB, Verstreate S, Wootton J (1986). Propranolol treatment of assaultive patients with organic brain disease. A double-blind crossover, placebo-controlled study. *J Nerv Ment Dis, 174*, 290–294.

Greenwood RJ, McMillan TM (1993). Models of rehabilitation programmes for the brain injured adult I: Current service provision. *Clin Rehab, 7*, 248–255.

Greenwood RJ, McMillan TM, Brooks DN, Dunn G, Brock D, Dinsdale S, Murphy L, Price J (1994). Effects of case management after severe head injury. *Br Med J, 308*, 1199–1205.

Griffiths R (1988). *Community care: An agenda for action*. London, HMSO.

Gronwall D (1986). Rehabilitation programmes for patients with mild head injury: Components, problems and evaluation. *J Head Trauma Rehab, 1*, 53–62.

Gronwall D, Wrightson P (1974). Delayed recovery of intellectual function after minor head injury. *Lancet, ii*, 605–609.

Gronwall D, Wrightson P (1975). Cumulative effects of concussion. *Lancet, ii*, 995–997.

Groswasser Z, Sazbon L (1990). Outcome in 134 patients with prolonged post-traumatic unawareness. Parts 1 and 2. *J Neurosurg, 72*, 75–84.

Gualtieri CT (1988). Pharmacotherapy and the neurobehavioural sequelae of traumatic brain injury. *Brain Injury, 2*, 101–129.

Gualtieri CT, Evans RW (1988). Stimulant treatment for the neurobehavioural sequelae of traumatic brain injury. *Brain Injury, 2*, 272–290.

Guide for the Uniform Data System for Medical Rehabilitation (Adult FIM), version 4.0 (1993). Buffalo, NY, State University of New York at Buffalo.

Hagen C, Malkmus D, Durham P (1972). *Levels of cognitive functioning*. Downer, CA, Ranch Los Amigos Hospital.

Haigh P, Ruess J (1990). Recovery from the vegetative state of six months duration associated with Sinemet. *Arch Phys Med Rehab, 71*, 1081–1083.

Hall KM (1997). Establishing a national traumatic brain injury information system based upon a unified data set. *Arch Phys Med Rehab, 78* (suppl 4), S5–S11.

Hall ME, MacDonald S, Young GC (1992). The effectiveness of directed multisensory stimulation versus non-directed stimulation in comatose CHI patients. *Brain Injury, 6*, 435–445.

Hall K, Mann N, High W, Wright K, Kreutzer J, Wood D (1996). Functional measures after traumatic brain injury: Ceiling effects of the FIM, FIM + FAM, DRS, and CIQ. *J Head Trauma Rehab, 11*, 27–39.

Harmon RL, Long DF, Jeannine S (1991). Treatment of post-traumatic midbrain resting-kinetic tremor with combined levodopa/carbidopa and carbamazepine. *Brain Injury, 5*, 213–218.

Hegel MT (1988). Application of a token economy with a non-compliant closed head injured male. *Brain Injury, 2*, 333–338.

Heinemann AW, Hamilton B, Linacre JM et al. (1995). Functional status and therapeutic intensity during inpatient rehabilitation. *Am J Phys Med Rehab, 74*, 315–326.

Hibbard MR, Uysal S, Kepler K, Bogdany J, Silver J (1998). Axis I psychopathology in individuals with traumatic brain injury. *J Head Trauma Rehab, 13*, 24–39.

Hickling EJ, Gillen R, Blanchard EB et al. (1998). Traumatic brain injury and post traumatic stress disorder: A preliminary investigation of neuropsychological test results in PTSD secondary to motor vehicle accidents. *Brain Injury, 12*, 265–274.

High WM Jr, Boake C, Lehmkuhl LD (1995). Critical analysis of studies evaluating the effectiveness of rehabilitation after traumatic brain injury. *J Head Trauma Rehab, 10*, 14–26.

High WM Jr, Hall KM, Rosenthal M, Mann N, Zafonte R, Cifu DX, Boake C, Bartha M, Ivanhoe C, Yablon S, Newton CN, Sherer M, Silver B, Lehmkuhl LD (1996). Factors affecting hospital length of stay and charges following traumatic brain injury of adults living in the community. *Brain Injury, 9*, 339–353.

Hillbom E (1960). After-effects of brain injuries. *Acta Psychiatr Neurol Scand, Suppl 142*, 1–195.

Holloway F (1991). Case management for the mentally ill: Looking at the evidence. *Int J Social Psychiatry, 37*, 2–13.

Horton AM, Howe NR (1981). Behavioural treatment of the traumatically brain injured: A case study. *Percept Motor Skills, 53*, 349–350.

Hunter M, Tomberlin J, Kirkikis C, Kuna ST (1990). Progressive exercise testing in closed head injured subjects: Comparison of exercise apparatus in assessment of a physical conditioning program. *Phys Ther, 70*, 363–371.

Jackson RD, Corrigan JD, Arnett JA (1985). Amitriptyline for agitation in head injury. *Arch Phys Med Rehab, 66*, 180–181.

Jankowski LW, Sullivan SJ (1990). Aerobic and neuromuscular training: Effect on the capacity, efficiency, and fatigability of patients with traumatic brain injuries. *Arch Phys Med Rehab, 71*, 500–504.

Jellinek HM, Harvey RF (1982). Vocational/education services in a medical rehabilitation facility: Outcomes in spinal cord and brain injured patients. *Arch Phys Med Rehab, 63*, 87–86.

Jenkins A, Teasdale G, Hadley MDM, MacPherson P, Rowan JO (1986). Brain lesions detected by magnetic resonance imaging in mild and severe head injuries. *Lancet, 2*, 445–446.

Jennett B (1975). *Epilepsy after non-missile head injuries*. 2nd edition. London, Heinemann.

Jennett B (1996). Epidemiology of head injuries. *J Neurol Neurosurg Psychiatry, 60*, 362–369.

Jennett B, Bond M (1975). Assessment of outcome after severe brain damage: A practical scale. *Lancet, 1*, 480–484.

Jennett B, Braakman R (1990). Severe traumatic brain injury. *J Neurosurg, 73*, 479.

Jennett B, MacMillan R (1981). Epidemiology of head injury. *Br Med J, 282*, 101–104.

Jennet B, Teasdale G (1981). *Measurement of head injury*. F.A. Davis and Co., Philadelphia.

Jennett B, Teasdale G, Braakman R (1979). Prognosis in a series of patients with severe head injury. *Neurosurgery, 4*, 283–289.

Jennett B, Snoek J, Bond M, Brooks N (1981). Disability after severe head injury: Observations on the use of the Glasgow Outcome Scale. *J Neurol Neurosurg Psychiatry, 44*, 285–293.

Jennett B, Teasdale G (1981). *Management of head injuries*. Philadelphia, FA Davis.

Johnson R, Gleave J (1987). Counting the people disabled by head injury. *Injury, 18*, 7–9.

Johnson SM, Omery A, Nikas D (1989). Effects of conversation on intracranial pressure in comatose patients. *Heart and Lung, 18*, 56–63.

Johnston MV (1991). Outcomes of community re-entry programmes for brain injury survivors. Part 2: Further investigations. *Brain Injury, 5*, 155–168.

Johnston MV, Keith RA (1983). Cost-benefits of medical rehabilitation: Review and critique. *Arch Phys Med Rehab, 64*, 147–154.

Johnston MV, Lewis FD (1991). Outcomes of community re-entry programmes for brain injury survivors. Part 1: Independent living and productive activities. *Brain Injury, 5*, 141–154.

Johnston S, Burgess J, McMillan TM, Greenwood RJ (1991). Management of adipsia by a behavioural modification technique. *J Neurol Neurosurg Psychiatry, 54*, 272–274.

Jorge RE, Robinson RG, Sarkstein SE, Arndt SV, Forrester AW, Geisler FH (1993). Secondary mania following traumatic brain injury. *Am J Psychiatry, 150*, 916–921.

Joseph S, Williams R, Yule W (1997). *Understanding post traumatic stress*. Chichester, John Wiley.

Karzmark P, Hall K, Englander J (1995). Late onset post-concussional symptoms after mild brain injury: The role of premorbid, injury related, environmental and personality factors. *Brain Injury, 59*, 21–26.

Katz RT, Haig AJ, Clarke BP et al. (1992). Long term survival, prognosis and life care planning for 29 patients with chronic locked-in syndrome. *Arch Phys Med Rehab, 73*, 403–408.

Kay T, Harrington DE, Adams A et al. (1993). Definition of mild traumatic brain injury. *J Head Trauma Rehab, 8,* 86–87.

Keenan M, Creighton J, Garland DE (1984). Surgical correction of spastic equinovarus deformity in the adult head trauma patient. *Foot Ankle, 5,* 35–41.

Keenan MA, Thomas ES, Stone C, Gersten LM (1990). Percutaneous phenol block of the musculocutaneous nerve to control elbow flexor spasticity. *J Hand Surg Am, 15,* 340–346.

Kelly R (1988). Headache after cranial trauma. In: A Hopkins (Ed.), *Headache: Problems in diagnosis and management.* Saunders, London, pp. 219–240.

Kibby MY, Long CJ (1996). Minor head injury: Attempts at clarifying the confusion. *Brain Injury, 10,* 159–186.

King NS (1997). Post traumatic stress disorder and head injury as a dual diagnosis: "Islands" of memory as a mechanism. *J Neurol Neurosurg Psychiatry, 62,* 82–84.

King NS, Crawford S, Wenden FJ, Moss NEG, Wade DT (1997). Interventions and service need following mild and moderate head injury: The Oxford Head Injury Service. *Clin Rehab, 11,* 13–27.

Klonoff PS, Lage GA (1995). Suicide in patients with traumatic brain injury: Risk and prevention. *J Head Trauma Rehab, 10,* 16–24.

Klonoff PS, Snow WG, Costa LD (1986). Quality of life in patients 2 to 4 years after closed head injury. *Neurosurgery, 19,* 735–743.

Koller WC, Wong GF, Lang A. (1989). Post-traumatic movement disorders: A review. *Mov Disord, 4,* 20–36.

Kraus JF, McArthur DL (1996). Epidemiological aspects of brain injury. *Neurol Clin, 14,* 435–448.

Kreuter M, Dahllof A-G, Gudjonsson G, Sullivan M, Siosteen A (1998). Sexual adjustment and its predictors after traumatic brain injury. *Brain Injury, 5,* 349–368.

Kreutzer JS, Zasler ND (1989). Psychosexual consequences of traumatic brain injury: Methodology and preliminary findings. *Brain Injury, 3,* 177–186.

Kreutzer JS, Wehman P, Morton MV, Stonnington HH (1988). Supported employment and compensatory strategies for enhancing vocational outcome following traumatic brain injury. *Brain Injury, 2,* 205–223.

LaChapelle DL, Finlayson MAJ (1998). An evaluation of subjective and objective measures of fatigue in patients with brain injury and healthy controls. *Brain Injury, 12,* 649–659.

Layton BS, Wardi-Zonna K (1995). Post traumatic stress disorder with neurogenic amnesia for the traumatic event. *The Clin Neuropsychol, 9,* 2–10.

Lazarus C, Logemann JA (1987). Swallowing disorders in closed head trauma patients. *Arch Phys Med Rehab, 68,* 79–84.

Leavitt SS, Beyer RD, Johnston TL (1972). Monitoring the recovery process *Ind Med, 41,* 25–30.

Levin HS, Mattis S, Ruff RM et al. (1987a). The Neurobehavioural Rating Scale: Assessment of the behavioural sequelae of head injury by the clinician. *J Neurol Neurosurg Psychiatry, 50,* 183–193.

Levin HS, Mattis S, Ruff RM, Eisenberg HM, Marshall LF, Tabaddor K, High WM, Frankowski RR (1987b). Neurobehavioural outcome after minor head injury: A three-centre study. *J Neurosurg, 66,* 234–243.

Levin HS, Williams DH, Eisenberg HM (1992). Serial MRI and neurobehavioural findings after mild to moderate closed head injury. *J Neurol Neurosurg Psychiatry, 55,* 255–262.

Levine AM (1988). Buspirone and agitation in head injury. *Brain Injury, 2,* 165–167.

Lewin W (1968). Rehabilitation after head injury. *Br Med J, 1,* 465–470.

Lewin J, Sumners D (1992). Successful treatment of episodic dyscontrol with carbamazepine. *Br J Psychiatry, 161,* 261–262.

Le Winn EB, Dimanescu MD (1978). Environmental deprivation and enrichment in coma. *Lancet, ii,* 156–157.

Lipper S, Tuchman MM (1976). Treatment of chronic post-traumatic organic brain syndrome with dextroamphetamine; first reported case. *J Nerve Ment Dis, 162,* 366–371.

Lishman, A (1998). *Organic psychiatry.* Blackwell, London.

Lloyd LF, Cuvo AJ (1994). Maintenance and generalisation of behaviours after treatment of persons with traumatic brain injury. *Brain Injury, 8,* 529–540.

MacFlynn G, Montgomery EA, Fenton GW et al. (1984). Measurement of reaction time after minor head injury. *J Neurol Neurosurg Psychiatry, 47,* 1326–1331.

Mackay LE, Bernstein BA, Chapman PE et al. (1992). Early intervention in severe head injury: Long term benefits of a formalised programme. *Arch Phys Med Rehab, 73,* 635–641.

Mahoney FI, Barthel DW (1965). Functional assessment. The Barthel index. *Maryland Med J, 14,* 61–65.

Malec JF, Smigielski JS, DePompolo RW, Thompson JM (1993). Outcome evaluation and prediction in a comprehensive-integrated post-acute outpatient brain injury rehabilitation programme. *Brain Injury, 7,* 15–29.

Malec JF, Buttington ALH, Moessner AM, Thompson JM (1995). Maximising vocational outcome after brain injury: Integration of medical and vocational hospital-based services. *Mayo Clin Proc, 70,* 1165–1171.

Manchester D, Hodgkinson A, Casey T (1997). Prolonged severe behavioural disturbance following traumatic brain injury: What can be done? *Brain Injury, 11,* 605–617.

Marsh NV, Smith MD (1995). Post-concussion syndrome and the coping hypothesis. *Brain Injury, 9,* 553–562.

Marshall LF, Gautille T, Klauber MR, Eisenberg HM, Jane JA, Luerssen TG, Marmarou A, Foulkes MA (1991). The outcome of severe head injury. *J Neurosurg, 75* (Suppl.), S28–S36.

Marshall M (1996). Case management: A dubious practice. *Br Med J, 312,* 523–524.

Matthews WB (1972). Footballers' migraine. *Br Med J, 2,* 326–327.

Max JE, Richards L, Hamdon-Allen G (1995). Case study: Antimanic effectiveness of dextro-amphetamine in a brain-injured adolescent. *J Am Acad Child Adolesc Psychiatry, 34,* 472–276.

McCaffrey RJ, Fairbank JA (1985). Behavioural assessment and treatment of accident-related post-traumatic stress disorder: Two case studies. *Behav Ther, 16,* 406–416.

McCorquodale Report (1965). London, HMSO, Cmd. 1867.

McDowell S, Whyte J, D'Esposito M (1998). Differential effect of a dopaminergic agonist on prefrontal function in traumatic brain injury patients. *Brain, 121,* 1155–1164.

McGrath J (1997). Cognitive impairment associated with post traumatic stress disorder and minor head injury: A case report. *Neuropsychol Rehab, 7,* 231–239.

McKeganey N, Hunter D (1986). 'Only connect': Tightrope walking and joint working in the care of the elderly. *Policy and Politics, 14,* 335–360.

McKeon J, McGuffin P, Robinson P (1984). Excessive compulsive neurosis following head injury. A report of four cases. *Br J Psychiatry, 144,* 190–192.

McKinlay WW, Brooks DN (1984). Methodological problems in assessing psychosocial recovery following severe head injury. *J Clin Neuropsychol, 6,* 87–99.

McMillan TM (1991). Post-traumatic stress disorder and severe head injury. *Br J Psychiatry, 159,* 431–433.

McMillan, TM (1996). Post traumatic stress disorder following minor and severe head injury: 10 single cases. *Brain Injury, 10,* 749–758.

McMillan TM (1997a). Neuropsychological assessment after extremely severe head injury in a case of life or death. *Brain Injury, 11,* 483–490.

McMillan TM (1997b). Minor head injury. *Curr Opin Neurol, 10,* 479–483.

McMillan TM, Glucksman EE (1987). The neuropsychology of moderate head injury. *J Neurol Neurosurg Psychiatry, 5,* 393–397.

McMillan TM, Greenwood RJ (1993). Models of rehabilitation programmes for the brain injured adult II: Model services and suggestions for change in the UK. *Clin Rehab, 7,* 346–355.

McMillan TM, Herbert CM (1999). Neuropsychological assessment of a potential euthanasia case: A five year follow-up. *Brain Injury, 14,* 197–204.

McMillan TM, Greenwood RJ, Morris JR, Brooks DN, Murphy L, Dunn G (1988). An introduction to the concept of head injury case management with respect to the need for service provision. *Clin Rehab, 2,* 319–322.

McMillan TM, Papadopoulos H, Cornall C, Greenwood RJ (1990). Modification of severe behaviour problems following herpes simplex encephalitis. *Brain Injury, 4,* 399–406.

McMillan TM, Jongen ELMM, Greenwood RJ (1996). Assessment of post-traumatic amnesia after severe closed head injury: Retrospective or prospective? *J Neurol Neurosurg Psychiatry, 60,* 422–427.

McMordie W, Barker SL, Paolo TM (1990). Return to work (RTW) after head injury. *Brain Injury, 4,* 57–69.

McNeil JE, Greenwood R (1996). Can PTSD occur with amnesia for the precipitating event? *Cog Neuropsychiatry, 1,* 239–246.

Medical Disability Society (1988). *Report of a working party on the management of traumatic brain injury*. London, The Development Trust for the Young Disabled.

Michals ML, Crismon ML, Roberts S, Childs A (1993). Clozapine response and adverse effects in nine brain-injured patients. *J Clin Psychopharmacol, 13*, 198–203.

Miller JD (1991). Changing patterns in acute management of head injury. *J Neurol Sci, 103*, S33–S37.

Miller JD, Jones PA (1985). The work of a regional head injury service. *Lancet, 1*, 1141–1144.

Minderhoud JH, Braakman R (1985). Het vegeterende bestaan. *Ned Tijdschr Geneeskd, 129*, 2385–2388.

Minderhoud JM, Boelens M, Huizenga J, Saan RJ (1980). Treatment of minor head injuries. *Clin Neurol Neurosurg, 82*,127–140.

Mitchell S, Bradley VA, Welch JL, Britton PG (1990). Coma arousal procedure: A therapeutic intervention in the treatment of head injury. *Brain Injury, 4*, 273–279.

Mittenberg W, Burton B (1994). A survey of treatments for post concussion syndrome. *Brain Injury, 8*, 429–437.

Mooney GF, Haas LJ (1993). Effect of methylphenidate on brain injury-related anger. *Arch Phys Med Rehab, 74*, 153–160.

Mueller J, Hopp M (1983). A demonstration of the cost-benefits of case management service for discharged mental patients. *Psychiatric Quart, 55*, 17–24.

Muller U, von Cramon DY (1994). The therapeutic potential of bromocriptine in neuropsychological rehabilitation of patients with acquired brain damage. *Prog Neuro-Psychopharmacol Biol Psychiatry, 18*, 1103–1120.

Multi-Society Task Force on PVS (1994). Medical aspects of the persistent vegetative state. *N Eng J Med, 330*, 1499–1508.

Murphy LD, McMillan TM, Greenwood RJ, Brooks DN, Morris JR, Dunn G (1989). Services for severely head injured patients in North London and environs. *Brain Injury, 4*, 95–100.

Mysiw WJ, Jackson RD, Corrigan JD (1988). Amitriptyline for post-traumatic agitation. *Am J Phys Med Rehab, 67*, 29–33.

National Center for Health Statistics (1997). *Data file documentation, National Hospital discharge survey, 1980–1995*. Rockville, MD, National Center for Health Statistics, Center for Disease Control and Prevention.

Newcombe F, Rabbitt P, Briggs M (1994). Minor head injury: Pathophysiological or iatrogenic sequelae? *J Neurol Neurosurg Psychiatry, 57*, 709–716.

Nickels JL, Schneider WN, Dombovy ML, Wong TM (1994). Clinical use of amantadine in brain injury rehabilitation. *Brain Injury, 8*, 709–718.

NIH Consensus Development Conference on Rehabilitation of Persons with Traumatic Brain Injury. *Panel Report (draft)*, August 1998.

Obeso JA, Narbona J (1983). Post-traumatic tremor and myoclonic jerking. *J Neurol. Neurosurg Psychiatry, 46*, 788.

Obeso JA, Artieda J, Rothwell JC, Day B, Thompson P, Marsden CD (1989). The treatment of severe action myoclonus. *Brain, 112*, 765–777.

Oddy M, Coughlan T, Tyerman A, Jenkins D (1985). Social adjustment after closed head injury: A further follow-up seven years after injury. *J Neurol Neurosurg Psychiatry, 48*, 564–568.

Oddy M, Bonham E, McMillan TM et al. (1990). A comprehensive service for the rehabilitation and long term care of head injury survivors. *Clin Rehab, 3*, 253–259.

Ohry A, Rattock J, Solomon Z (1996). Post traumatic stress disorder in brain injury patients. *Brain Injury, 10*, 687–695.

Olver JH, Ponsford JL, Curran CA (1996). Outcome following traumatic brain injury: A comparison between 2 and 5 years after injury. *Brain Injury, 10*, 841–848.

Oppenheimer DR (1968). Microscopic lesions in the brain following head injury. *J Neurol Neurosurg Psychiatry, 31*, 299–306.

Packard RC, Ham LP (1994). Post-traumatic headache. *J Neuropsychiatr Clin Neurosci, 6*, 229–236.

Paniak C, Toller-Lobe G, Durand A, Nagy J (1998). A randomised trial of two treatments for mild traumatic brain injury. *Brain Injury, 12*, 1011–1023.

Parker RS (1996). The spectrum of emotional distress and personality changes after minor head injury incurred in a motor vehicle accident. *Brain Injury, 10*, 287–302.

Pavesi G, Brianti R, Medici D, Mammi P (1998). Botulinum toxin type-A in the treatment of upper limb spasticity among patients with traumatic brain injury. *J Neurol Neurosurg Psychiatry, 64*, 419–420.

Pazzaglia P, Frank G, Frank F, Gaist G (1975). Clinical course and prognosis of acute post-traumatic coma. *J Neurol Neurosurg Psychiatry, 38*, 149–154.

Pearcy Report (1956). *Report of the Committee of Enquiry on the rehabilitation training and resettlement of disabled persons*. London, HMSO, Cmd. 9883.

Pettigrew LC, Jankovic J (1985). Hemidystonia: A report of 22 patients and a review of the literature. *J Neurol Neurosurg Psychiatry, 48*, 650–657.

Port MWM, de Bruin A, de Witte L, Schrijver A (1996). The SIP-68: A measure of health related functional status in rehabilitation medicine. *Arch Phys Med Rehab, 77*, 440–445.

Povlishock JT, Becker DT, Cheng CLY et al. (1983). Axonal change in minor head injury. *J Neuropathol Clin Neurol, 42*, 225–242.

Powell JH, Al-Adawi S, Greenwood RJ (1996). Motivational deficits after brain injury: Effects of bromocriptine on 11 patients. *J Neurol Neurosurg Psychiatry, 60*, 416–421.

Powell JH, Beckers K, Greenwood RJ (1998). Measuring progress and outcome in community rehabilitation after brain injury with a new assessment instrument – the BICRO-39 Scales. *Arch Phys Med Rehab, 79*, 1213–1225.

Prigatano GP (1986). Psychotherapy after brain injury. In: GP Prigatano (Ed.), *Neuropsychological rehabilitation after brain injury*. Johns Hopkins University Press, Baltimore.

Prigatano GP, Fordyce DJ (1986). *The neuro-psychological rehabilitation program at Presbyterian Hospital, Oklahoma City*. Johns Hopkins University Press, Baltimore.

Prigatano GP, Fordyce DJ, Zeiner HK et al. (1984). Neuropsychological rehabilitation after closed head injury in young adults. *J Neurol Neurosurg Psychiatry, 47*, 505–513.

Rader MA, Alston JB, Ellis DW (1989). Sensory stimulation of brain injury patients. *Brain Injury, 3*, 141–147.

Rao N, Woolsten DC (1985). Agitation in closed head injury haloperidol effects on rehabilitation outcome. *Arch Phys Med Rehab, 66*, 30–34.

Rappaport M, Hall KM, Hopkins K et al. (1982). Disability rating scale for severe head trauma: Coma to community. *Am Phys Med Rehab, 63*, 118–123.

Rappaport M, Herrero-Back C, Rappaport ML et al. (1989). Head injury outcome up to 10 years later. *Arch Phys Med Rehab, 70*, 885–892.

Ratey JJ, Leveroni CL, Miller AC et al. (1992). Low dose buspirone to treat agitation and maladaptive behaviour in brain-injured patients: Two case reports. *J Clin Psychopharmacol, 12*, 362–364.

Reeder KP, Rosenthal M, Lichtenberg P, Wood D (1996). Impact of age on functional outcome following traumatic brain injury. *J Head Trauma Rehab, 11*, 22–31.

Relander M, Troupp H, Bjorkesten G (1972). Controlled trial of treatment for cerebral concussion. *Br Med J, 4*, 777–779.

Richardson JC, Howes JL, Celinski MJ, Allman RG (1987). Kinesigenic choreoathetosis due to brain injury. *Can J Neurol Sci, 14*, 626–628.

Rimel RW, Giordiani B, Barth JT et al. (1981). Disability caused by minor head injury. *Neurosurgery, 9*, 221–228.

Roberts AH (1979). *Severe accidental head injury*. London, MacMillan Publishing Group.

Robertson III (1994). Methodology in neuropsychological rehabilitation research. *Neuropsychol Rehab, 4*, 1–6.

Robertson IH, North N, Geggie C (1992). Spatiomotor cueing in spatial neglect; three single case studies of its therapeutic effectiveness. *J Neurol Neurosurg Psychiatry, 55*, 799–805.

Robertson IH, Hogg K, McMillan TM (1998). Rehabilitation of unilateral neglect. *Neuropsychol Rehab, 8*, 19–29.

Ross ED, Stewart RM (1981). Akinetic mutism from hypothalmic damage: Successful treatment with dopamine agonists. *Neurology, 31*, 1435–1439.

Rowland TR, Mysiw WJ, Bogner JA (1992). Trazodone for post-traumatic agitation (abstract). *Arch Phys Med Rehab, 73*, 963.

Royal College of Physicians (1986). Physical disability in 1986 and beyond. *J Roy Col Phys Lond, 20*, 30–37.

Royal College of Psychiatrists (1991). Services for brain injured adults. *Psychiatric Bull, 15*, 513–518.

Ruff RM, Niemann H (1990). Cognitive rehabilitation versus day treatment in head-injured adults: Is there an impact on emotional and psychosocial adjustment? *Brain Injury, 4*, 339–347.

Ruff RM, Crouch JA, Troster AI et al. (1994). Selected cases of poor outcome following minor brain trauma: Comparing neuropsychological and positron emission tomography assessment. *Brain Injury, 8*, 297–308.

Ruff RM, Camenzuli L, Mueller J (1996). Miserable minority: Emotional risk factors that influence the outcome of a mild traumatic brain injury. *Brain Injury, 10*, 551–565.

Rusk HA, Loman EW, Block JM (1966). Rehabilitation of the patient with head injury. *Clinic Neurosurg, 12*, 312–323.

Rusk HA, Block JM, Loman EW (1969). Rehabilitation following traumatic brain damage. *Med Clin N Am, 53*, 677–684.

Russell WR (1932). Cerebral involvement in head injury: A study based on the examination of 200 cases. *Brain, 55*, 549–603.

Russell WR, Smith A (1964). Post-traumatic amnesia in closed head injury. *Arch Neurol, 5*, 4–29.

Rutherford WH, Merrett JD, MacDonald JR (1977). Sequelae of concussion caused by minor head injuries. *Lancet, i*, 104.

Rutherford WH, Merrett JD, MacDonald JR (1979). Symptoms at one year following concussion from minor head injuries. *Lancet, i*, 225.

Sahgal V, Heinemann A (1989). Recovery of function during inpatient rehabilitation for moderate traumatic brain injury. *Scand J Rehabil Med, 21*, 71–79.

Salazar AM, Jabbari B, Vance SC et al. (1985). Epilepsy after penetrating head injury. I. Clinical correlates: A report of the Vietnam Head Injury Study. *Neurology, 35*, 1406–1414.

Samie MR, Selhorst JB, Koller WC (1990). Post-traumatic midbrain tremors. *Neurology, 40*, 62–66.

Sandel ME, Williams KS, Dellapietra L, Derogatis LR (1996). Sexual functioning following traumatic brain injury. *Brain Injury, 10*, 719–728.

Saran AS (1985). Depression after minor closed head injury: Role of dexamethasone suppression test and antidepressants. *J Clin Psychiatry, 46*, 335–338.

Sarkstein SE, Maybury HS, Berthier ML et al. (1990). Mania after brain injury. *Ann Neurol, 27*, 652–659.

Sazbon L, Fuchs C, Costeff H (1991). Prognosis for recovery from prolonged post-traumatic unawareness: Logistic analysis. *J Neurol Neurosurg Psychiatry, 54*, 149–152.

Sazbon L, Groswasser Z (1991). Time related sequelae of TBI in patients with prolonged post-comatose unawareness (PC-U) state. *Brain Injury, 5*, 3–8.

Sbordone RJ, Liter JC (1995). Mild traumatic brain injury does not produce post-traumatic stress disorder. *Brain Injury, 9*, 405–412.

Scheffler LR, Ito VY, Philip PA (1994). Shunting in post-traumatic hydrocephalus: Demonstration of neurophysiologic improvement. *Arch Phys Med Rehab, 75*, 338–341.

Scherzer BP (1986). Rehabilitation following a severe head trauma: Results of a three year program. *Arch Phys Med Rehab, 67*, 366–374.

Schiffer RB, Herndon RM, Rudick RA (1985). Treatment of pathological laughing and weeping with amitriptyline. *N Engl J Med, 312*, 1480–1482.

Schrader H, Obelieniene D, Bovim G et al. (1996). Natural evolution of late whiplash syndrome outside the medicolegal context. *Lancet, 347*, 1207–1211.

Schwartz S (1974). Effect of neocortical lesions and early environmental factors on adult rat behaviour. *J Comp Physiol Psychol, 57*, 72–77.

Sechi GP, Zuddas M, Piredda M et al. (1989). Treatment of cerebellar tremors with carbamazepine: A controlled trial with long-term follow-up. *Neurology, 39*, 1113–1115.

Semlyen JK, Hurrell E, Carter S, Barnes MP (1996). The Newcastle Independence Assessment Form (Research): Development of an alternative functional measure. *J Neurol Rehab, 10*, 251–257.

Semlyen JK, Summers SJ, Barnes MP (1997). The predictive validity of the Newcastle Independence Assessment Form – Research (NIAF-R): Further development of an alternative functional measure. *J Neurol Rehab, 11*, 213–218.

Semlyen JK, Summers SJ, Barnes MP (1998). Traumatic brain injury: Efficacy of multidisciplinary rehabilitation. *Arch Phys Med Rehab, 79*, 678–683.

Shapiro LB (1939). Schizophrenia-like psychosis following head injury. *Illinois Med J, 76*, 2230–2254.

Sharp (1974). *Mobility of physically disabled people*. London, HMSO.

Shaw R (1986). Persistant vegetative state: Principles and techniques for seating and positioning. *J Head Trauma Rehab, 1*, 31–37.

SHHD. Scottish Health Services Council (1972). *Medical rehabilitation: A pattern for the future*. Scottish Home and Health Department, HMSO, Edinburgh.

Signorini DF, Andrews PJD, Jones PA et al. (1999). Predicting survival using simple clinical variables: A case study in traumatic brain injury. *J Neurol Neurosurg Psychiatry, 66*, 20–25.

Silver JM, Rattock J, Anderson K (1997). Post-traumatic stress disorder and brain injury. *Neurocase, 3*, 151–157.

Sisson R (1990). Effects of auditory stimulation on comatose patients with head injury. *Heart and Lung, 19*, 373–378.

Sloan R, Brown K, Pentland B (1992). Fluoxetine as a treatment for emotional lability after brain injury. *Brain Injury, 6*, 315–319.

Speech TJ, Rao SM, Osmon DC, Sperry LT (1993). A double-blind controlled study of methylphenidate treatment in closed head injury. *Brain Injury, 7*, 333–338.

Spettell CM, Ellis DW, Ross SE et al. (1991). Time of rehabilitation admission and severity of trauma: Effect on brain injury outcome. *Arch Phys Med Rehab, 72*, 320–325.

Spivack G, Spettell CM, Ellis DW, Ross SE (1992). Effects of intensity of treatment and length of stay on rehabilitation outcomes. *Brain Injury, 6*, 419–434.

Stanislav SW, Fabre T, Crismon ML, Childs A (1994). Busprione's efficacy in organic-induced aggression. *J Clin Psychopharmacol, 14*, 126–130.

Stapleton MB (1986). Maryland rehabilitation centre closed head injury study: A retrospective survey. *Cognit Rehab, 4*, 34–42.

Steadman JH, Graham JG (1970). Rehabilitation of the brain injured. *Proc Roy Soc Med, 63*, 23.

Stern JM, Sazbon L, Becker E, Costeff H (1988). Severe behavioural disturbance in families of patients with prolonged coma. *Brain Injury, 2*, 259–262.

Stern NJ, Stern B (1990). Psychotherapy in cases of brain damage. *Brain Injury, 4*, 297–304.

Stewart JT (1985). Carbamazepine treatment of a patient with Kluver–Bucy syndrome. *J Clin Psychiatry, 46*, 496–497.

Strauss DJ, Schavell ERM, Anderson TW (1998). Long term survival of children and adolescents after traumatic brain injury. *Arch Phys Med Rehab, 79*, 1095–1100.

Stuck AE, Aronow HU, Steiner A et al. (1995). A trial of annual in-home comprehensive geriatric assessments for elderly people living in the community. *N Engl J Med, 333*, 1184–1189.

Su-Ching L, Zasler ND, Kreutzer JS (1994). Male pituitary–gonadal dysfunction following severe traumatic brain injury. *Brain Injury, 8*, 571–577.

Sutton RL, Weaver MS, Feeney DM (1987). Drug-induced modifications of behavioural recovery following cortical trauma. *J Head Trauma Rehab, 2*, 50–58.

Taylor AE, Cox CA, Mailis A (1996). Persistent neuropsychological deficits following whiplash: Evidence for chronic mild traumatic brain injury? *Arch Phys Med Rehab, 77*, 529–535.

Teasdale GM, Nichol J, Fiddes H (1997a). Apolipoprotein E and outcome of head injury. *N Neurol Neurosurg Psychiatry, 63*, 123–131.

Teasdale TW, Christensen A-L, Pinner EM (1993). Psychosocial rehabilitation of cranial trauma and stroke patients. *Brain Injury, 7*, 535–542.

Teasdale TW, Skovdahl-Hansen H, Gade A, Christensen A-L (1997b). Neuropsychological test scores before and after brain injury rehabilitation in relation to employment. *Neuropsychol Rehab, 7*, 23–42.

Temkin NR, Dikmen SS, Wilensky AJ et al. (1990). A randomised, double-blind study of phenytoin for the prevention of post-traumatic seizures. *N Engl J Med, 323*, 497–502.

Temkin NR, Dikmen SS, Anderson G et al. (1997). Valproate for preventing late post-traumatic seizures (abstract). *Epilepsia, 38* (Suppl. 8), 102–103.

Thadani VM, Rimm DL, UrqHuart L et al. (1991). Locked in syndrome for 27 years following a viral illness. *Neurology, 41*, 222–223.

Thomsen IV (1987). Late psychosocial outcome in severe blunt head trauma: A review. *Brain Injury, 1*, 1131–1143.

Thurman DL, Jeppson L, Burnett CL et al. (1996). Surveillance of traumatic brain injuries in Utah. *West J Med, 165*, 192–196.

Tinklenberg JR, Taylor JL (1984). Assessments of drug effects on human memory functions. In: LR Squire, N Butters (Eds.), *Neuropsychology of memory*. New York, Guilford Press, pp. 213–223.

Tomlinson Report (1943). *Report of the Inter-departmental Committee on the Rehabilitation and Resettlement of Disabled Persons*. London, HMSO, Cmd. 64115.

Tunbridge Report (1972). *Rehabilitation report of a sub-committee of the standing medical advisory committee*. London, HMSO.

Tyler GS, McNeely HE, Dick ML (1980). Treatment of post-traumatic headache with amitriptyline. *Headache, 20*, 213–216.

Tzidkiahu T, Sazbon L, Solzi P (1994). Characteristic reactions of post-coma unawareness patients in the process of adjusting to loss. *Brain Injury, 8*, 159–165.

Udaka F, Yamao S, Nagata H et al. (1984). Pathologic laughing and crying treated with levodopa. *Arch Neurol, 41*, 1095–1096.

Van Reekum R, Bayley M, Garner S et al. (1995). N of 1 study: Amantadine for the amotivational syndrome in a patient with traumatic brain injury. *Brain Injury, 9*, 49–53.

Van Wimersam, Griedamus TJB, Jooles J, De Wied D (1985). Hypothalamic neuropeptides and memory. *Acta Neurochirurg, 75*, 99–105.

Van Woerkom TC, Teelken AW, Minderhond JM (1977). Difference in neurotransmitter metabolism in frontotemporal lobe contusion and diffuse cerebral contusion. *Lancet, 1*, 812–813.

Van Zomeren AH, Van Den Burg W (1985). Residual complaints of patients two years after severe head injury. *J Neurol Neurosurg Psychiatry, 48*, 21–28.

Vollmer DG, Torner JC, Jane JA et al. (1991). Age and outcome following traumatic coma: Why do older patients fare worse? *J Neurosurg, 75* (Suppl.), S37–S49.

Von Korff M, Gruman J, Schaefer J et al. (1997). Collaborative management of chronic illness. *Ann Intern Med, 127*, 1097–1102.

Wade D, Crawford S, Wenden FJ et al. (1997). Does routine follow up after head injury help? A randomised control trial. *J Neurol Neurosurg Psychiatry, 62*, 478–484.

Wade DT, King NS, Wenden FJ et al. (1998). Routine follow-up after head injury: A second randomised controlled trial. *J Neurol Neurosurg Psychiatry, 65*, 177–183.

Walker AE, Leuchs HK, Lechtape-Gruter H et al. (1971). Life expectancy of head injured men with and without epilepsy. *Arch Neurol, 24*, 95–100.

Walker-Batson B, Smith P, Curtis S (1995). Amphetamine paired with physical therapy accelerates motor recovery after stroke. Further evidence. *Stroke, 26*, 2254–2259.

Wall JR, Rosenthal M, Niemczura JG (1998). Community based retraining after acquired brain injury. *Brain Injury, 12*, 215–224.

Ware J, Sherbourne C (1992). The MOS36-item short-form health survey (SF-36). Conceptual framework and item selection. *Med Care, 30*, 473–483.

Wehman P, Kreutzer J, Wood W et al. (1989a). Helping traumatically brain injured patients return to work with supported employment: Three case studies. *Arch Phys Med Rehab, 70*, 109–113.

Wehman P, Kreutzer J, West M et al. (1989b). Employment outcome of persons following traumatic brain injury: Pre-injury, post-injury and supported employment. *Brain Injury, 3*, 397–412.

Wehman P, West M, Fry R et al. (1989c). Effect of supported employment on the vocational outcomes of persons with traumatic brain injury. *J Appl Behav Anal, 22*, 395–405.

Wehman P, Kreutzer JS, West MD et al. (1990). Return to work for persons with traumatic brain injury: A supported employment approach. *Arch Phys Med Rehab, 71*, 1047–1052.

Whetsell LA, Patterson CM, Young DH, Schiller WR (1989). Preinjury psycho-pathology in trauma patients. *J Trauma, 29*, 1158–1162.

Whiteneck GG, Charlifue SW, Gerhart KA, Overholser LA, Richardson GN (1992). Quantifying handicap: A new measure of long-term rehabilitation outcome. *Arch Phys Med Rehab, 73*, 519–526.

Whitlock JA (1992). Functional outcome of low-level traumatically brain injured admitted to an acute rehabilitation programme. *Brain Injury, 6*, 447–459.

Will BE, Rosenzweig MR (1976). Effects del'environment sur la recuperation functionelle apres lesions cerebrates chezles rats adultes. *Biol Behav, 1*, 5–16.

Willer B, Offenbacher KJ, Coad ML (1994). The community integration questionnaire. A comparative examination. *Am J Phs Med Rehab, 73*, 103–111.

Wilson B (1989a) Remediation of apraxia following an anaesthetic accident. In: J West, P Spinks (Eds.), *Case studies in clinical psychology*. London, John Wright and Son, pp. 178–183.

Wilson B (1989b). *Models of cognitive rehabilitation*. London, Chapman & Hall, pp. 17–141.

Wilson SLW, McMillan TM (1993). A review of the evidence for the effectiveness of sensory stimulation treatment for coma and vegetative states. *Neuropsychol Rehab, 3*, 149–160.

Wilson SL, Powell GE, Elliott K et al. (1993). Evaluation of sensory stimulation as a treatment for prolonged coma – seven single case studies. *Neuropsychol Rehab, 3*, 191–202.

Wilson SL, Powell GE, Elliott K, Thwaites H (1991). Sensory stimulation in prolonged coma; four single cases. *Brain Injury, 5*, 393–400.

Wilson SL, Cranny S, Andrews K (1992). The efficacy of music for stimulation in prolonged coma – four single case experiments. *Clin Rehab, 6*, 181–187.

Wilson SL, Powell GE, Brock D, Thwaites H (1996). Behavioural differences between patients who emerged from vegetative state and those who did not. *Brain Injury, 10*, 509–516.

Wilson DJ, Childers MK, Cooke DL, Smith BK (1997). Kinematic changes following botulinum toxin injection after traumatic brain injury. *Brain Injury, 11*, 157–167.

Wise RA (1980). The dopamine synapse and the notion of 'pleasure centres' in the brain. *Trends Neurosci, 3*, 91–95.

Wong JL, Regennitter RP, Barrios F (1994). Base rate and simulated symptoms of mild head injury among normals. *Arch Clin Neuropsychol, 9*, 411–426.

Wood RLl (1987). *Brain injury rehabilitation: A neurobehavioural approach*. London, Croom Helm.

Wood RLl (1991). Critical analysis of the concept of sensory stimulation for patients in vegetative states. *Brain Injury, 5*, 401–410.

Wood RLl, Winkowski T, Miller J (1993). Sensory regulation as a method to promote recovery in patients with altered states of conciousness. *Neuropsychological Rehabilitation, 3*, 177–190.

World Health Organization (1997). *ICIDH-2: International classification of Impairments, Activities, and Participation. A manual of disablement and functioning. Beta-1 draft for field trials*. Geneva, World Health Organization.

Wright JC, Telford R (1996). Psychological problems following minor head injury: A prospective study. *Br J Clin Psychol, 35*, 399–412.

Wright MT, Cummings JL, Mendez MF, Foti DJ (1997). Bipolar syndromes following brain trauma. *Neurocase, 3*, 111–118.

Wrightson P (1989). Management of disability and rehabilitation services after mild head injury. In: HS Levin, HM Eisenberg, AL Benton (Eds.), *Mild head injury*. New York: Oxford University Press, pp. 245–256.

Young B, Rapp RP, Norton JA et al. (1983). Failure of prophylactically administered phenytoin to prevent late post traumatic seizures. *J Neurosurg, 58*, 236–241.

Young RR (1989). Treatment of spastic paresis. *N Engl J Med, 320*, 1553–1555.

Youngson HA, Alderman N (1994). Fear of incontinence and its effects on a community based rehabilitation programme after severe brain injury. *Brain Injury, 8*, 23–36.

Yudofsky S, Williams D, Gorman J (1981). Propranolol in the treatment of rage and violent behaviour in patients with chronic brain syndromes. *Am J Psychiatry, 138*, 218–220.

Zablotney C (1987). Using neuromuscular electrical stimulation to facilitate limb control in the head injured patient. *J Head Trauma Rehab, 2*, 28–33.

Zafonte RD, Hammond FM, Mann NR et al. (1996). Relationship between Glasgow Coma Scale and functional outcome. *Am J Phys Med Rehab, 75*, 364–369.

Zafonte RD, Watanabe T, Mann NR (1998). Amantadine: A potential treatment for the minimally conscious state. *Brain Injury, 12*, 617–621.

Zencius A, Wesolowiski MD, Burke WH, Hough S (1990). Managing hypersexual disorders in brain injured clients. *Brain Injury, 4*, 175–181.

36. Stroke rehabilitation: The evidence

Derick T. Wade

INTRODUCTION

Successful stroke rehabilitation depends upon skill and knowledge. The skill is in undertaking the process of rehabilitation, and other parts of this book cover these matters. The knowledge required includes the evidence to guide the process of rehabilitation, and this knowledge covers several areas: prognosis, best screening assessments, effective interventions, local resources, etc.

This chapter on stroke rehabilitation focuses on evidence relating to the organisation of stroke rehabilitation and to specific interventions. It also highlights areas of likely change in emphasis over the next few years. The chapter starts with general issues, and then moves on to specific issues. It does so in relation to the stages of an individual patient's rehabilitation career. It is based on work undertaken in the development of the British National Clinical Guidelines for Stroke Management, which has been published by the Royal College of Physicians of London.

ORGANISATION—SPECIALIST UNIT WITH DISCHARGE PLANNING PROTOCOLS

All patients presenting with acute stroke should be managed within a specialist stroke service. The evidence for this is overwhelming (Table 36.1). It is worth stressing that the evidence suggests that the substantial benefits to patients: (1) do not require additional resources; and (2) last for many years. Moreover, the benefits apply to all patients, and there is no justification for denying the service to any subgroup of patients.

The characteristics of a specialist unit are that the staff:

- have expertise and experience in managing patients with stroke
- work together as a coordinated team
- undergo regular education and training.

It also seems probable that stroke units will use more standardised protocols, including undertaking a structured process of discharge planning. Both these features are probably associated

Table 36.1. Studies on organisation of stroke care: specialised services

Source	Design and sample	Intervention(s)	Conclusions
Stroke Unit Trialists' Collaboration, 1997	M/A; $n = 19$; RCTs, $n = 2060$ patients	Stroke unit care or general medical ward care	Stroke unit care reduces mortality and morbidity with no increase in length of stay
Kalra, 1994	RCT; $n = 141$; middle-band stroke patients	Stroke unit or general medical ward	Stroke unit patients recovered faster, and more, and had shorter LoS despite less total therapy time
Laursen et al., 1995	RCT; $n = 65$; acute stroke patients	Stroke unit or general ward	Stroke unit discharged fewer to nursing home
Logan et al., 1997	RCT; $n = 111$; stroke patients after discharge	Enhanced domiciliary OT; or normal Social Services OT service	Enhanced service reduced carer distress and improved patient function
Indredavik et al., 1997	RCT; $n = 220$; 5-year follow-up on acute patients	Specialist stroke unit or general medical ward	Stroke unit benefits sustained; less disability, more at home, fewer deaths
Dekker et al., 1998	S/R; $n = 7$; trials, $n = 1133$ patients	Day hospital out-patient rehabilitation or routine care/domiciliary care/nil	No firm conclusions can be drawn
Ronning & Guldvog, 1998a	RCT; $n = 251$; patients 7–14 days post-stroke	Organised specialist in-patient rehabilitation or community rehabilitation	Non-specialist, uncoordinated community rehabilitation associated with more mortality and morbidity
Ronning & Guldvog, 1998b	RCT*; $n = 550$; acute stroke patients admitted	Specialist stroke ward or general medical ward; both short-stay (< 14 days)	Specialist ward was more likely to intervene medically and reduced stroke recurrence
Indredavik et al., 1998	RCT; $n = 87$; 5-year follow-up on acute patients	Specialist stroke unit or general medical ward	Stroke unit associated with more social activities and less emotional distress

LoS, length of stay; M/A, meta-analysis (systematic review); OT, occupational therapy; RCT, randomised controlled trial (* = quasi-random by date of birth); S/R, systematic review (no meta analysis).

with a shorter length of stay and/or less morbidity and readmission (Tables 36.2 and 36.3).

Little more is currently known about the specific features that underlie the success of stroke units. However, until proven otherwise it seems reasonable to assume that the service should be staffed by a range of professions, including psychologists and social workers, and that the service should be based in a hospital with a specific geographic base. The extent to which the service is exclusive to stroke will depend upon local practical considerations, but it is likely that the service will have two

Table 36.2. Studies relating to use of protocols (note: not specific to stroke)

Source	Design and sample	Intervention(s)	Conclusions
Naylor, 1990	RCT	Comprehensive discharge planning protocol for elderly	Fewer readmissions
Lilford et al., 1992	RCT; $n = 2424$ first antenatal visits	Unstructured questionnaire (normal form); structured questionnaire; computer-based questionnaire	Structured questionnaire increased information obtained and increased number of effective actions
Naylor et al., 1994	RCT; $n = 276$ patients aged 70+ years	Comprehensive discharge planning protocol for elderly	Protocol led to shorter admission and fewer readmissions
Bowen & Yaste, 1994	CCT (before/after, and with/without); $n = 386$ acute stroke admissions	Protocol, with critical nursing pathway	Protocol led to lower hospital costs, and possible reduction in length of stay
Duncan et al., 1995	CCT (before/after); $n = 126$ patients; note review	Set-up of acute stroke unit with rehabilitation stroke unit, and protocols	Mortality reduced from 40% to 22%
Vissers et al., 1996	RCT; $n = 8$ doctors and 233 patients	Computer-given protocol for management of fracture, or normal management	Outcome improved by protocol *only if* correct diagnosis made initially
Vallet et al., 1997	RCT; $n = 24$ patients with COAD	Training programme individualised or standardised	Individualised protocol more effective
Kollef et al., 1997	RCT; $n = 357$ patients on mechanical ventilation	Protocol-directed or physician-directed weaning from ventilator	Protocol-direction safe and more efficient (quicker by 20%) (and saved $42,000)

CCT, controlled clinical trial; COAD, chronic obstructive airways disease; RCT, randomised clinical trial.

Table 36.3. Studies on discharge planning (note: not specific to stroke)

Source	Design and sample	Intervention(s)	Conclusions
Campion et al., 1983	CCT; $n = 132$ acute geriatric admissions	Geriatric consultation service in one ward; not in two	Increased use of rehabilitation services three times; no effect on LoS, readmissions or discharge placement
Ebrahim et al., 1987	Obs; $n = 183$ patients at home at 6 months	30% had not seen GP; under half had aids for extant problems	Planning and follow-up may be suboptimal
Kennedy et al., 1987; Neidlinger et al., 1987	RCT; $n = 80$ elderly acute admissions	Special nurse with special discharge protocol; or normal services	Reduced length of stay (2 days out of 10); less readmission. Cost-effectiveness shown
Victor & Vetter, 1988	Obs; $n = 1930$ patients 3 months after being discharged	Questionnaire on discharge planning	Under 50% had any discussion of needs prior to discharge; 40% had less than 24 hours notice but only 25% dissatisfied
Glennon & Smith, 1990	Obs; 46 case conferences, 45 patients, 213 questions	Record of questions asked by patient or family	Questions on discharge planning second most common (16%)
Naylor, 1990	RCT; $n = 40$ elderly patients	Comprehensive discharge planning protocol for elderly implemented by special nurse	Fewer readmissions, initial length of stay unchanged
Mamon et al., 1992	Obs; $n = 919$ discharges	Association between use or not of a single discharge coordinator	With a single person responsible, there are fewer unmet treatment needs at discharge, but care needs still unmet
Evans & Hendricks, 1993	RCT; $n = 835$ "high-risk" admissions	Discharge planning from day 3 of admission	Discharge planning increased discharge home, reduced readmission rate and total hospital stay, but did not affect initial length of stay
Naylor et al., 1994	RCT; $n = 276$ patients aged 70+ years with heart disease (medical) or heart surgery (surgical)	Comprehensive discharge planning protocol for elderly, executed by nurse specialist	Protocol led to shorter admission and fewer readmissions in medical (but not surgical) patients. Was cost-effective
Parfrey et al., 1994	RCT; $n = 1599$ acute patients (2 hospitals)	Questionnaire to identify patients for referral to professions	Shorter length of stay in one hospital; identification of patients needing help possible using questionnaire
Charles et al., 1994	Obs; $n = 4599$ patients seen after discharge	Interview to establish areas of dissatisfaction with hospital care	30–40% had complaints about discharge process; biggest area of dissatisfaction
Landefeld et al., 1995	RCT; $n = 651$ acutely ill hospital admissions aged 70+ years	Routine care, or special unit with: (a) good environment; (b) patient-centred care with protocols; (c) *discharge planning*; (d) specialist medical input	Specialised unit reduced dependence and discharge to nursing home
Wei et al., 1995	Obs; $n = 20,136$ discharged patients aged 65+ years	Relationship between factors documented at discharge and mortality or readmission	Absence of documented discharge planning associated with adverse outcomes after discharge

CCT, controlled clinical trial; LoS, length of stay; Obs, observational study; RCT, randomised clinical trial.

components: one for the relatively old patients, probably dominated by stroke; and one for the relatively young patients, offering specialised disability services to a wide range of neurologically disabled people (e.g. with head injury, multiple sclerosis, etc.).

The responsibility of the rehabilitation specialist is to ensure that every stroke patient is managed by a specialist service at least until the clinical situation is stable, probably at least until 6 months post-stroke. The precise arrangements will vary according to local circumstances, but it is important to ensure that the service provides for the different needs of younger patients.

HOSPITAL, DAY HOSPITAL, OR HOME

In practice, the majority of patients are admitted to hospital and this is probably the only practical way to ensure that all patients are managed by a specialist stroke service. Attempts to reduce the rate of admission have failed (Wade et al., 1985), and there is no good evidence to support acute hospital-at-home management (Shepperd et al., 1998a,b).

Once initial management has stabilised the patient, identifying and treating any treatable causes of the stroke, then early discharge can be considered (Table 36.4). However, it is vital that discharge is to a specialist service, as discharge to non-specialist domiciliary services is associated with a poor outcome (Ronning & Guldvog, 1998a,b). The specific role of day hospital rehabilitation is still uncertain (Table 36.5), but it is one way of offering a specialist service to people at home.

The rehabilitation specialist should ensure that all patients are managed by a specialist team throughout their period of rehabilitation, from the first day, if possible, to at least 6 months if necessary. It is particularly important to ensure that patients discharged needing further rehabilitation: (1) receive it; and (2) receive it from a specialist team and not from non-specialist isolated therapists.

ASSESSMENT

The "diagnosis" of the causes of disability, usually referred to assessment, is the essential first step in rehabilitation. Research into aspects of assessment is limited, but the available evidence (Table 36.6) suggests that assessment should:

- involve several professions
- be linked inextricably with treatment services
- be undertaken using agreed protocols.

Furthermore, it seems likely that early involvement of specialist rehabilitation is more effective.

Future research should hopefully investigate in more detail the most efficient and effective assessment protocols that ensure that problems are identified and analysed correctly.

GOAL PLANNING

The setting of goals is arguably the most important specific feature of specialist rehabilitation services. There has been little research into this aspect of rehabilitation specific to stroke, but the available evidence (Wade, 1998; Table 36.7) would suggest that:

- setting goals with the patient increases behavioural change
- goals should be set in both the short- and long-term
- goals set should be supported by appropriate specific interventions

Table 36.4. Organisation of care: early discharge to community services

Source	Design and sample	Intervention(s)	Conclusions
Rudd et al., 1997	RCT; $n = 331$; patients able to transfer	Specialist community team made available, compared with routine service	Disabled patients discharged 6 days earlier; no detriment and possible increase in satisfaction with hospital care
Rodgers et al., 1997	RCT; $n = 92$; discharged patients after acute stroke	Early supported discharge to specialist team, or routine servicers	Early discharge feasible, saving 9 days as in-patient, and no obvious detriment
Shepperd & Iliffe, 1999	M/A; $n = 5$ trials, 747 patients; very different groups, none stroke	Hospital-at-home or in patient hospital care	Insufficient evidence to warrant change of practice
Widen-Holmqvist et al., 1998	RCT; $n = 81$; acute stroke in hospital >5 days	Specialist, multidisciplinary outreach rehabilitation service, or routine care	Patients discharged 15 days earlier; disability levels the same, possibly more distress
Ronning & Guldvog, 1998a	RCT; $n = 251$; patients 7–14 days post-stroke	Organised specialist in-patient rehabilitation or community rehabilitation	Non-specialist, uncoordinated community rehabilitation associated with more mortality and morbidity
Shepperd et al., 1998a,b	RCT; $n = 538$ patients; need acute admission, *or* already in hospital	Hospital-at-home or in-patient hospital care	No differences in outcomes; no cost difference, but costs shifted to primary care
Richards et al., 1998; Coast et al., 1998	RCT; $n = 241$ patients, all in hospital	Hospital-at-home or in-patient hospital care	No differences in outcomes; hospital at home cheaper

M/A, meta-analysis (and systematic review); RCT, randomised controlled trial.

Table 36.5.   Use of day hospitals/domiciliary rehabilitation

Source	Design and sample	Intervention(s)	Conclusions
Smith et al., 1981	RCT; $n = 133$ patients discharged disabled, and fit enough to attend 5×/week	Three intensities DH: 5 days/week; 3 days/week; zero	Positive dose–response relationship found; DH specialist rehabilitation helped and sustained
Tucker et al., 1984	RCT; $n = 120$ patients needing rehabilitation (65 with stroke)	DH 2–3 days/week, 5 hours/day; 6–8 weeks or normal services	Unsustained increase in independence, sustained mood improvement; cost 30% more
Cummings et al., 1985	RCT; $n = 96$ people still disabled at discharge	Five days/week DH or routine in-patient rehabilitation	No difference in outcome; DH more cost-effective with some costing assumptions
Eagle et al., 1991	RCT; $n = 113$ patients with disability needing rehabilitation	DH or conventional geriatric out-patient service	No difference in outcome
Young & Forster, 1992, 1993	RCT; $n = 124$ patients discharged with disability	Specialist domiciliary therapy or specialist DH rehabilitation	Disability lessened more with home physiotherapy, which was also cheaper
Gladman et al., 1993; 1994; Gladman & Lincoln, 1994	RCT; $n = 327$ patients discharged with disability from 3 services: specialist elderly; general medical; or stroke unit	Specialist domiciliary rehabilitation, or routine day hospital or out-patient services	No overall difference in outcome (may be subgroup differences, but disappeared by 12 months); cost-differences varied between groups
Hui et al., 1995	RCT; $n = 120$ acute stroke patients	Neurology team (no DH) or geriatric team with DH	Faster achievement of independence at no greater cost
Corr & Bayer, 1995	RCT; $n = 110$ stroke patients at discharge from stroke unit	OT visits at home, or routine services	OT visits increased use of aids and reduced readmission rate
Dekker et al., 1998	S/R; $n = 6$ trials (all above)	DH rehabilitation for stroke	No conclusions as (1) no definition of DH; (2) varied outcome measures; (3) varied control groups

DH, day hospital; OT, occupational therapist; RCT, randomised controlled trial; S/R, systematic review (not a meta-analysis).

Table 36.6.   Studies on assessment (note: these are not specific to stroke)

Source	Design and sample	Intervention(s)	Conclusions
Stuck et al., 1993	M/A; $n = 28$ trials, 9871 elderly patients	CGA or routine medical care	CGA linked to coordinated management improved survival and function
Cunningham et al., 1996	Obs; $n = 30$ patients and 4 professions	Detection of disability outside own area	Low levels of agreement/detection between professions
Wikander et al., 1998	RCT; $n = 34$ acute stroke patients with urinary incontinence	Ward using structured assessment using FIM, or ward using Bobath clinical assessment	Structured assessment led to urinary continence being achieved more frequently

CGA, Comprehensive Geriatric Assessment; FIM, Functional Independence Measure; M/A, meta-analysis (following systematic review); Obs, observational study (comparing different groups); RCT, randomised controlled trial.

- patient involvement in goal setting increases its effectiveness
- goal setting can increase the long-term benefits of rehabilitation.

Recent research suggests that goal setting is not undertaken well, if at all. Therefore rehabilitation specialists should be active in helping rehabilitation teams develop the necessary skills. It is likely that more research will be undertaken in the next few years, and hopefully the skills needed to set goals will be taught more widely.

TREATMENT

How, and how much?

Two areas of current contention in stroke rehabilitation concern: (1) the best therapeutic approach; and (2) the importance of the amount of therapy given. The evidence concerning the type (quality) of therapy is currently equivocal (Table 36.8), but

it is my opinion that within 10 years the evidence will support a pragmatic, disability-level, task-oriented approach (i.e. practice the activity itself as soon as possible by any means). It must also be noted that the evidence from the stroke unit studies emphasises the need for well-educated, expert staff to be involved. The evidence concerning the amount of therapy is still also equivocal (Table 36.9), but again, is now suggesting that more therapy is associated with a greater benefit.

Specific problems

The essence of stroke rehabilitation is to identify problems, to determine their causes and then to intervene to reduce or get around the problems. Each patient will have their own unique combination of problems, and in many cases there is little or no evidence to guide the clinician in planning treatments. In this section the evidence relating to some common problems is reviewed.

Table 36.7. Studies relevant to goal setting in (stroke) rehabilitation (note: these are interventional studies, and are not specific to stroke)

Source	Design and sample	Intervention(s)	Conclusions
Greenfield et al., 1985	RCT; $n = 45$; patients with peptic ulcer	Routine education, or coaching with own medical records	Active, personal involvement reduced disability and handicap but not impairment
Berry et al., 1989	RCT; $n = 77$; enlisted military personnel	No instruction, or goal setting ± goal attainment	To achieve change must set goals and teach how to change
Kennedy et al., 1991	CCT; $n = 20$; patients with spinal injury	No goal planning, then goal planning	Goal planning associated with less time disengaged
Stenstrom, 1994	RCT; $n = 42$; patients with rheumatoid arthritis	Pain control techniques or goal setting techniques	Goal setting increased activity and decreased pain
Bar-Eli et al., 1994	RCT; $n = 80$; adolescents with disturbed behaviour	Long-term goals or long- and short-term goals	Adding short-term goals increased improvement in muscular performance
Webb & Glueckhauf, 1994	RCT; $n = 16$; head-injured patients	Low or high involvement in goal planning	Increased involvement led to maintenance of gains
van Vliet et al., 1995	CCT; $n = 5$ patients after stroke	Goal-directed or non-goal-directed movement (otherwise similar)	Goal-directed movement (reaching and grasping) more normal in kinematics
Landefeld et al., 1995	RCT; $n = 651$ acutely ill hospital admissions aged 70+ years	Routine care, or special unit with: (1) good environment; (2) patient-centred care with protocols; (3) discharge planning; (4) specialist medical input	Specialised unit reduced dependence and discharge to nursing home
Blair, 1995; Blair et al., 1996	RCT; $n = 79$; nursing-home residents	Routine care; or mutual goal setting ± behaviour modification	Combination of goal setting and behaviour modification reduced dependence in ADL.
Glasgow et al., 1996, 1997	RCT; $n = 206$; people with diabetes	Routine care, or patient-centred goal setting (20 min) aided by computer assessment	Goal setting led to prolonged change in dietary behaviour
Theodorakis et al., 1997	RCT; $n = 37$; injured sports students	Training alone, or setting specific goals and giving feedback	Performance (strength) improved more in trial group
Johnson et al., 1997	RCT; $n = 52$; people with learning disability	Strategy instruction ± goal setting ± self-instruction	Goal setting and self-instruction did not improve reading
Bar-Eli et al., 1997	RCT; $n = 346$; high-school students	Strength training with differing levels of target and differing practice intensity	Moderate/hard specific goals led to more strength gain than easy or unachievable goals or non-specific goals
Vallet et al., 1997	RCT; $n = 24$ people with chronic airway limitation	Standard (routine) goals or individualised goals for fitness training	Individualised goals more efficient and effective

ADL, activities of daily living; CCT, controlled clinical trial (not randomised); RCT, randomised controlled trial.

Table 36.8. Studies on therapeutic approaches

Source	Design and sample	Intervention(s)	Conclusions
Logigian et al., 1983	CCT; $n = 42$ acute stroke patients	Traditional therapy, or facilitatory (Bobath, Rood)	No differences found
Dickstein et al., 1986	CCT; $n = 131$ acute stroke patients	Functional, or PNF, or Bobath approach	No long-term differences seen (Bobath slower at regaining gait independence)
Lord & Hall, 1986	CCT; $n = 39$ patients in two centres	One centre was traditional, the other neuromuscular training technique	No difference seen
Basmajian et al., 1987	RCT; $n = 29$ stroke patients	Bobath approach or behavioural approach to arm therapy	Outcome the same; no differences seen
Jongbloed et al., 1989	RCT; $n = 90$; stroke within 12 weeks	Functional approach, or sensorimotor integrative approach to OT (Bobath/Rood)	No difference in outcome
Wagenaar et al., 1990	CCT; $n = 7$ acute stroke patients	Bobath and Brunnestrom approaches compared	No significant or systematic difference in effects
Richards et al., 1993 (see also Malouin et al., 1992)	RCT; $n = 27$ acute stroke patients	Early, intense conventional therapy; later less intense conventional therapy; early intense gait and muscle retraining	Early muscle retraining and gait retraining (on treadmill) facilitated gait recovery; no differences between conventional groups
Nelson et al., 1996	RCT; $n = 26$ post-stroke patients	Functional task (game, tipping dice) or exercise (identical rotation movement)	Functional task greatly increased supination of forearm
Dean & Shepherd, 1997	RCT; $n = 20$; stroke 1+ years ago	Training at reaching (functional), against cognitive training	Task-related training improved ability at similar tasks

CCT, controlled clinical trial; OT, occupational therapy; PNF, proprioceptive neuromuscular facilitation; RCT, randomised controlled trial.

Swallowing. Difficulty in swallowing (dysphagia) and poor nutrition are both easily overlooked problems of great importance. At present there is no good evidence to guide one on management (Tables 36.10 and 36.11), but it seems prudent to screen all patients for these problems so that further malnutrition is avoided if possible.

Aphasia. Aphasia is an impairment in the use of language. It is a common condition and is frequently not recognised. A standardised screening test such as the Frenchay Aphasia Screening Test should be used in all patients with left hemisphere stroke. The best management of aphasia is still uncertain (Table 36.12) and it is likely that the Cochrane Collaboration will soon publish

Table 36.9. Studies on intensity of therapy input

Source	Design and sample	Intervention(s)	Conclusions
Smith et al., 1981	RCT; n = 133 patients after discharge	Weekly visit from health visitor at home; or weekly or thrice weekly day hospital	Dose effect seen; many patients unable to tolerate it
Rapoport & Eerd, 1989	CCT; n = 273 (102 with acute stroke)	Physiotherapy over weekend (reorganisation of schedule, cost neutral)	Stroke patients had a shorter length of stay
Sunderland et al., 1992, 1994	RCT; n = 132 acute stroke patients	Routine therapy, or enhanced (more and different) therapy for arm	Faster recovery if some arm movement, but no long-term difference
Kwakkel et al., 1997	M/A; n = 9 trials, 1051 stroke patients	Daily rate of PT or OT	Higher rate of therapy associated with better outcome; but many confounding factors
Feys et al., 1998	RCT; n = 100 stroke patients 3–5 weeks post-stroke	Routine therapy with additional: attention only, or sensorimotor stimulation	Additional therapy reduced motor loss (impairment) but not arm disability

CCT, controlled clinical trial; M/A, meta-analysis (including systematic review); OT, occupational therapy; PT, physiotherapy; RCT, randomised controlled trial.

Table 36.10. Studies on dysphagia natural history and management

Source	Design and sample	Intervention(s)	Conclusions
DePippo et al., 1994	RCT; n = 115; patients with mild–moderate dysphagia 3–7 weeks post-stroke	One session explanation and advice, or prescribed diet and monitoring, or diet and therapy	Explanation and advice as effective as more intense SALT involvement
Odderson et al., 1995	CCT; n = 124; acute stroke admissions; historical controls	Use of a standardised protocol including dysphagia guidelines	Aspiration pneumonia risk reduced greatly
Norton et al., 1996	RCT; n = 30; dysphagia 14 days post-stroke	PEG feeding or NG feeding	PEG associated with better nutrition and better outcome (NB: many criticisms)
Teasell et al., 1996	Obs; n = 441; subacute stroke patients in rehabilitation	84 had aspiration on videofluoroscopy; 10/84 aspirators, 2/357 non-aspirators developed pneumonia	(Silent) aspiration asssociated with pneumonia
Smithard et al., 1996	Obs; n = 121; acute stroke patients	Dysphagia, detected clinically, associated independently with worse outcome	Dysphagia could be specific additional problem
Garon et al., 1997	RCT; n = 20; 4–17 days post-stroke and aspirating	Thickened fluids alone; or thickened fluids and free access to thin fluids	No additional risk with thin fluids, and possible faster recovery
Daniels et al., 1998	Obs; n = 55; not drowsy acute stroke patients	21 aspirated: 7 overtly and 14 silently	Silent aspiration is common
Perez et al., 1998	RCT; n = 17; patients with dysphagia 2 weeks post-stroke	Nifedipine slow-release, 30 mg or placebo	Trend towards improved swallow mechanism in treated group

CCT, controlled clinical trial; NG, nasogastric (tube feeding); Obs, observational study; PEG, percutaneous endoscopic gastrostomy (tube feeding); RCT, randomised controlled trial; SALT, speech and language therapist.

Table 36.11. Studies relating to nutrition after stroke

Source	Design and sample	Intervention(s)	Conclusions
Davalos et al., 1996	Obs; n = 104 acute stroke patients; assessed nutrition and 1 month disability	16% of admitted and 26% of 1 week surviving patients malnourished; outcome worse	Malnutrition is common and worsens in first week; may affect outcome
Finestone et al., 1996	Obs; n = 49 patients in stroke rehabilitation service	49% malnourished on admission; had slower rate of recovery	Malnutrition is common and slows recovery
Potter et al., 1998	M/A; n = 30 trials; 2062 patients, none stroke specific	Oral or enteral protein supplementation, or normal feeding	Routine supplementation of diet improved nutritional status

M/A, meta-analysis (and systematic review); Obs, observational study.

a meta-analytic review that will help. In the meantime, it is important that every patient is assessed by an experienced speech and language therapist both to guide the team and relatives on the best ways to communicate with the patient, and to consider treatment.

Hemiparesis. Poor motor control (hemiparesis) is perhaps the most characteristic impairment seen with stroke, and many studies have investigated the usefulness of biofeedback techniques and functional electrical stimulation (FES) as methods of improving or supporting motor control. Other studies have investigated the utility of "additional sensory input" (achieved through transcutaneous electrical nerve stimulation (TENS) or acupuncture). At present the evidence remains equivocal (Tables 36.13, 36.14, 36.15), insufficient to warrant widespread

Table 36.12. Studies on management of dysphasia

Source	Design and sample	Intervention(s)	Conclusions
Meikle et al., 1979	RCT; $n = 31$ patients with aphasia 3+ weeks post-stroke	Treatment from therapists or volunteers (after full SALT assessment and explanation)	Language and communication outcome same; volunteers did additional work
Di Carlo, 1980	RCT; $n = 14$ male stroke patients with long-term, severe aphasia	Speech therapy with additional filmed programmed instruction or attention only	No additional benefit shown for additional instruction
Wertz et al., 1981	RCT; $n = 67$ stroke patients with aphasia	Group therapy or individual therapy; 8 hours/week for weeks 4–48 post-stroke	Most measures no different; both groups improved; only difference in one measure favouring individual therapy
David et al., 1982	RCT; $n = 96$ stroke patients with aphasia	Assessment, then treatment by volunteer or therapist	No difference in outcome; assessment improved communication
Lincoln et al., 1982	RCT; patients with aphasia	Operant training or normal therapy	No difference in outcome
Shewan & Kertesz, 1984	RCT; $n = 100$ patients with recent onset post-stroke aphasia	Language-oriented therapy, stimulation-facilitation therapy, nurse support and communication	All patients improved, no detected differences related to type of therapy; type of therapy might not matter
Lincoln & Pickersgill, 1984	RCT; patients with aphasia	Programmed instruction and operant training or normal therapy	No difference in outcome
Lincoln et al., 1984, 1985a	RCT; $n = 327$ patients with aphasia 10 weeks post-stroke	Normal speech therapy service (0–48 hours) or nil	No difference in outcome for patients (communication or mood) or relatives (mood) associated with routine therapy service offered
Wertz et al., 1986	RCT; $n = 121$ patients with acute aphasia 2–24 weeks post-onset	Assessment then: immediate therapy from therapist, delayed therapy from therapist; or immediate therapy from volunteer	Patients improve naturally; treatment improves rate and extent of recovery; delaying treatment does not affect outcome; therapy from trained volunteers may be as effective as from therapists
Hartman & Landau, 1987	RCT; $n = 60$ patients with aphasia 4 weeks post-onset	Therapy from speech therapist or counselling from speech therapist	No difference in outcome; specific aspects of therapy do not influence outcome
Brindley et al., 1989	CCT; $n = 10$ patients with chronic aphasia	Intense therapy over 4 weeks	Improvement in communication occurred
Mackenzie, 1991	CCT; patients with chronic aphasia	Intense and group therapy	Improvement in communication occurred
Katz & Wertz, 1997	RCT; $n = 55$ patients with chronic aphasia	Computer reading programme, stimulation or nil	Specific computer-based treatment improves reading

CCT, controlled clinical trial; RCT, randomised clinical trial; SALT, speech and language therapist

use of any of these techniques on a routine basis. Functional electrical stimulation might have a limited role to play in some specific patients; biofeedback of balance might yet be shown to be helpful; and the jury is out on all forms of sensory stimulation.

Spasticity. This has been the focus of much therapeutic effort for years, with little evidence to support the techniques used. There remains little evidence for the routine use of drugs (Table 36.16), but there seems little doubt that evidence supporting the use of botulinum toxin will become extremely strong over the next few years (Table 36.17). At present, drugs should be used only sparingly, given the lack of evidence and their undoubted cognitive side-effects. On the other hand, there is no need to avoid the use of exercise as there is no evidence that exercise worsens spasticity (Table 36.16). The accumulating evidence on botulinum toxin should be reviewed regularly to establish its use: when (early or late); how given; to whom; and for what problems?

Painful shoulder. The development of a painful shoulder continues to be common, and at present there is no agreed best method for preventing or treating this complication. This probably reflects the lack of adequate evidence (Table 36.18). At present it is probably best to train staff to handle patients without stressing the shoulder and to consider triamcinolone injection if simple non-steroidal anti-inflammatory analgesic drugs are not sufficient.

Reduced mobility. This is perhaps the most common disability seen after stroke, and it is usually the one that patients wish to overcome most. Gait retraining probably is the major focus of most physiotherapy. The evidence to guide this effort is not large (Table 36.19) but currently supports a task-oriented approach possibly using a tread-mill and partial weight support if available. The value of ankle–foot orthoses has not been confirmed in group studies, although, clinically, it seems reasonable to try them in selected patients (Table 36.20).

Emotional changes. These are also common after stroke, although the precise frequency is uncertain because it is difficult to distinguish depression from misery. Despite its frequency, there are remarkably few studies investigating the best management (Table 36.21) and at present the most one can say is that antidepressants probably help reduce emotionalism after stroke (Table 36.22).

Post-discharge support. After discharge it has been suggested that providing social and emotional support could reduce patient and carer stress but again the evidence is equivocal (Table 36.23). However, there is reasonable evidence that further active rehabilitation late after stroke can lead to significant benefit (Table 36.24).

Table 36.13. Studies on technologically-assisted feedback including biofeedback (studies in meta-analyses also included)

Source	Design and sample	Intervention(s)	Conclusions
Schleenbaker & Mainous, 1993	M/A; n = 8 trials, 192 patients	BFB, arm or leg	BFB might be useful, but unproven
Moreland & Thomson, 1994	M/A; n = 5 trials, 135 patients	BFB relating to arm	No difference in outcome between BFB and conventional therapy
Glanz et al., 1995	M/A; n = 8 trials, 168 patients post-acute stroke	BFB (arm or leg)	Efficacy of BFB not established; insufficient data
Moreland et al., 1998	M/A; n = 8 trials	EMG BFB from leg, no or conventional therapy	EMG BFB increased ankle dorsiflexion strength (but little else)
Basmajian et al., 1975	RCT; n = 20 patients with footdrop following stroke 3+ months ago	Therapy with/without additional EMG BFB, over 5 weeks	Addition of BFB facilitated recovery from impairments
Lee et al., 1976	RCT; n = 18 patients with weak deltoid	True, false or absent BFB from deltoid muscle	No effect on strength of voluntary muscle contraction
Bowman et al., 1979	RCT; n = 30 stroke patients, recent onset	PFST to weak wrist, or routine therapy	Wrist extension strength greatly increased by PFST
Smith, 1979	RCT; n = 11 chronic stroke patients	EMG BFB on arm, 12 sessions in 6 weeks	More improvement, but not statistically significant
Greenburg & Fowler, 1980	RCT; n = 20 patients with some arm movement 1+ years post-onset	Normal OT, or audio-feedback on elbow extension	Both groups increased elbow extension; no differences between groups; BFB not helpful
Hurd et al., 1980	RCT; n = (1) 24 rehabilitation patients; and (2) 20 patients	(1) real or sham EMG BFB; (2) random muscle selection deltoid/anterior tibial	Possible effect to specific muscle targeted: functional change not assessed
Prevo et al., 1982	RCT; n = 18 chronic stroke patients	EMG BFB on arm, 28 sessions in 11 weeks	No benefit noted
Burnside et al., 1982	CCT; n = 22 patients late after stroke	EMG BFB or routine therapy for weak leg	EMG associated with greater and more sustained improvements
Basmajian et al., 1982	RCT; n = 37 stroke patients	EMG BFB or physiotherapy exercises	Minor differences
Winchester et al., 1983	RCT; n = 40 adult hemiparetic patients	Feedback stimulation training and electrical stimulation	Increased knee extension torque, but control no better
Inglis et al., 1984	RCT; n = 30 stroke patients 6 months post-stroke; (cross-over after treatment)	PT ± additional EMG BFB in arm muscles	Some possible minor additional benefit from EMG BFB
Skelly, 1985	CCT; n = 22 patients	EMG BFB on shoulder flexion	Trend towards more improvement in control group
John, 1986	RCT; n = 12 patients 12 weeks post-stroke	Additional EMG BFB on leg muscles	No additional benefit from BFB
Cozean et al., 1988	RCT; n = 36 acute stroke patients	PT/EMG BFB/FES/BFB and FES	Combined treatment of BFB and FES improved gait most
Crow et al., 1989	RCT; n = 40 acute stroke patients	Real or placebo EMG BFB on arm muscles	BFB improved speed of recovery, especially in severe impairment
Mandel et al., 1990	RCT; n = 37 stroke patients, 6+ months post-stroke	No therapy/BFB/rhythm and BFB	Gait improved with BFB; rhythmic pacing led to sustained improvement in gait
Svensson et al., 1992	RCT; n = 35 patients with facial palsy	Facial muscle retraining using EMG feedback	No benefits observed
Morris et al., 1992	RCT; n = 26	EMG BFB added to conventional therapy	EMG BFB enhanced reduction of knee hyperextension
Colborne et al., 1993	RCT; n = 8 patients 6+ months post-stroke	PT/EMG BFB/feedback on ankle angle	Both feedback methods improved gait
Wolf et al., 1994	RCT; n = 16 patients 1+ years post-stroke	EMG BFB to strengthen weak triceps	Both groups increased strength, no difference
Montoya et al., 1994	CCT; patients post-rehabilitation	Visual stimulation on step length with feedback	Asymmetry reduced/step length increased
Intiso et al., 1994	RCT; n = 16 stroke patients late post-stroke	BFB on ankle dorsiflexion muscles	Ankle dorsiflexion increased
Sukthankar et al., 1994	RCT; n = 12 patients; head injury or stroke	BFB on force of selected oral movements	Feedback increased control of oral muscles
Fanthome et al., 1995	RCT; n = 18; right hemisphere stroke with "neglect"	Feedback on eye movements into "neglected" visual field	No effect on neglect (eye movements may possibly have altered)
Dursun et al., 1996	CCT; n = 37 acute stroke patients	PT (2.5 hours/day) + feedback on sitting balance or additional 30 min PT	Feedback on sitting balance speeded recovery of balance and walking; hospital LoS shorter
Wong et al., 1997	RCT; n = 60 stroke (55) or head injury (5) patients with hemiplegia	Balance retraining by visual and auditory feedback or standard balance training	Stance symmetry improved greatly, and group difference maintained
Sackley & Lincoln, 1997	RCT; n = 26; 4–63 weeks post-stroke	Balance retraining by visual feedback	More rapid recovery of balance and reduction in disability, end result same
Bradley et al., 1998	RCT; n = 21 patients with acute stroke	Additional EMG feedback or sham EMG feedback	No differences

BFB, biofeedback; CCT, controlled clinical trial; EMG, electromyography (recording of electrical potential from contracting muscle); FES, functional electrical stimulation; LoS, length of stay; M/A, meta-analysis (and systematic review); PFST, positional feedback and muscle stimulation; PT, physiotherapy; RCT, randomised controlled trial.

Table 36.14. Studies on functional electrical stimulation (FES)

Source	Design and sample	Intervention(s)	Conclusions
Glanz et al., 1996	M/A; n = 4 trials, 132 patients	Electrostimulation ± BFB	FES decreases motor impairment (increases strength)
Cozean et al., 1988	RCT; n = 36 acute stroke patients	PT/EMG BFB/FES/BFB and FES	Combined treatment of BFB and FES improved gait most
Faghri et al., 1994	RCT; n = 26 patients	Routine PT ± additional FES to shoulder	Some benefits from FES on range of movement
Faghri & Rodgers, 1997	RCT; n = 26 patients with shoulder weakness post-stroke	Routine therapy ± FNS to deltoid	Improved active and passive range of motion with FNS
Burridge et al., 1997	RCT; n = 16 patients with chronic hemiplegia	ODFS or PT alone	ODFS improved gait while used, but not once stopped
Chae et al., 1998	RCT; n = 46 (28 complete) within 4 weeks of stroke	FES of wrist extensors, or minor skin stimulation	More motor recovery with FES, but many dropped out with pain/discomfort

BFB, biofeedback; FES, functional electrical stimulation; FNS, functional neuromuscular stimulation; M/A, meta-analysis (with systematic review); OFDS, Odstock dropped foot stimulator; PT, physiotherapy; RCT, randomised clinical trial.

Table 36.15. Studies on TENS and acupuncture

Source	Design and sample	Intervention(s)	Conclusions
Johansson et al., 1993	RCT; n = 78 acute stroke patients	Additional acupuncture twice weekly for 10 weeks	Additional acupuncture improved outcome
Hu et al., 1993	RCT; n = 30 acute stroke patients	Additional acupuncture three times weekly for 4 weeks	Acupuncture improved outcome, which was maintained
Sallstrom et al., 1996	RCT; n = 45 acute stroke patients	Additional acupuncture four times weekly for 6 weeks	Acupuncture improved outcome, including quality of life
Kjendahl et al., 1997	RCT; n = 41 acute stroke patients	Additional acupuncture (traditional Chinese approach) for 6 weeks	Additional acupuncture improved outcome in short- and long-term
Gosman-Hedstrom et al., 1998	RCT; n = 104 acute stroke patients	Acupuncture twice weekly for 10 weeks: deep, or superficial, or none	No differences in motor impairment or ADL seen
Levin & Hui, 1992	RCT; chronic hemiparetic patients	TENS or placebo over common peroneal nerve	Spasticity reduced and voluntary power increased
Tekeoolu et al., 1998	RCT; n = 60 patients subacute stroke	TENS or placebo–TENS	Greater increase in independence following TENS
Sonde et al., 1998	RCT; n = 44 patients 6–12 months post-stroke with weak arm	Routine therapy ± low frequency (1.7 Hz) TENS to weak arm	Motor control increased if some present initially; spasticity and pain unaffected

ADL, activities of daily living; Hz, Hertz (cycles/second); RCT, randomised controlled trial; TENS, transcutaneous electrical nerve stimulation.

Table 36.16. Studies in relation to spasticity

Source	Design and sample	Intervention(s)	Conclusions
Burt & Currie, 1978	RCT; n = 28 (initially 44), 2–27 months post-stroke	Baclofen or diazepam	Both drugs reduced spasticity; baclofen improved gait
Ketel & Kolb, 1984	CCT; n = 14; stroke patients with spasticity limiting rehabilitation	Change from dantrolene to placebo	Increased deficits on withdrawal of active drug; dantrolene beneficial
Medici et al., 1989	RCT; n = 30; stroke patients with spasticity	Tizanidine or baclofen, titrated dosage	Both reduced spasticity, slight favour for tizanidine
Katrak et al., 1992	RCT; n = 31; acute stroke, before spasticity	Dantrolene 200 mg/day or placebo	No benefits observed with routine use of dantrolene
Beckerman et al., 1996a,b	RCT; n = 60 acute stroke patients	AFO/PAFO, and thermocoagulation of tibial nerve or placebo coagulation	Thermocoagulation reduced spasticity but no benefit; AFO had no effect
Miller & Light, 1997	CCT; n = 9 patients with spastic left arm	Graded restive exercises given	No increase in spasticity; some decrease in cocontraction
Sharp & Brouwer, 1997	CCT; n = 15 patients 6 months post-stroke	40 min/day, 3 days/week, 6 weeks leg strengthening programme	Programme improved gait and strength without causing increase in spasticity
Brown & Kautz, 1998	CCT; n = 15; stroke > 6 months ago	Random variation in leg workload	No additional inappropriate muscle activity with exercise

AFO, ankle–foot orthosis (foot drop splint); CCT, controlled clinical trial; PAFO, placebo ankle–foot orthosis (foot drop splint); RCT, randomised controlled trial.

Table 36.17.   Studies on botulinum toxin and spasticity (includes non-stroke studies)

Source	Design and sample	Intervention(s)	Conclusions
Snow et al., 1990	RCT; $n = 9$ patients with stable MS	Botulinum toxin or placebo into adductor muscles	Toxin reduced spasticity and improved hygiene
Grazko et al., 1995	RCT; $n = 12$ patients with spasticity (3 with stroke)	Botulinum toxin into spastic muscles (no EMG guidance)	Botulinum toxin always reduced spasticity, for 2–4 months. Function often improved
Hesse et al., 1996	CCT; $n = 12$; leg spasticity 11+ months after stroke	Botulinum toxin into leg muscles; selective placement with EMG guidance	Improved gait in 9 out of the 12 patients
Simpson et al., 1996	RCT; $n = 39$; patients with arm spasticity 9+ months after stroke	Various doses of botulinum toxin including placebo	Tone was reduced by botulinum toxin
Bhakta et al., 1996	CCT; $n = 17$; over 1 year after stroke; spastic arm	Botulinum toxin in various arm muscles	Wide range of benefits, including in mobility, lasting one to eleven months
Burbaud et al., 1996	RCT; $n = 23$; patients with spastic leg after stroke	Botulinum toxin or placebo; cross-over at 90 days	Botulinum toxin improved gait speed and reduced spasticity
Childers et al., 1996	RCT; $n = 17$; patients with chronic hemiplegia after stroke	Botulinum toxin in one of two sites in calf (gastrocnemius): mid-calf or proximal calf	Injection to mid-calf no different from injection near muscle origin; site unimportant
Sampaio et al., 1997	CCT; $n = 19$; patients over 6 months post-stroke with spastic arms	Botulinum toxin into forearm muscles	Function improved and spasticity reduced after injection
Corry et al., 1997	RCT; $n = 14$; children with cerebral palsy and hemiplegia in arm	Botulinum toxin or saline intramuscular	Botulinum increased active movement and some functions, and decreased tone and associated movements
Reiter et al., 1998	RCT; $n = 18$; out-patient stroke with spastic foot 10+ months post-stroke	Botulinum toxin to calf with EMG guidance, or lower dose to tibialis posterior (no EMG guidance) with strapping for 3 weeks	Both groups walked better; no major differences observed; EMG guided injection not especially better
Hesse et al., 1998	RCT; $n = 24$ 6–11 months post-stroke	Botulinum or placebo; electrical stimulation or not; into arm flexor muscles	Botulinum toxin with additional stimulation at times increases effect of toxin and reduced disability
Corry et al., 1998	RCT; $n = 20$ children with cerebral palsy and spastic eequinus	Botulinum toxin or serial plaster casts	Equally effective; some possible advantages for botulinum toxin

CCT, controlled clinical trial; EMG, electromyography; MS, multiple sclerosis; RCT, randomised clinical trial.

Table 36.18.   Studies relating to shoulder pain after stroke

Source	Design and sample	Intervention(s)	Conclusions
Partridge et al., 1990	RCT; $n = 65$; patients with post-stroke shoulder pain	Cryotherapy or Bobath physiotherapy	No significant differences in pain outcome; both improved equally
Kumar et al., 1990	RCT; $n = 28$; patients in stroke rehabilitation unit	Physical RoM; skateboard RoM; overhead pulley RoM	Overhead pulley caused shoulder pain
Leandri et al., 1990	RCT; $n = 60$; patients with hemiplegic shoulder pain	TENS at intensity: zero, low, high	High intensity TENS led to prolonged pain relief and increase in RoM
Kotzki et al., 1991	RCT; $n = 42$; stroke rehabilitation unit patients	Postural support and FES; foam support; (Bobath) pillow support	Foam support ($\pm$ FES) was more effective at preventing shoulder pain than Bobath pillow
Ancliffe, 1992	CCT (alternating allocation); $n = 8$; patients admitted to hospital	Strapping of shoulder or no strapping	Strapping associated with many more days without pain
Dekker et al., 1997	RCT (single stroke case design, random start time); $n = 7$; stroke and shoulder pain	Three 40 mg intra-articular triamcinolone on days 1, 8, 22 post-start time	5 of 7 responded with reduction in pain, and 4 had improved range of movement
Braus et al., 1994	CCT; $n = 86$	Instructions to everyone, including family, on handling arm	Shoulder–hand syndrome reduced from 27% to 8%

CCT, controlled clinical trial; FES, functional electrical stimulation; RCT, randomised clinical trial; RoM, range of movement (or motion); TENS, transcutaneous electrical nerve stimulation.

Drugs.   There are a few studies on the direct benefits of drugs as a general or specific treatment when combined with active rehabilitation. These are interesting, and might eventually lead to better treatments, but at present the evidence is limited (Table 36.25). It is probably worth avoiding centrally acting drugs where possible, in case they impede recovery.

CONCLUSIONS

This brief review of some of the evidence shows that we can deliver an effective and efficient service without knowing precisely how we achieve this. A similar situation applies to many effective drug treatments, and should not deter purchasers from purchasing specialised stroke services. However, it is important that in any specific situation the clinician makes an effort to evaluate the utility of the proposed intervention if possible. In the meantime, every clinician needs to try and keep up-to-date, perhaps using the Cochrane Collaboration reviews. The situation is changing rapidly. By the time this chapter is published many important studies will have been published and, hopefully, when this chapter's third edition is written, there will be answers to many of the unanswered questions.

Table 36.19.   Studies on gait retraining: treadmill use and other studies

Source	Design and sample	Intervention(s)	Conclusions
Hesse et al., 1994	CCT; $n = 9$ patients 8+ weeks post-stroke with static gait ability	Treadmill training with partial bodyweight support	Further improvement in gait follows treadmill training
Hesse et al., 1995	CCT; $n = 7$ patients 3+ months post-stroke	Treadmill training and Bobath PT	Treadmill training improved gait, Bobath PT did not
Montoya et al., 1994	RCT; $n = 16$ patients with stroke	Treadmill training, ± feedback of length of stride, aiming for lighted target	Training to increase stride length lengthened stride
Macko et al., 1997	Obs; $n = 9$ patients with long-standing stroke	Treadmill training for 6 months	Low-intensity training improved cardiovascular fitness
Visintin et al., 1998	RCT; $n = 100$ patients with acute stroke	Treadmill gait training with 40% or 0% weight carried by harness	Partial support during training led to better gait, and a sustained advantage
Wall & Turnbull, 1987	RCT; $n = 20$ patients late after stroke	OP Bobath or home-based Bobath	Both groups improved; no differences
Weinstein et al., 1989	RCT; $n = 62$ subacute stroke patients	PT with or without visual feedback	Only difference was in weight distribution
Mandel et al., 1990	RCT; $n = 37$ stroke patients	Routine/BFB/rhythm and BFB music	Rhythmic pacing led to improved gait
Schauer et al., 1996	CCT; $n = 6$ patients with gait disability		Music decreased gait asymmetry.
Thaut et al., 1997	RCT; $n = 20$ patients as soon as took 5 steps	RAS, or normal (Bobath); 1 hour daily, 5 days/week, 6 weeks	RAS (music with beat) led to more and sustained improvement in gait

CCT, controlled clinical trial; Obs, observational study; OP, out-patient; PT, physiotherapy; RAS, rhythmic auditory stimulation; RCT, randomised clinical trial.

Table 36.20.   Studies on ankle–foot orthoses (AFOs)

Source	Design and sample	Intervention(s)	Conclusions
Corcoran et al., 1970	RCT; $n = 15$ patients 6+ months post-stroke	Metal or plastic AFO, or neither	AFOs increased speed and efficiency of gait
Beckerman et al., 1996a	RCT; $n = 60$ acute stroke patients	AFO/PAFO, and thermocoagulation of tibial nerve or placebo coagulation	Thermocoagulation reduced spasticity but no benefit; AFO had no effect
Beckerman et al., 1996b	RCT; $n = 60$ acute stroke patients	AFO/PAFO, and thermocoagulation of tibial nerve or placebo coagulation	AFO and thermocoagulation, individually or combined, did not improve walking

AFO, ankle–foot orthosis; CCT, controlled clinical trial; PAFO, placebo ankle–foot orthosis; RCT, randomised clinical trial.

Table 36.21.   Studies on treatment of depression after stroke

Source	Design and sample	Intervention(s)	Conclusions
Lipsey et al., 1984	RCT; $n = 34$	Nortriptyline compared with placebo in 6-week trial	3 nortriptyline and 1 placebo patient dropped out. Average 3 point lower scores on Hamilton DRS in nortriptyline group, but not intention-to-treat analysis
Reding et al., 1986	RCT; $n = 27$; in-patients in stroke rehabilitation unit	Trazodone compared with placebo, variable treatment duration average 32 days	Non-significant trend for Barthel ADL scores to improve more on trazodone. Depression outcomes not reported
Towle et al., 1989	RCT; $n = 44$; depressed stroke patients at home	Information ± additional social worker support	No difference in mood, equipment or services
Andersen et al., 1994	RCT; $n = 66$; stroke patients 2–52 weeks after stroke	6 weeks citalopram compared with placebo	6 citalopram and 1 placebo patient dropped out. Average 3 point lower scores on Hamilton DRS in citalopram group

ADL, activities of daily living; DRS, depression rating scale; RCT, randomised controlled trial.

Table 36.22. Evidence for treating emotionalism

Source	Design and sample	Intervention(s)	Conclusions
Lawson & McLeod, 1969	RCT; $n = 7$; subjects with organic emotionalism not all stroke	Imipramine 10 mg, imipramine 20 mg, phenobarbitone and placebo compared in a cross-over design	Imipramine in both doses, but not phenobarbitone or placebo, reduced crying and laughing
Schiffer et al., 1985	RCT; $n = 12$; in patients with MS	Amitriptyline compared with placebo using cross-over design	Amitriptyline more effective than placebo in reducing crying
Andersen et al., 1993	RCT; $n = 16$; subjects 6 days to > 2 years after stroke	Citalopram and placebo compared in a cross-over design	Citalopram reduced rate of crying more than placebo, in a 3 week trial
Robinson et al., 1993	RCT; $n = 54$; acute stroke and chronic cerebrovascular disease	Nortriptyline compared with placebo	Nortriptyline more effective than placebo in reducing crying. Unclear how much attributable to treating high rates of associated depression

MS, multiple sclerosis; RCT, randomised controlled trial.

Table 36.23. Studies on social support after discharge

Source	Design and sample	Intervention(s)	Conclusions
Towle et al., 1989	RCT; $n = 44$; depressed stroke patients at home	Information ± additional social worker support	No difference in mood, equipment or services
Hansen, 1990	RCT; $n = 100$; patients with neurological disease	Intensive social assistance at and after discharge	Many unmet needs at discharge. No differences in satisfaction, but readmission less, more problems solved
Friedland & McColl, 1992	RCT; $n = 88$; stroke patients at home after rehabilitation	Special Social Support Intervention, or nil (normal service)	No difference in social support or psychosocial function (GHQ, SIP)
Forster & Young, 1996	RCT; $n = 240$; patients at home after stroke	Specialist nurse visits (6+ over 6 months) or normal services alone	No beneficial effect on patient's disability, social activities, or mood; or carer's stress
Dennis et al., 1997	RCT; $n = 417$ patients 30 days post-stroke	FCW or standard care	FCW group more satisfied; but possible increase in patient helplessness; no other differences detected

FCW, family care worker; GHQ, general health questionnaire; RCT, randomised clinical trial; SIP, Sickness Impact Profile.

Table 36.24. Studies relevant to late rehabilitation after stroke

Source	Design and sample	Intervention(s)	Conclusions
Lehmann et al., 1975	CCT; $n = 114$; patients late after stroke	In-patient specialist multiprofessional input	Late rehabilitation reduced dependence in ADL
Tangeman et al., 1990	CCT; $n = 40$; patients over 1 year after stroke	Out-patient therapy; 2 hours/day, 4 days/week; 5 weeks	Reduced disability (ADL) and reduced impairment (balance performance)
Jongbloed & Morgan, 1991	RCT; $n = 40$; patients discharged from rehabilitation	Therapy from OT for leisure, or questions about leisure from OT	No differences in leisure activity or satisfaction with activity
Wade et al., 1992	RCT; $n = 92$; patients with reduced mobility 2–6 years after stroke	Home-based assessment and treatment from experienced PT	Therapy improved mobility for 3+ months, but when untreated, patients deteriorated
Dam et al., 1993	CCT; $n = 51$; patients 3 months after stroke	Out-patient rehabilitation for up to 2 years, on and off	Reduced disability
Werner & Kessler, 1996	RCT*; $n = 40$; patients >1 year after stroke	Nothing or 12 weeks of 4 days/week 2 hours/day therapy	Therapy reduced dependence and increased social function, and effect was maintained; control group deteriorated
Drummond & Walker, 1995	RCT; $n = 60$; patients 6 months after stroke	Occupational therapy, general or focused on leisure	Focused therapy improved leisure
Walker et al., 1996	RCT; $n = 15$; patients unable to dress 6 months post-stroke	Occupational therapy focused on dressing	Focused therapy improved independence in dressing

ADL, activities of daily living; CCT, controlled clinical trial (not randomised); OT, occupational therapist; PT, physiotherapist; RCT, randomised controlled trial (* = minor variation in design).

Table 36.25. Studies on drugs directly reducing impairment/disability

Source	Design and sample	Intervention(s)	Conclusions
West & Stockel, 1965	RCT; $n = 29$ people with post-stroke aphasia	Meprobamate or placebo; with speech therapy	No benefit observed
Sarno et al., 1972	RCT; $n = 16$ people with aphasia 3+ months post-stroke	Hyperbaric oxygen (100% at 2 atm) or air at 2 atm	No benefit on communication observed
Crisostomo et al., 1988	RCT; $n = 8$ acute stroke patients	Amphetamine (10 mg) or placebo once only; with physiotherapy	Motor recovery in subsequent therapy session greatly enhanced
Enderby et al., 1994	RCT; $n = 137$ acute stroke patients (67 with aphasia)	Piracetam 4.8 g/day for 12 weeks	Level of aphasia reduced more in piracetam group over 12 weeks; no other differences seen
Walker-Batson et al., 1995	RCT; $n = 10$ patients; 16–30 days after stroke	Amphetamine (10 mg) or placebo, every 4 days × 10; both with physiotherapy	Rate and extent of motor recovery enhanced and sustained 1 year
Goldstein, 1995	Obs; $n = 96$ acute stroke patients	Association between centrally-acting, "detrimental" drugs and outcome	Patients receiving detrimental drugs (e.g. benzodiazepines) did less well
Gupta et al., 1995	RCT; $n = 20$ patients with aphasia 13–200 months post-stroke	Bromocriptine, up to 15 mg/day or placebo	No benefits observed
Sabe et al., 1995	RCT; $n = 7$ patients with aphasia more than 1 year	Bromocriptine, up to 60 mg/day or placebo	No benefits observed
Huber et al., 1997	RCT; $n = 66$ patients with acute aphasia	Piracetam 4.8 g/day or placebo	Trend for greater improvement with piracetam

ADL, activities of daily living; atm, atmospheres; CCT, controlled clinical trial (not randomised); RCT, randomised controlled trial.

REFERENCES

Ancliffe J (1992) Strapping the shoulder in patients following a cerebrovascular accident (CVA): A pilot study. *Australian Journal of Physiotherapy* 1992; **38**: 37–41.

Andersen G, Vestergaard K, Rils JO (1993) Citalopram for post-stroke pathological crying. *Lancet* 1993; **342**: 837–839.

Andersen G, Vestergaard K, Lauritsen L (1994) Effective treatment of post-stroke depression with the selective serotonin uptake reinhibitor citalopram. *Stroke* 1994; **25**: 1099–1104.

Bar Eli M, Hartman I, Levy-Kolker N (1994) Using goal setting to improve physical performance of adolescents with behavior disorders: The effects of goal proximity. *Adapted Physical Activity Quarterly* 1994; **11**: 86–97.

Bar-Eli M, Tenenbaum G, Pie JS, Btesh Y, Almog A (1997) Effect of goal difficulty, goal specificity and duration of practice time intervals on muscular endurance performance. *Journal of Sports Sciences* 1997; **15**: 125–135.

Basmajian JV, Kulkulka CG, Narayan MG, Takebe K (1975) Biofeedback treatment of foot-drop after stroke compared with standard rehabilitation technique: Effects on voluntary control and strength. *Archives of Physical Medicine and Rehabilitation* 1975; **56**: 231–236.

Basmajian JV, Gowland CA, Brandstater ME, Swanson LR, Trotter JE (1982) EMG feedback treatment of upper limb in hemiplegic stroke patients: A pilot study. *Archives of Physical Medicine and Rehabilitation* 1982; **63**: 613–616.

Basmajian JV, Gowland CA, Finlayson MA, Hall AL, Swanson LR, Stratford PW, Trotter JE, Brandstater ME (1987) Stroke treatment: Comparison of integrated behavioural–physical therapy vs traditional physical therapy programs. *Archives of Physical Medicine and Rehabilitation* 1987; **68**: 267–272.

Beckerman H, Becher J, Lankhorst GJ, Verbeek ALM, Vogelaar TW (1996a) The efficacy of thermocoagulation of the tibial nerve and a polypropylene ankle–foot orthosis on spasticity of the leg in stroke patients: Results of a randomised clinical trial. *Clinical Rehabilitation* 1996; **10**: 112–120.

Beckerman H, Becher J, Lankhorst GJ, Verbeek ALM (1996b) Walking ability of stroke patients: Efficacy of thermocoagulation of tibial nerve blocking and a polypropylene ankle–foot orthosis. *Archives of Physical Medicine and Rehabilitation* 1996; **77**: 1144–1151.

Berry MW, Rinke WJ, Smicklas-Wright H (1989) Work-site health promotion: The effects of a goal-setting program on nutrition-related behaviours. *Journal of the American Dietetic Association* 1989; **89**: 914–920.

Bhakta BB, Cozens JA, Bamford JM, Chamberlain MA (1996) Use of botulinum toxin in stroke patients with severe upper limb spasticity. *Journal of Neurology, Neurosurgery and Psychiatry* 1996; **61**: 30–35.

Blair CE (1995) Combining behavior management and mutual goal setting to reduce physical dependency in nursing home residents. *Nursing Research* 1995; **44**: 160–165.

Blair CE, Lewis R, Vieweg V, Tucker R (1996) Group and single-subject evaluation of a programme to promote self-care in elderly nursing home residents. *Journal of Advanced Nursing* 1996; **24**: 1207–1213.

Bowen J, Yaste C (1994) Effect of a stroke protocol on hospital costs of stroke patients. *Neurology* 1994; **44**: 1961–1964.

Bowman BR, Baker LL, Waters RL (1979) Positional feedback and electrical stimulation: An automated treatment for the hemiplegic wrist. *Archives of Physical Medicine and Rehabilitation* 1979; **60**: 497–502.

Bradley L, Hart BB, Mandana S, Flowers K, Riches M, Sanderson P (1998) Electromyographic biofeedback for gait training after stroke. *Clinical Rehabilitation* 1998; **12**: 11–22.

Braus DF, Kraus JK, Strobel J (1994) The shoulder–hand syndrome after stroke: A prospective clinical trial. *Annals of Neurology* 1994; **36**: 728–733.

Brindley P, Copeland M, Demain C, Martyn P (1989) A comparison of the speech of ten chronic Broca's aphasics following intensive and non-intensive periods of therapy. *Aphasiology* 1989; **3**: 695–707.

Brown KW, Sloan RL, Pentland B (1998) Fluoxetine as a treatment for post-stroke emotionalism. *Acta Psychiatrica Scand* 1998, **98**. 455–458.

Burbaud P, Wiart L, Dubos JL, Gaujard E, Debelleix X, Joseph PA, Mazaux JM, Bioulac B, Barat M, Laqueny A (1996) A randomised, double-blind, placebo-controlled trial of botulinum toxin in the treatment of spastic foot in hemiparetic patients. *Journal of Neurology, Neurosurgery and Psychiatry* 1996; **61**: 265–269.

Burnside IG, Tobias HS, Bursill D (1982) Electromyographic feedback in the remobilisation of stroke patients: A controlled trial. *Archives of Physical Medicine and Rehabilitation* 1982; **63**: 217–222.

Burridge JH, Taylor PN, Hagan SA, Wood DE, Swain ID (1997) The effects of common peroneal stimulation on the effort and speed of walking: A randomised controlled trial with chronic hemiplegic patients. *Clinical Rehabilitation* 1997; **11**: 201–210.

Burt AA, Currie S (1978) A double-blind controlled trial of baclofen and diazepam in spasticity due to cerebrovascular lesions. In: Jukes AM (Ed), *Baclofen: Spasticity and Cerebral Pathology*. Cambridge: Cambridge Medical Publications. pp. 77–79.

Campion E, Jette A, Berkman B (1983) An interdisciplinary geriatric consultation service: A controlled trial. *Journal of the American Geriatric Society* 1983; **31**: 792.

Chae J, Bethoux F, Bohine T, Dobos L, Davis T, Friedl A (1998) Neuromuscular stimulation for upper extremity motor and functional recovery in acute hemiplegia. *Stroke* 1998; **29**: 975–979.

Charles C, Gauld M, Chambers L, O'Brien B, Haynes RB, Labelle R (1994) How was your hospital stay? Patients' reports about their care in Canadian hospitals. *Canadian Medical Association Journal* 1994; **150**: 1813–1822.

Childers MK, Stacy M, Cooke DL, Stonnington HH (1996) Comparison of two injection techniques using botulinum toxin in spastic hemiplegia. *American Journal of Physical Medicine and Rehabilitation* 1996; **75**: 462–469.

Coast J, Richards SH, Peters TJ, Gunnell DJ, Darlow MA, Pounsford J (1998) Hospital at home or acute hospital care? A cost minimisation analysis. *British Medical Journal* 1998; **316**: 1802–1806.

Colborne GR, Olney SJ, Griffin MP (1993) Feedback of ankle joint angle and soleus electromyography in the rehabilitation of hemiplegic gait. *Archives of Physical Medicine and Rehabilitation* 1993; **74**: 1100–1106.

Corcoran PJ, Jebsen RH, Brengelmann, Simons BC (1970) Effects of plastic and metal leg braces on speed and energy cost of hemiparetic ambulation. *Archives of Physical Medicine and Rehabilitation* 1970; **51**: 69–77.

Corr S, Bayer A (1995) Occupational therapy for stroke patients after hospital discharge—a randomised controlled trial. *Clinical Rehabilitation* 1995; **9**: 291–296.

Corry IS, Cosgrove AP, Walsh EG, McClean D, Graham HK (1997) Botulinum toxin A in the hemiplegic upper limb: A double-blind trial. *Developmental Medicine and Child Neurology* 1997; **39**: 185–193.

Corry IS, Cosgrove AP, Duffy CM, McNeill S, Taylor TC, Graham HK (1998) Botulinum toxin A compared with stretching casts in the treatment of spastic equinus: A randomised prospective trial. *Journal of Pediatric Orthopaedics* 1998; **18**: 304–311.

Cozean CD, Pease WS, Hubbell SL (1988) Biofeedback and functional electrical stimulation in stroke rehabilitation. *Archives of Physical Medicine and Rehabilitation* 1988; **69**: 401–405.

Cristomo EA, Duncan PW, Propst M, Dawson DV, Davis JN (1988) Evidence that amphetamine with physical therapy promotes recovery of motor function in stroke patients. *Annals of Neurology* 1988; **23**: 94–97.

Crow JL, Lincoln NB, Nouri FM, De Weerdt W (1989) The effectiveness of EMG biofeedback in the treatment of arm function after stroke. *International Disability Studies* 1989; **11**: 155–160.

Cummings V, Kerner JF, Arones S, Steinbock C (1985) Day hospital service in rehabilitation medicine: An evaluation. *Archives of Physical Medicine and Rehabilitation* 1985; **66**: 86–91.

Cunningham C, Horgan F, Keane N, Connoly P, Mannion A, O'Neil D (1996) Detection of disability by different members of an interdisciplinary team. *Clinical Rehabilitation* 1996; **10**: 247–254.

Dam M, Tonin P, Casson S et al. (1993) The effects of long-term rehabilitation therapy on post-stroke patients. *Stroke* 1993; **24**: 1186–1191.

Daniels SK, Brailey K, Priestly DH, Herrington LR, Weisberg LA, Foundas AL (1998) Aspiration in patients with acute stroke. *Archives of Physical Medicine and Rehabilitation* 1998; **79**: 14–19.

Davalos A, Ricart W, Gonzalez-Huix F, Soler S, Marrugat J, Molins A, Suner R, Genis D (1996) Effect of early malnutrition after acute stroke on clinical outcome. *Stroke* 1996; **27**: 1028–1032.

David R, Enderby P, Baniton D (1982) Treatment of acquired aphasia: Speech therapists and volunteers compared. *Journal of Neurology, Neurosurgery and Psychiatry* 1982; **45**: 957–961.

Dean CM, Shepherd RB (1997) Task-related training improves performance of seating reaching tasks after stroke. A randomised controlled trial. *Stroke* 1997; **28**: 722–728.

Dekker JHM, Wagenaar RC, Lankhorst GJ, de Jong BA (1997) The painful hemiplegic shoulder. Effects of intra-articular triamcinolone acetonide. *American Journal of Physical Medicine and Rehabilitation* 1997; **76**: 43–48.

Dekker R, Drost EAM, Groothof JW, Arendzen JH,van Gijn JC, Eisma WH (1998) Effects of day-hospital rehabilitation in stroke patients: A review of randomised clinical trials. *Scandinavian Journal of Rehabilitation Medicine* 1998; **30**: 87–94.

Dennis M, O'Rourke S, Slattery J, Staniforth T, Warlow C (1997) Evaluation of a stroke family care worker: Results of a randomised controlled trial. *British Medical Journal* 1997; **314**: 1071–1076.

DePippo KL, Holas MA, Reding MJ, Mandel FS, Lesser ML (1994) Dysphagia therapy following stroke: A controlled trial. *Neurology* 1994; **44**: 1655–1660.

Di Carlo LM (1980) Language recovery in aphasia: Effect of systematic filmed programmed instruction. *Archives of Physical Medicine and Rehabilitation* 1980; **61**: 41–44.

Dickstein R, Hocherman S, Pillar T, Shaham R (1986) Stroke rehabilitation. Three exercise therapy approaches. *Physical Therapy* 1986; **66**: 1233–1238.

Drummond AER, Walker MF (1995) A randomised controlled trial of leisure rehabilitation after stroke. *Clinical Rehabilitation* 1995; **9**: 283–290.

Duncan G, Ritchie LC, Jamieson DM, McLean MA (1995) Acute stroke in South Ayrshire: Comparative study of pre and post stroke units. *Health Bulletin* 1995; **53**: 159–166.

Dursuin E, Hamamci N, Donmez S, Tuzunalp O, Cakci A (1996) Angular biofeedback device for sitting balance of stroke. *Stroke* 1996; **26**: 1354–1357.

Eagle DJ, Guyatt GH, Patterson C, Turpie I, Sackett B, Singer J (1991) Effectiveness of a geriatric day hospital. *Canadian Medical Association Journal* 1991; **144**: 699–704.

Ebrahim S, Barer D, Nouri F (1987) An audit of follow-up services for stroke patients after discharge from hospital. *International Disability Studies* 1987; **9**: 103–105.

Enderby P, Broeckx J, Hospers W, Schildermans F, Deberdt W (1994) Effect of piracetam on recovery and rehabilitation after stroke: A double-blind, placebo-controlled study. *Clinical Neuropharmacology* 1994; **17**: 320–331.

Evans RL, Hendricks RD (1993) Evaluating hospital discharge planning: A randomised clinical trial. *Medical Care* 1993; **31**: 358–370.

Faghri PD, Rodgers MM (1997) The effects of functional neuromuscular stimulation-augmented physical therapy in the functional recovery of hemiplegic arm in stroke patients. *Clinical Kinesiology* 1997; **51**: 9–15.

Faghri PD, Rodgers MM, Glaser RM, Bors JG, Ho C, Akuthota P (1994) The effects of functional electrical stimulation on shoulder subluxation, arm function recovery, and shoulder pain in hemiplegic stroke patients. *Archives of Physical Medicine and Rehabilitation* 1994; **75**: 73–79.

Fanthome Y, Lincoln NB, Drummond A, Walker MF (1995) The treatment of visual neglect using feedback of eye movements: A pilot study. *Disability and Rehabilitation* 1995; **17**: 413–417.

Feys HM, De Weerdt WJ, Selz BE, Steck GAC, Spichiger R, Vereeck LE, Putman KD, van Hoydonck GA (1998) Effect of a therapeutic intervention for the hemiplegic upper limb in the acute phase after stroke. A single blind, randomised, controlled multicenter trial. *Stroke* 1998; **29**: 785–792.

Finestone HM, Greene-Finestone LS, Wilson ES, Teasell RW (1996) Prolonged length of stay and reduced functional improvement rate in malnourished stroke rehabilitation patients. *Archives of Physical Medicine and Rehabilitation* 1996; **77**: 340–345.

Forster A, Young J (1996) Specialist nurse support for patients with stroke in the community: A randomised controlled trial. *British Medical Journal* 1996; **312**: 1642–1646.

Friedland JF, McColl M (1992) Social support intervention after stroke: Results of a randomised trial. *Archives of Physical Medicine and Rehabilitation* 1992; **73**: 573–581.

Garon BR, Engle M, Ormiston C (1997) A randomised control study to determine the effects of unlimited oral intake of water in patients with identified aspiration. *Journal of Neurologic Rehabilitation* 1997; **11**: 139–148.

Gladman JRF, Lincoln NB (1994) Follow-up of a controlled trial of domiciliary stroke rehabilitation (Domino study). *Age Ageing* 1994; **23**: 9–13.

Gladman JRF, Lincoln NB, Barer DH (1993) A randomised controlled trial of domiciliary and hospital-based rehabilitation for stroke patients after discharge from hospital. *Journal of Neurology, Neurosurgery and Psychiatry* 1993; **56**: 960–966.

Gladman JRF, Whynes D, Lincoln NB (1994) Cost-comparison of domiciliary and hospital-based stroke rehabilitation. *Age Ageing* 1994; **23**: 241–245.

Glanz M, Klawansky S, Stason W, Berkey C, Shah N, Phan H, Chalmers TC (1995) Biofeedback therapy in post stroke rehabilitation: A meta-analysis of the randomised controlled trials. *Archives of Physical Medicine and Rehabilitation* 1995; **76**: 508–515.

Glanz M, Klawansky S, Stason W, Berkey C, Chalmers TC (1996) Functional electrostimulation in poststroke rehabilitation: A meta-analysis of the randomised controlled trials. *Archives of Physical Medicine and Rehabilitation* 1996; **77**: 549–553.

Glasgow RE, Toobert DJ, Hampson SE (1996) Effects of a brief office-based intervention to facilitate diabetes dietary self-management. *Diabetes Care* 1996; **19**: 835–842.

Glasgow RE, La Chance PA, Toobert DJ, Brown J, Hampson SE, Ridddle MC (1997) Long term effects and costs of brief behavioural dietary intervention for patients with diabetes delivered from the medical office. *Patient Education and Counseling* 1997; **32**: 175–184.

Glennon TP, Smith BS (1990) Questions asked by patients and their support groups during family conferences on inpatient rehabilitation units. *Archives of Physical Medicine and Rehabilitation* 1990; **71**: 699–702.

Goldstein LB (1995) Common drugs may influence motor recovery after stroke. The Sygen In Acute Stroke Study Investigators. *Neurology* 1995; **45**: 865–871.

Gosman-Hedstrom G, Claesson L, Klingenstierna U, Carlsson J, Olausson B, Frizell M, Fagerberg B, Blomstrand C (1998) Effects of acupuncture treatment on daily life activities and quality of life: A controlled prospective and randomised study of acute stroke patients. *Stroke* 1998; **29**: 2100–2108.

Grazko MA, Polo KB, Jabbari B (1995) Botulinum toxin A for spasticity, muscle spasms, and rigidity. *Neurology* 1995; **45**: 712–717.

Greenberg S, Fowler RS (1980) Kinesthetic biofeedback: A treatment modality for elbow range of motion in hemiplegia. *American Journal of Occupational Therapy* 1980; **34**: 738–743.

Greenfield S, Kaplan S, Ware JE (1985) Expanding patient involvement in care. Effects on patient outcomes. *Annals of Internal Medicine* 1985; **102**: 520–528.

Gupta SR, Mlcoch AG, Scolaro C, Moritz T (1995) Bromocriptine treatment of nonfluent aphasia. *Neurology* 1995; **45**: 2170–2173.

Hansen R (1990) Social intervention at discharge. Cooperation between a hospital department, general practice and the social sector. *Ugeskrift for Laeger* 1990; **152**: 2506–2510.

Hartman J, Landau WM (1987) Comparison of formal language therapy with supportive counselling for aphasia due to vascular accident. *Archives of Neurology* 1987; **44**: 646–649.

Hesse S, Bertelt C, Schaffrin A, Malezic M, Mauritz KH (1994) Restoration of gait in nonambulatory hemiparetic patients by treadmill training with partial body-weight support. *Archives of Physical Medicine and Rehabilitation* 1994; **75**: 1087–1093.

Hesse S, Bertelt C, Jahnke MT, Schaffrin A, Baake P, Malezic M, Mauritz KH (1995) Treadmill training with partial body weight support compared with physiotherapy in nonambulatory hemiparetic patients. *Stroke* 1995; **26**: 976–981.

Hesse S, Krajnik J, Luecke D, Jahnke MT, Gregoric M, Mauritz KH (1996) Ankle muscle activity before and after botulinum toxin therapy for lower limb extensor spasticity in chronic hemiparetic patients. *Stroke* 1996; **27**: 455–460.

Hesse S, Reiter F, Konrad M, Jahnke MT (1998) Botulinum toxin type A and short-term electrical stimulation in the treatment of upper limb flexor spasticity after stroke: A randomised, double-blind, placebo-controlled trial. *Clinical Rehabilitation* 1998; **12**: 381–388.

Hu HH, Chung C, Liu TJ, Chen RC, Chen CH, Chou P, Huang WS, Lin JC, Tsuei JJ (1993) A randomised controlled trial on the treatment for acute partial ischemic stroke with acupuncture. *Neuroepidemiology* 1993; **12**: 106–113.

Huber W, Willmes K, Poeck K, Van Vleymen B, Deberdt W (1997) Piracetam as an adjuvant to language therapy for aphasia: A randomised double-blind placebo-controlled pilot study. *Archives of Physical Medicine and Rehabilitation* 1997; **78**: 245–250.

Hui E, Lum CM, Woo J, Or KH, Kay RLC (1995) Outcomes of elderly stroke patients. Day hospital versus conventional medical management. *Stroke* 1995; **26**: 1616–1619.

Hurd WW, Pegram V, Nepomuceno C (1980) Comparison of actual and simulated EMG biofeedback in the treatment of hemiplegic patients. *American Journal of Physical Medicine* 1980; **59**: 73–82.

Indredavik B, Slordahl SA, Bakke F, Rokseth R, Haheim LL (1997) Stroke unit treatment. Long-term effects. *Stroke* 1997; **28**: 1861–1866.

Indredavik B, Bakke F, Slordahl SA, Rokseth R, Haheim LL (1998) Stroke unit treatment improves long-term quality of life. A randomised controlled trial. *Stroke* 1998; **29**: 895–899.

Inglis J, Donald MW, Monga TN, Sproule M, Young MJ (1984) Electromyographic biofeedback and physical therapy of the hemiplegic upper limb. *Archives of Physical Medicine and Rehabilitation* 1984; **65**: 755–759.

Intiso D, Santilli V, Grasso MG, Rossi R, Caruso I (1994) Rehabilitation of walking with electromyographic biofeedback in foot-drop after stroke. *Stroke* 1994; **25**: 1189–1192.

John J (1986) Failure of electrical myofeedback to augment the effects of physiotherapy in stroke. *International Journal of Rehabilitation Research* 1986; **9**: 35–45.

Johansson K, Lindgren I, Widner H, Wiklund I, Johansson BB (1993) Can sensory stimulation improve the functional outcome in stroke patients? *Neurology* 1993; **43**: 2189–2192.

Johnson L, Graham S, Harris KR (1997) The effects of goal setting and self-instruction on learning a reading comprehension strategy: A study of students with learning disabilities. *Journal of Learning Disabilities* 1997; **30**: 80–91.

Jongbloed L, Morgan D (1991) An investigation of involvement in leisure activities after stroke. *American Journal of Occupational Therapy* 1991; **45**: 420–427.

Jongbloed L, Stacey S, Brighton C (1989) Stroke rehabilitation: Sensorimotor integrative treatment versus functional treatment. *American Journal of Occupational Therapy* 1989; **43**: 391–397.

Kalra L (1994) The influence of stroke unit rehabilitation on functional recovery from stroke. *Stroke* 1994; **25**: 821–825.

Katrak PH, Cole AM, Poulos CJ, McCauley JC (1992) Objective assessment of spasticity, strength, and function with early exhibition of dantrolene sodium after cerebrovascular accident: A randomised, double-blind study. *Archives of Physical Medicine and Rehabilitation* 1992; **73**: 4–9.

Katz RC, Wertz RT (1997) The efficacy of computer-provided reading treatment for chronic aphasic adults. *Journal of Speech, Language, and Hearing Research* 1997; **40**: 493–507.

Kennedy L, Neidlinger S, Scroggins K (1987) Effective comprehensive discharge planning for hospitalised elderly. *The Gerontologist* 1987; **27**: 577–580.

Kennedy P, Walker L, White D (1991) Ecological evaluation of goal planning and advocacy in a rehabilitation environment for spinal cord injured people. *Paraplegia* 1991; **29**: 197–202.

Ketel WB, Kolb ME (1984) Long-term treatment with dantrolene sodium of stroke patients with spasticity limiting the return of function. *Current Medical Research and Opinion* 1984; **9**: 161–169.

Kjendahl A, Sallstrom S, Osten PE, Stanghelle JK, Borchgrevink CF (1997) A one year follow-up study on the effects of acupuncture in the treatment of stroke patients in the subacute stage. *Clinical Rehabilitation* 1997; **11**: 192–200.

Kollef MH, Shapiro SD, Silver P, St John RE, Prentice D, Sauer S, Ahrens TS, Shannon W, Baker-Clinkscale D (1997) A randomised, controlled trial of protocol-directed versus physician-directed weaning from mechanical ventilation. *Critical Care Medicine* 1997; **25**: 567–574.

Kotzki N, Pelissier J, Dusotoit C, Toulemonde M, Codine P, Enjalbert M, Daures P, Simon L (1991) Techniques de prévention du syndrome algodystrophique: Évaluation d'un protocole d'installation au lit. *Annales Réadaptation Médicine Physique* 1991; **34**: 351–355.

Kumar R, Metter EJ, Mehta AJ, Chew T (1990) Shoulder pain in hemiplegia. The role of exercise. *American Journal of Physical Medicine and Rehabilitation* 1990; **69**: 205–208.

Kwakkel G, Wagenaar RC, Koelman TW, Lankhorst GJ, Koetsier JC (1997) Effects of intensity of rehabilitation after stroke. A research synthesis. *Stroke* 1997; **28**: 1550–1556.

Landefeld CS, Palmer RM, Kresevic DM, Fortinsky RH, Kowal J (1995) A randomised trial of care in a hospital medical unit especially designed to improve the functional outcomes of acutely ill older patients. *New England Journal of Medicine* 1995; **332**: 1338–1344.

Laursen SO, Henriksen IO, Dons U, Jacobsen B, Gundertofte L (1995) Intensiv apopleksirehabilitering – et kontrolleret pilotstudie. *Ugeskr Laeger* 1995; **157**: 1996–1999.

Lawson IR, MacLeod RD (1969) The use of imipramine (Tofranil) and other psychotropic drugs in organic emotionalism. *British Journal of Psychiatry* 1969; **115**: 281–285.

Leandri M, Parodi CI, Corrieri N, Rigardo S (1990) Comparison of TENS treatments in hemiplegic shoulder pain. *Scandinavian Journal of Rehabilitation Medicine* 1990; **22**: 69–72.

Lee KH, Hill E, Johnston R, Smichorowski T (1976) Myofeedback for muscle retraining in hemiplegic patients. *Archives of Physical Medicine and Rehabilitation* 1976; **57**: 588–591.

Lehman JF, DeLateur BJ, Fowler RS et al. (1975) Stroke: does rehabilitation affect outcome? *Archives of Physical Medicine and Rehabilitation* 1975; **56**: 375–382.

Levin MF, Hui-Chan CW (1992) Relief of hemiparetic spasticity by TENS is associated with improvement in reflex and voluntary motor functions. *Electroencephalography and Clinical Neurophysiology* 1992; **85**: 131–142.

Lilford RJ, Kelly M, Baines A, Cameron S, Cave M, Guthrie K, Thornton J (1992) Effects of using protocols on medical care: Randomised trial of three methods of taking an antenatal history. *British Medical Journal* 1992; **305**: 1181–1184.

Lincoln NB, Pickersgill MJ (1984) The effectiveness of programmed instruction with operant training in the language rehabilitation of severely aphasic stroke patients. *Behavioural Psychotherapy* 1984; **12**: 237–248.

Lincoln NB, Pickersgill MJ, Hankey AI, Hilton CR (1982) An evaluation of operant training and speech therapy in the language rehabilitation of moderate aphasics. *Behavioural Psychotherapy* 1982; **10**: 162–178.

Lincoln NB, McGuirk E, Mulley GP, Lendrem W, Jones AC, Mitchell LRA (1984) Effectiveness of speech therapy for aphasic stroke patients: A randomised controlled trial. *Lancet* 1984; **1**: 1197–1200.

Lincoln NB, McGuirk E, Mulley GP (1985) Psychological effects of speech therapy. *Journal of Psychosomatic Research* 1985; **29**: 467–444.

Lipsey JR, Robinson RG, Pearlson GD, Rao K, Price TR (1984) Nortriptyline treatment of post-stroke depression: A double-blind study. *Lancet* 1984; **1**: 297–300.

Logan PA, Ahern J, Gladman JRF, Lincoln NB (1997) A randomised controlled trial of enhanced Social Services occupational therapy for stroke patients. *Clinical Rehabilitation* 1997; **11**: 107–113.

Logigian MK, Samuels MA, Falconer J (1983) Clinical exercise trial for stroke patients. *Archives of Physical Medicine and Rehabilitation* 1983; **64**: 364–367.

Lord JP, Hall K (1986) Neuromuscular reeducation versus traditional programs for stroke rehabilitation. *Archives of Physical Medicine and Rehabilitation* 1986; **67**: 88–91.

Mackenzie C (1991) An aphasia group intensive efficacy study. *British Journal of Disorders of Communication* 1991; **26**: 275–291.

Macko RF, DeSouza CA, Tretter LD, Silver KH, Smith GV, Anderson PA, Tomoyasu N, Gorman P, Dengel DR (1997) Treadmill aerobic exercise training reduces the energy expenditure and cardiovascular demands of hemiparetic gait in chronic stroke patients. *Stroke* 1997; **28**: 326–330.

Malouin F, Potvon M, Prevost J, Richards CL, Wood-Dauphinee S (1992) Use of an intensive task-oriented gait training program in a series of patients with acute cerebrovascular accidents. *Physical Therapy* 1992; **72**: 781–793.

Mamon J, Steinwachs DM, Fahey M, Bone LR, Oktay J, Klein L (1992) Impact of hospital discharge planning on meeting patient needs after returning home. *Health Services Research* 1992; **27**: 155–175.

Mandel AR, Nymark JR, Balmer SJ, Grinnell DM, O'Riain MD (1990) Electromyographic versus rhythmic positional biofeedback in computerised gait retraining with stroke patients. *Archives of Physical Medicine and Rehabilitation* 1990; **71**: 649–654.

Medici M, Pebet M, Ciblis D (1989) A double-blind, long-term study of tizanidine ("Sirdalud") in spasticity due to cerebrovascular lesions. *Current Medical Research and Opinion* 1989; **11**: 398–407.

Meikle M, Wechsler E, Tupper A, Benenson M, Butler J, Mulhall D, Stern G (1979). Comparative trial of volunteer and professional treatments of dysphasia after stroke. *British Medical Journal* 1979; **2**: 87–89.

Miller GJT, Light KE (1997) Strength training in spastic hemiparesis: Should it be avoided? *NeuroRehabilitation* 1997; **9**: 17–28.

Montoya R, Dupui P, Pages B, Bessou P (1994) Step-length biofeedback device for walk rehabilitation. *Medical Biological Engineering and Computing* 1994; **32**: 416–420.

Moreland J, Thompson MA (1994) Efficacy of electromyographic biofeedback compared with conventional physical therapy for upper-extremity function in patients following stroke: A research overview and meta-analysis. *Physical Therapy* 1994; **74**: 534–547.

Moreland JD, Thompson MA, Fuoco AR (1998) Electromyographic biofeedback to improve lower extremity function after stroke: A meta-analysis. *Archives of Physical Medicine and Rehabilitation* 1998; **79**: 134–140.

Morris ME, Matyas TA, Back TM, Goldie PA (1992) Electrogoniometric feedback: Its effect on genu recurvatum in stroke. *Archives of Physical Medicine and Rehabilitation* 1992; **73**: 1147–1154.

Naylor MD (1990) Comprehensive discharge planning for hospitalised elderly: A pilot study. *Nursing Research* 1990; **39**: 156–161.

Naylor M, Brooten D, Jones R, Lavizzo-Mourey R, Mezey M, Pauly M (1994) Comprehensive discharge planning for the hospitalised elderly. A randomised clinical trial. *Annals of Internal Medicine* 1994; **120**: 999–1006.

Neidlinger A, Scroggins K, Kennedy L (1987) Cost evaluation of discharge planning for hospitalised elderly. *Nursing Economics* 1987; **5**: 225–230.

Nelson DL, Konosky K, Fleharty K, Webb R, Newer K, Hazbourn VP, Fontane C, Licht BC (1996) The effects of an occupationally embedded exercise on bilaterally assisted supination in persons with hemiplegia. *American Journal of Occupational Therapy* 1996; **50**: 639–646.

Norton B, Homer-Ward M, Donnelly MT, Long RG, Holmes GK (1996) A randomised prospective comparison of percutaneous endoscopic gastrostomy and nasogastric tube feeding after acute dysphagic stroke. *British Medical Journal* 1996; **312**: 13–16.

Odderson IR, Keaton JC, McKenna BS (1995) Swallow management in patients on an acute stroke pathway: Quality is cost effective. *Archives of Physical Medicine and Rehabilitation* 1995; **76**: 1130–1133.

Parfrey PS, Gardner E, Vavasour H, Harnett JD, McManamon C, McDonald J, Dawe J (1994) The feasibility and efficacy of early discharge planning initiated by the admitting department in two acute care hospitals. *Clinical and Investigative Medicine* 1994; **17**: 88–96.

Partridge CJ, Edwards SM, Mee R, van Langenberghe HVK (1990) Hemiplegic shoulder pain: A study of two methods of physiotherapy treatment. *Clinical Rehabilitation* 1990; **4**: 43–49.

Perez I, Smithard DG, Davies H, Kalra L (1998) Pharmacological treatment of dysphagia in stroke. *Dysphagia* 1998; **13**: 12–16.

Potter J, Langhorne P, Roberts M (1998) Routine protein energy supplementation in adults: Systematic review. *British Medical Journal* 1998; **317**: 495–501.

Prevo AJH, Visser SL, Vogelaar TW (1982) Effect of EMG biofeedback on paretic muscles and abnormal co-contraction in the hemiplegic arm compared with conventional physical therapy. *Scandinavian Journal of Rehabilitation Medicine* 1982; **14**: 121–131.

Rapoport J, Eerd MJ (1989) Impact of physical therapy weekend coverage on length of stay in an acute care community hospital. *Physical Therapy* 1989; **69**: 32–37.

Reding MJ, Orto LA, Winter SW, Fortuna IM, DiPonte P, McDowell FH (1986) Anti-depressant therapy after stroke. A double blind study. *Archives of Neurology* 1986; **43**: 763–765.

Reiter F, Danni M, Lagalla G, Ceravolo G, Provinciali L (1998) Low-dose botulinum toxin with ankle taping for the treatment of spastic equinovarus foot after stroke. *Archives of Physical Medicine and Rehabilitation* 1998; **79**: 532–535.

Richards SH, Coast J, Gunnell DJ, Peters TJ, Pounsford J, Darlow MA (1998) Randomised controlled trial comparing effectiveness and acceptability of an early discharge, hospital at home scheme with acute hospital care. *British Medical Journal* 1998; **316**: 1796–1801.

Robinson RG, Parikh RM, Lipsey JR et al. (1993) Pathological laughing and crying following stroke: Validation of a measurement scale and a double blind treatment study. *American Journal of Psychiatry* 1993; **150**: 286–293.

Rogers H, Soutter J, Kaiser W, Pearson P, Dobson R, Skilbeck C, Bond J (1997) Early supported discharge following acute stroke: Pilot study results. *Clinical Rehabilitation* 1997; **11**: 280–287.

Ronning OM, Guldvog B (1998a) Stroke unit versus general medical wards, II: Neurological deficits and activities of daily living. A quasi-randomised controlled trial. *Stroke* 1998; **29**: 586–590.

Ronning OM, Guldvog B (1998b) Outcome of subacute stroke rehabilitation: A randomized controlled trial. *Stroke* 1998; **29**: 779–784.

Rudd AG, Wolfe CD, Tilling K, Beech R (1997) Randomised controlled trial to evaluate early discharge scheme for patients with stroke. *British Medical Journal* 1997; **315**: 1039–1044.

Sabe L, Salvarezza F, Garcia Cuerva A, Leiguarda R, Sarkstein S (1995) A randomised, double-blind, placebo-controlled study of bromocriptine in nonfluent aphasia. *Neurology* 1995; **45**: 2272–2274.

Sackley CM, Lincoln NB (1997) Single blind randomised controlled trial of visual feedback after stroke: Effects on stance symmetry and function. *Disability and Rehabilitation* 1997; **19**: 536–546.

Sallstrom S, Kjendahl A, Osten PE, Stranghella JH, Borchgrevink CF (1996). Acupuncture in the treatment of stroke patients in the subacute stage: a randomised controlled study. *Complementary Therapies in Medicine* 1996; **4**: 193–197.

Sampaio C, Ferreira JJ, Pinto AA, Crespo M, Ferro JM, Castro-Caldas A (1997) Botulinum toxin type A for the treatment of arm and hand spasticity in stroke patients. *Clinical Rehabilitation* 1997; **11**: 3–7.

Sarno MT, Sarno JE, Diller L (1972) The effect of hyperbaric oxygen on communication function in adults with aphasia secondary to stroke. *Journal of Speech and Hearing Research* 1972; **15**: 42–48.

Schauer M, Steingruber W, Mauritz K-H (1996) The effect of music on gait symmetry in stroke patients walking on the treadmill. *Biomedizinische Technik* 1996; **41**: 291–296.

Schiffer RB, Herndon RM, Rudick RA (1985) Treatment of pathologic laughing and weeking with amitriptyline. *New England Journal of Medicine* 1985; **312**: 1480–1482.

Schleenbaker RE, Mainous AG (1993) Electromyographic biofeedback for neuromuscular reeducation in the hemiplegic stroke patient – a meta-analysis. *Archives of Physical Medicine and Rehabilitation* 1993; **74**: 1301–1304.

Sharp SA, Brouwer BJ (1997) Isokinetic strength training of the hemiparetic knee: Effects on function and spasticity. *Archives of Physical Medicine and Rehabilitation* 1997; **78**: 1231–1236.

Shepperd S, Iliffe S (1999) Hospital-at-home versus in-patient hospital care (Cochrane review). In: *The Cochrane Library. Issue 2*. 1999. Oxford: Update Software.

Shepperd S, Harwood D, Jenkinson C, Gray A, Vessey M, Morgan P (1998a) Randomised controlled trial comparing hospital at home care with inpatient hospital care. I: Three month follow up of health outcomes. *British Medical Journal* 1998; **316**: 1786–1791.

Shepperd S, Harwood D, Gray A, Vessey M, Morgan P (1998b) Randomised controlled trial comparing hospital at home care with inpatient hospital care. II: Cost minimisation analysis. *British Medical Journal* 1998; **316**: 1791–1796.

Shewan CM, Kertesz A (1984) Effects of speech and language treatment on recovery from aphasia. *Brain and Language* 1984; **23**: 272–299.

Simpson DM, Alexander DN, O'Brien CF, Tagliati M, Aswad AS, Leon JM, Gibson J, Mordaunt JM, Monaghan EP (1996) Botulinum toxin type A in the treatment of upper extremity spasticity: A randomised, double-blind, placebo-controlled trial. *Neurology* 1996; **46**: 1306–1310.

Skelly M (1985) Biofeedback in stroke rehabilitation. *International Journal of Rehabilitation Research* 1985; **8**: 77.

Smith DS, Goldenberg E, Ashburn A, Kinsella G, Sheikh K, Brennan PJ, Meade TW, Zutshi DW, Perry JD, Reeback JS (1981) Remedial therapy after stroke: A randomised controlled trial. *British Medical Journal* 1981; **282**: 517–520.

Smith KN (1979) Biofeedback in strokes. *Australian Journal of Physiotherapy* 1979; **25**: 155–161.

Smithard DG, O'Neill PA, Park C, Morris J, Wyatt R, England R, Martin DF (1996) Complications and outcome after acute stroke. Does dysphagia matter? *Stroke* 1996; **27**: 1200–1204.

Snow BJ, Tsui JKC, Bhatt MH, Varelas M, Hashimoto SA, Calne DB (1990) Treatment of spasticity with botulinum toxin: A double-blind study. *Annals of Neurology* 1990; **28**: 512–515.

Sonde L, Fernaeus SE, Nilsson CG, Viitanen M (1998) Stimulation with low frequency (1.7 Hz) transcutaneous electric nerve stimulation (Low-TENS) increases motor function of the post-stroke paretic arm. *Scandinavian Journal of Rehabilitation Medicine* 1998; **30**: 95–99.

Stenstrom CH (1994) Home exercise in rheumatoid arthritis functional class II: Goal setting versus pain attention. *Journal of Rheumatology* 1994; **21**: 627–634.

Stroke Unit Trialist's Collaboration (1997) Collaborative systematic review of the randomised trial of organised inpatient (stroke unit) care after stroke. *British Medical Journal* 1997; **314**: 1151–1159.

Stuck AE, Siu AL, Wieland GD, Adams J, Rubenstein LZ (1993) Comprehensive geriatric assessment: A meta-analysis of controlled trials. *Lancet* 1993; **342**: 1032–1036.

Sukthankar SM, Reddy NP, Canilang EP, Stephenson L, Thomas R (1994) Design and development of portable biofeedback systems for use in oral dysphagia rehabilitation. *Medical Engineering and Physics* 1994; **16**: 430–435.

Sunderland A, Tinson DJ, Bradley EL, Fletcher D, Langton-Hewer R, Wade DT (1992) Enhanced physical therapy improves recovery of arm function after stroke. A randomised controlled trial. *Journal of Neurology, Neurosurgery and Psychiatry* 1992; **55**: 530–535.

Sunderland A, Fletcher D, Bradley L, Tinson D, Hewer RL, Wade DT (1994) Enhanced physical therapy for arm function after stroke: A one year follow-up study. *Journal of Neurology, Neurosurgery and Psychiatry* 1994; **57**: 856–858.

Svensson BH, Christiansen LS, Jepsen F (1992) Treatment of central facial nerve paralysis with electromyography biofeedback and taping of cheek. A controlled clinical trial. *Ugeskr Laeger* 1992; **154**: 3593–3596.

Tangeman PT, Banaitis DA, Williams AK (1990) Rehabilitation of chronic stroke patients: Changes in functional performance. *Archives of Physical Medicine and Rehabilitation* 1990; **71**: 876–880.

Teasell RW, McRae M, Marchuk Y, Finestone HM (1996) Pneumonia associated with aspiration following stroke. *Archives of Physical Medicine and Rehabilitation* 1996; **77**: 707–709.

Tekeoolu Y, Adak B, Goksoy T (1998) Effect of transcutaneous electrical nerve stimulation (TENS) on Barthel Activities of Daily Living (ADL) index score following stroke. *Clinical Rehabilitation* 1998; **12**: 277–280.

Thaut MH, McIntosh GC, Rice RR (1997) Rhythmic facilitation of gait training in hemiparetic stroke rehabilitation. *Journal of Neurological Sciences* 1997; **151**: 207–212.

Theodorakis Y, Beneca A, Malliou P, Goudas M (1997) Examining psychological factors during injury rehabilitation. *Journal of Sport Rehabilitation* 1997; **6**: 355–363.

Towle D, Lincoln NB, Mayfield LM (1989) Service provision and functional independence in depressed stroke patients and the effect of social work intervention on these. *Journal of Neurology, Neurosurgery and Psychiatry* 1989; **52**: 519–522.

Tucker MA, Davidson JG, Ogle S (1984) Day hospital rehabilitation – effectiveness and cost in the elderly: A randomised controlled trial. *British Medical Journal* 1984; **289**: 1209–1212.

Vallet G, Ahmaidi S, Serres I, Fabre C, Bourgouin D, Desplan J, Varray A, Prefaut C (1997) Comparison of two training programmes in chronic airway limitation patients: Standardised versus individualised protocols. *European Respiratory Journal* 1997; **10**: 114–122.

van Vliet P, Sheridan M, Kerwin DG, Fentem P (1995) The influence of functional goals on the kinematics of reaching following stroke. *Neurology Report* 1995; **19**: 11–16.

Victor CR, Vetter NJ (1988) Preparing the elderly for discharge from hospital: A neglected aspect of patient care? *Age Aging* 1988; **17**: 155–163.

Vissers MC, Hasman A, van der Linden CJ (1996) Impact of a protocol processing system (ProtoVIEW) on clinical behaviour of residents and treatment. *International Journal of Biomedical Computing* 1996; **42**: 143–150.

Visintin M, Barbeau H, Korner-Bitensky N, Mayo NE (1998) A new approach to retrain gait in stroke patients through body weight support and treadmill stimulation. *Stroke* 1998; **29**: 1122–1128.

Wade DT (1998) Evidence relating to assessment in rehabilitation. *Clinical Rehabilitation* 1998; **12**: 183–186.

Wade DT, Langton Hewer R, Skilbeck CE, Bainton D, Burns-Cox C (1985) Controlled trial of a home-care service for acute stroke patients. *Lancet* 1985; **i**: 323–326.

Wade DT, Collen FM, Robb GF, Warlow CP (1992) Physiotherapy intervention late after stroke and mobility. *British Medical Journal* 1992; **304**: 609–613.

Wagenaar RC, Meijer OG, van Wieringen PCW, Kuik DJ, Hazenberg GJ, Lindeboom J, Wichers F, Rijswijk H (1990) The functional recovery of stroke: A comparison between neuro-developmental treatment and the Brunnstrom method. *Scandinavian Journal of Rehabilitation Medicine* 1990; **22**: 1–8.

Walker MF, Drummond AER, Lincoln NB (1996) Evaluation of dressing practice for stroke patients after discharge from hospital: A crossover design study. *Clinical Rehabilitation* 1996; **10**: 23–31.

Walker-Batson D, Smith P, Curtis S, Unwin H, Greenlee R (1995) Amphetamine paired with physical therapy accelerates motor recovery after stroke. Further evidence. *Stroke* 1995; **26**: 2254–2259.

Wall JC, Turnbull GI (1987) Evaluation of out-patient physiotherapy and a home exercise program in the management of gait asymmetry in residual stroke. *Journal of Neurologic Rehabilitation* 1987; **1**: 115–123.

Webb PM, Glueckauf RL (1994) The effects of direct involvement in goal setting on rehabilitation outcome for persons with traumatic brain injuries. *Rehabilitation Psychology* 1994; **39**: 179–188.

Wei F, Mark D, Hartz A, Campbell C (1995) Are PRO discharge screens associated with post-discharge adverse outcomes? *Health Services Research* 1995; **30**: 489–506.

Werner RA, Kessler S (1996) Effectiveness of an intensive outpatient rehabilitation program for postacute stroke patients. *American Journal of Physical Medicine and Rehabilitation* 1996; **75**: 114–120.

Wertz RT, Collins MJ, Weiss D, Kurtzke JF, Friden T, Brookshire RH et al. (1981) Veterans Administration cooperative study on aphasia: A comparison of individual and group treatment. *Journal of Speech and Hearing Research* 1981; **24**: 580–594.

Wertz RT, Weiss DG, Aten JL, Brookshire RH, Garcia-Bunuel L, Holland AL et al. (1986) Comparison of clinic, home and deferred language treatment for aphasia. *Archives of Neurology* 1986; **43**: 653–658.

West R, Stockel S (1965) The effect of meprobamate on recovery from aphasia. *Journal of Speech and Hearing Research* 1965; **8**: 57–62.

Widen Holmqvist L, von Koch L, Kostulas V, Holm M, Widsell G, Tegler H, Johansson K, Almazan J, de Pedro-Cuesta J (1998) A randomised controlled trial of rehabilitation at home after stroke in southwest Stockholm. *Stroke* 1998; **29**: 591–597.

Wikander B, Ekelund P, Milsom I (1998) An evaluation of multidisciplinary intervention governed by functional independence measure (FIM sm) in incontinent stroke patients. *Scandinavian Journal of Rehabilitation Medicine* 1998; **30**: 15–21.

Winchester P, Montgomery J, Bowman B, Hislop H (1983) Effects of feedback stimulation training and cyclical electrical stimulation on knee extension in hemiparetic patients. *Physical Therapy* 1983; **63**: 1096–1103.

Wolf SL, Catlin PA, Blanton S, Edelman J, Lehrer N, Schroeder D (1994). Overcoming limitations in elbow movement in the presence of antagonist hyperactivity. *Physical Therapy* 1994; **74**: 826–835.

Wong AM, Lee MY, Kuo JK, Tang FT (1997) The development and clinical evaluation of a standing biofeedback trainer. *Journal of Rehabilitation Research and Development* 1997; **34**: 322–327.

Young JB, Forster A (1992) The Bradford community stroke trial: Results at six months. *British Medical Journal* 1992; **304**: 1085–1089.

Young J, Forster A (1993) Day hospital and home physiotherapy for stroke patients: A comparative cost-effectiveness study. *Journal of the Royal College of Physicians* 1993; **27**: 252–258.

37. The epilepsies

Pamela Thompson   Simon Shorvon   Dominic Heaney

INTRODUCTION

Epileptic seizures are common: the incidence of epilepsy in the developed world is 50–80 per 100,000 persons per year. The prevalence of active epilepsy is about 50–100 per 1000 persons and it is estimated that between 2 and 5% of the general population will suffer at least one non-febrile seizure during their lives (Sander & Shorvon, 1996). It is one of the most common neurological conditions in both children and adults. Although many patients have a mild condition, epilepsy has a particularly high prevalence in individuals with learning disabilities and also physical handicap. Furthermore, even if the epilepsy is mild and there are no additional physical handicaps, many individuals feel stigmatised and epilepsy carries with it potentially severe social disadvantage. The condition is responsible for considerable medical and social disturbance and there is a potential for rehabilitation in diverse areas; intervention may focus on medical, neuropsychological, psychiatric, and social aspects. The rehabilitation of physical disability is seldom the main issue and severe physical handicap uncommon, although when epilepsy and severe physical handicap do exist, disability and handicap is severe.

Epilepsy is a heterogeneous condition, varying considerably in regard to its severity, prognosis and extent of handicap and its aetiology. In about 60–70% of patients developing epilepsy, the condition remits and active epilepsy comprises a period of disability, which is usually relatively short (Goodridge & Shorvon, 1983). Such patients require little in the way of formal or specialised rehabilitation, although they do require a full medical evaluation and varying degrees of social and psychological support. For instance, driving restrictions following diagnosis can result in major social difficulties, influencing employment choices and social mobility. Intensive rehabilitation, however, is usually reserved for those patients whose epilepsy is intractable and in whom the condition is likely to continue and be a persistent handicap.

In a typical population of a million persons there will be about 5000 persons with active epilepsy. Of these, over half will have secondary generalised or partial seizures, and perhaps 30% will be having more than one seizure per week. Of the mass of patients with epilepsy, about 10% will have additional neurological disability and about half intellectual and/or behavioural disturbance. Thus, epilepsy comprises a spectrum. At one end are patients with mild seizures that are infrequent and not associated with other deficits. At the other end are patients with many seizures a day, frequently associated with intellectual or behavioural disturbance. The prognosis is poor in those patients with partial or mixed seizures, in those with structural or progressive disorders, those with psychiatric or behavioural disturbance, those with an early onset of seizures and those with a long history of epilepsy.

The overall cost of epilepsy has been estimated in several developed countries. A study performed in the USA used a model based on incidence and prognosis and estimated the lifetime cost of medical services provided for people with epilepsy to be $790 million (1990 prices) (Begley et al., 1994). This study also highlighted high "indirect" costs to society of lost "production" in the workplace and at home. With these costs the total cost of epilepsy in the USA was estimated to be $3 billion. A UK study using data on epidemiology and service utilisation estimated the total UK cost (including "indirect costs") to be £1.93 billion (1990 prices) (Cockerell et al., 1994). "Cost of illness" studies show that over half of the costs of epilepsy are due to the small group (15–30%) of individuals with poorly controlled epilepsy who require periods of hospitalisation or institutionalisation.

This chapter will primarily be considering patients at the severe end of the spectrum of epilepsy. For the purpose of rehabilitation, the most common patient group are those who are young, often in their 20s and early 30s. Academically, achievements are limited, with many individuals completing their education without obtaining any formal qualifications. Furthermore, for many, basic literacy skills might be poorly developed. Unemployment is common, although most young people have undertaken employment training schemes. The majority of individuals are single and live with their parents, where little is expected of them in the way of household management. Most do not have structured daily activity and might not have had for many years. The patient group is often socially isolated and relatively immature emotionally; the need for increased supervision during a childhood disrupted by epilepsy can contribute to this. For most patients, in contrast to other acquired neurological conditions, independent living skills have not been lost but rather have never been learned. The term "habilitation" is therefore more strictly applicable.

MODELS OF SERVICE PROVISION

Service provision for any disease depends on a number of factors. First, the epidemiological and demographic features of the disease and the population; second, the structure of the existing medical resources; and third, the extent to which financial and other resources are committed to the condition, this being a social and political decision. Clearly, for all these reasons care will vary from country to country, and in this section description of the structure of care for epilepsy in the UK will be given to illustrate these points. The emphasis here will be on the current facilities for rehabilitation, illustrated especially by activities at the Chalfont Centre for Epilepsy which is the largest epilepsy centre in the country.

Existing medical services in the UK

The basic medical care for epilepsy in the UK is provided by the GP on a long-term basis. Most patients with epilepsy, however, are referred to specialist hospital clinics for evaluation. In a community-based survey of unselected patients, 92% were referred to hospital, 40% attended a neurologist, 20% paediatricians, and 32% other medical specialists (Hart, 1992). Long-term follow-up is provided for a selected population of patients and re-referral is available for specific purposes. In a representative population of a million persons, there are approximately 5000 people with active epilepsy and currently such a population is served by approximately 550 GPs, five neurologists, one neurophysiologist, and two neurosurgeons. It is clearly not feasible for every patient with active epilepsy to be followed up at a specialist clinic. This having been said, it has been estimated that 20% of all out-patient consultations in adult neurology clinics are concerned with epilepsy (Stevens, 1989).

Special epilepsy clinics

In 1969, a government-sponsored committee published a report in which a recommendation was made that people with severe or complicated epilepsy should be under the care of specialised epilepsy clinics (Central Health Service Council, 1969). This recommendation has been endorsed by subsequent government and professional reports (Thompson, 1990). The epilepsy clinics were envisaged as being run by a consultant neurologist or paediatrician with access to other professionals who could provide information and counselling where appropriate. Epilepsy clinics were seen as a means of improving continuity of patient care, avoiding patients being seen by inexperienced junior doctors who would frequently not see the patient again at subsequent follow-up.

Unfortunately, numerous studies have shown epilepsy services to be deficient not only in the diagnosis and treatment of the condition (Goodridge & Shorvon, 1983; Hopkins & Scambler, 1977) but also in the organisation of care. People with epilepsy have faced, for example, long delays in obtaining first appointments or investigations (Betts, 1992), and poor follow-up and continuity of care between GPs and hospital specialists (Hopkins & Scambler, 1977; Lloyd-Jones, 1980). In a national General Practice Survey of people with active epilepsy, only 6% of patients claimed to have been seen in an epilepsy clinic (Hart, 1992).

Over recent years there is some evidence of an improvement in medical services provided for people with epilepsy. A more recent audit, which surveyed all consultant neurologists in the UK, revealed that over half of the major neurological centres represented in the survey had epilepsy clinics (Wallace et al., 1997). This audit also suggested that patients seen in epilepsy clinics were likely to have improved access to investigations, specialists, and provision of psychosocial support compared with those seen in general neurology clinics.

A more detailed comparison between the service provided by specialised clinics and general neurological services was made by Morrow (1990), who observed that special epilepsy clinics improved certain process outcomes of care. For example, they improved follow-up and continuity of care, there were fewer side-effects of medication, and greater patient satisfaction with the service. In an outcome audit of an epilepsy clinic, Tobias et al. (1994) also demonstrated improved seizure control and increased monotherapy following referral to the clinic. Although the results of these studies suggest that increasing the number of epilepsy clinics is likely to benefit patients, further evaluation of both their clinical and cost effectiveness on a larger scale is needed.

Nevertheless, epilepsy clinics have considerable potential to provide epilepsy education and counselling, particularly in cases where intensive rehabilitation programmes would not be necessary. Many of the techniques for assessments and approaches to rehabilitation discussed in the context of a specialist epilepsy centre in this chapter can be applied on an out-patient basis.

Special assessment centres

The government report of 1969 recommended the designation of special centres for "people with epilepsy whose management presents particular problems" (Central Health Service Council, 1969). The role of the special centres was seen as providing medical assessment, intervention, research and teaching facilities, and social and occupational rehabilitation. Following this recommendation, three centres were created. The largest of these is the Chalfont Centre for Epilepsy in Buckinghamshire.

The special assessment unit at the Chalfont Centre is administered jointly by the National Society for Epilepsy (the major epilepsy charity in the UK) and the National Hospital for Neurology and Neurosurgery (the largest specialised neurological hospital in the country). Patients admitted to the Chalfont

Centre for Epilepsy are representative of those requiring input of a rehabilitative nature. A summary of this patient group is given in Table 37.1. This group has severe epilepsy. The patients are usually young, with predominantly partial seizures that are frequent and take several forms, are on multidrug therapy, and have additional cognitive and other difficulties. Admission is not provided for patients with severe behavioural disorders, as rehabilitation measures in this group would be largely dictated by the control of the behavioural aspects rather than the epilepsy-related problem.

Table 37.1. Medical and demographic details of 100 assessment unit admissions (1996/1997)

Number	100
Males	48
Age (years)	
Mean	32
Standard deviation	10.2
Employment status	
Employed	16
Unemployed	72
Attends day centre	7
Full-time education	5
Diagnosis of seizures	
Epilepsy	67
Non-epileptic attack disorder	24
Both	9
Seizure classification	
Partial	58
Generalised	18
Aetiology	
Unknown	45
Perinatal injury	6
Post-traumatic	5
Hippocampal sclerosis	13
Postinfection	7
Other	24
Number of seizure types	
1	10
2	39
3+	27
Seizure frequency	
Yearly	4
Monthly	30
Weekly	42
Daily	24
Antiepileptic medications	
0	3
1	21
2	43
3	33
Drugs prescribed	
Carbamazepine	51
Carbamazepine Retard	15
Sodium Valproate	32
Lamotrigine	22
Phenytoin	20
Clobazam	16
Gabapentin	13
Diazepam	12
Clonazepam	9
Phenobarbitone	6
Topiramate	6
Vigabatrin	6
Other	5

The primary role of special assessment centres is to provide in a multidisciplinary setting a thorough assessment of medical, social, and psychological aspects of the patient's problem area and to make recommendations regarding rehabilitation. In the special assessment unit of the Chalfont Centre work can be divided into four main categories.

1. A comprehensive medical assessment. This aspect of work has become more prominent than envisaged in the Reid Report (Central Health Services Council, 1969), partly because of the failure of the hospital service to provide dedicated epilepsy clinics on a nationwide basis. This assessment includes a detailed scrutiny of previous medical history, electroencephalogram (EEG) monitoring, and treatment. Neuropsychological evaluation and other neurological investigations, including a magnetic resonance imaging (MRI) scan, are carried out. Seizures can be recorded on EEG videotelemetry and re-examined. During the admission diagnosis is clarified, treatment adjusted, and recommendations made about medication and surgical management after discharge.

2. A realistic appraisal of the patient's abilities in the educational, vocational, and psychosocial fields can be made. This assessment takes time to undertake and is only possible in those staying for more than a few weeks. This assessment can be vitally important when setting goals for young people at a time when they may be leaving the parental home and attempting to live independently.

3. Recommendations for long-term assistance. This includes recommendations regarding occupational choices, psychosocial health, and future rehabilitation and placement needs.

4. Postgraduate teaching and research activities are undertaken linked to the University Department at the Institute of Neurology, University College Hospital, London. These relate to clinical and non-clinical aspects.

Rehabilitation service

In addition to the Special Assessment Unit at Chalfont, which is a National Health Service facility, the National Society for Epilepsy also administers a separate rehabilitation unit, "Links". Individuals are admitted to the unit on a sponsored basis, specifically for psychosocial rehabilitation. Admission is usually for 12–18 months and, in the main, efforts are concentrated on psychological and social problems. The content of rehabilitation programmes is flexible, depending on an individual's assessed needs. However, the following aspects are usually covered.

1. Providing individuals and families with a better understanding of their epilepsy. The young adult with epilepsy might be overanxious because of misconceptions about the disorder. In some cases, epilepsy might have been used as an excuse for avoiding responsibility and opting out of activities.

2. Individuals are provided with practical opportunities to develop appropriate skills and knowledge pertinent for independent living and personal development. This might include instruction in the area of domestic management, social skills, personal relationships, and stress management.

3. Training is given to develop realistic attitudes towards seeking employment, taking into account skills, qualifications, and interests. Instruction is given on work preparation skills, including disclosure of epilepsy to potential employers. In many cases, young people need to explore alternatives to formal employment.

4. Towards the end of the rehabilitation programme, participants are assisted in finding independent or supported housing in the community.

In our experience of rehabilitation, both in the Special Assessment Unit and in Links, the rehabilitation facility forms the basis of the principles outlined in this chapter. We are confining our discussion to adults and the majority of subjects will be in young adult life, who, as is shown in Table 37.1, have epilepsy and additional handicaps. We will consider only those where epilepsy is the major handicap and not, for instance, those with a learning disability or a severe psychiatric disorder, in whom the problems caused by epilepsy are often less of concern than the other handicaps.

MEDICAL ASSESSMENT AND TREATMENT

Prior to any rehabilitation effort, a full medical assessment must be made. In general, this is essential to stabilise the medical condition before embarking on formal rehabilitation. In this way, one avoids the tendency to defer difficult rehabilitation choices with the excuse that medical changes may alter rehabilitation requirements. Several aspects of the medical assessment require comment.

Diagnosis

In all cases, the diagnosis of epilepsy should be reviewed. It has been estimated that perhaps 20% of patients attending epilepsy clinics with apparent intractable seizures do in fact have non-epileptic attacks (Lelliot & Fenwick, 1991) and this problem should not be underestimated. Of 100 consecutive admissions to the special assessment unit, one-third were diagnosed as having non-epileptic attacks solely, or in addition to, epileptic seizures (see Table 37.1).

Such attacks are more common in young females, although they also occur in males and in people of all ages. Suspicion of non-epileptic attacks should be raised in an individual with a history of frequent seizures, including episodes of status in the presence of normal routine EEGs. A detailed psychiatric history, including psychosexual aspects, can yield vital information as to the possible aetiology of attacks. Seizures are observed by trained staff. Features such as prolonged duration, non-stereotyped episodes, and bizarre motor phenomena should raise

suspicions. The measurement of blood prolactin can also help in differential diagnosis. Accurate diagnosis, particular in cases resembling partial seizures, might not be possible without further investigations, the most valuable of which is simultaneous video EEG monitoring.

Rehabilitative efforts in individuals with non-epileptic seizures should be directed at the psychological difficulties considered to underlie the episodes. For some individuals, the attacks represent a maladaptive reaction to stress. For such individuals, anxiety management techniques can be valuable. For other individuals, the attacks can be an expression of some more deep-seated problem, including past sexual traumas for which more long-term psychotherapy will be indicated. There is an increasing awareness that the outcome in managing non-epileptic attacks is variable, but it can be improved if the initial diagnosis is presented in a positive, non-judgemental manner.

Seizure type and aetiology

The epilepsy should be categorised in terms of seizure type and aetiology. A detailed seizure description is always important, including an understanding of the ictal and postictal phenomenology. Indeed, the postictal symptoms can be more distressing to a patient than those of the attack itself. Some gauge of the severity of an attack is also important, both in terms of its physical and psychological consequences. In the evaluation of people with epilepsy, seizure severity has until recently received scant attention in contrast to seizure frequency. At the Chalfont Centre, a scale has been developed to measure severity that can be easily applied in a routine clinical setting (O'Donoghue & Duncan, 1996). The scale was designed to be quick and easy to administer, with good reliability and validity. It is administered by a health-care professional during an interview with a patient and a witness to the seizures. It assigns scores according to aspects of the seizures, the higher the score the more severe the seizure. For example, a seizure where the attack starts without warning with the patient always falling to the floor having a "grand mal" convulsion, often being incontinent of urine and biting his tongue and taking 6 hours to recover fully would score 21 points out of a possible 27. Baker et al. (1991) have also developed a seizure severity scale. This instrument differs from the "Chalfont Scale" by focusing on the patient's perception of control and postictal effects.

Aetiology should be established. With modern imaging techniques, a substantial proportion of patients with apparent cryptogenic epilepsy can be shown to have an underlying cerebral structural abnormality, which might respond to surgical treatment (Fig. 37.1) (Duncan, 1997). If such abnormalities are found and are considered resectable, clearly rehabilitation should be instituted only after surgical treatment.

EEG

The EEG provides essential information for diagnosis and classification purposes (Fish, 1995). In addition, EEG recording can

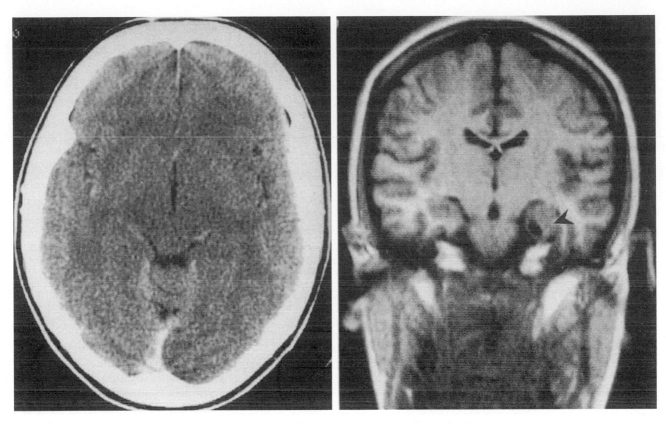

Figure 37.1. The CT scan (left) is normal but MR scanning (right) demonstrated a left medial temporal area of abnormal signal that was successfully removed at operation and proved pathologically to be a hamartoma.

reveal epileptogenic discharges that are not accompanied by any obvious seizure. Such events have been termed subclinical discharges and could have an impact on everyday functioning (see later). The occurrence of such activity could underlie difficulties in rehabilitation programmes if they go undetected and can be misinterpreted as lack of motivation or inability. In certain cases, antiepileptic drugs have been reported to result in a reduction in subclinical discharges to beneficial effect.

Ambulatory cassette recording EEG and video EEG recordings offer the means of more prolonged electrophysiological assessment (Fig. 37.2). These investigations can provide valuable information about the severity of the seizure disorder and also the timing of seizures. For instance, frequent nocturnal seizures can be missed without such recording. Their occurrence can help to explain drowsiness and variable daytime performance. An understanding of these aspects is important for setting rehabilitation goals.

Antiepileptic drug (AED) treatment

Several new AEDs were introduced during the 1990s. Thus, doctors treating epilepsy have a far greater selection of drugs from which to choose. These drugs can offer advantages in terms of their efficacy and side-effect profile when compared with the more established drugs. Nevertheless, the treatment of patients with chronic, intractable epilepsy remains a difficult area and specialist evaluation is appropriate (Duncan, 1991).

In all cases, a full treatment history should be obtained and a treatment programme devised. It is an interesting, but unconfirmed, observation that a patient's response to an individual drug is similar if the drug is introduced on different occasions over time. It is our practice when altering medication to use in rotation first-line drugs that have not been previously used in optimal doses (Table 37.2). These are usually given either in monotherapy or in two drug combinations. Prior to their introduction, it might be necessary to withdraw other antiepileptic drugs. If this fails, then second-line drugs can be considered, usually added to a single, first-line antiepileptic compound. The third stage in drug treatment is the use of new drugs undergoing special drug trials for evaluation; these are used only on a restricted basis.

The aim of this treatment programme is to ensure that the patient has had a trial of all first-line drugs at optimal doses, only at this stage is the epilepsy designated intractable. Monitoring of drug levels can be useful to guide dosing, particularly in the case of phenytoin, carbamazepine, ethosuximide, and barbiturates. AED levels can also be useful in cases of suspected toxicity or non-compliance. Nevertheless, the concept of therapeutic range should not be abused. Zealous adherence to quoted ranges is inappropriate and AED levels should always be interpreted in the light of clinical data.

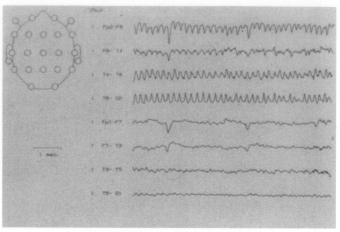

Figure 37.2. On the left, a patient is being recorded by video EEG telemetry. Behind the patient are the EEG machinery, video storage, and a computerized seizure detection device. The EEG leads can be seen in place on the patient's head and the cable from the machine is long enough to allow the patient to be freely mobile. On the right is an eight-channel paper recording of early EEG during a right temporal lobe epileptic attack that was recorded from this patient during a video EEG session.

Table 37.2.   Suggested first- and second-choice antiepileptic drugs*

Type of seizure	First choice	Second choice
Generalised seizures		
Tonic clonic	Carbamazepine	Acetozolamide
	Sodium valproate	Clobazam
	Lamotrigine	Clonazepam
		Gabapentin
		Phenytoin
		Phenobarbitone
		Topiramate
		Vigabatrin
Absence	Ethosuximide	Acetozolamide
	Valproate	Clonazepam
	Lamotrigine	
Myoclonic	Valproate	Acetozolamide
		Clobazam
		Lamotrigine
		Piracetam
Tonic clonic	Valproate	Acetozolamide
		Clobazam
		Gabapentin
		Lamotrigine
		Phenytoin
		Phenobarbitone
		Topiramate
		Vigabatrin
Partial seizures		
Simple partial and complex partial seizures	Carbamazepine Valproate	Acetozolamide Clobazam Gabapentin
Secondarily generalised partial onset seizures		Lamotrigine Phenytoin Phenobarbitone Topiramate Vigabatrin
Infantile spasms	ACTH	Vigabatrin Nitrazepam Clonazepam

*There is little consensus between epilepsy specialists regarding which drugs should be used as first or second choice, and indeed some authors argue that there is insufficient evidence to prescribe "rationally".

Surgical evaluation

Surgical treatment can offer considerable reduction in seizure frequency or cure for selected patients with epilepsy. All patients with chronic epilepsy should be considered for surgical treatment. Advances in anatomical and functional imaging have allowed surgically amenable lesions to be more clearly identified. In particular, MRI can demonstrate abnormalities of mesial temporal regions such as hippocampal sclerosis or other potentially epileptogenic lesions such as cavernomas. Video-monitored EEG and neuropsychology allows more accurate localisation of these lesions. Neuropsychology also allows prediction of postsurgical cognitive function. This is discussed later in this chapter. More invasive investigations, such as intracranial EEG monitoring and neuropsychological testing while patients are given intracarotid sodium amytal, might be required.

Surgery can involve "lesionectomy", which is the removal of an area that is thought to be epileptogenic. An example of this is the removal of a cavernoma. Lesionectomy can also involve the removal of the lesion and a volume of surrounding tissue as is the case in a temporal lobectomy or even hemispherectomy. Other surgery might be "functional". Examples of functional surgery include corpus callosotomy, multiple subpial transection, or, more controversially, insertion of vagal nerve stimulators. In many cases the aim of surgery is to abolish seizures completely, but in others the impact of epilepsy is so great on an individual's life that surgery is considered even to ameliorate seizure frequency or severity.

The timing of surgery is often difficult for both patient and doctor to decide. The risk of surgery, both in terms of complications and its uncertain outcome, can dissuade many patients who have not tried all the available AEDs or are "risk averse". However, the risk of surgery must be balanced against the evidence of recent epidemiological trials, which suggest that mortality rates for those individuals with chronic epilepsy are higher than those of the normal population and that this group have a particularly high incidence of SUDEP—sudden unexplained death in epilepsy (up to 0.5% per year in some groups).

COGNITIVE DYSFUNCTION

The majority of people with epilepsy have well-controlled seizures, with no significant cognitive difficulties. A minority has more problematic epilepsy and is likely to have disorganised brain function, even between overt clinical seizures. Poor seizure control almost always indicates interictal brain dysfunctioning, as indicated by abnormalities seen on EEG and brain imaging (Duncan et al., 1995).

Underlying brain damage

There are many reasons why individuals with intractable epilepsy are at elevated risk for cognitive difficulties (Thompson & Trimble, 1996). The most potent factor is underlying brain damage, which could have arisen from a variety of causes, e.g. head trauma, central nervous system infections, and vascular disease. Advances in MRI technology have resulted in the identification of hippocampal sclerosis and cortical dysplasias, which are now considered the most frequent causes of intractable seizures (Duncan, 1997). Many factors can modify the neuropsychological expression of underlying cerebral damage or development. These include the age of onset and the nature of the underlying pathology.

Seizures

Frequent, severe seizures will place an individual at risk for cognitive difficulties. Secondary atonic and tonic seizures can lead to falls and repeated minor head injuries, which can result in cognitive deterioration over the years. The frontal brain regions seem particularly vulnerable in such falls. Nocturnal seizures, which are often considered to be benign, can have an adverse effect on an individual's attentional capacity in the daytime, particularly if they are frequent, and can easily be overlooked.

Seizures can also result in transient cognitive difficulties. Seizure activity can be represented by a range of cognitive deficits of varying severity. Towards one end of the spectrum are brief epileptic seizures, which to an onlooker might have no obvious behavioural correlates, yet can be shown to underlie subtle short-lived impairments of cognition, the so-called phenomena of subclinical seizures (Binnie, 1991). Awareness that fleeting disturbance of cognition can arise in association with subclinical EEG discharges has increased over the last decade, largely due to technological developments which allow the synchronisation of EEG changes with neuropsychological test performance.

Over a number of years, Rugland and colleagues (1991) have developed computerised neuropsychological tests specifically to look at the impact of subclinical epileptic activity. It is clear from their studies that considerable individual variation exists as to whether impairment occurs and on which specific test deficits arise. The length of the discharge and the type of task influence whether cognitive impairments are observed in association with subclinical discharges. Those tasks requiring continuous attention seem to be particularly sensitive. Significant impairments of performance during discharges was seen in 61% of patients on either a simple reaction time test, a choice reaction time test, or both. Of in-patients with generalised discharges, 67% showed impaired performance compared to only 33% for patients with focal or marked asymmetrical discharges.

Theoretically, any cognitive deficit could be the manifestation of an ictal discharge. Language disturbance, including speech arrest and dysphasic difficulties, can occur with partial seizures arising from the frontal and dominant temporal lobes. Reports of ictal amnesia can also be found in the literature, defined as recurrent paroxysmal memory loss with no alteration of consciousness. During an attack the person would appear normal and continue activities, including speaking, and personal identity would be retained.

Episodes of non-convulsive status epilepticus can severely disrupt cognitive processing. However, despite the severity of the symptoms that can present, this cause of cognitive disturbance can be overlooked and many cases go undiagnosed for considerable periods of time. During absence status, a range of disturbances has been reported. Neuropsychological assessment during such episodes may reveal significant problems, particularly on tests of attention, and sequencing and organising skills. In reports of partial status, language disturbance is often predominant. In addition, cases of spatial disorientation, dysgraphia and perceptual deficits, ranging in severity up to cortical blindness, have been reported. Complex partial status has been associated with a range of deficits. During such periods, a patient might be confused and it is common for them to experience language difficulties, mental slowness and amnesia (Shorvon, 1996).

Recovery from seizures can be variable and, for some individuals, neuropsychological assessment undertaken in close proximity to complex partial seizures and generalised attacks can underestimate an individual's potential. Figure 37.3 illustrates this point. The total scores on a list-learning test are given for two individuals, who were tested on three occasions: (1) 2 hours after complex partial seizures of left temporal origin; (2) approximately 1 day later; and (3) a week after the complex partial seizure. Five other patients matched for ability level were also assessed at approximately the same time intervals. It can be seen that there is a considerable improvement in the two patients' performance over time, which cannot be adequately explained by practice effects or test familiarity. Patient AB shows the most dramatic gains and this individual had experienced more attacks prior to the assessment.

There are a number of case reports in the literature of specific cognitive processes inducing seizures. Some seizure precipitants reported include reading, writing, arithmetic, memorising, chess, and card playing (Antebi & Bird, 1992; Helmstaedter et al., 1992).

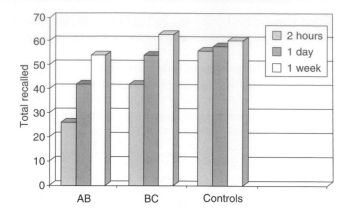

Figure 37.3. Scores on a list learning task (max = 75) in two patients following complex partial seizures arising from the temporal lobe. AB experienced three seizures in close succession and BC a single seizure.

AED medication

The majority of patients with epilepsy will be maintained for a number of years on AEDs. In recent years, there has been much research on the effects of these drugs on cognitive abilities, an area which has occasioned controversy. For most of the AEDs, favourable reports based mainly on subjective impressions are reported after their introduction. With more widespread use and with careful testing, adverse effects are usually detected. Indeed, there are reports in the literature of detrimental effects on cognitive function by most of the available antiepileptic drugs. The controversy in the literature is in part explained by variations in methodologies employed, dosages, and duration of the treatment, of the drugs administered (for a review, see Vermeulen & Aldenkamp, 1995). The clinical significance of the drug effects reported is sometimes questioned but they are generally sufficient to reduce peak efficiency at school, work, or during demanding daily activities, and can have implications for rehabilitation. Furthermore, unlike other causes of cognitive deterioration, such as underlying brain damage, drug effects are potentially reversible and if at all suspected should be explored further. It is not possible on the basis of one assessment to identify an effect that is attributable to drugs but rather, testing should take place on more than one occasion and with an appreciable gap between testing sessions. In the interval, changes can be made to medication and the impact of such changes can be evaluated by the second assessment. Of course, with some individuals a reduction in medication can result in a significant increase in seizures, which will in turn adversely impinge on cognitive abilities. In many people with intractable epilepsy, a balance has to be achieved between reasonable seizure control and minimal cognitive side-effects of medication.

Surgical treatment

Surgical treatment experienced a resurgence in the 1990s, stimulated in part by advances in MRI, which have resulted in the finding of brain abnormalities, most notably hippocampal sclerosis and cortical dysplasias. The most frequently undertaken surgical procedure is temporal lobectomy. There is a general consensus that surgery on the dominant temporal lobe (generally the left) will result in a decline in verbal memory; and surgery on the non-dominant temporal lobe (usually the right) will result in deficits in spatial memory (Trenerry, 1995). For individuals where preoperatively low scores were noted on both verbal and spatial memory tests, surgery can be expected to have an adverse impact on memory capacity, which will have implications for rehabilitative work. More extensive resections on the dominant hemisphere can also impact on language functioning, which can adversely effect not only cognitive capacity but also confidence and competence in social situations. It is our experience that psychosocial problems that exist before surgery generally persist following treatment. We have worked with a number of individuals within our rehabilitation facility who have previously undergone surgical treatment.

Other surgical procedures are undertaken less frequently but have been reported to have effects on cognition. Corpus callosotomy, which is generally undertaken only as a partial resection, has been associated with transient mutism, although there are some reports of more persistent language difficulties. Memory dysfunction has also been reported in some cases (Sass et al., 1992).

Neuropsychological assessment

There is no one cognitive deficit characteristic of people with epilepsy. Memory disturbance is the most frequent reason for referral and most commonly encountered in patients with intractable seizures of temporal lobe origin (Thompson, 1997). Any deficit is possible and a neuropsychological assessment for individuals being considered for further rehabilitation should tap a broad range of functions. Sometimes a person's complaints represent not a memory deficit *per se*, but a problem of concentration or perhaps a word-finding difficulty indicating expressive language problems. In our assessments, we are looking as much for areas of relative strength as for deficits. It is the former that can be positively harnessed in a rehabilitation programme. We frequently encounter individuals with significant cognitive problems that have not been recognised and that must have adversely effected their ability in school and in social settings, contributing to the psychosocial difficulties that they present as rehabilitation candidates. For a number of individuals, an assessment in the past could have involved just a global IQ measure, and the figure derived might have contributed to over- and/or under-expectations, as these figures tend to mask any unevenness in cognitive abilities. Furthermore, such measures miss important areas of cognition such as memory functioning. The cases below highlight the importance of a detailed neuropsychological assessment.

CASE NO. 1
Jackie, a 19-year-old woman, had had epilepsy from the age of 3. At the time of admission she was experiencing frequent nocturnal attacks and there was some uncertainty as to the diagnosis. She had attended mainstream schools and obtained three good GCSE passes in English

language, English literature, and history. On leaving school she had undertaken employment training in floristry, which had proved an unmitigated disaster. Assessment confirmed a diagnosis of complex partial seizures, originating in the right parietal region and a structural lesion was identified by scanning. Neuropsychological assessment revealed an individual of average intellectual ability, although she showed wide scatter, with individual subtest scores ranging from high average for verbal reasoning and word knowledge to mentally impaired on a measure of non-verbal problem solving (Block Design). Supplementary assessment of cognitive skills revealed her to have a mild constructional apraxia. In the context of these results it is not surprising she experienced difficulties with floristry, which is highly dependent on well-developed spatial skills, an area in which she was particularly deficient. Medication changes made during her admission to the Special Assessment Unit resulted in good seizure control. She was discharged 2 months later and at 6 months follow-up only occasional nocturnal seizures were reported. The results of the neuropsychological assessment were discussed with her and her family, emphasising her areas of strengths in the verbal and social spheres. On returning home she enrolled on another training scheme that involved working with the elderly. She encountered no difficulties with this and subsequently obtained full-time employment in the social care field.

CASE NO. 2

John, a 34-year-old man, had had epilepsy from his early teens. At the time of admission to the Special Assessment Unit his seizures were poorly controlled. He was living with his elderly parents and there was concern over his future. Neuropsychological assessment revealed significantly uneven abilities, his verbal and language skills being particularly weak relative to his ability to process and learn spatial information. He was considered to have the potential to benefit from a period of rehabilitation to learn to live more independently and move away from the parental home. Medication changes were made and he returned home for 3 months while waiting for a 2-week induction placement within Links, the rehabilitation facility. When he returned for his period of evaluation, it was evident that cognitive difficulties noted previously were much exacerbated. In the first few days, individuals working with him questioned his potential for rehabilitation. In particular, they reported significant slowness and great difficulty in expressing himself. For this reason, a re-evaluation was undertaken and this confirmed observations of a gross decline in his ability, including his already weak expressive language skills. He was reviewed by his consultant, who decided to reduce the recently introduced AED. Changes were initiated at Chalfont and he subsequently returned home for a further 3 months. Contact with his parents and with John during this period suggested a significant improvement was occurring in relation to the drug change and he returned for a second induction. Reassessment at this time showed substantial improvement, although he was not functioning quite at his original assessed level. Cognitive problems remained in his verbal reasoning and language skills but these were considered appropriate to tackle as part of his rehabilitation programme.

CASE NO. 3

Sam was admitted for a period of rehabilitation to the Links programme. His seizures had developed at the age of 17 years but had occurred only during sleep for the past 4 years. His past EEG demonstrated a left fronto/temporal focus but an MRI scan had revealed no structural abnormality. He had attended mainstream schools and achieved some GCSE passes. He had worked up to 2 years before in a clerical capacity but since then had been unemployed. He was assessed to be socially isolated, verging on being socially phobic. He lived in his own flat but was highly dependent on his parents. He was anxious and depressed and had

become increasingly verbally aggressive, particularly toward his two brothers and mother. His verbal IQ fell at a low average level (VIQ = 82) and his performance IQ at the upper end of the average range (PIQ = 108). Further assessment revealed significant expressive language difficulties. He described problems, beginning in his late teens, with word-finding difficulties and as a consequence he became embarrassed and withdrew from social settings. In his late teens he encountered difficulties at work, particularly when he was asked to do telephone duties, which exaggerated his communication problem and made him feel increasingly inadequate. Anger towards his family was often precipitated when they finished his sentences or spoke on his behalf. As part of his rehabilitation programme, work was undertaken with Sam and his family and the staff team on language problems. In addition, he was encouraged to undertake a computer course and to explore future work in this area.

Intervention

For some individuals, a neuropsychological assessment can be sufficient to identify problems that can be shared with the family and individual, as was the case for Case 1. For other individuals, cognitive difficulties encountered can benefit from additional intervention, which takes into account psychosocial factors, as was the case for Case 3.

Memory problems are frequently a target of our rehabilitation endeavours. Sessions can be offered to focus on strategies that might help to reduce the impact of a weak memory. Strategies are usually divided into internal and external measures (Wilson, 1995). The former include the use of visual imagery where individuals imagine mental pictures involving the information to be remembered. This can be useful for individuals with a verbal memory impairment, particularly where their assessed visual memory is good. Mental imagery can be helpful for remembering a few important names, e.g. a bizarre image can be made in association with a name. Other visual strategies include the method of loci and the peg method. Verbal rhymes and first letter mnemonics can be helpful for some people. In general, internal strategies can be mentally taxing and, in our experience, people find them difficult to employ in their everyday lives. However, it can be fun in rehabilitation sessions to focus on some of these strategies (Thompson, 1997).

More useful, in our experience, is adjusting people's expectations, together with the use of external memory aids. External aids can be divided into those that assist information storage and cueing devices that prompt people to remember to do things. It is surprising how many patients we encounter with impaired memory who do not use diaries. Training in the use of a diary or a personal organiser can have a major positive impact on their everyday lives. We find that at least daily reference to a diary is particularly beneficial in supporting a verbal memory deficit. In addition, a personal organiser has a certain status, which can have a positive impact on self-esteem. We have also found computerised diaries to be useful in some instances.

One of the most valuable external memory aids for people with epilepsy is a drug wallet. Many people find this device helps them remember to take their tablets, and also not to take too many. Drug wallets consist of seven small containers, one

John has significant memory difficulties; he finds it hard to remember things he has done and things he has talked about. Despite this, he possesses good planning and organisational skills.

Proposed management strategies

1. John is encouraged to take notes of key points of discussion during meetings so that he can remember the work he has done from one week to the next.
2. John now has a filofax/personal organiser, which has been personally tailored. This includes the following sections:
   - Programme sheets on which he records his daily activities alongside a record of his seizures.
   - "Don't forget" sheets on which he makes notes of things he needs/wants to remember to do.
   - A section in which he records the actions he agrees to do during programme review meetings.
   - A section in which he records key notes from meetings and workshops.
   - Account sheets on which he records his daily spending as part of his budget plan.
   - Names, addresses, and telephone numbers.

   John is encouraged to make frequent use of this organiser as a memory aid.
3. John has a number of identified places in which he keeps important papers/documents.
4. As John finds remembering large chunks of information difficult, important information should be presented in a simple, precise and sequenced way. Discussions should also be concluded by a summary of key points.
5. John needs structure to his day in order for things to become routine and so that the development of his organisational skills can be further encouraged.

Figure 37.4. Example of memory rehabilitation programme.

for each day of the week. The compartments can be filled once a week at set times. Individual containers are removable so that if a person goes out for the day they do not have to take the entire container with them. Drug wallets can be obtained from local chemists and are not expensive.

For others with memory difficulties, the results of the rest of the neuropsychological assessment can be of help. For instance, one young man had a very weak memory but was assessed to have good planning and organisation abilities. He undertook a year's residential placement in Links. On his rehabilitation programme, explicit steps were taken to support and improve his memory by capitalising on his good organisational skills (Fig. 37.4).

PSYCHOLOGICAL AND PSYCHIATRIC DISTURBANCE

Motivation, emotional resources, and degree of maturity affect the capacity to learn, to be trained, and to benefit from rehabilitation programmes. Psychological problems often present major barriers to the training involved in rehabilitating patients with epilepsy, as follows.

Anxiety

Anxiety can cause particular difficulties for rehabilitation. High levels of anxiety can make individuals reluctant to make social contacts. Anxiety in people with epilepsy is exacerbated by the unpredictability of the attacks, with the possibility that seizures will strike at uncertain times, places, or circumstances. Anxiety can be addressed in various ways, including increasing an individual's knowledge about epilepsy and about the mechanisms of anxiety, providing training in anxiety-reducing techniques, and by formal psychotherapy. Anxiolytic drugs can also be useful and clobazam, which has known anxiolytic and antiepileptic properties, might prove a good adjunct to other drug treatment. Reducing levels of anxiety can have a positive impact on an individual's confidence and interpersonal skills, but can, in some instances, also improve seizure frequency. It is generally accepted that stress and other environmental factors can trigger seizures in some individuals. Well controlled studies in the field are few, and indeed, difficult to undertake. However, existing findings suggest training in anxiety reduction techniques can have a beneficial impact on seizure control (Thompson & Baxendale, 1996).

Depression

Elevated levels of depression have been reported in people with epilepsy (Mendez, 1996). The episodic nature of epilepsy can predispose the individual towards passivity. The nature of the illness can prevent the person feeling in active control of his/her own behaviour. People with epilepsy can experience loss of control not only of their own behaviour but of other aspects of their lives. This seems particularly the case in adult onset epilepsy, when lifestyle and working practices are already established when the seizures present, as the following case illustrates.

CASE NO. 4
Peter, a 27-year-old man, was seen in our assessment unit. He left school at the age of 16 with two O levels. Between the ages of 16 and 21 he worked as a television repair engineer. At the age of 21 he married and began to buy his own home. At the age of 23, when on holiday in Spain, he developed a viral encephalitic illness. During this illness, several periods of status were documented and he was left with recurrent seizures that had proved intractable. Between the ages of 24 and 27 he lost his driving licence and his job, he experienced financial difficulties, his wife left, and he lost his home because he could not keep up with the mortgage payments. He moved back to live with his parents. On admission, his seizures were uncontrolled and he was experiencing weekly attacks and was assessed to be severely depressed. Medical assessment and intervention resulted in a marginal improvement in his seizure control. Considerable work was undertaken on his adjustment to a life with epilepsy, particularly to help him regain his confidence. During this time he became less depressed and was prepared to reassess his future. In particular, he accepted that the nature of his attacks seriously reduced his career options. On leaving the assessment unit at Chalfont he was accepted onto a sheltered employment scheme, working in a semi-skilled capacity as a bookbinder and moved into a housing association scheme specifically for young people with epilepsy. After 3 years within the scheme, he moved on to live independently in a council property in the locality.

Depression can be a significant obstacle to any rehabilitation work. People are not going to adjust to a diagnosis of epilepsy overnight and it can take several months or years to develop adaptive coping strategies (Upton & Thompson, 1992). For some people, it is sufficient to have contact with self-help organisations where they can receive support and practical guidance from fellow sufferers. For other individuals, where depression has firmly set in, it might be necessary to have some form of therapeutic input and sometimes antidepressant medication is appropriate, at least in the short term.

Aggression

Aggressive behaviour can pose particular problems for rehabilitation work. It has long been recognised that it can occur in association with epilepsy, however, the general consensus is that aggressive behaviour is less widespread than previously reported. Such behaviour can result more from underlying cerebral damage or immature cerebral development, from injudicious drug treatment or from social and psychological handicaps resulting from having epilepsy. Indeed, so interlinked are the problems that occasionally families are encountered who have come to accept verbal, and even physical, aggressive behaviour as part of the epileptic condition; by accepting this state of affairs over many years these difficult behaviours become more entrenched and thus difficult to redress.

Aggressive behaviour can be ictal or arise during a period of postictal confusion. This generally occurs when attempts are made to restrain the person or intervene before the seizure has run its course. Such aggression is clearly not a psychological issue but it is surprising how often this is unrecognised. Aggressive behaviour during a seizure, although rare, can be very frightening and this aspect might need specific counselling.

Clear descriptions of aggressive or difficult behaviour, and the situations in which these episodes arise in a particular individual, might be sufficient to decide whether an episode is ictal or interictal. Ictal aggressive episodes are likely to be stereotyped, to occur in the absence of environmental precipitants, not to be clearly directed toward a specific person or object, and not to involve planned or complicated motor actions. Prolonged EEG monitoring and audio cassette or video telemetry can also help identify the origins of an aggressive act, although violent actions can risk damage to sensitive and valuable equipment.

Aggressive and difficult behaviour encountered in a rehabilitation setting is more often the result of maladaptive coping strategies. Behavioural assessment taking into consideration the relationship of aggressive episodes to seizures is often productive, as the following case illustrates.

CASE NO. 5
A 34-year-old woman was admitted to the Chalfont Centre. On admission she was described as emotionally immature and difficult. It was believed many of her seizures were non-epileptic. In-patient assessment confirmed that her attacks were indeed epileptic and a right frontal focus was recorded on her EEG. Her AED medication was adjusted and there was a significant improvement in her

behaviour. For the next 10 years, during which she resided at the Centre, she did not present with any management problems. She was referred, however, at this time because of temper outbursts and on occasion caused injury to other individuals. Her assessment involved monitoring her outbursts of temper, observations by staff, scrutinising case records, EEG, and blood level monitoring. There was no association between her difficult behaviour and seizures, and indeed, she was experiencing good seizure control at the time of referral. There had been no recent medication changes and serum levels were within the therapeutic range and at levels she had previously tolerated. Daily monitoring revealed that outbursts of aggression occurred only in her home environment and never when she was working. At that time she undertook clerical duties in a part-time capacity. Rating scales of mood revealed her to be moderately depressed and she was preoccupied with a fear of mental decline. A major factor underlying her difficult behaviour seemed to be her living conditions. In fact, she was significantly more able than the majority of residents in her home environment. Care staff frequently expected her to help and assist with other less able residents and were very disapproving when she was not eager to do so. She was aware that a number of her living companions were deteriorating mentally and physically. The behavioural assessment suggested she was wrongly placed and that also she had the cognitive resources to exert some influence on her difficult behaviour. A subsequent move to an environment with more able individuals and short-term therapeutic intervention focusing on teaching anger management techniques resulted in a significant improvement in her behaviour and her mood. Indeed, she progressed very well and was considered not to require a residential placement. Currently she works in sheltered employment and is living independently with a partner in the community.

Sexual behaviour

Past research has suggested that reduced sexual drive and other sexual difficulties occur in people with epilepsy. Antiepileptic drugs have been implicated and there have been some reports of an improvement in sexual functioning following hormone treatment, but research in this area is inconclusive and environmental factors should not be underestimated as these can influence both libido and hormonal levels. In our experience, a common reason for sexual difficulties in young people with epilepsy is lack of, or inaccurate, knowledge. This can be addressed via sexual counselling and education and is an area that forms an essential part of our individual rehabilitation programmes.

Psychosis

The association between psychosis and epilepsy has attracted considerable interest over the years (Tandon & De Querdo, 1996). Psychosis can occasionally occur as an ictal phenomenon but is more usually interictal. During ictal psychotic episodes the patient can experience disturbing hallucinations and paranoid thoughts. Such behaviour can last several hours or longer and can be accompanied by abnormal EEG recordings. Antiepileptic drug treatment can result in a complete or substantial reduction in seizures and in these cases rehabilitation programmes are often appropriate. Where episodes are not well controlled, rehabilitative work can be difficult. We have experience of one individual with a history of ictal psychosis who embarked on the Links rehabilitation programme. However, although the episodes were infrequent, during them he placed himself at considerable risk and his behaviour had a disturbing and detrimental effect upon his living companions. Accordingly, his programme was terminated prematurely and currently he lives in a more sheltered setting, which has the staffing resources to cope with his psychotic episodes.

Studies of interictal psychosis suggest patients frequently have normal premorbid personalities and no history of schizophrenia, the psychosis developing in the decades following the onset of epilepsy. In cases of interictal psychosis, expert psychiatric evaluation and management is advised. Often, the psychotic disturbance is a greater problem than the epilepsy and these individuals are more appropriately placed on rehabilitation programmes within a psychiatric setting.

Non-epileptic attacks

There has been an increase in research interest in non-epileptic attacks in recent years. It is generally accepted that these can take a variety of forms. A major category are attacks that develop in response to a major traumatic episode or episodes and represent a specific form of post-traumatic stress syndrome. The most frequently cited cause is past sexual abuse, although other stressors have been identified (Gram et al., 1992; Kalogjera-Sackellares, 1996).

Rehabilitation candidates on the Links programme at Chalfont are generally psychologically complex; some have solely non-epileptic attacks, others non-epileptic attacks in addition to seizures. At the time of writing, four of the eight clients with non-epileptic attacks only have non-epileptic seizures, and in each case the attacks represented a significant management issue on referral. There has been some debate as to whether such individuals are appropriately placed on a programme geared for people with epilepsy. Certainly, some people with non-epileptic seizures, where these are longstanding and occur with additional signs of psychopathology, might not be considered good candidates. However, there are those individuals, including those where seizures are considered to be an "opting out" mechanism or a type of panic attack, or where they have developed in association with past traumas, who can do well when placed in such an environment. The advantage of a residential placement such as Links is that it provides an extended period of time to work on the attacks, and in particular on the individual's perception of them. It is often our experience that the attacks do not lessen until several months into the programme, and indeed, at some stages can increase in frequency, particularly when increased responsibility is placed on the young person as he or she progresses through the rehabilitation programme.

CASE NO. 6
Keith was admitted to the Special Assessment Unit at the age of 31. At that time he was experiencing at least daily attacks. Injuries were reported as frequent and for this reason he used a wheelchair to travel about. He had been living in a residential home for the physically disabled. He was admitted on five different AEDs, including large doses of clonazepam. Over a month's period his drugs were reduced to

two and seizure control improved such that, with encouragement, he "gave up" his wheelchair. Furthermore, the attacks that continued were diagnosed as non-epileptic. So dramatic was the improvement that he was considered suitable for a period of rehabilitation, something Keith himself was very keen to pursue. Part of his programme focused on his non-epileptic attacks. First, by increasing his understanding of how they occur and the role of psychological factors.
A major hurdle was for Keith to accept that by saying the attacks were psychological we were not implying he was "putting them on" or that he was "mad". Time was spent in helping Keith distinguish between epileptic and non-epileptic seizures and to keep records accordingly. In addition, he was shown a video recording of his seizures. He took to this system very quickly and his confidence increased noticeably as periods of freedom from non-epileptic seizures increased. Minimal fuss and no judgemental comment was made when the attacks did occur. Rather, much time and energy was devoted to his achievements on the programme. He was offered weekly therapy sessions to explore his feelings further and discuss issues that might underlie his attacks. Initially, anxiety was considered the trigger, however, over time this was not felt to be the key trigger but rather anger. This was generated in part from feeling inadequate and a failure within his family. The frequency of seizures dropped dramatically from 25 a week prior to admission to the Special Assessment Unit, to 12 a week during the assessment, to none during the third month of the rehabilitation programme. In the fourth and seventh months, some seizures occurred in conjunction with visits to the family home.

SOCIAL ASPECTS

It is important to identify areas of a client's family and social life that might create difficulties for the rehabilitation process. A detailed social history, including educational areas, is vital. The social needs of people with epilepsy are diverse and vary considerably between individuals. In our chapter in the previous edition, we bemoaned the lack of consistency and the involvement of different agencies with poor communication and no clear goals for young people. At that time, in the government White Paper *Caring for People* (HMSO, 1989), the role of the case manager was endorsed. These professionals were envisaged as having key coordinating roles in the community for individuals whose social and health care needs are complex. The case manager was seen as having a monitoring role, assessing interventions and outcome against assessed individual needs. People with problematic epilepsy, we suggested, would seem ideal candidates for supervision by such individuals, who were subsequently recruited by local authority Social Services as Care Managers. Unfortunately, it is our experience that it is becoming increasingly difficult to enlist Care Managers to take on cases, particularly where no ongoing "crisis" exists. Entry to our rehabilitation programme requires external funding, usually from local authority Social Services. An essential part of this process is a Care Manager to take on the client and support the proposal for a residential rehabilitation placement. Often the process is lengthened because of difficulty recruiting a local Care Manager. Indeed, for this very reason, we have just admitted one individual 4 years after admission to Links was recommended.

Some of the more frequently encountered social problems and issues are outlined below.

Employment

The group presenting for rehabilitation might be expected to have a high level of employment difficulties, with unemployment and underemployment over-represented (Chaplin & Thompson, 2001). The majority of young people who come through the assessment facilities at the Chalfont Centre for Epilepsy have not worked, or certainly not since developing epilepsy if the onset was in adulthood (see Table 37.1).

In a study of recently diagnosed cases of epilepsy, 70% of the sample rated their employment status as presenting some, or a serious problem (Chaplin et al., 1992), and in another study 80% of young people with epilepsy felt they had been actively discriminated against because of their epilepsy (Carroll, 1992). High rates of employment difficulties tend to be encountered at the intractable end of the epilepsy spectrum and research has demonstrated that where treatment is successful and seizure control good, then employment problems are less frequently encountered (Jacoby et al., 1995).

Employment problems

Qualifications.   People with epilepsy, especially those with longstanding, poorly controlled epilepsy, have inferior educational or academic qualifications when compared with the population without epilepsy. This is likely to have a detrimental effect on the chances of obtaining employment. In a long-term, prospective Finnish study, 55% of people had no vocational educational or academic qualifications. Similarly, Britten et al. (1986), found that 51% of people with epilepsy had fewer vocational qualifications when compared with a control group. Even with a good educational record, people with epilepsy can suffer difficulties in obtaining a job if employers harbour prejudices about the ability of people with epilepsy to cope with intellectual aspects of work.

Restrictions.   In the UK only a few occupations are barred by statutory provision from people with epilepsy, and these include working as an aircraft pilot, a merchant seaman, and in the armed services. There are also some occupations where difficulties can be experienced, although there are no statutory barriers concerning them. Examples of these are some teaching posts in state schools where laboratory work is required. There are also certain jobs that involve substantial risks if seizures are not fully controlled and therefore should not be recommended. These would include working at heights and working alone near open water. In order to hold a Heavy Goods Vehicle (HGV) or Passenger Carrying Vehicle (PCV) licence, an individual must have had no seizures or treatment for seizures for 10 years without treatment with AEDs (see later).

VDUs.   There is a common misconception among employers that people with epilepsy should not work on computers, as this will provoke a seizure. Indeed, many people with epilepsy report computers are a potential trigger (Millet et al., 1997). This is not the case. Only a small minority of individuals who have photo- or pattern-sensitive epilepsy are at risk for seizures when working at a VDU. For most people with epilepsy, computer-related work represents a safe working environment (Harding & Jeavons, 1994).

Shift work.   It has been suggested that adaptation to shift work will affect people with epilepsy, increasing the chances of a seizure. Shift work can cause persistent fatigue, sleep disturbance, and disruption of a routine, which some people with epilepsy might be particularly susceptible to. If a patient has more seizures in the context of lack of sleep or occasional missed tablets, then he or she might be vulnerable to seizures during shift work, as might individuals with well-established nocturnal seizures.

Seizures at work.   Stress is recognised as a possible seizure precipitant. Reports in the literature suggest that, during the first few weeks of a new job, the person with epilepsy will be particularly vulnerable. At this time, people who are keen to prove their worth and make a good impression might put themselves under the kind of stress that makes seizures likely to occur. This might particularly be the case where they have not disclosed their epilepsy. It has also been reported from a survey from the USA that as many as 80% of people with epilepsy reported that fear of having a seizure at work was a reason for not seeking or maintaining open employment (Chaplin & Thompson, 2001).

Accidents at work.   Only a few studies have been conducted looking at the experience of people with epilepsy at work. They tend to show that people with epilepsy do not tend to have more on the job accidents than anyone else. Of course, this could be due to less exposure to potentially risky situations, such as working at heights or driving vehicles, or perhaps accidents, when they occur 'particularly if relatively minor', are less likely to be reported. In one study of a sheltered workshop employing people with epilepsy, the accident rate was considered so impressively low that the company was awarded insurance premium reductions. It does seem that in many situations it should be possible to minimise the risk of accidents. The ineligibility of people with disabilities for employer's accident liability insurance has been used incorrectly as a reason for not employing someone with epilepsy. Employers are obliged to take out insurance to cover injury that might arise from work. The majority of insurance policies will treat anyone with a disability on the same terms as the rest of the workforce, providing the duties allocated take the disability into account. To ensure they are covered, employers might need to seek expert advice. In the UK this can be obtained from the Health and Safety Executives Employment Medical Advisory Service.

Pension schemes.   Many employers believe that high standards of health are required by new recruits to their pension schemes. This, however, is not the case. If a person is suitable for employment then that person is also suitable for a pension scheme. Large company schemes are usually based on a group policy with no requirement for individual health criteria to be met.

Disclosure.   Many people with epilepsy choose not to declare their epilepsy to their existing or prospective employers. Those who are more likely to have seizures during the working day are more likely to declare it than those whose epilepsy is in remission or occurs during sleep. The Health and Safety at Work Act (1974) requires both employers and employees to declare factors that might prejudice the safety of employees, and epilepsy is regarded as a relevant factor, such that a failure to declare can result in instant dismissal, which would not be considered unfair if brought before an industrial tribunal.

Overcoming employment disadvantages

Some protection from discrimination in employment is afforded by legislation that stipulates that people with disabilities are given equal rights to employment. In 1995, in line with several other European countries, the Disabilities Discrimination Act was introduced in the UK. It is too soon to judge the impact this will have on recruitment but similar legislation in the USA has been tested successfully in the courts by people with epilepsy.

Many factors need to be considered when assessing employment prospects. Too often, most focus is placed on seizure-related factors. Although the timing, frequency, and nature of attacks is important, these might actually not be the most relevant aspects of an individual. A person's work skills, qualifications, and work experience will be crucial. In addition, some inquiry into a person's understanding and attitude toward his or her epilepsy will be helpful. A person's ability to present seizures in an appropriate and reassuring way can do much to allay an employer's concerns. Difficulties obtaining relevant qualifications or maintaining employment can reflect an underlying cognitive difficulty. A thorough neuropsychological assessment, as highlighted earlier, can help to identify any problems that will be amenable to intervention, perhaps via a drug change, or can be taken into account when advising on career options.

Accurate guidance concerning career options can do much to prevent the development of unrealistic employment aspirations. Counselling and training is vital to provide input on job presentation skills and the role of psychosocial factors. Most people with epilepsy do not have access to specialist rehabilitation services and must rely on mainstream resources. In an attempt to improve the knowledge base of trainers in these sectors the first Transnational Epilepsy Training project (TET) was born. The project aims to assist trainers to acquire the information and skills they need to provide the most appropriate input to young people with epilepsy. As a consequence, a wealth of material has been developed, including a training video (National Society for Epilepsy, 1994).

Negative attitudes regarding the employment of people with epilepsy is often the result of ignorance and much can be accomplished by educating employers. To this end, the Employment Commission of the International Bureau for Epilepsy has produced a set of principles aimed at employers to improve awareness and hopefully employment practice. Attention is drawn to four key areas: health care, job suitability, recruitment and selection, and assistance at work. An adaptation from the Commission's set of principles is given in Fig. 37.5.

Driving

Restrictions on driving can have a significant impact on an individual's mobility, employment prospects (as discussed earlier), social functioning, and self-esteem. It is our experience that in young people with intractable epilepsy, the inability to drive represents one of the biggest disappointments they encounter. In the UK there has been a significant change in driving regulations in recent years, with the seizure-free period required being reduced from 2 years to 1 year for private driving licences. For those with nocturnal epilepsy, the seizure pattern must be established for 3 years (DVLA, 1994; Shorvon, 1995). For commercial driving licences, the restrictions are understandably stricter. For drivers of large goods vehicles (LGV) and for drivers of public service vehicles (PSV) with the capacity to carry more than nine passengers, no epileptic attacks must have occurred in the preceding 10 years and the driver remained unmedicated throughout this period. There is also a "no continuing liability to epileptic seizures" condition. This latter condition would exclude people from driving where a neurological condition exists or a surgical procedure has been undertaken that is potentially epileptogenic. There are few exceptions to the regulations in the UK. Arguments such as "I've never had an attack while driving" or "I will lose my livelihood", as undoubtedly many people do with adult onset epilepsy, cannot be used to overrule the regulations.

Single seizures, however, are not considered epilepsy by the DVLA unless a continuing liability can be demonstrated. Seizure type makes no difference. Thus, simple partial seizures and myoclonic jerks are seizures and their occurrence bans the person from driving. Arguments that an aura gives sufficient time to pull off the road and prevent an accident are not tolerated. Seizures occurring in the context of drug reductions will result in a driving ban whether the changes are intentional or accidental as the result of missed tablets. For individuals with a valid licence the DVLA recommends that driving be suspended for 6 months from the commencement of drug withdrawal. This is not covered by legislation and is purely advisory. It is also recommended that the individual should be clearly warned there is an overall 40% increased risk of seizure recurrence in the first year during withdrawal (DVLA, 1994).

If a person who already holds a driving licence has a seizure, the onus of responsibility is on them to notify the licensing authorities. The physician must be prepared to take time to highlight the risks to other motorists and pedestrians should a person continue to drive. It is advisable for a record to be made in the patient's case notes of such a discussion, or a copy of a letter that documents the main points raised. When there is a strong indication that a patient is continuing to drive in spite of clear advice to the contrary, the Medical Defence Union emphasises that it is a matter for each individual doctor's discretion as to whether patient confidentiality shall be breached. The General Medical Committee (GMC) acknowledges that exceptions to the confidentiality rule can arise when such disclosure is of public interest. If it comes to this, it is advisable to inform the patient of such intentions.

Health care

When assessing an employee or job applicant, the employer needs to understand some of the basic facts about epilepsy and its possible impact on work performance.

- Seizures can take many forms and many people have only one seizure in their lives. In such cases, a diagnosis of epilepsy is usually not made.
- When a seizure occurs for the first time there can be a detrimental effect on self-confidence and the person might require psychological support and education about epilepsy.
- In most cases recurrent seizures can be controlled completely with drug treatment.
- If they are prescribed properly, drugs for epilepsy should not produce any side-effects that have a noticeable effect on work performance.
- In such cases, assessment by a physician expert in epilepsy will often improve seizure control and reduce these side-effects.
- Employees with epilepsy should be provided with the same health and accident insurance cover as other employees.

Job suitability

The vast majority of jobs are suitable for people with epilepsy.

- When medical advice is sought about the suitability of particular jobs for people with epilepsy, the guidance given should take into account the known facts about epilepsy and seizures. Blanket prohibitions should be avoided.
- In those jobs known to carry a high physical risk to the individual worker or to others, the way the work practice is organised should be examined to reduce this risk to an acceptable level.
- Only in those situations where this cannot be done are restrictions on the employment of people with epilepsy justified.
- Where a person with epilepsy possesses the right qualifications and experience, job suitability should be assumed.

Recruitment and Selection

- When personal health information is required it should be processed separately from the job application form and evaluated by a skilled person.
- Interviews should focus on the capabilities of the individual and not on his or her real or assumed limitations.
- Suitability for a particular job should be decided by the employer before any implications arising from the job applicant's epilepsy are considered.
- If a medical opinion is sought, the guidance should be based on knowledge of the particular job and details of the individual's epilepsy.

Assistance at Work

When an employee has a seizure for the first time, the employer should respond fairly by giving the employee adequate opportunity to receive proper medical treatment before making any decisions about job suitability:

- If seizures are likely to occur at work, the employer should help the employee with epilepsy to disclose the epilepsy to work colleagues.
- Some first aid training, or other training, should be provided to those who might be involved should a seizure occur.
- If any special job restrictions are needed, there should be clearly stated policies about how they are to be implemented, reviewed or lifted in terms of set time periods.
- If, despite proper medical attention, redeployment to another job is necessary, appropriate counselling and vocational guidance and, if necessary, rehabilitation services should be made available at an early stage.

Figure 37.5. Principles for employing a person with epilepsy: good seizure control, work-related aptitudes and skills, and a positive approach to epilepsy are key factors in determining a person's employability (from IBE, 1991 with permission).

It is the exception that our rehabilitation candidates are eligible to drive. Rather, in our work with young people on rehabilitation programmes, time is taken to accustom them to the use of public transport, e.g. buses and trains. This can be quite complex, for example, the use of timetables. Using the 24-hour clock can be a cognitively complex activity for individuals with limited literacy and numeracy skills. Furthermore, when plans are made for an individual to move on, then a priority

is often a good transport facility with easy access to a range of shops.

The family

Work with the family is often an essential part of the rehabilitation process. Many rehabilitation candidates will be living in the parental home and many spend all of their time together, with little structured outside activity (Thompson & Upton, 1994). Often, inappropriate parenting styles such as overprotection and overindulgence have developed, which can lead to inappropriate and manipulative behaviours that need to be addressed as part of the rehabilitation process. Too often, parents are criticised for their past approach, however, they have generally acted within the available information their doctor and other professionals have provided. The distinction between being appropriately protective and overprotective, however, is by no means clear cut (Thompson, 2001).

Our task of encouraging independence is certainly easier because we have a residential programme and can keep parents at arm's length. Contact is maintained, however, throughout the programme and generally parents attend the 3-monthly reviews. At the onset of a rehabilitation programme, issues relating to risk management are confronted. For some individuals, seizure management plans are written. We also encourage the use of microwave ovens as opposed to gas or electric cookers and our flats are equipped with showers and not baths. Naturally, there are parental anxieties about the first unaccompanied trip on a bus or a train. Although we do our utmost to reduce the risk of injury from seizures, we cannot guarantee that the occasional injury will not occur, but such a possibility is discussed fully at the outset with the client and family members. Indeed, parents while endorsing greater independence often ask at the outset of the programme that their son or daughter inform them after completion of say a successful shopping trip to a nearby town, rather than forewarn them that this is to take place.

Social activities

Previous research shows that chronic epilepsy places individuals at risk of socially restricted lives and social isolation (Suurmeijer, 1995; Thompson, 2001). When epilepsy has developed in childhood, restrictions might have been placed on leisure activities. If a child is excluded from many normal social interactions and activities this will have an adverse impact on the development of social skills. Sometimes, appropriate interpersonal difficulties arise because of rejection from peers and not from the parental restrictions. Several of our young people have histories of significant bullying, which has eroded their confidence and caused them to withdraw from mixing with people of their own age. Social isolation in young people with epilepsy with poorly controlled seizures should be a matter of concern. Social participation and access to social support is regularly associated with the development of psychological or psychiatric disorders.

Many of the young people we consider for rehabilitation have difficulties forming friendships and developing social networks. The Links programme involves small group living and so interaction with peers becomes a necessity from day one. Input is given individually and in groups on social skills and forming relationships and, where anxiety and lack of confidence are felt to be important, then individual therapy and counselling sessions are offered. Appropriate interpersonal relationships often proves one of the more problematic areas of the programme. The linkworker might be the first person of a comparable age with whom the rehabilitee has had an opportunity to relate for many years.

Another approach is to encourage a range of leisure activities. Many young people with epilepsy tend to engage in passive leisure activities, such as watching television and reading books and magazines. In a Norwegian study the authors found participants with epilepsy were assessed to be only half as active physically as the general population. The authors also assessed individuals' physical health and condition and found this to be relatively poorer compared to the average Norwegian population matched for age and gender (Bjorholt et al., 1990). The authors suggested that the lack of fitness was the result of a sedentary lifestyle.

Most problems where epilepsy and leisure activities are concerned stem from misinformation, coupled with a general anxiety about taking risks. One-off accidents can happen to anyone whether epilepsy is present or not. One young man on a rehabilitation programme injured his leg—a suspected fracture of the ankle—while participating in weight training at the local gym. The injury occurred not because of a seizure but because he dropped a weight on his foot. This, fortunately, has not deterred him and he is anxious to return as soon as possible. The sessions at the gym have not only had a positive impact on his fitness level but also his self-esteem.

PHYSICAL ASPECTS

Perhaps 10% of people with severe epilepsy will have a physical handicap requiring rehabilitation measures. The most common handicaps are spastic hemiparesis, ataxia, and dysarthria. Hemiparesis can be acquired congenitally and the motor disturbance and the epilepsy can both be due to the same brain injury. The list of potential causes is long but the most common are perinatal injury, cerebral tumour, arterior venus malformation, abscess, and stroke. Hemiparesis dating from early life is often associated with limb shortening and atrophy. The principles of rehabilitation of motor weakness and spasticity are similar to those in cases without epilepsy and are outlined elsewhere in this volume. In a young person with partial epilepsy and a severe hemiparesis, hemispherectomy should be considered to control the seizures. This is usually only an option if the weakness of the arm is such that a pincer grip is impossible, and if there is little independent movement of the leg. Surgery in correctly selected patients can dramatically control seizures without worsening the functional motor deficit. Ataxia and dysarthria can be caused by permanent cerebral disease, but are often exacerbated by injudicious drug therapy, especially in intoxicating doses. Changes in antiepileptic drug regimens should therefore be considered. Thereafter, ataxia and dysarthria should be treated in the same manner as the subjects without epilepsy. Physical rehabilitation in epilepsy is generally required less often than is rehabilitation for psychosocial aspects of the condition, as outlined in this chapter.

CONCLUSION

Rehabilitation services for people with epilepsy, such as those outlined here, are unfortunately sparse. Service provision is at best fragmentary and many government departments can be involved, including health, education, and employment, as well as local authorities and voluntary bodies. As a group, people with intractable epilepsy often fall outside statutory provision, for example, services for those individuals with learning disabilities or the mentally ill, are not appropriate. A number of voluntary organisations provide support via personal contact and self-help groups (a list of useful addresses appears at the end of this chapter). These can also play an important role in public and professional education. Unless rehabilitative work is undertaken, many individuals will remain living in the parental home where dependency becomes a significant problem, particularly when parents are physically unable to continue as caretakers and potential fails to be maximised.

REFERENCES

Antebi D., Bird J. (1992). The facilitation and evocation of seizures. *British Journal of Psychiatry 160*: 154–164.

Baker G.A., Smith D.F., Dewey M. et al. (1991). The development of a seizure severity scale as an outcome measure in epilepsy. *Epilepsy Research 8*: 245–251.

Begley C.E., Annegers J.F., Lairson D.R. et al. (1994). Cost of epilepsy in the United States: a model based on incidence and prognosis. *Epilepsia 35*: 1230–1243.

Betts T. (1992). Epilepsy services: What people need and what they get. *Acta Neurologica 140*: 95–100.

Binnie C.D. (1991). Methods of detecting transient cognitive impairment during epileptiform discharges. In: Dodson W.E., Kinsbourne M., Hiltbrunner B. (eds). *The Assessment of Cognitive Functions in Epilepsy*. New York, Demos Publications p127–138.

Bjorholt P.G., Nakken K.O., Rohman K., Hansen H. (1990). Leisure time habits and physical fitness in adults with epilepsy. *Epilepsia 31*: 83–87.

Britten N., Morgan K., Fenwick P.B.C., Britten H. (1986). Epilepsy and handicap from birth to age thirty-six. *Developmental Medicine and Child Neurology 28*: 719–728.

Carroll D. (1992). Employment among young people with epilepsy. *Seizure 1*: 127–131.

Central Health Services Council (1969). People with epilepsy: report of the joint sub-committee and the advisory committee of the health and welfare of handicapped persons. London, HSMO.

Chaplin J.E., Yepez Lasso R., Shorvon S.D., Floyd M. (1992). National General Practice Study of Epilepsy: The social and psychological effects of a recent diagnosis of epilepsy. *British Medical Journal 304*: 1416–1418.

Chaplin J., Thompson P.J. (2001). Employment. In: Duncan J.S., Sisodiya, S., Smalls J.E. (eds). *Epilepsy 2001. From Science to Patient*. Edenbridge, Meritus Communications pp417–424.

Cockerell O.C., Hart Y.M., Sander J.W.A.S. et al. (1994). The cost of epilepsy in the United Kingdom: an estimation on the results of two population based studies. *Epilepsy Research 18*: 249–260.

Driving and Vehicle Licensing Agency (DVLA) (1994). *At a glance guide to the current medical standards to drive*. DVLA, Swansea.

Duncan J.S. (1991). Modern treatment strategies for patients with epilepsy: A review. *Journal of the Royal Society of Medicine 84*: 159–162

Duncan J.S., Shorvon S.D., Fish D.R. (1995). *Clinical Epilepsy*. New York, Churchill Livingstone.

Duncan J. (1997). Imaging and epilepsy. *Brain 120*(I) 339–378.

Fish D.R. (1995). The role of electroencephalography. In: Hopkins A., Shorvon S., Cascino G. (eds). *Epilepsy*, 2nd edition. London, Chapman Hall pp123–142.

Goodridge D.M., Shorvon S.D. (1983). Epileptic seizures in a population of 6000. *British Medical Journal 287*: 641–647.

Gram L., Johannessen SI., Osternan P.O., Sillenpaa M. (1993). *Pseudo-epileptic seizures*. Petersfield, Hampshire, Wrightson Biomedical Publishing Ltd.

Harding G.F.A., Jeavons P.M. (1994). Photosensitive Epilepsy. *Clinics in Developmental Medicine* No.133. London, MacKeith Press.

Hart YM (1992). *The early prognosis and medical care of people with epilepsy*. MD Thesis, University College London.

Helmstaedter C., Hufnagel A., Elger C.E. (1992). Seizures during cognitive testing in patients with temporal lobe epilepsy: Possibility of seizure induction by cognitive actuation. *Epilepsia 33*: 892–897.

HMSO (1989). *Caring for People. Community care in the next decade and beyond*. HMSO, London.

Hopkins A., Scambler G. (1977). How doctors deal with epilepsy. *Lancet i*: 183–186.

International Bureau for Epilepsy (IBE) (1991). *Epilepsy Education Manual*. IBE, Netherlands.

Jacoby A. et al. (1995). Impact of epilepsy on employment status: Findings from a UK study of people with well controlled epilepsy. *Epilepsy Research 21*: 125–132.

Kalogjera-Sackellares D. (1996). Psychological disturbances in patients with pseudoseizures. In: Sackellares J.C., Berent S. (eds). *Psychological Disturbance in Epilepsy*. Boston, Butterworth-Heinemann pp190–218.

Lelliot PT, Fenwick PBC (1991). Cerebral pathology in pseudo seizures. *Acta Neurological Scandinavica 83*: 129–132.

Lloyd-Jones A. (1980). Medical audit of care of patients with epilepsy in one group practice. *Journal of the Royal College of General Practioners 30*: 396–400.

Mendez M.F. (1996). Disorders of Mood and Affect in Epilepsy. In: Sackellares J.C., Berant S. (eds). *Psychological Disturbance in Epilepsy*. Boston, Butterworth-Heinemann pp125–142.

Millett C.J., Fish D., Thompson P.J. (1997). A survey of epilepsy patients' perception of video-game material/electronic screens and other factors as seizure precipitants. *Seizure 6*: 457–459.

Morrow J. (1990). Existing Care for Epilepsy. In: Chadwick D. (ed). *Quality of Life and Quality of Care in Epilepsy*. Royal Society of Medicine Round Table Series 23, pp96–103.

National Society for Epilepsy (1994). *Working with Epilepsy: A training resource pack for trainers* (1994). Transnational Epilepsy Training video (available from the National Society for Epilepsy, Chalfont Centre, Chalfont St Peter, Gerrards Cross, Buckinghamshire, SLQ ORJ).

O'Donoghue M.F., Duncan J.S., Sander J.W.A.S. (1996). The National Hospital Seizure Severity Scale: A Further development of the Chalfont Seizure Severity Scale. *Epilepsia 37* (6): 563–571.

Rugland A.L., Henrikson O., Bjornaes H. (1991). Computer-assisted neuropsychological assessment in patients with epilepsy. In: Dodson W.E., Kinsbourne M., Hiltbrunner B. (eds). *The Assessment of Cognitive Functions in Epilepsy*. New York, Demos Publications pp109–126.

Sander J.W.A.S., Shorvon S.D. (1996). Epidemiology of the epilepsies. *Journal of Neurology, Neurosurgery and Psychiatry 61*: 433–443.

Sass K.J., Spencer S.S., Westerveld M., Spencer D.D. (1992). The neuropsychology of corpus callosotomy for epilepsy. In: Bennett T.L. (ed). *The Neuropsychology of Epilepsy*. New York, Plenum Press pp291–308.

Shorvon S (1995). Epilepsy and driving. *British Medical Journal 310*: 885–886.

Shorvon S.D. (1996). *Status epilepticus. Its clinical features and treatment in children and adults*. Cambridge, Cambridge University Press.

Stevens DL (1989). Neurology in Gloucestershire: The clinical workload of an English neurologist. *Journal of Neurology, Neurosurgery and Psychiatry 52*: 439–446.

Suurmeijer T.P.B.M. (1995). The impact of epilepsy on social integration and quality of life: Family, peers and education. In: Aldenkamp A.P., Dreifuss F.E., Renier W.O., Suurmeijer T.P.B.M. (eds). *Epilepsy in Children and Adolescents*. Boca Raton, CRC Press Inc. pp251–270.

Tandon R., De Querdo J.R. (1996). Psychoses and Epilepsy. In: Sackellares J.C., Brent S. (eds). *Psychological Disturbance in Epilepsy*. Boston, Butterworth-Heinemann pp171–190.

Thompson P.J. (1990). The Cohen Report Onwards. In: Chadwick D. (ed). *Quality of Life and Quality of Care in Epilepsy*. Royal Society of Medicine Round Table Series 23, pp7–15. Royal Society of Medicine Services.

Thompson P.J., Upton D. (1994). Quality of Life in Epilepsy: The Family. In: Trimble M.R., Dodson W.E. (eds). *Epilepsy and Quality of Life*. New York, Plenum Press pp19–31.

Thompson P.J., Baxendale S. (1996). Non-pharmacological treatments for epilepsy. In: Shorvon S.D., Dreifuss F.E., Fish D.R., Thompson D.G.T. (eds). *The Treatment of Epilepsy*. Oxford, Blackwell Science pp345–356.

Thompson P.J., Trimble M.R. (1996). Neuropsychological aspects of epilepsy. In: Grant I., Adams K.M., (eds). *Neuropsychological Assessment of Neuropsychiatric Disorders*, 2nd Edition. Oxford, Oxford University Press, pp263–287.

Thompson P.J. (1997). Epilepsy and memory. In: Cull C., Goldstein L. (eds). *The Clinical Psychologist's Handbook of Epilepsy. Assessment and Management*. London, Routledge pp35–53.

Thompson P.J. (2001). Psychosocial aspects of epilepsy. In: Duncan J.S., Sisodiya S., Smalls J.E. (eds). *Epilepsy 2001. From Science to Patient*. Edenbridge, Meritus Communications, pp405–410.

Tobias E.S., Brodie A.F., Brodie M.J. (1994). An outcome audit at the epilepsy clinic. *Seizure 3*: 37–43.

Trenerry M.R. (1995). Clinical neuropsychology in epilepsy surgery. In: Hopkins A., Shorvon S., Cascino G. (eds). *Epilepsy*, 2nd edition London, Chapman Hall, pp269–282.

Upton D., Thompson P.J. (1992). Effectiveness of coping strategies employed by people with chronic epilepsy. *Journal of Epilepsy 5*: 119–127.

Vermeulen J., Aldenkamp A.P. (1995). Cognitive side effects of chronic antiepileptic drug treatment: A review of 25 years of research. *Epilepsy Research 22*: 65–95.

Wallace H.K., Shorvon S.D., Hopkins A. (1997). An audit of the organisation of adult epilepsy services in the United Kingdom. A comparative review of epilepsy and general neurology clinics. *Seizure 6*: 185–191.

Wilson B.A. (1995). Management and remediation of memory problems in brain injured adults. In: Baddeley A.D., Wilson B.A., Fraser F.N. (eds). *Handbook of Memory Disorders*. Chichester, John Wiley & Sons, pp428–451.

USEFUL ADDRESSES

Voluntary agencies

Irish Epilepsy Association, 249 Crumlin Road, Dublin 12, Eire.

British Epilepsy Association, Anstey House, 40 Hanover Square, Leeds LS3 1BE, England.

Epilepsie Cymru-Epilepsy Wales, Y pant teg Brynteg, Dolgellau, Gwynedd, LL40 1RP, Wales.

Epilepsy Association of Scotland, 48 Govan Road, Glasgow G51 1JL, Scotland.

National Society for Epilepsy, Chalfont St Peter, Gerrards Cross, Buckinghamshire SL9 ORJ, England.

Enlighten, Action for Epilepsy, Edinburgh Mid and East Lothian, 5 Coates Place, Edinburgh EH3 7AA, Scotland.

Assessment Centres and Epilepsy Clinics

The National Society for Epilepsy, Chalfont St Peter, Gerrards Cross, Buckinghamshire SL9 ORJ Tel: 01494 601300

Walton Hospital, Rice Lane, Liverpool L9 1AE Tel: 0151 5253611

University Hospital of Wales, Heath Park, Cardiff CF4 4XW Tel: 01222 747747

Birmingham University Neuropsychiatry & Seizure Clinic, Queen Elizabeth Psychiatric Hospital, Edgbaston, Birmingham B15 2TH Tel: 0121 47721311

Burden Neurological Hospital, Stapleton, Bristol BS16 1QT Tel: 0117 9567444

Bootham Park Hospital, Bootham, York YO3 7BY Tel: 01904 610777

David Lewis Centre, Alderley Edge, Cheshire SK9 7UD Tel: 01565 872613

Centre for Epilepsy, Maudsley Hospital, Denmark Hill, London SE5 8AZ Tel: 0171 703 6333

Manchester Royal Infirmary, Oxford Road, Manchester M13 9WL Tel: 0161 276.1234

Doncaster Royal Infirmary, Doncaster DN2 5LT Tel: 01302 796217

38. Parkinsonism and dystonia

Brian Pentland

INTRODUCTION

Despite dramatic improvements in drug therapy since the mid-1970s, the rehabilitation of Parkinson's disease and related syndromes is still a major challenge. Medication still does not offer a cure but provides symptom control and prolongs survival to give a life expectancy that is near to normal (Clarke, 1993). The aims of rehabilitation are to assist the individual to maintain optimal function, to prevent secondary complications, and to help and educate carers and patients in the process of adapting to problems as they develop.

The diagnosis of Parkinson's disease is far from straightforward (Quinn, 1995). It is important to distinguish idiopathic Parkinson's disease from other parkinsonian syndromes, which often follow a different course, can be unresponsive to dopaminergic drug treatment, and might show a different spectrum of disabilities (Table 38.1). The benefits of rehabilitation for disorders such as Steele–Richardson–Olszewski syndrome and multisystem atrophies are less well established but the need for careful assessment and support is as great.

PARKINSON'S DISEASE

Epidemiology

The prevalence of Parkinson's disease in Western countries is of the order of 150–120 per 100,000 with an incidence of about 18 per 100,000 (Wade & Langton Hewer, 1987). It is slightly more common in men and is predominantly a disease of the middle-aged and elderly, with an increasing prevalence with advancing age. However, the mean age of onset is 55 years, so that many people are employed at the time of onset.

Early features

The onset of Parkinson's disease is insidious and in the earliest stages the diagnosis is often difficult. Whereas tremor is the most common presenting symptom, it can be absent, and some individuals present with rather vague symptoms of fatigue, diffuse aches, pains or muscle cramps, or feelings of tension and restlessness. The components of hypokinesis (described later) can

Table 38.1. Causes of Parkinsonism

Iatrogenic
    Phenothiazines (e.g. chlorpromazine, fluphenazine, prochlorperazine)
    Butyrophenones (e.g. haloperidol, droperidol)
    Thioxanthenes (e.g. flupenthixol, zuclopenthixol)
    Fluspirilene, oxypertine, sulpiride
    Reserpine, metoclopramide, tetrabenazine
Toxic
    Manganese, carbon monoxide
Trauma
Tumour
Cerebrovascular disease, hypertensive encephalopathy
Encephalitis
Wilson's disease
"Parkinson-plus" syndromes
    Multiple system atrophy (e.g. Shy–Drager syndrome)
    Progressive supranuclear palsy (Steele–Richardson–Olszewski syndrome)
Corticobasal degeneration
Olivopontocerebellar atrophy
Hallevorden–Spatz disease

manifest singly, so that an individual can exhibit delay in starting a movement that appears simply as hesitancy or, alternatively, the individual might show only poverty of movement, which is misinterpreted as mild weakness. Slowness or clumsiness in upper or lower limb movements can be wrongly attributed to the effects of advancing years alone. Various parts of the body can be first affected and only with the passage of time and involvement of other functions does the diagnosis become obvious.

Principal diagnostic features

The cardinal features of Parkinson's disease are hypokinesis, rigidity, tremor, and impairment of postural reflexes (Ward, 1991). These disturbances underlie the major symptoms and signs found in the condition either alone or in combination.

Hypokinesis or "reduced movement". This includes a number of components: delay in initiation, poverty, imprecision and slowness of movement (bradykinesis), fatigue, and impairment of sequential actions. Automatically associated movements such as arm swing and facial expressions are reduced.

Rigidity. This is the increased resistance to passive muscle stretch found in the condition and, as it is present throughout the range of movement, it is classically described as "lead pipe" or "plastic". Anxiety, stress, and active use of the contralateral limb increase the tone in the limb being examined, the latter feature forming the basis of the "activated rigidity test" described by Webster (1968). Rigidity is present in axial as well as limb muscles and is most easily detected clinically in the muscles around the shoulders and neck. It is possibly this that is largely responsible for the stooped posture characteristic of the disease.

Tremor.   In Parkinson's disease, tremor is most commonly a slow, coarse rest tremor aggravated by stress with a frequency of 3.5–7 Hz. Clinically, in the early stages at least, the tremor is more of a social embarrassment than a functional problem, but as the disease progresses tremulous movements can interfere with manual activities.

Impaired postural reflexes.   These are included by some authors under the heading of hypokinesis. If the patient is standing and the examiner displaces his or her body, the patient is likely to have difficulty maintaining his or her stance. Thus, if pushed from in front the patient tends to stagger backwards (retropulsion); from behind, the patient stumbles forwards (propulsion); and a force displacing the patient sideways sends him or her off in the direction of that force (lateral propulsion). These findings of disequilibrium on examination are reflected in everyday difficulties in maintaining balance in busy streets, frequent falls, and the hurrying or festinating gait that is not uncommon with advancing disease.

Functional impairments

The face.   Several changes occur in the face: spontaneous movements of the muscles of facial expression and the eyes are reduced, as is blinking; the palpebral fissures might be widened; and, in advanced cases, the classic mask-like countenance and reptilian gaze can be seen. These changes can make the person with Parkinson's disease appear unemotional, hostile, or lacking in intelligence (Pentland et al., 1987). There is considerable social disability resulting from the reaction of others to the appearance of patients with Parkinson's disease (Pentland, 1991).

The hands.   Manual dexterity is reduced and can result in changes in handwriting, turning the pages of a book or newspaper, and later difficulty using door keys, fastening buttons, or tying shoe laces. The handwriting abnormality is classically described as micrographia. This is not simply script that is smaller than normal but includes changes such as loss of loops on l's and f's and flattening of m's and n's, resulting in a rather cramped and characterless form of writing. Alternating pronation and supination of the hands or repetitively touching each finger in turn rapidly with the thumb can reveal some or all of the features of hypokinesis, such as start hesitation, poverty, clumsiness, and slowness of movement.

Gait.   Loss of arm swing on one or both sides is often an early feature. In the feet, heel strike is lost and the individual tends increasingly to walk on the balls of the feet, with gradually reducing stride length eventually leading to the short, shuffling gait described as "marche à petit pas". The stooped, flexed posture and impaired postural reflexes can result in a festinating gait where the individual shuffles forward more and more quickly, as if chasing his or her centre of gravity. Pivotal or turning movements are often impaired, the individual appearing to move the whole body *en bloc*.

Gait can also be disturbed by the phenomenon of "freezing", where the patients' progress is suddenly stopped, as if the feet were stuck to the floor. This is particularly liable to occur at doorways, despite the door being open and there being no actual obstruction to the person's passage. Conversely, some individuals can run quite fast although they walk slowly, particularly under stress, in episodes of "kinesia paradoxica". A variety of other auditory and visual cues can improve gait problems, at least temporarily, and possibly prove therapeutically useful if applied consistently (Marchese et al., 2000).

Another fluctuating phenomenon that can affect gait is foot dystonia, which can occur in untreated as well as treated cases. The so-called "striatal foot deformity" refers to a unilateral equinovarus dystonic posture of the foot with dorsiflexion of the big toe (Jankovic & Fahn, 1988).

Speech.   Although attempts have been made to describe all the speech disturbances comprehensively in a single term this is not possible. Dysarthrophonia recognises the common features of defective articulation and impaired phonation, but there are also changes in the distribution of stress and intonation that comprise the melody of speech or prosody. The speech changes are usually considered to be largely attributable to the hypokinesis, but rigidity and tremor can contribute to the disturbances seen. The delay in initiation of movements can result in hesitant, almost stuttering, speech; the poverty is represented in monotony of pitch and loudness; the precision of articulation is often lacking, words might come in short rushes at variable rate and impaired breath control can give a breathy voice quality (Darley et al., 1975; Scott et al., 1985).

Mental state.   The personality, mood state, and cognitive function can all be altered in Parkinson's disease, although such changes are by no means universal and controversy exists as to the frequency of such disorders.

A "premorbid" personality has been suggested, although evidence is difficult to evaluate in a disease of insidious onset that can be present subclinically for some years before presentation. A large literature suggests that many parkinsonian patients exhibit emotional and attitudinal inflexibility, lack of affect, a tendency to depression, and introverted overcontrolled personality traits (Hubble & Koller, 1995; Todes & Lees, 1985). The finding of a high prevalence of Parkinson's disease in non-smoking teetotallers of rigid moralistic attitudes should not, however, be viewed as licence to adopt a libertine attitude to life.

Depression is common in Parkinson's disease and probably affects about half of all cases, although reported frequencies of the association vary from 20% to 90% (Gotham et al., 1986). Some of this variability is due to differences between hospital and community cases, studies of individuals at different stages of the disease, and—perhaps foremost—the diagnostic criteria for depression used (Hantz et al., 1994; Tandberg et al., 1996). The depression in Parkinson's disease is similar to that seen in arthritis, being characterised by pessimism and hopelessness, reduced drive and motivation, and increased concern with health, rather than negative feelings of guilt and worthlessness. There is some evidence that it correlates with severity of illness and degree of functional disability.

A vast literature exists on the incidence of dementia and cognitive impairments in the condition, with frequencies of dementia in Parkinson's disease being given as from less than 10% to over 80% (Brown & Marsden, 1984; Pirozzolo et al., 1988). Again, variation in diagnostic criteria used and patient selection methods help to explain the differences. The presence of depression and the effects of medication also significantly influence the diagnosis of dementia. The prevalence of dementia in Parkinson's disease is believed to be 20–30% (Brown & Marsden, 1984; Gibb, 1989).

Even in the absence of overt dementia there is considerable evidence that non-specific cognitive defects are fairly common in Parkinson's disease. Lees and Smith (1983) demonstrated difficulties in shifting conceptual sets and perseverative errors in patients with early Parkinson's disease and reviewed other reports of impairments in activities such as tracking tasks and predicting movements on visual tasks. The term "bradyphrenia" has been reintroduced to describe the subtle cognitive slowing that occurs in Parkinson's disease (Rogers et al., 1987). It is possible that such problems might underlie some of the mental inflexibility that is found.

Autonomic dysfunction. Seborrhoea and facial flushing occur in association with Parkinson's disease and blood pressure is often low. Postural hypotension can be found (often exacerbated by drug treatment), but profound hypotension suggests the Shy–Drager syndrome, one of the Parkinson-plus syndromes, which can also cause significant impairment of cardiovascular reflexes and other autonomic function tests.

Urinary bladder symptoms are reported in between 31% and 71% of people with Parkinson's disease, although these figures come from selected populations and many factors other than autonomic dysfunction might be responsible, for example cognitive impairment, physical immobility, concomitant urological conditions, and the effects of medications (Blaivas, 1988; Gray et al., 1995). Patients might report frequency, urgency, incontinence, or hesitancy and retention, and urodynamic evaluation is often necessary to identify the nature and so indicate the cause of the problem. Men with Parkinson's disease are sometimes submitted to unnecessary prostatectomies through failure to recognise that the disease causes bladder dysfunction.

Constipation is common and although autonomic dysfunction, with the added effect of anticholinergic drugs, might be responsible, other factors are involved. These include changes in diet due to feeding difficulties (see below), lack of exercise, and practical difficulties in getting to the toilet.

Feeding and nutrition. Problems with salivation occur in about 70% of cases, most commonly drooling, which causes considerable distress and social embarrassment. It might be a result of reduced rate of automatic swallowing, combined with the effects of flexed head posture and poor lip seal. There is no evidence of salivary hypersecretion but rather impaired transfer of saliva to the pharynx (Edwards et al., 1992). In some individuals the complaint is of a dry mouth. This is a common side-effect in those taking anticholinergic medication.

Feeding is often complicated by difficulties in handling cutlery as a result of hypokinesis or tremor. Chewing can also be impaired and dysphagia occurs much more commonly than in control populations. Videofluoroscopy has shown that even in those not complaining of dysphagia, silent aspiration can occur (Bird et al., 1994). Marked swallowing difficulties most commonly occur in advanced stages of the disease when other severe motor impairments are present.

Weight loss is common. Contributory factors include increased metabolic demand as a result of tremor, rigidity or dyskinesia, reduced appetite associated with feeding or swallowing difficulties, and depression, but the cause is not always apparent.

Sensory features and pain. Although sensory symptoms, in the form of parasthesias or pain, are not uncommon, sensory signs are absent. Cramp-like pains and diffuse aches and pains are common. These might be a secondary effect of rigidity or immobility or the result of osteoarthrosis, which accompanies the disease.

A number of patients do complain of severe, distressing pain either before the institution of treatment or, more commonly, when fluctuations in motor performance develop after therapy with levodopa (Quinn et al., 1986). These pains, which can involve the trunk or limbs, often fluctuate in parallel with the variations in motor function.

Sleep disturbance. Sleep disorders can be categorised as insomnias, excessive daytime somnolence, and parasomnias, and all occur commonly in Parkinson's disease (Nausieda, 1987). Insomnia in the form of inability to get off to sleep or early morning waking can occur as a result of concurrent anxiety or depression, respectively. The most common variety of insomnia, however, is "sleep fragmentation" characterised by recurrent waking (Stocchi et al., 1998). Patients often attribute this to joint pains, rigidity, tremor, or the desire to micturate but sleep studies suggest that spontaneous arousal is the initial event (Nausieda, 1987). The start of levodopa therapy can be associated with difficulty getting to sleep but tolerance to this effect usually develops fairly quickly. Sleep fragmentation sometimes improves with avoidance of late evening doses of levodopa.

Fatigue is common and patients often describe this as sleepiness. However, some individuals have true excessive somnolence during the day, which might or might not be accompanied by nocturnal wakefulness. Parasomnias are behavioural events such as nightmares, sleep-walking, or talking during sleep, and such problems usually relate to antiparkinsonian medication (Nausieda, 1987).

Sexual function. Sexual function and behaviour are very personal matters and people troubled with sexual dysfunction are often reluctant to mention it to their doctor, who in turn might not enquire about the possibility. The literature on sexual difficulties in the condition is limited but reveals a high frequency of difficulties in both sexes (Brown et al., 1990; Koller et al., 1990; Wermuth & Stenager, 1995). Apart from the adverse effects of anxiety, depression, and fatigue on libido, sexual function can be selectively impaired by the disease process. Certainly, improvement in libido with levodopa or selegiline treatment is recognised. Hypokinesis and rigidity impair body language, perhaps making the person with Parkinson's disease appear less attractive to others or, indeed, themselves, with loss of self-esteem. These physical impairments, by interfering with bodily movements, also cause mechanical difficulties in love-making, such as hindering pelvic movements or the adoption of a satisfactory sexual position. Simple counselling and sensitive advice can help couples overcome some of these problems.

A small proportion of men suffer erectile failure because of autonomic dysfunction. This is more likely in Shy–Drager syndrome, in which impotence without loss of libido can be the presenting feature (Duvoisin, 1984). Anticholinergic, beta-blocker, antidepressant, and hypnotic drugs can all contribute to impaired sexual performance and it is a useful rule to review medications whenever an individual describes sexual problems (see Chapter 22).

Social consequences.   Increasingly, physicians are exhorted to recognise the impact of illness on the individual in its effect on social functioning, and to direct their management towards reducing handicap rather than concentrating on physical impairments alone. Handicap is not easy to define, often difficult to measure, and frequently very difficult to influence. There is clear evidence of significant social repercussions from Parkinson's disease. A high proportion of people with Parkinson's disease take early retirement and report increasing social isolation (Mutch et al., 1986; Oxtoby, 1982; Singer, 1973). Outdoor leisure pursuits are abandoned in favour of home-based solitary activities, such as reading, radio, and television (Manson & Caird, 1985; Oxtoby, 1982). Many individuals and their spouses note a reduction in their social circle and a need for more company.

Explanations for these problems include the restriction in mobility, fatigue, communication difficulties, and the emotional and other mental accompaniments of the disease. Embarrassment resulting from tremors and dyskinesias and the reaction of others to the individual's general appearance and demeanour also contribute.

Driving.   Driving ability can be significantly impaired, especially in advanced stages of the disease (Dubinsky et al., 1991). However, with good drug control many patients are able to drive safely and efficiently for many years. In the UK, people with Parkinson's disease have a statutory obligation to notify the Driver and Vehicle Licensing Authority (DVLA) of the diagnosis, but should be specifically assessed for driving skills before advice not to drive is given to avoid unnecessary restriction with consequent aggravation of the social isolation. The lack of specific guidance to clinicians in assessing fitness to drive has been highlighted (Madeley et al., 1990).

Rating scales

Accurate clinical assessment of the patient is a fundamental part of the science of rehabilitation medicine. It is necessary to adequately identify the individual's problems in order to formulate an appropriate rehabilitation programme and to evaluate the efficacy of the programme once instituted. As drugs are a major component of the treatment, and all have significant side-effects, there is an added requirement to carefully monitor their effect. A large number of rating scales have been described and reviewed for use in Parkinson's disease (Marsden & Schachter, 1981; Martinez-Martin & Bermejo-Pareja, 1988). Many systems measure the signs and symptoms of the disease, and others attempt to evaluate functional aspects in terms of activities of daily living. The more commonly cited rating scales in the literature about Parkinson's disease are the Hoehn and Yahr (1967) classification for staging the disease and the Webster (1968) scale, which gives a rating of the major signs. These two are summarised in abbreviated form in Table 38.2. It should be emphasised, however, that although these scales might be superior to purely subjective methods of recording patient performance, there is considerable doubt about their validity and reliability (Martinez-Martin & Bermejo-Pareja, 1988). With regard to activities of daily living (ADL), the Northwestern University Disability scale is often recommended (Canter et al., 1961). This measures the following five activities: mobility, dressing, personal hygiene, eating and feeding, and speech, each being rated from 0 to 10, with 10 representing normal function. Although this scale might have some advantages over other ADL scales used routinely in a rehabilitation department when specific research into Parkinson's disease is being done, it is questionable as to whether it is necessary in routine use.

A further difficulty with most of these scales is that, as they have been in existence for many years, they do not take account of the problems of late fluctuation, which is common

Table 38.2.   Standard scales in Parkinson's disease

STAGING (Hoehn & Yahr, 1967)
I   Unilateral involvement: little or no functional impairment
II   Bilateral or midline involvement without impaired balance
III   First signs of impaired righting reflexes; some functional restriction but capable of independent living and may be able to work
IV   Fully developed, severely disabling disease; can stand and walk unaided
V   Confined to wheelchair or bed

DISEASE RATING (Webster, 1968)
A clinical rating (0–3) is given for each of the following 10 items with 0 = no involvement and 3 = severe (instructions being given for each):
1.   Bradykinesia of hands (including handwriting and pronation–supination)
2.   Rigidity: proximal and distal
3.   Posture: head flexion, "poker" spine and simian posture
4.   Upper extremity swing
5.   Gait: stride length, shuffling
6.   Tremor: amplitude and constancy
7.   Facies: mobility
8.   Seborrhoea
9.   Speech
10.   Self care

in levodopa-treated patients. One attempt to address this, and at the same time cover staging of the disease, rating of main signs, and ADL evaluation in a single measure is the Unified Parkinson's Disease Rating scale (Fahn et al., 1987a). This tool is predominantly used for research trial purposes.

Apart from assessing impairments and disabilities, there is increasing interest in gauging the handicap associated with chronic conditions like Parkinson's disease. One aspect of this is addressed by quality of life measures, of which there is a growing number of generic and disease-specific instruments from which to choose. In the latter category, the Parkinson's Disease Questionnaire (PDQ-39) and its associated PDQ-8 are gaining popularity (Jenkinson et al., 1995; Peto et al., 1998). Appropriate attention is also being given to the issue of measuring the effects of the disease on the quality of life of caregivers.

Management

Management is discussed here from the point of view of Parkinson's disease although many of the approaches are equally applicable to other parkinsonian syndromes.

Team approach to rehabilitation. As well as doctors, people with parkinsonism—and their families—can require the skills of a nurse, physiotherapist, occupational therapist, speech therapist, dietitian, clinical psychologist, and social worker, among others (Caird, 1991). In the UK, the professionals involved will commonly be determined by the availability of services rather than by needs. Many patients are not seen for regular medical review, about 15% might see a physiotherapist or occupational therapist, and 3–4% a speech therapist (Mutch et al., 1986; Oxtoby, 1982). Even when resources are scarce it should be possible to improve on this by organising services better. The use of group activities with a major educational component based in a day hospital, day centre, or other community setting, given in short pulses and repeated at intervals, looks promising and cost-effective (Gauthier et al., 1987; Robertson & Thomson, 1984). Alternatively, or even in conjunction with such a facility, professionals could be available to see patients in their own homes to advise on exercise, communication, practical problems, etc. This might be a cheaper alternative to using ambulance transport and could provide greater consumer satisfaction.

No matter which approach is taken, the patient's family should be involved in the process wherever possible. Professional input to the Parkinson's Disease Society can also prove mutually beneficial. The Society does much to disseminate appropriate professional advice to patients and their families, as well as acting as a source of support. It also promotes cross-fertilisation of ideas between professionals themselves.

Counselling. All patients and their families need counselling support. The time of diagnosis is critical, information must be delivered and subsequently reinforced, and time must be found for questions to be answered. In some centres, a social worker has been effective in a counselling role, supporting the work of the physician at diagnosis and subsequently (Baker & Smith, 1991). In other centres, a similar function is performed by a nurse.

Drug treatment. Full accounts of the clinical pharmacology of Parkinson's disease are widely available elsewhere (e.g. Marsden, 1995a; Koller & Tolosa, 1998), so only a few points of functional relevance will be emphasised here. Whatever drug is used, it is essential to base therapeutic decisions on knowledge of how the disease affects the person's lifestyle. Another obvious cardinal principle is that adverse effects, some of which are severe, must be avoided. The mainstay of treatment remains levodopa. There is still controversy about the long-term effects of beginning treatment earlier rather than later in the course of the disease (Lees, 1986; Markham & Diamond, 1986). Dopamine agonists such as bromocriptine, pergolide, and lisuride can be less likely to cause dyskinesia (Rinne, 1989) but are less effective than levodopa when used alone.

One of the major therapeutic challenges is preventing and managing the problems of treatment-related oscillations. Options include controlled-release levodopa preparations, the addition of selegiline, and apomorphine, which must be given by intermittent subcutaneous injection or as a continuous subcutaneous infusion (Frankel et al., 1990).

Several symptomatic drug treatments are useful in Parkinson's disease. For example, the judicious use of hypnotics for insomnia, antidepressants for confirmed depression, simple non-steroidal agents for musculoskeletal pains, and quinine for cramps should be considered.

Surgical treatment. A number of neurosurgical approaches were developed following the original work of Cooper (1953). The most common procedures were stereotactic pallidectomy and ventral thalamotomy, but there was significant morbidity (Mawdsley, 1975). There has been renewed interest in stereotactic neurosurgical procedures in recent years, including both ablative procedures and high-frequency electrical stimulation of three target areas: the thalamus, the subthalamic nucleus, and the globus pallidus (Bhatia et al., 1998). Implantation or neural grafting techniques to boost cerebral dopamine production have attracted much recent interest but require further evaluation (Marsden, 1995a; Olanow et al., 1994).

Management of autonomic dysfunction. Autonomic symptoms occur in Parkinson's disease (see earlier) but are more obvious and more troublesome in the Shy–Drager system (multisystem atrophy with dysautonomia). All forms of dysautonomia require the same general management approaches (for a review, see Polinsky, 1992). The aims of management of postural hypotension are to avoid syncopal episodes and to limit the disabling effects of hypotensive symptoms. The simplest measures, often discovered by patients for themselves, include the avoidance of abrupt changes in posture, straining, heavy meals, alcohol, and drugs that modify blood pressure. Physiological approaches—of relatively limited value—include restriction of intake of sodium and fluid, slight elevation of the head of the bed at night, and compressive garments. The dubious benefit of compressive garments is often outweighed by the difficulties they pose, particularly for people with neurological disabilities or bladder dysfunction. Drug treatment includes the use of fludro-cortisone, ephedrine, the peripheral-acting alpha-adrenergic drug midodrine, or desmopressin (Mathias & Kimber, 1998; Wright et al., 1998).

Nursing. Nurses are involved in the management of Parkinson's disease in hospitals, day hospitals, and in the community (Sharp, 1991). As they have the greatest direct contact with patients in hospital, they provide invaluable observations on the patient's functional performance throughout the day and night. The nurse has to show patience and understanding of the peculiar requirements of these patients, who might require a very long time to achieve self-care tasks and whose dependency can vary grossly from one part of the day to another. Flexibility in ward routines, such as meal times, is necessary. In the advanced and terminal stages of the disease, the nurse might have to assist with all activities of daily living as the person becomes increasingly immobile and uncommunicative.

There has been a welcome expansion of the nursing role with the appointment of Parkinson's disease nurse specialists or nurse practitioners. These nurses, who provide an invaluable link between the hospital and the patient's home, can fulfil a variety of tasks including education, psychological counselling, and practical advice on medication and access to local services. Visiting the individual and their carer in the home setting affords the opportunity to discuss sensitive issues, provide support for the family, and assess the person in a more realistic environment than the hospital clinic.

Physiotherapy. The value of physiotherapy for Parkinson's disease was recognised in the pre-levodopa era and one impressive study compared 100 patients who received physiotherapy with 100 who did not. After 10 years, significant disability was recorded in 13 of those treated compared with 55 of those not given physiotherapy (Doshay, 1962).

Since the introduction of modern drug therapy there have been few controlled studies of the effects of physiotherapy (Banks, 1991), and a Cochrane systemic review (Deane et al., 2000) identified only 11 trials comparing physiotherapy with placebo or no treatment.

It is perhaps not surprising that, with new drugs becoming available, it is difficult to identify suitable groups of patients and controls where the possible effects of physical therapy interventions can be separated from the effects of changes to drug regimes. As a result, most reported studies refer to small groups of patients. In addition, the question arises as to the appropriate outcome measures used. There is growing evidence that people with mild to moderate Parkinson's disease can tolerate and benefit from aerobic exercise (Canning et al., 1997) and that instruction in such exercise can slow the deterioration in mental and physical function (Bridgewater, 1996).

Much would appear to depend on: (1) the nature of the package of therapy provided; (2) its frequency and; in particular (3) the extent of follow-up. Although one early controlled study showed no measurable improvement in neurological impairment, it is doubtful whether this was a realistic goal in the first place (Gibberd, 1981). Modest functional benefit has been reported from individualised or group programmes in a number of studies of physical exercise (Dam et al., 1996; Franklyn et al., 1981; Palmer et al., 1986). Benefit from combinations of physiotherapy with other health professional input, such as occupational therapy and speech and language therapy, have also been reported (Comella et al., 1994; Gauthier et al., 1987; Patti et al., 1996). In contrast to such programmes, which are principally hospital based, Banks and Caird (1989) reported a sustained improvement in mobility and turning in bed following exercises taught in the home setting.

There is increasing recognition that early referral to physiotherapy, with repeated review or top-up instruction either on a group or individualised basis, is an effective method of helping the patient maintain optimal function. It would be unrealistic to expect such measures to reverse this progressive condition, a claim not even made for current drug therapy.

Speech therapy. As with physiotherapy, consumer satisfaction with speech therapy intervention is often high, but all too often the services of the speech therapist are either not requested or left until late in the disease. Controlled studies have, however, shown some promise (Scott, 1991). Having emphasised the importance of prosodic abnormalities in the speech of parkinsonian patients, Scott and Caird (1983) gave daily prosodic exercises at home for a short period and reported significant improvements in intonation, stress, and rhythm. Some of these improvements were maintained for up to 3 months. In a controlled study where intensive therapy was given to patients over a 2-week period with both group and individual attention, significant improvements in motor production of speech were found, which were continued for 3 months without further therapeutic intervention (Robertson & Thomson, 1984). The "package" of therapy in this study included group educational activities and videotaping patients' performance to take account of non-verbal as well as verbal aspects of communication.

The speech therapist, often working in concert with the dietitian and occupational therapist, can provide useful guidance to those troubled by dysphagia (see Chapter 25). Advice on posture and relaxation, and instruction in a feeding routine, is combined with consideration of food consistency and nutritional content. Crockery adapted to keep meals warm and the idea of taking several small meals through the day can be appropriate in some cases.

Occupational therapy. Although simple aids for activities of daily living such as feeding, dressing, bathing, toileting, and mobility are of proven value in the management of Parkinson's disease, they are often not provided (Beattie, 1991; Beattie & Caird, 1980; Oxtoby, 1982). This is usually the result of lack of occupational therapy input rather than parsimony on the part of health or social services. Home visits are one of the cornerstones of modern occupational therapy practice and the value of practical advice by an occupational therapist in the patient's own home cannot be understated. In such a setting, at a day centre or day hospital the opportunity can also be taken to address the vocational, leisure, and transport needs of the individual.

THE DYSTONIAS

The dystonias or dystonic syndromes are disorders characterised by sustained involuntary muscle contractions resulting in abnormal movements or postures. They can be present in childhood, adolescence, or adulthood, and can be idiopathic or symptomatic. Idiopathic dystonias can be divided into those that are familial, with a variety of inheritance patterns, and those that occur sporadically. The symptomatic group include those associated with hereditary neurological disorders, such as Wilson's disease, Huntington's disease, Parkinson-plus syndromes, and many others, and cases where a specific cause such as perinatal injury, encephalitis, head trauma, or vascular damage can be identified. Drug-induced dystonias account for a large proportion of symptomatic cases. Finally, there is the category of psychogenic dystonia. It is beyond the scope of this text to give more than a brief account of some of the more common conditions and make some general comments about management. For more detailed information the reader is directed to excellent reviews by Fahn and colleagues (Fahn et al., 1987b; Jankovic & Fahn, 1988).

In addition to classification according to age of onset and aetiology, these disorders are grouped according to the anatomic distribution of the movements into focal, segmental, multifocal, hemi- and generalised dystonias. These are summarised in Table 38.3.

Focal dystonias

Blepharospasm. This describes intermittent spasms of contraction of the orbicularis oculi. This occurs idiopathically in middle and old age, or can be secondary to Parkinson's disease, antiparkinsonian, and neuroleptic medication. Early symptoms can be experienced as excessive uncontrollable blinking, especially in bright light, but usually progress to irregular and prolonged episodes of eye closure. This effectively renders the patient intermittently blind in the presence of normal vision, as the eyelids are tightly closed. It stigmatises the patient and can cause significant problems in everyday life, for example driving.

Oromandibular dystonias. This involves the muscles of the jaw, tongue, and mouth causing the mouth to pull open or clamp closed with resulting disturbance of speech and swallowing.

Laryngeal dystonia (spasmodic dystonia or dystonic adductor dystonia). This is characterised by involuntary contractions of the laryngeal muscles resulting in impairment of speech, which can be strained or whispering in character, or temporarily lost altogether.

Spasmodic torticollis (wry neck or cervical dystonia). This is the most common focal dystonia, affecting the cervical muscles. Idiopathic spasmodic torticollis usually occurs in middle age, although the same syndrome can be secondary to neuroleptic drugs. Usually, the neck rotates to left or right, but it can flex (anterocollis), extend (retrocollis), or laterally flex (laterocollis). These syndromes often cause pain that is either located in the dystonic muscle or arises from soft tissues or joints. Spasms can interfere with any task requiring head control, such as eating, reading, walking, and driving. The distortion of facial features that often accompanies the twisting movements of the neck, with resulting loss of eye contact, can have profound effects on non-verbal communication. This can lead to low self-esteem or embarrassment, with distress to the individual and other members of the family.

Writer's cramp. This term is best restricted to a focal dystonia of the hand and forearm that occurs specifically on writing. Other occupational dystonias involving specific activities include typist's cramp, pianist's and musician's cramp, and golfer's "yips".

Segmental and generalised dystonias

Specific terms are used to describe different patterns of dystonia, according to distribution. "Generalised dystonia" is perhaps the least satisfactorily defined. The term is used to describe dystonia of at least one or both legs plus some other region of the body (Fahn et al., 1987a,b). Confusion is also caused by using the term synonymously for torsion dystonia or dystonia musculorum deformans, which were names previously used for the syndrome of trunk and limb dystonia, many cases of which would more accurately be classified as segmental crural dystonias.

Table 38.3. The dystonias

Classification	Name	Muscles involved
Focal	Blepharospasm	Eyelids
	Oromandibular	Jaw, tongue, mouth
	Laryngeal	Laryngeal
	Spasmodic torticollis	Neck
	Writer's cramp	Arm
Segmental	Cranial (Meige syndrome)	Cranial + neck
	Axial	Neck + trunk
	Brachial	Arm(s) + axial or cranial
	Crural	Leg(s) + trunk
Multifocal	Dystonia involving two or more non-contiguous body parts (e.g. torticollis + leg dystonia)	
Hemidystonia	Dystonia affecting arm and leg on the same side	
Generalised	Combination of crural and another segmental dystonia	

Management

Management of the dystonias can be described under four headings: specific measures, drug treatment, surgical procedures, and other therapies.

Specific measures.   Apart from withdrawal of the offending agent in drug-induced cases, specific treatment is possible only in a few instances, as in the use of D-penicillamine in Wilson's disease or the surgical removal of space-occupying lesions such as tumours or arteriovenous malformations (Fahn & Marsden, 1987). Even in these cases, symptomatic drug treatment is often necessary, at least temporarily.

Drug treatment.   No single class of drug is reliably effective in relieving dystonia and consequently an extensive list of agents has been recommended. Although uncommon, some cases of dystonia respond dramatically to levodopa. It is, therefore, wise to consider a therapeutic trial of levodopa to detect this dopa-responsive dystonia, as sustained improvement can result from low dose levodopa treatment (Nygaard et al., 1991). Anticholinergics, usually in large doses, are probably the most effective overall in other patients and, as well as orally, can be very effective intravenously for acute dystonias. There is some evidence to suggest that they should be started early after the onset of the disorder (Greene et al., 1988). As emphasised in relation to Parkinson's disease, the use of anticholinergics in elderly people is difficult. The muscle relaxant baclofen can be used orally or intrathecally. Other agents include benzodiazepines, neuroleptics, and tetrabenazine. The fact that both dopamine agonists and antagonists can prove beneficial highlights the complexity of the problem and emphasises the frequent need for careful therapeutic trials of different agents in individual patients.

Botulinum toxin, administered intramuscularly, is now recognised as a major advance in the treatment of focal dystonias. Numerous reports have indicated its efficacy in blepharospasm, cervical dystonia, and writer's cramp (Grandas et al., 1988; Jankovic & Schwartz, 1990; Turjanski et al., 1996; Van den Bergh et al., 1995). It also has a place in treating components of more generalised dystonias. In addition to reducing or abolishing the abnormal movements, this treatment can afford almost complete relief of pain in those reporting pain. Benefit lasts for about 3 months on average, although in some cases it extends to a year or more. Side-effects include dysphagia, neck weakness, nausea, and diarrhoea, and large doses can induce antibody production, rendering subsequent treatments ineffective.

Surgical procedures.   Surgical procedures for dystonias can be divided into stereotactic cerebral operations and peripheral surgery. As with Parkinson's disease, various stereotactic techniques have been used and, with improved imaging techniques and interoperative neurophysiological monitoring, even more sophisticated procedures are possible nowadays. There is general agreement that these operations are more successful for limb dystonias than for axial disorders and the indication for this approach is limited (Fahn & Marsden, 1987). Peripheral surgery in the form of orbicularis oculi myectomy and facial neurectomy for blepharospasm and posterior rhizotomy, or extraspinal peripheral denervation for torticollis can be successful in carefully selected cases (Jankovic & Fahn, 1988). The need for such approaches has, however, reduced with the increased use of botulinum toxin injection techniques.

Other therapy.   Finally, but certainly not least in importance, is the need for general support and consideration of non-invasive approaches to management. In the past, many patients with dystonic syndromes were erroneously diagnosed as suffering from hysteria. This is rarely the case, but in a few instances intensive psychological or psychiatric input can be appropriate. In most abnormal movement disorders, the condition is aggravated by fatigue and psychological stress or emotional upset. The reactions of other people to the patient's appearance can compound the distress already being suffered (Marsden, 1995b; Ward, 1993). Careful explanation of the nature of the disorder to the individual and, where possible, the family, with appropriate reassurance and advice on stress management, is essential and can considerably alleviate the situation. Most of the various methods of relaxation therapy such as hypnotherapy, aromatherapy, reflexology, and yoga are worth trying. Such instruction can be provided by a clinical psychologist, remedial therapist, or other health professional. Many individuals find contact with fellow sufferers through the Dystonia Society provides considerable comfort together with practical advice.

Biofeedback approaches have been tried with variable success, but even when improvement occurs it is rarely sustained (Fahn & Marsden, 1987). There is a very limited place for the use of orthotic devices or braces, which can, in fact, unless carefully prescribed, be detrimental.

Physiotherapy advice on appropriate rest and exercise routines and the use of certain sensory stimuli to reduce the severity of dystonia is worthwhile in most cases but aggressive approaches aimed at building up strength in antagonist muscles is not. Hydrotherapy can provide temporary relief but this is not sustained. Communication aids can be beneficial in some cases where speech is disrupted by the dystonia (Shahar et al., 1987), as can other practical aids to daily living in selected cases.

In focal dystonias especially, there is scope for adapting the environment to lessen the practical problems of dystonia, or even to lessen its severity. In writer's cramp, for example, the sitting posture, and the way in which the pen is held, can aggravate the dystonia, and alternative styles of writing or implements, and different types of seating, can sometimes be helpful. Similarly, more comfortable sitting postures can sometimes be found for people with spasmodic torticollis. Posture and exercise regimes can perhaps delay or prevent the onset of contractures.

REFERENCES

Baker M, Smith P (1991). The social worker. In: Caird FI (ed). *Rehabilitation of Parkinson's disease*. Chapman and Hall, London, p 107–119.

Banks MA (1991). Physiotherapy. In: Caird FI (ed) *Rehabilitation of Parkinson's disease*. Chapman & Hall, London, p 45–65.

Banks MA, Caird FI (1989). Physiotherapy benefits patients with Parkinson's disease. *Clinical Rehabilitation 3*: 11–16.

Beattie A (1991). Occupational therapy. In: Caird FI (ed) *Rehabilitation of Parkinson's disease*. Chapman and Hall, London, p 66–86.

Beattie A, Caird FI (1980). The occupational therapist and the patient with Parkinson's disease. *British Medical Journal 280*: 1354–1355.

Bhatia K, Brooks DJ, Burn DJ et al. (1998). Guidelines for the management of Parkinson's disease. *Hospital Medicine 59*: 469–480.

Bird MR, Woodward MC, Gibson EM, Phyland DJ, Fonda D (1994). Asymptomatic swallowing disorders in elderly patients with Parkinson's disease: a description of findings on clinical examination and videofluoroscopy in sixteen patients. *Age and Ageing 23*: 251–254.

Blaivas JG (1988). Urinary bladder problems in Parkinson's disease. *Current Opinion in Neurology and Neurosurgery 1*: 284–286.

Bridgewater KJ, Sharpe MH (1996). Aerobic exercise and early Parkinson's disease. *Journal of Neurological Rehabilitation 10*: 233–241.

Brown RG, Marsden CD (1984). How common is dementia in Parkinson's disease? *Lancet ii*: 1262–1265.

Brown RG, Jahan Shahi M, Quinn N, Marsden CD (1990). Sexual function in patients with Parkinson's disease and their partners. *Journal of Neurology, Neurosurgery and Psychiatry 53*: 480–486.

Caird FI (ed) (1991). *Rehabilitation of Parkinson's disease*. Chapman and Hall, London.

Canning CG, Alison JA, Allen NE, Groeller H (1997). Parkinson's disease: an investigation of exercise capacity, respiratory function, and gait. *Archives of Physical Medicine & Rehabilitation 78*: 199–207.

Canter GJ, De La Torre R, Mier M (1961). A method for evaluating disability in patients with Parkinson's disease. *Journal of Nervous and Mental Disease 133*: 143–147.

Clarke CE (1993). Mortality from Parkinson's disease in England and Wales 1921–89. *Journal of Neurology, Neurosurgery & Psychiatry 56*: 690–693.

Comella CL, Stebbins GT, Brown-Toms N, Goetz CG (1994). Physical therapy and Parkinson's disease. *Neurology 44*: 376–378.

Cooper IS (1953). Ligation of the anterior choroidal artery for involuntary movements of parkinsonism. *Psychiatric Quarterly 27*: 317–319.

Dam M, Tonin P, Casson S, Bracco F, Piron L, Pizzolato G, Battistin L (1996). Effects of conventional and sensory-enhanced physiotherapy on disability of Parkinson's disease patients. *Advances in Neurology 69*: 551–555.

Darley FL, Aronson AE, Brown JR (1975). *Motor speech disorders*. WB Saunders, Philadelphia.

Deane KHO, Jones A, Clarke CE, Playford ED, Ben-Shlomo Y (2000). Physiotherapy for patients with Parkinson's Disease (Cochrane review) 1: The Cochrane Library 4, Oxford: Update Software.

Doshay LJ (1962). Method and value of physiotherapy in Parkinson's disease. *New England Journal of Medicine 266*: 878–880.

Dubinsky RM, Gray C, Husted D et al. (1991). Driving in Parkinson's disease. *Neurology 41*: 517–520.

Duvoisin RC (1984). *Parkinson's disease: a guide for patient and family, 2nd edn*. Raven Press, New York.

Edwards LL, Quigley EMM, Pfeiffer RF (1992). Gastrointestinal dysfunction in Parkinson's disease: frequency and pathophysiology. *Neurology 42*: 726–732.

Fahn S, Marsden CD (1987). The treatment of dystonia. In: Marsden CD, Fahn S (eds) *Movement disorders*, vol 2. Butterworths, London, p 359–382.

Fahn S, Elton RL, Members of the UPDRS Development Committee (1987a). Unified Parkinson's Disease Rating Scale. In: Fahn S, Marsden CD, Calne DB, Coldstein M (eds) *Recent developments in Parkinson's disease*. Macmillan Healthcare Information, New Jersey, p 153.

Fahn S, Marsden CD, Calne DB (1987b). Classification and investigation of dystonia. In: Marsden CD, Fahn S (eds) *Movement disorders*, vol 2. Butterworths, London, p 332–358.

Frankel JP, Lees AJ, Kempster PA, Stern GM (1990). Subcutaneous apomorphine in the treatment of Parkinson's disease. *Journal of Neurology, Neurosurgery and Psychiatry 53*: 96–101.

Franklyn S, Kohout LJ, Stern GM, Dunning M (1981). Physiotherapy in Parkinson's disease. In: Rose FC, Capildeo R (eds). *Research progress in Parkinson's disease*. Pitman Medical, London, p 397–400.

Gauthier L, Dalziel S, Gauthier S (1987). The benefits of group occupational therapy for patients with Parkinson's disease. *American Journal of Occupational Therapy 41*: 360–365.

Gibb WRG (1989). Dementia and Parkinson's disease. *British Journal of Psychiatry 154*: 596–614.

Gibberd FB, Page NGR, Spencer KM et al. (1981). Controlled trial of physiotherapy and occupational therapy for Parkinson's disease. *British Medical Journal 292*: 1196.

Gotham A-M, Brown RG, Marsden CD (1986). Depression in Parkinson's disease: a quantitative and qualitative analysis. *Journal of Neurology, Neurosurgery and Psychiatry 49*: 381–389.

Grandas F, Elston J, Quinn N, Marsden CD (1988). Blepharospasm – a review of 264 patients. *Journal of Neurology, Neurosurgery and Psychiatry 51*: 767–772.

Gray R, Stern G, Malone-Lee J (1995). Lower urinary tract dysfunction in Parkinson's disease: changes relate to age and not disease. *Age and Ageing 24*: 499–504.

Greene P, Sahle H, Fahn S (1988). Analysis of open-label trials in torsion dystonia using high dosages of anticholinergics and other drugs. *Movement Disorders 3*: 46–60.

Hantz P, Caradoc-Davies G, Caradoc-Davies T, Weatherall M, Dixon G (1994). Depression in Parkinson's disease. *American Journal of Psychiatry 151*: 1010–1014.

Hoehn MM, Yahr MD (1967). Parkinsonism: onset, progression and mortality. *Neurology 17*: 427–442.

Hubble JP, Koller WC (1995). The Parkinsonian personality. *Advances in Neurology 65*: 43–48.

Jankovic J, Fahn S (1988). Dystonic syndromes. In: Jankovic J, Tolosa E (eds) *Parkinson's disease and movement disorders*. Urban and Schwarzenberg, Baltimore, p 283–314.

Jankovic J, Schwartz K (1990). Botulinium toxin injection for cervical dystonia. *Neurology 40*: 277–280.

Jenkinson C, Peto V, Fitzpatrick R, Greenhall R, Hyman N (1995). Self-reported functioning and well-being in patients with Parkinson's disease: comparison of the Short-form Health Survey (SF-36) and the Parkinson's Disease Questionnaire (PDQ 39). *Age and Ageing 24*: 505–509.

Koller WC, Tolosa E (1998). Current and emerging drug therapies in the management of Parkinson's disease. *Neurology 50 (Suppl 6)*: 1–48.

Koller WC, Vetere-Overfield B, Williamson A, Busenbark K, Nash J, Parrish D (1990). Sexual dysfunction in Parkinson's disease. *Clinical Neuropharmacology 13*: 461–463.

Lees AJ (1986). L-Dopa treatment and Parkinson's disease. *Quarterly Journal of Medicine 59*: 535–547.

Lees AJ, Smith E (1983). Cognitive deficits in the early stages of Parkinson's disease. *Brain 106*: 257–270.

Madeley P, Hulley JL, Wildgust H, Mindham RHS (1990). Parkinson's disease and driving ability. *Journal of Neurology, Neurosurgery and Psychiatry 53*: 580–582.

Manson L, Caird FI (1985). Survey of the hobbies and transport of patients with Parkinson's disease. *British Journal of Occupational Therapy 48*: 199–200.

Marchese R, Diverio M, Zucchi F, Lentino C, Abbruzzese G (2000). The role of sensory cues in the rehabilitation of parkinsonian patients: a comparison of two physical therapy protocols. *Movement Disorders 15*: 879–883.

Markham CH, Diamond SG (1986). Long-term follow-up of early dopa treatment in Parkinson's disease. *Annals of Neurology 19*: 365–372.

Marsden CD (1995a). Parkinson's disease. In: Wiles CM (ed) *Management of neurological disorders*. BMJ Publishing Group, London, p 179–203.

Marsden CD (1995b). Psychogenic problems associated with dystonia. *Advances in Neurology 65*: 319–326.

Marsden CD, Schachter M (1981). Assessment of extrapyramidal disorders. *British Journal of Clinical Pharmacology 11*: 129–151.

Martinez-Martin P, Bermejo-Pareja F (1988). Rating scales in Parkinson's disease. In: Jankovic J, Tolosa E (eds) *Parkinson's disease and movement disorders*. Urban and Schwarzenberg, Baltimore, p 235–242.

Mathias CJ, Kimber JR (1998). Treatment of postural hypotension. *Journal of Neurology, Neurosurgery and Psychiatry 65*: 285–289.

Mawdsley C (1975). Parkinson's disease. In: Matthews WB (ed) *Recent advances in clinical neurology*. Churchill Livingstone, Edinburgh, p 147.

Mutch WJ, Sturdwick A, Roy SK, Downie AW (1986). Parkinson's disease: disability, review, and management. *British Medical Journal 293*: 675–677.

Nausieda PA (1987). Sleep disorders. In: Koller WC (ed) *Handbook of Parkinson's disease*. Marcel Dekker, New York, p 371.

Nygaard TG, Marsden CD, Fahn S (1991). Dopa-responsive dystonia: long-term treatment response and prognosis. *Neurology 41*: 174–181.

Olanow CW, Marsden D, Lang AE, Goetz CG (1994). The role of surgery in Parkinson's disease. *Neurology, 44 (Suppl 1)*: S17–S20.

Oxtoby M (1982). *Parkinson's disease patients and their social needs*, Parkinson's Disease Society, London.

Palmer SS, Mortimer JA, Webster DD et al. (1986). Exercise therapy for Parkinson's disease. *Archives of Physical Medicine and Rehabilitation 67*: 741–745.

Patti F, Reggio A, Nicoletti F, Sellaroli T, Deinite G, Nicoletti F (1996). Effects of rehabilitation therapy on Parkinsonians' disability and functional independence. *Journal of Neurological Rehabilitation 10*: 223–231.

Pentland B (1991). Body language in Parkinson's disease. *Behavioural Neurology 4*: 181–187.

Pentland B, Pitcairn TK, Gray JM, Riddle WJR (1987). The effects of reduced expression in Parkinson's disease on impression formation by health professionals. *Clinical Rehabilitation 1*: 307–313.

Peto V, Jenkinson C, Fitzpatrick R (1998). PDQ-39: a review of the development, validation and application of a Parkinson's disease quality of life questionnaire and its associated measures. *Journal of Neurology 245*: S10–S14.

Pirozzolo FJ, Smihart A, Roy G, Jankovic J, Mortimer J (1988). Cognitive impairment associated with Parkinson's disease and other movement disorders. In: Jankovic J, Tolosa E (eds) *Parkinson's disease and movement disorders*. Urban and Schwarzenberg, Baltimore, p 425.

Polinsky RJ (1992). Autonomic dysfunction in neurological illness. In: Klawans HL, Goetz CG, Tanner CM (eds) *Textbook of clinical neuropharmacology*. Raven Press, New York, p 537–557.

Quinn N (1995). Parkinsonism – recognition and differential diagnosis. *British Medical Journal 310*: 447–452.

Quinn NP, Koller WC, Lang AE, Marsden CD (1986). Painful Parkinson's disease. *Lancet i*: 1366–1369.

Rinne UK (1989). Lisuride, a dopamine agonist in the treatment of early Parkinson's disease. *Neurology 39*: 336–339.

Robertson SJ, Thomson F (1984). Speech therapy in Parkinson's disease: a study of the efficacy and long term effects of intensive treatment. *British Journal of Disorders of Communication 19*: 213–224.

Rogers D, Lees AJ, Smith E et al. (1987). Bradyphrenia in Parkinson's disease and psychomotor retardation in depressive illness: an experimental study. *Brain 110*: 761–776.

Scott S (1991). Speech therapy. In: Caird FI (ed) *Rehabilitation of Parkinson's disease*. Chapman and Hall, London, p 87–106.

Scott S, Caird FI (1983). Speech therapy for Parkinson's disease. *Journal of Neurology, Neurosurgery and Psychiatry 46*: 140–144.

Scott S, Caird FI, Williams BO (1985). *Communication in Parkinson's disease*. Croom Helm, Beckenham, Kent.

Shahar E, Nowaczyk M, Tervo RC (1987). Rehabilitation of communication impairment in dystonia musculorum deformans. *Pediatric Neurology 3*: 97–100.

Sharp BK (1991). Nursing care. In: Caird FI (ed) *Rehabilitation of Parkinson's disease*. Chapman and Hall, London, p 25–44.

Singer E (1973). Social costs of Parkinson's disease. *Journal of Chronic Disease 26*: 243–254.

Stocchi F, Barbato L, Nordera G, Berardelli A, Ruggieri S (1998). Sleep disorders in Parkinson's disease. *Journal of Neurology 245*: S15–S18.

Tandberg E, Larsen JP, Aarsland D, Cummings JL (1996). The occurrence of depression in Parkinson's disease. *Archives of Neurology 53*: 175–179.

Todes CJ, Lees AJ (1985). The pre-morbid personality of patients with Parkinson's disease. *Journal of Neurology, Neurosurgery and Psychiatry 48*: 97–100.

Turjanski N, Pirtosek Z, Quirk J, Anderson TJ, Rivest J, Marsden CD, Lees AJ (1996). Botulinum toxin in the treatment of writer's cramp. *Clinical Neuropharmacology 19*: 314–320.

Van den Bergh P, Francart J, Mourin S, Kollman P, Laterre EC (1995). Five-year experience in the treatment of focal movement disorders with low-dose Dysport botulinum toxin. *Muscle & Nerve 18*: 720–729.

Wade DT, Langton Hewer R (1987). Epidemiology of some neurological diseases with special reference to work load on the NHS. *International Disability Studies 8*: 129–137.

Ward CD (1991). Parkinson's disease and related conditions. In: Swash M, Oxbury J (eds) *Clinical Neurology*. Churchill Livingstone, Edinburgh, p 1396–1424.

Ward CD (1993). Pathogenesis of focal and segmental dystonias: implications for rehabilitation. *Balliere's Clinical Neurology 2*: 159–177.

Webster DD (1968). Critical analysis of the disability in Parkinson's disease. *Modern Treatment 5*: 257–282.

Wermuth L, Stenager E (1995). Sexual problems in young patients with Parkinson's disease. *Acta Neurologica Scandinavica 91*: 453–455.

Wright RA, Kaufmann HC, Perera R, Opfer-Gehrking TL, McElligott MA, Sheng KN, Low PA (1998). A double-blind dose–response study of midodrine in neurogenic orthostatic hypotension *Neurology 51*: 120–124.

39. Multiple sclerosis

M. P. Barnes

INTRODUCTION

Multiple sclerosis is the most common cause of severe physical disability in young adults. The prevalence of the disease, combined with its progressive nature and the complexity of the disability, make multiple sclerosis one of the major challenges to the neurological rehabilitation team.

There is an ever-increasing literature on the aetiology, pathogenesis, and diagnosis of multiple sclerosis. This compares with a paucity of literature on the rehabilitation of a person with multiple sclerosis. This chapter concentrates on the management of disability at the expense of any detailed discussion regarding impairment. However, it is important to make a brief mention of points related to epidemiology, pathogenesis, and diagnosis that are of particular relevance to education of people with multiple sclerosis and their families.

EPIDEMIOLOGY

The geographical variation in prevalence of the disease has been well known for many years (Limburg, 1950). There is a strong trend for prevalence to increase with increasing latitude both north and south of the equator. This trend is even noticeable in a country the size of the UK, with lower prevalence rates in the southern part of the country compared with the very high rates reported in the northern Scottish islands (up to 258 per 100,000 population). Recent studies in the south of the UK have, however, shown prevalence rates higher than previously reported, at 118 per 100,000 in Cambridgeshire, 117 per 100,000 in south-east Wales, 115 per 100,000 in South London and 111 per 100,000 in Sussex (Robertson et al., 1995; Swingler & Compston, 1988; Williams & McKaren, 1986; Rice-Oxley, Williams & Ress, 1995). This might reflect a decline in mortality as well as an improvement in case ascertainment. A typical English Health District (population 250,000) will thus contain about 300–400 individuals with multiple sclerosis and a typical general practice in the UK (practice population 2000) will have 2–3 people with multiple sclerosis on the list.

The incidence rate in the UK has generally been reported to be between two and six per 100,000 population per annum (Swingler & Compston, 1988).

A more relevant statistic in the context of this chapter is the proportion of people with multiple sclerosis who are significantly disabled by the disease. A survey in Southampton showed that approximately two-thirds of the multiple sclerosis population in that city were moderately or severely disabled with scores of five or more on the Kurtzke Expanded Disability Status Scale (University of Southampton, 1989). This study confirmed the expected increasing degree of disability with disease duration. Over 80% of people were significantly disabled after 20 years. As the mean age of onset of multiple sclerosis is around 30, it follows that the burden of disability will fall in the fourth and fifth decades of life.

NATURAL HISTORY AND PREDICTION OF PROGNOSIS

Life expectancy is shortened in multiple sclerosis but mortality rates have undoubtedly declined in recent years. Kurtzke (1970) estimated median survival time was about 35 years from onset whereas more recent work by Weinschenker et al. (1989) demonstrated that the median survival time was greater than 40 years, with 88% not having died 40 years from onset. It is more relevant to look at the patterns of disease progression and whether such progression can be predicted at an early stage.

It is generally accepted that about two-thirds of people will have a relapsing remitting course at the onset of disease, with a further 15% having a progressive course with superimposed acute episodes. The remainder will have a chronically progressive course from onset (Weinschenker et al., 1989; Matthews et al., 1985). Eventually, most will convert to a progressive course; Weinschenker et al. (1989) demonstrated that 41% had done so by 10 years, 57% by 15 years and 65% by 25 years. There is probably a population of people in the order of 10% of the total multiple sclerosis population who do not convert to progressive disease but continue to have relapsing remitting disease and thus a relatively benign course (McAlpine, 1964). The time interval between onset and start of the progressive phase seems to be a useful prognostic indicator. Those people whose multiple sclerosis becomes progressive within a relatively short period are more likely to have an aggressive form of the disease (Compston, 1987).

The median time to reach Kurtzke Disability Status Scale (DSS) levels 3, 6, and 8 from the onset of the progressive phase was 1.4 years, 4.5 years, and 24 years in Weinschenker's (1989) study. This would seem to indicate that many people progress slowly once a level approximating to Kurtzke DSS 6 is reached.

The literature is rather confusing with regard to prediction of the course of the disease from the initial symptoms. As a generalisation, cerebellar symptoms and signs carry a poor prognosis, as does a polysymptomatic onset. Monosymptomatic onset and visual and early sensory symptoms are probably good prognostic indicators. The relative absence of pyramidal or cerebellar signs 5 years after onset is also a good indication of a benign course (Kraft et al., 1981). Increasing age of onset, particularly age of onset after 40, is another poor prognostic indicator (Poser et al., 1982). More recent work by Trojano and colleagues (1995) has confirmed that an age of onset greater than 25 years and the onset event giving a disability of ≥ 3 on the Kurtzke Expanded Disability Status Scale (EDSS) are the most unfavourable clinical indicators in terms of time taken to reach the secondary progressive phase. In a total of 69 people with the relapsing/progressive disease the time to reach severe disability (Kurtzke EDSS ≥ 6) was negatively influenced by a first interval between attacks shorter than 1 year, the number of bouts with a Kurtzke EDSS > 2 in the first 2 years and involvement of the pyramidal system at onset. Midgard and colleagues (1995) further confirm that young age of onset, initial remitting clinical course, and the presence of sensory symptoms at onset were significantly associated with longer survival in a study of 251 people in Norway.

The advent of greater knowledge regarding immunoregulatory mechanisms initially led to enthusiasm that markers of future disease activity might be found. Unfortunately these hopes have not yet been entirely realised. However, the wider availability of magnetic resonance image (MRI) has led to limited ability to predict prognosis. MRI lesion load at onset does seem to correlate with the development of clinically definite multiple sclerosis and disability over the next five years (Filippi et al., 1994). However, other studies have not shown a particularly good correlation of MRI changes with progression of disability. In a related study, Filippi and colleagues (1995) scanned 281 people and followed them for 2–3 years and found only a weak correlation ($r = .13$) between the number of new and enlarging lesions on T_2 weighted scans and an increase in disability. In the interferon-β-1b trial (IFNB Multiple Sclerosis Study Group, 1995) the correlation between disability and changes in T_2 lesion area over 4 years was a little higher but still did not achieve a useful level of significance. However, more advanced MRI techniques are beginning to be more helpful. Van Waldervein and colleagues (1995) followed a group of 19 people with multiple sclerosis for 2 years and did find a strong correlation between changes in disability and in hypointense lesion load on T_1 weighted images. It is hoped that further advances in MRI techniques will lead to more accurate prediction of prognosis over the next few years (Filippi & Miller, 1996).

DIAGNOSIS

The diagnosis of multiple sclerosis still rests largely on the traditional clinical skills of history and examination in an attempt to identify clinical lesions in the central nervous system at two or more different anatomical sites that have occurred on at least two separate occasions. The combination of clinical history and examination, cerebrospinal fluid examination with evidence of oligoclonal banding and increased immunoglobulin G (IgG) production, evoked potential examination, and neuroimaging (particularly MRI), now make earlier and more accurate diagnosis possible.

When should the individual be told of the diagnosis? In the past it has been common, at least in neurological practice in the UK, to impart the diagnosis of multiple sclerosis only at the time when the diagnosis is definite. In my opinion this approach is usually mistaken. The Southampton survey amply illustrated the problems associated with conveying the diagnosis (University of Southampton, 1989). Many individuals learnt their diagnosis inappropriately, 10% by accident. Many expressed feelings of relief when told of the diagnosis as this often expelled other concerns about psychosomatic illness or alternative conditions, such as cancer. The majority (59%) felt that they were not given sufficient information at the time of the diagnosis. It would seem that most people wish to know the diagnosis at an early stage, wish their family to be informed at the same time, and wish to be given adequate background information on the disease and a chance to ask their own questions. Diagnosis should be given in an unhurried atmosphere and it is particularly important to allow the person and family to return for a second consultation relatively quickly so that further questions can be answered. The importance of literature from support groups, such as the Multiple Sclerosis (Research) Charitable Trust and the Multiple Sclerosis Society, should be emphasised. Support groups can often act in a supporting and counselling role at such a time of stress and anxiety. It is often useful to refer people to literature that is written by those who have had multiple sclerosis (e.g. Forsythe, 1988).

GENETICS

It is now generally accepted that the percentage of cases in whose family there is at least one other member affected is about 10%. The increase in risk over that of the general population is difficult to interpret from the variety of studies on the subject but in general the risk to close family members of developing multiple sclerosis if one member of the family is already affected is in the order of 1%. In the UK this would equate to approximately a tenfold increase over that of the general population. The risk is slightly higher in parents and siblings and slightly less for sons and daughters. This increased risk extends to second and third degree relatives, but at diminishing levels.

The exception to these general guidelines is monozygotic twins, in whom the risk is considerably increased. An identical twin of someone with multiple sclerosis has about a 20–30% chance of developing the disease, whereas dizygotic twins have a risk in the order of 3–4% (Sadovnick et al., 1993; Mumford et al., 1994).

It has been known for many years that about 55% of people with multiple sclerosis are positive for the human leucocyte antigen (HLA) marker DR2. However, this is not particularly helpful in predicting genetic risks as the prevalence of this marker in the general population is in the order of 20%. More modern research has so far failed to find any definite association and linkage of a number of candidate genes in families in multiple sclerosis populations. Most such studies have shown negative or ambiguous results (Ebers, 1996).

Overall, there almost certainly is a genetic influence in multiple sclerosis, but the precise nature of that influence remains obscure and so far there is no genetic marker that can aid diagnosis or prognosis or family risk. An elegant study by Ebers et al. (1995) confirmed the view that familial aggregation is determined by genetic factors whilst environmental effects act at the level of populations.

PRECIPITATING AND AGGRAVATING FACTORS

Pregnancy

There is general agreement that the 9 months of pregnancy are a fairly safe time with regard to multiple sclerosis in terms of relapse. Several studies have shown a significant decrease in relapse rate particularly during the third trimester (Poser & Poser, 1983; Korn-Lubetzki et al., 1984). It would seem that there is a slightly increased relapse risk during the 3–6 months post partum (Korn-Lubetzki et al., 1984; Birk et al., 1990). However, not all studies agree with this and a recent work by Frith and McLeod (1988) showed no increased risk of relapse either during pregnancy or for at least 6 months post partum. A further encouraging study by Thompson et al. (1986) also demonstrated that long-term disability in women was no different whether they had no pregnancies, one pregnancy, or two or more pregnancies. Women who had initial symptom onset in pregnancy were found to have less subsequent disability than women whose symptoms began before or after pregnancy. They concluded that pregnancy per se, or the number of pregnancies, had no effect on subsequent disability. In 1993, Roullat et al. published the first prospective multiple sclerosis pregnancy study and confirmed an increase in relapse rate in the first 3 months of the puerperium and found in addition that post-partum relapses were more severe than those during pregnancy. The authors did not find that pregnancy led to increased disability.

There is also no evidence that oral contraceptives have a negative influence on the course of the disease (Poser et al., 1979), nor is there evidence that hormone replacement therapy in older women can have any adverse affect.

Stress and life events

Speculation that stressful life events can influence the onset and later course of multiple sclerosis has been discussed from the earliest days (Moxon, 1875). There are a number of anecdotal reports of an obvious temporal relationship between emotional shock and onset of disease (Adams et al., 1950) but larger scale studies are few and far between. A recent study by Grant et al. (1989) on 39 people with early multiple sclerosis and 40 matched non-patient volunteers found an excess of life adversity in the year prior to onset of symptoms in the people with multiple sclerosis. The excess stress was most evident in the 6 months before onset. Further work by Franklin et al. (1988) compared 20 relapsing people with multiple sclerosis to 35 non-relapsing people. They found that the people who experienced relapses did not differ from controls with regard to the number of stressful life events but those who had experienced "extreme" life events were 3.7 times more likely to develop a relapse than those not exposed to such events. They concluded that it was the quality rather than the quantity of stressful life events that appeared to be the important determinant of relapse in multiple sclerosis.

The reader is referred to an excellent review of the role of stress in multiple sclerosis by Warren (1990).

Infection, immunisation and temperature

There is only limited evidence that a systemic infection can precipitate the onset of multiple sclerosis but there is rather stronger evidence to suggest that infection can precede a relapse. Rapp and colleagues (1995) demonstrated that almost 50% of people with multiple sclerosis could have had an exacerbation of the disease in response to an infectious process. It seems quite possible that such findings could be explained by the increase of temperature commonly associated with such infections. It is well known that an increase of body temperature, such as the effects of a hot bath or exertion, can be associated with a temporary worsening of symptoms and occasionally with definite relapse (Uhthoff, 1889; Hopper et al., 1972). The effect of immunisation would appear to be very limited in multiple sclerosis and other than a few anecdotal reports to the contrary it would seem that vaccination is not detrimental to the course of the disease.

Trauma, including surgery

Once again, there are many anecdotal reports of significant trauma, including surgical operations, apparently precipitating both the onset of multiple sclerosis and the onset of a relapse of established disease. Controlled studies are fraught with difficulties and there are studies that both refute (Bamford et al., 1981) and confirm such an association (McAlpine & Compston, 1952). The association with trauma and surgery often poses difficult legal questions to which there are no definite answers. In general, the nearer the stressful event to the suspected outcome then the more convincing is the case for a causal relationship. Sibley et al. (1991) failed to show any significant correlation between trauma and disease activity. Indeed, they found a statistically significant negative correlation between traumatic episodes and exacerbations in 95 people due to less activity of the disease during a 3-month period following surgical procedures and fractures. Head injury was the only exception to this rule; it had a significant positive associated with exacerbation. Finally, they found no linkage between the frequency of trauma and progression of disability despite the fact that people with multiple sclerosis had two to three times more trauma than a control group.

The positive factors that need to be taken into account when considering a relationship between trauma and onset or exacerbation of multiple sclerosis are now generally agreed to be:

- close temporal relationship between the trauma and onset or exacerbation (certainly within 3 months)
- trauma actually involving the central nervous system
- close anatomical relationship between the presumed site of the multiple sclerosis, lesion, and the presumed anatomical site of the trauma.

It is now generally recommended that each case, from a legal point of view, is decided on its own merit as scientific "proof" from even very large-scale prospective studies would be extremely difficult, if not impossible, to obtain.

RATING SCALES

The essence of rehabilitation is multidisciplinary goal setting by the rehabilitation team. The setting of goals implies there must be some adequate measures of progress and in rehabilitation such progress is most appropriately measured in terms of disability (activity) and handicap (participation) rather than impairment. There is no need to employ a scale specifically designed for multiple sclerosis, and more general disability and handicap scales, as outlined in Chapter 5 are entirely acceptable. However, multiple sclerosis is one of the few specific diseases for which standardised scales have been developed. Most of the work on this subject has been carried out by Kurtzke, who published his first Disability Status Scale in 1955. This scale has been largely superseded by two further Kurtzke scales, the Incapacity Status Scale and the Expanded Disability Status Scale (Kurtzke, 1981, 1983).

In 1984, the International Federation of Multiple Sclerosis Societies published suggestions for a Minimal Record of Disability for Multiple Sclerosis, which included use of the Kurtzke Expanded Disability Status Scale as a measure of impairment, the Kurtzke Incapacity Status Scale as a measure of disability, and an Environmental Status Scale, which had been devised by Mellerup et al. in 1981 as a broad measure of handicap. These three scales, taken together, provide a wide-ranging categorisation of dysfunction on the WHO system. However, these scales have been criticised (Willoughby & Paty, 1988) on a number of grounds. First, the Disability Status Scale does not simply measure impairment but also, to some extent, disability and handicap. The Disability Status Scale also relies on a grading system

over eight functional systems (pyramidal, cerebellar, brainstem, sensory, bowel and bladder, visual and optic, mental or cerebral, and other), which in turn lack precision in definition and are open to differences in interpretation and scoring (Amato et al., 1988). There have been a number of suggestions for new scale systems and some have appeared over recent years (e.g. Illness Severity Score (Mickey et al., 1984); Neurological Rating Scale (Sipe et al., 1984)) but none have stood the test of time and, despite their drawbacks, the Kurtzke scales are still the most widely used in the international literature. Marolf and colleagues (1996) made a comparative study of the Functional Independence Measure (FIM), the Extended Barthel Index, and the Expanded Disability Status Scale (EDSS) and showed a very high correlation between the Extended Barthel Index and FIM; both scales correlated less well with the EDSS. The authors recommended the use of the Extended Barthel Index because it has a simpler rating scale than the FIM, but Granger et al. (1990) have demonstrated that the FIM is slightly superior to other scales in prediction of the physical care needs of people with multiple sclerosis. Most scales do suffer from ceiling effects and also from concentrating on disability (activity) rather than handicap (participation). The performance of more recently developed scales, for example the Newcastle Independence Assessment Form – Research (Semlyen et al., 1996), should be usefully evaluated in multiple sclerosis.

The Kurtzke Expanded Disability Status Scale is reproduced in Tables 39.1 and 39.2.

SYMPTOMS AND SIGNS

The purpose of the present chapter is to concentrate on the management of disability and handicap in multiple sclerosis. It is thus inappropriate to occupy too much space with details of impairment. However, a brief overview of the more common symptoms and signs is important, if only to emphasise the complexity of the disability management.

McAlpine (1972) reviewed published reports and found the following incidence of initial symptomatology:

- Weakness in one or more limbs—40%
- Optic neuritis—22%
- Paraesthesiae—21%
- Diplopia—12%
- Vertigo—5%
- Disturbance of micturition—5%
- Other—5%

About 55% of people presented with more than one symptom at the onset. Kurtzke et al. (1968), however, reported the involvement of a single major system at presentation in 13.7% of people, the remainder presenting with symptoms in at least one other major system.

It is characteristic that the combination of symptoms and signs becomes more complex as the disease progresses. In a series by Shepherd (1979) in people with a mean disease duration of 14.4 years there were signs of pyramidal disease in

Table 39.1. Kurtzke Expanded Disability Status Scale (Kurtzke, 1981)

0	Normal neurological exam (all grade 0 in functional systems (FS); cerebral grade 1 acceptable)
1.0	No disability, minimal signs in one FS (i.e. grade 1 excluding cerebral grade 1)
1.5	No disability, minimal signs in more than one FS (more than one grade 1 excluding cerebral grade 1)
2.0	Minimal disability in one FS (one FS grade 2, others 0 or 1)
2.5	Minimal disability in two FS (two FS grade 2, others 0 or 1)
3.0	Moderate disability in one FS (one FS grade 3, others 0 or 1), or mild disability in three or four FS (3/4 FS grade 2, others 0 or 1), although fully ambulatory
3.5	Fully ambulatory but with moderate disability in one FS (one grade 3) or one or two FS grade 2; or two FS grade 3; or five FS grade 2 (others 0 or 1)
4.0	Fully ambulatory without aid, self-sufficient, up and about some 12 hours a day despite relatively severe disability consisting of one FS grade 4 (others 0 or 1), or combinations of lesser grades exceeding limits or previous steps. Able to walk without aid or rest some 500 metres
4.5	Fully ambulatory without aid, up and about much of the day, able to work a full day, might otherwise have some limitation of full activity or require minimal assistance; characterised by relatively severe disability, usually consisting of one FS grade 4 (others 0 or 1) or combinations of lesser grades exceeding limits of previous steps. Able to walk without aid or rest some 300 metres
5.0	Ambulatory without aid or rest for about 200 metres; disability severe enough to impair full daily activities (e.g. to work full day without special provisions). (Usual FS equivalents are one grade 5 alone, others 0 or 1; or combination of lesser grades usually exceeding specifications for step 4.0.)
5.5	Ambulatory without aid or rest for about 100 metres; disability severe enough to preclude full day activities. (Usual FS equivalents are one grade 5 alone, others 0 or 1; or combinations of lesser grades usually exceeding those for step 4.0.)
6.0	Intermittent or unilateral constant assistance (cane, crutch, or brace) required to walk about 100 metres with or without resting. (Usual FS equivalents are combinations with more than two FS grade 3+.)
6.5	Constant bilateral assistance (canes, crutches or braces) required to walk about 20 metres without resting. (Usual FS equivalents are combinations with more than two FS grade 3+.)
7.0	Unable to walk beyond 5 metres even with aid, essentially restricted to wheelchair, wheels self in standard wheelchair and transfers alone; up and about in a wheelchair some 12 hours a day. (Usual FS equivalents are combinations with more than one FS grade 4+; very rarely, pyramidal grade 5 alone.)
7.5	Unable to take more than a few steps; restricted to wheelchair; may need aid in transfer; wheels self but cannot carry on in standard wheelchair for a full day; may require motorised wheelchair. (Usual FS equivalents are combinations with more than one FS grade 4+.)
8.0	Essentially restricted to bed or chair or perambulated in wheelchair, but may be out of bed itself much of the day; retains many self-care functions; generally has effective use of arms. (Usual FS equivalents are combinations, generally grade 4+ in several systems.)
8.5	Essentially restricted to bed much of the day; has some effective use of arm(s); retains some self-care functions. (Usual FS equivalents are combinations, generally 4+ in several systems.)
9.0	Helpless bed patient; can communicate and eat. (Usual FS equivalents are combinations, mostly grade 4+.)
9.5	Totally helpless bed patient; unable to communicate effectively or eat/swallow. (Usual FS equivalents are combinations, almost all grade 4+.)
10	Death due to multiple sclerosis

This scale should be scored in conjunction with Functional Systems scoring (Table 39.2).
FS, functional systems.

83.7%, sensory signs in 80.6%, cerebellar signs in 67%, brainstem involvement in 65%, sphincter involvement in 56.4%, and "mental" changes in 30.5%. More recently, Kraft et al. (1986) have reported the symptoms of 656 people with multiple sclerosis. They provide a useful subdivision into symptoms that are causing a disability and those that are causing no difficulty. The figures are reproduced in Table 39.3.

It is worth noting that epilepsy (about 2%; Matthews, 1962), deafness (Dix, 1965), dysphasia (Kahana et al., 1971), and respiratory failure (Yamamoto et al., 1989) are all uncommon features. Overt psychiatric symptoms such as psychosis and schizophrenia are also unusual features (Skegg et al., 1988) but are important to recognise as potential manifestations of multiple sclerosis. The list of symptoms and signs that have been associated with multiple sclerosis is protean and there are virtually no neurological features that should be regarded as incompatible with the diagnosis of multiple sclerosis.

THE MANAGEMENT OF MULTIPLE SCLEROSIS

Treatment to alter disease progression

Immunosuppression is the mainstay of treatment. This is based on the assumption that multiple sclerosis is an autoimmune disease in some way related to an environmental trigger (Giovannoni & Hartung, 1996). Immunosuppressive mechanisms would seem to play a role in modulating the disease and, until quite recently, treatment has been based on the empirical

success of steroids combined with the rather non-specific theory that immunosuppressive therapy would be helpful in a disease that exhibits inappropriate activation of the immune system. More rational therapy based on our increasing knowledge of immunoregulatory mechanisms is now beginning to be possible.

There follows a brief survey of treatments that are undergoing or have recently undergone clinical trials. However, a word of caution would be appropriate. The literature on multiple sclerosis is riddled with overinflated claims of success based on poorly designed trials, uncontrolled pilot studies, and inadequate numbers of people. Many therapies have been initially accepted on inadequate evidence and conversely it is likely that some therapies have been rejected too early. It is only quite recently that we have seen the advent of large-scale, multicentre studies with good quality trial design involving adequate patient numbers. It is only by such studies that genuine therapeutic progress will be made in such a highly variable disease.

Corticosteroids. Adrenocortisteroids were the first agents to be used effectively in the treatment of multiple sclerosis. One of the earliest double-blind, placebo-controlled trials involved a study of adrenocorticotrophic hormone (ACTH) and showed an improved short-term recovery following relapse, but without long-term benefit (Rose et al., 1970). The current favoured mode of steroid administration is intravenous methylprednisolone, which has been shown to produce a quicker improvement following relapse than ACTH, but again there was no longer term benefit (Barnes et al., 1985a). Milligan et al. (1987)

Table 39.2. Kurtzke functional systems (Kurtzke, 1981)

1. Pyramidal functions
0 – Normal
1 – Abnormal signs, no disability
2 – Minimal disability
3 – Mild or moderate paraparesis, hemiparesis, severe monoparesis
4 – Marked paraparesis or hemiparesis, moderate quadriparesis or monoplegia
5 – Paraplegia, hemiplegia, or marked quadriparesis
6 – Quadriplegia
V – Unknown

2. Cerebellar functions
0 – Normal
1 – Abnormal signs, no disability
2 – Mild ataxia
3 – Moderate truncal or limb ataxia
4 – Severe ataxia of all limbs
5 – No coordinated movements due to ataxia
V – Unknown
X – Is used throughout after each number if weakness (grade 3 or more on pyramidal) interferes with testing

3. Brainstem functions
0 – Normal
1 – Signs only
2 – Moderate nystagmus or other mild disability
3 – Severe nystagmus, marked weak EOM, moderate disability of other cranial nerves
4 – Marked dysarthria or other marked disability
5 – Inability to swallow or speak
V – Unknown

4. Sensory functions
0 – Normal
1 – Vibration or figure writing decreased in one or two limbs
2 – Position sense decreased in one or two limbs or vibration decreased in three or four
3 – Absent vibration sense or severe decrease in position sense or discrimination in one or two limbs or mild decrease of touch or pain
4 – Severe impairment of proprioception in three or four limbs or moderate decrease of touch or pain in at least one limb
5 – Loss of all modalities of sensation in one limb or decrease touch or pain over most of the body
6 – Loss of sensation below the head
V – Unknown

5. Bowel and bladder functions
0 – Normal
1 – Mild hesitation, urgency, or retention
2 – Moderate hesitation, urgency, or rare urinary incontinence
3 – Frequent incontinence
4 – In need of intermittent or indwelling catheterisation
5 – Loss of bowel and bladder function
V – Unknown

6. Visual or optic functions
0 – Normal
1 – Scotoma, visual acuity (corrected) better than 20/30
2 – Worse eye with scotoma, maximum visual acuity (corrected) of 20/30 to 20/59
3 – Worse eye with large scotoma or moderate defect in field but with maximum visual acuity (corrected) of 20/60 to 20/99
4 – Worse with marked defect of field and maximum visual acuity (corrected) of 20/100; grade 3 plus maximum acuity of better eye of 20/60 or less
5 – Worse eye with maximum visual acuity (corrected) less than 20/200; grade 4 plus maximum acuity of better eye of 20/60 or less
6 – Grade 5 plus maximum visual acuity of better eye of 20/60 or less
V – Unknown
X – Is added to grades 0–6 for presence of temporal pallor

7. Mental or cerebral functions
0 – Normal
1 – Mood alteration only—euphoria
2 – Mild decrease in mentation or judgement
3 – Moderate decrease in mentation, cannot abstract, recent memory loss
4 – Marked decrease in mentation
5 – Dementia, severe or incompetent
V – Unknown

EOM, extra-ocular movement

Table 39.3. Symptoms in 656 people with multiple sclerosis (from Kraft et al., 1986)

Symptom present	No ADL difficulty (%)	With ADL difficulty (%)	Total (%)
Fatigue	21	56	77
Balance problems	24	50	74
Weakness or paralysis	18	45	63
Numbness, tingling, or other sensory disturbance	39	24	63
Bladder problems	25	34	59
Increased muscle tension (spasticity)	23	26	49
Bowel problems	19	20	39
Difficulty remembering	21	16	37
Depression	18	18	36
Pain	15	21	36
Laugh or cry easily (emotional lability)	24	8	32
Double or blurred vision, partial or complete blindness	14	16	30
Shaking (tremor)	14	13	27
Speech and/or communication difficulties	12	11	23
Difficulty solving problems	12	9	21

ADL, activities of daily living.

have confirmed significant benefit with intravenous high dose methylprednisolone (500 mg) compared with placebo in acute relapse and also showed benefit in chronic progressive disease, largely secondary to improvement in pyramidal function and a positive effect on spasticity. Intravenous methylprednisolone would seem to shorten hospital admission and it is entirely possible to administer it on an out-patient basis. It is relatively free from serious side-effects, although some care would be wise in people with pre-existing history of psychosis or epilepsy. This work has recently been confirmed by Cazzato and colleagues (1995). Although intravenous methylprednisolone is a more common form of administration, it is interesting to note that Alam and colleagues (1993) found no difference between oral and intravenous administration of methylprednisolone. Precise dosages vary between 500 and 1000 mg of intravenous methylprednisolone given each day for about 5 days with or without a brief tailing-down course of oral steroids. A roughly equivalent oral course would also be 500 mg of methylprednisolone daily for 5 days.

There is no evidence that long-term treatment of multiple sclerosis with regular oral doses of corticosteroids has any positive effect, although most neurologists probably have one or two clients who seem to be steroid dependent with genuine functional decline on reducing steroid dosage.

Azathioprine.   There have been a large number of clinical trials using azathioprine, some of which have tentatively shown non-significant trends in favour of the drug (Mertin et al., 1982; Patzold et al., 1982). However, the results of a large study involving 354 people in the UK and the Netherlands showed a non-significant benefit in the azathioprine group and the authors could not generally recommend azathioprine as an immunosuppressive agent. A further major concern is the finding of a modest increase in the frequency of carcinoma in people who use aza-thioprine in the long term (British & Dutch Multiple Sclerosis Azathioprine Trial Group, 1988).

Cyclophosphamide.   There is now an accumulating body of evidence that suggests that cyclophosphamide is beneficial in multiple sclerosis and is an efficacious drug in the progressive phase of the disease (Carter et al., 1988). There is little consensus on a suitable regimen but a number of studies use a short induction period followed by maintenance intravenous boluses. As would be expected, a single initial treatment would seem to be capable of stabilising or improving disease for a short period of time but reprogression occurs at a later stage (at a mean time of 17 months in a recent study by Carter et al., 1988). Killian et al. (1988) have further shown that cyclophosphamide is useful in influencing the frequency and duration of relapses in multiple sclerosis using a monthly intravenous regimen for one year. The problems of long term toxicity have yet to be fully defined.

Glatiramer acetate (Copaxone).   This compound, formerly known as copolymer 1, is a mixture of synthetic basic polypeptides and is known to suppress experimental autoimmune encephalitis in a number of animal species (Teitelbaum et al., 1997). It is a compound that is now available for human use and is given by daily subcutaneous injection. Results of a phase III study in relapsing remitting disease have now been reported (Johnson et al., 1995; Wlinsky, 1995). The study demonstrated that the relapse rate of 125 treated people was reduced to 1.19 over 2 years, compared with 1.68 in a similar placebo group—a 29% (and significant) reduction. There was also a marginal reduction in the increase of the Kurtzke EDSS from baseline in the treated group compared to the placebo group. A more detailed analysis of the disability failed to show significant differences. However, in fairness, the Kurtzke scale is inadequate for demonstrating progression of disability and should be supplemented by more refined disability scales. Glatiramer acetate was well tolerated, with the main complication being pain at the injection site and systemic reactions soon after injection (chest pain, palpitations, and dyspnoea) occurring in about 15% of recipients. An open-label extension to the study continues and, at 6 years follow-up, 61% of the original 125 people randomised to treatment remain relapse-free and 70% of people on treatment for more than 5 years remain EDSS stable (Johnson et al., 2000). Further studies are required but the compound, which was licensed for relapsing remitting disease in the US in 1996 and awaits deliberations in the UK by the National Institute for Clinical Excellence (NICE), appears likely to be useful in the management of multiple sclerosis.

Methotrexate.   Methotrexate has been used for many years in the treatment of psoriasis and rheumatoid arthritis. An 18-month double-blind treatment with low dose oral methotrexate by Currier and colleagues (1993) showed it to be well tolerated and there was a suggestion of effectiveness in relapsing remitting multiple sclerosis, but not in relapsing progressive and chronic progressive forms. Efficacy was confirmed in a study by Goodkin and others (1995), who conducted a double-blind, placebo-controlled trial of low dose (7.5 mg) weekly oral methotrexate in 60 people with clinically definite progressive

multiple sclerosis. There was significantly less progression of impairment as measured by tests of arm function in the methotrexate treatment group without significant side-effect problems. Further studies are awaited.

Cyclosporin.   Cyclosporin acts primarily to prevent production of interleukin-2, which is necessary for T cell proliferation. A German multicentre study compared cyclosporin with azathioprine in long-term treatment and showed little difference between the two groups. The cyclosporin group had twice as many side-effects and the researchers concluded that cyclosporin should not be used as a single agent treatment in multiple sclerosis (Kappos et al., 1988). The potential side-effects and the need to give the drug on a continuous basis make cyclosporin an unlikely candidate for long term usage (Rudge et al., 1989). Troublesome side-effects have been further confirmed in a recent study by the Multiple Sclerosis Study Group (1990), but this study did confirm a statistically significant but clinically modest delay of progression of disability in the cyclosporin treated group.

Plasmapheresis and total lymphoid irradiation.   Plasmapheresis is an effective means of removing antibodies and the relative success of such treatment in Guillain–Barré syndrome and myasthenia gravis gives plasmapheresis a reasonable theoretical case in the treatment of multiple sclerosis. However, the results are conflicting. Some authors have found that long-term plasmapheresis, in combination with other immunosuppressive drug regimens (particularly cyclophosphamide and prednisolone), has produced considerable benefit in chronic progressive multiple sclerosis (Khatri, 1988). Other authors are less enthusiastic (Tindall, 1988). Once more, no clear conclusion can be reached at the present time. A meta-analysis of clinical studies of the efficacy of plasma exchange did find a significant reduction in the proportion of people who experienced neurological decline at 12 months follow-up (Vamakas et al., 1995). However, the authors still concluded that further clinical research was needed to refine the place of plasma exchange in the overall management of multiple sclerosis.

The same conclusion can be drawn from studies on total lymphoid irradiation. After initial enthusiasm more recent work has shown modest benefit (Cook et al., 1995) or no benefit (Wiles et al., 1994). The former study indicated that adding low dose prednisolone could enhance beneficial effect following total lymphoid irradiation.

Interferons.   Interferons are a group of naturally occurring proteins that modify the immune process. Interferon γ appears to stimulate immune response, whereas interferons α and β appear to be immunosuppressants. Studies have recently been published that demonstrate a benefit for people with multiple sclerosis following the administration of both interferon-β-1b and interferon-β-1a. Both these products have now been granted approval for usage in the US and throughout most of Europe. The first trial was a randomised control trial of interferon-β-1b. The study involved 372 people with clinically confirmed relapsing remitting disease in a multicentre, double-blind, placebo-controlled study comparing the dosages 1.6 or 8 million international units (miu) of interferon-β-1b given subcutaneously every other day against placebo. At a dose of eight miu every other day interferon-β-1b reduced the frequency and severity of relapses by about one-third whereas the lower dose did not differ from placebo. At the end of the second year the exacerbation rate in the placebo group had been 1.27 attacks per patient per year, whereas in the higher dose treatment group the attack rate was 0.84 attacks per patient per year ($p = .001$). This reduction of relapse persisted into the third and fourth years, although statistically significant, was not achievable because of the reduced number of people that it involved. MRI data supported these positive clinical findings. The annual median MRI lesion area continued to increase in the placebo group, whereas in those people receiving eight miu interferon-β-1b the MRI burden showed no significant increase. However, there was only a modest correlation between MRI and clinically detected change. A relatively large number of interferon-β-1b treated people developed neutralising antibodies (38% at 3 years), which effectively stopped the clinical benefit. Thus, it is possible that at least one-third of treated people can expect to derive only a short-term benefit. These studies also failed to demonstrate benefits with regard to long-term disability progression. However, this might be partly due to the lack of adequate disability measures used in the trial. Interferon-β-1b is currently mainly used for those with active, relapsing and remitting multiple sclerosis who have had at least two disabling attacks within the previous 2 years followed by recovery, which may or may not have been complete (IFNB Multiple Sclerosis Study Group, 1993, 1995; Paty et al., 1993).

There have been broadly similar results with interferon-β-1a (Jacobs et al., 1996). This study was a randomised, double-blind, controlled trial of 301 people for up to 2 years. Interferon-β-1a is administered intramuscularly once a week at a dose of 6 miu and thus has some advantage over the alternate daily administration of interferon-β-1b. The annual relapse rate was reduced from 0.82 in the placebo group to 0.67 in interferon recipients ($p = .04$) and, for the cohort completing 2 years in the study, it was reduced from 0.9 to 0.61 ($p = .002$). A reduction of approximately one-third is similar to that reported in the interferon-β-1b studies. MRI scans also showed significant reduction in disease activity as judged by the proportion of people suffering gadolinium DTPA-enhanced lesions at 2 years compared with baseline. Interferon-β-1a was well tolerated with no serious side-effects, in contrast with interferon-β-1b, which seems to have more troublesome side-effects, including skin reactions, flu-like symptoms, leukopenia, new or worsened depression, and new or worsened headache (Neilley et al., 1996). The interferon-β-1a study also seemed to indicate a significant delay in time to sustained EDSS progression; the proportion of people progressing by the end of 104 weeks was 34.9% in the placebo group and 21.9% in the interferon-treated group. Overall, interferon-β-1a seemed to have a significant beneficial impact on relapsing multiple sclerosis by reducing accumulation of permanent physical disability, exacerbation frequency, and disease activity (Jacobs et al., 1996).

More recently, studies have been completed that have examined the use of interferon-β-1b in secondary progressive MS (European Study Group on Interferon Beta-1B, 1998). A total of 718 people were involved in this study, 360 of whom were randomised to receive 8 miu interferon-β-1b and 358 randomised to receive placebo. The groups were well matched in terms of demographics and base line disease status. At the time of interim analysis all participants had completed at least 2 years in the study. Disability progression was delayed in people receiving interferon-β-1b compared to those receiving placebo. The delay in progress was significant at 12 months and still sustained at the end of the trial at approximately 33 months. After 12 months on the study progression was delayed by 9–12 months. Other secondary endpoints confirmed the delay in the time taken to become confined to a wheelchair and indeed reduction in the number of people requiring wheelchair use. Overall this was a positive and useful effect, and has now resulted in a licence for this indication. However, the more widespread introduction of interferon therapy in the UK is now awaiting the review by NICE. The recommendations of this group are expected to be published in 2002.

These positive results have major impact for overall disease management. The treatment has been enthusiastically accepted by some people with multiple sclerosis and by some neurologists, whereas in others the results of the studies are treated with much more caution. Both treatments are expensive, with a minimum cost of around £10,000 per annum. Thus, urgent studies are required on the health economics of these treatments and, until further studies regarding disability progression and cost-effectiveness are published then some influential bodies are not yet recommending the widespread use of either compound (Association of British Neurologists, 1994; Anonymous, 1996; Richards, 1996). There has been much debate on the politics of prescribing such an expensive compound and unfortunately this has meant that there is as yet no accepted protocol, and whether an individual receives the drug often depends on the vagaries of geographical location and the opinion of the treating neurologist (Walley & Barton, 1995; Rouse et al., 1996). Further and more definitive studies are awaited with interest.

Other disease-modifying treatments

The above resumé covers most of the current treatment regimens that are still under investigation. Multiple sclerosis research is littered with a variety of other treatments that have fallen by the wayside (Sibley, 1988). However, some other therapies are worthy of brief mention.

Hyperbaric oxygen. The use of hyperbaric oxygen dates back to 1970 but it was not until the late 1970s and early 1980s that dramatic claims of improvements began to emerge in the literature (Neubauder, 1980; Pallotta, 1982). The rationale of hyperbaric oxygen is probably secondary to an immunosuppressive effect, although other theories of mechanism of action have been proposed (James, 1982). Double-blind, placebo-controlled studies have generally failed to support the initial enthusiasm (Barnes et al., 1985b, 1987), although there have been modest improvements in bladder function and suggestions of retardation of disease progression. However, in general the therapy is time-consuming and extremely tiring for clients, and does not seem to confer great advantages over some of the other immunosuppressive therapies outlined above. Under careful supervision there are few side-effects but the treatment could not be recommended for general use. A review of control trials (Kleijnen & Knipschild, 1995) also concluded that hyperbaric oxygen could not be recommended for the treatment of multiple sclerosis.

Diet. Swank first proposed a link between dietary fat intake and multiple sclerosis in 1950. Deficiencies in the level of linoleic acid in people with multiple sclerosis have since been confirmed (Belin et al., 1971; Tswang et al., 1976). The rationale behind dietary manipulation was thus to add linoleic acid to the diet. A re-examination of data from three double-blind trials by Dworkin et al. (1984) showed some reduction in severity and duration of relapse at all levels of disability and treated people (particularly those with minimal or no disability at entry) seemed to have a slower disease progression than did the controls. A further study of dietary manipulation has been published (Bates et al., 1989). The study involved a total of 312 people treated for 2 years. One group was given dietary advice regarding intake of *n*-6 polyunsaturated fatty acids (linoleic acid), whereas the other group had the same dietary advice but their diet was further supplemented by *n*-3 fatty acids, mainly eicosapentaenoic and docosahexaenoic acids. The group supplemented with *n*-3 polyunsaturated fatty acids showed a non-significant trend towards shorter duration, reduced frequency, and severity of relapses. A trend was also revealed in those with mild multiple sclerosis at entry, who appeared to deteriorate less than the control group. In summary, dietary supplementation with polyunsaturated fatty acids in the form of vegetable oils further supplemented by polyunsaturated fatty acids of the *n*-3 group found in fish oils seems to have modest effects in disease progression and reduction of relapse rates.

Swank and Dugan (1990) have published the results of a 34-year follow-up study in 144 people. They found that those people who had adhered to a prescribed diet of less than 20 g of fat per day showed significantly less deterioration and much lower death rates than did those who consumed more fat than the prescribed level. Such diets have found favour in some people with multiple sclerosis and as this form of treatment is without significant side-effects and such a diet can provide other benefits too, for example, to the cardiovascular system, it is recommended by this author. In addition, people report that they feel they are actually doing something themselves to ameliorate the disease. In these circumstances the lack of statistically significant effect is probably less important than the psychological boost.

A variety of other diets have been suggested over the years for multiple sclerosis but none has been shown to be efficacious in double-blind controlled studies. No other dietary manipulation could be recommended at the present time.

Intravenous immunoglobulin. After some promising open-label experience with intravenous immunoglobulin (ivIg), larger-scale studies have now been carried out. Achiron and colleagues (1994) demonstrated that ivIg significantly reduced the number and severity of acute relapses and resulted in less neurological disability over a 3-year follow-up period. However, this is very preliminary work, and larger-scale double-blind, placebo-controlled studies will be required before any conclusion can be drawn regarding a place for intravenous immunoglobulin in the overall management of multiple sclerosis.

Monoclonal antibodies. So far, early results with monoclonal antibodies have not been particularly promising. Studies are ongoing with the use of humanised monoclonal antibody CAMPATH-1H (anti-CDw 52). Tentative evidence has indicated that lymphocyte depletion did reduce disease activity (Moreau et al., 1994). Another study of chimeric anti-CD 4 monoclonal antibodies involving 72 people showed no reduction in new lesions on MRI scanning, despite a marked and prolonged reduction in CD4-positive cells (Miller et al., 1995). Further work is clearly needed.

Mitoxantrone. Mitoxantrone is an anthracenedione antineoplastic agent that exerts a potent immunomodulating effect suppressing humoral immunity, reducing T cell numbers and enhancing suppresser function. Initial work has indicated favourable benefit (using 20 mg intravenously monthly) in combination with methylprednisolone (1 g iv monthly). This was effective in improving both clinical and MRI indices of disease activity over a 6-month period (Eadon et al., 1997). Once again, further double-blinded and long-term studies are required, particularly in relation to the progression of disability.

Cladribine. Cladribine has immunosuppressive effects and early work has also shown a stabilisation of the disease process in comparison to a placebo group in a 2-year placebo-controlled, double-blind, cross-over study (Beutler et al., 1996). Similar results have been produced previously by Sipe and colleagues (1994).

Linomide. Linomide is a synthetic immunomodulator (a quinoline-3-carboxamide), which has been shown to have an inhibitory influence in experimental autoimmune diseases. Results from a few small-scale studies have shown linomide to be well tolerated and suggest that it probably inhibits progression of the disease process, as well as reducing the appearance of new active lesions on MRI scans (Karussis et al., 1996). Larger-scale studies are now underway.

Ginkgolide B. Ginkgolide is a potent inhibitory platelet activating factor. A recent open-label pilot study showed a trend in favour of a group treated with ginkgolide towards an improvement in various mobility scores, but overall there was no clinical benefits seen for the treatment of acute exacerbations (Brochet et al., 1995).

Aminopyridines. Aminopyridines are potassium channel blockers that have been shown to improve nerve conduction in experimentally demyelinated nerves. Two such agents, 4-aminopyridine and 3-4-diaminopyridine, have been tested in people with multiple sclerosis. An improvement of function was found in a large randomised, double-blind, placebo-controlled, cross-over trial of 3 months of oral treatment in 68 people with multiple sclerosis with 4-aminopyridine. Similar benefits were shown in an open study of 3-4-diaminopyridine. It is possible that the aminopyridines could provide a new approach to the symptomatic treatment of multiple sclerosis (Bever, 1994; Bever et al., 1994).

FUTURE PROSPECTS

A major future area of research are therapies directed at the cytokine and adhesion molecule systems. The latter includes selectins, which are involved in the initial slowing and rolling of lymphocytes along the endothelium, and of integrins, which provide the main adhesive force between T cells and endothelium prior to transmigration in the central nervous system. For example, pentoxiphylline suppresses the production of tumour necrosis factor α, which is thought to be involved in the multiple sclerosis immune process. Other workers are developing antibodies against adhesion molecules. Exciting progress in this area is likely in the next few years (Thompson & Noseworthy, 1996).

MANAGEMENT OF MAJOR SYMPTOMS

The challenge for rehabilitation in multiple sclerosis is to unravel the complex interaction that lies behind a disability that often involves several different neuronal systems. There can be few other disorders that require so much active interdisciplinary cooperation from all members of the rehabilitation team.

Virtually no studies have looked at the best format for the clinical management of people with multiple sclerosis. However, there are studies that indicate a high level of dissatisfaction regarding a standard medical model of out-patient and in-patient management (University of Southampton, 1989). As the clinical management for people with multiple sclerosis rests so heavily on interdisciplinary cooperation, then there seems sense behind the creation of specific multiple sclerosis multidisciplinary clinics. These would facilitate interdisciplinary cooperation and provide an accessible range of professionals to offer advice and assistance to the person with multiple sclerosis and their family.

The needs of multiple sclerosis clients and their families would seem to focus on:

- *Time*—to discuss diagnosis, potential treatments, and more personal cognitive and emotional difficulties. The latter should include ready access to counselling facilities.
- *Information*—at the time of diagnosis and in the longer term to keep up to date with regard to research and potential treatments.
- *Practical help*—in terms of the provision of aids and equipment as well as access to personal help within the home (e.g. district nurses, care attendants, etc.).

- *Carer's needs*—an equal need for access to information, counselling, and support, as well as access to respite facilities.

These needs are most readily provided within the setting of a multidisciplinary clinic and it could have access not only to a range of health professionals but to information, self-help literature, and support groups. Such clinics should probably review multiple sclerosis clients on a regular basis and also allow quick access at times of crisis, either medical or social. Scheinberg et al. (1981) have described a comprehensive long-term care programme along these lines. Winters et al. (1989) have also described their experience in a multidisciplinary clinic that had a particular emphasis on the role of a nurse practitioner as clinic manager. Larocca (1990) has reviewed the importance of a comprehensive and multidisciplinary model of management in this disease.

Two randomised prospective evaluations of in-patient rehabilitation have been undertaken (Freeman et al., 1997; Solari et al., 1999). Such rehabilitation is frequently advocated but, until recently, there has been little scientific evidence to support the benefits. Freeman et al. (1997) carried out a stratified, randomised waiting-list-controlled study in progressive disease. Seventy people were selected from 112 people referred to a multidisciplinary assessment clinic. Treatment consisted of a period of goal-oriented in-patient neurorehabilitation lasting an average of 20 days. Solari et al. (1999) randomised 50 mobile patients to 3 weeks of in-patient rehabilitation or a home exercise programme after a 1-day session of instruction. In both studies, in-patient treatment resulted in significant improvements in function (FIM) and health status (SF-36), but not impairment (EDSS), which appeared to persist for up to several months (Freeman et al., 1999). These results are encouraging and will hopefully lead to replication in other centres and long-term trials. Integrated care pathways could facilitate these in-patient programmes and their audit (Rossiter & Thompson, 1995). The pathway consists of a document kept by the individual with multiple sclerosis with details of expected interventions over the in-patient stay, including the basic assessment, goal setting, review of the drug regime, and discharge planning. The whole process is client centred and multidisciplinary; it seems to facilitate communication between departments and disciplines, and with the client and his or her family.

Other units are now developing community multiple sclerosis teams. For example, Newcastle upon Tyne has developed such a team with the full-time involvement of a physiotherapist, occupational therapist, social worker, rehabilitation assistant, and administrator, and part-time input from a rehabilitation physician, psychologist, and counsellor. The role of the team is to identify everyone with multiple sclerosis in the city boundaries and offer information, advice and practical support and to act as a centre for onward referral to other health, social service, statutory, and voluntary agencies. The efficacy of this approach is being studied and the results awaited. The advent of interferon treatment has also stimulated the development of specialist multiple sclerosis nurses. Although such individuals were originally involved only in interferon treatment protocols, the role has in many cases been broadened to allow the nurse to be a key contact point between the multiple sclerosis family and the neurology service. Kirker and colleagues (1995) described the benefits from such a liaison nurse from the point of view of the family and primary care team.

Such studies need to be linked to a health economic analysis in order to determine the most cost effective method of service delivery. Health-care costs for this client group have been estimated up to $35,000 per year in the US and up to $1.2 billion per year for all patients in the UK (Bourdette et al., 1993; Holmes et al., 1995).

Mobility

Difficulty in walking is probably the most common symptom in multiple sclerosis and the frequency must approach 100% with time. Waking difficulty is often due to a combination of pyramidal weakness combined with spasticity, and with major secondary effects from fatigue, disuse, pain, ataxia, and sensory loss, particularly proprioceptive difficulties. Pyramidal weakness combined with spasticity can be extremely disabling. Other than the obvious disturbance of gait, the main consequence is the development of joint contractures, which in turn can exacerbate the spastic patterns, promote disuse, and thus cause further weakness. Prevention of contractures, although not always possible, is important and physiotherapy has an important and ongoing part to play in the management and maintenance of gait. A structured exercise programme, planned and supervised by a physiotherapist, can be of immense benefit to the individual. It is unfortunate that there are no controlled studies that confirm whether such exercise programmes can prevent or delay the onset of mobility problems or secondary complications.

Tourtellotte and Baumhefner (1983) have recommended the elements of such an exercise programme should include:

- Repetition of individual movements in order to increase strength.
- Passive stretching to reduce spasticity, improve range of movement, and prevent contractures.
- Exercises utilising activities of daily living to improve dexterity and coordination.
- Gait training using mobility aids (canes, walkers, orthoses) as necessary.
- Hydrotherapy as a further aid to increased activity and range of movement (with an additional antispastic effect).
- Use of intact vision to compensate for proprioceptive loss.

The management of spasticity (see Chapter 12) poses particular problems, and can involve a combination of some of the following approaches:

- Reduction of external stimuli (e.g. catheter repositioning, foot care, bowel management, active treatment of skin and urinary infections, etc.).
- Physiotherapy, including hydrotherapy.

- Proper attention to seating and posture, both in wheelchair and in leisure seating.
- Dynamic casting and correct use of orthoses.
- Pharmacological management.
- Peripheral nerve blocks and motor point blocks.
- Botulinum toxin injections.
- In more severe cases other techniques such as intrathecal baclofen and orthopaedic and neurosurgical procedures can be applied.

The use of mobility aids and a review of wheelchair and seating requirements as well as the use of orthoses are covered in Chapter 17. This chapter also includes a section on the essential importance of driving assessment for the continuing independence of people with mobility problems.

Two randomised studies have reported the effects of a physical therapy programme in chronic disease. Petajan and colleagues (1996) studied the effect of exercise in 54 people with multiple sclerosis. The group was randomly assigned to exercise or non-exercise groups and the exercise group underwent 15 weeks of aerobic training. The exercise group demonstrated significant increases in upper and lower extremity strength, reduced levels of depression and anger scores, less fatigue, and improvements for social interaction, emotional behaviour, home management, and involvement in recreation and pastimes on the Sickness Impact Profile. This useful study thus confirmed the benefits that can follow from a coordinated and structured exercise training programme. Wiles et al. (2001) compared the effects of either twice-weekly out-patient or domiciliary physiotherapy with no treatment, each for 8 weeks with 8-week "wash-out" periods, in 42 people with chronic multiple sclerosis, using a randomised crossover design. They found significant improvements in mobility, subjective well-being, and mood in the two treated groups, which were probably relatively short-lived, suggesting that sustained physiotherapy might be necessary to produce long-term benefit.

Upper limb function

The management of upper limb weakness and clumsiness in multiple sclerosis is again a complex problem. As with the leg, there is often a combination of pyramidal weakness combined with spasticity, and with ataxia as well as sensory disturbance. Many of the points mentioned above in the management of spasticity in the lower limb can be applied to the upper limb, and again, prevention of contractures secondary to spasticity must be a priority. The use of occupational therapy to promote function is often helpful but it is regrettable that the occupational therapy literature contains very few adequate studies demonstrating convincing evidence of the effectiveness of occupational therapy techniques. There can be little doubt, however, about the usefulness of aids to promote upper limb function both for use by the patient and to adapt the environment (Milward, 1984). There is now a remarkable range of practical devices to overcome most problems with regard to activities of daily living and in the UK, there is a network of Disabled Living Centres and

National Demonstration Centres where such equipment can be displayed and appropriate advice given (see Chapter 17).

The management of established severe spasticity or contractures in the upper limb is more difficult than in the lower limb. The limb is less accessible to peripheral nerve blocks and there is a higher risk of complication in the use of such blocks. Serial casting is a valid technique and occasionally orthopaedic procedures are necessary (see Chapter 12).

Cerebellar dysfunction

It is often the case that the main functional problem is in the arm secondary to cerebellar dysfunction. Cerebellar involvement is common in multiple sclerosis and is unfortunately difficult to treat. Various therapeutic techniques can be applied (see Chapter 13) but there is little convincing evidence of reliable improvement. Specific pharmacotherapy is also usually unrewarding but there are anecdotal reports of success from small-scale controlled studies with a variety of agents, particularly isoniazid, choline, benzodiazepines, and sodium valproate (Manyam, 1986). Adaptive equipment can be helpful and some patients report success with weighted bands on the wrists and other simpler aids such as large handled implements, plate guards and Velcro fastenings for buttoning and shoe laces, electric toothbrushes, electric page turners, etc. Troublesome titubation can be a major difficulty and the only success this author has ever had is in the use of fairly soft and shaped foam inserts around the headrests of a wheelchair.

In a few selected patients with severe intention tremor, cryothalamotomy can be helpful (Cooper, 1967). Tourtellotte and Baumhefner (1983) suggested the intriguing surgical selection procedure that if the patient can scratch his or her nose then surgery is not recommended.

Swallowing disorders

There is a surprising paucity of literature about swallowing problems in multiple sclerosis. Practical experience would indicate that it is not a common problem until later stages of the disease. However, bronchopneumonia is still the leading cause of death in multiple sclerosis and one wonders whether there is an underestimate of swallowing problems that might lead to aspiration in the final stages. Swallowing is now increasingly recognised as a highly complex motor sequence that requires expert evaluation by a speech therapist, dietician and radiographer. Videofluroscopy with a modified barium swallow is an essential prerequisite to proper evaluation of dysphagic problems. There is an increasing realisation that many of the neurological difficulties of swallowing are amenable to treatment. The reader is referred to Chapter 25 and also to the excellent review by Logemann (1981) and the discussion article by Hughes and colleagues (1994). Swallowing disorders raise ethical questions in the management of late-stage multiple sclerosis, as to how active such management should be. It is not uncommon for a person with multiple sclerosis to develop major swallowing difficulties

so that oral feeding is no longer practical or without a significant risk of aspiration. The author's experience is that if, despite dietary manipulation, there are still difficulties with oral feeding then a percutaneous endoscopic gastrostomy (PEG) should be considered sooner rather than later. This is a benign procedure and usually improves the quality of life.

Communication difficulties

Dysphasia is unusual in multiple sclerosis. The majority of communication problems arise from dysarthria (Farmakides & Boone, 1960; Darley et al., 1972). Although about one-quarter of people with multiple sclerosis are affected, a lesser proportion experience difficulty in communicating with strangers (about 4%; Benkleman et al., 1985). There is sometimes a reluctance to make speech therapy referrals in progressive disorders but such referrals can be useful in improving functional communication skills as is exemplified in the study by Farmakides and Boone (1960). Benkelman et al. (1985) estimated that less than 1% of people with multiple sclerosis required augmentative communication aids but the technological developments in this field now enable high quality communication and referral to appropriate centres should be borne in mind. In the UK there is a small network of Communication Aid Centres, which specialise in augmentative communication devices (see Chapter 17).

Continence

Urinary problems are extremely common in multiple sclerosis and are probably responsible for more handicap than any other disability. In a large series of 1528 males in the USA, Kurtzke (1970) found a 36% prevalence rate of urinary symptoms. In a smaller series of 52 people, Anderson and Bradley (1976) found bladder symptoms in 95% of subjects. Miller et al. (1965) noted bladder symptoms "at some time" in 78% of 197 people and longer term problems, with symptoms lasting over 6 months, in 52% of the series. These studies demonstrate a strong correlation between physical disability and bladder symptoms, which are less common in the early stages of the disease. Bladder symptoms occur in the first attack of multiple sclerosis only in about 5% of cases (Muller, 1949).

The most common symptom is urgency, which was reported in 71% of the people in Anderson and Bradley's 1976 series, followed by urge incontinence, which was present in about 50% of these people. Frequency is also common (38.5%; Anderson & Bradley, 1976). Symptoms associated with bladder hypoactivity (hesitancy, overflow incontinence, use of abdominal pressure when voiding, episodes of retention) are less usual but still occur in 20–30% of patients in most series (Miller et al., 1965; Anderson & Bradley, 1976; Hald & Bradley, 1982).

Urodynamic findings are in agreement that the most common cystometric abnormality is detrusor hyper-reflexia (Bradley et al., 1973; Blaivas et al., 1979; Petersen & Pedersen, 1984). Hyper-reflexia is normally associated with symptoms of frequency, urgency, and urge incontinence but there is by no means a reliable correlation between the symptoms and underlying urodynamic findings (see Chapter 21). About half the people with multiple sclerosis who have detrusor hyper-reflexia can also be shown to have detrusor sphincter dyssynergia (Anderson & Bradley, 1976). These authors found an incidence of 32.7% of detrusor areflexia, but Petersen and Pedersen (1984) found a lower incidence—at 16%. The incidence of upper urinary tract involvement in multiple sclerosis in older series is estimated to vary from 21% (Damanaski & Sutcliffe-Kerr, 1964) to 55% (Samellas & Rubin, 1965). However, more recent series have shown a lower incidence ranging from 10% (Petersen & Pedersen, 1984) to 0% (Anderson & Bradley, 1976), which probably reflects better pharmacological and/or surgical management in the early stages of the disease.

The management of continence difficulties in neurogenic bladder dysfunction is described in Chapter 21.

The advent of intermittent catheterisation has markedly improved management in many people. In an ideal world, urodynamic investigation is still necessary to determine the precise underlying pathophysiology. However, if a person with multiple sclerosis complains predominantly of frequency, urgency, and urge incontinence then the present author would initiate anticholinergic medication on an empirical basis in the first instance. The first choice is probably oxybutynin (dosage 2.5–3 mg bd, increasing to a maximum of 5 mg tds). If this is not tolerated then probanthine or imipramine can be tried. Another alternative is to administer oxybutyin intravesically. Intravesical capsaicin has also recently undergone successful studies. Night-time frequency and nocturnal enuresis can be helped by the use of a vasopressin analogue, desmopressin, which can be administered as an intranasal spray formulation at night (Eckford et al., 1994).

A determination of residual postmicturition volume is also necessary. This is preferably carried out by ultrasound, but if such a facility is not readily available then a postmicturition catheter volume is a reasonable alternative, albeit at a slight risk of inducing urinary infection. A residual volume of over 100 ml is probably an indication for catheterisation. This should preferably be performed by intermittent catheterisation either by the multiple sclerosis person or by a third party, although in many cases weakness, incoordination, adductor spasticity, or unavailability of a suitable carer still necessitates indwelling catheterisation in a number of people. The combination of anticholinergic medication and intermittent catheterisation can usually cope with most continence problems and it should now be in a minority of people that we need the more specialist techniques that are outlined in Chapter 21. Sirls and colleagues (1994) confirmed that medical management failed in only 7% of a study of 113 individuals with multiple sclerosis. They found that limited evaluation (voiding symptoms, postvoid residual, and cystometrography) was usually sufficient to formulate an effective treatment programme. Only 6.6% of their survey had hydronephrosis at presentation.

The psychological effects of urinary symptoms and incontinence should not be forgotten. In the UK there is now a reasonable network of specialist nurse continence advisors who will not only provide practical advice on aids and appliances but will often provide valuable psychological support and counselling. A modern approach to the overall management of bladder dysfunction in multiple sclerosis was recently outlined by Fowler (1994).

Bowel problems

Bowel function abnormalities in multiple sclerosis normally take the form of constipation, but more rarely can involve frequency and urgency (Glick et al., 1982). Hinds et al. (1990) confirmed constipation in 43% of an unselected out-patient population of 280 individuals. Faecal incontinence had occurred at least once in the preceding 3 months in 51% of these people and once per week or more frequently in 25% of people. The overall prevalence of bowel dysfunction in this population was 68% and this problem was common even in mildly disabled people. Chia and colleagues (1995) found that 36% of 77 consecutive people with clinically definite multiple sclerosis attending a uroneurology clinic had constipation; 20% had faecal incontinence, although another 30% had had at least one episode of faecal incontinence more than 3 months previously.

Medication should be avoided if at all possible and Levine (1985) suggests that attention should be paid to both the timing and the amount of time spent in defecation. Maximal use should be made of the gastrocolic reflex and defecation should be unhurried. Mechanical factors, including adoption of a flexed hip flexion, are important. Digital stimulation or abdominal pressure can be helpful. The diet should be high in fibre and supplemented, if needed, by bulking agents with an adequate water intake. If these measures still fail then stool softeners such as sodium docusate are helpful; only as a last resort should laxatives and enemas be applied.

Faecal incontinence (making sure this is not overflow secondary to constipation) can respond to anticholinergic agents in a similar way to bladder dysfunction. In more complicated cases, defecography is now possible to delineate the exact nature of the problem further and hopefully to initiate logical treatment (Gill et al., 1994).

Sexual function

Sexual dysfunction is common in multiple sclerosis and is probably still under-recognised by health professionals. Valleroy and Kraft (1984), in a large study on 217 people, reported that 75% of men and 56% of women had sexual difficulties. In women this centred mainly on fatigue and decreased sensation, libido, and orgasm (Hulter & Lundberg, 1995), whereas in men the main difficulty centred on achieving and maintaining erection (Kirkeby et al., 1988; Opsomer, 1996), combined with fatigue and decreased libido.

These figures are broadly in agreement with the few other studies of this subject (Lillus et al., 1976; Lundberg, 1978; Dupont, 1995). The management of sexual dysfunction should be a sensitive combination of physical and psychological intervention. Often, straightforward practical advice can be of great benefit. The timing of intercourse with regard to fatigue, optimisation of medication to reduce spasticity, correct advice on bladder management, and advice on positioning can all be helpful. It seems particularly common for problems to develop with regard to adductor spasticity. Physiotherapy and nerve block techniques can be helpful in this situation. Erectile dysfunction in the male can now normally be helped by self-injection of papaverine either alone or in combination with the α-adrenergic blocker phentolamine (Brindley, 1983; Betts et al., 1994; Matson et al., 1995). Other techniques are still needed occasionally and probably the most valuable of these are vacuum condom and venostricture devices, and occasionally the use of penile prostheses (see Chapter 22). The need for psychotherapy and psychosexual counselling should always be considered in combination with practical advice. Unfortunately, specialist psychosexual counselling for people with physical disabilities is difficult to obtain, at least in the UK. Problems are particularly common with regard to sexual attitude, sexual awareness, and self-image. The mainstay of counselling is to view sexuality in the broadest context, only a part of which is penetrative sexual intercourse.

There have been very few studies of fertility in multiple sclerosis but there is no evidence that fertility is impaired in women. It is possible that male fertility is slightly reduced by drawing comparison to such a reduction in spinal cord injured men. Electroejaculation techniques for sperm collection and artificial insemination should be borne in mind for couples who have difficulty in performing intercourse.

Pain and paroxysmal symptoms

Clifford and Trotter (1984) reviewed 317 people with multiple sclerosis and found that the incidence of clinically significant pain was 28.8%, excluding headache and paraesthesiae. Moulin et al. (1988) using a postal questionnaire on 159 people, found that 55% had either an acute or chronic problem with pain at some time during their disease; 15 people (9%) had acute pain at some stage, 7 trigeminal neuralgia, 4 l'Hermitte's phenomena, 2 paroxysmal burning pain, and 2 painful tonic seizures. All these people had an excellent response to anticonvulsant medication and the first choice would normally be carbamazepine. Archibold and colleagues (1994) found the prevalence of pain for the month preceding assessment was 53% in a sample of 85 individuals with multiple sclerosis. Disease duration and neurological symptoms of severity were significantly correlated with the number of hours of pain per week. People with pain reported poor mental health and more social handicap. Paroxysmal symptoms were well reviewed by Matthews (1975) and can include paroxysmal dysarthria, ataxia, diplopia, and itch as well as the painful paroxysms described above. In all paroxysmal attacks the response to carbamazepine is often dramatic. The management of chronic pain is more complex and will obviously depend on the underlying cause. The reader is referred to Chapter 19.

Pain is thus an increasingly recognised problem in multiple sclerosis and, if unrecognised or dismissed, can lead to major psychological difficulties. The advent of pain clinics with a combination of physical and cognitive strategies for pain management is a helpful development in the management of people with chronic pain conditions.

Visual disturbance

Optic neuritis is one of the main presenting symptoms of multiple sclerosis. The treatment of choice is corticosteroid therapy, and fortunately most recover normal vision. Occasionally, persistent monocular blindness or, more rarely, progressive bilateral visual loss occurs despite steroid therapy. More common problems are residual scotomas, diplopia, and oscillopsia. Visual rehabilitation is obviously difficult and referral to low vision clinics can sometimes be necessary. An interesting report by Traccis et al. (1990) documented successful treatment of acquired pendular nystagmus in multiple sclerosis with isoniazid and converging prisms. There is some evidence that botulinum toxin injections can be helpful for persistent oscillopsia (Lee et al., 1988).

General medical problems

The reader is referred to Chapter 15, which summarises the physical consequences of immobility. The prevention and, if necessary, management of pressure sores and the management of peripheral oedema are particularly relevant to multiple sclerosis. Lower limb immobility might be thought to give rise to a relatively high incidence of deep vein thrombosis but people with multiple sclerosis seem to have a low incidence of such complication (Kaufman et al., 1988).

Fatigue

Fatigue is probably the most common symptom in multiple sclerosis. It can have an overwhelming effect on patients' daily activities and be the predominant reason for handicap in terms of employment and leisure interests (Krupp et al., 1988). In the study by Krupp et al. the fatigue of multiple sclerosis seemed to be unrelated to either depression or degree of physical disability. However, depression should not be forgotten as a potential cause of fatigue. Studies also confirm the higher energy cost of walking in multiple sclerosis, which will probably also have a part to play in the causation of fatigue (Olgiati et al., 1988). However, most studies can find a central mechanism contributing to fatigue (Kersten & McLellan, 1996). Management depends on frequent rest periods during the day, often with more activities possible in the morning than the afternoon. A number of studies have shown the positive effect of amantidine (Murray, 1985; Cohen & Fisher, 1989). Krupp et al. (1995) confirmed that amantidine was significantly better than placebo in treating fatigue in multiple sclerosis, whereas pemoline was no better than placebo.

Ferini-Strambi and colleagues (1994) confirmed that people with multiple sclerosis had significantly reduced sleep deficiency and experienced more wakings during sleep. Periodic leg movements were found in 36% of their sample of 25 people with multiple sclerosis compared to 2 controls. Attention to sleep problems may reduce daytime fatigue.

MANAGEMENT OF PSYCHOLOGICAL DISABILITY

Cognitive dysfunction

Impairment of intellectual function in multiple sclerosis was recognised by such early authors as Charcot and l'Hermitte, and it is thus surprising that traditional teaching tends to underemphasise the importance of cognitive difficulties. There is now wide recognition that impairment of cognition is common in multiple sclerosis and makes an important contribution to disability and handicap.

Cognitive impairments are naturally more common in people with long-standing disease but several studies have now shown early cognitive deficits, even at a time when there is little physical disability (Grant et al., 1984; Van den Burg et al., 1987). Beatty et al. (1989) have confirmed that people with chronic progressive multiple sclerosis have greater impairments on cognitive testing than those with less severe relapsing remitting disease. However, in a related study they confirmed that no demographic or clinical variable (e.g. disease type, age, disease duration, and disability status) was able to predict cognitive performance with any degree of accuracy (Beatty et al., 1990).

The Southampton survey (McIntosh-Michaelis et al., 1991) demonstrated impairment of intellectual function (as measured by Folstein's Mini Mental State Examination) in 22% of their total survey of 147 people. There was a statistically significant trend for intellectual impairment to be more frequent in those with moderate or severe physical disability but they still found intellectual difficulties in 11% of those with mild physical disability. Intellectual impairment was not significantly associated with age, duration of multiple sclerosis, or the presence of depression. They found a high incidence of memory impairment, as measured by the Rivermead Behavioural Memory Test, at a rate of 34% of the whole sample compared with 12% of a control group of people with rheumatoid arthritis. Fifty per cent of those with severe physical disability had impaired memory but 19% of those with mild physical disability still had significant memory problems. Memory difficulties were significantly associated with increasing age and duration of multiple sclerosis. Although this is certainly true, it is important to remember that cognitive impairment can occur in earlier stages of multiple sclerosis. Amato and colleagues (1995) screened 50 people with multiple sclerosis with a mean duration of just over $1\frac{1}{2}$ years and significant cognitive impairments were found in a minority. It would seem that cognitive and neurological deficits do not develop in parallel and, whereas the chances of cognitive impairment obviously increase with disease duration, impairments in the early stages are entirely possible and need recognitive and appropriate referral.

Most other studies confirm these findings and a commonly described pattern is found to be problems with information processing speed, anterograde learning, and memory (Rao et al.,

1984; Litvan et al., 1988). Beatty and Goodkin (1990) suggest that the Minimental State Examination (Folstein et al., 1975) is a useful predictor of cognitive impairment, particularly in relapsing remitting people with relatively minor physical disabilities. Beatty and colleagues (1995) have suggested a readily administered brief screening battery, the Screening Examination for Cognitive Impairment (SEFCI). The performance on the SEFCI correctly identified 86% of people with impairment on any of the 11 measures from a longer neuropsychological test battery, and confirmed that the SEFCI was sensitive and easily administered and scored and might be an aid to a physician in deciding whether to refer someone with multiple sclerosis for a more complete neuropsychological assessment. Although an inadequate tool for detailed neuropsychological studies, it would appear to be a useful screening tool for the clinician. Anzola et al. (1990) and Rao et al. (1989) have both attempted to correlate neuropsychological findings with MRI with some success. This technique might be of increasing usefulness in the coming years.

It is important to recognise cognitive dysfunction as a common symptom of multiple sclerosis so that detailed neuropsychological assessment can be made and can lead to the design of appropriate rehabilitation and coping strategies. The reader is referred to a useful review of the neuropsychological and neurobehavioural aspects of multiple sclerosis by Rao (1990, 1995) and Beatty (1993).

Emotional problems

Although emotional problems are well recognised in multiple sclerosis, the literature on the subject is sparse and often contradictory. The prevalence of depression, for example, ranges from 6% to 54% in various studies (Minden & Schiffer, 1990). The literature has been reviewed by Sadovnick and colleagues (1996), who determined a life-time risk of depression of approximately 50% in a multiple sclerosis population of just over 220 people. In general, there is a trend for those with more severe disability to be more depressed, and for depression to be more common in elderly people. However, it is important to point out that depressive illness can occur at all stages of multiple sclerosis. Sullivan and colleagues (1995) screened 46 new referrals to a multiple sclerosis clinic using the Beck Depression Inventory and found that 40% had major depressive illness, 22% had an adjustment disorder with depressed mood, and only 37% of the entire sample showed no evidence of mood disorder.

Clinical anxiety is a further problem but in this instance the tendency is for it to be more common in younger people (McIntosh-Michaelis et al., 1991). However, even these facts are not clear cut, as demonstrated by the study by Dalos et al. (1983), who found that the presence of emotional disturbance was not related to age, sex, or other demographic variables, or to duration or severity of the disease, or the degree of disability.

Unfortunately, there is an increased risk of suicide in people with multiple sclerosis. It has been estimated that the risk of suicide is about 7.5 times greater in people with multiple sclerosis than the general population (Sadovnick et al., 1992). In a Danish study the risk of death by suicide was found to be higher in males with an onset before the age of 30, females with an onset after the age of 30, and within the first 5 years of diagnosis. In terms of the natural history of the disease, it is usually when the relapsing remitting phase becomes chronically progressive and the severity of disability and other symptoms are more obvious (Stenager et al., 1992).

The often-reported finding of euphoria in multiple sclerosis is probably not as common as first imagined, with estimates ranging from 0% to 63% (Herndon, 1990). There do not appear to have been studies of the prevalence of pathological laughing and crying, despite the fact that this is a particular problem for some people and is usually effectively and quickly treated by small doses of amitriptyline or imipramine.

Part of the difficulty of the present literature regarding emotional problems in multiple sclerosis is of widely varying standards for research and agreed definitions in instruments and measurement. Guidelines have been published (Minden & Schiffer, 1990; Peyser et al., 1990) and acceptance of these should lead to improvement in the quality of research in these difficult areas.

There is no evidence that affective disturbance in multiple sclerosis is more resistant to treatment than that occurring in any other disease states and it is important that it is recognised and treated promptly (Minden & Moes, 1990).

PARTICIPATION (HANDICAP)

Increased participation (reduction of handicap) is very dependent on national statutes and structures for rehabilitation and disability services. Local facilities are also extremely important and obviously variable. Health professionals should be acquainted with:

- local accessible leisure pursuits
- day-centre provision
- respite care provision
- how to access local rehousing and housing adaptation systems
- welfare rights advice
- employment rehabilitation services
- carers' support services
- information and advice service
- contact address of local and national multiple sclerosis society or other associated self-help groups.

Two particular points with regard to amelioration of handicap should be made in the context of this chapter. First, there is considerable psychological stress on the carers and close family of people with multiple sclerosis. The University of Southampton (1989) found 15% of carers to be depressed and 24% suffering from degrees of clinical anxiety. The stress of caring should be recognised and knowledge of local community support, including carers' self-help support groups, is important. Information regarding services, provision of practical help at home, and access to respite facilities would seem to be some of the more important factors that would relieve carers' stress. It must also be emphasised that multiple sclerosis can affect the whole family and, whereas the main emotional and physical burden will fall on the main carer, children and other close relatives are also at increased risk of psychological problems. There is clear value in the involvement of a counsellor or psychologist in the multidisciplinary multiple sclerosis team (Kalb & Scheinberg, 1992; Thompson, 1996).

The second point to emphasise is the importance of employment rehabilitation. O'Brien (1987) estimated the annual cost of multiple sclerosis in England and Wales was £125.4 million at 1986–87 prices. This included the cost of consultations, prescriptions, institutional and hospital care. However, £100 million of this figure represented the estimate of lost earnings. This emphasises the central importance of employment rehabilitation which, at least in the UK, is not often seen as a central part of a health-orientated rehabilitation service. Gronning et al. (1990) found that 51% of their group of 79 people with multiple sclerosis in Norway were unemployed. They found that particularly high-risk factors for unemployment included age of onset over 30, a non-remittent course and premorbid heavy physical work.

Burgeoning technology, described in other chapters of this book, now allows environmental access to people with even the most severe disabilities. This can lead to useful employment even at relatively late stages of the disease.

CONCLUSION

Multiple sclerosis is a common neurological disorder producing a complex interaction of physical, psychological, social, and vocational problems. There are no controlled studies of the best way to manage people with multiple sclerosis but a multidisciplinary approach is surely essential to identify the full range of abilities and disabilities and to design appropriate rehabilitation and support strategies. Progressive neurological disease still engenders an air of therapeutic nihilism. The rehabilitation team should rise to the challenge of multiple sclerosis.

REFERENCES

Achiron A, Gilad R, Margalit R. (1994) Intravenous gamma-globulin treatment in multiple sclerosis and experimental autoimmune encephalomyelitis: Delineation of usage and mode of action. *J Neurol Neurosurg Psychiatry, 57 (Suppl)*, 57–61.

Adams DK, Sutherland JM, Fletcher WB. (1950) Early clinical manifestations of disseminated sclerosis. *Br Med J, 2*, 431–436.

Alam SM, Kyriakides T, Lowden M, Newman PK. (1993) Methylprednisolone in multiple sclerosis: A comparison of oral with intravenous therapy at equivalent high dose. *J Neurol Neurosurg Psychiatry, 56*, 1219–1220.

Amato MP, Fratigliani L, Groppi C et al. (1988) Interrater reliability in assessing functional systems and disability on the Kurtzke scale in multiple sclerosis. *Arch Neurol, 45,* 746–748.

Amato MP, Ponziani G, Pracucci G et al. (1995) Cognitive impairment in early onset of multiple sclerosis. Pattern, predictors and impact on every day life in a four year follow-up. *Arch Neurol, 52,* 168–172.

Anderson JT, Bradley WE. (1976) Abnormalities of detrusor and sphincter function in multiple sclerosis. *Br J Urol, 48,* 193–198.

Anonymous. (1996) Interferon-β-1b – hope or hype? *Drug Ther Bull, 34,* 9–11.

Anzola GP, Bevilacqua L, Cappa SF et al. (1990) Neuropsychological assessment in patients with relapsing-remitting multiple sclerosis and mild functional impairment: Correlation with magnetic resonance imaging. *J Neurol Neurosurg Psychiatry, 53,* 142–145.

Archibold CJ, Macgrath PJ, Ritvo PG et al. (1994) Pain prevalence, severity and impact in a clinical sample of multiple sclerosis patients. *Pain, 58,* 89–93.

Association of British Neurologists. (1994) *New treatments for multiple sclerosis.* Association of British Neurologists, London.

Bamford CR, Sibley WA, Thies C. (1981) Trauma as an aetiologic and aggravating factor in multiple sclerosis. *Neurology, 31,* 1229–1234.

Barnes MP, Bateman DE, Cleland PG et al. (1985a) Intravenous methyl prednisolone for multiple sclerosis in relapse. *J Neurol Neurosurg Psychiatry, 48,* 157–159.

Barnes MP, Bates D, Cartlidge NEF et al. (1985b) Hyperbaric oxygen and multiple sclerosis: Short-term results of a placebo-controlled double blind trial. *Lancet, i,* 297–300.

Barnes MP, Bates D, Cartlidge NEF et al. (1987) Hyperbaric oxygen and multiple sclerosis: Final results of a placebo-controlled, double-blind study. *J Neurol Neurosurg Psychiatry, 50,* 1402–1406.

Bates D, Cartlidge NEF, French JM et al. (1989) A double-blind controlled trial of long chain *n*-3 polyunsaturated fatty acids in the treatment of multiple sclerosis. *J Neurol Neurosurg Psychiatry, 52,* 18–22.

Beatty WW. (1993) Cognitive and emotional disturbances in multiple sclerosis. *Behav Neurol, 11,* 189–204.

Beatty WW, Goodkin DE. (1990) Screening for cognitive impairment in multiple sclerosis: An evaluation of the Mini Mental State Examination. *Arch Neurol, 47,* 297–301.

Beatty WW, Goodkin DE, Manson N, Beatty PA. (1989) Cognitive disturbances in patients with relapsing-remitting multiple sclerosis. *Arch Neurol, 46,* 1113–1119.

Beatty WW, Goodkin DE, Hertsgaard D, Manson N. (1990) Clinical and demographic predictors of cognitive performance in multiple sclerosis. Do diagnostic type, disease duration and disability matter? *Arch Neurol, 47,* 305–308.

Beatty WW, Paul RH, Wilbanks SL et al. (1995) Identifying multiple sclerosis patients with mild or global cognitive impairment using the Screening Examination for Cognitive Impairment (SEFCI). *Neurology, 45,* 718–723.

Belin J, Pettet N, Smith AD et al. (1971) Linoleate metabolism in multiple sclerosis. *J Neurol Neurosurg Psychiatry, 34,* 25–29.

Benkelman DR, Kraft GH, Freal J. (1985) Expressive communicative disorders in persons with multiple sclerosis. *Arch Phys Med Rehabil, 66,* 675–679.

Betts CD, Jones SJ, Fowler CG, Fowler CJ. (1994) Erectile dysfunction in multiple sclerosis. Associated neurological and neurophysiological deficits and treatment of the condition. *Brain, 117 (Part 6),* 1303–1310.

Beutler E, Sipe JS, Romine JS. (1996) The treatment of chronic progressive multiple sclerosis with cladribine. *Proc Nat Acad Sci USA, 93,* 1716–1720.

Bever CT, Jr. (1994) The current status of studies of aminopyridines in patients with multiple sclerosis. *Ann Neurol, 36 (Suppl),* S118–121.

Bever CT, Jr, Young D, Anderson PA et al. (1994) The effects of 4-aminopyridine in multiple sclerosis patients: Results of a randomised, placebo-controlled, double-blind, concentration control cross-over trial. *Neurology, 44,* 1054–1059.

Birk K, Ford C, Smeltzer S et al. (1990) The clinical course of multiple sclerosis during pregnancy and the puerperium. *Arch Neurol, 47,* 738–742.

Blaivas JG, Bhimani G, Calib KV. (1979) Vesico-urethral dysfunction in multiple sclerosis. *J Urol, 122,* 342–347.

Bourdette DN, Prochazka AV, Mitchell W et al. (1993) Health care costs of veterans with multiple sclerosis: Implications for the rehabilitation of multiple sclerosis. *Arch Phys Med Rehab, 74,* 26–31.

Bradley WE, Logothetis JL, Timms GW. (1973) Cystometric and sphincter abnormalities in multiple sclerosis. *Neurology, 23,* 1131–1139.

Brindley GS. (1983) Cavernosal alpha blockade: A new technique for investigating and treating erectile impotence. *British Journal of Psychiatry, 143,* 332–337.

British & Dutch Multiple Sclerosis Azathioprine Trial Group. (1988) Double masked trial of Azathioprine in multiple sclerosis. *Lancet, ii,* 179–183.

Brochet B, Guinot P, Orgogozo JM et al. (1995) A double-blind, placebo-controlled, multi-centre study of ginkgolide B in the treatment of acute exacerbations in multiple sclerosis. The Ginkgolide Study Group in Multiple Sclerosis. *J Neurol Neurosurg Psychiatry, 58,* 360–362.

Carter JL, Hafler D, Dawson DM et al. (1988) Immunosuppression with high dose IV cyclophosphamide and ACTH in progressive multiple sclerosis: Cumulative six year experience in 104 patients. *Neurology, 38 (7 Suppl 2),* 9–14.

Cazzato G, Mesiano T, Antonello R et al. (1995) Double-blind, placebo-controlled, randomised, cross-over trial of high dose methylprednisolone in patients with a chronic progressive form of multiple sclerosis. *Eur Neurol, 35,* 193–198.

Chia YW, Fowler CJ, Kamm MA et al. (1995) Prevalence of bowel dysfunction in patients with multiple sclerosis and bladder dysfunction. *J Neurol, 242 (2),* 105–108.

Clifford DB, Trotter JI. (1984) Pain in multiple sclerosis. *Arch Neurol, 41,* 1270–1272.

Cohen RA, Fisher M. (1989) Amantadine treatment of fatigue associated with multiple sclerosis. *Arch Neurol, 46,* 676–680.

Compston DAS. (1987) Can the course of multiple sclerosis be predicted? In: Warlow CP, Garfield JS (Eds). *More dilemmas in neurology.* Churchill Livingstone, Edinburgh.

Cook SD, Devereux C, Troiano R et al. (1995) Combination total lymphoid irradiation and low dose corticosteroid therapy for progressive multiple sclerosis. *Acta Neurol Scand, 91,* 22–27.

Cooper IS. (1967) Relief of intention tremor of multiple sclerosis by thalamic surgery. *J Am Med Assoc, 119,* 689–694.

Currier RD, Haerer AF, Meydrech EF. (1993) Low dose oral methotrexate treatment in multiple sclerosis: A pilot study. *J Neurol Neurosurg Psychiatry, 56,* 1217–1218.

Dalos NP, Rabins PV, Brooks BR, O'Donnell P. (1983) Disease activity and emotional state in multiple sclerosis. *Ann Neurol, 13,* 573–577.

Damanaski M, Sutcliffe-Kerr A. (1964) Paraplegia of non-traumatic origin and disseminated (multiple) sclerosis: Urinary complications, their nature and treatment. *Acta Neurol Psychiat Belg, 64,* 495–519.

Darley FL, Brown JR, Goldstein NP. (1972) Dysarthria in multiple sclerosis. *J Speech Hearing Res, 15,* 229–233.

Dix MR. (1965) Observations upon the nerve fibre deafness in multiple sclerosis, with particular reference to the phenomena of loudness recruitment. *J Laryngol Otol, 69,* 608–616.

Dupont S. (1995) Multiple sclerosis and sexual function – a review. *Clin Rehab, 9,* 135–141.

Dworkin RH, Bates D, Millar JHD, Paty DW. (1984) Linoleic acid and multiple sclerosis: A re-analysis of three double-blind trials. *Neurology, 34,* 1441–1445.

Eadon G, Miller D, Clanet M. (1997) Therapeutic effect of mitoxantrone combined with methyl prednisolone in multiple sclerosis: A randomised multi-centre study of active disease using MRI and clinical criteria. *J Neurol Neurosurg Psychiatry, 62,* 112–118.

Ebers GC. (1996) Genetic epidemiology of multiple sclerosis. *Curr Opin Neurol, 9,* 155–158.

Ebers GC, Sadovnick AD, Risch NJ and the Canadian Collaborative Study Group. (1995) A genetic basis for familial aggregation in multiple sclerosis. *Nature, 377,* 150–151.

Eckford SD, Swami KS, Jackson SR, Abrams PH. (1994) Desmopressin in the treatment of nocturia and enuresis in patients with multiple sclerosis. *Brit J Urol, 74,* 733–735.

European Study Group on Interferon Beta-1B in Secondary Progressive Multiple Sclerosis. (1998) Placebo-controlled, multi-centre, randomised trial of interferon beta-1B in treatment of secondary progressive multiple sclerosis. *Lancet, 352,* 1491–1497.

Farmakides MN, Boone DR. (1960) Speech problems of patients with multiple sclerosis. *J Speech Hearing Dis, 25,* 385–389.

Ferini-Strambi L, Filippi M, Martinelli V. (1994) Nocturnal sleep study in multiple sclerosis: Correlations with clinical and brain magnetic resonance imaging findings. *J Neurol Sci, 125,* 194–197.

Filippi M, Miller DH. (1996) Magnetic resonance imaging in the differential diagnosis and monitoring of the treatment of multiple sclerosis. *Curr Opin Neurol, 9,* 178–186.

Filippi M, Horsfield MA, Morris SP et al. (1994) Quantitative brain MRI lesion load predicts the course of clinically isolated syndromes suggestive of multiple sclerosis. *Neurology, 44,* 635–641.

Filippi M, Paty DW, Cappos L et al. (1995) Correlations between changes and disability and T_2 weighted brain MRI activity in multiple sclerosis: A follow-up study. *Neurology, 45,* 255–260.

Folstein MF, Folstein FE, McHugh PR. (1975) Mini Mental State: A practical method for grading the cognitive state of patients for the clinician. *J Psychiatric Res, 12,* 189–198.

Forsythe E. (1988) *Multiple sclerosis: exploring sickness and health.* Faber and Faber, London.

Fowler C. (1994) Bladder dysfunction in multiple sclerosis: Causes and treatment. *Internat MS J, 1,* 98–107.

Franklin GM, Nelson LM, Heaton RK et al. (1988) Stress and its relationship to acute exacerbations in multiple sclerosis. *J Neurol Rehab, 2,* 7–11.

Freeman JA, Langdon DW, Hobart JC, Thompson AJ. (1997) The impact of rehabilitation on disability and handicap in progressive multiple sclerosis: A randomised controlled trial. *Ann Neurol, 42,* 236–244.

Freeman JA, Langdon DW, Hobart JL, Thompson AJ. (1999) Inpatient rehabilitation in multiple sclerosis: Do the benefits carry over into the community? *Neurology, 52,* 50–56.

Frith JA, McCleod JG. (1988) Pregnancy and multiple sclerosis. *J Neurol Neurosurg Psychiatry, 51,* 495–498.

Gill KP, Chia YW, Henry MM, Shorvon PJ. (1994) Defecography in multiple sclerosis patients with severe constipation. *Radiology, 191,* 553–556.

Giovannoni G, Hartung HP. (1996) The immunopathogenesis of multiple sclerosis and Guillain–Barré syndrome. *Curr Opin Neurol, 9,* 165–177.

Glick ME, Meshkinfoos H, Haldeman S. (1982) Colonic dysfunction in multiple sclerosis. *Gastroenterology, 83,* 1002–1006.

Goodkin DE, Rudick RA et al. (1995) Low dose (7.5 mg) oral methotrexate reduces the rate of progression in chronic progressive multiple sclerosis. *Ann Neurol, 37,* 30–40.

Granger CV, Cotter AC, Hamilton BB et al. (1990) Functional assessment scales: A study of persons with multiple sclerosis. *Arch Phys Med Rehab, 71,* 870–875.

Grant I, McDonald WI, Trimble MR et al. (1984) Deficient learning and memory in early and middle phases of multiple sclerosis. *J Neurol Neurosurg Psychiatry, 47,* 250–255.

Grant I, Brown GW, Harris T et al. (1989) Severely threatening events and marked life difficulties preceding onset of exacerbation of multiple sclerosis. *J Neurol Neurosurg Psychiatry, 52,* 8–13.

Gronning M, Hannisdal E, Millgren SI. (1990) Multivariate analysis of factors associated with unemployment in people with multiple sclerosis. *J Neur Neurosurg Psychiatry, 53,* 388–390.

Hald T, Bradley WE. (1982) Neurological disease in the urinary bladder. In: Hald T, Bradley WE (Eds). *The urinary bladder: neurology and dynamics.* Williams & Wilkins, Baltimore.

Herndon RM. (1990) Cognitive deficits and emotional dysfunction in multiple sclerosis. *Arch Neurol, 47,* 18.

Hinds JP, Eidelman BH, Wald A. (1990) Prevalence of bowel dysfunction in multiple sclerosis. A population survey. *Gastroenterology, 98,* 1538–1542.

Holmes J, Madgwick T, Bates D. (1995) The cost of multiple sclerosis. *Br J Med Econ, 8,* 181–193.

Hopper CL, Matthews CG, Cleland CS. (1972) Symptom instability and thermoregulation in multiple sclerosis. *Neurology, 22,* 142–148.

Hughes JC, Enderby PM, Langton-Hewer R. (1994) Dysphagia and multiple sclerosis: A study and discussion of its nature and impact. *Clin Rehab, 8,* 18–26.

Hulter BM, Lundberg PO. (1995) Sexual dysfunction in women with advanced multiple sclerosis. *J Neurol Neurosurg Psychiatry, 59,* 83–86.

IFNB Multiple Sclerosis Study Group. (1993) Interferon-β-1b is effective in relapsing remitting multiple sclerosis. 1. Clinical results of a multi-centre, randomised, double-blind, placebo-controlled trial. *Neurology, 43,* 655–661.

IFNB Multiple Sclerosis Study Group, The University of British Columbia MS/MRI Analysis Group. (1995) Interferon-β-1b in the treatment of multiple sclerosis: Final outcome of the randomised controlled trial. *Neurology, 45,* 1277–1285.

International Federation of Multiple Sclerosis Societies. (1984) Symposium of a minimal record of disability for multiple sclerosis. *Acta Neurol Scand, Suppl 101.*

Jacobs LD, Cookfair DL, Ruddick RA et al. (1996) Intramuscular interferon-β-1a for disease progression in relapsing multiple sclerosis. *Ann Neurol, 39,* 285–294.

James PB. (1982) Evidence for sub-acute fat embolism as the cause of multiple sclerosis. *Lancet, i,* 380–386.

Johnson KP, Brooks BR, Cohen JA et al. (1995) Copolymer 1 reduces relapse rate and improved disability in relapsing remitting multiple sclerosis. Results of a phase three multicenter double-blind, placebo-controlled trial. *Neurology, 45,* 1268–1276.

Johnson K, Brooks BR, Ford CC et al. (2000) Sustained clinical benefits of Glatiramer acetate in relapsing multiple sclerosis patients observed for 6 years. *Multiple Sclerosis, 6,* 255–266.

Kahana E, Leibowitz U, Alter M. (1971) Cerebral multiple sclerosis. *Neurology, 21,* 1179–1185.

Kalb RC, Scheinberg LC (Eds). (1992) *Multiple sclerosis and the family.* Demos, New York.

Kappos L, Patzold U, Dommasch D et al. (1988) Cyclosporin versus azathioprine in the long term treatment of multiple sclerosis – results of the German Multicenter Study. *Ann Neurol, 23,* 56–63.

Karussis DM, Miner Z, Lehmann D. (1996) Treatment of secondary progressive multiple sclerosis with the immunomodulator linomide: A double-blind, placebo-controlled pilot study with monthly magnetic resonance imaging evaluation. *Neurology, 47,* 341–346.

Kaufman J, Khatri BO, Riendl P. (1988) Are patients with multiple sclerosis protected from thrombophlebitis and pulmonary embolism? *Chest, 94,* 998–1001.

Kersten P, McLellan DL. (1996) Evidence for a central mechanism in the process of fatigue in people with multiple sclerosis. *Clin Rehab, 10,* 233–239.

Khatri BO. (1988) Experience with use of plasmapheresis in chronic progressive multiple sclerosis: The pros. *Neurology, 38 (7 Suppl 2),* 50–52.

Killian JM, Bressler RB, Armstrong RM, Huston DP. (1988) Controlled pilot trial of monthly intravenous cyclophosphamide in multiple sclerosis. *Arch Neurol, 45,* 27–30.

Kirkeby HJ, Poulsen EV, Petersen T, Dorup J. (1988) Erectile dysfunction in multiple sclerosis. *Neurology, 38,* 1366–1371.

Kirker SGB, Young E, Warlow CP et al. (1995) An evaluation of multiple sclerosis liaison nurse. *Clin Rehab, 9,* 219–226.

Kleijnen J, Knipschild P. (1995) Hyperbaric oxygen for multiple sclerosis. A review of controlled trials. *Acta Neurol Scand, 91,* 330–334.

Korn-Lubetzki I, Kahana E, Cooper G, Abramsky O. (1984) Activity of multiple sclerosis during pregnancy and puerperium. *Ann Neurol, 16,* 229–231.

Kraft GH, Freal JE, Coryll JK et al. (1981) Multiple sclerosis: early prognostic guidelines. *Arch Phys Med Rehab, 62,* 54–58.

Kraft GH, Freal JE, Coryll JK. (1986) Disability, disease duration and rehabilitation service needs in multiple sclerosis: patient perspectives. *Arch Phys Med Rehab, 67,* 164–178.

Krupp LB, Alvarez LA, Larocca NG, Scheinberg LC. (1988) Fatigue in multiple sclerosis. *Arch Neurol, 45,* 435–437.

Krupp LB, Coyle PK, Doscher S et al. (1995) Fatigue therapy in multiple sclerosis: Results of a double-blind, randomised, parallel trial of amantidine, pemoline and placebo. *Neurology, 45,* 1956–1961.

Kurtzke JF. (1955) A new scale for evaluating disability in multiple sclerosis. *Neurology, 5,* 580–583.

Kurtzke JF. (1970) Clinical manifestations in multiple sclerosis. In: Vinken PJ, Bruyn GW (Eds) *Handbook of Clinical Neurology (Vol 9).* Elsevier, Amsterdam.

Kurtzke JF. (1981) A proposal for a uniform minimal record of disability in multiple sclerosis. *Acta Neurol Scand, 64 (Suppl 87),* 110–129.

Kurtzke JF. (1983) Rating neurologic impairment in multiple sclerosis: An expanded disability status scale (EDSS). *Neurology, 33,* 1444–1452.

Kurtzke JF, Beebe GW, Nagler B et al. (1968) Studies on the natural history of multiple sclerosis 4: Clinical features of the onset bout. *Acta Neurol Scand, 44,* 467–499.

Larocca NG. (1990) A rehabilitation perspective. In: Rao SM (Ed) *Neurobehavioural aspects of multiple sclerosis.* Oxford University Press, Oxford.

Lee J, Elston J, Vickers S et al. (1988) Botulinum toxin therapy for squint. *Eye, 2,* 24–28.

Levine JS. (1985) Bowel dysfunction in multiple sclerosis. In: Maloney FP, Burks JS, Ringel SP (Eds) *Interdisciplinary rehabilitation of multiple sclerosis and neuromuscular disorders.* Lippincott, Philadelphia.

Lillus HG, Valtoneu EJ, Wikstrom J. (1976) Sexual problems in patients suffering from multiple sclerosis. *J Chron Dis, 29,* 643–647.

Limburg CC. (1950) Geographic distribution of multiple sclerosis and its estimated prevalence in the United States. *Proc Assoc Res Nervous Mental Dis, 28,* 15–24.

Litvan I, Grafman J, Vendrell P, Martinez JM. (1988) Slowed information processing in multiple sclerosis. *Arch Neurol, 45,* 281–285.

Logemann J. (1981) *The evaluation and treatment of swallowing disorders.* College Hill Press, San Diego.

Lundberg PO. (1978) Sexual dysfunction in patients with multiple sclerosis. *Sex Disabil, 1,* 218–223.

Manyam BV. (1986) Recent advances in the treatment of cerebellar ataxias. *Clin Neuropharm, 9,* 508–516.

Maroff MV, Vaney C, Konig N et al. (1996) Evaluation of disability in multiple sclerosis patients: A comparative study of the Functional Independence Measure, the Extended Barthel Index and the Expanded Disability Status Scale. *Clin Rehab, 10,* 309–313.

Matson D, Petrie M, Srivastava DK, McDermott M. (1995) Multiple sclerosis. Sexual dysfunction and its response to medications. *Arch Neurol, 52,* 862–868.

Matthews WB. (1962) Epilepsy and disseminated sclerosis. *Q J Med, 31,* 141–155.

Matthews WB. (1975) Paroxysmal symptoms in multiple sclerosis. *J Neurol Neurosurg Psychiatry, 38,* 617–623.

Matthews WB, Acheson ED, Batchelor JR, Weller RO. (1985) *McAlpine's multiple sclerosis.* Churchill Livingstone, Edinburgh.

McAlpine D. (1964) The benign form of multiple sclerosis: Results of a long term study. *Br Med J, 2,* 1029–1032.

McAlpine D. (1972) *Multiple sclerosis: a reappraisal.* Churchill Livingstone, Edinburgh.

McAlpine D, Compston ND. (1952) Some aspects of the natural history of disseminated sclerosis. *Q J Med, 21,* 135–167.

McIntosh-Michaelis SA, Roberts MH, Wilkinson SM et al. (1991) The prevalence of cognitive impairment in a community survey of multiple sclerosis. *Br J Clin Psychol, 30,* 333–348.

Mellerup E, Fog T, Raun N. (1981) The socio-economic scale. *Acta Neurol Scand, 64 (Suppl 87),* 130–138.

Mertin J, Rudge P, Kremer M et al. (1982) Double-blind, controlled trial of immunosuppression in the treatment of multiple sclerosis: Final report. *Lancet, ii,* 351–354.

Mickey MR, Ellison GW, Myers LW. (1984) An illness severity score for multiple sclerosis. *Neurology, 34,* 1343–1347.

Midgard R, Albrektsen G, Riise T et al. (1995) Prognostic factors for survival in multiple sclerosis: A longitudinal, population based study in More and Romsdal, Norway. *J Neurol Neurosurg Psychiatry, 58,* 417–421.

Miller DH, Lia HM, Llewellyn-Smith N. (1995) Phase 2 trial of anti-CD 4 antibodies in the treatment of multiple sclerosis. *J Neurol, 242 (Suppl 2),* S23.

Miller H, Simpson CA, Yates WK. (1965) Bladder dysfunction in multiple sclerosis. *Brit M J, 1,* 1265–1269.

Milligan NM, Newcombe R, Compston DAS. (1987) A double-blind, controlled trial of high dose methyl prednisolone in patients with multiple sclerosis: 1. Clinical effects. *J Neurol Neurosurg Psychiatry, 50,* 511–516.

Milward S. (1984) Practical help in multiple sclerosis. *Br Med J, 289,* 1441–1442.

Minden SL, Moes E. (1990) A psychiatric perspective. In: Rao SM (Ed) *Neurobehavioural aspects of multiple sclerosis.* Oxford University Press, Oxford.

Minden SL, Schiffer RB. (1990) Affective disorders in multiple sclerosis: Review and recommendations for clinical research. *Arch Neurol, 47,* 98–104.

Moreau T, Thorpe J, Miller D et al. (1994) Preliminary evidence from magnetic resonance imaging for reduction in disease activity after lymphocyte depletion in multiple sclerosis. *Lancet, 344,* 298–301.

Moulin DE, Foley KM, Ebers GC. (1988) Pain syndromes in multiple sclerosis. *Neurology, 38,* 1830–1834.

Moxon W. (1875) Eight cases of insular sclerosis of the brain and spinal cord. *Guy's Hospital Reports, 20,* 438–481.

Muller R. (1949) Studies on disseminated sclerosis with special reference to symptomatology, course and prognosis. *Acta Med Scand, 133 (Suppl 222),* 1–214.

Multiple Sclerosis Study Group. (1990) Efficacy and toxicity of cyclosporin in chronic progressive multiple sclerosis: A randomised double blinded placebo controlled clinical trial. *Ann Neurol, 27,* 591–605.

Mumford CJ, Wood NW, Kellar-Wood H et al. (1994) The British isles survey of multiple sclerosis in twins. *Neurology, 44,* 11–15.

Murray TJ. (1985) Amantadine therapy for fatigue in multiple sclerosis. *Can J Neurol Sci, 12,* 251–254.

Neilley LK, Gooding DS, Goodkin DE, Hauser SL. (1996) Side effect profile of interferon-β-1b in multiple sclerosis: Results of an open labelled trial. *Neurology, 46,* 552–554.

Neubauer RA. (1980) Exposure of multiple sclerosis patients to hyperbaric oxygen at 1.5–2 ATA. *J Florida Med Assoc, 67,* 498–504.

O'Brien B. (1987) *Multiple sclerosis.* Office of Health Economics, London.

Olgiati R, Burgunder JM, Mumenthaler M. (1988) Increased energy cost of walking in multiple sclerosis: effect of spasticity, ataxia and weakness. *Arch Phys Med Rehab, 69,* 846–849.

Opsomer RJ. (1996) Management of male sexual dysfunction in multiple sclerosis. *Sex Disabil, 14,* 57–63.

Pallotta R. (1982) La terapia iperbarica della sclerosis multipla. *Minerva Medica, 73,* 2947–2954.

Paty DW, Li DKB, UBS MS/MRI Study Group, IFNB Multiple Sclerosis Study Group. (1993) Interferon-β-1b is effective in relapsing remitting multiple sclerosis. 2. MRI analysis results of a multi-centre, randomised, double-blind, placebo-controlled trial. *Neurology, 43,* 662–667.

Patzold V, Hesker H, Pocklington P. (1982) Azathioprine in treatment of multiple sclerosis: Final results of a $4\frac{1}{2}$ year controlled study of its effectiveness covering 115 patients. *J Neurol Sci, 54,* 377–394.

Petajan JH, Gappmaier E, White AT et al. (1996) Impact of aerobic training on fitness and quality of life in multiple sclerosis. *Ann Neurol, 39,* 432–441.

Petersen T, Pedersen E. (1984) Neurourodynamic evaluation of voiding dysfunction in multiple sclerosis. *Acta Neurol Scand, 69,* 402–411.

Peyser JM, Rao SM, Larocca NG, Kaplan E. (1990) Guidelines for neuropsychological research in multiple sclerosis. *Arch Neurol, 47,* 94–97.

Poser S, Poser W. (1983) Multiple sclerosis and gestation. *Neurology, 33,* 1422–1427.

Poser S, Raun EN, Wikstrom J, Poser W. (1979) Pregnancy, oral contraceptives and multiple sclerosis. *Acta Neurol Scand, 55,* 108–118.

Poser S, Raun EN, Poser W. (1982) Age of onset, initial symptomatology and the course of multiple sclerosis. *Acta Neurol Scand, 66,* 355–362.

Rao SM (Ed). (1990) *Neurobehavioural aspects of multiple sclerosis.* Oxford University Press, Oxford.

Rao SM. (1995) Neuropsychology and multiple sclerosis. *Curr Opin Neurol, 8,* 216–220.

Rao SM, Hammeke TA, McQuillin MP et al. (1984) Memory disturbance in chronic progressive multiple sclerosis. *Arch Neurol, 41,* 625–631.

Rao SM, Leo GJ, Houghton UM. (1989) Correlation of magnetic resonance imaging with neuropsychological testing in multiple sclerosis. *Neurology, 39,* 161–166.

Rapp NS, Gilroy J, Learner AM. (1995) The role of bacterial infection in exacerbation of multiple sclerosis. *Am J Phys Med Rehab, 74,* 415–418.

Rice-Oxley M, Williams ES, Ress JE. (1995) A prevalence survey of multiple sclerosis in Sussex. *J Neurol Neurosurg Psychiatry, 58,* 27–30.

Richards RG. (1996) Interferon-β in multiple sclerosis: Clinical cost effectiveness falls at the first hurdle. *Br Med J, 313,* 1159.

Robertson N, Deans J, Fraser M, Compston DAS. (1995) Multiple sclerosis in the North Cambridgeshire Districts of East Anglia. *J Neurol Neurosurg Psychiatry, 59,* 71–76.

Rose AS, Kuzma JW, Kurtzke JF et al. (1970) Co-operative study in the evaluation of therapy and multiple sclerosis: ACTH versus placebo. *Neurology, 20 (5 pt 2),* 1–59.

Rossiter D, Thompson AJ. (1995) Introduction of integrated care pathways for patients with multiple sclerosis in an inpatient neurorehabilitation setting. *Dis Rehab, 17,* 443–448.

Roullet E, Verdier-Taillefer MH, Amarenco P et al. (1993) Pregnancy in multiple sclerosis: A longitudinal study of 125 remittent patients. *J Neurol Neurosurg Psychiatry, 56,* 1062–1065.

Rouse E, Coppel A, Howorth J, Noyce S. (1996) A purchaser experience of managing new expensive drugs: Interferon-β. *Br Med J, 313,* 1195–1196.

Rudge P, Koetsier JC, Mertin J et al. (1989) Randomised double-blind, controlled trial of cyclosporin in multiple sclerosis. *J Neurol Neurosurg Psychiatry, 52,* 559–565.

Sadovnick AD, Ebers GC, Wilson RW, Paty DW. (1992) Life expectancy in patients attending multiple sclerosis clinics. *Neurology, 42*, 991–994.

Sadovnick AD, Armstrong H, Rice GPA et al. (1993) A population based twin study of multiple sclerosis in twins: Update. *Ann Neurol, 33*, 281–285.

Sadovnick AD, Remick RA, Allen J et al. (1996) Depression and multiple sclerosis. *Neurology, 46*, 628–632.

Samellas W, Rubin B. (1965) Management of upper urinary tract infections in multiple sclerosis by means of a diversion to an ileo conduit. *J Urol, 93*, 548–552.

Scheinberg L, Holland NJ, Kirschenbaum MS. (1981) Comprehensive long term care of patients with multiple sclerosis. *Neurology, 31*, 1121–1123.

Semlyen JK, Hurrell E, Carter S, Barnes MP. (1996) The Newcastle Independence Assessment Form – Research: Development of an alternative functional measure. *J Neuro Rehab, 10*, 251–257.

Shepherd DI. (1979) Clinical features of multiple sclerosis in North East Scotland. *Acta Neurol Scand, 60*, 218–230.

Sibley WA. (1988) *Therapeutic claims in multiple sclerosis*, 2nd edn. Macmillan, London.

Sibley WA, Bamford CR, Clark K et al. (1991) A prospective study of physical trauma and multiple sclerosis. *J Neurol Neurosurg Psychiatry, 54*, 584–589.

Sipe JL, Knobler RL, Barkeny SL et al. (1984) A neurologic rating scale (NRS) for use in multiple sclerosis. *Neurology, 34*, 1368–1372.

Sipe JC, Romine JS, Koziol JA. (1994) Cladribine in treatment of chronic progressive multiple sclerosis. *Lancet, 344*, 9–13.

Sirls LT, Zimmeren PE, Leech GE. (1994) Role of limited evaluation and aggressive medical management in multiple sclerosis: A review of 113 patients. *J Urol, 151*, 946–950.

Skegg K, Corwin PA, Skegg DC. (1988) How often is multiple sclerosis mistaken for a psychiatric disorder? *Psychol Med, 18*, 733–736.

Solari A, Filippini G, Gnoco P et al. (1999) Physical rehabilitation has a positive effect on disability in multiple sclerosis patients. *Neurology, 52*, 57–61.

Stenager I, Stenager E, Koch-Henriksen N et al. (1992) Suicide and multiple sclerosis: An epidemiological investigation. *J Neurol Neurosurg Psychiatry, 55*, 542–545.

Sullivan MJ, Weinschenker B, Mikail S, Bishop SR. (1995) Screening for major depression in the early stages of multiple sclerosis. *Can J Neurol Sci, 22*, 228–231.

Swank RL. (1950) Multiple sclerosis. A correlation of its incidence with dietary fat. *Am J Med Sci, 220*, 421–430.

Swank RL, Dugan BB. (1990) Effect of low saturated fat diet in early and late cases of multiple sclerosis. *Lancet, 336*, 37–39.

Swingler RJ, Compston DAS. (1988) The prevalence of multiple sclerosis in South East Wales. *J Neurol Neurosurg Psychiatry, 51*, 1520–1524.

Teitelbaum D, Sela M. Arnon R. (1997) Copolymer 1 from the laboratory to FDA. *Israel J Med Sci, 33*, 280–284.

Thompson AJ, Noseworthy JH. (1996) New treatments for multiple sclerosis: A clinical prospective. *Cur Opin Neurol, 9*, 187–198.

Thompson DS, Nelson LM, Burns A et al. (1986) The effects of pregnancy in multiple sclerosis: A retrospective study. *Neurology, 36*, 1097–1099.

Thompson SBN. (1996) Providing a neuropsychology service for people with multiple sclerosis in an interdisciplinary rehabilitation unit. *Dis Rehab, 18*, 348–353.

Tindall R. (1988) A closer look at plasmapheresis in multiple sclerosis: The cons. *Neurology, 38 (7 Suppl 2)*, 53–56.

Tourtellotte WW, Baumhefner RW. (1983) Comprehensive management of multiple sclerosis. In: Hallpike JF, Adams CWM, Tourtellotte WW (Eds). *Multiple sclerosis: pathology, diagnosis and management*, 1st edn. Chapman & Hall, London.

Traccis S, Rosati G, Monaco MF et al. (1990) Successful treatment of acquired pendular elliptical nystagmus in multiple sclerosis with isoniazed and base-out prisms. *Neurology, 40*, 492–494.

Trojano M, Avolio C, Manzari C et al. (1995) Multivariate analysis of predictive factors of multiple sclerosis course with a validated method to assess clinical events. *J Neurol Neurosurg Psychiatry, 58*, 300–306.

Tswang WM, Berlin J, Munro JA. (1976) Relationship between plasma and lymphocyte linoleate in multiple sclerosis. *J Neurol Neurosurg Psychiatry, 39*, 767–771.

Uhthoff W. (1889) Untersuchen uber augenstorungen bei multipler herdsklerose. *Arch fur Psychiatrie und Nervenkrankheiten, 21*, 55–116.

University of Southampton. (1989) *Multiple sclerosis in the Southampton district*. Rehabilitation Unit & Department of Sociology & Social Policy, University of Southampton.

Valleroy MI, Kraft GH. (1984) Sexual dysfunction in multiple sclerosis. *Arch Phys Med Rehab, 65*, 125–129.

Vamakas EC, Pineda AA, Weinshenker BG. (1995) Meta-analysis of clinical studies of the efficacy of plasma exchange in the treatment of chronic progressive multiple sclerosis. *J Clin Apheresis, 10*, 163–170.

Van den Berg W, Van Zomeren AH, Minderhoud JM et al. (1987) Cognitive impairment in patients with multiple sclerosis and mild physical disability. *Arch Neurol, 44*, 494–501.

Van Waldervein MAM, Barkhof F, Hommes OR et al. (1995) Correlating MRI and clinical disease activity in multiple sclerosis: Relevance of hypointense lesions on short TR/short TE (T_1 weighted) spin echo images. *Neurology, 45*, 1684–1690.

Walley T, Barton S. (1995) A purchaser perspective of managing new drugs: interferon-β as a case study. *Br Med J, 311*, 796–799.

Warren S. (1990) The role of stress in multiple sclerosis. In: Rao SM (Ed) *Neurobehavioural aspects of multiple sclerosis*. Oxford University Press, Oxford.

Weinschenker BG, Bass B, Rice GPA et al. (1989) The natural history of multiple sclerosis: A geographically based study. *Brain, 112*, 133–146.

Wiles CM, Omar L, Swan AV et al. (1994) Total lymphoid irradiation in multiple sclerosis. *J Neurol Neurosurg Psychiatry, 57*, 154–163.

Wiles CM, Newcombe RG, Fuller KJ. (2001) Controlled randomised crossover trial of the effects of physiotherapy on mobility in chronic multiple sclerosis. *J Neurol Neurosurg Psychiatry, 70*, 174–179.

Williams ES, McKaren RO. (1986) Prevalence of multiple sclerosis in a South London borough. *Br Med J, 293*, 237–239.

Willoughby EW, Paty DW. (1988) Scales for rating impairment in multiple sclerosis: A critique. *Neurology, 38*, 1793–1798.

Winters S, Jackson P, Simms K, Magilvy J. (1989) A nurse managed multiple sclerosis clinic: Improved quality of life for persons with multiple sclerosis. *Rehab, Nurs, 14*, 13–22.

Wlinsky JS. (1995) Copolymer 1: A most reasonable alternative therapy for early relapsing remitting multiple sclerosis with mild disability. *Neurology, 45*, 1245–1247.

Yamamoto T, Imai T, Yamasaki M. (1989) Acute ventilatory failure in multiple sclerosis. *J Neurol Sci, 89*, 313–324.

40. Huntington's disease

C.D. Ward   N.R. Dennis

INTRODUCTION

Neurologists have an important role to play, along with others, in the support of people with Huntington's disease (HD) and of their families. After outlining the genetics and clinical and pathological features of HD, this chapter considers five groups of management and rehabilitation issues, corresponding to five stages which are often experienced successively by the same individual. In the first phase, a person at risk of HD requires primarily genetic advice. Those who are tested positive for the HD mutation enter a second phase during which they might have no clinical symptoms, but are very likely to do so. The process of establishing the diagnosis forms a third stage, and early and late HD comprise two further phases, each associated with some relatively distinctive issues. All too often, existing services are not merely inadequate but irrelevant, and we conclude the chapter by considering how to tailor services to the many different needs that HD families present.

EPIDEMIOLOGY

Recent estimates of prevalence in the UK are in the range 2 to 10 per 100,000 (Harper, 1991). Perhaps four times as many people are at 25% or 50% risk of HD. Genetic counseling has an impact on the epidemiology of HD (Quarrell et al., 1988).

The worldwide distribution of HD is irregular. The condition appears to be far more common in those of European descent than in other ethnic groups, and much of the variation in incidence outside Europe reflects patterns of European migration. There is, however, evidence of a separate mutational origin of HD in Japan (Masuda et al., 1995).

GENETICS

The genetics of HD must be understood by all those who work with HD patients and their families. HD is an autosomal dominant condition with virtually full penetrance, so that each offspring of an affected parent has a 1 in 2 risk of inheriting the mutant allele and of being affected, if he or she survives until the age of onset.

The HD gene (named IT15) was mapped to the tip of the short arm of chromosome 4 in 1983 (Gusella et al., 1983), and the responsible gene was identified in 1993 (Huntington's Disease Collaborative Research Group, 1993). The HD mutation is an expansion of a CAG repeat within the coding sequence of the gene, giving rise to an expanded polyglutamine tract in the protein product. The normal function of the HD gene product, huntingtin, is not yet known. In HD, and in several other progressive neurological disorders with the same mutational mechanism, CAG repeat expansion, occurring in different genes (Davies et al., 1998), appears to result from a new and actively deleterious property of the modified gene product (a so-called dominant negative effect) rather than a loss of its normal function. The pathogenesis of these conditions is probably related to the accumulation of polyglutamine-containing protein fragments, which are resistant to degradation, within the nuclei of neurones (Becher et al., 1998; Martindale et al., 1998).

Measurement of a subject's CAG repeat size by means of a polymerase chain reaction (PCR), using primers that hybridise to the sequences flanking the repeat region, is now a routine molecular test in genetic service laboratories. Because the repeat is polymorphic in the normal population, an unaffected individual's two copies of the gene will often have different repeat numbers. When this is not the case, and only a single normal sized signal is seen, the likeliest explanation is that the person has two chromosomes bearing CAG repeats of the same size. Because the efficiency of PCR falls with the length of the sequence being amplified, however, it might be advisable to carry out Southern blotting in such cases, to exclude an expansion that has not been detected by PCR.

Sensitivity and specificity of the mutational test for HD are very high, perhaps 100% (Kremer et al., 1994). When the test became available, over 95% of patients in whom a confident clinical diagnosis had been made were found to be carrying the mutation. Of the rest, a few were subsequently found to have an alternative well-characterised neurodegenerative disorder, such as dentatorubral and pallidoluysian atrophy, whereas in some of the remainder, the true diagnosis and its relationship to HD remains to be established (see, for example, Rosenblatt et al., 1998). Differential diagnosis is discussed later.

There is a positive correlation between the number of CAG repeats in the mutated copy of the gene and clinical severity, most easily expressed as an inverse correlation between repeat number and age of onset; however, apart from an association between juvenile HD and repeat numbers over 50, this is not very helpful clinically. At a neuropathological level, the correlation between repeat number and severity is closer (Penney et al., 1997).

The upper limit of CAG repeat number in the normal population is generally taken as 35, and values in the 30s are rare. Affected patients usually have one allele with over 40 CAG repeats. Alleles with 36–39 repeats might predispose to an atypically mild course with later onset, or apparent non-penetrance (Brinkman et al., 1997). Such alleles could expand further with transmission to offspring, and account for some cases of apparent "fresh mutation" (see later).

Intergenerational instability of repeat number is usually in an upwards direction, and is more marked with paternal than maternal transmission, accounting for the almost complete confinement of juvenile onset to offspring of affected fathers (De Rooji et al., 1993).

The mutation rate is low, and most new cases of HD have a parent with the HD gene. A parent surviving past middle age has usually been clinically affected by the time offspring develop symptoms (although occasionally the parent's symptoms develop later). If neither parent is affected, the likeliest explanation is non-paternity, the supposed father not being the biological parent.

PATHOLOGY AND NEUROIMAGING

HD is a degenerative disorder in which neuronal loss occurs especially in the caudate nucleus and putamen, with less involvement of cerebral cortex and other areas (Quarrell, 1991; Roos, 1986). Atrophy of the head of the caudate is a characteristic, but not universal, CT or MR scan finding. The severity of pathological changes is related to the number of CAG repeats (Furtado et al., 1996).

CLINICAL FEATURES

Natural history

In a South Wales series the peak age of onset was 41 years; onset was before age 20 in 4% and was 60 or above in 7% (Walker et al., 1981). However, onset is insidious (Penney et al., 1990; Young et al., 1986) and recorded age of onset depends on the sensitivity of assessment techniques. When the gene is inherited from the mother, the age of onset tends to be later than when the father is affected. Timing of onset is influenced by genetic factors so that variation in age of onset is greater between than within families, but this trend is not strong enough to be useful in predicting risks for individuals: an individual can develop HD at a later or earlier age than the age of onset in the parent. The time from diagnosis to death is typically 10–15 years (Walker et al., 1981) although the total duration of symptoms might be much longer. The spectrum of motor, psychiatric and cognitive impairments is relatively uniform but the order in which they evolve is variable. As the disease advances parkinsonism and dystonia become more prominent than chorea (Young et al., 1986).

Motor features

Involuntary movements including chorea are seen in most (but not all) patients at some stage in the disease. Patients often have little or no awareness of their movement disorder (Snowden et al., 1998). Chorea is a brief, flitting involuntary movement that can involve any muscle; in HD facial chorea is characteristic. Additional involuntary movements occur, and are often difficult to categorise. There is also failure to maintain sustained muscle contraction, sometimes termed motor impersistence. Gait is unsteady and has a dyspraxic quality. Apraxia can often be demonstrated in tests of upper limb and facial movement (Shelton & Knopman 1991). Dysarthria is present in the majority (Podoll et al., 1988; Young et al., 1986). Swallowing is impaired, a major factor being lack of coordination of the voluntary oral phase, so that the bolus is poorly formed and/or its transit to the automatic pharyngeal phase is mistimed (Hunt & Walker, 1989; Leopold & Kagel, 1985). Other motor signs include hyper-reflexia and abnormalities in both saccadic and slow pursuit eye movements. Parkinsonism tends to predominate in the early stages of juvenile HD but can also be prominent in adults.

Psychiatric disorders

Psychiatric disorders are almost universal. They can be the presenting problem and, as such, can lead to errors in diagnosis (Bolt, 1970; Dewhurst et al., 1970; Heathfield, 1967; Morris, 1991; Oliver, 1970; Pflanz et al., 1991). The severity of psychiatric manifestations is not correlated with the severity of other symptoms, or with the number of CAG repeats (Zappacosta et al., 1996).

Buxton (1976) differentiated three groups of symptoms: one group attributable to diffuse cerebral dysfunction; a second group, including amnesia and confusion, associated with dementia; and third, schizophrenia-like manifestations. Insidious changes in personality and behaviour often pre-date the first physical symptoms and then become increasingly obvious. Apathy can be a prominent feature, but a more common pattern is of irritability culminating in outbursts of verbal and physical aggression (Litvan et al., 1998). Outbursts are often triggered by trivial challenges to the patient's routine, and many patients display obsessional traits. A variety of sexual dysfunctions have been described, including excessive demands, violence, deviation, impotence and frigidity.

Major depressive illness is a common feature. There is increased risk of suicide, especially in the age group 50–69 (Schoenfield et al., 1984). Euphoria and manic episodes have been reported. There is also an increased incidence of schizophrenia-like psychotic illness (see Dewhurst et al., 1970;

Morris, 1991). This was the presenting syndrome in several members of one family (Lovestone et al., 1996).

Cognitive impairment

A wide range of cognitive impairments occur from the early stages of HD, severity being related to the number of CAG repeats (Jason et al., 1997; Lawrence et al., 1996). The rate and timing of cognitive decline varies considerably and is not reliably predicted by the severity of chorea (Girotti et al., 1988). Subtle intellectual decline, especially in executive function, is often detectable in carriers of the HD mutation before any symptoms are presented (Jason et al., 1997; Lawrence et al., 1998; Rosenberg et al., 1995). There is evidence that cognitive deterioration in HD is not uniform, and functions can be affected relatively selectively. This has important implications for rehabilitation.

In comparison with dementia of the Alzheimer type (DAT), HD has relatively little impact on language abilities (Aminoff et al., 1975; Butters et al., 1978; Podoll et al., 1988). However, spontaneous speech is often halting, punctuated by long pauses. There is markedly reduced verbal fluency, especially for production of words from initial letters (F, A, and S), and there are word-finding and naming difficulties, but frank aphasia is rare. Podoll et al. (1988) attribute deficits to a variety of non-linguistic factors such as impaired visual perception; they describe reduced conversational initiation. Reading is relatively preserved. Writing is impaired but specific dysgraphia is difficult to separate from many other contributory factors (Wallesch & Fehrenbach, 1988). Impairment in understanding the emotional content of speech has been reported (Speedie et al., 1990). As HD advances, the amount of functional communication decreases to the point that the patient usually becomes virtually mute in the late stages, when it is extremely difficult to gauge the extent of cognitive impairment.

Patients have been reported to have difficulty in planning, programming of cognitive and motor acts, and in shifting mental set and other tests of mental flexibility (Brandt & Butters, 1986). The pattern of deficits, with the absence of aphasia and agnosia, has led to the designation of HD as a subcortical dementia, although this concept is disputed.

Visuospatial tasks, such as map reading, and tasks that require attention and concentration seem to be performed more poorly in HD than in other dementing conditions (Butters et al., 1978). HD impairs performance in tests of procedural learning (Saint-Cyr et al., 1988), and hence the capacity for learning new skills might be less than in other memory disorders, for example following brain trauma, where procedural learning is relatively spared (see Chapter 10). However, this is a relative weakness, not an absolute one.

It is thought that impairment in memory is mainly due to defective recall rather than encoding (Butters et al., 1978). This too can have implications for management, such as the use of prompting and cueing strategies, although in clinical practice the picture can be complicated by apathy and attentional deficits.

Other clinical features

Incontinence of urine and faeces is a late complication, probably related to dementia rather than to other neurological factors. Seizures occur in a small minority of adults, but are more common in juvenile HD (Brackenridge, 1980).

PEOPLE AT RISK OF HD

Needs of people at risk of HD

It would be difficult to overestimate the severe psychological burdens imposed on individuals and on families by the risk of HD. Unaffected family members have an increased risk of suicide and of psychiatric disorders (Oliver, 1970). A familiar syndrome is the adolescent whose behaviour becomes disturbed and disruptive, with deterioration in school or work performance, frequent absences, and (potentially) promiscuity. The possibility is often raised that such abrupt changes in behaviour herald the onset of HD, but in many cases they are signals of distress that require a constructive response (Folstein et al., 1983b).

Perceptions of HD within families vary greatly: a close relative with severe physical impairments, or especially psychiatric illness, can produce a very negative image of HD in the family. There are likely to be overtones of fear, guilt, and social stigma. The result is that many people at risk of HD are reluctant to seek professional help. They could resort to a variety of coping mechanisms, which can be destructive. Martindale (1987) describes psychodynamic mechanisms that are adopted by HD families, including denial and rationalisation. Illustrative case histories are provided by Lam et al. (1988), Wolff (1988), and Hunt and Walker (1991). Irrational beliefs are common, for example a family might assume that one at-risk member is destined to be affected and that the others will be spared (Kessler, 1988). Individuals at risk for HD are liable to assume that they definitely are, or definitely are not, affected. They are liable to overinterpret trivial symptoms, and parents of at-risk children are similarly prone to "symptom-searching" (Korer & Fitzsimmons, 1981). Anxiety is often compounded by ignorance, and provision of reliable information is likely to be helpful for most people at risk of HD. The Huntington's Disease Association (see Useful Addresses) provides material geared to children, young adults, and older adults. The greatest need, however, is for committed case-work. Wolff (1988) suggests that a professional can provide a "third person" who is in a unique position to share some of the family's concerns and to facilitate positive responses.

Genetic counselling

People need genetic advice for a number of reasons. Some are concerned lest their own children develop HD, whereas others take the view that an illness that develops in middle age is offset by the possibility of a fulfilling life prior to, and even after, clinical symptoms of HD. In our experience, the latter attitude seems to be associated with families in which the psychological and behavioural effects of HD have been relatively mild or

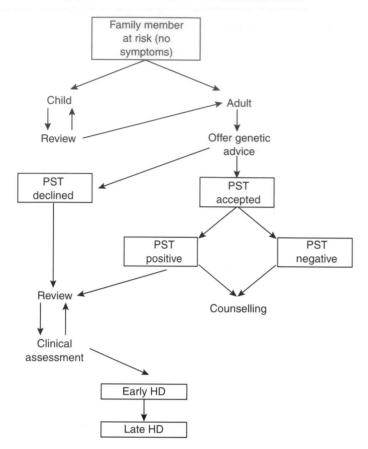

Figure 40.1. Management options for those at risk of Huntington's disease. PST, presymptomatic testing.

inconspicuous. By contrast, someone who has had severe social, psychological, or practical difficulties in childhood, adolescence, or later as a result of the illness of a parent might wish to be assured of a low risk lest such harrowing experiences be relived by his or her own children. Finally, the possibility of predictive testing motivates some people who wish to be relieved of uncertainty about their future. They might sometimes be gambling on a negative result with the expectation of despair if the risk is found to be high, or they might feel capable of accepting a high risk, wishing to plan their lives appropriately.

Figure 40.1 outlines the mangement of those at risk of HD, from the genetic point of view. The primary aim of the clinical genetics service is to provide an accessible and intelligible source of information to those at risk of HD, so that they can make informed choices, for example about the option of presymptomatic testing. Children can also benefit from genetic advice, but their needs must be clearly differentiated from those of adults and handled differently. The term "client" is used in this discussion, in preference both to "patient" (which the at-risk individual is not) and the unwieldy genetics jargon "consultand".

The first step following referral for genetic advice is to gather background information on:

1. *The family history*. A pedigree is constructed with as much detail as possible on at least first, second and third degree

relatives, extending further afield if appropriate. Names, dates of birth, whereabouts or place of death and affected/unaffected status, with clinical details if known, should be recorded.

2. *The client's concept of HD*. Recording the family history will often help one to explore this, as the client can be encouraged to recount his or her personal experience of the condition. The client's emotional responses to this process are often revealing. Misconceptions and important gaps in knowledge should be noted, as it might be important to correct them.

3. *The client's own background and agenda*. How long has he or she been aware of the genetic risk of HD in the family? Why has he or she come now? What are the main issues and questions, and how do these impinge on the client's immediate family?

4. *The basis for the diagnosis in the family*. Where only clinical descriptions of family cases are available, the diagnosis should not be accepted uncritically. Hospital records should show evidence of at least two of the following: (1) dementia; (2) motor impairments such as dyskinesia or speech impairment; and (3) psychiatric disturbance. Clear-cut caudate atrophy on a CT scan is helpful, but not pathognomonic. If an affected relative is thought to have had a molecular test, this should be noted and confirmation obtained. If a molecular test has not been carried out in the family, but a living affected person is available, it can be appropriate to suggest that a diagnostic test be carried out on that person, as good clinical practice. Where only deceased affected persons are known, neuropathological confirmation of the diagnosis should be sought, but even autopsy evidence is not always decisive in the absence of clinical data. The possibilities of extracting DNA from post-mortem tissue samples should be explored. If only fixed sections are available, the success rate, in our experience, is low. Where there is no molecular confirmation of the diagnosis in a family, it should be made clear to at-risk clients that diagnosis of HD is an assumption that is not fully proven, even if neuropathological evidence is available. This is obviously most important when anticipating how much reliance can be placed on a normal predictive test result.

The client should then be given some basic information about HD, including the natural history, variable age of onset and common clinical presentations. Any misapprehensions that have been noted should be corrected. These are common and include: that only one sex is at risk (if the pedigree appears to indicate this); that affected people are always violent; that there is an age, such as 50, beyond which at-risk people are no longer at risk.

The client's prior risk of carrying the mutation, based on the pedigree, should be discussed, as this is a common area for misunderstanding. The 50% risk to offspring of an affected parent falls progressively as long as the offspring remains asymptomatic, to around 30% in the mid-40s. The grandchildren of an affected person, whose at-risk parent remains unaffected in middle age, can be at lower risk than they imagine.

The general discussion of risk and prognosis, as outlined earlier, should take place before any specific discussion of presymptomatic testing. It should also be separated as far as possible from dealing with management of an affected relative, which is often simultaneously pressing. At-risk clients should feel that the consultation is theirs and not an adjunct to that of their affected relative. Dealing with their problems in a separate genetic clinic is helpful in this respect.

Presymptomatic testing

Presymptomatic testing for HD was the subject of much discussion between 1986, when an indirect approach using linked genetic markers became possible in a minority of families, and 1993, when the direct mutation test became available (Simpson & Harding, 1993). Similar discussions were taking place around testing for HIV, and in both situations there was general agreement that people should be helped to make an informed decision whether to take the test, together with professional concern about taking the responsibility for giving bad news to large numbers of well people (Craufurd & Tyler, 1992).

Research protocols were devised to assess the risk of adverse outcomes and identify prognostic factors. These, minus the collection of detailed psychometric data, have formed the basis for practice protocols in current use (Craufurd & Tyler, 1992; International Huntington Association and World Federation of Neurology, 1994). Experience has shown a low risk of morbidity following presymptomatic testing in previously psychiatrically well individuals, especially those who have known about their at-risk status for some months or years (Bundey, 1997). It was felt as helpful by some that presymptomatic testing using linked markers before 1993 imposed a delay, because a test could not be offered until samples had been collected from relatives and their informativeness assessed, allowing time for two or more pretest counselling sessions. The number of at-risk people undergoing presymptomatic testing remained low prior to 1993, probably because of the complicated nature of the test and the need to involve relatives, and increased rapidly once a "stand alone" test was available.

The United Kingdom Huntington's Prediction Consortium was set-up in 1990 (Craufurd & Tyler, 1992). It holds yearly meetings and compiles data on the number of tests carried out in the UK. In early 1999, approximately 3000 mutational predictive tests had been carried out since 1993, and the rate of testing seemed to be settling at 400–450 per year (R. Glew, personal communication). It also provides a forum in which difficult clinical issues can be discussed. It has been proposed that HD should be taken as a model for presymptomatic testing, and arrangements for that condition should be followed in other late onset neurological disorders. Although this might be appropriate for other conditions with progressive, ultimately severe, mental and physical disability, we feel that for milder conditions it might not be necessary; however, relevant experience is still slight and it seems wise to sound a note of caution in presymptomatic testing for any untreatable condition.

The presymptomatic testing protocol used by most clinical genetics service in the UK entails a series of sessions, usually shared between medical staff and specialist genetic nurses. This arrangement allows a great deal of flexibility, and also helps members of the team to support each other through difficult clinical decisions. Involvement of a rehabilitation neurologist in the presymptomatic testing process has the advantage of allowing continuity of follow-up for those who are tested positive and wish to be reviewed subsequently. The protocol typically includes:

- One or two sessions on the general features and inheritance of HD.
- Two sessions to concentrate on the issues of presymptomatic testing, at the second of which blood is taken if the client still wishes to go ahead.
- In some centres, one pretest session is routinely arranged with a psychiatrist, as a means of reducing the risk of a severe psychiatric reaction following the test. In other centres, pretest psychiatric advice is only offered to clients at increased risk, for example those with a past history of psychiatric disorder.
- A session at which the result is given, always done face to face, usually 3–4 weeks after the sample is taken.
- Appropriate follow-up arrangements. Follow-up is important because predictive testing can be stressful whether the result is negative or positive (Codori & Brandt, 1994). Counselling might be required following a negative result if it causes guilt through separation from other family members, such as siblings, who previously shared the same burden of risk. Follow-up arrangements will have been discussed before the test; we prefer to tailor arrangements to individual needs rather than follow a protocol. Contact is made within the week after giving the result, either by telephone or by means of a home visit by a genetic nurse specialist. After this, requirements for follow-up depend on the result of the test and on individual preferences.

The aim of pretest counselling sessions is to help clients make a choice that they will not regret, between knowledge and ignorance. It might be important to help them to examine their motives for requesting testing, and whether they have a realistic grasp of what it will be like to have a result. This might include the impact of the result on their close family relationships, something many people seem to take for granted. During these sessions it is worth reminding clients that remaining in ignorance is a valid option, and one that leaves them with a choice for the future; that they can withdraw from the test procedure at any time, right up to being given the result; that a positive result shows that they have the gene, but does not specify the age of onset; that the result is theirs and they are not obliged to share it with anybody, and that it is usually a mistake to take a test for someone else's sake if one does not wish it for oneself.

At-risk clients sometimes resent attending pre-test counselling sessions and waiting at least 2–3 months before being tested. These often seem to be people who have recently found out about their risk, and who are, effectively, gambling on a favourable result without having thought through the implications of having the gene. Although not advocating excessive paternalism, we feel it is usually in the client's interests to refuse demands for instant testing. One can do so in the knowledge that the client will find it extremely difficult to obtain an instant test through any clinical genetics unit in the UK, thanks to informal agreements on clinical protocols within the HD Predictive Testing Consortium, to which all units offering the test belong.

Some questions we have found useful in presymptomatic counselling sessions are as follows:

- Why are you requesting a test now?
- With whom, inside and outside your family, have you discussed this?
- With whom do you intend to share the result?
- Who will come with you to the remaining sessions, particularly the result session?
- What practical decisions will be altered by the result (especially career and reproduction)?
- Have you been worried that you might be showing signs of HD already?
- Have you imagined how it would feel to be told that you carry the gene?
- If you were found to carry the gene, would you want to be examined to see whether you were showing any signs of the condition?
- If the result will alter risks for existing children, are they aware you are being tested? If not, what do you propose to do if you are shown to have the gene?

Stress levels in spouses and partners are at least as high as in the primary clients, and sometimes higher; their needs must be fully considered (Quaid & Wesson, 1995).

Sometimes, a client who attends for presymptomatic testing is thought by the clinician almost certainly to be showing signs of early HD. As mentioned below, these can be very subtle, and are often unnoticed by both patients and their relatives. When testing was by linked markers with a possibility of a false negative result, it was important to exclude such clients, in case they were given false reassurance. The situation has now changed, and we feel that these requests can be taken at face value and managed as presymptomatic tests. This is often helpful in allowing the client to come to terms with the problem in two stages: first, possession of the gene is demonstrated, then, a choice can be offered between early detection of clinical signs and non-intervention until they become obvious. We do, however, ask clients, before carrying out the test, whether they think they are showing signs of the condition, whether they would like to be examined to look for these, and whether they would like to be examined if the test is positive. We also try to ascertain whether any accompanying relatives are suspicious. It is also important to identify tests in this category separately in collections of data on predictive testing.

Ethical issues in genetics

Predictive testing raises ethical problems that must be understood by all those who work with HD families (Tyler & Morris, 1990).

Children. The testing of children for late onset genetic disorders has been widely discussed and is the subject of a report from the Clinical Genetics Society (1994). The consensus among UK clinical geneticists is that presymptomatic testing for a condition like HD, for which there is no preventive measure or early treatment, should not be offered unless the subject can make a fully informed decision, and this excludes most young people under 16. In practice, requests for presymptomatic testing are rare under 20. When requests are received from teenagers, the most important criterion is the person's ability to understand the issues and reach an informed decision.

Confidentiality. Confidentiality is obviously of paramount importance at all stages in the process of genetic assessment and counselling. One common dilemma is posed when a person at risk of HD chooses not to inform other family members of his or her risks. A judgement must sometimes be made between the client's right to confidentiality and the rights of relatives to have the opportunity for genetic advice. Another dilemma can arise when a person's DNA test result is requested from a different centre to confirm the HD mutation in a family, without that person's knowledge. Ideally, the client would ask the affected relative for signed consent before results are released, and most genetics laboratories require such consent. Often, however, clients are reluctant to make the request.

Genetic registers for HD, comprising computerised lists of members of affected families, are kept by some regional clinical genetics centres. The aims of such registers are: (1) to ensure that individuals are assigned to the correct kindred, and avoid multiple registrations of a single family; (2) to help in identifying at-risk individuals who might benefit from the offer of genetic counselling and testing. An important subset of this group consists of at-risk children, who will require follow-up when they are older. Most genetic registers were established when issues of consent and confidentiality were less prominent than they are today, and the potential benefits and pitfalls of genetic registers might need to be reassessed (Dean et al., 1998).

Implications for a parent of a person tested positive for the HD mutation. If a person at 25% risk of HD is tested positive for the HD mutation, the mutation must also be present in the parent who was previously at 50% risk. Ethical difficulties therefore arise when presymptomatic testing is requested by the offspring of an at-risk person who is uncontactable or unwilling to be tested, or when the person requesting testing wishes to have this done without the knowledge of his or her parent. All reasonable steps should be taken to offer testing to the person who was originally at 50% risk. If this is rejected, or if contact is impossible or denied, and the client insists on his or her right to a test, one might have to proceed, after pointing out the potential drawbacks of generating a positive result on the parent without his or her consent.

Antenatal testing. A similar situation arises when an at-risk person requests testing of the fetus for the HD mutation during a pregnancy. In these cases, although time is often limited, it seems clear that the correct course of action is to offer testing to the at-risk parent and only to carry out antenatal diagnosis if the fetus is shown to be at risk.

The procedure known as exclusion testing can be used to show whether the fetus is at high (usually 50%) risk or at very low risk without revealing the genetic status of the at-risk parent. This depends on testing for linked genetic markers rather than for the HD mutation. The test shows whether the fetus has inherited, via its at-risk parent, a gene from its affected or its unaffected grandparent, without knowing whether the former is the affected grandparent's mutated or normal allele.

Although exclusion testing generated considerable interest in the early days of molecular testing for HD, there seems to have been little demand for it. The ethical rationale of the procedure is that couples agree to termination of pregnancy if there is a 50% risk that the fetus will be affected.

It is generally agreed that couples should be discouraged from antenatal testing for HD, whether mutational or exclusion testing, unless they express an intention to terminate the pregnancy if the fetus is shown to be affected (or at high risk). Otherwise, a predictive test will have been performed on an individual who is unable to give informed consent.

THE PRESYMPTOMATIC PHASE

As shown in Fig. 40.1, regular review might be requested by two groups of asymptomatic people: those who decline presymptomatic testing, and those who have tested positive for the HD mutation. As in the case of clinical assessment prior to presymptomatic testing (see earlier) it is important for the clinician and the client to have a clear understanding of the purposes of clinical review. Such clients might simply wish to obtain renewed confidence that they are *not* affected. This places the neurologist in a difficult dilemma, because the diagnosis depends on a constellation of features, none of which individually is a reliable predictor of HD. It is important for the client to understand that there can be genuine clinical uncertainty because of the subtlety of early clinical signs, and we normally discuss this before carrying out presymptomatic testing. Otherwise, the client might suspect that he or she is not being told everything. We believe that the physician has a responsibility to indicate to the client and family when HD is strongly suspected. However, the grounds for such suspicions must be concrete, as both the physician and the subject are easily swayed by subjective factors. Given the difficulty in judging when to make an unequivocal diagnosis, there are disadvantages in the practice of annually reviewing at-risk subjects and routinely assessing them for subtle symptoms and signs.

Nevertheless, there are potential advantages for the asymptomatic client who remains in regular contact with a rehabilitation-orientated physician. In the first place, the physician can sometimes provide unequivocal reassurance about symptoms that are clearly unrelated to HD. Second, early recognition of some symptoms (for example, mood disorders) can lead to more effective treatment. A third function of regular review is perhaps the most important: it allows a relationship of trust to build up between the client and the doctor. This is especially valuable when, as frequently occurs, the person has little insight into the importance of early symptoms that pose problems for a spouse or other family members. Such a person will sometimes accept advice from a familiar physician, but not from a stranger.

Making the diagnosis

As always in neurology, the process of diagnosis is inseparably linked with that of management, both of the patient and of the family as a whole. The needs of relatives place additional burdens on the physician when making the diagnosis of any genetic condition but never more so than in HD, because its dominant inheritance and relatively uniform clinical expression mean that the future prognosis of a large number of people is often in the balance.

Clinical diagnosis. In assessing the patient, a "gestalt" clinical impression, derived from such features as facial expression, speech, and chorea, together with knowledge of previous family history can be correct but is insufficiently specific. A basic diagnostic routine should allow most cases to be diagnosed and documented adequately by experienced non-neurologists. A minority require further assessment by a neurologist but a poorly documented diagnosis, even if made by a neurologist, is of limited value.

The history should include enquiries for early evidence of everyday cognitive failures or change in personality or behaviour. Among the most predictive physical signs are typical motor impersistence or chorea, defects in alternating voluntary saccades, and impaired heel–toe gait. These should be documented specifically and additional objective data such as handwriting specimens or video recordings are desirable. A Quantitative Neurological Examination (QNE) has been extensively used for research purposes (Folstein et al., 1983a) and the United Huntington Disease Rating Scale provides another research tool for monitoring progression (Huntington Study Group, 1996). A schedule for documenting functional capacities has been used extensively by Shoulson's group (e.g. Young et al., 1986) and is reproduced in Harper (1991).

Psychometry. Short cognitive screening tests, such as the "Mini-mental" are insufficiently sensitive, and more extensive cognitive testing is helpful in cases of diagnostic doubt (for example, in the absence of a clear family history). A more appropriate Dementia Rating Scale was used by Salmon et al. (1989). Group studies have shown cognitive impairments in early HD (Butters et al., 1978; Salmon et al., 1989). However, cognitive impairment in early HD can be equivocal. A recent study found no evidence of cognitive or emotional differences between individuals with and without genetic markers indicating high risk for HD (Strauss & Brandt, 1990). Serial neuropsychological testing is more useful diagnostically than any single test, because the presence or absence of progression over months or years can assist in the classification of doubtful cases. Psychometry is also, of course, useful in the assessment of abilities and disabilities for purposes of rehabilitation.

DNA testing as an aid to clinical diagnosis. Unlike some other genetic tests, which have exposed a previously unsuspected spectrum of disease, this one has not greatly altered our clinical concept of the condition. There have not been large numbers of clinically atypical cases diagnosed as HD. Nevertheless, the availability of a sensitive and specific molecular test for HD has inevitably led to its use in clinical situations where the prior probability of the diagnosis has not seemed high. It seems appropriate that highly sensitive and specific molecular diagnostic tests should take their place in the neurologist's repertoire, and be used early in the diagnostic process to avoid the use of more invasive and costly investigations. The proprietorial attitude often taken by clinical geneticists towards DNA testing can appear to be an attempt to stifle this trend. Many genetics laboratories have asked clinicians to sign a form before carrying out a diagnostic test for HD, confirming that: (1) the patient and family have been appropriately counselled about the implications of a positive diagnosis; and (2) the test is a diagnostic and not a presymptomatic one. Although it seems likely that clinical genetics will maintain its control of presymptomatic testing, neurologists might feel that they can be left to use their own judgement about what they tell patients and their families before carrying out an investigation with a low index of suspicion.

Differential diagnosis

Some conditions that can be confused with HD are shown in Table 40.1. Pedigrees in which dementia is not conspicuous are especially suspect because they can be confused with other causes of myoclonus, chorea, dystonia, or parkinsonism. However, dementia in HD can be inconspicuous for many years, and DNA testing has demonstrated the mutation in families where the presumptive clinical diagosis was idiopathic chorea (Brittan et al., 1995). The occurrence of parkinsonism or myoclonus in Alzheimer's disease is a source of potential difficulty. In one HD clinic, 9% of referrals had no family history; those found to have the HD mutation were more likely to have a lesser number of CAG repeats and to present solely with chorea (Nance et al., 1996). In another specialist clinic, patients with features similar to HD but without the mutation included a few who appeared to have a familial disease phenotypically indistinguishable from HD (Rosenblatt et al., 1998). Dentatorubropallidoluysian atrophy can produce a picture similar to HD. A high degree of intrafamilial variability, with cerebellar manifestations, euphoria and epilepsy, should raise suspicions.

Table 40.1. Differential diagnosis of HD

Main clinical features	Diagnosis
Dyskinesia	Chorea*
	Tardive dyskinesia
Dementia ± movement disorder	Alzheimer's disease*
	Prion disease*
	Neuroacanthosis**
	Tau body dementia
	Frontal lobe dementia
	Mitochondrial cytopathy
	Parkinson's disease*
	Multisystem atrophy**
	Dentatorubropallidoluysian atrophy*

* Sporadic or autosomal dominant, ** autosomal recessive.

Communicating the diagnosis and prognosis

Martindale (1987) points out that professionals, like patients and their families, are subject to psychological mechanisms that cloud the issue: for example, denial of the seriousness of the prognosis; evasion of problems through the assumption that HD is incurable and that nothing can be done; and omission of any reference to genetic implications. The needs of other relatives must always be considered and it is desirable that all branches of the family be given the opportunity to obtain professional advice about genetic risks.

The family's preconceptions must be kept in mind when communicating the prognosis following diagnosis. Emotive images of an affected parent often distort expectations and must be understood by the physician, as by others who might be involved at this stage. Quoting an average disease duration of 10–20 years gives little indication of how disability will evolve, and it should be remembered that most data are based on observations of groups of patients following symptomatic presentation, and give little idea of what to expect, for example, following predictive testing of an asymptomatic person who is shown to be at high risk.

Coming to terms with the diagnosis, and acquiring appropriate information, is a gradual process. An early goal of management is to identify a professional key-worker who is trusted by the patient and the family (Yale & Martindale, 1984). A social worker should become involved as early as possible, although sometimes an alternative key-worker, such as a genetic counsellor or a local nurse, might emerge. Many people with neurological disorders, and especially those with dementia, will reject such help but HD families are often markedly reclusive. In many cases this seems to be because of an unarticulated sense of social alienation caused by a disease that stigmatises the whole family.

There is a need for appropriate packages of information to be channelled to the patient and family and, equally importantly, community-based professionals such as the family physician, whose knowledge of HD is necessarily limited. For these purposes, an organisation such as the Huntington's Disease Association can be invaluable.

Detailed prognostication is often misleading, but the patient should understand in general terms the implications of HD, particularly as it affects employment and financial prospects. Psychometry can be useful in either confirming suspected deficits or in showing that abilities are preserved. A practical point is the need to consider the likelihood that driving will become impossible. Some families, if they are able to contemplate the likelihood of progressive dementia, might wish to consult a lawyer so that contingency plans can be made for assigning power of attorney when the need arises.

EARLY HD: PREVENTING COMPLICATIONS

As Lavers (1983) suggests, the emphasis in management of early HD should be preventive. Meeting the needs of patients and families requires regular, continuing contact and an ability to respond appropriately to the earliest signs of dysfunction. The involvement of other members of the professional team, including the family practitioner, the community nurse, the speech therapist, and the occupational therapist, will be more effective if coordinated by a key worker. The work of Korer and Fitzsimmons (1981) and of Yale and Martindale (1984) suggest that a social worker could often fulfill this role. In early HD the key worker can sometimes act to prevent too many overenthusiastic individuals becoming involved too quickly. However, it should be emphasised that the role of HD key worker is emotionally stressful and professionals working with HD must themselves have access to adequate support.

For many patients, the presenting problem is psychiatric (Dewhurst et al., 1970; Walker et al., 1981) and psychiatrists are often the most appropriate starting point for the management of family issues, as well as specific psychiatric symptoms. There is some scope for a preventive strategy. All those involved in the psychological support of patients and families need to understand the many functional as well as organic factors (Dewhurst et al., 1970; Martindale, 1987). Depression and anxiety can sometimes be related to obvious stresses such as the emotional trauma caused by the illness of a parent, and often of other relatives; the experience of being at risk for HD; the often appalling burden that follows the diagnosis; the anticipation of known and imagined future problems; and the experience of ensuing physical disabilities, communication impairment, and social problems. However, psychiatric disorders are often directly attributable to underlying cerebral changes. Deterioration in personality and behaviour can be obvious (and highly distressing) to the family, although sometimes difficult to describe.

The earliest evidence of dementia is often a decline in work performance, with lapses in memory and failure to plan efficiently. Evaluation of cognitive decline is complicated by parallel changes in mood and the first object of management is therefore to identify reactive depression and treat formal depressive illness appropriately. Neuropsychological assessment can assist in distinguishing between organic and functional factors but in many circumstances an empirical trial of an antidepressant drug can be justified. Early in the development of dementia the patient should be encouraged to establish routines such as the use of memory aids. Those who provide day and

respite care late in the disease, when communication is severely limited, often regret that they were not introduced to the patient at an earlier stage when relationships can more easily be formed and personality and preferences understood.

Social problems such as loss of employment and disruption of family life need to be anticipated. Korer and Fitzsimmons (1981) studied 12 HD families, including 44 children. Some families, categorised as "independently oriented" led an active life outside the home. Other, "HD oriented" families were introspective, insular, and socially isolated; they were dominated by considerations of HD. All the male patients had had manual occupations and all were out of work. One had lost his job because of repeated violence; another had crashed the bus he drove. All the families experienced some degree of financial hardship. Many of the families' experiences were similar to those encountered in other disabling disorders, for example changes in marital roles with increasing dominance of the unaffected spouse, and lack of outside help, partly as a result of appearing to cope despite severe psychological stresses within the home. It was sometimes feared that symptoms of HD in a child might be provoked by unrealistic "triggers", and this was given as a reason for failing to discipline children. A social worker with experience of HD will be able to help to prevent or at least mitigate many of these problems, working with the family, liaising with employers so as to maintain regular occupation if possible, and providing access to sources of information and support.

Neurologists, as opposed to psychiatrists, tend to see a population of patients in whom motor features are the presenting feature, although not necessarily the most important current problem. Involuntary movements are often first noticed by members of the family rather than by the patient, who in the early stages often seems to be neither embarrassed nor disabled by them. In this respect early HD resembles the milder forms of other dyskinesias caused by basal ganglia pathology, but in HD both the family and the patient are often aware of the momentous implications of even minor degrees of clumsiness or jerkiness. Tetrabenazine is often prescribed but its non-specific action as a depletor of catecholamines leads to parkinsonism and depression. Jankovic and Orman (1988) described the results of tetrabenazine treatment in a large series of patients, including a relatively small number with HD. Depression occurred in 10% of the series; the therapeutic response in HD was described as moderate. In our experience tetrabenazine rarely decreases functional disability.

Physical disability, as distinct from impairment, might not be conspicuous in the early years, and those without major psychiatric disturbance can retain normal occupations for some time. It is difficult to involve remedial therapists at a time that is neither too late to establish optimal practices, for example in speech and swallowing, nor too early to be accepted by the patient. Nutrition is one aspect of preventive care that most patients will readily accept: body weight should be charted, and early evidence of feeding or swallowing difficulties monitored.

Good preventive dentistry pays dividends later in the disease, removing avoidable contributions to both feeding difficulties and dysarthria. Mouth-breathing can cause drying of the mouth, which leads to increased swallowing difficulties, infection, and loose dentures.

In summary, goals of early management should be primarily preventive and should always include the patient as well as family members, who can benefit from a variety of services (Lavers, 1983; Shoulson & Behr, 1989). These include a system of preventive surveillance, coordinated by a key worker (probably a social worker); information and support from the Huntington's Disease Association; genetic advice, as desired; and prevention and treatment of primary and secondary psychiatric disorders. For the patient specifically, drug treatment of chorea and other complications is indicated only for functionally relevant goals. Promotion of optimal physical health includes monitoring of nutritional status and dental care. Links should be formed, if possible, with therapy and support services, partly as a means of increasing their acceptability at later stages of the disease.

ASPECTS OF REHABILITATION IN ADVANCED HD

Physical health and well-being

Dysphagia is the rule in late HD and swallowing should be assessed early, to prevent psychological aversion as well as physical complications. Although bolus formation is defective (Kagel & Leopold, 1992) the scope for remedial therapy is probably limited, especially as orofacial dyspraxia might be implicated. Therapy is likely to be directed towards changes in the environment, alleviation of anxieties of patient and carers, and adjustments to feeding routines and food consistency. Weighted cuffs were helpful in one patient (Lavers, 1983).

There is thought to be an increased caloric requirement, perhaps as a result of chorea or possibly because of neuroendocrine dysfunction. Daily intake as high as 5000 kcal per day may be required, and dietetic advice is needed.

Patients with severe chorea pose specific nursing problems. A patient of ours had severe chorea, requiring her at one stage to be strapped into her chair. Chorea caused damage to the plaster wall next to her bed (it is interesting that her adult sister had had parkinsonism rather than chorea; Hayden (1981) illustrates a similar pair of sisters). It is often preferable for the patient to sleep on a mattress on the floor. Specially designed cushioned seating, or bean-bags, may be needed (Lavers, 1983).

Preventing complications

Preventive management of nutritional problems is described above. Preventive physiotherapy is required because of the risk of contractures, as the patient tends progressively to adopt a flexed posture, especially in the late stages when chorea is less obvious. Hydrotherapy has been recommended (Sheaff, 1990). Inanition and contractures, and sometimes incontinence, add to the risk of pressure sores. Attempts to prevent contractures are sometimes in conflict with the desire for cushioned seating which may lead to poor sitting posture.

Independence

Mobility. Impaired gait and balance is an important source of disability and dependency. Mobility within and outside the home becomes dangerous because of falling, which the patient might take insufficient trouble to prevent. Walking aids are of little value because they tend to be used erratically (perhaps reflecting dyspraxia). The patient quickly loses competence in driving, and the process of seeking other modes of transport should begin early. The spouse should, of course, be encouraged to drive from the outset.

Self-care. Reduced manual dexterity causes difficulty in many everyday tasks. Physical disabilities are often compounded by cognitive factors, which limit the ability to follow a routine such as a recipe. Behavioural factors contribute greatly to dependency. It becomes difficult to leave the patient unsupervised because chores are left undone. Safety is an important consideration: smoking and other sources of flame are hazardous.

Few studies have evaluated the effectiveness of attempts to maintain or improve self-caring ability. One study used a single case design for 8 months in four patients with severe cognitive impairment, to assess the effect of occupational therapy on daily living skills during 16 weeks of treatment, but no improvement was found (Mason et al., 1991). This is in accord with the reported deficits in procedural learning (Saint Cyr, 1988) but does not reduce the need for occupational therapy involvement in planning the home environment.

Lifestyle

Communication and social participation. In addition to obtaining formal speech therapy advice, one of the aims of early management should be to increase the family's motivation to facilitate communication by some means. Silence should not automatically be attributed to severe dementia. Hearing should be assessed at an early stage. An effort should be made to introduce effective communication aids, but in practice these rarely seem to be useful, perhaps because of behavioural factors.

Mood and behaviour. There is little literature on the management of problems related to dementia in HD, for example disinhibited behaviour, sexual inappropriateness, and wandering, but the principles of management are similar to those required in other dementias. In the management of behaviour disorders attention must first be given to remediable factors such as impaired communication social isolation and family stresses (for which respite admissions might be helpful). Major tranquillisers must be used sparingly, to avoid both sedation and additional motor deficits.

Roles and occupations. The ending of employment should not mean the end of any form of meaningful occupation. Day centres designed for people with disabilities can provide appropriate occupations, social stimulation, and also much-needed respite for carers.

Social support

As HD advances, many families are placed under great strain and might be more able to cope with behavioural and physical problems if they receive increased levels of support. Some potential sources of advice and support are described in the next section. Respite care is often helpful and can sometimes be achieved in a residential unit for disabled adults, in a private nursing home, or occasionally in a psychiatric ward. At this stage, and when permanent residential care is needed, it is important that provision is based on the patient's needs rather than on diagnosis. Many residential units are wary of HD because of a minority of severely disruptive patients. In practice, many patients with advanced HD do not cause problems for units catering for people with a range of disabling disorders. The greatest difficulties are caused by patients who are confused but are still able to walk, and potentially to fall. Residential staff need to be educated about the special problems—including nutritional requirements—of people with HD.

DESIGNING SERVICES FOR HD

The nature of HD constrains the development of suitable services. There is as yet no satisfactory model for the provision of services to people with HD and what follows is an outline of three key issues: the geographical problem that arises with any relatively uncommon neurological disorder, the difficulty of providing for a wide range of needs, and the special requirements of HD families.

One group of problems arises from the relative rarity of HD. Patients and families need local expertise to coordinate teamwork, preventive surveillance, and continuity of care. Because HD is uncommon, family practitioners and other community personnel lack the necessary expertise. In the UK, specialist services are often separated from patients' and clients' homes by a journey of an hour or more and are not always accessible where they are most needed, in the community.

A second problem is that individuals' needs are very diverse, and change radically as the disease progresses. The gulf that separates early from late multiple sclerosis is no wider than that which separates the earliest from the latest forms of HD. No single service, and no single resource, would be acceptable to all patients and families at all stages. Moreover, there are needs that transcend boundaries between clinical genetics, neurology, medical rehabilitation, and psychiatry. Surveys of people with HD indicate high levels of unmet need (Skirton & Glendinning, 1997). In the UK, there is no service that comfortably accommodates the combination of physical disabilities, psychiatric illness, and cognitive impairment that affects many people in the late stages of HD. The lack of provision for so-called "multiple disability" is especially severe for middle-aged adults and also hampers the management of some survivors of severe closed head injury (see Chapter 35); however, there are difficulties in integrating sevices for people with head injury with services for a progressive condition such as HD.

A third consideration is that HD is a family problem. This is true of other disabling disorders in the sense that their impact is felt not only by the patient but also by other potential "clients" (see Chapter 2). In HD, however, there is a need for a scheme of management that meets the needs not only of carers, but also of those who are themselves at risk, a proportion of whom subsequently become affected. Rehabilitation of the patient with HD begins *before diagnosis*. Good management of asymptomatic people at risk for HD should contribute to quality of management following the onset of symptoms. Good management of the patient creates a better climate for the future management of other members of the family who subsequently become affected. For these reasons it is difficult, and undesirable, to separate genetic services from other aspects of rehabilitation. In practice, genetic counselling is much more than the assignation of genetic risks and must respond to the needs of the family as a whole, even if only to the extent of mobilising other resources, such as those of social work, neurology, and psychiatry. For the same reasons, doctors, therapists, social workers, and others who are involved in the rehabilitation of a patient with HD cannot be divorced from the genetic issues, and must be aware of the wider needs of the family.

Teamwork and professional resources

No single profession can meet all the needs of HD families, and a specialist HD team is desirable in order to establish efficient links with a wide range of services. Local circumstances will determine the core team's composition and leadership, but the essential components include:

- *Genetics.* The Regional Genetics Service provides genetic counselling, predictive testing, and information for patients and families within a population typically of 2–5 million. Genetics nurse specialists are key members of the team, contacting and supporting families throughout the process of assessment, counselling, and testing.
- *Neurology.* A neurologist with a special interest in HD can assist in assessing and advising those at risk, reviewing clients in the presymptomatic phase, establishing the diagnosis and supervising medical treatment thereafter.
- *Psychiatry.* A psychiatrist is an effective alternative to a neurologist for most of the above purposes and makes an invaluable contribution to the management of psychiatric and behavioural complications. These roles are better fulfilled by a psychiatrist with specific experience in HD and with experience in psychiatric rehabilitation than by a general psychiatrist.
- *Rehabilitation.* Various methods can be used to coordinate rehabilitation activities. One model that we have used is a joint clinic involving the genetics team and a rehabilitation consultant. This facilitates communication with other relevant professionals such as speech and language therapists and occupational therapists.

Key-working

A team is only fully effective if each client has an assigned key worker. The genetic nurse specialist provides a vital link between the clinic and the home environment and is often in the best position to hear and understand the concerns of patients and relatives. With the advent of predictive testing there has been an increased need for this service. Early discussions with adolescents and young people who are just learning of their at-risk status are facilitated if families can be offered a home visit rather than a clinic appointment, which teenagers in particular often find inhibiting.

Inevitably, genetics nurses have a key role in supportive counselling, but are easily drawn into time-consuming problems that are outside their province and that require an integrated rehabilitative approach. A few centres employ family support workers whose role overlaps with that of genetic counsellors. They might have a nursing, or preferably a social work background and act as key workers or case managers. Based at the centre, they reinforce the genetic counsellors' functions as an information resource and as part of the hospital-based clinic service. The Huntington's Disease Association also helps to fulfill the need for information and liaison through regional care advisors.

A centre-based key worker can coordinate services but must rely to a great extent on the support of community-based professionals. The key worker, together with the HD team, has an important educational role for less specialised workers and informal carers.

Data management

Comprehensive and systematic follow-up of HD families is facilitated by a computerised register, but this raises ethical difficulties (as discussed earlier).

CONCLUSION

HD poses management problems that involve close collaboration between several professionals and, despite its unique features, the disease provides a paradigm for multiprofessional rehabilitation of neurological disorders. Genetic services cannot be disentangled from neurological and rehabilitation services and an integrated approach is preferable. No single pattern of service is appropriate, however. The needs of at-risk relatives and patients change radically and require individual solutions. The greatest difficulties are also the greatest challenges; there are few conditions in which mismanagement can be so catastrophic, or in which so many avoidable pitfalls are to be found.

REFERENCES

Aminoff MJ, Marshall J, Smith EM, Wyke MA (1975). Pattern of intellectual impairment in Huntington's chorea. *Psychological Medicine, 5,* 169–172

Becher MW, Kotzuk JA, Sharp AH, Davies SW, Bates GP, Price DL, Ross CA (1998). Intranuclear neuronal inclusions in Huntington's disease and dentatorubral and pallidoluysian atrophy: Correlation between the density of inclusions and IT15 CAG triplet repeat length. *Neurobiology of Disease, 4,* 387–397

Bolt JMW (1970). Huntington's chorea in the west of Scotland. *British Journal of Psychiatry, 116,* 259–270

Brackenridge CJ (1980). Factors influencing dementia and epilepsy in Huntington's disease of early onset. *Acta Neurological Scandinavica, 62,* 305–311

Brandt J, Butters N (1986). The neuropsychology of Huntington's disease. *Trends in Neurosciences, 93,* 118–120

Brinkman RR, Mezei MM, Theilmann J, Almqvist E, Hayden MR (1997). The likelihood of being affected with Huntington disease by a particular age, for a specific CAG size. *American Journal of Human Genetics, 60,* 1202–1210

Britton JW, Uitti RJ, Ahlskog JE, Robinson RG, Kremer B, Hayden MR (1995). Hereditary late-onset chorea without significant dementia: Genetic evidence for substantial phenotypic variation in Huntington's disease. *Neurology, 45,* 443–447

Bundey S (1997). Few psychological consequences of presymptomatic testing for Huntington disease. *Lancet, 349,* 4

Butters N, Sax D, Montgomery K, Tarlow S (1978). Comparison of the neuropsychological deficits associated with early and advanced Huntington's disease. *Archives of Neurology, 35,* 585–589

Buxton M (1976). Diagnostic problems in Huntington's chorea and tardive dyskinesia. *Comprehensive Psychiatry, 17,* 325–333

Clinical Genetics Society (1994). *The genetic testing of children.* Report of a Working Party of the Clinical Genetics Society, Birmingham, UK

Codori A-M, Brandt J (1994). Psychological costs and benefits of predictive testing for Huntington's disease. *American Journal of Medical Genetics, 54,* 174–184

Craufurd D, Tyler A (1992). Predictive testing for Huntington's disease: Protocol of the United Kingdom Huntington's Prediction Consortium. *Journal of Medical Genetics, 29,* 915–918

Davies SW, Beardsall K, Turmaine M, DiFiglia M, Aronin N, Bates GP (1998). Are neuronal intranuclear inclusions the common neuropathology of triplet repeat disorders with polyglutamine expansions? *Lancet, 351,* 131–133

Dean JCS, Fitzpatrick DR, Farndon P, Kingston H (1998). Genetic registers in the UK: Where now? *Journal of Medical Genetics, 35* (Suppl. 1), SP53

De Rooji KE, De Koning Gans PAM, Skraastad MI, Belfroid RDM, Van Der Vlis MV, Roos RAC, Bakker E, Van Ommen GJB, Den Dunnen JT, Losekoot M (1993). Dynamic mutation in Dutch Huntington's disease patients: Increased paternal repeat instability extending to within the normal size range. *Journal of Medical Genetics, 30,* 996–1002

Dewhurst K, Oliver JE, McKnight AL (1970). Socio-psychiatric consequences of Huntington's disease. *British Journal of Psychiatry, 116,* 255–258

Folstein SE, Jensen B, Leigh JR, Folstein MF (1983a). The measurement of abnormal movement: Methods developed for Huntington's disease. *Neurobehavior Toxicology and Teratology, 5,* 605–609

Folstein SE, Franz ML, Jensen BA, Chase GA, Folstein M (1983b). Conduct disorder and affective disorder among offspring of patients with Huntington's disease. *Psychological Medicine, 13,* 45–52

Furtado S, Suchowersky O, Rewcastle NB, Graham L, Klimek ML, Garber A (1996). Relationship between trinucleotide repeats and neuropathological changes in Huntington's disease. *Annals of Neurology, 39,* 132–136.

Girotti F, Marano R, Soliveri P, Geminiani G, Scigliano G (1988). Relationship between motor and cognitive disorders in Huntington's disease. *Journal of Neurology, 235,* 454–457

Gusella JF, Wexler NS, Conneally PM, Naylor SL, Anderson MA, Tanzi RE, Watkins PC, Ottina K, Wallace MR, Sakaguchi AY, Young AB, Shoulson I, Bonilla E, Martin JB (1983). A polymorphic DNA marker genetically linked to Huntington's disease. *Nature, 306,* 234–238

Harper PS (Ed) (1991). *Huntington's disease.* WB Saunders, London

Hayden MR (1981). *Huntington's chorea.* Springer-Verlag, Berlin

Heathfield KWG (1967). Huntington's chorea. Investigation into the prevalence of this disease in the area covered by the North East Metropolitan Regional Hospital Board. *Brain, 90,* 203–232

Hunt V, Walker FO (1989). Dysphagia in Huntington's disease. *Journal of Neuroscience Nursing, 21,* 92–95

Hunt V, Walker FO (1991). Learning to live at risk for Huntington's disease. *Journal of Neuroscience Nursing, 23,* 179–182

Huntington Study Group (1996). United Huntington disease rating scale: Reliability and consistency. *Movement Disorders, 11,* 136–142

Huntington's Disease Collaborative Research Group (1993). A novel gene containing a trinucleotide repeat that is expanded and unstable on Huntington's disease chromosomes. *Cell, 72,* 971–983

International Huntington Association and World Federation of Neurology (1994). Guidelines for the molecular genetics predictive test in Huntington's disease. *Journal of Medical Genetics, 31,* 555–559

Jankovic J, Orman J (1988). Tetrabenazine therapy of dystonia, chorea, tics and other dyskinesias. *Neurology, 38,* 391–394

Jason GW, Suchowersky O, Pajurkova EM, Graham L, Klimek ML, Garber AT, Poirier-Heine D (1997). Cognitive manifestations of Huntington disease in relation to genetic structure and clinical onset. *Archives of Neurology, 54,* 1081–1088

Kagel MC, Leopold NA (1992). Dysphagia in Huntington's disease: A 16-year retrospective. *Dysphagia, 7,* 106–114

Kessler S (1988). Preselection: A family coping strategy in Huntington disease. *American Journal of Medical Genetics, 31,* 617–621

Korer J, Fitzsimmons JS (1981). The effect of Huntington's chorea on family life. *British Journal of Social Work, 15,* 581–597

Kremer B, Goldberg P, Andrew SE, Theilman J, Telenius H, Zeisler J, Squiteri F, Lin B, Bassett A, Almqvist E, Bird TD, Hayden MR (1994). A worldwide study of the Huntington's disease mutation. The sensitivity and specificity of measuring CAG repeat length. *New England Journal of Medicine, 330,* 1401–1406

Lam RW, Bloch M, Jones BD, Marcus AM, Fox S, Ammam W, Hayden MR (1988). Psychiatric morbidity associated with early clinical diagnosis of Huntington's disease in a predictive testing program. *Journal of Clinical Psychiatry, 49,* 444–447

Lavers A (1983). *Remedial involvement in the management of patients with Huntington's chorea.* The Association to Combat Huntington's Chorea, London

Lawrence AD, Sahakian BJ, Hodges JR, Rosser AE, Langes KW, Robbins TW (1996). Executive and mnemonic functions in early Huntington's disease. *Brain, 119,* 1633–1645.

Lawrence AD, Hodges JR, Rosser A, Kershaw A, ffrench-Constant C, Rubinsztein D, Robbins TW, Sahakian BJ (1998). Evidence for specific cognitive deficits in pre-clinical Huntington's disease. *Brain, 121,* 1329–1341

Leopold NA, Kagel MC (1985). Dysphagia in Huntington's disease. *Archives of Neurology, 42,* 57–60

Litvan I, Paulsen JS, Mega MS, Cummings JL (1998). Neuropsychiatric assessment of patients with hyperkinetic and hypokinetic movement disorders. *Archives of Neurology, 55,* 1313–1319

Lovestone S, Hodgson S, Sham P, Differ A-M, Levy R (1996). Familial psychiatric presentation of Huntington's disease. *Journal of Medical Genetics, 33,* 128–131

Martindale B (1987). Huntington's chorea: Some psychodynamics seen in those at risk and in the response of the helping professions. *British Journal of Psychiatry, 150,* 319–323

Martindale D, Hackam A, Wieczorek A, Ellerby L, Wellington C, McCutcheon K, Singaraja R, Kazemi-Esfarjani P, Devon R, Kim SU, Bredesden DE, Tufaro F, Hayden MR (1998). Length of huntingtin and its polyglutamine tract influences localisation and frequency of intracellular aggregates. *Nature Genetics, 18,* 150–154

Mason J, Andrews K, Wilson E (1991). Late stage of Huntington's disease: Effects of treating specific disabilities. *British Journal of Occupational Therapy, 54,* 4–7

Masuda N, Goto J, Murayama N, Watanabe M, Kondo I, Kanazawa I (1995). Analysis of triplet repeats in the huntingtin gene in Japanese families affected with Huntington's disease. *Journal of Medical Genetics, 32,* 701–705

Morris M (1991). Psychiatric aspects of Huntington's disease. In PS Harper (Ed), *Huntington's disease.* WB Saunders, London

Nance MA, Westphal B, Nugent S (1996). Diagnosis of patients presenting to a Huntington disease (HD) clinic without a family history of HD. *Neurology, 47,* 1578–1580

Oliver JE (1970). Huntington's disease in Northamptonshire. *British Journal of Psychiatry, 116,* 241–253

Penney JB, Young AB, Shoulson I et al. (1990). Huntington's disease in Venezuela: 7 years of follow-up on symptomatic and asymptomatic individuals. *Movement Disorders, 5,* 93–99

Penney JB, Vonsattel JP, MacDonald ME, Gusella JF, Myers RH (1997). CAG repeat number governs the development rate of pathology in Huntington's disease. *Annals of Neurology, 41,* 689–692

Pflanz S, Besson JA, Ebmeier KP, Simpson S (1991). The clinical manifestation of mental disorder in Huntington's disease: A retrospective record study of disease progression. *Acta Psychiatrica Scandinavica, 83,* 53–60

Podoll K, Caspary P, Lange HW, Noth J (1988). Language functions in Huntington's disease. *Brain, 111,* 1475–1503

Quaid KA, Wesson MK (1995). Exploration of the effects of predictive testing for Huntington disease on intimate relationships. *American Journal of Medical Genetics, 57,* 46–51

Quarrell O (1991). The neurobiology of Huntington's disease. In PS Harper (Ed), *Huntington's disease.* WB Saunders, London

Quarrell OW, Tyler A, Jones MP, Nordin M, Harper PS (1988). Population studies of Huntington's disease in Wales. *Clinical Genetics, 33,* 189–195

Roos RAC (1986). The neuropathology of Huntington's disease. In PJ Vinken, GW Bruyn, HL Klawans (Eds), *Handbook of clinical neurology,* vol. 49. Elsevier, Amsterdam

Rosenberg NK, Sorensen SA, Christensen A-L (1995). Neuropsychological characteristics of Huntington's disease carriers: A double blind study. *Journal of Medical Genetics, 32,* 600–604

Rosenblatt A, Ranen NG, Rubinsztein DC, Stine OC, Margolis RL, Wagster MV, Becher MW, Rosser AE, Leggo J, ffrench-Constant CK, Sherr M, Franz ML, Abbott MH, Ross CA (1998). Patients with features similar to Huntington's disease without CAG expansion in huntingtin. *Neurology, 51,* 215–220

Saint-Cyr JA, Taylor AE, Lang AE (1988). Procedural learning and neostriatal dysfunction in man. *Brain, 111,* 941–959

Salmon DP, Kwo-on-Yuen P, Heindel WC, Butters N, Thal LJ (1989). Differentiation of Alzheimer's disease and Huntington's disease with the dementia rating scale. *Archives of Neurology, 46,* 1204–1208

Schoenfield M, Myers RM, Cupples A, Berkman B, Sax DS, Clark E (1984). Increased rate of suicide among patients with Huntington's disease. *Journal of Neurology, Neurosurgery and Psychiatry, 47,* 1283–1287

Sheaff F (1990). Hydrotherapy in Huntington's disease. *Nursing Times, 86,* 46–49

Shelton PA, Knopman DS (1991). Ideomotor apraxia in Huntington's disease. *Archives of Neurology, 48,* 35–41

Shoulson I, Behr J (1983). Care of the patient and family with Huntington's disease: A guide for clinicians. Huntington's Disease Society of America Inc., New York

Simpson SA, Harding AE (1993). Predictive testing for Huntington's disease: After the gene. *Journal of Medical Genetics, 30,* 1036–1038

Skirton H, Glendinning N (1997). Using research to develop care for patients with Huntington's disease. *British Journal of Nursing, 6,* 83–90

Snowden JS, Craufurd D, Griffiths HL, Neary D (1998). Awareness of involuntary movements in Huntington disease. *Archives of Neurology, 55,* 801–805

Speedie LJ, Brake N, Folstein SE, Bowers D, Heilman KM (1990). Comprehension of prosody in Huntington's disease. *Journal of Neurology, Neurosurgery and Psychiatry, 53,* 607–610

Strauss ME, Brandt J (1990). Are there neuropsychologic manifestations of the gene for Huntington's disease in asymptomatic, at-risk individuals? *Archives of Neurology, 47,* 905–908

Tyler A, Morris M (1990). National symposium on problems of pre-symptomatic testing for Huntington's disease. *Journal of Medical Ethics, 16,* 41–42

Walker DA, Harper PS, Wells CEC, Tyler A, Davies K, Newcombe RG (1981). Huntington's chorea in South Wales, a genetic and epidemiological study. *Clinical Genetics, 19,* 213–221

Wallesch C, Fehrenbach RA (1988). On the neurolinguistic nature of language abnormalities in Huntington's disease. *Journal of Neurology, Neurosurgery and Psychiatry, 51,* 367–373

Wolff G (1988). Huntington disease carrier status and the problems involved for those affected. *Clinical Genetics, 34,* 172–175

Yale R, Martindale B, (1984). Social work with Huntington's chorea. *British Journal of Social Work, 14,* 157–171

Young AB, Shoulson I, Penney JB et al. (1986). Huntington's disease in Venezuela: Neurological features. *Neurology, 36*, 244–249

Zappacosta B, Monza D, Meoni C, Austoni L, Soliveri P, Gellera C, Alberti R, Mantero M, Penati G, Caraceni T, Girotti F (1996). Psychiatric symptoms do not correlate with cognitive decline, motor symptoms, or CAG repeat length in Huntington's disease. *Archives of Neurology, 53*, 493–497

USEFUL ADDRESSES

Huntington's Disease Association, 108 Battersea High Street, London SW11 3HP

Huntington's Disease Society of America, 140 West 22nd Street, New York, NY 10011

41. Rehabilitation in Alzheimer's disease and other dementias

Robert Woods

INTRODUCTION

Dementing conditions are seldom associated with any degree of therapeutic optimism. Despite the frequency with which they occur, it is only in the last few years that these conditions have attracted much attention from clinicians and researchers. Often, the diagnosis of dementia has signalled the end of the rehabilitative effort, rather than the starting point. It is now being recognised that conditions that afflict 0.1% of those under 65, and 5% of those over 65, deserve to be considered much more carefully. Realistically, what can be achieved? What are the most helpful approaches? This chapter seeks to clarify the goals of rehabilitation with these disorders, before describing some of the approaches used, and some of the basic issues raised by this work.

AIMS

Three features of the dementias pose particular problems for rehabilitation. First, dementia is usually defined as referring to a global impairment of function—intellect, memory and other high cortical functions, self-care and day-to-day problem-solving ability, perceptuomotor skills, emotional control, and judgement. When so many areas of function seem to be impaired, which should be addressed first? Are any preserved skills available to enable new strategies to be developed? The range of impairment is daunting, in comparison with, say, a more specific focal neurological deficit.

Second, many dementias have a natural history of progression; this is generally considered to be the case for Alzheimer's disease, which post-mortem studies suggest accounts for the majority of cases of dementia in both younger and older age groups. Typically, the person's condition will show further deterioration; there is no stable baseline from which to work; achieving a slower rate of decline might be considered an acceptable goal; programmes will need to be flexible, adapting to changes in the person's needs over time.

Third, the majority of patients will be in later life. The highest prevalence rates for dementing conditions are seen in people aged over 80, where up to one-fifth of the population might be affected. In the past, older people have at times been excluded from rehabilitation programmes, perhaps because of the apparent irrelevance of work-related programmes, or because such endeavours were often judged less worthwhile when older people were involved, perhaps because of their presumed inability to change or because of their assumed more restricted life-span, or because memory loss was seen as a normal part of ageing.

In the context of a wide-ranging, devastating disease, often progressive, mainly affecting older people, what can be achieved in rehabilitation? Complete recovery of function cannot be a realistic aim. Helping the person to retain preserved abilities for as long as possible would certainly be worthwhile. Keeping the person's dependency needs to a minimum could enable the person to function at a higher level for longer, perhaps remaining in his or her own home. If, on the other hand, dependency is actually encouraged (as Baltes (1988) suggests) then skills are likely to disappear even more rapidly. People who are encouraged to be actively involved in, say, their own self-care, and who are complimented on their appearance and smartness, could retain these skills longer than if passivity in dressing and washing were to be encouraged.

This raises the possibility that the person might show deficits over and above any arising directly from organic disease. These "excess disabilities" (see Holden & Woods, 1995, p. 32) reflect a discrepancy between actual and potential function. The aim can then go beyond prevention of decline to maximising function at each point in the dementing process, without any assumptions about the programme having an impact on the person's underlying neurological impairment or prognosis.

A third aim extends this further, with the goal of enhancing the quality of life. In many instances, maintaining functional abilities or achieving the best possible level of function can result in an improved quality of life for the person with dementia, but there might also be interventions that are of value, even though they have no impact on the person's level of function as such. This might apply particularly in the later stages of dementia, where ensuring the person continues to participate in valued, rewarding experiences becomes paramount. An enjoyable group session, where the person joins in reminiscing, singing, or whatever, can be valuable in its own right, even if it has no lasting impact.

Without this perspective, staff will feel continued failure and frustration in their efforts to work with people with dementia.

The progressive nature of dementia will require considerable adaptations to the goals of rehabilitation as time goes on. These disorders cover a number of stages—from the person with a very early memory disorder to the severely impaired immobile patient with limited communication ability. Any approach has to be flexible, changing over time as the person's needs change and abilities fluctuate. The great individual variation in patterns of dysfunction, and in rates of change, means that programmes have to be tailored individually.

The majority of people with dementia are not in hospitals or nursing homes but are cared for in the community by relatives, friends, or neighbours, often with relatively little support from statutory services. These informal carers often have high levels of strain (Morris, Morris, & Britton, 1988) as they experience what many describe as a "living bereavement", sustaining the loss of the person they once knew, while still coping with the daily physical and mental demands of caring for the apparent shadow of the person that remains. Their needs must also be addressed in any rehabilitation plan. Consideration must be given as to how best to involve them, without adding to their strain. Indeed, a valuable aim of work with people with dementia would be to reduce to a minimum the strain of those at the front-line of care, facing day-to-day difficult, frustrating, and at times irritating, problems in the midst of emotions of loss and grief.

REHABILITATION APPROACHES

Stimulation and activity

These approaches were amongst the first to be implemented and evaluated systematically. In the UK, Cosin, Mort, Post et al. (1958) introduced a wide-ranging programme of stimulation and activity, including full occupational therapy, social, and domestic activities. Increased purposeful, appropriate types of behaviour were noted in a group of dementing patients, in a controlled study. The improvement tended to be short-lived, being lost within a few weeks of the end of the stimulation programme.

More recently, more specific forms of stimulation have been assessed in patients with a severe degree of dementia. Norberg, Melin, and Asplund (1986) evaluated the effects of music, touch, and a variety of objects (such as hay, camphor, fur, and bread) with a potential impact on taste, touch, and smell, in two patients whose dementia was so severe that verbal communication was almost non-existent. A positive response to music was noted, but not to the objects or touch. Gaebler and Hemsley (1991) similarly identified a response to music in the majority of six patients with similarly advanced dementia. These results indicate that with careful, detailed observation a response to certain forms of sensory input can be found in patients with the severest levels of impairment. In less advanced cases, music provided on a regular basis was associated with positive changes in recall, mood, and social interaction compared with control groups involved in other activities (Lord & Garner, 1993).

Multisensory stimulation, usually involving sessions in a specially equipped room, exposing the person to a variety of auditory, visual, olfactory, and tactile stimulation, has proved popular in the UK. Arguably, the emphasis is on stimulation that relaxes, rather than on increasing arousal level. Several positive evaluations of this approach, often described as "Snoezelen", have been reported with patients with dementia (Baker, Dowling, Wareing, Dawson, & Assey, 1997; Spaull, Leach, & Frampton, 1998). In both studies, some benefits were evident outside the actual sessions. However, Brooker, Snape, Johnson, Ward, and Payne (1997), examining two of the components of this approach—aromatherapy and massage—in a series of four single cases, found that only one patient showed a positive response after the sessions, with some others tending to become more agitated.

Environmental adaptation

Clinically, it is often evident that the dementing person's behaviour is influenced by aspects of the environment. When taken from the hospital ward to a more normal social setting, such as a pub or a social club, it is not uncommon for a positive response to occur, for the person to seem more alert and interested. This might be because the more familiar setting offers many more cues and prompts to patterns of behaviour that are well-established enough to have survived the ravages of the dementia, but which need the most favourable conditions to be elicited. Some empirical studies reinforce this clinical impression (e.g. Sommer & Ross, 1958), although they differ greatly in the extent and type of environmental change that has been attempted. Several studies have reported wide-ranging changes, affecting both the physical and social environment. Melin and Gotestam (1981) introduced a series of changes in a ward of dementing patients with a high level of behavioural disability. Changes in social activity, eating skills, and activity levels were found when an approach emphasising independence and choice was implemented. Brane, Karlsson, Kihlgren, and Norberg (1989) trained staff in "integrity-promoting dementia care"; this involved achieving a more home-like atmosphere, with patients having their own clothes, possessions, and a domestic style of furnishing. Care was individualised, patients were given more time and encouraged to make choices and join in activities. The authors report that the treatment "induced a reduction of distractibility, confusion, anxiety and depressed mood, and improvement in motor performance" over a 3-month period, compared with a control group.

There is increasing interest in the effects of design and architecture on the life of the person with dementia (e.g. Benjamin & Spector, 1990; Keen, 1989; Netten, 1993). Internationally, the trend is for special-care units to be developed for people with dementia (Carr & Marshall, 1993), which in Europe and Australia have developed as "homely", small, local units built on a domestic scale, with domestic-style fittings and furnishings. In the UK, the prime example of these are the "domus" units; small, homely units for around ten people, with a philosophy geared towards meeting the specific needs of people with dementia. Evaluations reported by Dean, Briggs, and Lindesay (1993), Lindesay, Briggs, Lawes, Macdonald, and Herzberg (1991) and Skea and Lindesay (1996) of several such units indicate a number of positive benefits for patients, such as increased activity and interaction, and some functional improvements, related to replacing the traditional long-stay ward for people with dementia with this special-care unit model. In France (Ritchie et al., 1992) and in Sweden (Annerstedt, Gustafson, & Nilsson, 1993), again, some positive benefits have been associated with small, group-living units. However, they appeared less well able to manage the problems of very advanced cases, perhaps requiring transfer to alternative facilities such as a hospital or nursing home. This is in contrast to the domus units, which offered a "home for life", perhaps because they were originally designed to replace the hospital "end of the road" wards.

Reminiscence

Reminiscence sessions are popular in most facilities for people with dementia (Bornat, 1994; Schweitzer, 1998), particularly with patients where some social abilities and communication skills are regained. Reminiscence capitalises on the person's store of past memories, which, although not intact, contains enough overlearned and well-rehearsed information to enable some meaningful discourse. This is often aided by the use of prompts and memory triggers, of which a number are now commercially available—photographs, newspapers, artefacts, archive sound and film recordings, and popular music. Published evaluative studies have been slow to emerge; Thornton and Brotchie (1987) and Woods and McKiernan (1995) review the use of reminiscence with older people with dementia. Head, Portnoy, and Woods (1990) showed an increase in interaction in one group of dementing patients during reminiscence sessions compared with an alternative activity, but not in a second group attending a different centre, with a different range of competing activities. Baines, Saxby, and Ehlert (1987) similarly found that the effects of reminiscence sessions varied between groups; here some improvements were evident in one group on measures of verbal orientation and problem behaviour outside the sessions, but not in a second group. In both studies, reminiscence was very clearly an enjoyable activity for many people with dementia, and encouraged interaction and a positive response. However, other group activities might be just as enjoyable, and the evidence for effects on patients persisting after the sessions is mixed.

More individualised approaches to reminiscence, including the use of life-story books, are beginning to become more widely used. In prompting the person's autobiographical memory, these might have an important part to play in helping to support the person's sense of identity (Woods, 1998). Gibson (1994) reports the use of individualised reminiscence in developing individual care-plans in a series of five people with dementia showing challenging behaviour. The resulting care-plans were able to address the whole range of the person's needs much more effectively than plans based simply on the "here and now" aspects of the person's life, and led to increased sociability and decreased aggression in the patients.

Cognitive approaches

Reality orientation (RO) is the most thoroughly evaluated of the various cognitive approaches to be discussed. A number of descriptions of the techniques are available (e.g. Holden & Woods, 1995). Briefly, there are two major components: (1) RO sessions, where a small group meets on a regular basis, working on activities geared to increasing awareness of surroundings and of those around them; and (2) informal RO, or 24-hour RO, which involves staff and carers keeping the person in touch with current reality on an on-going basis, potentially in every interaction and encounter. The aims of RO can be summarised as helping the person with dementia to continue to experience success and achievement, to have an increased awareness of those aspects of the present reality of most personal significance, and to enhance communication and human personal contact with those around them.

There is reasonable evidence that regular RO sessions of, say, 30 minutes five times a week, are associated with statistically significant benefits in the area of verbal orientation compared with untreated control groups (Holden & Woods, 1995). More general changes in behaviour and function have been far more elusive, being shown in only a few studies. However, when specific training is given in finding the way around the ward or home (Hanley, McGuire, & Boyd, 1981), or where 24-hour RO has been used systematically to respond to patients' queries (Reeve & Ivison, 1985; Williams, Reeve, Ivison, & Kavanagh, 1987), positive results have been obtained.

RO has been criticised on the grounds that the "package" is so diverse that its essentials are difficult to define. There is now a welcome trend towards more individualised cognitive interventions, seeking to build on the person's preserved skills and identifying support for processes that are less well retained. Patients have been taught successfully to use external memory aids such as watches, calendars, and diaries (Camp, Foss, O'Hanlon, & Stevens, 1996; Hanley & Lusty, 1984; Woods, 1983). Bourgeois (1990, 1992) used a memory book with people with dementia, depicting past and current events in the person's life. Carers were encouraged to use the book with the person. Quality of interaction was assessed as significantly improved when the book was used as a focus for conversation. Arkin (1997) reports the successful use of memory tapes with patients with Alzheimer's disease. This involves the repetition of relevant information on an audiotape, with a quiz built into the tape to encourage active learning.

These interventions are founded on the growing literature on memory and learning processes in dementia (e.g. Bäckman, 1992; Miller & Morris, 1993). There is evidence that many people with dementia are able to learn and retain material, under the right conditions. Spaced retrieval appears to be a promising procedure (Camp et al., 1996). Here, one item at a time is taught to the person, with the retention interval gradually being increased as long as the person is able to correctly recall the item. Clare et al. (1999) describe the application of the principle of errorless learning to dementia. A patient was successfully taught a number of face–name associations using methods of prompting (and fading prompts) that sought to avoid the occurrence of any errors, which are thought to interfere with the learning of the correct association. There was evidence of generalisation to the real-life setting from this procedure.

Bäckman (1992) argues that persons with dementia require support at both the time of learning and at the point of retrieval. For example, Sandman (1993) demonstrated that when patients with dementia worked on devising questions about a TV programme they were watching, their recall improved, i.e. they were producing and utilising their own retrieval cues. In the same study, Sandman showed that patients' recall was greater regarding days when a memorable event occurred, even for items unconnected with the event itself. Implicit and procedural memory have also been recommended as pathways to enhance learning in people with dementia, through, for example, motor learning of actions and the use of prompts not requiring any "memorisation" as such (e.g. Josephsson et al., 1993; Zanetti et al., 1997).

Behavioural management

Much of the literature on behavioural methods in people with dementia is in the form of case reports, reflecting an emphasis on an individualised approach. However, larger series of such studies will be required before it will be clear how generally useful these methods might be. Using prompting and environmental manipulations to establish the conditions for the desired behaviour to occur have often been the most effective therapeutic techniques. Reinforcement has usually been social through staff or carer contact and attention, contingent on the desired behaviour. Studies have successfully increased participation in purposeful activities (Burton, 1980), mobility (Burgio, Burgio, Engel, & Tice, 1986), and shown improvements in dressing and self-care skills (Beck et al., 1997; McEvoy & Patterson, 1986; Rinke, Williams, Lloyd, & Smith-Scott, 1978).

The most promising work on incontinence is that reported by Schnelle et al. (1989), who have developed a "prompted voiding" technique, where patients are asked on a regular basis if they would like to go to the toilet, and are assisted with toileting if they answer positively. Patients were reinforced socially for being dry and for asking to go to the toilet. A clear treatment effect was demonstrated with 126 incontinent nursing home residents, many of whom had severe cognitive impairment. Improvements occurred immediately, on the first day of the implementation of the prompted voiding procedure. The authors stress that the patients were not then learning new continence-related skills, but "were responding to an environment that offered increased opportunity for toileting assistance and favourable reinforcement for continence". It should be noted that the aim was not independent toileting, but rather remaining dry. In many instances this is an attainable and worthwhile

goal, with benefits for patients and caregivers. Studies attempting to increase independent toileting skills have led to much less dramatic changes (e.g. Rona, Wylie, & Bellwood, 1986).

Reducing excesses of behaviour (e.g. shouting) has usually been tackled by increasing other, appropriate, behaviour and reducing any attention contingent on the actual problem as much as possible (e.g. Green, Linsk, & Pinkston, 1986). Increasing attention is now being given to efforts to reduce challenging behaviour, as its impact on caregiver strain and decisions regarding placement become more widely recognised (Stokes, 1996). Bird, Alexopoulos, and Adamowicz (1995) have described an individualised approach, based on careful assessment of the person, behaviour, and context. In several successful cases the person with dementia was taught to respond to a particular cue or prompt, which was then used to maintain the behaviour in the person's environment. For example, one patient who entered other people's rooms in a nursing home was taught not to enter rooms that had a particular sign outside.

Improving well-being

Anxiety, agitation, and depression contribute to excess disability and challenging behaviour in dementia, as well as reducing quality of life for the person with dementia. Some attempts to tackle these factors directly have been reported, in addition to approaches discussed above such as reminiscence, music therapy, and multisensory stimulation. Welden and Yesavage (1982) describe improvements in behavioural function and sleep patterns following a 3-month period of training in relaxation techniques for people with dementia.

Validation therapy (Feil, 1993) aims to establish communication at an emotional level with the person with dementia, in contrast with RO's more cognitive approach. Through empathic, non-judgemental listening, the person is enabled to express painful feelings, which through acknowledgement and validation are thought to decrease in strength. Although many dementia careworkers have found the validation approach to provide useful communication techniques (Bleathman & Morton, 1992), there is limited evidence for it having a measurable effect on the person with dementia's function and behaviour. The most thorough controlled study to date (Toseland, Diehl, Freeman, Manzanares, & McCallion, 1997) suggested that whereas nursing staff reported that those receiving validation therapy were less physically and verbally aggressive, and less depressed, these changes were not evident in independent ratings.

With greater awareness of Alzheimer's disease leading to earlier diagnosis, interest in psychological therapy has grown, in relation to depression and adjustment in the early stages of the condition. Psychotherapeutic approaches (e.g. Hausman, 1992; Sinason, 1992) have been described, and attention drawn to the diversity of coping strategies adopted in the face of developing cognitive impairment (Bahro, Silber, & Sunderland, 1995). Cognitive–behaviour therapy for depression in dementia has been advocated (Teri & Gallagher-Thompson, 1991), despite the presence of cognitive impairment, and Teri, Logsdon, Uomoto, and McCurry (1997) have shown that family caregivers can be taught to use these methods to reduce the level of depression in the person for whom they are caring, and that, in so doing, the carers' own level of depression is also reduced.

Pharmacological approaches

Since the discovery of a deficit in the cholinergic neurotransmission system in Alzheimer's disease, hopes have been raised that a therapeutic breakthrough might be achieved by enhancing the function of this system. The most encouraging approach currently involves the use of agents that inhibit the breakdown of acetylcholine by the enzyme acetylcholinesterase, resulting in an increase in the amount of available neurotransmitter.

Donepezil hydrochloride and rivastigmine are the first of these acetylcholinesterase (ACE) inhibitors to be licensed for use in Alzheimer's disease in the UK. A growing body of efficacy data is becoming available for these drugs (e.g. Ham, 1997; Rogers et al., 1998a, b). A proportion of patients show improvements in cognition and other function. The long-term impact has yet to be established. An earlier drug, tacrine, with similar presumed action was licensed for use in the USA, but not in the UK; the more recent compounds are thought to be less likely to show side-effects affecting liver function.

These approaches do not arrest the pathological process resulting in dementia by the production of amyloid β-peptides and disruption of the neuronal cytoskeleton (see Chapter 7), and can therefore only ever be partially successful in restoring function and preventing decline. Many further agents are in the process of development, including some for vascular dementia, where prophylactic aspirin has been the main pharmacological avenue available to date.

In practice, the most frequent pharmacological approach is still the prescription of psychotropic drugs in response to the behavioural problems that so often bring people with dementia to the attention of service providers (DeLeo, Stella, & Spagnoli, 1989). Indeed, a cursory study of drug charts in residential and nursing homes might lead to the conclusion that Alzheimer's disease is related to a phenothiazine deficiency (see, for example, Furniss, Craig, & Burns, 1998; Thacker & Jones, 1997)! Sunderland and Silver (1988) have reviewed 20 double-blind or placebo-controlled studies of neuroleptics in dementia, involving 1207 patients. In 60% of the double-blind studies some positive results were obtained, although in most studies only a relatively small proportion showed a marked clinical improvement. Symptoms of excitement, agitation, hallucinations, and hostility were found to be most responsive to neuroleptics, which tended to be more effective than other drugs such as benzodiazepines. Schneider, Pollock, and Lyness (1990) report a meta-analysis, concluding that the therapeutic effects of neuroleptics in this context were modest, giving an improvement of only 18% over placebo. Side-effects are a particular concern, and neuroleptic malignant syndrome is a major risk in Lewy body dementia (McKeith, Fairbairn, Perry, Thompson,

& Perry, 1992). This form of dementia is particularly associated with hallucinations and delusions, which might attract neuroleptic medication. Lewy body dementia might be present in up to one-quarter of older people with dementia (Shergill, Mullan, D'Ath, & Katona, 1994). Studies such as that reported by Findlay, Sharma, McEwen et al. (1989), showing few effects when thioridazine was withdrawn from a group of dementing patients, suggest that their use with a particular patient should be reviewed regularly to monitor whether the drug is still required.

Sleep problems are particularly troublesome where the person is being cared for at home by his or her family. Sometimes the difficulty can be helped by keeping the person more active during the day, by reducing the amount of daytime sleep, and by establishing a calming routine in the period leading up to bedtime. This can be combined with a hypnotic, the dosage of which is carefully monitored to avoid hangover effect the following morning. Benzodiazepines are amongst the most common drugs used as hypnotics. Withdrawal of them has been shown to improve cognitive function in older people resident in nursing homes (Salzman et al., 1992); it is likely that they also have a deleterious effect on cognitive function in dementia. In institutional settings, the problem at night sometimes relates to unrealistic expectations of how long the person needs to sleep. It is not surprising if someone who is put to bed at 19:00 h awakes at 03:00 h, having had 8 hours sleep! Daytime sleep often results from a lack of structured activity. When prompting and encouragement to join in an activity are given, the amount of daytime sleep is reduced (Burton, 1980).

Work with families

Family caregivers can benefit from training in certain of the techniques described above. This can have beneficial effects on the carers because they now have something positive to do in a situation where previously they felt helpless. Pinkston and Linsk (1984) taught a wife to reinforce her dementing husband's positive statements with praise, and to selectively ignore his "worried statements". These had troubled his wife greatly, and reduction was accompanied by an improvement in her subjective level of burden in caring for him at home. The positive effects on family carers of being trained to reduce depression in their relative was mentioned earlier (Teri et al., 1997).

A second strategy is to work directly on the carer's level of stress. For example, Sutcliffe and Larner (1988) report the successful use of psychological stress management techniques, focusing on the control of both anxiety and anger, with a small sample of carers. Greater reductions in strain were found using this procedure than in a control group who was simply given information about dementia.

A third group of approaches is being developed, which have as a focus the carers' perception of their situation. Carers' attributions about what is happening, their sense of control, and the meaning they give to the patient's actions and to their own position as a carer have been related to levels of strain or depression (Morris et al., 1988). Cognitive therapies are beginning to be used, teaching coping and problem-solving skills to help carers achieve more a sense of control over their situation. Gallagher-Thompson and Steffen (1994) report the successful use of both cognitive–behaviour therapy and brief psychodynamic therapy in improving mood in depressed family caregivers. The former was more effective where the caregiving had been going on for some years, whereas brief psychodynamic therapy showed particular efficacy earlier in the caregiving career.

There is evidence that certain types of support from the various statutory services, and from family and friends, are helpful to carers (Moriarty, 1998; Moriarty & Levin, 1993). Care management schemes (Challis, Chessum, Chesterman, Luckett, & Woods, 1988) that use skilled case management to set up a flexible, tailored package of care, with relatives being encouraged to set clear limits on their involvement, can usefully help the carer to become part of a network of care.

Some studies of groups offering a mix of these approaches have been reported. Chiverton and Caine (1989) found positive effects from a brief series of three 2-hour educational sessions with spouse caregivers, compared with untreated controls, and Toseland, Rossiter, and Labrecque (1989) found significant improvements in psychological functioning in carers attending eight 2-hour sessions where the emphasis was particularly on problem-solving skills. Carers in these groups increased the size of their social support networks during the course. Brodaty and Gresham (1989) report an intensive programme where carer and patient are brought into hospital together. The carers received training in coping with the problems of dementia, and the patients had memory retraining sessions. Compared with carers who had enjoyed an equivalent period of respite care, with the patient going into hospital alone, the carers who received training reported less strain a year later, and maintained the patient at home for a longer period. This differential benefit in admission rates has been maintained over a period of 8 years (Brodaty, Gresham, & Luscombe, 1997). A family support and counselling programme in New York has also reported positive outcomes, both in terms of carer depression (Mittelman et al., 1995) and reduced admissions to institutional care (Mittelman, Ferris, Shulman, Steinberg, & Levin, 1996). This programme offers family meetings and support groups, as well as access to counsellors as required by the caregiver.

CONCLUSIONS

A number of general points emerge from the various approaches reviewed.

Attitudes

People with dementia are often at risk of being subjected to indignity, and having their full range of human needs denied. Attitudes that find expression in statements such as "it doesn't matter what you do or say to him, he doesn't know what's going on" are antithetical to any rehabilitation approach. The notion that people with dementia simply need physical care

is pervasive and often resistant to change. Holden and Woods (1995) discuss the issue of attitude change in more detail, and show how negative attitudes can distort some of the positive approaches discussed above. Kitwood (1997a) has highlighted the way in which social environments for people with dementia often serve to dehumanise, depersonalise, and invalidate, reducing the person's level of function and perhaps accelerating the process of decline. It should be emphasised that this does not occur because caregivers are generally malicious, abusive people; on the contrary, they are often highly caring. The problem is that too often caregivers, family, and professionals see the dementia—the neurological condition—but not the person, and so lose sight of the individual's needs, preferences, and potential. Kitwood has written extensively regarding person-centred care in dementia, and the conditions needed for its development. Without attention to the human value, needs, and rights of the person with dementia, any rehabilitation approach will be misdirected.

Learning—is it possible?

Many of the possibilities for rehabilitation described above do not involve new learning on the part of the person with dementia—environmental manipulations or tapping-in to preserved areas of function are generally more useful strategies. However, the possibility of some learning ability should be noted (Little, Volans, Hemsley, & Levy, 1986). The cognitive rehabilitation approaches described earlier are beginning to delineate the most favourable conditions for learning to occur. As with amnesic patients, cueing with the initial letters of words to which the person was previously exposed has been shown to reduce the memory impairment with respect to normal controls (Miller & Morris, 1993), suggesting at least a priming effect, even if, as Downes (1987) suggests, this cannot be considered as remembering in any conventional sense. Case studies on verbal and ward orientation have shown a clear learning effect, for example, Lam and Woods (1986) used an ABAB design to demonstrate the ability of an 80-year-old dementing patient to learn her way around a ward, with brief, simple daily training sessions.

Clinical relevance

Is the effort worthwhile? Are the results obtained clinically significant? Here the answer lies in careful selection of rehabilitation goals, so they are of maximum benefit to the individual patient and his or her carers. An individual approach is vital, rather than one that assumes, for example, that knowing the name of the week or reminiscing is necessarily of value for every person (Woods & Bird, 1999).

Maintenance and generalisation

The weight of evidence suggests that once a programme stops, any improvements are lost fairly rapidly. Some attempts to improve maintenance by teaching the person to use memory aids should be mentioned (e.g. Bird et al., 1995; Hanley & Lusty, 1984; Woods, 1983). This emphasises the importance of environmental manipulations, which, by their very nature, can become a long-standing component of the rehabilitation programme.

Similarly, changes tend to be quite specific, and not to generalise readily from one area to another. For example, Woods (1983) showed that the learning of verbal orientation material was fairly specific to what was actually taught; the patient mentioned earlier in Lam and Woods' study—who learned her way around a ward—needed additional training sessions when moved to a residential home. As far as possible, work has to be where the person actually will be, not in a special training environment, and must focus fairly precisely on the actual goals of relevance to that person.

A further complication is that staff might not persist with an approach, even when it is demonstrably effective. For example, Schnelle et al. (1993) have had to develop on-going monitoring systems to ensure that their highly effective prompted voiding programme is continued once the research input is withdrawn. Burgio and Burgio (1990) review the staff training literature in this field and illustrate the difficulty in producing and maintaining change in staff behaviour.

A way forward

An individualised, flexible approach is clearly called for in work with people with dementia, founded on positive attitudes that recognise the human worth and needs of the person with dementia. The individual care-planning approach emphasises a careful assessment of the person's strengths and needs, and should make possible the identification of excess disabilities. Goals of clinical relevance to the quality of life of each patient are set out in the care plan, aiming to use the person's strengths more fully and to meet more of the person's needs. Regular monitoring and review of the plan provides the mechanism for a flexible response to the changing clinical picture. Barrowclough and Fleming (1986) show that it is quite feasible to train care staff to devise and use individual care plans. There is considerable scope for evaluative research to identify key components of the approach, and to increase the repertoire of methods of tackling common needs, but this individualised system provides the best available framework within which to tackle rehabilitative work in dementia. In residential settings there is much to be said, in addition, for regular detailed audit of the quality of care, focusing on the individual patient's experience. Dementia care mapping (Kitwood & Bredin, 1992) provides one such approach, and feedback of the results allows staff to develop action plans to improve both the overall quality of care and the quality of their approach to individual residents (Brooker, Foster, Banner, Payne, & Jackson, 1998).

Organisation of care

A variety of forms of help are likely to be needed by the person with dementia and those who care for him or her.

Diagnosis. Many carers are left in the dark, not even knowing the name of the condition that has transformed their loved one. A diagnostic assessment is also essential to exclude other, potentially treatable, conditions that might present with a similar clinical picture. Assessment might have to continue over a period of time before the diagnosis becomes clear, and might need to be repeated later, perhaps if there is a sudden deterioration that could be related to an acute confusional state. There is much debate at present as to whether or not the person with dementia should be told the diagnosis (Maguire et al., 1996; Rice & Warner, 1994). Family caregivers often do not want the person to be told, even though they report that they themselves would want to be told if in that position. There is recognition that the way in which the diagnostic process is handled can have a major impact on coping and adaptation by both the family and the person with dementia.

Information. Carers need accurate information about the condition with which they are coping, relevant to their own situation, and in a form that they can assimilate and use. Many books and booklets are currently available (the Alzheimer's Society can provide a list), but these should be viewed as complementary to access to an informed, knowledgeable person, who can adapt the generalisations of the books to the particular individuals involved.

Practical help. Reliable, flexible assistance tailored to individual needs, available when required (even out of office hours and at weekends) is invaluable. The key is in changing the question from "What of the help we have available do you want?" to "What help do you need and want us to find for you?" Consistency is also helpful, so that a person with dementia and the carer can get to know and trust the careworker, and so that the careworker can get to know the person as an individual, with a unique life-story, preferences, interests, and needs.

Relief. Being with a person with dementia for long periods of time can be a great strain, and yet often the person cannot safely be left alone. A break from caring is usually near the top of any list of carers' needs (Moriarty, 1998), but for the carer to actually feel relief, the substitute care has to be seen as being of high quality. Many forms of relief are in operation—day care, sitting services, short stays in hospital or at a home—and now night shelters are beginning to be set up, on the basis that night-time disturbance is a particular difficulty for carers to manage.

Emotional help. Some carers will find emotional support within their families. For others, especially where the person would previously have been a major confidant, outside help might be needed. Many carers find support groups very helpful, sharing with and learning from other carers. Others need individual counselling, perhaps in dealing with the feelings of loss involved in what is often described by carers as a living bereavement.

Acceptable alternatives to home care. When continuing care at home becomes impossible, carers need to feel that the person can be placed in an environment where his or her needs will be met adequately, and that avoids the worst connotations of institutional care. Small, homely units for people with dementia are now beginning to be established (see earlier); many more will be needed.

Currently, there is much concern to separate "health" from "social" care. In the above list, only diagnosis would fall fully into the health-care category. Memory clinics are being established in many areas to assist with the challenge of early diagnosis, but also provide an excellent starting point for psychosocial interventions (Moniz-Cook & Woods, 1997). Whereas the responsibility for ensuring care management operates effectively falls to local authority Social Services departments, the other forms of help are likely to come from a diverse range of service providers, including private and voluntary agencies. In particular, the domination of institutional care provision by Health and Social Services departments has now been broken in the UK by the rapid growth of the independent sector, encouraged initially by favourable funding arrangements.

Many challenges remain (Woods, 1995). There is concern that community care packages are not being developed creatively and flexibly enough to meet the needs of people with dementia; in some areas, if the cost of the package of care required to keep the person at home exceeds a relatively low threshold then the person will be placed in a residential or nursing home, with the person having little choice in the matter. Where there is a carer living with the person, services appear to give the situation a lower priority. There are also concerns regarding the quality of some residential and nursing home provision. There are increasing differences in service provision from area to area. However, some welcome areas of development can also be identified. It is being recognised that younger people with dementia have specific needs, which can be difficult for services for older people to meet; for example, younger people might feel out of place in a day centre or home catering mainly for older people. Specialist nursing services for people with dementia and their carers are being developed, which might help to compensate for the tendency of members of community mental health teams for the elderly to focus on the non-dementing cases on their caseload (Brown, Challis, & von Abendorff, 1996). Social worker care managers have also been shown to provide a valuable on-going support to people with dementia and their carers, reducing the rate of admission to residential care (Challis, von Abendorff, & Brown, 1997).

There is now much more awareness of the importance of recognising the perspective of the person with dementia, of his or her experience of the condition (Kitwood, 1997b) and of the support received and desired. If rehabilitation approaches are to be useful in this condition it is vital that we continue to seek greater understanding of individual patients, their priorities, needs, and preferences. We need to explore further ethical issues in this work, particularly those relating to informed consent (Kitwood, 1995). More generally, voluntary agencies such as the Alzheimer's Society have a vital role in advocating the needs of people with dementia of all ages to those responsible for planning, commissioning, and providing services.

REFERENCES

Annerstedt, L., Gustafson, L., & Nilsson, K. (1993). Medical outcome of psychosocial intervention in demented patients: one-year clinical follow-up after relocation into group living units. *International Journal of Geriatric Psychiatry, 8*, 833–841.

Arkin, S. M. (1997). Alzheimer memory training: Quizzes beat repetition, especially with more impaired. *American Journal of Alzheimer's Disease, 12*, 147–158.

Bäckman, L. (1992). Memory training and memory improvement in Alzheimer's disease: Rules and exceptions. *Acta Neurologia Scandinavica, Supplement 139*, 84–89.

Bahro, M., Silber, E., & Sunderland, T. (1995). How do patients with Alzheimer's disease cope with their illness? A clinical experience report. *Journal of American Geriatrics Society, 43*, 41–46.

Baines, S., Saxby, P., & Ehlert, K. (1987). Reality orientation and reminiscence therapy: A controlled cross-over study of elderly confused people. *British Journal of Psychiatry, 151*, 222–231.

Baker, R., Dowling, Z., Wareing, L. A., Dawson, J., & Assey, J. (1997). Snoezelen: Its long-term and short-term effects on older people with dementia. *British Journal of Occupational Therapy, 60*(5), 213–218.

Baltes, M. M. (1988). The etiology and maintenance of dependence in the elderly: Three phases of operant research. *Behavior Therapy, 19*, 301–319.

Barrowclough, C., & Fleming, I. (1986). Training direct care staff in goal-planning with elderly people. *Behavioural Psychotherapy, 14*, 192–209.

Beck, C. K., Heacock, P., Mercer, S. O., Walls, R., Rapp, C. G., & Vogelpohl, T. S. (1997). Improving dressing behavior in cognitively impaired nursing home residents. *Nursing Research, 46*(3), 126–132.

Benjamin, L. C., & Spector, J. (1990). The relationship of staff, resident and environmental characteristics to stress experienced by staff caring for the dementing. *International Journal of Geriatric Psychiatry, 5*, 25–31.

Bird, M., Alexopoulos, P., & Adamowicz, J. (1995). Success and failure in five case studies: Use of cued recall to ameliorate behaviour problems in senile dementia. *International Journal of Geriatric Psychiatry, 10*, 305–311.

Bleathman, C., & Morton, I. (1992). Validation therapy: Extracts from 20 groups with dementia sufferers. *Journal of Advanced Nursing, 17*, 658–666.

Bornat, J. (Ed.) (1994). *Reminiscence reviewed: perspectives, evaluations, achievements.* Buckingham: Open University Press.

Bourgeois, M. S. (1990). Enhancing conversation skills in patients with Alzheimer's disease using a prosthetic memory aid. *Journal of Applied Behavior Analysis, 23*, 29–42.

Bourgeois, M. S. (1992). *Conversing with memory impaired individuals using memory aids: A memory aid workbook.* Bicester: Winslow Press.

Brane, G., Karlsson, I., Kihlgren, M., & Norberg, A. (1989). Integrity-promoting care of demented nursing home patients: Psychological and biochemical changes. *International Journal of Geriatric Psychiatry, 4*, 165–172.

Brodaty, H., & Gresham, M. (1989). Effect of a training programme to reduce stress in carers of patients with dementia. *British Medical Journal, 299*, 1375–1379.

Brodaty, H., Gresham, M., & Luscombe, G. (1997). The Prince Henry Hospital dementia caregivers' training programme. *International Journal of Geriatric Psychiatry, 12*, 183–192.

Brooker, D. J. R., Snape, M., Johnson, E., Ward, D., & Payne, M. (1997). Single case evaluation of the effects of aromatherapy and massage on disturbed behaviour in severe dementia. *British Journal of Clinical Psychology, 36*(2), 287–296.

Brooker, D., Foster, N., Banner, A., Payne, M., & Jackson, L. (1998). The efficacy of Dementia Care Mapping as an audit tool: Report of a 3-year British NHS evaluation. *Aging & Mental Health, 2*(1), 60–70.

Brown, P., Challis, D., & von Abendorff, R. (1996). The work of a community mental health team for the elderly: Referrals, caseloads, contact history and outcomes. *International Journal of Geriatric Psychiatry, 11*(1), 29–39.

Burgio, L. D., & Burgio, K. L. (1990). Institutional staff training and management: A review of the literature and a model for geriatric, long-term care facilities. *International Journal of Aging & Human Development, 30*(4), 287–302.

Burgio, L. D., Burgio, K. L., Engel, B. T., & Tice, L. M. (1986). Increasing distance and independence of ambulation in elderly nursing home residents. *Journal of Applied Behavior Analysis, 19*, 357–366.

Burton, M. (1980). Evaluation and change in a psychogeriatric ward through direct observation and feedback. *British Journal of Psychiatry, 137*, 566–571.

Camp, C. J., Foss, J. W., O'Hanlon, A. M., & Stevens, A. B. (1996). Memory interventions for persons with dementia. *Applied Cognitive Psychology, 10*, 193–210.

Carr, J. S., & Marshall, M. (1993). Innovations in long-stay care for people with dementia. *Reviews in Clinical Gerontology, 3*, 157–167.

Challis, D., Chessum, R., Chesterman, J., Luckett, R., & Woods, R. (1988). Community care for the frail elderly: An urban experiment. *British Journal of Social Work, 18* (Suppl.), 13–42.

Challis, D., von Abendorff, R., & Brown, P. (1997). Care management and dementia: An evaluation of the Lewisham intensive case management scheme. In S. Hunter (Ed), *Dementia: Challenges and new directions* (pp. 139–164). London: Jessica Kingsley.

Chiverton, P., & Caine, E. D. (1989). Education to assist spouses in coping with Alzheimer's disease: A controlled trial. *Journal of American Geriatrics Society, 37*, 593–598.

Clare, L., Wilson, B. A., Breen, K., & Hodges, J. R. (1999). Errorless learning of face–name associations in early Alzheimer's disease. *Neurocase, 5*, 37–46.

Cosin, L. Z., Mort, M., Post, F., Westropp, C., & Williams, M. (1958). Experimental treatment of persistent senile confusion. *International Journal of Social Psychiatry, 4*, 24–42.

Dean, R., Briggs, K., & Lindesay, J. (1993). The domus philosophy: A prospective evaluation of two residential units for the elderly mentally ill. *International Journal of Geriatric Psychiatry, 8*, 807–817.

DeLeo, D., Stella, A. G., & Spagnoli, A. (1989). Prescription of psychotropic drugs in geriatric institutions. *International Journal of Geriatric Psychiatry, 4*, 11–16.

Downes, J. (1987). Classroom RO and the enhancement of orientation – a critical note. *British Journal of Clinical Psychology, 26*, 147–148.

Feil, N. (1993). *The validation breakthrough: simple techniques for communicating with people with "Alzheimer's type dementia"*. Baltimore: Health Professions Press.

Findlay, D. J., Sharma, J., McEwen, J., Ballinger, B.R., MacLennan, W.J., & MacHarg, A.M. (1989). Double-blind controlled withdrawal of thioridazine treatment in elderly female in-patients with senile dementia. *International Journal of Geriatric Psychiatry, 4*, 115–120.

Furniss, L., Craig, S. K. L., & Burns, A. (1998). Medication use in nursing homes for elderly people. *International Journal of Geriatric Psychiatry, 13*(7), 433–439.

Gaebler, H. C., & Hemsley, D. R. (1991). The assessment and short-term manipulation of affect in the severely demented. *Behavioural Psychotherapy, 19*, 145–156.

Gallagher-Thompson, D., & Steffen, A. M. (1994). Comparative effects of cognitive–behavioral and brief psychodynamic psychotherapies for depressed family caregivers. *Journal of Consulting & Clinical Psychology, 62*, 543–549.

Gibson, F. (1994). What can reminiscence contribute to people with dementia? In J. Bornat (Ed), *Reminiscence reviewed: Evaluations, achievements, perspectives* (pp. 46–60). Buckingham: Open University Press.

Green, G. R., Linsk, N. L., & Pinkston, E. M. (1986). Modification of verbal behavior of the mentally impaired elderly by their spouses. *Journal of Applied Behavior Analysis, 19*, 329–336.

Ham, R. J. (1997). Clinical efficacy of donepezil hydrochloride in patients with Alzheimer's disease: Case studies. *Advances in Therapy, 14*, 223–233.

Hanley, I. G., & Lusty, K. (1984). Memory aids in reality orientation: A single-case study. *Behaviour Research & Therapy, 22*, 709–712.

Hanley, I. G., McGuire, R. J., & Boyd, W. D. (1981). Reality orientation and dementia: A controlled trial of two approaches. *British Journal of Psychiatry, 138*, 10–14.

Hausman, C. (1992). Dynamic psychotherapy with elderly demented patients. In G. Jones & B. M. L. Miesen (Eds), *Care-giving in dementia: Research and applications* (pp. 181–198). London: Routledge.

Head, D., Portnoy, S., & Woods, R. T. (1990). The impact of reminiscence groups in two different settings. *International Journal of Geriatric Psychiatry, 5*, 295–302.

Holden, U. P., & Woods, R. T. (1995). *Positive approaches to dementia care* (3rd ed). Edinburgh: Churchill Livingstone.

Josephsson, S., Backman, L., Borell, L., Bernspang, B., Nygard, L., & Ronnberg, L. (1993). Supporting everyday activities in dementia: An intervention study. *International Journal of Geriatric Psychiatry, 8*, 395–400.

Keen, J. (1989). Interiors: Architecture in the lives of people with dementia. *International Journal of Geriatric Psychiatry, 4*, 255–272.

Kitwood, T. (1995). Exploring the ethics of dementia research: A response to Berghmans and ter Meulen. *International Journal of Geriatric Psychiatry, 10*, 655–657.

Kitwood, T. (1997a). *Dementia reconsidered: The person comes first*. Buckingham: Open University Press.

Kitwood, T. (1997b). The experience of dementia. *Aging & Mental Health, 1*, 13–22.

Kitwood, T., & Bredin, K. (1992). A new approach to the evaluation of dementia care. *Journal of Advances in Health & Nursing Care, 1*, 41–60.

Lam, D. H., & Woods, R. T. (1986). Ward orientation training in dementia: A single-case study. *International Journal of Geriatric Psychiatry, 1*, 145–147.

Lindesay, J., Briggs, K., Lawes, M., Macdonald, A., & Herzberg, J. (1991). The domus philosophy: A comparative evaluation of a new approach to residential care for the demented elderly. *International Journal of Geriatric Psychiatry, 6*, 727–736.

Little, A. G., Volans, P. J., Hemsley, D. R., & Levy, R. (1986). The retention of new information in senile dementia. *British Journal of Clinical Psychology, 25*, 71–72.

Lord, T. R., & Garner, J. E. (1993). Effects of music on Alzheimer patients. *Perceptual & Motor Skills, 76*, 451–455.

Maguire, C. P., Kirby, M., Coen, R., Coakley, D., Lawlor, B. A., & O'Neill, D. (1996). Family members' attitudes toward telling the patient with Alzheimer's disease their diagnosis. *British Medical Journal, 313*, 529–530.

McEvoy, C. L., & Patterson, R. L. (1986). Behavioral treatment of deficit skills in dementia patients. *Gerontologist, 26*, 475–478.

McKeith, I., Fairbairn, A., Perry, R., Thompson, P., & Perry, E. (1992). Neuroleptic sensitivity in patients with senile dementia of Lewy body type. *British Medical Journal, 305*, 673–678.

Melin, L., & Gotestam, K. (1981). The effects of rearranging ward routines on communication and eating behaviours of psychogeriatric patients. *Journal of Applied Behavior Analysis, 14*, 47–51.

Miller, E., & Morris, R. (1993). *The psychology of dementia*. Chichester: Wiley.

Mittelman, M. S., Ferris, S. H., Shulman, E., Steinberg, G., Ambinder, A., Mackell, J. A., & Cohen, J. (1995). A comprehensive support program: Effect on depression in spouse-caregivers of AD patients. *Gerontologist, 35*, 792–802.

Mittelman, M. S., Ferris, S. H., Shulman, E., Steinberg, G., & Levin, B. (1996). A family intervention to delay nursing home placement of patients with Alzheimer's disease: A randomized controlled trial. *Journal of American Medical Association, 276* (21), 1725–1731.

Moniz-Cook, E., & Woods, R. T. (1997). The role of memory clinics and psychosocial intervention in the early stages of dementia. *International Journal of Geriatric Psychiatry, 12*, 1143–1145.

Moriarty, J. (1998). Community care reviewed. *Journal of Dementia Care, 6* (4), 33–37.

Moriarty, J., & Levin, E. (1993). Interventions to assist caregivers. *Reviews in Clinical Gerontology, 3*, 301–308.

Morris, R. G., Morris, L. W., & Britton, P. G. (1988). Factors affecting the emotional well-being of the caregivers of dementia sufferers. *British Journal of Psychiatry, 153*, 147–156.

Netten, A. (1993). *A positive environment? Physical and social influences on people with senile dementia in residential care*. Aldershot: Ashgate.

Norberg, A., Melin, E., & Asplund, K. (1986). Reactions to music, touch and object presentation in the final stage of dementia: An exploratory study. *International Journal of Nursing Studies, 23*, 315–323.

Pinkston, E. M., & Linsk, N. L. (1984). *Care of the elderly – a family approach*. New York: Pergamon.

Reeve, W., & Ivison, D. (1985). Use of environmental manipulation and classroom and modified informal reality orientation with institutionalized, confused elderly patients. *Age & Ageing, 14*, 119–121.

Rice, K., & Warner, N. (1994). Breaking the bad news: What do psychiatrists tell patients with dementia about their illness? *International Journal of Geriatric Psychiatry, 9,* 467–471.

Rinke, C. L., Williams, J. J., Lloyd, K. E., & Smith-Scott, W. (1978). The effects of prompting and reinforcement on self-bathing by elderly residents of a nursing home. *Behavior Therapy, 9,* 873–881.

Ritchie, K., Colvez, A., Ankri, J., Ledesert, B., Gardent, H., & Fontaine, A. (1992). The evaluation of long-term care for the dementing elderly: A comparative study of hospital and collective non-medical care in France. *International Journal of Geriatric Psychiatry, 7,* 549–557.

Rogers, S. L., Doody, R. S., Mohs, R. C., Friedhoff, L. T., & Donepezil Study Group (1998a). Donepezil improves cognition and global function in Alzheimer disease: A 15-week, double-blind, placebo-controlled study. *Archives of Internal Medicine, 158,* 1021–1031.

Rogers, S. L., Farlow, M. R., Doody, R. S., Mohs, R., Friedhoff, L. T., & Donepezil Study Group (1998b). A 24-week, double-blind, placebo-controlled trial of donepezil in patients with Alzheimer's disease. *Neurology, 50,* 136–145.

Rona, D., Wylie, B., & Bellwood, S. (1986). Behaviour treatment of day-time incontinence in elderly male and female patients. *Behavioural Psychotherapy, 14,* 13–20.

Salzman, C., Fisher, J., Nobel, K., Glassman, R., Wolfson, A., & Kelley, M. (1992). Cognitive improvement following benzodiazepine discontinuation in elderly nursing home residents. *International Journal of Geriatric Psychiatry, 7,* 89–93.

Sandman, C. A. (1993). Memory rehabilitation in Alzheimer's disease: Preliminary findings. *Clinical Gerontologist, 13,* 19–33.

Schneider, L. S., Pollock, V. E., & Lyness, S. A. (1990). A meta-analysis of controlled trials of neuroleptic treatment in dementia. *Journal of American Geriatrics Society, 38,* 553–563.

Schnelle, J. F., Traughber, B., Sowell, V. A., Newman, D. R., Petrilli, C. O., & Ory, M. (1989). Prompted voiding treatment of urinary incontinence in nursing home patients: A behavior management approach for nursing home staff. *Journal of American Geriatrics Society, 37,* 1051–1057.

Schnelle, J. F., Newman, D., White, M., Abbey, J., Wallston, K. A., Fogarty, T., & Ory, M. G. (1993). Maintaining continence in nursing home residents through the application of industrial quality control. *Gerontologist, 33,* 114–121.

Schweitzer, P. (Ed). (1998). *Reminiscence in dementia care.* London: Age Exchange.

Shergill, S., Mullan, E., D'Ath, P., & Katona, C. (1994). What is the clinical prevalence of Lewy body dementia? *International Journal of Geriatric Psychiatry, 9* (11), 907–912.

Sinason, V. (1992). The man who was losing his brain. In V. Sinason (Ed), *Mental handicap and the human condition: New approaches from the Tavistock* (pp. 87–110). London: Free Association Books.

Skea, D., & Lindesay, J. (1996). An evaluation of two models of long-term residential care for elderly people with dementia. *International Journal of Geriatric Psychiatry, 11,* 233–241.

Sommer, R., & Ross, H. (1958). Social interaction on a geriatric ward. *International Journal of Social Psychiatry, 4,* 128–133.

Spaull, D., Leach, C., & Frampton, I. (1998). An evaluation of the effects of sensory stimulation with people who have dementia. *Behavioural & Cognitive Psychotherapy, 26,* 77–86.

Stokes, G. (1996). Challenging behaviour in dementia: A psychological approach. In R. T. Woods (Ed), *Handbook of the clinical psychology of ageing* (pp. 601–628). Chichester: Wiley.

Sunderland, T., & Silver, M. A. (1988). Neuroleptics in the treatment of dementia. *International Journal of Geriatric Psychiatry, 3,* 79–88.

Sutcliffe, C., & Larner, S. (1988). Counselling carers of the elderly at home: A preliminary study. *British Journal of Clinical Psychology, 27,* 177–178.

Teri, L., & Gallagher-Thompson, D. (1991). Cognitive-behavioural interventions for treatment of depression in Alzheimer's disease. *Gerontologist, 31,* 413–416.

Teri, L., Logsdon, R. G., Uomoto, J., & McCurry, S. M. (1997). Behavioral treatment of depression in dementia patients: A controlled clinical trial. *Journal of Gerontology, 52B,* P159–P166.

Thacker, S., & Jones, R. (1997). Neuroleptic prescribing to the community elderly in Nottingham. *International Journal of Geriatric Psychiatry, 12* (8), 833–837.

Thornton, S., & Brotchie, J. (1987). Reminiscence: A critical review of the empirical literature. *British Journal of Clinical Psychology, 26,* 93–111.

Toseland, R. W., Rossiter, C. M., & Labrecque, M. S. (1989). The effectiveness of peer-led and professionally led groups to support family caregivers. *Gerontologist, 29,* 465–471.

Toseland, R. W., Diehl, M., Freeman, K., Manzanares, T., & McCallion, P. (1997). The impact of validation group therapy on nursing home residents with dementia. *Journal of Applied Gerontology, 16* (1), 31–50.

Welden, S., & Yesavage, J. A. (1982). Behavioral improvement with relaxation training in senile dementia. *Clinical Gerontologist, 1,* 45–49.

Williams, R., Reeve, W., Ivison, D., & Kavanagh, D. (1987). Use of environmental manipulation and modified informal reality orientation with institutionalized confused elderly subjects: A replication. *Age & Ageing, 16,* 315–318.

Woods, R. T. (1983). Specificity of learning in reality orientation sessions: A single-case study. *Behaviour Research & Therapy, 21,* 173–175.

Woods, R. T. (1995). Dementia care: Progress and prospects. *Journal of Mental Health, 4,* 115–124.

Woods, R. T. (1998). Reminiscence as communication. In P. Schweitzer (Ed), *Reminiscence in dementia care* (pp. 143–148). London: Age Exchange.

Woods, R. T., & Bird, M. (1999). Non-pharmacological approaches to treatment. In G. Wilcock, K. Rockwood, & R. Bucks (Eds), *Diagnosis and management of dementia: A manual for memory disorders teams* (pp. 311–331). Oxford: Oxford University Press.

Woods, R. T., & McKiernan, F. (1995). Evaluating the impact of reminiscence on older people with dementia. In B. K. Haight & J. Webster (Eds), *The art and science of reminiscing: Theory, research, methods and applications* (pp. 233–242). Washington DC: Taylor & Francis.

Zanetti, O., Binetti, G., Magni, E., Rozzini, L., Bianchetti, A., & Trabucchi, M. (1997). Procedural memory stimulation in Alzheimer's disease: Impact of a training programme. *Acta Neurologica Scandinavica, 95,* 152–157.

42. The young adult with neurological disabilities with particular reference to cerebral palsy and spina bifida

Christian Murray-Leslie   Peter Critchley

INTRODUCTION

This chapter discusses the needs and resources available for a hitherto much neglected group, viewed largely from a UK perspective. The first part of the chapter focuses on two important congenital neurological conditions, cerebral palsy and spina bifida. Cerebral palsy (CP) is the most common cause of severe disability among school leavers. Spina bifida (SB), often associated with hydrocephalus, is a less frequent cause of severe physical disability since the advent of prenatal screening and folate supplementation (Wald & Bower, 1995) and since less aggressive surgical management has been used (Lorber & Salfield, 1981). However, some children are still born with varying degrees of impairment and the nature and the pattern of those produced by SB are very different from those produced by CP.

The second part of the chapter discusses more general aspects of the rehabilitation of disabled adults. The intention is to consider the problems presented particularly among young people aged 16–30 years, taking into account what has happened in the earlier years and what lies ahead in later life.

CEREBRAL PALSY

The term cerebral palsy (CP) was first used by William Osler in 1889 but William Little in 1862 is credited with first describing and classifying the motor syndromes of CP. Little suggested that the syndromes were caused by abnormal parturition, premature birth, or asphyxia neonatorum, ideas that have influenced thinking on aetiology to the present time (Ingram, 1984)

DEFINITION

CP is a disorder of posture or movement, which is persistent but not necessarily unchanging and is caused by a non-progressive lesion(s) of the brain acquired at the time of rapid brain development (Hall, 1989). Epidemiological definitions include brain damage occurring at any time from conception up to 1 month post-partum, although it has been suggested that post-neonatal cases should be counted separately (Paneth & Kiely, 1984).

CLASSIFICATION

Classifications of CP based on aetiology and the time of occurrence are unsatisfactory because, in many cases, these characteristics are unknown. Classifications based on the distribution of neurological impairments and on clinical syndromes are generally used for clinical and epidemiological purposes (Ingram, 1984). Even so, problems remain in that the cut-off points between syndromes are often not precisely defined (and probably cannot be), overlap syndromes are common, and mixed patterns of tone occur. The classification that will be used here is shown in Table 42.1.

AETIOLOGY AND PATHOLOGY

CP is an umbrella term for a group of clinical syndromes and is therefore neither a single clinicopathological entity nor a single syndrome with different aetiologies.

For many years it was believed that birth trauma was the main cause of CP, but improved imaging techniques have failed to provide much evidence for this assumption and it is now estimated that intra partum hypoxia accounts for only around 10% of cases of cerebral palsy (Badawi et al., 1998; Nelson, 1988). There is a relatively poor correlation between Apgar scores and the subsequent development of CP (Nelson & Ellenberg, 1981). Prenatal causes are now thought to be

Table 42.1. A classification for CP

CP syndrome	Main features	Parts affected	Estimated percentage cases of CP
Hemiplegic	Spasticity and/or dystonia	One side of the body	34
Diplegic	Spasticity and/or dystonia	Both sides of the body, mainly the legs	44
Quadriplegic	Spasticity and/or dystonia	Whole body	7
Ataxic	Cerebellar ataxia	Both sides of the body	6
Dyskinetic	Athetosis and other involuntary movements	Whole body	9

most important. These include genetic malformations, *in utero* infections (rubella, cytomegalovirus, toxoplasmosis), and vascular problems sometimes secondary to placental insufficiency. Most cases with severe mental retardation are prenatal rather than perinatal in origin (Hagberg, 1979; Nelson & Ellenberg, 1981). Prematurity and low birth weight are risk factors not only because they increase the risk of perinatal brain damage but also because they can reflect developmental deficits that also give rise to CP. Postnatal causes, accounting for about 10% of cases (Paneth & Kiely, 1984) are usually readily identified. They include infection, especially *Escherichia coli* or streptococcal B meningitis, prolonged convulsions, and cerebral ischaemia sometimes associated with respiratory distress syndrome (RDS). When postnatal brain damage is excluded, there is a strong positive association between normal birth weight cases of CP and lower social class (Dowding & Berry, 1990).

Some clinical manifestations are associated with particular aetiologies, for example, ataxia with recessive inheritance and athetoid dyskinesias with kernicterus (now rare) or with birth asphyxia. Hemiplegia is often associated with a cerebrovascular event in the internal carotid or middle cerebral artery territory. Diplegia is caused by damage around the lateral portions of the lateral ventricles (periventricular leucomalacia) from relatively localised ischaemia and is associated with both prematurity and low birth weight (Alberman, 1963; McDonald, 1964). Quadriplegia is associated with more widespread bilateral brain damage and generalised brain malformation.

The most important forms of cerebral damage in both premature and full-term infants are haemorrhagic and ischaemic lesions (Pape & Wigglesworth, 1979). Subependymal/intraventricular haemorrhage develops in about 40–50% of all infants with a birth weight less than 1500 g. This can be present at birth or might develops in the first 3 days of life in association with respiratory distress syndrome (Hambleton & Wigglesworth, 1976). Ventricular clots of varying size can form with little cerebral damage, but equally there could be considerable white matter destruction or obstruction of the circulation of cerebrospinal fluid (CSF). These haemorrhagic changes might be associated with varying degrees of ischaemic damage.

The periventricular region in the preterm infant represents a vascular boundary zone between the blood vessels passing in towards the ventricles from the cerebral cortex and those that penetrate up close to the ventricles from the base of the brain and supply the ependyma and adjacent subependymal tissue. This area is very metabolically active and therefore especially sensitive to ischaemic damage either from intra-partum asphyxia or placental dysfunction. The resulting areas of brain damage are referred to as periventricular leucomalacia.

Other areas especially sensitive to generalised anoxia in the preterm infant are the midbrain nuclei, basal ganglia, and thalamus, because these areas remain more metabolically active and require greater blood flow up to term (Leech & Alvord, 1977; Pape & Wigglesworth, 1979).

EPIDEMIOLOGY AND NATURAL HISTORY

The incidence of CP is about 2.5 cases per 1000 live births. Several authors draw attention to the trend towards increased survival of low birth weight babies with an overall static or slightly increased incidence of CP, with an increased proportion of more severely affected children (Bhusan et al., 1993; Hagberg et al., 1989; Mutch et al., 1992). Improvements in obstetric care have apparently had little effect on the incidence of perinatal CP.

Hemiplegic CP has the best prognosis and, not surprisingly, those with total body involvement the worst. The prognosis for walking, which can be a major preoccupation to parents of young children, cannot reliably be given under the age of 1 year (Nelson & Ellenberg, 1982). Guidance on predicting walking achievement has been given by the studies of Bleck (1987), Nelson and Ellenberg (1982), Beales (1966), Sala and Grant (1995). Mental handicap *per se*, unless profound, is not a predictor of walking ability. Surveys referred to above show that adults with CP have a very high frequency of musculoskeletal problems. The risk of developing hip problems or dislocation can be predicted from the radiological status of the hips in at-risk children at the age of 30 months (Scrutton & Baird, 1997).

Overall survival rates are 86–89% at 20 years (Hutton et al., 1994); but the 20-year survival rate is only 50% for those with severely impaired manual dexterity, ambulation, and cognition (Hutton et al., 1994). Adverse factors for survival are spastic quadriplegia, epilepsy, and severe mental retardation, all of which are frequently associated (Crichton et al., 1995; Eyman et al., 1993; Hutton et al., 1994).

CLINICAL FEATURES

Motor signs can first be recognised up to the age of 2 years. Although the underlying disorder is non-progressive, its expression can change; children who are initially hypotonic can develop spastic quadriparesis, dystonia, dyskinesias, or rigidity. Severe structural changes can occur with the passage of time in muscles, bones, and joints. Children who walk at 2 or 3 years might cease to make further improvement after the age of seven or eight, and some may stop walking altogether in their teens, either through choice or necessity as their growth exceeds their strength. In later life, chronic effects of CP cause musculoskeletal problems. These were found in 76% of moderately and severely disabled adults with CP aged 16–74 years, causing symptoms before the age 50 years in 63% (Murphy et al., 1995). Robson (1968) has described continuing slow deterioration in scoliosis in a population of 152 individuals with CP aged 11–40 years, of whom 70 were over the age of 16 years.

Hemiplegic CP

This common form of CP has a prevalence of 0.66 per 1000 live births (Uvebrant, 1988). There is unilateral involvement, with the arm usually affected more than the leg. Spasticity is the most common feature but dystonic posturing of the arm also occurs. A child's motor asymmetry is often recognised by the parents as early as 3–4 months of age. Most cases are due to prenatal vascular damage. Those with unilateral ventricular enlargement on CT scan usually have only moderate disability; cortical and subcortical cavities frequently indicate severe disability, including mental retardation and epilepsy.

Motor impairment is mild in 50% and severe in 19%, with additional impairments (mental retardation, epilepsy, impaired vision, hearing and speech, and perceptual and behavioural problems) present in 42% (Uvebrant, 1988). The affected arm and leg is frequently underdeveloped. Scoliosis sometimes occurs, either functionally in relation to a shortened leg or as a structural feature, but is seldom severe.

The severity of lower limb involvement has been classified by means of gait analysis into four types reflecting increasing severity of proximal involvement (Gage, 1991). Children with hemiplegic CP usually walk between 18 and 21 months (Bleck, 1987). As these children have one good hand and arm, most become fully independent and potentially employable provided the associated problems of epilepsy (often delayed for several years and usually confined to partial seizures), mental retardation, and behavioural disturbance are not too severe.

Diplegic CP (Little's disease)

This condition is bilateral, although often asymmetrical. The lower limbs are affected much more than the arms. The frequency of learning disabilities is linked to the severity of arm involvement (Beales, 1966). The condition is associated with low birth weight and preterm birth and results from relatively localised damage to the corticospinal fibres in the periventricular regions. Preterm children usually have a better prognosis than those born at term. The muscles are usually spastic, but there can be accompanying ataxia. Spasticity can cause growth abnormalities in the long bones, especially femoral and tibial torsion, and the hip can sublux or even dislocate (Scrutton & Baird, 1997). Epilepsy and mental retardation are infrequent complications but optic atrophy and strabismus are often present.

The child's mother might first notice difficulty with changing nappies through adductor spasticity. There might be difficulty in attaining sitting but most often the problem becomes fully apparent when the child attempts standing, which is often considerably delayed. Most children manage some steps with support but often only eventually function as household walkers, when they frequently need an anterior or posterior walking aid. These children have frequently been the object of intensive physiotherapy and surgical programmes and—unfortunately—in the past inappropriately segregated education, as they often have normal intelligence.

Quadriplegia (whole body)

In this form of CP there is severe bilateral hemispheric damage causing involvement of all four limbs, the trunk, and head and neck, often associated with mental retardation and generalised epilepsy. Seizures often start in the first year of life. Motor

impairment is noticed early, especially in the most severely affected children. Muscle tone can be either spastic or mixed and persisting primitive reflexes, such as the asymmetric tonic neck reflex or symmetric tonic neck reflex, and severe extensor thrusting can make positioning, feeding, and care-giving very difficult. Coordination of swallowing and airway protection can be severely impaired (Rogers et al., 1994), often complicated by gastro-oesophageal reflux and oesophagitis (Sullivan & Rosenbloom, 1996).

Communication difficulties can result both from mental retardation and from bulbar muscle dysfunction. Optic atrophy and squints are often present and hearing is frequently impaired. Major scoliosis is very common, as is pelvic obliquity, both of which might be associated with subluxation or dislocation of one or both hips (Black & Griffin, 1997; Letts et al., 1984). Supportive seating is particularly important in this group of people. Hip dislocation is a very disabling problem, which is difficult to treat once it has occurred and which has significant long-term consequences (Cornell, 1995). Cooperman et al. (1987) reported that 50% of adults with dislocated hips continue to have pain. Scruton and Baird (1997) have described surveillance measures for at-risk children based on their radiological survey of a population of children with bilateral CP (diplegia and quadriplegia). Cornell (1995) has made a detailed review of the extensive literature on the hip in CP.

Ataxic CP

This relatively uncommon form of CP is characterised by bilateral cerebellar signs with disturbance of balance and incoordination, with a high stepping gait, intention tremor in the arms, dysarthria, hypotonia especially of the trunk, and sometimes nystagmus. The early motor milestones are frequently delayed but the majority of children with ataxia alone acquire independence in walking and other aspects of life, as their intelligence is often not impaired. Epilepsy is relatively common in this group. Most cases are genetic in origin but a combination of ataxia and spasticity can occur in a diplegic pattern as a result of hypoglycaemia.

Dyskinetic CP

This form of CP is due to extrapyramidal system damage in the basal ganglia and was previously mainly caused by kernicterus, but is now thought to result from perinatal anoxia. Involuntary movements occur at rest and increase with volitional effort, and consist of athetoid writhing movements and choreiform jerks combined with dystonic posturing. All four limbs and the head, neck and trunk are involved and a degree of spasticity might also be present. Hearing is often impaired. The problem is often first noticed when a floppy child first starts to have difficulty executing movements. There is frequently persistence of primitive mass reflexes such as the asymmetrical tonic neck reflex (ATNR) and there is poor trunk control; most children do not achieve independent walking. Dystonia can be severe and can lead to marked scoliosis and pelvic misalignment. People with this type of CP are often thin because of the energy expenditure associated with the continuous writhing movements and increased muscle tension. Many experience pain in muscles and joints, but also from reflux oesophagitis, the latter sometimes significantly increasing involuntary movements.

Intellectual function is often intact but communication can be difficult as a result of dysarthria, inability to write, and occasionally because of visual and hearing impairment. People with this form of CP can often be helped by assistive technology for communication, environmental, and wheelchair control.

MANAGEMENT OF CP

The wider needs of the cerebral palsied child and adolescent should be taken into account in planning any therapeutic programme including surgical management. The need for health care to be integrated with education and social activities has already been discussed. Unfortunately, in trying to help their child, parents can sometimes become unduly focused on a physical objective such as walking (Bleck, 1987). This can lead to the relentless pursuit of training and treatment programmes so that the child's other needs are neglected. It is not uncommon for parents to take their child to one or more specialist centres, where a particular therapeutic creed is practised with more or less intensity. This can place considerable demands on the parents and child. The various therapeutic schools, including Bobath, Conductive Education, Doman Delacato, Portage and Vojta, have been reviewed in detail by Bower (1993). Bower and McLellan (1992) have suggested a holistic, child-centred approach to the management of CP, where the goals of therapy are negotiated with the child and carers. They point out that motor skills are achieved only if the child is at the appropriate developmental age and the skills are associated with daily functional activities, which are understood and desired by the child and do not require increased assistance from others.

Given that brain damage cannot be reversed, improvement in function is unlikely to occur other than by maturation or compensatory movement. Consequently, the most important aims of treatment are to delay or prevent deformity and to promote the psychological well-being and optimal social functioning of the child (Bower, 1993).

Physiotherapy and positioning

It is doubtful whether physiotherapy can reduce spasticity other than temporarily. However, stretching muscle appears to prevent or limit muscle shortening due to spasticity. In childhood, muscle shortening through spasticity and inhibition of muscle growth is worsened by the continuing growth of the adjacent long bones. Maintaining function and muscle length and allowing muscle growth to occur is therefore an important aspect of therapy. Tardieu et al. (1988) found that no progressive contracture developed in the soleus provided that this muscle was stretched for at least 6 hours a day (the same as is likely to occur in an able-bodied child). Lespargot et al. (1994) have shown that a stretching regime benefited the hip adductor muscles.

The gastrocnemius and soleus are among the first muscles to shorten and attempts to prevent this are made through regular stretching exercises (with the stretching often carried out by parents), periods of sustained stretching in below-knee casts and encouragement of weight bearing through the feet. Weight bearing can be achieved by a child standing in a static frame or walking (either independently or assisted) and often wearing ankle/foot orthoses (AFOs) to discourage equinus. Siebel et al. (1998), in a randomised comparative trial in 69 children aged 4–11 years found that wearing a below-knee cast for 4 weeks was as effective as botulinum toxin injected into the calf muscles in diminishing dynamic spasticity. Both treatment groups showed statistically significant improvement in ankle position at initial ground contact and in maximum dorsiflexion during stance and swing phase.

Fulford and Brown (1976) have emphasised the role of gravity alone as opposed to spasticity in the very young child in influencing the development of asymmetrical deformity and Scrutton (1989) advised that cerebral palsied children at a risk of hip and spine problems need early and persistent positional control of posture. A further reason for encouraging weight bearing is the risk of osteoporosis, which can lead to pathological fractures (of the femur in particular; Brunner & Doederlein, 1996; Hobbs & Wynne, 1995; Lingam & Joester, 1994). Positioning in seating is regarded by many as being extremely important in preventing contracture in the hip adductors and hip deformities (Bower, 1990; Clarke & Redden, 1992; Scrutton, 1989) with positioning in lying also important to prevent contracture of the psoas muscle and the hip adductors (Nakamura & Ohamu, 1980).

Various modular support systems are available for supporting a child or adult in lying in as comfortable and symmetrical a position as possible. The principles of seating assessment and provision have been described by Green and Nelham (1991) and by Bardsley (1993). The effort of balancing in an unstable body position can be considerable and instability in sitting can lead to an increase in muscle tone and abnormal movements. In addition to any effects on preventing hip contractures, an appropriate seating system can be of critical importance in assisting feeding, preventing extensor thrusting, and allowing the use of the arms. At the simplest level, the accommodation of fixed deformity by an accurately conforming seating system can improve comfort and reduce points of high pressure and shearing. Abnormal mass reflexes can be inhibited by positioning, for example the prevention of involuntary neck extension by positioning the body in a forward and flexed position can aid swallowing and reduce the risk of aspiration of food (Morton et al., 1993; Robinson & McCarthy, 1994). Stabilising the pelvis will assist trunk stability and thereby the function of the arms and head. Stabilising the trunk itself will further assist function in the upper limbs in a floppy child.

Oral medication

Oral antispasticity drugs that are used routinely in adults with acquired spasticity are used much less frequently in children with spasticity. The side-effects seem to outweigh any useful effects (Bleck, 1987, p. 196). Diazepam can be very effective in reducing spasticity in muscle, but does so at the cost of marked sedation. It might, however, be useful on occasions for the treatment of postoperative spasms (Gage, 1991).

Intrathecal baclofen

This has been used for some years for the treatment of severe spasticity in adults with spinal cord injuries and multiple sclerosis. It has already been reported to be of benefit in children with CP for the relief of spasticity (Albright et al., 1991) and for dystonia (Albright et al., 1998). In the 1991 study by Albright and colleagues, 17 children with spastic CP were injected with varying doses of baclofen or placebo. Those receiving baclofen were reported to have a reduction in lower limb spasticity within 2 hours of injection, with this persisting for 8 hours. In the 1998 study, which was inspired by dramatic improvement from intrathecal Baclofen in a single dystonic adult, 12 patients with dystonic CP had continuous infusion of intrathecal Baclofen by means of an external pump. All 12 patients were reported to have had a reduction in dystonia, with 8 going on subsequently to have a programmable pump implanted. These reports encourage some hope that certain hitherto more or less untreatable patients with severe torsional dystonias can be prevented from progressing to major spinal deformities and might be able to enjoy a better quality of life. Major problems reported with intrathecal baclofen treatment include sudden overdosage, catheter infections and blockage, and CSF leakage.

Botulinum toxin

Studies by Cosgrove and colleagues have awakened great interest in the use of botulinum toxin (BTX) in the treatment of CP. These authors first demonstrated that the early injection of BTX into the gastrocnemius muscle of the hereditary spastic mouse prevented contracture from developing (Cosgrove & Graham, 1994). In a second study, which was open and uncontrolled, BTX was injected into gastrocnemius, hamstrings, or sometimes both in a group of 26 children without obvious muscle contracture. These children were aged between 2 and 17 years of age and reduction in muscle spasticity occurred within a few days in all but one of the muscles injected and resulted in considerable functional improvement in 14 children. In particular it was noted that ankle dorsiflexion improved—mainly in children under 7 years of age—suggesting that muscle-shortening not amenable to BTX might have already occurred in the older patients (Cosgrove et al., 1994). Koman et al. (1994), in a very small, randomised, double-blind study, demonstrated that BTX was superior to placebo in the treatment of dynamic ankle equinus and Corry et al. (1997), in another small, double-blind study showed that BTX was superior to placebo in the treatment of upper limb spasticity in children with CP, although the actual functional gain was very small.

Neville (1994) has emphasised the need for larger randomised, controlled studies, pointing out the high cost of BTX and its potential for misuse, but also the considerable possibilities for its beneficial application in the cerebral palsies. In addition to the need for more substantial evidence for the efficacy of BTX, we need answers to questions such as: "What is the optimum muscle dose, dilution, frequency of injection?" "How should BTX be used in conjunction with splinting, physiotherapy and surgery?" "For how long can it be given and what is its long-term effect on the muscles and neuromuscular junctions of growing children?"

Rhizotomy

The practice of selective dorsal root rhizotomy (SDR) for the treatment of severe spasticity in cerebral palsied children has been promoted by Peacock and others, especially in South Africa and the USA, where its use has become widespread. The best results have been reported in children with diplegia, normal intelligence, and "capable" families, and when the procedure has been carried out before fixed contractures have developed (Peacock & Arens, 1982; Peacock & Staudt, 1991). There seems to be little doubt that spasticity is reduced (Boscarino et al., 1993; Peacock & Staudt, 1991; Peter & Arens, 1997), and it has been reported that, if performed in younger children, rhizotomy can reduce the need for orthopaedic surgery (Chicoine et al., 1997). Provided that the surgery is selective, i.e. not more than 30% of rootlets are sectioned at each level and the surgery is carried out between L1 and S2 (and not below), and the spinal laminae are replaced, the morbidity is reported to be low (Peacock et al., 1991). Problems that have been noted in the short term from less selective procedures include muscle weakness, severe hypotonia, crouch posture and valgus feet, sensory loss and hypersensitivity of the feet and legs. The longer-term effects are not known and there are concerns about the potential for spinal deformity, hip dislocation (Greene et al., 1991; Park et al., 1994), and neuropathic joints.

It has unfortunately become very difficult to carry out longterm controlled evaluations of SDR in the USA because the current popularity of the operation makes it impossible to sustain a control group (Neville, 1997). Nevertheless, three trials have been reported comparing SDR combined with intensive physiotherapy against intensive physiotherapy alone, with conflicting results. McLaughlin et al. (1994) found no difference in gross motor function measure (GMFM; Russell et al. 1989) between the two treatment groups at 2 years, whereas Steinbok et al. (1997) and Wright et al. (1998) found improvement in the GMFM at 9 months and 12 months, respectively.

Orthopaedic surgery

Orthopaedic surgery is carried out during childhood and less commonly during adult life. Surgery attempts to reduce and ameliorate the consequences of spasticity, but cannot address its causes. It is also known to be less successful in those patients with dystonia and mixed tonal patterns, and in those who have ataxia or dystonia. Operative objectives include lengthening of tendons, release of fascial attachments, redirection of muscles, reorientation of bones, and fusion of joints. In non-ambulatory children with quadriplegia, surgery is usually directed towards the treatment of the hip (adductor or psoas release, or bony surgery for acetabular dysplasia/hip subluxation or dislocation) or for the correction of scoliosis. The objectives of such surgery are usually to promote comfort in sitting, ease of hygiene, to maintain the hip joint in the socket, or to relieve pain.

Clearly, very marked muscle weakness can militate against successful surgery in those who walk.

Children who walk and have either hemiplegia and diplegia might have both bony and soft tissue procedures carried out to assist walking function. Although most hemiplegic children simply require surgery at the ankle, usually a single operation to lengthen gastrocnemius or tibialis posterior or both, those with diplegia frequently require multilevel surgery to ankle, hip, and knee to produce a balanced effect on the lower limb as a whole (Gage, 1991). This can involve correction of bony torsions, reorientation of the long bones in the direction of progression, joint fusions (especially in the feet to provide a stable base for walking), and soft tissue surgery to balance or redirect muscle forces. In the past children were subjected to a series of operations termed "the birthday syndrome" by Rang (1990), as the children spent most of their childhood either having operations or recovering from them with huge social and educational disruption. More recently it has become increasingly accepted that multilevel surgery should be carried out at the same time (Gage, 1991, p.192; Nene et al., 1993). It has been suggested that this surgery should be after the age of seven because at this age gait is fully matured to the adult pattern and the child is likely to have reached a plateau in motor development (Bleck, 1987; Nene et al., 1993).

Lengthening muscles can on occasion have quite markedly deleterious effects. Excessive elongation of the tendo Achilles can result in a very unpleasant deformity of the hindfoot known as calcaneus, with the child developing a crouching planovalgus gait. The risk of this occurring is greater in those with diplegia and greatest in those with quadriplegia and when surgery has been attempted before the age of 8 years (Borton et al., 1998). Selective lengthening of gastrocnemius by fascial section is believed to be a better operation than lengthening the heel cord (Gage, 1991) but is associated with a greater recurrence rate. Hip adductor lengthening can in some circumstances lead to wind-sweeping (deformity of the hips) and, when performed in dystonic children, to an abducted externally rotated position of the thigh. The more widespread use of instrumented three-dimensional gait analysis allowing full kinematic, kinetic and electromyographic (EMG) recordings has allowed more careful evaluation of surgical procedures and better surgical planning.

Upper limb surgery has a limited place in the management of CP and is usually carried out for cosmetic reasons in hemiplegic patients.

Cerebellar stimulation

Cerebellar stimulation through an implanted electrode was described by Davis et al. (1980) and Cooper et al. (1976). This treatment was based on the observations of Sherington, who found that stimulating the anterior cerebellar cortex in decerebrate animals reduced extensor tone. However, there appears to be little evidence in the literature for worthwhile benefit and these procedures appear to have been largely abandoned.

Stereotactic surgery for movement disorder

Stereotactic lesions have been produced in the basal ganglia for the treatment of involuntary movement (Gornall et al., 1975; Speelman & Manen, 1989; Trejos & Araya, 1990). The results appear to differ considerably, perhaps indicating the lack of case definition and agreement on the precise nature of and indications for these procedures. In addition, the benefits in relation to the risks posed do not seem to have been adequately assessed and these procedures do not appear to be widely carried out.

SPINA BIFIDA AND HYDROCEPHALUS

The aetiology of neural tube defects is uncertain. Genetic factors are important, although the recurrence rate to a couple with an affected child is less than 25%. Environmental factors are also important. It has recently been demonstrated that the recurrence rate of spina bifida can be decreased if the mother takes folate before and during pregnancy (as reported by the MRC Vitamin Study Research Group, 1991; Wald & Bower, 1995). Screening in pregnancy for neural tube defects is via serum alpha-fetoprotein estimations and ultrasound scanning, particularly in those at risk (e.g. previous congenital malformation or maternal epilepsy being treated with an anticonvulsant such as carbamazepine or sodium valproate). These methods have reduced the prevalence of spina bifida and hyrocephalus.

SPINA BIFIDA

Spina bifida (SB) occurs in two forms: occulta and cystica. Spina bifida occulta is a bony defect in which the normal cord covered with meninges remains within the spinal canal. There is an overlying cutaneous stigma such as a hairy naevus or lipoma. As an incidental radiological diagnosis this has been found in up to 5% of lumbar spine X-rays in some series. Spina bifida occulta is rarely associated with a tethered cord producing a progressive neurological deficit in one foot with pes cavus, requiring surgical release.

Spina bifida cystica (SBC), i.e. meningocoele or myelomeningocoele, has a prevalence of approximately 5 in 2000 births, with a slight female preponderance. Meningocoele (which accounts for 10% of SBC) is present when dura and arachnoid form a cystic swelling protruding through the bony defect, but the cord remains within the spinal canal. A meningocoele is a relatively benign form of SBC. If treated surgically within 24 hours there is usually no neurological deficit, but 20% of subjects have an associated hydrocephalus. In myelomeningocoele, neural tissue (cauda equina and spinal cord) and the dura are in the cystic swelling protruding through the bony defect. This defect is almost invariably associated with neurological deficit in the sphincters and legs. There is, in addition, a risk of further injury from birth trauma and subsequent infection (ventriculitis and meningitis).

The neurological deficit in SBC depends not only on the level of the lesion, but also on its nature. Type 1 lesions show a complete loss of function below the upper level of the lesion, with a flaccid paralysis and areflexia, anaesthesia, and sphincter involvement. A type 2 lesion shows a lower motor lesion at one or more levels with an upper motor neuron lesion below. In some type 2 lesions there can be a partial cord lesion with limited voluntary movement distally. Rarely, SBC affects one side of the cord and not the other, i.e. a hemimyelomeningocoele. There might be an associated kyphoscoliosis and shortening of the affected leg.

Bladder and bowel involvement is common to all lesions except hemimyelomeningocoele. The bladder can be denervated together with the sacral roots, or it can show an upper motor neurone pattern with reflex activity, with associated detrusor instability with trabeculations and reflux. Bowel motility is impaired and constipation, with the need for laxatives, enemas, and manual evacuations, is almost invariable. Secondary musculoskeletal abnormalities are frequent depending upon the level of the lesion and include spinal deformities (kyphosis, hyperlordosis, scoliosis), hip deformities (dislocation, subluxation, and dysplasia), and deformities at the knees and feet. The combined effects of flaccid paralysis, spinal and musculoskeletal problems, sensory impairment, and incontinence create a very high risk of skin breakdown (McCarthy et al., 1984). Vasomotor changes are seen in the affected legs, with mottled blue cold legs, which, together with anaesthesia, make for a high risk of ulceration. There might be additional congenital abnormalities, including severe kyphoscoliosis, hemivertebrae, anomalous ribs, renal malformations in up to 20%, and an associated hydrocephalus in 85–90%.

HYDROCEPHALUS

Hydrocephalus can occur in congenital form as an isolated finding or together with SBC, or it can occur as an acquired disorder in infancy following, for example, meningitis or subarachnoid haemorrhage. The two important types of congenital hydrocephalus are the Dandy–Walker syndrome and the Arnold–Chiari malformation.

The Dandy–Walker syndrome is characterised by failure of development of the midportion of the cerebellum and obstruction of outflow of CSF from the fourth ventricle as the foraminae of Luschka and Magendie are blocked. There might also be a deficient or absent corpus callosum with enlargement of the aqueduct, third, and lateral ventricles.

The Arnold–Chiari malformation, like SBC, is divided into two principal types, type 1 without and type 2 with a myelomeningocoele. The medulla and pons are elongated, the aqueduct is narrowed, and the medulla and the cerebellar tonsils are herniated through the foramen magnum. In type 2 there might also be lower cranial nerve palsies. Type 2 presents in infancy whereas type 1 might not present until adolescence or early adult life, with hydrocephalus and/or syringomyelia.

Some people with congenital hydrocephalus are of normal intelligence and physical function, the diagnosis being made when a CT scan is performed for some other reason, but in general hydrocephalus is associated with impaired intelligence and learning difficulties. Sometimes there are associated cranial nerve palsies, and a combination of pyramidal and cerebellar dysfunction in arms and legs.

PROGNOSIS AND OUTCOME

A high proportion of children with the severest spinal lesions and greatest mental handicap die within the first 5 years, and many within the first year, of life despite surgery to the spine and relief of hydrocephalus. As would be anticipated, the degree of overall disability is strongly associated with the sensory level (Hunt & Poulton, 1995). The most severely disabled survivors with type 1 SBC and associated hydrocephalus grow into dependent adults with learning difficulties, paraplegia, and no voluntary control over bladder or bowels. They require physical help with activities of daily living throughout childhood and adult life (Hunt, 1990).

Hunt and Poulton (1995) followed up a consecutive series of 117 babies (50 male) with SBC, born between 1963 and 1970, and who were referred to a Regional Neurosurgical Unit. All had their backs closed within 48 hours of birth irrespective of the severity or level of the lesion, with 3 proving to have meningoceles only and with 95 also having placement of a ventriculoatrial shunt. At follow-up in 1992, there were 61 survivors aged 22–28 (mean 25 years). Of these, 43 had normal intelligence (IQ 80–137, including all the 9 survivors who had never required a CSF shunt); 41 were wheelchair users, of whom 30 were able to transfer independently; 20 survivors were able to walk 50 metres and of these 10 were able to walk more than one mile; 25 had succeeded in passing their driving test; 16 were continent of urine and did not require an appliance; 12 used intermittent self-catheterisation; 6 required an indwelling catheter (urethral or suprapubic); 6 used a penile sheath; 1 had an artificial urethral sphincter; 8 had a supravesical urinary diversion performed; and 12 used padding only. Nineteen had evidence of renal damage and 9 of these were on antihypertensive therapy; 5 had problems with faecal incontinence.

Of the 33 survivors regarded as having the potential to live independently, 14 (all with normal intelligence) were doing so, although 28 needed supervision only or varying degrees of help with their personal care.

Thirteen adults were in open employment, 12 in sheltered employment and 4 were full-time students. Four young women had become mothers.

MANAGEMENT OF SPINA BIFIDA AND HYDROCEPHALUS

Current practice in the management of SBC and hydrocephalus involves selective management pre- and postdelivery. This selectivity of surgical treatment has led to a marked decline in the prevalence of children and young adults with severe physical disability and cognitive impairment, relative to the cohort treated unselectively who are now in their twenties or older. Surgical practice is derived from studies of unselective treatment (Hunt, 1990), and other studies of selective treatment (Lorber & Salfield, 1981; Evans et al., 1985). Those with the most severe lesions and the worst outcomes can sometimes be identified antepartum and the pregnancy terminated, or alternatively identified at birth and not treated surgically. Recommended exclusion criteria for surgical treatment include:

- Level of lesion above L3.
- Head circumference 2 cm or more over the 90th centile.
- Birth injury, haemorrhage, or prematurity.
- Other major congenital malformations such as kyphoscoliosis.

Progressive obstructive hydrocephalus is treated by shunting (usually ventriculoperitoneal) in the first few days of life. Shunts can become infected or blocked, and might need revision. In some there is an arrest in the progress of hydrocephalus after some years; these people can survive with a blocked shunt. Regular follow-up in neurosurgical clinics and urology clinics (with annual or biannual renograms) is appropriate (with others attending orthopaedic or scoliosis clinics). Children usually attend a general paediatric clinic for the overall coordination of health care, with transfer to young adult services at 16–19 years of age.

Carr et al. (1983) reported that 47% of 132 12-year-olds with spina bifida had had pressure ulcers within the preceding 5 years. Although loss of sensation seemed to be the fundamental predisposing cause, ill-fitting appliances, footwear, or seating were important contributory causes. Prevention of skin pressure damage in people with spina bifida is therefore an important priority. The many improvements in the management of SBC, in particular of the neuropathic bladder and hydrocephalus, might improve mortality and morbidity but seem to have no effect on the level of physical disability present in adults, which is determined by the extent of neurological deficit present at birth (Hunt & Poulton, 1995).

PREVALENCE OF DISABILITY IN YOUNG ADULTS

There are some 340,000 disabled young people in the UK, representing about 2.5% of those aged 16–29 years (Martin, White & Metzer, 1988). Of these, 20,000 were found to be living in residential care or communal establishments with half having very severe disability (category 7 or above) (Hirst, 1990; Martin et al., 1988). In addition to CP and SB, causes of severe disability among young people include muscular dystrophy, spinal muscular atrophy, cerebellar ataxia, Rett's syndrome, and brain damage acquired through infection (meningitis), trauma, or anoxia. It should be noted that although many inherited neurological diseases are rare, together they form a significant group with many common features and needs, which can be inferred from a knowledge of the two conditions described in this chapter and from muscular dystrophy (described in Chapter 49). Non-neurological causes of disability in young adults include juvenile onset arthritis, cystic fibrosis, congenital heart disease, congenital dysmorphisms, and growth disorders, which can produce many of the psychological and social needs described in this chapter.

DEFICIENCIES IN CURRENT SERVICE PROVISION

Much has been written about the deficiencies and fragmentation of medical and other services for disabled school leavers as compared with those services available to them during their schooling (Beardshaw, 1988; Castree & Walker, 1981; Chamberlain et al., 1993; Stevenson et al., 1997; Thomas et al., 1989) and led to Gloag (1984) describing the provision of services for young adults in the UK as being the worst in Europe. It is unfortunate that this lack of support and service occurs at the time of adolescence, when young people are seeking to consolidate their identity, achieve independence from their parents, establish adult relationships outside the family, and find a vocation (Hardoff & Chigier, 1991). Achieving these goals is always difficult, but especially so for those with disabilities (Warnock, 1978).

Following leaving school there is evidence of a lack of basic health-care provision and supervision, especially for those in greatest need (Parker & Hirst, 1987; Thomas et al., 1989); poor health screening, especially amongst those with severe learning disabilities (Wilson & Haire, 1990; Murphy et al., 1995); lack of help for psychological and relationship problems for those living in the community (Wadsworth & Harper, 1993); and a lack of genetic and sexual counselling (Court Report, 1976; Warnock, 1978).

Hirst (1983) found that 81% of those who had regularly seen a physiotherapist at school no longer did so when they left, and Thomas et al. (1989), in addition to confirming this loss of physiotherapy, also reported a lack of occupational therapy and speech therapy services. Beardshaw (1988), in her review of community health services for people with physical disabilities, highlighted the lack of information and advice services then available and accessible to disabled school leavers.

However, not all is doom and gloom. In the UK, progress has been made through a series of reports and through legislation that is paving the way for better services (see Appendix). Hirst and Baldwin (1994), in their study of a population of young adults with disabilities who had been identified in the OPCS Survey (Martin, White, & Metzer) and who they compared with a sample of non-disabled young adults of the same age, found grounds for optimism as well as pessimism. They noted that substantial numbers of disabled people were moving towards adulthood without major disruption or widespread unhappiness and could not be distinguished in these respects from their able-bodied peers. Nevertheless, there were significant social and economic differences between the two groups and they estimated that between 30 and 40% of disabled young people would have great difficulty in attaining a degree of independence as an adult compared to people who were not disabled.

THE NEEDS OF DISABLED SCHOOL LEAVERS

The needs of disabled young people at the time of transition between children's and adult services will vary greatly depending on the nature, number, and complexity of their impairments and disabilities and the resulting handicaps. For example, a young person with mild hemiplegic cerebral palsy (CP) and normal intelligence might be expected to lead a more or less normal life, to need very few services, and to have relatively few difficulties compared with a person who has quadriplegic (whole body involvement) CP and severe learning disabilities, who is likely to remain highly dependent on others. The needs of a 16-year-old with a comparatively rapidly deteriorating condition, such as Duchenne muscular dystrophy, and the emotional needs of the parents and carers will also be very different. Disabled young adults potentially need information and advice, some times with assessment and practical help, over a wide range of issues. These can include the provision of technical aids and equipment, transport, mobility, access, housing, employment, further education, leisure, health care, and personal and emotional issues.

Integration into society and progress towards independence

In the UK there has been considerable progress towards the integration of disabled children into mainstream schools, disabled adults into further and higher education, setting up Physically Handicapped and Able Bodied (PHAB) clubs, and improvement in public attitudes towards disability. All the same, young people with anything more than mild disabilities will tend to have much less personal experience of life and relationships and be generally less mature than their able-bodied peers (Hirst & Baldwin, 1994; Wadsworth & Harper, 1993). In addition, parents, knowing the vulnerability of their children, the general lack of service provision, and poor coordination and liaison, tend to "hang on" to their parental role for too long, discouraging attempts by the disabled young person to become more financially and socially independent. Disabled people wish, and indeed need, to be integrated into mainstream life—living and working, taking their leisure and socialising with "able bodied" people, and participating as far as possible in everyday ordinary activities. The Living Options Principles (Fiedler, 1990) support the development of individual autonomy and independence

so that services and agencies respond to the needs, wishes, and aspirations of the individual and so that disabled people can make informed choices based on good quality and accessible advice and information.

Social and vocational considerations on leaving school

Leaving school can be a disaster for some young people with disabilities unless there is good forward planning and support such as intended by the 1981 Education Act and recommended by the Warnock Report (1978). School often provides the main and most coherent structure in many young people's lives and some, particularly those with learning disabilities, might be just at the point of making real progress when they have to leave. Thus, for some, leaving school can increase social isolation (Anderson & Clarke, 1982).

There is now an increasing trend for young people aged 16 and over to stay in full time education, reflecting the changing patterns of employment and government policy; currently the figure staying in education is put at about 70% (McCarthy, 1997). Similarly, disabled school leavers are seldom equipped to go straight into employment and some further education and/or life skills or vocational training is usually necessary.

A number of options exist. In the UK, Local Education Authorities have an obligation to provide education between 16 and 19 for those who desire it. Further education can be provided locally in a Further Education college or, more remotely, in a Residential Training College. Banstead Place in Surrey, Portland College in Nottingham and St Loye's College in Exeter take disabled students exclusively. They are well resourced and provide a good range of education/training options and generally have considerable expertise and experience in these regards. They do, however, require the students to be termly or weekly boarders (which might be helpful to some but by no means all).

Unfortunately, there can be a vacuum when people finish college unless there is good local support to build on what has been learned and to continue to help people into independent or supported independent living and vocational activities. Parents might need counselling and support at this stage to help them with the process of "letting go".

There is little doubt the provision of skilled and appropriate/adequately trained disabled (peer) counsellors can be very helpful in assisting disabled young people address the emotional and relationship problems with which they may be confronted in growing up and becoming independent. Benefits advice is important and many disabled peoples' organisations and Social Services departments employ Welfare Rights Advisors, who can assist in the crucial matter of filling in the forms to trigger the necessary help, and also help with tribunals and appeals.

THE NEEDS OF CARERS

The need for respite for families who continue to look after more severely disabled people, especially those with learning disabilities, has been increasingly recognised. In the UK this has been recognised by the Disabled Persons (Services Consultation and Representation) Act of 1986. Very few young people even with very severe learning difficulties are now cared for in a chronic hospital setting; the majority are either looked after by their parents or by professional carers in small group homes or hostels. When the health care of such young people passes from paediatric to adult services there may be fewer facilities for their short-term residential placement. There is also a need for good quality day care facilities to provide an appropriately structured day with opportunities for learning life skills, socialisation and recreation, and ongoing training programmes.

HEALTH-RELATED NEEDS

The literature referred to earlier indicates that young people with multiple complex difficulties have many health-related needs and that there is ample room for improvement in the services for these. In the past, inactivity in this area has resulted from a lack of interest and rather poor attitudes among doctors, but the social model of disability when adopted too rigidly has sometimes discouraged specialist medical involvement, assuming that all health matters will be dealt with by primary care, or even led to health-care needs being overlooked altogether. Unfortunately, apart from emergency and other reactive "health care", regular health checks for prevention of illness and avoidance of complications have often not been available for young adults with complex disabilities (Murphy et al., 1995; Thomas et al., 1989).

Young adults with congenital neurological disabilities commonly have medical or health-related needs requiring active management, maintenance, and prevention in the following broad areas:

- musculoskeletal functioning
- feeding and digestion
- dental care
- the management of incontinence
- sexual function and relationships
- the management of epilepsy and hydrocephalus
- communication problems, including hearing and vision
- psychological adjustment to disability
- the maintenance of general cardiovascular and respiratory fitness
- prevention of ill health and further disability.

Musculoskeletal functioning

Musculoskeletal problems, as already described for CP and SB, give rise to pain, loss of function, or deformity. They are common in association with chronic neurological impairments, especially when these are acquired early in life or are congenital (Bleck, 1987; Murphy et al., 1995; Thomas et al., 1989; Turk et al., 1997). Musculoskeletal problems are a common cause of disturbed sleep and the need for night-time attention can impose an additional burden on carers (Thomas et al., 1989).

Added to all this there is the effect of ageing and abnormal loading on normal joints or on established peripheral joint and spinal deformities, causing premature degenerative change. Lundberg (1984) has shown that the physical working capacity of people with physical disabilities decreases with age as a result of poor mechanical efficiency. Thomas et al. (1989) reported that many young people in their survey, especially those with CP, had stated that their physical condition had deteriorated after they left school and in particular they had become less mobile and their joints more fixed.

In addition to physiotherapy and other measures to relieve musculoskeletal discomfort, including measures to treat abnormal muscle tone, young adults will have a continuing need for orthoses to support peripheral joints or the spine, appropriate footwear, and adequately supportive seating. As already stated, pressure ulcers are a major problem for those with spina bifida.

Feeding and digestion

Problems with nutrition and swallowing tend to occur in those with multiple physical and learning disabilities from CP (Dahl et al., 1996; Rogers et al., 1994). Oral feeding can be a slow and difficult business, requiring patience and some expertise on the part of the carer, with the individual being maintained in the correct body posture and food needing to be of the right consistency and to be presented correctly. Clearly, this can be difficult to ensure in a day care or respite setting. Morton et al. (1993) demonstrated the value of videofluoroscopy in the assessment of feeding disorders in a group of severely impaired children with mainly quadriplegic CP. Thomas et al. (1989) found 11% of their sample of 111 disabled young adults were emaciated (mostly those with CP) and 20% obese (mostly those with spina bifida). Low body weight results from an inadequate food intake due to slow feeding and reduction of appetite from chronic respiratory infections due to aspiration. Occasionally there is excessive energy expenditure in some dyskinetic, hypertonic states (Johnson et al., 1997).

In the event of failure to maintain a satisfactory body weight or when aspiration of food or fluids is becoming a problem, a gastrostomy might be required. This procedure is not without risk and is known to make gastro-oesophageal reflux worse in some, although it can prove to be life saving in others (Chang et al., 1987; McGrath et al., 1992). Monitoring of body weight by regular weighing is obviously important and a Nutritional Assessment Rating Scale exists for those with learning disabilities (Bryan et al., 1997).

Gastro-oesophageal reflux causing pain and vomiting with the risk of aspiration and haematemesis in addition to dysphagia is not infrequently found in those most severely affected with quadriplegic CP who have major swallowing difficulties. It requires appropriate medical or surgical management (Catto-Smith et al., 1991).

Dental care

People with severe physical disabilities tend to have more periodontal disease and poorer oral hygiene than the general population. Thomas et al. (1989) noted that 12% of 111 disabled young adults in their survey were in need of dental treatment and that 41% never saw a dentist. They also found that poor dental health care seemed to be a particular problem in those with CP. Physically disabled people can have difficulty accessing dental premises and dentists sometimes have little expertise for treating them, and indeed might have little incentive to do so (Gill & Garcia-Moreno, 1983; Hirschmann, 1997). Other factors that could contribute to poor dental health include: (1) sugar containing liquid medication; (2) a poor diet high in sugar; (3) drugs that dry the mouth, such as tricyclic antidepressants, oxybutynin, and anticholinergic drugs used for treatment of extrapyramidal symptoms; (4) difficulty with teeth cleaning due to spasticity or oral hypersensitivity; or (5) "difficult" behaviour in those with learning disabilities. Whereas poor oral hygiene and dental disease can cause no more than discomfort and bad breath, dental pain can lead to difficult behaviour in those with learning disabilities or possibly to malnutrition. In some circumstances, such as the presence of congenital heart disease or an intracranial shunt for hydrocephalus, dental infection can lead to potentially life-threatening systemic infection.

Although it would be hoped that those with mild physical and learning disabilities would be treated by a local dental practitioner, those with multiple complex needs and learning disabilities would be probably better seen by the Community Health Services Dental Service. In some cases, dental treatment and scaling and polishing of teeth might need to be carried out under endotracheal anaesthesia.

Drooling of saliva can be a very troublesome practical and social problem for some young people with CP, and can be difficult to manage. This topic has been reviewed by Blasco (1996). Drooling is a normal phenomenon in infancy, but should not persist during wakefulness beyond the age of 3–4 years (Crysdale, 1989). Its reported causes include oral motor dysfunction with retention of saliva in the mouth and inadequate lip seal, reduced sensation in the mouth, but also decreased awareness of saliva on the skin in those with learning disabilities. Drooling is likely to represent part of a continuum of feeding, swallowing, speech, and upper respiratory functional impairment (Brody, 1977). Several modalities of treatment have been suggested, including various therapies, behavioural and postural approaches, medications to dry-out secretions, surgery to alter or eliminate salivary gland function, and even radiation. None is universally successful and no comparative studies have been done (Blasco, 1996).

Bowel management can be problematical in those with CP and severe learning disabilities, who are inactive and take constipating medications and who might have required laxatives for many years. Clayden (1996) has reviewed the causes of constipation in disabled children and its management. There is high prevalence of faecal incontinence of at least some degree of severity in people with spina bifida owing to poor anal tone and sensation, but the situation can usually be effectively managed by planned bowel evacuations (McCarthy, 1984).

The management of incontinence

Urinary incontinence is an important cause of social handicap in a significant proportion of young adults with congenital neurological impairments. Thomas et al. (1989) found 56% of their survey of disabled young adults were incontinent of urine, compared with 54% incontinent of faeces, and that incontinence occurred most commonly in those with spina bifida, where 94% were incontinent of urine and 83% incontinent of faeces.

In spina bifida, the bladder is affected chiefly, if not entirely, by lower motor neurone lesions of the sacral nerves, which involve the afferent as well as the parasympathetic motor control of the detrusor and internal sphincter so that there can be incomplete bladder emptying, detrusor/sphincter dyssynergia with ureteric reflux in addition to incontinence. Formerly, many young people with spina bifida progressed to renal failure and hypertension, but the introduction of intermittent, clean, self catheterisation has been revolutionary in improving the quality of life and preserving the kidneys of these patients (Hunt et al., 1996; Lindenhall et al., 1991; Uehling et al., 1995). There might also be weakness of the pelvic floor muscles.

In CP, urinary incontinence tends to be associated with learning disabilities, especially when severe, but urinary retention and ureteric reflux is not a characteristic feature and therefore urinary tract screening is probably not warranted (Brodak et al., 1994). However, Mayo (1992) reported that in a group of 23 adults and children with CP who had been referred for lower urinary tract symptoms, half had difficulty urinating due to lack of voluntary control and hypertonus of the pelvic floor (with only one older person having classical detrusor/sphincter dyssynergia), and half had urge incontinence, which was nearly always due to hyper-reflexia.

Faecal continence can be a problem in CP where the upper motor lesion leaves the reflex arc intact but voluntary control can be impaired or lacking. People with CP are more easily managed than those with SBC, in whom the sacral deficit might be lower motor neuron in type, where a flaccid compliant rectum can retain large quantities of hard stool (Edwards-Beckett & King, 1996).

The management of urinary incontinence has hitherto left a lot to be desired (Bradshaw & Lawton, 1978; Thomas et al., 1980). However, there has been considerable improvement since the establishment of District Continence Services and Nurse Continence Advisors, who are frequently community based and could have links with Urological or Medicine for the Elderly Departments (Rhodes & Parker, 1993). Raising of general awareness by such events as National Continence weeks, the first of which took place in 1994, has also helped and good quality advice and literature is now available to patients and carers. Improved understanding of urodynamics and the availability of drugs such as oxybutynin, for bladder irritability, and desmopressin, for reduced nocturnal secretion of urine, along with better behavioural management, especially toilet training programmes in adults with learning disabilities, have also contributed to better management and reduced social handicap.

Sexual function and relationships

Disabled people have been frequently disadvantaged in their attempts to emerge as sexual beings by traditional public attitudes towards sexuality in disabled people, lack of appropriate sex education, and lack of appropriate counselling and advice regarding sexuality and relationship difficulties. These are combined with the problems of social isolation and lack of opportunity to discuss such matters both with their peers and professional people (Blum et al., 1991; Brown, 1980; Hirst & Baldwin, 1994; Thomas et al., 1989). These problems were highlighted in the Court Report, in 1976, which recommended that "much wider recognition should be given to the handicapped adolescent's need for genetic and psychosexual counselling to prepare him/her for adulthood" and also in the Warnock Report (Warnock, 1978), which found that "sex education and counselling for the handicapped tended to be handled very poorly in schools". It is not uncommon for physically disabled teenagers to worry about their sexuality. Dorner (1976) found in his study of 46 adolescents with spina bifida, that girls worried about their capacity to conceive and boys about their potency, but very few had consulted anyone or received any advice. It is not surprising, given all these problems, that close relationships and dating are less frequent among disabled young people than amongst their able-bodied peers (Blum et al., 1991; Hirst & Baldwin, 1994)

Management of epilepsy and hydrocephalus

Epilepsy.   Epilepsy is a common accompaniment of congenital neurological conditions and all seizure types are seen, ranging from focal seizures in people with mild hemiparesis and normal intellect to severe generalised epilepsy in people who have severe physical and learning disabilities (Hadjipanayis et al., 1997).

Epilepsy and its treatment have a direct bearing on major aspects of lifestyle, such as education and employment prospects, car driving, the use of alcohol, relationships, contraception, and parenthood. Compliance with drug treatment is a particular problem in adolescence (Smith, 1998). Overall, about 20–30% of people with learning disabilities have epilepsy, but some groups with mental retardation, for example those with tuberose sclerosis, have an extremely high frequency. Thomas et al. (1989) found in their survey of young adults that 33% of those with CP, 22% of those with spina bifida, and 33% of their remaining group of 45 individuals with "other" diagnoses had epilepsy, and that primarily epilepsy occurred in individuals who had both physical and learning disabilities. The same authors also noted that the management of epilepsy in young adults was particularly poor, with many not having had specialist review for more than 10 years (some more than 15 years) and

with much polypharmacy involving antiepileptic drugs (AEDs) and tranquillisers. In view of the known effects of AEDs on cognition and behaviour, and the relationship of psychiatric and behavioural problems to seizures themselves (Fenwick, 1995), together with the communication, psychological, and behavioural problems that can arise in people with learning disabilities, it is particularly important that seizure management is optimal. This might not be easy because of the inherent communication difficulties present in people with mental retardation with the consequent problems of distinguishing epileptic and non-epileptic phenomena, and recognising insidious drug-related side-effects. It is clearly important to advise disabled people on the possible effects of AEDs on oral contraception and on fetal malformations (Wallace, Shorvon, Hopkins, & O'Donoghue, 1997; Smith, 1998). Some patients with poorly controlled epilepsy might be suitable for surgical treatment and this can be curative.

Hydrocephalus.   Eighty per cent of people with spina bifida have hydrocephalus, which is also occasionally seen in relation to CP and other forms of congenital brain pathology. The management of shunts is neurosurgical and good practice includes regular—usually annual—review and the establishment of an emergency hotline number by the local Neurosurgical department to provide urgent advice and help in the event of a problem or complication with the shunt, such as blockage or infection.

Communication problems, including hearing and vision

Articulatory and language disorders are relatively common in people with congenital neurological disorders who have multiple and complex disabilities. Thomas et al. (1989) found that severe communication disorders were predominantly associated with CP (44%) as opposed to spina bifida (11%). The major cause is the associated learning difficulty. Frequency of these rose with increasing severity of the learning disability.

Dysarthria also occurs, and can range from a complete inability to articulate words and be understood, to lesser problems of intelligibility, which can be readily amenable to therapeutic help. Others will have a failure of development of language function, and some can have a combination of both.

About 25–30% of young people with spina bifida and hydrocephalus present as chatterers, showing a fluent type of conversation known as the "cocktail party syndrome", which can give the false impression of high intelligence, when cognitive testing reveals impairments, particularly in relation to perception and reasoning ability (Spain, 1974; Tew, 1979; Tew & Laurance, 1972).

Hearing.   The presence of severe hearing impairment will have a major impact on the development of language function. Overall, hearing impairment does not seem to be especially common in populations of disabled adolescents. Thomas et al. (1989) found mild hearing problems in 21% of their sample, with severe problems in only 1%.

Speech therapists can help with the intelligibility of speech and advise on alternative methods of communication using aids.

Communication may be word- or symbol-based, involving gesture, pointing, or operating a simple switch, touch-sensitive board, or keyboard (Rhyner, 1988). Improvements in switch technology and computer software has greatly extended the available options.

Vision. Visual problems are fairly common in young adults with physical disabilities and can include disorders of visual acuity, disordered eye movements such as strabismus or nystagmus, or impairment of visual fields, attention, or perception. Amblyopia is a visual impairment developing in childhood and affecting 1–4% of the general population. It is usually unilateral and is associated with misalignment of the eyes (strabismus) or in a difference in refraction of the two eyes (anisometropia). It is treatable only in childhood and requires early detection (Woodruff, 1995). Thomas et al. (1989) found visual problems most marked in CP, where 30% of individuals were affected. Those with hydrocephalus characteristically have impairment of visual perception (Miller & Sethi, 1971), which can present particular difficulties when individuals try to learn skills such as car driving (Sims, 1989)

Psychological adjustment to disability

Some of the problems the adolescent with disabilities has to face have already been alluded to or discussed, in particular with regard to difficulties in forming relationships. In addition, a disabled person has to develop considerable emotional resilience to cope with all the implications of disability. Several studies have shown that depression, low confidence, and low self-esteem are common, particularly in girls (Dorner, 1975; Kashani, 1986; McAndrew, 1979). Others have shown that those with severe disabilities and those with disabilities most easily noticed by others have the greatest psychological difficulty (Anderson et al., 1982; Offer et al., 1984). Overall, girls have been found to exhibit more marked psychological problems than boys, in particular depression and anxiety, although boys are more likely to show antisocial behaviour (Anderson et al., 1982). The World Health Organisation (1977) has suggested that all "at-risk adolescents" should be identified and that "counselling" should be offered through multidisciplinary teams and be available on a long-term basis (see the section "Service Models").

Maintenance of cardiovascular and respiratory fitness

Maintenance of respiratory and circulatory health can be difficult for many disabled people, who have poor neuromuscular function, skeletal deformities, and a sedentary lifestyle. The maintenance of bone mass is also a problem of immobility. This area has been generally neglected by health professionals in the past but is being increasingly addressed in day centres and leisure centres. The benefits of training programmes on the physical work performance of ambulatory subjects with CP has been documented by Fernandez and Piletti (1993). As already stated, obesity can be a problem, particularly with young adults with spina bifida, and needs attention as part of good preventive health care.

Prevention of ill health and disability

In common with maintaining bodily fitness, prevention of illness and injury is an essential component in any rehabilitation strategy or holistic health plan and will encompass such aims as preventing pressure ulcers, falls, contractures, or medication-associated problems. For physically disabled adults in the community it remains an all too frequently neglected area although "reactive" or emergency care is usually satisfactory (Murphy et al., 1995).

Routine health checks tend not to be done on those with moderately severe learning disabilities and insidious conditions such as chronic anaemia and hypothyroidism can be missed, and in addition signs of malignancy not noted. Women in particular need to have routine cervical and breast screening carried out.

SERVICE MODELS TO SUPPORT YOUNG ADULTS

It is evident that services set up to assist disabled school leavers and to fill the traditional post-16 vacuum differ considerably (Chamberlain et al., 1993) and it is not clear what is necessarily the best model.

The structure and working of well coordinated multidisciplinary Young Adult Services have been described by Baines and Chamberlain (1994) and Aung et al. (1994). It has been suggested that the core members of such teams should be a social worker, psychologist, secretary, nurse, and career officer/disability advisor (Ward & Chamberlain, 1997). To address more specific health-related needs, variable amounts of input might be required from a doctor with rehabilitation expertise, physiotherapist, occupational therapist, and speech and language therapist. It should almost go without saying that a goal-oriented, client-centred approach should be used, and that the service should be readily accessible yet flexible in its approach towards helping individuals.

APPENDIX: PRINCIPAL LEGISLATION AND REPORTS RELEVANT TO THE NEEDS OF DISABLED SCHOOL LEAVERS IN THE UK

A number of UK Reports and Acts of Parliament have important implications for disabled school leavers, reflecting changing attitudes to disability and these will be briefly reviewed.

Chronically Sick and Disabled Persons Act (1970)

Under this Act, local authority Social Services Departments are required to provide a range of services to disabled people. They are required to establish the numbers of disabled people living in their areas and compile and maintain a register of them (this is not easy to do if disabled people are not asking for services or move from one district to another).

Court Report (1976)

This provided a comprehensive review of Child Health Services in the UK and stressed the significance of social factors in children's health; the importance of family involvement in child health and social care; and the interrelationship between the health, educational, and social needs of children. The report also noted that children most in need of health care used health care least, and noted that the problems were likely to be greatest at the time of transition from childhood to adolescence. This report led to the setting up of local District Handicap teams or Child Development teams.

NHS Act (1977)

This Act states that the Secretary of State for Health has a duty to provide a comprehensive health service (including rehabilitation) and by subordinate legislation under the Act, Health Authorities are required to provide this on behalf of the Secretary of State for their local population.

Warnock Report (1978)

This influential report recommended a change in the system of special educational provision from that based on broad categories of disablement to that directed to the specific needs of the individual child. In addition, the report recommended that local educational authorities (LEAs) be required to identify and assess children who have special educational needs and to provide a statement of these needs.

Education Act (1981)

This legislation adopted the recommendations of the Warnock Report and partly replaced or amended the requirements of the Education Act (1944) regarding the provision of special educational needs (SEN). In particular, it stated that the provision of SEN should be met in as ordinary a school as possible. It laid down the procedure for the assessment and statementing of children with SENs from the age of 2 years, and for parental involvement in the process. It should be noted that a complete re-assessment takes place between the ages of 13 and 14 years and that the purpose of this is not only to determine the pupil's needs for his of her final years in school but also to plan for postschool provision. In addition, it should be realised that not all disabled children with health and social care needs will have a statement, and will not come under the terms of the Act, which is purely educational in intent.

Disabled Persons (Services Consultation) Act (1986)

This Act requires that local authority Social Services departments (SSDs) must, in reaching decisions about the need for services, have regard to the ability of the disabled person's carer to provide care on a continuing basis. Importantly, the Act lays down a procedure for liaison and formal notification between SSDs and LEAs (not Health Authorities) so that disabled school leavers are identified and are assessed for appropriate social services to assist their transition to adult life. Under this legislation, Social Services Committees are also required to consult with organisations for disabled people whenever an individual with special knowledge of the needs of disabled people is appointed or coopted. *Note*: this is an endorsement of the Living Options Principles (Fiedler, 1990).

Children Act (1989)

Central to this Act is the interest of the child, but the need to fully involve parents and carers in decision making is also recognised as being crucial. Nevertheless, it is parental responsibility for the child's benefit rather than parental proprietorial rights and duties that is the guiding principle (Tuke, 1991). The Act rationalises previous legislation so that children with disabilities are seen as children in need, and requires local authorities to provide services to minimise children's disabilities and to enable them to lead lives that are as near normal as possible. It seeks to encourage coordinated planning of services between local authorities, SSDs, Health Authorities, LEAs, and voluntary organisations. It provides for the planning and review of services for the individual child. These responsibilities extend until the age of 18 years, following which the needs of those young people who require continuing services are covered by the NHS and Community Care Act of 1990.

NHS and Community Care Act (1990)

This Act has had the most far-reaching effects to date on the assessment of all disabled people's needs, in that SSDs as the lead agencies in community care have a duty to ensure a qualified person carries out the assessment of need without regard to available resources and services. This is clearly not the same thing as having to meet those needs in full and it will be noted that although the responsibilities of SSDs have been progressively increasing with successive legislation, their funding has often been progressively reduced by central government capping of rates, council tax, etc. The assumed obligation and responsibility for SSDs to provide services irrespective of funding has been successfully challenged in the courts by Gloucestershire County Council.

The main principle underlying NHS reforms is the separation of commissioning (purchasing) of services from their provision. This has been mirrored in the reforms in the functioning of Social Services departments and the Act as a whole seeks to encourage a greater community emphasis and continue to move away from traditional institutional settings for care and rehabilitation.

Disability Discrimination Act (1995)

This Act creates rights of non-discrimination for disabled people in the areas of employment, access to goods and services, provision of financial services, and sale and letting of property, along with the right of access to transport infrastructure such as railways and bus stations. It requires that schools, colleges, and universities provide information for disabled people about accessibility to their facilities. A National Disability Council has been set up to monitor and advise government on the operation of the Act, but no enforcement body has been established

(unlike the Equal Opportunities Act and Race Relations Act). The Act is regarded by disabled people's organisations as being a step in the right direction, but is considered to be insufficiently comprehensive, effective or enforceable (RADAR, 1995). The Americans with Disabilities Act is more satisfactory in these respects.

REFERENCES

Alberman ED (1963). Birthweight and length of gestation in cerebral palsy. *Developmental Medicine and Child Neurology, 5,* 388–394

Albright AL, Cervi A, Singletary J (1991). Intrathecal baclofen for spasticity in cerebral palsy. *Journal of the American Medical Association, 265,* 1418–1422

Albright AL, Barry MJ, Painter MJ, Shultz B (1998). Infusion of intrathecal baclofen for generalised dystonia in cerebral palsy. *Journal of Neurosurgery, 88,* 73–76

Anderson EM, Clarke L, Spain B (1982). *Disability in adolescence.* London: Methuen

Aung TS, Boughey AM, Ward AB (1994). A study of the North Staffordshire Young Adult Services for physically disabled school leavers and young adults. *Clinical Rehabilitation, 8,* 147–153

Badawi N, Kurinczuk JJ, Keogh JM et al. (1998). Intrapartum risk factors for new born encephalopathy. *British Medical Journal, 317,* 1554–1558

Baines P, Chamberlain MA (1994). The physically disabled adolescent – service provisions in the community. *Maternal and Child Health Journal, January,* 10–19

Bardsley G (1993). Seating. In Bowker P, Condie DN, Bader DL, Pratt DJ (Eds), *Biomechanical basis of orthotic management.* Oxford: Butterworth Heinemann

Beales RK (1966). Spastic paraplegia and diplegia: An evaluation of non-surgical and surgical factors influencing prognosis for ambulation. *Journal of Bone and Joint Surgery, 48A,* 827–846

Beardshaw V (1988). *Last on the list: Community services for people with physical disability.* London: King's Fund Institute

Bhusan V, Paneth N, Kiely J (1993). Impact of improved survival of very low birth weight infants on recent secular trends in the prevalence of cerebral palsy. *Pediatrics, 91,* 1094–1100

Black BE, Griffin PP (1997). The cerebral palsied hip. *Clinical Orthopaedics and Related Research, 338,* 42–51

Blasco PA (1996). Drooling. In Sullivan PB, Rosenbloom L (Eds), *Feeding the Disabled Child. (Clinics in developmental medicine, no. 140.)* London: MacKeith Press

Bleck EE (1987). *Orthopaedic management in cerebral palsy. (Clinics in developmental medicine, no. 99/100).* Oxford: MacKeith Press

Blum RW, Resnick MD, Nelson R, St. Germaine A (1991). Family and peer issues amongst adolescents with spina bifida and cerebral palsy. *Pediatrics, 88,* 280–285

Borton DC, Walker K, Radda J, Starr R, Nattrass G, Graham HK (1998). Calf lengthening in cerebral palsy: Risk factors outcome analysis. *Gait and Posture, 8,* 75–76

Boscarino LF, Ounpuu S, Davis RB, Gage JR, De Luca PA (1993). Effects of selective dorsal rhizotomy on gait in children with cerebral palsy. *Journal of Pediatric Orthopaedics, 13,* 174–179

Bower E (1990). Hip abduction and spinal orthosis in cerebral palsy. *Physiotherapy, 76,* 658–659

Bower E (1993). Physiotherapy for cerebral palsy: A historical review. In Ward CD (Ed), *Rehabilitation of motor disorders. Ballière's clinical neurology vol. 3,* pp. 29–55

Bower E, McLellan DL (1992). Effect of increased exposure to physiotherapy on skill acquisition of children with cerebral palsy. *Developmental Medicine and Child Neurology, 34,* 25–39

Bradshaw J, Lawton D (1978). Tracing the causes of stress in families with handicapped children. *British Journal of Social Work, 8,* 181–192

Brodak PP, Scherz HC, Packer MG, Kaplan GW (1994). Is urinary tract screening necessary for patients with cerebral palsy? *Journal d'Urologie, 152* (51), 1586–1587

Brody GS (1977). Control of drooling by translocation of the parotid duct and extirpation of mandibular duct. *Developmental Medicine and Child Neurology, 19,* 514–517

Brown H (1980). Sexual knowledge and education of ESN students in centres of further education. *Sexuality and Disability, 3,* 215–220

Brunner R, Doederlein L (1996). Pathological fractures in patients with cerebral palsy. *Journal of Pediatric Orthopaedics, 5,* 232–238

Bryan F, Jones JM, Russell L (1997). Reliability and validity of a nutritional screening tool to be used with clients with learning difficulties. *Journal of Human Nutrition and Dietetics, 11,* 41–50

Carr J, Pearson A, Halliwell M (1983). The effect of disability on family life. *Zeitschrift fur Kinderchirurgie, 38* (Suppl. 2), 103–106

Castree BJ, Walker JH (1981). The young adult with spina bifida. *British Medical Journal, 283,* 1040–1042

Catto-Smith AG, Machida H, Butzner JD, Gall DG, Scott RB (1991). The role of gastroesophageal reflux in paediatric dysphagia. *Journal of Paediatric Gastroenterology and Nutrition, 12,* 159–165

Chamberlain MA, Guthrie S, Kettle M, Stowe J (1993). *An assessment of health and related needs of physically handicapped young adults.* London: Department of Health

Chang JHT, Coln CD, Strickland AD, Andersen JM (1987). Surgical management of gastro-oesophageal reflux in severely mentally retarded children. *Journal of Mental Deficiency Research, 31,* 1–7

Chicoine MR, Park TS, Kaufman BA (1997). Selective dorsal rhizotomy and rates of orthopaedic surgery in children with spastic cerebral palsy. *Journal of Neurosurgery, 86,* 34–39

Clarke AM, Redden JF (1992). Management of hip posture in cerebral palsy. *Journal of the Royal Society of Medicine, 85,* 150–151

Clayden G (1996). Constipation in disabled children. In Sullivan PB, Rosenbloom L, Bosma JF (Eds), *Feeding the disabled child. (Clinics in Developmental Medicine, no. 140.)* London: MacKeith Press

Cooper IS, Riklan M, Amin I, Watz JM, Cullinan T (1976). Chronic cerebellar stimulation in cerebral palsy. *Neurology, 26,* 744–753

Cooperman DR, Bartucci E, Dietrick E, Millar EA (1987). Hip dislocation in spastic cerebral palsy. Long term consequences. *Journal of Pediatric Orthopaedics, 7,* 268–276

Cornell MS (1995). The hip in cerebral palsy. *Developmental Medicine and Child Neurology, 37,* 3–18

Corry IS, Cosgrove AP, Walsh EG, MacLean D, Graham HK (1997). Botulinum toxin A in the hemiplegic upper limb: A double blind trial. *Developmental Medicine and Child Neurology, 39,* 185–193

Cosgrove AP, Graham HK (1994). Botulinum toxin prevent the development of contractures in the hereditary spastic mouse. *Developmental Medicine and Child Neurology, 36,* 379–385

Cosgrove AP, Corry IS, Graham HK (1994). Botulinum toxin in the management of the lower limb in CP. *Developmental Medicine and Child Neurology, 36,* 386–396

Court Report (1976). *Fit for the future – the report of the Committee on Child Health Services,* Cmnd 6684. London: HMSO

Crichton JU, Mackinnon M, White CP (1995). Life expectancy of persons with cerebral palsy. *Developmental Medicine and Child Neurology, 37,* 567–576

Crysdale WS (1989) Management options for the drooling patient. *Ear, Nose and Throat Journal, 68,* 820–830

Dahl M, Thommessen M, Ramussen M, Selberg T (1996). Feeding and nutritional characteristics in children with moderate and severe cerebral palsy. *Acta Paediatrica, 85* (6), 697–701

Davis R, Barolat-Romana G, Engle H (1980). Chronic cerebellar stimulation for cerebral palsy – 5 year study. *Acta Neurochirurgica, Suppl. 30,* 317–322

Dorner S (1975). The relationship of physical handicap to stress in families with an adolescent with spina bifida. *Developmental Medicine and Child Neurology, 17,* 765–776

Dorner S (1976). Adolescents with spina bifida: How they see their situation. *Archives of Disease in Childhood, 51*, 439–444

Dowding VM, Berry C (1990). Cerebral palsy. Social class differences in prevalence in relation to birth weight and severity of disability. *Journal of Epidemiology and Community Health, 44* (3), 191–195

Edwards-Beckett J, King H (1996). The impact of spinal pathology on bowel control in children, *Rehabilitation Nursing, 21*, 292–297

Evans R, Tew B, Thomas M, Ford J (1985). Selective surgical management of neural tube malformations. *Archives of Disease in Childhood, 60*, 415–419

Eyman RK, Grossman HJ, Chaney RH, Call TL (1993). Survival of profoundly handicapped people with severe mental retardation. *American Journal of Disease of Children, 147*, 329–336

Fenwick P (1995). Psychiatric disorder and epilepsy. In Hopkins, Shorvon Cascino (Eds), *Epilepsy*, 2nd edition. London: Chapman and Hall

Fernandez JE, Piletti KH (1993). Training of ambulatory individuals with cerebral palsy. *Archives of Physical Medicine and Rehabilitation, 74*, 468–472

Fiedler B (1990). *A frame for action: Developing services for people with severe physical and sensory disabilities. Living options in practical projects*. London: King's Fund Institute

Fulford GE, Brown JK (1976). Position as a cause of deformity in children with cerebral palsy. *Developmental Medicine and Child Neurology, 18*, 305–314

Gage JR (1991). Principles of treatment in cerebral palsy. In Gage JR (Ed), *Gait analysis in cerebral palsy*. Oxford: MacKeith Press, pp. 13–14

Gill M, Garcia-Moreno C (1983). *The health needs of severely mentally handicapped adults in Hammersmith and Fulham* (Internal Report). London: Hammersmith and Fulham District Health Authority

Gloag D (1984). Unmet need in chronic disability. *British Medical Journal, 289*, 211–212

Gornall P, Hitchcock E, Kirkland IS (1975). Stereotaxic neurosurgery in the management of cerebral palsy. *Developmental Medicine and Child Neurology, 17*, 279–286

Green EM, Nelham R (1991). Development of sitting ability, assessment of children with a motor handicap and prescription of appropriate seating system. *Prosthetics and Orthotics International, 15*, 203–216

Greene WB, Dietz FR, Goldberg MJ, Gross RH, Miller F, Sussman MD (1991). Rapid progression of hip subluxation in CP after selective posterior rhizotomy. *Journal of Pediatric Orthopaedics, 11*, 494–497

Hadjipanayis A, Hadjichristocloulou C, Youroukos S (1997). Epilepsy in patients with CP. *Developmental Medicine and Child Neurology, 39*, 659–663

Hagberg B (1979). Epidemiological and preventative aspects of cerebral palsy and severe mental retardation in Sweden. *European Journal of Pediatrics, 130*, 71–78

Hagberg B, Hagberg G, Olow I, Wend TL (1989). The changing panorama of cerebral palsy in Sweden. The birth year period 1979–1982. *Acta Paediatrica Scandinavica, 78*, 283–290

Hall D (1989). Birth asphyxia and cerebral palsy. *British Medical Journal, 291*, 279–282

Hambleton G, Wigglesworth JS (1976). Origin of intraventricular haemorrhage in the pre-term infant. *Archives of Disease in Childhood, 51*, 651–659

Hardoff D, Chigier E (1991). Developing community based services for youth with disabilities. *Paediatrician, 18*, 157–162

Hirschmann PN (1997). Dental care. In Goodwill CJ, Chamberlain MA, Evans C (Eds), *Rehabilitation of the physically disabled adult*. Cheltenham: Stanley Thornes

Hirst MA (1983). Young people with disabilities: What happens at 16? *Child Care, Health and Development, 9*, 273–284

Hirst MA (1990). *National survey of young people with disabilities matching and weighing samples*. DHSS 531 Social Policy Research Unit Working Paper. York: University of York

Hirst MA, Baldwin S (1994). *Unequal opportunities – growing up disabled*. London: Social Policy Research Unit, HMSO

Hobbs CJ, Wynne JM (1995). Spontaneous fractures in cerebral palsy. *British Medical Journal, 310*, 873–874

Hunt G (1990). Open spina bifida: Outcome for a complete cohort treated unselectively and followed into adulthood. *Developmental Medicine and Child Neurology, 32*, 108–118

Hunt GM, Poulton A (1995). Open spina bifida – a complete cohort reviewed 25 years after closure. *Developmental Medicine and Child Neurology, 37*, 19–29

Hunt GM, Oakeshott P, Whitaker RH (1996). Intermittent catheterisation: Simple, safe and effective but underused. *British Medical Journal, 312*, 103–107

Hutton JL, Cooke T, Pharoah POD (1994). Life expectancy in children with cerebral palsy. *British Medical Journal, 309*, 431–435

Ingram TTS (1984). A historical review of the definition and clarification of the cerebral palsies. In Stanley F, Albernan E (Eds), *The epidemiology of the cerebral palsies. (Clinics in developmental medicine, no 87.)* London: Blackwell Scientific, pp. 1–11

Johnson RK, Hildreth HG, Contompasis SH, Goran MI (1997). Total energy expenditure in adults with cerebral palsy as assessed by doubly labelled water. *Journal of American Dietetic Association, 97* (9), 966–970

Kashani JH (1986). Self esteem of handicapped children and adolescents. *Developmental Medicine and Child Neurology, 28*, 77–83

Korman AL, Mooney JF, Smith BP, Goodman A, Mulvaney T (1994). Management of cerebral palsy with Botulin A toxin: Report of a preliminary randomised double blind trial. *Journal of Pediatric Orthopaedics, 14*, 297–303

Leech RW, Alvord EC (1977). Anoxic–ischaemic encephalopathy in the human neonatal period: The significance of brain stem involvement. *Archives of Neurology, 34*, 109–113

Lespargot A, Renaudin E, Khouri N, Robert M (1994). Extensibility of hip adductors in children with cerebral palsy. *Developmental Medicine and Child Neurology, 36*, 930–988

Letts M, Shapiro L, Mulder K, Klassen O (1984). The windblown hip syndrome in Total Body Cerebral Palsy. *Journal of Pediatric Orthopedics, 4*, 55–62

Lindenhall B, Claesson H, Hjalmas K, Jodal U (1991). Effect of clean intermittent catheterisation on radiological appearance of the upper urinary tract in children with myelomeningocele. *British Journal of Urology, 67*, 415–419

Lingam S, Joester J (1994). Spontaneous fractures in children and adults with cerebral palsy. *British Medical Journal, 309*, 265

Lorber J, Salfield SAW (1981). Results of selective treatment of spina bifida cystica. *Archives of Disease in Childhood, 56*, 822–830

Lundberg A (1984). A Longitudinal study of physical working capacity of young people with spastic cerebral palsy. *Developmental Medicine and Child Neurology, 26*, 328–334

Martin J, White A, Metzer H (1988). The prevalence of disability amongst adults. Report 1 OPCS Survey of Disability in Great Britain. London: HMSO

Mayo ME (1992). Lower urinary tract dysfunction in cerebral palsy. *Journal d'Urologie, 147* (2), 419–420

McAndrew I (1979). Adolescents and young people with spina bifida. *Developmental Medicine and Child Neurology, 21*, 619–629

McCarthy GT (1984). Spina bifida and hydrocephalus in the physically handicapped child – an Interdisciplinary Approach to Management. London: Faber and Faber

McCarthy J (1997). Providing training for employment. In Goodwill CJ, Chamberlain MA, Evans C (Eds), *Rehabilitation of the physically disabled Adult*. Cheltenham: Stanley Thornes

McDonald AD (1964). The aetiology of spastic diplegia. *Developmental Medicine and Child Neurology, 6*, 277–285

McGrath SJ, Splaingard ML, Alba HM, Kaufman BH, Glicklich M (1992). Survival and functional outcome of children with severe cerebral palsy following gastrostomy. *Archives of Physical Medicine and Rehabilitation, 73*, (2) 133–137

McLaughlin JF, Bjornson KF, Astley SJ, Hays RM, Hoffinger SA, Armantrout E, Roberts TH (1994). The role of selective dorsal rhizotomy in cerebral palsy; critical evaluation of a prospective series. *Developmental Medicine and Child Neurology, 36*, 755–769

Miller E, Sethi L (1971). The effects of hydrocephalus on perception. *Developmental Medicine and Child Neurology, Suppl. 25*, 77–81

Morton RE, Bonas R, Fourie B, Minford J (1993). Videofluoroscopy in the assessment of feeding disorders of children with neurological problems. *Developmental Medicine and Child Neurology, 35*, 388–395

MRC Vitamin Study Research Group (1991). Prevention of neural tube defects; results of the MRC vitamin study. *Lancet, 338*, 132–137

Murphy KP, Molner GE, Lankaskey K (1995). Medical and functional status of adults with cerebral palsy. *Developmental Medicine and Child Neurology, 37* (12), 1075–1084

Mutch L, Alberman E, Hagberg B, Kodana K, Perat MV (1992). Cerebral palsy epidemiology: Where are we now and where are we going? *Developmental Medicine and Child Neurology, 34*, 547–551

Nakamura T, Ohamu M (1980). Hip abduction splint for use at night for scissor legs of cerebral palsy patients. *Orthotics and Prosthetics, 34*, 13–18

Nelson K (1988). What proportion of cerebral palsy is related to birth asphyxia? *Journal of Pediatrics, 112*, 572–574

Nelson KB, Ellenberg JH (1981). Apgar scores as predictors of chronic neurological disability. *Pediatrics, 68*, 36–44

Nelson KB, Ellenberg JH (1982). Children who outgrow cerebral palsy. *Pediatrics, 69*, 529–536

Nene AV, Evans GA, Patrick JH (1993). Simultaneous multiple operations for spastic diplegia. *Journal of Bone and Joint Surgery, 75-B*, 488–494

Neville B (1994). Botulinum toxin in the cerebral palsies – grounds for cautious optimism. *British Medical Journal, 309*, 1526–1527

Neville B (1997). *Dorsal rhizotomy: The case against in interventions for cerebral palsy*. Abstract of MacKeith Meeting at Royal Society of Medicine

Offer DI, Ostrov E, Howard KI (1984). Body Image, self perception and chronic illness in adolescents. In Blum RW (Ed), *Chronic illness and disabilities in childhood and adolescence*. Orlando, FL: Grune and Stratton

Paneth N, Kiely J (1984). The frequency of cerebral palsy: A review of population studies in industrialized nations since 1950. In Stanley F, Alberman E (Eds), *The epidemiology of the cerebral palsies. (Clinics in developmental medicine, no. 87.)* London: SIMP with Blackwell Scientific, pp. 46–56

Pape K, Wigglesworth JS (1979). *Haemorrhage ischaemia and the perinatal brain. (Clinics in Developmental Medicine, nos. 69/70.)* London: SIMP with William Heinemann Medical Books, pp. 69–70

Park TS, Volger GP, Lawrence H, Phillips LH, Kaufman BA, Ortman MR, McClure SM, Gaffney PE (1984). Effects of selective dorsal rhizotomy for spastic diplegia on hip migration in cerebral palsy. *Pediatric Neurosurgery, 20*, 43–49

Parker G, Hirst M (1987). Continuity and change in medical care for young adults with disabilities. *Journal of the Royal College of Physicians of London, 21*, 129–133

Peacock WJ, Arens LJ (1982). Selective posterior rhizotomy for relief of spasticity in cerebral palsy. *South African Medical Journal, 62*, 119–124

Peacock WJ, Staudt MS (1991). Functional outcome following selective posterior rhizotomy in children with cerebral palsy. *Journal of Neurosurgery, 74*, 380–385

Peter JC, Arens LJ (1997). Selective lumbo-sacral rhizotomy for the management of cerebral palsy patients. A 10-year experience. *South Africa Medical Journal, 83*, 745–747

RADAR (1995). Disability Discrimination Act: An overview. London: Royal Association for Disability and Rehabilitation

Rang M (1990). Cerebral palsy. In Morrissey RT (Ed), *Pediatric orthopaedics*, 3rd edition. Philadelphia: JB Lippincott, pp. 465–506

Rhodes P, Parker G (1993). The role of continence advisers in England and Wales. York: Social Policy Research Unit, University of York

Rhymer PM (1988). Graphic symbol and speech training of young children with Down's syndrome: Some preliminary findings. *Journal of Childhood Communication Disorders, 12*, 25–47

Robinson RO, McCarthy GT (1984). Cerebral palsy. In McCarthy GT (Ed), *The physically handicapped child*. London: Faber and Faber

Robson P (1968). The prevalence of scoliosis in adolescents and young adults with cerebral palsy. *Developmental Medicine and Child Neurology, 10*, 447–452

Rogers B, Arvedson J, Buck G, Smart P, Msall M (1994). Characteristics of dysphagia in children with cerebral palsy. *Dysphagia, 9* (1), 69–73

Russell DJ, Rosenbaum Cadman DT, Gowland C, Hardy S, Jarvis S (1989). The gross motor function measure. A means to evaluate the effect of physical therapy. *Developmental Medicine and Child Neurology, 31*, 341–352

Sala DA, Grant AD (1995). Prognosis for ambulation in CP. *Developmental Medicine and Child Neurology, 37*, 1020–1026

Scrutton D (1989). The early management of hips in cerebral palsy. *Developmental Medicine and Child Neurology, 31*, 108–116

Scrutton D, Baird G (1997). Surveillance measures of the hip of children with bilateral cerebral palsy. *Archives of Disease in Childhood, 56*, 381–384

Siebel A, Metaxiotis Accles W, Doderlein L (1998). Botulinum toxin and short leg casting – 2 different treatments in cerebral palsy equinus feet. *Gait and Posture, 8*, 61–81

Sims B (1989). Driver education: The needs of the learner driver with spina bifida and hydrocephalus. *Zeitschrift fur Kinderchirurgie, 44*, 35–37

Smith PEM (1998). The teenager with epilepsy. *British Medical Journal, 317*, 960–961

Spain B (1974). Verbal and performance ability in pre-school children with spina bifida. *Developmental Medicine and Child Neurology, 16*, 773–780

Speelman JD, Van Manen J (1989). Cerebral palsy and stereotactic neurosurgery: Long term results. *Journal of Neurology, Neurosurgery and Psychiatry, 52*, 23–30

Steinbok P, Reiner AM, Beauchamp R, Armstrong RW, Cochrane DD (1997). A randomised clinical trial to compare selective posterior rhizotomy plus physiotherapy with physiotherapy alone in children with spastic cerebral palsy. *Developmental Medicine and Child Neurology, 39*, 178–184

Stevenson CJ, Pharoah POD, Stevenson R (1997). Cerebral palsy – the transition from youth to adulthood. *Developmental Medicine and Child Neurology, 39* (5), 336–342

Sullivan PB, Rosenbloom L (1996). An overview of the feeding difficulties experienced by disabled children. In Sullivan PB, Rosenbloom L (Eds), *Feeding the disabled child. (Clinics in Developmental Medicine, no 140.)* London: MacKeith Press

Tardieu C, Lespargol A, Tabary C, Bret MD (1988). For how long must the soleus muscle be stretched each day to prevent contracture? *Developmental Medicine and Child Neurology, 30*, 3–10

Tew BJ (1979). The cocktail party syndrome in children with hydrocephalus and spina bifida. *British Journal of Disorders of Communication, 14*, 89–101

Tew BJ, Laurence KM (1972). The ability and attainment of spina bifida patients born in South Wales between 1956 and 1962. *Developmental Medicine and Child Neurology, 14* (Suppl. 27), 124–131

Thomas AP, Bax MCO, Smythe DPL (1989). The health and social needs of young adults with physical disabilities. *(Clinics in Developmental Medicine, no 106.)* London: MacKeith Press

Thomas TM, Plymat KR, Blannin J, Meade TW (1980). The prevalence of urinary incontinence. *British Medical Journal, 281*, 1243–1245

Trejos H, Araya R (1990). Stereotactic surgery for cerebral palsy. *Stereotactic and Functional Neurosurgery, 54–55*, 130–135

Tuke J (1991). Doctors and the Children Act. *British Medical Journal, 303*, 868–869

Turk MA, Gerenski CA, Rosenbaum PF, Weber RJ (1997). The health status of women with cerebral palsy. *Archives of Physical Medicine and Rehabilitation, 78* (Suppl. 12), 10–17

Uehling D, Smith J, Meyer J, Bruskewitz R (1985). Impact of intermittent catheterisation programme on children with myelomeningocele. *Pediatrics, 76*, 892–895

Uvebrant P (1988). Hemiplegic cerebral palsy. Aetiology and outcome. *Acta Paediatrica Scandinavia, 345* (Suppl. 77), 6–100

Wadsworth JS, Harper DC (1993). The social needs of adolescents with cerebral palsy. *Developmental Medicine and Child Neurology, 35*, 1015–1024

Wald NJ, Bower C (1995). Folic acid and the prevention of neonatal tube defects. *British Medical Journal, 310*, 1019–1020

Ward AB, Chamberlain MA (1997). Enabling the young disabled adult. In Goodwill CJ, Chamberlain MA, Evans C (Eds), *Rehabilitation of the physically disabled adult*. Cheltenham: Stanley Thornes

Wallace H, Shorvon SD, Hopkins A, O'Donoghue M (1997). *Adults with poorly controlled epilepsy*. London: Royal College of Physicians

Warnock HM (1978). Report of the Committee of Enquiry into the education of handicapped young people. London: HMSO

Wilson DN, Haire A (1990). Health care screening for people with mental handicap living in the community. *British Medical Journal, 301*, 1379–1381

Woodruff G (1995). Amblyopia: Could we do better? *British Medical Journal, 310*, 1153–1154

World Health Organization (1977). *Health needs of adolescents*. Report of WHO Expert Committee, Technical Report Series no 609. Geneva: WHO

Wright VW, Sheil EMH, Drake JM, Wedge JH, Naumann S (1998). Evaluation of selective dorsal rhizotomy for the reduction of spasticity in cerebral palsy; a randomised controlled trial. *Developmental Medicine and Child Neurology, 40*, 239–247

43. Malignant cerebral gliomas: Rehabilitation and care

Elizabeth Davies   Charles Clarke

I don't want to delay his death if it is inevitable. What I want to do is to make sure his quality of life is the best it can be until he dies. I don't want him to live two weeks longer in pain.

(Wife of a 59-year-old glioma patient)

All our enquiries seemed to receive the message: Brain damage from accidents. Think: 'rehabilitation'. Brain damage from terminal malignancy. Read: 'nothing to offer'.

(Chappell, 1997)

INTRODUCTION

The rapid and devastating consequences of cerebral gliomas on physical, psychological, and social well-being often leave clinicians who possess a strong curative approach with the feeling that they have little positive to offer in what is an increasingly difficult situation. This chapter discusses how a rehabilitative approach, understood in the widest sense as helping patients and their families adapt to change, might make the situation easier for all to manage. The chapter reviews survival following different treatments, and looks at current debates and guidelines for management. It also considers psychological aspects of diagnosis and treatment, the adaptation that patients and their families undergo, and changes in family roles that can occur. We suggest how to initiate in some modest way changes that address and attempt to maintain quality of life and discuss the need to develop new models of care and rehabilitation models for these patients.

EPIDEMIOLOGY, PRESENTATION, AND DIAGNOSIS

Although cerebral gliomas form a significant part of the work of a neurosurgical unit, they are generally seen as uncommon in the general population. Recent work, however, suggests that the incidence of primary brain tumours, and their impact on adults of working age, have almost certainly been underestimated (Grant, 1996a). A meta-analysis has shown those epidemiological studies undertaking thorough and prospective case ascertainment within defined populations indicate the real incidence of these tumours. Well-conducted studies performed in the post-CT era report incidences between 4.2 and 7.7 per 100,000 population per year for cerebral glioma (Counsell & Grant, 1998). However,

some of the highest incidences have been found by studies in the Lothian region of Scotland (Counsell et al., 1996) and South West England (Poberskin & Chadduck, 2000), where cancer registries were found to have missed a significant number of cases (Counsell et al., 1997). Since the 1970s, the recorded incidence of primary brain tumours has increased in developed countries by 1–2% each year, particularly amongst the elderly. This finding has attracted attention because it hints at the possibility of identifying new aetiological factors. However, improved diagnosis as a result of CT and MR scanning and better case-finding cannot yet be excluded as a cause. Although a large number of possible risk factors have been investigated, the aetiology of the majority remains elusive and only a small proportion can be explained by genetic syndromes. Ionising and therapeutic radiation, N-nitroso compounds, and nitrates remain possibilities. The effect of mobile phones has attracted publicity and is being investigated, although there are no data to support their role in causation.

There are few comprehensive studies of the presentation of cerebral glioma and few comparing the likelihood of this diagnosis given symptoms to those seen in general practice, general medical, or neurological practice. One retrospective review of diagnosed cases at Queen Square between 1955 and 1975—before imaging was available—found that the most common recorded clinical presentations were epilepsy (38%), headache (35%), mental change (17%), and hemiparesis (10%). By the time patients reached specialist assessment, the frequency of these symptoms had increased; mental change was reported in 52% and epilepsy in 54% (McKeran & Thomas, 1980). A Scottish study of the management of intracranial tumours identified by CT scan showed a wide variation in referral pathways, investigation, and subsequent treatment (Grant et al., 1996b). A Working Group recently attempted to define standard criteria for the urgent referral and assessment of such patients in England and Wales (Department of Health, 1999). Although there is no evidence that delay in diagnosis affects survival, it must be recognised that no studies have directly addressed this question. Data from registered cases suggests a gradual modest improvement in survival for astrocytoma between the 1970s and the 1990s but not for glioblastoma (Davis et al., 1998), and this

Table 43.1. Classification systems for the grading of gliomas

Kernohan (Kernohan & Sayre, 1952)	WHO (Zulch, 1979)	Brain tumour study group (Walker et al., 1978, 1980)
Grade I	Grade 1 and 2	Astrocytoma
Grade II and III	Grade 3	Anaplastic astrocytoma (Malignant astrocytoma)
Grade III and IV	Grade 4	Glioblastoma multiforme

could be explained by earlier diagnosis. After some early debate about the accuracy of image diagnosis alone, it is now generally recognised that the diagnosis must usually be confirmed by stereotactically guided surgical biopsy. The real benefits of an accurate diagnosis are seen to be the exclusion of curable infective lesions and tumours with better prognoses, providing accurate information to patients and their families, developing a coherent plan for treatment and care, and comparing outcomes after different treatments (Davies & Hopkins, 1997; Porter & Thomas, 1997a).

Knowledge of tumour grade helps to predict the duration of survival, although the use of different classification systems can create confusion. Here we concentrate on the clinical course of the histological diagnoses of glioblastoma multiforme and anaplastic astrocytoma, highly malignant tumours as used by the Brain Tumour Study Group (Walker et al., 1978, 1980) that are equivalent to grades 3 and 4 in the WHO scheme (Zulch, 1979) and grades II, III, and IV of the Kernohan scheme (Kernohan & Sayre, 1952) (see Table 43.1). Another scheme that is increasingly used in the UK is the Daumas-Duport classification (Daumas-Duport, 1988). Patients with lower grade tumours (Walker et al., 1978, 1980) have a better prognosis and 43% of cases with Kernohan grades I and II survive up to 10 years (North et al., 1990). The prognosis of those with the third or fourth grades of either classification is poor, and most patients will not be alive 2 years from diagnosis.

EVIDENCE FOR SURVIVAL FOLLOWING DIFFERENT TREATMENTS

There is a large volume of literature covering experimental treatments; much of it in non-randomised designs and involving selected patient populations. The Cochrane database, which collects and develops high quality systematic reviews of trial evidence, does not yet include any reviews on glioma treatment. A Cochrane neuro-oncology subgroup is proposed (R. Grant, personal communication) and, if successful, this should do much to bring clarity to the area. However, a number of reviews on the Database of Reviews of Effectiveness (DARE) cover the three main treatments of surgery, radiotherapy, and chemotherapy, assessed as meeting a number of clear methodological criteria and these are summarised here.

Quigley and Maroon (1991) reviewed the role of surgery using the results of 20 published series including over 5000 patients. They found that no series properly compared biopsy with surgery. Patients selected for surgery tended to be those who already possessed good prognostic factors, such as young age, histological status, and good performance status. Most series also did not show evidence that more extensive surgery improved survival compared to subtotal resection. The effects of these selection biases could not be ruled out, although there remained a suggestion that it might have a favourable effect in some subgroups. Ten years later Metcalfe again could find no published trials (Metcalfe, 2000).

Blomgren (1996) reviewed evidence for the effectiveness of radiotherapy from three randomised controlled trials that compared radiotherapy to surgery alone. Radiotherapy was given to the whole brain and/or to a wide margin around the tumour. The review found that doses of 45–60 Gy significantly improved survival by several weeks to several months. Further randomised trials showed that survival could be only marginally improved by varying the absorbed dose, fractionation, irradiated tissue volume, and radiation quality. No benefits were found for increasing the radiation dose over 60 Gy, for treating the whole brain rather than the tumour volume alone to up to below 60 Gy, nor did the addition of substances thought to potentiate the toxic effects of radiotherapy help. The review concludes that radiotherapy extends life with good quality survival and is therefore valuable as palliative therapy. Brachytherapy was considered experimental due to the lack of studies that included control subjects (Blomgren, 1996). A slightly later review (Stuschke & Thames, 1997) peformed a meta-analysis of three trials of hyperfractioned radiotherapy and found a trend for increased survival compared to conventional radiotherapy.

A final review (Fine et al., 1993) concerns the effectiveness of chemotherapy demonstrated by trials of nitrosoureas and other drug classes published up to 1989. This meta-analysis included 16 randomised controlled trials of patients receiving radiotherapy alone or radiotherapy plus chemotherapy. The results showed a 10% higher survival rate at 12 months and 8.6% at 2 years amongst patients receiving chemotherapy. Fine and colleagues concluded that chemotherapy should be considered as part of standard treatment, although more studies were needed to define subgroups of patients most likely to gain real benefit.

PROGNOSIS FOR PATIENT SUBGROUPS

The median survival for patients in randomised controlled trials following radiotherapy is around 10 months, compared with 3 months after surgery alone. Although the prognosis is poor, there is some variability in survival. A prognostic index incorporating the variables of age, performance status, presence of epilepsy and extent of surgery was developed using data from patients entered into two Medical Research Council (MRC) trials (MRC Brain Tumour Working Party, 1990) and seemed to predict survival well (see Table 43.2). The usefulness of the index when applied to patients treated largely outside of clinical trials has been confirmed (Davies et al., 1996a; Latif et al., 1998a) and the inclusion of information about tumour grade or the presence of necrosis to the index can help further (Latif et al., 1998a). Two studies including small samples of disabled

Table 43.2. The MRC prognostic index

Category	Score
Age (years)	
<45	0
45–59	6
>60	12
Clinical performance status	
0–1 (little disability)	0
2	4
3–4 (severe disability)	8
Extent of neurosurgery	
Complete resection	0
Partial resection	4
Biopsy	8
History of fits	
>3 months	0
<3 months	5
None	10

Index = sum of scores for each factor.

Table 43.3. The Karnofsky performance index

Description	Scale (%)
Normal, no complaints	100
Able to carry on normal activities; minor signs or symptoms of disease	90
Normal activity with effort. Cares for self. Unable to carry on normal activity or do active work	80
Requires occasional assistance but able to care for most of needs	70
Requires considerable assistance and frequent medical care	60
Disabled; requires special care and assistance	50
Severely disabled; hospitalisation indicated although death not imminent	40
Very sick. Hospitalisation necessary	30
Active supportive treatment necessary	20
Moribund	10
Dead	0

Table 43.4. The WHO clinical performance status

Grade	Description
0	Capable of all normal activity
1	No strenuous activity but able to carry out light work
2	Capable of all self care but no work; up and about more than half of the time
3	Limited self-care. In bed or chair more than half of the time
4	No self care, confined to bed or chair

patients with in Clinical Performance Status of 3 before radiotherapy suggest such patients derive little benefit from treatment (Davies et al., 1996a; Ford et al., 1997)

STUDIES OF FUNCTION OR PERFORMANCE STATUS

Until recently, the glioma literature has concentrated on treatment and survival rather than on psychosocial aspects of the disease or its impact on family members. Studies that have considered function have tended to use the Karnofsky Index or a modified version of this scale and initially tended to equate this with quality of life (see Table 43.3). For example, Shapiro and Young (1976) used the scale to show that quality of life was not affected by chemotherapy, although the scale does not cover the subjective issues that would be considered in the decision to prescribe chemotherapy. Such subjective factors might include time spent visiting hospital, the distress of nausea, vomiting, and occasional herpes zoster—or indeed dismay, the consequence of false hope.

The Karnofsky Index was originally developed to assess nursing needs among oncology patients, the clinician deciding on one of ten numbered categories (Karnofsky & Burchenal, 1949). It was popular for some time, and probably remains so in some quarters because of its simplicity and speed of administration, the fact that it relates to the prognosis and perhaps the spurious "scientific" sense given by being able to focus on a number. There has also been a temptation to treat this categorical scale as a continuous numerical one and to begin calculating mean "scores" for a patient sample, without thinking too clearly about the properties of the scale, or comparing it to other measures to assess neurological disability. In reality, comparison of ratings made by clinic staff show these tend to be overoptimistic compared to those made after home visits (Yates et al., 1980). Interrater reliability between different clinicians assessing case histories of glioma patients is at best moderate and fails to reflect handicap such as that, for example,

due to epilepsy (Macleod et al., 1995). Mackworth and colleagues (1992) compared Karnofsky ratings for 200 patients with patients' own questionnaire ratings about quality of life. They showed that the top range of the Karnofsky scale did not predict questionnaire measures of well-being or depression, but that it was more useful in the middle range, although highly sensitive to age. There have now also been efforts to explore the use of established measures of disability. For example, Thomas et al. (1995) and Brazil et al. (1997) adapted the original Barthel score (Mahoney & Barthel, 1965) for glioma patients to include an item on dysphasia and found the scale was sensitive to change, correlated with the Karnofsky, and had prognostic value. These authors suggested it might be a useful measure to evaluate palliation. In our own studies, we used the WHO clinical performance status rather than the Karnofsky to assess patient function (see Table 43.4). We used information from the unadapted Barthel (Mahoney & Barthel, 1965) and Nottingham Extended Activities of Daily Living (Nouri & Lincoln, 1987) scales to decide in which category patients should be placed (Davies, 1996a). We also used the Barthel score to identify the point at which patients began to deteriorate and experience severe disability (Davies et al., 1996a). Other workers have begun to develop more specific measures of neurological impairment. The Edinburgh Functional Impairment Tests—a battery of upper and lower limb function, memory, and a rating scale for dysphasia—aims to measure more the degree of disability, being quick, easy to administer and correlating with patient assessment of handicap (Clyde et al., 1998; Grant et al., 1994).

STUDIES OF QUALITY OF LIFE

Once it was acknowledged that a measure of performance, or even disability, is insufficient to describe quality of life (QOL) from the patient's perspective, a number of self-report questionnaire measures began to be used or developed to try and capture this elusive concept. Some researchers have tested out existing cancer or quality of life questionnaires on patients with brain tumours. For example, Giovaglioni and colleagues (1996) used the Functional Living Index for Cancer, Whitton and colleagues (1997) the Health Utilities Index, and Weitzner and colleagues (1996) the Ferrans and Powers Quality of Life for Cancer and the Psychosocial Adjustment to Illness Scale— Self Report. However, as pointed out by Weitzner and Meyers (1997), depending on their original purpose, such questionnaires are likely to be measuring different aspects of quality of life. Other groups have therefore developed brain-tumour-specific scales or modules, for example, the Functional Assessment of Cancer Therapy—Brain (FACT-BR) (Weitzner et al., 1995), the European Organisation for the treatment of Cancer (EORTC) brain subscale (Osoba et al., 1996), and the Preston Profile (Lyons, 1996).

These questionnaires take a multidimensional approach to QOL, asking questions about different domains such as physical state or symptoms, social or family aspects, functional well-being, and emotional well-being. Patients choose the point on a five-point scale they feel best describes their state, and these scores are correlated or compared with other ratings, or to disability or cognitive problems. So far, studies have mostly focused on the psychometric evaluation of the scales' properties and comparison with other measures of physical function, performance, or disability. For example, Osoba et al. (1996, 1997) report that EORTC QOL scores appear to reflect Karnofsky scores and showed differences between patients at diagnosis and at recurrence. They also found that deteriorating neurological status was associated with a marked increase in emotional distress and future uncertainty. Sneeuw et al. (1997a) have compared patients' ratings to those made by close relatives or carers. Although there was reasonable agreement, the carers tended to rate the patient as having a lower QOL than the patients themselves, particularly when patients had been judged as mentally confused. These authors argue that caregiver ratings can add important information (Sneeuw et al., 1997b, 1998). The results so far indicate that although QOL scores might *relate* to performance or disability measures, there is not a one-to-one relationship between the two. To our knowledge, such QOL measures have not yet been reported as outcome measures in trials of new treatments for malignant cerebral glioma, or used to decide on the efficacy of that treatment. However, an EORTC trial of two doses of radiotherapy (59 versus 45 Gy) for patients with low-grade glioma suggested that those receiving higher doses reported reduced QOL in terms of questionnaire ratings of decreased function and fatigue, and no improved survival (Kiebert et al., 1998).

Such measures, therefore, begin to give an indication of some of the experiences of these patients, although of course not in the detail that face-to-face accounts provide. Nor are these measures explicitly grounded in the personal accounts and explanations of patients. Although these questionnaires were developed after interviews or discussions with patients and relatives, issues defined by medical staff were also included and the process of reduction to questionnaire items is not described. Lyons (1996) observed in her study that interviews with patients or their carers elicited considerably more information than questionnaires, and that some patients found the concentration needed for questionnaires too demanding. One of the few qualitative studies that reports interview results and discussions with 23 patients exploring what the term "quality of life" meant to them, found this was a term only a few used spontaneously. Others found it difficult to define or talk about. Some talked instead about "living their lives", "living at all costs" and a few associated the term QOL with a situation of approaching death where no further treatment was possible (Fox & Lantz, 1998).

GUIDELINES AND DEBATES ABOUT MANAGEMENT

In the 1990s a few groups began to develop guidelines for the management of patients with malignant glioma in the US (Anonymous, 1997), and a multidisciplinary group was established in the UK (Davies & Hopkins, 1997). Both sets of guidelines present a consensus view rather than one based on systematic review of the literature and explicit grading of evidence for recommendations, but make similar recommendations about initial treatment. The UK guidelines considered the role of psychosocial and palliative care in more depth. An independent appraisal of the UK guidance concluded that it was a useful attempt at improving multidisciplinary care, although the method for developing the guidelines needed further work (HCEU, 1998). The UK guidance and some debates that remain are considered before discussing more recent work on the role of rehabilitation.

The UK guidelines pointed to the lack of evidence that surgical resection affected survival (Porter & Thomas, 1997b; Quigley & Maroon, 1991), and suggested that a randomised trial of surgery and biopsy for patients falling into each surgeon's area of uncertainty might be justified (Davies & Hopkins, 1997). Such a trial has been discussed for a long time (see, for example, Punt, 1984) and would be difficult to set up, but not impossible (Garth Cruickshank, personal communication, 2001). A recent study found no survival advantage for patients operated on by surgical neuro-oncologists compared to other neurosurgeons (Latif et al., 1998b), but the more important issue might be whether surgery can affect morbidity and patient function, and therefore the quality of remaining life. For example, studies have shown about 20% of patients deteriorating following an attempted maximal resection and 80% remained the same or improved (Fadul et al., 1988; Vecht et al., 1990). One recent prospective study by 40 patients with left-sided tumours, however, has demonstrated improved language after resection for those with dysphasia (Whittle et al., 1998).

It is perhaps the role of radiotherapy that has generated most disagreement—both overt and covert. The UK guidelines recognised evidence for the survival advantage of radiotherapy over steroids alone for selected patients and recommended clearly defined and well-planned treatment volumes (Davies & Hopkins, 1997; Gregor, 1997). Previous debates had followed observations at one large UK centre that neurologists were tending to treat patients with steroids alone and not refer for radiotherapy (Wroe et al., 1986a). These authors reported similar outcomes in the two patient groups and suggested that a policy of no treatment might be ethically justified. Their paper generated some considerable correspondence and criticism in the *British Medical Journal* (Bucy, 1986; Davies et al., 1986; Miller et al., 1986; Wroe et al., 1986b). Ten years later we presented data from a follow-up study of 92 patients receiving radiotherapy outside a trial setting from seven neurosurgery and radiotherapy units in London over 2 years (Davies et al., 1996a,b). We aimed to explore the quality of these patients' lives and record their problems in more detail. We made home interviews to see patients and their relatives and undertook disability assessments and in-depth interviews to ask about their experience. Our study confirmed the poor outlook for these patients, with a 12-month survival of 39% despite radiotherapy. Patients severely disabled at the outset gained little from radiotherapy, and nearly 70% of those who were less severely disabled experienced either clinical deterioration or severe tiredness after treatment; effects that were related to radiation dose and field size (Davies et al., 1996a). However, overall, assessed by their own reports, we found that 40% of patients achieved a period of stability or remission, and most did not express any strong dissatisfaction with radiotherapy. We also explored, during the interviews with patients as they began treatment, their perception of the prognosis. We judged that only one-quarter of patients were aware of the poor outlook as they commenced radiotherapy, compared with three times that number in the relatives (Davies et al., 1996b).

Again, our paper questioning the benefit of radiotherapy and suggesting adverse effects generated considerable criticism. In our study we sought to explore the effects of treatment outside a trial setting, that is in the reality of general neurosurgery and radiotherapy units within London, rather than within oncology centres specialising in brain tumour therapy. Not unnaturally, writers from specialist centres argued that better treatment techniques could have been given (Brada et al., 1996; Burnet & Taylor, 1997) but, at the same time, they seemed to us to have difficulty in accepting the reality of the day-to-day management of the patients we had actually studied. The claim of improved quality of life following radiotherapy made by Blomgren (1996) is based on trials that used whole brain irradiation and judged outcome using clinician assessment of performance status rather than a patient-based assessment of morbidity. The slow emergence of data suggesting neuropsychological deficits as a late effect of radiation is partly explained by the rarity of these cases, but it also suggests that the long-term evaluation of outcome was not well organised. Considering the radical nature of the treatment being undertaken this is disappointing, and might explain some of the earlier scepticism of neurologists about radiotherapy. Nevertheless, the results of our study show that most of the patients who were aware of the prognosis wished to undergo radiotherapy for the chance of extra survival (Davies et al., 1996b). MRC trials attempting to randomise patients with gliomas presenting with epilepsy to early or delayed intervention and treatment have found it difficult to recruit patients once the possibility of delayed treatment has been explained (Porter & Thomas, 1997b). These observations suggest that a neurologist's decision to avoid or delay referring patients for radiotherapy might not be the choice that an informed patient would make.

The UK guidelines also considered the role of chemotherapy. Rampling (1997) pointed out that the survival gain for chemotherapy demonstrated by the earlier meta-analysis (Fine et al., 1993) is modest and occurs only when the median survival for the majority has passed. No studies have really addressed the issue of quality of life in a systematic fashion. The UK guidance therefore recommended that adjuvant treatment should not be given at diagnosis, particularly to patients with a poor prognosis. This might be considered for palliative treatment after relapse or treated within experimental protocols where outcome and quality of life could be carefully evaluated. Equally, patients should also receive experimental treatment only within well-designed treatment protocols (Davies & Hopkins, 1997). Further evidence has since emerged from phase II trials of temozolamide (Temodal) for treating patients after recurrence. A multicentre trial has shown that of 103 patients treated, 11% of patients responded and 47% remained stable (Bower et al., 1997). More studies to define the role of this drug after diagnosis are needed, but the National Institute for Clinical Excellence (NICE) in the UK has recommended its use after other chemotherapy has failed (Dinnes et al., 2001; NICE, 2001). NICE will also be co-ordinating the development of new, national guidance, which will consider the full range of care for patients with brain tumours as part of the NHS Cancer Plan.

PSYCHOSOCIAL ASPECTS OF DIAGNOSIS AND TREATMENT

Turning from the purely medical aspects of treatment, we now consider psychosocial aspects of care. Some of these areas such as breaking bad news, models of follow-up, support of patients and their relatives, and palliative care were considered by recent UK guidance. Other areas we discuss include psychological aspects of the diagnosis of a life-threatening illness for patient and family, neuropsychological and psychiatric problems, rehabilitation, and finally handling death and bereavement. In these areas there is either less evidence or new evidence now emerging.

Breaking bad news

*It was very psychologically done, they're sort of giving you the soft
sell along the line—kind of letting you down gently.*

(40-year-old woman with a parietal tumour)

There are few worse tasks in medicine than conveying the news
of a fatal prognosis and, consequently, it is often avoided either
deliberately or by default. It is also well recognised that, often,
much of the content of consultations involving bad news is not
recalled. This is probably partly because too much information is
given too quickly and partly because the human mind is well able
to minimise threatening information. A few studies have investigated the views of general cancer patients about their disease,
comparing this with what their oncologists believe they have disclosed (Bernheim et al., 1987). Although the majority of patients
affirm that they have cancer, their views on prognosis often do
not tally with those of their doctors. In one study, half were more
optimistic about prognosis, and one-third of those who were
being treated palliatively believed they were being treated for a
cure (MacKillop et al., 1988). A study using hypothetical clinical cases suggests that such reworking of information is most
likely a normal response to life-threatening disease (Slevin et al.,
1990). Cancer patients, when compared with medical staff and
a general population sample, were overwhelmingly more likely
to accept as worthwhile treatment plans with very low odds for
success in either palliation or cure—and also treatments with
many more side-effects.

In our own study, as mentioned earlier, many seemed wholly
unaware of the likely poor prognosis or the palliative aim of
treatment. However, they did not become dissatisfied, despite
many experiencing side-effects (Davies et al., 1996b). A separate qualitative interview study in the Netherlands, however,
judged that *most* (11 of 19) of a sample of patients with malignant cerebral glioma were aware of the possibility that their
disease could be fatal (Salander et al., 1996). These authors
used a psychoanalytic framework to describe how patients used
a variety of psychological strategies to minimise this threat. In
our study, we based our judgement on interviews with patients,
the radically different awareness of close relatives, and poor
documentation of discussions in the medical records (Davies,
1997a). We suggested that relatives and medical staff were not
explicit about prognosis and often protected patients from this
news. A further problem, which we found evidence for, is that
because clinicians varied in the details they told patients, teams
could, without realising it, contradict or fail to amend the contribution of a previous team. Salander and colleagues (1997)
criticised our interview assessment of awareness of prognosis,
which they felt might be confounded by the patient's successful coping. However, whereas we reported patient awareness
of the *strong probability* that the disease would be fatal using
scales we tested for interrater reliability, Salander and colleagues
(1996) recorded knowledge of the *possibility* that the disease
could be fatal and did not report the reliability of their judgements. The methods might explain the differing results between
the two studies, but it might also be a matter of context and staff

attitudes. Interestingly, an Italian study of stable patients after
treatment at one centre between 1995 and 1997 recently reported
that it was the centre's policy not to tell any of its patients about
the prognosis, so as not to remove hope (Giovaglioni, 1999).
Another study of a sample of 40 patients with a range of benign
and malignant brain tumours treated in an organised Scottish
neuro-oncology centre assessed patient awareness of the prognosis (Anderson et al., 1999). These authors made their ratings
from interviews with relatives rather than patients, and judged
that 95% of patients had full or partial knowledge of their prognosis. They did not confirm our finding that aware patients were
more distressed, but clearly many of their patients had far better prognoses and were not directly comparable to our sample.
None the less, these findings suggest some variation in practice, which does not seem unlikely given the range of individual
clinicians' views, expressed whenever the question is debated.

There cannot be much doubt that doctors tend to present an
optimistic gloss on the most unfavourable prognosis. A recent
study of doctors' predictions about the prognosis of 468 patients
referred for hospice care found that, overall, the referring doctors
overestimated survival by a factor of more than five (Christakis
et al., 2000). Doctors might also wish to convey that something can be done about a disease. Perhaps this occurs more
with gliomas than other cancers because few neurologists or
neurosurgeons have specific training in the methods of communication used in oncology. Clinicians can, however, be seen as
polarising between those who wish to enable patients to "get
their life in order", and those who wish to withhold the harshest
facts in an effort to maintain hope and morale. The dilemma
of how to maintain hope without seeming dishonest, or without
creating greater future anguish, is particularly pressing when
dealing with the patient with a glioma. When remission is likely
to be short it is perhaps not an unreasonable fear that, should too
much be disclosed, precious time would be spent in the depths
of despair. On the other hand, failure to warn of a future decline
can mean an eventual greater plunge into despair. Hope for the
patient, however, is not a cost-free option, although a cheerful
display can hide this from the clinician. Maintenance of hope
can put a family under considerable strain, and can result in
the failure of the patient as breadwinner to make adequate provision for them and, of course, leave many things unsaid and
undone. And at whatever point the truth emerges, we should not
fail to recognise the support and counselling that both patient
and family will need in coming to terms with the diagnosis—in
and out of hospital (Chappell, 1997; North, 1997). The UK consensus guidelines covered communication in some detail and
considered research from other areas of cancer care. It was
recommended that centres identify critical points in the pathway where patients needed to receive information, ensure that
news was imparted in a private place by experienced and trained
clinicians, if possible with a nurse or counsellor present to stay
and clarify information and provide support. It was also suggested that specific details of what had been told should always be
recorded for other staff to see and so maintain a consistent message, and that patients be routinely given written information

to back-up consultations. The aim should be to give patients, as far as possible, sufficient information to be able to make an informed decision about treatment (Davies & Hopkins, 1997).

Information for the family

I had to keep going back and asking the surgeon to repeat what he had told me [about my husband]. I wanted to get it right, but I couldn't believe what he had told me. I thought I must be getting it wrong—that my mind was playing tricks on me because I was so tired.

(wife of a 46-year-old glioma patient)

He told me if he operated she might have 6 months, maybe a year, so I told him if she had a chance to go ahead. But no, I didn't tell *her* that. I thought if she got that chance she wouldn't need to know.

(husband of a 60-year-old glioma patient)

I knew at once when he [the doctor] said it was serious, but I didn't ask any more. I just want to take one day at a time. I don't want to know what's going to happen, and I've said to my children, I don't want him to know either.

(wife of a 59-year-old glioma patient)

As these verbatim comments illustrate, once a patient is unable to appreciate much that is happening, the well spouse will tend to take the responsibility both for information-seeking and for deciding what the patient is told. In our study, we found that relatives were three times more likely to be aware of the poor prognosis than patients, and had often deliberately sought out this information (Davies et al., 1996b). It is often easier and less painful for the doctor to reveal information to an apparently robust carer (who in any case can appear more likely to retain information), and then to assume that the family will deal with the task of breaking bad news themselves. But, as our study shows, information will not necessarily be conveyed as expected, and the clinician can later be put in the uncomfortable position of being asked to collude with the family in evading a patient's questions. A balance of joint and separate interviews for disclosing the prognosis can avoid such entanglements and mean that all parties are reasonably aware of each other's knowledge (Davies & Hopkins, 1997).

Cognitive and psychological change

The task of coming to terms with the implications of the diagnosis can be different for glioma patients than for patients with other types of cancer because the tumour site, anticonvulsants, and steroids can all affect cognitive skills and behaviour. Gliomas are associated with a higher incidence of mental change than meningiomas, which might be partly related to their faster growth rate (Lishman, 1998). Attempts to isolate particular syndromes are difficult because of the large variation in the clinical picture both between individuals and over time, but early clinical studies classified typical syndromes of focal lesions reviewed by Lishman (1998). Frontal tumours, for example, cause intellectual deterioration, with those on the left leading a greater loss of linguistic skills. Memory failure is often present, together with profound apathy, lack of spontaneity, and indifference. Personality change, including irritability and lack of

reserve, is well known, and there can be an indifference to or even denial of the diagnosis. Temporal lobe tumours are associated with the highest incidence of psychiatric disturbance and epilepsy. Emotional changes include blunting of affect and occasionally psychotic states. Parietal tumours are associated with depression; non-dominant tumours can produce disorders of visuospatial perception and body image disturbance, and dysphasia in dominant hemisphere tumours makes the mental state difficult to assess. Occipital tumours cause less specific mental symptoms but affect vision.

Most of the early studies of psychological changes in patients with brain tumours are, however, concerned with mental state at presentation, and are the result of clinical observation rather than systematic measurement of psychiatric, psychological, or cognitive function. Many observations were made prior to modern brain imaging techniques or the use of steroids. Following treatment with steroids, neurological deficits improve as oedema surrounding the tumour regresses. Premorbid personality and coping are likely to become more important and, as Lishman (1998) points out, individual reactions to the diagnosis itself have so far been overlooked as a distinct cause of mental change in patients with brain tumours and much could be an understandable response to physical impairment. Recently, workers have begun to describe the psychological state of patients following debulking and decompression. Pringle and colleagues (1999) compared 109 patients with brain tumours with 20 patients undergoing spinal surgery. These authors found that 30% of patients were anxious and 16% were depressed. Patients with meningiomas expressed the highest levels of psychological distress, but overall patients with brain tumours expressed no more distress than those undergoing spinal surgery. Anderson and colleagues (1999) classified 20% of their sample of patients with a range of primary brain tumours as depressed or anxious and found that this was related to increased physical and cognitive disability. Both samples, however, included patients with a range of benign and malignant tumours. The responses of patients with malignant glioma have not yet been fully charted and their possible complexity is illustrated by the case history below.

CASE NO. 1
A 40-year-old male solicitor presented with a 1-month history of headache, intellectual decline, and disorientation in time. A right temporal glioblastoma multiforme was partially excised and dexamethasone commenced. His mental state improved, and both he and his wife were told in a series of interviews that his tumour would definitely come back within 1–2 years. At this point he described feeling exhilarated that he had escaped the ensuing coma and said he saw every day as a bonus. Not wishing to leave any practical problems for his family, he was active in planning his finances and recontacted his local church to make arrangements for his burial. Nevertheless, he intended to fight his disease as far as he could. During radiotherapy a consultant radiotherapist gave him—quite clearly—more optimistic figures for survival, including a 30% chance of "success". Two months later, at the end of his treatment, still on dexamethasone because of some headache, he described a milder feeling of elation. He was now convinced that he would survive the disease and had consequently not settled his finances. His wife described his irritability when she tried

to discuss the information they had received initially and which they had originally discussed openly. She considered his optimistic personality to have become exaggerated, although at times she felt she was living with an entirely different person. After his radiotherapy treatment the patient was able to return fully to work for 6 months, continuing on dexamethasone, and believed he might be cured. Eight months after diagnosis, when he developed further headaches, a recurrence was diagnosed and he chose to begin chemotherapy. He and his wife were again clearly told the prognosis, but his wife described his unwillingness to discuss this with her and his angry and increasingly paranoid outbursts at home. Seen alone, shortly before his death, he appeared sad and disappointed by his situation. He reported that he had sought counselling and had acknowledged his feelings of anger at his death. He said he now planned to talk with his wife about the future, but died suddenly before he could.

As well as the complexity of psychological and behavioural responses to the diagnosis, often in a situation where one seems to have "come back from the dead", this case raises the possibility of steroid-induced psychiatric disorder. Apart from the more obvious steroid-induced psychosis, a whole range of psychological changes have been reported in patients receiving high dose steroids for other conditions such as vasculitis. These range from euphoria and feelings of well-being to irritability and depression. In a review of the literature, Bell (1991) points out that many of these states, which typically fall short of the clinically obvious, often go unrecognised, and can, with euphoria, simply be seen as a beneficial side-effect. However, in our study of patients after the diagnosis, we found that awareness of the diagnosis was unrelated to steroid dose at the time of the interview (Davies et al., 1996b). It is a common clinical observation that patients with gliomas are more optimistic than other cancer patients about their prognosis. We do not know whether mood-elevating effects of steroids, in combination with deficits in the processing of new information, can help to explain this, but any tendency towards undue optimism is exacerbated when clinicians fail to reinforce information, vary amongst themselves in the details they choose to impart, and work within an environment where every action gives the appearance of being orientated towards a cure.

Concerns about treatment

Radiotherapy normally takes place over 6 weeks, often on an out-patient basis. If the patient is already disabled or lives some distance away, treatment can be completed in hospital. Although the daily ritual of radiotherapy can provide structure and support to the patient, it can also be frightening. A mask is made for each patient to carry markings to guide treatment. The patient's head is strapped down for several minutes while radiation is administered and all personnel leave the room. A few patients find this claustrophobic and feel anxious. However, a small study of 10 patients found that they rated physical side-effects such as tiredness and hair loss as most distressing aspects of treatment (Irvine & Jodrell, 1990). The few studies that have specifically asked patients about tiredness or fatigue have found much higher levels of these symptoms than are recorded as side-effects in any trials of radiotherapy. For example, in our study we found

42% of the group of patients who were least disabled as they began treatment experienced severe tiredness or somnolence sufficient to limit leisure or domestic activities severely during or after treatment (Davies et al., 1996a). Faithfull (1991) also documented the emergence of somnolence during treatment using daily patient diaries and found that 16 of 19 patients developed symptoms including drowsiness, lethargy, and fatigue (Faithfull & Brada, 1998). Lovely and colleagues (1999) investigated fatigue and QOL scores in 60 patients with glioblastoma before and after radiotherapy and found fatigue scores increased following radiotherapy and were associated with poorer overall QOL scores. The UK guidance recommends pretreatment information to allay fears and to warn of possible side-effects. Planned appointment systems and joint neuro-oncology clinics can also help to ameliorate time spent waiting as this, combined with travelling, can take up the best part of each day.

Models of follow-up

At the end of radiotherapy, responsibility for follow-up should be established. The patient and family will, we found, frequently be given a series of appointments with a neurosurgeon, radiotherapist, and a neurologist, and sometimes an oncologist in addition (Davies, 1997b). Quite apart from involving a major feat of coordination on the part of the family in journeys to tertiary centres, everyone can be left wondering who is actually in charge, and hence to whom to address problems. In reality, medical intervention is usually limited. At one tertiary center, Steele and colleagues (1997) retrospectively reviewed the content of follow-up visits for 36 patients with malignant glioma. They found that the main areas of clinic activity were adjustment of steroids; discussions about work, leisure, driving, and rehabilitation; and organising CT scan results. In all instances, tumour recurrence had been detected by the patient or relative prior to the visit and rather than *at* the clinic. A prospective study of a further 24 patients confirmed that visits were taken up by neurological examination, discussing clinical and psychosocial issues, and ordering scans rather than detecting recurrence (Steele et al., 1997). Developing services that reflect and respond to patient need rather than traditional pattern of hospital follow-up is a challenge for neuro-oncology. One approach has been for specialist nurses in tertiary centres to provide support and advice after radiotherapy and to maintain contact with patients and their families by telephone (Brada & Guerrero, 1997; James et al., 1994). This approach appears to be acceptable to patients and is efficient of both patient and medical staff time. The development of a specialist nurse who can be dedicated to these patients is widely recommended (Davies & Hopkins, 1997) but sadly funding is not widely available for such posts. In other circumstances, the interested UK neurologist, with a catchment area including the home town and the tertiary centre, might be able to carry out this role and to refer the patient back for assessment for possible future treatment after recurrence. In any event, the key worker in the case should be defined clearly. The general practitioner will also be faced with many of the day-to-day problems and anxieties of the family, and early liaison is therefore essential to provide the necessary continuity of care and to ensure that this local role is not undermined by specialised services (Davies, 1997c). Other important links are patient support organisations that provide information and local support for patients and their relatives or carers. Treatment centres should hold information about such sources and point these out as possibilities to patients and their families (Davies & Hopkins, 1997). A list of useful addresses is given at the end of this chapter.

REMISSION AND ADAPTATION TO CHANGE

The course of the illness

Despite the interest in measures of performance and disability, there seems little descriptive information about the course of the illness or the needs of patients at different stages. Shapiro and Young (1976) showed that the postoperative Karnofsky reflected the patient's likely function for some 70% of the time he or she survived. Another retrospective analysis of 74 patients with glioblastoma multiforme who were well enough to receive carmustine (BCNU) maintained their postoperative functioning level for an average of 8 months. Some 40% were able to perform some kind of work and 70% to care reasonably well for themselves (Hochberg et al., 1979). A prospective trial of 118 patients with anaplastic astrocytoma and glioblastoma multiforme who received radiotherapy and bleomycin showed that more than half were able to work in some capacity 6 months after diagnosis, and between two-thirds and three-quarters were able to look after themselves (Kristiansen et al., 1981). This kind of data is of some value in considering how the care of the patient with a glioma might be organised, bearing in mind that the needs of patients and their families will vary at different points of the illness.

Improvement can be expected to level-off after radiotherapy, and a point reached when the patient will be at his or her fittest. Intensive treatment aims to create just such a plateau—a median period of increased life expectancy of some 24 weeks for glioblastoma multiforme, but maybe up to 100 weeks in anaplastic astrocytoma. The clinician might or might not choose to communicate the likely length and nature of this remission, but there is certainly a case to be made for actively encouraging as full a life as possible. During this time the patient also has the task of adapting to disability and of assimilating the implications of this into their own plans and that of their family. This adaptation involves coming to terms with a series of changes—typically experienced as losses, both real and potential.

Changes to body and mind

Partial loss of hair after surgery will become virtually total following external radiotherapy. Men rarely openly admit this as a problem, although many prefer to wear a cap and find that their children, if quite young, take time to become used to the change. Hair does begin to grow back after 6 months, but it is sometimes patchy and thin, and some never regain their full head of hair.

By contrast, loss of hair for women is often highly distressing, despite prior warning, and can be catastrophic for self-esteem. The early and sensitive provision of wigs should therefore be a routine facet of treatment, as well as questioning about any restriction of social activities caused by hair loss.

Steroids cause weight gain and fat redistribution and, when even facial features change, patients can wonder if anything about their appearance is to remain the same. There is also sometimes a ravenous hunger. Although typically borne stoically in the cause of treatment, weight gain can be the cause of much hidden distress. Acknowledging this sympathetically can help but the message that steroid dosage should be reduced as much and as soon as possible can only be underlined. Although lifesaving in the early stages of the disease, steroids tend to be overused during remission and, as already discussed, can lead to additional psychiatric symptoms. Furthermore, muscle loss and weight gain caused by the steroids will only make any disability in walking or moving more difficult to overcome (Dropcho & Soong, 1991).

Memory loss, a common preoccupation of patients, tends, we find, to be glossed over by medical staff. At first, patients often complain of being unable to remember details of their hospital stay, of forgetting names, and of slowness with arithmetic. Frontal and temporal tumours are most likely to lead to this intellectual deterioration and can make return to work impossible. Cognitive losses around the time of diagnosis and treatment have been less studied than the problems of patients who survive longer period. However, it is thought that the cognitive deficits due to tumours are different from those due to stroke because of the more gradual neuronal and the plasticity of other areas as tumours grow (Anderson et al., 1990). One way of responding to such difficulties is to emphasise what patients can do. Formal assessment of memory in itself can provide some reassurance, and this might well be done as part of planning a realistic assessment of employment possibilities. Advice about memory aids can provide comfort, as can the knowledge that the loss is not so severe. Some patients become preoccupied by modest defects that those around them see as no more than normal forgetfulness.

There have been more studies of the cognitive problems of patients who survive longer periods after treatment and who develop brain damage due to the delayed effects of radiation. Studies of relatively small case series suggested generalised cortical dysfunction and deterioration over time (Hochberg & Slotnick, 1980; Imperato et al., 1990) leading to problems with memory and difficulty coping with new situations (Archibald et al., 1994). In the largest study to date Scheibel and colleagues (1996) assessed the performance of 245 glioma patients after treatment on a range of neuropsychological tests. They found that patients with left-sided lesions scored lower on verbal tests and those with right-sided lesions found tests of facial recognition more difficult. Test scores were not related to the grade of the original tumour but were related to the treatment patients had received. Those treated with radiotherapy or radiotherapy and chemotherapy showed lower graphomotor speeds. These deficits are best prevented by careful radiotherapy techniques.

However, some centres in the US have also begun to develop rehabilitation programmes, discussed later, that attempt to help patients and their families cope with these problems.

Family and leisure

After a hospital stay and operation, many patients seem to have received that curious advice to "take it easy". It is rarely clear what this means, especially if the patient feels well enough to do most things. The family, who have seen the patient in a confused or even moribund state before treatment, might—understandably—wish him or her to rest and might try to limit activity. In fact, there is little to be said for resting as such, unless dictated by disability or fatigue. A clear statement by the clinician of a short rest period following surgery will avoid any tendency to sit at home until cured, or to put off resuming normal life until ill-defined medical events such as "after the results of the next scan". The beneficial effect of activity should be emphasised and fears about initiating seizures or encouraging disease progression discussed. Resuming independent activity can increase enjoyment and morale, as well as decreasing family tensions.

It is our impression that couples rarely acknowledge openly for long, or discuss in depth, the prospect of early death, even if one of them (usually the spouse) has actively sought information about prognosis. Many prefer to cope with practical problems on a day-to-day basis, continuing to hold future cure as a possibility, or with the well partner adopting the view that they'll deal with the death and its aftermath when it comes (Davies et al., 1996b). Couples are often brought closer by severe illness that brings into focus their mutual dependence. One sometimes senses that such closeness can help to make the distressing aspects of the illness more tolerable. Some emphasise coming closer as a surprisingly positive feature of the disease. However, even in successful marriages, the inevitable "role reversal" that the disease leads to is a potential source of tension. It is in this context that the clinician has the goal of enabling the patient to get as much enjoyment as possible out of life, and to prevent future regret on the part of the survivor that the last months together were not better spent. Some clinicians try and play an active role in helping a couple come to terms jointly with the prognosis, whereas others see this as outside their skills and remit, preferring to take their cues for supplying information from the patient and family rather than volunteering information themselves. These issues remain controversial and no simple answers can be supplied (see Rait & Lederberg (1989) for a review). One area that can be addressed is sexual difficulties. Complete upper motor neurone lesions impair capacity for orgasm in both sexes. In males, ejaculation can be impaired, although erection remains possible. Enquiry, however, can reveal that a fall in libido followed awareness of diagnosis, rather than physical presence of the tumour and, in this situation, it is likely that the drop in sexual activity accompanies depression or anxiety. It might therefore be possible to give simple reassurance about the normality of this response. Occasionally, increased libido occurs as part of disinhibition.

At a practical level, hospital appointments must not be allowed to interfere with holidays because a telephone call ahead plus a letter and contact telephone number will deal with most needs for consultation or admission. Even exotic journeys are possible. A man with a glioma took part in an expedition to Mount Everest and survived; another, a weightlifter competed internationally for a short period. Although there are, of course, elements of risk, it would be all too easy to discourage such activities on medical grounds. Insurance companies and airlines need to be contacted but they are normally cooperative. Airlines are, however, sometimes initially reluctant to accept patients as passengers on longhaul flights in the 3 months following brain surgery.

Work and social roles

It's being at home all day with nothing to do that really is the most difficult thing.

(50-year-old man with occipital tumour)

The peak age incidence of cerebral gliomas is such that it mainly involves individuals who are at or near their maximum earning capacity. A proportion will be able to return to full-time work briefly, and others would be able to return if some kind of accommodation were made in the workplace. Because some degree of cognitive impairment is often present, it is an advantage to make some assessment of this before return to work. Indeed, the avoidance of stigmatising rejection from the workforce could be seen as an important clinical goal. Quite apart from the fact of having a brain tumour, the loss of a job and ability to support self or family is capable of provoking depression and feelings of shame, yet this is just one of a whole series of losses that the patient will have to undergo. Furthermore, although most firms allow full pay for a few months, a reduction in pay might coincide with a deterioration in clinical state. It is worth noting that the well partner might need to give up his or her own job to care for "their other half" and that this will lead to additional financial problems.

The self-employed are particularly vulnerable because their businesses rely on them taking on a variety of organisational and accounting tasks, and they might not have the benefit of a full permanent health insurance for sick pay. Such information, obtained at the time of making the diagnosis, will give the social worker a chance to attempt some solution and so head-off feelings of failure about supporting the family. In the UK there are a number of payments available, such as Attendance Allowance and Severe Disablement Allowances. The relative might be entitled to Invalid Care Allowance if constant care is required. All these will often need to be pointed out. At a time when finances are already stretched, weight gain due to steroids can necessitate new clothes and extra expense.

In the UK, drivers should advise the DVLA of the diagnosis. Recent surgery for glioma leads to automatic licence withdrawal. After 2 years, reissue will be considered on an individual basis if there is evidence of prolonged remission, without epilepsy of any kind. Medical support will also usually be required.

Models of rehabilitation

Although many patients will have contact with hospital and community physiotherapists or occupational therapists at some point, few are offered formal rehabilitation programmes. This has probably been due to the rarity of long-term survivors, a lack of awareness of these patients' difficulties, and a perception that nothing useful could be offered (see Chappell, 1997, for a relative's view). A few studies now begin to emerge from centres in the US, which have built on an assessment of patients' problems to suggest possible strategies for rehabilitation. Meyers and Boake, 1993 report that relatives or carers most often report as problems the fact that the patient does not return to work, that they are forgetful, help less around the house, and sit a lot during the day. Following-up these findings, programmes include assessment of the patient at home or work, taking into account the reports of relatives, and the results of neuropsychological tests to determine the patients' problems and their full impact on their lives. Interventions include training the patient to use a daily organiser; family education and counselling; individual and group work with psychologists, speech, and occupational therapists; and help looking for employment and starting off in a new work environment (Sherer et al., 1997). Other groups have compared the outcomes of patients with brain tumours with those of other patients undergoing rehabilitation programmes. A few studies suggest that those patients referred to services seem to have comparable outcomes to those with stroke (O'Dell et al., 1998) and shorter length of stay than patients with head injury (Huang et al., 1998). One survey in the UK suggests the need for more education for professionals in the UK about the needs of these patients (Cruickshank & Wilkinson, 1998). One area highlighted by the independent appraisal of the UK guidelines was the omission of guidance for rehabilitation. This is clearly an area where more research is needed to see how best to help these patients.

RECURRENCE AND DETERIORATION

Home care and disability aids

I felt so depressed this morning; I thought I've got to get out of this blasted bed, wobble down to the bathroom, get downstairs and do the things of the day.

(59-year-old man with a parietal tumour)

This final stage of the disease is heralded by an increasing neurological deficit and disability, despite the reintroduction of full-dose steroids, and occasionally by epileptic fits. Optimistic attitudes are now difficult to maintain. Questions of reoperation, further treatment with, for example radioactive implants or chemotherapy, or the unusual possibility that deterioration is due to irradiation necrosis need to be addressed. Once these options have been excluded, it remains to make it as easy as possible to accomplish the basic tasks of every day living. Urgent occupational therapy referral, backed-up by personal contact to hurry things along, will almost certainly be necessary if aids and adaptions are to arrive in time to be of use. The maintenance of

independence and dignity must be the clinical goal. The provision of disability aids is discussed elsewhere in this volume. If delays do occur, and finances permit, self-purchasing might need to be explored. Some insurance companies will release funds from life insurance if there is terminal illness and, when the patient is aware of the outcome, this can be explored positively. Again, this will necessitate the clinician in charge liaising with the appropriate body.

In the few cases where epilepsy is not fully controlled, the family will need counselling about what they should do, when to seek medical advice and when not to. Onlookers often assume that death is occurring during the first fits they witness. Reassurance that this is not likely to be a great risk will prevent many dramatic emergency visits to hospital, as will simple practical advice, such as the use of diazepam suppositories for repeated seizures.

Psychological care of the family

Although the situation for the patient is severe, that of the close relative or carer is also very difficult. In our study we found that close relatives or carers appeared to show more distress than the patients after diagnosis (Davies et al., 1996b). Other authors have also recognised the difficulty for relatives of later watching the patient deteriorate (Salander, 1996). From their experience with working with families in a neuro-oncology service, Passik and colleagues (1994) identify a range of issues with which relatives have to cope. These include their grief at losing their previous relationship, and—because of personality change—beginning to mourn the patient before he or she dies, difficulty in communicating with the patient; the unpredictability of the patient's cognitive state; feelings of anger and guilt at feeling overburdened by the patient; and coping with changes of responsibility, such as having to adopt a parent-like role. Horowitz and colleagues (1996) also describe setting up a self-help group for close relatives or carers to help reduce their isolation and provide informal support. Such groups might not be appropriate for all but are generally described positively by those who do attend. The Useful Addresses section at the end of this chapter lists organisations that provide fact sheets and booklets for patients and relatives at all stages of the illness and identify useful contacts and local support groups; others can be reached via NHS Direct (www.nhsdirect.nhs.uk).

Palliative care

If contact has been maintained with local services from the outset, care can probably be organised at the community level and the patient remain at home (Davies & Hopkins, 1997; Minton, 1997). When this is done, the carer will often need help with physical demands and to be given a chance to talk about his or her distress. Insomnia, for example, is common with steroids; this will tend at times to disturb the spouse as well, and a night nurse can bring great respite. Personality and severe cognitive change in a loved one is particularly distressing—whatever the cause—as underlined by studies of those looking after patients at home in the context of stroke, dementia, and head injury (see Chapter 34). Psychological distress can be prominent in both patient and carer during the final deterioration—sometimes for different reasons. Palliative care teams have experience in disentangling the various physical and psychological sources of distress and in facilitating communication among family members, and their help might be sought. In our study, we found that patients and relatives praised highly the care given by palliative care teams at this stage (Davies, 1997b). If the family has chosen to have the patient cared for in hospital; the family doctor should be quickly informed once death has occurred.

It is worth emphasising to family members the usual mode of death, i.e. in apparently peaceful coma. Severe headache, or apparent anguish is unusual, although when present these problems are particularly difficult to manage. Diamorphine in regular, adequate doses, and/or midazolam are of value (Minton, 1997). Drug therapy might need review, especially as there is a tendency to prescribe increasing doses of dexamethasone during decline, with decreasing effect. Some clinicians maintain a policy of withdrawing steroids altogether in the final stages so that the patient does not linger long in an unconscious state.

Bereavement

Following death, one suggested practice is that a letter of condolence is sent by the consultant in charge with an offer to discuss the case. About half of relatives respond. Some ask for an appointment and often wish to ascertain that everything possible was done for the patient or to discuss other forms of therapy. Frequent questions concern whether the outcome would have been any different if the diagnosis had been made earlier, or whether the condition runs in the family. It is not exceptional for a family to wait between 1 and 2 years after death to take up these offers.

Bereavement counselling should be offered to all families. Generally, at 3–4 months an assessment can be made as to whether grief is beginning to resolve or is running a protracted course. Although we cannot consider in detail here the full process of mourning and forms of counselling available, we mention it as a way in which the clinician's role can be extended. Like the spouse or relatives, the attending clinician must feel that as much as was sensible to offer was provided, and so maintain his or her own morale and confidence in dealing with future cases. Studies of adult bereavement are increasingly suggesting that the survivor's grief is more likely to run a disabling and chronic course if they received little or no warning of imminent or likely death, had not discussed death with their spouse, and had felt helpless to deal with distressing symptoms (Ransford & Smith, 1991). The suggestion that forewarning allows the spouse to come to terms with death, and the fact that the clinical course of gliomas allows for this, might offer some compensation amidst the devastation of this diagnosis.

SUMMARY

We have put forward the view that intensive treatment programmes for cerebral glioma need to be matched by concern for the psychological and social well-being of patients and their families. This is best achieved by a key worker, specialist nurse, or clinician liaising between tertiary and community settings, drawing on the resources of counselling, occupational therapy, support care, and "if necessary" psychiatric services. Much of what we have discussed might seem at some distance from traditional medical practice, but we would argue that cerebral glioma is a uniquely devastating disease, often dealt with suboptimally, and demands new approaches to both medical and social management.

There is clearly controversy surrounding the care of patients with gliomas. Our own detailed study and others reveal areas where management could be improved, and raise questions about established practices. There is little doubt that, outside neuro-oncology centres where thought has been given to the specific needs of these patients and their families, the delivery of care can become fragmented and, perhaps by being spread between specialities, even adds to the difficulties families endure.

ACKNOWLEDGEMENTS

The work on which this chapter is based was carried out in the Department of Neurological Sciences, St Bartholomew's Hospital, London and the former Research Unit of the Royal College of Physicians, supported by the Cancer Research Campaign (Grant no. CP1017) and the Central Audit Fund of the Department of Health.

REFERENCES

Anderson SW, Damasio H, Tranel D (1990). Neuropsychological impairments associated with lesions caused by tumour or stroke. *Archives Neurology, 47*, 397–405.

Anderson SI, Taylor R, Whittle IR (1999). Mood disorders in patients after treatment for primary intracranial tumours. *British Journal of Neurosurgery, 13* (5), 480–485.

Anonymous (1997). NCCN Adult brain tumour practice guidelines. *Oncology, 11* (11A), 237–277.

Archibald YM, Lunn D, Ruttan LA, Macdonald DR, del Maestro RF, Hugh W, Barr WK, Warwick Pexman JH, Fisher BJ, Gaspar LE, Cairncross JG (1994). Cognitive functioning in long-term survivors of high-grade glioma. *Journal of Neurosurgery, 80*, 247–253.

Bell G (1991). Steroid-induced psychiatric disorders. *Nordisk Psykiartriask (Nordic Journal of Psychiatry), 45*, 437–441.

Bernheim JL, Ledure G, Souris M, Razavi D (1987). Differences in perception of disease and treatment between cancer patients and their physicians. In: Aaronson NK and Beckman J (Eds), *The quality of life of cancer patients*. Raven, New York.

Blomgren H (1996). For SBU, the Swedish Council on Technology Assessment in Health Care. Brain tumours. *Acta Oncologica, 35* (Suppl. 7), 16–21.

Bower M, Newlands ES, Bleehan NM, Brada M, Begent RJ, Calvert H, Colquhoun I, Lewis P, Brampton MH (1997). Multicentre CRC phase II trial of temozolamide in recurrent progressive high-grade glioma. *Cancer Chemotherapy and Pharmacology, 40* (6), 484–488.

Brada M, Guerrero D (1997). One model of follow-up care. In: Davies E, Hopkins A (Eds), *Improving care for patients with malignant cerebral glioma*. RCP Publications, London.

Brada M, Thomas D, Rampling R, Crawford P, Burnet N, Byrne P, Sokal M (1996). Letter. *British Medical Journal, 314*, 899.

Brazil L, Thomas R, Laing R, Hines F, Guerrero D, Ashley S, Brada M (1997). Verbally administered Barthel Index as functional assessment in brain tumour patients. *Journal of Neuro-oncology, 34*, 187–192.

Bucy PC (1986). Letter. *British Medical Journal, 293*, 1505.

Burnet NG, Taylor RE (1997). Letter. Modern radiotherapy techniques are needed to spare normal tissue. *British Medical Journal, 314*, 900.

Chappell J (1997). Breaking bad news: The perspective of relatives. In: Davies E, Hopkins A (Eds), *Improving care for patients with malignant cerebral glioma*. RCP Publications, London.

Christakis NA, Lamont EB (2000). Extent and determinants of error in doctors' prognoses in terminally ill patients: prospective cohort study. *British Medical Journal, 320*, 469–473.

Clyde Z, Chataway SJ, Signorini D, Gregor A, Grant R (1998). Significant change in tests of neurological impairment in patients with brain tumours. *Journal of Neuro-oncology, 39*, 81–90.

Counsell CE, Grant R (1998). Incidence studies of primary and secondary intracranial tumours: A systematic review of their methodology and results. *Journal of Neuro-oncology, 37*, 241–250.

Counsell CE, Collie DA, Grant R (1996). The incidence of intracranial tumours in the Lothian region of Scotland 1989–90. *Journal of Neurology, Neurosurgery and Psychiatry, 61*, 143–150.

Counsell CE, Collie DA, Grant R (1997). Limitations of using a cancer registry to identify incident primary intracranial tumours. *Journal of Neurology, Neurosurgery and Psychiatry, 63*, 94–97.

Cruickshank GS, Wilkinson SC (1998). Speech and language services for patients with malignant brain tumours: A regional survey of providers. *Health Bulletin, 56* (3), 659–666.

Daumas-Duport C, Scheithauer B, O'Fallon J, Kelly P (1988). Grading of astrocytomas: A simple and reproducible method. *Cancer, 62*, 2152–2165.

Davies E (1997a). Breaking bad news: The perspective of health professionals. In: Davies E, Hopkins A (Eds), *Improving care for patients with malignant cerebral glioma*. RCP Publications, London.

Davies E (1997b). Patients' perceptions of follow-up services. In: Davies E, Hopkins A (Eds), *Improving care for patients with malignant cerebral glioma*. RCP Publications, London.

Davies E (1997c). What general practitioners want to know. In: Davies E, Hopkins A (Eds), *Improving care for patients with malignant cerebral glioma*. RCP Publications, London.

Davies E, Hopkins A (1997). Good practice in the management of adults with malignant cerebral glioma: Clinical guidelines. *British Journal of Neurosurgery, 11* (4), 318–330.

Davies E, Clarke C, Hopkins A (1996a). Malignant cerebral glioma I: Survival, disability and morbidity after radiotherapy. *British Medical Journal, 313*, 1507–1512.

Davies E, Clarke C, Hopkins A (1996b). Malignant cerebral glioma II: Perspectives of patients and relatives on the value of radiotherapy. *British Medical Journal, 313*, 1512–1516.

Davies KG, Walters KA, Weeks RD (1986). Letter. *British Medical Journal, 293*, 1236.

Davis FG, Freels S, Grutsch J, Barlas S, Brem S (1998). Survival rates in patients with primary malignant brain tumours stratified by patient age and tumour histological type: An analysis based on surveillance, epidemiology and end results (SEER) data, 1973–1991. *Journal of Neurosurgery, 88*, 1–10.

Department of Health (1999). *Referral guidelines for suspected cancer – consultation document*. Department of Health, London.

Dinnes J, Cave C, Huang S, Major K, Milne R (2001). The effectiveness and cost-effectiveness of temozolamide for the treatment of recurrent malignant glioma: A rapid and systematic review. *Health Technology Assessment, 5* (13), 1–73.

Dropcho EJ, Soong SJ (1991). Steroid-induced weakness in patients with primary brain tumours. *Neurology, 44*, 675–680.

Fadul CD, Wood J, Thaler H, Galicich J, Patterson RH, Posner JB (1988). Morbidity and mortality of craniotomy for excision of supratentorial gliomas. *Neurology, 38*, 1374–1379.

Faithfull S (1991). Patients' experiences following cranial radiotherapy: A study of the somnolence syndrome. *Journal of Advanced Nursing, 16*, 936–946.

Faithfull S, Brada M (1998). Somnolence syndrome in adults following cranial irradiation for primary brain tumours. *Clinical Oncology (Royal College of Radiologists), 10* (4), 250–254.

Fine HA, Dear KB, Loeffler JS (1993). Meta-analysis of radiation therapy with or without adjuvant chemotherapy for malignant gliomas in adults. *Cancer, 71*, 2585–2597.

Ford JM, Stenning SP, Boote DJ, Counsell R, Falk SJ, Flavin A, Laurence VM, Bleehan NM (1997). A short fractionation radiotherapy treatment for poor prognosis patients with high-grade glioma. *Clinical Oncology, 9*, 20–24.

Fox S, Lantz C (1998). The brain tumour experience and quality of life: A qualitative study. *Journal of Neuroscience Nursing, 30* (4), 245–252.

Giovagnoli AR (1999). Quality of life in patients with stable disease after surgery, radiotherapy, and chemotherapy for malignant brain tumour. *Journal of Neurology, Neurosurgery and Psychiatry, 67*, 358–363.

Giovagnoli AR, Tanburini M, Boiardi A (1996). Quality of life in brain tumour patients. *Journal of Neuro-Oncology, 30*, 71–80.

Grant R, Slattery J, Gregor A, Whittle IR (1994). Recording neurological impairment in clinical trials of glioma. *Journal of Neuro-Oncology, 19* (1), 37–49.

Grant R, Collie DA, Counsell CE (1996a). The incidence of cerebral glioma in the working population: A forgotten cancer? *British Journal of Cancer, 73*, 252–254.

Grant R, Collie DA, Gregor A, Ironside JW (1996b). Referral pattern and management of patients with malignant brain tumours in South East Scotland. *Health Bulletin, 54* (3), 212–222.

Gregor A (1997). Radiotherapy. In: Davies E, Hopkins A (Eds), *Improving care for patients with malignant cerebral glioma*. RCP Publications, London.

HCEU (1998). *Independent appraisal of "Davies E, Hopkins A (1997) Improving care for patients with malignant cerebral glioma" on behalf of the NHS Executive*. Health Care Evaluation Unit, Department of Public Health Sciences, St George's Hospital Medical School, London.

Hochberg FH, Linggood R, Wolfson L, Baker WH, Kornblith P (1979). Quality and duration of survival in glioblastoma multiforme. Combined surgical, radiation and lomustine therapy. *Journal of the American Medical Association, 241*, 1016–1018.

Hochberg FH, Slotnick B (1980). Neuropsychological impairment in astrocytoma survivors. *Neurology, 30*, 172–177.

Horowitz, S, Passik SD, Malkin MG (1996). "In sickness and in health": A group intervention for spouses caring for patients with brain tumours. *Journal of Psychosocial Oncology, 14* (2), 43–56.

Huang ME, Cifu DX, Keyser-Marcus L (1998). Functional outcome after brain tumour and acute stroke: A comparative analysis. *Archives of Physical Medicine and Rehabilitation, 79*, 1386–1390.

Imperato JP, Paleologos NA, Vick NA (1990). Effects of treatment on long-term survivors with malignant astrocytomas. *Annals of Neurology, 28*, 818–822.

Irvine L, Jodrell N (1999). The distress associated with cranial irradiation: A comparison of patient and nurse perceptions. *Cancer Nursing, 22* (2), 126–133.

James ND, Guerrero D, Brada M (1994). Who should follow up cancer patients? Nurse specialist based out-patient care and the introduction of a phone clinic system. *Clinical Oncology, 6*, 283–287.

Karnofsky DA, Burchenal JH (1949). The clinical evaluation of chemotherapeutic agents in cancer. In: Macleod CM (Ed), *Evaluation of chemotherapeutic agents in cancer*. Columbia University Press, New York.

Kernohan JW, Sayre GP (1952). Tumours of the central nervous system. *Atlas of Tumour Pathology, Section 10, Fascicle 35*. Armed Forces Institute of Pathology, Washington.

Kiebert GM, Curran D, Aaronson NK, Bolla M, Menten J, Rutten EH, Nordman E, Silvestre ME, Pierart M, Karim AB (1998). Quality of life after radiation therapy of cerebral low-grade gliomas of the adult: Results of a randomised phase III trial on dose response (EORTC trial 22844). EORTC Radiotherapy Co-operative Group. *European Journal of Cancer, 34* (12), 1902–1909.

Kristiansen M, Hagan S, Kollevold T, Torvik A, Holme I, Nesbakken R, Hatlevoll R, Lingren M, Brun A, Lingred S, Notter G, Anderson AP, Elgen K (1981). Combined modality therapy of operated astrocytomas grades III and IV. Confirmation of the value of irradiation and lack of differentiation of bleomycin on survival time. *Cancer, 47*, 647–654.

Latif AZB, Signorini D, Gregor A, Grant R, Ironside J, Whittle IR (1998a). Application of the MRC Prognostic index to patients with malignant glioma not managed in a randomised control trial. *Journal of Neurology, Neurosurgery and Psychiatry, 64,* 747–750.

Latif AZB, Signorini DF, Whittle IR (1998b). Treatment by a specialist surgical neuro-oncologist does not provide any survival advantage for patients with a malignant glioma. *British Journal of Neurosurgery, 12* (1), 29–32.

Lishman WA (1998). *Organic psychiatry. The psychological consequences of cerebral disorder,* 3rd edition. Blackwell Scientific Publications, Oxford.

Lovely MP, Miaskowski C, Dodd M (1999). Relationship between fatigue and quality of life in patients with glioblastoma multiforme. *Oncology Nursing Forum, 26* (5), 921–925.

Lyons GJ (1996). The "Preston Profile" – the first disease-specific tool for assessing quality of life in patients with malignant glioma. *Disability and Rehabilitation, 18* (9), 460–468.

Mackillop WJ, Stewart WE, Ginsberg AD, Stewart SS (1988). Cancer patients' perception of their disease and its treatment. *British Journal of Cancer, 58,* 355–358.

Mackworth N, Fobair P, Prados MD (1992). Quality of life self-reports from 200 brain tumour patients: Comparisons with Karnofsky performance scores. *Journal of Neuro-oncology, 14,* 243–253.

Macleod M, Slattery J, Grant R (1995). The effect of tumour associated epilepsy on performance/handicap scales used in cerebral glioma. *British Journal of Neurosurgery, 9,* 653–657.

Mahoney FI, Barthel DW (1965). Functional evaluation: The Barthel Index. *Maryland Medical Journal, 14,* 61–65.

McKeran RO, Thomas DGT (1980). The clinical study of gliomas. In: Thomas DGT, Graham DI (Eds), *Brain tumours. Scientific basis, clinical investigation and current therapy.* Butterworths, London.

Medical Research Council (MRC) Brain Tumour Working Party (1990). Prognostic factors for high-grade malignant glioma: Development of a prognostic index. *Journal of Neuro-oncology, 9,* 47–55.

Metcalfe SE (2000). Biopsy versus resection for malignant glioma. *Cochrane Database Syst Rev (2):* CD002034.

Meyers CA, Boake C (1993). Neurobehavioural disorders in brain tumour patients: Rehabilitation strategies. *The Cancer Bulletin, 45* (4), 362–364.

Miller JD, Miller ES, Todd NV, Whittle IR (1986). Letter. *British Medical Journal, 293,* 1236.

Minton M (1997). Palliative care in the community. In Davies E, Hopkins A (Eds), *Improving care for patients with malignant cerebral glioma.* RCP Publications, London.

National Institute for Clinical Excellence (2001). *Guidance on the use of temozolamide for the treatment of recurrent malignant glioma (brain cancer). Technology Appraisal Guidance No. 23* NICE, London.

North CA, North RB, Epstein JA, Piantadosi S, Wharam MD (1990). Low-grade cerebral astrocytomas. Survival and quality of life after radiation therapy. *Cancer, 66,* 6–14.

North J (1997). The need for support of patients and their relatives or carers. In: Davies E, Hopkins A (Eds), *Improving care for patients with malignant cerebral glioma.* RCP Publications, London.

Nouri FM, Lincoln NB (1987). An extended activities of daily living. *Clinical Rehabilitation, 1,* 301–305.

O'Dell MW, Barr K, Spanier D, Warnick RE (1998). Functional outcome of inpatient rehabilitation in persons with brain tumours. *Archives of Physical Medicine and Rehabilitation, 79,* 1530–1534.

Osoba D, Aaronson NK, Muller M, Sneeuw K, Hsu MA, Yung WKA, Brada M, Newlands E (1996). The development and psychometric validation of a brain cancer quality of life questionnaire for use in combination with general cancer specific questionnaires. *Quality of Life Research, 5,* 139–150.

Osoba D, Aaronson NK, Muller M, Sneeuw K, Hsu MA, Yung WKA, Brada M, Newlands E (1997). Effects of neurological dysfunction on health-related quality of life in patients with high-grade glioma. *Journal of Neuro-oncology, 34,* 263–278.

Passik SD, Malkin MG, Breitbart WS, Horowitz MSW (1994). Psychiatric and psychosocial aspects of neuro-oncology. *Journal of Psychosocial Oncology, 12* (1/2), 101–122.

Poberskin LH, Chadduck JB (2000). Incidence of brain tumours in two English counties: A population-based study. *Journal of Neurology, Neurosurgery and Psychiatry, 69,* 464–471.

Porter D, Thomas D (1997a). Confirming the diagnosis after imaging. In: Davies E, Hopkins A (Eds), *Improving care for patients with malignant cerebral glioma.* RCP Publications, London.

Porter D, Thomas D (1997b). Surgical treatment of malignant gliomas. In: Davies E, Hopkins A (Eds), *Improving care for patients with malignant cerebral glioma.* RCP Publications, London.

Pringle AM, Taylor R, Whittle IR (1999). Anxiety and depression in patients with an intracranial neoplasm before and after tumour surgery. *British Journal of Neurosurgery, 13* (1), 46–51.

Punt J (1984). Does biopsy or any surgery influence the outcome in patients with supratentorial gliomas? In Warlow C, Garfield J (Eds), *Dilemmas in the management of the neurological patient.* Churchill Livingstone, London.

Quigley JR, Marroon JC (1991). The relationship between survival and the extent of resection in patients with supratentorial malignant gliomas. *Neurosurgery, 29,* 385–389.

Rait D, Lederberg M (1989). The family of the cancer patient. In: Holland J, Rowland J (Eds), *Handbook of psychooncology – psychological care of the patient with cancer.* Oxford University Press, New York.

Rampling R (1997). Chemotherapy. In: Davies E, Hopkins A (Eds), *Improving care for patients with malignant cerebral glioma.* RCP Publications, London.

Ransford HE, Smith ML (1991). Grief resolution among the bereaved in hospice and hospital wards. *Social Science and Medicine, 32,* 295–304.

Salander P (1996). Brain tumour as a threat to life and personality: The spouse's perspective. *Journal of Psychosocial Oncology, 14* (3), 1–18.

Salander P, Bergenheim T, Henriksson R (1996). The creation of protection and hope in patients with malignant brain tumours. *Social Science and Medicine, 42,* 985–996.

Salander P, Bergenheim AT, Henriksson R (1997). Letter. *British Medical Journal, 314,* 900.

Scheibel RS, Meyers CA, Levin VA (1996). Cognitive functioning surgery for intracranial glioma: Influence of histopathology, lesion location, and treatment. *Journal of Neuro-oncology, 30,* 61–69.

Shapiro WR, Young DF (1976). Treatment of malignant glioma. *Archives of Neurology, 33,* 494–500.

Sherer M, Meyers CA, Bergloff P (1997). Efficacy of postacute brain injury rehabilitation for patients with primary malignant brain tumours. *Cancer, 80* (2), 250–257.

Slevin M, Stubbs L, Plant H, Wilson P, Gregory WM, Armes PJ, Downer SM (1990). Attitudes to chemotherapy: Comparing views of patients with cancer with those of doctors, nurses and the general public. *British Medical Journal, 300,* 1458–1460.

Sneeuw KCA, Aaronson NK, Osoba D, Muller MJ, Hsu MA, Yung A, Brada M, Newlands ES (1997a). The use of significant others as proxy raters of the quality of life of patients with brain cancer. *Medical Care, 35* (5), 490–506.

Sneeuw KCA, Aaronson NK, Sprangers MAG, Detmar SB, Wever LDV, Schornagel JH (1997b). Value of caregiver ratings in evaluating the quality of life of patients with cancer. *Journal of Clinical Oncology, 15* (4), 1206–1217.

Sneeuw KC, Aaronson NK, Sprangers MAG, Detmar SB, Wever LDV, Schornagel JH (1998). Comparison of patient and proxy EORTC QLQ-C30 ratings in assessing the quality of life of cancer patients. *Journal of Clinical Epidemiology, 51* (7), 617–631.

Steele J, Sibtain A, Brada M (1997). The content and efficacy of conventional methods of follow-up in neuro-oncology: The need for new strategies. *Clinical Oncology (Royal College of Radiologists), 9* (3), 168–171.

Stuschke M, Thames HD (1997). Hyperfractionated radiotherapy of human tumours: Overview of the randomised trials. *Journal of Radiation Oncology Biology and Physics, 37,* 259–267.

Thomas R, Guerrero D, Hines F, Ashley S, Brada M (1995). Modifying the Barthel Performance Index Score for use in patients with brain tumours. *European Journal of Cancer Care, 4,* 63–68.

Vecht CHJ, Avezzaat CJJ, van Putten WLJ, Eijkenboom WMH, Stefanko SZ (1990). The influence of the extent of surgery on the neurological function and survival in malignant glioma. A retrospective analysis in 243 patients. *Journal of Neurology, Neurosurgery and Psychiatry, 53,* 466–471.

Walker MD, Alexander E, Hunt WE, MacCarty CS, Mahaley J, Norrell HA, Owens G, Ransohoff J, Wilson CB, Gehan EA, Strike TA (1978). Evaluation of BCNU and/or radiotherapy in the treatment of anaplastic gliomas. A co-operative clinical trial. *Journal of Neurosurgery, 49,* 333–343.

Walker MD, Green SB, Byar DP, Alexander E, Batzdorf U, Brooks WH, Hunt WE, MacCarty CS, Mahaley MS, Mealey J, Owens G, Ransohoff J, Robertson JT, Shapiro WR, Smith KK, Wilson CB, Strike TA (1980). Randomized comparisons of radiotherapy and nitrosoureas for the treatment of malignant glioma after surgery. *New England Journal of Medicine, 303* (2), 1323–1329.

Weitzner M, Meyers CA (1997). Cognitive functioning and quality of life in malignant glioma: A review of the literature. *Psycho-oncology, 6,* 169–177.

Weitzner MA, Meyers CA, Byrne K (1996). Psychosocial functioning and quality of life in patients with primary brain tumours. *Journal of Neurosurgery, 84,* 29–34.

Weitzner MA, Meyers CA, Gelke CK, Byrne KS, Cella DF, Levin V (1995). The functional assessment of cancer therapy (FACT) scale: Development of a brain subscale and revalidation of the general version of FACT in patients with primary brain tumours. *Cancer, 75* (5), 1151–1161.

Whittle IR, Pringle AM, Taylor R (1998). Effects of resective surgery for left-sided intracranial tumours on language function: A prospective study. *Lancet, 351,* 1–14–18.

Whitton AC, Rhydderch H, Furlong W, Feeny D, Barr RD (1997). Self-reported comprehensive health status of adult brain tumour patients using the health utilities index. *Cancer, 80* (2), 258–265.

Wroe SJ, Foy PM, Shaw MD, Williams IR, Chadwick DW, West C, Towns G (1986a). Differences between neurological and neurosurgical approaches to the management of malignant brain tumours. *British Medical Journal, 293,* 1015–1018.

Wroe SJ, Foy PM, Shaw MD, Williams IR, Chadwick DW, West C, Towns G (1986b). Letter. *British Medical Journal, 293,* 1373.

Yates JW, Chalmer B, McKegney P (1980). Evaluation of patients using the Karnofsky performance status. *Cancer, 45,* 2220–2224.

Zulch KJ (1979). *Histological typing of tumours of the nervous system.* World Health Organisation, Geneva.

USEFUL ADDRESSES

Brain Tumour Action
   30 Woodburn Terrace, Edinburgh EH10 4SS. Tel: 0131 447 2476
Brain Tumour Foundation
   PO Box 162, New Malden, Surrey KT3 3YN. Tel: 0208 336 2020, e-mail: Btf.uk@virgin.net
British Brain and Spine Foundation
   7 Winchester House, Kennington Park, Cranmer Road, London SW9 6EJ. Tel: 0207 793 5900, Helpline: 0808 808 1000, e-mail: Info@bbsf.org.uk

Cancerlink
   11–21 Northdown Street, London N1 9BN. Tel: 0207-833-2818
Cancer BACUP
   3 Bath Place, Rivington Street, London EC2A 3JR. Tel: 0808 800 1234, Helpline: 0207 613-2121

44. Spinal injury

James Allibone   Benjamin Taylor   Frederick Middleton

INTRODUCTION

The Edwin Smith papyrus, written 4000 years ago and the first known account of spinal injury, documents six cases of injury to the vertebral column. Two of the cases had limb paralysis with urinary incontinence and were considered "an ailment not to be treated", but there is no clear evidence of an understanding of the anatomical basis of the injury at this time (Breasted, 1922; Hughes, 1988). Hippocrates discussed vertebral dislocation and its relationship to paralysis of the apparently still, but did not appreciate the role of the spinal cord (Adams, 1849). In the first century AD, Celsus (Spencer, 1935) noted that death followed quickly when the cervical cord was injured, but a century followed before Galen showed experimentally that interruption of the spinal cord caused paralysis and loss of sensation (Walker, 1951).

Attempts at spinal decompression are recorded even in early records, but without much success or enthusiasm. In 1814, Cline decompressed a thoracic fracture-dislocation (Cline, 1815). The patient died and for almost a century this was used as an argument against surgery. Although operation was still used and limited success reported, critics were numerous and included people of such stature as Charles Bell. The effect of such eminent opinion was to retard spinal surgery for many years.

The occurrence of two world wars in the twentieth century exposed the inadequacy of the management of spinal injuries. During the First World War, 80% of spinal cord injury (SCI) casualties died within 3 years (Thompson-Walker, 1937). For those who survived, the outlook was bleak, with little incentive or encouragement to return to useful life. During the Second World War, twelve special units were created in the UK for the management of spinal injuries: initially this did little to improve the lot of these patients, as the need for a dedicated multidisciplinary team had not been recognised. In 1943 Ludwig Guttman assumed control of the Spinal Injuries Centre at the Ministry of Pensions Hospital in Stoke Mandeville, where he introduced the doctrine of comprehensive care of the spinal-cord-injury patient. His pioneering approach marked the beginning of a new era in the management of spinal cord injury.

EPIDEMIOLOGY

Worldwide, the incidence of spinal cord injury (SCI) lies between 9.2 and 50 patients per 1,000,000 population, which results in a multibillion dollar annual health-care problem (Green et al., 1987). In the UK there are 10–15 cases per 1,000,000 population per year (Grundy, 1993). The majority of these occur in the second, third, and fourth decades of life, with males being four times more likely than females to be injured. Road traffic accidents are the most common cause; falls, sporting injury, and industrial accidents account for the majority of the rest. Worldwide, the aetiology varies; Greenland has a high incidence due to suicide attempts (26%), whereas in Nigeria 41% are the result of falls from palm trees (Okonkwo, 1988; Pederson et al., 1989).

THE VERTEBRAL COLUMN INJURY

Level of injury

In 1927, Jefferson found the incidence of vertebral column injuries peaked at three levels: C1/C2, the low cervical region, and the thoracolumbar junction. This observation reflects the areas of greatest mobility within the spine. SCI occurs in 10–14% of thoracolumbar injuries (Riggins, 1977) but in 40% of those in the cervical region (Bohlman, 1979). Multiple, non-contiguous vertebral injury has been reported in 7–9% of cases of SCI (Gupta & Masri, 1989). However, modern MRI reveals non-contiguous bone injury in a much greater proportion.

Classification of thoracolumbar fractures

A number of systems of fracture classificaion have been described (Table 44.1). That of Dennis (1983) is descriptive and based on his three-column model. This model has achieved wide acceptance:

1. Anterior column: the anterior longitudinal ligament, anterior half of the annulus fibrosus, and the anterior half of the vertebral body.

Table 44.1. Classification of fractures

Cervical spine fractures
Atlantoaxial region
   Atlantooccipital dislocation
   Jefferson fracture
   Odontoid fracture
   C2 body fracture
   Hangman's fracture
Lower cervical spine
   Flexion   compressive
               distractive
   Extension compressive
               Distractive
   Vertical compression
   Lateral flexion

Thoracolumbar fractures
Descriptive
   Compression
   Burst
   Flexion/distraction
   Fracture/dislocation
Mechanistic
   Flexion   compressive
               distractive
               torsional
   Extension distractive
   Vertical compression
   Lateral flexion
   Translational

2. Middle column: the posterior longitudinal ligament, posterior half of the annulus fibrosus, and the posterior half of the vertebral body.
3. Posterior column: the facet joints, ligamentum flavum, and interspinous ligament.

One of the principal aims of classification is to identify those injuries, which are inherently unstable. Biomechanical instability is present when two or more of the columns are disrupted (Haher et al., 1989). Others have a mechanistic approach.

1. Compression: failure of the anterior column; wedging of the body occurs.
2. Burst: compressive failure of the anterior and middle columns.
3. Flexion/distraction: a distraction injury of the middle and posterior columns, hinging around the anterior column.
4. Fracture/dislocation.

The comprehensive AO classification of thoracic and lumbar injuries was described in 1994 and is based primarily on patho-morphological criteria (Magerl et al., 1994).

When assessing the spine, pain radiographs of all suspect levels are required and if vertebral injury is confirmed the whole spine should be imaged to exclude non-contiguous injuries. The cord and vertebral canal are assessed with MRI (Kerslake et al., 1991). CT will give additional useful information in the planning of treatment in some cases.

Ligamentous injury can be inferred from the pattern of bony injury on plain X-ray e.g. compressive failure of the anterior column of >25% in the presence of a preserved middle column implies posterior ligamentous rupture. In addition, MR allows direct imaging of the soft tissues; rupture of the posterior ligament complex appearing as high signal in the interspinous region on sagittal T2 weighted MRI.

Classification of cervical injuries

A number of well-known patterns of injury are described in the atlantoaxial region. Those in the lower cervical spine are usually classified by mechanism (Table 44.1).

THE SPINAL CORD INJURY

Primary and secondary cord injury

In a non-penetrating injury, the spinal cord can be damaged by compression, contusion, stretching, or puncture by bone fragments. In most cases the cord is anatomically in continuity. Following the primary injury, local biochemical events are initiated that, by adverse effects on cell metabolism, membrane permeability, and the accumulation of toxic metabolites produce secondary neural injury. Reduced tissue perfusion and hypoxia consequent on systemic hypotension caused by hypovolaemia and/or neurogenic shock will contribute to these mechanisms. It is this secondary injury which is potentially avoidable and which is the target of treatment.

Grading of the neurological injury

In 1992 the American Spinal Injury Association (ASIA), along with the International Medical Society of Paraplegia (IMSOP), published the International Standards for Neurological and Functional Classification of Spinal Cord injury (Table 44.2; ASIA/IMSOP, 1992). This is based on the Frankel classification of 1969, with modifications from Tator et al. (1982) and Waters et al. (1991).

The degree of injury–complete versus incomplete injury

The SCI is termed complete if there is no motor or sensory function in the lowest sacral segment and incomplete if sensory or motor function is preserved in the lowest sacral segment (Waters et al., 1991). For example, if a patient has normal function at C5 but no function below, including the lowest sacral segment, the patient will be classified as C5 complete. The zone of partial preservation refers to those dermatomes and myotomes below the level of a complete injury that remain partially innervated. Sacral sensation includes deep anal sensation as well as sensation at the anal mucocutaneous junction. Motor function of the lowest sacral segment is assessed by presence or absence of voluntary contraction of the external anal sphincter on digital examination. Because of the width of the canal only 16% of injuries at the atlanto-axial level produce a neurological deficit.

In the early 1970s, approximately one-third of SCI presenting to rehabilitation units were incomplete and two-thirds complete.

Table 44.2. ASIA/IMSOP impairment scale

Grade	Clinical findings below the injured level
A – Complete	No motor or sensory function in sacral segments S4 and S5
B – Incomplete	Sensory function preserved below the lesion
C – Incomplete	Motor function preserved below the lesion. The majority of key muscles have a muscle grade < 3
D – Incomplete	Motor function preserved below the lesion. The majority of key muscles have a muscle grade > or equal to 3
E – Normal	Normal neurology

Muscle grade based on Medical Research Council Grade. *Source*: ASIA (1992). *Standards for neurological classification of spinal injury patients*. ASIA, Chicago.

This has now changed, and two-thirds of SCI presenting to rehabilitation units are incomplete. The reasons for this change include improved prehospital and initial hospital care.

Assessment of the level of injury

In accordance with the new ASIA classification, the level of injury is determined by neurological examination of a key sensory point in each of 28 dermatomes (Fig. 44.1) and of a key muscle in each of 10 myotomes on each side of the body (Table 44.3, Fig. 44.1). The level of injury is defined as the most caudal segment of the spinal cord with normal motor and sensory function on both sides of the body. The sensory level is the most caudal level with normal sensation; the motor level is the most caudal level with normal motor function. In this context normal motor function means at least MRC grade 3 strength, providing that the segments above are intact (i.e. MRC grade 5) (MRC, 1943). The reason for this is that most muscles are innervated by more than one spinal cord segment. If a muscle has at least grade 3 it is considered that the more rostral of the innervating segments is intact. The skeletal level refers to the level of greatest vertebral damage as determined by radiographic examination.

Spinal shock

During the acute phase of the injury, in addition to motor and sensory loss, the patient may show limb flaccidity with loss of tendon reflex activity and sphincter function. This is termed spinal shock. The underlying biochemical mechanisms of this evolve over a period of hours to weeks, during which the functioning of less injured spinal nerves is marked. Its duration is variable and its presence has no long-term prognostic significance. With resolution of spinal shock there is a change to limb hypertonicity and hyperreflexia as segmental reflexes recommence. The delayed plantar response is normally the first to recover, usually within a few days of injury, followed by the bulbocavernosum and cremasteric reflex (Ko et al., 1999). Deep tendon reflexes recover in 1 to 2 weeks. Spinal shock should not be confused with neurogenic shock (vide infra).

Reversible, transient spinal injury syndromes

These have been described particularly in young male athletes. Hyperflexion or, more usually, hyperextension of the neck without bony injury is the usual mechanism. Motor changes from mild weakness to complete paralysis have been reported along with dysaesthetic pain, especially in the hands, and sensory loss. This deficit is transitory, resolving over minutes to hours. Radiographs can show pre-existing spinal stenosis, congenital vertebral anomalies, or intervertebral disc herniation. Such patients are best advised to avoid future contact sports, although the evidence that they are predisposed to permanent neurological injury is inconclusive (Torg, 1995).

SCIWORA

In children, Spinal Cord Injury Without Radiological Abnormality (SCIWORA) represents a significant proportion of SCI. The incidence reduces with age and SCIWORA is uncommon in adults. In young children SCIWORA accounts for approximately one-third of spinal cord injuries (Dickman et al., 1991). The usual mechanism is a spontaneously reduced subluxation or distraction injury made possible by the increased elasticity of the paediatric spine. Instability must be excluded and immobilisation with a collar, halo, or surgery used as appropriate (Pang & Wilberger, 1982).

Patterns of incomplete injury

Incomplete injuries tend to conform to a pattern dependent on the anatomical location of the injury within the cord, possibly reflecting the cord blood supply. Motor fibres tend to be more susceptible to trauma so that incomplete injuries always have sensory preservation with or without motor preservation.

Anterior cord syndrome. The distribution of clinical findings is similar to that seen with anterior spinal artery infarction with loss of the spinothalamic (pain and temperature sensation) and motor tracts (Schneider, 1955). The dorsal columns (vibration sense, proprioception, and some touch sensation) are preserved. The prognosis for motor recovery is poorer than in other incomplete injury syndromes.

Central cord syndrome. The neurological picture is of quadraparesis and sensory loss, disproportionately affecting the upper limbs (Schneider et al., 1954). Because proprioceptive loss in the lower limbs can be marked, regaining the ability to walk can be difficult, even with reasonable motor recovery. Overall, the prognosis for independent ambulation is about 50%, but recovery is age related and 97% of those under 50 ambulated compared to 41% of those over 50 in one study (Penrod et al., 1990). Recovery of distal upper limb function is less good

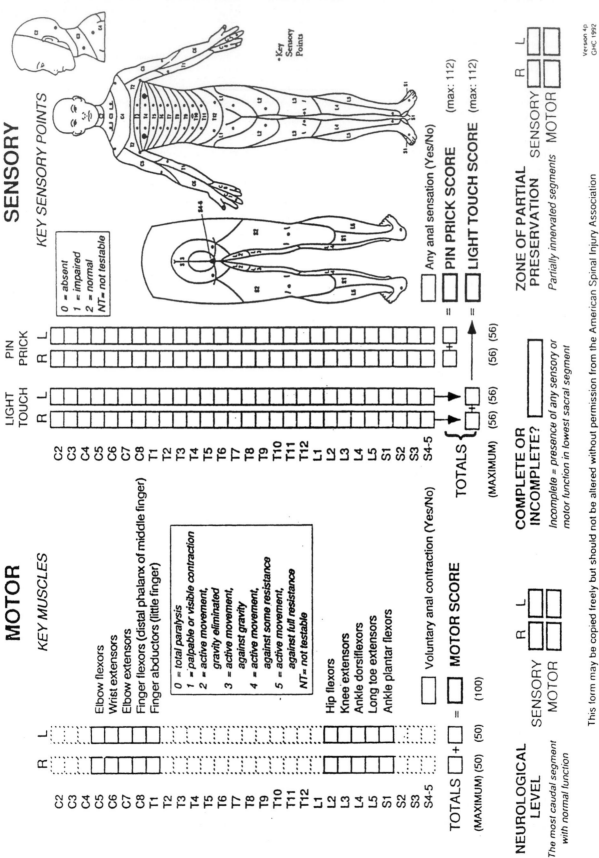

Figure 44.1. ASIA summary chart.

Table 44.3. Assessment of sensory level

0	Absent
1	Impaired
2	Normal
NT	Not testable

Source: ASIA (1992). *Standards for neurological classfication of spinal injury patients.* ASIA, Chicago.

Table 44.4. Assessment of motor level

C1–4	Sensory level and diaphragm
C5	Elbow flexion
C6	Wrist extension
C7	Elbow extension
C8	Middle finger distal phalanx flexion
T1	Small finger abduction
T2–L1	Sensory level (and Beevor's sign)
L2	Hip flexion
L3	Knee extension
L4	Ankle dorsiflexion
L5	Big toe extension
S1	Ankle plantar flexion
S2–5	Sensory level and sphincter ani

Source: ASIA (1992). *Standards for neurological classification of spinal injury patients.* ASIA, Chicago.

(Mesard, 1978). This pattern of injury is most commonly seen in the elderly with underlying spondylosis, who have suffered a cervical hyperextension injury. In this group the prognosis is less good. One study showed that only 31% ambulate, with a mean age of 65 years (Foo, 1986).

Posterior cord syndrome. Rare, this involves injury to the dorsal columns alone. Despite this, the loss of proprioception can be as disabling as a motor deficit.

Hemicord (Brown–Séquard) syndrome. Ipsilateral loss of motor and dorsal column function with contralateral loss of pain and temperature sensation. It has been described in association with most mechanisms of injury. The prognosis, in general, is good with a 90% chance of good recovery (Mesard, 1978). Almost all walk successfully.

Individual root lesions. These can occur at the level of the injury and, in general, carry a good prognosis, if the root is in continuity.

Injuries of the conus and cauda equina

Injuries to the conus are frequent because the relative mobility of the thoracolumbar junction predisposes it to trauma. Lesions higher in the conus produce a clinical picture of paraplegia with mixed upper and lower motor neurone features. If the lower end of the conus is injured the exiting lumbar roots might be unaffected and the legs relatively spared. The patients have saddle sensory loss and flaccid sphincters. Lesions to the cauda equina produce a lower motor neurone picture with varying degrees of bowel and bladder dysfunction, impotence, and sensory loss. The prognosis for cauda equina lesions is better because the

lumbar roots seem more resistant to trauma, having fewer secondary injury mechanisms and greater regenerative capacity than the cord. The sacral roots, however, are very delicate and recovery is usually poor following injury.

Chronic post-traumatic cord syndromes

Following the initial injury, liquefaction of haematoma and necrosed cord tissue can lead to cyst formation and further neurological deterioration. This can be in the form of microcystic degeneration or a syrinx. The pathogenesis of syrinx formation and extension is poorly understood (Silberstein & Hennessy, 1992; Williams, 1990). Syringomyelia causing a worsening neurological deficit occurs in about 3% of cord injuries, although MRI demonstrates syringomyelia in up to 22% of SCI (Squier & Lehr, 1994) and the incidence of asymptomatic cysts in the injured cord might be as high as 60%. Cysts can form within weeks of the injury, although typically they cause symptoms beginning months to years after the injury, usually heralded by causalgic-type pain and followed by neurological deterioration that can spread rostrally with some rapidity. A high index of suspicion for post-traumatic syringomyelia is needed. Regular and frequent follow-up of the spinally injured patient on a yearly or alternate-year basis is the best way to prevent the potentially devastating effects of this complication (Biyani & el Masry, 1994).

Arachnoiditis can also be a cause of symptoms. Even minor injuries can result in florid arachnoiditis, which can extend rostrally and caudally some distance from the original level of injury and be associated with delayed neurological deterioration.

MANAGEMENT OF THE SPINALLY INJURED PATIENT

The initial steps in the management of a patient with acute SCI are resuscitation and the prevention of further harm to the spinal cord. In recent years this has improved considerably. The "ABC" of trauma management is now in general well known and there is greater awareness of the importance of preventing hypoxia and hypotension and of the need for early immobilisation of the spine.

Initial management goals in spinal cord injury

1. *Prevention of secondary injury and neurological deterioration.* The key to recovery is the number and quality of surviving axons traversing the injured segment. The spine should be immobilised. Secondary neuronal injury will be minimised by maintaining spinal cord perfusion and oxygenation. SCI causes a "functional sympathectomy", the results of which are vasodilatation, increased venous capacitance and relative hypovolaemia, all of which contribute to hypotension and reduced cord perfusion. Above T4 the sympathetic drive to the heart is also lost resulting in loss of the ability to increase cardiac output in response to hypotension. This neurogenic shock may be exacerbated by hypovolaemia due to other injuries

(Kiss & Tator, 1983). Good oxygenation should be maintained with ventilatory support as required. Systemic hypotension should be corrected by volume replacement and vasopressors to maintain the mean systemic arterial pressure at 90 mm Hg, and central venous pressure at 5–10 mm (Levi et al., 1993; Vale et al., 1997). Neurogenic shock may be distinguished from hypovolaemic shock secondary to associated injuries by the presence of warm peripheries and bradycardia.

2. *Identification and management of associated injuries.* Over 60% will have associated systems injuries. Major injuries to the head, chest, and abdomen will occur in approximately 15%, 10% and 5%, respectively. The history and examination will give clues to both these and the pattern of spinal injury that is to be expected. The presence of head injury, limb fractures, peripheral nerve injury, and spinal shock can make an accurate neurological examination impossible during the initial assessment.

3. *Determination of the degree and extent of neurological injury*:
   (a) Sensory examination: at each of the key dermatomal points (see Fig. 44.1). Two aspects of sensation are examined: pin prick and light touch. Sensation is scored as absent (0), impaired (1), or normal (2) (Table 44.3) and a total score calculated (see Fig. 44.1). Anal sensation is assessed by digital examination. Joint position sense can also be recorded.
   (b) Motor examination: each of the key myotomes is assessed (Table 44.4) using the MRC 6-point scale.
   The results of these examinations are recorded on the standard ASIA form (see Fig. 44.1)

Treatment of the spinal injury itself is directed towards two parallel concerns: restoration of spinal alignment/stability and promotion of neurological recovery. These two aims are not independent; restoration of alignment is important not only in preventing subsequent painful and progressive deformity but also in facilitating neurological recovery (Holdsworth & Hardy, 1953).

Conservative management

The basis of conservative management is fracture reduction and bed-rest until the fracture is stable enough for mobilisation. Only 4 of a cohort of 612 patients treated in this way subsequently developed spinal instability (Frankel et al., 1969) and it is this benchmark against which surgical intervention should be judged. However, to date, studies of conservative treatment are limited to noncontrolled retrospective analyses. In the cervical spine reduction can be achieved and maintained with traction, whereas in the thoracolumbar spine recumbency and appropriately positioned bolsters are used. Following mobilisation, stability can be maintained by an external orthosis.

The role of chemotherapeutic neuroprotection

A variety of pharmacological substances have been tested in animal models of SCI. Methyl prednisolone (MP) has been the most extensively investigated (Otani et al., 1994; Tator & Fehling, 1999). NASCIS-2 showed that MP started within 8 hours of spinal injury and given for 24 hours improved neurological recovery compared with both a placebo group and with a second treatment group that received naloxone (Bracken et al., 1990). NASCIS-3 showed that if administration was begun within 3 hours of injury, there was no additional benefit to prolonging the treatment after 24 hours, however, if commencement of MP was delayed to between 3 and 8 hours postinjury then improved outcome was seen by continuing MP therapy for 48 hours (Bracken et al., 1997). But patients who received MP for 48 hours experienced a higher incidence of severe sepsis and pneumonia than those who received treatment for 24 hours. Since these trials, the majority of patients with SCI in North America have received MP according to the NASCIS-2 recommendations (an initial intravenous dose of 30 mg/kg followed by 5.4 mg/kg/hour for the next 23 hours).

The NASCIS results have been subjected to a number of methodological, scientific and statistical criticisms (Hurlbert, 2000; Short et al., 2000). The overall benefit was negative, positive benefits were only seen in a subpopulation following post-hoc analysis and no improvement in survival or improved quality of life was demonstrated. An increased risk of wound infection, hyperglycaemia, pneumonia, gastrointestinal haemorrhage and sepsis was seen and has been confirmed by others (Galendiuk, 1993). Recently, several reviews of the available evidence for methylprednisolone have been published. One concluded that MP was safe and modestly effective if given within 8 hours of injury (Bracken, 2001) whilst several others concluded that the available medical evidence does not support the use of methylprednisolone in SCI (Short et al., 2000; Hurlbert, 2001; Appuzzo, 2002). The use of methylprednisolone following spinal injury remains controversial.

A number of other, potentially neuroprotective, agents have also been investigated. M-1 is a bovine glycolipid that enhances neuronal sprouting and regeneration and counteracts some secondary injury processes. In the initial human trial, a statistically significant beneficial result was achieved (Geisler et al., 1991). Unfortunately, in a subsequent, large multi-centre randomised controlled trial the overall results were negative, although there were some modestly beneficial effects (Geisler et al., 2001). TRH, an antagonist of endogenous opioids (Pitts et al., 1995), Gacyclidine and n-methyl-D-aspartate receptor antagonist (Tadie et al., 1995) and Nimodipine (Petitjean et al., 1995), used for neuroprotection in subarachnoid haemorrhage, have not been shown to confer any benefit.

Assessment of the vertebral column injury

A detailed history of the mechanism of injury should be taken. Plain radiographs of all suspect levels are required and, if vertebral injury is confirmed, the whole spine should be imaged to

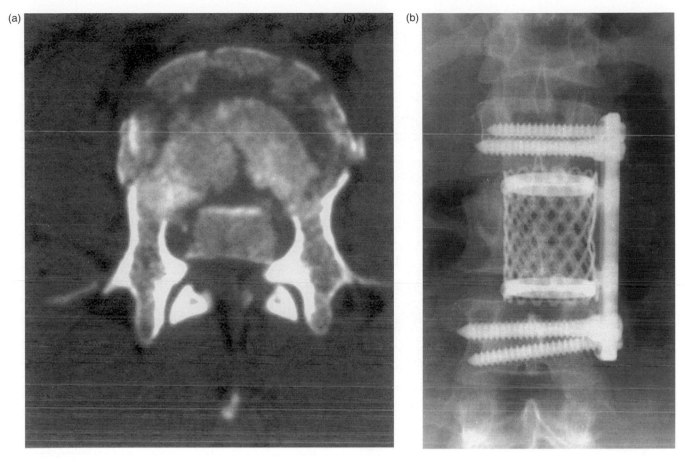

Figure 44.2. Major burst fracture of L2. (a) A large bone fragment is filling the canal. (b) Reconstruction using a MOSS cage and anterior screw plate construct.

exclude non-contiguous injuries. The cord and vertebral canal are assessed with MRI (Kerslake et al., 1991). CT will give additional useful information in the planning of treatment in some cases.

SURGICAL MANAGEMENT

The role of surgical fixation

Opinion as to the role of surgery remains divided, as a number of studies have shown no significant difference in neurological outcome irrespective of surgical intervention (Bohlmann et al., 1985). A major consideration, however, is that entry into the active rehabilitation process only fully takes place once the spine is stable and recumbent management typically requires 8–12 weeks bedrest to achieve this. Surgery offers certain advantages over recumbent care: it allows correction and immediate stabilisation of the deformity and more rapid mobilisation of the patient, while avoiding the hindrance of an external orthosis and minimising the problems of recumbency (Benze & Kesterson, 1989). In addition, some injuries will not reduce without surgery, whereas some are intrinsically highly unstable. Surgery can reduce the incidence of post-traumatic kyphosis compared to recumbent, conservative management (Denis et al., 1984). It

decreases rehabilitation time (Jacobs et al., 1980) and can also improve neurological outcome.

Although some units retain a conservative policy to many of these injuries, there has been a move towards early surgery in many spinal units. The relative safety, flexibility, and ease of use of modern instrumentation systems have promoted this trend. The surgical approach, timing, and type of instrumentation remain controversial, but in general modern surgical technique aims to preserve as many motion segments as possible by short segment fusion.

The role and timing of decompressive surgery

The timing and role of decompressive surgery is even more controversial. The single widely accepted indication for decompression is progressive neurological deterioration due to spinal cord compression. There is strong evidence from animal models that early decompression improves neurological recovery after SCI (Fehlings et al., 2001) but, in humans, there is no Class I evidence for surgery and no consensus on the role and timing of decompression. Even in the presence of an incomplete injury, the evidence for neurological benefit from surgical intervention is not incontrovertible. The only randomised trial of the timing of decompression showed no difference between early and

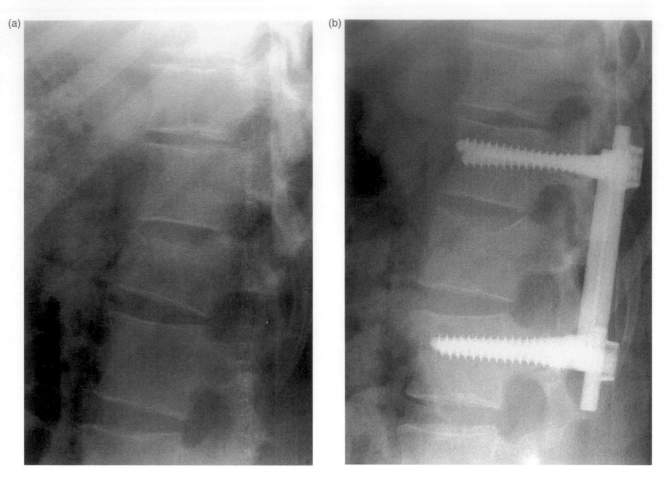

Figure 44.3. (a) Minor burst fracture of L3. (b) Reconstruction using pedicle screw rod construct. This provides an internal splint during bone healing. The construct is removed at 6 months with the aim of minimising the number of fused spinal segments.

delayed surgery (Vaccaro et al., 1997), however, the cut-off time was 72 hours and the relevant time frame when decompression might be beneficial remains unclear.

A number of authors have reported neurological benefit from surgical decompression (Hu, 1993; Kiwerski, 1993) even after considerable delay, confirming that ongoing cord compression can be a contributor to neuronal dysfunction (Bohlman, 1979). Because of the lack of evidence a conservative approach is acceptable, but we would in general advocate cord decompression I an attempt to improve neurological recovery even in those who are not deteriorating. Intuitively, early surgery is attractive; it is safe and there is evidence to support that it is efficacious (Vaccoro et al., 1997; Tator et al., 1987).

Surgery for thoracic and thoracolumbar fractures

Denis's three-column model is useful in planning the surgical approach. Surgery aims to leave uninjured segments unfused. If the vertebral canal is significantly compromised then decompression should be considered. If the compression is predominantly anterior then an anterior approach is usually most appropriate, although in some cases an adequate decompression can be achieved through a posterolateral approach. Reconstruction of the anterior column is usually achieved through implantation of a cage device containing bone graft via an anterior approach (Fig. 44.2) which provides structural support until bone union is achieved (Crockard & Ransford, 1990). A number of cage devices are now available in stainless steel, titanium, and even carbon fibre; experience is showing them to be safe and effective in experienced hands. Cages require additional stabilisation either using an anterior plate or rods or using posterior instrumentation to give circumferential stabilisation.

Immediate stabilisation of the posterior column is most satisfactorily achieved using a pedicle screw construct that provides rigid segmental fixation. Posterior instrumentation can be used as part of the circumferential stabilisation of a three-column injury but posterior stabilisation alone is sufficient for some injuries. For example, we use a short pedicle screw construct without formal fusion as an "internal brace" (Fig. 44.3) for the management of some minor burst fractures without neural compromise. The instrumentation is removed at 6 months. This allows reconstitution of the normal anatomy without loss of motion segments.

Surgery for cervical fractures

The same general principles apply in the cervical spine as in the thoracolumbar spine. The compressive load on the cervical vertebra is much lower than in the thoracolumbar spine and autologous tricortical bone graft from the iliac crest has sufficient mechanical strength to withstand this load. For this reason reconstruction of the anterior column in the neck is usually achieved using iliac crest graft alone, although if insufficient structural bone is available a cage might still be required. An anterior plate will be required to maintain stability until bony union occurs (Fig. 44.4).

Pedicle screw fixation in the cervical spine is technically difficult and not without risk of neurovascular compromise. The lateral masses, however, offer an excellent fixation point for posterior segmental instrumentation and a number of instrumentation systems are available that exploit this (Fig. 44.5). A variety of techniques can be used for fixation of fractures of the atlantoaxial complex.

Surgery for late deformity

Deformity, either scoliosis or kyphosis, can occur in the non-fused spine following trauma. Many of these deformities are non-progressive, although some will progressively deform (Denis et al., 1984). Progression is more common in the young, with fracture at the thoracolumbar junction and in those that have had decompressive laminectomy. Deformity can be painful (Osti, 1986; Young, 1973), functionally disabling, and cosmetically unsatisfactory. All of these can be improved by surgery. Children, in particular, need regular follow-up for avoidance or early detection of these complications. The correction and stabilisation of progressive deformity following injury can be technically difficult and prevention by early surgery is preferable. A detailed description of the surgical techniques is beyond the scope of this chapter but the principles of surgery are deformity correction while fusing the minimal number of motion segments. Patients who develop progressive deformity or pain at the level of injury should be referred for a surgical opinion.

Surgery for late neurological deterioration

Delayed neurological deterioration can be related to residual or progressive spinal deformity, syrinx formation, intrinsic cord damage, or arachnoiditis. The advent of MRI has led to an increase in the identification of post-traumatic syringomyelia. The creation of a pseudomeningocoele with or without a syrinx shunt draining to the subarachnoid space or pleura might be required for progressive syrinx dilatation. The surgical management of microcystic degeneration or arachnoiditis is unrewarding.

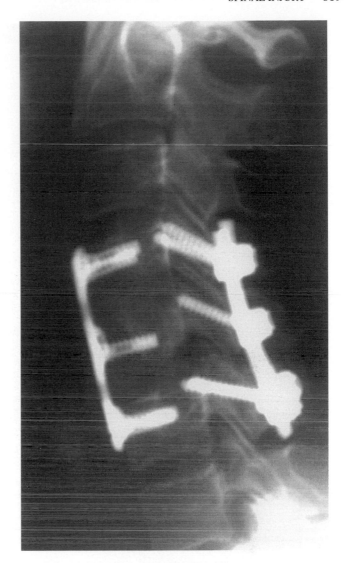

Figure 44.4. Circumferential cervical fixation using anterior unicortical screw plate and lateral mass screw rod constructs.

SYSTEMIC SEQUELAE AND THEIR MANAGEMENT IN COMPLETE SPINAL INJURIES

Cardiovascular/autonomic

The sympathetic outflow from the cord is from between T1 and L2. Cervical and thoracic trauma can disrupt this, leading to the loss of vasomotor tone. Lesions above T4 also cause loss of the cardiac sympathetic drive. The parasympathetic outflow delivered predominantly via the vagus nerve remains intact. The resultant cardiovascular instability can result in episodes of bradycardia and hypotension. During the initial assessment of the trauma victim, neurogenic shock can be distinguished from hypovolaemic shock secondary to associated injuries by the presence of warm peripheries and bradycardia.

During the early period following SCI, hypotension and bradycardia (and even asystole) are easily triggered. Pulse

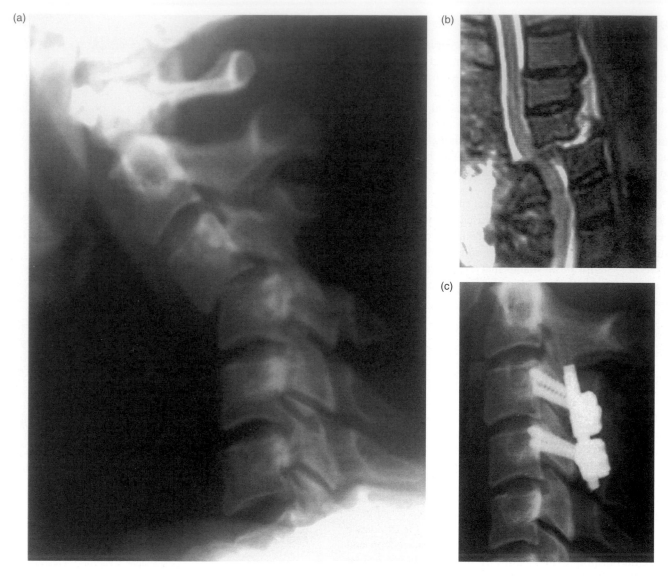

Figure 44.5. (a) Bilateral jumped cervical facets. (b) MRI T2-weighted showing canal narrowing at the level of subluxation. (c) Reduction and fixation with lateral mass screws rod construct.

monitoring must be maintained during catheterisation, airway suction, bowel evacuation, and patient turning, and atropine should be available or given before any such procedure. This usually settles after 1 month but can persist indefinitely. Postural hypotension can interfere with rehabilitation and is best managed by gradually increasing tolerance to head-up tilt using a tilt table (Fig. 44.6) (Mathias, 1987) or sitting the patient in a chair.

Peripheral vasodilatation causes fluctuations in temperature regulation and excessive sweating. Core temperature can fall to as low as 32°C and periods of pyrexia can also occur. Careful control of the ambient temperature is required.

Autonomic dysreflexia is one of the few causes of postacute mortality. It is unusual before 3 months and is most likely between 3 and 18 months. It then tends to diminish, although it can recur at any stage. It is seen in 48–80% of patients who have lesions at or rostral to T6 and comprises peripheral vasoconstriction triggered by (usually visceral) afferent stimulation (Lindan et al., 1980). This results in a marked rise in blood pressure with a subsequent parasympathetically mediated reflex bradycardia. Other features include pounding headache, sweating, and flushing above the level of the cord lesion, pupillary dilatation, cold hands and feet, and a feeling of dread. Removal of the precipitating factor and sitting the patient up is virtually always successful in relieving the problem. Sublingual nifedipine can be used prophylactically during procedures such as catheterisation or to relieve an attack. Following a precipitating event some patients have repeated but less dramatic rises in blood pressure for hours or days, which are usually controlled with nifedipine; an α-blocker can also be used (Vaidyanathan et al., 1998). Most patients nowadays are aware of this problem but education is imperative as several cerebral haemorrhages and

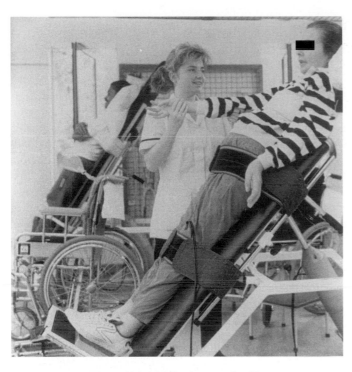

Figure 44.6. Mobilisation on a tilt table.

deaths occur each year in the UK as a result of unrecognised or untreated dysreflexia.

Respiratory

Patients with high thoracic/low cervical lesions have compromised ventilatory ability due to loss of innervation of the intercostals and accessory abdominal musculature. Injuries at C3 and above can render the patient dependent on mechanical ventilation due to loss of the phrenic nerves. Atelectasis and pneumonia are problems in these patients. Injuries at C6 and above often require temporary ventilation due to diaphragmatic fatigue during the first 24 to 72 hours.

Skin care

Regular turning is required in the early recumbent phase for protection of pressure areas. Avoidance of pressure ulcers is very important as they can take a long time to heal and have a markedly deleterious effect on rehabilitation. Care of pressure areas does not stop with mobilisation and in the rehabilitation phase all patients should be taught methods to relieve pressure points. An appropriate wheelchair cushion is very important. When sitting, pressure relief should be performed every 10 to 15 minutes and techniques to achieve this, such as leaning from side to side, should be taught to the patient.

Nutrition

The ileus associated with spinal shock usually passes off within a few weeks, although it can last longer. During this time, nasogastric drainage might be required. H_2 antagonists reduce the risk of gastric ulceration in the first few weeks following injury. Dramatic weight loss is common in the first weeks following SCI associated with high catabolism and reduced intake. A high-protein diet (4000 kcal daily) is required. Later, this is replaced with a balanced, low-calcium diet.

Bowel

Most patients achieve predictable reflex bowel emptying on a regular basis (usually alternate days) using suppositories or digital anal stimulation. With a flaccid bowel, regular enemas might be required.

Bladder

The overall aims of treatment are continence and the protection of renal function. In general, bladder dysfunction after SCI falls into two categories: upper motor neuron syndrome and lower motor neuron syndrome. Lower motor neuron syndrome is characterised by bladder flaccidity requiring passive drainage. Upper motor neuron syndrome is considerably more complex. Initially, following complete SCI, the bladder is flaccid and is managed with an indwelling urethral catheter. As the patient improves a program of self intermittent catheterisation (SIC) can be commenced (Guttman & Frankel, 1966). This provides the mainstay of bladder rehabilitation for most patients (Maynard, 1993). Indwelling urethral or suprapubic catheters should only be used as a last resort as an increased incidence of infection, stones, and bladder carcinoma is well documented. Relative detrusor over-activity in those using SIC may lead to episodic incontinence for which anticholinergics are usually helpful. Impaired coordination of detrusor contractions with relaxation of the bladder sphincter is termed bladder–sphincter dyssynergia. The bladder contracts against an outlet obstruction which leads to elevated bladder pressures and vesico-uretic reflux. Over time the elevated pressure predisposes to complications (hydronephrosis, pyelonephritis, stone formation, amyloidosis and renal failure) which used to the main cause of mortality in SCI (de Vivo et al., 1993). In addition, overdistention can lead to potentially life-threatening autonomic dysreflexia.

Anticholinergics for detrusor relaxation and α-blockers to relax the bladder neck and sphincters will reduce bladder pressures (Burns et al., 2001). Intravesicial capsaicin and botulinum toxin A can also be used to reduce detrusor hyperreflexia (de Deze et al., 1999; Schurch et al., 2000). If medication fails to work, surgery may be needed. The options available include: bladder augmentation to increase bladder compliance (Mundy & Stephenson, 1985), bladder neck division to reduce outflow resistance and urinary diversion by ileal conduit. Implantable anterior sacral roof stimulators (Brindley et al., 1982;

Brindley, 1994) have shown improvements in continence, bladder compliance, bladder emptying, and prevention of ureteric reflux and upper tract dilatation, resulting in improved renal function.

Recurrent UTIs are a common problem. Bacteriuria in itself does not warrant antibiotic treatment unless systemic effects occur. The most effective method of preventing recurrent UTIs is adequate bladder drainage. A maximum residual bladder volume of 75ml is acceptable. With care, long periods of urinary sterility can often be achieved.

There are a number of options for bladder management. The use of urodynamics has led to a more rational approach and it is important that the most suitable technique is chosen for each patient. Follow-up monitoring of the bladder, upper tracts and serum creatinine should be performed annually.

Sexual function

Despite the loss of genital sensation many of those with SCI injury enjoy active sex lives. Sexual function and fertility is usually maintained in females, although it could be 6–9 months before the normal ovulating cycle is re-established. Pregnancy and delivery are relatively straightforward apart from complications such as deep vein thrombosis (DVT), urinary tract infection (UTI), and constipation, but autonomic dysreflexia may occur.

The majority of men with SCI are infertile because of a combination of ejaculatory dysfunction, impaired spermatogenesis, and poor semen quality. Males with an intact sacral cord will usually experience reflex erections. In some patients they will be sustained enough for intercourse, although erectile function might not return for 6–12 months following injury. For those in which it does not drugs, surgery, or mechanical devices may achieve restoration. Viagra (sildenafil citrate), a phosphodiesterase type 5 inhibitor has become the treatment of choice. It facilitates non-adrenergic, non-cholinergic smooth muscle relaxation in the corpora cavernosa. Experience suggests it to be effective and well tolerated in SCI. A recent trial has shown that 78% of SCI patients had improved erections and 80% had improved ability to have sexual intercourse with sildenafil (Giuliano et al., 1999).

Ejaculation is rare in SCI. Useful semen can be obtained in 80% of SCI men by use of a vibrator at the root of the penis or in nearly 100% by transrectal electrode stimulation (Perkash et al., 1990). Although electrostimulation is the more successful (Seager & Halstead, 1993), vibratory stimulation has the benefit of being possible in the home.

The reasons for poor semen quality remain unclear, but UTIs can impair spermatogenesis and cause ductal blockage, resulting in semen that is inadequate. Techniques of sperm enhancement can be useful, but intracytoplasmic sperm injection offers the best chance for those who cannot conceive because of poor sperm quality. Fertilisation can be improved from 30% to 88% (Hultling et al., 1997). It is, however, expensive.

Spasticity

Spasticity is defined as both abnormal increase in tone and velocity-dependent increased resistance to muscle stretch. The degree of an individual's spasticity can be extremely variable, being altered by bodily changes such as constipation and intercurrent illness (sepsis in particular) and also by changes in ambient temperature, noise, and emotional state. A reasonable level of spasticity is beneficial, maintaining muscle bulk, providing some support during transfer, and aiding venous return from the legs. However, excessive spasticity inhibits function, disturbs sleep, is painful and risks the development of contractures. Physiotherapy, exercises, and passive stretching are important in preventing contractures and maintaining joint ranges of motion. Splinting in the position of function is important for the hands and might also be needed for the ankles. The shoulders of a tetraplegic patient also need attention to prevent adhesive capsulitis. For problematic spasticity oral baclofen is the treatment of choice and in contrast to the treatment of pain is effective in most patients. Intrathecal baclofen delivered by a pump implanted in the anterior abdominal wall (Penn & Kroin, 1985; Zirski et al., 1988) can give very good results although the devices are expensive and not without complications (Gardner et al., 1995). For localised spasticity botulinum toxin may be useful whilst some contractures may require surgery in the form of a tenotomy or soft tissue release. Ablative procedures such as rhizotomy and myelotomy were once the main stays of treatment. They are effective procedures that should still be considered in refractory cases (Putty & Shapiro, 1991), especially those that are not functionally reliant on a degree of spasticity.

Venous thrombosis

Deep venous thrombosis is common and pulmonary embolus is a common cause of mortality in SCI. Classic symptoms can be absent; unexplained fever can be the only clue. Subcutaneous heparin prophylaxis can be given for the first 3 months if there is no contraindication.

Pain

The International Association for the Study of Pain has proposed a scheme for characterising SCI pain (Siddall et al., 2000). It defines two types of pain: nociceptive and neuropathic. Nociceptive pain is divided into musculoskeletal and visceral pain. Neuropathic pain is usually described as sharp, shooting, burning, or electrical, and there is usually abnormal sensory responsiveness (hyperaesthesia or hyperalgesia). Psychological factors clearly play a role in all types of chronic pain and are not separately categorised.

The incidence of pain in SCI has been reported to be as high as 90% (New, 1997) and in many patients is severe. Treatment can be a frustrating experience, as oral therapy for severe pain is relatively ineffective. Opioids, antidepressants and antiepileptics all have a role. Intrathecal drug therapy holds some promise, perhaps through combinations of agents such as morphine,

Table 44.5. Areas in which goals should be considered for each patient

Mobility
Transfer
Activities of daily living
Carer
Residence
Social
Psychological
Education
Vocation

clonidine, and baclofen, or innovative agents, such as gabapentin (Burchiel et al., 2001). The development of late onset pain at the injured level warrants a surgical opinion as pseudarthrosis or a damaged intervertebral disc are pain sources that may be relieved by surgical fusion. The delayed onset of pain may also signal extension of an underlying syrinx. For medically intractable pain, surgical procedures may be of value: destructive lesions of the dorsal root entry zone, of peripheral nerves and of the thalamus have all been used. For some patients with incomplete lesions, the implantation of a spinal cord stimulator may provide an answer, although poor results have been reported with complete lesions (Cioni et al., 1995).

Mortality

The mortality rate continues to decrease (Geisler, 1983). Life expectancy is usually quoted as being reduced by 5–8 years for paraplegics and by 8–15 years for tetraplegics, but for an individual with on SCI occurring today, the life expectancy might well be normal. There has been a marked reduction in deaths due to renal disease, but at the same time there has been a relative increase in deaths due to suicide and liver disease.

THE REHABILITATION PROCESS

Rehabilitation is primarily a learning experience which aims to restore the individual to his or her full potential (Mair, 1972). The ideal setting is a comprehensive spinal injuries unit using a multidisciplinary approach. The process should run in parallel with management of the vertebral column injury, the spinal cord injury and their systemic sequelae. The critical outcome goal is reintegration into the community with an acceptable degree of physical, psychological and social independence. This is achieved by acquisition of skills and knowledge along with physical and psychological adaptation.

Timing

Spinal, neural, and autonomic stability are usually achieved within weeks; resolution of the social factors such as housing, relationships, and employment can take months; and psychological adaptation to the injury can take many years. Discharge from the spinal unit can be delayed by many months by unresolved social problems and the lack of provision of appropriate accommodation with wheelchair access. Long in-patient stays are common in the UK, the average being 6 months for a paraplegic 9–12 months for a tetraplegic.

Goal setting

The first goal is the preservation or restoration of maximum neurological function, the primary determinant of which is the neurological level. All members of the multidisciplinary team should assess the patient and realistic and achievable goals should be set (Table 44.5). The individual management plan is one of the most important parts of the rehabilitation process. Each individual is allocated a case manager who administers and coordinates the program.

Recovery and functional outcome

There is good evidence that the majority of patients will make some neurological recovery, although the potential for this is much greater in those with incomplete injuries. The distinction between incomplete and complete injury is crucial from a prognostic point of view. If the patient shows no signs of recovery below the level of injury within the first 24–48 hours then the chance of useful distal motor recovery is only 3–4%, regardless of further treatment (Suwanwela et al., 1962).

The biological basis for recovery includes resolution of secondary injury processes (hypoxia, toxic metabolite accumulation, neurotransmitter changes), restoration of normal microvasculature and longer-term processes such as axonal regeneration and remyelination. Following a complete injury neurological recovery is greater for injuries in the cervical region than in the thoracic region whereas following an incomplete lesion cervical and thoracic injuries show a similar degree of recovery. Recovery is worse for injuries at the thoraco-lumbar junction for both incomplete and complete lesions (Tator, 1983).

In most cases the long-term outcome is predictable within a week of their initial injury (Ditunno et al., 1999). It is important that this information about prognosis is conveyed to the patient and their family, to ensure the pursuit of realistic goals by all concerned.

Expected functional outcome can usually be predicted from the level of injury (Table 44.6). In complete tetraplegia more than 90% of muscles with grade 1 or 2 power from at 1 month after injury will eventually recover to at least grade 3 power. The chance of recovering an additional motor level varies in studies from 27 to 85%. Muscles two levels below the most caudal level with motor function regain grade 3 power in only 1% of cases (Ditunno et al., 1992; Waters et al., 1993; Ditunno et al., 2000). The gain of even one extra level can be highly significant in terms of function especially between C4 and C8.

Most recovery in complete patients occurs during the first 6 to 9 months. The rate of improvement then drops off with a plateau being reached 12 to 18 months following injury. Incomplete injuries are more likely to recover and may do so over a longer time period.

Table 44.6. Typical functional goals for complete spinal injuries (Hussey, 1988)

Level	Wheelchair	Ambulation	Driving	Transfer	ADL and dress	Bowel care	Bladder care	Attendant care
C1/2	Electric W/C	N/A	No	Dependent	Dependent	Dependent	Dependent	Full time
C3/4/5	Electric W/C	N/A	No	Dependent	Dependent	Dependent	Dependent	Full time
C6	Manual W/C	N/A	Specially adapted van	?Dependent	Assistance	Dependent	Dependent	Part time
C7	Manual W/C	N/A	Car with hand controls	Independent	Independent	Dependent	Assistance	Part time
C8/T1	Manual W/C	N/A	Car with hand controls	Independent	Independent	Assistance	Assistance	Minimum
T2–T10	Manual W/C	N/A	Car with hand controls	Independent	Independent	Independent	Independent	None
T11–L2	Manual W/C	Indoors with orthoses	Car with hand controls	Independent	Independent	Independent	Independent	None
L3–S3	Manual W/C	Community with orthoses	Car with hand controls	Independent	Independent	Independent	Independent	None

N/A, not applicable; w/c, wheelchair.

Lower limb function and prognosis for ambulation

The aim of most SCI patients, at least initially, is to achieve their previous level of mobility and walking is usually the goal towards which they direct most effort. Currently, the Functional Independence Measure defines community ambulation as the ability to ambulate 150 feet. To be an effective community ambulatory, one needs at least grade 3 strength in the hip flexors on one side, grade 3 strength in the quadriceps on the other side and intact proprioception. In theory, with appropriate orthoses, any patient with a thoracic SCI can be taught to walk (Hussey & Stauffer, 1973). Some patients with lesions below T12 may be fitted with calipers and achieve swing-to gait over short distances. Some may achieve a reasonable gait with a lesion above L1 using reciprocating gait orthoses (RGO) (Figure 44.7). Despite this it has been clearly established that patients with complete spinal cord injuries rarely walk following discharge (Cemy et al., 1980) and the majority will be wheelchair users. Patients who are incomplete have a better prognosis for walking. 76% of incomplete paraplegics will become community ambulators compared to only 46% of incomplete tetraplegics. This difference largely relates to the ability to use crutches (Waters, 1993). Preservation of pinprick below the level of injury is also significant. At 72 hours post injury 89% of motor complete patients with preserved pinprick will ambulate compared to 11% of those with preserved light touch but no pinprick (Crozier, 1991). Age is another factor. For patients with ASIA C tetraplegia, recovery of ambulation is significantly less likely if age is 50 years or older. In one study 91% of ASIA C patients younger than 50 years of age became ambulatory by discharge, versus 42% ASIA C patients age 50 or older. All patients initially classified as ASIA D became ambulatory by discharge (Burns et al., 1997). Independent transfer required greater than grade 3 power of elbow extension and shoulder adduction; without this transfer will need assistance or be totally dependent.

The selection of a wheelchair and adaptation to the particular needs of the patient are very important, especially as many patients in the UK have to purchase their own or obtain funds from charities. Rapid progress in basic chair skills and bed to chair transfer should be the aim. Advanced skills such as kerb negotiation and floor to chair transfer usually take from 3 to 6 months. With lesions above C6 wheelchair pushing is impractical, as is pressure relief by lifting and an electric chair will

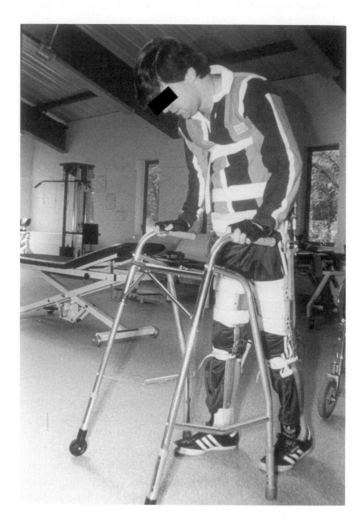

Figure 44.7. Walking using a reciprocating gait orthosis and frame.

be required. In fact, electrical chairs are increasingly being prescribed, even for those who can manually propel themselves. The reason for this is protection of the shoulders from long-term injury. Electrical chairs with an appropriate control system (e.g. mouth or breath) will be needed for lesions above C4.

Encouragement should be given to drive an appropriately modified car. In the past patients with lesions above C6 have been precluded by an ability to transfer in and out of the car, but the provision of lifts has now made even this possible. The future lies with restoration of neural function and reconstitution of the motor cortex to muscle fibre link. Functional electrical stimulation (FES) to achieve standing and walking remains in the early stages of development and is not yet a practical proposition for most patients (Barr et al., 1989).

Upper limb function in tetraplegia

C1 to C4 tetraplegics have no functional upper limb use and are dependent for activities of daily living (ADLs). Patients with C5 lesions have functional use of the biceps. Appropriate splinting can improve functional ability significantly and, with a variety of assist devices, C5 tetraplegics can feed themselves after set-up, assist with dressing, and perform simple orofacial hygiene. C6 tetraplegics have wrist extension. The use of appropriate orthoses can allow self-catheterisation and wheelchair independence on level terrain. Nevertheless, most still require assistance for ADLs, bed mobility, and transfers. Functional use of triceps (C7 tetraplegia) greatly enhances transfer, mobility, and participation in self-care. C8 tetraplegics, although not having normal hand function can usually achieve total independence in a wheelchair. They can also independently transfer their wheelchair into a car. With an injury at T1 upper limb and hand function is normal.

Tendon transfers can restore some function to the upper limbs; for example, posterior deltoid transfer to the olecranon can achieve elbow extension. They are usually performed 12–18 months after injury to allow maximum recovery of the spinal cord.

Although it has not yet proved particularly useful in the lower limbs, FES of paralysed muscles is one approach that has demonstrated significant benefit in restoring grasp and release. In a recent study, 50% of C5 or C6 ASIA A, B, or C patients (11.7% of all tetraplegic individuals) were felt suitable for a neuroprosthetic hand-grasp system (Gorman & Wuolle, 1997). Under this protocol, and given the prevalence of tetraplegia, approximately 12,200 Americans would be candidates for and could benefit from a FES hand grasp system. Grasp, "pinch", and "key" grip can be restored. A number of additional surgical procedures can be performed to enhance the function provided with electrical stimulation. Examples of such procedures include tendon transfers, side-to-side tendon anastomoses, arthrodesis of the interphalangeal joint of the thumb, and rotational osteotomy of the radius.

Functional Independence Measure (FIM)

LEVELS		
	7 Complete Independence (Timely, Safely) 6 Modified Independence (Device)	No Helper
	Modified Dependence 5 Supervision 4 Minimal Assist (Subject = 75%+) 3 Moderate Assist (Subject = 50%+) **Complete Dependence** 2 Maximal Assist (Subject = 25%+) 1 Total Assist (Subject = 0%+)	Helper

	ADMIT	DISCH
Self Care		
A. Eating		
B. Grooming		
C. Bathing		
D. Dressing-Upper Body		
E. Dressing-Lower Body		
F. Toileting		
Sphincter Control		
G. Bladder Management		
H. Bowel Management		
Mobility		
Transfer:		
I. Bed, Chair, Wheelchair		
J. Toilet		
K. Tub, Shower		
Locomotion		
L. Walk/wheelChair	W / C	W / C
M. Stairs		
Communication		
N. Comprehension	A / V	A / V
O. Expression	V / N	V / N
Social Cognition		
P. Social Interaction		
Q. Problem Solving		
R. Memory		
Total FIM		

NOTE: Leave no blanks; enter I if patient not testable due to risk

COPY FREELY - DO NOT CHANGE

RESEARCH FOUNDATION OF THE STATE UNIVERSITY OF NEW YORK

Figure 44.8. Functional Independence Measure.

Functional outcome and patient scoring

The ASIA score is assessed during rehabilitation and, in addition, comprehensive muscle charting might be performed by the physiotherapist. To fully describe the impact of SCI on an individual and to evaluate progress during rehabilitation a measure of a number of functional activities is necessary. The Functional Independence Measure (FIM) is one approach that is becoming widely accepted (International Standards For Neurological And Functional Classification Of Spinal Cord Injury, 1992; McKinley et al., 1998). It focuses on six areas of functioning: self-care, sphincter control, mobility, locomotion, communication, and social cognition. Within each area, a number of specific activities are evaluated. This gives a total of 18 activities that are evaluated in terms of independence of function using a seven-point scale (Fig. 44.8). Patients are assessed at admission, regularly during their stay and at discharge.

Figure 44.9. A variety of sports are now accessible to those with spinal cord injury.

Independence

For the paraplegic there should be few limitations to the activities of daily living. Many improvements have been made to improve access to shops, places of employment and culture, and public transport (although there are many places where access remains unsatisfactory). Independence will be maximised by the provision of personnel and equipment (such as special plates and cutlery). Tetraplegics will inevitably be more limited but it is possible to make even a high level tetraplegic independent within a specific environment using environmental control systems. The balance between the provision of equipment and the provision of personnel will vary from individual to individual.

Some patients never achieve independence. In particular there is a small group of patients with high cervical lesions who require long-term ventilatory support (30 per year in the UK). It is now possible for approximately 50% of these to manage at home; the rest require long-term hospitalisation. Phrenic nerve stimulation might provide a solution for some of these individuals (Mayr et al., 1993; Sharkey et al., 1989).

The value of competitive sport was recognised by Ludwig Guttman. A variety of sports are now accessible, to both paraplegics and tetraplegics (Fig. 44.9) and are increasingly becoming integrated with non-disabled sports.

Community support

In the community, in addition to aids and equipment, appropriately trained support personnel will be required. Considerable skills are required, particularly for the care of tetraplegics and unfortunately there may be insufficient adequately trained people available. This may result in otherwise avoidable complication. Community services are often overstretched and the patient may increasingly rely on the main carer and family, compounding the difficulties of the carer/patient and family/patient relationships. Breakdowns in carer arrangements are common and may occasionally result in the need for long-term residential care. Flexible care arrangements with periods of short-term, respite care may help (Griffiths, 1988).

ADJUSTMENT

There can be few more emotive things to be told than that one is paralysed and there will be many difficulties in adjusting to such a major life event. The initial realisation of paralysis will be frightening The patient will then be subjected to a series of unfamiliar and, for most people, threatening environments and medical interventions in the casualty department and ITU. The ability to absorb information in the first few weeks is impaired. Initially the patient may go through a period of denial. They then may wish to prove the doctors to be wrong. Unrealistic recovery goals are common. Once the acute medical and surgical problems are dealt with the patient will move to a rehabilitation unit. It is not uncommon for there to be anxiety and ambivalence about moving to a lower level of care. In the rehabilitation unit, the patient has to accept their loss of bladder, bowl and limb functions and the invasion of privacy may cause them to become irritable and aggressive. Conflicts with family members may also develop. A raft of emotions may overwhelm the patient's and their relatives ability to cope. It is important that the whole rehabilitation team forms an integral part of the psychological support for both the patient and their relatives. Psychologists must play an early, integral role.

Discharge from the rehabilitation unit is the next hurdle. The patient must confront the physical, social and occupational limitations that their disability will inflict on them in the outside world. They may have to move accommodation, if appropriate modifications cannot be made. They may be unable to return to their job. Depression is common as are drug and alcohol abuse

and there is a higher divorce rate following SCI (de Vivo et al., 1995). For these reasons, psychological and social support must continue after discharge.

The ultimate goal is to return the spinal cord injured individual to independence; if the patient and family cannot adapt to the injury, then reintegration into the community will fail.

REFERENCES

Adams F (transl) (1849). *The Genuine Works of Hippocrates*. The Sydenham Society, London

Anthes DL, Theriault E, Tator CH (1996). Ultrastructural evidence for arteriolar vasospasm after spinal cord trauma. *Neurosurgery, 39*, 804–814

ASIA/IMSOP (1992). International Standards For Neurological And Functional Classification Of Spinal Cord Injury. Revised 1992. American Spinal Injury Association/International Medical Society of Paraplegia (ASIA/IMSOP), Chicago

Barr RMD, Moffat B, Bayley JIL, Middleton FRI (1989). Evaluation of the effects of functional electrical stimulation on muscle power and spasticity in spinal cord injury patients. *Clin Rehabil, 3*, 17–22

Benze EC, Kesterton L (1989). Posterior cervical interspinous wiring and fusion for mid to low cervical spine injuries. *J Neurosurg, 70*, 893–899

Biyani A, el Masry WS (1994). Post-traumatic syringomyelia: A review of the literature. *Paraplegia, 32* (11), 723–731

Bohlman HH (1979). Acute fractures and dislocations of the spine. *JBJS, 61A*, 1119–1142

Bohlman HH, Freehager A, Dejak J (1985). The results of treatment of acute injuries of the upper thoracic spine with paralysis. *Journal of Bone and Joint Surgery, 67*, 360–369

Bracken MB (2001). Methylprednisolone and acute spinal cord injury: an update of the randomised evidence. *Spine, 26* (24S), S47–54

Bracken MB, Collins WF, Freeman DF et al. (1984). Efficacy of methylprednisolone in acute spinal cord injury. *JAMA, 251*, 45–52

Bracken MB, Shepard MJ, Hellenbrand KG et al. (1985). Methylprednisolone and neurological function 1 year after spinal cord injury. Results of the National Acute Spinal Cord Injury Study. *J Neurosurg, 63*, 704–713

Bracken MB, Shepard MJ, Collins WF, et al. (1990). A randomized controlled trial of methylprednisolone or naloxone in the treatment of acute spinal cord injury. Results of the Second National Acute Spinal Cord Injury Study. *New Engl J Med, 322*, 1405–1411

Bracken MB, Shepard MJ, Holford TR et al. (1997). Administration of methylprednisolone for 24 or 48 hours or tirilazad mesylate for 48 hours in the treatment of acute spinal cord injury. Results of the Third National Acute Spinal Cord Injury Randomized Controlled Trial. *JAMA, 277*, 1597–1604

Breasted JH (1922). The Edwin Smith surgical papyrus. *Quarterly Bulletin, New York Historical Society, 6*, 1–31

Brindley GS (1994). The first 500 patients with sacral anterior root stimulation implants: General description. *Paraplegia, 32*, 795–805

Brindley GS, Polkey CE, Rushton DN (1982). Sacral anterior root stimulators for bladder control in paraplegia. *Paraplegia, 20*, 365–381

Burchiel KJ, K Hsu FP (2001). Pain and spasticity after spinal cord injury: mechanisms and treatment. *Spine, 26* (24S), S146–160

Burns SP, Golding DG, Rolle WA, Graziani V, Ditunno JF (1997). Recovery of ambulation in motor-incomplete tetraplegia. *Arch Phys Med Rehabil, 78* (11), 1169–1172

Burns AS, Rivas DA, Ditunno JF (2001). The management of neurogenic bladder and sexual dysfunction after spinal cord injury. *Spine, 26* (24S), S129–136

Cerny K, Waters R, Hislop H, Perry J (1980). Walking and wheelchair energetics in persons with paraplegia. *Phys Ther, 60*, 1133–1139

Cioni B, Meglio M, Pentimalli L, et al. (1995). Spinal cord stimulation in the treatment of paraplegic pain. *J Neurosurg., 82*, 35–39

Cline HJ (1815). Cited by Hayward G (1815). In: An account of a case of a fracture and dislocation of the spine. *New Eng J Med, 4*, 1–3

Crockard HA, Ransford AO (1990). Stabilisation of the spine. *Adv Tech Stand Neurosurg, 17*, 160–617

Crozier KS, Graziani V, Ditunno JF Jr, et al. (1991). Spinal cord injury: prognosis for ambulation based on sensory examination in patients who are initially motor complete. *Arch Phys Med Rehabil, 72*, 119–121

De Deze M, Wiart L, Ferriere J, et al. (1999). Intravesical instillation of capsaicin in urology: a review of the literature. *Eur Urol, 36*, 267–277

Denis F (1983). The three column spine and its significance in the classification of acute thoracolumbar spinal injuries. *Spine, 8*, 817–831

Denis F, Armstrong GWD, Searls K, Matta L (1984). Acute thoracolumbar burst fractures in the absence of neurological deficit. *Clin Orthop, 189*, 142–149

De Vivo MJ, Black KJ, Stover SL (1993). Causes of death during the first 12 years after spinal cord injury. *Arch Phys Med Rehabil, 74*, 248–254

De Vivo MJ, Hawkins LN, Richards JS, Go BK (1995). Outcomes of post-spinal cord injury marriages. *Arch Phys Med Rehabil, 76* (2), 130–138 (erratum *Arch Phys Med Rehabil, 76* (4), 397)

Dickman CA, Zabramski JM, Hadley MN, Rekate HL, Sonntag VK (1991). Pediatric spinal cord injury without radiographic abnormalities: Report of 26 cases and review of the literature. *J Spinal Disord, 4* (3), 296–305

Ditunno JF Jr (1999). The John Stanley Coulter Lecture. Predicting recovery after spinal cord injury: a rehabilitation imperative. *Arch Phys Med Rehabil, 80*, 361–364

Ditunno JF Jr, Cohen ME, Hauck WW, et al. (2000) Recovery of upper–extremity strength in complete and incomplete tetraplegia: a multicenter study. *Arch Phys Med Rehabil, 81*, 389–393

Ditunno JF, Stover SL, Freed MM, et al. (1992). Motor recovery of the upper extremities in traumatic quadriplegia: a multicenter study. *Arch Phys Med Rehabil, 73*, 431–436

Farkash AE, Portenoy RK (1986). The pharmacological management of chronic pain in the paraplegic patient (review). *J Am Paraplegia Soc, 9*, 41–50

Fehlings MG, Sekhon LHS, Tator C (2001). The role and timing of decompression in acute spinal cord injury: what do we know? What should we do? *Spine, 26* (24S), S101–110

Foo D (1986). Spinal cord injury in forty-four patients with cervical spondylosis. *Paraplegia, 24*, 301–306

Frankel H, Hancock D, Hyslop G, et al. (1969). The value of postural reduction in he initial management of closed injuries of the spine with paraplegia and tetraplegia: part 1. *Paraplegia, 7*, 179–182

Galen. *Oeuvres anatomiques, physiologiques et médicales de Galien*. (Trans. C Dremberg, 1854.) Paris, JB Ballières

Galendiuk S, Raque G, Appel S, Polk HC Jr (1993). The two edged sword of large dose steroids for spinal trauma. *Ann Surg, 218*, 419–425

Gardner B, Jamous A, Teddy P, Bergstrom E, Wang D, Ravichandran G, Sutton R, Urquart S (1995). Intrathecal baclofen—a multicentre clinical comparison of the Medtronics Programmable, Cordis Secor and Constant Infusion Infusaid drug delivery systems. *Paraplegia, 33* (10), 551–554

Geisler FH, Coleman WP, Grico G, et al. (2001). The Sygen® multicenter acute spinal cord injury study. *Spine, 26* (suppl 1), S87–98

Geisler FH, Dorsey FC, Coleman WP (1991). Recovery of motor function after spinal-cord injury—a randomized, placebo-controlled trial with GM-1 ganglioside. *New Engl J Med, 324*, 1829–1838

Geisler FH, Dorsey FC, Patarnello F et al. (1998). SYGEN acute spinal cord injury study (Abstract). *J Neurotrauma, 15*, 868

Geisler KWO, Jousse AT, Wynn-Jones M, Breithaup D (1983). Survival in traumatic spinal cord injury. *Paraplegia, 21*, 364–371

Gorman PH, Wuolle KS, Peckham H, Heydrick D (1997). Patient selection for an upper extremity neuroprosthesis in tetraplegic individuals. *Spinal Cord, 35* (9), 569–573

Green BA, Eismont FJ, O'Heir JT (1987). Pre-hospital management of spinal cord injuries. *Paraplegia, 25*, 229–238

Griffiths R (1988). *Community care agenda for action. A report to the secretary for social services.* HMSO, London

Grundy D, Swain A (1993). ABC of spinal cord injury, 2nd edition. BMA Publishing, London

Guiliano F, Hultling C, El Masry WS, Smith MD, Osterloh IH, Orr M, Maytom M (1999). Randomized trial of sildenafil for the treatment of erectile dysfunction in spinal cord injury. Sildenafil Study Group. *Ann Neurol, 46* (1), 15–21

Gupta A, Masri WS (1989). Multilevel spinal injuries. Incidence, distribution and neurological patterns. *JBJS, 71B*, 692–695

Guttman L, Frankel H (1966). The value of intermittent catheterisation in the early management of paraplegia and tetraplegia. *Paraplegia, 4*, 63–83

Haher TR, Felmy W, Baruch H, Devlin V, Welin D, O'Brien M, Ahmed J, Valenza J, Parish S (1989). The contributions of the three columns of the spine to rotational stability. *Spine, 14*, 663–669

Hansebout RR (1988). A comprehensive review of methods of improving cord recovery after acute spinal cord injury. In: Tator CH (Ed), *Early management of acute spinal injury*. Raven Press, New York, pp. 139–155

Heathcote PS, Galloway NTM, Lewis DC, Stephenson TP (1987). An assessment of the complications of the Brantley Scott artificial sphincter. *B J Urol, 60*, 119–121

Holdsworth FW, Hardy A (1953). Early treatment of paraplegia from fractures of the thoracolumbar spine. *JBJS, 35B*, 540–550

Hu SS, Capen DA, Rimoldi RL, Zigler JE (1993). The effect of surgical decompression on neurologic outcome after lumbar fractures. *Clin Orth Rel Res, 288*, 166–173

Hughes JT (1988). The Edwin Smith surgical papyrus: An analysis of the first case reports of spinal cord injuries. *Paraplegia, 26*, 71–82

Hultling C, Rosenlund B, Levi R, Fridstrom M, Sjoblom, Hillensio T (1997). Assisted ejaculation and in-vitro fertilization in the treatment of infertile spinal cord-injured men: The role of intracytoplasmic sperm injection. *Human Reprod, 12* (3), 499–502

Hurlbert RJ (2001). The role of steroids in acute spinal cord injury: and evidence-based analysis. *Spine, 26* (24S), S39–46

Hussey RW (1988). Rehabilitation after spinal cord injuries. In: Dee R, Mango E, Hurst L (Eds), *Principles of orthopaedic practice*. McGraw-Hill, New York

Hussey RW, Stauffer ES (1973). Spinal cord injury: Requirements for ambulation. *Arch Med Rehab, 54*, 544–547

Jacobs RR, Asher MA, Snider RK (1980). Thoracolumbar injuries: A comparative study of recumbent and operative treatment in 100 patients. *Spine, 5*, 463–477

Jefferson G (1927). Discussion on spinal injuries. *Proc R Soc Med, 21*, 625

Kerslake RW, Jaspan T, Worthington BS (1991). Magnetic resonance imaging of spinal trauma. *B J Radiol, 64*, 386–402

Kiss ZHT, Tator CH (1983). Neurogenic shock. In: Geller ER (Ed), *Shock and resuscitation*. McGraw-Hill, New York, pp. 421–440

Kiwerski J (1993). Hyperextension-dislocation injuries of the cervical spine. *Br J Accident Surg, 24*, 674–677

Ko HY, Ditunno JF Jr, Graziani V, et al. (1999). The pattern of reflex recovery during spinal shock. *Spinal Cord, 37*, 402–409

Levi L, Wolf A, Belzberg H (1993). Hemodynamic parameters in patients with acute cervical cord trauma: Description, intervention, and prediction of outcome. *Neurosurgery, 33* (6), 1007–1016; discussion 1016–1017

Lindan R, Joiner E, Freehafer EE, Hazel C (1980). Incidence and clinical features of autonomic dysreflexia in patients with spinal cord injury. *Paraplegia, 18*, 285–292

McKinley W, Cifu D, Keyser-Marcus L, Wilson K (1998). Comparison of rehabilitation outcomes in violent versus non-violent traumatic SCI. *J Spinal Cord Med, 21* (1), 32–36

Magerl F, Aebi M, Gertzbein SD, Harms J, Nazarian S (1994). A comprehensive classification of thoracic and lumbar injuries. *Eur Spine J, 3*, 184–201

Mair A (1972). *Medical rehabilitation: The pattern for the future*. Scottish Home and Health Department, Scottish Health Services Council, HMSO, Edinburgh

Mathias CJ (1987). Autonomic dysfunction. *Br J Hosp Med, 38*, 238–243

Maynard FM (1993). Long-term management of the neurogenic bladder: Intermittent catheterisation. *Phys Med Rehab Clin North Am, 4*, 299–310

Mayr W, Bijak M, Girsch W, Holle J, Lanmuller H, Thoma H, Zrunek M (1993). Multichannel stimulation of phrenic nerves by epineural electrodes. Clinical experience and future developments. *ASAIO J, 39* (3), M729–M735

Mesard L (1978) Survival after spinal cord trauma. *Arch Neurol, 35*, 78–86

MRC (1943). Aids to investigation of peripheral nerve injuries. Medical Research Council War Memorandum, 2nd edition. London: HMSO

Mundy AR, Stephenson TP (1985). 'Clam' ileocystoplasty for the treatment of refractory urge incontinence. *J Urol, 57*, 641–646

New P (1997). A survey of pain during rehabilitation after acute spinal cord injury. *Spinal Cord, 35*, 658–663

Okonkwo CA (1988). Spinal cord injuries in Enugu, Nigeria – preventable accidents. *Paraplegia, 26*, 12–18

Osti O, Fraser RD, Cornish BL (1986). Fractures and fracture dislocations in the lumbar spine. *JBJS, 68B*, 34

Otani K, Abe H, Kadoya S et al. (1994). Beneficial effect of methylprednisolone sodium succinate in the treatment of acute spinal cord injury. *Sekitsui Sekizui J, 7*, 633–647

Pang D, Wilberger JE Jr (1982). Spinal cord injury without radiographic abnormalities in children. *J Neurosurg, 57* (1), 114–129

Pedersen V, Muller PG, Biering-Sorenson F (1989). Traumatic spinal cord injuries in Greenland 1965–1986. *Paraplegia, 27*, 345–349

Penn RD, Kroin JS (1985). Continuous intrathecal baclofen for severe spasticity. *Lancet, 20*, 2(8447), 125–127

Penrod LE, Hegde SK, Ditunno JF (1990). Age effect on prognosis for functional recovery in acute, traumatic central cord syndrome. *Arch Phys Med Rehabil, 71*, 963–968

Perkash I, Martin DE, Warner H, Speck V (1990). Electroejaculation in spinal cord injury patients: Simplified new equipment and technique. *J Urol, 143*, 305–307

Petitjean ME, Pointillart V, Daverat P et al. (1995). Administration of methylprednisolone or nimodipine or both versus placebo at the acute phase of spinal cord injury (Abstract). *J Neurotrauma, 12*, 456

Pitts LH, Ross A, Chase GA, Faden AI (1995). Treatment with thyrotropin-releasing hormone (TRH) in patients with traumatic spinal cord injuries. *J Neurotrauma, 12*, 235–243

Putty TK, Shapiro SA (1991). Efficacy of dorsal longitudinal myelotomy in treating spinal spasticity: a review of 20 cases. *J Neurosurg, 75*, 397–401

Riggins RS, Kraus JF (1977). The risk of neurological damage with fractures of the vertebrae. *J Trauma, 17*, 126–133

Schneider RC (1955). The syndrome of acute anterior spinal cord injury. *J Neurosurg, 12*, 95–122

Schneider RC, Cherry GL, Pantek HF (1954). The syndrome of acute central cervical spinal cord injury. *J Neurosurg, 11*, 546–577

Schurch B, Stohrer M, Kramer G (2000) Botulinum-A toxin for treating detrusor hyperreflexia in spinal cord injured patients: a new alternative to anticholinergic drugs? Preliminary results. *J Urol, 164*, 692–697

Seager SW, Halstead LS (1993). Fertility options and success after spinal cord injury. *Urol Clin N Am, 20* (3), 543–548

Sharkey PC, Halter JA, Nakajima K (1989). Electrophrenic respiration in patients with high quadriplegia. *Neurosurgery, 24* (4), 529–535

Short DJ, El Masry WS, Jones PW (2000). High dose methylprednisolone in the management of acute spinal cord injury: a systematic review from a clinical perspective. *Spinal Cord, 38*, 273–286

Silberstein M, Hennessy O (1992). Cystic cord lesions and neurological deterioration in spinal cord injury: Operative considerations based on magnetic resonance imaging. *Paraplegia, 30*, 661–668

Spencer WG (trans) (1935). *Da Mecina*. Harvard University Press, Cambridge Mass

Squier MV, Lehr RP (1994). Post-traumatic syringomyelia. *J Neurol Neurosurg Psychiatry, 57* (9), 1095–1098

Suwanwela C, Alexander E, Davis CH (1962). Prognosis in spinal cord injury with special reference to patients with motor paralysis and sensory preservation. *J Neurosurg, 19*, 220–227

Tadie M, Jin O, Lui S et al. (1995). Experimental and clinical study of an inhibitor of NMDA receptors in the early treatment of the spinal cord injuries (Abstract). *J Neurotrauma, 12*, 349

Tator CH (1983). Spine–spinal cord relationships in spinal cord trauma. *Clin Neurosurg, 30*, 479–494

Tator CH, Duncan EG, Edmonds VE, et al. (1987). Comparison of surgical and conservative management in 208 patients with acute spinal cord injury. *Can J Neurol Sci, 14*, 60–69

Tator CH, Fehlings MG (1999). Review of clinical trials of neuroprotection in acute spinal cord injury. *Neurosurg Focus, 6* (1), Article 8

Tator CH, Rowed DW, Schwartz ML (1982). Sunnybrook cord injury scales for assessing neurological injury and neurological recovery. In: Tator CH (Ed), *Early management of acute spinal cord injury*. Raven Press, New York, pp. 7–24

Thompson-Walker J (1937). The treatment of the bladder in spinal injuries in war. *Proc Roy Soc Med, 30*, 1233–1240

Torg, JS (1995). Cervical spinal stenosis with cord neurapraxia and transient quadriplegia. *Sports Med, 20* (6), 429–434

Vaccaro AR, Daugherty RJ, Sheehan TP, et al. (1997). Neurologic outcome of early versus late surgery for cervical spinal cord injury. *Spine, 22*, 2609–2613

Vaidyanathan S, Soni BM, Sett P, Watt JW, Oo T, Bingley J (1998). Pathophysiology of autonomic dysreflexia: Long-term treatment with terazosin in adult and paediatric spinal cord injury patients manifesting recurrent dysreflexic episodes. *Spinal Cord, 36* (11), 761–770

Vale FL, Burns J, Jackson AB et al. (1997). Combined medical and surgical treatment after acute spinal cord injury: Results of a prospective pilot study to assess the merits of aggressive medical resuscitation and blood pressure management. *J Neurosurg, 87*, 239–246

Velhahos GC, Kern J, Chan LS, et al. (2000). Prevention of venous thromboembolism after injury: an evidence-based report: II. Analysis of risk factors and evaluation of the role of vena caval filters. *J Trauma, 49*, 140–144

Walker AE (1951). *A history of neurological surgery*. Baillière, Tindall and Cox, London

Waters RL, Adkins RH, Yakura JS (1991). Definition of complete spinal cord injury. *Paraplegia, 9*, 573–581

Waters RL, Adkins RH, Yakura JS, et al. (1993). Motor and sensory recovery following complete tetraplegia. *Arch Phys Med Rehabil, 74*, 242–247

Wilmot CB, Cope DN, Hall KM, Acker M (1985). Occult head injury: Its incidence in spinal cord injury. *Arch Phys Med Rehabil, 66*, 227–231

Williams B (1990). Post-traumatic syringomyelia, an update. *Paraplegia, 20*, 296–313

Young MH (1973). Long term consequences of stable fractures of the thoracic and lumbar vertebral bodies. *JBJS, 55B*, 295–300

Zierski J, Muller H, Dralle D, Wurdinger T (1988). Implanted pump systems for treatment of spasticity. *Acta Neurochir Suppl. (Wien), 43*, 94–99

45. Non-traumatic myelopathies

Jagdish C. Chawla   E.D. Playford

INTRODUCTION

The management of acute traumatic spinal cord lesions is a well established area of disability medicine (Young & Sarkarati, 1992). As experience in management of these injuries increased it became possible to predict the likely functional outcome of a patient with an acute complete spinal cord lesion by accurately assessing the level of the cord damage (Ozer, 1988). Although the basic care of spinal injury is equally applicable to patients with non-traumatic myelopathy, the outcome for this group is less certain. In part this arises from lack of detailed study, and in part because the conditions are very varied. Lesions can be acute (e.g. anterior spinal artery occlusion) or slowly progressive (e.g. spinal meningioma), can occur in the young (e.g. spina bifida) or the old (e.g. cervical myelopathy), can be partial or more rarely complete, and can occur in any site from the low thoracic cord to the high cervical cord. These different conditions, not surprisingly, have different potential for functional improvement.

Patients with complete lesions are conveniently managed in spinal injuries units, but patients with incomplete lesions can also be managed in a neurological rehabilitation unit. The majority of cases of non-traumatic myelopathy are incomplete, and more likely to be insidious or subacute in onset, associated with cognitive deficit, and seen in older patients. Complete lesions above T6 are rare in non-traumatic myelopathy and should be managed in spinal injuries units, where there is greater expertise in managing autonomic dysreflexia.

AETIOLOGY

Moore and Blumhardt (1997) found that of 585 patients referred for investigation of spastic paraparesis or tetraparesis over a 3-year period from UK population of 3 million, diagnosis after MRI remained uncertain in 18.6%. The most common diagnosis was cervical spondylotic myelopathy (23.6%), followed by extrinsic neoplasm (16.4%), multiple sclerosis (17.8%), motor neurone disease (4.1%), intrinsic neoplasm (2.5%), syrinx (2.4%), and congenital spinal or foramen magnum abnormalities (1.9%). Other conditions were rare but included abscess, rheumatoid disease, other infections, hereditary disorders, and

Table 45.1. Common causes of non-traumatic myelopathies

Compressive	Neurodegeneration/movement disorders
Cervical and thoracic spondylosis	Cerebral palsy
Tumours	Dystonias
Developmental abnormalities	Tourette's
Extradural abscess	Motor neurone disease
Haematoma	Non-metastatic tumour effects
Skeletal abnormalities, e.g. in rheumatoid	Familial spinal cord disease
Arthritis	
Inflammatory	**Vascular**
Multiple sclerosis	Arteriovenous malformations
Infections:	Extradural haemorrhage
Bacterial:	Aortic haemorrhage
pyogenic	Aortic trauma or dissection
tuberculosis	Anterior spinal artery occlusion
syphilis	
brucellosis	**Physical agents**
Lyme disease	Radiation
herpes simplex	Electric injury
Viral:	Caisson disease
Postinfective	Arachnoiditis
Sarcoid	
Beçhet's	
Lupus	

arachnoiditis. There are reports in the literature of other yet rarer causes. Table 45.1 lists some of the potential causes of myelopathy, and this chapter will describe the presentation and management of the more common causes, particularly cervical spondylotic myelopathy.

EPIDEMIOLOGY

The world incidence of spinal cord injury varies from 9 to 53 per million per year (Buchan et al., 1972; Minaire et al., 1978; Shingu et al., 1994). In European studies, non-traumatic lesions form 25 to 39% of all spinal cord lesions (Minaire et al., 1978). An estimate of the incidence of non-traumatic spinal cord injury from the Netherlands was 16 per million per year (Schonherr et al., 1996). Non-traumatic incomplete spinal cord injury accounts for at least 1.2% of all new neurology out-patient consultations (Perkin, 1989).

For traumatic spinal cord injury, the male to female ratio is known to be about 10:1, although the proportion of female patients is rising. For non-traumatic spinal cord injury the ratio is probably of the order of 2 : 1 (Schonherr et al., 1996). The ratio of non-traumatic to traumatic injuries increases with increasing age, so that in one study based in a rehabilitation unit, three-quarters of the patients over the age of 40 had a non-traumatic cause (Schonherr et al., 1996).

SIGNS AND SYMPTOMS

The signs and symptoms of spinal cord lesions depends on the lesion site. Four main patterns are recognised (Clarke & Robinson, 1956):

1. the complete lesion
2. the anterior cord syndrome
3. the central cord syndrome
4. the Brown–Sèquard syndrome.

Recognising these different syndromes is important because, in part, they point to the aetiology.

In complete transverse lesions, at the level of the injury there is involvement of the anterior horn cell, motor root, and sensory root, resulting in a flaccid paralysis of muscles and anaesthesia or sometimes pain at the level of the affected segment. Below the level of the lesion there is involvement of the long tracts, resulting in loss of all motor, sensory and autonomic function, and a spastic paraplegia. When the onset is acute there is usually an initial period of spinal shock where the paraplegia is flaccid.

The anterior cord syndrome commonly occurs as a result of a vascular insult resulting in infarction of the anterior spinal artery territory. This results in a lesion that spares the posterior columns leading to a characteristic pattern of sensory loss in which pin-prick and temperature perception is impaired but perception of vibration and proprioception are intact.

The central cord syndrome is most commonly recognised in the cervical cord when it affects the upper limbs more severely than the lower limbs, leading to numb, clumsy hands and mild spasticity in the legs. Classically, the result of a syrinx in association with a foramen magnum anomaly, this syndrome can also occur after hyperextension injury in older patients with cervical spondylosis, when arterial insufficiency in the watershed area between the central and radial arterial systems of the cervical cord probably explains the characteristic pattern of neurological deficit (Romano et al., 1996).

The classic Brown–Sèquard syndrome resulting from hemisection of the cord is rare. There is involvement of the ipsilateral anterior horn cells, and motor and sensory roots, resulting in a flaccid paralysis of muscles and anaesthesia of the ipsilateral affected segment. In addition, there is ipsilateral posterior column and corticospinal tract involvement leading to ipsilateral weakness and loss of proprioception and vibration perception, and contralateral spinothalamic tract involvement leading to loss of pin-prick and temperature perception.

Foramen magnum lesions result in a spastic quadriparesis, cerebellar ataxia, dysarthria, and nystagmus, which can be down-beating. Wasting of the hand muscles can occur.

Two index conditions will be described in detail, the myelopathy due to cervical spondylosis and ischaemic myelopathy. Cervical spondylotic myelopathy is insidious in onset, progressive, and occurs in an older population; ischaemic myelopathy is usually sudden in onset and often initially nearly complete, yet there is some recovery. These two conditions illustrate different aspects of the management of non-traumatic spinal cord injury.

CERVICAL SPONDYLOTIC MYELOPATHY

The cervical and lumbar spine are the most mobile areas of the vertebral column and are therefore most prone to suffer degenerative changes. Osteoarthritis was originally considered as a cause of compression of the spinal cord and its roots in 1911 by Bailey and Casamajor, and established as a cause of cervical myelopathy by Brain and colleagues (Brain et al., 1952; Wilkinson, 1971).

With advancing age, the disc space narrows; the annulus fibrosus bulges beyond the line of the vertebral bodies; the nucleus pulposus shrinks; and anterior, lateral, and posterior osteophytes form opposite the disc spaces. The ligmentum flavum thickens and hypertrophy of laminal arches and pedicles occurs. The sagittal diameter of the canal thus decreases. Sometimes the myelopathy is largely the result of extensive ossification of the posterior longitudinal ligaments (Yang et al., 1992). Spinal column movement also causes dynamic changes in the anatomy of the contents of the spinal canal, including the spinal cord. There can be intermittent block of the spinal subarachnoid space when the neck is flexed or extended. During extension, there is thickening of the cord and narrowing of spinal canal (Breig, 1960). In flexion, the tension on the cord increases because of tethering of the cord by the ligamentum, and there is a decrease in the cord's anteroposterior diameter (Breig, 1978). At autopsy, the spinal cord is distorted and compressed (Hughes, 1978). The presence of local areas of necrosis and cyst formation, and occasional rapid neurological recovery following surgery, implicate both a vascular and a compressive aetiology (Bohlman & Emery, 1988).

Cervical spondylotic myelopathy is now recognised to be the most common cause of spinal cord dysfunction in middle aged and older males. The onset of symptoms is insidious. The clinical picture is variable and depends on the site, extent, severity, and rate of evolution of local disease of the cervical spine and/or involvement of the spinal cord and/or other involvement of the roots. Ferguson and Caplan (1985) described four distinct but overlapping syndromes:

1. lateral or radicular when there is root involvement only
2. medial when the cord is involved
3. combined medial and lateral when there is both root and cord involvement
4. vascular when the pattern is that of the central cord syndrome.

The evolution and age of onset of the myelopathy is particularly determined by the congenital dimensions of the spinal canal.

Myelopathy seldom develops in a capacious canal (Ogino et al., 1983). The cervical cord is at its largest at C5/C6, the canal is at its narrowest at C5/6, C6/7, and C4/C5, and thus the levels most frequently involved are C5/C6, C6/C7, C4/C5, and C7/T1 in descending order of frequency. Multiple level involvement is common. Reflexes are absent or diminished at the level of the lesion and brisk below. The pattern of muscle weakness, reflex change, and sensory loss can identify the level of compression. Diagnosis involves differentiating cervical spondylotic myelopathy, particularly from motor neurone disease, multiple sclerosis, and spinal cord tumour, and also cerebral causes of a gradually increasing gait disturbance, including an arrested or communicating hydrocephalus and cerebrovascular disease, with which it might coexist. The investigation of choice is magnetic resonance imaging, which demonstrates changes both intrinsic and extrinsic to the cord.

The course of cervical spondylotic myelopathy is very variable. Often, there is a lengthy period of stability after which an exacerbation of symptoms take place. In general, one-third of patients will improve after initial presentation, one-third stabilise, and one-third deteriorate (Nagat et al., 1996). Motor symptoms can persist or progress, whereas sensory and bladder symptoms might be transient. Minor trauma can lead to a sudden clinical deterioration. Older patients can deteriorate more rapidly than those who are younger. Objective description of the impairment can be difficult, so that relative minor changes in signs can go unnoticed apart from their impact upon function. In patients with an insidious development of problems, adaptation to the impairment can be very successful, so that there is little apparent disability. Various quantitative measures have been used in cervical myelopathy and are described later.

Patients who present with minor disability can improve when the neck is immobilised (Campbell & Phillips, 1960). Collars can either immobilise the cervical spine or provide temporary support and limit excessive movements. The selection of either a hard or soft collar depends on the degree of immobilisation required. If a hard collar is worn during the day, a soft collar should be worn at night. The collar should be worn continuously for 3 months and then intermittently. Once worn intermittently, patients should be advised to wear the collar when travelling as the minor trauma encountered as a passenger may exacerbate symptoms.

In general terms, surgical intervention should be considered (Ebersold et al., 1995) if there is:

- progression of symptoms with underlying MRI evidence of cord compression, including high signal change within the cord
- failure of medical treatment
- acute myelopathy following midline disc herniation.

Following decompression, 20–50% of patients have sustained improvement (Ebersold et al., 1995). The patient should not deteriorate further at the level of the decompression and there might be slow neurological recovery. Late deterioration at other levels can occur. After operative intervention the patient might benefit from a period of in-patient multidisciplinary rehabilitation.

Symptomatic management will include treatment of headache and neck pain due to local disease in the cervical spine, producing ill-defined aching or stiffness of the neck, which might be helped by a cervical collar. Neck movements might be restricted and there might be a suboccipital headache due to spasm of neck muscles caused by irritation of nerve roots. Simple analgesics can alleviate this type of pain. Often, the myelopathy proceeds in the absence of any local discomfort. Root pain is present in 50% of patients and is often an asymmetric, unpleasant neuropathic pain with a burning and aching quality; it can be exacerbated by neck movements. Simple analgesics are rarely of any benefit and amitriptyline should be considered. Sensory disturbance is often present in the upper limbs and can result in clumsiness of hand function or, less often, injury by burning when cooking or using hot water. Weakness is usually the result of radicular involvement causing difficulties with shoulder abduction (C5), elbow flexion (C5/C6), elbow extension (C7/C8), finger flexion (C7/C8), and small hand muscles (T1). Persson et al. (1997) randomised 81 patients with radicular pain, weakness, or sensory loss to physiotherapy, nerve root decompression, or the use of a cervical collar, and found that surgical treatment resulted in less pain, weakness, and sensory loss 4 months after starting treatment, but that at 12 months there was no difference in outcome between the three groups.

A spastic paraparesis is rarely severe in cervical myelopathy, but many patients will have difficulty walking, an effortful gait, a tendency to trip over uneven surfaces, and difficulty with stairs. This will be exacerbated by disturbances of dorsal column sensation in the legs. Approximately half of all patients will have urinary frequency, urgency, and incomplete bladder emptying (Brain et al., 1952). In older patients it is worth excluding additional factors such as outflow obstruction due to prostatic hypertrophy or pelvic floor weakness. Bladder dysfunction that disturbs sleep or social activity, or that results in incontinence, should be treated. Bowel dysfunction is reportedly rare.

ISCHAEMIC MYELOPATHY

Ischaemic myelopathy can result from spontaneous thrombotic or embolic anterior spinal artery occlusion, an aortic dissecting aneurysm or traumatic rupture or surgical manipulation of the aorta, or as a result of severe hypotension, for example after myocardial infarction (Henson & Parsons, 1967; Kim et al., 1988). It can be difficult to distinguish from a transverse myelitis, which can be infective, the presenting symptom of multiple sclerosis, or idiopathic, and it is extremely important to exclude a compressive lesion, particularly an epidural abscess (Bouchez et al., 1985).

The symptoms and signs are usually those of an anterior spinal artery occlusion but the whole cord can infarct. A spontaneous thromboembolic anterior spinal artery occlusion usually presents acutely, often with pain at the level of the lesion. A flaccid paraplegia develops rapidly, with loss of pain and temperature perception and sparing of joint position and vibration sense. There is loss of function of bowel and bladder sphincters. In 50% of cases, flaccidity of the lower limbs persists and, not surprisingly, an incomplete spastic paraparisis has a better prognosis than a complete flaccid paraplegia (Kim et al., 1988). Following aortic surgery, cord dysfunction is usually immediately apparent postoperatively. In about 25% of patients, the neurological deficit develops over 24 hours after surgery, probably due to reperfusion injury (Lintott et al., 1998).

Conventional textbooks claim that significant recovery following spinal cord infarction is unusual unless there is significant recovery in the first 24 hours (Geldmacher & Nager, 1989). Pelser and Gijn (1993), however, described improvements in power in all eight of their patients with spinal cord infarction, and Waters et al. (1993) found that patients with partial motor function at 1 month continued to recover for 1 year. However, a paraplegia might not improve and some patients can develop profound spasticity. This should be managed actively from onset with correct positioning in bed and appropriate seating, supported by oral drug management. A significant proportion of patients with complete lesions will remain flaccid. This poses less of a management problem. Bladder dysfunction is common, typically at presentation, taking the form of urinary retention with overflow. Approaches to management are outlined later. Bowel dysfunction is characterised by constipation, followed by faecal incontinence, which might be due to reflex bowel emptying or overflow.

REHABILITATION

Unlike traumatic spinal cord injury, which is often complete and stable, outcome in non-traumatic spinal cord injury cannot be predicted from the level of lesion. The reasons for this are multiple but include related systemic and neurological conditions, sparing of some activity below the lesion, and the fact that the disorders are not static. Some will continue to deteriorate, for example the patient with a hereditary spastic paraparesis or with a transverse myelitis who develops multiple sclerosis. Patients with non-traumatic myelopathies are often middle-aged or elderly. A lengthy period of bedrest is not often required and they can therefore be mobilised early in a wheelchair. However, an active and aggressive rehabilitation programme might not be feasible because there could be associated medical problems likely to interfere with the rehabilitation programme, and older patients are much more likely to require rehabilitation. Rehabilitation goals will depend upon life expectancy, social backup, and employment needs. The young person with spinal cord dysfunction has needs that are very different from those of the older person. Management thus requires not only accurate assessment of physical capacity, disabilities, handicaps, psychological make-up, and social environment, but also knowledge of the long-term prognosis of the primary disorder and associated comorbidities.

Surgical intervention, if appropriate, can result in neurological gain, and continued recovery of the spinal cord and of function, even after infarction, can occur over many months. Continued assessment and therapy is therefore important as minor changes in impairment can lead to significant changes in functional status. A UK study observed that all patients made functional gains during their rehabilitation but that this was greatest in patients in whom there was neurological recovery (Stevenson et al., 1996). A Portuguese study of nine patients with spinal brucellosis demonstrated that a rehabilitation programme resulted in improvement in sphincter control, activities of daily living, and walking ability (Faria & Viegas, 1995). Schonherr et al. (1996) compared the rehabilitation of patients with non-traumatic and traumatic spinal cord injury in a rehabilitation unit in the Netherlands. Not surprisingly, the duration of rehabilitation was shorter in patients with non-traumatic spinal cord injury at 85 days rather than 205 days. This contrasts with a study in the UK in which the average duration of stay for in-patient rehabilitation was 42 days (Stevenson et al., 1996). In the Dutch study, only 79% of patients with non-traumatic spinal cord injury were discharged home, compared with 88% of patients with traumatic spinal cord injury. This might occur because patients with metastatic disease causing compression are more likely to be discharged to nursing homes.

Symptomatic management

Pain. Spinal pain can be due to involvement of bone, nerve roots, and/or spinal cord. In metastatic vertebral disease, pain, whether bony or radicular, usually responds to a combination of radiotherapy, chemotherapy, and steroids. Surgical stabilisation might be indicated if the pain is persistent and can dramatically improve pain (Baldini et al., 1979). Radicular pain is usually referred along the dermatomal distribution of the nerve. Multisegmental pain can be seen in degenerative disease of the spine due to chronic compression of nerve roots. Such pain can respond to rest, analgesics with or without non-steroidal anti-inflammatory drugs, physical and other therapies described in Chapter 19, and occasionally surgical decompression should be considered (Philips, 1973). The use of amitriptyline requires careful supervision in the middle-aged or elderly. Occasionally, pain can be due to peripheral muscle spasms, which might respond to antispastic agents (see Chapter 19).

Sensory disturbances. These can range from parasthesiae to complete sensory loss in a dermatomal distribution. If severe, patients can be at risk of injuring themselves by burning when cooking or using hot water. Patients should be made aware of the risks and use other approaches to gauging temperature, such as a thermometer. Postural sensory loss in the upper limbs contributes to difficulty in self-care, accurate placing of objects, and a tendency for a limb to be trapped or injured. With practice, it can be compensated for using other stimuli, mainly visual. Rooms should therefore be well lit.

Weakness. Difficulty with shoulder abduction can lead to problems brushing hair, putting items away on high shelves, and hanging up washing. Assisted active shoulder movements should be carried out daily to prevent the development of a painful frozen shoulder. Weakness of elbow flexion and extension causes difficulties with heavy housework, shopping, driving, transferring in and out of the bath, grooming, washing, and dressing, as well as with instrumental activities of daily living. Weakness of hand muscles can cause problems with writing, eating, and holding tools. Splints might be required to prevent finger flexion. The arm can develop dependent oedema, which can be treated with a flowtron or by elevation of the arm in a sling, although this must not be positioned so that it aggravates a spastic posture.

Spasticity. Patients can develop profound spasticity (see Chapter 12). This should be actively managed from onset with correct positioning in bed and appropriate seating. When spasticity starts to interfere with functional activity, or causes pain and discomfort, it requires treatment. Passive or active stretching, combined with range of motion exercises, can sometimes reduce spasticity enough to eliminate the need for drugs (Young et al., 1997). Regular standing in alignment is helpful using sticks, backslabs, or a standing frame (Bromley, 1981). The aims of management are to maintain function, minimise pain, prevent contractures, and maintain a full range of joint movement. The limbs below the level of the lesions should be properly positioned. Gentle passive range of movements can help prevent contractures. Drug management with baclofen (Duncan, 1976), dantrolene (Behan, 1982), or tizanidine (Nance et al., 1994) can follow. Specific muscle groups can be helped by phenol nerve blocks (Wood, 1978) or by intramuscular botulinum toxin (Snow et al., 1990). If the spasticity causes severe pain, difficulties with seating or transferring, or difficulty with care despite optimum management, then intrathecal baclofen could be considered (Azouvi et al., 1996). This has been shown to result in a decrease in tone and associated spasms, improvement in function (particularly for bathing, lower body dressing, and, in some cases, walking), increased ease of nursing, and comfort. A more destructive procedure in patients with no remaining lower limb function, bowel or bladder control is the use of intrathecal phenol (Iwatsubo et al., 1994). Tone in a significant proportion of patients with complete lesions will remain flaccid. This poses less of a management problem.

Bladder function. Approximately half of all patients with cervical myelopathy will have urinary frequency, urgency and incomplete bladder emptying. In patients with complete cord lesions all will be affected by a neurogenic bladder (see Chapter 21). In older patients it is worth excluding outflow obstruction due to prostatic hypertrophy and pelvic floor weakness.

Bladder dysfunction that disturbs sleep or social activity, or that results in incontinence, can be treated by a combination of bladder relaxants with intermittent self-catheterisation, provided hand function is good enough, or, alternatively, with an indwelling catheter. Urinary urgency can be treated with intravesical capsaicin (Hussain & Fowler, 1998). Woman who are electively catheterised should be considered for a suprapubic catheter.

A number of approaches have been described in men with significant detrusor sphincter dyssynergia, including the use of botulinum toxin A into the external urethral sphincter (Schurch, 1997), and the use of a wire mesh prosthesis in the external sphincter (Chancellor et al., 1993). Other approaches to management include the use of anterior sacral nerve root stimulation with posterior rhizotomy, which can result in an improvement in the degree of continence and bladder capacity (Brindley, 1994).

Bowels. Bowel dysfunction is reportedly rare in cervical myelopathy but is likely to become an increasingly severe problem over time with patients with complete cord lesions. Mobilisation should be encouraged in patients with progressive lesions, as should the use of a high-fibre diet with adequate fluid intake so that a regular bowel habit is established. If this proves inadequate then defecation might need to be stimulated by the use of digital stimulation, simple suppositories, or, if necessary, laxatives. This approach can be augmented by the use of a stimulant laxative the previous day. Cisapride has been reported to be useful in severe constipation and is associated with an increase in small bowel motility (Hellstrom et al., 1990). Occasionally, the anal sphincter can become so spastic that it leads to a cramp-like pain. Intramural neurolysis can control the spasticity and enable better bowel evacuation (Optiz & Lutness, 1985). Drugs that aggravate constipation should be kept to a minimum.

Sexual function. Sexual desire usually remains unaltered in the presence of a spinal cord lesion but sexual function is impaired in both men and women. Common problems include erectile and ejaculation dysfunction in men and problems with vaginal lubrication in women. Both men and women have difficulties with decreased sensation and achieving orgasm. Satisfaction with the sexual relationship usually decreases and depends on a number of factors, including confidence about urinary and faecal continence, perception of a partner's satisfaction, and having a varied repertoire of rewarding sexual expressions, including the ability to have intercourse. Erectile dysfunction can be treated with vacuum erection devices, penile prostheses, intracavernous injections, or alprostidil. Ejaculatory failure can respond to vibratory stimuli (Pryor, 1995). The re-establishment and maintenance of an active sexual life will depend on specific sexual impairment, general levels of disability, the individual's perception of his or her own sexuality, and the relationship with the partner (Althof & Levine, 1993).

Pressure ulcers. The risk factor for pressure ulcers in patients with spinal cord disease include immobility and sensory loss. Further factors such as obesity, emaciation, and vascular changes (for example secondary to diabetes), can aggravate the situation. It is the responsibility of the clinical team caring for the patient to ensure that appropriate seating and bedding is available at home at all times (including in the toilet and at meal times). Carers need to understand that attention to detail is important, so that sheets should be clean and uncreased and clothing flat and not creased, that shearing skin during poorly executed transfers is dangerous, and that rubbing the skin is contraindicated. Patients who are anaesthetic to heat should not be placed near to heaters, hot water bottles, and electric blankets.

Reflex sympathetic dystrophy. This is a rare complication of non-traumatic spinal cord injury and must be considered in patients with an incomplete tetraparesis presenting with unexplained pain in the hand and shoulder, or with hand oedema, vasomotor instability, and reduced range of finger movements (Philip, 1990). It is important because the additional disability caused by this syndrome can have a devastating effect upon functional recovery. The early recognition and treatment of the condition are the most important factors in the effective management of reflex sympathetic dystrophy. Early mobilisation facilitates recovery and reduces physical disability. Other management approaches include the use of steroids in the acute phase, and adequate pain control using regional sympathetic blocks.

Heterotopic ossification (HO). This complication is more commonly seen in acute traumatic spinal cord injury but is reported in paraparesis and tetraparesis due to tumours and transverse myelitis. It is associated with hip contractures, an increased risk of pressure sores, and prolonged hospitalisation (Knudsen et al., 1992). Limited range of hip movement can prevent sitting, transfers, standing from sitting, and walking. To prevent HO it is important to examine the patient with a new paraparesis or tetraparesis regularly for hip mobility, thigh circumference, and alkaline phosphatase. Management is controversial (see Chapter 15) but many authors advocate gentle mobilisation of the joint during the acute phase and subsequently more intensive joint exercises once the signs of inflammation have settled (e.g. Knudsen et al., 1982).

Arm function. Upper limb function can be impaired as a result of pain, paraesthesiae, distal weakness of small muscle of the hands and forearms, contractures (Figs 45.1 and 45.2), which are usually preventable, or loss of postural sensation, especially in the fingers. The patient with clumsy hands might not be able to write, hold eating implements, or perform activities that require hand dexterity. Self-care skills can be affected. Appropriate training, with or without the help of devices or adaptations, can enable the patient to achieve improved function (Nicholas, 1971). The arm should be rested in a sling because dependency can produce swelling of the hands. Assisted active shoulder movements should be carried out daily to avoid development of a painful frozen shoulder. The hands need special attention because there is a tendency for contractures to occur. Splints might be required to prevent finger flexion. If sympathetic dystrophy is diagnosed, regional sympathetic blocks, either by reserpine or quanethidine, might be helpful. Care must be taken to prevent injury to desensitised skin when splints are prescribed. With postural sensory loss, the patient can be taught to use visual or auditory stimuli to compensate for the loss. Upper limb function can be improved by provision of a flexor hinge splint or a mobile arm support (Figs 45.3 and 45.4).

Mobility. In the context of normal cognitive function, mobility is the foundation on which various skills of daily living are based. They in turn form the basis of activities such as work, leisure, and social interaction. Where mobility cannot be maintained, the rehabilitation team should attend to these aspects of daily life so that they can be as normal as possible in

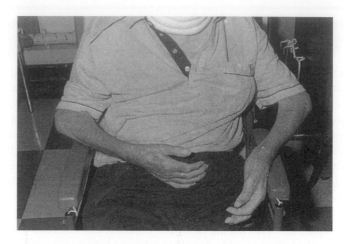

Figure 45.1. Flexor contractures of the elbows and weak hands in a patient with a C5 lesion.

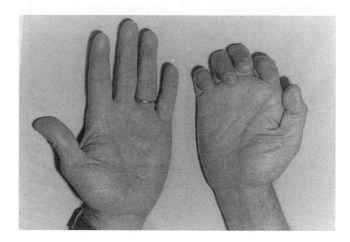

Figure 45.2. Fixed flexion contractures of the fingers of the right hand in a patient with a central cord syndrome.

the presence of restricted or modified mobility. Loss of mobility contributes to contractures and fixed deformity, obesity, muscle wasting, pressure ulcers, constipation, respiratory problems, venous thrombosis, hypothermia, prolonged hospitalisation, loss of self-care skills, social isolation, and dependency on others (Millaszo & Resh, 1982).

Many patients will have difficulty walking, with an effortful gait, a tendency to trip over uneven surfaces, and difficulty with stairs. These difficulties are the result of various combinations of weakness, spasticity, loss of dorsal column sensation, and comorbidities, particularly degenerative disease of the hips and knees in older patients. The use of high sticks can compensate for poor balance and encourage an upright posture. Ankle–foot orthoses can be useful to prevent a disabling foot drop. Spasticity will need to be controlled, muscle strength improved, and trunk stability achieved. If functional walking is not possible, patients should nevertheless be encouraged to stand because this helps tone management, improves bowel and bladder drainage, prevents osteoporosis, and encourages good respiratory function. An appropriate wheelchair should be prescribed, with attention paid to posture, comfort, pressure relief, and mobility. If

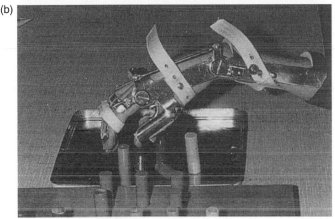

Figure 45.3. To show use of a flexor hinge splint to enable the patient to pick up medium-sized or large objects.

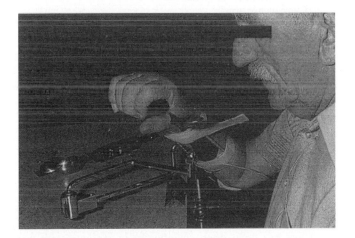

Figure 45.4. Mobile arm support enabling the patient to bring the hand to the face and therefore feed independently when set up.

the patient is unable to self-propel then an electrically powered indoor or outdoor/indoor chair should be considered. Patients must be taught how to use the wheelchair safely, with particular attention paid to transfers. Community mobility needs must also be addressed.

Mood. Little has been written about the incidence of depression in patients with non-traumatic spinal cord injury. Studies after traumatic spinal cord injury suggest that depression occurs in approximately one-third of patients early after an acute insult such as an ischaemic injury, but usually resolves within 3 months (Kishi, 1994). In this case the severity of the depression could be related to the severity of the deficit; late or persisting depression is more commonly due to inadequate social support. Premorbid factors such as a pre-existing depressive illness are important in the aetiology of depression in this group. Depression is less common in patients with more predictable and slowly progressive diseases such as cervical spondylosis.

Parenting. No specific studies of parenting have been performed in patients with non-traumatic spinal cord injury but studies of adults with traumatic lesions suggest that the physical aspects of spinal cord pathology do not prevent people assuming responsibility for childcare and successful parenting (Westgren & Levi, 1994). Children did not perceive their mothers as different because of the disability, identifying their support for and interest in their activities as important. Children often identified some practical problems, such as their mothers not being able to reach high-placed items.

Dying. Patients with malignant compression of the cord might have a short life expectancy but can still gain in terms of quality life from appropriate management. The main aim of a management programme should be to establish a successful discharge, and this will include ensuring adequate analgesia, and teaching the family/carers to transfer the patient successfully and to gain skills in skin, catheter and bowel care.

OUTCOME MEASURES

The objective assessment of cervical myelopathy can be particularly difficult. Various clinical grading systems have been proposed for the assessment of rheumatoid and spondylotic cervical myelopathy. Ranawat's (1979) classification (Table 45.2) is a simple four-point grading system but mixes impairment and disability and, unfortunately, makes it difficult to decide between classes II and IIIA, which are the areas of most interest to the surgeon. Steinbrocker's (1994) four-point scale to measure of functional ability has been adopted by the American College of Rheumatologists, but is perhaps too insensitive for use in rehabilitation. As difficulty in walking is the most common initial symptom, Nurick (1972) has classified disability on the basis of gait (see Table 45.2). This classification is, however, weighted heavily on lower limb function and does not consider the disability caused by sphincter disturbance or upper limb function. The evaluation system proposed by the Japanese Orthopaedic Association in 1976 (Hayashi, 1988; Table 45.3) considers these factors but mixes impairments and disabilities and has to be modified for a Western population. A more recent scoring system based on the Stanford Health Assessment Questionnaire has been developed by Casey and colleagues (1996) for patients with rheumatoid arthritis with cervical myelopathy. This simple ten-item, four-point questionnaire has four items relating to upper

Table 45.2.   Three early classifications of disablement in spondylotic and rheumatoid myelopathy

Nurick's (1972) classification of disability in spondylotic myelopathy

Grade 0	Root signs and symptoms No evidence of cord involvement
Grade I	Signs of cord involvement Normal gait
Grade II	Mild gait involvement Able to be employed
Grade III	Gait abnormality prevents employment
Grade IV	Able to ambulate only with assistance
Grade V	Chair bound or bedridden

Ranawat's (1979) classification of disability of rheumatoid myelopathy

I	No neurological deficit (normal neurological condition)
II	Subjective weakness with hyper-reflexia and dysaesthesia
IIIA	Objective weakness and long tract signs but able to walk
IIIB	Quadriparetic and non-ambulatory

Steinbrocker's (1994) classification of disability in rheumatoid myelopathy

I	Complete ability to carry out all the usual duties without handicaps
II	Adequate for normal activities despite handicap of discomfort or limited motion of one of the joints
III	Limited to little or none of the duties of usual occupation or self-care
IV	Incapacitated, largely or wholly bed-ridden or confined to a wheelchair with little or no self-care

Table 45.3.   The assessment scale proposed by the Japanese Orthopaedic Association (1976) (Hukuda et al. 1985)

Motor dysfunction of the upper extremity
0   Unable to feed onself
1   Unable to handle chopsticks, able to eat with
        a spoon
2   Handles chopsticks with much difficulty
3   Handles chopsticks with slight difficulty
4   None

Motor dysfunction of the lower extremity
0   Unable to walk
1   Walk on the flat floor with walking aid
2   Up and/or down the stairs with handrail
3   Lack of stability and smooth reciprocation
4   None

Sensory deficit
A.   Upper extremity
        0   Severe sensory loss or pain
        1   Mild sensory loss
        2   None
B.   Lower extremity, same as A
C.   Trunk, same as A

Sphincter dysfunction
0   Unable to void
1   Marked difficulty in micturition (retention,
        stranguria)
2   Difficulty in micturition (frequency, nocturia)
3   None

Table 45.4.   The measure validated by Casey et al. (1996) for rheumatoid cervical myelopathy. From Casey et al. (1996) with permission from the BMJ Publishing Group

Rising: are you able to:
    Stand up from an armless straight chair?
    Get in and out of bed?
Eating: are you able to:
    Cut up your meat?
    Lift a full cup or glass to your mouth?
Walking: are you able to:
    Walk outdoors on flat ground?
    Climb up five steps?
Hygiene: are you able to:
    Wash and dry your entire body?
    Get on and off the toilet?
Grip: are you able to:
    Open jars that have previously been opened?
Activities: are you able to:
    Get in and out of a car?

Each item is rated on a 4-point scale: without *any* difficulty (0); with *some* difficulty (1); with *much* difficulty (2); unable to do (3). Requirement for aids or assistance scores 2. Range 0–30. Final score is expressed as a percentage.

limb function and four relating to lower limb function. It was shown to be a reliable and sensitive measure of disability in these patients, as well as an accurate predictor of functional outcome following surgery.

Health-related functional status in both traumatic and non-traumatic spinal cord injury has been studied using the short version of the Sickness Impact Profile (SIP-68) and has been demonstrated to be valid and reliable (Post et al., 1996). Little other work has been done specifically in patients with non-traumatic myelopathy, but many generic measures have face validity and have been shown to be reliable and sensitive in other causes of neurological disability. The Barthel index (Mahoney & Barthel, 1965; Wade & Collin, 1988), Functional Independence Measure (Dodds et al., 1993), SF-36 (Garratt et al., 1993; Jenkinson et al., 1993), 9-hole peg test (Mathiowetz et al., 1995), and many other measures, can all be of use in this condition to monitor progress and the results of treatment.

REFERENCES

Althof SE, Levine SB (1993). Clinical approaches to the sexuality of patients with spinal cord injury. *Urologic Clinics of North America, 20*, 527–534

Azouvi P, Mane M, Thiebaut JB, Denys P, Remy-Neris O, Bussel B (1996). Intrathecal baclofen administration for control of severe spinal spasticity: Functional improvement and long term follow up. *Archives of Physical Medicine and Rehabilitation, 77*, 35–39

Bailey P, Casamajo L (1911). Osteoarthritis of the spine as a cause of compression of the spinal cord and its roots. *Journal of Nervous and Mental Diseases, 38*, 588–596

Baldini M, Tonnarelli GP, Princi L, Vivenza C, Nizzdi V (1979). Neurological results in spinal cord metastases. *Neurochirurgia (Stuttg), 22*, 159–165.

Behan PO (1982). An evaluation of low dose dantrolene sodium (Dantrium) therapy in the treatment of ambulatory patients with spasticity. *Clinical Trials Journal, 19*, 1–8

Bohlman HH, Emery EE (1988). The pathophysiology of cervical spondylosis and myelopathy. *Spine, 13*, 839–846

Bouchez B, Arnott G, Delfosse JM (1985). Acute spinal epidural abscess. *Journal of Neurology, 231*, 343–344

Brain WR, Northfield DW, Wilkinson M (1952). The neurologic manifestations of cervical spondylosis. *Brain, 75*, 187–225

Breig A (1960). *Biomechanics of the central nervous system.* Almquist and Wiksel, Stockholm

Breig A (1978). *Adverse mechanical tension in the central nervous system.* John Wiley, New York

Brindley GS (1994). The first 500 patients with sacral anterior root stimulator implants: General description. *Paraplegia, 32*, 795–805

Bromley I (1981). Complications. In: Bromley I (Ed), *Tetraplegia and paraplegia: A guide for physiotherapists.* Churchill Livingstone, Edinburgh, pp. 219–223

Buchan AC, Fulford GE, Harris P, Jellinek E, Kerr WG, Kirkland I, Newsman JE, Stark GD (1972). A preliminary survey of the incidence and aetiology of spinal paralysis. *Paraplegia, 10*, 23–28

Campbell AMG, Phillips DG (1960). Cervical disc lesions with neurological disorder. *British Medical Journal, 2*, 481–485

Casey ATH, Bland JM, Crockard HA (1996). Development of a functional scoring system for rheumatoid arthritis patients with cervical myelopathies. *Annals of Rheumatic Diseases, 55*, 901–906

Chancellor MB, Karusick S, Erhard MJ, Abdill CK, Liu J-B, Goldber BB, Staas WE (1993). Placement of a wire mesh in the external urinary sphincter of men with spinal cord injuries. *Radiology, 187*, 551–555

Clarke E, Robinson PK (1956). Cervical myelopathy: A complication of cervical spondylosis. *Brain, 79*, 483–510

Dodds TA, Martin DP, Stolov WC, Deyo RA (1993). A validation of the functional independence measure and its performance among rehabilitation patients. *Archives of Physical Medicine and Rehabilitation, 74*, 531–536

Duncan GW, Shahani BT, Young RR (1976). An evaluation of baclofen treatment for certain symptoms in patients with spinal cord symptoms. *Neurology, 26*, 441–446

Ebersold MJ, Pare, Quasr LM (1995). Surgical treatment for cervical spondylotic myelopathy. *Journal of Neurosurgery, 82*, 745–751

Faria F, Viegas F (1995). Spinal brucellosis: A personal experience of nine patients and a review of the literature. *Paraplegia, 33*, 294–295

Ferguson RJL, Caplan LR (1985). Cervical spondylotic myelopathy. *Neurologic Clinics of North America, 3*, 40–51

Garratt AM, Ruta DA, Abdalla MI, Buckingham JK, Russell IT (1993). The SF36 health survey questionnaire: An outcome measure suitable for routine use within the NHS. *British Medical Journal, 306*, 1440–1444

Geldmacher DS, Nager BJ (1989). Spinal cord vascular disease. In: Bradley WG, Daroff RB, Fenichel GM, Marsden CD (Eds), *Neurology in clinical practice,* vol 2. Butterworth Heinemann, Boston, pp. 983–988

Hayashi H, Okada K, Hashimoto J et al. (1988). Cervical spondylotic myelopathy in the aged patient. *Spine, 113*, 618–625

Hellstrom PM, Aly A, Johannsson C (1990). Cisapride stimulates small intestinal motility and relieves constipation in myelopathy due to cervical stenosis: Case report. *Paraplegia, 28*, 261–264

Henson RA, Parsons M (1967). Ischaemic lesions of the spinal cord: An illustrated review. *Quarterly Journal of Medicine, 36*, 205–211

Hughes JT (1978). *Pathology of the spinal cord,* 2nd edition. Lloyd Luke, London

Hukuda S, Mouchizuki T, Ogata M et al. (1985). Operation for cervical spondylotic myelopathy. *Journal of Bone and Joint Surgery, 67B*, 609–615

Hussain IF, Fowler CJ (1998). Use of the intravesical capsaicin for urge incontinence and irritative voiding syndromes. *Current Opinion in Urology, 8*, 293–296

Iwatsubo E, Okada E, Takehara T, Tamada K, Akatsu T (1994). Selective intrathecal block to improve activities of daily living in patients with spastic quadriplegia. A preliminary report. *Paraplegia, 32*, 489–492

Jenkinson C, Coulter A, Wright L (1993). Short form 36 (SF36) health survey questionnaire: Normative data for adults of working age. *British Medical Journal, 306*, 1437–1440

Kim SW, Kim RC, Choi BH, Gordon SK (1988). Non traumatic ischaemic myelopathy. *Paraplegia 26*, 262–263

Kishi Y, Robinson RG, Forrester AW (1994). Prospective longitudinal study of depression following spinal cord injury. *Journal of Neuropsychiatry and Clinical Sciences, 6*, 237–244

Knudsen L, Lundberg D, Ericson G (1982). Myositis ossificans circumscripta in para/tetraplegics. *Scandinavian Journal of Rheumatology, 11*, 27–31

Lintott P, Hafez HM, Stansby G, (1998). Spinal cord complications of thoracoabdominal aneurysm surgery. *British Journal of Surgery, 85*, 5 15

Mahoney FI, Barthel DW (1965). Functional evaluation: The Barthel Index. *Maryland State Medical Journal, 14*, 61–65

Mathiowetz V, Weber K, Kashman N, Volland G (1985). Adult norms for the nine hole peg test of finger dexterity. *Occupational Therapy Journal of Research, 5*, 24–38

Millazo V, Resh C (1982). Kinetic nursing – a new approach to the problems of immobilisation. *Journal of Neurological Nursing, 14*, 120–123

Minaire P, Castainer R, Girard R, Berard E, Deidier C, Bourret J (1978). Epidemiology of spinal cord injury in the Rhone–Alpes region, France, 1970–1975. *Paraplegia, 16*, 76–87

Moore AP, Blumhardt LD (1997). A prospective study of the causes of non-traumatic spastic paraparesis and tetraparesis in 585 patients. *Spinal Cord, 35*, 361–367

Nagat K, Ohashi T, Abe J, Morita M, Inoue A (1996). Cervical myelopathy in elderly patients: Clinical results and MRI findings before and after decompression surgery. *Spinal Cord, 34*, 220–226

Nance PW, Bugaresti J, Shellenberger K et al. (1994). Efficacy and safety of tizanidine in the treatment of patients with spinal cord injury. *Neurology, 44* (Suppl. 9), S44–S52

Nicholas PJR (1971). *Rehabilitation of the severely disabled.* Butterworth, London, pp. 405–433

Nurick S (1972). The pathogenesis of the spinal cord disorder with cervical spondylosis. *Brain, 95*, 101–108

Ogino H, Tader K, Okada K et al. (1983). Canal diameter, antero-posterior compression ratio and spondylotic myelopathy of the cervical spine. *Spine, 8*, 1 15

Optiz JL, Lutness MP (1985). Motor point blocks in the treatment of symptomatic anorectal dyssynergia in the paraplegic male. *Archives of Physical Medicine and Rehabilitation, 66*, 559 560

Ozer MN (1988). *The management of persons with spinal cord injury.* Demos, New York

Pelser H, Van Gijn J (1993). Spinal infarction: A follow-up study. *Stroke, 24*, 896–898

Penington GR (1986). Management of non-traumatic paraplegia. *The Medical Journal of Australia, 144*, 364–365

Perkin GD (1989). An analysis of 7836 successive new out-patient referrals. *Journal of Neurology, Neurosurgery and Psychiatry, 52*, 447–448

Persson LCG, Moritz U, Brandt L, Carlsson CA (1997). Pain, muscular tenderness, cervical and shoulder mobility in patients with cervical radiculopathy randomly treated with surgery, physiotherapy or a cervical collar. *European Spine Journal, 6*, 256–266

Philip PA, Philip M, Monga T (1990). Reflex sympathetic dystrophy in central cord syndrome; case report and review of the literature. *Paraplegia, 28*, 48–54

Phillips DG (1973). Surgical treatment of myelopathy with cervical spondylosis. *Journal of Neurology, Neurosurgery and Psychiatry, 36*, 819–824

Post MWN, de Bruin A, de Witte L, Schrijvers A (1996). The SIP68: A measure of health related functional status in rehabilitation medicine. *Archives of Physical Medicine and Rehabilitation, 77*, 440–445

Pryor JL, LeRoy RC, Nagel TC, Hensleigh HC (1995). Vibratory stimuli for the treatment of anejaculation in quadriplegic men. *Archives of Physical Medicine and Rehabilitation, 76*, 59–64

Ranawat C, O'Leary P, Pellici P, Tsairis P, Marcheisello P, Dort L (1979). Cervical fusion in rheumatoid arthritis. *Journal of Bone and Joint Surgery of America, 61A*, 1003–1010

Romano JG, Bradley WG, Green B (1996). High cervical myelopathy presenting with the numb clumsy hand syndrome. *Journal of the Neurological Sciences, 140*, 137–140

Schonherr MC, Groothoff JW, Mulder GA, Eisma WH (1996). Rehabilitation of patients with spinal cord lesions in The Netherlands: An epidemiological study. *Spinal Cord, 34*, 679–683

Schurch B, Hodler J, Rodic B (1997). Botulinum A toxin as a treatment of detrusor–sphincter dyssynergia in patients with spinal cord injury: MRI controlled transperineal injections. *Journal of Neurology, Neurosurgery and Psychiatry, 63*, 474–476

Shingu H, Ikata T, Katoh S, Akatsu T (1994). Spinal cord injuries in Japan: A nation-wide epidemiological survey in 1990. *Paraplegia, 32*, 3–8

Snow BJ, Tsui JK, Bhatt MH, Varelas M, Hashimoto SA, Calne DB (1990). Treatment of spasticity with botulinum toxin: A double blind study. *Annals of Neurology, 28*, 512–515

Steinbocker O, Traeger CH, Batterman RC (1994). Therapeutic criteria in rheumatoid arthritis. *Journal of American Medical Association, 140*, 659–662

Stevenson VL, Palyford ED, Langdon DW, Thomspon AJ (1996). Rehabilitation of incomplete spinal cord pathology: Factors affecting prognosis and outcome. *Journal of Neurology, 243*, 344–347

Wade DT, Collin C (1988). The Barthel ADL index: A standard measure of physical disability? *International Disability Studies, 10*, 64–67

Waters RL, Sie I, Yakura J, Adkins R (1993). Recovery following ischaemic myelopathy. *Journal of Trauma, 35*, 837–839

Westgren N, Levi R (1994). Motherhood after traumatic spinal cord injury. *Paraplegia, 32*, 517–523

Wilkinson M (Ed) (1971). *Cervical spondylosis: Its early diagnosis and treatment*. Heinemann, London

Wood KM (1978). The use of phenol as a neurolytic agent: A review. *Pain, 5*, 205–229

Yang DY, Wang Y Ch, Lee Ch Sh, Chou DY (1992). Ossification of the posterior cervical longitudinal ligaments. *Acta Neurochirugica (Wien), 115*, 15–19

Young RR, Emre M, Nance PW, Schapiro R, Barnes M (1997). Current issues in spasticity management. *The Neurologist, 3*, 261–275

Young RR, Sarkarti M (1992). Acute and long term care of patients with spinal cord injury or impairment. In Young RR, Delwaide PJ (Eds). *Principles and practice of restorative neurology*. Butterworth Heinemann, Oxford, pp. 125–135

46. Motor neurone disease

Pamela J. Shaw

INTRODUCTION

The precise cause(s) of the selective neurodegenerative process in motor neurone disease (MND) remain unknown. For individuals afflicted with the disease, there is progressive unremitting paralysis, leading to death usually within 3–5 years. Several aspects relating to the clinical course of MND can create difficulties both for families coming to terms with the disease and for their medical attendants. First, the progression often occurs over a rapid time course, so that the patient can no sooner have adapted to one level of disability when a new set of problems has to be faced. Second, because of the progression of disability, the optimum period for the provision of aids and appliances can be relatively short, and this aspect of patient care needs to be finely judged and organised quickly. Third, the majority of patients afflicted by MND retain normal cognitive function and full conscious appreciation of their worsening disability, and ultimately of their impending death. Feeling powerless to influence this distressing and tragic disease, the doctor might hesitate to discuss the diagnosis with the patient and to offer continuing medical care and support. However, even though there is no curative treatment for MND, and as yet no treatment that has a major effect on clinical and pathological progression, there is much that can be done to alleviate distress and maximise independence and quality of life for patients and their carers during the course of the disease. This provides a significant challenge to the physician, who must combine diagnostic skills, compassion, and the ability to manage a rehabilitative programme with skill in providing information and counselling to families appropriate for the stage of the disease. This chapter outlines the practical measures to be taken by doctors and other health-care professionals to help patients to achieve the highest possible quality of life during the course of MND.

MOTOR NEURONE DISEASES

The World Federation of Neurology classification of motor neurone diseases is based on heredity and presumed causes (De Jong, 1991). A simplified clinical classification is shown in Table 46.1. Adult-onset MND is sporadic in 90% of cases, and familial, usually with an autosomal dominant mode of inheritance, in

Table 46.1. Clinical classification of motor neurone diseases

Sporadic motor neurone disease
  Amyotrophic lateral sclerosis (ALS)
  Progressive bulbar palsy (PBP)
  Progressive muscular atrophy (PMA)
  Primary lateral sclerosis (PLS)

Familial motor neurone disease
  SOD[1] (Cu/Zn superoxide dismutase) related (20%)
  Alsin—autosomal recessive juvenile-onset
  Genetic locus unknown (80%)

Other inherited forms of motor neurone degeneration
  Kennedy's disease
  Vialetto van Laere syndrome

Western Pacific amyotrophic lateral sclerosis/parkinsonism/ dementia complex

Juvenile onset MND with intracytoplasmic inclusions

Motor neurone diseases with definable causes
  Post-polio syndrome
  Heavy metal intoxication
  Hexosaminidase-A deficiency

approximately 10% of cases; 20% of familial cases have a mutation in the gene on chromosome 21 encoding Cu/Zn superoxide dismutase (SOD1) (Rosen et al., 1993). The genetic alterations underlying the remaining 80% of cases of familial MND remain unknown. There are several clinical and pathological variants of sporadic MND. Approximately two-thirds of patients present with the amyotrophic lateral sclerosis (ALS) variant; 25% present with progressive bulbar palsy (PBP), 8% with progressive muscular atrophy (PMA), and 2% with primary lateral sclerosis (PLS) (Caroscio et al., 1984). In the most common ALS variant, there are signs of both upper and lower motor neurone dysfunction, which eventually involve both somatic and bulbar musculature. Diagnostic criteria with various levels of certainty have been developed for classical ALS (World Federation of Neurology El Escorial Criteria) (Brooks, 1994).

In progressive bulbar palsy, the initial symptoms begin in those muscles controlling speech, chewing, and swallowing that are innervated by motor neurone groups in the pons and medulla. At presentation, there might be no symptoms or signs of limb involvement and the disease can remain confined to the bulbar muscles for several years. Eventually, however, the disease usually progresses to more generalised muscle weakness, i.e.

the ALS variant. In patients with the progressive muscular atrophy variant, the initial symptoms are due to degeneration of lower motor neurones in the spinal cord, without evidence of upper motor neurone or bulbar features. Primary lateral sclerosis is the least common variant of MND. The patient presents with progressive motor dysfunction involving the limb and bulbar musculature, which is associated with evidence of only upper motor neurone degeneration. There are no lower motor neurone features on clinical examination or neurophysiological assessment. A degree of sphincter dysfunction might be present (Pringle et al., 1992). The PLS form of MND tends to be relatively slow in its progression. Lower motor neurone features can become apparent as long as 8–10 years after presentation.

The lower motor neurones alone are affected in a number of less common, adult-onset motor neurone disorders. These are generally not so rapidly progressive or as uniformly fatal as classical ALS. They include Kennedy's disease, an X-linked disorder due to expansion of a trinucleotide repeat in the androgen receptor gene (La Spada et al., 1991); the post-poliomyelitis syndrome (Sonies & Dalakas, 1991); an ill-defined group of spinal muscular atrophies, some of which have a genetic basis; and multifocal motor neuropathy with conduction block sometimes associated with anti-ganglioside antibodies (Pestronk et al., 1988).

EPIDEMIOLOGY

Studies on the epidemiology of MND can be difficult to interpret because of uncertainties in the criteria used for making the diagnosis. The reported worldwide incidence rates for MND are in the region of 1–2/100,000 population (Tyler & Shefner, 1991), with prevalence rates of 4–6/100,000 (Tandan & Bradley, 1985). Such a prevalence would suggest that approximately 5000 patients in the UK are affected with MND. The incidence and prevalence rates are largely comparable in populations of different ethnic origins. There are, however, geographical foci where disease incidences 50–100 times higher than the global average have been reported (see later).

MND is primarily a disease of late middle age. The average age of onset varies in different series from 52 to 66 years (Tyler & Shefner, 1991). In most studies of age-specific rates, the incidence is very low until the age of 40, then rises sharply to a maximum at approximately 65 years (Jokelainen, 1977; Kurland et al., 1973; Kurtzke, 1982). There is some controversy concerning age-specific incidence rates in older age groups. Most studies have found a reduced age-specific incidence rate in the eighth and ninth decades (Kondo, 1995).

In all studies, the incidence of MND is greater in males than in females, with a male : female ratio of approximately 1.6 : 1. Males are more likely to sustain physical injury, a suspected risk factor for MND, but this alone does not adequately explain the male predominance. The average duration of disease from the onset of symptoms is approximately 2–3 years (Kondo, 1975). Survival tends to be longer in younger patients. In one study the mean disease duration was found to decline

from 45 months for patients with disease onset in the fourth and fifth decades, to 20–25 months for those with onset in the eighth decade (Kondo, 1975). The rate of disease progression can vary markedly. Appel and co-workers (1987), using a quantitative scale to measure disease progression, found a 20–60-fold difference in the rate of progression between the fastest- and slowest-progressing patients. Patients presenting with bulbar dysfunction tend to have a worse prognosis than individuals with limb-onset disease (Jokelainen, 1977).

Among potential risk factors, age is undoubtedly a contributory factor. A decline in the number of surviving motor neurones in the elderly can contribute to this finding (Tomlinson, 1973). A history of prior physical trauma, electrical injury, a high level of athleticism, or occupational exertion have been reported to be more common in MND patients than in controls (Deapen & Henderson, 1986; Felmus et al., 1976; Gawel et al., 1983; Kondo & Tsubaki, 1981; Kurtzke & Beebe, 1980). An excess of MND has been reported in leather workers and in those exposed to heavy metals and solvents (Gunnarson & Linberg, 1989; Hawkes & Fox, 1981; Roelofs-Iverson et al., 1984). Occasional cases have been linked to excessive pesticide exposure (Pall et al., 1987). No consistent dietary risk factors have been established.

High-incidence foci

Three high-incidence foci of MND have been documented. These sites have been extensively studied and include the Western Pacific island of Guam; several villages in the Kii peninsula of Japan, and the Irian Jaya area of West New Guinea, where incidence rates as high as 147/100,000 have been reported (Arnold et al., 1953; Gadjusek & Salazar, 1982; Mulder et al., 1954). These areas are isolated ecosystems. The native residents are relatively primitive, impoverished, inbred, and engaged in local primary industries and in the production of their staple diet. In Guam and the Kii peninsula, the onset of MND tends to occur at a young age, is clinically atypical, and is associated with the presence of a parkinsonism–dementia complex affecting other individuals in the same areas. The cases in West New Guinea are less well documented. The high incidence of MND in Guam and the Kii peninsula has rapidly declined in recent years. It seems likely that the traditional life-style of the indigenous population of these areas contained risk factors that are still unknown, but that are being gradually eliminated as a consequence of recent profound socioeconomic changes.

AETIOLOGICAL HYPOTHESES

MND, as with other diseases, is the consequence of an interplay between host factors and environmental factors. Neurones are fixed postmitotic cells that are no longer capable of replication and thus have limited life-spans. The cumulative effects of somatic mutations and oxidative stress with age could contribute to neuronal injury. The function of any neuronal system must decline with age because of a reduction in neuronal numbers, and possibly also as a result of declining function in the surviving neurons. The primary pathogenetic processes underlying MND are likely to be multifactorial and the precise mechanisms underlying selective cell death in the disease are at present unknown. Current understanding of the neurodegenerative process in MND suggests that there could be a complex interplay between genetic factors, toxic activation of glutamate receptors, oxidative stress, and damage to critical target proteins (Brown, 1995). The relative importance of these factors may vary in different subgroups of patients.

Genetic factors. The single most important advance in research into MND in recent years has been the identification of mutations in the Cu/Zn superoxide dismutase (SOD1) gene, which underlie 20% of autosomal dominant familial MND cases, or 2% of MND cases as a whole (Rosen et al., 1993). More than 90 different mutations, affecting all five exons of the SOD1 gene, have been described (Siddique et al., 1996). The normal role of SOD1 is to scavenge or dismutate superoxide free radicals produced during normal cellular metabolism. The bulk of the scientific evidence that has emerged, including data from SOD1 transgenic mice, suggests that motor neurone injury results from a toxic gain of function of the mutant protein, rather than simply a reduction of oxygen free radical scavenging capacity (Brown, 1995). A leading hypothesis for the toxic gain of function is that the active site of the mutant enzyme which contains the Cu^{2+} and Zn^{2+} atoms, is more open and less well shielded than normal. The resulting abnormal accessibility to the active site of peroxynitrite and hydrogen peroxide might result, respectively, in nitration of tyrosine residues of cellular proteins and abnormal production of highly reactive hydroxyl radicals, which can cause cumulative damage to cellular constituents.

Other genetic clues to motor system degeneration have been reported. Thus, cases of MND screened for mutations in neurofilament genes revealed five individuals with apparently sporadic disease who had deletions in the KSP repeat sequence of the neurofilament heavy gene (Figlewicz et al., 1994). It is uncertain whether such mutations are directly responsible for MND or whether they simply represent a susceptibility gene or genetic risk factor. Of related interest are the reports by two research groups describing motor system degeneration in transgenic mice engineered to overexpress neurofilament proteins (Julien et al., 1995; Wong et al., 1995).

Two genes on chromosome 5q, the survival motor neurone (SMN) gene and the neuronal apoptosis inhibitory protein (NAIP) gene, have been shown to be associated with spinal muscular atrophy. These genes have been investigated as candidates for susceptibility genes in MND, but so far no definite link has been shown (Jackson et al., 1996).

Kennedy's disease, which can mimic the PMA form of MND, is associated with expansion of a CAG trinucleotide repeat sequence in the androgen receptor gene on the X chromosome. Affected males can have clinical features of androgen insensitivity, such as gynaecomastia and reduced fertility (Harding et al., 1982). Because of the slower progression and better prognosis of Kennedy's disease, it is important to distinguish this condition from classic MND.

Glutamatergic toxicity. The circumstantial evidence that inappropriate activation of glutamate receptors can contribute to motor neurone injury in MND has been reviewed (Shaw, 1994; Shaw & Ince, 1997; Zeman et al., 1994) and is summarised in Table 46.2. Modulation of glutamatergic neurotransmission is a potential therapeutic strategy for retarding clinical and pathological progression of the disease (Lacomblez et al., 1996). It is of interest that separate studies have shown that a similar proportion of cases of MND have: (1) marked reduction in the expression of the glial glutamate transporter EAAT2 in motor cortex (Rothstein et al., 1995); (2) increased levels of glutamate in the CSF (Shaw et al., 1995); and (3) increased excitability of the motor cortex on transcranial magnetic stimulation (Eisen et al., 1993; Mills et al., 1995). The first of these is a marker for clearing glutamate from the synaptic cleft and terminating its excitatory signal. The second two factors could reflect the consequences of impaired glutamate reuptake, resulting in an elevated level of glutamate in the extracellular fluid and a lower threshold for receptor activation. Definitive studies are needed to determine whether these observations apply to the same subgroup of MND patients and to correlate these parameters with response to anti-glutamate therapies.

Oxidative stress. The possibility that oxygen free-radical-mediated neurotoxicity contributes to the pathogenesis of MND has been strengthened by the discovery of SOD1 mutations underlying some cases of familial disease. There is close clinical and pathological similarity between familial and sporadic MND, suggesting they might share common pathophysiological

---

Table 46.2. Evidence for disturbance of glutamatergic neurotransmission in MND

Elevation of CSF glutamate levels
Decreased CNS tissue levels of glutamate
Abnormalities of glutamate reuptake transport
Abnormalities of glutamate receptor binding sites in MND spinal cord and motor cortex
Motor system disorders due to dietary ingestion of glutamate-agonist toxins, e.g. lathyrism
Experimental and animal models of glutamate neurotoxicity:
   CSF of MND patients is toxic to neurones in culture
   Chronic blockade of glutamate transport *in vitro* causes motor neurone degeneration
   Antisense oligonucleotide inhibition of glutamate-transporter protein synthesis causes motor neurone degeneration *in vitro* and *in vivo*
PET scanning studies of the motor cortex in MND shows abnormally widespread activation (i.e. excess of excitatory over inhibitory activity)
Transcranial magnetic stimulation of the motor cortex in MND shows hyperexcitability
Antiglutamate therapy (riluzole) shows a modest effect in prolonging the survival of MND patients

mechanisms. Several lines of evidence have emerged that oxidative stress could contribute to motor neurone injury in sporadic MND: (1) protein carbonyls, which are formed by oxidative modification of certain amino acid residues in protein, are elevated in the spinal cord (Shaw et al., 1995) and frontal cortex (Bowling et al., 1993) of MND patients; and (2) biochemical indices present in the CNS of MND patients have also been reported, which could reflect a compensatory response to oxidative stress. Thus, the content of selenium and the activity of the selenium containing the free-radical-scavenging enzyme glutathione peroxidase, are increased in the spinal cord of MND cases compared with controls (Ince et al., 1994). SOD1 mRNA has been shown to be increased in individual motor neurones from sporadic MND cases (Bergeron et al., 1994). Immunohistochemical studies in human spinal cord have shown increased glial immunoreactivity for the free-radical-scavenging enzymes SOD1, Mn SOD, and catalase in MND in the vicinity of the corticospinal tracts and/or in the neuropil of the ventral horn (Shaw et al., 1997). Increased expression of metallothionein, which is employed in the detoxification and storage of metals, as well as the scavenging of free radicals, has been reported in the postmortem spinal cord from MND patients (Sillevis-Smitt et al., 1994).

Glutamatergic neurotransmission and the generation of oxygen free radicals are interlinked processes, which could generate an escalating cascade of motor neurone injury (Coyle & Puttfarcken, 1993; Shaw & Ince, 1997). Both of these processes are major potential targets for therapeutic intervention in the neuroprotection of motor neurones.

PATHOLOGY

The cell death process in MND is relatively selective for upper motor neurones, a proportion of which are represented by Betz cells in the fifth layer of the motor cortex, and for lower motor neurones in the ventral horn of the spinal cord and brainstem. Motor neurones innervating the extraocular muscles, and those in Onuf's nucleus in the sacral spinal cord innervating the pelvic floor muscles, tend to be spared, which explains the preservation of eye movements and sphincter control in MND patients (Mannen et al., 1977). However, the selective vulnerability of motor neurones is relative, and there is increasing evidence from pathological (Ince et al., 1996; Iwanaga et al., 1997; Williams et al., 1995) and clinical (Chari et al., 1996; Kew et al., 1993; Subramaniam et al., 1990) studies that extramotor-system involvement commonly occurs and that MND is in fact a multisystem disorder in which the most severe damage affects the motor system. Experience from countries where clinical practice includes the use of ventilatory support to prolong life beyond the stage of the disease when death would normally occur, has revealed very extensive multisystem pathological changes in advanced MND (Hayashi & Kato, 1989; Sasaki et al., 1992).

The degenerating motor neurones in MND are characterised by the presence of ubiquitinated inclusion bodies (Leigh et al., 1988; Lowe et al., 1988). The inclusions can be hyaline, Lewy body-like, or skein-like (Fig. 46.1a,b). In most circumstances the major protein constituent of the fibrils comprising these inclusions is unknown, although the most promising candidates are neurofilament epitopes. In some cases of SOD1-related familial MND, dramatic hyaline conglomerate inclusions have been observed, which demonstrate intense immunoreactivity for both phosphorylated and non-phosphorylated neurofilament epitopes (Ince et al., 1998) (Fig. 46.1c).

Death of lower motor neurones denervates muscle fibres, which can, in time, be reinnervated by collateral sprouts from the axons of surviving motor neurones. In the earlier stages of the disease this reinnervation compensates for the progressive loss of motor neurones. Later in the disease, the extent of motor neurone loss is such that the few surviving neurones are incapable of reinnervating the very large number of denervated muscle fibres. Thus, the rate of clinical progression of weakness in MND is determined not only by the rate of neuronal degeneration, but also by the effectiveness of collateral reinnervation.

At autopsy, gross examination can reveal atrophy of the precentral gyrus of the cerebrum, thin hypoglossal nerves, and atrophied ventral roots emanating from the spinal cord. There can be shrinkage and sclerosis of the anterolateral tracts of the spinal cord.

Histologically, there is extensive neuronal loss with a degree of reactive gliosis in the ventral horns of the spinal cord and in some of the cranial nerve nuclei. The pathological changes are usually most pronounced in the cervical enlargement and in the X, XI, and XII cranial nerve nuclei. There can be discernible depletion of Betz cells in layer V of the motor cortex.

Demyelination and axonal loss can be traced in the crossed and uncrossed corticospinal tracts. The anterolateral pathways of the spinal cord often show reduction in staining for myelin, in contrast to the usually preserved posterior columns (Fig. 46.2). However, pathological changes can be observed in the posterior column sensory pathways and in the ascending spinocerebellar tracts in some cases.

Histological studies of muscle in MND have revealed the features of fatty infiltration of muscle (Lawyer & Netsky, 1953), and the features of denervation atrophy, with groups of angular atrophic muscle fibres. Axonal sprouting has been demonstrated from residual intramuscular nerve fibres, and increased segmentation and volume of the motor end-plate has been reported (Bjornskov et al., 1975). Enzyme histochemistry shows muscle fibre type grouping (Hughes, 1982).

CLINICAL FEATURES AT DIAGNOSIS

Upper limb symptoms are the presenting feature in 40–50% of patients, lower limb symptoms in approximately 25–40%, and bulbar symptoms in 20–30% (Swash & Schwartz, 1995). Motor weakness in the absence of sensory loss is the most common presenting feature, although occasionally the first complaint can be of muscle cramps, fasciculations, or wasting. These early symptoms are usually asymmetrical and frequently involve

(a)

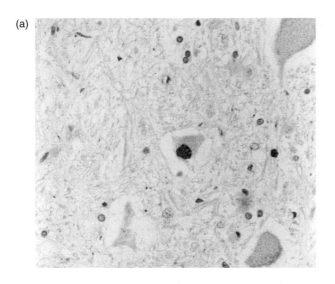

(b)

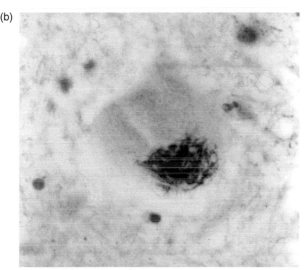

(c)

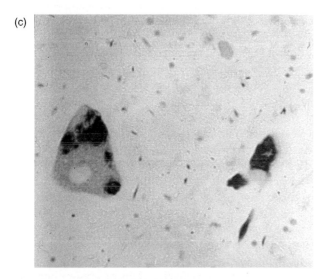

Figure 46.1. Ubiquitinated inclusions in surviving motor neurones in MND. **(a)** Hyaline inclusion. **(b)** Skein-like inclusion. **(c)** Hyaline conglomerate inclusions showing positive neurofilament immunoreactivity in case of familial MND with an I113T SOD1 mutation.

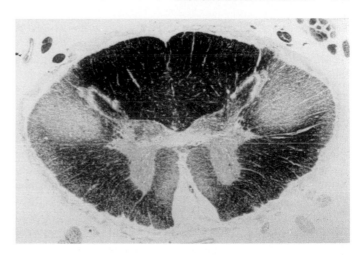

Figure 46.2. Spinal cord from a case of MND, showing marked depletion of motor neurones from the ventral horn, and loss of myelin staining in the lateral and anterior corticospinal pathways.

only one limb. Weight loss, paraesthesia, or breathlessness are uncommon presenting complaints. Where upper motor neurone involvement is prominent, the presenting complaints can be of stiffness, spasticity or ankle clonus.

Limb weakness. In the upper limbs there is often a characteristic pattern of muscle involvement. Distally in the upper limb, weakness and wasting tends to most prominently affect the thenar muscles, interossei, and wrist and finger extensors, with relative sparing of the wrist and finger flexors. A frequent early symptom is of difficulty in manipulating objects with the fingers of one hand and activities such as writing, turning keys, or unscrewing tops from jars can prove difficult. More proximally, the biceps, deltoid, and infraspinatus tend to be affected first, with relative sparing of triceps. In the lower extremities weakness frequently initially involves hip flexion and ankle dorsiflexion. Plantar flexion and the quadriceps muscles are often relatively spared. Frequent early symptoms are of dragging of one leg, unilateral foot drop, or simply of a tendency to trip.

Fasciculation. Fasciculations are fine, rapid twitching movements of muscle due to spontaneous contractions of the fibres belonging to a single motor unit. The pathogenesis of this phenomenon remains uncertain. In general, the larger the muscle, the larger the size of the fasciculations, and they tend to be most readily observed in the bulky proximal limb musculature. Patients are often aware of fasciculations, but do not usually find them painful or distressing.

Cramps. Muscle cramp is an abrupt, involuntary, and painful shortening of muscle, which is accompanied by a visible or palpable knotting of the muscle, relieved by massage or stretching. Muscle cramp is a frequent complaint and is often observed during the clinical examination when muscle power is being assessed. Cramps can predate the onset of other symptoms in MND by several years (Fleet & Watson, 1986). Cramps are most commonly experienced in the legs, but the hands, proximal upper limb muscles, neck, jaw, abdomen, chest, and even the tongue can also be involved. The cause of cramp in MND is not well understood.

Fatiguability. The neuromuscular junctions in muscles undergoing denervation and reinnervation are electrophysiologically unstable, which can cause fatigue on repetitive muscle contraction. Fatiguability is a common symptom in MND and can occasionally be sufficiently prominent to cause confusion with myasthenia gravis. The fatigue will often relate to specific symptoms, for example increasing dysarthria at the end of the day or after talking for a period, or decreased ability to walk more than a certain distance without tiring. Fatigue can often be demonstrated electrophysiologically in MND, using repetitive stimulation.

Bulbar dysfunction. The first sign of bulbar involvement is usually a problem of articulation due to impairment of tongue movement. Initial complaints include an inability to shout or sing, a weakening of the voice, or slurring of speech. Paresis of the vocal cords can result in hoarseness. Weakness of the palate allows air to escape into the nose, which imparts a nasal quality to the voice. Spasticity of the bulbar muscles lends an effortful, tight, strangled quality to the speech and difficulty with repetitive movements of the lips, tongue, and pharynx. Progression to complete anarthria is common.

Dysphagia is often noticed once dysarthria becomes significant. Manipulating food inside the mouth becomes difficult because of tongue weakness. Liquid can regurgitate into the nose because of nasopharyngeal incompetence. Weakness and incoordination of swallowing movements can trigger coughing. When the cough reflex is impaired because of accompanying weakness of the pharyngolaryngeal and respiratory muscles, aspiration into the airway can occur.

Patients with bulbar MND frequently complain of drooling of saliva, which is a cause of considerable distress and social embarrassment. This problem results from reduction in spontaneous automatic swallowing, which normally clears excessive saliva from the mouth.

Facial weakness, with especially involving of orbicularis oculi and orbicularis oris, can be present as an early feature. Weakness of the muscles controlling jaw movements can develop later in the course of the disease.

Patients with upper motor neurone bulbar features can develop emotional lability, with inappropriate crying or laughter. This is due to bilateral damage of the corticobulbar tracts connecting to the bulbar nuclei.

Examination of the patient with bulbar dysfunction will often reveal a combination of upper and lower motor neurone signs. Facial weakness and reduced voluntary movement of the palate can be apparent. The tongue often shows fasciculation, wasting, and bilateral weakness, together with spasticity. The jaw jerk is usually pathologically brisk.

Tone and reflex abnormalities. Some evidence of upper motor neurone involvement is the rule in the most common ALS variant of MND. Often, upper motor neurone abnormalities are not as functionally significant as the accompanying lower motor neurone features. The tendon reflexes are frequently brisk in the presence of significant muscle atrophy. Less often, tone can be markedly increased and severe spasticity can be the major cause of disability in occasional patients. Extensor plantar reflexes might be present, although this sign can be less common in MND than in other diseases affecting the pyramidal tracts.

Neck weakness. Weakness of the neck extensor muscles can result in a tendency of the head to fall forwards. In more advanced disease, the head can adopt a completely flexed posture, resulting in limitation of the field of vision, as well as interference with feeding and respiratory function.

Respiratory symptoms. Many patients with MND have a degree of impairment of respiratory function at the time of presentation, although this is seldom symptomatic. Later in the course of the disease, exertional dyspnoea might be reported. In some patients with MND, diaphragmatic weakness is a relatively early feature, resulting in symptomatic breathlessness in the supine position. On rare occasions, patients present with impending respiratory failure (Nightingale et al., 1982). As the first manifestation of MND, this symptom is associated with a very grave prognosis. Some patients require immediate respiratory support in an intensive care unit at the time of presentation, and this can result in some delay in reaching the correct diagnosis.

Weight loss. Progressive muscle wasting and reduced caloric intake due to dysphagia or loss of appetite can cause progressive weight loss in patients with MND. Occasionally, weight loss is far more profound than expected. This phenomenon has been called ALS cachexia, and is associated with a poor prognosis.

UNCOMMON MANIFESTATIONS OF MND

Dementia. The traditional view of MND is that cognitive function remains unaffected. However, it has been estimated that dementia, typically of frontal lobe type, occurs in approximately 3% of patients and this can occasionally be the presenting feature of the disease (Hudson, 1981). Reports on MND patients with overt dementia suggest a characteristic pattern of cognitive dysfunction, with marked attention deficits, particularly on tasks requiring sustained effort or the ability to shift from one line of thinking to another. Confrontation naming, verbal fluency, insight, and judgement are also impaired. In contrast, verbal and non-verbal memory and spatial abilities are usually well preserved (Neary et al., 1990; Peavy et al., 1992). Detailed neuropsychological testing in MND patients without overt dementia has shown that a mild degree of cognitive disturbance is more common than previously recognised (Chari et al., 1996).

Sensory impairment. Although sensory abnormalities are not normally considered part of the clinical syndrome of MND, patients might complain of sensory symptoms, particularly early in the disease. However, objective signs of sensory impairment on examination are virtually never found. Detailed morphological studies of cutaneous sensory nerves and dorsal root ganglia, as well as electrophysiological assessment and quantitative sensory testing, have shown that subclinical involvement of the sensory system is common in MND (Jamal et al., 1985; Subramanium & Yiannikas, 1990).

Autonomic function is generally normal in MND, at least to clinical examination. Patients with MND do not commonly develop pressure ulcers, even with periods of prolonged bed rest in the terminal stages of the disease. This feature is consistent with sparing of sensation and autonomic regulation of skin blood flow.

As a clinical rule, even the totally paralysed and bedfast patient retains bowel and bladder control and ocular movements, unless the course of the disease is prolonged by ventilatory support measures. However, detailed analysis of bladder function (Hattori, 1984) and ocular motility (Mitsumoto, 1988) can reveal subtle subclinical abnormalities in MND patients.

DIAGNOSIS AND INVESTIGATION

The diagnosis of MND is essentially clinical, as there is no specific diagnostic test. The major features supporting the diagnosis are the presence of upper and lower motor neurone signs in a distribution extending beyond a discrete spinal level or peripheral nerve, usually with spontaneous fasciculation, and without sensory abnormalities. A series of investigations might be necessary to allow the confident exclusion of other diagnoses; neurophysiological assessment is particularly useful. Neurophysiological evidence of denervation and reinnervation in muscles of at least two limbs, not corresponding to a single nerve root or peripheral nerve distribution, is strongly suggestive of a diagnosis of MND. Motor conduction is normal or slightly slowed, with no evidence of conduction block, and sensory conduction velocities are normal. Neuroimaging with magnetic resonance imaging (MRI) or computerised tomography (CT) might be necessary to exclude other intracranial or spinal disorders. Most biochemical investigations are normal in patients with MND. The blood creatine kinase level may be elevated 2–3-fold in approximately 50% of patients (Williams & Bruford, 1970). A minor elevation of CSF protein may be found. Approximately 5% of MND patients have an IgG or IgM paraprotein band. The paraprotein is usually present at a low concentration and no causal association with motor neurone dysfunction has been demonstrated to date. Oligoclonal bands are also occasionally noted in the CSF of patients with MND and were found in 12% of patients in one series (Younger et al., 1990).

The major conditions to be considered in the differential diagnosis of MND are listed in Table 46.3.

PROGRESSION OF DISABILITY AND PROGNOSIS

Although the disability due to weakness is often trivial in the early stages of the disease, relentless progression of limb and bulbar weakness is the rule, ultimately producing extreme disability. Temporary stabilisation sometimes occurs. Occasional cases have been described where the disease appears to remit (Tucker et al., 1991), but this is so rare that it should not be

Table 46.3. Differential diagnosis of MND

Benign cramp/fasciculation syndrome
Degenerative spinal disease—radiculomyelopathy
Motor neuropathies, e.g. multifocal motor neuropathy with conduction block
Myasthenia gravis
Myopathies, e.g. inclusion body myopathy
Multifocal cerebrovascular disease
Post-polio syndrome
Spinal muscular atrophy
Kennedy's disease (X-linked bulbospinal neuronopathy)
Syringomyelia/syringobulbia
Endocrine disease, e.g. hyperthyroidism, hyperparathyroidism
Heavy metal intoxication

proposed as a likely prospect when the diagnosis of MND is made. Limb weakness, even if it starts in a single limb, usually progresses to involve all four limbs. Early involvement of paravertebral muscles is rare but, as the disease progresses, head droop into flexion can interfere with vision, feeding, and breathing. Weakness of trunk muscles can prevent voluntary turning in bed. Significant diaphragmatic weakness usually occurs in the wake of considerable bulbar or limb muscle weakness. Bulbar symptoms eventually develop in approximately 80% of patients with MND. Speech difficulties can progress to anarthria. Communication difficulties can be compounded by the loss of facial expression due to facial muscle weakness and loss of upper limb function causing difficulty in writing and typing. Dysphagia can also progress to a severe level, with the potential complications of dehydration, malnutrition and aspiration pneumonia.

Approximately 50% of patients with MND die within 3–4 years of the onset of symptoms, 20% live for 5 years, 10% live for 10 years, and a few individuals live for as long as 20 years (Mulder, 1982). Life expectancy is shorter in older individuals and in those whose initial symptoms involve bulbar or respiratory muscles. In contrast, patients who have onset of disease at a young age, or where the disease involves exclusively the upper motor neurones (PLS) or lower motor neurones (PMA), have a better prognosis (Mortara et al., 1984; Younger et al., 1988). The cause of death in MND is usually respiratory failure, which can be accompanied by bronchopneumonia. Occasionally, patients die as a result of trauma following falls.

REHABILITATIVE MANAGEMENT

Giving the diagnosis

Making the diagnosis of MND is relatively straightforward in 80% of cases and an experienced neurologist can often make the diagnosis within a few minutes of meeting the patient. In about 10% of individuals the diagnosis is more difficult and in 10% it might not be possible to make the diagnosis until several months have elapsed. Difficulties can occur particularly when the symptoms and signs are initially relatively localised or when only upper or lower motor neurone signs are present.

Patients and their families have to bear a period of great anxiety while the cause of the progressive muscle weakness is being investigated. This can be one of the most distressing times in the whole course of the disease, when symptoms worsen, with no adequate explanation. Telling patients and family members of the diagnosis of MND, although painful for all concerned, rids the afflicted families of the anguish of uncertainty. The experience of many physicians, and of sufferers (Carus, 1980), suggests that the great majority of sufferers wish to have accurate information about the diagnosis and its implications as soon as a firm diagnosis has been made. As in the case of other fatal diseases, to be informed about the illness does not seem to be associated with increased emotional distress in the long term but, on the contrary, facilitates adjustment to the illness. Only by knowing what lies ahead can the individual make decisions regarding home, family, money, work, and other outstanding commitments.

Patients and their relatives can find it difficult to assimilate the profound implications of a diagnosis of MND when they are first told about the condition, particularly if there is little or no associated disability at this time. Opportunity should be given for staged discussion of the implications of the disease, guided by the particular evolution of the disease course in a given individual.

The way the diagnosis is given sets the whole tone for ongoing clinical care. It is clear that, in the past, families have often been unhappy with the communication of the diagnosis. Reported problems have included: no diagnosis was given or a euphemistic term was employed; the diagnosis was given in a brusque, uncaring fashion; the diagnosis was given with the implication that "nothing could be done"; no follow-up care plan was arranged and, initially, families had to cope alone following diagnosis; insufficient time was given to answer questions and concerns.

In giving the diagnosis of MND, the physician must appreciate the impact of giving the bad news and the patient's emotional reactions, and must overcome the fear of being blamed for the message, as well as the sense of failure for not being able to improve the situation. There is a paucity of detailed information about the best way of giving the diagnosis in MND. However, guidelines have emerged to facilitate breaking bad news to patients and their families facing other serious illnesses (Garg et al., 1997; Meininger, 1993; Ptacek & Eberhardt, 1996).

The approach used personally by the author encompasses these principles and appears to work well in practice, although it has not been audited formally. The diagnosis is usually explained at the time of admission to hospital for diagnostic investigations. The setting chosen is a quiet room, free from interruptions, with the patient and whichever family members the patient would like to be present. Initial discussion uncovers what the patient knows or suspects about the medical problem and also what the patient wants to know. The results of the investigations that indicate damage to the motor neurones and the diagnosis of motor neurone disease are then explained. A brief description is then given of the role of motor neurones and the reason for the symptoms, using clear language understandable to a lay person. This is followed by a discussion, aligned to the individual's level of comprehension, about current understanding of the causes of motor neurone damage. Some information about what can be expected during the course of the disease is then conveyed, attempting to be honest without destroying hope. It is important that the patient and the family understand that the symptoms will progress with time, that there is no cure for the illness, and no treatment that will allow recovery of existing symptoms. However, this "negative" information is balanced by more positive information including: (1) the emphasis that many aspects of neurological function, including vision, hearing, intellect, sensation, and bowel and bladder control will remain intact; (2) that the rate of progression of symptoms is very variable and that some patients have a slowly progressive course with survival for years; (3) that treatments and aids and appliances can help certain symptoms; (4) that there is a great deal of research investigating mechanisms of motor neurone injury and that there are now at least some prospects for therapies to help to slow disease progression; and (5) that medical care will continue and practical help will be available throughout the illness. A plan for follow-up care and support is then outlined. It is important to make a professional and personal commitment to the ongoing care of the patient at this time, and to make clear this commitment to the patient and the family. Any practical measures that might be helpful to the patient are then implemented, for example, the introduction of symptomatic therapies or input from paramedical professionals. The opportunity is then given to the family for further questions and discussion. Following this discussion with the physician, a specialist MND nurse will visit the patient 30–60 minutes later for further discussion, if required. A postdiagnosis visit or telephone contact is made by the specialist nurse 2 weeks after hospital discharge and the first out-patient clinic visit is arranged for 4 weeks.

Social and financial aspects

Employment. So long as work is enjoyed, it should be continued. However, difficulties in travelling, weakness, fatigue, stumbling, loss of manual skills, dysarthria, and dysphonia can all be impediments to work. Advice from the physician is needed about what should be said to employers, when it is best said, and how to plan for finishing work and receiving a pension. Advice from the Disability Services Team at the Department of Employment will bring the assistance of a Disability Employment Advisor both to the worker and to the employer. Financial help might be given towards the higher costs of journeys to and from work. Aids, such as computers or electrically powered wheelchairs can be provided to enable disabled people to continue working. Financial assistance can be provided for the employer to obtain equipment and carry out structural alterations to the workplace. The employer might agree to a flexible working day, to shorter working hours, or to a change from manual to sedentary work. The patient's experience might make it possible to move to new roles in supervision, training or consultancy, or to work from home.

Income and benefits. It is essential to ensure that the patient and his or her family receive all the financial allowances to which they are entitled by the state. When appropriate, the patient should be seen by a hospital- or community-based social worker so that he or she can be registered with the local Social Services department and the provision of home care assistants, meals-on-wheels, day centre attendance, and play schemes for dependent children can be arranged as soon as the need arises.

Those receiving Income Support, and their dependants, are eligible for certain health benefits including free National Health Service prescriptions and dental treatment, as well as reimbursement of travel costs to hospital. Fact sheets covering all these benefits are available from local Benefits Agency (Social Security) Offices and Post Offices.

Help from voluntary organisations. In addition to statutory benefits, charities can be asked to consider helping with unexpected expenses or funding aids to improve communication or mobility. Professional and trade benevolent funds, ex-service organisations, and the Motor Neurone Disease Organisation can all be approached for such support.

The Motor Neurone Disease Association (MNDA). The association is a registered charity, founded in 1979. The aims are first to further research into both the cause and management of MND; second to provide advice, support, information, and equipment that is not available through statutory services to sufferers and their carers, and third to provide links between families coping with the effects of MND, to provide information on research progress and to bring MND to public attention. The association employs 12 regional care advisors, who each work with a number of volunteer visitors and act as facilitators to ensure that MND patients receive the attention they need. More recently, the MNDA has helped to establish a number of specialist clinics for MND within Care and Research Centres, set up in several regions in England and Wales.

Home alterations. As the disease progresses, consideration will need to be given to the necessity of altering the MND patient's home, for example to allow access and space for a wheelchair and to circumvent problems with stairs or the use of bathroom facilities. Sometimes, moving to a ground-floor flat or bungalow accommodation is the most feasible option. Those offering advice on housing or home alterations must be familiar with the patient's home and have some notion of the likely course and duration of the disease as it affects the particular individual. In the UK, assessment is carried out by a Social-Services-based occupational therapist, and a means-tested Disabled Facilities Grant is available for housing alterations and improvements. These can include improved means of access, adaptations to kitchens and bathrooms, and equipment such as lifts, floor-mounted bathroom hoists, and electric hoists with ceiling tracking. Further information on the grants, the criteria for qualification, and how to apply can be obtained from the local district council offices.

The NHS can supply environmental control systems for patients with MND. This equipment can provide call, alarm intercommunication, and release of the front door lock; a telephone with memory-stored numbers; and control of up to five 13 amp sockets. Steeper's environmental control fulfills the needs of most MND patients. The Possum 2000PSU6 has the additional facilities of electronic typewriter, word processor, and computer, if required. Applications are made to a designated team that includes a medical assessor and an occupational therapist. It is often possible to obtain environmental control equipment as a priority for patients with MND and keep the delay for provision short. It is increasingly feasible to supply electronic environmental control systems that also serve as communication aids.

Using a car. As soon as the person with MND is aware of disability that will persist, he or she is obliged to notify the Driver and Vehicle Licensing Centre (DVLA). With medical evidence of fitness to continue driving, the licence will be renewed for a limited period. Drivers with MND can benefit from joining one of the organisations for disabled motorists. There are several regional mobility centres in the UK offering advice and information on the choices of car, accessories, and conversions, as well as functional assessment, for disabled drivers.

The Orange Badge scheme grants parking concessions to disabled drivers and passengers. Cars displaying an orange badge can park free and without limit at on-street meters and in areas where waiting is limited. To qualify for an orange badge, a person must receive Mobility Allowance or have very considerable difficulty in walking. Medical evidence might be required in support of the application to the local Social Services department.

Summoning help. A telephone is a vital line of communication in emergencies and for social contact. By dialling 100 and asking for Freephone Telephone Sales, advice can be obtained about the different telephone systems that can be hired or bought. Most local authorities operate Community Alarm or Careline services. The patient wears a portable pendant and the main unit replaces the current telephone.

Professional resources and technologies

There is currently much debate within the UK, Europe, and the US about standards of care and management guidelines, as well as quality of life issues for patients with MND. The management of MND poses considerable ethical, logistical, and educational problems (Carey, 1986). Ethical issues are involved in aspects of management including the use of artificial methods of feeding, ventilatory support, the use of drugs such as riluzole, which has a modest effect in prolonging survival in MND, and the use of narcotic drugs in the terminal phase of the disease. The logistical and educational problems arise from the relative rarity of MND and the fact that many health-care professionals have little experience in dealing with the rapidly progressive weakness and bulbar and respiratory failure that can occur during the course of the disease. Patients and their relatives should be able to obtain efficient professional help throughout the course of the disease from diagnosis to death. A possible solution is to concentrate the care of MND patients in specialist centres, with the staff of these centres taking on the role of helping to educate other medical and paramedical staff in the care of patients.

The multidisciplinary team. The coordinated action of multiple health-care professionals can lessen the difficulties experienced by patients with MND and by their carers and families. Conversely, the uncoordinated activities of different specialists can fragment the delivery of care and bring anxiety and confusion. The care plan should be coordinated by the physician, often the neurologist, who can ensure the timely delivery of services as appropriate. The personal view of the author is that patients with MND should remain under the care of a physician with neurological expertise in partnership with the general practitioner. The main roles of the neurologist in follow-up care are:

1. To manage symptomatic therapy.
2. To coordinate paramedical services and the provision of aids and appliances quickly once the patient has need of them. The timing of discussion and the provision of these measures is very important—too early can be as bad for the morale of the patient as too late.
3. To educate and counsel patients and their families as appropriate for the stage of the disease. This is particularly important in MND, where the patient might not have time to adapt to one level of disability before the condition worsens.
4. To offer patients the opportunity to participate in therapeutic trials or clinical research projects where possible.

There is a growing tendency in the UK for patients with MND to be managed in specialist clinics, with input from nursing staff with specialist training. Other paramedical staff whose expertise can be of great value in the care of MND patients include the physiotherapist, the occupational therapist, the speech therapist, the dietician, the social worker and the orthotist.

Nursing care. The nurse plays a very important role in giving comfort, emotional support, and practical assistance to patients with MND. In MND patients with bulbar dysfunction, careful attention should be paid to oral hygiene. Weakness of the muscles of the tongue and face impedes the clearing of particles of food from around the teeth and gums. The saliva can change in consistency and gingivitis, candidiasis, and foetor oris can occur. Nursing advice should be given on the cleaning of the teeth and mouth after every meal. Nursing input might also be required to advise on skin care, including gastrostomy sites, constipation, and the lifting and handling of the patient with MND.

In the Newcastle Motor Neurone Disease Care and Research Centre, the specialist nurse also contributes to the care of MND patients and their families in the following ways:

1. The provision of extra contact time and support around the time of diagnosis.
2. The servicing of a helpline for patients, families, and other health-care professionals. Many of the queries that come through the helpline can be dealt with effectively by the specialist nurse, with the opportunity for support and input from medical staff when necessary.

3. Liaison with health-care personnel in the community to facilitate the delivery of community support services and enhance the flexibility of care.
4. The provision of improved support at crisis times and for patients whose level of disability prevents attendance at the hospital clinic. A combination of telephone contact, domiciliary visits, and encouraging families to make use of the helpline ensures the ongoing provision of care.
5. Liaison with, and the provision of advice to, hospice and residential nursing home staff.
6. The education of both hospital-based and community nursing staff about specific aspects of the care of MND patients.

Physiotherapy. The physiotherapist can be called upon to advise about exercise, correction of posture, prevention of contractures and stiffness of joints (particularly the shoulders and hands), preservation of functional independence, mobility aids, coping with falling, repiratory care and the management of choking, and lifting and handling.

A drooping head and flexed trunk are common problems in MND due to weakness of the extensor muscles of the neck and spine. The physiotherapist can provide advice on the provision of collars or head supports (Fig. 46.3). The physiotherapist can teach carers passive exercises to prevent stiffness and pain in joints. These exercises should become part of the daily routine at home. Falls are common with the onset of lower limb weakness and can be particularly hazardous when upper limb weakness prevents the arms being used to break the fall. A foot-drop splint can reduce the tendency to trip in the presence of ankle dorsiflexion weakness. As the disease advances, a succession of aids might be required including a walking stick, elbow crutches, a walking-frame, and eventually a wheelchair. Advice might also be required on the best way of tackling the stairs. A gentle exercise regime can be taught to the patient with the aim of preserving limb and respiratory function, encouraging mobility and preventing contractures.

In the later stages of the disease the physiotherapist can provide advice on transferring, positioning in bed and chair, elevation to reduce distal oedema in paralysed limbs, and on the management of coughing and breathing difficulties. A portable suction machine (Fig. 46.4) and Yankauer catheter can be useful in clearing secretions from the mouth and pharynx. The patient can be shown breathing exercises to maintain maximal ventilation. Carers can be taught how to achieve postural drainage of secretions from the chest and manoeuvres to assist coughing (Fig. 46.5).

Occupational therapy. The hospital-based occupational therapist, attached to a specialist MND centre, can contribute advice and expertise regarding the use of specific items of equipment, for example mobile arm supports (Fig. 46.6). The community occupational therapist forms a personal link between the family, health services, the local authority, and the Disablement Resettlement Officer. The occupational therapist is informed about housing, aids, and the equipment required to

(a)

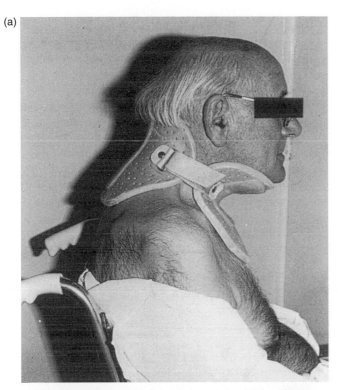

(b)

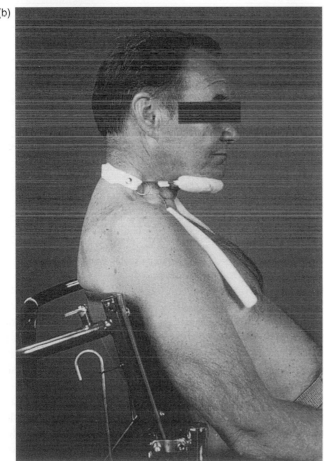

Figure 46.3. Head supports that can be useful in MND. **(a)** Reinforced plastazote head support. **(b)** Spring-steel head support.

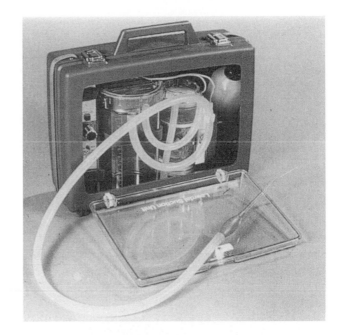

Figure 46.4. Portable suction machine.

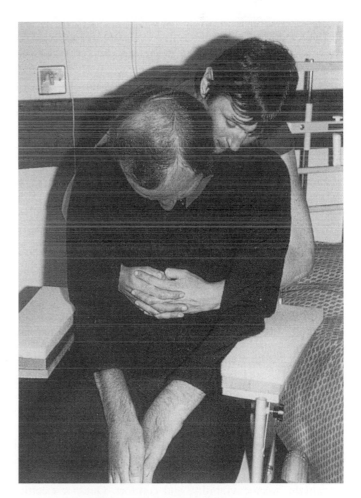

Figure 46.5. Assistance with coughing.

(a)

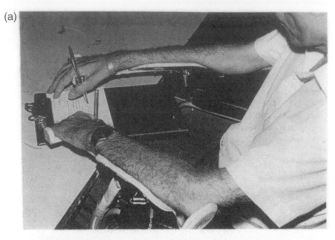

(b)

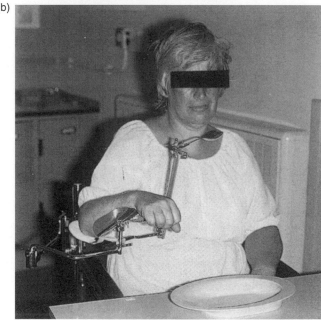

Figure 46.6. **(a)** Mobile arm support. **(b)** Augmented mobile arm support.

Table 46.4. Aids and appliances commonly required by patients with MND

Upper limb
Writing implements
Adapted cutlery
Devices to aid activities, e.g. key turning, tap turning, kettle lifting
Mobile arm supports:
    wheelchair attached
    free standing
    table attached
Other devices to help feeding, e.g. Neater-eater system
Page turner
Splints

Lower limb
Ankle–foot orthosis
Walking aids:
    walking stick
    elbow crutches
    walking frame
Wheelchairs:
    hand propelled
    electrically powered
Rails
Ramps

Bulbar
Communication aids
Suction machine
Blender
Flexiflow pump for enteral feeding

Other
Hoists/slings
Stair-lift/through floor lift
Bath aids, e.g. Manga bath lift
Transfer boards
Back-rest
Adjustable bed/bed elevator
Environmental controls:
    possum
    steeper
Riser–recliner chair
Urinal bottle
Toilet adaptation with washing/drying facility
Commode
Collars
Pressure care:
    Spenco
    Roho cushions/mattresses
    Quatro
    Pegasus
Personal alarm system

preserve independence and make the task of caring easier for others. The therapist should visit regularly, alert to changing requirements as the patient's condition deteriorates. A flexible system for supply of equipment can be established for the immediate and short-term loan of a stock of aids and appliances which may be required. Table 46.4 lists aids and appliances that are commonly needed during the course of MND.

Wheelchairs. In the UK, wheelchairs can be obtained in two ways: either loaned and maintained free within the NHS, or bought privately. A wide range of wheelchairs, cushions, seating, accessories and adaptations is available within the NHS. The most suitable equipment is selected by a rehabilitation engineer and occupational therapist within the district or regional wheelchair service. The private purchase of a wheelchair allows an extended personal choice in design quality, performance, low weight, manoeuvrability, and comfort. Outdoor electrically powered wheelchairs, controlled by the user, can only be

bought privately or through Motability, a voluntary organisation that helps disabled people to use their Mobility allowance to obtain an electric wheelchair or car. Various types of pressure-distributing cushions are available for use with a wheelchair for comfort, relief of pressure, postural support, hygiene, and ventilation. The choice most suitable for the individual patient is made by trial and error.

Rehabilitation engineering. Engineers produce all the aids that are manufactured commercially: hand-propelled and electrically powered wheelchairs, hoists, lifts and stair riders, individually made supporting seats, and electronic aids for communication and environmental control. Functional orthoses can be supplied to counter weakness and increase the range of controlled movement. The rehabilitation engineer can adapt existing aids, instal equipment and instruct in its use and make minor alterations to the patients' homes.

Technical Equipment for Disabled People is a voluntary organisation with over 100 branches across the country. It specialises in designing, manufacturing, and supplying equipment to satisfy a particular need. Each branch attracts the voluntary services of engineers and industrial designers to cooperate with the medical and social services.

Speech therapy.   The majority of patients with MND experience dysphagia, drooling, choking, dysarthria, and failure of oral communication during the course of the disease. For the management of dysphagia, the speech therapist can provide advice on swallowing technique and food consistency. Sucking ice cubes before meals and iced drinks during meals can reduce the tone of spastic muscles, with improvement in the coordination of the swallowing reflex. Smooth food with an even texture tends to be easiest for the patient to swallow. A thickening agent can facilitate the swallowing of liquids. Foods containing lumps or with a crumbly or stringy texture can precipitate coughing spells. Certain food items with sharp or strong flavours, for example citrus fruits, spices, or alcoholic spirits are sometimes poorly tolerated by MND patients with bulbar dysfunction.

The speech therapist can also provide useful information to the dysarthric patient, to maximise the clarity of speech. Specific exercises can be useful to improve tongue placement and precision of lip movements. Other strategies include slowing the rate of speech, using key words only, and increased pausing. Some patients find that sucking ice cubes can improve the quality of speech. The individual with mainly upper motor neurone bulbar dysfunction should relax to reduce spasm, whereas the individual with flaccid dysarthria might gain from speaking forcefully.

Communication aids.   The interests of the principal listener should be considered, especially if there is visual or hearing impairment. Many patients will initially complement speech by writing, for as long as this is possible. When manual dexterity declines, a direct select aid such as the Canon Communicator or the Memowriter (Fig. 46.7a) can be used. A Lightwriter is another useful communication aid, and has the advantage that the keys are larger and more widely spaced (Fig. 46.7b). Communicators that incorporate voice synthesisers are also available. When weakness is severe, a scanning aid can be introduced in which each letter is identified by a cursor light that can be stopped by a switch. A keyboard head pointer, any keyboard emulator, or a mouse can be used to provide direct access to a computer. The range of available computers, computer software, and environmental controls is being extended very rapidly (Cochrane, 1990).

Dietetics.   The dietitian will be called upon to provide advice to achieve the best possible nutritional status for the patient. In the early stages of bulbar dysfunction, advice about the use of dietary items to maximise energy and protein intake can be useful. Later, nutritional supplements of liquid or "pudding" consistency can be employed. A variety of brands are available in fruit, sweet, and savoury flavours. The patient can be introduced

(a)

(b)

Figure 46.7. Communication aids that can be useful for MND patients with significant dysarthria. (**a**) Memowriter. (**b**) Lightwriter.

to a variety of different supplements so that the most palatable brand can be chosen. In patients who eventually require enteral feeding via a gastrostomy or nasogastric tube, the dietitian will advise on the staged introduction and maintenance of adequate nutritional and fluid intake. Nutrition in liquid form can be given intermittently as bolus feeding with a syringe, or over a more continuous period via a flexiflow pump. The energy requirement is calculated by the Harris–Benedict equation, which takes into account the individual's height, weight, and level of activity.

Equipment to facilitate eating and drinking.   People want to feed themselves, not to be fed. Various devices can help to preserve independence in feeding. Crockery can be stabilised on Dycem non-slip mats. A plate guard will save "chasing" food around the plate. The handles of cutlery can be enlarged, angled, or shaped. The overall shaped dishes of Manoy have a concave "wall" at one end for scooping food on to a spoon. Flexible straws can be bent to any angle to facilitate drinking, and when

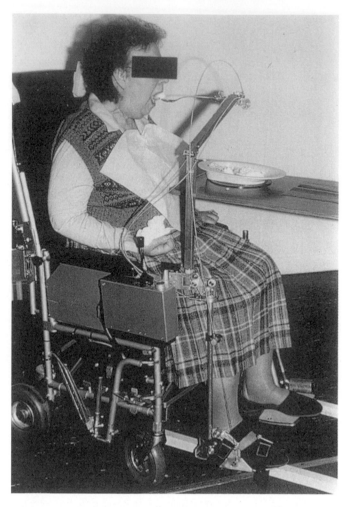

Figure 46.8. Magpie, a foot-operated feeding device.

Table 46.5. Symptoms that can require medical intervention in MND

Symptom	Therapies
Cramp	Quinine sulphate (baclofen, diazepam, phenytoin)
Fatigue	Occasionally pyridostigmine
Spasticity	Baclofen, diazepam, tizanidine
Dysphagia	Nutritional supplements, liquid thickeners, PEG
Drooling	Hyoscine patches, atropine, amitriptyline, suction machine, parotid gland irradiation
Constipation	Ispaghula, methyl cellulose, lactulose, glycerol suppositories
Emotional lability	Amitriptyline, imipramine (L-dopa preparations)
Depression	Tricyclic agents or serotonin reuptake inhibitors
Insomnia	Address underlying cause, fluorazepam, diphenhydramine
Pain	Address underlying cause
Dyspnoea	Antibiotics for aspiration pneumonia, chest physiotherapy, sublingual lorazepam for acute attacks of dyspnoea. Consider NIPPV if dyspnoea occurs early in the disease. Morphine for end-stage respiratory distress

sucking is feeble a Pat Saunders drinking straw with a non-return valve can be helpful.

Mobile arm supports cradle the forearm in a trough, and depression of the elbow by movements of the trunk and shoulder bring the hand to the mouth (see Fig. 46.6a,b). Modifications to the basic mobile arm support are available for those who have paralysis of the hands or loss of proximal upper limb function. When the upper limbs are paralysed but there is preservation of lower limb function, a foot-operated manipulator (Magpie) makes it possible to feed, reach, or turn a page without asking for help (Fig. 46.8). The basic concept is to translate four independent leg and foot movements to four movements of the manipulator by means of simple mechanical linkages and cables (Evans, 1985).

Controlling physical symptoms

Symptomatic therapy aimed at alleviating the distressing symptoms that often arise during the course of MND can do much to improve the quality of life for the patient. Some of the common symptoms that can require medical attention are shown in Table 46.5 and discussed in this section.

Cramps.   Painful muscle cramps are common in MND, particularly in the early stages of the disease. This symptom often responds to quinine sulphate in a dose of 200–400 mg per day. Other therapies that can be useful in alleviating cramp include phenytoin, baclofen and diazepam.

Weakness and fatigue.   Muscle weakness is the hallmark of MND and generalised weakness will eventually develop. Fatigue is a common symptom and can be sufficiently intrusive so that even slight exertion seems to cause more weakness. Several studies have shown that this is due to a failure of neuromuscular transmission or a myasthenic state, although with significant differences from myasthenia gravis. MND patients with marked fatigue can obtain temporary benefit from anticholinesterase medication such as pyridostigmine, although the beneficial effect is likely to recede within a few months. In patients with prominent involvement of the muscles of respiration, aminophylline can be used. This has been shown to strengthen the contractility of the diaphragm (Aubier et al., 1981). With the exception of these two measures, however, there is little that can be done pharmacologically to alleviate weakness in MND.

In the early stages of MND, foot-drop can impair walking balance and increase the tendency to fall, with the attendant risk of major injury. A moulded ankle–foot orthosis will alleviate this problem. Physiotherapy is important in the care of patients with MND, particularly as weakness progresses and the patient becomes unable to move the major joints (Janiszewski et al., 1983). Passive range of motion treatment should be administered several times each day to prevent the development of painful joint contractures. The shoulders and small hand joints require particular attention. Simple exercises can be learned quickly by the patient's carers. A night-time splint can be useful to prevent contractures of the wrists and fingers.

Weakness of neck extension is a common problem in MND. This results in the head falling forwards so that the chin rests on the chest. This is uncomfortable for the patient, impairs eye contact, and results in problems with eating and swallowing. A variety of supporting collars can be used to alleviate this problem, and the patient might be most comfortable seated in a chair with a reclining back. Occasionally, the best solution is a supporting band around the head, which is attached to an upright stay attached either to the patient's trunk or to the wheelchair.

Weakness of the trunk muscles can make it difficult for the patient to maintain an upright sitting posture and can impair respiratory function. Side supports or a moulded back cushion for the wheelchair might be required.

Spasticity. Spasticity can be a management problem in some cases of MND. Frequently, however, lower motor neurone features predominate and spasticity is insufficiently prominent to require therapy. The use of muscle relaxants to treat spasticity can be valuable in some patients. However, many patients are intolerant of such therapy because reduction of tone in the limbs increases the sensation of weakness and reduces mobility. If spasmolytic therapy is required, baclofen, tizanidine or a benzodiazepine such as diazepam can be used. Dantrolene, which acts peripherally by reducing the release of calcium from the sarcoplasmic reticulum during muscle contraction, can lead to profound weakness in some patients with MND and is probably best avoided (Rivera et al., 1975). Other measures, such as motor point blocks to reduce severe spasticity of the hip adductors, are rarely necessary in patients with MND.

Dysarthria. One of the most distressing consequences of MND is the progressive impairment of the ability to communicate by speech. Approximately 80% of patients will have major problems with speech during the course of MND (Saunders et al., 1981). Most patients with MND have both lower motor neurone and upper motor neurone components to their bulbar dysfunction. This results in a "mixed" dysarthria characterised by flaccid and spastic elements. The early problems involve palatal weakness, poor lip seal, and impaired tongue movement (Enderby & Langton Hewer, 1987). Later, impaired control of the vocal cords and respiratory difficulties contribute to the speech problem. Advice from a speech therapist can help to improve the clarity of the patient's speech. Decreasing the speed of speech and the use of key words and short phrases may improve intelligibility. When speech becomes unintelligible, communication aids of varying sophistication will be required, as described earlier.

Dysphagia. Dysphagia eventually becomes a problem in most patients with MND. Other factors can contribute to inadequate caloric intake, including loss of appetite and difficulties with food preparation or feeding due to upper limb weakness.

Feeding and swallowing begins with the prebuccal phase, which involves the act of getting the food or fluid into the mouth and requires correct positioning of the relevant anatomical parts, and continues with four phases of swallowing—the oral preparatory, oral, pharyngeal, and oesophageal phases (see Chapter 25). Any of these phases of swallowing can be impaired in MND. Abnormal posture or upper limb weakness can impair the prebuccal phase. Weakness of lip closure can allow oral contents to escape. Tongue weakness can result in slowness and incoordination in the passage of the bolus from mouth to pharynx. Poor elevation of the palate can cause nasal regurgitation of oral contents. Pooling of material in the vallecula

and pyriform recesses can occur. Failure or incoordination of laryngeal elevation can result in tracheal aspiration of swallowed material. Spasticity of the cricopharyngeal sphincter can hinder the entry of the food bolus into the oesophagus.

In early dysphagia, a few simple principles can be helpful to patients in coping with swallowing difficulties. Dysphagia can be increased by anxiety and social embarrassment resulting from slowness in eating, dribbling, and choking. Patients should be encouraged to eat in as relaxed and comfortable an environment as possible. Sucking ice prior to a meal can help reduce spasticity of the bulbar muscles. Attention to food consistency is important and the family should receive advice from a dietician, as described earlier. If the patient is continuing to lose weight, then nutritional supplements of liquid or semisolid consistency can be helpful. Attention should be paid to concomitant problems that might exacerbate dysphagia, e.g. loose-fitting dentures or oropharnygeal candidiasis.

More active therapeutic intervention for the dysphagia should be considered when the following problems are apparent: (1) continuing weight loss (more than 20% of the normal body weight) despite the above measures; (2) dehydration; (3) aspiration with resultant respiratory infections; or (4) oral food intake has become intolerable due to frequent choking spells. For patients with terminal disease, a fine-bore nasogastric feeding tube might be appropriate. The disadvantages are nasal and oropharyngeal irritation and, for some patients, this solution is unacceptable on aesthetic grounds. For long-term enteral feeding, percutaneous endoscopic gastrostomy (PEG) is the procedure of choice (Fig. 46.9). This is one of the major advances in symptomatic care for patients with MND. The placement of a PEG is a relatively straightforward procedure that can be performed under a local anaesthetic. The puncture site is identified through an endoscope inserted into the patient's stomach. A stab wound is then made through the abdominal wall using a large-bore needle, through which a guidewire and subsequently the feeding tube is passed into the stomach. Water can be introduced into the PEG tube after 12 hours. Thereafter, a full-strength feeding regime providing 1500–2000 calories per day can be introduced over 48 hours. Feeding can be managed by syringe boluses at normal meal times, or by continuous infusion by pump. Complications of PEG include local and peritoneal infections. However, the PEG site usually heals well and is easily maintained with minimal daily care. When the PEG tube has been in place for 3 months it can be replaced with a "button" system, which is cosmetically superior (Fig. 46.9b). The PEG procedure should not be postponed until the patient has severely compromised respiratory function. At this stage in the disease, the patient could develop respiratory failure following the procedure, resulting from basal atelectasis due to pressure of the air-inflated stomach against the weakened diaphragm.

No patient likes the idea of a PEG when the concept is first mentioned, and the procedure is best discussed in stages as the degree of dysphagia progresses. After PEG placement, many patients report great relief and increased well-being, although as yet no large scale quality of life studies have been conducted

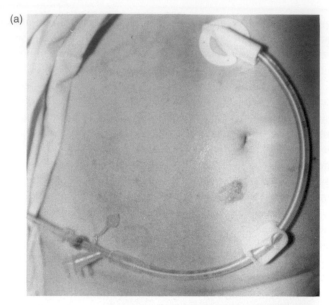

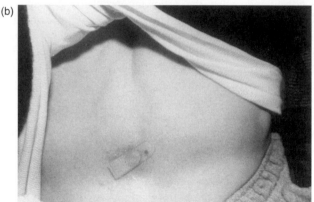

Figure 46.9. Percutaneous endoscopic gastrostomy (PEG) used for the management of dysphagia in MND. **(a)** Standard PEG tube. **(b)** Button PEG tube.

Whether early PEG placement results in increased duration of survival has not yet been convincingly demonstrated (Mazzini, 1995).

Drooling of saliva.   Drooling of saliva is one of the most distressing problems confronting a patient with MND. A normal person produces approximately 1500–2000 ml saliva per day and will swallow automatically about 600 times per day (Langton Hewer, 1995). Salivation is stimulated principally by the parasympathetic nervous system. On clinical grounds, the main factors contributing to drooling appear to be weakness of lip closure and reduction in swallowing capacity. There is no reason to suspect that excess saliva is being produced, although this question has not been carefully studied. The mainstay of therapy is the use of anticholinergic medication. The most commonly used medications are amitriptyline, atropine, and hyoscine skin patches. Other drugs that could be considered include benzhexol and propantheline. A portable suction device, which can be used by either the patient or the carer to remove pools of saliva, might be useful. Carbocisteine is recommended by some physicians to reduce the viscosity of secretions (Borascio & Volz, 1997). If the above measures do not control the problem successfully, then staged, low-dose parotid irradiation can be considered in some patients.

Choking.   Choking is a distressing accompaniment of dysphagia in bulbar MND and occurs mainly with liquids. The severity of choking depends on the amount of material entering the laryngeal inlet and the strength of the patient's cough. The patient and the carer should be given general advice regarding the types and consistency of nutritional intake, as well as instructions on how to manage a severe episode of choking. The patient's mouth should be emptied with a suction machine, if available. The patient should be encouraged to lean forwards in the chair and to breathe slowly. The carer can be taught to exert pressure on the abdomen in time with the patient's attempts at coughing. In extreme circumstances a Heimlich manoeuvre will be required. Frequent choking episodes can indicate the need to consider cessation of oral feeding.

Constipation.   Constipation can be a major and distressing problem in MND. Contributory factors include inability to adequately perform a Valsalva manoeuvre due to weakness of the abdominal muscles, spasticity of the pelvic floor muscles, immobility, dehydration, dietary alterations with reduced fibre intake, and medication including anticholinergics and opiates. Severe constipation and abdominal distension can exacerbate the problem of compromised respiratory function. If possible, the dietary fluid and fibre intake should be increased and the patient's medication adjusted. Laxative preparations including the bulk-forming agents ispaghula and methyl cellulose, and osmotic agents such as lactulose, can be helpful, as can glycerol suppositories. Professional nursing help might be required to relieve faecal impaction using sodium citrate enemas or manual evacuation.

Sleep disturbance.   Sleep disturbance is a common problem in patients with MND, and can also have a significant impact on the well-being of the carer. Multiple factors can contribute to insomnia. Muscle weakness and the resultant impairment of mobility both reduces or prevents customary physical activities during the day and interferes with postural adjustments at night. A pressure-relieving mattress or an electrically powered bed can be helpful. Various types of pain interfere with sleep, including painful cramps, joint stiffness, and discomfort due to pressure effects or poor positioning. Pain management is discussed later. Anxiety and depression can also contribute to insomnia and a night-time prescription of amitriptyline can be helpful, for both its sedative and antidepressant actions. Dysphagia with aspiration of saliva can also be a contributory problem. Attention to sleeping position, the use of anticholinergic medication and provision of a suction machine can also be useful. Respiratory insufficiency (see later) with hypoxia and dyspnoea can render the patient fearful of going to sleep. Care should be taken in prescribing sedative medication to patients with MND because respiratory depression can occur. All of the benzodiazepines can suppress respiration and flurazepam is perhaps the best tolerated preparation (Norris, 1994). Diphenhydramine is a sedative preparation well tolerated by older individuals, which has the added benefit of reducing muscle cramps. In the later stages of the disease, where the carer is suffering from repeated sleep interruptions, consideration should be given to hospice attendance for spells of respite care, or the provision of night-time assistance in the home for one or two nights per week.

Pain.   Pain is not usually present in the early stages of MND but is common in the later stages of the disease. One study of 42 patients reported that pain was a major feature in 64% (Newrick & Langton-Hewer, 1985). Saunders et al. (1981) evaluated 100 patients in a hospice setting and found that 45% had pain. The major identifiable problems were: stiffness of joints, muscle cramps, skin pressure, immobility requiring external help, severe spasticity, and constipation.

Effort should be made to establish the site and reason for the patient's pain. This can prove a challenge in the late stages of the disease, with its concomitant communication difficulties. Non-steroidal anti-inflammatory agents and physiotherapy will help to control pain arising from joint stiffness. Pharmacological agents can be employed to alleviate cramps, spasticity, and constipation, as described earlier. Special attention should be given to nursing care to ensure that the patient achieves the most comfortable position both during the day and at night. Hoists for transfers, riser–recliner chairs, pressure-relieving mattresses, and adjustable beds can all be helpful.

Emotional and psychological problems

Psychological problems.   Almost all patients with MND undergo a period of anxiety and reactive depression surrounding the time of diagnosis. Adequate support and counselling is important at this time. Many patients subsequently shift into a more settled emotional phase of acceptance, particularly if their level of disability is not showing rapid progression. Anxiety and depression are common problems throughout the course of MND. Antidepressant or anxiolytic therapy will be required for some patients. These problems can also be alleviated to some extent by ensuring that the main carer is adequately supported. Severe depression, however, appears to be surprisingly uncommon, occurring in 2.5% in one series of 40 patients (Houpt et al., 1977). Whereas suicidal thoughts are common, particularly arising from the patient's fear of becoming a burden on the family, suicide attempts are uncommon. The psychological state of patients with MND has been shown to correlate with survival (McDonald, 1994) and it is therefore important that clinically significant mood changes should be looked for and treated at all stages of the disease.

Emotional lability.   Emotional lability or pathological tearfulness and laughter can be disturbing for the patient in social situations. The underlying pathological substrate for this behaviour is thought to be bilateral degeneration of corticobulbar pathways resulting in loss of cortical inhibition of the brainstem. It can be reassuring for the patient and the carer to have an explanation for the development of this problem. Emotional lability often responds to amitriptyline or imipramine therapy;

L-dopa and lithium preparations have also been reported to be of benefit to some patients (Borascio & Volz, 1997).

Respiratory failure

The majority of patients with MND die from respiratory failure due to weakness of the respiratory muscles, with or without concomitant pneumonia. It is unusual for respiratory failure to develop before the onset of significant disability due to limb or bulbar weakness. Occasionally, diaphragmatic function is affected early and patients occasionally present with breathlessness or respiratory failure (Nightingale et al., 1982). The principal factors that can lead to respiratory complications include: diaphragmatic weakness, impaired cough, aspiration, and intercurrent respiratory infection. Weakness of the diaphragm and external intercostal muscles results in decreased inspiratory pressures and volumes. Weakness of the internal intercostal and abdominal wall muscles, as well as weakness and incoordination of the glottis, results in decreased expiratory pressures and volumes and ineffective cough. Fatigue of the respiratory muscles can also be a significant problem (Howard et al., 1989; Kreitzer et al., 1978).

The symptoms of respiratory muscle weakness in MND include dyspnoea on mild exertion or when lying flat; difficulty with coughing and talking; daytime somnolence; difficulty falling asleep, interrupted sleep, and nightmares; morning headaches; nervousness, tremor, increased sweating, tachycardia, and anorexia. When the vital capacity approaches 30–40% of the predicted value, there is a risk of sudden, life-threatening respiratory failure (Oppenheimer, 1993).

The management of the respiratory complications of MND includes the following general measures. Attention should be given to the detection and prevention of aspiration pneumonia. Antibiotic therapy should be used at the first hint of a chest infection. Chest physiotherapy and postural drainage, which can be taught to the carer, should be used when the patient has difficulty in clearing secretions from the chest. Patients will breathe more comfortably if positioned in an upright position, using several pillows or a backrest, at night. When patients experience bouts of severe dyspnoea, accompanied by extreme anxiety or panic, a small dose of lorazepam (0.5–1 mg) sublingually can be helpful (Borascio & Volz, 1997). If breathlessness causes distress during the later stages of the disease, the use of small amounts of morphine will be useful. The depression of respiration can usually be avoided if the initial dose is small and increments are gradual (Saunders et al., 1981).

Assisted ventilation, coupled with appropriate nutritional support, could theoretically extend the patient's life indefinitely, and the implications of initiating such respiratory support must be thought through clearly and discussed with each patient. There are considerable international differences in the use of assisted ventilation to manage respiratory failure in MND. Estimates from a regional survey in the American mid-west suggested that up to 8% of MND patients are placed on artificial ventilation (Moss et al., 1993). In Japan, until recently, physicians did not tend to tell patients of their diagnosis or prognosis and many MND patients were placed on ventilators without knowing the implications (Hayashi et al., 1994). In UK clinical practice, the progressive nature of MND has acted as a deterrent for the active management of respiratory dysfunction in many MND patients, particularly when other motor disabilities are extensive. However, as discussed earlier, some patients present with respiratory failure as an early feature of their disease, when limb and bulbar function are relatively well preserved. Full 24-hour intermittent positive-pressure ventilation via a tracheostomy is an option that is only rarely chosen by fully informed patients. The costs, in terms both of financial resources and the caregiver support required, are substantial. This course of action would be considered in UK practice only in exceptional circumstances. Non-invasive intermittent positive-pressure ventilation (NIPPV) via a mask is the most practical form of assisted ventilation usually considered (Fig. 46.10). The equipment is portable and relatively inexpensive. Because this equipment cannot be used continuously, the risk of "ventilator entrapment" is avoided. Use of ventilatory support during sleep can lead to subjective improvement in sleep, resolution of morning headache,

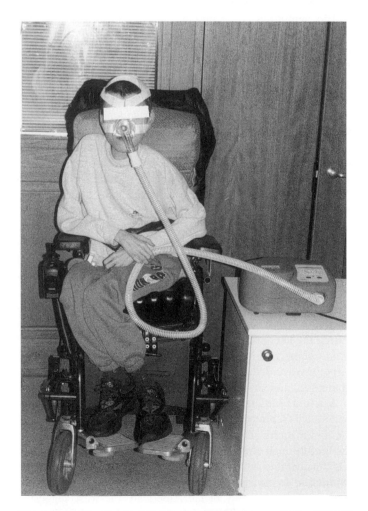

Figure 46.10. Non-invasive intermittent positive-pressure ventilation (NIPPV) via a mask, which can be used as a means of respiratory support in MND.

and improvement in exercise tolerance, mobility, respiratory function, and fatigue during the day (Howard et al., 1989).

Practical problems in using the NIPPV system include skin trauma resulting from the tight-fitting mask, distension of the abdomen due to air entering the oesophagus if the cricopharygeal sphincter is weak, and air leak through the mouth in the presence of facial muscle weakness.

Negative pressure ventilation by cuirass, Tunnicliffe jacket, or tank respirator are much more cumbersome to apply than NIPPV and generally require the assistance of an able caregiver.

Terminal care

In the absence of ventilatory support, the majority of patients with MND die from respiratory failure, often during their sleep. The only aim of medical intervention in the terminal phase of the disease is to ensure that the patient is comfortable. Morphine therapy should be administered as required to alleviate discomfort or dyspnoea. This can be given via the PEG, by the subcutaneous or intravenous routes or via a nebuliser. Diazepam or chlorpromazine can be given to alleviate anxiety. Many patients will wish to die at home, and every attempt should be made to provide the necessary medical and nursing support from the community. Terminal care in the hospital or hospice setting will be necessary for some patients. This should ideally involve staff previously known to the family, and family members should be allowed to stay with the patient as they wish.

THERAPIES DESIGNED TO RETARD DISEASE PROGRESSION

The precise sequence of events underlying cell death in MND remains unknown, but progress in understanding the pathophysiology of the disease has been made in recent years. No currently available therapy has a dramatic effect in slowing disease progression. However, some small steps have now been taken towards this ultimate goal. A detailed critique of all the recent therapeutic trials is beyond the scope of this chapter, and the principal results only will be highlighted.

In 1988, Plaitakis et al. reported in a pilot study that branched-chain amino acid therapy, which might modulate glutamatergic neurotransmission, could slow the rate of deterioration in MND (Plaitakis et al., 1988). This result was not confirmed in a large pan-European multicentre, double-blind, placebo-controlled, randomised, parallel-group trial involving 760 patients (data unpublished).

Subsequently, other trials of antiglutamate therapy have taken place. Riluzole is a sodium channel blocker that inhibits glutamate release, and has several other potentially neuroprotective effects. Two double-blind, placebo-controlled clinical trials of riluzole have been carried out in more than 1100 patients with MND (Bensimon et al., 1994; Lacomblez et al., 1996). The results of both studies show a modest (and statistically significant) benefit in prolonging survival in MND. These results have led to the licensing of this drug for use in MND in Europe and the US. Unfortunately, the trials did not include a quality of life measure, although there is no evidence that riluzole prolongs the stage of severe disability in MND patients. In addition, in the second larger trial, no statistically significant benefit was seen in secondary parameters, including the deterioration of muscle strength. Riluzole therapy is relatively expensive (approximately £3700 per patient per year) and the average survival benefit to be expected is modest, but against this must be weighed the arguments that the patient population requiring the drug is relatively small, and that these patients are facing a lethal disease for which no other therapy is available. At present it is unknown whether the modest overall therapeutic effect conceals responders and non-responders.

Gabapentin, an anticonvulsant drug with antiglutamate activity has been evaluated in MND in a pilot therapeutic trial (Miller et al., 1996a). No statistically significant benefit was seen but there was a trend suggesting a possible slowing in the rate of decline of limb strength as assessed by MVIC (maximum voluntary isometric contraction) equipment. A further trial, using higher doses of gabapentin failed to confirm a significant neuroprotective effect.

No large-scale trials of anti-oxidant therapy have yet been conducted in MND. A trial of acetylcysteine therapy in 110 Dutch patients showed a trend towards improved survival in patients with limb-onset disease, which just failed to reach statistical significance ($p = .06$) (Louwerse et al., 1995). In transgenic mice bearing SOD1 mutations associated with familial MND, the anti-oxidant vitamin E, delays the onset of the disease, although it does not influence disease duration (Gurney et al., 1996). The effect in human patients is unproven, although many patients are empirically prescribed anti-oxidant therapy with vitamin C and vitamin E because of the emerging evidence that free radicals could contribute to motor neurone injury.

Several neurotrophic factors administered by subcutaneous injection have also been assessed in recent trials. Ciliary neurotrophic factor (CNTF) showed no therapeutic benefit when administered by this route in MND, and actually appeared to have a detrimental effect in the high-dose group (Miller et al.,

1996b). In the US, recombinant human insulin-like growth factor 1 (IGF-1), in a trial involving 266 patients, slowed progression of functional impairment (assessed by the Appel ALS rating scale total score) by 26% over 9 months ($p = .01$) and also slowed the decline in health-related quality of life (assessed by the Sickness Impact Profile) (Lai et al., 1997). However, a similar trial conducted in Europe has failed to replicate this result and, as yet, IGF-1 has not been licensed for use in MND. The published results of several other trials of neurotrophic factors, including brain-derived neurotrophic factor (BDNF) and glial-derived neurotrophic factor (GDNF), are awaited. Concern has been expressed about the half-life and access to motor neurones of neurotrophic factors administered by the subcutaneous route, and pilot studies are underway exploring the potential for using intrathecal administration. A multinational trial of the orally active agent SR57746A, which appears to have neurotrophic-like effects on motor neurones, has recently been completed and published results are awaited.

CONCLUSIONS

In several ways MND is a disease that is uniquely challenging to medical and health-care professionals. Rapidly progressive disability, without periods of remission, and usually in the presence of preserved intellectual function, make MND a particularly difficult disease for patients and their families to face. A nihilistic approach from medical attendants can add to the distress and suffering of these families. There is much that can be done during the course of the disease to alleviate symptoms, maximise functional independence, and counsel and support these families. A coordinated, multidisciplinary approach is the best way of managing the disease, with the development of links between hospital-based, community, and palliative-care personnel. At the present time, drug therapies are becoming available that have a modest effect in slowing the progression of MND and prolonging survival. Quality of life issues will be important in the evaluation of the place in management of these new neuroprotective therapies.

REFERENCES

Appel, V., Stewart, S. S., Smith, G., & Appel, S. H. (1987). A rating scale for amyotrophic lateral sclerosis: Description and preliminary experience. *Ann Neurol, 22,* 328 333.

Arnold, A., Edgran, D. C., & Palladino, V. S. (1953). Amyotrophic lateral sclerosis: Fifty cases observed in Guam. *J Nerv Ment Dis, 117,* 135.

Aubier, A., De Troyer, M., Sampson, P., Macklem, T., & Roussos, C. (1981). Aminophylline improves diaphragmatic contractility. *New Engl J Med, 305,* 249–252.

Bensimon, G., Lacomblez, L., Meininger, V., & Group, A. R. S. (1994). A controlled trial of riluzole in amyotrophic lateral sclerosis. *New Engl J Med, 330,* 585–591.

Bergeron, C., Muntasser, S., Somerville, M. J., Weyer, L., & Percy, M. E. (1994). Copper/zinc superoxide dismutase mRNA levels are increased in sporadic amyotrophic lateral sclerosis motorneurons. *Brain Res., 659* (1–2), 272–276.

Bjornskov, E. K., Dekker, N. P., Norris, F. H., & Stuart, M. E. (1975). End-plate morphology in amyotrophic lateral sclerosis. *Arch Neurol, 32,* 711–712.

Borascio, G. D., & Volz, R. (1997). Palliative care in amyotrophic lateral sclerosis. *J Neurol, 244* (Suppl. 4), S11–S17.

Bowling, A. C., Schulz, J. B., Brown, R. H., & Beal, M. F. (1993). Superoxide dismutase activity, oxidative damage and mitochondrial energy metabolism in familial and sporadic amyotrophic lateral sclerosis. *J Neurochem, 61,* 2322–2325.

Brooks, B. (1994). El Escorial World Federation of Neurology criteria for the diagnosis of amyotrophic lateral sclerosis. *J Neurol Sci, 124,* 96–107.

Brown, R. H. (1995). Amyotrophic lateral sclerosis: Recent insights from genetics and transgenic mice. *Cell, 80,* 687–692.

Carey, J. S. (1986). Motor neurone disease – a challenge to medical ethics: Discussion paper. *J Roy Coll Med, 79,* 216–220.

Caroscio, J. T., Calhoun, W. F., & Yahr, M. D. (1984). Prognostic factors in motor neuron disease – a prospective study of longevity. In F. C. Rose (Ed.), *Research progress in motor neuron disease* (pp. 34–43). London, Pitman.

Carus, R. (1980). Motor neuron disease: A demeaning illness. *Br Med J, 280,* 455–456.

Chari, G., Shaw, P. J., & Sahgal, A. (1996). Non-verbal visual attention, but not recognition memory or learning processes are impaired in motor neurone disease. *Neuropsychologica, 34*, 377–385.

Cochrane, G. M. (1990). *Communication. Equipment for disabled people*. Oxford, Oxfordshire Health Authority.

Coyle, J. T., & Puttfarcken, P. (1993). Oxidative stress, glutamate and neurodegenerative disorders. *Science, 262*, 689–695.

Deapen, D. M., & Henderson, B. E. (1986). A case-control study of amyotrophic lateral sclerosis. *Am J Epidemiol, 123*, 790–799.

DeJong, J. M. B. V. (1991). The World Federation of Neurology classification of spinal muscular atrophies and other disorders of motor neurons. In P. J. Vinken, G. W. Bruyn, H. L. Klawans, & J. M. B. V. DeJong (Eds.), *Handbook of clinical neurology: Diseases of the motor system* (vol. 59, pp. 1–13). Amsterdam, Elsevier.

Eisen, A., Pant, B., & Stewart, H. (1993). Cortical excitability in amyotrophic lateral sclerosis: A clue to pathogenesis. *Can J Neurol Sci, 20*, 11–16.

Enderby, P., & Langton Hewer, R. (1987). Communication and swallowing: Problems and aids. In G. M. Cochrane (Ed.), *The management of motor neurone disease* (pp. 22–47). Edinburgh, Churchill Livingstone.

Evans, M. (1985). *Magpie: A lower limb manipulator. Annual Report of the Oxford Orthopaedic Engineering Centre*, p. 64. Oxford, Nuffield Orthopaedic Centre.

Felmus, M. T., Patten, B. M., & Swanke, L. (1976). Antecedent events in amyotrophic lateral sclerosis. *Neurology, 26*, 167–172.

Figlewicz, D. A., Krizus, A., Martinoli, M., Meininger, V., Dib, M., Rouleau, G. A., & Julien, J.-P. (1994). Variants of the heavy neurofilament subunit are associated with the development of amyotrophic lateral sclerosis. *Hum Mol Genet, 3*, 1757–1761.

Fleet, W. S., & Watson, R. T. (1986). From benign fasciculations and cramps to motor neurone disease. *Neurology, 36*, 997–998.

Gajdusek, D. C., & Salazar, A. M. (1982). Amyotrophic lateral sclerosis and parkinsonian syndromes in high incidence among the Auyw and Jakai people of West New Guinea. *Neurology, 32*, 107–126.

Garg, A., Buckman, R., & Kason, Y. (1997). Teaching medical students how to break bad news. *Can Med Assoc J, 156*, 1159–1164.

Gawel, M., Zaiwalla, A., & Rose, F. C. (1983). Antecedent events in motor neuron disease. *J Neurol Neurosurg Psychiatry, 46*, 1041–1043.

Gunnarson, L. G., & Lindberg, G. (1989). Amyotrophic lateral sclerosis in Sweden 1970–1983 and solvent exposure. *Lancet, i*, 958.

Gurney, M. E., Cutting, F. B., Zhai, P. et al. (1996). Benefit of vitamin E, riluzole and gabapentin in a transgenic model of familial amyotrophic lateral sclerosis. *Ann Neurol, 39*, 147–158.

Harding, A. E., Thomas, P. K., Baraitser, M., Bradbury, P. G., Morgan-Hughes, J. A., & Ponsford, J. R. (1982). X-linked recessive bulbospinal neuropathy: A report of 10 cases. *J Neurol Neurosurg Psychiatry, 45*, 1012–1019.

Hattori, T. (1984). Negative symptoms and signs of amyotrophic lateral sclerosis: Disturbance of micturition. *Rinsho Sinkeigaku, 24*, 1254–1256.

Hawkes, C. H., & Fox, A. J. (1981). Motor neurone disease in leather workers. *Lancet, i*, 507.

Hayashi, H. (1994). Long-term, in-hospital ventilatory care for patients with amyotrophic lateral sclerosis. In H. Mitsumoto & F. H. Norris (Eds.), *Amyotrophic lateral sclerosis. A comprehensive guide to management* (pp. 127–138). New York, Demos Publications.

Hayashi, H., & Kato, S. (1989). Total manifestations of amyotrophic lateral sclerosis. *J Neurol Sci, 93*, 19–35.

Houpt, J. L., Gould, B. S., & Norris, F. H. (1977). Psychological characteristics of patients with amyotrophic lateral sclerosis. *Psychsom Med, 39*, 299–303.

Howard, R. S., Wiles, C. M., & Loh, L. (1989). Respiratory complications and their management in motor neuron disease. *Brain, 112*, 1155–1170.

Hudson, A. J. (1981). Amyotrophic lateral sclerosis and its association with dementia, Parkinsonism and other neurological disorders: A review. *Brain, 104*, 217–247.

Hughes, J. T. (1982). Pathology of amyotrophic lateral sclerosis. In L. P. Rowland (Ed.), *Human motor neuron diseases* (pp. 61–74). New York, Raven Press.

Ince, P. G., Shaw, P. J., Candy, J. M. et al. (1994). Iron, selenium and glutathione peroxidase activity are elevated in sporadic motor neuron disease. *Neurosci Lett, 183*, 87–90.

Ince, P. G., Shaw, P. J., & Lowe, J. (1998). Motor neurone disease: Recent advances in molecular pathology, pathogenesis and classification. *Neuropathol Appl Neurobiol, 24*, 104–117.

Ince, P. G., Shaw, P. J., Slade, J. Y., Jones, C., & Hudgson, P. (1996). Familial amyotrophic lateral sclerosis with a mutation in exon 4 of the Cu/Zn superoxide dismutase gene: Pathological and immunocytochemical changes. *Acta Neuropath, 92*, 395–403.

Iwanaga, K., Hayashi, S., Oyake, M. et al. (1997). Neuropathology of sporadic amyotrophic lateral sclerosis of long duration. *J Neurol Sci, 146*, 139–143.

Jackson, M., Morrison, K. E., Al-Chalabi, A., Bakker, M., & Leigh, P. N. (1996). Analysis of chromosome 5q13 genes in amyotrophic lateral sclerosis: Homozygous NAIP deletion in a sporadic case. *Ann Neurol, 39*, 796–800.

Jamal, G. A., Weir, A. I., Hansen, S., & Ballantyne, J. P. (1985). Sensory involvement in motor neurone disease: Further evidence from automated thermal threshold detection. *J Neurol Neurosurg Psychiatry, 48*, 906–910.

Janiszewski, D. W., Caroscio, J. T., & Wisham, L. H. (1983). Amyotrophic lateral sclerosis: A comprehensive rehabilitation approach. *Arch Phys Med Rehab, 64*, 304–307.

Jokelainen, M. (1977). Amyotrophic lateral sclerosis in Finland. 1: An epidemiological study. *Acta Neurol Scand, 56*, 185–192.

Julien, J.-P., Cote, F., & Collard, J.-F. (1995). Mice overexpressing the human neurofilament heavy gene as a model of ALS. *Neurobiol Aging, 3*, 487–492.

Kew, J. J. M., Leigh, P. N., Playford, E. D., Passingham, R. E., Goldstein, L. H., Frackowiak, R. S. J., & Brooks, D. J. (1993). Cortical function in amyotrophic lateral sclerosis: A positron emission tomography study. *Brain, 116*, 644–680.

Kondo, K. (1975). Clinical variability of motor neuron disease. *Neurol Med, 2*, 11–16.

Kondo, K. (1995). Epidemiology of motor neuron disease. In P. N. Leigh & M. Swash (Eds.), *Motor neuron disease* (pp. 19–34). London, Springer-Verlag.

Kondo, K., & Tsubaki, T. (1981). Case-control studies of motor neuron disease: Association with mechanical injuries. *Arch Neurol, 38*, 220–226.

Kreitzer, S. M., Saunders, N. A., Tyler, H. R., & Ingram, R. H. (1978). Respiratory muscle function in amyotrophic lateral sclerosis. *Am Rev Respir Dis, 117*, 437–447.

Kurland, L. T., Kurtzke, J. F., & Goldberg, I. D. (Eds.), (1973). *Epidemiology of neurologic disorders. Vital and health statistics monographs. American Public Health Association*. Boston, Harvard University Press.

Kurtzke, J. F. (1982). Epidemiology of amyotrophic lateral sclerosis. In L. P. Rowland (Ed.), *Human motor neuron diseases* (pp. 281–302). New York, Raven Press.

Kurtzke, J. F., & Beebe, G. W. (1980). Epidemiology of amyotrophic lateral sclerosis. 1. A case-control comparison based on ALS death. *Neurology, 30*, 453–462.

La Spada, A. R., Wilson, E. M., Lubahn, D. B., Harding, A. E., & Fischbeck, K. H. (1991). Androgen receptor gene mutations in X-linked spinal and bulbar muscular atrophy. *Nature, 352*, 77–79.

Lacomblez, L., Bensimon, G., Leigh, P. N. et al. (1996). Dose-ranging study of riluzole in amyotrophic lateral sclerosis. *Lancet, 347*, 1425–1432.

Lai, E. C., Felice, K. J., Festoff, B. W. et al. (1997). Effect of recombinant human insulin-like growth factor-I on progression of ALS. A placebo-controlled study. *Neurology, 49*, 1621–1630.

Langton Hewer, R. (1995). The management of motor neuron disease. In P. N. Leigh & M. Swash (Eds.), *Motor neuron disease. Biology and management* (pp. 375–406). London, Springer-Verlag.

Lawyer, T., & Netsky, M. G. (1953). Amyotrophic lateral sclerosis: A clinicopathological study of 53 cases. *Arch Neurol Psychiatr, 69*, 171–192.

Leigh, P. N., Anderton, B., Dodson, A., Gallo, J.-M., Swash, M., & Power, D. (1988). Ubiquitin deposits in anterior horn cells in motor neurone disease. *Neurosci Lett, 93*, 197–203.

Louwerse, E. S., Weverling, G. J., Bossuyt, P. M. M., Posthumus Meyjes, F. E., & de Jong, J. M. B. V. (1995). Randomized, double-blind controlled trial of acetylcysteine in amyotrophic lateral sclerosis. *Arch Neurol, 52*, 559–564.

Lowe, J., Lennox, G., Jefferson, D. et al. (1988). A filamentous inclusion within anterior horn cell neurones in motor neurone disease defined by immunocytochemical localisation with ubiquitin. *Neurosci Lett, 93*, 202–210.

Mannen, T., Iwata, M., Toyakura, Y. et al. (1977). Preservation of a certain motorneurone group of the sacral cord in amyotrophic lateral sclerosis. *J Neurol Neurosurg Psychiatry, 40*, 464–469.

Mazzini, L., Corra, T., Zaccala, M., Mora, G., M., D. P., & Galante, M. (1995). Percutaneous endoscopic gastrostomy and enteral nutrition in amyotrophic lateral sclerosis. *J Neurol, 242*, 695–698.

McDonald, E. R., S.A., W., Hillel, A., Carpenter, C. L., & Walter, R. A. (1994). Survival in amyotrophic lateral sclerosis: The role of psychological factors. *Arch Neurol, 51*, 17–23.

Meininger, V. (1993). Breaking bad news in amyotrophic lateral sclerosis. *Palliative Medicine, 7* (Suppl. 2), 37–40.

Miller, R. G., Moore, D., & Young, L. A. (1996a). Placebo-controlled trial of gabapentin in patients with amyotrophic lateral sclerosis. *Neurology, 47*, 1383–1388.

Miller, R. G., Petajan, J. H., Bryan, W. W. et al. (1996b). A placebo-controlled trial of recombinant human ciliary neurotrophic (rhCNTF) factor in amyotrophic lateral sclerosis. *Ann Neurol, 39*, 256–260.

Mills, K. R. (1995). Motor neurone disease: Studies of the corticospinal excitation of single motoneurons by magnetic brain stimulation. *Brain, 118*, 971–982.

Mitsumoto, H., Hanson, M. R., & Chad, D. A. (1988). Amyotrophic lateral sclerosis: Recent advances in pathogenesis and clinical trials. *Arch Neurol, 40*, 189–202.

Mortara, P., Chio, A., Rossa, M. G. et al. (1984). Motor neuron disease in the province of Turin, Italy 1966–1980. *J Neurol Sci, 66*, 165–173.

Moss, A. H., Casey, P., Stocking, C. B., Roos, R. P., Brooks, B. R., & Siegler, M. (1993). Home ventilation for amyotrophic lateral sclerosis patients: Outcomes, costs, and patient, family and physician attitudes. *Neurology, 43*, 438–443.

Mulder, D., Kurland, L., & Iriarte, L. (1954). Neurologic diseases on the island of Guam. *US Armed Forces Med J, 5*, 1724–1739.

Mulder, D. W. (1982). Clinical limits of amyotrophic lateral sclerosis. In L. P. Rowland (Ed.), *Human motor neuron diseases* (pp. 15–29). New York, Raven Press.

Neary, D., Snowden, J. S., Mann, D. M. A., Northen, B., Goulding, P. J., & Macdermott, N. (1990). Frontal lobe dementia and motor neuron disease. *J Neurol Neurosurg Psychiatry, 53*, 23–32.

Newrick, P. G., & Langton Hewer, R. (1985). Pain in motor neuron disease. *J Neurol Neurosurg Psychiat, 48*, 838–840.

Nightingale, S., Bates, D., Bateman, D., Hudgson, P., Ellis, D. A., & Gibson, G. J. (1982). Enigmatic dyspnoea: An unusual presentation of motor neurone disease. *Lancet, i*, 933–935.

Norris, F. H. (1994). Care of the amyotrophic lateral sclerosis patient. In H. Mitsumoto & F. H. Norris (Eds.), *Amyotrophic lateral sclerosis. A comprehensive guide to management* (pp. 29–42). New York, Demos Publications.

Oppenheimer, E. A. (1993). Decision making in the respiratory care of amyotrophic lateral sclerosis patients: Should home mechanical ventilation be used? *Palliative Med, 7* (Suppl. 2), 49–64.

Pall, H. S., Williams, A. C., Waring, R. et al. (1987). Motor neurone disease as a manifestation of pesticide toxicity. *Lancet, ii*, 685.

Peavy, G. M., Herzog, A. G., Rubin, N. P., & Mesulam, M. M. (1992). Neuropsychological aspects of the dementia of motor neurone disease: A report of two cases. *Neurology, 42*, 1004–1008.

Pestronk, A., Cornblath, D. R., Ilyas, A. A. et al. (1988). A treatable multifocal motor neuropathy with antibodies to GM1 ganglioside. *Ann Neurol, 24*, 73–78.

Plaitakis, A., Mandeli, J., Smith, J., & Yahr, M. D. (1988). Pilot trial of branched-chain amino acids in amyotrophic lateral sclerosis. *Lancet, i*, 1015–1018.

Pringle, C. E., Hudson, A. J., Munoz, D. G., Kiernan, J. A., Brown, W. F., & Ebers, G. C. (1992). Primary lateral sclerosis. Clinical features, neuropathology and diagnostic criteria. *Brain, 115*, 495–520.

Ptacek, J. T., & Eberhardt, T. L. (1996). Breaking bad news. A review of the literature. *JAMA, 276*, 496–502.

Rivera, V. M., Breitbach, W. B., & Swanke, L. (1975). Dantrolene in amyotrophic lateral sclerosis. *JAMA, 223*, 863–864.

Roelofs-Iverson, R. A., Mulder, D. W., Elveback, L. R. et al. (1984). ALS and heavy metal: A pilot case-control study. *Neurology, 34*, 393–395.

Rosen, D. R., Siddique, T., Patterson, D. et al. (1993). Mutations in Cu/Zn superoxide dismutase are associated with familial amyotrophic lateral sclerosis. *Nature, 362*, 59–62.

Rothstein, J. D., Van Kammen, M., Levey, A. I., Martin, L. J., & Kuncl, R. W. (1995). Selective loss of glial glutamate transporter GLT-1 in amyotrophic lateral sclerosis. *Ann Neurol, 38*, 73–84.

Sasaki, S., Tsutsumi, Y., Yamane, K., Sakuma, H., & Maruyama, S. (1992). Sporadic amyotrophic lateral sclerosis with extensive neurological involvement. *Acta Neuropathologica, 84*, 211–215.

Saunders, C. M., Walsh, T. D., & Smith, M. (1981). Hospice care in motor neuron disease. In S. C. M. (Ed.), *Hospice: The living idea* (pp. 126–155). London, Edward Arnold.

Shaw, P. J. (1994). Excitotoxicity and motor neurone disease: A review of the evidence. *J Neurol Sci, 124* (Suppl.), 6–13.

Shaw, P. J., Chinnery, R. M., Thagesen, H., Borthwick, G., & Ince, P. G. (1997). Immunocytochemical study of the distribution of the free radical scavenging enzymes Cu/Zn superoxide dismutase (SOD1), Mn superoxide dismutase (Mn SOD) and catalase in the normal human spinal cord and in motor neurone disease. *J Neurol Sci, 147*, 115–125.

Shaw, P. J., Forrest, V., Ince, P. G., Richardson, J. P., & Wastell, H. J. (1995). CSF and plasma amino acid levels in motor neuron disease: Elevation of CSF glutamate in a subset of patients. *Neurodegeneration, 4*, 209–216.

Shaw, P. J., & Ince, P. G. (1997). Glutamate, excitotoxicity and amyotrophic lateral sclerosis. *J Neurol, 244* (Suppl. 2), S3–S14.

Shaw, P. J., Ince, P. G., Falkous, G., & Mantle, D. (1995). Oxidative damage to protein in sporadic motor neuron disease spinal cord. *Ann Neurol, 38*, 691–695.

Siddique, T., Nijhawan, D., & Hentat, A. (1996). Molecular genetic basis of familial ALS. *Neurol, 47* (Suppl. 2), S27–S35.

Sillevis-Smitt, P. A. E., Mulder, T. P. J., Verspaget, H. W., Blaauwgeers, H. G. T., Troost, D., & de Jong, J. M. B. V. (1994). Metallothionein in amyotrophic lateral sclerosis. *Biol Signals, 3* (4), 193–197.

Sonies, B. C., & Dalakas, M. C. (1991). Dysphagia in patients with the post-polio syndrome. *New England Journal of Medicine, 324*, 1162–1167.

Subramaniam, J. J., & Yiannikas, C. (1990). Multimodality evoked potentials in motor neurone disease. *Arch Neurol, 47*, 989–994.

Swash, M., & Schwartz, M. S. (1995). Motor neuron disease: The clinical syndrome. In P. N. Leigh & M. Swash (Eds.), *Motor neuron disease: Biology and management* (pp. 1–18). London, Springer-Verlag.

Tandan, R., & Bradley, W. G. (1985). Amyotrophic lateral sclerosis: Part 1. Clinical features, pathology and ethical issues in management. *Ann Neurol, 18*, 271–280.

Tomlinson, B. E., Irving, D., & Rebeiz, J. J. (1973). Total numbers of limb motor neurons in the human lumbosacral cord and an analysis of the accuracy of various sampling procedures. *J Neurol Sci, 20*, 313–327.

Tucker, T., Layzer, R. B., Miller, R. G., & Chad, D. (1991). Subacute, reversible motor neuron disease. *Neurology, 41*, 1541–1544.

Tyler, H. R., & Shefner, J. (1991). Amyotrophic lateral sclerosis. In P. J. Vinken, G. W. Bruyn, H. L. Klawans, & J. M. B. V. DeJong (Eds.), *Handbook of clinical neurology: Diseases of the motor system* (vol. 59, pp. 169–215). Amsterdam, Elsevier.

Williams, E. R., & Bruford, A. (1970). Creatine phosphokinase in motor neuron disease. *Clin Chim Acta, 27*, 53–56.

Williams, T. L., Shaw, P. J., Lowe, J., Bates, D., & Ince, P. G. (1995). Parkinsonism in motor neuron disease: case report and literature review. *Acta Neuropathol, 89*, 275–283.

Wong, P. C., Marszalek, J., Crawford, T. O., Xu, Z., Hsieh, S.-T., Griffin, J. W., & Cleveland, D. W. (1995). Increasing neurofilament subunit NF-M expression reduces axonal NF-H, inhibits radial growth, and results in neurofilamentous accumulation in motor neurons. *J Cell Biol, 130*, 1413–1422.

Younger, D. S., Chou, S., Hay, S. A. P. et al. (1988). Primary lateral sclerosis: A clinical diagnosis re-emerges. *Arch Neurol, 45*, 1304–1307.

Younger, D. S., Rowland, L. P., Latov, N. et al. (1990). Motor neuron disease and amyotrophic lateral sclerosis. Relation of high CSF protein content to paraproteinaemia and clinical syndromes. *Neurology, 40*, 595–599.

Zeman, S., Lloyd, C., Meldrum, B., & Leigh, P. N. (1994). Excitatory amino acids, free radicals and the pathogenesis of motor neuron disease. *Neuropathol Appl Neurobiol, 20*, 219–231.

47. Management of brachial plexus injuries

Rolfe Birch

INTRODUCTION

There have been considerable advances in understanding of traction lesions to the brachial plexus in adults and in children since the last edition of this book was published in 1997: to what extent these are translated into therapeutic benefits and rehabilitation remains to be seen.

Severe lesions of the brachial plexus are the most serious of all injuries to the peripheral nerves and the aims of treatment include: elucidation of diagnosis, and so of prognosis, for function and for pain; improvement in prognosis by intervention, nerve repair, or other methods of re-innervation; improvement of prognosis by reconstruction, which is operation other than re-innervation; the treatment of residual or intractable pain; restoration of function by orthoses or prostheses; return to normal life in study or employment. Three types of injury will be described: that to the plexus in adults or children from missile or other wound or from closed traction force; the iatropathic injury, including post-irradiation neuropathy; and finally the obstetric brachial plexus palsy.

SOME ANATOMICAL FEATURES

The roots of the brachial plexus are formed from the dorsal and ventral rootlets, which join the spinal cord at, respectively, the posterolateral and the anterolateral sulcus. The change from central to peripheral nervous tissue lies outside the cord, in the transitional zone described by Berthold et al. (1993). In the central tissue, neurones are supported in a network of oligodendrocytes and atrocyte processes with very little extra cellular space. In the peripheral tissue axon—Schwann cell units are suspended in a collagen-rich extracellular space. A cone of central tissue projects into the base of each rootlet. As Berthold et al. (1993) say "each transitional region can be subdivided into an axial central nervous system compartment and the surrounding peripheral nervous system compartment".

The intraspinal course of the spinal roots of the brachial plexus is increasingly oblique from above down. The fifth, sixth, and seventh cervical nerves are supported by transverse radicular ligaments; the eighth cervical and first thoracic nerves are not. Proximal branches pass from the ventral primary rami to the phrenic nerve (C5), to the nerve to serratus anterior (C5, C6, and C7), and to the scalene muscles (C5, C6). These anatomical arrangements offer some protection against traction to the upper roots of the brachial plexus. There are potential areas of tethering or compression: at the posterior margin of scalenus anterior, between an accessory rib or the first thoracic rib and the clavicle, deep to the pectoralis minor. The suprascapular and circumflex nerves pass quite sharply away laterally and posteriorly from the main axis; so too, to a lesser degree, do the musculocutaneous and radial nerves. These nerves are selectively vulnerable to rupture in those traction lesions principally affecting the infraclavicular plexus.

It seems that there are between 120,000 and 150,000 myelinated nerve fibres (MNF) in the adult plexus and that fully 25% of these pass to the shoulder girdle (Bonnel, 1989; Narakas, 1978; Slingluff et al., 1987). C5 and T1 are the smallest, containing between 15,000 and 20,000 MNF; C8 is the largest, containing about 30,000. Harris (1904) thought that the proportion of motor fibres was highest in C5 than in C8; and that the sensory contribution was highest in C6 followed by C7. A considerable degree of functional segregation is established proximally: the suprascapular nerve can be traced to an anterolateral bundle within C5 at the level of the anterior tubercle, and one bundle innervating the radial wrist extensors can be consistently identified within the posterior division of the upper trunk by stimulation during operation. Schady and colleagues (1983) confirmed functional segregation in their microneurographic examination of the median nerve of volunteers.

The formation and functional distribution of the plexus and its branches varies between individuals. Occasionally C4 makes a major contribution to scapulohumeral muscles and, on one occasion, I have seen the musculocutaneous nerve arising directly from that spinal nerve. However, some general observations can be made. The cutaneous distribution of C5 does not extend below the elbow; C6 consistently innervates the skin of the thumb; C7 innervates the index, middle, and ring fingers (Gu & Shen, 1994). T1 does not innervate the skin of the hand. C5 regularly controls extension, abduction, and lateral rotation of the shoulder. C6 usually controls elbow flexion and pronosupination and the radial wrist extensors; C7 is widely distributed throughout the upper limb. When this nerve alone is damaged there is a rather diffuse loss of function without complete anaesthesia or paralysis of any significant muscle group. C8 innervates the extensor muscle of fingers and thumb in at least one-third of cases: T1 does this and also innervates triceps in at least 10% of cases. These variations need to be remembered when evaluating clinical and neurophysiological evidence. The variations of supply between the spinal nerves forming the brachial plexus are far more significant than pre- or postfixation, and this is particularly true for C7, C8 and T1.

The extraspinal plexus is richly supplied by branches from the subclavian and vertebral arteries (Abdulla & Bowden, 1960). These are damaged in missile wounds and in the more severe traction injuries, and thrombosis of the subclavian and axillary artery is, of course, a complication of irradiation (Barros d'Sa, 1992b; Butler et al., 1980). The vertebral artery passes anterior to the root of the brachial plexus in especially close relation to C5, C6, and C7, to which it contributes radicular vessels. Bleeding from these can be profuse: in one case urgent tracheostomy was necessary because of compression from bleeding radicular vessels after avulsion of the 7th cervical nerve. Communication between the radicular vessels and the anterior spinal artery can explain the development of Brown–Séquard syndrome in about 5% of cases of complete avulsion injury, and also the occasional catastrophic spinal cord lesion seen after brachial plexus block. Domisse (1975) examines these and other important anatomical variations in arterial supply to the spinal cord.

Among the most relevant of the anatomical arrangements are those that enhance the selective vulnerability of the rootlets and intraspinal roots to injury when compared with the peripheral nerves. These include the less robust blood supply (Yoshizawa et al., 1991). The connective tissue sheath is thinner, and as Sunderland and Bradley (1961) showed, the resistance to a load before rupture is far higher in peripheral nerves than it is in the intraspinal segments; it was found to be least in the ventral roots.

THE CLOSED TRACTION LESION IN ADULTS

Over 500 adults suffer permanent disability from traction lesion to the supra- and infraclavicular plexus in a year (Goldie & Coates, 1992). Road traffic accidents account for the great majority. Rosson (1987) studied 102 patients with severe injuries to the brachial plexus caused by motor cycle accidents. These were treated in one hospital in the years 1985 and 1986. He found a mean age of 21 years, injury to the dominant upper limb in 65 cases, and severe associated injuries in half these patients. At 1 year, one-third remained unemployed and two-thirds were still in severe pain. Despite the pioneering work of Bonney in diagnosis and repair, many patients in the UK are still treated by neglect. Diagnosis is not confirmed and little attempt is made to improve prognosis. Ransford and Hughes (1977) showed that few patients treated by early amputation and prostheses actually used that prosthesis. Wynn Parry et al. (1987) followed patients with injury to the brachial plexus in whom no operation was ever performed for up to 30 years and found that 48 of

122 patients continued to endure severe pain 3 years after injury. The management and rehabilitation of these patients is complex and requires:

1. Prompt and accurate diagnosis of level and extent of the lesion.
2. Operations to promote re-innervation of the limb and to provide improved function by appropriate muscle transfers or other reconstructive modes.
3. A closely supervised scheme of rehabilitation, which has as its central aim return to normal work and normal life as soon as possible against a background of staged withdrawal of support. This course should include a multidisciplinary retraining programme, the provision of specialised splinting and the recognition and treatment of pain.

In the first description of traction lesion in an adult, Flaubert (1827) recorded the outcome after attempted closed reduction of long-standing dislocation of the shoulder; the patient died. At necropsy, C5 was ruptured; there was avulsion of C7, C8, and T1 with rupture of the subclavian artery. The radicular vessels had been torn and there was a haematoma within the spinal cord. Before death, Flaubert detected a Claude Bernard–Horner syndrome and clinical evidence of cord affliction.

The twentieth century saw many innovative and pioneering efforts towards the repair of traction lesions of the brachial plexus. This work gained a rational basis in the distinction between pre- and postganglionic rupture by Bonney (1954), the latter being amenable to repair and the former not so. Physiological methods distinguishing between these two were based on the fact that afferent fibres do not degenerate because they remain connected to their parent neurones within the dorsal root ganglion: hence the histamine test and the recording of sensory action potentials by Bonney and Gilliatt (1958). The first attempted replantation of avulsed spinal nerves was performed by Bonney and Jamieson in 1979, when the dorsal roots of C7 and C8 were reattached to the spinal cord. "It was clear that the rupture had taken place just distal to the surface of the cord: little stumps of rootlets were visible" (Bonney 1998a). Recognition of the differing levels of rupture of roots and of dura has led Bonney to refining the concept of the preganglionic injury. We now see true avulsion as distinct from rupture of the rootlets. The latter is potentially irreparable; the former can be treated by reimplantation. Furthermore, it is clear that selective rupture of ventral or of dorsal rootlets does occur, and this observation is particularly significant in analysis of obstetric brachial plexus palsy (Table 47.1).

Diagnosis

The cause of injury is distraction of the forequarter from the axis: the extent of that violence and the line of application of force can be deduced by the history given either by the patient or witnesses. In one case, a rugby player went into a low tackle on a particularly burly opponent and recollected intense shooting pain coursing down the upper limb into the thumb at the moment

Table 47.1. Preganglionic injury

A		Roots torn from central to transitional zone. True avulsion
B		Roots torn distal to transitional zone
	Type 1	Dura torn within spinal canal, DRG displaced into neck
	Type 2	Dura torn at mouth of foramen, DRG more or less displaced
	Type 3	Dura not torn, DRG not displaced
	Type 4	Dura not torn, DRG not displaced, either ventral or dorsal roots intact

DRG, dorsal root ganglion.

his right shoulder collided with his opponent's shin. There was paralysis of muscles of the shoulder and of the elbow. At operation 2 days later, the 5th and 6th cervical nerves were shown avulsed from the spinal cord. Similar histories have been given by tobogganists, skiers, mountaineers, and racing cyclists. One patient with a total avulsion described how a ten foot wall had collapsed onto her shoulder, missing her head, and she felt as if the arm had been "torn off". At least three impacts occur during a road traffic accident: the first is with the other vehicle, there is then a secondary impact with the bonnet or windscreen, and, last, further impact with the road. In the usual case, of high speed motor cycle accidents, additional impacts occur.

The urgent onset of pain is characteristic, indeed diagnostic. Constant crushing or burning pain in the insensate hand indicates a total lesion of the plexus. Such pain can be reasonably described as deafferentation pain. Sharp convulsive pain shooting down the limb, often into specific digits, tell of the intradural injury to the relevant spinal nerve. Simple observations provide clear evidence of the line of application of force. Deep bruising in the posterior triangle of the neck, a focal ecchymosis from collision with an object, linear abrasions on the skin of the face and the shoulder, show that distraction was added to direct contusion. Detection of rupture of subclavian or axillary artery is elementary. The extent of the neurological lesion is described by the area of sensory loss and paralysis; its depth by sympathetic paralysis. A Bernard–Horner sign is usually, but not invariably, indicative of avulsion of C8 and T1. Loss of sensation above the clavicle, paralysis of the ipsilateral hemidiaphragm, and of serratus anterior with weakness of trapezius muscle, suggests a similar injury for C4, C5, and C6. A strong Tinel sign, with radiation into the cutaneous territory of a spinal nerve, is very strong evidence of a postganglionic rupture of that spinal nerve. Indeed, the more painful the Tinel sign, the more likely it is that there is a reparable rupture. Tinel (1917) described this "as a rule it appears only about the fourth to sixth week after the wound . . ." but in these cases a Tinel sign can be elicited within hours of the injury. Landi and Copeland (1979) studied the value of this simple but important piece of clinical evidence (Figs 47.1–47.4).

Patterns of injury

It is convenient to separate supraclavicular from retroclavicular and infraclavicular lesions. The supraclavicular lesion is the most common: it is caused by distraction of the head from the upper limb and is characterised by a high incidence of rupture or

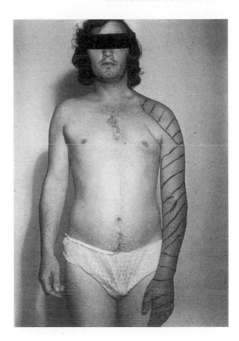

Figure 47.1. Preganglionic injury C5–T1. Note weakness of trapezius and loss of sensation above the clavicle.

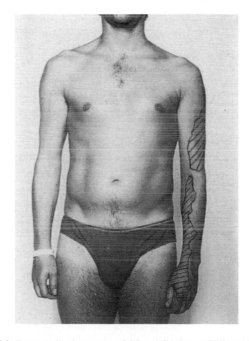

Figure 47.2. Postganglionic rupture of C5 and C6. Intact C7/8 and T1. The sensory loss is typical of this lesion.

of preganglionic injury to the spinal nerves forming the plexus. Rupture of the subclavian artery occurs in about 50% of these cases; damage to the spinal cord is found in 5% of complete lesions. The retroclavicular lesion is surprisingly infrequent: it involves the divisions of the brachial plexus and there is a high incidence of associated arterial injury. In the infraclavicular injury there is rupture of the axillary artery in nearly 30% of

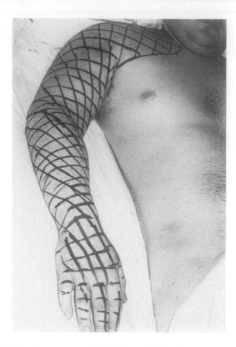

Figure 47.3. Complete preganglionic lesion C5–T1. Note the sensory loss and swelling with bruising above the clavicle.

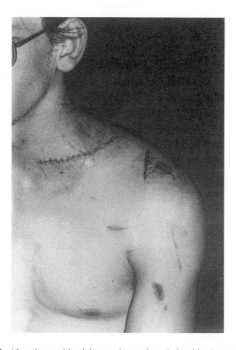

Figure 47.4. Abrasion and bruising at the neck and shoulder in a patient with complete preganglionic lesion C5–T1.

Table 47.2. Operations for injuries of the brachial plexus 1976 to 1996, showing the incidence of open and vascular injuries (from Birch et al. (1998a))

	Total	Vascular
Supraclavicular		
Complete avulsion (C4) C5 to T1. No repair	148	48
Incomplete or recovering lesions. No repair	262	20
Repairs in complete or partial lesions	687	42
Repairs by vascularised ulnar nerve graft	65	5
Total	1162	115
Infraclavicular		
Involving suprascapular and circumflex nerves	126	6
Caused by shoulder dislocation, no nerve rupture	26	2
Caused by shoulder dislocation, with vascular injury but no nerve rupture, in older persons	8	8
Multiple ruptures of nerves (the true infraclavicular lesion)	282	62
Total	442	78
Penetrating missile injury		51

lesion is that associated with anterior dislocation of the shoulder, although even here there can be rupture of nerves in particular, of the circumflex (Table 47.2, Fig. 47.5).

The distinction by level is to some extent artificial: there is overlap between these categories, with double lesions of supraclavicular lesion combined with more distal rupture occurring in about 10% of cases. Alnot (1988) and Narakas (1984a) found this double lesion in 8.5–15% of their cases. None the less, it is reasonable to take the infraclavicular lesion as a distinct entity. It is caused by violent hyperextension at the shoulder; there is almost always fracture of shaft of humerus or injury to the glenohumeral joint; the incidence of vascular injury is much higher; the level of proximal rupture of the nerve is deep to pectoralis minor, which acts as a guillotine on the neurovascular bundle (Tables 47.3–47.5).

Special investigations

Plain radiographs are useful, a fracture dislocation of the first rib points to an avulsion of the roots, whereas elevation of the ipsilateral hemidiaphragm indicates similar injury to C5. Roaf (1963) described tilting of the spine away from the side of injury, a feature of the most violent traction injuries. In one group of patients the radiological features are quite characteristic, showing depression of the shoulder girdle and lateral displacement of the scapula. This is the worst of all injuries to the brachial plexus. Avulsion of C4 to T1 is usually found and rupture of the subclavian artery is almost inevitable (Fig. 47.6).

Myelography. Earlier work (Davis et al., 1966; Yeoman, 1968) with oil-based media has been extended using water-soluble agents. Nagano et al. (1989) reviewed 90 cases where metrizamide myelography was compared with the findings at

cases and the neural injury is complex and variable with ruptures of cords or of the terminal branches. The proximal nerve stumps are usually found at the level of the coracoid deep to pectoralis minor. In about 20% of the infraclavicular group there is associated preganglionic injury to the lower-most roots of the brachial plexus. In general, the mildest form of infraclavicular

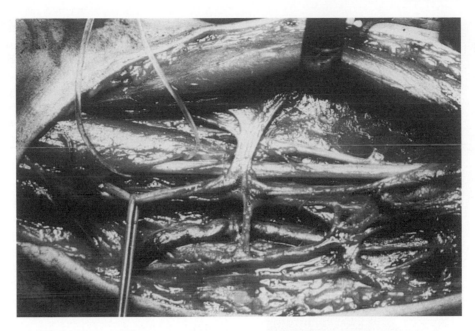

Figure 47.5. A case of infraclavicular lesion, showing the exposure of the distal injury in the brachial bundle of the arm. The retracted distal stump of the ulnar nerve is seen below. The axillary artery and musculocutaneous and ulnar nerves were ruptured at the level of the coracoid.

Table 47.3. Patterns of injury in 300 consecutive operated supraclavicular lesions, 1989–1993

Complete lesions: Pre- and postganglionic injury	
Ruptures upper nerves C5 (C6,C7), intradural lower nerves (C6, C7, C8) T1	83
Ruptures middle nerves (C6) C7 (C8), intradural above and below	5
Ruptures lower nerves C8, T1, intradural upper nerves C5, C6, C7	1
Rupture C5, T1, intradural C6, C7, C8	7
Total intradural C5–T1	52
Total	148
Incomplete lesions: some roots intact	
Damage C5, C6 (C7), recovering or intact (C7) C8, T1	117
Damage C6, C7, T1, recovering or intact C5, T1	23
Damage C7, C8, T1, recovering or intact C5, C6	13
Total	153

Table 47.4. Common patterns of intradural injury seen in 300 consecutive operated cases 1989–1993

Intradural injury of nerves	Number
C5–T1	52
C6–T1	39
C7–T1	54
C8–T1	10
C6	10
C7	13
C5–C6	21
C5–C6–C7	21
C6–C7–C8	10

Table 47.5. Injuries to individual spinal nerves in 300 consecutive operated cases, 1989–1993

	Intact or lesion in continuity (LIC)	Rupture	Intradural
C5	41	154	105
C6	39	90	171
C7	76	24	200
C8	105	15	180
T1	133	7	170
Total	394	290	826

operation and confirmed that the water-soluble medium does allow more precise delineation of the spinal nerves within the spinal canal. Introduction of computerised tomographic (CT) scanning with contrast enhancement improved definition, and

Marshall and de Silva (1986) compared the CT scan with the myelograph and the findings at operation in 16 cases, confirming that CT scan with contrast enhancement was a good deal more accurate, particularly for C5 and C6, than the standard myelograph. In some of their cases the dorsal and ventral rootlets could plainly be seen. Our preferred method of radiological investigation remains CT-myelography. Magnetic resonance imaging (MRI) is of great value in displaying lesions of the spinal cord but, as yet, it has been disappointing in demonstrating the intradural rootlets. However, the capacity of MRI to show major nerve trunks (magnetic resonance neurography) is revealed by Fahr and Sauser (1988), Taylor et al. (1993), and Filler et al. (1993). West et al. (1994) showed changes of signal in denervated muscles. Using fast spin-echo magnetic resonance imaging, Francel et al. (1995) have been able to shorten the time of the procedure sufficiently to permit examination of infants with birth lesions of the brachial plexus. A further and particularly important contribution from the Seattle Group appeared in 1996 (Dailey et al., 1996) and used a phased array coil system to obtain high resolution images of the cervical spine

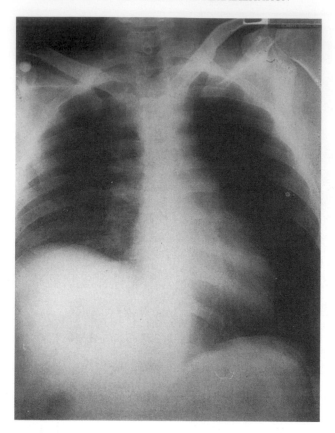

Figure 47.6. Paralysis of the right hemidiaphragm in a case of preganglionic injury C4/5/6/7.

and spinal nerves in three patients with cervicobrachial pain and one control subject aged 38 years. No doubt continuing advances in the application of MRI will prove of great value in the analysis of injuries to the brachial plexus: so Filler et al. (1993) define magnetic resonance neurography as "tissue-selective imaging directed at identifying and evaluating characteristics of nerve morphology: internal fascicular pattern, longitudinal patterns in signal intensity and calibre, and connections and relations to other nerves and plexuses".

Physiological investigations.   Bonney (1954) and Bonney and Gilliatt (1958) described two investigations that distinguished between pre- and postganglionic injury. When the dorsal rootlets of the spinal nerves are torn from the spinal cord, afferent fibres are in continuity with the dorsal root ganglion and do not degenerate. The normal flair from intradermal histamine persists—the axon reflexes unimpaired. Sensory potentials are detectable in the median and ulnar nerve on stimulation of the appropriate digits. The two investigations are useful from about 3 weeks, when Wallerian degeneration will have occurred distal to postganglionic ruptures. Celli and Rovesta (1987) combined EMG examination of paravertebral muscles with pre- and intra-operative sensory evoked potential recordings to determine the level of lesion and the found evidence indicating selective avulsion of ventral or dorsal rootlets. Landi et al. (1980) extended this

work by recording cortical evoked potentials through scalp electrodes from stimulation to nerve stumps displayed at operation. They found the investigations particularly helpful in diagnosing the extent of injury to the fifth cervical nerve. Sugioka and Nagano (1989) described detailed analysis of pre- and intra-operative neurophysiological recordings with the findings at operation demonstrating examples of combined pre- and postganglionic injury. These techniques are valuable in diagnosis before and during operation.

The introduction of electrophysiological process during operation has brought massive advantages, in particular in determining neural continuity across a lesion in continuity, determining the site of conduction block, determining which part of the nerve has suffered axonal interruption, and determining whether an apparently intact component of the brachial plexus has intact central connections. Such intraoperative electrophysiological investigation has been central to our diagnosis in lesions of the plexus in both adults and in children for over 20 years. The whole matter is considered at length by Smith (1998).

Indications for operation: Results

Operation is indicated when there are good clinical grounds for suspecting rupture or avulsion of the spinal nerves forming the brachial plexus. The intervention should be performed as an emergency where there is rupture of subclavian or axillary artery; open wounds from sharp objects or penetrating missiles should be treated with similar alacrity. The timing of operation in the closed traction lesion remains a matter of quite needless controversy. Exploration should be done as soon as the patient's condition permits, assuming that adequate facilities are available. Of course, life-threatening injuries to the central nervous system, the chest or the viscera are obvious contraindications to such urgent exploration (Fig. 47.7)

Details of techniques, of methods, of measurement of recovery, and of results of repair in over 700 cases are described at length elsewhere (Birch, 1998a). The following statements are based on this experience:

1. The outlook for patients with preservation of function in C8 and T1 is immeasurably better than for those with total lesions, assuming prompt re-innervation of the damaged nerve trunks either by graft in postganglionic lesions or by selective nerve transfers in the pre-ganglionic lesion of the upper nerves of the brachial plexus.
2. Nerve transfers of particular value in the preganglionic injury include: re-innervation of the nerve to serratus anterior by an intercostal nerve; re-innervation of the suprascapular nerve by the spinal accessory; and re-innervation of the biceps by a fascicle from the ulnar nerve.
3. There is an inexorable decline in the results with delay. The only adult patients presenting with complete lesions in whom some useful hand function was regained by nerve

and Norén (1995); this work has since been extended. There can be no doubt that functional recovery from the spinal cord to the periphery is possible. Much remains to be done—improvements in access to the spinal cord, the possibility of repair directly to the torn stumps of central roots, and the problem of sensory recovery through the repaired dorsal rootlets.

Rehabilitation

Early and accurate diagnosis is an essential first step towards achieving as normal an existence as is possible with the minimum of dependence. Early nerve repair gives the best prospect of improving prognosis. Although overoptimism is a danger, the writer's experience is that too many of these patients are told that nothing can be done and are effectively cast aside. The great majority of these patients show great courage when the news is severe and are willing to take any chance to improve their state and get themselves back to normal life. The patients' understanding of their condition and their cooperation in further treatment is essential for successful rehabilitation. As Petry and Merle (1989) comment, from their experience in Nancy "La Collaboration du patient est essentielle et seva d'autant étroite qu'il sera tenu informé et conseillé" ["Patient cooperation is essential, and will be all the more active as he will be well informed and well advised."]

The object of rehabilitation after serious damage to the brachial plexus are:

1. The objective assessment of disability and the accurate measurement of the outcome of treatment.
2. The reduction of the degree of disability by physical and other therapies.
3. The return of the patient to his or her original work, to the original work modified, or to suitable other work for the restoration of the patient's ability to live in his or her own home, to enjoy recreation and social intercourse and to be independently mobile.

It is now possible, in most cases of serious injuries to the brachial plexus, to measure with some accuracy the likely end state, to inform the patient accordingly, and to plan ahead with his or her cooperation for return to work and ordinary life. This process, begun with diagnosis and repair, is continued soon after recovery from operation. At about 6 weeks after operation the patient will be admitted for 1 or 2 weeks for a planned process of rehabilitation. Progress is monitored; if necessary, one or more further admissions for planned treatment can be arranged. In cases in which a patient is seen some months after injury and in which contractures have developed and morale has deteriorated it might be necessary to admit for preliminary rehabilitation before operation. We strongly believe that physiotherapy and occupational therapy should be for short but intensive periods. Occasional attendance at therapy departments stretching over months is self-defeating. We have had patients saying they have not returned to work because they must continue to attend for treatment two or three times a week for many months.

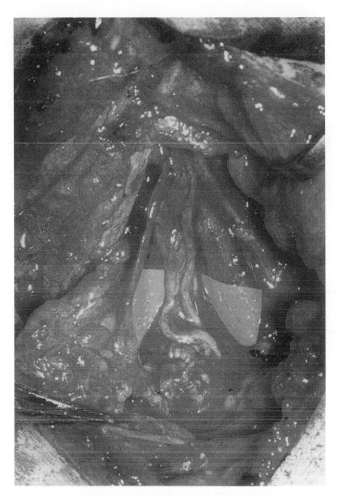

Figure 47.7. Rupture of C5 and C6; intact C7/8 and T1. Preparation of grafts from stumps of spinal nerves to divisions of the upper trunk and suprascapular nerve.

repair (and there are few enough of these) were operated within 3 weeks of injury. The proportion of failures of nerve repair in those cases operated within 3 weeks was about 20%. This rose to about 40% in those operated between 3 and 6 months and to over 60% in those operated after 6 months (Figs 47.8–47.10).

Repair of the intradural injury. Prompted by the earliest attempt at re-implantation, Jamieson and Eames (1980) demonstrated regeneration of axons through re-attached ventral roots in the dog. Thomas Carlstedt and his colleagues have gone very much further in a lengthy series of experiments and in clinical application. In 1986 came the demonstration of functional recovery after re-implantation of the ventral root in rats (Carlstedt et al. 1986). Functional reintegration between motor neurones and skeletal muscle after ventral root implantation was demonstrated in experiments on the spinal cord of the cat by Culheim et al. (1989). In 1995 came the first report of successful restoration of function in the adult human by re-implantation of avulsed spinal nerves in a case of total avulsion by Carlstedt, Grane, Hallin,

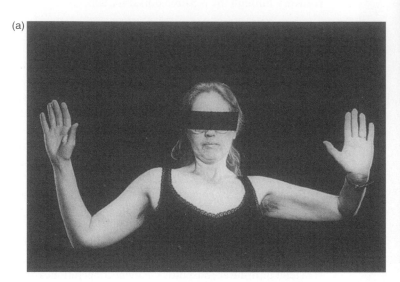

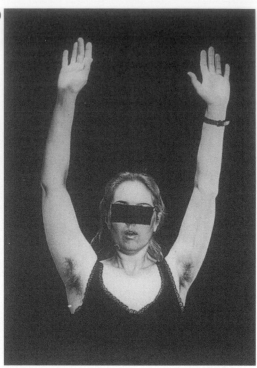

Figure 47.8. The same patient as Fig. 47.7—outcome 3 years after repair.

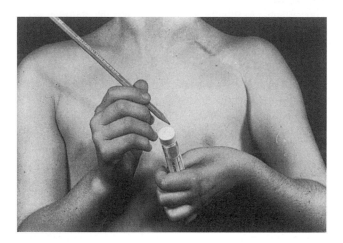

Figure 47.9. The outcome 4 years after extensive repair of a complete lesion of the brachial plexus in a 4-year-old child. There was preganglionic injury to C7 and C8, and postganglionic rupture of C5/6 and T1. Repair used the free vascularised ulnar nerve in addition to conventional graft.

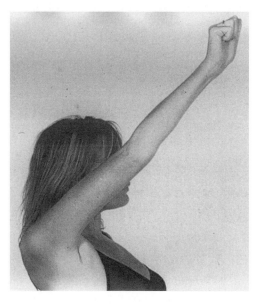

Figure 47.10. The result 2 years after preganglionic injury C5 and C6, intact C7/8 and T1. The repair was accessory to suprascapular and intercostals to musculocutraneous transfer. Power of elbow flexion exceeded 5 lb.

Patients are admitted to a low-dependency ward run by experienced nurses who are in a good position to recognise psychological and social problems and who are also responsible for making serial plaster of Paris splints for the correction of deformity and after tendon transfer. Physiotherapists work to overcome deformity and to develop strength and coordination. Intensive physiotherapy is used after restraining bandages are removed at 6 weeks following operations of nerve repair and, again, both before and after operations of muscle or tendon transfer. Patients are taught their own exercise programmes and are advised how to maintain their passive range of movement. Physiotherapists have a valuable role in treating the consequences of other severe injuries of the limbs: major fractures or dislocations occur in half of our patients. Finally, physiotherapists are responsible for implementing and monitoring transcutaneous nerve stimulation for pain. It is particularly difficult to maintain a full range of movement of the metacarpophalangeal and glenohumeral joints.

It is indeed remarkable how fixed-extension deformity of the former and the medial rotation deformity of the latter develop in spite of what appears to be careful and continuing treatment. There must be a considerable tendency to neglect the paralysed limb, and to rely on the treatment given in the hospital. It is the business of a responsible clinician, so far as possible, to change such an attitude and to impress upon the patient that the key to the avoidance or mitigation of permanent disability is in his or her hands. Spared muscle and recovering muscle are exercised; the patient is instructed about care for a limb to avoid accidental injury and the effects of disuse. The paralysed limb is especially sensitive to cold; patients might be tempted to warm an ice-cold limb by applying heat of a degree that would hardly be tolerated by healthy limbs. Anaesthesia of the skin allows exposure to such heat without the warning of pain; the disorder of vasomotor control certainly alters the reaction of the skin to such heat. Patients should be encouraged to protect the paralysed limb against external cold.

Once recovery of motor function begins, passive movements give way to active exercises. In the early stages, gravity-assisted exercises on the plinth and exercises in a pool are best. Immersion in warm water assists weak muscles; in the later stages water serves usefully as resistance. In these early stages, techniques of proprioceptive neuromuscular facilitation are particularly useful. The action of the weak biceps brachii can be enhanced by combined movement of adduction, flexion, and medial rotation.

Once muscles are strong enough to move joints against gravity, resistance can progressively be introduced: first against the hand of the physiotherapist; later against springs and weights. Isokinetic machines represent an extension of this principle; "cardiovascular training" has been useful in restoring morale and in general fitness, especially in older patients. Pressure garments are useful for swollen and hyperaesthetic limbs.

"Biofeedback", in which the contraction of the muscles are antagonist are visually recorded, is useful in the recovery phase, especially in cases of "co-contraction" of agonist and antagonist.

The occupational therapists continue functional training within a department that is equipped with many of the features found in the workplace. They continue to work towards improvement in range of motion, of power, and of stamina. They assess the need for special instruments, or adaptations, and supply these if they are necessary. Occupational therapists are responsible for fitting and training in the use of orthoses. The standard Royal National Orthopaedic Hospital modes of assessment for sensory function of peripheral nerve injuries is often useful in patients with partial lesions of the brachial plexus.

Pyschologists and speech therapists contribute in the treatment of those recovering from associated head injury—some 10% of out patients. Chronic pain and long-lasting disability are certain in some cases to produce depression. In such cases the advice of a clinical psychologist is likely to be helpful, but much of the burden of maintaining and improving morale must rest on those who are in daily contact with the patient.

Functional training and functional splinting

The elbow lock splint is useful in the absence of active control of the elbow (C5 and C6 lesions). The gauntlet splint is useful when there is major and lasting loss of function in the forearm and hand (C7, C8, and T1 lesions). The flail arm splint is used when there is irreparable and irrecoverable damage to the whole plexus (C5–T1 lesions) (Figs 47.11 and 47.12). The simplest of these is, of course, the elbow lock splint. The flail arm splint includes an elbow hinge and a wrist platform to which can be attached various devices, such as the split hook that is opened and closed by a cable and operated by the opposite shoulder. It

(a) 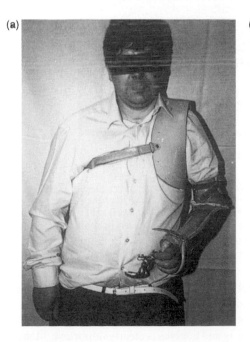 (b) 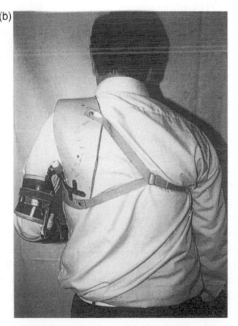 (c)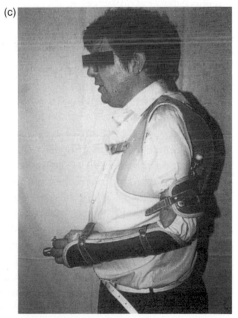

Figure 47.11. The full flail arm splint.

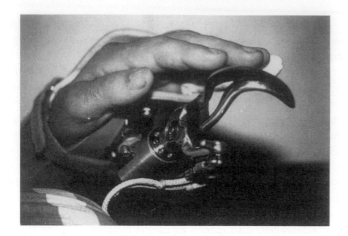

Figure 47.12. The standard curved hook appliance.

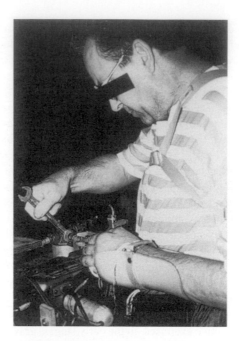

Figure 47.13. Using the plier attachment.

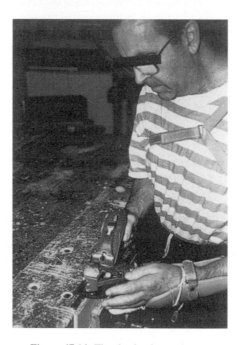

Figure 47.14. The chuck grip attachment.

is, in effect, an artificial limb over the paralysed limb. It consists of a shoulder support piece, an elbow ratchet that allows flexion in five different positions, and the forearm trough to which the appliance is fitted. The lower part of the splint—in effect the gauntlet—comes in three sizes. Adjustment by the orthotist and training by the occupational therapist takes about 10 days. The most useful devices are the tool holder, the split hook, and the appliance for steadying a sheet of paper. Although "success" is measured by continuing use of the splint, fitting and instruction are justified if:

1. The temporary use of a splint carries the patient usefully through a period of recovery.
2. Function confirmed by temporary splintage gives sufficient function to distract the patient from his or her pain.
3. Temporary use gives the patient the motivation to start and to continue rehabilitation.

Wynn Parry et al. (1987) were able to review 103 of 211 patients with flail arm splints. Sixty eight had continued to use these splints. It is probable that most of those failing to respond also failed to continue use of their splints (Figs 47.13–47.15).

Of 446 patients fitted between 1980 and July 1996 at the Royal National Orthopaedic Hospital, 205 responded to a questionnaire and 107 of these continued to use the splint; a "take-up" rate of perhaps one-quarter. The "take-up" rate was roughly the same for all three types of splints. Further examination of the design of these splints could result in the failure rate being reduced.

Between 1986 and 1993, 324 patients who underwent operations for supraclavicular injury of the brachial plexus were followed for at least 30 months; all had a period of admission for rehabilitation. Five parameters of response to rehabilitation were examined: (i) usefulness of the admission; (ii) continued use of splints; (iii) value of transcutaneous nerve stimulation; (iv) return to work or study; and (v) time off work. The results are shown in Tables 47.6–47.9. These are important figures, showing again the rather frequent failure of the splints in their present state; the general appreciation of a period of admission, and the rather high rate of return to work. A review of

the use of flail arm splints over 1 year from April 1995 confirmed the rather low rate of continued use (probably, 14 from 35). One of our patients with brachial plexus lesions works in the Orthotics Unit at Stanmore; two more are studying orthotics (Figs 47.16–47.19).

It is important not to offer the splint too early, before the patient grasps the reality of his or her disability, nor too late, before the patient has become functionally one armed. Respect for the patient's interests and hobbies is clearly important. Many

Figure 47.15. The straight pincer attachment.

Table 47.6. 324 supraclavicular lesions of the brachial plexus, usefulness of admission (patients' assessment)

Useful	301
Not useful	23
Benefits*	
Mobilisation of limb	
Adaptation to disability	
Meeting others with same type of injury	
Enhancement of morale	

*40% of all patients referred to all four of these benefits.

Table 47.7. 324 supraclavicular lesions of the brachial plexus, use of splint and TENS

	Yes	No
Splint used for more than 1 year (not fitted in 47)	87	195
TENS used for more than 1 year	48	
Never useful	168	

Table 47.8. 324 supraclavicular lesions of the brachial plexus, return to work or study

Return to work or study	249
Did not return	75
Same occupation as before injury	54
Different occupation	195
Formal retraining	81

Table 47.9. 324 supraclavicular lesions of the brachial plexus, time off work

Time off work (months)	Number of patients
< 3	19
4–6	44
7–12	60
13–18	32
19–30	28
> 31	18
Total	201

Return to work

It seems that the rate of return to work after serious injury of the brachial plexus is encouragingly high, but the findings that four out of five return to a different job indicates the importance of retraining and assistance with information about employment. Apart from physical disability, several factors militate against an early return to work. The patient might feel that, for a time, he or she has had enough and deserves a rest. If the question of compensation is raised, solicitors might well advise their client against an early return to work, apprehending that the chief item in any sum awarded is likely to relate to loss of earnings. It must, however, be recalled that from any sum awarded for loss of earnings the Department of Social Security will deduct welfare payments made in the period of invalidity.

The attitude of employers to disabled applicants is often unhelpful: the 1990s ethos of a long day's work for the lowest acceptable pay is inimical to the employment of persons who make special demands. However, recent changes in the medical criteria of unfitness for work might oblige many persons to resume work who otherwise would be content to rely on social security payments. Formerly, employees of more than 20 persons were obliged to include a percentage of disabled people within their workforce; this obligation was widely disregarded. The Disability Discrimination Act of 1996 introduces radical changes. Disability is defined as a physical or mental impairment that has a substantial and long-term adverse effect on a person's ability to carry out normal day-to-day activities. People who have a disability, and people who have had a disability but no longer have one, are covered by the Act. It is now unlawful for employers with 20 or more staff to discriminate against current or prospective employees with disability because of reasons relating to this disability, and they also have to make a readjustment if their employment arrangements or premises substantially disadvantage a disabled employee or a disabled applicant. Unlawful discrimination is defined; circumstances are defined in which less favourable treatment of a disabled person is justified. This includes those serving in the Armed Forces. As Bonney (1998b) notes "one may speculate that, had these regulations been enforced 200 years ago, the victor of the Nile, Copenhagen, and Trafalgar would not have come as he did to his triumph and his death". Evidently, the balance has been altered decisively and the employer is no longer obliged to include a proportion of disabled persons in the workforce; rather, it is for the disabled person refused a job to show that the

have been helped by being able to go back to fishing or gardening, even though they do not use the splint for work itself. In a small number of patients engaged in heavy manual work, it soon becomes clear that the modular model of the flail arm splint is insufficiently robust. For these patients, a custom-made "heavy duty" orthosis is supplied.

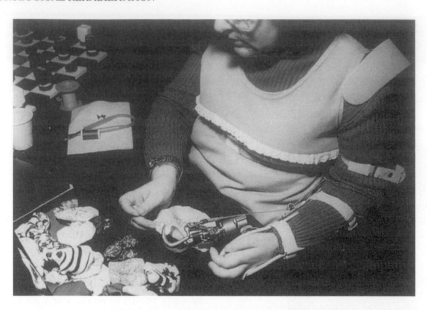

Figure 47.16. The curved hook in fine work.

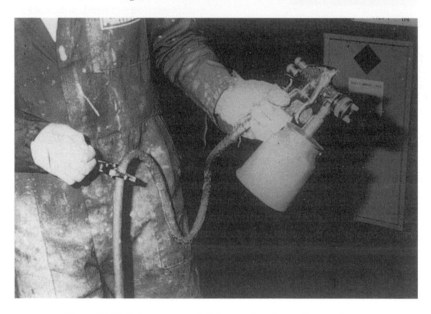

Figure 47.17. Paint sprayer at full-time work, using a plier attachment.

refusal stemmed from discrimination because of his or her disability. Cox (1996) comments quite sharply that the guidance notes published to help interpretation of the provisions of the Act "signal a contentious time ahead for health professionals".

Success in returning the patient to work depends on the capacity and motivation of the patient, on the efforts of whoever is in charge of treatment, and on the availability of employment. At Job Centres, Disablement Resettlement Officers are available to advise on possibilities of return to work. A hospital-based Employment Advisor has also been in post at the Royal National Orthopaedic Hospital since 1969 and advises generally about the problems associated with return to work. There is little difficulty for a patient with minor residual disability, for those having easy access to transport, or for those working in an assured job that

is not physically demanding. For the majority who are not so favourably placed, the hospital Employment Advisor is available to help while the patient is in hospital. Problems can be discussed and, in favourable cases, difficulties can be resolved before discharge. With the patient's permission, the Advisor makes contact with the employer and discusses the job situation and any adjustments that will be required to accommodate the patient's disability. Best, of course, is return to the original work, but if that is not possible then alternative employment with the same firm may be available. Employers are given an incentive to make suitable provision by access to government grants of up to 80% of costs between £300 and £10,000, and 100% of costs over £10,000, for the adaptation of premises or provision of special equipment.

In cases of severe permanent disability, precluding a return to anything like the original work, retraining offers a way forward. The Employment Advisor can arrange for such patients to be seen at one of the numerous employment assessment centres. That can lead to a specialised training course, either locally or at one of the four residential training colleges maintained in Durham, Exeter, Leatherhead, and Nottingham. The Employment Advisor can also help in the matter of transport and mobility: patients with serious disability of one upper limb are able to handle a car fitted with an automatic gear box and adjustments for the steering wheel and hand brake. Modifications are also available for the patient whose disability affects the lower limb.

IATROPATHIC AND POSTIRRADIATION NEUROPATHY

Although it has been traditional to describe injuries produced by doctors as "iatrogenic", this term indicates "doctor-producing" rather than "produced by or derived from a doctor". Bonney proposed "iatrogenous" in 1986 and then proposed the term "iatropathic" in his outstanding review of this field in 1998 (Bonney, 1998c). Most of what follows is drawn from that review. It seems that iatropathic injury of peripheral nerves is a serious problem and it is probably on the increase. Since the mid-1990s there has been a three-fold increase in the number of patients seen in the Peripheral Nerve Injury Unit with substantial damage to nerves incurred during operations. Bonney suggested a number of mechanisms of iatropathic injuries:

1. Drugs causing neuropathy.
2. Drugs interfering with blood coagulation, and so causing intra- or extraneural haemorrhage.
3. Injection of agents into or near a main nerve.
4. Pressure from haematoma following accidental or deliberate arterial puncture.
5. The production of or failure to recognise and treat ischaemia of a limb.
6. Closed pressure or traction during general anaesthesia.

Figure 47.18. Full-time gardener who uses a variety of attachments for his tools.

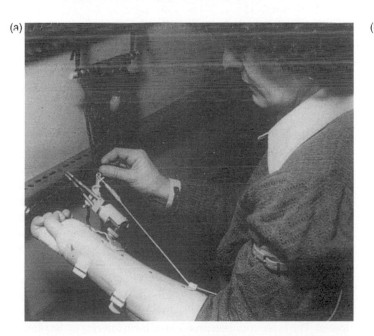

(a)

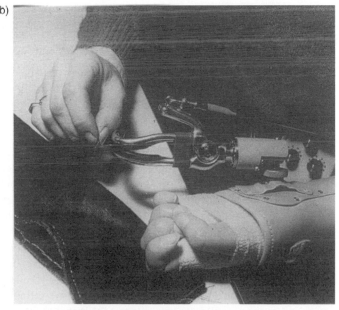

(b)

Figure 47.19. The gauntlet splint in a patient with irreparable lesion C6/7/8 and T1.

7. Traction during manipulation under anaesthesia or during delivery.
8. Direct damage from pressure, traction, heat, clamping, or cutting within the field of operation.
9. Ionising radiation.

We will now consider those mechanisms that are particularly significant in the causation of lesions to the brachial plexus before going on to consider post-irradiation neuropathy, pain, and obstetric brachial plexus palsy.

Injection injury

Experimental studies indicate the relative neurotoxicity of various agents and stress particular danger of intrafascicular injection (Gentili et al., 1979; MacKinnon & Dellon, 1984). Hudson (1984) suggested that harm arose from intraneural injection rather than from diffusion from adjacent injection, although more recent work (Kline & Hudson, 1995) supports this mechanism too. The benefits from successful regional blocks are so considerable that it seems carping to speak of hazard. Nevertheless, our experience of 52 cases of significant neural deficit following regional blockade warrants closer inspection. There were three patterns of injury. In the first (38 cases) there was direct injury to the nerve trunk by needle, and this injury was compounded by the injection of an anaesthetic agent into the nerve, on occasions within the perineurium of individual fascicles. Recovery in these cases was generally good for the A-alpha and A-beta fibres: it seemed to be worst for the A-delta and C-fibres so that spontaneous pain, dysaesthesia, hyperalgesia and even allodynia persisted. These symptoms often proved resistant to treatment. Inspection at operation was delayed in most of these cases and the intervention was usually fruitless. Findings suggested fibrosis within the nerve trunk, within and between the fascicles and also between the nerve trunk and enveloping fascial sleeves. Obliteration of longitudinal epineural vessels over the fibrosed segment was a constant feature.

In the second group (eight cases) the neural lesion developed as a consequence of laceration of an axial artery, usually the axillary. The presentation was dramatic and characteristic. Evolution and progression of the nerve deficit followed the pattern seen in false aneurysm: deepening over the course of 24 hours or so, generally afflicting the largest fibres most deeply, and accompanied by severe pain. The prognosis for this group was good when intervention was performed early, when the arterial lesion was treated adequately, and when the nerve trunk was not intimately involved by the sac of the false aneurysm. When the epineurium was breached and the nerves involved within the sac, persisting pain and deficit was the rule.

In the final group (six cases) the damage to the spinal cord, and to spinal and cranial nerves, was substantial and permanent. These catastrophes followed interscalene block. The common factor in these seemed to be the interference with the vertebral artery and/or the radicular vessels entering the spinal canal with the 7th and 8th cervical nerves.

CASE STUDY
A 4-year-old boy suffered a closed fracture of the right clavicle. Operative reduction and internal fixation were done. A right interscalene injection of 10 ml 0.5% marcaine (Bupivicaine) was given. There was a lesion of the cord and the brainstem with right facial weakness, deviation of the uvula, left abducens paresis, right Bernard–Horner syndrome, and sensory and motor paralysis of the right upper limb. There was, probably, recurrent laryngeal nerve paralysis and phrenic nerve palsy. Magnetic resonance imaging 2 days after the operation showed swelling of the right side of the brainstem and cervical spinal cord. Vertebral angiography showed no abnormality. It is likely that the responsible lesion here was a true spasm of the right vertebral artery, causing an ipsilateral lesion of the spinal cord and brainstem.

CASE STUDY
A patient suffered lasting and severe spinal cord lesion from interscalene block performed at the end of an operation for reconstruction of the rotator cuff. Initially there was weak paraparesis and a dense bilateral lesion of the 7th and 8th cervical and first thoracic nerves. There was some recovery of function into both lower limbs but this was complicated by severe diffuse burning pain and there was no recovery for the skeletal efferents passing through C8 and T1 in either upper limb.

The studies of Dommisse (1975) show that although the vertebral artery does not contribute directly to the anterior spinal artery below the third cervical segment, radicular branches support the blood supply of the cord below that level by contributing to the longitudinal anastomosis. Radicular vessels passing with the 7th and 8th cervical nerves were often substantial.

Closed pressure and traction during general anaesthesia

The use of shoulder rests to support patients in the Trendelenberg position was formerly a common cause of lesion to the brachial plexus (Bonney, 1947). These now seem to be very uncommon but the brachial plexus is vulnerable during operations in which the upper limb is abducted and laterally rotated at the shoulder, a position adopted during operations within the abdomen, in transaxillary operations on the sympathetic chain, and in operations for removal of the first rib. The lesions are nearly always caused by transient ischaemia or by local demyelination and they usually recover, although the period of recovery can be long and the disability tiresome. When possible, abduction of the shoulder should be limited to 70 degrees, and lateral rotation and extension of the glenohumeral joint should be avoided. Traction upon the lower trunk of the brachial plexus seems unavoidable during open heart surgery from the movement of the upper hemithorax on the axial skeleton. Parks (1973) studied peripheral neuropathy after no less than 50,000 operations. Three of the 28 cases of injury to the brachial plexus followed open heart operations. Birch and colleagues (1991b) reported on three cases in which the brachial plexus was damaged during manipulation of the shoulder for "frozen shoulder". In one case the plexus was explored, there was no rupture, and recovery followed. The more common problem of birth injuries to the plexus is considered later.

Direct damage in the field of operation

The brachial plexus and its branches are at risk during operations within the posterior triangle of the neck, the axilla, for excision of the first thoracic or accessory ribs, and during sympathectomy. We have seen cases where a major part, and in one case where the whole of the plexus, have been transected in operations for the excision of "lymph node" or "lump". Severe pain is a constant feature in all of these cases, quite apart from the neural defect.

CASE STUDY
A 27-year-old man, otherwise fit, suffered from constant and severe burning pain throughout the left upper limb as a consequence of an injury to the cervical spine during rugby 5 years previously. Transthoracic endoscopic sympathectomy was done and was complicated by haemorrhage; the lower trunk of the brachial plexus was transected while attempting to control haemorrhage. For 9 weeks the burning pain disappeared, but it was then replaced by severe lancinating pain with intense paraesthesae in the ulnar border of the forearm and hand. The defect in the lower trunk was grafted, the lancinating pain disappeared within days of the operation. The treatment for causalgia was complicated by post-traumatic neuralgia—this was eased by repair of C8 and T1.

The spinal accessory nerve is too often divided during lymph node biopsy. Seddon (1975) reported 14 cases from a clinical practice extending over 40 years. We have now seen close on 100 cases in 10 years; 30 more cases have been seen in connection with civil process being taken by victims and in only very few of these had repair even been attempted. Williams and colleagues (1996) reported 40 cases and commented "injury to the accessory nerve results in a characteristic group of symptoms and signs—reduced shoulder abduction, drooped shoulder and pain. Repair of the nerve improves the symptoms in most cases. A sound grasp of the surgical anatomy, together with the use of the nerve stimulator, ought to prevent this serious complication of surgery in the neck". Two pitfalls are common: (i) the apparent winging of the scapula is mistakenly attributed to paralysis of serratus anterior perhaps from neuralgic amyotrophy; and (ii) the almost constant finding of polyphasic units or some motor units under voluntary control at electromyographic examination of the middle and lower fibres is taken as evidence of recovery.

Although some allowance can be made for the damage to nerves incurred during operation, in some cases, little or no allowance can be permitted for failure to recognise the fact of the nerve injury; failure to diagnose the depth of the affection, its nature, and the extent of injury; and failure to take appropriate action. An early paper on this subject (Birch et al., 1991a) showed a delay in diagnosis from seconds to 40 months. In nearly half the patients, diagnosis was delayed for more than 6 months. A subsequent report (Khan & Birch, 2001) showed that the situation was, if anything, actually worse than this.

POST-IRRADIATION NEUROPATHY (IN)

The onset of pain, sensory disturbance, and weakness in the arm following radiotherapy to the neck and axilla for cancer can be taken as evidence of recurrent disease, but direct injury to the brachial plexus by irradiation is an important differential diagnosis. Furthermore, the late development of malignant peripheral nerve sheath tumours after irradiation is now clearly established (Ducatman & Scheithauer, 1983; Sordillo et al., 1981).

Interest in the field of radiation neuropathy, and in particular of that of neuropathy after treatment of breast cancer, goes back at least 30 years. There has been much difficulty. Until recently it could be difficult to convince some radiotherapists of the condition, and disclosure of the details of the dosage and duration of treatment was sometimes difficult to find. Next, it is difficult to understand why one patient treated for breast cancer should develop irradiation neuropathy whereas another treated in an apparently similar manner should not. Third, the great interval, up to 24 years, between the treatment and onset of symptoms is an important obstacle to investigation. Hospital Authorities and Trusts are commonly averse to spending money on the storage and retrieval of records and policies of routine destruction after 6 years or so are common. Last, is the continuing uncertainty about the value of operation in IN: the only definite conclusion about its value is as a method of distinguishing between recurrence and neuropathies. The situation of the clinician directing the radiotherapy is one of particular difficulty. Radiation must be sufficient to destroy tumour cells; on the other hand it should not be enough, nor so directed, as to cause serious damage to normal tissues, and in particular to nerves. The long latency between treatment and symptoms only adds to these difficulties.

Pathogenesis

Cavanagh (1968a,b) investigated the effects of radiation on the sciatic nerves of rats. He found significant nuclear abnormalities in the Schwann cells after exposure to as little as 200 rads (2 Gy) and he further found that cellular proliferation after crush injury was seriously impaired if the limb had been previously subjected to 1900 rads (19 Gy) of irradiation. Spiess (1972) showed there were changes in the axons and in the myelin sheath and these, together with vasculitis, led to fibrosis. Stoll and Andrews (1966) reported a high incidence of neuropathy in patients receiving 63 Gy by megavoltage radiation over 25 to 28 days after radical operation. Mumenthaler (1964), Maruyama and colleagues (1967), and Burns (1978) described cases with onset of symptoms many years after completion of radiation. However, Castaigne and colleagues (1969) referred to a case of metastatic neuropathy 26 years after the completion of treatment of a primary breast cancer. In two of our cases, metastatic neuropathy became evident at 10 and 14 years after treatment of the primary tumour.

The difficulties in differentiation of radiation and metastatic neuropathy were addressed by Steiner and colleagues (1971) and by Thomas and Colby (1972). Both recommended surgical exploration of the brachial plexus in those cases in which diagnosis was uncertain. Both agreed that a long interval between the primary treatment and the onset of symptoms of neuropathy was no certain indicator of damage by irradiation. Kori (1981) proposed a clinical distinction from findings in 100 patients. Pain, affliction of the lower part of the plexus and Bernard–Horner syndrome were more common in metastatic neuropathy than in radiation neuropathy. These impressions were supported by Lederman and Wilbourn (1984), who suggested that fasciculation in radiation neuropathy was the "most useful diagnostic criteria". Roth et al. (1988) also showed the value of the physiological findings of myokymic discharges as an indicator of radiation neuropathy and indicated a connection with conduction block. Harper and colleagues (1989) were able to confirm the more common finding of myokymic discharges in radiation rather than in metastatic neuropathy. In 1994, De Lisa and colleagues defined myokymia as "continuous quivering and undulation of the surface and overlying skin . . . associated with spontaneous, repetitive discharge of motor unit potentials".

The role of CT and MRI in distinguishing between metastases and IN has been investigated by a number of workers. Castagno and Shuman (1987) concluded that "MR may have substantial clinical utility in evaluating patients with suspected brachial plexus tumours, particularly in patients with suggestive neurological signs and symptoms". Certainly, MRI was of critical importance in the diagnosis of three of our cases of post-irradiation malignant peripheral nerve sheath tumour. Cooke and colleagues (1988) thought that CT scanning could be useful in distinguishing metastatic disease from IN and Glazer and colleagues (1985) found that radiation fibrosis, like muscle, "usually remained low in signal intensity on T2-weighted images, while tumours demonstrated higher signal intensity". Rapaport and colleagues (1988) correlated findings on MRI with pathological findings and appearances on computer tomography: MRI was found to be more accurate than computer tomography. Posniak and colleagues (1993) found that the value of magnetic resonance imaging remained unclear "because hypo-intensive and hyper-intensive lesions on T2-weighted images had been described in radiation fibrosis. Biopsy may be required to make a definitive diagnosis".

Incidence of irradiation neuropathy

Kogelnik (1977) concluded that the development of IN of cranial nerve and of brachial plexus was closely related to the total dose applied, the number and size of individual doses per fraction, and overall time. Barr and Kissin (1987) found that six out of 250 patients treated by local excision and irradiation at the Royal Marsden Hospital between 1980 and 1983 developed IN at intervals of from 4 to 24 months. Olsen and colleagues (1990) found that chemotherapy increased the incidence of neuropathy after radiotherapy, and, in a later, major, study (Olsen et al., 1993) examined 161 recurrence-free breast cancer patients for radiation plexopathy after a median follow-up period of 50 months; 5% and 9% of patients receiving radiotherapy had disabling and mild radiation plexopathy, respectively. This was more common in patients receiving chemotherapy and in younger patients and they concluded that fractions of 2 Gy or less were advisable.

The Royal College of Radiologists (London) has made valuable contributions towards clarifying the morass that surrounds work on IN. In part, this was a response to a group action taken by the Radiation Action Group Exposure (RAGE). An independent review by Bates and Evans (1995) established a number of findings, which included:

1. The association of neuropathy with movement of the patient between the treatment of the chest wall and the treatment of the lymph nodes.
2. The very high incidence of neuropathy in patients receiving high doses of treatment coupled with moderate movement during treatment.

The Royal College set up a committee to review the "management of adverse effects following radiotherapy". This is a wide ranging study of the nature, diagnosis, natural course, and response to treatment of radiation neuropathy of the brachial plexus, and Spittle (1995) performed a valuable service in bringing these reports to the notice of wider audience.

Pathology and natural course

The lesion is sclerotic and there is occlusion of small vessels, but sudden and severe defects can be related to the occlusion of large vessels as reported by Butler (1980), Barros d'Sa (1992a), and Gerard and colleagues (1989), who demonstrated segmental thrombosis within the subclavian artery 22 years after irradiation and radical mastectomy (Fig. 47.20). Superimposed upon the primary neural lesion is external compression from sclerosis of such muscles as the scalenus anterior and medius, the subclavius and pectoralis minor. The prevertebral fascia, the axillary sheath, and the fat pads in the supra- and infraclavicular fossae also become fibrosed. Merle and colleagues (1988) described these as "Syndromes canalaires créés par la nécrose du petit pectoral et du sous-clavier". ["Entrapment syndromes caused by fibrosis of the pectoralis minor and subclavius muscles."]

Narakas et al. (1987) described the evolution of the lesion in 126 patients in whom operations were performed. Three stages of increasing neural deficit with pain were recognised. Our own experience of more than 70 cases shows, almost always, steady deterioration. The initial symptom is usually that of paraesthesae in the fingers and it is at this stage that a diagnosis of carpal tunnel syndrome or cervical radiculopathy is commonly made. Muscle weakness and pain are less common as initial symptoms. There is then progression to severe alteration of sensibility and motor paralysis; sometimes pain develops or progresses to become constant and severe. Salner and colleagues (1981) described cases of spontaneous remission. Killer and Hess (1990) found that the condition progressed without remission in all of their cases.

Post-irradiation malignant peripheral nerve sheath tumour is marked by a definite change in the nature and in the evolution of symptoms, most especially by the onset of severe pain and by rapidly progressive loss of function within a segment of the

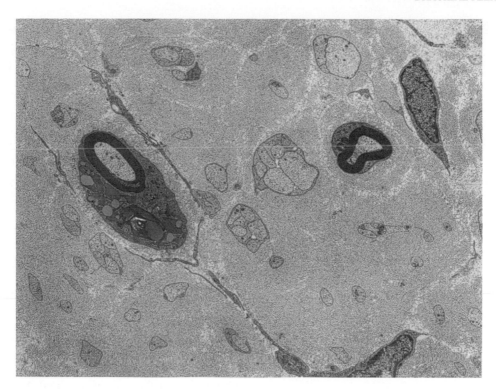

Figure 47.20. Electron micrograph (×5000) of bundle biopsy, lateral cord of brachial plexus, IN. Note the extensive endoneurial fibrosis, scanty myelinated nerve fibres and abnormal Schwann cell cytoplasm.

brachial plexus. MR scanning will reveal a mass before it is palpable.

Treatment

Mondrup and colleagues (1990), reporting from Denmark, stated bleakly: "because the treatment of brachial plexopathy is unsuccessful, prevention is warranted". Opinion is certainly divided. For a number of years we recommended and practised exploration and biopsy, externally by neurolysis and occasionally by epineurotomy for confirmation of diagnosis and in the hope of giving relief, an attitude shared by Fallet and colleagues (1967) in Geneva, Steiner and colleagues (1971), and Merle (1988) in Nancy. There is no very clear evidence supporting the use of steroids that have been given on empirical grounds, nor for the use of actihaemyl (Albert & Mackert, 1970). A prospective clinical trial of hyperbaric oxygen is currently being undertaken.

The bold aim of revascularising the plexus, or at least surrounding it with healthy tissue by enveloping it in revascularised omentum was proposed by Kiricuta (1963), Uhlschmid and Clodius (1978), and Narakas (1984b). Narakas thought that omentoplasty was most likely to succeed if used early; he achieved a "functional result" in only 20% of cases. Le Quang (1989) made careful observations from a wide practical experience and concluded that operations should be performed in radiation plexitis; that they should be performed as soon as possible; and that selective neurolysis should be completed by a pedicled omentoplasty. Le Quang stated clearly the limitations

of operation. Our own experience with omentoplasty has been discouraging, but outstandingly good results have been achieved in three cases in which a pedicle graft of the latissimus dorsi muscle was used; these operations were done in collaboration with Professor Roy Sanders (Mount Vernon Hospital). In all three cases there was dramatic relief of pain and significant recorded improvement in sensation and in muscle power.

CASE STUDY

A man born in 1972 was treated at the ages of 3, 6 and 8 years for "lesions" of the left pectoral region, later thought to be those of malignant fibrocycteocytoma. In 1992 a recurrent tumour was widely excised and the site was irradiated (60 Gy in 18 fractions over 18 weeks). Symptoms and radiation neuropathy began soon after treatment and progressed until, at 6 months, there was serious severe pain with deep affection of motor and sensory functions and serious damage to the skin over the clavicle. Electrophysiological examination confirmed severe affection of the medial and posterior cords; in particular, there were frequent fibrillations and positive sharp waves in the left first dorsal interosseous muscle. At operation in 1994, 2 years after radiotherapy, an extensive neurolysis of the plexus was done, with division of the scaleni, pectoralis minor, and clavicular head of pectoralis major. Stimulation of roots and recording from cords showed the potentials had diminished amplitude and velocity (medial cord 25 metres per second, posterior cord 10 metres per second). Professor Sanders then elevated and placed a pedicle musculocutaneous flap of latissimus dorsi and overlying skin to replace the burnt skin and surround the plexus. There was early relief of pain; 2 years after operation there was good recovery of motor and sensory function.

Overall, our experience with 55 traced patients who underwent operation for IN suggest that the likelihood of relief of

Table 47.10.   Irradiation neuropathy: outcomes

	Number of patients
Irradiation neuropathy: operation	
Women	
Breast cancer	45
Lymphoma	3
Cancer of the thyroid	1
Skin malignancy	1
Total	50
Men	
Lymphoma	3
Malignant fibrous histiocytoma (one received neutron therapy and later had amputation)	2
Total	5
Operations	
"Decompression"	46
Pedicled latissimus dorsi	5
Free latissimus dorsi	2
Omental transfer	2
Outcome of operation	
Relief of pain with neurological improvement	5
Relief of pain with stabilisation of neurological state	24
Transient or no relief	26
Recurrence of cancer confirmed	3
Complications	
Amputation (arterial necrosis)	1
Thrombosis of the subclavian artery	1
Delayed healing with necrosis of clavicle	1
Death (CVA 3 months after operation)	1
Irradiation neuropathy: no operation	
Women	
Lumbosacral (pelvic cancer)	1
Cancer of the breast (very severe radiation effects)	5
Cancer of the breast: spontaneous remission (10-year observation)	1
Total	7

pain and regression of the neurological abnormality is low (5 patients); 24 patients obtained relief of pain and stabilisation of their neurological state; 25 obtained no relief. Recurrence of carcinoma was confirmed in three cases; remarkably there was substantial relief of pain in two of these after operation. There were a number of serious complications. In one, necrosis of the artery led to amputation; in another there was thrombosis of the subclavian artery; in one there was delayed healing with necrosis of part of the clavicle; and one patient died from cerebrovascular accident 3 months after operation. In one undoubted case of radiation neuropathy there was spontaneous remission over a period of 10 years (Table 47.10).

It is a pity that the place of operation in the treatment of radiation neuropathy remains uncertain in spite of all that has been done and has been published. Operation is probably indicated in three circumstances: (i) to establish diagnosis, and in particular the diagnosis of radiation-induced malignant tumour of the peripheral nerve sheath; (ii) in cases of severe and persisting pain; and (iii) in cases where there is rapid and progressive loss of function.

PAIN

Severe pain is usual in patients after preganglionic injury, and for some it is an overwhelming problem that dominates their life. All units treating a significant number of such patients will know of those who have become hopelessly addicted to opiates or who have committed suicide. The pain is usually immediate in onset and, typically, it has two components. First, there is the constant pain, which is usually felt in the insensate hand and which is described as crushing or boring, bursting, or burning. Superimposed on this are lightning-like shooting pains that course down the whole of the limb. These last a few seconds, they can occur up to 30 or 40 times every hour, and they are exceptionally severe in intensity. It is usually the case that patients will report the distribution of these pains within the territory of avulsed nerves. The shooting pain is not experienced in those parts of the limb that have not been denervated. Any intellectual construct that seeks to explain the source of this pain must take into account the clearly defined characteristics of the two types of pain, the immediacy of onset and the modulation or exacerbation of that pain by other factors. It is usually worse in cold weather, if the patient is otherwise ill, or when the patient is stressed or depressed. A hypothesis that seeks to explain these observations on the basis of structural changes occurring within the central nervous system, over a period of some weeks, will not account for the immediacy of onset.

In 1911, Frazier and Skillern set out to perform dorsal rhizotomy in a patient—a physician with intractable pain from closed traction lesion of the brachial plexus. They exposed the spinal cord by laminectomy and found the anterior and posterior rootlet of C6, C7, and C8 absent: "the roots evidently had been torn completely from the cord". The patient's description of the pain was characteristic: "the pain is continuous, it does not stop a minute, either day or night. It is either burning or compressing . . . in addition, there is, every few minutes, a jerking sensation similar to that of pain by touching . . . a Leyden jar. It is like a zigzag made in the sky by a stroke of lightning. The upper part of the arm is mostly free of pain; the lower part from a little above the elbow to the tips of the fingers, never."

Of some relevance here perhaps is the observation made by Bonney and Jamieson in 1976 that, in a human spinal cord observed 24 hours after avulsion of the roots of the brachial plexus, the level of separation was in fact about 1 mm proud of the surface of the cord (Bonney & Jamieson, 1979). Later histological studies confirm that in many cases of preganglionic injury the line of separation is within the peripheral nerve, through or distal to the transitional zone. The lesion is akin to rhizotomy. In more extreme cases, however, the rootlets are torn from within the spinal cord, and fragments of this are seen attached to those rootlets when they are exposed within the posterior triangle of the neck. This is true avulsion (Schenker, 1998).

Bonney (1973) suggested that the pain arose in the spinal cord because of damage and later gliosis in the substantia gelatinosa. This has been confirmed in the lumbar spinal cord of the cat after dorsal rhizotomy or avulsion (Ovelmen-Levitt et al., 1982). There were differences in the morphological and the electrophysiological response between these two groups. Ovelmen-Levitt et al. (1982) found a different pattern of neuropeptides within the damaged dorsal horn after rhizotomy or avulsion.

The intradural rupture or rhizotomy is, in effect, an injury of the peripheral nerves; an avulsion is an injury of the central nervous system. Bristol and Fraher (1989) observed that most of the myelinated fibres within the ventral roots of rat spinal nerves ruptured at the transition zone junction. Hoffman et al. (1993) recorded changes in the spinal cord of the cat at different intervals after avulsion of the cervical ventral root. They showed a progressive degeneration of motor axons between the ventral horn cell and the surface of the cord. In the first few weeks there was evidence of proximal motor axons entering a phase of regeneration by forming "terminal clubs", an observation made earlier by Cajal (1928).

An extreme example of the anatomical damage following avulsion is the rare complication of post-traumatic syrinx. Taylor (1962) and Richter and Schachenmayr (1984) demonstrated cyst formation in the region of the posterior horn and interomediolateral (Lissauer's) tract long after avulsion, and Taylor produced instant and lasting relief of pain by excision of the cyst.

The severe traction lesion of the brachial plexus brings about loss of all afferent input, disruption of the descending central inhibitory pathways, and damage to both dorsal and ventral horns. The neurophysiological sequelae of deafferentation were described by Loeser and Ward (1967) and Anderson et al. (1977), who showed that experimental deafferentation produced spontaneous firing in laminae 1 and 5 of the posterior horn—the sites of relay of the nociceptor fibres. This spontaneous firing began a few days after the lesion and gradually increased to reach a maximum at about 1 month. Two varieties of activity were observed: (i) a continuous barrage; and (ii) superimposed paroxysmal bursts of high frequency firing. Micro-electro recordings made from the deafferented cords of human subjects showed paroxysmal discharges that coincided with the occurrence of painful flexor spasms. Albé-Fessard and Lombard (1983) showed experimentally that spontaneous firing found in the posterior horn after experimental section of the roots was gradually transmitted more rostrally. Some months after injury, impulses could be detected in the thalamus. If transcutaneous stimulation was applied before and immediately after the lesion was inflicted, spontaneous firing could be reduced considerably. Rinaldi et al. (1991) recorded electrical activity from single cells in the thalamus in ten patients with chronic pain associated with deafferentation. One of these had suffered a traction injury to the brachial plexus; lesions of peripheral nerves accounted for seven others. Spontaneous activity in neurones in the Lateral Ventral Posterior nucleus (of the thalamus) (VPL) was demonstrated, but also, and for the first time in humans, hyperactivity within the medial thalamus. They commented "the findings of a dual representation of neuronal hyperactivity in the lateral and medial thalamus is perhaps not surprising in view of the fact that these are the two primary thalamic targets for the pain related

relays from the spinal cord carried by the neo-spino-thalamic and paleo-spino-thalamic systems".

Although it is tempting to suggest that the constant crushing element of brachial plexus pain is a reflection of deafferentation, and is associated with the rhizotomy lesion, and that the shooting or the convulsive element indicates true avulsion, it must be admitted that the paucity of light or electron microscopic evidence about the state of the human spinal cord and of its posterior horn makes it very difficult to define the cause or to determine why some have pain, why some lose it, and why some have no pain at all. The knowledge of spontaneous firing of neurones in the substantia gelatinosa, and of the inhibitory impulses in the posterior columns, makes the theory of "deafferentation pain" attractive. Further observations on human subjects are required.

Birch and Bonney (1998) classed pain after nerve injury as follows:

1. Causalgia (complex regional pain syndrome type 2).
2. Reflex sympathetic dystrophy (complex regional pain syndrome type 1).
3. Post-traumatic neuralgia, which can be divided between that following major injury to a major nerve trunk and that following injury to a nerve of cutaneous sensation.
4. Pain due to persistent compression, distortion, or ischaemia. We have called this pain neurostenalgia, from ὅτενος (stenos) a strait as in stenosis added to νευρου (neuron) a nerve or tendon. It is agreeable that the verb ὅτενω means to moan or groan, so that there is a dual reference to the idea of pain. This group undoubtedly contains many examples of Seddon's "irritative" lesions.
5. Central pain. This too can be divided between that following rupture of spinal nerves at the level of the transitional zone leading to pure deafferentation and that following avulsion of roots of a limb plexus from the spinal cord itself, a lesion that is truly an injury of the central nervous system.
6. Pain maintained either deliberately or subconsciously by the patient in response to a challenge, such as the wish to obtain compensation or because of resentment against a public body such as an insurance company, or other provocation.

Although central pain is by far the most common of the severe states following injury to the brachial plexus, the distinctive qualities of certain others and their response to correct surgical intervention deserves mention.

Causalgia

We have treated 14 patients who presented with this, the most severe of neuropathic pain states. Penetrating missile injury was the cause in every case and in seven cases there was associated false aneurysm or arteriovenous fistula. Notwithstanding uncertainties about the role of the sympathetic nervous system in pain states previously considered "sympathetically maintained", causalgia remains as clearly defined as the pain after pregangli-onic injury of the brachial plexus. Diagnosis is made from the history alone. There has been a wound to the proximal part of the upper limb; there has been partial damage to the brachial plexus. There is spontaneous persistent pain, very often of a burning nature; pain is localised principally in the distribution of the nerve or nerves affected, but spreading beyond that dis-tribution; pain is aggravated by physical and emotional stimuli; there is association of pain with hyperaesthesia and hyperal-gesia of the skin and the distribution of the nerves affected; and there is association with disturbances of circulation and of sweat-ing. Allodynia and hyperpathia are present. Analgesic drugs are rarely effective.

The following description is typical. One of our patients, a 28-year-old man, was shot in the axilla by a shotgun in the course of a robbery while he was working in his bank. He experienced immediate and intense searing pain in the hand, the forearm, and the arm. We first saw him at 6 weeks, he had lost weight and was clearly exhausted from lack of sleep. No examination of the affected arm was tolerated. The hand itself was swollen, mottled, blue, and cold. There was profuse sweating, the nails were coarse and the hair on the back of the hand had overgrown.

An injection of local anaesthetic into the cervical sympathetic chain brought relief within minutes, soon after this showing a Bernard–Horner sign, and a short while before vaso- and sudo-motor paralysis appeared in the hand. At operation, a partial transection of the medial and posterior cords was displayed. There was an arteriovenous fistula, between the axillary artery and vein. The damaged nerves and vessels were repaired and an indwelling catheter was retained for 2 weeks to permit infu-sion of local anaesthetic about the brachial plexus of the cervical sympathetic chain. There was early and permanent relief of pain.

Patients with causalgia should be treated urgently. The core of the treatment is operative, directed towards diagnosis and rec-tification of the prime cause of the injured nerve and vessels. Sympathetic block is invaluable both in diagnosis and in treat-ment and, although the indications for formal sympathectomy seem less than before, a successful block does strengthen the case for operation.

Neurostenalgia

Patients in this group, together with those suffering from true causalgia, are the most rewarding to treat by operation. Chronic compression or distortion or chronic ischaemia of the nerve will produce pain. In most cases the nerve trunk is intact, the lesion is neurapraxia, prolonged conduction block or, at worst, axonot-mesis. The nerve is in some way irritated, tethered, compressed, or ischaemic. Treatment of the cause relieves pain. Over 50 patients who presented with severe pain from lesions of the brachial plexus caused by a displaced spike of bone from a fracture, or by a retained foreign body as, for example, a shot-gun pellet, or by an encircling suture, were greatly relieved by the appropriate operation. It might perhaps be right to think of

certain cases of thoracic outlet syndrome as expressing neuros-tenalgia because of the distraction of the lower and middle trunks of the brachial plexus by an accessory rib or musculotendinous band.

Post-traumatic neuralgia

Post-traumatic neuralgia (PTN) is pain after nerve injury that is not sympathetically maintained. Writing of such patients, Sed-don (1975) came to "an aspect of peripheral nerve injury that is profoundly unsatisfactory: the painful syndromes lacking the distinctive features of causalgia"; the situation remains unsat-isfactory. Even when the cases of central pain from traction injury to the brachial plexus and those of obvious continuing irritation are taken out, there remain patients with pain, hyper-aesthesia, hyperalgesia, and even hyperpathia and allodynia that are resistant to all forms of treatment. Occasionally, a cutaneous neuroma goes unrecognised for years and the value of accurate diagnosis and of simple operation is exemplified by one of our patients whose treatment course included psychiatric referral. Fortunately, the psychiatrist insisted that there must be an injury to a peripheral nerve.

CASE STUDY
A 34-year-old woman had severe pain in the left side of her face, neck, arm, and chest for 8 years after internal fixation of fracture of the clavicle. There was allodynia, but there was also a well localised area of exquisite tenderness just above the scar of earlier incisions. Movements of the neck brought on pain: the patient adopted a position of torticollis. At operation we displayed a neuroma of the supraclavicular nerve, 8 mm in diameter, which was tethered to the clavicle. The neuroma was excised and the stump was placed deep to the fat pad. Pain was abolished.

Post-traumatic neuralgia following direct injury to the nerves or trunks of the brachial plexus or to the spinal accessory nerve is all too common, and was alluded to in "iatropathic injuries".

Central pain

The natural history of this pain has been studied by a number of authors. Bonney (1959) followed 25 patients for over 2 years. Twelve of these, who had no recovery, remained in severe pain several years after their injuries. Wynn-Parry has made detailed studies in several large series that described the characterist-ics, the onset, and the relation between extent of neural injury, and the effect for better or worse of such factors as cold, ill-ness, psychological state, and occupation. In 1980 he reported on 122 cases of avulsion of at least one spinal nerve; of these, 112 had severe pain. Cold, worry, or current illness deepened the pain. Distraction by work, play, or conversation consider-ably improved the pain in most cases. Pain remained severe at 3 years or more in 48 cases, whereas it had spontaneously abated in 28; 15 of those who obtained spontaneous improve-ment noted it within 12 months of injury, a further 11 between 12 and 36 months after injury. Wynn Parry (1989) later followed 404 patients with known avulsion lesions over periods of 3 to 35 years to clarify the natural history of the condition. In just over half the patients, pain subsided over 3 years; in one-third the pain lasted for more than 3 years, but after that time was accepted and did not interfere with daily life; in 20% severe pain persisted unchanged for many years and continued seriously to affect the lives of sufferers; in only 1% was there no pain at all. The first thoracic nerve was avulsed in every patient with severe pain persisting for more than 3 years: the whole plexus was also damaged in 48 of these. Bruxelle et al. (1988) described outcome in 118 patients who were followed from 3 to 14 years after different forms of treatment. They discussed their indications and results from dorsal root end zone (DREZ) lesion.

Certain conclusions can be drawn from the writings of these authors. Pain develops on the day of injury in one-half of patients. The majority of patients with preganglionic injury describe it as severe, interfering with concentration and with sleep. There is some improvement in pain in perhaps one-half of patients where no operation for nerve repair is performed but, if pain persists for 3 years, then it will be permanent. The severity of pain is in proportion to the number of spinal nerves suffering preganglionic injury and it is worse where the 8th cervical and first thoracic nerves are so damaged. The majority find that pain is worst in cold weather and when they are otherwise ill or at times of emotional disturbance. About 80% of patients find that distraction at work or at play eases the pain. This one factor seems to be more effective in easing pain than any other and it is an overwhelmingly strong argument for assisting, and indeed firmly encouraging, return to some form of occupation.

Treatment by methods short of operation

The first and best method is to create distraction by appropriate rehabilitation designed to bring the patient back as soon as possible to work and recreation.

Transcutaneous nerve stimulation. Transcutaneous nerve stimulation (TNS or TENS) is an offshoot of the proposal by Melzac and Wall (1965) of the gate theory of pain. It was argued that the addition of a sensory input by another root would diminish the painful effect of "deafferentation". The basis of this is to increase input to the posterior columns and thereby to promote inhibitory impulses inhibiting rostral transmission of impulses from the dorsal horn. Since January 1995, 281 in-patient episodes have been studied in the Physiotherapy Department of the Royal National Orthopaedic Hospital. High intensity/low frequency stimulation was found to be preferable, in bursts or continuously for "stretching" pain; low intensity/high frequency stimulation, again in bursts or continuously was preferable for "neuralgic" pain. Transcutaneous nerve stimulation was not useful in the treatment of hyperaesthesia. About 80% of patients with plexus lesions gained relief, but the results deteriorated after 3 to 6 months in more than half the patients. As Wynn Parry and colleagues (1987) point out, it will not do simply to give the patient a TENS machine and tell him or her to get on with it. All our patients are admitted to the rehabilitation ward, a pain history is taken, and a diary recorded. Various positions of the stimulator and variations of frequencies, duration, and amplitude of pulse are tried. Patients are encouraged to wear the stimulator for many hours a day and for at least 2 weeks. Effective use on daily activity, drug intake, and subjective feelings are all recorded.

There seems to be no relation between the relation of symptoms and the effectiveness of the stimulator. An extreme case is that of the patient who had been in pain for some 50 years, whose pain was almost completely relieved by 2 days of treatment. There is no relation between the type of lesion and effectiveness. The particular advantage of transcutaneous nerve stimulation is, of course, that it is non-invasive, simple, has no side-effects and is considerably cheaper than long-term treatment with drugs. Sindou and Keraval (1980) commented that nerve stimulation cannot work if the fibres of the dorsal columns are wholly degenerate; the technique can only work in postganglionic lesions or in cases where some of the fibres are preserved.

Drugs. The usual analgesics are virtually useless in avulsion pain. Occasionally some relief is given by co-proxamol or codeine derivatives. Controlled drugs such as morphine and the synthetic opiates have little effect on this pain, so it is, in our experience, rare to find addicts amongst these patients. However, Nashhold and Ostdahl (1979), commenting on 17 patients with pain after avulsion of the plexus, noted that addiction to narcotics played "a major role" in nearly half their cases. Carbamazepine, phenytoin and sodium valproate, known for their use in controlling seizures in epilepsy, are worth trying in patients in whom shooting pains predominate. Carbamazepine is given in doses rising to a daily intake of 0.8–1.2 g. It has fewer side effects than phenytoin, but drowsiness can limit its use. Eighteen of our patients obtained from its use relief sufficient to justify taking it regularly. Antidepressants have a central effect on pain by their effects on the serotonin mechanism and Triptafen (amitriptylline and perphenazine) has proved the most useful. It is important to make sure that the patient does not think that the clinician thinks the pain is imaginary, and the rationale for giving an antidepressant should, whenever possible, be explained. Much the most successful drug for controlling plexus pain is cannabis. Many patients have told of relief by smoking the substance. It is unfortunate that its mild hallucinogenic effect, at present inseparable from its analgesic action, prevents its regular use. At the time of writing it has no approved medicinal use and it cannot be prescribed by doctors.

Amputation and sympathectomy

It is hardly necessary to say that amputation of the affected limb has no part in the treatment of central pain: the origin of the pain is not in the affected limb. However, this is not to say that amputation has no place in rehabilitation: it certainly does. Fletcher (1981) found that 90% of his 80 patients, who were very carefully selected, used their prostheses, and 63% of them found them particularly useful. Most of Fletcher's patients were back at work; one, working on the training ship *Sir Winston Churchill*, used his prosthesis to climb rigging. We have found that amputations ease pain, but this is usually the dragging pain of the paralysed shoulder, not deafferentation pain. Although Taylor (1962) reported relief of pain by cervicothoracic sympathectomy in one case of avulsion of the plexus, our early experience firmly suggests otherwise.

Relief of pain by re-innervation of the limb

The relation between pain and recovery of function following operative repair remains obscure, but there is increasing evidence that repair by graft or by nerve transfer is indeed useful, and it seems increasingly to be the most important treatment of all. Narakas (1981) and Bonnard and Narakas (1985) have reported to this effect. The pain from ruptures was eased in 90% of their cases. Of the patients with avulsions, 17% continued with disturbing pain at 3 years or more from neurotisation, compared with 25% among those who had not been operated on. Berman and Taggart (1995) have gone further in detailed prospective studies. In the first of these, 116 patients with root avulsions were followed for over 12 years. The diagnosis had been established at operation. In one-third of the patients the whole plexus had been avulsed; in the remainder there was a mixed pre- and postganglionic pattern of injury. In all cases the limb was affected by nerve transfer and where possible supplemented by nerve grafting. All 116 patients experienced significant pain at first presentation, and this was graded as follows:

1. *Severe*. Continued disturbance of daily life, of work, of study and of sleep (visual analogue scale (VAS 0–10) (9–10)).
2. *Significant*. Able to sleep but unable to work or study, nor enjoy hobbies (VAS 7–8).
3. *Moderate*. Able to work, but pain sometimes so severe the patient has to take time off (VAS 4–6).
4. *Mild*. Patient is aware of pain but leads a normal life (VAS 0–3).

Eighty-eight per cent of these patients described their pain as being severe at some time during their course. In 62% of patients the pain began within 24 hours of injury and the mean time to onset was 13 days (0–180 days). Pain was at its most intense, on average, at 6 months from injury. The proximal pain was never experienced in the absence of constant pain and the intensity of the pain was closely related to the extent of deafferentation of the spinal cord. It was exceptionally severe in cases of avulsion of C4 to T1. No clear relation between the depth of pain and the extent of the associated injuries was shown. A measurable decrease in pain was noted at a mean time of over 6 months after operation. In 34% of cases pain remained moderate or severe at 3 years or more from that operation.

It seems reasonable to compare Berman and Taggart's study with that of Wynn Parry (1980). All these patients attended the same institution, The Royal National Orthopaedic Hospital. Those seen before 1980 did not have nerve transfers; all those studied by Berman and Taggart did. In 1996, Berman et al. described the outcome in 19 patients in whom intercostal transfers were performed at more than 1 year from injury with the sole purpose of relieving pain. The introduction of this application of the operation was prompted by earlier experience with patients who reported substantial relief in pain at about the same time as muscular function was restored by intercostal nerve transfer to the musculocutaneous nerve in cases of proven avulsion of C5, C6, and C7. These unexpected findings prompted us to use the operation for the treatment of intractable pain and, of course, at an interval of more than 1 year from injury such transfers cannot possibly restore muscular function.

All the 19 patients studied had avulsion of at least two roots. Seven had avulsion of five roots; six had avulsion of four roots; four had avulsion of three roots and two had avulsion of two roots. In five patients a limited repair by graft was possible in addition to the intercostal transfer. T3, T4, and T5 were transferred to the lateral cord or its derivative branches in nine cases and to the medial cord or its branches in ten more. The choice of the recipient nerve was made on the basis of the location of the pain in the hand and the extent of recovery from either nerve graft or intact roots. The results were startling and unexpected: 16 of 19 patients reported significant relief of pain at an average of 8 months after intercostal transfer. Before operation 18 patients had severe pain, one had significant pain; in ten cases pain dropped from severe to mild and in six more it reduced from severe to moderate. The time between the intercostal nerve transfer and pain relief ranged from 3 days to 3 years, the average being 8 months.

Berman et al. (1996) outlined possible explanations for these surprising results. The concept of two distinct types of preganglionic injury, of intradural rupture distal to the transitional zone, and in more severe cases of avulsion from the cord itself, was adumbrated. The constant pain probably arises from disinhibition of neurones within the substantia gelatinosa, which fire spontaneously (Loeser et al., 1968). The convulsive pain that can respond to such anticonvulsants as phenytoin or carbamazepine arises from sudden outbursts of ectopic electrical activity in the damaged part of the dorsal horn. Transfer of healthy intercostal nerves into the trunk nerves of the upper limb inhibits this abnormal electrical activity. The rationale for the use of intercostal nerve transfers for the relief of pain is that it restores the input from the damaged limb, from receptors in muscle or skin. However, such an explanation is untenable in those cases in which pain is modified before any reinnervation could have occurred. Further, it could be argued that the input was there all along, from receptors of the skin of the chest and intercostal muscle. Further proposals were made: pain relief could depend on cortical inhibition initiated by the site of activity in the formally paralysed limb. It is well known that distraction regularly relieves pain during the period in which it operates. This explanation cannot apply to those cases where no muscular function was regained.

Pain relief can be a purely non-specific effect of operation, depending on the anaesthetic, the postoperative pain, and the use of analgesics or on suggestion alone. Against this view is the fact that the operations of former days often produced transient relief of pain, never permanent alleviation. Finally, the pain relief in these cases might have been produced by sectioning of functioning (but disconnected) axons on the posterior root system, impulses from which have, in some way, been reaching the central nervous system.

Berman et al. 1998 went some way further in answering some of these questions from a prospective study of 14 cases of severe traction lesion of the brachial plexus. In all patients, the diagnosis was confirmed by display at operation and by intra-operative neurophysiological studies. In all, at least one spinal nerve had been avulsed on the spinal cord and some form or other of repair was performed. A strong correlation and temporal relationship between reduction in pain and successful nerve repair was found. "All five patients with motor recovery experienced significant relief of deafferentation pain, while in the seven patients with persistent pain, none had motor recovery". No correlation was shown between pain relief and the recovery of cutaneous sensation, indeed, none of these 14 patients demonstrated recovery sensory or sympathetic cutaneous axon reflexes. The conclusion of this study was that nerve repair can reduce pain from spinal root avulsions and that the mechanism can involve successful regeneration and/or restoration of peripheral connections prior to their function, possibly in muscles. Berman commented "This decrease in pain appears to accompany or slightly precede the first sign of recovery of function. As the capsaicin-induced flares did not show any signs of recovery at the time of the last follow-up, the reduction in pain scores appears to be associated with returning large fibre function rather than A delta or C fibre function". This is an important observation and suggests a different mechanism for pain relief from that following late intercostal transfer.

Interventions on the spinal cord

The first serious attempts to relieve brachial plexus pain by operation arose from the identification of the cord in the site of origin of the symptoms and the refinements of cordotomy introduced in this country by Lipton (1968), which made that procedure far safer than it had formally been. "Percutaneous" cordotomy became a standard treatment in cases of intractable pain in the terminal stages of malignant disease. It was tried in a few cases of plexus pain: the early results were good, but it soon became apparent that a procedure applicable in case of terminal disease was inapplicable in the case of otherwise healthy young persons. There was recurrence of pain within a year. This disadvantage was additional to the theoretical one of intervening on the healthy side of the cord already damaged unilaterally.

With the increase of knowledge of inhibitor mechanisms Shealy et al. (1967) introduced posterior column stimulators in some cases. There were technical difficulties and this method fell for a time into disfavour. Technical advances have again brought it to the fore. Watkins and Koeze (1993) gave an account of the present status of this method as used with the advantages of improved technology. Bennet and Tai (1994) found lasting and significant pain relief in their five cases of pain after traction lesions of the brachial plexus. These injuries had occurred between 5 and 16 years earlier. Electrodes were inserted under radiological control in the conscious patient, usually in the D6–D7 interspace and then advanced cranially to the lower cervical spine cord. The stimulation pattern was adjusted accordingly to the patient's experience.

Sindou (1972) performed an operation of selective posterior rhizotomy of the DREZ by microsurgical technique, which rested on the topographical distribution of afferent fibres in the dorsal root injury zone. The technique was extended for the treatment of plexus pain and experience of this technique was reviewed by Sindou and Mertens (1993). Nashold and Osdahl (1979) related experience with coagulation of the DREZ on the basis that this procedure destroyed part of the grey matter in which the spontaneous firing was occurring, namely the substantia gelatinosa. Good results were obtained in 13 of 21 patients but in 11 cases there was some degree of residual weakness of the ipsilateral lower limb or, occasionally, both lower limbs. Nashold (1981) reports modification of the duration of coagulation, amplitude of current, and depth of penetration, which have reduced the incidence of long tract damage.

The principal objection to coagulation of the entry zone is that it inflicts another lesion on the damaged side of an already damaged cord. Thomas and Jones (1984) found evidence of subclinical affection of the posterior columns in 50% of their patients with avulsion of the brachial plexus coming to operation for relief of pain. The potential complications are serious: damage to the ipsilateral corticospinal tract; damage to the ipsilateral posterior columns; impotence; and unpleasant paraesthesiae. There is an incidence of failure of around 40% and some evidence of late recurrence. Thomas and Kitchen (1994) provided a long-term review of this operation in 44 patients at a minimum of interval of 63 months from DREZ lesion for brachial plexus pain: 35 patients found significant and lasting pain relief, eight cases (18%) had persisting neurological deficit, which was usually mild.

Central operations of this sort, and entry zone coagulation in particular, must be reserved for those patients who continue to have very severe and intractable pain persistently marring their lives. It should be considered for those who failed to respond to a full range of treatment short of operation, who have failed to show spontaneous improvement after 3 years, and who have failed to experience any relief after an otherwise successful neurotisation. The hazards of entry zone coagulation must be made clear and patients addicted to controlled drugs are not suitable subjects for central operation.

OBSTETRIC BRACHIAL PLEXUS PALSY (OBPP) OR THE BIRTH LESION (OPL)

The incidence of this condition is not known with precision. Seddon's comment (1975) "where Sever, an American writing in 1925, could report 1100 cases, my own experience is limited to under 50 cases over a period of almost 40 years" suggests that it is rare. Our experience suggests otherwise: nearly 1000 new cases have been seen since 1985 and new referrals to the Peripheral Nerve Injury Unit now match, or even exceed, the number of adult cases. A prospective study has been set up by the British Paediatric Association and this might at last give real information about incidence: supported and extended for at least 3 years it could provide the first national measure of natural history. Published figures from other countries suggest a range from less than 0.1% to 4% of live births. Greenwald and colleagues (1984) found 61 cases among 30,000 consecutive live births from a single group of hospitals in the US. Camus and colleagues (1995) saw only 19 from over 30,000 live births in the Pitié Hospital over a 10-year period. In Singapore, Tan (1973) recorded an incidence of 0.14% in vertex deliveries, rising to 22.4% per 1000 in breech deliveries. The significance of breech delivery was further underlined by Boo and colleagues (1991) in Malaysia, who recorded an incidence of 0.16% in vertex deliveries compared with 0.86% in breech deliveries.

One does encounter, from time to time, the term "congenital", which is wholly inappropriate when used in those cases, which are the great majority, in which the damage plainly occurred during birth. Congenital aplasia is exceptionally rare. There is, however, quite convincing evidence that the damage to the plexus occurred *in utero* in a small number of children. Dunn and Engel (1985) and Jennett and colleagues (1992) collated evidence incriminating oligohydramnios, abnormal intrauterine posture, and uterine abnormalities. The report from Paradiso and colleagues (1997) is particularly interesting. An 18-day-old infant was examined by electromyography. The evidence suggested that axonal injury occurred several weeks before delivery. Serious study of the disorder began over 150 years ago, significantly earlier than equivalent work in the adult lesions. It fell to Duchenne (1872) to confirm that the lesion of the brachial plexus was caused during birth, and that it was not congenital. Erb (1876) defined the level of lesion at the formation of the upper trunk. Klumpke (1885) described lesions of the lower nerves of the brachial plexus also emphasising the significance of Bernard–Horner sign. Trombetta (1880) found that two groups are particularly at risk: the heavy baby and the baby born by breech. Duval and Guillain (1898) performed experiments showing the mechanism of injury. Boyer (1911) demonstrated damage to the spinal cord itself at necropsy in a 41-year-old woman.

Evidently, breech delivery is a particularly significant factor in causation. The best account comes from Slooff and Blaauw (1995), who reviewed 40 of their cases. The injuries were often bilateral, often associated with phrenic palsy, and the damage to the uppermost groups of the brachial plexus was particularly severe; these nerves were often avulsed from the spinal cord. The babies in this series were small and were often premature. By contrast, it is the heavy baby that is at risk in cephalic deliveries. Zancolli and Zancolli (1993) recorded a mean birth weight of 4.55 kg in their series of 512 patients. Gilbert (1993) found a mean birth weight of 4.3 kg. Giddins and colleagues (1994) took the matter further forwards in two studies of risk factors, the first in 230 consecutive babies, the second in 775. Four main groups of factors were studied. Those relating to the parents, those occurring during pregnancy, those occurring during labour, and those relating to the child. There was no significant correlation between social class. There was a trend towards the mother being heavier and shorter than the national average and also excessive weight gain during pregnancy, but none of these factors could be shown to be significant in statistical terms. The one factor of overwhelming significance was the weight of the baby: the mean weight in these two series was 4.5 kg against the mean for the North West Thames Region of 3.88 kg. There was, furthermore, a correlation between severity of lesion and increasing weight of the baby. Shoulder dystocia was recorded as a complication of birth in some 70% of these cases.

One explanation for the apparent increase in OPL is given by Power (1994), who showed a mean annual increase in birth weight of 0.4% in Scotland over the years 1991–1992 and a mean annual increase of 0.35% in England and in Wales until 1986, after which time statistical information about heavier babies was no longer kept, presumably because such data has no place in a "market-driven national health service".

The diagnosis is usually straightforward but fracture of the clavicle or humerus can cause immobility mimicking paralysis. Neonatal sepsis of the glenohumeral joint has been taken for OPL and we have seen cases of cerebral palsy, arthrogryposis, and ischaemic injury to the cord mimicking OPL.

The natural history of the disorder is not at all clear. Few published series describe the course to spontaneous recovery in unselected cases. Bennet and Harrold (1976) reported a favourable outcome in over 80%. Hardy (1981), Jackson and colleagues (1988), Donn and Faix (1983), Gordon and colleagues (1973), and Specht (1975) were similarly optimistic. Michelow et al. (1994) studied the natural history of spontaneous recovery in 66 children, of whom 38 had involvement of the whole of the plexus; there was spontaneous recovery in 61. However, Sharrard (1971) saw poor recovery in one-half of children born with a complete lesion. Gjörup (1965) followed 103 patients for over 33 years, finding 22 with a poor result and 40 of those with useful recovery considered that they had some persisting significant disability. Eng (1971) and Eng et al. (1978) made particularly detailed observations in a series of 135 children, noting severe and persisting problems in 30%, the deformities of the shoulder and elbow proving particularly resistant to prevention by physiotherapy. One notable finding in these series was the demonstration of neurapraxia in eight children with paralysed muscles but normal electromyogram. Narakas (1987) analysed the outcome in 460 patients and found that few babies born with complete paralysis made good recovery at the shoulder, but that 90% of these children regained useful hand function.

The matter of the natural history in OPL requires much closer study, because otherwise indications for exploration and repair of the neurological lesion must remain in doubt save in the most clear-cut circumstances. One particularly useful clinical advance is the introduction of the system of classification, proposed by Narakas (1987) and by Gilbert and Tassin (1984). This system is best applied at between 2 and 4 weeks from birth, by which time simple conduction block lesions should have recovered. It permits clear definition of the extent of injury to the brachial plexus and offers a broad guide to prognosis. However, it is not, in itself, an indication for operation. It does not recognise Klumpke's lesion of damage confined to the 8th cervical and first thoracic nerves, nor does it define that not uncommon pattern of injury in which the middle nerves, the 7th and 8th cervical nerves, are severely damaged, whereas those above and below go on to good recovery. Brunelli and Brunelli (1991) described this as the fourth type of brachial plexus lesion.

Our interpretation of this system is as follows:

Group 1.   The 5th and 6th cervical nerves are damaged. There is paralysis of deltoid and elbow flexor muscles. About 90% of babies proceed to full spontaneous recovery when there is clinical evidence of that recovery at no later than 2 months.

Group 2.   The 5th, 6th, and 7th cervical nerves are damaged so that there is paralysis at the shoulder, at the elbow, and of the extensor muscles of the wrist and the digits. Perhaps 65% of these children make full spontaneous recovery, the remainder persisting with serious defects in control of the shoulder.

Group 3.   Paralysis is virtually complete, although there is some flexion of the fingers at, or shortly after, birth. Full spontaneous recovery occurs in less than half of these children, most are left with substantial impairment of function at the shoulder and elbow with deficient rotation of the forearm. Wrist and finger extension does not recover in about one-quarter.

Group 4.   The whole plexus is involved. Paralysis is complete. The limb is flaccid and there is a Bernard–Horner syndrome. In most children the spinal nerves have been either ruptured or avulsed from the spinal cord and there is permanent and serious defect within the limb: we have seen a few instances of quite unexpected spontaneous recovery to a very high level.

Damage to the spinal cord occurs in some of the Group 4 babies, it presents as delayed and unsteady walking and, in later years, a smaller ipsilateral foot. Shortening of the digits and atrophy of their pulps is important evidence of denervation, and this becomes evident at between 4 and 6 weeks (Table 47.11, Figs 47.21–47.23).

Treatment

This rests on delineation of the extent and the prognosis of neurological injury. There is, later, the problem of deformities secondary to the neural lesion. On the whole, palliative procedures for these are unsatisfactory. The results of musculotendinous transfers in OPL are far inferior to those following good nerve regeneration and, generally, to those from analogous operations in simple peripheral nerve injuries. The indications of operation upon the plexus itself remains a field of serious controversy.

Table 47.11.   Lesions by Gilbert and Tassin grading, 680 babies seen between 1986 and 1995

	Number (babies)
Group 1	118
Group 2	259
Group 3	200
Group 4	103
Total	**680**
Brachial plexus explored	147
Palliative operations performed	347
No operations necessary	298
More than one operation necessary	112

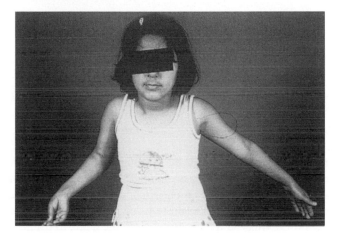

Figure 47.21. 5-year old child with group 3 OPL. Poor shoulder function, flexion, and supination deformity of the forearm and shortening of the limb are all evident.

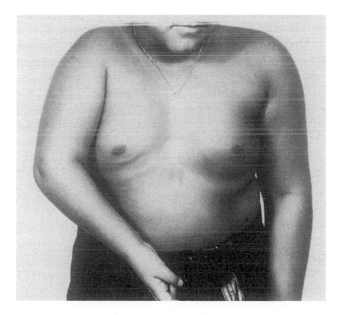

Figure 47.22. 14-year-old with group 4 OPL. The head of the humerus was dislocated posteriorly.

Regular and gentle exercises are essential in the prevention of fixed deformity, and the best physiotherapist is the mother or father or both. Parents must be involved in the treatment of the child from the outset. The chief aim is to maintain full passive

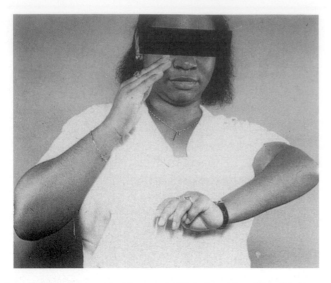

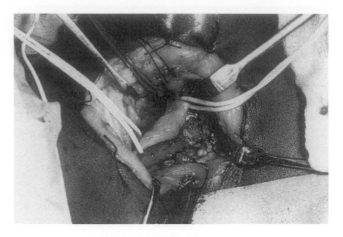

Figure 47.24. The plexus exposed in a 4-month-old baby. The two upper slings mark C5 and C6. Preganglionic injury to C5 is evident.

Figure 47.23. 22-year-old with group 4 OPL lesions. The afflicted limb was used as no more than a passive helpmate in this highly motivated patient.

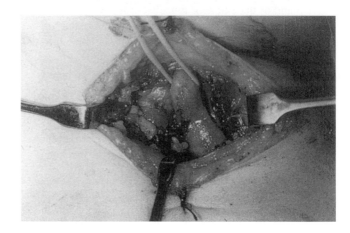

Figure 47.25. Rupture of upper trunk in a group 2 lesion in a 6-month-old baby.

rotation with full abduction at the glenohumeral joint. To achieve this, both upper limbs must be worked together. This is particularly important, to work on one limb at a time merely moves the scapulothoracic joint and the twisting movements of the fretful child can mislead the observer. A simple guide to parents is that these exercises should be performed for 2–3 minutes before every meal. For medial and lateral rotation, the shoulder is first adducted, then stretched into full lateral and medial rotation, and then elevated into abduction. The inferior glenohumeral angle is maintained by gently holding the scapula against the chest wall while abducting the arm; the posterior glenohumeral angle maintained by holding the scapula against the ribs while flexing and medially rotating the arm. Many severe fixed deformities can be prevented by this simple regime. The progress of recovery, or lack of it, in the first 8 weeks, is critical. In favourable lesions, parents report powerful grasp at 2 weeks and then flexion at shoulder and elbow at between 6 and 8 weeks. Return of a grasp within 4 weeks virtually guarantees that the child will regain good hand function. Gilbert and Tassin (1984) emphasised that early recovery signals a good prognosis, and in their cases with a favourable outcome, all had elbow flexion and shoulder abduction at 3 months. Gilbert (1993, 1995) has acquired immense experience in the treatment of OBPP and his recommendations, which are drawn from careful analysis of this experience, must be noted. They include, among others: failure of recovery of flexion of the elbow by the age of 3 months is an indication for exploration and repair of the upper trunk of the brachial plexus; in cases of avulsion of C8 and T1 the only possible chance of regaining any hand function is by re-innervation of these two nerves, and for this use of an adjacent postganglionic rupture of, say, C6 or C7 is far preferable than re-innervation by nerve transfer (Figs 47.24 and 47.25).

The value of radiological investigations remains controversial. Gilbert (1995) found that myelography was useful in the detection of avulsion. Slooff and Blaauw (1995) described the advantages of CT scanning and of MRI in showing haematoma within the spinal canal, and atrophy and denervation of muscle. Francel et al. (1995) felt that MRI provided high-speed, non-invasive imaging sufficient to permit clinicians "to evaluate pre-ganglionic nerve root injuries without the use of general anaesthesia and lumbar puncture". This sounds a promising development but my own view is that no radiological investigation affords sufficient resolution to define lesions of the rootlets of the spinal nerves; nor do they clearly demonstrate ruptures within the posterior triangle. Preoperative neurophysiological investigations have proven to be remarkably accurate in predicting the extent of injury and so prognosis for individual spinal nerves, and this method is now the mainstay of our assessment for operation. For more detailed discussion of the application of the technique and interpretation of findings the reader is referred to Smith (1998).

The close observations of Gilbert, Slooff, and Raimondi, together with the neurophysiological evidence given by Smith, persuades this author to side firmly with those who argue that operation for diagnosis and repair is amply justified in three circumstances:

1. When the natural history of a Group 4 lesion is bad and intervention is justified when electrophysiological evidence suggests multiple ruptures and avulsions.
2. In cases of damage to the upper portion of the brachial plexus associated with phrenic nerve palsy (Sloof & Blaauw, 1995).
3. If there is no clinical evidence of recovery in deltoid and in biceps in children falling into Groups 1, 2, and 3 by 3 months, and if this is supported by adequate electrophysiological evidence. Gilbert (1995) reported the largest series, with 178 cases followed for 3 years or more. Results for function at the shoulder and the elbow were generally good, but of particular importance was the outcome in the 64 children with total lesions in whom the lower trunk of the brachial plexus was re-innervated; 75% of these children recovered useful finger flexion and useful intrinsic function was obtained in 50%.

Measurement of outcome

Analysis of outcome after intervention is impossible without some agreement about the systems of measurement used by different Units engaged in this work. Those used by the Peripheral Nerve Injury Unit are set out in Tables 47.12–47.16. They incorporate the methods developed and used by Gilbert (Paris) and Raimondi (Legnano) cited by Birch (1998b). All are defective but, taken as a whole, provide a simple and reliable measure of clinical progress, or lack it. Their application in analysis of 65 repairs in OPL is set out in Table 47.17.

There are important differences between the adult lesion and OPL. There are more partial intradural lesions in OPL. The definition of injury to the nerves in the posterior triangle is less abrupt, there is a spectrum from the lesion in continuity to the neuroma and so to the rupture. There is almost always some conducting tissue across the lesion, a fact that might have contributed to other workers' disenchantment with the value of EMGs. The recognition of prolonged conduction block in about 15% of cases is a most important advance because it explains the unexpectedly favourable progression in some children who start recovery late (no earlier than 9 months) and then go on to make a full recovery.

It does seem that pain is very rare in children. In fact, no case of central pain from avulsion injury has been encountered in any child. This might be a reflection of the rarity of complete sensory loss in the hand in OPL. The posterior columns are not myelinated in neonates. A possible alternative explanation comes from the anatomical arrangement of the spinal cord in infancy; perhaps the transitional zone is more vulnerable than in adults. In the infant, the spinal cord fills the cervical spine and the spinal roots emerge at, or near to, a right angle from the cord; separation is more likely at the transitional zone than true avulsion. The adult system for analysis of sensation has become accustomed to input along the posterior columns and

Table 47.12. Shoulder paralysis (reprinted from Gilbert, 1993, Copyright 1993, with permission from Elsevier Science)

Stage	Description
0	Flail shoulder
I	Abduction or flexion to 45 degrees, No active lateral rotation
II	Abduction < 90 degrees, lateral rotation to neutral
III	Abduction = 90 degrees—weak lateral rotation
IV	Abduction < 120 degrees—incomplete lateral rotation
V	Abduction > 120 degrees—active lateral rotation

The suffix + is added to indicate sufficient medial rotation permitting the hand to come against the opposite shoulder.

Table 47.13. Elbow recovery (from Gilbert & Raimondi, 1996)

Flexion	
Nil or some contraction	1
Incomplete flexion	2
Complete flexion	3
Extension	
No extension	0
Weak extension	1
Good extension	2
Extension deficit	
0 to 30 degrees	0
30 to 50 degrees	−1
More than 50 degrees	−2

Table 47.14. Hand evaluation scale (from Raimondi, 1993)

Stage	Description
0	Complete paralysis or slight finger flexion of no use; useless thumb—no pinch; some or no sensation
I	Limited active flexion of fingers; no extension of wrist or fingers, possibility of thumb lateral pinch
II	Active flexion of wrist with passive flexion of fingers (tenodesis)—passive lateral pinch of thumb
III	Active complete flexion of wrist and fingers—mobile thumb with partial abduction—opposition. Intrinsic balance—no active supination; good possibilities for palliative surgery
IV	Active complete flexion of wrist and fingers; active wrist extension—weak or absent finger extension. Good thumb opposition with active ulnaris intrinsics. Partial pronosupination
V	Hand IV with finger extension and almost complete pronosupination

so responds to its abolition or diminution by giving rise to pain whereas no such acclimatisation has taken place in the neonates.

The rate of recovery is slow considering the distance through which new axons must grow. Furthermore, recovery, although usually good, is never complete. This might be a reflection of loss of ventral horn cells; such changes are more severe in the young than in the mature animal. Of itself, this is a considerable argument for early intervention in cases in which a secure diagnosis can be established. At present this is possible only in the two unfavourable types of lesion: Groups 1 and 2 with phrenic nerve palsy, and Group 4 with Bernard–Horner syndrome.

Table 47.15. The peripheral nerve injury unit OBP assessment chart

Name	Tassin	D.O.O	X-rays	EMG	Operation	Surgical pathology
					On BP: On shoulder:	Of plexus: Of shoulder: 1. Dislocation 2. Subluxation 3. Contracture 4. Flail
Seen by OT: Before operation: After operation:	Mallett score Before operation: After operation:				Gilbert grading (shoulder) Before operation: After operation:	Raimondi grading (hand) Before operation: After operation:

Table 47.16. The Peripheral Nerve Injury Unit OBP assessment chart

Range of movement																							
FF		ER		GH angle		ABD		IR		Rotation forearm		FF		ER		GH angle		ABD		IR forearm		Rotation	
Ac	Pa	Ac	Pa	Ac	Pa	Ac	Pa	Ac	Pa	Ac	Pa	Ac	Pa	Ac	Pa	Ac	Pa	Ac	Pa	Ac	Pa	Ac	Pa

ABD, Abduction; Ac, Active; ER, External rotation; FF, Forward flexion; GH, Glenohumeral; IR, Internal rotation; Pa, Passive

Table 47.17. Results of repairs in 65 cases with minimum follow up of 30 months

Lesion	Shoulder		Elbow		Hand
	Gilbert	Mallett			
Group I: C5, C6	1	6–7	0	1	0	1	0
One or two roots	2	8–9	0	2	0	2	0
grafted	3	10–11	0	3	0	3	0
	4	12–13	1	4	1	4	0
Total cases = 6	5	14–15	5	5	5	5	6
Group II: C5, C6,	1	6–7	0	1	0	1	0
and C7	2	8–9	0	2	0	2	0
Two or three roots	3	10–11	8	3	5	3	0
grafted	4	12–13	11	4	9	4	12
Total cases = 25	5	14–15	6	5	11	5	13
Groups III and IV: C5,	1	6–7	0	1	1	1	0
C6, C7, C8, and T1	2	8–9	7	2	4	2	4
Two or three roots	3	10–11	13	3	6	3	10
grafted, with intra- or	4	12–13	8	4	18	4	20
extraplexual transfer	5	14–15	6	5	5	5	0
Total cases = 34							

This excludes four cases of avulsion of C5 and C6, and 11 cases of late re-innervation (older than 2 years).

Secondary deformities: the medial rotation contracture at the shoulder

The medial rotation contracture at the glenohumeral joint is by far and away the most common and the most serious of all secondary deformities in OPL. In the majority of cases the deformity is provoked by muscular imbalance, and that muscular imbalance is caused by the neurological injury. The subscapularis muscle, the most powerful muscle within the rotator cuff and the most powerful medial rotator of the shoulder, is innervated by the C7 and C8. In lesions of C5, C6, and C7 the muscle either works from the outset or it recovers rapidly and overwhelms the weaker abductors and lateral rotators innervated by the 5th and 6th cervical nerves. Unnoted or unchecked, the deformity progresses to posterior subluxation or posterior dislocation of the head of the humerus from the glenoid cavity and, in far too many cases, neurological recovery is seriously marred by this development. Increasing diminution of the range of passive lateral rotation at the shoulder, which fails to respond to adequate stretching, is a strong indication for the appropriate operation and subluxation of the head of the humerus is virtually an absolute indication. The natural history of this

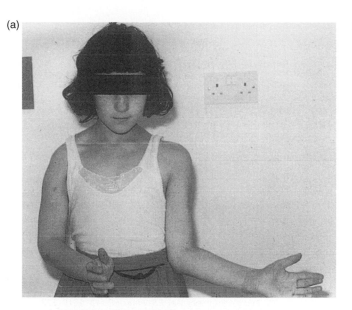

Figure 47.26. 6-year-old child with group 2 OPL. Posterior dislocation of the head of the humerus. Note the loss of external rotation and impaired abduction.

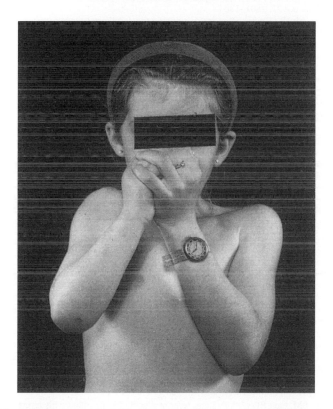

Figure 47.27. 4-year-old child with group 3 OPL lesion. The afflicted hand can be brought to the mouth only with the other hand. Note the shortening of the forearm. The head of the humerus is dislocated posteriorly.

deformity, the radiological changes and the techniques of operation are described at some length by Birch (1998b) (Figs 47.26 and 47.27).

ACKNOWLEDGEMENTS

None of the work outlined in this chapter would have been possible without the great contributions made by many colleagues and it is a pleasure now to acknowledge some of them.

I thank nursing colleagues, particularly Evelyn Hunter and her staff, and Moira Nurse, head of the Rehabilitation Ward. In dealing with physiotherapy and occupational therapy, I thank Alison Somek and her staff, Sara Probert, Manuelle Scheutte, Annette Leong, and Lydia Dean; from the Department of Physiotherapy Miss Pam Barsby and Miss Helen Gray gave much help in matters of transcutaneous nerve stimulation and in the assessment and treatment of children with birth lesions. Uta Boundy and Dirk De Camp in the Photographic Department of the Institute of Orthopaedics provided us with figures and Dr Peter Smith, Librarian of the Institute of Orthopaedics, gave much help with references. Mr Peter Cozens, Employment Officer to the Royal National Orthopaedic Hospital gave much advice from his knowledge in all aspects of the field of disability and employment legislation.

Mrs Margaret Taggart (Research Co-ordinator of the Peripheral Nerve Injury Unit, RNOH) provided the analysis and the basis for analysis of much of the work set out here, devised and maintained prospective programmes of measurement of outcome in cases of injury to the brachial plexus, initiated work on pain, rehabilitation and the birth lesion and edited and typed the manuscript. George Bonney, co-author of *Surgical Disorders of the Peripheral Nerves*, generously gave full approval to refer to his work and to use the tables set out in that work.

REFERENCES

Abdulla S, Bowden REM (1960). The blood supply of the brachial plexus. *Proc Royal Soc Med 53*: 203–205

Albe-Fessard D, Lombard MC (1983). Use of an animal model to evaluate the origin of and protection against deafferentation pain. In: Bonica JJ,

Lindblom U, Iggo A (Eds), *Advances in pain research and therapy*, vol. 5. Raven Press, New York, pp. 691–700

Albert HH von, Mackert B (1970). Eine neue Behandlungsmöglichkeit strahlenbedingter Armplexusparesen nach Mammakarzinomoperation. *Deutsche Medinizinische Wochenscrift 95*: 2119–2122

Alnot JY (1988). Traumatic brachial plexus palsy in the adult. *Clin Orth Rel Res 237*: 9–16

Anderson SD, Basbaum AI, Fields HI (1977). Response of medullary raphe neurons to peripheral stimulation and to systemic opiates. *Brain Res 123*: 363–368

Barr LC, Kissin MW (1987). Radiation-induced brachial plexus neuropathy following breast conservation and radical radiotherapy. *Br J Surg 74*: 855–856

Barros d'Sa AAB (1992a). Arterial injuries. In: HHG Eastcott (Ed), *Arterial surgery*, 3rd edition. Churchill Livingstone, Edinburgh, pp. 355–413

Barros d'Sa AAB (1992b). Radiation injury of arteries. In: Eastcott HHG. (Ed), *Arterial surgery*, 3rd edition. Churchill Livingstone, Edinburgh, pp. 359

Bates T, Evans RGB (1995). *Brachial neuropathy following radiotherapy for breast cancer*. Report of the independent review commissioned by the Royal College of Radiologists

Bennet CC, Harrold AJ (1976). Prognosis and early management of birth injuries to the brachial plexus. *Br Med J 1*: 1520–1521

Bennett MI, Tai YMA (1994). Cervical dorsal column stimulation relieves pain of brachial plexus avulsion. *J Roy Soc Med 87*: 5–7

Berman J, Anand P, Chen L, Taggart M, Birch R (1996). Pain relief from preganglionic injury to the brachial plexus by later intercostal transfer. *J Bone and Joint Surg 78B*: 759–760

Berman J, Birch R, Anand P (1998). Pain following human brachial plexus injury with spinal cord root avulsion and the effect of surgery. *Pain 75*: 199–207

Berthold CH, Carlstedt T, Corneliuson O (1993). Anatomy of the mature transitional zone. In: Dyck PJ, Thomas PK, Griffin JW, Low PA, Poduslo JF (Eds), *Peripheral neuropathy*, 3rd edition. WB Saunders, Philadelphia, pp. 75–80

Birch R (1998a). Traumatic lesion of the brachial plexus In: Birch R, Bonney G, Wynn Parry CB (Eds), *Surgical disorders of the peripheral nerves*. Churchill Livingstone, London, pp. 157–207

Birch R (1998b). Obstetric palsy. In: Birch R, Bonney G, Wynn Parry CB (Eds), *Surgical disorders of the peripheral nerves*. Churchill Livingstone, London, pp. 209–233

Birch R, Bonney G (1998). Classification of pain. In: Birch R, Bonney G, Wynn Parry CB (Eds), *Surgical disorders of the peripheral nerves*. Churchill Livingstone, London, p. 338

Birch R, Bonney G, Dowell J, Hollingdale J (1991a). Iatrogenic injuries of peripheral nerves. *J Bone Joint Surg 73B*: 280–282

Birch R, Jessop J, Scott G (1991b). Brachial plexus palsy after manipulation of the shoulder. *J Bone and Joint Surg 73*: 172

Bonnard C, Narakas A (1985). Syndromes douloureux et lesions post-traumatiques du plexus brachial. *Helv Chir Acta 52*: 621–632

Bonnel F (1989). Anatomie du plexus brachial chez le nouveau-né et l'adulte. In: Alnot J-Y, Narakas A (Eds), *Les paralysies du plexus brachiale*. Monographies du groupe d'étude de la main. Expansion Scientifique Francaise, Paris, pp. 3–13

Bonney V (1947). *A textbook of gynaecological surgery*, 5th edition. Cassell, London, p. 55

Bonney G (1954). The value of axon responses in determining the site of lesion in traction lesions of the brachial plexus. *Brain 77*: 588–609

Bonney G (1959). Prognosis in traction lesions of the brachial plexus. *J Bone Joint Surg 41B*: 4–35

Bonney G (1973). Causalgia. *Br J Hosp Med 9*: 593–596

Bonney G (1998a). Reimplantation of avulsed spinal nerves. The first clinical case (1997). In: Birch R, Bonney G, Wynn Parry CB (Eds), *Surgical disorders of the peripheral nerves*. Churchill Livingstone, London, pp. 200–202

Bonney G (1998b). Rehabilitation. In: Birch R, Bonney G, Wynn Parry CB (Eds), *Surgical disorders of the peripheral nerves*. Churchill Livingstone, London, p. 463

Bonney G (1998c) Iatropathic. In: Birch R, Bonney G, Wynn Parry CB (Eds), *Surgical disorders of the peripheral nerves*. Churchill Livingstone, London pp. 293–333

Bonney G, Gilliatt RW (1958). Sensory nerve conduction after traction lesion of the brachial plexus. *Proc Coll Med 51*: 365–367

Bonney G, Jamieson A (1979). Communication au Symposium sur le plexus brachial; reimplantation of C7 and C8. Lausanne 1978 (Abstract). *Int Microsurg 1*: 103–106

Boo NY, Lye MS, Kanchanala M, Ching CL (1991). Brachial plexus injuries in Malaysian neonates. *Incidence and Associated Risk Factors 37*: 327–330

Boyer GF (1911). The complete histopathological examination of the nervous system of an unusual case of obstetrical paralysis 41 years after birth and a review of the pathology. *Proc Roy Soc Med 5 (Neurol section)*: 31–58

Bristol DC, Fraher JP (1989). Experimental traction injuries of ventral spinal nerve roots. A scanning electron microscopic study. *Neuropathol Appl Neurobiol 15*: 549–561

Brunelli GA, Brunelli GR (1991). A fourth type of brachial plexus lesion: the intermediate (C7) palsy. *J Hand Surg 16*: 492–494

Bruxelle J, Travers V, Theibaut JB (1988). Occurrence and treatment of pain after brachial plexus injury. *Clin Orthop Rel Res 237*: 87–95

Burns RJ (1978). Delayed radiation-induced damage to the brachial plexus. *Clin Exp Neurol 15*: 221–227

Butler MJ, Lane RHS, Webster JHH (1980). Irradiation injury to large arteries. *Br J Surg 67*: 341–343

Cajal RY (1928). *Degeneration and regeneration in the nervous system*. Translated and edited by RM May. Oxford University Press, London

Camus M, Lefebure G, Veron P, Darbois Y (1995). Traumatisme obstétrique du nouveau né. *J Gynecol Obstet Biol Reprod 14*: 1033–1044

Carlstedt T, Lindå H, Cullheim S, Risling M (1986). Reinnervation of hind limb muscles after ventral root avulsion and implantation in the lumbar spinal cord of the adult rat. *Acta Physiol Scand 128*: 645–646

Carlstedt T, Crane P, Hallin RG, Noren G (1995). Return of function after spinal cord implantation of avulsed spinal nerve roots. *Lancet 346*: 1323–1325

Castagno AA, Shuman WP (1987). MR imaging in clinically suspected brachial plexus tumor. *Am J Roentgenol 148*: 1219–1222

Castaigne P, Laplane D, Augustin P, Degos J-D, Ammouni J-A (1969). A propos des paralysies du plexus brachial après cancer du sein. *Presse Médicale 77*: 1801–1804

Cavanagh JB (1968a). Prior irradiation and the cellular response to nerve crush: duration and effect. *Exp Neurol 22*: 253–258

Cavanagh JB (1968b). Effects of irradiation on the proliferation of cells in peripheral nerve during Wallerian degeneration. *Br J Radiol 41*: 275–281

Celli L, Rovesta C (1987). Electrophysiologic intraoperative evaluations of the damaged root in traction of the brachial plexus. In: Terzis JK (Ed), *Microreconstruction of nerve injuries*. WB Saunders, Philadelphia, pp. 473–482

Chokroverty S, Sachdeo R, Dilullo J, Duvoisin RC (1989). Magnetic stimulation in the diagnosis of lumbosacral radiculopathy. *J Neurol Neurosurg Psychiatry 52*: 767–772

Cooke J, Powell S, Parsons C (1988). The diagnosis by computed tomography of brachial plexus lesions following radiotherapy for carcinoma of the breast. *Clin Radiol 39*: 602–606

Cox RAF (1996). Avoiding discrimination against disabled people. *Br Med J 313*: 1346–1347

Culheim S, Carlstedt T, Lindå H, Risling M, Ulfhake B (1989). Motorneurons reinnervate skeletal muscle after ventral root implantation into the spinal cord of the cat. *Neuroscience 29*: 725–733

Dailey AT, Tsumuda JS, Goodkin R, Haynor DR, Filler AG, Hayes CE, Maravilla KR, Kliot M (1996). Magnetic resonance neurography for cervical radiculopathy: a preliminary report. *Neurosurgery 38*: 488–492

Davis ER, Sutton D, Bligh AS (1966). Myelography in brachial plexus injury. *Br J Radiol 39*: 362–371

De Lisa JA, Lee HJ, Baran EM, Lai K-S, Spielholz N, Mackenzie K (1994). Macroelectromyography. In: De Lisa JA (Ed.) *Manual of nerve conduction velocity and clinical neurophysiology*, 3rd edition. Lippincott Williams & Wilkins, New York, p. 465

Dommisse GF (1975). *The arteries and veins of the human spinal cord from birth*. Churchill Livingstone, Edinburgh

Donn SM, Faix RG (1983). Long term prognosis for the infant with severe birth trauma. *Clin Perinatol 10*: 507–520

Ducatman BS, Scheithaeur BW (1983). Post irradiation neurofibrosarcoma. *Cancer 51*: 1028–1033

Duchenne GBA (1872). *De l'élèctrisation Localisée et de son application à la pathologie et à la thérapeutique*, 2nd edition. JB Ballière Paris, pp. 357–362

Dunn DW, Engle WA (1985). Brachial plexus palsy: intrauterine onset. *Paediatr Neurol 1*: 367–369

Duval P, Guillain G (1898). Pathogénie des accidents nerveux consécutifs aux luxations et traumatisme de l'épaule. Paralysies radiculaires traumatiques du plexus brachial. *Archives Générales Médicine 2*: 143–191

Eng G (1971). Brachial plexus palsy in new born infants. *Paediatrics 48*: 18–28

Eng GD, Koch B, Smokvina MD (1978). Brachial plexus palsy in neonates and children. *Arch Phys Med Rehab 59*: 458–464

Erb WH (1877). Uber eine eigenthümliche localisation von Lähmungen im Plexus Brachialis. *Verh Naturh-Med Ver (Heidelberg) NF Bd. 1*: 130–136

Fahr LM, Sauser DD 1988. Imaging of peripheral nerve lesions. *Orthop Clin N Am 19*: 27–41

Fallet GH, Moody J-F, Roth G, Boussina I (1967). Lésions du plexus brachial survénant après radiothérapie pour cancer du sein. *Rhumatologie 19*: 199–204

Filler AG, Howe FA, Hayes CE, Kliot M, Winn HR, Bell BA, Griffiths JR, Tsuruda JS (1993). Magnetic resonance neurography *Lancet 341*: 659–661

Flaubert AC (1827). Mémoire sur plusiers cas de luxations dans les efforts pour la réduction ont été suivis d'accidents graves. *Répertoire Générale d'Anatomie et de Physiologie Pathologique 3*: 55–79

Fletcher I (1981). Amputations of the upper limb. In: Wynn Parry CB (Ed), *Rehabilitation of the hand*, 4th edition. Butterworths. London, pp. 331–354

Francel PC, Koby M, Park TS, Lee BCP, Noetzel MJ, Mackinnon SE, Henegar MM, Kaufman BA (1995). Fast spin-echo magnetic resonance imaging for radiological assessment of neonatal brachial plexus injury. *J Neurosurg 83*: 461–466

Frazier CH, Skillern PG (1911). Supraclavicular subcutaneous lesions of the brachial plexus not associated with skeletal injuries. *J Am Med Assoc 57 (25)*: 1957–1963

Gentili F, Hudson A, Kline DG, Hunter D (1979). Peripheral nerve injection: an experimental study. *Neurosurgery 4*: 244–253

Gerard JM, Franck N, Moussa Z, Hildebrand J (1989). Acute ischaemic brachial plexus neuropathy following radiation therapy. *Neurology 39*. 450–451

Giddins GEB, Birch R, Singh D, Taggart M (1994). Risk factors for obstetrical brachial plexus palsies. *J Bone Jt Surg Suppl II/III*: 156

Gilbert A (1993). Obstetrical brachial plexus palsy. In: Tubiana R (Ed), *The hand*, vol. 4. WB Saunders, Philadelphia, pp. 576–601

Gilbert A (1995). Paralysie obstetricale du plexus brachial. In: Alnot J-Y, Narakas A (Eds), *Les paralysies du plexus brachial*, 2nd édition. Monographie de la Société Français de Chirurgie de la Main, Expansion Scientifique Français, Paris, pp. 270–281

Gilbert A, Raimondi P (1996). *Evaluation of results in obstetrical brachial plexus plasy. The elbow*. Paper to the International Meeting on Obstetric Brachial Plexus Palsy Heerlen.

Gilbert A, Tassin JL (1984). Réparation chirurgicale de plexus brachial dans la paralysie obstétricale. *Chirurgie (Paris) 110*: 70–75

Gjörup L (1965). Obstetrical lesion of the brachial plexus. *Acta Neurol Scand 42 (Suppl. 18)*: 9–38

Glazer HS, Lee JKT, Levitt RG, Heiken JP, Ling D, Totty WG, Balfe DM, Emani B, Wasserman TH, Murphy WA (1985). Radiation fibrosis: differentiation from recurrent tumor by MR imaging. *Radiology 156*: 721 726

Goldie BS, Coates CJ (1992). Brachial plexus injuries a survey of incidence and referral pattern. *J Hand Surg 17B*: 86–88

Gordon M, Rich H, Deutschberger J, Green M (1973). The immediate and long term outcome of obstetric birth trauma. 1. brachial plexus paralysis. *Am J Obst Gynaecol 117*: 51–56

Greenwald AG, Schute PC, Shively JL (1984). Brachial plexus palsy: a 10 year report on the incidence and prognosis. *J Paediatr Orthop 4*: 639–692

Gu YD, Shen LY (1994). Electrophysiological changes after severance of the C7 nerve root. *J Hand Surg 19B*: 69–71

Hardy AE (1981). Birth injuries of the brachial plexus. *J Bone Joint Surg 63B*: 98–101

Harper CM, Thomas JE, Cascino TL, Litchy WJ (1989). Distinction between neoplastic and radiation induced brachial neuropathy, with emphasis on the role of EMG. *Neurology 39*: 502–512

Harris W (1904). The true form of the brachial plexus and its motor distribution *J Anat Physiol 38*: 399–422

Hoffman CFE, Choufoer H, Marani E et al. (1993). Ultrastructural study on avulsion effects of the cat cervical motor-axonal pathways in the spinal cord. *Clin Neurol Neurosurg 95 (Suppl.)*: S39–S47

Hudson AR (1984). Injection injuries of nerves. In: Dyck PJ, Thomas PK, Lambert EH, Burge R (Eds), *Peripheral neuropathy*, 2nd edition. WB Saunders, Philadelphia, pp. 429–431

Jackson ST, Hoffer MM, Parish N (1988). Brachial-plexus palsy in the newborn. *J Bone Joint Surg 70A (8)*: 1217–1220

Jamieson A, Eames RA (1980). Reimplantation of avulsed brachial plexus roots: an experimental study in dogs. *Int J of Microsurg 2*: 75–80

Jennett RJ, Tarby TJ, Kreinick CJ (1992). Brachial plexus palsy: an old problem revisited. *Am J Obst Gynaecol 166*: 1637–1677

Khan R, Birch R (2001). Latropathic injuries of peripheral nerves. *J Bone Jt Surg, 83B*: 1145–1148.

Killer HE, Hess K (1990). Natural history of radiation induced brachial plexopathy compared with surgically treated patients. *J Neurol 237*: 247–250

Kiricuta I (1963). L'emploi du grand épiploon dans la chirurgie du sein cancéreux. *Presse Médicale 71*: 15–17

Kline DG, Hudson AR (1995) *Nerve injuries, injection injury*. WB Saunders, Philadelphia, pp. 46–50

Klumpke A (1885). Contribution a l'etude des paralysies radiculaires du plexus brachial: paralysies radiculaires totales. *Rev Med (Paris) 5*: 591–616

Kogelnik HD (1977). Einfluss der Dosis-Relation auf die Pathogenese der peripheren Neuropathie. *Strahlentherapie 153*: 467–469

Kori SH, Foley KM, Osner JB (1981). Brachial plexus lesions in patients with cancer. *Neurology 31*: 45–50

Landi A, Copeland S (1979) Value of the Tinel sign in brachial plexus lesions. *Ann Roy Coll Surg Engl 61*: 470–471

Landi A, Copeland SA, Wynn Parry CB, Jones SJ (1980). The role of somatosensory evoked potentials and nerve conduction studies in the surgical management of brachial plexus injuries. *J Bone Joint Surg 62B*: 492–496

Le Quang C (1989). Post irradiation lesions of the brachial plexus. *Hand Clinics 5*: 23–32

Lederman JR, Wilbourn AJ (1984). Brachial plexopathy: recurrent cancer or radiation? *Neurology 34*: 1331–1335

Lipton S (1968). Percutaneous electrical cordotomy in relief of intractable pain. *Br Med J 2*: 210–212

Loeser JD, Ward AA (1967). Some effects of deafferentation on neurons of the cat spinal cord. *Arch Neurol 17*: 629–636

Loeser JD, Ward AA, White LE (1968). Chronic deafferentation of human spinal cord neurons. *J Neurosurg 39*: 48–50

Mackinnon SE, Dellon AL, Hudson AR, Hunter DA (1984). Chronic nerve compression – an experimental model in the rat. *Ann Plastic Surg 13*: 112–120

Marshall RW, de Silva RD (1986). Computerised tomography in traction lesions of the brachial plexus. *J Bone Joint Surg 68B*: 734–738

Maruyama Y, Mylrea MM, Logothetis J (1967). Neuropathy following radiation. *Am J Roentgenol 101*: 216–219

Melzack R, Wall PD (1965). Pain mechanisms: A new theory. *Science 150*: 971–979

Merle M, Duprez K, Delandre D et al. (1988). La neurolyse microchirurgicale des plexites brachiales postradiothérapiques. *Chirurgie 114*: 421–423

Michelow BJ, Clarke HM, Curtis CG, Zuker RM, Seifs Y, Andrews DF (1994). The natural history of obstetrical brachial plexus palsy. *Plastic Reconstruct Surg 94*: 675–680

Mondrup K, Olsen NK, Pfeiffer P, Rose C (1990). Clinical and electro-diagnostic findings in breast cancer patients with radiation-induced brachial plexus neuropathy. *Acta Neurol Scand 81*: 153–158

Mumenthaler M (1964). Armplexus paresen in Anschluss an Röntgenbestrahlung. Mitteilung von 8 eigenen Beobachtungen. *Schweizerische Medizinische Wochenschrift 94*: 399–406

Nagano A, Ochiai N, Sugioka H et al. (1989). Usefulness of myelography in brachial plexus injuries. *J Hand Surg 14B*: 59–64

Narakas AO (1978). Surgical treatment of traction injuries of the brachial plexus. *Clin Orthop Rel Res 133*: 71–90

Narakas AO (1981). The effects on pain of reconstructive neurosurgery in 160 patients with traction and/or crush injury to the brachial plexus. In: Siegfried J, Zimmerman M (Eds), *Phantom and stump pain*. Springer Verlag, Berlin, p. 126

Narakas AO (1984a). Traumatic brachial plexus lesions. In: Dyck PJ, Thomas PK, Lambert EH, Bunge R (Eds), *Peripheral neuropathy*, 2nd edition. WB Saunders, Philadelphia, pp. 1394–1409

Narakas AO (1984b). Operative treatment for radiation induced and metastatic brachial plexopathy in 45 cases, 15 having omentoplasty. *Bull Hosp Joint Dis Orthop Inst 44*: 354–375

Narakas AO (1987). Obstetrical brachial plexus injuries. In: Lamb D.W. (Ed), *The paralysed hand*. Churchill Livingstone, Edinburgh, pp. 116–135

Narakas AO, Brunelli G, Clodius L, Merle M (1987). Traitement chirurgical des plexopathies postactinique. In: Alnot J-Y, Narakas A (Eds), *Les paralysies du plexus brachial.* Mongraphies du groupe d'etude de la main, no. 15. Expansion Scientifique Francaise, Paris pp. 240–249

Nashold BS (1981). Modification of lesion of DREZ technique. *J Neurosurg 55*: 1012

Nashold BS, Osdahl RH (1979). Dorsal root entry zone lesions for pain relief. *J Neurosurg 51*: 59–69

Olsen NK, Pfeiffer P, Mondrup K, Rose C (1990). Radiation-induced brachial plexus neuropathy in breast cancer patients. *Acta Oncol 29*: 885–895

Olsen NK, Pfeiffer P, Johannsen L, Schroder H, Rose C (1993). Radiation-induced brachial plexopathy: neurological follow-up in 161 recurrence-free breast cancer patients. *Int J Radiation Oncol Biol Physics 26*: 43–49

Ovelmen Levitt J, Blumenkopf B, Sharpe R, Lee KH, Nashold BS (1982). Electrical activity and neuropeptide localization in the lumbar dorsal horn after dorsal root avulsion and rhizotomy in the cat. *Soc Neurosci Abst. 8*: 94

Paradiso G, Grañana N, Maza E (1997). Prenatal brachial plexus injury. *Neurology 49*: 261–262

Parks BJ (1973). Postoperative peripheral neuropathies. *Surgery 74*: 348–357

Petry D, Merle M (1989). Le réinsertion sociale des blessés atteints de paralysie traumatique du plexus brachial. In: Alnot J-Y, Narakas A (Eds), *Les paralysies du plexus brachial.* Mongraphies du groupe d'etude de la main, no. 15. Expansion Scientifique Francaise, Paris, pp. 224–227

Posniak HV, Olson MC, Dudiak CM, Wisniewski R, O'Malley C (1993). MR imaging of the brachial plexus. *Am J Roentgenol 161*: 373–379

Power C (1994). National trends in birth weight. *Br Med J 308*: 1270–1271

Raimondi P (1993). *Evaluation of results in obstetric brachial plexus palsy. The hand.* Paper to the International Meeting on obstetric brachial plexus palsy, Heerlen.

Ransford AO, Hughes SPF (1977). Complete brachial plexus lesions. *J Bone Joint Surg 59B*: 417–442

Rapoport S, Blair DN, McCarthy SM, Dewer TS, Hammers LW, Sostman HD (1988). Brachial plexus: correlation of MR imaging with CT and pathological findings. *Radiology 167*: 161–165

Richter HP, Schachenmayr W (1984). Is the substantia gelatinosa the target in dorsal root entry zone lesions? An autopsy report. *Neurosurgery 15*: 913–916

Rinaldi PC, Young RF, Albe-Fessard D, Chodakiewitz J (1991). Spontaneous neuronal hyperactivity in the medial intralaminar thalamic nuclei of patients with deafferentation pain. *J. Neurosurg 74*: 415–421

Roaf R (1963). Lateral flexion injuries of the cervical spine. *J Bone Joint Surg 45B*: 36

Rosson JW (1987). Disability following closed traction lesions of the brachial plexus sustained in motor cycle accidents. *Hand Surg 12B*: 353–355

Roth G, Magistris MR, Le Fort D, Desjaques P, Della Snata D (1988). Plexopathies post-radique. Bloc de conduction persistants. Décharges myokimiques et crampes. *Revue Neurologique 144*: 173–180

Salner AL, Botnik LE, Herzog AG, Goldstein MA, Harris JR, Levene MB, Hellman S (1981). Reversible brachial plexopathy following primary radiation therapy for breast cancer. *Cancer Treat Rep 65*: 797–802

Schady W, Ochoa JL, Torebjork HE (1983). Peripheral projections of fascicles in the human median nerve. *Brain 106*: 745

Schenker M (1998). *Analysis of avulsed roots in traction injury of the human brachial plexus.* MSc thesis, University College London

Seddon HJ (1975). *Surgical disorders of peripheral nerves,* 2nd edition. Churchill Livingstone, Edinburgh

Sharrard WJW (1971). *Paediatric orthopaedics and fractures,* 2nd edition. Blackwell, Oxford

Shealy CN, Mortimer JT, Reswick JB (1967). Electrical inhibition of pain by stimulation of the dorsal columns. *Anaesth Analg 46*: 489–491

Sindou M (1972). *Étude de la jonction radiculo-médullaire postérieure. La radicellotomie postérieure sélective dans la chirurgie de la douleur.* Thése Med, Lyons

Sindou M, Keravel Y (1980). Analgésie par la méthode d'électrostimulation transcutanée: résultats dans les douleurs neurologiques à propos de 180 cm. *Neurochirurgie 26*: 153–157

Sindou M, Mertens P (1993). Neurosurgical treatment of pain in the upper limb. In: Tubiana R (Ed), *The Hand,* vol. 4. WB Saunders, Philadelphia, pp. 858–870

Slingluff CL, Terzis JK, Edgerton MT (1987). The quantitative microanatomy of the brachial plexus. In: Terzis JK (Ed), *Microreconstruction of nerve injuries.* WB Saunders, Philadelphia, pp. 285–324

Slooff ACJ, Blaauw G (1995). Aspects particuliers. In: Alnot J-Y, Narakas A (Eds), *Les paralysies du plexus brachial.* Monographie du groupe d'etude de la main, no. 15. Expansion Scientifique Francaise, Paris, pp. 282–284

Smith SJM (1998). Electrodiagnosis. In: Birch R, Bonney G, Wynn Parry CB (Eds), *Surgical disorders of the peripheral nerves.* Churchill Livingstone, London

Sordillo PP, Helson L, Hajdu SL, Margill GD, Kosloff C, Golbey RB, Beattie EJ (1981). Malignant schwannoma – clinical characteristics, survival and response to therapy. *Cancer 47*: 2503–2509

Specht DD (1975). Brachial plexus palsy in the newborn: incidence and prognosis. *Clin Orthop 110*: 32–34

Spiess H (1972). Schädigungen am peripheren Nervensystem durch iioniserende Strahlen. In: *Schriftenreihe neurologie, Band 10.* Springer Verlag, New York

Spittle MF (1995). Brachial plexus neuropathy after radiotherapy for breast cancer. *Br Med J 311*: 1516–1517

Steiner RC, Fallet GH, Moody J-F, Roth G, Maurice PA, Alberto P, Paunier J-P (1971). Lésions du plexus brachial survénant après radiothérapie pour cancer du sein. *Schweizerische Medizinische Wochenschrift 101*: 1846–1848

Stoll BA, Andrews JT (1966). Radiation-induced peripheral neuropathy. *Br Med J I*: 834–837

Sugioka H, Nagano A (1989). Électrodiagnostic dans l'évaluation des lésions par élongation du plexus brachial. In: Alnot J-Y, Narakas A (Eds), *Les Paralysies du plexus brachial.* Mongraphies du groupe d'etude de la main, no. 15. Expansion Scientifique Francaise, Paris, pp. 123–129.

Sunderland S, Bradley KC (1961) Stress – strain phenomenon in human spinal nerve roots. *Brain 84*: 125

Tan KL (1973). Brachial palsy. *J Obs Gynaecol Br Commonwealth 80*: 60–62

Taylor PE (1962). Traumatic intradural avulsion of the nerve roots of the brachial plexus. *Brain 85*: 579–602

Taylor TE, Wills BA, Kazembe P, Chisale M, Wirima JJ, Ratsma EYEC, Molyneux ME (1993). Magnetic resonance neurography *Lancet 341*: 659–661

Thomas JE, Colby MY (1972). Radiation-induced or metastatic brachial plexopathy. *J Am Med Assoc 222*: 1392–1395

Thomas DGT, Jones SJ (1984). Dorsal root entry zone lesions (Nashold's procedure) in brachial plexus avulsion. *Neurosurgery 15*: 966–968

Thomas DGT, Kitchen ND (1994). Long term follow up of dorsal root entry zone lesions in brachial plexus avulsion. *J Neurol Neurosurg Psychiatry 57*: 737–738

Tinel J (1917). *Nerve Wounds.* Ballière Tindall and Cox, London. Authorised translation by F Rothwell; revised and edited by CA Joll

Trombetta A (1880). *Sullo stiramento dei nervi.* Frat D'Angelo, Messina

Uhlschmid G, Clodius L (1978). Eine Neue Anwendung des frei Transplantation Omentums. *Der Chirurg 49*: 714–718.

Watkins ES, Koeze TH (1993). Spinal cord stimulation and pain relief. *Br Med J 307*: 462

West GA, Haynor DR, Goodkin R, Tsuruda JS, Bronstein AD, Kraft G, Winter T, Kliot M (1994). Magnetic resonance imaging signal changes in denervated muscles after peripheral nerve injury. *Neurosurgery 35*: 1077–1086

Williams WW, Twyman RS, Donell ST, Birch R (1996). The posterior triangle and the painful shoulder – spinal accessory nerve injury. *J Bone Joint Surg 73B (Suppl. 1)*: 60

Wynn Parry CB (1980). Pain in avulsion lesions of the brachial plexus. *Pain 9*: 41–53

Wynn Parry CB (1989). Pain in avulsion of the brachial plexus. *Neurosurgery 15*: 960–965

Wynn Parry CB, Frampton V, Monteith A (1987). Rehabilitation of patients following traction lesion of the brachial plexus. In: Terzia JK (Ed), *Microreconstruction of nerve injuries.* WB Saunders, Philadelphia, pp. 483–495

Yeoman PM (1968). Cervical myelography in traction injuries of the brachial plexus. *J Bone Joint Surg 50B*: 253–260

Yoshizawa H, Kobayashi S, Hachiya Y (1991). Blood supply of nerve roots and dorsal root ganglia. *Orthop Clin N Am Rel Res 22*: 195–211

Zancolli EA, Zancolli ER (1993) Palliative surgical procedures in sequelae of obstetrical palsy [English transl] In: Tubiana R (Ed). *The hand,* vol. 4. WB Saunders, Philadelphia, pp. 602–623

48. Disorders of the peripheral nerves

Mary Reilly   Richard J. Greenwood

INTRODUCTION

The rehabilitation of patients with a peripheral neuropathy is directed by the type and the severity of the disorder, and by the age of the patient. Although peripheral neuropathies are heterogeneous, with various aetiologies and natural histories, almost all patients have impaired limb function (which can be severe), whereas the intellect is spared. These two features govern the broad approach to the rehabilitation of these patients.

Specific treatment of both acute and chronic neuropathies continues to advance. For example, manipulation of the immune system is helpful in inflammatory neuropathy (Dalakas & Engel, 1981; Guillain–Barré Study Group, 1985; Van Der Meche et al., 1992), and chronic inflammatory demyelinating neuropathy (CIDP) can relapse if treatment is stopped. Refsum's disease can respond to dietary manipulation (Stokke & Eldjarn, 1984) whereas the neuropathies caused by vitamin E or B12 deficiency will improve dramatically with replacement. Although various specific treatments can be very effective, there is often residual impairment requiring rehabilitation.

Other neuropathies are untreatable. Relentless deterioration can lead to a sense of hopelessness, which can retard effective rehabilitation; such patients offer a major challenge to the rehabilitation team. Focal mononeuropathies can produce less impairment than generalised forms but a surprising degree of handicap can develop, despite what might appear to be a restricted impairment.

Many of these points will be expanded upon in the rest of the chapter, which will not be concerned with peripheral nerve trauma.

FACTORS GOVERNING THE GENERAL APPROACH

In patients with generalised neuropathies, management is dictated by the rate of progression of the disease. In acute neuropathies, severe impairment develops rapidly; this can result in considerable anxiety in both patient and family members. For the majority of patients, the maintenance of ventilation, care of bowel and bladder, and nutrition are often crucial issues during the early stages of a severe and acute neuropathy, and it is important to provide physiotherapy to prevent contractures and

avoid pressure sores by careful positioning and regular turning. Incomplete recovery can lead to long-term disability, requiring rehabilitation and adaptation of lifestyle to minimise handicap.

This situation is not unlike that following severe spinal cord trauma. By contrast, in chronic neuropathies the rehabilitation team will first encounter the patient when abilities are at their greatest; adaptations must be planned in the light of progressive deterioration, which is frequently accompanied by anxiety and depression.

Improvement is sometimes not as rapid or complete as expected. Clearly, specific medical reasons for this must be considered (such as adequacy of immunosuppression in CIDP) but the situation can be more complex. Although negative factors such as weakness and sensory loss are apparent on clinical examination, positive phenomena such as pain and paraesthesiae are less readily apparent to the examiner, but can be more disturbing and debilitating to the patient. Contractures, pressure ulcers, poor sleep, cardiorespiratory deconditioning, fatigue, and respiratory weakness can all retard the effective rehabilitation of such patients, and must be kept in mind.

MEASUREMENTS OF PROGRESS AND OUTCOME

The history and physical examination give a good picture of the patient's present level of impairment, disability, and likely handicap. This can be refined further by various means. For example, electromyography (EMG) can demonstrate extensive denervation, thus predicting prolonged and possibly incomplete recovery (Raman & Taori, 1976); conversely, evidence of re-innervation (and improved prognosis) might be apparent on EMG before it is apparent clinically. In a slowly developing or deteriorating neuropathy, it is difficult to detect change using the standard neurological examination. The MRC grading scheme (Medical Research Council, 1976) for muscle power is subjective and non-linear. It might fail to detect small changes in power that are nevertheless important (Karni et al. 1984). Questioning patients about the changes in their level of functional disability can be more revealing. Some of this uncertainty can be avoided by the use of simple, objective testing of muscle power (Wiles & Karni, 1983). Reproducible, sensitive, and accurate measurements can be made with a lightweight, hand-held myometer suitable for use at the bedside, in the out-patient department, or at home.

It is more difficult to measure sensation objectively (Lindblom & Tegner, 1989). Thermal threshold testing and visual analogue scales can give an approximate guide to progress. In this way, problems such as neuropathic ulceration or falling due to proprioceptive loss can be anticipated and minimised, or avoided by early intervention such as skin care, chiropody, or walking aids.

MANAGEMENT

Weakness

Even in the early stages of acute neuropathies, active limb movements can be feasible with careful positioning to minimise the effects of gravity; passive movements of limbs will prevent contractures. Functional splinting can restore function to weak upper limbs. Foot drop, with its dangers of tripping and secondary injuries, is compensated for by tilt of the pelvis away from the foot drop with increased hip and knee flexion. Passive dorsiflexion by an ankle–foot orthosis will correct the abnormal gait and prevent falls. Surgical procedures such as tendon transfers, osteotomies, or arthrodeses can be of value in more chronic cases.

Exercise can retrain patients to use muscles or joints using methods developed for patients with poliomyelitis (Knapp, 1955). Isometric and isotonic exercises increase muscle power (Einarsson, 1991; Milner Brown & Miller, 1988) and exercise tolerance (Carroll et al., 1979; Hagberg et al., 1980) in patients with myopathy or after poliomyelitis; there are remarkably few data concerning the value of such therapy in peripheral neuropathy. Milner Brown and Miller (1988) showed increased muscle strength in one patient with an "idiopathic peripheral neuropathy" but Florence and Hagberg (1984) failed to show increased exercise tolerance in two patients with Charcot–Marie–Tooth disease in contrast to six patients with myopathies. This lack of data concerning the efficacy of exercise training in peripheral neuropathy is surprising and worthy of further study, as exercise can allow a patient to carry out a useful function that was previously impossible. Once improved function is achieved, the new functions can be repeated and improvement maintained. To prevent patients exercising to the point of overuse in the expectation that recovery will be faster, it is important to emphasise that although exercise can hasten functional recovery and reduce disability, the rate of recovery of the underlying neuropathy will not be affected. There is some experimental evidence that electrical stimulation of denervated muscle can retard atrophy in animals but this is unproven in man (Sunderland, 1991); even if effective, its use is impractical in any condition more extensive than single nerve lesions, for example Bell's Palsy to traumatic mononeuropathies, in which eventual reinnervation is expected.

In patients with permanent weakness, adaptations to the environment such as ramps, lifts, special utensils, and mobility aids such as crutches or wheelchairs (patients with upper limb weakness might need electric wheelchairs) can reduce disability and allow patients to retain independence. Increasingly, sophisticated electronic systems can be installed in the home for more severely affected patients.

Sensory loss

Loss of normal sensation carries the risk of unnoticed trauma to the skin with dangers of neuropathic ulceration and neuropathic arthropathy. Patients must be educated to examine the areas of abnormal sensation regularly, and appropriate footwear and careful chiropody in more disabled patients are valuable. Sensory ataxia can incorrectly be attributed to cerebellar dysfunction or even weakness; careful examination allows the real nature of the problem to be identified with subsequent emphasis on the use of visual cues in physiotherapy.

Pain

In some patients, an abnormal gait and posture can lead to secondary musculoskeletal pain, which is readily treated in most cases. Non-steroidal anti-inflammatory agents, local heat, physiotherapy, orthoses, and mobility aids might be required. Neuropathic pain is usually more resistant to therapy. Sometimes, the intensity of such pain or dysaesthesia can completely dominate the clinical situation. Typically, there is a constant, deep aching or superficial pains in one or more limbs. Neuropathic pain is seen mostly in axonal neuropathies, particularly if small fibres are involved (e.g. hereditary sensory neuropathy, alcoholic, amyloid, or diabetic neuropathies, or Fabry's disease) although some large fibre neuropathies can be painful (Scadding, 1989). The judicious use of anticonvulsants and tricyclic drugs, local or regional sympathetic blockade and, in some diabetic patients, adjusted glycaemic control (Lancet, 1985) can be helpful.

General measures

Acute or progressive physical impairments, neuropathic pain, and disability can lead to depression that can, if unrecognised, significantly increase disability and retard or prevent rehabilitation. Secondary complications of severe peripheral neuropathy, such as pressure ulcers, scoliosis, and contractures can require surgical treatment. In some cases, arthrodeses can stabilise unstable joints and improve function.

SPECIFIC EXAMPLES

To illustrate the rehabilitation process in the context of peripheral nervous system disorders, three syndromes will be discussed in detail: acute neuropathies, exemplified by critical illness polyneuropathy and the Guillain–Barré syndrome (GBS), postpolio syndrome, and chronic neuropathies, illustrated by hereditary motor and sensory neuropathy (HMSN or Charcot–Marie–Tooth disease).

Critical illness polyneuropathy

Critical illness polyneuropathy (CIP), first described by Bolton et al. in 1984, results from the systemic inflammatory response syndrome (SIRS), and is seen in patients admitted to intensive care in the context of severe sepsis or multiple trauma (Zochodne & Bolton, 1996). Nerve conduction studies and nerve biopsy reveal an axonal neuropathy with reduction of compound motor and sensory action potentials and evidence of denervation on sampling. There is usually a good long-term prognosis and functional recovery in the majority of patients. However, CIP is now well recognised to sometimes prolong hospital stay, and thus lead to inpatient rehabilitation after intensive care. In addition, poor recovery with significant long-term deficit in a small percentage of patients is now well documented.

Coakley et al. (1993) recruited 23 patients after more than 7 days of intensive care and found that hospital discharge was delayed for between 1 and 2 months in six of nine patients who had severe limb weakness at discharge from intensive care. Leijten et al. (1995) studied 50 consecutive patients ventilated on an ITU for more than 7 days. Of 24 patients who survived the intensive care period and could be evaluated for a polyneuropathy, eight of twelve with a critical illness polyneuropathy, and only one of twelve without, had not achieved full muscle strength and the ability to walk 50 metres more than 4 weeks after achieving complete ventilatory independence. Five of the eight, 22% of all 1-year survivors, had "severe residual functional handicap", which was not described in more detail, at 1 year; all these patients were said to have conduction slowing on electrophysiological testing, and four of the five also had evidence of denervation on sampling. Recovery to walking unassisted in the six survivors of 24 patients described by Latronico et al. (1996), all of whom developed a neuromyopathy after being admitted comatose to intensive care, took between 115 and 210 days (median 142 days).

Thus, whereas most patients who are referred for in-patient rehabilitation as a result of critical illness neuromyopathy achieve good independence, at least in personal and domestic functional activities, some can have long-term residual mobility problems, as illustrated by the four patients described in detail by Jarrett and Mogelof (1995), and prediction about outcome early on in severe cases might need to be somewhat circumspect. The long-term prognosis in occasional patients with a necrotising myopathy, usually seen after severe respiratory illness (especially asthma), and the prescription of steroids, seems similar to those with a polyneuropathy. Thus, the three surviving patients of the four reported by Hanson et al. (1997) walked without crutches after 2, 5, and 8 months. Whether electrophysiological findings help to predict those who will have significant residual deficit, as suggested by Leijten et al. (1995), deserves further study.

Rehabilitation programmes for severe cases follow the principles described below for the Guillain–Barré syndrome. Coakley et al. (1993) and Latronico et al. (1996) found neurogenic and/or myopathic changes on muscle biopsy in 22 of 23,

and 23 of 24 patients, respectively. How often critical illness neuromyopathy delays a return to full activity after intensive care, rather than merely delaying discharge from hospital or the ability to walk 50 metres, has never been examined. The weakness must add to the detraining effect of immobility and recumbency associated with severe illness (see Chapter 15), and possibly also the fatigue associated with early attempts to achieve full fitness.

Guillain–Barré syndrome (GBS)

GBS or acute inflammatory polyradiculoneuropathy (AIP) produces a variable degree of acute or subacute quadriparesis; this is frequently severe. GBS affects between 0.75 and 2.0 persons per 100,000 per year (Ropper, 1992). These incidence figures have more recently been confirmed in the UK (Rees et al., 1998). Patients often become unable to walk and there can be associated respiratory, bulbar, and autonomic failure. Admission to an intensive therapy unit is sometimes needed and about 20% of patients require artificial ventilation (Ropper, 1992). In a UK series prior to the use of immunomodulatory treatment (Winer et al., 1988), 13% of patients died and, at 12 months, 20% were left significantly disabled, whereas 67% had recovered completely; 88% lost the ability to walk at the height of the illness. Plasma exchange (Ropper, 1992) or intravenous IgG (Van Der Meche et al., 1992) effectively attenuate the severity of GBS if commenced within 2 weeks of the onset. Such therapy is indicated in patients who are unable to walk or have significant bulbar or respiratory weakness. Intravenous IgG infusion is currently the preferred treatment because of the ease of application (Hahn, 1998). In a recent UK study, 68% of patients with GBS had immunomodulatory treatment. At 1 year, 8% of all patients had died, 62% had made a complete or almost complete recovery, 4% remained bedbound or ventilator dependent, 9% were unable to walk unaided, and 17% were unable to run (Rees, 1998).

This highlights the fact that a significant minority of patients remain disabled despite immunomodulatory treatment and require continuing rehabilitation. However, many aspects of the management in both the acute and more chronic stages require a multidisciplinary approach, which is applicable to all patients with GBS.

At an early stage, various prognostic factors can be used to predict the likely degree and duration of disability (Winer et al., 1988). Older age, small compound muscle action potentials on nerve conduction tests, inability to walk within 4 days, onset after campylobacter infection (Rees et al., 1995), or the need for artificial ventilation all predict a poor outcome. Reliable and reproducible functional measures of severity are useful; a lack of demonstrable improvement in the first few weeks suggests a poor outlook with prolonged or permanent disability.

From the outset, high priority must be given to the prevention of complications if long-term disability is to be minimised. In severely affected patients, close monitoring of respiratory, cardiovascular, and bulbar function (on an intensive therapy unit) is vital to prevent potentially lethal complications. Attention to positioning, posture, bowel and bladder function, and chest physiotherapy can prevent pressure ulcers, peripheral nerve damage, constipation, urinary infection, and chest infections. Passive limb movements and moulded limb splints can avoid contractures. In this regard, the use of a tilt table to prevent contractures should be supervised closely because of the dangers of severe postural hypotension in patients with autonomic involvement. Compression stockings (and probably subcutaneous heparin) are aimed at the prevention of venous thromboembolism. Pain, perhaps mediated by nervi nervorum in inflamed nerve roots (Thomas, 1979), can be severe and should be borne in mind, especially in the ventilated patient. It can be resistant to all treatments apart from intrathecal opioids. Attention to positioning and limb support, passive movements, cold or heat, vibration or transcutaneous neural stimulation (TNS) can be helpful.

The psychological impact of GBS can be devastating (Rice, 1977) and depression is common (Ropper, 1992). Reassurance, explanation, and attention to a frequently deranged sleep pattern are important. Support from ex-patients can be enlisted from the local branch of the Guillain–Barré Support Group (see the section useful addresses at the end of the chapter). During recovery a full range of movement should be maintained in all joints. Muscle strengthening will initially involve movements that are assisted and can exclude the effect of gravity. Hydrotherapy can have a place here. Later, active movement against gravity will target trunk and head control, sitting, unsupported, kneeling, standing from sitting and walking. In most patients, the use of special seating (including head support), walking aids, and functional splinting will be more or less temporary. Activities of daily living will be gradually reintroduced. Graduated strengthening exercises, and exercises to improve balance and coordination will also be started at around this time. The relative value of the various techniques in use is entirely unexplored.

Patients often fatigue early: both exercise regimes and a patient's daily routine must take this into account. Fatigue can continue even when power has returned to normal on clinical testing. This can be shown to be due to residual motor, rather than psychological, factors by myometry (Nicklin et al., 1987).

Postpolio syndrome (PPS)

Although substantial progress towards the "global eradication of poliomyelitis by the year 2000" has been achieved, with an 88% reduction in the number of reported cases globally since 1988 (when the WHO member states adopted this goal), polio is still endemic in some countries (Tangermann et al., 1997). When paralysis occurs it is often confined to the legs. The RNA enterovirus (picornavirus) responsible for the disease affects the anterior horn cells, sparing sensory function. It has been postulated recently that the poliovirus targets motor neurones by entering the axon through recently described poliovirus receptors at the nerve–muscle interface and then migrates to the nerve cell body in the anterior horn of the spinal cord (Halstead, 1998).

Recovery can continue for over a year. It results from a number of adaptive processes, particularly sprouting of terminal axons of surviving motor units, probably in response to the expression of neural cell adhesion molecules by denervated myofibres (Cashman et al., 1987).

Hypertrophy of innervated fibres and fibre transformation from fast-twitch glycolytic type 2 to slow-twitch oxidative type I fibres also occurs (Borg et al., 1988). Exercise of weak muscles can be started safely within 4 weeks of the onset of the illness and can produce increased endurance during the recovery phase (Russell & Fisher-Williams, 1954). This might well be useful to patients, even though it seems unlikely that there is an appreciable influence on final muscle strength.

Polio is now rare in the UK. However, there are a large number of disabled people who were affected when the disease was still common. Many became ill at an early age. The physical development of such people will have been influenced by the physical impairments caused by polio. Lifestyle and environment will have developed in the light of ability rather than having been modified because of a more recently acquired disability. In the authors' experience, also noted by others (Kohl, 1987), many of these patients do not readily acknowledge that they are disabled and resent any suggestion that they are not merely "different". This can affect their willingness to accept help and change in the light of late deterioration (see later). The British Polio Fellowship (see the section useful addresses) was founded in 1939 to "provide a personal welfare service to polio-disabled persons living in the UK, whether members or not". There are local groups, a regular newsletter and active fundraising; many patients gain a great deal from membership.

Late deterioration after polio is well described and typically occurs from 30–40 years after the acute illness. The most commonly used term to describe this late deterioration is the postpolio syndrome (PPS). This is defined by various authors as the development of new neuromuscular symptoms (fatigue, muscle/joint pain, new weakness, atrophy, functional loss, or cold intolerance) at least 15 years after reaching maximum recovery from acute paralytic poliomyelitis, when these symptoms are not due to other medical causes. The term "postpolio muscular atrophy" (PPMA) is used specifically for new muscle weakness and new muscle atrophy (Dalakas et al., 1984). Another term, "post-polio muscular dysfunction" (PPMD) has also been introduced for new or increased muscle weakness found in patients with prior polio (Workshop Report, 1996). It is very difficult to get an accurate estimate of the true incidence of PPS or PPMA because it depends on how vigorously other medical causes have been excluded. The constellation of new symptoms of progressive weakness, fatigue, aches and pains, and cold intolerance are quoted as occurring in 25–40% of survivors (Codd et al., 1985; Spier et al., 1987). Two recent studies of patients with previous poliomyelitis failed to detect any cases of PPMA making this a rare diagnosis (Windebank et al., 1996; Kidd et al., 1997). In the study by Kidd et al., 239 patients were studied who had a late deterioration which was associated with orthopaedic disorders in 170 cases, neurological disorders (e.g. cervical radiculopathy/myelopathy, lumbar radiculopathy, or entrapment neuropathies) in 35, respiratory disorders in 19, and other disorders in 15. This highlights the importance of looking for the other causes of a late deterioration. The orthopaedic complications are particularly common. In some patients the abnormal physical development will have caused abnormal stresses to joints with premature degenerative changes. This can cause disproportionate disability because of the lack of functional reserve in already disabled persons; the scope for functional re-education by physiotherapists and occupational therapists is therefore reduced. In patients with symptoms attributable to the effects of late neuromuscular deterioration, the symptoms happen sooner in those with more severe pre-existing disease (Halstead et al., 1985). The deterioration can be subtle and slowly progressive. There can be increased severity of a pre-existing scoliosis and increased difficulty with tasks that were performed adeptly in the past—most frequently ambulation and stair climbing (Einarsson & Grimby, 1990). There might be a late decline in respiratory function (Kidd et al., 1997). To these problems can be added the effects of weight gain, occurring in over 60% of postpolio patients in one study (Agre et al., 1989), or disuse weakness, sometimes resulting from incidental immobilisation.

It is now clear that the symptoms and the muscle atrophy that can occur in PPS do *not* represent a form of motor neurone disease, as was suggested by Mulder et al. (1972). Individual muscle fibre loss occurs as a result of degeneration of individual nerve terminals in an "overextended" motor neurone, rather than the group atrophy due to loss of whole motor units seen in motor neurone disease (Dalakas et al., 1986; Hayward & Seaton, 1979; Kidd et al., 1997; Weichers & Hubbell, 1981). This deterioration is very slow; it occurs at a rate of about 1% of muscle strength per year and functional clinical thresholds are crossed at intervals of over a year. A recent 8-year longitudinal study in individuals with late polio showed muscle strength decreased during the 8-year follow up by 9–15%, endurance decreased, and EMG studies showed evidence of on-going denervation–re-innervation as well as failing capacity to maintain large motor units (Grimby et al., 1998). It has also been suggested that some of the fluctuating symptoms in PPS could be due to defective synthesis or release of acetylcholine, which might explain the occasional reports of a response to pyridostigmine (Halstead, 1998).

Diagnostic tests for PPS, including EMG and muscle biopsies, are limited as they often show the same abnormalities in polio survivors with PPS as in those without it.

Berthy et al. (1991) have found that management should include explanation, reassurance, and advice about methods of conserving energy and avoiding fatigue, including work simplification and appropriate prescription of equipment. Depression occurred in 23 of their 86 patients. Mild exercise increased fatigue in 48% of cases, possibly in part because of the cardiorespiratory deconditioning that occurs in postpolio patients, and which can be reversed by aerobic training (Jones et al., 1989). Einarsson (1991), however, showed that training increased

muscle strength but that fatigue was not improved; 6–12 months after training, strength was maintained but fatigue had increased. This emphasises the importance of managing fatigue in these patients by performing exercise or physical work at intervals rather than to exhaustion, a technique that decreases symptoms and improves function (Agre et al., 1989). An interesting study quantifying voluntary activation and strength of the elbow flexors showed that, compared with control subjects, patients with prior polio had impaired voluntary activation both when the elbow flexors were not fatigued and during fatiguing submaximal exercise. Central and peripheral fatigue were more marked in those with PPS (Allen et al., 1994). Another recent study shows that physical activity in daily life is related to pain in individuals with late effects of polio (Willen & Grimby, 1998). The authors recommended that patients with late effects of polio, experiencing aching and especially cramping pain, modify their level of physical activity.

As a result of these changes people might have to turn to the rehabilitation team for help. At the same time, they might be unwilling to acknowledge that they are (and have been) disabled. Well-intentioned advice might be rejected. The long-term poliomyelitis patient is often an excellent example of how well a disabled person can cope with a complex society. Occasional patients respond to the suggestion that if there is a refusal to acknowledge the true situation there is a lost opportunity to demonstrate the fact that disabled people can cope so well in society. In this way, such patients are failing to support the wish expressed by those within the disabled community to be treated more normally. If the patient is willing to be helped, a full range of orthoses, equipment and adaptations to home and workplace can be considered. Therapeutic exercise programmes should be tailored individually to exercise some muscles and not others, and thus avoid fatigue and overuse. The long-term poliomyelitis sufferer might be persuaded to use a wheelchair out of doors or to display a disabled driver's permit, thereby continuing to work, maintain independence, and to socialise. Sometimes a patient will only accept attention to one problem—a painful shoulder, for example—rejecting other offers of assistance. Perhaps the painful shoulder can be thought of as a separate condition, unrelated to the effects of poliomyelitis.

Finally, it is important to emphasise that the usual progression of symptoms in PPS is fairly slow and the overall prognosis is good unless there are severe breathing or swallowing difficulties.

Hereditary motor and sensory neuropathy

The hereditary motor and sensory neuropathies (HMSN), more commonly known as Charcot–Marie–Tooth (CMT) disease in the genetic literature, are a heterogeneous group of genetically determined disorders. The most common are HMSN I (demyelinating), HMSN II (axonal), and HMSN III (severe demyelinating). Other forms of HMSN are well known but rare.

In HMSN I there is demyelination and hypertrophic change in peripheral nerve. Foot drop, distal wasting in the legs, and sensory loss develop with onset before the age of 10 years in two-thirds of patients (Buchthal & Behse, 1977). Sensory loss can be severe (Thomas et al., 1974) and some patients have associated scoliosis, tremor, and ataxia (Roussy–Lévy syndrome). All affected individuals have abnormal nerve conduction studies (median nerve motor conduction velocity < 38 m/second), but this bears no relation to clinical severity, which is variable even within families.

Severe disability (defined as considerable difficulty walking by the fourth decade) is rare, seen in about 5% of cases, but marked foot drop is seen in one-third; 20% of affected relatives are asymptomatic (Harding & Thomas, 1980a,b).

In HMSN II there is axonal degeneration in peripheral nerve. Two-thirds or more of patients develop symptoms after the age of 10 years and one-third after the age of 40 (Buchthal & Behse, 1977; Harding & Thomas, 1980a). Sensory loss, upper limb involvement, scoliosis, and foot deformity are less common than in HMSN I and 60% have no clinically detectable sensory loss. Median motor conduction velocity is normal (> 38 m/second) and absent sural sensory nerve action potentials might be the only means of distinguishing HMSN II from distal spinal muscular atrophy (Bundey, 1985). Forty-four per cent of affected relatives are asymptomatic but nerve conduction studies are not reliable as a means of detecting affected relatives in contrast to HMSN I. The risk of severe disease is about 5% as in HMSN I.

HMSN III (Dejerine–Sotas disease (DSD)) is characterised by a severe demyelinating/hypomyelinating neuropathy with extremely slow motor conduction velocities; the median nerve motor conduction velocity is usually less than 6 m/second. Onset is in childhood, with delayed motor development and often severely impaired walking. Autosomal recessive inheritance was originally thought to be the most common form of inheritance in this condition but molecular genetic studies have shown that new mutations in both of the genes involved in HMSN I (see later) account for many of the patients clinically thought to have HMSN III. HMSN III therefore probably represents the severe end of the spectrum of hereditary demyelination neuropathies and should probably be considered as a severe form of HMSN I.

Genetic studies have shown that autosomal dominant (AD) HMSN I is genetically heterogeneous, involving at least four gene loci. HMSN IA (CMT 1A) is the most common form of HMSN I and is due to a large DNA duplication within chromosome 17p11.2 (Lupski et al., 1991; Timmerman et al., 1990) containing the gene peripheral myelin protein 22 (PMP-22). Rarely, HMSN IA is due to point mutations of PMP-22. HMSN IB (CMT 1B) is also autosomal dominant and results from point mutations of the human myelin protein zero gene (P0) on chromosome 1 (Chance et al., 1990; Hayasake et al., 1993). Recently, a family with AD HMSN I was found to have a mutation in the early growth response 2 gene (Warner et al., 1998) but it remains to be seen whether this gene is responsible for the disease in other families. There remain rare families with AD HMSN I in whom the genetic loci is not known. X-linked HMSN I (CMT X1) is now well documented and usually results from a mutation in the gene located on Xq13.1 for the gap junction protein connexin 32 (Berghofen et al., 1993; Hahn et al., 1990).

There are no genes described in HMSN II (CMT 2), although three genetic loci have already been described (Reilly, 1998) suggesting that HMSN II is very heterogeneous. It is of interest that one family with a HMSN II phenotype have a point mutation in P0, a gene involved in myelination and usually seen in HMSN I families (Marrosu et al., 1998).

HMSN III usually results from new mutations in the genes causing HMSN I, PMP-22 and P0 but mutations in EGR2 have also recently been described in two families with a congenital hypomyelinating neuropathy (Warner et al., 1998). There are also families with autosomal recessive (AR) HMSN I, HMSN II, and HMSN III. A recent attempt in the genetic literature to classify all autosomal recessive forms of HMSN as CMT 4 is not satisfactory as it has already failed to include two recently described loci. Linkage has been described to four loci in AR demyelinating neuropathies but no genes have yet been identified (Reilly, 1998). There are no genes described for AR axonal neuropathies.

No cure is available for HMSN, so management centres around provision of information and explanation to patients and relatives (especially genetic counselling), reduction of disability and handicap, and avoidance of secondary complications. The benign prognosis for the majority of those affected should be emphasised. Available relatives should be offered genetic counselling and diagnostic electrical, genetic tests, or predictive genetic testing where requested. Predictive testing is not usually offered to those below the age of 18. Patients with unaffected relatives or incomplete family histories should also be offered

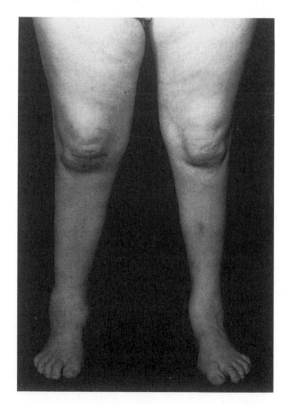

Figure 48.1. Distal wasting in HMSN with early toe and varus hind foot deformities.

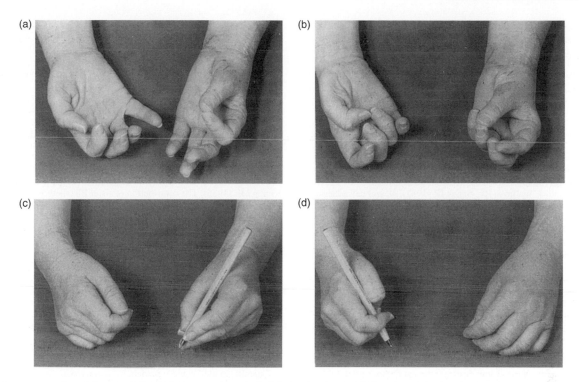

Figure 48.2. Improvement in and function following opponensplasty to the left thumb using the FDS tendon of the ring finger (Mr D. Elliot). In this case a 40-year-old patient with HMSN type I, tip pinch (a), opposition (b) and key pinch (c, d) of the operated left thumb compared with similar movements of the non-operated right side (prior to a similarly successful procedure on the right).

genetic counselling with respect to risks to siblings and off-spring, although exact risks might not always be able to be calculated.

Weakness of small foot muscles and ankle dorsiflexiors with relative preservation of the calf muscles results in dorsiflexion of the proximal phalanx on the metatarsal head, plantar flexion of the distal phalanges, and shortening with secondary contracture of the longitudinal foot arch and varus deformity of the hind foot (Fig. 48.1) (Mann & Missirian, 1988). Clawing of the toes, pes cavus, and corns, calluses, and an inability to find properly fitting shoes are the eventual results of these conditions. Special footwear and regular chiropody will then be required, perhaps incorporating drop-foot supports and foot care if sensory loss is severe. Later, surgical correction might be necessary (Alexander & Johnson, 1989). This can involve Achilles tendon lengthening, plantar fasciotomy, and posterior tibial, long flexor and extensor tendon transfers. Arthrodeses and osteotomies can have a place. Kyphoscoliosis can be a major problem, and might require bracing and special seating to be considered, or surgery might be necessary (Daher et al., 1986).

Upper limb deterioration often may not prove to be a problem and tends not to be significant until at least middle life, though there are exceptions, mainly seen in HMSN I. In these cases, surgical procedures such as opponensplasty (Fig. 48.2) can helpfully restore some function (Reid & McGouther, 1986). Such patients might benefit from a short in-patient stay, during which the members of the entire team will assess the patient separately, and then meet with the patient to discuss what measures might be helpful. This can be a lot more effective than asking the patient to attend several different out-patient sessions.

Conclusion

In the context of a peripheral neuropathy, as in other causes of persisting neurological disablement, it is important to appreciate how much can be done to limit handicap in the face of severe impairment. Neither failure of a disease process to recover, nor even progressive deterioration, should mean that a patient's disabilities are ignored.

REFERENCES

Agre JC, Rodriguez AA, Sperling KB (1989). Symptoms and clinical impressions of patients seen in a postpolio clinic. Archives of Physical Medicine and Rehabilitation 70: 367–370

Alexander IJ, Johnson KA (1989). Assessment and management of pes cavus in Charcot–Marie–Tooth disease. Clinical Orthopaedics 246: 273–281

Allen GM, Gandevia SC, Neering IR, Hickie I, Jones R, Middleton J (1994). Muscle performance, voluntary activation and perceived effort in normal subjects and patients with prior poliomyelitis. Brain 117: 661–667

Berghoffen J, Scherer SS, Wang S, Scott MO, Bone LJ, Paul DL, Chen K, Lensch MW, Chance PF, Fischbeck KH (1993). Connexin mutations in X-linked Charcot–Marie–Tooth disease. Science 262: 2039–2042.

Berthy MH, Strauser WW, Hall KM (1991). Fatigue in post polio syndrome. Archives of Physical Medicine and Rehabilitation 72: 115–118

Bolton CF, Gilbert JJ, Hahn AF, Sibbald WJ (1984). Polyneuropathy in critically ill patients. Journal of Neurology, Neurosurgery and Psychiatry 47: 1223–1231

Borg K, Borg J, Eistrom L, Grimby L (1988). Effects of excessive use of remaining muscle fibres in prior polio and left ventricular lesion. Muscle and Nerve 11: 1215–1230

Buchthal F, Behse F (1977). Peroneal muscular atrophy (PMA) and related disorders I. Clinical manifestations as related to biopsy findings, nerve conduction and electromyography. Brain 100: 41–46

Bundey S (1985). Genetics and neurology. Churchill Livingstone, Edinburgh, pp. 194–222

Caroll JE, Hagberg JM, Brooke MH, Shumate JB (1979). Bicycle ergometry and gas exchange measurements in neuromuscular diseases. Archives of Neurology 36: 457–461

Cashman NR, Corault J, Wollman RL, Sanes JR (1987). Neural cell adhesion molecule in normal, denervated and myopathic human muscle. Annals of Neurology 21: 481–489

Chance PF, Bird TD, O'Connell P et al. (1990). Genetic linkage and heterogeneity in type I Charcot–Marie–Tooth disease (hereditary motor and sensory neuropathy type I). American Journal of Medical Genetics 47: 915–925

Coakley JH, Nagendran K, Honavar M, Hinds CJ (1993). Preliminary observations on the neuromuscular abnormalities in patients with organ failure and sepsis. Intensive Care Medicine 19: 323–328

Codd MB, Mulder DW, Kurland LT, et al. (1985). Poliomyelitis in Rochester MN 1935–1955; epidemiology and long term sequel: a preliminary report. In Halstead LS, Weikers DO (Eds), Late effects of poliomyelitis. Symposia Foundation, Miami, pp. 121–134

Daher YH, Lonstein JE, Winter RB, Bradford DS (1986). Spinal deformities in patients with Charcot–Marie–Tooth disease. Clinical Orthopaedics 202: 219–222

Dalakas MC, Engel WK (1981). Chronic relapsing (dysimmune) polyneuropathy: pathogenesis and treatment. Annals of Neurology 9: S134–S145

Dalakis MC, Sever JL, Madden DL et al. (1984). Late postpoliomyelitis muscular atrophy: clinical, virologic and immunologic study. Review of Infectious Diseases 6 (Suppl 2): S562–S567

Dalakas MC, Elder G, Hallett M, et al. (1986). A long term follow up study of patients with post poliomyelitis neuromuscular symptoms. New England Journal of Medicine 314: 959–963

Einarsson G (1991). Muscle conditioning in late poliomyelitis. Archives of Physical Medicine and Rehabilitation 72: 11–14

Einarsson G, Grimby G (1990). Disability and handicap in late poliomyelitis. Scandinavian Journal of Rehabilitation Medicine 22: 113–121

Florence JM, Hagberg JM (1984). Effect of training on exercise responses of neuromuscular disease patients. Medicine and Science in Sports and Exercise 16: 460–465

Grimby G, Stalberg E, Sandberg A, Stilbrant Sunnerhagen K (1998). An 8 year longitudinal study of muscle strength, muscle fibre size, and dynamic electromyogram in individuals with late polio. Muscle Nerve 21: 1428–1437

Guillain–Barré Study Group (1985). Plasmapheresis and acute Guillain–Barré syndrome. Neurology 35: 1096–1104

Hagberg JM, Carroll JE, Brooke MH (1980). Endurance exercise training in a patient with central core disease. Neurology 30: 1242–1244

Hahn FH (1998). Guillain–Barré syndrome. Lancet 352: 635–641

Hahn AF, Brown WF, Koopman WJ, Feasby TE (1990). X-linked dominant hereditary motor and sensory neuropathy. Brain 113: 1511–1525

Halstead L (1998). Post-polio syndrome. Scientific American 278: 42–47.

Halstead LO, Weichers DO, Rossi CD (1985). Late effects of poliomyelitis. Part II: Results of a survey of 201 polio survivors. Southern Medical Journal 78: 1281–1287

Hanson P, Dive A, Brucher J-M, Bisteau M, Dangoisse M, Deltombe, T (1997). Acute corticosteroid myopathy in intensive care patients. Muscle and Nerve 20: 1371–1380

Harding AE, Thomas PK (1980a). The clinical features of hereditary motor and sensory neuropathy types I and II. Brain 103: 259–280

Harding AE, Thomas PK (1980b). Genetic aspects of hereditary motor and sensory neuropathy (types I and II). Journal of Medical Genetics 17: 329–336

Hayasake K, Himoro M, Sato W, Bird T, Connealy PM, Chance PF (1993). Charcot–Marie–Tooth disease type 1B associated with mutations of the myelin P0 gene. Nature Genetics 5: 31–34

Hayward M, Seaton D (1979). Late sequelae of paralytic poliomyelitis: a clinical and electro myographic study. Journal of Neurology, Neurosurgery and Psychiatry 42: 117–122

Jarrett SR, Mogelof JS (1995). Critical illness neuropathy: 1995 diagnosis and management. Archives of Physical Medicine and Rehabilitation 76: 688–691

Jones DR, Speier J, Canine K et al. (1989). Cardiorespiratory responses to aerobic training by patients with post poliomyelitis sequelae. Journal of the American Medical Association 261: 3255–3258

Karni Y, Archdeacon L, Mills KR, Wiles CM (1984). Clinical assessment and physiotherapy in Guillain–Barré syndrome. Physiotherapy 70: 288–292

Kidd D, Howard RS, Williams AJ, Heatley FW, Panayiopoulos CP, Spencer GT (1997). Late functional deterioration following paralytic poliomyelitis. Quarterly Journal of Medicine 90: 189–196

Knapp ME (1955). The contribution of sister Elizabeth Kenny to the treatment of poliomyelitis. Archives of Physical Medicine and Rehabilitation 36: 510–517

Kohl SJ (1987). Emotional responses to the later effects of poliomyelitis. Birth Defects 23: 135–143

Lancet (1985). Editorial. Lancet i: 83–84

Latronico N, Fenzi F, Recupero D, Guarneri B, Tomelleri G, Tonin P, De Maria G, Antonini L, Rizzuto N, Candiani A (1996). Critical illness myopathy and neuropathy. Lancet 347: 1579–1582

Leijten FSS, Havinck-de-Weerd JE, Poortvlier DCJ, de weed A1 W (1995). The role of polyneuropathy in motor convalesence after prolonged mechanical ventilation. Journal of the American Medical Association 274: 1221–1582.

Lindblom U, Tegner R (1989). Quantification of sensibility in mononeuropathy, polyneuropathy, and central lesions. In: Munsat TL (Ed), Quantification of neurologic deficit. Butterworths, Stoneham, pp. 171–185

Lupski JR, de Oca-Luna RM, Slaugenhaupt S (1991). DNA duplication associated with Charcot–Marie–Tooth disease type Ia. Cell 66: 219–232

Mann RJ, Missirian J (1988). Pathophysiology of Charcot–Marie–Tooth disease. Clinical Orthopaedics 234: 221–228

Marrosu MG, Vaccargiu S, Marrosu G, Vannelli A, Cianchetti C, Muntoni F (1998). Charcot–Marie–Tooth disease type 2 associated with mutation of the myelin protein zero gene. Neurology 50: 1397–1404

Medical Research Council (1976). Aids to the examination of the peripheral nervous system. Memorandum No. 45. HMSO, London

Milner Brown HS, Miller RG (1988). Muscle strengthening through high resistance weight training in patients with neuromuscular disorders. Archives of Physical Medicine and Rehabilitation 69: 14–19

Mulder DW, Rosenbaum RA, Layton DO (1972). Late progression of poliomyelitis or forme fruste amyotrophic lateral sclerosis? Mayo Clinic Proceedings 47: 756–761

Nicklin J, Karni Y, Wiles CM (1987). Shoulder abduction fatigability. Journal of Neurology, Neurosurgery and Psychiatry 50: 423–427

Raman PT, Taori GM (1976). Prognostic significance of electrodiagnosis studies in Guillain–Barré syndrome. Journal of Neurology, Neurosurgery and Psychiatry 39: 163–170.

Rees JH, Soudain SE, Gregson NA, Hughes RAC (1995). Campylobacter jejuni infection and Guillain–Barré syndrome. The New England Journal of Medicine 333: 1374–1379

Rees JH, Thompson RD, Smeeton NC, Hughes RAC (1998). Epidemiological study of Guillain–Barré syndrome in south east England. Journal of Neurology, Neurosurgery and Psychiatry 64: 74–77

Reid DAC, McGrouther DA (1986). Surgery of the thumb. Butterworth, London, pp. 47–154

Reilly MM (1998). Genetically determined neuropathies. Journal of Neurology 245: 6–13

Rice D (1977). Landry–Guillain–Barré syndrome: personal experience of acute ascending paralysis. British Medical Journal 1: 1330–1332

Ropper AH (1992). The Guillain–Barré syndrome. New England Journal of Medicine 326: 1130–1136

Russell WR, Fischer Williams M (1954). Recovery of muscle strength after poliomyelitis. Lancet i: 330–333

Scadding JW (1989). Peripheral neuropathies. In Wall PD, Melzack R (Eds), A textbook of pain, 2nd edn. Churchill Livingstone, Edinburgh, pp. 522–534

Speier JL, Owen RR, Knapp M, Canine JK (1987). Occurrence of post-polio sequelae in an epidemic population. Birth Defects 23: 39–48

Stokke O, Eldjarn L (1984). Biochemical and dietary aspects of Refsum's disease. In Dyck PJ, Lambert EH, Thomas PK, Bunge R (Eds), Peripheral neuropathy, WB Saunders, Philadelphia, pp. 1685–1693

Sunderland S (1991). Nerve injuries and their repair: a critical appraisal. Churchill Livingstone, Edinburgh, pp. 251–254

Tangerman RH, Aylward B, Birmingham M, Horner R, Olive JM, Nkowane BM, Hull HF, Burton A (1997). Current status of the global eradication of poliomyelitis. World Health Statistics Quarterly 50: 188–194

Thomas PK (1979). Painful neuropathies. In: Bonica JJ, Lieberkind JC, Albe-Fessard DG (Eds), Advances in pain research and therapy 3. Raven Press, New York, pp. 103–110

Thomas PK, Calne DB, Stewart G (1974). Hereditary motor and sensory polyneuropathy (peroneal muscular atrophy). Annals of Human Genetics 38: 111–153

Timmerman V, Paemaekers P, De Jonghe P et al. (1990). Assignment of the Charcot–Marie–Tooth neuropathy type I (CMT Ia) gene to chromosome 17p11.2-p12. American Journal of Human Genetics 47: 680–685

Van Der Meche FG, Schmitz PI (1992). A randomized trial comparing intravenous immune globulin and plasma exchange in Guillain–Barré syndrome. New England Journal of Medicine 326: 1123–1129

Warner LE, Manicas P, Butler IJ, McDonald CM, Keppen L, Kobb KG, Lupski JR (1998). Mutations in the early growth response 2 (EGR2) gene are associated with hereditary myelinopathies. Nature Genetics 18: 382–384

Weichers DO, Hubbell SL (1981). Late changes in the motor unit after acute poliomyelitis. Muscle and Nerve 4: 524–528

Wiles CM, Karni Y (1983). The measurement of muscle strength in patients with peripheral neuromuscular disorders. Journal of Neurology, Neurosurgery and Psychiatry 46: 1006–1013

Willen C, Grimby G (1998). Pain, physical activity, and disability in individuals with late effects of polio. Archives of Physical Medical Rehabilitation 79: 915–919

Windebank AJ, Litchy WJ, Daube JR, Iverson RA (1996). Lack of progression of neurologic deficit in survivors of paralytic polio: a 5 year prospective population based study. Neurology 46: 80–84

Winer JB, Hughes RAC, Osmond C (1988). A prospective study of acute idiopathic neuropathy. I. Clinical features and their prognostic value. Journal of Neurology, Neurosurgery and Psychiatry 51: 605–612

Workshop Report (1996). Post-polio muscle dysfunction, 29th ENMC Workshop. Neuromuscular Disorders 6: 75–80

Zochodne DW, Bolton CF (1996). Neuromuscular disorders in critical illness. In: Bolton CF, Young GB (Eds), Bailliére's Clinical Neurology vol 5, no 3. Bailliére Tindall, London

USEFUL ADDRESSES

Guillan–Barré Support Group
Foxley, Holdingham, Sleaford, Lincolnshire NG34 8NR
British Polio Fellowship
Bell Close, West End Road, Ruislip, Middlesex HA4 6LP

49. Muscle disorders

Nicholas Davies George Cochrane Michael Hanna

INTRODUCTION—THE CLASSIFICATION OF MUSCLE DISEASE AND THE MULTIDISCIPLINARY APPROACH TO PATIENT CARE

Muscle diseases can be broadly divided into those that are genetically determined and those that are acquired (Table 49.1). The most common genetically determined muscle disorders are the muscular dystrophies, and the most common acquired form of muscle diseases are the inflammatory myopathies.

Although there are many different types of muscle disease, patients often experience similar difficulties and complications. The optimum care of such patients should be multidisciplinary.

Table 49.1. A classification of muscle diseases

Genetic muscle disease
The muscular dystrophies
    Dystrophinopathies (Duchenne and Becker)
    Fascioscapulohumeral muscular dystrophy
    Emery–Dreifuss muscular dystrophy
    Limb girdle muscular dystrophy
    Myotonic dystrophy

Metabolic myopathies
    Glycogenolytic myopathies, e.g. McArdle's disease
    Lipid myopathies, e.g. carnitine palmitoyltransferase II deficiency
    Mitochondrial myopathies

Skeletal muscle ion channel disorders
    The periodic paralyses
    Myotonia congenita

Congenital myopathies
    Nemaline myopathy
    Central core disease

Acquired muscle disease
Inflammatory muscle disease
    Polymyositis
    Dermatomyositis
    Inclusion body myositis

Endocrine myopathies
    Thyrotoxicosis
    Cushing's disease

Drug-induced and toxic myopathies
    Corticosteroids
    Lipid lowering drugs (HMG CoA reductase inhibitors)
    Alcohol

In practice, this often centres around a muscle clinic run by a neurologist collaborating with other physicians (e.g. gastroenterologists, chest physicians, geneticists), surgeons, and a range of therapists (physiotherapists, occupational therapists, speech therapists, dietitians, and genetic counsellors) as necessary. At different stages in the natural history of muscle diseases one or more of the following broad categories of management strategies might be required: physical therapy, respiratory therapy, cardiac therapy, dietary/feeding therapy, surgery and orthotics, or genetic counselling. The multidisciplinary approach with the neurologist as the coordinator facilitates the most appropriate management at any given time. Although there are presently no curative drug therapies for the genetic myopathies, drug therapy can have a significant benefit in certain inflammatory myopathies. Therefore, patients with such inflammatory myopathies not only require many of the therapeutic strategies outlined above, but also require careful monitoring of often complex immunosuppressive drug regimes. "Inflammatory muscle disease clinics" held in collaboration with rheumatologists are often helpful in managing this group of patients. The involvement of neuromuscular charitable organisations is often invaluable for patients affected with these muscle diseases. Details of such charities should always be made available to interested patients.

This chapter first describes the general clinical and investigative approach to muscle disease and then focuses upon the dystrophies and the inflammatory myopathies. In view of major developments in molecular genetics, the group of disorders known as the skeletal muscle channelopathies has also been included. For each disease, the clinical and diagnostic approach is considered and the key areas relevant to long-term management of these patients are described, emphasising the multidisciplinary approach.

HISTORY AND EXAMINATION

A detailed history in conjunction with a clinical examination is essential when assessing a patient with suspected muscle disease. The information obtained can then be used to determine which patients need further investigation. Although a muscle biopsy is usually needed to determine the precise type of muscle disease, the history and examination are usually sufficient to determine whether a muscle disease is present or absent. As many muscle diseases are genetically determined it is particularly important to consider the family history; a careful drug history is also essential.

Although a wide variety of diseases can affect skeletal muscle (see Table 49.1), there are three main symptoms with which patients can present: (i) muscular pain; (ii) muscular weakness; and (iii) fatiguability. A further important, but less common, symptom is darkening of the urine (pigmenturia) due to release of myoglobin from damaged muscle. This occurs in certain muscle diseases such as the metabolic myopathies. Unless pigmenturia has been dramatic patients might not volunteer this symptom unless asked.

Muscle pain is a common symptom but in only approximately one-third of patients presenting with this symptom will an underlying muscle disease be identified. In those without a definable muscle disease, a high proportion are usually suspected to have a psychogenic cause for their muscle pain, although some could have as yet undefined disorders of muscle metabolism. It can sometimes be difficult for the patient and the physician to distinguish between pain originating in muscle and pain originating in joints or bones. Certain rheumatological diseases can result in both joint pain and muscle pain. For example, systemic lupus erythematosis (SLE) can cause arthritis and polymyositis.

Muscle pains can take the form of cramps, which are involuntary contractions of muscle groups. Simple muscle cramps are not uncommon in the elderly and are frequently nocturnal. In such cases there is usually no underlying muscle disease but drugs such as diuretics, which induce hypokalaemia, might be implicated. In younger patients, muscle cramps can be the presenting feature of a metabolic muscle disease such as McArdle's disease. Muscle pain brought on by exertion is a particular feature of some of the metabolic muscle diseases. Muscle contractures may also be a source of muscle pain in patients with metabolic myopathies. Patients experience a pain similar to a cramp but unlike a cramp a contracture is electrically silent on electromyography (EMG).

Muscle weakness is a common feature in muscle diseases. The distribution of weakness in most muscle diseases is in the proximal limb muscles. Many muscle diseases affect the limb musculature in a relatively symmetrical fashion, although there are important exceptions to this. For example, one of the common autosomal dominant muscular dystrophies—fascioscapulohumeral muscular dystrophy (FSHD)—often affects the limb muscles in an asymmetrical fashion. Some muscle diseases affect the facial musculature as well as the limb musculature. Progressive external ophthalmoplegia is a particular feature found in patients with mitochondrial myopathies. Respiratory muscle involvement can occur in many forms of muscle disease (e.g. Duchenne, polymyositis), usually when the limb weakness is well established. In certain muscle diseases, respiratory failure can be the presenting feature (e.g. myotonic dystrophy, nemaline myopathy, acid maltase deficiency). It is important to determine the natural history of muscle weakness. In most genetically determined muscle diseases, weakness progresses slowly, often over years, although occasionally the patient can experience attacks of weakness separated by periods when they seem to have normal strength, as in the periodic paralyses. The muscle weakness in the inflammatory muscle diseases usually develops more rapidly, typically over several weeks.

Fatiguability is defined as an increase in weakness with exercise. Patients might explain that they can start a particular physical activity but that the longer they continue the weaker they become; they might also complain that they become weaker as the day goes on. Myasthenia gravis, a disorder of neuromuscular transmission, is the major condition that causes fatiguability. In patients with myaesthenia gravis, fatiguability can usually be demonstrated on examination at the bedside. Patients with metabolic muscle diseases, such as the mitochondrial myopathies, can also experience fatiguability.

The examination of a patient with muscle disease can be broadly divided into two areas. First, examination is made to establish whether there are any clues to the cause of the muscle disease. In this context the general examination is very important. Particular attention is paid to eliciting signs that might indicate an underlying endocrine or rheumatological disorder. For example, signs of hyper- or hypothyroidism, or of rheumatological disorders such as SLE. Inspection of the skin might reveal the rash of dermatomyositis.

The second part of the examination involves examining the muscular system itself. This will determine the extent and severity of the muscle disease and might, in addition, give further clues to the aetiology. The muscles are inspected for any atrophy or hypertrophy (as occurs in some muscular dystrophies) or for any spontaneous activity of the muscle fibres (e.g. fasciculations that might indicate an anterior horn cell disorder). The muscles can then be palpated for any tenderness or swelling that might occur in inflammatory muscle diseases. Myotonia is a delayed relaxation of muscle after contraction. This can be observed by asking patients to clench their fist, and then to open it rapidly. A patient with myotonia is unable to rapidly open the clenched fist due to an inability to relax the contracted muscles quickly. Myotonia might also be evident on percussion of muscle. The examination of muscle power is performed systematically, starting with the cranial musculature and then proceeding to the upper and then lower limbs. The degree of weakness is assessed with reference to the MRC grading scale (0–5). The distribution of weakness is also noted, as different muscle diseases have characteristic patterns of weakness. Bedside assessment of respiratory muscles, including the diaphragm, is also important, although detailed assessment of these muscles requires formal spirometry. Finally, the tendon reflexes are elicited. These are generally preserved in acquired muscle diseases, except when there is advanced weakness, but can be lost relatively early in some dystrophies.

Investigations (Mastaglia & Laing, 1996; Pourmand, 2000)

Blood tests. The muscle enzyme creatine kinase (CK) is a marker of muscle fibre damage. It tends to be very high in rhabdomyolysis (> 100 times normal) but is markedly raised (50–100 times normal) in some of the dystrophies (Duchenne muscular dystrophy, dysferlinopathy) and inflammatory myopathies (polymyositis). Mild elevation can cause confusion because although in most cases it indicates a primary muscle problem, it can also result from chronic neurogenic disorders, or even be the result of exercising normal muscle. CK is frequently used as a marker of disease activity when monitoring therapy in inflammatory muscle disorders. In any patient with a raised aspartate transaminase (AST) it is important to check the CK to avoid unnecessary liver investigations.

Other blood tests can suggest a cause for muscle symptoms, for instance an underlying inflammatory disorder (erythrocyte sedimentation rate (ESR), autoantibody screen) or endocrine disorder (thyroid function).

The forearm exercise test (FET) involves 1 minute of isometric exercise followed by the measurement of blood lactate and ammonia levels at intervals over 10 minutes (this replaces the ischaemic lactate test, which can be dangerous in carbohydrate metabolism disorders). The FET can be useful in distinguishing between different metabolic myopathies. A reduced or absent elevation in lactate is seen in the glycogenoses. Resting lactate can be elevated in mitochondrial myopathies. This can be confirmed by an exaggerated elevation of lactate after exercise.

Electromyography (EMG). This can help to confirm the clinical suspicion of a muscle disorder, although it can be normal even in the presence of certain muscle diseases (e.g. some metabolic myopathies). It can help in the choice of muscle for biopsy. Nerve conduction studies serve to exclude neurogenic disorders that may mimic myopathies.

The typical myopathic features on EMG include motor unit action potentials that are polyphasic, of short duration and of low amplitude, termed myopathic potentials. The interference pattern is usually full at low resistance. In some of the inflammatory myopathies, and less so in the dystrophies, increased "muscle irritability" is seen on EMG. This manifests as positive sharp waves, fibrillation potentials, and occasionally complex repetitive discharges. Myotonic discharges might be evident in myotonic dystrophy and in the non-dystrophic myotonias.

Some disorders characteristically show mixed myopathic and neuropathic features (inclusion body myositis, mitochondrial disorders). Repetitive stimulation and single fibre studies are performed if a neuromuscular transmission disorder is suspected, e.g. myasthenia gravis or Lambert–Eaton myasthenic syndrome.

Electrocardiogram (ECG)/echocardiogram. These are useful in detecting asymptomatic cardiac muscle or conduction pathway dysfunction, enabling early intervention. In familial cases these techniques can be used to screen carriers, e.g. Emery–Dreifuss muscular dystrophy.

Muscle biopsy. Even with the advent of molecular genetic techniques, this procedure is still often necessary for a definitive diagnosis. In planning a muscle biopsy attention should be given to the site of the biopsy, the type of biopsy, and the handling of the specimen. In patients with a long history of weakness it is important to choose a muscle that is mildly rather than severely affected to avoid non-diagnostic biopsies simply demonstrating end-stage muscle pathology. In contrast, if the history is very short, the weakest muscle will be more likely to reveal the causative insult. Commonly selected muscles include the lateral quadriceps, the biceps, and the triceps. Although debatable, these authors prefer open biopsy to needle biopsy in terms of diagnostic yield. The specimen should be handled as little as possible and delays in transit to the pathology laboratory avoided. Ideally, part of the sample should be snap frozen (with isopentane) in the operating room. A wide variety of staining, histoenzymatic, and immunocytochemical techniques are available. Close collaboration between the neurologist and the pathologist is essential in deciding the most appropriate techniques to apply and in interpreting the biopsy in the context of the clinical presentation.

Muscle imaging. Plain X-rays are of very limited value, perhaps assisting in the diagnosis of cysticercosis or confirming calcification in dermatomyositis. Muscle ultrasound is used frequently in paediatric myology practice but not usually in adults. Computerised tomography (CT) and, more recently, magnetic resonance imaging (MRI) can be used to delineate the extent of a particular muscle disease. These techniques can also be useful in distinguishing inflammatory processes from other causes of muscle diseases. Magnetic resonance spectroscopy (MRS) with an exercise test can be useful in distinguishing between certain metabolic myopathies and, in future, might prove a practical, non-invasive tool for monitoring therapeutic response in certain metabolic muscle diseases.

Molecular genetics. Developments in this field have led to the greatest advances in the diagnosis of muscle disorders. In certain conditions, DNA analysis can obviate the need for muscle biopsy, e.g. myotonic dystrophy, fascioscapulohumeral dystrophy (FSHD). Genotype–phenotype relationships have emerged so that some information about prognosis can be given to patients and prospective parents. Prenatal diagnosis is available for several muscle disorders and is most commonly used in Duchenne muscular dystrophy families. In the past, carrier detection in such a family was less precise relying on an elevation of CK. Such detection can now be achieved reliably with DNA analysis.

It is important to be aware of the limitations of molecular genetic analysis. The role of the geneticist in the multidisciplinary approach is critical in conveying genetic information accurately to patients and families. For example, one might need to consider whether a particular muscle disorder exhibits reduced penetrance. That is, is it possible that an individual harbouring a mutation within the particular gene will never develop symptoms? It is also worth noting that most laboratories offer screening procedures rather than exhaustive whole-gene sequencing because many of the muscle proteins are encoded by huge genes. This introduces the possibility of false negative tests.

MUSCULAR DYSTROPHIES

This inherited group of muscle disorders was originally characterised by their inheritance pattern, age of onset, degree and distribution of muscle weakness/wasting, and the presence of additional features (e.g. cardiac involvement, contractures, myotonia). This clinical diagnostic classification has proved useful in many cases (Walton & Nattrass, 1954). However, as molecular genetic advances have been made, it has become evident that there is significant phenotypic overlap between genetically distinct disorders (e.g. limb girdle muscular dystrophies). In addition, considerable variation in phenotype has been observed within families with the same disorder (e.g. facioscapulohumeral dystrophy). The current classification relies on the underlying molecular genetic basis of the disorder but careful clinical evaluation is still necessary to direct genetic analysis.

It has been established that many of the muscular dystrophies result from genetic defects in structural proteins of the muscle cell, its cell membrane or the supporting extracellular matrix. Diagnostic accuracy has been greatly improved by the development of immunocytochemical techniques for assessing the expression of these proteins.

Duchenne and Becker muscular dystrophy

Both disorders are X-linked and are due to defects within the same gene encoding the muscle membrane protein, dystrophin

(Fig. 49.1). Becker muscular dystrophy can usually be distinguished from Duchenne on clinical grounds as its onset is later and its course milder (Hoffman, 1996).

Duchenne muscular dystrophy (DMD)

This disorder is often first noticed when the boy starts walking. Typically, there is a clumsy gait and the affected boy might have to use his arms to rise from the floor (Gower's manoeuvre). By 5 years of age, difficulty in climbing stairs is apparent and spontaneous falls can occur. The child cannot run and may be observed to toe-walk. Independent walking is lost by 10 years and the child often requires a wheelchair to get around. This can be prolonged to age 12 by physiotherapy and orthopaedic procedures (*Note*: in Becker muscular dystrophy ambulation can be maintained beyond 16 years). Once wheelchair-bound, the child is at greater risk of developing contractures, scoliosis, and respiratory insufficiency. These complications, or the cardiac muscle involvement, leads to death in the early 20s. Some DMD patients have a slower progression despite early onset, the so-called outlier or intermediate group. In this group, the cardiomyopathy is more commonly the cause of death. It is now clear that there is a correlation between the severity of the phenotype and the quantity of dystrophin protein in skeletal muscle (Hoffman, 1996). Additional features in DMD can include mental retardation, muscle pain (although not prominent), and urinary/faecal incontinence.

Examination initially reveals hypertrophic calf muscles that have a rubbery consistency. Proximal weakness, especially around the hip, is usual and there is shortening of the Achilles

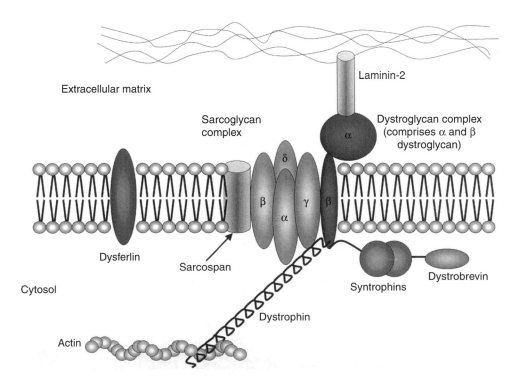

Figure 49.1. Components of dystrophin–glycoprotein complex (DGC) spanning the skeletal muscle fibre membrane. This chain of structural proteins are interdependent. Loss of one of the proteins results in breakdown of the entire complex.

tendons. As the disorder progresses, a Gower's manoeuvre is required to get out of a chair and the gait becomes waddling with hyperextended knee joints and marked lumbar lordosis.

Most female carriers of DMD are not symptomatic. The 10% of carriers that do manifest always have very mild symptoms and a normal life expectancy. In rare instances, females can present with a DMD phenotype because of biased X chromosome inactivation or Turner's syndrome.

Blood. CK is often extremely high, up to 100 times normal. In the past, elevation of CK was used for carrier detection within a DMD family. This proved to be unreliable as some confirmed carriers had CK levels within the normal range, and it has been superseded by molecular genetic analysis.

EMG. This is myopathic. In advanced cases the interference pattern can be reduced because of replacement of muscle fibres with fibrosis or fat.

ECG/echocardiogram. This can confirm a dilated cardiomyopathy. The ECG commonly shows large R waves in the right precordial leads and deep Q waves in the left precordial leads.

Muscle biopsy. This demonstrates degeneration and regeneration. Increased fibre size variation, necrotic fibres, hypercontracted opaque fibres, and increased connective tissue are seen. Internal nuclei might be present but are not as numerous as in Becker muscular dystrophy (BMD). Groups of basophilic regenerating fibres can be prominent. Occasional inflammatory cells are observed, particularly in the early stages of the disease. Variable amounts of fat are seen, depending on the stage at which the biopsy is taken. Immunocytochemistry is performed using three antibodies that react with three regions of the dystrophin molecule. This technique demonstrates an absence of staining for dystrophin on the sarcolemma. It is important to note that a secondary reduction in staining for the sarcoglycans is common in DMD. In cases of patchy or mosaic staining for dystrophin, Western blot analysis should be performed.

Molecular genetics. The gene encoding dystrophin lies on chromosome Xp21 (Koenig et al., 1987). As with many of the genes encoding structural muscle proteins, the DMD gene is large, consisting of 79 exons, making mutation detection time consuming. Genetic diagnosis is made more difficult by the fact that 30% of cases represent new mutations (Hoffman, 1996). Most cases of DMD or BMD are caused either by a deletion or duplication of part of the gene and there are a few hot spots that can be screened initially. In general, those deletions/duplications that cause a change in the reading frame (frameshift mutation) cause a severely truncated protein resulting in DMD, and those that do not result in BMD. This is a useful prognostic indicator but is not absolute, as up to 16% of BMD have been shown to have a frameshift mutation. The size of deletion is not helpful in assessing prognosis.

Genetic analysis of an individual with a DMD phenotype and absent dystrophin immunostaining on muscle biopsy is straightforward if it is due to a known duplication/deletion within the dystrophin gene. The difficulty arises in the 30% with new point mutations as no hot spots have been identified to target gene analysis.

Table 49.2. Physical management in Duchenne muscular dystrophy

1. **Promotion of ambulation**
   Weight control
   Active and passive exercises
   Tenotomies
   Orthoses

2. **Prevention of deformities**
   Correction of posture, support, and orthoses
   Exercises and stretchings
   Surgery

3. **Observation of respiratory function**
   Incentive spirometry and exercises
   Antibiotics, suction, and physical treatment
   Respiratory support (including intermittent positive pressure ventilation)

Treatment. DMD is not curable but much can be done to improve the boy's quality of life by maintaining his general health, stimulating activity, avoiding excess gain in weight, preventing contractures, and preserving respiratory function (Table 49.2). Obesity is a risk because food intake usually exceeds the reduced energy demand and is aggravated by overeating and indulging. A well-balanced, low calorie, and high-fibre diet is recommended. Obesity hampers movements, ambulation, self-care, lifting and carrying by others, and ultimately cardiac function. Adequate intake of dietary fibre guards against frequent problems with constipation. Oral hygiene is important and early and regular use of an electric toothbrush is recommended.

Physical activities are psychologically beneficial to boys and their parents and should be encouraged, e.g. recreational sports—especially swimming because the buoyancy of the water makes movements easier. Prolonged rest in bed for any intercurrent infection, following surgery or fracture, should be avoided. Passive stretching exercises daily, perhaps after a nightly bath, can prevent or at least delay the development of muscle contractures and can be reinforced by night splints to prevent contractures at the ankle and knee joints, but only if they are tolerated and do not interfere with sleep. Once contractures have developed, such passive stretchings are ineffective, cause pain, are resented, and, if much force is applied, can cause injury. More emphasis should then be put upon respiratory exercises.

Chest physiotherapy encompasses deep breathing exercises, positioning and postural drainage, manual techniques of percussion and vibration, coughing and assisted coughing, and suction when there is pooling of secretions in the pharynx. Chest excursion becomes limited and breathing shallower, compliance of the lungs and chest wall is reduced and with hypoventilation there is microatelectasis and predisposition to infection. To induce deeper inspiration the boy is encouraged to cough and, several times in succession, to sustain maximum inspiration for 3s. Incentive spirometers encourage maximum inspiration. These range from small, inexpensive flow-sensitive devices to more expensive, electronic, volume-sensitive spirometers with breath-hold indication, which encourages sustaining maximum inspiration. For all active and passive exercises it is essential to

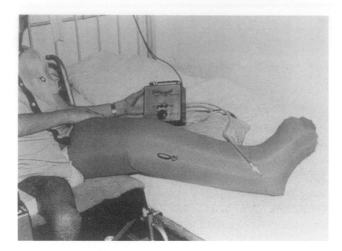

Figure 49.2. Flowtron splint ("yellow wellie").

Figure 49.3. Light-weight knee–ankle–foot orthosis (KAFO).

gain the understanding and compliance of the boy and his parents by careful instruction, practice, reviewing, and measuring. There are doubts concerning the physical benefits of exercises, and in particular chest physiotherapy, and a paucity of well-designed trials. A single-blind crossover study failed to find any significant changes in vital capacity, mean total ventilation, and maximum static inspiratory pressure after inspiratory resistance training (Smith et al., 1988). Kyphoscoliosis diminishes pulmonary function. Use of a spinal brace might slightly slow the progression of the spinal deformity but does not ultimately prevent severe scoliosis, and spinal bracing reduces vital capacity (Miller, 1985).

Unequal weakness in agonist and antagonist muscle, habitual posture, and gravity lead to contractures, which are most severe in muscles that span two joints. Passive movements complemented by intermittent compression splinting using Flowtron (Fig. 49.2) for about 1 h, and individually made, comfortable light orthoses (Fig. 49.3) for walking, delay contractures, and spinal deformities. Sitting and lying with hips and knees flexed accelerate progression of flexion contractures at weight-bearing joints.

Prolongation of ambulation.   Success in prolonging walking without pharmaceutical intervention, perhaps by 18 months, depends on correct timing, the enthusiasm of the boy and his parents, the presence of a physiotherapist at school, intelligence within the normal range, and well-fitting knee–ankle–foot orthoses (KAFOs) (Heckmatt et al., 1985). The orthosis should be provided while the boy can still walk short distances independently and takes 10 s to walk 8 m unsupported. Before fitting the orthosis, hip flexors, tensor fasciae latae, and calf muscles that are too short are lengthened by tenotomies. Achilles tenotomy can be performed percutaneously. Long leg plasters are applied temporarily and the boy stands and takes paces on the day after operation. Orthoses should be ready for fitting within a week of surgery. Surgical procedures have been advocated at progressively earlier stages of the disease with prophylactic tenotomies of the superficial hip flexors and of the

flexors of the knees, lengthening of the Achilles tendons and aponeurectomies of the thighs between 4 and 5 years old (Rideau et al., 1985). Walking is resumed within a week without plaster casts or orthoses and the boy is fully mobile within 4 weeks. Subsequently, the agility and mobility of the boys have been impressive, but the analysis and presentation of the data have lacked scientific precision.

Some therapists have preferred dynamic elastic bracing to hinged and locking KAFOs. The trunk component is joined on each leg to knee pads and KAFOs by spiral elastic traces, assisting extension at the hips and knees. Alternatively, the swivel walker (Fig. 49.4) will enable a boy to continue to stand and move short distances indoors; modifications have been proposed to accept contractures at the knees and ankles and to bring the feet closer together (Sibert et al., 1987).

When a boy is too weak to walk he can continue to stand in a frame (Fig. 49.5) if flexion contractures do not prevent this. Stand-up wheelchairs, like the Levo and Crest, serve the same purpose.

Fractures.   Because of osteoporosis and falls or accidents in handling, fractures of long bones occur not infrequently. They heal normally and should be treated with minimal splintage and early resumption of usual activities.

Scoliosis.   When a boy loses the ability to stand, contractures and soliosis follow (Fig. 49.6). Lumbar lordosis has been conspicuous in standing but in sitting he slumps with kyphosis. Hyperlordosis persists in a small proportion, with increasing stiffness throughout the spine from fibrosis of the paraspinal

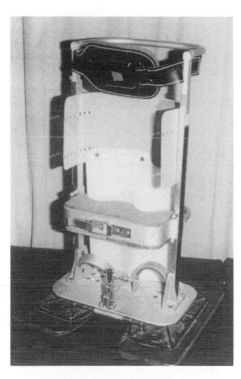

Figure 49.4. Swivel walker.

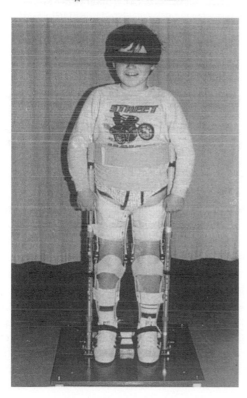

Figure 49.5. A standing frame.

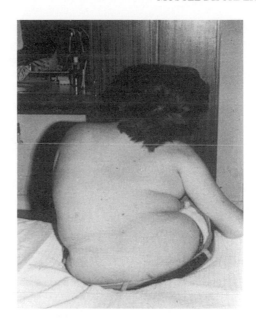

Figure 49.6. Scoliosis.

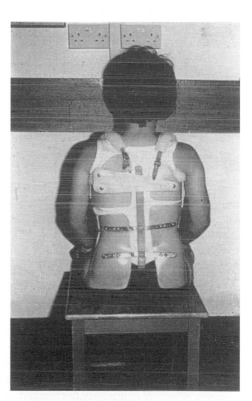

Figure 49.7. Modified Calot spinal brace.

muscles, and fewer retain almost normal spinal curves. In the majority there is progressive paralytic scoliosis, with one arm dedicated to propping; asymmetric loading on the ischia causes discomfort. Compression of the sciatic nerve results in tingling and altered sensation in the lower leg and foot. Pulmonary ventilation diminishes as intercostal muscles weaken and is made worse by progressive thoracic deformity.

Wearing a thoracolumbosacral orthosis, such as a block leather jacket or modified Calot brace (Fig. 49.7), and imposing a lumbar lordosis will retard but not prevent the development of scoliosis because the forces applied to the trunk are limited.

The surgical correction of scoliosis by Luque's segmental stabilisation, wiring each vertebrum to stainless steel rods extending from the sacrum to the upper thorax, has proved successful (Sussman, 1985). The operation must be timed precisely and preoperative assessment must be scrupulous. At every 4-monthly review the spine must be examined and the respiratory function measured. Changes in posture can be monitored by annual radiographs of the spine or as reliably, without radiation and quickly at every attendance, by the optical technique of the integrated shape imaging system (ISIS), which produces three-dimensional images of the back shape with pictorial and numerical records (Bogie et al., 1988). The forced vital capacity falls gradually from its peak value at 11 years of age. Progressive cardiomyopathy is inevitable, with interstitial fibrosis beginning in the posterobasal part and becoming more diffuse in the left ventricle.

There is a time between the curve developing and the vital capacity falling below 50% during which spinal surgery should be performed. If the boy wears a spinal brace this "window" will be narrowed, because the progression of the scoliosis will be temporarily slowed while pulmonary function continues to deteriorate. Sinus tachycardia, atrial and ventricular fibrillation, and cardiac arrest can occur during surgery. Succinylcholine should be avoided because it has been implicated in rhabdomyolysis. During the early postoperative days, intensive paediatric care must be given because of the hazards of weak respiratory muscles and retained bronchial secretions, gastric dilatation, myoglobinuria and hyperkalaemia.

By the fourth day, the boy is able to sit in his wheelchair. No longer able to stoop to his plate he has to lift food higher to his mouth and, during the early weeks, he might use mobile arm supports or need to be fed. Subsequently, he has no recollection of postoperative discomfort, affirms pleasure at the outcome and commends the operation to others similarly affected. Respiratory function has improved a little, comfort in sitting is more readily achieved and the carer finds that lifting is easier.

Respiratory insufficiency and respiratory failure (see Chapter 23). The vital capacity is a prognostic index and closely reflects the degree of respiratory disability. Around the age of 11 years, the higher the peak value is above 1.21, the better the prognosis. Gradually, the strength of the respiratory muscles diminishes and the load on the pump increases. There are three potentially reversible load factors: scoliosis, obesity, and diminished compliance of the chest wall and lungs. A fourth factor is chronic aspiration, which is commonly overlooked; in muscular dystrophies silent aspiration has not been fully investigated. Inability to swallow competently is combined with ineffectual coughing.

Sleep, when central drive is reduced, can be the time when respiratory failure is first evident and posture is a major factor: lying reduces lung compliance and the abdominal contents displace a weak diaphragm upwards. A vital capacity that is lower lying than sitting indicates that the diaphragm is weak. A patient with diaphragm weakness sleeps propped up or lying on one side. Respiratory failure can be sudden, precipitated by infection, but usually has been preceded by insidious nocturnal hypoxia, which might have been overlooked. Its features are restless sleep, morning confusion and headache, daytime sleepiness, and mental dulling. The physician should be alert to incipient failure if there is breathlessness without obvious reason, positive "sniff sign", weak cough, and difficulty in speaking continuously. The more that those at risk are asked about symptoms, the more likely it becomes that symptoms will be revealed. Sleep hypoventilation is confirmed by overnight oximetry. Arterial puncture is very difficult in boys with DMD and earlobe or finger oximetry detects important abnormalities in oxygen saturation.

In advanced DMD, the boys are at risk of hypoxaemia during rapid eye movement (REM) sleep. Loss of intercostal activation is a feature of the transition to REM sleep. In the presence of respiratory muscle weakness the ventilatory response to hypoxaemia and hypercapnia is reduced. Assistance with intermittent positive-pressure ventilation can normalise blood gases, lessen recurrent arousals, relieve symptoms, and benefit the boy and his carers (Heckmatt et al., 1990). All involved with muscular dystrophy should be aware of respiratory failure and the benefits that result from night ventilation. The decision to introduce nocturnal assisted ventilation should be made jointly by the physician, patient, and relatives after discussing the indications, potential benefits, practical inconveniences, and the possibility that, as the respiratory muscles weaken, assisted ventilation will be required continuously. The decision in DMD is easier because cardiomyopathy is inevitable. The wishes of the patient are paramount. Ordinarily, two forms of assisted ventilation are practicable: nasal intermittent positive-pressure ventilation (NIPPV) and negative pressure ventilation by cuirasse or Tunnicliffe jacket; both are non-invasive, portable, convenient, and allow independence. Except for young children and those unable to tolerate a mask, NIPPV is chosen as it is readily available and does not require individual shaping.

Adolescence and leaving school. As soon as the nature of the disease, course of events, and likely outcome are clear, the parents need information, counselling, confidence, and encouragement to be actively involved in their son's care. Remember, the boy's sisters might be carriers of the gene (see earlier). After initial distress there might be unrealistic hopes of cure. Physical and emotional strain, too little time for discussion, and not enough time for themselves can alienate parents and break up the home. In a survey of 25 families of children with DMD, over half the parents had serious marital problems and one-quarter were divorced (Buchanan et al., 1979). The success of treatment is to be measured by the accomplishments of the child, the behaviour of the parents and siblings, and the integrity of the family.

Asked about the major difficulties the parents encountered, the practical problems in daily care were conspicuous (Firth et al., 1983). Most frequent was lifting (47%), housing (28%), bathing and toileting (19%), and lack of sleep due to attending their son at night (9%). This study identified a need to improve the techniques for handling and lifting and transferring, with seats at the right height and grab rails, Trans-sit lifting seat, individual wheelchair seating (Fig. 49.8), shower/commode

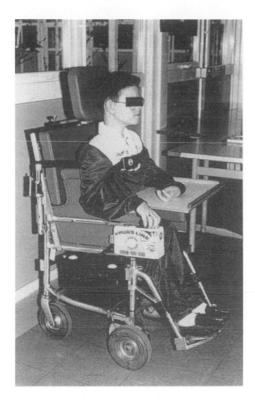

Figure 49.8. Wheelchair seating for Duchenne muscular dystrophy.

wheelchair and bed of adjustable heights. Difficulties in the home are appreciated by a physical or occupational therapist seeing the limited access and space, the needs of others in the family, the bathroom and lavatory, the use made of equipment that has been supplied, and the deficiencies. Plans should be laid for when the boy will be unable to walk. His own groundfloor bedroom/study is ideal, with TV and personal computer, to do as he chooses. His parents need advice about state benefits, statutory services, voluntary agencies, and sources of information. The Muscular Dystrophy Campaign has literature in the form of leaflets, and also has a website (www.muscular-dystrophy.org). People need to know all that is available to them and how they can obtain what they want. The Disability Information Trust publishes 14 books about every form of equipment. Coordination and communication between health authority and local authority education, housing and welfare services are often lacking, and especially so at the time of leaving school. In part, this can be corrected by regional neuromuscular centres sponsored by the Muscular Dystrophy Campaign with emphasis on the team approach. The regional centre bonds the clinicians, family care officer and neuropathology, genetic and research laboratories, with the family doctor, the district hospital, and departments of the local authority. As the boy becomes increasingly incapacitated the stress falls not only on him and his parents but on the entire family. Counselling is less available than professionals concede and the need continues through the terminal stage, dying, and bereavement.

Steroid treatment in DMD. Steroid therapy is now advocated in DMD and has been shown to delay the loss of independent ambulation by up to 3 years (Fenichel et al., 1991). Recent studies have suggested that deflazacort (a synthetic steroid) is the steroid drug of choice as it appears to have fewer side-effects than other drugs. In particular, it results in less weight gain and less severe loss of bone mineral density than prednisolone (Bonifati et al., 2000). Most practitioners delay therapy until 5 years of age.

Future treatments—gene therapy. Since the discovery of the molecular basis for DMD the possibility of genetic intervention has been studied. Initially, myoblast transfer was attempted, but with little success. It was postulated that fusion of a healthy myoblast with a dystrophic fibre would introduce a normal copy of the dystrophin gene. Unfortunately, expression levels of the protein were not sufficient to affect the disease (Mendell et al., 1995).

More recently, attention has focused on whether upregulation of another muscle membrane protein, utrophin, could attenuate disease progression in DMD. Utrophin has a similar structure to dystrophin but is normally expressed only in the sarcolemma at neuromuscular junctions. In degenerative and inflammatory muscle fibres, this expression was noted to be increased. It was suggested that this represented some form of compensatory mechanism. Work with the mdx mouse (an animal model of DMD) reinforced this theory. Transgenic mdx mice induced to upregulate utrophin so that it was expressed throughout the sarcolemma did not develop dystrophic features (Tinsley et al., 1996). However, this effect has yet to be demonstrated in humans.

A further possibility is a new form of genetic therapy. Direct transfer of the dystrophin gene into the dystrophic muscle fibre is achievable by means of a viral vector. This technique proved successful in the mouse model and recently the first human trial began, but was stopped prematurely because of a single fatality (Wang et al., 2000).

Becker muscular dystrophy (BMD) and other dystrophin allelic variants

This allelic disorder has a milder course than DMD and muscle weakness tends to be first noticed from age five. Cases have been reported with onset in the 30s and 40s. One of the main distinctions between BMD and DMD is that ambulation is maintained after the age of 16 in the former. Patients tend not to become wheelchair-bound until their 20s or 30s. Otherwise, the distribution of weakness is similar, and calf hypertrophy is often prominent (Fig. 49.9). Muscle pain is a common feature, often more pronounced in the legs and worsened or triggered by exercise. The patients do not develop mental retardation. Even with early onset, survival into the 40s and 50s is not unusual. Cardiomyopathy is frequent and might necessitate transplant in patients with only mild skeletal muscle involvement.

Quadriceps myopathy is considered to be a forme fruste of BMD. Individuals develop isolated wasting and weakness of the

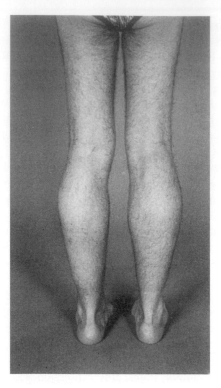

Figure 49.9. Becker muscular dystrophy: hypertrophy of calf muscles.

quadriceps muscles in their teens or later and the calves are noted to be hypertrophied. Other patients included in the BMD group include those who experience muscle cramps and myoglobinuria with exertion but do not develop muscle weakness. Clinical examination features in BMD are similar to those in DMD. Most investigations in BMD yield results indistinguishable from DMD.

Blood.   The CK is often markedly raised but in the milder phenotypes and especially the late onset cases may only be moderately elevated.

Muscle biopsy.   Reveals degenerative and regenerative changes but also more frequent internal nuclei. Immunocytochemistry demonstrates reduced staining for dystrophin. Western blot analysis confirms that the dystrophin is reduced but also that it may be of abnormal size. The dystrophin is detected with both the C-terminal and the N-terminal antibodies.

Molecular genetics.   BMD is usually associated with in-frame deletions or duplications of part of the dystrophin gene on Xp21. Genetic counselling is important in patients with BMD.

Treatment.   Many of the treatments outlined for DMD apply in BMD but are required later in life. Steroids are not generally used in this disorder. Regular cardiac screening is important.

Fascioscapulohumeral dystrophy (FSHD)

FSHD is inherited as an autosomal dominant trait. Typically, weakness of the facial and periscapular muscles begins in adolescence and progresses slowly (Tawil et al., 1998). There is wide variation in expression within families and, indeed, some family members consider themselves asymptomatic until subtle facial weakness or scapula-winging is identified by careful clinical examination. Others might be severely disabled by dysarthria and weakness in school years and are unable to walk after adolescence. This disorder should always be considered when dealing with any predominantly upper limb girdle dystrophy with autosomal dominant inheritance. Facial muscle weakness is the usual additional clue to the diagnosis, but can occasionally be subtle or even absent.

Although facial muscle weakness is usually the first sign, it is more likely that the patient will present when shoulder girdle weakness and deformity occur. Onset in infancy is rare but does occur. More commonly, the onset is between 5 and 30 years of age. There is often a descending sequence of muscle involvement from the face to the shoulder girdle to biceps and triceps and then the pelvic girdle. A jump from shoulder girdle to anterior tibial/peroneal muscle involvement frequently occurs. In fact, a few individuals with FSHD first present with foot-drop. The muscle weakness and wasting in this disorder is commonly asymmetric, so much so that other myopathies/dystrophies should be considered if the distribution is symmetric. Most patients will show progression of the disorder over many years. Some experience a slowing or halt in progression that can last several years. Pain is now recognised as a common symptom in FSHD. This is usually localised to the shoulder girdle or can be interscapular. The pathogenesis of this symptom is not clear but the possibilities include the inflammatory element of the condition (see below) or mechanical pain secondary to the shoulder muscle weakness and deformity.

Other systems are commonly involved in FSHD. Many patients have been shown to have subclinical retinal vascular abnormalities. These can be in the form of telangiectatic vessels or exudates. Importantly, patients are at risk of sight-threatening exudate. An ophthalmology opinion should be sought in any FSHD patient, and perhaps more particularly in those with early onset of symptoms and/or a family history of retinal complications. When dealing with young patients with FSHD the association with sensorineural deafness is particularly important. In sporadic cases, infants with facial weakness and deafness can be erroneously diagnosed as having mental retardation. In most patients with FSHD, although there is audiological evidence of hearing loss, this is not usually symptomatic. No convincing evidence exists to suggest cardiac involvement in FSHD and the condition does not limit life span.

Examination reveals facial muscle weakness but there is sparing of temporalis and masseter muscles. The patient often cannot close the eyes forcefully, cannot whistle and, when smiling, the mouth appears to move transversely. Observing the shoulder girdle, in the early stages the only sign might be that of asymmetrical scapular winging on abduction or elevation of the arms. Later, because of further weakness of the scapular fixators, the scapulae are displaced upwards causing the trapezius muscles to look hypertrophied. Characteristically, the deltoid muscle is spared (unlike the sarcoglycanopathies). Wasting around the shoulder girdle becomes apparent, as does wasting of pectoralis major. In the arms, the biceps and triceps gradually become weaker but, notably, wrist extensors can also be involved. Abdominal muscle weakness leads to a protuberant abdomen with a positive Beevor's sign. In the lower limbs, anterior tibial and peroneal muscle wasting and weakness is often apparent in the initial stages of the disorder, but can sometimes be detected only by asking the patient to walk on his/her heels. Pelvic girdle involvement occurs much later.

Blood. CK is often elevated, but not markedly. In older onset cases it can be normal.

EMG. This has no specific features but is often myopathic.

ECG/echocardiogram. This is usually normal.

Muscle biopsy. This shows evidence of degeneration and regeneration. Increased variation in fibre size, a few necrotic fibres, and increased connective tissue is seen. There is an increased number of internal nuclei. Often, biopsies from patients with FSHD show quite a prominent inflammatory infiltrate and can occasionally be confused with polymyositis. This perivascular and endomysial infiltrate consists mainly of lymphocytes and macrophages but it is not usually accompanied by the extensive muscle fibre destruction typical of inflammatory myopathies. There is no specific immunocytochemical profile in FSHD. Other muscle disorders that cause a scapuloperoneal syndrome with or without facial muscle involvement can usually be distinguished histologically or by means of immunocytochemistry (e.g. nemaline myopathy, centronuclear myopathy, sarcoglycanopathies).

Molecular genetics. This autosomal dominant condition has 95% penetrance by the age of 20 years but, as mentioned, clinical expression is variable. The disorder has been linked to a region close to the telomere of chromosome 4q but, to date, the gene responsible has not been identified (Wijmenga et al., 1990). Most cases of FSHD are associated with a deletion of an integral number of tandem repeat sequences each 3.3 kb long (denoted D4Z4), on chromosome 4q 35. In general, the larger the deletion the more severe the disorder. Although evidence of clinical anticipation (i.e. a more severe phenotype occurring in subsequent generations) has been documented in some families with FSHD, this cannot be attributed to the size of the deleted fragment, which remains constant in transmission from generation to generation. Males tend to be more severely affected than females.

It is not clear how the deletions cause the disorder because no gene has been found in this region. In view of this, and the fact that the region is not transcribed, it is hypothesised that a positional effect is exerted by the deleted fragment on a gene that lies more proximally on 4q.

The genetic diagnosis in FSHD is complicated by the fact that there is a homologous repeat sequence fragment on chromosome 10q and this crosses over with the 4q region in 20% of normal individuals. The molecular genetic technique for diagnosis involves two separate restriction enzyme digestions (double digest) and sensitive means of electrophoretic separation (pulsed field gel electrophoresis) (Fitzsimons, 1999).

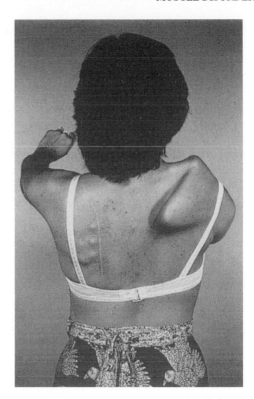

Figure 49.10. Gain in abduction of arm after thoracoscapular fusion.

The other complicating factor is that 30% of cases are new mutations or probably represent germ-line mosaicism in one of the parents. These cases often have a more severe phenotype.

Treatment. As with other dystrophies, supportive treatments are the mainstay in FSHD. Ophthalmological complications such as exposure keratitis can be readily treated with minor surgical procedures, including placing gold implants in the upper lids. The aesthetic and mechanical effects of scapular winging can be remedied by scapular fixation. This is by no means a minor procedure and patients should be aware of its limitations. It should improve shoulder abduction and scapular winging but, as yet, it is not certain whether it reduces the typical shoulder pain (Copeland et al., 1999) (Fig. 49.10). As with any patient with foot-drop, ankle–foot orthoses can be beneficial.

As yet, there is no accepted medical therapy to halt disease progression in FSHD. In view of the inflammatory element in the muscle biopsies of some of these patients, the effect of steroid therapy has been studied in a small number of patients. It does not seem to be of any long-term benefit. Hopes were raised by a pilot study of the β_2-agonist, albuterol but a large trial of this drug in FSHD failed to demonstrate a significant effect (Kissel et al., 2001).

Emery–Dreifuss muscular dystrophy (EDMD)

This disorder has X-linked, autosomal dominant and autosomal recessive variants (Emery, 2000); the X-linked form (XL-EDMD) is the most common. The genes for the X-lined and dominant forms have been discovered recently.

XL-EDMD is a childhood onset disorder. Contractures are an early sign and develop before the onset of weakness. Typically, the elbows, Achilles tendons, and spine are affected first. The latter can lead to difficulty with neck flexion. Later in the course of the disease, flexion contractures of the fingers can develop. The accompanying slowly progressive muscle wasting and weakness tends to start in a humeroperoneal distribution. This can give the false impression of enlarged forearms (reminiscent of "Popeye"). Gradually, the shoulder and then the pelvic girdle become affected. It should be noted that facial muscle weakness can also occur. Muscle hypertrophy is not a feature.

A cardiac conduction defect is almost invariable in XL-EDMD but ventricular dysfunction can also occur. Importantly, the conduction defect often affects female carriers who should have careful cardiological screening.

Blood.   CK is moderately elevated.

EMG.   This usually shows myopathic features, but could have neurogenic elements.

ECG/echocardiogram.   This often demonstrates atrioventricular block/bundle branch block; echocardiogram might demonstrate left ventricular dysfunction.

Muscle biopsy.   This shows a dystrophic pattern but immunocytochemistry demonstrates a reduction or absence of staining for emerin (see later).

Molecular genetics.   XL-EDMD is caused by a deficiency of a ubiquitous nuclear membrane protein called emerin. This is encoded by a gene (STA) on chromosome Xq (Bione et al., 1994).

Treatment.   Early insertion of a pacemaker might be required. This is often also the case in carrier females. Supportive measures to help to slow progression of contractures are of benefit.

The features of AD-EDMD overlap considerably with those previously attributed to an autosomal dominant limb girdle dystrophy (LGMD1B). They are both known to be due to mutations within the gene encoding another nuclear membrane protein, lamin A/C. The onset tends to be later than XL-EDMD and the variants include a slowly progressive limb girdle dystrophy with heart block and later onset of contractures, a syndrome with similar features to XL-EDMD, and cardiac involvement with little or no skeletal muscle manifestations (Bonne et al., 2000). Cardiac failure is a more frequent complication than with XL-EDMD. Some patients might require an implantable defibrillator as a pacemaker is often inadequate.

Muscle biopsy.   This shows similar changes to those in XL-EDMD but emerin staining is normal.

Molecular genetics.   The gene encoding lamin A/C (LMNA) is located on chromosome 1q. Mutations in this gene have also been identified in the recessive form of EDMD (Bonne et al., 1999; Di Barletta et al., 2000).

Limb girdle muscular dystrophies (LGMD)

This molecular basis of this group of disorders was ill defined until the discovery of some of the components of the dystrophin–glycoprotein complex (DGC). This protein complex lies within the muscle fibre membrane and has a critical structural role linking intracellular dystrophin to the extracellular matrix (see Fig. 49.1). Linkage analysis and positional cloning of genes encoding some of these proteins has led to the current classification of LGMD. It is now apparent that the different forms of LGMD are caused by mutations in genes for the different components of the DGC. The current classification system divides LGMD into autosomal dominant and autosomal recessive inheritance forms, termed LGMD1 and LGMD2 respectively (Bushby, 1999). Although there are some clinical clues that indicate which subtype of LGMD1 or LGMD2 a patient has, immunocytochemical and molecular genetic techniques are required to provide a definitive diagnosis. As mentioned above, any individual with an autosomal dominant limb girdle muscular dystrophy should have FSHD excluded first, as other causes are uncommon. Treatment of this group of disorders is currently limited to supportive measures.

Sarcoglycanopathies

Five members of this family of transmembrane glycoproteins, all of which are components of the DGC, have been identified (α-, β-, δ-, γ- and ϵ-sarcoglycan). Mutations within the genes encoding four of the sarcoglycans are established causes of LGMD. As yet there is no clear clinical distinction between these disorders. Although adult-onset cases have been described, most cases develop symptoms in childhood and are therefore more likely to present to paediatric neurologists.

The most common disorder in this group is α-sarcoglycanopathy (LGMD2D). It usually begins in the first decade of life, although early motor milestones are usually normal. Presenting features include difficulty running and ascending stairs. Calf hypertrophy is common but, unlike the dystrophinopathies, so is scapular winging. This can cause confusion with FSHD but in α-sarcoglycanopathy the deltoid is affected and facial weakness is rare. Cardiac involvement is unusual but can be a feature. Contractures are a late feature in this disorder.

Blood.   The CK is often mildly elevated.

EMG.   This has no distinctive features but is often myopathic.

ECG/echocardiogram.   This is usually normal.

Muscle biopsy.   Demonstrates dystrophic features, but the diagnosis relies on an absence of immunostaining for α-sarcoglycan. It is important that antibodies to the four sarcoglycans are used together with those for dystrophin. If not, patients with a sarcoglycan deficiency might be incorrectly diagnosed as Duchenne carriers because of the secondary reduction in dystrophin staining. In equivocal cases multiplex Western blotting is suggested.

Molecular genetics.   This is an autosomal recessive disorder. The transmembrane protein α-sarcoglycan is encoded by a gene on chromosome 17q.

Dysferlinopathy (LGMD2B)

Interestingly, two distinct phenotypes are associated with mutations in the gene encoding the sarcolemmal protein, dysferlin, which is also part of the DGC complex. The first is a limb girdle syndrome that starts in the teens or young adulthood (LGMD2B). Muscle weakness is first noticeable around the hip girdle but calf hypertrophy is not usual. In fact, the calves can become a little wasted and typically the patient has difficulty walking on tiptoe.

The second phenotype is known as Miyoshi myopathy, in which the posterior compartment of the lower leg becomes wasted and weak early in the disease course. Ankle jerks can be diminished or absent. Onset is at a similar age to LGMD2B. As the disease progresses the hand muscles are affected and a proximal myopathy might also develop. A further variant has been reported with involvement of the anterior tibial and peroneal muscles. Some patients with Miyoshi myopathy are initially diagnosed as having a hereditary neuropathy. Cardiac involvement does not occur in any of the variants.

Blood.   CK is often markedly raised and could be more than 100 times normal. This is a useful test if a hereditary neuropathy is amongst the differential diagnoses.

EMG.   This shows myopathic features with occasional neurogenic elements in Miyoshi myopathy.

ECG/echocardiogram.   These are normal.

Muscle biopsy.   This reveals a dystrophic picture, but with normal immunostaining for dystrophin and the sarcoglycans. Specific immunostaining with antibodies to dysferlin confirms the diagnosis. Very occasionally rimmed vacuoles may be present.

Molecular genetics.   The disorders are inherited in an autosomal recessive manner. The gene for dysferlin (DYSF) has been mapped to chromosome 2p. The same mutation can result in either LGMD2B or Miyoshi myopathy, even within the same family. This is a large gene, which hinders mutation identification.

Calpainopathy (LGMD2A)

This is the most common cause of autosomal recessive limb girdle dystrophy (approximately 40% of cases). Calpain 3 deficiency is the cause of LGMD2A. In contrast to the other LGMDs, calpain 3 is not a structural protein but is a muscle-specific, calcium-activated protease. The mechanism by which this causes a dystrophy is still under investigation.

Onset of disease is usually in adolescence or early teens, but patients have been described with onset in their 40s. The first sign is proximal lower limb weakness with difficulty running and ascending stairs. Contractures are common mainly affecting the Achilles tendons but can also involve the spine. Characteristically, the hip abductors are spared early on. Most patients have mild scapular winging and weak abdominal muscles leading to some confusion with FSHD, but facial muscles are not affected. Muscle hypertrophy is not usually a feature. Cardiac involvement has not been reported. The course is variable

but some patients can become wheelchair bound 10–20 years after onset.

Blood.   CK is moderately elevated, sometimes greater than 10 times normal.

EMG.   This is myopathic, but there are no specific features.

ECG/echocardiogram.   These are normal.

Muscle biopsy.   Dystrophic changes. Immunocytochemistry is not reliable in demonstrating calpain 3 staining. Western blot analysis is diagnostic, however, revealing either a reduction or a complete loss of the protein in this disorder.

Molecular genetics.   The gene encoding calpain 3 (CAPN3) is located on chromosome 15q.

Myotonic dystrophy

This autosomal dominant disorder is the most common muscular dystrophy and, in its classical form, is easily distinguishable from the other dystrophies. It is a multisystem disorder and its manifestations vary from a late onset mild variant to a severe congenital form. This marked phenotypic variability can be observed within the same family.

The most common presentation is in early adult life with muscle weakness and stiffness (Harper, 1989). Unlike the other muscular dystrophies, the weakness in this disorder is distal initially. The patient notices weak grip and might trip because of foot drop. The stiffness is a manifestation of the myotonia (myotonia classically describes delayed muscle relaxation after contraction). Patients often do not volunteer this, as the myotonia is not profound (unlike the non-dystrophic myotonias) and just describe muscle stiffness. These symptoms gradually progress and are accompanied by other symptoms depending on the other tissues involved (Table 49.3).

As the disorder progresses, other muscle groups are affected, including the respiratory muscles. This, in combination with dysphagia, puts the patient at great risk of aspiration. Regular ECG analysis should be undertaken to identify presymptomatic conduction defects.

Examination findings depend on the stage at which the patient is examined. Mental slowing might be prominent and frontal balding is frequently seen. Ocular examination reveals bilateral ptosis and cataracts (extraocular muscle weakness can be detected in advanced cases). There is a myopathic facies with facial muscle weakness and wasting that includes the temporalis and masseter muscles (unlike FSHD, see earlier). Characteristically, the sternocleidomastoid muscles are wasted and neck flexion

Table 49.3.   Systemic manifestations of myotonic dystrophy

Central nervous system	Cognitive decline, hypersomnia
Eye	Cataract, retinal degeneration
Heart	Atrioventricular block, arrhythmias, cardiomyopathy
Gastrointestinal tract	Pharyngeal/oesophageal dysmotility
Endocrine	Diabetes mellitus, pituitary dysfunction, testicular dysfunction

is weak. In later stages of the disorder there might be a nasal dysarthria as palatal weakness ensues.

Although initial wasting and weakness is localised to distal muscles in the upper and lower limbs, most muscles become involved. The calf muscles, hamstrings and pelvic girdle are spared in many cases.

The diagnosis is often revealed when myotonia is sought specifically. This can be achieved by testing grip relaxation time or by percussing a muscle, commonly the thenar eminence. Deep tendon reflexes tend to be reduced or absent. It is important to remember that in some family members, cataracts can be the only manifestation of the disease.

Congenital myotonic dystrophy is a severely disabling, sometimes fatal disorder. This syndrome seems to occur only with maternal transmission (see later). The mothers are often only mildly affected with the disease themselves. The first indications might be lack of fetal movements or polyhydramnios. The neonate is floppy, has poor sucking, and might require mechanical ventilation. If the baby survives, the facial weakness becomes apparent ("carp mouth"). There is usually marked delay in cognitive and motor development. With improvements in neonatal care over 50% of these cases now survive.

Blood.   CK can be normal or mildly elevated. Oral glucose tolerance test may be of benefit in identifying glucose intolerance early on.

EMG.   This demonstrates myopathic features plus high frequency discharges that wax and wane in frequency and amplitude (myotonic discharges).

ECG/echocardiogram.   Reveal heart block, and echocardiography can confirm ventricular dysfunction. An annual ECG is recommended in all cases.

MRI head.   This has been reported to show periventricular white matter lesions in some patients.

Muscle biopsy.   Since the development of a reliable molecular genetic test for myotonic dystrophy, muscle biopsy is not usually necessary. Typically, muscle biopsy shows increased fibre size variation, numerous internal nuclei, ringed fibres and a relative loss of type I fibres. No immunocytochemical techniques are specific.

Slit lamp examination.   This demonstrates the cataracts.

Molecular genetics.   This disorder is fully penetrant and is caused by an expansion of trinucleotide repeats (CTG) in an untranslated region (3′UTR) of a gene encoding a serine/threonine kinase on chromosome 19q (denoted DMPK). Several hypotheses exist as to how this mutation causes the disorder but none are proven. It is possible that the lack of kinase activity leads to a change in phosphorylation states of other enzymes. Another suggestion is that the expansion has an effect on a distant gene(s) on 19q (Thornton, 1999). Diagnosis now relies on a PCR-based technique that detects an expansion of these repeats. Normal alleles comprise 5 to 37 CTG repeats, whereas those associated with the disease vary from 50 to several 1000. The greater the number of repeats, the earlier the onset and the more severe the disorder. Individuals in subsequent generations tend to get the disorder earlier and more severely

(i.e. anticipation). The expansion is unstable when transmitted from generation to generation. In general, in transmission from a male the expansion contracts, whereas with transmission from a female there is further expansion. This is thought to be the basis for congenital myotonic dystrophy. A mildly affected female with a moderate expansion transmits a massively expanded repeat sequence to her offspring. Genetic counselling is therefore particularly important for affected females of childbearing age. Prenatal diagnosis is available but except in cases with either massive or very minimal expansions disease severity in offspring cannot be predicted with certainty.

Treatment.   This is generally supportive, as no therapeutic agent has yet been shown to prevent progressive muscle weakness in this disorder. Myotonia is usually a minor symptom but responds to antimyotonic therapies such as phenytoin and mexiletine (*Note*: these agents are hazardous in those patients with heart block).

Patients with myotonic dystrophy are prone to ventilatory problems following general anaesthesia. Close monitoring of respiratory function is therefore required. The obstetric patient with myotonic dystrophy is also a case for specialist care due to the likelihood of complications for both the mother and the baby.

Proximal myotonic myopathy

Several families have been described with similar features to myotonic dystrophy but with a proximal distribution of weakness and a less progressive course. None of the cases had an expanded CTG repeat in the DM gene. Linkage analysis suggested a locus on chromosome 3q (DM2) and this syndrome is known as proximal myotonic myopathy (PROMM) (Ranum et al., 1998; Ricker et al., 1999). Onset is usually in the 20s to 40s. Difficulty rising from a seat, difficulty ascending stairs, muscle stiffness, and pain are common symptoms. The myotonia can be symptomatic but is often intermittent. Cataracts are common. Endocrine and cardiac involvement can occur and some patients develop sensorineural deafness. Examination often reveals little wasting and the calves can be hypertrophied. Facial weakness and wasting if present is minimal. Percussion and grip myotonia are not always elicitable (Meola, 2000).

Blood.   CK can be up to 10 times normal but can be normal. For reasons that remain unclear, an elevated hepatic γ-GT is common and might help to distinguish from myotonic dystrophy.

EMG.   This usually demonstrates myotonic discharges but might need to be repeated to detect these.

ECG/echocardiogram.   In a minority of cases these can reveal heart block. However, an annual ECG seems a sensible precaution.

MRI head.   In a few families, periventricular white matter lesions have been described.

Muscle biopsy.   Shows numerous internal nuclei but is not specific for the disorder.

Molecular genetics.   The disorder(s) is inherited in an autosomal dominant manner, most are linked to 3q. This disorder is now known to be due to a CCTG tetranucleotide repeat expansion in the ZNF9 gene.

There is further genetic heterogeneity in this disorder as families with a PROMM phenotype have been described that do not link to either the DM locus on 19q or the DM2 locus on 3q.

Treatment. Supportive therapies with or without anti-myotonic treatment if necessary.

INFLAMMATORY MYOPATHIES

This section will focus on the three most common inflammatory myopathies: polymyositis, dermatomyositis, and inclusion body myositis. These disorders can usually be distinguished from each other by their clinical features. A significant proportion of cases of polymyositis and dermatomyositis respond to immunosuppressive therapy. Inflammatory changes in muscle can accompany some muscular dystrophies (especially FSHD) and this can cause diagnostic difficulties. Such diagnostic problems can usually be overcome with careful clinical, genetic, and immunocytochemical analysis. If doubt persists a trial of immunosuppressive treatment may be appropriate.

Polymyositis

This disorder often presents in a subacute manner between the ages of 40 and 60. Less commonly, cases with a more rapidly progressive course or with childhood onset have been described. The typical initial symptoms are due to proximal muscle weakness, particularly the shoulder girdle, hip girdle, and the neck extensors and flexors. The muscle involvement can be remarkably focal and, in a few cases, respiratory or paraspinal muscle weakness can be the presenting feature with no evidence of limb weakness. Dysphagia is frequent and occasionally facial muscle weakness is observed. In contrast to the dystrophies, deep tendon reflexes tend to be preserved in polymyositis unless particularly severe. The muscle involvement in polymyositis also helps to distinguish it from certain dystrophies, i.e. the deltoid is not spared, scapular winging is rare, as is weakness

and wasting of brachioradialis and pectoralis major (Amato & Barohn, 1997).

Other systems can be affected in polymyositis and the cardiac complications include peri- and myocarditis. In a small number of cases this leads to cardiac failure. Interstitial lung disease occurs in about 10% of cases so the onset of breathlessness can be related to this complication rather than respiratory muscle weakness.

Additional features can be present if there is an underlying connective tissue disorder (an overlap syndrome). In contrast to dermatomyositis, the association between polymyositis and underlying malignancy is not strong. It is advisable, however, to screen for malignancy in elderly patients with refractory myositis, particularly if there are numerous necrotic fibres on muscle biopsy.

Blood. CK is often markedly raised (up to 50 times normal), although cases of biopsy-proven active polymyositis with normal CK are recognised. In the more slowly progressive cases the CK might be only mildly elevated. Anti-Jo-1 antibodies are present in about 20% of cases. Their presence increases the likelihood of interstitial lung disease and tends to indicate a worse prognosis. An elevated antinuclear antibody (ANA) is common but, if raised, the dsDNA, Scl-70, ENA, and U1-RNP antibodies should be checked to identify an overlap syndrome (i.e. for SLE, scleroderma, Sjögren's syndrome, and mixed connective tissue disease, respectively) (Ioannou, 1999).

EMG. Demonstrates a myopathic picture but, unlike most of the dystrophies, there is marked irritability in the early stages of the disease. This manifests as fibrillation potentials, positive sharp waves, complex repetitive discharges, and occasional myotonic runs.

ECG/echocardiogram. This can show asymptomatic changes, including varying degrees of heart block, and ventricular dysfunction has been reported.

Muscle biopsy. There is evidence of degeneration and regeneration with muscle fibre necrosis. There is an endomysial inflammatory infiltrate with invasion of non-necrotic and necrotic fibres. The infiltrate consists predominantly of CD8-positive (cytotoxic) lymphocytes and macrophages.

Table 49.4. The muscular dystrophies

Disorder	Inheritance	Chromosome	Protein	Site
Duchenne/Becker muscular dystrophy	XL	Xp21	Dystrophin	Sarcolemma
Facioscapulohumeral dystrophy	AD	4q35	—	—
Emery–Dreifuss muscular dystrophy	XL	Xq28	Emerin	Nuclear membrane
Emery–Dreifuss muscular dystrophy	AD	1q11	Lamin A/C	Nuclear membrane
α-sarcoglycanopathy (LGMD2D)	AR	17q12	α-sarcoglycan	Sarcolemma
Dysferlinopathy (LGMD2B)	AR	2p13	Dysferlin	Sarcolemma
Calpainopathy (LGMD2A)	AR	15q15	Calpain	Cytosol and nucleus
Myotonic dystrophy	AD	19q13	Serine/threonine protein kinase	Ubiquitous
Proximal myotonic myopathy (PROMM)	AD	3q	ZFN9 (RNA-binding protein)	Ubiquitous

Treatment. Prednisolone, despite the lack of good trial data, is usually first-line therapy at a starting dose of 1–2 mg/kg. In fulminant cases, intravenous methylprednisolone can be used. Various second-line steroid-sparing agents have been used but the current authors' preference is for azathioprine and then methotrexate, or in combination; cyclosporin and cyclophosphamide are other options. Although good data are lacking, intravenous immunoglobulins can be useful in treating relapses (Mastaglia et al., 1999).

Dermatomyositis

Some authors divide this disorder into a more common childhood form and an adult form. The underlying muscle pathology is very similar but there are some differences in clinical manifestations.

A vague prodromal illness is followed by a subacute weakness of the proximal muscles, as in polymyositis. Focal muscle weakness is not usually a feature. The muscles can be tender but muscle pain is prominent in only the childhood variant. Dysphagia does occur and can occasionally be the presenting symptom. As the disease progresses, other muscles can be involved and, infrequently, more severe cases are complicated by respiratory muscle weakness (Callen, 2000).

The typical rash of dermatomyositis can develop prior to the onset of muscle involvement. This might be limited to the violaceous heliotrope rash around the eyes with accompanying periorbital oedema and red/purple Gottron's papules over the knuckles. In other cases, the rash becomes more extensive and oedematous, covering the face, neck, upper chest, and upper back with papules over the knees and elbows. If the nail beds are viewed under magnification, characteristic capillary abnormalities are seen, including thromboses and marked dilatation and looping. Subcutaneous calcification is common in the more chronic childhood cases. Children with dermatomyositis are at risk of a systemic vasculitis that can affect any organ but seems to have a predilection for the gastrointestinal tract. Complications in the adult form depend on whether there is an underlying connective tissue or neoplastic disorder. The associated malignancies include breast, lung, ovary, stomach, prostate, and lymphoma. Screening for these should be undertaken, especially in elderly patients. It should not be forgotten that the presentation of dermatomyositis can precede that of the neoplasm by a number of years, therefore serial screening might be required.

As with polymyositis, any patient with dermatomyositis is at risk of developing cardiac complications and interstitial lung disease (see earlier).

Blood. CK can be elevated up to > 10 times normal. Anti-Jo-1 antibodies are less frequent than in polymyositis but have the same consequences. Overlap syndromes should be sought, as outlined earlier.

EMG. This is usually indistinguishable from polymyositis with myopathic features and irritability.

ECG/echocardiogram. Asymptomatic heart block and arrhythmias are frequently detected. Ventricular dysfunction is unusual but has been reported.

Muscle biopsy. The inflammation principally affects small vessels, leading to microinfarction, and, typically, the perifascicular region bears the brunt of this early on (leading to perifascicular atrophy). Endomysial inflammation is uncommon. B and CD4-positive (helper) lymphocytes predominate in the infiltrate. Complement membrane attack complex (MAC) deposition within blood vessel walls is often an early pathological sign and is not seen in polymyositis. Necrotic fibres are seen but inflammatory infiltration of non-necrotic fibres is unusual.

Treatment. Similar to polymyositis. There is evidence that ivIg is of significant benefit in dermatomyositis (Dalakas, 1999).

Inclusion body myositis and myopathy (Table 49.5)

Sporadic inclusion body myositis (sIBM)

This is the most common inflammatory myopathy presenting in patients over the age of 50. There is a male preponderance (male : female 3 : 1). Typically, a slowly progressive weakness and wasting is first apparent in the long finger flexors, wrist flexors, and quadriceps muscles. Dysphagia is also a presenting symptom and occurs in over 30% of cases. Gradually, more proximal muscles in the upper limbs and more distal muscles in the lower limbs are affected. Deep tendon reflexes can be reduced (the knee jerks particularly) and there are occasionally sensory signs of a peripheral neuropathy. Patients can lose independent mobility within 10 years of onset (Askanas et al., 1998). Cardiac or interstitial lung pathology complications do not occur. There is evidence to suggest a slightly increased incidence of some autoimmune diseases in sIBM (type II diabetes and pernicious anaemia). An autoimmune basis for sIBM has been supported by its association with HLA-DR3. No relationship with underlying malignancy has emerged. Often, some of the distinctive clinical and pathological features of sIBM are absent, leading to some confusion with polymyositis. Any elderly patient with refractory polymyositis should be considered as potentially having sIBM.

Blood. CK can be mildly elevated or normal.

EMG. This does not reliably distinguish sIBM from the other inflammatory myopathies. Many cases of sIBM do, however, have a neurogenic element on their EMG and can also have evidence of an axonal sensorimotor neuropathy on nerve conduction studies.

Table 49.5. Features of inclusion body myositis and myopathy

	sIBM	hIBM
Age at onset	50+	30s
Distribution	Finger/wrist flexors, quadriceps	Distal leg, quads sparing
Muscle pathology	Inflammatory infiltrate, RRFs	No inflammation, no RRFs
HLA association	DR3	None

ECG/echocardiogram.   Normal.

Muscle biopsy.   The cellular infiltrate (endomysial, CD8-positive lymphocytes) and invasion of non-necrotic fibres is very similar to that in polymyositis. In contrast, fibre-type grouping and angulated fibres are more typical of sIBM as a consequence of the neuropathic element of the disorder. In addition, there are filamentous neuronal and intracytoplasmic inclusions and rimmed vacuoles. These vacuoles are not specific, however, as they can occur in other muscle disorders, e.g. oculopharyngeal muscular dystrophy. Additional pathological features are important in confirming the diagnosis. For instance, in sIBM there are abnormal accumulations of proteins within the fibre, including β-amyloid precursor protein, prion protein, and ubiquitin. An excess of ragged red fibres (RRFs) and cytochrome-oxidase-deficient (COX negative) fibres is common. Characteristically, electron microscopy demonstrates two sizes of paired helical filaments (15–21 nm and 6–10 nm in diameter) in both the cytoplasm and the nucleus.

Treatment.   There are no rigorous trial data that show that either steroids or ivIgG are of significant long-term benefit in sIBM. In some centres, both can be given a trial if significant inflammatory infiltrate is observed on muscle biopsy. A long cricopharyngeal myotomy has been successful in treating dysphagia in sIBM.

Hereditary inclusion body myopathy (hIBM)

In most families reported with this disorder the disease segregates in an autosomal recessive manner, but autosomal dominant inheritance has also been described.

In the recessive form, onset is before 30 years, with a slowly progressive distal leg weakness with quadriceps sparing (see Table 49.5). Recent genetic analysis suggests that the disorder distal myopathy with rimmed vacuoles (DMRV), first described in Japan, and hIBM are allelic disorders (Tome & Fardeau, 1998). In the largest family with the dominant condition, early contractures, proximal weakness, and ophthalmoplegia were prominent.

Muscle biopsy.   Many of the pathological hallmarks are the same as in sIBM. However, inflammatory infiltrate, RRFs and mitochondrial DNA deletions are not features of hIBM.

Molecular genetics.   Most autosomal recessive cases are linked to chromosome 9 and recently mutations in the GNE gene have been identified in some of these families. The Swedish kindred with the dominant form demonstrated linkage to chromosome 17p.

SKELETAL MUSCLE CHANNELOPATHIES

Recent significant advances in cellular electrophysiology and molecular genetics have led to the current understanding of this group of disorders. They are all caused by alterations in the excitability of the muscle cell membrane through dysfunction of membrane bound ion channels (Davies & Hanna, 1999), hence the term "channelopathies".

Myotonia congenita

Myotonia describes the phenomenon of delayed muscle relaxation after contraction. Myotonia congenita can exhibit either autosomal dominant or autosomal recessive inheritance. The clinical features of the dominant and recessive forms overlap but there are some differences. Autosomal dominant myotonia congenita (Thomsen's disease) is generally thought to be less common than the recessive type, and has its onset in infancy or early childhood; the condition tends to plateau after adolescence. The muscles can be hypertrophied but not usually as markedly as in the autosomal recessive form. The myotonia shows a predilection for the face, tongue, and arms rather than the legs. The myotonia demonstrates a definite "warm up" with exercise. There is no paradoxical myotonia (see later) but any form of myotonia will worsen a little with the cold (Table 49.6). Transient or progressive muscle weakness is not a feature of Thomsen's disease. In contrast to patients with paramyotonia congenita, patients with this disorder do not develop profound cold sensitivity or weakness.

The more common autosomal recessive myotonia congenita (Becker's generalised myotonia) usually presents between the ages of 4 and 12 years. It tends to be more progressive than Thomsen's disease and symptoms might not plateau until the 30s or 40s. Proximal weakness can develop in some patients. Muscle hypertrophy, especially in the lower limbs, is often marked and patients can initially be diagnosed as having a muscular dystrophy. In its early stages, the muscle stiffness has a predilection for the legs but slowly progresses to involve the arms, neck, and face over years. The myotonia eases with exertion ("warm up" phenomenon) and is not exacerbated profoundly by cold. Characteristically, patients with Becker's generalised myotonia notice a very transient weakness when attempting to initiate movement after rest. Patients with either disorder should be advised of the theoretical risk of a malignant hyperthermia-like reaction if exposed to volatile anaesthetic or muscle relaxing agents (see later) (Becker, 1977).

Blood.   CK can be mildly to moderately raised (up to 5–10 times normal).

EMG.   This often demonstrates profuse myotonic discharges, which characteristically wax and wane in amplitude and frequency which may sound like "revving a motorbike" or a "dive-bomber". EMG does not reliably distinguish between the Thomsen and Becker myotonia.

ECG/echocardiogram.   Normal.

Muscle biopsy.   This is now not necessary but typically reveals absent type IIb fibres and tubular aggregates.

Molecular genetics.   Work in an animal model of myotonia congenita (the myotonic goat) demonstrated reduced muscle cell membrane chloride conductance. Genetic analysis linked both recessive and dominant myotonia congenita to the gene encoding the skeletal muscle voltage-gated chloride channel (CLCN-1) on chromosome 7q. Mutations within this gene cause both the recessive and dominant disorder (George et al., 1993; Koch et al., 1992). Genetic counselling of patients with myotonia congenita

Table 49.6. Features of paramyotonia congenita and myotonia congenita

	Paramyotonia congenita	Myotonia congenita	
		Thomsen's	Becker's
Inheritance	Dominant	Dominant	Recessive
Onset	Birth/infancy	Early childhood	First decade
Distribution	Face, tongue and arms	Face, arms > legs	Legs > face, arms
Myotonia features	Paradoxical worsening	"Warm up" phenomenon	"Warm up" phenomenon
Precipitants	Cold and exertion	Rest	Rest
Additional symptoms	Cold-induced weakness and some with periodic paralysis	None	Transient weakness, some progressive weakness
Routine neurophysiology	Myotonic discharges on EMG	Myotonic discharges on EMG	Myotonic discharges on EMG
Cold immersion neurophysiology	CMAP amplitude decrement with cooling	No CMAP amplitude decrement with cooling	No CMAP amplitude decrement with cooling
Treatment	Mexiletine, acetazolamide	Mexiletine, phenytoin	Mexiletine, phenytoin
Channel affected	Na^+ channel	Cl^- channel	Cl^- channel

CMAP, compound muscle action potential.

is complex, as a mutation can behave in a recessive, a dominant or an incomplete dominant manner

Treatment.   Advice about avoiding precipitants, e.g. staying warmed up when playing sport, can help to prevent profound muscle stiffness. It is important to rule out underlying hypothyroidism and check that the patient is not on medication that might exacerbate these disorders (e.g. propanolol, clofibrate, HMG CoA reductase inhibitors).

In contrast to myotonic dystrophy, patients with myotonia congenita are often disabled by their muscle stiffness. Few good trials have been performed but in our experience the antiarrhythmic drug mexiletine is the drug of choice (100–150 mg bd, titrating up to a maximum of 1000 mg a day, in divided doses). Other drugs, such as phenytoin and procainamide, can also be of benefit (Davies & Hanna, 2001).

Hyperkalaemic periodic paralysis, potassium aggravated myotonia, and paramyotonia congenita

These disorders are inherited in an autosomal dominant manner. Electrophysiological analysis demonstrated that they resulted from a common underlying defect of muscle membrane excitability. They are now known to be allelic disorders caused by mutations in the voltage-gated skeletal muscle sodium ion channel gene SCN4A (Hudson et al., 1995).

Hyperkalaemic periodic paralysis (hyperPP) has its onset in late childhood to adolescence with attacks of weakness rather than complete paralysis (Table 49.7). The episodes last 30 minutes to a few hours and can result in generalised limb weakness or sometimes remarkably focal weakness. Common precipitants include rest after a period of exercise, stress, and cold. Patients can also complain of symptoms suggesting elements of potassium aggravated myotonia (PAM) or paramyotonia, as the conditions frequently overlap. Although attack frequency can decline with age, a fixed proximal myopathy can develop and, in some patients, this results in significant disability. Potassium loading tests have been used in the past to provoke an attack but these are not usually necessary and can be dangerous. Genetic analysis is now obviating the need for these in the majority of patients.

Table 49.7. Features of the periodic paralyses

	Hyperkalaemic periodic paralysis	Hypokalaemic periodic paralysis
Onset of symptoms	First decade	Second decade
Triggers	Rest after exercise, cold	As for hyperPP and carbohydrate load
Length of attack	Minutes to hours	Hours to days
Severity of attack	Mild to moderate weakness, can be focal	Moderate to severe weakness
Additional symptoms	Myotonia or paramyotonia	None
Serum K^+	Usually high, can be normal	Usually low, seldom normal
Interictal EMG	Myotonic discharges in some	None show this
Treatment	Acetazolamide/thiazide	Dichlorphenamide or acetazolamide
Ion channel	Na^+ channel	Ca^{2+} channel (L-type)

The onset of paramyotonia congenita (PMC) can be as early as the first few days of life. The muscle stiffness in PMC is unlike that in the chloride channel myotonias because it characteristically worsens with activity—paradoxical myotonia (see Table 49.6). The muscle stiffness becomes profound in cold weather and weakness can also develop in cold environments. The hands, face, and tongue seem to bear the brunt of these symptoms. Common complaints include the tongue and jaw "seizing up" after eating ice cream and difficulty opening the eyes or the face "sticking" in a smile in the cold. In those with an overlap syndrome (sometimes termed paramyotonia paralysis periodica PPP) periodic paralysis can develop in adolescence.

The diagnosis of potassium aggravated myotonia (PAM) is important as it can mimic myotonia congenita (see earlier). As the name suggests, symptoms in this disorder are provoked by potassium ingestion. Rest after exercise can also provoke an attack, as in hyperPP. The conditions previously known as myotonia fluctuans, myotonia permanens, and acetazolamide-sensitive myotonia are now known as PAM. The mild phenotype involves extremely variable muscle stiffness, with symptom-free periods of days or weeks (myotonia fluctuans). The severe phenotype includes permanent and profound muscle stiffness, with hypertrophy of neck and shoulder muscles and possibly respiratory difficulty because of intercostal muscle stiffness. An intermediate phenotype that includes mild but persistent myotonia with painful muscle spasms or cramps is particularly responsive to acetazolamide therapy.

Any patients with a skeletal muscle sodium channel disorder should be advised of the theoretical risk of a malignant hyperthermia-like reaction when exposed to certain anaesthetic and muscle relaxing agents (see later).

Blood. CK can be mildly to moderately elevated. In hyperPP, serum potassium during an attack might be elevated to about 6 mmol/l but can also be normal, particularly if measured late in the attack.

EMG. Neurophysiological tests do not always distinguish between hyperPP and hypokalaemic periodic paralysis (hypoPP), but the EMG might reveal subclinical myotonic discharges in some cases of hyperPP; these do not occur in hypoPP. During an attack, EMG indicates that the muscle fibre membrane is in a partially depolarised inexcitable state. Exercise testing and neurophysiological tests postexercise can be helpful in diagnosis.

Routine EMG does not distinguish between myotonia and paramyotonia but cold immersion neurophysiology is more useful. This frequently demonstrates a fall in compound muscle action potential (CMAP) amplitude in PMC when the muscle is cooled, a phenomenon that does not occur in myotonia congenita.

ECG/echocardiogram. Between attacks, the ECG is normal but during a hyperPP attack they might show tenting of the T wave.

Muscle biopsy. If undertaken, this might demonstrate vacuolar change or tubular aggregates but this does not distinguish between hypoPP and hyperPP.

Molecular genetics. The underlying electrophysiological defect in patients with hyperPP and PMC was found to be impaired skeletal muscle sodium channel inactivation. The gene encoding the alpha subunit of the adult skeletal muscle voltage-gated sodium channel (SCN4A) was identified on chromosome 17q (George et al., 1990, 1991). Mutations in this gene cause hyperPP, PMC, and PAM. Some mutations have a consistent genotype–phenotype correlation whereas others exhibit both inter- and intrafamilial phenotypic variability.

Treatment. Regular carbohydrate intake, a low potassium diet, and avoidance of particularly vigorous activities can prevent or reduce attacks in hyperPP. Decreasing exposure to the cold can benefit patients with hyperPP and PMC. Thyrotoxicosis should be excluded in patients with PMC, as this will exacerbate their symptoms.

Mexiletine is effective in PMC but might not reduce attack frequency in hyperPP. Acetazolamide (125 mg bd up to 1000 mg daily in divided doses) will alleviate the symptoms of PAM and can be beneficial in some, but not all, patients with PMC.

An acute attack of hyperPP can be averted by eating a chocolate bar or by exercising gently. It might also respond to a single dose of either acetazolamide or a thiazide diuretic. It has also been shown that inhaled beta adrenergic agents are of benefit in the acute phase of an attack (two doses of 100 µg of inhaled salbutamol). Prevention of attacks is achieved with thiazide diuretics, acetazolamide, or dichlorphenamide (Davies & Hanna, 2001).

Andersen's syndrome

This syndrome is characterised by periodic paralysis, ventricular arrhythmia, and dysmorphism (Andersen et al., 1971; Sansone et al., 1997). The dysmorphic features are often minor and can be easily overlooked. These include clino- or syndactyl, hypoplastic mandible, hypertelorism, and low-set ears. The patients are usually of small stature. Both hypokalaemic and hyperkalaemic periods of paralysis have been described in this syndrome but, typically, potassium loading will provoke an attack. Importantly, the arrhythmias can be asymptomatic in the early stages of the disorder. Later, they present as palpitations and/or syncope. The electrocardiograph often reveals a bidirectional ventricular tachycardia when symptomatic. At other times, the ECG might show a long QT interval, bigeminy, or it might be normal. Several families have been described in which Andersen's syndrome segregates in an autosomal dominant manner but with marked intrafamilial phenotypic variation. Of note is that other family members might have an asymptomatic long QT syndrome without any other manifestations. Recognition of this disorder is important because the patients are at risk of sudden death associated with malignant ventricular arrhythmias. The proband should have thorough cardiological investigation with follow up, as should first degree relatives (even if asymptomatic). Any patient presenting with periodic paralysis with, or even without, features suggestive of Andersen's syndrome should at least have a routine ECG.

Blood. CK might be mildly raised.

EMG. Does not show myotonia. Neurophysiological tests postexercise might be abnormal, as in hypoPP and hyperPP.

ECG/echocardiogram. The most common abnormality is a prolonged QT interval.

Muscle biopsy. May show vacuolar change and/or tubular aggregates.

Molecular genetics. Andersen's syndrome is now known to be caused by mutations in the gene encoding an inward rectifying potassium channel (KCNJ2) on chromosome 17q.

Treatment. Conventional antiarrhythmics are frequently ineffective in controlling the cardiac rhythm disturbance in Andersen's syndrome. Anecdotally, imipramine might be of benefit in reducing the ventricular arrhythmias. Pacemaker insertion or implantable defibrillator might be necessary. In contrast to hyperPP, the periodic paralysis in Andersen's syndrome might not be responsive to acetazolamide, and thiazide diuretics can exacerbate symptoms. Case reports suggest that dichlorphenamide is the drug of choice.

Hypokalaemic periodic paralysis

This disorder is inherited in an autosomal dominant manner and is more common than hyperPP. Unlike hyperPP, approximately one-third of cases represent new dominant mutations, so the absence of a family history is not uncommon. It presents a little later (second decade) and penetrance is reduced in females. Weakness involves the legs and arms and is usually more profound and prolonged (hours to days) than in hyperPP. As with hyperPP, rest after exercise and cold are common precipitants to attacks (Rudel et al., 1999). However, in contrast to hyperPP, carbohydrate loading can precipitate or worsen an attack in hypoPP. A progressive, mainly proximal myopathy can also occur in this disorder. Serum potassium levels during an attack are often between 2 and 3 mmol/l, but can occasionally be normal (see Table 49.7). To differentiate between the periodic paralyses, a provocative test involving glucose and insulin administration has been used in the past. In our practice, DNA analysis has now negated the need for this rather hazardous investigation in most patients.

Secondary causes of hypokalaemia should be considered in any patient suspected of suffering from primary hypoPP. Iatrogenic, gastrointestinal, and renal tubular disorders can result in hypokalaemia and paralysis as can thyrotoxicosis.

Any patients with hypoPP should be advised of the theoretical risk of a malignant hyperthermia-like reaction when exposed to certain anaesthetic and muscle relaxing agents.

Blood. CK might be mildly to moderately elevated.

EMG. As for hyperPP.

ECG/echocardiogram. Usually normal. During an attack it might show small T waves and prominent U waves.

Muscle biopsy. As for hyperPP.

Molecular genetics. Three mutations were discovered in the gene encoding the alpha-1 subunit of the dihydropyridine-sensitive (L-type) voltage-gated calcium channel (denoted CACNA1S) on chromosome 1q (Fontaine et al., 1994; Ptacek et al., 1994). Two of the mutations account for nearly all the cases. More recently, we and others have discovered that a small number of cases of hypoPP are actually due to mutations within SCN4A.

Treatment. As with hyperPP, patients with hypoPP should be educated to avoid precipitating factors. These measures include avoiding vigorous exercise and high carbohydrate meals. In an acute attack, oral potassium chloride (not intravenous) is the treatment of choice (2–10 g, repeated after 4 hours if necessary). To prevent attacks a carbonic anhydrase inhibitor is often the drug of choice. Dichlorphenamide is preferable to acetazolamide in this disorder (Davies & Hanna, 2001). Potassium-sparing diuretics, lithium, and calcium channel blockers occasionally prove helpful in refractory cases.

ACKNOWLEDGEMENT

Dr NP Davies is a Wellcome Trust clinical research fellow.

REFERENCES

Amato AA, Barohn RJ (1997). Idiopathic inflammatory myopathies. *Neurologic Clin*; 15: 615–648.

Andersen ED, Krasilnikoff PA, Overvad H (1971). Intermittent muscular weakness, extrasystoles and multiple developmental anomalies: a new syndrome? *Acta Paediat Scand*; 60: 559–564.

Askanas V, Serratrice G, Engel WK (Eds) (1998). *Inclusion-body myositis and myopathies*. Cambridge, Cambridge University Press.

Becker PE (1977). *Myotonia congenita and syndromes associated with myotonia*. Georg Thieme, Stuttgart.

Bione S, Maestrini E, Rivella S et al. (1994). Identification of a novel X-linked gene responsible for Emery–Dreifuss muscular dystrophy. *Nat Genet*; 8: 323–327.

Bogie K, Cochrane GM, Turner-Smith AR, Bader DL (1988). *Monitoring back shape in Duchenne muscular dystrophy*. Annual report of Oxford Orthopaedic Engineering Centre, Oxford, pp. 42–44.

Bonifati MD, Ruzza G, Bonometto P et al. (2000). A multicenter, double-blind, randomised trial of deflazacort versus prednisolone in Duchenne muscular dystrophy. *Muscle Nerve*; 23: 1344–1347.

Bonne G, Di Barletta MR, Varnous S et al. (1999). Mutations in the gene encoding lamin A/C cause autosomal dominant Emery–Dreifuss muscular dystrophy. *Nat Genet*; 21: 285–288.

Bonne G, Mercuri E, Muchir A et al. (2000). Clinical and molecular genetic spectrum of autosomal dominant Emery–Dreifuss muscular dystrophy due to mutations of the lamin A/C gene. *Ann Neurol*; 48: 170–180.

Buchanan DC, Larbarera CJ, Roelofs R et al. (1979). Reactions of families to children with Duchenne muscular dystrophy. *General Hospital Psychiatry*; 1: 262–269.

Bushby KM (1999). Making sense of the limb-girdle muscular dystrophies. *Brain*; 122: 1403–1420.

Callen JP (2000). Dermatomyositis. *Lancet*; 355: 53–57.

Copeland SA, Levy O, Warner GC et al. (1999). The shoulder in patients with muscular dystrophy. *Clin Orthop*; 368: 80–91.

Dalakas MC (1999). Controlled studies with high-dose intravenous immunoglobulin in the treatment of dermatomyositis, inclusion body myositis and polymyositis. *Neurology*; 51 (Suppl. 5): S37–S45.

Davies NP, Hanna MG (1999). Neurological channelopathies: diagnosis and treatment into the next millennium. *Ann Med*; 31: 406–420.

Davies NP, Hanna MG (2001). The neurological channelopathies. In: Scolding NJ (Ed), *Contemporary treatments in neurology*. Butterworth-Heinemann, pp. 398–440.

Di Barletta MR, Ricci E, Galluzzi G et al. (2000). Different mutations in the LMNA gene cause autosomal dominant and autosomal recessive Emery–Dreifuss muscular dystrophy. *Am J Hum Genet*; 66: 1407–1412.

Emery AEH (2000). Emery–Dreifuss muscular dystrophy – a 40 year retrospective. *Neuromuscul Disord*; 10: 228–232.

Fenichel GM, Florence JM, Pestronk A et al. (1991). Long-term benefit from prednisolone therapy in Duchenne muscular dystrophy. *Neurology*; 41: 1874–1877.

Firth M, Gardner-Medwin D, Hosking G, Wilkinson E (1983). Interview with parents of boys suffering Duchenne muscular dystrophy. *Developmental Medicine and Child Neurology*; 25: 466–471.

Fitzsimons RB (1999). Facioscapulohumeral muscular dystrophy. *Curr Opin Neurol*; 12: 501–511.

Fontaine B, Vale-Santos JM, Jurkat-Rott K et al. (1994). Mapping of hypokalaemic periodic paralysis (HypoPP) to chromosome 1q31-q32 by genome-wide search in three European families. *Nat Genet*; 6: 267–272.

George AL Jr, Kallen RG, Barchi RL (1990). Isolation of a human skeletal muscle sodium channel cDNA clone. *Biophys J* (abstract); 57: 108a.

George AL Jr, Ledbetter DH, Kallen RG et al. (1991). Assignment of a human skeletal muscle sodium channel alpha subunit gene (SCN4A) to 17q23.1-25.3. *Genomics*; 9: 555–556.

George AL Jr, Crackower MA, Abdalla JA et al. (1993). Molecular basis of Thomsen's disease (autosomal dominant myotonia congenita). *Nat Genet*; 3: 305–310.

Harper PS (1989). *Myotonic dystrophy*. London, Saunders.

Heckmatt JZ, Hyde SA, Florence J et al. (1985). Prolongation of walking in Duchenne muscular dystrophy with lightweight orthoses: review of 57 cases. *Developmental and Child Neurology*; 27: 149–154.

Heckmatt JZ, Loh L, Dubowitz V (1990). Night-time nasal ventilation in neuromuscular disease. *Lancet*; 335: 579–582.

Hoffman EP (1996). The muscular dystrophies. In: Rosenberg RN, Prusiner SB, DiMauro S, Barchi RL (Eds), *The molecular and genetic basis of neurological disease* (2nd edition). Boston, Butterworth-Heinemann, pp. 877–912.

Hudson J, Ebers GC, Bulman DE (1995). The skeletal muscle sodium and chloride channel diseases. *Brain*; 118: 547–563.

Ioannu Y, Sultan S, Isenberg DA (1999). Myositis overlap syndromes. *Curr Opin Rheumatol*; 11: 468–474.

Kissel JT, McDermott MP, Natarajan R et al. (1998). Pilot trial of albuterol in facioscapulohumeral muscular dystrophy. *Neurology*; 50: 1402–1406.

Koch MC, Steinmeyer K, Lorenz C et al. (1992). The skeletal muscle chloride channel in dominant and recessive human myotonia. *Science*; 257: 797–800.

Koenig M, Hoffman EP, Bertelson CJ et al. (1987). Complete cloning of the Duchenne muscular dystrophy (DMD) cDNA and preliminary genomic organisation of the DMD gene in normal and affected individuals. *Cell*; 50: 509–517.

Mastaglia FL, Laing NG (1996). Investigation of muscle disease. *J Neurol Neurosurg Psychiatry*; 60: 256–274.

Mastaglia FL, Phillips BA, Zilko PJ (1999). Inflammatory myopathy. *Curr Treat Options Neurol*; 1: 263–272.

Mendell JR, Kissel JT, Amato A et al. (1995). Myoblast transfer in the treatment of Duchenne's muscular dystrophy. *NEJM*; 333: 832–838.

Meola G (2000). Clinical and genetic heterogeneity in myotonic dystrophies. *Muscle Nerve*; 23: 1789–1799.

Miller G (1985). Spinal bracing and respiratory function in Duchenne muscular dystrophy. *Clinical Paediatrics*; 24: 94.

Pourmand R (2000). Metabolic myopathies. In: *Neurologic Clinics*; 18 (1): 1–13.

Ptacek LJ, Tawil R, Griggs RC et al. (1994). Dihydropyridine receptor mutations cause hypokalaemic periodic paralysis. *Cell*; 77: 863–868.

Ranum LP, Rasmussen PF, Benzow KA et al. (1998). Genetic mapping of a second myotonic dystrophy locus. *Nat Genet*; 19: 196–198.

Ricker K, Grimm T, Koch MC et al. (1999). Linkage of proximal myotonic myopathy to chromosome 3q. *Neurology*; 52: 170–171.

Rideau Y, Dupont G, Marie-Agnes Y et al. (1985). Traitment de dystrophie musculaire. Resultats d'une cooperation Franco-Italienne. *Semaine des Hospitaux*; 63: 438.

Rudel R, Hanna MG, Lehmann-Horn F (1999). Muscle channelopathies: malignant hyperthermia, periodic paralyses, paramyotonia and myotonia. In: Schapira AHV, Griggs RC (Eds), *Muscle diseases*. Boston, Butterworth Heinemann, pp. 135–175.

Sansone V, Griggs RC, Meola G et al. (1997). Andersen's syndrome: a distinct periodic paralysis. *Ann Neurol*; 42: 305–312.

Sibert JR, Williams V, Burkinshaw R et al. (1987). Swivel walkers in Duchenne muscular dystrophy. *Arch Dis Child*, 62. 471–472.

Smith PEM, Coabley JH, Edwards RHT (1988). Respiratory muscle training in Duchenne muscular dystrophy. *Nerve*; 11: 784–785.

Sussman MD (1985). Treatment of scoliosis in Duchenne muscular dystrophy. *Dev Med Child Neurol*; 27: 522–524.

Tawil R, Figelwicz DA, Griggs RC et al. (1998). Facioscapulohumeral dystrophy: a distinct regional myopathy with a novel molecular pathogenesis. FSH Consortium. *Ann Neurol*; 43: 279–282.

Thornton C (1999). The myotonic dystrophies. *Semin Neurol*; 19: 25–33.

Tinsley JM, Potter AC, Phelps SR et al. (1996). Amelioration of the dystrophic phenotype of mdx mice using a truncated utrophin transgene. *Nature*; 384: 349–353.

Tome FMS, Fardeau M (1998). Hereditary inclusion body myopathies. *Curr Opin Neurol*; 11: 453–459.

Walton JN, Nattrass FJ (1954). On the classification, natural history and treatment of the myopathies. *Brain*; 77: 169–231.

Wang B, Li J, Xiao X (2000). From the cover: adeno-associated virus vector carrying human minidystrophin genes effectively ameliorates muscular dystrophy in mdx mouse model. *Proc Natl Acad Sci USA*; 97: 13714–13719.

Wijmenga C, Frants RR, Brouwer OF et al. (1990). Location of facioscapulohumeral muscular dystrophy gene on chromosome 4. *Lancet*; 336: 651–653.

Index